WORLD POPULATION AND HUMAN CAPITAL IN THE TWENTY-FIRST CENTURY

About IIASA (International Institute for Applied Systems Analysis)

Founded in 1972, IIASA is an international scientific institute that conducts policy-oriented research into problems that are too large or too complex to be solved by a single country or academic discipline. Problems like climate change that have a global reach and can be resolved only by international cooperative action. Or problems of common concern to many countries that need to be addressed at the national level, such as energy security, population ageing, and sustainable development. Our findings provide valuable options to policy makers to shape the future of our changing world. IIASA is independent and funded by scientific institutions in the following twenty-two member countries: Australia, Austria, Brazil, China, Egypt, Finland, Germany, India, Indonesia, Japan, Republic of Korea, Malaysia, Mexico, Netherlands, Norway, Pakistan, Russian Federation, South Africa, Sweden, Ukraine, USA, and Vietnam.

More information: <http://www.iiasa.ac.at>

IIASA

WORLD POPULATION AND HUMAN CAPITAL IN THE TWENTY-FIRST CENTURY

Edited by
WOLFGANG LUTZ, WILLIAM P. BUTZ,
and
SAMIR KC

OXFORD
UNIVERSITY PRESS

OXFORD
UNIVERSITY PRESS

Great Clarendon Street, Oxford, OX2 6DP,
United Kingdom

Oxford University Press is a department of the University of Oxford.
It furthers the University's objective of excellence in research, scholarship,
and education by publishing worldwide. Oxford is a registered trade mark of
Oxford University Press in the UK and in certain other countries

First Edition published in 2014

Impression: 2

Published in the United States of America by Oxford University Press
198 Madison Avenue, New York, NY 10016, United States of America

British Library Cataloguing in Publication Data
Data available

Library of Congress Control Number: 2013956087

ISBN 978-0-19-870316-7

As printed and bound by
CPI Group (UK) Ltd, Croydon, CR0 4YY

Dedicated to the memory of Nathan Keyfitz on the occasion of his 100th birth year, 2013.

> Forecasting is one of the oldest of demographic activities, and yet it has never been fully integrated with the main body of demographic theory and data.
>
> (Nathan Keyfitz in Lutz, W. (ed.) 1994 *The Future Population of the World. What Can We Assume Today?* Earthscan: London, Foreword)

Acknowledgements

The editors' most substantial debt is to the 26 lead authors who, working with us as a team, planned and produced the population projections that form the core of this book. This multifaceted three-year effort culminated in the initial chapters describing the methodological and substantive foundations for our projections assumptions, as well as the later chapters that explore the patterns and implications of the projections.

Our second debt is to the 46 contributing authors, who have helped, with their expertise, to enrich the substantive background chapters through specific pieces of analysis. Their names are listed in the chapters to which they contributed.

We are also grateful to the 62 experts who took the time and effort to attend the five substantive meta-expert meetings that helped to convert the state of knowledge and the input from the hundreds of source experts into numerical assumptions. These meetings on five continents were attended as follows.

- *Workshop on the Likely Future Trajectories of International Migration, 3–5 October 2011, Boulder, CO, USA*: Guy Abel, Ayla Bonfiglio, William Butz, Joel Cohen, David Coleman, Hugo Graeme, Siew-Ean Khoo, Jeffrey Passel, James Raymer, Philip Rees, Fernando Riosmena, Andrei Rogers, and Nikola Sander.
- *Workshop on the Likely Future Trajectories of Fertility in High Fertility Countries, 7–9 November 2011, Kathmandu, Nepal*: Mohammad-Jalal Abbasi-Shavazi, William Butz, Youssef Courbage, Regina Fuchs, Anne Goujon, K.S. James, Gavin Jones, Samir KC, Wolfgang Lutz, John May, Vinod Mishra, and Bruno Schoumaker.
- *Workshop on the Likely Future Trajectories of Fertility in Low Fertility Countries, 1–2 December 2011, Vienna, Austria*: Alicia Adsera, Margareth Arilha, Bilal Barakat, Stuart Basten, Jan van Bavel, Francesco C. Billari, William Butz, Minja Kim Choe, Joshua R. Goldstein, K.S. James, Leiwen Jiang, Samir KC, Tomáš Kučera, Wolfgang Lutz, Elsie Pamuk, Dimiter Philipov, Anna Rotkirch, Warren C. Sanderson, Vegard Skirbekk, Tomáš Sobotka, Olivier Thévenon, and Kryštof Zeman.
- *Workshop on the Likely Future Trajectories of Mortality in High Mortality Countries, 10–11 February, 2012, Cape Town, South Africa*: Rob Dorrington, Alessandra Garbero, Michel Garenne, Kenneth Hill, Harold Lentzner, Wolfgang Lutz, Tom Moultrie, Elsie Pamuk, Francois Pelletier, and Ian Timaeus.
- *Workshop on Alternative Assumptions of Future Mortality in Low Mortality Countries, 21–22 February 2012, San Jose, Costa Rica:* Gilbert Brenes, Graziella Caselli, Sven Drefahl, Michel Guillot, Wolfgang Lutz, Marc Luy, France Mesle, Arodys Robles, Richard Rogers, Sergei Scherbov, and Edward Tu.

We are also grateful to the many hundreds of source experts who responded from around the globe to the online survey that provided the initial knowledge base for the projections. We thank Mr Iain Stewart, Head of the International Institute for Applied Systems Analysis (IIASA) Communications Department, for his guidance; Mr James Dawson for his tireless editing at several levels; and Mr Matthew Cantele and Ms Ekaterina Scherbov for their valued assistance. Coordinating these authors' and editors' work through to a publishable manuscript fell, at the beginning, to Dr Heike Barakat and then to Ms Stefanie Andruchowitz in the middle and final stages. Their essential contributions merit a title: Associate Editors.

This research was made possible by a European Research Council (ERC) Advanced Grant to Wolfgang Lutz on the theme 'Forecasting Societies' Adaptive Capacities to Climate Change', Grant Agreement No. ERC-2008-AdG 230195-FutureSoc. We are also grateful to IIASA, the Austrian Academy of Sciences, and the Vienna University of Economics and Business (the three pillar institutions of the Wittgenstein Centre for Demography and Global Human Capital) for providing support for this study.

Contents

List of Contributors

Wolfgang Lutz, Founding Director of the Wittgenstein Centre for Demography and Global Human Capital (a collaboration between the International Institute for Applied Systems Analysis (IIASA), the Vienna Institute of Demography/Austrian Academy of Sciences (VID/ÖAW), and the Vienna University of Economics and Business (WU)). Program Director of the World Population Program at IIASA; Director of the Vienna Institute of Demography of the Austrian Academy of Sciences since 2002; Full Professor of Applied Statistics (part-time) at the WU since 2008; Professorial Research Fellow at the Oxford Martin School for 21st Century Studies.

Univ. Prof. Mag. MA PhD: Philosophy, Theology, Mathematics, and Statistics at the Universities of Munich, Vienna, and Helsinki. He holds a PhD in Demography from the University of Pennsylvania (1983) and a second doctorate (Habilitation) in Statistics from the University of Vienna.

Research focus: He has worked on family demography, fertility analysis, population projections, and the interactions between population and environment. He has been conducting a series of in-depth studies on population–development–environment interactions in Mexico, several African countries, and Asia. He is author of the series of world population projections produced at IIASA and has developed approaches for projecting education and human capital. He is also principal investigator of the Asian MetaCentre for Population and Sustainable Development Analysis. Wolfgang Lutz is author and editor of 28 books and more than 200 refereed articles, including seven in *Science* and *Nature*. In 2008, he received a European Research Council (ERC) Advanced Grant; the Mattei Dogan Award of the International Union for the Scientific Study of Population (IUSSP) in 2009; and the Wittgenstein Prize in 2010, the highest Austrian science award.

William P. Butz, Senior Research Scholar, World Population Program, IIASA and Director of Coordination and Outreach at the Wittgenstein Centre (IIASA, VID/ÖAW, WU). From October 2003 to February 2011, he was president and chief executive officer of the Population Reference Bureau (PRB), based in Washington, DC, USA. Before joining PRB, he was senior economist at the RAND Corporation; associate director of the US Census Bureau, where he was in charge of household surveys, international activities, and population estimates and projections; and division director for social and behavioural sciences at the National Science Foundation. His undergraduate and graduate educations were at Indiana University and the University of Chicago, respectively, where he studied economics, statistics, and demography. Mr Butz has taught economic development at the University of California, Los Angeles and the University of

California, Santa Barbara; served on numerous commissions and boards; and written more than 80 research and policy papers on a variety of topics related to economic demography, nutrition and health, and statistical and science policy. Since 2001, he has served on the board of reviewing editors of *Science* magazine, where his responsibilities include the social sciences, the policy forum, and the education forum.

Samir KC, Leader of Modelling Human Capital Project, World Population Program, IIASA and part of the Wittgenstein Centre (IIASA, VID/ÖAW, WU). KC's master's degree in statistics is from Tribhuvan University, Nepal (1997). Subsequently, he taught university statistics in Kathmandu and worked as a biostatistician at the Nepal Health Research Council. KC received his PhD from the University of Groningen, the Netherlands (2009), and has worked as a Research Scholar at the World Population Program at IIASA since 2005. His major research interests are developing and applying multi-state population models in demographic analysis and projections with a particular focus on modelling human capital formation in education and health; and differential vulnerability to natural disasters. KC has published in *Science* (2011) and other peer-reviewed journals.

Lead Author Details

Guy J. Abel, Research Scientist; Wittgenstein Centre (IIASA, VID/ÖAW, WU), Vienna Institute of Demography/ÖAW

Research focus: international migration, statistical demography

PhD: University of Southampton, 2009

Bilal F. Barakat, Research Scientist; Wittgenstein Centre (IIASA, VID/ÖAW, WU), International Institute for Applied Systems Analysis

Research focus: education policy and development, modelling

DPhil: University of Oxford, 2009

Stuart Basten, Associate Professor in Social Policy, Department of Social Policy and Intervention, University of Oxford

Research focus: population and policy in Asia

PhD: University of Cambridge, 2008

Ramon Bauer, Research Scientist; Wittgenstein Centre (IIASA, VID/ÖAW, WU), Vienna Institute of Demography/ÖAW

Research focus: human capital, spatial demography, urban diversity

PhD: in process at the University of Vienna

Graziella Caselli, Honorary Professor; University of Rome 'La Sapienza'

Research focus: Population longevity and ageing; mathematical models for analysing socio-economic differences in mortality; analysis of the role of socio-demographic factors on the future of the welfare state; elderly health and survival; projections and forecast models for mortality by cause; longitudinal studies of Sardinian longevity

Sven Drefahl, Post-doctoral Fellow; Department of Sociology, Stockholm University and Karolinska Institute

Research focus: old age mortality, determinants of mortality

PhD: University of Rostock, 2010

Rachel E. Durham, Research Scientist; Wittgenstein Centre (IIASA, VID/ÖAW, WU), Vienna University of Economics and Business

Research focus: educational policy, inequality, school processes

PhD: Pennsylvania State University, 2007

Regina Fuchs, Research Scholar; Wittgenstein Centre (IIASA, VID/ÖAW, WU), IIASA

Research focus: high fertility and demographic transition; household energy consumption and emissions

PhD: Vienna University of Economics and Business, 2012

Alessandra Garbero, Econometrician; International Fund for Agricultural Development (IFAD)

Research focus: economics of HIV and AIDS impacts; vulnerability differentiation; monitoring and evaluation; missing data and econometric methods

PhD: London School of Hygiene and Tropical Medicine, 2011

Anne Goujon, Senior Research Scholar and Research Group Leader; Wittgenstein Centre (IIASA, VID/ÖAW, WU), IIASA

Research focus: population projections by education or religion

PhD: University of Vienna, 2003

Marc Luy, Senior Research Scholar and Research Group Leader; Wittgenstein Centre (IIASA, VID/ÖAW, WU), VID/ÖAW

Research focus: health and mortality

PhD: University of Rostock, 2004

Elsie Pamuk, Visiting Scholar; IIASA

Research focus: health, mortality, and education

PhD: University of Pennsylvania, 1989

Michaela Potančoková, Research Scientist; Wittgenstein Centre (IIASA, VID/ÖAW, WU), IIASA

Research focus: education, fertility and family formation processes

PhD: Charles University in Prague, 2009

Fernando Riosmena, Assistant Professor; Population Program Institute of Behavioral Science (IBS) and Geography Department, University of Colorado at Boulder

Research focus: Demographic processes associated with spatial and social mobility, well-being, and development in Latin American societies and immigrant communities in the ISA

PhD: University of Pennsylvania, 2005

Nikola Sander, Research Scholar; Wittgenstein Centre (IIASA, VID/ÖAW, WU), VID/ÖAW

Research focus: internal and international migration, data visualization

PhD: The University of Queensland, Brisbane, 2011

Warren C. Sanderson, Professor of Economics and Professor of History; Stony Brook University in New York, and Research Scholar; Wittgenstein Centre (IIASA, VID/ÖAW, WU), IIASA

Research focus: economic demography

PhD: Stanford University, 1974

Sergei Scherbov, Director of Demographic Analysis, Project Leader and Research Group Leader; Wittgenstein Centre (IIASA, VID/ÖAW, WU), IIASA

Research focus: population projections; analysis of fertility and mortality; measuring ageing in ways that take life expectancy changes into account; computer methods in demographic analysis; issues related to human capital; modelling disability; multi-state demography

PhD: All-Union Research Institute for Systems Studies of the USSR Academy of Sciences, 1983

Vegard Skirbekk, Project Leader; Wittgenstein Centre (IIASA, VID/ÖAW, WU), IIASA

Research focus: measures of beliefs and values; health and cognition; life cycle and cohort change; childbearing; age and productivity

PhD: University of Rostock, 2005

Tomáš Sobotka, Research Group Leader; Wittgenstein Centre (IIASA, VID/ÖAW, WU), VID/ÖAW

Research focus: fertility, family changes, postponement of childbearing, measurement

PhD: University of Groningen, the Netherlands, 2004

Erich Striessnig, Research Assistant; Wittgenstein Centre (IIASA, VID/ÖAW, WU), IIASA

Research focus: demographics of economic growth, optimal fertility, education and disaster vulnerability

PhD: in progress, Vienna University of Economics and Business

Christian Wegner-Siegmundt, Research Scientist; Wittgenstein Centre (IIASA, VID/ÖAW, WU), VID/ÖAW

Research focus: differential mortality and morbidity, formal demography

PhD: University of Rostock, 2014

Kryštof Zeman, Research Scientist; Wittgenstein Centre (IIASA, VID/ÖAW, WU), VID/ÖAW

Research focus: demography of Central and Eastern Europe, family formation processes

PhD: Charles University in Prague, 2004

CHAPTER 1

INTRODUCTION

WOLFGANG LUTZ AND WILLIAM P. BUTZ

This book addresses systematically and quantitatively the role of educational attainment in global population trends and models. By adding education to the traditional demographic characteristics of age and sex, this distinguishing feature substantially alters the way we look at changes in populations and how we project them into the future. In most societies, particularly during the process of demographic transition, women with more education have fewer children, both because they want fewer and because they find better access to birth control. And better educated men and women in virtually all societies have lower mortality rates and their children have a better chance of survival. Migration flows also differ by level of education, and better educated migrants integrate more easily into receiving societies.

These pervasive demographic differentials by level of education matter greatly for population dynamics. When we explicitly address this important source of population heterogeneity the projected future population trends are different from those based on the conventional stratifications that include only age and sex. In addition, the future educational attainment levels of the adult population are of great interest in their own right as a key determinant of outcomes ranging across economic growth, quality of governance, and adaptive capacity to environmental change.

Traditionally in demography, the sex of a person is considered the most fundamental characteristic because it is essential for studying the process of reproduction. Mortality and migration also show significant variation by gender. Age is another key characteristic because it is the main driver of biological maturation at an early age and is directly related to school attendance, labour force entry, and retirement, all landmarks that are important for social institutions. Because there are distinct age-related patterns of fertility, mortality, and migration intensities, gender and age are considered the most fundamental demographic dimensions. In addition, demographers frequently take into account other biological, social, and economic characteristics, including place of residence (especially urban or rural), citizenship, marital status, race, migration status, employment status, health/disability status, and educational attainment. These additional characteristics are not systematically considered in every study, but tend to appear in corresponding topical studies.

With respect to highest educational attainment level, the argument has recently been put forward that among all of the demographic characteristics, it is the most important source of observable population heterogeneity after age and sex, and should therefore be routinely added to many types of population analyses (Lutz and KC, 2011). This assertion is made on the basis of three criteria that an additional standard characteristic should meet: (i) it should be feasible in terms of available data and methodology; (ii) it should be of such importance that it can alter population dynamics; and (iii) it should be of interest in its own right in terms of its social and economic implications. This book is dedicated to systematic assessments of the first two criteria by demonstrating the feasibility of introducing educational attainment for all countries in the world and showing how this alters the global population outlook. At the end in Chapter 12 and the Epilogue we will also discuss a fourth criterion—the central relevance of education for sustainable development beyond its effect on a population. Through the systematic addition of the education dimension, this approach can be thought of as adding a 'quality' dimension to the consideration of population numbers.

When measuring education it is important to distinguish conceptually between education 'flows' and 'stocks'. Flows refer to the process of education, to schooling, and, more generally, the production of human capital, which may consist of formal and informal education. This process of education is the central focus of pedagogics and education science, where the usual statistical indicators are school enrolment rates, student–teacher ratios, drop-out rates, and grade level repetition rates. Human capital refers to the stock of educated adult people, which is the result of recent education flows for younger adults, and flows from the more distant past for older adults. This stock is typically measured in terms of the quantity of formal education (highest level of attainment or mean years of schooling), but the quality (the general knowledge and cognitive skills people actually have), content, and direction of education also matter. Content is more important for higher education than basic education, where the focus is on acquisition of literacy skills and basic numeracy.

In economics, the quantity of formal education is often measured by the mean years of schooling of the adult population above the ages of either 15 or 25. This measurement has the advantage of capturing the entire human capital of a population at one moment in time in a single number (or two, distinguishing between men and women). But there is much to be gained from decomposing this highly aggregated indicator into the full distribution of educational attainment categories (which also captures the inequality in education) and into different age groups (capturing intercohort changes that drive many of the social and economic consequences of improving human capital over time).

The toolbox of technical demographers contains the powerful methods of multidimensional (multi-state) population dynamics, which are tailor-made for the task of integrating the processes of human capital formation with those of fertility, mortality, and migration to arrive at a comprehensive, analytically consistent, and directly applicable model of these processes. This demographic model is also more appropriate than standard economic approaches for studying changes in aggregate human capital because it can readily accommodate the fact that fertility, mortality, and migration all tend to differ by level of education. Accordingly, this book takes the decisive step of translating these multidimensional methods and new insights about the role of education into applied population projections for all countries in the world by combining them with the best available expert knowledge about the drivers of fertility, mortality, and migration.

This new effort is a logical next step in the tradition of multidimensional and probabilistic population forecasting at the World Population Program of the International Institute for Applied Systems Analysis (IIASA). This project is also the first major joint research effort of the recently established Wittgenstein Centre for Demography and Global Human Capital (WIC), a collaboration between IIASA's World Population Program, the Vienna Institute of Demography of the Austrian Academy of Sciences, and the WU–Vienna University of Economics and Business. The collaboration started in 2011 as a consequence of the 2010 Wittgenstein Award (the most prestigious science prize in Austria, and which also gives the Centre its name) being awarded to Wolfgang Lutz. This book draws on the broad knowledge base of the WIC scientists, with many of them serving as lead authors of the substantive reviews.

This study also builds on the long-standing research focus on global environmental change of several other IIASA programs with which the World Population Program has closely interacted in the production of comprehensive scenarios for the twenty-first century. Most recently, we collaborated in the production of the 'human core' of a new set of broadly agreed upon Shared Socioeconomic Pathways (SSPs). These will be the common point of reference for a broad range of research activities on climate change, particularly in the context of integrated assessment models and vulnerability, risk, and adaptation studies. A detailed description of this new set of scenarios appears in Chapter 12.

1.1 A BRIEF HISTORY OF WORLD POPULATION PROJECTIONS AND THE IIASA TRADITION OF PRODUCING INTERNATIONAL PROJECTIONS SINCE 1988

The oldest known long-term world population projection was published in 1696 by British statistician Gregory King (1973), who projected that the world population would reach 630 million in 1950 and 780 million in 2050. The method used by King, as well as by Pearl (1924, 1923) and Knibbs (1976) in the 1920s, was simple: combine an estimate of current world population size with assumed future rates of population growth. These early projections have been described by Frejka (1996), who states that the projections published by Pearl in 1924 gave a total world population of 1.96 billion for 2000 and a roughly constant population of 2 billion for 2050 and 2100. Knibb's projections published only four years later, in 1928, evidently assumed a much higher growth rate that resulted in a projection of 3.9 billion in 2000 and 15.6 billion for the 2169. The current United Nations (UN) estimate for the year 2000 is 6.1 billion. This latest estimate demonstrates that all of the early world population projections up to the year 2000 were far too low.

American demographer Frank Notestein was the first to apply the methods of cohort component projections to international population projections. Notestein's projections were based on the population stratified by sex and five-year age groups, along with the assumption of future age- and sex-specific mortality, fertility, and migration rates. This method was originally developed by the English economist Edwin Cannan in 1895 (O'Neill et al., 2001) and further formalized by the demographer Pascal Whelpton (1936) and P.H. Leslie (1945) for international projections. Notestein first applied this method to the countries of Europe and the Soviet Union in a projection commissioned by the League of Nations (Notestein et al., 1944) and soon thereafter for the entire world population (Notestein, 1945). These first global cohort component projections went only to the year 2000 and were, for the first time, based on a wealth of newly available population statistics from around the world. The projections foresaw a world population of 3.3 billion in 2000. Hence, over a projection horizon of only 55 years these projections underestimated population growth during the second half of the twentieth century by almost a factor of two. This was mostly a consequence of mortality assumptions that were too pessimistic.

The UN population projections of the 1950s and 1960s followed Notestein's model, but refined it and incorporated newly available statistical information. From 1955 onward the UN used a set of model life tables along with models of fertility trends. The UN projections of the late 1950s projected world populations ranging from 4.9 to 6.9 billion for the year 2000. A set of long range scenarios to 2100 was produced by Frejka in (1973). Unlike the earlier UN projections that aimed at providing projections that are 'as accurate as possible' (Frejka, 1996, p. 7), Frejka presented alternative pathways based on different assumptions on when a net reproduction rate of 1.0 would be reached (and assumed to be constant thereafter). Depending on whether it would be reached in 1970 or 2040, the world population in 2000 was projected to range from 4.7 billion to 6.6 billion and in 2100 from 5.7 billion to 15.1 billion. As Frejka (1996) stressed, these projections were merely intended to demonstrate the momentum of population growth and were not forecasts.

Over the last few decades the UN has also published longer-term projections at irregular intervals. In the 1978 projection the medium variant projected 6.2 billion for 2000, 9.8 billion for 2050, and 10.5 billion for 2100. The 1992 UN long-term projection was somewhat higher, giving 10.0 billion for 2050 and 11.2 billion for 2100. The 2002 UN assessment was quite a bit lower, with the medium variant reaching 8.9 billion in 2050 and 9.0 billion in 2100. Several experts have noted that the UN projections are remarkably accurate in projecting populations up to the present (Bongaarts and Bulatao, 2000).

This is true in terms of total population size. But a closer look reveals that there were rather significant errors in the assumptions for both fertility and mortality trends that tended to compensate for each other on total population size, but reinforced each other on population ageing. Systematic comparisons of past UN projections to the actual trends in birth and death rates (Keilman, 1998) show that in the industrialized countries in particular, births rates declined faster and to lower levels than anticipated, while at the same time life expectancy increased to higher levels than expected. A study by Khan and Lutz (2008) differentiated between projection errors based on wrong baseline information and erroneous assumptions about future trends for a number of Asian countries for the period 1975–80 to 1995–2000, as projected in the 1978 assessment. In terms of assumed fertility trends, the projection was on target in some countries, such as the Philippines. In other countries, such as Vietnam, the projection was far too high (a projected total fertility rate (TFR) for 1995–2000 of 4.39 compared with an observed rate of only 2.50) because of an error in the assumed change. In Thailand the projection was far too high (a projected TFR for 1995–2000 of 3.28 compared with an observed one of only 1.90) owing to a high estimate of the 1975–80 baseline and an underestimate of the speed of decline. While it is instructive to study past projection errors, we would learn more if the publications not only listed the assumed numbers, but also described the reasoning underlying the assumptions. This explicit scientific underpinning of assumptions made about the future is a distinguishing feature of the IIASA population projections that will be discussed in the remainder of this section.

Other agencies, including the World Bank, the US Census Bureau, and the US-based Population Reference Bureau (PRB), also produce on regular or occasional-basis longer-term global population projections. The World Bank had published regular country-level population projections since 1978, but recently began producing them for internal use only. The US Census Bureau has regularly published projections under just one set of assumptions for all countries since 1985 (O'Neill et al., 2001), and PRB presents its projections (only total population size without age structures or underlying fertility and mortality assumptions) annually as part of its World Population Data Sheet. Like the UN, none of these global population projections describe the substantive reasoning behind the assumptions made.

The IIASA in Laxenburg, Austria, was established in 1972 as an international research institute (with mostly national academies of sciences as constituent members) to address global change in a forward-looking manner with an emphasis on quantitative systems modelling. While IIASA's main focus has always been on energy and global environment change, IIASA had a demography group from the beginning, first under the leadership of Andrei Rogers (1973–84) and then Nathan Keyfitz (1984–94). The focus in the early years was on developing the methods of multidimensional mathematical demography. These methods incorporate a generalization of the conventional life table and cohort-component approach to population forecasting in which the population is stratified by demographic dimensions beyond age and sex.

Based on these interactions with the environmental modelling groups at IIASA, Wolfgang Lutz, who has led IIASA's World Population Program since 1994, worked with colleagues to translate the alternative scenario approach into sets of systematic numerical population projections. The first such set of numerical population scenarios for Europe was produced by Douglas Wolf, Babette Wils, Lutz, and Sergei Scherbov (1988) in response to a request from IIASA's environmental programs for population scenarios as part of their broader scenarios.

In producing such alternative scenarios, strong efforts were made to bridge the apparent disconnect between the extensive substantive analyses of the drivers of fertility, mortality, and migration trends, and the available numerical projections whose producing agencies typically made little effort to justify their assumptions substantively. In the words of Nathan Keyfitz: 'Forecasting is one of the oldest of demographic activities, and yet it has never been fully integrated with the main body of demographic theory and data' (p. xii, in Lutz, 1994a). Consequently, much of the first book of what turned out to become a series of books on projections, entitled *Future Demographic Trends in Europe and North America: What Can We Assume Today?* (Lutz, 1991), consisted of substantive chapters by leading demographers. The description of projection results was short, making up less than 10 per cent of the pages. The same emphasis characterized the next volume, entitled *The Future Population of the World. What Can We Assume Today?* (Lutz, 1994a), which presented a large number of alternative scenarios to 2050 with extensions to 2100 at the level of 12 world regions.

Because the large number of scenarios (27 scenarios from combining three sets of fertility, mortality, and migration assumptions, plus some special scenarios) was difficult to summarize and the plotted results looked like uncertainty distributions, a methodology was formalized that translated the expert-defined ranges into a set of stochastic population projections by assuming normal distributions for each component and each region. As a result, in 1996, IIASA was the first to produce global-level probabilistic population projections (Lutz, 1996).

All three rounds of probabilistic assessments produced thus far by IIASA have been published in *Nature*. Their titles, 'Doubling of World Population Unlikely' (Lutz et al., 1997), 'The End of World Population Growth' (Lutz et al., 2001), and 'The Coming Acceleration of Global Population Ageing' (Lutz et al., 2008b), illustrate the changing substantive focus, as well as changing public concerns. IIASA and its collaborators also organized broad assessments of methodological issues involved in population projections in general, and probabilistic forecasting in particular. These are summarized in a special issue of *Population and Development Review* entitled 'Frontiers of Population Forecasting' (Lutz et al., 1999b), and a special issue of the *International Statistical Review* entitled 'How to Deal with Uncertainty in Population Forecasting?' (Lutz and Goldstein, 2004).

The IIASA team also developed and began using the multidimensional population projections model to explicitly model population heterogeneity with respect to the level of educational attainment. The model's methodological basis is not only the previously mentioned work of Keyfitz and Rogers, but also relates to the groundbreaking IIASA work of Jim Vaupel and Anatoli Yashin on the dynamics of heterogeneous populations (Vaupel and Yashin, 1985). The first empirical application of this model to treat educational attainment as a key source of observable population heterogeneity was an in-depth analysis of population-development–environment interactions on the island of Mauritius (Lutz, 1994b). The model was further developed and applied to other populations (Lutz et al., 1999a). Over recent years, this approach has been applied to more than 120 countries, producing systematic reconstructions of populations by age, sex, and educational attainment back to 1970 (Lutz et al., 2007), as well as projections (KC et al., 2010). The demographic reconstructions of the age/cohort structure of human capital provided the first consistent time series data of improvements on education by five-year cohorts for most countries of the world. Hence, they formed the basis for major reassessments of the returns to education ranging from economic growth (Lutz et al., 2008a) to the quality of governance and democracy (Lutz et al., 2010). Two recent reviews deal with this methodology for forecasting population heterogeneity (Lutz and KC, 2010, 2011).

IIASA researchers, particularly in the Institute's Energy Program, have a long tradition of producing global long-term scenarios in the context of the Intergovernmental Panel on Climate Change assessments. The Special Report on Emissions Scenarios (Nakicenovic et al., 2000) for the twenty-first century developed and published by IIASA have, for the last decade, served as the main point of reference for environmental modelling communities around the world. Currently, a new generation of scenarios is being developed by the international Integrated Assessment (IA) and Vulnerability and Adaptation scientific communities at IIASA, and elsewhere under the name of SSPs. The SSPs will replace the previous generation of scenarios that had total population size (as a scaling parameter) and gross domestic product (GDP) per-capita as the only socio-economic variables. The new and richer set of socio-economic information provided by these scenarios highlights the independent roles of the gender, age, and education dimensions in sustainable development. This more comprehensive picture is complemented by internally consistent assumptions for GDP trends, which also reflect the impact of human capital and age structure on economic growth. The population and education core of the new SSPs that are likely to form the international point of reference for modelling over the coming decade and beyond will be based on the methodology, numerical assumptions, and results described in this book. For this reason, Chapter 12 will describe our projection results in the context of the SSP framework.

The new global population projection effort presented in this book significantly extends the state of the art by advancing two key priorities of the IIASA population forecasting tradition. First, this effort substantially broadens the basis for incorporating into population projections the best substantive knowledge available in the international scientific community through the systematic involvement of more than 500 population experts around the world. Second, this effort explicitly and systematically incorporates population heterogeneity by level of education, thereby illustrating how educational attainment can and should be routinely added to age and sex as a third demographic dimension. Chapter 2 addresses these key aspects.

Our ambition in this volume is to provide the most comprehensive scientific review of what is known today about the drivers of fertility, mortality, and migration both in the recent past and near future. We demonstrate the feasibility of systematically adding education to age and sex, and therefore make population projections more relevant. We believe that the data and analyses presented here represent one of the most significant integrated and future-oriented scientific efforts of its kind. Leaving aside some encyclopedic volumes on population, the iconic 1973 'Determinants and Consequences of Population Trends' (UN, 1973) summarized global population trends from early human history onward, together with the state of knowledge about these trends. But the 1973 volume says little about human capital and about likely trends in the twenty-first century. These are the topics of the current volume.

1.2 Plan of the book

As our major theme throughout this book is the importance of education, we begin by establishing in Chapter 2 the causal links between educational attainment and the outcomes we examine. This requires discussion of the conditions for causality in the social sciences and the presentation of evidence that these education links satisfy those conditions. Much of this material has not been presented before. It is collected here for the benefit of readers who have not considered the role of education in demography, or who have thought about it but doubted its causal influence because of concerns about reverse causality or selectivity.

Chapter 2 then turns to the role of substantive knowledge in formulating assumptions on which population projections are constructed. We treat these links more formally and comprehensively than has been done before. How these links are handled in this book is summarized here. Details follow in the six background chapters.

The first five of these, Chapters 3–7, cover the traditional demographic components of fertility, mortality, and migration. Fertility and mortality each get two chapters, one for the countries in which fertility or mortality is low, and the other for the countries in which they are high. The low fertility countries—defined as having a current TFR of below 2.5—come first (Chapter 3) because this is the condition to which every country in the world is trending, however haltingly for a minority of them. Indeed 'low,' or at least lower, fertility is our projection by 2050 for every country. Chapter 4 takes up the current high fertility countries, summarizing what we know about the conditions that are driving the likely timing and speed of future fertility decline.

Chapters 5 and 6 follow the same sequence of low mortality countries followed by high mortality countries, and for the same reason: first the state to which all belong or are trending, and then those with the most distance to go, according to the cut-off of a current child mortality rate of above 40/1,000.

Within each of these four chapters, the authors first summarize past trends, comparing and contrasting regional experiences and drawing on the examples of particular countries to illuminate recent developments. They then turn within their respective chapters to theories that purport to explain the trends, casting the net broadly to catch social, economic, political, geographic, and, where relevant, biological and climate theories. From the published research, they bring to bear diverse evidence regarding these theories' contributions, pointing toward the likely courses of future trends.

Each of these chapters then describes in some detail the procedures we employed—surveys and meetings of experts—to solicit expert judgement on arguments about the forces that will likely influence future trends. The authors build on the more general discussion in Chapter 2 of the roles of information and assumptions in population forecasting. Finally, these chapters present the results of the IIASA–Oxford survey, present the outcomes of the deliberations in the thematic expert meetings, and introduce the numerical assumptions that then will be used in the projections. Building from the raw materials constituted of past trends, theories, evidence, and expert judgement, these alternative scenarios for future fertility and mortality are translated into the projections described and analysed in the latter chapters, and summarized numerically in the country appendices.

Chapter 7 deals with international migration. Because migration and the data that describe it are different from fertility and mortality, the structure and content of this chapter are somewhat different. The authors begin with the forces that influence international migration, and then move directly to the severe problems of data availability and comparability. This leads to presentation of a new methodology for deriving international migration flow data from the available stock data, and discussion of the resulting set of bilateral migration flow tables of past movements between all countries. The authors then describe the expert judgement solicitation method and results for migration, and present their derived future scenarios, which become an integral component of the book's overall population projections.

In any projections presentation up to now, these subjects—fertility, mortality, and migration—would together likely complete the core components of the exercise. Here there is another component—education—which we argue is a necessary addition. Chapter 8 covers education worldwide. This chapter, along with the foundational background in Chapter 2 and the projection results, puts on the table a proposal for education to join age and sex as basic dimensions in the study of demography and in the production of demographic projections.

From a description of commonalities in historical education trends, the authors turn to an analytical synthesis of theoretical approaches to this experience and the empirical evidence that helps distinguish among them on the basis of their predictive content. They then present a new projection model for global educational attainment, along with a detailed discussion of its characteristics. Finally, they define alternative education scenarios for the future and discuss their implications for projecting populations.

These six chapters present the core background material from which our projections assumptions and scenarios emerged. The chapters may thereby serve as short, albeit intense, guides to current theory and evidence across the expanse of core demographic investigations.

Amassing the historical and baseline data, the sheer numbers for transforming these scenarios into quantitative projections for 195 countries, by five-year age groups, to the year 2100, by age, sex, and educational level is a substantial effort of sleuthing, comparing, adjusting, standardizing, and coordinating. Chapter 9, which is on data and methods, although quite detailed in its description of our work, is still only a summary. From the chapter, however, readers should be able to assess how the baseline data were constructed, how particular questions of inconsistency, comparability, and completeness were answered, and how the trade-offs between systematic modelling and in-process adjustments were handled.

The alternative scenarios as defined and calculated here for 195 countries for 2010 to 2100, and for five-year age groups for men and women, result in more than five million data points, which are all given in the online data base <http://www.wittgensteincentre.org/dataexplorer>. Some of the most important data are provided in the country-specific appendix tables at the end of the book (Appendix II), which highlight results from the different scenarios at different points in time. The verbal summary of these results is structured into three separate chapters that deal with three specific topics and approaches.

Chapter 10 begins by describing the results of the medium scenario that combines medium fertility, mortality, and migration assumptions with the middle-of-the-road global education trends scenario, and can hence be considered as the most likely scenario. While this scenario is slightly higher than previous IIASA projections owing to a slower than expected fertility decline in parts of Africa, it still shows world population as peaking in the second half of the century, followed by a slight decline. The scenario confirms the previously published notion of an 'end of world population growth' (Lutz et al., 2001). The second part of the chapter illustrates the significant effects of different education scenarios on projected population outcomes, even when the same sets of education-specific fertility and mortality trajectories are assumed.

Chapter 11 addresses population ageing. It begins by questioning the conventional ways of measuring and depicting age and ageing in times of increasing life expectancies and better health conditions at any given age. The chapter introduces the concepts of prospective median age (as opposed to conventional median age) and prospective proportion elderly, where being old is not defined as the proportion above age 65, but rather as the proportion at ages where the remaining life expectancy is 15 years or less. The chapter describes projected future trends in the conventional measures, as well as the new indicators of ageing for all continents and for selected countries. It shows that the ageing trend is universal and pervasive, but that the speed and degree of ageing depend greatly on the indicators chosen.

Chapter 12 puts the new population projections into the context of global sustainable development. The international modelling community in the field of IA and Vulnerability, Risk, and Adaptation has recently agreed to refer to a common set of SSPs that describe alternative future worlds with respect to social and economic mitigation and adaptation challenges. This effort has been conducted in parallel with the population projections exercise described here. In the end, both efforts were merged such that the medium scenario of our projections is identical to SSP2, which is the middle-of-the-road SSP scenario. The other four SSP scenarios span a wide range of future population and education trajectories that combine high and low education-specific fertility, mortality, and migration scenarios with different education scenarios. The chapter concludes with a special set of rather extreme scenarios that try to capture possible catastrophic events, such as serious mortality crises or mass migration induced by the consequences of climate change. More than others, this chapter explicitly addresses the interdependencies between population trends and environmental change.

The book concludes with an Epilogue that synthesizes some of the key findings while pointing at broader implications that go beyond the more technical focus on population and human capital projections. The title 'With education the future looks different' is interpreted in three different ways: education changing our perception of the future; explicit accounting of education heterogeneity resulting in a different projection of the future; and improvements in education leading to a better outlook for the future in terms of health, wealth, democracy, and resilience to environmental change.

References

Bongaarts, J. and Bulatao, R.A. (eds.) 2000 *Beyond Six Billion: Forecasting the World's Population, Panel on Population Projections, Committee on Population, Commission on Behavioral and Social Sciences and Education*. National Academy Press: Washington, DC.

Frejka, T. 1973 *The Future of Population Growth: Alternative Paths to Equilibrium*. John Wiley & Sons: New York.

Frejka, T. 1996 'Long-range Global Population Projections: Lessons Learned'. In: Lutz, W. (ed.) *The Future Population of the World. What Can We Assume Today?*, pp. 3–13 Earthscan: London.

KC, S., Barakat, B., Goujon, A., Skirbekk, V., Sanderson, W.C. and Lutz, W. 2010 'Projection of Populations by Level of Educational Attainment, Age, and Sex for 120 Countries for 2005–2050', *Demographic Research*, 22: 383–472.

Keilman, N. 1998 'How Accurate are the United Nations World Population Projections?' In: Lutz, W., Vaupel, J.W. and Ahlburg, D.A. (eds) *Frontiers of Population Forecasting. A Supplement to Vol. 24, 1998, Population and Development Review*, pp. 15–41. The Population Council: New York.

Khan, H.T.A. and Lutz, W. 2008 'How Well did Past UN Population Projections Anticipate Demographic Trends in Six South-east Asian Countries?' *Asian Population Studies*, 4: 77–95.

King, G. 1973 'Natural and Political Observations and Conclusions Upon the State and Condition of England 1696'. In: Laslett, P. (ed.) *The Earliest Classics: John Graunt and Gregory King*, pp. 31–73. Gregg International, Farnborough.

Knibbs, S.G.H. 1976 [1928] *The Shadow of the World's Future, or, the Earth's Population Possibilities and the Consequences of the Present Rate of Increase of the Earth's Inhabitants*. Reprint edn. Arno Press: New York.

Leslie, P.H. 1945 'On the Use of Matrices in Certain Population Mathematics', *Biometrika*, 33: 213–45.

Lutz, W. (ed.) 1991 *Future Demographic Trends in Europe and North America: What Can We Assume Today?* Academic Press: London.

Lutz, W. (ed.) 1994a *The Future Population of the World. What Can We Assume Today?* Earthscan: London.

Lutz, W. (ed.) 1994b *Population, Development, Environment: Understanding Their Interactions in Mauritius*. Springer-Verlag: Berlin.

Lutz, W. (ed.) 1996 *The Future Population of the World. What Can We Assume Today?* Revised edn. Earthscan: London.

Lutz, W. and Goldstein, J. (eds) 2004 'How to Deal with Uncertainty in Population Forecasting?', *International Statistical Review*, 72: 1–106, 157–208.

Lutz, W. and KC, S. 2010 'Dimensions of Global Population Projections: What do we Know About Future Population Trends and Structures?', *Philosophical Transactions of the Royal Society B: Biological Sciences*, 365: 2779–91.

Lutz, W. and KC, S. 2011 'Global Human Capital: Integrating Education and Population', *Science*, 333: 587–92.

Lutz, W., Sanderson, W.C. and Scherbov, S. 1997 'Doubling of World Population Unlikely', *Nature*, 387: 803–5.

Lutz, W., Goujon, A. and Doblhammer-Reiter, G. 1999a 'Demographic Dimensions in Forecasting: Adding Education to Age and Sex', *Population and Development Review*, 24: 42–58.

Lutz, W., Vaupel, J.W. and Ahlburg, D.A. (eds) 1999b 'Frontiers of Population Forecasting'. A Supplement to Vol. 24, 1998, Population and Development Review. The Population Council: New York.

Lutz, W., Sanderson, W.C. and Scherbov, S. 2001 'The End of World Population Growth', *Nature* 412: 543–5.

Lutz, W., Goujon, A., KC, S. and Sanderson, W.C. 2007 Reconstruction of Populations by Age, Sex and Level of Educational Attainment for 120 Countries for 1970–2000', *Vienna Yearbook of Population Research*, 5: 193–235.

Lutz, W., Crespo Cuaresma, J. and Sanderson, W.C. 2008a 'The Demography of Educational Attainment and Economic Growth', *Science* 319: 1047–8.

Lutz, W., Sanderson, W.C. and Scherbov, S. 2008b 'The Coming Acceleration of Global Population Ageing', *Nature* 451: 716–19.

Lutz, W., Crespo Cuaresma, J. and Abbasi-Shavazi, M.J. 2010 'Demography, Education, and Democracy: Global Trends and the Case of Iran', *Population and Development Review*, 36, 253–81.

Nakicenovic, N., Alcamo, J., Grubler, A., Riahi, K., Roehrl, R.A., Rogner, H.-H. and Victor, N. 2000 *Special Report on Emissions Scenarios (SRES), A Special Report of Working Group III of the Intergovernmental Panel on Climate Change, IPCC Special Reports on Climate Change*. Cambridge University Press: Cambridge.

Notestein, F.W. 1945 'Population: The Long View'. In: Schultz, T.W. (ed.) *Food for the World*, pp. 36–69. University of Chicago Press: Chicago, IL.

Notestein, F.W., Taeuber, I.P., Dudley, K., Coals, A.J. and Kiser, L.E. 1944 *The Future Population of Europe and the Soviet Union: Population Projections, 1940–1970*. League of Nations: Geneva.

O'Neill, B.C., Balk, D., Brickman, M. and Ezra, M. 2001 'A Guide to Global Population Projections', *Demographic Research*, 4: 203–88.

Pearl, R. 1923 *The Rate of Living*. Alfred Knopf: New York.

Pearl, R. 1924 *Studies in Human Biology*. Williams & Wilkins: Baltimore, MD.

United Nations 1973 *The Determinants and Consequences of Population Trends*. Vol. 1. United Nations: New York.

Vaupel, J.W. and Yashin, A.I. 1985 'Heterogeneity's Ruses: Some Surprising Effects of Selection on Population Dynamics', *The American Statistician*, 39: 176–85.

Whelpton, P.K. 1936 'An Empirical Method of Calculating Future Population', *Journal of the American Statistical Association*, 31: 457–73.

Wolf, D., Wils, B., Lutz, W. and Scherbov, S. 1988 'Population Futures for Europe: An Analysis of Alternative Scenarios' (IIASA Working Paper No. WP-88-046). International Institute for Applied Systems Analysis (IIASA): Laxenburg.

CHAPTER 2

HOW EDUCATION DRIVES DEMOGRAPHY AND KNOWLEDGE INFORMS PROJECTIONS

WOLFGANG LUTZ AND VEGARD SKIRBEKK[1]

2.1 Introduction

This chapter provides the background necessary for understanding our approach to projecting population and human capital. First, we investigate the proper place of education in demographic analysis and the evidence for an underlying causal relationship between education and demographic outcomes. Second, we emphasize the importance of explicit assumptions undergirding population projections and detail our procedures for incorporating the views of hundreds of experts into sets of assumptions that drive the Wittgenstein Centre (WIC) projections. Subsequent chapters build on this background in their detailed discussions of trends and arguments in fertility, mortality, migration, and education.

2.2 Adding education as a demographic dimension in global population projections

A major innovative feature of this volume is the systematic addition of educational attainment as a standard demographic dimension in addition to age and sex for demographic analyses, particularly for projections. The underlying assumption is that

[1] Section 2.1 was mainly written by Wolfgang Lutz with input from Vegard Skirbekk, Sections 2.2 and 2.3 have been mainly written by Vegard Skirbekk with input from Wolfgang Lutz.

educational attainment is not just one of many socio-economic factors that matter for population, as it is often viewed in conventional demographic analysis, but is the single most important source of empirically observable population heterogeneity next to age and sex.

The suggestion of routinely adding educational attainment as a dimension of demographic analysis is not new. It was first proposed in a *Population and Development Review* article by Lutz et al. (1998), entitled 'Adding Education to Age and Sex'. More recently, the idea of adding the education factor to demographic analysis was discussed by Lutz (2010) in a commentary entitled, 'Education Will be at the Heart of 21st Century Demography'. It has also been the focus of two recent articles by Lutz and KC, one published in *Philosophical Transactions* entitled, 'Dimensions of Global Population Projections' (2010), and a review article published in *Science* entitled, 'Global Human Capital: Integrating Education and Population' (2011). In the latter paper they argue that an additional demographic dimension should be added routinely to age and sex in population analyses and projections according to three criteria: (i) its explicit consideration should be feasible in terms of available data and methodology; (ii) it should matter substantially in terms of altering population dynamics; and (iii) it should be of interest in its own right in terms of its social and economic implications. Lutz and KC (2010, 2011) address these criteria systematically, reaching the conclusion that educational attainment is the only additional demographic dimension that meets all three of these criteria and should hence be routinely and systematically included as a standard demographic dimension. On a more substantive level, this systematic addition of educational attainment can be viewed as adding a 'quality' dimension to the consideration of the quantity of people.

Before a detailed discussion of the effects of educational attainment on demographic and other outcomes, it is useful to examine the more conventional standard demographic dimensions of age and sex. One counter-argument to giving educational attainment such prominent standing is that age and sex are natural determinants, while education is a purely social construction. But let us look critically at the 'naturalness' of these two characteristics. Our thinking about age is dominated by what can be called 'fixed chronological age', defined as the time measured in years that has elapsed since birth. However, there are many different ways of looking at age and ageing as referring not just to chronological age, but to biological, mental, and social maturity. These different conceptions are not only constructs by scientists, but are deeply embedded in traditional cultures. For example, demographers in Australia had problems constructing life tables for the aboriginal population because in that culture individuals often did not know their chronological age. Age and ageing were seen as a succession through different life cycle phases that varied in length depending on different dimensions of maturity as assessed by the elders. Another example is the frequent occurrence of 'age heaping' in the censuses of developing countries in which people are not able to state their precise age. The 'heaping' often approximates age to a round number, such as 40 or 50.

Even in modern Western societies it has become fashionable to point to the many shortcomings of the deeply engrained concept of chronological age as a basic determinant of behaviour and social organization. This is reflected in recent anti-age discrimination legislation that makes it illegal to use chronological age as a decisive criterion for many relevant decisions. Even universities are turning from chronological age as a criterion for support of 'young' scientists to duration-defined criteria such as 'time since doctorate'. The European courts recently decided that, as a matter of principle, 'seniority based earnings systems' are illegitimate because they represent a form of age discrimination. As to public perception of the issue, probably the most relevant change has been the rethinking of the meaning of age with respect to health status and remaining life expectancy. It has become a frequent saying that '60 is the new 50' or '70 is the new 60,' implying that people aged 70 today are in many important dimensions equivalent to those aged 60 some time ago. There is scientific evidence supporting this popular perception.

Demographers are slowly picking up these new ideas about redefining age and ageing. But the idea of adjustment is not new; Ryder (1975) and Shryock and Siegel (1993) have made suggestions in this direction, and Fuchs (1984) even made the more general point that ages should be adjusted for changing life expectancy routinely in the same way that financial variables are adjusted for inflation. Lutz et al. (2008) have applied these ideas to recalculating adjusted ageing indicators on a global level. Sanderson and Scherbov (2010) have published such adjustments based on trends in age-specific disability rates rather than just mortality. They write:

> Disability-free life expectancies, which describe how many years of life are spent in good health, have also been increasing, often as fast as unconditional life expectancies, because of decreases in age-specific disability rates. For example, in the United States, the proportion disabled in the age group 65 to 74 declined from 14.2% in 1982 to 8.9% in 2004–5. Thus, fixed chronological ages do not work well in evaluating the effect of age structure changes on health care costs, because most of those costs occur in the last few years of life, which happen at ever later ages as life expectancies increase. (p. 1287).

Although measures of age-specific functioning based on disability may be biased by, for instance, social and cultural influences—which could potentially bias comparisons across cohorts and nations—research also based on objective measures of performance, including assessments of cognitive functioning based on standardized tests, show that there are, in fact, improvements across subsequent cohorts among those aged 50 and above (Gerstorf et al., 2011; Skirbekk et al., 2013). Such gains are likely to have taken place earlier in some countries than in others, partly as educational expansions have taken place at different periods, which thereby could contribute to differences in in age-specific cognitive functioning across countries. This could be a reason why many countries that are chronologically young, such as India, have been found to be cognitively 'older' than demographically older regions such as the Nordic countries (Skirbekk et al., 2012).

Chapter 11 presents the results of our new projections in terms of indicators based on different definitions of 'age'. Here it suffices to say that the measurement and interpretation of age is neither natural nor uncontested, and clearly contains important elements of social construction. As discussed in the Epilogue, this also has far-reaching consequences for future social and economic policies.

As to the second standard differentiation in demographic analysis and forecasting, gender or sex, the ubiquitous distinction between men and women, has also been losing some of its self-evident nature and is increasingly understood to be, at least in part, a social construction. Even the purely biological distinction between the two sexes is not as clear as it was assumed to be. An increasingly vocal transgender lobby is complaining about being forced to make choices that are perceived as violations of the group's human rights. In Australia, the courts recently ruled that in all official documents persons must not be forced to state their sex as either male or female, but can also choose 'indeterminate, intersex, or unspecified'. Similarly, Nepal's Supreme Court has ordered the government to alter passports so that transgender persons no longer have to describe themselves as male or female. With respect to the more socially determined gender roles and norms, there is little doubt that the traditional male/female distinction is increasingly blurred, while female behavioural patterns and lifestyles have become less distinguishable from those of males. This is also reflected in the changing sex differentials in mortality and migration. In many countries, female smoking behaviour now mirrors that of men (and in some cases increases, while male smoking declines). Indeed, the male–female difference in life expectancy is, in some cases, less pronounced than the educational differences. This will be discussed in detail in Chapter 4. A similar change in traditional sex differentials can also be observed for migration, where increasing female labour force participation is leading to more female labour migration.

In sum, in twenty-first-century demography traditional age and gender distinctions are losing their previously unquestioned 'natural' and absolute deterministic power, while at the same time educational attainment is increasingly recognized as a key determinant of people's behaviour and life course outcomes, with significant educational differentials from cradle to grave (Lutz, 2010). Hence, we no longer face a situation in which there are presumably natural factors (age and sex) that are on an ontologically different level from other factors that are assumed to be merely socially constructed (e.g. educational attainment). We now understand that all three factors have elements of social construction, as well as real physiological differences. The fact that there also is a physiological impact of education on the synaptic structure of our brains with consequences for our perception, memory, personality, and behaviour is not well-known among social scientists and will be discussed in section 2.2.1.

2.2.1 Functional causality in the context of intervention sciences

An important prerequisite for suggesting the addition of educational attainment as a third demographic dimension is the assumption that the effects of education on demographic behaviour and outcomes are not spurious associations, but real and causal in nature. A comprehensive review of the ongoing and controversial social science debate about what constitutes causality and under which conditions it can be assumed or rejected is beyond our scope. Instead, we present our working definition of causality that is employed in this book. This definition includes a brief discussion of the new epistemological concept of 'intervention sciences' and the associated concept of 'functional causality'. In presenting these concepts, we specify three criteria that need to be met in order to consider the effect of educational attainment on demographic outcomes as causal, and discuss the extent to which we see these criteria as being met.

An important starting point is the view that the assessment of causality in the social sciences is context-specific. In this book the context is the field of demographic analysis and, more specifically, the field of population forecasting. As discussed above, it is conventionally taken for granted in this field that a person's age and sex have direct and stable causal relationships to many different demographic outcomes (births, deaths, migrations, etc.), and therefore changing age and sex structures of populations can be meaningfully used to forecast future trends in demographic outcomes. This is the basic paradigm that underlies the cohort–component projection model of population projections which, as discussed in Chapter 1, is the virtually unchallenged and universally used approach to population forecasting. In this specific context we propose that educational attainment should henceforth be routinely added to age and sex using the well-established methods of multidimensional cohort–component projection.

Another relevant epistemological consideration in this context is a distinction between 'identity sciences' and 'intervention sciences,' as recently suggested by Lutz (2012). Under this view of the social sciences and humanities there is a basic distinction that depends on the goal of the analysis. *Identity sciences*, on the one hand, address the questions of 'Who are we?' and 'Where are we coming from?', both at the micro-level of individuals and at the macro-level of societies. These questions, which can include both qualitative and quantitative components, relate to a more general view of how the world functions, and do not refer to any specific goal of forecasting or directly influencing the course of events. *Intervention sciences*, on the other hand, try to understand how the most important forces of change function in order to predict the future evolution of the system. The predictions can be based on no intervention, or on alternative interventions and their likely consequences. As human systems are not strictly deterministic, all such assessments need to consider uncertainty, either probabilistically or in the form of alternative scenarios, as is done in this volume. In the research effort presented here, we clearly take an intervention sciences approach. This implies an understanding of causality. We are satisfied with *functional causality,* which is based on plausible and not contradicted functional relationships between forces that can be assumed to hold for the societies and for the periods to which they are applied. This is distinguished from *strong causality,* which is harder to assess in the social sciences and typically can only be tested through planned randomized or natural experiments. This approach has been inspired by the work on interventions and functional causal models of Pearl (2000).

The specific distinction between functional and strong causality in the context of intervention sciences is first introduced here and will be elaborated elsewhere by the first author of this chapter. We note only that strong causality, as it is often assumed in the natural sciences, is almost impossible to establish in the social sciences. This is partly owing to the difficulty of conducting planned experiments with human subjects and societies without violating human rights, and also to the fact that, unlike in the natural sciences, it cannot be assumed that all individuals and all societies around the world behave and react in the same ways, even if the external conditions are the same. In a comprehensive review on causation in demography Bhrolcháin and Dyson (2007) specify ten criteria that are supportive of causal inference regarding demographic change. The three criteria that will be discussed have been inspired by their work.

The following review of the literature about the effects of education on health/mortality and fertility cites many findings from so-called natural experiments. When such experiments support causality for one specific population group in one country at one time, it is far from clear that this demonstrated relationship also holds in very different cultures at different stages of social and economic development. Such observations can strengthen the case for assuming more generally valid causality, but they cannot prove it for all societies and all times. Hence, in order to use such relationships as a basis for projections for all countries in the world we do not attempt to demonstrate strong causality, but focus on establishing functional causality through assessing the following three criteria:

(a) There must be *strong empirically observed associations* between the two factors studied, and those associations should hold across different societies and for different subgroups of the population, and for different points in time (considering the appropriate lag structures). The case for a causal relationship is significantly strengthened if this association is observed both at the individual level (across people and households) and the aggregate level (across societies), in particular when it can be found in longitudinal cohort studies. As stated earlier, the presence of the effect in (natural) experiments further strengthens the case for general functional causality, although this does not automatically imply validity across all societies. In this and the following chapters we present empirical evidence regarding such empirical associations.

(b) There must be a *plausible narrative about the mechanisms* through which one force influences the other. This explanation must tend to the sequence and timing of events according to the general principle that the cause must always lie before the consequence. In the social sciences it is important to consider that the expectation of a coming event, not just the event itself, qualifies as a cause of behaviour. We discuss what is known about how education influences the brain and behaviour. The more specific mechanisms through which changes in level of education affect fertility and health/mortality will be the topic of the following sections.

(c) *Other obvious competing explanations* of the observed associations should be explicitly and systematically studied, and ruled out as playing dominant roles. We examine the two principal alternative explanations of the observed associations between educational attainment and various outcomes, which are self-selection and reverse causality.

Self-selection would imply, in the case of the education–health/mortality link, for example, that the observed strong association is explained by the genetic endowment of some individuals with both better health and higher intelligence, resulting in both better educational attainment and greater longevity. We will review several natural experiments that test this hypothesis at the individual level. First, there is an aggregate-level argument that provides strong evidence against self-selection as the cause of the strong association between education and health. Assuming, for the purpose of argument, a time-invariant distribution of genetic predispositions in any population, then an expansion of educational attainment to broader segments of the population should lead to a reduction in the health/mortality advantage, if self-section were a dominant factor. Moving from an elitist educational structure in which only a very select group of people could get educated to a more inclusive one, people from the bottom part of the distribution would move to the educated category, thus reducing the degree of selectivity. However, empirical evidence from around the world clearly shows that in virtually all populations an expansion of education (in some cases even a very rapid expansion, such as in South Korea) has resulted in significant increases in overall health and a continuation of the relative health advantage of the better-educated people.

In comprehensive global assessments of the relationship between education and adult health and mortality KC and Lentzner (2010) and Baker et al. (2011) also show that at a given time (thus implying a similar global frontier knowledge in medical technology) on all continents (i.e. for very different levels of socio-economic development) for all adult ages and for men and women alike, the less educated segments of the population have significantly higher mortality and morbidity (measured in terms of activities of daily living) than those who are better educated. This evidence is inconsistent with the proposition that self-selection explains the general patterns of association between educational attainment and related outcomes. The other alternative explanation, reverse causality, is largely irrelevant with respect to mortality because most adult deaths happen after completion of education and, by definition, mortality removes people from the study population. If health is considered instead of mortality the pattern becomes more complex because children with health problems may be less likely to attend school and more likely to experience premature death. While this may be the case in some developing countries, the evidence from highly developed countries where even children with serious health problems receive the best possible education also shows strong education gradients in mortality.

The reverse causality argument could be more relevant for fertility. For example, girls dropping out of school because of pregnancy, or being discouraged from further education because of the presence of young children, might well have lower educational attainment. While this undoubtedly happens, the relative importance of this factor can be tested empirically for higher education that happens after the beginning of reproductive age. But for basic education the causality can only go from basic education to fertility because the basic education of girls is generally completed before reproductive age. Accordingly, the empirical evidence presented in this volume and other major surveys (e.g. Bongaarts, 2010) shows significant and robust negative associations between education received before reproductive age and subsequent levels of fertility. Hence, reverse causation is unlikely to play a dominant role in explaining the strong empirical associations between education, on the one hand, and fertility and mortality, on the other.

Before discussing more deeply the empirical evidence concerning the causal effects of education on health/mortality and fertility-related behaviour, we address the beginning of the causal chain, the basic biological mechanisms through which learning and, in particular, systematic learning through formal education changes the physiology of the brain. Modern brain research leaves no doubt that every learning experience, and especially repeated experiences, changes our brains physiologically by building new synapses that store the information about our experiences, and thus produce learning. Eric Kandel, who received the 2000 Nobel Prize in Medicine and Physiology for his path-breaking work on memory, remarked: 'Let us repeat this point once more and now it is stored in your brains, and when you walk out through this door you are physiologically a different person from when you walked into the room' (Austrian Science Day, New York, 10 September 2011). In his book *In Search of Memory* (2007), Kandel provides a systematic account of what is known about the storage of information in the brain and how learning experiences change brain structures for the rest of a person's life. He notes that even twins with identical genes have different brains because of different life experiences (p. 218). Because such physiological changes are difficult to show anatomically in humans, Kandel studied them primarily in Aplysia (a sea slug with particularly large neurons), for which he could demonstrate that learning experiences (such as repeated stimuli of the tail) led to the growth of new synaptic connections, anatomical change that involves the synthesis of new protein (p. 256). In humans, specialized learning and repeated activity changes the size of certain parts of the brains and reduces the energy used for certain activities once routine has been gained (Elbert et al., 1995; Jenkins et al., 1990). While neuroscience is still far from a full understanding of the process of learning, neurological studies have confirmed that neurological structures, brain volumes, and cortical thickness can be affected by additional education (Mårtensson et al., 2012; Richards and Hatch, 2011).

If it is accepted that education changes our brains and how we process and store information, which, according to Kandel (2007), is also the basis for our sense of personality, then it follows that education also changes other cognitive dimensions, including our perception of the environment, our view of the future, our degree of rationality, and ultimately our behaviour resulting from these mental processes. Indeed, empirical studies show that better educated individuals tend to have a longer investment horizon, be more risk averse, and have fewer mental health problems (Meijer et al., 2009; Murphy and O'Leary, 2010; van der Pol, 2011). Psychosocial factors, such as a sense of control, anxiety, depression, social isolation, and stress are also linked to school attainment level (Matthews et al., 2010).

Regarding general cognitive functioning, several studies that assess the effects of exogenous changes in compulsory education show that cognitive functioning is related to the length of schooling and give strong evidence that this effect is causal. Brinch and Galloway (2011) investigated the lengthening of Norwegian compulsory schooling and found that it caused a growth in general intelligence by more than a fifth of a standard deviation for male conscripts. Glymour et al. (2008) examined extensions to compulsory schooling laws in the USA and found that these reforms improved cognitive function among seniors. Schneeweis et al. (2014) investigated the long-term effects of extensions to education on mental ability among seniors in Europe, finding that these education reforms significantly improved functioning at several cognitive ability levels, including immediate recall.

2.2.2 Effects of education on health and mortality

Moving from the effect of education on general cognitive functioning to the effects on health-related behaviour and mortality, we first note two recent comprehensive assessments and then a larger number of specific studies. Baker et al. (2011) offer a meta-analysis of the education effect on adult mortality with data from 29 studies with a total of 69 reported effects covering a sample of more than 20 million adults. All studies consistently showed that less education was associated with higher likelihood of death. The pooled education effect showed that people with low education (lower secondary or less) had a 46 per cent higher probability of dying than people with high school or higher education. This study stressed that these effects are likely causal, pointing, in particular, to the neurological and cognitive impact of schooling as a mechanism. The aforementioned survey by KC and Lentzner (2010) illustrates the effect of education on health and disability, using data primarily from the World Health Survey. They show that consistently and across all ages and continents, for both men and women separately, higher education is associated with lower rates of disability. The association across four education categories is in all cases monotonic, with the change from no education to primary usually showing the strongest impact on health. They also provide an extensive review of the possible mechanisms by which education influences health and mortality (including behavioural risk factors, psychosocial factors, and multifactor models), which strongly suggests that these are, indeed, causal mechanisms at work.

In terms of more specific studies, between 1949 and 1962 Sweden implemented a one-year increase in compulsory schooling where each year children in a number of municipalities were exposed to the reform and others were kept as controls ($N = 1{,}247{,}867$, of whom 92,351 died). A study based on the resulting data found that this one-year extension reduced both-sex mortality risk from overall cancer, lung cancer, and accidents. In addition, women reduced their risk of cardiovascular disease mortality and men reduced their death risk from external causes (Lager and Torssander, 2012). Overall, there was significantly lower mortality in the group that took the longer compulsory schooling, and this group had lower mortality from causes known to be related to education, such as smoking. Similarly, Lleras-Muney (2005) found that variation in compulsory schooling in the USA is causally associated with adult mortality, such that an additional year of education lowers the probability of dying in the next 10 years by 3–6 percentage points.

However, effects are not uniform across all studies. In France, Albouy and Lequien (2009) studied the effects of the increase in minimum school leaving age from 13 to 14 for cohorts born after 1923, and later for an additional two years for cohorts born after 1953. Based on regression discontinuity and two-stage estimation approaches, the authors found that these reforms did not result in significant declines in mortality. Changes in compulsory schooling in England were identified as reducing morbidity levels in one study (Silles, 2009); however, Clark and Royer (2010) failed to find effects of the English compulsory schooling extensions of 1947–53 on mortality. In Sweden, an extension of schooling from seven or eight years, depending on municipality, to nine years nationally, affecting cohorts born between 1946 and 1957, reduced male mortality up to age 50 for those assigned to the reform, but the gains were erased by increased mortality later on (Meghir et al., 2012). An analysis of several European school reforms found that the beneficial educational effects tended to be concentrated among men, with few effects for women (Gathmann et al., 2012).While these studies of changes in the length of compulsory education provide good examples of natural experiments that avoid some of the concerns about self-selection and generally support (and never contradict) the case for assuming a causal relationship of varying strength from length of schooling to health, they only refer to small changes in length of schooling in industrialized countries with high levels of public health services.

A recent study on differential trends in life expectancy in the USA actually finds widening differences by level of education (Olshansky et al., 2012). Drawing from a range of data sources, they find that in 2008 US adult men and women with fewer than 12 years of education had life expectancies not much better than that of all adults in the 1950s and 1960s. They find that since then the education differentials have widened, and their analysis suggests that in addition to its indirect effects through giving access to better jobs and higher incomes, education also has a direct effect on both health and duration of life. As a consequence, they suggest policies of educational enhancements for all segments of the population.

Now we turn to the broader global pattern.

There is ample empirical evidence of a pervasive pattern in which mortality levels tend to decrease with the level of education over time, both at the individual and aggregate levels, and in both poorer settings with high income inequality and richer, more egalitarian nations (Govingdasamy and Ramesh, 1997; KC and Lentzner, 2010; Murphy et al., 2006). Education has been found in many countries to correlate with longer lives, better health, and improved physical and mental functioning (Dikshit et al., 2012; Mackenbach et al., 1999; Sachan et al., 2012; Shkolnikov et al., 2012). Although most of the research into education effects on morbidity or mortality has focused on Western countries, negative relationships of education with morbidity have also been identified in South Korea, Japan, and other countries (Khang et al., 2004; Kondo, 2012). Educational differences in health are often larger in poorer nations; for example, child mortality differentials by maternal education are relatively high in sub-Saharan Africa and Asia (Monden and Smits, 2012). An extensive multi-level study covering all recent Demographic and Health Surveys (DHS) showed that maternal education is the single most important determinant of child survival at all levels and that its effects on child survival are clearly stronger than those of household wealth or income (Fuchs et al., 2010;

Pamuk et al. 2011). There are also large differences in health by human capital for seniors in developing countries, as evidenced in India, where self-rated health is significantly positively related to education (Alam and Karan, 2011).

Larger data sets that go beyond the analysis of specific surveys that have limited sample size can improve the knowledge base and increase the ability to identify causal effects. Administrative registration data with high or full national coverage spanning longer time periods allow large-scale population-based research to be carried out with a decreased risk of sample bias. Such datasets are increasingly available for research purposes in a number of nations, including the Nordic countries. Such data sources have been used to investigate the effect of education on lifetime outcomes, including analysing the effects of schooling on morbidity and lifespans. Some of the largest available studies, including those with full population coverage and a relatively broad set of control variables, suggest a strong positive association of education with longevity (Brønnum-Hansen et al., 2004; Remes et al., 2010; Strand et al., 2010).

Another important source of information is panel surveys based on repeated interviews of a sample of individuals and containing in-depth questions and tests. These data sets facilitate a significantly better understanding of causal mechanisms by allowing for control of additional individual characteristics beyond what is usually found in register data. However, such surveys often lack the size of administrative national registers and their coverage can, potentially, be biased. For instance, ageing surveys such as SHARE exclude the institutionalized population in the base sample (Börsch-Supan et al., 2008), which could create a sample bias and limit the general validity and reliability of estimates of the effects of education on health. However, such surveys can follow changes in health and function over time in more detail than administrative data registers. Several analyses of these surveys find that education has a positive effect on health and cognitive functioning, even after controlling for ability levels early in life (Richards et al., 2004; Whalley and Deary, 2001).

Finally, analyses of pairs of monozygotic twins to identify the effects of education represent an important approach as they can control for inherited influences. When comparing twins with the same genetic make up and shared prenatal influences, one can isolate and measure the environmental effects of education, while the role of nature (and the prenatal environment) is held constant. There are, however, limitations to twin studies such as relatively small sample size and the possibility that twins could be a selected group, so that the effects may be less representative of the whole population. Still, studies of monozygotic twins represent an important way of identifying the effects of education after controlling for genetic influences. Several twin studies have found a strong positive effect of education on, for instance, mental health (Haworth et al., 2008; Rodgers et al., 2008).

The evidence discussed here of strong positive associations between education and health in different countries and at different points in time, combined with the pervasive evidence from several natural experiments, makes it very plausible to assume that there are clear functional causal mechanisms connecting education to better health and lower mortality. These mechanisms can be assumed to remain valid in the future in the context of population projections by level of education. And, as discussed in section 2.2.1, there is strong evidence to doubt that this consistent and strong empirical association is dominated by a self-selection effect.

2.2.3 Effects of education on fertility

Turning to the effects of education on fertility, the pattern is more complex. Because survival is a universally shared value, people prefer to survive and see their family members survive. Hence, higher empowerment through education can be expected to translate into better survival with a clear unidirectional effect. It is not the same with fertility, where ideal/desired family size is, to a large degree, culturally determined and where higher empowerment of women through education may lead either to lower fertility (under conditions in which actual fertility is higher than desired) or to higher fertility (where desired exceeds actual fertility). The case is further complicated by the fact that couples have children, and disagreements can arise between the man and woman, the outcomes of which are influenced by female education. Female education changes the power of the relationship, and tends to be associated with postponement of childbearing during the finite fertile segment of the female lifecycle. Finally, for higher levels of education there is the possibility of reverse causation, that is, young women dropping out of education because of a pregnancy. In spite of this complexity, the negative association is pervasive for almost all societies, except premodern ones and the most advanced egalitarian ones.

Because the effect of education on fertility is expected to vary over the long-term course of demographic transition, it is instructive to start with the long-term historic trends in fertility differentials. Skirbekk (2008) provides a comprehensive meta-analysis of available data sets on historical differentials by level of education and/or social status from 1300 to the present. His analysis illustrates that relative wealth (typically of the man) or position in a social hierarchy was positively associated with the level of fertility in the pre-demographic transition era. A plausible explanation for this is that under the prevalence of very high fertility norms—as can be found in virtually all traditional pre-transition societies—higher social status facilitates a better achievement of these ideals. Furthermore, higher social status women tended to have better health status and receive more support from nannies so that they could physically have more children.

Over time, however, this positive effect of social status on fertility became less pronounced, particularly in the latter half of the twentieth century. Indeed, female education has been negatively associated with fertility for as long as education has been measured. Particularly in developing countries that are still in the midst of the fertility transition, the negative association is very strong. In Ethiopia, for example, the DHS data show that women without formal education have more than six children, on average, whereas women with secondary or higher education have only two children.

Increasing education levels are widely considered a key cause of fertility decline during the demographic transition (Basu, 2002; Cleland, 2002; Martin and Juarez, 1995). Education tends to be associated with a delay in the onset of childbearing and lower fertility outcomes. A close examination of the mechanisms at work suggests that these effects are causal and not solely driven by selection into schooling (e.g. those who would have fewer children in any case attain a higher education). Education has been found to depress fertility preferences, raise female autonomy, increase contraceptive practice, raise the opportunity costs of having children, and postpone the timing of childbearing (Gustafsson, 2001; Jejeebhoy, 1995; Kravdal, 2002).

In a comprehensive review of the evidence for sub-Saharan Africa, Bongaarts (2010) examines the factors that contribute to this pervasive negative association. Looking at data from DHS surveys in 30 countries, he demonstrates that education levels are positively associated with demand for, and use of, contraception and negatively associated with fertility and desired family size. He also finds that as education rises, fertility is lower at a given level of contraceptive use, contraceptive use is higher at a given level of demand, and demand is higher at a given level of desired family size. He concludes that the most plausible explanations for these shifting relationships are that better educated women marry later and less often, use contraception more effectively, have more knowledge about and access to contraception, have greater autonomy in reproductive decision-making, and are more motivated to implement demand because of the higher opportunity costs of unintended childbearing. Given this convincing narrative it is indicative that Bongaarts chose to give his paper the title 'The Causes of Educational Differences in Fertility in Sub-Saharan Africa'.

Regarding the possibility of reverse causation in high fertility countries, the most likely case is young women stopping their education because of an early pregnancy resulting in a birth. While a pattern has been found, particularly in some African contexts, it is only a minor factor and cannot explain the overall pattern. This can be demonstrated by looking at educational differentials up to junior secondary education, that is, before reproductive age, where the differentials are most pervasive. Alternatively, one can restrict the sample to women who only started childbearing after age 18 or 22; within this sub-sample the association appears to be equally strong. Some of this empirical analysis will be discussed in Chapter 3.

In many developing countries age at marriage is another important intermediate variable in the relationship. There is strong evidence that early basic education is associated with later age at marriage. In Vietnam, for instance, longer education has been found to increase marital choice. Using household data, where war disruptions and spatial indicators of schooling supply act as statistical instruments, it is estimated that a year of additional schooling reduces the probability of an arranged marriage by about 14 percentage points (Smith et al., 2009).

As mentioned earlier, in low fertility industrialized countries the differentials tend to be smaller, but the association with female education is still clearly negative in most cases. This also seems to be related to the timing of the onset of childbearing. Education could also have self-reinforcing effects on fertility timing, where increasing levels of education create a race where one needs to have more and more schooling in order to be 'on par' or better than others of the same sex-cohort group (Lutz et al., 2006; Skirbekk and KC, 2012). This can imply that education results in fertility being increasingly postponed for each successive generation, as education levels gradually increase and more years of schooling are needed to reach a given percentile in the educational distribution. Several natural experiments suggest causal effects from educational extensions to a delay in the age of fertility in early adulthood. This phenomenon has been identified in very different contexts where school reforms have taken place, for instance in Norway and Turkey (Kýrdar et al., 2011; Monstad et al., 2008).

One study (Skirbekk et al., 2004) uses Swedish school age laws that cause variation in the school leaving age based on birth month (those born in January exit school at an age 11 months older than those born in December). As all children born in a calendar year enter and exit school at the same time, and their month of birth is random, the resulting variation in the school leaving age is not likely to be related to other individual characteristics. Skirbekk et al. (2004) found that this variation in school leaving age had strong effects on parental age at the first childbirth. The difference of 11 months in the age at leaving school between women who were born in the two consecutive months December and January implied a delay in the age at first birth of 4.9 months. This may be explained by the fact that there exists a relatively rigid sequencing of demographic events in early adulthood, and the age at graduation from school emerges as an important factor in determining the timing of family formation. These findings are also relevant for studying the level of fertility because postponement of childbearing not only depresses aggregate period fertility measures through the tempo effect, but tends to reduce cohort fertility through apparent tempo-quantum interactions (Kohler et al., 2006).

The global empirical evidence concerning the association between female education and fertility is comprehensively reviewed and discussed in Chapters 3, 4, and 9. Here it suffices to say that the assumptions used in our projections assume a gradual narrowing of educational fertility differentials with the progress in demographic transitions. But the assumptions also consider country- and culture-specific differences, taking account, in particular, of certain countries where differentials are already very low.

In conclusion, we emphasize the convincing narrative of a causal effect of female education on the advance of the fertility transition in terms of the famous three preconditions of a lasting fertility decline as identified by Ansley Coale (1973). First, fertility must be regarded as being within the realm of conscious choice. It is evident that the transition from a more fatalistic attitude to a more rational planning attitude is closely associated with the transition from illiteracy to a more educated status. Second, there must be objective advantages to lower fertility. This is where the higher opportunity costs for more educated women come into play. Moreover, educated women tend to have higher aspirations for the education of their children and understand that they will be better able to afford this if they have fewer children. This corresponds to Gary Becker's (1981) point of a quantity–quality transition. Third, Coale stresses that acceptable means of fertility regulation must be readily available. Here, again, there is ample evidence from all societies that more educated women find better and easier access to family planning services and contraception than less educated women, and are better empowered to overcome possible objections from their husbands and extended families. Surveys show that in every society, from least developed Mali and Niger to the socially most developed Nordic countries, less educated women have a higher rate of unwanted pregnancies than more highly educated women.

All of the literature and evidence presented in this section suggest that all three of the specified criteria are being met to assume functional causality from higher education to better health, and thus lower mortality for both men and women, and from higher female education to lower fertility, at least over the course of the demographic transition. This causal presumption, in turn, underlies the assumptions and scenarios that are the foundation for the population projections presented in this book. We now turn to the knowledge base of these assumptions and to the way they can be derived through expert argumentation.

2.3 How are the assumptions for population projections defined?

'Can Knowledge Improve Forecasts' was the title of a famous paper by Nathan Keyfitz (1982), in which he expresses the view that demographic trends are easier to forecast than many social and economic trends, which are often seen as drivers of fertility and mortality. But how should the demographic trends themselves be forecast? What should be the basis for assumptions about future fertility, mortality, and migration trends? Ahlburg and Lutz (1999), in the introduction to a special issue of *Population and Development Review* on the topic 'Frontiers of Population Forecasting' (Lutz et al., 1999), interpret this view of Keyfitz (after discussions with Nathan Keyfitz at the International Institute for Applied Systems Analysis (IIASA)) by suggesting that demographic trends should not be entirely derived from other forecasts (as in the World 3 Model of the 'Limits to Growth' by Meadows et al., 1972), or based on blind extrapolation or replication of past trends. Instead, they suggest summarizing the scientific community's knowledge base concerning future demographic trends through a structured process of expert solicitation. This view was also inspired by the influential work of Armstrong and colleagues on forecasting outside the realm of demography (Collopy and Armstrong, 1992), which demonstrated that structured judgement outperforms either judgement alone or a statistical model alone (Ahlburg and Lutz, 1999). This insight guides the approach chosen in this study.

In parallel to the scientific discussion, the practice in statistical offices has been moving in this direction of using structured expert judgement for defining the assumptions. Virtually all national statistical agencies in the world, as well as inter-governmental agencies, such as the United Nations (UN) (until recently) and Eurostat, have been producing regular population projections by age and sex, following the cohort–component projection method with assumptions on future fertility, mortality, and migration based on expert judgement.

It is worth noting here that the UN Population Division recently (since the 2010 assessment) decided to go in a very different direction, which bases assumptions largely on a statistical model using only past national level time series within the context of a particular structure, and disregards whatever substantive knowledge there exists in the international scientific community about the country- and region-specific factors influencing future fertility, mortality, and migration trends. A detailed comparison of the approach chosen in this volume with the new UN approach is currently in progress and will be published elsewhere. At this point, is suffices to say that the two approaches follow quite different forecasting philosophies. While the new UN approach essentially assumes that the best we can assume is that the future will see a replication of past trends interpreted within the framework of their model we chose to follow the alternative path of making the substantive arguments upon which our forecasts rest explicit. We did this by improving the structured procedures for soliciting country-specific expert knowledge and significantly enlarging the number of experts involved in the process to over 500. And, as will be described in detail in the following chapters, the substantive expert assessment of alternative arguments relevant for the future trends is blended with formal statistical models much in the spirit recommended by Collopy and Armstrong (1992).

In this section we first review the current practice of statistical agencies in the European region and note a survey that indicated near consensus on the need for improving the procedures by which expert knowledge is assessed as the basis for making assumptions. The main result of the survey was that the offices charged with making population projections would welcome more structured interactions with the demographic research community. We then discuss the proposal for a systematic argument-based approach to making demographic assumptions that was developed under the European Commission's 'MicMac' project ('Bridging the Micro–Macro Gap in Population Forecasting', <http://www.nidi.nl/micmac>) and has been operationalized for the projections presented in this volume.

In 2005, all national statistical offices (NSOs) of the European Union (EU) countries were asked to provide information on their procedures for producing their most recent population projections. Each office received from Eurostat an IIASA-designed questionnaire, which 21 out of 25 NSOs returned. The results of this survey were documented in Prommer and Wilson (2006) and Lutz (2009). The most common procedure was to create scenarios that cover a 'plausible' range of future fertility, mortality, and migration. The involvement of external experts and meetings was generally considered very important, but all NSOs suggested that the methods used to make assumptions could use further improvements.

As the most desirable procedure, one NSO explicitly stated: 'We base our assumption on facts and reasoning. We try to present as many facts as possible and we also try to specify where we are uncertain and show how and why we have decided in a certain way. We also try to describe the reasoning behind the assumptions thoroughly in the publication about the population projection'.

The NSOs were also asked about the best directions for such improvements. The following three improvement options were most frequently endorsed: (i) 'have a more systematic review of all the substantive arguments behind the assumptions'; (ii) 'have some structured interactions with the European demographic research community about the state of the art in our knowledge about future demographic trends'; and (iii) 'involve more experts'.

In a nutshell, this extensive and informative enquiry among EU national statistical offices shows that all national offices consider the current practice for defining the assumptions for population projections as suboptimal and needing further improvement. The results further indicate the direction in which to move: have a more systematic review of the substantive arguments behind the assumptions in the form of a structured interaction with the demographic research community, which also facilitates the involvement of more experts.

This important view from the practitioners of population projections, together with the theoretical insights discussed earlier, provided the basis for the new expert argument-based approach that was developed at IIASA and has now been broadly applied to defining the assumptions for the set of global population projections presented in this volume. This process involved more than 500 population experts from around the world who answered the IIASA–Oxford online questionnaire or participated in one of the five meta-expert meetings. Before describing the design and conduct of this exercise, it is useful to step back and discuss some of the general problems associated with any kind of expert solicitation regarding future trends, and with the general reluctance of academics to make statements about the future.

2.3.1 The meta-science of expert knowledge

Given the public prominence and substantive importance of likely future demographic trends in virtually all countries of the world, we find it surprising how little systematic attention the scientific community has given to the evaluation of arguments underlying the assumptions of future fertility, mortality, and migration trends. While the described survey shows that national statistical offices place hope in input from the demographic research community, this topic has largely been confined to the statistical agencies. As these offices cannot avoid making choices about assumptions in order to fulfil their mandate of producing population projections, they cannot escape this challenging task as easily as academics seem to be able to. Our approach attempts to translate the vast body of relevant research in the demographic community and other related research communities into specific sets of science-based assumptions for projections. This follows earlier work by Lutz et al. (2000), which explicitly discusses some of the shortcomings of expert-based procedures. Such procedures typically follow the tradition of Delphi methods, which have been developed and extensively documented elsewhere (Linstone and Turoff, 2002).

The main problem with expert opinions is that they tend to be opinionated; this can result in undesirable biases and distortions that do not necessarily reflect the state of knowledge. There is abundant evidence that experts tend to hold strong beliefs about the future that are at the level of emotions and intuitions (Lutz, 2009). Hence, the approach proposed here goes beyond opinion-based Delphi to embody a more objective science-based procedure. Of course, whenever one relies on the views of people, the result cannot be fully objective, but one can move toward objectivity by making the process inter-subjective and applying the standard scientific tools of peer review and critical evaluation. In order to make progress there must be something on the table to be evaluated and analytically reviewed. Hence, our argument-based approach puts specific arguments on the table that are directly relevant for the future course of the demographic force under consideration and which can be critically assessed.

In designing this new argument-based approach, we collaborated with P. Saariluoma, an experimental psychologist working in the field of cognitive science, who is an expert on experts. We learned that one important contribution that meta-science can make to any scientific approach is to investigate problems in the way arguments are built in particular scientific fields. Such an investigation can help applied scientists find a more analytical way of thinking in their own fields. It is important to understand that all scientific argumentation ends somewhere, and from that point on the operation of intuitive assumptions begins. Infinite chains of arguments are impossible. Being aware of this, one should reflect on when to end the chain of argumentation. This point might be right next to the object of observation, in which case there is no argumentative foundation at all. It can also be too far away from the object, in which case the arguments considered and the objects are linked only tentatively. The choice of this cut-off point needs to be based on expert judgement. But this is judgement at the meta-level rather than at the level of the object itself. Such judgement must be based on some sense of plausibility or intuition, as it is typically called in cognitive science and foundational analysis. Hence, intuitions in the foundations of scientific ways of thinking are unavoidable. We cannot get around them; we have to learn to live with them, and the best way to do so is to be cognizant of the known traps and fallacies and to be entirely transparent about the choices made.

2.3.2 The systematic inquiry of expert arguments chosen for this study

Based on these considerations and principles, a team at IIASA and the Vienna Institute of Demography designed an online questionnaire with separate segments for fertility, mortality, and migration. The questionnaire was developed gradually, first only with respect to mortality when it was tested with a group of 17 mortality experts in the context of the aforementioned MicMac project (Lutz, 2009). It was then further operationalized and programmed in Excel by the National Office of Statistics in the UK, which used it for systematically collecting expert-based assessments on fertility, mortality, and migration for population projections. A team at IIASA further developed the questionnaire for its broader use for all countries. For each of the three segments the arguments were grouped according to selected major forces that were defined to be as independent from each other as possible.

For fertility and mortality six such major forces were identified, and for international migration five. They are given as follows.

Major forces on which future fertility (F) will depend:

F1. Changing cultural and social forces in fertility ideals, norms and desires
F2. Changing patterns of partnerships and gender differences
F3. Changing roles of government policies (childcare facilities, housing, etc.)
F4. The changing environment in terms of employment and the economy
F5. Changing biomedical conditions (sperm quality and counts, female fecundability, new methods for assisted conception, etc.)
F6. Changes in educational attainment.

Major forces on which the future of life expectancy (L) will depend:

L1. Progress in biomedical technology
L2. Changes in the effectiveness of health care systems
L3. Changes in health-related behaviour
L4. Possible new infectious diseases and resurgence of old diseases
L5. Environmental change, disasters, and wars
L6. Changes in population composition and differential trends in population subgroups.

Major forces influencing international migration (M):

M1. Trends in economic development as a driver of international migration
M2. Climate change and conflict as possible drivers of international migration
M3. Demographic factors as a possible driver of international migration
M4. Changes in the costs of migration (in the broader sense)
M5. Trends in migration regimes and policies.

For each of these 17 major forces up to ten specific arguments were listed, with responding experts invited to add additional self-defined arguments. These specific arguments are listed and discussed in the next five chapters dealing with fertility, mortality, and migration.[2] For each of the arguments the experts were asked to judge the degree of correctness based on the scientific evidence. They were given five predefined choices about the validity of the argument ('very likely to be right', 'more right than wrong', 'do not know/ambivalent', 'more wrong than right', 'very likely to be wrong'). As can be seen from Figure 2.1, which provides a screen shot of one of the argument assessment pages, these answers were translated into a numerical factor (in parentheses) ranging from 0.0 for 'very likely to be wrong' to 1.0 for 'very likely to be right'.

Whether the argument is right is not all that matters; the relevance of the argument for influencing the future course of the force under consideration is also important.

[2] The full IIASA–Oxford survey can be found at <http://webarchive.iiasa.ac.at/Research/POP/ExpertSurveySandbox/> (accessed 15 January 2014).

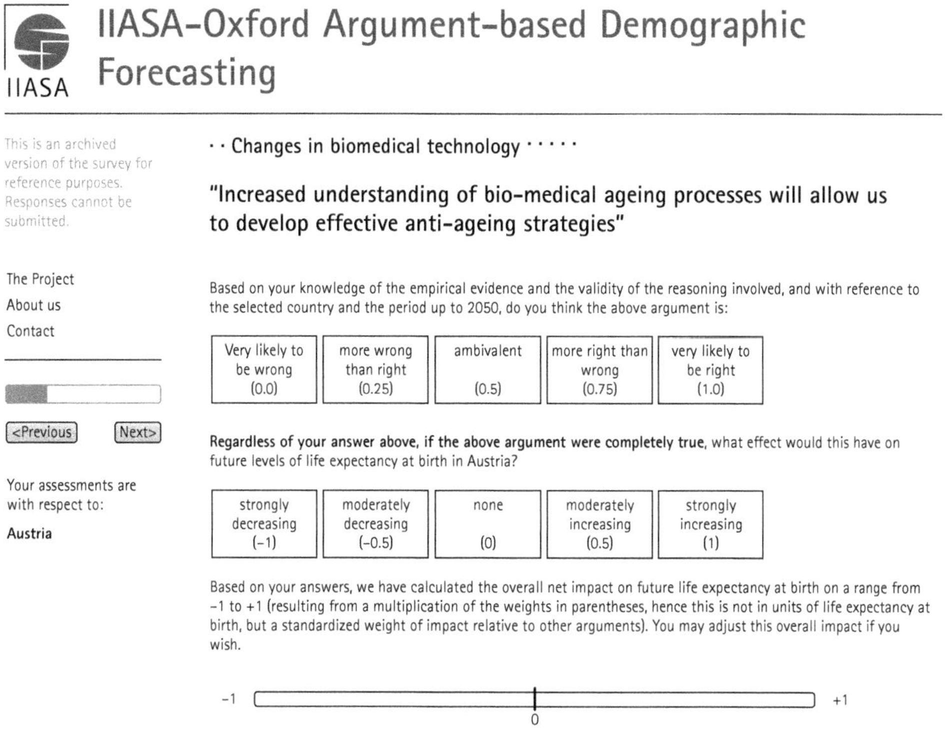
IIASA
IIASA-Oxford Argument-based Demographic Forecasting
This is an archived version of the survey for reference purposes. Responses cannot be submitted.
The Project
About us
Contact
<Previous
Next>
Your assessments are with respect to:
Austria
Changes in biomedical technology
"Increased understanding of bio-medical ageing processes will allow us to develop effective anti-ageing strategies"
Based on your knowledge of the empirical evidence and the validity of the reasoning involved, and with reference to the selected country and the period up to 2050, do you think the above argument is:
Very likely to be wrong (0.0)
more wrong than right (0.25)
ambivalent (0.5)
more right than wrong (0.75)
very likely to be right (1.0)
Regardless of your answer above, if the above argument were completely true, what effect would this have on future levels of life expectancy at birth in Austria?
strongly decreasing (-1)
moderately decreasing (-0.5)
none (0)
moderately increasing (0.5)
strongly increasing (1)
Based on your answers, we have calculated the overall net impact on future life expectancy at birth on a range from -1 to +1 (resulting from a multiplication of the weights in parentheses, hence this is not in units of life expectancy at birth, but a standardized weight of impact relative to other arguments). You may adjust this overall impact if you wish.
-1
0
+1

FIGURE 2.1 Screen shot from a sample page of the online questionnaire listing one argument on future life expectancy under the force 'changes in biomedical technology'.

Some arguments may likely be true but completely irrelevant for the question under consideration. Hence, experts were asked a second question concerning the likely impact of each argument on the demographic component (see Figure 2.1), which says, 'Regardless of your answer above, if the above argument were completely true, what effect would this have on the future of…' Again, the user could choose among five answers ranging from 'strongly decreasing' (assigned a factor of –1.0) to 'strongly increasing' (assigned a factor of +1.0). If the respondent believes that the factor has no effect on the demographic outcome considered, then this answer is assigned zero.

In a final assessment, the two factors stated for any given argument are multiplied, with the total argument impact score automatically shown, as in the scale at the bottom of Figure 2.1. This multiplicative assessment of the degree of the statement's correctness and of its impact if correct can thus range from a strong negative impact, given by –1.0 (when the statement is considered correct and to have a strong negative impact), to a strong positive impact given by +1.0 (when the statement is considered incorrect and to have a strong positive impact). If the statement is either considered to be wrong or right but having no impact the total impact score (resulting from the multiplication of the two scores) is zero. These scores have then been further processed as described in the following substantive chapters.

In mid-2011 all members of international population associations (International Union for the Scientific Study of Population, Population Association of America, European Association for Population Studies, Asian Population Association, and all other regional population associations) were invited to participate in the online survey. More than 550 responses were submitted. The lead authors of this volume, most of whom are affiliated with the Wittgenstein Centre for Demography and Global Human Capital (IIASA, VID/ÖAW, WU), systematically analysed the responses and led a series of five meta-expert meetings to review and focus them. These specialized workshops consisted of groups of 8–12 leading experts in the respective fields. Between October 2011 and February 2012 the meetings were held on five continents: 'Migration' (Boulder, CO, USA.), 'Low Fertility' (Vienna, Austria), 'High Fertility' (Kathmandu, Nepal), 'Low Mortality' (San Jose, Costa Rica), and 'High Mortality' (Cape Town, South Africa). Based on these meetings, we defined alternative fertility, mortality, and migration assumptions for all countries, as is described in detail in the following chapters.

Acknowledgements

We acknowledge support by a Starting Grant of the European Research Council, Grant Agreement 241003-COHORT.

References

Ahlburg, D.A. and Lutz, W. 1999 'Introduction: The Need to Rethink Approaches to Population Forecasts'. In: Lutz, W., Vaupel, J.W. and Ahlburg, D.A. (eds) *Frontiers of Population Forecasting. A Supplement to Vol. 24, 1998, Population and Development Review*, pp. 1–41. The Population Council: New York.

Alam, M. and Karan, A. 2011 'Elderly Health in India Dimension, Differentials and Determinants' (BKPAI Working Paper No. 3). United Nations Population Fund: New Dehli.

Albouy, V. and Lequien, L. 2009 'Does Compulsory Education Lower Mortality?' *Journal of Health Economics*, 28: 155–68.

Baker, D.P., Leon, J., Smith Greenaway, E.G., Collins, J. and Movit, M. 2011 'The Education Effect on Population Health: A Reassessment'. *Population and Development Review*, 37: 307–32.

Basu, A.M. 2002 'Why Does Education Lead to Lower Fertlity? A Critical Review of Some of the Possibilities'. *World Development*, 30: 1779–90.

Becker, G.S. 1981 *A Treatise on the Family*. Harvard University Press: Cambridge, MA.

Bhrolcháin, M.N. and Dyson, T. 2007 'On Causation in Demography: Issues and Illustrations'. *Population and Development Review*, 33: 1–36.

Bongaarts, J. 2010 'The Causes of Educational Differences in Fertility in Sub-Saharan Africa'. *Vienna Yearbook of Population Research*, 8: 31–50.

Börsch-Supan, A., Brugiavini, A., Jürges, H., Kapteyn, A., Mackenbach, J., Siegrist, J. and Weber, G. 2008 *First Results from the Survey of Health, Ageing and Retirement in Europe (2004–2007): Starting the Longitudinal Dimension*. Mannheim Research Institute for the Economics of Aging (MEA): Mannheim.

Brinch, C.N. and Galloway, T.A. 2011 'Schooling in Adolescence Raises IQ scores'. *Proceedings of the National Academy of the United States of America*, 109: 425–30.

Brønnum-Hansen, H., Andersen, O., Kjøller, M. and Rasmussen, N.K. 2004 'Social Gradient in Life Expectancy and Health Expectancy in Denmark'. *Social and Preventative Medicine*, 49, 36–41.

Clark, D. and Royer, H. 2010 'The Effect of Education on Adult Health and Mortality: Evidence from Britain (Working Paper No. 16013)'. National Bureau of Economic Research: Cambridge, MA.

Cleland, J. 2002 'Education and Future Fertility Trends with Special Reference to Mid-Transitional Countries (Background Papers No. 48/49), Completing the Fertility Transition'. United Nations: New York.

Coale, A.J. 1973 'The Demographic Transition Reconsidered'. Presented at the International Population Conference, Committee on South-North Migration, International Union for the Scientific Study of Population, Liege, pp. 53–72.

Collopy, F. and Armstrong, J.S. 1992 'Rule-based forecasting: development and validation of an expert systems approach to combining time series extrapolations'. *Management Science*, 38: 1394–414.

Dikshit, R., Gupta, P.C., Ramasundarahettige, C., Gajalakshmi, V., Aleksandrowicz, L., Badwe, R., et al. 2012 'Cancer Mortality in India: a Nationally Representative Survey'. *The Lancet*, 379: 1807–16.

Elbert, T., Pantev, C., Wienbruch, C., Rockstroh, B. and Taub, E. 1995 'Increased Cortical Representation of the Fingers of the Left Hand in String Players'. *Science*, 270: 305–7.

Fuchs, V.R. 1984 '"Though Much is Taken": Reflections on Aging, Health, and Medical Care'. *The Milbank Memorial Fund Quarterly. Health and Society*, 62: 143–66.

Fuchs, R., Pamuk, E. and Lutz, W. 2010 'Education or Wealth: Which Matters More for Reducing Child Mortality in Developing Countries?' *Vienna Yearbook of Population Research*, 8: 175–99.

Gathmann, C., Jürges, H. and Reinhold, S. 2012 'Compulsory Schooling Reforms, Education and Mortality in Twentieth Century Europe' (SSRN Scholarly Paper No. ID 2020246). Social Science Research Network: Rochester, NY.

Gerstorf, D., Ram, N., Hoppmann, C., Willis, S.L. and Schaie, K.W. 2011 'Cohort Differences in Cognitive Aging and Terminal Decline in the Seattle Longitudinal Study'. *Developmental Psychology*, 47, 1026–41.

Glymour, M.M., Kawachi, I., Jencks, C.S. and Berkman, L.F. 2008 Does childhood schooling affect old age memory or mental status? Using state schooling laws as natural experiments. *Journal of Epidemiology and Community Health*, 62: 532–7.

Govingdasamy, P. and Ramesh, B.M. 1997 'Maternal Education and the Utilization of Maternal and Child Health Services in India' (National Family Health Survey Subject Reports vol.5). International Institute for Population Sciences and Macro International Inc.: Mumbai, India, and Calverton, MD.

Gustafsson, S. 2001 'Optimal Age at Motherhood. Theoretical and Empirical Considerations on Postponement of Maternity in Europe'. *Journal of Population Economics*, 14: 225–47.

Haworth, C., Daleb, P. and Plomin, R. 2008 'A Twin Study into the Genetic and Environmental Influences on Academic Performance in Science in Nine Year Old Boys and Girls'. *International Journal of Science Education*, 30: 1003–25.

Jejeebhoy S. 1995 *Women's Education, Autonomy and Reproductive Behaviour: Experience from Developing Countries*. Clarendon Press: Oxford.

Jenkins, W.M., Merzenich, M.M., Ochs, M.T., Allard, T. and Guíc-Robles, E. 1990 'Functional Reorganization of Primary Somatosensory Cortex in Adult Owl Monkeys After Behaviorally Controlled Tactile Stimulation'. *Journal of Neurophysiology*, 63: 82–104.

Kandel, E.R. 2007 *In Search of Memory: The Emergence of a New Science of Mind*. W.W. Norton & Co.: New York.

KC, S. and Lentzner, H. 2010 'The Effect of Education on Adult Mortality and Disability: A Global Perspective'. *Vienna Yearbook of Population Research*, 8: 201–35.

Keyfitz, N. 1982 'Can Knowledge Improve Forecasts?' *Population and Development Review*, 8: 729–51.

Khang, Y.H., Lynch, J.W., Yun, S. and Lee, S.I. 2004 'Trends in Socioeconomic Health Inequalities in Korea: Use of Mortality and Morbidity Measures'. *Journal of Epidemiology and Community Health*, 58: 308–14.

Kohler, H.-P., Billari, F.C. and Ortega, J.A. 2006 'Low Fertility in Europe: Causes, Implications and Policy Options'. In: Harris, F.R. (ed.) *The Baby Bust: Who Will Do the Work? Who Will Pay the Taxes?*, pp. 48–109. Rowman & Littlefield Publishers: Lanham, MD.

Kondo, N. 2012 'Socioeconomic Disparities and Health: Impacts and Pathways'. *Journal of Epidemiology*, 22: 2–6.

Kravdal, Ø. 2002 'Education and Fertility in Sub-Saharan Africa: Individual and Community Effects'. *Demography*, 39: 233–50.

Kýrdar, M.G., Dayýoglu Tayfur, M. and Koç, Ý. 2011 'The Effect of Compulsory Schooling Laws on Teenage Marriage and Births in Turkey' (IZA Discussion Papers No. 5887). Institute for the Study of Labor (IZA): Bonn.

Lager, A.C.J. and Torssander, J. 2012 'Causal Effect of Education on Mortality in a Quasi-experiment on 1.2 Million Swedes'. *Proceedings of the National Academy of Science of the United States of America*, 109: 8461–6.

Linstone, H.A. and Turoff, M. (eds) 2002 *The Delphi Method: Techniques and Applications, Digital Reproduction of the Original 1975 Version*. New Jersey Institute of Technology: Newark, NJ.

Lleras-Muney, A. 2005 'The Relationship between Education and Adult Mortality in the United States'. *The Review of Economic Studies*, 72: 189–221.

Lutz, W. 2009 'Toward a Systematic, Argument-Based Approach to Defining Assumptions for Population Projections' (IIASA Interim Report No. IR-09-037). International Institute for Applied Systems Analysis (IIASA): Laxenburg.

Lutz, W. 2010 'Education Will be at the Heart of 21st Century Demography'. *Vienna Yearbook of Population Research*, 8: 9–16.

Lutz W. 2012 'Identity Sciences und Intervention Sciences: Was die Geistes- und Sozialwissenschaften leisten können'. *Thema*, 11: 3.

Lutz, W., KC, S. 2010 'Dimensions of Global Population Projections: What do we Know about Future Population Trends and Structures?' *Philosophical Transactions of the Royal Society B*, 365: 2779–91.

Lutz, W., KC, S. 2011 'Global Human Capital: Integrating Education and Population'. *Science*, 333: 587–92.

Lutz, W., Goujon, A. and Doblhammer-Reiter, G. 1998 'Demographic Dimensions in Forecasting: Adding Education to Age and Sex'. *Population and Development Review*, 24: 42–58.

Lutz, W., Vaupel, J.W. and Ahlburg, D.A. (eds) 1999 *Frontiers of Population Forecasting. A Supplement to Vol. 24, 1998, Population and Development Review*. The Population Council: New York.

Lutz, W., Saariluoma, P., Sanderson, W.C. and Scherbov, S. 2000 'New Developments in the Methodology of Expert- and Argument-Based Probabilistic Population Forecasting'

(IIASA Interim Report No. IR-00-020). International Institute for Applied Systems Analysis (IIASA): Laxenburg.

Lutz, W., Skirbekk, V. and Testa, M.R. 2006 'The Low-fertility Trap Hypothesis: Forces That May Lead to Further Postponement and Fewer Births in Europe'. *Vienna Yearbook of Population Research*, 2006: 167–92.

Lutz, W., Sanderson, W.C. and Scherbov, S. 2008 'The Coming Acceleration of Global Population Ageing'. *Nature*, 451: 716–19.

Mackenbach, J.P., Kunst, A.E., Groenhof, F., Borgan, J.K., Costa, G., Faggiano, F., et al. 1999 'Socioeconomic Inequalities in Mortality Among Women and Among Men: an International Study'. *American Journal of Public Health*, 89: 1800–6.

Mårtensson, J., Eriksson, J., Bodammer, N.C., Lindgren, M., Johansson, M., Nyberg, L. and Lövdén, M. 2012 'Growth of Language-related Brain Areas after Foreign Language Learning'. *NeuroImage*, 63: 240–4.

Martin, T.C. and Juarez, F. 1995 'The Impact of Women's Education on Fertility in Latin America: Searching for Explanations'. *International Family Planning Perspectives*, 21: 52–80.

Matthews, K.A., Gallo, L.C. and Taylor, S.E. 2010 'Are Psychosocial Factors Mediators of Socioeconomic Status and Health Connections?' *Annals of the New York Academy of Sciences*, 1186: 146–73.

Meadows, D.H., Meadows, D.L., Randers, J. and Behrens, W.W., III 1972 *The Limits to Growth: A Report for the Club of Rome's Project on the Predicament of Mankind*. Universe Books: New York.

Meghir, C., Palme, M. and Simeonova, E. 2012 'Education, Health and Mortality: Evidence from a Social Experiment' (Working Paper No. 17932). National Bureau of Economic Research: Cambridge, MA.

Meijer, W.A., van Boxtel, M.P.J., Van Gerven, P.W.M., van Hooren, S.A.H. and Jolles, J. 2009 'Interaction Effects of Education and Health Status on Cognitive Change: A 6-year Follow-up of the Maastricht Aging Study'. *Aging & Mental Health*, 13: 521–9.

Monden, C.W. and Smits, J. 2012 'Maternal Education is Associated With Reduced Female Disadvantages in Under-five Mortality in Sub-Saharan Africa and Southern Asia. *International Journal of Epidemiology*, 42: 211–18.

Monstad, K., Propper, C. and Salvanes, K.G. 2008 'Education and Fertility: Evidence from a Natural Experiment'. *Scandinavian Journal of Economics*, 110: 827–52.

Murphy, M. and O'Leary, E. 2010 'Depression, Cognitive Reserve and Memory Performance in Older Adults'. *International Journal of Geriatric Psychiatry*, 25: 665–71.

Murphy, M., Bobak, M., Nicholson, A., Rose, R. and Marmot, M. 2006 'The Widening Gap in Mortality by Educational Level in the Russian Federation, 1980–2001'. *American Journal of Public Health*, 96: 1293–9.

Olshansky, S.J., Antonucci, T., Berkman, L., Binstock, R.H., Boersch-Supan, A., Cacioppo, J.T., et al. 2012 'Differences in Life Expectancy due to Race and Educational Differences are Widening, and Many may not Catch up'. *Health Affairs*, 31: 1803–13.

Pamuk, E.R., Fuchs, R., and Lutz, W. 2011. 'Comparing relative effects of education and economic resources on infant mortality in developing countries'. *Population and Development Review*, 37: 637–64.

Pearl, J. 2000 *Causality: Models, Reasoning, and Inference*. Cambridge University Press: Cambridge and New York.

Prommer, I. and Wilson, C. 2006 'Analytical Summary of the Current Practices of Definition of Assumption Making in Population Projections' (Report prepared for the European Commission 6th Framework Project 'Bridging the Micro-Macro Gap in Population

Forecasting' (MicMac), Contract No. SP23-CT-2005-006637 No. deliverable D14.). International Institute for Applied Systems Analysis (IIASA): Laxenburg.

Remes, H., Martikainen, P. and Valkonen, T. 2010 'Mortality Inequalities by Parental Education Among Children and Young Adults in Finland 1990–2004'. *Journal of Epidemiology and Community Health*, 64: 130–5.

Richards, M. and Hatch, S.L. 2011 'Good News About the Ageing Brain'. *British Medical Journal*, 343: d6288.

Richards, M., Shipley, B., Fuhrer, R. and Wadsworth, M.E.J. 2004 'Cognitive Ability in Childhood and Cognitive Decline in Mid-life: Longitudinal Birth Cohort Study. *British Medical Journal*, 328: 552–4.

Rodgers, J.L., Kohler, H.-P., McGue, M., Behrman, J.R., Petersen, I., Bingley, P. and Christensen, K. 2008 'Education and Cognitive Ability as Direct, Mediating, or Spurious Influences on Female Age at First Birth: Behavior Genetic Models Fit to Danish Twin Data'. *American Journal of Sociology*, 114(Suppl.): 202–32.

Ryder, N.B. 1975 'Notes on Stationary Populations'. *Population Index*, 41: 3–28.

Sachan, B., Idris, M., Jain, S., Kumari, R. and Singh, A. 2012 'Social Determinants and its Influence on the Prevalence of Morbidity Among Adolescent Girls'. *North American Journal of Medical Sciences*, 4: 474–8.

Sanderson, W.C. and Scherbov, S. 2010 'Remeasuring Aging'. *Science*, 329: 1287–8.

Schneeweis, N., Skirbekk, V. and Winter-Ebmer, R. (2014) 'Does Education Improve Cognitive Performance Four Decades After Finishing School? *Demography*, 51: 619–43.

Shkolnikov, V.M., Andreev, E.M., Jdanov, D.A., Jasilionis, D., Kravdal, Ø., Vågerö, D. and Valkonen, T. 2012 'Increasing Absolute Mortality Disparities by Education in Finland, Norway and Sweden, 1971–2000'. *Journal of Epidemiology and Community Health*, 66: 372–8.

Shryock, H.S. and Siegel, J.S. 1993 *The Methods and Materials of Demography, 8th edn., Studies in Population*. US Government Printing Office: Washington, DC.

Silles, M.A. 2009 'The Causal Effect of Education on Health: Evidence from the United Kingdom'. *Economics of Education Review*, 28: 122–8.

Skirbekk, V. 2008 'Fertility Trends by Social Status'. *Demographic Research*, 18: 145–80.

Skirbekk, V. and KC, S. 2012 'Fertility-reducing Dynamics of Women's Social Status and Educational Attainment'. *Asian Population Studies*, 8: 251–64.

Skirbekk, V., Kohler, H.-P. and Prskawetz, A. 2004 'Birth Month, School Graduation, and the Timing of Births and Marriages'. *Demography*, 41: 547–68.

Skirbekk, V., Loichinger, E. and Weber, D. 2012 'Variation in Cognitive Functioning as a Refined Approach to Comparing Aging Across Countries'. *Proceedings of the National Academy of Sciences of the United States of America*, 109: 770–4.

Skirbekk, V., Stonawski, M., Bonsang, E. and Staudinger, U.M. 2013 'The Flynn Effect and Population Aging'. *Intelligence*, 41: 169–77.

Smith, S.C., Emran, M.S. and Maret, F. 2009 'Education and Freedom of Choice: Evidence from Arranged Marriages in Vietnam' (Working Paper No. 2009-15). The George Washington University, Institute for International Economic Policy: Washington, DC.

Strand, B.H., Groholt, E.-K., Steingrimsdottir, O.A., Blakely, T., Graff-Iversen, S. and Naess, O. 2010 'Educational Inequalities in Mortality Over Four Decades in Norway: Prospective Study of Middle Aged Men and Women Followed for Cause Specific Mortality, 1960–2000'. *BMJ*, 340: c654.

Van der Pol, M. 2011 'Health, Education and Time Preference'. *Health Economics*, 20: 917–29.

Whalley, L.J. and Deary, I.J. 2001 'Longitudinal Cohort Study of Childhood IQ and Survival up to age 76'. *BMJ*, 322: 819.

CHAPTER 3

FUTURE FERTILITY IN LOW FERTILITY COUNTRIES

STUART BASTEN, TOMÁŠ SOBOTKA, AND KRYŠTOF ZEMAN

Contributing authors:[1]

M. Jalal Abbasi-Shavazi, Alicia Adsera, Jan Van Bavel, Caroline Berghammer, Minja Kim Choe, Tomas Frejka, Henri Leridon, Melinda Mills, S. Philip Morgan, Ronald R. Rindfuss, Louis Rosero-Bixby, Anna Rotkirch, Warren C. Sanderson, Maria Rita Testa, Olivier Thévenon, and Zhongwei Zhao

[1] The contributing authors have drafted considerable parts of sections 3.1.4 and 3.2. They were selected as lead experts in respective topics and regions. Specifically, they have provided texts to the following sections: M. Jalal Abbasi-Shavazi to section 3.1.4.8 ('The Middle East'); Alicia Adsera to sections 3.1.4.7 ('Southern Europe') and 3.2.4 ('Employment, economic uncertainty, and fertility'); Jan Van Bavel and Ronald R. Rindfuss to section 3.2.8 ('Education'); Caroline Berghammer to section 3.2.3.2 ('Religion'); Minja Kim Choe to section 3.1.4.9 ('East Asian countries and territories') and Box 3.2 ('Living arrangements, gender roles, and their relationship to fertility in East Asia'); Melinda Mills to section 3.2.3.3 ('Gender equality'); S. Philip Morgan to section 3.1.4.1 ('The USA, Australia, Canada, and New Zealand'); Anna Rotkirch to section 3.1.4.6 ('Nordic countries'); Warren C. Sanderson to section 3.5.2 ('Long-term futures: preparing fertility scenarios beyond 2050'); Louis Rosero-Bixby to section 3.1.4.2 ('Latin America'); Maria Rita Testa to section 3.2.3.1 ('Fertility intentions'); Olivier Thévenon to section 3.2.5 ('Family policies'); and Zhongwei Zhao to sections 3.1.4.10 ('China') and Box 3.1 ('Finding China's period fertility rate'). Henri Leridon reviewed section 3.2.7 ('Biomedical factors'). Tomas Frejka provided detailed comments on the first draft of the chapter and produced regional cohort fertility estimates. The lead authors have modified these texts in order to achieve higher uniformity and reduce overlaps, and consulted with the contributing authors and book editors over these modifications. In addition, the whole chapter has been distributed to selected experts for additional comments and revisions.

3.1 Introduction and Summary of Past Trends: Beyond the Fertility Transition

3.1.1 Introduction

3.1.1.1 *The future of the low fertility world*

The ongoing transition to low fertility is, alongside the long-term expansion of life expectancy, the key force reshaping populations around the world. It has sweeping economic and social repercussions as it affects labour markets, intergenerational ties, gender relations, and public policies. Many middle-income countries, including China, Brazil, Iran, and Turkey, have joined the expanding list of low fertility countries. Consequently, low fertility is no longer an exclusive feature of rich Western societies. As close to half of the global population now lives in regions with below replacement fertility, low fertility has become a truly global phenomenon.

What are the key ingredients of this 'revolutionary' change? Expanding education, rising income, the rise of gender equality, female labour force participation, ideational changes, consumerism, urbanization, family disintegration, economic uncertainty, globalization, modern contraception, and many other complementary or contrasting forces are often highlighted. But how will these drivers shape the long-term future of fertility? Will fertility in most countries stabilize at around the replacement level threshold, as implied by the demographic transition theory, or will it decline below this level? Is very low fertility merely a 'passing phenomenon', a sign of a temporary imbalance between rapid social and economic changes and opportunities on the one hand, and family, gender relations, and reproduction on the other?

3.1.1.2 *Outline of this chapter*

This chapter aims to present both a comprehensive overview of the forces shaping contemporary reproductive behaviour in low fertility countries and an exploration of possible future scenarios based upon a new IIASA–Oxford survey of international experts introduced in Chapter 2 of this volume.[2] We begin with a presentation of recent trends in fertility in low fertility settings followed by a review of the particular recent histories of fertility change in North America, Europe, and the emerging low fertility settings in East Asia, Latin America, and the Middle East. We then explore the theoretical and empirical evidence that has been cited in the literature as underpinning these past trends and possible future scenarios. As well as 'meta-theories' such as the Second Demographic Transition (SDT), section 3.2 considers the roles played by cultural, biomedical, and economic factors, family policies, economic uncertainty, education, and the contribution of migrants' fertility.

[2] An extended version of this chapter containing expanded references, as well as additional background information about the survey of experts, is available as a working paper (Basten et al., 2013).

The concise summaries of underlying drivers of recent fertility trends presented in section 3.2 pave the way for the overview of the main results of the expert survey in section 3.3. While most demographers, as well as the global projection scenarios by the United Nations (UN), expect that fertility will continue declining in countries with currently higher fertility rates (Chapter 4), there are many uncertainties about the future of fertility in the low fertility world. Some of these uncertainties have been addressed in the IIASA–Oxford global survey of population experts, which included a module on the future of fertility in low fertility countries and the main factors likely to drive these future trends. In section 3.3, therefore, we outline the raison d'être for the expert survey, its design, and evaluation, and present the results of the qualitative element of the survey—namely the subjective appraisal of a series of forces shaping future trends of fertility in low fertility settings.

In section 3.4 we present the results of the quantitative component of the survey. Here, experts were invited to provide point and range estimates of period total fertility rates (TFRs) in 2030 and 2050. In addition to summarizing these figures, we compare them to the assumptions used by the UN in their global population projections. Section 3.5 takes all of the information gathered throughout the exercise, as well as the arguments of the experts participating in the Vienna meeting, and demonstrates how we then produce a series of fertility projections scenarios—medium-term until 2050, and very long-term until 2200—to be integrated into the Wittgenstein Centre (WIC) global population projections. In particular, we attempt to integrate education-specific futures into our projection scenarios.

Compared to many existing studies on low fertility, this chapter is innovative in several respects. First, in line with the evidence that low fertility has become a global phenomenon, it covers both the 'traditional' low fertility world (Europe, Japan, North America, Australia, and New Zealand) and the more recent and emerging low fertility regions. Thus, it also bridges the increasingly artificial distinction that is still often made between 'developing' and 'developed' countries. Second, the discussion about likely future developments is shaped by the views of experts who represented in their responses as many as 42 low fertility countries. This is an important step forward in overcoming the limitations of traditional population projections, where a few carefully selected experts formulate national and global fertility scenarios. It also allows incorporation of 'nonconformist' voices that might otherwise be disregarded (Lutz et al., 1999a). One way to find out that our approach does make a difference from the more traditional projection-making exercise was to compare the projected future fertility trends with those of the 2010 World Population Prospects by the UN (see section 3.4.2). Third, many contributing authors and collaborators have been involved in drafting selected sections of the chapter and also in reviewing its early drafts. Finally, the special focus on education brings to the fore a dimension that can be quantified, has been neglected in the past population analyses and projections, and, at the same time, has been suggested as 'a key factor, if not the single most important determinant in development' (Lutz et al., 1999b, p. 45; see also Chapter 2). Specifically, we argue that rising education level, among women, is the most important factor contributing to the observed global fertility trends in the last decades, especially the decline of fertility in higher fertility countries, and the postponement of parenthood to higher childbearing ages in affluent countries with low fertility. In addition, the inclusion of education is also adding a 'quality' dimension to the otherwise quantitative study of population changes (Lutz and KC, 2011).

3.1.2 The ongoing fertility transition in East Asia, the Middle East, and Latin America

Half a century ago, the global fertility map was polarized, reflecting the traditional division between 'developed' and 'developing' countries. The group of the 'more developed countries' (MDC; defined by the UN for statistical purposes as Europe, Northern America, Japan, Australia, and New Zealand) had experienced relatively low fertility by the early 1950s and saw gradual, but continuing, fertility reduction from the late 1960s through the 1990s, when the period TFR[3] in the region fell below 1.6 (UN, 2011; Figure 3.1a). In contrast, the group of the 'less developed countries' (LDC)—that is, all other regions not listed earlier—had high and stable fertility rates at about six births per woman throughout the 1950s and 1960s: more than double the level of the MDC group. However, in the early 1970s, sustained fertility declines across much of the LDC group had begun, with the whole set of countries reaching a TFR level of 2.6 by 2010 (PRB, 2012)—a level reached by European countries in the 1950s and early 1960s. The continuous and strong fertility declines in the LDC group led to the gradual reduction in fertility differences between major world regions that began in the early 1970s, with only sub-Saharan Africa and parts of Asia recording fertility rates above four births per woman in 2010 (PRB, 2012).

Three regions covered in this chapter—Latin America, East Asia, and parts of the Middle East—have undergone dramatic fertility transformation since the 1960s. The breathtaking pace of fertility decline in the largest countries in these regions is illustrated in Figure 3.1b. In 1960–65, fertility in these countries ranged from a TFR of 5.6 in China and South Korea to 6.8 in Mexico and 6.9 in Iran. Rapid fertility declines then ensued, with fertility rates typically falling by a half in the course of 2–3 decades. This surprising pace of fertility transitions is partly attributed to government action concerning family planning, whether through explicit restrictions in China (see section 3.1.4.10), effective campaigns in Korea and elsewhere in East Asia (Choe and Park, 2006), or the sanctioning of family planning by religious authorities in Iran (Abbasi-Shavazi et al., 2009a). However, the remarkable similarity of fertility transitions, with all of the

[3] The period TFR is a widely available, but also problematic, indicator that is affected by changes in the timing of births and parity composition of the female population of reproductive ages (Bongaarts and Feeney, 1998; Sobotka and Lutz, 2011; see also section 3.2.1). In conformity with its dominance in the literature and data sources we employ it frequently in this chapter, but also complement it with cohort fertility indicators, as well as alternative measures of period fertility.

compared countries experiencing fertility rates in 2005–10 ranging from 1.45 in China to 2.4 in Mexico, indicates that while targeted government action might have facilitated or accelerated observed changes, fertility change was driven by a host of other factors related to socio-economic development, modern contraception, and new values and norms favouring small family sizes (e.g. Cai, 2010 for China). Caldwell (2001, p. 109) sees this transformation as a manifestation of a 'globalisation of fertility attitudes and behaviour'.

As the boundaries between MDC and many LDC countries are becoming increasingly blurred with regard to demographic and socio-economic characteristics, so it is with fertility behaviour. Many 'less developed' countries, including China, Cuba, and Iran, have lower fertility today than some of the countries traditionally belonging to the club of the 'most developed' countries with low fertility, such as Sweden, France, and the USA. Indeed, more than 45 per cent of the global population lives in countries with below replacement fertility levels, and when regions of India are taken into account, more than half of humanity lives in below replacement fertility settings (Wilson and Pison, 2004). Low fertility is no longer an issue confined to the most affluent societies, but has become an important topic for public discussion and a motivation for development of government policies. On the one hand, a few countries have even reversed their policies and become explicitly pro-natalist either through limiting family-planning programmes (as in Turkey and Iran) or through extensive, explicitly pro-natalistic family policy interventions (e.g. Singapore, Taiwan, South Korea) (section 3.1.4.8). On the other

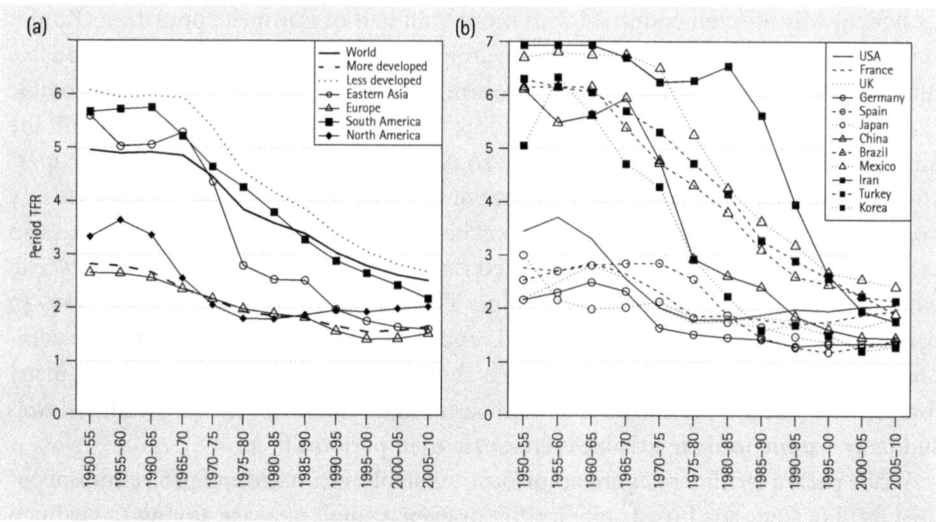

FIGURE 3.1(a, b) Period total fertility rate (TFR) in major world regions and in largest countries covered in this chapter, 1950–55 to 2005–10.

Note: Period TFR in China in 1990–2010 is likely to be overestimated in the official statistics and the UN data (see Box 3.1); data shown are based on Zhao and Zhang (2010, p. 490, Table 6).

Data source: UN (2011, Table A.22).

hand, the Chinese government has been slow to respond to demographers' arguments calling for the dismantling of China's fertility restrictions, which limit the authorized number of births per couple (Wang et al., 2013).

With this transformation in fertility regimes, many new questions arise. Where will fertility decline stop? Will East Asia retain the position of the lowest-fertility region globally? Will the Middle East and Latin America follow and experience decades of very low fertility? Can previous experience of post-transitional fertility trends in Europe, the USA, Japan, and other rich societies serve as a guide to what might happen elsewhere? Will many non-European countries experience protracted postponement of family formation to ever-later ages, depressing period fertility levels for many decades to come (Bongaarts, 1999)?

3.1.3 Europe, the USA, Japan, and other highly developed countries

The USA, Canada, Japan, and most European countries have a long history of low fertility rates. In the 1930s, in the context of economic crises and shifts in values and attitudes towards family, many Western countries, including Austria, Germany, Sweden, and Great Britain, temporarily experienced TFRs falling below two births per woman (Kirk, 1946; Van Bavel, 2010a). In the 1970s and 1980s ever more developed countries experienced what were thought to be irreversible falls of fertility to sub-replacement levels, while, in the 1990s, a phenomenon of 'lowest-low fertility' with a TFR declining below 1.3 temporarily affected countries with more than half of Europe's population (Kohler et al., 2002; Sobotka, 2004a). Beginning in around 2000, however, declines in period fertility halted and an upturn took place across most low-fertility regions, with the notable exception of East Asia (Goldstein et al., 2009; OECD, 2011). The upturn lasted until the onset of the global economic recession in 2008 (see also Box 3.3). This fertility recuperation was largely an expected consequence of the slowing-down in the pace of fertility postponement and the associated tempo effect (Bongaarts and Sobotka, 2012; see also section 3.2.2). It marked the first concerted rise in fertility across the developed world, with many countries registering an absolute TFR increase of 0.3–0.6, or around 20–40 per cent in absolute terms (Goldstein et al., 2009). Moreover, this fertility increase demonstrated that there is nothing inevitable about extreme low fertility rates, as many former state-socialist countries that were seemingly 'stuck' at very low fertility levels suddenly experienced remarkable increases in their period TFRs.[4]

While period fertility rates are notoriously unstable, estimates and projections of cohort fertility suggest a broad stabilization or even a small increase among the women

[4] The most remarkable TFR upturn took place in Eastern Germany (former German Democratic Republic) where period TFR plummeted well below 1.0 after German unification in the early 1990s and then almost doubled, reaching 1.46 in 2010 (Goldstein and Kreyenfeld, 2011; see also section 3.1.4.5).

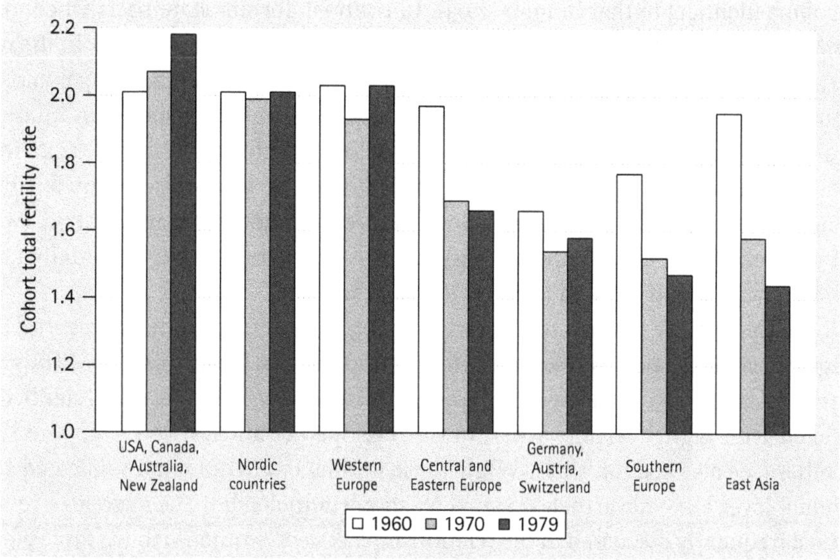

FIGURE 3.2 Observed and projected completed fertility rate in major regions of Europe, East Asia, and English-speaking countries outside Europe; women born in 1960, 1970, and 1979.

Notes: Completed fertility is partly projected in the cohorts born in 1970 and 1979. Regional data are weighted by population size in 2012 of all countries in a given region. The region 'Central and Eastern Europe' includes all former 'state-socialist' countries of Europe, including the former Soviet Union (except Latvia), but excluding most of the former Yugoslavia, where only Slovenia was included (data not available for other countries). 'East Asia' includes Japan, South Korea, Singapore, and Taiwan.

Sources: Computations based on cohort fertility data and projections presented by Myrskylä et al. (2013, Table 2).

born in the 1970s in most European countries, as well as the USA, Australia, Canada, Japan, and New Zealand (Myrskylä et al., 2013). Figure 3.2 presents observed and projected completed cohort fertility rates (CFR) for larger regions in Europe and East Asia among women born in 1960–79, based on the computations of Myrskylä et al. (2013).[5] Although the data for the most recent cohort, 1979, are still subject to possible downward revisions owing to the recent recession-induced period fertility declines (section 3.2.4; see also Box 3.3), the contrasts in regional fertility trends are sizeable and robust. Among women born in 1960, five out of seven analysed regions had fertility rates very close to two children per woman; only Southern Europe (CFR at 1.77) and the three predominantly German-speaking countries in Central Europe (Austria, Germany, and Switzerland, CFR at 1.66) showed an early spread of fertility well below replacement. Subsequently, regional cohort fertility trajectories diverge. The English-speaking countries outside Europe show a modest increase to cohort fertility slightly above replacement in the 1979 cohort (CFR at 2.18), chiefly because of the projected fertility increase in the USA (CFR at 2.23). Nordic countries have a flat fertility trend at around a CFR of 2.01. Western Europe shows a slight U-shaped trend, with a projected CFR in the

[5] Regional data weighted by 2012 population size of all the countries in each region.

1979 cohort identical to that in 1960 (2.03). In contrast, former state-socialist countries of Central and Eastern Europe (CEE) display sizeable falls in cohort fertility in the 1960s cohorts, with the projected CFR down to 1.66 in the 1979 cohort; even stronger and continuous declines are projected for East Asia (Japan, Korea, Singapore, and Taiwan), where the projected CFR falls to the lowest level of all regions analysed (1.44). Finally, cohort fertility in the two regions with earlier onset of sub-replacement fertility is expected to decline as well, moderately in the three German-speaking countries (with a slight recovery in the 1970s cohorts) and more in Southern Europe, eventually falling below the 1.5 threshold (CFR of 1.47 in the 1979 cohort).

Prior to the fertility upturns of the early twenty-first century, a notable reversal in an aggregate correlation between socio-economic and cultural indicators and fertility rates occurred (Castles, 2003). Factors traditionally associated with low fertility rates became associated with higher fertility when most developed countries were compared with each other (see also section 3.2.1). While these findings were often not replicated at the individual level, they nevertheless signal an important change. The aggregate reversal was most frequently discussed in the relationship between women's labour force participation and fertility (Brewster and Rindfuss, 2000; Engelhardt and Prskawetz, 2004). More recently, it has been suggested that at advanced levels of development, further increases in development no longer translate into lower fertility, but could instead lead to rising fertility rates (Myrskylä et al., 2011, 2009; OECD, 2011; section 3.2.1).

3.1.4 Summary of past trends and key factors in major low fertility regions

In this section we outline recent trends in fertility by region.[6] We use regions that are distinct geographically, economically, culturally, and demographically. In Europe we distinguish smaller regions that mirror particular histories of low fertility and family patterns.

3.1.4.1 *The USA, Australia, Canada, and New Zealand*

The USA, Australia, Canada, and New Zealand have shared similar fertility patterns for much of the post-World War II period, including a relatively a pronounced baby boom in the 1950s and early 1960s. Between 1960 and 1980, these countries experienced fertility declines from around 3.5 (higher in New Zealand) to sub-replacement TFRs ranging from 1.8 in Canada to 2.0 in New Zealand (Preston, 1986). In the USA, fertility decline bottomed out in 1976 when the TFR reached 1.75, the lowest level recorded to date.

[6] For details regarding the selection of countries for the low and high fertility modules, respectively, see Appendix 3.1. To keep text concise and informative, we focus especially on main countries in each region and pay only marginal attention to small countries and territories, especially those with a population below 1 million.

Since 1980, fertility has remained relatively stable. While the USA experienced gradual increases, Canada's fertility decline continued through to 2000 when it briefly dropped below 1.5. By then, the fertility contrast between Canada and the USA surpassed half a birth (TFRs of 1.49 and 2.05 respectively). Most recently, US fertility declined most following the onset of the recession, while Canada's TFR showed continued slow recovery. The period TFR in 2011 ranged from below 1.6 in Canada through 1.9 in Australia and the USA up to a 'high' value of 2.1 in New Zealand. The lower fertility in Canada is illustrated in differences in cohort fertility among women born in 1970, which declined below 1.8 in Canada, but remained above 2.0 in the other three countries, reaching 2.02 in Australia, 2.11 in the USA, and 2.17 in New Zealand (Myrskylä et al., 2013; see Table 3.2).

The USA has relatively high fertility compared with most other developed countries, which, combined with its population size of 314 million, warrants special attention. Different explanations have been proposed to explain the USA's 'exceptionalism' in fertility, including higher fertility rates among specific migrant and minority groups, especially Hispanics; a slower trend toward delayed childbearing; stronger importance of religion; and highly flexible labour markets combined with ample availability of cheap private childcare (Frejka, 2004; Hayford and Morgan, 2008; McDonald and Moyle, 2010). But, arguably, the key factor in the higher fertility in the USA is the closeness of intended and realized family size, with the level of intended fertility being only slightly higher than observed period TFRs despite considerable inconsistency in the number of children individual women intend and actually bear (Morgan and Rackin, 2010; see also section 3.2.3.1). In other words, a large number of women 'miss their target,' but approximately equal numbers miss low and high. The primary reason many women exceed intended parity is a high frequency of unplanned pregnancies—especially among teenagers and low educated and economically disadvantaged social groups (resulting in unintended and unwanted births) (Finer and Zolna, 2011; Musick et al., 2009). Almost half of all pregnancies (49 per cent in 2006) in the USA are unintended, with very high shares among never-married young women. In contrast, Canadian completed fertility is more than 0.3 births per woman lower despite evidence of a 'remarkable stability of fertility intentions reported by Canadian women' averaging 2.1 births (Edmonston et al., 2010, p. 320). While high teenage childbearing has been a general characteristic of English-speaking countries, this is less true for Canada, where the mean age of childbearing has increased to nearly 30 years, similar to Western Europe. Thus, Canadian women, as in much of Europe, have low fertility because, in the language used earlier, many more 'miss low than high'. The Canadian and US difference may also represent different effects of immigrant fertility (see also section 3.2.6). The flow of Hispanics (especially Mexicans) into the USA increases fertility (Frank and Heuveline, 2005); immigrants to Canada (primarily from Asia) often exhibit higher fertility initially (with a notable exception of Chinese immigrants who display low fertility early on), but their fertility quickly falls to the levels of natives (Woldemicael and Beaujot, 2012). Among the second generation, fertility among migrants is, in fact, lower (Adsera and Ferrer, 2010).

If one compares 2010 non-Hispanic whites' TFR in the USA with overall Australian TFR, the rates are very similar (1.8 and 1.9 respectively). Australia's selective immigration policy reduces the impact of immigrant fertility. In contrast, the higher TFR seen in New Zealand—in 2010 the second highest after Iceland (2.2) among the most developed countries—partly reflects the higher fertility rates of Māori and Pacific women (New Zealand Government, 2010).

3.1.4.2 *Latin America and the Caribbean*

The most recent UN estimates show a TFR in the Latin America and Caribbean (LAC) region of 2.3 births per woman in 2005–10, with a falling trend of about 0.2 every 5 years (UN, 2011).[7] As such, by the time of publication it is highly likely that period TFR in this region has fallen to replacement rate.

Brazil and Mexico are key to understanding the trends in LAC given that their populations make up about 50 per cent of the region's population. Brazil has recently reached sub-replacement fertility with an estimated 2009 TFR of 1.94 (IBGE, 2010). In Mexico, meanwhile, the TFR is estimated at 2.4 births per woman in 2005–10 (UN, 2011). In both countries this represents a fall of over four births per woman since the onset of the fertility transition in the 1960s. Fertility decline in Brazil accelerated in the 2000s (Potter et al., 2010), concurrent with rapid economic growth and broadening of the middle class. Brazilian fertility is clearly heading to levels substantially lower than replacement, especially if Brazil experiences an intensive postponement of childbearing similar to that experienced in European and East Asian countries in recent decades. By contrast, fertility decline in Mexico has slowed down: its TFR estimate for 2005–10 was corrected upward by 0.2 in the light of the 2010 census results. The anticipation of the Mexican government of reaching the replacement level by 2005 (Tuiran et al., 2002) will only be fulfilled at least a decade later.

The highest fertility in LAC occurs in the two countries with the largest indigenous ethnic groups (CELADE, 2012): Guatemala (41 per cent indigenous) and Bolivia (62 per cent) with a TFR of 4.1 and 3.5, respectively, as well as in Haiti, the poorest country in the region, which has a TFR of 3.5. The onset of the fertility transition arrived in these countries later—in the 1970s and 1980s—but their fertility decline has been faster in the first decade of the twenty-first century, by about one birth per woman compared to the LAC average of 0.4 (UN, 2011). There is no reason to believe that the fertility decline in these 'laggard' countries will stop before reaching the replacement level.

Cuba has the lowest TFR in LAC, estimated at 1.8 in 2011 (ONE, 2012), following an upturn from a low of 1.4 in 2006. But even in Cuba, adolescent fertility remains

[7] Although the lack of reliable vital statistics in most LAC countries limits monitoring demographic trends in a timely way, data from population censuses of 2010 and 2011 make estimates for 2005–10 robust in most countries. The *2012 World Population Datasheet* estimates the region's TFR level at 2.2 (PRB, 2012).

relatively high at 57 births per thousand women aged 15–19 in 2011. This high adolescent fertility is a characteristic of the whole region, with an average rate of 73 per 1000 (Rodríguez, 2011). Closely related are the statistics revealing that women in Latin America also report very high shares of unwanted pregnancies and births, ranging from 21 per cent in Paraguay to 60 per cent in Bolivia in the early 2000s (Casterline and Mendoza, 2009, Figure 1). However, recent census and survey data suggest both teenage fertility rates and unwanted fertility rates have declined in the region, fuelling, to a large extent, the observed fertility decline (Casterline and Mendoza, 2009). The social imperative of early motherhood and motherhood in general, which has long prevailed in the region, is weakening in young cohorts (Rosero-Bixby et al., 2009). An increase in voluntary childlessness coupled with further reductions in unwanted fertility and the trend towards childbearing postponement would facilitate the occurrence of lowest-low fertility levels, similar to those in Southern Europe, in many LAC countries.

3.1.4.3 *Western Europe*

Western European countries (Belgium, France, Ireland, Luxembourg, the Netherlands, and the UK)—alongside the Nordic countries—generally exhibit higher fertility than other parts of Europe. They share family and fertility patterns typical of an advanced stage of the SDT, marked by a late timing of childbearing, high rates of extramarital childbearing, and a high labour force participation of women (see section 3.2.1). In Western Europe, the trend toward late childbearing had already begun in the early 1970s, but slowed after 2000. This led to a pronounced cycle of fertility decline after 1970s and a gradual fertility recovery in more recent years, especially between the late 1990s and 2008 when period and cohort fertility levels converged to similar values. Once changes in fertility timing are taken into account, period and cohort fertility levels in Western Europe have been remarkably stable during recent decades despite the ongoing trend to later childbearing, rapid family transformations, rising tertiary education, female labour participation, and more competitive labour markets (section 3.1.3).

Fertility outside marriage has been increasingly accepted since the 1970s, so that by 2011 between 34 per cent (Ireland) and 55 per cent (France) of births took place outside marriage, mostly in cohabiting unions. This broad acceptance of cohabiting unions and childbearing outside marriage may arguably have a positive impact on fertility (section 3.2.1).

France and the UK have similar fertility levels, with the period TFR close to 2.0 in 2010, and cohort fertility of women born in 1970 at the same level for France and a slightly lower level of 1.9 in the UK (VID, 2012). But this similarity masks contrasts with respect to birth timing, order-specific fertility, and social status differences in fertility, which partly reflect different institutional conditions, including family policies, norms, and contraceptive use. The French fertility pattern, similarly to the Nordic countries, can be characterized as 'egalitarian', with low childlessness and relatively low differentials by social status (Ekert-Jaffé et al., 2002; Rendall et al., 2009). This can be explained, in part, by an active family policy introduced in France in the 1940s and adapted in the 1980s to accommodate women's entry into the labour force. Pro-natalist in nature, this active set of policies seems to have created especially positive attitudes towards two- or three-child families in France (Toulemon et al., 2008).

The fertility pattern in the UK can be seen as 'polarized', marked by high childlessness of around 20 per cent (especially among women with a university education), a higher share of women with four or more children, high social status differentials (Ekert-Jaffé et al., 2002), and, similar to the USA, higher rates of both teenage and unintended pregnancies. Since reaching a low point of 1.6 in 2001, period TFR in the UK has increased as a consequence of the diminishing importance of the tempo effect, higher fertility among immigrants, and, arguably, the introduction of a raft of more 'family-friendly' policies (Sigle-Rushton, 2008).

Ireland, until recently a more conservative Catholic country than others in Western Europe, has been an outlier in Western Europe in maintaining a high TFR above 3.0 until the mid-1970s and barely falling below 2.0 in the period 1994–2006. In contemporary Ireland a strong preference for larger families seems to be in evidence (Testa, 2012). In fact, Ireland now has the highest TFR level in Europe of 2.11 in 2011, followed by Iceland (2.04 in 2012) and France (2.00 in 2012).

The Benelux countries (Belgium, the Netherlands, and Luxembourg) also experienced sharp declines in fertility in the 1970s and 1980s, followed by a gradual recovery. In the Netherlands TFR briefly fell below 1.5 in the early 1980s, but a subsequent recovery brought it back to about 1.7 by the turn of the millennium, a rate similar to Belgium and to the completed fertility in both countries. In the Netherlands, a combination of work and family life is facilitated by a wide adherence to part-time work, which is very common among women with children, and also of some significance among men (Yerkes, 2009). In Belgium, a relatively high and stable cohort fertility (just above 1.8 for the 1950s–1970s cohorts) went hand-in-hand with reversals in the educational gradient in fertility, with tertiary educated women having above average fertility levels since the 1950s cohorts (Neels and De Wachter, 2010).

3.1.4.4 *Central and Eastern Europe*

CEE is an economically, culturally, and demographically heterogeneous region composed of countries that belonged to a state-socialist political system that collapsed between 1989 and 1991. Fertility rates in the region fell to relatively low levels in the late 1950s following legalization of abortion and a push to dramatically expand women's labour force participation. Unlike many other parts of Europe, CEE did not experience a distinct baby boom in the 1950s and 1960s, instead recording some of the lowest fertility rates globally, with some countries, including Croatia, Hungary, Romania, Russia, and Ukraine, experiencing sub-replacement TFR levels (Sobotka, 2011). In response, governments started stimulating fertility in the form of social, housing, and family policies, as well as more restrictive measures, especially limiting access to abortion (David, 1999).

By the late 1990s the CEE countries stood out as a result of their almost universal and relatively early marriage and childbearing, a strong adherence to the two-child family norm, and high abortion and divorce rates, especially in parts of the former Soviet Union (Sobotka, 2003). Political regime change in 1990 resulted in a long and painful period of economic and social transformation toward a market economy, parliamentary democracy, and, in the case of central Europe, Bulgaria, and Romania, eventual entry to the European Union (EU) (Heyns, 2005). Fertility and family have changed profoundly, with marriage and fertility trends best characterized by later, fewer, less universal, and—with respect to social status differential—more heterogeneous. A rapid shift toward later timing of births generated a sizeable tempo effect, which exacerbated the fertility decline in the 1990s, leading to extreme low levels of period fertility rates across the whole region at the end of the decade (Goldstein et al., 2009; Sobotka, 2003). The multifaceted nature of fertility changes fuelled discussion of both positive and negative aspects, including falling living standards, expanding tertiary education, new opportunities, the spread of modern contraception, and new attitudes typical of the SDT. Because these changes proceeded simultaneously, it is impossible to single out the effects of individual factors that drove fertility decline and postponement (Philipov and Dorbritz, 2003; Sobotka, 2011).

After recovering somewhat in the decade since 2000, fertility rates in CEE still remain relatively low, with a period TFR ranging between 1.3 in Latvia and Hungary and 1.5–1.67 in Estonia, Belarus, Lithuania, Russia, and Slovenia in 2010. The lowest levels of completed fertility rates among women born in 1970 were recorded in Russia (1.6) and Ukraine (1.55; VID, 2012). Fertility and family patterns grew much more differentiated, with Central European countries, especially the Czech Republic, Estonia, Hungary, former German Democratic Republic (East Germany), and Slovenia experiencing particularly rapid postponement of first births and also the shift away from marriage to cohabitation and single living, including single motherhood, especially among socially disadvantaged women (Perelli-Harris et al., 2012). The prolonged experience of very low fertility rates led to renewed concerns about low fertility and population decline, and to the resurgence of explicit top-down pro-natalism in parts of Eastern Europe, especially in Belarus and Russia, where achieving higher birth rates is seen as a matter of national interest and a key for achieving 'demographic security' (e.g. Heino, 2012; Ministry of Labour, 2010).

3.1.4.5 *Germany, Austria, and Switzerland ('German-speaking' countries)*

A number of distinct fertility developments in Austria, Switzerland, and Germany can be pointed out. First, fertility has been lower in these three countries than in most of Europe since the 1920s, and the fall in fertility rates after 1964 took place with greater intensity than in neighbouring regions. The Federal Republic of Germany (Western Germany) was the first European country to experience a TFR fall below 1.5 in 1975 and a brief decline below 1.3 a decade later. Second, fertility has remained at similar low levels since the mid-1970s, little affected by the shifts typical for many other parts of Europe

(Dorbritz, 2008; Prskawetz et al., 2008). In 2011 the period TFR ranged from 1.36 in Germany to 1.52 in Switzerland, slightly above the lows reached between 1994 and 2001; the adjusted TFR that aims to eliminate influences of the changes in the timing of births (section 3.2.2) has remained around 0.2 higher. Third, low fertility in Austria, Switzerland, and Western Germany is largely attributable to high childlessness, especially among university educated women. Finally, low fertility appears to be linked to low family size intentions and ideals, in contrast to North America (Goldstein et al., 2003; Sobotka, 2009).

In Germany, low fertility has resulted in a negative balance between births and deaths since 1972. The data for Germany hide persistent contrasts in fertility patterns and their underlying institutional conditions between the eastern and western parts of the country (Basten et al., 2011; Goldstein and Kreyenfeld, 2011; Kreyenfeld, 2010). However, differences in fertility levels diminished after the post-unification 'demographic shocks' in Eastern Germany (Conrad et al., 1996) when a record low TFR level of 0.77 was reached in 1993–94 (Goldstein and Kreyenfeld, 2011).

As the three countries were relatively little affected by the recent economic recession, fertility rates remained stable after 2008. Projections suggest a stabilization in completed fertility rates among Austrian women born after 1970 at a level of 1.6 and a slight rise among (West) German women, who reached the lowest cohort fertility in Europe of 1.5 in the 1968 cohort (Myrskylä et al., 2013; VID, 2012).

3.1.4.6 *Nordic countries*

The five Nordic countries (Denmark, Sweden, Norway, Finland, and Iceland) are characterized by stable and relatively high fertility, with completed cohort fertility of postwar generations consistently around two children per woman (Andersson et al., 2009). In Finland, for example, two surviving children per mother has been the dominant pattern for well over a century (Liu et al., 2012). Women born in the 1960s had their first child 2–3 years later than those born in the 1950s, and mean age at first birth is now around 29 years. There has also been a steady increase in childlessness, reaching around 15 per cent for women born in the 1960s (Andersson et al., 2009). The great majority of Nordic women wish to have two or three children, and voluntary childlessness stands at less than 5 per cent (Miettinen, 2010).

The period TFR increased modestly after the early 1980s, peaking in 2008–10, and then began declining, arguably as a result of the recent economic recession. Apart from Iceland, which retained a TFR around replacement level (reaching 2.23 in 2009, but declining thereafter), Norway has the highest completed fertility (Andersson et al., 2009), as well as lowest ages at first birth and lowest proportion of childless women (around 12 per cent for women born in the late 1960s). Denmark had the lowest fertility in the 1980s with the TFR falling briefly below 1.4, but is now close to Finland with a TFR of 1.73 in 2012. Finland exhibits higher childlessness, around 19 per cent for the youngest cohorts now completing their fertility (Miettinen, 2010). Projections by national statistical offices published in 2012–13 assume fertility rates just below replacement levels by mid-century, reaching—in 2050—1.89 in Norway, 1.91 in Sweden, and 2.00 in Iceland, according to the medium variant (online databanks of Statistics Sweden, Statistics Norway, and Statistics Iceland, accessed 20 June 2013).

Higher fertility in Nordic countries is often explained by generous family policies and high levels of gender equality (Rønsen and Skrede, 2010; see also section 3.2.5). Availability of local childcare has been shown to increase fertility at all parities (Rindfuss et al., 2010), while family policy in the form of childcare allowance buffered Finnish fertility at higher parities during the severe economic recession in the early 1990s (Vikat, 2004). Gender equality also appears to promote family formation in the region, but not necessarily progression to third or later births (Duvander et al., 2010). The relationship between socio-economic status and number of children is positive among men, and neutral or positive among mothers (Kravdal and Rindfuss, 2008; Lappegård et al., 2011).

3.1.4.7 *Southern Europe*

Fertility in Southern Europe has undergone major changes during recent decades. Fertility rates remained among the highest in developed countries well into the late 1970s. In 1975 the TFR ranged from 2.80 in Spain and 2.75 in Portugal to 2.32 in Greece and 2.21 in Italy. Since the mid-1980s, however, all these countries experienced a dramatic fertility decline. After 1992, Italy and Spain became the first countries in Europe to experience 'lowest-low fertility'—a TFR below 1.3 (Kohler et al., 2002)—with Greece joining them in the late 1990s. The decrease was initially more moderate in Portugal. Tempo effects associated with the rapid expansion in educational attainment and subsequent entry of women into the labour market are estimated to have depressed TFR by about 0.3 during the late 1990s, although this influence decreased thereafter (for Spain, see VID, 2012).

Furthermore, high unemployment rates during the late 1980s and early 1990s contributed to fertility postponement (Adsera, 2011a); indeed, the mean age at first birth in Spain and Italy, about 30, is now among the highest in Europe. Childlessness has been rising rapidly but still remains at less than 20 per cent. Surveys on fertility intentions indicate only a low proportion of women desiring no children (Testa, 2012). Since the 1990s almost all Southern European countries have experienced a rapid increase in the share of out-of-wedlock children, an uncommon occurrence until recently (Delgado et al., 2008). However, this trend is very unevenly distributed—in 2011 non-marital births comprised 43 per cent of all births in Portugal, 37 per cent in Spain, and 23 per cent in Italy, but only 7 per cent in Greece.

The consequences of the dramatic decline in fertility are evident in the age composition of the population (OECD, 2012). The current imbalance between births and deaths was compensated by large immigration flows between the mid-1990s and late 2000s, particularly to Spain and Italy, reversing the migration outflows of the 1960s and 1970s. Although migrants display, on average, higher fertility than natives, this difference diminishes over time and gives only a minor boost, if any, to the TFR (Roig Vila and

Castro-Martín, 2008; see also section 3.2.6). The recent economic crisis has had a strong impact in Southern Europe—particularly among recent migrants. Fertility is down from 2008 levels (see also Box 3.3), accompanied by a decrease in immigration flows or even net outflows in Spain.

3.1.4.8 *The Middle East*

In 1950, the TFR in the Middle East stood at 7.0, higher than in other world regions, including sub-Saharan Africa. The lowest TFR was recorded in Lebanon (5.7), while the highest was in Yemen, which had fertility above eight children per woman. The figures for such countries as Iran, Turkey, Kuwait, United Arab Emirates, and Qatar were also remarkably high at around 7.0 (Dyer, 2008; UN, 2011). High fertility rates prevailed in the region throughout the 1950s and 1960s, and were noted by Kirk (1966), who argued that Muslim countries as a group were experiencing only the early stages of demographic transition.

Fertility decline in the Middle East commenced in the mid-1960s, and by 1980 the period TFR had slightly declined to around 6.3 in the region as a whole. However, many countries experienced an accelerated decline during the 1980s, so that by 2010 the TFR in the region was below 3.0. But the regional average masks wide cross-country differences: Iran's sharp fertility decline since the mid-1980s is, for example, unique—the TFR declined from around 6.5 in 1985 to around 2.0 in 2000, and further decreased to around 1.8 in 2006 (Abbasi-Shavazi et al., 2009b, p. 209), stabilizing thereafter and estimated at 1.9 in 2012 (PRB, 2012). The recent fertility levels in several other countries in the region have also been much lower than those recorded in the 1980s. For example, during 2005–10 the TFR in Qatar (2.2) and Turkey (2.2) was slightly higher than the figure in United Arab Emirates (2.0) and Lebanon (1.6); all of these countries have reached fertility around or below replacement. In contrast, Yemen (4.9) and Iraq (4.4) still retained very high TFR levels (UN, 2013). Indeed, many of these countries are included in Chapter 4, which deals with 'higher' fertility settings.

The high Muslim fertility observed in the past led some scholars to believe that religion and fertility were more closely correlated for Muslims than for other religious groups (Jones and Karim, 2005). However, the sharp and accelerated fertility decline of recent decades does not support this hypothesis (Abbasi-Shavazi and Jones, 2005, pp. 35–6; Eberstadt and Shah, 2012).[8] The decline of fertility in recent decades appears to be much more clearly linked to urbanization, advancement of women's education (Abbasi-Shavazi and Torabi, 2012; Lutz et al., 2010), and rising aspirations for women who seek employment (Jones, 2012), as well as an accentuation of children's education

[8] Courbage (1999) argued that high fertility in some of the Middle East countries has been linked to their oil-driven economy, which allowed governments to establish subsidies leading to the reduction of the costs associated with children and reinforcing preferences for large families. The fall of the oil price in the 1980s, followed by cut-backs in subsidies, also coincided with the fall of fertility in these countries.

and opportunities, access to media, changing family ideals, decline of infant mortality, and the introduction of effective contraception. Finally, there are indications that universality of marriage is also being questioned (Rashad et al., 2005; Torabi et al., 2012), with divorce rising in most countries (Singerman, 2007).

Fertility trends in Israel warrant special attention—it is a society more developed and more affluent than many countries in Europe and East Asia, yet it shows a persistence of high fertility and high fertility intentions, with the period TFR stabilizing around 3.0 since the mid-1980s (CBS, 2011). This is achieved through a unique combination of pronatalism (policies supporting large families), cultural, ethnic, and religious diversity, and competition. Some population subgroups, especially the 'ultra-religious' Jews, maintain traditional values in tandem with very high fertility (Bystrov, 2012; DellaPergola, 2007). Such unique conditions will not be repeated elsewhere, but the same elements may contribute to higher fertility and possibly also a return of more traditional values in some post-transitional settings in the future.

The diversity of the region implies that Middle Eastern countries will retain different fertility patterns, although recent trends and the experience of other countries suggest that further declines in fertility are likely. Some countries in the region, especially Iran and Turkey have reverted to actively pro-natalist rhetoric and policies (Roudi, 2012), which—if fully implemented—could interrupt or partly reverse fertility decline.

3.1.4.9 *East Asian countries and territories*

Fertility decline in Asia began in the late 1940s in Japan where the TFR dropped from 4.5 in 1947 to 2.0 in 1957. It continued a slow decline to 1.5 in 1994 and 1.3 in 2002 (Retherford and Ogawa, 2006). Fertility was high in Singapore, South Korea, and Taiwan in 1960 with TFRs of around 6.0, but declined rapidly in the 1970s and 1980s (Tsuya et al., 2009). In Singapore, fertility dropped to replacement level by 1975, below 1.5 in 1998, and below 1.3 in 2003 (Yap, 2009). TFR in South Korea and Taiwan reached below replacement level about a decade later than in Singapore, in 1983 and 1984 respectively. The decline then proceeded rapidly, and the TFR fertility in these four countries dipped below 1.3 in the early 2000s. Since then, the TFR in Japan climbed slightly to 1.4 in 2010, but it remained at an ultra-low level in other countries, reaching 1.2 in Singapore and South Korea, and 0.9 in Taiwan and the Special Administrative Region of Hong Kong (statistical offices: various countries and years). Indeed, national statistical offices in the region assume that fertility in the region will stay very low (Basten, 2013a). Fertility trends are considerably less certain in North Korea, where only limited data are irregularly released by the government and official institutions; Spoorenberg and Schwekendiek (2012) show the period TFR around replacement level in two census years, 1993 (2.16) and 2008 (2.00), with a possible intermediate dip during the periods marked by famine and economic collapse.

Rapid economic development, increasing level of education among women leading to increasing labour force participation, and effective national family planning programmes initiated in the 1960s (excluding Japan) are considered to be major forces behind the rapid fertility decline in all of these countries (Choe, 2006; McDonald, 2009; Tsuya et al., 2009). Fertility declines in recent decades are mostly due to delayed onset of childbearing, resulting, in part, from increasing age at first marriage combined with still low levels of non-marital births (Bumpass et al., 2009; Jones, 2007). Persistent gender inequality marked by limited involvement of men in household work and childrearing have contributed to these trends (see Box 3.2).

The importance of having a son while fertility levels were falling to below replacement level, combined with modern medical technology that allowed parents to identify the sex of the fetus and easy access to induced abortions, produced an unusually high sex ratio at birth in South Korea, Taiwan, and Singapore before the preference for boys began to weaken (Chung and Das Gupta, 2007). In contrast, fertility behaviour in Japan is not associated with son preference.

In Japan, South Korea, Taiwan, and Singapore, higher education for men is associated with higher probability of marrying, but also results in a slower pace of marriage. Among women, higher education is associated with lower probability of ever marrying and slower pace of marriage. As a result, a large proportion of men with low levels of education and women with high levels of education remain unmarried into their late 30s.[9] Education differentials in marriage notwithstanding, fertility decline proceeded almost simultaneously in most social groups. Especially in South Korea there was a remarkable convergence in fertility by education, indicating that rising education level contributed only a little to the observed fertility decline (Yoo, 2013). At the same time, Anderson and Kohler (2012) argued that under competitive conditions typical for East Asia, the desire of parents to provide their children with a top education makes children very costly in terms of both time and money. This 'education fever' constitutes an important force behind very low fertility in the region.

3.1.4.10 *China*

While a notable fertility reduction had already been observed in some Chinese cities in the 1950s and 1960s (Lavely and Freedman, 1990), nationwide fertility decline did not begin until the early 1970s under the 'Later, Longer, Fewer' family planning policy, which encouraged 'later' childbearing, 'longer' birth intervals, and 'fewer' total births. During that decade, China's TFR fell from about 6.0 to about 2.5 children per woman. In the 1980s, following the enactment of more proscriptive family planning regulations, the TFR fluctuated between 2.3 and 2.9 (Yao, 1995). These fluctuations were largely observed in period TFR, whereas cohort fertility continued to decline during this period (Zhao and Guo, 2010). China's fertility recorded another sharp reduction in the early 1990s when the TFR fell below replacement. It declined further to around 1.6 in 2000. While many studies have suggested that China's fertility has remained that low or has fallen to a lower level in

[9] Since the late 1990s new marriage behaviour has emerged in Taiwan, Singapore, and South Korea where men, especially with lower levels of education, are increasingly marrying foreign-born women (Kim, 2007).

the first decade of the twenty-first century (Cai, 2008; Retherford et al., 2005; Scharping, 2005; Zhao and Zhang, 2010), there is some controversy over the 'true' fertility rates of China (Box 3.1). Morgan et al. (2009) estimate that the 1976–80 birth cohorts will reach fertility well below replacement threshold and will have about 1.7 births per woman.

China's unique history of family planning regulations has undoubtedly affected its recent demographic history. The 'Later, Longer, Fewer' family planning programme played a major part in driving down fertility in the 1970s. However, some scholars have recently argued that the macro-level effect of the restrictive 'one-child policy', introduced in 1978 and applied in 1979, has been overstated (Cai, 2010). First, the policy was not universally implemented, with many exceptions made for rural areas, ethnic minorities, or couples with a daughter. Indeed, Gu et al. (2007) show that in the late 1990s 11 per cent of couples were allowed to have two or three children, and as many as 54 per cent were allowed a second child if their only child was a girl.[10] Second, the fertility decline seen in China echoes that seen elsewhere in East Asia (see section 3.1.4.9). As such, economic and social development can be argued to be a major driver as much as policy (Wang et al., 2013). Despite this, there is currently a significant policy debate regarding ending or at least reforming the family planning restrictions.

In East Asia and in China in particular, growing evidence indicates a deviation from the two-child norm prevalent in Europe and North America. In China, 2001 national data show a mean desired number of children among married women aged 20–29 of 1.50 for urban areas and 1.75 for rural women (Zhang, 2004). A number of regional surveys in both urban and rural settings have reported ideal family sizes around these figures (Basten and Gu, 2013). In Taiwan and Hong Kong, surveys of young people indicate levels similar to China, of around 1.5–1.7 (Basten, 2013b). While deliberate under-reporting of fertility ideals is widespread in China, the similarities to Hong Kong and Taiwan are indicative of such low ideals being 'genuine' in China.

China's fertility is likely to stay at current low levels—or decline further—even if family planning restrictions are relaxed (Zheng et al., 2009). Like many other populations in East Asia, China is experiencing a significant change in its reproductive culture. China's traditional marriage patterns are going through a great transition, with age at marriage and proportion remaining single having increased and likely to increase further. Divorce, sex outside marriage, and same sex partnering are likely to become ever more acceptable (Wang and Zhou, 2010). These changes are likely to spread from urban to rural areas. All of these factors could lower fertility, although some of the fertility declines may be caused by the temporary effect of rising age at childbearing (Box 3.1).

[10] This has not prevented, however, the spread of sex-selective abortion, leading to skewed sex ratios at birth (SRB) estimated at around 120 males per hundred females in 2005–7 (Das Gupta et al., 2009, Figure 1). Mini-census data for 2005 show that in 5 out of 31 provinces there were over 125 males per 100 females born as of 2005, while only three provinces reported 'normal' SRBs of around 105 (Eberstadt, 2011).

Box 3.1 Finding China's Period Fertility Rate

While the low fertility rates reported in the text are supported by the preliminary results of China's 2010 census, which was of a high quality according to the National Bureau of Statistics (Ma, 2011), the rates differ markedly from those reported by China's National Population and Family Planning Commission, which suggests that China's total fertility rate (TFR) has been 1.8 since the mid-1990s (National Strategy on Population Development Research Group, 2007). The UN's 2010 World Population Prospects (WPP) stated that China's TFRs were 1.80, 1.70, and 1.64 for 1995–2000, 2000–05, and 2005–10 respectively (UN, 2011). However, China's 2010 census recorded only 222 million children aged 0–14. If these results were, indeed, accurate, China's TFRs for 1996–2010 would be significantly lower than those suggested by both the Chinese government and the United Nations Population Division (Cai, 2011; Zhao and Chen, 2011). In line with that, the 2012 WPP released in 2013 lowered the estimate of the TFR in China in 2000–05 to 1.55 (UN, 2013).

This confusion arises partly from the fact that China's demographic data were often collected by different government departments for different purposes, which resulted in some inconsistencies. In addition, the sharp fertility reduction in the early 1990s was not expected at the time, which led government officials and researchers to believe that the reported low fertility was caused by serious under-registration (Zeng, 1996). Some demographers questioned this notion and further examined China's fertility decline in recent years (Cai, 2008; Zhao and Zhang, 2010). Similar changes in how the data are viewed have not yet been observed among policymakers. Officially endorsed fertility figures are most likely to have over-estimated China's fertility for more than a decade.

3.1.5 Regional trends: common issues and key factors

This overview of regional fertility developments shows that a trend toward low fertility has become a defining feature of the demographic landscape in a number of countries whose fertility levels were considered to be 'too high' only two or three decades ago. With the notable exception of sub-Saharan Africa, all major global regions appear to be firmly set on a path to low fertility. Furthermore, the epicentre of lowest fertility moved away from the 'Western World' to East Asia and some formerly communist countries in Central and Eastern Europe.

Paradoxically, some of the countries that were at the forefront of the march to sub-replacement fertility in the 1960s–70s, especially the Nordic countries and the USA, now register close-to-replacement and relatively stable (or even slightly rising) CFRs (Myrskylä et al., 2013; see also section 3.1.4). This evidence gives rise to the possibility that countries with very low fertility may eventually witness a recovery to levels close to replacement once broader societal conditions become more conducive to having children (Myrskylä et al., 2011), especially if the predominant family size ideal remains fixed at around two children. Equally possible, however, are other alternative scenarios, either of a continuing diversity in low fertility as currently seen in Europe, or a global move to very low fertility levels, with widespread childlessness and a widespread one-child family ideal (see also section 3.5.2).

Having outlined major trends in contemporary low fertility settings, section 3.2 explores some of the key factors driving these patterns as highlighted by the experts and the literature.

3.2 Explaining past and future fertility trends: theories and empirical evidence

3.2.1 'Meta-theories' of low fertility and family changes

There are many overarching theories that have been employed to explain recent fertility patterns and differences in the countries covered in this chapter. The very basic contour of the global fertility decline has been provided by the concept of the demographic transition. This 'theory' of population, which has been applied, adjusted, and critiqued continually since it was first proposed in the mid-1940s (Notestein, 1945), envisages a shift from high mortality and high fertility to stabilization at low levels of mortality and fertility around replacement rate. However, the presence of below replacement fertility both before and after the publication of the theory suggests that it has relatively little—in its unmodified form—to say concerning currently low fertility settings.

One of the most widely used concepts is an overarching narrative of the 'Second Demographic Transition' (SDT) (Lesthaeghe, 2010, 1995; van de Kaa, 1987). This theory links dramatic changes in family behaviour—including sustained below replacement fertility, extensive postponement of marriage and childbearing, and the rapid rise of cohabitation and births outside of wedlock—with a transformation in values, emphasis on individual self-fulfilment, the massive rise in higher education, and changing gender roles. A closer investigation of the link between the progression of the SDT and fertility revealed a strong correlation with childbearing at higher reproductive ages (the 'recuperation' component; Lesthaeghe, 2010), and an unexpected positive correlation between the SDT and the level of period fertility rates in Europe (Sobotka, 2008a). The SDT was also shown to be closely associated with the approval of voluntary childlessness (Merz and Liefbroer, 2012).

The decline in marriage and the rise in partnership instability have been surprisingly little connected with fertility declines, at least in Europe. In most of the traditional low-fertility countries (with the important exception of Japan), marriage has become ever less relevant for reproduction and childbearing has increasingly shifted outside marriage, especially to cohabiting unions. In 2011, almost 40 per cent of births in the EU took place outside marriage; in the USA the corresponding share was 41 per cent in 2010. Eight European countries, including Bulgaria, France, Sweden, and Slovenia, registered more than half of all births outside marriage; in Spain, where only one out of ten births took place outside wedlock in the early 1990s, 37 per cent births were extramarital in 2011. European countries with high shares of non-marital births have, on average, higher fertility rates, suggesting that permissive attitudes to less conventional living arrangements go hand in hand with more opportunities for women and couples to form a family (Billari and Kohler, 2004; see also section 3.1.4.3, 'Western Europe'). The spread of less stable family forms together with rising divorce rates and, in some countries, a higher frequency of single motherhood, increased the exposure of children to the experience of living with one parent only, typically with the mother (Heuveline et al., 2003; Perelli-Harris et al., 2012). The evidence on the impact of union instability on fertility is mixed or slightly negative (Bélanger et al., 2010; Thomson et al., 2012), as three contrasting mechanisms can be identified. Union break-up means a disruption in family life, which negatively affects the likelihood of having another child in the subsequent period when most of the women and men live without a partner. However, the formation of a new union provides an opportunity to have another child, a decision which also signals the commitment of the new partners to each other and is often expected to 'cement' their relationship (Griffith et al., 1985). At younger ages, partnership instability may lead to the delay of family formation, as many women and men are unable or unwilling to form a lasting union, which is often seen as a precondition for parenthood. On balance, the aggregate effect of union instability depends on the age at first union formation, family stage (and age) at which divorce or dissolution takes place, the share of women who re-partner after separation, and the speed with which these new partnerships are formed (e.g. Beaujouan and Solaz, 2012; Thomson et al., 2012).

The finding on the positive correlation between SDT progression and fertility rates is also related to the debate on the possible reversal of the relationship between economic and social development and fertility, fuelled by the studies suggesting that at advanced levels of development (as measured by the gross domestic product (GDP) level or by the Human Development Index (HDI)) fertility decline stops or even reverses. These studies (see Luci and Thévenon, 2011; Myrskylä et al., 2009) have turned on its head the widely accepted notion that more development generally equals lower fertility. However, the hypothesis on the reversals between development and fertility is not universally accepted: the study by Myrskylä et al. (2009) has been criticized for the indicators used, countries omitted from the analysis, for relying on the period TFRs that are affected by tempo effect, lack of robustness, and other data issues (e.g. Furuoka, 2009; Harttgen and Vollmer, 2013). Luci and Thévenon (2011) and Luci-Greulich and Thévenon (2013) highlight the key role of institutional changes that make it possible for women to combine career and fertility in most developed settings. In a more recent study revisiting their earlier work, Myrskylä et al. (2011) indicate that the development–fertility reversal can also be traced with the completed fertility rates for women born in 1970. Furthermore, they show that the positive effect of development (HDI) on fertility is limited to childbearing at later ages (30+), suggesting that there is a positive association between development and the recuperation of the previously postponed births. This link is conditioned by the level of gender equity in the society, with countries scoring low on gender equality registering declining fertility even at very advanced levels of development (see also section 3.2.3.3).

Another influential notion in most international projections is the concept of convergence between countries of fertility to a given level. This idea has, for many decades, informed some long-term population projections produced by the UN (which envisioned that fertility will universally rise towards the replacement level) and prevailed in long-term fertility scenarios beyond 2050 by the WIC, as described in section 3.5.2.

Related to the previous concept is an idea of 'feedback' effect. Demeny (2004, p. 142) observed that the UN's medium projections 'implicitly assume that the trend toward lower birth rates... will elicit negative feedbacks that by the middle of the twenty-first century will bring fertility back to near-replacement levels everywhere'. This is derived from an implicit assumption of a homeostatic response by humans to ensure a continuity in (at least) replacement levels of population. However, Demeny also observed that positive feedbacks were 'equally plausible...reinforcing a tendency for further falls in fertility'. As a consequence of population ageing, individuals needing to provide for their old age have an increased incentive to accumulate human capital and savings, and to acquire pension benefits. This could result in the institutionalization of many of the elements discussed earlier that are driving low fertility in East Asia. Indeed, such a situation has been formalized in the so-called 'Low Fertility Trap' hypothesis (Lutz, 2006). First, population decline fuelled by sustained low fertility leads to fewer women of reproductive age and, hence, fewer births. Second, through socialization and social learning, family size ideals are influenced by the experiences of young people who grow up in an environment with few children (e.g. few siblings, absence of larger families). Hence, children will figure less prominently in their own image of a desirable life. Finally, rapidly ageing societies drive pessimism among the young regarding their own economic opportunities. This, combined with widening consumption opportunities, can lead to an ever greater gap between aspirations and income—a gap which childbearing would only further exacerbate. Should each of these conditions be met, then reversing fertility decline would prove to be extremely difficult.

When considering heterogeneous concepts, including those outlined earlier, it is important to examine the contribution of more specific drivers in fertility change—in other words, the issues which underlie these grand theories and how they interact with choices over the life course such as timing of fertility. For example, many features of the SDT are barely nascent in much of East Asia. Therefore, we explore in greater depth some of the main issues and determinants behind the fertility changes outlined in section 3.1 and, ultimately, those further explored in the IIASA–Oxford survey of experts. These include the effect of fertility postponement; cultural factors relating to ideals and intentions, religion, and gender equality; family policies; immigration; and biomedical aspects and education. Before we do so, however, it is crucial to consider the effect of fertility postponement upon how we measure contemporary fertility.

3.2.2 Fertility postponement and its impact on period fertility

Across the developed world, parenthood has been shifted to ever-higher ages (Kohler et al., 2002; Sobotka, 2004b). In Western, Northern, and Southern Europe, as well as Japan, the mean age of mothers at first birth has reached 28–30 years, 4–6 years later than in the early 1970s (Schmidt et al., 2012). The frequency of childbearing has increased most rapidly at advanced reproductive ages, including women aged over 40.

This postponement transition (Kohler et al., 2002) has multiple roots. The expansion of higher education and the resulting later age of completing education and entering of the labour market (as well as the concomitant increase in the share of women entering the labour market) have been repeatedly identified as important factors (Blossfeld and Huinink, 1991; Goldin, 2006; Ní Bhrolcháin and Beaujouan, 2012). Other factors include the spread of hormonal contraception, rising economic and employment uncertainty in young adulthood, decline of marriage, the rise of more unstable forms of partnerships, and the spread of new values incompatible with parenthood (Blossfeld et al., 2005; Goldin and Katz, 2002; Goldin, 2006; Kohler et al., 2002; Mills et al., 2011; Sobotka, 2004a).

This fertility postponement temporarily affected period fertility rates, as some births that would otherwise have taken place in a given year were shifted into the future, potentially leading to more dramatic assessments of fertility change than would otherwise be the case. The resulting tempo effect (or tempo distortion), which is the difference between the observed and hypothetical fertility in the absence of birth postponement, has become widely debated in the literature (Luy, 2011) and has emerged as one of the key explanations for the very low fertility levels observed in many rich societies (Bongaarts and Sobotka, 2012; Kohler et al., 2002; Sobotka, 2004b). A number of methods have been proposed to account for the tempo effect and compute tempo-adjusted period fertility rates (e.g. Bongaarts and Feeney, 1998; Bongaarts and Sobotka, 2012; Kohler and Ortega, 2002). The Bongaarts and Feeney (1998) method became most prominent (although not universally accepted; see, e.g., Schoen, 2004). As a result of tempo effect, depressed period fertility rates are often incorrectly interpreted as implying similarly low levels of cohort fertility in the future. Sobotka and Lutz (2011) demonstrate that these interpretations may lead to dramatic assessments of fertility trends. Empirical analysis based on tempo-adjusted period fertility indicators suggests that in the absence of the shifts in fertility timing, the period TFR in the EU around 2008 would have been by almost 0.2 higher, at 1.77, than the observed TFR of 1.59 (VID, 2012). Large cross-country differences exist, however, in the estimated size of this effect (Bongaarts and Sobotka, 2012; Goldstein et al., 2009).

Fertility trends will continue to be affected by changes in the timing of births. In Europe the pace of increase in the mean age at first birth diminished after 2000 and the 'postponement transition' was seemingly coming to an end in some countries by 2008 (Bongaarts and Sobotka, 2012). However, the recent economic recession has brought a renewed postponement of births, leading to additional downward pressure on period fertility (see section 3.2.4 and also Box 3.3). In contrast, developing and middle-income countries with low fertility typically report earlier ages at childbearing with most only beginning to experience a shift towards later parenthood, which may depress their period TFRs for decades to come (Bongaarts, 1999; Rosero-Bixby et al., 2009).

Postponement of childbearing has a critical biological dimension. The higher a woman's age when she attempts to become pregnant, especially above 35 years, the longer the waiting time for a pregnancy to occur, resulting in a lower chance of achieving a pregnancy and a higher risk of miscarriage if there is a pregnancy (Menken, 1985; see also section 3.2.7.1). Furthermore, men's age has been identified as an independent risk factor for infertility (section 3.2.7.2). Consequently, couples delaying childbearing face an increased risk of not realizing their childbearing plans through either lower completed fertility or higher involuntary childlessness (Leridon, 2008; te Velde et al., 2012; sections 3.2.7.1 and 3.2.7.3).

Rising infertility at higher childbearing ages implies an increase in the demand for assisted reproduction technology (ART), as well as elevated multiple birth rates (section 3.2.7.3). In addition, higher maternal and paternal ages are linked to an increased risk of pregnancy complications and adverse reproductive outcomes. However, positive influences of rising age at childbearing include psychological maturity, lower income loss for the mothers, and a higher level of happiness among the parents (Miller, 2011; Myrskylä and Margolis, 2012).

3.2.3 Cultural and social forces in fertility ideals, intentions, and behaviour

3.2.3.1 *Fertility intentions*

Where modern contraception makes it easy for couples to prevent unwanted pregnancies, fertility preferences are key determinants of reproductive behaviour and fertility trends (Bongaarts, 2001; Schoen et al., 1999). Yet, the number of children individuals intend to have often surpasses the number they actually achieve by the end of their reproductive career (Testa, 2012). Constraints on meeting intentions include not having a suitable partner, experiencing partnership instability, fecundity impairments, and unexpected events that may lead to a downward revision of reproductive intentions (Iacovou and Tavares, 2011; Liefbroer, 2009). While childbearing intentions can also move upward, especially as family size grows, these shifts are less frequent than downward adjustments.

A two-child family appears to be the dominant ideal of Europeans, which has become entrenched over time according to the Eurobarometer surveys conducted in 2001, 2006, and 2011 (Testa, 2012, 2006). The mean intended family size is also concentrated at around two children in all European countries, with the notable exception of Austria and Germany, which show, according to some surveys, below replacement ideal and intended family sizes (Goldstein et al., 2003). The temporal trend is marked by a remarkable stability, with the exception of Greece and Portugal, where an abrupt and pervasive decline in family size ideals has been observed between 2006 and 2011. This decrease is most likely linked to the recent economic recession, which was particularly severe in these countries (Testa and Basten, 2012).

The Eurobarometer survey, which is only cross-sectional, shows that more than one third of European women and men stop childbearing with fewer children than initially desired (Testa, 2012). In addition, the share of people reporting a family bigger than the size actually desired amounts to 10–15 per cent. Hence, the use of lifetime fertility intentions for forecasting purposes has its limits owing to considerable challenges in measuring both intentions and (un)certainty (Morgan, 2001). Negative reproductive intentions (not wishing to have a child) are usually more reliable predictors of subsequent behaviour than the positive ones (Rovi, 1994).

Because of a lack of adequate data, most studies on fertility are based upon the female perspective. However, some evidence on gender differences in intentions exists. In Europe, women generally indicate a slightly larger family size ideal than men, and they also display smaller inconsistency between ideal and actual family size (Testa, 2012). Studies based on couple data show that men and women have equal influence over the final reproductive decision (Thomson, 1997) and therefore have equal power in negotiation if a conflict arises between them (Jansen and Liefbroer, 2006). In settings characterized by low gender equality where women have the main or the sole responsibility for childcare, such as in Italy and Austria, women also have a greater influence on childbearing decisions than men in the early stages of the family formation process (i.e. at parities zero and one) (Testa et al., 2011). This may also be the case in countries with a high acceptance of single mothers, such as the Nordic countries, where women may decide to have a child 'on their own'. Typically, the disagreement between partners favours the one who does not want to have a child. This couple approach increases the predictive power of fertility intentions (Beckman et al., 1983).

In the USA, the aggregate correspondence between intended and actual fertility is generally higher than in Europe, largely owing to a high share of unplanned pregnancies and unintended births (section 3.1.4.1). Furthermore, there is growing evidence in East Asia that the two-child norm that is dominant in Europe may be much more fluid in that region (Basten et al., 2013). This could have profound consequences for future fertility trends (section 3.1.4.10).

3.2.3.2 *Religion*

A review of studies referring to the 1950s and early 1960s documented the higher fertility of Catholics compared with other religious groups and the non-affiliated for Western countries (Jones and Nortman, 1968). This was mainly attributed to the prohibition of artificial contraception by the Catholic Church. Marked fertility differences by religious affiliation had, by and large, disappeared by the 1970s (Derosas and van Poppel, 2006; Westoff and Jones, 1979), but a gap with the non-affiliated persists (Philipov and Berghammer, 2007). Moreover, some religious minorities diverge from average fertility levels (Skirbekk et al., 2010). Muslims have a higher number of children than members of other religions in Europe, but there is convergence over time (Pew Research Center, 2011; Westoff and Frejka, 2007). Religious affiliation is an important correlate of family size in parts of Asia (Morgan et al., 2002), but less so in some Latin American countries (Heaton, 2011). Higher levels of fertility are observed in countries with Muslim majorities, even though they have fallen in recent decades (Pew Research Center, 2011). Abbasi-Shavazi and Jones (2005) and Abbasi-Shavazi and Torabi (2012) argue that the high fertility recorded until recently in many predominantly Muslim countries could be largely explained by their socio-economic and cultural characteristics. In some contexts, religious differences in fertility behaviour have a crucial impact on the future religious composition of a population (Hout et al., 2001).

Studies report clear fertility differences by religious intensity for Western countries, often measured by church attendance or self-assessed religiosity (Philipov and Berghammer, 2007; Zhang, 2008). In explaining why religious people have larger families, scholars refer to the influence of religious teaching, the role of church-based social networks, and the coping function of religion (Chatters and Taylor, 2005). The socio-economic traits of adherents also matter, as does the status of the religion within the social and economic order of society (McQuillan, 2004).

In some contexts, religious fertility differences have a crucial impact on the future religious composition of a population (Hout et al., 2001; Kaufmann, 2010; Skirbekk et al., 2010). The way in which the share of religious people in a country is related to fertility rates is, however, unknown. One may argue that the erosion of religion should have a negative effect on fertility, but examples of secular countries with higher fertility rates (e.g. Sweden and France) and vice versa suggest that the link may be more complex.

3.2.3.3 *Gender equality*

At the societal or institutional level, gender equality includes whether women and men are offered similar opportunities for educational attainment, economic participation, health and survival, and political empowerment. When women are offered similar educational and employment opportunities as men but these opportunities are severely restricted by having children, women react by having fewer children and having them later in life. In a large meta-analysis of the central reasons for birth postponement in advanced societies, Mills et al. (2011) suggest that gender equality plays a key role. Although empirical evidence connecting gender equality at the societal level to fertility faces methodological challenges (Mills, 2010) and has been less rigorous, there is evidence that institutional factors affect fertility.

Gender equality can be examined at the societal (political empowerment), institutional (provision of childcare and parental leave), household (division of labour), and individual level (gender role attitudes). In the latter two cases, the term 'gender equity' is often used, referring to 'fairness and opportunity rather than strict equality of outcome' (McDonald, 2013, p. 983). A number of aggregate indices measuring the status of women and different aspects of gender equality have been proposed since the

Box 3.2 Living Arrangements, Gender Roles, and their Relationship to Fertility in East Asia

Current family behaviour, including marriage, childbearing, gender roles, and living arrangements, in Japan, China, South Korea, Singapore, and Taiwan reflect both the influence of the Confucian family tradition and the rapid economic and social changes of the second half of the twentieth century.

The family system based on Confucian ideals emphasizes proper roles and relationships based on gender, generation, and age. The basic purpose and function of the family was preservation of lineage and prosperity. Under a family system based on patrilineal descent, the most important obligation of a person was to marry and produce a son. Marriage was mandatory, and early marriage was common. Co-residence with parents was the norm for both men and women until marriage, and for the eldest sons even after marriage. A woman's position in a family changed drastically from being a daughter to being a daughter-in-law with low status upon marriage; however, a married woman attained a high status within the family by bearing and rearing a son (Choe, 2006; Tsuya et al., 1991).

Meiji restoration in Japan in the nineteenth century and the establishment of republics in other East Asian countries in the twentieth century provided the legal basis for equal rights for women. It took until the second half of the twentieth century, however, for substantial changes in family behaviour and gender roles to occur, in tandem with rising levels of education for women, rapid economic growth, urbanization, and greater geographic mobility. Now, women and men are marrying at increasingly later ages, and the proportion of people who never marry is rising (Jones, 2007). Typical family size has decreased to two or fewer children, and it has become less common for grown children to reside with their parents. Most women work outside home before marriage, and a substantial proportion continue to work after marriage and having children.

However, the persistence of traditional norms in East Asian countries has resulted in patterns of family behaviour different from those experienced in the West. The strong patrilineal and patriarchal family traditions, for example, have kept out-of-wedlock childbearing at very low levels (Bumpass and Choe, 2004; Jones, 2007), with the civil code in Japan requiring registration of a birth of a child in his/her father's family registry. In South Korea, the family law was changed in 2005, abolishing the household headship system and making birth registration a stand-alone document. However, it is not yet possible to see whether this has had a large effect on the attitude and behaviour of the general public. A child whose father is unidentified experiences serious social stigma. The divorce rate was low until the 1990s. Although women, including married women, are participating in paid employment at increasingly higher levels, men rarely take on domestic roles (Rindfuss, 2004; Tsuya et al., 2005). In addition, long-standing preferences for boys combined with very low fertility and the spread of sex-selective abortion led to an emergence of distorted sex ratios at birth in China, Korea, and Taiwan (section 3.1.4.9). Finally, participation in housework and childcare responsibilities has remained persistently low among Asian men, which some scholars have suggested plays a role in discouraging partnership formation and childbearing for (increasingly better educated) women (Ishii-Kuntz et al., 2004).

mid-1980s (Bericat, 2012). Gender systems determine the division of labour and responsibilities between the sexes, as well as the rights and responsibilities allocated to men and women, and are therefore considered crucial for understanding fertility patterns (Mason, 1997; McDonald, 2000).

The literature on household gender equity stems largely from Becker's (1981) argument that women's increased economic independence results in higher relative opportunity costs of childbearing via foregone earnings during childbearing and care periods, thereby generally lowering fertility. Unequal gender roles in the household and specifically the perpetuation of the male breadwinner/female homemaker model, force women to choose between a career without children or remaining in the home (Cooke, 2004; Mills et al., 2008; Oláh, 2003). The lack of sustained improvement in gender inequality in the household is considered as a core underlying determinant of very low fertility (McDonald, 2000), particularly in East Asia (Box 3.2). This discrepancy between new public opportunities and sustained domestic obligations is sometimes referred to as the 'incomplete gender revolution' (Esping-Andersen, 2009).

Empirical results linking egalitarian gender role attitudes to fertility are mixed, particularly in relation to men (Goldscheider et al., 2010; Westoff and Frejka, 2007). Some studies suggest that men's more gender-egalitarian roles result in higher fertility (Kaufman, 2000; Puur et al., 2008), while others find the opposite (Westoff and Higgins, 2009), and still others identify a U-shaped effect, where men with either traditional or egalitarian views report higher ideal family sizes (Miettinen et al., 2011) (Box 3.2).

3.2.4 Employment, economic uncertainty, and fertility

The fertility literature has long highlighted the relevance of both aggregate and individual economic conditions for the timing and number of births. Economic events and economic uncertainty alter current and future demand for children among couples (De Cooman et al., 1987). Sobotka et al. (2011) note that, overall, fertility has exhibited a pro-cyclical relationship with economic growth for more than a hundred years. However, the effect is small and difficult to identify as most recessions have been short-lived and fertility developments were often dominated by stronger and longer-lasting shifts, including the fall of fertility to low and very low levels in most European countries and East Asia in the 1970s–90s. This section highlights general findings on the links between economic uncertainty and fertility; more detailed examination of fertility changes during the recent economic recession is provided in Box 3.3.

As noted earlier, Becker's (1981) microeconomic model of fertility offers a good analytical tool to explain the conflicting impacts of economic conditions on childbearing decisions. Childbearing is time-intensive relative to other activities, and its associated opportunity cost can be measured by the potential wage of the mother. Whereas increases in men's work mainly entail an income effect that raises the demand for children, higher female wages give rise to a combination of income and substitution effects as they result in an increase in the cost of a child relative to other 'goods'. Accordingly, women (particularly those with high potential wages) may restrict their fertility and trade-off children for less time-demanding alternatives if the substitution effects are important.

In this context, a woman's temporary unemployment is a good time for childbearing, and fertility should be counter-cyclical, as in the USA during the 1960s and early 1970s when contraceptive access also improved (Butz and Ward, 1979). However, most analyses have found a negative relationship between different measures of unemployment and first births both in long time series (Rindfuss et al., 1988) and for recent periods (Adsera, 2011a; Kravdal, 2002; Myrskylä et al., 2013; Neels et al., 2013). The association between unemployment and fertility is complex and heterogeneous across age, parity, institutional frameworks (labour regulation, types of contracts, unemployment benefits), and the length and acuteness of economic shocks, as these factors mediate opportunity costs of having children. In a recession, women who are at a point in their life cycle when human capital accumulation is crucial may postpone childbearing to acquire more work experience or education. The pervasive long-term and youth unemployment characterized by the most recent recession is bound to have had a large negative impact on household permanent income. It may render childbearing unattractive not only for those directly affected by unemployment but also for those threatened by it—as documented for the Great Depression era (Becker, 1981; Murphy, 1992) and for the periods of high unemployment in Europe during the 1980s and 1990s (Adsera, 2011b). While the majority of short-lived recessions only seem to affect the tempo of fertility (Lee, 1990), severe crises have also had an impact on the quantum of fertility as women who postponed childbearing for lengthy periods of time did not have all the children they intended (Sobotka et al., 2011). In addition, with persistent unemployment, partnership formation is delayed (and with it, childbearing), particularly in Southern Europe or East Asia where fertility outside marriage was, and still is, relatively rare. Likewise, parents may invest more per child and reduce their family size to improve their future outlook (Easterlin, 1976), and young adults may prolong their educational training (Kohler et al., 2002).

The association between employment and fertility is weaker in countries where the family trade-offs are minimized by the availability of permanent public employment, and support for working mothers through flexible work schedules, generous leaves, or abundant and affordable childcare (as in Scandinavia) (D'Addio and d' Ercole, 2005; Matysiak and Vignoli, 2008). Conversely, the short-term contracts with meagre provisions and high turnover that expanded rapidly during the 1990s, particularly among the young in Southern Europe owing to previous strict regulation and dualization of the labour market, do not offer any of those guarantees and are associated with further depression of fertility (Adsera, 2011b). Both individual unemployment experience and aggregate economic shocks matter (Adsera, 2011a), and in some places the latter matter the most (for Norway, see Kravdal, 2002).

Box 3.3 The Impact of the Recent Economic Recession

The economic recession that started in 2008 has marked an end to the first concerted increase in period total fertility across the developed world since the Baby Boom era of the 1950s–60s, which occurred between the late 1990s and 2008 (Bongaarts and Sobotka, 2012; Goldstein et al., 2009). The early evidence for the years 2008–11 suggests that in many countries total fertility rates (TFRs) stopped rising in 2009–10 and subsequently declined in 2011 (Lanzieri, 2013; Myrskylä et al., 2013; VID, 2012). This is in line with a pro-cyclical association between economic trends and fertility rates that characterized developed countries in recent decades (Adsera, 2011a; Neels et al., 2013; Sobotka et al., 2011). However, there was considerable variation in fertility changes by country, age, and birth order, which suggests that different segments of the population responded differently to the early stage of the recession (Lanzieri, 2013; Myrskylä et al., 2013).

This trend reversal in fertility has thus far been limited to Europe, the USA, Australia, and Canada—regions affected by the economic downturn. Moreover, large cross-country differences can be observed in recent fertility trends. The USA shows a clear pattern of reversal, with a period TFR peaking at 2.1 in 2007—the highest level since 1971—before falling to 1.90 in 2011 (Livingston and Cohn, 2012), while in Europe the evidence is mixed. An average TFR for the 37 European countries shows period TFR stabilizing at 1.58–1.59 in 2008–10 and subsequently declining to 1.55 in 2011 (Figure 3.3a,b, left panel). Of these 37 countries, as many as 26 experienced a decline by 0.02 or stronger, four had stagnating fertility rates (between −0.01 and + 0.01) and only seven recorded some fertility increase (+ 0.02 or more). If countries with problematic data are removed (i.e. countries where post-2011 census revisions of population data made time series incomparable between 2010 and 2011; see note below Figure 3.3a,b), only three European countries (Belarus, Malta, and Ukraine) experienced rising fertility in 2011. This decline strongly contrasts with the situation before the onset of the recession: in 2008, 35 countries experienced rising fertility and only two saw a stable trend.

The trend towards fertility decline has been more pronounced in countries and regions that experienced stronger economic downturns and faster increases in unemployment (Livingston, 2011 for the states of the USA; Sobotka et al., 2011). Figure 3.3a,b plots the TFR trends in 2000–11 in the most populous European countries (with population over 20 million), as well as Australia, Canada, and the USA. It illustrates clearly the heterogeneity in fertility 'responses' during the initial stage of the economic recession. Among these large countries, only the USA, Romania, Spain, and, to a smaller extent, Australia and Canada have seen a reversal in the previous trend of increasing fertility. A more common pattern, with the pre-recession fertility increase subsequently coming to a halt, was typical of many large European countries, including France, Italy, and the UK. Finally, Germany stands out for its stable period TFR and Russia for its continuous fertility increase, partly fuelled by pro-natalist policies established since 2007. This heterogeneity makes it difficult to incorporate explicitly the possible future effects of the recession into fertility scenarios for the next five years (see section 3.5.1 and Appendix 3.1).

In the past, economic recessions typically induced postponement of childbearing rather than a permanent decline of fertility that would also affect cohort fertility rates (Neels et al., 2013). The current evidence suggests the same pattern for the recent recession. Fertility decline has been largely concentrated among women younger than 25 and, in most countries, confined especially to first birth rates (Lanzieri, 2013; Myrskylä et al., 2013). Also, the rise in the mean age at first birth, slowing before 2008, accelerated thereafter, suggesting that tempo effect was largely responsible for the observed declines in period TFRs.

(*continued*)

Box 3.3 Continued

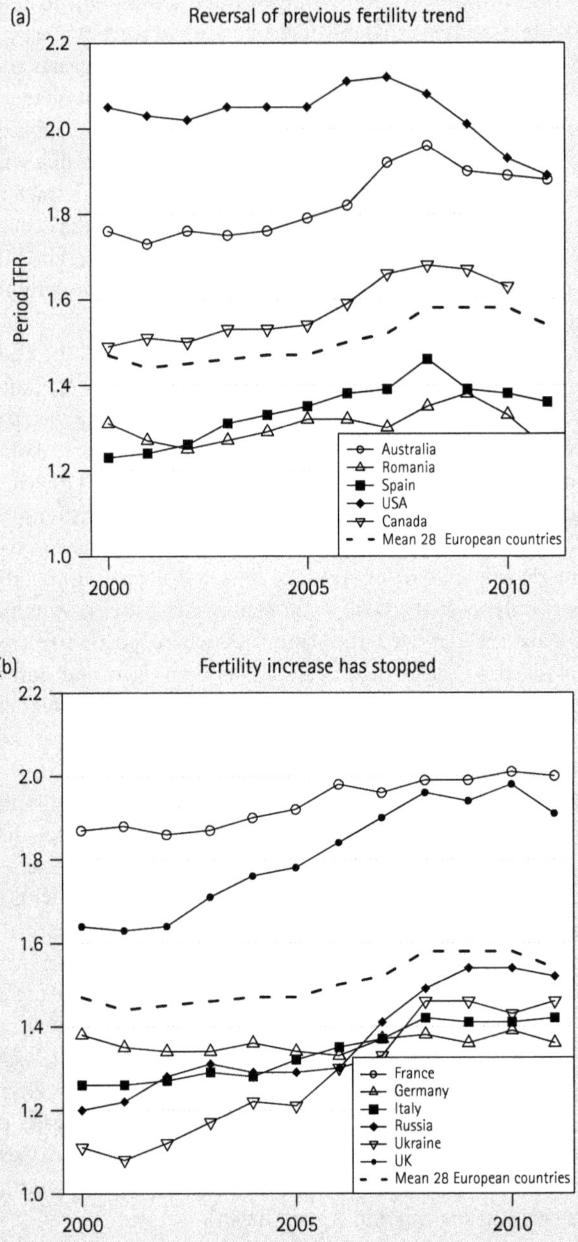

FIGURE 3.3(a, b) Period total fertility rate (TFR) in selected European countries, Australia, Canada, and the USA, 2000–11.

Notes: Average values for 28 European countries constitute a simple average that is not weighted by population size; data include countries with available data on TFR in 2011 and population size > 1 million. In addition, countries with a series break in 2011 due to post-census adjustments were excluded (Bulgaria, Latvia, Lithuania, Slovakia, the UK). The 2011 fertility decline in the line representing UK data might be artificial as a new post-census round of population estimates was used in the computation of 2011 data, making them incomparable to the data series up to 2010.

Sources: Eurostat statistical database (2012) and national statistical offices (data reported until February 2013).

A major challenge for this literature is to find the appropriate way to measure economic conditions, both aggregate and individual. Declines in GDP tend to be associated with corresponding declines in fertility (Goldstein et al., 2009). However, once other covariates are introduced, such as unemployment, the relationship weakens or disappears (for Latin America, see Adsera and Menendez, 2011). Arguably, this is partly caused by the effects that family and social policies have in offsetting some of the adverse effects of the recession. While measures of consumer sentiment or perception of the crises fit better, unemployment appears to be the most enduring relationship (Sobotka et al., 2011). Recent papers have employed new methods to deal with the problem of endogeneity of unemployment measures. Del Bono et al. (2012) use unexpected plant closings in Austria as a statistical instrument to study fertility changes after job displacement, and find fertility decline in the short and medium term, mostly due to the impact of career interruption rather than income changes.

3.2.5 Family policies

Family-related policies cover a spectrum of interventions that range from explicitly pronatalist measures through 'softer' regulations that help people to balance work and family life and have the number of children they desire. Policies that help parents balance work and family are central to mobilizing female labour supply, promoting gender equity, increasing the labour income of couples, and ensuring the financial sustainability of the welfare states (OECD, 2011; Saraceno et al., 2012). Furthermore, family policy interventions can play a role in combating child poverty and ensuring equal opportunities for children from different backgrounds (Bradshaw and Mayhew, 2006).

A key differentiating characteristic of policies across countries is whether they emphasize financial assistance, entitlements to leave work after a birth, or the provision of childcare services (OECD, 2011). There is no convincing evidence of cross-national convergence in family policies (Gauthier, 2002). Different mixes of these three policy instruments are rooted in welfare state histories, as well as prevailing attitudes towards families, the government's role, and current family patterns. Thévenon (2011) provides an in-depth description of cross-country differences and similarities in the policy mix created to support families in OECD countries. The Nordic countries (Denmark, Finland, Iceland, Norway, and Sweden) provide comprehensive support for working parents with very young children (under the age of three) through a combination of generous leave arrangements after the birth of a child and widely available childcare services (Björklund, 2006). While English-speaking countries (Ireland, the UK, Australia, New Zealand, and, to some extent, Canada and the USA) provide much less support in time and in-kind for working parents with very young children, financial support is more generous—if primarily targeted to low-income families and preschool children (McDonald and Moyle, 2010). Not all of these countries offer the same level of support, with Canada and the USA lagging behind the others. Western and Eastern European countries form a more heterogeneous group occupying an intermediate position.

Among these countries, France and Hungary stand out by offering rather generous support for working parents compared with the other countries in their respective groups. In East Asia, policy provision ranges from the laissez-faire approach of Hong Kong up to the more comprehensive measures enacted in Japan and Taiwan (Chin et al., 2012; Frejka et al., 2010). However, across the region, the relatively low tax rates and, in some cases, high public budget deficits mean that investment in family policy is often limited.

Not all policies succeed in promoting the conditions necessary for individuals to start or enlarge their families. The evidence on the effect of family policies on fertility is inconclusive (Gauthier, 2007). Interestingly, the increase in fertility rates prior to the onset of the recent economic recession has been steeper in countries where female labour market participation has also risen markedly and where women have more opportunities to combine work and childbearing. Hence, fertility rates are now higher in countries with high rates of female employment, while the opposite situation prevailed 30 years ago (Billari and Kohler, 2004; Engelhardt and Prskawetz, 2004; OECD, 2011). Recent research has emphasized the contribution of family policies to this reversal (D'Addio and d' Ercole, 2005; Hilgeman and Butts, 2009; Luci-Greulich and Thévenon, 2013). In particular, policies that help parents balance work and family life (leave entitlements, but especially the availability of childcare services for children below the age of 3, and part-time work) are found to encourage fertility (for a literature review see Thévenon and Gauthier, 2011).

3.2.6 Migrants' fertility

With generally rising mobility, migration has contributed to population increase in many low-fertility countries that would otherwise be experiencing declining population (Coleman, 2009). Around 2005, births to immigrant women accounted for 15–25 per cent of all births in the USA and many Western European countries, including the Netherlands, France, the UK, and Sweden (Sobotka, 2008b).

In most low fertility countries migrants have higher fertility than the native-born women (Sobotka, 2008b).[11] This difference can be quite substantial, reaching as high as one child per woman, when measured with the conventional period TFR. Migrant women in France had a high TFR level, estimated at 2.89 in 2008 compared with 1.89 for women born in France (Pla and Beaumel, 2012). Similarly, migrants in the USA, especially Hispanics, have had higher fertility rates for many decades—although recently the notion of high Hispanic fertility has been contested (Parrado, 2010). There are also massive differences between groups of migrants. For instance, in Sweden, where detailed statistics are available for the main groups of migrants, the TFR among immigrants in

[11] One of the main well-documented exceptions is Australia where most migrant groups showed fertility below the level recorded among Australian-born women between 1977 and 1991 (Abbasi-Shavazi and McDonald, 2000).

2009 ranged from below 1.8 among women born in Bosnia-Herzegovina, Finland, or Thailand up to 4.0 for women born in Somalia (SCB, 2010, Table 2.2.14).

Despite having, on average, higher fertility rates, migrant women in many low fertility countries have achieved sub-replacement fertility. According to the data for 2007–11, all migrant or foreign women combined had a period TFR below 2.0 in Austria, Germany, the Netherlands, Spain, and Denmark (national statistical offices; see also Figure 3.4). In contrast, migrant fertility remained at about, or slightly above, the replacement level (2.0–2.3) in Italy, Greece (data for 2005; Tsimbos, 2008), Norway, Sweden, and the UK (national statistical offices and Tromans et al., 2009), whereas it stayed above 2.6 in the USA in 2010 (estimate based on Livingston and Cohn, 2012) and approached the high level of three births per woman in France in 2008 (Pla and Beaumel, 2012). Indeed, in most low fertility countries the fertility of migrants has declined considerably since the early 1980s (Figure 3.4), contributing to a gradual fertility convergence between migrant and 'native' women. Moreover, the recent economic recession has negatively affected the fertility rates of migrants more than those of 'native women' and in several countries, including Denmark, Spain, the UK, and the USA migrant fertility fell sharply between 2008 and 2011 (Livingston and Cohn, 2012, Figure 4).

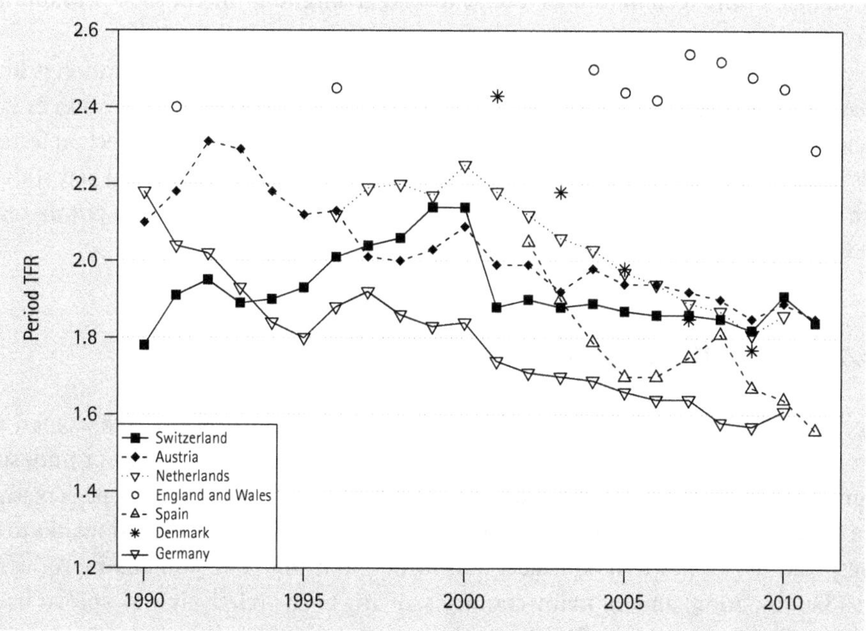

FIGURE 3.4 Period total fertility rate (TFR) among immigrant (or foreign) women in selected European countries, 1990–2011.

Notes: Data pertain to immigrant women in Denmark, England and Wales, the Netherlands, and Austria since 2002. Other data pertain to women with foreign citizenship. Data for Denmark are for five-year-periods centred in a given year and exclude migrants of Danish origin.

Sources: national statistical offices, Sobotka (2008b).

In many low fertility countries there is a common misconception that birth rates among immigrants have a significant influence on fertility rates (e.g. Héran, 2004). Also, the increase in fertility in Europe in the early 2000s has been often falsely interpreted as an outcome of high immigration. These views are not supported by the evidence as fertility rates in that period increased the most among native-born women, while they often stagnated or even declined among immigrants (Figure 3.4). In most European countries with sizeable immigration, the fertility of migrants had a small positive effect on country TFR in 2007–08, ranging from 0.03 in Germany to 0.13 in England and Wales in absolute terms. In smaller regions with high immigration, this effect was often much stronger: in Vienna, in 2009, fertility of immigrant women lifted the overall TFR for all women by 0.28 in absolute terms (Zeman et al., 2011). In contrast, in the Netherlands, the fertility of migrants and women born in the country (including the second generation) has broadly converged, and in at least one country—Denmark—migrants' fertility has fallen below that of the native-born women as of 2008. Finally, the daughters of immigrants, representing the second generation of immigrants, typically have fertility rates similar to fertility among the women without migrant origin. This rapid convergence to the fertility patterns of the host country has been illustrated even for higher-fertility populations of Turkish and Moroccan origin in the Netherlands (Garssen and Nicolaas, 2008). One important exception is the elevated fertility among the second- and third-generation of Mexican-origin migrants in the USA (Frank and Heuveline, 2005).

Little is known about the fertility effect of emigration. Short-term migration is likely to have a negative effect on fertility as many couples face temporary separation or have to relocate. Long-term emigration probably does not have a significant effect on fertility rates among the women staying in a country, but it could distort official statistics on birth and fertility, especially in countries with sizeable emigration that is poorly registered (Sobotka, 2013, section B).

3.2.7 Biomedical factors

Huge individual variability in fecundability (Dunson et al., 2002) presents women and men of reproductive ages with two contrasting challenges: how to prevent undesired pregnancies from occurring, and how to achieve pregnancy if and when one is ready to have a child. Current low fertility rates in rich countries have been reached thanks to the widespread use of modern contraception throughout much of women's reproductive lives (Skouby, 2004) and, in many countries, owing to the relatively widespread use of abortion (Sedgh et al., 2012). Still, given that 47 per cent of pregnancies and 22 per cent of births in the more developed countries are estimated as unintended, it is clear that not all sexually active women and men consistently use reliable contraception when not planning to bear children (Singh et al., 2010).

This section reviews three key issues where biomedical factors and assisted reproduction (AR) influence fertility rates: (i) infertility and its age pattern, (ii) the notion of deteriorating male reproductive capacity, and (iii) AR and its potential role in fertility trends at higher childbearing ages.

3.2.7.1 *Infertility and sterility*

Analysing trends and variation in infertility and sterility is difficult as different concepts and definitions are used and modified over time; also, medical, epidemiological, and demographical definitions of infertility vary (Habbema et al., 2004; Leridon, 2007; Mascarenhas et al., 2012a). It is now common in the medical field to define as 'infertile' a couple that has been unable to conceive after a defined exposure to unprotected intercourse. This period may vary from 12 months to 5 years. It would be more appropriate to report explicitly 'one-year infertility rates' or 'five-year infertility rates', but this is rarely the case. In this section we will use the word 'infertility' in this broad sense.

Data on infertility have mostly been collected for higher-fertility, less-developed countries. Boivin et al. (2007), using a wider definition of infertility that includes women reporting current 'difficulties in carrying a child' ('subfecundity'), showed that in selected rich countries current prevalence of infertility ranged from 3.5 per cent in Australia (1988) to 16.7 per cent in Russia (1998). Lifetime infertility prevalence in these countries varied even more, from 6.5 per cent in Norway (1985–95) to 26.4 per cent in the UK (1993). These estimates vary so widely in part because infertility definitions differ, and because infertility is affected by different age patterns of childbearing across countries. Mascarenhas et al. (2012b) produced global and regional standardized estimates of primary (absence of a first live birth) and secondary infertility (absence of a live birth among women with at least one child) cumulated for couples over a five-year period of unprotected intercourse. Using these definitions, primary infertility was very low and amounted in 2010 to 1.5 per cent globally (1.9 per cent among child-seeking women), with little variation by country and region. Secondary infertility varied considerably more: the global average was 2.9 per cent for all women and 10.2 per cent for child-seeking women (Mascarenhas et al., 2012b). These data also show that very few women experience infertility from an early age on. While infertility prevalence is often computed for women, male-factor infertility strongly contributes to observed infertility of couples (CDC, 2011; Thonneau et al., 1991).

Relatively few studies have examined infertility trends over time. Mascarenhas et al. (2012b) showed there were no strong shifts globally and in high-income countries between 1990 and 2010, especially when age-standardized data were used. Rich evidence exists on infertility trends in the USA. Mosher and Pratt (1985) reported a decline in infertility between 1965 and 1982, whereas more recent analysis by Stephen and Chandra (2006) covering the period 1982–2002 found a gradual infertility decline up until 1995, which was particularly pronounced among older childless couples. These and other studies do not lend support to the notion of a general increase in infertility over time.

The key factor in infertility is age. Among men, fertility is usually maintained until high age, but it is negatively affected by age-related degenerative changes to sperm and testes, as well as erectile dysfunction (e.g. Kühnert and Nieschlag, 2004; Sartorius and Nieschlag, 2010). As a result, male age has an independent effect on couple's fecundity, and higher male age (>40) has detrimental effects, especially in combination with advanced reproductive age of the woman (de la Rochebrochard and Thonneau, 2003). For women, age imposes much stricter limits to their ability to reproduce as the number and the quality of their oocytes (eggs) decline rapidly (Broekmans et al., 2007). Infertility, sterility, the frequency of miscarriages, and pregnancy complications increase gradually among women aged 30–39 and then surge after age 40. By age 40 almost 17 per cent of women are permanently sterile, while as many as 35 per cent of women will remain childless if starting their first pregnancy effort at that age, mainly because the rate of foetal wastage increases rapidly after age 35 (Leridon, 2008).

3.2.7.2 *Male reproductive health*

Carlsen et al. (1992, p. 609) stated in a meta-analysis of studies published between 1938 and 1990 that 'there has been a genuine decline in semen quality over the past 50 years', a finding partly confirmed in a more sophisticated analysis by Swan et al. (2000). Regional studies from Europe and Asia have demonstrated heterogeneity in the results (Iwamoto et al., 2007; Jørgensen et al., 2002). The European Science Foundation's Science Policy Briefing (ESF, 2010, p. 7), prepared by some of the leading scientists in the field, voiced concern about 'significant adverse trends in reproductive health problems in young men'. The research suggesting decline in sperm quality has, however, been challenged by some studies that question the methods and data, particularly of the meta-reviews (Fisch, 2008; Lerchl, 1995). The few studies based on the measurement of the time to conception, notably in the UK (Joffe, 2000) and Sweden (Scheike et al., 2008), have not found evidence of a declining trend in fecundity. Overall, there are many conflicting findings and no consensus on this issue (Bonde et al., 2011; Fisch and Braun, 2013; Merzenich et al., 2010).

The reported risk factors for declining semen quality (measured by sperm counts, motility, and morphology) include the effect of chemicals such as xeno-oestrogens and lifestyle effects of tobacco, obesity, and stress (He and Ju, 2008; Jensen et al., 2004; Sharpe and Skakkebaek, 1993). Declining sperm quality could play an important role in shaping levels of reproductive success within certain subgroups of society and, eventually, affect aggregate fertility rates (ESF, 2010). Furthermore, increasing age of fatherhood is a significant determinant of declining semen quality and reproductive success (Frattarelli et al., 2008). In the context of increasing age of first birth and a generally greater social acceptance of older fathers, this factor could play a prominent role in the future.

3.2.7.3 *Fertility postponement and assisted reproduction*

Data on AR, although incomplete for many countries, indicate continuing increase in its use, including by women at higher reproductive ages (Ferraretti et al., 2012). According to AR registries in European countries, between 0.5 per cent (Turkey) and 4.6 per cent (Denmark) of children born in 2008 were conceived via AR (Ferraretti et al., 2012); the average for European countries with available data was 1.6 per cent, comparable to the USA (1.5 per cent in 2009). AR has a very minor positive effect on aggregate fertility rates in rich countries (Habbema et al., 2009; Sobotka et al., 2008) although its 'net impact' is difficult to estimate as some of its users would otherwise achieve a spontaneous conception (Pinborg et al., 2009).

To what extent can AR compensate for infertility linked to postponing childbearing to higher reproductive ages? The contribution of AR using women's own oocytes is relatively small. A simulation by Leridon (2004) showed that an ability of AR to overcome age-related infertility falls dramatically with age. Fewer than 30 per cent of the births 'lost' by postponing conception attempt from age 35 to age 40 could eventually be 'compensated' by *in vitro* fertilization. In the USA in 2009, only 18.1 per cent of AR cycles using non-donor oocytes at age 42 resulted in pregnancy, with 8.6 per cent resulting in a live birth. Leridon and Slama (2008) simulated population-level impact on fertility of additional postponement of childbearing and 'compensatory' use of ART. In the contemporary French population, an additional shift in age at pregnancy attempts by 2.5 years was estimated to lead to a 5 per cent decline in fertility rate (from 2.00 to 1.90), of which only one fifth (0.02) would later be made up through AR use. Despite this evidence, many women erroneously believe that AR can help them to overcome infertility at high reproductive ages (Maheshwari et al., 2008).

Much higher success rates have been achieved with AR using donor oocytes from healthy young women. However, relying on donors implies women will have offspring who carry someone else's genetic endowment. Recently, oocyte cryopreservation (OC), or 'egg freezing', has emerged as a major breakthrough (Setti et al., 2012) that may give women more autonomy in reproductive decisions and erode the age boundaries of reproductive ages (Wyndham et al., 2012). Ideally, women using OC would have their oocytes harvested at prime reproductive ages, and cryopreservation would then preserve them for possible later use with the help of AR. AR using oocytes vitrified at younger ages, especially until a woman's early 30s, achieves similar success rate as AR with donor oocytes (Cobo et al., 2011). Although the number of births after OC has increased (Noyes et al., 2009), there is still a lack of long-term data about success rates and possible drawbacks of using AR with OC after many years of cryopreservation.

3.2.8 Education

Conventional demographic wisdom holds that fertility levels among women have a negative relationship to educational attainment (e.g. Castro Martin, 1995; Skirbekk, 2008). The causal direction of the relationship seemed clear because education was typically completed prior to the time when women started having children. Now, in low fertility countries, where massive expansion of high education has taken place and the education process has extended well into the fecund years, the causality question has become murkier and the education–fertility association has become more varied (Andersson et al., 2009; Kravdal and Rindfuss, 2008; Neels and De Wachter, 2010).

The expansion of higher education in developed countries, particularly among women, has been a major factor behind the postponement of parenthood and the emergence of very low period TFRs in the final decades of the twentieth century (Billari and Kohler, 2004; Ní Bhrolcháin and Beaujouan, 2012). First, there is a normative expectation that women still in school are not ready for motherhood. In this context, the ever expanding time spent in education further delays first births (Blossfeld and Huinink, 1991). As a result, women with higher levels of education have a later mean age at childbearing (Andersson et al., 2009; Mills et al., 2011) and, during the transition from lower to higher levels of education, the associated fertility postponement leads to lower levels of period fertility. Second, a higher level of education entails enhanced human capital and a higher earnings potential, which women may want to capitalize on in the labour market. This implies that higher educated women have more to lose by staying at home to provide childcare—a situation aggravated by the persistence of traditional gender role division, particularly in East Asia (see Box 3.2). These higher opportunity costs of childbearing may contribute both to the delay and decline of fertility (Kravdal, 2004; Lappegård and Rønsen, 2005). But education effects are likely not confined to financial issues. Higher levels of education prepare one for jobs and careers that are more interesting, creative, and intrinsically rewarding. An increased orientation toward careers in the labour market may motivate educated women to further postpone motherhood until they have gained work experience, established their position in the labour market, and accumulated sufficient material resources to afford starting a family (Kravdal and Rindfuss, 2008; Mills et al., 2011). Third, field of study can also be important for fertility timing. One reason is that different subject areas imply differential earning potentials in the labour market after graduation (e.g. fine art compared to engineering). The choice of study discipline also tends to both reflect and mould a person's attitudes, including those related to family formation (Hoem et al., 2006; Martín-García and Baizán, 2006; Van Bavel, 2010b). Postponement has been more limited among graduates from disciplines in which stereotypical attitudes about gendered family roles prevail and in which a large share of the graduates are female (Van Bavel, 2010b).

Whereas the effects of education on the timing of entry into parenthood are well documented and reasonably consistent, the effect on fertility quantum is much less clear (Kravdal and Rindfuss, 2008). The aforementioned postponement effect, higher opportunity costs of childrearing, and stronger career orientation should lead to lower levels of completed fertility, and there has been empirical support for this effect (e.g. Kohler et al., 2002). However, women with higher levels of education are more likely to be able to afford the costs associated with raising children, even more so if they are partnered with a highly educated male (which is usually the case).

The empirical record on the relationship between educational attainment and completed fertility is little studied. In the Nordic countries, the fertility gradient by level of education has almost disappeared for women, and parity progression ratios to a second and third child are positively associated with women's education level (Andersson et al., 2009; Kravdal and Rindfuss, 2008). In Belgium, Neels and De Wachter (2010) reported crossovers in fertility and education association, with above average completed fertility found among women with tertiary education born in the 1950s. There are also difference by parity, with Adsera (2011a) observing a U-shaped relationship between educational attainment and third births across the EU. However, when parity-specific patterns are disregarded, research, in most countries, shows a continuation of the negative education–fertility differentials for women (Davie and Mazuy, 2010; Musick et al., 2009; Sobotka, 2012; van Agtmaal-Wobma and van Huis, 2008). We review the empirical evidence on trends and cross-country variation in education–fertility differentials in low-fertility countries in sections 3.5.3.1–3.5.3.5.

Our expectation is that countries that have the least developed institutional support for a combination of motherhood and employment will have both the steepest negative education–fertility gradient and the lowest levels of completed fertility. The evidence suggests that the relation between education and the number of children strongly depends on the social context. A key factor here is the practical availability and cultural acceptability of non-family childcare, which differs dramatically across countries for children below the age of three (Liefbroer and Merz, 2010; OECD, 2011). Childcare facilities may greatly mitigate the opportunity costs of childbearing, which are known to be highest for highly educated women (Kravdal and Rindfuss, 2008). It has been found that formal childcare availability has a positive effect on second birth rates in Europe, but only for highly educated women (Van Bavel and Różańska-Putek, 2010). The development of organized childcare and other institutions promoting gender equity in family life has probably contributed to the diminishing gradient between women's level of education and their fertility (Kravdal and Rindfuss, 2008).

3.2.9 Limitations and moving to the future

In sections 3.1 and 3.2 we have outlined the prior quantitative trends, as well as a set of socio-economic and cultural determinants of fertility, in a varied set of countries characterized by low fertility. We have also highlighted what we believe to be some of the key underlying themes and issues that have shaped these trends over the last few generations.

Although we have attempted to give a comprehensive overview of all the major factors shaping fertility, our review has limitations. We have paid relatively scant attention to the slowly accumulating literature on male fertility determinants, levels, and patterns. Some potentially relevant factors were not discussed because the literature is relatively undeveloped, the evidence on their relevance is limited, or simply because the lack of space precludes discussing every possible driver of fertility. Examples of such 'neglected' factors include type of settlement and the potential role of urban–rural differentials, population density, and environmental and climate-related factors. Similarly, this chapter has not covered widely enough the ongoing transformation in family and living arrangements, and its multiple links to childbearing behaviour. Also, we have not discussed potentially important psychological factors operating at both societal and individual levels, such as how the degree of trust, insecurity, sense of control, and, more generally, ideologies, fads, and fashions related to childlessness or having children, influence fertility decisions. With the exception of economic uncertainty and the more specific case of anomie during the post-communist transition in CEE (Philipov et al., 2006), the literature is very limited and usually dated. Of potential relevance as a fertility-limiting factor in the future may be the ideology of intensive mothering prevalent in many affluent countries. In the long-run, the increased 'price of parental time' may clash with the widespread notion that parenthood, especially motherhood, should be child-centred, emotionally involving, and time-consuming (Arendell, 2000).

We have also provided only a limited discussion of the links between different determinants of fertility, in particular, of how micro-, meso-, and micro-level factors interact to generate broader fertility trends (for a useful discussion, see Balbo et al., 2013).[12]

We would like to highlight two broader issues that deserve more attention in future research. First, more attention should be paid to analysing and discussing family size norms and ideals in different settings and population subgroups. Coleman (1998) suggests that besides normative factors there are no pertinent theoretical arguments suggesting that fertility and fertility preferences should be higher than zero. Other contributions that take for granted that parenthood and nurturing care about offspring provide a unique experience that is desirable for most individuals suggest that the preference for having one child might be the most rational outcome, also considering the emphasis on the 'quality' of children (Foster, 2000). Yet the overwhelming evidence for the majority of countries indicates a surprisingly strong and stable persistence of two-child family norms and ideals. Given that the actual fertility in rich countries with widespread use of modern contraception is usually lower than fertility ideals and intentions, it is important to study the experience of urban China and other settings with an emerging dominant preference for one-child families, which might herald an era of 'ultra-low' fertility in these places (Basten and Gu, 2013).

Second, more attention should be given to the unfolding 'postponement transitions' (Kohler et al., 2002) in middle-income countries that have seen fertility rates falling close to the replacement level. There, the empirical experience of the countries with a long history of low fertility shows that such fertility tempo transitions can negatively affect period fertility rates for decades, often contributing to the temporary spells of very low fertility (Bongaarts, 2002; Goldstein et al., 2009; Sobotka, 2004a). Thus, the key question is whether couples in countries such as Brazil, China, India, Iran, Mexico, and South Africa will embark on a similar trend of having children at ever later ages. If they do, perhaps in part as a consequence of an expansion of tertiary education there, these countries may see decades of very low fertility, significantly below the current levels. But differently from the case of the normative shifts towards low ideal family size, some recovery of fertility can be expected once the postponement transition comes to an end and the age patterns of childbearing eventually stabilize.

[12] As one of the contributing authors observed, 'this topic is an unresolvable dilemma. Knowledge is continuously accumulating on specific factors and mechanisms operating to shape fertility trends. In hindsight, we appear to be reasonably successful in analysing various specific situations. But a definitive comprehensive model that can be used to determine future trends is eluding us'.

When we look to the future, however, how can we discern the likely track of fertility rates? Furthermore, which of the forces and issues discussed in section 3.2 will have the most impact on such future trends? In this context, we employed a 'low fertility' module within the IIASA–Oxford survey discussed in Chapter 2 to elicit both quantitative information regarding likely future trends and qualitative information regarding the validity and potential effect of possible drivers of these trends. In section 3.3 we discuss the design of the survey module and outline the findings.

3.3 Expert survey and results of expert meeting: summary of findings

3.3.1 Introduction

The low fertility module (LFM) of the IIASA–Oxford survey sought to gather information regarding numeric estimates of future fertility, as well as its underlying determinants, in countries defined as having low fertility. For a full discussion of the selection procedure, as well as the list of countries involved, see Appendix 3.2. First, respondents were presented the baseline TFR estimate for 2010 as published by the Population Reference Bureau (PRB) (PRB, 2012) and asked to provide point projection and 80 per cent uncertainty interval (CI) range for the TFR in 2030 and 2050. These estimates are at the heart of fertility scenarios prepared for the low-fertility countries as described in section 3.4. Second, respondents were asked to assess the impact and validity of a series of qualitative statements regarding future drivers of fertility. Finally, respondents were asked whether they wished to reassess their initial TFR forecasts after performing the qualitative exercise. Experts could add additional countries or regions for which their assessment was valid; they could also comment on the survey or on individual arguments.

In this section we outline the design and construction of the LFM, followed by a description of the characteristics of respondents. We then introduce the qualitative statements regarding likely drivers of future trends of fertility and analyse the responses in total by region and in some cases by individual country. Given the emphasis on education and human capital in this project, we analyse responses pertaining to education-related arguments separately in section 3.3.4.

3.3.2 The IIASA–Oxford survey

3.3.2.1 *Survey design and evaluation*

The broad tenets and workings of the survey are outlined in Chapter 2. Here, we briefly outline the main concepts and how they have been adapted for use in the LFM.

Each module of the expert survey comprised numerous arguments. These arguments took the form of a statement on future trends that might affect population dynamics. The statements were formulated in a neutral way, without explicitly referring to their likely consequence on fertility, mortality, or migration. It was deemed important not to give respondents preconceived judgements about the way diverse social, cultural, biomedical, health, policy, and economic developments may affect population. For instance, one argument in the LFM of the survey reads: 'Men and women will increasingly share the burden of housework and childcare'.[13] Each argument is grouped into a series of forces. These are the broad themes that encompass most of the main determinants of low fertility and broadly reflect the discussion in section 3.2.[14] These forces (and respective number of arguments) in the LFM were:

- cultural and social forces in fertility ideals, norms, and desires (9)
- partnerships, living arrangements, and gender differences (9)
- role of policies (9)
- employment and economy (9)
- biomedical and timing of parenthood (7)
- education (3).

For each argument, respondents were asked to gauge its expected future likelihood or validity and its impact pertaining to the year 2050. These are defined and interpreted as follows.

1. Validity, ranging from 0.0 to 1.0, gives an indication whether a given argument is likely to be true, based on five predefined response options and the validity score attached to them. The complete phrasing and response options are illustrated in the following example:

Module: low fertility countries

Force: role of policies

Argument: government will take an increasingly pro-natalist stance (e.g. through communication campaigns and family policies)

Based on your knowledge of the empirical evidence and the validity of the reasoning involved, and with reference to the selected country and the period up to 2050, do you think the above argument is:

Very likely to be wrong (0.0)	More wrong than right (0.25)	Ambivalent (0.5)	More right than wrong (0.75)	Very likely to be right (1.0)

2. Impact, also called conditional impact, represents an assessment of the hypothetical influence of a given trend on fertility (mortality, migration). The predefined range

[13] For a complete list of all of the arguments, see Appendix 3.4.

[14] The order of the arguments was randomized within the forces, and the order of the forces was also randomized to minimize the fatigue effect.

was from –1 (strongly negative) to +1 (strongly positive). Specifically, the respondents were asked:

Regardless of your answer above, if the above argument were completely true, what effect would this have on future levels of cohort fertility in country?

Strongly decreasing (–1.0)	Moderately decreasing (–0.5)	None (0.0)	Moderately increasing (0.5)	Strongly increasing (1.0)

3. Finally, validity and conditional impact are assessed in combination to define a net impact. This was computed in two steps. First, the validity score and conditional impact score were multiplied resulting in a net impact which is, by definition, smaller or equal to the conditional impact, and can range from –1.0 (strongly negative) to +1.0 (strongly positive), with the results presented on-screen.[15] Subsequently, the experts were allowed to adjust the net impact so that it better reflected their expectations. Thus, we have frequently obtained two alternative measures of the net impact for each argument, one computed in a standardized fashion and the other adjusted by the respondent. We use the latter measure in our analyses and further computations as it better reflects respondents' views.

Mean likelihood, mean conditional impact, and mean net impact on fertility were calculated for each argument for the set of all analysed countries for regions and for selected countries. These were calculated as simple averages over all respondents for a given country or region. Alternative approaches, such as weighting responses of experts by the population size of their countries of expertise, were rejected, as this could give disproportionately strong influence to experts from large countries with a very small expert base.

In the analysis of responses in the LFM, a complementary indicator—an index of disagreement—was computed for each of the three main indicators. It gauges the level of consensus among the experts over the validity and impact of different arguments. When all responses point in one direction, the index of disagreement falls towards 0.0; when the experts are split into two opposing groups of the same size, the index reaches a maximum value of 1.0. The cut-off point for delineating two diverging groups was set at 0.5 for the validity measure (recall that responses ranking below 0.5 signal disagreement with the argument's validity and vice versa), and 0.0 for impact and net impact. The index of disagreement is computed by relating the number of respondents holding a minority view (either positive or negative) to the number of respondents supporting a majority view.

Finally, we calculated indicators pertaining to the broad forces. First, force weights express the relative importance of a given force or cluster of arguments, as assessed by

[15] A zero net impact is achieved either because the respondent considered the given argument invalid ('very likely to be wrong') or expected that the argument would have no impact on fertility. For the example given, the net impact would be calculated as $0.75 \times 0.50 = 0.375$.

the respondents. This sums up to 100 per cent (or 1.0) for all clusters combined. Again, we compute mean cluster weights overall and by regions and countries as a simple average across all experts in a given country or region. Aggregate net impact represents a sum of net impacts computed for each expert across all 46 arguments. The more negative the score, the more arguments were suggested to have a negative impact on future fertility, and vice versa. Combined net impact, in contrast, summarizes net impact across different arguments by country, region, or for all analysed countries. It is computed either for individual forces or for all arguments combined. We computed it as a simple sum of the net impact for all the arguments considered. It can therefore reach values outside of the range of the net impact for individual responses (−1.0 to +1.0).

We then analysed experts' estimates pertaining to the future level of period TFRs in 2030 and 2050. These mean values are computed for countries and regions, as well as globally. They differ from the indicators above in that they are weighted by population size of the countries in each region in order to better reflect expected regional and global fertility levels. Finally, voluntary data regarding respondent's age, gender, country of origin, and place/nature of work were collected, as well as comments concerning either missing arguments or the structure of the survey. The survey as a whole was extensively tested with an estimated completion time of about 20–30 minutes.

3.3.2.2 *Feedback and testing for bias*

A number of respondents left valuable feedback that helped us evaluate the exercise. In terms of the survey itself, some respondents found it too long, and there were concerns that some arguments were missing[16] or of limited relevance to particular countries and regions. However, the latter concern could easily be addressed by rating these arguments as unlikely to be correct or as having no potential impact on fertility. Conceptually, some respondents expressed concern about making period TFR estimates for the future and about the time scale involved. Generally, however, most feedback was positive.

One method by which we could evaluate the broader consistency and integrity of responses by individual respondents was to compare the aggregate argument score (see section 3.3.2.1) for each expert with their estimate of the expected change in the period TFR between 2010 and 2050. It can be expected that the experts who thought that many of the factors presented will negatively affect future fertility should also, on average, forecast that fertility levels will decline. This 'internal logic' is, indeed, in evidence in Figure 3.5, which depicts a good correspondence between the direction and the strength of the aggregate argument score on the one side and expected fertility change on the other side (correlation coefficient is 0.38).

[16] Several broader factors have been repeatedly mentioned as missing in the IIASA–Oxford survey: ethnic and socio-economic population diversity within a country, urban–rural differences, changes in family planning policies, adolescent fertility, microeconomic cycles and economic crises, and climate change and environmental disasters.

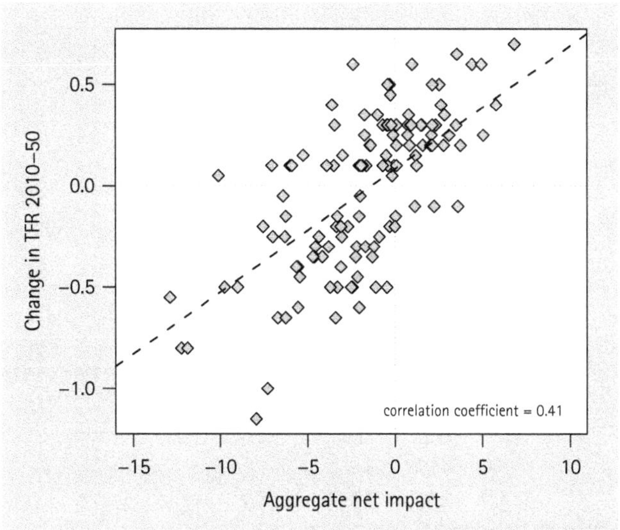

FIGURE 3.5 Aggregate net impact and estimated total fertility rate (TFR) change in 2010–50 (individual experts, all low fertility countries combined).

We were also concerned that the implied trajectory, or direction, of the arguments should be as balanced as possible, that is, that a similar number of arguments pointed towards higher and lower fertility. One method of testing for any systematic bias was to analyse the extent to which respondents altered their initial estimates of TFR in 2050 as a consequence of performing the qualitative exercise. If experts disproportionately lowered their estimates, for example, then it would suggest that our arguments may have been geared towards a negative impact on fertility, potentially biasing projection scenarios that were largely based on expert's expectations (see section 3.4). If the arguments were disproportionately leading in one direction, this could fundamentally alter the total projection exercise and create either a downward or upward bias.

A changed estimate of TFR in 2050 was found in 32 of the 184 questionnaires. However, as Figure 3.6 demonstrates, the directionality is far from uniform. Indeed, the number of respondents who revised their estimates up or down is almost identical. This suggests that our arguments were generally not biased towards indicating either lower or higher fertility futures.

A final check was performed by examining the net impact of the 46 arguments. Overall, 26 were deemed to have a negative effect, while 20 were suggested to have a positive impact.

3.3.2.3 *Respondents*

Altogether, 184 questionnaires on the LFM of the survey were completed by more than 170 experts (some experts chose to make two or more assessments; 110 experts revealed their full names). Appendix 3.3 gives a full breakdown of the respondents' profiles. The vast majority come from an academic background. Altogether, for 14 countries, 5 or

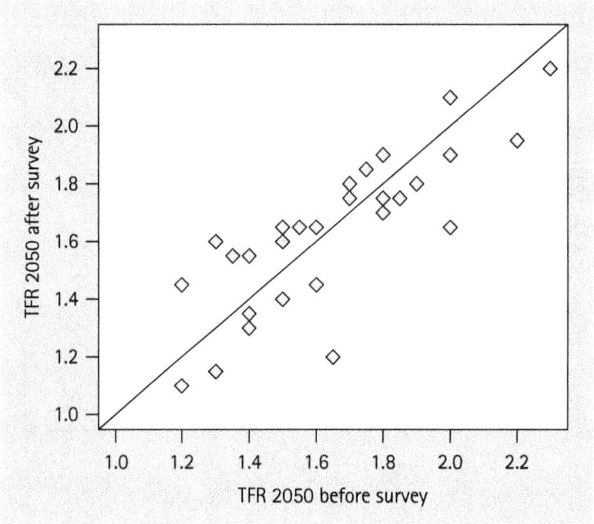

FIGURE 3.6 Respondents who altered their total fertility rate (TFR) estimates for 2050 *ex post.*

more experts have provided assessments, with the USA by far the most popular country (22 assessments), followed by China (14 assessments), Italy (12), and Germany (9). A number of experts have assessed countries outside the traditional low fertility regions of Europe, Northern America, Japan, Australia, and New Zealand. Clearly, despite uneven coverage of some countries—with no expertise provided for France with a population of 64 million and 7 assessments for Sweden with a population of 9 million—the assessments mirror quite well the wide geographical spread of low fertility today, with particularly good coverage of China, Brazil, Japan, Mexico, Turkey, and Iran.

3.3.3 Results

3.3.3.1 *An overview using CIRCOS plots*

In Figure 3.7 we summarize the general results of the survey using a Circos plot (Krzywinski et al., 2009). Around the plot are abbreviated versions of the arguments and their associated code (for the complete list of all arguments, see Appendix 3.4). The arguments are clustered into their associated forces, which are labelled in the centre (e.g. 'Education' and 'Culture').

3.3.3.2 *The relative importance of different forces (width of sections)*

When considering the 'overall' forces alone, respondents felt that forces 1 and 4, namely, 'Cultural and social forces in fertility ideals, norms, and desires' and 'Employment and economy' were the most pertinent for shaping future fertility trends. These forces were weighted as 0.230 and 0.221 respectively. Forces 2, 3, and 6 concerning 'Partnerships, living arrangements, and gender differences', 'Role of policies', and 'Education', respectively, are gathered together in a second-tier cluster (weights 0.162, 0.156, and 0.156 respectively), while force 5, which concerns issues relating to biomedicine (including infertility and AR) and the timing of parenthood, was ranked last (0.077).

In Figure 3.7, these weights are translated into the width of the segments devoted to each force irrespective of the number of constituent arguments. Note, for example, the different sizes of the 'Culture' and 'Biomedical' forces. In terms of directionality, of the six groups only 'Policies', broadly defined, were deemed to have a positive net impact on fertility, while 'Partnerships, living arrangements, and gender differences' were expected to have the most depressing effect. However, without further exploring the impact of individual arguments, which often run in the opposite direction within each broad force, this general finding is difficult to interpret. Finally, there are sizeable regional differences in terms of the net impact of both the entire forces and individual arguments by region. We address the regional differences in arguments later in Figure 3.8 and in Table 3.2.

3.3.3.3 *Mean net impact (outer circle)*

As discussed earlier, the mean net impact of an argument is derived from a combination of the stated validity of a given argument with its conditional impact (i.e. the impact it would have if it were completely true). In Figure 3.7 those arguments that were deemed to have a positive net impact are shaded in lighter grey, while those perceived to have a negative impact are shaded darker.

Across the entire survey, the arguments perceived to have the strongest net positive impact on fertility related to immigration from higher fertility countries, increasing flexibility in work practices, the provision of universal childcare and other family policies, and increased gender equity in the performance of housework. Regarding the strongest net negative impact, uncertainty in individual life course planning and the related arguments concerning job instability among the young and an inability to find the right partner were key. Two related arguments of spending more years in education and the postponement of childbearing were also expected to place a downward pressure on fertility, suggesting that most respondents expected continuation of the trend towards later timing of childbearing in the coming decades.[17] Finally, the argument that 'Women will follow lifestyles incompatible with motherhood' also had strong negative mean net impact on fertility. This suggests that different facets of increased gender equality may have contrasting impacts on fertility that largely offset one another: while, on balance, a stronger engagement of men in household tasks is expected to give some boost to

[17] The respondents were explicitly asked to consider the effects of the given argument on cohort fertility—in that case it might be argued that they expected that the negative influence of prolonged education and postponed childbearing will be permanent, also affecting cohort fertility quantum (e.g. via increased infertility related to shifting childbearing to late reproductive ages). It is likely, however, that some of the respondents focused on period fertility, expecting that education and the related fertility postponement will temporarily reduce it, mainly through the tempo effect.

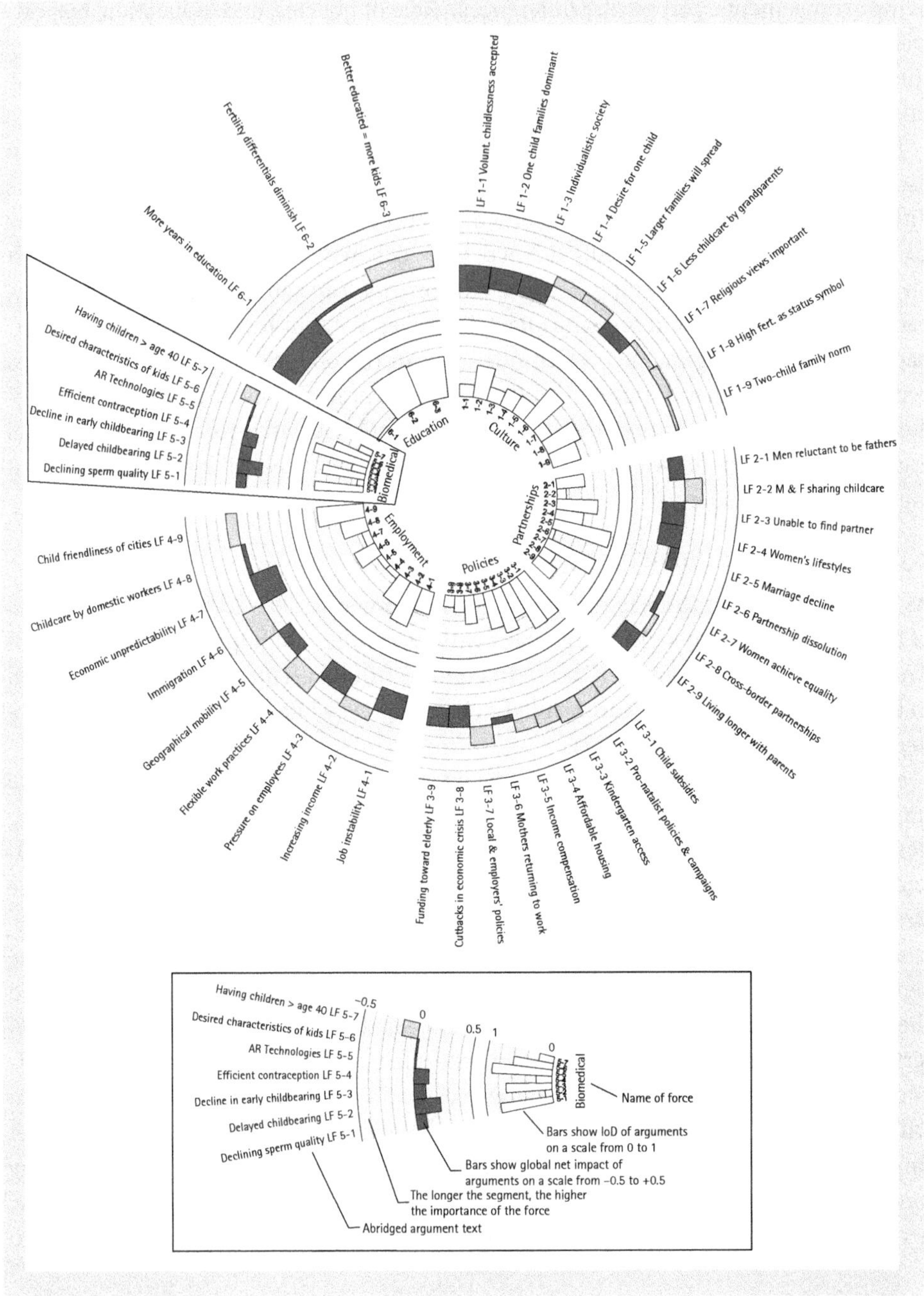

FIGURE 3.7 Global mean Net Impact and Index of Disagreement (IoD) for all arguments about future fertility in low fertility countries. AR: artificial reproduction; M: male; F: female fert.: fertility; volunt.: voluntary.

fertility, women's more independent lifestyles are likely to put a downward pressure on fertility rates.

3.3.3.4 *Validity of arguments and the index of disagreement (inner circle)*

The validity of an argument is key to determining its net impact, as well as giving useful evidence of the confidence that respondents have in the continuation of key social, cultural, and economic processes affecting fertility.

The continuation of two related trends towards ever longer time spent in education and delayed childbearing were deemed to be the most valid arguments, followed by partnership dissolution and re-partnering, increased flexibility in work practices, geographical mobility, and the growing acceptability of voluntary childlessness. In contrast, respondents thought that the role of religion in shaping family attitudes and the share of large families (defined relatively) were the least valid arguments, followed by the statement that 'men are increasingly reluctant to become fathers'.[18]

To demonstrate the importance of measuring both validity and impact, it is worth considering a particular argument in Table 3.1. Argument 2.6 'Partnership dissolution and re-partnering will become more common' was deemed very valid, but its mean net impact was precisely 0.0.[19]

More interesting, however, is the extent to which respondents disagreed over the validity of a given argument. This is measured by the index of disagreement in the inner circle of Figure 3.7. The index ranges from 0.0, which would imply that all of the experts shared a similar view (either joint agreement or joint disagreement with the statement), up to 1.0, which implies half of the respondents agreed and half disagreed (section 3.3.2.1). As Figure 3.7 shows, the arguments with the highest indices of disagreement of 0.84 or above were related to the further decline of marriage (argument 2.5, index of disagreement 0.94), continued barriers to AR (5.5), the elimination of gender inequalities in the public sphere (2.7), and the role of governments through taking an explicitly pro-natalist stance (3.2) and increasing spending on child subsidies and tax benefits (3.1).

Clearly, there was significant disagreement among respondents concerning the institution of marriage, the accessibility of AR, and the likelihood that women achieve equality with men. Respondents were also divided on the likelihood of governmental intervention. In each of these cases, the mean net impact is minimal.

[18] Note, however, that there is considerable variability in answers to the presented questions, and even the arguments generally deemed as 'most likely to be wrong' were found 'likely to be right' by a significant share of respondents. For instance, regarding the third 'most invalid argument' that men will be increasingly reluctant to become fathers, almost a quarter of respondents (22 per cent) thought it is more right than wrong and another quarter (27 per cent) indicated that it is as likely to be right as it is to be wrong.

[19] As we discuss in the next section, there was a very high level of disagreement among experts over the conditional impact of this likely trend and therefore mean net impact happened to average out at zero.

Table 3.1 Arguments Deemed Most and Least Valid

Argument (abbreviated, see full version in Appendix 3.4)			
Most likely to be right	**Group**	**Validity score**	**Mean net impact**
6.1'More young adult years enrolled in education and training'	6 (Education)	0.78	-0.26
5.2 'Delayed childbearing yet more common'	5 (Biomedical)	0.75	-0.23
2.6 'Partnership dissolution and re-partnering more common'	2 (Partnership)	0.73	0.00
4.4 'Work practices will become more flexible'	4 (Economy)	0.71	0.19
4.5 'Geographical mobility will increase'	4 (Economy)	0.70	-0.14
1.1 'Voluntary childlessness increasingly accepted'	1 (Culture)	0.70	-0.24
Most likely to be wrong			
1.7 'Religious views on family will gain importance'	1 (Culture)	0.33	0.06
1.5 'The share of groups with larger families will increase'	1 (Culture)	0.36	0.09
2.1 'Men increasingly reluctant to become fathers'	2 (Partnership)	0.41	-0.14

These disagreements can also reflect regional differences in the responses on important factors shaping contemporary fertility. In the next section we examine differences by region in terms of both forces and arguments.

3.3.3.5 *Regional differences in net impact of arguments*

Figure 3.8 represents the responses to each argument differentiated by the relevant region. This should be read in conjunction with Table 3.2, which shows the two arguments that respondents deemed to have the strongest positive and negative impact on future fertility trends for each individual region (see Appendix 3.3 for listing of all the countries with at least one respondent within each region). Table 3.2 also shows the net impact of all forces combined for each region, that is, the overall general direction in which the responses suggest fertility will go.

Regional variation concerning 'Cultural and social forces in fertility ideals, norms, and desires', and 'Partnerships, living arrangements, and gender differences' was broadly similar, with respondents for Latin America reporting a strong association between these forces and future rates of fertility compared with Europeans (excluding CEE), who felt these forces would contribute to either only a small decrease or, in the case of Western Europe, a very small increase. Interestingly, respondents for Japan stated that 'Partnerships, living arrangements, and gender differences' was the force that would have the most depressing effect on future fertility—a feature that concurs with our discussion on gender roles in section 3.2, especially Box 3.2.

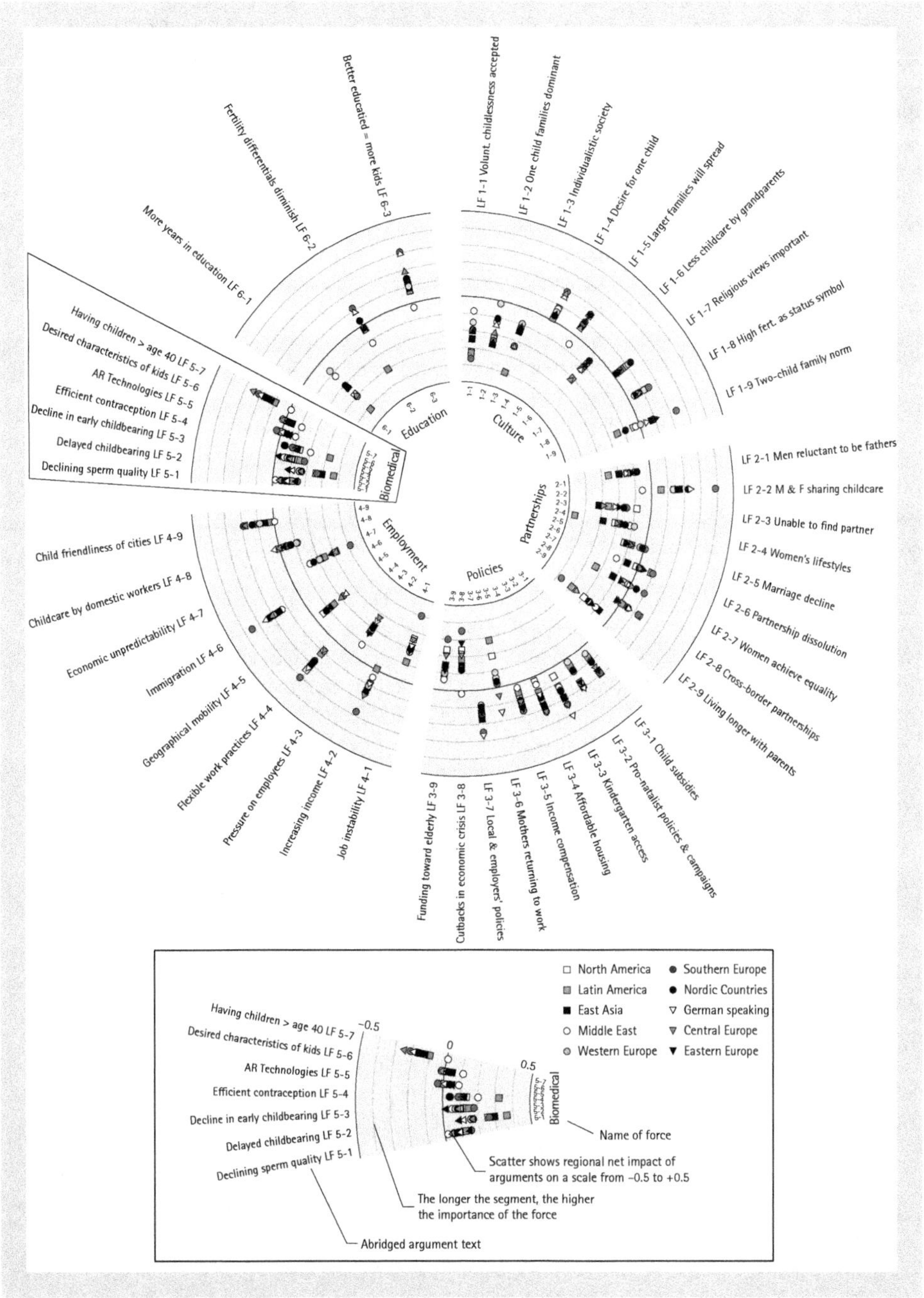

FIGURE 3.8 Mean net impact by region for all arguments about future fertility in low fertility countries. AR: artificial reproduction; M: male F: female fert.: fertility; volunt.: voluntary.

Table 3.2 Top Two Arguments Deemed by Respondents to Have the Strongest Mean Net Impact on Future Trends of Fertility, Either Positive or Negative

Region and net impact of all forces combined	Code	Abbreviated argument*	Mean net impact
North America (−2.20)	4.4	Work practices become more flexible	+0.24
	4.6	Immigration from high fertility countries will increase	+0.20
	1.1	Voluntary childlessness is increasingly socially accepted	−0.32
	4.7	Economic unpredictability means uncertain life course planning	−0.32
Latin America (−4.55)	4.6	Immigration from high fertility countries will increase	+0.15
	3.7	Increased family-related policies by local governments and employers	+0.14
	6.1	Ever more years of life enrolled in education	−0.41
	2.4	Women will pursue lifestyles not compatible with motherhood	−0.46
East Asia (−1.47)	4.4	Work practices become more flexible	+0.20
	3.3	Government will provide universal nursery/kindergarten access	+0.19
	5.2	Delayed childbearing will become yet more common	−0.30
	2.3	Harder to find the right partner to form a family	−0.31
Western Asia/Middle East (Iran and Turkey) (−1.86)	3.2	Government will take an increasingly pro-natalist stance	+0.17
	4.6	Immigration from high fertility countries will increase	+0.13
	4.1	Unemployment and job instability among under-30s will increase	−0.19
	5.4	Broad availability and use of efficient contraception	−0.20
Western Europe (−0.31)	4.6	Immigration from high fertility countries will increase	+0.19
	5.7	Assisted reproduction will allow routine childbearing at ages 40+	+0.17
	4.3	Employers will put more pressure on their employees	−0.18
	4.7	Economic unpredictability means uncertain life course planning	−0.21
Nordic countries (−0.37)	4.6	Immigration from high fertility countries will increase	+0.23
	2.2	Men and women will increasingly share housework and childcare	+0.22
	6.1	Ever more years of life enrolled in education	−0.20
	4.3	Employers will put more pressure on their employees	−0.20
Southern Europe (−0.32)	2.2	Men and women will increasingly share housework and childcare	+0.39
	4.6	Immigration from high fertility countries will increase	+0.35
	4.1	Unemployment and job instability among under-30s will increase	−0.40
	4.7	Economic unpredictability means uncertain life course planning	−0.41
Austria, Germany, Switzerland ('German-speaking') (+0.26)	3.3	Government will provide universal nursery/kindergarten access	+0.32
	6.3	Better educated women will want more children and pursue a career	+0.30
	4.3	Employers will put more pressure on their employees	−0.25
	4.7	Economic unpredictability mean uncertain life course planning	−0.32

(continued)

Region and net impact of all forces combined	Code	Abbreviated argument*	Mean net impact
Central Europe (−1.07)	5.7	Assisted reproduction will allow routine childbearing aged 40+	+0.25
	3.3	Government will provide universal nursery/kindergarten access	+0.24
	2.3	Harder to find the right partner to form a family	−0.29
	4.7	Economic unpredictability means uncertain life course planning	−0.31
Eastern Europe (−0.89)	4.4	Work practices become more flexible	+0.19
	3.4	Increased provision of affordable housing for families/young adults	+0.18
	3.8	Retrenchment of family support when economic conditions worsen	−0.28
	4.7	Economic unpredictability means uncertain life course planning	−0.28

* See Appendix 3.4 for full text of all arguments.

The role of policies was felt to have a potentially depressing effect upon fertility among respondents for North America, perhaps mirroring widespread scepticism about the possibility of launching a more comprehensive set of family-related policies there, but a generally positive effect among respondents for Europe and Asia. We explore the causes of this contrast later in this section. The net impact of employment and economy was generally small across the regions (with the exception of Mexico and Iran), with the opposing impacts of individual arguments largely cancelling out. Biomedicine and the timing of parenthood were held to have a universally depressing effect on fertility across the regions, with Latin America (−0.90) and Western Europe (−0.18) as high- and low-impact extremes.

In terms of positive impacts, immigration from higher fertility countries was among the top two arguments in six regions, including the Middle East, but not German-speaking countries. Increasing flexibility in work practices was among the top two factors in North America, East Asia, and Eastern Europe. Policy is clearly deemed as important, with three related arguments concerning childcare provision, social housing, and the role of local government and employers reported as a leading argument in five regions. Indeed, within German-speaking countries, there is logical consistency between the top two arguments of 'Government will provide universal nursery/kindergarten access' and 'Better educated women will want more children and pursue a career'. Respondents in Iran and Turkey emphasized the expected role of government pro-natalism, mirroring the new emphasis given to supporting higher birth rates there (section 3.1.4.8). Curiously, respondents for Nordic countries and Southern Europe—traditionally at different ends of the domestic gendered division-of-labour—both agreed that an increase in male contribution to childcare and housework is likely to positively influence fertility in the future. Finally, for Western and Central Europe, the role of ART was deemed as important.

Box 3.4 Expert Views on Current Economic Uncertainty by Country

In terms of expected negative effects on fertility, the role of economic uncertainty and job security in general, and the current economic recession explicitly, are clearly highlighted by the respondents. At least one of the related arguments of 'Economic unpredictability means uncertain life course planning' and 'Unemployment and job instability among the under-30s will increase', ranked among the top two arguments in all regions except for East Asia, Latin America, and Nordic countries. It is no coincidence that these are the regions that have escaped from the recent recession relatively unscathed. Likewise, it is no surprise that these two arguments resonated particularly well in Southern Europe, where economic uncertainty is expected to have the strongest negative impact on fertility.

We can disaggregate further by examining the responses for particular countries. Table 3.3 shows responses to the two arguments mentioned for countries with four or more respondents. Clearly, the experts for Italy and Spain were the most pessimistic, while those for Brazil, China, and Iran appear generally less concerned. Japan is an interesting example in that the emphasis was especially placed upon job security for the under-30s rather than the more general economic uncertainty and life planning. It is curious that Austria and Germany should score so high, especially given that both countries have weathered the recent economic recession relatively well.

Table 3.3 Impact of Economic Uncertainty Upon Future of Fertility, Mean Net Impact

4.1 'Unemployment and job instability among the under-30s will increase'		4.7 'Economic unpredictability mean uncertain life course planning'	
Italy (N12)	-0.52	Italy (N12)	-0.53
Japan (N6)	-0.28	Spain (N7)	-0.36
USA (N22)	-0.26	Austria (N7)	-0.35
Austria (N7)	-0.26	Germany (N10)	-0.35
Turkey (N5)	-0.26	Mexico (N6)	-0.34
Sweden (N9)	-0.25	USA (N22)	-0.31
Spain (N7)	-0.22	Australia (N5)	-0.26
Germany (N10)	-0.20	Czech Republic (N6)	-0.23
Czech Republic (N6)	-0.19	China (N14)	-0.20
Mexico (N6)	-0.18	Turkey (N5)	-0.18
Iran (N9)	-0.14	Brazil (N7)	-0.15
China (N14)	-0.10	Iran (N9)	-0.14
Brazil (N7)	-0.10	Japan (N6)	-0.10
Australia (N5)	-0.08	Sweden (N9)	-0.08

Aside from the economy, the more generic argument concerning delayed childbearing was prominent in East Asia and the Middle East, while in Latin America and Central Europe the related issue of ever more years spent in education was also cited. Other unique, region-specific arguments include the growing acceptability of voluntary childlessness in the USA; work-related geographical mobility in German-speaking countries; the pursuit of lifestyles by women that are incompatible with childbearing in Latin America; and the increasing inability to find the right partner in East Asia. Each of these top-ranking arguments 'makes sense', especially when linked back to our thematic and region-specific reviews in sections 3.1 and 3.2.

In conclusion, there are large differences between regions in terms of the validity and impact of different arguments, of which we highlight only the most prominent features. Several key themes can be detected across the regions, especially regarding immigration, family policy, and economic uncertainty, which is further explored in Box 3.4. However, there are also unique factors that are particularly salient for a given region.

3.3.4 A focus on education

As discussed in Chapter 2, a key element of this exercise is to examine the role of education in shaping population futures. This will be seen in both section 3.5 and Chapter 9, which present population projections by age, sex, and educational level. In this section, we explore the arguments concerning education in greater depth and consider their significance.

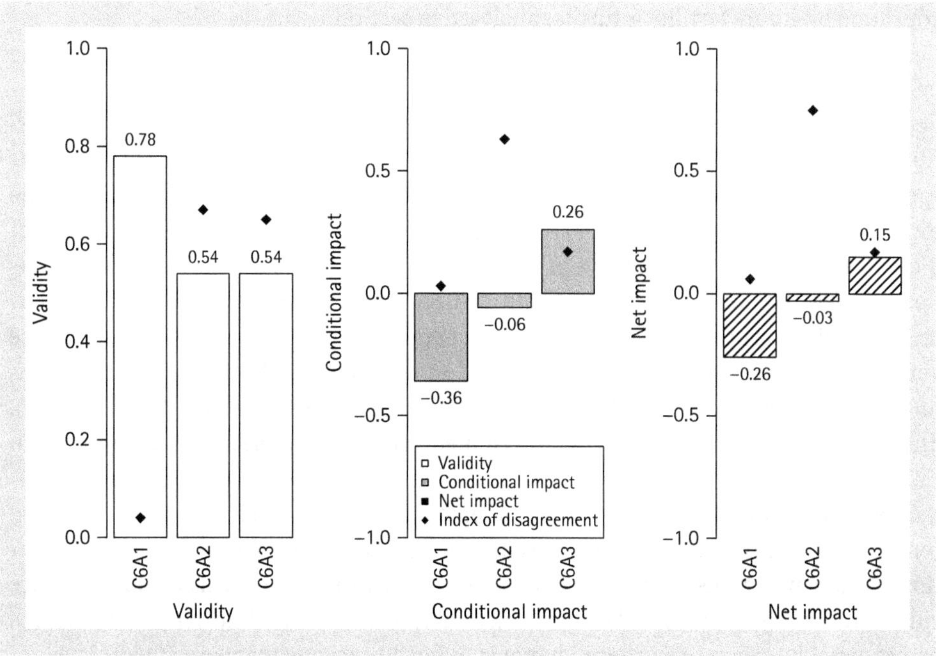

FIGURE 3.9 Validity, impact, and net impact (with indices of disagreement as black dots) for all countries in low fertility data set.

Taken together as an overall force consisting of three arguments, education appears to have a relatively marginal negative impact at the global level, returning a net impact on fertility of −0.14 (recall that this number does not pertain to any specific indicator). There are, however, important regional differences. For example, in Latin America the net impact of the education force is −0.64, indicating an expected massive fertility-depressing effect of rising educational level in the region (compared to −0.06 for the group of arguments pertaining to policies and −0.40 for employment and the economy). Meanwhile, in German-speaking Europe education had a positive effect of + 0.19—second only to the policy cluster, in fact indicating an expectation that high levels of education will increasingly be compatible with motherhood.

3.3.4.1 *Education arguments*

The education component of the survey contained three arguments:

- 6.1 'People will spend ever more years of their young adult life enrolled in education and professional training on the job'
- 6.2 'Fertility differentials by level of female education will diminish'
- 6.3 'There will be a new trend for better educated women to have more children and simultaneously pursue a professional career'.

The validity of these arguments and their conditional, as well as net, impacts are depicted for all low fertility countries in Figure 3.9, while the net impact is also shown by region in Figure 3.8. Regional variation in expert expectations regarding the impact of education on future fertility is further analysed in section 3.5.3.5.

The intimation in argument 6.1 is that as more and more people spend increasing periods of their adult life enrolled in education (usually tertiary education), which is frequently perceived as being incongruous to raising children, a depressing effect on fertility could ensue. Generally, there was very strong agreement that the amount of time spent by young people in education would increase. Indeed, on a global level this was the most likely scenario across all the arguments. Not surprisingly, most respondents predicted this would have a negative effect on fertility. The global mean net impact was −0.26. After 'Individual life-course planning becoming ever more uncertain', this argument had the strongest individual net impact among the 46 arguments in the exercise and was negative in all regions. With regard to regional variation, this argument was found to have smaller impact in Western Europe (−0.08) and the Middle East (−0.12). The strongest negative impact was envisioned for Latin America (−0.41) and South Europe (−0.30).[20]

The second and third educational arguments (6.2–6.3) approach the widely discussed topic of the possible convergence of fertility among women with different levels of education (argument 6.2, discussed in sections 3.2.7 and 3.5.3.1–3.5.3.5). This could take place either because higher educated women will be able to have more children (argument 6.3), or, presumably, owing to further reductions in fertility among women with low levels of education. Unlike argument 6.1, 6.2 saw significant levels of disagreement among the

[20] For regional differences in validity and conditional impact, see Figure 3.15.

respondents in terms of both validity and impact, suggesting considerable ambiguity among them on whether achieved level of education will remain an important differentiating factor in fertility. For argument 6.3, meanwhile, most respondents agreed on the conditional impact of the argument if true, but there was significant disagreement on the likelihood that highly educated women will achieve higher fertility in the future.

As Figure 3.8 shows, the regional variation within responses to argument 6.2 is relatively slight, with a congregation around no overall impact, with the exception of Latin America and the Middle East. Argument 6.3, meanwhile, revealed some interesting regional variations. Respondents in Southern Europe and German-speaking Europe reported the highest net impact of better educated women having more children combined with a career (both about 0.3). When we compare this to East Asia, Latin America, and the Middle East, where the net impact was perceived to be virtually non-existent, we might conclude that the expected positive impact of education on fertility is strongest in the two European regions envisioned to progress through Esping-Andersen's (2009) 'incomplete gender revolution,' with the East Asian countries trailing well behind.

3.4 Quantitative forecasts of future fertility levels: experts' views

3.4.1 Introduction

The development of assumptions for the projection exercise was a multi-stage process. In step one, respondents to the survey were asked to provide point (main) and range (covering 80 per cent CI) estimates for period TFR in 2030 and 2050. In step two, these estimates were analysed and interpreted by an invited group of experts in low fertility at a meeting in Vienna in December 2011.[21] These experts focused on discussing the likely

[21] Altogether, the organizers (Basten, Sobotka, and Zeman) and 20 invited experts participated in the meeting, of which 12 were from abroad and 8 from the Vienna area (researchers from the Wittgenstein Centre for Demography and Global Human Capital (WIC), a collaboration among the International Institute for Applied Systems Analysis, IIASA; the Vienna Institute of Demography of the Austrian Academy of Sciences, VID/ÖAW; and the Vienna University of Economics and Business, WU). Here we provide the complete list of all participants and their institutional affiliation at the time of the meeting: Alicia Adsera, Princeton University; Margareth Arilha, Universidade Estadual de Campinas (Brazil); Bilal Barakat, WIC (IIASA, VID/ÖAW); Jan Van Bavel, University of Leuven; Francesco Billari, Bocconi University, Milan; Stuart Basten, University of Oxford; William Butz, WIC (IIASA, VID/ÖAW); Minja Kim Choe, East West Center, Hawaii; Joshua R. Goldstein, Max Planck Institute for Demographic Research, Rostock; K.S. James; Institute for Social and Economic Change (India); Leiwen Jiang, National Center for Atmospheric Research. Boulder; Samir K, WIC (IIASA); Tomáš Kučera, Charles University, Prague; Wolfgang Lutz, WIC (IIASA, VID/ÖAW, WU); Elsie Pamuk, WIC (IIASA); Dimiter Philipov, VID; Anna Rotkirch, Population Research Institute, Helsinki; Warren C. Sanderson, State University of New York at Stony Brook, WIC (IIASA); Tomáš Sobotka, WIC (VID/ÖAW); Vegard Skirbekk, WIC (IIASA); Olivier Thévenon, Institute National Etudes Démographiques, Paris, and Organisation for Economic Co-operation and Development, Paris.

long-term fertility trends through 2050 in major low fertility countries such as China, the USA, Brazil, Japan, Russia, Germany, and Iran, as well as in countries representing broader regions (e.g. Sweden for the Nordic countries). They also discussed possible factors and mechanisms influencing fertility in the very long-term horizon through 2200. Finally, in step three, numerous adjustments to the projections have been made jointly by the WIC teams working on low fertility countries, high fertility countries, databases (including data on education–fertility differentials), and defining and implementing projection scenarios (see section 3.5 and Chapter 9). During this process, future fertility rates have been forecasted for every country in the 'low fertility' group (see Appendix 3.2), including the countries with no expert evaluation or expert discussion, by means of implementing regional averages. To assure consistency in projections within broad geographical regions, future fertility in Latin America, South East Asia, and most of West Asia and the Middle East (except Iran, Israel, and Turkey) was projected using a forecasting model applied by the researchers analysing 'high fertility countries' (Chapter 4). In addition, the scenarios of fertility by level of education have been specified (section 3.5.3.5). In this section we concentrate on presenting the opinions of the respondents in the survey.

One of the key elements of the exercise was to obtain predictions of period TFRs by the respondents for 2030 and 2050. These not only form the basis for the projection scenarios, especially the main variant, but are also a means of providing a local expert-based 'bottom-up' comparison to the model-derived assumptions from the UN World Population Prospects (UN, 2011).[22] In this section we outline some of the key findings, presented as global results across all analysed countries, for world regions, and selected countries. Regional means were created as population-weighted averages for all countries within each region with available responses by at least two experts. We use final point projections of the TFR that the experts had a chance to revise after assessing all the arguments pertaining to the future fertility trends.

3.4.2 Overall trends

3.4.2.1 *Global trends*

The overwhelming global message from the survey is that respondents expect that fertility will stay below the replacement level to 2050, even should the current negative tempo effect eventually lose relevance. As Table 3.4 shows, among the experts who changed at least some of the predefined future TFR values (point, low, or high estimate; $N = 174$ out of the total of 184), the overwhelming majority thought fertility would remain below replacement to 2050, with about one-sixth expecting it to reach a very low level of 1.3 or below. Even in the high variant—or the expert-defined upper level of the

[22] For more details on deriving the UN set of probabilistic fertility projections, see Alkema et al. (2011), Raftery et al. (2012), and the supporting documentation to the UN population projections (UN, 2012).

Table 3.4 Experts' Projection of the Period Total Fertility Rate (TFR) in 2050 (Final Main Estimate of All Low Fertility Countries in Survey; Selected Results)

	N (experts)	% (*N* = 174)
Point estimate of the TFR in 2050		
≥ 2.0	26	15.2
...of which > 2.1	13	7.6
≤ 1.5	53	30.5
...of which < 1.3	24	13.8
TFR in 2050 will be...		
Lower than in 2010	61	35.1
...of which by ≤ 0.5	19	10.9
Higher than in 2010	75	43.1
...of which by ≥ 0.5	11	6.3
Same as in 2010	38	21.8

80 per cent CI—over one-third of experts anticipated that fertility would remain below two children per woman. Because recent fertility rates were very low in many countries, more experts expected a TFR increase between 2010 and 2050 ($N = 75$) than expected a decline ($N = 61$). Only few expected that these increases or declines would be of a large magnitude of 0.5 or higher.

These expectations differ considerably from the higher TFR values projected by the 2010 round of the UN population projections (UN, 2011). Figure 3.10 shows the mean point projections of the TFR in 2050 for each country with at least two participating experts, as contrasted with the UN medium projection. In 27 out of 31 countries the experts expected lower fertility in the future than the UN projection; the four exceptions are Argentina, Brazil, Mexico, and Georgia. In as many as 12 countries the experts expect the TFR to be at least 0.3 lower than the median UN projection in 2050; this discrepancy surpasses 0.5 for Japan and 0.4 for Russia and Romania. The experts expect sizeable fertility declines (by 0.2 or more) and/or stagnation at a low level (1.6 or lower) for the majority of the most populous low-fertility countries, including China, Iran, Russia, Turkey, Italy, and Japan (see also Table 3.5). These expectations paint a picture of a rich- and medium-income world where many smaller countries may retain fertility rates relatively close to the replacement levels, but some of the major countries experience persistent low fertility. Overall, the UN model predicts TFRs for the total group of analysed countries of 1.70 in 2030 and 1.84 in 2050; the respondents' mean projection is 1.58 and 1.57 respectively.[23] Overall, the number of countries with a TFR below 1.5 is expected to diminish, and most countries are expected eventually to fall in a broad range between 1.50 and 1.99

[23] Population-weighted average (using 2010 population size) for 31 countries with two or more respondents; see Table 3.5 for an alternative estimate of future TFR trends based on a simple average across all experts.

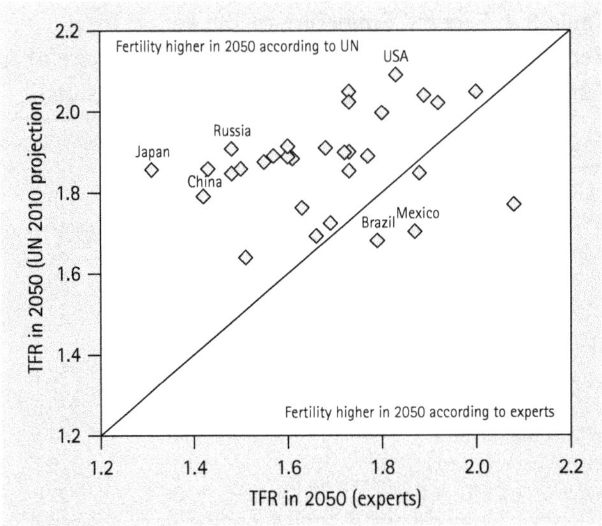

FIGURE 3.10 Projected period total fertility rate (TFR) in 2050; mean point estimate of the experts as compared with the United Nations (UN) medium value, 31 countries with at least two expert assessments.

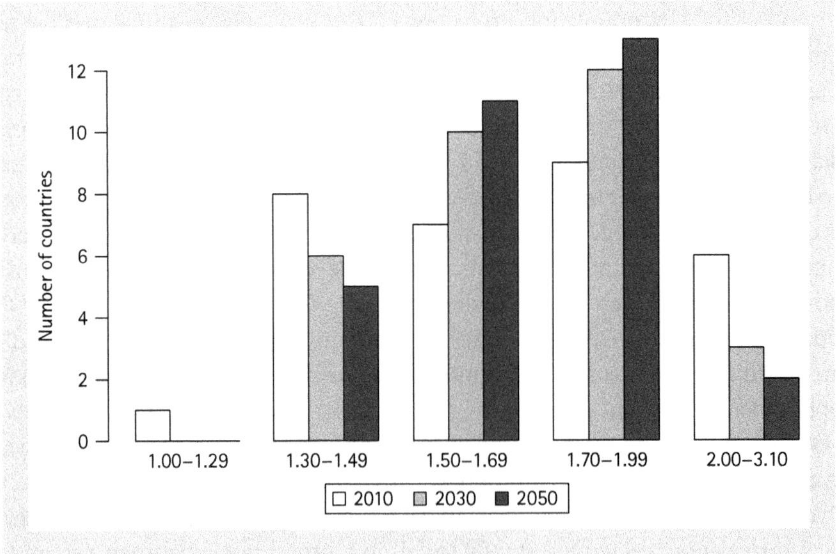

FIGURE 3.11 Distribution of the observed (2010) and projected (2030 and 2050) period total fertility rate in 31 low fertility countries with at least two expert assessments (point estimate, mean value across all experts for each country).

(Figure 3.11), with 11 out of 31 countries belonging to the low fertility group (1.50–1.69) and another 13 to moderately low fertility group (1.70–1.99) as of 2050. The diminishing number of countries expected to retain very low (TFR below 1.5) or around replacement fertility (TFR at 2.0 or higher) indicates that the experts envision a gradual trend towards convergence to moderate sub-replacement fertility for most countries. This is illustrated in Figure 3.12, which depicts a close correlation between the observed TFR level in 2010 and the expected TFR change between 2010 and 2050. Almost all countries with a TFR at 1.7 or lower are expected to experience an increase in fertility, while almost all countries with the currently higher TFR level are expected to see future fertility declines.

Figure 3.13 presents a further comparison to the UN's 2010 assumptions, showing both the medium assumption and the 80 per cent CIs for all low fertility countries with at least two experts in 2030 and 2050. The UN probabilistic projection is remarkably similar to the WIC projection in its upper boundary of the 80 per cent CIs, but it shows progressively higher values of the main TFR estimates, as well as of the lower boundary of the 80 per cent CIs, especially after 2025.

Turning to a country level confirms the expectation of a low fertility future. Among the large countries, two East Asian giants, China and Japan, are ranked at the bottom of the expected future TFR levels, with the point estimates of their TFR in 2050 of 1.31 and 1.42 respectively (see section 3.4.2.2). These expectations contrast with much higher projected values by the UN. Given China's high share of the population of low fertility countries and, indeed, of the global population, these low expected fertility rates have strongly contributed to overall low projected TFR across the entire group of analysed countries.

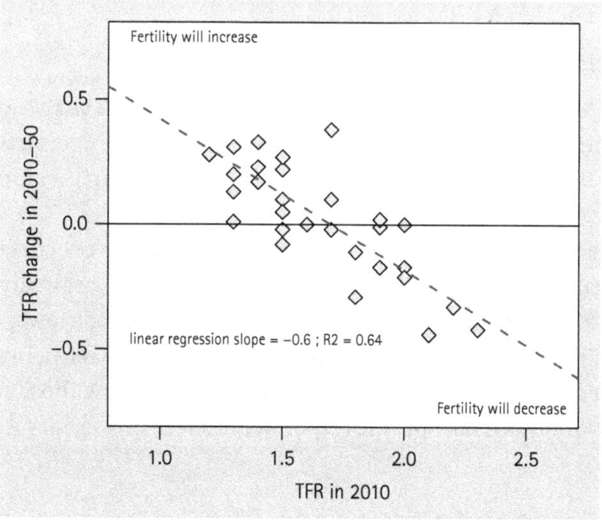

FIGURE 3.12 Projected period total fertility rate (TFR) in 2050; mean point estimate of the experts as compared with the 2010 value, 31 countries with at least two expert assessments.

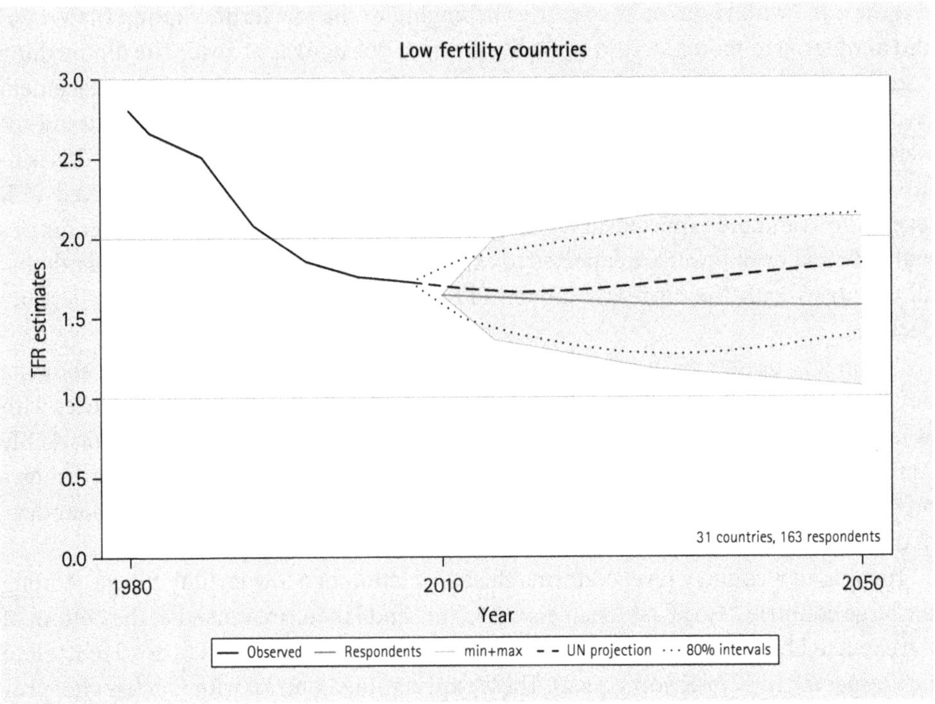

FIGURE 3.13 Total fertility rate (TFR) estimates and assumptions (including 80% uncertainty intervals) for all low fertility countries combined, 1980–2050 as derived from United Nations (UN) 2010 World Population Prospects (probabilistic scenarios) and expert survey.

Notes: Only countries with at least two expert assessments included. Global mean weighted by population size of countries included. See Appendix 3.5 for similar graphs by regions.

3.4.2.2 *Regional trends*

In Appendix 3.5 we present graphs for each low fertility region analysed in this chapter (data are weighted by population size). Here, we give a brief overview of the general trends (see also Table 3.5; the list of countries included in each region is provided in Appendix 3.3).[24]

For Western and Nordic Europe, the respondents broadly concurred with the UN projections of stabilization, with the predictions centred on marginally below replacement fertility (TFR approximately 1.9 by 2050). Meanwhile, in the lower fertility areas of Europe a more mixed picture emerges. The respondents for 'German-speaking' countries predicted a constant increase in TFR to 2050, albeit below those predicted by the UN. Similarly, in Southern Europe, the respondents envisaged a general increase in TFR

[24] Note that the experts focused in their assessment on individual countries, and regional trends are subsequently built up from these country-specific trajectories that can also be seemingly inconsistent and moving in opposite directions.

Table 3.5 Observed Period Total Fertility Rate (TFR) in 2010 and Projected Period TFR in 2050 in Largest Low Fertility Countries and in Selected Countries Representing Broader Regions; Expert's Expectations (Mean Value of Point Estimates and 80% Uncertainty Interval (UI)) and United Nations World Population Prospects (UN WPP) 2010 Medium Projection Variant

Country	N[‡]	2010: observed TFR[§]	2030: mean		2050		
			Expert	UN WPP 2010	Expert: mean	80% CI: min.–max.[¶]	UN WPP 2010: mean
USA	22 (19)	1.93	1.93	2.09	1.83	1.38–2.30	2.09
China	13 (7)	1.45	1.41	1.61	1.42	0.93–2.09	1.79
Australia	5 (4)	1.89	1.83	2.01	1.73	1.48–2.06	2.05
Brazil	7 (2)	1.94	1.83	1.61	1.79	–	1.68
Mexico	5 (1)	2.30	1.95	1.80	1.92	–	1.70
Iran	8 (1)	1.90	1.77	1.36	1.54	–	1.64
Japan	6 (2)	1.39	1.30	1.68	1.31	–	1.86
Turkey	5 (2)	2.04	1.82	1.74	1.66	–	1.69
Czech Republic	6 (6)	1.49	1.63	1.74	1.72	1.39–2.28	1.90
Germany	9 (4)	1.39	1.57	1.71	1.58	1.23–2.06	1.89
Italy	12 (7)	1.40	1.55	1.72	1.57	1.30–1.92	1.89
Russia	4 (2)	1.54	1.46	1.76	1.48	–	1.91
Spain	6 (4)	1.39	1.58	1.74	1.68	1.34–2.12	1.90
Sweden	7 (6)	1.99	1.90	2.00	1.89	1.47–2.23	2.04
UK	4 (4)	1.98	1.99	1.96	1.92	1.31–2.65	2.02
All countries–weighted*	31 countries	1.64	1.58	1.70	1.57	1.07–2.13	1.84
All countries–average[†]	174 (105)	1.69	1.70	1.77	1.68	1.27–2.21	1.88

* These data show global mean TFR for all the countries with at least two expert evaluations (see Appendix 3.3), weighted by population size of these countries in 2010; these computations are based on 163 expert assessments.

[†] These data show simple average across all experts participating in the IIASA-Oxford survey and the corresponding value for the UN projection (weighted by the number of respondents in each country).

[‡] Number of respondents giving valid 80 per cent uncertainty interval shown in brackets.

[§] 2010 TFR values are based on VID (2012), Eurostat, national statistical offices, and, for China, on Zhongwei Zhao's estimate. Note that the experts participating in the online survey were shown slightly different values published by Population Reference Bureau (PRB, 2011); see Appendix 3.1, Section A1.1 for more details.

[¶] Figures shown only for countries with at least four respondents providing CIs.

to 2030 and 2050, although again generally not at the speed predicted by the UN. Central Europe also sees notable increases in TFR, which are more closely matched to the UN model. In Eastern Europe the experts predicted a general stagnation or very slight increase in fertility. For Russia and Ukraine, the respondents expected a slight decline in TFR to 2030 followed by recuperation to 2010 levels by 2050.

For North America, 22 of the 25 respondents made predictions for the USA. For both 2030 and 2050, while the UN predicts stagnation at around replacement level, the respondents predicted an overall slight TFR decline from 2.0 in 2010 to the means of 1.93 in 2030 and 1.83 by 2050. The lower boundary of 80 per cent CI in 2050 (1.38) was predicted to be significantly lower than the low variant of the UN model (1.59).

In East Asia, the respondents generally predicted either stagnation or decline in TFR. In particular, the views of these respondents are at odds with the UN model for 2050, in that almost all the survey responses predicted a lower TFR than the UN. The 13 respondents for China generally expected stagnation at or around 1.4–1.5, while the UN's medium variant is 1.79 and the low variant 1.31. Respondents for Japan were even more sceptical about the possibility of future fertility increases, and with the mean predicted TFR of 1.31 in 2050 they differed most from the UN medium variant projection of 1.86.

Finally, for the rather heterogeneous group of Latin America (15 responses, 3 countries), there is a general concurrence with the UN model of continuing fertility decline.

3.5 Projecting future fertility

The preparation of fertility scenarios involved a complex decision-making process engaging several research teams working on the WIC projections, as well as multiple interactions with selected experts outside the teams. The key decisions concerned defining the main variant of the period TFR in 2030 and 2050, agreeing on long-term fertility pathway through 2200, projecting fertility trajectories by level of education, formulating low and high variants of fertility scenarios for each educational category, and, finally, coordinating the teams working on the low and high fertility countries in order to achieve a degree of uniformity in the methods used and data analysed. This section describes the development of these fertility scenarios, as well as contrasts to the fertility scenario-making for the countries with higher fertility levels. More detailed materials and descriptions appear as appendices.

3.5.1 Formulating main scenario point projections for 2030 and 2050

This section outlines the process of deriving the main TFR projection scenario for 2030 and 2050 for all countries and regions covered in this chapter except for Latin America and parts of the Middle East (only Iran, Israel, and Turkey are projected here), which are projected following the model employed for the higher fertility countries (see Chapters 4 and 9). Additional information is provided in Appendix 3.1. The observed TFR data for the base year of the projection, 2010, originate from a variety of sources. For most low fertility countries, these data were derived from the PRB database or national vital statistics, and are relatively precise, computed annually, and usable without further adjustments, given good and practically complete vital statistics coverage. Only in a few cases, such as Iran and the Caucasus countries, is data coverage patchy, meaning the initial TFR data should be treated as 'qualified estimates', based mostly on the UN (2011) and PRB (2011) databases. The most notable exception from relatively good data coverage is the most populous country, China, where past numbers of births and fertility rates remain highly uncertain (see Box 3.1).

The point estimates of the period TFR in 2030 and 2050 (main scenario) were derived in several steps. Following experts' predictions gathered in the IIASA–Oxford online survey and at the Vienna meeting where the TFR scenarios for the key countries were settled, the coordinating team (i.e. the three main authors of this chapter), in collaboration with other teams, formulated the point estimates for all low fertility countries. This was done by selecting one or two key countries in each region for which the fertility rates in 2030 and 2050 were defined by experts. Within each region, countries for which no projected TFRs were available by the online survey experts (at least two per country) or invited experts were assumed to follow an identical TFR trajectory as one of the key countries in that region. For instance, countries in Central Europe for which no future TFR were available from the experts survey were assumed to follow the same trajectory as either the Czech Republic (a higher fertility pathway) or Hungary (lower fertility pathway); the definition of the key countries and the decision to which 'key country' each individual country was attached was mostly done by the low fertility coordinating team (see details on deriving future TFR trends by country in Appendix 3.1 and in Basten et al., 2013).

Finally, a complete TFR trajectory has been constructed for five-year periods from 2010–14 to 2045–49, assuming a linear trend between the starting year value and the two years for which the TFR was already projected, 2030 and 2050. However, the initial five-year projection period, 2010–14, constitutes an exception whereby in countries with an increasing TFR trajectory through 2030, the rise occurs only after 2015 and the TFR in 2010–14 remains identical with the most recent observed data, usually for 2011 and, in some cases, for 2012. This is a simple effort to account partly for the effect of the recent economic recession, during which fertility rates were likely falling in most countries (see section 3.2.4). As there was heterogeneity of country-specific TFR trends in Europe during the recession (see Box 3.3) and the future course of the recession and economic recovery were unknown at the time fertility scenarios were developed, a 'conservative' strategy was employed, assuming no TFR increase in the initial period rather than modelling its potential temporary decline.

To derive uncertainty intervals around the main (point) TFR estimates, two possibilities were considered. First, the more flexible and less standardized option was to define low and high projected TFR representing 80 per cent CI on the basis of experts' assessment of country-specific CI in 2030 and 2050 (see sections 3.4.2.1 and 3.4.2.2). The second option followed quite 'traditional' solutions, providing a standardized and easily-derived estimate for all countries, namely using either a relative or a fixed absolute interval around the main TFR estimate. Initially, the first option was selected, which allows both reflecting the experts' views and mirroring the likely future regional differences in uncertainty about fertility trends, which should be higher in regions undergoing rapid fertility changes in recent decades, such as the Middle East. However, this solution became impractical owing to low response rates in some countries where many respondents did not provide assessments of the likely future uncertainty in their TFR estimates, and also owing to implausibly high variation of these estimates between some countries belonging to the same region. As a result, a standardized (although somewhat simplistic) solution has been chosen, assuming a low versus high TFR interval of 20 per cent around the main TFR projection in 2030, increasing to 25 per cent in 2050 (see also Chapter 9, section 9.3.6). This roughly reflects the uncertainty interval in 2050 averaged across all experts providing its assessment (Table 3.5, last line): starting with an average TFR value of 1.68 predicted by the experts for that year, a 25 per cent range around that mean, representing 80 per cent CI gives a TFR from 1.26 to 2.10 compared with the average of expert-defined 80 per cent CI of 1.27–2.21. To reflect an initial sharp increase in projection uncertainty in the early projection period, further exacerbated by unstable fertility rates during the economic recession after 2008, two thirds of the estimated 80 per cent CI observed by 2030 would open up during the first projection period, 2010–14.

The outlined TFR projections differ considerably from how projection scenarios have been derived for the countries with high fertility, which relied less on the online survey of experts and more on the input given at an expert meeting in Kathmandu and on the modelling of future TFR trajectories. This modelling was based on the most recent observed fertility level and on the previous trajectories of fertility decline in the presently low fertility countries (Chapter 4, section 4.5.3). As we have been able to collect comprehensive expert input covering most low fertility regions, and also given that there are no systematic experiences of long-term TFR changes in post-transitional societies with low fertility on which such a model can be based, the scenarios for low fertility countries did not utilize such a model. However, to prevent coherent geographical regions from following two different projection set-ups, all Latin American and most Middle East and East-Asian countries were merged and their future TFR scenarios modelled by the team covering high-fertility countries (Chapter 4).

3.5.2 Long-term futures: preparing fertility scenarios beyond 2050

Fertility forecasting has been dominated by the paradigm of the demographic transition. Fertility was thought to fall from a high comparatively stable level to a low comparatively stable level. This transition was considered to be irreversible, so once a low enough level of fertility was achieved it would never increase. The textbook versions of the demographic transition generally show a crude birth rate and crude death rate converging, leading to a cessation of natural population growth (Caldwell, 1976). This homeostatic convergence towards long-term stationary population would imply, given current and projected very low (and further declining) mortality levels, fertility rates stabilizing at around two births per woman.

However, this stylized model does not fit the empirical evidence on post-transitional fertility and, arguably, gives no guidance about future fertility trends (Lutz, 2006). In one country after another, this post-transitional stage has been associated with at least a brief, but often persistent, era of fertility being below the replacement threshold (see section 3.1). Therefore, achieving a long-term equilibrium of fertility and mortality levels remains very uncertain.[25] The key issue is whether below replacement fertility is a temporary phenomenon or whether the long-term future of most rich countries features a continuation of low fertility rates.

Four arguments are commonly put forth to suggest that fertility rates may eventually increase in countries with low rates. First, period TFR declines to very low levels have been, to a large extent, fuelled by the postponement of childbearing to higher ages (Kohler et al., 2002; see section 3.2.2). This postponement will eventually come to an end, paving the way for a modest rise in period TFRs fuelled by fertility increases ('recuperation') at higher childbearing ages (Frejka, 2011; Sobotka, 2004a), as observed in many rich countries between the late 1990s and 2008 (Goldstein et al., 2009). Second, CFRs in most countries with low fertility never declined to such low levels as period TFRs did. Indeed, recent fertility trends for some countries could be extrapolated into slight increases in the completed cohort fertility of women born in the 1970s (Myrskylä et al., 2013; see section 3.1.3). Third, intended family size among men and women of reproductive ages in Europe, as well as North America, remains remarkably stable at or slightly above two children (Testa 2012; see sections 3.2.3.1 and 3.1.4.1); if couples were to fully realize their fertility intentions, fertility rates would increase. Finally, low fertility rates may be seen as a transitory stage during which society adjusts to the host of factors associated with the SDT (Lesthaeghe, 2010). Once societies adapt to this new reality by, for instance, promoting gender equality and developing policies, institutions, and norms that allow an easier combination of work and childrearing for couples, and possibly also medical interventions expanding the biological limits of human reproduction, fertility rates may recover (Esping-Andersen, 2009, Myrskylä et al., 2011).

There are more general arguments and mechanisms that explain why fertility may rise, including long-term fertility cycles, changes in population composition through migration or fertility differentials, and the concept of homeostasis, which suggests that 'demographic systems' tend to converge in the long run towards an equilibrium that assures their maintenance and survival (Billari and Dalla-Zuanna, 2012; Lutz, 2006). There are also many cogent arguments succinctly summarized by Lutz (2006) of why fertility

[25] Other macro-level uncertainties—some of which are referred to in section 3.2.9—contribute to this. Furthermore, in the long-run, climate change might also affect fertility trends with a varied impact in different settings. However, considering uncertainties about its progression, potential (often yet unforeseen) adaptations to it, and diverse pathways of how it might affect fertility and reproduction, we have not produced explicit scenarios linking climate change and projected fertility.

rates may fall further or remain at very low levels for extended periods of time. The most prominent among these arguments is the 'Low Fertility Trap' hypothesis, which suggests that the long-term experience of low fertility may generate a downward spiral of declining family size ideals, births, and fertility rates determined through both the normalization of small family sizes and a political realignment towards the needs of increasingly older populations (Lutz et al., 2006; see also section 3.2.1). Other potential determinants of low fertility in the future, including current trajectories of female educational attainment, are examined in sections 3.2, 3.3.2, 3.3.4, and 3.5.3.

Despite a wealth of arguments and hypotheses highlighted here and in other parts of this chapter, there exists little settled theory concerning the long-term future of fertility, especially in the period beyond 2050 when generations not yet born will be responsible for the reproduction of future generations. The main scenarios of global population projections produced by the UN continue to embrace the idea that, in the long term, fertility rates in different global regions will fluctuate around the replacement level and eventually stabilize. The 2010 medium projection variant envisions that in the more developed regions period TFR will reach 1.97 in 2045–50 and 2.07 in 2095–2100 (UN, 2011, p. 11, Table ii.1). Also, the probabilistic projection model of fertility developed on behalf of the UN by Alkema et al. (2011, 2010) assumes that global fertility change proceeds in distinct phases, which include a spell of sub-replacement fertility and an eventual recovery, leading to a final convergence and an oscillation around the replacement level.

The debate with selected experts in November 2011 in Vienna on the long-term future of fertility addressed two possible alternative futures: Will most countries become more like the USA or Sweden today, with close-to-replacement fertility levels, or will they follow the path of South Korea, reaching very low fertility levels at advanced stages of development? By definition, the long time horizon selected makes the nature of fertility scenarios highly speculative and limits the forecasters' ability to draw lessons and conclusions from the currently observed fertility trends and determinants, as well as those predicted in the next decades. Besides the arguments and evidence highlighted earlier, the following facts and considerations informed the discussion on long-term fertility future.

- The cohort fertility forecasts by Myrskylä et al. (2013) showed that the average completed cohort fertility of women in 37 developed countries born in 1979 would be 1.77 (see section 3.1.3 for more details). This figure is well above the period TFRs experienced in many of these countries during the last few decades. More importantly, Myrskylä et al. showed that cohort completed fertility had either stopped falling or that its decline had slowed significantly in developed countries in every region of the world, with the exception of East Asia and some countries in Southern Europe and CEE.
- The consensus among the experts participating in the online survey was that fertility rates in most of the low fertility countries will stay below the replacement level threshold by 2050. The overall average of the projected TFR in 2050 (main scenario) across all experts reached 1.68, that is, 20 per cent below the replacement

level. These expectations deviated strongly from the UN World Population Prospects 2010 projection model (section 3.4.2).

- It is unlikely that fertility levels will be the same across different countries or that fertility will remain at a stable level in one country over an extended period of time (Bongaarts and Bulatao, 2000). However, in the absence of a commonly agreed unifying theory on how fertility will differ between countries or how will it change over time in a distant future, a simplistic assumption of long-term cross-country convergence and eventual stabilization can be justified.

These considerations resulted in two competing scenarios based on the notions of long-term convergence and stabilization: one of a convergence to the fertility level of 2.0 children per woman by 2200, that is, close-to-replacement fertility level, and the other of a convergence to 1.75 by 2200, that is, a fertility level that remains moderately below the replacement level.[26] The idea that fertility could fall and stabilize at very low levels close to 1.5 or below did not find support as a main scenario. Following a short discussion, a majority of experts participating in the Vienna meeting chose the scenario with a fertility level at 1.75, corresponding roughly to current cohort fertility levels, as well as the projected TFRs in 2050 in the set of countries analysed. This projected 'target' TFR served for projecting the fertility trajectories between 2050 (an endpoint of the expert-based projection, differentiated by region and country) and 2200, using linear interpolation.[27] The long-run TFR level of 1.75 might be consistent with keeping populations in many countries stable if they experience further increases in life expectancy and modest levels of in-migration. Myrskylä et al. (2012), using mortality rates forecasted by the UN, show that Europe would be able to keep its population stable by bringing in one migrant for every seven live births. The mortality rates for developed countries that we use in our forecasts are generally lower than those forecasted by the UN, so population stability would be reached with even fewer immigrants.

A plausible higher scenario is suggested by the analysis in Myrskylä et al. (2012). They show, using the World Economic Forums' Global Gender Gap Index, that gender inequality is a good predictor of cohort completed fertility among younger cohorts

[26] There has been much debate regarding the justification of convergence as a 'belief' in the specific course of future global population trends as opposed to a computational tool. In some ways, the deployment of convergence takes elements of both of these uses and interpretations. In our exercise, we embrace the latter interpretation, acknowledging that the future variance in fertility across countries will be underestimated. The debate on the global convergence in fertility levels during the last half century has been inconclusive, partly depending on the measurement and methods used (see Dorius, 2008; Wilson, 2011).

[27] To some observers, projecting fertility and population change up to 2200 seems to encompass an absurdly long time horizon. One of the contributing authors, reviewing this chapter stated 'there are limits to our imagination. When we think in 2013 about fertility in 2200 we are in the same position as Malthus trying to make forecasts for 2000'. Because of this huge uncertainty about the very long-term future, most of our projection exercise focuses on the time horizon through 2050. Likewise, education–fertility differentials are not projected beyond 2050, as their longer-term development in low fertility countries is very uncertain.

analysed. This is consistent with the arguments made by our source experts. In the scenario where gender gaps slowly disappear in the future, TFRs would converge to a higher level of around-replacement fertility, which is consistent with that currently observed in countries with low gender gaps. A lower scenario could be driven by improvements in contraception. This is also consistent with the arguments made by the source experts reflecting remarkably high rates of unintended pregnancies in some regions, including the USA and Latin America (sections 3.1.4.1 and 3.1.4.2). Improvements in contraceptive technologies would reduce the number of unintended pregnancies and result in fewer births. However, it is impossible to say precisely what the effects of improved contraception would be.

3.5.3 Defining TFR assumptions by level of education

This empirically oriented section complements a more theoretical discussion on the relationship between education and fertility in section 3.2.8 and gives background analysis informing fertility projection scenarios by level of education. We also discuss evidence for Latin America and the Middle East, regions for which projection scenarios are formulated separately using the model for high fertility countries (except for Iran, Israel, and Turkey).[28]

3.5.3.1 *Education-fertility differentials in low fertility settings: empirical evidence*

In order to produce global population projections differentiated by level of education, it was necessary to quantify current and the likely future educational differentials in fertility. Given limited data availability and the fact that education categories are often not readily comparable between countries (see Chapter 9), we have mostly focused on three broad education categories: 'Low' (International Standard Classification of Education (ISCED) levels 0–2),[29] 'Medium' (ISCED 3 or 3–4), and 'High' education (ISCED 5–6). When possible, especially in countries with a high proportion of women with primary or lower level of education, we have divided the 'Low' category into 'Very low' education (ISCED 0–1) and 'Lower secondary' education (ISCED 2). To increase data comparability between countries, we primarily used data on completed or almost completed cohort fertility collected from censuses, large-sample surveys, or registry data, using the data sets for the most recent five-year cohorts aged 40–44 or 45–49 and over (see also Appendix 6 in Basten et al., 2013 and Chapter 9 for more details about data and data sources). This allowed us to avoid problems inherent in estimating period fertility data by level of education, especially

[28] For an analysis of fertility differentials in (mostly) higher fertility settings based on Demographic and Health Survey data, see KC and Potančoková (2013).

[29] In the group of countries with high fertility and generally lower levels of education, this broad category has been subdivided into four distinct categories (Chapter 4).

the instability of the data over time; problems with classifying educational categories at younger ages, especially for women still in education; and tempo distortions that vary by level of education. However, the use of cohort data brings an obvious drawback: these data pertain to women whose prime childbearing period was 10–20 years ago and who therefore may not represent the most recent trend. We first focus on analysing the existing differentials in fertility by level of education, which serve as a baseline for the formulation of projection scenarios, as well as for the assessments of the likely future trends in countries that still have above replacement fertility levels. Rather than analysing absolute fertility levels, we are primarily interested in relative fertility differentials. For each country and cohort (or calendar year) analysed, we computed relative fertility indexes (RFI), which are related to the group of women with medium education (RFI = 1). Our main questions and findings are summarized in the next three sub-sections.

3.5.3.2 *Do fertility differentials by level of education vary by region?*

Table 3.6 features the RFI for broader regions, computed for recent cohorts past prime reproductive age, as simple averages across all countries with available data (see Appendix 6 in Basten et al. 2013 for further details about data coverage by country, region, cohorts, and/or period). The expected fertility gradient shows up in all regions except Nordic countries, where the three categories analysed have identical fertility levels. Furthermore, the fertility gradient is relatively small in Western Europe, 'German-speaking' countries, and Southern Europe, especially for women with higher education. In the USA, women

Table 3.6 Relative Fertility Index by Level of Education in Major Low Fertility Regions; Evidence for Female Birth Cohorts Past Reproductive Age

Region	# Countries	Education category				
		Low	of which:		Medium	High
			Very low	Lower secondary		
North America	1 (USA)	1.34	–	–	1.00	0.97
Latin America	8	1.44	1.63	1.20	1.00	0.81
East + South East Asia (except China)	3	1.29	–	–	1.00	0.89
Middle East	3	1.51	1.57	1.18	1.00	0.89
Western Europe and German-speaking	5	1.15	–	–	1.00	0.96
Nordic countries	3	1.01	–	–	1.00	0.98
Southern Europe	2	1.16	1.24	1.11	1.00	0.91
Central Europe	8	1.22	1.23	1.22	1.00	0.85
Eastern Europe	4	–	1.47	1.39	1.00	0.85

See more details about the data and countries included in Appendix 6 in Basten et al. (2013). Regretfully, no data are available for China.

with low education have elevated fertility levels that contrast strongly with the other two categories. The strongest education gradient in fertility is observed in Latin America and the Middle East which are in the late stage of fertility transition. In these regions highly-educated women still form a select group the low fertility of which contrasts starkly with much higher fertility among women with primary or lower education.

3.5.3.3 *Is there a distinct trend in education–fertility differentials once the overall fertility declines below a threshold of 2.2?*

This question is important for the formulation of education–fertility scenarios in the higher fertility countries that are expected to undergo a transition to sub-replacement fertility in the coming decades. The empirical evidence can be elucidated on two levels. First, purely cross-sectional data from recent surveys and censuses (figures available upon request) suggest that the differentials tend to diminish. But the correlation is weak and the spread is wide; for instance, a cohort TFR level around 1.8 is associated with a RFI of the lower-educated women of between 1.0 and 1.4. The same 'weak' evidence of diminishing differential applies to women with higher education.

Second, more valid evidence comes from the analysis of changes in fertility differentials across cohorts experiencing declining fertility. We have assembled data for nine European countries. Focusing on what happens when completed cohort fertility declines from around 2.3 to around 1.7, the data suggest diminishing distinctiveness of the low-education group (with smaller 'surplus' fertility as the overall fertility level declines)

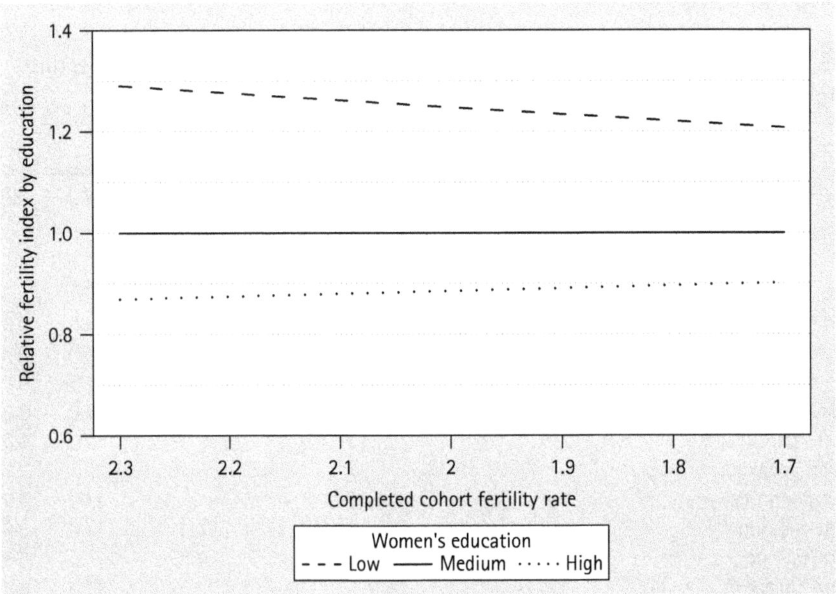

FIGURE 3.14 Relationship between overall fertility level and relative fertility index by level of education, based on cohort fertility data for nine countries (exponential regression, cohorts born in the 1920s–60s).

and a minor trend of diminishing distinctiveness of the higher-educated category (but with very weak significance; data and graphs available upon request). Exponential trends[30] are shown in Figure 3.14.

3.5.3.4 *Is there a distinct trend in education–fertility differentials across cohorts?*

This question is addressed in Figure 3.15 with an expanded data set for 19 countries in 3 broader regions. In parallel to the evidence on gradually declining education–fertility differentials with declining fertility level described earlier, there is a continuous RFI decline among the lower-educated women in each of the three regions analysed. This fall was particularly impressive in Singapore, where the RFI fell from above 1.6 in the cohorts born around 1935 to below 1.2 in the cohorts born around 1960. A similar trend occurred in the Republic of Korea, although from a lower initial RFI level. Also, in some countries of CEE, especially Hungary, the RFI fell rapidly across cohorts. However, this region retains elevated fertility among women with low education, with the mean RFI still above 1.3 in the cohorts born around 1955. In contrast, the mean RFI in Western and Northern Europe (including Austria, Germany, and Switzerland, as well as Greece; no data available for other Southern European countries), has fallen below 1.1.

The RFI trends are less uniform when women with higher education are analysed in comparison with those having medium levels of educational attainment. The average mean trend in the analysed regions can be best described as a stable differential, with highly educated women having slightly lower fertility. A few countries in Western and Northern Europe (especially Belgium and Austria) registered a rapid rise in the RFI, leading in Belgium to a crossover whereby fertility among the higher-educated surpassed that of women with a medium level of education (data exclude immigrant women). In the cohorts born around 1955 the average RFI among women with higher education oscillates around 0.9 in many countries and at a lower level closer to 0.8 in CEE. Romania shows a particularly steep gradient in education–fertility differentials, with relative fertility falling to very low levels among the higher-educated women.

3.5.3.5 *Expected and projected future trends in education–fertility differentials*

Are future education–fertility differentials likely to diminish? A simple extrapolation of cohort trends described earlier suggests that in most countries the fertility rates of women with low levels of education may eventually converge with those with a medium level (upper secondary) education. The trend is much less clear-cut for tertiary-educated women, with a slight (but incomplete) convergence in Western, Northern Europe, and East Asia, and mixed trends, mostly marked by a slight rise of the negative gradient, in CEE.

[30] Exponential trend of RFI (related to 1) can be understand as linear trend of logarithm of RFI (related to 0) with intercept at [0;0], which prevents the crossover and enforces the convergence of RFIs.

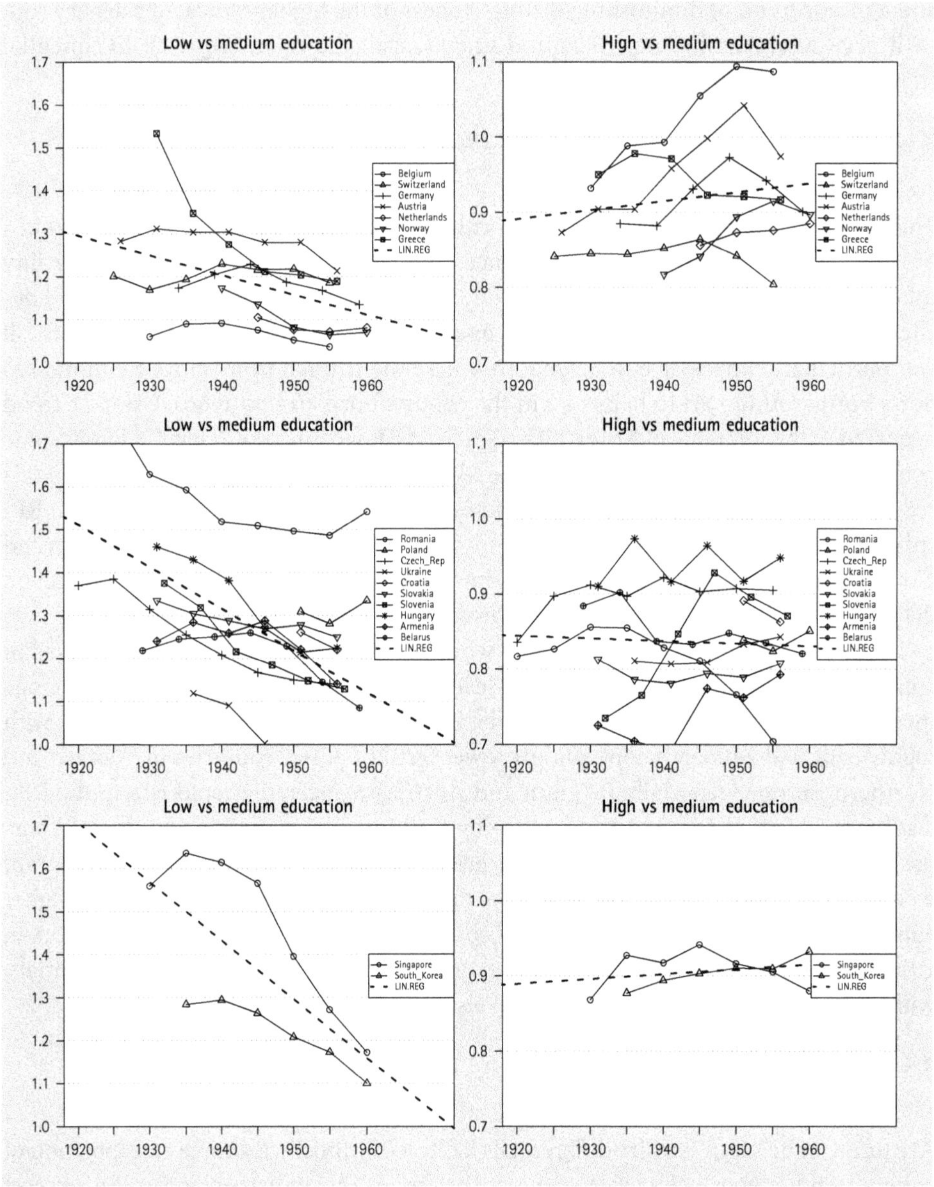

FIGURE 3.15 Trends in relative fertility index by cohort in three broader regions (Western and Northern Europe, Central and Eastern Europe, and East Asia); low- and high- vs medium-educated women.

The experts' views about regional trends are summarized in Figure 3.16 (see section 3.4.1 for a global overview). The experts expect diminishing education–fertility differentials especially in Latin America, the Middle East, and Southern Europe. In the former two regions, these differentials are still pronounced (Table 3.6; KC and Potančoková, 2013) and the experts expect that they will diminish through a decline in

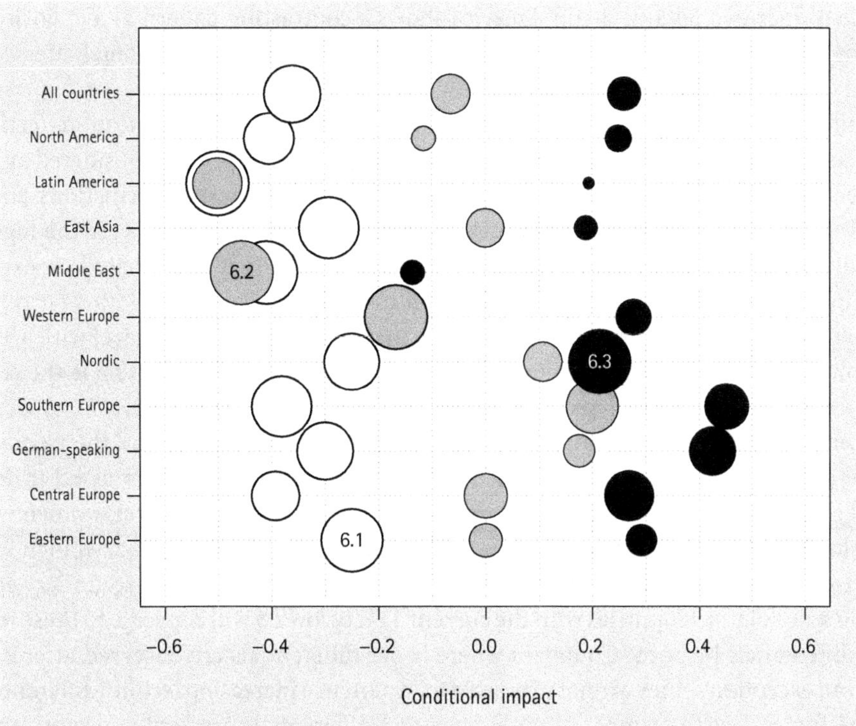

FIGURE 3.16 Validity and conditional impact of education-related arguments 6.1–6.3 by region. Diameter of the bubbles corresponds to squared value of the validity of each argument (ranging from 0.32 to 0.82).

Note:

- Argument 6.1 (white bubbles with bold border): people will spend ever more years of their young adult life enrolled in education and professional training on the job.
- Argument 6.2 (light-grey bubbles): fertility differentials by level of female education will diminish.
- Argument 6.3 (dark bubbles): there will be a new trend for better educated women to have more children and simultaneously pursue a professional career.

fertility among lower educated women, bringing a negative pressure on the overall fertility rate. In contrast, in Southern Europe the experts expect that a reduced education–fertility differential will materialize owing to an increase in the fertility of the women with tertiary education, which will have a positive effect on fertility. Additionally, experts indicated that a convergence in educational–fertility differentials is unlikely in the USA (argument validity of 0.39). More specific responses about the possibility of better educated women having higher fertility in the future while pursuing their career depict a strong agreement (validity = 0.75) among experts on the Nordic countries (where tertiary-educated women already record relatively high fertility; Table 3.6 and Figure 3.15) and also considerable agreement in selected other regions of Europe, German-speaking countries, Southern Europe, and Central Europe (validity index above 0.6). A rather strong positive net impact of this trend on overall fertility is expected in the former two regions. Latin America shows a contrasting pattern as a majority of experts there disagreed with the expectation of increasing fertility among better-educated women (validity = 0.32).

Different possibilities of how to combine the observed trends in education–fertility differentials by region with the experts' insights and expectations were considered by the project's coordinating team. Given regional variation in experts' expectations and a need to produce a global set of projections (lacking expert assessments for the higher fertility countries analysed in Chapter 4), a simple model that is not based on expert opinion was produced (see also Chapter 9). It assumes that countries with a currently higher fertility level will converge by the time they reach a low fertility level with a TFR around 1.8 to average education–fertility differentials experienced at present in the set of low fertility countries analysed here. The model combines the most recent observed education–fertility differentials in low fertility countries (Table 3.6) and the trends in these differentials at sub-replacement fertility levels (Figure 3.14). Expressed in RFI, fixed at the level of 1.00 among the women with high (tertiary) education, women with very low education (completed primary and lower) will have a RFI of 1.42, women with lower secondary education will have a RFI of 1.35, and those with upper secondary education a RFI of 1.14. Countries with the current TFR below 1.8 will converge to these relative differentials by 2030. Countries where lower differentials are observed at present form an exception—they are not projected to experience increasing fertility differentials in the future, but their most recently observed differentials are kept constant in the projection.

3.6 Conclusion

In this chapter, we have attempted to present a comprehensive, state-of-the-art overview of both the regional context of fertility decline in currently low fertility settings and the possible contributions of the theoretical and empirical drivers that underpin them. Many sections have demonstrated that the locus of low fertility is increasingly moving away from 'Old Europe' and towards the rapidly developing economies of East Asia, Latin America, and the Middle East. In this respect, any understanding of the forces behind recent fertility decline needs to take into account changes in these settings and their particular contexts.

In view of the wide variation of fertility levels in contemporary rich and middle-income countries, a global convergence of fertility to around replacement level appears unlikely. Either continuing bifurcation in future trends of low fertility or a stronger movement towards the low fertility rates seen in East Asia—especially in rapidly developing settings—is a possible future scenario. In absolute terms, contemporary variation in post-transitional fertility in the order of one birth per woman is small. In relative terms, a period TFR of 2.0–2.1 in France, New Zealand, and, until recently, the USA, is almost twice as high as the period TFR of 1.0–1.2 recently recorded in Hong Kong, Korea, and Taiwan. This range between East Asia on one side and France and New Zealand on the other side also roughly corresponds to the global average of the 80 per cent CI of the period TFR in 2050 predicted by the experts participating in the online survey, which ranged from 1.07 to 2.13 (data weighted by population size).

These vast relative differences, if they persist, will have negative repercussions for the group of lowest fertility countries, which will face accelerated population ageing and protracted population declines, especially if they do not attract sizeable immigration. Even if period fertility rates recover somewhat, as they did in much of Europe in the early 2000s, replacement level is seen by many experts as an upper boundary for the post-transitional fertility levels. However, a return of above replacement fertility cannot be completely ruled out, although it seems incompatible with contemporary economic uncertainty, as well as lifestyles, career, and consumer aspirations of the majority of populations in rich countries. Past experience shows that baby booms may occur unexpectedly, taking demographers by surprise.

Acknowledgements

The completion of this chapter would not have been possible without the committed involvement of different contributors—researchers, contributing authors, experts participating in the IIASA–Oxford survey, and those participating in the expert meeting in Vienna—who have organized the survey of experts or contributed to it, were involved in the debates on fertility scenarios presented here, and who have directly contributed to this chapter, or helped in checking and reviewing it.

Special thanks are due to Bilal Barakat, who helped design the survey of experts and provided first analyses of survey results; Michaela Potančoková who helped us collect data on the education–fertility differentials analysed in sections 3.5.3.1–3.5.3.4; Nikola Sander who operationalized the Circos plots used in Figures 3.7 and 3.8; Bill Butz, Josh Goldstein, and Tomas Frejka who provided detailed comments on the first draft of this chapter; and Jim Dawson and Jayne MacArthur who copyedited the draft.

Sobotka and Zeman's contribution was funded by the European Research Council (ERC) under the EU's Seventh Framework Programme (FP7/2007-2013)/ERC Grant agreement no. 284238. Basten's contribution was funded by the ERC Advanced Investigator Grant entitled 'Forecasting Societies' Adaptive Capacities to Climate Change' (ERC-2008-AdG 230195-FutureSoc), and the UK Economic and Social Research Council's 'Future Research Leader' Grant, no. ES/K001434/1.

APPENDIX 3.1

Defining the initial total fertility rates values in 2010 and formulating main scenario point projections for 2030 and 2050

We discuss only countries and regions for which Wittgenstein Centre for Demography and Global Human Capital (WIC) projections scenarios were formulated using input provided by experts on low fertility countries. Fertility scenarios for Latin American countries, for most of the Middle East region (except Iran, Israel, and Turkey), and for some other low fertility countries have been formulated jointly with the higher fertility countries, using a scenario model described in Chapters 4 and 9. As a result, the following low fertility countries are not discussed here: Thailand, all Latin American and Caribbean countries, Algeria, Tunisia, Mauritius, Brunei, Kuwait, Qatar, United Arab Emirates, and Lebanon. Here we provide a condensed description; full details can be found in Appendix 1 of the working paper by Basten et al. (2013).

A3.1.1 The initial total fertility rate in 2010

Most of the total fertility rate (TFR) data for European countries were computed by the Vienna Institute of Demography for the European Demographic Data Sheet 2012; for a few countries, the TFR data originate from Eurostat or national statistical offices.

For most non-European countries, the 2010 TFR data are based on the 2010 edition of the World Population Data Sheet published by the Population Reference Bureau (PRB, 2011). Additional data sources for some countries are listed in Basten et al. (2013).

A3.1.2 Deriving medium (point) total fertility rate estimates

The derivation of the 'medium' (point) TFR estimates proceeded in several steps described as follows. First, simple data cleaning took place to exclude data where the experts left the expected TFR values for 2030 and 2050 at the predefined values (which were identical to the 'starting' values for 2010). These exclusions occurred only for the experts who did not change any of the six projected TFR values (minimum, maximum, and median for 2030 and 2050), assuming that they did not want to deal with this empirical part of the survey or could not effectively manipulate the sliders with TFR estimates on their computer. For experts who changed at least one of these predefined TFR values, the medium TFR estimates were counted, even when they were identical with the predefined values.

A3.1.2.1 *The representative countries*

The 'representative countries' were the 13 most populous countries or countries with distinct fertility patterns representative of the broader region (and with at least four respondents per country): China, the USA, Japan, Iran, Turkey, Russia, Italy, Spain, Germany, the UK, Sweden, the Czech Republic, and Australia.

Mean values of experts' responses to the online survey were presented at the expert meeting in Vienna. These values were either accepted or revised, if a sufficient number of participating experts thought there was a strong case for such revision. Most efforts concentrated on settling the 2050 values, while less attention was paid to the 2030 values. Revisions were mostly upwards, except for Spain. All values were rounded to the nearest 0.05. Most changes were small, except for Russia (0.30). Further details are provided in Basten et al. (2013).

A3.1.2.2 *The countries with at least one expert response (additional 26 countries)*

The average across experts of the expected TFR in 2030 and 2050 was assessed. It was left the same if it fit well the broader regional pattern or was close to the regional 'representative country', as defined in section A3.2.1. It was also left the same if it differed from some other countries in the region, but represented well a specific pattern of a given country or more countries in the region.

The coordinating team changed the projected TFRs suggested by experts in cases where the projected TFRs for a given country differed from a broader regional pattern (as defined by the 'representative countries' discussed at the Vienna workshop, but also from other countries in the region) or when it diverged from the overall higher and lower boundaries expected for the medium estimates of the future TFR.

Specifically, the following rule was applied: the medium TFR estimate in 2030 and 2050 will fall between 1.4 and 2.00 (except in Israel).

For 11 countries, the coordinating team made minor adjustments (generally, by <0.20) to the initial experts' mean values for 2030, 2050, or both (see Basten et al., 2013 for details).

A3.1.2.3 *The countries that were not assessed by experts*

The remaining low fertility countries were 'attached' to a representative country for a broader region, and their projected TFR values for 2030 and 2050 defined as identical to this representative country (see Table A3.1.1 listing all countries by region).

A3.1.3 Projecting the TFR values in 2010–15

The recent economic recession, which hit, in particular, the most developed countries, and the subsequent cuts in government spending have led to a huge increase in economic and employment uncertainty. This uncertainty affects, in particular, younger men and women, and is likely to negatively influence their childbearing decisions and thus also aggregate fertility rates, as evidenced in many European countries and the USA (see Box 3.3). As of 2013, many low fertility countries remained characterized by high unemployment and an uncertain economic outlook. Consequently, it is unlikely their period fertility rates will resume an increasing trajectory in the near future.

In light of this evidence, our projections assume that in the countries where a TFR rise is expected between 2010 and 2030, the TFR will initially remain at the most recent observed level (for 2011 or 2012) until 2015, and only then follow a linear increase up to the projected values for 2030. In countries where a TFR decline is expected between 2010 and 2030, it is assumed to follow a linear trajectory, without any recession-induced interruption or acceleration between 2010 and 2015. A more sophisticated set of fertility assumptions for the near future, reflecting sizeable cross-country differences in their economic trends and experiences of economic recession, was ruled out because it would require separate assessments of each individual country.

Table A3.1.1 List of Low Fertility Countries for which Projection Scenarios were Formulated Here (Countries Listed by Reference Region; Representative Countries Shown in Bold)

Reference region	Country	Reference region	Country
North America	**USA**	Southern Europe (high)	**Italy**
	Canada		Cyprus
Australia and Oceania	**Australia**		Greece
	New Caledonia		Malta
	New Zealand	Southern Europe (low)	**Spain**
East Asia (high)	**Japan**		Portugal
	Korea PDR	Central Europe (high)	**Czech Republic**
	Republic of Korea		Estonia
	Singapore		Lithuania
East Asia (low)	**Hong Kong SAR**		Slovenia
	Macao SAR	Central Europe (low)	**Hungary**
	Taiwan		Latvia
	China		Poland
Middle East	**Turkey**		Slovakia
	Iran		**Croatia**
	Israel	Eastern Europe (high)	**Bulgaria**
			Ukraine
			Belarus
Western Europe (high)	**UK***		Macedonia
	Ireland		Montenegro
	France†		Serbia
Western Europe (low)	**Netherlands**	Eastern Europe (low)	**Romania**
	Belgium		Albania
	Luxembourg		Bosnia-Herzegovina
German-speaking	**Austria**		Republic of Moldova
	Germany		**Russian Federation**
	Switzerland	Caucasus	**Georgia**
Nordic countries	**Sweden**		Armenia
	Denmark		Azerbaijan
	Finland		
	Iceland		
	Norway		

SAR: Special Administrative Region.
* Including Channel Islands.
† Including French Polynesia, Guadeloupe, Martinique, and Réunion.

A3.1.4 Projecting TFR values beyond 2050

The WIC projections extend beyond the year 2050, which was the endpoint in the online expert survey. The Vienna workshop with invited experts discussed such long-range scenarios. A simple method has been proposed, assuming a uniform global convergence in medium TFR to a sub-replacement level of 1.75 by 2200 (section 3.5.2). Using a linear approximation between the projected medium value for 2050 and this 'target' endpoint in 2200, the medium TFR can be derived for any period between these two years.

APPENDIX 3.2

SELECTION OF COUNTRIES INTO THE 'LOW FERTILITY' MODULE

Two sets of arguments pertaining to fertility have been formulated within the WIC project on argument-based global population projections: one for low fertility settings with more advanced levels of development, and another for higher fertility settings with a lower level of development. This division is somewhat subjective, with a number of countries potentially falling on the border between the two groups. We used the period TFRs estimated for the period of 2005–10 by the United Nations (UN) World Population Prospects 2010 and the UN Human Development Index (HDI) for 2010 to rank the countries by their levels of fertility and development.[31] The main motivation behind considering an additional selection criterion based on human development was the need to differentiate between the more affluent and more developed set of countries and all other countries in order to formulate suitable sets of arguments pertaining to likely future fertility trends. For instance, some of the questions the experts were asked on low fertility countries pertained to immigration, assisted reproduction or family policies, and were largely irrelevant in less developed settings. Similarly, the questions on the role of child's and mother's health and child survival are largely irrelevant in higher income settings with very low maternal and child mortality, even when they register above replacement fertility, such as Israel.

The following criteria were used to divide countries into the 'low fertility, higher development' (90 countries and territories) and 'higher fertility, lower development' (100 countries and territories) groups.

The former group of countries with low fertility includes:

- Countries with sub-replacement period fertility (total fertility rate (TFR) <2.10) and moderate or high level of development (HDI at ≥0.650 or higher). Only three countries with a TFR <2.10 had a HDI level <0.65 (Maldives, Myanmar, and Vietnam) and were therefore included in the higher fertility group analysed in Chapter 4.
- Countries with moderate period fertility (TFR between 2.10 and 2.49) and a higher level of development (HDI at ≥0.670). The following countries with a TFR between 2.10 and 2.49 were included: Brunei, New Zealand, Uruguay, Turkey, Azerbaijan, Argentina, Kuwait, Algeria, Mexico, Jamaica, Qatar, and Colombia.
- Countries with moderate period fertility (TFR between 2.10 and 2.49) and unknown level of the HDI (which has not been computed for them). The following countries and territories with the TFR between 2.10 and 2.49 were included: Guadeloupe, French Polynesia, New Caledonia, and Réunion.

[31] Note that the series of the period total fertility rates (TFR) used for this selection differed from the estimates of the period TFR used in the survey to provide the initial TFR level for all countries in 2010. For the latter purpose, the more recent (2010) estimates published by Population Reference Bureau (PRB) (2010, <http://www.prb.org/pdf10/10wpds_eng.pdf>) were used. However, the division of countries into the higher and lower fertility groups would remain identical if the PRB data were used instead of the UN estimates.

- Countries with higher period fertility (TFR at ≥2.50) and with very high level of development (HDI >0.85). Only one country, Israel, was included on this basis.

All other countries fall into the high fertility group, which therefore comprises:

- All countries with a TFR at ≥2.50 except Israel.
- Countries with a TFR between 2.10 and 2.49 and HDI <0.670: Indonesia, Guyana, Salvador, Sri Lanka, Morocco, Bangladesh, Suriname, and Uzbekistan.
- Three countries with a TFR <2.10 with low HDI values (<0.65): Maldives, Myanmar, and Vietnam.

Table A3.2.1 ranks all the countries by their TFR (ranking from the lowest fertility up) and lists their TFR in 2005–10, their HDI in 2010, and their distribution into the low or high fertility module of the survey.

Table A3.2.1 Country Ranking by the Period Total Fertility Rate (TFR) in 2005–10 (from the Lowest Level to the Highest) and their Inclusion into the 'Low Fertility' Module Only Countries with a TFR <2.50 and Israel are Listed)

	Country	Period TFR (UN) 2005–10	HDI, 2010	Fert. mod.		Country	Period TFR (UN) 2005–10	HDI, 2010	Fert. mod.
1	Hong Kong SAR	0.99	0.900	Low	50	Finland	1.84	0.871	Low
2	Macao SAR	1.02	n.a.	Low	51	Denmark	1.85	0.866	Low
3	Bosnia-Herzegovina	1.18	0.710	Low	52	United Arab Emirates	1.86	0.815	Low
4	Singapore	1.25	0.846	Low	53	Lebanon	1.86	0.743	Low
5	Slovakia	1.27	0.818	Low	54	Vietnam	1.89	0.572	High
6	Republic of Korea	1.29	0.905	Low	55	Sweden	1.90	0.885	Low
7	Poland	1.32	0.795	Low	56	Brazil	1.90	0.699	Low
8	Japan	1.32	0.884	Low	57	Chile	1.90	0.783	Low
9	Malta	1.33	0.815	Low	58	Maldives	1.90	0.602	High
10	Romania	1.33	0.767	Low	59	Bahamas	1.91	0.784	Low
11	Hungary	1.34	0.805	Low	60	Martinique	1.91	n.a.	Low
12	Germany	1.36	0.885	Low	61	Costa Rica	1.92	0.725	Low
13	Portugal	1.36	0.795	Low	62	Norway	1.92	0.938	Low
14	Italy	1.38	0.854	Low	63	Australia	1.93	0.937	Low
15	Austria	1.38	0.851	Low	64	France	1.97	0.872	Low
16	Slovenia	1.39	0.828	Low	65	Netherlands Antilles	1.98	n.a.	Low
17	Belarus	1.39	0.732	Low	66	Tunisia	2.04	0.683	Low

	Country	Period TFR (UN) 2005–10	HDI, 2010	Fert. mod.		Country	Period TFR (UN) 2005–10	HDI, 2010	Fert. mod.
18	Ukraine	1.39	0.710	Low	67	North Korea	2.05	n.a.	Low
19	Czech Republic	1.41	0.841	Low	68	USA	2.07	0.934	Low
20	Lithuania	1.41	0.783	Low	69	Myanmar	2.08	0.451	High
21	Spain	1.41	0.863	Low	70	Ireland	2.10	0.895	Low
22	Latvia	1.41	0.769	Low	71	Iceland	2.10	0.869	Low
23	Croatia	1.42	0.767	Low	72	Brunei	2.11	0.805	Low
24	Russian Federation	1.44	0.719	Low	73	Uruguay	2.12	0.765	Low
25	Bulgaria	1.46	0.743	Low	74	New Zealand	2.14	0.907	Low
26	Switzerland	1.46	0.874	Low	75	Guadeloupe	2.14	n.a.	Low
27	Greece	1.46	0.855	Low	76	Turkey	2.15	0.679	Low
28	Macedonia	1.46	n.a.	Low	77	Azerbaijan	2.16	0.713	Low
29	Cuba	1.50	0.775	Low	78	French Polynesia	2.16	n.a.	Low
30	Moldova	1.50	0.652	Low	79	Indonesia	2.19	0.600	High
31	Cyprus	1.51	0.810	Low	80	New Caledonia	2.19	n.a.	Low
32	Barbados	1.53	0.788	Low	81	Argentina	2.25	0.775	Low
33	Georgia	1.58	0.698	Low	82	Kuwait	2.32	0.771	Low
34	Albania	1.60	0.719	Low	83	Guyana	2.33	0.611	High
35	Luxembourg	1.62	0.852	Low	84	Salvador	2.35	0.659	High
36	Serbia	1.62	0.735	Low	85	Sri Lanka	2.36	0.658	High
37	Thailand	1.63	0.654	Low	86	Morocco	2.38	0.567	High
38	Estonia	1.64	0.812	Low	87	Bangladesh	2.38	0.469	High
39	China	1.64	0.663	Low	88	Algeria	2.38	0.677	Low
40	Trinidad and Tobago	1.64	0.736	Low	89	Réunion	2.40	n.a.	Low
41	Canada	1.65	0.888	Low	90	Jamaica	2.40	0.688	Low
42	Mauritius	1.67	0.701	Low	91	Qatar	2.40	0.803	Low
43	Montenegro	1.69	0.769	Low	92	Mexico	2.41	0.750	Low
44	Armenia	1.74	0.695	Low	93	Suriname	2.42	0.646	High
45	Netherlands	1.75	0.890	Low	94	Colombia	2.45	0.689	Low
46	Iran	1.77	0.702	Low	95	Uzbekistan	2.46	0.617	High
47	Belgium	1.79	0.867	Low	...	...		...	...
48	Puerto Rico	1.83	n.a.	Low	119	Israel	2.91	0.872	Low
49	UK	1.83	0.849	Low					

UN: United Nations; HDI: Human Development Index; Fert. mod.: fertility module; SAR: Special Administrative Region; n.a.: not available.

Note: Taiwan is missing from the list as it is a territory not recognized by the UN; also excluded are all countries and territories with populations below 100,000 and the following countries and territories with populations over 100,000: Aruba, the Channel Islands, Grenada, Saint Lucia, and Saint Vincent and the Grenadines. The ranking of countries by period TFR in 2005–10 was based on the UN (2011) data set released with the World Population Prospects 2010.

APPENDIX 3.3

PROFILE OF RESPONDENTS AND COUNTRY RESPONSES

Total respondents: 184	Country (and region) of projection:		
Gender:	Central Europe (15)	Czech	6
81: Male		Republic	
62: Female		Hungary	3
41: Blank		Poland	2
		Croatia	2
Field:		Slovenia	1
135: Academia		Lithuania	1
14: Government	Eastern Europe (13)	Russia	4
11: Think tanks/Policy Institute		Romania	3
5: Other		Ukraine	2
2: National NGO		Bulgaria	2
1: NGO		Georgia	2
16: Blank	Southern Europe (21)	Italy	12
		Spain	6
Country of work:		Greece	1
26: USA		Portugal	1
14: Austria	Western Europe (9)	UK	4
7: Australia, France, Italy, Spain, Sweden		Netherlands	4
6: Brazil, Germany		Belgium	1
5: China, Iran, UK	Nordic (14)	Sweden	7
4: Canada, Netherlands, Turkey		Norway	2
3: Argentina, Japan, Mexico, Romania		Finland	2
2: Belgium, Czech Republic, Hungary,		Iceland	1
Poland, Switzerland, Thailand	German-speaking (10)	Germany	9
1: Colombia, Croatia, Finland, Georgia,		Austria	7
Greece, Lithuania, New Zealand, Portugal,		Switzerland	3
Russia, Slovenia, Ukraine, Uruguay	East Asia	China	14
34: Blank	(including Thailand, 27)	Japan	6
		Thailand	4
Age of respondents (y):		Korea (Rep.)	2
25–29: 8		Hong Kong SAR	1
30–34: 21	Latin America (18)	Brazil	7
35–39: 20		Mexico	5
40–44: 20		Argentina	3
45–49: 15		Uruguay	1
50–54: 4		Colombia	1
55–59: 20	North America and Australia	USA	22
60–64: 8	(31)	Australia	5

65–69: 16		Canada	4
70–74: 3	Western Asia/Middle east (14)	Iran	8
75+: 4		Turkey	5
	Others (2)	Algeria	1
		Israel	1

NGO: non-governmental organization; SAR: special administrative region.

APPENDIX 3.4

Complete list of arguments and their groupings by major factors in the low fertility module of the IIASA–Oxford survey

1. Cultural and social forces in fertility ideals, norms, and desires

1.1 Voluntary childlessness is becoming increasingly socially accepted
1.2 One-child families will become a dominant cultural norm
1.3 Society will become yet more individualistic
1.4 It is a human constant that people will always desire at least one surviving child in order to 'continue living' in the future
1.5 The share of population groups with larger families will increase
1.6 The availability of grandparents for childcare and family care will decline
1.7 Religious views on family and reproduction will gain importance
1.8 High fertility will become a status symbol among the wealthy
1.9 Globally, there will be a convergence of all populations towards a two-child family as an ideal and actual family size

2. Partnerships, living arrangements, and gender differences

2.1 Men are increasingly reluctant to become fathers, even when they live with a partner
2.2 Men and women will increasingly share the burden of housework and childcare
2.3 People are increasingly unable to find the right partner to form a family
2.4 Women will increasingly pursue lifestyles and activities not compatible with motherhood
2.5 Marriage will further decline and will become a minority experience
2.6 Partnership dissolution and 're-partnering' will become yet more common among women of reproductive age
2.7 Women will achieve complete equality with men with respect to their education, employment, career, and income
2.8 Cross-border partnership and marriage migration will increase in importance
2.9 Adults in their 20s, and even 30s, will spend ever longer periods of life living with their parents

3. Role of policies (in this case, 'government' entails national government unless stated otherwise)

3.1 Government will raise child subsidies and tax benefits, or introduce birth bonuses
3.2 Government will take an increasingly pro-natalist stance (e.g. through communication campaigns and family policies)
3.3 Government will provide universal nursery/kindergarten access
3.4 Provision of affordable housing for families and young adults will become an important part of social policies
3.5 New policies will allow young parents to significantly reduce their working hours for several years with some compensation of income
3.6 Mothers will be increasingly expected and encouraged to return to work, even when their children are small
3.7 Family-related policies, including childcare provision, will be increasingly pursued by local governments and employers
3.8 Governments will cut back on family support when economic conditions worsen.
3.9 As populations age government funds will become increasingly directed toward the elderly and away from the young

4. Employment and economy

4.1 Unemployment and job instability among the under-30s will further increase
4.2 Increasing average household income will lead to higher fertility
4.3 Employers will put more pressure on their employees in terms of higher working hours and more work commitments
4.4 Work practices will become more flexible in the future (e.g. telecommuting, working from home, flexi-time, part-time)
4.5 Geographical mobility, especially work-related, will further increase
4.6 Immigration from high fertility countries will increase
4.7 Continuing economic unpredictability will make individual life course planning ever more uncertain
4.8 Informal childcare will shift from grandparents to paid domestic workers
4.9 Cities will become more child-friendly

5. Biomedicine and the timing of parenthood

5.1 Men are becoming less fecund owing to declining sperm counts or quality
5.2 Delayed childbearing will become yet more common among women
5.3 Having children under the age of 25 will be rare
5.4 The broad availability and use of efficient contraception, including post-coital methods, will make mistimed and unwanted pregnancies rare
5.5 Financial, normative, and institutional barriers to assisted reproductive technologies (ART) will keep their application limited
5.6 Assisted reproduction and selective abortion will be increasingly used to achieve a desired sex composition, as well as other characteristics of children
5.7 The technology and availability of ART will improve sufficiently that women in their 40s who want a child will routinely be able to have one

6. Education

6.1 People will spend ever more years of their young adult life enrolled in education and professional training on the job

6.2 Fertility differentials by level of female education will diminish

6.3 There will be a new trend for better educated women to have more children and simultaneously pursue a professional career

APPENDIX 3.5

Regional graphs of expected TFR trends up to 2050: a comparison of the global survey of experts and the 2010 United Nations (UN) projection (probabilistic fertility scenarios)

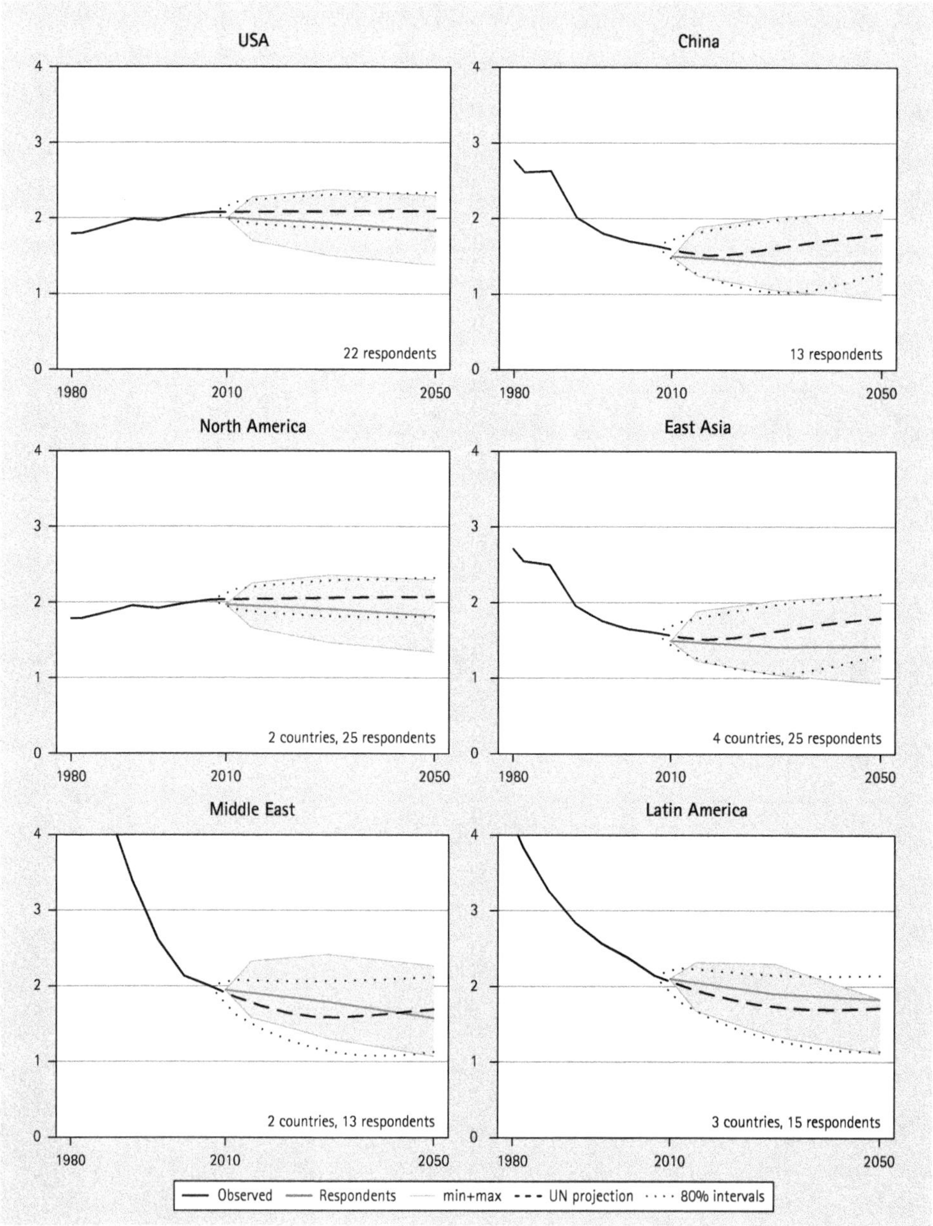

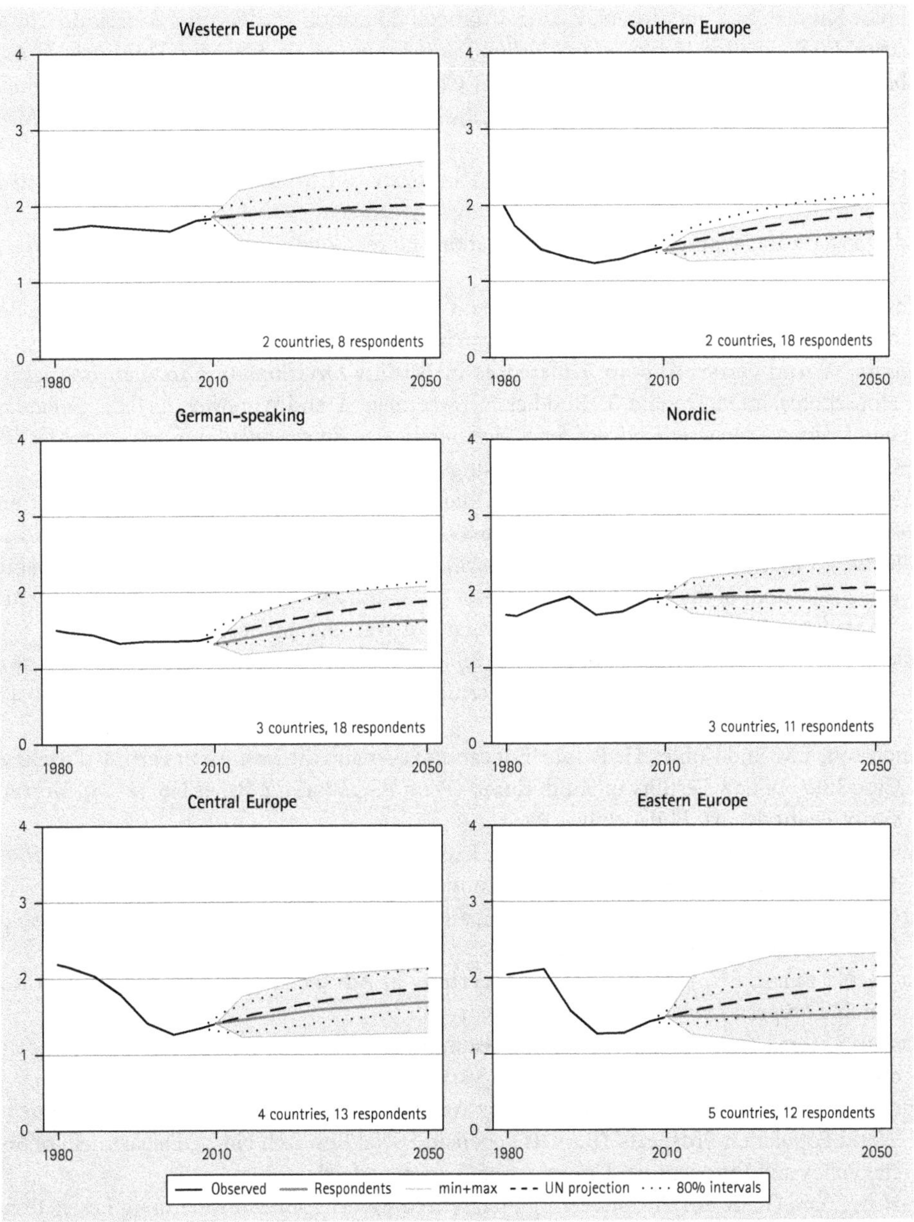

References

Abbasi-Shavazi, M.J. and Jones, G.W. 2005 'Socio-economic and Demographic Setting of Muslim Populations'. In: Jones, G.W. and Karim, M.S. (eds) *Islam, the State and Population*, pp. 9–39. Hurst and Co.: London.

Abbasi-Shavazi, M.J. and McDonald, P. 2000 'Fertility and Multiculturalism: Immigrant Fertility in Australia, 1977–1991'. *International Migration Review*, 34: 215–242.

Abbasi-Shavazi, M.J. and Torabi, F. 2012 'Women's Education and Fertility in Islamic Countries'. In: *Population Dynamics in Muslim Countries*, pp. 43–62. Springer: Dordrecht.

Abbasi-Shavazi, M.J., Morgan, S.P., Hosseini-Chavoshi, M. and McDonald, P. 2009a 'Family Change and Continuity in Iran: Birth Control Use Before First Pregnancy'. *Journal of Marriage and Family*, 71: 1309–24.

Abbasi-Shavazi, M.J., McDonald, P. and Hosseini-Chavoshi, M. 2009b *The Fertility Transition in Iran: Revolution and Reproduction*. Springer: Dordrecht.

Adsera, A. 2011a 'Where Are the Babies? Labor Market Conditions and Fertility in Europe'. *European Journal of Population*, 27: 1–32.

Adsera, A. 2011b 'The Interplay of Employment Uncertainty and Education in Explaining Second Births in Europe'. *Demographic Research*, 25: 513–44.

Adsera, A. and Ferrer, A. 2010 'Differences in Fertility Decisions of Canadian Immigrant Households'. In: McDonald, T., Ruddick E., Sweetman, A. and Worswick, C. (eds) *Canadian Immigration Economic Evidence for a Dynamic Policy Environment*, pp. 283–309. McGill-Queen's University Press: Montreal and Kingston.

Adsera, A. and Menendez, A. 2011 'Fertility Changes in Latin America in Periods of Economic Uncertainty'. *Population Studies*, 65: 37–56.

Alkema, L., Raftery, A.E., Gerland, P., Clark, S.J., Pelletier, F. and Buettner, T. 2010 'Probabilistic Projections of the Total Fertility Rate for all Countries' (Working Paper No. 97). Center for Statistics and the Social Sciences University of Washington: Seattle, WA.

Alkema, L., Raftery, A.E., Gerland, P., Clark, S.J., Pelletier, F., Buettner, T. and Heilig, G.K. 2011 'Probabilistic Projections of the Total Fertility Rate for all Countries'. *Demography*, 48: 815–39.

Anderson, T.M. and Kohler, H.-P. 2012 'Education Fever and the East Asian Fertility Puzzle: A Case Study of Low Fertility in South Korea' (Penn PSC Working Paper No. 12–07). University of Pennsylvania: Philadelphia, PA.

Andersson, G., Rønsen, M., Knudsen, L.B., Lappegård, T., Neyer, G., Skrede, K., et al. 2009 'Cohort Fertility Patterns in the Nordic Countries'. *Demographic Research*, 20: 313–52.

Arendell, T. 2000 'Conceiving and Investigating Motherhood: The Decade's Scholarship'. *Journal of Marriage and Family*, 62: 1192–207.

Balbo, N., Billari, F.C. and Mills, M. 2013 'Fertility in Advanced Societies: A Review of Research'. *European Journal of Population*, 29: 1–38.

Basten, S. 2013a 'Comparing Projections Assumptions of Fertility in Advanced Asian Economies; or "Thinking Beyond the Medium Variant"'. *Asian Population Studies*, 9: 322–331.

Basten, S. 2013b 'Re-Examining the Fertility Assumptions for Pacific Asia in the UN's 2010 World Population Prospects' (Barnett Papers in Social Research No. 1). Department of Social Policy and Intervention, University of Oxford: Oxford.

Basten, S. and Gu, B. 2013 'Childbearing Preferences, Reform of Family Planning Restrictions and the Low Fertility Trap in China' (Working Paper No. 61). Department of Social Policy and Intervention, University of Oxford: Oxford.

Basten, S., Huinink, J. and Klüsener, S. 2011 'Spatial Variation of Sub-national Fertility Trends in Austria, Germany and Switzerland'. *Comparative Population Studies*, 36, 573–614.

Basten, S., Sobotka, T. and Zeman, K. 2013 'Future Fertility in Low Fertility Countries' (VID Working Papers 5/2013). Vienna Institute of Demography: Vienna.

Beaujouan, E. and Solaz, A. 2012 'Racing Against the Biological Clock? Childbearing and Sterility Among Men and Women in Second Unions in France'. *European Journal of Population*, 29: 39–67.

Becker, G.S. 1981 *A Treatise on the Family*. Harvard University Press: Cambridge, MA.

Beckman, L.J., Aizenberg, R., Forsythe, A.B., Day, T. 1983 'A theoretical analysis of antecedents of young couples' fertility decisions and outcomes'. *Demography* 20, 519–33.

Bélanger, A., Morency, J.-D. and Spielauer, M. 2010 'A Microsimulation Model to Study the Interaction between Fertility and Union Formation and Dissolution: An Application to Canada and Quebec'. *Canadian Studies in Population*, 37: 339–73.

Bericat, E. 2012 'The European Gender Equality Index: Conceptual and Analytical Issues'. *Social Indicators Research*, 108: 1–28.

Billari, F.C. and Dalla-Zuanna, G. 2012 'Is Replacement Migration Actually Taking Place in Low Fertility Countries?' *Genus*, 67: 105–23.

Billari, F.C. and Kohler, H.-P. 2004 'Patterns of Low and Lowest-low Fertility in Europe'. *Population Studies*, 58: 161–76.

Björklund, A. 2006 'Does Family Policy Affect Fertility?' *Journal of Population Economics*, 19: 3–24.

Blossfeld, H.P. and Huinink, J. 1991 'Human Capital Investments or Norms of Role Transition? How Women's Schooling and Career Affect the Process of Family Formation'. *American Journal of Sociology*, 97: 143–68.

Blossfeld, H., Klijzing, E., Mills, M. and Kurz, K. 2005 *Globalization, Uncertainty and Youth in Society*. Routledge Advances in Sociology Series: London and New York.

Boivin, J., Bunting, L., Collins, J.A. and Nygren, K.G. 2007 'International Estimates of Infertility Prevalence and Treatment-seeking: Potential Need and Demand for Infertility Medical Care'. *Human Reproduction*, 22: 1506–12.

Bonde, J.P., Ramlau-Hansen, C.H. and Olsen, J. 2011 'Commentary: Trends in Sperm Counts: The Saga Continues'. *Epidemiology*, 22: 617–19.

Bongaarts, J. 1999 'The Fertility Impact of Changes in the Timing of Childbearing in the Developing World'. *Population Studies*, 53: 277–89.

Bongaarts, J. 2001 'Fertility and Reproductive Preferences in Post-transitional Societies'. *Population and Development Review*, 27: 260–81.

Bongaarts, J. 2002 'The End of the Fertility Transition in the Developed World'. *Population and Development Review*, 28: 419–43.

Bongaarts, J. and Feeney, G. 1998 'On the Quantum and Tempo of Fertility'. *Population and Development Review*, 24: 271–91.

Bongaarts, J. and Bulatao, R.A. (eds) 2000 *Beyond Six Billion: Forecasting the World's Population, Panel on Population Projections, Committee on Population, Commission on Behavioral and Social Sciences and Education*. National Academy Press: Washington, DC.

Bongaarts, J. and Sobotka, T. 2012 'A Demographic Explanation for the Recent Rise in European Fertility'. *Population and Development Review*, 38: 83–120.

Bradshaw, J. and Mayhew, E. 2006 'Family Benefit Packages'. In: Bradshaw, J. and Hatland, A. (eds) *Social Policy, Employment and Family Change in Comparative Perspective*, pp. 97–117. Edward Elgar Publishing: Cheltenham.

Brewster, K.L. and Rindfuss, R.R. 2000 'Fertility and Women's Employment in Industrialized Nations'. *Annual Review of Sociology*, 26: 271–96.

Broekmans, F.J., Knauff, E.A., te Velde, E.R., Macklon, N.S. and Fauser, B.C. 2007 'Female Reproductive Ageing: Current Knowledge and Future Trends'. *Trends in Endocrinology and Metabolism*, 18: 58–65.

Bumpass, L.L. and Choe, M.K. 2004 'Attitudes Relating to Marriage and Family Life'. In: Tsuya, N.O. and Bumpass, L.L. (eds) *Marriage, Work, and Family Life in Comparative Perspective: Japan, South Korea, and the United States*, pp. 19–38. University of Hawai'i Press: Honolulu, HI.

Bumpass, L.L., Rindfuss, R.R., Choe, M.K. and Tsuya, N.O. 2009 'The Institutional Context of Low Fertility: The Case of Japan'. *Asian Population Studies*, 5: 215–35.

Butz, W.P. and Ward, M.P. 1979 'Will US Fertility Remain Low? A New Economic Interpretation'. *Population and Development Review*, 5: 663–88.

Bystrov, E. 2012 'The Second Demographic Transition in Israel: One for All?' *Demographic Research*, 27: 261–98.

Cai, Y. 2008 'An Assessment of China's Fertility Level Using the Variable-r Method'. *Demography*, 45: 271–81.

Cai, Y. 2010 'China's Below-Replacement Fertility: Government Policy or Socioeconomic Development?' *Population and Development Review*, 36: 419–40.

Cai, Y. 2011 'United Nations Population Projection still Overestimated China's Fertility Level'. *First Caijing Daily*, 23 May 2011.

Caldwell, J.C. 1976 'Toward a Restatement of Demographic Transition Theory'. *Population and Development Review*, 2: 321–66.

Caldwell, J.C. 2001 'The Globalization of Fertility Behavior'. *Population and Development Review*, 27: 93–115.

Carlsen, E., Giwercman, A., Keiding, N. and Skakkebæk, N.E. 1992 'Evidence For Decreasing Quality Of Semen During Past 50 Years'. *British Medical Journal*, 305: 609–13.

Casterline, J.B. and Mendoza, J.A. 2009 'Unwanted Fertility in Latin America: Historical Trends, Recent Patterns'. In: Cavenaghi, S. (ed.) *Demographic Transformations and Inequalities in Latin America*, pp. 193–218. ALAP: Rio de Janeiro.

Castles, F.G. 2003 'The World Turned Upside Down: Below Replacement Fertility, Changing Preferences and Family-friendly Public Policy in 21 OECD Countries'. *Journal of European Social Policy*, 13: 209–27.

Castro Martin, T. 1995 'Women's Education and Fertility: Results from 26 Demographic and Health Surveys'. *Studies in Family Planning*, 26: 187–202.

CBS 2011 *Statistical Abstract of Israel 2011. Chapter 3: Vital Statistics (No. 62)*. The Central Bureau of Statistics: Jerusalem.

CDC 2011 'Assisted Reproductive Technology Success Rates 2009. National Summary and Fertility Clinic Reports'. Center for Disease Control and Prevention, American Society for Reproductive Medicine, Society for Assisted Reproductive Technology: Atlanta, GA.

CELADE 2012 Sistema de Indicadores Sociodemográficos de Poblaciones y Pueblos Indígenas (SISPPI) (Electronic database). Latin American Demography Center CELADE.

Chatters, L.M. and Taylor, R.J. 2005 'Religion and Families'. In: Bengtson, V.L., Acock, A.A., Allen, K.R., Dilworth-Anderson, P. and Klein, D.M. (eds) *Sourcebook of Family Theory and Research*, pp. 517–41. Sage: London.

Chin, M., Lee, J., Lee, S., Son, S. and Sung, M. 2012 'Family Policy in South Korea: Development, Current Status, and Challenges'. *Journal of Child and Family Studies*, 21: 53–64.

Choe, M.K. 2006 'Modernization, Gender Roles and Marriage Behavior in South Korea'. In: Chang, Y.-S., and Steven, H. L. (eds) *Transformations in Twentieth Century Korea*, pp. 291–309. Routledge: London.

Choe, M.K. and Park, K.-A. 2006 'Fertility Decline in South Korea: Forty Years of Policy-Behavior Dialogue'. *Korea Journal of Population Studies*, 29: 1–26.

Chung, W. and Das Gupta, M. 2007 'The Decline of Son Preference in South Korea: The Roles of Development and Public Policy'. *Population and Development Review*, 33: 757–83.

Cobo, A., Remohí, J., Chang, C.-C. and Nagy, Z.P. 2011 'Oocyte Cryopreservation for Donor Egg Banking'. *Reproductive Biomedicine*, 23: 341–6.

Coleman, D.A. 1998 'Reproduction and Survival in an Unknown World: What Drives Today's Industrial Populations, and to What Future?' (No. 5) NIDI Hofstee Lecture Series. Netherlands Interdisciplinary Demographic Institute (NIDI): The Hague.

Coleman, D. 2009 'Migration and its Consequences in 21st Century Europe'. *Vienna Yearbook of Population Research*, 7: 1–18.

Conrad, C., Lechner, M. and Werner, W. 1996 'East German Fertility After Unification: Crisis or Adaptation?' *Population and Development Review*, 22: 331–58.

Cooke, L.P. 2004 'The Gendered Division of Labor and Family Outcomes in Germany'. *Journal of Marriage and Family*, 66: 1246–59.

Courbage, Y. 1999 'Economic and Political Issues of Fertility Transition in the Arab World—Answers and Open Questions'. *Population and Environment*, 20: 353–79.

D'Addio, A.C. and d' Ercole, M.M. 2005 'Trends and Determinants of Fertility Rates: The Role of Policies (No. 27)'. OECD Social, Employment and Migration Working Papers. OECD Publishing: Paris.

Das Gupta, M., Chung, W. and Shuzhuo, L. 2009 'Evidence for an Incipient Decline in Numbers of Missing Girls in China and India'. *Population and Development Review*, 35: 401–16.

David, H.P. 1999 *From Abortion to Contraception: A Resource to Public Policies and Reproductive Behavior in Central and Eastern Europe from 1917 to the Present*. Greenwood Publishing Group: Westport, CT.

Davie, E. and Mazuy, M. 2010 'Women's Fertility and Educational Level in France: Evidence from the Annual Census Surveys'. *Population (English Edition)*, 65: 415–49.

De Cooman, E., Ermisch, J. and Joshi, H. 1987 'The Next Birth and the Labour Market: A Dynamic Model of Births in England and Wales'. *Population Studies*, 41: 237–68.

De la Rochebrochard, E. and Thonneau, P. 2003 'Paternal Age ≥40 Years: An Important Risk Factor for Infertility'. *American Journal of Obstetrics and Gynecology*, 189: 901–5.

Del Bono, E., Weber, A. and Winter-Ebmer, R. 2012 'Clash of Career and Family: Fertility Decisions After Job Displacement'. *Journal of the European Economics Association*, 10: 659–83.

Delgado, M., Meil, G. and Zamora López, F. 2008 'Spain: Short on Children and Short on Family Policies'. *Demographic Research*, 19: 1059–104.

DellaPergola, S. 2007 'Actual, Intended, and Appropriate Family Size in Israel: Trends, Attitudes and Policy Implications: A Preliminary Report'. Avraham Harman Institute of Contemporary Jewry: Jerusalem.

Demeny, P. 2004 'Population Futures for the Next Three Hundred Years: Soft Landing or Surprises to Come?' *Population and Development Review*, 30: 507–17.

Derosas, R. and van Poppel, F.W.A. 2006 *Religion and the Decline of Fertility in the Western World*. Springer: Dordrecht.

Dorbritz, J. 2008 'Germany: Family Diversity with Low Actual and Desired Fertility'. *Demographic Research*, 19: 557–98.

Dorius, S.F. 2008 'Global Demographic Convergence? A Reconsideration of Changing Intercountry Inequality in Fertility'. *Population and Development Review*, 34: 519–37.

Dunson, D.B., Colombo, B. and Baird, D.D. 2002 'Changes with Age in the Level and Duration of Fertility in the Menstrual Cycle'. *Human Reproduction*, 17: 1399–403.

Duvander, A.-Z., Lappegård, T. and Andersson, G. 2010 'Family Policy and Fertility: Fathers' and Mothers' use of Parental Leave and Continued Childbearing in Norway and Sweden'. *Journal of European Social Policy*, 20, 45–57.

Dyer, P.D. 2008 'Demography in the Middle East: Implications and Risks'. In: Laipson, E. and Pandya, A. (eds) *Transnational Trends: Middle Eastern and Asian Views*, pp. 62–90. The Henry L. Stimson Center: Washington, DC.
Easterlin, R.A. 1976 'The Conflict Between Aspirations and Resources'. *Population and Development Review*, 2: 417–25.
Eberstadt, N. 2011 'The Global War Against Baby Girls'. *The New Atlantis*, 33: 3–18.
Eberstadt, N. and Shah, A. 2012 'Fertility Decline in the Muslim World, *c.* 1975–*c.* 2005: A Veritable Sea-Change, Still Curiously Unnoticed'. In: Groth, H. and Sousa-Poza, A. (eds) *Population Dynamics in Muslim Countries: Assembling the Jigsaw*, pp. 11–27. Springer: Dordrecht.
Edmonston, B., Lee, S.M. and Wu, Z. 2010 'Fertility Intentions in Canada: Change or No Change?' *Canadian Studies in Population*, 37: 297–337.
Ekert-Jaffé, O., Joshi, H., Lynch, K., Mougin, R., Rendall, M.S. and Shapiro, D. 2002 'Fertility, Timing of Births and Socio-economic status in France and Britain: Social Policies and Occupational Polarisation'. *Population (English Edition)*, 57: 475–507.
Engelhardt, H. and Prskawetz, A. 2004 'On the Changing Correlation Between Fertility and Female Employment Over Space and Time'. *European Journal of Population*, 20: 35–62.
ESF 2010 'Male Reproductive Health. Its Impacts in Relation to General Wellbeing and Low European Fertility Rates (No. 40). Science Policy Briefings. European Science Foundation: Strasbourg.
Esping-Andersen, G. 2009 *The Incomplete Revolution: Adapting Welfare States to Women's New Roles*. Polity Press: Cambridge.
Eurostat 2012 Data on Period Total Fertility Rate (Eurostat Statistics Database). Eurostat: Luxembourg.
Ferraretti, A.P., Goossens, V., de Mouzon, J., Bhattacharya, S., Castilla, J.A., Korsak, V., et al., 2012 'Assisted Reproductive Technology in Europe, 2008: Results Generated from European Registers by ESHRE'. *Human Reproduction*, 27: 2571–84.
Finer, L.B. and Zolna, M.R. 2011 'Unintended Pregnancy in the United States: Incidence and Disparities, 2006'. *Contraception*, 84: 478–85.
Fisch, H. 2008 'Declining Worldwide Sperm Counts: Disproving a Myth'. *Urology Clinics of North America*, 35: 137–46.
Fisch, H. and Braun, S.R. 2013 'Trends in Global Semen Parameter Values'. *Asian Journal of Andrology*, 15: 169–73.
Foster, C. 2000 'The Limits to Low Fertility: A Biosocial Approach'. *Population and Development Review*, 26: 209–34.
Frank, R. and Heuveline, P. 2005 'A Crossover in Mexican and Mexican-American Fertility Rates: Evidence and Explanations for an Emerging Paradox'. *Demographic Research*, 12: 77–104.
Frattarelli, J.L., Miller, K.A., Miller, B.T., Elkind-Hirsch, K. and Scott Jr, R.T. 2008 'Male Age Negatively Impacts Embryo Development and Reproductive Outcome in Donor Oocyte Assisted Reproductive Technology Cycles'. *Fertility and Sterility*, 90: 97–103.
Frejka, T. 2004 'The "Curiously High" Fertility of the USA: Discussion of Paper "Explanations of the Fertility Crisis in Modern Societies: A Search for Commonalities"', *Population Studies*, 58: 77–94.
Frejka, T. 2011 'The Role of Contemporary Childbearing Postponement and Recuperation in Shaping Period Fertility Trends'. *Comparative Population Studies*, 36: 927–58.
Frejka, T., Jones, G.W. and Sardon, J.-P. 2010 'East Asian Childbearing Patterns and Policy Developments'. *Population and Development Review*, 36: 579–606.

Furuoka, F. 2009 'Looking for a J-shaped Development–Fertility Relationship: Do Advances in Development Really Reverse Fertility Declines?' *Economics Bulletin*, 29: 3067–74.

Garssen, J. and Nicolaas, H. 2008 'Fertility of Turkish and Moroccan Women in the Netherlands: Adjustment to Native Level Within One Generation'. *Demographics Research*, 19: 1249–80.

Gauthier, A.H. 2002 'Family Policies in Industrialized Countries: Is There Convergence?' *Population (English Edition)*, 57: 447–74.

Gauthier, A.H. 2007 'The Impact of Family Policies on Fertility in Industrialized Countries: A Review of the Literature'. *Population Research and Policy Review*, 26: 323–46.

Goldin, C. 2006 'The Quiet Revolution That Transformed Women's Employment, Education, and Family'. *American Economic Review*, 96: 1–21.

Goldin, C. and Katz, L.F. 2002 'The Power of the Pill: Oral Contraceptives and Women's Career and Marriage Decisions'. *Journal of Political Economy*, 110: 730–70.

Goldscheider, F., Oláh, L.S. and Puur, A. 2010 'Reconciling Studies of Men's Gender Attitudes and Fertility'. *Demographics Research*, 22: 189–98.

Goldstein, J.R. and Kreyenfeld, M. 2011 'Has East Germany Overtaken West Germany? Recent Trends in Order-specific Fertility'. *Population and Development Review*, 37: 453–72.

Goldstein, J.R., Lutz, W. and Testa, M.R. 2003 'The Emergence of Sub-replacement Family Size Ideals in Europe'. *Population Research and Policy Review*, 22: 479–96.

Goldstein, J.R., Sobotka, T. and Jasilioniene, A. 2009 'The End of "Lowest-low" Fertility?' *Population and Development Review*, 35: 663–99.

Griffith, J.D., Koo, H.P. and Suchindran, C.M. 1985 'Childbearing and Family in Remarriage'. *Demography*, 22: 73–88.

Gu, B., Wang, F., Zhigang, G. and Erli, Z. 2007 'China's Local and National Fertility Policies at the End of the Twentieth Century'. *Population and Development Review*, 33: 129–48.

Habbema, J.D.F., Collins, J., Leridon, H., Evers, J.L. and Lunenfeld, B. 2004 'Towards Less Confusing Terminology in Reproductive Medicine: A Proposal'. *Human Reproduction*, 19: 1497–501.

Habbema, J.D.F., Eijkemans, M.J.C., Nargund, G., Beets, G., Leridon, H. and te Velde, E.R. 2009 'The Effect of In Vitro Fertilization on Birth Rates in Western Countries'. *Human Reproduction*, 24: 1414–19.

Harttgen, K. and Vollmer, S. 2013 'A Reversal in the Relationship of Human Development With Fertility?' *Demography*. DOI: 10.1007/s13524-013-0252-y.

Hayford, S.R. and Morgan, P.S. 2008 'Religiosity and Fertility in the United States: The Role of Fertility Intentions'. *Social Forces*, 86: 1163–88.

He, J. and Ju, W. 2008 'Influence of Cigarette Smoking on Semen Quality in Males'. *Chinese Journal of Andrology*, 22: 31–7.

Heaton, T.B. 2011 'Does Religion Influence Fertility in Developing Countries'. *Population Research and Policy Review*, 30: 449–65.

Heino, E. 2012 'Concern Over the Future of the Nation–A Discourse Analytical Study on Changes in Russian Demographic Policy in the Years 2000–2010'. *Finnish Yearbook of Population Research*, 47: 65–89.

Héran, F. 2004 'Five Immigration Myths'. *Population and Societies*, 397: 1–4.

Heuveline, P., Timberlake, J.M. and Furstenberg Jr, F.F. 2003 'Shifting Childrearing to Single Mothers: Results from 17 Western Countries'. *Population and Development Review*, 29: 47–71.

Heyns, B. 2005 'Emerging Inequalities in Central and Eastern Europe'. *Annual Review of Sociology*, 163: 163–97.

Hilgeman, C. and Butts, C.T. 2009 'Women's Employment and Fertility: A Welfare Regime Paradox'. *Social Science Research*, 38: 103–17.

Hoem, J.M., Neyer, G. and Andersson, G. 2006 'Educational Attainment and Ultimate Fertility among Swedish Women Born in 1955–59'. *Demographic Research*, 14: 381–404.

Hout, M., Greeley, A. and Wilde, M.J. 2001 'The Demographic Imperative in Religious Change in the United States'. *American Journal of Sociology*, 107: 468–500.

Iacovou, M. and Tavares, L.P. 2011 'Yearning, Learning, and Conceding: Reasons Men and Women Change Their Childbearing Intentions'. *Population and Development Review*, 37: 89–123.

IBGE 2010 'Síntese de Indicadores Sociais. Uma Análise das Condições de Vida da População Brasileira 2010. Estudos e Pesquisas (No. 27)'. Informação Demográfi ca e Socioeconômica. Instituto Brasileiro de Geografi a e Estatística: Rio de Janeiro.

Ishii-Kuntz, M., Makino, K., Kato, K. and Tsuchiya, M. 2004 'Japanese Fathers of Preschoolers and Their Involvement in Child Care'. *Journal of Marriage and Family*, 66: 779–91.

Iwamoto, T., Nozawa, S. and Yoshiike, M. 2007 'Semen Quality of Asian Men'. *Reproductive Medicine and Biology*, 6: 185–93.

Jansen, M. and Liefbroer, A.C. 2006 'Couples' Attitudes, Childbirth, and the Division of Labor'. *Journal of Family Issues*, 27: 1487–511.

Jensen, T.K., Jørgensen, N., Punab, M., Haugen, T.B., Suominen, J., Zilaitiene, B., et al. 2004 'Association of In Utero Exposure to Maternal Smoking with Reduced Semen Quality and Testis Size in Adulthood: A Cross-Sectional Study of 1,770 Young Men from the General Population in Five European Countries'. *American Journal of Epidemiology*, 159: 49–58.

Joffe, M. 2000 'Time Trends in Biological Fertility in Britain'. *The Lancet*, 355: 1961–5.

Jones, G.W. 2007 'Delayed Marriage and Very Low Fertility in Pacific Asia'. *Population and Development Review*, 33: 453–78.

Jones, G.W. 2012 'Where are all the Jobs? Capturing the Demographic Dividend in Islamic Countries'. In: Groth, H. and Sousa-Poza, A. (eds) *Population Dynamics in Muslim Countries*, pp. 31–42. Springer: Dordrecht.

Jones, G.W. and Nortman, D. 1968 'Roman Catholic Fertility and Family Planning: A Comparative Review of the Research Literature'. *Studies in Family Planning*, 1: 1–27.

Jones, G.W. and Karim, M.S. 2005 *Islam, the State and Population*. C. Hurst & Co. Publishers: London.

Jørgensen, N., Carlsen, E., Nermoen, I., Punab, M., Suominen, J., Andersen, A.-G., et al. 2002 'East–West Gradient in Semen Quality in the Nordic–Baltic Area: A Study of Men from the General Population in Denmark, Norway, Estonia and Finland'. *Human Reproduction*. 17: 2199–208.

Kaufman, G. 2000 'Do Gender Role Attitudes Matter? Family Formation and Dissolution Among Traditional and Egalitarian Men and Women'. *Journal of Family Issues*, 21: 128–44.

Kaufmann, E. 2010 *Shall the Religious Inherit the Earth? Demography and Politics in the Twenty-First Century*. Profile Books: London.

KC, S. and Potančoková, M. 2013 'Differential Fertility by Level of Education in DHS Countries'. Presented at the 2013 Annual Meeting of the Population Association of America, New Orleans, 11–13 April 2013, New Orleans, LA, USA.

Kim, D.-S. 2007 *Cross-Border Marriage: Process and Dynamics*. Hanyang University: Seoul.

Kirk, D. 1946 *Europe's Population in the Interwar Years*. League of Nations and Princeton University Press, Princeton, NJ.

Kirk, D. 1966 'Factors Affecting Moslem Natality'. In: Berelson, B. (ed.) *Family Planning and Population Programs: A Review of World Developments,* pp. 573–8. University of Chicago Press: Chicago, IL.

Kohler, H.-P. and Ortega, J.A. 2002 'Tempo-Adjusted Period Parity Progression Measures, Fertility Postponement and Completed Cohort Fertility'. *Demographic Research,* 6: 91–144.

Kohler, H.-P., Billari, F.C. and Ortega, J.A. 2002 'The Emergence of Lowest-Low Fertility in Europe During the 1990s'. *Population and Development Review,* 28: 641–80.

Kravdal, Ø. 2002 'The Impact of Individual and Aggregate Unemployment on Fertility in Norway'. *Demographic Research,* 6: 263–94.

Kravdal, Ø. 2004 'An Illustration of the Problems Caused by Incomplete Education Histories in Fertility Analyses'. *Demographic Research,* Special 3: 135–54.

Kravdal, Ø. and Rindfuss, R.R. 2008 'Changing Relationships between Education and Fertility: A Study of Women and Men Born 1940 to 1964'. *American Sociology Review,* 73: 854–73.

Kreyenfeld, M. 2010 'Uncertainties in Female Employment Careers and the Postponement of Parenthood in Germany'. *European Sociology Review,* 26: 351–66.

Krzywinski, M., Schein, J., Birol, İ., Connors, J., Gascoyne, R., Horsman, D., et al. 2009 'Circos: An Information Aesthetic for Comparative Genomics'. *Genome Research,* 19: 1639–45.

Kühnert, B. and Nieschlag, E. 2004 'Reproductive Functions of the Ageing Male'. *Human Reproduction Update,* 10: 327–39.

Lanzieri, G. 2013 'Towards a 'Baby Recession' in Europe? Differential Fertility Trends During the Economic Crisis (Statistics in Focus No. 13)'. Statistics in Focus. Eurostat: Luxembourg.

Lappegård, T. and Rønsen, M. 2005 'The Multifaceted Impact of Education on Entry into Motherhood'. *European Journal of Population,* 21: 31–49.

Lappegård, T., Rønsen, M. and Skrede, K. 2011 'Fatherhood and Fertility'. *Fathering,* 9: 103–20.

Lavely, W. and Freedman, R. 1990 'The Origins of the Chinese Fertility Decline'. Demography, 27: 357–67.

Lee, R. 1990 'The Demographic Response to Economic Crisis in Historical and Contemporary Populations'. *Population Bulletin of the United Nations,* 29: 1–15.

Lerchl, A. 1995 'Evidence for Decreasing Quality of Sperm. Presentation of Data on Sperm Concentration was Flawed'. *British Medical Journal,* 311: 569.

Leridon, H., 2004 'Can assisted reproduction technology compensate for the natural decline in fertility with age? A model assessment'. *Human Reproduction* 19, 1548–53.

Leridon, H. 2007 'Studies of Fertility and Fecundity: Comparative Approaches from Demography and Epidemiology'. *Comptes Rendus Biologies,* 330: 339–46.

Leridon, H. 2008 'A New Estimate of Permanent Sterility by Age: Sterility Defined as the Inability to Conceive'. *Population Studies,* 62: 15–24.

Leridon, H. and Slama, R. 2008 'The Impact of a Decline in Fecundity and of Pregnancy Postponement on Final Number of Children and Demand for Assisted Reproduction Technology'. *Human Reproduction,* 23: 1312–19.

Lesthaeghe, R.J. 1995 'Second Demographic Transition in Western Countries: An Interpretation'. In: Mason, K.O. and Jensen, A.-M. (eds) *Gender and Family Change in Industrialized Countries,* pp. 17–62. Clarendon Press: Oxford.

Lesthaeghe, R.J. 2010 'The Unfolding Story of the Second Demographic Transition'. *Population and Development Review,* 36: 211–51.

Liefbroer, A.C. 2009 'Changes in Family Size Intentions Across Young Adulthood: A Life-Course Perspective'. *European Journal of Population*, 25: 363–86.

Liefbroer, A.C. and Merz, E.-M. 2010 'Report on Analysis of ESS Data on Cross-national Differences in Perceived Norms Concerning Fertility-related Behaviour'. REPRO project Deliverable 6.16. Available at: <http://vidrepro.oeaw.ac.at/wp-content/uploads/Norms_fertility-behaviour.pdf> (accessed 29 January 2014).

Liu, J., Rotkirch, A. and Lummaa, V. 2012 'Maternal Risk of Breeding Failure Remained Low Throughout the Demographic Transitions in Fertility and Age at First Reproduction in Finland'. *PLoS ONE*, 7: e34898.

Livingston, G. 2011 'In a Down Economy, Fewer Births'. *Pew Research Center Social & Demographic Trends*, 2011: 1–14.

Livingston, G. and Cohn, D. 2012 'U.S. Birth Rate Falls to a Record Low; Decline is Greatest Among Immigrants'. *Pew Research Center Social & Demographic Trends*, 2012: 1–20.

Luci, A. and Thévenon O. 2011 'Does Economic Development Explain the Fertility Rebound in OECD Countries?' (INED Working Paper 481). INED: Paris.

Luci-Greulich, A. and Thévenon, O. 2013. 'The Impact of Family Policies on Fertility Trends in Developed Countries'. *European Journal of Population*, 29: 387–416.

Lutz, W. 2006 'Fertility Rates and Future Population Trends: Will Europe's Birth Rate Recover or Continue to Decline?' *International Journal of Andrology*, 29: 25–33.

Lutz, W. and KC, S. 2011 'Global Human Capital: Integrating Education and Population'. *Science*, 333: 587–92.

Lutz, W., Goujon, A. and Doblhammer-Reiter, G. 1999a 'Demographic Dimensions in Forecasting: Adding Education to Age and Sex'. *Population and Development Review*, 24: 42–58.

Lutz, W., Sanderson, W. and Scherbov, S. 1999b 'Expert-Based Probabilistic Population Projections'. *Population and Development Review*, 24: 139–55.

Lutz, W., Skirbekk, V. and Testa, M.R. 2006 'The Low-fertility Trap Hypothesis: Forces that may Lead to Further Postponement and Fewer Births in Europe'. *Vienna Yearbook of Population Research*, 4: 167–92.

Lutz, W., Cuaresma, J.C. and Abbasi-Shavazi, M.J. 2010 'Demography, Education, and Democracy: Global Trends and the Case of Iran'. *Population and Development Review*, 36: 253–81.

Luy, M. 2011 'Tempo Effects and their Relevance in Demographic Analysis'. *Comparative Population Studies*, 35: 415–46.

Ma, J. 2011 'Ma Jian-Tang Explains China's Sixth National Population Census'. *News* 163: May 2011.

McDonald, P. 2000 'Gender Equity, Social Institutions and the Future of Fertility'. *Journal of Population Research*, 17: 1–16.

McDonald, P. 2009 'Explanations of low fertility in East Asia'. In: Straughan, P., Chan, A. and Jones, G. (eds) *Ultra-low Fertility in Pacific Asia: Trends, Causes and Policy Issues*, pp. 23–39. Routledge: Oxon.

McDonald, P. 2013 'Societal foundations for explaining fertility: Gender equity'. *Demographic Research*, 28: 981–94.

McDonald, P. and Moyle, H. 2010 'Why do English-speaking Countries Have Relatively High Fertility?' *Journal of Population Research*, 27: 247–73.

McQuillan, K. 2004 'When Does Religion Influence Fertility?' *Population and Development Review*, 30: 25–56.

Maheshwari, A., Porter, M., Shetty, A. and Bhattacharya, S. 2008 'Women's Awareness and Perceptions of Delay in Childbearing'. *Fertility and Sterility*, 90: 1036–42.

Martín-García, T. and Baizán, P. 2006 'The Impact of the Type of Education and of Educational Enrolment on First Births'. *European Sociology Review*, 22: 259–75.

Mascarenhas, M.N., Cheung, H., Mathers, C.D. and Stevens, G.A. 2012a 'Measuring Infertility in Populations: Constructing a Standard Definition for Use with Demographic and Reproductive Health Surveys'. *Population Health Metrics*, 10: 17.

Mascarenhas, M.N., Flaxman, S.R., Boerma, T., Vanderpoel, S. and Stevens, G.A. 2012b 'National, Regional, and Global Trends in Infertility Prevalence Since 1990: A Systematic Analysis of 277 Health Surveys'. *PLoS Medicine*, 9: e1001356.

Mason, K.O. 1997 'Explaining Fertility Transitions'. *Demography*, 34: 443–54.

Matysiak, A. and Vignoli, D. 2008 'Fertility and Women's Employment: A Meta-analysis'. *European Journal of Population*, 24: 363–84.

Menken, J. 1985 'Age and Fertility: How Late Can You Wait?' *Demography*, 22: 469–83.

Merz, E.M. and Liefbroer, A.C. 2012 'The Attitude Toward Voluntary Childlessness in Europe: Cultural and Institutional Explanations'. *Journal of Marriage and Family*, 74: 587–600.

Merzenich, H., Zeeb, H. and Blettner, M. 2010 'Decreasing Sperm Quality: A Global Problem?' *BMC Public Health*, 10: 24.

Miettinen, A. 2010 'Voluntary or Involuntary Childlessness? Socio-demographic Factors and Childless Intentions Among Childless Finnish Men and Women Aged 25–44'. *Finnish Yearbook of Population Research*, 45: 5–24.

Miettinen, A., Basten, S. and Rotkirch, A. 2011 'Gender Equality and Fertility Intentions Revisited'. *Demographic Research*, 24: 469–96.

Miller, W.B. 2011 'The Relationship between Childbearing Motivations and Attitude Toward Abortion among Married Men and Women'. *Family Planning Perspectives*, 26: 165–8.

Mills, M. 2010 'Gender Roles, Gender (In)equality and Fertility: An Empirical Test of Five Gender Equity Indices'. *Canadian Studies of Population*, 37: 445–74.

Mills, M., Mencarini, L., Tanturri, M.L. and Begall, K. 2008 'Gender Equity and Fertility Intentions in Italy and the Netherlands'. *Demographic Research*, 18: 1–26.

Mills, M., Rindfuss, R.R., McDonald, P., te Velde, E.R. and Force, E.R.S.T. 2011 'Why do People Postpone Parenthood? Reasons and Social Policy Incentives'. *Human Reproduction Update*, 17: 848–60.

Ministry of Labour 2010 *National Demographic Security Programme of the Republic of Belarus, 2011–2015*. Ministry of Labour and Social Protection: Minsk.

Morgan, S.P. 2001 'Should Fertility Intentions Inform Fertility Forecasts?' In: Spencer, G.K. (ed.) *The Direction of Fertility in the United States, Proceedings of US Census Bureau Conference, Session III*, pp. 153–70. US Census Bureau: Washington, DC.

Morgan, S.P. and Rackin, H. 2010 'The Correspondence Between Fertility Intentions and Behavior in the United States'. *Population and Development Review*, 36: 91–118.

Morgan, S.P., Stash, S., Smith, H.L. and Mason, K.O. 2002 'Muslim and Non-Muslim Differences in Female Autonomy and Fertility: Evidence from Four Asian Countries'. *Population and Development Review*, 28: 515–37.

Morgan, S.P., Zhigang, G., Hayford, S.R. 2009 'China's Below-Replacement Fertility: Recent Trends and Future Prospects'. *Population and Development Review*, 35: 605–29.

Mosher, W.D. and Pratt, W.F. 1985 'Fecundity and Infertility in the United States, 1965–82, Advance Data from Vital and Health Statistics'. National Center for Health Statistics: Hyattsville, MD.

Murphy, M. 1992 'Economic Models of Fertility in Post-war Britain—A Conceptual and Statistical Re-interpretation'. *Population Studies* 46, 235–58.

Musick, K., England, P., Edgington, S. and Kangas, N. 2009 'Education Differences in Intended and Unintended Fertility'. *Social Forces*, 88: 543–72.

Myrskylä, M., Goldstein, J.R. and Cheng, Y.A. 2012 'New Cohort Fertility Forecasts for the Developed World'. (MPIDR Working Paper No. 2012-014). Max Planck Institute for Demographic Research: Rostock.

Myrskylä, M., Goldstein, J.R. and Cheng, Y.A. 2013 'New Cohort Fertility Forecasts for the Developed World: Rises, Falls, and Reversals'. *Population and Development Review*, 39: 31–56.

Myrskylä, M., Kohler, H.-P. and Billari, F.C. 2009 'Advances in Development Reverse Fertility Declines'. *Nature*, 460: 741–3.

Myrskylä, M., Kohler, H.-P. and Billari, F.C. 2011 'High Development and Fertility: Fertility at Older Reproductive Ages and Gender Equality Explain the Positive Link' (PSC Working Papers Series No. 10-3-2011). Population Studies Center, University of Pennsylvania: Pennsylvania, PA.

Myrskylä, M. and Margolis, R. 2012 'Happiness: Before and After the Kids' (MPIDR Working Paper No. 2012013). Max Planck Institute for Demographic Research: Rostock.

National Strategy on Population Development Research Group 2007 *The General Report on China's National Strategy on Population Development*. Beijing: China Population Publishing House [in Chinese].

Neels, K. and De Wachter, D. 2010 'Postponement and Recuperation of Belgian Fertility: How are They Related to Rising Female Educational Attainment?' *Vienna Yearbook of Population Research*, 8: 77–106.

Neels, K., Theunynck, Z. and Wood, J. 2013 'Economic Recession and First Births in Europe: Recession-induced Postponement and Recuperation of Fertility in 14 European Countries Between 1970 and 2005'. *International Journal of Public Health*, 58: 43–55.

New Zealand Government 2010 'The Social Report': Wellington.

Ní Bhrolcháin, M. and Beaujouan, É. 2012 'Fertility Postponement is Largely Due to Rising Educational Enrolment'. *Population Studies*, 66: 311–27.

Notestein, F.W. 1945 'Population: The Long View'. In: Schultz, T.W. (ed.) *Food for the World*, pp. 36–69. University of Chicago Press: Chicago, IL.

Noyes, N., Porcu, E. and Borini, A. 2009 'Over 900 Oocyte Cryopreservation Babies Born with no Apparent Increase in Congenital Anomalies'. *Reproduction Biomedicine Online*, 18: 769–76.

OECD 2011 *Doing Better for Families*. OECD Publishing: Paris.

OECD 2012 *OECD Population Pyramids in 2000 and 2050*. OECD Publishing: Paris.

Oláh, L.S. 2003 'Gendering Fertility: Second Births in Sweden and Hungary'. *Population Research and Policy Review*, 22: 171–200.

ONE 2012 *Anuario Demográfico de Cuba 2011. Capitulo II. Nacimientos*. Oficina Nacional de Estadísticas: Havana.

Parrado, E. 2010 'How High is Hispanic/Mexican Fertility in the U.S.? Immigration and Tempo Considerations' (PSC Working Paper No. 10–04). University of Pennsylvania: Philadelphia, PA.

Perelli-Harris, B., Kreyenfeld, M., Sigle-Rushton, W., Keizer, R., Lappegård, T., Jasilioniene, A., et al. 2012 'Changes in Union Status During the Transition to Parenthood in Eleven European Countries, 1970s to Early 2000s'. *Population Studies*, 66: 167–82.

Pew Research Center 2011 *The Future of the Global Muslim Population. Projections for 2010–2030*. Pew Research Center: Washington, DC.

Philipov, D. and Dorbritz, J. 2003 *Demographic Consequences of Economic Transition in Countries of Central and Eastern Europe, Population Studies*. Council of Europe: Strasbourg.

Philipov, D. and Berghammer, C. 2007 'Religion and Fertility Ideals, Intentions and Behaviour: A Comparative Study of European Countries'. *Vienna Yearbook of Population Research*, 5: 271–305.

Philipov, D., Spéder, Z. and Billari, F.C. 2006 'Soon, Later, or Ever? The Impact of Anomie and Social Capital on Fertility Intentions in Bulgaria (2002) and Hungary (2001)'. *Population Studies*, 60: 289–308.

Pinborg, A., Hougaard, C.O., Nyboe Andersen, A., Molbo, D. and Schmidt, L. 2009 'Prospective Longitudinal Cohort Study on Cumulative 5-year Delivery and Adoption Rates Among 1338 Couples Initiating Infertility Treatment'. *Human Reproduction*, 24: 991–9.

Pla, A. and Beaumel, C. 2012 *Bilan démographique 2011: la fécondité reste élevé*. Insee Première: Paris.

Potter, J.E., Schmertmann, C.P., Assunção, R.M. and Cavenaghi, S.M. 2010 'Mapping the Timing, Pace, and Scale of the Fertility Transition in Brazil'. *Population and Development Review*, 36: 283–307.

PRB 2011 *2011 World Population Data Sheet*. Population Reference Bureau: Washington, DC.

PRB 2012 *2012 World Population Data Sheet*. Population Reference Bureau: Washington, DC.

Preston, S.H. 1986 'Changing Values and Falling Birth Rates'. *Population Development and Review*, 12: 176–95.

Prskawetz, A., Bloom, D.E. and Lutz, W. 2008 *Population Aging, Human Capital Accumulation, and Productivity Growth*. Population Council: New York.

Puur, A., Oláh, L.S., Tazi-Preve, M.I. and Dorbritz, J. 2008 'Men's Childbearing Desires and Views of the Male Role in Europe at the Dawn of the 21st Century'. *Demographic Research*, 19: 1883–912.

Raftery, A.E., Li, N., Ševčíková, H., Gerland, P. and Heilig, G.K. 2012 'Bayesian Probabilistic Population Projections for all Countries'. *Proceedings of the National Academy of Sciences of the United States of America*, 109: 13915–21.

Rashad, H., Osman, M. and Roudi-Fahimi, F. 2005 *Marriage in the Arab World*. Population Reference Bureau: Washington, DC.

Rendall, M.S., Ekert-Jaffé, O., Joshi, H., Lynch, K. and Mougin, R. 2009 'Universal Versus Economically Polarized Change in Age at First Birth: A French-British Comparison'. *Population and Development Review*, 35: 89–115.

Retherford, R.D. and Ogawa, N. 2006 'Japan's Baby Bust: Causes, Implications, and Policy Responses'. In: Harris, F.R. (ed.) *The Baby Bust: Who Will Do the Work? Who Will Pay the Taxes?* pp. 5–47. Rowman and Littlefield: Boulder, CO.

Retherford, R.D., Choe, M.K., Chen, J., Li, X. and Cui, H. 2005 'Fertility in China: How Much has it Really Declined'. *Population and Development Review*, 19: 57–84.

Rindfuss, R.R. 2004 'The Family in Comparative Perspective'. In: Tsuya, N.O. and Bumpass, L.L. (eds) *Marriage, Work, and Family Life in Comparative Perspective: Japan, South Korea, and the United States*, pp. 134–44. University of Hawai'i Press: Honolulu, HI.

Rindfuss, R.R., Morgan, S.P. and Swicegood, G. 1988 *First Births in America*. University of California Press: London.

Rindfuss, R.R., Guilkey, D.K., Morgan, S.P. and Kravdal, Ø. 2010 'Child-care Availability and Fertility in Norway'. *Population and Development Review*, 36: 725–48.

Rodríguez, J. 2011 'High Adolescent Fertility in the Context of Declining Fertility in Latin America'. Presented at the United Nations Expert Group Meeting on Adolescents, Youth and Development, Population Division, Department of Economic and Social Affairs, United Nations Secretariat, 21–22 July 2011, New York.

Roig Vila, M. and Castro-Martín, T. 2008 'Childbearing Patterns of Foreign Women in a New Immigration Country'. *Population (English Edition)*, 62: 351–79.

Rønsen, M. and Skrede, K. 2010 'Can Public Policies Sustain Fertility in the Nordic Countries? Lessons from the Past and Questions for the Future'. *Demographic Research*, 22: 321–46.

Rosero-Bixby, L., Castro-Martín, T. and Martín-García, T. 2009 'Is Latin America Starting to Retreat from Early and Universal Childbearing?' *Demographic Research*, 20: 169–94.

Roudi, F. 2012 'Iran Is Reversing Its Population Policy (Viewpoints No. 7)'. Wilson Center: Washington, DC.

Rovi, S.L. 1994 'Taking 'no' for an Answer: Using Negative Reproductive Intentions to Study the Childless/Childfree'. *Population Research and Policy Review*, 13: 343–65.

Saraceno, C., Lewis, J. and Leira, A. 2012 *Families and Family Policies*. Edward Elgar Publishing: Cheltenham.

Sartorius, G.A. and Nieschlag, E. 2010 'Paternal Age and Reproduction'. *Human Reproduction Update*, 16: 65–79.

SCB 2010 *Tabeller över Sveriges befolkning 2009*. Statistics Sweden: Stockholm.

Scharping, T. 2005 'Chinese Fertility Trends 1979–2000: A Comparative Analysis of Birth Numbers and School Data'. *Population Research*, 29: 1–12.

Scheike, T.H., Rylander, L., Carstensen, L., Keiding, N., Jensen, T.K., Stromberg, U., et al. 2008 'Time Trends in Human Fecundability in Sweden'. *Epidemiology*, 19: 191–6.

Schmidt, L., Sobotka, T., Bentzen, J.G. and Nyboe Andersen, A. 2012 'Demographic and Medical Consequences of the Postponement of Parenthood'. *Human Reproduction Update*, 18: 29–43.

Schoen, R. 2004 'Timing Effects and the Interpretation of Period Fertility'. *Demography*, 41: 801–19.

Schoen, R., Astone, N.M., Kim, Y.J., Nathanson, C.A., Fields, J.M. and Fields, M. 1999 'Do Fertility Intentions Affect Fertility Behavior?' *Journal of Marriage and Family*, 61: 790–9.

Sedgh, G., Singh, S., Shah, I.H., Åhman, E., Henshaw, S.K. and Bankole, A. 2012 'Induced Abortion: Incidence and Trends Worldwide from 1995 to 2008'. *Obstetrics and Gynecological Survey*, 67: 341–2.

Setti, P.E.L., Desgro, M., Vaiarelli, A. and Patrizio, P. 2012 'Oocyte Cryopreservation: Who, how and what to Expect'. *Journal of Fertilization: In Vitro* 2: e118.

Sharpe, R.M. and Skakkebaek, N.E. 1993 'Are Oestrogens Involved in Falling Sperm Counts and Disorders of the Male Reproductive Tract?' *The Lancet*, 341: 1392–6.

Sigle-Rushton, W. 2008 'England and Wales: Stable Fertility and Pronounced Social Status Differences'. *Demographic Research*, 19: 455–502.

Singerman, D. 2007 'The Economic Imperatives of Marriage: Emerging Practices and Identities Among Youth in the Middle East' (Middle East Youth Initiative Working Paper).

Singh, S., Sedgh, G. and Hussain, R. 2010 'Unintended Pregnancy: Worldwide Levels, Trends, and Outcomes'. *Studies in Family Planning*, 41: 241–50.

Skirbekk, V. 2008 'Fertility Trends by Social Status'. *Demographic Research*, 18: 145–80.

Skirbekk, V., Kaufmann, E. and Goujon, A. 2010 'Secularism, Fundamentalism, or Catholicism? The Religious Composition of the United States to 2043'. *Journal for the Scientific Study of Religion*, 49: 293–310.

Skouby, S.O. 2004 'Contraceptive Use and Behavior in the 21st Century: A Comprehensive Study Across Five European Countries'. *European Journal of Contraception and Reproductive Health*, 9: 57–68.

Sobotka, T. 2003 'Tempo-quantum and Period-cohort Interplay in Fertility Changes in Europe. Evidence from the Czech Republic, Italy, the Netherlands and Sweden'. *Demographic Research*, 8: 151–214.

Sobotka, T. 2004a 'Is Lowest-low Fertility in Europe Explained by the Postponement of Childbearing?' *Population and Development Review*, 30: 195–220.

Sobotka, T. 2004b 'Postponement of Childbearing and Low Fertility in Europe'. PhD Thesis. University of Groningen, Amsterdam.

Sobotka, T. 2008a 'Does Persistent Low Fertility Threaten the Future of European Populations?' In: Surkyn, J., Deboosere, P. and van Bavel, J. (eds) *Demographic Challenges for the 21st Century. A State of Art in Demography*, pp. 27–89. VUBPRESS: Brussels.

Sobotka, T. 2008b 'The Rising Importance of Migrants for Childbearing in Europe'. *Demographic Research*, 19: 225–48.

Sobotka, T. 2009 'Sub-Replacement Fertility Intentions in Austria'. *European Journal of Population*, 25: 387–412.

Sobotka, T. 2011 'Fertility in Central and Eastern Europe After 1989: Collapse and Gradual Recovery'. *Historical Social Research*, 36: 246–96.

Sobotka, T. 2012 'Fertility in Austria, Germany and Switzerland: Is There a Common Pattern?' *Comparative Population Studies*, 36: 263–304.

Sobotka, T. 2013 'Pathways to Low Fertility: European Perspectives' (Expert Paper No. 2013/8). United Nations, Department of Economic and Social Affairs, Population Division.: New York.

Sobotka, T. and Lutz, W. 2011 'Misleading Policy Messages from the Period TFR: Should We Stop Using It?' *Comparative Population Studies*, 35: 637–64.

Sobotka, T., Hansen, M.A., Jensen, T.K., Pedersen, A.T., Lutz, W. and Skakkebæk, N.E. 2008 'The Contribution of Assisted Reproduction to Completed Fertility: An Analysis of Danish Data'. *Population and Development Review*, 34: 79–101.

Sobotka, T., Skirbekk, V. and Philipov, D. 2011 'Economic Recession and Fertility in the Developed World'. *Population and Development Review*, 37: 267–306.

Spoorenberg, T. and Schwekendiek, D. 2012 'Demographic Changes in North Korea: 1993–2008'. *Population and Development Review*, 38: 133–58.

Stephen, E.H. and Chandra, A. 2006 'Declining Estimates of Infertility in the United States: 1982–2002'. *Fertility and Sterility*, 86: 516–23.

Swan, S.H., Elkin, E.P. and Fenster, L. 2000 'The Question of Declining Sperm Density Revisited: An Analysis of 101 Studies Published 1934–1996'. *Environmental Health Perspectives*, 108: 961.

Te Velde, E., Habbema, D., Leridon, H. and Eijkemans, M. 2012 'The Effect of Postponement of First Motherhood on Permanent Involuntary Childlessness and Total Fertility Rate in Six European Countries Since the 1970s'. *Human Reproduction*, 27: 1179–83.

Testa, M.R. 2006 'Childbearing Preferences and Family Issues in Europe (Special Eurobarometer No. 253/Wave 65.1—TNS Opinion & Social)'. European Commission: Brussels.

Testa, M.R. 2012 'Family sizes in Europe. Evidence from the 2011 Eurobarometer survey.' *European Demographic Research Papers* 2012, No. 2. Vienna Institute of Demography, Austrian Academy of Sciences.

Testa, M.R. and Basten, S.A. 2012 'Have Lifetime Fertility Intentions Declined During the "Great Recession"?' VID Working Papers No. 9/12, Vienna Institute of Demography, Austrian Academy of Sciences.

Testa, M.R., Cavalli, L. and Rosina, A. 2011 'Couples' Childbearing Behaviour in Italy: Which of the Partners is Leading it?' *Vienna Yearbook of Population Research*, 9: 157–78.

Thévenon, O. 2011 'Family Policies in OECD Countries: A Comparative Analysis'. *Population and Development Review*, 37: 57–87.

Thévenon, O. and Gauthier, A.H. 2011 'Family Policies in Developed Countries: A "Fertility-booster" with Side-effects'. *Community, Work & Family*, 14: 197–216.

Thomson, E. 1997 'Couple Childbearing Desires, Intentions, and Births'. *Demography*, 34: 343–54.

Thomson, E., Winkler-Dworak, M., Spielauer, M. and Prskawetz A. 2012 'Union Instability as an Engine of Fertility? A Microsimulation Model for France'. *Demography*, 49: 175–95.

Thonneau, P., Marchand, S., Tallec, A., Ferial, M.-L., Ducot, B., Lansac, J., et al. 1991 'Incidence and Main Causes of Infertility in a Resident Population (1 850 000) of Three French Regions (1988–1989)'. *Human Reproduction*, 6: 811–16.

Torabi, F., Baschieri, A., Clarke, L. and Abbasi-Shavazi, M.J. 2012 'Marriage Postponement in Iran: Accounting for Socio-economic and Cultural Change in Time and Space'. *Population, Space and Place*, 19: 258–74.

Toulemon, L., Pailhé, A. and Rossier, C. 2008 'France: High and Stable Fertility'. *Demographic Research*, 19: 553–6.

Tromans, N., Natamba, E. and Jefferies, J. 2009 'Have Women Born Outside the UK Driven the Rise in UK Births Since 2001?' *Population Trends*, 136: 28–42.

Tsimbos, C. 2008 'Immigrant and Native Fertility in Greece: New Estimates and Population Prospects (2005–2025)'. *Population Review*, 47: 67–84.

Tsuya, N.O., Choe, M.K. and Daigaku, N. 1991 *Changes in Intrafamilial Relationships and the Roles of Women in Japan and Korea*. Nihon University, Population Research Institute: Tokyo.

Tsuya, N.O., Bumpass, L.L., Choe, M.K. and Rindfuss, R.R. 2005 'Is the Gender Division of Labour Changing in Japan?' *Asian Population Studies*, 1: 47–67.

Tsuya, N.O., Choe, M.K. and Wang, F. 2009 'Below-replacement Fertility in East Asia: Patterns, Factors, and Policy Implications'. Presented at the IUSSP International Population Conference, Marrakech, Morocco.

Tuiran, R., Partida, V., Mojarro, O. and Zúñiga, E. 2002 'Fertility in Mexico: Trends and Forecast'. Report of the United Nations Population Division. UN 2011 *World Population Prospects: The 2010 Revision. Volume 1: Comprehensive Tables*. United Nations, Department of Economic and Social Affairs, Population Division: New York.

UN 2012 *Probabilistic Population Projections based on the 2010 Revision of the World Population Prospects (Data, Documentation and Supplementary Materials)*. United Nations, Department of Economic and Social Affairs, Population Division: New York.

UN 2013 *World Population Prospects: The 2012 Revision, Key Findings and Advance Tables*. United Nations, Department of Economic and Social Affairs, Population Division: New York.

Van Agtmaal-Wobma, E. and van Huis, M. 2008 'De relatie tussen vruchtbaarheid en opleidingsniveau van de vrouw'. *Bevolkingstrends*, 56: 32–41 (in Dutch).

Van Bavel, J. 2010a 'Subreplacement Fertility in the West Before the Baby Boom: Past and Current Perspectives'. *Population Studies*, 64: 1–18.

Van Bavel, J. 2010b 'Choice of Study Discipline and the Postponement of Motherhood in Europe: The Impact of Expected Earnings, Gender Composition, and Family Attitudes'. *Demography*, 47: 439–58.

Van Bavel, J. and Różańska-Putek, J. 2010 'Second Birth Rates Across Europe: Interactions Between Women's Level of Education and Child Care Enrolment'. *Vienna Yearbook of Population Research*, 8: 107–38.

Van de Kaa, D.J. 1987 'Europe's Second Demographic Transition'. *Population Bulletin*,.42: 1–59.

VID 2012 *European Demographic Data Sheet 2012*. Vienna Institute of Demography: Vienna.

Vikat, A. 2004 'Women's Labor Force Attachment and Childbearing in Finland'. *Demographic Research*, 3: 175–212.

Wang, Q. and Zhou, Q. 2010 'China's Divorce and Remarriage Rates: Trends and Regional Disparities'. *Journal of Divorce and Remarriage*, 51: 257–67.

Wang, F., Cai, Y. and Gu, B. 2013 'Population, Policy, and Politics: How Will History Judge China's One-Child Policy?' *Population and Development Review*, 38: 115–29.

Westoff, C.F. and Jones, E.F. 1979 'The End of "Catholic" Fertility'. *Demography*, 16: 209–17.

Westoff, C.F. and Frejka, T. 2007 'Religiousness and Fertility among European Muslims'. *Population and Development Review*, 33: 785–809.

Westoff, C.F. and Higgins, J. 2009 'Relationships Between Men's Gender Attitudes and Fertility'. *Demographic Research*, 21: 65–74.

Wilson, C. 2011 'Understanding Global Demographic Convergence Since 1950'. *Population and Development Review*, 37: 375–88.

Wilson, C. and Pison, G. 2004 'More than Half of the Global Population Lives Where Fertility is Below Replacement Level'. *Population and Society*, 405: 1–4.

Woldemicael, G. and Beaujot, R. 2012 'Fertility Behavior of Immigrants in Canada: Converging Trends'. *Journal of International Migration and Integration*, 13: 325–41.

Wyndham, N., Marin Figueira, P.G. and Patrizio, P. 2012 'A Persistent Misperception: Assisted Reproductive Technology can Reverse the "Aged Biological Clock"'. *Fertility and Sterility*, 97: 1044–7.

Yao, X. 1995 *Fertility Data of China*. China Population Publishing House: Beijing.

Yap, M.T. 2009 'Ultra-low Fertility in Singapore: Some Observations'. In: Jones, G., Tay-Straughan, P. and Chan, A. (eds) *Ultra-low Fertility in Pacific Asia: Trends, Causes and Policy Dilemmas*, pp. 160–80. Routledge: London.

Yerkes, M. 2009 'Part-time Work in the Dutch Welfare State: The Ideal Combination of Work and Care?' *Policy and Politics*, 37: 535–52.

Yoo, S.H. 2013 'Was Fertility Decline in Korea Driven by Educational Expansion? A Cohort Analysis'. Presented at the Annual Meeting of the Population Association of America, New Orleans, LA, USA.

Zeman, K., Sobotka, T., Gisser, R., Winkler-Dworak, M. and Lutz, W. 2011 'Geburtenbarometer Vienna: Analysing Fertility Convergence between Vienna and Austria' (VID Working Paper 7). VID: Vienna.

Zeng, Y. 1996 'Is Fertility in China in 1991–1992 Far Below Replacement Level?' *Political Studies*, 50: 27–34.

Zhang, G. 2004 'Does the Family Planning Program Affect Fertility Preferences? The Case of China'. Presented at the Australian Population Association 12th Biennial Conference, Canberra, Australia.

Zhang, L. 2008 'Religious Affiliation, Religiosity and Male and Female Fertility'. *Demographic Research*, 18: 233–62.

Zhao, Z. and Chen, W. 2011 'China's Far Below Replacement Fertility and its Long Term Impact: Comments on the Preliminary Results of the 2010 Census'. *Demographic Research*, 25: 819–36.
Zhao, Z. and Guo, Z. 2010 'China's Below Replacement Fertility: A Further Exploration'. *Canadian Studies in Population*, 37: 525–62.
Zhao, Z. and Zhang, X. 2010 'China's Recent Fertility Decline: Evidence from Reconstructed Fertility Statistics'. *Population (English Edition)*, 65: 451–78.
Zheng, Z., Cai, Y., Wang, F. and Gu, B. 2009 'Below-replacement Fertility and Childbearing Intention in Jiangsu Province, China'. *Asian Population Studies*, 5: 329–47.

CHAPTER 4

FUTURE FERTILITY IN HIGH FERTILITY COUNTRIES

REGINA FUCHS AND ANNE GOUJON

Contributing authors:[1]

Donatien Beguy, John Casterline, Teresa Castro-Martin, Youssef Courbage, Gavin Jones, Samir KC, James K.S., John F. May, Blessing Mberu, Michaela Potančoková, Zeba Sathar, Bruno Schoumaker, David Shapiro, Laura Wong, and Brenda Yepez-Martinez

4.1 Introduction: Summary of Past Trends

Beginning in 1960, a phenomenon occurred that John Caldwell named the 'global fertility transition' (Caldwell, 1997), in which fertility declines have become the general rule throughout the world, including in the majority of the less developed countries. This is important partly because fertility is in many circumstances negatively associated with socio-economic development (Bryant, 2007). From 1970–75 to 2005–10, the average total fertility rate (TFR) for the developing world fell by half, from 5.4 to 2.7

[1] The contributing authors were selected as lead experts in respective topics and regions. Specifically, they have provided texts to the following sections: Donatien Beguy to section 4.2.1.3 ('Uganda'); John Casterline to Box 4.2 ('A focus on the unmet need for family planning'); Teresa Castro-Martin to section 4.2.4.1 ('Guatemala'); Youssef Courbage to section 4.2.3.2 ('Yemen') and 4.2.3.3 ('Morocco'); Gavin Jones to section 4.2.2.3 ('Indonesia'); Samir KC to section 4.3.7 ('The impact of education in the course of demographic transition—empirical evidence'); James K.S. to section 4.2.2.1 ('India'); John F. May to section 4.2.1 ('Sub-Saharan Africa') and 4.2.1.1 ('Niger'), and Box 4.4.3 ('A focus on population policies'); Blessing Mberu to section 4.2.1.3 ('Uganda'); Michaela Potančoková to section 4.3.7 ('The impact of education in the course of demographic transition—empirical evidence'); Zeba Sathar to section 4.2.2.2 ('Pakistan'); Bruno Schoumaker to Box 4.1 ('A focus on stalling fertility'); David Shapiro to section 4.2.1.2 ('Democratic Republic of Congo'); Laura Wong to section 4.2.4.3 ('Bolivia'); Brenda Yepez-Martinez to section 4.2.4.2 ('Venezuela').

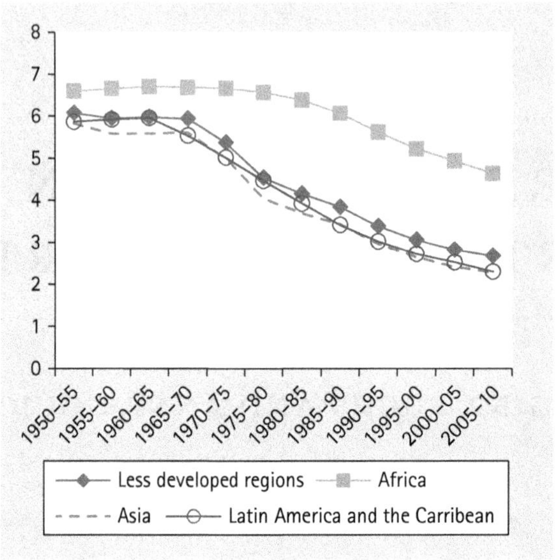

FIGURE 4.1 Total fertility rates (TFR) among major regions of the world and for the less developed countries over time.

Source: United Nations (2011).

births per woman on average (United Nations, 2011). However, global figures hide important differences in fertility levels among the different regions. In Asia and Latin America, the reproductive behaviour of women reflected the pattern of change noted by Caldwell, halving the TFR in the last 35 years. In Africa, on the contrary, fertility stagnated at 6.2–6.4 from 1950 to 1985, and then began a decline that was much slower than in other developing regions (see Figure 4.1). As a whole, the TFR of sub-Saharan Africa has, for decades, been higher than the fertility levels elsewhere. This was the case in 1950 and 1975, and remains so today.

Fertility differences among countries are now larger than ever because transitions to replacement fertility have not yet started in some subpopulations of Western and Middle Africa, but have already been completed in others (e.g. in the economically most advanced countries of Asia, especially East Asia, as well as in many countries in Latin America and the Caribbean). As a result, the observed TFRs of (former) developing countries in 2005–10 range from a high of 7.1 in Niger[2] to a low of 1.0 in Hong Kong.[3]

All regions of the world experience wide variations in their TFRs. For instance, East Asia has experienced a faster fertility decline than countries like Pakistan in south-central Asia. Moreover, fertility levels can show significant variations within a single country. This is the case in India, where Northern and Southern patterns of fertility are

[2] The latest survey carried out in 2012 even points at a fertility increase to 7.6 children—see section 4.2.1.1.

[3] According to the classification of countries by the United Nations. See <http://esa.un.org/unpd/wpp/Excel-Data/definition-of-regions.htm> (accessed 16 April 2013).

very different. Overall, regional variations are most apparent in sub-Saharan Africa. Southern Africa, which represents only 7 per cent of the sub-Saharan Africa population, has a TFR of 2.5, whereas Eastern Africa has a TFR of 5.1, and Western Africa and Middle Africa have TFRs of 5.4 and 5.9 respectively.

The future world population will depend substantially on the speed of the fertility decline in the subregions that still follow high patterns of fertility. The topic generates conflicting views. Although the mechanisms behind the fertility decline are well known—particularly in terms of education, family planning, female empowerment, and urbanization—their spread and future intensity are not certain, and the relationships between the causal factors and the fertility reductions are not linear.

The first part of this chapter analyses the trends in the fertility decline in the remaining world regions with high fertility, and focuses on the historical and present fertility trends in a few countries in each region. The second part presents the theoretical framework explaining the fertility path, which is dominated by demographic transition theory. This theory assesses fertility decline as part of development as societies transition from traditional to modern ones. We also examine fertility stalls, which are counter-examples to that theory. The third and fourth parts adopt a forward-looking perspective that provides insights into future fertility trends. In the third part, we present and analyse results of the IIASA–Oxford survey and meta-expert meeting that provided input into the projection process carried out by the Wittgenstein Centre for Demography and Global Human Capital (WIC) and reported in this book. In the fourth part, we explain how we translated the analysis of past and present trends, and the expert views of the future into fertility assumptions for the WIC projections. We conclude the chapter with a section on the future fertility differentials by education. Education is a common thread in all sections of this chapter as it is an important indicator of 'development', having a strong influence on women's fertility.

4.2 Different world experiences

The transition to lower fertility has occurred at different speeds, and some countries and regions are still in its midst. In the following subsections we review the main trends at the regional level in sub-Saharan Africa, the Middle East, and North Africa (MENA), Asia, and Latin America. We also present case studies of three countries within each region that either exemplify or diverge from the general picture.

4.2.1 Sub-Saharan Africa

With the exception of Southern Africa, sub-Saharan Africa is experiencing the demographic transition much later than all other world regions. Some rural regions of several sub-Saharan countries have not yet started their fertility transition in earnest, for example in the three case studies presented in the next sections: Niger (section 4.2.1.1), the Democratic Republic of Congo (D.R. Congo) (section 4.2.1.2), and Uganda (4.2.1.3). Even in sub-Saharan Africa countries where fertility has declined, the pace of fertility reduction has usually been very slow (see Box 4.1). The current prospects for rapid fertility decline in this area are therefore less promising than the experience in other regions, and the future trajectory of fertility in sub-Saharan Africa might be much slower than anticipated in the current United Nations (UN) population projections (United Nations, 2011), where the TFR is declining from 4.8 (in 2010–15) to 2.1 by the end of the century in the medium variant.

The reasons are manifold, including poor socio-economic outcomes, the high level of desired fertility (even among the educated population), and the timid policy approaches to the issue of rapid population growth on the part of African leaders and elites. Female literacy rates are still very low in sub-Saharan Africa, and so are income per capita and labour force participation in the formal sector. Organized programmes of family planning have generally also been weak. The latent demand (unmet need) for contraceptive use is also low (around 25 per cent on average), and the pace of increase of contraceptive coverage has been very slow, Rwanda being a noteworthy exception (Westoff, 2013). Some countries have even experienced a reversal in overall contraceptive coverage, sometimes accompanied by a decline in the percentage of women in unions[4] using modern contraception since 2000. This is particularly true in Guinea, D.R. Congo, and Chad.[5] Because the future of population growth in sub-Saharan Africa hinges on fertility, the key research question is how soon fertility could decline, especially in the three sub-Saharan Africa subregions (Western, Eastern, and Middle Africa) where the TFR is still above five children per woman. Traditional social norms favouring high fertility and poor access to family planning services may prevent fertility from declining rapidly.

4.2.1.1 *Niger*

Between 1950 and 2010 the population of Niger in Western Africa grew from 2.4 million to 15.5 million—a sixfold increase (United Nations, 2011). The mortality decline that induced this growth could accelerate in the future, fuelling further population growth, unless episodes of famine become more frequent. International migration could reduce population growth somewhat, with an estimated 166,000 Nigeriens leaving the country every year (République du Niger, 2012), although it seems that many Nigeriens have recently returned from foreign countries (e.g. from Libya). Niger has one of the highest fertility rates in the world and fertility has declined only very slowly in the past, with the most recent round of Demographic and Health Survey (DHS) even showing an increase in the TFR from 7.1 in 2006 to 7.6 in 2012 (DHS Niger, 2006, 2012). Desired fertility

[4] In most countries where fertility is high, childbearing primarily occurs inside marriage. Hence, interviews in surveys on fertility are often conducted only with married women.

[5] As can be seen from the database on contraceptive prevalence rate (Millennium Development Goals): <http://www.un.org/en/development/desa/population/theme/mdg/index.shtml> (accessed 18 April 2013).

remains very high, including among women with five children, of whom only nine per cent do not desire an additional birth. This is the case even among the more educated: people with secondary schooling still want six children, according to the 2006 DHS (DHS Niger, 2006, 2012). Although the use of any contraceptive method has increased slightly from 11 to 14 per cent in the last 6 years (DHS Niger, 2006, 2012), the demand for contraceptives and the resulting unmet need for family planning remain modest. Women, especially in rural areas, have little information on family planning methods and, as a result, have difficulty making an informed choice concerning family planning methods.

The UN estimates that the TFR in Niger will decrease to 4.2 children per woman by 2050 (United Nations, 2011). However, some experts (Guengant and May, 2011) doubt that this will happen if age at marriage remains very low, if social norms do not change, and if the contraceptive prevalence rate does not increase more rapidly. The future of fertility decline in Niger will depend on these factors, along with the age at first birth, success in empowering women, efforts to promote female education, and political commitment to set up organized family planning programmes. Among these factors, addressing the prevalence of 'child marriage' might not be feasible, as public authorities may not be able to muster the political will to combat traditions that have long been culturally entrenched.

4.2.1.2 *D.R. Congo*

D.R. Congo is a high-fertility country in Middle Africa with little evidence of fertility decline at the national level (Romaniuk, 2011). Its population has increased from 12 million in 1950 to 66 million in 2010 (United Nations, 2011). At the same time, the D.R. Congo's capital, Kinshasa, the second-largest city in sub-Saharan Africa with about nine million inhabitants, has seen its fertility decline by half between 1975 and 2007 (Shapiro, 2012).

The history of fertility is shown in Figure 4.2. Data from a large national survey carried out in the 1950s indicate that the TFR at the national level was 5.9, while the TFR for Kinshasa was estimated at 7.5 (Romaniuk, 1967, 1968). The higher fertility of the city reflects in large part the incidence of venereal disease in the countryside, resulting in high levels of sterility in the north, which was part of a Central African infertility belt (Retel-Laurentin, 1974; Romaniuk, 1961).

Following independence in 1960, a major demographic survey was carried out in the mid-1970s in the western part of the country, a national census was done in 1984, a DHS was completed in 2007, and three national Multiple Indicator Cluster Surveys (MICS) were conducted in 1995, 2001, and 2010. These many surveys suggest first that for at least the two decades after independence, fertility in D.R. Congo rose somewhat owing, in part, to public health campaigns that reduced the incidence of sterility in the north. Another factor in the increase was the initiation of some modernizing behaviours in the population, reducing the impact of traditional restraints such as post-partum sexual abstinence and prolonged breastfeeding, thereby contributing to higher fertility (Romaniuk, 1980). In 2007, the overall TFR in the D.R. Congo was estimated to be 6.3. The rural TFR was 7.0 compared with an urban TFR of 5.4 (Ministère

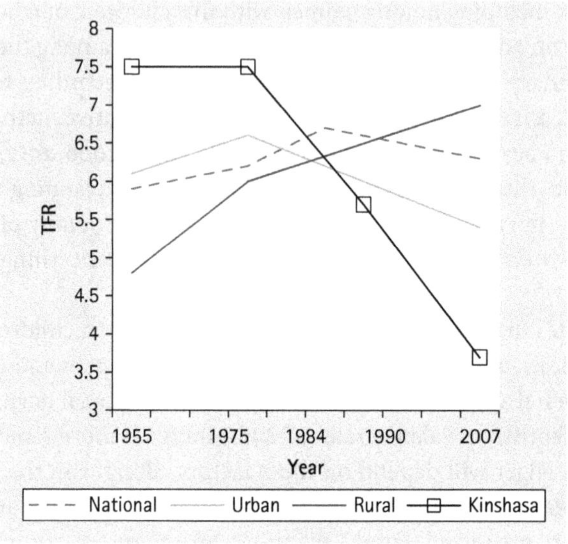

FIGURE 4.2 Total fertility rate (TFR) by place of residence, D.R. Congo.

Source: different sources.

du Plan and Macro International, 2008). The TFR for Kinshasa was 3.7; the TFR for other urban areas was 6.3. The 2010 MICS showed mostly similar numbers: an overall TFR of 6.3, with 7.1 at the rural level, 4.8 at the urban level, and 3.5 for Kinshasa (Institut National de la Statistique et Fonds des Nations Unies pour l'Enfance, 2011). While allowances should be made for sampling variability across data sets, these numbers suggest that a fertility decline is ongoing in Kinshasa, at best only beginning in other urban settings, and not yet evident in rural areas or for the country as a whole.

In considering determinants and correlates of fertility as part of the process of understanding the fertility transition, Romaniuk (2011) emphasizes the desirability of a balanced approach that takes into account both the forces of tradition that typically hinder fertility decline and the forces of modernization that tend to foster fertility transition. For the D.R. Congo overall, the forces of tradition are clearly stronger at present than the forces of modernization. Even for Kinshasa, where a fertility decline has taken place, it appears that the decline is less a consequence of the strong forces of modernization than a reaction to the extended persistence of economic hardship (Shapiro, 2012). Hence, at least in the near-term, future fertility in the D.R. Congo will likely remain high.

4.2.1.3 *Uganda*

Uganda has one of the highest TFRs in sub-Saharan Africa. Accordingly, the country's population has grown rapidly in recent decades, increasing from 9.5 million in 1969 to 24.2 million in 2002, and reaching 32.9 million in mid-2011 (Uganda Bureau of Statistics, 2012). Still, data from four rounds of nationally representative Uganda DHSs show a marginal decrease (9 per cent) in the country's fertility rates, declining from 7.4 children per woman in 1988 to 6.7 in 2006/2007 (DHS Uganda, 2012).

As a result of lower mortality but still high fertility, Uganda has developed one of the world's youngest age structures, with half of its population aged 15 or younger (Haub and Gribble, 2011). The country's population will continue to grow, as large numbers of people are either currently of childbearing age or will soon enter that age group. If current fertility levels persist, the country's population is projected to reach 70 million by 2031 and could attain 100 million after 2040, a near tripling of its current size (Haub and Gribble, 2011).

While fertility has remained at pre-transition levels over the last 20 years, there are signs of decline within particular subgroups of women, namely the most educated and those living in urban areas and in the central region. Conversely, fertility hovers around seven children per woman in some areas, particularly the eastern region where TFR increased from 7.4 in 2000 to 7.6 by 2006/2007 (DHS Uganda, 2012). Consequently, there are calls for specific actions to reverse increasing levels of desired family size and growing negative attitudes toward family planning. There are also calls to address high levels of unmet need for family planning (34 per cent in 2011) and high levels of unintended pregnancies (44 per cent in 2011) (DHS Uganda, 2012).

4.2.2 Asia

Asia has been characterized by large fertility declines over the second half of the twentieth century, starting with Eastern Asia. Japan's early transition began in the 1930s, followed by Hong Kong, Taiwan, and Singapore in the 1960s. Rapid industrialization, economic wealth, the spread of education (particularly among women), and the diffusion of contraceptive use in the context of strong political commitments have played a significant role in bringing about a rapid pace of fertility decline in most South East Asian countries, one of the most rapid in the developing world. Indonesia (see section 4.2.2.3) belongs to those countries that began their fertility transition at higher levels of socio-economic development and have progressed much faster in approaching replacement-level fertility. These countries were able to reap the demographic dividend that was arising from having the largest share of the population of working age, faster than other countries, mostly in South Asia, that are at different stages of this transition. In India (see section 4.2.2.1), although fertility has been rapidly declining, some states have seen less substantial fertility declines than others. However, ideational change and the wish for smaller families are underway in all states, and family planning diffusion will certainly facilitate further declines. The picture is slightly different in Pakistan (see section 4.2.2.2), where increasing female education and meeting the unmet demand for family planning will be key challenges.

4.2.2.1 *India*

India experienced a modest decline in fertility during the second half of the twentieth century. The pace of decline has, however, quickened over the last two decades. According to the Sample Registration System data available since 1970, TFR has declined at 1.5 per cent per annum until around the early 1990s. While TFR was around 5.2 in the early 1970s, it reached a level of 2.5 by 2010. Given this pace of decline, India is expected to reach replacement fertility levels toward the second half of this decade (Office of the Registrar General of India, 2006).

Interestingly, the fertility transition has been quite uneven across the regions and states in the country. Among the 20 largest states, 11 (home to nearly 48 per cent of India's population of 1 billion) have already achieved replacement fertility (James, 2011). In eight states, the TFR is hovering around 1.8 children. In contrast, in the nine states constituting more than 50 per cent of India's population, fertility levels are above replacement. Still, the pace of fertility decline has quickened everywhere in the last few years. Even the state with the highest fertility, Bihar, has recorded a strong decline, from 4.3 in 2005 to 3.7 in 2010 (Office of the Registrar General of India, 2012).

The desired number of children has also come down significantly over the recent period, reaching replacement level according to the 2005–06 DHS. The total 'wanted' fertility rate (calculated as the difference between desired number of children and actual number born) was only 1.9, lower by 0.8 child than the TFR of 2.7, based on the most recent DHS. The decline in the desired number of children among illiterate women, from 3.2 in 1992–93, to 2.2 in 2005–06, is an example of such a change.

At the same time, marriage remains nearly universal in India. The weakening of the institution of marriage, which is one of the major routes of sustaining below replacement fertility, has not affected India to any significant extent. The mean age at marriage has risen slowly. Therefore, it is still unclear how low the Indian TFR will go, given the country's socio-cultural context.

India's fertility transition has been unique in many respects. Most notably, the transition has occurred without notable improvements in socio-economic conditions. Indeed, the Indian fertility decline has been mainly among illiterate women (Mari Bhat, 2002). With the female literacy rate remaining low, the only way to achieve drastic fertility reduction has been diffusion among illiterate women of the idea of having only a few children. The experience of the recent decades gives credence to the fact that the country has been successful in spreading this small-family message (Dreze and Murthi, 2001; Guilmoto and Rajan, 2001). At the same time, the educational gradient of fertility still remains significant. Illiterate women bear, on average, around 3.4 children compared with 1.8 for those with graduate and higher educational levels.

On the whole, it appears that India is on a course of rapid fertility change and approaching replacement-level fertility. With the narrowing of fertility differences across states and across educational categories, fertility is even likely to fall below replacement level. However, it is still not clear whether the country will achieve the very low fertility of many European countries, given India's rigid religious and cultural context.

4.2.2.2 *Pakistan*

Pakistan, a country that has seen its population more than double from 60 to 174 million between 1980 and 2010 (United Nations, 2011), stands apart from other populous countries in South Asia that have already experienced substantial declines in fertility. In the

1980s and 1990s there was a wide divergence of opinion about levels of fertility, mainly reflecting the findings of various surveys that followed different approaches. There is consensus, however, on the beginning of fertility decline in Pakistan (Feeney and Alam, 2003; Sathar and Casterline, 1998), based on 1990s data that show a distinct decline.

Considered together, estimates imply a considerable decline of around 1.5 births per woman from the late 1980s through the 1990s (Sathar and Zaidi, 2011). The decline in fertility from the Pakistan Demographic and Health Survey (PDHS) 1990–91 (National Institute of Population Studies, 1992) was from 5.8 births to 4.8 births in 2000, according to the Pakistan Reproductive Health and Family Planning Survey (National Institute of Population Studies, 1992). The annual Pakistan Demographic Survey (PDS) showed a sharper decline (starting higher) from 6.2 births per woman in 1990 to 4.5 births per woman by 2000 (Feeney and Alam, 2003).

Demographers were optimistic about the speed of further fertility decline in Pakistan after 2000; however, the decline did not continue at the same pace. The 2008 PDHS (National Institute of Population Studies, 2008) shows a decline from 4.1 to 3.7 births in the period 2001–07, while the fertility surveys show TFR declining from 4.8 (Hakim et al., 2001) to 4.1 births per woman for the period. While there is still a divergence in rates between the two types of surveys, it is much narrower than in earlier years. The preliminary report of the most recent PDHS (Measure DHS, 2013) estimates a TFR of 3.9.

The speed and timing of the decline are very different for urban and rural areas. Urban areas experienced the fertility transition earlier and much more rapidly. The TFR in urban areas declined by almost two births, from 5.6 births per woman in the 1980s to 4.9 in 1990, and 3.8 births per woman by 2000. On the one hand, however, in the last decade the urban fertility decline has slowed, with TFR at only 3.3 by 2007. On the other hand, rural fertility remained above 6 births per woman until the mid-1990s, at which time it declined from 6.3 births per woman (Ministry of Population Welfare, 1995) to 5.4 births per woman by 2000 (Hakim et al., 2001), and to 4.5 births per woman by 2006–07. Consequently, there has been some narrowing of the rural–urban differential from the initial 1.7 births in 2000 to 1.2 births by 2007.

Prospects for future fertility decline have kept changing in Pakistan. Demographers were first encouraged by the rapid fertility decline of the 1990s and then cautioned by the unexpected slowing in the last decade. Pakistan lacks national fertility estimates after 2007. The various scenarios of fertility decline depend on the priority that the Government of Pakistan, other policymakers in the development sector, and donors assigned to the expansion and improvement of family planning services. With improvements in such services, there is huge potential for meeting unmet demand for family planning in the country and thus for fertility to decline at a more rapid pace. Otherwise, fertility will decline slowly and possibly erratically over the next two decades.

4.2.2.3 *Indonesia*

Indonesia experienced a relatively rapid decline in its TFR, from about 5.4 in 1970, with a population of 118 million, to about 2.4 in 2010—when the population doubled from its 1970 level of 240 million (United Nations, 2011). While far less spectacular than those of

Singapore and Thailand, this decline was almost as rapid as in the Latin American countries with the most rapid fertility declines (Mexico, Brazil, and Costa Rica), and was notable for having occurred in a country with a low level of per capita income and a relatively high proportion of the population living in rural areas. The decline was characterized by less urban–rural difference than was the case for many other countries and less difference by educational background, but substantial regional differences.

What were the underlying causes of this decline? Comparing the situation in 2010 with that in 1970, notable changes had occurred in every aspect of economic and social conditions. Relatively high rates of economic growth had been achieved, punctuated by short periods of economic crisis, the most severe of which was the Asian financial crisis of 1997–98. By 2010, almost 50 per cent of the population was living in urban areas, per capita income in purchasing power parity terms was much higher than in 1970, and the infant mortality rate had fallen from slightly over 100 per 1,000 live births in 1970 to about 27 in 2010. The gross secondary school enrolment ratio had risen from about 15 in 1970 to about 79 over the same period. Between 1970 and the late 1990s, an effective family planning programme was mounted by the government, which, to some extent, lost its way after the economic crisis and the new regional autonomy programmes adopted after 2001. These undercut the centralized direction and management of the programme, which had been an important element in its success.

Generally accepted explanations for the Indonesian fertility decline are based on rapid socio-economic development and on the role of the family planning programme. However, these could be called into question by comparing the decline with that of Myanmar, where the trend in TFR was remarkably similar to that in Indonesia, despite Myanmar's poor record of economic and social development over the same period. Myanmar also lacked a family planning programme, with government officials showing some hostility toward family planning during the earlier part of the period. However, the onus of providing a persuasive explanation of the fertility decline seems to rest more on the case of Myanmar than on that of Indonesia.

Indonesia has the largest Muslim-majority population in the world, with Muslims making up 87 per cent of its 240 million population. Although the sharp decline in fertility in a number of Muslim-majority countries has undercut the long-standing belief that Muslim populations are inherently resistant to fertility decline, a potential resistance to family planning by local-level Islamic leaders was certainly anticipated and effectively neutralized by the Indonesian family planning programme operating in the context of strong control over Islamic political forces during the Suharto era. This stands in sharp contrast to the failure to neutralize Islamic opposition to family planning in countries such as Pakistan.

More recently, however, the Indonesian fertility decline has slowed, albeit at a level of TFR that is not much above replacement level. Over the decade 2000–10, the TFR has fallen only slightly, although sources differ on the extent of the decline and the exact numbers involved. The DHS and contraceptive prevalence surveys yield higher TFR estimates than do the census and other major socio-economic surveys. Hull and Hartanto (2009) demonstrate effectively that the DHS 2007 under-sampled single women living outside their parents' household. Accordingly, they suggest an adjustment of the DHS TFR for 2005–07 from 2.6 to 2.3. While the deceleration in fertility decline is often attributed to the problems facing the family planning programme, it seems to be related more to an upturn in Islamic religiosity and a related emphasis on marriage and family-building (Sakai and Fauzia, 2014). Over the period from 2006 to 2010, the mean age at marriage has fallen, the first such decline recorded in recent decades anywhere in South East Asia. The future trajectory of such a trend in religiosity is hard to predict but needs to be kept in mind as an influence on future trends in Indonesian fertility. Concerns that a major upsurge in fertility will take place appear to be unfounded, however, given the continuing rapid pace of socio-economic development and the lack of evidence of fertility upturns in other Muslim-majority countries.

4.2.3 Middle East and North Africa

The fertility transition is well underway in most countries of the MENA region, although in the 1980s it was considered to be one of the main counter-examples to demographic transition theory, as the region was experiencing strong improvements in health and general development without showing significant signs of fertility decline. In 2010, a number of countries approached replacement fertility, particularly in North Africa (Morocco, Algeria, and Libya), or had already reached below-replacement levels. These countries included Tunisia, Lebanon, Bahrain, Kuwait, and the United Arab Emirates. Morocco (see section 4.2.3.3), which is one of the least developed countries in the Arab world, anticipated the movement of fertility decline ahead of many other MENA countries. In the other Eastern Mediterranean countries, such as Egypt, Jordan, and Syria, fertility is also declining significantly. Only the Palestinian Territories and Iraq still exhibited a TFR above 3.5 children in the 2005–10 period (United Nations, 2011).

If decreased nuptiality and marriage postponement were the main factors in the fertility decline so far, progress in contraceptive prevalence rates and educational levels among the young female population are pointing to further declines. However, as Egypt shows (see section 4.2.3.1), the norm in terms of number of children desired by couples might be an obstacle to more rapid fertility declines. In the less developed Arab countries, such as Mauritania, Sudan, and Yemen, the fertility transition started less than 20 years ago and fertility levels remain high (see section 4.2.3.2), with an uncertain future.

4.2.3.1 *Egypt*

In comparison to other Arab countries, the decline in fertility in Egypt was quite slow, comparable to that in Sudan, Bahrain, and Yemen, among others (United Nations Economic and Social Commission for Western Asia, 2005), leading to substantial increase in the population from 40 to 81 million between 1975 and 2010 (United Nations, 2011). There were two main phases in the Egyptian fertility decline. It was quite rapid between 1980 and the mid-1990s, when the TFR declined from 5.3 children per woman (1979–80) to 3.3 (1995–97). Between 1995 and 2005, the fertility decline slowed, and two DHSs even indicated an increase in TFRs around 1998 and 2000 (Eltigani, 2003; El-Zanaty and Way, 2004). However, Engelhardt (2005) hypothesized that the indicated increase could have been spurious. According to Eltigani (2003), households with higher education and income were responsible for the stalling of fertility at a time when women in other education categories also experienced a levelling off of their fertility. The fertility of women with a secondary education and higher has been constant during the last 15 years, at about 3.0 children per woman between 1992 and 2005. A survey conducted by the Cairo Demographic Center (2006) showed that the gender bias toward boys and the desire to have three children, in addition to peer pressure, are the main reasons for having more than two children among the more highly educated. In the same way, Casterline and Roushdy (2007), while studying fertility desires in an analysis of differences between current fertility levels and replacement-level fertility, revealed the absence of a vanguard group of young, educated, and/or wealthy persons who would have adopted the two-child norm in Egypt. Replacement fertility is not yet a desirable goal for a substantial majority of the Egyptian population. The last DHS surveys (DHS Egypt, 2009, 2006, 2004) point to the return of a general fertility decline, homogenously across regions, although at a very slow pace. The TFR in 2008 was estimated at 3.0 children per woman in the whole of Egypt, down from 3.1 in 2005.

The future of fertility rates in Egypt is highly uncertain. There are several obstacles on the pathway to replacement-level fertility in the near future, some having to do with the difficulty of limiting unwanted fertility, estimated at 1.0 child in 2005. It has been observed that women do not feel committed to their goal of wanted fertility of two children (Casterline and El-Zeini, 2005). Other obstacles have to do with desired family size, which remains between two and three with no visible changes between the older and younger generations of women. The Arab Spring and the resulting political and economic crisis are other sources of uncertainty regarding the future of fertility in Egypt.

4.2.3.2 *Yemen*

There are two ways to look at fertility in Yemen. The pessimistic evaluation sees Yemen as one of the most fertile countries in the world with about five children[6] per woman in 2010, and a doubling of its population in the 20 years since 1990 to 24 million. The more optimistic view emphasizes the achievement of reducing the fertility rate by almost half in the last 30 years, a task that is even more impressive because it was done in the context of a remote and mountainous country with some 70 per cent of the population living in rural areas (Courbage and Todd, 2011). In spite of a long history of outmigrations that sent Yemenis to Indonesia, the USA, and the coasts of Eastern Africa, most migrants went to neighbouring countries like Saudi Arabia, where they were exposed to more conservative values than Arab Maghreb migrants experienced in the European world.

[6] Estimates for present fertility diverge greatly: the TFR is 5.0 according to estimates by Courbage, 5.2 according to the Population Reference Bureau (2012), 4.9 according to the UN for 2010–15 (2011), and 4.3 according to the US Census Bureau for 2013.

The Yemeni fertility transition started in the middle 1990s, later than most other Arab countries, and at a time when female literacy levels were low. Even now, more than half of women aged 15–24 are illiterate, whereas illiteracy has been eradicated in most other Arab countries. Male literacy is much higher, approaching 95 per cent. Hence, males may have taken the lead and could have triggered a significant fertility decline. However, it would be reasonable to imagine that female education will instead become the leading cause of fertility decline in Yemen. The illiteracy rate among the youngest females—those who will soon reach marriage and reproduction ages—is decreasing at a rate of 3.7 per cent per annum.

As important as education is, it does not tell the whole story. In many Arab countries, Yemen in particular, other determinants of fertility may also be important. First, a competition over population size[7] is taking place between the two giants of the Arabian Peninsula, Yemen and Saudi Arabia. Yemen currently has the larger population, mostly because of its expatriate population. However, Yemen still experiences internal conflicts between the North and the South that might impact fertility behaviour, partly because of tribalism and the different kinds of Islam practised across the country, such as the Shiite Yemeni community called *zaidi*, which is active in North Yemen.

The Arab Spring, which has led to the exile of Yemen's 'president for life', might change the course of fertility trends. Women took to the streets of the capital, and their newly gained political presence might well be followed by an improved access to education, hence pushing fertility to lower levels.

4.2.3.3 *Morocco*

Morocco, one of the least developed Arab countries, anticipated fertility transition ahead of the 20 or so other countries of the MENA region, excluding two small ones, Lebanon and Tunisia. Despite an official family planning programme launched by King Hassan II in 1966, fertility started to increase rather than decrease, from 7.2 children in 1962, to 7.4 in 1973. As in other countries in the region, revenues from mineral wealth redistributed by the state consolidated large family norms. Morocco's entry into the demographic transition was brought by two political and economic events: the Western Sahara crisis pushed military expenditures forward in 1975 and, at the same time, phosphate prices fell. As a result, the state lost its main source of family planning funding and, moreover, compensated the drop in state revenues by increasing household taxes. This prompted many women to join the labour force and abandon their traditional role at home a decade ahead of the Arab world (Courbage, 1999). Consequently, fertility fell to 5.9 in 1977. Between 1960 and 1995, young women joined the labour force, their share nearly quadrupling from a mere 10 to 37 per cent over that time period. The resulting new work patterns influenced marriage and reproduction by creating new time constraints and a weakening of family networks. Since then, fertility has continued to decline at unprecedented rates. Each census or survey held since the World Fertility

[7] The battle of numbers could be also fuelled by the fact that Yemen has claims over the Asir, a Yemeni populated region lost during the war of 1934, to the benefit of the Saudis.

Survey in 1977 has revealed yet another decline: to 4.5 in 1988, 3.0 in 1999, and 2.2 in 2009–10.

Therefore, economic and labour market factors among other determinants of fertility—decline in infant and childhood mortality, urbanization, increase of the service sector in the economy, and female education—were decisive in triggering Morocco's fertility decline (Courbage and Todd, 2011). However, the impacts of these factors should not be over-estimated. This is particularly true for female education. The Moroccan fertility transition has gone a long way, whereas female illiteracy is still high (39 per cent among women aged 15–24 years).

The gap between Morocco's fertility trends and those in the richer and better educated Middle East—Egypt, Syria, Jordan, or the Arabian Peninsula—is not explained by referring to demographic transition theory. Population origins, geography, and colonial and post-colonial history have shaped Morocco in a particular way reflected in its demography. Morocco's family patterns have been influenced by the interdependence with colonial powers France and Spain. Even after independence in 1956, Morocco's identity has had a strong European imprint. Even more significant is the impact of the 2.5 million Moroccan diaspora living in Western Europe. In the 1960s migrants followed the large family size model. One or two generations later, they became agents of the small nuclear family model. There are no convincing reasons to anticipate a fertility stall in the coming decades; fertility will most likely fall to levels comparable to other countries on the Mediterranean coast.

4.2.4 Latin America

The demographic transition that started in the 1960s in most Latin American countries originated in radical changes in the socio-economic environment and in people's attitudes towards fertility regulation when contraception availability was increasing (Guzman et al., 1996). As usual, the global trends hide important differences between and within the countries of the region. This is apparent when comparing in Figure 4.3 the TFR at the beginning of the transition in 1965–70, when 36 out of 37 countries of the region had a TFR above 3.0 (except Uruguay, where women had, on average, 2.8 children), and in 2005–10, when only six countries had fertility above 3.0 children. In two-thirds of the countries, the current fertility rate is below 2.5 (United Nations, 2011). The regional average TFR is 2.2 children per women. Most interesting are the countries in which the TFR was still above three children in 2005–10.

Presently, Guatemala is among a small group of countries that have the highest fertility rates in Latin America and the Caribbean region. The other such countries are Haiti, Bolivia (see section 4.2.4.3), Honduras, French Guiana, and Paraguay. The lesson from case studies is that countries experience varied reproductive patterns according to socio-demographic factors such as place of residence, education, and ethnicity. For some of these groups particularly, the transition has not yet been completed, even in countries like Venezuela where it is well underway.

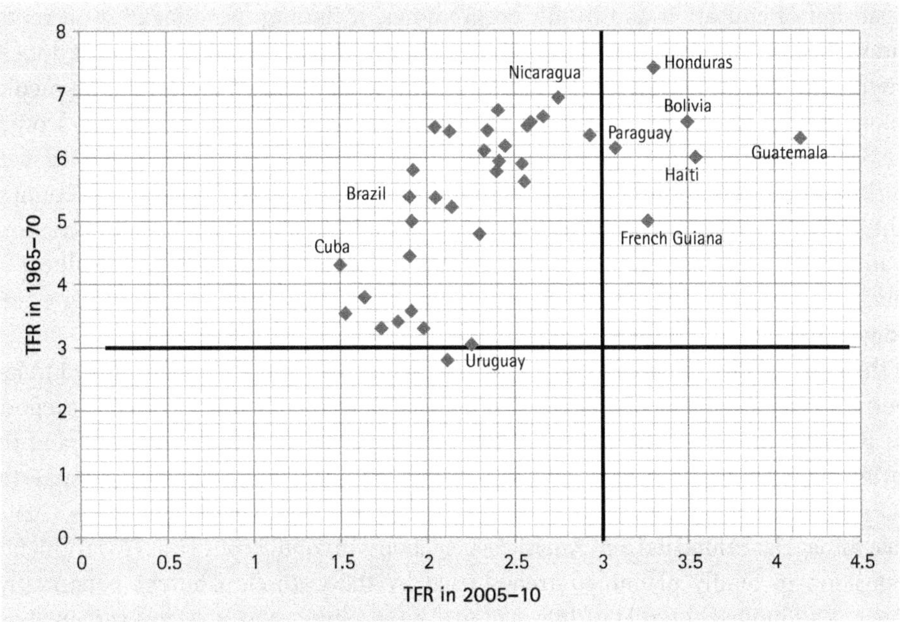

FIGURE 4.3 Total fertility rate (TFR) in 1965–70 vs TFR in 2005–10 (United Nations, 2011).

4.2.4.1 *Guatemala*

According to the most recently available survey data (ENSMI, 2008/09), Guatemala's TFR is 3.6 children per woman. Stalled social and economic development is part of the explanation for the relatively slower decline in Guatemala. The country ranks 131 out of 187 countries on the UN Development Programme Human Development Index (UNDP, 2011) and maintains the second lowest score—after Haiti—in the Latin America and the Caribbean region. Despite being classified as a middle-income country by the World Bank, Guatemala has one of the highest poverty rates and most unequal income distributions in Latin America. The slow pace of fertility decline is not surprising in a country where 51 per cent of the population live in rural areas and 20 per cent have no access to electricity, 31 per cent of adult women and 20 per cent of adult men are illiterate, maternal and infant mortality remain high, and nearly half of all children under five suffer from chronic malnutrition (World Bank, 2011). Large socio-economic differentials are reflected in wide fertility gaps, particularly related to education. The TFR of women with no formal education is 5.2 children compared with 2.3 children among women with secondary education or more.

Guatemala's population of 14 million (United Nations, 2011) is also varied by ethnicity and language. Indigenous Mayans, who belong to 23 different linguistic groups, make up about half of the population. The vast majority of Mayans live in poverty in rural areas, experience high rates of maternal and infant mortality, and have high illiteracy rates. The violence they suffered during the civil war (1960–96), which dominated the second half of the twentieth century, caused extensive societal disruption and halted the expansion of education and health programmes, including those focused on reproductive health. The civil war also sowed distrust towards government-sponsored social programmes, including family planning. About 40 per cent of indigenous women in union use contraception compared with 63.3 per cent of non-indigenous women (ENSMI, 2008/09). The high proportion of indigenous population combined with marked social, economic, and political inequality has resulted in a two-tier country. Ethnic divides are strongly correlated with geographical location and socio-economic stratification. The stratification is also manifest in fertility differentials, with the TFR being 4.5 among Mayans compared with 3.1 among 'ladinos', the Spanish-speaking non-indigenous population (ENSMI, 2008/09).

The high fertility of Guatemala within the context of Latin America is linked to low contraceptive prevalence rates. Fifty-four per cent of women in union use contraception (44 per cent modern contraception), whereas the average in Latin America and the Caribbean region is 72.9 per cent (67 per cent modern contraception). Despite the establishment of a dynamic private family planning association in the mid-1960s, Guatemala still lags far behind its Latin American neighbours in contraceptive use. Governmental opposition to family planning, strengthened by the Catholic Church's conservative stance, also limited the role of international programmes and non-governmental aid organizations in the area of family planning. Guatemala was one of the few nations that did not fully endorse the Plan of Action of the 1994 International Conference on Population and Development in Cairo.

Despite earlier views that considered Guatemala's fertility transition stalled, recent data reveal a steady decline in fertility and a parallel increase in contraceptive use, particularly since the turn of the twenty-first century. Guatemala has increased public social spending since the Peace Accords of 1996, but the country still has a long way to go before its economic and social indicators match those of other comparable countries in the region. Future efforts to eradicate extreme poverty, redress the discrimination and marginalization of indigenous population, and to invest in youth's health and education will be crucial for shaping fertility trends and the well-being of future generations.

4.2.4.2 *Venezuela*

The transition to low fertility in Venezuela—from 5.0 children per woman in 1970 to 2.49 in 2010—has happened mostly through increases in levels of education and women's employment, and delays in the age of cohabitation or marriage. Venezuela's family planning policies were implemented during the transition to democracy after the end of the Pérez Jimenez dictatorship in 1958. However, family planning efforts never became particularly strong after promising efforts in the 1960s. Programmes were restricted to public initiatives and were later embedded in more general health programmes (Parrado, 2000).

Venezuela's rapid economic development and modernization was closely tied to its export- and oil-based economy. Oil nationalization created the wealth that was conducive to fertility reduction, which is not the case for all oil-based economies, as can be seen from the case of Algeria. In the middle of the twentieth century, Venezuela attracted a large number of migrants from Southern Europe (mainly Portugal, Italy, and Spain), which led to the diffusion of smaller family norms and family ideals (Van Roy, 1987).

Even though Venezuela is the most urbanized country in Latin America with more than 93 per cent of the population living in cities (World Bank, 2012), persistent differentials still exist by education and place of residence. While TFR is down to 1.9 in the Capital district, TFR was found to be as high as 4.9 in Delta Amacuro in 2010,[8] where the population is composed of indigenous people called the Warao.

4.2.4.3 *Bolivia*

Bolivia, one of the poorest countries in the region, belongs to the last group of Latin American countries to experience the onset of the fertility transition. According to the latest census (Instituto Nacional de Estadística (INE), 2013), the total population was 10.4 million compared with only 2.7 in 1950. The country currently has one of the highest fertility levels: 3.5 children in 2008. The TFR was above seven children per woman in the first half of the twentieth century and, as opposed to other countries in the region, remained at relatively high levels through the second half of the century. According to the UN (2011), the TFR stayed at five children through the 1990s. It is only in the last decade (2000–10) that Bolivian fertility showed significant signs of a decline.

Although the fertility transition has definitively started in Bolivia, there are no indications that the country will follow the Latin American pattern, especially because of two peculiarities regarding reproductive behaviour in the context of extremely wide socio-economic gaps, consistently high teenage fertility, and low contraceptive prevalence.

The fertility rate of women 15–19 was about 90 per 1,000 women in 2008 compared with 70 at the regional level, having increased from the 2000 value of 85 (ECLAC, 2010). The proportion of adolescents who are mothers among young women with a low formal education is nearly five times higher than that of young women who have received a secondary or higher education, according to data from 1998 and 2003. The same is true when comparing the lowest and highest wealth quintiles. This gap shows no signs of narrowing: in 2008, while the proportion of mothers in the wealthiest quintile was 5.5 per cent, the equivalent proportion among the poorest quintile was 26.6 per cent. The gap according to educational differences was even wider.

The absence of a sustainable fertility decline is also related to the relatively low prevalence of modern contraception. Whereas some neighbouring countries like Brazil show a near 80 per cent prevalence rate in the use of modern contraception methods among married women, the prevalence in Bolivia was 35 per cent in 2003 and in 2008. Once again, the disparities by education and wealth are significant, with twice as many women who use modern contraception among the secondary and higher educated women compared to women with less than secondary education. The same degree of difference is observed among the lowest and highest wealth quintiles. There is no evidence of a narrowing gap in recent years (DHS Bolivia, 2009).

[8] According to the National Statistical Institute (INE, 2011).

4.2.5 Conclusions

The experience of individual countries shows that if the transition to low fertility seems to be the general rule globally, its speed and intensity vary greatly across geographical areas (continents, countries, and subregions), cultural factors (religion, ethnicity), and socio-economic characteristics (such as education, income, and place of residence) at the individual level. Other macro-level factors, such as the political environment (active policy support for family planning) and the economic setting—for instance whether the economy is built on the exploitation of raw materials—are also key in explaining fertility declines.

While these examples document the diversity of fertility trends, they lack a theoretical framework with explanatory power. That framework is the aim of the next section, which will also allow evaluation of the potential future fertility trends in the different countries based on analysis of the current main drivers of change.

4.3 State of the theory explaining past and future trends

4.3.1 Introduction

In the first part of this chapter, we investigate country- and region-specific fertility patterns and trends. Although we identify considerable differences in their stages of demographic transition, within, as well as across, regions, almost all countries have entered at least the early stages of fertility transition. Although the speed of consecutive transition pathways is not known, research has shown that it depends on many factors, including improvements in infant and child mortality, changing norms and values of desired fertility, meeting the unmet need for family planning, further education progress, political reforms, and environmental pressure.

Demographic transition theory was developed to describe the passage of populations from the status of traditional societies where both fertility and mortality rates are high to the status of modern societies where both fertility and mortality rates are low. The model elaborated by Notestein in 1945, based on earlier work by Landry, consists of four stages: (1) equilibrium at high fertility and mortality levels; (2) a phase of rapid population growth as death rates begin to fall because of improvements in living standards, food supply, and health, particularly increasing child survival owing to immunization and better hygiene; (3) a fertility decline that follows the mortality decline, which leads to (4) a stage of quasi-equilibrium between low birth and death rates (Notestein, 1945).

Contrary to the European demographic transition that was long-lasting and accompanied by slow population growth, the transition from high birth and mortality rates to low birth and mortality rates in Asia, Latin America, and African countries only started in the second half of the twentieth century. This transition was more rapid and accompanied by higher growth rates of the population, up to 3–4 per cent per year, and is still underway in most developing countries.

The general trend toward declining fertility rates in the majority of countries is undisputed, and a large number of countries in Asia and Latin America have experienced substantial declines or even reached replacement fertility (Bongaarts, 2008). However, the pace of the fertility decline in many countries in sub-Saharan Africa and South Asia has been slower than expected as socio-economic development, a key driver of fertility decline, stagnated for many decades (Bongaarts and Casterline, 2013; Bulatao and Lee, 1983). In particular, the process of demographic transition in sub-Saharan Africa and periods of stalling fertility are discussed among demographers (Bongaarts, 2006; Schoumaker, 2009; see Box 4.1). Current theoretical and empirical contributions to the field centre around the question of whether we can observe an alternative type of fertility transition in Africa, as compared to transition pathways observed elsewhere (Bongaarts and Casterline, 2013; Caldwell et al., 1992; Moultrie et al., 2012).

The underlying causes of sluggish fertility transitions in Africa are multidimensional. In a number of countries, the unmet needs for contraception are stalled at high levels because family planning programmes received little attention at the beginning of the twenty-first century (Blanc and Tsui, 2005; Cleland et al., 2006; see Box 4.2). However, positive development can be observed; for example Rwanda committed to an extensive expansion of its family planning programmes and educational efforts (Bongaarts and Casterline, 2013; Westoff, 2013), which led to rapid improvement of reproductive health indicators. Acknowledging the consequences of population growth and raising awareness at the national political level seems to be a powerful tool to improve women's and children's health in the long run. Also, following the London Family Planning Summit in 2012, international donor agencies recognized the undersupply of funds for programmes supporting reproductive health and, as a result, new funding schemes are being established.

Nonetheless, from a theoretical perspective, it remains an open question whether conventional demographic transition theory can be applied to countries at the high ends of the current fertility spectrum, and if these countries will ever converge to levels around replacement fertility. In their recent contribution, Bongaarts and Casterline argue that family size ideals in almost all countries in sub-Saharan Africa are higher than in other countries at similar stages of fertility transition in Asia, Latin America, or North Africa. Also, fertility transition is slower than observed elsewhere (Bongaarts and Casterline, 2013). In contrast, fertility in Addis Ababa had already reached below replacement levels at the turn of the twenty-first century (Sibanda et al., 2003). Thus, the variation in demographic indicators, historical and political circumstances—within and across countries, regions, and ethnicities—is notable.

The next section identifies the most important determinants and conditions for further fertility decline across high fertility regions and assesses their relevance for expected future fertility trajectories. We start with a section on stalling fertility, followed by the impact of family size ideals, and matters of reproductive health, female autonomy, economic circumstances, and the impact of policies. Given the importance of education mediating a vast majority of factors relevant for fertility decline, each part will specifically refer to the role of education as a driver of fertility change. The final section will introduce empirical evidence of differential fertility by educational attainment. This review of theoretical and empirical literature created the theoretical basis for designing the questionnaire, which will be introduced in the next section.

Box 4.1 A Focus on Stalling Fertility

Fertility stalls, corresponding to an interruption of the fertility decline before the end of the transition, were, until recently, considered rare (Bongaarts, 2006). In the last 15 years, however, the number of countries experiencing stalls has grown substantially, even though the genuineness of several of these stalls has been debated (Machiyama, 2010; Schoumaker, 2009).

Early literature on this topic described stalls in Costa Rica and South Korea (Gendell, 1989, 1985). More recently, stalls or reversals of fertility declines have been found and analysed in a variety of countries. Bongaarts (2006) identified seven developing countries with stalling fertility in the 1990s, namely Bangladesh, Colombia, Dominican Republic, Ghana, Kenya, Peru, and Turkey. The list of countries with fertility stalls increased quickly in the early 2000s, with new surveys showing interruptions in fertility transitions in sub-Saharan Africa. As of today, as many as 14 sub-Saharan African countries have experienced stalls in fertility transition, although the list of countries varies according to the authors and the methods used to identify stalls (Bongaarts, 2008; Garenne, 2007; Machiyama, 2010; Schoumaker, 2009; Shapiro and Gebreselassie, 2008). Stalls have also been described in Egypt (Eltigani, 2003) and Jordan (Cetorelli and Leone, 2012). In short, stalls no longer appear to be an exception.

Research on the causes of stalls in fertility transitions has focused mainly on the influence of family planning programmes, the role of demand for children (desired family size), and the impact of socio-economic development. Overall, studies on the causes have provided mixed results and, as stated by Moultrie et al., 'no consensus exists about the causes of such stalls' (2008, p. 44).

The role of family planning programmes has received considerable attention and generated diverse findings. Gendell (1985) noted the deterioration of the family planning programme in the late 1970s as a possible cause for the long stall in Costa Rica during that period. Recent studies in sub-Saharan Africa have suggested that shortages of contraceptive supplies (in Kenya, see Westoff and Cross, 2006) and slowdowns of investments in family planning programmes were partly responsible (for Ghana, see Agyei-Mensah, 2007; for Kenya and Tanzania, see Ezeh et al., 2009; Sinding, 2008). In contrast, Bongaarts' study (2006, p. 13) on the causes of stalls in seven countries concluded that there is 'little support for the hypothesis that declining access to contraception is a main cause of stalling fertility'.

The demand for children (desired family size) has been shown to be correlated to fertility stalls in several contexts. Bongaarts (2006) found stalls in decreases of wanted fertility in the seven countries in his study. In one of these countries, Kenya, Westoff and Cross (2006) also showed a reversal in the declining trend of desired family size. In Egypt, Eltigani

(2003) highlighted a stall in desired family size as a possible explanation. However, the reasons for the stalls in desired family size are not, themselves, fully understood. In Kenya, increasing child mortality may have changed fertility preferences and contributed to the stall (Westoff and Cross, 2006). In some countries, desired family size may also be influenced by preferences for sex composition, which contributes to stalls. For instance, Menken et al. (2009) suggest that in Bangladesh the 'desire for at least one child of each sex, especially boys, and a preference for two boys and a girl may have inhibited the fall in fertility'.

Regarding socio-economic development, no clear pattern has emerged from research. In some countries, for example Kenya, stalls in fertility corresponded to levelling off in development as measured by gross domestic product (GDP) per capita, female schooling, and child survival (Bongaarts, 2006). Yet other countries (e.g. Turkey and Bangladesh) have experienced stalls while socio-economic development was proceeding apace (Bongaarts, 2006). In sub-Saharan Africa, Garenne (2007) found mixed results regarding the relationship between fertility and GDP growth in the cases of stalling fertility.

Finally, another possible 'explanation' for the stalls, especially in sub-Saharan Africa, is that they are spurious. This hypothesis was explored in sub-Saharan Africa by Schoumaker (2009) and Machiyama (2010). According to these authors, several of the stalls actually reflect data quality problems (omissions and displacements of births and problems with sampling frames across surveys). The most obvious example is Nigeria, where the stall between the late 1990s and early 2000s is almost certainly due to a substantial underestimation of fertility in the late 1990s.

What do these stalls imply for the future of the fertility transition? In most cases that have been studied, stalls lasted 5–10 years, followed by a renewed fertility decline. Hence, stalls appear as relatively short breaks in the course of the transition, delaying the time when these countries reach low fertility. Given that some countries were advanced in their fertility transition before the stall (their fertility was lower than expected as predicted by their level of development; see Bongaarts, 2006), countries that have experienced fertility stalls are not necessarily late in their transitions compared with other countries. Still, relatively long stalls have been identified in some countries (for Jordan, see Cetorelli and Leone, 2012) and should these stalls last, their impact on population growth could be significant.

4.3.2 Desired family size and ideational change

Early stages of demographic transition are characterized by declining rates of infant and child mortality. Assuming that parents are seeking to optimize their number of surviving children, they adapt to increased survival of their offspring by adjusting the number of live births. This process has been extensively described in most countries that have undergone the transition (Dyson, 2010). Families plan their children sequentially, often only after they have already experienced birth, illness, and death, and have learned about their own fecundity. Women in societies little influenced by family planning through mass media, social workers, or their network of peers often answer the question about their desired family size with 'up to God,' or give unreasonably large numbers of children they consider as optimal. Although researchers have challenged this concept of 'natural' fertility (Mason, 1997) and argued that pre-transitional societies have controlled fertility well before entering the process of industrialization and modernization (Coale and Watkins, 1986), fertility desires remain an important determinant for predicting actual fertility.

The relationships between education, fertility desires, and actual fertility are well documented (Castro Martin, 1995; Castro Martin and Juarez, 1995; Cochrane, 1979; Jejeebhoy, 1995). Women with some, but less than primary, education at the beginning of the demographic transition experience lower rates of foetal mortality and better levels of health in general, and thus show even higher levels of fertility than women with no formal education at all. In contrast, women with at least completed primary schooling incorporate fewer child deaths into their planning and behaviour, and, in addition, consider fewer children as desirable. Educational differences in fertility can be observed throughout the demographic transition and tend to be larger in early rather than in later stages of the transition. An important relationship is that women with higher educational attainment are, on average, better able to exercise family planning and control their fertility (Hayford and Agadjanian, 2012). Unwanted children and education are inversely related (Bongaarts, 2003).

In a transitional society, attitudes toward children change mainly through the import of Western culture through two main vehicles: mass education and the mass media. Caldwell (1982) distinguishes between modernization and Westernization, noting that Westernization may occur before or without modernization. Sri Lanka is an example of a country where fertility and mortality have both experienced substantial declines due to the Westernization of institutions, values, and aspirations without a corresponding degree of economic modernization. The presence of mass education in a country will increase the impact of education in lowering fertility rates. In those countries, even a small amount of education will be associated with a decline in fertility. The introduction of mass education is a sign of a changing society moving toward modernity in the Western sense of the word—an industrial, urban, monetized economy with lower community childbearing norms.

For decades it had been argued that compared to other world regions, women and men in sub-Saharan Africa show unusually high numbers of desired children and exceptionally high levels of actual fertility. Nonetheless, in African countries with still high levels of fertility, women with some degree of education desire fewer children than their uneducated counterparts. To the extent that the process of fertility decline can be regarded as a diffusion of new, progressive ideas and modes of behaviour, the existence of substantial group differences in fertility may be temporary, and without profound theoretical significance. It is hardly surprising that those segments of the population most exposed to new ideas, by reason of their education or geographical location, will form the vanguard of change (Bongaarts, 2011). Thus, theoretical considerations about the determinants of desired family size and their interaction with educational attainment still hold for sub-Saharan countries, even if desired family size has been higher than in Western countries before they entered the fertility transition. These levels could converge to levels higher than replacement fertility.

Modern theories of fertility transition explicitly incorporate the idea of ideational change (Cleland and Wilson, 1987; Lesthaeghe and Surkyn, 1988), and the spread of norms and ideals within and across societies. Cultural factors, family organization, and parents' education are more important for the diffusion of new family ideals than economic well-being and female employment. Beyond investigating micro-level characteristics of women and men, it is important to analyse higher-order characteristics, including peers in the community, regional factors, ethnicity, and country-specific indicators. These higher-order characteristics enhance the predictive power of fertility transitions. Empirically, the challenge is 'to find out whether education at the aggregate level has any effects on a woman's fertility above and beyond that of her own education' (Kravdal, 2000, p. 2). The importance of mass education creates a 'spillover' from other people's education so that, for instance, uneducated women living in an educated society could have different fertility behaviour than uneducated women living in an uneducated society. Hence, the depressing effect of education on fertility could be stronger than individual data on women's education would suggest, through the effect of aggregate education.

In recent years, a large body of empirical research has focused on the transmission of changing norms and ideals. It has been shown that family size norms and ideals tend to spread within and across all societal clusters, and should always be considered when analysing fertility behaviour. Social learning is relevant for contraceptive prevalence (Kohler, 1997); proximity to schools and ethnicity have effects on fertility (Axinn and Barber, 2001); and local, regional, and global interactions affect the global fertility transition (Bongaarts and Watkins, 1996; Kravdal, 2012, 2002, 2000; Moursund and Kravdal, 2003; Rosero-Bixby and Casterline, 1993).

Regarding family planning programmes, mass media are frequently employed for changing attitudes toward contraception. A recent study by Mwaikambo et al. (2011) provides an extensive review of family planning programmes and their success in changing knowledge, use, and attitudes regarding contraception. Employing mass media for information, education, and communication has proven to be a successful strategy of inducing behavioural change towards contraception and 'talk down fertility' (Robinson and Ross, 2007). Since the 1970s, the effectiveness of family planning programmes has greatly improved. Some early family planning programmes were poorly managed and offered few alternatives to sterilization (see India, Nepal, etc.). As a result, together with failing political commitment, many programmes did not succeed initially. Nonetheless, carefully designed programmes appropriately embedded in social settings and respecting cultural frameworks are still considered state-of-the-art measures that can trigger changes in attitudes towards modern means of contraception and bring down actual fertility. A recent study of 40 countries with high fertility indicates that about half of the difference in birth rates across countries can be attributed to family planning efforts. Family planning programmes are most successful in favourable social settings with already decreasing infant mortality rates and improving female education. However, the effects of family planning programmes, education, and infant mortality on fertility weaken in settings outside of sub-Saharan Africa, where fertility rates are, on average, lower (Jain and Ross, 2012).

Concerning the literature on religion's impacts on fertility, three main classical paradigms introduced by Goldscheider (1971) and others are in competition. The first, the 'characteristics approach', denies the existence of a link between religious affiliation and fertility, and assumes that other socio-economic factors, such as education and place of residence, predominantly explain changes in fertility within and across countries. The fertility decline in European countries and Turkey are examples of this approach. This is consistent with the finding that religion loses influence once the fertility of couples is within the calculus of conscious choice (Lynch, 2006). A second paradigm, the 'particularized theology hypothesis', emphasizes the influence of teaching and spread of values related to fertility behaviour for explaining fertility differences (McQuillan, 2004) that remain after controlling for socio-economic factors. It has been shown that religious intensity plays an important role in explaining fertility differences, with highly religious people being more likely to want and have more children than less religious and secular people. The reasons for this go beyond religious teaching to the impact of social networks and social capital (Adsera, 2004; Philipov and Berghammer, 2007). A third paradigm, called the 'minority status hypothesis', emphasizes that communities that are a minority in a country may adopt a particular fertility behaviour (Day, 1984; Goldscheider and Uhlenberg, 1969), as shown by Muslims in India (Kulkarni and Alagarajan, 2005) and the Palestinian territories, or Catholics in Northern Ireland. Given competing hypotheses at play, it remains unknown if, where, and when religions and religious beliefs will play an increasing role in shaping future fertility in high fertility countries.

The range of fertility levels in the set of high fertility countries is huge. Fertility ranges from slightly above or above replacement level to fertility close to 7. While many countries are still in the early stages of fertility transition and struggle with low levels of female education, high infant mortality, and high desired family size, there is a range of countries in all parts of the world, including Peru, Colombia, Morocco, Algeria, India, and the Philippines, that experience levels of fertility less than 3. They are most likely to attain replacement fertility in the next decade, and, as a result, a different set of factors will be important for continuing fertility decline than the drivers in the highest fertility countries. Postponement of parenthood and non-marital childbearing—indicators of the second demographic transition (Lesthaeghe, 1995; van de Kaa, 1987, 2001)—are expected to gain momentum in countries now close to replacement level fertility. Nonetheless, even though fertility has reached low levels in countries like India and the Philippines, cultural components of fertility preferences (such as son preference) and ideals should be considered carefully when predicting further fertility decline.

4.3.3 Health and reproductive health

Davis and Blake (1956) analysed the biological and behavioural dimensions of human fertility. They linked the two dimensions through a set of proximate determinants or intermediate fertility variables. These proximate determinants have a direct influence on fertility. Socio-economic factors and health and nutrition influence the proximate determinants. Education was found to influence controlled fertility through its proximate determinants: marriage, contraception, and induced abortion. This framework was further used and extended by Bongaarts (1980) and Bongaarts and Potter (1983). In a study of eight countries, Bongaarts and Potter found marital fertility to be lowest among better educated women, but with some notable exceptions, for example among women with no education in Kenya and Indonesia. Higher education is associated with later age at marriage and increased contraceptive use in all studied countries.

Since the seminal work of Caldwell (1979) in Nigeria, the relationship of education to infant mortality has been subject to a great deal of research, which has found, in part, that favourable child health outcomes are generally positively correlated with female education (Hobcraft, 1993; Mensch et al., 1985). As a consequence of the negative association of foetal mortality and female education, it had been shown that in selected countries women with some education show higher rates of fertility than women without formal education (Jejeebhoy, 1995). Clearly, living in a wealthier, more developed environment with better health services and improved sanitation increases the chances of child survival. Nonetheless, recent literature shows that education of the mother and women in the community has a stronger effect on infant health outcomes than household income and community wealth (Pamuk et al., 2011). Thus, with increasing proportions of women gaining access to formal education, positive diffusion effects from living in a better educated community can be expected to further boost the speed of mortality decline.

Given the predictive power of infant and child mortality for the fertility transition, it is of particular interest to observe recent developments in this area. A recent study by Rajaratnam et al. (2010) collects data from all available sources on infant and child mortality from 187 countries since the 1970s. The researchers find accelerating rates of mortality decline from 2000 to 2010 compared with the period from 1990 to 2000 for many world regions, including sub-Saharan Africa. Only in countries with high prevalence of HIV/AIDS in Southern Africa (South Africa, Swaziland, and Lesotho) do they find oscillating and even increasing rates of under-five mortality. Countries in Latin America and North Africa show the fastest rates of decrease in the period from 1970 to 2010, while yearly declines have been smaller in South and South East Asia and smallest in sub-Saharan Africa. Comparing the share of neonatal deaths to infant and child deaths worldwide, regions with low child mortality are characterized by a high share of neonatal births out of the total number of child deaths. Only in Africa does the proportion of infant and child deaths caused by pneumonia, malaria, diarrhoea, or other infectious diseases remain above 70 per cent and 62 per cent, respectively, as a proportion of all deaths (Black et al., 2010). Nonetheless, these findings confirm the general trend of decreasing child mortality and, in turn, suggest further reductions in fertility. While countries in Southern Africa are challenged by the HIV/AIDS epidemic, most countries in East and West Africa have experienced steadily decreasing infant and child deaths.

Elements of the proximate determinants of fertility as defined by Bongaarts (1987) are closely linked to marriage patterns in early stages of fertility transition. Demographic transition theory predicts increasing levels of age at marriage. Child marriage (marriage under the age of 18) is associated with an increasing level of mortality and morbidity of children under five, but also leads to high levels of fertility, multiple unwanted pregnancies, higher levels of pregnancy termination, and sterilization (Raj et al., 2009, 2010). These results persist when controlling for socio-economic characteristics. Still, a majority of women who married before the age of 18 receive little-to-no education and live in the poorest households. Empirical evidence shows slowly increasing age at first marriage in many, but not all, high-fertility countries in sub-Saharan Africa (Marston et al., 2009; Westoff, 2003). Age at first marriage remains a valuable indicator leading to further improvements in under-5 mortality and reproductive health.

While the proportion of teenage marriage is consistently declining in Latin America, age at first birth is stable or even declining in some Latin American countries (Colombia and the Dominican Republic). Even though both the availability of contraception and educational attainment have increased, adolescents are now more sexually active (Blanc et al., 2009; Westoff, 2003). In contrast to Latin America, trends in the percentage of unmarried, sexually active females aged 15–19 are down in many countries in sub-Saharan Africa in recent decades (Blanc et al., 2009), although sexual activity is increasing among 15–19 year olds in Ghana, Mali, Nigeria, Ethiopia, and Madagascar. Sexual activity is negatively related to female education, but shows no clear association with male education (Doyle et al., 2012). Contraceptive prevalence has grown faster for adolescents than for older women, but reported method failure discontinuation rates are higher. Women who are sexually active but unmarried are more likely to use contraception than their married counterparts. Still, most adolescent sexually active women are married (Blanc et al., 2009). Through increasing contraceptive use together with lower desired family sizes, today's young cohorts from high fertility backgrounds may well display distinct patterns of contraceptive use and thus fertility behaviour throughout their reproductive careers compared with their mothers' generation. In Latin America, adolescents are freeing themselves from traditional marriage patterns by showing increasing rates of sexual activity and childbearing outside of marriage. In sub-Saharan Africa and Asia, the general pattern is less clear, but many indicators are moving in the same direction.

Research shows that in regions with high prevalence of unmet need (see Box 4.2), high abortion rates prevail (Westoff, 2006). From 1995 to 2003 as unmet need has declined worldwide, abortion rates have therefore fallen. The majority of abortions (55 per cent) are unsafe in developing regions, including 38 per cent in Asia, 94 per cent in Latin America, and 98 per cent in Africa (Sedgh et al., 2007). Highly restrictive abortion laws are generally not connected to low abortion incidence; instead, abortion is practised unsafely. The root cause of abortion is unintended pregnancy, and there is a clear

Box 4.2 A Focus on the Unmet Need for Family Planning

Women with an 'unmet need for contraception' are those who want to avoid pregnancy (at least for the time being), but are not using contraception. These are women at risk of an unintended pregnancy, either mistimed or unwanted.

Although the concept of unmet need is straightforward, measurement is complicated because the concept joins together fertility preferences and contraceptive use; hence, estimates of unmet need are derived by comparing survey responses on preferences and use. Additional challenges are posed by women who are pregnant or amenorrhoeic at the time of the survey. The estimation approach should accommodate these women because unintended pregnancies are the outcome of an unmet contraceptive need. The estimation approach must also allow for the fact that women who are sexually inactive or infecund do not have a contraceptive need. (For detailed discussion of the measurement task and the current approach used by the Demographic and Health Survey (DHS), see Bradley et al., 2012.) Usual practice is to distinguish an unmet need for *limiting* fertility (i.e. absence of contraceptive use among those who wish to have no more children) from an unmet need for *spacing* (i.e. absence of contraceptive use among those who wish to postpone the next birth). The potential impact on fertility of satisfying an unmet need for limiting is probably far larger than the impact of satisfying an unmet need for spacing (Bradley et al., 2012).

The global percentage of currently married women who have unmet need (limiting and spacing), according to recent estimates from the United Nations (UN) (Alkema et al., 2013), was 12.3 per cent in 2010. This is a 3.1 percentage point decline from the estimate of 15.4 per cent for 1990. In 2010, among subregions consisting largely or entirely of countries not yet post-transition, unmet need was lowest in South America (8.9 per cent) and Central America (12.0 per cent), and highest in Eastern, Middle, and Western Africa (26.3 per cent, 26.1 per cent, and 25.9 per cent respectively). Unmet need is far more common in sub-Saharan Africa than in other regions, with more than half of sub-Saharan African countries (28 of 48) having more than a quarter of currently married women with an unmet need. Outside of this region, subregional averages are less than 20.0 per cent. But certain countries in other regions also have a high unmet need, including Afghanistan, Nepal, and Pakistan in Southern Asia (29.5 per cent, 26.3 per cent, and 25.9 per cent respectively), Timor-Leste in South Eastern Asia (29.0 per cent), and Guyana and Haiti in the Caribbean (29.4 per cent and 35.5 per cent respectively). According to the UN estimates, in the period from 1990 to 2010, unmet need declined in all subregions, with the notable exception of Western Africa. As would be expected, variation in rates of unintended fertility follows the same pattern across regions and countries (Singh et al., 2010).

The relatively low levels of unmet need outside of sub-Saharan Africa are the result of substantial decline over the last few decades, as is plainly evident from the UN estimates (Alkema et al., 2013) and from within-country comparisons of successive DHS surveys (Bradley et al., 2012). It is important to appreciate that trends in the prevalence of unmet need are typically not monotonically downward. Instead, unmet need often declines only slightly for an extended period of time, and sometimes increases slightly, before experiencing a steady and marked decline (Bongaarts et al., 2012). The initial resistance to decline occurs where change in fertility preferences—decline in the desired number of children—proceeds as rapidly (or more rapidly) as contraceptive adoption, resulting in an initial stage of fertility transition during which the fraction of women who wish to avoid

(*continued*)

Box 4.2 Continued

pregnancy but are not using contraception remains relatively stable over time, despite an increase in contraceptive prevalence. In fact, DHS surveys reveal that this has been a common pattern in sub-Saharan Africa countries during the last two decades (especially in Western Africa).

Whatever the trends in unmet need, increasing contraceptive prevalence by satisfying unmet need results in fertility decline, *ceteris paribus.* Among the countries with a recent DHS, entirely (and instantaneously) eliminating unmet need for limiting would, hypothetically, reduce fertility (total fertility rate (TFR)) by one-quarter, with the fertility reduction ranging from one-tenth in West and Central Africa, the Middle East, and North Africa to one-third in the Latin American and Caribbean countries (Bradley et al., 2012). These estimated reductions are based on the country-level regression relationship between contraceptive prevalence and the TFR. Alternatively, employing more sophisticated reproductive models, one can project a gradual satisfaction of unmet need and calculate the resulting impact on both the TFR and total population size. Moreland et al. (2010) performed this exercise for the developing world and calculated that satisfaction of unmet need would result in a TFR that, as of 2050, would fall below the UN medium variant projection (TFR = 1.65 if unmet need is satisfied, as against TFR = 2.05 under medium variant), and total population in 2050 that would be about 300 million smaller (5.97 billion if unmet need is satisfied, as against 6.27 billion under the medium variant). That is, meeting unmet need is a more than sufficient means of achieving the UN medium variant projections of fertility and population size. By any calculus, the potential demographic consequences of substantial reduction in unmet need are enormous (Bongaarts et al., 2012; Singh and Darroch, 2012). How to achieve a reduction in unmet need? Improving access to family planning services (preferably low-cost and high-quality) is the most direct programmatic strategy, and there is little doubt that in many settings this has been, or could be, the key (Bongaarts et al., 2012). However, lack of convenient access to quality family planning services is but one of the obstacles to contraceptive use that have been identified through in-depth research on the causes of unmet need (Bongaarts et al., 2012; Casterline and Sinding, 2000). Other major obstacles include:

- Lack of knowledge of modern contraception, of where to obtain supplies, of how to use contraception.
- Belief that contraceptive protection is not required (e.g. low perceived risk of conceiving).
- Health concerns, especially fear of side effects from using contraception, but also fear of infertility.
- Opposition from husbands and other family members.
- Concerns about the social and moral acceptability of practising contraception.

correlation between increasing contraceptive use and declining rates of abortion. Unsafe abortion laws can lead to a high burden of maternal deaths that can be several hundred times higher than if abortion is performed professionally under safe conditions (WHO, 2004). Meeting the unmet need for family planning in high fertility countries will thus potentially lead to lower abortion rates and declining maternal mortality caused by unsafe abortion. In general, maternal mortality has declined substantially from 1980 to 2008 worldwide (Hogan et al., 2010). Factors associated with lower maternal mortality—decreasing fertility, higher income, better sanitary and health conditions, female educational attainment, and higher proportions of skilled birth attendance—have been improving on a global level, albeit region and country-specific variations persist. HIV/AIDS, in particular, is putting pressure on economic development in Southern Africa.

4.3.4 Status of women in family and society

Karen Oppenheim Mason (1987) describes the impact of female autonomy on the supply of and demand for children, as well as on contraceptive uptake. She argues that the societal position of women is affecting all dimensions of reproductive behaviour, including nuptiality, breastfeeding, gender preferences of children, the value and cost of children, and the use of contraception. Many of these factors involved in fertility decisions are closely related to female educational enrolment and attainment. Female education acts as a driver for autonomy and changing fertility decisions. On the supply side of fertility, education is expected to increase women's influence on fertility decisions and decrease the probability of an arranged marriage. Age at marriage tends to be higher for romantically contracted marriages. School enrolment may prevent arranged marriage by altering women's attitudes towards marriage, as well as their desired family size. Furthermore, the size of dowry or other marriage-related expenses is positively associated with female education, so that the age of marriage increases through the need to accumulate sufficient assets.

On the demand side of fertility, female autonomy acts through many different channels. For one, the existence of gender preferences in fertility behaviour is expected to be stronger in societies with lower female autonomy (Das Gupta et al., 2003). Thus, son preference can be an influential driver in raising the desire for another child (Jayaraman et al., 2009). Also, bearing children, and especially sons, is often connected to an improved position of women in family and society. Probably one of the most important factors relates female autonomy to the costs of children. It had been argued that the concept of opportunity costs may not apply to women in the least developed countries because women employed in rural, agricultural jobs often bring along their children or have family childcare available, while domestic servants take care of minors of women employed in modern sector jobs (Mason, 1987). In light of a globally changing environment, rapid rates of urbanization and increasing female educational attainment, this line of argumentation will not necessarily hold for future generations of women in today's highest fertility countries.

Female autonomy and gender equality are associated with a more egalitarian husband–wife relationship. Spousal communication is often limited (Ijadunola et al., 2011), with men preferring shorter birth intervals than women (Gebreselassie and Mishra, 2011). However, women with greater decision autonomy are more likely to discuss family planning with their partners and experience higher rates of contraceptive prevalence (Link, 2011). Many studies have shown that female autonomy and education translate into lower fertility rates (Jejeebhoy, 1995; Moursund and Kravdal, 2003; Saleem and Bobak, 2005). To ensure further improvements in female autonomy and gender equality it will be important to close the gender gap in educational attainment globally.

While education does not automatically guarantee an improved standing of women vis-à-vis their partners and families, it can act as a mediating variable and trigger ideational changes in the society as a whole. Although a little education can make a difference in desired family size and actual fertility outcomes, providing only primary education will not be sufficient for sustainable progress in gender equity (Jeffery and Basu, 1996).

4.3.5 Economic costs and benefits

Through the work of Easterlin and Crimmins (Easterlin, 1975, 1985; Easterlin and Crimmins, 1985), fertility transition and behaviour was placed in a market context, where children enter the model as consumption goods (Schultz, 1997). They single out one subset of proximate determinants having to do with deliberate fertility control variables while de-emphasizing exposure to intercourse, fecundability, duration of post-partum infecundability, spontaneous intrauterine mortality, and sterility. Instead, they emphasize regulation costs and demand and supply, thereby introducing links between modernization and fertility. In their approach, all the determinants are assumed to work through three categories: the demand for children, the supply of children, and the costs of fertility regulation.

Education is recognized by the two authors as the most pervasive factor influencing fertility control behaviour compared with other factors such as rural–urban residence, occupational structure, wives' work status before marriage, innovations in public health and medical care, urbanization, and the introduction of new goods. Education operates on all three of the intervening variables, in the following ways:

(a) *On the supply of children.* Although education increases age at marriage, it also breaks down traditional beliefs (e.g. post-partum and lactational abstinence, as well as customs such as long duration breastfeeding) that increase birth spacing and limit fertility. Education also improves health conditions by diffusing improved knowledge, which lowers child and maternal mortality, and it leads to a higher standard of childcare, with more emphasis on child quality than quantity.

(b) *On the demand for children.* Education shifts preferences away from a large number of children and decreases the price of goods relative to children; it improves the income-earning possibilities of women and thus increases the opportunity cost of the mother's childrearing time; it increases the relative cost of children by reducing the possible contribution of child labour to family income; it decreases the intensity of the desire for children (associated with 'old goods') relative to new goods (new lifestyles put forward by education). It also decreases the preference for sons over daughters.

(c) *On the costs and obstacles to contraceptive use.* Education increases information about various means of fertility control, alters cultural norms opposed to the use of fertility control, and increases spousal communication.

Caldwell's research on 'wealth flows' stresses factors affecting the demand for children (Caldwell, 1982). He argues that fertility decline began when there was a reversal of the net flow of resources from parents to children, rather than from children to parents. This economic change was the result of social changes that concentrate greater family concern on the children. Hence, it is often argued that in the absence of pension systems and social security networks, healthy, surviving children guarantee old age support, and the wealth flow from children to parents would persist. Thus, as long as no pension schemes are implemented, couples would not feel safe limiting their fertility. While there are discussions of whether declining fertility is causing policymakers to establish public pension systems or vice versa (Entwisle and Winegarden, 1984), fertility regimes in Africa differ from developed countries in their kinship systems, social organization, polygyny, child fostering, and related characteristics, such that conventional demographic transition theory may not apply (Lesthaeghe, 1989). Certainly, development of social security networks and pension regimes entails positive effects on old age morbidity and mortality; however, it is not clear whether such reforms are necessary to bring down fertility in the currently high fertility countries.

Since Gary Becker's contributions on the trade-off between quantity and quality of children (Becker, 1991; Becker et al., 1960), the association of the demand for children with respect to income has been an integral part of explaining the shifting demand for children with rising income. While early demographic transition theory focused on the aggregate level of development and modernization, Becker offered a new approach focusing on individual preferences for children. In this approach, the utility function parents seek to maximize depends indirectly on the price of children relative to the price of other commodities. Partly because the costs of having children are less in rural than in urban areas owing to lower costs of food and housing, family sizes in rural areas are larger than in urban areas. As populations become richer and better educated, positive income effects are counteracted by rising opportunity costs of women gaining higher education and working in the labour market, thus raising the relative costs of rearing children. Becker therefore relates declines in fertility to income growth and especially the earning power of women.

Following Becker, economists usually argue that income and the cost of children are the most important factors in shaping future fertility. A related recent contribution hypothesizes that the changing demand for human capital in the course of modernization and technological change has been an important cause of smaller family sizes (Galor, 2011). In addition, globalization is causing high degrees of specialization in the production process, requiring a highly skilled labour force. The production of unskilled goods is outsourced to developing countries, where, as a consequence, incentives to educate the labour force are missing and fertility remains at high levels (Galor, 2011). This market pressure, caused by international division of labour, is a factor typically not accounted for in classical demographic transition theory.

Differences in fertility by income are observed worldwide. While there is a negative association for most developing countries, patterns of U-shaped fertility are observed in several developed countries. As the correlation of educational attainment and income is high in general, it is hard to disentangle the effects. The educational gradient tends to be steeper than the income gradient, and the causal mechanism of positive and negative income effects as drivers of fertility in the course of demographic transition are still disputed. The Princeton Project, which investigated the decline of fertility in Europe, emphasized the role of changing norms and values and diffusion of new ideals rather than income as the most important factors in fertility decline (Coale and Watkins, 1986).

4.3.6 Other factors

Many developing countries are facing rapid and uncontrolled urbanization. Deforestation, droughts, population pressure, education, and poverty are among the causes, compelling individuals' search for a better life away from rural areas. The consequences of urbanization for fertility remain unclear. On the one hand, fertility in urban areas was traditionally connected to lower levels of infant mortality, desired fertility, and actual fertility. Indeed, health outcomes in urban areas, even in poor urban settlements, often indicate improvements owing to upgraded infrastructure, for example water and sanitation (Butala et al., 2010). On the other hand, unplanned migration to urban areas without public infrastructure and any provision of government services will result in subpopulations vulnerable to infectious diseases and extreme climatic events. Accordingly, informal settlements of Nairobi experience higher rates of infant mortality than rural areas (Patel and Burke, 2009). Even when the cost of raising children in urban settings is high and housing scarcity discourages couples from raising children, modern values and ideals may not diffuse rapidly in the poorest socio-economic communities, for example in the shantytowns of Africa. Future impacts of urbanization on fertility will thus depend strongly on political commitment of urban planning and servicing of women and couples migrating to urban settlements. Population policies have also been an important factor in determining fertility (see Box 4.3).

4.3.7 The impact of education in the course of demographic transition: empirical evidence

In the framework of the demographic transition, education received much attention because it was found to increase the likelihood and the pace of the transition through its impact on both fertility and mortality. This is especially true of female education. More educated women are healthier and bear fewer and healthier children than women with

Box 4.3 A Focus on Population Policies

After World War II, government efforts in developing countries were geared at reducing high mortality levels, especially among infants and children. These efforts were initially focused on public hygiene (e.g. sanitation and water adduction), but later evolved into programmes aimed at controlling, and sometimes eradicating, specific diseases (e.g. smallpox). Thereafter, governments launched large immunization campaigns (e.g. against poliomyelitis) with considerable logistical means and funding levels. These programmes helped to improve health outcomes and reduce mortality levels.

The survival of large numbers of people as a result of sanitation and disease control accelerated the rate of demographic growth. In many developing countries, fertility levels were still high and there was no indication that they would decline in the foreseeable future. These demographic trends lasted until the late 1960s and made the need to address the issue of rapid population growth and high fertility, particularly in Asia, more compelling. Several vanguard countries, such as Japan, enacted fertility reduction measures or, in the case of India, initiated broad family planning programmes (India prepared the first formal population policy in 1952[9]). Other countries, mostly in Asia, also launched family planning programmes. International know-how and funding—under what is known as the *Population Movement*—helped to expand these programmes, which became better organized and widespread in developing countries. This heralded the beginning of the worldwide contraceptive revolution, which occurred in most regions with the exception of the least developed countries and, in particular, sub-Saharan Africa. As a result, these countries did not launch organized family planning programmes as had been done in Asia, Latin America, and the Caribbean.

These family planning programmes succeeded in reducing fertility levels by a factor estimated to be between half a child and one and a half children. However, family planning programmes were not successful everywhere. In Pakistan, for instance, efforts to reduce fertility failed initially, whereas similar efforts succeeded in Bangladesh (which was part of Pakistan until 1971). It became clear that family planning programmes per se were not sufficient to trigger fertility declines and needed to be complemented by broader interventions, such as female education and female participation in the labour force. Moreover, policymakers sometimes became frustrated by the lack of progress of family planning programmes, to the extent that they resorted to coercion. This happened in India in 1975–77 during the Emergency period, and when China enacted the one-child policy in 1979. Concomitantly, feminists and women groups led a growing concern about the issue of human rights as a fundamental prerequisite for socio-economic development. This reproductive rights movement gained pre-eminence internationally in the late 1980s and early 1990s.

[9] Population policies are 'actions taken explicitly or implicitly by public authorities, in order to prevent, delay, or address imbalances between demographic changes, on the one hand, and social, economic, and political goals, on the other' (May, 2012). Population policies are implemented through policy levers, i.e. entry points or instruments to implement the policy interventions. Initially, population policies were focused on the reduction of fertility levels, which were deemed to be too high.

(*continued*)

Box 4.3 Continued

The main paradigm shift occurred at the 1994 International Conference on Population and Development in Cairo, Egypt, where an agenda was crafted based on reproductive rights and reproductive health (human rights in the area of reproduction had already been highlighted at the Tehran International Conference of 1968). However, after the Cairo conference, the contraceptive revolution lost its initial momentum (this was caused, in part, by the success of family planning programmes in several countries, which led donors to turn to other priorities). Moreover, family planning suffered from the vagaries of US domestic politics (linked to the debate about abortion), such that family planning became a contentious issue internationally and the USA withdrew funding to the United Nations Population Fund. In the early 1990s, the international community also became concerned with a host of new issues, such as the HIV/AIDS epidemic, good governance, climate change, and the food crisis. As international assistance was redirected to combat the threat of HIV/AIDS, family planning programmes became less adequately funded. In addition, the Millennium Development Goals (MDGs) adopted in 2000 did not include family planning (this was done only in 2005, with the addition of Target 5b to achieve, by 2015, universal access to reproductive health). Today, there are still about 222 million couples in need of family planning services (Singh and Darroch, 2012).

At the July 2012 London Summit on Family Planning, the international community formally pledged to rekindle its efforts in this critical area. To this end, a number of countries, mostly the least developed countries in sub-Saharan Africa, need either to trigger a fertility decline or accelerate their ongoing fertility declines, which have generally been very slow. In this respect, Western and Middle Africa are the subregions where the needs are the greatest. In order to make a difference, voluntary family planning will need to be complemented with far-reaching interventions in the areas of female education, female empowerment and autonomy, and youth employment. Moreover, social norms favouring high fertility levels will also need to change. A major additional challenge will be the coordination of the support—technical and financial—provided on the ground by a host of donors and stakeholders. Finally, the development framework that will replace the MDGs after 2015 will need to highlight the need for expanded access to family planning services, as this remains an unfinished agenda.

To conclude, policy efforts in the area of population and development will need to be pursued consistently and over several decades. The implementation of these policy efforts cannot be accomplished without a strong commitment on the part of the leadership of individual countries. Several sub-Saharan Africa countries have now embarked on broad and organized family planning programmes with some success, as was demonstrated recently in Rwanda. It is only by acting with a sense of urgency that one might hope to reach a stage of sustainable demographic growth in a timeframe of two or three decades.

little or no education. In the previous sections several models have been put forward to explain the factors through which education affects fertility behaviour. The next few paragraphs will summarize recent empirical evidence on fertility differentials by educational attainment, in a regional framework.

Since the 1970s, the commonly held view had been that increasing the education of a population would contribute to fertility decline. This view was consistent with the theory of demographic transition, stating that a steady decline of fertility would take place with increasing levels of socio-economic development. Cochrane (1979) disproved this notion and found an inverted 'U'-shape relationship in several developing countries, challenging the common knowledge of a uniform inverse association between fertility and education. With the advent of the World Fertility Surveys, a largely negative association between education and fertility was confirmed. The strength of this relationship was deemed to be a function of the level of socio-economic development and cultural factors (Castro Martin, 1995).

The influential paper by Castro Martin showed evidence from 26 DHS surveys and emphasized that 'the pattern of association between education and fertility is not static over the course of the demographic transition' and that 'considerable diversity existed in the magnitude of the gap between upper and lower educational strata and in the strength of the association across countries' (Castro Martin, 1995, p. 187). Jejeebhoy (1995) analysed education differentials in fertility using a large set of DHS data and concluded that with higher levels of education, fertility declines. Using 57 DHS data sets Bongaarts (2003) documented empirical education differentials at different phases of the fertility decline, and concluded that educational differentials were marginally larger in countries in the earlier stages of the transition and that they were likely to remain when less developed countries reach the end of their transitions.

The findings presented in this section contribute to the debate and inform the assessment of future fertility by education in different projection scenarios. Unlike the case of low fertility countries (see Chapter 3), we assess education-specific fertility looking at period-specific fertility rates. Completed fertility has the advantage of overcoming problems caused by tempo distortions as more educated women tend to postpone childbearing, but in dynamically changing societies it is beneficial to capture recent trends. Owing to often huge differences between educational attainments of women of fertile age compared with women with completed fertility, we focus on period fertility rates, as completed fertility may show outdated magnitudes of education differentials in childbearing. Owing to increasing education, women with at least secondary education are becoming a less selective group compared with 20 years ago.

The DHSs are a unique source of detailed fertility data for many high fertility countries. We used the two most recent waves of the survey carried out in the late 1990s and 2000s, or the most recent survey only for the countries that did not have more than one survey after 1995, to reassess fertility differentials by education attainment. We have thoroughly harmonized education to correspond to the definition of six categories used in the WIC projections (see Chapter 9.1 for the definition of the categories): no education (no formal schooling), incomplete primary (International Standard Classification of Education (ISCED) level 1 not completed), completed primary (ISCED 1), lower secondary (ISCED 2), upper secondary (ISCED 3), and post-secondary (ISCED 4, 5, or 6). Chapter 9 contains a more detailed look at the effort to arrive to comparable education categories. In 26 out of 54 samples for sub-Saharan African countries with very low educational attainments of women and small samples of post-secondary educated women, it was necessary to aggregate upper secondary and post-secondary into a single category.

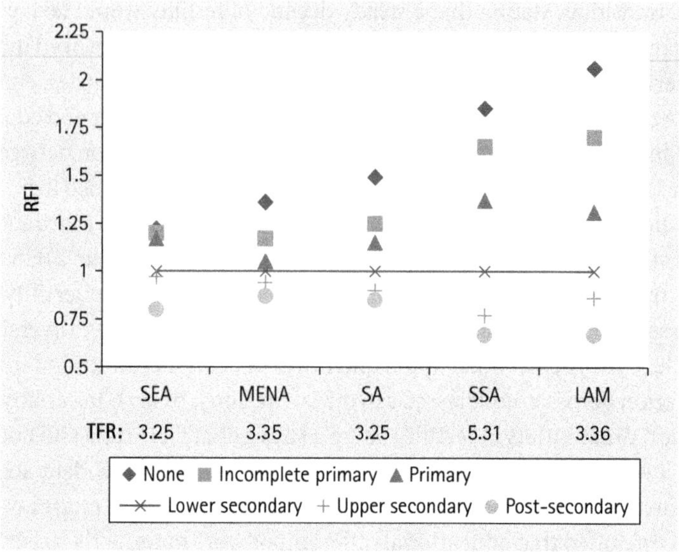

FIGURE 4.4 Relative fertility index (RFI) by levels of education and region. SEA: South East Asia; MENA: Middle East and North Africa; SA: Southern Africa; SSA: sub-Saharan Africa; LAM: Latin America; TFR: total fertility rate.

We have computed education-specific TFRs for 58 countries (94 samples). High fertility countries differ largely in terms of their fertility levels and stage in demographic transitions. Therefore, we focus on relative fertility differentials rather than education-specific TFRs. Relative fertility indexes (RFI), used to analyse fertility differentials by education, are presented by using the group of women with lower-secondary education (ISCED 2) as a reference category.

The results shown in Figure 4.4 highlight considerable heterogeneity across TFR levels and differentials by education categories. However, some empirical regularity can be isolated. For instance, we find the usual negative relationship between TFR and female education, without crossovers in the education categories. We find that RFI tend to be more pronounced in countries that are in the middle of the demographic and education transition, as best illustrated by Latin America. The differential tends to narrow only when TFR drops below four children per woman. This pattern is caused by increased education of women and the known depressing effect of higher education on family size. In countries where most women have very little education and only very few achieve post-secondary level, the differential is pronounced, but it is still narrower than in countries where more women have at least completed upper secondary education (KC and Potančoková, 2013). This demonstrates that highly educated women are the trendsetters in preference for smaller families.

4.3.8 Conclusions

The theoretical and empirical literature on the main drivers shaping future fertility suggests many factors that will potentially play a role in further fertility decline in today's high fertility countries. While differences are important, all countries and regions will sooner or later pass through the process of demographic transition. How fast they do so, how long they remain in each stage, and whether there will be major disruptions will also depend on unpredictable shocks such as extreme climatic events, political instability, and wars. The expert survey reported in the next section offers country-specific perspectives on future fertility declines. The arguments in this IIASA–Oxford survey include main elements from the literature discussed here. From analysing the experts' predictions about major drivers of fertility decline and their numerical estimates of future fertility levels, we create scenarios for projecting the demographic future of countries from a high fertility background.

4.4 Results from the questionnaire

4.4.1 Introduction

The high fertility module (HFM) was sent in summer 2011 as part of questionnaires on all demographic determinants to members of the International Union for the Scientific Study of Population, the Population Association of America, and other professional organizations. The module sought to collect information on numerical estimates of expected fertility transition, as well as to identify the main underlying drivers of fertility transition within a list of potential known factors, for countries classified as having high fertility. The complete list of countries within this categorization can be found in Chapter 3, Appendix 3.2.

In a first step, respondents were presented for their self-selected country of expertise the baseline fertility estimates for the period from 2005 to 2010, published by the UN (United Nations, 2011), and asked to provide estimates for TFR in 2030 and 2050, respectively, as well as an 80 per cent uncertainty interval range. These estimates informed the fertility scenarios, which will be outlined in the next section. In a second step, respondents were asked to assess the impact and validity of a sample of qualitative statements referring to expected drivers of fertility decline. Finally, respondents were given the opportunity to alter their numerical estimates for 2030 and 2050. The respondents could name other countries for which their numerical and qualitative estimates were also valid and could provide comments on the questionnaire or individual questions.

This section begins with an introduction to the IIASA–Oxford survey design, followed by a description of the survey respondents. We then present and analyse the qualitative statements on expected fertility decline and show the results from the questionnaire. The last part focuses on education-related outcomes from the respondents.

4.4.2 Survey design

The HFM was embedded in a global survey on the future of fertility, mortality, and migration. A description of the overall questionnaire design can be found in Chapter 2.

This section provides a short description of the survey structure and indicators used to describe the results.

Each module of the survey consists of a number of *arguments*, clustered in *forces*. These arguments are centred on drivers of fertility decline for the countries in the HFM, as identified in the literature review, and are organized within five *forces*:

- cultural change
- health and child survival
- status of women
- economic costs and benefits
- reproductive health.

The *arguments*, clustered in *forces* standing for a broader theme, aim to capture the majority of factors/drivers influencing expected fertility transition in the future. The drivers, acting through improvements in reproductive health, child survival, ideational change, and economic factors are formulated in a neutral fashion. In contrast to the low fertility module, the *arguments* mostly point to the direction of declining fertility. Although there are arguably countries where fertility is stalling or increasing slightly, there is broad scientific consensus that demographic transition is underway, even in the highest fertility regions of Africa (see section 4.2.1). Within the long-term horizon of our projection period, all countries and subregions would enter fertility transition and converge to lower levels of fertility. The formulation of the questions is neutral, for example the argument 'More women will decide to stay unmarried', does not refer to the consequences for fertility, nor make a value judgement on the outcome of such a development. In total, 30 *arguments* were selected for the high fertility questionnaire and grouped within five forces.

For each *argument*, respondents were asked to gauge its expected future likelihood, or *validity*, and its *impact* pertaining to the year 2050. These are defined and interpreted as follows.

1. Validity, ranging from 0 to 1, refers to the likelihood that an argument will be true. Respondents were asked to select from five predefined responses; each response was labelled with an attached validity score. By clicking on one of the responses, the box was visually highlighted. An example is illustrated as follows:

Module: High fertility countries

Force: Economic costs and benefits

Argument: The participation of women in the labour force will increase

Based on your knowledge of the empirical evidence and the validity of the reasoning involved, and with reference to the selected country and the period up to 2050, do you think the above argument is:

Very likely to be wrong (0.0)	More wrong than right (0.25)	Ambivalent (0.5)	More right than wrong (0.75)	Very likely to be right (1.0)

2. Impact, sometimes also called *conditional impact,* represents the hypothetical influence on fertility if the above stated argument was true. The predefined values ranged from –1 (strong negative effect on fertility) to 1 (strong positive effect on fertility).

Regardless of your answer above, if the above argument were completely true, what effect would this have on future levels of cohort fertility in *country?*

Strongly decreasing (–1)	Moderately decreasing (0.5)	None (0)	Moderately increasing (0.5)	Strongly increasing (1)

3. Finally, validity and impact were combined by multiplication to yield the *(mean) net impact.* Even though the likelihood score (*validity*) and *conditional impact* are interesting results as such, the interpretation of the argument might change dramatically when merging the indicators. Depending on the framing of the question and the country considered, an argument could 'very likely be right', but at the same time have no expected effect on fertility. The resulting value was presented to the respondents and they were allowed to alter the value by repositioning the slider on a bar ranging from –1 to +1. About ten per cent of respondents altered their initial judgements.[10]

Based on your answers, we have calculated the overall net impact on future cohort fertility on a range from –1 to +1 (resulting from a multiplication of the weights in parentheses, hence this is not in units of cohort fertility, but a standardized weight of impact relative to other arguments). You may adjust this overall impact if you wish.

All indicators (mean likelihood, mean conditional impact, and mean net impact) were calculated for each argument, as well as for selected regions and countries. All summary measures were calculated as simple means, without applying population weights. Given the unequal distribution of population sizes across our set of high fertility numbers, responses for a small number of countries would have disproportionately dominated the overall results.

Aggregate arguments scores represent the sum of net impacts for all 30 arguments by each respondent. The *combined net impact* summarizes the net impact across selected arguments, countries, or regions. Again, the values are combined by summation and created for separate arguments, forces, or regions. Numerical estimates for 2030 and 2050 were calculated using population weights within each region.

The next sections present the results from the experts' assessment. We start with a description of the respondent's background characteristics, then proceed with results

[10] A number of respondents reported that they had difficulties moving the slider on the horizontal bar. Other respondents misunderstood the handling and meaning of the slider and set all the values to 0. For these reasons the adjusted net impact was replaced by the calculated values (validity times conditional impact) if values were missing or faulty.

from their qualitative statements. Finally, numerical expectations for 2030 and 2050 will be presented across regions and selected countries. A full description of the arguments, as well as the numerical estimates can be found in Appendix 4.1.

4.4.3 Demographic characteristics of experts

Altogether, 140 experts completed the high fertility questionnaire that was sent to members of professional organizations in 2011.[11] Most experts provided an assessment for one high fertility country, while two experts answered for two countries. The respondents were allowed to provide information that could be compiled into a demographic profile. The typical respondent was male, 42 years old, and working in academia. Sixty-nine per cent were men; 31 per cent were women. Most experts were employed in academia (56 per cent), 11 per cent worked in international non-governmental organizations (NGOs; Population Reference Bureau, Africa Population Health Research Center, Futures Group, Population Council, etc.), and the remaining 33 per cent were distributed equally between national NGOs, governments, and think tanks. There were three experts below the age of 25, with a majority (22.6 per cent) aged 35–45. The oldest expert was 76 years old at the time of the survey.

4.4.3.1 *Countries of analysis*

Most experts filled out the questionnaire for south-central Asian countries (Figure 4.5). India, with 37 experts, leads the ranking of countries analysed. While there are only 28 experts from India, 9 experts originating from outside India (mostly from the USA) filled out the questionnaire on India. Twelve more experts filled the questionnaire on Nepal, twelve on Bangladesh and Pakistan, and one each on Afghanistan, Bhutan, the Maldives, and Sri Lanka. South East Asia is quite well covered with 14 experts on Indonesia, Malaysia, the Philippines, and Vietnam.

In Africa, we received 16 expert judgements for 8 distinct countries in Eastern Africa: Ethiopia, Kenya, Malawi, Mozambique, Rwanda, Tanzania, Uganda, and Zambia. Most respondents on Western Africa are experts on Ghana (12) and Nigeria (7), and fewer responded for Burkina Faso, Mali, Niger, and Senegal. Out of seven experts on Northern Africa, five are on Egypt, and one each on Sudan and Morocco. The coverage on Southern Africa (4) is poor, with only two experts completing the questionnaire on South Africa, one on Lesotho, and one on Botswana.

The Latin American and Caribbean region where few countries with a high fertility remain is under-represented, as only eight experts filled the questionnaire: Haiti (1), Panama (1), Bolivia (1), Ecuador (1), Peru (1), Suriname (2), and Venezuela (2). Similarly, there was only one expert for Oceania (Papua New Guinea). These regions are not represented by a large enough number of experts to derive statistically reliable conclusions.

[11] About 15 per cent of respondents did not supply their demographic characteristics. The percentages presented here are based on the total of all available information within each subcategory.

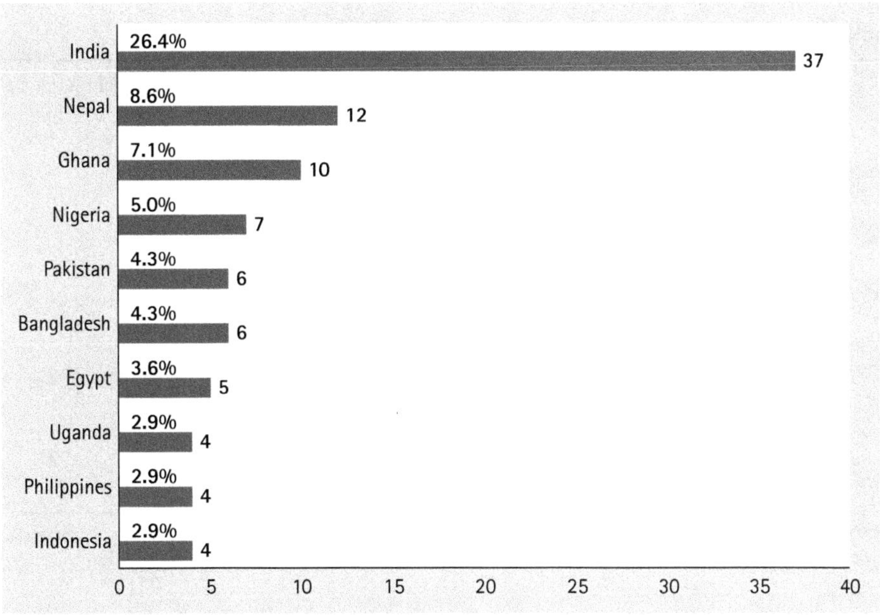

FIGURE 4.5 Number (and share) of experts for the top countries of analysis.

4.4.4 Forces

Before analysing the results in more detail, Table 4.1 summarizes the main findings across forces. 'Mean weight' describes the weight of each force relative to the other forces. The sum of mean weights across clusters is 1. Even though the experts evaluated the force 'Economic cost and benefit' as the most powerful driver for shaping future fertility (0.24), the overall difference in terms of weight between the different forces is small, with the 'health and child survival' and 'reproductive health' forces scoring lowest, relative to the other forces (0.17). All forces seemed of equal importance to the experts, even when investigating regions separately.

Averaging the expert likelihood scores across countries, the resulting mean likelihood score is presented here. It can be interpreted as the predicted 'degree of truth', or how likely it is that the suggested statement will come true. For high fertility countries, the experts valued arguments in the second force, 'Health and child survival', as most likely to come true, whereas this force was evaluated lowest in the relative importance across clusters. Experts believing in improvements in health and child survival (most arguments were formulated positively), regardless of rapidly decreasing fertility, would be an extreme interpretation of the phenomenon. The lowest likelihood score was attributed to the 'reproductive health' force, which also results in the lowest 'conditional impact on fertility'.

On the contrary, the 'conditional impact on fertility' is highest for the force related to the 'status of women in family and society'. Thus, experts expect changes in female status

Table 4.1 Main Findings Across Forces

Force	Mean weight of force	Likelihood score	Conditional impact on fertility	Net impact on fertility
1. Cultural change in ideal family size (cultural)	0.19	0.64	-0.35	-0.22
2. Health and child survival (health)	0.17	0.80	-0.39	-0.28
3. Status of women in family and society (status)	0.22	0.78	-0.47	-0.32
4. Economic cost and benefit (cost)	0.24	0.76	-0.41	-0.28
5. Reproductive health (RP health)	0.17	0.57	-0.30	-0.22

to have potentially the strongest depressing effects on fertility. Multiplying the 'likelihood score' with the 'conditional impact' on fertility yields the 'net impact on fertility'. Hence, by generating the product of the likelihood of an event with its impact, we derive a combined measure of expected changes in fertility, weighted by its expected chances to come true. The 'net impact' on fertility shows that the status of women is thought to have the largest depressing effect on fertility.

Overall, the different scores calculated for the forces reinforce the first impression that the experts tend to think that no one force could be responsible for a decline in fertility, but rather a balanced mixture of all forces, with one force emerging occasionally as slightly more important, but not substantially so. That is why it is interesting to identify a general trend in the expert's evaluations and more informative to investigate individual argument scores rather than summary measures across forces. Single arguments within forces could drive average net impact scores up or down, even if the other arguments show strong overall effects. This is discussed in the next section.

4.4.5 Analysis of likelihood scores

Table 4.2 displays the arguments resulting in the highest and lowest likelihood scores, independent of the expected net impact on fertility shown in Figure 4.6. For the experts, these statements are very likely to come true (or most likely to be wrong), regardless of their effect on fertility. Most arguments were phrased positively, meaning that the general indicators of development, health, supply of contraceptives, and so on, would improve. As a consequence, there are few arguments with low likelihood scores.

The experts seem to agree with the theory developed in Section 4.3 about the main drivers of fertility decline in developing countries: female education, urbanization, and

Table 4.2 Details About the Five Arguments Most Likely to be Right and Most Likely to be Wrong

Force	Argument	Likelihood score	Conditional impact on fertility	Net impact on fertility	Mean weight of force
Most likely to be right					
Status	Female educational enrolment rates will increase	0.91	-0.58	-0.45	0.22
Cost	The cost of raising children in urban settings will increase	0.88	-0.55	-0.41	0.24
Cost	Parents put increasing value on good education of their children	0.88	-0.52	-0.38	0.24
Status	Age at first marriage will continue to increase	0.87	-0.55	-0.40	0.22
Health	Parents will expect that most of their children survive to adulthood	0.86	-0.38	-0.29	0.17
Most likely to be wrong					
Status	More women will decide to stay unmarried	0.56	-0.36	-0.19	0.22
Cultural	Childlessness will become socially acceptable	0.52	-0.35	-0.15	0.19
Reproductive (RP) health	Traditional methods of family planning will remain/become widespread	0.42	-0.13	-0.09	0.17
Cultural	Religions and religious beliefs will become more important for fertility decisions	0.34	0.02	-0.01	0.19
RP health	Modern contraception will be banned for religious, political, or other reasons	0.14	0.18	-0.01	0.17

the costs of raising children. The experts assigned the highest likelihood to the argument 'female educational enrolment rates will increase'. A second argument, connected to the force on female status in family and society, 'The age at first marriage will continue to increase', is among the top five arguments most likely to be right. Also top ranked are two arguments relating to economic cost and benefit. These arguments state that the cost of raising children in urban settings will increase, and parents put increasing value on good education of their children. There is a strong belief among experts that education not only plays a major role in further developments, but also that governments will be committed to further invest and improve educational systems.

Further arguments with high likelihood scores are linked to health, including birth spacing, decreasing infant mortality, and improved access to sanitation and health care. There is little disagreement on the positive development of health-related factors. With regard to reproductive health, experts are convinced that the availability of modern family planning services will significantly increase and do not foresee a ban on modern contraception for religious, political, or other reasons.

There is some disagreement relating to cultural factors. Most experts have positive expectations for the further adoption of modern contraceptives and increased autonomy of couples in fertility decisions. Also, relatively few experts believe that religions and religious beliefs will become more important for those making fertility decisions (0.34). Nonetheless, the disagreement with the statement is not as strong as for banning modern contraceptives. The value lies between 'more likely to be wrong than right' and 'ambivalent'.

4.4.6 Analysis of net impact scores

The next sections of this chapter show global results, as well as results for sub-Saharan Africa and south-central Asia. The majority of respondents (114) picked a country within these regions. Thus, owing to the low number of respondents, we do not specifically refer to countries outside of these two regions. Figure 4.6 displays the net impact scores of all arguments across forces for all countries. Results for south-central Asia and sub-Saharan Africa are labelled with markers.

As discussed earlier, as fertility is expected to decline, most phrases were framed positively, such that net impact scores for all arguments across all countries were negative, implying fertility decline. The experts expect effects to be larger for countries in sub-Saharan Africa than for regions in south-central Asia, because starting values of fertility are higher in Africa. In fact, as shown in Figure 4.6, almost all net impact scores were larger in sub-Saharan Africa than in south-central Asia. However, in 4 of the 30 arguments in the questionnaire, the expected net impact on fertility was larger in the Asian than in the African subregion. The argument on 'son preference' is particularly interesting: although the effects were expected to have a significant impact on fertility decline in both regions, the effect in south-central Asia was particularly large, relative to the other arguments. In contrast, the argument was not ranked very highly in comparison with the other arguments in sub-Saharan Africa.

Not surprisingly and consistent with the high likelihood shown in the previous section, Figure 4.6 shows that three out of five arguments with the strongest depressing impact on fertility belong to the third force, related to the status and autonomy of women. Increasing female educational enrolment is ranked first (HF3-2), and increasing age at first marriage (HF3-4) and the participation of women in the labour force (HF3-5) are ranked fourth and fifth respectively. Arguments related to women's status with the lowest net impact on fertility are arranged marriage (HF3-1) and an increasing share of unmarried women (HF3-6). Bearing in mind that arranged marriage is still an important factor in nuptiality, especially in South Asia, other forces are considered more important for immediate changes in fertility behaviour.

Furthermore, the arguments on the cost of raising children in urban settings (HF4-4) belong to the set of most important drivers of fertility decline. Urbanization as driver of fertility decline is at the root of modern demographic transition theory, and the experts identify it as a driving factor for fertility transition in our high fertility sub-sample. The arguments relating to female employment (HF4-3) and the closing gender gap in educational enrolment (HF4-5) were also assigned high net impact scores. As mentioned earlier, the belief in establishing public pension funds and social security systems is weak (HF4-1). The experts do not expect large impacts of decreasing prevalence of child labour on fertility behaviour.

Almost uniformly, experts worldwide think that improving access to family planning services (HF5-1) is one of the most important drivers of fertility decline. Rather than switching from modern means of contraception to traditional methods to escape potential side effects, the experts expect the development and distribution of modern contraceptives without side effects.

The experts are strongly convinced that individualism will gain momentum and thus decisions about family size will increasingly be made by couples themselves, with less pressure from members of the extended family or the community (HF1-1). The argument with the largest expected impact on fertility, however, refers to diminishing negative attitudes towards contraception (HF1-5). Given current high educational differentials in desired family size, argument HF1-7 relates to a decreasing educational gradient as demographic transition progresses. The experts rank this argument third in its expected likelihood and net impact on fertility across all arguments on changing family size ideals.

The resulting scores from the health cluster are relatively homogenous. While the experts assign the smallest likelihood to a lower percentage of teenage pregnancies (HF2-1), the lowest net impact on fertility is expected to result from improved access to health care and sanitation for mothers and their children (HF2-2). The highest net impact on fertility is expected to arise from increasing birth intervals (HF2-4).

The two least important factors for fertility decline are, as already identified in the likelihood ratings, religions and religious beliefs for fertility decisions (HF1-2), and banning modern contraception for religious or other reasons (HF5-5). Even though the experts assign a positive conditional impact to these arguments, the overall net impact is negligible.

Two arguments related to economic cost and benefits are ranked among the arguments with the weakest impact on shaping future fertility. They are declining prevalence of child labour (HF4-6), and pension funds and social security systems replacing family support in old age (HF4-1). Neither of those factors is expected to have significant impact on fertility. The experts assign low likelihoods, as well as low conditional impacts, to both arguments. This result is remarkable, for while the experts strongly believe in

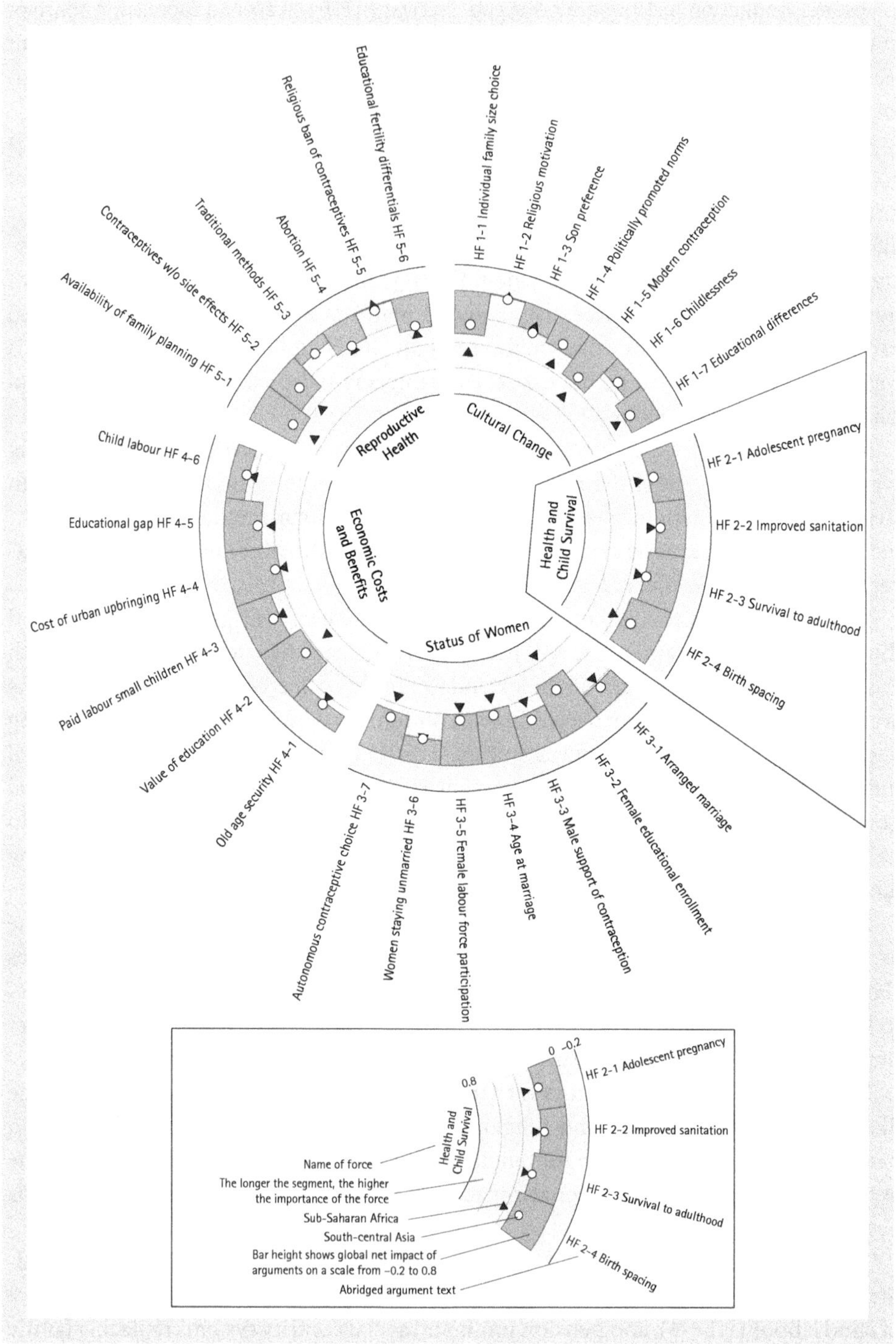

FIGURE 4.6 Global mean net impact and region-specific impact for sub-Saharan Africa and south-central Asia for all arguments about future fertility in high fertility countries.

further improvements of educational systems, female autonomy, and improving supply and acceptance of modern contraceptives, there is little belief in changing policies against child labour or policies establishing social security systems. Even if there was a significant likelihood of changing systems, the experts assign relatively low impact on fertility to the arguments.

4.4.7 Regional differences

Given the current high levels of fertility, compared to most countries outside of these two regions, the countries find themselves at very different stages of demographic transition. As a result, expected fertility declines might be caused by distinct mechanisms that vary regionally. Tables 4.3 and 4.4 list the arguments with highest net impact on fertility in and outside sub-Saharan Africa. The average level of net impact scores is lowest in sub-Saharan Africa. Assuming a negative relationship between net impact scores and the expected fertility decline in Africa, the experts thus predict larger decreases of fertility in sub-Saharan Africa than in the other high fertility countries by 2050. This is consistent with demographic transition theory, which holds that higher rates of decrease are expected at earlier stages of fertility transition than in later phases.

In sub-Saharan Africa, two out of three highest ranked arguments concern education. Experts are confident about subsequent improvements in female enrolment and parents' educational investment in their offspring. These measures are expected to have strong impacts on future fertility. The argument on increasing availability of modern contraception also shows up consistently atop rankings by country or region. The experts have strong beliefs in future investments and government commitment in satisfying the unmet need for family planning. Easing the access and improving the supply of modern contraception tops the agenda of many development agencies (see, e.g., Bill & Melinda Gates Foundation).

Interestingly, the experts assigned the argument on increasing costs of raising children in urban settings the largest net impact score. Further increasing rates of urbanization in many Asian countries (i.e. Bangladesh, India) put pressure on governments with regards to urban planning, with rapidly growing mega-cities leading to housing shortages and growing urban slums. It can be argued that sub-Saharan African countries are not yet at this stage of development. While Africa is also experiencing rapid rates of urbanization, industrialization and educational systems are far more developed in Asia and certainly Latin America countries.

Outside of sub-Saharan countries, the experts assign the second largest weight to the depressing effect of increasing female labour participation on fertility. It has been shown that women employed in poorly paid agricultural work are often able to bring along their children, and that the positive income effect of female employment outweighs the negative effect of higher opportunity costs. In contrast, for women in the

Table 4.3 The Arguments with Highest Net Impact on Fertility in Sub-Saharan Africa (SSA)

Force	Argument	Net impact on fertility	Likelihood score	Conditional impact on fertility
Status	Female educational enrolment rates will increase	−0.65	0.92	−0.74
Cost	Parents put increasing value on good education of their children	−0.53	0.88	−0.63
Reproductive (RP) health	The availability of modern family planning services will significantly increase	−0.52	0.82	−0.67
Cultural	Negative attitudes towards modern methods of contraception will diminish	−0.50	0.83	−0.63
Status	Age at first marriage will continue to increase	−0.49	0.85	−0.61
Cultural	Family size decisions will increasingly be made by couples themselves rather than surrounding networks	−0.47	0.81	−0.60
Status	Women will increasingly be able to decide on their own about using contraceptives	−0.45	0.82	−0.59
Status	Participation of women in the labour force will increase	−0.45	0.85	−0.58
Cost	The cost of raising children in urban settings will increase	−0.44	0.85	−0.59
RP health	Convenient contraceptives without side effects will become broadly available	−0.43	0.78	−0.61
Health	Mothers will increasingly see the benefits of birth spacing	−0.40	0.82	−0.50
Status	Male partners will become more supportive of modern contraceptive use	−0.38	0.79	−0.53
Cost	The gap in access to education of boys and girls will be removed	−0.38	0.78	−0.48
Cultural	The government will take leadership in promoting the idea of small family size	−0.34	0.67	−0.53
Health	Parents will expect that most of their children survive to adulthood	−0.33	0.83	−0.45

Health	Adolescent pregnancy will become less frequent	−0.33	0.69	−0.44
Cultural	Educational differentials in desired family size will diminish	−0.32	0.65	−0.48
Cost	Mothers will increasingly return to paid employment even when their children are small	−0.30	0.75	−0.43
RP health	Educational differentials in actual fertility will diminish	−0.30	0.59	−0.49
Health	There will be increasing access to improved sanitation and health care for mothers and children	−0.28	0.82	−0.35
RP health	Abortion (whether legal or illegal) will be more widely practised than today	−0.23	0.58	−0.39
Status	Marriage arranged by parents or relatives will lose ground	−0.23	0.84	−0.29
Status	More women will decide to stay unmarried	−0.19	0.59	−0.26
Cost	The prevalence of child labour will decline	−0.18	0.73	−0.28
Cost	Pension funds and social security systems will replace family support in old age	−0.18	0.54	−0.30
Cultural	The traditional preference for boys will eventually disappear	−0.15	0.58	−0.23
Cultural	Childlessness will become socially acceptable	−0.12	0.41	−0.30
RP health	Traditional methods of family planning will remain/ become widespread	−0.08	0.39	−0.09
Cultural	Religions and religious beliefs will become more important for fertility decisions	0.00	0.30	0.05
RP health	Modern contraception will be banned for religious, political, or other reasons	0.01	0.13	0.22

Table 4.4 The Arguments with Highest Impact on Fertility Outside of Sub-Saharan Africa (SSA)

Force	Argument	Net impact on fertility	Likelihood score	Conditional impact on fertility
Cost	The cost of raising children in urban settings will increase	−0.40	0.90	−0.54
Status	Participation of women in the labour force will increase	−0.37	0.86	−0.51
Reproductive (RP) health	The availability of modern family planning services will significantly increase	−0.37	0.82	−0.53
Status	Age at first marriage will continue to increase	−0.37	0.88	−0.52
Status	Female educational enrolment rates will increase	−0.36	0.91	−0.50
Cost	Parents put increasing value on good education of their children	−0.32	0.88	−0.46
Cultural	Negative attitudes towards modern methods of contraception will diminish	−0.31	0.81	−0.45
Health	Mothers will increasingly see the benefits of birth spacing	−0.31	0.84	−0.46
Status	Women will increasingly be able to decide on their own about using contraceptives	−0.30	0.75	−0.47
Cost	Mothers will increasingly return to paid employment even when their children are small	−0.28	0.75	−0.42
Cultural	Family size decisions will increasingly be made by couples themselves rather than surrounding networks	−0.27	0.81	−0.40
RP health	Convenient contraceptives without side effects will become broadly available	−0.27	0.76	−0.40
Health	Parents will expect that most of their children survive to adulthood	−0.27	0.87	−0.35
Cost	The gap in access to education of boys and girls will be removed	−0.27	0.79	−0.40

Status	Male partners will become more supportive of modern contraceptive use	-0.26	0.77	-0.44
RP health	Educational differentials in actual fertility will diminish	-0.25	0.69	-0.41
Cultural	Educational differentials in desired family size will diminish	-0.22	0.71	-0.36
Health	There will be increasing access to improved sanitation and health care for mothers and children	-0.22	0.83	-0.35
Health	Adolescent pregnancy will become less frequent	-0.22	0.70	-0.31
Cultural	The traditional preference for boys will eventually disappear	-0.21	0.64	-0.35
RP health	Abortion (whether legal or illegal) will be more widely practised than today	-0.20	0.61	-0.38
Status	More women will decide to stay unmarried	-0.19	0.55	-0.41
Cultural	The government will take leadership in promoting the idea of small family size	-0.18	0.66	-0.33
Cultural	Childlessness will become socially acceptable	-0.17	0.57	-0.38
Status	Marriage arranged by parents or relatives will lose ground	-0.17	0.68	-0.30
Cost	The prevalence of child labour will decline	-0.13	0.69	-0.23
Cost	Pension funds and social security systems will replace family support in old age	-0.13	0.58	-0.25
RP health	Traditional methods of family planning will remain/become widespread	-0.09	0.44	-0.16
RP health	Modern contraception will be banned for religious, political, or other reasons	-0.02	0.14	0.16
Cultural	Religions and religious beliefs will become more important for fertility decisions	-0.01	0.36	0.01

industrial sector, rising opportunity costs dominate the income effect, and increasing proportions of women in the labour force have depressing effects on aggregate fertility.

However, even with differences in the ranking of arguments across countries and regions, there is a high degree of homogeneity in the experts' judgement of relevant determinants of future fertility. The magnitude of expected future changes in fertility vary by the level of current fertility, with experts predicting larger negative effects on fertility for still very high fertility countries, and smaller decreases for countries in the middle of demographic transition. Apart from the several questions on the impact of religious beliefs on family size norms and banning modern contraception, all arguments were considered more or less relevant for shaping future fertility. The experts, almost uniformly, believe in the path suggested by demographic transition theory. Accordingly, there is no reason to assume on this basis that sub-Saharan Africa will enter or remain in a phase of stalling fertility. Expected improvements in health, female autonomy, norms, and values, and their impact on fertility were largest in this region.

4.4.8 Numerical estimates

This section assesses the numerical estimates of fertility levels predicted by the experts.[12] Given the current level of fertility, the experts were asked to provide a prediction for 2030 and 2050 for their country of choice. Figure 4.7 shows population-weighted numerical predictions of the TFR in 2030 and 2050 for all experts. Data for 2010 represent UN 2010 period estimates for 2005–10.

Across all countries in the expert sample in sub-Saharan Africa, experts predict average fertility to decline from 5.2 in 2005–10 to 3.8 in 2030. By 2050 they expect the TFR to reach a value of 3.2.

Owing to the high population weight of India, the numerical predictions in south-central Asia are biased towards the Indian experts. By 2050, fertility is expected to fall from a TFR of 2.9, by almost one child, to 2.0. While we observe a large range of fertility outcomes (Afghanistan 2005–10: 6.3; Maldives 2005–10: 1.8) in the base year, all experts expect fertility to drop significantly, including in today's highest fertility countries (Afghanistan 2030: 4; 2050: 1.9). Detailed estimates for all countries can be found in Appendix II.

India is by far the most populous country in the subsample of high fertility countries. Its development is crucial to world population growth. After dropping unreasonable responses[13] from the numerical estimates, 30 experts remain for India. The mean value

[12] This section exclusively deals with *point* estimates derived from the high fertility questionnaires. Minima and maxima were discarded because of technical problems reported by respondents using the Internet Explorer browser.

[13] See footnote 9.

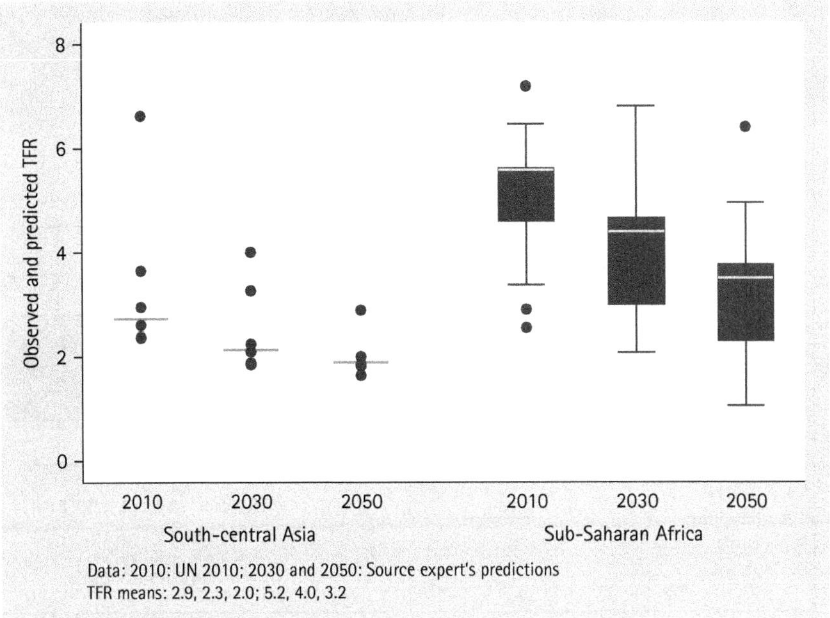

FIGURE 4.7 Population weighted numerical predictions of total fertility rate (TFR) in 2030 and 2050 for all experts, and 2010 estimated TFR, south-central Asia and sub-Saharan Africa. UN: United Nations.

of TFR predicted for 2030 and 2050 is 2.1 and 1.9 respectively. However, Figure 4.8a shows that the experts' opinions on India's future are quite widely distributed. The values for 2030 range from 1.5 to 2.5 in 2030, and 1.05 to 2.45 in 2050.

While Ghana cannot be compared to India in its contribution to world population growth, it is the country with the largest number of expert predictions in sub-Saharan Africa ($n = 10$ after cleaning). Experts for Ghana provide a wide range of estimates, with the minimum and maximum estimates varying importantly (see Figure 4.8b). The numerical estimates from India and Ghana underline the necessity of having large enough expert samples for using expert predictions in the assumption-making process. Country-specific predictions originating from a small number of source experts should be evaluated with a higher degree of uncertainty when making fertility scenarios compared to countries with many experts.

Even though we only show a selected subset of numerical predictions, the general tendency is clear: there is little-to-no disagreement about the downward trend of fertility. With few exceptions, the experts predict fertility to decline—to a higher degree in still very high fertility regions (sub-Saharan Africa), and to a smaller degree in regions that are further along in the process of demographic transition (Latin America). The experts, on average, follow the stereotypical descent of a country in fertility transition. While there are more pessimistic experts for several countries in sub-Saharan Africa

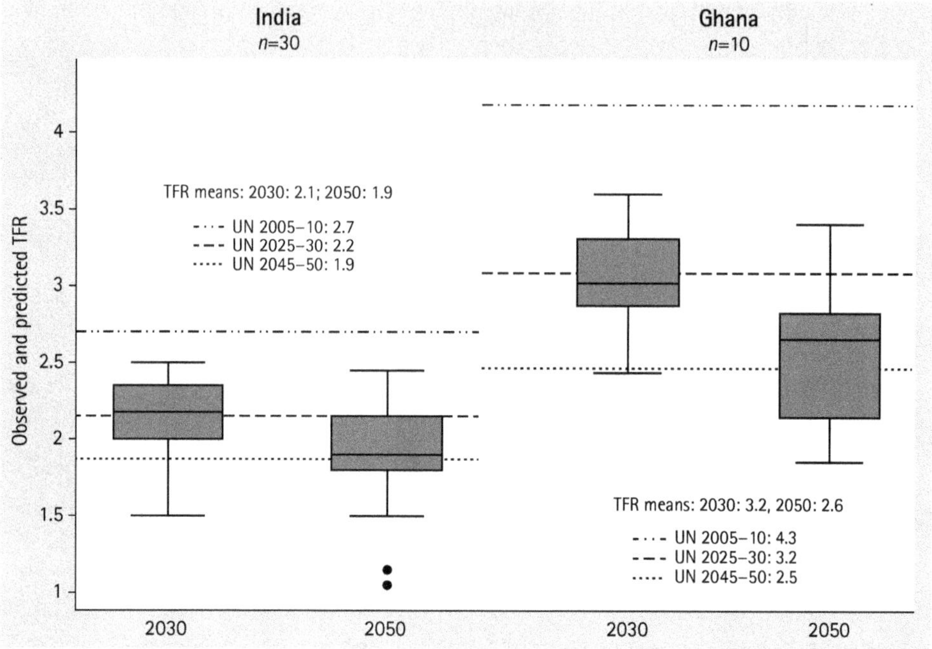

FIGURE 4.8(a, b) Numerical estimates by experts for 2030 and 2050, Ghana and India. TFR: total fertility rate; UN: United Nations.

(see Burkina Faso, Mozambique, and Niger) than for others (see Ethiopia, Ghana, and Senegal), the number of experts predicting relatively slow/fast fertility decline is too small to automatically assume slow descents for a given country or region.

4.5 High fertility assumptions

4.5.1 Introduction

Policymakers, NGOs, and the informed public make frequent use of future population scenarios produced by demographers. Conventional methods of projecting future trajectories are based upon the judgements of few experts, sometimes supported by time series, logistic regressions, and other models. The WIC projections are an attempt to overcome the limitations of standard assumption-making by soliciting the views of a large number of experts and then having a group of meta-experts reflect on the questionnaire results, and combining those expert opinions with a theoretical model, as well as data on country-specific historical fertility declines. This section discusses the assumption-making process for countries in today's high fertility world.

4.5.2 Results from the meta-expert meeting

The meta-expert meeting on high fertility took place in Dhulikhel, Nepal, 7–9 November 2011.[14] After considering results of the expert questionnaire, the meta-experts held a general discussion to identify the most important drivers of fertility. They designed high and low fertility storylines for three major regions (Africa, Asia, the Middle East and North Africa; see Box 4.4). Assuming a pessimistic or optimistic level of development, these storylines picture potential fertility outcomes in the respective regions. After creating the storylines, the experts discussed country-specific fertility futures.

4.5.2.1 *Main drivers of fertility and country-specific meta-expertise*

While the expansion of education could be the main driver of fertility decline in many countries (as seen in Singapore and South Korea) and a necessary condition for changing fertility norms and behaviours, the experts argued that it might not be sufficient under certain fertility regimes and given other socio-economic conditions. While many sub-Saharan countries have promoted education, especially educating girls and women (Ethiopia, Ghana), variation in the quality of education remains large. Furthermore, it has been shown that education does not necessarily (as in Nigeria) lead to upward mobility. Despite ambitious education policies in such countries as Kenya, economic development is lagging behind, resulting in high levels of unemployment. In Egypt, despite the increasing education of younger cohorts, unemployment is high and the share of women participating in the labour force remains low. In India, education-specific fertility rates declined uniformly in the past; however, more recently, the most rapid decline has been occurring among the poorly educated, whose fertility is converging to the level of their highly educated counterparts. Pakistan is following the trend of India, with further declines in fertility expected as Pakistan continues its substantial increase in education investments. In South Asia, despite a declining quality of education and decelerating economic growth in the Philippines, overall labour force participation by women is relatively high compared with women in India or Pakistan. As a result, it is likely that fertility will further decrease in Indonesia and the Philippines. Similarly to Egypt or Kenya, economic progress is not proceeding at the same pace as improvements in education, and labour markets cannot fully absorb young, well-educated cohorts. Nonetheless, fertility ideals seem to continue decreasing, in spite of, or even because of, economic uncertainty.

Political commitment is a crucial factor in demographic transition and fertility decline (e.g. contraceptive prevalence and programme efforts in Bangladesh). Such

[14] Experts attending the meeting were Mohammad-Jalal Abbasi-Shavazi, Australian National University; Youssef Courbage, Institute National d'Etudes Démographiques; K.S. James, Institute for Social and Economic Change, Bangalore; Gavin Jones, Asia Research Institute, National University of Singapore; John F. May, World Bank; Vinod Mishra, UN Population Division; and Bruno Schoumaker, Université Catholique de Louvain. The meeting was moderated by five researchers from the Wittgenstein Centre: Bill Butz, Regina Fuchs, Anne Goujon, Samir KC, and Wolfgang Lutz.

commitment will be a key element, especially in sub-Saharan Africa where accelerated fertility decline could be foreseen, if governments and international organizations commit more resources to family planning programmes. In the case of Rwanda, Ethiopia, and Madagascar, contraceptive prevalence rates have increased recently as a consequence of political efforts. In contrast, in the Western African countries of Nigeria, Niger, Senegal, Chad, and Mali, political commitment to family planning is weak and, as a result, contraceptive prevalence and infant/child mortality are high. In the high fertility regions of Nigeria, contraceptive prevalence rates are extremely low and only increasing very slowly. The same is true of other indicators such as infant and child mortality rates, which suggests that fertility is not going to experience a major decline in the foreseeable future, given the lack of support from governments in the region for family planning and/or socio-economic development. While important steps were made to bring down infant and child mortality in Niger, the recurrence of a food crisis could counter the current efforts to reduce the infant and child mortality rates.

Ghana serves as a positive role model for West Africa, having experienced income growth and fertility decline in the last decade. Its fertility rate is expected to decline more rapidly than in most other countries in the region. However, the fertility decline and related family planning efforts in Ghana have relied, to a certain extent, on abortion more than adoption of contraception. In Ghana, as well as in many other African countries, patterns of contraceptive use are disconnected from fertility behaviour, as large proportions of men are living abroad and women are therefore not exposed to pregnancy.

Political commitment in East Africa is framed by opposites. In Ethiopia there is serious commitment to family planning, and many volunteers promote contraception across the country. The reverse is true in Uganda, where the current leadership is pushing pro-natalist policies that experts expect will slow the fertility decline that has been underway. The situation in Egypt is ambiguous, with pro-natalist attitudes prevalent among the population and the authorities. The importance of the Muslim Brotherhood could impede progress in fertility decline as the organization is one of the providers of social services and encourages early marriage and large families.

Many states of India, including the most fertile (Uttar Pradesh, Bihar, and Punjab), have low fertility in urban areas (1.3 children in Calcutta) and show strong declines that point to further declines in many states where fertility is still high. Although political commitment to family planning is strong, norms and marriage patterns change slowly, and it is unlikely that fertility will fall below 2.0 children in India in the near future. Even in Bangladesh where family planning programmes are very strong, there are still large pockets of high fertility in slums and in some remote places with few services. Other indicators, such as age at first marriage (very low) and abortion rates (very high), could also have an inhibiting impact on further rapid fertility decline. Thus, uncertainty is larger in India because the country could either go down the East Asian road of rapid fertility decline or else pursue a different path. Publicity for family planning has been very active and successful in Nepal, similar to programmes carried out in Bangladesh. However, improvements in reproductive health are lagging behind the family planning efforts as shown by infant and child mortality indicators. Also, the single mean age at marriage is still very low (about 18 years). In nearby Pakistan, levels of education and contraceptive prevalence are low and, unlike in Nepal, there is little support for family planning.

In Indonesia, signs seem to point to a decline in fertility rather than a further stall or increase. Increasing postponement of fertility, decreasing rates of breastfeeding, increasing divorce rates, and a rising share of the better educated are underway. Nonetheless, religiosity is high and people have conservative views about family, contrasting with high labour force participation by women. Hence, there are reasons to believe that Indonesia will follow the Indian example of fertility decline. In the Philippines there is strong political will to bring fertility down, and the traditional impact of religiosity on fertility is weakening. Still, there are high rates of unmet needs in the women's health field, and the supply of contraceptives is unsatisfactory. Given the political commitment in the Philippines, however, fertility is likely to decrease even further.

The importance of politically motivated fertility, especially in the Middle East, should not be underestimated, as shown in Syria, Palestine, and Israel, and potentially in Egypt, Algeria, and Tunisia. Rather than stopping fertility decline, so-called 'war fertility' is most likely to slow it down. For example, the main obstacles to a fast decline in Nigeria are related to a widespread practice of regional fertility behaviours that are connected to ethnic and religious differences that maintain high fertility. Also, Yemen is divided politically, regionally, and ethnically, and is one of the few countries where consanguinity (or kinship) increased across generations. The commitment to progress toward lowering fertility seems very low at the societal and governmental level.

Outmigration of an active labour force is an important factor in the Philippines, as there are large migration streams to Western Asia and Europe. In Nepal, internal and international migration plays a role in fertility and should be kept in mind in any analysis of fertility rates. The dominant trait of demographic change in recent years had been streams of people moving out of the hills and mountains to live in the valleys and plains. For those migrating out of Nepal, the movement has been predominantly to the Gulf states and India. Remittances are very high and account for a quarter of the gross domestic product. Urbanization rates have been steadily increasing (currently above 55 per cent) and urban fertility is very low, with a TFR of 1.6. The situation is comparable to Ethiopia, where population pressure on the highlands pushes urbanization and constrains fertility. In Ethiopia's urban settings, fertility is already below replacement level. The pressures from a growing population can also be observed in Egypt, where the country faces acute shortages of both land and water. However, Egypt has managed to increase arable land in the desert along the Nile River. Despite the trends in Egypt, however, the role of population pressures should not be overestimated in their importance for fertility decline. Countries like Java, Bangladesh, and North Vietnam face population pressures similar to Egypt, yet have been successful at reducing fertility rates.

Having identified education, overall political commitment, and politically motivated fertility programmes as key forces in further fertility decline, researchers must also consider other norms, values, and events when analysing fertility. Among these are ethnic diversity, kinship systems, globalization, national and international conflicts, population pressure, poverty, economic development, and investments in health. While demographic transition follows similar patterns across world regions, most countries in Asia find themselves at levels of fertility very different from the majority of countries in sub-Saharan Africa. With few exceptions, demographic transition in South Asia is well ahead of economic development in sub-Saharan Africa, especially West Africa. Kinship systems, strong preferences for large families, HIV/AIDS, weak governments, and ethnic conflicts are some of the factors that explain differences in fertility and the speed of fertility decline within and across these two regions. The following sections sketch potential demographic futures with low and high fertility, respectively, for Asia, MENA, and sub-Saharan Africa.

4.5.3 Fertility scenarios: data and methods

Our assumption-making process consists of a three-stage modelling approach. First, we estimate a model using a country's level and decrease of fertility during the last five-year period. Second, we estimate the expected decrease of fertility, employing information gathered in the questionnaire. And third, numerical point estimates, supplied by the experts, are utilized to estimate future fertility decline. Combining information from three different sources, from qualitatively very different sets of data, we are able to provide a new set of fertility assumptions to feed into the WIC projections.

4.5.3.1 *Model 1: historical analogy*

While countries experience fertility declines at many different paces, patterns of fertility decline had been generalized extensively in the demographic transition literature (Dyson, 2010; Kirk, 1996). In early stages of fertility transition, owing to improvements in child mortality, patterns of breastfeeding, improvements in fecundity, and other factors, fertility tends to increase moderately before couples anticipate the increasing health and survival of their offspring. Women with higher average education generally act as forerunners, as formal schooling pushes advancements in female and child health, and new norms regarding family size emerge. The early stage of fertility transition is followed by a period of rapid fertility decline, which tends to slow before fertility reaches replacement level. Exploring historical data broadly confirms this over-simplified description of phases in fertility transition. However, variation across countries in the original level of fertility, the speed of transition, and the duration of stay in each phase of transition, is enormous. Country-specific characteristics determine patterns in demographic transition, including political commitment to family planning, changes in educational systems, economic performance, fertility preferences, female autonomy, gender equity, old age security, and kinship systems. Nonetheless, cross-country similarities dominate cross-country variation, so it is advantageous to learn from the past experiences of countries that have already gone through demographic transition.

Box 4.4 Storylines for World Regions by Meta-experts

Asia

High Fertility Storyline: Cultural/familial/gender norms remain unchanged, with the norm of low age at marriage persisting, and divorce and remarriage remaining largely unacceptable. The desired number of children remains high, and access to family planning information and services remain stagnant. Pro-natalist religious/ethnic ideologies persist. Religious and political leaders play an essential role in preserving traditional societal regimes. Female education and labour force participation stagnate, as well as improvements in health care and child survival.

Low Fertility Storyline: The region witnesses rapid changes in cultural, familial, and gender norms. Values are in place that include marriage choice, individualism, and gender empowerment. Provision of safe, effective, affordable, and acceptable methods of family planning becomes universal. Secularization and decline in religiosity weakens pro-natalist attitudes and reduces the influence of religious and political leaders. Universal secondary education for females and rapid increase in opportunities for gainful employment empowers women to participate fully in the economy. Health care expands rapidly, and child survival increases significantly.

Middle East and North Africa

High Fertility Storyline: The increasing influence of cultural and political minorities slows the process of fertility decline. This trend is exacerbated by religious–political agendas, explicit or hidden. Slowing international migration to the Western world and/or increasing migration to more conservative settings slow the pace of fertility decline. Oil-based economies reduce the individual costs of having children and thus maintain higher levels of fertility.

Low Fertility Storyline: Increasing educational levels, particularly for women, combined with increasing urbanization, raises the status of women, the cost of children, and the desirability and necessity of having jobs prior to marriage and childbearing. Simultaneous globalization leads to ideational change, including smaller family size. International migration to modern countries accelerates this process.

Africa

High Fertility Storyline: Progress in education is slow and there is little spill over from high to low socio-economic strata. There is no progress in gender inequity. Weak governance and social conflicts result in slow health improvements and little progress in delivery and access to family planning services. Governments do not commit to fertility reduction. Inevitable globalization and the negative consequences of population growth mean there is less available land. The result is the slow onset of fertility decline in most of the densely populated areas.

Low Fertility Storyline: Strong political efforts raise education and increase social mobility. The impact of education increases and leads to further fertility reduction. Sex education becomes part of the school curriculum and adolescent pregnancies become rare. Women become increasingly autonomous. Governments are fully committed to reducing family size, and the countries witness rapid improvements in the provision of health and family planning services. Awareness is raised through media campaigns advocating for small families, as well as public debates, and advertisements for condoms and contraceptive use. The secondary effects of AIDS campaigns that urge condom use and 'safe sex' thinking lead to an increasing use of contraceptives. Strong interaction with the more developed world, including international migration, reinforces and spreads ideational change.

Employing past levels and decreases of fertility across countries, we developed a model of historical analogy. The overarching idea can be summarized as follows: take a country's level and decrease of fertility in the past five-year interval and compare it to all countries that have undergone similar levels and decreases of fertility in the period since 1970. As greater access to and adoption of modern means of contraception, as well as family planning programmes, were limited across many world regions in the period before 1970 (Freedman and Berelson, 1976), we disregard earlier records. We are aware of the argument that the world today, with its political systems, mortality and morbidity influenced by HIV/AIDS, globalization, and the emergence of family planning, cannot be compared to circumstances in 1970. Utilizing information across a time-horizon of 40 years might not be the optimal way to learn from past experience; however, we decided in favour of drawing from a larger set of countries going through a similar process as compared to shortening the time-horizon or even dropping historical observations.

Historical time series were taken from UN World Population Prospects, 2010 (UN, 2011). Employing total fertility estimates for five-year intervals, we generated percentage changes in fertility decline for adjacent periods. The predicted percentage change of fertility for country *i1* in projection period t_1 can be described as the median percentage decrease of all countries *j*, in any period *s*.

$$\%\Delta TFR_{i1,t1} = \frac{TFR_{i1,t1} - TFR_{i1,t1-1}}{TFR_{i1,t1-1}} = Median\left(\frac{TFR_{j,s} - TFR_{j,s-1}}{TFR_{j,s-1}}\right)$$

$$\forall j \neq i1, j = 1,\ldots,n, s = 1,\ldots,n$$

$$s.t. 0.9 \times TFR_{i1,t1-1,} > TFR_{j,s} < 1.1 \times TFR_{i1,t1-1},$$

$$\%\Delta TFR_{i1,t1-1} - 0.05 > \left(\frac{TFR_{j,s-1} - TFR_{j,s-2}}{TFR_{j,s-2}}\right) < \%\Delta TFR_{i1,t1-1} + 0.05$$

$$where$$

$$j = Afghanistan, Albania, \ldots, Zimbabwe =$$
$$= all\ countries\ where\ UN\ POP\ provides\ historical\ estimates,$$
$$s = (1970-1975), (1975-1980), \ldots, (2005-2010)$$
$$i1 = Afghanistan,\ i2 = Algeria, \ldots,\ in = Zimbabwe$$
$$== set\ of\ high\ fertility\ countries$$

$$t1 = (2010-2015), t2 = (2015-2020), \ldots, tn = (2095-2100)$$

The first constraint guarantees that a country's predicted decrease of fertility is exclusively compared to countries that have experienced a similar level of fertility (± 10 per cent) at any period *s*. The second constraint refers to considering only countries that were exposed to comparable decreases in fertility (± 5 percentage points) in period *s*. By restricting the set of countries used for predictions to a subset of countries with a similar level and decrease of fertility, we hoped to achieve a sufficiently high degree of commonalities relative to countries from which we 'borrowed' percentage fertility decrease. Defining the interval of ± 10 per cent of a country's fertility level was chosen after comparing current fertility estimates of different sources (UN vs Population Reference Bureau 2010). Differences in 2010 account for an average of 7 per cent across our set of high fertility countries and can be as high as 54 per cent (for Western Sahara). Choosing ±5 percentage points for the second constraint in comparing past percentage decrease arose as a trade-off between ensuring a sufficiently large number of countries to borrow from, and a constraint strict enough to be binding. In the first projection period, the average number of countries for estimating fertility decline in each country is almost 83. By 2100 the number drops to 23. If a country fulfilled both constraints in several periods, we took the mean decrease across periods to avoid over-representation of individual countries. The prediction is repeated stepwise for each period until 2100.

4.5.3.2 *Model 2: questionnaire results*

Having received 140 responses to the HFM in the expert questionnaire, we developed a model that translates responses from arguments to respective changes in fertility. Respondents were invited to evaluate the arguments toward 2050. As described in Chapter 3, responses from the experts are weighted by their validity and summed to an aggregate argument score for each expert. Experts were also asked to provide numerical estimates for their country of choice in 2030 and 2050. The construction of the arguments allows the drawing of a positive association between the expected decrease in fertility and the value of the aggregate argument score. In other words, the lower the aggregate argument score (AGGSCORE), the stronger the expected decrease in fertility.

For modelling the expected relative decrease in fertility, we calculated the median response across experts p within each country i. Countries with multiple experts entered the regression with a weight w, which represents the number of experts available in the respective country. The regression was estimated using the 'analytic' weights function STATA 12, where the variance was assumed to be σ^2/w_i, meaning that the weight is inversely related to the variance of the ith observation. Using the 'analytic' weights function is a common method to overcome heteroskedastic errors.[15]

We formulated the following model:

$$\%\Delta \boldsymbol{TFR} = \beta_1 \times \boldsymbol{AGGSCORE} + \varepsilon$$
$$\textit{where } AGGSCORE = median\ (AGGSCORE_p)$$

The resulting β_1(0.15(0.009)) (see Figure 4.9) can be interpreted as the average predicted relative change in fertility from 2010 to 2050. By applying the regression coefficient β_1, we calculated the predicted percentage change in TFR, using the median aggregate argument score for each country. It would be desirable to estimate this regression separately

[15] Further details can be found here: <http://www.stata.com/support/faqs/stat/crc36.html> (accessed 3 January 2014).

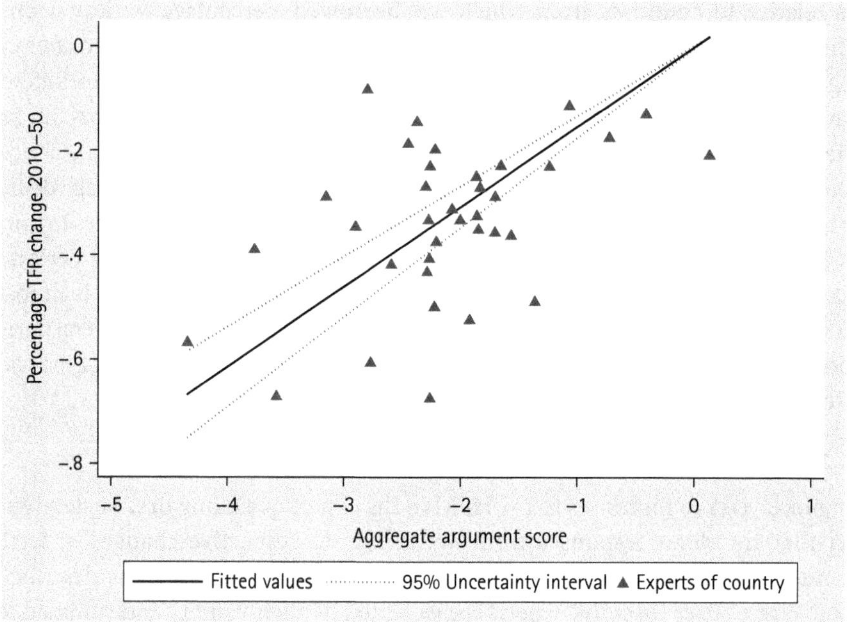

FIGURE 4.9 Predicted percentage change in total fertility rate (TFR), 2010–50, $\%\Delta TFR =$ 0.150.009 × AGGSCORE; adjusted R2 = 0.87.

for countries, starting at higher levels of fertility in 2010, compared to countries already close to replacement level. However, owing to the relatively small number of countries (37), it was not possible to run the regression for smaller subsets of data.

Finally, we decomposed the predicted change in TFR from 2010 to 2050 in compound rates of decrease, yielding eight five-year rates of change r for each country i.

$$TFR_{2010} \times \hat{\beta}_{1i} = TFR_{2050,\ experts}$$
$$\hat{\beta}_{1i} = (1+r_i)^8$$

4.5.3.3 *Model 3: meta-expertise*

During the meeting with meta-experts in Dhulikhel, Nepal, we not only gained further insights into the most important drivers of fertility across world regions, but also formulated numerical estimates of fertility for 14 countries in 2030 and 2050 (Bangladesh, Egypt, Ethiopia, Ghana, India, Indonesia, Nepal, Niger, Nigeria, Pakistan, Philippines, South Africa, Uganda, and Yemen). Unlike the model from the experts, we calculated two rates of decrease, one from 2010 to 2030 (r_1) and another from 2030 to 2050 (r_2).

$$TFR_{2010} \times (1+r_{1i})^4 = TFR_{2030,meta-experts}$$
$$TFR_{2030,meta-experts} \times (1+r_{2i})^4 = TFR_{2050,meta-experts}$$

4.5.4 Combining the models

In a final step, we developed a method of combining estimated fertility decreases of all three models. While the model of historical analogy can be implemented in all countries in the cluster of high fertility countries, we estimated rates of fertility change for 37 countries from the expert questionnaire model, and another 14 trajectories from the meta-expert model (the models partially overlap). Thus, for countries where we did not have an expert model, we applied only the model of historical analogy. The following weighting scheme yielded a percentage change in fertility for five-year periods from 2010 to 2050.

	Historical analogy %ΔTFR_1	Expert model %ΔTFR_2	Meta-expert model %ΔTFR_3
	α_1	α_2	α_3
Relative Weight	1	1	0.2 × # of experts

For each projection period, we first calculated model 1, weighted the percentage decline with results from models 2 and 3, and then deducted the weighted percentage change from TFR_{t-1}.

$$TFR_t = TFR_{t-1} + \alpha_1\%\Delta TFR_1 + \alpha_2\%\Delta TFR_2 + \alpha_3\%\Delta TFR_3$$
$$\alpha_1 + \alpha_2 + \alpha_3 = 1$$

This process was repeated for all *t* until 2045–50. After 2050, only model 1 applied. If a country's fertility reached 1.6 or below in the period 2010–2100, the model estimates were replaced by linear convergence towards 1.75 in 2200. If a country did not yield ≤1.6 by 2100, we implied linear convergence to 1.75, starting in the period 2100–05. The benchmark of 1.6 was chosen after calculating mean fertility of all countries below replacement level that had experienced positive growth rates in the successive five-year interval period. Alongside, we observed minimum fertility of all countries that reached sub-replacement fertility. Countries that had experienced positive growth rates entered the sample only once because if a country showed alternate fertility patterns (i.e. short recovery followed by a successive decrease and recovery) only the first period before the first recovery was considered. The resulting average fertility was 1.67 and can be interpreted as the mean level of sub-replacement fertility, before positive growth rates were measured in the next five-year interval. In applying this method we disregarded countries that have not yet experienced a fertility recovery and face further declines: China was not included in the calculation of the turning point. Calculating minimum fertility of all countries below replacement level yielded a value of 1.57. Given that in the calculation of minimum fertility, 29 countries in the sample had not yet experienced a fertility recovery and fertility

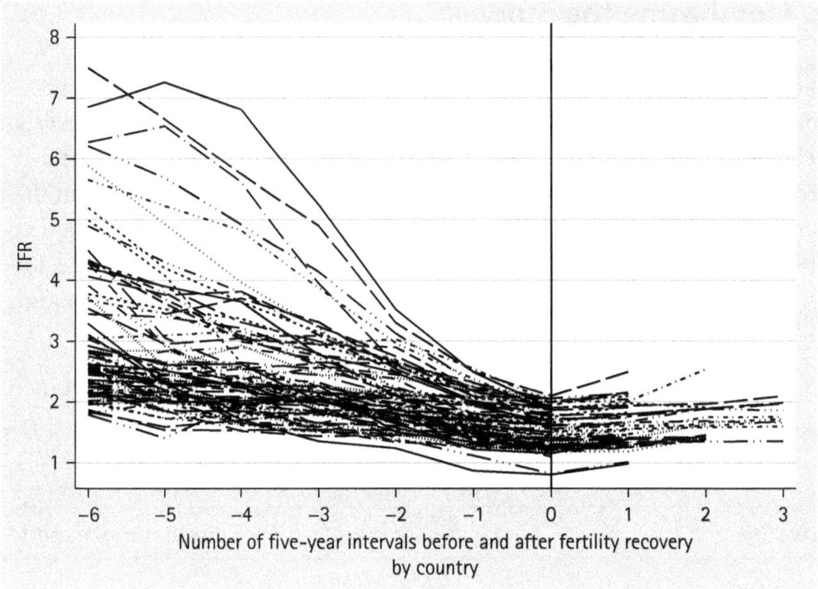

FIGURE 4.10 Pathways of fertility decline and recovery, by country. TFR: total fertility rate.

Sources: United Nations (2011); own calculations.

could possibly decline further, we decided to adopt 1.6, a value closer to the minimum observed fertility.

Figure 4.10 displays fertility transition pathways of all countries that have experienced levels below replacement fertility followed by a period of increasing fertility rates. Choosing the benchmark of 1.6 followed the same reasoning as modelling rates of fertility decline in the model of historical analogy (model 1). Rather than picking an arbitrary level of fertility, the benchmark was a result of analysing historical fertility trajectories worldwide. The sample of countries that had at some point experienced below replacement fertility, followed by a period of positive growth rates, covered 55 countries across all continents. Generating minimum fertility of all countries below replacement fertility included 84 countries.

4.5.5 Results

Here, we show results from this model. As discussed, the fertility scenarios were constructed from a model of historical analogy and a model from the expert questionnaire and the meta-experts' estimates. All figures presented here show historical fertility records since 2000. While the model employs observations of fertility since 1970, the graphs disregard records before 2000. The UN (United Nations, 2011) five-year period fertility is labelled with squared markers. In the first interval, we produced fertility scenarios

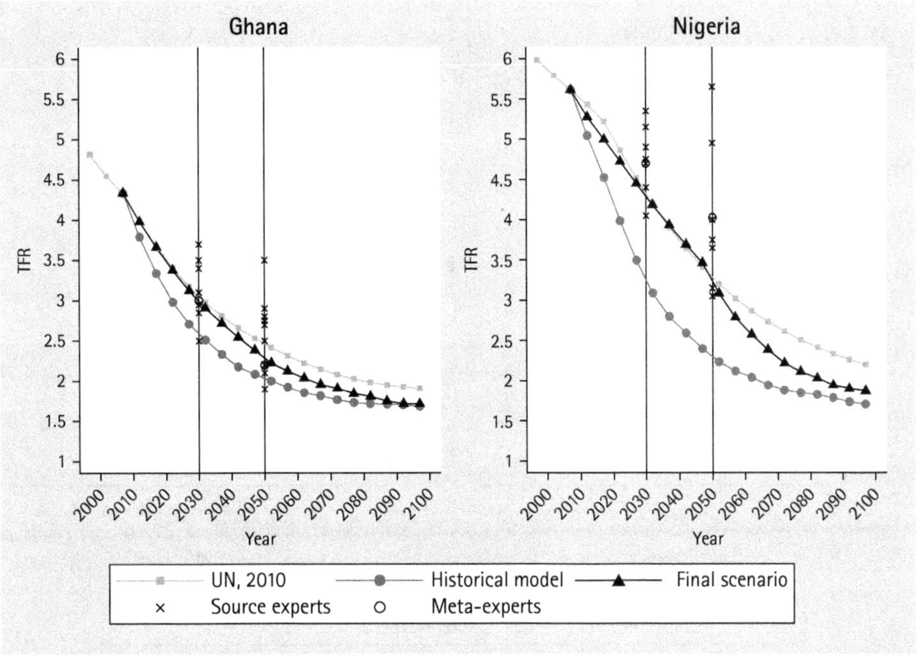

FIGURE 4.11 Historical fertility and fertility scenarios for Ghana and Nigeria, 1990–2100. TFR: total fertility rate.

for 2010–15. Baseline model results, generating a scenario without expert judgement, produces fertility estimates labelled with round markers. The final fertility scenario, combining model results and expert model estimations, is displayed with diamond markers.

Figure 4.11 shows model outcomes for two countries in West Africa, Ghana and Nigeria. Fertility in the period 2005–10 is 4.3 for Ghana and 5.6 for Nigeria. The historical model outcomes suggest rapid fertility decline; values in the period 2025–30 are 2.7 for Ghana and 3.5 for Nigeria. Completing the model with estimates from experts and meta-experts decelerates the expected speed of decline from the baseline model. On average, experts on Ghana suggest a slower fertility decline compared with the historical model. Relative to other countries, experts evaluated socio-economic change with regard to fertility more conservatively than in other countries (values of aggregate score from the questionnaire are not shown here). The meta-experts also gave values of fertility that were higher than the model results. As a consequence, the original historical model results were shifted up, resulting in fertility scenarios close to the UN's fertility estimates until 2050. The situation in Nigeria is similar. Relative to the historical model, experts and meta-experts suggest substantively slower fertility decline in Nigeria and thus the combination of all three models results in higher fertility.

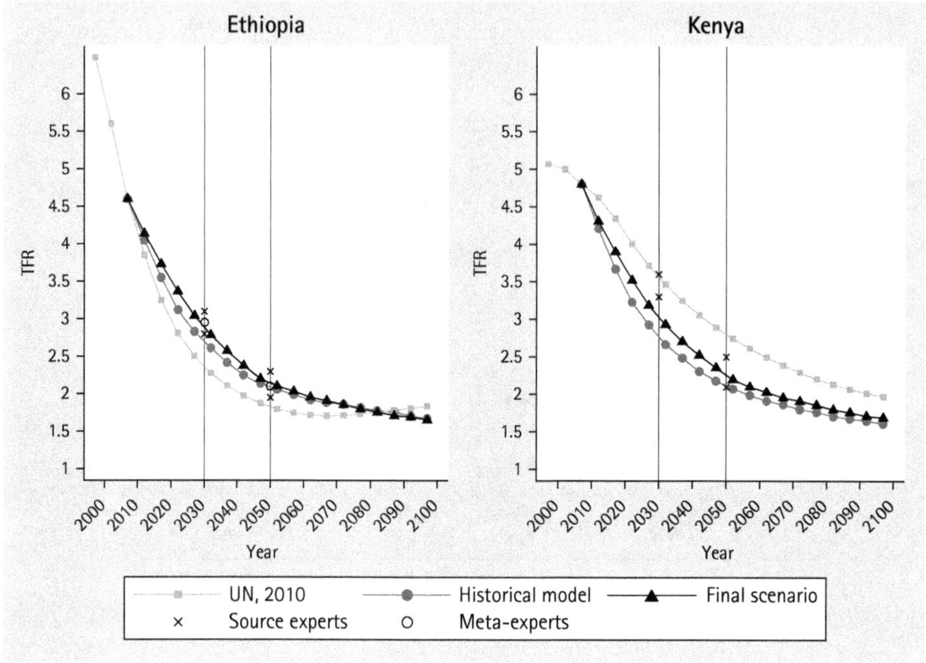

FIGURE 4.12 Historical fertility and fertility scenarios for Ethiopia and Kenya, 1990–2100. TFR: total fertility rate.

Figure 4.12 displays fertility scenarios for the East African countries Ethiopia and Kenya. Compared to the UN's fertility scenarios, our joint models produce fertility that is higher than both the historical model and the UN estimates. In Kenya, there are no numerical estimates from the group of meta-experts, thus the final fertility scenario is only constructed by weighting the historical model and the two source experts, resulting in an increase in the fertility estimates.

Comparing the results in Figures 4.11 and 4.12 shows results from countries with a varying number of experts. While there are only two source experts for Ethiopia and Kenya, we are able to employ questionnaire results from six experts for Ethiopia and nine experts for Ghana. By definition of the weighting scheme in combining the models, source experts for Nigeria and Ghana have a much higher joint weight than in Ethiopia and Kenya, relative to the historical model and the meta-experts. Keep in mind that the relative weights for meta-experts' estimates and the historical model are 1 each. That means, for example, that in Ghana the expert weight is $0.47 = 1.8/3.8$ (9 experts $\times\ 0.2/(1+1+1.8)$), and in Ethiopia the respective value is $0.17 = 0.4/2.4$ (2 experts $\times\ 0.2/(1 + 1 + 0.4)$). The weighting scheme explicitly reflects the number of experts answering the questionnaire. Fertility trajectories of countries with large numbers of experts predominantly rely on the expert judgement from the questionnaire. For countries where we have little expert knowledge we instead put more weight on the historical model and the meta-expert estimates.

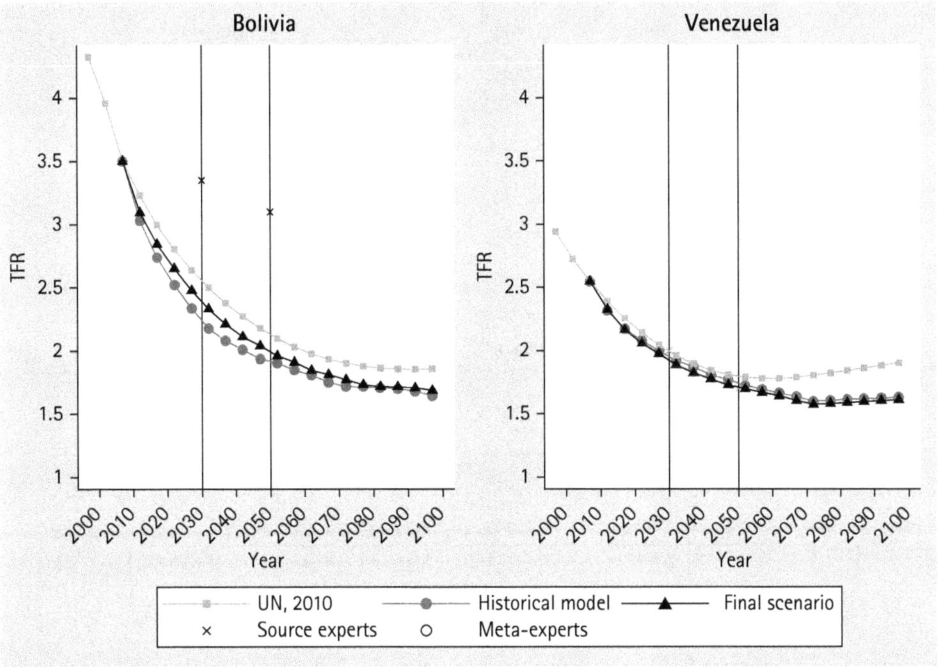

FIGURE 4.13 Historical fertility and fertility scenarios for Bolivia and Venezuela, 1990–2100. TFR: total fertility rate.

Having discussed Latin America's advanced stage in fertility transition in the first section of this chapter, we now show potential pathways of completing demographic transition for Bolivia and Venezuela. Venezuela begins at 2.5 in the period from 2005 to 2010, while the UN estimate of Bolivia's fertility in the same period is 3.5. For both Bolivia and Venezuela only one expert filled out a questionnaire. As a result, the expert's weight is limited and has little impact on the overall trajectory of fertility transition. In the case of Venezuela, the expert model generates a slightly faster fertility decrease than we get from the historical model. The expert in Bolivia left us with very high fertility estimates for 2030 and 2050, and together with the judgement from the arguments, fertility decline is expected to happen at a slower pace than calculated from the historical model. The fertility scenarios suggest level sub-replacement fertility by the 2020–25 period in Venezuela, and by the 2045–50 period in Bolivia (Figure 4.13).

Fertility scenarios for India and Bangladesh are shown in Figure 4.14. India is characterized by a large number of experts (25). While meta-experts estimated India's fertility sub-replacement levels before 2030, the large number of experts and their less progressive views produce, through combining the models, fertility estimates of 2.2 in the period 2025–30 and 1.88 in 2045–50. In contrast, expert and meta-expert models drive model estimates downward in Bangladesh. Fertility drops below 2 in the period 2015–20 and reaches 1.65 in 2045–50.

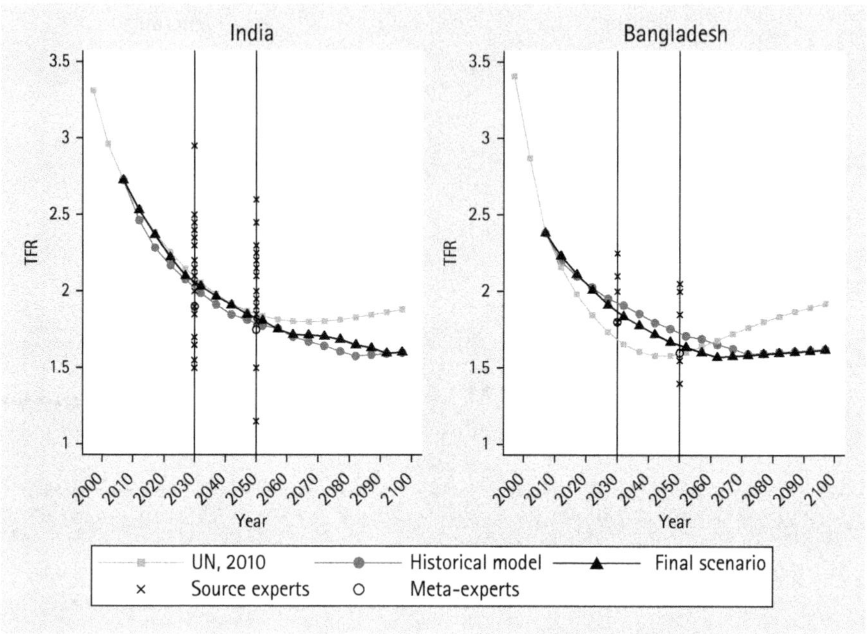

FIGURE 4.14 Historical fertility and fertility scenarios for India and Bangladesh, 1990–2100. TFR: total fertility rate.

4.6 Conclusions

About half the world's population currently lives in countries where women of childbearing age have below replacement fertility (United Nations, 2011). The key for future population growth lies with the other women, those in high or intermediate fertility countries where fertility is still above replacement levels. With a 30-year time lag between the moment the world reaches below replacement fertility and the time population starts declining, these women's fertility will largely determine if, when, and at which level the world population will finally peak. We have shown in this chapter that most regions of the world have yet to reach intermediate levels of fertility, and that the last two regions with high levels of fertility are sub-Saharan Africa and South Asia. Africa is the most problematic, and the evidence indicates that the socio-economic conditions in many countries in terms of political governance, low levels of education, and under-performing economies do not favour rapid future declines in fertility. On the contrary, the experts consulted for this exercise anticipated further declines in fertility rates in other regions as they considered the continuous spread of women's education, modern family planning, and rapid urbanization as factors inducing further reductions.

In the theoretical section of this chapter, we highlight women's education as the main influence on their fertility. At the middle stage of the demographic transition, where the several society strata are spread out across different stages of transition, the role of education is most pronounced, with the highly educated having considerably lower fertility than the less and not educated. As the fertility transition proceeds to low levels of childbearing, the differentials then tend to disappear, which was pointed out by Cleland (2002) when describing the association between education and fertility as a transient phenomenon. Nevertheless, the impact of education will prevail for several decades as many countries find themselves at, or approaching, the mid-transitional stage. Also, as described in Chapter 3, differential fertility by education does not entirely disappear in many countries and is not expected to do so in the future.

The future fertility assumptions developed in this book are based on a model that takes the level and recent trends in fertility into consideration, and is further informed by the numerical estimates of experts obtained through an online questionnaire and a meeting. Beyond the argumentation on the predictors of future fertility declines, the results show that out of the 117 countries that had strictly above replacement fertility in 2010—set conventionally at 2.1—there would be only 71 in 2030 and 42 in 2050. In 2060, out of the 17 countries where women are expected to bear more than 2.1 children, only 5 will experience fertility above 2.5. Four are in sub-Saharan Africa (Niger, Nigeria, Uganda, and Malawi) and one is in South Asia (Afghanistan). Two-thirds of the countries that had very high levels of fertility in 2010 are expected to converge to below replacement fertility in 2060.

APPENDIX 4.1

Table A4.1 List of Qualitative Statements (Arguments) in the High Fertility Questionnaire

CL 1 Cultural change in ideal family size (CULTURAL)	
HF1-1	Family size decisions will increasingly be made by couples themselves rather than surrounding networks
HF1-2	Religions and religious beliefs will become more important for fertility decisions
HF1-3	The traditional preference for boys will eventually disappear
HF1-4	The government will take leadership in promoting the idea of small family size
HF1-5	Negative attitudes towards modern methods of contraception will diminish
HF1-6	Childlessness will become socially acceptable
HF1-7	Educational differentials in desired family size will diminish
CL 2 Health and child survival (HEALTH)	
HF2-1	Adolescent pregnancy will become less frequent
HF2-2	There will be increasing access to improved sanitation and health care for mothers and children
HF2-3	Parents will expect that most of their children survive to adulthood
HF2-4	Mothers will increasingly see the benefits of birth spacing

(continued)

Table A4.1 Continued

CL 3 Status of women in family and society (STATUS)	
HF3-1	Marriage arranged by parents or relatives will lose ground
HF3-2	Female educational enrolment rates will increase
HF3-3	Male partners will become more supportive of modern contraceptive use
HF3-4	The age at first marriage will continue to increase
HF3-5	The participation of women in the labour force will increase
HF3-6	More women will decide to stay unmarried
HF3-7	Women will increasingly be able to decide on their own about using contraceptives
CL 4 Economic costs and benefits (COST)	
HF4-1	Pension funds and social security systems will replace family support in old age
HF4-2	Parents put increasing value on good education of their children
HF4-3	Mothers will increasingly return to paid employment even when their children are small
HF4-4	The cost of raising children in urban settings will increase
HF4-5	The gap in access to education of boys and girls will be removed
HF4-6	The prevalence of child labour will decline
CL 5 Reproductive Health (RP HEALTH)	
HF5-1	The availability of modern family planning services will significantly increase
HF5-2	Convenient contraceptives without side effects will become broadly available
HF5-3	Traditional methods of family planning will remain/become widespread
HF5-4	Abortion (whether legal or illegal) will be more widely practised than today
HF5-5	Modern contraception will be banned for religious, political, or other reasons
HF5-6	Educational differentials in actual fertility will diminish

Table A4.2 Numerical Estimates by Country and Number of Respondents in 2030 and 2050

Country	# Respondents	TFR 2030	TFR 2050	Country	# Respondents	TFR 2030	TFR 2050
Afghanistan	1	4.0	1.9	Nepal	9		1.8
Bangladesh	6	1.9	1.6	Nepal	10	2.2	
Bhutan	1	2.1	1.9	Niger	1	6.8	6.4
Bolivia	1	3.4	3.1	Nigeria	6	4.7	3.8
Botswana	1	2.8	1.1	Oman	1	2.5	2.0
Burkina Faso	1	5.7	5.0	Pakistan	4	3.3	
Ecuador	1	2.2	2.0	Pakistan	5		2.9
Egypt	5	2.4	2.0	Papua New Guinea	1	3.1	2.5
Ethiopia	2	3.0	2.1	Peru	1	2.1	1.9
Ghana	10	3.2	2.6	Philippines	3	2.8	2.4
Haiti	1	3.2	2.8	Rwanda	2	4.0	3.5
India	30	2.1	1.9	Senegal	1	3.5	2.5
Indonesia	4	2.1	1.8	South Africa	2	2.1	1.9
Kenya	2	3.5	2.3	Sri Lanka	1	1.9	2.0

Lesotho	1	2.8	2.6	Sudan	1	3.8	3.2
Malawi	3	4.5	3.2	Suriname	2	2.0	1.9
Malaysia	3	2.1	2.0	Tanzania	1	4.4	3.5
Mali	1	3.0	2.9	Uganda	4	5.3	4.3
Mongolia	1	2.4	2.4	Venezuela	1	2.0	1.7
Morocco	1	1.8	1.8	Vietnam	3	1.7	1.4
Mozambique	1	4.8	4.4	Zambia	1	5.1	3.6

TFR: total fertility rate. Estimates are based on numerical responses after statistical cleaning. Selected respondents for Nepal and Pakistan provided numerical estimates for 2030 or 2050, only.

References

Adsera, A. 2004 'Changing Fertility Rates in Developed Countries. The Impact of Labor Market Institutions'. *Journal of Population Economics*, 17: 17–43.

Agyei-Mensah, S. 2007 'New Times, New Families: The Stall in Ghanaian Fertility'. Presented at the African Population Conference, Union for African Studies, Arusha, Tanzania.

Alkema, L., Kantorova, V., Menozzi, C. and Biddlecom, A. 2013 'National, Regional, and Global Rates and Trends in Contraceptive Prevalence and Unmet Need for Family Planning Between 1990 and 2015: A Systematic and Comprehensive Analysis'. *The Lancet*, 381: 1642–52.

Axinn, W.G. and Barber, J.S. 2001 'Mass Education and Fertility Transition'. *American Sociological Review*, 66: 481–505.

Becker, G.S. 1991 *A Treatise on the Family*. Harvard University Press: Cambridge, MA.

Becker, G.S., Duesenberry, J.S. and Okun, B. 1960 *An Economic Analysis of Fertility*. Columbia University Press: New York.

Black, R.E., Cousens, S., Johnson, H.L., Lawn, J.E., Rudan, I., Bassani, D.G., et al. 2010 'Global, Regional, and National Causes of Child Mortality in 2008: A Systematic Analysis'. *The Lancet*, 375: 1969–87.

Blanc, A.K. and Tsui, A.O. 2005 'The Dilemma of Past Success: Insiders' Views on the Future of the International Family Planning Movement'. *Studies in Family Planning*, 36: 263–76.

Blanc, A.K., Tsui, A.O., Croft, T.N. and Trevitt, J.L. 2009 'Patterns and Trends in Adolescents' Contraceptive Use and Discontinuation in Developing Countries and Comparisons With Adult Women'. *International Perspectives on Sexual Reproduction and Health*, 35: 63–71.

Bongaarts, J. 1980 'Does Malnutrition Affect Fecundity? A Summary of Evidence'. *Science*, 208: 564–9.

Bongaarts, J. 1987 'The Proximate Determinants of Fertility'. *Technology in Society*, 9: 243–60.

Bongaarts, J. 2003 'Completing the Fertility Transition in the Developing World: The Role of Educational Differences and Fertility Preferences'. *Population Studies*, 57: 321–36.

Bongaarts, J. 2006 'The Causes of Stalling Fertility Transitions'. *Studies in Family Planning*, 37: 1–16.

Bongaarts, J. 2008 'Fertility Transitions in Developing Countries: Progress or Stagnation?' *Studies in Family Planning*, 39: 105–10.

Bongaarts, J. 2011 'Can Family Planning Programs Reduce High Desired Family Size in Sub-Saharan Africa?' *International Perspectives on Sexual and Reproductive Health*, 37: 209–16.

Bongaarts, J. and Potter, R.G. 1983 *Fertility, Biology, and Behavior: An Analysis of the Proximate Determinants*. Academic Press: New York.

Bongaarts, J. and Watkins, S.C. 1996 'Social Interactions and Contemporary Fertility Transitions'. *Population and Development Reviews*, 22: 639–82.

Bongaarts, J. and Casterline, J. 2013 'Fertility Transition: Is Sub-Saharan Africa Different?' *Population and Development Reviews*, 38: 153–68.

Bongaarts, J., Cleland, J., Townsend, J.W., Bertrand, J.T. and Das Gupta, M. 2012 *Family Planning Programs For the 21st Century*. Population Council: New York.

Bradley, S.E., Croft, T.N., Fishel, J.D. and Westoff, C.F. 2012 'Revising Unmet Need for Family Planning' (No. AS25). ICF International: Calverton, MD.

Bryant, J. 2007 'Theories of Fertility Decline and the Evidence From Development Indicators'. *Population and Development Review*, 33: 101–27.

Bulatao, R.A. and Lee, R.D. 1983 *Determinants of Fertility in Developing Countries*. National Academic Press: New York.

Butala, N.M., VanRooyen, M.J. and Patel, R.B. 2010 'Improved Health Outcomes in Urban Slums Through Infrastructure Upgrading'. *Social Science & Medicine*, 71: 935–40.

Cairo Demographic Center 2006 *Exploring Reasons for the Relatively High Fertility of Educated Women in Egypt*. Cairo Demographic Center: Cairo.

Caldwell, J.C. 1979 'Education as a Factor in Mortality Decline an Examination of Nigerian Data'. *Population Studies*, 33: 395–413.

Caldwell, J.C. 1982 *Theory of Fertility Decline*. Academic Press: London.

Caldwell, J.C. 1997 'The Global Fertility Transition: The Need for a Unifying Theory'. *Population and Development Review*, 23: 803–12.

Caldwell, J.C., Orubuloye, I.O. and Caldwell, P. 1992 'Fertility Decline in Africa: A New Type of Transition?' *Population and Development Review*, 18: 211–42.

Casterline, J.B. and Sinding, S.W. 2000 'Unmet Need for Family Planning in Developing Countries and Implications for Population Policy'. *Population and Development Review*, 26: 691–723.

Casterline, J. and El-Zeini, L.O. 2005 'Fertility Decline in Egypt: Current Status, Future Prospects'. Presented at the XXV International Population Conference, Tours, France.

Casterline, J.B. and Roushdy, R. 2007 'Slow Fertility Transition in Egypt' (Research Report). Population Council: Cairo.

Castro Martin, T. 1995 'Women's Education and Fertility: Results from 26 Demographic and Health Surveys'. *Studies in Family Planning*, 26: 187–202.

Castro Martin, T. and Juarez, F. 1995 'The Impact of Women's Education on Fertility in Latin America: Searching for Explanations'. *International Family Planning Perspectives*, 21: 52–80.

Cetorelli, V. and Leone, T. 2012 'Is Fertility Stalling in Jordan?' *Demographic Research*, 26: 293–318.

Cleland, J. 2002 'Education and Future Fertility Trends with Special Reference to Mid-Transitional Countries (Background Papers No. 48/49), Completing the Fertility Transition'. United Nations: New York.

Cleland, J.G. and Wilson, C. 1987 'Demand Theories of the Fertility Transition: An Iconoclastic View'. *Population Studies*, 41: 5–30.

Cleland, J., Bernstein, S., Ezeh, A., Faundes, A., Glasier, A. and Innis, J. 2006 'Sexual and Reproductive Health 3—Family Planning: The Unfinished Agenda'. *The Lancet*, 368, 1810–27.

Coale, A.J. and Watkins, S.C. 1986 *The Decline of Fertility in Europe*. Princeton University Press: Princeton, NJ.

Cochrane, S.H. 1979 *Fertility and Education. What Do We Really Know?* Johns Hopkins University Press: Baltimore, MD.

Courbage, Y. 1999 'Issues in Fertility Transition in the Middle East and North Africa' (Working Paper No. 9903). Economic Research Forum: Cairo.

Courbage, Y. and Todd, E. 2011 *A Convergence of Civilizations: The Transformation of Muslim Societies Around the World*. Columbia University Press: New York.

Das Gupta, M., Zhenghua, J., Bohua, L., Zhenming, X., Chung, W. and Hwa-Ok, B. 2003 'Why is Son Preference so Persistent in East and South Asia? A Cross-country Study of China, India and the Republic of Korea'. *Journal of Development Studies*, 40: 153–87.

Davis, K. and Blake, J. 1956 'Social Structure and Fertility: An Analytic Framework'. *Economic Development and Cultural Change*, 4: 211–35.

Day, L.H. 1984 'Minority-group Status and Fertility: A More Detailed Test of the Hypothesis'. *The Sociological Quarterly*, 25: 456–72.

DHS Bolivia 2009 *Bolivia Demographic and Health Survey*. Central Statistical Agency, ICF International: Calverton, MD.

DHS Egypt 2004 *Egypt Demographic and Health Survey 2003*. Central Statistical Agency, ICF International: Addis Ababa and Calverton, MD.

DHS Egypt 2006 *Egypt Demographic and Health Survey 2005*. Central Statistical Agency, ICF International: Addis Ababa and Calverton, MD.

DHS Egypt 2009 *Egypt Demographic and Health Survey 2008*. Central Statistical Agency, ICF International: Addis Ababa and Calverton, MD.

DHS Niger 2006 *Niger Demographic and Health Survey 2006*. ICF International: Calverton, MD.

DHS Niger 2012 *Niger Demographic and Health Survey 2012*. ICF International: Calverton, MD.

DHS Uganda 2012 *Uganda Demographic and Health Surveys 1988–2012*. ICF International: Calverton, MD.

Doyle, A.M., Mavedzenge, S.N., Plummer, M.L. and Ross, D.A. 2012 'The Sexual Behaviour of Adolescents in Sub-Saharan Africa: Patterns and Trends From National Surveys'. *Tropical Medicine and International Health*, 17: 796–807.

Dreze, J. and Murthi, M. 2001 'Fertility, Education, and Development: Evidence From India'. *Population and Development Review*, 27: 33–63.

Dyson, T. 2010a *Population and Development: The Demographic Transition*. Zed Books: London.

Easterlin, R.A. 1975 'An Economic Framework for Fertility Analysis'. *Studies in Family Planning*, 6: 54–63.

Easterlin, R.A. 1983 'Modernization and Fertility: A Critical Essay'. In: Bulatao, R.A. and Lee R. D. (eds) *Determinants of Fertility in Developing Countries, Volume 2: Fertility Regulation and Institutional Influences*, pp. 562–86, Academic Press: New York.

Easterlin, R.A. and Crimmins, E.M. 1985 *The Fertility Revolution: A Supply-Demand Analysis*. University Of Chicago Press: Chicago, IL, and London.

ECLAC 2010 'Population and Health in Latin America and the Caribbean: Outstanding Matters, New Challenges (No. LC/L.3216 (CEP.2010/3))'. ECLAC Ad Hoc Committee on Population and Development: Santiago.

Eltigani, E. 2003 'Stalled Fertility Decline in Egypt, Why?' *Population and Environment*, 25: 41–59.

El-Zanaty, F. and Way, A.A. 2004 *Egypt Interim Demographic and Health Survey 2003*. National Population Council, El-Zanaty and Associates and ORC Macro, Ministry of Health and Population: Cairo.

Engelhardt, H. 2005 'Recent Trends and Components of Change in Fertility in Egypt' (IIASA Interim Report No. IR-05-024). International Institute for Applied Systems Analysis (IIASA): Laxenburg.

ENSMI 2008 *Encuesta Nacional de Salud Materno Infantil.* Ministerio de Salud Pública y Asistencia Social (MSPAS), Instituto Nacional de Estadística (INE), Centros de Control y Prevención de Enfermedades (CDC): Guatemala.

Entwisle, B. and Winegarden, C.R. 1984 'Fertility and Pension Programs in LDCs: A Model of Mutual Reinforcement'. *Economic Development and Cultural Change*, 32: 331–54.

Ezeh, A.C., Mberu, B.U. and Emina, J.O. 2009 'Stall in Fertility Decline in Eastern African Countries: Regional Analysis of Patterns, Determinants and Implications'. *Philosophical Transactions of the Royal Society B*, 364: 2991–3007.

Feeney, G. and Alam, I. 2003 'New Estimates and Projections of Population Growth in Pakistan'. *Population and Development Review*, 29: 483–92.

Freedman, R. and Berelson, B. 1976 'The Record of Family Planning Programs'. *Studies in Family Planning*, 7: 1–40.

Galor, O. 2011 'The Demographic Transition: Causes and Consequences'. *Cliometrica* 6: 1–28.

Garenne, M. 2007 'Situations of Fertility Stall in Sub-Saharan Africa'. *African Population Studies*, 23: 173–88.

Gebreselassie, T. and Mishra, V. 2011 'Spousal Agreement on Preferred Waiting Time to Next Birth in Sub-Saharan Africa'. *Journal of Biosocial Science*, 43: 385–400.

Gendell, M. 1985 'Stalls in Fertility Decline in Costa Rica, Korea, and Sri Lanka'. *Population Today*, 13: 8–10.

Gendell, M. 1989 'Stalls in the Fertility Decline in Costa Rica and South Korea'. *International Family Planning Perspectives*, 15: 15–21.

Goldscheider, C. 1971 *Population, Modernization, and Social Structure*. Little Brown: Boston, MA.

Goldscheider, C. and Uhlenberg, P.R. 1969 'Minority Group Status and Fertility'. *American Journal of Sociology*, 74: 361–72.

Guengant, J.-P. and May, J. 2011 'Proximate Determinants of Fertility in Sub-Saharan Africa and Their Possible Use in Fertility Projections' (Expert Paper No. 2011/13). United Nations: New York.

Guilmoto, C.Z. and Rajan, S.I. 2001 'Spatial Patterns of Fertility Transition in Indian Districts'. *Population and Development Review*, 27: 713–38.

Guzman, J.M., Singh, S., Rodriguez, G. and Pantelides, E.A. 1996 *The Fertility Transition in Latin America*. Clarendon Press: Oxford.

Hakim, A., Sultan, M. and Uddin, F. 2001 'Pakistan Reproductive Health and Family Planning Survey (2000–01)' (Preliminary Report). National Institute for Population Studies: Islamabad.

Haub, C. and Gribble, J. 2011 'The World at 7 Billion (Population Bulletin 66 No. 2)'. Population Reference Bureau: Washington, DC.

Hayford, S.R. and Agadjanian, V. 2012 'From Desires to Behavior'. *Demographic Research*, 26: 511–42.

Hobcraft, J.N. 1993 'Women's Education, Child Welfare and Child Survival: A Review of the Evidence'. *Health Transitiion Review*, 3: 159–73.

Hogan, M.C., Foreman, K.J., Naghavi, M., Ahn, S.Y., Wang, M., Makela, S.M., et al. 2010 'Maternal Mortality for 181 Countries, 1980–2008: A Systematic Analysis of Progress Towards Millennium Development Goal 5'. *The Lancet*, 375: 1609–23.

Hull, T.H. and Hartanto, W. 2009 'Resolving Contradictions in Indonesian Fertility Estimates'. *Bulletin of Indonesian Economic Studies*, 45: 61–71.
Ijadunola, M.Y., Abiona, T.C., Ijadunola, K.T., Afolabi, O.T., Esimai, O.A. and OlaOlorun, F.M. 2011 'Male Involvement in Family Planning Decision Making in Ile-Ife, Osun State, Nigeria'. *African Journal of Reproductive Health*, 14: 43–50.
INE, 2011 *Tasa de fecundidad corregida por grupo de edad de la madre, según entidad federal, 2011*. Available at: <http://www.ine.gov.ve/> (accessed 18 April 2013).
Institut National de la Statistique et Fonds des Nations Unies pour l'Enfance 2011 'Enquête par Grappes à Indicateurs Multiples en République Démocratique du Congo' (Final Report No. MICS-RDC 2010). Institut National de la Statistique et Fonds des Nations Unies pour l'Enfance: Kinshasa.
Instituto Nacional de Estadística (INE) 2013 *Boletín Informativo—Censo Nacional de Población y Vivienda 2012*. Instituto Nacional de Estadística (INE): La Paz.
Jain, A.K. and Ross, J.A. 2012 'Fertility Differences Among Developing Countries: Are They Still Related to Family Planning Program Efforts and Social Settings?' *International Perspectives in Sexual Reproductive Health*, 38: 15–22.
James, K.S. 2011 'India's Demographic Change: Opportunities and Challenges'. *Science*, 333: 576–80.
Jayaraman, A., Mishra, V. and Arnold, F. 2009 'The relationship of Family Size and Composition to Fertility Desires, Contraceptive Adoption and Method Choice in South Asia'. *International Perspectives in Sexual Reproductive Health*, 35: 29–38.
Jeffery, R. and Basu, A.M. 1996 'Schooling as Contraception?' In: *Girls' Schooling, Women's Autonomy and Fertility Change in South Asia*, pp. 15–47. Sage: New Delhi.
Jejeebhoy, S.J. 1995 *Women's Education, Autonomy, and Reproductive Behaviour: Experience from Developing Countries*. Clarendon Press: Oxford.
KC, S. and Potančoková, M. 2013 'Differential Fertility by Level of Education in DHS Countries'. Presented at the 2013 Annual Meeting of the Population Association of America, New Orleans, 11–13 April 2013, New Orleans, LA, USA.
Kirk, D. 1996 'Demographic Transition Theory'. *Population Studies*, 50: 361–87.
Kohler, H.-P. 1997 'Learning in Social Networks and Contraceptive Choice'. *Demography*, 34: 369–83.
Kravdal, Ø. 2000 'A Search for Aggregate-level Effects of Education on Fertility, Using Data From Zimbabwe'. *Demographic Research* 3.
Kravdal, Ø. 2002 'Education and Fertility in Sub-Saharan Africa: Individual and Community Effects'. *Demography*, 39: 233–50.
Kravdal, Ø. 2012 'Further Evidence of Community Education Effects on Fertility in Sub-Saharan Africa'. *Demographic Research*, 27: 645–80.
Kulkarni, P.M. and Alagarajan, M. 2005 'Population Growth, Fertility and Religion in India'. *Economic and Political Weekly*, 40: 403–10.
Lesthaeghe, R.J. 1989 *Reproduction and Social Organization in Sub-Saharan Africa*. University of California Press: Berkeley and Los Angeles, CA.
Lesthaeghe, R.J. 1995 'Second Demographic Transition in Western Countries: An Interpretation'. In: Mason, K.O. and Jensen, A.-M. (eds) *Gender and Family Change in Industrialized Countries*, pp. 17–62. Clarendon Press: Oxford.
Lesthaeghe, R. and Surkyn, J. 1988 'Cultural Dynamics and Economic Theories of Fertility Change'. *Population and Development Review*, 14: 1–45.

Link, C.F. 2011 'Spousal Communication and Contraceptive Use in Rural Nepal: An Event History Analysis'. *Studies in Family Planning*, 42: 83–92.

Lynch, K. 2006 'Theoretical and Analytical Approaches to Religious Beliefs, Values, and Identities during the Modern Fertility Transition'. In: Derosas, R. and Van Poppel, F (eds) *Religion and the Decline of Fertility in the Western World Religion and the Decline of Fertility in the Western World*, pp. 21–39 Springer: Dordrecht.

Machiyama, K. 2010 'A Re-examination of Recent Fertility Declines in Sub-Saharan Africa' (DHS Working Papers No. 68). ICF Macro: Calverton, MA.

McQuillan, K. 2004 'When Does Religion Influence Fertility?' *Population and Development Review*, 30: 25–56.

Mari Bhat, P. 2002 'Returning a Favor: Reciprocity Between Female Education and Fertility in India'. *World Development*, 30: 1791–803.

Marston, M., Slaymaker, E., Cremin, I., Floyd, S., McGrath, N., Kasamba, I., et al. 2009 'Trends in Marriage and Time Spent Single in Sub-Saharan Africa: A Comparative Analysis of Six Population-based Cohort Studies and Nine Demographic and Health Surveys'. *Sexually Transmitted Infections*, 85: i64–71.

Mason, K.O. 1997 'Explaining fertility transitions'. *Demography*, 34: 443–54.

Mason, K.O. 1987 'The Impact of Women's Social Position on Fertility in Developing Countries'. *Sociology Forum*, 2: 718–45.

May, J.F. 2012 *World Population Policies—Their Origin, Evolution, and Impact*. Springer: Dordrecht, New York and London.

Measure DHS 2013 'Pakistan: DHS 2012–13—Preliminary Report (No. PR 35)'. Macro International Inc.: Calverton, MD.

Menken, J., Khan, N. and Williams, J. 2009 'The Stalled Fertility Transition in Bangladesh: The Effects of Sex and Number Preferences'. Presented at the XXVI International Population Conference, Marrakech, Morocco.

Mensch, B., Lentzner, H. and Preston, S. 1985 *Socio-economic Differentials in Child Mortality in Developing Countries*. United Nations: New York.

Ministère du Plan and Macro International 2008 *Enquête Démographique et de Santé, République Démocratique du Congo 2007*. Ministère du Plan and Macro International: Calverton, MA.

Ministry of Population Welfare 1995 *PCPS 1994-1995: Pakistan Contraceptive Prevalence Survey: Main Findings, 1994-95*. Ministry of Population Welfare: Islamabad.

Moreland, S., Smith, E. and Sharma, S. 2010 *World Population Prospects and Unmet Need for Family Planning*. Futures Group: Washington, DC.

Moultrie, T.A., Hosegood, V., McGrath, N., Hill, C., Herbst, K. and Newell, M.-L. 2008 'Refining the Criteria for Stalled Fertility Declines: An Application to Rural KwaZulu-Natal, South Africa, 1990–2005'. *Studies in Family Planning*, 39: 39–48.

Moultrie, T.A., Sayi, T.S. and Timæus, I.M. 2012 'Birth Intervals, Postponement, and Fertility Decline in Africa: A New Type of Transition?' *Population Studies*, 66: 241–58.

Moursund, A. and Kravdal, Ø. 2003 'Individual and Community Effects of Women's Education and Autonomy on Contraceptive Use in India'. *Population Studies*, 57: 285–301.

Mwaikambo, L., Speizer, I.S., Schurmann, A., Morgan, G. and Fikree, F. 2011 'What Works in Family Planning Interventions: A Systematic Review'. *Studies in Family Planning*, 42: 67–82.

National Institute of Population Studies 2008 *Pakistan Demographic and Health Survey* 2006–07. Macro International Inc.: Calverton, MD.

National Institute of Population Studies 2001 *Pakistan Reproductive Health and Family Planning Survey* 2000–2001. Islamabad.

National Institute of Population Studies 1992 *Pakistan Demographic and Health Survey 1991–92*. Macro International Inc.: Calverton, MD.

Notestein, F.W. 1945 'Population: The Long View'. In: Schultz, T.W. (ed.) *Food for the World*, pp. 36–69. University of Chicago Press: Chicago, IL.

Office of the Registrar General of India 2006 *Population Projections for India and States, 2001–2026*. Office of the Registrar General and Census Commissioner of India: New Delhi.

Office of the Registrar General of India 2012 *Sample Registration System 2010*. Office of the Registrar General and Census Commissioner of India: New Delhi.

Pamuk, E.R., Fuchs, R. and Lutz, W. 2011 'Comparing Relative Effects of Education and Economic Resources on Infant Mortality in Developing Countries'. *Population and Development Review*, 37: 637–64.

Parrado, E.A. 2000 'Social Change, Population Policies, and Fertility Decline in Colombia and Venezuela'. *Population Research and Policy Review*, 19: 421–57.

Patel, R.B. and Burke, T.F. 2009 'Urbanization—An Emerging Humanitarian Disaster'. *New England Journal of Medicine*, 361: 741–3.

Philipov, D. and Berghammer, C. 2007 'Religion and Fertility Ideals, Intentions and Behaviour: A Comparative Study of European Countries'. *Vienna Yearbook of Population Research*, 5: 271–305.

Raj, A., Saggurti, N., Balaiah, D. and Silverman, J.G. 2009 'Prevalence of Child Marriage and its Effect on Fertility and Fertility-control Outcomes of Young Women in India: A Cross-sectional, Observational Study'. *The Lancet*, 373: 1883–9.

Raj, A., Saggurti, N., Winter, M., Labonte, A., Decker, M.R., Balaiah, D. and Silverman, J.G. 2010 'The Effect of Maternal Child Marriage on Morbidity and Mortality of Children Under 5 in India: Cross Sectional Study of a Nationally Representative Sample'. *British Medical Journal*, 340: b4258.

Rajaratnam, J.K., Tran, L.N., Lopez, A.D. and Murray, C.J.L. 2010 'Measuring Under-five Mortality: Validation of New Low-cost Methods'. *PLoS Medicine*, 7: e1000253.

République du Niger 2012 *Enquête nationale sur la migration au Niger (2011)*. Ministère des Finances, Institut National de la Statistique: Niamey.

Retel-Laurentin, A. 1974 *Infécondité en Afrique noire: Maladies et conséquences sociales*. Masson: Paris.

Robinson, W.C. and Ross, J.A. (eds) 2007 *The Global Family Planning Revolution: Three Decades of Population Policies and Programs*, 1st ed. World Bank Publications: Washington, DC.

Romaniuk, A. 1961 *L'Aspect démographique de la stérilité des femmes congolaises*. Studia Universitatis 'Lovanium,' Institut de Recherches Economiques et Sociales, Editions de l'Université: Léopoldville.

Romaniuk, A. 1967 *La Fécondité des populations congolaises*. Mouton: Paris.

Romaniuk, A. 1968 'The Demography of the Democratic Republic of the Congo'. In: Brass, W. (ed.) *The Population of Tropical Africa*, pp. 241–341. Princeton University Press: Princeton, NJ.

Romaniuk, A. 1980 'Increase in Natural Fertility During the Early Stages of Modernization: Evidence From an African Case Study, Zaire'. *Population Studies*, 34: 293–310.

Romaniuk, A. 2011 'Persistence of High Fertility in Tropical Africa: The Case of the Democratic Republic of the Congo'. *Population and Development Review*, 37: 1–28.

Rosero-Bixby, L. and Casterline, J.B. 1993 'Modelling Diffusion Effects in Fertility Transition'. *Population Studies*, 47: 147–67.

Sakai, M. and Fauzia, A. 2014 'Islamic Orientations in Contemporary Indonesia: Islamism on the Rise?' *Asian Ethnicity*, 15: 41–61.

Saleem, S. and Bobak, M. 2005 'Women's Autonomy, Education and Contraception Use in Pakistan: A National Study'. *Reproductive Health*, 2: 8.

Sathar, Z. and Casterline, J. 1998 'The Onset of Fertility Transition in Pakistan'. *Population and Development Review*, 24: 773–96.

Sathar, Z. and Zaidi, B. 2011 'Fertility Prospects in Pakistan' (Expert Paper No. 2011/07). United Nations Department of Economic and Social Affairs, Population Division: New York.

Schoumaker, B. 2009 'Stalls in Fertility Transitions in Sub-Saharan Africa: Real or Spurious?' (Document de Travail No. 30). Département des sciences de la population et du développement, Université catholique de Louvain: Louvain.

Schultz, T.P. 1997 'Demand for Children in Low Income Countries'. In: Rosenzweig, M.R. and Stark, O. (eds) *Handbook of Population & Family Economics, Handbooks in Economics*, pp. 349–430. Elsevier Science: Amsterdam.

Sedgh, G., Henshaw, S., Singh, S., Åhman, E., Shah, I.H. 2007 'Induced Abortion: Estimated Rates and Trends Worldwide'. *The Lancet*, 370: 1338–45.

Shapiro, D. 2012 'Enduring Economic Hardship, Women's Education, and Fertility Transition in Kinshasa' (Working Paper). Department of Economics, Pennsylvania State University: State College, PA.

Shapiro, D. and Gebreselassie, T. 2008 'Fertility Transition in Sub-Saharan Africa: Falling and Stalling'. *African Population Studies*, 23: 3–23.

Sibanda, A., Woubalem, Z., Hogan, D.P. and Lindstrom, D.P. 2003 'The Proximate Determinants of the Decline to Below-replacement Fertility in Addis Ababa, Ethiopia'. *Studies in Family Planning*, 34: 1–7.

Sinding, S.W. 2008 'Will Africa's Fertility Decline?' (Transcripts of online interview (10 December 2008)). Population Reference Bureau: Washington, DC.

Singh, S., Sedgh, G. and Hussain, R. 2010 'Unintended Pregnancy: Worldwide Levels, Trends, and Outcomes'. *Studies in Family Planning*, 41: 241–50.

Singh, S. and Darroch, J.E. 2012 *Adding It Up: Costs and Benefits of Contraceptive Services*. Guttmacher Institute. UNFPA: New York.

Uganda Bureau of Statistics 2012 'Population of Uganda'. Available at: <http://www.ubos.org/index.php> (accessed 8 January 2014).

UNDP 2011 *Human Development Index (HDI)*. United Nations Development Program: New York.

United Nations 2011 *World Population Prospects: The 2010 Revision*. Department of Economic and Social Affairs, Population Division: New York.

United Nations Economic and Social Commission for Western Asia 2005 *Annual Review of Developments in Globalization and Regional Integration in the Countries of the ESCWA Region*. United Nations Economic and Social Commission for Western Asia: Beirut.

Van de Kaa, D.J. 1987 'Europe's Second Demographic Transition'. *Population Bulletin*, 42: 1–59.

Van de Kaa, D.J. 2001 'Postmodern Fertility Preferences: From Changing Value Orientation to New Behavior'. *Population and Development Review*, 27: 290–331.

Van Roy, R. 1987 'La población clandestina en Venezuela: resultados de la Matrícula general de extranjeros'. In: Centro de estudios de pastoral y asistencia migratoria, *Migraciones internacionales en las Américas*, number 2, pp. 47–66. CEPAM: Caracas.

Westoff, C.F. 2003 'Trends in Marriage and Early Childbearing in Developing Countries' (DHS Comparative Reports 5). ORC Macro: Calverton, MD.

Westoff, C.F. 2006 'New Estimates of the Unmet Need and the Demand for Family Planning' (No. 14), DHS Comparative Reports. ORC Macro: Calverton, MD.
Westoff, C.F. 2013 'The Recent Fertility Transition in Rwanda'. *Population and Development Review*, 38: 169–78.
Westoff, C.F. and Cross, A.R. 2006 'The Stall in the Fertility Transition in Kenya' (DHS Analytical Studies No. 9). Macro International Inc.: Calverton, MD.
WHO 2004 'Unsafe Abortion. Global and Regional Estimates of the Incidence of Unsafe Abortion and Associated Mortality in 2000' (4th edition). WHO: Geneva.
World Bank 2011 *World Development Indicators: Guatemala*. World Bank: Washington, DC.
World Bank 2012 *World Development Indicators (WDI)*. World Bank: Washington, DC.

CHAPTER 5

FUTURE MORTALITY IN LOW MORTALITY COUNTRIES

GRAZIELLA CASELLI, SVEN DREFAHL, CHRISTIAN WEGNER-SIEGMUNDT, AND MARC LUY

Contributing authors:[1]
Michel Guillot, France Meslé, Arodys Robles, Richard G. Rogers, Edward Jow-Ching Tu, and Zhongwei Zhao

5.1 Introduction

This chapter provides an overview of past and expected future trends in life expectancy in populations with low levels of mortality. High and low mortality populations were separated on the basis of the level of child mortality in the year 2010 according to the revised estimates of the United Nations Inter-agency Group for Child Mortality Estimation (2011), with the threshold being 40 deaths per 1,000 children below the age of 5 years. The low mortality population is comprised of 132 countries including Europe, North America, most of Oceania and Latin America, large parts of Asia (excluding the high mortality area in Central and Southern Asia), and Northern Africa (see Figure 5.1).

The populations of these countries are already engaged in an advanced phase of the demographic and 'epidemiologic transition'. Because they previously experienced strong decreases in infant mortality, the future mortality trends are driven mainly by

[1] The contributing authors have drafted considerable parts of section 5.2. They were selected as lead experts in respective topics and regions. Specifically, they have provided texts to the following sections: Michel Guillot to section 5.2.6 (Former Soviet Republics of Central Asia and the Caucasus) and to section 5.2.5 (The Middle East and Northern Africa); France Meslé to section 5.2.1 (Europe); Arodys Robles to section 5.2.3 (Latin America and the Caribbean); Richard G. Rogers to section 5.2.2 (North America and Mexico); Zhongwei Zhao and Edward Jow-Ching Tu to section 5.2.4 (East Asia, South East Asia, and Oceania).

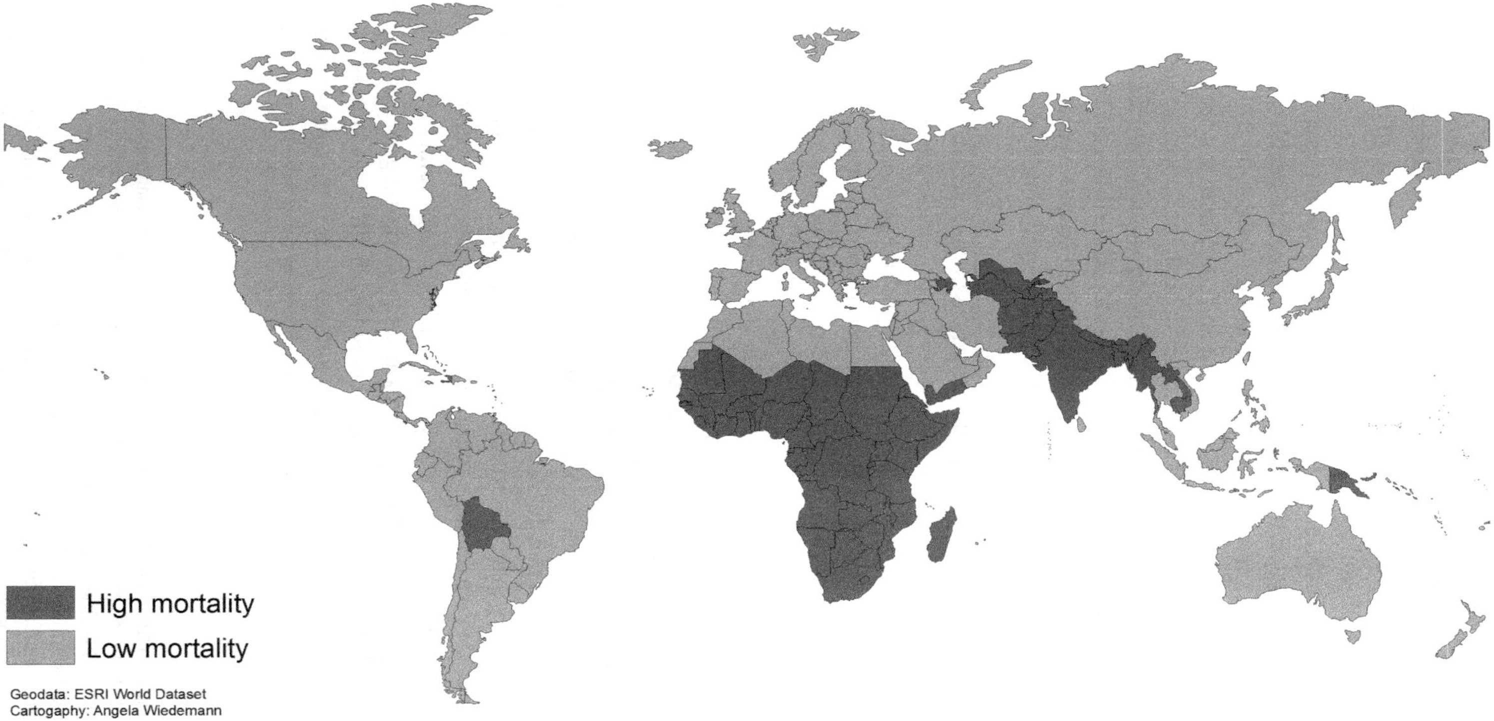

FIGURE 5.1 Today's low and high mortality countries defined on the basis of child mortality (below the age of 5) below or equal to and above 40 deaths per 1,000 persons.

mortality in adult ages, primarily the old and oldest-old. Although the data sources on which the existing estimates of life expectancy for these populations are based vary considerably (owing to differences in the death registration systems and the estimation techniques, see, e.g., Luy, 2010), we have relatively good knowledge of past and current mortality levels and trends and their causes.

Despite the similar general trends, today's low mortality countries are very heterogeneous in various aspects, including medical standards, access to health care, and behavioural risk factors, such as smoking prevalence. These diversities are strongly related to the populations' stages of economic development and contribute to a broad variance of life expectancy levels. Among men, life expectancy at birth for the years 2005–10 ranges between 60.2 in Kazakhstan and 79.5 in Iceland. Among women, the range is between 67.8 in the Solomon Islands and 86.1 in Japan.[2] To demonstrate this relationship between economic development and life expectancy we classified countries according to their current per capita income as an indicator of the economic development level of the populations. We used the World Bank classification, which groups countries into high income (≥$12,276 annually), upper middle income ($3,976–$12,275), lower middle income ($1,006–$3,975), and low income (≤$1,005).[3] As current low mortality populations are mainly clustered in the high and upper middle income groups, we reclassified the countries into the two groups of high- and medium-income populations. The first is identical to the World Bank classification, while the latter includes all remaining low mortality countries.[4]

Figure 5.2 shows for each low mortality country the life expectancy at birth for males (x-axes) and females (y-axes). The medium-income populations are marked by grey diamonds and the high-income countries by black, filled circles. The graph reveals the strong correlation between life expectancy and the level of economic development for both sexes. High-income countries are characterized by female life expectancy of >75 years, with Oman, Saudi Arabia, and Trinidad and Tobago being the only exceptions with slightly lower levels of female life expectancy. In contrast, medium-income countries are characterized by male life expectancy <75 years. Here, the only exceptions are Chile, Cuba, and Costa Rica. In these countries, life expectancy for men ranges between 75.5 and 76.5 years. The average life expectancy for both sexes combined in high- and medium-income populations differs by approximately 6 years, ranging from 72.1 to 78.0 years. In low mortality populations women enjoy higher life expectancies than men, with an average advantage of 5.3 years in high-, and 6.0 years in medium-income countries. The exception is Qatar, where men outlive women by 0.8 years in terms of life expectancy at birth.

[2] The numbers refer to the estimates of the 2010 revision of the United Nations World Populations Prospects (United Nations, 2011) to which all data in this chapter refer, if not stated otherwise.

[3] More details about this classification can be found on the World Bank's website at <http://data.worldbank.org/about/country-classifications> (accessed 6 January 2014).

[4] In fact, only three of today's low mortality countries are classified by the World Bank as low-income countries, namely the Democratic People's Republic of Korea, Kyrgyzstan, and the Solomon Islands.

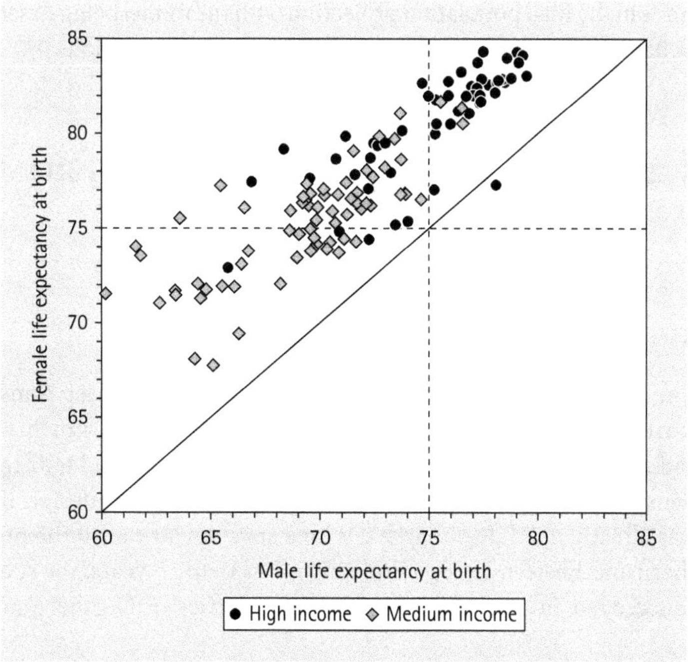

FIGURE 5.2 Female and male life expectancy at birth in low mortality countries by income group, United Nations (UN) estimates for the period 2005–10.

Note: categories of per capita income according to actual World Bank classification (see footnote 3), data on life expectancy from UN (2011); because no data on per capita income are available French Guinea, Guadeloupe, Martinique, and Occupied Palestinian Territories are excluded from the graph.

We begin this chapter with an overview of the life expectancy trends in current low mortality countries from 1950 forward (section 5.2). The figures refer only to the overall and sex-specific populations, and do not provide insights into the mechanisms behind the trends. Such insights could be gained by investigating life expectancy trends at specific ages or for specific causes of death (see, e.g., Meslé and Vallin, 2011). Section 5.3 provides the background for the project's expert survey and the subsequent meta-experts meeting that was held in San José, Costa Rica on 21–22 February 2012 to formulate the assumptions for WIC projections of future trends in life expectancy. The section starts with a description of past trends in mortality in light of the so-called 'epidemiologic transition' (section 5.3.1). Then the most likely determinants of mortality in coming decades and their corresponding impacts on future life expectancy are presented (section 5.3.2). The end of section 5.3 summarizes the mainstream expectations regarding future mortality trends, which can be divided into pessimistic (the 'Olshansky School') and optimistic (the 'Vaupel School') outlooks (section 5.3.3), and develops a conceptual framework for projecting future trends in life expectancy (section 5.3.4). The expert survey and the corresponding results are presented in section 5.4. Section 5.5 summarizes the optimistic and pessimistic storylines for future trends in life expectancy as they were developed at the meta-experts meeting. These storylines are the final basis for the assumed future mortality trends in the final population projection with the model being described in section 5.6. The chapter ends with a brief summary of the main conclusions.

5.2 Life expectancy trends from 1950 to 2010

5.2.1 Europe

Since 1950, the European life expectancy pattern has undergone deep transformations (Luy et al., 2011b; Mackenbach, 2013; Vallin and Meslé, 2001). The north-western part of Europe had much higher life expectancy levels in 1950 than the Mediterranean and eastern regions in which the standards of living were generally inferior. By 1965, this difference was already much less marked, with a spectacular rise in the life expectancies of Southern and Eastern Europe. Indeed, in less than 20 years, the south and east had nearly succeeded in catching up with the countries of Northern and Western Europe.

In the early 1960s, this transformation seemed to be in compliance with Abdel Omran's pattern of 'epidemiologic transition' (1971; see section 5.3.1). European life expectancies were all converging toward a seeming maximum, which Sweden had almost reached. However, from the mid-1960s, the situation changed completely. The countries of Eastern Europe, then governed by Communist regimes, were struck by a health crisis that considerably hampered their progress toward longer life expectancy. Indeed, in some cases, life expectancy even declined, especially among men. At the same time, after a period of stagnation in the 1960s, life expectancy in Western Europe began to increase thanks to new advances in the treatment of cardiovascular diseases. By 1995, this divergent movement between east and west had transformed the European life expectancy map, and the new line of separation corresponded with that of the former Iron Curtain.

This new divergence was caused by two major events (Meslé and Vallin, 2002). First, advances in health care were not limited to infectious diseases, as stated by Omran (1971). Progress in the treatment of cardiovascular disease and some forms of cancer, as well as advances in preventing 'man-made' diseases, such as alcoholism, smoking, and accidents, favoured the increase in life expectancy. Consequently, in the whole of Western Europe life expectancy continued to rise. At the same time, the communist countries, which had progressed very quickly in the field of infectious diseases, were unable to follow the new trends under way in the west. Thus, in 1995, after 30 years of near-stagnation among women and a decline among men, life expectancy in Russia was 10 years below that of Sweden for women and almost 20 years below for men.

Since the last decade of the twentieth century, trends in life expectancy in European countries have taken a new turn. Most Central and Eastern European countries have enjoyed the cardiovascular revolution and embarked on a new phase of convergence (Luy et al., 2011b; Vallin and Meslé, 2004). At the very beginning of the 1990s the Czech Republic was the first of these countries to re-establish progress toward longer lifespans, followed by Poland, Slovakia, and Hungary, among others (Meslé, 2004). In recent years, some progress has appeared in Russia, but it is too early to say if it will be sustainable. Southern European countries have continued to progress and are now the leaders of life expectancy in Europe.

European countries are now facing the challenging issue of the degenerative diseases that come with advanced age, especially neurodegenerative conditions like Alzheimer's disease. Future progress in life expectancy will depend on the ability of societies to efficiently manage the increasing medical burdens of people who live into very old age (see section 5.3).

5.2.2 North America and Mexico

The USA and Canada have witnessed tremendous increases in life expectancy since the 1950s through slow, yet steady, gains. Between 1950–55 and 2005–10, Americans experienced a 9.3 year gain in life expectancy (or 0.17 years per calendar year), whereas Canadians experienced a 11.6 year gain (or 0.21 years per calendar year). Compared with Americans, Canadians have experienced greater gains in life expectancy over the last almost 6 decades: they had slightly higher life expectancies at birth in 1950–55 (69.0 compared with 68.6 years), but substantially higher life expectancies by 2005–10 (80.5 compared with 78.0 years). The life expectancy gap between the Americans and Canadians has grown from 0.4 years in 1950–55 to 2.5 years in 2005–10. Furthermore, Americans' life expectancy at birth has also lagged behind other high-income nations (Woolf and Aron, 2013).

Life expectancy at birth has increased for the overall populations, and for both men and women in the USA and Canada. Between 1950–55 and 2005–10, life expectancy at birth increased from 65.8 to 75.4 among American men, 71.7 to 80.5 among American women, 66.6 to 78.2 among Canadian men, and 71.5 to 82.8 among Canadian women. In every year, life expectancy at birth is higher for Canadian than American men. In the quinquennium 1950–55, life expectancy at birth is higher for American than Canadian women, but from 1955–60 through 2005–10, life expectancy at birth is greater for Canadian women.

These descriptive comparative trends are illustrative. We can speculate, but cannot offer definitive evidence on the mechanisms that have produced these trends (see section 5.3). Trends in life expectancy for the overall and sex-specific populations are most likely due to health behaviours, especially smoking; health conditions, especially obesity; and structural factors, including health care access and insurance (Rogers et al., 2010). Compared with Canada, the USA has higher prevalence rates of smoking, obesity, and violence, along with limited access to health care, all of which most likely contributes to higher overall life expectancies in Canada. Further, the USA has had a longer history of cigarette consumption, especially among men, which has contributed to lower male life expectancies and larger sex gaps in life expectancy compared with Canada (Pampel, 2005).

In summary, three major findings stand out: (1) life expectancy at birth for both men and women in the USA and in Canada has experienced remarkable gains since the 1950s; (2) today, compared with Americans, Canadians enjoy higher life expectancies at birth for the overall population, and for men and women; (3) some of the differences between Canadian and American life expectancy are likely due to higher rates of smoking, obesity, and limited health insurance coverage in the USA.

The remarkable increases in life expectancy in the USA and Canada have been surpassed by Mexico's even more dramatic increases. Between 1950–55 and 2005–10, life expectancy at birth increased by a staggering 25.5 years in Mexico, from 50.7 to 76.2 years. Mexico has substantially narrowed, but not completely eliminated, the life expectancy gap with Canada and the USA. Still, in 2005–10, the 1.8-year life expectancy gap between Mexico and the USA is smaller than the 2.5-year gap between the USA and Canada.

5.2.3 Latin America and the Caribbean

This section refers to the populations of Latin America and the Caribbean, excluding Mexico and the high mortality countries Bolivia, Haiti, and Guyana (see Figure 5.1). From the early 1950s to the mid-1980s, two characteristics of life expectancy in the region were the existence of significant differences in both the size and pace of the yearly gains in life expectancy at birth. In 1950–55 two sets of countries are clearly distinguishable: those where mortality declined during the first half of the twentieth century, and those with high levels of mortality that had experienced very little change over this period. The former group includes Argentina and Uruguay, where mortality had been declining since the late nineteenth century (Palloni, 1990; Palloni and Pinto-Aguirre, 2011; Pérez-Brignoli, 2010), and Brazil, Costa Rica, Colombia, Cuba, and Panama, which showed evidence of declines prior to the introduction of modern medical technologies (Palloni, 1990). Among those countries, life expectancy in 1950–55 ranged from 54.8 in Chile to 66.0 in Uruguay. The latter group of countries with high levels of mortality and small gains in life expectancy ranged from Honduras, with 41.6, to Ecuador, with 48.4 years.

Up to the 1960s, countries that reached the highest life expectancies were those in which the gains were related not so much to medical technology, but to improvements in standards of living, strengthened institutions, and favourable conditions in international economic markets (Palloni, 1990; Pérez-Brignoli, 2010). Even though declines in mortality slowed for countries such as Argentina and Uruguay, they still maintained the highest life expectancy. For the rest of the countries, there is evidence that after the 1950s exogenous changes, particularly in medical technologies, and vertical programmes (i.e. public health measures aimed at particular diseases) were behind the gains in life expectancy (Guzmán, 2006; Palloni, 1990).

Beginning in the 1970s, the relationship between life expectancy and socio-economic conditions became stronger in Latin America and the Caribbean (Palloni, 1990). This is probably owing to the fact that countries such as Chile, Costa Rica, and Cuba, with sustained gains in life expectancy, expanded social services and access to health care and infrastructure for their populations. The average gains that decreased beginning in the 1970s for all the countries became more pronounced after the mid-1980s.

Until the early 1980s differences in life expectancy between countries in this geographical area remained large. The difference of approximately 24 years between the countries with highest and lowest life expectancies in the early 1950s decreased only slightly to 17 years in the early 1980s. However, as more countries reached life expectancy levels above 70 years, differences between countries declined. During the 1980s, the gains in life expectancy slowed down at the same time as a significant debt crisis occurred in all Latin American countries. Since that time, average gains in life expectancy have decreased steadily and considerably until today. Current levels of life expectancy for the quinquennium 2005–10 range in Latin America from a high of 78.9 years for Costa Rica to a low of 68.7 in Guyana.

A common characteristic throughout the different periods is that the pace of gains in life expectancy is not linked to original levels. While there is a group of countries that lagged behind the others throughout the 60-year period (Guatemala, Nicaragua, Honduras, El Salvador, and up to the year 2000, Peru), others lost their former leading position in the life expectancy ranking (Argentina, Uruguay, and Paraguay), or moved from lower to top positions (Costa Rica and Cuba). Costa Rica and Cuba were the first countries in Latin America to achieve life expectancy levels above 70 years in the late 1970s, and today their life expectancy is even higher than in the USA. El Salvador is an outlier, the only Latin American country that showed for some years a decrease in life expectancy, above all among men. This negative trend is due primarily to the armed conflicts that ravaged the country in the late 1970s and the 1980s.

Caribbean countries show a different pattern. In the early 1950s almost all reached a life expectancy above 50 years (with the Dominic Republic being the only exception) and differences were rather small. They had high gains during the early 1950s, and by 1960 their life expectancy was comparable to the forerunners of Latin America. During the subsequent 50-year period their pattern of change is also remarkably similar. Today's life expectancy levels range from a high of 80.1 in Martinique to a low of 69.4 in Trinidad and Tobago.

5.2.4 East Asia, South East Asia, and Oceania

From the mid-twentieth century onwards, East and South East Asia have experienced the most spectacular mortality decline in the world. In 1950–55 life expectancies were

46.4 years for East Asia and 42.4 years for South East Asia—notably lower than the world average of 47.7 years. By 2005–10, life expectancy for the world population increased by slightly more than 20 years and reached 67.9 years. In contrast, life expectancy rose about 27 years in both East Asia and South East Asia, and reached 74.0 years and 69.3 years respectively. During this period, the most impressive mortality reductions took place in Vietnam and South Korea, where life expectancies increased by 33.9 years and 32.1 years respectively.

There were significant variations in mortality in East and South East Asia in the early 1950s. Life expectancies were already over 60 years in Japan and three small urban populations in Hong Kong, Macao, and Singapore. At the same time, life expectancy was below 40 years in Indonesia. Although this gap has narrowed in recent years, the difference between high life expectancies (82.7 years for Japan, 81.6 years for Hong Kong, and 80.6 years for Singapore) and low life expectancies (67.9 years for Indonesia, 67.8 years for the Philippines, and 67.3 years for Mongolia) remains significant.

It is noteworthy that in the early 1950s, life expectancy in East and South East Asia was much lower than in the developed regions of the world. The gap between those Asian regions and much of the developed world was more than 20 years. That has changed significantly during the last six decades. In comparison with what has been achieved in developed countries, life expectancy for South East Asia is now about eight years lower, and the life expectancy for East Asia is less than three years behind. It is particularly noteworthy that Japan and Hong Kong have been leading the world in mortality decline in recent years. Life expectancies in South Korea and Taiwan have also increased rapidly (Zhao, 2011; Zhao and Kinfu, 2005). The currently highest life expectancy in the world can be found among Japanese women (see section 5.1). If these trends continue, female life expectancies in some East Asian populations could reach 90 years by 2025, and perhaps even 100 years by 2060, as indicated by Oeppen and Vaupel (2002; see section 5.3.3.2).

Australia also belongs to the countries with the highest life expectancies in the world, with a level of 81.7 years in 2005–10. In the early 1950s, life expectancy in Australia was already at a relatively high level (69.4 years) and showed very strong increases until today, above all in the periods after the mid-1970s. New Zealand exhibited similar levels of life expectancy until this time. However, mortality in New Zealand did not decrease at a similar pace as in Australia. But still, the population of New Zealand also reached a life expectancy of more than 80 years in the most recent period 2005–10 (80.2 years). The other low mortality countries of Oceania lag behind by some years of life expectancy, but they all showed similar, and almost parallel, increases during the middle of the twentieth century. At the top of these populations is Guam, where life expectancy increased from 57.1 years in 1950–55 to 77.4 years in 2005–10. At the lower end is Kiribati, with a life expectancy of 43.5 in 1950–55 and 67.2 in 2005–10. The only population of Oceania showing a less steep increase in life expectancy is that of the Solomon Islands. Here, life expectancy increased during the same period from 45.4 to only 66.4 years, mainly owing to a period of decreasing life expectancy during the late 1980s.

5.2.5 The Middle East and Northern Africa

The vast majority of countries in this region are defined today as low mortality countries. Only Sudan and Yemen are excluded because they have child mortality levels above the defined threshold at the beginning of this chapter (see Figure 5.1). However, the Middle East and Northern Africa (MENA) region is vast and encompasses a range of different mortality-relevant experiences, with values of life expectancy for the period 2005–10 ranging from 67.3 years in Iraq to 80.7 years in Israel.

Most countries in this region have experienced significant increases in life expectancy during the last 60 years, with the most impressive trajectories observed in the Gulf States, especially Bahrain and the United Arab Emirates (Omran and Roudi, 1993; Roudi, 2001). These two countries saw life expectancy increases from about 45 years in 1950–55 to 70 years in 1980–85 (an average increase of about 0.8 year per year). However, progress in life expectancy in the Gulf states has slowed since the late 1980s. In 2005–10, life expectancy values in these countries were about 75 years. Similarly, Syria and Jordan show relatively fast increases in the 1950s, 1960s, and 1970s, followed by slower increases in the 1980s and thereafter. After a period of stagnation in the 1950s and 1960s, Turkey experienced increases in life expectancy from 49.0 years in 1965–70 to 73.0 years in 2005–10.

Progress has been more gradual in countries of Northern Africa. Starting from life expectancy values of about 43 years in 1950–55, these countries have experienced a slower, but near linear, increase in life expectancy, with little sign of slowdown in recent years. Life expectancy values in this region for the period 2005–10 range from 71.2 in Morocco to 74.0 in Libya. Egypt and Morocco experienced trends similar to those in Turkey.

The MENA region includes some outliers to the described trends. In Iran and Iraq, increases in life expectancy were abruptly interrupted in the early 1980s as a result of the war between the two countries, which generated many casualties. Recovery has been impressive in Iran, with a life expectancy of 72.1 years for the period 2005–10. Iraq, by contrast, has lost ground since the early 1990s, in part because of subsequent conflict in that country. With a value of 67.3 years in 2005–10, life expectancy in Iraq is actually lower than in 1990–95. Progress in Lebanon has also been hampered by conflict. In the 1950s and 1960s, Lebanon enjoyed one of the highest levels of life expectancy in the region. Progress has slowed significantly since the 1970s, and in 2005–10, with a life expectancy of 72.0 years, Lebanon is in the lower range among countries of the region.

Israel is another outlier in the region, with a life expectancy trajectory similar to those observed in Western Europe or North America (Na'amnih et al., 2010). Having started from a level of 68.9 years in 1950–55, life expectancy in Israel has increased in a near linear fashion, reaching a value of 80.7 in 2005–10, which is the highest life expectancy in the MENA region.

5.2.6 Former Soviet Republics of Central Asia and the Caucasus

Only four countries in this region are defined as low mortality countries: Armenia, Georgia, Kazakhstan, and Kyrgyzstan. Kazakhstan and Kyrgyzstan were experiencing life expectancy values of 55.0 years and 52.9 years, respectively, in 1950–55. Such values were among the lowest in the Soviet Union and were due to relatively high levels of infant mortality. Kazakhstan and Kyrgyzstan subsequently experienced notable increases in life expectancy, primarily driven by reductions in infant mortality. The two countries experienced virtually linear increases in life expectancy until the late 1980s, reaching values of 67.4 years and 66.0 years, respectively, for the period 1985–90. This progress ended with the break-up of the Soviet Union in 1991. The two countries experienced some deterioration in life expectancy during the 1990s, and levels for the period 2005–10 increase similarly to those of the period 1985–90 (Guillot, 2007).

Values of life expectancy in Armenia and Georgia in 1950–55 (62.8 years and 60.6 years, respectively) were more favourable than in Central Asia and closer to the experience of Russia. However, in these two republics life expectancy started stagnating as early as the 1970s, with values oscillating around 70 years. As in Kazakhstan and Kyrgyzstan, Armenia and Georgia experienced declines in life expectancy in the 1990s (Duthé et al., 2010), but have experienced some mortality recovery during the first decade of the twenty-first century, with values of life expectancy around 73 for the period 2005–10.

5.3 Expectations for future changes in life expectancy

5.3.1 The 'epidemiologic transition' and recent changes in mortality

Section 5.2 provided an overview of the trends in life expectancy in today's low mortality populations since the middle of the twentieth century. In most of these populations, the mortality decrease started some 50 years earlier, at the close of the nineteenth century. These changes in mortality were the basis of the theory of demographic transition and led to considerable interest from economists, medical doctors, and epidemiologists (e.g. Caselli, 1995, 1989). In the field of epidemiology, trends by cause of death gave rise to the formulation of the theory of 'epidemiologic transition' by Omran (1971), who attempted to account for the extraordinary advances in health care made in industrialized countries since the eighteenth century.

Omran defined three epidemiologic 'ages,' with the first corresponding to the period of high mortality, in which infectious diseases were the primary cause of death. The second age is the transition period between the first and third age. The latter defines a new regime with constant low mortality in which degenerative and man-made diseases act as the primary cause of death (see section 5.2.1). At the time Omran developed his theory of 'epidemiologic transition', most medical specialists, as well as United Nations (UN) health experts, saw life expectancies generally converging toward a maximum age. Moreover, the most advanced countries were supposed to be already close to this limit. According to the projections of the UN (1975) at that time, the assumed point of convergence was a life expectancy of 75 years. Therefore, the 'epidemiologic transition' proposed by Omran was an apt description of the mortality developments until the end of the 1960s, when the incidence of infectious diseases in the developed countries had been so far reduced that any further reduction could not lead to further significant gains in the average life expectancy.

Omran failed, however, to predict the so-called 'cardiovascular revolution' that started in the 1970s and launched a new period of decreasing mortality (Omran, 1983). Olshansky and Ault (1986) followed by Rogers and Hackenberg (1987), without criticizing the basic premises of the theory of 'epidemiologic transition', introduced the idea of a fourth stage during which the maximum point of convergence of life expectancies would seem to increase as a consequence of achievements in the treatment of cardiovascular diseases (Caselli et al., 2002).[5] Olshansky et al. (1990) set this new maximum at 85 years, the same as that chosen by the UN (1989) for all total populations in their projections at the end of the 1980s (82.5 years for men and 87.5 years for women).

In recent years, the 85-year threshold has been strongly criticized by many authors who believe that such a limit cannot be determined (Carey and Judge, 2001; Vaupel, 2001). The validity of the threshold is also being challenged by the presence of populations that have already surpassed the 85-year maximum in female life expectancy at birth (see section 5.1). With the dawn of the twenty-first century, the decline in mortality in some developed countries has given fresh impetus to achieving new maxima in life expectancy, particularly for women. Estimating these potentials requires an assessment of the most likely determinants of future mortality, that is, the most important risk factors, as well as the factors that might cause further reductions in mortality. We summarize some of these in the following subsections.

5.3.2 Most likely determinants of future mortality

Based on past experience in today's low mortality countries, smoking and obesity are major factors that can be individually influenced and have high potential to affect future mortality. Beside these health behavioural factors, biomedical progress and the influence of environmental changes are likely to become main drivers in future mortality trends, as described in this section. Another likely determinant is socio-economic status, including individual educational attainment, occupation, income, and wealth. Within the prevalent societal, economic, and disease environment individuals can

[5] Only Olshansky and Ault (1986) called that additional stage the 'fourth stage of the epidemiologic transition'. The other authors defined this age as the 'new' or 'hybristic' stage.

improve their socio-economic situation and can, consequently, experience a longer life time.

5.3.2.1 *Smoking*

An abundance of studies have identified smoking as a major health hazard and one of the most important factors that contribute to mortality differences between individuals and populations. Tobacco consumption has been linked to a variety of diseases and negative health outcomes, including adverse reproductive effects and mortality. Smoking increases the risk of death from at least ten types of malignant neoplasm's (cancer), with lung cancer being the leading smoking-related fatal form of cancer (U.S. Department of Health and Human Services, 2004). Smoking also causes cardiovascular and respiratory diseases, of which ischaemic heart disease and chronic airway obstruction are the most important in terms of number of deaths (U.S. Department of Health and Human Services, 2004). Smoking-related mortality is considered to peak some decades after the peak in smoking prevalence. Beyond being hazardous to smokers, second-hand smoke has also been shown to cause deaths in non-smokers, especially from heart diseases and lung cancer (U.S. Department of Health and Human Services, 2004). In fact, smoking-related mortality has been shown to be responsible for the less favourable developments in life expectancy in Denmark, the Netherlands, and the USA (Christensen et al., 2010; Preston et al., 2010; Staetsky, 2009).

Widespread smoking was first observed in the USA. In the 1950s Americans had higher levels of cigarette consumption than any other population (Forey et al., 2002). In the following years smoking prevalence increased steadily in both the USA and most other countries. Cigarette consumption in the USA peaked in the mid-1960s and started to decline thereafter; in many other countries a similar decline was observed during the 1970s. Today, cigarette consumption is still receding, although some European countries and Japan now have a higher smoking prevalence than the USA (Crimmins et al., 2011).

It has been shown that the trend in smoking prevalence in a population follows the spread pattern of an epidemic and involves a diffusion process across socio-economic strata (Lopez et al., 1994). The emergence of smoking has first been observed among groups of high socio-economic status and then spreads to the rest of the population. Similarly, the decline in smoking prevalence begins among groups of high socio-economic status, who are typically the first to become concerned with the harmful effects of smoking (Pampel, 2005). Today, smoking is much more common among groups of low socio-economic status. These processes can be observed among both sexes, with higher prevalence rates in men and a time lag of 20–30 years between men and women.

A similar diffusion process has been observed in sex differences in smoking. Recent studies identified the major role of this process in the widening and narrowing of the sex gap in life expectancy (e.g. Pampel, 2002, 2005; Preston and Wang, 2006). The onset and peak of smoking prevalence in women has been considerably later than for men in almost all developed countries, which first contributed significantly to the widening and then to the narrowing in the sex gap in life expectancy in recent decades. Smoking is expected to contribute to a further narrowing in the gap between men and women (e.g. Preston and Wang, 2006).

For the USA, Wang and Preston (2009) predicted that the changes toward lower smoking prevalence will lead to a faster mortality decline than anticipated by most experts. These conclusions are supported by the projections of Bongaarts (2006) and King and Soneji (2011). In many low mortality countries, national health policies are currently conducting intensive anti-smoking campaigns that can be expected to lead to further decreases of smoking rates among women and men. It has been shown for several populations that these efforts have already led to significant reductions in smoking prevalence and lung cancer mortality among men (Ádám et al., 2013).

5.3.2.2 *Obesity*

Obesity is another major factor that has been identified as a health hazard with possible consequences for the future development of life expectancy in developed countries. According to the World Health Organization, a person is considered obese if he or she has a body mass index (BMI) of 30 or more. The proportion of obese individuals has increased in the last 50 years in the USA (Crimmins et al., 2011, p. 44). In 1960–62 about 11 per cent of adult men and 16 per cent of adult women were categorized as obese; by 2007–08 the proportion was 33 per cent for adult men and 36 per cent for adult women (Flegal et al., 2001, 2010). Increases in obesity rates have also been observed for many developed countries, although obesity levels and trends vary considerably by country (Alley et al., 2010). In Anglo-Saxon countries the rise has been more rapid and the overall prevalence has been higher than in most other countries, while Japan and Italy experienced the lowest prevalence and slowest increase in obesity (Alley et al., 2010). In very recent years there is an indication that obesity rates in the USA are levelling off, while, at the same time, they continue to increase for many other countries (Crimmins et al., 2011). Recent evidence for the USA suggests that obesity reduces the life expectancy at age 50 by 1.54 years for women and 1.85 years for men (Preston and Stokes, 2011). The authors argue that the high prevalence of obesity in the USA contributes substantially to its bad performance in terms of life expectancy compared with many other developed countries (see section 5.2).

Obesity is associated with a variety of diseases of the circulatory system (e.g. high blood pressure), diabetes, and certain cancers (colorectal, breast, endometrial, cancers of the kidney, pancreas, liver, and gallbladder). However, the consequences of increased obesity on a population's life expectancy have been a matter of debate (see also section 5.3.3). Olshansky et al. (2005) suggested that the growing prevalence of obesity could lead to a potential decline in life expectancy in the future. Using a different forecasting method, Reither et al. (2011) confirmed that obesity may have an impact on death rates that is far worse than generally anticipated, especially for younger cohorts. In contrast, other recent studies indicate that the relationship between obesity and mortality is rather complex and that earlier studies have probably overestimated the effects. This is partly because the relationship between obesity and mortality varies by age and cause of death, and is confounded by smoking (Alley et al., 2010). Another reason recently brought forward is earlier data limitations. Almost all studies that showed a strong relationship between obesity and mortality used data collected before 1990 (Mehta and Chang, 2011). Studies that used more recent data suggest a rather modest relation between mortality and obesity on the population level (e.g. Alley et al., 2010; Finkelstein et al., 2010). The relation is stronger in individuals with severe obesity (BMI ≥35) (Prospective Studies Collaboration, 2009) and becomes stronger with age (Masters et al., 2013). Evidence for differences between men and women is mixed (Alley et al., 2010; Flegal et al., 2013).

Some studies even suggest that mortality associated with obesity has been declining over time (e.g. Flegal et al., 2005, 2010; Mehta and Chang, 2011). The association seems to have particularly changed for moderate obesity (BMI 30.0–34.9). Using three different data sources, Mehta and Chang (2011) found no relationship between mortality and moderate obesity for more recent years. For severe obesity results have been mixed, suggesting no significant change in the relationship between mortality and obesity for individuals with a BMI of 35 and above (Mehta and Chang, 2011). The impact of the complex and changing relationship between different levels of obesity and mortality on future life expectancy is not yet clear. Recent projections for the USA indicate that the negative impact of the rise of obesity may be much lower than the expected gains in life expectancy owing to the reductions in smoking prevalence (King and Soneji, 2011).

5.3.2.3 *Biomedical progress*

A major source of uncertainty for forecasts of life expectancy in the developed countries is the contribution of biomedical technology to the biology of ageing and extending lifespans. To our knowledge there have been no studies that investigate the possible impact of these technologies on extending human longevity. A recent review by Sierra et al. (2009) addresses the state of knowledge regarding the biological mechanisms that underlie the ageing process. The study notes that several processes have been found to extend the lifespan of animals. At least one, caloric restriction, is now being investigated in humans, and others are being tested in animals with unknown prospects for human application.[6] The study also suggests that genetic manipulation of humans in order to extend lifespan is unlikely in the foreseeable future (Sierra et al., 2009).

Although it seems unlikely that complex biological mechanisms will be completely understood for many years to come, biomedical technology may contribute in the near future to the treatment of degenerative diseases and syndromes such as dementia. Dementia has been recognized as one of the most important medical problems in the elderly. Alzheimer's disease is the most prevalent and most studied subtype of dementia, accounting for 50–56 per cent of all cases. Patients diagnosed with Alzheimer's disease typically die within 3–9 years of diagnosis (Querfurth and LaFerla, 2010). The incidence of Alzheimer's disease is highly related to age and doubles every 5 years after age 65.

[6] Note, however, that caloric dietary restriction (40 per cent food intake reduction) has been shown to lengthen lifespans in some strains of mice, but it can shorten lifespans in other strains of mice (see Liao et al., 2010).

After age 85, the odds of being diagnosed with Alzheimer's disease is higher than one in three (Querfurth and LaFerla, 2010). The apolipoproteine E gene (*APOE*) has been identified as a major determinant for the risk of onset of this disease. There is currently no treatment for the disease, and existing disease-modifying drugs yield only modest effects. The same is true for most drugs that are currently in the development pipeline, and a significant advance in secondary prevention will likely take one or two decades (see van Marum, 2008 for more details).

Although research in the field is increasing, understanding of the basic biological mechanisms of ageing is still limited, and it is unclear if knowledge of these mechanisms can significantly contribute to increases in life expectancy in the near future. Similarly, it is impossible to assess whether a major breakthrough in the treatment or prevention of degenerative diseases will take place in the near future. Nevertheless, progress in understanding the underlying mechanisms of these diseases could, in fact, lead to increases in longevity even in the upcoming decade.

5.3.2.4 *Environmental changes*

The impact of environmental conditions on the health and mortality of a population has long been a matter of study and concern. Climatic conditions affect the body and directly trigger either biomedical reactions such as infections, or affect the body through intervening social factors such as housing conditions, exposure to outdoor cold and heat, and other conditions. Air pollution is also discussed in this context as a possible risk factor for mortality (see, e.g., Wen and Gu, 2012).

Some aspects of climate and environmental effects on the mortality level of a population have been investigated in the context of seasonal changes in the risk of dying. These studies show that mortality varies systematically within the year; in most European countries and the USA, higher mortality is observed during the winter (Healy, 2003; McKee, 1989). The amplitude of these seasonal variations has decreased over time, and it differs between countries (Rau, 2004; Rau and Doblhammer, 2003). Surprisingly, countries with the mildest winters, such as Portugal, Greece, Spain, Ireland, and the UK, experience the highest seasonal fluctuations in mortality, while seasonal excess mortality is lower in Northern and Central Europe (Healy, 2003). These differences were largely attributed to differences in housing standards. An important implication was drawn from these observations: the key factor explaining the differences in seasonal excess mortality was the ability of the population to protect itself from environmental stress (Healy, 2003).

A great deal of public, political, and scientific attention is devoted to the observed changes in the earth's environmental conditions. Climate change, resulting in a warming of the earth's surface, has been observed for some decades, and an overwhelming majority of the world's climate scientists agree that human activities contribute substantially to this ongoing development (Intergovernmental Panel on Climate Change (IPCC), 2007; Richardson et al., 2011). The increases in the average temperature have been accompanied by extreme weather conditions—especially heatwaves, storms, fires, and floods. However, the injuries and deaths caused by such events rarely have a direct impact on a population's life expectancy, especially not on the long-term trends as experienced with several naturally caused mortality crises during the last centuries (Browning et al., 2011).

Indirect pathways of climate change can include water and food insecurity, and the spread of infectious diseases (Gollin and Zimmermann, 2012; McMichael and Lindgren, 2011). As water and food insecurity is predicted to be more devastating in developing countries, climate change may increase population displacement and migration to the less affected countries (see Chapter 7). Assessment of the impact of climate changes on mortality in developed societies has just begun. Even recent pessimistic projections for the impact of climate change on US mortality yield only a modest increase in age-adjusted mortality of about 3 per cent by the end of the twenty-first century (Deschênes and Greenstone, 2011). However, such projections do not take into account the likelihood that humans will be able to adapt to the new climatic situation, for instance by developing new lifestyles and technologies, especially in light of the increases in the overall level of education (see section 5.3.2.5).

5.3.2.5 *Socio-economic status*

Socio-economic status has four main components: educational attainment, occupation, income, and wealth. These components are often combined to define social class. The relationships between mortality and socio-economic determinants are well documented (see, e.g., Valkonen, 2006). The influence of variables such as occupational status and social class on cardiovascular mortality has been long established, and later studies added hypertension or hypercholesterolemia to the mortality–social class relationship.

In the last few decades several studies have indicated an inverse relationship between mortality and educational attainment. The differences vary in their extent between countries (Corsini, 2010; Kunst, 1997) and, in general, they are larger among men than among women (Ross et al., 2012). Figures 5.3a and 5.3b show the trends in life expectancy between the education subgroups with highest and lowest mortality levels for selected populations, separated by sex. The data stem from different studies on education-specific life expectancy with the estimates referring to different countries, ages, and calendar year periods between 1970 and 2006 (see notes below Figures 5.3a and 5.3b). Among men (left panel in Figure 5.3a) these maximum differences in life expectancy by education varied at the initial observation time of these studies (denoted 'time 1' in Figure 5.3a) between 1.3 and 7.8 years. In most populations, the differences increased over time ranging from 2.5 years to 13.1 years at the time of second observation (time 2). Reductions in education-specific mortality differences in these studies were reported only for Austrian men between 1991 and 2001 and between 2001 and 2006, with decreases in the life expectancy gap from 6.0 to 5.7 years and from 5.7 to 5.2 years respectively (Klotz, 2010). Among women (right panel in Figure 5.3b), the differences in life expectancy by education are smaller and more populations show decreases in education-specific mortality differentials. However, the overall range of the differences also increased. At time 1, the maximum differences in life expectancy by education varied between 1.3 and 5.7 years, while at time 2 the differences ranged from 0.7 to 10.2 years. Among both sexes, the highest differences are reported for Eastern European

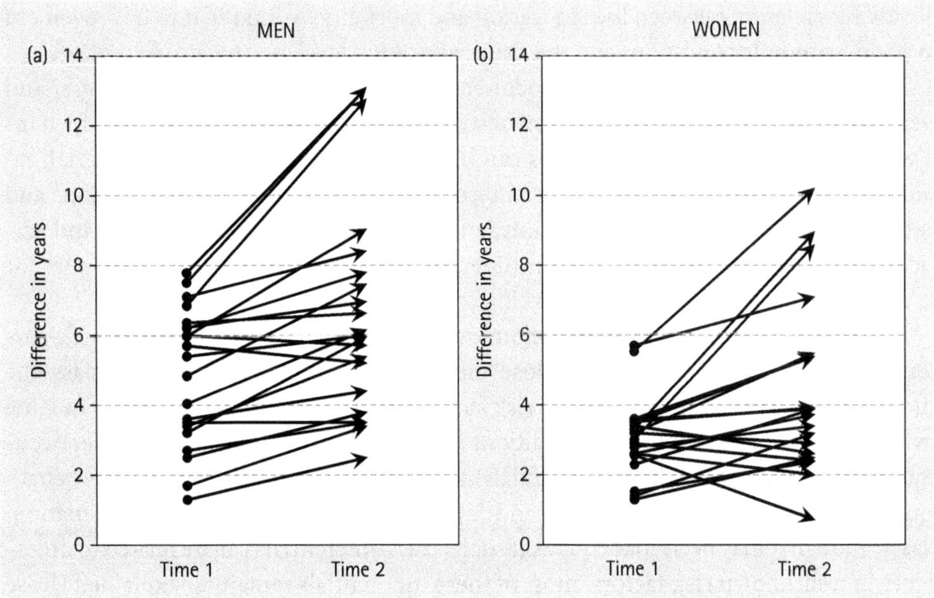

FIGURE 5.3(a, b) Trends in life expectancy differences between population subgroups with highest and lowest education levels from different countries and at different ages and time periods.

Notes: Estimates refer to Austria 1981–91, 1991–01, 2001–06 (Klotz, 2010); Belgium 1991–01 (Deboosere et al., 2009); the Czech Republic 1984–99 (Shkolnikov et al., 2006); Estonia 1989–2000 (Leinsalu et al., 2003), 1988–99 (Shkolnikov et al., 2006); Finland 1988–99 (Shkolnikov et al., 2006); Germany 1990–96 (Luy et al., 2010); Italy 1982–87 (men only), 1987–92 (Luy et al., 2011a); Russia 1979–89 (Shkolnikov et al,. 1998), 1988–99 (Shkolnikov et al., 2006); and the USA 1970–80, 1980–90 (Crimmins and Saito, 2001), 1982–90 (Manton et al., 1997), 1981–90, 1990–00 (Meara et al., 2008).

populations, such as Russia and Estonia, and the lowest for Western populations and higher age groups.

Despite the fact that the education gradient in mortality is a universal phenomenon, the role of education within the network of factors comprising the socio-economic status of persons is still unclear. Most studies consider educational attainment a mediating factor that helps individuals to acquire, develop, and use a set of resources, such as information about health behaviours, social psychological resources, access to and utilization of health care, and other types of socio-economic attainment.

The twentieth century saw revolutionary improvements in educational attainment. Younger cohorts have acquired higher and higher levels of education, shifting the entire educational distribution upward (see Lutz et al., 2007). These cohorts have been educated about the hazards of unhealthy lifestyles and have learned to deal with increasing complexities, while learning how to educate themselves using new forms of communication. These ongoing changes in the educational distribution are important when considering the impact of socio-economic factors in the future. The mentioned inverse relationship between educational level and mortality is complex and the importance of different explanatory pathways has changed over time. Consequently, explaining the positive correlation between low education and mortality by linking it to improvement in socio-economic conditions and the rise of education level may be insufficient.

The other main components of socio-economic status—occupation, income, and wealth—are central to the stratification of society and represent the degree to which individual characteristics and resources can be converted into other, often material, resources. Individuals with more material resources are able to pay for medications and better health care, food of better quality, and other health-promoting goods and services. Research also shows education differentials with respect to social support for stress, particularly stress linked to working conditions.

The main components of socio-economic status are often primary indicators of a person's social status, a concept that is closely linked to social class. As to social class, the classical explanation is that the health risk factor of lower classes is linked to low income (which itself determines housing conditions and poor eating habits) and to higher occupational risk, such as accidents. Stressful living conditions may induce unhealthy behaviours such as alcoholism, smoking, and lack of physical exercise. This explanation, classic though it may be, is inadequate. If social class differentials can be related to differences in well-known risk factors, most of these differentials remain unexplained (Rose and Marmot, 1981; Thiltgès et al., 1995).

We note that the impact of socio-economic status on mortality is not just a question of an individual's performance in this network of factors. The societal, political, and disease environment in which an individual lives is also important (e.g. Johansson, 1991). This is likely an important mediator between socio-economic status and individual health outcomes which could explain why socio-economic status has different effects in different populations at different times.

5.3.3 The debate between optimists and pessimists

The previous descriptions of the most likely drivers of future longevity illustrated that their impacts on mortality are complex and difficult to assess. For this reason, predicting the development of life expectancy is a matter of deep disagreement among demographers, epidemiologists, and other population scientists. In recent years, two schools of thought have developed that dominate the discussion about the most likely trends of future life expectancy (for the most recent dispute see Olshansky and Carnes, 2013, and Vaupel and Rau, 2013). Both agree that mortality will continue to decrease, lifespan will increase, and life expectancy records will continue to be broken. Thus, the difference of opinion between the two schools about likely future trends in life expectancy 'appears to be smaller than is widely presumed' (Bongaarts, 2006, p. 608; see also Wilmoth, 2001). They differ, however, in their opinions on the time course and magnitude of these improvements.

5.3.3.1 *Pessimistic view: the 'Olshansky School'*

The first school of thought is represented by Olshansky and colleagues who argue that future progress in life expectancy is likely to be much smaller than in the past. Their view is derived from several lines of reasoning. The first is that future increases in life expectancy are more difficult to achieve than in the past. As already mentioned in section 5.1, the rapid increase in life expectancy during the first half of the twentieth century was mainly driven by mortality reductions at childhood and early adult ages. Today's mortality levels at these ages are very low and any further mortality decline will only yield small increases in life expectancy in the future (Olshansky et al., 2001). In 1990, Olshansky and colleagues calculated that eliminating all mortality before the age of 50 would lead to an increase in life expectancy of only 3.5 years (Olshansky et al., 1990). Because of this, most of the recent increase in life expectancy has been achieved in older ages and likewise, any future increases must be fuelled by mortality reductions in the elderly population. Saving an elderly life, however, has a smaller impact on life expectancy than saving the life of a newborn, which is why life expectancy is becoming less sensitive to changes in death rates (Olshansky et al., 1990). Thus, the increases in life expectancy may only continue at the present pace if death rates at older ages can be reduced much faster than in the past (Olshansky et al., 2001).

A second, closely related line of reasoning argues that extrapolations of past trends in life expectancy are flawed because the mortality experience of today's cohorts is fundamentally different from that of earlier cohorts (Carnes and Olshansky, 2007). The authors argue that not only did the age pattern that caused the rise in life expectancy shift upward during the 'epidemiologic transition', but the cause of death pattern has also dramatically changed. The early mortality regime was characterized by high mortality in younger ages, with deaths often caused by infectious diseases. Today's deaths occur at a late age and are caused by long-term processes that originate and progress within each individual (Carnes and Olshansky, 2007). With these fundamental, and to a large extent unforeseeable, regime changes of the past in mind, it is likely that the future regime of mortality may also depart from the known patterns (Carnes and Olshansky, 2007; Miech et al., 2011).

The third line of reasoning refers to the emergence of new threats to further increases in life expectancy. One of those threats is obesity (Olshansky, 2005), which has been increasing for several decades in many developed countries, most prominently in the USA. As already outlined in section 5.3.2.2, obesity has been associated with several negative health outcomes, such as diabetes, and may lead to a shortened life. Despite the mixed empirical evidence, Olshansky and colleagues assume that obesity alone may lead to a levelling off or even a decline of life expectancy in the USA. Infectious diseases are another major threat to further increases in life expectancy. They are still a leading cause of death in many low-income countries and they are re-emerging and increasing in the developed countries (Olshansky et al., 1997). Most of the increase has been fuelled by the AIDS epidemic, but other sources of infectious diseases, ranging from hospital-acquired infectious diseases to antibiotic resistant pathogens, have also increased (Olshansky, 2005). Moreover, according to Olshansky (2005), today's societies are much more vulnerable to global pandemics, such as influenza.

A fourth line of reasoning is based on the fundamental evolutionary theory that human bodies are not capable of infinite functioning and thus the duration of life is finite (Carnes et al., 2013). The most prominent scholar who advocates the limited lifespan perspective is James Fries. In his most influential paper he argued that the length of life is ultimately fixed and that the average maximum lifespan will be approximately 85 years (Fries, 1980).

On the basis of these considerations, Olshansky and colleagues conclude that life expectancy for both sexes combined will—in accordance with Fries' approach—unlikely exceed age 85 (see also section 5.3.1), although this limit is considered a 'soft one' (Couzin-Frankel, 2011). They argue that unless the ageing process itself can be modified, life expectancy gains will become increasingly difficult in the future and will likely 'be measured in days or months rather than years' (Olshansky et al., 2001, p. 1492).

5.3.3.2 *Optimistic view: the 'Vaupel School'*

A second school of thought is represented by James W. Vaupel and colleagues, who have long argued against the limited lifespan paradigm, mainly directed against the 'Fries limit' of 85 years. Collecting and using high-quality empirical data, Vaupel and colleagues present evidence indicating that the limited lifespan paradigm as proposed by Fries is wrong (Kannisto, 1988, 1994, 1996; Kannisto et al., 1994). The optimists' arguments on the future of life expectancy are heavily based on evidence derived from available empirical data on past trends in mortality.

A first set of evidence shows that mortality rates at older ages have decreased for several decades for all developed countries that have reliable data (e.g. Kannisto, 1994; Kannisto et al., 1994). Recent data illustrate that these trends have continued in many countries, although the pace of decrease varies (Rau et al., 2008). Mortality reduction for the extreme ages has also been shown for countries such as France and Japan (Robine and Saito, 2003), indicating that survival rates even at the highest ages can be modified. This is further supported by mortality data on the German elderly before and after reunification of East and West Germany. Before 1990, mortality of East and West Germans increasingly diverged. After unification, East German mortality dropped close to West German levels within a very short time (Luy, 2004), most strikingly even for men and women who were 80 years and older at the time of unification (Vaupel et al., 2003). These empirical observations strengthen the view that human mortality is highly plastic (see also Burger et al., 2012, and Gage, 1994), and that future improvement in living conditions and medical progress can have a large effect on the lifespans of individuals at all ages.

A second set of evidence is female period life expectancy in the country where women live the longest, first published by Oeppen and Vaupel (2002) and recently modified by Vallin and Meslé (2009). The so-called 'record life expectancy' has increased for more than 170 years, most of its time at an almost linear pace with an increase of approximately 2.5 years per decade. Shkolnikov et al. (2011) showed that record cohort life expectancy also increased more or less linearly until today, with an even stronger pace of 4.3 years per decade. Vaupel and colleagues reason that if a limit of life expectancy was being approached—either a limit that could not be overcome with medical technology or an absolute limit on the human body's lifespan—the pace of increase in the record-holding country would begin to slow down. As of today there is no sign of a deceleration in the increase of female record life expectancy (Christensen et al., 2009). This perspective has been supported recently by alternative investigations of trends in life expectancy by Cohen and Oppenheim (2012) and Rossi et al. (2013). A similar study by White (2002) revealed that the linear life expectancy increase not only holds for the world's record life expectancy, but also for the average life expectancy of high-income countries as demonstrated for the years 1955–96.

A third set of evidence is based on findings in non-human species. Vaupel and colleagues refuted Fries' prediction that death rates should rise rapidly at advanced ages. Studies in large populations of Medflies showed that their age trajectory of mortality reached a maximum and then declined (Carey et al., 1992). Mortality decelerations were also found for other insects and species, such as nematode worms (e.g. Curtsinger et al., 1992). Later on, laboratory research confirmed that changes in environmental factors such as diet, as well as genetic factors, can have a large impact on the age trajectory of mortality for some species (e.g. Mair et al., 2003).

Based on these different types of empirical observations, Vaupel and colleagues conclude that there is no convincing evidence that life expectancy is approaching a limit or that the increase in life expectancy is decelerating (Vaupel, 2010). They argue that as long as life expectancy continues to increase with no sign of deceleration, it is reasonable to assume that future progress in life expectancy will continue to be similar to the progress of the past. Extrapolating the observed life expectancy trends to the future with a similar pace as record life expectancy yields impressive results. Median cohort survival time, which is the age until half of the cohort will survive, will be above 100 years of age for recently born cohorts in many developed countries (Christensen et al., 2009). In these projections, Japan will continue to be the leading country in terms of life expectancy, with more than half of the babies born in 2007 becoming at least 107 years of age (Christensen et al., 2009).

5.3.4 A 'conceptual framework' for assessing the potential of future life expectancy

The previous sections made it clear that today almost no progress in life expectancy can be made by further reductions of mortality at young ages. However, summarizing all empirical evidence and theoretical considerations, additional gains in life expectancy are still possible owing to further reductions of mortality at older ages. Achieving these gains requires an understanding of the best strategies and preventions against the main risk factors. This could lead, above all, to further decreases in mortality from cardiovascular diseases, particularly from ischaemic heart diseases, and cancer.

Another key function for increasing longevity lies in people's increased awareness of their own health status. This increases the chances for an early diagnosis of severe diseases, enhances the efficacy of new treatments, and—with the introduction of healthier lifestyles—lessens a number of other risks. However, it is difficult to establish whether the greater attention paid to the health status of more recent cohorts is a direct result of health education policies (e.g. early cancer prevention measures for women, anti-smoking campaigns to combat lung cancer) that have only been implemented in some countries, or the outcome of a change in the social and economic structure that affects most populations of today's low mortality countries. The latter seems plausible given that the proportion of more highly educated people has risen during this century and hence provided more and more individuals with access to better health information and the development of preventive lifestyles.

All these arguments indicate that enormous potentials for further increases of longevity exist, and they might be the milestones of the path our post-industrial society will follow toward a truly new phase in health transition. Without overlooking the effects of economic change on a society's mortality level, the possibility for this new phase to become a reality depends on the interplay between a new health culture and further discoveries in treatment, therapy, and bio-genetic and biomedical techniques. The former would act on the individual and social control over risk factors and the possibility of making an early diagnosis; the latter would provide more prompt and effective structures and treatment. Consequently, the continuing decline in mortality in more developed countries appears to justify hope for further significant gains in life expectancy.

Population scientists, including demographers and epidemiologists, have long been aware that the diversity in mortality levels and patterns across individuals and populations is the net result of a host of interactions between societal, environmental, biological, and behavioural variables, the mechanisms of which remain elusive (Lopez et al., 1995). A death above the age of 30 generally results from a number of associated and competing pathologies, and is rarely the result of a single morbid condition or injury. Demographic and descriptive epidemiological studies have typically assessed health patterns and trends in terms of the immediate medical cause of death. A broader and more relevant concept is that of 'determinants of mortality' that may affect several medical causes of death, for example smoking as a cause of lung cancer.

Considering the causality, some determinants have a negligible impact on adult mortality in industrialized countries. Rather, their impact is much more likely to be felt through interactions that are often synergistic with individual health behaviour (e.g. smoking) and can substantially alter the risk of death from certain causes. Besides acting directly and indirectly, determinants of mortality also operate dynamically throughout an individual life course. Each individual's life course starts with a basic situation at birth, to which various careers are added (e.g. Graham, 2002; Kuh and Shlomo, 2004; Kuh et al., 2003). Each of these careers is defined by different states and events, and can influence the individual risk of dying either immediately or through an accumulation of factors. Studies of mortality then have to incorporate temporal variation exposures, with conceptual frameworks for adults having to take into account the life history of individuals (Caselli et al., 1987, 1991; Caselli, 1991; Caselli and Lopez, 1996). In particular, studies have demonstrated that the life conditions experienced in infancy and childhood have an impact on mortality at old ages (Bengtsson and Lindström, 1989, 2000; Doblhammer, 2004; Montez and Hayward, 2011).

In today's developed countries, individual lifestyle (smoking, alcohol and drug abuse, and obesity) is a dominant factor in the survival of adults. An important contribution can also be attributed to socio-economic status, as outlined in section 5.3.2.5 (see also Marmot, 1995), or educational level, possibly deriving from relative wealth (e.g. availability and use of health services). Genetic factors and selection effects may also play an important role in determining the longevity of the elderly, in part through interactions with adverse health behaviour. Understanding all of the determinants of mortality and their interactions and changes over time is a complex undertaking. The problem is made even more difficult by the consideration that the evolving economic, social, environmental, and cultural situation in the developed world could, with time, produce new risks factors (such as obesity or drug overdoses), create new pathologies (e.g. the emergence of AIDS), or lead to the spread of others (such as Alzheimer's and other neurodegenerative diseases). However, if the passage from the mortality patterns of the ancient regime to those emerging in a modern industrial society permitted average life expectancy to double, it is reasonable to expect that this new emergent phase is characteristic of a modern knowledge-based, post-industrial society and will lead to further increases in life expectancy. A more difficult question is to assess if the pace of life expectancy increases will continue.

5.4 Expert survey on future trends of life expectancy in low mortality countries

In 2011, a global Internet survey on likely future trends in fertility, mortality, migration, and the main factors behind them (i.e. their relevance and impact) was conducted among the members of major population associations and selected other professional organizations. The survey, a collaboration between the International Institute for Applied Systems Analyisis' (IIASA) World Population Program and Oxford University, is the basis for new population forecasts by age, sex, and level of education for most of the world's countries, as presented in this book. For the survey, experts selected a country for which, as part of their assessment, they provided numerical estimates of the likely range of the gain in life expectancy between 2020 and 2030, and between 2040 and 2050 ('best guess' estimates plus 80 per cent uncertainty intervals). The experts could add additional countries or regions for their assessments. Altogether, the low mortality module was completed for 30 countries by 75 experts. To summarize the results in this section we grouped the countries into five regions. Table 5.1 presents, for each region, the included countries and the corresponding number of experts who assessed the mortality trends for these countries. The highest number of assessments was provided for the USA (20 experts), while most other countries were assessed by 3 or fewer experts. There is one exception to the regional composition of section 5.2, as we include Israel in Western Europe because its mortality level is more comparable to the Western European countries than to the selected Asian countries (see section 5.2.5). The expert assessments were

Table 5.1 Number of Experts and Assessed Countries in the IIASA-Oxford Survey

North America		Western Europe		Asia	
Canada	3	Austria	3	China	1
USA	20	Germany	2	Indonesia	3
		Italy	4	Iran (Islamic Republic of)	3
		Netherlands	1	Japan	1
		Norway	1	Palestine	1
		Spain	1	Philippines	1
		Sweden	2	Thailand	3
		Israel	*1*	Vietnam	1
Latin America		**Eastern Europe**		**Total**	
Argentina	3	Bulgaria	1	Countries	30
Brazil	5	Czech Republic	3	Experts	75
Costa Rica	3	TFYR Macedonia	1		
Cuba	1	Romania	1		
Mexico	2	Russian Federation	1		
		Serbia	1		
		Ukraine	1		

analysed along two key dimensions: (1) estimates for future trends in life expectancy, and (2) rankings of the relevance and impact of individual arguments pertaining to the expected main factors behind future trends.

The following results refer to the experts' final projections of life expectancy at birth, illustrated alongside the empirical trends since 1950–55 and comparisons to the projections of the 2010 revision of the UN World Populations Prospects until 2050–55 (United Nations, 2011). Hence, the experts' estimates refer to the decades 2020–30 and 2040–50 respectively. The gains in life expectancy for the 2005–20 and the 2030–40 time periods are derived from interpolating the decadal estimates related to the initial values of the period in 2005. The grey areas around the expert trend indicate the range of the 80 per cent uncertainty intervals assessed by the experts. The regional and global estimates were further weighted by the population sizes of the countries based on the actual UN data and the corresponding medium variant predictions until 2050–55 (United Nations, 2011). For comparing the regional mortality trends estimated by the experts with those by the UN, we selected only those countries for which the experts have assessed the future gain in life expectancy.

After providing numerical estimates for the decadal gains in life expectancy, the experts were asked to assess the validity and relevance of alternative arguments about the forces that could shape future mortality trends in the country or region they chose. In total, the survey contains 34 arguments that were grouped into 6 clusters: (1) changes in biomedical technology; (2) effectiveness of health care systems; (3) behavioural changes related to health; (4) possible new infectious diseases and resurgence of old diseases; (5)

environmental change, disasters, and wars; (6) changes in population composition and differential trends in population subgroups (all single arguments can be found in Appendix 5.1). For each argument the experts could assess its likelihood, its conditional impact, and its net impact. The validity was measured along the following response scale: very likely wrong; more likely wrong than right; ambiguous; more likely right than wrong; and very likely right. The conditional impact gives the respondents' assessments regarding the consequences of the argument for future life expectancy, if it becomes true. The scale comprises five categories for the arguments' effect on future life expectancy: strongly decreasing; moderately decreasing; none; moderately increasing; and strongly increasing. Validity and conditional impact were then used to determine an argument's net impact on future life expectancy. In the survey, these net impacts were predefined as a combination (multiplication) of an argument's validity and its conditional impact, but the experts were free to change the calculated mean net impacts if they wished to do so. At the end of the questionnaire the experts could assign each cluster of arguments its relative importance for future trends in life expectancy.

Figure 5.4 presents the net impact of each argument. Each segment of the plot presents one cluster, with the size of the segment depending on the importance of the cluster, as assessed by the experts. The most significant clusters include arguments about behavioural changes related to health (25 per cent importance), effectiveness of health care system (20 per cent importance), and changes in biomedical technology (19 per cent importance). Beyond the relevance of those clusters, the displayed segments also contain the arguments with the highest net impact for all considered low mortality countries. A positive impact on future mortality is mainly expected from reduction in smoking prevalence (LD3-1), breakthrough in the understanding of carcinogenic processes (LD1-2), and progress in preventive medicine (LD2-5). The highest negative impact is expected to come from limited access to medical treatments due to the growing elderly population (LD2-3), increasing drug resistance to known infectious diseases (LD4-2), and more intensive heat waves during summer (LD5-3).

Another way of analysing the expected impact of arguments is presented by ranking net impact in relation to the relevance of the underlying clusters. As the net impact of an argument can be either positive or negative, we used the absolute value in the characterization of the overall ranking. In the left panel of Figure 5.5 each cluster is represented by one circle, with the size of the circle symbolizing the importance of the cluster. Moreover, the location of the circle along the *y*-axis shows the mean net impact of the argument with the highest assessed importance on future life expectancy within the specific cluster. Circles located in the positive area indicate a positive impact of future survival conditions and vice versa.

Figure 5.5 shows that the arguments with the highest net impact are included in the most relevant clusters. This pattern is reflected in the left panel of the graph. The group of behavioural arguments (third circle) is assessed as the most important cluster for future life expectancy, with the most important argument being the decrease in the prevalence of smoking (LD3-1). The second rank is occupied by changes in biomedical technology (first circle). Within this cluster, expected breakthroughs in understanding

FIGURE 5.4 Global mean net impact for all arguments about future mortality in low mortality countries.

Data sources: International Institute for Applied Systems Analysis–Oxford Demographic Expert Survey; own calculations.

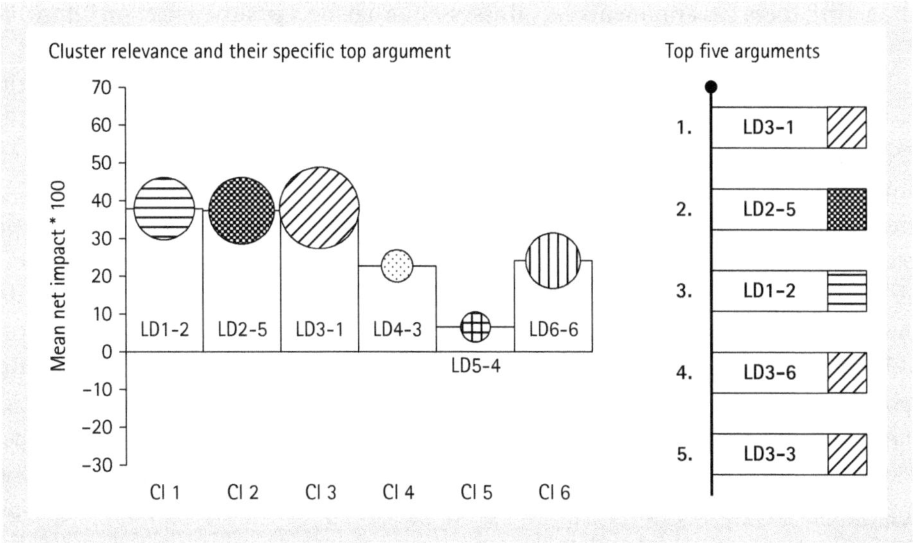

FIGURE 5.5 Cluster relevance and the ranking of highest impact arguments for all low mortality countries.

Data sources: IIASA–Oxford survey; own calculations.

of carcinogenic processes (LD1-2) have the highest impact on future life expectancy. The effectiveness of the health care system (second circle) places third in the ranking. The greatest influence on future survival, based on the arguments that make up this cluster, is expected progress in preventive medicine (LD2-5). Figure 5.5 also presents the rankings of the other clusters and their most relevant argument. The cluster concerning changes in population composition and differential trends in population subgroups (sixth circle) holds fourth place. Within this group, reduction of the sex differential in mortality (LD6-6) has the highest impact. But the value of the net impact is distinctly lower than the arguments of the three main clusters. The last ranked clusters include arguments about the possibility of new infectious diseases and the resurgence of old diseases (fourth circle), as well as the influence of environmental changes, disasters, and wars (fifth circle). The main arguments within these clusters are increased capability of early detection and control to avoid the spread and impact of new infectious diseases (LD4-3), and the minor positive effect of less extreme winters on survival of the elderly (LD5-4).

The combination of the cluster balance and the net impact of single arguments allows a further total ranking of all arguments. The right panel of Figure 5.5 presents the five arguments with the highest assessed impact on future life expectancy weighted by the cluster relevance. This ranking is mainly dominated by behavioural factors. The argument ranked first, decreasing smoking prevalence (LD3-1), is supplemented by two arguments of the same cluster: increasing mental and social activities to prolong lifetime among the elderly (LD3-6, fourth rank) and expected increased awareness of the importance of physical activity to counteract obesity (LD3-3, fifth rank). The second-ranked argument, however, is dedicated to progress in preventive medicine (LD2-5), while breakthrough in carcinogenic processes (LD1-2) occupies the third rank.

Altogether, these top arguments are all assessed as having a positive effect on future life expectancy.

The assumed global trend in future life expectancy is presented in Figure 5.6. In the past, life expectancy increased from 54.0 years in 1950–55 to 73.4 years in 2005–10. The UN (2011) estimates in their medium variant a further increase to 80.8 years in 2050–55. However, the experts assessed a constant gain in life expectancy of two years for the decades 2020–30 and 2040–50. Consequently, the predicted life expectancy is 83.3 years and thus 2.6 years higher than the UN projection. The uncertainty range assessed by the experts presents a wide range of 67.5 to 89.1 years by the end of the projection period. Note, however, that this uncertainty reflects the fact that several experts did not modify the wide limits of the uncertainty range set in the online survey. Figure 5.6 also shows the optimistic linear trend of life expectancy as proposed by Oeppen and Vaupel (2002). These authors have derived a yearly increase in life expectancy of about 0.25 years per year for countries with the highest life expectancy (see section 5.3.3.2). This assumption implies that the life expectancy for the last projection period 2050–55 increases to almost 85 years, 1.6 years higher than the experts' assessment. These results reflect a global perspective on future life expectancy, calculated as the averages of the expert assessments for different countries and regions. These global estimates indicate that the experts' best guess expectations lie below the optimistic linear pattern suggested by Oeppen and Vaupel (2002), a relationship that is valid for most of the regions.

An extreme example of this difference between the 'Oeppen/Vaupel line' and the experts' assessments is North America. Figure 5.7 shows that the trend predicted by the experts for 2050–55 is 85.6 years, 1.8 years higher than the UN estimate of 83.8 years. But the optimistic trend (Oeppen/Vaupel line) for North America suggests a much stronger increase to 89.5 years, almost 4 years higher than the estimate put forward by the experts. For the European and Asian regions, however, the difference between the expert assessments and the optimistic line is significantly lower compared with North America.

Another interesting point is the ranking of the underlying arguments for future survival in North America (Figure 5.8). Biomedical improvement (first circle) was assessed as being the most important cluster. Within this group, as well as compared with the arguments of all other clusters, innovative medicine and its expected containable effect on life threatening diseases (LD1-3) is assumed to have the highest positive impact on life expectancy. The group of arguments related to changes in health-related behaviour (third circle) holds second rank. The decline in smoking prevalence (LD3-1) has the highest expected impact on life expectancy within this cluster. Changes in population composition (sixth circle) are ranked third. The greatest influence on future survival is expected from convergence of mortality among ethnic minorities to mortality of the indigenous population (LD6-1).

Although the assessed impact of further progress in preventive medicine on life expectancy (LD2-5) is higher than that of population composition and, surprisingly, of reduction in smoking, the entire cluster concerning effectiveness of the health care system ranks only fourth. The last-ranked clusters include arguments about influence of environmental changes, resurgence of old infectious diseases, and the possibility of new infectious diseases.

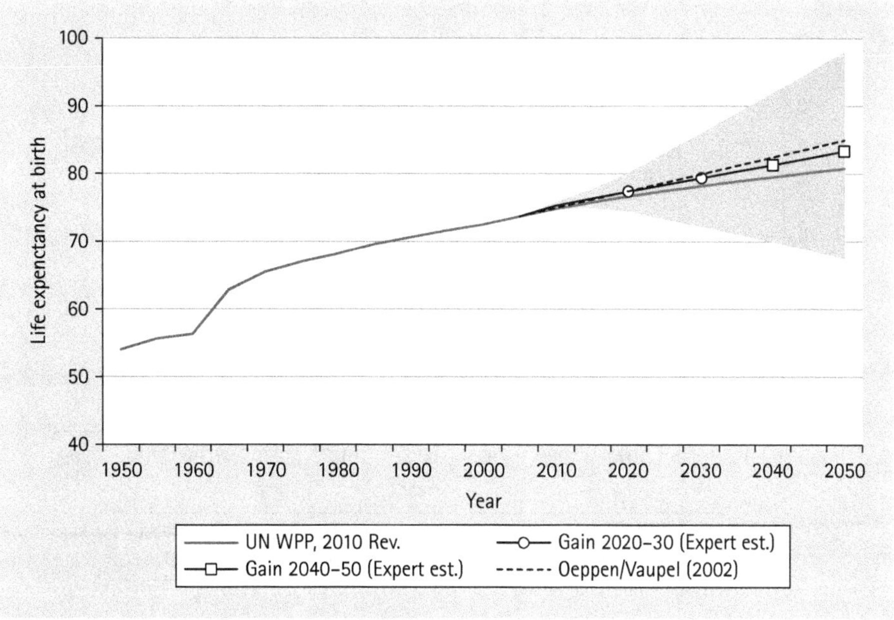

FIGURE 5.6 Previous and expected future global trend in life expectancy at birth.

Data sources: IIASA–Oxford survey, United Nations (UN) World Population Prospects, 2010 Revision (UN, 2011); own calculations.

Although the cluster ranking almost follows the global one, the ranking of the top arguments (right panel of Figure 5.8) is dominated by the cluster about biomedical technology. Thus, progress in innovative medication (LD1-3, first rank), expected breakthrough in cancer treatment (LD1-2, second rank), development of effective anti-ageing strategies (LD1-1, fourth rank), and improvements in surgery including transplants and implants (LD1-4, fifth rank) are expected to be the major drivers of future increases in life expectancy in North America. Only the third rank is not dedicated to the progress of biomedical technology, but to health behavioural changes. As in the global perspective, ongoing decrease of smoking prevalence (LD3-1) is assessed to reduce future mortality.

Only for the Latin American region did the experts assume a linear trend in life expectancy, reflecting almost exactly the optimistic 'Oeppen/Vaupel line' (see Figure 5.9). While the UN predicts an increase in life expectancy from 74.0 years in 2005–10 to 81.0 years in 2050–55, the experts expect an increase to 86.0 years in the last projection period. An interesting consequence of this linear increase is that Latin America is expected to become the region with the second highest life expectancy in 2050–55. Only Western Europe is assumed to have a higher life expectancy of 90.1 years. The life expectancy in all other regions is expected to be lower, with 85.6 years in North America, 82.1 years in Asia, and 79.0 years in Eastern Europe.

Alongside the exceptional trend in life expectancy, the experts also assessed different cluster relevancies for Latin America. The most important cluster is, again, related to changes in health-related behaviour (third circle), as illustrated by the biggest circle in the left panel of Figure 5.10. Reduction of smoking prevalence (LD3-1) is expected to

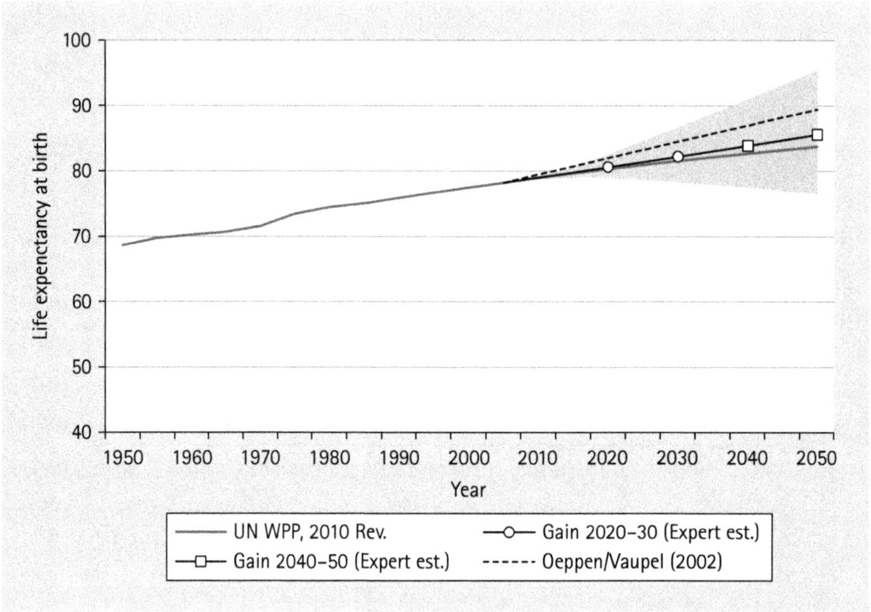

FIGURE 5.7 Previous and expected future trend in life expectancy at birth for North America.

Data sources: IIASA–Oxford survey, United Nations (UN) World Population Prospects, 2010 Revision (UN, 2011); own calculations.

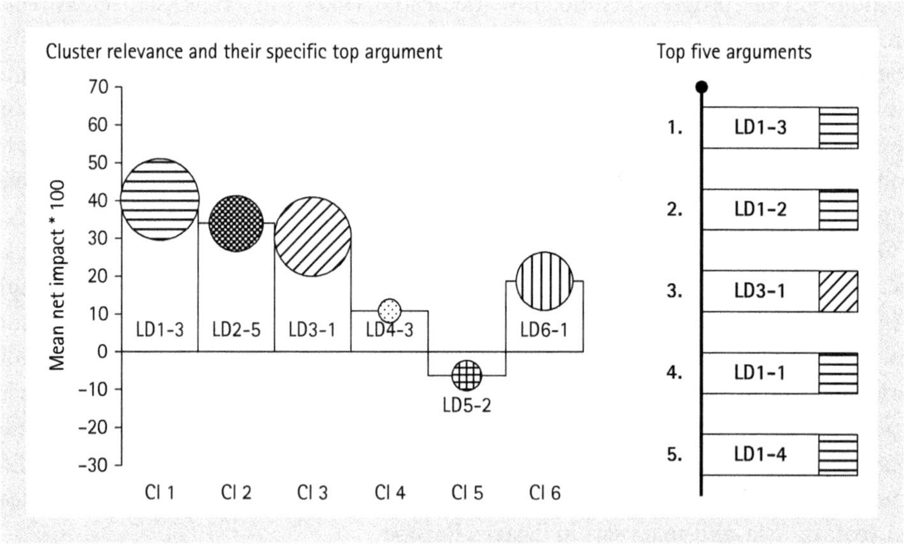

FIGURE 5.8 Cluster relevance and the ranking of highest impact arguments for North America.

Data sources: IIASA–Oxford survey; own calculations.

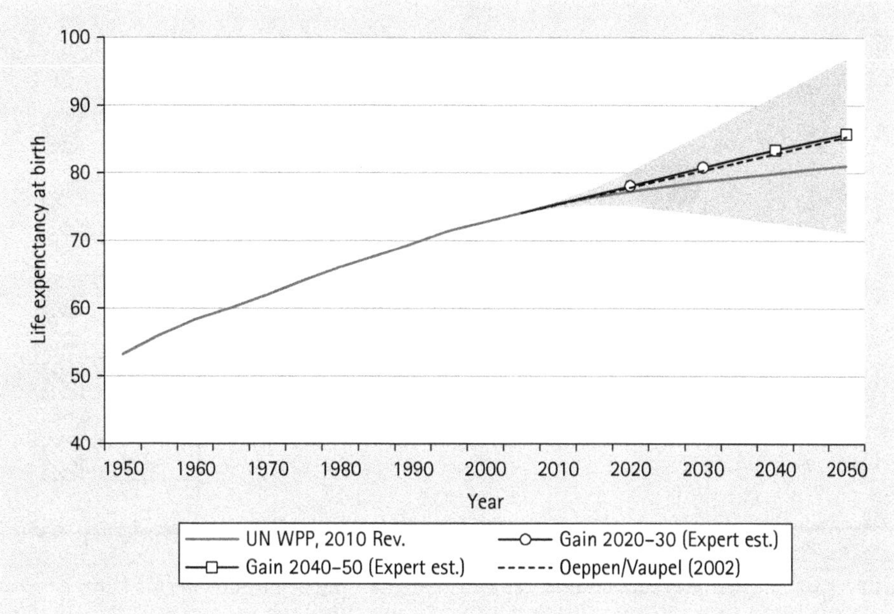

FIGURE 5.9 Previous and expected future trend in life expectancy at birth for Latin America.
Data sources: IIASA–Oxford survey, United Nations (UN) World Population Prospects, 2010 Revision (UN, 2011); own calculations.

play the most important role. The second ranked cluster includes all arguments about the effectiveness of health care systems (second circle). The main argument within this cluster is further progress in preventive medicine (LD2-5), which has a net impact 15 points higher than decline in smoking prevalence. The third rank is occupied by the cluster about changes in population composition and differential trends in population subgroups (sixth circle). It is only in Latin America and Asia that the experts ranked this cluster within the top three, with the most important arguments being the reduction of sex differentials in mortality (LD6-6). In all other regions, the three main clusters refer to health behavioural changes, progress in biomedical technologies, and effectiveness of the health care system. A further interesting characteristic for Latin America is the relatively high net impact compared with other regions of the expected improvement of earlier detection and control of the occurrence of new infectious diseases (LD4-3), although the related cluster is only ranked fourth.

The top five ranking of arguments for Latin America (right panel of Figure 5.10) is composed of the expected ongoing effectiveness of health care systems and health behavioural factors. The first rank is occupied by future progress in preventive medicine (LD2-5). Moreover, the presence of effective and easily affordable new technologies (LD2-2, third rank) is expected to improve future survival conditions. All other arguments in the top five belong to the cluster about changes in health behaviour. The decrease in smoking prevalence (LD3-1, second rank) is expected to reduce future mortality. The other

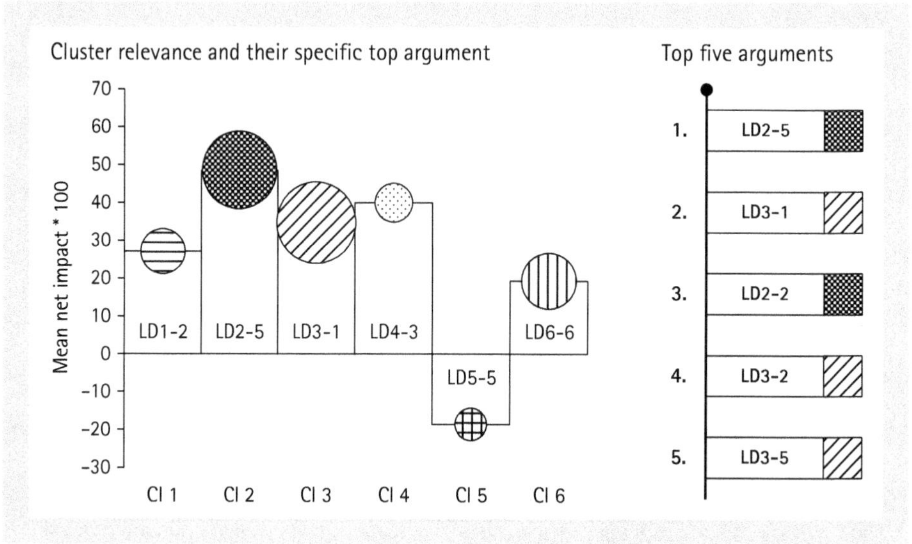

FIGURE 5.10 Cluster relevance and the ranking of highest impact arguments for Latin America.
Data sources: IIASA–Oxford survey; own calculations.

arguments related to alcohol and drug abuse (LD3-2, fourth rank) and increasing stress levels (LD3-5, fifth rank) are assessed as being factors that will increase future mortality.

The dominance of behavioural factors in the ranking of the top five arguments is also valid for Europe and Asia. In particular, a decrease in smoking prevalence is assumed to be the key factor for the future trend in European life expectancy. Both Eastern and Western Europe share the same pattern of cluster relevance, the one seen in the global perspective. However, this does not hold for Asia, where the importance of clusters and the top ranked arguments are different from the other regions. Analysis of the cluster relevance, illustrated in the left panel of Figure 5.11, shows the almost identical importance of each group of arguments. Although behavioural factors play a major role in the experts' expectations for Asia's future life expectancy, the other clusters, especially the ones related to the occurrence of new infectious diseases as well as environmental changes, disasters, and wars have a higher relevance than the assessments for the other regions. This pattern could be caused by the heterogeneous composition of countries within this region, which includes both Japan, with the highest worldwide life expectancy, and the Occupied Palestinian Territory, where life expectancy is around 10 years lower.

As in most regions, the highest ranked arguments in Asia are dominated by health behavioural factors (right panel of Figure 5.11). However, the most relevant argument is not decrease in smoking prevalence as in the global perspective, but positive impact of increasing mental and social activities among the elderly (LD3-6). Reduction of smoking prevalence (LD3-1) is ranked second. The third rank is held by expected better and faster medical and health information dissemination (LD2-6), which aims to improve the effectiveness of future health care systems. The fourth and fifth ranks again refer to health behaviour. Increased awareness of the importance of nutrition (LD3-4) and

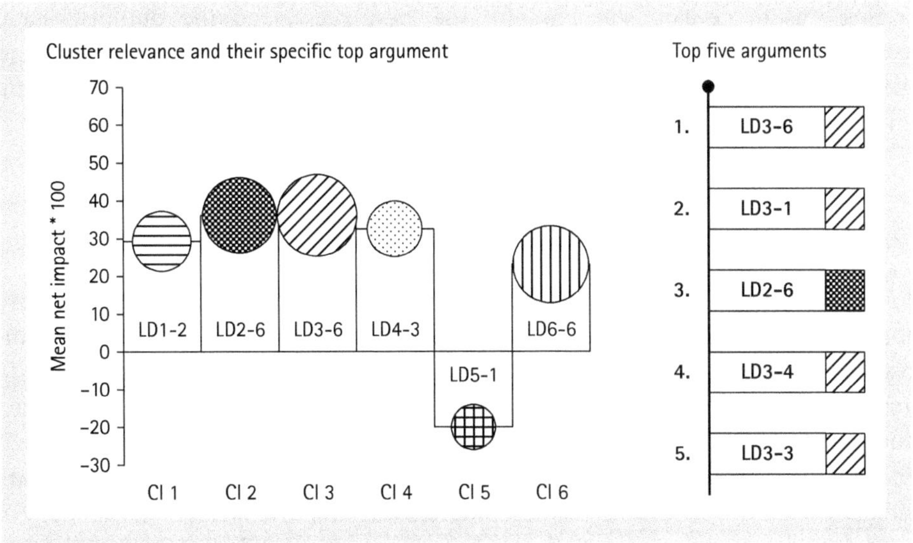

FIGURE 5.11 Cluster relevance and the ranking of highest impact arguments for Asia.
Data sources: IIASA–Oxford survey; own calculations.

increase of physical activities (LD3-3) are assessed as having a positive effect on future life expectancy. The last two factors also play a major role in the future trend of life expectancy in Western and Eastern Europe.

The main conclusions of the expert assessments for low mortality countries can be summarized as follows: Life expectancy is assumed to increase more strongly compared with the UN estimations. In the case of Latin America, the predicted trend is identical to the optimistic linear increase in life expectancy by 0.25 years per year according to the 'Oeppen/Vaupel line'. However, for all regions the range of uncertainty always includes both the UN estimations and the linear trend proposed by Oeppen and Vaupel (2002). The experts' assessments also show that the future trend in life expectancy is expected to be influenced mainly by health behavioural factors (above all the reduction of smoking prevalence), effectiveness of health care systems (with the ongoing progress of preventive medicine as the major argument), and progress in biomedical technologies (most importantly the understanding and treating of carcinogenic processes).

5.5 Meta-experts' assessment of future life expectancy trends

The information in the previous sections provided the basis for the meta-experts meeting that took place in San José, Costa Rica on 21–22 February 2012.[7] The primary purpose of the

[7] Participants of the meta-experts meeting: Gilbert Brenes, Central American Population Center, University of Costa Rica; Graziella Caselli, University of Rome La Sapienza, Italy; Sven Drefahl,

meeting was to develop storylines for the 'best guess', and the 'optimistic' and 'pessimistic' scenarios for future life expectancy trends in low mortality populations. This section summarizes the outcomes of these storylines for Europe, North and Latin America, and Asia.

5.5.1 Storylines for Europe

Most experts believe that life expectancy in Europe will continue to increase. To achieve substantial gains in life years until 2050, several conditions have to be fulfilled. Most importantly, behavioural changes, especially reductions in smoking, need to continue. To continue over time, behavioural changes would have to be supported by a continued educational expansion. In Eastern Europe people would also have to decrease their alcohol consumption, and countries in the region would have to improve their health care systems. For Europe as a whole, medical progress will have to contribute substantially to increasing life expectancy, especially through progress against diseases such as cancers and neurodegenerative diseases such as dementia.

European life expectancy may also increase more slowly or even start to stagnate. Such a scenario is possible in Eastern Europe if the current lifestyle issues remain unchanged for a long period. In the rest of Europe the most hazardous lifestyle characteristic is smoking. If the smoking epidemic in women continues or the reduction of smoking prevalence in men stops, life expectancy increase would be dampened. Economic stagnation or an economic crisis could have a similar effect, especially if there is an increase in the number of people without significant resources. Another problem could occur if the European health systems, which stand out for their universal availability, do not have the means to function as desired. Other factors that could contribute to a slower increase in life expectancy are more speculative and include the development of drug resistance in existing diseases, the appearance of new diseases, and the creation of new technologies and materials that might prove dangerous.

5.5.2 Storylines for North and Latin America

Similar to Europe, most experts believe that life expectancy in the Americas will continue to increase. In such positive scenarios life expectancy at birth could reach 90 years by 2050, which corresponds to a decadal increase of about 2.5 years. It is expected that the factors contributing to this positive scenario are similar to those for the countries of

Stockholm University, Sweden; Michel Guillot, University of Pennsylvania, USA; Wolfgang Lutz, Wittgenstein Centre, Austria; Marc Luy, Wittgenstein Centre, Austria; France Meslé, Institut National d'Etudes Démographiques, Paris, France; Arodys Robles, Central American Population Center, University of Costa Rica; Richard G. Rogers, University of Colorado at Boulder, USA; Sergei Scherbov, Wittgenstein Centre, Austria; and Edward Tu, Hong Kong University of Science and Technology.

North America and Latin America. The most important factors expected to increase life expectancy in North America are continued improvements in health behaviours, including further decreases in smoking, drinking, and drug abuse, as well as increases in physical activity to counteract trends in obesity. These changes are closely linked with continued progress in educational attainment. For Latin America, health behaviours are expected to be the second most important factor; only improvements in preventive medicine, including the early detection of chronic diseases like hypertension and obesity, are considered more influential. The experts agree that biomedical research also must contribute significantly to allow life expectancy to increase rapidly.

Conversely, negative health behaviours, violence (especially homicides and suicides) and reductions in government support, including reductions in Social Security, Medicare, and Medicaid, could slow gains in life expectancy considerably, especially in North America. This negative trend could be even stronger if the health care system loses its effectiveness when larger proportions of the population begin to reach old age. Vulnerability of the elderly may increase because many may not be able to rely on family support owing to increased divorces, fewer children, and other changes in family structure. The effect of environmental changes is much less predictable; however, natural disasters could occur more frequently and affect life expectancy, especially in Latin America. Infectious diseases might also play an increasingly important role in some parts of Latin America.

5.5.3 Storylines for Asia

If it is true that current human life expectancy is far from a biological limit, better health behaviours fuelled by the rapid increase in education may also play an important role in Asia's future life expectancy. However, if life expectancy is to continue to rise at a quick pace, smoking prevalence must decrease and the number of smoking women must remain small. Further improvements in democratization and public health, as well as new medical interventions, will also play an important role in rapidly increasing life expectancy.

However, if women adopt the smoking behaviour of Asian men and thus smoking incidence remains stable, developments will be less positive. Negative health behaviours that imitate the lifestyle in Russia may also lead to only slow progress in Central Asia. Similarly, political turmoil and uncertainty are factors that may lead to only modest increases or even stagnation in life expectancy, particularly in East Asian and Muslim countries.

5.5.4 Expected convergence and optimistic future trends

At the end of the meeting, meta-experts expressed their expectations for future trends in life expectancy, indicating whether they support the optimistic or pessimistic views as described in section 5.3.3. The majority identified themselves as optimists, expecting further increases of life expectancy during the coming decades with the changes being at least close to the increase described by Oeppen and Vaupel (2002). Moreover, the meta-experts expect that the differences between countries will further decline in the future, and they proposed using a convergence model for the projections of future life expectancy with regional convergence processes.

5.6 Combining Expert Assessments and Model Forecasts to Define Forecasting Assumptions

The procedure for defining the final assumptions for overall mortality levels for each country are isomorphic to those described in Chapter 4 for the fertility assumptions. The outcomes of a model-based forecast were blended with the assessments of the surveyed experts and with results of the meta-expert meeting in San José (Costa Rica). Our procedure follows the principle described in Chapter 2: the best way of defining forecasting assumptions is to combine a statistical model with structured expert judgement.

While the results of the survey of individual experts and the results of the meta-expert meeting are documented elsewhere in this chapter, the statistical model is summarized in Chapter 9 and presented in detail in Appendix I. This model explicitly assumes convergence in the decadal increase of life expectancy. The model also takes into account country-specific heterogeneity in the historical trajectories of life expectancy, as well as between-country heterogeneity in terms of increases in life expectancy. This reflects the view that national mortality trends should be viewed in a larger international context rather than being analysed and projected individually (Lee, 2006). Our model also follows the argument of Torri and Vaupel (2012) that life expectancy across different countries tends to be positively correlated, so that forecasts for particular countries can be carried out by forecasting the best-practice level of life expectancy and then the gap between this best-practice level and the particular country's performance. The model used here builds upon this approach by varying the speed of convergence, taking into account differential rates of linear increase in life expectancy across groups of countries. As described in detail in Appendix I, this is operationalized by choosing Japan as the global forerunner with a long-term increase of life expectancy of two years per decade. A set of regional forerunners is then assumed to converge to this Japanese speed of improvement. In a second round, the model then defines the convergence of all countries to their respective regional forerunners. This statistical model results in a consistent set of projections for all high and low mortality countries except for some countries with high AIDS prevalence that required special assumptions, as described in Chapter 6.

The added value of this convergence model lies partly in the fact that it is based on empirical data. In addition, it takes into account the heterogeneous country-specific historical experiences, as well as differences in gains between forerunners and laggards over time and across regions. Thus, it accounts for structural, as well as stochastic, components that contribute to life expectancy trends over time and can generate unbiased parameters upon which the new forecasts are based. Building further, the model-based forecasts were adjusted to incorporate source experts' and meta-experts' arguments and assessments about future gains in life expectancy in individual countries up to 2050. This was done by merging the results of the statistical model the weight of 1.0, the average of the meta-experts' responses with the assumptions of experts where available (for more details see Appendix I). The final step consisted of modifying the future trajectories (2050–95) based on the new trend implied by the reweighted forecasts up to 2050, as described in detail in Appendix I. This procedure is applied to female life expectancy, from which male life expectancy is derived by assuming the sex differentials in mortality used in the 2010 UN assessment.

The resulting mortality assumptions for each country are listed in Appendix II for all countries for selected years and in the online material <http://www.wittgensteincentre.org/dataexplorer> for all years. The high and low mortality assumptions were derived for all low mortality countries by the same procedure under the simple assumption that the decadal gain of the frontrunner is 1.0 years higher or lower than in the medium assumption. Education-specific trajectories of life expectancy were then derived by the procedure described in Chapter 9, based on the assumption that the medium trend in overall life expectancy (across all education groups) reflects the educational attainment change over time that is implied by the Global Education Trend scenario. Together with the assumption of certain given relative differences in education-specific mortality, this procedure produces unique iteratively derived sets of education-specific mortality trends for each educational attainment category.

It is worth noting that using different education scenarios together with identical sets of education-specific mortality trajectories produces a trajectory of overall future life expectancy that is different because the different education structure of the population implies different weights for the sub-populations that each have different education-specific mortality rates. In this way the assumed future of education trends is also a direct determinant of the future trajectory of the overall level of mortality. This is illustrated in Chapters 10–12, which discuss the projection results.

5.7 Conclusions

The evidence presented in this chapter indicates that that the positive influences on human mortality and life expectancy will likely outweigh the negative risk factors, thus supporting the optimists' perspective on future trends in life expectancy. The possibility that new risk factors and/or new diseases will occur in the future cannot be excluded, as outlined by the views of the pessimists and discussed in section 5.3. However, the experience of how people in the past have dealt with such impacts provides reason to believe that future societies will profit from increasing education levels and thus be able to adapt to coming threats and challenges. The expectations gathered by both the expert survey (section 5.4) and the meta-experts meeting (section 5.5) pointed in this same optimistic direction, toward increases in future life expectancy in today's low mortality countries that are close to or somewhat below the 2.5 years per decade increase as indicated by the so-called 'Oeppen/Vaupel line' (see section 5.3.3.2). Moreover, the meta-experts agreed that the differences in life expectancy between countries are likely to narrow further in the future, suggesting a regional convergence process for projections of future life expectancy.

Acknowledgements

Section 5.6 was provided by Samir KC to summarize the projection assumptions and methods. More details can be found in Chapter 9 and in Appendix I. Marc Luy and Christian Wegner-Siegmundt received support from the European Research Council (ERC Starting Grant agreement No. 262663).

APPENDIX 5.1

List of arguments for assessing future mortality trend in low-mortality countries:

Module 1: Progress in biomedical technology	
LD1-1	Increased understanding of biomedical ageing processes will allow us to develop effective anti-ageing strategies
LD1-2	Breakthroughs in the understanding of carcinogenic processes will lead to substantial changes in mortality from cancers
LD1-3	Innovative medication will make hitherto life threatening diseases containable
LD1-4	Improvements in surgery, including transplants and implants, will improve longevity
LD1-5	Unintended adverse consequences of new biomedical technologies will outweigh their benefits
Module 2: Health care system	
LD2-1	The cost of new treatments will be prohibitive to large segments of the population
LD2-2	There will be some very effective and easily affordable new technologies
LD2-3	Because of the growing elderly population there will be limited access and increased waiting times for treatment
LD2-4	Society will be able and willing to afford expensive new treatments
LD2-5	Progress in preventive medicine (e.g., screening, genetic testing) will decrease death rates
LD2-6	Better and faster medical and health information dissemination will improve longevity
LD2-7	Changing living arrangements will improve the health of the population, above all the elderly

Module 3: Health-related behaviour	
LD3-1	Smoking prevalence will decline
LD3-2	Substance abuse (alcohol and drugs) will lead to more premature mortality and accidents
LD3-3	Increased awareness of the importance of physical activity will lead people to exercise more
LD3-4	Increased awareness of the importance of nutrition will lead people to adopt healthier diets
LD3-5	Increased stress levels will contribute to increased morbidity
LD3-6	Increasing mental and social activities at old age will increase longevity
Module 4: Infectious diseases	
LD4-1	There will be a growth in infectious diseases leading to increases in overall mortality
LD4-2	Increasing drug resistance to known infectious diseases will increase mortality
LD4-3	Increased capability of early detection and control will help to contain the spread and impact of new infectious diseases
LD4-4	A major flu epidemic (avian or other) is likely to occur over the next 25 years
Module 5: Environment, disasters, and wars	
LD5-1	Increased frequency and intensity of natural disasters (such as flooding and strong storms) will increase mortality
LD5-2	Global warming will lead to the spread of Malaria
LD5-3	More intensive heat waves during summer will increase mortality among the elderly
LD5-4	Less extreme cold spells during winter will decrease mortality among the elderly
LD5-5	Increased pollution including nuclear contamination will increase mortality
LD5-6	This country is unlikely to experience wars in the future
Module 6: Population composition	
LD6-1	For ethnic minority groups already resident in this country and their descendants, mortality rates will converge to those for the indigenous population, thereby reducing mortality
LD6-2	The majority of new immigrants will come from countries where mortality rates are higher than in this country, thereby raising mortality
LD6-3	Emigration of low mortality populations from this country will raise mortality rates
LD6-4	Due to the considerably decreased levels of mortality in the young and youngest age groups, less health selection occurs and thus more frail people will reach middle and high adult ages, thereby increasing mortality at those ages
LD6-5	Mortality differentials between higher and lower education groups will increase
LD6-6	Mortality differences between men and women will decline

References

Ádám, B., Molnár, Á., Gulis, G. and Ádány, R. 2013 'Integrating a Quantitative Risk Appraisal in a Health Impact Assessment: Analysis of the Novel Smoke-free Policy in Hungary'. *European Journal of Public Health*, 23: 211–17.

Alley, D.E., Lloyd, J. and Shardell, M. 2010 'Can Obesity Account for Cross-national Differences in Life Expectancy Trends?' In: Crimmins, E.M., Preston, S.H. and Cohen, B. (eds) *International Differences in Mortality at Older Ages*, pp. 164–92. The National Academies Press: Washington, DC.

Bengtsson, T. and Lindström, M. 2000 'Childhood Misery and Disease in Later Life: The Effects on Mortality in Old Age of Hazards Experienced in Early Life, Southern Sweden, 1760–1894'. *Population Studies*, 54: 263–77.

Bongaarts, J. 2006 'How Long Will We Live?' *Population and Development Review*, 32: 605–28.

Browning, C., Bjornstrom, E.E. and Cagney, K.A. 2011 'Health and Mortality Consequences of the Physical Environment'. In: Rogers, R.G. and Crimmins, E.M. (eds) *International Handbook of Adult Mortality*, pp. 441–64. Springer: New York.

Burger, O., Baudisch, A. and Vaupel, J.W. 2012 'Human Mortality Improvement in Evolutionary Context'. *Proceedings of the National Academy of Science*, 109: 18210–14.

Carey, J.R. and Judge, D.S. 2001 'Principles of Biodemography with Special Reference to Human Longevity'. *Population: An English Selection*, 13: 9–40.

Carey, J.R., Liedo, P., Orozco, D. and Vaupel, J.W. 1992 'Slowing of Mortality Rates at Older Ages in Large Medfly Cohorts'. *Science*, 258: 457–61.

Carnes, B.A. and Olshansky, S.J. 2007 'A Realist View of Aging, Mortality, and Future Longevity'. *Population and Development Review*, 33: 367–81.

Carnes, B.A., Olshansky, S.J. and Hayflick, L. 2013 'Can Human Biology Allow Most of us to Become Centenarians?' *The Journals of Gerontology Series A: Biological Sciences and Medical Sciences*, 68: 136–42.

Caselli, G. 1989 'Transition sanitaire et structure par cause de la mortalité. Anciennes et nouvelles causes'. *Annales de Démographie Historique*: 55–77.

Caselli, G. 1991 'The Quest for an Interpretation of Mortality Differences: Socio-economic Background and Adult Mortality'. In: INED, INSEE, CICRED (eds) *Socio-economic Differential Mortality in Industrialized Societies (No. 7)*, pp. 229–41. Anon: Paris.

Caselli, G. 1995 'The Key Phases of the European Health Transition'. *Polish Population Review*, 7: 73–102.

Caselli, G. and Lopez, A.D. 1996 'Health and Mortality among the Elderly: Issues for Assessment'. In: Caselli, G. and Lopez, A.D. (eds) *Health and Mortality Among the Elderly: Issues for Assessment*, pp. 3–20. Clarendon Press: Oxford.

Caselli, G., Duchêne, J. and Wunsch, G. 1987 'L'apport de la démographie à l'explication de la mortalité différentielle'. In: Duchêne, J., Wunsch, G. and Vilquin, E. (eds) *L'explication En Science Sociales. La Recherche Des Causes En Démographie*, pp. 41–50. Ciaco: Brussels.

Caselli, G., Duchêne, J., Egidi, V., Santini, A. and Wunsch, G. 1991 'A Matter of Life and Death: Methodologies for the Life History Analysis of Adult Mortality'. In: INED, INSEE, CICRED (eds) *Socio-economic Differential Mortality in Industrialized Countries (No. 7)*, pp. 242–77. Anon: Paris.

Caselli, G., Meslé, F. and Vallin, J. 2002 'Epidemiologic Transition Theory Exceptions'. *Genus*, 58: 9–51.

Christensen, K., Doblhammer, G., Rau, R. and Vaupel, J.W. 2009 'Ageing Populations: The Challenges Ahead'. *The Lancet*, 374: 1196–208.

Christensen, K., Davidson, M., Juel, K., Mortensen, L.H., Rau, R. and Vaupel, J.W. 2010 'The Divergent Life-Expectancy Trends in Denmark and Sweden—and Some Potential Explanations'. In: Crimmins, E.M., Preston, S.H. and Cohen, B. (eds) *International Differences in Mortality at Older Ages: Dimensions and Sources*, pp. 385–407. The National Academies Press: Washington, DC.

Cohen, J. E. and Oppenheim, J. N. 2012 'Is a Limit to the Median Length of Human Life Imminent?' *Genus*, 68: 11–40.

Corsini, V. (ed.) 2010 *Highly Educated Men and Women Likely to Live Longer. Life Expectancy by Educational Attainment. Statistics in Focus*. Eurostat: Brussels.

Couzin-Frankel, J. 2011 'A Pitched Battle over Life Span'. *Science*, 333: 549–50.

Crimmins, E.M. and Saito, Y. 2001 'Trends in Healthy Life Expectancy in the United States, 1970–1990: Gender, Racial, and Educational Differences'. *Social Science & Medicine*, 52: 1629–41.

Crimmins, E.M., Preston, S.H. and Cohen, B. (eds) 2011 *Explaining Divergent Levels of Longevity in High-income Countries*. The National Academies Press: Washington, DC.

Curtsinger, J.W., Fukui, H.H., Townsend, D.R. and Vaupel, J.W. 1992 'Demography of Genotypes: Failure of the Limited Life-span Paradigm in *Drosophila melanogaster*'. *Science*, 258: 461–3.

Deboosere, P., Gadeyne, S. and Oyen, H.V. 2009 'The 1991–2004 Evolution in Life Expectancy by Educational Level in Belgium Based on Linked Census and Population Register Data'. *European Journal of Population*, 25: 175–96.

Deschênes, O. and Greenstone, M. 2011 'Climate Change, Mortality, and Adaptation: Evidence From Annual Fluctuations in Weather in the US'. *American Economic Journal-Applied Economics*, 3: 152–85.

Doblhammer, G. 2004 *The Late Life Legacy of Very Early Life*. Springer: Berlin and Heidelberg.

Duthé, G., Badurashvili, I., Kuyumjyan, K., Meslé, F. and Vallin, J. 2010 'Mortality in the Caucasus: An Attempt to Re-estimate Recent Mortality Trends in Armenia and Georgia'. *Demographic Research*, 22: 691–732.

Finkelstein, E.A., Brown, D.S., Wrage, L.A., Allaire, B.T. and Hoerger, T.J. 2010 'Individual and Aggregate Years-of-life-lost Associated with Overweight and Obesity'. *Obesity (Silver Spring)*, 18: 333–9.

Flegal, K.M., Carroll, M.D., Ogden, C.L. and Johnson, C.L. 2002 'Prevalence and Trends in Obesity Among US Adults, 1999–2000'. *Journal of the American Medical Association*, 288: 1723–7.

Flegal, K.M., Graubard, B.I., Williamson, D.F. and Gail, M.H. 2005 'Excess Deaths Associated With Underweight, Overweight, and Obesity'. *Journal of the American Medical Association*, 293: 1861–7.

Flegal, K.M., Carroll, M.D., Ogden, C.L. and Curtin, L.R. 2010 'Prevalence and Trends in Obesity Among US Adults, 1999–2008'. *Journal of the American Medical Association*, 303: 235–41.

Flegal, K.M., Kit, B.K., Orpana, H. and Graubard, B.I. 2013 'Association of All-cause Mortality with Overweight and Obesity Using Standard Body Mass Index Categories: A Systematic Review and Meta-analysis'. *Journal of the American Medical Association*, 309: 71–82.

Forey, B., Hamling, J. and Lee, P. (eds) 2002 *International Smoking Statistics: A Collection of Historical Data from 30 Economically Developed Countries*. Oxford University Press: London, Oxford, and New York.

Fries, J.F. 1980 'Aging, Natural Death, and the Compression or Morbidity'. *The New England Journal of Medicine*, 303: 130–5.

Gage, T.B. 1994 'Population Variation in Cause of Death: Level, Gender, and Period Effects'. *Demography*, 31: 271–6.

Gollin, D. and Zimmermann, C. 2012 'Global Climate Change, the Economy, and the Resurgence of Tropical Disease'. *Mathematical Population Studies*, 19: 51–62.

Graham, H. 2002 'Building an Inter-disciplinary Science of Health Inequalities: The Example of Lifecourse Research'. *Social Science & Medicine*, 55: 2005–16.

Guillot, M. 2007 'Mortality in Kyrgyzstan Since 1958: Real Patterns and Data Artifacts'. *Espace Populations Sociétés*, 1: 113–26.

Guzmán, J.M. 2006 'The Demography of Latin America and the Caribbean Since 1950'. *Population (English Edition)*, 61: 519–620.

Healy, J.D. 2003 'Excess Winter Mortality in Europe: A Cross Country Analysis Identifying Key Risk Factors'. *Journal of Epidemiology and Community Health*, 57: 784–9.

Intergovernmental Panel on Climate Change (IPCC) 2007 *Climate Change 2007: Physical Science Basis. Contribution of Working Group I to the Fourth Assessment Report of the Intergovernmental Panel on Climate Change*. Cambridge University Press: Cambridge and New York.

Johansson, S.R. 1991 'Welfare, Mortality, and Gender. Continuity and Change in Explanations for Male/Female Mortality Differences Over Three Centuries'. *Continuity and Change*, 6: 135–77.

Kannisto, V. 1988 'On the Survival of Centenarians and the Span of Life'. *Population Studies*, 42: 389–406.

Kannisto, V. 1994 *Development of Oldest-Old Mortality, 1950–1990: Evidence from 28 Developed Countries*. Odense University Press: Odense.

Kannisto, V. 1996 *The Advancing Frontier of Survival*. Odense University Press: Odense.

Kannisto, V., Lauritsen, J., Thatcher, A.R. and Vaupel, J.W. 1994 'Reductions in Mortality at Advanced Ages—Several Decades of Evidence from 27 Countries'. *Population and Development Review* 20: 793–810.

King, G. and Soneji, S. 2011 'The Future of Death in America'. *Demographic Research*, 25: 1–38.

Klotz, J. 2010 'Convergence or Divergence of Educational Disparities in Mortality and Morbidity? The Evolution of Life Expectancy and Health Expectancy by Educational Attainment in Austria in 1981–2006'. *Vienna Yearbook of Population Research*, 8: 139–74.

Kuh, D. and Shlomo, Y.B. 2004 *A Life Course Approach to Chronic Diseases Epidemiology*, 2nd edn. Oxford University Press: Oxford and New York.

Kuh, D., Shlomo, Y.B., Lynch, J., Hallqvist, J. and Power, C. 2003 'Life Course Epidemiology'. *Journal of Epidemiology and Community Health*, 57: 778–83.

Kunst, A.E. 1997 *Cross-national Comparisons of Socio-economic Differences in Mortality*. Department of Public Health, Erasmus University: Rotterdam.

Lee, R. 2006 'Mortality Forecasts and Linear Life Expectancy Trends'. *Social Insurance Studies*, 3: 19.

Leinsalu, M., Vågerö, D. and Kunst, A.E. 2003 'Estonia 1989–2000: Enormous Increase in Mortality Differences by Education'. *International Journal of Epidemiology*, 32: 1081–7.

Liao, C.-Y., Rikke, B.A., Johnson, T.E., Diaz, V. and Nelson, J.F. 2010 'Genetic Variation in the Murine Lifespan Response to Dietary Restriction: From Life Extension to Life Shortening'. *Aging Cell*, 9: 92–5.

Lopez, A.D., Collishaw, N.E. and Piha, T. 1994 'A Descriptive Model of the Cigarette Epidemic in Developed Countries'. *Tobacco Control*, 3: 242–7.

Lopez, A.D., Caselli, G. and Valkonen, T. 1995 'Moving from Description to Explanation of Adult Mortality: Issues and Approaches'. In: Valkonen, T., Caselli, G. and Lopez, A.D. (eds) *Adult Mortality in Developed Countries: From Description to Explanation*, pp. 3–20. Clarendon Press: Oxford.

Lutz, W., Goujon, A., KC, S. and Sanderson, W.C. 2007 'Reconstruction of Populations by Age, Sex and Level of Educational Attainment for 120 Countries for 1970–2000'. *Vienna Yearbook of Population Research*, 5: 193–235.

Luy, M. 2004 'Mortality Differences Between Western and Eastern Germany Before and After Reunification—A Macro and Micro Level Analysis of Developments and Responsible Factors'. *Genus*, 60: 99–141.

Luy, M. 2010 'A Classification of the Nature of Mortality Data Underlying the Estimates for the 2004 and 2006 United Nations' World Population Prospects'. *Comparative Population Studies—Zeitschrift für Bevölkerungswissenschaft*, 35: 315–34.

Luy, M., Di Giulio, P. and Caselli, G. 2010 'Gender-specific Mortality Differences by Education in Germany and Italy. Indirect Orphanhood-based Estimates with GGP-data'. Paper presented at the Annual Conference of the German Society for Demography in collaboration with the Italian Association for Population Studies, 3–5 March 2010, Rostock.

Luy, M., Di Giulio, P. and Caselli, G. 2011a 'Differences in Life Expectancy by Education and Occupation in Italy, 1980–94: Indirect Estimates From Maternal and Paternal Orphanhood'. *Population Studies*, 65: 137–55.

Luy, M., Wegner, C. and Lutz, W. 2011b 'Adult Mortality in Europe'. In: Rogers, R.G. and Crimmins, E.M. (eds) *International Handbook of Adult Mortality*, pp. 49–82. Springer: New York.

Mackenbach, J.P. 2013 'Political Conditions and Life Expectancy in Europe, 1900–2008'. *Social Science & Medicine*, 82: 134–46.

McKee, C.M. 1989 'Deaths in Winter: Can Britain Learn from Europe?' *European Journal of Epidemiology*, 5: 178–82.

McMichael, A.J. and Lindgren, E. 2011 'Future Risks to Health, and Necessary Responses'. *Journal of Internal Medicine*, 270: 401–13.

Mair, W., Goymer, P., Pletcher, S.D. and Partridge, L. 2003 'Demography of Dietary Restriction and Death in *Drosophila*'. *Science*, 301: 1731–3.

Manton, K.G., Stallard, E. and Corder, L. 1997 'Education-specific Estimates of Life Expectancy and Age-specific Disability in the U.S. Elderly Population: 1982 to 1991'. *Journal of Aging and Health*, 9: 419–50.

Marmot, M.G. 1995 'Regional Differences in Mortality: The Whitehall Studies'. In: Lopez, A.D., Caselli, G. and Valkonen, T. (eds) *Adult Mortality in Developed Countries: From Description to Explanation*, pp. 243–60. Clarendon Press: Oxford.

Masters, R.K., Powers, D.A. and Link, B.G. 2013 'Obesity and US Mortality Risk Over the Adult Life Course'. *American Journal of Epidemiology*, 177: 431–42.

Meara, E., Richards, S. and Cutler, D. 2008 'The Gap Gets Bigger: Changes in Mortality and Life Expectancy, by Education, 1981–2000'. *Health Affairs*, 27: 350–60.

Mehta, N.K. and Chang, V.W. 2011 'Secular Declines in the Association Between Obesity and Mortality in the United States'. *Population and Development Review*, 37: 435–51.

Meslé, F. 2004 'Mortality in Central and Eastern Europe: Long Term Trends and Recent Upturns'. *Demographic Research (Special Collection)*, 2: 45–70.

Meslé, F. and Vallin, J. 2002 'Mortality in Europe: The Divergence Between East and West'. *Population*, 57: 157–97.

Meslé, F. and Vallin, J. 2011 'Historical Trends in Mortality'. In: Rogers, R.G. and Crimmins, E.M. (eds) *International Handbook of Adult Mortality*, pp. 9–47. Springer: London and New York.

Miech, R., Pampel, F., Kim, J. and Rogers, R.G. 2011 'The Enduring Association Between Education and Mortality: The Role of Widening and Narrowing Disparities'. *American Sociological Review*, 76: 913–34.

Montez, J.K. and Hayward, M.D. 2011 'Early Life Conditions and Later Life Mortality'. In: Rogers, R.G. and Crimmins, E.M. (eds) *International Handbook of Adult Mortality*, pp. 187–206. Springer: New York.

Na'amnih, W., Muhsen, K., Tarabeia, J., Saabneh, A. and Green, M.S. 2010 'Trends in the Gap in Life Expectancy Between Arabs and Jews in Israel Between 1975 and 2004'. *International Journal of Epidemiology*, 39: 1324–32.

Oeppen, J. and Vaupel, J.W. 2002 'Broken Limits to Life Expectancy'. *Science*, 296: 1029–31.

Olshansky, S.J. 2005 'Projecting the Future of U.S. Health and Longevity'. *Health Affairs*, 24(Suppl. 2): W5R86–89.

Olshansky, S.J. and Ault, A.B. 1986 'The Fourth Stage of the Epidemiologic Transition: The Age of Delayed Degenerative Diseases'. *The Milbank Quarterly*, 64: 355–91.

Olshansky, S.J. and Carnes, B.A. 2013 'Zeno's Paradox of Immortality'. *Gerontology*, 59: 85–92.

Olshansky, S.J., Carnes, B.A. and Cassel, C. 1990 'In Search of Methuselah: Estimating the Upper Limits to Human Longevity. *Science*, 250: 634–40.

Olshansky, S.J., Carnes, B., Rogers, R.G. and Smith, L. 1997 'Infectious Diseases—New and Ancient Threats to World Health'. *Population Bulletin*, 52: 1–52.

Olshansky, S.J., Carnes, B.A. and Désesquelles, A. 2001 'Prospects for Human Longevity'. *Science*, 291: 1491–92.

Olshansky, S.J., Passaro, D.J., Hershow, R.C., Layden, J., Carnes, B.A., Brody, J., et al. 2005 'A Potential Decline in Life Expectancy in the United States in the 21st Century'. *New England Journal of Medicine*, 352: 1138–45.

Omran, A.R. 1971 'The Epidemiologic Transition. A Theory of the Epidemiology of Population Change'. *Milbank Memorial Fund Quarterly*, 49: 509–38.

Omran, A.R. 1983 'The Epidemiologic Transition Theory. A Preliminary Update'. *Journal of Tropical Pediatrics*, 29: 305–16.

Omran, A.R. and Roudi, F. 1993 'The Middle East Population Puzzle'. *Population Bulletin*, 48: 1–40.

Palloni, A. 1990 'Fertility and Mortality Decline in Latin America'. *Annals of the American Academy of Political and Social Science*, 510: 126–44.

Palloni, A. and Pinto-Aguirre, G. 2011 'Adult Mortality in Latin America and the Caribbean'. In: Rogers, R.G. and Crimmins, E.M. (eds) *International Handbook of Adult Mortality*, pp. 101–32. Springer: New York.

Pampel, F.C. 2002 'Cigarette Use and the Narrowing Sex Differential in Mortality'. *Population and Development Review*, 28: 77–104.

Pampel, F.C. 2005 'Forecasting Sex Differences in Mortality in High Income Nations: The Contribution of Smoking'. *Demographic Research*, 13: 455–84.

Pérez-Brignoli, H. 2010 'América Latina en la transición demográfica, 1800–1980'. *Población y Salud en Mesoamérica*, 7: 1–29.

Preston, S.H., Glei, D.A. and Wilmoth, J.R. 2010 'A New Method for Estimating Smoking-attributable Mortality in High-income Countries'. *International Journal of Epidemiology*, 39: 430–8.

Preston, S.H. and Wang, H. 2006 'Sex Mortality Differences in the United States: The Role of Cohort Smoking Patterns'. *Demography*, 43: 631–46.

Preston, S.H. and Stokes, A. 2011 'Contribution of Obesity to International Differences in Life Expectancy'. *American Journal of Public Health*, 101: 2137–43.

Prospective Studies Collaboration 2009 'Body-mass Index and Cause-specific Mortality in 900 000 Adults: Collaborative Analyses of 57 Prospective Studies'. *The Lancet*, 373: 1083–96.

Querfurth, H.W. and LaFerla, F.M. 2010 'Alzheimer's Disease'. *New England Journal of Medicine*, 362: 329–44.

Rau, R. 2004 'Winter Mortality in Elderly People in Britain: Lack of Social Gradient in Winter Excess Mortality is Obvious in Denmark'. *British Medical Journal*, 329: 976–7.

Rau, R. and Doblhammer, G. 2003 'Seasonal Mortality in Denmark: The Role of Sex and Age'. *Demographic Research*, 9: 197–222.

Rau, R., Soroko, E., Jasilionis, D. and Vaupel, J.W. 2008 'Continued Reductions in Mortality at Advanced Ages'. *Population and Development Review*, 34: 747–68.

Reither, E.N., Olshansky, S.J. and Yang, Y. 2011 'New Forecasting Methodology Indicates More Disease and Earlier Mortality Ahead for Today's Younger Americans'. *Health Affairs*, 30: 1562–8.

Richardson, K., Steffen, W. and Liverman, D. (eds) 2011 *Climate Change: Global Risks, Challenges and Decisions*. Cambridge University Press: Cambridge.

Robine, J.M. and Saito, Y. 2003 'Survival Beyond Age 100: The Case of Japan'. *Population and Development Review*, 29: 208–28.

Rogers, R.G. and Hackenberg, R. 1987 'Extending Epidemiologic Transition Theory: A New Stage'. *Biodemography and Social Biology*, 34: 234–43.

Rogers, R.G., Everett, B.G., Saint Onge, J.M. and Krueger, P.M. 2010 'Social, Behavioral, and Biological Factors, and Sex Differences in Mortality'. *Demography*, 47: 555–78.

Rose, G. and Marmot, M.G. 1981 'Social Class and Coronary Heart Disease'. *British Heart Journal*, 45: 13–19.

Ross, C.E., Masters, R.K. and Hummer, R.A. 2012 'Education and the Gender Gaps in Health and Mortality'. *Demography*, 49: 1157–83.

Rossi, I.A., Rousson, V. and Paccaud, F. 2013 'The Contribution of Rectangularization to the Secular Increase of Life Expectancy: An Empirical Study'. *International Journal of Epidemiology*, 42: 250–8.

Roudi, F. 2001 *Population Trends and Challenges in the Middle East and North Africa*. Population Reference Bureau: Washington, DC.

Shkolnikov, V.M., Leon, D.A., Adamets, S., Andreev, E. and Deev, A. 1998 'Educational Level and Adult Mortality in Russia: An Analysis of Routine Data 1979 to 1994'. *Social Science & Medicine*, 47: 357–69.

Shkolnikov, V.M., Andreev, E.M., Jasilionis, D., Leinsalu, M., Antonova, O.I. and McKee, M. 2006 'The Changing Relation Between Education and Life Expectancy in Central and Eastern Europe in the 1990s'. *Journal of Epidemiology and Community Health*, 60: 875–81.

Shkolnikov, V.M., Jdanov, D.A., Andreev, E.M. and Vaupel, J.W. 2011 'Steep Increase in Best-practice Cohort Life Expectancy'. *Population and Development Review*, 37: 419–34.

Sierra, F., Hadley, E., Suzman, R. and Hodes, R. 2009 'Prospects for Life Span Extension'. *Annual Review of Medicine*, 60: 457–69.

Staetsky, L. 2009 'Diverging Trends in Female Old-age Mortality: A Reappraisal'. *Demographic Research*, 21: 885–914.

Thiltgès, E., Duchêne, J. and Wunsch, G. 1995 'Causal Theories and Models in the Study of Mortality'. In: Valkonen, T., Caselli, G. and Lopez, A.D. (eds) *Adult Mortality in Developed Countries: From Description to Explanation*, pp. 21–36. Clarendon Press: Oxford.

Torri, T. and Vaupel, J.W. 2012 'Forecasting Life Expectancy in an International Context'. *International Journal of Forecasting*, 28: 519–31.

U.S. Department of Health and Human Services 2004 'The Health Consequences of Smoking: A Report of the Surgeon General'. U.S. Department of Health and Human Services, Centers for Disease Control and Prevention, National Center for Chronic Disease Prevention and Health Promotion, Office on Smoking and Health: Washington, DC.

United Nations 1975 *World Population Prospects, 1970–2000, as Assessed in 1973*. United Nations: New York.

United Nations 1989 *World Population Prospects 1988*. United Nations: New York.

United Nations 2011 *World Population Prospects: The 2010 Revision*. United Nations: New York.

United Nations Inter-agency Group for Child Mortality Estimation 2011 *Levels & Trends in Child Mortality*. Report 2011. United Nations Children's Fund: New York.

Valkonen, T. 2006 'Social Inequalities in Mortality'. In: Caselli, G., Vallin, J. and Wunsch, G. (eds) *Demography: Analysis and Synthesis. Volume 2: A Treatise in Population Studies*, pp. 195–206. Academic Press: London.

Vallin, J. and Meslé, F. 2001 'Trends in Mortality in Europe Since 1950: Age-, Sex- and Cause-Specific Mortality'. In: Vallin, J., Meslé, F. and Valkonen (eds) *Trends in Mortality and Differential Mortality, Population Studies*, pp. 31–184. Council of Europe: Strasbourg.

Vallin, J. and Meslé, F. 2004 'Convergences and Divergences in Mortality. A New Approach to Health Transition'. *Demographic Research (Special Collection)*, 2: 11–44.

Vallin, J. and Meslé, F. 2009 'The Segmented Trend Line of Highest Life Expectancies'. *Population and Development Review*, 35: 159–87.

Van Marum, R.J. 2008 'Current and Future Therapy in Alzheimer's Disease'. *Fundamental & Clinical Pharmacology*, 22: 265–74.

Vaupel, J.W. 2001 'Demographic Insights into Longevity'. *Population*, 13: 245–59.

Vaupel, J.W. 2010 'Biodemography of Human Ageing'. *Nature*, 464: 536–42.

Vaupel, J.W. and Rau, R. 2013 'Research Versus Rhetoric'. *Gerontology*, 59: 95–6.

Vaupel, J.W., Carey, J.R. and Christensen, K. 2003 'Aging. It's Never too Late'. *Science*, 301: 1679–81.

Wang, H. and Preston, S.H. 2009 'Forecasting United States Mortality Using Cohort Smoking Histories'. *Proceedings of the National Academy of Sciences of the United States of America*, 106: 393–8.

Wen, M. and Gu, D. 2012 'Air Pollution Shortens Life Expectancy and Health Expectancy for Older Adults: The Case of China'. *Journals of Gerontology A: Biological Sciences and Medical Sciences*, 67: 1219–29.

White, K.M. 2002 'Longevity Advances in High-Income Countries, 1955–96'. *Population and Development Review*, 28: 59–76.

Wilmoth, J.R. 2001 'How Long Can we Live? A Review Essay'. *Population and Development Review*, 27: 791–800.

Woolf, S.H. and Aron, L. (eds) 2013 *U.S. Health in International Perspective: Shorter Lives, Poorer Health. Panel on Understanding Cross-National Health Differences among High-Income Countries*. The National Academic Press: Washington, DC.

Zhao, Z. 2011 'Adult Mortality in Asia'. In: Rogers, R.G. and Crimmins, E.M. (eds) *International Handbook of Adult Mortality*, pp. 133–50. Springer: New York.

Zhao, Z. and Kinfu, Y. 2005 'Mortality Transition in East Asia'. *Asian Population Studies*, 1: 3–30.

CHAPTER 6

FUTURE MORTALITY IN HIGH MORTALITY COUNTRIES

ALESSANDRA GARBERO AND ELSIE PAMUK

Contributing authors:[1]
Michel Garenne, Bruno Masquelier, and François Pelletier[2]

6.1 Introduction

The theory and empirical basis of the demographic transition includes the important role played by mortality declines in generating a societal shift from high mortality and high fertility to low mortality and low fertility. In particular, it is the improved survival of children into adulthood that initially produces increasingly large populations with a very young age structure. Because the level of childhood mortality is strongly linked to fertility levels (Angeles, 2010; Becker and Barro, 1988) and adult mortality rates, the definition of a high mortality country used in the IIASA–Oxford survey reported in this

[1] The contributing authors have drafted considerable parts of section 6.4. They were selected as lead experts in respective topics and regions. Specifically, they have provided texts to the following sections: Michel Garenne contributed to section 6.4.4 ('Behavioural changes related to health'), section 6.4.5 ('Other infectious diseases: role of neglected and emerging diseases'), and short paragraphs in sections 6.4.1 ('HIV and AIDS'), 6.4.7 ('Mortality due to crises'), and 6.4.8 ('Differential trends of population subgroups'); Bruno Masquelier provided child mortality data and contributed to section 6.3 ('Adult mortality'); François Pelletier 6.4.1 ('HIV and AIDS'), and 6.4.7 ('Mortality due to crises'). The views and opinions expressed by François Pelletier are those of the author and do not necessarily represent those of the United Nations (UN). This chapter has not been formally edited or cleared by the UN.

[2] **Acknowledgements and disclaimer**: The authors are grateful to Patrick Gerland and the volume's editors for helpful discussions and insightful comments.

book is in terms of the level of childhood mortality, that is, the probability of death before the age of five (${}_5q_0$ in the life table designation).

In accordance with recent practice at the World Health Organization (WHO) and UNICEF in monitoring progress toward the Millennium Development Goals, we use a cutoff point of 40 deaths before age 5 per thousand live births to designate a country as having high mortality (Hill et al., 2012). In 2010, the under-5 mortality rate exceeded 40 in one-third of the 193 member countries of United Nations (UN), and in only one of these countries did life expectancy at birth exceed 70 years (Azerbaijan, $e_0 = 70.1$) (United Nations, 2011a). Despite its relatively low under-five mortality rate (estimated at 0.025 in 2011), Botswana is also considered here as a country with high mortality because its life expectancy is estimated at 53 years (United Nations, 2011a). The geographic distribution of these countries is shown in Figure 6.1, while Table 6.1 lists all 65 high mortality countries, along with current estimates of life expectancy, child mortality, and the change in life expectancy between the periods 1995–2005 and 2005–2010.

As shown, high mortality countries include all of sub-Saharan Africa except the island nations of Cape Verde, Mauritius, Mayotte, and Réunion. Most of South Asia meets the criterion of high mortality, including the populous countries of India, Pakistan, and Bangladesh.

6.1.1 Past trends and current levels

Many demographers have, over the last 50 years, predicted a general convergence worldwide toward low mortality and fertility resulting in higher levels of life expectancy. The presumption of global convergence in mortality was based on analyses of mortality data, primarily from developed countries, starting from the 1960s (McMichael et al., 2004). These data revealed the occurrence of a common pattern, named the 'epidemiological transition' (Omran, 1971), broadly indicating not only that declines in death rates from infectious diseases (affecting mainly children and younger adults) cause increases in life expectancy, but also leave the remaining mortality as primarily due to non-communicable diseases, largely occurring in old age. The apparent pervasiveness of this pattern gave some expectation of a rapid decline of mortality in high mortality countries, while countries that had already achieved a relatively low level of mortality would find future increases in life expectancy harder to achieve.

However, the idea of a global convergence in mortality has been challenged by the occurrence of mortality reversals during the last two decades. These reversals took place in countries that experienced conflict (i.e. Rwanda, Angola, Sierra Leone, Liberia, and Somalia), failure of health systems (i.e. Kazakhstan and Zimbabwe), or HIV and AIDS epidemics (Reniers et al., 2011). In 2004, HIV and AIDS was the fourth leading cause of death in low-income countries, followed by deaths from lower respiratory infections, ischemic heart disease, and diarrhoeal diseases (Mathers et al., 2008). Increases in malaria and tuberculosis (TB) have also been partly responsible for mortality trend reversals in the last two decades in sub-Saharan Africa and in other regions.

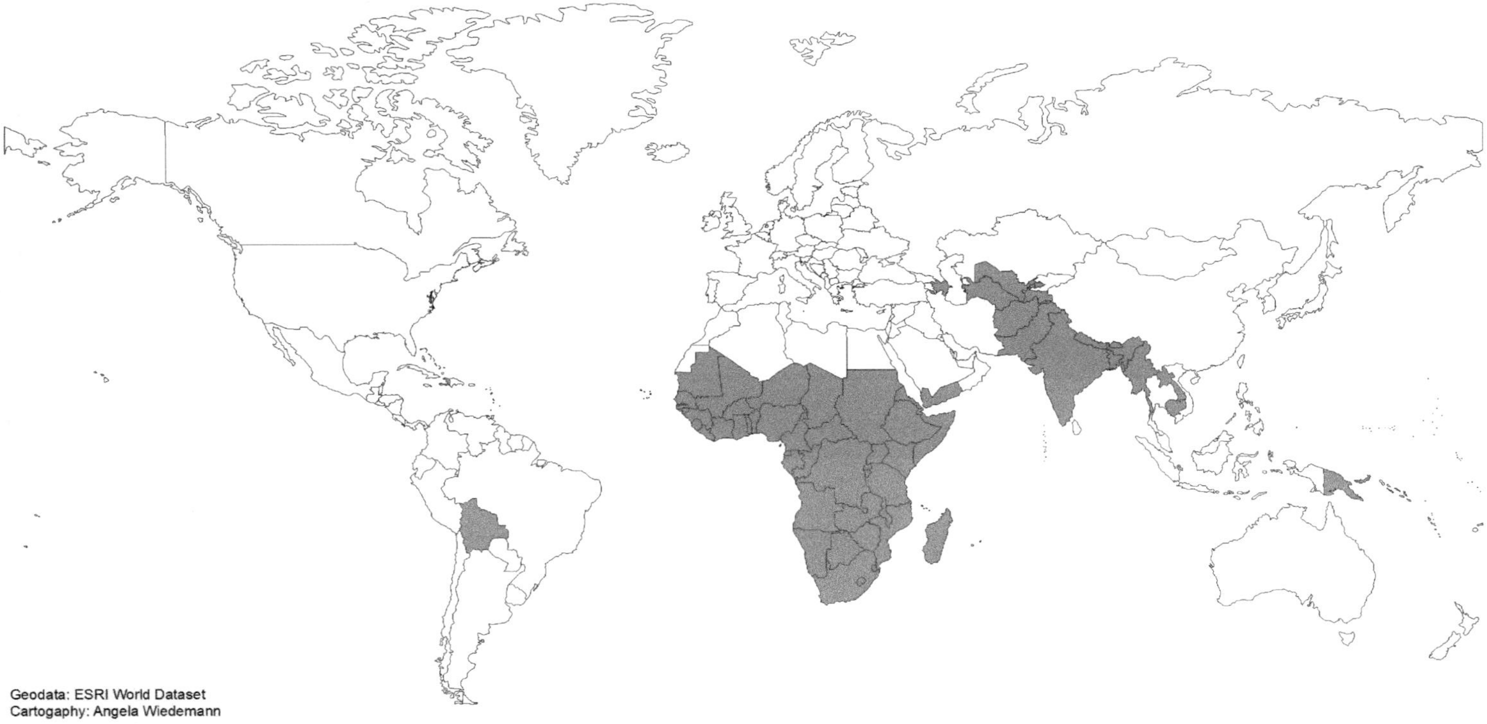

FIGURE 6.1 Geographic distribution of high mortality countries discussed in this chapter.

Table 6.1 Countries with High Mortality

Selection criterion = ${}_5q_0$>40/1,000				Life expectancy (e_0) in years (both sexes)		Under-5 mortality (${}_5q_0$) per 1,000 live births (both sexes)
				UN–WPP 2010		IGME
e_0 rank	Country	Population (thousands) 2010	HIV-affected	Decadal change in e_0 (1995–2005 to 2005–10)	2005–10	2011
Africa—Eastern						
4	Zimbabwe	12,571	HIV	−1.6	46.6	67.1
6	Zambia	13,089	HIV	4.3	46.9	82.9
11	Mozambique	23,391	HIV	2.0	48.8	103.1
12	Burundi	8,383	HIV	3.4	48.8	139.1
17	Somalia	9,331		3.4	50.2	180.0
20	Malawi	14,901	HIV	5.4	51.6	82.6
21	Uganda	33,425	HIV	7.2	52.2	89.9
27	Rwanda	10,624	HIV	12.3	53.9	54.1
30	Kenya	40,513	HIV	1.1	55.0	72.8
31	United Republic of Tanzania	44,841	HIV	5.7	55.4	67.6
34	Djibouti	889	HIV	3.4	56.6	89.5
35	Ethiopia	82,950	HIV	6.7	57.2	77.0
39	Comoros	735		2.3	59.7	79.3
40	Eritrea	5 254	HIV	5.5	60.0	67.8
57	Madagascar	20,714		8.5	65.8	61.6
Africa—Middle and Northern						
1	Central African Republic	4,401	HIV	1.3	45.9	163.5
9	Democratic Republic of Congo	65,966	HIV	2.3	47.4	167.7
10	Chad	11,227	HIV	−0.7	48.5	169.0
13	Angola	19,082	HIV	6.3	49.6	157.6

14	Cameroon	19,599	HIV	-1.0	50.0	127.2
16	Equatorial Guinea	700	HIV	1.5	50.1	118.1
33	Congo	4,043	HIV	1.7	56.0	98.8
45	Gabon	1,505	HIV	0.7	61.3	65.6
50	Sao Tome and Principe	165		1.8	63.8	88.8
41	Sudan	43,552		4.9	60.3	86.0
Africa—Southern						
2	Lesotho	2,171	HIV	-6.5	46.0	86.0
8	Swaziland	1,186	HIV	-5.4	47.4	103.6
19	South Africa	50,133	HIV	-6.5	51.2	46.7
25	Botswana	2,007	HIV	-1.6	53.3	25.9
44	Namibia	2,283	HIV	1.6	61.1	41.5
Africa—Western						
3	Sierra Leone	5,868	HIV	8.2	46.3	185.3
5	Guinea-Bissau	1,515	HIV	2.5	46.8	160.6
15	Mali	15,370	HIV	3.4	50.0	175.6
18	Nigeria	158,423	HIV	5.0	50.3	124.1
22	Guinea	9,982	HIV	5.8	52.4	125.8
23	Côte d'Ivoire	19,738	HIV	2.7	53.0	114.9
24	Niger	15,512		6.7	53.1	124.5
26	Burkina Faso	16,469	HIV	4.3	53.9	146.4
28	Liberia	3,994	HIV	11.0	54.4	78.3
29	Benin	8,850	HIV	2.7	54.6	106
32	Togo	6,028	HIV	1.2	55.7	110.1
36	Gambia	1,728	HIV	3.0	57.3	106
37	Mauritania	3 460		0.7	57.5	112.1
38	Senegal	12,434		3.2	58.2	64.8
48	Ghana	24,392	HIV	4.9	62.7	77.6

(continued)

Table 6.1 Continued

Selection criterion = ${}_5q_0$>40/1,000				Life expectancy (e_0) in years (both sexes)		Under-5 mortality (${}_5q_0$) per 1,000 live births (both sexes)
				UN–WPP 2010		IGME
e_0 rank	Country	Population (thousands) 2010	HIV-affected	Decadal change in e_0 (1995–2005 to 2005–10)	2005–10	2011
Asia—Southern						
7	Afghanistan	31,412		2.8	47.3	101.1
52	India	1,224,614	HIV	3.5	64.2	61.3
54	Pakistan	173,593		2.0	64.6	72.0
58	Bhutan	726		6.9	65.8	53.7
61	Nepal	29,959		7.8	67.4	48.0
63	Bangladesh	148,692		4.4	67.8	46.0
Asia—South East						
42	Timor-Leste	1,124		7.0	60.8	54.1
47	Cambodia	14,138		4.8	61.5	42.5
49	Myanmar	47,963		2.4	63.5	62.4
59	Lao People's Democratic Republic	6,201		6.1	66.1	41.9
Asia—Central and Western						
55	Turkmenistan	5,042		1.1	64.6	52.5
60	Tajikistan	6,879		3.6	66.4	63.3

62	Uzbekistan	27,445		0.7	67.4	48.6
51	Yemen	24,053		5.7	63.9	76.5
65	Azerbaijan	9,188		4.1	70.1	44.7
Latin America						
43	Haiti	9,993	HIV	3.0	61.0	70.0
56	Bolivia (Plurinational State of)	9,930		3.5	65.6	50.6
Oceania						
46	Papua New Guinea	6,858		3.5	61.5	57.8
64	Micronesia (Fed. States of)	111		1.3	68.3	41.5
53	Kiribati	100		4.6	64.4	47.4
		Range =		-6.5 to 12.3	45.9–70.1	25.6–185.3

UN: United Nations; WPP: World Population Prospects; IGME: Inter-agency Group for Child Mortality Estimation.

In addition, progress toward reducing infant and child mortality has stagnated or slowed in many countries, due not only to HIV/AIDS and conflicts, but also to increases in malaria-related mortality and stalls in immunization rates in the 1990s. Other factors contributing to this divergent trend are the growing burden of injuries and non-communicable diseases, as well as health risks due to environmental changes, induced or not by human pressures. Often, several factors combine to adversely affect mortality trends. For example, life expectancy has been severely affected in Haiti (Farmer et al., 2003) as a consequence of aid restrictions in a context of widespread poverty and a failed health system.

A serious problem in estimating past trends and projecting the future course of life expectancy in high mortality countries is the lack of reliable data on age-specific mortality rates, particularly for adults. Among the 65 countries considered here, only Azerbaijan, Turkmenistan, Uzbekistan, and São Tomé and Príncipe have vital registration systems covering at least 90 per cent of deaths.[3] The coverage of death registration in South Africa hovers around 85 per cent, and, until recently, vital registration data could also be used in Zimbabwe (Feeney, 2001). In other countries, either the coverage is far too low to estimate mortality or vital statistics are not compiled and transferred to national statistical offices (Mathers et al., 2005). Because of this lack of registration-type data, trends in child mortality are generally obtained from direct or indirect methods making use of mothers' reports on the survival of their children, as collected in censuses and large-scale surveys (Demographic and Health Survey (DHS), Multiple Indicator Cluster Survey, etc.). For adult mortality, no equivalent approach has proved entirely satisfactory (Hill et al., 2005). Converting the cohort attrition between two census age distributions into measures of adult mortality poses several difficulties, mainly due to age misreporting, differences in the completeness of the censuses, and migrations (Preston, 1983). Several death distribution methods have been designed to evaluate and potentially adjust (upwards) mortality rates computed from recent household deaths or incomplete vital registration (Hill, 1987), but these methods are hard to apply when net migration is substantial, and they are based on rather stringent assumptions (such as a constant under-reporting of deaths over a certain age limit). A third series of methods makes use of survey and census reports on the survival status of close relatives, that is, first spouses, siblings, or parents (Hill, 1987; Hill and Trussell, 1977). The rare studies that exploited data on the survival of first spouses were not very encouraging (Makinson, 1993; Timaeus, 1987), and the method has since fallen into disuse. Probabilities of dying inferred from data on orphanhood also tend to under-estimate adult mortality and they can be heavily distorted by HIV-related biases. By contrast, the data on the survival of siblings that have been collected in more than 100 DHS are emerging as a major source of estimates of adult mortality in developing countries. The main advantage of sibling survival data is that they provide occurrence-/exposure-type mortality rates

[3] Source: United Nations Statistics Division (n.d) 'Coverage of Birth and Death Registration'. Available at: <http://unstats.un.org/unsd/demographic/CRVS/CR_coverage.htm> (accessed 7 November 2012).

when full sibling histories are collected from adult household members. Limited modelling is required to derive age- and period-specific mortality rates (Timaeus and Jasseh, 2004), yet substantial biases can also affect these retrospective data (Helleringer et al., 2014; Masquelier, 2013).

Against this backdrop of paucity and poor quality of data on mortality, the next section describes what is known about trends in child and adult mortality in high mortality countries, using the best data available, for the 65 countries classified as having high mortality in 2010.

6.2 Child mortality: current levels and past trends

An advantage of using early childhood mortality as the defining criterion for designating a country as having high mortality is that considerable effort is being made by the UN's Inter-agency Group for Child Mortality Estimation (IGME) to form the most reliable estimates for every country in the world. The IGME collects and assesses the quality of all available data, then uses acceptable data and recognized statistical methods to form time series estimates of mortality before the age of 5. New estimates for countries and world regions through 2011 have recently been made available (Hill et al., 2012), and provide the basis for the description of current levels and past trends contained in the next section.

Since 1990, the global under-5 mortality rate has dropped by 41 per cent—from 87 deaths per 1,000 live births in 1990 to 51 in 2011 (UNICEF, 2012). In the majority of countries, including many developing countries, the under-5 mortality rate has been cut in half in the last two decades. At the same time, however, the disparity between areas where child mortality remains high and the rest of the world has increased. As shown in Figure 6.1, child mortality is increasingly concentrated in sub-Saharan Africa and South Asia; over 80 per cent of child deaths in 2011 occurred in these two regions. Yet even within this group of high mortality countries, the level of child mortality varies considerably. The under-5 mortality rate in Sierra Leone, the country with the highest rate in 2011, was 4.5 times greater than the rates for Micronesia, Lao People's Democratic Republic (PDR), and Namibia, and 7.0 times greater than that for Botswana (Table 6.1).

The difficulty involved in making accurate projections of future trends in life expectancy for countries with high levels of mortality is illustrated by examining the trends in child mortality within these countries over the last three decades, time periods for which reasonably reliable estimates of child mortality levels have been made (You et al., 2011).

Figures 6.2–6.7 show the trends in the under-5 mortality rate for countries separated by region. For regions with many high mortality countries, the overall trend and distribution is indicated by a series of boxplots accompanied by examples of different country-specific trends to indicate the range of variation in the patterns. The countries shown

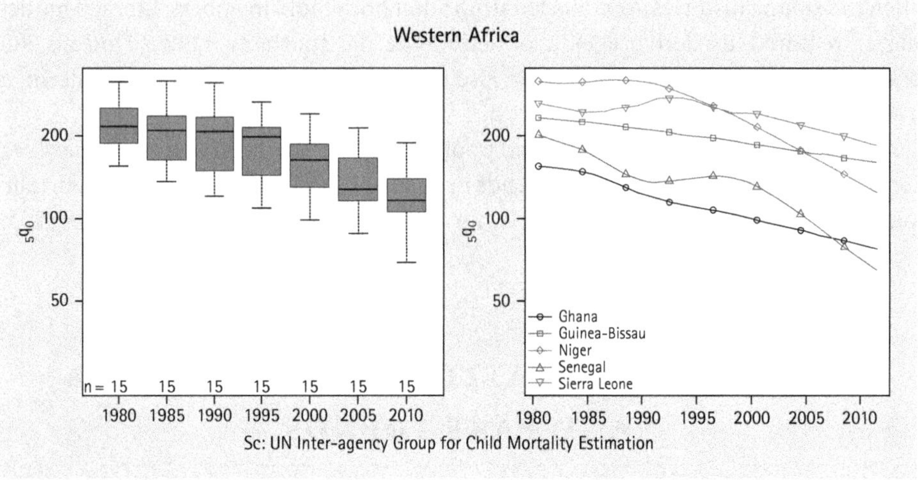

FIGURE 6.2 Trends in the under-5 mortality rate, Western Africa.

in the right-hand panel are those with the greatest and slowest rate of change between 1980 and 2011, those with the highest and lowest mortality rates in 2011, and examples of atypical trends.

In 1980 the 15 countries of Western Africa experienced very high child mortality, averaging 226 (deaths of children aged <5 years for every 1,000 live births) and ranging from a high of 317 in Niger to a low of 155 in Ghana (Figure 6.2). Over the next three decades, the rate of child mortality declined in every country, but the amount of decline varied from 67–68 per cent in Liberia and Senegal to just 29–30 per cent in Mauritania and Sierra Leone. For many Western African countries, the declines in child mortality have been steady, albeit at different rates, as typified by Ghana and Guinea-Bissau (Figure 6.2, right panel). However, for Sierra Leone, Niger, Liberia, and Nigeria, little or no progress was made between 1980 and the mid-to-late 1990s, followed by much more rapid declines in the last decade. By 2011, the average child mortality rate for these countries was 120 and ranged from 185 in Sierra Leone to 65 in Senegal, but the variation in the pattern and pace of decline produced a quite different ranking of countries by level of child mortality in 2011 compared with 1980.

Figure 6.3 shows a generally similar overall pattern for the 15 countries of Eastern Africa. In 1980 child mortality in these countries averaged 182 and ranged from 256 in Malawi to a low of 104 in Zimbabwe. By 2011 child mortality had declined by an average of 52 per cent to 88 child deaths per 1,000 live births. However, the variation in the pace of decline across these 15 countries was even more striking than in Western Africa. Estimates of declines ranged from 75 per cent in Rwanda to only 30 per cent in Burundi and to no change in Somalia. In most countries of Eastern Africa, the pace of decline in child mortality was slow or non-existent until the mid-to-late 1990s (Figure 6.3). The recent declines have tended to be more rapid in countries where child mortality was higher initially, resulting in less variation across the region in 2011 than in 1980–2000. By 2011 all but three of the Eastern African countries had estimated child mortality rates between 54 and 90.

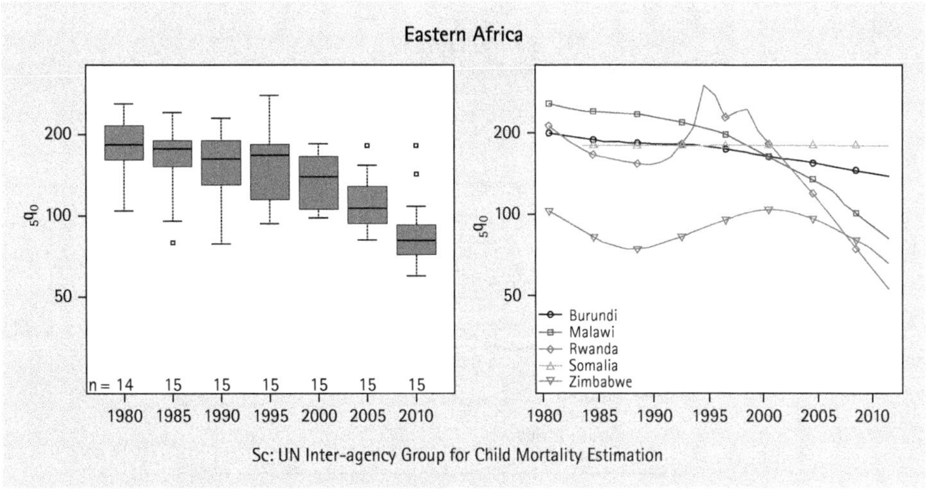

FIGURE 6.3 Trends in the under-5 mortality rate, Eastern Africa.

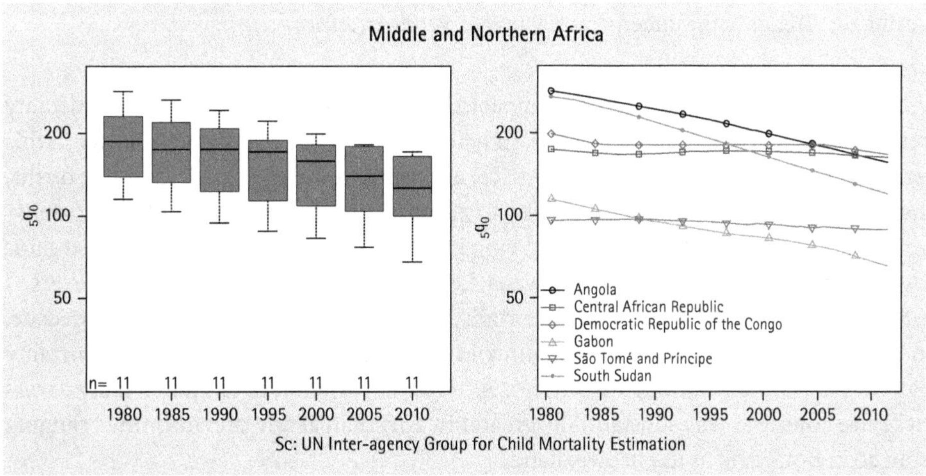

FIGURE 6.4 Trends in the under-5 mortality rate, Middle and Northern Africa.

Overall, the 11 countries of Middle and Northern Africa have seen less progress in reducing child mortality (Figure 6.4). In 1980 the average child mortality rate was 186, ranging from 286 in Angola to 96 in São Tomé and Príncipe. By 2011 the average had fallen to 124, a decline of just 33 per cent. The greatest decline was estimated to have occurred in South Sudan (56 per cent), while only minimal declines were seen for the Central African Republic (7 per cent) and São Tomé and Príncipe (8 per cent). Although declines tended to be more substantial for countries with higher child mortality in 1980, such as Angola and South Sudan, the reduction in variation was not as great as that seen in Eastern Africa. In 2011, under-5 mortality rates ranged from 66 in Gabon to 166 in the Democratic Republic of Congo (D.R. Congo).

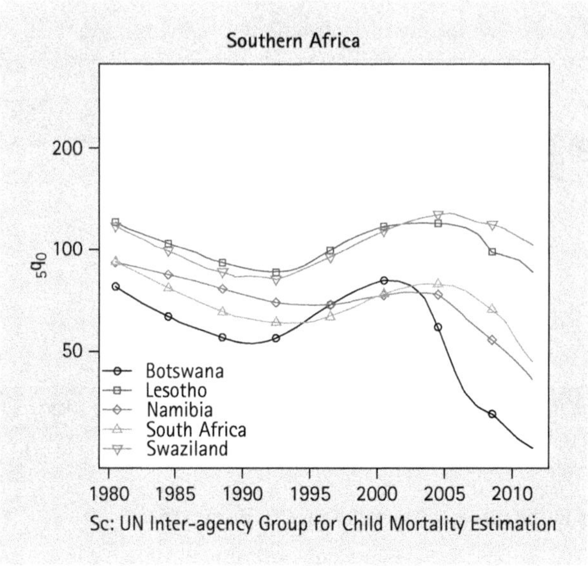

FIGURE 6.5 Trends in the under-5 mortality rate, Southern Africa.

It is in Southern Africa that the impact of the AIDS epidemic on child mortality trends is the most obvious (Figure 6.5). In 1980, child mortality was already lower in this region than the rest of sub-Saharan Africa, averaging 100 deaths per 1,000 live births, and ranging only between 121 in Lesotho to 78 in Botswana. In addition, child mortality continued to decline between 1980 and 1990 in all five countries, but by 2000 these gains had been completely reversed in Botswana, Lesotho, and Swaziland, and nearly reversed in South Africa and Namibia. Child mortality has started to fall again in the last decade, and at a more rapid rate in the countries that already had lower child mortality (Botswana, Namibia, and South Africa). As a result, variation in child mortality across these five countries was substantially greater in 2011 than at any previous time, ranging from 26 in Botswana to 104 in Swaziland.

In general, declines in child mortality were much larger and more consistent in the high mortality countries in Asia. The five high mortality countries of Central and Western Asia have each seen their child mortality rates decline by between 49 and 61 per cent since 1980 (Figure 6.6). The declines in child mortality in Southern Asia have been even greater, averaging 67 per cent since 1980. However, it is notable that child mortality declined less in India and Pakistan, the countries with the lowest levels in 1980, than in all other countries in the region. By 2011, Afghanistan was the only country in South Asia with higher child mortality than India and Pakistan. Progress has been even more striking in the remaining high mortality countries of South East Asia (Figure 6.7). Since 1982, the child mortality rate has been reduced by 77 per cent in Lao PDR and Timor-Leste, and by 72 per cent in Cambodia, despite the period of stagnation between 1985 and 1998. Even in Myanmar, the child mortality rate is estimated to have fallen by more than 50 per cent since 1982.

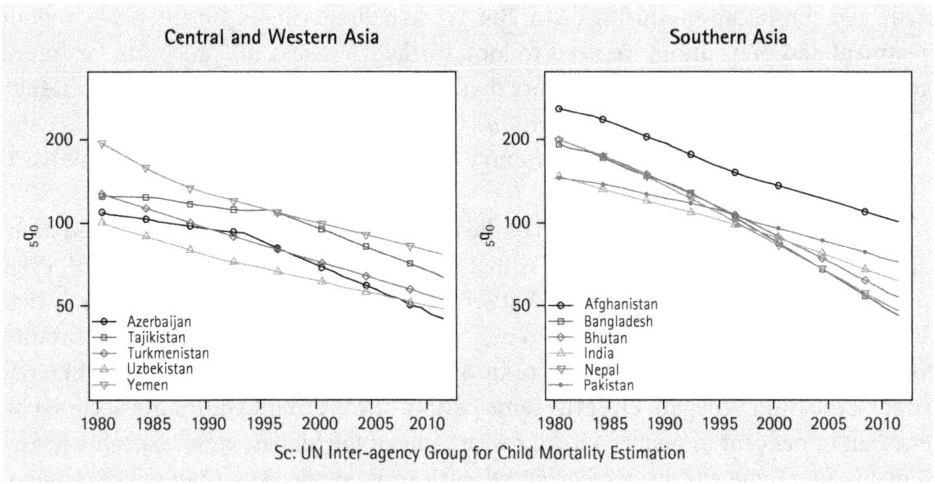

FIGURE 6.6 Trends in the under-5 mortality rate, Central, Western and Southern Asia.

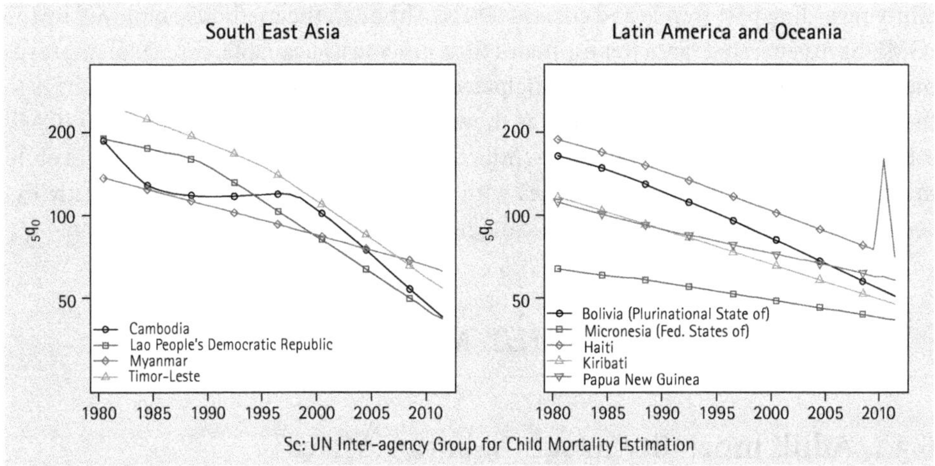

FIGURE 6.7 Trends in the under-5 mortality rate, South East Asia, Latin America, and Oceania.

The remaining 'high' mortality countries are divided between Latin American and Oceania (Figure 6.7). The two Latin American countries, Bolivia and Haiti, have seen child mortality decline by more than 60 per cent since 1980, despite the 2010 earthquake in Haiti. Declines in childhood mortality have been less steep in the three island nations of Oceania. The disparity across the 'high' mortality countries in these 30-year trends in child mortality reinforces the difficulty of making predictions about the future course of life expectancy without linking these predictions to the forces determining the progress—or lack thereof—in combating the underlying determinants of both child and adult mortality peculiar to each of these countries. The direct causes of childhood death in high mortality countries are predominately pneumonia, diarrhoea, malaria, pre-term birth, and complications during birth. But as these direct causes are amenable to both treatment and prevention, we need to look further to assess the prospects for future trends. The UN has estimated that more than a third of deaths of children under the age of 5 can be attributed to under-nutrition (UNICEF, 2012). In turn, many underlying forces affect the extent to which a country can provide adequate nutrition and basic health services for its children.

What is clear from an examination of the most recent decadal changes in child mortality in all high mortality countries is that rapid improvement can be achieved, even under less than ideal circumstances. Between 2000 and 2011, the IGME estimates that the child mortality rate declined by 30 per cent or more in 29 of the 66 high mortality countries and by 50 per cent or more in 6 (Rwanda, Botswana, Cambodia, Liberia, Timor-Leste, and Senegal). Over the same period, however, child mortality declined by less than 10 per cent in many countries with some of the highest child mortality levels: Somalia, São Tomé and Príncipe, Central African Republic, Mauritania, D.R. Congo, Congo, Cameroon, and Swaziland.

Adding to the challenges of predicting future trends in child mortality is the uncertainty regarding past trends and current levels. Although the methods employed by the IGME have generated far better estimates than previously available, continual improvement in both data and methods is anticipated. Each improvement results in changes to the existing 'best available' estimates, as shown by a comparison of 2010 and 2011 IGME estimates for high mortality countries. Still, our knowledge of levels and trends in child mortality for high mortality countries with inadequate death registration greatly exceeds that for adult mortality in these same countries, as shown in the next section.

6.3 Adult mortality

6.3.1 Adult mortality in sub-Saharan Africa

African nations are experiencing the heaviest burden of adult mortality worldwide. In the period 2005–10, all countries in which the life expectancy at age 15 was lower than 50 years were located in sub-Saharan Africa, with the notable exception of Afghanistan (United Nations, 2011a). This summary measure of adult mortality varied from 38 years in Zimbabwe to 56 years in Madagascar. Its average value, estimated at 48 years, remained almost 10 years below the corresponding value for South East Asia (57). In addition, whereas the life expectancy at age 15 increased by about 5 years in the last 25 years in South East Asia, it has remained virtually unchanged in sub-Saharan Africa. Only a handful of countries have benefited from substantial improvements in adult survival (Eritrea, Ethiopia, and Madagascar), whereas life expectancy in adults aged 15 years and over has declined since the 1980s in about 20 countries.

A detailed account of trends in adult mortality in the region remains elusive because of the lack of reliable and comprehensive data sources. As mentioned earlier, the partial absence of comprehensive registration systems forces demographers to resort to indirect techniques: intercensal survival methods, death distribution methods, and approaches based on orphanhood or sibling data. However, the resulting estimates are often discrepant and refer only to a few points in time. In addition, the development of these techniques often predates the emergence of AIDS as a major cause of death. The epidemic has since introduced serious breaches in many of the assumptions underpinning these techniques. For most African countries, the UN's Population Division (UNPD) thus resorts to the long-standing tradition of combining child mortality rates with model mortality schedules, and making ad hoc adjustments for HIV/AIDS (Masquelier et al., 2013). First, a complete life table that pertains to the population not infected by HIV (also referred to as the background mortality) is estimated. Then, for countries where HIV prevalence ever exceeded two per cent, estimates of background mortality are supplemented by AIDS deaths calculated via an epidemiological multistate model. This model is analogous to the Spectrum model used by UNAIDS (Stover et al., 2010, 2008). The resulting estimates of overall mortality are then compared to existing empirical data. When important discrepancies with model outputs are apparent, the background mortality is revised and the procedure is repeated until a reasonable agreement is achieved (United Nations, 2005). Likewise, the WHO employs estimates of AIDS deaths from UNAIDS and adds them to the background mortality rates derived from child mortality estimates and a modified Brass logit model (Murray et al., 2003). Recently, the Institute for Health Metrics and Evaluation has also produced its own set of mortality estimates for the Global Burden of Disease 2010 Study (Rajaratnam et al., 2010). The calculation of age- and sex-specific mortality rates was performed in three steps (Wang et al., 2012). First, empirical measurements of the probabilities of dying in childhood ($_5q_0$) and between the age of 15 and 60 ($_{45}q_{15}$) were extracted from survey, census and vital registration data, and adjusted for various biases. Second, trends in these two summary indices were fitted through a method known as Gaussian process regression, with a series of covariates, including education and lagged distributed income. Third, a complete life table was derived from fitted trends in $_5q_0$ and $_{45}q_{15}$ by using yet another relational life table system. Some important differences with the methods used by the UNPD or the WHO are the use of covariates and the reliance on survey data on the survival of siblings, which often provide lower levels of adult mortality, as will be shown in the following paragraphs.

The UNPD mortality rates are probably the most reliable estimates to date, mainly because they are subject to a careful comparison with other existing data and they are obtained by ensuring consistency with other components of the demographic dynamic (fertility and migration). That said, they are underpinned by a complex modelling of the HIV epidemic that involves several parameters known to have large uncertainties, such as the HIV incidence by age and sex, or, more recently, the coverage of antiretroviral therapies (ART). In addition, in a majority of high mortality countries, trends in non-AIDS mortality are inferred from child mortality, which can be misleading if adult and child mortality have not evolved in concert.

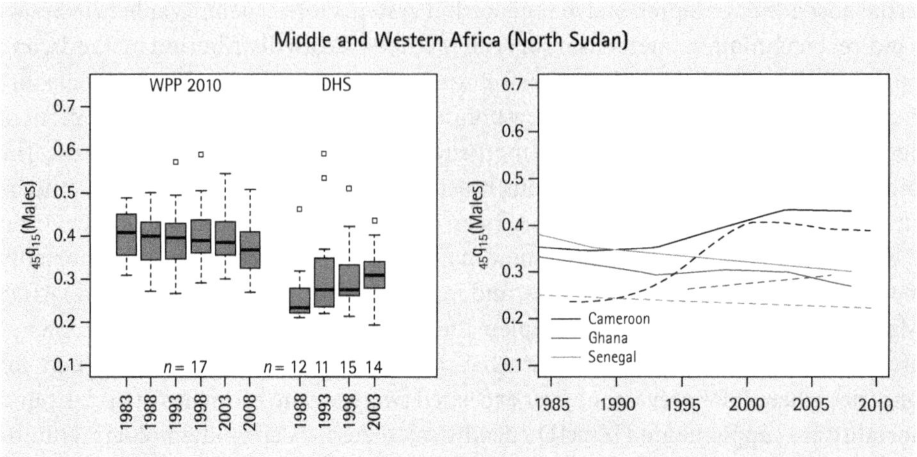

FIGURE 6.8 Trends in the probability of a man dying between the age of 15 and 60 years in 18 countries in Middle, Western Africa, and North Sudan, from the 2010 revision of the *World Population Prospects* (WPP; United Nations, 2011a) and Demographic and Health Survey (DHS) sibling histories.

Data on sibling survival collected in DHS provide useful counterpoints to these estimates. Masquelier et al. (2013) compared the probability of dying between the age of 15 and 60 ($_{45}q_{15}$) from the 2010 revision of the *World Population Prospects* (*WPP*) and sibling survival data for sub-Saharan Africa. We summarize here their main observations and present a brief overview of mortality trends in the following plots, also applying their estimation method to DHS conducted outside of sub-Saharan Africa.

The boxplot in Figure 6.8 displays the probability of a man dying between the age of 15 and 60 ($_{45}q_{15}$) in 18 countries located in Western and Middle Africa (plus North Sudan),[4] in which at least one set of sibling survival data was collected in the DHS. Trends from the 2010 revision of the *WPP* (United Nations, 2011a) are presented alongside estimates derived from DHS. Sibling estimates largely fare as lower-bound estimates. The right-hand side of Figure 6.8 singles out some countries and compares WPP estimates (solid lines) with DHS estimates (dashed lines). In Senegal, for example, the male probability $_{45}q_{15}$ for 2004 is about 35 per cent higher in the *WPP* than in the DHS. Large discrepancies are also found in Cameroon prior to 2000, while there is a better agreement in Ghana.

Estimates in Eastern and Southern Africa can also be quite discrepant, as illustrated by Malawi (Figure 6.9), for which sibling-based estimates are lower in the pre-AIDS

[4] North Sudan is the only country from Northern Africa covered by sibling data (apart from Morocco, which is not included here) because South Sudan was not covered in the 1989–90 DHS. The 2010 *WPP* estimates refer to the former Sudan. Estimates for Rwanda in 1993 or 1998 are not included in the graphs owing to the extremely high mortality levels related to the genocide. DHS estimates for Middle and Western Africa are only presented up to 2003 because few countries have conducted a DHS with sibling histories after 2008.

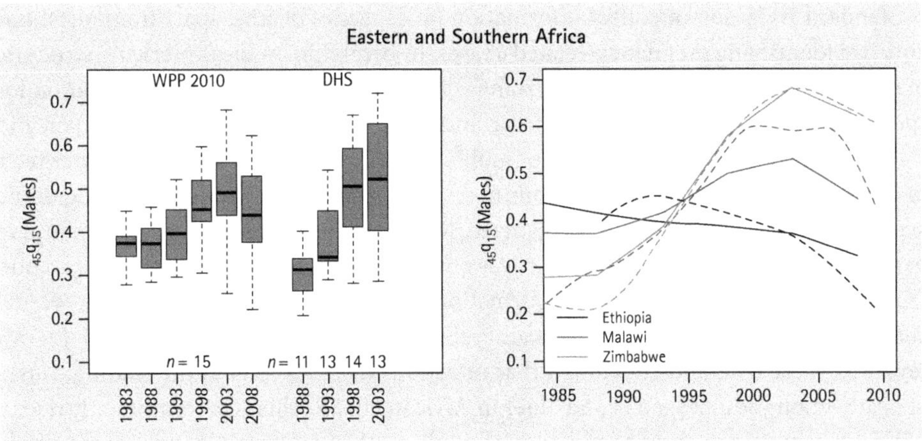

FIGURE 6.9 Trends in the probability of a man dying between the age of 15 and 60 years in 15 countries in Eastern and Southern Africa, from the 2010 revision of the *World Population Prospects* (WPP; United Nations, 2011a) and Demographic and Health Survey (DHS) sibling histories.

period, but higher in recent years. Reniers et al. (2011) noted that discrepancies between *WPP* and DHS estimates are larger in settings with small HIV prevalence, especially in the Sahelian countries. They speculated about the reasons for this and suggested that recall errors could be more pervasive in surveys conducted in Western Africa because of greater complexity of family structures (owing to higher fertility rates and polygyny). Another explanation is that sibling histories underestimate mortality irrespective of the region, but this is obfuscated in countries affected by HIV/AIDS. This could be the case if *WPP* estimates were themselves too low in these countries, potentially because of recent downward revisions of HIV prevalence (Reniers and Eaton, 2009). However, this explanation needs to be supported by further investigations.

Despite these methodological issues, some common trends can be isolated from both sources (Figures 6.8 and 6.9; Table 6.2). In Middle and Western Africa, adult mortality mostly stagnated at relatively high levels. Increases in mortality have also occurred since 1985 in a few countries, either because of high HIV prevalence (in the case of Cameroon and Côte d'Ivoire) or civil unrest (D.R. Congo). According to the DHS, the post-civil war period in Congo-Brazzaville is the only case in this region where adult mortality declined sharply during the 1990s.

In Eastern and Southern Africa, with the exceptions of Ethiopia, Madagascar, and Burundi (in the period post-2000), all countries covered by DHS sibling histories have experienced mortality increases. These have been the largest in Lesotho, Malawi, Namibia, Rwanda (during the genocide), Swaziland, Uganda, Zambia, and Zimbabwe. In several cases, however, mortality rates have peaked and seem to be declining. Some of these peaks occurred before the rapid scale-up of ART programmes (Zimbabwe, Zambia, Tanzania, Uganda). In Southern Africa, adult mortality levels are still on the rise in Lesotho, Namibia, and Swaziland.

Standard DHS do not collect information on causes of deaths, apart from questions aimed at identifying pregnancy-related causes. Information on the underlying structure of causes of death thus come either from (1) hospital records, (2) death registration for specific areas, such as in South Africa and some urban centres (Waltisperger and Meslé, 2005), or (3) Health and Demographic Surveillance sites (HDSS). The latter refer to geographically localized populations in which a recurrent collection of demographic events (e.g. every four months) is organized. More than 20 sites exist in Africa (many are part of the INDEPTH Network) and cover populations ranging from 50,000 to 200,000 (Kinyanjui and Timaeus, 2010). Information on causes of death come from 'verbal autopsies' conducted with caregivers and relatives of the deceased. Adjuik et al. (2006) reviewed these data and concluded that infectious diseases remain the leading causes of death among adults aged 15 and older in African HDSS. This is predominantly due to AIDS (causing as much as 53 per cent of adult deaths in Africa Centre Demographic Information System (ACDIS), KwaZulu-Natal (Tanser et al., 2007)), TB (ranging from 2 per cent of deaths in Nouna, Burkina Faso, to 19 per cent in Butajira, Ethiopia), and malaria (causing about a quarter of adult deaths in Niakhar, Senegal). Evidence is also accumulating that sub-Saharan Africa is facing an epidemic of non-communicable diseases (Dalal et al., 2011), including cardiovascular disease, cancer, and metabolic diseases. Rather than the expected transition from communicable diseases to non-communicable diseases, the sub-continent thus faces a double burden.

6.3.2 Adult mortality in Asia

The measurement of adult mortality has also proven to be difficult in Asia. Mortality data simply did not exist in most Asian countries until the mid-to-late twentieth century (Zhao, 2011). Data from only 11 Asian populations contributed to the development of the UN's Model Life Tables for Developing Countries in the early 1980s (United Nations, 1982). Since then, the frequency of censuses increased, but Asia is still lagging behind in terms of data quality. Demographic and health surveys have also played an important role and managed to fill some of the data gaps. In addition, as in the African region, the UNPD and the WHO have made considerable efforts to evaluate and adjust available data, and correct for under-reporting and enumeration errors.

The first three plots in Figure 6.10 (a, b) present adult mortality estimates for men in Asian countries that fall within our classification criterion. These are based on estimates from the *WPP* (solid lines). The corresponding regions are Southern Asia, South East Asia, and a few countries in Central and Western Asia. For countries in these regions, the estimates of the probability ${}_{45}q_{15}$ in the *WPP* are only available for the period 1995–2010.[5] Data on sibling survival have only been collected in Afghanistan, Nepal, Bangladesh, Cambodia, and Timor-Leste. The corresponding estimates appear with dashed lines.

[5] Estimates are available from 1980 onwards for countries for which an explicit modelling of HIV/AIDS is made by the UNPD, as is the case in most African countries.

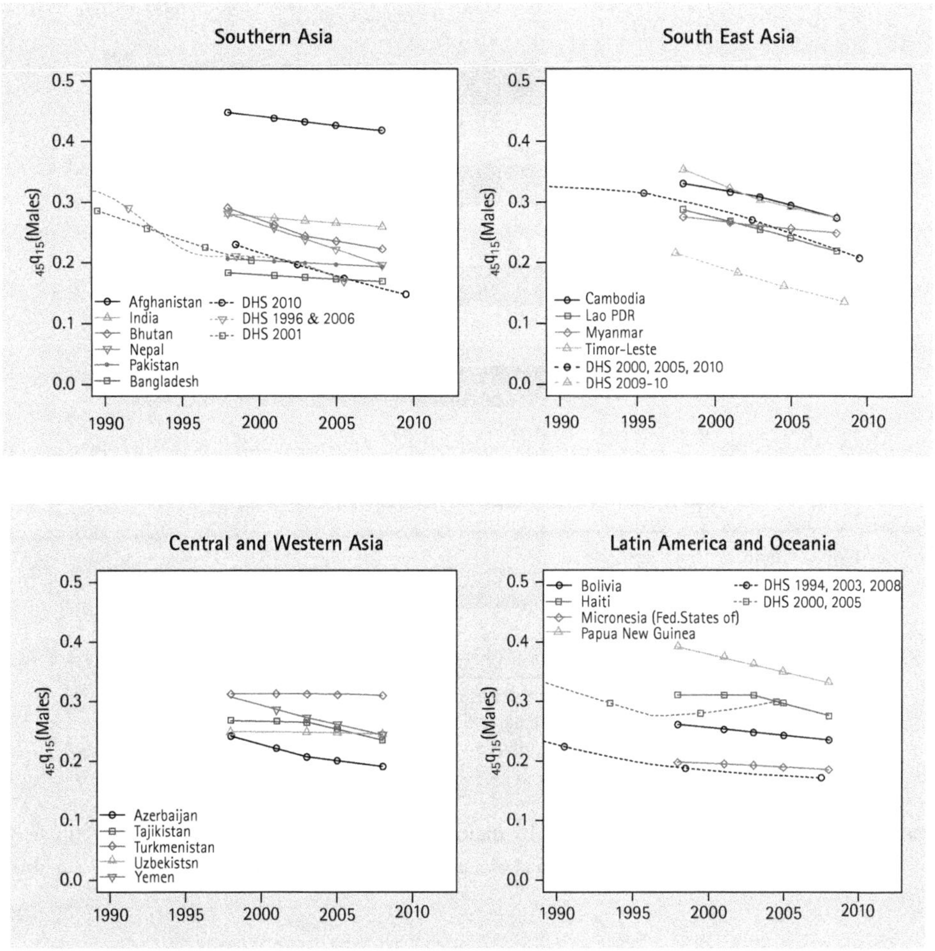

FIGURE 6.10(a, b) Trends in the probability of a man dying between the age of 15 and 60 years, by region, from the 2010 revision of the *World Population Prospects* (WPP; United Nations, 2011a) and Demographic and Health Survey (DHS) sibling histories.

A number of countries, mostly in the Southern and Central region, have experienced either a slow decline or no remarkable change in the level of adult mortality in the period 1990–2005, as portrayed by these most recent estimates by the UN. Such countries are Afghanistan, Pakistan, India, Turkmenistan, and Uzbekistan. Afghanistan is the country where life expectancy was estimated at 47 years in 2005–10 according to the 2010 revision of the *WPP*, faring as the lowest life expectancy at birth in Asia (United Nations, 2011a). But there are large uncertainties around these mortality estimates. In the recently released 2012 revision of the *WPP*, mortality rates for Afghanistan have been revised downwards, with life expectancy reaching 58 years in 2005–10. This revision was based on the 2010 Afghanistan Mortality Survey, in which low levels of child and adult mortality were reported. For example, the trend in adult

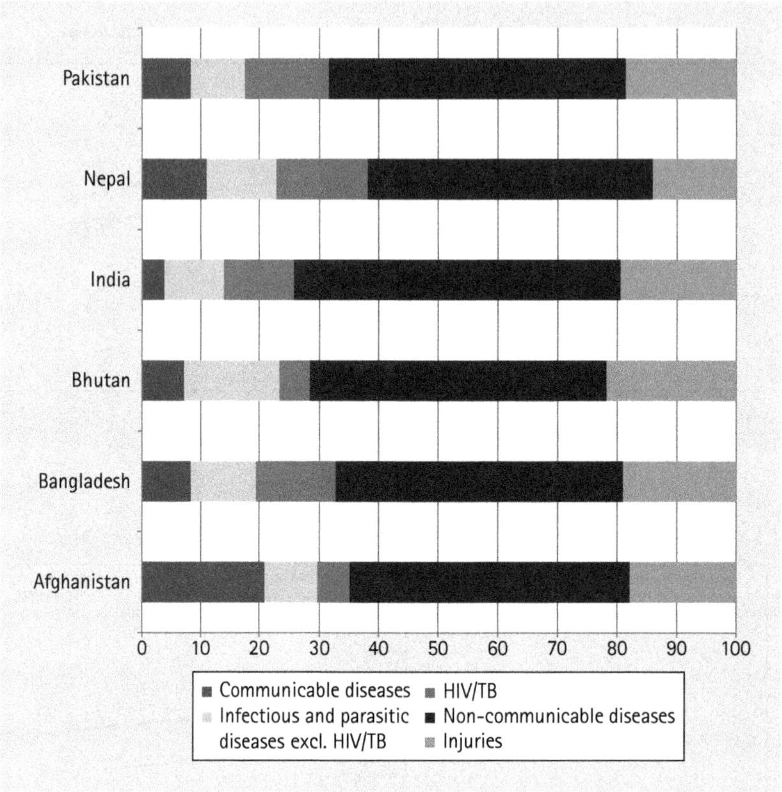

FIGURE 6.11 Distribution of adult deaths by major cause (%), Southern Asia. TB: tuberculosis.

Note: Authors' own calculations based on World Health Organization 2011 data.

mortality inferred from sibling data collected in this survey are presented in Figure 6.10 (a, b). These estimates should not be taken at face value, however, as several indicators point to poor data quality, such as very high sex ratios of reported siblings and a large fraction of deaths reported as having occurred exactly ten years prior to the survey. In addition, approximately 13 per cent of the population was not surveyed because of security or other issues.

In order to shed light on the heterogeneous cause-of-death structure that is characteristic of Asia, the per cent distribution of adult deaths by cause is displayed in Figures 6.11 and 6.12 for both sexes based on the 2008 WHO estimates of deaths due to diseases and injury (World Health Organization, 2011). Adult deaths (ages 15–59) were disaggregated by cause according to the major *International Classification of Diseases-10* groupings (World Health Organization, 1992), that is, communicable, non-communicable, and injury deaths. Deaths from 'infectious and parasitic diseases' were extracted from communicable diseases to understand their role in the countries under study. HIV and AIDS, and TB-related deaths were also isolated from the subgroup 'infectious and parasitic diseases' to show their weight in the countries under study.

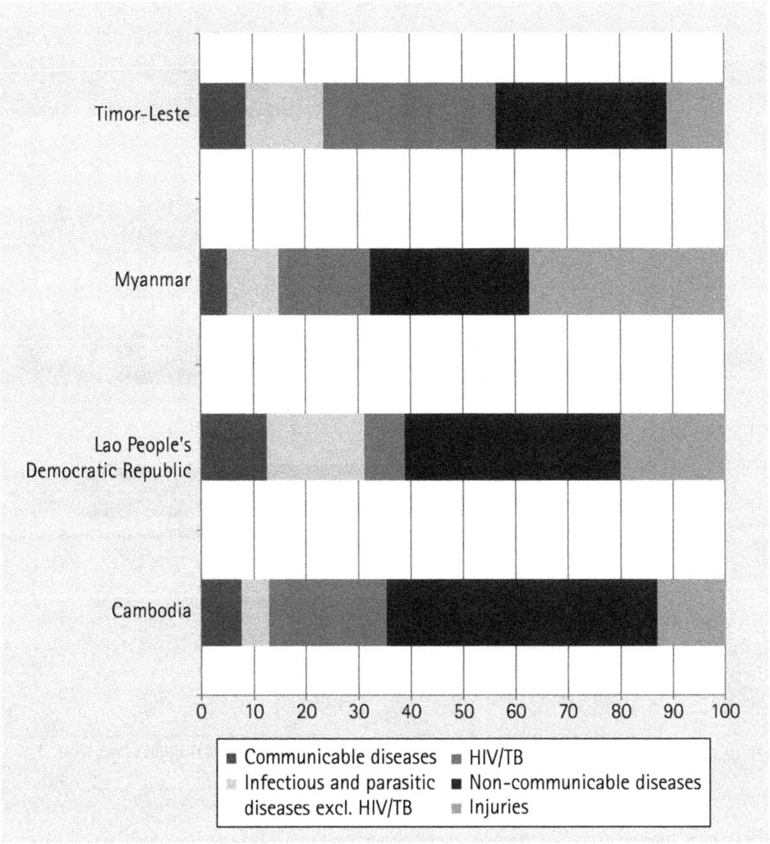

FIGURE 6.12 Distribution of adult deaths by major cause (%), South East Asia. TB: tuberculosis.

Note: Authors' own calculations based on World Health Organization 2011 data.

In general in high mortality Asian countries, factors that have contributed to these high adult mortality trends are wars, social unrest, the collapse of the USSR, the spread of HIV and AIDS and, to a certain extent, a low level of socio-economic development.

In Southern Asia (Figure 6.11), although these countries are still in the later stage of the epidemiological transition, the high levels of adult mortality can be attributed to non-communicable diseases, although communicable diseases as a whole (including infectious and parasitic diseases) still account for a large share.

In South East Asia (Figure 6.12), communicable diseases—particularly infectious and parasitic diseases—prevail, with Timor-Leste and Cambodia showing a large burden due to HIV and TB-related adult deaths. Cambodia and Lao PDR also exhibit a large share of adult deaths due to non-communicable diseases. A significant burden from injury deaths is present in Myanmar.

In Central and Western Asia (Figure 6.13), adult deaths from non-communicable diseases represent the major killer, according to WHO estimates. Countries that belong

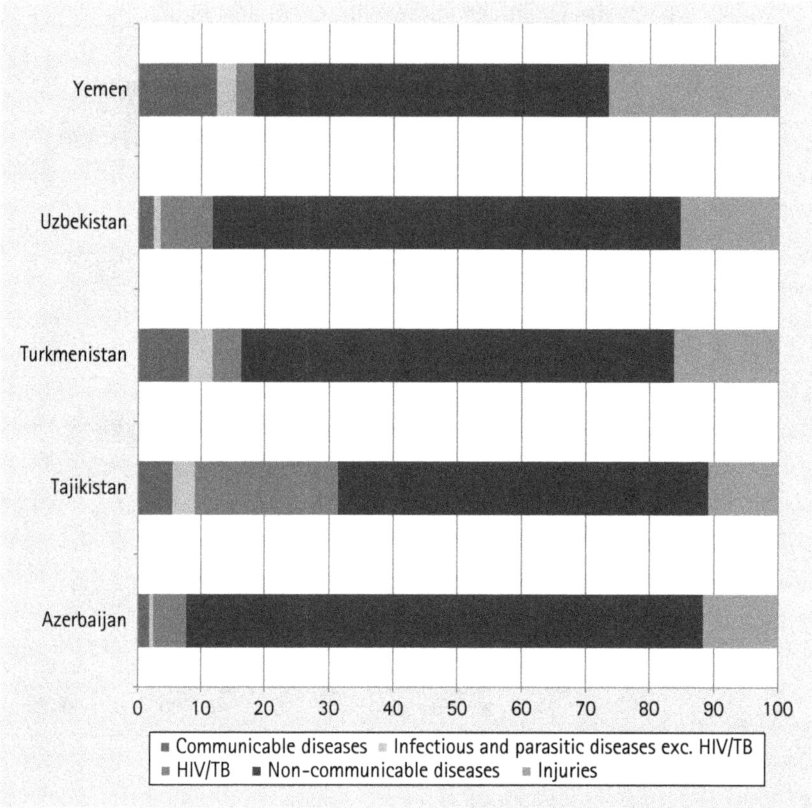

FIGURE 6.13 Distribution of adult deaths by major cause (%), Central and Western Asia. TB: tuberculosis.

Note: Authors' own calculations based on World Health Organization 2011 data.

to this group are Azerbaijan, Tajikistan, Turkmenistan, Uzbekistan, and Yemen. HIV and AIDS, and TB-related deaths occupy the largest share in Tajikistan.

6.3.3 Adult mortality in other countries: Latin America and Oceania

Two Latin American countries, Bolivia and Haiti, fall within our classification criteria (Figure 6.10b). UN estimates of adult mortality for Bolivia indicate a downward trend, while siblings estimates are substantially lower.

In Bolivia, the burden of adult deaths can be largely attributed to non-communicable and injury deaths, which seem to predominate. In Haiti, social conditions deteriorated in recent years owing to failure of the state and the lack of capacity to cope with the existing humanitarian crisis generated by the aid embargo and coupled with the health care system failure. The WHO data portray a large share of adult deaths due to infectious and parasitic diseases.

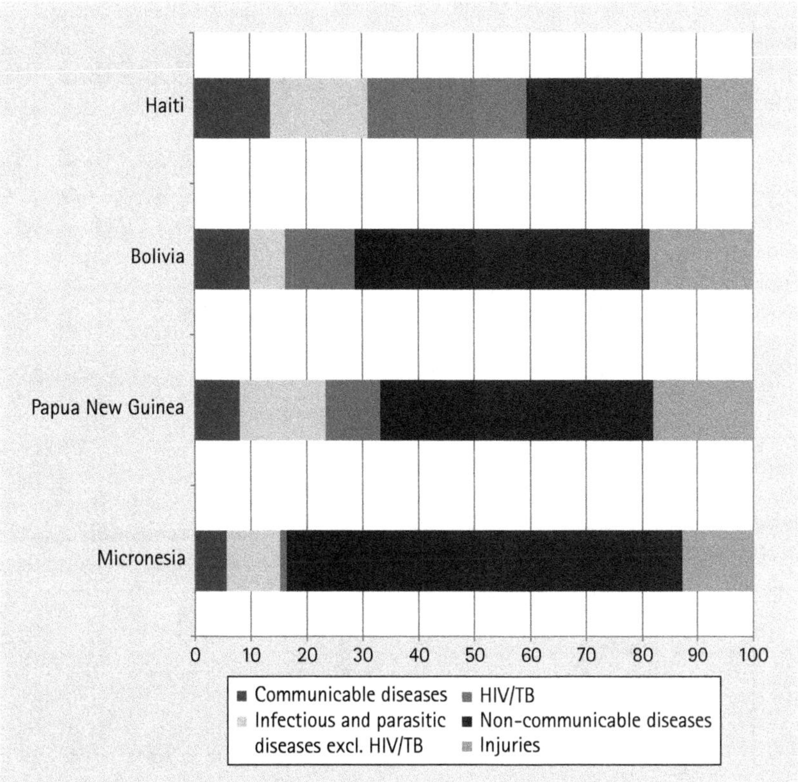

FIGURE 6.14 Distribution of adult deaths by major cause (%), for selected countries in Latin America and Oceania. TB: tuberculosis.

Note: Authors' own calculations based on World Health Organization 2011 data.

Turning to the selected countries in the Oceanian region, that is, Micronesia and Papua New Guinea (Figure 6.10b), UN adult mortality estimates present a stalled trend for Micronesia; UN estimates for Papua New Guinea indicate a downward trend instead. In the latter, the breakdown by cause of death (Figure 6.14) shows that communicable diseases—particularly infectious disease, including HIV and TB—account for a large share of the estimates, followed by non-communicable diseases. The burden of non-communicable diseases is instead predominant in Micronesia.

6.4 Forces affecting the future of mortality in high mortality countries

Over the last 50 years, mortality changes in high mortality countries have varied considerably, sometimes with major and rapid declines, sometimes with slow, but regular, declines, sometimes with stagnations, and occasionally with major increases. The determinants of

Table 6.2 Probabilities of Dying Between the Age of 5 and 60 Years, Disaggregated by Sex, From the United Nation's (UN) 2010 Revision of the *World Population Prospects* and Estimates Based on Siblings' Histories Collected in Demographic Health Surveys (DHS)

	Men						Women					
Country	DHS 1998	DHS 2003	DHS 2008	UN 1998	UN 2003	UN 2008	DHS 1998	DHS 2003	DHS 2008	UN 1998	UN 2003	UN 2008
	Central and Western Asia											
Azerbaijan				0.24	0.21	0.19				0.12	0.12	0.09
Tajikistan				0.27	0.26	0.24				0.15	0.15	0.14
Turkmenistan				0.31	0.31	0.31				0.17	0.17	0.16
Uzbekistan				0.25	0.25	0.24				0.14	0.14	0.14
Yemen				0.31	0.27	0.24				0.26	0.23	0.20
	South East Asia											
Cambodia	0.30	0.26	0.22	0.33	0.31	0.27	0.23	0.20	0.16	0.29	0.28	0.24
Lao People's Democratic Republic				0.29	0.26	0.22				0.24	0.21	0.18
Myanmar				0.28	0.26	0.25				0.23	0.22	0.20
Timor-Leste	0.21	0.17	0.14	0.35	0.30	0.27	0.24	0.20	0.16	0.31	0.27	0.24
	Southern Asia											
Afghanistan	0.23	0.19	0.15	0.45	0.43	0.42	0.20	0.17	0.14	0.42	0.40	0.39
Bangladesh	0.21			0.18	0.18	0.17	0.18			0.18	0.16	0.15
Bhutan				0.29	0.24	0.22				0.24	0.20	0.17
India				0.28	0.27	0.26				0.22	0.20	0.18
Nepal	0.21	0.19		0.28	0.24	0.20	0.20	0.18		0.26	0.22	0.17
Pakistan				0.21	0.20	0.19				0.18	0.17	0.16
	Latin America											
Bolivia	0.19	0.18		0.26	0.25	0.24	0.17	0.16		0.20	0.19	0.18
Haiti	0.28	0.29		0.31	0.31	0.28	0.32	0.35		0.27	0.28	0.25

	Oceania										
Kiribati											
Micronesia				0.20	0.19	0.19				0.18	0.17	0.16
Papua New Guinea				0.39	0.36	0.33				0.3	0.28	0.25
	Middle and Northern Africa										
Angola				0.45	0.42	0.40				0.40	0.37	0.35
Cameroon	0.39	0.41	0.39	0.39	0.43	0.43	0.32	0.32	0.31	0.35	0.39	0.40
Central African Republic				0.51	0.54	0.51				0.45	0.50	0.48
Chad	0.32	0.34		0.36	0.39	0.38	0.26	0.24		0.30	0.33	0.33
Congo	0.51	0.44		0.39	0.38	0.35	0.38	0.32		0.35	0.35	0.32
Democratic Republic of **Congo**	0.33	0.36		0.44	0.42	0.42	0.25	0.28		0.39	0.38	0.36
Equatorial Guinea				0.39	0.39	0.39				0.33	0.34	0.34
Gabon	0.43			0.29	0.32	0.30	0.25			0.25	0.29	0.27
São Tomé and Príncipe				0.25	0.25	0.24				0.21	0.21	0.20
Sudan (Former Sudan)				0.34	0.29	0.28				0.28	0.24	0.22
	Western Africa										
Benin	0.29	0.31		0.38	0.37	0.34	0.22	0.21		0.30	0.30	0.29
Burkina Faso	0.35	0.31	0.25	0.39	0.36	0.31	0.26	0.25	0.23	0.32	0.30	0.26
Côte d'Ivoire	0.41	0.48		0.43	0.45	0.41	0.29	0.33		0.38	0.42	0.38
Gambia				0.34	0.32	0.31				0.28	0.27	0.26
Ghana	0.27	0.29		0.30	0.30	0.27	0.24	0.25		0.27	0.27	0.24
Guinea	0.28	0.33		0.42	0.40	0.37	0.27	0.32		0.37	0.35	0.32
Guinea-Bissau				0.44	0.43	0.42				0.38	0.38	0.37

(continued)

Table 6.2 Continued

	Men						Women					
Country	DHS 1998	DHS 2003	DHS 2008	UN 1998	UN 2003	UN 2008	DHS 1998	DHS 2003	DHS 2008	UN 1998	UN 2003	UN 2008
Liberia	0.22	0.28		0.49	0.44	0.38	0.23	0.30		0.43	0.39	0.34
Mali	0.27	0.25		0.42	0.40	0.37	0.32	0.29		0.35	0.33	0.31
Mauritania				0.31	0.30	0.30				0.24	0.23	0.23
Niger	0.24	0.23		0.38	0.35	0.33	0.24	0.23		0.34	0.31	0.28
Nigeria	0.28	0.28		0.45	0.44	0.41	0.26	0.27		0.41	0.40	0.38
Senegal	0.24	0.23	0.23	0.33	0.31	0.30	0.17	0.17	0.16	0.28	0.26	0.25
Sierra Leone	0.26	0.31		0.59	0.55	0.48	0.22	0.27		0.55	0.52	0.46
Togo				0.35	0.36	0.36				0.30	0.31	0.31
	Eastern Africa											
Burundi	0.65	0.46	0.31	0.48	0.47	0.44	0.54	0.37	0.24	0.43	0.43	0.40
Comoros				0.32	0.31	0.29				0.27	0.26	0.25
Djibouti				0.37	0.36	0.34				0.32	0.32	0.30
Eritrea				0.45	0.40	0.37				0.36	0.32	0.28
Ethiopia	0.41	0.36	0.24	0.39	0.37	0.32	0.37	0.33	0.22	0.34	0.32	0.28
Kenya	0.38	0.42		0.42	0.47	0.41	0.33	0.36		0.38	0.44	0.39
Madagascar	0.28	0.28		0.30	0.26	0.22	0.25	0.26		0.26	0.21	0.18
Malawi	0.57	0.59	0.49	0.50	0.53	0.45	0.54	0.52	0.40	0.45	0.51	0.44
Mozambique	0.39			0.46	0.49	0.50	0.27			0.38	0.42	0.45
Rwanda	0.67	0.40	0.31	0.54	0.43	0.36	0.57	0.29	0.18	0.50	0.40	0.32
Somalia				0.41	0.38	0.38				0.35	0.33	0.32
Uganda	0.51	0.52	0.44	0.54	0.50	0.42	0.43	0.42	0.32	0.49	0.48	0.41
United Republic of Tanzania	0.42	0.39	0.34	0.45	0.45	0.40	0.36	0.35	0.32	0.41	0.42	0.38

Zambia	0.60	0.65		0.60	0.61	0.50	0.56	0.60		0.56	0.60	0.50
Zimbabwe	0.59	0.68	0.62	0.58	0.68	0.62	0.50	0.60	0.55	0.55	0.69	0.66
	Southern Africa											
Botswana				0.44	0.58	0.51				0.40	0.57	0.54
Lesotho	0.50	0.72	0.73	0.44	0.62	0.60	0.37	0.58	0.60	0.40	0.61	0.62
Namibia	0.50	0.61		0.35	0.42	0.35	0.34	0.47		0.30	0.40	0.34
South Africa				0.42	0.53	0.55				0.31	0.46	0.52
Swaziland	0.52	0.71		0.44	0.59	0.57	0.43	0.61		0.4	0.57	0.57

Note: Estimates referring to DHS data are based on authors' computations.

these changes are complex, and can be studied at various levels. The following sections review the literature on forces affecting the future course of mortality, with particular reference to those aspects relevant to high mortality populations. In assessing the capability of specific forces to substantially affect future trends in child mortality, it is important to bear in mind that, as childhood mortality declines, infant mortality as a share of childhood mortality increases, especially mortality during the first month after birth. By 2010, half of all deaths under the age of 5 occurred in neonates in South Asia, and in sub-Saharan Africa the neonatal share of child mortality was 30 per cent.

6.4.1 HIV and AIDS

The AIDS epidemic is considered the most important factor affecting the survival prospects of adults and children in most of the high mortality countries. The future of HIV and AIDS rests primarily on hope for the development of a preventive vaccine that is 'safe, simple, highly effective and affordable' (Hemelaar et al., 2006, p. 2). However, the effectiveness of a global vaccine is threatened by the genetic and antigenic variability of the virus (HIV-1). The impact of ART and viral drug resistance are also important factors that could determine the future of the pandemic (Mahy et al., 2010). Beside the 'ABC' strategy, which promotes abstinence, being faithful, and condom use, and therefore safer behaviours, the most effective intervention coming as close to a lifetime effective protection similar to a vaccine has been found to be circumcision (about 60 per cent effectiveness based on randomized trials) (Auvert et al., 2005).

According to the most recent epidemic update by UNAIDS (2010), the overall growth of the HIV epidemic seems to have stabilized: the annual number of new HIV infections has been declining since the 1990s. In addition, the number of AIDS deaths has also been decreasing, a consequence of the scale-up of ART, resulting in an increasing trend in prevalence (defined as all currently infected individuals). In sub-Saharan Africa, where the epidemic has been particularly severe, UNAIDS estimated the number of new infections in 2009 at 1.8 million, lower than the previous 2.2 million estimated for 2001. Five countries—Botswana, South Africa, Tanzania, Zambia, and Zimbabwe—have shown a significant decline in new infections among young men and women according to national surveys, a decline largely attributed to changes in sexual behaviour.

In a recent paper, Bongaarts et al. (2011) present trends in AIDS mortality from 1980 to 2030 using the UNPD estimates and projections. According to the authors, nearly all of the epidemics have reached their plateau, a consequence of both behavioural change and the natural course of the epidemic (i.e. saturation of high-risk groups, as well as decline in the average infectiousness of individuals because fewer are in the post-infection state, or because of higher levels of ART).

According to UNAIDS, an estimated 33.3 million people in the world were living with HIV in 2009 (UNAIDS, 2010). In the 2010 revision of the *WPP*, the demographic impact of the HIV/AIDS epidemic was explicitly taken into account when estimating and projecting mortality levels in 48 countries. Figure 6.15 shows the estimated and projected

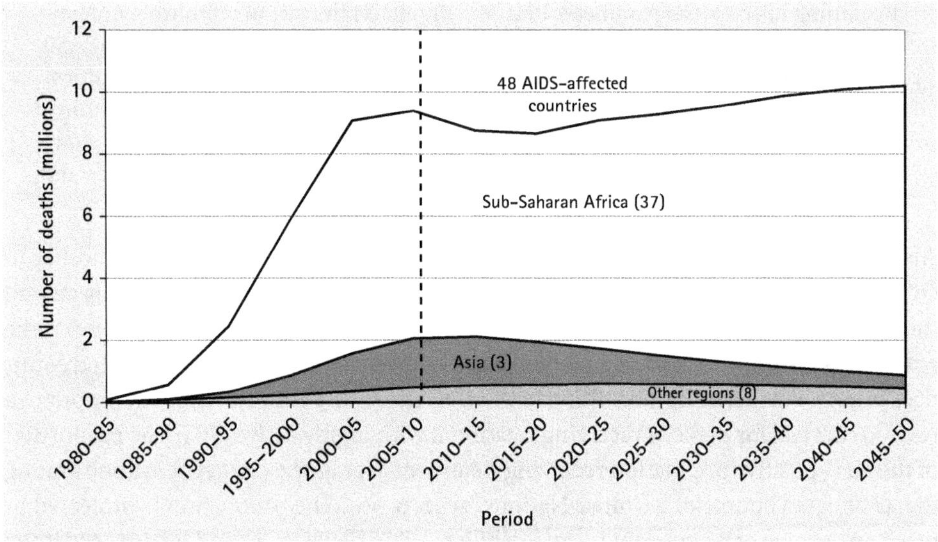

FIGURE 6.15 Estimated and projected number of deaths due to AIDS by region, per quinquennium, 48 AIDS-affected countries, 1980–2050.

number of deaths due to AIDS for selected groups of countries or regions based on those 48 countries (values are per five-year period). Together, these countries account for a substantial portion of all AIDS-related deaths in the world, but the numbers shown here should not be taken as estimates for the world. For these countries as a whole, particularly for the sub-Saharan countries, a sharp increase in number of AIDS-related deaths took place beginning in the mid-1980s and continuing to 2000. From that point on, the number of deaths plateaued at about 9 million deaths per quinquennium, with a peak of 9.4 million for the period 2005–10. During the projection period, the total number of deaths is expected to decline slightly and subsequently increase slowly to about 10 million in 2045–50. This projected increase is driven partly by population growth, but also by some of the assumptions made regarding parameters of the epidemic simulation model, and the treatment coverage (see discussion in the following paragraph). Cohort effects are also at play. Out of the 48 countries for which the impact of HIV/AIDS epidemic was explicitly incorporated in the mortality estimates, 37 are in sub-Saharan Africa, 3 are in Asia (including both China and India), and 8 pertain to other regions of the world. The vast majority of AIDS-related deaths occur in sub-Saharan Africa, and the share of AIDS-related deaths in that region is projected to rise from about 76 per cent in 2010–15 to about 90 per cent in 2045–50 (United Nations, 2012). In the three Asian countries, the number of AIDS-related deaths is expected to decline.

Considering that some assumptions made about parameters of the epidemic simulation model and the treatment coverage partly determine future trends, it is important to discuss some of these assumptions. As noted in the UN's Mortality Report (United Nations, 2012, p. 30),

> Beginning in 2009, the parameter PHI, which reflects the rate of recruitment of new individuals into the high-risk or susceptible group, is projected to decline by half every twenty years. The parameter R, which represents the force of infection, is projected to decline by half every thirty years. The reduction in R reflects the assumption that changes in behavior among those subject to the risk of infection, along with increases in access to treatment for those living with HIV, will reduce the chances of HIV transmission.

Also, coverage levels of interventions to prevent transmission of HIV from mother to child were projected in the 2010 revision to reach, on average, 74 per cent by 2015 among the affected countries, varying between 40 per cent and 95 per cent. After 2015, the coverage is assumed to remain constant at the level reached in each of the affected countries in 2015. Furthermore, according to the UN report, 'the 2010 Revision incorporates a revised survival for persons receiving treatment with highly active ART. The proportion of the HIV-positive population receiving treatment averaged 64 per cent in 2009 among the 48 affected countries' (United Nations, 2012, p. 30). The proportion is projected to reach an average of 84 per cent in 2015, while ranging between 40 and 99 per cent at the country level. Coverage levels are assumed to remain constant thereafter. For further details regarding the assumptions, we refer readers to individual UN publications (United Nations, 2011a, 2012).

While looking at the same total number of AIDS-related deaths, this time broken down by broad age groups (Figure 6.16), it can be said that AIDS mortality predominantly affects the 'adult' population at the age of 15–59. 'Since the turn of the millennium, about 85 per cent of all AIDS deaths in those 48 countries have occurred at ages 15–59

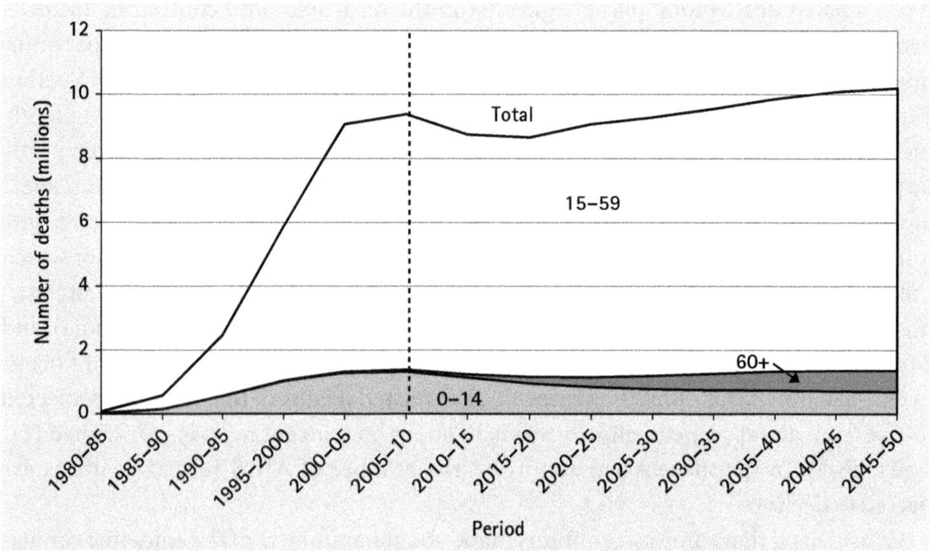

FIGURE 6.16 Estimated and projected number of deaths due to AIDS by broad age groups, per quinquennium, 48 AIDS-affected countries, 1980–2050.

Sources: United Nations (2011a) DEMOBASE extract (special tabulations), and United Nations (2012).

and that proportion is expected to only slightly increase by 2045–2050' (United Nations, 2012, p. 31). As for children under the age of 15 who die from AIDS-related causes, a decline in both absolute and relative terms is anticipated in the following decades. When taking into account the recent achievements that were made with respect to the reduction in mother-to-child transmission of HIV, one could expect even sharper reductions in the number of AIDS-related deaths of children (United Nations, 2012).

Based on the results of the estimates and projections for the group of countries described earlier, it is quite evident that when doing mortality projections for countries affected by the HIV/AIDS epidemic, especially those with very high prevalence levels, one needs to adopt special procedures that take into account the current and future impact of HIV on mortality indicators. Clearly, the trajectories in the projected levels of life expectancy at birth, and other mortality indicators, should differ from those in non-affected or very low HIV prevalence countries. Furthermore, considering the differential impact across age groups, the age patterns of mortality should also encompass distinct shapes over time. Lastly, considering the timing of the onset of the epidemic and the phasing-in of treatment, there is a substantial cohort effect in the impact of HIV on mortality levels and patterns. In this regard, special attention should be given to countries with prevalence levels above 10 per cent, mainly in Southern and Eastern Africa.

Again, based on the results of the 2010 Revision of the *WPP*, and while measuring the mortality impact of the HIV/AIDS epidemic by comparing the mortality between the medium variant ('with AIDS') and the no-AIDS scenario ('without AIDS') in 2010–15, researchers can get a sense of the impact of HIV/AIDS on specific mortality indicators. For instance, based on this comparison, AIDS more than doubled the probability of dying between the age of 15 and 60 in seven countries, namely Botswana, Lesotho, Malawi, Namibia, South Africa, Swaziland, and Zimbabwe. AIDS can also significantly increase mortality among children, especially in the absence of treatment. For the period 2010–15, the largest absolute impact in child mortality was estimated to be in Swaziland, where excess under-5 mortality due to AIDS amounted to 20 deaths per 1,000 live births. The highest relative impact (33 per cent) occurred in South Africa, where the competing risks from other causes are lower than in Swaziland. In all countries of the Southern African region, the relative impact on under-5 mortality exceeded 25 per cent. Outside the sub-Saharan African region, most countries have experienced absolute impacts on under-5 mortality of 5 deaths per 1,000 or less, while the relative impact has exceeded 10 per cent in some countries with relatively low mortality (United Nations, 2012).

Consequently, the increased mortality among adults and children may translate into severe reductions in life expectancy at birth. The largest impact in 2010–15 was found to be in Botswana, where life expectancy at birth was estimated to be 17 years lower in the medium variant than in the no-AIDS scenario. The loss in life expectancy due to AIDS was estimated to exceed ten years in eight other countries, namely Lesotho, Malawi, Mozambique, Namibia, South Africa, Swaziland, Zambia, and Zimbabwe, and was found to be between five and ten years in seven other countries (Cameroon, Central Africa Republic, Côte d'Ivoire, Gabon, Kenya, Uganda, and the United Republic of Tanzania).

The very high HIV prevalence levels encountered in Southern and Eastern African countries have not been found in other regions of the world, and thus the impact on life expectancy for other regions is lower (United Nations, 2012).

For the reasons outlined earlier, the WIC projections have adopted mortality forecasts where the medium scenario coincides with the UN/*WPP* 2010 medium variant up to 2050 for sub-Saharan Africa, Haiti, and Afghanistan. Details on the methodology can be found elsewhere (Garbero and Sanderson, 2012).

6.4.2 Changes to biomedical technology

Another determinant of mortality trends is health technology (preventive and curative medicine), as well as population coverage. For instance, the development of vaccines against childhood diseases (measles, whooping cough, tetanus, poliomyelitis, pneumonia, etc.) was instrumental in controlling the targeted diseases in high mortality countries and reducing their mortality. However, the demographic impact was most visible when the vaccination campaigns reached the whole population and became sustained, especially after the major effort led by UNICEF and other international organizations that began in 1985.

The development of drugs had a huge impact on mortality. Drug development started after 1945 with antimalarial drugs and antibiotics, and more recently has seen the use of antiretroviral drugs and numerous other new medicines. These drugs have strongly reduced mortality from malaria, bacterial diseases, and, more recently, HIV/AIDS. In the field of nutrition, major improvements were also made through the creation of new strategies for treating and preventing severe malnutrition.

However, there remains a number of diseases for which treatments are ineffective. That is particularly true for many cancers and other non-communicable diseases.

Changes in biomedical technology encompass a range of developments, each of which has the potential to substantially reduce mortality. These technology changes include the development of new drugs and vaccines and their associated delivery mechanisms and diagnostic tools, as well as improvements in medical techniques, health care management, and improved software and communication tools. Yet the promise and almost certain introduction of new biotechnology developments in the future must be tempered by acknowledgment of the barriers to technological innovation and implementation that exist in resource-poor settings. Such barriers include deficiencies in both infrastructure (power, water, roads) and personnel (skilled technicians and practitioners), as well as public mistrust and competing priorities for even minimal resources (Malkin, 2007). In the past, financial incentives for developing biomedical technology appropriate for resource-poor populations have come predominantly from wealthier countries—either governments or private foundations—and the extent to which this will be necessary in the future is likely to differ dramatically across the current high mortality countries. Large countries, such as India with its substantial highly trained research and technical workforce, have already demonstrated the capability of generating appropriate new biomedical technologies. Smaller countries with fewer trained personnel are less likely to develop this capacity (Coloma and Harris, 2004).

An international focus on reducing childhood mortality, with a recent emphasis on improving both maternal and newborn outcomes during delivery and immediately post-partum, might provide the impetus needed to bring important changes in medical care and treatment to resource-poor areas. Examples of technological innovations that show promise include treatment of post-partum haemorrhage with misoprostol or pre-packaged injectable oxytocin (Buekens and Althabe, 2010; Winikoff et al., 2010), use of antenatal steroids to prevent death associated with premature delivery (Mwansa-Kambafwile et al., 2010), use of chlorhexidine to prevent umbilical cord infections (McClure et al., 2007), administration of ART to prevent mother-to-child transmission of HIV/AIDS, new pneumococcal and rotavirus vaccines, and remote imaging from rural health clinics.

6.4.3 Effectiveness of health care systems

All of the high mortality countries have relatively high levels of both maternal mortality and neonatal mortality. These two adverse outcomes are strongly linked, and their levels reflect the effectiveness of health care systems. A country's overall health system and the number of health personnel, in particular, are key determinants of mortality decline. Countries with a high proportion of physicians per capita have low mortality, as in Botswana before 1990. In contrast, when physicians leave a country, mortality tends to rise, as in Ghana between 1978 and 1983 (Garenne, 2010a).

As child mortality declines, neonatal mortality will assume a larger share of the remaining mortality burden. Reducing neonatal mortality will depend on improving and increasing access to antenatal care, skilled birth attendants, and available care for complications arising during pregnancy and delivery. Data from the DHS around 2008 indicate that the per cent of births attended by a skilled provider varied considerably over the high mortality countries, from less than 25 per cent in Bangladesh, Nepal, and Lao PDR to almost 100 per cent in Turkmenistan (World Health Organization, 2010).

Efforts to increase access to skilled health providers for delivery have been both numerous and varied in these countries, especially over the last decade. Increases in institutional deliveries occurred in both Ghana and Rwanda after government initiatives to reduce user fees as a barrier by paying providers directly for services and, in the case of Rwanda, to improve the quality of service provided. Other countries have focused on upgrading the skills of traditional midwives or providing incentives for private doctors to deliver services in underserved areas (World Health Organization, 2010). The successes and failures of these various programmes can guide future health systems investments in other high mortality countries where health care resources are limited. However, progress toward cost-effective rationalization of reproductive health services delivery is hampered by a lack of data on the current level and quality of services provided.

6.4.4 Behavioural changes related to health

Behavioural changes related to health are also important determinants of mortality, especially related to the rise of non-communicable diseases in developing countries.

With respect to nutrition, the quantity and quality of the diet has generally improved over the last 50 years, which has had an impact on the mortality of children and adults. There are exceptions to the overall improvement, especially in Africa, which has been plagued by political turmoil, wars, and extensive government mismanagement. And while people in much of the developing world struggle to get enough food, the problem of obesity is emerging in Southern Africa, especially among women. The problem is linked not only to consuming too much food, but eating unhealthy food (e.g. some industrially-produced products), as well as diets based on fried food and saturated fat. Economic and social changes are typically accompanied by changes in health behaviours, especially with respect to hygiene, disease prevention, and the use of appropriate health services when sick. However, economic and social change is sometimes associated with negative behaviours, such as smoking, substance abuse, lack of physical exercise, and risky sexual behaviour. These behaviours can lead to significant increases in mortality from cancers and other non-communicable diseases.

6.4.5 Other infectious diseases: role of neglected and emerging diseases

In the 1960s, the widely held belief around the globe was that infectious diseases were under control in terms of prevention and treatment, and that their effect on mortality would become negligible. Since that time, a number of diseases have emerged or re-emerged, sometimes with significant impacts on mortality levels and trends. The WHO defines an emerging disease as 'one that has appeared in a population for the first time, or that may have existed previously but is rapidly increasing in incidence or geographic range'.

The dynamics of such diseases are largely independent of economic development, level of education, or socio-economic status, and are almost impossible to predict. They are determined by a variety of factors, including evolutionary factors (jumping the species barrier); natural selection (pressure of antibiotics or other drugs); ecological factors (appearance of a new niche or a new vector); demographic factors (population density, migration); and behavioural factors (e.g. sexual behaviour). The mortality impact of these diseases depends on their spread in general populations, their lethality, their latency period (e.g. the length of the asymptomatic phase) and the absence of prevention or treatment. The National Institute of Allergy and Infections Diseases lists around 20 recent emerging/re-emerging diseases, and more are likely to come in the future.

Among the emerging/re-emerging diseases in the last 40 years in high mortality countries, three stand out as having a major mortality impact: HIV/AIDS, TB, and malaria.

HIV/AIDS started to spread in general populations in the early 1980s and soon became a leading cause of death among young adults and children. The disease was almost always lethal for the first 20 years of the epidemic. The course of the epidemic changed in about 2000, when prevention efforts (condom use and reducing casual partners) came into effect. Since that time HIV prevalence has stabilized and tended to decline in most infected countries. Its mortality impact changed radically at about the same time, with the massive use of ART. Even in highly infected countries such as South Africa, mortality started declining after years of increase. South Africa experienced 15 years of increases in mortality before a decline began in 2005, which was the start of a fast-paced new trend.

Emerging diseases such as HIV/AIDS have not only an impact on mortality from infectious diseases, but also on non-communicable diseases (cancers) and even on maternal mortality. For instance, in South Africa, indirect causes of maternal deaths increased fourfold because of HIV and TB, and direct causes increased twofold, partly because of the diseases themselves (causing puerperal infections), and partly because ART treatments induced hypertension, causing death by eclampsia.

TB also re-emerged in a number of places for two reasons: first, it is an opportunistic infection of HIV/AIDS, so the HIV/AIDS epidemic induced a large increase in the number of TB cases; second, the use of antibiotics was so extensive that it led to an increase in resistant strains of diseases, which increased their lethality. In recent years, however, new combination treatments are bringing the disease under control.

Malaria re-emerged in Africa in the 1980s and 1990s, mostly as a result of the pressure of treatment with chloroquine, leading to massive resistance and increased mortality (Trape, 2001). However, since 2000, the disease is again on the path to be controlled, in part because of new and more efficient treatments (in particular with Artemisinin combination therapy), and owing to new prevention efforts, particularly insecticide impregnated bed nets.

Infectious agents for a host of diseases, such as influenza, meningitis, and diarrhoeal diseases, are constantly evolving and responding to drugs by developing resistance. As a result, the long-term effect of these diseases on mortality can only be estimated with a large degree of uncertainty.

6.4.6 Environmental changes

The impact of climate change on human life and health is an area of intense scientific scrutiny. The pathways through which climate change may affect health and mortality can be partitioned into four broad groups: (1) increased frequency and intensity of heat waves, floods, and droughts, for example climate stress; (2) a reduction in cold-related deaths; (3) changes in the distribution of vector-borne and infectious diseases; and (4) increased risks of disasters and malnutrition (Haines et al., 2006). The overall balance across these factors is likely to be negative, with populations in developing countries likely to be greatly affected by the adverse impacts of climate change. For instance, the direct impacts will result in changes in water distribution and agricultural production, including food. Rising temperatures leading to changes in the distribution of vector-borne diseases are believed to be responsible for changes in the incubation period of the pathogen within the vector, resulting in increased risks of malaria, Dengue fever, Lyme disease, and Ross River Virus (Strand et al., 2010). The evidence shows that high-income countries are also likely to be affected, with possible examples being the 2003 heat wave in Europe, hurricane Katrina in the USA in 2005, and the Melbourne (Australia) bushfires in 2009. Indirect impacts of rising temperature include increased sea level and ocean acidity.

Public health strategies and improved surveillance are essential to improve adaptation to climate change, especially in low-income countries. Reducing the use of fossil fuels and increasing the use of renewable energy technologies should improve health in the near term by reducing exposure to air pollution and therefore mitigating the negative impacts of climate change (McMichael et al., 2004; Tanser et al., 2003; World Health Organization, 2006).

6.4.7 Mortality due to crises

The political stability of the state, or national government, and its investment in the health sector are likely to be key ingredients of a positive transition to low mortality. Conversely, political instability often leads to an increase in mortality. An example of the first scenario is Senegal, a country with virtually no economic growth and a low level of education, which yet has experienced a dramatic decline in under-5 mortality since 1960. A counter-example is Uganda, where a major political crisis induced by a coup d'état in the 1970s and years of civil war led to a large increase in mortality (Garenne and Gakusi, 2006).

Crises resulting from conflicts, violence, famine, or natural disasters (including tsunamis, earthquakes, floods, and hurricanes, etc.) may not only lead to overall increases in mortality, but also affect segments of the population in ways that may translate into distinct patterns of excess mortality by age and sex. Excess deaths from these crises can be caused directly by violence or natural disasters, but may moreover be associated with indirect effects, such as damage to infrastructure, interruption of services (water, sanitation, health care), and harm to production and marketing of food. Consequently, mortality risks may continue to be higher after the period of an actual crisis. Furthermore, crisis-induced morbidity and malnutrition could also have long-term negative effects on the health and mortality of a given population.

Such crises can lead to important deviations in the trend of mortality decline that is considered typical in most projections of mortality levels and therefore need to be taken into account while doing such an exercise. Though it is clear that many different types of crises will occur in the following decades, predicting such events in specific geographic settings is not feasible. However, our knowledge of current crises and post-conflict situations can be taken into account when generating feasible assumptions regarding short- or medium-term projections of mortality decline. Clearly, countries that are now in the midst of a crisis should be subject to different patterns than countries that have recently faced one. On the one hand, the projected increase in life expectancy at birth should be more conservative in a country that is currently in the midst of conflict or civil strife. Such considerations should be taken into account for countries like Afghanistan, Somalia, Sudan, and Syria. On the other hand, a country that has recently come out of a severe crisis may be experiencing outstanding progress in mortality declines, and researchers should be cautious in extrapolating the resulting trends into the future. For example, Rwanda, a country that experienced tremendous mortality spikes in the mid-1990s due to the genocide and other crises has been experiencing exceptional declines in mortality, partly as a result of the recovery one would anticipate following a mortality shock.

Outside interventions following a shock can benefit the survival prospects of populations. Though it is not easy to measure precisely the role of each event (recovery vs interventions), it is clear that the outcome of such a unique combination of events should not be extrapolated into the future; the pace of decline in mortality is likely to slow down. Furthermore, not all countries that have undergone a mortality crisis due to a conflict, civil strife, or other events have experienced fast declines in mortality in the aftermath of the crisis. Following a crisis, government capabilities to make proper interventions are sometimes limited or compromised, which may result in slow progress in survival improvements. The same may apply to countries that have been facing a long-term crisis. One could anticipate, for the following years, slow improvements in the level of life expectancy at birth, if any, in countries that are no longer in the midst of a crisis but are still facing economic and other challenges.

6.4.8 Differential trends in population subgroups

This section briefly reviews important relationships between a variety of causes and conditions, on the one hand, and mortality trends in particularly affected populations, on the other. Economic development and income per capita are important determinants of mortality decline, and periods of economic growth are usually associated with the latter, whereas periods of economic crises are often associated with increased mortality. An example of the first scenario is Gabon before 1990, a relatively wealthy country that reached relatively low levels of mortality. A counter-example is Zambia, which has been ruined by an economic crisis that struck in 1975 and led to a major increase in mortality. Higher household income also has a direct effect on health through improved nutrition, causing major declines in income to be associated with worsening nutritional status (Waltisperger and Meslé, 2007).

Pockets of extreme poverty have emerged in numerous large cities, with serious health consequences. For instance, in the slums of Nairobi, Kenya, under-5 mortality has doubled over the last 20 years because of inadequate hygiene conditions, violence, and lack of infrastructure and personnel (Garenne, 2010b).

A high level of education at the national and household levels is usually associated with lower mortality because education is closely associated with knowledge, attitudes, and behaviours—all determinants of a person's health status.

Familial socio-economic status has been found through extensive research to be a primary determinant of infant and child survival across virtually all societies, regardless of the overall standard of living. In addition, the independent effect of maternal education on infant and child survival has received special consideration beginning with the pioneering work of John Caldwell (1979). While the majority of empirical research has shown a strong, independent effect of maternal education on family economic resources, variation in the strength of this effect has been observed across countries and over time. Recent research has demonstrated that some of this variation may be due to the overall level of educational attainment of women at both the community and societal levels. Thus, as a higher proportion of women attain secondary or higher levels of education, infant and child survival appears to improve even for women with less education and fewer economic resources. In projecting the impact of subgroup differentials on future trends in infant and child mortality, the extent of social and economic integration across the country as a whole, and particularly between rural and urban areas, is likely to have a large influence on the rapidity of improvement in child survival (Pamuk et al., 2011).

Evidence has shown that increasing levels of educational attainment are likely to be correlated with decreasing levels of mortality, morbidity, and disability among adults (for a survey see KC and Lentzner, 2010). In North America and Europe, the literature has documented the existence of an education gradient in mortality, specifically a strong inverse relationship between education and mortality among adults (Kunst and Mackenbach, 1994; Ross and Mirowsky, 1999, 2006; Zajacova, 2006).

The relevant literature outside of developed countries, particularly sub-Saharan Africa, is scarce. A few studies in Asia document the usual negative relationship, with some exceptions, primarily related to women's survival and breast cancer mortality (KC and Lentzner, 2010).

In sub-Saharan Africa, where HIV and AIDS has been ravaging populations for the last 20 years, evidence of an education gradient in mortality is mixed, implying a high degree of heterogeneity, especially as far as the link between HIV infection and education is concerned (Fortson, 2008). A number of authors (Gregson et al., 2001; Over and Piot, 1993) have documented a positive relationship, particularly at the beginning of the epidemic, where highly educated individuals were more likely to engage in risky sexual behaviours given the availability of casual sex and the means to pay for it. Fortson (2008) shows evidence of a robust positive education gradient in HIV infection, after controlling for a rich set of confounders and non-response bias in HIV testing, where adults with six years of schooling were more likely to be HIV-positive than adults with no education. Other authors (Glynn et al., 2004) found no evidence of increased risk of HIV infection associated with education, hypothesizing that the more educated might be responding more adequately to behavioural change programmes.

Based on an analysis of maternal mortality modules across 84 DHS surveys conducted in high mortality countries, Masquelier and Garbero (2012) looked at educational differentials in adult mortality (defined as the probability of dying between the age of 25 and 40) based on siblings estimates. The analyses were based on surveys conducted in high mortality countries such as in sub-Saharan Africa (70 DHS), Haiti, Afghanistan, Bangladesh, Nepal, Cambodia, Timor-Leste, and Bolivia. In this study, the authors examined the relationship between the living sister level of educational attainment and adult deaths in the household. The critical assumption is that educational outcomes are correlated among siblings; therefore, the level of educational attainment of the living sibling acts as a proxy for the level of educational attainment of the deceased sisters (Graham et al., 2004).

The results confirm the large heterogeneity of country-specific trends by level of educational attainment, particularly for those countries with several DHS and reliable adult mortality trends (namely Bolivia, Kenya, Madagascar, Namibia, Uganda, Rwanda, Zambia, and Zimbabwe). This heterogeneity is both a function of the overall level of adult mortality and the stage and size of the HIV epidemic. Specifically, in countries with a relatively low level of adult mortality such as Bolivia and Madagascar, the negative expected gradient was found, that is, significantly higher risks of dying for uneducated women versus those of women with lower secondary education or higher. In some of the remaining countries, an opposite gradient was found, although not statistically significant. Other countries presented instead an evolving gradient that highlights the important role of HIV as a confounding factor in the positive relationships between educational attainment and survival gains (Masquelier and Garbero, 2012). Further research using supplementary data sets should both aim at triangulating these results and also exploring the causal mechanisms that drive the relationship between education and mortality, and which lie behind such gradients.

6.5 Expert survey on the future of life expectancy in high mortality countries

This section presents the results of the 2011 survey module on future trends in life expectancy in high mortality countries. Survey respondents provided numerical predictions of future trends in life expectancy through 2050 and an assessment of factors producing these trends for a country of their choice. They were also asked to indicate additional countries or regions for which their assessment was valid. Altogether, only 28 questionnaires in the high mortality module of the survey were completed, with results pertaining to a total of 14 countries. The paucity of responses corroborates both the uncertainty that revolves around the estimation of mortality trends in high mortality countries and the lack of experts' confidence in making predictions about the future of mortality in such countries. The following figures combine responses for all 14 countries in the high mortality questionnaire sample (n = 28), as well as for the 10 countries of sub-Saharan Africa (n = 17) and the 4 countries of South Asia (n = 11) separately (Table 6.3).

Table 6.3 Survey Respondents According to Country and Region of Projection Provided, Country of Work, Field of Expertise, Gender, and Age

Country (and region of projection)	No. of experts	Country of work	No. of experts
Eastern Africa			
Kenya	1	Austria	1
Malawi	1	Belgium	1
Tanzania	1	Burkina Faso	3
Uganda	1	Congo	2
Zimbabwe	1	India	5
Middle Africa		Kenya	1
Cameroon	3	Lesotho	1
Congo (Demoratic Republic of)	3	Nepal	1
Southern Africa		Nigeria	2
Lesotho	1	Pakistan	1
Western Africa		South Africa	1
Burkina Faso	3	Uganda	1
Nigeria	2	USA	2
South-Central Asia		Missing	6
Bangladesh	1	Total	28
India	8		
Nepal	1	**Gender**	**No.**
Pakistan	1	Female	6
Total responses	**28**	Male	16
		Missing	6
Field of expertise		**Total**	**28**
Data collection and analysis	1		
Demography	1	**Age group (years)**	**No.**
Economics	1	20–24	1
Epidemiology	1	25–29	2
Fertility, ageing, reproductive health	1	30–34	2
Health economics	1	35–39	5
Mortality	1	45–49	3
Maternal and childhood mortality	1	50–54	2
Migration	3	55–59	3
Migration and health	1	60–64	2
Monitoring and evaluation	1	65+	1
Population and health	1	Missing	7
Population studies	1	**Total**	**28**
Population, family planning, reproductive health	1		
Quantitative demography/projections	2		
Reproductive health and development	1		
Social demography	3		
Economic demography, fertility, health	1		
Reproductive health	1		
Missing	4		
Total	28		

One of the key elements of this exercise was to obtain predicted decadal gains in life expectancy at birth from respondents for 2010–30 and 2030–50 ('best guess' estimates plus 80 per cent uncertainty intervals). After providing a numerical estimate for the decadal gain in life expectancy, experts were asked to assess the validity and relevance of alternative arguments about the forces (clusters) that will shape these future trends. Then, having worked through the arguments of the questionnaire, experts were asked whether they wanted to alter their initial projections. Most experts kept their projections unaltered. If the respondent did not alter the preset default value for the point estimate, minimum, or maximum, these responses were set to 'missing'. The following figures show the experts' final projections of life expectancy at birth, along with the official UN estimated trend since 1950 and projections revised in 2010 (United Nations, 2011a). The gains in life expectancy for 2005–20 and for the decade 2030–40 are derived from interpolating the decadal estimations related to the start of the period in 2005. The grey areas around the expert trend indicate the range of the 80 per cent uncertainty intervals assessed by the experts (Figure 6.17). The regional and global estimations were further weighted by the population sizes of the countries, based on UN data and medium variant prediction until 2050/55. For comparing the regional mortality trend of the experts with the UN estimation, we selected only those countries for which the experts assessed the future gain in life expectancy.

The gains in life expectancy since 1950 in these high mortality countries represent one of the major achievements of the latter half of the twentieth century. Between 1950 and 1975, the UN estimates that life expectancy at birth increased from 39 to 53 years in

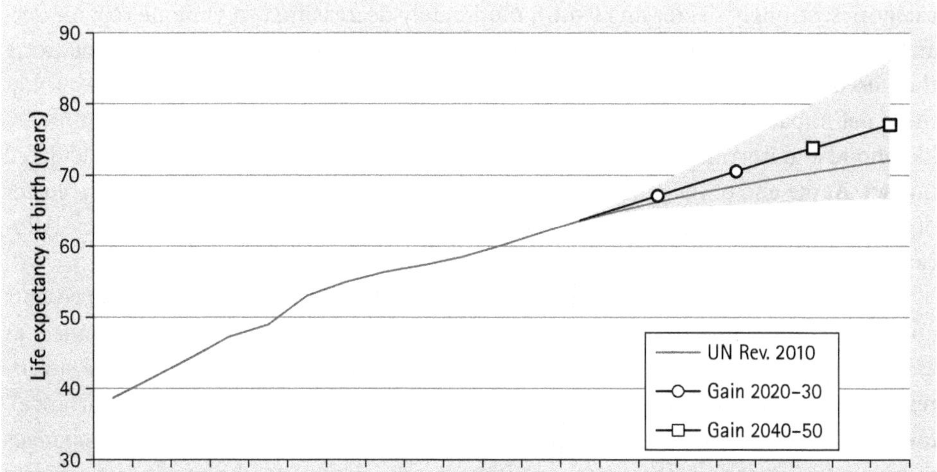

FIGURE 6.17 Previous and expected future trend in life expectancy at birth for all high mortality countries.

Note: Authors' own calculations.

these countries. However, the impact of the HIV/AIDS epidemic resulted in a dramatic slowing of the previous pace of improvement. Between 1975 and 2000, life expectancy at birth increased by only seven years. More recently, the pace of improvement appears to have again accelerated slightly, with life expectancy at birth reaching 63.6 in 2010. The UN medium variant, however, projects a future gain of only two years each decade between 2010 and 2050, implying life expectancy at birth of only 72 years by mid-century. The experts responding to our survey were more optimistic, predicting decadal gains of over three years, implying a life expectancy at birth of 70.5 in 2030 and 77.1 in 2050. Despite this general optimism, the range of uncertainty was quite high, with lower values representing only a 3-year gain between 2010 and 2050, and higher values indicating a 20-year gain.

The survey respondents were also asked to assess the validity and relevance of alternative arguments about the forces that could shape future mortality trends in the country or region they chose. Survey respondents for high mortality countries were given a list of 39 arguments grouped according to 7 underlying forces, forming the following clusters: changes in biomedical technology; effectiveness of health care systems; behavioural changes related to health; infectious diseases and resurgence of old diseases; environmental change, disasters, and wars; changes in composition and differential trends in population subgroups; and HIV/AIDS.

For each argument the experts could assess the likelihood, the conditional impact, and the net impact. The likelihood or validity of an argument was defined across the following response scale: very likely wrong = 0; more likely wrong than right = 0.25; ambiguous = 0.5; more likely right than wrong = 0.75; very likely right = 1.0. The conditional impact gives the respondents' assessment regarding the consequences of the argument for future life expectancy, if the argument becomes true. The scale contains five categories: strongly decreasing (–1.0); moderately decreasing (–0.5); none (0); moderately increasing (0.5); strongly increasing (1.0). Likelihood and conditional impact were then used to derive an argument's net impact on future life expectancy. In the survey, these net impacts were predefined as a combination (multiplication) of an argument's likelihood and its conditional impact, but the experts were free to change the calculated impact. At the end of the questionnaire the experts could allocate points to each cluster of arguments based on its relative importance for future trends in life expectancy. Allocations were made so that the sum of distributed points totaled 100 per cent.

Figure 6.18 shows the net impact of each argument. Each segment of the plot presents one cluster (cl), while the size of the segment depends on the cluster importance, as assessed by the experts. The cluster of arguments deemed most important by the survey respondents related to the effectiveness of health care systems (24 per cent importance), followed by behavioural changes related to health (17 per cent importance) and changes in biomedical technology (15 per cent importance). However, the specific arguments having the greatest net impact on life expectancy in the high mortality countries under consideration were not necessarily in those clusters of forces deemed to have the greatest importance. Within each cluster, the net impact of individual arguments is shown in the outer grey ring. Arguments could be interpreted to have either a positive or negative influence on life expectancy, as indicated by the position of the bars. The

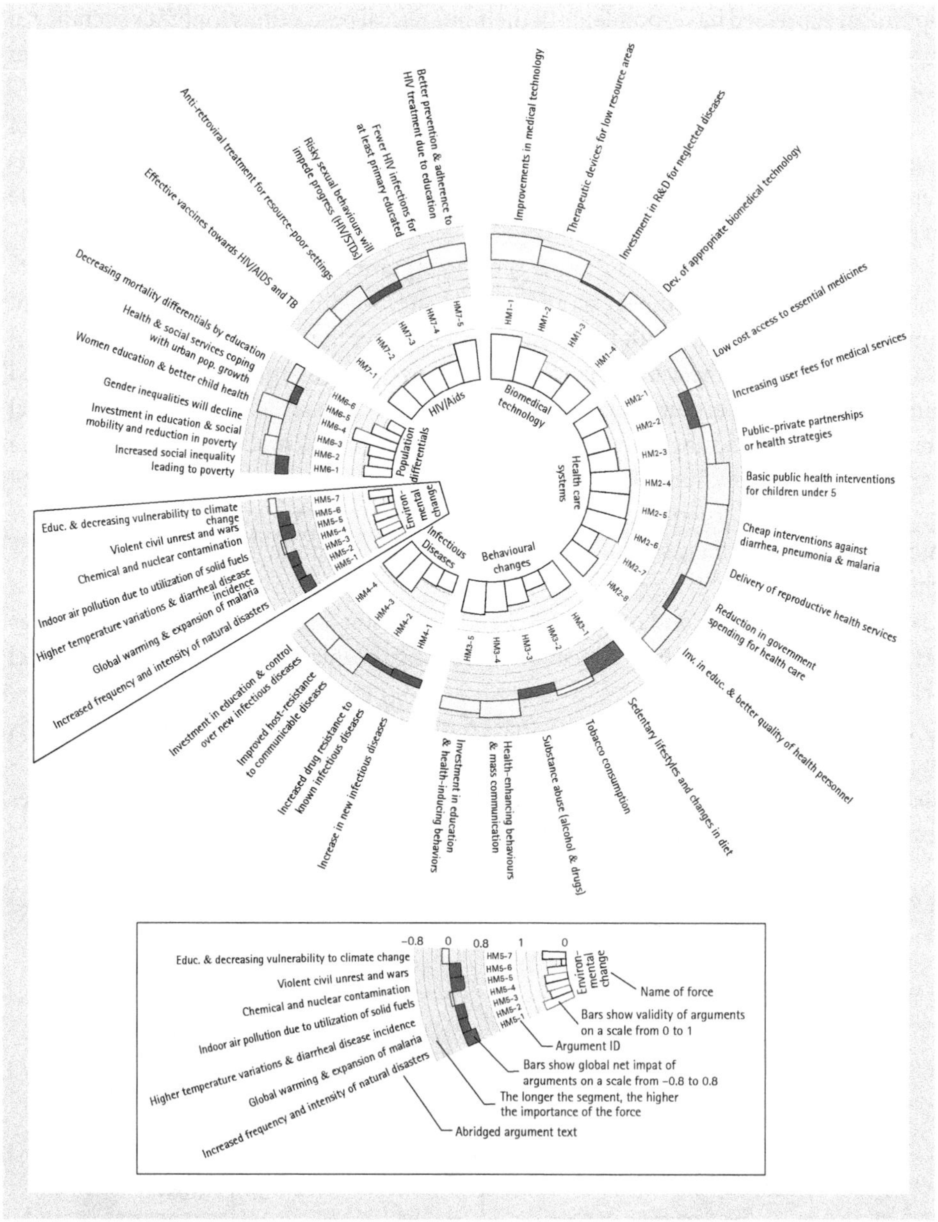

FIGURE 6.18 Global mean net impact and validity for all arguments about future mortality in high mortality countries.

optimism expressed by respondents in their numerical predictions for life expectancy at birth is reflected in the larger net impact values for arguments with positive influences compared with arguments with negative influence.

The average relative importance given to each cluster is shown on the left side of Figure 6.19, here indicated by the size of the circle. The position of the circle on the *y*-axis represents the absolute value of the argument with the highest net impact on future life expectancy within that cluster.

The right side of Figure 6.19 ranks specific arguments by multiplying the absolute value of their mean net impact score by the cluster weight. So although the argument 'Improvements in the education of women will improve the health of children' (HD 6-4) was assigned the highest net impact score of any specific argument, it is not ranked among the top five arguments. This is because, overall, factors related to differential trends in population subgroups are not considered to have as much impact on future life expectancy as other forces. By contrast, the importance allocated to the effectiveness of health care systems combined with relatively high net impact scores means that the four highest ranked arguments come from this cluster: basic public health interventions for children under 5 (HD 2-4); expansion of coverage for inexpensive interventions against diarrhoea, pneumonia, and malaria (HD 2-5); extension of reproductive health services (HD 2-6); and investments in education increasing the quality of health care personnel (HD 2-8).

As noted previously, the countries that continue to experience high mortality levels are concentrated in sub-Saharan Africa and Asia, with African countries disproportionately affected by the HIV/AIDS epidemic. We therefore examine the survey responses for African and Asian countries separately.

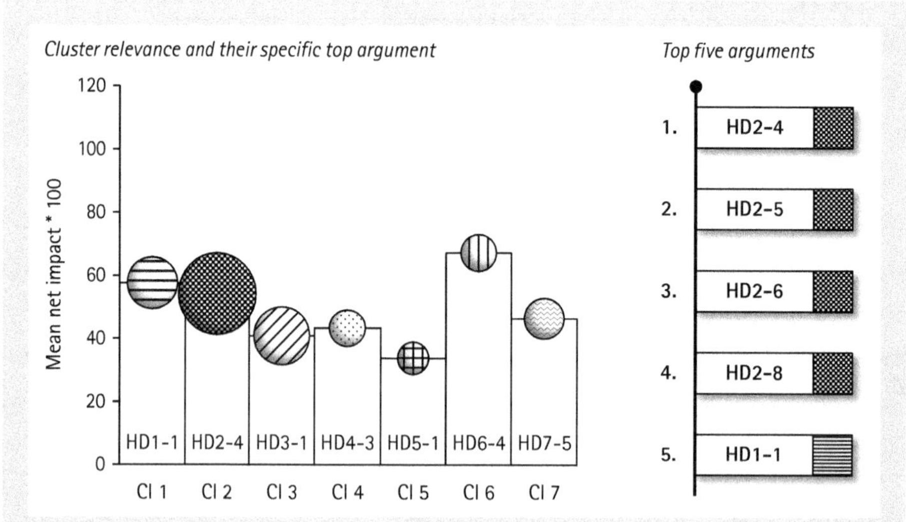

FIGURE 6.19 Cluster relevance and the ranking of highest impact arguments for all high mortality countries (global trend).

Data Source: IIASA–Oxford survey, own calculation

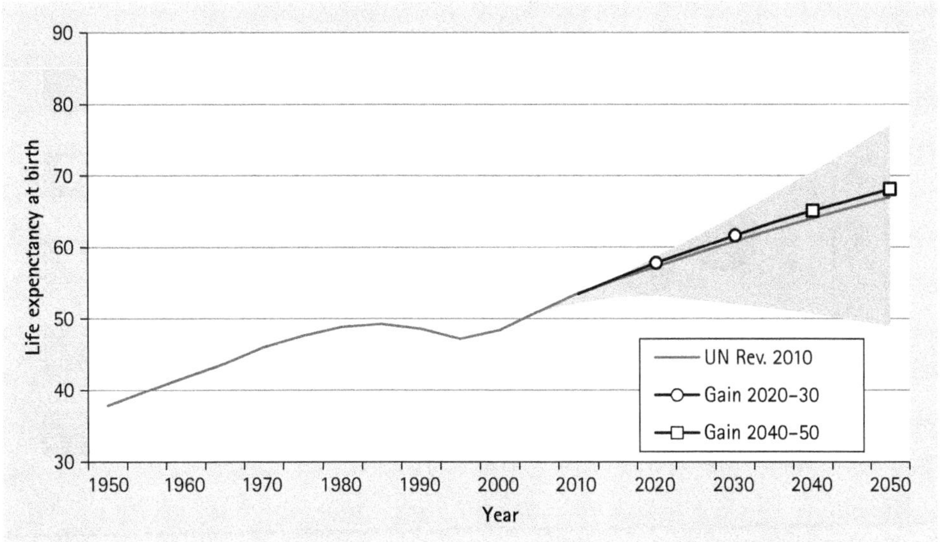

FIGURE 6.20 Previous and expected future trend in life expectancy at birth for Africa.

As shown in Figure 6.20, the increase in life expectancy at birth since 1950 has been less dramatic in the 10 African countries for which we obtained survey responses than for all 14 high mortality countries. In addition, the HIV/AIDS epidemic resulted in a decline in life expectancy between 1985 and 1995, but the recent resumption of continual improvement in survival has been quite dramatic. Still, by 2010 life expectancy at birth in these African countries was estimated to be only 53.6 years.

The increase in life expectancy predicted by the survey respondents exceeded the UN projections only slightly; the UN medium variant projects a gain of 7.2 years for 2010–20 and a gain of 6.2 years for 2020–50, while the survey respondents predicted, on average, gains of 8.1 years and 6.4 years for these same periods. However, the degree of uncertainty expressed by the survey respondents was substantial; the lower bound reflects a decline in life expectancy of 4.6 years by 2050, while the upper bound indicates a gain of 23.4 years.

Figure 6.21 shows that survey respondents for African countries regarded a number of underlying forces as important in determining the future course of life expectancy: the effectiveness of health care systems (Cl-2, 26 per cent influence), HIV/AIDS (Cl-7, 17 per cent influence), changes to biomedical technology (Cl-1, 16 per cent influence), and behavioural changes related to health (Cl-3, 15 per cent influence). With respect to specific arguments, 'Improvements in the education of women will improve the health of children' (HD 6-4) and 'Improvements in medical technology will contribute to declining mortality' (HD 1-1) were considered to have the greatest net impact on life expectancy. Still, the combination of the greater cluster weight and relatively high net impact scores given to specific arguments means that arguments related to the effectiveness of health care systems dominated the list of top five arguments for African countries (Figure 6.21, right side).

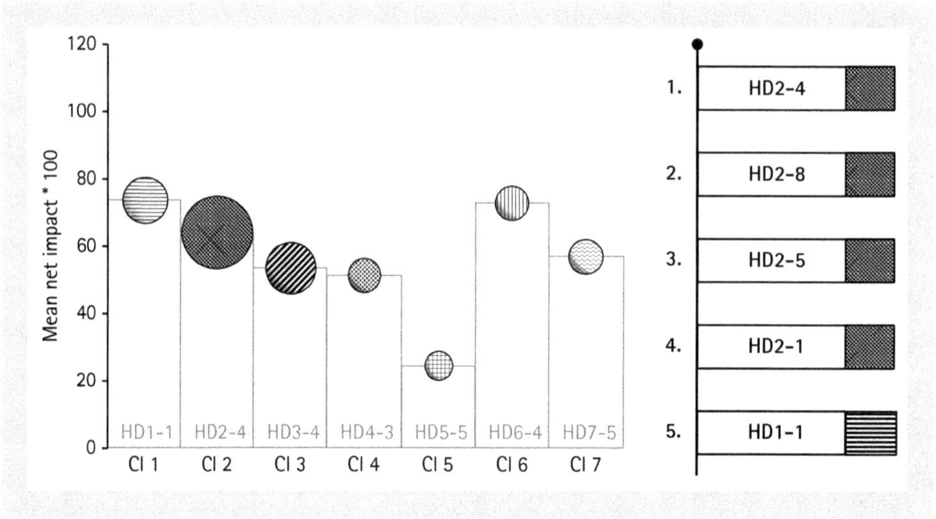

FIGURE 6.21 Cluster relevance and the ranking of highest impact arguments for Africa.

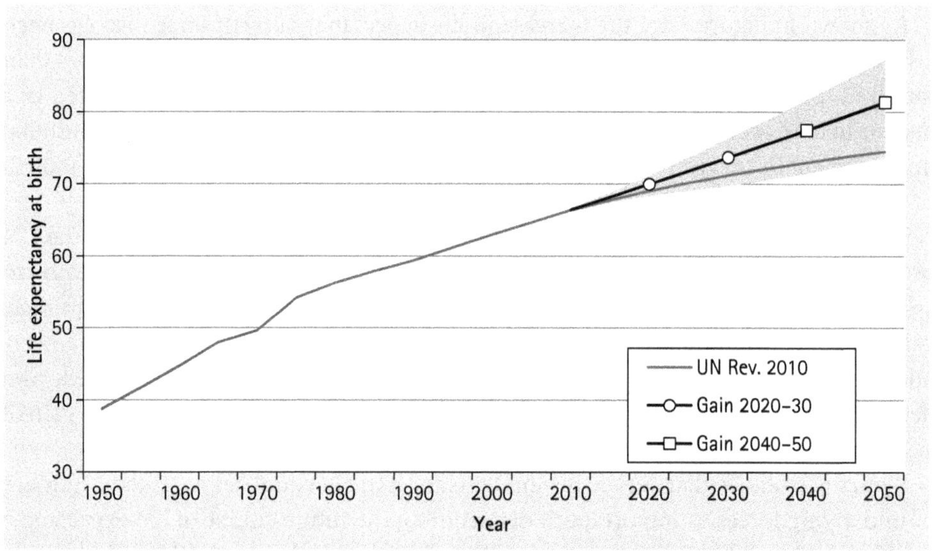

FIGURE 6.22 Previous and expected future trend in life expectancy at birth for Asia.

As shown in Figure 6.22, life expectancy at birth increased dramatically after 1950 in the four populous Asian countries of India, Pakistan, Bangladesh, and Nepal. The period between 1950 and 1975 saw an increase of 15 years, and even as the pace of increase slowed somewhat since 1975, life expectancy continued to rise by nearly 3.5 years per decade, reaching 66 years by 2010. After 2010, the UN medium variant assumes a slowing in life expectancy gains in these four countries, projecting a decadal gain of only 2.5 years between 2010 and 2030 and a decadal gain of only 1.5 years between 2030 and 2050. The survey respondents for these countries were considerably more optimistic, expecting an average increase of 3.8 years per decade, producing a life expectancy at birth of 81.4 by mid-century. In addition, the level of confidence expressed for these predictions was substantially greater than for Africa. The upper bound indicates a gain of 21 years by 2050, resulting in life expectancy at birth reaching 87.2 years. It is interesting to note that the lower confidence bound given by survey respondents indicated a pattern and level of life expectancy gain only slightly less than the UN medium variant projection, resulting in a projected life expectancy for 2050 of 73.5 years, while the UN projection is for life expectancy to reach 74.6 years.

Another difference is that respondents for Asian countries tended to attribute importance more evenly across the underlying forces affecting life expectancy than respondents for Africa, as reflected in the more similar sizes of the circles in Figure 6.23.

Respondents for Asian countries still attributed the most importance to the effectiveness of health care systems (Cl-2, 22 per cent importance), changes in behaviours affecting health (Cl-3, 19 per cent importance), and changes in biomedical technology (Cl-1, 15 per cent importance). But in contrast to respondents for Africa, more importance was attached to differential trends in population subgroups and less to HIV/AIDS.

Still, the top five arguments again reflected the importance attached to the effectiveness of health care systems, but with 'Delivery of reproductive health services, including antenatal care services and family planning programmes, will be extended' (HD 2-6) ranked highest. Concern with chronic disease as a cause of death in Asia is reflected in the argument 'Sedentary lifestyles and changes in diet leading to chronic disease risk will increase' (HD 3-1) appearing among the top five. 'Improvements in the education of women will improve the health of children' (HD 6-4) again had the greatest mean net

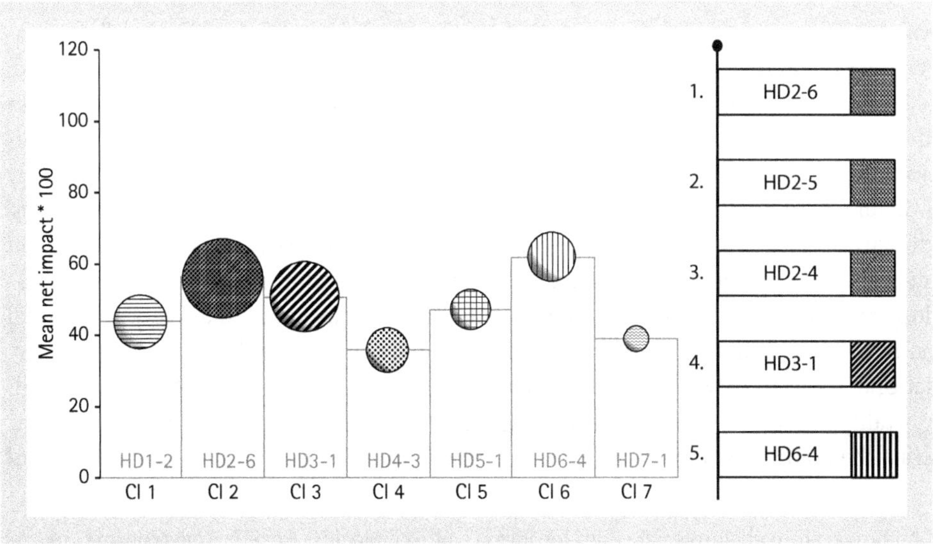

FIGURE 6.23 Cluster relevance and the ranking of highest impact arguments for Asia.

impact score of all the specific arguments, and the greater importance assigned to the population subgroup cluster (Cl-6) for Asia resulted in this argument's appearance among the top five.

6.6 Meta-experts' assessments of future life expectancy trends

On 10–11 February 2011, a meeting of experts was held in Cape Town, South Africa, to review, synthesize, and critique the survey results and to develop alternative scenarios—most likely, optimistic, and pessimistic—for future mortality trends in high mortality countries.[6] The initial discussion focused on the unique issues in projecting mortality for countries with high mortality: the lack of data for determining past trends and current levels of life expectancy, and the inability to predict emergent threats and their impacts on future trends. An example of the latter is the difficulty posed by the HIV/AIDS epidemic, not just with respect to predicting the epidemic, but also in modelling its future impact. As a group, these experts felt that attempting specific projections for individual countries was unwieldy and likely to yield inconsistent results, and that the mortality projections should be based on a classification of countries that would follow similar trajectories into the future. The most obvious starting point for this classification was to separate high mortality countries according to their prevalence of HIV/AIDS.

6.6.1 Storylines for low HIV/AIDS prevalence countries

An optimistic scenario for countries that continue to have high mortality implies a convergence of forces that would act to dramatically reduce death in infancy and childhood, accompanied by improvements in mortality among working-aged men and women. In most of these countries, this could be maximally achieved by the development of a vaccine and improved treatments for malaria that would be both effective and made widely available. This, in combination with broad implementation of current 'best practices' known to reduce deaths from pneumonia, diarrhoeal diseases, and under-nutrition (pneumonia vaccination, oral rehydration therapies, food and vitamin supplementation) and injuries (especially road accidents), could translate into a five-year decadal gain in life expectancy. Achievement of this optimal scenario would imply that the international community would continue, at a minimum, its current level of funding for high mortality countries. In addition, the high mortality countries would have to demonstrate the political will to utilize external funding appropriately and to provide internal

[6] The meeting participants were Rob Dorrington and Tom Moultrie from the University of Cape Town; Ian Timaeus from the London School of Hygiene and Tropical Medicine; Michel Garenne from Institut Pasteur; and Francois Pelletier for the UNPD.

resources to improve health services infrastructure, and increase and improve education. Improvements in education are crucial as education increases motivation to improve health at the individual level, providing benefits over the entire life course. With respect to chronic, as opposed to infectious diseases, the most optimistic scenario would occur if these high mortality countries benefit from the experience of low mortality countries by preventing increases in the behavioural risk factors for chronic disease (smoking, obesity, drug and alcohol use).

The pessimistic scenario was described essentially as the opposite of the optimistic scenario. The negative scenario could occur as a consequence of increased isolation and reductions in aid from wealthier nations to high mortality countries. Within a high mortality country, lowering mortality could be set back by economic stagnation or decline. An economic crisis could lead to a reduction in standards of living and, in more extreme cases, increased internal or external conflicts. In addition, easy solutions would not materialize in the form of long-lasting 'magic bullets': newly developed vaccines would prove to be ineffective when scaled up, drug-resistance would develop to existing treatments, and non-compliance with treatment regimens would increase. Along with this failure to effectively combat mortality from infectious diseases, unhealthy behaviours leading to chronic diseases (poor dietary habits, drug and alcohol use, and smoking) could increase. The group felt that this scenario would result, on average, in a 0.1-year increase in life expectancy over a decade, but that this could vary significantly across countries with some countries experiencing declines in life expectancy.

Regionally, all of the high mortality countries outside of Africa have relatively low AIDS prevalence, with the exception of Haiti. Even without a high HIV/AIDS prevalence, South Asia represents a disproportionate share of the world's mortality because of its large population size. The meeting participants agreed that the most likely scenarios for the most populous countries in this region would be determined by progress in reducing infant and child mortality. In general, the meeting participants were somewhat less optimistic than the survey experts with respect to the likely future scenario for India. These meta-experts felt that it was unlikely that mortality decline would continue at as rapid a pace once substantial reductions in child mortality had been achieved. The group agreed that a four-year increase for 2020–30 seemed reasonable, somewhat less for 2040–50, and that a best case scenario would be an increase of five years in both decades. The worst case scenario would be decadal gains of 1.5 years. For Bangladesh, the consensus was that the recent rapid increase in life expectancy was likely to continue into the near future, in line with the UN projection. A pessimistic scenario for Bangladesh would be only a one-year gain per decade, while an optimistic scenario would not be much better than the UN projection, as mortality is now low enough that gains will be slower. The consensus opinion regarding the most likely course for Pakistan was much less positive. Meeting participants noted that education gains in Pakistan have stalled, especially for girls. The probable scenario was seen as a slow improvement in life expectancy equal to the UN projection of two years per decade. A pessimistic scenario would be a loss of one year per decade, while the optimistic scenario would produce a three year per decade gain.

6.6.2 Storylines for high HIV/AIDS prevalence countries

The most optimistic scenario for countries severely affected by the HIV/AIDS epidemic would imply the development, in the near future, of an effective vaccine that could be made available at a reasonable cost. Barring this, a lesser, but still optimistic, scenario could be achieved by maintaining international support for antiretroviral development and treatment. As the effectiveness of currently available antiretroviral drugs is less than 100 per cent, even an optimistic scenario would mean that there would still be many AIDS deaths in 30 years, but perhaps not in 50 years. However, the meeting participants agreed that current methods for the prevention of mother-to-child transmission of HIV could, under optimal circumstances, mean that childhood AIDS could be eliminated. This, combined with a broader reduction of infectious disease mortality, especially in childhood, could produce decadal life expectancy gains of five years through 2050.

A pessimistic scenario would imply a continuance of mother-to-child transmission and childhood AIDS. Adult AIDS mortality could even increase if funding for ART diminishes and/or host resistance to these drugs increases. An added problem would be that advances against chronic disease mortality could be constrained by expanding resources on HIV/AIDS so that little is left for prevention and control of other diseases.

The region most affected by the HIV/AIDS epidemic is Southern Africa. According to UNAIDS, the average prevalence rate in 2009 for these five countries was 21 per cent, ranging from 13 per cent in Namibia to 26 per cent in Swaziland. In terms of the most likely scenario for future life expectancy in this region, the general consensus was that an effective AIDS vaccine was unlikely to be available in less than ten years. South Africa, the most populous country in the region, was seen as likely to experience a three year per decade increase in life expectancy. A pessimistic scenario would result in life expectancy stagnating, while an optimistic scenario would result in rapid short-term gains allowing South Africa to catch up to the UN non-AIDS projection and then follow that trajectory. The meta-experts generally felt that Lesotho was likely to follow the pattern set by South Africa, but that Botswana and Swaziland would be different, but in ways that were difficult to predict owing to the lack of data.

Eastern Africa is the region with the next highest AIDS prevalence; the average across these 15 countries is 5.7 per cent, but the range extends from 0.1 per cent in Comoros to 14.3 per cent in Zimbabwe. The situation in Zimbabwe illustrates the difficulty with making country-specific projections. Recent data indicate that both HIV/AIDS prevalence and mortality have been falling, but explanations for this decline remain elusive. Speculation for the cause range from the dire economic situation resulting in less travel and less risky behaviour overall, to previous high mortality years eliminating many HIV-infected persons. It was suggested that Kenya would likely follow a pattern similar to South Africa because the lower HIV/AIDS prevalence (estimated to be 6.3 per cent in 2009) would permit effective implementation of antiretroviral drug treatment programmes. Ethiopia, the largest country in Eastern Africa, also presents difficulties owing to the paucity of data. The trend projected by the UN for Ethiopia is heavily dependent on the future course of child mortality, which appears to have declined steadily, with some recent acceleration in the rate of decline. The consensus was that the probable trend for Ethiopia was likely to be somewhat better than the UN projection.

On average, the countries of Middle and Northern Africa have a somewhat lower HIV/AIDS prevalence (3.5 per cent in 2009), ranging from a low of 1 per cent in Sudan to 5 per cent in Cameroon. The meta-experts felt unable to project a specific probable course for mortality for this region as a whole or for any of the constituent countries owing to a lack of data and the history of recent civil conflicts.

Western Africa has, on average, the lowest HIV/AIDS prevalence in sub-Saharan Africa (1.8 per cent in 2009). Even so, projecting mortality for these countries must be done in the context of uncertainty. Nigeria, the largest country in the region, epitomizes this problem. The high levels of child mortality in Nigeria imply the potential for dramatic decreases, but the meta-experts felt that there was enough uncertainty in the Nigerian data to question their use as the basis for future projections. The general sense among the meeting participants was that a decadal gain of four years in life expectancy was very optimistic, that a gain of only one year somewhat pessimistic, and the most likely scenario would be decadal gains of two years.

6.7 Combining Expert Assessments and Model Forecasts to Define Scenario Assumptions

For high and low mortality countries the same procedure was applied for defining the final assumptions for overall mortality levels for each country. The procedure is summarized in Chapter 9 and detailed in Appendix I. For the high mortality countries, outcomes of the model-based forecast were blended with the assessments of the surveyed experts as described in this chapter and with the results of the meta-expert meeting in Cape Town, South Africa.

In sum, the statistical model used explicitly assumes convergence in the decadal increase of life expectancy. The model also takes into account country-specific heterogeneity in the historical trajectories of life expectancy, as well as between-countries heterogeneity in terms of increases in life expectancy. This reflects the view that 'national mortality trends should be viewed in a larger international context rather than being analysed and projected individually' (Lee, 2003). Our model also follows the argument of Torri and Vaupel (2012) that life expectancy across different countries tends to be positively correlated, so that forecasts for particular countries can be carried out by forecasting the best-practice level of life expectancy and then the gap between this best-practice level and the particular country's performance. The model used here builds upon this method by varying the speed of convergence, taking into account differential rates of linear increase in life expectancy across groups of countries. As described in detail in Appendix I, this is operationalized by choosing Japan as the global forerunner with a long-term increase of life expectancy of two years per decade. A set of regional forerunners is then assumed to converge to this Japanese speed of improvement. In a second round, the model then defines the convergence of all countries to their respective regional forerunners. This statistical model results in a consistent set of projections for all high and low mortality countries except for some countries with high AIDS prevalence that required special assumptions, as described in technical Appendix I.

The added value of this convergence model lies partly in the fact that it is based on empirical data. In addition, it takes into account the heterogeneous country-specific historical experiences, as well as differences in gains between forerunners and laggards over time and across regions. Thus, it accounts for structural, as well as stochastic, components that contribute to life expectancy trends over time and can generate unbiased parameters upon which the new forecasts are based. Building further, the model-based forecasts were adjusted to incorporate source experts' and meta-experts' arguments and assessments about future gains in life expectancy in individual countries up to 2050. This was done by assigning the results of the statistical model a weight of 1.0, the average of the meta-experts' responses a weight of 1.0, and the specification of each individual source expert who made a statement on a given country the weight of 0.2. The final step consisted of modifying the future trajectories (2050–95) based on the new trend implied by the reweighted forecasts up to 2050, as described in detail in Appendix I. This procedure is applied to female life expectancy, from which male life expectancy is derived by assuming the sex differentials in mortality used in the 2010 UN assessment. For countries seriously affected by the HIV/AIDS epidemic, the UN's medium scenario, which explicitly models the impact of HIV and AIDS with an epidemiological model (Alkema et al., 2007; Brown et al., 2010; Raftery and Bao, 2010), is used up to 2050. After 2050 life expectancies to the end of the century were projected using the model with Namibia as the forerunner country for this group of countries. A comparison with the UN assumptions for this period showed very close results.

The resulting mortality assumptions for each country are listed in Appendix II for selected years and in the online material for all years. The high and low mortality assumptions were derived for all low mortality countries by the same procedure under the simple assumption that the decades gain of the front-runner is 1.0 years higher or lower than in the medium assumption. For countries (mostly in sub-Saharan Africa) with a high prevalence of HIV/AIDS, larger uncertainty intervals were assumed for the nearer-term future. In the first decade of the projections, life expectancy is assumed for those countries to be five years lower or higher than in the medium. After 2020, the 'high' mortality scenario for those countries assumes a one year lower decadal gain than in the medium scenario. The 'low' mortality scenario assumes an additional two years gain per decade on top of the gain from the medium scenario until 2050, and one year additional gain thereafter. This procedure was only applied to the high HIV/AIDS countries in order to reflect the particularly large uncertainties with respect to speed for recovering from AIDS, which is also directly linked to the future funding of ART.

Education-specific trajectories of life expectancy were then derived by the procedure described in Chapter 9, based on the assumption that the medium trend in overall life expectancy (across all education groups) as discussed in this chapter reflects the educational attainment change over time that is implied by the global education trend scenario. Together with the assumption of certain given relative differences in education-specific mortality, this procedure produces unique, iteratively-derived sets of education-specific mortality trends for each educational attainment category.

It is worth noting that using different education scenarios together with identical sets of education-specific mortality trajectories produces a resulting trajectory of overall future life expectancy that is different, because the different education structure of the population implies different weights for the sub-populations that each have different education-specific mortality rates. In this way the assumed future of education trends is also a direct determinant of the future trajectory of the overall level of mortality. This is illustrated in Chapters 10–12, which discuss the projection results.

6.8 Conclusion

This chapter has highlighted the challenges that attend the estimation of past trends, as well as the projection of the future course of life expectancy in high mortality countries. The challenges revolve around the presence of a large degree of uncertainty that encompasses several dimensions.

First is the uncertainty that surrounds the empirical basis for the estimation of past trends and current levels, namely the lack of reliable data on age-specific mortality rates, particularly for adults, in this subset of countries. Although the methods employed have generated far better estimates than previously available, continual improvement in both data and methods is anticipated.

Second, there is uncertainty that points towards the heterogeneity of trends and pathways across this group of countries; in other words, the disparity in terms of past trends reinforces the difficulty in making predictions about the future course of life expectancy without linking these predictions to the forces determining the progress—or lack thereof—in combatting the underlying determinants of both child and adult mortality peculiar to each of these countries.

Third, there is uncertainty that revolves around the use of demographic and epidemiological models to predict the future of life expectancy in high mortality countries, as well as the assumptions regarding the parameters that are at the basis of these models. This is particularly true for countries affected by HIV and AIDS, where assumptions about coverage and efficacy of treatment are key determinants of these predictions.

Fourth, there is uncertainty around expert opinions vis-à-vis the importance and the role of the forces that will shape the future of life expectancy and the direction and magnitude of life expectancy gains. This uncertainty is reflected both in the small number of source-experts who provided answers to the high mortality questionnaire, and in the meta-experts' mostly dichotomist view of the future of life expectancy in high mortality countries, which could be summarized as a radical versus a more conservative view around their vision of the effectiveness of ART, continued progress towards reducing child and infant mortality, and increasing behavioural health risk factors.

Taking stock of these considerations, the model used to project life expectancy in this book incorporates the various levels of uncertainty through blending an expert-based approach with a model-based approach as described in detail in Appendix I.

Acknowledgements

Portions of section 6.4.1 draw partly on publications of the UN, Department of Economic and Social Affairs, Population Division: *World Mortality Report 2011* (2012) and *World Population Prospects, The 2010 Revision: Highlights and Advance Tables* (United Nations, 2011b). Portions of section 6.4.7 are partly drawn upon from the UN, Department of Economic and Social Affairs Population Division: *United Nations Expert Group Meeting on Mortality Crises: Conflicts, Violence, Famine, Natural Disasters and the Growing Burden of Non-communicable Diseases, Report of the meeting* (United Nations, 2011c).

APPENDIX 6.1

List of arguments for assessing future mortality trend in high mortality countries:

Module 1: **Changes in biomedical technology**	
HM1-1	Improvements in medical technology will contribute to declining mortality
HM1-2	Medical care will improve due to therapeutic and diagnostic devices developed specifically for low resource areas
HM1-3	There will be little financial incentive for private pharmaceutical companies to invest in research and development for new treatments for neglected diseases
HM1-4	Investing in education and in-country research will favour in-country development of appropriate biomedical technology
Module 2: **Health care systems**	
HM2-1	Low cost access to essential medicines for broad segments of the population will improve
HM2-2	Increasing user fees for medical services will restrict access to effective and timely treatment
HM2-3	Public–private partnerships will be created for development and implementation of successful health strategies
HM2-4	Basic public health and nutrition interventions (e.g., immunization, breastfeeding, vitamin A supplementation, and safe drinking water) will be expanded to cover more children under the age of 5
HM2-5	Coverage of inexpensive interventions against diarrhea, pneumonia, and malaria will be expanded

HM2-6	Delivery of reproductive health services, including antenatal care services and family planning programmes, will be extended
HM2-7	Competing demands will reduce government spending for health care systems
HM2-8	Investments in education will increase the quality of health personnel
Module 3: **Behavioural changes**	
HM3-1	Sedentary lifestyles and changes in diet leading to chronic disease risk will increase
HM3-2	Tobacco consumption will decrease
HM3-3	Substance abuse (alcohol and drugs) will increase
HM3-4	Health-enhancing behaviours will spread widely due to mass communication
HM3-5	Investments in education will lead people toward more health-inducing behaviours
Module 4: **Infectious diseases**	
HM4-1	There will be an increase in new infectious diseases
HM4-2	There will be increasing drug resistance to known infectious diseases
HM4-3	Increasing standard of living, hygiene and nutrition will improve host-resistance to communicable diseases
HM4-4	Investments in education will increase capability of early detection and control to contain the spread and impact of new infectious diseases
Module 5: **Environment, disasters, and wars**	
HM5-1	The frequency and intensity of natural disasters (such as flooding and strong storms) will increase
HM5-2	Global warming will lead to an expansion of the malaria zone
HM5-3	Higher temperature variations will lead to increased diarrheal disease incidence
HM5-4	Indoor air pollution due to utilization of solid fuels, including biomass (wood, dung, and crop residues) and coal, will decrease
HM5-5	Chemical and nuclear contamination will be a major health threat in the future
HM5-6	There will be more violent civil unrest and wars
HM5-7	Better education will contribute to decreasing vulnerability to climate change
Module 6: **Population differentials**	
HM6-1	Increased social inequality will lead to higher prevalence of poverty, distrust, violence, and crime
HM6-2	Investing in education will favour upward social mobility and reduce poverty
HM6-3	Gender inequalities will decline and will lead to narrowing health gaps between men and women
HM6-4	Improvements in the education of women will improve the health of children
HM6-5	Health and social services in urban areas will not keep pace with urban population growth
HM6-6	Mortality differentials by level of education will diminish
Module 7: **HIV/AIDS**	
HM7-1	Effective vaccines towards HIV and AIDS and TB will be developed within 20 years
HM7-2	Anti retroviral treatment will be effectively implemented to meet the needs of populations living in resource-poor settings

(*continued*)

Module 7: **HIV/AIDS Continued**

HM7-3	Risky sexual behaviours will impede progress towards reducing the risk of HIV and sexually transmitted infections (STDs)
HM7-4	HIV infection rates will decline most among people with primary and post-primary education
HM7-5	More education (not just sexual education but also basic education) will favour better prevention and adherence to treatment

REFERENCES

Adjuik, M., Smith, T., Clark, S., Todd, J., Garrib, A., Kinfu, Y., et al. 2006 'Cause-specific Mortality Rates in Sub-Saharan Africa and Bangladesh'. *Bulletin of the World Health Organization*, 84: 181–8.

Alkema, L., Raftery, A.E. and Clark, S.J. 2007 'Probabilistic Projections of HIV Prevalence Using Bayesian Melding'. *Annals of Applied Statistics*, 1: 229–48.

Angeles, L. 2010 'Demographic Transitions: Analyzing the Effects of Mortality on Fertility'. *Journal of Population Economics*, 23: 99–120.

Auvert, B., Taljaard, D., Lagarde, E., Sobngwi-Tambekou, J., Sitta, R. and Puren, A. 2005 'Randomized, Controlled Intervention Trial of Male Circumcision for Reduction of HIV Infection Risk: The ANRS 1265 Trial'. *PLoS Medicine*, 2: e298.

Becker, G.S. and Barro, R.J. 1988 'A Reformulation of the Economic Theory of Fertility'. *Quarterly Journal of Economics*, 103: 1–25.

Bongaarts, J.P., Pelletier, F. and Gerland, P. 2011 'Global Trends in AIDS Mortality'. In: Rogers, R.G. and Crimmins, E.M. (eds) *International Handbook of Adult Mortality, International Handbooks of Population*, pp. 171–83. Springer: Amsterdam.

Brown, T., Bao, L., Raftery, A.E., Salomon, J.A., Baggaley, R.F., Stover, J. and Gerland, P. 2010 'Modelling HIV Epidemics in the Antiretroviral Era: The UNAIDS Estimation and Projection Package 2009'. *Sexually Transmitted Infections*, 86: ii3–10.

Buekens, P. and Althabe, F. 2010 'Post-partum Haemorrhage: Beyond the Confrontation Between Misoprostol and Oxytocin'. *The Lancet*, 375: 176–8.

Caldwell, J.C. 1979 'Education as a Factor in Mortality Decline an Examination of Nigerian Data'. *Population Studies*, 33: 395–413.

Coloma, J. and Harris, E. 2004 'Innovative Low Cost Technologies for Biomedical Research and Diagnosis in Developing Countries'. *British Medical Journal*, 329: 1160–2.

Dalal, S., Beunza, J.J., Volmink, J., Adebamowo, C., Bajunirwe, F., Njelekela, M., et al. 2011 'Non-communicable Diseases in Sub-Saharan Africa: What We Know Now'. *International Journal of Epidemiology*, 40: 885–901.

Farmer, P., Smith Fawzi, M.C. and Nevil, P. 2003 'Unjust Embargo of Aid for Haiti'. *The Lancet*, 361: 420–3.

Feeney, G. 2001 'The Impact of HIV/AIDS on Adult Mortality in Zimbabwe'. *Population and Development Review*, 27: 771–80.

Fortson, J.G. 2008 'The Gradient in Sub-Saharan Africa: Socioeconomic Status and HIV/AIDS'. *Demography*, 45: 303–22.

Garbero, A. and Sanderson, W.C. 2012 'Forecasting Mortality Convergence Up to 2100' (Interim Report No. IR-12-013). International Institute for Applied Systems Analysis (IIASA): Laxenburg.

Garenne, M. 2010a 'La récupération après les crises sanitaires: Etudes de cas sur les tendances de la mortalité des jeunes enfants en Afrique sub-saharienne'. Presented at the Chaire Quetelet 2010: Ralentissements, résistances et ruptures dans les transitions démographiques, Institut de Recherche pour le Développement (IRD): Paris.

Garenne, M. 2010b 'Urbanisation and Child Health in Resource Poor Settings With Special Reference to Under-five Mortality in Africa'. *Archives of Disease in Childhood*, 95: 464–8.

Garenne, M. and Gakusi, E. 2006 'Health Transitions in Sub-Saharan Africa: Overview of Mortality Trends in Children Under 5 Years Old (1950–2000)'. *Bulletin of the World Health Organization*, 84: 470–8.

Glynn, J.R., Caraël, M., Buvé, A., Anagonou, S., Zekeng, L., Kahindo, M., et al. 2004 'Does Increased General Schooling Protect Against HIV Infection? A Study in Four African cities'. *Tropical Medicine & International Health*, 9: 4–14.

Graham, W., Fitzmaurice, A., Bell, J. and Cairns, J. 2004 'The Familial Technique for Linking Maternal Death With Poverty'. *The Lancet*, 363: 23–7.

Gregson, S., Waddell, H. and Chandiwana, S. 2001 'School Education and HIV Control in Sub-Saharan Africa: From Discord to Harmony?' *Journal of International Development*, 13: 467–85.

Haines, A., Kovats, R.S., Campbell-Lendrum, D. and Corvalan, C. 2006 'Climate Change and Human Health: Impacts, Vulnerability, and Mitigation'. *The Lancet*, 367: 2101–9.

Helleringer, S., Pison, G., Kanté, M., Duthé, G. and Andro, A. 2014 'Reporting Errors in Survey Data on Adult Mortality: Results From a Record Linkage Study in Senegal'. *Demography*, 51:387–411.

Hemelaar, J., Gouws, E., Ghys, P.D. and Osmanov, S. 2006 'Global and Regional Distribution of HIV-1 Genetic Subtypes and Recombinants in 2004'. *AIDS*, 20: W13–23.

Hill, K. 1987 'Estimating Census and Death Registration Completeness'. *Asian and Pacific Population Forum*, 1: 8–13, 23–4.

Hill, K. and Trussell, J. 1977 'Further Developments in Indirect Mortality Estimation'. *Population Studies*, 31: 313–34.

Hill, K., Choi, Y. and Timaeus, I. 2005 'Unconventional Approaches to Mortality Estimation'. *Demographic Research*, 13: 281–300.

Hill, K., You, D., Inoue, M., Oestergaard, M.Z., Technical Advisory Group of the United Nations Inter-agency Group for Child Mortality Estimation 2012 'Child Mortality Estimation: Accelerated Progress in Reducing Global Child Mortality, 1990–2010'. *PLoS Medicine*, 9: e1001303.

KC, S. and Lentzner, H. 2010 'The Effect of Education on Adult Mortality and Disability: A Global Perspective'. *Vienna Yearbook of Population Research*, 8: 201–35.

Kinyanjui, S. and Timaeus, I.M. 2010 'The International Network for the Demographic Evaluation of Populations and Their Health (INDEPTH), the Importance of Core Support'. *Sida Review*, 11.

Kunst, A.E. and Mackenbach, J.P. 1994 'The Size of Mortality Differences Associated With Educational Level in Nine Industrialized Countries'. *American Journal of Public Health*, 84: 932–7.

Lee, R. 2003 'Mortality Forecasts and Linear Life Expectancy Trends'. Available at: <http://www.demog.berkeley.edu/~rlee/papers/Lund4b.pdf> (accessed 30 January 2014).

McClure, E.M., Goldenberg, R.L., Brandes, N., Darmstadt, G.L. and Wright, L.L. 2007 'The Use of Chlorhexidine to Reduce Maternal and Neonatal Mortality and Morbidity in Low-resource Settings'. *International Journal of Gynaecology and Obstetrics*, 97: 89–94.

McMichael, A.J., McKee, M., Shkolnikov, V. and Valkonen, T. 2004 Mortality trends and setbacks: global convergence or divergence? *The Lancet*, 363: 1155–9.

Mahy, M., Stover, J., Stanecki, K., Stoneburner, R. and Tassie, J.-M. 2010 'Estimating the Impact of Antiretroviral Therapy: Regional and Global Estimates of Life-years Gained Among Adults'. *Sexually Transmitted Infections*, 86: ii67–71.

Makinson, C. 1993 'Estimates of Adult Mortality in Burundi'. *Journal of Biosocial Science*, 25: 169–86.

Malkin, R.A. 2007 'Design of Health Care Technologies for the Developing World'. *Annual Review of Biomedical Engineering*, 9: 567–87.

Masquelier, B. 2013 'Adult Mortality From Sibling Survival Data: A Reappraisal of Selection Biases'. *Demography*, 50: 207–28.

Masquelier, B. and Garbero, A. 2012 'A Familial Approach to Estimating Education-based Differentials in Adult Mortality in Developing Countries'. Presented at the 2012 Quetelet Seminar, Louvain-la-Neuve.

Masquelier, B., Reniers, G., Pison, G. 2013 'Divergences in Child and Adult Mortality Trends in Sub-Saharan Africa: Survey Evidence on the Survival of Children and Siblings'. *Population Studies*. Epub ahead of print. DOI: 10.1080/00324728.2013.856458.

Mathers, C.D., Ma Fat, D., Inoue, M., Chalapati, R. and Lopez, A.D. 2005 'Counting the Dead and What They Died From: An Assessment of the Global Status of Cause of Death Data'. *Bulletin of the World Health Organization*, 83: 171–7c.

Mathers, C., Boerma, T. and Fat, D.M. 2008 *The Global Burden of Disease: 2004 Update*. World Health Organization: Geneva.

Murray, C.J.L., Ferguson, B.D., Lopez, A.D., Guillot, M., Salomon, J.A. and Ahmad, O. 2003 'Modified Logit Life Table System: Principles, Empirical Validation, and Application'. *Population Studies*, 57: 165–82.

Mwansa-Kambafwile, J., Cousens, S., Hansen, T. and Lawn, J.E. 2010 'Antenatal Steroids in Preterm Labour for the Prevention of Neonatal Deaths Due to Complications of Preterm Birth'. *International Journal of Epidemiology*, 39(Suppl. 1): i122–33.

Omran, A.R. 1971 'The Epidemiologic Transition. A Theory of the Epidemiology of Population Change'. *Milbank Memorial Fund Quarterly*, 49: 509–38.

Over, M. and Piot, P. 1993 'HIV Infection and Sexually Transmitted Diseases'. In: Jamison, D.T., Mosley, W.H., Measham, A.R. and Bobadilla, J.L. (eds) *Disease Control Priorities in Developing Countries*, pp. 455–527. Oxford University Press: New York.

Pamuk, E.R., Fuchs, R. and Lutz, W. 2011 'Comparing Relative Effects of Education and Economic Resources on Infant Mortality in Developing Countries'. *Population and Development Review*, 37: 637–64.

Preston, S.H. 1983 'An Integrated System for Demographic Estimation from Two Age Distributions'. *Demography*, 20: 213–26.

Raftery, A.E. and Bao, L. 2010 'Estimating and Projecting Trends in HIV/AIDS Generalized Epidemics Using Incremental Mixture Importance Sampling'. *Biometrics*, 66: 1162–73.

Rajaratnam, J.K., Marcus, J.R., Levin-Rector, A., Chalupka, A.N., Wang, H., Dwyer, L., et al. 2010 'Worldwide Mortality in Men and Women Aged 15–59 Years from 1970 to 2010: A Systematic Analysis'. *The Lancet*, 375: 1704–20.

Reniers, G. and Eaton, J. 2009 'Refusal Bias in HIV Prevalence Estimates From Nationally Representative Seroprevalence Surveys'. *AIDS*, 23: 621.

Reniers, G., Masquelier, B. and Gerland, P. 2011 'Adult Mortality in Africa'. In: Rogers, R.G. and Crimmins, E.M. (eds) *International Handbook of Adult Mortality, International Handbooks of Population*, pp. 151–70. Springer: Amsterdam.

Ross, C.E. and Mirowsky, J. 1999 'Parental Divorce, Life-Course Disruption, and Adult Depression'. *Journal of Marriage and Family*, 61: 1034.

Ross, C.E. and Mirowsky, J. 2006 'Sex Differences in the Effect of Education on Depression: Resource Multiplication or Resource Substitution?' *Social Science & Medicine*, 63: 1400–13.

Stover, J., Johnson, P., Zaba, B., Zwahlen, M., Dabis, F. and Ekpini, R.E. 2008 'The Spectrum Projection Package: Improvements in Estimating Mortality, ART Needs, PMTCT Impact and Uncertainty Bounds'. *Sexually Transmitted Infections*, 84: i24–30.

Stover, J., Johnson, P., Hallett, T., Marston, M., Becquet, R. and Timaeus, I.M. 2010 'The Spectrum Projection Package: Improvements in Estimating Incidence by Age and Sex, Mother-to-child Transmission, HIV Progression in Children and Double Orphans'. *Sexually Transmitted Infections*, 86: ii16–21.

Strand, L.B., Tong, S., Aird, R. and McRae, D. 2010 'Vulnerability of Eco-environmental Health to Climate Change: The Views of Government Stakeholders and Other Specialists in Queensland, Australia'. *BMC Public Health*, 10: 441.

Tanser, F.C., Sharp, B. and le Sueur, D. 2003 'Potential Effect of Climate Change on Malaria Transmission in Africa'. *The Lancet*, 362: 1792–98.

Tanser, F., Hosegood, V., Barnighausen, T., Herbst, K., Nyirenda, M., Muhwava, W., et al. 2007 'Cohort Profile: Africa Centre Demographic Information System (ACDIS) and Population-Based HIV Survey'. *International Journal of Epidemiology*, 37: 956–62.

Timaeus, I. 1987 'Estimation of Fertility and Mortality from WFS Household Surveys'. In: Cleland, J.G. and Scott, C. (eds) *The World Fertility Survey: An Assessment*, pp. 93–128. Oxford University Press: London.

Timaeus, I. and Jasseh, M. 2004 'Adult Mortality in Sub-Saharan Africa: Evidence From Demographic and Health Surveys'. *Demography*, 41: 757–72.

Torri, T. and Vaupel, J.W. 2012 'Forecasting Life Expectancy in an International Context'. *International Journal of Forecasting*, 28: 519–31.

Trape, J.F. 2001 'The Public Health Impact of Chloroquine Resistance in Africa'. *American Journal of Tropical Medicine and Hygiene*, 64: 12–17.

UNAIDS 2010 *Report on the Global AIDS Epidemic*. UNAIDS: Geneva.

UNICEF 2012 *Levels & Trends in Child Mortality: Estimates Developed by the UN Inter-agency Group for Child Mortality Estimation*. UNICEF: New York.

United Nations 1982 'Model Life Tables for Developing Countries (No. ST/ESA/SER.A/77)'. United Nations: New York.

United Nations 2005 'World Population Prospects: The 2004 Revision'. Department of Economic and Social Affairs, Population Division: New York.

United Nations 2011a 'World Population Prospects: The 2010 Revision'. Department of Economic and Social Affairs, Population Division: New York.

United Nations 2011b 'World Population Prospects: The 2010 Revision, Highlights and Advance Tables' (No. Working Paper ESA/P/WP. 220). Department of Economic and Social Affairs, Population Division: New York.

United Nations 2011c 'United Nations Expert Group Meeting on Mortality Crises: Conflicts, Violence, Famine, Natural Disasters and the Growing Burden of Non-communicable Diseases, Report of the Meeting'. Department of Economic and Social Affairs Population Division: New York.

United Nations 2012 'World Mortality Report 2011' (No. ST/ESA/SER.A/324). Department of Economic and Social Affairs Population Division: New York.

Waltisperger, D. and Meslé, F. 2005 'Crise économique et mortalité: Le cas d'Antananarivo 1976–2000'. *Population*, 60: 243–75.

Waltisperger, D. and Meslé, F. 2007 'Economic Crisis and Changes in Mortality Due to Infectious and Parasitic Diseases in Antananarivo, Madagascar'. In: Caraël, M. and Glynn, J. (eds) *HIV, Resurgent Infections and Population Change in Africa*, pp. 79–99. Springer: Dordrecht.

Wang, H., Dwyer-Lindgren, L., Lofgren, K.T., Rajaratnam, J.K., Marcus, J.R., Levin-Rector, A., et al. 2012 'Age-specific and Sex-specific Mortality in 187 Countries, 1970–2010: A Systematic Analysis for the Global Burden of Disease Study 2010'. *The Lancet*, 380: 2071–94.

Winikoff, B., Dabash, R., Durocher, J., Darwish, E., Ngoc, N.T.N., León, W., et al. 2010 'Treatment of Post-partum Haemorrhage With Sublingual Misoprostol Versus Oxytocin in Women Not Exposed to Oxytocin During Labour: A Double-blind, Randomised, Non-inferiority Trial'. *The Lancet*, 375: 210–16.

World Health Organization 1992 *International Statistical Classification of Diseases and Related Health Problems (ICD 10) 10th ed.* World Health Organization: Geneva.

World Health Organization 2006 *Scientific Working Group Report on Dengue*. World Health Organization: Geneva.

World Health Organization 2010 *Countdown to 2015 Decade Report (2000–2010)*. World Health Organization: Washington, DC.

World Health Organization 2011 *Disease and Injury Country Estimates*. World Health Organization: Geneva.

You, D., Jones, G. and Wardlaw, T. 2011 *Level of Trends in Child Mortality: Report 2011*. United Nations Children's Fund: New York.

Zajacova, A. 2006 'Education, Gender, and Mortality: Does Schooling Have the Same Effect on Mortality for Men and Women in the US?' *Social Science & Medicine*, 63: 2176–90.

Zhao, Z. 2011 'Adult Mortality in Asia'. In: Rogers, R.G. and Crimmins, E.M. (eds) *International Handbook of Adult Mortality, International Handbooks of Population*, pp. 133–50. Springer: Amsterdam.

CHAPTER 7

THE FUTURE OF INTERNATIONAL MIGRATION

NIKOLA SANDER, GUY J. ABEL, AND FERNANDO RIOSMENA

Contributing authors:[1]
Ayla Bonfiglio, Graeme Hugo, Lori Hunter, Siew-Ean Khoo, Douglas Massey, and Philip Rees

7.1 Introduction

MIGRATION is a key means by which human beings act to preserve or enhance their well-being. Since *Homo sapiens* first emerged in Africa about 200,000 years ago, geographic mobility has been a prominent strategy for human adaptation and improvement (Cavalli-Sforza et al., 1994). In modern societies, people most commonly migrate to further their economic position or to join family members who migrated before them (Massey et al., 1993). Yet, many others move, both temporarily and permanently, with the more explicit purpose of reducing social, economic, political, or environmental vulnerability (Bardsley and Hugo, 2010; Hunter, 2005; Lundquist and Massey, 2005). All of these forms of human mobility frequently span international borders, oftentimes despite substantial barriers to transborder movement.[2]

Estimates of migration flows are the expression of these heterogeneous motivations. As the drivers of migration also vary conspicuously across nations (Clark et al., 2004;

[1] The contributing authors have drafted considerable parts of sections 7.1 ('Introduction') and 7.2 ('Migration Forces'). They were selected as lead experts in respective topics and regions.

[2] Although international mobility may be particularly costly (and thus less common than intranational movement), in no small part due to restrictive immigration policies and practices, transnational movement may still be likely and possible for individuals with access to various forms of human, financial, and social capital that can support and facilitate lawful and extralegal moves.

Massey and Sana, 2003) and evolve over time within countries (Lindstrom and Ramírez, 2010; Massey, 1990; Massey et al., 1994), they are particularly difficult to forecast. As we show in this chapter, even developing a homogeneous series of baseline estimates at a global level is very complex (Abel, 2013a), further complicating forecasting efforts. Reliable baseline estimates are hard to obtain, for instance, given differences in the definitions across countries of what is an international migrant (Kupiszewska and Nowok, 2008) and owing to the presence of sizable irregular or unauthorized flows in some nations (e.g. Passel et al., 2009).

Notwithstanding these difficulties, international migration has increasingly become, and will remain, a crucial component of the population dynamics of many sending and receiving nations. While only 2 per cent of the world's population lives outside of their country of birth,[3] this figure is above 10 per cent for nationals of countries like Mexico and El Salvador. Foreign-born shares are also substantial relative to the population of many migrant-receiving countries, with levels above 10 per cent (in some cases well above) in North America, most of Western Europe and Oceania, and parts of South East Asia. At the extreme, this share has reached levels of 60–80 per cent in some age groups in the oil-producing nations of the Gulf Cooperation Council (GCC).[4] Furthermore, the origins and destinations of international migrants have become more diverse in the last four decades (Abel and Sander, 2014; Özden et al., 2011).

These shares imply the increasing importance of international migration as a component of national population growth (Zlotnik, 2004), reproduction (Ediev et al., 2007; Preston and Wang, 2007), and (to a lesser extent) the age structure of immigrant-receiving nations (Espenshade, 2001; Wu and Li, 2003).[5] Because of the increased demographic relevance of international migration, developing plausible quantitative central and conditional 'what if' scenarios has become increasingly important. The inclusion of realistic assumptions is hindered by the difficulties in measuring past migration flows required to quantify future levels of movements for projection models. Consequently, the accurate and realistic projection of longer-term migration (through both immigration and emigration rates) is one of the most difficult, but unavoidable, challenges in population forecasting.

[3] Note that many of the people included in this count are 'statistical migrants', such as ethnic Russians living in former Soviet Republics. These people became foreigners not because they moved but because the nation of their birth ceased to exist. Another large share of the world's foreigners consists of displaced persons fleeing civil violence or natural disaster. Such people generally lack the resources to migrate internationally and proceed instead to the closest safe haven, usually within their own or an adjacent country. Leaving aside statistical migrants and displaced persons, only about 1.5 per cent of the world's foreigners are immigrants in the conventional sense—people who emigrated deliberately as part of a conscious strategy to enhance well-being.

[4] All figures come from the United Nation's International Migrant Stock: 2008 Revision, available at <http://esa.un.org/migration/> (accessed 15 August 2012).

[5] As a result of this relevance, ignoring the addition or subtraction of population due to migration can distort traditional calculations of net reproduction rates in both sending and destination countries (Ediev et al., 2007; Preston and Wang, 2007). Under some circumstances, emigration and immigration can also have a significant effect on the age structure of a nation (Coleman, 2002; Espenshade, 2001; Keyfitz, 1971).

This chapter outlines our approach for meeting this challenge. We first present an overview of the economic, climate, political, policy, and socio-demographic forces that affect migration. In section 7.3, we outline the available data to study international migration. We describe our methodology to estimate a set of bilateral migration flow tables of past movements between all countries, which seeks to address the lack of comparable migration statistics at the global level. The spatial patterns of contemporary migration, as revealed by our estimates of bilateral flows, are summarized in section 7.3.3. These estimated flow tables serve as base data for the bi-region population projection model discussed in section 7.4. In section 7.5, we outline how scenarios for the projection model are constructed. This includes details on how expert views expressed in an online survey and meta-expert meetings were combined with the baseline data estimates to develop three future migration scenarios. Section 7.6 sets out the medium scenario and two alternative 'what if' scenarios derived from expert judgement. Selected results of the Wittgenstein Centre (WIC) population projections regarding projected numbers of migrants and different spatial scales are presented in section 7.7.

7.2 Migration forces

For this book's scenario-based approaches, it is important to consider what kinds of forces have affected migration in the past and might in the foreseeable future.[6] We classify these in a relatively straightforward manner distinguishing between economic, demographic, migration policy, environmental, and political factors, although migration, as noted previously, is the outcome of interaction among these factors, such that distinguishing the relative importance of each force is often difficult.[7] Before that, we introduce a more general overview of the volume of international migration flows.

7.2.1 The geography and timing of the initiation of international migration flows

As mentioned earlier, international movement is strongly motivated by economic forces. Although the commonplace idea of an international migrant is one moving

[6] While this overview may also be useful for informing and guiding other forms of forecasting taking them into account in practice is generally extremely difficult (and, oftentimes, counterproductive) given the difficulty in itself in forecasting economic, social, political, and environmental change at both national and global scales.

[7] We present these forces (as opposed to a review of theories) because the migration response to these forces could be consistent with several theories in non-mutually exclusive ways. Further, it may be less problematic to assume that a given force (e.g. wage differentials) may continue to have an effect on migration in the future than to assume that a whole theory (i.e. the combination of a set of forces acting in a particular way, such as the notion that wage differentials net of a specific set of migration costs) will continue to have a similar effect on migration in the future.

from less developed to more developed countries, the magnitude of 'north–north' and, especially 'south–south', movement has increased in recent decades. Scholars estimate that 'south–south' movement may be larger than (or at least almost up to par with) 'south–north' movement (Ratha and Shaw, 2007). Examples of this movement include that of Nicaraguans to Costa Rica (Gindling, 2009; Lundquist and Massey, 2005); Haitians to the Dominican Republic (Grasmuck, 1982); Bolivians and Paraguayans to Argentina (Aide and Grau, 2004; Parrado and Cerrutti, 2003); Bangladeshis to India; and Filipinos to Malaysia (Sadiq, 2009); as well as cross-border labour migration to South Africa (McDonald, 2000).[8]

Uneven processes of development, in their broadest sense, are at the core of factors that explain the initiation of large international migration flows between two given countries. Differences in living standards between sending and destination areas suggest that economic conditions have a preponderant role in stimulating international migration in most corridors, including those with large amounts of intra-regional 'south–south' migration (Clark et al., 2004; Massey et al., 1998). Yet, 'pioneer' migrants move and choose their destinations not only on the basis of where they can achieve the largest present net wage gains; the establishment of most migration 'corridors' is clearly facilitated by prior relations of trade and exchange. That is, although substantial wage differentials are generally a necessary condition for jumpstarting sizable international movements, wage disparities alone are not a sufficient driver of movement. As suggested by the fact that the poorest people from the poorest countries are generally not the most likely to migrate, nor do those moving go to the richest nations necessarily, many other economic and non-economic factors play a role in influencing the timing and geography of international migration flows.[9]

For instance, several kinds of active private and public recruitment efforts have set in motion corridors such as Turkish migration to Germany (Abadan-Unat, 1995); Mexican migration to the USA (Calavita, 1992); Puerto Rican migration to the continental USA (Duany, 2011; Rivera-Batiz and Santiago, 1996); Caribbean migration to the UK, France, and the Netherlands (Grosfoguel, 1997); Middle Eastern, South Asian, Indonesian, and Filipino migration to the Persian Gulf (e.g. Ling, 1984); and ethnic Japanese migration from Brazil, Peru, and Colombia to Japan (e.g. Tsuda, 2003). All of these flows increased only after recruitment took place, despite the fact that persistent income differentials between these sending and destination areas existed well before recruitment began.

In addition to the timing, the choice of specific countries where to recruit from (and thus the pairing of particular sending and destination areas) was further structured by

[8] Note, however, that bilateral migrant stocks within developing countries had risen by 1990, but have flat-lined since then. The big rise since 1970 was in developing country migrants in developed countries (Özden et al., 2011; Figure 1).

[9] While this may not be convincing evidence against the power of wage differentials per se, it does suggest at the very least that other factors mediate the role of wage disparities (for instance, by entering the migration decision as costs (Todaro and Maruszko, 1987)). As such, one of course needs to understand these other factors.

historical connections between places. The labour-importing countries directed recruitment efforts to the less developed nations mentioned earlier not only because of mere propinquity (which played a role in the Mexico–USA case, but only after railroad networks connected the south-western USA with central-western Mexico, (Cardoso, 1980), but owing to colonial (Caribbean–UK/France/the Netherlands; Algeria–France) and cultural/religious ties (Middle East/South/South East Asia–Persian Gulf, ethnic 'return migration' from Latin America to Japan).

In flows where active recruitment was not at play, similar kinds of translocal and transnational connections had a role in influencing the initiation of migration flows and their timing. For instance, military interventions in South East Asia explain the beginning of migration from these countries to the USA (Rumbaut, 1994). US involvement in Latin America and the Caribbean also explains flows from countries such as the Dominican Republic (Grasmuck and Pessar, 1991), Cuba (Duany, 2011), and Nicaragua (Lundquist and Massey, 2005), among others (see Mitchell, 1989).

7.2.2 The continuation of migration flows

Whatever the original motivation for international migration, it tends to set in motion a series of social and economic changes in both sending and receiving societies that facilitate migration and make additional migration more likely. For instance, international migration is facilitated by different institutions and 'industries' facilitating either legal or 'irregular' movement (Spener, 2009). Particularly deep transformations of place lead to a process known as cumulative causation (Massey, 1990). The translocal, transnational exchanges associated with the migration process change life in sending and destination areas in many ways (e.g. Levitt, 1998; Levitt and Lamba-Nieves, 2011), some of which motivate migration even after the conditions originally motivating migration are mitigated (for a more detailed account of cumulative causation processes, see Massey et al., 1998: Chapter 2). One of these mechanisms takes place when migrants remit to their families or bring back large amounts of money that help shift the income distribution of sending areas, motivating the subsequent emigration of individuals from 'non-migrant' households in the wake of their newfound relative deprivation (Stark and Taylor, 1991). Another process of cumulative causation is related to the creation of a 'culture' of migration that perpetuates mobility by making it a rite of passage (e.g. Kandel and Massey, 2002).

The most powerful form of cumulative causation appears to be social capital formation, which occurs through the progressive expansion and elaboration of migrant networks. Social capital is created within a migrant's social network whenever he/she gains access to employment in a high-wage country. Friends and relatives thereby acquire a tie to someone who can lower the costs of movement and overcome the barriers to entry, thus increasing their likelihood of migrating (e.g. Massey and Aysa-Lastra, 2011). Each new departure from the source country expands the migrant network further, creating more social capital that prompts others to emigrate, further expanding the network and creating more social capital, particularly in the context of labour migration and under relatively favourable economic conditions in destinations. Under these circumstances, migrant networks can sometimes operate as informal recruitment mechanisms for employers (Krissman, 2000), linking the processes with labour demand and economic development. After this brief overview of how migration flows initiate and continue, let us now turn to discussing the different types of forces and drivers associated with international migration flows in more detail.

7.2.3 Economic forces, development, and emigration

International migration is mostly driven by economic development and the penetration of markets into non-market societies. The creation of markets for land, labour, and capital, the mechanization of agriculture, and the industrialization of production powerfully transform societies, displacing large numbers of people from more 'traditional' ways of life in the process. The entry of nations into the global regime of trade, production, and exchange thus creates populations of people highly motivated to look for new ways of securing their material well-being. Economic development, at least in its early stages, may produce, rather than inhibit, migration (Sassen, 1998).

Under conditions of economic transformation, international migration becomes an 'attractive' strategy that people can deploy in order to adapt to changes set in motion by globalization and development. In the absence of international recruitment, most of those displaced by market penetration may move within their own countries, either to urban destinations or to rural areas with commercial primary sector production. Those who do move internationally are either highly selected with respect to risk-taking, ambition, and motivation, or have access to forms of capital that can support and facilitate an international move, including the social capital discussed in section 7.2.2.

In seeking to move internationally, migrants adopt one of two basic economic strategies. Those with access to human or financial capital seek to maximize material well-being by relocating to a more affluent nation in search of higher wages (Todaro and Maruszko, 1987) and greater returns to capital. These moves tend to be permanent, or at least of longer duration, and often involve the 'tied' migration of dependent family members (Cerrutti and Massey, 2001; Zlotnik, 2005). The costs and barriers to international movement are lower for those with access to human or financial capital, as many nations have policies to encourage the entry of skilled, educated, and wealthy immigrants.

Apart from maximizing earnings, another motivation for international migration is to overcome the non-existence or malfunctioning of markets at places of origin (Stark and Bloom, 1985). By sending family members to work in high-wage countries, households can also generate remittance streams to smooth consumption in the absence of credit markets, accumulate savings to fund investments in the absence of capital markets, and overcome capital and crop losses in the event of climatic variability in the absence of insurance markets. By sending different family members to different geographic locations, households can also self-insure against other risks to income (e.g. due to unemployment) by diversifying their labour portfolios and generating multiple earnings streams.

Whereas a migration strategy aimed at maximizing individual earnings may suit skilled workers who move for purposes of settlement or long-term employment, migration decisions in the wake of market failure and volatility in sending areas are oftentimes temporary and collective, involving households sending out unskilled workers for shorter periods of foreign labour to generate funds that can solve economic problems at home. This latter motivation seems to predominate in many international flows (Massey et al., 1998), partly, perhaps, as it responds to several forms of economic, social, and environmental change.

7.2.4 Migration as an adaptation strategy to climate and environmental change

The effects of environment and environmental change are complex (Hugo, 1996) and mediated not only by the severity and nature of environmental change but also by the vulnerability, resilience, resources, and situation of affected communities. As a whole, research on the environmental drivers of migration suggests that environmental factors act in concert with socio-economic, political, and cultural considerations to shape migration decision-making (e.g. Black et al., 2011). In some cases, environmental scarcity may constrain some types of mobility (e.g. Gray, 2009) as natural resources provide the capital necessary for livelihood diversification (e.g. Nawrotzki et al., 2012).[10] Overall, short-distance mobility is typically more common than international movement among drought- and/or poverty-stricken populations (e.g. Gray and Mueller, 2012; Henry et al., 2003).

Stojanov (2008) has classified environmentally-induced migrations according to the nature of their causes, distinguishing between environmental migrations initiated by dramatic and sudden environmental events, such as tsunamis, hurricanes, and volcanic eruptions, and those of slow onset, with gradual, but cumulative, environmental forces. This is an important distinction as both the mobility responses and the policies relating to them are different.[11] Sudden disasters can be very destructive and cause major displacement of population, but that displacement is usually temporary. For

[10] Access to productive land also positively predicts outmigration in some settings (e.g. Gray, 2009; VanWey, 2005).

[11] The sudden environmental hazard impact attracts the most attention among policymakers and researchers, while the latter has been neglected, particularly with regard to international migration (see Hunter et al., 2013).

instance, most people displaced by the Asian Tsunami of 2004 eventually returned and rebuilt their communities (Laczko and Collett, 2005). Indeed, the influx of resources and the magnitude of the task of rebuilding can lead to an immigration of additional workers (Laczko and Collett, 2005). In contrast, migration associated with slow-onset environmental change can be much more varied because residents of areas affected by this kind of deterioration are generally able to deploy a larger variety of in situ adaptations.

Yet, specific types of migration may indeed take place in response to slow-onset environmental change, particularly if this in situ adaptive capacity worsens. For instance, a common initial response to perceptions of food shortages associated with environmentally-induced crop failure is temporary circular migration of some of a family's labourers to work in areas not affected by the famine, such as cities. If the famine is prolonged and it becomes unsustainable to remain in the area, this gradually gives way to displacement of entire families on both temporary and permanent bases. In extreme cases, where the entire food resources of an area are exhausted, the result may be mass distress migration (Black et al., 2011).

Drought has dramatic impacts on livelihoods, especially in rural, agriculturally-dependent regions such as northern Africa. Yet, evidence suggests that ongoing adaptation through livelihood diversification often reduces rural household vulnerability. In northern Ethiopia, for example, households with more diverse livelihoods involving animals, non-agricultural income, and/or migrant remittances have more options for coping with drought. Still, there seems to be a threshold above which rainfall deficits force even diversified peasant households to migrate (Meze-Hausken, 2000). Similarly, residents of dry regions of Burkina Faso are more likely to engage in both temporary and permanent migrations (Henry et al., 2003), perhaps related to diversification of origin incomes through remittances.

Historical research in the US Great Plains also links outmigration in the early 1900s to rainfall deficits in agriculturally-dependent regions and in periods of particularly poor weather (Deane and Gutmann, 2003; Gutmann et al., 2005). Indeed, migration has long been a human strategy in the face of climate constraints, with some scholars making use of historical analogues to consider future climate impacts (McLeman and Hunter, 2010; McLeman and Smit, 2006).

As mentioned earlier, some types of moves (urban-oriented, short distance, internal) may be more likely to take place under these conditions. Although it has been argued that many of the processes shaping internal and international migration are similar (King and Skeldon, 2010; Skeldon, 2006), the fact remains that the controls exerted over migration between countries are much greater than those within countries. Internal migration is usually a more available option than international migration, involving smaller distances, lower costs, ease of travel, and less economic, social, and cultural disruption. Accordingly, in most contexts, the rates of internal migration are greater than international movement (Bardsley and Hugo, 2010).

International migration is a much less likely response to these kinds of environmental forces. Migration across national boundaries is not an easy undertaking—and resource scarcity may inhibit costly diversification strategies. For example, people in dryer regions of Burkina Faso were less likely to emigrate to international locales (Henry et al., 2003). Yet, international migration can be a response to environmental stress in some circumstances, in the presence, for example, of pre-established international migrant networks. This is the case in rural Mexican communities with a longstanding history of migration to the USA, where rainfall deficits are associated with higher international migration (Hunter et al., 2013). Still, 'climate-related migration' out of these Mexican communities seems to be an exception to a pattern of low international outmigration in the wake of slow-onset environmental change.

The increased focus on environmental drivers of migration has stemmed largely from the recognition that human-induced climate change is one of the most significant global challenges of the twenty-first century. Part of the burgeoning global discourse on climate change has focused on its potential effects in displacing populations. While it has long been recognized that changes in environmental conditions can have an important effect on migration (Hugo, 1996), this relationship has been oversimplified in much of the recent discourse on the impact of climate change. Much of this discussion assumes that there is a simple deterministic effect whereby environmental change results, inevitably, in population displacement. For example, the most authoritative Fourth Assessment of the Intergenerational Panel on Climate Change (2007) stated: 'Stresses such as increased drought, water shortages and riverine and coastal flooding will affect many local and regional populations. This will lead in many cases to relocation within and between countries, exacerbating conflicts and imposing migration pressures'.

Accordingly, there have been a number of 'projections' of future population displacement that largely assume all people in areas severely affected by climate change will move. Hence, there are pronouncements, which have been given wide currency, that climate change, and especially associated sea level rises, will result in the displacement of hundreds of millions of people between countries (Christian Aid, 2007; Myers, 2002). These 'projections' are not based on a detailed analysis of future trends in climate patterns (McLeman, 2011) nor on an understanding of drivers of migration (Bardsley and Hugo, 2010). The reality is that the relationship between migration and environmental change is complex, and that this complexity must be taken into account in any assessment of future effects of climate change on migration.

7.2.5 Shocks to the system? Violence, political upheaval, and displacement

Shocks are extreme disturbances that affect social systems. In addition to the types of sudden-onset environmental events discussed earlier, dislocation associated with war and political turmoil can cause vast population displacements out of conflict zones, including refugees. These more forced migrations oftentimes take place against a backdrop of more voluntary movement undertaken for reasons related to work, family, education, and retirement. In this section we provide a brief outline of international political events and conflicts that have generated migrant flows around the world.

At the global level, the 1960–2000 time series of intercountry migration indicate a great deal of politically generated migration. The United Nations High Commissioner for Refugees (UNHCR) (2012) estimated that at the end of 2010 there were an estimated 33.9 million people 'of concern'. These included 10.6 million refugees, 838,000 asylum seekers, 14.7 million internally displaced persons protected or assisted by UNHCR, 3.5 million stateless persons, and 1.3 million in 'other' dire circumstances. As the focus of this chapter is on international movement, we do not focus on internal displacement that is common in conflict situations, which (as the quoted figures suggest) is in many cases more common than refugee outflows (also see International Displacement Monitoring Centre (IDMC), 2013).

Domestic and international conflicts in North Africa and West Asia have been numerous. Since 1960 there have been wars involving Afghanistan (1979–89, 2003–12), Algeria (1954–62), Iraq/Iran (1980–88), Iraq/Kuwait/USA coalition (1990–91), Iraq/USA coalition (2003–11), Israel/Jordan/Egypt/Syria (1967), Israel/Lebanon (1982–85, 2006), Libya (2011), Syria (2012–), and Yemen (1994). These conflicts all generated political refugees—several millions in the case of Afghanistan. It is likely that violence will continue in the decades ahead as political, religious, and ethnic divides continue to be sources of conflict.

In South Asia, massive international movement was spurred by population exchanges between India and Bangladesh after the secession of East Bengal from Pakistan; by the India/Pakistan wars; and by the decades-long Tamil–Singhalese conflict in Sri Lanka. South East Asia saw a quarter century of war (roughly between 1950 and 1975) in Vietnam, Cambodia, and Laos, leading to large refugee flows into the USA and Europe (Rumbaut, 1989). In Burma/Myanmar the civil war between the military and ethnic minorities has persisted for decades, leading to the emigration of several thousand people to neighbouring Thailand (Lang, 2002). East Asia experienced large refugee flows during the Korean War.

West Africa has seen civil wars in Nigeria, Sierra Leone, Ivory Coast, Mali, and Liberia. Central and East Africa have seen decades of conflict in the Republic of the Congo, Rwanda, Burundi, Uganda, South Sudan, and Sudan. Southern Africa has experienced refugee flows as a result of wars of independence in Mozambique and Angola, and consequent to the economic collapse in Zimbabwe. Latin America has also experienced civil wars displacing people out of Guatemala, El Salvador, and Nicaragua (Coutin, 2003; Lundquist and Massey, 2005), as well as a large exodus of political refugees from Cuba (Duany, 2011). Most of the refugees from Latin America relocated to the USA.

Europe also saw large refugee flows during the twentieth century, including the massive movement of people during World Wars I and II, and the exodus of individuals of Jewish descent out of Eastern and Central Europe. During the Cold War, refugees trickled out of Warsaw Pact nations, with larger outflows observed in times of unrest, such as in Czechoslovakia (1968) and Poland (1980–89). Although the break-up of the Soviet Union and the fall of the Iron Curtain, a structural break that was a shock to the political and social systems, did not lead to major refugee flows per se, it did greatly facilitate the migration of Eastern and Central Europeans of Jewish descent to Israel and of ethnic Germans (*Aussiedler*) into the newly reunified Germany.[12] In addition to the relocation of Russians, Kazakhs, Uzbeks, and people from other former Soviet Republics back to their ethnic/national homelands, several million of them were classified as international migrants by virtue of the break-up of the Soviet Union and their location in a country different to their ethnic/national homeland (Zlotnik, 1998, p. 446–9).

Unfortunately, it is expected that these flows will continue in the future as turmoil continues in much of the world. This complicates projection exercises as it is, indeed, difficult to forecast international flows that include a non-trivial component of movement related to conflict and other types of shocks, not only in terms of magnitude, but also in terms of timing and directionality. Yet, with hardened refugee and asylum policies around the world, it is likely that many displaced individuals will not leave their countries of origin, but will be increasingly classified as internally displaced (hopefully while still protected by organizations such as UNHCR). Since 1951, the asylum regime has gone through several global policy shifts, giving preference to third-country resettlement to the USA, Canada, and Australia until the late 1950s; integration in the country of first asylum or voluntary repatriation from the 1960s to 1980s; and preventing refugee flows from occurring or confining them to their region of origin since the 1980s (Crisp, 2000). We now turn to policies influencing different forms of immigration flows, where we also discuss asylum policies.

7.2.6 The effects of migration policies on migration dynamics

Political theorists and migration scholars have posited that the ability to exert control over a bounded territory and determine who is allowed to enter and remain in it is one of the foremost defining features of a state (Gibney, 2004; see also Haddad, 2003; Held, 1995; Zolberg et al., 1989). Broadly conceived, policy is one of the most important barriers to and facilitators of migration. For instance, intraregional movement has been facilitated by bilateral and regional agreements allowing the free movement of people, such as in the case of the European Union and envisaged and currently underway for the Economic Community of West African States and the East African Community. Yet, movement to and from nation-states may be affected not only by migration policies, but also by what Czaika and de Haas (2011) term 'non-migration' policies. Migration policies are laws or regulations that have the express aim of regulating the size and structure of migration flows, such as the British Alien Act of 1844 or Uganda's Control of Alien Refugees Act of 1960. Non-migration policies are laws and regulations that carry no such direct (or even intended) aim, but nevertheless affect the size or structure of

[12] The reunification of the German Democratic and Federal Republics into a single nation also led to massive (but, in this case, internal) population redistribution.

migration flows because they influence migration determinants, such as the UK's Welfare Reform Act 2010–12 (Czaika and de Haas, 2011; Haddad, 2003).[13]

Non-migration policies may have a greater effect on migration flows than migration policies in terms of magnitude and long-term trends, as they may be linked to structural determinants of migration, such as macroeconomic and political conditions (e.g. labour demand in countries of destination; social and development policies in sending areas). Migration policies, however, target specific aspects of migration and categories of migrants (Czaika and de Haas, 2011, p. 5). The effects of such policies on flows are easier to evaluate than the effects of non-migration policies.

The effect of a migration policy can be ascertained by its effectiveness in influencing the size or composition (e.g. gender, nationality, age, education, skill distribution) of migration flows. Migration policies can affect migration in both intended and unintended ways. Typically, if a migration policy yields an unexpected outcome, it is because (1) the policy interacted with powerful non-migration policies or macrolevel migration determinants in ways unforeseen by policymakers, (2) the policy was comprised of contradictory and self-undermining aims, or (3) a gap existed between the discourse surrounding the policy and the actual policy measures and the implementation of the policy (Czaika and de Haas, 2011; Ellermann, 2006).

De Haas (2011) posits that there are four types of unintended migration policy effects or 'substitution effects': spatial, categorical, inter-temporal, and reverse flow. Spatial substitution refers to migration flows diverted to other locations, rather than being disrupted, as in the case of Chinese migrants 'diverting' into the north-west of Mexico and other parts of Latin America at the advent of the 1882 Chinese Exclusion Act in the USA (Lee, 2003, p. 157). Categorical substitution occurs when migrants shift to different legal or unauthorized migration channels after a particular channel is targeted by control policies, as in the interplay between overstaying tourist visas and crossing borders without authorization. Inter-temporal substitution occurs when migrants anticipate a tightening of migration policies, prompting them to migrate en masse, as in the 1980 Mariel boatlift out of Cuba (Duany, 2011). Last, reverse flow substitution takes place when return migration flows decrease as a result of increasing migration restrictions, as with the decreasing return rates of undocumented Mexicans in the aftermath of increased US border enforcement in the 1990s (Angelucci, 2012; Reyes, 2004).

Before exploring specific types of migration policies and their effects, it is important to acknowledge that although migration policies can have an observable impact on migration flows, they are not an independent migration determinant. Rather, migration policies are, to some degree, endogenously determined by prior migration flows and can reflect existing migration patterns, which are, in turn, affected by the effectiveness of past migration policies.

[13] The line between migration and non-migration policies is at times difficult to draw, for laws regarding citizenship or labour market policies may have elements that seek to address migration issues (Czaika and de Haas, 2011).

7.2.6.1 *Immigration policies*

The empirical literature on the effects of immigration policies suggests that restrictive immigration policies reduce the flows of people and, more generally, that migration policies affect migration flows in the intended 'direction', but not necessarily in the fully intended manner (Czaika and de Haas, 2011, p. 17; see also Green and Green, 1995; Mayda, 2010; Ortega and Peri, 2009). Additionally, the effects of structural migration determinants in sending or receiving countries in constraining or promoting migration are larger when coupled with more restrictive or open immigration policies respectively. Hence, the positive effect of increasing gross domestic product per capita on immigration flows is more pronounced during times of relatively open immigration policies. Compared with macro-level migration determinants like economic growth, labour demand in receiving countries, conflict, or youth cohort size in sending countries, immigration policies appear to have a small effect on flows, particularly on undocumented, 'illegal', or irregular migration (Angelucci, 2012; Cornelius and Salehyan, 2007; Czaika and de Haas, 2011; Spilimbergo and Hanson, 1999).

7.2.6.2 *Asylum policies*

The right to seek asylum from persecution was established in the Universal Declaration of Human Rights in 1948 and formed the basis of the 1951 Refugee Convention. At its core, this right allows any non-citizen to enter a territory, either through authorized or unauthorized channels, and apply for asylum without the threat of being forcibly returned to his or her country of origin before a status determination is made and before it can be established that the non-citizen would not return to cruel or inhuman treatment. Although the concept of asylum from persecution is established in international law, some states and regions have adopted more expansive asylum policies that include generalized violence and individuals fleeing conflict (see the 1969 Organisation of African Unity (OAU) Convention and 1984 Cartagena Declaration). Furthermore, while the right to seek asylum from persecution is well established, the right to settle in a country is not.

As a result, states and regions uphold the right to asylum and settlement through their own policies and procedures, including status determination waiting periods, resettlement quotas, detention practices, and welfare benefits. Thus, it is possible to observe the effects of different asylum policies on migration flows. For example, some studies have found that increasingly restrictive asylum policies in Europe have reduced immigration flows (Hatton, 2004; Holzer et al., 2000; Thielemann, 2005). In contrast, it is unclear in the USA whether the tightening of asylum policies reduced immigration or only pushed flows into irregular forms of movement (e.g. Coutin, 2003).

7.2.6.3 *Emigration policies*

In examining the impact of policies on migration, few studies explore the effects of policies designed to control emigration or of non-migration policies issued by 'sending' countries (de Haas and Vezzoli, 2011; Kureková, 2011). Emigration policies that encourage or restrict emigration often aim to control the migration of specific groups of individuals, based on gender, skill level, education, or ethnic affiliation. We know of no empirical studies of the effects of these policies on contemporary migration flows (de Haas and Vezzoli, 2011; Fitzgerald, 2009; Kureková, 2011), perhaps because of the tendency in the literature to emphasize other forms of immigration; the lack or low quality of emigration data; the relatively small amount of emigration policymaking compared with immigration; and the fact that the right to leave one's country is internationally recognized.

7.2.7 Socio-demographic factors

Demographic factors that can affect the level of migration include not only the size and growth rate of the population per se, but its age and sex structure, all of which are the expression of past demographic rates (e.g. Preston et al., 1989). There are two main types of migration related to demographic factors. The first refers to how population growth and, especially, age structure imbalances influence relative labour supply and labour migration patterns. The second relates to how the age–sex structure of the population shapes marriage markets and stimulates marriage migration.

7.2.7.1 *The demography of labour demand and supply as drivers of labour migration*

High population growth rates resulting from high fertility and low mortality rates lead to a young population and, potentially, to excess labour supply, which can increase unemployment rates and curb wage growth. A large cohort of people in the mobile young adult ages is a potential source of migrants (e.g. in the case of Mexico–USA migration; see Hanson and McIntosh, 2010), particularly when sending nations face challenging economic or political conditions (e.g. Coleman, 1993), although the lack of development per se does not necessarily yield the highest emigration rates.

By the same token, slower population growth, stability, or decline, when combined with the appropriate structural and institutional conditions, can also affect migration and even lead to immigration. Fertility decline and slower population growth lead to fewer young people in the mobile age groups, thus reducing the supply of potential emigrants. Some former migrant-sending nations, mainly in East and South East Asia, and Southern and Western Europe, have undergone this kind of demographic transition while also having solid social, political, and economic institutions, and experiencing high economic growth and expansion due to investments in human capital and infrastructure (Bloom and Canning, 2008; Paldam, 2003).

This prosperity might have not only led them to reap fiscal and economic benefits of having a population heavy in the middle-age groups, but could also explain their transition from sending to receiving nations.[14] Population and labour force ageing can result in a shortage of workers, which is most likely to be felt in the service sectors. Countries experiencing a short supply of either skilled or unskilled labour have turned to importing labour from other countries with a more abundant supply of workers (Piore, 1980). For example, labour demand and supply issues have been important drivers of Australia's immigration programme since the 1950s and in the current context of below replacement fertility rates since the 1980s. Labour issues will continue to be important drivers of immigration policy with the impending retirement of the baby boom cohorts in the next two decades (McDonald and Temple, 2008).

The likelihood of population decline in industrialized countries with very low fertility rates has led the United Nation's (UN) Population Division to project the scale of migration needed to prevent population decline, to maintain a constant population in the working ages, and to maintain a constant ratio of older persons to persons of working age (United Nations, 2000). These projections are illustrative of the role of demographic factors as drivers of migration if countries decide to consider migration as a policy instrument for addressing the issue of future population and labour force declines (see also Coleman, 2002; Espenshade, 2001).

7.2.7.2 *Socio-demographic drivers of marriage migration*

Demographic factors can also affect the availability and choice of marriage partners, stimulating cross-border marriage migration. The sex ratio of the population in the marriage ages is a function of changing fertility, sex-selective mortality, and migration in younger ages, and imbalances in the sex ratio at birth. In most societies, men usually marry younger women. In a population experiencing declining fertility rates, the size of younger cohorts of women would be smaller than those of older cohorts of men, implying that some of these older men may have difficulty finding a spouse in the 'appropriate age group'. Demographers refer to these circumstances as a 'marriage squeeze'. Advances in female education and other social and cultural factors affecting people's preferences in the choice of a marriage partner can exacerbate the problem.

In addition, the contemporary increase in sex ratios at birth in several Asian countries (e.g. Coale and Banister, 1994; Guilmoto, 2007) to figures well above the 'normal' ratio of 103–107 male per 100 female births (e.g. to 110–117) also has the potential to exacerbate the problem in future. A marriage squeeze can lead to men looking abroad for potential

[14] Demography may have a role in the current status of China and India as two of the top source countries of migration. These two most populous countries in the world currently have a relatively large proportion of people in the peak migration age groups and have emerged as significant sources of migrants to countries such as Australia, Canada, and the USA. They have been the largest sources of immigrant arrivals in Canada since 1996 (Statistics Canada, 2006); the first and third largest sources of immigrants to Australia in 2010–11 (Department of Immigration and Citizenship, 2011); and the second and third largest sources of legal permanent resident admissions in the USA (Office of Immigration Statistics, 2010).

marriage partners (Davin, 2007; Guilmoto, 2007), particularly when cross-border marriage migration is facilitated by cheap transport and communication.

In addition to marriage migration motivated by age–sex structure imbalances, newly established migrant or ethnic communities (which, in some cases, may have an unbalanced sex ratio in the marriage age groups, such as an excess of young single men) may further stimulate marriage migration from the country of origin if there is a preference for a marriage partner of the native ethnic origin (among the first or second-plus generations), or there are other barriers to intermarriage with local residents, as in the case of some ethnic communities in Australia, Europe, and North America (e.g. Telles and Sue, 2009).

7.2.7.3 *Beyond drivers: the relevance of understanding the demographic profile of migrants*

Although demographic factors are generally not the main drivers of international migration flows, it is important to understand them for better estimation and forecasting of migration. In addition to their mild influence on the magnitude of flows, understanding the composition of migrants and their socio-demographic selectivity is also useful for surmising some of the root causes and potential consequences of migration for sending and receiving areas, and for investigating them further. Given the paucity of detailed data for many immigrant groups, socio-demographic profiles of both emigrants and return migrants have helped scholars understand migration trends, particularly at the regional and global levels (e.g. Fassmann and Munz, 1992; Zlotnik, 1998).

Demographic characteristics can also be useful for the indirect estimation and forecasting of migration, given that many migration flows exhibit relatively stable demographic patterns (Rogers et al., 2010). This is particularly true in the case of age patterns of directional migration flows (e.g. Rogers and Castro, 1981; Rogers et al., 2007), which have remarkable stability, which is also the case in other demographic events. We take advantage of these regularities in our estimations and projections of global international migration flows, as explained in section 7.3.

7.3 Global estimates of international migration flow data

International moves are typically enumerated in a demographic context using a measure of either migrant stocks or migration flows. A migrant stock is defined as the total number of international migrants present in a given country at a particular time. A migration flow is defined as the number of persons arriving or leaving a given country over the course of a specific period of time. Flow measures reflect the dynamics of the migration process, but are harder to estimate and less available than stock measures (Bilsborrow et al., 1997).

Flow data have several desirable qualities. Information on migration patterns from studying stocks can potentially provide a poor indication of contemporary international migration flows in relation to the forces outlined in section 7.2. In countries where there are significant return migrations or mortality among foreign population, migrant stock data can yield a misleading portrait of the current migration system (Massey et al., 1998). Flow data provide a quantifiable measure of the number of movements over a specified time period, along with rates of births and deaths, by population projections models.

In this section, existing statistics on international migration flow data for global movements produced by national statistics agencies and the UN are discussed first. Currently, detailed flow data required for advanced projection models tend to be available only for more developed nations. In response to this demand, we outline a methodology to estimate bilateral migration flows between all countries. The methodology, fully detailed in Abel and Sander (2014) and Abel (2013a), allows a number of different detailed migration measures to be used from the resulting estimates. It also allows additional regularities by age and other factors to be incorporated into the disaggregation of estimated migration flows by age and sex, as required by advanced projection models. An outline of the estimation procedure is followed by a discussion of the estimated trends in migration in recent decades.

7.3.1 International migration flow data

International migration flow data often lack adequate measurements of volumes, direction, and completeness, making cross-national comparisons difficult. The lack of comparability in flow data can be traced to a number of causes. First, migration is a multi-dimensional process involving a transition between two states. Consequently, movements can be reported by sending or receiving countries. When data collection methods or measurements for countries differ, the reported counts do not match. Second, international migration flow data are typically collected by national statistics institutes in each country, where measures have been designed to suit domestic priorities. Data are often produced within a legal framework, and hence alterations to their collection are difficult to implement. Finally, in many countries, migration data collection systems do not exist. In other countries, collection methods such as passenger surveys may provide inadequate detail for some data users.

These problems have motivated demographers to estimate migration flows, rather than rely on incomplete and non-comparable sets of government migration statistics. To date, at the global level, the only recognized set of flow estimates for all countries is the set of net migration flows over five-year periods produced by the UN Population Division (UNPD, 2011).

These estimates are based predominately on scaled annual flows derived from either migration records or through demographic accounting. They provide an important set of base data for most global projection models. However, as with any net migration measure, they suffer from a number of problems. Net migration measures can often confound insights into migration patterns and migrant behaviours, as they provide no detail on the scale of movements in and out of a country. Hence, it can be difficult to fully disentangle the effect of various forces on the level of migration. The use of estimates of net international migration flows in global forecasting exercises often runs the risk of well-documented problems when using net measures in projection models (see, e.g., Rogers, 1990, 1995). This can often lead to distinctly different projections than might be obtained from using immigration and emigration measures with the same net migration. Net migration is also more difficult to forecast and could potentially lead to greater uncertainty in the population projections (Raymer et al., 2012), as net migration tends to be more volatile than alternative measures of migration flows.

In order to address these problems, we developed a set of estimated bilateral migration flow tables that not only provide values on total immigration and emigration (from which a net migration figure can be derived), but also provide details on the origin and destinations of migrants.

7.3.2 Estimating global migration flow tables

A full exposition of the methodology to estimate global bilateral flow tables is given in Abel and Sander (2014) and Abel (2013a). This section consists of a brief overview of the general concept in order to allow the reader to understand how further disaggregations of the bilateral flow table, by age and sex required for the projection model, are possible.

The estimation of global migration flow tables is based upon linking sequential migrant stocks tables to derive the flow estimates that are consistent with changes in the stocks. Basing estimated migration flows upon stocks has a number of potential advantages. First, bilateral migration flow tables can be considered as part of a wider accounting of demographic data. Rees (1980) noted that national account statistics of financial stocks and flows have served economists well in their modelling activities, encouraging users to compare data for consistency, check for inadequacies, and attempt to match available data with a conceptual model. He suggested that a similar system of demographic accounts in migration stocks and flows would likely lead to similar improvements. Second, stock data are, in comparison to international migration flow data, far easier to measure and more widely available, both across time and countries. This is reflected in World Bank migration stock data, which include bilateral records from more than 200 nations and 4 decades (Özden et al., 2011). In comparison, the 2010 revision of bilateral international migration flow data released by the UN (Henning and Hovy, 2011; UNPD, 2009) covers only 29 nations, predominately developed world countries, from the last two decades. The greater availability of migrant stock data makes them an invaluable source of information on migrant patterns that can, as will be illustrated next, be used as a basis to estimate global bilateral migration flow tables.

7.3.2.1 *Methodology*

Bilateral migration data are commonly represented in square tables. Values within a table vary, depending on definitions used in data collection or the research question. Values in non-diagonal cells represent some form of movement, for example a migration flow or a foreign-born stock between a specified set of regions or areas. Values in diagonal cells represent some form of non-moving population, or those that move within a region, and are sometimes not presented.

Consider two migrant stock tables in consecutive time periods (t and $t+1$) in Table 7.1. Regions A–D represent places of birth in the rows, and place of residence in the columns. Hence, non-diagonal entries represent the number of foreign-born migrants in each area of residence, while diagonal entries contain the number of native-born residents. In this hypothetical example there are no births or deaths. This results in two noticeable features. First, the row totals in each time period remain the same, as the number of people born in each region cannot increase or decrease. Second, differences in cells must implicitly be driven solely by migration flows. These movements occur by individuals changing their place of residence (moving across columns), while their place of birth (row) characteristic remains fixed.

To derive a corresponding set of flows that are constrained to meet the stocks tables, one can alternatively consider the data in Table 7.1 as a set of four birthplace-specific migration flow tables where the marginal totals are known, shown in Table 7.2. These are formed by considering each row of the two consecutive stock tables as a set of separate margins of a migration flow table. Place of residence totals at time t from the stock data now become origin margin (row) totals for each birthplace-specific population. Similarly, place of residence totals at time $t+1$ from the stock data now become destination margin (column) totals for each birthplace-specific population. As the row totals from the stock tables are equal, the sum of the row and column marginal totals in each of the birthplace-specific migration flow tables in Table 7.2 are also equal.

Within each birthplace-specific table in Table 7.2, missing non-diagonal cells represent the migrant transition flows between a chosen origin and destination, within time period t to $t+1$ and categorized by birthplace. In order to estimate the missing migrant

Table 7.1 Dummy Example of Place of Birth Migrant Stock Data in Stock Table Format

		Place of residence (t)							*Place of residence* (t + 1)				
		A	B	C	D	Sum			A	B	C	D	Sum
Place	A	1,000	100	10	0	1,110	*Place*	A	950	100	60	0	1,110
of	B	55	555	50	5	665	*of*	B	80	505	75	5	665
birth	C	80	40	800	40	960	*birth*	C	90	30	800	40	960
	D	20	25	20	200	265		D	40	45	0	180	265
	Sum	1,155	720	880	245	3,000		Sum	1,160	680	935	225	3,000

Table 7.2 Dummy Example of Place of Birth Migrant Stock Data in Flow Table Format

	Place of birth = A						*Place of birth = B*				
	Destination						*Destination*				
	A	B	C	D	Sum		A	B	C	D	Sum
Origin A	950				1,000	*Origin* A	55				55
B		100			100	B		505			555
C			10		10	C			50		50
D				0	0	D				5	5
Sum	950	100	60	0	1,110	Sum	80	505	75	5	665
	Place of birth = C						*Place of birth = D*				
	Destination						*Destination*				
	A	B	C	D	Sum		A	B	C	D	Sum
Origin A	80				80	*Origin* A	20				20
B		30			40	B		25			25
C			800		800	C			0		20
D				40	40	D				180	200
Sum	90	30	800	40	960	Sum	40	45	0	180	265

transition flows an assumption is made about the non-movers on the diagonal entries. Abel (2013a) proposed to fix the diagonal elements to their maximum possible values that do not violate their corresponding marginal constraints in the row and column sum totals. These values, also illustrated in Table 7.2, allow the missing cells to correspond to the minimum number of migrant flows required to match the known marginal stock totals.

The remaining missing (non-diagonal) cells in Table 7.2 can be estimated using indirect model-based methods. These involve adoption of an underlying model. In Abel (2013a) a log-linear model is chosen to allow the imputations of all missing cells in Table 7.2 to maintain both the marginal and diagonal constraints. The parameters in the model are chosen to match the known data, and hence include terms for origins (rows), destinations (columns), and non-movers (cell-specific). Similar approaches have been previously applied to estimate internal migration flow tables with known marginal totals (see, e.g., Willekens, 1990 or Raymer et al., 2007). An iterative set of equations to estimate the parameters is derived by maximizing the Poisson likelihood of the log-linear model. A program to perform this estimation is available in the *migest* R package (Abel, 2013b). Running the program on the data in Table 7.2 gives the complete estimates of all migration flows by birthplace in the top panel of Table 7.3. These detailed estimates can be summed over to derive traditional origin to destination migration flow tables in the bottom panel of Table 7.3 (having deleted the non-movers from the principle diagonals

Table 7.3 Estimates of Migrant Transition Flow Tables Based on Stock Data in Table 7.2

Estimates of origin-destination-birthplace flow tables

Place of birth = A

		Destination				
		A	B	C	D	Sum
Origin	A	950	0	50	0	1,000
	B	0	100	0	0	100
	C	0	0	10	0	10
	D	0	0	0	0	0
	Sum	950	100	60	0	1,110

Place of birth = B

		Destination				
		A	B	C	D	Sum
Origin	A	55	0	0	0	55
	B	25	505	25	0	555
	C	0	0	50	0	50
	D	0	0	0	5	5
	Sum	80	505	75	5	665

Place of birth = C

		Destination				
		A	B	C	D	Sum
Origin	A	80	0	0	0	80
	B	10	30	0	0	40
	C	0	0	800	0	800
	D	0	0	0	40	40
	Sum	90	30	800	40	960

Place of birth = D

		Destination				
		A	B	C	D	Sum
Origin	A	20	0	0	0	20
	B	0	25	0	0	25
	C	10	10	0	0	20
	D	10	10	0	180	200
	Sum	40	45	0	180	265

Estimates of origin-destination flow tables

		Destination				
		A	B	C	D	Sum
Origin	A		0	50	0	50
	B	35		25	0	60
	C	10	10		0	20
	D	10	10	0		20
	Sum	55	20	75	0	150

and margins of each birthplace table). Estimates represent the number of migrant transition flows from each origin to each destination within the time period t to $t+1$.

In reality, changes in migrant stock populations from births and deaths occur, which ensure that the row totals of sequential stock tables, such as those in Table 7.1, are not equal. However, these changes can be controlled for using demographic procedures outlined in Abel and Sander (in press). Using data on the total number of births and deaths for each country available from the UN Population Division (UNPD, 2011), the stock tables are altered to adjust for changes due to births and deaths during the interval. This procedure allows the estimated bilateral flow table to have the same net migration during the period as implied by application of demographic accounting in each country (Abel and Sander, 2014).

7.3.2.2 *Application of the methodology to obtain global flow table estimates by sex*

As discussed in Abel and Sander (2014), bilateral migrant stock data published by the UN (2012) provide bilateral migrant stock tables by sex at the start of each of the last three decades (1990, 2000, and 2010) for 230 countries. Data are primarily based on place of birth or citizenship responses to census questions, or details collected from population registers or nationally representative surveys. In order to create a complete data set the UN undertook a number of estimation steps, which are now briefly described (for full details the reader is referred to UNPD, 2012). For countries where there are no place of birth data available, data on citizenship are used as approximate measures of place of birth totals. In countries where neither place of birth nor citizenship measure were available, missing values were addressed using various propensity and interpolation methods. These were based on either historical or future data when a measure in a specific period was missing, or using available data from model countries chosen to reflect similar criteria for enumerating migrants, geographical proximity, and migration experience. Estimates of refugee populations from other UN agencies were included in the final stock totals. Some bilateral cells in the published tables are empty. These represent—for the most part—small, foreign-born populations. Aggregations of these cells are provided in two additional places of birth rows labelled 'Other north' and 'Other south'. These counts represent less than 5 per cent of the total foreign-born populations in almost all countries.

In order to estimate five-year migrant transitions flows by sex during the base year period, 2005–10, using the methodology outlined in Abel and Sander (in press) and Abel (2013a), two further steps were taken to prepare the data. First, the diagonal elements in each stock table of the native-born male or female population totals in each place of residence j, ($P_j^{k=j}$), not provided by the UN, were estimated. This was calculated as a remainder ($P_j^{k=j} = P_j^{+} - \Sigma_{k \neq j} P_j^k$) using annual male and female population totals from the UN Population Division (2011), (P_j^{+}), and the column sums of the foreign-born populations in each place of residence ($\Sigma_{k \neq j} P_j^k$). This procedure constrained the column totals of the stock tables to meet those of the reported male and female populations at the start of each decade. Second, in order to estimate five-year transition flows, a bilateral migrant stock table was required in 2005. The mid-decade table was estimated using a similar procedure used by the UN to calculate partially missing migrant stock data. The proportions of each foreign-born stock in the bilateral flow table were interpolated to their mid-decadal values. The proportions were then multiplied by the population total in 2005.[15]

Demographic data on the number of births and deaths by sex in each country, which are controlled for when estimating the flows from the stocks, were also taken from the UN Population Division (2011). In addition, data on the geographic distances between

[15] Note, we set all missing values (of small, foreign-born populations discussed in the previous paragraph) to zero.

all capital cities were also used in the estimation procedure, as outlined in Abel and Sander (2014) and Abel (2013a). These were taken from the Centre d'Etudes Prospective et d'Informations Internationales data by Mayer and Zignago (2012).

The conditional maximization routine was then run to calculate the migration flow tables for men and women in the five-year period between 2005 and 2010 using the ffs routine in the *migest* R package (Abel, 2013b). This resulted in a single bilateral table of migrant transitions from mid-2005 to mid-2010 for each sex.

7.3.2.3 *Disaggregation by age*

As with other components of demographic change, populations have been found to have considerable regularities in age-specific rates of migration. A typical migration age schedule is shown by the solid grey line in Figure 7.1.

Migration rates among infants and young children are relatively high, similar to those of their parents and other young adults in their 20s and early 30s. Migration rates of adolescents are low, but exceed those of young teens, for whom the lowest migration rate is about age 15. Rates rise to a peak after the completion of education and then fall monotonically with age to retirement years. Rogers and Castro (1981) proposed a mathematical representation of migration age schedules, $M(x)$, for age x using seven parameters:

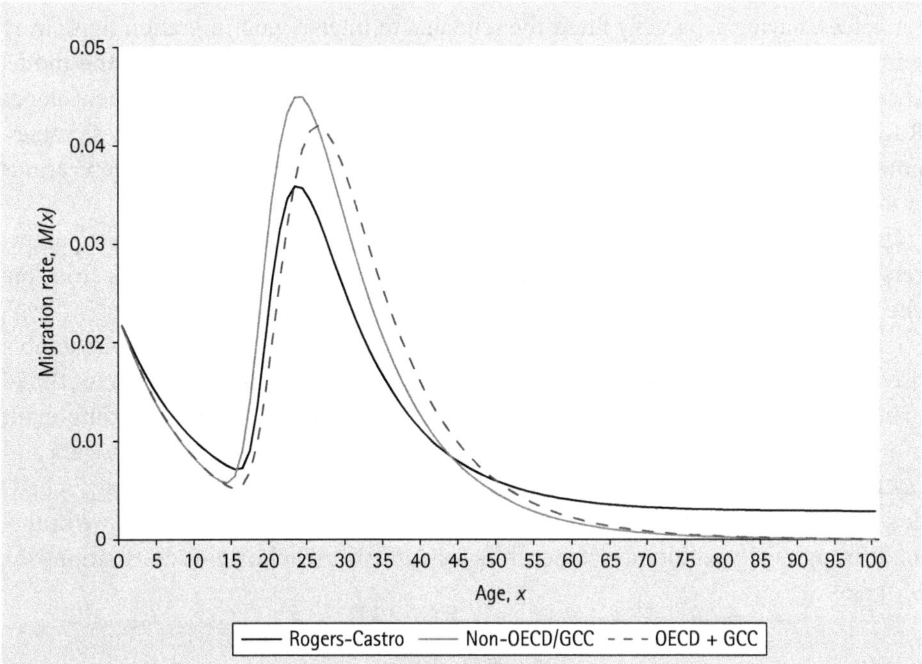

FIGURE 7.1 Model migration schedules. OECD: Organisation for Economic Co-operation and Development; GCC: Gulf Cooperation Council.

Table 7.4 The Parameters of the Model Migration Schedule for the Standard Rogers–Castro and Our Two Custom Schedules

Parameter	Rogers–Castro	Non-OECD/GCC	OECD + GCC
α_1	0.02	0.015	0.015
α_1	0.10	0.10	0.10
α_2	0.06	0.06	0.06
λ_2	0.40	0.30	0.25
μ_2	20	20	22.5
α_2	0.10	0.10	0.10
c	0.003	0	0

OECD: Organisation for Economic Co-operation and Development; GCC: Gulf Cooperation Council.

$$M(x) = a_1\exp(-\alpha_1 x) + a_2\exp\{-\lambda_2(x-\mu_2) - \alpha_2(x-\mu_2)\} + c$$

The first exponential in the schedule controls the rate of descent in the prelabour force component. The second exponential controls the shape of the labour force peak. In the first half, the exponential term, λ_2, represents the rate of ascent in the peak, while in the second half, the α_2 parameter controls the descent. The μ_2 term controls the location of the peak.

Rogers and Castro (1981) proposed a unisexual standard set of fundamental parameter values, having separately fitted the schedule to inter-region migration flows in 17 countries and then averaging. Later studies have proposed extensions to the model schedule, adding more parameters to include retirement peaks, post-retirement slopes (Rogers and Little, 1994), and entry into higher education (Wilson, 2010). These values, shown in the first column of Table 7.4, imply a number of simple ratios between various parts of the age schedule (see Rogers and Castro, 1981, for further details).

The migration schedule formed by entering the fundamental parameter set parameters into $M(x)$ is plotted in the solid grey line of Figure 7.1. The estimates from the schedule have been scaled to fix the area under the curve to be unity.

As there was no information on migrant stock populations by age, we were unable to estimate age-specific flows using the flows-from-stock methodology outlined earlier. In order to derive estimates by age groups, required for cohort component projection models, we relied upon the seven-parameter age schedule of Rogers and Castro to disaggregate each estimated flow in our bilateral table. Given the age schedules, where the sum of the age-specific migration rates summed to unity, we multiplied through age-specific rates at each five-year interval to each origin–destination–sex (m_{ijs}) table:

$$m_{ijxs} = m_{ijs} M(x)$$

This resulted in an array of origin–destination migration flow tables by sex and age.

In order to account for differences between internal migration (from which the fundamental parameters were derived) and our international migration application, we altered some values of the fundamental parameter set used to derive the age-specific rates, depending on the country of origin. For flows from countries outside the Organisation for Economic Co-operation and Development (OECD) and GCC countries, we applied a migration schedule with a larger labour force peak, shown in Figure 7.1. This schedule is based on the parameter set given in the second column of Table 7.4, and then scaled to set the age-specific rates to sum to unity. Only three parameters differ from those in the fundamental parameter set. First, the α_1 parameter was reduced to lower the relative amount of child migration flows in relation to young adults entering the labour force. Second, the rate of ascent in the labour force peak was lowered to average over differing ages of entrance into the labour force across multiple countries. Third, the *c* parameter was set to zero, lowering elderly international migration intensities to very low levels.

Flows that originated from OECD and GCC countries were assumed to follow a migration age schedule with a later peak, shown in Figure 7.1. This schedule is based on the parameter set given in the third column of Table 7.4 and then scaled to set the sum of the age-specific rates to unity. Two parameters differ from the schedule used for the non-OECD/GCC nations. First, the ascent of the labour force peak is further reduced. Second, the location of the peak is shifted by 2.5 years. Both alterations reflected an assumption of moves after longer periods of education and later entry into the education market in these countries, while also allowing return migration of temporary workers from non-OECD/GCC countries at older ages.

7.3.3 Current trends in global migration flows

In the absence of adequate data on bilateral migration flows, the number of net migrants and the stock of foreigners present in a given country are commonly used as proxy measures for the global flow of people. Consequently, progress towards understanding the complex patterns of country-to-country migration flows has been slow. Our unique new bilateral data on the contemporary global flow of people outlined in Abel and Sander (2014) and summarized in section 7.3.2 allow us to paint a comprehensive picture of recent intensities and patterns. Our interactive online visualization 'The Global Flow of People' is available at: <http://www.global-migration.info>.

Here, we present estimates of international migration flows disaggregated by sex that capture the number of men and women who changed residence over the five-year interval from mid-2005 to mid-2010. According to our estimates, 41.5 million people (or 0.61 per cent of the world population in 2005) moved between countries over the period 2005–10 (Abel and Sander, 2014). Of these, 21.7 million (or 55 per cent) were men. Hence, the migration rate among men was, with 0.66 per cent of population in 2005, higher than the rate for women (0.55 per cent).

Table 7.5 Estimated Numbers of Migrants (in 1,000) Within and Between Regions, 2005–10

	Europe	North America	Latin America	Africa	Former Soviet Union	West Asia	South Asia	East Asia	South East Asia
Europe	2,401	61	16	138	38	136	0	5	134
North America	1,216	96	277	47	113	130	0	39	94
Latin America	1,763	3,628	879	23	11	39	0	112	39
Africa	2,108	541	12	3,142	5	673	0	3	157
Former Soviet Union	609	21	1	2	1,871	22	0	6	1
West Asia	450	169	9	99	68	927	14	0	43
South Asia	1,390	1,508	7	61	16	4,902	1,308	74	873
East Asia	469	1,058	35	17	65	3	0	781	424
South East Asia	772	1,000	8	29	13	881	59	386	2,167

At the regional level,[16] Table 7.5 shows that just under 5 million people moved from South Asia to West Asia (mostly the oil-rich Gulf States), while 3.6 million people moved from Latin America to North America. Europe and North America recorded substantial numbers of migrants moving to and from many other regions, whereas migration in South Asia and Africa was mostly occurring within the region.

The spatial patterns of international migration flows hidden in Table 7.5 can be visualized effectively using circular migration plots (Abel and Sander, 2014). Figure 7.2 illustrates the key elements of our new method for visualizing complex flow data. A detailed discussion of these plots and how to create them is provided in Sander et al. (2014).

Figure 7.2 gives a snapshot of our flow estimates in 2005–10, aggregated into four major world regions (Abel and Sander, 2014). Compared to the widely available data on migrant stocks (i.e. people living outside their country of birth) (UNPD, 2012), our estimates suggest fewer movements in Europe and more movements within and from Asia.

The overall pattern of migration flows depicted in Figure 7.2 is one of substantial movements within each continent, as well as migration from Asia to the USA and Europe. The counter-flows from the USA and Europe to Asia are negligible in size, highlighting the substantial impact of migration on the redistribution of population (Abel and Sander, 2014).

16 Based on regional classification of the UN, South East Asia, including Oceania.

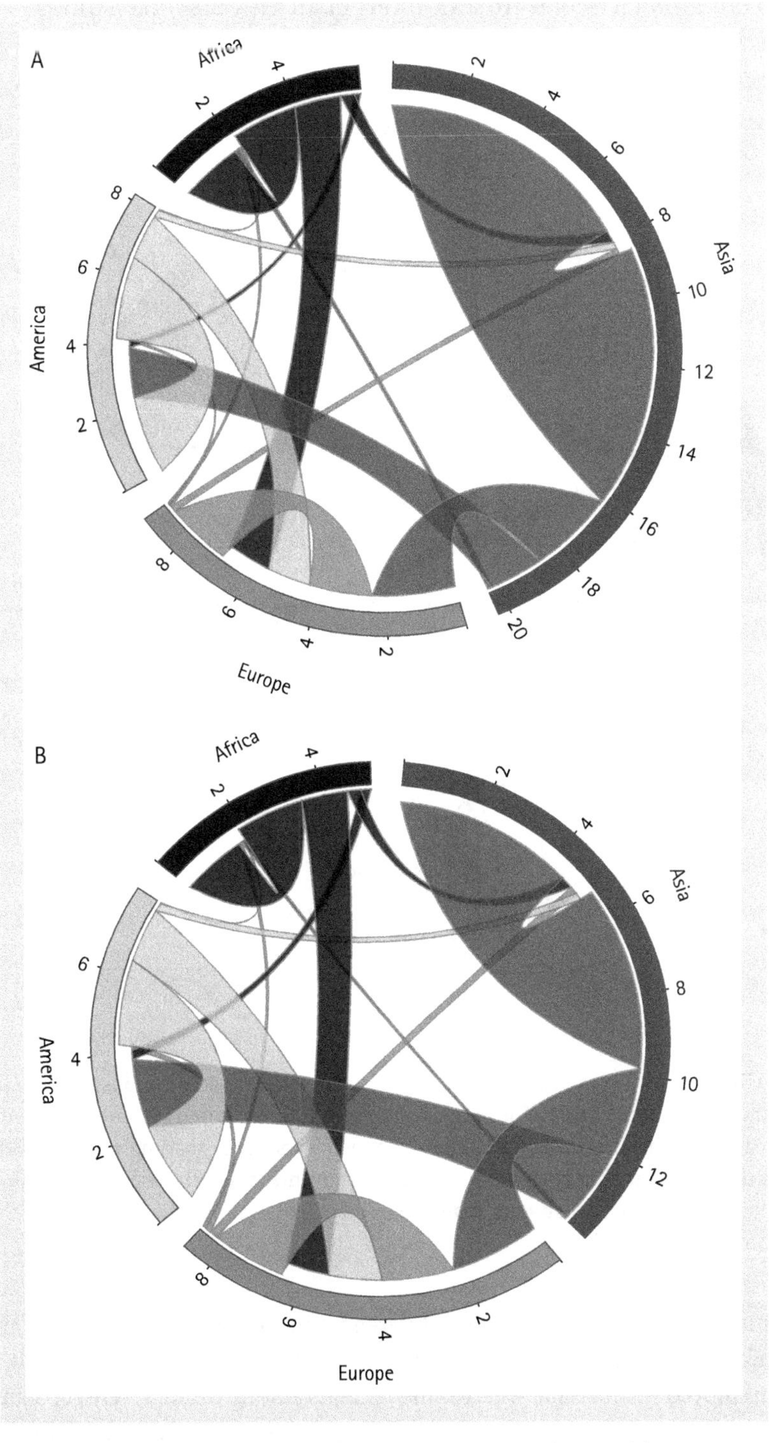

FIGURE 7.2 Circular plots of migration flows between and within world regions in 2005–10 for **(A)** males and **(B)** females (see Abel and Sander, 2014 for details). The origins and destinations of migrants (Africa, Asia, Europe, and America) are represented by the circle's segments. The direction of the flow is encoded by both the shading and a gap between the flow and the destination's segment. The volume of movement is indicated by the width of the flow. Tick marks on the circle segments show the number of migrants in millions.

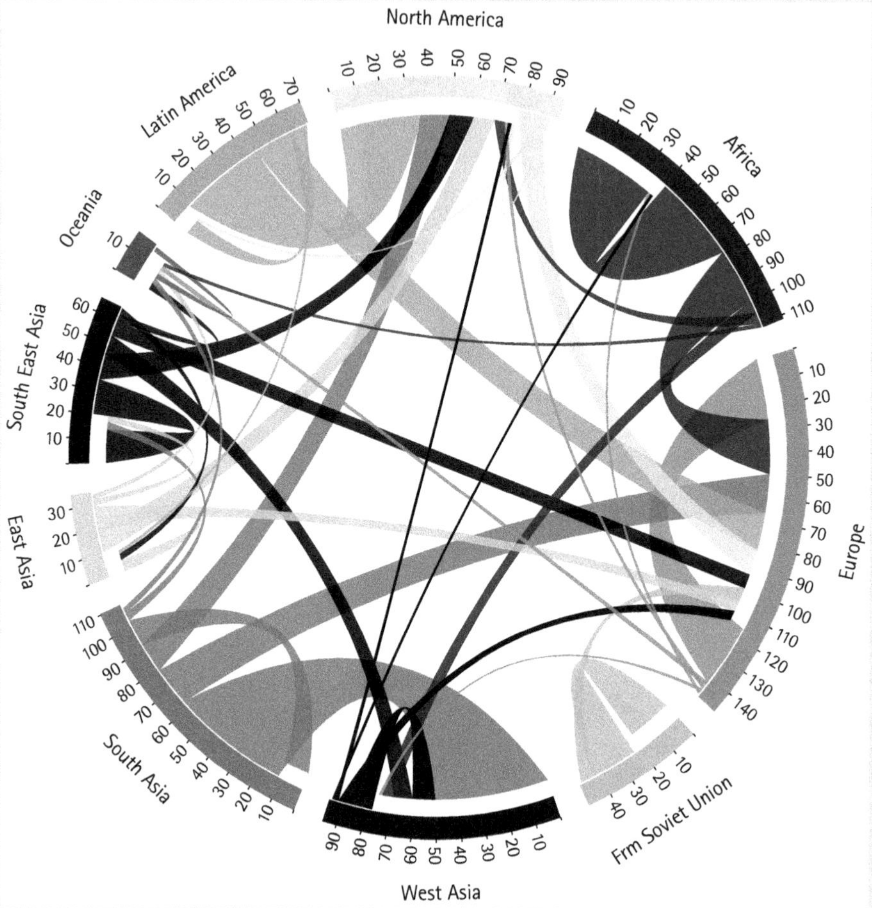

FIGURE 7.3 Circular plots of migration flows between and within world regions in 2005–10 (see Abel and Sander, 2014 for details). The origins and destinations of migrants are represented by the circle's segments. The direction of the flow is encoded by both the shading and a gap between the flow and the destination's segment. The volume of movement is indicated by the width of the flow. Tick marks on the circle segments show the number of migrants in millions. Only the largest 75 per cent of flows are shown.

Our estimates point to strong gender differences in migration, especially in movements within and from Asia. An estimated 7.7 million men (or 35 per cent of all flows among men) moved within Asia, whereas movements among women were substantially lower, with 4.6 million (or 25 per cent of all flows among women). In contrast, migration from Asia to the USA was characterized by a higher share of women (1.8 million women vs 1.5 million men). Substantial movements of female nurses and doctors from countries such as the Philippines to the USA and Canada may go some way to explain the female dominance of migration from Asia to the USA (Clark et al., 2006).

Figure 7.3 depicts our estimates of bilateral migration flows within and between ten regions in 2005–10. The high volume of migration within Asia appears to be mostly due to substantial movements from South Asia and India to the oil-rich Gulf States in West Asia. The patterns of movements between regions confirm earlier observations based on European harmonized flow data (Beer et al., 2010; Raymer et al., 2011), as well as fragmented data on migrant stocks and international flows for selected countries (see, e.g. Zlotnik, 1999). This earlier work demonstrated the dominance of migration from less to more developed countries in North America, Oceania, Europe, and—at increasing rates—the Gulf States in West Asia, alongside movements between developing countries.

The comprehensive overview of contemporary global migration flows as shown in Figure 7.3 uncovers several important features of international migration (for details, see Abel and Sander, 2014). First, the dominance of within-region flows in Africa over movements to a different continent. Second, the high spatial concentration of migrants in a relatively small number of flows from South Asia to other regions, especially to West Asia and to North America. And, third, a number of longer distance intercontinental movements through the centre of the circular migration plot.

Little attention has been paid in the literature to the gendered nature of international migration flows, owing largely to the lack of adequate data. Figure 7.4 confirms the presumption that movements to the Gulf States in West Asia are dominated by male migrants, whereas migration flows from South Asia to North America and Europe (most prominently the UK) are dominated by female migrants. The data underlying the migrant flows shown in Figure 7.4 are the same as those in Figure 7.3. The only difference between the figures pertains to the colouring of the bilateral flows. In Figure 7.4, flows are coloured based on the sex ratio (women/men) of each bilateral flow. All flows with a sex ratio of 0.5 or lower (suggesting a male-dominated flow) are coloured dark grey, whereas flows with a sex ratio of 1.5 or higher (suggesting a female-dominated flow) are coloured black. All flows with a more even sex ratio (0.5 to 1.5) are coloured light grey.

Migration within and between Africa, Europe, and Latin America is characterized by a remarkably even sex ratio, whereas migration from South Asia shows substantial differences in the sizes of flows by gender, which are strongly dependent on the destination of migrants. Movements from South Asia to North America are comprised of mostly women, whereas migration flows from South Asia to West Asia and from South East Asia to West Asia are dominated by male migrants.

What explains the movements among women from South Asia to North America? Canadian immigration statistics on the composition of immigrants by origin, occupation, visa category, and gender suggest substantial movements of female health care professionals from South Asia to Canada (Clark et al., 2006). Figure 7.5 provides some empirical evidence for the notion of skilled female labour migration to North America, Singapore, and the UK. Showing the ten largest country-to-country migration flows for women with origins and destinations of these flows arranged based on gross national income per capita in PPP (constant 2005 international $), Figure 7.5 highlights the dominance of flows from lower- to higher-income countries (UN, 2012). Not surprisingly, the largest female migrant flow (800,000 migrants) in 2005–10 went from Mexico to the

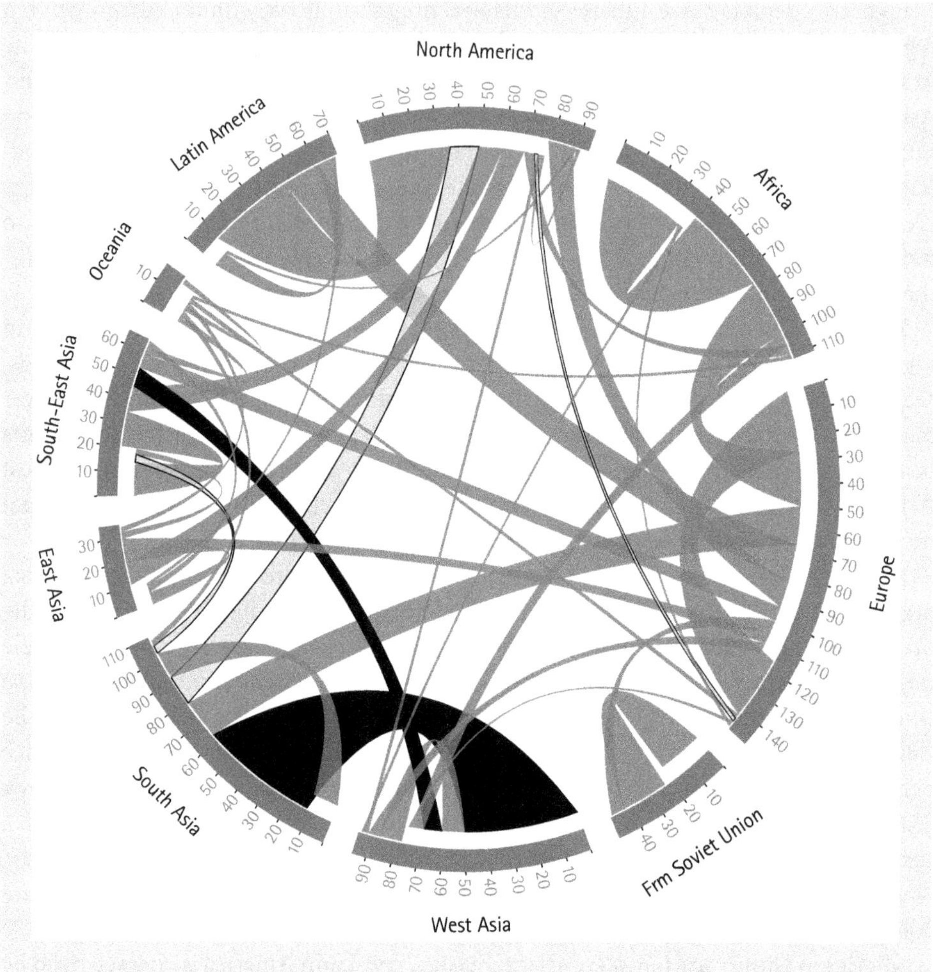

FIGURE 7.4 Circular plots of migration flows between and within world regions in 2005–10. The colour of the flow indicates the sex ratio (female/males) of the bilateral flow: black shading indicates less than 0.5 women for each men moving; grey shading indicates a sex ratio between 0.5 and 1.5; and light grey shading indicates more than 1.5 women moving for each men. The direction of the flow is encoded by a gap between the flow and the destination's segment. The volume of movement is indicated by the width of the flow. Tick marks on the circle segments show the number of migrants in millions. Only the largest 75 per cent of flows are shown.

USA, followed by 320,000 women moving from India to the USA, and just under 300,000 women moving from India to the United Arab Emirates.

The Philippines and China are also important origins of female migrants moving to the USA, confirming earlier findings about large volumes of Philippino nurses moving to more developed countries that are experiencing shortages of health care professionals (Clark et al., 2006). Noteworthy is the one-way nature of the ten largest female migrant flows, with India being the only country that is both an origin and a destination of these flows.

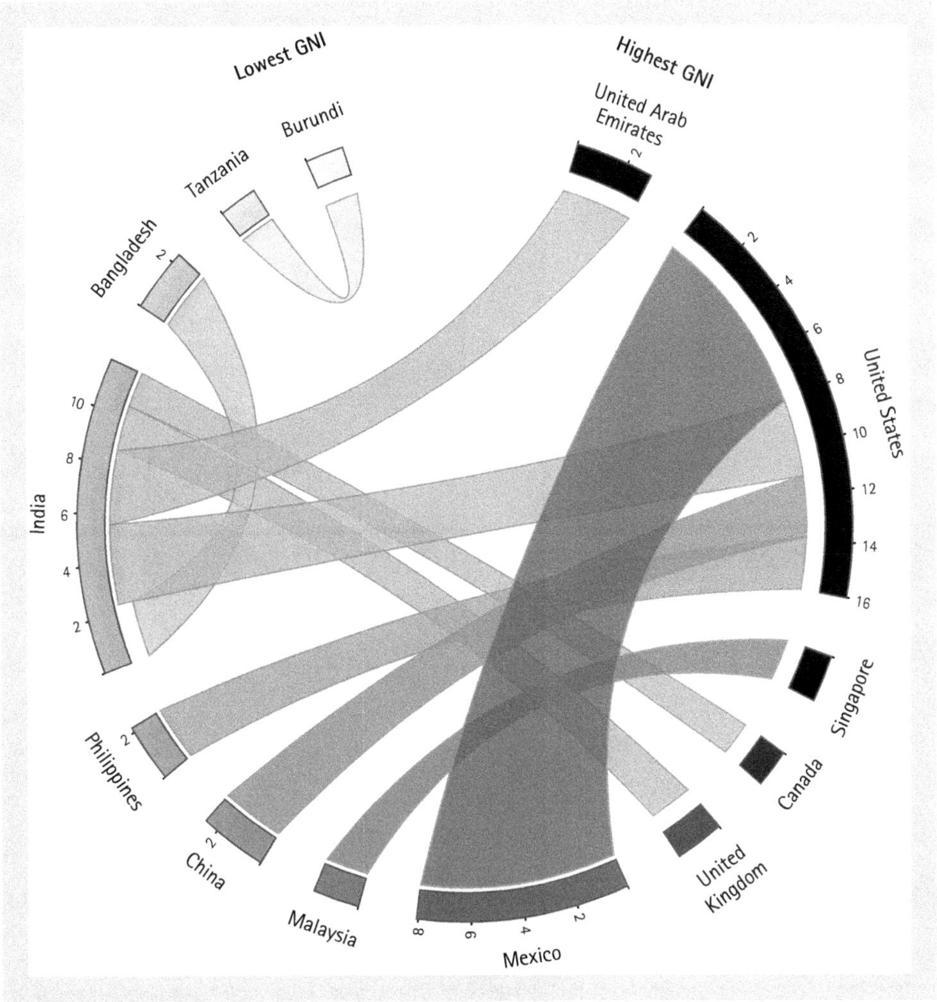

FIGURE 7.5 Circular plots of the 10 largest bilateral migration flows in 2005–10 for females. The direction of the flow is encoded by the shading and a gap between the flow and the destination's segment. The volume of movement is indicated by the width of the flow. Tick marks on the circle segments show the number of migrants in 100,000s.

The ten largest international migrant flows among men reveal a remarkably different picture compared with that for women. Figure 7.6 shows that, for men, the USA is a less prominent destination, owing largely to the attractiveness of the Gulf States for male labour migrants.

Among the ten largest flows in the world, only two went to the USA (originating in Mexico and China), whereas the Gulf States were the destinations of five of the largest flows. The origins of large male migrant flows differed substantially from those of women. For example, flows from Bangladesh to India and to the Gulf contained 1.3 million men, but only 200,000 women.

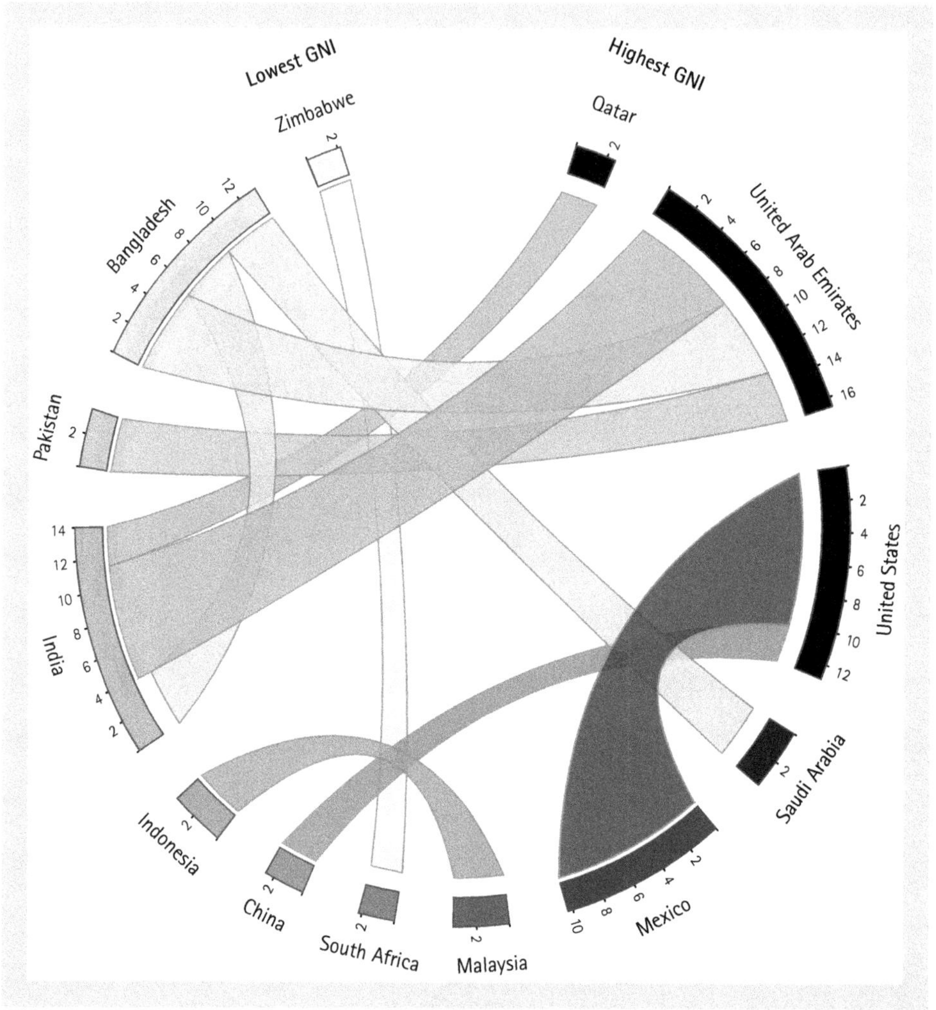

FIGURE 7.6 Circular plots of the 10 largest bilateral migration flows in 2005–10 for males. The direction of the flow is encoded by the shading and a gap between the flow and the destination's segment. The volume of movement is indicated by the width of the flow. Tick marks on the circle segments show the number of migrants in 100,000s.

For the new set of WIC projections, we extracted from our flow estimates information on the intensity of immigration and emigration for each country in the period 2005–10 disaggregated by age and sex. These immigration and emigration rates serve as the basis for our assumptions about future migration. Owing to lack of space, we present in Figures 7.7 and 7.8 only the ten countries in the more developed world (left) and the less developed world (right) with the highest immigration and emigration intensities in 2005–10. Rates were calculated using each country's population in 2005.

Figure 7.8 depicts the more and less developed countries with the highest emigration rates in 2005–10. The overall pattern is one of much lower emigration rates compared

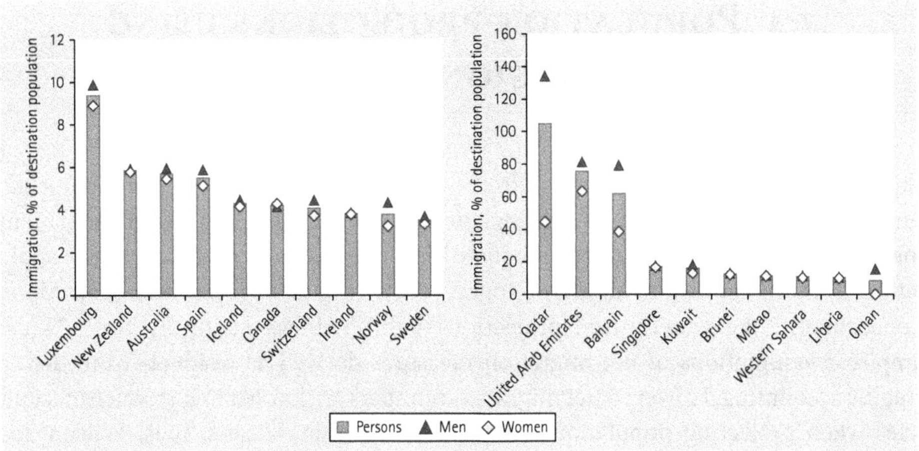

FIGURE 7.7 The top ten *immigration* countries (in per cent of population) among more developed (left) and less developed (right) countries in 2005–10.

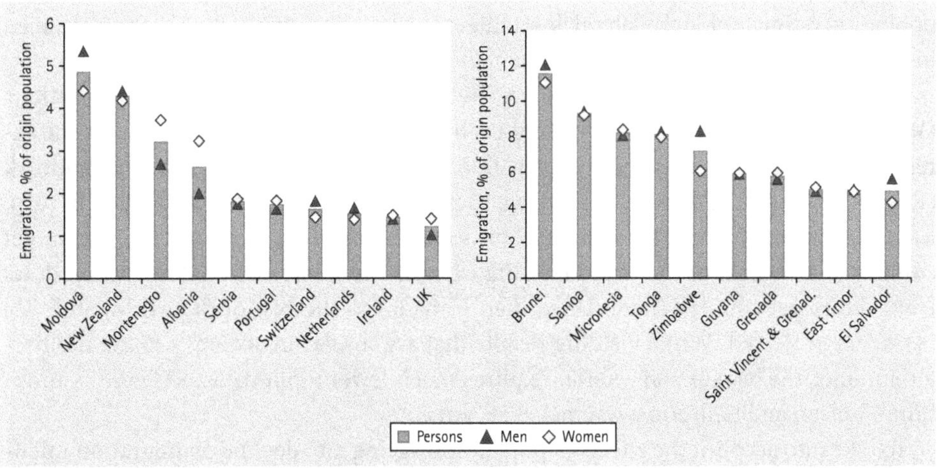

FIGURE 7.8 The top ten *emigration* countries (in per cent of population) among more developed (left) and less developed (right) countries in 2005–10.

with the immigration rates shown in Figure 7.7. Moreover, gender differences are stronger for emigration from more developed countries than from less developed ones (with the exception of Zimbabwe, which records strong male labour migration to South Africa). High intensities of emigration from several Eastern European countries (e.g. Moldova, Montenegro, Albania, and Serbia) can be expected to accelerate population ageing and decline in these countries. As we discuss in section 7.5, the projected size of populations in these countries strongly depends on whether assumptions about future trends are made in terms of absolute numbers of emigrants or in terms of emigration rates.

7.4 Population projections using a bi-regional model

The accurate projection of migration in the long run is one of the most difficult challenges in population forecasting. The high temporal volatility in net migration in many countries coupled with the lack of adequate bilateral flow data has hindered the application of multiregion flow models (Rogers, 1995) in global population projections. Consequently, the widely used projections published biannually by the UN use simplistic assumptions of net migration measures derived as residuals from demographic accounting. However, net migration numbers are known to introduce inaccuracies when projecting populations (Raymer et al., 2012; Rogers, 1995; Wilson and Bell, 2004).

The global population WIC projections presented in this volume depart from the common practice of focusing on a convergence of net migration rates towards zero. Instead, we apply a multiregion projection model to forecast global population. The baseline migration data for the projection model are obtained from the application of a methodology to estimate global bilateral flow tables from known migration stock totals detailed in section 7.3. A more detailed discussion of the methodology is given in Abel (2013a).

Multiregional projection models are frequently used in subnational projections (Wilson, 2011). Rather than projecting each country-to-country flow, we use the bi-regional model as a spatial aggregation of the full multiregional framework (Rogers, 1995). In the bi-regional setting, each country in the world is handled in turn. Migration to and from each country is projected by dividing the world into the target country and the rest of the world (see Figure 7.9). Then, international migration flows from the target country (here: USA, then Canada) to the rest of the world, and vice versa, are projected. While yielding results that are similar in accuracy to the multiregion model, the bi-regional version requires much fewer input data and fewer assumptions (Wilson and Bell, 2004; Raymer et al., 2012).

To take into account the effects of population ageing and decline on migration intensities, our migration assumptions correspond to probabilities rather than absolute numbers. The assumption of constant probabilities rather than constant absolute numbers of migrants can, over time, produce changes in the absolute flows as a function of changing national population size (for emigration) or world population size (for immigration). Using a transitions framework, we compute emigration probabilities in 2005–10 using the origin population in 2005, conditional upon survival to 2010. Immigration probabilities for a given country are calculated using the population in the rest of the world in 2005, conditional upon survival to 2010. Directional migration flows are then projected as the product of migration probabilities and the population in the origin (for emigration) and the rest of the world (for immigration). As with all bi-regional models, a small adjustment is made at each five-year projection step to ensure that total emigration across all countries equals total immigration.

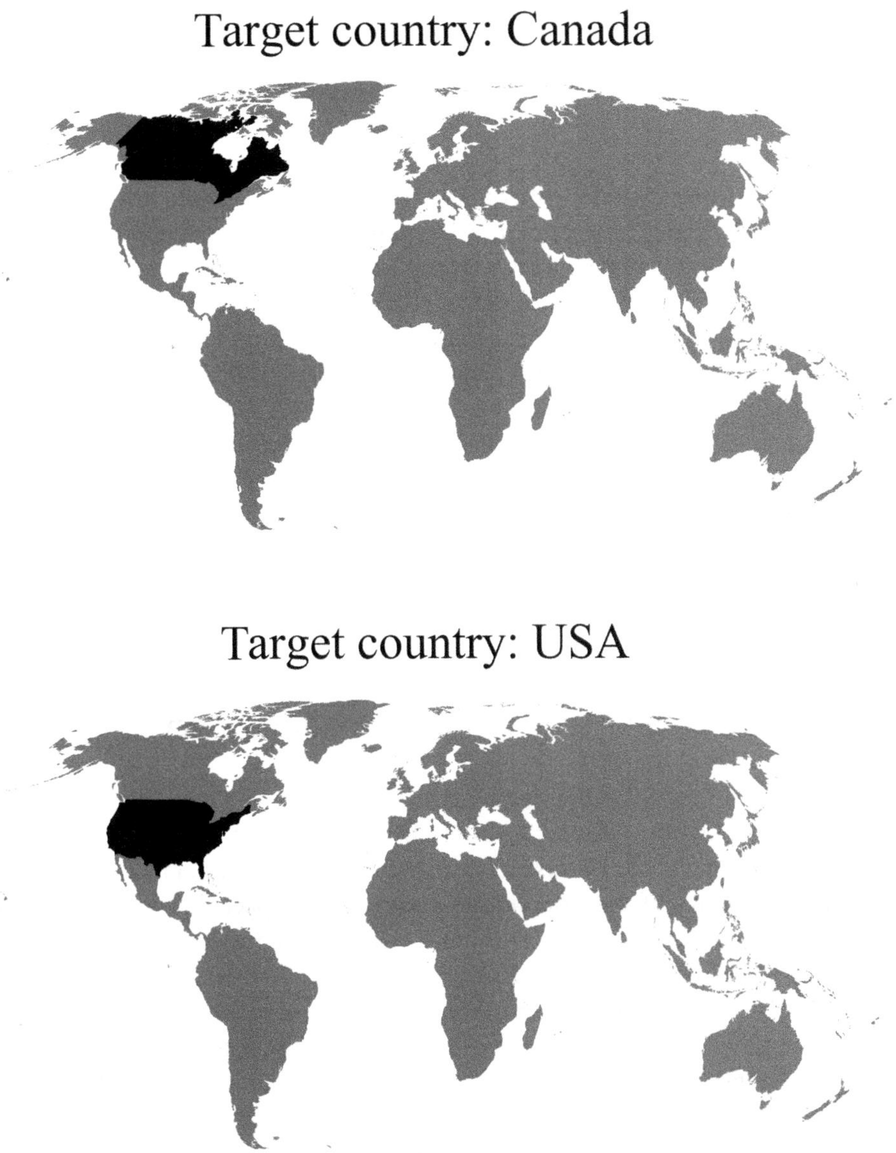

FIGURE 7.9 Dividing the world in a target country and the rest-of-the-world in the bi-regional model using USA and Canada as examples.

7.5 Expert views on the future of migration

Future intensities and spatial patterns of international migration will be shaped by myriad forces, ranging from economic development to policy interaction to demographic trends. Such complexities render any approach to projecting global migration trajectories naturally difficult and lead to a large degree of uncertainty about future trends. Consequently, international projection-making agencies commonly use simplistic assumptions of net-migration converging to zero over the projection horizon, despite sustained increases in net migration in many developed countries.

The bi-regional projection model allows us to circumvent the aforementioned problems by making assumptions for immigration and emigration flows. We tackle the challenging task of making plausible assumptions about future international migration by drawing on expert views about the future trajectory of migration, which were collected using a structured online survey (referred to as source experts' views hereafter) and a two-day expert group meeting (referred to as meta-experts' views hereafter).

7.5.1 Source experts' views from the online survey

The IIASA–Oxford online survey was sent to all members of international population associations in mid-2011.[17] The survey's objective was to obtain source experts' views on the likely impact of various factors on future immigration and emigration levels to/from a particular country of the respondent's choice. The impact that economic, demographic, environmental, and policy factors may have on migration combine the various pull and push forces prevailing in more developed and less developed countries, and were formulated as neutral arguments. For example, one argument on economic growth reads: 'Remittances will become more important for the economic development of migrant-sending countries'. A full list of the arguments pertaining to five different forces is given in Appendix 7.1.

For each of the 30 arguments, the experts were asked:

'Based on your understanding of current scientific knowledge and with reference to the period up to 2030, do you think the argument is... (very likely to be wrong to very likely to be right)'

'If the above argument were completely true, what effect would this have on future levels of immigration? (strongly decreasing to strongly increasing)'

'If the above argument were completely true, what effect would this have on future levels of emigration? (strongly decreasing to strongly increasing)'

[17] See Chapter 2 for a detailed discussion on the online survey.

Three key indicators are provided as follows.

1. Validity, ranging from 0 to 1.0, indicates whether a given argument is likely to be true, based on five predefined response options and the validity score attached to them.
2. Impact, assessing the hypothetical influence of a given trend on migration. The predefined range was from −1.0 (strongly negative) to +1.0 (strongly positive).
3. Net impact, assessing validity and impact in combination. This was calculated by multiplying the validity score with the impact score.

The respondents were also asked to give a point estimate for the number of net migrants they expect the country of their choice to gain or lose. Unfortunately, the directional flow estimates presented in Abel and Sander (2014) and summarized in section 7.3 were not yet finalized at the time the IIASA–Oxford survey was distributed. Thus, we relied on the UN estimates of net numbers of migrants as the only migration data set available for the period 2005–10 that covered all countries in the world. The results from this section of the survey were inconclusive, reflecting the dearth of migration theory that could provide guidance in determining future trajectories, and the fact that scientific endeavour into thinking about future international migration has lagged behind fertility and mortality. Moreover, respondents noted problems with setting the 80 per cent range using the web interface, which may explain a large degree of disagreement among respondents about future net migration levels for individual countries. Given that the bi-regional projection model requires assumptions for immigration and emigration flows, rather than net migration, we found the assessment of the impact of arguments more beneficial than the point estimates for setting migration assumptions.

The 30 arguments pertaining to economic, demographic, climatic, and policy impacts on migration were grouped into five clusters. Towards the end of the survey, respondents were asked to assign weights of relative importance to each of these clusters. The weights sum to 100 per cent for all clusters combined. We computed the mean cluster weights over all respondents and countries, as they showed only minor regional differences.

Overall, we obtained 122 responses in the migration module of the survey. Table 7.6 shows the distribution of the responses across regions for which responses were given. There was a reasonable spread across regions, with a considerable share of responses for North America and Europe.

Figures 7.10 and 7.11 summarize source experts' views on the likely future trajectory of global migration flows over the period 2010–30. The figures indicate the relative weight of each of the five clusters and the mean net impact of each argument at region level. The relative weight of each cluster is indicated by the slice of the circle devoted to them. For example, the largest slice of the circle is devoted to the cluster of arguments on economic factors as this cluster was expected to have the strongest relative impact. Within each cluster, the arguments are arranged based on their identification (ID). The net impact, calculated simply by multiplying the impact score with the validity score pertaining to each argument, is shown on a scale from −0.8 to 0.8. Values below 0 (inside of the solid black line) cause the intensity of migration to decrease; values above 0 (outside of the solid black line) cause migration to increase. To aid visual examination of the survey

Table 7.6 IIASA–Oxford Survey Responses by Region

Region	Responses
North America	29
Latin America	17
Europe	36
Former Soviet Union	1
West Asia	5
South Asia	9
East Asia	3
South East Asia	7
Oceania	6
Africa	9
Total	122

results, the argument ID and an abridged version of the argument text are shown on the outside of the circular graph.

Figure 7.10 depicts the net impact of each argument on future immigration, calculated as region-specific mean net impact. The effect that each argument is expected to have on immigration varies substantially across regions, reflecting the well-established pattern of sending and receiving countries. For example, argument M 1–7 'Economic recession' has a negative impact on immigration to North America and Europe, and a positive impact on immigration to Africa. The latter effect appears to be primarily driven by return movements of African migrants as a result of less demand for migrant workers in North America and Europe. The overall picture is one of more positive than negative effects of arguments on future immigration. Arguments pertaining to climate and migration costs are expected to increase migration levels, although the relative importance attributed to these two clusters is low, as indicated by the small slice of the circle.

Arguments pertaining to economic forces are expected to have the strongest impact on immigration levels. Immigration is expected to increase if remittances become increasingly important for economic development in sending countries, if income differentials between countries further widen, and if population ageing results in increasing labour and skill shortages in more developed countries. At the other end of the spectrum, immigration to North America and Europe would decline if foreign direct investment in developing countries as a stimulus to economic growth rectifies the imbalance between supply and demand in the labour markets in those countries (M 1-5), or if global wage levels converge in the long run (M 1-8). The strongest negative impact is given to economic recessions in industrialized countries and the resulting decline in demand for migrants (M 1-7).

The impact of each argument on future emigration (see Figure 7.11) reveals larger differences between regions than for immigration. The impacts are expected to be very strong for Africa (white circle) and East Asia (light grey triangle), whereas the

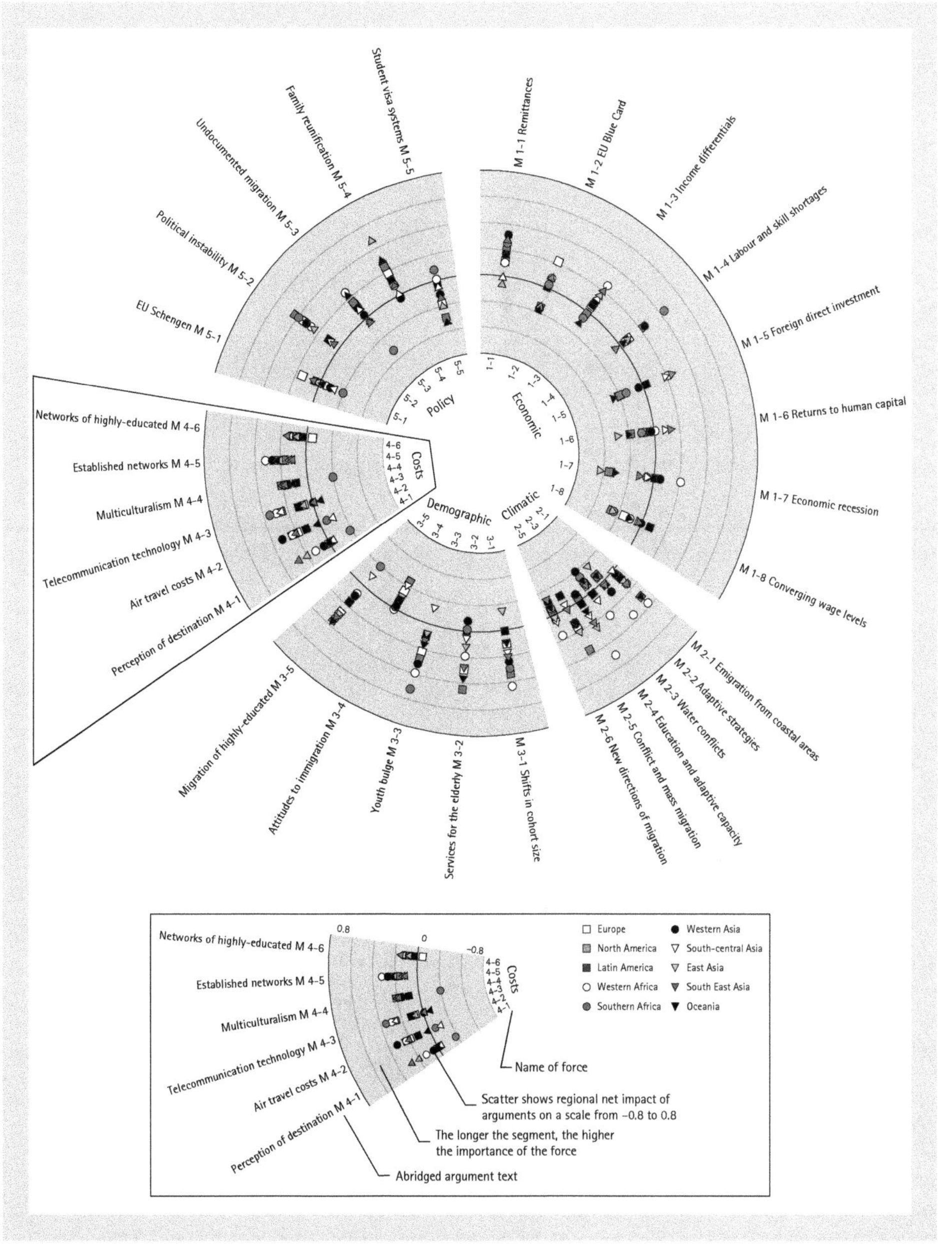

FIGURE 7.10 Mean net impact by region for all arguments about future immigration. EU: European Union.

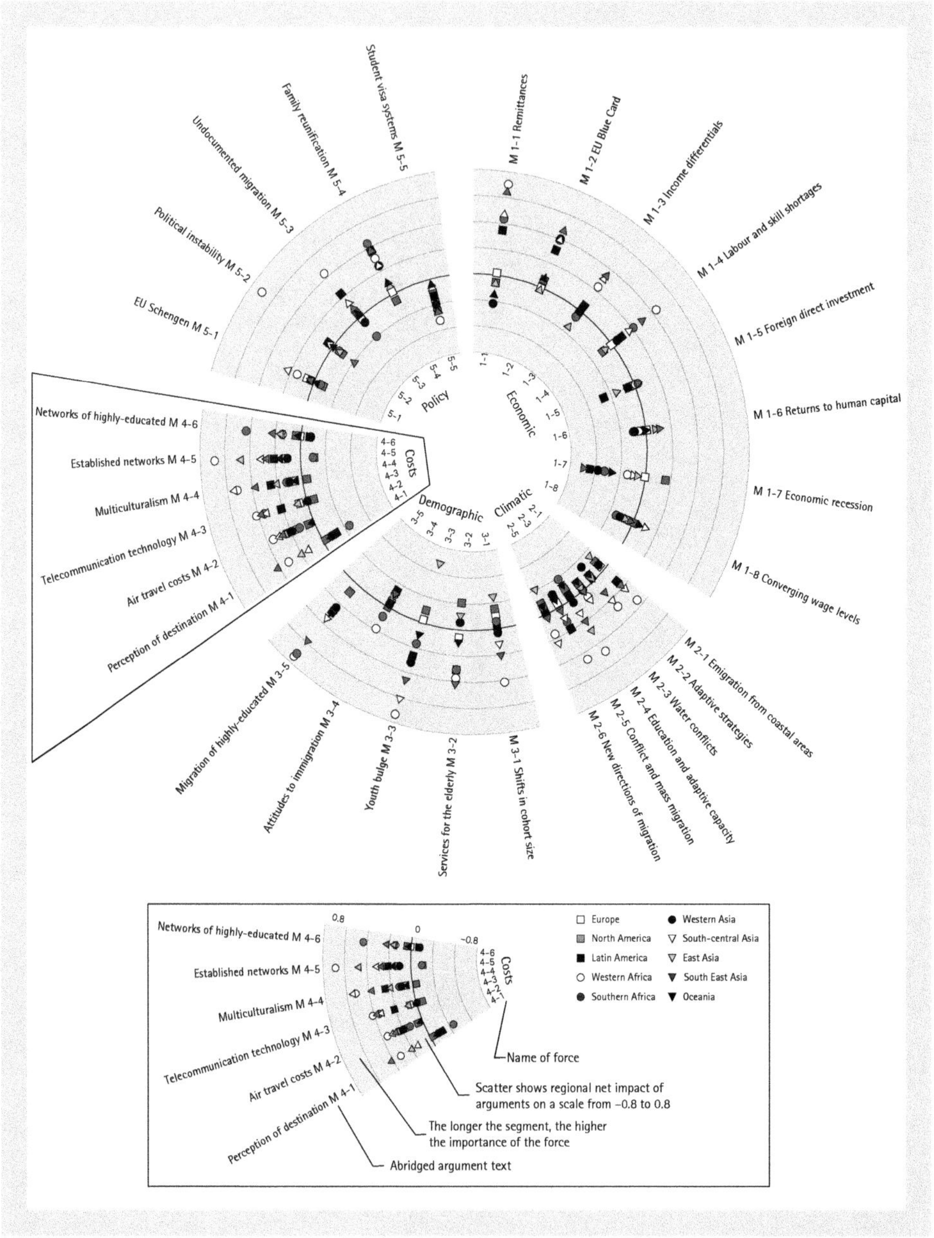

FIGURE 7.11 Mean net impact by region for all arguments about future emigration. EU: European Union.

expected impact on emigration from Europe and North America is closer to zero for most arguments. Noteworthy are the strong positive impacts of arguments on remittances (M 1-1), a demographic youth bulge (M 3-3), education differentials (M 3-5), and family reunification (M 5-4) on emigration.

In summary, it appears that overall trends in future migration will be driven mostly by economic and demographic developments, as well as selected policy-related factors. Environmental forces are expected to have a strong impact, but the validity scores of the arguments within this cluster were the lowest of all 30 arguments, and the relative weight of the cluster was the smallest of all clusters. These results partly reflect the large degree of uncertainty about potential negative impacts of climate change on migration, with most environmentally-induced migration expected to be within countries rather than across borders.

7.5.2 Meta-expert's views

These results from the IIASA–Oxford survey were complemented by an expert group meeting held at the University of Colorado at Boulder, USA, in the autumn of 2011. The participants, representing different geographic regions, scientific disciplines, and areas of expertise included nine meta-experts, one representative of the University of Colorado, and three representatives of the Wittgenstein Centre for Demography and Global Human Capital (WIC).[18] Selected results from the survey were presented to the meeting participants to serve as a basis for discussion. All participants stressed the importance of departing from convergence to zero assumptions and making plausible assumptions about future migration flows. They also emphasized the need for more adequate data on contemporary migration flows. The lack of flow data and the dominance of zero convergence scenarios in existing global population projections meant that discussing future levels of immigration and emigration for each country in the world was too ambitious a task.

In considering the issues related to the dearth of existing migration projections that could have served as a basis for discussions about future numbers of migrants, the aim of the meeting was to elaborate in qualitative, rather than quantitative, terms the likely future trajectory of migration flows to and from the major regions. The meta-experts were asked to identify the arguments from the survey that, in their opinion, best capture the key determinants of migration that are likely to be most influential in shaping future trends. The seven arguments identified by the participants are shown in Figures 7.12 and 7.13, and listed in Table 7.7. In several round table discussions, we then elaborated how these arguments will shape migration to and from major regions. Experts expressed their views on whether arguments would increase, decrease, or have no impact on immigration and emigration. Figures 7.12 and 7.13 depict the outcomes of the roundtable discussions and provide a comparison with the results of the survey. The meta-experts were

[18] Meta-experts participating in the meeting were Ayla Bonfiglio, Philip Rees, James Raymer, Andrei Rogers, Graeme Hugo, Siew-Ean Khoo, Joel Cohen, David Coleman, Guy Abel, Bill Butz, Fernando Riosmena, Nikola Sander and Jeffrey Passel.

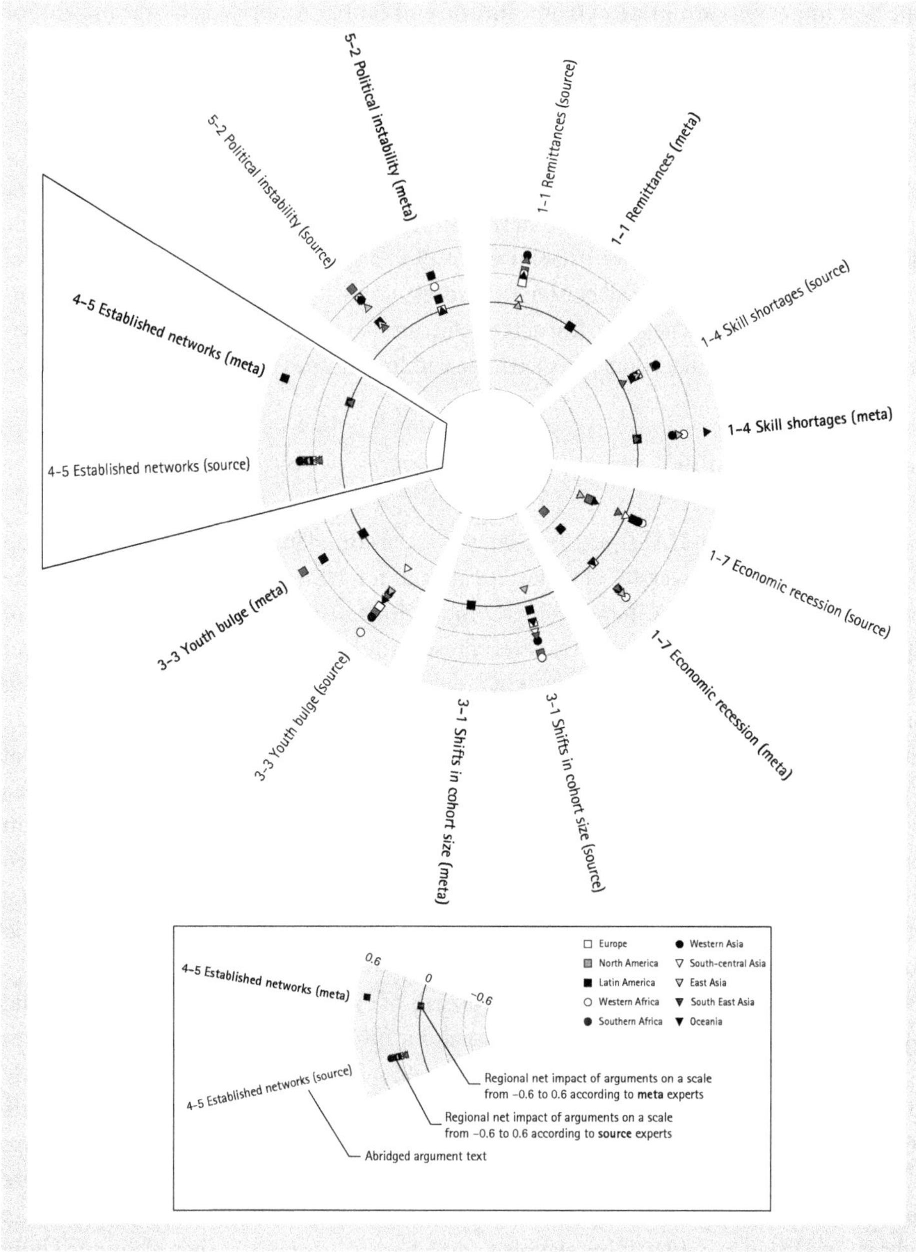

FIGURE 7.12 Expert views on future immigration among source experts (normal font) and meta-experts (bold font) for seven arguments identified by meta-experts as having a strong impact on future trends. Results for source experts are identical to those shown in Figure 7.10. EU: European Union.

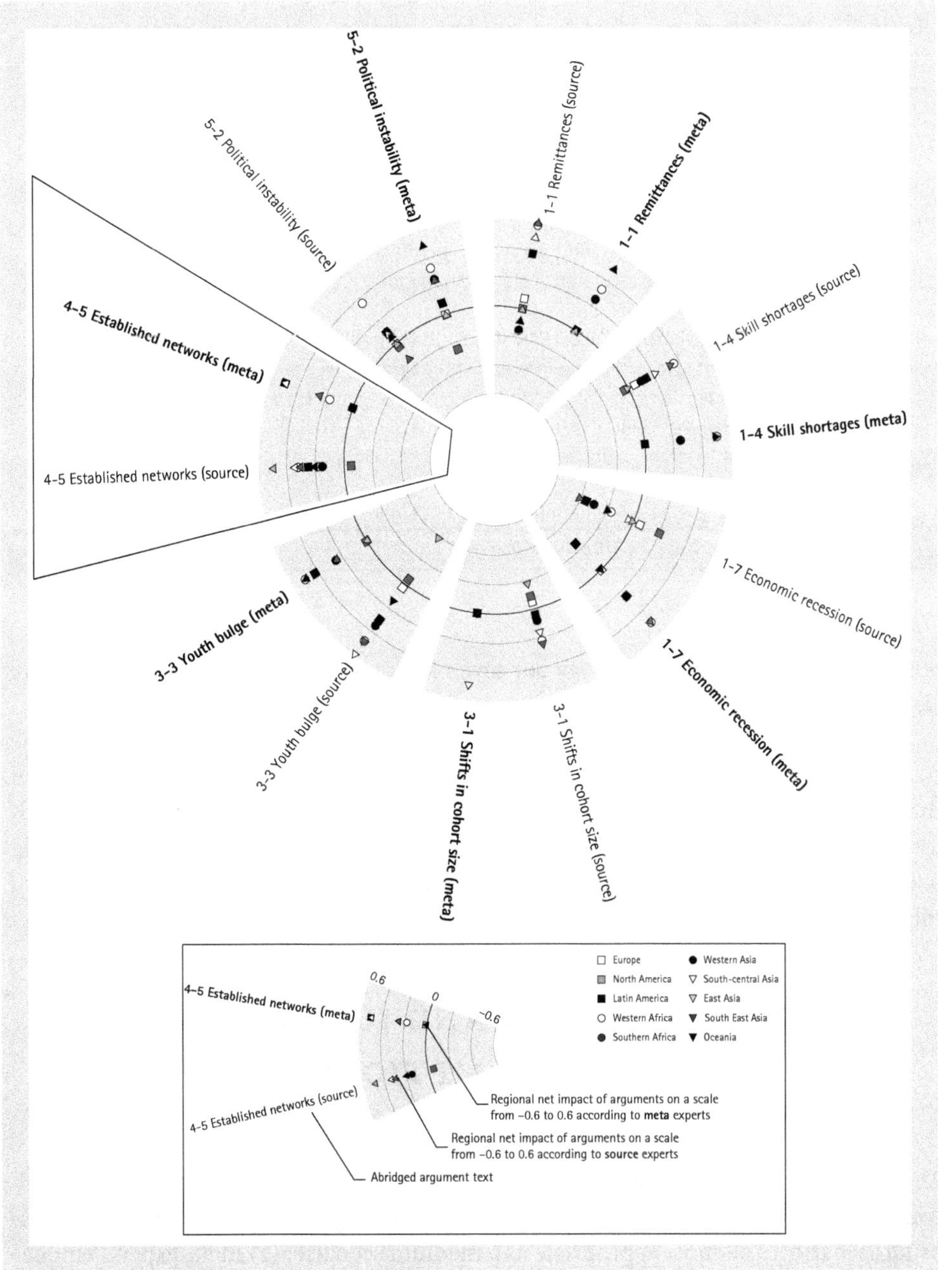

FIGURE 7.13 Expert views on future emigration among source experts (normal font) and meta-experts **(bold font)** for seven arguments identified by meta-experts as having a strong impact on future trends. Results for source experts are identical to those shown in Figure 7.11. EU: European Union.

Table 7.7 Key Arguments Identified by Meta-experts as Having a Strong Impact on Future Trends

Identification	Argument text
1-1	Remittances will become more important for the economic development of migrant-sending countries.
1-4	Temporary labour migration will increasingly compensate for skills shortages in developed countries and thus replace permanent migration.
1-7	Major economic recessions/stagnation in industrialized countries will lead to less demand for migrants.
3-1	Shifts in cohort size, especially related to the baby boom and bust, will play an important role in shaping international migration levels.
3-3	The propensity to move abroad among 15-29-year-olds will be particularly high in countries with a large 'youth bulge'.
4-5	International migration will mostly follow established paths and existing migrant networks.
5-2	Political instability and oppression in African and Middle Eastern countries will result in more people seeking political asylum in democratic countries.

broadly in agreement about the way our seven key arguments are likely to shape future trends.

The overall pattern of expert views suggests that prolonged economic recession in the traditional migrant-receiving countries in the developed world is the only argument that may cause immigration to the receiving countries and emigration from the traditional sending countries to decrease. All other arguments, especially those pertaining to cohort size and occurrence of a youth bulge, are expected to lead to higher volumes of migration.

7.6 Specification and Justifications of Assumptions

The development of assumptions for future immigration and emigration for each country in the world was primarily based on (1) meta-experts suggesting a 'business-as-usual scenario' to be most appropriate as a medium scenario; (2) meta-experts emphasizing the importance of accounting for changes in the size and age structure of origin populations through assumptions for migration rates rather than numbers; and (3) the net impact scores for the seven key arguments identified by the meta-experts.

The expert views collected in the IIASA–Oxford survey and subsequent discussions with meta-experts focused on the period 2010–60. Likely trends for the period 2060–2100 were not considered in the meeting because of major uncertainties concerning migration trends in the second half of the century. In light of this uncertainty, we assume a gradual convergence to zero net migration over the period 2060–2100. This is achieved by converging each country's immigration and emigration flows towards their average, so that each country's net migration reaches zero in the last projection period, 2095–2100.

7.6.1 The medium scenario

A 'business-as-usual' scenario assuming jump-off period rates to remain constant was suggested during the expert group meeting. A constant rates scenario was therefore preferred over a time series forecast, the assumption of turning points, or a projection model based on other projected covariates.

Our medium scenario therefore assumes immigration and emigration rates estimated for the period 2005–10 to remain constant throughout the projection horizon until 2060.[19] We make assumptions for rates rather than absolute numbers to take into account changes in the population size and age structure of origin populations. For example, using migration rates assumptions, we ensure that emigration from strongly ageing and weakly growing populations in Eastern Europe will decrease over the projected period. Adjustments are made to the constant rates assumption for 25 countries where rapid changes to migration trends occurred in the last decade (e.g. immigration to Spain), which are unlikely to persist until the year 2060 (Table 7.8).

7.6.2 Two alternative 'what if' scenarios

We drew on expert views regarding the impact of a set of arguments for future migration patterns and intensities for developing alternative immigration and emigration assumptions. The net impacts of seven key arguments for migration identified by the meta-experts as being most relevant in shaping future trajectories were translated into two 'what if' scenarios. The number of scenarios had to be limited to two so that the migration scenarios could be readily combined with the high and low scenarios for fertility and mortality. A key distinction between the two migration scenarios had to be that one results in lower levels of global migration flows, whereas the other results in higher global volumes. We therefore based the first scenario on the net impact scores of all key arguments that cause immigration to the traditional receiving countries and emigration from the traditional sending countries to decrease. The second scenario was based on the net impact scores of all key arguments that yield higher immigration to the receiving countries. The resulting scenarios can be summarized as follows.

The 'rise of the east' (referred to as RE scenario hereafter) scenario assumes economic stagnation in Europe and North America, resulting in restrictive migration policies.

[19] A table with the assumed immigration and emigration rates for each country is given in Appendix II.

Table 7.8 Percentage Change in Assumed Rates of Immigration and Emigration Over the First Two Projection Periods Under the Medium Scenario for Countries Where the Constant Rates Assumption Appears Not to be Plausible. For Example, Immigration Into Australia is Assumed to Decrease by 20 Per Cent in the Period 2010–15 to 2015–20

Country	Immigration	Emigration
Australia	-0.20	–
Austria	-0.20	–
Bahrain	-0.65	0.20
Burundi	-0.20	–
Czech Republic	-0.20	–
Greece	-0.20	–
Iceland	-0.20	–
Ireland	-0.20	–
Italy	-0.65	–
Kuwait	-0.20	–
Liberia	-0.20	–
Luxembourg	-0.20	–
Macao	-0.20	–
Micronesia	–	-0.20
Norway	-0.20	–
Qatar	-0.65	0.20
Samoa	–	-0.20
Singapore	-0.65	–
Spain	-0.65	–
Sweden	-0.20	–
Switzerland	-0.20	–
Tonga	–	-0.20
United Arab Emirates	-0.65	0.20
UK	-0.20	–
Zimbabwe	–	-0.20

South and South East Asia become increasingly attractive destinations, resulting in a shift in global migration patterns. Assumptions under this scenario are based on the mean net impact of argument 1–7, 'economic recession'.

The 'intensifying global competition' scenario (referred to as IGC scenario hereafter) assumes dynamic economic growth and social development, resulting in growing competition among governments and the private sector for (skilled) labour and natural resources, as well as between the traditional activities of agriculture and mining and industry, residential development and recreational activities. Economic growth in the developing world contributes towards rising levels of global mobility, which is paralleled by liberal immigration policies in the more developed world. Assumptions under this scenario are based on the mean net impact of arguments 1–4 'labour and skill shortages', 2–3 'water conflicts', 3–3 'youth bulge', 4–5 'established networks', and 5–2 'political instability'.

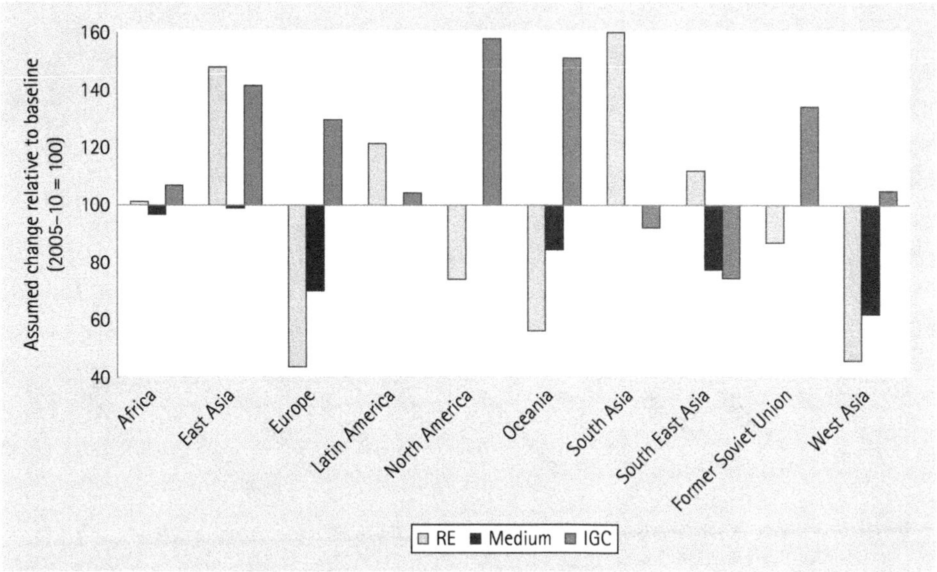

FIGURE 7.14 Translating expert views on future *immigration* into alternative scenarios. The assumed relative change in immigration volumes by region under the 'rise of the east' (RE), medium, and 'intensifying global competition' (IGC) scenarios. Immigration volumes in the jump-off period 2005–10 are set to 100.

The mean net impact scores were translated into a set of multipliers, which cause the global volume of flows to decrease under the RE scenario and to increase under the IGC scenario. The multipliers were region-specific and applied to all countries in a given region in the first two projection periods (2010–15 and 2015–20). After 2020, rates are then kept constant until 2055–60. Figures 7.14 and 7.15 show assumed region-specific changes in immigration and emigration between 2005–10 and 2015–20 under alternative scenarios. For most countries, migration intensities are assumed to stay constant under the medium scenario, with some exceptions in Europe, Oceania, South East Asia, and West Asia.

The traditional receiving countries in Europe, North America, and Oceania are assumed to record lower immigration volumes under the RE scenario and higher volumes under the IGC scenario. At the other end of the spectrum, East Asia, South Asia, and South East Asia are assumed to experience higher levels of immigration under the RE scenario. In East Asia, immigration volumes are assumed to rise under both the RE and the IGC scenarios, reflecting the sustained pattern of strong economic growth and hence the growing attractiveness of the region as a migrant destination.

To illustrate how expert opinion was translated into immigration and emigration assumptions for each of the 195 countries in the age–sex projections, Figure 7.16 shows the assumptions on future immigration for Austria.

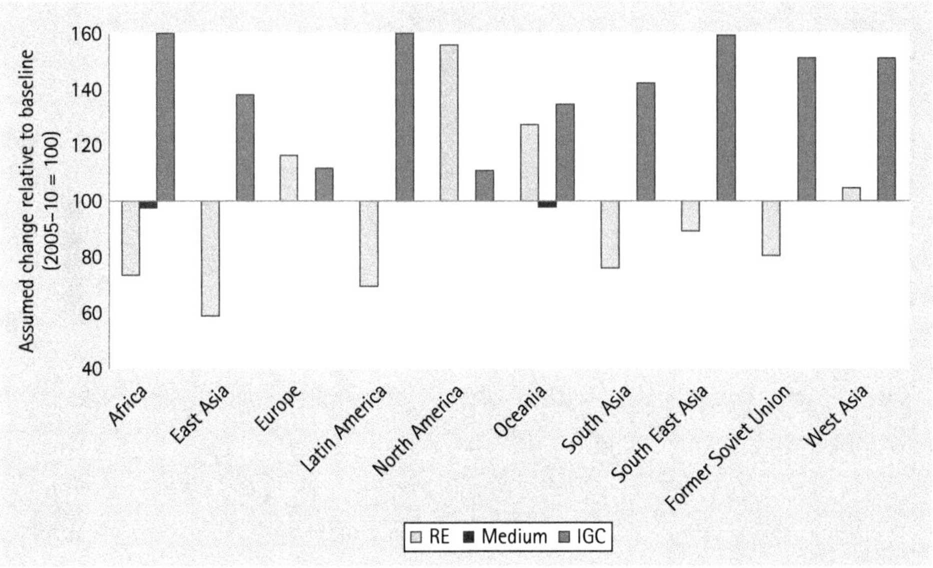

FIGURE 7.15 Translating expert views on future *emigration* into alternative scenarios. The assumed relative change in emigration volumes by region under the 'rise of the east' (RE), medium, and 'intensifying global competition' (IGC) scenarios. Emigration volumes in the jump-off period 2005–10 are set to 100.

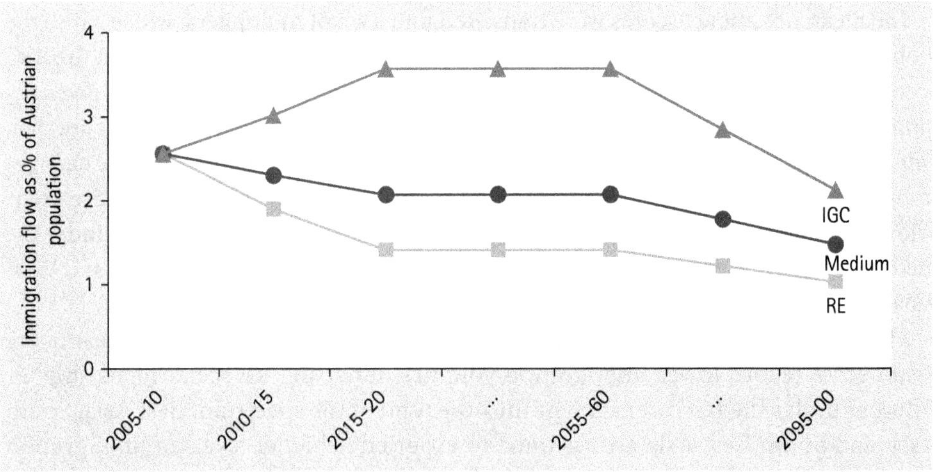

FIGURE 7.16 Assumed rates of immigration for Austria under alternative scenarios. Expert-based multipliers cause the estimated intensity of immigration in 2005–10 to decline under the 'rise of the east' (RE) scenario and to increase under the 'intensifying global competition' (IGC) scenario until 2015–20. Under the medium scenario, the estimated intensity in 2005–10 is assumed to decline slightly over the first two projected periods. All rates are assumed to remain constant over the period 2020–60. A gradual convergence to zero net migration is assumed for the period 2060–2100.

7.7 Projected numbers of migrants

This section presents selected results of the bi-regional cohort-component population projections by age and sex for 195 countries. We focus on the projected numbers of migrants at world, region, and country levels. A detailed discussion of the overall results of the population WIC projections for 195 countries and the human capital projections for 171 countries is provided in Chapters 10–12.

Figure 7.17 shows the projected number of global migrants under three alternative scenarios. In the 5-year period 2005–10, an estimated 40 million people changed their country of residence. Under the medium scenario, this number is projected to decline to 32 million in 2015–20 owing to the correction factors we applied under the medium scenario for the periods 2010–15 and 2015–20 to lower assumed volumes of immigration in selected countries. Because we draw on a bi-regional flow model to project migration, our assumption of decreasing immigration flows to countries like Spain and Singapore over the first two projected periods results in less emigration from the origin countries (e.g. Latin America for Spain and Malaysia for Singapore) and thus smaller numbers of global migrants. Under the IGC scenario, global migration volumes are projected to increase substantially compared with the medium scenario, whereas the decline under the RE scenario is more subtle. The decline in global migration under the RE scenario is small because of the assumed shift in spatial patterns of global migration. Destinations in Europe and North America become less attractive, whereas destinations in Asia become increasingly popular.

Under all three scenarios, the global number of migrants is projected to peak in the period 2040–45, with population ageing combined with our assumed Rogers–Castro

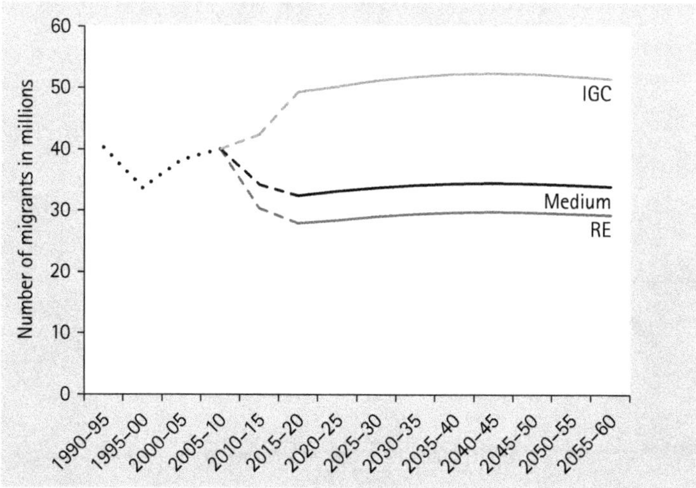

FIGURE 7.17 Estimated (1990–95 to 2005–10) and projected (2010–15 to 2055–60) number of global migrants moving over five-year periods under alternative scenarios. RE: 'rise of the east' scenario; IGC: 'intensifying global competition' scenario.

migration schedule causing numbers to decline thereafter. The dawning of an era of mass migration seems to be rather unlikely if current trends continue as assumed under the medium scenario.

Figures 7.18–7.20 depict the projected numbers of immigrants, emigrants, and resulting net migration by region under alternative scenarios. Differences between scenarios are most pronounced in the traditional destination regions in North America, West Asia, and Europe (for immigration) and the sending regions in South Asia and Africa (for emigration). Under the medium scenario, sub-Saharan population growth is projected to boost emigration numbers, although at lower rates than commonly assumed. Population ageing in many parts of the world, including East Asia, Latin America, and Europe, is projected to result in lower volumes of emigration from these ageing regions.

The overall pattern is one of projected increases in emigration from South Asia and Africa, much reduced losses in East Asia, smaller gains in West Asia and stable gains in North America and Europe. Since in the bi-regional model, immigration is projected as the product of the assumed immigration rate and population in the rest of the world, one could have expected a substantial increase in immigration numbers to North America and Europe as a result of global population growth. Figure 7.18 shows that the positive effect of population growth in the less developed world will be offset by widespread population ageing, which, under the assumption of a Rogers–Castro migration schedule, results in lower numbers of projected migrants.

Figure 7.21 shows the projected numbers of migrants for Austria until 2060. The results can be readily compared to the assumed immigration rates shown in Figure 7.16.

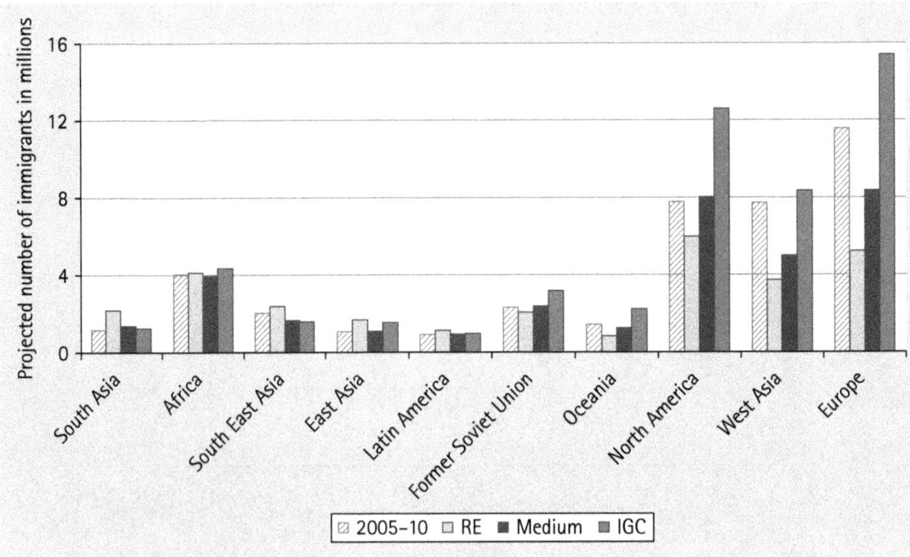

FIGURE 7.18 Estimated (2005–10) and projected (2055–60) number of *immigrants* moving over five-year periods under alternative scenarios, by region. RE: 'rise of the east' scenario; IGC: 'intensifying global competition' scenario.

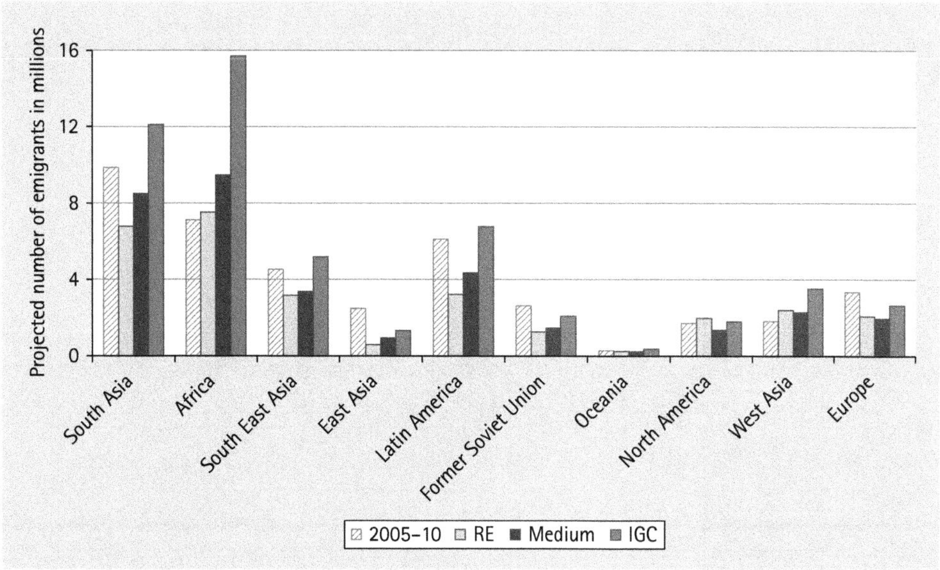

FIGURE 7.19 Estimated (2005–10) and projected (2055–60) number of *emigrants* moving over five-year periods under alternative scenarios, by region. RE: 'rise of the east' scenario; IGC: 'intensifying global competition' scenario.

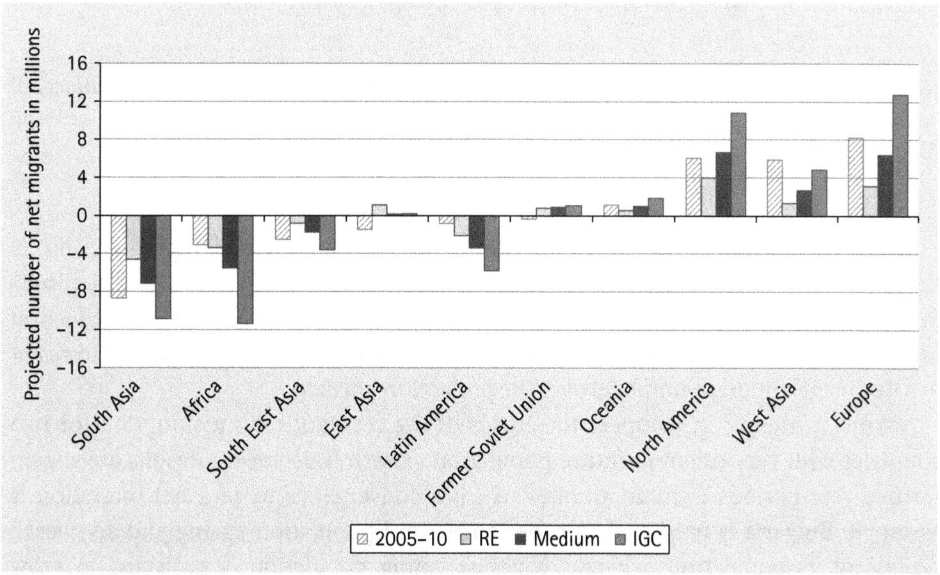

FIGURE 7.20 Estimated (2005–10) and projected (2055–60) number of *net migrants* under alternative scenarios, by region. RE: 'rise of the east' scenario; IGC: 'intensifying global competition' scenario.

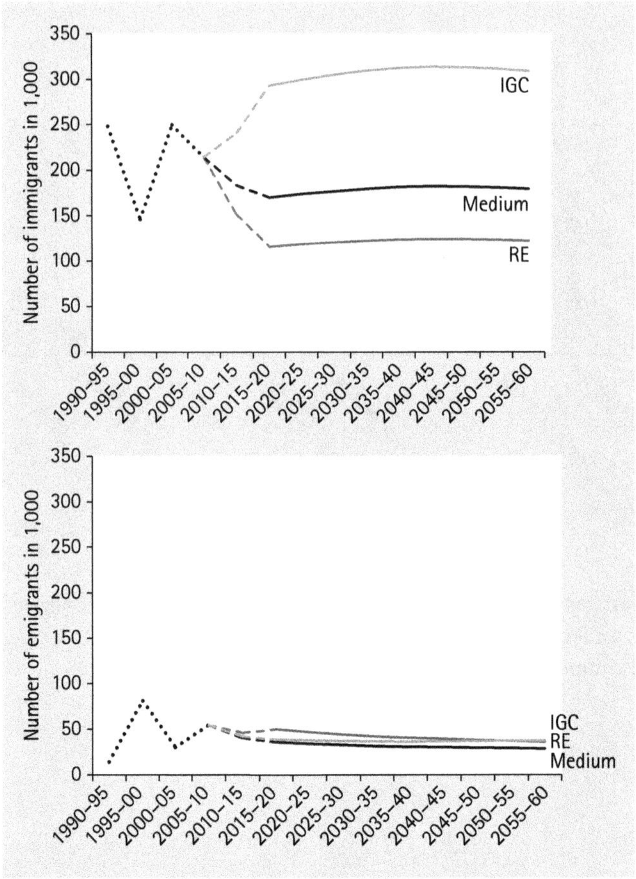

FIGURE 7.21 Estimated (1990–95 to 2005–10) and projected (2010–15 to 2055–60) numbers of *immigrants* and *emigrants* under alternative scenarios, Austria. RE: 'rise of the east' scenario; IGC: 'intensifying global competition' scenario.

Using a projection model based on rates rather than numbers highlights the effects that changes in population size and age structure have on migrant numbers. The results for Austria demonstrate that sub-Saharan population growth has no visible effect on projected numbers of immigrants. In contrast, population ageing is projected to result in a decline in emigrant numbers over the projection horizon.

Figures 7.22 and 7.23 compare the effects of the constant rates assumption for two countries with very different future population growth trajectories. Results are shown for five-year periods until 2060, after which a convergence to zero net migration is assumed. Bulgaria is predicted to experience rapid population ageing and an overall decline of its population, whereas Nigeria's young population is projected to grow strongly. The predicted number of emigrants is predicted to decline substantially in Bulgaria, whereas emigration from Nigeria is set to increase. Immigration to both countries is projected to be almost stable over the projection horizon.

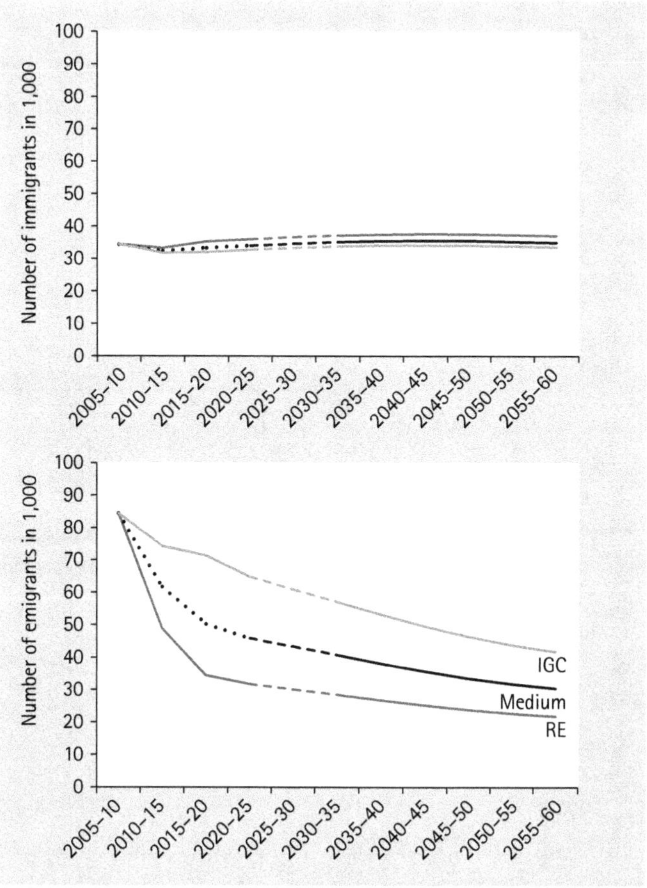

FIGURE 7.22 Estimated (2005–10) and projected (2010–15 to 2055–60) numbers of *immigrants* and *emigrants* under alternative scenarios, Bulgaria. RE: 'rise of the east' scenario; IGC: 'intensifying global competition' scenario.

7.8 Conclusions

International migration has increasingly become, and is likely to remain, a crucial component of the population dynamics of many sending and receiving nations. This chapter presented a comprehensive overview of the economic, climate, political, policy, and socio-demographic forces that affect migration. Drawing on new estimates of global international migration flows (Abel and Sander, 2014) allowed us to overcome the lack of comparable statistics that has thus far hindered the application of multiregion flow models at the global scale. The discussion of contemporary trends in global bilateral migration flows presented in Abel and Sander (2014) has pointed to stable intensities of the global flow of people since the mid-1990s.

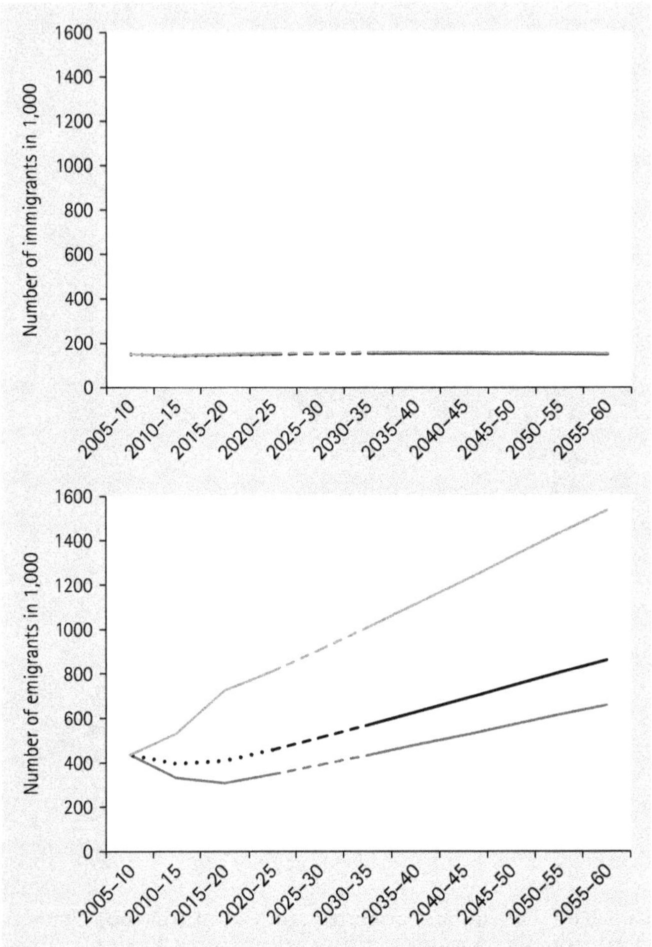

FIGURE 7.23 Estimated (2005–10) and projected (2010–15 to 2055–60) numbers of *immigrants* and *emigrants* under alternative scenarios, Nigeria.

We circumvented the difficulties associated with making ad hoc assumptions about future migration by drawing on expert judgement. The online survey revealed a strong agreement among experts about the factors most likely to shape future migration. Based on the respondents' collective judgement, we are more likely to see an increase in global migration levels than a decrease, unless current economic stagnation does not improve. Assuming a continuation of current trends as the most likely outcome and translating expert views into two alternative 'what if' scenarios allowed us to explore likely future migration trends.

The results of our population projections suggest that the global number of migrants will start declining in about 30 years. This is mostly because in the bi-regional flow model, slowed population growth and substantial population ageing result in fewer emigrants if a constant age schedule is assumed. The results also point to strong effects of population decline and ageing on projected emigration flows in many European countries, and they highlight differences in the future level and distribution of populations around the globe between the constant rates and two 'what if' scenarios. Using a medium scenario based on rates rather than numbers emphasizes the effects that changes in population size and age structure tend to have on emigration numbers.

APPENDIX 7.1

List of clusters of arguments in the migration module of the IIASA–Oxford survey:

Cluster	Argument	Cluster name	Cluster key	Argument text
1	1	Economic development	Economic	Remittances will become more important for the economic development of migrant-sending countries.
1	2	Economic development	Economic	The EU 'Blue Card' skilled immigration scheme will attract more highly-qualified migrant workers from non-EU countries on a temporary basis.
1	3	Economic development	Economic	Per capita income differentials between Asian countries will further widen.
1	4	Economic development	Economic	Temporary labour migration will increasingly compensate for skills shortages in developed countries and thus replace permanent migration.
1	5	Economic development	Economic	Foreign direct investment in developing countries as a stimulus to economic growth will rectify the imbalance between supply and demand in the labour market in those countries.
1	6	Economic development	Economic	There will be a global convergence in returns to human capital.
1	7	Economic development	Economic	Major economic recessions/ stagnation in industrialized countries will lead to less demand for migrants.
1	8	Economic development	Economic	Global wage levels will converge in the long run.

(*continued*)

Continued

Cluster	Argument	Cluster name	Cluster key	Argument text
2	1	Climate change	Environment	International migration from low-lying coastal areas and small islands in the developing world will increasingly be driven by the negative impacts of climate change.
2	2	Climate change	Environment	Populations in the Mediterranean region that are negatively affected by climate change will be successful in developing adaptive strategies.
2	3	Climate change	Environment	Governments of North Africa and the Middle East will find peaceful resolutions to intensifying water and land use conflicts.
2	4	Climate change	Environment	Relatively better educated populations will have a higher adaptive capacity to the negative impacts of climate change.
2	5	Climate change	Environment	Climate change will lead to conflict in poor countries and mass migration of asylum seekers to countries in the north.
2	6	Climate change	Environment	Climate change will lead to new directions of migration such as from India or the Middle East to Siberia.
3	1	Demographic factors	Demographic	Shifts in cohort size, especially related to the baby boom and bust, will play an important role in shaping international migration levels.
3	2	Demographic factors	Demographic	Strategies for ensuring the provision of adequate health and care services to the growing elderly populations in OECD countries will increasingly draw on immigrant workers.
3	3	Demographic factors	Demographic	The propensity to move abroad among 15–29-year-olds will be particularly high in countries with a large 'youth bulge'.
3	4	Demographic factors	Demographic	Ageing societies will be less open to immigration from different cultures.
3	5	Demographic factors	Demographic	More highly educated people will be more likely to migrate.

4	1	Cost of migration	Costs	Populations in developing countries will develop a more realistic perception of life in developed countries through information technology.
4	2	Cost of migration	Costs	Air travel and international freight will become less expensive, thus reducing the financial costs of migration.
4	3	Cost of migration	Costs	Communication technologies will be a viable alternative to face-to-face communication with friends and relatives left behind, thus reducing the physical cost of migration.
4	4	Cost of migration	Costs	Increasing multiculturalism in developed countries will reduce the linguistic and cultural barriers to migration.
4	5	Cost of migration	Costs	International migration will mostly follow established paths and existing migrant networks.
4	6	Cost of migration	Costs	Migrant networks are not as relevant for the migration of more educated people.
5	1	Migration regimes and policy	Policy	Among countries of the EU, freedom of movement will make it impossible for governments to influence migration.
5	2	Migration regimes and policy	Policy	Political instability and oppression in African and Middle Eastern countries will result in more people seeking political asylum in democratic countries.
5	3	Migration regimes and policy	Policy	Developed countries will be largely unsuccessful in reducing undocumented migration through the tightening of immigration policies and the strengthening of border controls.
5	4	Migration regimes and policy	Policy	Family reunification policies in Western societies will support the right of a family to live together in the destination country.
5	5	Migration regimes and policy	Policy	Rich countries will tighten their student visa systems.

EU: European Union; OECD: Organisation for Economic Co-operation and Development.

References

Abadan-Unat, N. 1995 'Turkish Migration to Europe'. In: Cohen, R. (ed.) *The Cambridge Survey of World Migration*, pp. 279–84. Cambridge University Press: Cambridge.

Abel, G.J. 2013a 'Estimating Global Migration Flow Tables Using Place of Birth Data'. *Demographic Research*, 28: 505–46.

Abel, G.J. 2013b 'migest: Useful R code for the Estimation of Migration'. Available at: <http://cran.r-project.org/web/packages/migest/> (accessed 25 April 2013).

Abel, G.J. and Sander, N. 2014 'Quantifying Global International Migration Flows'. *Science*, 343: 1520–22.

Aide, T.M. and Grau, H.R. 2004 'Ecology. Globalization, Migration, and Latin American Ecosystems'. *Science*, 305: 1915–16.

Angelucci, M. 2012 'US Border Enforcement and the Net Flow of Mexican Illegal Migration'. *Economic Development and Cultural Change*, 60: 311–57.

Bardsley, D.K. and Hugo, G.J. 2010 'Migration and Climate Change: Examining Thresholds of Change to Guide Effective Adaptation Decision-making'. *Population and Environment*, 32: 238–62.

Beer, J. de, Raymer, J., Erf, R. van der and Wissen, L. van 2010 'Overcoming the Problems of Inconsistent International Migration data: A New Method Applied to Flows in Europe'. *European Journal of Population*, 26: 459–81.

Bilsborrow, R.E., Hugo, G., Oberai, A.S. and Zlotnik, H. 1997 *International Migration Statistics: Guidelines for Improving Data Collection Systems*. International Labour Office: Geneva.

Black, R., Kniveton, D. and Schmidt-Verkerk, K. 2011 'Migration and Climate Change: Towards an Integrated Assessment of Sensitivity'. *Environment and Planning A*, 43: 431–50.

Bloom, D.E. and Canning, D. 2008 'Global Demographic Change: Dimensions and Economic Significance'. *Population and Development Review*, 34: 17–51.

Calavita, K. 1992 *Inside the State: The Bracero Program, Immigration, and the INS*. Routledge: New York.

Cardoso, L.A. 1980 *Mexican Emigration to the United States, 1897–1931: Socio-economic Patterns*. University of Arizona Press: Tucson, AZ.

Cavalli-Sforza, L.L.L., Menozzi, P. and Piazza, A. 1994 *History And Geography Of Human Genes*. Princeton University Press: Princeton, NJ.

Cerrutti, M. and Massey, D.S. 2001 'On the Auspices of Female Migration from Mexico to the United States'. *Demography*, 38: 187–200.

Christian Aid 2007 *Human Tide: The Real Migration Crisis*. Christian Aid: London.

Clark, X., Hatton, T.J. and Williamson, J.G. 2004 'What Explains Emigration Out of Latin America?' *World Development*, 32: 1871–90.

Clark, P.F., Stewart, J.B. and Clark, D.A. 2006 'The Globalization of the Labour Market for Health-care Professionals'. *International Labour Review*, 145: 37–64.

Coale, A.J. and Banister, J. 1994 'Five Decades of Missing Females in China'. *Demography*, 31: 459–79.

Coleman, D.A. 1993 'Contrasting Age Structures of Western Europe and of Eastern Europe and the Former Soviet Union: Demographic Curiosity or Labor Resource?' *Population and Development Review*, 19: 523–55.

Coleman, D.A. 2002 'Replacement Migration, or Why Everyone is Going to Have to Live in Korea: A Fable For Our Times From the United Nations'. *Philosophical Transactions of the Royal Society B*, 357: 583–98.

Cornelius, W.A. and Salehyan, I. 2007 'Does Border Enforcement Deter Unauthorized Immigration? The Case of Mexican Migration to the United States of America'. *Regulation & Governance*, 1: 139–53.
Coutin, S.B. 2003 *Legalizing Moves: Salvadoran Immigrants' Struggle for US Residency*. University of Michigan Press: Ann Arbor, MI.
Crisp, J. 2000 'Managing Forced Migration: Evolving International Responses to the Refugee Problem'. In: Conference on International Migration and Foreign Policy, Wilton Park UK.
Czaika, M. and de Haas, H. 2011 'The Effectiveness of Immigration Policies: A Conceptual Review of Empirical Evidence' (IMI/DEMIG Working Paper). International Migration Institute, University of Oxford: Oxford.
Davin, D. 2007 'Marriage Migration in China and East Asia'. *Journal of Contemporary China*, 16: 83–95.
De Haas, H. 2011 'The Determinants of International Migration: Conceptualizing Policy, Origin and Destination Effects' (IMI Working Paper). International Migration Institute, University of Oxford: Oxford.
De Haas, H. and Vezzoli, S. 2011 'Leaving Matters: The Nature, Evolution and Effects of Emigration Policies' (IMI Working Paper 34, DEMIG Project Paper 4). International Migration Institute, University of Oxford: Oxford.
Deane, G. and Gutmann, M.P. 2003 'Blowin' Down the Road: Investigating Bilateral Causality Between Dust Storms and Population in the Great Plains'. *Population Research and Policy Review*, 22: 297–331.
Department of Immigration and Citizenship 2011 *Immigration Update, 2010–11*. Department of Immigration and Citizenship: Canberra.
Duany, J. 2011 *Blurred Borders: Transnational Migration between the Hispanic Caribbean and the United States*. University of North Carolina Press: Chapel Hill, NC.
Ediev, D., Coleman, D.A. and Scherbov, S. 2007 *Migration as a Factor of Population Reproduction*. Vienna Institue of Demography: Vienna.
Ellermann, A. 2006 'Street-level Democracy: How Immigration Bureaucrats Manage Public Opposition'. *West European Politics*, 29: 293–309.
Espenshade, T.J. 2001 'Replacement Migration from the Perspective of Equilibrium Stationary Populations'. *Population and Environment*, 22: 383–9.
Fassmann, H. and Munz, R. 1992 'Patterns and Trends of International Migration in Western Europe'. *Population and Development Review*, 18: 457–80.
Fitzgerald, D. 2009 *A Nation of Emigrants: How Mexico Manages its Migration*. University of California Press: Berkeley, CA.
Gibney, M.J. 2004 *The Ethics and Politics of Asylum: Liberal Democracy and the Response to Refugees*. Cambridge University Press: Cambridge.
Gindling, T.H. 2009 'South–South Migration: The Impact of Nicaraguan Immigrants on Earnings, Inequality and Poverty in Costa Rica'. *World Development*, 37: 116–26.
Grasmuck, S. 1982 'Migration within the Periphery: Haitian Labor in the Dominican Sugar and Coffee Industries'. *International Migration Review*, 16: 365–77.
Grasmuck, S. and Pessar, P.R. 1991 *Between Two Islands: Dominican International Migration*. University of California Press: Berkeley, CA.
Gray, C. 2009 'Environment, Land, and Rural Out-migration in the Southern Ecuadorian Andes'. *World Development*, 37: 457–68.
Gray, C. and Mueller, V. 2012 'Drought and Population Mobility in Rural Ethiopia'. *World Development*, 40: 134–45.

Green, A.G. and Green, D.A. 1995 'Canadian Immigration Policy: The Effectiveness of the Point System and Other Instruments'. *The Canadian Journal of Economics*, 28: 1006–41.

Grosfoguel, R. 1997 'Colonial Caribbean Migrations to France, The Netherlands, Great Britain and the United States'. *Ethnic and Racial Studies*, 20: 594–612.

Guilmoto, C.Z. 2007 *Sex-ratio Imbalance in Asia: Trends, Consequences and Policy Responses.* LPED/IRD: Paris.

Gutmann, M.P., Parton, W.J., Cunfer, G. and Burke, I.C. 2005 *Population and Environment in the US Great Plains.* National Research Council Population, Land Use, and Environment. National Academies Press: Washington, DC.

Haddad, E. 2003 'The Refugee: The Individual Between Sovereigns'. *Global Society*, 17: 297–322.

Hanson, G.H. and McIntosh, C. 2010 'The Great Mexican Emigration'. *Review of Economics and Statistics*, 92: 798–810.

Hatton, T.J. 2004 'Seeking Asylum in Europe'. *Economic Policy*, 19: 5–62.

Held, D. 1995 *Democracy and the Global Order: From the Modern State to Cosmopolitan Governance.* Stanford University Press: Palo Alto, CA.

Henning, S. and Hovy, B. 2011 'Data Sets on International Migration'. *International Migration Review*, 45: 980–5.

Henry, S., Schoumaker, B. and Beauchemin, C. 2003 'The Impact of Rainfall on the First Out-Migration: A Multi-level Event-History Analysis in Burkina Faso'. *Population and Environment*, 25: 423–60.

Holzer, T., Schneider, G. and Widmer, T. 2000 'The Impact of Legislative Deterrence Measures on the Number of Asylum Applications in Switzerland (1986–1995)'. *International Migration Review*, 34: 1182–216.

Hugo, G.J. 1996 'Environmental Concerns and International Migration'. *International Migration Review*, 30: 105–31.

Hunter, L.M. 2005 'Migration and Environmental Hazards'. *Population and Environment*, 26: 273–302.

Hunter, L.M., Murray, S. and Riosmena, F. 2013 'Rainfall Patterns and U.S. Migration from Rural Mexico'. *International Migration Review*, 47: 874–909.

International Displacement Monitoring Centre (IDMC) 2013 'Global Overview 2012: People Internally Displaced by Conflict and Violence'. Available at: <http://www.internal-displacement.org/assets/publications/2013/2012-global-overview-corporate-en.pdf> (accessed 31 January 2014).

Kandel, W. and Massey, D.S. 2002 'The Culture of Mexican Migration: A Theoretical and Empirical Analysis'. *Social Forces*, 80: 981–1004.

Keyfitz, N. 1971 'Migration as a Means of Population Control'. *Population Studies*, 25: 63–72.

King, R. and Skeldon, R. 2010 '"Mind the Gap!" Integrating Approaches to Internal and International Migration'. *Journal of Ethnic and Migration Studies*, 36: 1619–46.

Krissman, F. 2000 'Immigrant Labor Recruitment: US Agribusiness and Undocumented Migration From Mexico'. *Immigration Research For a New Century: Multidisciplinary Perspectives*, 277–300.

Krzywinski, M., Schein, J., Birol, İ., Connors, J., Gascoyne, R., Horsman, D., et al. 2009 'Circos: An Information Aesthetic for Comparative Genomics'. *Genome Research*, 19: 1639–45.

Kupiszewska, D. and Nowok, B. 2008 'Comparability of Statistics On International Migration Flows in the European Union'. In: Willekens, F. and Raymer, J. (eds) *International Migration in Europe: Data, Models and Estimates*, pp. 41–73. Wiley: Chichester.

Kureková, L. 2011 'From Job Search to Skill Search: Political Economy of Labour Migration in Central and Eastern Europe'. PhD Thesis. Department of International Relations and European Studies, Central European University, Budapest.

Laczko, F. and Collett, E. 2005 *Assessing the Tsunami's Effects on Migration*. International Organization for Migration: Geneva.

Lang, H.J. 2002 *Fear and Sanctuary: Burmese Refugees in Thailand*. SEAP Publications: Ithaca, NY.

Lee, E. 2003 *At America's Gates: Chinese Immigration During the Exclusion Era, 1882–1943*. University of North Carolina Press: Chapel Hill, NC.

Levitt, P. 1998 'Social Remittances: Migration Driven Local-level Forms of Cultural Diffusion'. *International Migration Review*, 32: 926.

Levitt, P. and Lamba-Nieves, D. 2011 'Social Remittances Revisited'. Journal of Ethnic and Migration Studies, 37: 1–22.

Lindstrom, D.P. and Ramírez, A.L. 2010 'Pioneers and Followers: Migrant Selectivity and the Development of U.S. Migration Streams in Latin America'. *The Annals of the American Academy of Political and Social Science*, 630: 53–77.

Ling, L.H.-M. 1984 'East Asian Migration to the Middle East Causes, Consequences and Considerations'. *International Migration Review*, 18: 19–36.

Lundquist, J.H. and Massey, D.S. 2005 'Politics or Economics? International Migration During the Nicaraguan Contra War'. *Journal of Latin American Studies*, 37: 29–53.

McDonald, D.A. 2000 *On Borders: Perspectives on International Migration in Southern Africa*. Palgrave MacMillan: Basingstoke.

McDonald, P. and Temple, J. 2008 'Demographic and Labour Supply Futures for Australia'. Report for the Department of Immigration and Citizenship. Available at: <http://www.immi.gov.au> (accessed 14 January 2014).

McLeman, R. 2011 'Settlement Abandonment in the Context of Global Environmental Change'. *Global Environmental Change*, 21(Suppl. 1): S108–20.

McLeman, R. and Smit, B. 2006 'Migration as an Adaptation to Climate Change'. *Climatic Change*, 76: 31–53.

McLeman, R. and Hunter, L.M. 2010 'Migration in the Context of Vulnerability and Adaptation to Climate Change: Insights From Analogues'. *Wiley Interdisciplinary Reviews: Climate Change*, 1: 450–61.

Massey, D.S. 1990 'Social Structure, Household Strategies, and the Cumulative Causation of Migration'. *Population Index*, 56: 3.

Massey, D.S. and Aysa-Lastra, M. 2011 'Social Capital and International Migration from Latin America'. *International Journal of Population Research* 2011: 834145.

Massey, D.S., Arango, J., Hugo, G.J., Kouaouci, A., Pellegrino, A. and Taylor, J.E. 1993 'Theories of International Migration: A Review and Appraisal'. *Population and Development Review*, 19: 431–66.

Massey, D.S., Goldring, L. and Durand, J. 1994 'Continuities in Transnational Migration: An Analysis of Nineteen Mexican Communities'. *American Journal of Sociology*, 99: 1492–533.

Massey, D.S., Arango, J., Hugo, G.J., Kouaouci, A., Pellegrino, A. and Taylor, J.E. 1998 *Worlds in Motion: Understanding International Migration at the End of the Millennium*. Oxford University Press: New York.

Massey, D.S. and Sana, M. 2003 'Patterns of U.S. Migration from Mexico, the Caribbean, and Central America'. *Migraciones Internacionales*, 2: 5–39.

Mayda, A.M. 2010 'International Migration: A Panel Data Analysis of the Determinants of Bilateral Flows'. *Journal of Population Economics*, 23: 1249–74.

Mayer, T. and Zignago, S. 2012 'Notes on CEPII's Distances Measures: The GeoDist Database' (CEPII Working Paper No. 2011–25). Available at: <http://mpra.ub.uni-muenchen.de/36347/2/MPRA_paper_36347.pdf> (accessed 15 April 2014).

Meze-Hausken, E. 2000 'Migration Caused by Climate Change: How Vulnerable Are People in Dryland Areas?' *Mitigation and Adaptation Strategies for Global Change*, 5: 379–406.

Mitchell, C. 1989 'International Migration, International Relations and Foreign Policy'. *International Migration Review*, 23: 681.

Myers, N. 2002 'Environmental Refugees: A Growing Phenomenon of the 21st Century'. *Philosophical Transactions of the Royal Society B*, 357: 609–13.

Nawrotzki, R., Hunter, L.M. and Dickinson, T.W. 2012 'Natural Resources and Rural Livelihoods'. *Demographic Research*, 26: 661–700.

Office of Immigration Statistics 2010 *2009 Yearbook of Immigration Statistics*. U.S. Department of Homeland Security: Washington, DC.

Ortega, F. and Peri, G. 2009 'The Causes and Effects of International Migrations: Evidence from OECD Countries 1980–2005' (Working Paper No. 14833). National Bureau of Economic Research: Cambridge, MA.

Özden, C., Parsons, C.R., Schiff, M. and Walmsley, T.L. 2011 'Where on Earth is Everybody? The Evolution of Global Bilateral Migration 1960–2000'. *The World Bank Economic Review*, 25: 12–56.

Paldam, M. 2003 'Economic Freedom and the Success of the Asian Tigers: An Essay on Controversy'. *European Journal of Political Economy*, 19: 453–77.

Parrado, E.A. and Cerrutti, M. 2003 'Labor Migration between Developing Countries: The Case of Paraguay and Argentina 1'. *International Migration Review*, 37: 101–32.

Passel, J.S., Cohn, D. and Center, P.H. 2009 *Mexican Immigrants: How Many Come? How Many Leave?* Pew Hispanic Center Washington: Washington, DC.

Piore, M.J. 1980 *Birds of Passage: Migrant Labor and Industrial Societies*. Cambridge University Press: Cambridge.

Preston, S.H., Himes, C. and Eggers, M. 1989 'Demographic Conditions Responsible for Population Aging'. *Demography*, 26: 691–704.

Preston, S.H. and Wang, H. 2007 'Intrinsic Growth Rates and Net Reproduction Rates in the Presence of Migration'. *Population and Development Review*, 33: 357–666.

Ratha, D. and Shaw, W. 2007 *South-South Migration and Remittances*. World Bank Publications: Washington, DC.

Raymer, J., Abel, G. and Smith, P.W. 2007 'Combining Census and Registration Data to Estimate Detailed Elderly Migration Flows in England and Wales'. *Journal of the Royal Statistical Society: Series A (Statistics in Society)*, 170: 891–908.

Raymer, J., Beer, J. de and Erf, R. van der 2011 'Putting the Pieces of the Puzzle Together: Age and Sex-Specific Estimates of Migration amongst Countries in the EU/EFTA, 2002–2007'. *European Journal of Population*, 27: 185–215.

Raymer, J., Abel, G.J. and Rogers, A. 2012 'Does Specification Matter? Experiments With Simple Multiregional Probabilistic Population Projections'. *Environment and Planning A*, 44: 2664.

Rees, P. 1980 'Multistate Demographic Accounts: Measurement and Estimation Procedures'. *Environment and Planning A*, 12: 499–531.

Reyes, B.I. 2004 'Changes in Trip Duration for Mexican Immigrants to the United States'. *Population Research and Policy Review*, 23: 235–57.

Rivera-Batiz, F.L. and Santiago, C.E. 1996 *Island Paradox: Puerto Rico in the 1990s*. Russell Sage Foundation: New York.

Rogers, A. 1990 'Requiem for the Net Migrant'. *Geographical Analysis*, 22: 283–300.

Rogers, A. 1995 *Multiregional Demography: Principles, Methods and Extensions*. John Wiley: Chichester.

Rogers, A. and Castro, L.J. 1981 'Model Migration Schedules' (IIASA Research Report RR-81-030). International Institute for Applied Systems Analysis (IIASA): Laxenburg.

Rogers, A. and Little, J. 1994 'Parameterizing Age Patterns of Demographic Rates With the Multiexponential Model Schedule'. *Mathematical Population Studies*, 4: 175–95.

Rogers, A., Jones, B., Partida, V. and Muhidin, S. 2007 'Inferring Migration Flows From the Migration Propensities of Infants: Mexico and Indonesia'. The Annals of Regional Science, 41: 443–65.

Rogers, A., Little, J. and Raymer, J. 2010 The Indirect Estimation of Migration: Methods for Dealing with Irregular, Inadequate, and Missing Data. Springer: Dordrecht.

Rumbaut, R.G. 1989 'The Structure of Refuge: Southeast Asian Refugees in the United States, 1975–1985' (SSRN Scholarly Paper No. ID 1886685). Social Science Research Network: Rochester, NY.

Rumbaut, R.G. 1994 'Origins and Destinies: Immigration to the United States Since World War II'. *Sociology Forum*, 9: 583–621.

Sadiq, K. 2009 'When Being Native is Not Enough: Citizens as Foreigners in Malaysia'. *Asian Perspective*, 33: 5–32.

Sander, N., Abel, G. J., Bauer, R. and Schmidt, J. 2014 'Visualising Migration Flow Data With Circular Plots' (VID Working Paper 02/2014). Vienna Institute of Demography: Vienna.

Sassen, S. 1998 *The Migration of Capital and Labour*. Cambridge University Press: Cambridge.

Skeldon, R. 2006 'Interlinkages Between Internal and International Migration and Development in the Asian Region'. *Population, Space and Place*, 12: 15–30.

Spener, D. 2009 *Clandestine Crossings: Migrants and Coyotes on the Texas-Mexico Border*. Cornell University Press: Ithaca, NY.

Spilimbergo, A. and Hanson, G.H. 1999 'Illegal Immigration, Border Enforcement, and Relative Wages: Evidence from Apprehensions at the U.S.-Mexico Border'. *American Economic Review*, 89: 1337–57.

Stark, O. and Bloom, D.E. 1985 'The New Economics of Labor Migration'. *The American Economic Review* 75, 173–8.

Stark, O. and Taylor, J.E. 1991 'Migration Incentives, Migration Types: The Role of Relative Deprivation'. *The Economic Journal*, 101: 1163.

Statistics Canada 2006 *Immigration and Citizenship, 2006 Census*. Statistics Canada: Ottawa.

Stojanov, R. 2008 *Environmental Factors of Migration, in: Development, Environment and Migration. Analysis of Linkages and Consequences*. Palacky University: Olomouc.

Telles, E.E. and Sue, C.A. 2009 'Race Mixture: Boundary Crossing in Comparative Perspective'. *Annual Review of Sociology*, 35: 129–46.

Thielemann, E. 2005 'Does Policy Matter? On Governments' Attempts to Control Unwanted Migration' (SSRN Scholarly Paper No. ID 495631). Social Science Research Network: Rochester, NY.

Todaro, M.P. and Maruszko, L. 1987 'Illegal Migration and US Immigration Reform: A Conceptual Framework'. *Population and Development Review*, 13: 101–14.

Tsuda, T. 2003 *Strangers in the Ethnic Homeland: Japanese Brazilian Return Migration in Transnational Perspective*. Columbia University Press: New York.

UN 2012 'International Human Development Indicators'. Available at: <http://hdr.undp.org/en/data> (accessed 30 January 2014).

UNHCR 2012 *Statistical Yearbook 2011: Ten Years of Statistics*. United Nations: New York.

United Nations 2000 'Millennium Development Goals Indicators'. Available at: <http://mdgs.un.org/unsd/mdg/Host.aspx?Content=Indicators/OfficialList.htm> (accessed 14 January 2014).

UNPD 2009 *International Migrant Flows To and From Selected Countries: The 2008 Revision*. United Nations Population Division: New York.

UNPD 2011 *World Population Prospects: The 2010 Revision*. United Nations Population Division: New York.

UNPD 2012 *Trends in International Migrant Stock: Migrants by Destination and Origin*. United Nations Population Division: New York.

VanWey, L.K. 2005 'Land Ownership as a Determinant of International and Internal Migration in Mexico and Internal Migration in Thailand'. *International Migration Review*, 39: 141–72.

Willekens, F. 1999 'Modeling Approaches to the Indirect Estimation of Migration Flows: From Entropy to EM'. *Mathematical Population Studies*, 7: 239–78.

Wilson, T. 2010 'Model Migration Schedules Incorporating Student Migration Peaks'. *Demographic Research*, 23: 191–222.

Wilson, T. 2011 'A Review of Sub-Regional Population Projection Methods' (Working Paper). The University of Queensland.

Wilson, T. and Bell, M. 2004 'Comparative Empirical Evaluations of Internal Migration Models in Subnational Population Projections'. *Journal of Population Research*, 21: 127–60.

Wu, Z. and Li, N. 2003 'Immigration and the Dependency Ratio of a Host Population'. *Mathematical Population Studies*, 10: 21–39.

Zlotnik, H. 1998 'International Migration 1965–96: An Overview'. *Population and Development Review*, 24: 429–68.

Zlotnik, H. 1999 'Trends of International Migration since 1965: What Existing Data Reveal'. *International Migration*, 37: 21–61.

Zlotnik, H. 2004 'Population Growth and International Migration'. *International Migration*, 13–34.

Zlotnik, H. 2005 'International Migration Trends Since 1980'. Selected papers of the UNFPA Expert Group Meeting, pp. 13–28. UNFPA: New York.

Zolberg, A.R., Suhrke, A. and Aguayo, S. 1989 *Escape From Violence: Conflict and the Refugee Crisis in the Developing World*. Oxford University Press: New York.

CHAPTER 8

FUTURE EDUCATION TRENDS

BILAL F. BARAKAT AND
RACHEL E. DURHAM

8.1 Introduction

Education is an inherently long-term endeavour. Not only in the sense that formal schooling alone may last a significant part of a lifetime, but also because part of the reason for spending this time in school is the promise of benefits for decades to come. This is true at both the individual and societal levels.

For the underlying educational systems, the long-term nature of education is felt more keenly than at the individual level. Schools are built to serve multiple generations of students, and teachers are often hired for life as civil servants. A newly trained teacher of today will, towards the end of her/his career, teach students who, in turn, may well still be in the active labour force 100 years from now.

Educators themselves also hold expectations about the long-term future. Part of why we care whether a Dalit boy gets some form of early childhood education is because we expect that, as a consequence, his increased chances to complete school will benefit him not only for the next 10 or 15 years, to the end of our programme intervention or planning horizon, but for the rest of his life. His own education may even make it more likely that he will send his own children to school. If he sends a daughter to school, her education will possibly lead her to wait until she is in her late 20s to bear her first child, when she is better able to provide care. That 'delayed benefit' of the Dalit boy going to school now might not occur until sometime in the 2050s.

To insist that we 'learn for life, not for school' is a cliché, yet there are strikingly few attempts to look ahead—much less project quantitatively—how today's students will contribute to the educational composition of tomorrow's population, and the implications for their personal life course and the challenges of their generation. Some of the key contemporary policy debates concern very long-term issues. Among these are the sustainability of pensions, the provision of health care, and response to environmental degradation. For all of these, the education of the concerned populations matters. Conversely, these debates have serious consequences for education today, such as public funding cuts motivated by the aspiration to reduce future public debt.

Informing these debates from a perspective of educational futures requires an attempt to abstract away the vagaries of never-ending educational policy reforms that, at first glance, appear to render any concrete attempts to look into the future an exercise in speculation. Yet, given the proven difficulty of achieving set objectives through deliberate policy changes, it is all too easy to overstate the problem they cause for projection. Even less successful than long-term forecasts of education have been predictions of its imminent radical change.

On a different level, tremendous differences exist in what nominally equivalent school qualifications in different settings actually mean, either in terms of knowledge and skills, or in terms of societal reward. On educational grounds, we have no reason to expect nominal attainment levels to distinguish groups of people with identifiably distinct, and generalizable, demographic behaviours; yet mark such distinctions they do, as the empirical evidence presented in other chapters in this book demonstrates. For marking such distinctions, and as a characteristic that is stable over the life course, taking an interest in the educational attainment profile of future populations is prudent. Not least, the demographic consequences of educational expansion are relatively predictable compared to projections of economic and poverty impacts (Hannum and Buchmann, 2005).

Forecasting in the sense of predicting is certainly impossible. And there is no possibility of conducting meaningful *planning* over such a generational time horizon. Not because this would necessarily require predictions as inputs—it does not—but because, in any case, there can be no credible commitments that far into the future. What is possible is to place explicit bounds on what we can and do know about the future; within those bounds we can form reasonable expectations, even if the expectations remain open to further revision. Indeed, some of the potential benefits of thinking systematically about the future of educational attainment lie not in the results, but in potentially highlighting contradictions in our thinking. The education development community generally asserts that a 'GDP economic growth first' development strategy cannot substitute for an active education policy. From such a position, it would be inconsistent to deny the relevance of long-term projections of education by arguing that schooling will anyhow become virtually universal within our lifetime owing to increasing wealth.

Such ambivalence reflects long-standing, and unresolved, debates among educationalists between the poles of seeing structural 'periodicity and process' (Archer, 1982, p. 3) in educational expansion, and calling such generalizations into question with reminders of the importance of accounting for contextual and historical specificity when assessing a concrete educational policy challenge. We believe the latter perspective is essential for well-grounded educational action. Nevertheless, we do not think it invalidates the effort to seek 'stabilities and governing principles' in the 'emergence and development of educational systems' (Ericson, 1982, p. 300). Indeed, the international consensus surrounding the quintessential elements of a public school system appears to be shifting from being almost universal to being truly so.

Today, of the 199 countries on which United Nations Educational Scientific and Cultural Organization (UNESCO) reports, 98 per cent require children to attend school (UNESCO, 2012, pp. 18–19), up from 90 per cent in 2002 (Benavot et al., 2006).This fact reflects a widespread belief that formal education should be, at least up to a basic level, provided or supported by the state. The motivations for formalizing education and developing state-sponsored systems of mass education have varied by context. Widely different pressures, goals, and priorities have supported public education development across time and place. Yet despite such differences, the pattern and structures of educational development exhibit remarkable similarity in many societies.

Education by the most liberal definition is at least as old as civilization, but here we are not addressing informal learning occurring in the home, provided by families or the immediate community, or even learning occurring in the workplace after graduation. While these forms of education are fundamental to individual development, the current discussion refers only to formal, systematized schooling. Thus, the following sections will briefly examine the history of educational expansion with respect to formal schooling, focusing on commonalities and differences in its structures and progress across time and place, as well as theories regarding the motivations and processes of educational development in different contexts. In a novel step, we then derive the predictive content of these empirical patterns and theoretical frameworks. Section 8.3 presents a specific statistical projection model based on these insights.

8.2 Dynamics of educational expansion

8.2.1 Historical overview

Similarities across time and place in educational structures, as well as the motivations for educational expansion, have long been noted. Until modern times, formal education was—in practice and intention—a privilege of only the elite classes of society, for example those serving as civil or religious authorities. Trades and skills were passed down over generations within families or through apprenticeships. While a handful of ancient societies supported systems of formal education, mass literacy—especially with any sense of gender parity—was a rare occurrence until relatively recently. Literacy education was traditionally linked to social privilege, and there are numerous instances in history where the withholding of literacy education was a means of oppression.

However, over the last two centuries, a level of expansion in mass schooling has occurred that indicates the emergence of an alternative paradigm. Societies worldwide appear to recognize that providing basic education—fundamental skills in literacy and numeracy—improves quality of life for persons of disparate social and economic backgrounds and, by eliminating inequality, benefits the whole of society. The historic motivations to offer formal basic education have varied widely and signified local social, economic, and political concerns (Benavot et al., 2006). In the West, the Reformation brought forward the belief that all individuals must have the capability to read and interpret scripture for themselves; as a result, basic education came to be seen as a fundamental requirement. This is one reason why churches were often the initial stewards of educational instruction across Europe. In part, this was because monasteries had been the only providers of schooling and literate material for centuries (Cordasco, 1976). Literacy for religious purposes is still a motivating factor in the organization of formal education in areas like Northern Africa, where Qur'anic schools, in addition to instruction in local languages, teach Arabic literacy for scriptural understanding, as has been done for centuries.

During the eighteenth and nineteenth centuries, education was also seen as a means to provide moral instruction to emergent citizenries, as the role of the church as moral leader declined during this period of rapid secularization and modernization. Because the formalization of mass education systems coincided with industrialization, some analysts have theorized that education systems were created to provide the necessary skills for a productive workforce and create a rational sorting mechanism for employers. We also see evidence that nation-states elect to formulate mass education systems as a means of generating legitimacy on the world stage, often adopting the formal structures of other nations' educational systems and creating identical systems of symbolic links between the individual and society (Meyer, 1992). This motivation is plausible, as in many cases, the formal education system appeared at the same time that the nation-state emerged.

In the contemporary era, the initiation of a formal, mass educational system typically involves several signals of commitment (Boli et al., 1985). Although in some cases a formal education system predates an official statute (and in some cases a system predates the nation-state), nation-states have commonly begun by adopting laws regarding compulsory education, which often mandate an age at which education must begin and the years of duration to reach a required minimum level of schooling. Ministries of education are also commonly authorized, whose function is to implement programmes, set benchmarks, develop curricula, and to monitor and report progress. Education entities also tend to adopt uniform, hierarchical systems, that is, primary education that leads to secondary education, which, in turn, is required for entry to tertiary education. This is enabled by standardization, which tends to coincide with centralization of the educational system.

Importantly, educational expansion has followed rather typical patterns across all world regions (Wils and Goujon, 1998). Initially, there is a focus on primary or 'basic' education that provides fundamental skills such as literacy and numeracy. Once a stable level of primary educational participation is achieved, expansion into secondary schooling occurs, where the curriculum is characterized by greater skill specificity. However, expansion of secondary education does not necessarily follow universal primary enrolment. In some cases, for example in Africa and Latin America, secondary education has developed even in the midst of high levels of illiteracy and low levels of primary completion. In such contexts where primary educational expansion is growing slowly, secondary education enrolment is confined to the more economically advantaged echelons of society. For instance, prior to World War II secondary education in Europe was relatively selective and was considered to serve primarily as preparation for university. After World War II, however, a new political climate in Europe led to increased inclusiveness and longer periods of free, compulsory education, resulting in virtually universal secondary participation.

Then, as nations mature and secondary enrolment levels rise, tertiary enrolment expands. Although university education is at least 1,000 years old, this stage of educational development is still underway, and the final shape that global tertiary expansion will take is still being determined. For many centuries, tertiary education served only a very small minority, such as clerical, medical, or legal specialists, but over the last century enrolments have grown tremendously. During the twentieth century tertiary enrolments increased by a factor of 200, from around half a million people of college age, to more than 100 million (UNESCO 2004, cited in Schofer and Meyer, 2005), and between 1950 and 1970 enrolments in higher education grew faster than at any other level (Meyer et al., 1977). Schofer and Meyer (2005) found that higher education enrolments grew rapidly in conjunction with global democratization, scientization, growth in human rights, and involvement in development planning. These variables proved more important than secondary enrolments, inequality, research and development levels, or economic development at the country level (although country-level secondary enrolments were positively related to tertiary enrolments). Moreover, higher education institutions tend to be similar worldwide, both in what is taught and how the curriculum is delivered. This suggests that the recent expansion of higher education is the result of global cultural and symbolic forces emphasizing the value of advanced forms of knowledge and its potential to generate capital in many forms—economic, social, and intellectual. Countries invest in higher education to meaningfully participate in, and integrate into, the global discourse of progress and human development. Boxes 8.1–8.3 examine some illustrative country case studies of expansion at different levels of education.

8.2.2 Theoretical perspectives

The body of research examining educational expansion has considered the timing and pace of formal education's development along with antecedents of historical context and socio-political conditions. The different themes in the historical overview—social privilege, nationalism, and industrialization—have served as organizing principles for different theories to explain the diverse conditions under which educational expansion has taken place. While points of overlap exist, to date these theories largely remain as competing explanations, and a 'grand theory' of educational growth that would reconcile the different explanatory paradigms remains elusive.

Box 8.1 The Example of the Republic of Korea

The education system in the Republic of Korea (henceforth Korea) expanded greatly over the course of the second half of the twentieth century. As can be seen in Figure 8.1, while absolute enrolments in primary schooling, which was virtually universal, started declining in the 1970s owing to shrinking cohort size, secondary enrolments more than doubled in 15 years. In relative terms (Figure 8.2), this was the result of extending the secondary franchise from a minority of children to virtual universality. The overall shape of the expansion of secondary attainment also provides an excellent example of the theoretical sigmoid pattern (i.e. an s-shape). Increasing public and private investments in education grow even more, with the education sector as a whole increasing more than 100-fold in real gross domestic product between 1960 and 1980 (Kim, 2012, p. 3).

While such dynamics appear to point to a determined 'all-out' effort to maximize educational attainment, these figures must be interpreted in context. After decades of a slowly increasing share, Korea's Ministry of Education's budget only reached 20 per cent of the total government budget in 1985, an unremarkable percentage in international comparison. The state's development strategy was not fully based on rational human capital planning to the extent that is often assumed. On the contrary, Jeong and Armer argue that the state's shift in economic policy 'from light manufacturing to heavy, chemical, and high-tech industries [. . .] spurred a transformation of the South Korean economy, [but] it largely ignored the nation's comparative advantage in skilled labour' (Jeong and Armer, 1994, p. 535).

While tertiary enrolments grew more than tenfold between 1970 and 2010, Figure 8.1 clearly shows that this growth occurred in distinct spurts, reflecting the policy-driven process of expansion and an education system that lacked autonomy. Indeed, up until the late 1970s, the tertiary sector was rather small, as the military junta was concerned about over-education and actively limited growth at the higher level (Jeong and Armer, 1994). Indeed, most of the higher education in the early 1970s was private rather than public

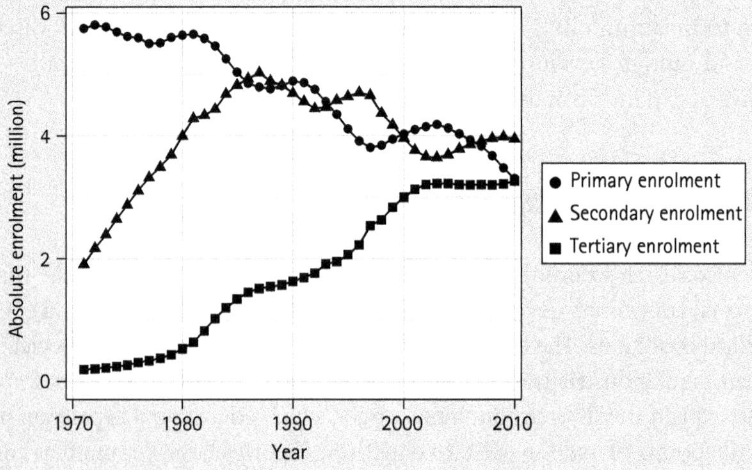

FIGURE 8.1 Absolute enrolments over time.

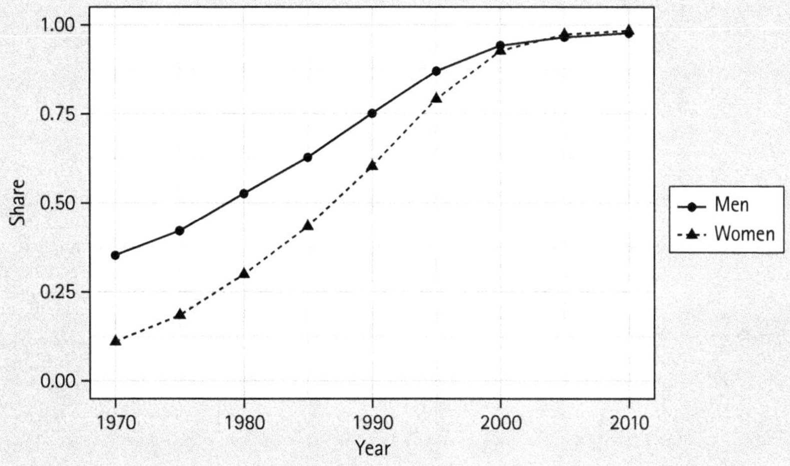

FIGURE 8.2 Upper secondary attainment at age 30–34.

(Kim, 2012). When tertiary expansion did eventually take off, it was 'in response to political and class forces rather than economic needs' (Jeong and Armer, 1994, p. 539).

Indeed, the argument has been made that educational expansion at the secondary and higher level in Korea occurred as an unintended consequence of a bipolar dynamic between government policy and society. It was precisely the state's earlier efforts to *contain* expansion at the post-primary level that 'intensified entrance examination competitions, stimulated demand for education, [...] and mobilized private resources for education' (Kim, 2012, p. 14). Ironically, when the state did react to popular demand during a political legitimacy crisis by taking over funding responsibilities for private secondary schools, it 'laid [the] foundation for universal secondary education and, as such [...] reached far beyond what the public had demanded' (Kim, 2012, p. 13). This observation provides an example of a 'self-propelled' dynamic in educational expansion that is elaborated in section 8.2.3.

Box 8.2 The Example of the USA

With a focus on the latter part of the twentieth century when primary education was universal and high school completion stable at a relatively high level in the USA, the main dynamic in the education sector, in addition to overall growth to keep pace with population growth, has been at the post-secondary and tertiary levels. Figure 8.3 shows how tertiary enrolments, while undergoing sometimes decade-long periods of stagnation, more than doubled in total between 1970 and 2010. This dynamic is not immediately evident in the attainment distribution at age 30–34, though (Figure 8.4). This is partly because the latter is lagged relative to enrolments, and does not yet fully reflect the enrolment expansion that has occurred since 2000.

Enrolments only translate into attainment if students successfully complete their courses. In this context, parts of the enrolment growth driven by community colleges that enjoy lower completion rates than academic four-year colleges contribute proportionally

Box 8.2 Continued

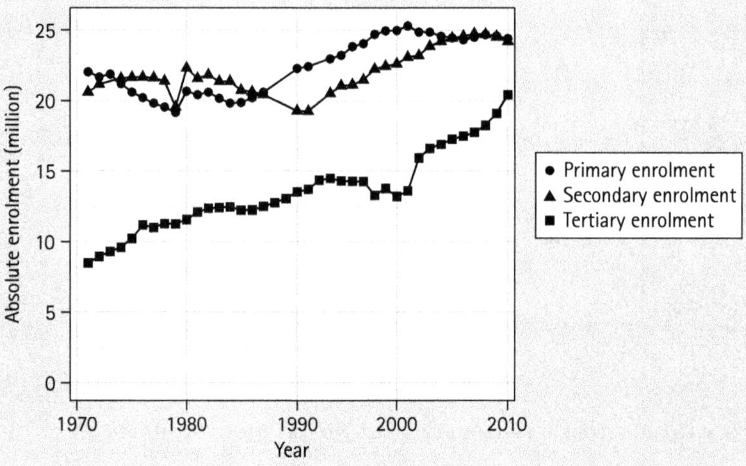

FIGURE 8.3 Absolute enrolments over time.

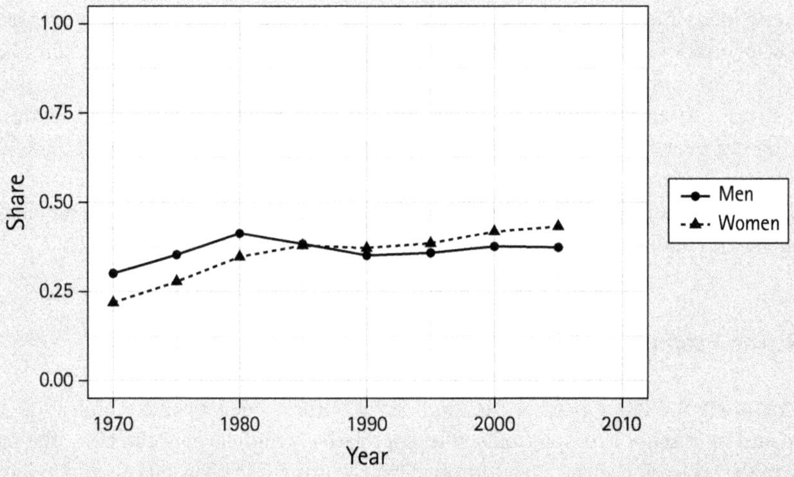

FIGURE 8.4 Post-secondary attainment at age 30–34.

less to attainment growth. Another reason that growth in tertiary completion rates in the USA may slow somewhat is that, compared with other developed countries, the financial cost of a college education in the USA is substantial and growing rapidly. In 2007–08, the average full-time 4-year college enrolee spent $19,100 a year (including room, board, tuition, and materials). This figure represented a 22 per cent increase over the cost just 8 years prior in 1999–00. More recent estimates suggest that tuition in some places has nearly doubled in 10 years. While this trend may, in fact, stratify options across different socio-economic groups (e.g. poor minorities less likely to enrol), innovative means by which to pay for college are growing.

In addition, composition effects depress the expansion of US post-secondary and tertiary attainment as a result of population heterogeneity. Growth in college completion rates over the last 30 years has not occurred uniformly across demographic groups. Between 1971 and 2009, white students' bachelor degree completion share increased from 19 per cent to 37 per cent. For black students it increased from 7 per cent to 19 per cent; for Hispanics from 5 per cent to only 12 per cent. Thus, although college completion is increasing for all three groups, minority groups' college completion has not increased as fast as for white students. At the same time, this supports the view that, in the long run, further expansion can be expected, as college completion is increasing for all subgroups.

Labour market dynamics continue to encourage further upgrading of qualifications, as income differentials by educational attainment remain high. In 2010, an employee with a college education earns, on average, 66 per cent more in weekly earnings than an employee with only a high school diploma (Bureau of Labor Statistics, 2012a). In the next decade, occupations requiring some post-secondary education are projected to grow the most (i.e. management, scientific, technical consulting, and computer systems design), while those requiring secondary or less will decline the most (i.e. manufacturing and retail trade) (Bureau of Labor Statistics, 2012b).

Box 8.3 The Example of Brazil

While the relative stability in primary enrolments over the last few decades (Figure 8.5) already reflects the Brazilian fertility transition, the education system as a whole expanded greatly during that time, with secondary and tertiary enrolments increasing fivefold, despite the presence of a 'lost decade' from the mid-1980s to mid-1990s (Burton, 2011). Even at the primary level, the relatively recent successes in expanding participation can

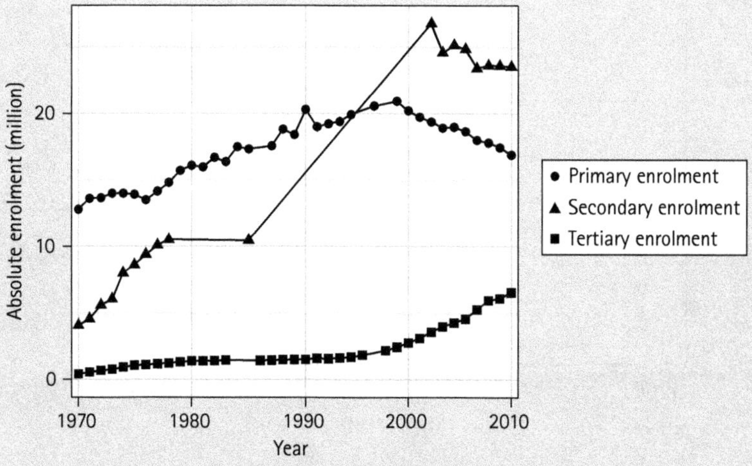

FIGURE 8.5 Absolute enrolments over time.

still be observed in the attainment of the 30–34 age group. While only a minority of both men and women of this age had completed primary school in 1970, this share is steadily approaching universality (Figure 8.6).

Brazil has shown a strong reduction in inequality in educational participation as a result of policies and programmes intended to increase both the supply and demand for education. At the starting point, the 1970s were characterized by top-down supply-driven programmes, such as the implementation of a law that made school mandatory for all children aged 7–14 (the previous law only required schooling for children aged 7–10), and a corresponding investment in construction of new schools in order to support new entrants. By the 1980s, investments in education stalled, and a number of studies have shown evidence of a close relationship between the deep economic crisis (faced by Brazil and other countries in Latin America) and poor educational outcomes (Duryea et al., 2007; Torche, 2010). Indeed, Figure 8.5 demonstrates a slow pace of expansion during that decade. From the point of view of social justice, the 1980s were actually a success, as the most disadvantaged children were catching up faster with the most advantaged children. This indicates that the convergence toward a more balanced attainment distribution between groups occurred at the expense of a reduction in the aggregate level of education.

From the mid-1990s onward, sustained educational policies, which were maintained and expanded especially after the Brazilian government transition in 2003, extended schooling to even the poorest and most geographically remote children. Among the most influential programmes were FUNDEF (Fund for the Maintenance and Development of Basic Education and Teacher Appreciation), the education finance equalization strategy that increased expenditures in the poorest Brazilian regions (north and north-east), and Conditional Cash Transfer Programs that tied the payment of benefits to households to the school attendance of their children.

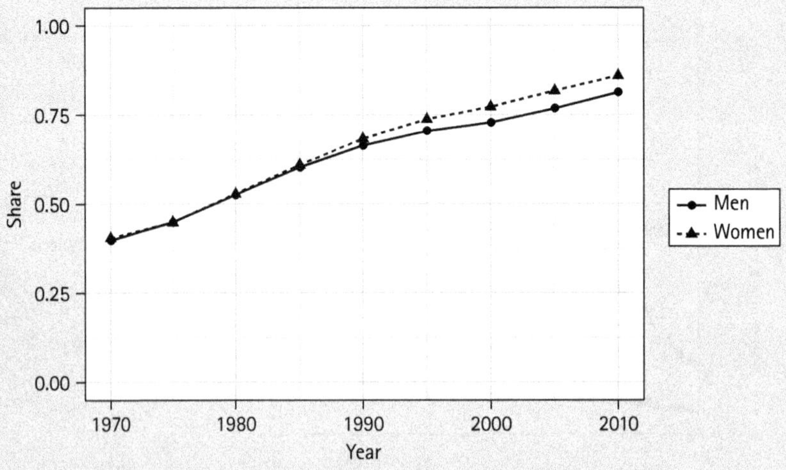

FIGURE 8.6 Upper secondary attainment at age 30–34.

The main theories range from functional–structural perspectives that emphasize the development of education as a response to society's social needs, or to maintain existing power relationships, to systemic theories that frame educational expansion as a feature of an emergent, self-reinforcing world culture.

8.2.2.1 *Technological progress and economic transformations*

Within the functionalist paradigm, formal education serves an important function in the labour market, where mass schooling systems lead to credentials that allow employers to differentiate potential workers in a systematic and objective manner. Credentials may legitimate claims of skills learned, but, importantly, education provides a skills-differentiated workforce for the industrial labour force. As a result, economic transformations, beginning with the industrial revolution, but including more recent shifts towards a service economy, create a demand for the output of the education system. In many cases, this pressure has been expansionary and spurred an upgrading of qualifications. But while economic development has been considered a prerequisite to the emergence of mass schooling, its relationship to educational expansion is certainly not straightforward, especially as this relationship is not limited to the labour market. For one, the distribution of wealth weighs on the demand for education because demand seems to be proportionally related to household income. Population growth (or decline) also affects enrolment rates, as educational infrastructure must be able to keep pace with the size of entering cohorts (Colclough and Al-Samarrai, 2000). Secondary and tertiary educational expansion may be especially affected by economic development for reasons related to both supply and demand. When increased industrialization and development of technical infrastructure occur, employers seek out workers with more highly specialized skills, such as those provided in secondary or tertiary programmes (Meyer et al., 1977). At the same time, development can provide resources to be invested in the educational infrastructure, creating openings for more enrolments.

While research has examined the extent to which economic development has spurred the growth in educational enrolments, to a large extent the motivation behind external aid efforts for developing countries' education sectors historically has revolved around the belief that increasing educational enrolments itself leads to economic growth (Corrales, 2006; Resnik, 2006). Recent discourse has additionally emphasized the power of education to eliminate poverty and promote sustainable development (Hannum and Buchmann, 2003). The process whereby education leads to improved economic conditions, however, is not well understood and is widely debated, not least because empirical verification of the causal relationship is challenging (see the discussion of causality between education and selected outcomes in Chapter 2). To some extent, the relationship is one of mutual feedback mechanisms.

Increasing amounts of education within a population might seem clearly related to a country's economic growth potential, but there are many correlates of both higher enrolment rates and economic development. For example, higher levels of female primary enrolment are associated with lower fertility rates, and lower fertility rates are positively correlated with economic growth. Economic growth is also strongly correlated with the openness of the economy and stability, which also likely relate strongly to educational investment. Moreover, countries with low initial levels of both human capital and GDP tend to grow faster than more developed countries, as a result of their lower starting place, which gives the impression that education enrolment growth per se causes economic development (Barro and Lee, 2001). And educational quality, as measured by cognitive ability on internationally normed tests in reading, mathematics, and science, may matter for economic growth as much as enrolment or attainment shares. Studies indicate that aggregate cognitive ability affects economic development via a better trained labour force, higher individual incomes, and a more equitable distribution of wealth (Barro and Lee, 2001; Hanushek and Kimko, 2000; Hanushek and Woessmann, 2008). In effect, 12 years of schooling in one country is not necessarily the same as 12 years in another country in terms of actual learning. Learning is also not only the purview of the school, as it occurs in the home, in the community, and among peers—the features of which also vary across countries. Furthermore, internal efficiency (i.e. school quality) may not coincide with expansion, nor may enrolment growth necessarily lead to appreciable increases in attainment shares. Rapid expansion in enrolment is sometimes characterized by an initial decrease in school quality, as stocks of qualified teachers must accumulate and funds must be properly allocated in response to where needs are greatest. Poor quality can, in turn, depress overall attainment and cognitive ability. Finally, improvements in schooling change the existing population stock of human capital only slowly; the contribution of educational expansion to economic development, taking age structural effects into account, has been analysed only recently (Lutz et al., 2008).

8.2.2.2 *Nation-states and the imperatives of nationalism*

Despite the strong linkages between educational expansion and industrial development, the observation that mass educational systems pre-date industrialization, for example in Europe and the USA (Boli et al., 1985; Meyer, 1992; Meyer et al., 1977), and that mass educational systems arose only after the appearance of the nation-state, point to a dominant role of the latter. Indeed, the earliest modern instances of state-sponsored mass education systems explicitly served the purpose of creating citizens for the emergent nation-states. In this way, mass formal education is viewed as necessary for the development of a coherent, nationalistic, and unifying identity. For instance, in Prussia, which, in the late 1700s, was characterized by geographically isolated city-states, a unifying curriculum was perceived as particularly useful for national security and consensus building (for a good review of European national education systems, see Ramirez and Boli (1987)). Even before being legally instituted, some societies provided formal education because of normative beliefs about its value as a socializing agent for children (Benavot et al., 2006). Over time, as labour markets diversified and populations became increasingly diverse in terms of language, norms, and religious belief, the home as a primary learning environment came to be seen as inadequate.

Public schools were instituted to offer not just basic skills, but also an orientation to normative civically and socially responsible behaviour and abilities. Furthermore, public schools were viewed as a way to equalize learning opportunities across populations of disparate socio-economic and cultural backgrounds. In some countries, state-run systems of mass schooling were legally established to enhance the power of the state, and in many cases to simultaneously diminish the historical power of the Church (Archer, 1982).

However, neither a strong centralized effort by a nation-state to define its educational system, nor nation-wide standardization (of credential and curricula) is necessary. England, the USA, Switzerland, and Belgium have fairly de-centralized national education systems (Benavot et al., 2006). Significantly, Green (1980) notes that the structure of an educational system tends to reflect the philosophy and exigencies of the country. Systems in South East Asia, for instance, educate vastly diverse linguistic and ethnic groups, which necessitates a higher degree of centralization. However, other nations with diverse populations place a higher value on autonomy than unification. The USA, for example, has a long tradition of federalism (i.e. states' rights), which is reflected in its widely-varying state education agencies.

The dominant role of the state in the effective supply of schooling is uncontested, even if the question of whose interests it serves is. In addition, however, at all but the most advanced levels of educational development, the state apparatus likewise influences the demand. In European countries well into the 1970s, the labour market for tertiary graduates was essentially limited to the public sector and publicly-regulated professions. Similar patterns can be observed in many developing countries, where the prospect of a public sector civil service job may be a dominant motivation for seeking formal schooling.

8.2.2.3 *Social privilege, status, and conflict*

Functionalist accounts, whether explicitly applied to a global pattern or to a country-level trend towards modernization, are sharply contradicted by theories locating the driving force behind school expansion in social conflict. This view posits that schooling expands 'to legitimate present inequalities, allowing advantaged classes to retain their jobs and cultural forms through a seemingly fair, meritocratic system. Here, the central state does not functionally expand mass schooling to pursue society's "common good." Instead, political actors, captured by elites, serve to reinforce and reproduce economic and cultural differences' (Fuller and Rubinson, 1992, p. x). More specifically, some argue that mass educational systems are organized to reproduce existing inequalities over generations and serve the priorities of the elite by creating a skilled and obedient working class capable of performing the labour that keeps those with the means of production wealthy (Bernstein, 1971; Bowles and Gintis, 1976; Collins, 1971). In a related vein, cultural theories argue that educational credentials offered by formal mass educational systems offer a way for individuals to signal their privileged status within social realms (e.g. social class membership, eligibility for marriage) or the field of labour (e.g. entitlement to authority) (Bourdieu, 1986).

Support for this perspective comes from the fact that one of the most important predictors of an individual's educational attainment continues to be his or her parents' educational attainment (Clemens, 2004). Parents' education is an essential determinant of family socio-economic status (SES), and home and community SES, in turn, determines a child's educational and occupational aspirations (Sewell and Hauser, 1980). Countless studies also emphasize how important family background is to academic performance. Not only does the home environment created by more educated parents stimulate higher cognitive ability, it also conditions children's attitudes toward schooling and beliefs about the inherent value of education. Thus, parents with relatively high educational attainment tend to raise more educated children.

Despite the fact that these patterns suggest a great deal of intergenerational transfer of status, an inherent amount of individual competition leads, at the same time, to self-sustaining levels of education within a population: as one generation becomes more educated, the higher the probability that the next generation will be *at least* as highly educated. Higher levels of participation can create an intrinsic, self-reinforcing demand. This is not just true of industrialized societies. A body of research aimed towards understanding the reasons for educational expansion grew rapidly during the 1970s, when the world was witnessing tremendous expansion in mass schooling systems in developing nations across Latin America, South East Asia, and sub-Saharan Africa. These studies explored a number of contextual differences in economic development, political and social modernization, and economic dependencies. The contexts examined also varied according to ethnic and linguistic diversity, governmental authority (e.g. democracy vs authoritarianism), and degree of centralization. The results suggested that educational development within a country is often a self-generating process, whereby underlying levels of education create increasing demand over cohorts as higher levels of educational attainment become normative.

At the same time, *different dimensions* or *stages* of educational growth respond to different processes of social negotiation. Archer (1982), for example, suggests that 'external transactions' result in increased provision of schooling (e.g. private universities in Latin America), while 'internal initiation' results in longer schooling for the privileged (e.g. when teachers press for greater differentiation to reflect rising professionalization), in contrast to 'political manipulation' of the system leading to wider access (e.g. the movement towards desegregation of schools in the USA). 'The fact which accounts for the extremely high growth rate is that these three processes of negotiation take place conjointly and their effects reinforce each other' (Archer, 1982, p. 25).

Furthermore, processes of 'political manipulation' do not necessarily move directly from inequality toward greater equality. As a case in point, we can consider the unintended consequences of school desegregation efforts in the USA. During the 1960s and 1970s, after the decision of *Brown v. Board of Education* led to efforts to better balance the racial composition of public schools in recognition of the fact that minority concentration was associated with inherently unequal school outcomes, families of more affluent backgrounds reacted in ways that ultimately countered such efforts (Massey, 1990). In some cases, parents withdrew their children from the local public schools and re-enrolled them in private schools. In other cases, parents left inner cities in search of more favourable residential areas where minorities were far less concentrated. In fact, this de facto segregation is still a major factor in educational inequality (Kozol, 1991). Schools are primarily funded by local property taxes, and local property tax revenue reflects the local tax base, resulting in vast disparities in revenue across locales. Children are most often assigned to the school district closest to their homes, and neighbourhood segregation is a phenomenon not so easily legislated away. But again, in response, 'school choice' initiatives have been implemented in an attempt to allow families in less affluent neighbourhoods to select schools in more prosperous areas; however, it is often the case that families from the most disadvantaged backgrounds have been the least likely to exercise this choice, or 'choice schools' in segregated areas have failed to attract a diverse student population, both of which have resulted in further concentration of disadvantage in schools (Frankenberg et al., 2010).

8.2.2.4 *Emerging global norms*

In the contemporary, globally-connected world, the needs of nation-states are not limited to creating favourable conditions within their own borders, but include successful participation in international systems of political and economic cooperation. The state's engagement in education, therefore, is guided not just by the considerations outlined in the preceding sections, of achieving specific outcomes in the form of well-educated citizens and productive workers; it is also guided by the desire to signal its adherence to emerging global norms. In other words, 'mass schooling spreads like a social movement, allowing the state to signal that it is modern and efficacious' (Fuller and Rubinson, 1992, p. x). Systemic theories (i.e. world culture theories) positing the emergence or existence of a world system, a world society, or a world culture, as they refer to educational development, all point to the inherent desire of nation-states to legitimize themselves on the world stage via the adoption of common ideologies, institutions, and organizational systems. This 'isomorphization' is seen as a way for countries to signal their validity to proximate nation-states, as they adopt the same symbolic systems of legitimation as their peers (DiMaggio and Powell, 1983; Meyer, 1992). A system of mass schooling is an essential institution that can communicate a country's position in the world order. Problems with these theories have been discussed elsewhere (Fuller and Rubinson, 1992), but perhaps the biggest problem is that they lack specificity as to whether development results from actions of individuals, interest groups, or states, though it is likely that they are interactive (Jónasson, 2003). For instance, states may invest in educational infrastructure based on ideals promoted by power elites, but individuals or their families must act to enrol.

Furthermore, it is undeniable that international organizations have played a major role in the expansion of mass educational systems worldwide. One of the most important milestones in global educational expansion was the establishment in 1946 of UNESCO, which was granted the authority to make policy recommendations and provide technical assistance concerning educational progress in specific countries, and to inform efforts undertaken by other international economic organizations (Chabbott, 1998). The sustained commitment of groups like UNESCO, the United Nations Children's Education Fund (UNICEF), the World Bank, United Nations Development Programme (UNDP), and other country-specific aid organizations (e.g. U.S. Agency for International Development, Canadian International Development Agency) have given rise to an enormous field of research and associated professional communities devoted to educational development. These organizations have initiated several international conferences intended to advance a framework for universal literacy, universal primary enrolment, and gender equality within education (i.e. Education for All), or the Millennium Development Goals. Such efforts have built off other initiatives, such as Health for All, and infer authority from the Universal Declaration of Human Rights and the Rights of Children.

The fundamental tension between World Culture Theory and conflict-based accounts of educational dynamics becomes evident when the former is characterized as being predicated on two assumptions: 'the existence of significant commonality across societies (convergence) and, by implication, the view of change as primarily a derivative of consensual cultural processes (consensus)' (Carney et al., 2012, p. 373). World Culture Theory emphasizes that 'the fact that the system may originally have been pieced together by elites is no longer the salient point. Now everyone accepts the credibility of modern schools, states, and workplaces: These provide understood rules for achievement, common paths towards higher status, and seemingly just ways of distributing material goods' (Fuller and Rubinson, 1992, p. x). However, while at some level, the occurrence of convergence is an empirical question, it cannot be fully decided by empirical observation alone because superficial convergence in form does not necessarily entail 'deep' normative convergence.

However, identifying global processes as driving educational growth does not imply that such processes are necessarily consensus-driven. At their best, the efforts of international aid organizations reflect a sincere belief in promoting better outcomes in people's lives globally. But others argue that these efforts reflect pre-World War II colonial dependencies and Western biases, create unintentional structural problems, and lack necessary oversight and accountability (Corrales, 2006; de Moura Castro, 2002; Heyneman, 2003). Indeed, there is evidence that supply-side interventions ill-adapted to local conditions have not had the desired impact, particularly when demand has been assumed to be universal but is, in fact, insufficient. In other words, externally-led efforts are unlikely to achieve their desired results when they fail to account for barriers to quality schooling or attendance, or fail to account for labour market characteristics, local cultural characteristics, or the dynamics that shape demand for education within the population.

Among the most important determinants of increased educational demand are labour market demand and household economic factors, which are often more influential than supply-side inputs, such as school availability or distance to school (for an interesting review, see Clemens, 2004). Developing countries seeking external aid for various educational efforts have generally been in a vulnerable position. Given the appeal of the loans on offer, and the desire for recognition in the world community, such countries face strong incentives to commit to any number of externally-mandated reforms (e.g. the decentralization of education systems and devolution of authority to local community-centred education agencies), despite the social, economic, or demographic realities these countries confront (McNeely, 1995). As a result, oft-stated commitments to certain principles may not translate into actual results. Further, the structural reforms to which countries conditionally agree have sometimes had unintended and unfortunate consequences. These conditions are otherwise known as 'Structural Adjustment Programs', which typically require countries to cut expenditures on sectors seen by outside organizations as inefficient, such as public health or public employment. Countries may also be required to privatize certain public-good industries. Geo-Jaja and Mangum (2001) note the irony in expecting that de-funding public services would have a positive effect on development, as previous international aid programmes that actually improved economic conditions heavily funded the social service sectors (e.g. the Marshal Plan, the New Deal, etc.). In any case, the purposes of these loans provided are arguably too broad. Often, goals are non-specific or poorly matched to local conditions. Geo-Jaja and Mangum (2001) suggest that educational development plans should be better aligned with actual labour market needs and should take into account the changes to the market occurring in a re-structured economy.

8.2.2.5 *Autonomous systemic dynamics of the education sector*

In contrast to functional–structural explanations, a different explanatory framework focuses on 'the internal laws of the system [in order] to ask from a fresh perspective whether its behaviour is controlled or guided by its relation to the surrounding society or whether it is in fact the other way—that the relation of the system to its society is determined by its own internal necessities' (Green, 1980, p. 112). This approach does not deny the ties between the education system and other social structures, but notes that the larger the education system itself, the greater its autonomy (Ericson, 1982, p. 306). The positive feedback relation through parents' ambitions for their children, for example, becomes merely one in a number of feedback relations, most of which are considered to be intrinsic to the education system itself. This is based not least on the observation that frequently, and particularly at early stages of development, the education sector tends to be the largest single employer of its own graduates, and thereby increasingly able to tailor the system to its own needs.

Based on empirical analysis, Müller-Benedict (1991) affirms the latter interpretation and concludes that the autonomous dynamics of the education system are logically prior to functional relationships with other social systems. Evidence in favour of this claim is his analysis of university enrolment time series for Germany. Disregarding the long-term growth and looking only at fluctuations around the overall trend, internal dynamics in terms of two kinds of cycles explain 75 per cent of the remaining variance in this case. The first type of cycle is characterized by a wavelength (a period between peaks) that corresponds roughly to the length of a professional working life, namely in the range of 25–40 years. This can intuitively be recognized as fluctuations in replacement demand resulting from an uneven age structure within a profession and the resulting regular occurrence of large retirement waves. The second regular fluctuation is shorter and reflects the anti-cyclical entry behaviour into training. In other words, a peak (trough) in graduates in a given field entering the labour market encourages a corresponding trough (peak) in entrants into training through the feedback mechanism of observed career chances. As the distance between neighbouring peaks and troughs is the approximate duration of the relevant training, the wavelength of this fluctuation is approximately twice the training duration, namely 8–15 years. From a slightly different perspective, these can be interpreted as the response of entry flows to observed changes in the stock on the one hand, and to changes in the flows of the profession being trained for on the other. While the existence of 'long' cycles in educational growth is controversial, the explanatory power with respect to short-term fluctuations actually provides a stronger rationale for considering educational dynamics as being largely autonomous. Moreover, under certain conditions the short cycles of twice the duration of study experience a destabilizing feedback. Mathematically, this leads to an arbitrarily increasing amplitude. In practice, of course, this will not occur because pressure on the labour market will result in an increase in the number of skilled positions (Müller-Benedict, 1991).

The tight feedback between past and future output of an education system naturally hinges on the availability of qualified teachers. Despite external funding efforts, one of the most difficult internal constraints on educational expansion is the lack of a qualified teaching force. Without an infusion of foreign personnel, a native population must build its teaching corps from the underlying stock of qualified persons, and in countries with historically low enrolment and fast population growth, this is particularly challenging. In a systematic analysis of teacher shortages, Wils and O'Connor (2004) examined the links between gross primary enrolment and a number of country-level characteristics, including adult educational attainment, gross national product (GNP) per capita, and per cent of GNP spent on education. They found that the single largest correlate of primary enrolment was the proportion of adults with secondary education. Moreover, in countries with a relatively low proportion of adults with secondary education, a very large share worked as teachers, implying that a serious impediment to enrolment was low educational attainment among the adult population. The authors point out, however, that increasing enrolment is a 'chicken versus egg' problem (p. 8) in the sense that an increased share of adults qualified to teach primary and secondary education is necessary to increase enrolment, while at the same time increasing adult education levels requires earlier sustained success with primary and secondary enrolment. In sub-Saharan Africa the problem of teacher shortage is particularly stark. Children in such education systems may have teachers with barely more education than they have themselves. This may either result from efforts to avoid large classes at the expense of low teacher qualifications, or occur in addition to large classes. In this sense, poor teacher quality could be a self-reinforcing process.

An emphasis on feedback relations and autonomous behaviour driven more by systemic logic than by external factors does not mean that the behaviour of the education system is in any way 'automatic'. What it does mean is that, to a large extent, it is the result of the behaviour of actors within the system applying 'practical arguments' (Green, 1980) that are rational with respect to their situation within the education sector, not necessarily with respect to the education sector's functional relationship with other social systems.

8.2.2.6 *A tentative synthesis*

'Mono-causal factors [such] as status-group conflict, the social reproduction of the class structure, or the homogenizing characteristics of an evolving world system [are] superficially appealing, but inadequate' (Craig and Spear, 1982, p. 154). Instead, the different general theories 'can be seen as simultaneous oscillating processes, each operating within a given society but with varying strength over long stretches of time' (Fuller and Rubinson, 1992, p. 12). With a slightly different focus, Archer cautioned that 'the possibility/probability that different theories (or theoretical modifications) may be needed for different stages of socio-educational development is never even considered' (Archer, 1982, p. 5).

Overall, the debate has not advanced significantly in elaborating the conditions under which different effects are operative or how their relative importance varies either over time or at different levels of development. Instead, the debate has become stuck in disagreements about fundamental premises underlying different explanations, and the meaning and causal attribution of expansion. At the same time, the different theoretical approaches do not necessarily stand in conflict. For example, while not focusing on the political aspects of social competition, Green's systems perspective serves to further explicate why educational expansion does not resolve class conflict. This perspective implies that as an attainment level is universalized, the last to reach it 'will be disappointed because as they attain their target... they will not gain the relative benefits that others have secured. They will only have avoided a disaster that is uniquely their own' (Green, 1980, p. 111). This is both empirically confirmed and conceptually echoed more recently by Raftery and Hout and their notion of 'maximally maintained inequality' (1993).

We argue that the different accounts of educational dynamics are not mutually contradictory, but could be interpreted as focusing on, respectively, the demand for entry (sociological), demand for the product (economic), supply (nation-state), and the self-interested internal logic of the education sector. Undoubtedly, all these processes are at work. *For the purpose of educational projection, which is the central programme of this chapter and book, the key question is not which of them dominates, but which has stable long-term implications, and which result in fluctuations that may be characterized as statistical noise.*

A unified perspective, at least on the macro-dynamics, appears possible if the hints are taken seriously as to conditions under which each theory applies. For example, individualistic status competition for attainment may not be keenly felt in a setting where educational participation is extremely low and does not differentiate members of the vast majority. It seems likely that 'take-off' is driven by an economic need for more skilled manpower, and the ensuing rapid expansion to levels over and beyond societal needs is driven by status competition, while universalization to the last marginalized groups can only be achieved through state intervention under normative pressure.

This perspective is not pursued any further here. Rather than arbitrating between competing explanations, of greatest interest for present purposes is to identify overlaps in their implications for future developments, especially in what they identify as deep underlying trends, as opposed to fluctuating actions. The different explanations need not stand in conflict in terms of their qualitative implications for future expansion. The next section attempts to extract such insights.

8.2.3 Predictive content of the theoretical models

The theories outlined earlier have been formulated by their proponents as explanations of observed patterns of expansion, not as vehicles for generating predictions. Nevertheless, examining their statements about conditions conducive to educational expansion and considering conditions we may expect to prevail in the future provide some basis to expect overall sustained expansion in the long run.

Indeed, one implication of Green's framework is that 'there are reasons to believe that the system will expand, even when there is a decline in resources for it and a decline in the demand for its services', termed the 'Principle of Uniform Growth' (Green, 1980, p. 17). One of the reasons is the upgrading of qualification requirements within the education system itself in response to either an undersupply or oversupply of graduates. This leads to the expectation that, in the long run, everyone within the system will have the highest credentials. A consequence of the systemic nature of the education sector is that growth at one level tends to stimulate growth at another. This applies both in 'upstream' and 'downstream' directions. An upgrading of early childhood education, for example, leads to an expansion in post-secondary or even tertiary training of early childhood specialists and teachers. Conversely, high targets for tertiary attainment stimulate expansion at lower levels in order to supply the pool of candidates so selectivity can be maintained at the tertiary stage. Importantly, 'this principle is not a prediction that the system is always, in fact, expanding or that qualifications for positions within it are always, in fact, increasing' (Green, 1980, p. 74), but that other behaviours can only occur in response to outside influence.

Even where internal system dynamics do not provide the propulsion for expansion, they can create an upward drift by acting as an expansion 'valve' (Müller-Benedict, 1991, p. 144). Several factors serve to ensure that the system has a tendency to react only to growth pressures, but not to contract when demand falls. On the face of it, a difference between a constant expansionary drift on the one hand, and such a one-way 'valve' effect on the other, is that the latter only leads to increasing size of the education system in terms of its capacity, not necessarily its output. However, in practice, non-decreasing capacity means that eventual demand increases can always be accommodated, so an upward drift in output still follows.

It is important to note that projections of continued expansion are intended as descriptive, not prescriptive, accounts of future developments. Indeed, Green and colleagues describe how system momentum drives attainment at any level towards universality, but explicitly argue that from an equity point of view, a more appropriate policy target would be 55–60 per cent high school attainment (which they argue would force the labour market to offer valid opportunities to those without a high-school diploma, whose number would be too large to ignore). The same applies to not only the final level, but also the pace of expansion. Descriptively, we can assert that expansion slows down at high levels, while in terms of social equity, it would be desirable to reach between 75 and 100 per cent participation as quickly as possible 'in order to minimize the hardships that will have to be endured by the decreasing percentage of non-attainers' (Seidman, 1982, p. 285); at the intermediate stage, non-attainment is already a liability. Archer likewise diagnoses 'unguided growth' of the system as 'an unintended consequence, sought by no-one and welcomed nowhere' (Archer, 1982, p. 55).

For projections to be meaningful, we need neither an unfounded belief that the spread of formal attainment is necessarily 'effective, efficient, and equitable' (Carney et al., 2012, p. 383), nor an assumed inevitability of continued attainment expansion in a way that is consistent with past patterns. Indeed, the partial disagreement Archer expressed with Green's model was not about the regularity in expansion it describes, but about whether this regularity reflects an 'ineluctable logic' or whether there are merely 'good reasons, founded in social interactions, why these conditions [leading to expansion] are approximated to in reality' (Archer, 1982, p. 53).

We recognize the contingency of expansion on these conditions (hierarchical organization of attainment levels and educational credentials as sorting mechanisms), but we also note that their persistence is likely, or at least provides a defensible baseline hypothesis. It seems more likely that our projections will be falsified because the very meaning, or modality, of 'formal schooling' changes than because formal attainment growth radically changes its dynamic. It would be misguided to deny the meaningfulness of projections by pointing out that policy represents a deliberate and purposeful attempt to direct the educational process, and that projections cannot account for such future policy changes. We may think of policy and crises as 'non-deterministic deviations' from a deterministic expectation. Here, 'deterministic expectation' does not mean that we expect a deterministic trajectory, but that whatever our expectation is we do not form it by tossing coins

This hypothesis of sustained expansion does not contradict the fact that when development advocates have attempted to 'scale up' successful interventions from one place to others, they have found that the contingencies of the context matter tremendously.

This suggests that interactions between population growth, social demand, economic development, and the existing stock of human capital are complex and do not necessarily allow the imposition of one particular policy of schooling expansion onto any setting (Mennerick and Najafizadeh, 1987). However, locating the driver of expansion in conditions the education system is likely to endogenously create in the long run explains, rather than contradicts, the difficulty of bringing about change through external policy stimulus. Historical evidence supports this. 'In Europe, since the late eighteenth century...prior enrollment levels predict subsequent school expansion more strongly than the appearance of novel forces, such as rapid commercial growth, industrial job demand, and the modern state's rise and penetration into the hinterlands' (Fuller and Rubinson, 1992, pp. 23–4). In any case, as changes in the external input and output relations with other systems do not create corresponding changes in the education system directly, but only by triggering an autonomous response within the system, they are transformed into internal dynamics. The implication is that it is sufficient to study only the dynamics of the education system itself, without explicit consideration of external factors such as economic development because the consequences of relevant impacts have already been absorbed (Müller-Benedict, 1991, p. 255).

In summary, in terms of their implications for future developments, there is overlap among different theories seeking to explain past attainment growth. This overlap points to continued expansion in the long term; a trend towards (not necessarily complete) global convergence; the qualitatively similar expansionary behaviour at higher education levels now and lower levels before (to the extent that expansion is driven by competition and not the substantive benefits directly linked to the educational content); and accelerating expansion as a given level of attainment becomes more common. This final point occurs because the 'cycles of positive reinforcement operating between supply and demand, context and environment, and microscopic and macroscopic action' are, in general, speeding up (Archer, 1982, p. 42). The systems-theoretical accounts specifically, as well as the empirical evidence, justify a model seeking to project educational attainment endogenously based only on past and current attainment levels.

8.3 A projection model for global educational attainment

Our overall approach consists of two parts: fitting a model of educational development trajectories to the empirical development of attainment over the course of recent decades, and projecting attainment by extending these trajectories into the future.

The specifics of both parts are interdependent. Estimating the model is logically prior, as it is meaningful without attempting a projection, but the converse is not true, and the feasible characteristics of the model constrain the form of the projection. Conversely, the intended primary purpose of the model as a projection input determines the requirements. On the one hand, the model must be of a kind that can be extrapolated in a meaningful and consistent way; on the other hand, it need only capture temporally robust associations, not causal explanations. The model is fit to reconstructed educational attainment data for 178 countries for the period 1970–2010.

8.3.1 Fitting past expansion

The first question is which measure(s) to model directly, and which to derive. In the present context, educational growth could conceivably be modelled by projecting the number of people attaining each level, or the shares of different attainment groups among each cohort, or transitions between levels. There are arguments in favour of each choice. Modelling absolute numbers accounts for some of the absolute constraints on capacity expansion in the education sector, and might suggest a view that educational development is supply-driven. Transition rates between attainment levels arise naturally from the common approach to modelling within-school flows in terms of entry, promotion, repetition, and dropout rates. We choose to focus on attainment shares among (five-year) cohorts as the measure to be modelled directly. The distinct advantages are three-fold. First, in a world of declining fertility, supply-side constraints are expected to lose importance relative to social demand, especially at levels below tertiary, and normalizing the education model by population size makes it possible to specify it independently from the overall population growth model and its fertility assumptions. This breaks a potentially troublesome feedback loop in the projection method. Second, in contrast to transitions, attainment is directly a property of persons, and represents the outcome of the education model required for inclusion in the overall population projection (this also serves as an argument against examining enrolments, which are, indeed, a person characteristic, but not a stable one). Moreover, shares at different levels can be interpreted independently, whereas transitions are cumulative and their implications for attainment can only be understood as an ensemble.

Having settled on attainment shares as the principal measure, the question of whose attainment to model directly arises or, more specifically, which age group to focus on. It would be possible, of course, to separately model the attainment at different ages, but the possibility of contradictory results makes it an unattractive approach. Using a single reference age group, however, calls for a balancing act: younger ages reflect more closely the recent developments in the education system, while at older ages there is a greater chance of accurately capturing the maximal lifetime attainment. Here, we use the attainment share at ages 30–34 as the benchmark, in a compromise between these two concerns.

An additional question concerns the levels to model explicitly. Separate models for different attainment levels risk creating inconsistent results, where the share of those with upper secondary or higher attainment is projected to be greater than the share with lower secondary or higher attainment, for example. This risk is greater the closer the levels in question are to each other. Instead of attempting a complex joint model that imposes ordering constraints, we estimate independent models for the sufficiently separated levels of completed primary, upper secondary, and tertiary education, which results in projections without inconsistent crossovers. We then interpolate the intermediary levels of lower secondary and incomplete primary education, with no education calculated as the residual. Specifically, the share of these intermediary levels among those with completed primary, but less than completed upper secondary schooling (in the case of lower secondary), and among those with less than completed primary schooling (in the case of incomplete primary), respectively, is held constant at the most recent value observed.

Based on the discussion in section 8.2.3, the model is designed to capture the intrinsic dynamics of the education sector, rather than the effect of external predictors (such as economic growth), that would then, in turn, need to be projected, raising additional questions of data reliability and endogeneity.

The model assumed here effectively relates the growth over time in the share of 30–34-year-olds having reached a given attainment level or higher to the current level of said share. The relationship is such that growth is slowest for both very low and very high shares, and fastest at middle levels, resulting in a sigmoid trajectory over time. In the present case, this shape is parameterized as an (inverse) probit curve. The probit curvature was found during exploratory investigations to match the empirical patterns more closely than a logistic specification.

Concretely, the observed data on the highest attainment are transformed into reversely-cumulated attainment shares such as 'percentage with upper secondary or higher' and correspondingly for other attainment levels. These figures in the interval [0,1] are probit-transformed into unbounded numbers. An exact inverse-probit sigmoid curve would be perfectly linearized as a result, turned, in other words, into a straight line. Accordingly, a linear fit to the transformed data corresponds to an inverse-probit sigmoid curve fitted to the original data. The linear predictor is taken to consist of an overall global component g, as well as region- and country-specific elements (r and c), all time-invariant, as well as random residuals epsilon at the level of country–year dyads. Formally:

$$\text{participation}_{it} = \Phi(x_{it} + \varepsilon_{it})$$

$$x_{it} = x_{i(t-1)} + g + r_i + c_i \tag{8.1}$$

Because we are not interested in lateral shifts in time, the data can be centred so that participation is 50 per cent at time $t0$ for estimation purposes. In order to obtain distributional results to aid scenario creation, the given specification is estimated within a Bayesian framework. The priors for all parameters are normally distributed with zero means and half-Cauchy priors for the variances. The outcomes of the estimation are posterior probability distributions for the overall global-, regional-, and country-specific rates of educational growth.

For the post-secondary education level, the attainment share is re-scaled so that complete saturation corresponds to 90 per cent of a cohort attaining post-secondary education. This reflects the fact that, unlike lower levels of schooling, universalizing post-secondary education is a policy target nowhere, and, on the contrary, the current frontrunners, such as Singapore, are debating whether to actively limit post-secondary expansion.

Figure 8.7 shows the empirical pattern of attainment growth by level. The dashed line is a locally weighted scatterplot smoother (LOESS). The solid line displays the predicted growth based on only the global average term *g* in equation 8.1. In other words, this represents the global average inverse probit-shaped expansion path. In terms of implied trajectories of educational growth over time, Figure 8.8 displays the observed country paths at the original scale, arranged around the hypothetical global average trajectory. As is evident, even this simple, purely endogenous, model does a credible job of approximating the pattern in the data.

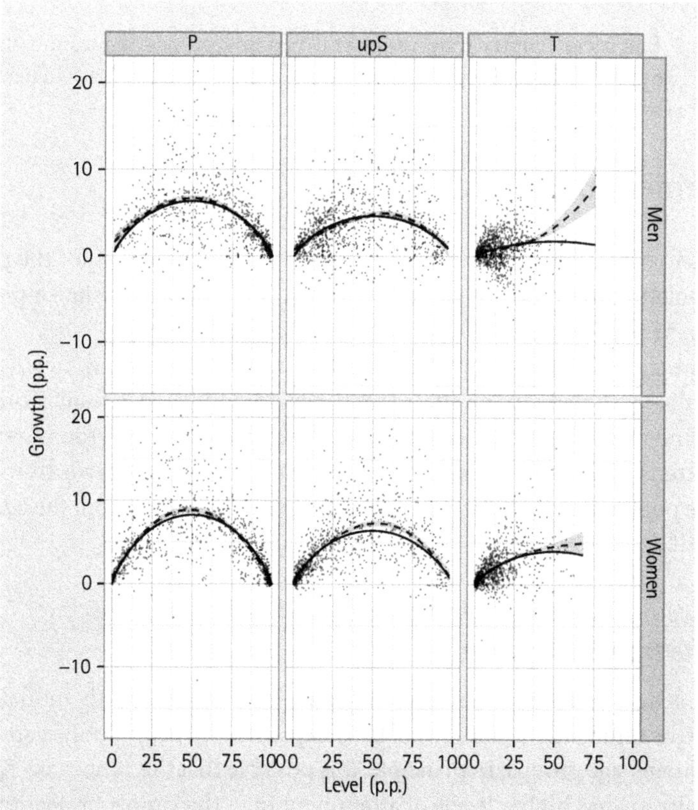

FIGURE 8.7 Observed (dots), smoothed (dashed), and predicted (solid) five-year attainment growth (in percentage points) as a function of attainment share already achieved.

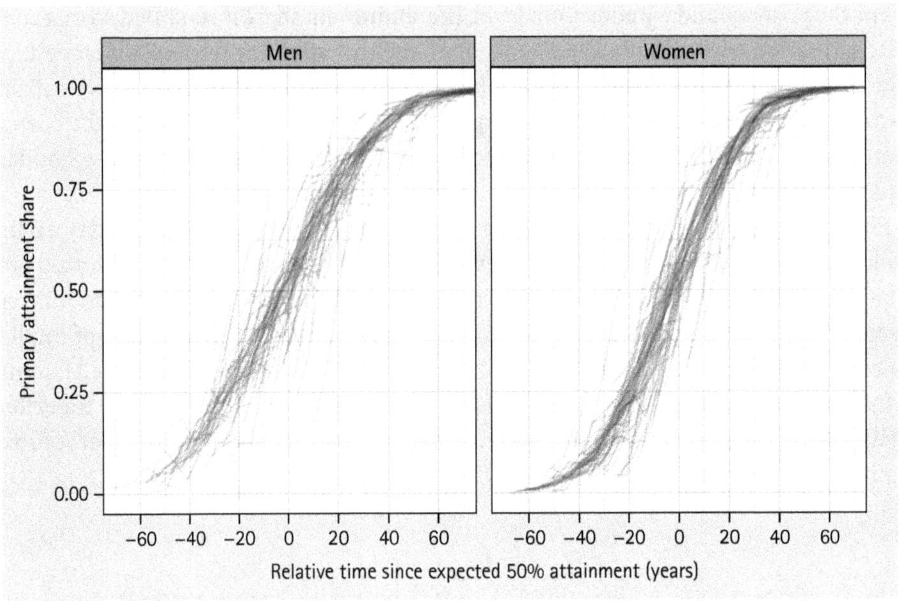

FIGURE 8.8 Empirical country trajectories of expanding primary education attainment in the 30–34 age group, arranged around global average time since reaching 50 per cent attainment share (see section 8.3).

8.3.2 Projected diffusion

Our aim is to obtain projected attainment levels for all age groups for the period 2010–60. Extrapolating the model given in section 8.3.1 in the first instance provides these only for 30–34-year-olds.

Given the simplifying assumption that educational attainment is mostly complete by the age of 30–34, changes in the attainment shares at higher ages result from differential mortality and migration behaviour between different education groups, rather than attainment transitions. Accordingly, the shares at higher ages derive from the general multi-state population projection and require no further input from the education projection itself.

8.3.2.1 *Reconciliation of observations and projections during the transition phase*

Because it is time series of attainment at age 30–34 that is explicitly modelled and projected into the future, there is potential for disagreement with the observations of attainment at younger age groups. In principle, it is possible that the cohort 25–29 years in the base year already has higher levels of attainment than the simple projection implies for the age group 30–34 five years later.

This affects only the first three projection steps, as the individuals who in the base year are located in the age groups 25–29, 20–24, and 15–19 have observed attainment shares that might be inconsistent with their projected attainment at age 30–34 based on the simple projection. Beginning with the cohort that is aged 10–14 in the base year, there are no observations that could be at odds with the projected attainment at later ages.

A two-step process ensures consistency along two directions. The first is along cohort lines. As the highest level of education attained is non-decreasing with age, this is a logical requirement. It is achieved by adjusting the projection so that the share having achieved a given education level in a cohort is, at all ages, at least as high as the share observed in the base year (Figure 8.9).

The second step ensures that the application of the first step does not result in fluctuations over time in attainment at a given age. While this is not a logical necessity as educational stagnation and even decline across cohorts are certainly possible in reality, this is done in the interest of coherence. Fluctuations around the central trend are possible, but the entire model is set up to project the long-term central trend, not short-term fluctuations. Accordingly, the maximum is taken of the values resulting from (1) the simple projection of attainment at age 30–34 over time, starting in the base year; and (2) the attainment of younger age groups observed in the base year, brought forward along cohort lines.

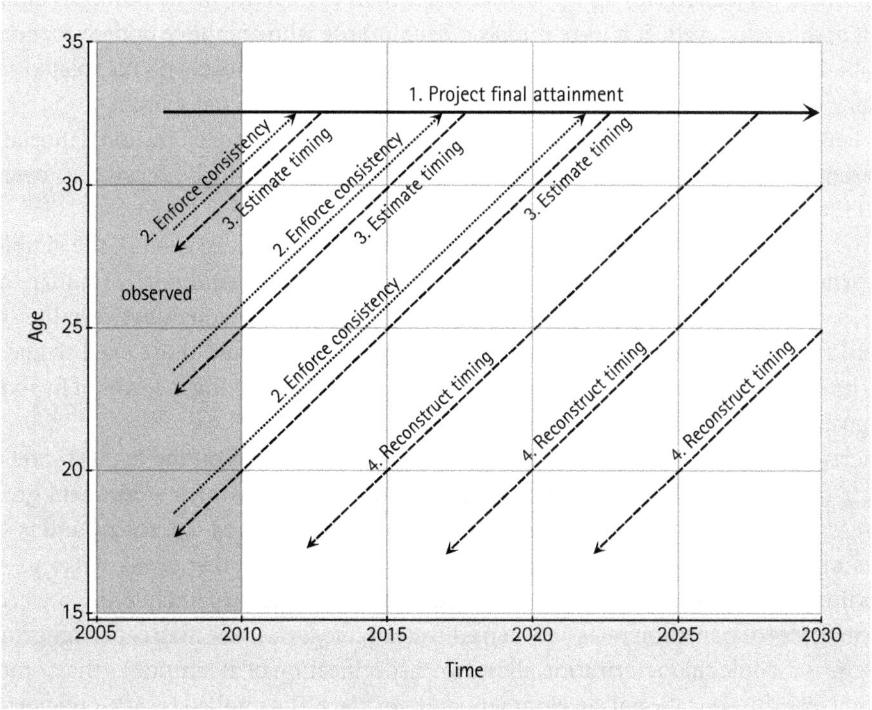

FIGURE 8.9 Short-term reconciliation between projected attainment at age 30–34 and observed attainment at younger ages.

In effect, the local maximization approach to the first step corresponds to the assumption that, as far as possible, inconsistencies should be reconciled by adjusting the assumed timing of attainment, rather than the final level. Consider, for example, a situation in which the observed attainment at age 20–24 is higher than the projected attainment at this age, but lower than the projected final attainment at age 30–34. Our approach reconciles this by adjusting the timing of attainment so that sufficiently many attainment transitions are assumed to have occurred earlier than initially assumed, but without changing the overall number of transitions to higher levels. In principle, it would be equally possible to fix the timing schedule, in other words the assumed relationship between attainment at age 20–24 and final attainment at age 30–34, but to adjust the assumed final level so that the back-projected attainment at the younger age no longer falls below the observed level. The choice between the two approaches (and against a mixture of them) was dictated by the principle that the least certain parts of the model should be the first to be adjusted to accommodate contradictory information. In the present case, the timing schedules are reasonable a priori assumptions, while, by contrast, the projected final attainment levels at age 30–34 also incorporate modelling assumptions and hence are also data-driven.

8.3.2.2 *Transition schedules below the age of 30*

Attainment projections for age groups younger than 30 depend on the timing of attainment at different levels. If it were the case that all those who complete upper secondary school do so by the age of 24 at the oldest, then the share of those with completed secondary schooling among 25–29-year-olds is equal to their projected share as 30–34-year-olds five years later. These relations are only strict in the absence of educational mortality differentials. The error induced by ignoring mortality is marginal, however, as overall mortality at young adult ages is low.

The aggregation into five-year age groups complicates matters: even in the simplest case where everyone completes the upper secondary level at the nominally standard age of 18, for example, the age group 15–19 would include both individuals between the ages 15 and 17 who will complete the level, but only in the future, and those aged 18 and 19 who have already graduated. The specification of attainment timing in terms of five-year age groups should take this into account.

Here, the system of attainment age schedules is conditioned on the highest level attained by the age of 30–34. This means the schedules specify which attainment group those with post-secondary degrees by age 30–34 were in at ages 25–29, 20–24, and 15–19, and similarly for those with upper secondary attainment and other levels at age 30–34. Conditional on the shares at age 30–34, these schedules could, in principle, be converted into matrices of transition rates between education categories, one matrix per age group. The age–schedule characterization allows for a specification of assumptions that is more natural from an educational development point of view. The implied transition matrices are effectively parameterized by five parameters with a natural interpretation (the ultimate attainment shares). Many entries are either logically predetermined or straightforward to specify: the monotonicity of highest attainment over the life course implies a number of structural zeroes.

The transition schedules are estimated for each country by taking the short-term projections for the age group 30–34 as given, and comparing them with the observed attainment at ages 25–29, 20–24, and 15–19 in the baseline year. Specifically, if 30 per cent are projected to have completed post-secondary attainment or higher by age 30–34 in 2015, and 20 per cent are observed to do so among 25–29-year-olds in 2010, then the implied schedule is that, of those completing post-secondary, two-thirds do so between the ages of 25–29 and 30–34. A similar comparison is made for the age group 30–34 in 2020 and the age group 20–24 in 2010, and for the age group 30–34 in 2025 and the age group 15–19 in 2010.

These schedules are not guaranteed to be consistent from a cohort perspective. In a second step, schedules are determined through optimization techniques that satisfy logical consistency constraints and are closest in absolute difference (over the entries) to the raw schedules found earlier. More precisely, a weighted average distance is minimized between the raw country-specific schedules and a standard set of schedules described in the next paragraph, with weights of 0.7 on the country-specific schedule and 0.3 on the standard schedules. This regularization step avoids some undesirable transition behaviour that can occur in the raw schedules in countries in which baseline population attainment at younger ages is highly irregular owing to rapid educational change, declining attainment, or possibly migration.

The assumed schedules are designed to correspond to nominal graduation ages based on school entry at age 6, with a stylized school system of 6 + 3 + 3 for primary, lower, and upper secondary schooling, and three years for a first post-secondary degree, while taking into account the age spread within five-year age groups. At the same time, it must be recognized that at the post-secondary level, there is no consensus that a 'regular' education career requires higher education studies to immediately follow the completion of upper secondary schooling. Indeed, 'late' post-secondary attainment, even above the age of 35, is substantial in some countries, including the USA.

The sensitivity of the Wittgenstein Centre for Demography and Global Human Capital (WIC) projections with respect to the assumptions concerning attainment timing is expected to be greater in the case of fertility than for mortality. Overall mortality is generally lowest at the young adult ages at which the assumptions apply. The greatest impact is expected to be on fertility and migration. However, this impact is moderated by the fact that absolute educational fertility differentials are smallest in the countries with high levels of post-secondary attainment and largest in those countries where the share of post-secondary graduates, and therefore the share of those whose attainment timing is most difficult to estimate, is relatively low. In general, the specification of assumptions in terms of age schedules conditional on ultimate attainment means that, in contrast to the alternative of specifying transition rates, specification errors do not cumulate.

8.3.2.3 *Convergence*

Owing to the specification of the model, where countries' expansion parameters are estimated as coming from a shared statistical distribution (by gender and education level), the basic country estimates and, by implication, their projected trajectories, are not independent. Some 'shrinkage' towards the overall mean occurs, reflecting the fact that a country with an exceptionally fast/slow historical expansion path may be assumed to have experienced a particularly fast/slow incidental spell in addition to having a fast/slow intrinsic momentum.

However, the estimation model does not assume that countries become more similar over time. This is, nonetheless, something that may be assumed as a projection assumption. Here, it is the rates of change in probit-transformed attainment that undergo convergence, not the attainment levels directly. In other words, even if complete convergence were assumed, countries would still differ in attainment, and—owing to the non-linear sigmoid expansion model—would still expand at different rates on the original scale of attainment shares because even with identical rates on the transformed scale, countries at middle levels of attainment would increase their attainment share more rapidly than countries close to saturation.

The case for assuming a weak convergence over a very long time horizon is different from the case for assuming relatively rapid complete convergence (within a few decades). The first is a 'regularization' of the projection, rather than a reflection of a strong assumption of mechanisms leading to convergence. In the absence of any convergence, countries that have undergone a recent decline in educational attainment would be projected to undergo an educational collapse if the decline was extrapolated without a corrective. Assuming a slight level of convergence to the global median ensures that such countries' trajectories are merely stagnant. Accordingly, a slow convergence in rates, namely complete convergence by 2100, is assumed for all scenarios. By contrast, the central scenario is one where globalization trends in educational development result in a convergence in rates by 2060.

A separate issue is that of convergence of educational attainment of men and women within a given country. The initial estimates of the trajectories are independent for each gender. Indeed, historical patterns show that large gender differences in attainment can occur and remain for decades at all education levels. Gender difference in primary school attendance in countries with low educational development in sub-Saharan Africa, South Asia, and elsewhere are systematically highlighted by international development agencies. But large gaps at the post-compulsory stage can also be observed in industrialized countries. Nevertheless, for projection purposes, it is appropriate to include some degree of linkage between female and male attainment levels in a given country to avoid a situation where gaps are projected that fall outside the range of precedent. Here, male and female attainment, in terms of the share attaining or exceeding each level of education, is projected to converge to the gender-averaged attainment by the end of the projection horizon in 2060.

8.3.3 Scenario definition

Basing the projection on the median estimates of the country slopes corresponds to a 'business-as-usual' setting. One of the aims of the exercise is to investigate the possible consequences of more rapid, or on the contrary more laggard, educational growth.

8.3.3.1 *Central scenario: global education trend*

In the global education trend scenario, the attainment profile of future cohorts is based on the median parameter estimates of the model estimated in section 8.3.2. In that sense, while not interpretable as the 'most likely' scenario in a probabilistic sense, it can be interpreted as the scenario that reality is equally likely to exceed or fall short of.

In policy terms, this may be interpreted as 'business-as-usual'. This does not, however, imply a static perspective. On the contrary, even if the pace of educational expansion statistically depends on the level already attained in an endogenous fashion, the theoretical discussion in section 8.2 makes it clear that this expansion, though statistically unsurprising, nevertheless has to be actively produced by the actors involved. It is therefore a scenario of sustained effort. At the same time, being based on the average performance of the most recent decades, including at the country-specific level, this scenario does factor in the inevitable setbacks and mismatches between ambitious policy targets and actual change 'on the ground'.

Accordingly, the assumed and implied overall development will continue to have both light and shade. Steady progress may be achieved in terms of overall education participation, but some groups will not benefit as much economic and less tangible rewards from the schooling they receive as they could owing to low quality of education. As a result, increasing educational aspirations from generation to generation cannot be taken as a given. Technological progress and social innovation will continue to be made, but their diffusion is uneven.

8.3.3.2 *High scenario: fast benchmark*

In this scenario, the most rapid country-specific expansion parameters are applied to all countries throughout the projection period. In other words, all countries follow the educational development paths taken in the past by the frontrunners in East and South East Asia.

Note that owing to the non-linearity in the expansion paths, this does not mean that all countries proceed at the same pace on the original scale of attainment shares, much less that all countries have identical attainment profiles at the end of the projection.

In policy terms, this corresponds to a scenario where there is an immediate and concerted global effort to supply a sufficient number of schools, expand teacher training, and pursue the enrolment and retention of marginalized and disadvantaged subpopulations. At the global level, assuming that all countries simultaneously and successfully replicate the educational growth of the Republic of Korea or Singapore is, of course, implausible. This scenario therefore purely serves the function of supplying an upper bound on the effect educational expansion could possibly exert on overall projection outcomes.

As educational development is locked into a tight relationship of mutual feedback with overall socio-economic change, such a scenario of rapid educational expansion can only be meaningfully interpreted in an assumed context of substantial transformation of global society, partly as a prerequisite and partly as an effect of explosive educational growth. It may therefore be assumed, in the context of the fast benchmark scenario, that a focused global effort is made not only to finally achieve the 'Education for All' aims initially set by the international community for 2015 in terms of universalizing primary education, but that similar schemes follow at the secondary level. The unconditional success of such schemes on a global level would facilitate the achievement of other development goals relating to poverty reduction and global health. In particular, the scenario implies the essential disappearance of female disadvantage in education, with significant implications for female empowerment and possibly the ease of diffusion for social innovation. This scenario also assumes a substantial reduction in the occurrence of man-made crises and conflicts that have set back educational development in the past.

8.3.3.3 *Low scenarios*

Constant enrolment rates

For the constant enrolment rates (CER) scenario, the attainment shares at age 30–34 of future cohorts are fixed at the levels observed in the base year (but adjusted where necessary if younger age groups in the base year already exhibit higher than predicted attainment).

While in general terms, this is a lower bound scenario that is likely to be exceeded in most places, it is not necessarily a 'worst case' scenario. Indeed, in countries where cohort-on-cohort population growth remains high, schooling even a constant proportion of increasing successive cohorts may require substantial investments in capacity expansion. It is quite possible for an actual country trajectory to fall behind even the CER scenario if the education system is under pressure from population growth, disasters, emergencies, or conflict. Nevertheless, constant rates at the global level would correspond to an unprecedented period of stagnation.

Constant enrolment numbers

Under the constant enrolment numbers (CEN) scenario, the absolute numbers of individuals in each five-year age cohort that complete a given level of schooling by age 30–34 remains constant.

To give it a substantive interpretation, such a scenario may be approximated if educational growth is limited by capacity constraints. A given number of university places for example, coupled with an underdeveloped private sector to cater to potential excess demand for them, means student numbers may be stable regardless of the size of school-leaving cohorts. In contrast to the CER scenario, where fixed participation rates imply that absolute enrolments fluctuate as a function of cohort size, under CEN the reverse is true: absolute numbers are fixed, and together with cohort sizes they determine the rates.

Structurally, CEN is a pessimistic scenario in that the education category that is not subject to the constancy constraint, and that therefore expands or contracts to accommodate changing cohort sizes, is the category of 'no education'. However, in some circumstances, this case may lead to greater educational growth than the CER scenario, specifically when birth cohorts are becoming successively smaller. However, because the educationally least developed countries are, at the same time, among those with the highest fertility, the CEN scenario is particularly negative at the low end. In these countries, the implied participation rates amount to a deterioration of current conditions.

An actual path close to either the CER or CEN scenarios would likely represent a major obstacle to socio-economic development. A parent generation with a stagnant or even increasing share of the poorly-educated would not help the further diffusion of improving child health, for example. And an increasing supply of unskilled labour would at the same time provide little incentive for a modernization of the national economy and also depress wages at the low end.

8.4 Implications

At the country level, there is no lack of policy questions that can benefit from an informed estimate of future educational attainment. A few examples among many will suffice here. The question of how many older persons there will be relative to the number of school children and students in higher education will be a crucial part of the political economy context for education spending in the future. Anticipating when and where public support is likely to shift away from public education as a spending priority towards public provision of services for the elderly is a crucial strategic parameter for educators. The education profile of the senior majority itself is also likely to matter, as will their family relationships, that is, whether the higher education students are still disproportionately members of families that contain the most politically active and sophisticated seniors, or whether, owing to a combination of demography (the poor have more children) and educational progress, the student body does not seem like kin to these seniors.

The future education profile of the population will also matter in terms of how, through ageing of the generations that benefited from the rapid expansion in higher education, the average 'vintage' of degrees and qualifications in the population will increase. In partially predictable ways, the importance of life-long learning vis-à-vis formal schooling for the young will increase almost automatically, simply because there will be relatively more older adults, and more of them than today will be in knowledge industries and qualified by degrees that have a shorter 'half-life'.

Teacher recruitment is another case in point. To base recruitment on present (or worse: recent!) teacher shortages is to lag eternally behind. Matters are worse regarding recruiting students into teacher training. Ideally, human resource planning for the teaching force would take into account demand in the coming 40 years (as well as estimates of retirement, attrition, etc.). Even ignoring the students, aligning teacher recruitment purely with current needs rather than taking a sufficiently long-term view would risk creating problems that are both foreseeable and avoidable. For example, if an unbalanced age structure among the teaching force is created, the situation may arise where there is a shortage of head teachers (because the pool of potential candidates who are neither too old nor too inexperienced is small), even if there is an oversupply of teachers overall.

There are also theoretical implications at the aggregate level. On average, educational expansion tends to follow a sigmoid diffusion pattern. Taken at face value, this implies that a cluster of countries with similarly, but not exactly equally, low levels of educational attainment, will, by this measure, move apart before moving closer again, as one passes the 'take-off' point before the other. In other words, it is not unreasonable to expect that inequality between countries that are only beginning to embark on a path towards universalizing schooling will initially increase, even if all of them are on (the same) track. This has implications for the direction of international support.

Moreover, extreme cases illustrate the benefit of projecting long-term scenarios, even if they are purely hypothetical and not intended as reasonable forecasts, because they provide bounds on what can be achieved. Even if Niger stepped up to the extraordinary pace of South Korea, given its current stocks, it would still be far behind the international average even two generations from now (Figure 8.10).

In fact, together with only a handful of other countries, in relative terms Niger would be even further behind than it is now, because the global benchmark may well move faster than the latecomers. This means we have to acknowledge what it means to be 'in it for the

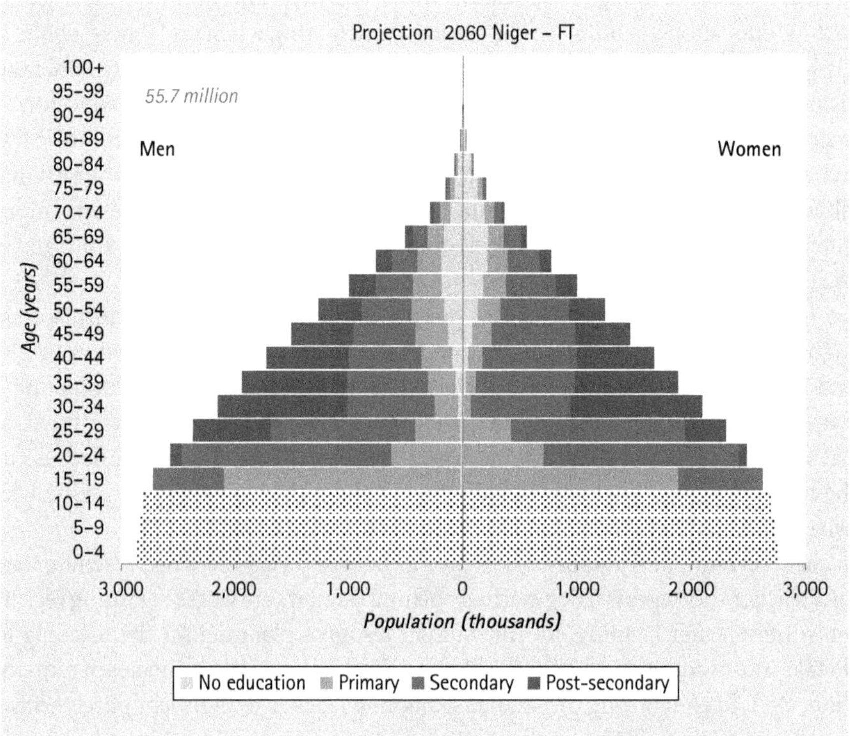

FIGURE 8.10 Projected education composition of Niger in 2060 under the fast benchmark scenario.

long haul'. This example also raises the question of how much momentum is likely to remain behind international support for educational expansion once it has become a minority problem of a few marginalized nations. It also means that, eventually, adult education will have to become a bigger part of educational development work than initial schooling.

References

Archer, M. 1982 'Theorizing about the Expansion of Educational Systems'. In: Archer, M. (ed.) *The Sociology of Educational Expansion: Take-off, Growth and Inflation in Educational Systems*, pp. 3–64. Sage: Beverly Hills, CA.

Barro, R.J. and Lee, J. 2001 'International Data on Educational Attainment: Updates and Implications'. *Oxford Economic Papers*, 53: 541–63.

Benavot, A., Resnick, J. and Corrales, J. 2006 *Global Educational Expansion: Historical Legacies and Political Obstacles*. American Academy of Arts and Sciences: Cambridge, MA.

Bernstein, B. 1971 *Class, Codes and Control: Theoretical Studies Towards a Sociology of Language*. Routledge: London.

Boli, J., Ramirez, F.O. and Meyer, J.W. 1985 'Explaining the Origins and Expansion of Mass Education'. *Comparative Education Review*, 29: 145.

Bourdieu, P. 1986 'The Forms of Capital'. In: Richardson, J. (ed.) *Handbook of Theory and Research for the Sociology and Education*. Greenwood: New York.

Bowles, S. and Gintis, H. 1976 *Schooling in Capitalist America: Educational Reform and the Contradictions of Economic Life*. Basic Books: New York.

Bureau of Labor Statistics 2012a. *Employment Projections*. U.S. Department of Labor: Washington, DC.

Bureau of Labor Statistics 2012b *Employment Projections: 2010–2020 Summary*. U.S. Department of Labor: Washington, DC.

Burton, G. 2011 'Brazil's Lost Decade in Education, 1985–1994: How to Account for the Lack of Reform in the New Republic?' *Jornal de Políticas Educacionais*, 4(7).

Carney, S., Rappleye, J. and Silova, I. 2012 'Between Faith and Science: World Culture Theory and Comparative Education'. *Comparative Education Review*, 56: 366–93.

Chabbott, C. 1998 'Constructing Educational Consensus: International Development Professionals and the World Conference on Education For All'. *International Journal of Educational Development*, 18: 207–18.

Clemens, M. 2004 'The Long Walk to School: International Education Goals in Historical Perspective' (Working Paper 37). Centre for Global Development: Washington, DC.

Colclough, C. and Al-Samarrai, S. 2000 'Achieving Schooling For All: Budgetary Expenditures on Education in Sub-Saharan Africa and South Asia'. *World Development*, 28: 1927–44.

Collins, R. 1971 'Functional and Conflict Theories of Educational Stratification'. *American Sociological Review*, 36: 1002–19.

Cordasco, F. 1976 *A Brief History of Education: A Handbook of Information on Greek, Roman, Medieval, Renaissance, and Modern Educational Practice*. Rowman & Littlefield: Paterson, NJ.

Corrales, J. 2006 'Political Obstacles to Expanding and Improving Schooling in Developing Countries'. In: Cohen, J. E., Bloom, D. E. and Malin, M. B. (eds). *Educating All Children Well: A Global Agenda*, pp. 231–99. MIT Press: Cambridge, MA.

Craig, J.E. and Spear, N. 1982 'Explaining Educational Expansion: An Agenda for Historical and Comparative Research'. In: Archer, M.S. (ed.) *The Sociology of Educational Expansion*, pp. 133–57. Sage: Beverly Hills, CA.

De Moura Castro, C. 2002 'The World Bank Policies: Damned if You do, Damned if You Don't'. *Comparative Education*, 38: 387–99.

DiMaggio, P.J. and Powell, W.W. 1983 'The Iron Cage Revisited: Institutional Isomorphism and Collective Rationality in Organizational Fields'. *American Sociological Review*, 48: 147–60.

Duryea, S., Lam, D. and Levison, D. 2007 'Effects of Economic Shocks on Children's Employment and Schooling in Brazil'. *Journal of Development Economics*, 84: 188–214.

Ericson, D.P. 1982 'The Possibility of a General Theory of the Educational System'. In: Archer, M. (ed.) *The Sociology of Educational Expansion: Take-off, Growth and Inflation in Educational Systems*, pp. 293–313. Sage: Beverly Hills, CA.

Frankenberg, E., Siegel-Hawley, G. and Wang, J. 2010 'Choice without Equity: Charter School Segregation and the Need for Civil Rights Standards'. (Civil Rights Project No. ED509773). University of California: Los Angeles, CA.

Fuller, B. and Rubinson, R. 1992 *The Political Construction of Education: The State, School Expansion, and Economic Change*. Praeger: New York.

Geo-Jaja, M.A. and Mangum, G. 2001 'Structural Adjustment as an Inadvertent Enemy of Human Development in Africa'. *Journal of Black Studies*, 32: 30–49.

Green, T.F. 1980 *Predicting the Behaviour of the Educational System*. Syracuse University Press: Syracuse, NY.

Hannum, E. and Buchmann, C. 2003 *The Consequences of Global Educational Expansion: Social Science Perspectives*. American Academy of Arts and Sciences: Cambridge, MA.

Hannum, E. and Buchmann, C. 2005 'Global Educational Expansion and Socio-Economic Development: An Assessment of Findings from the Social Sciences'. *World Development*, 33: 333–54.

Hanushek, E.A. and Kimko, D.D. 2000 'Schooling, Labor-force Quality, and the Growth of Nations'. *American Economic Review*, 90: 1184–208.

Hanushek, E.A. and Woessmann, L. 2008 'The Role of Cognitive Skills in Economic Development'. *Journal of Economic Literature*, 46: 607–68.

Heyneman, S.P. 2003 'The History and Problems in the Making of Education Policy at the World Bank 1960–2000'. *International Journal of Education Development*, 23: 315–37.

Jeong, I. and Armer, J.M. 1994 'State, Class, and Expansion of Education in South Korea: A General Model'. *Comparative Education*, 38: 531–45.

Jónasson, J.T. 2003 'Does the State Expand Schooling? A Study Based on Five Nordic Countries'. *Comparative Education Review*, 47: 160–83.

Kim, K.S. 2012 'Developmental State Policy, Educational Development, and Economic Development: Policy Processes in South Korea (1961–1979)'. *Education Policy Analysis Archives*, 20.

Kozol, J. 1991 *Savage Inequalities: Children in America's Schools*. Broadway Paperbacks: New York.

Lutz, W., Crespo Cuaresma, J. and Sanderson, W.C. 2008 'The Demography of Educational Attainment and Economic Growth'. *Science*, 319: 1047.

McNeely, C.L. 1995 'Prescribing National Education Policies: The Role of International Organizations'. *Comparative Education Review*, 39: 483–507.

Massey, D.S. 1990 'Social Structure, Household Strategies, and the Cumulative Causation of Migration'. *Population Index*, 56: 3.

Mennerick, L. A. and Najafizadeh, M. 1987 'Observations on the Missing Linkage Between Theories of Historical Expansion of Schooling and Planning for Future Educational Development'. *International Review of Education*, 33: 87–102.
Meyer, J.W. 1992 'World Expansion of Mass Education, 1870–1980'. *Sociology of Education*, 65: 128–49.
Meyer, J.W., Ramirez, F.O., Rubinson, R. and Boli-Bennett, J. 1977 'The World Educational Revolution, 1950–1970'. *Sociology of Education*, 50: 242–58.
Müller-Benedict, V. 1991 *Akademikerprognosen und die Dynamik des Hochschulsystems, Campus Forschung*. Campus-Verl.: Frankfurt/Main.
Raftery, A. and Hout, M. 1993 'Maximally Maintained Inequality: Expansion, Reform, and Opportunity in Irish Education, 1921–75'. *Sociology Education*, 66: 41–62.
Ramirez, F.O. and Boli, J. 1987 'The Political Construction of Mass Schooling: European Origins and Worldwide Institutionalization'. *Sociology Education*, 60: 2–17.
Resnik, J. 2006 'International Organizations, the Education–Economic Growth Black Box, and the Development of World Education Culture'. *Comparative Education Review*, 50: 173–95.
Schofer, E. and Meyer, J.W. 2005 'The Worldwide Expansion of Higher Education in the Twentieth Education Century'. *American Sociological Review*, 70: 898–920.
Seidman, R.H. 1982 'The Logic and Behavioral Principles of Educational Systems: Social Independence or Dependence'. In: Archer, M. (ed.) *The Sociology of Educational Expansion: Take-off, Growth and Inflation in Educational Systems*, pp. 267–92. Sage: Beverly Hills, CA.
Sewell, W.H. and Hauser, R.M. 1980 'The Wisconsin Longitudinal Study of Social and Psychological Factors in Aspirations and Achievements'. In: *Research in Sociology of Education and Socialization*, pp. 59–99. JAI Press: Greenwich, CN.
Torche, F. 2010 'Economic Crisis and Inequality of Educational Opportunity in Latin America'. *Sociology of Education*, 83: 85–110.
UNESCO 2012 *EFA Global Monitoring Report 2012: Youth and Skills—Putting Education to Work*. UNESCO: Paris.
Wils, A. and Goujon, A. 1998 'Diffusion of Education in Six World Regions, 1960–90'. *Population and Development Review*, 24: 357–68.
Wils, A. and O'Connor, R. 2004 'Teachers Matter: Teacher Supply as a Constraint on the Global Education Transition' (Working Paper WP-04-01). Education Policy and Data Center: Washington, DC.

CHAPTER 9

DATA AND METHODS

SAMIR KC, MICHAELA POTANČOKOVÁ, RAMON BAUER, ANNE GOUJON, AND ERICH STRIESSNIG

9.1 Introduction

The preceding chapters have all contributed to building the knowledge base for the actual Wittgenstein Centre for Demography and Global Human Capital (WIC) projections that will be presented and discussed in the second part of this book. This chapter stands as a bridge between the two parts. Its focus is the translation and operationalization of the empirical evidence and the substantive arguments presented so far into specific population projections by age, sex, and level of educational attainment for all countries in the world. This is a complex exercise in which data and methodology play the crucial roles. The cohort–component multidimensional projections presented in this volume require a large amount of information, ranging from base-year data on population disaggregated by levels of educational attainment by age and sex, to data on fertility, mortality, and migration by age, sex, and education for the base year, and, finally, to the assumed numerical values of these determinants according to the different scenarios.

This new set of expert argument-based projections by age, sex, and educational attainment presents an important new step at the forefront of international population projections. As discussed in Chapter 1, this is a logical next step in the tradition of international population projections by the World Population Program of the International Institute for Applied Systems Analysis (IIASA). This effort also goes beyond what the United Nations (UN) and other agencies have been doing in two important ways: it provides the most comprehensive and systematic summary of expert knowledge on future fertility, mortality, and migration to date—including the input of hundreds of demographers from around the world—and it translates this into the most comprehensive set of human capital projections for 195 countries. The WIC projections cover all countries in the world with more than 100,000 inhabitants.

In this effort, the study builds on and significantly expands earlier IIASA reconstructions and projections of the population by age, sex, and educational attainment for 120 countries published in 2007 and 2010 (KC et al., 2010; Lutz et al., 2007). These data have already been used by researchers and planners, for example, to analyse the age dimension of the relationship between human capital and economic growth (Chappuis and Walmsley, 2011; Eberstadt, 2012; Lutz et al., 2008); to understand the impacts of natural disasters (Cavallo and Noy, 2010) and vulnerability to natural disasters (Pichler and Striessnig, 2013; Striessnig et al., 2013); to study demographic and health-related issues (KC and Lentzner, 2010; Prettner et al., 2012); to predict armed conflict (Hegre et al., 2013); and to include education as an important dimension of population projections for measuring demographic heterogeneity as shown in Lutz and KC (2011; see also 2010).

Compared with these earlier population projections, three important changes were implemented regarding data structure and coverage in the current WIC projections: the projection base year data were updated to the year 2010 instead of 2000, the number of education categories was increased from four to six to encompass a broader range and more variability in levels of attainment, and more countries were added—from 120 to 195[1] to cover virtually the entire world population. The result is a global picture of educational attainment levels today and alternative scenarios for their evolution over the rest of the century. In addition to the assumptions regarding the future of fertility, mortality, migration, and educational attainment that are described in the preceding chapters, education differentials in fertility, mortality, and migration are also based on our estimations that rely on census and survey data, and on the available literature. Various methods of dealing with schooling variability have been fine-tuned and some additional complexities have been introduced (e.g. allowing child mortality to depend on the education of the mother).

This chapter is structured in three parts. The first details the procedure used to arrive at a consistent 2010 base year population by age, sex, and education. The second summarizes the assumptions developed for the WIC projections, which are also detailed in Appendix II and online (<http://www.wittgensteincentre.org/dataexplorer>). The third part walks the reader through the projection methodology.

9.2 The base year population

9.2.1 Introduction

Internationally comparable data on levels of educational attainment of the adult population consistent across time and space cannot be found in a nationally aggregated form by age and sex. This is a serious data deficiency because level of educational attainment

[1] Based on empirical data for the education structure for 171 countries and approximation for the remaining 24 countries as explained in section 9.4.10.

of the working-age population is the main indicator of human capital used in many models relating to economics, information technology, and health. A comprehensive data set, including detailed and accurate data on educational attainment comparable across countries, is also crucial for the Wittgenstein Centre for Demography and Global Human Capital (WIC) projections presented in this book. It does not make sense to keep the data as close as possible to directly available data sets because most of the existing collections of education data suffer from severe flaws and tend to take the collected data at face value. In particular, constructing an appropriate data set for the starting year for projections can be highly problematic, requiring much harmonizing and mapping of levels of education within and across sources.

In general, data on human capital stocks are much more difficult to obtain than data on education flows, such as school attendance, completion, and dropout rates. These data on schooling are typically collected by the school authorities and suffer in many countries from over-reporting of enrolment, for example in India (see Kingdon, 2007). Censuses and surveys are alternative sources of information. Information from these sources is available for the population of school age or those who were enrolled in education or training at the time of the census or survey. Most censuses and surveys also provide information on the educational composition (i.e. highest level attained) of the adult population by age and sex. But this theoretical availability of attainment data stands in stark contrast to the actual availability of useful internationally comparable data based on common definitions. This is surprising, given the efforts of UNESCO in this field and given that evidence on human capital stocks by educational attainment contains valuable information about social change that is relevant for human capital research and policy formulation, particularly in an internationally comparative perspective

Toward our original goal of collecting data on shares of the population by age, sex, and educational attainment for 195 countries with a population of at least 100,000, we managed to collect and harmonize data for 171 countries (88 per cent of all countries), covering 97.4 per cent of the world population in 2010. This makes the data set the most comprehensive in comparison to other widely used data sets, such as that of Barro and Lee (2013), which covers 146 countries. Another advantage of the WIC projections is the application of transparent procedures in cross-national harmonization of educational data across the globe based on International Standard Classification of Education (ISCED) 1997 classification.

9.2.2 Data sources

Collecting and harmonizing data by education undertaken under the current round of WIC projections is not the first such effort. Major international institutions (UNESCO, EUROSTAT) publish data obtained from the national statistical offices, which they tend to accept at face value. These collections are flawed owing to different categorization approaches that lead to inconsistencies and affect data quality.

Collections of data from various data sources (Education Policy and Data Center, <http://www.epdc.org/>, Barro and Lee, 2013) build on the data sets already compiled by international bodies and thus suffer from the same problems. Finally, survey data (e.g. Demographic and Health Survey (DHS) or Multiple Indicator Cluster Surveys) can raise sampling issues and, because they can be designed for national context surveys, are not always immediately comparable across countries.

To collect the most reliable and up-to-date data on population shares by age, sex, and educational attainment, we sought data sources for populations aged 15 years and older by five-year age groups that contain detailed information on the highest level attained and highest grade attended. This approach allows disentangling the latent ambiguity between completed and incomplete levels of educational attainment. In general, first we looked for register or census data, which usually comply with all requirements. Because appropriate register data are only rarely available, data collection efforts primarily focused on the census data. Accordingly, we collected census data from several sources (IPUMS, EUROSTAT, CELADE, National Statistical Agencies, etc.).

Whenever census data were of poor quality, not available, or outdated, we turned to surveys (Figure 9.1). To keep the quality of the whole data set high, we excluded countries with poor data (see Table 9.1).

9.2.3 Data harmonization

A thorough harmonization of data on educational attainment is necessary to ensure the high quality of the data set. Owing to the variety of nationally distinct educational systems, UNESCO designed the ISCED to make education statistics comparable across countries. We base our six educational categories on ISCED 1997 (UNESCO, 2006). The categories are also in line with the new ISCED 2011 (UNESCO, 2012), which becomes effective in 2014.

For the allocation of country-specific educational categorizations into ISCED 1997, we developed standardized procedures to differentiate between completed and incomplete level, and to allocate categories as precisely as possible. Table 9.2 summarizes the definitions of the six categories, their correspondence to ISCED 1997, and the main allocation rules. More detailed information about our data harmonization methodology can be found in Bauer et al. (2012).

We have developed standardized procedures to deal with certain obstacles during the process of allocating educational categories. Discrepancies between the surveyed categories and ISCED 1997 definitions are numerous, and determining how to treat these discrepancies was not always clear cut. Accurate allocation of such fuzzy categories was often possible only with particular knowledge of the type of programme concerned, using codebooks from national statistical institutes, or relying on the knowledge of local experts. Distinguishing between completed and incomplete post-secondary education was problematic, in particular for post-secondary education in DHS. To solve the problem, we used ISCED mappings and assumed that persons who indicated fewer

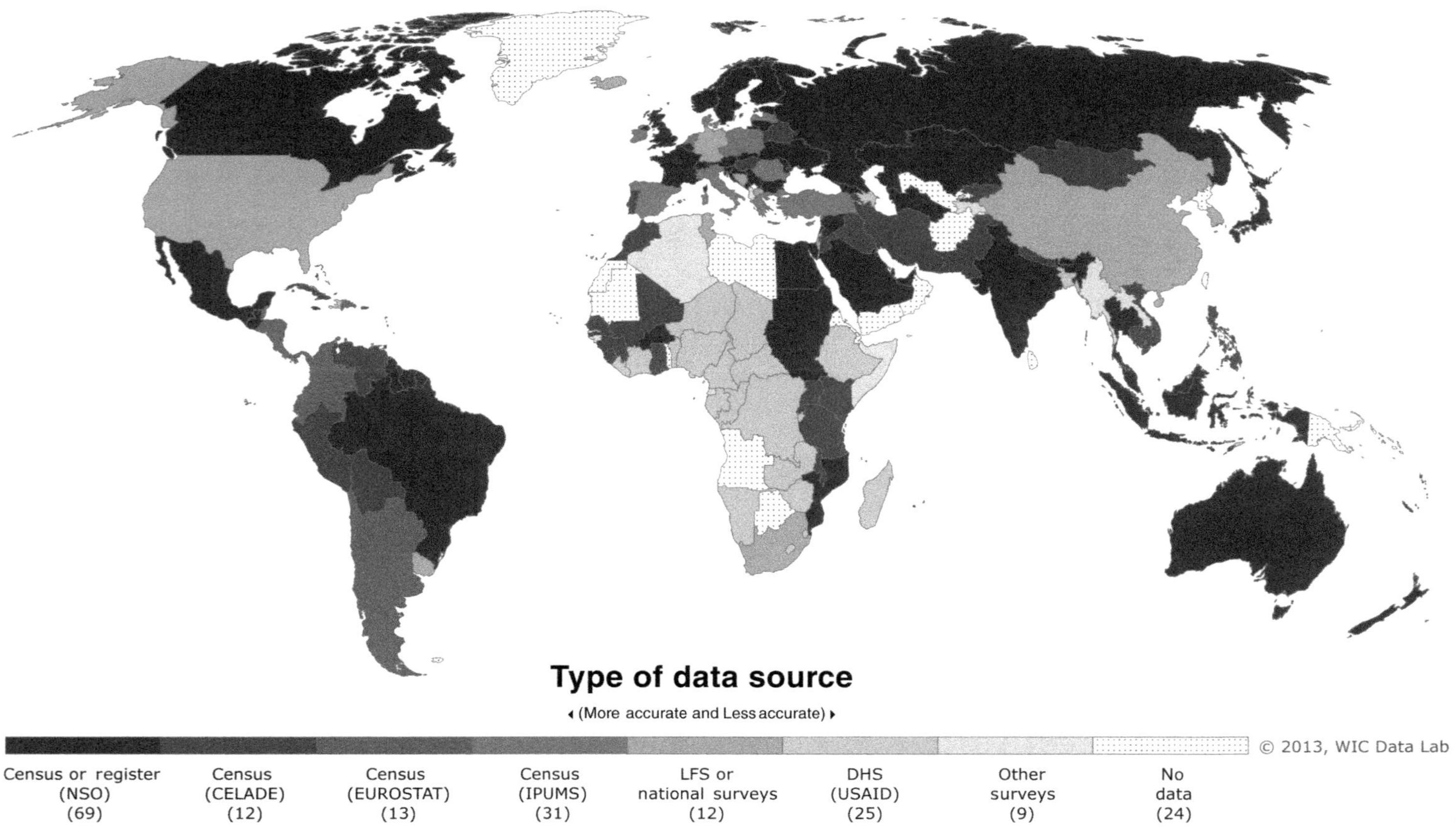

FIGURE 9.1 Data sources on educational attainment (effective December, 2012). NSO: National Statistical Office; LFS: Labour Force Survey; DHS: Demographic and Health Survey; USAID: U. S. Agency for International Development.

Table 9.1 Country Coverage of the WIC Projections by United Nations (UN) Region

UN region	All countries	Countries covered	Countries covered (%)	Population covered (%)	Missing countries
Europe	39	39	100	100	
Asia	50	43	86.0	96.9	Afghanistan, Brunei, North Korea, Oman, Sri Lanka, Uzbekistan, Yemen
Africa	55	46	83.6	95.7	Angola, Botswana, Djibouti, Eritrea, Libya, Mauritania, Mayotte, Togo, Western Sahara
Northern America	2	2	100	100	
Latin America	37	34	91.9	98.9	Barbados, Grenada, Virgin Islands
Oceania	12	7	58.3	75.8	Fiji, Papua New Guinea, Solomon Islands, Micronesia, Guam
World	195	171	87.7	97.4	

Note: Data collection focused on 195 countries with populations of at least 100,000 in 2010.

years studied at the post-secondary level than the duration of shortest post-secondary programme existing in the country could not have completed higher education

Allocation of categories of religious education was especially challenging when religious schooling exists alongside a public school system. It was difficult to allocate Koranic or Buddhist schools and educational programmes. Religious education may provide education at all kinds of ISCED levels, from pre-primary to post-secondary education. At Koranic schools, which are common in many Arabic, Maghreb, and sub-Saharan countries, as well as in Southern Asia, contents and standards of educational programmes vary from memorizing the Koran in traditional schools to curricula similar to public schools in modern Koranic schools called madrasa (Demonsant and Andre, 2012; Easton et al., 1997; UNESCO/UNICEF Co-operative Programme, 1985). When recording problematic cases, we used studies evaluating the quality of religious schools in a particular country, following the advice given by experts with country-specific knowledge.

Yet another challenge emerged owing to changes in education systems over time. Some countries change their education systems fairly frequently, some do not. Since 1970, for example, Cambodia has had four different systems, while Mozambique and the Ukraine reformed their educational systems three times, resulting in modified durations of schooling at primary and secondary levels. Such changes in national education systems are often poorly documented and difficult to identify. We benefited from a compendium of documented changes compiled by UNESCO[2] and whenever possible adjusted the educational attainment of corresponding cohorts to the system in which

[2] UNESCO Institute for Statistics collects evidence on past educational systems. This information can be found online at: <http://stats.uis.unesco.org/unesco/TableViewer/tableView.aspx?ReportId=163> (accessed January 2013).

Table 9.2 Categories of Educational Attainment and Allocation Rules

Categories	ISCED 1997 level	Allocation rules
No education	No level or ISCED 0 Grade 1 of ISCED 1 not completed	Illiterates and persons who have never attended school; persons who were attending first grade of primary education at time of survey; persons attending adult literacy courses at time of survey; khalwa (first level of traditional Koranic schools)
Incomplete primary	Incomplete ISCED 1	Persons attending last grade of ISCED 1 at time of survey; persons who indicated an unknown number of grades/ years at ISCED 1 level; traditional Koranic schools above khalwa level
Primary	Completed ISCED 1 Incomplete ISCED 2	Completed last grade of ISCED 1 level or grades below the last grade of ISCED 2 level; persons attending last grade of ISCED 2 at time of survey; persons who indicated an unknown number of grades at ISCED 2 level
Lower secondary	Completed ISCED 2 Incomplete ISCED 3	Completed last grade of ISCED 2 level or grades below the last grade of ISCED 3 level; persons attending last grade of ISCED 3 at time of survey; persons who indicated an unknown number of grades at ISCED 3 level
Upper secondary	Completed ISCED 3 Incomplete ISCED 4 or 5	Completed last grade of ISCED 3 level; completed number grades or years below the standard duration at ISCED 4 or ISCED 5 level; persons who indicated an unknown number of grades at ISCED 4 or 5 level
Post-secondary	ISCED 4 and 5B (first diploma, shorter post-secondary courses) ISCED 5A and 6 (longer post-secondary courses, postgraduate level)	Persons who have completed number of years or grades corresponding to standard duration of ISCED 4 or ISCED 5B programmes; persons holding degrees corresponding to ISCED 4, ISCED 5B, ISCED 5A, and ISCED 6 levels

Note: The post-secondary level encompasses non-tertiary and tertiary. The category is broad because some data sources (e.g. DHS) lacked the level of detail necessary to differentiate between tertiary and non-tertiary higher education. ISCED: International Standard Classification of Education.

they were most likely actually enrolled. Sensitivity analyses showed that adjusting the data makes a great deal of difference, as shown for Cambodia in Bauer et al. (2012). The example demonstrates that educational attainment is much lower for persons who were actually enrolled in an older system with shorter primary education if the current education classification is applied. Including information on changing duration of schooling is a step forward in estimating the actual educational attainment of older cohorts who did not study under the updated educational system that was used for measurement at time of survey.

As a result, the estimates presented in the data set may deviate from data published by UNESCO, National Statistical Agencies, other data sets, or publications on educational attainment. However, our data set has the advantage of better comparability across the countries.

9.2.4 Data validation

We have placed considerable emphasis on validation of this new data set on global educational attainment. From the beginning, we have collected data on educational attainment from a wide variety of sources and validated them against each other to determine which was the most reliable. If only one source met the criteria, we validated aggregated information against a different data source such as from UNESCO or from the UN Statistical Division.

An example of the benefits of this method can be seen in comparisons of DHS and census data for selected African and Asian countries. The comparisons revealed that uneducated populations tend to be less represented in DHS as compared to censuses, with proportions of those showing incomplete or completed primary education being higher than in censuses. But the educational attainment information collected in censuses is also not without problems, in particular when the information is provided by census enumerators or heads of big households without direct inquiry of the individuals themselves. This implies caution in comparisons, as populations of DHS countries may appear better educated than what the census data might indicate.

To get a comprehensive overview of the harmonized data on global educational attainment, we examined the new data set first by the simple, but effective, method of map comparisons. Comparing educational compositions of the population aged 25 years and older of different countries, we detected eye-catching discrepancies by looking at the share of the lower educated population (with ISCED 1 and lower). This is especially relevant when comparing countries with a lower human development index (HDI), and looking at the share of the post-secondary educated population, which is relevant when comparing countries with higher HDIs.

In a second step, we applied principal component analysis to classify and compare countries by two dimensions (components): the level of education and the variation between the six educational categories. Both exercises enabled us to identify outliers with suspiciously high concentrations in one or another educational category. Such concentrations were often country-specific particularities in national education systems (e.g. related to different length of compulsory education), or inherent in UNESCO's ISCED mappings of national educational categories. Overall, validation leads to more accurate description of educational composition of many countries and increased accuracy of the data set.

9.2.5 Data adjustments

Various sources used to build the data set differed by accuracy and level of detail. Therefore, adjustments were inevitable in order to estimate missing educational categories (see Bauer et al. 2012 for a full list of adjustments). Predominately in more developed countries, where the share of the lower educated population is generally small, but still significant, in older cohorts there was a lack of detail in the lower education levels (below ISCED 2 or ISCED 1 level). Less detailed information about lower education categories made it difficult to capture the educational attainment of (often less educated) immigrants from developing countries. In a few cases we estimated ISCED 2 and ISCED 3 levels from information on secondary education. We used either additional information from other sources or data on populations with similar educational compositions and education systems to split these broader categories or distinguish between fuzzy original categories. To maintain the high quality of the data set, we refrained from any 'guesstimation' beyond solid evidence. As a consequence, the data set includes a few countries with less than the intended six categories of educational attainment.

Interpolations were used to estimate five-year age groups when original data were organized into broader or uneven age groups, and extrapolations were applied to extend the oldest age group to 100 years and older for all countries. In doing so, we followed the procedure described in section 4.4 of Lutz et al. (2007).

9.2.6 From education shares to the 2010 base year population

The data set on the educational composition of the population of 171 countries extends through the 12-year period from 1998 to 2010, with only a few countries outside this range (1995–97: Central African Republic, Comoros, Guinea, Iraq, and Turkmenistan). For each country with available data from a year not ending with 0 or 5, a simple rounding was done such that the shares from years 1 and 2 were assigned to 0 and from years 3 and 4 were assigned to 5. As the projection base year is 2010, population distribution by age, sex, and education for countries with data source years other than 2010 were first projected to 2010 by applying the UN's estimates of fertility, mortality, and migration in order to provide the absolute population by age, sex, and education.

9.3 Summary of Projection Assumptions

9.3.1 Introduction

The assumptions about future trends in fertility, mortality, and migration that underlie our projections are a combination of the application of statistical models, the scientific input of hundreds of source experts who responded to the online questionnaire and assessed the validity of alternative arguments that impact on these trends, and the intensive discussions at five meta-expert meetings held on five continents in which the available knowledge was systematically assessed. The detailed descriptions of this process and the substantive arguments that led to the assumptions are given in the preceding chapters. Here we will only provide a concise summary of how the assumptions were derived and what was actually assumed in numerical terms.

As no international empirical time series exist on education-specific fertility, mortality, and migration trends over the last few decades and the expert knowledge on education-specific trends is very limited, the process of defining assumptions initially focused on defining the numerical values for overall fertility, mortality, and migration levels, that is, for the aggregate population across all educational attainment levels. Once these values were assessed, education-specific fertility and mortality assumptions over time were derived by assuming certain relative differentials between the vital rates of the different education groups and by assuming that the medium global education trend (GET) scenario describes the future educational attainment trend that underlies the assumed aggregate level trends in vital rates.

As mentioned earlier, this procedure is an improvement over an earlier projection by level of education for 120 countries (KC et al., 2010). This earlier projection was done by four levels of educational attainment: never been to school, some primary education, secondary school, and tertiary education. The baseline data were for 2000. We now describe the new improved procedures in comparison to the earlier procedures described in KC et al. (2010)

9.3.2 Fertility assumptions

Chapters 3 and 4 describe in detail the process that led to the assumptions of specific trajectories. Because the drivers of future fertility are very different between countries that are still in the process of fertility transition and those that are already toward the end of this global transition, two separate exercises dealt with these two sets of countries. The primary criterion for placing a country in the high or low fertility group was the level of total fertility rate (TFR) as estimated for the period 2005–10 by the UN (United Nations, 2011), with 2.1 as the main cut-off point. As a secondary criterion we used the UN Development Programme's HDI for 2010 to rank the countries by their levels of development. As period fertility levels can show some peculiarities, an additional selection criterion based on human development was necessary in order to differentiate between the more developed set of countries and all others in formulating suitable sets of arguments to underlie likely future fertility trends.

For the definition of fertility assumptions for the medium scenario, formulated in terms of TFRs for five-year periods for all countries, three different sources of information were merged. The results of a statistical model were blended with the assessments of the source experts who had replied to the online questionnaire and with the outcome of two separate meta-expert meetings held in Dhulikhel (Nepal) and Vienna (Austria). (The participants in these meta-expert meetings are listed in the Acknowledgements.) For fertility (as well as for mortality, as described in section 9.3.3), the procedures were inspired by the view discussed in Chapter 2 that the best way of making assumptions about the future is by combining statistical models with structured expert judgement.

The procedures chosen to derive the fertility trajectories differed somewhat between the high and low fertility groups. For the high fertility countries, the assumption-making process merged three different sources of information. First, a statistical model was defined to predict a country's future decrease in fertility. This was calculated by comparing its current level of fertility to countries that have experienced a similar level of fertility (± 10 per cent) at any five-year period between 1970 and 2005. Historical time series for this exercise were taken from United Nations (2011). In addition, only countries that experienced comparable decreases in fertility (± 5 percentage points) relative to the previous period were considered in the calculation of the expected fertility decline. The mean fertility decline for all countries fulfilling these two constraints was then taken to predict the expected fertility decline for the following five-year period for every country. This model is quite similar to what the UN assumed until 2010. It is described in detail in Chapter 4.

The second source of information was the results of the online questionnaire. From the 140 responses to the high fertility module of the questionnaire, the aggregate impact scores of all the different arguments that were assessed by the experts were related to their respective numerical values of likely future fertility levels via a regression analysis. This general relationship was then used to convert, for every country, the argument scores given by the experts into numerical point estimates for 2030 and 2050. A third source of information was the numerical point estimates of fertility in 2030 and 2050 for 14 big developing countries that were assumed to be representative for their regions, provided by meta-experts at the meeting in Nepal.

Model results, meta-expert assumptions, and source expert score-based values were then weighted in the ratio 1:1:0.2 (where the sum of all source experts could not get a weight of >1 even when they were >5). For countries that by this procedure reached a TFR of ≤1.6 in any period before 2100, the procedure chosen by the low fertility group was enacted, implying a slow convergence towards a TFR of 1.75.

For the low fertility countries, point estimates of the period TFR in 2030 and 2050 (medium scenario) were derived in several steps. Following the source experts' judgements gathered in the IIASA-Oxford online survey and the agreements reached during the discussions of the meta-expert meeting in Vienna, TFR scenarios for a number of the key countries were derived. Based on these, the point estimates for all remaining low fertility countries were derived by analogy. This process and the reasoning behind it are described in detail in Chapter 3.

For the near term, a special effort was made to account for the effect of the ongoing economic recession. This was done by combining the most recent information about annual fertility trends with the assumption that fertility rates were likely to fall somewhat in the most affected countries and that no country would see a fertility increase in the period 2010–15.

For the long range assumptions for the second half of the century, it was assumed that period TFR levels in low fertility countries would slowly converge to an average value of 1.75, with the convergence point in the year 2200. The reasoning behind this choice is described in Chapter 3. The resulting TFR for 195 countries is presented in Table 9.3.

For deriving the age-specific fertility rates (ASFR) corresponding to these assumed fertility trajectories, the period-specific age schedules as used in the UN medium variant were chosen. The UN generated ASFR schedules by linearly interpolating between the current fertility pattern and model patterns to be reached by a certain time that varies by region. For a detailed description of their methodology see United Nations (2006).

Country-specific differentials in fertility by level of education for the base year were obtained from the literature and from census and survey data. Table 9.4 lists these differentials and a detailed description of the data sources is given in KC and Potančoková (2013). Over time, the education differentials are assumed to converge to ratios of TFRs of 1.42, 1.42, 1.42, 1.35, 1.14, and 1 for the different education levels relative to post-secondary education. These values are assumed to be reached by the time TFR reaches 1.8 children per woman. For countries where the maximum differential is <1.42 in the base year, the relative ratios (RRs) are kept constant at those lower levels.

9.3.3 Mortality assumptions

As with fertility, the mortality assumptions are based on a combination of a statistical model and country-specific expert assessments. Accordingly, the results of model-based forecast were blended with the assessments of individual experts and the results of the meta-expert meetings, following the principle described in Chapter 2, that is, the best way of defining forecasting assumptions is to combine a statistical model with structured expert judgement. Accordingly, our model specifies the assumptions for female life expectancy at birth for the entire female population across all education groups. Male life expectancy, as well as education-specific trajectories of life expectancy, are derived from this model, as described later in this section.

The mortality model is described in detail in Appendix I. Here we provide a brief summary of the method. As discussed in the two mortality chapters (Chapters 5 and 6), the model is based on the general assumption of convergence. This was a decision made at the meta-expert meeting in Costa Rica. Although the idea of a global mortality convergence is widely acknowledged (Wilson 2001), there have been relatively few attempts to deal with convergence explicitly (Heuveline 1999; Wilson 2001; Oeppen 2006). However, the concept of convergence has been widely employed in the economics literature, particularly in the empirical literature on economic growth (Barro and Sala-I-Martin 1995; Landau et al. 1996). There are two main concepts of convergence in this literature; the first, beta-convergence, occurs when the growth rate of the variable of interest (normally the growth rate in gross domestic product) depends negatively on its prior value.

Table 9.3 Medium Assumptions for Aggregate Total Fertility Rate for 2010–2100

Country	2005–2010	2010–2015	2015–2020	2020–2025	2025–2030	2030–2035	2035–2040	2040–2045	2045–2050	2050–2055	2055–2060	2060–2065	2065–2070	2070–2075	2075–2080	2080–2085	2085–2090	2090–2095	2095–2100
Afghanistan	6.6	6.2	5.8	5.3	4.9	4.5	4.0	3.6	3.2	2.9	2.7	2.5	2.3	2.2	2.1	2.0	1.9	1.8	1.8
Albania	1.4	1.4	1.4	1.5	1.5	1.5	1.5	1.5	1.5	1.5	1.5	1.5	1.5	1.5	1.5	1.6	1.6	1.6	1.6
Algeria	2.4	2.2	2.1	2.0	1.9	1.9	1.9	1.9	1.8	1.8	1.7	1.7	1.7	1.6	1.6	1.6	1.6	1.6	1.6
Angola	5.8	5.3	4.7	4.2	3.7	3.2	2.9	2.7	2.5	2.3	2.2	2.1	2.0	1.9	1.9	1.9	1.8	1.8	1.7
Argentina	2.3	2.1	2.1	2.0	2.0	1.9	1.9	1.9	1.8	1.8	1.7	1.7	1.7	1.6	1.6	1.6	1.6	1.6	1.6
Armenia	1.6	1.5	1.6	1.6	1.7	1.7	1.7	1.7	1.7	1.7	1.7	1.7	1.7	1.7	1.7	1.7	1.7	1.7	1.7
Aruba	1.7	1.6	1.6	1.5	1.5	1.5	1.5	1.5	1.4	1.5	1.5	1.5	1.5	1.5	1.5	1.5	1.5	1.5	1.5
Australia	1.9	1.9	1.9	1.9	1.9	1.8	1.8	1.8	1.8	1.8	1.8	1.8	1.8	1.8	1.8	1.8	1.8	1.8	1.8
Austria	1.4	1.4	1.5	1.5	1.5	1.5	1.5	1.6	1.6	1.6	1.6	1.6	1.6	1.6	1.6	1.6	1.6	1.6	1.6
Azerbaijan	1.9	2.4	2.2	2.0	1.8	1.7	1.7	1.7	1.7	1.7	1.7	1.7	1.7	1.7	1.7	1.7	1.7	1.7	1.7
Bahamas	1.9	1.8	1.7	1.7	1.7	1.7	1.7	1.7	1.7	1.7	1.7	1.6	1.6	1.6	1.6	1.6	1.6	1.6	1.6
Bahrain	2.6	2.4	2.2	2.1	2.0	1.9	1.9	1.9	1.8	1.8	1.7	1.7	1.7	1.7	1.6	1.6	1.6	1.6	1.6
Bangladesh	2.4	2.2	2.1	2.0	1.9	1.8	1.8	1.7	1.7	1.6	1.6	1.6	1.6	1.6	1.6	1.6	1.6	1.6	1.6
Barbados	1.5	1.4	1.4	1.4	1.4	1.4	1.4	1.4	1.4	1.5	1.5	1.5	1.5	1.5	1.5	1.5	1.5	1.5	1.5
Belarus	1.5	1.5	1.5	1.5	1.5	1.5	1.5	1.6	1.6	1.6	1.6	1.6	1.6	1.6	1.6	1.6	1.6	1.6	1.6
Belgium	1.8	1.8	1.8	1.8	1.8	1.8	1.8	1.8	1.8	1.8	1.8	1.8	1.8	1.8	1.8	1.8	1.8	1.8	1.8
Belize	2.9	2.6	2.4	2.2	2.1	2.0	2.0	1.9	1.9	1.8	1.8	1.8	1.7	1.7	1.7	1.6	1.6	1.6	1.6
Benin	5.5	4.9	4.4	3.9	3.4	3.0	2.7	2.5	2.3	2.2	2.1	2.0	1.9	1.9	1.9	1.8	1.8	1.7	1.7
Bhutan	2.6	2.4	2.2	2.1	2.0	1.9	1.9	1.9	1.8	1.8	1.7	1.7	1.7	1.7	1.6	1.6	1.6	1.6	1.6
Bolivia	3.5	3.1	2.8	2.7	2.5	2.3	2.2	2.1	2.0	2.0	1.9	1.8	1.8	1.8	1.7	1.7	1.7	1.7	1.7
Bosnia and Herzegovina	1.8	1.3	1.4	1.4	1.5	1.5	1.5	1.5	1.5	1.5	1.5	1.5	1.5	1.5	1.5	1.6	1.6	1.6	1.6
Botswana	2.9	2.6	2.4	2.2	2.1	2.0	1.9	1.8	1.8	1.7	1.7	1.7	1.7	1.6	1.6	1.6	1.6	1.6	1.6
Brazil	1.9	1.8	1.8	1.8	1.7	1.7	1.7	1.6	1.6	1.6	1.6	1.6	1.6	1.6	1.6	1.6	1.6	1.6	1.6
Brunei Darussalam	2.1	1.9	1.9	1.8	1.8	1.8	1.7	1.7	1.7	1.7	1.7	1.6	1.6	1.6	1.6	1.6	1.6	1.6	1.6
Bulgaria	1.5	1.4	1.5	1.5	1.6	1.6	1.6	1.6	1.6	1.6	1.6	1.6	1.6	1.6	1.6	1.6	1.6	1.6	1.6

Burkina Faso	5.9	5.5	5.1	4.7	4.2	3.8	3.5	3.1	2.9	2.6	2.4	2.3	2.2	2.1	2.0	1.9	1.9	1.8	1.8
Burundi	4.7	4.1	3.6	3.2	2.9	2.6	2.4	2.3	2.2	2.1	2.0	1.9	1.9	1.8	1.8	1.7	1.7	1.7	1.7
Cambodia	2.8	2.5	2.3	2.2	2.1	2.0	1.9	1.9	1.9	1.8	1.8	1.7	1.7	1.7	1.6	1.6	1.6	1.6	1.6
Cameroon	4.7	4.1	3.6	3.2	2.9	2.6	2.4	2.3	2.2	2.1	2.0	1.9	1.9	1.9	1.8	1.8	1.7	1.7	1.7
Canada	1.7	1.6	1.6	1.7	1.7	1.7	1.7	1.8	1.8	1.8	1.8	1.8	1.8	1.8	1.8	1.8	1.8	1.8	1.8
Cape Verde	2.6	2.4	2.2	2.1	2.0	1.9	1.9	1.9	1.8	1.8	1.8	1.7	1.7	1.7	1.6	1.6	1.6	1.6	1.6
Central African Republic	4.8	4.3	3.7	3.3	3.0	2.7	2.5	2.3	2.2	2.1	2.0	1.9	1.9	1.8	1.8	1.7	1.7	1.7	1.6
Chad	6.2	5.7	5.3	4.8	4.3	3.8	3.4	3.0	2.7	2.5	2.3	2.2	2.1	2.0	1.9	1.9	1.9	1.8	1.8
Channel Islands	1.6	1.6	1.6	1.6	1.6	1.6	1.6	1.6	1.6	1.6	1.6	1.6	1.6	1.6	1.6	1.6	1.6	1.6	1.6
Chile	1.9	1.8	1.7	1.7	1.7	1.6	1.6	1.6	1.5	1.5	1.5	1.6	1.6	1.6	1.6	1.6	1.6	1.6	1.6
China	1.5	1.4	1.4	1.4	1.4	1.4	1.4	1.4	1.4	1.4	1.4	1.4	1.4	1.5	1.5	1.5	1.5	1.5	1.5
Colombia	2.5	2.3	2.2	2.1	2.0	1.9	1.9	1.9	1.8	1.8	1.8	1.7	1.7	1.6	1.6	1.6	1.6	1.6	1.6
Comoros	5.1	4.5	4.0	3.4	3.0	2.8	2.5	2.4	2.2	2.1	2.0	1.9	1.9	1.8	1.8	1.7	1.7	1.7	1.6
Congo	4.6	4.1	3.6	3.1	2.9	2.6	2.4	2.3	2.2	2.1	2.0	1.9	1.9	1.9	1.8	1.8	1.7	1.7	1.7
Costa Rica	1.9	1.8	1.7	1.7	1.7	1.7	1.7	1.7	1.7	1.7	1.7	1.6	1.6	1.6	1.6	1.6	1.6	1.6	1.6
Cote d'Ivoire	4.6	4.1	3.6	3.1	2.9	2.6	2.4	2.3	2.2	2.0	2.0	1.9	1.9	1.8	1.8	1.7	1.7	1.7	1.6
Croatia	1.5	1.4	1.4	1.5	1.5	1.5	1.5	1.5	1.5	1.6	1.6	1.6	1.6	1.6	1.6	1.6	1.6	1.6	1.6
Cuba	1.5	1.4	1.4	1.4	1.4	1.4	1.4	1.4	1.4	1.4	1.4	1.4	1.4	1.5	1.5	1.5	1.5	1.5	1.5
Cyprus	1.5	1.3	1.4	1.5	1.6	1.6	1.6	1.6	1.6	1.6	1.6	1.6	1.6	1.6	1.6	1.6	1.6	1.6	1.6
Czech Republic	1.5	1.5	1.5	1.6	1.6	1.7	1.7	1.7	1.7	1.7	1.7	1.7	1.7	1.7	1.7	1.7	1.7	1.7	1.7
Denmark	1.9	1.7	1.8	1.9	2.0	2.0	2.0	2.0	2.0	2.0	2.0	2.0	2.0	2.0	2.0	1.9	1.9	1.9	1.9
Djibouti	4.0	3.4	2.9	2.7	2.5	2.3	2.2	2.1	2.0	1.9	1.9	1.8	1.8	1.7	1.7	1.7	1.6	1.6	1.6
Dominican Republic	2.7	2.4	2.3	2.1	2.1	2.0	1.9	1.9	1.9	1.8	1.8	1.7	1.7	1.6	1.6	1.6	1.6	1.6	1.6
D. R. Congo	6.1	5.6	5.1	4.6	4.1	3.6	3.1	2.8	2.6	2.4	2.3	2.2	2.1	2.0	1.9	1.9	1.9	1.8	1.8
Ecuador	2.6	2.4	2.2	2.1	2.0	2.0	1.9	1.9	1.8	1.8	1.7	1.7	1.7	1.7	1.7	1.6	1.6	1.6	1.6
Egypt	2.9	2.7	2.5	2.4	2.3	2.2	2.1	2.0	1.9	1.9	1.8	1.8	1.8	1.7	1.7	1.7	1.6	1.6	1.6
El Salvador	2.3	2.2	2.1	2.0	1.9	1.9	1.9	1.8	1.8	1.7	1.7	1.7	1.6	1.6	1.6	1.6	1.6	1.6	1.6

(continued)

Table 9.3 Continued

Country	2005–2010	2010–2015	2015–2020	2020–2025	2025–2030	2030–2035	2035–2040	2040–2045	2045–2050	2050–2055	2055–2060	2060–2065	2065–2070	2070–2075	2075–2080	2080–2085	2085–2090	2090–2095	2095–2100
Equatorial Guinea	5.4	4.8	4.2	3.7	3.2	2.9	2.7	2.5	2.3	2.2	2.1	2.0	1.9	1.9	1.9	1.8	1.8	1.7	1.7
Eritrea	4.7	4.1	3.6	3.2	2.9	2.7	2.5	2.3	2.2	2.1	2.0	1.9	1.9	1.8	1.8	1.7	1.7	1.6	1.6
Estonia	1.6	1.5	1.6	1.6	1.6	1.7	1.7	1.7	1.7	1.7	1.7	1.7	1.7	1.7	1.7	1.7	1.7	1.7	1.7
Ethiopia	4.6	4.1	3.7	3.4	3.0	2.8	2.6	2.4	2.2	2.1	2.0	2.0	1.9	1.9	1.8	1.8	1.7	1.7	1.7
Fiji	2.8	2.5	2.3	2.2	2.1	2.0	1.9	1.9	1.8	1.8	1.7	1.7	1.7	1.7	1.7	1.6	1.6	1.6	1.6
Finland	1.9	1.8	1.9	1.9	2.0	2.0	2.0	2.0	2.0	2.0	2.0	2.0	2.0	2.0	2.0	1.9	1.9	1.9	1.9
France	2.0	2.0	2.0	2.0	2.0	2.0	2.0	1.9	1.9	1.9	1.9	1.9	1.9	1.9	1.9	1.9	1.9	1.9	1.9
French Guiana	3.3	2.8	2.6	2.4	2.2	2.1	2.0	1.9	1.9	1.8	1.8	1.8	1.7	1.7	1.7	1.6	1.6	1.6	1.6
French Polynesia	2.1	2.1	2.1	2.0	2.0	2.0	2.0	1.9	1.9	1.9	1.9	1.9	1.9	1.9	1.9	1.9	1.9	1.9	1.9
Gabon	3.4	2.9	2.6	2.4	2.2	2.1	2.1	2.0	1.9	1.9	1.9	1.8	1.8	1.7	1.7	1.7	1.6	1.6	1.6
Gambia	5.1	4.5	4.0	3.5	3.1	2.8	2.6	2.4	2.2	2.1	2.0	2.0	1.9	1.8	1.8	1.8	1.8	1.7	1.7
Georgia	1.9	1.6	1.7	1.7	1.7	1.7	1.7	1.7	1.7	1.7	1.7	1.7	1.7	1.7	1.7	1.7	1.7	1.7	1.7
Germany	1.4	1.4	1.4	1.5	1.5	1.6	1.6	1.6	1.6	1.6	1.6	1.6	1.6	1.6	1.6	1.6	1.6	1.6	1.6
Ghana	4.3	4.0	3.7	3.4	3.1	2.9	2.7	2.5	2.4	2.2	2.1	2.0	2.0	1.9	1.8	1.8	1.7	1.7	1.7
Greece	1.5	1.4	1.5	1.5	1.6	1.6	1.6	1.6	1.6	1.6	1.6	1.6	1.6	1.6	1.6	1.6	1.6	1.6	1.6
Grenada	2.3	2.1	2.1	2.0	1.9	1.9	1.9	1.8	1.8	1.7	1.7	1.7	1.6	1.6	1.6	1.6	1.6	1.6	1.6
Guadeloupe	2.2	2.2	2.1	2.1	2.0	2.0	2.0	1.9	1.9	1.9	1.9	1.9	1.9	1.9	1.9	1.9	1.9	1.9	1.9
Guam	2.5	2.3	2.2	2.1	2.0	1.9	1.9	1.8	1.8	1.7	1.7	1.6	1.6	1.6	1.6	1.6	1.6	1.6	1.6
Guatemala	4.2	3.6	3.1	2.8	2.6	2.4	2.3	2.2	2.1	2.0	1.9	1.9	1.9	1.8	1.8	1.7	1.7	1.6	1.6
Guinea	5.5	4.9	4.3	3.8	3.4	3.0	2.7	2.5	2.3	2.2	2.1	2.0	1.9	1.9	1.8	1.8	1.7	1.7	1.7
Guinea-Bissau	5.3	4.7	4.2	3.6	3.2	2.9	2.7	2.5	2.3	2.2	2.1	2.0	1.9	1.9	1.8	1.8	1.7	1.7	1.7
Guyana	2.3	2.2	2.1	2.0	1.9	1.9	1.9	1.8	1.8	1.7	1.7	1.7	1.6	1.6	1.6	1.6	1.6	1.6	1.6
Haiti	3.5	3.1	2.7	2.5	2.3	2.2	2.1	2.0	1.9	1.9	1.8	1.8	1.7	1.7	1.6	1.6	1.6	1.6	1.6
Honduras	3.3	2.9	2.6	2.4	2.3	2.2	2.1	2.0	1.9	1.9	1.9	1.8	1.8	1.7	1.7	1.7	1.6	1.6	1.6
Hong Kong	1.1	1.3	1.2	1.2	1.2	1.2	1.3	1.3	1.4	1.4	1.4	1.4	1.4	1.5	1.5	1.5	1.5	1.5	1.5
Hungary	1.3	1.2	1.3	1.4	1.4	1.5	1.5	1.5	1.5	1.6	1.6	1.6	1.6	1.6	1.6	1.6	1.6	1.6	1.6

India	2.7	2.5	2.4	2.2	2.1	2.0	2.0	1.9	1.8	1.8	1.8	1.7	1.7	1.7	1.7	1.6	1.6	1.6	1.6
Indonesia	2.2	2.0	1.9	1.8	1.8	1.7	1.6	1.6	1.5	1.5	1.5	1.5	1.5	1.6	1.6	1.6	1.6	1.6	1.6
Iran	1.8	1.9	1.8	1.8	1.7	1.7	1.6	1.6	1.5	1.5	1.5	1.5	1.5	1.5	1.5	1.6	1.6	1.6	1.6
Iraq	4.9	4.3	3.7	3.3	3.0	2.7	2.5	2.3	2.2	2.1	2.0	1.9	1.9	1.8	1.8	1.8	1.7	1.7	1.7
Ireland	2.1	2.0	2.0	2.0	2.0	2.0	2.0	1.9	1.9	1.9	1.9	1.9	1.9	1.9	1.9	1.9	1.9	1.9	1.9
Israel	3.0	3.0	2.9	2.8	2.7	2.7	2.6	2.6	2.5	2.5	2.5	2.4	2.4	2.4	2.4	2.3	2.3	2.3	2.3
Italy	1.4	1.4	1.5	1.5	1.6	1.6	1.6	1.6	1.6	1.6	1.6	1.6	1.6	1.6	1.6	1.6	1.6	1.6	1.6
Jamaica	2.4	2.2	2.1	2.0	2.0	1.9	1.9	1.8	1.8	1.8	1.8	1.7	1.7	1.6	1.6	1.6	1.6	1.6	1.6
Japan	1.4	1.4	1.4	1.4	1.4	1.4	1.4	1.4	1.4	1.4	1.4	1.4	1.4	1.5	1.5	1.5	1.5	1.5	1.5
Jordan	3.3	2.9	2.6	2.4	2.2	2.1	2.0	2.0	1.9	1.9	1.8	1.8	1.8	1.7	1.7	1.7	1.6	1.6	1.6
Kazakhstan	2.5	2.3	2.2	2.1	2.0	1.9	1.8	1.8	1.7	1.7	1.7	1.7	1.6	1.6	1.6	1.6	1.6	1.6	1.6
Kenya	4.8	4.3	3.9	3.5	3.2	2.9	2.7	2.5	2.4	2.2	2.1	2.0	2.0	1.9	1.9	1.8	1.8	1.7	1.7
Kuwait	2.3	2.2	2.1	2.0	1.9	1.9	1.9	1.8	1.8	1.7	1.7	1.7	1.7	1.7	1.6	1.6	1.6	1.6	1.6
Kyrgyzstan	2.7	2.4	2.3	2.2	2.0	2.0	1.9	1.9	1.8	1.8	1.7	1.7	1.7	1.7	1.6	1.6	1.6	1.6	1.6
Laos	3.0	2.7	2.4	2.3	2.2	2.1	2.0	1.9	1.9	1.9	1.8	1.8	1.7	1.7	1.7	1.7	1.7	1.6	1.6
Latvia	1.2	1.3	1.3	1.4	1.4	1.5	1.5	1.5	1.5	1.6	1.6	1.6	1.6	1.6	1.6	1.6	1.6	1.6	1.6
Lebanon	1.9	1.7	1.7	1.7	1.7	1.7	1.6	1.6	1.6	1.6	1.6	1.6	1.6	1.6	1.6	1.6	1.6	1.6	1.6
Lesotho	3.4	2.9	2.7	2.5	2.3	2.2	2.1	2.0	1.9	1.8	1.8	1.8	1.8	1.7	1.7	1.6	1.6	1.6	1.6
Liberia	5.4	4.9	4.3	3.8	3.4	3.0	2.7	2.5	2.3	2.2	2.1	2.0	1.9	1.9	1.9	1.8	1.8	1.7	1.7
Libya	2.7	2.5	2.3	2.2	2.1	2.0	1.9	1.9	1.9	1.8	1.8	1.8	1.7	1.7	1.6	1.6	1.6	1.6	1.6
Lithuania	1.6	1.6	1.6	1.6	1.6	1.7	1.7	1.7	1.7	1.7	1.7	1.7	1.7	1.7	1.7	1.7	1.7	1.7	1.7
Luxembourg	1.6	1.5	1.6	1.7	1.8	1.8	1.8	1.8	1.8	1.8	1.8	1.8	1.8	1.8	1.8	1.8	1.8	1.8	1.8
Macao	1.1	1.1	1.1	1.2	1.2	1.2	1.3	1.3	1.4	1.4	1.4	1.4	1.4	1.5	1.5	1.5	1.5	1.5	1.5
Madagascar	4.8	4.2	3.7	3.3	3.0	2.7	2.5	2.3	2.2	2.1	2.0	1.9	1.9	1.9	1.8	1.8	1.7	1.7	1.7
Malawi	6.0	5.6	5.2	4.9	4.5	4.1	3.8	3.4	3.1	2.8	2.6	2.4	2.3	2.1	2.1	2.0	1.9	1.9	1.9
Malaysia	2.7	2.5	2.4	2.2	2.1	2.0	1.9	1.9	1.8	1.8	1.7	1.7	1.7	1.7	1.6	1.6	1.6	1.6	1.6
Maldives	1.9	1.8	1.7	1.7	1.7	1.7	1.6	1.6	1.6	1.6	1.6	1.6	1.6	1.6	1.6	1.6	1.6	1.6	1.6
Mali	6.5	6.0	5.4	4.9	4.3	3.8	3.3	3.0	2.7	2.5	2.3	2.2	2.1	2.0	1.9	1.9	1.9	1.8	1.8

(continued)

Table 9.3 Continued

Country	2005–2010	2010–2015	2015–2020	2020–2025	2025–2030	2030–2035	2035–2040	2040–2045	2045–2050	2050–2055	2055–2060	2060–2065	2065–2070	2070–2075	2075–2080	2080–2085	2085–2090	2090–2095	2095–2100
Malta	1.4	1.5	1.5	1.5	1.6	1.6	1.6	1.6	1.6	1.6	1.6	1.6	1.6	1.6	1.6	1.6	1.6	1.6	1.6
Martinique	2.0	2.0	2.0	2.0	2.0	2.0	2.0	1.9	1.9	1.9	1.9	1.9	1.9	1.9	1.9	1.9	1.9	1.9	1.9
Mauritania	4.7	4.1	3.6	3.2	2.9	2.7	2.5	2.3	2.2	2.1	2.0	1.9	1.9	1.8	1.8	1.7	1.7	1.7	1.6
Mauritius	1.5	1.5	1.5	1.6	1.7	1.7	1.7	1.7	1.7	1.7	1.7	1.7	1.7	1.7	1.7	1.7	1.7	1.7	1.7
Mayotte	4.3	3.7	3.3	3.0	2.7	2.5	2.3	2.2	2.1	2.0	1.9	1.9	1.8	1.8	1.7	1.7	1.7	1.7	1.7
Mexico	2.4	2.3	2.2	2.1	2.0	2.0	1.9	1.9	1.8	1.8	1.7	1.7	1.7	1.7	1.6	1.6	1.6	1.6	1.6
Micronesia	3.6	3.1	2.8	2.5	2.3	2.2	2.1	2.0	1.9	1.9	1.9	1.8	1.8	1.7	1.7	1.6	1.6	1.6	1.6
Moldova	1.2	1.3	1.3	1.4	1.5	1.5	1.5	1.5	1.5	1.5	1.5	1.5	1.5	1.5	1.5	1.6	1.6	1.6	1.6
Mongolia	2.5	2.4	2.3	2.2	2.1	2.1	2.0	1.9	1.9	1.9	1.8	1.8	1.7	1.7	1.6	1.6	1.6	1.6	1.6
Montenegro	1.7	1.6	1.6	1.6	1.6	1.6	1.6	1.6	1.6	1.6	1.6	1.6	1.6	1.6	1.6	1.6	1.6	1.6	1.6
Morocco	2.4	2.2	2.1	2.0	2.0	1.9	1.9	1.8	1.8	1.7	1.7	1.7	1.6	1.6	1.6	1.6	1.6	1.6	1.6
Mozambique	5.1	4.5	4.0	3.5	3.1	2.8	2.6	2.4	2.2	2.1	2.1	2.0	1.9	1.9	1.9	1.8	1.8	1.7	1.7
Myanmar	2.1	1.9	1.8	1.7	1.7	1.7	1.7	1.6	1.6	1.6	1.6	1.6	1.6	1.6	1.6	1.6	1.6	1.6	1.6
Namibia	3.4	2.9	2.6	2.4	2.2	2.1	2.0	2.0	1.9	1.8	1.8	1.7	1.7	1.7	1.7	1.6	1.6	1.6	1.6
Nepal	2.9	2.7	2.5	2.3	2.2	2.1	2.0	1.9	1.9	1.8	1.8	1.7	1.7	1.7	1.7	1.6	1.6	1.6	1.6
Netherlands	1.8	1.7	1.7	1.8	1.8	1.8	1.8	1.8	1.8	1.8	1.8	1.8	1.8	1.8	1.8	1.8	1.8	1.8	1.8
Netherlands Antilles	2.0	1.8	1.8	1.7	1.7	1.7	1.7	1.7	1.7	1.7	1.7	1.7	1.7	1.7	1.7	1.7	1.7	1.6	1.6
New Caledonia	2.2	2.2	2.1	2.0	1.9	1.8	1.8	1.8	1.8	1.8	1.8	1.8	1.8	1.8	1.8	1.8	1.8	1.8	1.8
New Zealand	2.2	2.1	2.0	1.9	1.9	1.8	1.8	1.8	1.8	1.8	1.8	1.8	1.8	1.8	1.8	1.8	1.8	1.8	1.8
Nicaragua	2.8	2.5	2.3	2.2	2.1	2.0	1.9	1.9	1.8	1.8	1.7	1.7	1.7	1.7	1.7	1.6	1.6	1.6	1.6
Niger	7.2	6.8	6.4	5.9	5.5	5.2	4.8	4.5	4.1	3.6	3.2	2.9	2.7	2.5	2.3	2.2	2.1	2.0	1.9
Nigeria	5.6	5.3	5.0	4.7	4.4	4.2	3.9	3.7	3.5	3.1	2.8	2.6	2.4	2.2	2.1	2.0	1.9	1.9	1.9
North Korea	2.0	1.9	1.8	1.6	1.5	1.4	1.4	1.4	1.4	1.4	1.4	1.4	1.4	1.5	1.5	1.5	1.5	1.5	1.5
Norway	2.0	1.9	1.9	1.9	2.0	2.0	2.0	2.0	2.0	2.0	2.0	2.0	2.0	2.0	2.0	1.9	1.9	1.9	1.9
Oman	2.5	2.3	2.2	2.1	2.0	1.9	1.9	1.8	1.8	1.7	1.7	1.7	1.7	1.7	1.7	1.7	1.7	1.7	1.7
Pakistan	3.7	3.3	3.1	2.8	2.7	2.5	2.4	2.3	2.2	2.1	2.0	1.9	1.8	1.8	1.8	1.8	1.7	1.7	1.6

Palestine	4.6	4.1	3.6	3.1	2.9	2.6	2.4	2.3	2.2	2.0	2.0	1.9	1.9	1.8	1.8	1.7	1.7	1.7	1.6
Panama	2.6	2.3	2.2	2.1	2.0	1.9	1.9	1.8	1.8	1.8	1.7	1.7	1.7	1.6	1.6	1.6	1.6	1.6	1.6
Papua New Guinea	4.1	3.5	3.1	2.8	2.6	2.4	2.2	2.1	2.0	1.9	1.8	1.8	1.7	1.7	1.7	1.7	1.7	1.6	1.6
Paraguay	3.1	2.7	2.5	2.3	2.2	2.1	2.0	1.9	1.9	1.8	1.8	1.7	1.7	1.7	1.7	1.7	1.6	1.6	1.6
Peru	2.6	2.4	2.2	2.1	2.0	1.9	1.9	1.8	1.8	1.8	1.7	1.7	1.7	1.7	1.6	1.6	1.6	1.6	1.6
Philippines	3.3	3.0	2.7	2.5	2.3	2.2	2.1	2.0	1.9	1.9	1.9	1.8	1.8	1.7	1.7	1.7	1.6	1.6	1.6
Poland	1.4	1.3	1.4	1.5	1.6	1.7	1.7	1.7	1.7	1.7	1.7	1.7	1.7	1.7	1.7	1.7	1.7	1.7	1.7
Portugal	1.4	1.3	1.3	1.4	1.5	1.5	1.6	1.6	1.7	1.7	1.7	1.7	1.7	1.7	1.7	1.7	1.7	1.7	1.7
Puerto Rico	1.8	1.7	1.7	1.7	1.6	1.6	1.6	1.5	1.5	1.5	1.5	1.5	1.6	1.6	1.6	1.6	1.6	1.6	1.6
Qatar	2.4	2.2	2.1	2.0	2.0	1.9	1.8	1.8	1.8	1.8	1.7	1.7	1.6	1.6	1.6	1.6	1.6	1.6	1.6
Réunion	2.3	2.3	2.2	2.1	2.0	2.0	2.0	1.9	1.9	1.9	1.9	1.9	1.9	1.9	1.9	1.9	1.9	1.9	1.9
Romania	1.3	1.3	1.3	1.4	1.5	1.5	1.5	1.5	1.5	1.5	1.5	1.5	1.5	1.5	1.5	1.6	1.6	1.6	1.6
Russian Federation	1.5	1.6	1.6	1.5	1.5	1.5	1.6	1.6	1.7	1.7	1.7	1.7	1.7	1.7	1.7	1.7	1.7	1.7	1.7
Rwanda	5.4	5.0	4.5	4.1	3.7	3.4	3.1	2.8	2.7	2.5	2.3	2.2	2.1	2.0	1.9	1.9	1.8	1.8	1.7
Saint Lucia	2.0	1.9	1.8	1.7	1.7	1.7	1.6	1.6	1.6	1.6	1.6	1.6	1.6	1.6	1.6	1.6	1.6	1.6	1.6
Saint Vincent and the Grenadines	2.1	2.0	1.9	1.9	1.8	1.8	1.7	1.7	1.7	1.7	1.7	1.6	1.6	1.6	1.6	1.6	1.6	1.6	1.6
Samoa	4.0	3.4	3.0	2.7	2.5	2.3	2.2	2.1	2.0	1.9	1.9	1.9	1.8	1.8	1.7	1.7	1.7	1.7	1.6
São Tomé and Principe	3.9	3.3	2.9	2.6	2.5	2.3	2.2	2.1	2.0	1.9	1.9	1.9	1.8	1.8	1.7	1.7	1.7	1.6	1.6
Saudi Arabia	3.0	2.7	2.5	2.3	2.2	2.1	2.0	1.9	1.9	1.9	1.8	1.8	1.7	1.7	1.7	1.6	1.6	1.6	1.6
Senegal	5.0	4.5	4.1	3.6	3.3	3.0	2.7	2.6	2.4	2.2	2.1	2.0	2.0	1.9	1.9	1.8	1.8	1.7	1.7
Serbia	1.4	1.4	1.4	1.5	1.6	1.6	1.6	1.6	1.6	1.6	1.6	1.6	1.6	1.6	1.6	1.6	1.6	1.6	1.6
Sierra Leone	5.2	4.6	4.1	3.6	3.2	2.9	2.6	2.4	2.3	2.2	2.1	2.0	1.9	1.9	1.8	1.8	1.7	1.7	1.7
Singapore	1.2	1.3	1.3	1.3	1.4	1.4	1.4	1.4	1.4	1.4	1.4	1.4	1.4	1.5	1.5	1.5	1.5	1.5	1.5
Slovakia	1.4	1.4	1.5	1.6	1.6	1.7	1.7	1.7	1.7	1.7	1.7	1.7	1.7	1.7	1.7	1.7	1.7	1.7	1.7
Slovenia	1.6	1.6	1.6	1.6	1.6	1.7	1.7	1.7	1.7	1.7	1.7	1.7	1.7	1.7	1.7	1.7	1.7	1.7	1.7
Solomon Islands	4.4	3.8	3.4	3.0	2.7	2.5	2.3	2.2	2.1	2.0	1.9	1.9	1.9	1.8	1.8	1.7	1.7	1.7	1.7

(continued

Table 9.3 Continued

Country	2005–2010	2010–2015	2015–2020	2020–2025	2025–2030	2030–2035	2035–2040	2040–2045	2045–2050	2050–2055	2055–2060	2060–2065	2065–2070	2070–2075	2075–2080	2080–2085	2085–2090	2090–2095	2095–2100
Somalia	6.4	6.0	5.5	4.9	4.4	3.9	3.4	3.0	2.7	2.5	2.3	2.2	2.1	2.0	1.9	1.9	1.8	1.8	1.7
South Africa	2.6	2.4	2.3	2.1	2.0	2.0	1.9	1.9	1.8	1.8	1.7	1.7	1.7	1.6	1.6	1.6	1.6	1.6	1.6
South Korea	1.2	1.3	1.3	1.4	1.4	1.4	1.4	1.4	1.4	1.4	1.4	1.4	1.4	1.5	1.5	1.5	1.5	1.5	1.5
Spain	1.4	1.3	1.4	1.4	1.5	1.5	1.6	1.6	1.7	1.7	1.7	1.7	1.7	1.7	1.7	1.7	1.7	1.7	1.7
Sri Lanka	2.4	2.2	2.1	2.0	1.9	1.8	1.8	1.7	1.7	1.7	1.6	1.6	1.6	1.6	1.6	1.6	1.6	1.6	1.6
Sudan	4.6	4.1	3.6	3.2	2.9	2.7	2.5	2.3	2.2	2.1	2.0	1.9	1.9	1.9	1.8	1.8	1.7	1.7	1.7
Suriname	2.4	2.3	2.2	2.1	2.0	2.0	1.9	1.9	1.9	1.9	1.8	1.8	1.7	1.7	1.7	1.7	1.6	1.6	1.6
Swaziland	3.6	3.1	2.8	2.5	2.4	2.2	2.1	2.0	1.9	1.9	1.9	1.8	1.8	1.7	1.7	1.6	1.6	1.6	1.6
Sweden	2.0	1.9	1.9	2.0	2.0	2.0	2.0	2.0	2.0	2.0	2.0	2.0	2.0	2.0	2.0	1.9	1.9	1.9	1.9
Switzerland	1.5	1.5	1.6	1.6	1.7	1.7	1.7	1.7	1.7	1.8	1.8	1.8	1.8	1.8	1.8	1.8	1.8	1.8	1.8
Syria	3.1	2.7	2.5	2.3	2.2	2.1	2.0	1.9	1.9	1.8	1.8	1.7	1.7	1.7	1.7	1.7	1.6	1.6	1.6
Tanzania	5.6	5.1	4.6	4.1	3.7	3.3	3.0	2.7	2.5	2.4	2.2	2.1	2.0	1.9	1.9	1.9	1.9	1.8	1.8
Tajikistan	3.5	3.0	2.7	2.5	2.3	2.2	2.1	2.0	1.9	1.9	1.9	1.8	1.8	1.7	1.7	1.7	1.7	1.6	1.6
Thailand	1.6	1.6	1.6	1.5	1.5	1.5	1.5	1.5	1.5	1.5	1.5	1.5	1.5	1.6	1.6	1.6	1.6	1.6	1.6
Timor-Leste	6.5	6.1	5.6	5.1	4.7	4.1	3.6	3.2	2.9	2.7	2.5	2.3	2.2	2.1	2.0	1.9	1.8	1.8	1.8
Togo	4.3	3.8	3.3	3.0	2.7	2.5	2.3	2.2	2.1	2.0	1.9	1.9	1.8	1.8	1.7	1.7	1.7	1.7	1.7
Tonga	4.0	3.5	3.0	2.7	2.5	2.3	2.2	2.1	2.0	1.9	1.9	1.9	1.8	1.8	1.7	1.7	1.7	1.6	1.6
Trinidad and Tobago	1.6	1.5	1.5	1.5	1.5	1.5	1.4	1.4	1.4	1.4	1.4	1.5	1.5	1.5	1.5	1.5	1.5	1.5	1.5
Tunisia	2.0	1.9	1.8	1.7	1.7	1.7	1.6	1.6	1.6	1.6	1.6	1.6	1.6	1.6	1.6	1.6	1.6	1.6	1.6
Turkey	2.2	2.0	2.0	1.9	1.8	1.8	1.7	1.7	1.6	1.6	1.6	1.6	1.6	1.6	1.6	1.6	1.6	1.6	1.6
Turkmenistan	2.5	2.3	2.2	2.1	2.0	1.9	1.9	1.8	1.8	1.7	1.7	1.7	1.6	1.6	1.6	1.6	1.6	1.6	1.6
TFYR Macedonia	1.6	1.5	1.5	1.5	1.6	1.6	1.6	1.6	1.6	1.6	1.6	1.6	1.6	1.6	1.6	1.6	1.6	1.6	1.6
Uganda	6.4	5.9	5.5	5.0	4.6	4.2	3.9	3.5	3.2	2.9	2.7	2.5	2.3	2.2	2.1	2.0	1.9	1.8	1.8
Ukraine	1.4	1.5	1.5	1.5	1.5	1.5	1.5	1.6	1.6	1.6	1.6	1.6	1.6	1.6	1.6	1.6	1.6	1.6	1.6
United Arab Emirates	1.9	1.7	1.7	1.7	1.6	1.6	1.6	1.5	1.5	1.5	1.5	1.5	1.5	1.6	1.6	1.6	1.6	1.6	1.6
United Kingdom	2.0	2.0	2.0	2.0	2.0	2.0	2.0	1.9	1.9	1.9	1.9	1.9	1.9	1.9	1.9	1.9	1.9	1.9	1.9

United States of America	1.9	1.9	1.9	1.9	1.9	1.9	1.9	1.9	1.9	1.9	1.9	1.9	1.9	1.9	1.9	1.9	1.9	1.9	1.9
Uruguay	2.1	2.0	1.9	1.8	1.8	1.7	1.7	1.7	1.6	1.6	1.6	1.6	1.6	1.6	1.6	1.6	1.6	1.6	1.6
Uzbekistan	2.5	2.3	2.1	2.1	2.0	1.9	1.9	1.9	1.8	1.8	1.7	1.7	1.7	1.6	1.6	1.6	1.6	1.6	1.6
Vanuatu	4.0	3.5	3.0	2.7	2.5	2.3	2.2	2.1	2.0	1.9	1.9	1.8	1.8	1.7	1.7	1.6	1.6	1.6	1.6
Venezuela	2.5	2.3	2.2	2.1	2.0	1.9	1.8	1.8	1.7	1.7	1.7	1.6	1.6	1.6	1.6	1.6	1.6	1.6	1.6
Virgin Islands	2.1	1.9	1.8	1.7	1.7	1.7	1.7	1.6	1.6	1.6	1.6	1.6	1.6	1.6	1.6	1.6	1.6	1.6	1.6
Viet Nam	1.9	1.8	1.7	1.7	1.6	1.6	1.5	1.5	1.4	1.4	1.5	1.5	1.5	1.5	1.5	1.5	1.5	1.5	1.5
Yemen	5.5	4.9	4.4	3.9	3.5	3.2	2.9	2.7	2.5	2.4	2.2	2.1	2.0	1.9	1.9	1.8	1.8	1.7	1.7
Zambia	6.2	5.7	5.3	4.8	4.4	3.9	3.5	3.1	2.8	2.6	2.4	2.3	2.1	2.0	2.0	1.9	1.9	1.8	1.8
Zimbabwe	3.5	3.0	2.7	2.5	2.3	2.2	2.1	2.0	1.9	1.8	1.8	1.8	1.8	1.7	1.7	1.6	1.6	1.6	1.6

Table 9.4 Fertility Differentials by Education in the Base Period

Country	No Education	Incomplete primary	Completed primary	Low secondary	Upper secondary	Post-secondary
Afghanistan	2.59	2.36	1.94	1.39	1.00	0.87
Albania	1.47	1.47	1.47	1.39	1.00	0.80
Algeria	1.57	1.57	1.57	1.18	1.00	0.89
Angola	2.67	2.66	2.11	1.51	1.00	0.71
Argentina	1.54	1.54	1.54	1.19	1.00	0.90
Armenia	1.12	1.12	1.12	1.14	1.00	0.79
Aruba	1.79	1.46	1.27	1.13	1.00	0.88
Australia	1.23	1.23	1.23	1.23	1.00	0.87
Austria	1.27	1.27	1.27	1.27	1.00	1.04
Azerbaijan	1.12	1.12	1.12	1.14	1.00	0.79
Bahamas	1.63	1.63	1.63	1.20	1.00	0.79
Bahrain	3.08	1.70	1.53	0.86	1.00	1.09
Bangladesh	1.41	1.39	1.26	1.15	1.00	1.05
Barbados	1.63	1.63	1.63	1.20	1.00	0.79
Belarus	1.13	1.13	1.13	1.35	1.00	0.84
Belgium	1.04	1.04	1.04	1.04	1.00	1.06
Belize	2.09	1.83	1.54	1.00	1.00	1.06
Benin	1.96	1.61	1.26	0.99	1.00	0.86
Bhutan	1.66	1.39	1.28	1.11	1.00	0.95
Bolivia	2.33	2.15	1.75	1.35	1.00	0.73
Bosnia and Herzegovina	1.47	1.47	1.47	1.39	1.00	0.80
Botswana	2.09	1.84	1.55	1.26	1.00	0.87
Brazil	1.97	1.97	1.97	1.23	1.00	0.83
Brunei Darussalam	1.57	1.57	1.57	1.18	1.00	0.89
Bulgaria	1.47	1.47	1.47	1.39	1.00	0.80
Burkina Faso	2.21	1.68	1.33	0.70	1.00	0.86
Burundi	2.56	2.30	1.89	1.33	1.00	0.87
Cambodia	1.26	1.24	1.20	1.03	1.00	0.82

Cameroon	2.54	2.48	1.86	1.19	1.00	0.99
Canada	1.26	1.26	1.26	1.26	1.00	1.04
Cape Verde	2.09	1.84	1.55	1.26	1.00	0.87
Central African Republic	2.33	2.35	2.12	1.22	1.00	0.86
Chad	2.15	2.25	1.95	1.39	1.00	0.86
Channel Islands	1.15	1.15	1.15	1.15	1.00	0.96
Chile	1.63	1.63	1.63	1.20	1.00	0.79
China	1.21	1.21	1.21	1.21	1.00	0.89
Colombia	2.21	1.89	1.48	1.23	1.00	0.74
Comoros	4.10	3.16	3.68	2.69	1.00	0.86
Congo	2.56	2.30	1.89	1.33	1.00	0.87
Costa Rica	1.63	1.63	1.63	1.20	1.00	0.79
Côte d'Ivoire	3.44	2.86	2.04	1.24	1.00	0.86
Croatia	1.22	1.22	1.22	1.22	1.00	0.86
Cuba	1.63	1.63	1.63	1.20	1.00	0.79
Cyprus	1.24	1.24	1.24	1.11	1.00	0.91
Czech Republic	1.13	1.13	1.13	1.13	1.00	0.88
Denmark	1.02	1.02	1.02	1.02	1.00	0.98
Djibouti	2.56	2.30	1.89	1.33	1.00	0.87
Dominican Republic	1.90	1.37	1.37	1.09	1.00	0.74
D. R. Congo	1.96	1.94	1.94	1.47	1.00	0.90
Ecuador	2.01	1.81	1.54	1.23	1.00	0.82
Egypt	1.05	1.02	0.90	0.86	1.00	0.80
El Salvador	1.84	1.69	1.42	1.19	1.00	0.87
Equatorial Guinea	2.56	2.30	1.89	1.33	1.00	0.87
Eritrea	2.56	2.30	1.89	1.33	1.00	0.87
Estonia	1.14	1.14	1.14	1.14	1.00	0.77
Ethiopia	4.67	4.02	2.72	1.96	1.00	0.86
Fiji	1.95	1.65	1.41	1.19	1.00	0.87
Finland	0.96	0.96	0.96	0.96	1.00	0.97

(continued)

Table 9.4 Continued

Country	No Education	Incomplete primary	Completed primary	Low secondary	Upper secondary	Post-secondary
France	1.29	1.29	1.29	1.29	1.00	1.00
French Guiana	2.39	1.97	1.53	1.16	1.00	0.78
French Polynesia	1.86	1.54	1.33	1.15	1.00	0.88
Gabon	1.90	2.06	1.60	1.13	1.00	1.14
Gambia	2.56	2.30	1.89	1.33	1.00	0.87
Georgia	1.12	1.12	1.12	1.14	1.00	0.79
Germany	1.10	1.10	1.10	1.10	1.00	0.89
Ghana	2.78	2.17	1.94	1.48	1.00	0.66
Greece	1.21	1.21	1.21	1.09	1.00	0.92
Grenada	1.88	1.57	1.35	1.16	1.00	0.88
Guadeloupe	1.85	1.54	1.33	1.15	1.00	0.88
Guam	1.92	1.61	1.38	1.17	1.00	0.87
Guatemala	2.67	2.20	1.60	1.25	1.00	0.58
Guinea	1.53	1.29	1.10	0.96	1.00	0.58
Guinea-Bissau	2.56	2.30	1.89	1.33	1.00	0.87
Guyana	2.60	1.88	1.43	1.41	1.00	0.66
Haiti	2.83	2.15	1.43	1.10	1.00	1.12
Honduras	2.23	2.01	1.44	1.01	1.00	0.84
Hong Kong	1.21	1.21	1.21	1.21	1.00	0.89
Hungary	1.22	1.22	1.22	1.22	1.00	0.95
Iceland	1.01	1.01	1.01	1.01	1.00	0.98
India	2.18	1.50	1.54	1.37	1.00	1.25
Indonesia	1.06	1.15	1.18	1.12	1.00	1.14
Iran	1.80	1.80	1.80	1.24	1.00	0.83
Iraq	1.58	1.52	1.45	1.20	1.00	0.84
Ireland	1.15	1.15	1.15	1.15	1.00	0.96

Israel	1.49	1.49	1.49	1.13	1.00	0.94
Italy	1.27	1.27	1.27	1.13	1.00	0.89
Jamaica	1.16	1.16	1.16	1.16	1.00	0.57
Japan	0.99	0.99	0.99	0.99	1.00	0.87
Jordan	1.09	1.25	1.12	1.15	1.00	0.95
Kazakhstan	1.11	1.11	1.11	1.09	1.00	0.81
Kenya	2.24	2.01	1.66	1.57	1.00	0.80
Kuwait	1.57	1.57	1.57	1.18	1.00	0.89
Kyrgyzstan	0.92	0.92	0.92	1.01	1.00	0.71
Laos	1.86	1.80	1.73	1.36	1.00	1.00
Latvia	1.22	1.22	1.22	1.22	1.00	0.85
Lebanon	1.57	1.57	1.57	1.18	1.00	0.89
Lesotho	1.76	1.61	1.36	1.10	1.00	0.56
Liberia	3.18	2.90	2.39	1.66	1.00	0.86
Libya	2.12	1.69	1.45	1.26	1.00	1.03
Lithuania	1.22	1.22	1.22	1.22	1.00	0.85
Luxembourg	1.15	1.15	1.15	1.15	1.00	0.96
Macao	1.21	1.21	1.21	1.21	1.00	0.89
Madagascar	2.87	2.47	1.63	1.30	1.00	0.91
Malawi	2.52	2.30	2.01	1.67	1.00	0.77
Malaysia	1.26	1.24	1.20	1.03	1.00	0.82
Maldives	1.66	1.39	1.28	1.11	1.00	0.95
Mali	2.26	2.08	1.67	1.10	1.00	0.86
Malta	1.24	1.24	1.24	1.11	1.00	0.91
Martinique	1.82	1.49	1.29	1.14	1.00	0.88
Mauritania	2.28	2.01	1.68	1.29	1.00	0.87
Mauritius	1.23	1.23	1.23	1.23	1.00	0.87
Mayotte	1.95	1.65	1.41	1.18	1.00	0.87

(*continued*)

Table 9.4 Continued

Country	No Education	Incomplete primary	Completed primary	Low secondary	Upper secondary	Post-secondary
Mexico	1.86	1.86	1.86	1.25	1.00	0.85
Micronesia	2.10	1.81	1.53	1.23	1.00	0.87
Moldova	1.47	1.47	1.47	1.39	1.00	0.80
Mongolia	1.91	1.60	1.38	1.17	1.00	0.88
Montenegro	1.47	1.47	1.47	1.39	1.00	0.80
Morocco	2.12	1.69	1.45	1.26	1.00	1.03
Mozambique	2.61	2.36	1.87	1.38	1.00	0.86
Myanmar	2.06	1.94	1.61	1.28	1.00	0.72
Namibia	2.36	1.73	1.41	1.17	1.00	0.81
Nepal	2.06	1.74	1.39	0.99	1.00	0.96
Netherlands	1.08	1.08	1.08	1.08	1.00	0.88
Netherlands Antilles	1.63	1.63	1.63	1.20	1.00	0.79
New Caledonia	1.23	1.23	1.23	1.23	1.00	0.87
New Zealand	1.23	1.23	1.23	1.23	1.00	0.87
Nicaragua	2.27	1.71	1.29	0.99	1.00	0.71
Niger	2.29	2.28	1.68	1.40	1.00	0.86
Nigeria	1.74	1.59	1.46	1.24	1.00	0.74
North Korea	1.21	1.21	1.21	1.21	1.00	0.89
Norway	1.05	1.05	1.05	1.05	1.00	0.97
Pakistan	1.51	1.36	1.15	1.03	1.00	0.70
Palestine	1.30	1.42	1.34	1.16	1.00	0.87
Panama	1.95	1.80	1.45	1.18	1.00	0.76
Papua New Guinea	2.18	1.90	1.60	1.26	1.00	0.87
Paraguay	1.82	2.00	1.54	1.28	1.00	1.09
Peru	2.32	1.97	1.55	1.16	1.00	0.79

Philippines	1.40	1.38	1.31	1.09	1.00	0.71
Poland	1.39	1.39	1.39	1.39	1.00	0.79
Portugal	1.24	1.24	1.24	1.11	1.00	0.91
Puerto Rico	1.63	1.63	1.63	1.20	1.00	0.79
Oman	1.92	1.61	1.38	1.17	1.00	0.87
Qatar	1.43	1.43	1.43	1.18	1.00	0.90
Réunion	1.90	1.58	1.36	1.17	1.00	0.88
Romania	1.81	1.81	1.81	1.42	1.00	0.77
Russian Federation	1.47	1.47	1.47	1.39	1.00	0.80
Rwanda	2.18	2.06	1.71	1.33	1.00	0.83
Saint Lucia	2.39	1.97	1.53	1.16	1.00	0.78
Saint Vincent and the Grenadines	2.39	1.97	1.53	1.16	1.00	0.78
Samoa	2.16	1.88	1.58	1.25	1.00	0.87
São Tomé and Principe	1.71	1.82	1.57	1.09	1.00	1.00
Saudi Arabia	2.00	1.70	1.45	1.20	1.00	0.87
Senegal	3.06	2.49	1.91	1.93	1.00	0.86
Serbia	1.47	1.47	1.47	1.39	1.00	0.80
Sierra Leone	2.74	2.47	2.04	1.39	1.00	1.35
Singapore	1.21	1.21	1.21	1.21	1.00	0.89
Slovakia	1.25	1.25	1.25	1.25	1.00	0.81
Slovenia	1.14	1.14	1.14	1.14	1.00	0.87
Solomon Islands	2.23	1.95	1.64	1.27	1.00	0.87
Somalia	2.56	2.30	1.89	1.33	1.00	0.87
South Africa	2.08	1.72	1.53	1.19	1.00	0.88
South Korea	1.21	1.21	1.21	1.21	1.00	0.89
Spain	1.24	1.24	1.24	1.11	1.00	0.91
Sri Lanka	1.66	1.39	1.28	1.11	1.00	0.95
Sudan	1.39	1.30	1.32	1.24	1.00	0.79

(continued)

Table 9.4 Continued

Country	No Education	Incomplete primary	Completed primary	Low secondary	Upper secondary	Post-secondary
Suriname	2.39	1.97	1.53	1.16	1.00	0.78
Swaziland	1.78	1.61	1.45	1.23	1.00	0.77
Sweden	1.01	1.01	1.01	1.01	1.00	0.98
Switzerland	1.11	1.11	1.11	1.11	1.00	0.86
Syria	2.01	1.71	1.46	1.20	1.00	0.87
Tajikistan	1.11	1.11	1.11	1.09	1.00	0.81
Tanzania	2.69	2.34	2.02	1.07	1.00	0.86
TFYR Macedonia	1.47	1.47	1.47	1.39	1.00	0.80
Thailand	1.21	1.21	1.21	1.21	1.00	0.89
Timor-Leste	1.28	1.30	1.38	1.13	1.00	0.66
Togo	2.56	2.30	1.89	1.33	1.00	0.87
Tonga	2.16	1.89	1.59	1.25	1.00	0.87
Trinidad and Tobago	1.63	1.63	1.63	1.20	1.00	0.79
Tunisia	1.57	1.57	1.57	1.18	1.00	0.89
Turkey	2.55	1.70	1.50	1.02	1.00	0.76
Turkmenistan	1.11	1.11	1.11	1.09	1.00	0.81
Uganda	2.81	2.60	2.05	1.45	1.00	1.33
Ukraine	1.47	1.47	1.47	1.39	1.00	0.80
United Arab Emirates	1.57	1.57	1.57	1.18	1.00	0.89
United Kingdom	1.15	1.15	1.15	1.15	1.00	0.96
United States of America	1.42	1.42	1.42	1.42	1.00	0.90

Uruguay	1.63	1.63	1.63	1.20	1.00	0.79
Uzbekistan	1.11	1.11	1.11	1.09	1.00	0.81
Vanuatu	2.16	1.88	1.58	1.25	1.00	0.87
Venezuela	2.07	1.86	1.51	1.23	1.00	0.77
Viet Nam	1.45	1.04	1.14	0.96	1.00	0.89
Virgin Islands	1.84	1.52	1.31	1.15	1.00	0.88
Yemen	2.40	2.15	1.78	1.33	1.00	0.87
Zambia	3.07	2.84	2.32	1.72	1.00	1.04
Zimbabwe	1.25	1.45	1.29	1.14	1.00	0.70

Controlling for the influence of other factors, this produces conditional convergence, where the level of convergence depends on those other factors. The second concept is sigma-convergence, which occurs when the dispersion of the indicator decreases. This is merely a description, without any assumption about the functional relationship, in contrast to beta-convergence. There are different sub-concepts of sigma convergence in the literature (Anand and Ravallion 1993; Bidani and Ravallion 1997). Using the concept of sigma convergence in absolute terms, this model produces female life expectancy forecasts for all countries covered by this study. Exceptions were made for HIV/AIDS-affected countries (owing to specific requirement of treating mortality-related HIV/AIDS) where UN assumptions (medium variant; United Nations, 2011) were assumed until 2050, after which the models and the rules of convergence were applied.

Our model also takes into account country-specific heterogeneity in the historical trajectories of life expectancy, as well as between-countries heterogeneity with respect to gains in life expectancy. This reflects the view that national mortality trends should be viewed in a larger international context, rather than being analysed and projected individually (Lee 2003).The model also follows the argument given by Torri and Vaupel (2012), that life expectancy in different countries tends to be positively correlated, such that life expectancies of particular countries can be forecast by forecasting the best practice level and then the gap between the national performance and the best practice level.

This convergence procedure was implemented in five steps. First, Japan was identified as the current global forerunner in female life expectancy. Under the medium scenario the life expectancy at birth of Japanese females is assumed to grow by 2 years per decade from 86.1 years in 2005–10 to 104.2 in 2095–2100. Regional forerunners (22 regions) were identified, wherein female life expectancies were projected so that the change in life expectancies converges to the assumed change in Japan, that is, by 2 years per decade. This was implemented by applying the following dynamic panel data model, autoregressive of order 1 with fixed effects, which was estimated with two-step generalized method of moments over the period 1980–2005. This specification was estimated:

$$\Delta e_0 c_{t,t-1} = \gamma \Delta e_{0\,i,t,t-1} + \beta(e_{0\,i,t-1} - e_{0\,c,t-1}) + \varepsilon_{c,t} + \in_c \tag{9.1}$$

where $e_{0\,i,t}$ is the female life expectancy at birth for the forerunner *i* at time *t*; $e_{0\,c,t}$ is the female life expectancy at birth for the country *c* at time *t*; $\Delta e_0 c_{t,t-1}$ is the change in female life expectancy at birth for the country *c* between *t* and *t–1*; $\Delta e_0 i_{t,t-1}$ is the change in female life expectancy at birth for the forerunner *i* between t and *t–1*; $\varepsilon_{c,t}$ is the time-varying error component; and $\in_c$ are country-specific fixed effects.

The equilibrium is reached when:

$$(e_{0\,i,t-1} - e_{0\,c,t-1}) = \frac{(\gamma - 1)\Delta e_{0\,it,t-1} + \in_c}{\beta} \tag{9.2}$$

Once the life expectancies for regional forerunners were projected, a similar model was applied for countries within each region that were assumed to follow their regional forerunners. This convergence model has the advantage that it is based on empirical data. In addition, it takes into account the heterogeneous country-specific historical experiences, as well as differences in gains between forerunners and laggards over time and across regions. Thus, it takes into account structural, as well as stochastic, components that contribute to life expectancy trends over time, and it is able to generate unbiased parameters upon which the new forecasts are based

In the third step, for HIV-affected countries and two high mortality countries (Haiti and Afghanistan) the UN medium-variant life expectancies (United Nations, 2011) were assumed until the period 2045–50. Because we did not aspire to independently develop a specific AIDS forecasting model of the kind that underlies the UN mortality projections, we decided to refer to this well referenced model up to 2050 by which time the AIDs-specific effects are assumed to have become insignificant. After 2050 life expectancies to the end of the century were projected using the model with Namibia as the forerunner country for this group of countries. A comparison with the UN assumptions for this period showed very close results.

In the fourth step, the model results were blended with the country-specific expert assessments. This was done by a weighting procedure that used country-specific assessments of individual source experts until the period 2045–50 (as extensively described in Chapters 5 and 6), as well as the results of the meetings of meta-experts as described in Chapters 3–7. The gains in life expectancies at birth were thus calculated as a weighted average of three different sources of information on this gain, assigning the results of the statistical model the weight of 1.0, the average of the meta-experts the weight of 1.0, and the specification of each individual source expert who made a statement on a given country the weight of 0.2.

In the final step, the model net gains for the period 2050–2100 were re-estimated and modified using the new parameters obtained from the weighted net gains during 2010–50.

Similar steps were repeated for the high and low mortality scenarios. There, it was assumed that life expectancy would increase by one year per decade faster or slower than in the 'medium' case. For countries, mostly in sub-Saharan Africa, with a high prevalence of HIV/AIDS, larger uncertainty intervals were assumed for the nearer-term future. In the first decade of the projections, life expectancy is assumed for those countries to be five years lower or higher than in the medium. After 2020, the 'high' mortality scenario for those countries assumes a one year lower decadal gain than in the medium scenario. The 'low' mortality scenario assumes an additional two years gain per decade on top of the gain from the medium scenario until 2050, and one year additional gain thereafter. This procedure for deriving mortality assumptions is described in detail in Appendix I.

The resulting mortality assumptions for each country are listed in Appendix II for all countries for selected years and in the online material <http://www.wittgensteincentre.org/dataexplorer> for all years. To illustrate the resulting mortality assumptions for a specific example, Figure 9.2 gives the assumed trends in overall female life expectancy (across all education groups) at birth for global forerunner Japan, the South Asian

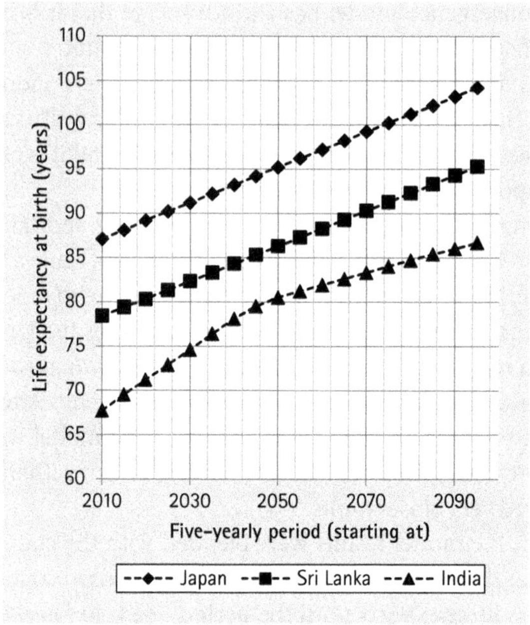

FIGURE 9.2 Medium scenario for life expectancy at birth for women.

regional forerunner Sri Lanka, and India as an arbitrarily chosen big country in the South Asia region. While Sri Lanka quickly converges to the two-year decadal increase assumed for Japan and hence draws parallel to Japan, India shows, at first, more rapid increases drawing closer to Sri Lanka, but the rate of improvement is visibly slowed during the second half of the century as a consequence of rather pessimistic expert assessments about the longer-term rate of mortality improvement. Despite a few such cases of country-specific assumptions resulting in less convergence, the overall pattern is that of slow but steady convergence in overall levels of life expectancy.

Figure 9.3 shows the trend in standard deviation (SD) of the assumed levels of female life expectancy at birth across all countries. This SD declines from around 10.5 years today to 8.5 years by the end of the century. This illustrates the results of the chosen model of convergence in terms of assumed national mortality trends for the rest of the century.

Once life expectancies at birth for five-year periods during 2010–2100 were modelled for women in 195 countries (see Table 9.5), life expectancies for men were derived by applying the difference between the female and overall life expectancy in the UN medium variant (United Nations, 2011). For a given sex-specific e_0, life tables were derived by interpolating and extrapolating (when the values were higher than the highest in the UN Medium variant) using country-specific life tables used in the UN-medium variant.

We introduce gender-specific education differentials in mortality as differences in life expectancy at age 15. In doing so, we follow the literature. The difference in life expectancy at age 15 between the 'no education' category and the tertiary-educated population is assumed to be of 6 years for men and 4 years for women. Between these extreme points, among men

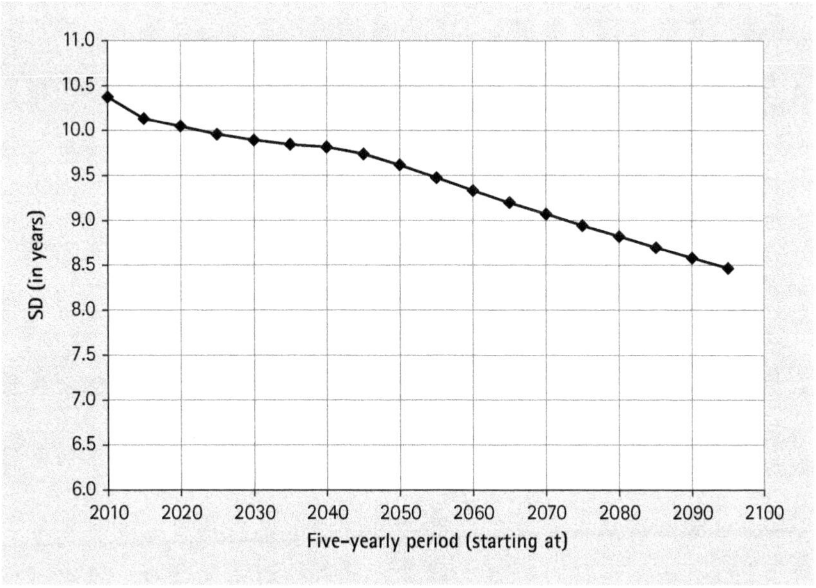

FIGURE 9.3 Standard deviation (SD) of the assumed medium levels of female life expectancy at birth across all countries 2010–2100.

we assume two years difference between 'completed primary' and 'completed lower secondary', and one year for the remaining levels of attainment. Likewise, for women, we proportionally adjust to the lower assumption of a four-year differential overall.

Finally, for children up to the age of 15 the differential mortality is introduced through the mother's education. We assume that the differentials in terms of RR of mortality rates with respect to the completed upper secondary category are 1.8, 1.7, 1.6, 1.4, 1.0, and 0.8, in ascending order of educational attainment. These values are based on the averages of under-five mortality rates in the DHS countries (see the DHS website: <http://www.measuredhs.com/Data/>).

9.3.4 Migration assumptions

The migration component of the WIC projections represents a significant innovation in the way migration is handled in global population projections. The limitations of the conventional approach of using net migration models were overcome by drawing on a first-of-a-kind set of bilateral migration flow estimates (see Chapter 7 and, for a detailed discussion of the estimation method, Abel, 2013). These estimates of country-to-country migration flows for five-year periods allow us to use a bi-regional cohort–component projection model where flows, rather than net numbers, are projected. The total number of emigrants and immigrants by sex in the period 2005–10 is presented in Table 9.6.

Table 9.5 Life Expectancy at Birth for Women

Country	2005–2010	2010–2015	2015–2020	2020–2025	2025–2030	2030–2035	2035–2040	2040–2045	2045–2050	2050–2055	2055–2060	2060–2065	2065–2070	2070–2075	2075–2080	2080–2085	2085–2090	2090–2095	2095–2100
Afghanistan	47.5	49.5	51.4	53.3	55.4	57.4	59.4	61.5	63.4	65.2	67.0	68.5	69.9	71.2	72.4	73.5	74.5	75.5	76.4
Albania	79.7	80.7	81.8	82.8	83.8	84.8	85.8	86.8	87.8	88.8	89.8	90.8	91.8	92.8	93.8	94.8	95.8	96.8	97.8
Algeria	73.7	75.2	76.5	77.7	78.8	79.9	80.9	81.9	82.9	83.9	84.9	85.9	86.9	88.0	89.0	90.0	91.0	92.0	93.0
Angola	51.0	53.2	55.2	56.6	57.9	59.2	60.4	61.5	62.8	64.2	65.6	67.1	68.5	69.9	71.3	72.7	74.2	75.6	77.0
Argentina	79.1	80.1	81.1	82.1	83.0	83.9	84.8	85.6	86.6	87.6	88.7	89.8	91.0	92.1	93.2	94.3	95.4	96.5	97.7
Armenia	76.7	77.4	78.2	79.1	80.0	81.0	82.0	82.9	83.9	84.9	85.9	86.9	87.9	88.9	89.9	90.9	91.9	92.9	93.9
Aruba	77.1	78.7	80.1	81.3	82.4	83.5	84.5	85.5	86.6	87.6	88.6	89.6	90.6	91.6	92.6	93.6	94.6	95.6	96.6
Australia	83.8	85.0	86.1	87.2	88.3	89.3	90.3	91.3	92.3	93.3	94.3	95.3	96.3	97.3	98.3	99.3	100.3	101.3	102.3
Austria	82.9	84.1	85.2	86.3	87.4	88.6	89.8	91.0	92.1	93.1	94.0	94.9	95.8	96.7	97.6	98.5	99.4	100.3	101.3
Azerbaijan	73.1	73.9	74.8	75.7	76.7	77.7	78.6	79.6	80.6	81.6	82.6	83.6	84.6	85.6	86.6	87.6	88.6	89.6	90.6
Bahamas	77.8	78.8	79.8	80.7	81.7	82.7	83.7	84.6	85.6	86.6	87.6	88.6	89.6	90.6	91.6	92.6	93.6	94.6	95.6
Bahrain	75.4	76.9	78.3	79.5	80.6	81.7	82.7	83.7	84.8	85.8	86.8	87.8	88.8	89.8	90.8	91.8	92.8	93.8	94.8
Bangladesh	68.3	70.4	72.1	73.6	75.0	76.3	77.5	78.6	79.8	80.9	82.0	83.1	84.2	85.2	86.3	87.4	88.5	89.6	90.7
Barbados	79.5	81.1	82.4	83.6	84.7	85.7	86.8	87.8	88.8	89.8	90.8	91.8	92.8	93.8	94.8	95.8	96.8	97.8	98.8
Belarus	75.5	76.9	78.1	79.2	80.3	81.4	82.4	83.4	84.4	85.5	86.5	87.5	88.5	89.5	90.5	91.5	92.5	93.5	94.5
Belgium	82.5	83.8	84.9	86.0	87.1	88.1	89.2	90.2	91.2	92.2	93.2	94.2	95.2	96.2	97.2	98.2	99.2	100.2	101.2
Belize	76.8	78.2	79.4	80.6	81.7	82.8	83.8	84.9	85.9	86.9	87.9	88.9	89.9	90.9	91.9	92.9	93.9	94.9	95.9
Benin	56.5	58.7	60.7	62.1	63.4	64.6	65.8	66.8	67.9	69.1	70.4	71.6	72.9	74.1	75.3	76.6	77.8	79.1	80.3
Bhutan	67.8	69.9	71.9	73.7	75.3	76.9	78.3	79.7	80.9	82.2	83.4	84.5	85.7	86.8	87.9	88.9	90.0	91.0	92.1
Bolivia	67.7	68.7	69.8	70.9	71.9	72.9	74.0	75.0	76.0	77.0	78.0	79.0	80.0	81.0	82.0	83.0	84.0	85.0	86.0
Bosnia and Herzegovina	77.7	78.9	80.1	81.1	82.2	83.2	84.3	85.3	86.3	87.3	88.3	89.3	90.3	91.3	92.3	93.3	94.3	95.3	96.3
Botswana	52.5	51.3	52.0	53.3	54.6	55.9	57.1	58.4	59.8	61.4	63.0	64.7	66.3	67.8	69.4	71.0	72.6	74.1	75.7
Brazil	75.9	77.3	78.6	80.0	81.3	82.6	83.9	85.2	86.3	87.3	88.2	89.0	90.0	90.9	91.8	92.7	93.6	94.5	95.4
Brunei Darussalam	80.0	81.5	82.8	84.0	85.1	86.1	87.2	88.2	89.2	90.2	91.2	92.2	93.2	94.3	95.3	96.3	97.3	98.3	99.3
Bulgaria	76.3	77.3	78.3	79.3	80.4	81.4	82.4	83.5	84.5	85.6	86.6	87.7	88.8	89.9	90.9	92.0	93.1	94.2	95.2
Burkina Faso	54.8	57.0	59.1	60.5	62.0	63.4	64.7	66.0	67.2	68.5	69.7	71.0	72.2	73.5	74.7	76.0	77.2	78.4	79.7

Burundi	50.0	52.6	54.8	55.9	57.0	58.1	59.1	60.0	61.2	62.6	64.1	65.6	67.1	68.6	70.1	71.6	73.1	74.5	76.0
Cambodia	62.6	65.6	67.9	69.7	71.2	72.6	73.8	74.9	76.0	77.1	78.1	79.2	80.2	81.2	82.2	83.2	84.2	85.2	86.2
Cameroon	50.9	53.6	55.7	57.0	58.2	59.4	60.5	61.6	62.9	64.2	65.6	67.0	68.4	69.8	71.2	72.6	74.0	75.3	76.7
Canada	82.8	83.7	84.6	85.7	86.7	87.7	88.8	89.9	90.9	92.0	93.1	94.2	95.3	96.4	97.5	98.5	99.6	100.7	101.8
Cape Verde	77.4	78.1	79.0	79.9	80.9	81.9	82.9	83.9	84.9	85.9	86.9	87.9	89.0	90.0	91.1	92.1	93.2	94.2	95.3
Central African Republic	47.3	51.3	54.4	55.8	57.1	58.2	59.3	60.3	61.5	62.9	64.4	65.9	67.4	68.9	70.4	71.9	73.4	74.9	76.3
Chad	49.9	51.6	53.3	54.7	56.1	57.4	58.6	59.9	61.2	62.7	64.2	65.7	67.2	68.7	70.1	71.6	73.1	74.6	76.1
Channel Islands	81.6	82.8	84.0	85.1	86.1	87.1	88.2	89.2	90.2	91.2	92.2	93.2	94.2	95.2	96.2	97.2	98.2	99.2	100.2
Chile	81.7	82.9	84.2	85.3	86.4	87.5	88.5	89.5	90.5	91.5	92.5	93.5	94.5	95.5	96.5	97.5	98.5	99.6	100.6
China	74.4	75.7	76.9	78.0	79.1	80.1	81.1	82.1	83.2	84.2	85.2	86.2	87.2	88.2	89.2	90.2	91.2	92.2	93.2
Colombia	76.7	78.0	79.3	80.5	81.6	82.7	83.7	84.7	85.8	86.8	87.8	88.8	89.8	90.8	91.8	92.8	93.8	94.8	95.8
Comoros	61.0	62.0	62.9	63.8	64.7	65.6	66.5	67.3	68.2	69.3	70.4	71.5	72.6	73.8	74.9	76.0	77.1	78.2	79.3
Congo	57.2	59.3	61.2	62.3	63.4	64.5	65.5	66.4	67.4	68.6	69.8	71.1	72.3	73.6	74.8	76.0	77.3	78.5	79.8
Costa Rica	81.4	82.2	83.1	84.0	84.9	85.7	86.5	87.3	88.2	89.3	90.3	91.4	92.5	93.5	94.6	95.7	96.7	97.8	98.8
Croatia	79.5	80.7	81.8	82.9	83.9	85.0	86.0	87.0	88.0	89.0	90.0	91.0	92.0	93.0	94.0	95.0	96.0	97.0	98.0
Cuba	80.5	81.7	82.9	83.9	84.9	86.0	87.1	88.2	89.2	90.2	91.2	92.1	93.1	94.1	95.0	96.0	96.9	97.9	98.9
Cyprus	81.1	82.4	83.7	84.8	85.9	86.9	87.9	89.0	90.0	91.0	92.0	93.0	94.0	95.0	96.0	97.0	98.0	99.0	100.0
Czech Republic	80.2	81.4	82.6	83.8	85.0	86.2	87.4	88.6	89.7	90.6	91.5	92.4	93.3	94.2	95.1	96.0	96.9	97.8	98.7
Côte d'Ivoire	54.0	57.7	60.6	61.9	63.2	64.3	65.3	66.2	67.2	68.4	69.6	70.9	72.1	73.4	74.6	75.9	77.1	78.4	79.6
Denmark	80.5	81.7	82.8	83.8	84.9	85.9	86.9	87.9	88.9	89.9	90.9	91.9	92.9	93.9	94.9	95.9	96.9	97.9	98.9
Djibouti	58.0	60.0	62.3	63.5	64.6	65.7	66.8	67.8	68.9	70.0	71.2	72.5	73.7	74.9	76.1	77.4	78.6	79.8	81.0
Dominican Republic	75.4	76.8	77.9	79.0	80.0	81.1	82.1	83.1	84.1	85.1	86.1	87.1	88.1	89.1	90.1	91.1	92.1	93.1	94.1
D. R. Congo	48.9	50.6	52.2	53.5	54.8	56.0	57.3	58.5	59.9	61.4	62.9	64.4	66.0	67.5	69.0	70.5	72.0	73.5	75.0
Ecuador	78.1	79.2	80.4	81.5	82.5	83.6	84.6	85.6	86.6	87.6	88.6	89.7	90.7	91.7	92.7	93.7	94.7	95.7	96.7
Egypt	74.3	75.1	76.0	76.9	77.9	78.8	79.8	80.8	81.8	82.8	83.8	84.8	85.8	86.8	87.8	88.8	89.8	90.8	91.8
El Salvador	76.1	77.4	78.6	79.8	80.9	82.0	83.0	84.0	85.0	86.0	87.1	88.1	89.1	90.1	91.1	92.1	93.1	94.1	95.1
Equatorial Guinea	51.5	52.9	54.4	55.7	57.0	58.3	59.5	60.7	62.0	63.4	64.9	66.4	67.8	69.3	70.7	72.2	73.6	75.1	76.5

(*continued*)

Table 9.5 Continued

Country	2005–2010	2010–2015	2015–2020	2020–2025	2025–2030	2030–2035	2035–2040	2040–2045	2045–2050	2050–2055	2055–2060	2060–2065	2065–2070	2070–2075	2075–2080	2080–2085	2085–2090	2090–2095	2095–2100
Eritrea	62.2	64.4	66.3	67.3	68.4	69.3	70.2	70.9	71.8	72.8	73.9	75.0	76.1	77.2	78.3	79.4	80.6	81.7	82.8
Estonia	79.2	79.9	80.7	81.7	82.6	83.6	84.5	85.5	86.5	87.5	88.5	89.5	90.5	91.5	92.5	93.5	94.5	95.5	96.5
Ethiopia	58.7	61.6	63.6	64.8	66.1	67.2	68.2	69.2	70.2	71.3	72.4	73.6	74.7	75.9	77.1	78.2	79.4	80.5	81.7
Fiji	71.9	73.2	74.3	75.4	76.4	77.5	78.5	79.5	80.5	81.5	82.5	83.5	84.5	85.5	86.5	87.5	88.5	89.5	90.5
Finland	82.8	83.9	85.1	86.1	87.2	88.2	89.2	90.3	91.3	92.3	93.3	94.3	95.3	96.3	97.3	98.3	99.3	100.3	101.3
France	84.3	85.6	86.7	87.8	88.9	89.9	90.9	91.9	93.0	94.0	95.0	96.0	97.0	98.0	99.0	100.0	101.0	102.0	103.0
French Guiana	79.9	81.1	82.3	83.4	84.5	85.5	86.6	87.6	88.6	89.6	90.6	91.6	92.6	93.6	94.6	95.6	96.6	97.6	98.6
French Polynesia	77.1	77.8	78.8	79.8	80.7	81.7	82.7	83.7	84.7	85.7	86.7	87.7	88.7	89.7	90.7	91.7	92.7	93.7	94.7
Gabon	62.3	64.3	66.0	67.0	68.0	68.9	69.8	70.6	71.5	72.5	73.7	74.8	75.9	77.1	78.2	79.3	80.5	81.6	82.7
Gambia	58.5	60.3	61.9	63.1	64.2	65.3	66.3	67.3	68.3	69.5	70.7	71.9	73.1	74.4	75.6	76.8	78.1	79.3	80.5
Georgia	76.5	77.7	78.9	80.0	81.0	82.0	83.0	84.1	85.1	86.1	87.1	88.1	89.1	90.1	91.1	92.1	93.1	94.1	95.1
Germany	82.4	83.4	84.5	85.5	86.6	87.6	88.6	89.7	90.7	91.7	92.7	93.8	94.8	95.8	96.9	97.9	98.9	100.0	101.0
Ghana	63.6	65.8	67.4	68.3	69.2	70.0	70.8	71.5	72.4	73.4	74.5	75.7	76.8	77.9	79.0	80.2	81.3	82.4	83.5
Greece	82.0	83.5	84.8	86.0	87.1	88.2	89.2	90.2	91.2	92.3	93.3	94.3	95.3	96.3	97.3	98.3	99.3	100.3	101.3
Grenada	76.8	77.8	78.8	79.8	80.8	81.8	82.8	83.8	84.8	85.8	86.8	87.8	88.8	89.8	90.8	91.8	92.8	93.8	94.8
Guadeloupe	82.9	84.1	85.2	86.3	87.3	88.3	89.4	90.4	91.4	92.4	93.4	94.4	95.4	96.4	97.4	98.4	99.4	100.4	101.4
Guam	77.9	79.3	80.4	81.4	82.4	83.4	84.4	85.4	86.4	87.4	88.4	89.4	90.4	91.4	92.4	93.4	94.4	95.4	96.4
Guatemala	73.8	74.6	75.5	76.5	77.5	78.5	79.5	80.5	81.5	82.5	83.5	84.5	85.5	86.5	87.5	88.5	89.5	90.5	91.5
Guinea	54.0	56.4	58.5	59.9	61.3	62.6	63.9	65.0	66.3	67.5	68.8	70.1	71.4	72.7	74.0	75.3	76.6	77.9	79.2
Guinea-Bissau	48.2	50.4	52.4	53.8	55.1	56.5	57.8	59.0	60.4	61.9	63.5	65.0	66.5	68.0	69.5	71.0	72.5	74.0	75.5
Guyana	71.9	72.5	73.3	74.2	75.1	76.1	77.1	78.0	79.0	80.0	81.0	82.0	83.0	84.0	85.0	86.0	87.0	88.0	89.0
Haiti	62.0	63.9	65.4	66.9	68.4	69.9	71.3	72.4	73.5	74.6	75.6	76.5	77.4	78.2	79.0	79.8	80.5	81.3	82.0
Honduras	74.5	75.8	77.0	78.2	79.3	80.4	81.4	82.4	83.4	84.5	85.5	86.5	87.5	88.5	89.5	90.5	91.5	92.5	93.5
Hong Kong	84.3	85.6	86.7	87.8	88.9	89.9	90.9	92.0	93.0	94.0	95.0	96.0	97.0	98.0	99.0	100.0	101.0	102.0	103.0
Hungary	77.6	78.7	79.8	80.8	81.8	82.8	83.8	84.8	85.8	86.8	87.8	88.8	89.8	90.8	91.8	92.8	93.8	94.8	95.8
Iceland	83.1	84.3	85.5	86.6	87.6	88.7	89.7	90.7	91.7	92.7	93.7	94.7	95.7	96.7	97.7	98.7	99.7	100.7	101.7
India	65.7	67.7	69.5	71.2	72.9	74.6	76.4	78.1	79.5	80.5	81.2	81.9	82.6	83.3	84.0	84.7	85.4	86.0	86.7

Indonesia	69.4	70.8	72.2	73.5	74.7	76.0	77.4	78.7	79.8	80.9	81.8	82.7	83.6	84.5	85.4	86.3	87.2	88.1	89.0
Iran	73.9	75.8	77.5	79.0	80.6	82.0	83.3	84.6	85.8	87.0	88.2	89.4	90.5	91.7	92.8	94.0	95.1	96.3	97.4
Iraq	71.7	74.1	75.9	77.5	78.8	80.0	81.1	82.2	83.2	84.2	85.3	86.3	87.3	88.3	89.3	90.3	91.3	92.3	93.3
Ireland	82.0	83.0	84.1	85.1	86.1	87.1	88.1	89.1	90.1	91.1	92.1	93.1	94.1	95.1	96.1	97.1	98.1	99.1	100.1
Israel	82.9	84.0	85.1	86.2	87.2	88.2	89.2	90.2	91.2	92.2	93.1	94.1	95.0	96.0	96.9	97.9	98.9	99.8	100.8
Italy	84.0	85.1	86.2	87.3	88.3	89.4	90.4	91.4	92.4	93.4	94.4	95.4	96.4	97.5	98.5	99.5	100.5	101.5	102.6
Jamaica	75.0	76.5	77.7	78.9	80.0	81.0	82.1	83.1	84.1	85.1	86.1	87.1	88.1	89.1	90.1	91.1	92.1	93.1	94.1
Japan	86.1	87.1	88.1	89.2	90.2	91.2	92.2	93.2	94.2	95.2	96.2	97.2	98.2	99.2	100.2	101.2	102.2	103.2	104.2
Jordan	74.3	75.8	77.1	78.3	79.4	80.5	81.5	82.6	83.6	84.6	85.6	86.6	87.6	88.6	89.6	90.6	91.6	92.6	93.6
Kazakhstan	71.5	73.8	75.2	76.3	77.4	78.4	79.4	80.4	81.4	82.4	83.4	84.4	85.4	86.4	87.4	88.4	89.4	90.4	91.4
Kenya	55.9	59.2	61.0	62.2	63.3	64.3	65.2	66.0	67.0	68.1	69.3	70.6	71.8	73.1	74.3	75.5	76.8	78.0	79.2
Kuwait	75.2	76.8	78.1	79.3	80.4	81.5	82.5	83.6	84.6	85.6	86.6	87.6	88.6	89.6	90.6	91.6	92.6	93.6	94.6
Kyrgyzstan	71.0	72.3	73.7	74.9	76.0	77.1	78.2	79.2	80.3	81.3	82.3	83.3	84.3	85.3	86.3	87.3	88.3	89.3	90.3
Laos	67.3	68.1	69.0	69.8	70.7	71.6	72.6	73.6	74.5	75.5	76.5	77.5	78.5	79.5	80.5	81.5	82.5	83.5	84.5
Latvia	77.4	78.6	79.8	80.9	81.9	82.9	84.0	85.0	86.0	87.0	88.0	89.0	90.0	91.0	92.0	93.0	94.0	95.0	96.0
Lebanon	74.2	75.5	76.6	77.7	78.8	79.8	80.8	81.8	82.8	83.8	84.8	85.8	86.8	87.8	88.8	89.8	90.8	91.8	92.8
Lesotho	45.2	48.1	49.3	50.7	52.1	53.5	54.7	56.0	57.3	58.8	60.2	61.7	63.1	64.5	65.9	67.3	68.8	70.2	71.6
Liberia	55.3	58.6	61.1	62.4	63.7	64.8	65.9	66.9	68.0	69.1	70.3	71.5	72.7	73.9	75.2	76.4	77.6	78.8	80.0
Libya	76.9	78.5	79.9	81.1	82.3	83.4	84.4	85.4	86.5	87.5	88.5	89.5	90.5	91.5	92.5	93.5	94.5	95.5	96.5
Lithuania	77.2	78.7	80.0	81.1	82.2	83.3	84.3	85.4	86.4	87.4	88.4	89.4	90.4	91.4	92.4	93.4	94.4	95.4	96.4
Luxembourg	82.0	83.2	84.4	85.5	86.5	87.6	88.6	89.6	90.6	91.6	92.6	93.6	94.6	95.6	96.6	97.6	98.6	99.6	100.6
Macao	82.6	83.8	85.0	86.1	87.1	88.2	89.2	90.2	91.2	92.2	93.2	94.2	95.2	96.2	97.2	98.2	99.2	100.2	101.2
Madagascar	67.3	70.4	72.4	73.2	74.0	74.7	75.5	76.3	77.2	78.3	79.3	80.4	81.4	82.5	83.5	84.6	85.6	86.7	87.7
Malawi	51.5	55.2	57.0	58.6	60.2	61.7	63.0	64.3	65.6	66.9	68.2	69.4	70.7	72.0	73.3	74.6	75.8	77.1	78.4
Malaysia	75.7	77.3	78.6	79.8	80.9	81.9	83.0	84.0	85.0	86.0	87.1	88.1	89.1	90.1	91.1	92.1	93.1	94.1	95.1
Maldives	76.5	79.1	81.4	83.4	85.3	87.0	88.6	90.0	91.4	92.7	94.0	95.2	96.4	97.5	98.6	99.7	100.8	101.9	102.9
Mali	51.0	53.1	55.1	56.7	58.2	59.6	61.0	62.4	63.8	65.2	66.6	67.9	69.3	70.7	72.0	73.4	74.7	76.1	77.4
Malta	81.2	82.4	83.6	84.7	85.7	86.8	87.8	88.8	89.8	90.8	91.8	92.8	93.8	94.8	95.8	96.8	97.8	98.8	99.8
Martinique	83.2	83.7	84.5	85.5	86.5	87.5	88.5	89.5	90.5	91.5	92.5	93.5	94.5	95.5	96.5	97.5	98.5	99.5	100.5
Mauritania	59.2	59.8	60.7	61.8	62.9	63.9	64.8	65.7	66.9	68.5	70.3	72.1	73.8	75.5	77.2	78.9	80.6	82.3	84.0

(continued)

Table 9.5 Continued

Country	2005–2010	2010–2015	2015–2020	2020–2025	2025–2030	2030–2035	2035–2040	2040–2045	2045–2050	2050–2055	2055–2060	2060–2065	2065–2070	2070–2075	2075–2080	2080–2085	2085–2090	2090–2095	2095–2100
Mauritius	76.2	77.6	78.8	79.9	81.0	82.1	83.1	84.1	85.2	86.2	87.2	88.2	89.2	90.2	91.3	92.3	93.3	94.3	95.3
Mayotte	81.1	82.4	83.6	84.7	85.8	86.8	87.9	88.9	89.9	90.9	91.9	92.9	93.9	94.9	95.9	96.9	97.9	98.9	99.9
Mexico	78.6	79.8	81.0	82.0	83.1	84.1	85.0	85.9	86.9	87.9	88.9	90.0	91.0	92.1	93.1	94.2	95.2	96.2	97.3
Micronesia	69.1	70.3	71.5	72.6	73.7	74.7	75.8	76.8	77.8	78.8	79.8	80.8	81.8	82.8	83.8	84.8	85.8	86.8	87.8
Moldova	72.1	73.5	74.7	75.9	76.9	78.0	79.0	80.1	81.1	82.1	83.1	84.1	85.1	86.1	87.1	88.1	89.1	90.1	91.1
Mongolia	71.5	71.8	72.3	73.1	73.9	74.8	75.8	76.7	77.7	78.7	79.7	80.7	81.7	82.7	83.7	84.7	85.7	86.7	87.7
Montenegro	76.5	78.6	80.2	81.6	82.9	84.0	85.1	86.2	87.2	88.2	89.2	90.3	91.3	92.3	93.3	94.3	95.3	96.3	97.3
Morocco	73.4	74.8	76.0	77.1	78.1	79.2	80.2	81.2	82.2	83.2	84.2	85.2	86.2	87.2	88.2	89.2	90.2	91.2	92.2
Mozambique	49.9	51.8	54.1	55.5	57.0	58.3	59.6	60.8	62.1	63.4	64.9	66.3	67.7	69.1	70.5	71.9	73.3	74.7	76.0
Myanmar	65.0	66.3	67.4	68.4	69.5	70.5	71.5	72.5	73.5	74.5	75.5	76.5	77.5	78.5	79.5	80.5	81.5	82.5	83.5
Namibia	61.6	63.0	62.6	63.6	64.7	65.6	66.5	67.3	68.2	69.3	70.5	71.7	72.8	73.9	75.0	76.1	77.2	78.4	79.5
Nepal	68.0	71.4	74.0	75.8	77.6	79.3	80.8	82.3	83.6	84.6	85.4	86.2	87.0	87.8	88.6	89.4	90.1	90.9	91.7
Netherlands	82.2	83.1	84.0	85.0	86.0	87.0	88.0	89.0	90.1	91.1	92.2	93.3	94.4	95.5	96.6	97.7	98.8	99.9	101.0
Netherlands Antilles	79.4	81.0	82.3	83.5	84.6	85.7	86.7	87.7	88.7	89.7	90.8	91.8	92.8	93.8	94.8	95.8	96.8	97.8	98.8
New Caledonia	78.7	79.3	80.2	81.1	82.1	83.1	84.1	85.1	86.1	87.1	88.1	89.1	90.1	91.1	92.1	93.1	94.1	95.1	96.1
New Zealand	82.2	83.3	84.4	85.5	86.5	87.5	88.6	89.6	90.6	91.6	92.6	93.6	94.6	95.6	96.6	97.6	98.6	99.6	100.6
Nicaragua	76.1	76.7	77.6	78.5	79.4	80.4	81.4	82.3	83.3	84.3	85.3	86.3	87.3	88.3	89.3	90.3	91.3	92.3	93.3
Niger	53.5	56.2	58.0	59.1	60.1	61.2	62.1	63.1	64.1	65.3	66.6	67.9	69.1	70.4	71.7	72.9	74.2	75.5	76.7
Nigeria	51.0	53.4	55.6	56.9	58.2	59.3	60.3	61.2	62.4	63.7	65.2	66.7	68.2	69.6	71.1	72.5	74.0	75.4	76.9
North Korea	71.8	73.6	75.2	76.5	77.7	78.9	79.9	81.0	82.0	83.0	84.0	85.0	86.1	87.1	88.1	89.1	90.1	91.1	92.1
Norway	82.7	83.6	84.6	85.7	86.7	87.7	88.8	89.8	90.8	91.8	92.9	94.0	95.0	96.1	97.1	98.2	99.2	100.3	101.3
Oman	74.8	76.9	78.5	79.9	81.1	82.3	83.4	84.4	85.5	86.5	87.5	88.5	89.5	90.5	91.5	92.5	93.5	94.5	95.5
Pakistan	65.4	66.5	67.6	68.7	69.9	71.0	72.1	73.1	74.2	75.3	76.4	77.5	78.7	79.8	80.9	82.0	83.1	84.2	85.4
Palestine	73.8	74.8	76.0	77.2	78.5	79.8	81.1	82.5	83.7	84.8	85.7	86.7	87.6	88.5	89.4	90.4	91.3	92.2	93.1
Panama	78.2	79.5	80.8	82.0	83.1	84.2	85.2	86.2	87.2	88.2	89.3	90.3	91.3	92.3	93.3	94.3	95.3	96.3	97.3
Papua New Guinea	63.7	65.0	66.2	67.4	68.4	69.5	70.5	71.5	72.5	73.5	74.5	75.5	76.5	77.5	78.5	79.5	80.5	81.5	82.5
Paraguay	73.9	75.0	76.1	77.1	78.2	79.2	80.2	81.2	82.3	83.3	84.3	85.3	86.3	87.3	88.3	89.3	90.3	91.3	92.3
Peru	75.9	76.8	77.8	78.8	79.8	80.8	81.8	82.8	83.8	84.8	85.8	86.8	87.8	88.8	89.8	90.8	91.8	92.8	93.8

Philippines	71.3	72.2	73.2	74.3	75.3	76.3	77.3	78.4	79.4	80.5	81.6	82.6	83.7	84.8	85.9	87.0	88.0	89.1	90.2
Poland	79.8	80.8	81.8	82.8	83.8	84.8	85.8	86.8	87.8	88.8	89.8	90.8	91.8	92.8	93.8	94.8	95.8	96.8	97.8
Portugal	81.8	83.1	84.2	85.3	86.4	87.5	88.5	89.5	90.5	91.5	92.5	93.5	94.5	95.5	96.5	97.5	98.5	99.5	100.5
Puerto Rico	82.7	83.9	85.0	86.1	87.1	88.1	89.1	90.1	91.1	92.1	93.1	94.1	95.1	96.1	97.1	98.1	99.1	100.1	101.1
Qatar	77.3	78.7	79.9	81.1	82.1	83.2	84.2	85.3	86.3	87.3	88.3	89.3	90.3	91.3	92.3	93.3	94.3	95.3	96.3
Romania	76.8	78.3	79.6	80.7	81.9	83.0	84.1	85.2	86.2	87.1	88.0	88.9	89.9	90.8	91.7	92.6	93.5	94.4	95.3
Russian Federation	74.0	75.0	76.0	77.0	78.1	79.0	80.0	80.9	81.9	82.9	84.0	85.1	86.2	87.3	88.3	89.4	90.5	91.6	92.7
Rwanda	55.1	57.1	58.7	59.9	61.1	62.2	63.3	64.2	65.3	66.6	67.9	69.3	70.6	72.0	73.3	74.6	76.0	77.3	78.7
Réunion	81.1	82.1	83.2	84.2	85.2	86.2	87.2	88.2	89.2	90.2	91.2	92.2	93.2	94.2	95.2	96.2	97.2	98.2	99.2
Saint Lucia	76.6	77.9	79.0	80.0	81.1	82.1	83.1	84.1	85.1	86.1	87.1	88.1	89.1	90.1	91.1	92.1	93.1	94.1	95.1
Saint Vincent and the Grenadines	73.8	75.6	77.1	78.3	79.5	80.6	81.6	82.6	83.7	84.7	85.7	86.7	87.7	88.7	89.7	90.7	91.7	92.7	93.7
Samoa	74.9	76.1	77.2	78.3	79.3	80.3	81.4	82.4	83.4	84.4	85.4	86.4	87.4	88.4	89.4	90.4	91.4	92.4	93.4
São Tomé and Principe	65.1	66.1	66.9	67.8	68.6	69.4	70.3	71.1	72.0	73.1	74.2	75.3	76.4	77.5	78.6	79.7	80.8	81.9	83.0
Saudi Arabia	74.4	76.0	77.3	78.5	79.6	80.7	81.7	82.8	83.8	84.8	85.8	86.8	87.8	88.8	89.8	90.8	91.8	92.8	93.8
Senegal	59.1	60.6	61.9	63.1	64.3	65.4	66.4	67.3	68.5	70.0	71.6	73.2	74.7	76.3	77.9	79.4	81.0	82.5	84.1
Serbia	76.3	77.3	78.3	79.3	80.4	81.4	82.4	83.5	84.5	85.5	86.6	87.7	88.7	89.8	90.8	91.9	93.0	94.0	95.1
Sierra Leone	46.9	48.9	50.8	52.3	53.8	55.3	56.8	58.3	59.8	61.3	62.8	64.3	65.8	67.2	68.7	70.2	71.6	73.1	74.6
Singapore	82.7	83.5	84.4	85.4	86.4	87.4	88.4	89.4	90.4	91.4	92.4	93.4	94.4	95.4	96.4	97.4	98.4	99.4	100.4
Slovakia	78.7	79.8	81.0	82.0	83.1	84.1	85.1	86.2	87.2	88.2	89.2	90.2	91.2	92.2	93.2	94.2	95.2	96.2	97.2
Slovenia	82.0	82.9	83.8	84.8	85.8	86.8	87.8	88.8	89.8	90.8	91.8	92.8	93.8	94.8	95.8	96.8	97.8	98.8	99.8
Solomon Islands	67.8	68.0	68.5	69.1	69.9	70.8	71.7	72.7	73.6	74.6	75.6	76.6	77.6	78.6	79.6	80.6	81.6	82.6	83.6
Somalia	51.8	53.3	54.6	55.8	57.0	58.1	59.0	59.9	61.1	62.6	64.2	65.9	67.5	69.0	70.6	72.2	73.8	75.3	76.9
South Africa	52.1	54.1	55.8	57.2	58.5	59.8	61.0	62.3	63.6	65.0	66.4	67.8	69.1	70.5	71.9	73.2	74.6	75.9	77.3
South Korea	83.3	84.1	85.0	85.9	86.9	87.9	88.8	89.8	90.8	91.8	92.8	93.8	94.8	95.8	96.8	97.8	98.8	99.8	100.8
Spain	83.8	84.7	85.7	86.8	87.8	88.9	89.9	90.9	91.9	93.0	94.1	95.2	96.2	97.3	98.4	99.5	100.6	101.7	102.7
Sri Lanka	77.4	78.4	79.4	80.3	81.3	82.3	83.3	84.3	85.3	86.3	87.3	88.3	89.3	90.3	91.3	92.3	93.3	94.3	95.3
Sudan	62.0	63.9	65.2	65.9	66.6	67.3	68.1	68.8	69.7	70.6	71.6	72.6	73.6	74.6	75.6	76.6	77.6	78.6	79.6
Suriname	73.1	74.5	75.7	76.9	78.0	79.1	80.2	81.2	82.2	83.2	84.2	85.2	86.2	87.2	88.2	89.2	90.2	91.2	92.2

(*continued*)

Table 9.5 Continued

Country	2005–2010	2010–2015	2015–2020	2020–2025	2025–2030	2030–2035	2035–2040	2040–2045	2045–2050	2050–2055	2055–2060	2060–2065	2065–2070	2070–2075	2075–2080	2080–2085	2085–2090	2090–2095	2095–2100
Swaziland	47.0	48.5	47.7	49.4	51.2	52.8	54.3	55.7	57.2	58.9	60.7	62.4	64.1	65.7	67.4	69.0	70.7	72.4	74.0
Sweden	82.9	83.7	84.5	85.5	86.5	87.5	88.5	89.5	90.5	91.6	92.6	93.7	94.8	95.9	97.0	98.1	99.2	100.3	101.4
Switzerland	84.1	85.4	86.5	87.6	88.7	89.7	90.7	91.8	92.8	93.8	94.8	95.8	96.8	97.8	98.8	99.8	100.8	101.8	102.8
Syria	76.8	78.2	79.4	80.5	81.6	82.6	83.7	84.7	85.7	86.7	87.7	88.7	89.7	90.7	91.7	92.7	93.7	94.7	95.7
Tajikistan	69.9	70.7	71.7	72.7	73.8	74.8	75.8	76.8	77.8	78.8	79.8	80.8	81.8	82.8	83.8	84.8	85.8	86.8	87.8
Tanzania	56.2	60.3	63.3	64.5	65.8	66.9	67.9	68.8	69.8	70.9	72.0	73.1	74.3	75.4	76.6	77.7	78.8	80.0	81.1
TFYR Macedonia	76.3	77.2	78.3	79.4	80.6	81.8	83.0	84.2	85.3	86.3	87.3	88.3	89.2	90.2	91.2	92.1	93.1	94.0	95.0
Thailand	77.1	77.6	78.1	78.8	79.5	80.1	80.7	81.3	81.9	82.6	83.4	84.1	84.8	85.6	86.3	87.1	87.8	88.5	89.3
Timor-Leste	61.7	63.1	64.3	65.4	66.5	67.5	68.5	69.6	70.6	71.6	72.6	73.6	74.6	75.6	76.6	77.6	78.6	79.6	80.6
Togo	57.1	59.4	61.7	63.0	64.2	65.3	66.4	67.3	68.4	69.6	70.8	72.1	73.3	74.5	75.8	77.0	78.3	79.5	80.8
Tonga	74.7	76.0	77.2	78.3	79.4	80.4	81.4	82.5	83.5	84.5	85.5	86.5	87.5	88.5	89.5	90.5	91.5	92.5	93.5
Trinidad and Tobago	72.9	74.8	76.3	77.6	78.8	79.9	80.9	82.0	83.0	84.0	85.0	86.0	87.0	88.0	89.0	90.0	91.0	92.0	93.0
Tunisia	76.0	76.7	77.6	78.6	79.6	80.6	81.6	82.6	83.6	84.6	85.6	86.6	87.6	88.6	89.6	90.6	91.6	92.6	93.6
Turkey	75.3	76.0	76.8	77.7	78.7	79.6	80.6	81.6	82.6	83.6	84.5	85.5	86.5	87.5	88.5	89.5	90.5	91.5	92.5
Turkmenistan	68.9	70.0	71.2	72.4	73.5	74.5	75.6	76.6	77.6	78.6	79.6	80.6	81.6	82.6	83.6	84.6	85.6	86.6	87.6
Uganda	52.7	55.4	57.0	58.3	59.6	60.8	62.0	63.1	64.3	65.6	66.9	68.3	69.6	70.9	72.2	73.5	74.9	76.2	77.5
Ukraine	73.5	74.1	74.9	75.9	77.0	78.0	78.9	79.9	80.9	82.0	83.2	84.3	85.5	86.6	87.8	88.9	90.0	91.2	92.3
United Arab Emirates	77.0	78.4	79.6	80.7	81.8	82.8	83.9	84.9	85.9	86.9	87.9	88.9	89.9	90.9	91.9	92.9	93.9	94.9	95.9
United Kingdom	81.7	82.9	84.0	85.1	86.2	87.2	88.2	89.2	90.2	91.2	92.2	93.2	94.2	95.2	96.2	97.2	98.2	99.2	100.2

United States of America	80.5	81.2	81.9	82.8	83.6	84.5	85.4	86.3	87.3	88.4	89.5	90.7	91.8	93.0	94.1	95.3	96.4	97.6	98.7
Uruguay	79.8	81.1	82.2	83.4	84.4	85.5	86.5	87.5	88.5	89.6	90.6	91.6	92.6	93.6	94.6	95.6	96.6	97.6	98.6
Uzbekistan	70.7	72.0	73.3	74.5	75.7	76.8	77.8	78.9	79.9	80.9	81.9	82.9	83.9	84.9	85.9	86.9	87.9	88.9	89.9
Vanuatu	72.1	73.1	74.1	75.1	76.1	77.1	78.1	79.1	80.1	81.1	82.1	83.1	84.1	85.1	86.1	87.1	88.1	89.1	90.1
Venezuela	76.8	78.1	79.3	80.5	81.6	82.7	83.7	84.8	85.8	86.8	87.8	88.8	89.8	90.8	91.8	92.8	93.8	94.8	95.8
Viet Nam	76.2	77.9	79.2	80.3	81.4	82.5	83.5	84.4	85.4	86.5	87.6	88.7	89.7	90.8	91.9	93.0	94.1	95.1	96.2
Virgin Islands	82.0	83.6	84.8	86.0	87.1	88.2	89.2	90.2	91.2	92.2	93.2	94.2	95.2	96.2	97.2	98.2	99.2	100.2	101.2
Yemen	65.4	66.3	67.3	68.3	69.3	70.3	71.3	72.3	73.2	74.2	75.2	76.2	77.2	78.2	79.2	80.2	81.2	82.2	83.2
Zambia	47.3	50.0	51.3	52.7	54.0	55.3	56.4	57.6	58.9	60.5	62.1	63.8	65.5	67.1	68.7	70.3	72.0	73.6	75.2
Zimbabwe	45.4	52.7	56.9	58.1	59.2	60.3	61.4	62.4	63.6	65.0	66.5	68.0	69.4	70.9	72.4	73.8	75.3	76.8	78.2

Table 9.6 Current Level of In and Out Migration (2005–10) (Number, All Ages)

	Emigration		Immigration		Net migration	
Country	Female	Male	Female	Male	Female	Male
Afghanistan	197	195	6	8	-191	-187
Albania	49	30	16	15	-34	-14
Algeria	85	111	24	32	-61	-79
Angola	0	1	37	46	37	46
Argentina	142	136	38	41	-104	-95
Armenia	49	50	23	1	-26	-49
Aruba	0	0	2	2	2	2
Australia	17	23	561	604	544	581
Austria	21	32	103	110	81	78
Azerbaijan	11	3	26	42	15	38
Bahamas	0	0	3	4	3	3
Bahrain	0	0	120	328	120	328
Bangladesh	788	2173	1	62	-787	-21,11
Barbados	2	1	2	1	0	0
Belarus	57	52	31	28	-26	-24
Belgium	7	11	109	108	103	97
Belize	4	4	4	3	0	-1
Benin	19	10	34	45	15	36
Bhutan	1	1	4	15	3	14
Bolivia	104	90	13	16	-91	-74
Bosnia and Herzegovina	16	14	11	10	-5	-5
Botswana	9	10	17	21	8	11
Brazil	251	257	2	3	-248	-254
Brunei Darussalam	23	24	25	26	2	2
Bulgaria	41	43	16	18	-26	-24
Burkina Faso	172	215	129	134	-43	-81
Burundi	0	0	183	187	183	187
Cambodia	105	150	0	0	-105	-149
Cameroon	31	23	17	18	-13	-4
Canada	172	127	718	680	546	553
Cape Verde	13	8	2	2	-12	-6
Central African Republic	18	16	20	20	2	4
Chad	71	78	31	44	-40	-34
Channel Islands	2	1	4	4	2	2
Chile	40	31	54	47	14	16
China	1,003	1,012	73	53	-930	-959
Colombia	63	77	9	11	-54	-66
Comoros	5	5	0	0	-5	-5
Congo	0	0	24	26	24	26
Costa Rica	20	23	55	65	34	42
Côte d'Ivoire	277	289	92	116	-185	-173
Croatia	14	14	18	20	4	6
Cuba	101	89	0	0	-101	-89

Cyprus	1	1	18	28	16	28
Czech Republic	0	0	96	145	96	145
Denmark	8	12	55	55	47	43
Djibouti	2	1	1	1	0	0
Dominican Republic	103	102	29	37	-74	-65
D. R. Congo	56	44	27	50	-29	7
Ecuador	129	130	67	72	-62	-58
Egypt	147	249	24	29	-123	-220
El Salvador	134	161	2	2	-133	-159
Equatorial Guinea	0	0	8	12	8	12
Eritrea	0	0	28	28	28	28
Estonia	4	1	4	1	0	0
Ethiopia	166	131	0	0	-166	-131
Fiji	18	13	1	1	-17	-12
Finland	0	0	33	40	33	40
France	120	133	363	391	243	258
French Guiana	1	2	4	5	3	3
French Polynesia	1	0	0	1	-1	0
Gabon	15	15	16	20	1	4
Gambia	13	24	8	16	-5	-8
Georgia	70	82	1	1	-69	-81
Germany	319	471	671	670	351	199
Ghana	142	169	118	144	-24	-25
Greece	36	23	106	106	71	84
Grenada	3	3	1	0	-3	-2
Guadeloupe	2	3	1	1	-1	-2
Guam	3	3	3	3	0	0
Guatemala	81	125	3	3	-78	-122
Guinea	154	149	2	2	-151	-148
Guinea-Bissau	9	9	4	5	-5	-5
Guyana	22	22	2	2	-20	-20
Haiti	110	131	1	1	-109	-130
Honduras	56	44	0	1	-56	-43
Hong Kong	69	79	196	129	126	50
Hungary	5	4	42	42	37	38
Iceland	1	2	6	7	5	5
India	1,750	1,954	283	510	-1,466	-1,444
Indonesia	381	895	1	0	-381	-895
Iran	235	241	142	151	-93	-90
Iraq	75	74	0	0	-75	-73
Ireland	35	33	83	84	49	52
Israel	48	42	194	170	146	127
Italy	13	1	879	1,135	865	1,134
Jamaica	52	51	1	1	-50	-50
Japan	97	74	229	211	131	138
Jordan	72	105	178	203	106	98
Kazakhstan	193	141	165	176	-28	35

(continued)

Table 9.6 Continued

	Emigration		Immigration		Net migration	
Country	Female	Male	Female	Male	Female	Male
Kenya	133	136	47	34	-86	-102
Kuwait	35	85	129	268	95	183
Kyrgyzstan	64	69	0	0	-63	-68
Laos	39	37	0	0	-38	-36
Latvia	6	5	0	0	-6	-4
Lebanon	45	54	39	47	-6	-7
Lesotho	11	10	1	1	-10	-10
Liberia	10	12	159	163	150	151
Libyan Arab Jamahiriya	14	42	16	20	3	-23
Lithuania	20	17	0	0	-19	-16
Luxembourg	0	0	21	22	20	22
Macao	0	4	28	28	28	23
Madagascar	5	4	2	1	-3	-3
Malawi	24	14	12	7	-12	-8
Malaysia	253	383	291	431	38	48
Maldives	0	0	0	0	0	0
Mali	52	64	7	9	-45	-55
Malta	0	0	2	3	2	3
Martinique	2	2	1	1	-1	-1
Mauritania	4	7	8	13	4	6
Mauritius	5	4	5	4	0	0
Mayotte	2	2	2	1	0	-1
Mexico	850	1,076	58	65	-792	-1,011
Micronesia	5	4	0	0	-5	-4
Moldova	88	95	1	10	-86	-86
Mongolia	10	6	0	1	-10	-5
Montenegro	12	9	11	7	-1	-2
Morocco	254	423	1	1	-253	-421
Mozambique	70	65	60	55	-9	-10
Myanmar	181	321	4	0	-177	-321
Namibia	11	10	10	10	-1	-1
Nepal	77	120	98	1	21	-119
Netherlands	115	132	139	158	24	26
Netherlands Antilles	1	2	6	5	5	3
New Caledonia	0	0	4	3	4	3
New Zealand	90	92	124	123	34	31
Nicaragua	91	109	1	0	-91	-109
Niger	24	35	17	15	-7	-20
Nigeria	217	219	75	77	-143	-142
North Korea	14	9	10	10	-4	1
Norway	4	0	76	100	72	99
Oman	45	16	0	214	-45	198
Pakistan	788	1,245	14	30	-774	-1,215

Palestine	45	45	0	0	–45	–45
Panama	12	6	15	14	3	8
Papua New Guinea	3	3	2	5	–1	2
Paraguay	21	25	5	2	–17	–23
Peru	370	354	0	0	-370	-354
Philippines	584	679	15	17	-569	-662
Poland	6	31	44	48	38	18
Portugal	91	74	161	155	69	81
Puerto Rico	83	64	1	1	-82	-63
Qatar	7	2	124	742	118	739
Réunion	2	2	2	2	0	0
Romania	72	70	20	23	–52	–48
Russian Federation	148	119	706	696	558	577
Rwanda	29	17	35	27	5	10
Saint Lucia	1	1	1	1	0	–1
Saint Vincent and the Grenadines	3	3	0	0	–3	–2
Samoa	8	9	1	1	–7	–8
São Tomé and Principe	4	4	1	0	–3	–3
Saudi Arabia	26	224	514	794	487	569
Senegal	58	92	8	10	-50	-82
Serbia	91	84	90	85	–1	1
Sierra Leone	8	7	38	37	30	30
Singapore	0	0	351	371	351	371
Slovakia	4	0	15	25	11	25
Slovenia	1	2	11	14	9	13
Solomon Islands	0	1	0	1	0	0
Somalia	154	146	0	0	–154	–146
South Africa	54	43	344	454	290	411
South Korea	59	51	46	35	–14	–16
Spain	71	87	1143	1265	1072	1178
Sri Lanka	132	131	13	0	–118	–131
Sudan	34	30	86	114	52	85
Suriname	4	3	1	0	–3	–2
Swaziland	7	10	6	6	–2	–4
Sweden	26	27	153	166	127	139
Switzerland	56	67	142	163	87	96
Syria	193	254	212	179	19	–74
Tajikistan	125	171	0	0	–125	–171
Tanzania	192	175	31	36	–161	–138
TFYR Macedonia	9	7	10	8	1	1
Thailand	26	0	224	295	198	295
Timor-Leste	24	26	0	0	–24	–26
Togo	10	7	7	6	–3	–2
Tonga	4	4	0	0	–4	–4
Trinidad and Tobago	9	12	1	0	–9	–11
Tunisia	15	14	4	5	–11	–9

(continued)

Table 9.6 Continued

	Emigration		Immigration		Net migration	
Country	Female	Male	Female	Male	Female	Male
Turkey	82	79	52	59	-29	-20
Turkmenistan	29	28	1	1	-28	-27
Uganda	82	65	6	8	-76	-57
Ukraine	227	196	204	178	-23	-17
United Arab Emirates	0	0	815	2262	815	2261
United Kingdom	429	289	911	827	482	539
United States of America	663	779	3,219	3,181	2,557	2,401
Uruguay	25	28	2	2	-23	-27
Uzbekistan	266	260	4	4	-262	-256
Vanuatu	0	0	0	0	0	0
Venezuela	37	35	50	62	13	28
Viet Nam	272	178	5	15	-267	-163
Virgin Islands	2	2	0	0	-2	-2
Western Sahara	0	0	21	26	21	26
Yemen	91	120	34	44	-57	-76
Zambia	65	62	21	22	-44	-41
Zimbabwe	384	516	0	0	-384	-516

As described in Chapter 7, we assume the age profile of migration flows to follow a modified Rogers–Castro standard age schedule.

Migration assumptions were developed by the team working on global migration flows and, as required by the bi-regional model, were formulated as probabilities of immigration and emigration (see Chapter 7 for a discussion of the bi-regional model). As the risk populations for emigration rates are the national populations, whereas for immigration rates they are the global populations and both populations can develop differently, the level of net migration is not constant, even under constant immigration and emigration rates as is assumed in the medium scenarios for the coming half century. The assumption of a continuation of current trends until the year 2060 marks the most important outcome of the meta-experts meeting on migration (see Chapter 7). After 2060, immigration and emigration flows gradually converge to their average. As a result, net migration for each country is zero in the last period of the projection, 2095–2100.

For the WIC projections, an additional state is added to the bi-regional framework to project age-, sex-, and education-specific immigration and emigration flows. In the absence of a harmonized data set on the education composition of global bilateral migration flows, we assume that the education composition of migration flows is equal to that in the origin country.

9.3.5 Education assumptions

For education, we used the GET scenario as our medium scenario. As explained in Chapter 8, this is based on a Bayesian model that estimates the most likely future trajectory in education-specific progression rates to higher levels from the cumulative experience of all countries over the last 40 years. The GET scenario was combined with the medium demographic scenarios summarized earlier to project the population by age, sex, and educational attainment to 2100.

The distribution by six levels of educational attainment in the age group 30–34 was first extracted (see Table 9.7) from the Bayesian model as a median trajectory of thousands of iterations (Chapter 9). It represents the final education distribution of a particular cohort that will remain unchanged—apart from changes due to education differentials in mortality and migration—over the cohort's remaining lifetime. In order to calculate the education distribution under the age of 30, the education-specific proportions in the age group 30–34 were back-casted to 15–19, 20–24, and 25–29, such that attainment in younger age groups follows country-specific experience in the past. We imposed convergence in cases where attainment progressions in certain education groups were occurring in late ages. For example, we expect that the completion of primary education—typically four years in duration—will eventually occur by the age of 15. These sets of education distributions were prepared for each sex separately and for all periods from 2010 to 2100. As will be described in section 9.4.3, these proportions for four age groups were directly implemented in distributing the population by education once the population has been projected forward in five-year steps.

In addition to the medium GET scenario, three alternative scenarios were defined. These scenarios are used to explore the sensitivity of the population projections to our education assumption (Chapter 10). The results suggest that altering education can result in differences in the projected population by almost one billion by 2060. The three scenarios are defined as follows.

Fast benchmark or fast track: In this scenario, the most rapid country-specific expansion parameters are applied to all countries throughout the projection period. In other words, all countries follow the educational development paths taken in the past by the frontrunners in East and South East Asia.

Constant enrolment rates (CER): For this scenario, the attainment shares at age 30–34 of future cohorts are fixed at the levels observed in the base year (but adjusted where necessary if younger age groups in the base year already exhibit higher than predicted attainment).

Constant enrolment numbers (CEN): This scenario differs from CER, as country-specific attainment by age (under the age of 35) and sex is kept constant at the absolute levels observed in the base year. While CER is a pessimistic low scenario, CEN could be either lower than CER for countries with larger size of younger cohorts, or higher than CER in countries with a smaller size of younger cohorts.

Table 9.7 Distribution by Level of Education Among Age Group 30–34 in 2010, 2030, and 2060 Under the Global Education Trend Scenario

	2010						2030						2060					
Country	No education	Incomplete primary	Primary	Lower secondary	Upper secondary	Post-secondary	No education	Incomplete primary	Primary	Lower secondary	Upper secondary	Post-secondary	No education	Incomplete primary	Primary	Lower secondary	Upper secondary	Post-secondary
Albania	0.00	0.00	0.02	0.33	0.53	0.10	0.00	0.00	0.01	0.18	0.67	0.13	0.00	0.00	0.01	0.06	0.73	0.21
Algeria	0.08	0.03	0.09	0.33	0.32	0.15	0.01	0.00	0.05	0.19	0.49	0.25	0.00	0.00	0.01	0.04	0.52	0.43
Argentina	0.01	0.05	0.23	0.16	0.36	0.19	0.00	0.01	0.16	0.11	0.44	0.28	0.00	0.00	0.06	0.04	0.47	0.42
Armenia	0.00	0.00	0.01	0.04	0.71	0.25	0.00	0.00	0.00	0.01	0.70	0.29	0.00	0.00	0.00	0.00	0.62	0.38
Aruba	0.03	0.03	0.20	0.30	0.12	0.32	0.01	0.01	0.12	0.23	0.18	0.46	0.00	0.00	0.05	0.09	0.22	0.63
Australia	0.00	0.00	0.03	0.09	0.45	0.43	0.00	0.00	0.01	0.04	0.42	0.53	0.00	0.00	0.00	0.01	0.33	0.66
Austria	0.00	0.00	0.02	0.13	0.50	0.35	0.00	0.00	0.01	0.06	0.45	0.49	0.00	0.00	0.00	0.01	0.33	0.66
Azerbaijan	0.00	0.00	0.04	0.07	0.69	0.19	0.00	0.00	0.01	0.02	0.76	0.20	0.00	0.00	0.00	0.00	0.74	0.25
Bahamas	0.00	0.01	0.10	0.62	0.12	0.14	0.00	0.00	0.09	0.54	0.19	0.18	0.00	0.00	0.06	0.35	0.33	0.26
Bahrain	0.05	0.07	0.09	0.20	0.37	0.22	0.00	0.01	0.07	0.15	0.44	0.34	0.00	0.00	0.03	0.06	0.42	0.49
Bangladesh	0.24	0.24	0.19	0.16	0.07	0.10	0.10	0.10	0.27	0.23	0.14	0.17	0.03	0.03	0.20	0.17	0.26	0.31
Belarus	0.00	0.00	0.00	0.01	0.76	0.23	0.00	0.00	0.00	0.00	0.69	0.31	0.00	0.00	0.00	0.00	0.56	0.44
Belgium	0.01	0.00	0.02	0.11	0.37	0.49	0.00	0.00	0.00	0.03	0.33	0.63	0.00	0.00	0.00	0.00	0.24	0.76
Belize	0.04	0.31	0.31	0.16	0.04	0.13	0.03	0.20	0.33	0.17	0.09	0.19	0.01	0.05	0.28	0.14	0.21	0.31
Benin	0.53	0.24	0.09	0.08	0.04	0.02	0.30	0.13	0.23	0.20	0.10	0.03	0.12	0.05	0.27	0.23	0.26	0.07
Bhutan	0.45	0.23	0.02	0.18	0.04	0.08	0.17	0.09	0.04	0.44	0.13	0.14	0.02	0.01	0.03	0.38	0.32	0.24
Bolivia	0.06	0.16	0.17	0.20	0.23	0.18	0.01	0.03	0.13	0.18	0.40	0.26	0.00	0.00	0.05	0.07	0.48	0.40
Bosnia and Herzegovina	0.01	0.01	0.06	0.19	0.61	0.12	0.00	0.00	0.01	0.03	0.78	0.18	0.00	0.00	0.00	0.00	0.73	0.27
Brazil	0.05	0.11	0.20	0.17	0.33	0.13	0.02	0.03	0.12	0.16	0.48	0.19	0.00	0.00	0.05	0.06	0.57	0.31
Bulgaria	0.00	0.00	0.03	0.09	0.61	0.27	0.00	0.00	0.01	0.03	0.61	0.35	0.00	0.00	0.00	0.00	0.52	0.48
Burkina Faso	0.67	0.13	0.07	0.06	0.04	0.02	0.52	0.10	0.13	0.12	0.10	0.03	0.23	0.04	0.21	0.19	0.26	0.06
Burundi	0.35	0.27	0.30	0.04	0.03	0.03	0.21	0.17	0.37	0.13	0.07	0.05	0.06	0.05	0.45	0.16	0.18	0.10
Cambodia	0.25	0.18	0.28	0.20	0.08	0.02	0.08	0.13	0.37	0.22	0.16	0.05	0.02	0.02	0.33	0.19	0.33	0.11
Cameroon	0.13	0.17	0.38	0.14	0.12	0.05	0.03	0.05	0.43	0.15	0.26	0.08	0.00	0.00	0.25	0.09	0.51	0.14
Canada	0.00	0.00	0.01	0.03	0.30	0.66	0.00	0.00	0.00	0.01	0.24	0.75	0.00	0.00	0.00	0.00	0.17	0.83

Cape Verde	0.03	0.47	0.19	0.20	0.06	0.04	0.01	0.17	0.30	0.32	0.14	0.05	0.00	0.04	0.27	0.29	0.32	0.09
CAR	0.23	0.25	0.34	0.11	0.05	0.02	0.09	0.09	0.49	0.15	0.14	0.03	0.01	0.01	0.41	0.13	0.36	0.08
Chad	0.58	0.22	0.10	0.05	0.03	0.02	0.47	0.17	0.16	0.09	0.09	0.03	0.27	0.09	0.20	0.11	0.27	0.06
Chile	0.01	0.03	0.13	0.17	0.46	0.21	0.00	0.01	0.07	0.09	0.52	0.31	0.00	0.00	0.02	0.02	0.48	0.47
China	0.02	0.00	0.11	0.58	0.17	0.12	0.00	0.00	0.08	0.43	0.27	0.22	0.00	0.00	0.04	0.19	0.36	0.41
Colombia	0.04	0.11	0.22	0.09	0.31	0.22	0.01	0.03	0.14	0.06	0.41	0.34	0.00	0.00	0.04	0.02	0.41	0.52
Comoros	0.19	0.15	0.36	0.14	0.06	0.09	0.05	0.04	0.44	0.18	0.14	0.16	0.00	0.00	0.28	0.12	0.32	0.28
Congo	0.02	0.10	0.48	0.22	0.11	0.06	0.00	0.01	0.46	0.21	0.22	0.10	0.00	0.00	0.27	0.12	0.43	0.17
Costa Rica	0.01	0.07	0.41	0.13	0.19	0.19	0.00	0.01	0.33	0.10	0.29	0.27	0.00	0.00	0.15	0.05	0.39	0.41
Côte d'Ivoire	0.38	0.22	0.15	0.12	0.04	0.08	0.19	0.11	0.25	0.19	0.13	0.12	0.03	0.02	0.23	0.18	0.32	0.22
Croatia	0.00	0.00	0.01	0.10	0.70	0.19	0.00	0.00	0.00	0.03	0.72	0.25	0.00	0.00	0.00	0.00	0.64	0.36
Cuba	0.00	0.01	0.07	0.26	0.52	0.14	0.00	0.00	0.03	0.13	0.62	0.21	0.00	0.00	0.01	0.03	0.61	0.35
Cyprus	0.00	0.00	0.03	0.06	0.43	0.49	0.00	0.00	0.01	0.01	0.34	0.64	0.00	0.00	0.00	0.00	0.23	0.77
Czech Republic	0.00	0.00	0.00	0.04	0.77	0.19	0.00	0.00	0.00	0.01	0.74	0.24	0.00	0.00	0.00	0.00	0.64	0.36
Denmark	0.00	0.00	0.00	0.16	0.51	0.32	0.00	0.00	0.00	0.08	0.50	0.42	0.00	0.00	0.00	0.02	0.42	0.55
Dominican Republic	0.01	0.12	0.10	0.33	0.25	0.20	0.00	0.03	0.07	0.24	0.34	0.31	0.00	0.00	0.03	0.10	0.38	0.49
D. R. Congo	0.11	0.19	0.15	0.30	0.19	0.05	0.04	0.06	0.17	0.33	0.33	0.08	0.00	0.00	0.10	0.20	0.57	0.13
Ecuador	0.03	0.09	0.27	0.14	0.21	0.26	0.01	0.02	0.18	0.09	0.28	0.42	0.00	0.00	0.06	0.03	0.30	0.62
Egypt	0.26	0.05	0.04	0.05	0.42	0.18	0.07	0.01	0.03	0.04	0.57	0.28	0.01	0.00	0.01	0.01	0.53	0.45
El Salvador	0.10	0.21	0.13	0.21	0.21	0.14	0.04	0.09	0.12	0.19	0.32	0.23	0.01	0.01	0.06	0.10	0.43	0.40
Equatorial Guinea	0.06	0.07	0.17	0.38	0.24	0.08	0.02	0.03	0.15	0.31	0.35	0.14	0.00	0.00	0.09	0.17	0.48	0.25
Estonia	0.00	0.00	0.00	0.03	0.56	0.40	0.00	0.00	0.00	0.00	0.50	0.49	0.00	0.00	0.00	0.00	0.40	0.60
Ethiopia	0.55	0.22	0.11	0.03	0.05	0.03	0.24	0.21	0.26	0.11	0.11	0.08	0.06	0.05	0.32	0.14	0.28	0.14

(continued)

Table 9.7 Continued

Country	2010						2030						2060					
	No education	Incomplete primary	Primary	Lower secondary	Upper secondary	Post-secondary	No education	Incomplete primary	Primary	Lower secondary	Upper secondary	Post-secondary	No education	Incomplete primary	Primary	Lower secondary	Upper secondary	Post-secondary
Finland	0.00	0.00	0.00	0.16	0.33	0.50	0.00	0.00	0.00	0.12	0.33	0.55	0.00	0.00	0.00	0.05	0.33	0.62
France	0.01	0.00	0.07	0.08	0.42	0.42	0.00	0.00	0.02	0.03	0.37	0.57	0.00	0.00	0.00	0.00	0.26	0.73
French Guiana	0.14	0.00	0.28	0.13	0.26	0.18	0.08	0.00	0.20	0.15	0.35	0.23	0.02	0.00	0.11	0.09	0.45	0.33
French Polynesia	0.02	0.01	0.06	0.23	0.45	0.24	0.00	0.00	0.03	0.11	0.52	0.34	0.00	0.00	0.01	0.03	0.48	0.48
Gabon	0.03	0.09	0.44	0.24	0.13	0.07	0.00	0.01	0.41	0.22	0.26	0.10	0.00	0.00	0.23	0.12	0.47	0.17
Gambia	0.38	0.10	0.12	0.22	0.10	0.07	0.18	0.04	0.17	0.30	0.18	0.12	0.04	0.01	0.15	0.25	0.34	0.21
Georgia	0.00	0.00	0.01	0.03	0.35	0.60	0.00	0.00	0.00	0.01	0.30	0.68	0.00	0.00	0.00	0.00	0.23	0.77
Germany	0.01	0.00	0.02	0.10	0.45	0.41	0.00	0.00	0.01	0.08	0.39	0.53	0.00	0.00	0.00	0.03	0.31	0.66
Ghana	0.34	0.04	0.09	0.31	0.17	0.06	0.17	0.02	0.11	0.38	0.25	0.07	0.03	0.00	0.09	0.32	0.44	0.12
Greece	0.00	0.00	0.08	0.10	0.50	0.31	0.00	0.00	0.03	0.03	0.48	0.47	0.00	0.00	0.00	0.00	0.35	0.64
Guadeloupe	0.01	0.02	0.14	0.12	0.45	0.25	0.00	0.00	0.04	0.06	0.53	0.35	0.00	0.00	0.01	0.01	0.47	0.51
Guatemala	0.19	0.27	0.22	0.12	0.13	0.07	0.11	0.16	0.26	0.14	0.23	0.11	0.03	0.04	0.21	0.12	0.42	0.20
Guinea	0.64	0.04	0.11	0.12	0.04	0.04	0.43	0.02	0.14	0.24	0.10	0.07	0.13	0.01	0.19	0.30	0.24	0.13
Guinea-Bissau	0.45	0.12	0.15	0.15	0.12	0.02	0.28	0.07	0.18	0.18	0.28	0.03	0.08	0.02	0.15	0.15	0.54	0.06
Guyana	0.02	0.02	0.11	0.30	0.43	0.13	0.00	0.00	0.08	0.19	0.56	0.16	0.00	0.00	0.03	0.08	0.66	0.23
Haiti	0.10	0.30	0.17	0.21	0.14	0.07	0.04	0.11	0.17	0.21	0.35	0.11	0.00	0.01	0.08	0.09	0.60	0.22
Honduras	0.11	0.20	0.38	0.09	0.15	0.08	0.04	0.07	0.42	0.10	0.24	0.13	0.01	0.01	0.29	0.07	0.40	0.23
Hong Kong	0.00	0.01	0.04	0.16	0.38	0.41	0.00	0.00	0.01	0.04	0.35	0.59	0.00	0.00	0.00	0.00	0.23	0.77
Hungary	0.00	0.00	0.01	0.12	0.70	0.17	0.00	0.00	0.00	0.03	0.73	0.23	0.00	0.00	0.00	0.00	0.65	0.35
Iceland	0.00	0.00	0.24	0.00	0.33	0.43	0.00	0.00	0.15	0.00	0.29	0.56	0.00	0.00	0.07	0.00	0.25	0.68
India	0.29	0.07	0.15	0.14	0.24	0.12	0.14	0.03	0.15	0.14	0.36	0.18	0.03	0.01	0.09	0.08	0.50	0.30
Indonesia	0.03	0.04	0.33	0.21	0.29	0.10	0.00	0.01	0.17	0.15	0.49	0.18	0.00	0.00	0.04	0.04	0.56	0.35
Iran	0.08	0.05	0.18	0.23	0.29	0.17	0.01	0.01	0.12	0.15	0.42	0.31	0.00	0.00	0.03	0.03	0.41	0.53
Iraq	0.09	0.06	0.30	0.10	0.19	0.25	0.02	0.01	0.22	0.07	0.28	0.39	0.00	0.00	0.07	0.02	0.31	0.59

Ireland	0.00	0.00	0.03	0.13	0.23	0.61	0.00	0.00	0.01	0.04	0.21	0.74	0.00	0.00	0.00	0.00	0.16	0.84
Israel	0.01	0.02	0.12	0.21	0.35	0.30	0.00	0.00	0.09	0.15	0.44	0.31	0.00	0.00	0.04	0.07	0.51	0.38
Italy	0.00	0.00	0.03	0.29	0.51	0.18	0.00	0.00	0.01	0.13	0.60	0.26	0.00	0.00	0.00	0.03	0.55	0.42
Jamaica	0.00	0.01	0.08	0.60	0.12	0.19	0.00	0.00	0.07	0.48	0.19	0.27	0.00	0.00	0.04	0.27	0.29	0.40
Japan	0.00	0.00	0.01	0.04	0.38	0.57	0.00	0.00	0.00	0.01	0.25	0.74	0.00	0.00	0.00	0.00	0.16	0.84
Jordan	0.06	0.03	0.11	0.21	0.27	0.33	0.01	0.00	0.06	0.12	0.32	0.50	0.00	0.00	0.02	0.03	0.28	0.66
Kazakhstan	0.00	0.00	0.01	0.09	0.63	0.28	0.00	0.00	0.00	0.02	0.56	0.41	0.00	0.00	0.00	0.00	0.45	0.54
Kenya	0.05	0.09	0.15	0.27	0.37	0.06	0.01	0.01	0.09	0.16	0.63	0.10	0.00	0.00	0.02	0.03	0.76	0.19
Kuwait	0.13	0.29	0.03	0.17	0.19	0.19	0.01	0.02	0.06	0.34	0.30	0.28	0.00	0.00	0.04	0.19	0.35	0.42
Kyrgyzstan	0.00	0.00	0.00	0.04	0.80	0.15	0.00	0.00	0.00	0.01	0.81	0.18	0.00	0.00	0.00	0.00	0.73	0.27
Laos	0.17	0.19	0.26	0.22	0.10	0.06	0.07	0.08	0.30	0.25	0.24	0.07	0.01	0.02	0.23	0.19	0.44	0.11
Latvia	0.00	0.00	0.00	0.04	0.56	0.39	0.00	0.00	0.00	0.01	0.50	0.49	0.00	0.00	0.00	0.00	0.37	0.62
Lebanon	0.02	0.01	0.19	0.32	0.21	0.25	0.00	0.00	0.10	0.16	0.30	0.44	0.00	0.00	0.03	0.04	0.28	0.65
Lesotho	0.10	0.27	0.35	0.10	0.11	0.07	0.03	0.10	0.38	0.15	0.24	0.11	0.00	0.01	0.24	0.10	0.46	0.19
Liberia	0.73	0.09	0.05	0.07	0.04	0.02	0.55	0.07	0.11	0.16	0.09	0.02	0.21	0.03	0.19	0.28	0.24	0.05
Lithuania	0.00	0.00	0.00	0.02	0.43	0.55	0.00	0.00	0.00	0.00	0.34	0.65	0.00	0.00	0.00	0.00	0.24	0.75
Luxembourg	0.05	0.00	0.07	0.20	0.36	0.33	0.01	0.00	0.05	0.13	0.38	0.43	0.00	0.00	0.02	0.05	0.35	0.58
Macao	0.00	0.02	0.09	0.26	0.28	0.35	0.00	0.00	0.05	0.14	0.28	0.53	0.00	0.00	0.01	0.03	0.22	0.73
Madagascar	0.22	0.45	0.22	0.07	0.03	0.02	0.15	0.33	0.32	0.13	0.04	0.04	0.06	0.13	0.45	0.18	0.12	0.06
Malawi	0.24	0.24	0.15	0.22	0.13	0.02	0.11	0.15	0.17	0.28	0.26	0.03	0.03	0.04	0.14	0.23	0.50	0.06
Malaysia	0.02	0.02	0.06	0.21	0.45	0.24	0.00	0.00	0.02	0.07	0.50	0.40	0.00	0.00	0.00	0.01	0.37	0.62
Maldives	0.03	0.18	0.25	0.43	0.03	0.08	0.00	0.02	0.27	0.46	0.10	0.14	0.00	0.00	0.17	0.28	0.29	0.26
Mali	0.76	0.07	0.07	0.05	0.04	0.01	0.60	0.06	0.12	0.10	0.11	0.02	0.29	0.03	0.19	0.15	0.31	0.04
Malta	0.00	0.00	0.01	0.56	0.11	0.31	0.00	0.00	0.01	0.35	0.16	0.48	0.00	0.00	0.00	0.13	0.19	0.67
Martinique	0.00	0.02	0.10	0.11	0.47	0.30	0.00	0.00	0.03	0.05	0.51	0.41	0.00	0.00	0.00	0.01	0.42	0.57
Mauritius	0.01	0.22	0.41	0.18	0.14	0.04	0.00	0.06	0.41	0.18	0.29	0.06	0.00	0.01	0.25	0.11	0.52	0.11
Mexico	0.03	0.09	0.21	0.34	0.16	0.17	0.01	0.02	0.13	0.30	0.27	0.27	0.00	0.00	0.05	0.13	0.37	0.45
Moldova	0.00	0.00	0.02	0.23	0.58	0.17	0.00	0.00	0.01	0.10	0.69	0.20	0.00	0.00	0.00	0.02	0.69	0.28
Mongolia	0.00	0.01	0.06	0.19	0.62	0.12	0.00	0.00	0.04	0.10	0.71	0.15	0.00	0.00	0.02	0.04	0.71	0.24

(continued)

Table 9.7 Continued

Country	2010						2030						2060					
	No education	Incomplete primary	Primary	Lower secondary	Upper secondary	Post-secondary	No education	Incomplete primary	Primary	Lower secondary	Upper secondary	Post-secondary	No education	Incomplete primary	Primary	Lower secondary	Upper secondary	Post-secondary
Montenegro	0.01	0.00	0.01	0.12	0.68	0.18	0.00	0.00	0.00	0.04	0.72	0.24	0.00	0.00	0.00	0.00	0.64	0.35
Morocco	0.31	0.13	0.18	0.19	0.10	0.09	0.12	0.05	0.20	0.23	0.23	0.17	0.01	0.01	0.11	0.13	0.41	0.34
Mozambique	0.61	0.19	0.04	0.11	0.05	0.01	0.44	0.13	0.08	0.23	0.10	0.02	0.17	0.05	0.12	0.37	0.24	0.05
Myanmar	0.04	0.05	0.42	0.23	0.13	0.14	0.01	0.01	0.36	0.20	0.17	0.25	0.00	0.00	0.23	0.13	0.22	0.42
Namibia	0.06	0.15	0.12	0.33	0.24	0.09	0.02	0.04	0.10	0.29	0.41	0.14	0.00	0.00	0.04	0.13	0.59	0.23
Nepal	0.38	0.06	0.12	0.09	0.28	0.06	0.14	0.02	0.13	0.10	0.49	0.11	0.01	0.00	0.05	0.04	0.67	0.22
Netherlands	0.02	0.00	0.03	0.14	0.46	0.34	0.01	0.00	0.02	0.07	0.46	0.44	0.00	0.00	0.01	0.02	0.39	0.58
Netherlands Antilles	0.00	0.03	0.32	0.33	0.23	0.09	0.00	0.01	0.26	0.26	0.34	0.12	0.00	0.00	0.15	0.15	0.50	0.20
New Caledonia	0.02	0.01	0.04	0.20	0.42	0.32	0.00	0.00	0.01	0.08	0.45	0.46	0.00	0.00	0.00	0.01	0.36	0.63
New Zealand	0.00	0.00	0.03	0.10	0.47	0.40	0.00	0.00	0.01	0.04	0.45	0.49	0.00	0.00	0.00	0.01	0.36	0.63
Nicaragua	0.15	0.23	0.24	0.11	0.16	0.11	0.07	0.11	0.25	0.11	0.28	0.19	0.01	0.02	0.16	0.07	0.41	0.33
Niger	0.73	0.13	0.07	0.04	0.01	0.01	0.58	0.10	0.16	0.09	0.04	0.02	0.28	0.05	0.30	0.16	0.16	0.05
Nigeria	0.29	0.05	0.19	0.07	0.24	0.15	0.11	0.02	0.11	0.10	0.39	0.27	0.01	0.00	0.03	0.03	0.44	0.49
Norway	0.00	0.00	0.00	0.18	0.37	0.45	0.00	0.00	0.00	0.12	0.31	0.57	0.00	0.00	0.00	0.04	0.25	0.70
Pakistan	0.50	0.05	0.11	0.11	0.18	0.07	0.30	0.03	0.13	0.13	0.30	0.11	0.08	0.01	0.10	0.10	0.51	0.19
Palestine	0.03	0.06	0.17	0.28	0.21	0.25	0.00	0.00	0.09	0.15	0.32	0.43	0.00	0.00	0.02	0.03	0.30	0.66
Panama	0.04	0.06	0.24	0.13	0.29	0.25	0.01	0.02	0.14	0.12	0.35	0.37	0.00	0.00	0.05	0.04	0.36	0.55
Paraguay	0.02	0.16	0.32	0.16	0.19	0.16	0.01	0.05	0.28	0.14	0.28	0.24	0.00	0.00	0.15	0.07	0.38	0.39
Peru	0.03	0.09	0.12	0.08	0.39	0.30	0.01	0.02	0.07	0.05	0.44	0.40	0.00	0.00	0.02	0.01	0.41	0.56
Philippines	0.01	0.07	0.19	0.05	0.33	0.34	0.00	0.02	0.10	0.02	0.38	0.48	0.00	0.00	0.02	0.01	0.32	0.64

Poland	0.00	0.00	0.00	0.05	0.67	0.28	0.00	0.00	0.00	0.01	0.63	0.36	0.00	0.00	0.00	0.00	0.52	0.48
Portugal	0.01	0.01	0.07	0.43	0.28	0.20	0.00	0.01	0.12	0.19	0.38	0.29	0.00	0.00	0.05	0.07	0.43	0.44
Puerto Rico	0.01	0.00	0.04	0.06	0.46	0.43	0.00	0.00	0.01	0.02	0.40	0.57	0.00	0.00	0.00	0.00	0.28	0.72
Qatar	0.03	0.24	0.22	0.12	0.23	0.16	0.01	0.10	0.18	0.13	0.29	0.28	0.00	0.02	0.13	0.08	0.33	0.44
Réunion	0.01	0.03	0.17	0.16	0.40	0.24	0.00	0.00	0.05	0.09	0.51	0.34	0.00	0.00	0.01	0.01	0.47	0.50
Romania	0.01	0.00	0.03	0.12	0.68	0.17	0.00	0.00	0.01	0.03	0.76	0.20	0.00	0.00	0.00	0.00	0.72	0.28
Russian Federation	0.00	0.00	0.00	0.02	0.74	0.24	0.00	0.00	0.00	0.00	0.71	0.29	0.00	0.00	0.00	0.00	0.61	0.39
Rwanda	0.21	0.35	0.30	0.06	0.07	0.01	0.11	0.19	0.44	0.08	0.16	0.02	0.03	0.04	0.41	0.08	0.38	0.06
Saint Lucia	0.01	0.01	0.32	0.21	0.27	0.19	0.00	0.00	0.21	0.13	0.39	0.26	0.00	0.00	0.08	0.05	0.47	0.40
Saint Vincent and the Grenadines	0.01	0.02	0.42	0.17	0.24	0.14	0.00	0.00	0.31	0.12	0.37	0.20	0.00	0.00	0.15	0.05	0.49	0.31
Samoa	0.00	0.00	0.29	0.40	0.13	0.17	0.00	0.00	0.23	0.31	0.22	0.23	0.00	0.00	0.13	0.17	0.35	0.35
São Tomé and Principe	0.04	0.51	0.29	0.11	0.04	0.01	0.02	0.20	0.43	0.22	0.11	0.03	0.00	0.02	0.46	0.23	0.21	0.07
Saudi Arabia	0.05	0.03	0.10	0.21	0.23	0.38	0.00	0.00	0.04	0.08	0.29	0.59	0.00	0.00	0.00	0.01	0.22	0.77
Senegal	0.55	0.08	0.20	0.08	0.06	0.04	0.34	0.05	0.32	0.12	0.11	0.06	0.10	0.01	0.37	0.14	0.25	0.13
Serbia	0.00	0.00	0.02	0.13	0.68	0.17	0.00	0.00	0.01	0.04	0.73	0.22	0.00	0.00	0.00	0.01	0.66	0.33
Sierra Leone	0.55	0.13	0.09	0.11	0.08	0.04	0.39	0.09	0.15	0.17	0.13	0.06	0.14	0.03	0.20	0.23	0.27	0.13
Singapore	0.00	0.01	0.02	0.04	0.13	0.80	0.00	0.00	0.00	0.00	0.11	0.88	0.00	0.00	0.00	0.00	0.10	0.90
Slovakia	0.00	0.00	0.00	0.05	0.79	0.17	0.00	0.00	0.00	0.01	0.77	0.22	0.00	0.00	0.00	0.00	0.66	0.34
Slovenia	0.00	0.00	0.00	0.09	0.66	0.24	0.00	0.00	0.00	0.04	0.64	0.32	0.00	0.00	0.00	0.01	0.55	0.44
Somalia	0.49	0.05	0.24	0.04	0.15	0.03	0.26	0.03	0.34	0.06	0.26	0.06	0.05	0.00	0.32	0.06	0.44	0.13
South Africa	0.02	0.08	0.09	0.37	0.38	0.05	0.00	0.02	0.07	0.29	0.55	0.07	0.00	0.00	0.03	0.12	0.72	0.13
South Korea	0.00	0.00	0.00	0.01	0.33	0.65	0.00	0.00	0.00	0.00	0.18	0.82	0.00	0.00	0.00	0.00	0.12	0.88
Spain	0.00	0.01	0.08	0.32	0.28	0.31	0.00	0.00	0.04	0.16	0.34	0.47	0.00	0.00	0.01	0.04	0.31	0.64
Sudan	0.61	0.08	0.07	0.06	0.11	0.08	0.33	0.08	0.17	0.03	0.25	0.14	0.08	0.02	0.15	0.03	0.46	0.26
Suriname	0.00	0.04	0.22	0.45	0.22	0.08	0.00	0.01	0.18	0.37	0.34	0.10	0.00	0.00	0.10	0.21	0.52	0.17

(continued)

Table 9.7 Continued

Country	2010						2030						2060					
	No education	Incomplete primary	Primary	Lower secondary	Upper secondary	Post-secondary	No education	Incomplete primary	Primary	Lower secondary	Upper secondary	Post-secondary	No education	Incomplete primary	Primary	Lower secondary	Upper secondary	Post-secondary
Swaziland	0.05	0.15	0.24	0.15	0.28	0.14	0.01	0.04	0.15	0.10	0.48	0.22	0.00	0.00	0.04	0.02	0.56	0.38
Sweden	0.00	0.00	0.02	0.08	0.41	0.48	0.00	0.00	0.00	0.04	0.37	0.59	0.00	0.00	0.00	0.01	0.28	0.72
Switzerland	0.00	0.00	0.01	0.13	0.55	0.31	0.00	0.00	0.01	0.06	0.52	0.41	0.00	0.00	0.00	0.02	0.42	0.56
Syria	0.10	0.32	0.24	0.10	0.11	0.13	0.04	0.14	0.28	0.11	0.19	0.23	0.01	0.02	0.19	0.08	0.30	0.40
Tajikistan	0.03	0.00	0.02	0.15	0.67	0.14	0.01	0.00	0.01	0.05	0.75	0.18	0.00	0.00	0.00	0.01	0.73	0.26
Tanzania	0.07	0.04	0.76	0.08	0.02	0.02	0.01	0.00	0.80	0.09	0.07	0.03	0.00	0.00	0.63	0.07	0.22	0.08
TFYR Macedonia	0.01	0.04	0.03	0.31	0.49	0.12	0.00	0.00	0.02	0.11	0.66	0.20	0.00	0.00	0.00	0.02	0.69	0.28
Thailand	0.02	0.04	0.31	0.24	0.20	0.19	0.00	0.00	0.20	0.15	0.31	0.34	0.00	0.00	0.06	0.04	0.35	0.55
Timor-Leste	0.26	0.14	0.17	0.10	0.25	0.08	0.04	0.03	0.11	0.16	0.51	0.15	0.00	0.00	0.02	0.04	0.66	0.28
Tonga	0.01	0.00	0.08	0.57	0.18	0.16	0.00	0.00	0.06	0.42	0.29	0.23	0.00	0.00	0.03	0.20	0.41	0.36
Trinidad and Tobago	0.01	0.01	0.14	0.49	0.28	0.07	0.00	0.00	0.10	0.37	0.43	0.10	0.00	0.00	0.05	0.17	0.61	0.17
Tunisia	0.10	0.00	0.39	0.19	0.16	0.17	0.01	0.00	0.02	0.34	0.26	0.37	0.00	0.00	0.01	0.08	0.31	0.60
Turkey	0.03	0.01	0.44	0.11	0.28	0.13	0.00	0.00	0.29	0.07	0.43	0.20	0.00	0.00	0.09	0.02	0.54	0.35
Turkmenistan	0.00	0.00	0.00	0.02	0.84	0.15	0.00	0.00	0.00	0.00	0.83	0.17	0.00	0.00	0.00	0.00	0.75	0.25
Uganda	0.17	0.35	0.30	0.11	0.03	0.04	0.10	0.20	0.42	0.14	0.08	0.06	0.02	0.05	0.43	0.15	0.23	0.12
Ukraine	0.00	0.00	0.00	0.04	0.75	0.21	0.00	0.00	0.00	0.01	0.73	0.26	0.00	0.00	0.00	0.00	0.63	0.37
United Arab Emirates	0.08	0.12	0.12	0.18	0.32	0.18	0.01	0.01	0.12	0.18	0.40	0.29	0.00	0.00	0.07	0.10	0.40	0.43
United Kingdom	0.00	0.00	0.10	0.39	0.14	0.37	0.00	0.00	0.07	0.28	0.18	0.47	0.00	0.00	0.03	0.12	0.23	0.61

United States of America	0.00	0.00	0.02	0.07	0.48	0.42	0.00	0.00	0.01	0.05	0.44	0.50	0.00	0.00	0.00	0.01	0.37	0.61
Uruguay	0.00	0.03	0.32	0.33	0.15	0.16	0.00	0.00	0.28	0.28	0.20	0.23	0.00	0.00	0.17	0.17	0.30	0.35
Vanuatu	0.12	0.20	0.34	0.18	0.13	0.04	0.04	0.08	0.34	0.24	0.24	0.06	0.00	0.01	0.25	0.18	0.46	0.10
Venezuela	0.02	0.07	0.26	0.15	0.23	0.26	0.01	0.02	0.20	0.11	0.28	0.38	0.00	0.00	0.09	0.05	0.32	0.54
Viet Nam	0.05	0.13	0.35	0.29	0.09	0.10	0.01	0.03	0.23	0.34	0.24	0.14	0.00	0.01	0.16	0.23	0.39	0.22
Zambia	0.05	0.15	0.33	0.25	0.15	0.07	0.01	0.03	0.35	0.26	0.25	0.10	0.00	0.00	0.23	0.17	0.43	0.16
Zimbabwe	0.01	0.06	0.17	0.14	0.55	0.07	0.00	0.00	0.06	0.05	0.77	0.11	0.00	0.00	0.01	0.00	0.78	0.21

This scenario is of particular interest in regard to the question of what happens when no further capacities are generated in schools and universities in the future.

9.3.6 Other scenarios

The medium demographic scenario, incorporating the GET scenario for education, is considered as the most likely scenario of global population development. This means that the future population is equally likely to be either higher or lower than the medium scenario. This scenario is the basis for the WIC projections by age, sex, and education reported in this book. In addition to this medium scenario, some further scenarios are also of interest. These scenarios combine alternative assumptions for fertility, mortality, migration, and education. The three alternative education scenarios were described in the previous section; here we define two alternative scenarios each for fertility, mortality, and migration.

The 'high' and 'low' fertility scenarios are defined as gradual increases to a point of 20 per cent higher and lower, respectively, than the 'medium' by 2030, and 25 per cent different by 2050 and thereafter. These numbers are based on averages of the inputs given by the experts in the IIASA–Oxford online survey when they were asked to provide a number covering an 80 per cent range of uncertainty in 2030 and 2050 respectively. (Refer to Chapter 3 for details.)

For the 'high' and 'low' mortality scenarios we assume that life expectancy would increase by one year per decade faster or slower than in the 'medium' case.

For countries—most in sub-Saharan Africa—with a high prevalence of HIV/AIDS, larger uncertainty intervals are assumed for the nearer-term future. In the first decade of the projections, life expectancy is assumed to be five years lower or higher than in the medium. This takes into account serious developmental and food insecurity problems, high vulnerability to climate change, and possible feedbacks from very high population growth.

After 2020, the 'high' mortality scenario for those countries assumes a one year lower decadal gain than in the medium scenario. The 'low' mortality scenario, assumes an additional two-year gain per decade on top of the gain from the medium scenario until 2050, and one year additional gain thereafter.

The alternative migration scenarios are simple modifications of the medium scenario. The 'high' scenario assumes a 50 per cent higher and the 'low' migration scenario a 50 per cent lower net migration than in the medium scenario. A gradual decline in the first three of the five-year time steps is assumed. In addition, two alternative migration scenarios were developed based on expert views (see Chapter 7 for details) by the team working on global migration flows. The 'rise of the East' assumes economic stagnation in Europe and North America, and restrictive migration policies, resulting in lower levels of global migration flows. South and South East Asia become increasingly attractive destinations, resulting in a shift in global migration patterns. The 'steady global growth' scenario assumes dynamic economic growth and social development, resulting in growing competition of (skilled) labour and liberal immigration policies in the more developed world. Economic growth in the developing world also contributes towards rising levels of global mobility.

In Chapters 10–12, combinations of these different variants are used to illuminate questions in contemporary demographic, economic, environmental, and policy discussions. Chapter 12 defines a specific set of five scenarios that refer to the story lines of the Shared Socio-economic Pathways as they have been defined by a group of international research institutes in the context of climate change modelling. These five distinct scenarios have been composed by combining different elements of the high and low scenarios described earlier. Chapter 12 also defines and illustrates two different special disaster scenarios that show the consequences of some possible future mortality crises that are much more extreme than the high mortality scenarios described earlier.

In the remainder of this chapter, we present the methodological advancements and challenges in introducing education as an additional dimension in the projection of population distributions.

9.4 Summary of Methods Used and Steps in Computation

9.4.1 Introduction

As described earlier in this chapter, since the first publication of projections by age, sex, and educational attainment for 120 countries (KC et al., 2010) a number of steps have been taken to improve the accuracy of the underlying base-year distributions (section 9.1), the assumptions (section 9.2), and the methodology of the computations. Here we deal with the most significant of those changes and provide a brief summary of the methodological challenges in introducing education as an additional dimension in the evolution of population distributions.

Most notably, various methods of dealing with the education differentials in fertility, mortality, and migration have been fine-tuned and some additional complexities introduced (e.g. allowing child mortality to depend on the education of the mother). Also, the education projections were improved by going beyond global trends and allowing country and regional trends to influence future attainment.

9.4.2 Projecting population by age and sex

Using the standard cohort component method, as a first step the population distribution by sex and five-year age groups is projected to the next five-year period, applying

ASFR, sex-specific life tables, and age- and sex-specific immigration and emigration rates corresponding to the medium assumptions regarding fertility (see Chapters 3 and 4), mortality (see Chapters 5 and 6), and total number of immigrants and emigrants (see Chapter 7, as well as Abel, 2013).

Age- and sex-specific survival ratios are applied to the population distribution at the beginning of each five-year interval. In parallel, age- and sex-specific migration flows are calculated by applying the assumed period-specific rates (kept constant until 2060 in the medium scenario and converging to zero net migration by the end of 2100) to the same initial population distribution. Emigration rates are applied to the population of origin, and the immigration rates are applied to the population in the rest of the world. Owing to changes in the population structure, the overall age- and sex-specific net flows are different from zero at the global level. To ensure zero net migration at the global level, age- and sex-specific adjustment factors were applied. These sets of global level adjustment factors were applied to adjust the flows in all countries.

At that point, we have, for every country, a population consisting of those aged 5 years and above who survived and who did not emigrate in the last five years, plus those who immigrated in the last five years and are still alive. We calculate the number of births, applying ASFRs on the mid-period population (calculated as an average of the population at the beginning and the end of the period) of women aged 15–49 in the respective age group. The total number of births is then divided into males and females using the sex ratios at birth assumed in the UN's medium variant and sex-specific survival ratios. These steps are repeated until the end of the century.

9.4.3 Adding educational attainment to age and sex

As a second step, the level of educational attainment is added to the base year population distribution by age and sex. On this basis the age- and sex-specific proportions implied by the earlier described GET scenario are projected in five-year steps along cohort lines, applying the education-specific mortality differentials described in section 9.4.5. This procedure then results in the medium projections of the populations by age, sex, and level of education for all countries, as resulting from the GET education scenario and the earlier described assumptions about overall fertility, mortality, and migration trends.

This procedure of starting with a two-dimensional projection by age and sex alone and then converting it into a three-dimensional projection by level of education is a consequence of the fact that there is no basis (either in terms of past time series or of specific expert knowledge) for directly defining assumptions for education-specific fertility, mortality, and migration trends. Instead, these education-specific trends that are implicit in overall projections following the GET scenario are made explicit only in a second stage through the iterative procedures described in section 9.4.4, applied in one five-year step after another. Once the full set of education-specific rates has been derived, they can be freely altered and combined in different ways to form other scenarios that differ in their assumptions from the earlier described medium case.

9.4.4 Education-specific ASFRs

The methodology underlying the fertility section of the model has changed very little and technical details are explained in KC et al. (2010). The major novelty consists of assuming convergence in the RR of TFRs for different education subcategories that were previously assumed to remain constant. Using those education-specific RRs derived from censuses (IPUMS), surveys (e.g. DHS) and the existing literature (see Chapters 2 and 3), as well as the future overall TFRs suggested by the experts, we derive education-specific ASFRs by applying Brass's relational logit model involving a Gompertz transformation of the standard fertility schedule (UN estimate of global ASFR pattern for the period 1995–2000).

The idea is that by applying an empirically determined transformation of the age axis, the cumulative schedule of the standard fertility schedule can be described by a Gompertz function. Based on that reference ASFR distribution, we specify a new set of ASFRs corresponding to the expert-given TFR. Booth (1984) has shown that there is a linear relationship between the reference distribution and the new set of ASFRs, with the intercept (alpha) describing the age of first birth and the slope parameter (beta) corresponding to the spread or the kurtosis of the ASFR distribution.

Our goal is to express the education-specific ASFRs in terms of a particular country's overall relationship to the global ASFR pattern. KC et al. (2010) found a significant relationship between beta and the TFR; however, the general relationship with alpha was not clear. We know that education has a postponing effect on fertility comparable to the postponement that is observable during the demographic transition. But it is not possible to simply predict new sets of ASFRs corresponding to different levels of educational attainment exploiting the information that is available for countries at different stages of the demographic transition. Instead, we apply whatever alpha we found to relate overall TFR and ASFRs within a certain country, anchor this countrywide alpha within one specific education category, and assume certain differentials in alphas by education.

As a next step, we apply an iterative procedure varying the education-specific levels of fertility, while enforcing the RR. Setting the difference in the known number of births from the projection by age and sex as a target, we run this procedure until the predicted number of births by age, sex, and education sums up to the same value. The education-specific alphas implied by this distribution of fertility over education categories and (transformed) age describe a country's (transformed) fertility pattern at different levels of TFR in the most accurate possible way.

Finally, we reverse the transformations to get six series of education-specific ASFRs corresponding to the global reference distribution in ASFR, the given overall TFR, and the RR (e.g. for Kenya in Figure 9.4). Residual births following from unavoidable estimation error are distributed proportionally across education groups. This procedure is repeated for every country in every period. Table 9.8 presents education-specific, as well as overall, TFRs for the periods 2010–15 and 2055–60.

9.4.5 Education-specific life tables

Education differentials in mortality are important in the reconstruction and projection of population by age, sex, and educational attainment. The main idea has not changed much from what was done in earlier projections (KC et al., 2010). However, we have made an effort to improve the mortality part of our model, especially the optimization procedure.

In line with the previous set of projections, we derive education-specific survival ratios for six education categories. We use 15 as the cut-off age, assuming that education attained later in life does not affect mortality at lower ages. Instead, mother's education matters for the survival of those under age 15. Education-specific survival ratios are then derived from the total population's survival ratios and the education-differentials (d^i) in life expectancy at the age of 15, which are based on the literature. Taking into account the gender difference in life expectancy, the difference in life expectancy between women from the highest and the lowest education category is now six years, whereas for men it is only four years.

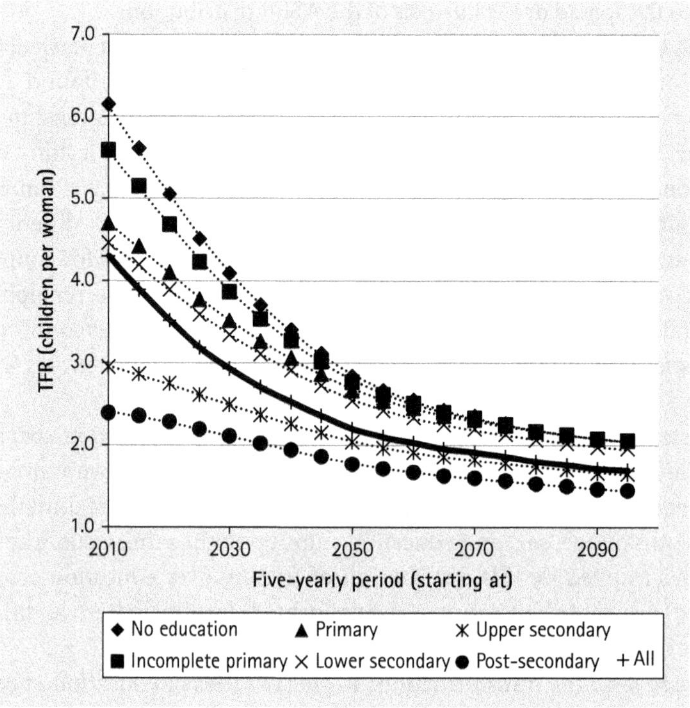

FIGURE 9.4 An example of education-specific total fertility rates (TFRs) predicted from the aforementioned procedure (country: Kenya).

Table 9.8 Overall and Education-specific Total Fertility Rates for the Periods 2010–15 and 2055–60 for 171 Countries

Country	2010–15							2055–60						
	No education	Incomplete primary	Primary	Lower secondary	Upper secondary	Post-secondary	All	No education	Incomplete primary	Primary	Lower secondary	Upper secondary	Post-secondary	All
Albania	1.79	1.79	1.79	1.69	1.25	1.01	1.41	1.86	1.86	1.86	1.77	1.49	1.31	1.51
Algeria	2.80	2.80	2.80	2.27	1.91	1.70	2.20	2.22	2.22	2.22	2.12	1.78	1.57	1.72
Argentina	2.73	2.73	2.73	2.22	1.87	1.68	2.14	2.12	2.12	2.12	2.02	1.69	1.49	1.72
Armenia	1.76	1.76	1.76	1.77	1.54	1.24	1.50	2.19	2.19	2.19	2.09	1.75	1.55	1.70
Aruba	2.51	2.11	1.88	1.69	1.48	1.30	1.61	1.83	1.84	1.84	1.75	1.47	1.30	1.47
Australia	2.38	2.38	2.38	2.38	1.94	1.69	1.88	2.36	2.36	2.36	2.36	1.93	1.70	1.80
Austria	1.68	1.68	1.68	1.68	1.36	1.39	1.43	1.89	1.89	1.89	1.89	1.67	1.55	1.61
Azerbaijan	2.67	2.67	2.67	2.69	2.33	1.88	2.38	2.12	2.12	2.12	2.02	1.69	1.49	1.70
Bahamas	2.43	2.43	2.43	1.84	1.54	1.23	1.80	1.94	1.94	1.94	1.85	1.56	1.37	1.68
Bahrain	5.13	3.31	3.08	2.15	2.18	2.19	2.37	2.23	2.24	2.24	2.13	1.79	1.57	1.74
Bangladesh	2.49	2.46	2.27	2.10	1.82	1.85	2.23	1.82	1.82	1.82	1.75	1.51	1.35	1.60
Belarus	1.75	1.75	1.75	2.02	1.52	1.28	1.52	2.09	2.09	2.09	1.98	1.67	1.47	1.61
Belgium	1.82	1.82	1.82	1.82	1.76	1.85	1.81	1.88	1.88	1.88	1.88	1.82	1.79	1.80
Belize	3.44	3.12	2.76	2.04	1.92	1.91	2.63	2.06	2.05	2.05	1.94	1.63	1.44	1.81
Benin	5.72	4.82	3.93	3.18	3.11	2.70	4.91	2.34	2.29	2.24	2.11	1.79	1.58	2.08
Bhutan	2.71	2.40	2.27	2.04	1.79	1.65	2.36	2.02	2.02	2.02	1.92	1.61	1.42	1.74
Bolivia	4.76	4.44	3.72	2.99	2.28	1.73	3.09	2.47	2.44	2.39	2.23	1.86	1.62	1.91
Bosnia and Herzegovina	1.80	1.80	1.80	1.71	1.26	1.02	1.32	1.93	1.93	1.93	1.84	1.55	1.36	1.51
Brazil	2.67	2.67	2.67	1.76	1.44	1.20	1.83	1.88	1.88	1.88	1.80	1.51	1.33	1.59
Bulgaria	1.96	1.96	1.96	1.85	1.36	1.11	1.40	2.08	2.08	2.08	1.98	1.67	1.47	1.61
Burkina Faso	6.10	4.75	3.84	2.21	2.91	2.52	5.47	2.81	2.65	2.54	2.24	2.01	1.76	2.44
Burundi	4.57	4.15	3.52	2.62	2.01	1.75	4.10	2.17	2.14	2.10	1.95	1.63	1.43	1.98
Cambodia	2.64	2.61	2.56	2.26	2.10	1.77	2.53	1.96	1.96	1.96	1.86	1.57	1.38	1.75
Cameroon	5.21	5.10	4.02	2.79	2.35	2.27	4.11	2.32	2.31	2.25	2.09	1.75	1.55	1.98

(continued)

Table 9.8 Continued

Country	2010–15							2055–60						
	No education	Incomplete primary	Primary	Lower secondary	Upper secondary	Post-secondary	All	No education	Incomplete primary	Primary	Lower secondary	Upper secondary	Post-secondary	All
Canada	1.93	1.93	1.93	1.93	1.57	1.60	1.61	2.13	2.13	2.13	2.13	1.90	1.77	1.80
Cape Verde	2.97	2.69	2.38	2.03	1.64	1.43	2.33	1.96	1.96	1.96	1.86	1.57	1.38	1.76
Central African Republic	4.49	4.53	4.14	2.62	2.15	1.87	4.24	2.18	2.18	2.15	1.97	1.66	1.46	1.99
Chad	5.87	6.13	5.37	3.91	2.86	2.48	5.73	2.56	2.59	2.52	2.29	1.89	1.66	2.34
Chile	2.58	2.58	2.58	1.96	1.64	1.31	1.79	1.94	1.94	1.94	1.85	1.56	1.37	1.54
China	1.53	1.53	1.53	1.53	1.26	1.12	1.42	1.69	1.69	1.69	1.69	1.40	1.24	1.41
Colombia	3.83	3.36	2.78	2.38	1.95	1.51	2.26	2.18	2.18	2.18	2.08	1.75	1.54	1.75
Comoros	5.46	4.30	4.94	3.69	1.54	1.34	4.51	2.35	2.26	2.31	2.12	1.66	1.46	2.00
Congo	5.49	4.99	4.24	3.15	2.43	2.11	4.08	2.30	2.27	2.23	2.07	1.73	1.52	1.99
Costa Rica	2.22	2.22	2.22	1.68	1.41	1.12	1.81	1.99	1.99	1.99	1.90	1.60	1.41	1.68
Côte d'Ivoire	5.06	4.29	3.20	2.10	1.71	1.49	4.09	2.37	2.31	2.22	2.04	1.71	1.50	1.98
Croatia	1.70	1.70	1.70	1.70	1.40	1.21	1.40	1.96	1.96	1.96	1.96	1.61	1.41	1.56
Cuba	2.07	2.07	2.07	1.57	1.31	1.05	1.42	1.73	1.73	1.73	1.65	1.39	1.22	1.42
Cyprus	1.75	1.75	1.75	1.58	1.41	1.28	1.35	2.12	2.12	2.12	2.03	1.74	1.55	1.61
Czech Republic	1.68	1.68	1.68	1.68	1.47	1.30	1.45	2.05	2.05	2.05	2.05	1.75	1.59	1.70
Denmark	1.78	1.78	1.78	1.78	1.74	1.71	1.73	2.07	2.07	2.07	2.07	2.00	1.97	1.99
Dominican Republic	3.84	2.99	3.00	2.51	2.24	1.75	2.42	2.15	2.15	2.15	2.04	1.72	1.51	1.76
D. R. Congo	6.45	6.37	6.39	4.94	3.45	3.10	5.57	2.66	2.65	2.65	2.45	2.01	1.77	2.25
Ecuador	3.51	3.24	2.85	2.38	1.95	1.63	2.37	2.12	2.12	2.12	2.02	1.70	1.50	1.73
Egypt	2.92	2.84	2.57	2.47	2.72	2.23	2.67	2.23	2.23	2.24	2.15	1.87	1.71	1.85
El Salvador	2.82	2.66	2.35	2.06	1.73	1.51	2.16	1.99	1.99	1.99	1.90	1.59	1.40	1.69

Equatorial Guinea	7.20	6.53	5.51	4.06	3.11	2.70	4.75	2.62	2.58	2.52	2.33	1.94	1.70	2.07
Ethiopia	5.04	4.38	3.05	2.25	1.23	1.07	4.14	2.56	2.47	2.30	2.10	1.68	1.48	2.04
Estonia	1.89	1.89	1.89	1.89	1.64	1.29	1.52	2.21	2.21	2.21	2.21	1.81	1.59	1.70
Finland	1.82	1.82	1.82	1.82	1.87	1.81	1.83	2.07	2.07	2.07	2.07	2.00	1.97	1.99
France	2.45	2.45	2.45	2.45	1.93	1.90	2.00	2.35	2.35	2.35	2.35	2.01	1.82	1.89
French Guiana	4.54	3.88	3.18	2.57	2.20	1.78	2.85	2.22	2.21	2.19	2.08	1.75	1.54	1.83
French Polynesia	3.57	3.05	2.70	2.39	2.06	1.80	2.09	2.77	2.61	2.50	2.32	1.97	1.73	1.89
Gabon	3.36	3.56	2.99	2.37	2.05	2.13	2.87	2.04	2.05	2.03	1.92	1.62	1.43	1.85
Gambia	5.64	5.12	4.32	3.18	2.44	2.12	4.53	2.46	2.43	2.38	2.20	1.83	1.61	2.05
Georgia	2.06	2.06	2.06	2.08	1.81	1.45	1.65	2.30	2.30	2.30	2.19	1.84	1.62	1.70
Germany	1.54	1.54	1.54	1.54	1.39	1.25	1.36	1.91	1.91	1.91	1.91	1.67	1.54	1.61
Ghana	5.69	4.51	4.06	3.15	2.18	1.49	3.98	2.83	2.64	2.57	2.33	1.88	1.59	2.12
Greece	1.72	1.72	1.72	1.57	1.43	1.31	1.42	2.02	2.02	2.02	1.94	1.69	1.54	1.61
Guadeloupe	3.64	3.10	2.73	2.41	2.08	1.82	2.17	2.46	2.46	2.47	2.35	1.98	1.74	1.89
Guatemala	5.11	4.30	3.27	2.64	2.13	1.36	3.60	2.35	2.28	2.20	2.06	1.72	1.48	1.92
Guinea	5.25	4.52	3.94	3.48	3.52	2.17	4.87	2.30	2.26	2.22	2.10	1.80	1.53	2.08
Guinea-Bissau	5.43	4.92	4.15	3.05	2.34	2.03	4.70	2.45	2.42	2.36	2.18	1.82	1.60	2.08
Guyana	4.18	3.21	2.60	2.54	1.89	1.36	2.15	2.06	2.08	2.08	1.98	1.67	1.47	1.69
Haiti	4.44	3.60	2.69	2.24	1.98	2.05	3.04	2.11	2.10	2.09	1.99	1.67	1.48	1.79
Honduras	4.01	3.70	2.87	2.21	2.07	1.77	2.89	2.11	2.10	2.07	1.95	1.65	1.45	1.85
Hong Kong	1.51	1.51	1.51	1.51	1.24	1.11	1.25	1.85	1.85	1.85	1.85	1.53	1.36	1.42
Hungary	1.47	1.47	1.47	1.47	1.21	1.14	1.23	1.88	1.88	1.88	1.88	1.60	1.45	1.56
Iceland	2.08	2.08	2.08	2.08	2.05	2.00	2.04	2.07	2.07	2.07	2.07	2.00	1.97	1.99
India	3.43	2.59	2.64	2.39	1.82	2.06	2.53	2.16	2.16	2.16	2.05	1.72	1.52	1.75
Indonesia	1.98	2.12	2.16	2.07	1.88	2.08	2.05	1.57	1.57	1.57	1.55	1.52	1.49	1.53
Iran	2.62	2.62	2.62	1.89	1.53	1.28	1.87	1.94	1.94	1.94	1.86	1.56	1.37	1.51
Iraq	5.16	4.99	4.81	4.09	3.42	2.90	4.27	2.53	2.52	2.52	2.37	1.99	1.75	2.01
Ireland	2.28	2.28	2.28	2.28	2.00	1.90	1.98	2.23	2.23	2.23	2.23	1.99	1.86	1.89

(continued)

Table 9.8 Continued

Country	2010–15							2055–60						
	No education	Incomplete primary	Primary	Lower secondary	Upper secondary	Post-secondary	All	No education	Incomplete primary	Primary	Lower secondary	Upper secondary	Post-secondary	All
Israel	4.11	4.11	4.11	3.25	2.85	2.66	3.00	3.13	3.13	3.13	2.99	2.51	2.21	2.46
Italy	1.74	1.74	1.74	1.56	1.37	1.22	1.39	2.08	2.08	2.08	1.99	1.67	1.47	1.61
Jamaica	2.51	2.51	2.51	2.51	2.13	1.37	2.21	2.05	2.05	2.05	2.05	1.68	1.48	1.76
Japan	1.48	1.48	1.48	1.48	1.47	1.29	1.37	1.61	1.61	1.61	1.61	1.47	1.40	1.42
Jordan	3.03	3.38	3.08	3.12	2.72	2.56	2.86	2.27	2.26	2.27	2.18	1.90	1.72	1.84
Kazakhstan	2.73	2.73	2.73	2.67	2.42	1.99	2.32	2.19	2.19	2.19	2.09	1.78	1.59	1.70
Kenya	6.12	5.57	4.70	4.46	2.96	2.41	4.30	2.68	2.63	2.55	2.43	1.97	1.72	2.10
Kuwait	2.74	2.74	2.74	2.23	1.88	1.67	2.15	2.12	2.12	2.12	2.02	1.70	1.49	1.71
Kyrgyzstan	2.50	2.50	2.50	2.61	2.47	1.87	2.45	2.17	2.17	2.17	2.06	1.73	1.53	1.72
Laos	3.02	2.94	2.85	2.38	1.83	1.75	2.66	2.08	2.08	2.08	1.97	1.65	1.46	1.82
Latvia	1.63	1.63	1.63	1.63	1.34	1.14	1.30	2.02	2.02	2.02	2.02	1.66	1.46	1.56
Lebanon	2.37	2.37	2.37	1.85	1.56	1.39	1.74	2.06	2.06	2.06	1.96	1.65	1.45	1.58
Lesotho	3.76	3.49	3.05	2.55	2.28	1.44	2.93	2.09	2.08	2.08	1.97	1.66	1.45	1.81
Liberia	5.17	4.75	3.97	2.87	1.81	1.57	4.85	2.33	2.30	2.23	2.04	1.66	1.46	2.08
Lithuania	2.04	2.04	2.04	2.04	1.68	1.43	1.60	2.24	2.24	2.24	2.24	1.83	1.61	1.70
Luxembourg	1.70	1.70	1.70	1.70	1.49	1.42	1.52	2.07	2.07	2.07	2.07	1.85	1.72	1.80
Macao	1.29	1.29	1.29	1.29	1.06	0.94	1.11	1.80	1.80	1.80	1.80	1.49	1.33	1.41
Madagascar	5.35	4.69	3.31	2.74	2.15	1.95	4.24	2.20	2.16	2.08	1.96	1.63	1.44	2.00
Malawi	6.96	6.39	5.62	4.69	2.89	2.27	5.59	3.42	3.32	3.17	2.90	2.24	1.92	2.63
Malaysia	3.17	3.14	3.07	2.69	2.53	2.12	2.52	2.34	2.35	2.35	2.23	1.88	1.65	1.75
Maldives	2.32	2.00	1.87	1.65	1.46	1.37	1.78	1.83	1.83	1.83	1.75	1.47	1.29	1.59
Mali	6.36	5.88	4.80	3.29	2.96	2.57	5.97	2.55	2.52	2.44	2.23	1.89	1.66	2.28
Malta	1.73	1.73	1.73	1.57	1.40	1.26	1.45	2.03	2.03	2.03	1.94	1.66	1.48	1.61

Martinique	3.35	2.83	2.51	2.24	1.95	1.71	2.00	2.45	2.46	2.46	2.35	1.97	1.73	1.89
Mauritius	1.56	1.56	1.56	1.56	1.27	1.11	1.50	1.90	1.90	1.90	1.90	1.55	1.37	1.70
Mexico	3.13	3.13	3.13	2.23	1.80	1.55	2.29	2.13	2.13	2.13	2.02	1.70	1.50	1.74
Moldova	1.68	1.68	1.68	1.59	1.17	0.95	1.27	1.89	1.89	1.89	1.80	1.52	1.34	1.51
Mongolia	4.04	3.47	3.06	2.67	2.27	1.99	2.37	2.29	2.27	2.26	2.14	1.80	1.58	1.80
Montenegro	2.30	2.30	2.30	2.17	1.60	1.30	1.65	2.06	2.06	2.06	1.96	1.65	1.46	1.61
Morocco	2.78	2.29	2.01	1.78	1.43	1.43	2.20	2.03	2.03	2.04	1.94	1.63	1.43	1.70
Mozambique	5.00	4.57	3.74	2.88	2.14	1.85	4.53	2.33	2.30	2.24	2.08	1.73	1.52	2.05
Myanmar	2.79	2.66	2.24	1.81	1.43	1.06	1.89	1.92	1.93	1.93	1.84	1.55	1.37	1.61
Namibia	4.69	3.70	3.19	2.75	2.35	1.95	2.91	2.17	2.16	2.16	2.05	1.72	1.52	1.80
Nepal	3.72	3.24	2.71	2.08	2.00	1.88	2.71	2.19	2.18	2.18	2.07	1.74	1.53	1.80
Netherlands	1.92	1.92	1.92	1.92	1.76	1.57	1.72	2.11	2.11	2.11	2.11	1.86	1.73	1.80
Netherlands Antilles	2.31	2.31	2.31	1.75	1.46	1.17	1.84	2.00	2.00	2.00	1.91	1.60	1.41	1.71
New Caledonia	2.60	2.60	2.60	2.60	2.11	1.85	2.15	2.32	2.32	2.32	2.32	1.91	1.68	1.79
New Zealand	2.57	2.57	2.57	2.57	2.09	1.83	2.05	2.35	2.35	2.35	2.35	1.93	1.69	1.80
Nicaragua	3.87	3.07	2.47	2.02	1.94	1.47	2.48	2.02	2.02	2.03	1.93	1.62	1.43	1.73
Niger	7.05	7.04	5.28	4.41	3.19	2.76	6.81	3.66	3.66	3.26	2.97	2.38	2.08	3.20
Nigeria	6.67	6.14	5.67	4.84	3.92	2.95	5.27	3.98	3.85	3.74	3.42	2.84	2.38	2.79
Norway	1.99	1.99	1.99	1.99	1.89	1.84	1.88	2.12	2.12	2.12	2.12	2.02	1.96	1.99
Pakistan	3.80	3.48	3.01	2.74	2.59	1.90	3.32	2.44	2.40	2.35	2.22	1.90	1.63	1.99
Palestine	4.62	4.94	4.73	4.19	3.59	3.13	4.09	2.53	2.55	2.54	2.40	2.02	1.78	1.98
Panama	3.56	3.34	2.86	2.44	2.06	1.64	2.33	2.13	2.13	2.13	2.03	1.71	1.50	1.71
Paraguay	3.34	3.58	2.98	2.59	2.07	2.11	2.71	2.11	2.11	2.11	2.01	1.69	1.48	1.76
Peru	4.17	3.66	3.04	2.42	2.07	1.69	2.37	2.20	2.20	2.21	2.10	1.77	1.56	1.71
Philippines	4.05	4.00	3.85	3.29	2.96	2.21	2.96	2.46	2.46	2.45	2.32	1.96	1.71	1.87
Poland	1.85	1.85	1.85	1.85	1.35	1.08	1.30	2.19	2.19	2.19	2.19	1.80	1.58	1.70
Portugal	1.48	1.48	1.48	1.34	1.20	1.08	1.26	2.12	2.12	2.12	2.03	1.73	1.55	1.70

(continued)

Table 9.8 Continued

Country	2010–15							2055–60						
	No education	Incomplete primary	Primary	Lower secondary	Upper secondary	Post-secondary	All	No education	Incomplete primary	Primary	Lower secondary	Upper secondary	Post-secondary	All
Puerto Rico	2.76	2.76	2.76	2.10	1.76	1.41	1.72	1.98	1.98	1.98	1.89	1.59	1.40	1.54
Qatar	2.75	2.75	2.75	2.37	2.01	1.79	2.22	2.09	2.09	2.09	1.99	1.67	1.47	1.70
Réunion	3.64	3.14	2.79	2.45	2.09	1.83	2.26	2.62	2.53	2.46	2.31	1.94	1.71	1.89
Romania	2.02	2.02	2.02	1.62	1.17	0.91	1.25	1.90	1.90	1.90	1.81	1.53	1.35	1.51
Russian Federation	2.28	2.28	2.28	2.15	1.58	1.29	1.58	2.19	2.19	2.19	2.09	1.76	1.55	1.70
Rwanda	5.75	5.45	4.60	3.66	2.79	2.33	4.97	2.67	2.64	2.54	2.34	1.93	1.68	2.28
Saint Lucia	3.67	3.08	2.45	1.92	1.65	1.31	1.88	1.96	1.97	1.98	1.89	1.59	1.40	1.59
Saint Vincent and the Grenadines	3.75	3.15	2.51	1.97	1.69	1.34	1.97	2.02	2.02	2.03	1.94	1.63	1.44	1.68
Samoa	5.28	4.73	4.14	3.44	2.79	2.44	3.45	2.33	2.31	2.29	2.16	1.81	1.59	1.90
São Tomé and Principe	3.45	3.61	3.25	2.49	2.22	2.13	3.30	2.04	2.04	2.03	1.91	1.61	1.42	1.88
Saudi Arabia	4.14	3.65	3.25	2.80	2.34	2.05	2.68	2.41	2.40	2.39	2.27	1.91	1.68	1.81
Senegal	5.41	4.47	3.52	3.54	1.96	1.70	4.53	2.53	2.43	2.32	2.23	1.76	1.55	2.12
Serbia	1.89	1.89	1.89	1.79	1.31	1.07	1.35	2.05	2.05	2.05	1.95	1.65	1.45	1.61
Sierra Leone	5.21	4.78	4.07	2.99	2.24	2.72	4.64	2.33	2.31	2.27	2.11	1.76	1.59	2.07
Singapore	1.66	1.66	1.66	1.66	1.37	1.22	1.28	1.89	1.89	1.89	1.89	1.57	1.39	1.42
Slovakia	1.82	1.82	1.82	1.82	1.46	1.20	1.45	2.15	2.15	2.15	2.15	1.76	1.55	1.70
Slovenia	1.83	1.83	1.83	1.83	1.59	1.40	1.56	2.09	2.09	2.09	2.09	1.77	1.59	1.70
Somalia	6.96	6.27	5.23	3.77	2.86	2.48	5.96	2.85	2.79	2.69	2.45	2.03	1.79	2.34

South Africa	3.78	3.23	2.95	2.40	2.02	1.77	2.38	2.06	2.06	2.06	1.97	1.65	1.45	1.71
South Korea	1.65	1.65	1.65	1.65	1.36	1.21	1.30	1.86	1.86	1.86	1.86	1.54	1.37	1.41
Spain	1.60	1.60	1.60	1.45	1.29	1.17	1.32	2.19	2.19	2.19	2.10	1.79	1.60	1.70
Sudan	4.31	4.08	4.13	3.89	3.16	2.55	4.08	2.33	2.32	2.32	2.21	1.85	1.62	1.98
Suriname	4.10	3.47	2.81	2.25	1.92	1.54	2.27	2.30	2.25	2.20	2.06	1.74	1.52	1.84
Swaziland	3.97	3.67	3.38	2.96	2.43	1.95	3.09	2.28	2.27	2.26	2.14	1.80	1.58	1.86
Sweden	1.96	1.96	1.96	1.96	1.93	1.89	1.91	2.07	2.07	2.07	2.07	2.01	1.97	1.99
Switzerland	1.73	1.73	1.73	1.73	1.54	1.33	1.52	2.14	2.14	2.14	2.14	1.82	1.65	1.75
Syria	3.52	3.11	2.77	2.39	1.99	1.74	2.72	2.10	2.10	2.10	1.99	1.68	1.47	1.77
Tajikistan	3.24	3.24	3.24	3.16	2.86	2.36	2.97	2.29	2.29	2.29	2.19	1.87	1.67	1.87
Tanzania	6.57	5.78	5.06	2.88	2.66	2.30	5.06	2.49	2.42	2.36	2.08	1.77	1.55	2.19
TFYR Macedonia	1.91	1.91	1.91	1.81	1.33	1.08	1.46	2.04	2.04	2.04	1.94	1.64	1.44	1.61
Thailand	1.73	1.73	1.73	1.73	1.43	1.27	1.56	1.89	1.89	1.89	1.89	1.56	1.39	1.53
Timor-Leste	6.61	6.67	7.05	5.87	5.16	3.50	6.11	3.06	3.06	3.09	2.87	2.43	2.05	2.46
Tonga	5.55	4.98	4.36	3.62	2.93	2.56	3.47	2.40	2.38	2.36	2.23	1.87	1.64	1.91
Trinidad and Tobago	2.11	2.11	2.11	1.60	1.34	1.07	1.54	1.74	1.74	1.74	1.66	1.40	1.23	1.45
Tunisia	2.31	2.31	2.31	1.80	1.52	1.35	1.86	2.06	2.06	2.06	1.97	1.65	1.45	1.59
Turkey	3.83	2.66	2.38	1.69	1.62	1.26	2.02	1.99	2.01	2.01	1.92	1.61	1.42	1.61
Turkmenistan	2.62	2.62	2.62	2.56	2.32	1.91	2.31	2.10	2.10	2.10	2.01	1.71	1.53	1.69
Uganda	7.26	6.77	5.45	4.00	2.83	3.57	5.93	3.19	3.13	2.97	2.68	2.19	2.06	2.67
Ukraine	2.09	2.09	2.09	1.98	1.45	1.18	1.46	2.07	2.07	2.07	1.97	1.66	1.46	1.61
United Arab Emirates	2.42	2.42	2.42	1.89	1.60	1.42	1.73	1.91	1.91	1.91	1.82	1.53	1.35	1.53
United Kingdom	2.13	2.13	2.13	2.13	1.86	1.77	1.96	2.14	2.14	2.14	2.14	1.91	1.78	1.89

(continued)

Table 9.8 Continued

Country	2010–15							2055–60						
	No education	Incomplete primary	Primary	Lower secondary	Upper secondary	Post-secondary	All	No education	Incomplete primary	Primary	Lower secondary	Upper secondary	Post-secondary	All
United States of America	2.41	2.41	2.41	2.41	1.89	1.67	1.88	2.57	2.57	2.57	2.57	2.00	1.77	1.89
Uruguay	2.53	2.53	2.53	1.92	1.61	1.28	1.96	1.86	1.86	1.86	1.78	1.50	1.32	1.60
Vanuatu	4.43	3.96	3.47	2.88	2.33	2.04	3.44	2.09	2.08	2.07	1.96	1.65	1.45	1.85
Venezuela	3.92	3.57	2.96	2.47	2.02	1.59	2.32	2.03	2.03	2.04	1.95	1.64	1.44	1.67
Viet Nam	2.38	1.82	1.95	1.69	1.68	1.49	1.78	1.71	1.71	1.71	1.63	1.37	1.20	1.45
Zambia	7.99	7.43	6.13	4.67	2.82	2.87	5.74	3.07	3.01	2.88	2.62	2.09	1.88	2.43
Zimbabwe	3.29	3.68	3.37	3.05	2.64	1.97	2.98	2.25	2.25	2.25	2.14	1.80	1.58	1.81

Table 9.9 Education-specific Survival Ratio for Men Between the Age of 60 and 64 for the Periods 2010–15 and 2055–60 for 171 Countries

Country	2010–15						2055–60					
	No Education	Incomplete primary	Primary	Lower secondary	Upper secondary	Post-secondary	No education	Incomplete primary	Primary	Lower secondary	Upper secondary	Post-secondary
Albania	0.87	0.88	0.89	0.91	0.92	0.93	0.94	0.95	0.95	0.97	0.97	0.98
Algeria	0.88	0.89	0.90	0.92	0.93	0.94	0.92	0.93	0.94	0.95	0.96	0.97
Argentina	0.86	0.87	0.88	0.90	0.91	0.92	0.92	0.93	0.94	0.95	0.95	0.96
Armenia	0.81	0.83	0.84	0.86	0.87	0.89	0.89	0.90	0.91	0.93	0.94	0.95
Aruba	0.87	0.88	0.89	0.91	0.92	0.93	0.94	0.95	0.95	0.97	0.97	0.98
Australia	0.92	0.93	0.94	0.95	0.96	0.96	0.97	0.97	0.98	0.98	0.99	0.99
Austria	0.90	0.91	0.92	0.93	0.94	0.95	0.97	0.97	0.97	0.98	0.98	0.99
Azerbaijan	0.80	0.82	0.83	0.85	0.87	0.88	0.87	0.89	0.90	0.92	0.93	0.94
Bahamas	0.87	0.88	0.89	0.91	0.92	0.93	0.92	0.93	0.94	0.95	0.96	0.97
Bahrain	0.88	0.89	0.90	0.92	0.93	0.94	0.94	0.95	0.96	0.97	0.97	0.93
Bangladesh	0.87	0.88	0.89	0.91	0.92	0.93	0.91	0.92	0.93	0.95	0.95	0.95
Belgium	0.90	0.91	0.92	0.94	0.94	0.95	0.96	0.96	0.97	0.98	0.98	0.93
Belize	0.91	0.92	0.93	0.94	0.95	0.95	0.96	0.96	0.97	0.98	0.98	0.93
Benin	0.84	0.85	0.86	0.87	0.88	0.89	0.87	0.88	0.89	0.90	0.91	0.92
Bhutan	0.88	0.89	0.90	0.91	0.92	0.93	0.93	0.94	0.94	0.96	0.96	0.97
Bolivia	0.85	0.86	0.87	0.89	0.90	0.90	0.89	0.90	0.91	0.92	0.93	0.94
Bosnia and Herzegovina	0.86	0.87	0.88	0.90	0.91	0.92	0.94	0.94	0.95	0.96	0.97	0.97
Brazil	0.88	0.89	0.89	0.91	0.91	0.92	0.93	0.94	0.95	0.95	0.96	0.96
Bulgaria	0.81	0.82	0.83	0.86	0.87	0.88	0.90	0.91	0.92	0.94	0.95	0.95
Burkina Faso	0.83	0.84	0.85	0.87	0.88	0.89	0.86	0.87	0.88	0.90	0.91	0.92
Burundi	0.83	0.84	0.84	0.86	0.87	0.87	0.87	0.87	0.88	0.89	0.90	0.91
Belarus	0.76	0.77	0.78	0.80	0.81	0.82	0.87	0.88	0.90	0.91	0.92	0.93

(continued)

Table 9.9 Continued

Country	2010–15						2055–60					
	No Education	Incomplete primary	Primary	Lower secondary	Upper secondary	Post-secondary	No education	Incomplete primary	Primary	Lower secondary	Upper secondary	Post-secondary
Cambodia	0.83	0.84	0.85	0.87	0.88	0.89	0.87	0.88	0.89	0.92	0.93	0.93
Cameroon	0.83	0.84	0.85	0.86	0.87	0.87	0.86	0.86	0.87	0.88	0.89	0.90
Canada	0.90	0.91	0.92	0.93	0.94	0.95	0.96	0.96	0.97	0.98	0.98	0.93
Cape Verde	0.87	0.88	0.89	0.91	0.92	0.93	0.93	0.94	0.95	0.96	0.97	0.97
Central African Republic	0.82	0.83	0.84	0.85	0.86	0.86	0.85	0.86	0.86	0.88	0.89	0.89
Chad	0.82	0.83	0.84	0.86	0.86	0.87	0.85	0.86	0.87	0.89	0.89	0.90
Chile	0.90	0.90	0.91	0.93	0.94	0.94	0.95	0.95	0.96	0.97	0.97	0.98
China	0.86	0.87	0.89	0.91	0.92	0.92	0.92	0.93	0.94	0.95	0.96	0.96
Colombia	0.89	0.90	0.91	0.92	0.92	0.93	0.94	0.94	0.95	0.96	0.96	0.97
Comoros	0.82	0.83	0.84	0.86	0.87	0.88	0.83	0.84	0.85	0.87	0.88	0.89
Congo	0.85	0.85	0.86	0.87	0.88	0.89	0.86	0.87	0.88	0.89	0.90	0.91
Costa Rica	0.91	0.92	0.93	0.94	0.95	0.95	0.95	0.95	0.96	0.97	0.97	0.98
Côte d'Ivoire	0.85	0.86	0.86	0.88	0.88	0.89	0.87	0.88	0.89	0.90	0.91	0.91
Croatia	0.84	0.85	0.86	0.88	0.90	0.91	0.93	0.94	0.95	0.96	0.97	0.97
Cuba	0.90	0.91	0.92	0.93	0.94	0.95	0.95	0.95	0.96	0.97	0.97	0.98
Cyprus	0.90	0.91	0.92	0.94	0.94	0.95	0.96	0.96	0.97	0.98	0.98	0.98
Czech Republic	0.85	0.86	0.87	0.89	0.90	0.91	0.94	0.95	0.96	0.97	0.97	0.98
Denmark	0.88	0.89	0.90	0.92	0.93	0.94	0.95	0.96	0.96	0.97	0.97	0.98
Dominican Republic	0.89	0.89	0.90	0.91	0.92	0.92	0.93	0.93	0.94	0.95	0.95	0.96
D. R. Congo	0.81	0.81	0.82	0.84	0.84	0.85	0.84	0.85	0.85	0.87	0.88	0.88
Ecuador	0.91	0.92	0.92	0.94	0.94	0.95	0.95	0.95	0.96	0.97	0.97	0.97
Egypt	0.86	0.87	0.88	0.91	0.92	0.93	0.90	0.91	0.92	0.94	0.95	0.96

El Salvador	0.89	0.89	0.90	0.91	0.91	0.92	0.93	0.93	0.94	0.95	0.95	0.95
Equatorial Guinea	0.82	0.83	0.83	0.85	0.85	0.86	0.85	0.86	0.86	0.88	0.88	0.89
Ethiopia	0.86	0.87	0.87	0.89	0.90	0.90	0.88	0.89	0.89	0.91	0.92	0.93
Estonia	0.81	0.82	0.83	0.85	0.86	0.87	0.90	0.91	0.92	0.94	0.94	0.95
Finland	0.89	0.90	0.91	0.93	0.93	0.94	0.96	0.96	0.97	0.97	0.98	0.98
France	0.92	0.92	0.93	0.94	0.95	0.96	0.97	0.97	0.97	0.98	0.98	0.99
French Guiana	0.87	0.88	0.89	0.91	0.92	0.93	0.95	0.95	0.96	0.97	0.98	0.98
French Polynesia	0.84	0.86	0.87	0.89	0.90	0.91	0.91	0.92	0.93	0.95	0.95	0.96
Gabon	0.87	0.88	0.88	0.90	0.90	0.91	0.88	0.89	0.90	0.91	0.92	0.93
Gambia	0.79	0.80	0.81	0.84	0.85	0.86	0.83	0.84	0.85	0.87	0.88	0.89
Georgia	0.83	0.84	0.85	0.88	0.89	0.90	0.91	0.92	0.93	0.94	0.95	0.96
Germany	0.89	0.90	0.91	0.93	0.94	0.94	0.96	0.97	0.97	0.98	0.98	0.98
Ghana	0.87	0.87	0.88	0.90	0.90	0.91	0.88	0.89	0.90	0.91	0.92	0.93
Greece	0.92	0.92	0.93	0.95	0.95	0.96	0.96	0.97	0.97	0.98	0.98	0.98
Guadeloupe	0.90	0.91	0.92	0.93	0.94	0.94	0.95	0.96	0.96	0.97	0.97	0.98
Guatemala	0.90	0.90	0.91	0.92	0.93	0.93	0.93	0.94	0.94	0.95	0.96	0.96
Guinea	0.84	0.85	0.85	0.87	0.88	0.88	0.87	0.88	0.88	0.90	0.91	0.91
Guinea-Bissau	0.82	0.82	0.83	0.84	0.85	0.86	0.85	0.85	0.86	0.88	0.88	0.89
Guyana	0.83	0.84	0.85	0.87	0.88	0.89	0.87	0.88	0.89	0.91	0.92	0.93
Haiti	0.84	0.85	0.86	0.88	0.89	0.90	0.88	0.89	0.90	0.91	0.92	0.93
Honduras	0.90	0.91	0.91	0.93	0.94	0.94	0.94	0.94	0.95	0.96	0.96	0.97
Hong Kong	0.91	0.92	0.93	0.94	0.95	0.96	0.96	0.96	0.97	0.98	0.98	0.98
Hungary	0.81	0.82	0.84	0.86	0.87	0.88	0.91	0.91	0.92	0.94	0.95	0.95
Iceland	0.92	0.93	0.94	0.95	0.96	0.96	0.97	0.97	0.98	0.98	0.99	0.99
India	0.82	0.83	0.84	0.86	0.88	0.89	0.89	0.90	0.91	0.93	0.94	0.94
Indonesia	0.84	0.85	0.86	0.88	0.89	0.90	0.91	0.92	0.92	0.94	0.94	0.95
Iran	0.90	0.90	0.91	0.93	0.93	0.94	0.95	0.95	0.96	0.97	0.97	0.98

(continued)

Table 9.9 Continued

Country	2010–15						2055–60					
	No Education	Incomplete primary	Primary	Lower secondary	Upper secondary	Post-secondary	No education	Incomplete primary	Primary	Lower secondary	Upper secondary	Post-secondary
Iraq	0.87	0.88	0.89	0.91	0.92	0.93	0.92	0.93	0.94	0.95	0.96	0.97
Ireland	0.91	0.92	0.92	0.94	0.95	0.95	0.96	0.96	0.97	0.98	0.98	0.93
Israel	0.91	0.92	0.93	0.94	0.95	0.96	0.96	0.97	0.97	0.98	0.98	0.93
Italy	0.92	0.93	0.94	0.95	0.96	0.96	0.97	0.97	0.98	0.98	0.98	0.99
Jamaica	0.89	0.90	0.90	0.92	0.92	0.93	0.93	0.94	0.95	0.96	0.96	0.97
Japan	0.91	0.92	0.93	0.94	0.95	0.96	0.96	0.97	0.97	0.98	0.98	0.93
Jordan	0.88	0.89	0.90	0.91	0.92	0.93	0.93	0.93	0.94	0.95	0.96	0.97
Kazakhstan	0.76	0.77	0.78	0.80	0.81	0.82	0.85	0.86	0.88	0.90	0.91	0.92
Kenya	0.85	0.86	0.86	0.87	0.88	0.89	0.86	0.87	0.87	0.89	0.89	0.90
Kuwait	0.88	0.89	0.90	0.92	0.93	0.94	0.95	0.95	0.96	0.97	0.97	0.98
Kyrgyzstan	0.78	0.79	0.80	0.82	0.83	0.84	0.87	0.88	0.89	0.91	0.92	0.93
Laos	0.83	0.84	0.86	0.88	0.89	0.90	0.85	0.87	0.88	0.90	0.91	0.92
Latvia	0.80	0.81	0.82	0.84	0.85	0.86	0.90	0.91	0.92	0.94	0.94	0.95
Lebanon	0.86	0.87	0.88	0.90	0.91	0.92	0.91	0.92	0.93	0.95	0.95	0.96
Lesotho	0.83	0.84	0.84	0.85	0.86	0.86	0.83	0.84	0.84	0.85	0.86	0.87
Liberia	0.82	0.83	0.84	0.86	0.87	0.88	0.85	0.86	0.87	0.89	0.90	0.91
Lithuania	0.80	0.81	0.82	0.84	0.85	0.86	0.90	0.91	0.92	0.93	0.94	0.95
Luxembourg	0.90	0.91	0.92	0.93	0.94	0.95	0.96	0.97	0.97	0.98	0.98	0.98
Macao	0.92	0.93	0.94	0.95	0.96	0.96	0.97	0.97	0.97	0.98	0.98	0.99
Madagascar	0.88	0.89	0.90	0.91	0.92	0.93	0.92	0.92	0.93	0.94	0.95	0.96
Malawi	0.85	0.86	0.87	0.88	0.89	0.89	0.88	0.89	0.89	0.91	0.91	0.92
Malaysia	0.87	0.88	0.89	0.91	0.92	0.93	0.93	0.94	0.95	0.96	0.97	0.97
Maldives	0.91	0.92	0.93	0.95	0.95	0.96	0.98	0.98	0.98	0.99	0.99	0.99
Mali	0.80	0.81	0.82	0.84	0.85	0.86	0.85	0.86	0.86	0.88	0.89	0.90
Malta	0.90	0.91	0.92	0.94	0.95	0.95	0.95	0.96	0.97	0.97	0.98	0.98

Martinique	0.92	0.92	0.93	0.94	0.95	0.96	0.96	0.96	0.97	0.97	0.98	0.98
Mauritius	0.85	0.86	0.87	0.89	0.90	0.91	0.92	0.93	0.94	0.95	0.96	0.96
Mexico	0.91	0.91	0.92	0.94	0.94	0.95	0.95	0.95	0.96	0.97	0.97	0.97
Moldova	0.77	0.78	0.79	0.82	0.83	0.84	0.87	0.88	0.89	0.91	0.92	0.93
Mongolia	0.81	0.82	0.83	0.84	0.85	0.86	0.84	0.86	0.87	0.89	0.90	0.91
Montenegro	0.84	0.85	0.86	0.88	0.89	0.91	0.93	0.94	0.95	0.96	0.97	0.97
Morocco	0.88	0.89	0.90	0.92	0.93	0.94	0.92	0.93	0.94	0.95	0.96	0.97
Mozambique	0.85	0.85	0.86	0.87	0.87	0.88	0.87	0.87	0.88	0.89	0.90	0.90
Myanmar	0.82	0.83	0.84	0.86	0.87	0.88	0.84	0.85	0.86	0.89	0.90	0.91
Namibia	0.85	0.86	0.87	0.88	0.89	0.89	0.87	0.87	0.88	0.89	0.90	0.91
Nepal	0.86	0.87	0.88	0.91	0.92	0.93	0.93	0.94	0.95	0.96	0.97	0.97
Netherlands	0.90	0.91	0.92	0.94	0.95	0.95	0.96	0.97	0.97	0.98	0.98	0.98
Netherlands Antilles	0.89	0.90	0.91	0.92	0.93	0.94	0.95	0.96	0.96	0.97	0.97	0.98
New Caledonia	0.84	0.86	0.87	0.89	0.90	0.90	0.91	0.92	0.93	0.94	0.95	0.95
New Zealand	0.91	0.92	0.93	0.94	0.95	0.95	0.96	0.97	0.97	0.98	0.98	0.98
Nicaragua	0.89	0.90	0.91	0.92	0.93	0.93	0.93	0.94	0.94	0.95	0.96	0.96
Niger	0.82	0.83	0.84	0.86	0.87	0.88	0.85	0.86	0.87	0.89	0.90	0.91
Nigeria	0.83	0.84	0.84	0.86	0.86	0.87	0.85	0.85	0.86	0.87	0.88	0.89
Norway	0.90	0.91	0.92	0.94	0.94	0.95	0.96	0.97	0.97	0.98	0.98	0.98
Pakistan	0.86	0.87	0.88	0.90	0.91	0.92	0.88	0.89	0.90	0.92	0.93	0.94
Palestine	0.86	0.87	0.88	0.90	0.91	0.92	0.92	0.93	0.94	0.95	0.96	0.97
Panama	0.91	0.91	0.92	0.94	0.94	0.95	0.95	0.95	0.96	0.97	0.97	0.98
Paraguay	0.89	0.90	0.90	0.92	0.93	0.93	0.93	0.93	0.94	0.95	0.96	0.96
Peru	0.88	0.89	0.89	0.91	0.92	0.93	0.92	0.93	0.93	0.94	0.95	0.96
Philippines	0.81	0.82	0.83	0.85	0.86	0.87	0.89	0.90	0.91	0.92	0.93	0.94
Poland	0.83	0.84	0.85	0.87	0.88	0.89	0.92	0.93	0.94	0.95	0.96	0.96

(continued)

Table 9.9 Continued

Country	2010–15						2055–60					
	No Education	Incomplete primary	Primary	Lower secondary	Upper secondary	Post-secondary	No education	Incomplete primary	Primary	Lower secondary	Upper secondary	Post-secondary
Portugal	0.92	0.93	0.94	0.95	0.96	0.96	0.96	0.97	0.97	0.98	0.98	0.98
Puerto Rico	0.89	0.90	0.91	0.92	0.93	0.94	0.95	0.95	0.96	0.97	0.97	0.97
Qatar	0.91	0.92	0.93	0.95	0.95	0.96	0.96	0.97	0.97	0.98	0.98	0.99
Réunion	0.89	0.90	0.90	0.92	0.92	0.93	0.94	0.94	0.95	0.95	0.96	0.96
Romania	0.83	0.84	0.85	0.87	0.88	0.89	0.92	0.93	0.93	0.95	0.96	0.96
Russian Federation	0.77	0.78	0.79	0.81	0.81	0.82	0.85	0.87	0.88	0.90	0.91	0.92
Rwanda	0.85	0.85	0.86	0.87	0.88	0.89	0.87	0.88	0.88	0.90	0.90	0.91
Saint Lucia	0.86	0.87	0.88	0.90	0.91	0.92	0.92	0.93	0.94	0.95	0.95	0.95
Saint Vincent and the Grenadines	0.86	0.87	0.88	0.90	0.91	0.92	0.93	0.94	0.95	0.96	0.96	0.97
Samoa	0.81	0.83	0.84	0.87	0.88	0.89	0.90	0.91	0.92	0.94	0.94	0.95
São Tomé and Principe	0.86	0.87	0.88	0.90	0.91	0.91	0.88	0.89	0.90	0.92	0.92	0.93
Saudi Arabia	0.88	0.89	0.90	0.92	0.93	0.94	0.93	0.94	0.94	0.96	0.96	0.97
Senegal	0.79	0.80	0.82	0.84	0.85	0.87	0.84	0.85	0.87	0.89	0.90	0.91
Serbia	0.82	0.84	0.85	0.87	0.88	0.90	0.92	0.92	0.93	0.95	0.95	0.96
Sierra Leone	0.71	0.72	0.73	0.76	0.77	0.78	0.80	0.81	0.82	0.84	0.85	0.86
Singapore	0.89	0.90	0.91	0.93	0.94	0.95	0.94	0.95	0.96	0.97	0.97	0.97
Slovakia	0.82	0.83	0.84	0.87	0.88	0.89	0.92	0.93	0.94	0.95	0.96	0.96
Slovenia	0.87	0.88	0.89	0.91	0.92	0.93	0.94	0.95	0.96	0.97	0.97	0.98
Somalia	0.82	0.83	0.83	0.85	0.86	0.87	0.85	0.85	0.86	0.88	0.89	0.89

South Africa	0.77	0.77	0.78	0.79	0.80	0.81	0.81	0.81	0.82	0.84	0.85	0.85
South Korea	0.90	0.91	0.92	0.93	0.94	0.95	0.95	0.95	0.96	0.97	0.97	0.98
Spain	0.92	0.93	0.93	0.95	0.95	0.96	0.97	0.97	0.97	0.98	0.98	0.99
Sudan	0.86	0.87	0.88	0.90	0.90	0.91	0.87	0.88	0.88	0.90	0.91	0.92
Suriname	0.84	0.85	0.86	0.88	0.89	0.89	0.91	0.92	0.93	0.94	0.95	0.95
Swaziland	0.83	0.83	0.84	0.85	0.85	0.86	0.80	0.81	0.82	0.83	0.83	0.84
Sweden	0.91	0.92	0.93	0.94	0.95	0.96	0.96	0.97	0.97	0.98	0.98	0.93
Switzerland	0.91	0.92	0.93	0.95	0.95	0.96	0.97	0.97	0.98	0.98	0.99	0.99
Syria	0.90	0.91	0.92	0.94	0.95	0.95	0.95	0.96	0.96	0.97	0.98	0.93
Tajikistan	0.78	0.80	0.81	0.83	0.84	0.86	0.85	0.86	0.88	0.90	0.91	0.92
Tanzania	0.86	0.87	0.88	0.89	0.89	0.90	0.89	0.89	0.90	0.91	0.92	0.93
TFYR Macedonia	0.84	0.86	0.87	0.89	0.91	0.92	0.93	0.94	0.94	0.96	0.96	0.97
Thailand	0.89	0.90	0.91	0.92	0.93	0.93	0.91	0.92	0.92	0.94	0.94	0.95
Timor-Leste	0.83	0.84	0.85	0.87	0.88	0.89	0.82	0.83	0.84	0.87	0.88	0.89
Tonga	0.81	0.83	0.84	0.86	0.88	0.89	0.90	0.91	0.92	0.94	0.94	0.95
Trinidad and Tobago	0.83	0.84	0.85	0.87	0.88	0.89	0.91	0.91	0.92	0.94	0.94	0.95
Tunisia	0.89	0.90	0.91	0.93	0.94	0.94	0.92	0.93	0.94	0.96	0.96	0.97
Turkey	0.85	0.87	0.88	0.90	0.91	0.92	0.91	0.92	0.93	0.95	0.95	0.96
Turkmenistan	0.78	0.79	0.80	0.82	0.83	0.84	0.85	0.86	0.87	0.89	0.90	0.91
Uganda	0.85	0.85	0.86	0.87	0.88	0.88	0.87	0.87	0.88	0.89	0.90	0.91
Ukraine	0.76	0.77	0.78	0.79	0.80	0.81	0.85	0.86	0.87	0.89	0.90	0.91
United Arab Emirates	0.87	0.89	0.90	0.92	0.93	0.94	0.95	0.95	0.96	0.97	0.97	0.98
United Kingdom	0.91	0.92	0.93	0.94	0.95	0.96	0.96	0.97	0.97	0.98	0.98	0.98
United States of America	0.89	0.89	0.90	0.92	0.92	0.93	0.94	0.95	0.95	0.96	0.97	0.97

(continued)

Table 9.9 Continued

Country	2010–15						2055–60					
	No Education	Incomplete primary	Primary	Lower secondary	Upper secondary	Post-secondary	No education	Incomplete primary	Primary	Lower secondary	Upper secondary	Post-secondary
Uruguay	0.87	0.88	0.89	0.91	0.92	0.93	0.94	0.95	0.95	0.96	0.97	0.97
Vanuatu	0.85	0.86	0.87	0.90	0.91	0.92	0.90	0.91	0.92	0.94	0.95	0.96
Venezuela	0.89	0.89	0.90	0.92	0.92	0.93	0.94	0.94	0.95	0.96	0.96	0.97
Viet Nam	0.90	0.91	0.91	0.93	0.94	0.94	0.95	0.96	0.96	0.97	0.97	0.93
Zambia	0.83	0.84	0.84	0.85	0.86	0.87	0.85	0.85	0.86	0.87	0.88	0.83
Zimbabwe	0.86	0.86	0.87	0.88	0.88	0.89	0.87	0.88	0.88	0.89	0.90	0.90

1. We begin by initializing education-specific life expectancy at age 15 (e_{15}), subject to the constraint given by the empirical differentials in education-specific mortality d^{i}_{15}.

$$e^{i}_{15} = e_{15} + d^{i}_{15} \tag{9.3}$$

2. At the same time, e_{15} can be described as the population-weighted mean of e^{i}_{15}, where *i* refers to education categories E1, E2,…, E6

$$e_{15} = \sum p^{i}_{15}\, e^{i}_{15} \tag{9.4}$$

3. From the life table corresponding to overall e_{15}, we get a standard mortality schedule for a given country in a given year.
4. Using the two relations described in (1) and (2), we apply the Gompertz relational model in accordance with the methodology applied in estimating education-differentials in fertility.
5. Using an iterative procedure, we minimize the difference between the total number of age- and sex-specific deaths and the sum of deaths by age and sex from the individual education categories.
6. The death rates minimizing that difference correspond to a mortality schedule for each education subgroup.
7. This procedure is repeated for every country in every period, assuming that the survival ratio during a five-year period depends on the education status at the beginning of the interval. Table 9.9 shows, as an example, resulting education specific survival ratios for men between the age of 60 and 64 for the periods 2010–15 and 2055–60 for 171 countries.

9.4.6 Mortality of children under 15

We add an additional layer of sophistication to the mortality section by deriving the mortality of children (under 15) by their mothers' education. The education differentials are taken from a review of the literature and from our own estimates based on surveys. Holding the differentials constant, we minimize the difference between overall age-specific deaths under 15, and the sum of age- and sex-specific deaths by education category. This marks a further methodological improvement compared with the 2010 version of the projections, where children under the age of 15 were assumed to be exposed to the same risk of dying, irrespective of their mothers' education.

9.4.7 Education scenarios

Once the population is projected to the end of a five-year period applying the described education-specific survival ratios, education transitions are implemented to match a predefined set of education profiles corresponding to the medium population scenario for the 15–34 age group (see Chapter 8). We assume there are no education transitions between the six education states after the age of 34. Once a certain level of educational attainment has been reached, there is no way of falling below this level, that is, transitions go only in one direction. The problem is that the ages at transitions from E1 to E6 vary greatly between countries. While the timing of the transitions to E4 will only require some assumptions about the age group 15–19, the transitions to tertiary education clearly require more consideration as they can take place over a wider range of age groups depending on particular features of national school systems, such as the official age of entry, the number of grades in primary and lower secondary school, and so on. A detailed description of how education transitions are dealt with in different scenarios can be found in Chapter 8.

9.4.8 Education-specific migration flows

In the absence of data on the education composition of global bilateral migration flows, we make the commonly used assumption that the education structure of emigration flows is proportional to the origin country's education structure. However, this assumption is not valid in the case of immigration flows, which are rarely proportional to the education structure of the destination country. Hence, we calculate net numbers of migrants in each projected period based on the results of the age–sex projection and then assume that the education distribution of net migrants is proportional to a country's education distribution.

9.4.9 Alternative scenarios

As noted earlier, we developed several alternative scenarios in addition to the medium scenario. For all of the alternatives, 2010 is defined as the base year for all countries, and the distribution of population by age, sex, and educational attainment in that year is taken as given. For the future levels of fertility, mortality, migration, and education, alternative trajectories are then defined.

Scenarios in the first set of three alternative scenarios in Chapter 10 differ only with respect to the education future, while education-specific fertility, mortality, and migration rates are the same as in the medium scenario. Rather than recalculating the education-specific rates for alternative scenarios, we directly apply those rates derived from the medium scenario and apply the new education scenario at the end of each step. The population composition will change owing to the changes in education composition, enabling us to analyse the sensitivity of our model to changes in the education assumptions.

In Chapters 10 and 12, several scenarios are developed by introducing 'low' and 'high' variants of fertility, mortality, and migration. For the high and low mortality scenarios, a projection similar to that done for the medium scenario was conducted with medium fertility, no migration, and the GET education scenario so that high and low education-specific survival ratios were generated. For high and low fertility, the education-specific age schedules were kept the same as in the medium scenario. For high and low migration scenarios, and for two additional scenarios ('shifts' and 'divergence'), the age- and sex-specific migration rates for the period 2010–2100 were derived by running the age–sex projection (summarized in section 9.4.2) with medium mortality, fertility, and scenario-specific migration assumptions in the form of multipliers that were applied to the previous period's age–sex migration rates. As summarized in section 9.3.5, we also defined four different education scenarios.

In summary, any combination of demographic and education assumptions could be projected with the aforementioned inputs. A detailed description of all these scenarios is provided in Chapters 10–12.

9.4.10 Expanding education projection to 24 countries with no education data

The population projection by age and sex is done for 195 countries of the world. The population projection by age, sex, and educational attainment is done for 171 countries, or 97 per cent of the world's population, for which the distribution of population by education was available (explained in section 9.1). For 24 of the 195 countries with populations larger than 100,000 in the year 2010, no data on education distribution are available. Therefore, we present the population projection by education for the 171 countries with education distribution in the base period(s) (see Appendix I for all countries).

It was necessary, however, to also provide the projection at the regional and global levels, for which some estimation of the distribution of education in the base year for the remaining 24 countries is required. For the sake of simplicity, we assumed the distribution of education to be same as the overall distribution in the subregions these countries belong to. With the assumed baseline distribution by education, the population projection was derived for these 24 countries separately in a manner similar to the process used for the 171 countries for which data were available. While doing so, the education scenario for the future is derived from region-specific distributions obtained from the projection of 171 countries. Final results of these projections are used in presenting the results at the regional and global levels.

9.4.11 Mean years of education

The frequently used indicator of mean years of schooling (MYS) has the advantage of approximating the distribution of educational attainment in a single number. It is therefore often used for cross-country comparisons, as well as in economic and environmental models as the unique indicator of educational attainment and human capital stock. The computation of MYS from a given educational attainment distribution is complex for two main reasons. First, the standard duration of different levels of schooling varies from country to country, and within countries each school level can have different lengths in different studies, for example studies of general secondary as opposed to vocational secondary. Second, the calculation is biased by the presence of pupils/students who do not complete the full course at any level, which can amount to a substantial share in some countries. To contravene these difficulties, the methodology used and detailed in this section computes MYS as the weighted mean of six educational levels (defined in section 9.1). Our procedure takes into account country-specific educational systems, as well as changes in these systems over time. Information on duration of schooling of completed ISCED levels is taken from the UNESCO Institute of Statistics (UIS) database. For the cohorts that studied prior to 1970, which is the last year for which UIS provides information, we assume that durations are the same as in the last year of observation. For the projected periods we use durations for 2010.

Although the majority of persons with completed primary, lower secondary, or upper secondary level of attainment did not study any further, each of these categories includes a small fraction of individuals who studied some years longer at the next higher level, but did not complete it. As data on the six aggregate levels of education do not include detailed information by levels and grades studied, we needed to estimate duration of schooling for incomplete primary level in each country using correction factors for completed primary, lower secondary, and upper secondary education. For post-secondary education, which is a broad category comprising non-university and university education, as well as postgraduate education, we apply years of schooling equivalent to four years in all countries with the exception of Singapore, where the post-secondary category consisted of some people with duration equivalent to that in the upper secondary. Age- and sex-specific proportions of these persons at the post-secondary level were estimated and used to correct the average years of schooling.

Earlier methods to convert distributions into MYS (KC et al., 2010; Lutz and KC, 2011; Lutz et al., 2007) estimated average durations in these categories using the official definition of the duration weighted by the educational distribution above and below each category. For example, a person with completed primary education might have spent time in school that ranges from the duration of primary to one day less than the duration of lower secondary. An average is obtained from the middle 50 per cent of this range, such that the average years of schooling will be larger if the proportion below the specific education category is lower than the proportion above. This method, although intuitive, was found to overestimate average years of schooling when compared with the average years of schooling computed directly from the census micro-data and from surveys.

In our new approach,[3] duration of schooling at the incomplete primary level is estimated using a set of simple models for five broad regions: Latin America, South East

[3] For more details see Potančoková, M., KC, S., Goujon, A. 2014. *Global Estimates of Mean Years of Schooling: A New Methodology*. IIASA Interim Report IR-14-005. Please see <http://www.iiasa.ac.at/publication/more_IR-14-005.php> for details.

Asia, South Asia, sub-Saharan Africa, and Arab countries. The regional distribution was chosen because of distinct differences in the slopes of the regression function. Trends in education are more similar for countries with a shared history and culture. The models are built using detailed data on duration of schooling by grades completed within primary level for 57 countries (using micro-data from the IPUMS and DHS).We expected to find a relationship between the duration of schooling at primary level and educational attainment composition because we assumed that in countries with low educational attainment and attendance pupils would be more likely to drop out earlier than in societies with high educational attainment, where dropouts are rather exceptional and would occur at higher grades as children are supported to stay in education longer. The analysis we performed confirmed this hypothesis.

We also found that this assumption holds not only across countries, but also across cohorts within individual countries: duration of schooling within the incomplete primary level is shorter for older (less educated) cohorts. Therefore, for countries and cohorts with nearly universal primary education, we find higher duration of incomplete primary among the fraction that has dropped out of primary. This relationship holds for both genders. Figure 9.5 depicts the model for Latin America. The results are similar in the four other broad regions mentioned earlier. South Asia is an exception; the model has better explanatory power using simple proportions with incomplete primary rather than cumulative proportion as in the other regions. For the regions where the necessary data were not available, like Europe, North America, Australia, Oceania, and the ex-Soviet countries in central Asia,[4] we assume the same relationship as in Latin America, that is, rather high duration of schooling for those with incomplete primary as these regions benefit from high levels of educational attainment. The fraction of the incomplete primary education category in these regions is negligible overall, even for older cohorts.

In the projection, duration of schooling for incomplete primary was calculated using the aforementioned relationship for a given (projected) cumulative proportion with incomplete primary.

For primary, lower, and upper secondary levels, we have estimated correction factors to inflate average duration of schooling to take into account the fraction of persons who enrolled into the next higher level—for example, in upper secondary education for those who have completed lower secondary education—but did not complete it to the highest grade. The correction factors were estimated for three broad regions—Latin America, Asia, and Africa—observing changes across different age groups. Differences between the regions are relatively small and therefore we estimated the correction factors for only three broader regions. For primary level, we observe a trend across age groups (Figure 9.6), which we use to adjust the average duration of primary education by age groups. For example, if standard duration of schooling for age group 25–29 is 6

[4] Early introduction of universal lower secondary education translated into high completion of this level and negligible proportion of persons with lower educational attainment, which makes these countries distinctly different from other countries in the region.

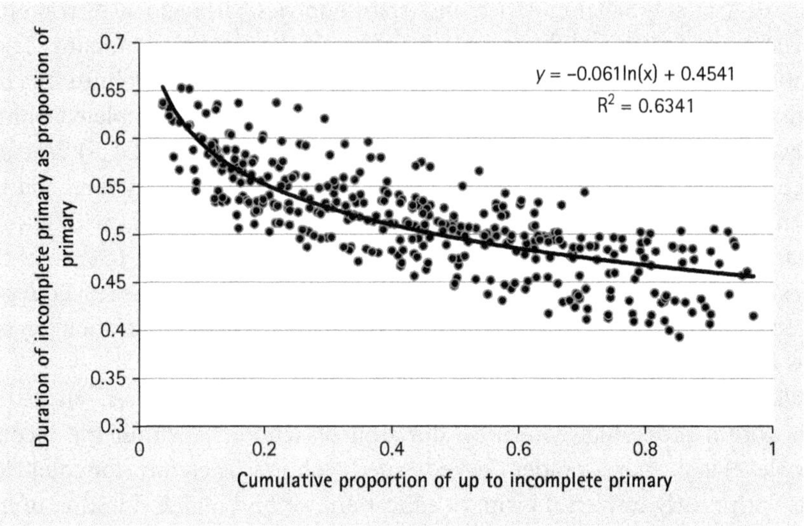

FIGURE 9.5 Relationship between duration of incomplete primary education (International Standard Classification of Education 1) and cumulative proportion of up to incomplete primary by cohorts aged 25–80+ in 16 Latin American countries.

years in an African country we apply the correction factor of 1.15 to adjust for the fraction of population with incomplete lower secondary education. The correction factor declines with increasing age. In the WIC projections, these correction factors were applied to respective cohorts, such that at each step, the youngest cohort has the same correction factor as that of the youngest cohort in the baseline.

For lower and upper secondary we could not identify any trend and therefore use a single value for all age groups: 1.05 for Latin America, 1.04 for Africa and 1.00 for Asia.[5] For Europe, North America, ex-Soviet countries, and Australia and Oceania we use the values for Latin America. For those education categories, the single factor is calculated as the average across age groups because the variation across ages is small and heaping, rather than following a clear trend.

9.5 CONCLUSION

Despite the importance of education as a key indicator for appraising the level of socio-economic development of a country's population and for modelling interactions with other parameters strongly correlated with education, educational

[5] The value is close to 1 in Asia because most students in countries like India or Nepal, which have educational systems based on the British system, complete tenth grade (ISCED 3C) and only a small fraction completes twelfth grade (ISCED 3A).

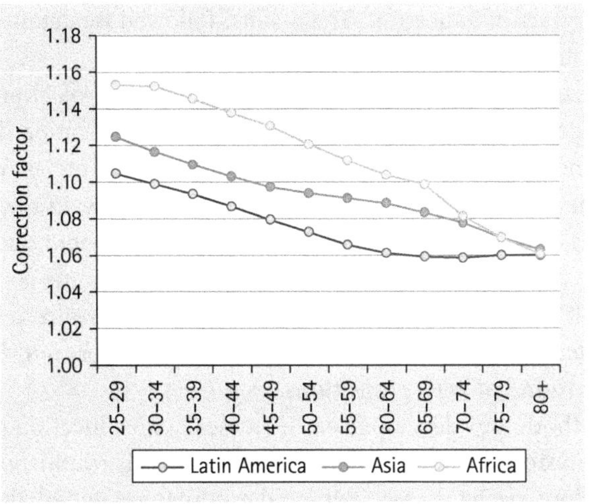

FIGURE 9.6 Correction factors for the average duration of completed primary level for three broad regions.

Note: Smoothed using five-year moving average.

attainment has always suffered from measurement problems. The many attempts to standardize levels of educational attainment have not been successful in removing all important discrepancies across countries, not to mention across age and time. The efforts undertaken in the course of this exercise address the main issues and incorporate clear and systematic measures to overcome the earlier deficiencies. The resulting base-year data set is the most comprehensive collection of harmonized data on educational attainment by age and sex for as many as 171 countries. The strength of our approach also lies in the exhaustive documentation (see also Bauer et al., 2012) that will facilitate replication and enhancement. Hence, we are one step closer to the harmonization of levels of educational attainment of the global population. What remains to be done by national and international organizations is to enhance the data collection and classification efforts.

In addition to the base year distribution, the traditional cohort–component model of population projection requires particular assumptions about the future levels of fertility, mortality, and migration. Here, we summarized the approach and the procedures that were applied to combine statistical models with expert judgement about the validity of alternative arguments that matter for future trends and with the synthesizing assessments of meta-expert meetings. The outcome of this process in terms of overall TFR, life expectancy at birth, and narratives for future migration assumptions were used in the cohort–component model to project the future.

As a final step, education was introduced in the model by including education differentials in fertility and mortality, along with specific education scenarios for the future. Using the multidimensional population projection model, population by age, sex, and educational attainment for 171 countries for the period 2010–2100 are generated for several scenarios. At the same time, we have introduced a new, empirically-based way of calculating mean years of education. The results, followed by detailed discussions, are presented in Chapters 10–12.

In introducing the education dimension in population projections, we confronted two main challenges. First, the empirical data on current education differentials in fertility, mortality, and migration are not available in many countries. While we successfully estimated the differentials in fertility for most countries, in the case of mortality, data on differentials by education was not available and we could only rely on generalizations about the differentials reported in the literature for some countries. Migration is the most difficult among the three in this regard. Although we are developing methods for estimating differential migration by education level, we were not able to apply such a differential in this round of WIC projections.

Second, the methodology developed earlier to deal with education in population projections (KC et al. 2010) was modified and improved in this round. Some shortcomings in the earlier versions are fixed and additional modules are added, the most important being the mortality differentials among children according to their mothers' education. Summing up, the main modelling challenge has been to generate the education-specific mortality, fertility, and migration rates. Given the data constraints, specifically in terms of age and sex, several optimization procedures were developed that can be considered the methodological core of the current projection model.

References

Abel, G.J. 2013 'Estimating Global Migration Flow Tables Using Place of Birth Data'. *Demographic Research*, 28: 505–46.

Anand, S. and Ravallion, M. 1993 'Human Development in Poor Countries: On the Role of Private Incomes and Public Services'. *Journal of Economic Perspectives*, 7: 133–50.

Bauer, R., Potančoková, M., Goujon, A. and KC, S. 2012 'Populations for 171 Countries by Age, Sex, and Level of Education around 2010: Harmonized Estimates of the Baseline Data for the Wittgenstein Centre Projections' (IIASA Interim Report IR-12-016). International Institute for Applied Systems Analysis (IIASA): Laxenburg.

Barro, R.J. and Sala-i-Martin, X. 1995 *Economic Growth*. McGraw-Hill: New York.

Barro, R.J. and Lee, J.W. 2013 'A New Data Set of Educational Attainment in the World, 1950–2010'. *Journal of Developmental Economics*, 104: 184–98.

Bidani, B. and Ravallion, M. 1997 'Decomposing Social Indicators Using Distributional Data'. *Journal of Econometrics*, 77: 125–39.

Booth, H. 1984 'Transforming Gompertz's Function for Fertility Analysis: The Development of a Standard for the Relational Gompertz Function'. *Population Studies*, 38: 495–506.

Cavallo, E. and Noy, I. 2010 'The Economics of Natural Disasters: A Survey' (IDB Working Paper Series No. IDB-WP-124). Inter-American Development Bank: New York.

Chappuis, T. and Walmsley, T.L. 2011 *Projections for World CGE Model Baselines*. Center for Global Trade Analysis, Department of Agricultural Economics, Purdue University: West Lafayette, IN.

Demonsant, J.-L. and Andre, P. 2012 'Koranic Schools in Senegal: A Real Barrier to Formal Education?' (CEPS/INSTEAD Working Paper Series No. 2012-34). CEPS/INSTEAD: Esch-sur-Alzette.

Easton, P., Peach, M., Bah, I.L., Doumboula, E.B., Barry, M.L., Bayo, M.L., et al. 1997 'The Practical Applications of Koranic Learning in West Africa'. ABEL Project (1989–1994), Center for Human Capacity Development, Bureau for Global Programs, Field Research and Support, U.S. Agency for International Development: Washington, DC.

Eberstadt, N.N. 2012 'Looking Towards 2030: A New World Coming into Focus'. *Economic Affairs*, 32: 17–25.

Hegre, H., Nygård. H.M., Strand, H., Urdal, H. and Karlsen, J. 2013 'Predicting Armed Conflict, 2010–2050'. *International Studies Quarterly*, 57: 250–70.

Heuveline, P. 1999 'The Global and Regional Impact of Mortality and Fertility Transitions 1950–2000'. *Population and Development Review*, 25: 681–702.

KC, S. and Lentzner, H. 2010 'The Effect of Education on Adult Mortality and Disability: A Global Perspective'. *Vienna Yearbook of Population Research*, 8: 201–35.

KC, S. and Potančoková, M. 2013 'Differential Fertility by Level of Education in DHS Countries'. Presented at the 2013 Annual Meeting of the Population Association of America, 11–13 April 2013, New Orleans, LA, USA.

KC, S., Barakat, B., Goujon, A., Skirbekk, V., Sanderson, W.C. and Lutz, W. 2010 'Projection of Populations by Level of Educational Attainment, Age, and Sex for 120 Countries for 2005–2050'. *Demographic Research*, 22: 383–472.

Kingdon, G.G. 2007 'The Progress of School Education in India'. *Oxford Review of Economic Policy*, 23: 168–95.

Landau, R., Taylor, T. and Wright, G. (eds) 1996 *The Mosaic of Economic Growth*, 1st edn. Stanford University Press: Stanford, CA.

Lee, R. 2003 'Mortality Forecasts and Linear Life Expectancy Trends. In: Bengtsson, T. (ed.) *Perspectives on Mortality Forecasting, III. The Linear Rise in Life Expectancy: History and Prospects. Social Insurance Studies* 3, pp. 19–40. Swedish Social Insurance Agency: Stockholm.

Lutz, W. and KC, S. 2010 'Dimensions of Global Population Projections: What do we Know About Future Population Trends and Structures?' *Philosophical Transactions of the Royal Society B*, 365: 2779–91.

Lutz, W. and KC, S. 2011 'Global Human Capital: Integrating Education and Population'. *Science*, 333: 587–92.

Lutz, W., Goujon, A., KC, S. and Sanderson, W.C. 2007 'Reconstruction of Populations by Age, Sex and Level of Educational Attainment for 120 Countries for 1970–2000'. *Vienna Yearbook of Population Research*, 2007: 193–235.

Lutz, W., Crespo Cuaresma, J. and Sanderson, W. C. 2008 'The Demography of Educational Attainment and Economic Growth'. *Science*, 319: 1047–8.

Oeppen, J. 2006 'Life Expectancy Convergence Among Nations Since 1820: Separating the Effects of Technology and Income'. In: Bengtsson, T. (ed.) *Perspectives on Mortality Forecasting-III. The Linear Rise in Life Expectancy: History and Prospects*, pp. 55–82. Swedish Social Insurance Agency: Försäkringskassan.

Pichler, A. and Striessnig, E. 2013 'Differential Vulnerability to Hurricanes in Cuba, Haiti and the Dominican Republic: The Contribution of Education'. *Ecology and Society*, 18: 31

Potančoková, M., KC, S. and Goujon, A. (2014) *Global Estimates of Mean Years of Schooling: A New Methodology* (Interim Report No. IR-14-005). International Institute for Applied Systems Analysis (IIASA): Laxenburg. Available at: <http://www.iiasa.ac.at/publication/more_IR-14-005.php> (accessed 16 April 2014).

Prettner, K., Bloom, D.E. and Strulik, H. 2012 'Declining Fertility and Economic Well-being: Do Education and Health Ride to the Rescue?' (PGDA Working Paper No. 8412). Program on the Global Demography of Aging.

Striessnig, E., Lutz, W. and Patt, A.G. 2013 'Effects of Educational Attainment on Climate Risk Vulnerability'. *Ecology and Society*, 18: 16.

Torri, T. and Vaupel, J.W. 2012 'Forecasting life expectancy in an international context'. *International Journal of Forecasting*, 28: 519–31.

UNESCO 2006 *International Standard Classification of Education: ISCED 1997 (Reprint)*. UNESCO Institute for Statistics: Montreal.

UNESCO 2012 *International Standard Classification of Education, ISCED 2011*. UNESCO Institute for Statistics: Montreal.

UNESCO/UNICEF Co-operative Programme 1985 'Koranic Schools in Sudan as a Resource for UPEL: Results of a Study on Khalwas in Rahad Agricultural Project'. UNESCO-UNICEF Co-operative Programme.

United Nations 2006 *World Population Prospects: The 2006 Revision, Volume III: Analytical Report*. Department of Economic and Social Affairs, Population Division: New York.

United Nations 2011 *World Population Prospects: The 2010 Revision*. Department of Economic and Social Affairs, Population Division: New York.

Wilson, C. 2001 'On the Scale of Global Demographic Convergence 1950–2000'. *Population and Development Review*, 27: 155–71.

CHAPTER 10

THE RISE OF GLOBAL HUMAN CAPITAL AND THE END OF WORLD POPULATION GROWTH

WOLFGANG LUTZ AND SAMIR KC

10.1 How human capital improves along cohort lines

This is the first of three chapters that present the population projections by age, sex, and level of educational attainment for all countries in the world with a time horizon of 2060, and extensions to 2100. Before discussing the Wittgenstein Centre for Demography and Global Human Capital (WIC) projections, however, it is worth stepping back to consider how social structures change over time. While understanding the evolution of social structures is important under the conventional demographic approach that breaks down populations by age and sex, a more in-depth understanding of the changes in human capital requires that the interplay between different levels of schooling over time (the flow variable), and the changing educational attainment composition of the adult population (the stock variable) be taken into account.

Societies can be stratified along several dimensions. In conventional social science the divisions studied refer to social class, race, or ethnicity. Demographers routinely break down populations by age and sex. Another important demographic dimension is that of birth cohorts or generations, that is, persons born and socialized during the same historical period. Particularly during periods of rapid social change, young cohorts tend to differ from older ones in important respects, and the demographic process of generational replacement is a powerful driver of socio-economic change. This process is analytically described by the theory of 'Demographic Metabolism', recently introduced as a generalized predictive demographic theory of socio-economic change by the first author (Lutz, 2013), building on earlier work by Mannheim (1952) and Ryder (1965). Ryder, who introduced the notion of Demographic Metabolism in a qualitative way, saw it as the main force of social change. While this theory applies to many stable human characteristics that are acquired at young age and remain invariant over a lifetime, it is particularly appropriate for studying and modelling the dynamics of the change in the distributions of highest educational attainment by age and sex over time.

This perspective on human capital formation is the main focus of this book. This first of the three results chapters will highlight the results with respect to future population numbers by level of education in different parts of the world. Before presenting those results, however, we will look at one vivid example of how human capital changes along cohort/generational lines.

The Demographic Metabolism for educational attainment has been particularly dramatic in some Asian societies that, since the 1960s, have experienced a massive expansion in schooling. When the first author visited Singapore during the mid-1990s, he saw one of the world's most modern, technologically advanced societies where virtually all the young people he met were highly educated. They were acquainted with the most recent technologies, spoke like native English-speakers, had good incomes, and high aspirations. But under the surface was a second Singapore, one of elderly people who were mostly uneducated, spoke little English, and seemed rather helpless in the high tech world that swirled about them. Most also did not appear to be of high economic standing. The society seemed to be stratified into two classes, with the divisions not being along social classes (each containing people from different generations), but separated by cohort lines, the older being mostly uneducated and the younger ones highly educated.

This pattern of Singapore's society in 1995 is clearly reflected in the age and education pyramid depicted in Figure 10.1. The shadings show four levels of educational attainment for each age group, separated for men and women. It shows that, to a large degree, women older than 60 years never attended school, yet somehow managed to survive in a modern society. At the other extreme, young women, aged 25–29, were among the best educated women in the world. More than 90 per cent of them had secondary or higher education, and more than half had completed the first level of tertiary education.[1] How could it be that in the same city at the same moment in time the education structure of the young population resembled that of the most advanced Scandinavian society, whereas the education profile of the older population looked like an undeveloped country in Africa? What appears to be a puzzle, is actually understandable when considered in the context of the very rapid expansion of education in Singapore that began in the 1950s. The power of that expansion is bolstered by the fact that educational attainment tends to be achieved at young ages and, typically, remains invariant for the rest of life.

[1] As discussed in Chapter 9, throughout this book the highest educational category, which is often labelled as 'tertiary', refers to all persons with any kind of completed post-secondary education. Both labels are used interchangeably in this book.

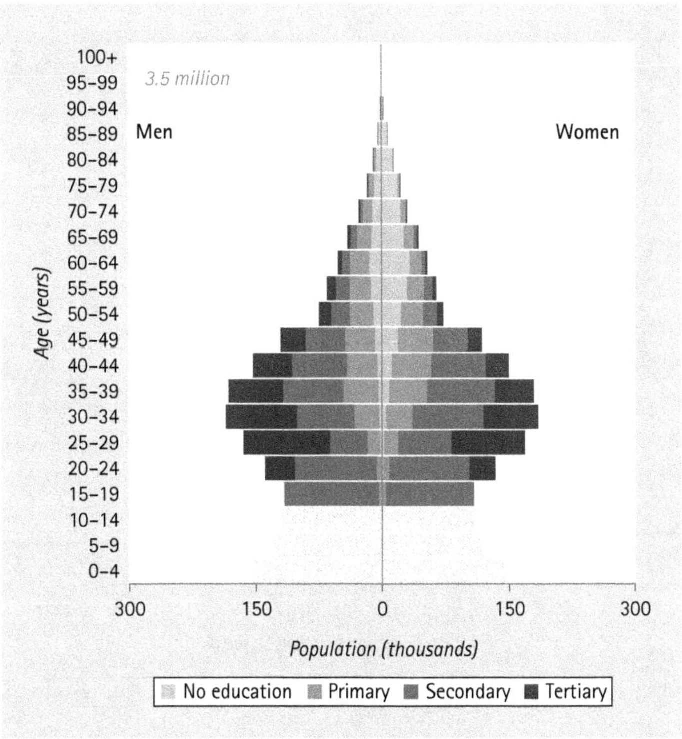

FIGURE 10.1 Education and age pyramid of Singapore in 1995.

This fact becomes evident when one looks at the reconstructed education and age pyramid of Singapore for 1970, just a few years after independence. Here we clearly see that the large majority of the female population above the age of 35 (the same cohort that was 60 years old in 1995) had never been to school. For the women older than 55, virtually none of them had ever seen a school from the inside. But Figure 10.2 also illustrates the first fruits of the massive government investment in school expansion since the late 1950s. Within 15 years of the expansion, Figure 10.2 shows that essentially all men aged 15–19 had received some education, as well as more than 90 per cent of all women in the same age group. This achievement is all the more remarkable if one considers that, owing to the very high fertility rates of the 1950s when the total fertility rate (TFR) was above 6.5, the cohorts that needed to be educated were much larger than previous ones. But education did not stop at primary or junior secondary level, continuing on to further education—mostly technical and commercial training—at the tertiary level because of the demand for skilled labour in the rapidly expanding economy.

Figure 10.2 shows that by the 1970s some men aged 20–39 had received tertiary education, while for women a comparable expansion happened a few years later. During the subsequent years, as better and better educated cohorts entered the labour market and took over the leadership in companies and public life, Singapore experienced its now-legendary rates of economic growth. The question of whether the human capital

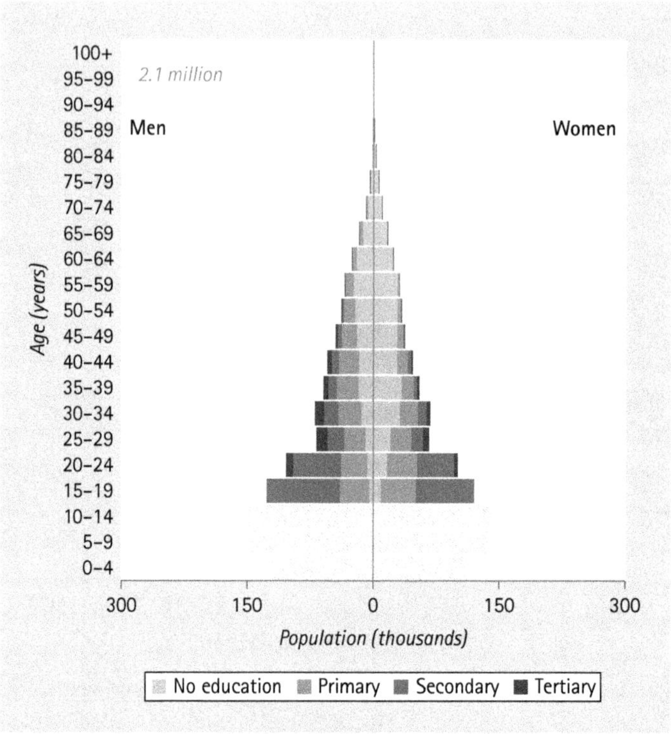

FIGURE 10.2 Education and age pyramid of Singapore in 1970.

expansion drove the economic growth, or vice versa, will be discussed in more detail in the Epilogue. Here it suffices to note that the expansion of basic education clearly came before the onset of the rapid economic growth, whereas the expansion of tertiary education occurred more or less in parallel. Furthermore, the societal improvements that happened in conjunction with the expansion of human capital were not limited to economic success. In 1983, after an intense malaria eradication programmes that lasted only seven years, Singapore was declared by the World Health Organization as being malaria-free. The disease has not reappeared—a rare success in the fight against malaria in a tropical climate.

While Figure 10.2 stepped back 25 years from the initial pyramid of 1995, Figure 10.3 steps 25 years into the future and shows the pyramid as projected for 2020. This pattern can be projected with high certainty because all of the cohorts (above the age of 15) shown in the pyramid have already been born and most have reached their highest educational attainment. The only uncertainties remaining are with respect to migration over the coming years, and the further expansion of school enrolment among the youngest cohorts. Now, 50 years after the picture shown in Figure 10.2, there remain only a very few very old people who have never attended school. In essence, everybody below the age of 50 has at least completed junior secondary education. While the achievement of post-secondary education was still a privilege for a minority among those over the

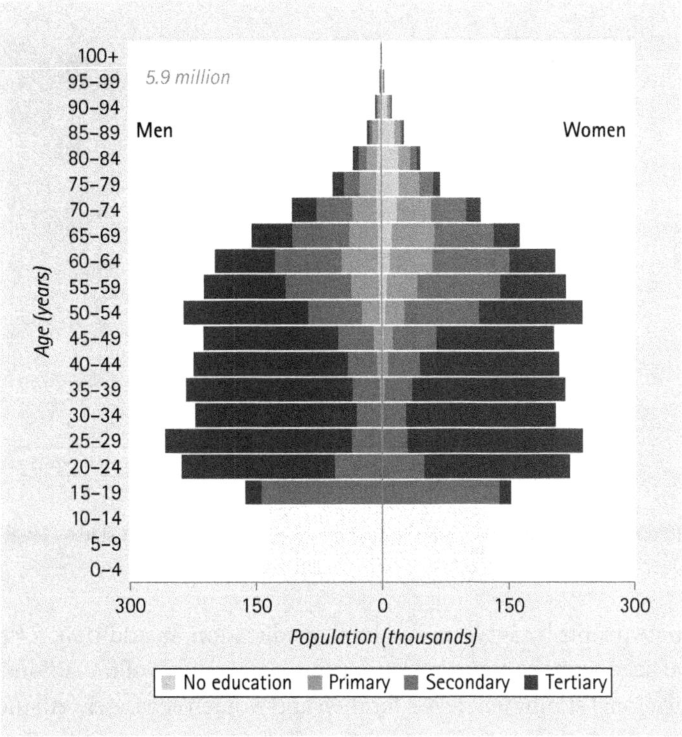

FIGURE 10.3 Education and age pyramid of Singapore as projected to 2020 under the global education trend scenario.

age of 35 in 1995, now nearly 80 per cent of the younger population has enjoyed at least some post-secondary education.

Figures 10.2 and 10.3 seem to show two very different countries, but, in fact, show the same society just 50 years apart. This transition from a largely uneducated poor society to a highly educated and rich one can be well described and modelled through the multi-dimensional cohort–component model of population dynamics. The main driver of this change is the gradual replacement of less educated older cohorts with better educated younger ones. This is a good example of Demographic Metabolism, which describes how societies change as a function of the changing composition of the population by age cohort and other important characteristics that, once achieved, tend to be sticky over the rest of the life cycle. In the case of highest educational attainment this clearly observable individual characteristic is, by definition, invariant once it has been achieved, which typically happens at younger ages. Hence, this model of cohort replacement is not only appropriate for reconstructing the educational attainment distributions by age and sex, but also for projecting them into the future.

When projecting the educational attainment distribution into the future, several assumptions must be made in addition to the earlier described process of gradual cohort replacement. We need to make assumptions about future mortality, fertility, and migration

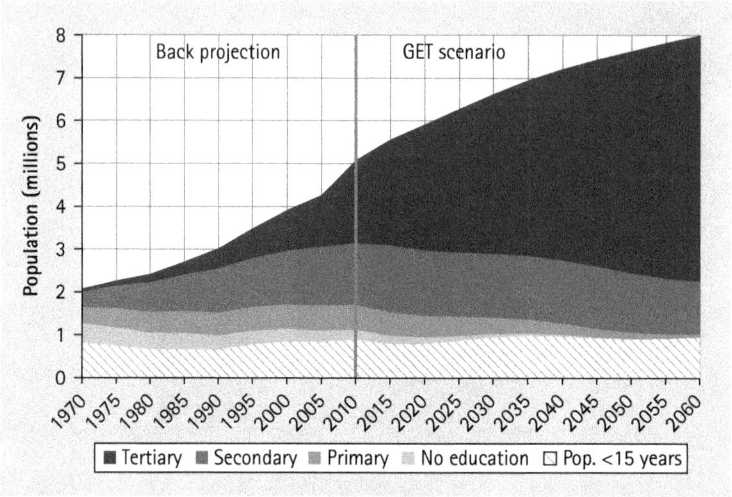

FIGURE 10.4 Reconstructed and projected trend of changing population size by level of education in Singapore over the period 1970–2060. GET: global education trend.

that differentiate people by age, sex, and level of education. In addition, for the younger age groups we need to make assumptions for the future course of transitions from lower to higher educational attainment levels for men and women separately. All these assumptions were discussed in the previous chapters. In this chapter we describe the results. Figure 10.4 gives the long-term trend as reconstructed and projected under the previously described global education trend (GET) scenario for population size by level of education for the example of Singapore for 1970–2060. The figure shows one of the most rapid expansions of human capital that has yet occurred and can hence serve as a useful benchmark for the following discussion of global human capital projections.

In this book we present a number of different scenarios reflecting different assumptions about future trends in education, fertility, mortality, and migration. These assumptions have been discussed in detail and substantively justified in Chapters 3–8. In these chapters, the main focus is on the assumptions considered as most likely based on today's knowledge. The assumptions were assessed through the extensively documented process of expert argumentation and the series of meta-expert meetings involving more than 500 population experts from around the world. The combination of these most likely fertility, mortality, migration, and education assumptions results in the medium, or most likely, scenario. This is identical to the second of the five Shared Socio-economic Pathways (SSPs) that have been agreed among major global climate change research groups. The SSPs are presented more fully in Chapter 12.

This chapter focuses on the results of combining the most likely (or medium) assumptions on future fertility, mortality, and migration with alternative assumptions about future education trends. Chapter 12 will discuss a broader range of scenarios that reflect alternative education-specific fertility, mortality, and migration assumptions and their implications for future trends in global population ageing (Chapter 11) and interactions with the changing global environment (Chapter 12). Section 10.2 of this chapter focuses on the GET scenario, as it is considered to reflect the most likely assumptions about future school enrolment and educational transitions. Section 10.3 compares these results to those of other education scenarios, in particular the constant enrolment rates (CER) and the fast track (FT) scenarios. These comparisons are carried out at the level of the world, continents, and selected bigger countries. As we explicitly consider education-specific fertility and mortality trends, these alternative education scenarios result in different sizes of the respective education groups and hence in different weights for aggregating education groups to the total population. These education scenario-induced differences in the global population outlook are the topic of section 10.4.

10.2 The medium path of future world population and human capital

The results of these WIC projections for all countries by five-year age groups, sex, and six education categories for five-year steps in time over the twenty-first century constitute such a large volume of data that any written description can hope, at best, to pick up some interesting highlights. Hence, we focus mostly on the global level, the results by continents, and some selected bigger countries from different parts of the world at different stages of demographic transition. Appendix II contains figures and tables for each country and for continents and the world. These appendix data provide standardized tables that can be compared across countries, although they cover only a miniscule fraction of the total numerical information. More extensive information is accessible in a database on the WIC website (<http://www.oeaw.ac.at/wic/>).

Figure 10.5 illustrates that in 1970 the world population stood at 3.7 billion, of whom around 1.4 billion were children below the age of 15. The remaining 2.3 billion adults were distributed roughly equally among those who never attended school, those with some primary education, and those with at least completed junior secondary school, but incomplete post-secondary education. Those with tertiary/post-secondary education are hardly visible in Figure 10.5 in 1970. There were only about 90 million persons with tertiary education in the entire world in 1970, which has increased by a factor of almost 7 to 617 million in 2010 and is likely to further increase to 3.07 billion by the end of the century. Figure 10.5 summarizes the combined processes of world population growth and increasing average educational attainment. Tables 10.1 and 10.2 will separately address these two issues.

Table 10.1 shows that according to the medium scenario (GET), which is considered most likely, the world population will increase from 6.90 billion in 2010 to 7.64 billion by 2020, and 8.29 billion by 2030.

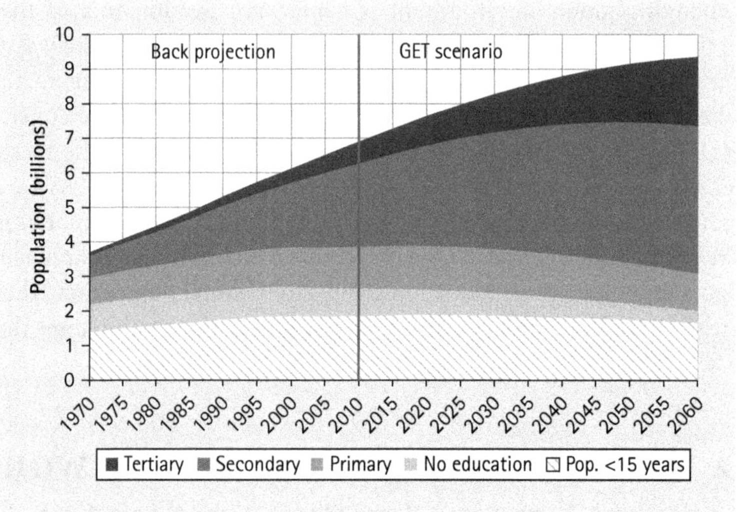

FIGURE 10.5 Reconstructed and projected trend of changing world population size by level of education 1970–2060. Most likely scenario (corresponds to Shared Socio-economic Pathway 2). GET: global education trend.

This is an increase of 1.4 billion people over the 20-year period starting in 2010. By 2050, world population growth is expected to slow, with only 0.8 billion likely to be added over this second 20-year period. Beyond 2050, the medium scenario shows a further levelling-off of world population growth, with the peak around 2070 at a level of 9.4 billion people. Over the rest of the century we expect world population to begin a slow decline, with total world population reaching a level of somewhat below 9.0 billion by 2100.

This picture of a likely end of world population growth before the end of the century reconfirms earlier population projections by Lutz et al. (2001, 2004, 2008) and Scherbov et al. (2011), who studied the end of world population growth in a probabilistic context. These studies indicate that there is a more than 80 per cent chance the world population will peak and start to decline before the end of the century. A more detailed comparison of our new scenarios by level of education to these and other recent global population projections (by age and sex) is given in section 10.2 and Box 10.1.

The breakdown of population trends by continents, which is given in the lower parts of Table 10.1, clearly indicates that most of the expected population growth over the

Table 10.1 Projections of Total Population Size for World and Continents to 2100 (Under the Most Likely Global Education Trend Scenario)

	2010	2020	2030	2040	2050	2060	2070	2080	2090	2100
Population (in millions)										
World	6,896	7,639	8,286	8,804	9,174	9,375	9,431	9,369	9,207	8,981
Africa	1,022	1,268	1,527	1,782	2,019	2,217	2,378	2,499	2,579	2,622
Asia	4,164	4,557	4,855	5,049	5,135	5,111	4,999	4,826	4,611	4,380
Europe	738	748	753	755	755	750	741	730	717	703
Latin America	590	651	702	738	758	762	754	737	712	684
N. America	345	372	400	426	447	470	491	506	516	521
Oceania	37	42	48	53	57	61	64	66	67	67

coming decades will occur in Africa and Asia. The population of Africa is expected to double from 1.02 billion in 2010 to 2.02 billion in 2050. The population of Asia is expected to increase by 1.0 billion, from 4.16 billion in 2010 to 5.14 billion in 2050. Although the expected absolute increase of 1.0 billion is practically identical for both continents, the relative increase in Asia is only 24 per cent compared with 100 per cent in Africa. Moreover, as the more detailed national analysis provided later in this section will show, most of this Asian increase is expected in Southern and Western Asia, with Eastern Asia already experiencing population decline by the middle of the century. Accordingly, for the second half of the century Africa is expected to continue its growth, albeit at a slowing rate, reaching 2.6 billion in 2100. Asia is expected to decline from a peak of 5.14 billion to about 4.4 billion. As for the other continents, North America and Oceania are expected to experience fairly slow population increases over the entire century owing primarily to continued migration gains. Europe is expected to peak in 2040–50 and Latin America in 2050–60, at about the same level of 750–760 million, and then enter a slow decline for the rest of the century. In Europe the picture is rather heterogeneous and much of the expected population increase will be due to migration, as is discussed in this section.

Box 10.1 Comparing the Wittgenstein Centre for Demography and Global Human Capital's World Population Projections to Other Recent Projections

Several groups have a tradition of producing world population projections. Some do so on a regular basis for all countries, others only occasionally and at the level of world regions. The United Nations (UN) Population Division (UNPD) has the longest tradition of producing systematic population projections, which are the most widely used global projections. The UNPD has traditionally produced three variants (high, medium, and low) based on alternative fertility assumptions while using identical mortality and migration assumptions. The time horizon of the UN assessments published every two years was 2050 with only occasional extensions to 2150 or 2300, until the 2010 assessment, which goes to 2100. Since 2010, the UN has used a different approach for defining its medium fertility assumptions and since 2012 for its medium mortality assumptions. These are now derived from a probabilistic forecasting model with the median for each country serving as the assumption of the medium variant. The high and low variants are still assumed to be 0.5 children higher and lower than the medium assumption.

Other agencies that have regularly published global-level population projections in recent years are the US Census Bureau (USCB) and the Population Reference Bureau (PRB). They present only one variant for all countries, with a time horizon to 2050. Their numbers have typically been very close to those of the UN. As described in Chapter 1, the International Institute for Applied Systems Analysis' (IIASA) World Population Program has published probabilistic world population projections at the level of world regions since 1997. The most recent such projection was published in 2008 (Lutz et al., 2008). In 2012, the Club of Rome (Randers, 2012) published a global population projection to 2052 that, although based on a simple method of trend extrapolation, received wide coverage in the international media and is, for this reason, also included in the comparison.

Figure 10.6 plots the results of nine world population projections published by these agencies over the last decade and compares them to the new Wittgenstein Centre for Demography and Global Human Capital (WIC) projections presented in this volume. To simplify matters, Figure 10.6 shows only the trajectories considered the most likely in the different projections (medium in case of the UN, median in case of IIASA's probabilistic projections, and the only ones given in case of USCB, PRB, and the Club of Rome). The plot shows the projected size of the total world population from 2010 to 2050.

While there are already minor differences in the population size assumed for 2010, Figure 10.6 shows only little divergence among the different projections until around 2030. In 2030 the spread ranges from 8.0 to 8.5 billion people. By 2050, however, the spread increases to 1.5 billion, from a low of 8.0 billion (Club of Rome) to a high of 9.6 (PRB-2012). While the projection of the Club of Rome peaks in 2040 and then starts to decline, all other projections are on an increasing trajectory up to the middle of the century. The four UN projections that have been included in this comparison show considerable variation over time. The UN long-range projections published in 2003 (and based on the 2002 revision) show the lowest trajectory, with a projected world population of 8.9 billion in 2050. The most recent UN-2012 revision gives a world population size of 9.6 billion in 2050. In comparison, the WIC projections presented in this book shows 9.2 billion for the middle of the century, which is almost exactly the middle of the two UN projections, but higher than the median of the IIASA-2008 projections, which was 8.8 billion (with an 80 per cent uncertainty range from 7.8 to 9.9 billion).

Table 10.2 compares the results of the WIC projections described in this volume to other projections that have been made with a time horizon to the end of the century. These are the UN long range projections of 2003, as well as the UN 2010 and 2012 assessments. Table 10.2 also lists the underlying total fertility rate (TFR) assumptions that are the main driver of the differences among projections. This illustrates that the UN long-range projections of 2003 and the WIC projections come out lower than the two most recent UN assessments primarily because of their differing assumptions about longer-term fertility levels. But there are also effects of differing baseline data. Without space to compare the fertility assumptions in any detail, we only highlight that the three main reasons for these sizable differences lie in the long-term fertility levels for current low fertility countries (where

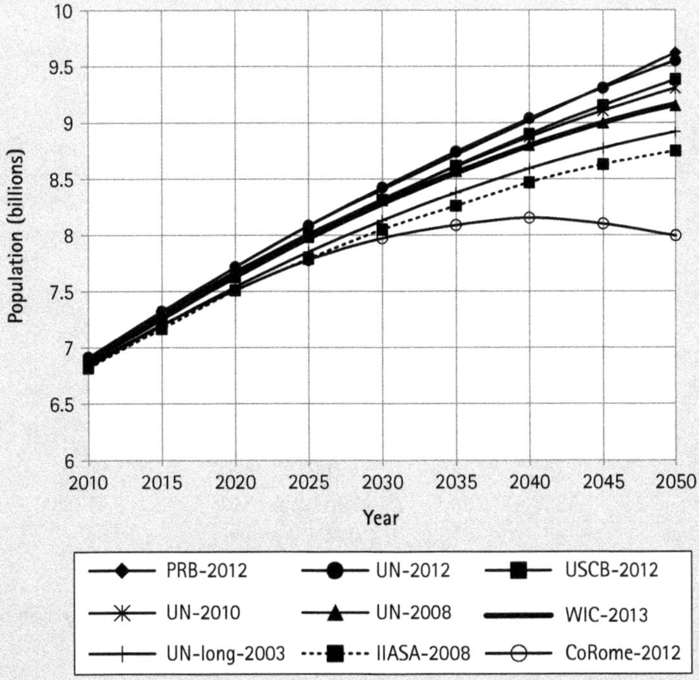

FIGURE 10.6 Comparison of different world population projections published over the last decade with a time horizon to 2050. PRB: Population Reference Bureau; UN: United Nations; USCB: US Census Bureau; WIC: Wittgenstein Centre for Demography and Global Human Capital; IIASA: International Institute for Applied Systems Analysis; CoRome: Club of Rome.

(continued)

Box 10.1 Continued

WIC assumes very long-term convergence around a TFR of 1.75, while for UN-2010 it is 2.1), a lower fertility level for China currently and in the near term future (which, because of the high weight of China, makes a significant global level difference), and in the assumed future speed of decline (as well as, in some cases, current fertility levels) in major African countries.

To illustrate the latter point, Table 10.2 details the fertility assumptions and projected population sizes for Nigeria. Nigeria is not only a big country but also very problematic in terms of population statistics, with experts holding very different views about current fertility and mortality levels and even more so about likely future trends. As described in Chapter 4 the experts involved in defining the WIC projections discussed Nigeria at length, with the resulting baseline estimates and assumptions being lower than those assumed by UN-2012 and more similar to those of UN-2010. The most recent data from the Nigeria Demographic and Health Survey 2013 (which became available in Spring 2014 after the completion of the projections) give a TFR of 5.5 for the three years preceding the survey, which is directly in line with the WIC assumptions.

Table 10.2 Assumptions and Results of Different Medium Projections for Nigeria

	Population (millions)			Total fertility rate (period)		
World	2010	2050	2100	2005–10	2045–50	2095–2100
WPP2012	6,916	9,551	10,854	2.53	2.24	1.99
WPP2010	6,896	9,306	10,125	2.52	2.17	2.03
UN-Long Range	6,830	8,919	9,064	2.50	1.96	1.92
WIC	6,896	9,162	8,963	2.52	2.00	1.68
Nigeria						
WPP2012	160	440	914	6.00	3.79	2.18
WPP2010	158	390	730	5.61	3.41	2.20
UN-Long Range	146	258	302	4.31	2.05	1.85
WIC	158	371	576	5.61	3.46	1.87

WPP: World Population Prospects; UN: United Nations; WIC: Wittgenstein Centre for Demography and Global Human Capital.

Table 10.3 Changes in Educational Attainment of the Future Population of the World and the Continents by Age and Sex for the Period 2010–60 und the Mostly Likely (Global Education Trend) Scenario

		Proportion 25+ (%)				Proportion (%)	Mean years of schooling		
Region	Year	No education	Primary	Secondary	Tertiary	ALS 20–39	25 +	25–29	60–64
Men									
World	2010	13	25	47	15	7	9.8	10.8	9.0
World	2030	8	19	53	19	77	11.0	12.0	10.2
World	2060	4	13	54	28	87	12.7	13.8	12.1
Africa	2010	31	31	30	8	47	7.0	8.4	4.7
Africa	2030	19	29	41	11	58	9.1	10.0	7.5
Africa	2060	8	24	50	18	74	11.5	12.3	10.3
Asia	2010	14	27	46	12	71	9.0	10.5	7.7
Asia	2030	9	20	53	18	79	10.5	11.9	9.5
Asia	2060	4	13	55	28	90	12.4	14.0	11.8
Europe	2010	1	11	66	22	96	13.2	14.0	12.8
Europe	2030	0	6	67	27	98	14.1	14.8	13.6
Europe	2060	0	2	58	40	99	15.1	15.5	15.1
LAC	2010	8	39	39	13	65	9.3	10.9	7.6
LAC	2030	4	28	49	18	80	11.1	12.7	9.8
LAC	2060	1	16	55	29	93	13.1	14.7	12.6
N. America	2010	1	5	56	38	96	14.9	15.0	15.1
N. America	2030	0	3	54	43	98	15.2	15.4	15.1
N. America	2060	0	1	46	53	99	15.7	15.9	15.6
Oceania	2010	2	14	55	29	88	13.8	15.2	13.1
Oceania	2030	1	9	55	35	90	14.8	15.7	13.9
Oceania	2060	0	6	48	46	95	15.7	16.0	15.7
Women									
World	2010	22	25	39	13	65	8.5	10.2	7.3
World	2030	14	21	46	19	75	10.3	11.9	8.9
World	2060	6	14	51	28	87	12.4	13.7	11.9
Africa	2010	48	26	21	5	37	4.9	6.9	2.1
Africa	2030	28	28	34	9	54	7.7	9.5	5.0
Africa	2060	11	24	48	17	74	11.1	12.3	9.7
Asia	2010	27	28	35	9	63	7.3	9.7	5.4
Asia	2030	16	23	46	15	76	9.4	11.8	7.8
Asia	2060	7	14	53	27	90	12.0	14.0	11.4
Europe	2010	1	14	63	22	97	12.7	14.5	12.1
Europe	2030	1	7	62	30	98	14.0	15.2	13.7
Europe	2060	0	2	55	43	99	15.1	15.5	15.3
LAC	2010	10	38	38	15	69	9.2	11.4	7.0

(*continued*)

Table 10.3 Continued

		Proportion 25+ (%)				Proportion (%)	Mean years of schooling		
Region	Year	No education	Primary	Secondary	Tertiary	ALS 20–39	25 +	25–29	60–64
LAC	2030	5	27	47	21	83	11.2	13.2	9.9
LAC	2060	1	15	52	31	93	13.2	14.7	13.0
N. America	2010	1	5	57	38	97	14.9	15.3	14.9
N. America	2030	0	2	50	47	99	15.4	15.6	15.3
N. America	2060	0	1	42	57	99	15.7	15.9	15.7
Oceania	2010	3	18	48	31	89	13.4	15.4	12.3
Oceania	2030	2	11	48	40	91	14.7	15.8	13.9
Oceania	2060	1	6	44	50	95	15.7	16.0	15.9

ALS: at least lower secondary completed; LAC: Latin America and Caribbean.

As depicted in Figure 10.5, the world population, in addition to growing by more than two billion, is also expected to experience a marked increase in average human capital over the coming half century. This increase is clearly more pronounced for women than for men. Because of these important gender differences, Table 10.3 provides the educational attainment information separately for men and women. Here, as in the rest of this book, the detailed projections for age, sex, and education are only tabulated for the 50-year period up to 2060 because they are more sensitive to specific assumptions and therefore more uncertain in the very long term than projections of the aggregate population.[2]

Table 10.3 shows that in 2010 about 13 per cent of adult men (above the age of 25) were without any formal education, while among women the proportion was about 22 per cent. This situation is expected to improve significantly over the next five decades so that under the GET scenario in 2060, only 6 per cent (1 out of 17) of adult women will have never been to school. This major improvement is a result of both the improving school enrolment rates assumed under this scenario, and of the fact that in virtually every country in the world young women today are already better educated than older ones. The better educated women will, over the years, move up the age pyramid and replace the less educated cohorts, reflecting the Demographic Metabolism, as described earlier for Singapore. A comparison to the CER scenario (see Table 10.6) helps to quantify this aspect. Under the GET scenario the female proportion without education declines from 22 per cent in 2010 to 14 per cent in 2030, while the decline under the CER scenario is

[2] Although the specific results are not given here, the scenarios had to be extended by level of education up to the end of the century in order to produce consistent time series of results at the aggregate population level.

only to 17 per cent. Hence, in the next two decades more than half of this change (five of the eight percentage points of decline) will be due to the momentum in educational change that is already embedded in today's age structure of education. In the longer term, however, this momentum results in only slight improvement: by 2060 the female proportion without education declines only marginally to 16 per cent under the CER scenario compared with 6 per cent under GET. Thus, in the longer run it is clear that the expected future expansion of education makes the most difference.

Table 10.3 makes clear that Africa is the laggard in terms of education. In Africa in 2010 almost half of all adult women (48 per cent, see lower part of Table 10.3) had never been to school. But the data also show that there has been recent progress in expanding education, so that even in Africa women aged 30–34 tend to be better educated than older ones, with, on average, 5.8 years of education compared with 2.1 years for older women. Hence, even in the hypothetical case of no further increases in enrolment (CER scenario), the overall proportion of women without schooling is pre-programmed to decline from the current 48 per cent to, at the slowest, 36 per cent by 2030 and 31 per cent by 2050 (see Table 10.6). Under the more likely assumption of a continuation of the school expansion trend (GET scenario), this proportion will fall to 28 per cent in 2030 and only 10 per cent in 2060. In terms of mean years of schooling (MYS) under this scenario, younger women in Africa are expected to see a marked increase to 11.1 years by 2060, which is higher than the level among younger women in Latin America or the world average today. The relative increase in MYS will be most dramatic for elderly African women, increasing by a factor of more than 4 from currently 2.1 to 8.6 years of schooling in 2060. In Asia the average education of women aged 60–64 will also more than double from 4.6 years to 9.9 years in 2060. This increase is due to the recent expansion of education among younger women.

African adult men are only slightly better educated than African adult women today. Table 10.3 shows that their educational attainment is uniformly distributed (30–31 per cent each) over the three education categories: no education, some primary education, and completed junior secondary education. Eight per cent of African men have some post-secondary education, while only 5 per cent of women have such education. In the coming decades the education of African men is expected to increase significantly, with the proportion of men without formal education declining from 31 per cent in 2010 to 19 per cent in 2030, and only 8 per cent in 2050. The proportion with post-secondary education increases from 8 per cent to 18 per cent over the next half century under the likely GET scenario. As a consequence, the MYS of men aged 30–34 is likely to increase from 7.3 years to 11.1 years by 2060, while that of men aged 60–64 will more than double from 4.3 to 9.2 years. This is slightly above the average level of education that younger Asian men have today (8.7 MYS). Viewed across all age groups the average education of adult African men (above the age of 25) in 2030 (8.1 MYS) will be slightly higher than that of Asian men today (on average, 7.8 years of schooling). At the level of entire continents this shows that Africa is about two decades behind the average of Asia in the development of its human capital. This is also apparent in comparisons of the following education pyramids.

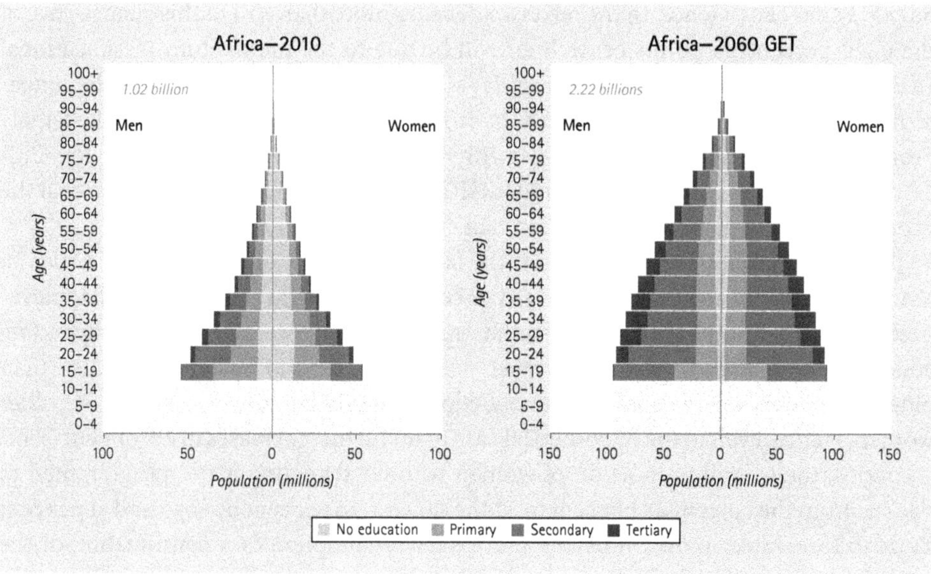

FIGURE 10.7 Age and education pyramids for Africa in 2010 and projected to 2060 under the most likely global education trend (GET) scenario.

The age and education pyramid for Africa (Figure 10.7) still shows the shape of a pyramid, with each successive cohort being larger than the previous one—a consequence of the continuing high level of fertility that averages just slightly below five children per woman. The total population of Africa in 2010 was about 1 billion people, with about 40 per cent children below the age of 15 years and only 3 per cent above the age of 65. The picture also illustrates the significant progress in education that has been described numerically. While the vast majority of the elderly population are without any formal education, the majority of the younger generations have already received some schooling. The graph also illustrates that female education lags behind male education, although the gap has been narrowing recently. The graph also shows that despite the rapid population growth, the education system in Africa managed to significantly expand school enrolment in most countries over the last two decades. This past achievement lays the groundwork for future human capital in Africa. The right hand-side of Figure 10.7 shows the age and education pyramid under the most likely GET scenario for 2060. Although population size will have increased by a factor of more than 2, to 2.2 billion, the number of Africans without any formal education will have significantly declined, with most of the uneducated concentrated in the older age groups. As a consequence of the expected fertility decline, the largest age groups will shift from children to young adults. Under this scenario, the vast majority of Africans of working age will have junior secondary or higher education. Given the positive consequences of education, this is, indeed, a rather optimistic outlook for Africa.

In Asia (Figure 10.8), by far the most populous continent with about 4.2 billion inhabitants, the population pyramid has already significantly deviated from its traditional

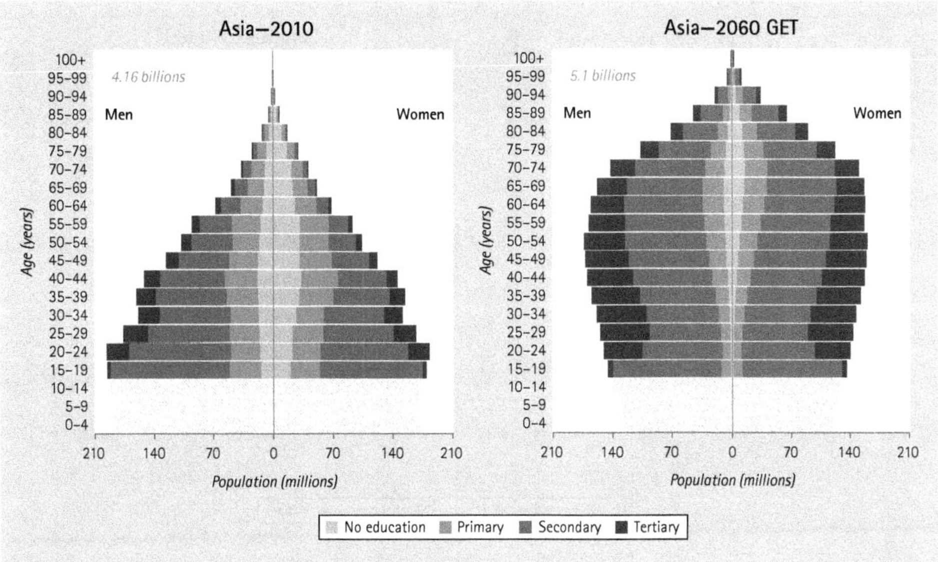

FIGURE 10.8 Age and education pyramids for Asia in 2010 and projected to 2060 under the most likely global education trend (GET) scenario.

pyramid shape. This is mostly owing to the very strong recent fertility decline in China. As consequence, currently the largest age group is that of 20–24-year-old men and women. And, as the shadings in Figure 10.8 indicate, these young adults are already reasonably well educated, with more than three quarters having received junior secondary or higher education. Figure 10.8 also shows that women lag behind men in their education, a pattern that is greatly influenced by the Indian situation, as discussed later in this section. By 2060, under the GET scenario, the Asian education pyramid is likely to look rather similar to that of Europe today, with the biggest age group being about 50–54, featuring very high education levels among the working age population.

The pyramid for Europe (extending from Portugal to Russia) shows that Europe is the oldest continent today in terms of age structure (Figure 10.9). Owing to the decline of fertility to very low levels in recent decades, the base of the pyramid has become much smaller than the middle section. The pyramid also shows that there are many more elderly women than men in Europe, which results from gender differences in life expectancy, and, to a minor extent, from World War II for the oldest cohorts. As is the case on every other continent, younger cohorts in Europe are, on average, better educated than older ones. Among those below the age of 35, women are better educated than men. This is an interesting reversal of traditional gender differences in education. Table 10.3 shows that MYS among women aged 60–64 in Europe (10.3 years) is lower than that of men (10.9 years). For women aged 30–34 schooling is higher (12.2 years) than for men of the same age group (11.8 years). Over the coming half century the average educational attainment among Europeans is expected to continue to increase under this likely GET scenario to more than 14 average years of schooling, while total population size will stay

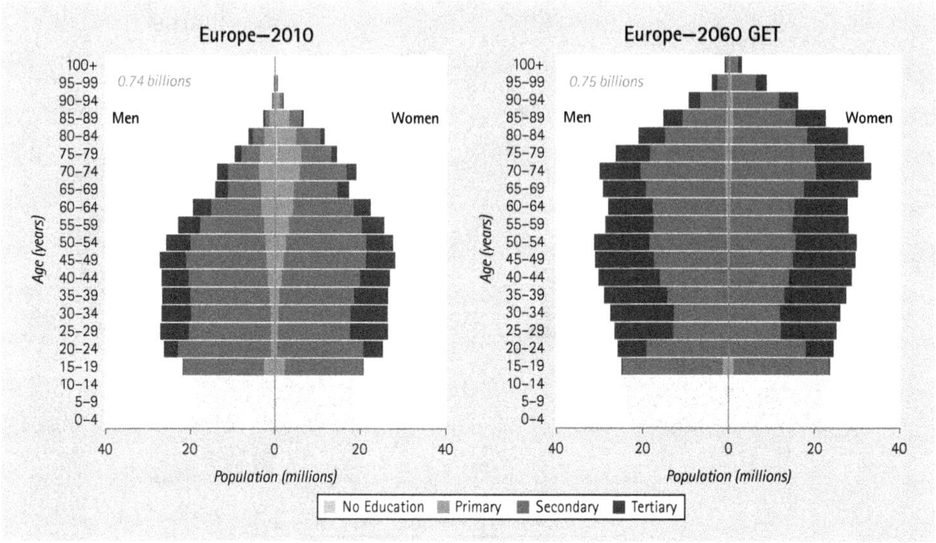

FIGURE 10.9 Age and education pyramids for Europe in 2010 and projected to 2060 under the most likely global education trend (GET) scenario.

about the same or increase slightly from 738 million to 750 million. At the same time, the proportion of the elderly will be increasing significantly. It is important to note that the elderly of the future will be much better educated than the elderly today, which may have important positive implications for their health, cognitive functioning, and ability to continue contributing to society.

It is worth noting that in all tables in this chapter that list MYS for different age groups there is an interesting pattern appearing in the case of several low fertility countries and continents. By the middle of the century MYS 25+ (i.e. the MYS for the entire population above the age of 25) can turn out to be lower than those for the elderly age group 60–64. This may seem strange, particularly under the assumption of rapid education expansion among the younger cohorts. The reason, however, lies in the fact that in those countries the proportion of elderly above the age of 65 is already very significant and their on average much lower level of education depresses the MYS 25+. This fact also cautions against the uncritical use of this indicator (MYS 25+), which, among economists, is by far the most often used human capital indicator. The patterns derived from age-specific education indicators can hence be quite different than those derived from MYS 25+, which also includes the very old cohorts who tend to have much lower education and typically no longer contribute to economic productivity. The implications of these different indicators for the assessment of the contribution of human capital to economic growth will be further discussed in the Epilogue.

Because the earlier described patterns for entire continents tend to mask significant differentials among countries in those continents, the following discussion focuses on describing the results for a set of 14 selected bigger countries from different parts of the world. The corresponding data for all 171 countries for which education-specific projections could be carried out are in the country-specific appendix tables (Appendix II) at the end of the book.

Among the 14 selected countries listed in Table 10.4, very different trends in future population size during the twenty-first century are visible: China, Germany, Russia, and South Korea are on a clearly declining trajectory; Egypt, India, Kenya, Nigeria, and the USA are on a clearly increasing trajectory; Indonesia, Iran, South Africa, and Spain have only minor changes in population size. This surprising grouping of countries is the consequence of different starting conditions combined with different assumed trajectories in fertility, migration, and—particularly in the case of South Africa—mortality. Spain is not shrinking despite very low fertility owing to high assumed migration. Migration is also the main reason for the expected 50 per cent increase in the US population over the course of this century.

Table 10.4 also includes the two population billionaires—China and India. Although the current population of China is more numerous than that of India, by 2020 India will have surpassed China and reached a total population of 1.385 billion. The trajectories of these countries are projected to continue diverging, with India continuing to grow to a peak population of around 1.75 billion in about 2060, and then experiencing a moderate decline resulting in 1.6 billion by the end of the century. China, under this scenario, will start declining in the 2020s, with the decline accelerating during the second half of the century and population size falling to 0.75 billion, only a bit more than half of its peak population size. These very different trajectories in total population size are associated with, and are in part the consequence of, very different levels of human capital.

Table 10.4 Trends in Total Population Size 2010–2100 for 14 Selected Bigger Countries According to the Most Likely Global Education Trend Scenario

	2010	2020	2030	2040	2050	2060	2070	2080	2090	2100
Population (in millions)										
Brazil	195	211	223	231	233	230	223	212	201	189
China	1,341	1,379	1,378	1,334	1,255	1,154	1,045	939	839	754
Egypt	81	95	107	118	126	133	136	137	136	134
Germany	82	82	81	80	79	77	75	73	71	69
India	1,225	1,385	1,521	1,632	1,715	1,755	1,752	1,716	1,652	1,569
Indonesia	240	261	276	285	285	280	269	255	240	225
Iran	74	84	90	95	98	98	95	91	86	81
Kenya	41	51	61	71	80	87	92	96	98	98
Nigeria	158	202	253	310	371	425	475	517	550	576
Russia	143	142	138	135	132	129	126	122	119	115
South Africa	50	55	59	61	63	64	64	63	61	59
South Korea	48	50	50	49	46	43	39	36	33	30
Spain	46	48	49	51	52	52	51	50	49	47
USA	310	334	359	381	400	420	438	452	461	466

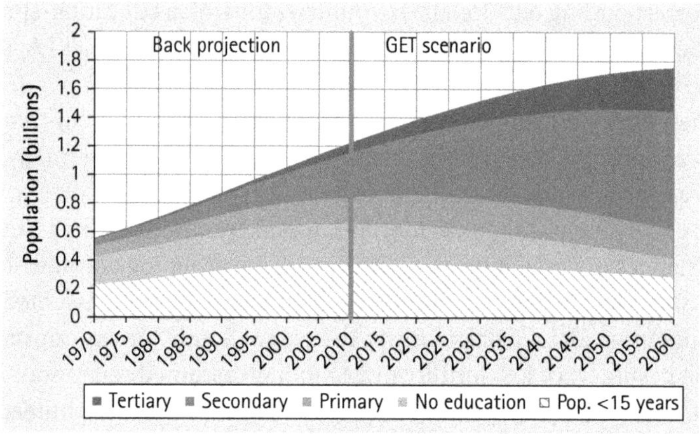

FIGURE 10.10 Line chart of population by educational attainment 1970–2060 for India as reconstructed and projected under the global education trend (GET) scenario.

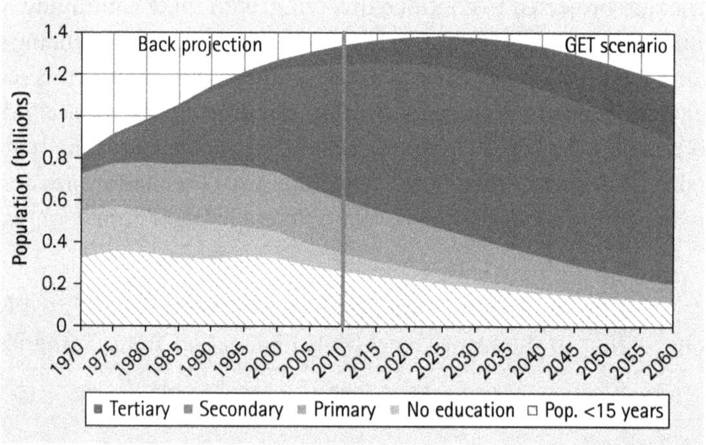

FIGURE 10.11 Line chart of population by educational attainment 1970–2060 for China as reconstructed and projected under the global education trend (GET) scenario.

Figures 10.10 and 10.11 illustrate the differences in educational attainment trends in India and China. In the 1970s, China had only a minor advantage over India in the educational attainment of its adult population. But during the 1980s and 1990s China massively invested in near-universal basic education of its young population, while India's educational investments focused on narrow elites, leaving about half of the adult population without any formal schooling. As a consequence of this educational inequality, China and India both have about 6 per cent of their female populations with tertiary education, while the MYS of the entire female adult population is only 4.2 years in India compared with 6.8 in China. By 2010, 51 per cent of Indian women above the age of 25 were without any formal education, while in China this proportion had declined to only 15 per cent (see Table 10.5). Under the likely GET scenario, India will need 40–50 years to reach a similarly low level of uneducated adult women. Hence, in terms of universal basic education, India lags about four decades behind China, despite recent efforts by the Indian government to increase school enrolments.

Among the countries listed in Table 10.5, Egypt has the most polarized education distribution. Although half (49 per cent) of all adult women aged 25 and above are without any formal education, 42 per cent have secondary or higher education. The middle group of women with primary education is only 8 per cent. This clearly shows the great division in Egyptian society. It also illustrates why looking at the MYS alone is not enough because this aggregate indicator hides the distribution and the associated inequality. In Table 10.5, Nigeria (49 per cent) and India (51 per cent) have similarly high proportions of women without any formal education, but they also have significantly lower proportions of women with secondary or tertiary education. As a consequence, the mean years of education of all adult women in Egypt currently lies at 5.7 years compared with 4.8 years in Nigeria and only 4.2 years in India. Another summary indicator of educational attainment that captures the distributional aspect better than years of schooling is also listed in Table 10.5: the proportion of women with secondary or higher education among all women. Here this proportion is given for women of main reproductive age (20–39 years) whose education is most important for a country's fertility level. While Nigeria and India have only 42 and 45 per cent of younger women in this higher education category, Egypt has already achieved 67 per cent of younger women with at least secondary education. These recent improvements in female education can also be seen by comparing the last two columns of Table 10.5. Women aged 30–34 in Egypt today have, on average, 7.8 years of schooling, which is almost three times that of women aged 60–64 (2.7 MYS). Hence, the data for 2010 show a complex pattern for female education in Egypt: in a context of very high inequality in the education distribution, Egypt has recently seen significant improvements in average education of women, which tend to diminish the inequalities. This is seen in more detail in the education pyramids for 2010 and 2060 (Figure 10.12).

Nigeria is one of the most rapidly growing countries in the world. In 1950 it had 38 million inhabitants, far fewer than Italy and similar countries. During the last 60 years its population has already more than quadrupled, to 158 million in 2010, and is expected to surpass the USA in population size by about 2050 and further increase to about 720 million by the end of the century. This will not be far below the 830 million projected for China for 2100, resulting in Nigeria likely becoming the third most populous country in the world, just behind India and China. But whether this expected phenomenal growth in population size will also be associated with a major increase in its economic muscle globally or instead result in disastrous overpopulation will be very much dependent on its human capital development. As shown in Figure 10.13, our most likely GET scenario does, indeed, suggest that average educational attainment would increase substantially with, for example, the MYS of adult women increasing from 4.8 years

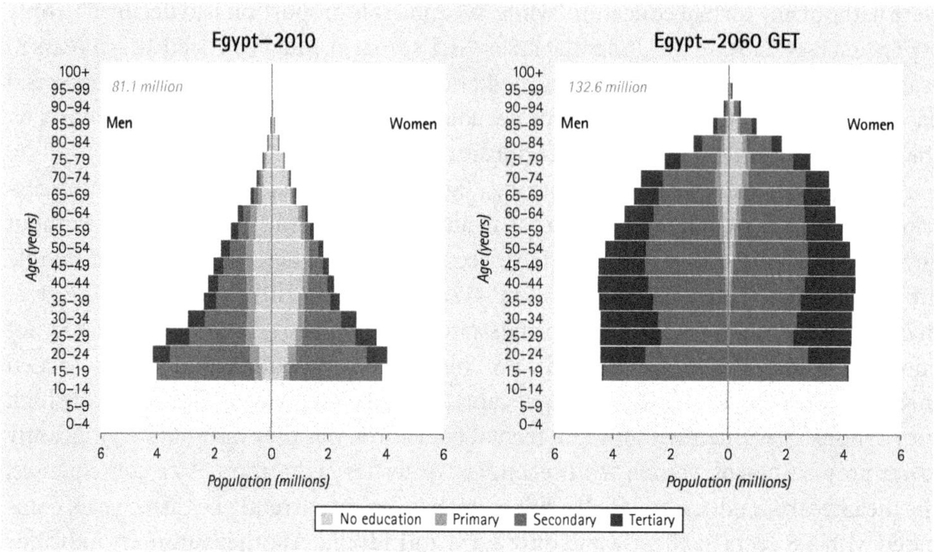

FIGURE 10.12 Age and education pyramids for Egypt in 2010 and projected to 2060 under the most likely global education trend (GET) scenario.

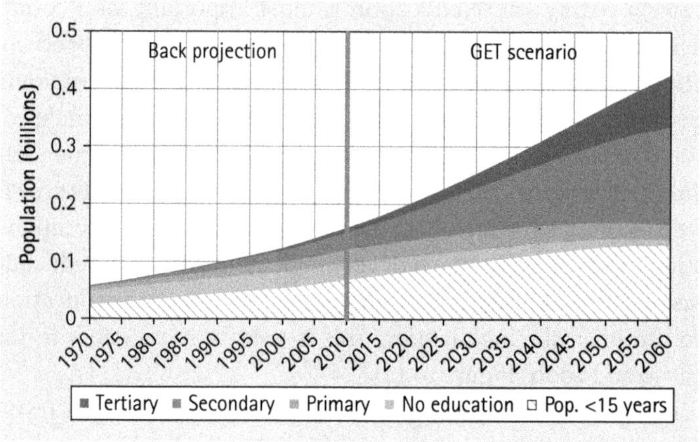

FIGURE 10.13 Line chart of population by educational attainment 1970–2060 for Nigeria as reconstructed and projected under the global education trend (GET) scenario.

today to 12.3 years by 2060. The possible effects of alternative education scenarios are discussed in the section 10.3.

In contrast to these two African countries, South Korea has, like Singapore, seen one of the most impressive expansions of educational attainment in human history. Today, 100 per cent of young South Korean women have achieved secondary or higher education levels. Only in the elderly cohorts are there still women with lower levels of education. The improvements still possible for the future relate to the proportions of the population with tertiary education. Currently, 30 per cent of adult women in Korea have tertiary

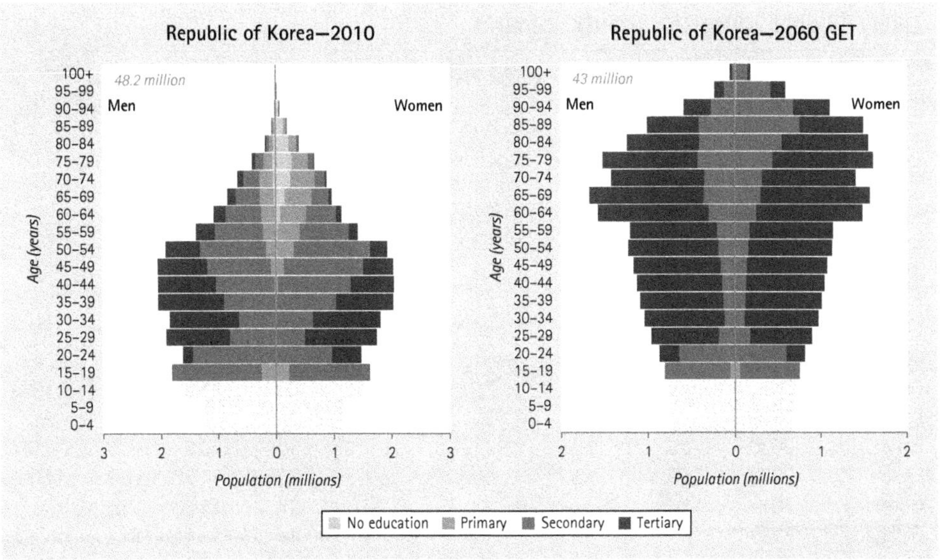

FIGURE 10.14 Age and education pyramids for South Korea in 2010 and projected to 2060 under the most likely global education trend (GET) scenario.

education, a proportion that is expected to increase to 72 per cent by 2060. But, in part because of the phenomenal expansion of female education, the associated lower level of fertility results in significant population ageing and decline over the course of the century. This is apparent in the pyramids in Figure 10.14 as from Table 10.4, which shows that the total population of South Korea is likely to decrease from 50 to about 30 million by the end of the century. This very low fertility results in significant population ageing as is described in the Chapter 11. The right-hand side of Figure 10.14 dramatically illustrates that South Korea in 2060 will be much older, but much better educated. Hence, a key question for Korea and many other highly educated, low fertility countries is whether higher human capital can compensate in economic terms for the smaller size of the younger labour force. This topic is explored in the Epilogue.

This section presents the results for the mostly likely, or medium, scenario that combines medium fertility, mortality, and migration assumptions with the most likely education scenario (the GET scenario). As the title of this chapter indicates, however, the most important trend in the coming decades is likely to be significant improvements in human capital in virtually all countries of the world. That trend is already embedded in today's educational attainment distributions by age cohorts. In addition, we are likely to experience an end of world population growth during the second half of the century. Owing to the momentum of population growth and high fertility rates in parts of South Asia and sub-Saharan Africa, world population is still likely to increase by slightly more than 2 billion. But this increase will slowly level off so that by the end of the century world population will, under this scenario, already have declined to around 9 billion after having reached a peak of about 9.4 billion in 2060–70.

Table 10.5 Changes in Educational Attainment of the Future Female Population for Selected Countries by Age and Sex for the Period 2010–60 Under the Most Likely (Global Education Trend) Scenario

		Proportion 25+ (%)				Proportion (%)	Mean years of schooling		
Country	Year	No education	Primary	Secondary	Tertiary	ALS 20–39	25 +	25–29	60–64
Brazil	2010	11	37	40	13	71	8.5	11.0	6.1
Brazil	2030	5	26	52	17	86	10.4	12.6	9.0
Brazil	2060	2	14	61	23	95	12.3	14.0	12.3
China	2010	15	30	48	6	83	8.0	10.8	5.7
China	2030	5	22	61	13	91	9.9	12.2	8.8
China	2060	1	10	65	25	96	11.9	13.8	11.9
Egypt	2010	49	8	30	12	67	6.5	10.8	2.9
Egypt	2030	26	7	47	20	90	10.5	14.5	6.5
Egypt	2060	7	3	56	34	99	14.2	15.8	14.0
Germany	2010	1	3	71	25	97	15.5	16.6	15.1
Germany	2030	1	2	60	37	99	16.4	17.3	16.4
Germany	2060	0	1	45	53	100	17.3	17.7	17.4
India	2010	51	20	22	6	45	4.8	7.9	2.6
India	2030	32	20	36	11	67	7.8	11.1	4.5
India	2060	13	15	51	21	89	11.4	14.3	10.5
Indonesia	2010	13	47	33	7	62	8.6	11.2	5.3
Indonesia	2030	5	34	49	13	83	11.0	13.5	9.3
Indonesia	2060	1	16	60	24	95	13.5	15.2	13.2
Iran	2010	29	28	32	11	67	7.4	11.4	2.5
Iran	2030	13	23	44	19	87	10.5	14.0	6.9
Iran	2060	3	13	50	34	97	13.5	15.4	13.7
Kenya	2010	21	32	44	3	67	7.6	9.9	2.6
Kenya	2030	6	19	69	5	88	10.9	12.0	8.1
Kenya	2060	1	6	81	12	98	13.7	13.3	12.8
Nigeria	2010	49	24	18	8	42	5.4	7.8	2.0
Nigeria	2030	25	19	37	18	73	9.6	12.2	6.0
Nigeria	2060	6	8	49	38	95	14.0	15.1	12.2
South Korea	2010	7	16	47	30	100	12.7	16.0	10.0
South Korea	2030	2	8	42	48	100	14.6	16.1	15.3
South Korea	2060	0	0	27	73	100	15.9	16.1	16.1
Russia	2010	0	5	73	22	100	12.7	14.0	12.7
Russia	2030	0	1	72	27	100	13.8	14.4	13.2
Russia	2060	0	0	66	33	100	14.5	14.5	14.7
South Africa	2010	10	28	56	5	83	9.5	11.5	6.9
South Africa	2030	4	16	73	7	92	11.3	12.3	10.3
South Africa	2060	0	6	84	10	97	12.8	13.1	12.4
Spain	2010	2	31	46	21	93	10.3	13.5	8.7
Spain	2030	1	16	51	33	97	12.3	14.5	12.0
Spain	2060	0	5	46	50	99	14.0	14.8	14.5
USA	2010	1	4	59	36	97	14.9	15.3	15.0
USA	2030	0	3	53	45	99	15.3	15.6	15.2
USA	2060	0	1	44	54	99	15.7	15.8	15.7

ALS: at least lower secondary.

In section 10.3 we go beyond the most likely GET scenario to study the consequences of alternative education assumptions, while still maintaining the medium fertility, mortality, and migration assumptions. These different education scenarios have a large impact beyond educational distributions, resulting in different trends in total population size and age structure.

10.3 Alternative education scenarios

So far we have only discussed the results of education assumptions following the GET scenario. Now we turn to the CER and FT scenarios. The CER is a useful benchmark scenario that allows us to understand how much of the expected future increase in human capital is a consequence of the momentum already embedded in today's cross-cohort improvements in education. When assuming constant future enrolment rates we essentially freeze the transitions from lower to higher levels of education at their current levels, which results in a constant distribution of the members of younger cohorts over the educational attainment categories. But as older cohorts still have different (and typically lower) levels of education, the process of demographic metabolism in which the less educated older cohorts are successively replaced by the better educated younger ones means that even under this CER scenario, the average educational attainment of the entire adult population will continue to improve for decades. This is the momentum of educational improvement that can be quantified with reference to this CER scenario.

The FT scenario depicts the fastest possible expansion scenario and makes explicit reference to a specific country that, at a certain given level of education, has been the best performing of all countries. Hence, although for any given country in, for example, Africa, it may be unlikely that over the coming five years the school enrolment rates will expand at a rate similar to the unprecedented expansion in South Korea in the 1960s, it is at least theoretically possible because it has actually occurred in the historical experience of at least one country. The 'fast track' name of this scenario is derived from the Fast Track Initiative of the World Bank, launched in 2002, which has recently made major investments in educational expansion at the fastest possible rate for a small number of least developed countries.

Tables 10.6 and 10.7 give the same information as Table 10.3, but on the basis of the CER and FT scenarios. Again, this is first shown for the world and the continents and then for sets of selected countries. Figure 10.15 shows four age and education pyramids for the world: the empirical pyramid as given for 2030, the projected pyramid under the most likely GET scenario, and then the pyramids resulting from the alternative scenarios FT and CER.

The comparison between the results of the FT and CER scenarios by 2060 shows two very different worlds. The only thing these two pictures have in common is that in both cases the world population will be bigger and older than it is today. Otherwise the

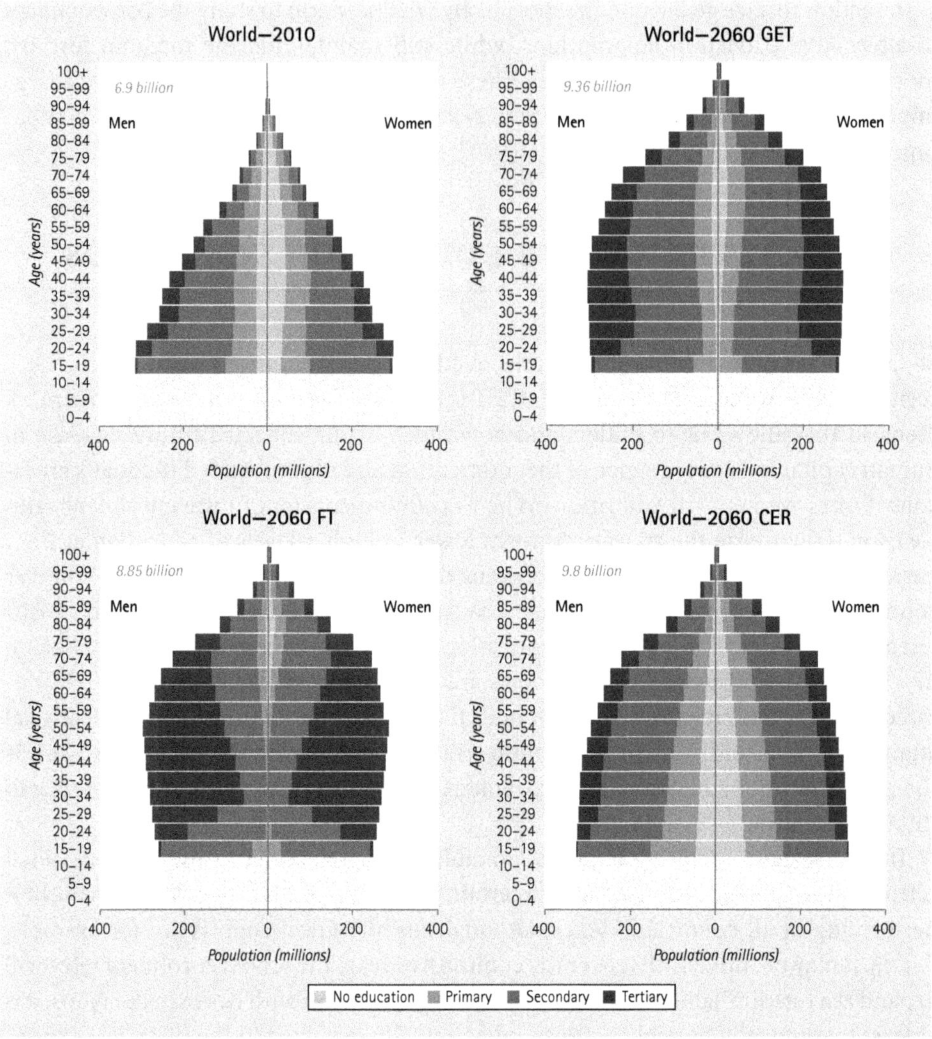

FIGURE 10.15 Age and education pyramids for the world in 2010 and projected to 2060 under the global education trend (GET), fast track (FT), and constant enrolment rate (CER) scenarios.

assumption of constant school enrolment rates in each country leads, at the global level, to an actual increase in the number of people with no education, particularly among the younger cohorts. This is because in the least educated countries fertility rates remain much higher than in the better educated countries, and therefore these less educated segments of the world population are increasing more rapidly. This increase causes a higher proportion of younger persons in the world to remain without any education. In Table 10.6 this worsening trend among younger cohorts is shown by a declining mean years of education of men and women aged 30–34, which, in the CER scenario, declines from 9.1 years in 2010 to 8.8 years in 2060 for men, and from 8.5 to 8.0 years for women over the same period. For the entire adult population above the age of 25, however, the average educational attainment is still on an increasing trajectory, even under this pessimistic scenario, owing to past education improvements and momentum. For women, at the global level, this expected increase in the MYS is from 7.4 years now to 8.5 years by 2060. This is reflected in a declining proportion of adult women without any formal education, which even under the CER scenario would decrease from the current 22 per cent to 16 per cent by 2060.

Under the FT scenario, however, the given momentum is significantly augmented by much better education of the younger cohorts. As a result, the global proportion of women without any education would decline from 22 per cent to only 2 per cent by 2060. Correspondingly, among adult women the MYS would increase from 7.4 years to 13.3 years between 2010 and 2060. As the age and education pyramid in Figure 10.15 shows, large majorities of both young men and women at the global level would have post-secondary education by 2060.

Tables 10.6 and 10.7 provide these data at the level of continents. They show that the global patterns largely result from alternative assumed trends in Africa and Asia. On these two continents the momentum effects due to past improvements are strong and further enhanced through the alternative future trends in school enrolment. In North America, Europe, Latin America, and Oceania the differences are less pronounced owing to a longer history of high levels of average educational attainment of both men and women. Of these continents, Latin America had the highest recent expansion of female education and therefore the strongest momentum of pre-programmed increase. This is shown by the increase in MYS of adult women from 7.9 years now to 9.7 years by 2060, even under the assumption of constant school enrolment rates in the CER scenario.

At the level of individual countries, Table 10.8 gives the results for females of the CER scenario and Table 10.9 those of the FT scenario. For China, the world's most populous country, the recent improvements in female education have created such strong momentum that even the assumptions of constant enrolment rates will lead to significantly higher levels of average education. The MYS of the female adult population will increase from 6.8 years now to 8.2 in 2030, and further to 9.2 years by 2060. In terms of the educational attainment distribution, the proportion of adult women without any formal education will decline from its current level of 15 per cent to only 1 per cent by 2060. The only way this can happen under assumptions of constant enrolment is for those without formal education to be virtually all elderly women who will die over the coming decades and be replaced by better educated younger cohorts. This process is a good illustration of demographic metabolism at work.

For India and Nigeria, Figures 10.16 and 10.17 also provide full sets of age and education pyramids. These two countries are likely to be first and third in terms of population size in the second half of the century. For China, owing to past achievements, the uncertainty of future trends relates to the proportion of the population with tertiary education (14–48 per cent depending on scenario). India, however, is still at a crossroads with respect to its future human capital trajectory and future economic standing. The MYS

Table 10.6 Results for World and Continents According to the Constant Enrolment Scenario

		Proportion 25+ (%)				Proportion (%)	Mean years of schooling		
Region	Year	No education	Primary	Secondary	Tertiary	ALS 20–39	25+	25–29	60–64
Men									
World	2010	13	25	47	15	70	9.8	10.8	9.0
World	2030	10	22	52	16	68	10.5	10.3	10.2
World	2060	10	21	52	17	63	10.6	10.0	10.8
Africa	2010	31	31	30	8	47	7.0	8.4	4.7
Africa	2030	22	32	37	9	45	8.1	8.1	7.5
Africa	2060	20	33	38	9	44	8.3	8.0	8.5
Asia	2010	14	27	46	12	71	9.0	10.5	7.7
Asia	2030	10	22	53	15	69	10.0	10.2	9.5
Asia	2060	10	20	54	16	66	10.4	10.0	10.5
Europe	2010	1	11	66	22	96	13.2	14.0	12.8
Europe	2030	1	6	69	24	95	13.8	13.9	13.6
Europe	2060	0	4	69	26	95	14.1	13.9	14.1
LAC	2010	8	39	39	13	65	9.3	10.9	7.6
LAC	2030	5	33	48	15	67	10.4	10.8	9.8
LAC	2060	3	29	52	15	66	10.9	10.7	11.0
N. America	2010	1	5	56	38	96	14.9	15.0	15.1
N. America	2030	0	3	57	39	96	15.1	14.9	15.1
N. America	2060	0	3	57	40	96	15.1	14.9	15.1
Oceania	2010	2	14	55	29	88	13.8	15.2	13.1
Oceania	2030	2	10	58	30	87	14.5	15.0	13.9
Oceania	2060	2	9	59	31	87	15.0	15.0	15.1
Women									
World	2010	22	25	39	13	65	8.5	10.2	7.3
World	2030	17	23	45	15	61	9.5	9.5	8.9
World	2060	16	22	46	16	56	9.8	9.0	9.9
Africa	2010	48	26	21	5	37	4.9	6.9	2.1
Africa	2030	36	30	28	6	36	6.2	6.6	5.0
Africa	2060	31	32	30	6	34	6.7	6.4	6.9
Asia	2010	27	28	35	9	63	7.3	9.7	5.4
Asia	2030	19	25	44	12	61	8.6	9.2	7.8
Asia	2060	17	22	48	14	57	9.3	8.9	9.4
Europe	2010	1	14	63	22	97	12.7	14.5	12.1
Europe	2030	1	7	65	27	96	13.7	14.3	13.7
Europe	2060	0	4	65	31	96	14.4	14.3	14.5
LAC	2010	10	38	38	15	69	9.2	11.4	7.0
LAC	2030	5	31	47	17	72	10.5	11.3	9.9
LAC	2060	3	26	53	19	70	11.3	11.2	11.4
N. America	2010	1	5	57	38	97	14.9	15.3	14.9
N. America	2030	0	3	54	43	97	15.2	15.2	15.3
N. America	2060	0	2	52	46	97	15.3	15.2	15.3
Oceania	2010	3	18	48	31	89	13.4	15.4	12.3
Oceania	2030	2	11	51	36	88	14.5	15.3	13.9
Oceania	2060	1	8	51	39	88	15.3	15.4	15.4

ALS: At least lower secondary completed; LAC: Latin America and Caribbean.

Table 10.7 Results for World and Continents According to the Fast Track Scenario

		Proportion 25+ (%)				Proportion (%)	Mean years of schooling		
Region	Year	No education	Primary	Secondary	Tertiary	ALS 20–39	25+	25–29	60–64
Men									
World	2010	13	25	47	15	70	9.8	10.8	9.0
World	2030	6	15	48	31	91	12.2	14.0	10.2
World	2060	1	5	36	58	99	14.6	15.2	14.5
Africa	2010	31	31	30	8	47	7.0	8.4	4.7
Africa	2030	13	22	42	23	78	10.8	12.6	7.5
Africa	2060	3	9	37	52	96	14.3	14.8	13.3
Asia	2010	14	27	46	12	71	9.0	10.5	7.7
Asia	2030	6	15	49	29	94	11.8	14.2	9.5
Asia	2060	1	5	37	57	99	14.4	15.2	14.5
Europe	2010	1	11	66	22	96	13.2	14.0	12.8
Europe	2030	0	5	57	38	99	14.5	15.6	13.6
Europe	2060	0	1	34	65	100	15.6	15.8	15.9
LAC	2010	8	39	39	13	65	9.3	10.9	7.6
LAC	2030	3	23	45	28	92	12.0	14.3	9.8
LAC	2060	1	8	37	55	99	14.6	15.6	14.8
N. America	2010	1	5	56	38	96	14.9	15.0	15.1
N. America	2030	0	2	45	53	100	15.5	15.9	15.1
N. America	2060	0	0	25	74	100	16.0	16.0	16.1
Oceania	2010	2	14	55	29	88	13.8	15.2	13.1
Oceania	2030	1	8	47	44	95	15.0	16.0	13.9
Oceania	2060	0	2	31	67	99	15.9	16.1	16.1
Women									
World	2010	22	25	39	13	65	8.5	10.2	7.3
World	2030	11	16	44	29	92	11.5	14.1	8.9
World	2060	2	5	36	57	99	14.5	15.2	14.8
Africa	2010	48	26	21	5	37	4.9	6.9	2.1
Africa	2030	22	20	40	19	78	9.7	12.4	5.0
Africa	2060	4	7	40	50	97	14.2	14.8	13.3
Asia	2010	27	28	35	9	63	7.3	9.7	5.4
Asia	2030	12	17	44	26	94	10.9	14.3	7.8
Asia	2060	3	5	37	55	99	14.2	15.2	14.8
Europe	2010	1	14	63	22	97	12.7	14.5	12.1
Europe	2030	1	6	53	40	100	14.3	15.7	13.7
Europe	2060	0	1	31	68	100	15.5	15.9	16.0
LAC	2010	10	38	38	15	69	9.2	11.4	7.0
LAC	2030	4	21	43	32	97	12.3	14.9	9.9
LAC	2060	1	6	33	60	99	14.8	15.7	15.5
N. America	2010	1	5	57	38	97	14.9	15.3	14.9
N. America	2030	0	2	42	56	100	15.6	16.0	15.3
N. America	2060	0	0	22	77	100	16.0	16.0	16.1
Oceania	2010	3	18	48	31	89	13.4	15.4	12.3
Oceania	2030	1	9	41	49	96	14.8	16.0	13.9
Oceania	2060	0	2	26	71	100	15.8	16.1	16.1

ALS: at least lower secondary completed; LAC: Latin America and Caribbean.

Table 10.8 Results for Selected Bigger Countries for Women Under the Constant Enrolment Rates Scenario

Region	Year	Proportion 25+ (%)				Proportion (%)	Mean years of schooling		
		No education	Primary	Secondary	Tertiary	ALS 20–39	25+	25–29	60–64
Brazil	2010	11	37	40	13	71	8.5	11.0	6.1
Brazil	2030	5	28	52	15	78	10.0	11.1	9.0
Brazil	2060	3	20	61	16	78	11.0	11.1	11.2
China	2010	15	30	48	6	83	8.0	10.8	5.7
China	2030	6	22	62	10	87	9.6	10.9	8.8
China	2060	1	13	72	14	87	10.7	10.9	10.9
Egypt	2010	49	8	30	12	67	6.5	10.8	2.9
Egypt	2030	29	9	48	15	76	9.6	11.7	6.5
Egypt	2060	16	9	58	17	76	11.5	11.7	11.7
Germany	2010	1	3	71	25	97	15.5	16.6	15.1
Germany	2030	1	2	63	34	98	16.2	16.7	16.4
Germany	2060	1	1	56	42	98	16.7	16.7	16.8
India	2010	51	20	22	6	45	4.8	7.9	2.6
India	2030	39	23	31	7	44	6.3	7.3	4.5
India	2060	31	24	36	8	44	7.3	7.3	7.4
Indonesia	2010	13	47	33	7	62	8.6	11.2	5.3
Indonesia	2030	5	36	48	10	73	10.6	11.9	9.3
Indonesia	2060	2	27	59	12	73	11.8	11.9	12.0
Iran	2010	29	28	32	11	67	7.4	11.4	2.5
Iran	2030	15	26	45	13	72	9.6	11.3	6.9
Iran	2060	7	23	54	16	72	11.1	11.3	11.3
Kenya	2010	21	32	44	3	67	7.6	9.9	2.6
Kenya	2030	13	34	51	3	55	8.3	8.3	8.1
Kenya	2060	10	33	54	3	55	8.5	8.3	8.6
Nigeria	2010	49	24	18	8	42	5.4	7.8	2.0
Nigeria	2030	34	22	32	11	50	7.7	8.6	6.0
Nigeria	2060	28	21	39	12	50	8.7	8.6	8.9
Russia	2010	0	5	73	22	100	12.7	14.0	12.7
Russia	2030	0	1	75	24	99	13.6	14.0	13.2
Russia	2060	0	0	74	25	99	14.1	14.0	14.2
South Africa	2010	10	28	56	5	83	9.5	11.5	6.9
South Africa	2030	4	19	72	5	86	10.8	11.4	10.3
South Africa	2060	1	13	81	5	86	11.5	11.4	11.5
South Korea	2010	7	16	47	30	100	12.7	16.0	10.0
South Korea	2030	2	8	45	46	100	14.5	16.0	15.3
South Korea	2060	0	1	35	65	100	15.9	16.0	16.0
Spain	2010	2	31	46	21	93	10.3	13.5	8.7
Spain	2030	1	18	55	26	90	11.8	13.0	12.0
Spain	2060	0	9	58	32	90	12.9	13.0	13.0
USA	2010	1	4	59	36	97	14.9	15.3	15.0
USA	2030	0	3	56	41	97	15.2	15.2	15.2
USA	2060	0	2	54	43	97	15.3	15.2	15.3

ALS: at least lower secondary completed.

for adult women in 2060 differs by more than a factor of two depending on scenario: 6.2 years under the CER and 13.3 years under the FT. For adult women without any formal education, there is some positive momentum due to past school extension that should bring the proportion down from the current 51 per cent to 31 per cent in 2060. But under the FT scenario the proportion of uneducated women would shrink to only 5 per cent, mostly elderly women. For adult women with tertiary education, the difference in 2060 between the alternative futures depicted by the two scenarios is huge: 8 per cent under the CER scenario compared with 57 per cent under the FT scenario. These scenarios would result in very different societies and economies, with substantial differences in the levels of health, well-being, and political empowerment. A comparison of the two bottom pyramids in Figure 10.16 illustrates this difference between the two futures for India in 2060.

For Nigeria the stakes are even higher because of higher levels of fertility and resulting population growth. Regarding average female education, Nigeria, where the MYS of adult women is currently 4.8 years, is actually slightly ahead of India, which has a mean of only 4.2 years. Regarding younger women with junior secondary or higher education, India, at 45 per cent, is slightly ahead of Nigeria, at 42 per cent. But Nigeria has more educational momentum owing to rapid recent expansion (50 per cent in 2060 under the CER scenario compared with 44 in India). Under the FT scenario both countries will see similarly impressive rates of growth in human capital. To keep its education efforts moving forward, Nigeria must avoid keeping its enrolment rates constant, but instead expand the school system as the population grows. As we will see in the following discussion, if no new schools are being built in Nigeria, population growth could more than eat up the existing positive momentum and result in the proportion of young women with at least junior secondary education falling to only 18 per cent by 2060.

As discussed earlier, the CER scenario assuming constant school enrolment rates is rather pessimistic, but under conditions of population growth it still assumes that absolute school enrolment is being expanded in parallel with the increasing number of children. There have been instances in some African countries where this expansion could not be managed and school enrolment rates actually fell during certain time periods. For illustrative purposes we calculated a fourth scenario that is more pessimistic than CER, assuming constant absolute enrolment numbers (CEN). As this scenario only makes sense for rapidly growing populations, its results are only presented for a few such countries.

Table 10.10 lists the results of this CEN scenario for women in Kenya and Nigeria, two of the larger countries in Africa that are still experiencing rapid growth. The results in terms of worsening overall educational attainment are indeed dramatic: In Kenya the proportion of adult women without any formal education would fall from 21 per cent now to a low of 13 per cent by 2030 (as a consequence of the momentum induced by past school expansion), but then dramatically increase to 34 per cent by 2060. This increase in relative proportions of the population without education is simply due to population growth under the assumption that no new schools are built between now and 2060.

Table 10.9 Results for Selected Bigger Countries for Women Under the Fast Track Scenario

Region	Year	Proportion 25+ (%)				Proportion (%)	Mean years of schooling		
		No education	Primary	Secondary	Tertiary	ALS 20–39	25+	25–29	60–64
Brazil	2010	11	37	40	13	71	8.5	11.0	6.1
Brazil	2030	5	21	48	27	97	11.3	14.2	9.0
Brazil	2060	1	7	39	53	100	13.8	14.9	14.7
China	2010	15	30	48	6	83	8.0	10.8	5.7
China	2030	5	19	56	20	98	10.7	14.0	8.8
China	2060	1	5	46	48	100	13.4	14.9	14.3
Egypt	2010	49	8	30	12	67	6.5	10.8	2.9
Egypt	2030	22	5	40	33	96	11.6	15.4	6.5
Egypt	2060	4	1	31	64	99	15.2	15.9	15.8
Germany	2010	1	3	71	25	97	15.5	16.6	15.1
Germany	2030	1	2	55	43	100	16.6	17.8	16.4
Germany	2060	0	1	31	68	100	17.6	17.9	18.0
India	2010	51	20	22	6	45	4.8	7.9	2.6
India	2030	24	12	38	26	93	10.3	14.6	4.5
India	2060	5	4	34	57	99	14.7	15.7	15.3
Indonesia	2010	13	47	33	7	62	8.6	11.2	5.3
Indonesia	2030	4	28	46	21	95	11.8	14.8	9.3
Indonesia	2060	1	9	40	51	100	14.8	15.8	15.3
Iran	2010	29	28	32	11	67	7.4	11.4	2.5
Iran	2030	13	19	40	28	97	11.4	15.7	6.9
Iran	2060	3	8	35	55	100	14.5	16.1	15.6
Kenya	2010	21	32	44	3	67	7.6	9.9	2.6
Kenya	2030	6	13	63	18	98	12.5	13.6	8.1
Kenya	2060	0	2	46	52	100	15.5	14.9	15.5
Nigeria	2010	49	24	18	8	42	5.4	7.8	2.0
Nigeria	2030	19	15	39	27	87	11.1	14.0	6.0
Nigeria	2060	2	3	32	63	98	15.3	15.6	14.9
Russia	2010	0	5	73	22	100	12.7	14.0	12.7
Russia	2030	0	1	58	41	100	14.0	14.9	13.2
Russia	2060	0	0	30	69	100	14.8	15.0	15.1
South Africa	2010	10	28	56	5	83	9.5	11.5	6.9
South Africa	2030	3	12	66	20	99	12.5	13.8	10.3
South Africa	2060	0	1	46	53	100	14.7	14.7	14.8
South Korea	2010	7	16	47	30	100	12.7	16.0	10.0
South Korea	2030	2	8	41	50	100	14.6	16.1	15.3
South Korea	2060	0	0	24	75	100	15.9	16.1	16.1
Spain	2010	2	31	46	21	93	10.3	13.5	8.7
Spain	2030	1	15	45	40	100	12.6	15.0	12.0
Spain	2060	0	3	31	66	100	14.4	15.1	15.1
USA	2010	1	4	59	36	97	14.9	15.3	15.0
USA	2030	0	2	43	54	100	15.6	16.0	15.2
USA	2060	0	0	23	76	100	16.0	16.0	16.1

ALS: at least lower secondary completed

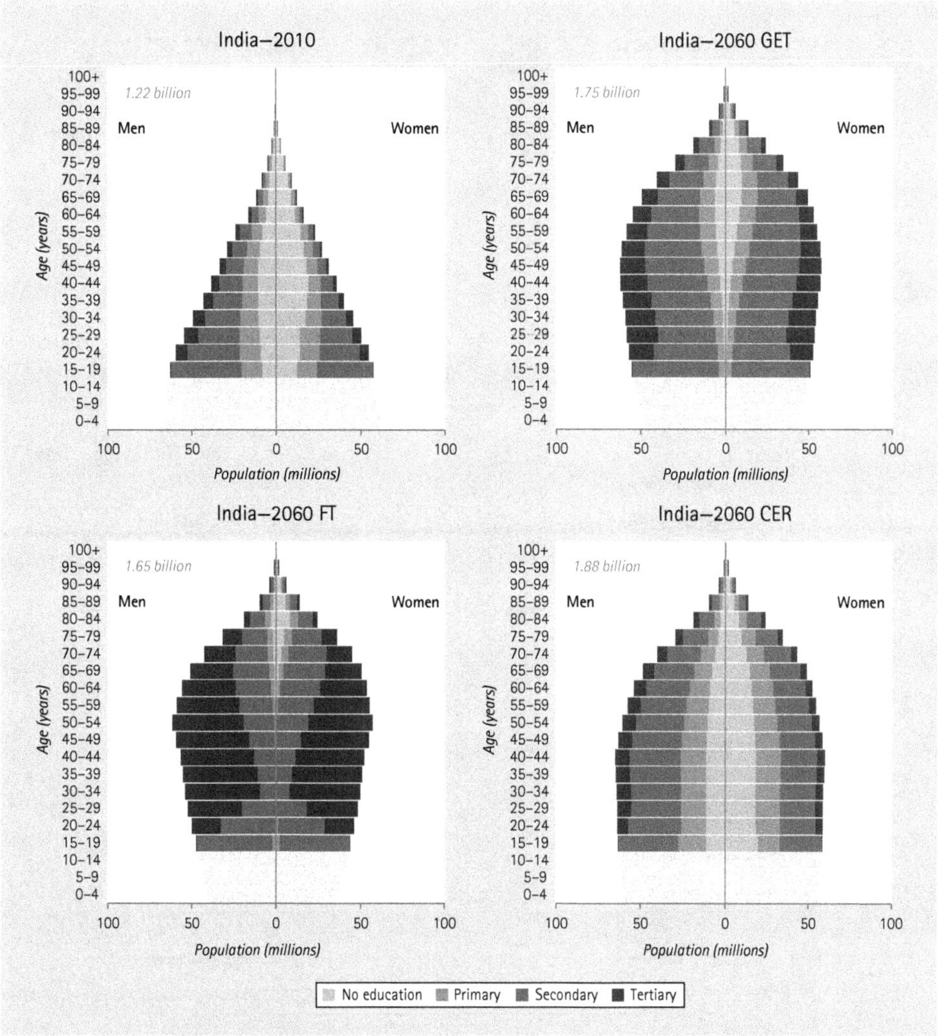

FIGURE 10.16 Age and education pyramids for India in 2010 and projected to 2060 under the global education trend (GET), fast track (FT), and constant enrolment rate (CER) scenarios.

Table 10.10 also shows that the proportion of young women (aged 20–39) with junior secondary or higher education would fall from 67 per cent now to a low 36 per cent by 2060. For Nigeria the resulting pattern is similar, but at an even lower level of education. If Nigeria stopped building new schools, the proportion of adult women without any schooling would fall from its current level of 49 per cent to 37 per cent, and then increase to 55 per cent by 2060. The proportion of young women with junior secondary or higher education would fall to a very low 18 per cent by 2060. This clearly illustrates that educational momentum can be easily lost over the course of a few decades if no further improvements in the education system take place.

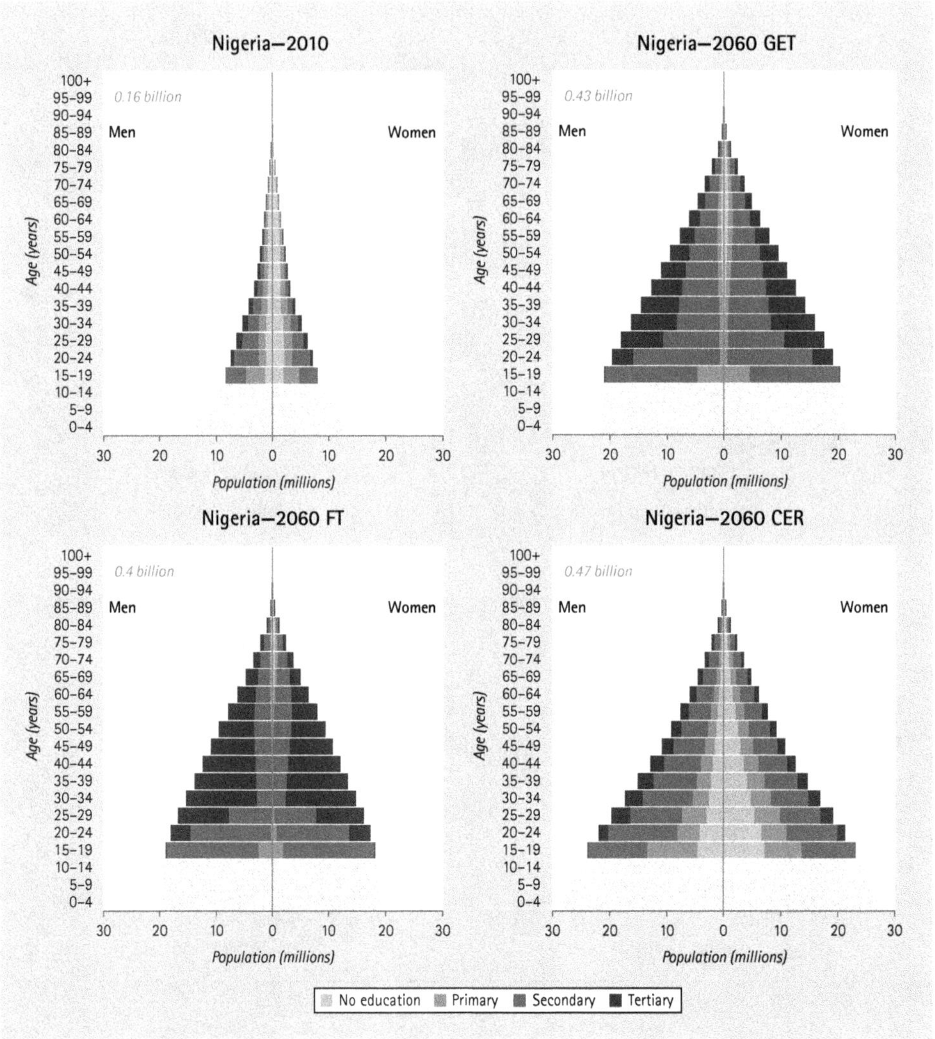

FIGURE 10.17 Age and education pyramids for Nigeria in 2010 and projected to 2060 under the global education trend (GET), fast track (FT), and constant enrolment rate (CER) scenarios.

Figure 10.18 illustrates the dramatic consequences of building no new schools under conditions of high fertility for Nigeria. The GET scenario in Figure 10.17 describes a fast improvement in the educational attainment of the country from a low level today to that of a middle-income country 50 years in the future. The FT scenario shows the potential transformation to a highly educated modern country over a half century. But the CEN scenario shows a case of completely stalled development with an increasing proportion of the younger population being without any formal education. Also, the shape of the pyramid is different because in our model less education also implies higher fertility and significantly higher child mortality. These directly demographic consequences of alternative education scenarios are analysed in more detail in section 10.4.

Table 10.10 Results for Women in Kenya and Nigeria Under the Constant Enrolment Numbers Scenario

		Proportion 25+ (%)				Proportion (%)	Mean years of schooling		
Region	Year	No education	Primary	Secondary	Tertiary	ALS 20–39	25+	25–29	60–64
Kenya	2010	21	32	44	3	67	7.6	9.9	2.6
Kenya	2030	14	28	56	3	56	8.7	7.4	8.1
Kenya	2060	35	19	44	2	36	6.5	4.7	8.9
Nigeria	2010	49	24	18	8	42	5.4	7.8	2.0
Nigeria	2030	37	25	30	9	37	6.9	6.2	6.0
Nigeria	2060	56	17	22	5	18	4.8	3.0	7.4

ALS: at least lower secondary completed.

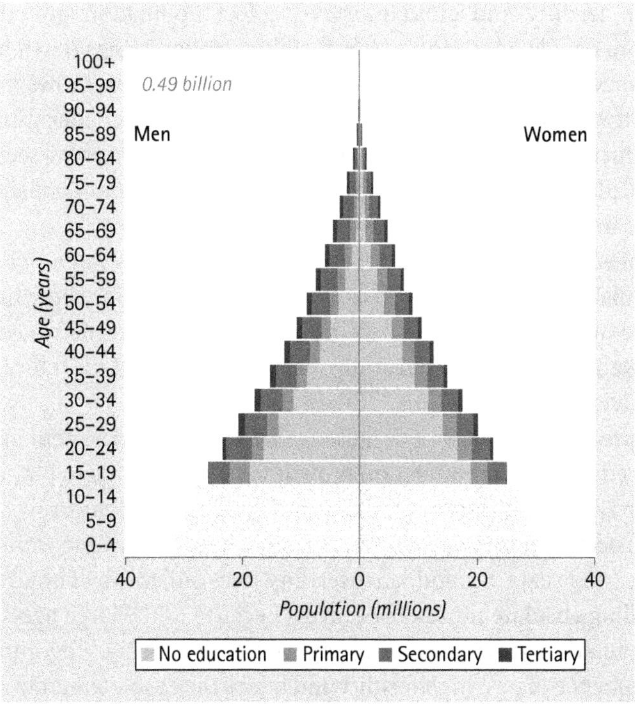

FIGURE 10.18 Age and education pyramid for Nigeria as projected to 2060 under the constant enrolment rate scenario.

10.4 How female education scenarios affect population growth and child mortality

In Chapters 2 and 9 we demonstrated that in virtually all countries, and at different levels of development, there is a strong negative association between the level of female education and the levels of fertility rates and child mortality rates. We also argued that there is a strong case for assuming a direct causal effect from the empowerment of women through basic education to changes in attitudes, behaviour, and the relative standing of women in their partnership, extended family, and society, and that this causal effect results in the observed lower levels of fertility and child mortality rates.

Given this clear relationship between female education and demographic outcomes, we should expect that alternative scenarios about future education trends of women will result in different levels of fertility and mortality. The following tables and graphs quantify these effects. It is important when looking at the data to understand that the aggregate effects on fertility and child mortality affect population growth in different directions. More female education in low fertility settings brings down birth rates and improves the survival of children. But the following calculation shows that the fertility factor by far outweighs the improved survival. As a result, better education is associated with a clear reduction in population growth. For this reason, universal secondary female education—in addition to its many other positive implications—is likely an effective way to slow the world's population growth (Cohen, 2008).

This effect of education on future population growth is illustrated in Figure 10.19 for the world population and in Figure 10.20 for Africa. The figures show future trends in population size by level of education according to the four alternative education scenarios, while assuming identical education-specific fertility and mortality trajectories at the level of individual countries.

When interpreting comparisons of these scenarios, it should be kept in mind that the effect of better education on population growth takes a long time to play out because of two factors. First, if more girls are entering primary education tomorrow, the main effect on fertility will occur some 15 or more years later, when these young women are in their prime child-bearing years. Second, once fertility rates fall, this will not translate immediately into falling absolute numbers of births because of the large age-structural momentum of population growth. More young women will be moving into reproductive ages as a consequence of past high fertility and hence the absolute number of births may still increase, even though the number of births per woman declines. Even in the unlikely case of instant replacement-level fertility, young populations would continue to grow substantially for decades.

For these reasons, the differences among the four scenarios shown in Figure 10.19 only become visible after a few decades. But by 2060 very clear differences show up. As can be expected, the differences are most pronounced between the FT scenario and the scenarios assuming constant school enrolment. The difference in total population size by 2060 is already about a billion people at the global level. In other words, identical education-specific fertility and mortality assumptions result in total world population of 8.89 billion under the FT scenario compared with 9.87 billion under the CER scenario.

For Africa the effect of alternative education trajectories on population growth is even more pronounced owing to the higher levels of fertility and greater absolute differentials in education-specific fertility rates. As shown in Figure 10.20, under the FT scenario the total population of Africa would 'only' increase to 2.02 billion by 2060, whereas under the CEN scenario it would increase to 2.44 by 2060. As can be seen from the shadings in Figure 10.20, these scenarios also envision very different future compositions of the population. While under the CEN scenario the population without any formal schooling is on a rapidly increasing trajectory (due to falling school enrolment rates when keeping the in-school population constant under conditions of population growth), the FT scenario will bring Africa a future that is not so different from the recent experience of Eastern Asia, at least in terms of human capital trends.

Table 10.11 shows the different demographic outcomes as a consequence of different education scenarios for a number of least-developed countries. For Ethiopia, Table 10.11 shows that population, under the most likely GET scenario, will increase from 83 million in 2010 to 172 million by 2060, which is more than a doubling of population due to the current high fertility rates and a very young age structure. Under the FT scenario, the

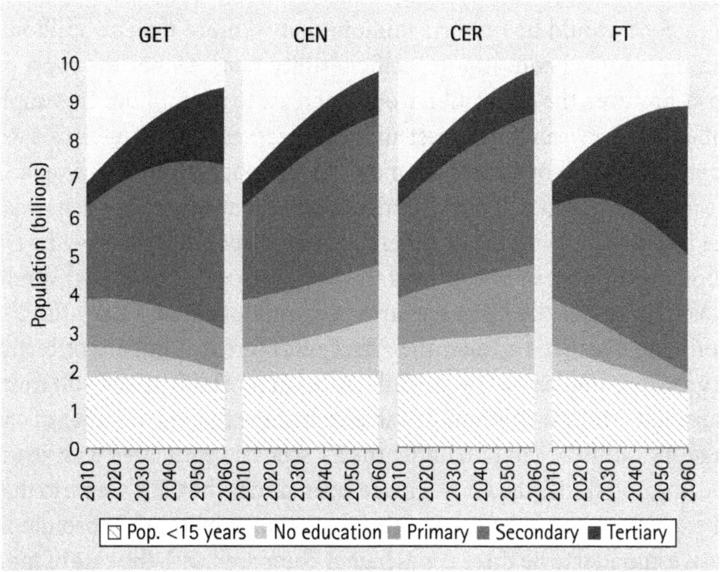

FIGURE 10.19 World population scenarios by level of education according to four alternative education scenarios while assuming identical education-specific fertility and mortality trajectories at the level of individual countries. GET: global education trend; CEN: constant enrolment numbers; CER: constant enrolment rate; FT: fast track.

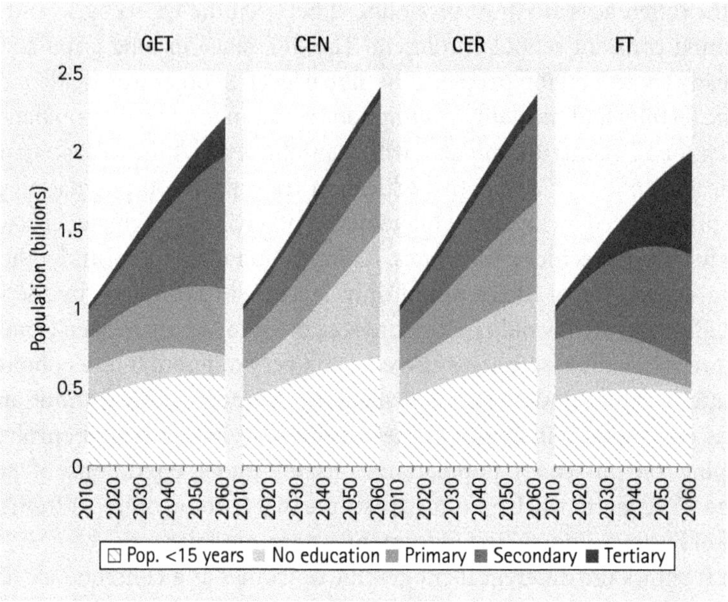

FIGURE 10.20 Scenarios for Africa by level of education according to four alternative education scenarios while assuming identical education-specific fertility and mortality trajectories at the level of individual countries. GET: global education trend; CEN: constant enrolment numbers; CER: constant enrolment rate; FT: fast track.

population in 2060 would be only 151 million, that is, more than 20 million less, even when assuming identical education-specific fertility rates. Under the most pessimistic CEN scenario, however, the population would increase to 194 million. This implies that by 2060 the difference between the highest and the lowest education scenarios would be 43 million people, which is more than half of the current population of Ethiopia. Table 10.11 also lists the absolute number of births under the different education scenarios, which illustrates the reasons for these major differences in the population growths trajectories. By about 2060 the number of births (over the five-year period 2060–65) would be more than twice as high under the CEN scenario (1.77 million) than under the FT scenario (0.88 million). As discussed earlier, the effect of different numbers of births on total population growth is moderated by the differences in mortality that result from different levels of education. The last columns of Table 10.11 show that the number of child deaths under the age of 5 would be 120,000 under the FT scenario compared with 363,000 under the CER and 403,000 under the CEN. Hence, even under the CER scenario that assumes that school expansion can keep pace with population growth, the absolute number of child deaths is estimated to be three times higher compared with the case of the fastest expansion of schooling. In this sense, the expansion of female education does not only have significant consequences for population growth and development in general, but it also has massive direct effects on one of the most important humanitarian goals, namely reducing premature mortality and, in particular, child mortality.

Table 10.11 Different Demographic Outcomes as a Consequence of Different Education Scenarios for a Number of Least-developed Countries (Medium Fertility Assumptions)

		Population (in millions)				Births (in '00,000)*				Deaths under age 5 (in '000)*			
	Year	GET	CER	FT	CEN	GET	CER	FT	CEN	GET	CER	FT	CEN
Benin	2010	9	9	9	9	18	18	17	18	114	116	112	115
Benin	2030	14	14	14	14	19	20	17	20	83	95	67	97
Benin	2060	21	22	19	22	17	19	13	20	38	52	23	55
Burkina Faso	2010	16	16	16	16	36	37	35	36	270	275	262	272
Burkina Faso	2030	27	28	26	28	43	48	35	48	220	252	160	251
Burkina Faso	2060	43	47	37	47	40	49	28	49	98	142	54	143
Burundi	2010	8	8	8	8	15	15	15	15	123	122	120	122
Burundi	2030	13	13	13	13	15	16	13	16	96	105	77	105
Burundi	2060	19	19	17	19	14	15	10	15	46	58	27	60
Chad	2010	11	11	11	11	26	26	26	26	261	263	257	262
Chad	2030	18	18	18	18	30	32	27	32	230	249	187	250
Chad	2060	27	29	25	29	26	30	20	30	112	151	71	153
D.R. Congo	2010	66	66	66	66	151	154	148	154	1444	1473	1396	1469
D.R. Congo	2030	107	109	104	109	170	186	151	191	1301	1561	1007	1642
D.R. Congo	2060	160	169	149	171	145	174	118	181	671	1000	444	1113
Ethiopia	2010	83	83	83	83	140	142	139	143	722	727	710	731
Ethiopia	2030	124	127	120	128	149	166	121	172	526	608	391	633
Ethiopia	2060	172	188	151	194	129	166	88	177	234	363	120	403
Guinea	2010	10	10	10	10	19	19	18	19	137	139	129	137
Guinea	2030	13	14	13	14	17	19	15	18	86	102	64	98
Guinea	2060	16	17	15	17	12	14	9	14	34	49	21	47
Haiti	2010	10	10	10	10	13	13	12	13	52	53	50	53
Haiti	2030	12	12	12	12	11	12	10	12	26	33	21	32
Haiti	2060	13	14	13	14	8	10	7	9	8	13	6	13
Madagascar	2010	21	21	21	21	36	36	35	36	93	91	89	92
Madagascar	2030	33	33	32	34	40	42	35	44	66	70	49	75

(*continued*)

Table 10.11 Continued

		Population (in millions)				Births (in '00,000)*				Deaths under age 5 mortality (in '000)*			
	Year	GET	CER	FT	CEN	GET	CER	FT	CEN	GET	CER	FT	CEN
Madagascar	2060	50	51	44	53	37	40	26	43	34	40	17	45
Malawi	2010	15	15	15	15	34	34	33	35	204	207	200	209
Malawi	2030	26	27	25	27	48	52	40	56	204	238	152	268
Malawi	2060	48	53	42	57	52	67	38	77	141	223	86	285
Mali	2010	15	15	15	15	36	37	35	37	321	326	309	323
Mali	2030	26	26	25	26	42	45	34	45	259	294	186	292
Mali	2060	40	43	35	43	36	43	26	43	120	171	64	171
Mozambique	2010	23	23	23	23	43	44	41	43	290	292	277	290
Mozambique	2030	34	35	33	35	44	49	38	49	186	217	136	218
Mozambique	2060	46	49	41	49	38	46	27	46	84	124	47	127
Niger	2010	16	16	16	16	40	40	39	40	284	286	278	285
Niger	2030	30	30	29	30	63	67	54	67	330	360	266	362
Niger	2060	62	67	54	67	78	92	58	93	250	331	150	340
Rwanda	2010	11	11	11	11	22	22	21	22	138	141	131	139
Rwanda	2030	17	17	16	17	24	27	20	27	113	133	80	135
Rwanda	2060	26	28	23	28	23	28	17	29	58	86	32	91
Senegal	2010	12	12	12	12	23	24	22	24	107	110	100	107
Senegal	2030	19	20	18	20	25	29	20	28	81	99	52	96
Senegal	2060	27	31	23	30	22	29	15	29	31	50	15	49
Sierra Leone	2010	6	6	6	6	11	11	11	11	93	94	89	93
Sierra Leone	2030	9	9	8	9	12	12	10	13	68	78	50	79
Sierra Leone	2060	12	13	11	13	10	12	7	12	33	46	19	48
Somalia	2010	9	9	9	9	20	20	19	20	174	177	170	176
Somalia	2030	13	14	13	14	21	23	17	24	146	175	107	181
Somalia	2060	17	19	15	19	15	20	11	20	64	107	37	113

Sudan	2010	44	44	44	44	71	71	70	71	331	329	322	330
Sudan	2030	65	65	64	65	74	78	68	80	267	309	212	325
Sudan	2060	88	91	84	92	63	75	53	78	148	233	103	256
Uganda	2010	33	33	33	33	80	83	76	81	480	495	456	486
Uganda	2030	60	62	57	62	111	125	93	127	488	582	349	600
Uganda	2060	109	122	93	123	120	154	88	160	278	419	162	459
Tanzania	2010	45	45	45	45	91	94	88	93	396	407	382	402
Tanzania	2030	73	75	70	75	107	117	91	120	273	314	207	330
Tanzania	2060	114	122	99	124	100	117	71	123	145	190	82	209
Zambia	2010	13	13	13	13	30	31	28	31	207	217	194	213
Zambia	2030	21	22	20	22	37	43	29	44	187	234	120	250
Zambia	2060	33	38	28	39	34	46	24	50	96	157	52	185
Bangladesh	2010	149	149	149	149	154	154	152	154	406	408	390	406
Bangladesh	2030	179	179	177	179	128	133	119	132	164	187	128	182
Bangladesh	2060	189	194	182	193	88	102	75	100	49	70	34	65
Cambodia	2010	14	14	14	14	16	16	16	16	58	58	57	58
Cambodia	2030	17	17	17	17	14	14	13	14	22	24	18	24
Cambodia	2060	19	19	18	19	10	11	8	12	7	10	4	10
Laos	2010	6	6	6	6	7	7	7	7	21	21	20	21
Laos	2030	8	8	8	8	7	7	6	7	13	14	9	14
Laos	2060	9	9	8	9	5	6	4	6	5	6	3	6
Myanmar	2010	48	48	48	48	40	40	38	40	147	147	139	146
Myanmar	2030	52	52	51	52	32	34	27	33	77	86	51	80
Myanmar	2060	47	49	44	48	23	27	18	25	24	34	14	28
Nepal	2010	30	30	30	30	38	40	37	39	64	69	60	66
Nepal	2030	42	43	41	43	37	43	34	42	24	35	20	33
Nepal	2060	55	61	52	60	31	43	27	41	9	19	7	18

GE: global education trend; CER: constant enrolment rates; FT: fast track; CEN: constant enrolment numbers. DR: Congo. Democratic Republic of the Congo.
*For period measures the year is the beginning of the five-year period (e.g. 2060 refers to 2060–65).

So far, all discussions of the impact of alternative education scenarios have been combined with medium (the most likely) education-specific fertility and mortality assumptions. But the positive effects of education can be expected to be even stronger than indicated because future education-specific fertility rates would follow a higher trajectory owing to the higher absolute differences between the birth rates of the different education categories. In Table 10.12 we briefly discuss the consequences of this case with the example of the two countries already examined. In Ethiopia, under the high fertility scenario (discussed in previous chapters), total population size would increase from 83 million to between 178 and 238 million in 2060, depending on the education scenario used. Not surprisingly, this is much higher overall population growth than is given for the most likely GET scenario with medium fertility, which was 172 million instead of 208 million under the high fertility assumption. Population growth under the FT scenario, combined with high fertility, would be roughly comparable with that of the GET scenario under medium fertility (178 million compared with 172 million). But in terms of child deaths the FT scenario (higher fertility: 186,000 child deaths) would be better than the GET scenario (medium fertility: 234,000 child deaths). Under the most pessimistic education scenario, CEN combined with high fertility, not only would population growth go to the extremely high level of 238 million by 2060, but child mortality would be catastrophically high, with 638,000 child deaths.

Nepal is a smaller country than Ethiopia and the birth rates are somewhat lower, as can be seen from relating the number of births to total population size in Table 10.12. In terms of the TFR, the previous chapters showed that they are currently (2010–15) 4.14 and 2.71 for Ethiopia and Nepal respectively. As a consequence of these higher fertility levels, Ethiopia is expected to grow more rapidly than Nepal. For Nepal, the difference between the total population size in 2060 under the FT and CER scenarios is 12 million people, still more than a third of the population size today. But owing to rather high levels of child mortality, the consequences of better female education for the number of projected child births are dramatic. Under the CER and CEN scenarios, almost three times as many children will be dying in 2060–65 than under the most optimistic FT scenario. Again, these differences are induced simply by assuming alternative education scenarios while using the same sets of education-specific fertility and mortality assumptions.

These results dramatically illustrate how important progress in female education is for reducing the otherwise rapid increase in the number of births and avoiding a high number of child deaths. It can even be argued that these numbers are likely to underestimate the effect of education on population growth and child mortality because they only consider the individual level effects and not the community-level impacts of education. The literature has shown (Fuchs et al., 2010; Pamuk et al., 2011) that there are typically spill-over effects—normative change in favour of family limitation, and better availability of reproductive health services in communities with better educated women.

Finally, it needs to be pointed out that the interaction between education and population growth goes both ways. The discussion of the CEN scenario showed that under conditions of high population growth due to high birth rates, the increase in the school age population is such that even maintaining current school enrolment rates can be an

Table 10.12 Different Demographic Outcomes as a Consequence of Different Education Scenarios for a Number of Least-developed Countries (High Fertility Assumptions)

		Population (in millions)				Births (in '00,000)*				Deaths under age 5 (in '000)*			
	Year	GET	CER	FT	CEN	GET	CER	FT	CEN	GET	CER	FT	CEN
Ethiopia	2010	83	83	83	83	148	150	146	150	747	754	737	758
Ethiopia	2030	131	134	126	135	183	204	148	211	641	742	476	774
Ethiopia	2060	208	230	178	238	201	258	137	279	361	562	186	638
Nepal	2010	30	30	30	30	40	42	39	41	67	72	63	69
Nepal	2030	44	45	43	45	46	53	42	52	30	43	24	41
Nepal	2060	64	73	61	72	49	69	43	67	15	30	12	31

GE: global education trend; CER: constant enrolment rates; FT: fast track; CEN: constant enrolment numbers.
*For period measures the year is the beginning of the five-year period (e.g. 2060 refers to 2060–65).

uphill battle. In several African countries during the 1980s, the proportions of young cohorts in school actually declined, presumably because of economic and political problems, and very rapid population growth resulting in an increase in the school-age population (Malik and Kugler, 2013). The stall of the fertility decline observed in some African countries around 2000 was associated with this stall in education of the relevant female cohorts. Although female education is an important force in lowering fertility, rapid growth in the number of children in a society in which resources do not grow at the same pace is an obstacle to the expansion of education. For this reason, it is most effective from a policy perspective to try to increase female education while at the same time improving access to family planning programmes.

References

Cohen, J.E. 2008 'Make Secondary Education Universal'. *Nature*, 456, 572–3.

Fuchs, R., Pamuk, E. and Lutz, W. 2010 'Education or wealth: Which Matters More for Reducing Child Mortality in Developing Countries?' *Vienna Yearbook of Population Research*, 8: 175–99.

Lutz, W. 2013 'Demographic Metabolism: A Predictive Theory of Socioeconomic Change'. *Population and Development Review*, 38: 283–301.

Lutz, W., Sanderson, W. C. and Scherbov, S. 2001 'The End of World Population Growth'. *Nature*, 412: 543–5.

Lutz, W., Sanderson, W.C. and Scherbov, S. (eds) 2004 *The End of World Population Growth in the 21st Century: New Challenges for Human Capital Formation and Sustainable Development*. Earthscan: London.

Lutz, W., Sanderson, W.C. and Scherbov, S. 2008 'The Coming Acceleration of Global Population Ageing'. *Nature*, 451: 716–19.

Malik, K. and Kugler, M. 2013 'Human Progress and the Rising South' (UNDP Human Development Report). Available at: <http://hdr.undp.org/sites/default/files/human_progress_and_the_rising_south.pdf>(accessed 3 February 2014).

Mannheim, K. 1952 'The Problem of Generations'. In: Kecskemeti, P. (ed.) *Essays on the Sociology of Knowledge by Karl Mannheim*, pp. 157–85. Routledge & Kegan Paul: New York.

Pamuk, E.R., Fuchs, R. and Lutz, W. 2011 'Comparing Relative Effects of Education and Economic Resources on Infant Mortality in Developing Countries'. *Population and Development Review*, 37: 637–64.

Randers, J. 2012 *2052: A Global Forecast for the Next Forty Years*. Chelsea Green Publishing Company: White River Junction, VT.

Ryder, N.B. 1965 'The Cohort as a Concept in the Study of Social Change'. *American Sociological Review*, 30: 843–61.

Scherbov, S., Lutz, W. and Sanderson, W.C. 2011 'The Uncertain Timing of Reaching 8 Billion, Peak World Population, and Other Demographic Milestones'. *Population and Development Review*, 37: 571–8.

CHAPTER 11

RE-MEASURING TWENTY-FIRST CENTURY POPULATION AGEING

SERGEI SCHERBOV, WARREN C. SANDERSON, SAMIR KC, AND WOLFGANG LUTZ

11.1 Introduction

Probably the most famous demographic riddle of all time is the one that the Sphinx was said to have posed to travellers outside the Greek city of Thebes: 'Which creature walks on four legs in the morning, two at noon, and three in the evening?' Unfortunate travellers who could not answer the riddle correctly were immediately devoured. Oedipus, fresh from killing his father, was the first to have got the answer right. The correct answer was 'humans'. People crawl on their hands and knees as infants, walk on two feet in adulthood, and walk with a cane in old age.

We easily recognize the three ages of humans. Humans are born dependent on the care of others. As they grow, their capacities and productivities generally increase, but eventually these reach a peak. After a while, capacities and productivities decline and, eventually, if they are lucky enough to survive, people become elderly, often again requiring transfers and care from others. The human life cycle is the basis of all studies of population ageing, and so we cannot begin to study population ageing without first answering the Sphinx's riddle.

However, answering the Sphinx's riddle is not enough to get us started on a study of population ageing. We must take two more steps before we begin. First, we must recognize that not all people age at the same rate. As seen in Chapter 5, nowadays more educated people tend to have longer life expectancies than less educated people. Second, we must realize that there is no natural generalization of the Sphinx's riddle to whole populations. Populations cannot be categorized into the stages of infancy, adulthood, and old age.

Indeed, if the Sphinx was reborn today, we might find her sitting near another city and posing an equally perplexing riddle, one especially relevant for our times: 'What can grow younger as it grows older?' Answering this riddle correctly is the central challenge of this chapter and the key to understanding population ageing in the twenty-first century.

11.2 A New Way of Thinking About Ageing is Needed

As individuals, we care about ageing for personal reasons. At advanced enough ages, consumption generally exceeds labour income. The difference between the two is made up through capital income, the sale of assets, and through transfers from family members, other private sources, and governments (Lee and Mason, 2011). For those we care about and for ourselves, we need to ensure that this gap between an acceptable standard of consumption in old age and labour income is covered.

It is incorrect, however, to think that the defining feature of old age is a positive difference between consumption and labour income. Billionaires normally consume far more than their labour incomes because their incomes come mainly from returns to capital and capital gains. We cannot categorize all billionaires as old simply because only a small share of their consumption is supported by their labour incomes. Young people who stay at home taking care of children likewise have consumption that is greater than their labour incomes. Their consumption is often supported by transfers from their partners. Intra- and interfamily transfers are normal for young people, as well as for the elderly.

Sometimes, a vague argument is made that the elderly are more dependent on others than younger people. This argument is bolstered by a commonly used measure of ageing, the old age dependency ratio. However, old age dependency is not a clearly defined concept. Nowadays, few people produce the food that they eat. The rest are dependent on farmers. In modern societies, we are all dependent on the activities of many thousands of other people for our survival, health, and well-being. Older people use a different mix of goods and services than younger people, but we could hardly define old age dependency based on one's consumption basket.

As adults age, their capacities and productivities generally diminish gradually, usually at different speeds. A person can be physically fit, but have mental difficulties, or vice versa. There is never a precise moment at which some index of an individual's characteristics passes a particular threshold and the person enters the state of being old. Ageing presents people with a set of challenges to adapt to their changing physical, mental, economic, social, and emotional conditions. New challenges arrive more rapidly for the elderly and, on a personal level, we are concerned with how we and our loved ones will cope with them.

Also, on a social level, we are concerned about how populations cope with the problems of growing older. But, as with individuals, the notion of what it means for a society to grow older is complex. Over time, the age and education distributions of populations can change simultaneously (see Chapter 10). Older, more educated populations are likely to be different from young, less educated populations in important ways. For example, older, more educated people may be healthier than young, less educated people (Olshansky et al., 2012). A study of ageing has to be about more than just how old people are. It must also be about how capable, productive, and healthy people are, features that differ at each age by education, as well as by other characteristics that change over time (Chapter 10).

It is useful for many purposes to distinguish elderly people as a group from the rest of a population, even though as individuals they differ greatly from one another in their characteristics. In more developed countries a portion of the costs of supporting the elderly is socialized through governmental provision of pensions, health care, and other services. In this case, there must be clear criteria for public support eligibility, and these become the public finance definition of the onset of old age. These age thresholds are sometimes generated by a complex set of rules. In Sweden, income-based pensions may be taken at age 61 or above, and there is no specified full pension age (Ministry of Health and Social Affairs, 2011). For those aged 65 or older whose income-based pensions fall below a prescribed level, a guaranteed minimum pension is available. In the USA, public pensions can be taken starting at the age of 62 with restrictions, and at the age of 66 without them (SSA, 2013a). Eligibility for subsidized health care for the elderly begins at the age of 65. In the USA, the full pension age is scheduled to rise to 67 for those born in 1960 and later, but fixed pension ages do not imply fixed pension costs relative to contributions because of future changes in the life expectancy of pensioners.

Different pension plans generate different levels of concern about population ageing. The Swedish pension system is designed to be flexible with respect to changes in life expectancy and economic growth. Different speeds of change in the Swedish age structure will generate different paths of pension payouts, with a pension system designed to be sustainable. In contrast, the US national pension system (the Social Security System) is, on the basis of current legislation, going to be bankrupt in around three decades (SSA, 2013b). After that, the system would be able to pay out only about two-thirds of expected benefits.

At the societal level, the effects of an ageing population depend not only on the changing capacities and productivities of people, but on the interactions of these with the social and political structures. For example, in a society without a public pension system, the cost of supporting the elderly comes from their savings, their private pension plans, their children, other relatives, and many other sources. It is meaningless to ask whether it is feasible to raise taxes high enough to support them. There is also no reason to have a mandated age at which people become old enough to receive a public pension. In most wealthy countries, however, some of the costs of supporting the elderly are socialized. But even if none of the costs of supporting the elderly were socialized, they would still be important to consider because they would still have to be paid one way or another.

Public provision of health care is another reason to care about ageing. In countries that subsidize the health care costs of their populations, ageing is likely to cause health care costs to rise because older people require more health care than younger ones. As each year passes, people of a given age are superseded by people born one year later. Where educational attainments are increasing, the people born later are likely to be more educated, on average, than the people born earlier. Evidence suggests that more educated people tend to be healthier, holding age constant, than less educated people. But as populations grow healthier, age-specific costs could decline. Changes in health care costs, therefore, have two offsetting components, the age composition change of the population and the effects of changes in the health status of people of particular ages, which is likely to be driven, in part, by their increasing levels of education. The net effect of the two is unclear a priori (Sanderson and Scherbov, 2010). Ageing will affect health care costs, but we cannot make an estimate of those costs simply based on the chronological age of people, without also taking into account the dynamics of education and health status change.

Given the complexity of defining and measuring population ageing, researchers and policymakers have fallen back on an expedient and simplistic approach. They have formalized the Sphinx's three phases: young extends to age 14 (or sometimes 20), adulthood usually to age 64, and old age begins after that.

These threshold ages are then treated as constants that do not change over time. Thus, traditional measures of ageing assume people became 'old' at age 65 in 1900 and will become 'old' at age 65 in 2100. This time invariance is assumed, although there have been substantial changes in the life expectancy of 65-year-olds, their health, their education, and a host of other characteristics. While this approach is computationally simple, it is certainly inadequate for a full, even useful, understanding of population ageing. Population ageing has two main sources, reductions in fertility and increases in life expectancy, both of which are frequently associated with increases in average levels of education. In a situation where education is an important cause of ageing, assuming that the characteristics of older people do not change is inconsistent and implies inappropriate policy guidance.

11.3 A NEW APPROACH TO QUANTIFYING POPULATION AGEING

The study of ageing is not primarily about studying changes in the distribution of people by age. It is about studying how the distributions of important characteristics change. Many important characteristics, such as health status, change not only with age, but with other factors, such as education. If we want to know something about the evolution of the average health status of adults, we would need to look both at changes in age and at other relevant factors affecting health.

The first step in the new approach to quantifying population ageing is to think more deeply about the meaning of age itself. In theory, we would like to redefine age so that it corresponds to some relevant characteristic of people. In the conventional approach to population ageing, people at the same age have had the same number of birthdays. But the number of birthdays a person has had is only one of their characteristics. Other relevant characteristics include remaining life expectancy, health status, and eligibility for a full public pension. The conventional approach defines everyone who has had the same number of birthdays as having the same age. Here, alternatively, we define people who have the same remaining life expectancy as having the same age. We use the term 'prospective' to denote measures of age and ageing that use remaining life expectancy as the defining characteristic because they are forward-looking measures.

In this chapter, for simplicity, we compare conventional measures of ageing only with their prospective counterparts. In previous research, we have found, more broadly, that remaining life expectancy is a useful summary measure of people's productivities and capacities (Sanderson and Scherbov, 2013). Remaining life expectancy at specific ages changes at the societal level because of two factors: a generalized country-specific path of improvement and the mix of people by educational attainment. When we come to look at different education scenarios, we hold the generalized country-specific path of life expectancy constant and allow age-specific remaining life expectancies to vary because of variations in the education composition of the population at each age. Within an education scenario, overall life expectancy of a society at different ages reflects the past history of educational attainments because these are influenced by the education distribution of the population at each age.

Nevertheless, remaining life expectancy is only one important characteristic of people that changes over time, and it only incorporates one dimension of the demographic effect of education on ageing. Education also affects disability rates, health status, and retirement age. If we were interested in forecasting the future cost of health care or future pension costs, for example, we might use other characteristics. No single measure provides us with all the information that we need to study ageing. But the conventional approach, by ignoring changing age-specific characteristics of people, is surely misleading. Contrasting conventional measures of ageing with one that takes changing life expectancy into account provides us with a rough assessment of how misleading the conventional measures could be.

Figure 11.1 shows the difference between chronological and prospective ages for French women in 1952 and 2005. Panels A and B show bars, the lengths of which represent people's lifetimes. Each bar is divided into two segments. The segment on the left shows the number of years a person has already lived, and the one on the right the expected number of years left to live. Panel A shows the conventional view of age. The left parts of the bars indicate that the women were both 30 years old, so those parts are of equal length. Remaining life expectancies, however, are different and therefore the right parts of the bars have different lengths. The 30-year-old woman in 1952 had a remaining life expectancy of 44.7 years, while her counterpart in 2005 had a remaining life expectancy of 54.4 years.

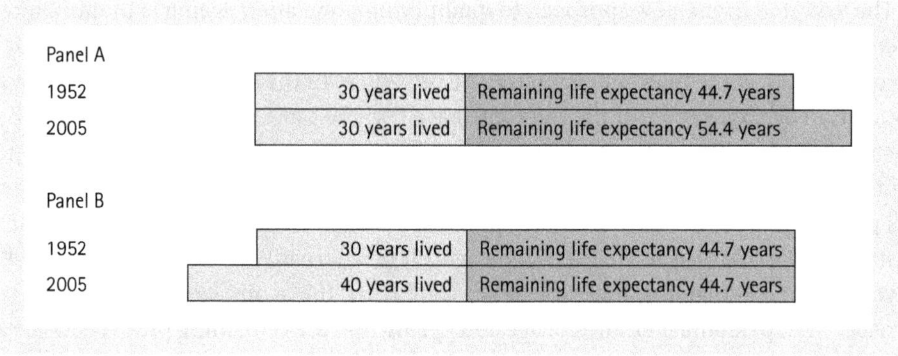

FIGURE 11.1 Remaining life expectancy among french women, 1952 and 2005.

Source: University of California, Berkeley, and Max Planck Institute for Demographic Research, Human Mortality Database (<http://www.mortality.org> and <http://www.humanmortality.de>).

The new approach to establishing age equivalence emphasizes the length of the right-hand portions of the bar. This is done in panel B. Here, the remaining life expectancy in 1952 and 2005 is 44.7 years. However, when the right-hand portions of the bars are of the same length, the left-hand sides are generally of different length. In this example, a 30-year-old woman in 1952 and a 40-year-old woman in 2005 have the same remaining life expectancy, and therefore have the same characteristic-based age. In this example, 40 is the new 30 for French women in 2005 when compared with women in 1952, or to put the matter more technically, the prospective age of 40-year-old French women in 2005 is 30 when 1952 is the base year.

Our first application of the new meaning of age is to compare prospective median ages with their conventional counterparts by world region and for selected countries, using our central projections. Prospective median age is just the prospective age of median-aged people. Table 11.1 shows conventional and prospective median ages for the world's population at decadal intervals from 2010 to 2090 (for technical reasons, prospective median ages for 2100 cannot be computed). Median ages are computed for three education scenarios, the general education trend scenario (GET), the constant enrolment rate scenario (CER), and the fast track scenario (FT). These are described in Chapter 8. All the tables in this chapter use our medium fertility, mortality, and migration assumptions.

The median age of the world's population in 2010 was 28.4 years. In the GET scenario, it would increase to 46.4 years in 2090, about the same as the median age of Germany at the time of writing. In contrast, the prospective median age rises only to 34.9 in that scenario, close to the current median (and prospective median) age of China. Over the eight decades the median age of the world's population increases by 18.0 years, while the perspective median age rises by only 6.5 years. This substantial difference in the extent of measured ageing arises from the fact that the prospective median age takes increases in life expectancy into account, while the conventional approach does not.

Table 11.1 World Conventional (MA) and Prospective Median Ages (PMA) by Education Scenario

	GET		CER		FT	
Panel A: levels						
Year	MA	PMA	MA	PMA	MA	PMA
2010	28.4	28.4	28.4	28.4	28.4	28.4
2020	31.2	29.4	31.0	29.3	31.3	29.5
2030	33.9	30.5	33.4	30.2	34.4	31.0
2040	36.2	31.4	35.3	30.7	37.3	32.2
2050	38.5	32.3	37.1	31.2	40.2	33.6
2060	40.7	33.3	38.7	31.9	42.9	35.0
2070	42.7	34.0	40.1	32.3	45.2	36.0
2080	44.5	34.5	41.4	32.4	47.3	36.8
2090	46.4	34.9	42.7	32.5	49.2	37.4
Panel B: decadal changes						
Start year						
2010	2.8	1.0	2.6	0.9	3.0	1.1
2020	2.7	1.1	2.4	0.9	3.1	1.5
2030	2.3	0.8	1.9	0.5	2.8	1.2
2040	2.3	0.9	1.7	0.5	2.9	1.4
2050	2.2	1.0	1.7	0.7	2.7	1.3
2060	2.0	0.7	1.4	0.4	2.4	1.0
2070	1.8	0.5	1.3	0.2	2.1	0.8
2080	1.8	0.4	1.3	0.1	1.9	0.6

GET: global education trend; CER: constant enrolment rate; FT: fast track.

The time patterns of changes in median and prospective median ages are also different. Decadal changes in the median age tend to decline over time. The speed of change in the prospective median age does not change much over the next few decades. Only beginning in 2060 do we see a significant reduction in the speed of ageing.

The different education scenarios have two kinds of effects on the median ages. First, because education affects fertility and mortality, as discussed in Chapters 3–6, it changes the age distribution of the population, causing the median age to change. Second, eventually the different education scenarios change the education composition of people at the median age and therefore their remaining life expectancy. In the CER scenario, where fertility is higher and life expectancy lower than in the GET scenario, ageing is slower. Indeed, toward the end of this century, the prospective median age barely changes. Ageing is faster in the FT scenario, with its lower fertility and higher life expectancy. In that scenario, the increase in the conventional median age from 2010 to 2090 is 20.8 years and the increase in the prospective median age is 9.0 years. In 2090, the differences between the CER and FT scenarios result in a difference of 6.5 years in the world's median age and a difference in 4.9 years in its prospective median age.

The evolution of population ageing will be quite different on different continents. Tables 11.2 and 11.3 show the situations for Africa and Europe. In the GET scenario, the median age of Africans increases from 19.6 years in 2010 to 37.9 years in 2090. The prospective median age increases much more slowly, only to 25.7 years in 2090. So adjusting for life expectancy improvements reduces the median age in 2090 by 12.2 years. Without adjustment for life expectancy change, the African median age increases over time, then stabilizes at a decadal gain of 2.7 years after 2060. The pattern of change in the prospective median age is somewhat different. It decreases between 2010 and 2020, then after 2030 changes at a roughly constant pace to 2090. Hence, the education scenario chosen has a substantial effect on the speed of ageing. The decadal changes in the prospective median age are almost twice as fast in the FT scenario as in the CER scenario.

Europe's population is much older than Africa's. Even in 2090, Africa's population will not be as old as Europe's is in 2010. The median age of Europe's population in 2010 was 40.2 years. Under the GET scenario, it is forecast to increase to 51.7 years in 2090. But the prospective median age in Europe shows a dramatically different evolution. The prospective median age rises from 40.2 years in 2010 to 41.1 years in 2040 and then decreases. The prospective median age of Europeans in 2090 is only 34.9 years, 5.3 years

Table 11.2 Africa Conventional (MA) and Prospective Median Ages (PMA) by Education Scenario

	GET		CER		FT	
Panel A: levels						
Year	MA	PMA	MA	PMA	MA	PMA
2010	19.6	19.6	19.6	19.6	19.6	19.6
2020	20.8	19.1	20.7	19.0	21.1	19.1
2030	22.7	19.6	22.1	19.3	23.5	19.9
2040	24.9	20.6	23.8	20.0	26.3	21.3
2050	27.2	21.6	25.8	20.8	29.2	22.7
2060	29.8	22.6	27.9	21.5	32.2	23.9
2070	32.5	23.7	30.1	22.3	35.2	25.3
2080	35.2	24.7	32.3	23.0	38.1	26.6
2090	37.9	25.7	34.6	23.5	40.8	27.8
Panel B: decadal changes						
Start year						
2010	1.3	−0.5	1.1	−0.5	1.5	−0.4
2020	1.8	0.5	1.4	0.2	2.4	0.8
2030	2.2	1.0	1.7	0.7	2.8	1.4
2040	2.4	1.0	2.0	0.8	2.9	1.4
2050	2.6	1.0	2.1	0.7	3.0	1.2
2060	2.7	1.1	2.2	0.8	3.0	1.4
2070	2.7	1.0	2.3	0.7	2.9	1.3
2080	2.7	1.0	2.2	0.5	2.7	1.1

GET: global education trend; CER: constant enrolment rate; FT: fast track.

Table 11.3 Europe Conventional (MA) and Prospective Median Ages (PMA) by Education Scenario

	GET		CER		FT	
Panel A: levels						
Year	MA	PMA	MA	PMA	MA	PMA
2010	40.2	40.2	40.2	40.2	40.2	40.2
2020	42.5	40.2	42.5	40.1	42.5	40.2
2030	45.1	40.7	45.0	40.7	45.3	40.9
2040	47.4	41.1	47.1	40.9	47.8	41.5
2050	47.8	39.4	47.2	39.0	48.4	40.1
2060	48.6	38.2	47.8	37.6	49.5	39.1
2070	49.6	37.1	48.5	36.3	50.8	38.2
2080	50.5	35.8	49.1	34.8	51.8	37.1
2090	51.7	34.9	50.1	33.7	53.1	36.2
Panel B: decadal changes						
Start year						
2010	2.3	0.0	2.3	−0.1	2.4	0.0
2020	2.7	0.6	2.6	0.6	2.8	0.7
2030	2.3	0.3	2.1	0.2	2.5	0.5
2040	0.4	−1.7	0.1	−1.9	0.7	−1.4
2050	0.8	−1.2	0.6	−1.4	1.1	−1.0
2060	1.0	−1.1	0.7	−1.3	1.3	−0.8
2070	0.9	−1.3	0.6	−1.5	1.0	−1.2
2080	1.2	−0.9	1.0	−1.1	1.3	−0.9

GET: global education trend; CER: constant enrolment rate; FT: fast track.

lower than it was in 2010. Once we incorporate the effects of life expectancy change into our measurement of age, we see that Europe will be ageing slowly between 2010 and 2040, and then will become effectively younger.

The difference between thinking of ageing on a personal level and on a population or societal level can be envisioned as the difference between moving along a fixed piece of string and moving along a rubber band that is being stretched. An individual life can be viewed as movement along a fixed piece of string. The farther one is from birth the closer one is to death. In the case of populations with increasing life expectancies, though, ageing is like moving along a stretching rubber band. It is possible, as the rubber band stretches, for the median-aged person both to be farther from birth and simultaneously farther from death. If we think chronological age is a good proxy for our productivities and capacities then, after a certain age, moving farther from birth means that our productivities and capacities have, on average, declined. However, if we think that our remaining life expectancy is a good proxy for our productivities and capacities, then, after a certain age, being farther from our death implies that our productivities and capacities have, on average, increased. A falling prospective median age in Europe means that median-aged Europeans will, after 2040, have more and more years ahead of them.

As people and societies adjust to these longer remaining lifetimes, we may well see consistent changes in behaviour and policy.

As we would expect, the difference between prospective median ages in the CER and FT scenarios is smaller in Europe than in Africa. In 2090, the difference in prospective medians in Africa is 4.3 years, while in Europe it is 2.5 years. Education attainment levels are already high in Europe and there is less difference there between the two scenarios than there is for Africa. Nevertheless, the difference of 2.5 years shows that, even in Europe, faster education improvements can still matter.

In Table 11.4, we limit our attention to the GET education scenario and focus on ageing as measured by forecasted conventional and prospective median ages in African, Asia, Europe, Latin America and the Caribbean (LAC), and North America. One interesting feature of Table 11.4 is the pattern of ageing in North America. The median age there in 2010 was 37.2 years, after which it rises in every decade reaching a peak of 48.5 years in 2090. In contrast, the prospective median age in North America falls in every decade, except between 2020 and 2030, when it remains roughly constant. While median-aged people in North America are growing older over time in the conventional sense, they are also having longer average lifetimes ahead of them. As the century progresses, median-aged North Americans will have experienced more birthdays and simultaneously have more future birthdays left to enjoy.

In Table 11.4, the oldest population group in 2010 was the Europeans, with a prospective median age of 40.2 years. By 2090, they will no longer be the oldest under this scenario. Their prospective median age will have declined to 34.9 years. Europeans will, effectively, be younger in 2090 than they are today. In Asia and in the LAC region, however, populations age relatively rapidly. In Asia, the prospective median age rises from 28.5 years in 2010 to 37.8 years in 2090. The increase in the LAC region is similar, from 27.4 years in 2010 to 37.4 years in 2090. Europe is currently a relatively old region that, over time, will become effectively younger. Asia and the LAC region are relatively young regions today that will become effectively older.

Table 11.4 Median (MA) and Prospective Median Ages (PMA) by Continent

	Africa		Asia		Europe		LAC		North America	
	MA	PMA	MA	PMA	MA	PMA	MA	PMA	MA	PMA
2010	19.6	19.6	28.5	28.5	40.2	40.2	27.4	27.4	37.2	37.2
2020	20.8	19.1	32.0	30.2	42.5	40.2	30.9	28.8	38.4	36.9
2030	22.7	19.6	35.6	32.1	45.1	40.7	34.4	30.3	40.1	37.0
2040	24.9	20.6	38.8	33.6	47.4	41.1	38.0	32.1	41.5	36.7
2050	27.2	21.6	41.6	34.9	47.8	39.4	41.3	33.8	42.6	35.8
2060	29.8	22.6	44.2	36.3	48.6	38.2	44.4	35.2	43.5	34.5
2070	32.5	23.7	46.5	37.2	49.6	37.1	47.2	36.2	44.9	33.8
2080	35.2	24.7	48.3	37.6	50.5	35.8	49.6	37.0	46.7	33.5
2090	37.9	25.7	49.9	37.8	51.7	34.9	51.8	37.4	48.5	33.1

LAC: Latin America and the Caribbean.

If we exclude Africa, the gap in prospective median ages across the remaining four regions in 2010 is 12.8 years (27.4 in LAC and 40.2 in Europe). In 2090, the gap is much smaller, only 4.7 years (33.1 in North America and 37.8 in Africa.) For a number of reasons this convergence is likely exaggerated compared with what may actually transpire. For one thing, we have considered in Table 11.4 only a single education scenario. It is likely that there will be more education variation than assumed here. Also, our calculations used only the central fertility and mortality assumptions. Inevitably, variability in our fertility, mortality, and education assumptions would result in less convergence. Nevertheless, as more and more countries complete their demographic and education transitions, we think that prospective median ages across continents will slowly become more similar.

Table 11.5 shows conventional and prospective median ages for 2010, 2050, and 2090 for 11 selected countries. For simplicity, we present figures based on only a single scenario that uses our medium assumptions with respect to fertility, mortality, migration, and education. When we look at the conventional median age measures, we obtain the traditional view of population ageing. Median ages rise in each interval for all of the 11 countries. However, when we take life expectancy increases into account, the picture changes substantially.

The traditional view occurs in only 4 of our 11 countries: Egypt, Kenya, India, and Indonesia. In the other seven countries, the prospective median age falls in at least one

Table 11.5 Conventional (MA) and Prospective Median Ages (PMA): Selected Countries

Country	MA			PMA		
	2010	2050	2090	2010	2050	2090
Africa						
Egypt	24.4	36.1	47.3	24.4	30.0	34.1
Kenya	18.5	27.4	38.6	18.5	22.1	25.5
Nigeria	18.4	23.1	34.1	18.4	17.6	21.2
South Africa	24.9	33.2	41.9	24.9	24.7	23.4
Asia						
China	34.6	51.6	58.4	34.6	45.0	44.9
India	25.1	38.0	48.2	25.1	29.4	35.4
Indonesia	27.7	42.3	51.7	27.7	34.1	37.4
Republic of Korea	37.9	55.4	60.5	37.9	48.4	46.1
Europe						
Germany	44.3	52.2	55.3	44.3	44.2	39.2
Russian Federation	37.8	44.6	48.7	37.8	36.4	31.6
North America						
USA	36.9	42.3	48.2	36.9	35.6	32.9

of the intervals. The prospective median age falls in both intervals, 2010–50 and 2050–90, in South Africa, Germany, the Russian Federation, and the USA. South Africa is a particularly interesting example of this pattern. Its median age rises from 24.9 years in 2010 to 41.9 years in 2090. When we do not take increasing life expectancy into account, it appears that South Africa should plan for substantial ageing. However, when we do take increasing life expectancy into account, the median age of South Africans in 2090 is not expected to be very different from what it is today. More generally, Table 11.5 shows that when we measure ageing while ignoring the effects of the life expectancy changes that are built into our forecasts, we get a picture of uniformity that is unjustified. Taking those life expectancy changes into account yields a far more nuanced picture, with some countries having increasing prospective median ages, some having decreasing ones, and some where the prospective median age goes up in one period and down in another.

11.4 How old do you have to be to be 'old'?

One use of prospective ages is to provide an old age threshold, analogous to the age of 65, but adjusted for changes in life expectancy. This use was first proposed by Ryder (1975):

> To the extent that our concern with age is what it signifies about the degree of deterioration and dependence, it would seem sensible to consider the measurement of age not in terms of years elapsed since birth but rather in terms of the number of years remaining until death.... We propose that some arbitrary length of time, such as 10 years, be selected and that we determine at what age the expectation of life is 10 years, that age to be considered the point of entry into old-age... (p. 16)

With this insight Ryder redefined the old age threshold, not with another fixed number, but with remaining life expectancy, a characteristic of people that changes over time and is closely related to changing age structure. Essentially, Ryder's idea was to take a constant value of a characteristic that defines the threshold of old age and transform it into a time-varying age.

Sanderson and Scherbov (2005) came independently to the same conclusion, but with the old age threshold at 15 years of remaining life. They preferred 15 years because it was the remaining life expectancy of 65-year-olds in many low mortality countries in the 1960s. Table 11.6 shows our old age thresholds for the world and for the five continents using our medium assumptions. These correspond to chronological ages in forecasted life tables where remaining life expectancy is exactly 15 years. Using this criterion for the world as a whole, people would be classified as 'old' in 2010 when they reached the age of 67.0. We compute that the old age threshold for the world would increase to 72.6 years of age in 2050 and to 77.8 years in 2090.

The continent with the highest old age threshold in 2010 was North America where a person would have to be 70.8 years old. It was lowest in Africa, where the threshold value was 62.6 years of age. These thresholds change at different speeds on different continents.

We expect it to grow particularly slowly in Africa. Because of this and because of the increasing proportion of the world's population that will be in Africa as the century progresses, the world's old age threshold increases less rapidly than it does for all the continents except Africa. The speed at which the old age threshold increases is especially rapid in Europe, where the threshold increases by 14.6 years over the 8 decades covered in Table 11.6.

Table 11.7 shows the old age thresholds for selected countries. In Germany, the statutory pension age is scheduled to increase by two years, from 65 to 67, between 2010 and 2034. The old age threshold increases from 70.8 in 2010 to around 75 in 2034, an increase of 4.2 years. Clearly, the old age threshold is expected to rise about twice as fast as the statutory pension age. If Germans retire at the age of 67 in 2034, they are still likely to have more years of pension support than the 65-year-olds who retired in 2010, and they will have 8 years of retirement before they would be categorized as being old. By contrast, the old age threshold increases least rapidly in Kenya in the medium term. There, people entered 'old age' at 63.1 years in 2010 and are forecast to enter that group at age 64.9 in 2050. In 2090, Kenya remains the country with the lowest threshold age in our table.

Table 11.7 also shows old age thresholds diverging over time. In 2010, the difference between the highest (Germany) and lowest (South Africa) threshold ages was 9.6 years. By 2090 we expect that the difference between the highest (Germany) and the lowest (Nigeria) would balloon to 17.5 years.

Tables 11.6 and 11.7 provide a sharp contrast to the notion that people all over the world become 'old' at the age of 65. Using the criterion that people become 'old' when life expectancy at their age falls to 15 years, old age thresholds vary dramatically by continent, by country, and especially over time. We are interested in ageing because the characteristics of people differ by age, and, of course, these characteristics differ for many reasons. When ages represent productivities and capacities, not just the number of birthdays people have had, the new measures of ageing match the interests in ageing more closely.

Table 11.6 Threshold Ages for Becoming 'Old'

Year	World	Africa	Asia	Europe	LAC	North America
2010	67.0	62.6	65.7	69.2	69.1	70.8
2020	68.5	63.5	67.3	71.2	70.9	72.2
2030	69.9	64.3	68.7	72.9	72.6	73.4
2040	71.3	65.2	70.2	74.6	74.1	74.6
2050	72.6	66.1	71.7	76.4	75.5	76.2
2060	73.8	67.1	73.0	78.1	77.0	78.0
2070	75.0	68.1	74.2	79.7	78.6	79.8
2080	76.4	69.1	75.5	81.7	80.1	81.7
2090	77.8	70.3	77.0	83.8	81.7	83.7

LAC: Latin America and the Caribbean.

Table 11.7 Old Age Thresholds

Countries	2010	2020	2030	2040	2050	2060	2070	2080	2090
Africa									
Egypt	64.5	65.7	66.9	68.4	70.0	71.7	73.3	74.9	76.7
Kenya	63.1	63.2	63.8	64.2	64.9	66.0	67.2	68.6	69.9
Nigeria	61.2	61.8	62.4	63.0	63.6	64.2	65.1	66.3	67.6
South Africa	61.5	63.0	63.3	63.9	64.7	65.8	66.8	68.0	69.3
Asia									
China	65.6	67.2	68.8	70.2	71.9	73.5	75.1	76.7	78.5
India	63.4	64.8	66.5	68.5	70.2	71.3	72.4	73.5	74.5
Indonesia	63.4	65.3	67.1	69.0	70.5	71.9	73.2	74.6	76.0
Republic of Korea	70.6	72.1	73.8	75.3	77.1	78.8	80.5	82.4	84.2
Europe									
Germany	70.8	72.6	74.3	76.1	77.6	79.5	81.3	83.2	85.1
Russian Federation	65.0	66.6	68.0	69.3	70.9	72.7	74.3	76.2	78.1
North America									
USA	70.7	72.0	73.2	74.4	76.0	77.8	79.5	81.4	83.4

11.5 The proportion of the population who are 'old'

Tables 11.6 and 11.7 demonstrate that the threshold for becoming 'old' varies across space and over time. In this section, we use these thresholds to compute the proportions of populations who are 'old'. Table 11.8 shows proportions 'old' for the world using the two threshold ages, one assuming people always become 'old' at the age of 65 and one based on prospective age (see Table 11.6).

In the world as a whole in our GET scenario, 7.6 per cent of the population was 65+ years old in 2010. That figure increases to 17.5 per cent by 2050 and then to 27.4 per cent in 2090. Using the prospective age criterion, the proportion of the world's population who are old increases much more slowly, from 6.5 per cent in 2010 to 10.3 per cent in 2050 and to 13.2 per cent in 2090. The percentage 'old' roughly doubles between 2010 and 2090, even using prospective age to define who is 'old', but the conventional percentage increases by much more, about 3.6 times over that period.

Table 11.8 shows the proportions 'old' using our prospective definition for three education scenarios. Changes in educational policies after 2010 have only modest effects on this measure of ageing in the short and medium term. Increases in educational attainments for women decrease fertility and the number of children in the population. This has a small effect on the total size of the world's population, which is

Table 11.8 World Conventional (Conv.) and Prospective (Prosp.) Proportions 'Old' by Education Scenario

	GET		CER		FT	
Panel A: levels						
Year	Conv.	Prosp.	Conv.	Prosp.	Conv.	Prosp.
2010	0.076	0.065	0.076	0.065	0.076	0.065
2020	0.094	0.068	0.093	0.068	0.094	0.069
2030	0.119	0.080	0.118	0.079	0.121	0.081
2040	0.149	0.092	0.145	0.090	0.153	0.094
2050	0.175	0.103	0.169	0.099	0.183	0.107
2060	0.206	0.113	0.194	0.109	0.219	0.119
2070	0.228	0.124	0.210	0.118	0.250	0.134
2080	0.252	0.128	0.225	0.120	0.281	0.143
2090	0.274	0.132	0.241	0.120	0.305	0.152
Panel B: decadal changes						
Start year						
2010	0.018	0.003	0.017	0.003	0.018	0.004
2020	0.025	0.012	0.024	0.011	0.027	0.012
2030	0.030	0.012	0.028	0.011	0.032	0.013
2040	0.026	0.011	0.023	0.009	0.030	0.012
2050	0.031	0.011	0.026	0.009	0.037	0.012
2060	0.023	0.011	0.016	0.009	0.031	0.015
2070	0.023	0.004	0.015	0.002	0.031	0.009
2080	0.022	0.004	0.016	0.001	0.024	0.009

GET: global education trend; CER: constant enrolment rate; FT: fast track.

reflected in our data as early as 2020. The main effect of changing educational attainments beginning in 2010 happens only after a lag of about 70 or more years, when the people born after the changes in educational policy become old enough to be considered elderly.

Table 11.9 presents the proportions 'old' by continent, again using our medium assumptions about fertility, mortality, migration, and education. In 2010, the proportion 'old' in Africa is 3.5 per cent using the age of 65 as the old-age threshold and 4.4 per cent using the prospective old-age threshold. Africa is the only region where the proportion 'old' is higher when measured using the prospective criterion. This occurs because in Africa in 2010, life expectancy at the age of 65 is less than 15 years.

In Europe, the picture of ageing is far different when we adjust the proportion elderly for changes in life expectancy. In Europe in 2010, 16.2 per cent of the population was 'old' using the age of 65 as a threshold. This figure rises rapidly to 28.9 per cent by 2050 and then continues upward to 35.0 per cent in 2090. These kinds of figures underlie current public and policy discussions of rapid population ageing in Europe. However, taking increasing life expectancy into account, the per cent of the population 'old' increases only

Table 11.9 Conventional (Conv.) and Prospective (Prosp.) Proportions 'Old' by Continents

	Africa		Asia		Europe		LAC		North America	
	Conv.	Prosp.	Conv.	Prosp.	Conv.	Prosp.	Conv.	Prosp.	Conv.	Prosp.
2010	0.035	0.044	0.067	0.063	0.162	0.126	0.069	0.049	0.069	0.049
2020	0.039	0.045	0.088	0.070	0.190	0.120	0.090	0.053	0.090	0.053
2030	0.045	0.048	0.117	0.085	0.229	0.132	0.123	0.064	0.123	0.064
2040	0.053	0.053	0.158	0.104	0.261	0.145	0.161	0.081	0.161	0.081
2050	0.068	0.062	0.191	0.119	0.289	0.148	0.202	0.097	0.202	0.097
2060	0.087	0.073	0.232	0.135	0.309	0.151	0.243	0.112	0.243	0.112
2070	0.107	0.084	0.261	0.151	0.314	0.154	0.282	0.126	0.282	0.126
2080	0.132	0.096	0.288	0.158	0.331	0.142	0.313	0.137	0.313	0.137
2090	0.159	0.108	0.312	0.162	0.350	0.134	0.342	0.145	0.342	0.145

LAC: Latin America and the Caribbean.

from 12.6 per cent in 2010 to 14.8 per cent in 2050. In 2090, the per cent elderly becomes 13.4 per cent, 1.4 percentage points less than in 2050. This is hardly a picture of exceptionally rapid ageing. Indeed, between 2010 and 2050, the prospective measure of the proportion elderly increases less rapidly in Europe than on any other continent except Africa.

Comparing the speed of ageing in North America with Europe is also interesting. In North America, the prospective percentage of the elderly population increases from 4.9 in 2010 to 9.7 in 2050. North America begins the period younger than Europe and it remains younger throughout most of the century, but it is expected to age much more rapidly. The ageing of North America is so much faster than in Europe that, by 2090, Europe is actually younger than North America. Outside of Africa, Europe would have the youngest population among the other four continents in 2090.

Asia provides a clear example of the effects of adjusting the measurement of the proportion elderly for changes in life expectancy. In 2010, the conventional and the prospective proportions are nearly the same, but by 2090 the conventional proportion is nearly twice as high.

Table 11.10 presents conventional and prospective proportions 'old' for our selected countries for 2010, 2050, and 2090. Using the prospective measure, the proportion 'old' in Germany increases from 14.0 per cent in 2010 to 18.7 per cent in 2050. In the second half of the century, this proportion decreases. In 2090, the proportion is barely higher than in 2010. Germany provides a good example of countries where ageing in the first half of the century will progress much faster than in the second half. Other countries with this pattern of ageing include the Republic of Korea, the Russian Federation, and the USA. In China, ageing will also slow after the middle of the century. In some countries, the pattern will be the reverse. These include Egypt, Kenya, Nigeria, South Africa, and India, where ageing will be more rapid during the second half of the century. The difficulties involved in adjusting to older populations depend, importantly, on the speed of ageing; in these countries those difficulties will become more pressing later in the century.

Table 11.10 Conventional and Prospective Proportions 'Old': Selected Countries

Country	Conventional			Prospective		
	2010	2050	2090	2010	2050	2090
Africa						
Egypt	0.050	0.138	0.281	0.053	0.088	0.140
Kenya	0.027	0.063	0.165	0.032	0.063	0.117
Nigeria	0.034	0.048	0.112	0.048	0.054	0.090
South Africa	0.046	0.092	0.189	0.065	0.094	0.141
Asia						
China	0.082	0.282	0.416	0.078	0.190	0.225
India	0.049	0.146	0.282	0.057	0.095	0.163
Indonesia	0.056	0.194	0.329	0.063	0.127	0.183
Republic of Korea	0.111	0.370	0.445	0.070	0.194	0.200
Europe						
Germany	0.204	0.338	0.388	0.140	0.187	0.153
Russian Federation	0.128	0.239	0.310	0.128	0.153	0.145
North America						
USA	0.130	0.224	0.309	0.086	0.117	0.117

11.6 Tomorrow's older population will not be like today's

Tomorrow's ≥65-year-old populations will not be like today's. We demonstrate this in two ways. First, we look at the proportion of the 65+ population who would be 'old' according to our prospective definition. Second, we consider the projected proportions of older populations by level of education.

If we follow Ryder in stipulating that the old age category should not start at the age of 65 (or any other fixed chronological age), but should depend on the characteristics of people such as their remaining life expectancy, then a new question arises: What fraction of the 65+ population is 'old'? The answer for the world and its continents is in Table 11.11, based again on our medium assumptions.

For the world as a whole, 85 per cent of the 65+ population was 'old' in 2010. This percentage falls over time, such that between 2080 and 2090 only a minority of the 65+ population of the world will be 'old'. North America has the lowest percentage of its 65+ population 'old' in 2010. Between 2050 and 2060, only a minority of 65+ year old people will be 'old'. This transition to a minority of 65+ year olds being 'old' happens first in the LAC region. There, a minority of 65+ years old are 'old' from 2040 onwards. In Africa,

Table 11.11 Proportion of ≥65-Year-Old Populations 'Old'

	World	Africa	Asia	Europe	LAC	North America
2010	0.85	1.00	0.94	0.78	0.71	0.65
2020	0.73	1.00	0.80	0.63	0.59	0.55
2030	0.67	1.00	0.72	0.57	0.52	0.54
2040	0.62	0.99	0.66	0.56	0.50	0.58
2050	0.59	0.90	0.62	0.51	0.48	0.52
2060	0.55	0.84	0.58	0.49	0.46	0.44
2070	0.54	0.78	0.58	0.49	0.45	0.42
2080	0.51	0.73	0.55	0.43	0.44	0.40
2090	0.48	0.68	0.52	0.38	0.42	0.37

LAC: Latin America and the Caribbean.

Table 11.12 Proportions of 65+ Populations Who Are 'Old': Selected Countries

Country	2010	2020	2030	2040	2050	2060	2070	2080	2090
Africa									
Egypt	1.00	0.94	0.85	0.77	0.64	0.62	0.58	0.53	0.50
Kenya	1.00	1.00	1.00	1.00	1.00	0.92	0.82	0.75	0.71
Nigeria	1.00	1.00	1.00	1.00	1.00	1.00	0.99	0.90	0.81
South Africa	1.00	1.00	1.00	1.00	1.00	0.94	0.88	0.81	0.74
Asia									
China	0.95	0.80	0.73	0.67	0.67	0.59	0.60	0.57	0.54
India	1.00	1.00	0.88	0.74	0.65	0.63	0.61	0.59	0.58
Indonesia	1.00	0.98	0.82	0.71	0.66	0.64	0.60	0.58	0.56
Republic of Korea	0.63	0.56	0.47	0.51	0.53	0.51	0.48	0.49	0.45
Europe									
Germany	0.69	0.61	0.51	0.53	0.55	0.48	0.45	0.43	0.40
Russian Federation	1.00	0.87	0.81	0.76	0.64	0.64	0.64	0.49	0.47
LAC									
Brazil	0.69	0.55	0.48	0.48	0.45	0.46	0.46	0.46	0.45
North America									
USA	0.66	0.56	0.55	0.58	0.52	0.45	0.43	0.41	0.38

LAC: Latin America and the Caribbean.

however, all of the ≥65-year-olds are 'old' in 2010. By 2090, 68 per cent will be 'old'. All over the world, fewer and fewer ≥65-year-olds will be 'old' in the future.

Table 11.12 presents the data for our selected countries. In the Russian Federation in 2010, all people aged 65+ will be classified as 'old', but this percentage declines over time so that around 2080, less than half of those 65+ would fall into this category. In the three sub-Saharan African countries all people aged 65+ would be considered 'old' through to the middle of the century. After that, a smaller percentage will be 'old', but a comparatively high percentage would still be classified as being old in 2090. Of the 12 countries in Table 11.12, five have 50 per cent or less of the 65+ population in the 'old' category by 2090. Only three have percentages 'old' above 60 per cent in 2090. Clearly, as the century progresses, being above the age of 65 becomes an ever worse predictor of whether a person is 'old'.

When thinking about population ageing, it is natural to envision a situation where there are more people in the population who are similar to older people alive today. But this is not a good model of future ageing populations. As we just discussed, one way in which people age 65+ in the future will be different from people of that age today is that a smaller percentage of them will be 'old'. A related way in which they will differ is in their level of education. Tomorrow's older population will be much more educated and therefore much more capable and productive than today's older population.

Table 11.13 (a, b) shows the education distribution of the population aged 65+ and of the 'old' population using our prospective definition. Table 11.13 presents the proportions of those two groups with some secondary schooling or more for the world and the

Table 11.13a Proportion of 'Old' Population with Some Secondary or Higher Education

	World	Africa	Asia	Europe	LAC	North America
2010	0.37	0.11	0.23	0.62	0.22	0.87
2020	0.46	0.17	0.34	0.72	0.30	0.92
2030	0.55	0.26	0.46	0.82	0.41	0.95
2040	0.63	0.34	0.55	0.88	0.51	0.96
2050	0.69	0.44	0.64	0.92	0.60	0.96
2060	0.75	0.53	0.71	0.95	0.68	0.97
2070	0.79	0.59	0.77	0.97	0.76	0.98
2080	0.83	0.65	0.81	0.98	0.81	0.99
2090	0.86	0.69	0.85	0.98	0.85	0.99

LAC: Latin America and the Caribbean.

Table 11.13b Proportion of 65+ Population with Some Secondary or Higher Education

	World	Africa	Asia	Europe	LAC	North America
2010	0.38	0.09	0.23	0.65	0.24	0.89
2020	0.48	0.16	0.36	0.77	0.35	0.94
2030	0.57	0.25	0.48	0.86	0.46	0.95
2040	0.64	0.34	0.58	0.91	0.56	0.96
2050	0.70	0.44	0.66	0.94	0.65	0.97
2060	0.76	0.53	0.73	0.96	0.73	0.98
2070	0.79	0.60	0.78	0.97	0.79	0.98
2080	0.83	0.65	0.82	0.98	0.84	0.99
2090	0.86	0.70	0.86	0.99	0.88	0.99

LAC: Latin America and the Caribbean.

five continents. Thirty-seven per cent of the 'old' population of the world had secondary education or higher in 2010. Between 2020 and 2030 a majority of the world's 'old' population will be in that group. By 2050, the figure rises to 68 per cent and, by 2090, to 86 per cent. In the LAC region and Asia, the proportion of the 'old' population with secondary or higher education roughly quadruples from 2010 to 2090, ending that period at 85 per cent. In Africa, 11 per cent of the 'old' population had this level of education in 2010. According to our medium assumption, this will rise to 69 per cent by 2090. Toward the end of this century under these assumptions, the 'old' in Africa will be more educated than the 'old' were in Europe in 2010. All over the world, tomorrow's 'old' will be more educated than today's. The education distributions of those aged 65+ are almost identical. In this particular comparison, choosing between the prospective definition of who is 'old' and the conventional definition makes almost no difference.

Table 11.14 presents the same kinds of data for individual countries under our three education scenarios. A striking feature of the GET scenario is its implications for the evolution of education levels of the elderly in Africa. In Egypt, Kenya, and Nigeria, the proportion of the 'old' who have some secondary or higher education was less than 20 per cent in 2010. In 2050, it is over 50 per cent, increasing to more than 90 per cent by

Table 11.14 Proportions of 'Old' Populations with Some Secondary Education or More: Selected Countries

Country	2010	2020	2030	2040	2050	2060	2070	2080	2090
Africa									
Egypt									
GET	0.17	0.27	0.39	0.50	0.62	0.75	0.84	0.90	0.94
CER	0.17	0.27	0.39	0.50	0.62	0.74	0.80	0.81	0.81
FT	0.17	0.27	0.39	0.50	0.62	0.81	0.92	0.97	0.99
Kenya									
GET	0.14	0.22	0.34	0.54	0.72	0.82	0.88	0.93	0.96
CER	0.14	0.22	0.34	0.54	0.64	0.64	0.63	0.63	0.63
FT	0.14	0.22	0.34	0.54	0.75	0.89	0.96	0.98	0.99
Nigeria									
GET	0.09	0.15	0.27	0.40	0.55	0.68	0.78	0.86	0.91
CER	0.09	0.15	0.27	0.40	0.53	0.60	0.63	0.63	0.63
FT	0.09	0.15	0.27	0.40	0.59	0.77	0.91	0.97	0.99
South Africa									
GET	0.32	0.39	0.51	0.66	0.79	0.87	0.91	0.94	0.95
CER	0.32	0.39	0.51	0.66	0.79	0.85	0.87	0.87	0.87
FT	0.32	0.39	0.51	0.66	0.82	0.92	0.97	0.99	1.00
Asia									
China									
GET	0.19	0.33	0.51	0.65	0.75	0.85	0.90	0.92	0.94
CER	0.19	0.33	0.51	0.65	0.75	0.84	0.89	0.90	0.90
FT	0.19	0.33	0.51	0.65	0.75	0.86	0.93	0.97	0.98

India									
GET	0.18	0.25	0.31	0.38	0.47	0.56	0.65	0.72	0.78
CER	0.18	0.25	0.31	0.38	0.47	0.53	0.56	0.56	0.56
FT	0.18	0.25	0.31	0.38	0.47	0.69	0.86	0.94	0.98
Indonesia									
GET	0.13	0.21	0.31	0.43	0.56	0.67	0.77	0.83	0.88
CER	0.13	0.21	0.31	0.43	0.56	0.67	0.74	0.76	0.76
FT	0.13	0.21	0.31	0.43	0.56	0.71	0.84	0.92	0.97
Republic of Korea									
GET	0.28	0.46	0.68	0.86	0.95	0.99	1.00	1.00	1.00
CER	0.28	0.46	0.68	0.86	0.95	0.99	1.00	1.00	1.00
FT	0.28	0.46	0.68	0.86	0.95	0.99	1.00	1.00	1.00
Europe									
Germany									
GET	0.96	0.97	0.97	0.97	0.97	0.97	0.98	0.99	0.99
CER	0.96	0.97	0.97	0.97	0.97	0.97	0.98	0.98	0.99
FT	0.96	0.97	0.97	0.97	0.97	0.97	0.99	0.99	1.00
Russian Federation									
GET	0.81	0.93	0.98	0.99	0.99	1.00	1.00	1.00	1.00
CER	0.81	0.93	0.98	0.99	0.99	0.99	0.99	0.99	0.99
FT	0.81	0.93	0.98	0.99	0.99	1.00	1.00	1.00	1.00
LAC									
Brazil									
GET	0.20	0.27	0.38	0.48	0.56	0.66	0.75	0.82	0.87
CER	0.20	0.27	0.38	0.48	0.56	0.66	0.74	0.78	0.79
FT	0.20	0.27	0.38	0.48	0.56	0.66	0.74	0.78	0.79
North America									
USA									
GET	0.88	0.93	0.95	0.96	0.96	0.97	0.98	0.99	0.99
CER	0.88	0.93	0.95	0.96	0.96	0.97	0.98	0.98	0.98
FT	0.88	0.93	0.95	0.96	0.96	0.97	0.99	1.00	1.00

GET: global education trend; CER: constant enrolment rate; FT: fast track; LAC: Latin America and the Caribbean.

2090. Even in a few decades, the characteristics of the 'old' in Africa as a whole will be substantially different from what it is today.

The laggard in the table is India. In 2010, only 17 per cent of 'old' Indians had some secondary or higher education. By 2050, we expect this to rise by 30 percentage points and then to increase to 78 per cent by 2090. Of course, the education of the 'old' late in the century depends on recent, current, and near-term enrolment patterns. Good data on enrolments exist today, so the lagging position of the 'old' in India toward the end of the century is already a reasonably settled matter.

Because we are considering the educational distributions of the elderly, changes emerge only toward the end of the century. The largest such effects of moving from the CER to the FT scenario occur for India. In 2090, the proportion of the 'old' population there with some secondary education or higher is 56 per cent under the CER scenario and 98 per cent under the FT scenario. Large differences between those two scenarios also appear for Kenya, Nigeria, and Indonesia. In the other countries, the difference between the CER and FT scenarios is modest.

11.7 Retiring the Old Age Dependency Ratio

Standard demographic forecasting emphasizes two key dimensions of human heterogeneity: age and sex. The central message of this book is that a third dimension, education, must be added. However, when studying ageing, we must take another step and recognize that age itself needs to be re-conceptualized. The characteristics that determine when a person becomes 'old' change over time. Yes, toward the end of a person's life he/she might walk with a cane, but now, in an era when hip replacements and sophisticated spinal surgeries for older people are commonplace, the age at which that happens becomes later and later. The addition of education to the standard set of dimensions in population forecasting and the re-conceptualization of age taken together imply that the commonly used measurement of population ageing, the old age dependency ratio, is so misleading that it should now, itself, be retired.

The conventional old age dependency ratio has in its numerator the number of people aged 65 years and older. Age 65 is taken as the invariant age at which people make the transition to being 'old'. Figures 11.2–11.5 show conventional old age dependency ratios

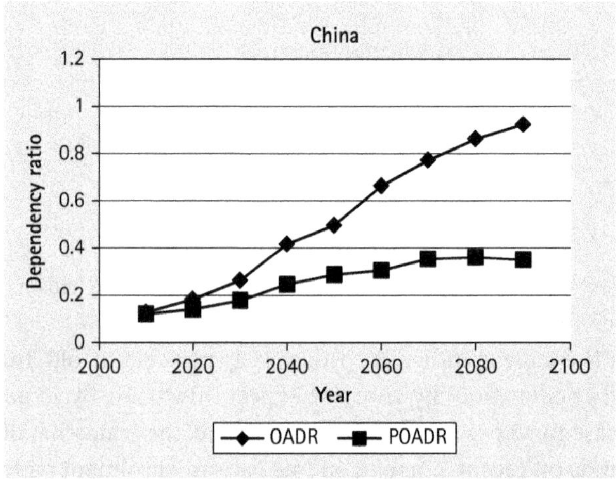

FIGURES 11.2 Comparison of conventional old age dependency ratios (OADR) and prospective old age dependency ratios (POADR) (China).

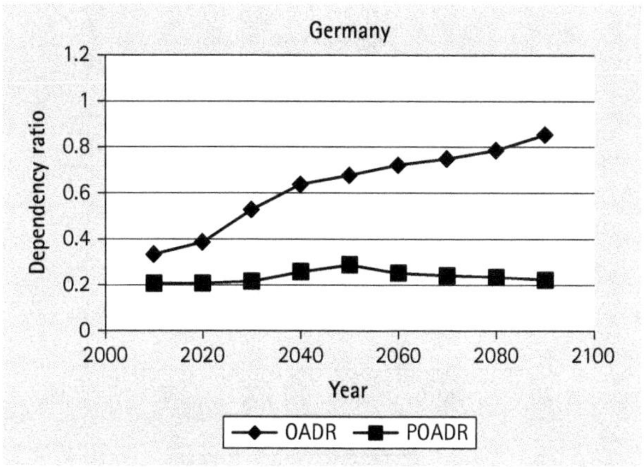

FIGURE 11.3 Comparison of conventional old age dependency ratios (OADR) and prospective old age dependency ratios (POADR) (Germany).

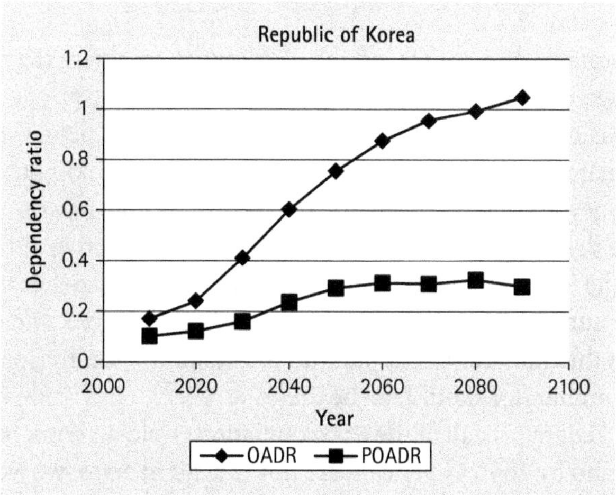

FIGURE 11.4 Comparison of conventional old age dependency ratios (OADR) and prospective old age dependency ratios (POADR) (Republic of Korea).

along with prospective old age dependency ratios where the old age thresholds are adjusted for changes in remaining life expectancy (Table 11.7). Four countries are represented: China, Germany, the Republic of Korea, and the Russian Federation. The time profiles of the prospective old age dependency ratios differ substantially from the unadjusted ones. In Germany and the Russian Federation, the prospective old age dependency ratios are hardly different in 2090 from what they were in 2010. In China and the Republic of Korea, although the conventional old age dependency ratio keeps increasing throughout the century, the prospective old age dependency ratio eventually reaches a plateau. In all cases, ageing measured by the conventional old age dependency ratio rises dramatically faster than when adjusted for changes in life expectancy.

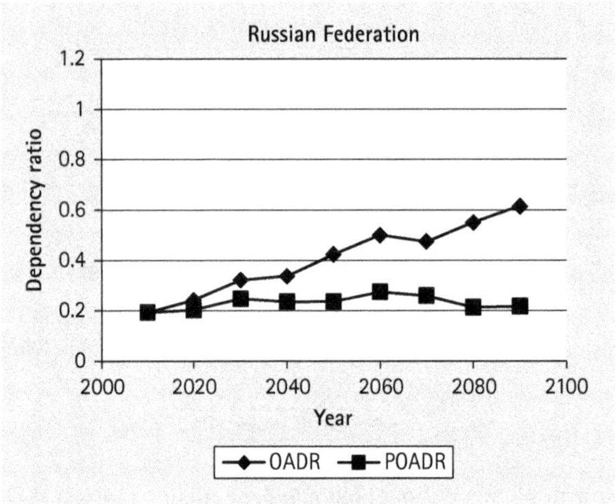

FIGURE 11.5 Comparison of conventional old age dependency ratios (OADR) and prospective old age dependency ratios (POADR) (Russian Federation).

Table 11.15 examines the source of the differences between the prospective and unadjusted old age dependency ratios. In 2010, the prospective old age dependency ratio in China was 0.12 and the unadjusted ratio was 0.13. Ninety-five per cent of the people in the numerator of the unadjusted ratio were 'old', so to compute the prospective old age dependency ratio, 5 per cent of the people would have to move from the numerator to the denominator. In 2050 in China, the prospective old age dependency ratio is 0.29 and the unadjusted ratio is 0.50. This difference arises because 33 per cent of the people in the numerator of the conventional ratio are not 'old' and should therefore be removed from the numerator and put into the denominator. By 2090, 46 per cent of the people in the numerator should not be there.

In the Russian Federation, all of the 65+ population is 'old' in 2010, but by 2050 36 per cent are not 'old' and by 2090 53 per cent are not 'old'. So in 2090, we would have to take more than half of the population in the numerator of the conventional old age dependency ratio and transfer that number to the denominator. By 2090, in Germany, the Republic of Korea, and the Russian Republic, more than half of the number of people who were 65+ would no longer be counted as 'old' after adjusting for changes in remaining life expectancy. Similarly, in China, 46 per cent would not be counted as 'old' by 1990.

The conventional old age dependency ratio suffers mightily from its definition of 'old' being invariant to time and place. It does not matter how long people live, how healthy they are, or how productive they are; everyone becomes old at the age of 65. Adjusting for this, as is done with the prospective old age dependency ratio, changes the measure of ageing considerably.

This is not the only serious problem with the conventional old age dependency ratio. It also does not account for changes in the education composition of the population. In China, 95 per cent of the population aged 65+ was 'old' in 2010. Only 19 per cent of those who were 'old' had secondary or higher education. By 2050 under all three education

Table 11.15 Problems With Old Age Dependency Ratios (OADR)

	2010	2020	2030	2040	2050	2060	2070	2080	2090
China									
OADR	0.13	0.18	0.26	0.42	0.50	0.66	0.77	0.86	0.92
POADR	0.12	0.14	0.18	0.25	0.29	0.30	0.35	0.36	0.35
Per cent 65+ 'old'	0.95	0.80	0.73	0.67	0.67	0.59	0.60	0.57	0.54
Per cent 'old' with secondary education or higher	0.19	0.33	0.51	0.65	0.75	0.84	0.90	0.93	0.94
Germany									
OADR	0.33	0.39	0.53	0.64	0.68	0.72	0.75	0.79	0.85
POADR	0.21	0.21	0.22	0.26	0.29	0.25	0.24	0.23	0.22
Per cent 65+ 'old'	0.69	0.61	0.51	0.53	0.55	0.48	0.45	0.43	0.40
Per cent 'old' with secondary education or higher	0.96	0.97	0.97	0.97	0.98	0.97	0.98	0.98	0.99
Republic of Korea									
OADR	0.17	0.24	0.41	0.60	0.76	0.87	0.96	0.99	1.05
POADR	0.10	0.12	0.16	0.24	0.29	0.31	0.31	0.32	0.30
Per cent 65+ 'old'	0.63	0.56	0.47	0.51	0.53	0.51	0.48	0.49	0.45
Per cent 'old' with secondary education or higher	0.28	0.47	0.68	0.86	0.95	0.99	1.00	1.00	1.00
Russian Federation									
OADR	0.19	0.24	0.32	0.34	0.43	0.50	0.47	0.55	0.61
POADR	0.19	0.20	0.25	0.24	0.24	0.27	0.26	0.21	0.22
Per cent 65+ 'old'	1.00	0.87	0.81	0.76	0.64	0.64	0.64	0.49	0.47
Per cent 'old' with secondary education or higher	0.82	0.94	0.98	0.99	0.99	1.00	1.00	0.99	1.00

POADR: prospective old age dependency ratio.

scenarios, a revolution has occurred in the education of China's elderly population. Among the 67 per cent of the post-65 population who are 'old', a full 75 per cent have secondary or higher education. Even though the old age threshold is rising over time, 94 per cent of the Chinese who will be 'old' in 2090 will have secondary or higher education. Even more spectacularly, in the Republic of Korea, 28 per cent of the 'old' population had secondary or higher education in 2010, a figure that rises to 95 per cent in 2050.

So the education levels of the 'old' population change everywhere over time. In some places they change rapidly and in some, like Germany where the elderly are already quite well educated, they change more slowly. Of course, the educational attainments of the people in the denominator of the prospective dependency ratio also change. Neither the unadjusted old age dependency ratio nor the prospective measure take these denominator changes into account. Some research has been done that focuses on adding education to old age dependency ratios, but at the time of writing there is no definitive way to do it. As there will be massive changes in education distributions in many countries of the world and there is as yet no clear way to adjust for this, we know that even the prospective old age dependency ratio will provide misleading signals about the extent and speed of ageing.

The difficulty of adjusting the old age dependency ratio for education arises, in part, because of the term 'dependency'. Warren Buffet is one of the world's richest people. He was born in 1930, so he would certainly be considered 'old'. Very little of his extensive income comes from labour earnings. Most of it comes from returns to capital and capital gains. If Warren Buffet's consumption were greater than his labour income, would he properly be considered an old age dependent? He is certainly dependent on others for his food and his medical care. He might even have people who clean his house, do his laundry, plan his diet, help keep him limber, and arrange for his taxes to be paid. But does this make him an old age dependent? Intuitively, it does not seem sensible to categorize Buffet as an old age dependent.

Old age dependency is not a clearly defined concept. One definition might be the ratio of adults who are not in the labour force to those who are, but this is very different from either the conventional old age dependency ratio or the prospective one. Instead, this is a variant of the economic dependency ratio that omits children. To make a forecast of how this economic dependency ratio would evolve over time would require forecasts of age-specific labour force participation rates, which would naturally depend on changes in educational attainments. But even this definition is fraught with problems. If Warren Buffet retired and was no longer in the labour force, would he immediately become an economically-dependent old person?

It would be more natural to define dependency as referring to people over half of whose consumption is financed through transfers from others, including governments. This would solve the Warren Buffet question. We could then define a new adult economic dependency ratio as the ratio of adults who require transfers to finance more than half of their consumption to those who do not. This ratio would not require the explicit specification of an old age threshold and would have a firm conceptual foundation. It would, however, be much more difficult to compute and forecast.

11.8 Conclusions

Greek mythology is silent on the matter of whether the Sphinx had any demographic training, but if she had and she followed current practice her question might have been stated a bit differently: What creature walks on four legs until 6 o' clock in the morning, walks on two legs until 7 o' clock in the evening and thereafter walks on three? Those invariant times are the analogues of the fixed ages used in most current measures of population ageing. For studies of population ageing in the twenty-first century, we have argued in this chapter that using chronological age as an indicator of people's productivities, capacities, and interactions with political and social institutions is certainly not appropriate. Assuming that the productivities, capacities, and interactions with political and social institutions are the same today as they were a century ago, which is the underlying assumption for a traditional unadjusted measures of ageing, defies both history and biology.

In many parts of the world, the twentieth century saw an education revolution. This revolution is continuing and it is changing the behaviour of people in myriad ways. Older people of tomorrow will be different from older people today. Their much higher levels of education will allow them to prepare for old age differently. Education, however, is only one part of the story of how people in the future will not be like people today. If the twenty-first century is like the last one, people of the future will enjoy the fruits of scientific, technological, and medical advances. They are likely to live longer and have lower age-specific rates of severe disabilities. Ageing is driven, in part, by changes in life expectancy. Those changes, in turn, are the result of increases in educational attainments and improvements in medical knowledge and practice. We cannot, on one hand, take the age structure effects of life expectancy changes into account, and, on the other hand, ignore the effects of life expectancy changes on the characteristics of people. This kind of gross inconsistency produces scientifically inappropriate results.

If the Sphinx were around today, she might pose a different riddle: 'What can grow younger as it grows older?' The answer to this riddle is human populations. Because of education changes and scientific advances, human populations can grow in productivity, creativity, and remaining life expectancy, even as the median age of the population increases. Functionally, human populations can become younger even as they grow older chronologically. This is the key to understanding what ageing will really be like in the twenty-first century.

References

Lee, R.D. and Mason, A. 2011 *Population Aging and the Generational Economy: A Global Perspective.* Edward Elgar Publishing: Cheltenham.

Ministry of Health and Social Affairs 2011 'Pensions in Sweden'. Available at: <http://www.government.se/sb/d/15473/a/183496> (accessed 29 January 2014).

Olshansky, S.J., Antonucci, T., Berkman, L., Binstock, R.H., Boersch-Supan, A., Cacioppo, J.T., et al. 2012 'Differences in Life Expectancy Due to Race and Educational Differences are Widening, and Many May Not Catch Up'. *Health Affairs*, 31: 1803–13.

Ryder, N.B. 1975 'Notes on Stationary Populations'. *Population Index*, 41: 3–28.

Sanderson, W.C. and Scherbov, S. 2005 'Average Remaining Lifetimes Can Increase as Human Populations Age'. *Nature*, 435: 811–13.

Sanderson, W.C. and Scherbov, S. 2010 'Remeasuring Aging'. *Science*, 329: 1287–8.

Sanderson, W.C. and Scherbov, S. 2013 'The Characteristics Approach to the Measurement of Population Aging'. *Population and Development Review*, 39: 673–85.

SSA 2013a 'Retirement Planner: Benefits by Year of Birth'. Available at: <http://www.ssa.gov/retire2/agereduction.htm> (accessed 23 June 2013).

SSA 2013b 'The 2013 Annual Report of the Board of Trustees of the Federal Old-Age and Survivors Insurance and Federal Disability Insurance Trust Funds' (Annual Report). US Social Security Administration: Washington, DC.

CHAPTER 12

ALTERNATIVE SCENARIOS IN THE CONTEXT OF SUSTAINABLE DEVELOPMENT

SAMIR KC AND WOLFGANG LUTZ

12.1 INTRODUCTION: POPULATION–ENVIRONMENT INTERACTIONS

THE number of people inhabiting the earth has fluctuated significantly over the course of human history, in response to both natural changes in the environment and stresses to local habitats created by the populations themselves. From the first appearance of *Homo sapiens* some 200,000 years ago in Africa until about 35,000 years ago, the world's human population was well under one million, a number that meant the threat of extinction was always looming (Biraben, 2002). Only after the Neolithic Revolution, which introduced agriculture, did the world population increase significantly, surpassing 100 million about 7,000 years ago. But it was in the nineteenth century that population growth began to accelerate in what are now the world's most industrialized countries. This rapid population increase was a consequence of declining death rates owing to better nutrition and hygiene, more accessible fresh water supplies, and advances in preventive medicine. Immediately after World War II, death rates began a precipitous fall, owing primarily to the development of antibiotics and other medical advances. For several decades after the war, birth rates remained very high (and in some cases increased owing to the better health of women) because high fertility norms had been deeply imbedded in most traditional cultures and religions. Such norms tend to change only slowly, and, as a consequence, the world population experienced a dramatic increase, from 2.5 billion in 1950 to more than 7 billion today.

The previous chapters have detailed what we now expect about the future of global population trends over the course of the twenty-first century. But in presenting this analysis, we have only occasionally made explicit reference to the fact that all human life depends on functioning environmental life support systems. This 'support system' aspect of human life was included in the expert meeting and IIASA–Oxford survey described in Chapters 2–7, with some of the predefined arguments explicitly referring to the possible effects of environmental change on future trends in health, mortality, and migration.

With a time horizon of up to 2050, these possible effects of environmental change on the population outlook were seen by the experts as having only marginal impacts. This may be owing to the fact that the international population experts included in the survey were almost exclusively social scientists who rarely deal with environmental issues, and consider social and economic factors as the key drivers in their analysis. Another dampening factor on the rating of environmental change is that even though climate change is already ongoing the more dramatic impacts that might significantly affect mortality levels are unlikely to happen in the nearer future. The significant changes in sea level rise and regional temperature and precipitation patterns could, potentially, have serious implications for future health and migration patterns, but probably not yet within the next few decades. This chapter will address the environmental change issue directly by analysing the global population and human capital outlook for the rest of this century in a broader context of sustainable development and global environmental change. In doing so, we will consider both the effects of human population on the natural environment and the vulnerability of human populations to such possible future changes.

Figure 12.1 depicts how the interactions between population change and climate change can be conceptualized. It shows that the changing size and structure of human populations enter into our concerns about climate change at both the beginning and the end of the causal chain. Humans have been causing the emissions that trigger climate change. In turn, climate change sets in motion forces that can threaten humans' well-being. In the past, most research and policy focus has been on mitigating greenhouse gas (GHG) emissions, but, more recently, the emphasis has been shifting to strategies for strengthening adaptive capacities for coping with unavoidable climate change. This shift opens important new areas of analysis for demographers. Although efforts to quantify the contribution of population changes to climate change have been outside the realm of demography and have proven difficult, efforts to address adaptive capacity by studying and forecasting differential vulnerability are well-suited to what the powerful demographic toolbox has to offer (Lutz, 2009).

Climate change is of concern principally because it is dangerous to human well-being. The notion of 'dangerous' has a specific importance with respect to climate change because the only globally binding agreement, the 1992 Framework Convention on Climate Change, postulates in its core sentence to 'avoid dangerous interference with the climate system'. This convention has become the fundamental document supporting every international effort to combat or adapt to climate change. In principle,

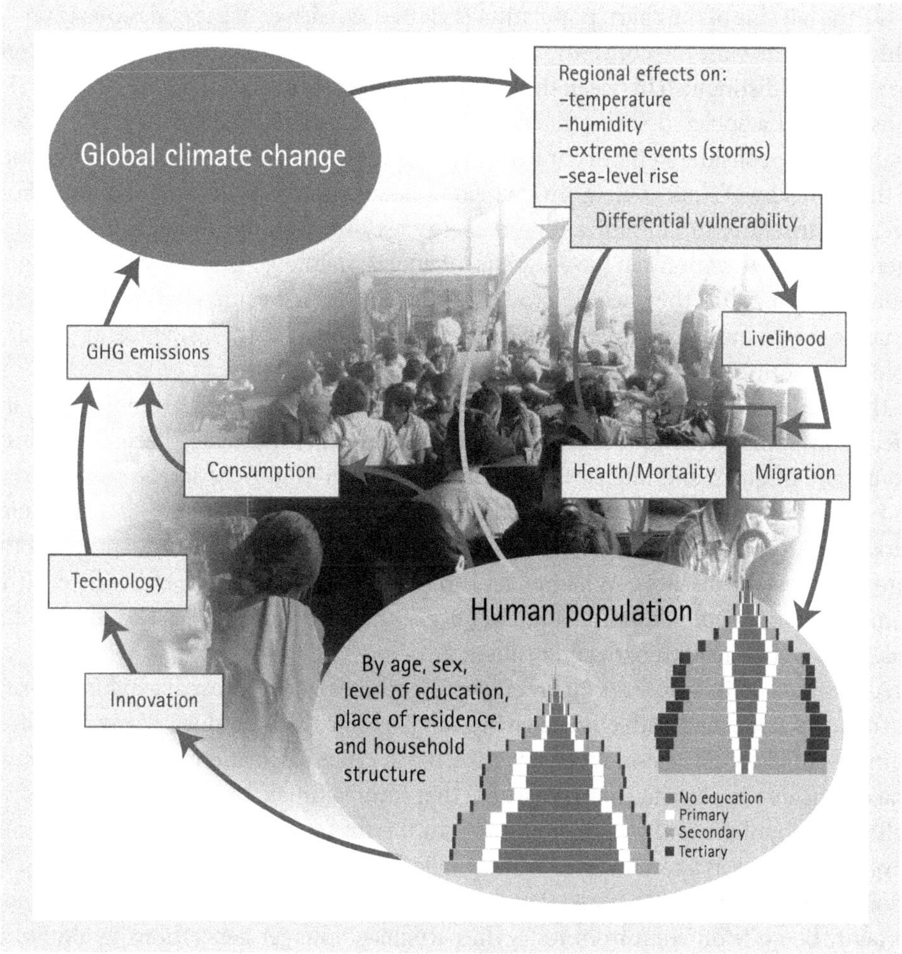

FIGURE 12.1 Chart depicting how the human population influences climate change and is, in turn, affected by the consequences of climate change. GHG: greenhouse gases.

Source: Lutz (2009).

every assessment of the dangers associated with alternative emissions trajectories would have to anticipate the consequences of the resulting climate change on human well-being. This is impossible in practice because not enough is known about what changes will occur in the bio-physical conditions or how future populations will be able to cope with those changes. The European Union and the Copenhagen Climate Summit have defined a simple, clear goal in mitigating climate change: limiting the warming to not more than 2 °C in global mean temperature. This pragmatic definition of dangerous climate change, however, does not address the role of adaptation in moderating the impacts on human well-being. This path of causation is depicted on the right-hand side of the chart at the bottom of Figure 12.1.

On the left side of the chart, population is viewed as a driver of the emissions of GHG, which is in line with the conventional view: the I = PAT model (Ehrlich and Holdren, 1971) tried to distinguish between the supposedly separate effects of population size (P), consumption associated with affluence (A), and technological efficiency (T). Recent analyses have considered more complex effects and the possibility of interactions, such as the model by O'Neill et al. (2010), which includes the effects of changing household size, age structure, and urbanization on energy use. The findings show that population ageing and urbanization can have significant effects on total emissions with the magnitudes depending on the specific model definitions. In the same chart, the changing structure of the human population by age, sex, education, place of residence, and household size also appear as drivers of consumption levels.

The right-hand side of Figure 12.1 indicates that the human population is also being affected by climate change. People will likely be exposed to increasing hazards resulting from more frequent and intensive extreme events, such as storms, floods, sea level rise, and changing regional and temporal patterns of temperature and humidity. The temperature and humidity changes are expected to affect agricultural production and the spread of certain diseases. Whether and to what extent these hazards will result in human fatalities depends on the vulnerability of the people affected. That vulnerability is dependent on their strength and resiliency.

Assessment of likely future vulnerability presents the biggest research gap for assessing the dangers associated with climate change and is difficult to conduct. Many published estimates of likely climate-induced fatalities, for instance calculations of additional malaria deaths due to climate change, assume that future climate conditions (e.g. in 2070) will affect populations that will continue into the future with similar socio-economic development and, as a result, have similar public health capabilities as they have today. As previous chapters have illustrated, however, societies are not stationary and will almost certainly be quite different from today. In particular, younger generations in almost all countries are, on average, better educated than the older ones, which will result in improvements in the average education of the future adult population. Economic growth and public health governance will also strengthen resilience. In addition to mortality and morbidity directly inflicted by such hazards, many of the expected consequences of climate change arise from climate-induced threats to traditional livelihoods. 'Loss of livelihood' may constitute a push factor for migration or, in the worst case, lead to mortality—both demographic factors that change a population's structure.

As demonstrated in the previous chapters, we not only know that societies change over time as a function of changing age, sex, education, and other structures, but we also have a unique toolkit (multi-state cohort component methods) to model and project those changing structures with relatively small uncertainties over several decades. Furthermore, demographers have long studied a wide variety of differentials, particularly differential vulnerability to threats such as infant mortality, adult mortality, morbidity, and disability. We can also study differentials in education and other empowerment factors that enhance the adaptive capacity of individuals, households, and communities.

12.2 Defining the Shared Socio-economic Pathways scenarios

The multi-state cohort component approach has substantial potential for studying climate change mitigation and adaptation. Accordingly, the most recent international effort to develop a shared set of socio-economic scenarios included a more detailed population component than previous efforts. For more than a dozen years the Intergovernmental Panel on Climate Change (IPCC) modelling community has used a set of emissions scenarios as defined in Nakicenovic et al. (2000). While these Special Report on Emissions Scenarios (SRES) were very detailed on the energy, technology, and emissions side, they included only total population size and gross domestic product per capita as indicators. Population was only used as a scaling variable.

More recently, the climate change research community began development of a new framework for the creation and use of scenarios to improve interdisciplinary analysis and assessment of climate change, its impacts, and response options (O'Neill et al., 2014).

This process, as formulated at an IPCC workshop in 2007, includes a set of forcing pathways, known as the Representative Concentration Pathways (RCPs), to be combined with alternative socio-economic development pathways (Moss et al., 2010). The development of RCPs has been completed and the pathways documented in a special issue of *Climatic Change* (Vuuren et al., 2011). The development of the socio-economic scenarios, known as Shared Socio-economic Pathways (SSPs) was completed in late 2012.

The SSPs were designed to include both a qualitative component in the form of a narrative on global development (see sections 12.2.1–12.2.5), and a quantitative component that includes numerical pathways for certain variables (Arnell et al., 2011). Narratives were developed for basic versions of five SSPs, illustrated in Figure 12.2, with respect to socio-economic challenges to mitigation and adaptation. This range of the SSPs is broad enough, in principle, to contain a large number of socio-economic pathways that represent various combinations of challenges to mitigation and adaptation. The SSPs, as presented here, are single pathways that are representative of the types of socio-economic pathways that could occupy particular domains within the overall range. The following definitions of the narratives are based on O'Neill et al. (2014). In the following list, we present the overall storyline and then translate this general view of future global trends into specific assumptions for future fertility, mortality, migration, and education trends as they have been developed at the International Institute for Applied Systems Analysis (IIASA) in consultations with the global SSP community (see Table 12.1). Three groups of countries are considered: 'high fertility countries', as defined by a total fertility rate (TFR) of more than 2.9 in 2005–10; 'low fertility countries', including all countries with a TFR of $\leq$2.9 that are not included in the third category; 'rich-OECD countries', defined

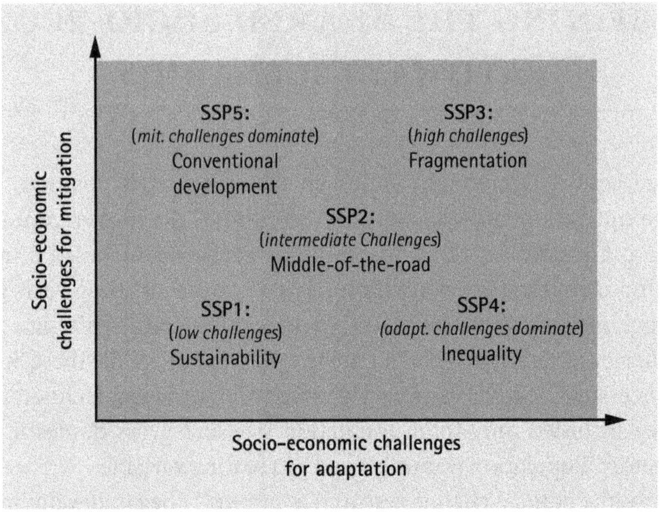

FIGURE 12.2 Location of five Shared Socio-economic Pathways (SSPs) in space spanned by differing degrees of socio-economic challenges for adaptation (adapt.) and mitigation (mit.).

Source: O'Neill et al., 2013

by Organisation for Economic Co-operation and Development (OECD) membership and the World Bank category of high-income countries (see Appendix 12.1). It is important to note that for this set of general SSPs, countries are assumed to stay in their initial grouping throughout the process. This may be unrealistic for countries that are, for example, in the midst of a fertility decline and may move soon into the low fertility group of countries. Because there are a seemingly infinite number of ways in which countries could change groupings, we decided that this should be left to users who want to define their country-specific SSPs.

Although the SSP process and the effort reported in Chapters 1–11 were independent processes, they now have been merged in the sense that the medium scenario of the earlier described new WIC population projections is identical in every respect to the SSP2 as described in section 12.2.2. Similarly, the different education scenarios and the high and low fertility, mortality, and migration assumptions used in the SSP scenarios are directly derived from the analysis presented in this book. In this way, the SSP community can benefit from the scientific effort that produced this new set of WIC projections.

12.2.1 SSP1: sustainability

This world is making relatively good progress toward sustainability, with ongoing efforts to achieve development goals while reducing resource intensity and fossil fuel dependency. Elements that contribute to this progress are a rapid development of low-income countries, a reduction of inequality (globally and within economies), rapid technology development, and a high level of awareness regarding environmental degradation. Rapid economic growth in low-income countries reduces the number of people below the poverty line. The world is characterized by an open, globalized economy, with rapid technological change directed toward environmentally friendly processes, including clean energy technologies and innovations that enhance agricultural output. Consumption is oriented toward low material growth and energy intensity, with a relatively low level of consumption of animal products. Significant investments in education coincide with low population growth, and both government and private institutions are working together to promote public policy solutions and economic development. The Millennium Development Goals (MDG) are achieved within the next decade or two, resulting in educated populations with access to safe water, improved sanitation, and medical care. Other factors that reduce vulnerability to climate and other global changes include the implementation of stringent policies to control air pollutants and rapid shifts toward universal access to clean and modern energy in the developing world.

12.2.1.1 *Population component of SSP1: rapid development*

This storyline assumes that educational and health investments accelerate the demographic transition, leading to a relatively low world population. This implies assumptions of low mortality and high education for all three country groups. With respect to fertility assumptions, the story is more complex. For rich OECD countries the emphasis on quality of life is assumed to make it easier for women to combine work and family, making further fertility declines unlikely. For this reason the medium fertility assumption was chosen for this group of countries. Low fertility assumptions were chosen for all other countries as implied by the assumed rapid continuation of demographic transition. Migration levels were assumed to be medium for all countries under this SSP.

12.2.2 SSP2: Middle of the road—continuation of trends

In this SSP2 world, trends typical of recent decades continue, with some progress toward achieving development goals, historic reductions in resource and energy intensity, and slowly decreasing fossil fuel dependency. Development of low-income countries proceeds unevenly, with some countries making relatively good progress, while others are left behind. Most economies are politically stable with partially functioning and globally connected markets. A limited number of comparatively weak global institutions exist. Per capita income levels grow at a medium pace on the global average, with slowly converging income levels between developing and industrialized countries. Intra-regional income distributions improve slightly with increasing national income, but disparities remain high in some regions. Educational investments are not high enough to rapidly slow population growth, particularly in low-income countries. Achievement of the MDG at the country level is delayed by several decades, leaving populations without access to safe water, improved sanitation, or medical care. Similarly, there is only intermediate success in addressing air pollution and improving energy access for the poor.

12.2.2.1 *Population component of SSP2: medium*

This is the middle of the road scenario that that can also be seen as the most likely path for each country. It combines for all countries medium fertility with medium mortality, medium migration, and the global education trend (GET) scenario. This corresponds exactly to the medium scenario of the Wittgenstein Centre for Demography and Global Human Capital (WIC) projections described in the previous chapters.

12.2.3 SSP3: Fragmentation

This narrative is an opposite of sustainability. The world is separated into regions characterized by extreme poverty, with pockets of moderate wealth. In the majority of countries, the struggle is to maintain living standards for rapidly growing populations. Regional blocks of countries have re-emerged with little coordination between them. This is a world failing to achieve global development goals and with little progress in reducing resource intensity and fossil fuel dependency. Environmental concerns, such as air pollution, are not being addressed. Countries in this scenario focus on achieving energy and food security goals within their own region. The world has de-globalized, and international trade, including energy resource and agricultural markets, is severely restricted. The lack of international cooperation combined with low investments in technology development and education slow down economic growth in high-, middle-, and low-income regions. Population growth in this scenario is high as a result of the education and economic trends, and the growth in urban areas in low-income countries is often in unplanned settlements. Unmitigated emissions are relatively high, driven by the high population growth, use of local energy resources, and slow technological change in the energy sector. Governance and institutions are weak and lack cooperation, consensus, or effective leadership. Investments in human capital are low and inequality is high. A regionalized world leads to reduced trade flows, and institutional development is unfavourable, leaving large numbers of people vulnerable to climate change because of their low adaptive capacity. Policies are oriented towards security, including barriers to trade.

12.2.3.1 *Population component of SSP3: stalled development*

In demographic terms this is a world with a stalled demographic transition. Fertility is assumed to be low in the rich OECD countries and high in the other two country groups. Population growth is assumed to be high in developing countries and low in industrialized countries. Accordingly, this scenario assumes high mortality and low education for all three country groupings. Owing to the emphasis on security and barriers to international exchange, migration is assumed to be low for all countries.

12.2.4 SSP4: inequality

This pathway envisions a highly unequal world, both within and across countries. A relatively small, rich global elite is responsible for much of the emissions, while a larger, poorer group contributes little to emissions and is vulnerable to impacts of climate change in both industrialized and developing countries. In this world, global energy corporations use investments in research and development as hedging strategy against potential resource scarcity or climate policy, developing and applying low-cost alternative technologies. Mitigation challenges are therefore low owing to a combination of low reference emissions and/or high latent capacity to mitigate. Governance and globalization are effective for and controlled by the elite, but are ineffective for most of the population. Access to high quality education, health services, and family planning is also limited, leading to high population growth in low-income countries. Challenges to adaptation are high owing to relatively low income and low human capital among the poorer population, and ineffective institutions.

12.2.4.1 *Population component of SSP4: inequality*

In order to best reflect the inequality in education, we developed a special scenario that differs from the standard education scenarios used in the rest of the book in that it produces a more polarized education distribution in every country. There is a group with very high education levels (which is bigger in the rich OECD countries) and large groups with low education levels. In terms of fertility, the national averages imply continued high fertility in today's high fertility countries and continued low fertility in both groups of low fertility countries. The high fertility countries are assumed to suffer from high levels of mortality, whereas the other two groups have medium mortality. Migration is assumed to be at the medium level for all countries.

12.2.5 SSP5: conventional development

This storyline envisions a world that stresses conventional development oriented toward economic growth as the solution to social and economic problems through the pursuit of enlightened self-interest. The preference for rapid conventional development leads to an energy system dominated by fossil fuels, resulting in high GHG emissions and challenges to mitigation. Lower socio-environmental challenges to adaptation result from attainment of human development goals, robust economic growth, highly engineered infrastructure with redundancy to minimize disruptions from extreme events, and highly managed ecosystems.

12.2.5.1 *Population component of SSP5: conventional development*

This world of conventional development features high education assumptions and low mortality assumptions across all countries. For fertility, the pattern is strongly

Table 12.1 Matrix with Shared Socio-economic Pathway (SSP) Definitions

	Country groupings	Fertility	Mortality	Migration	Education
SSP1:	HiFert	Low	Low	Medium	High (FT-GET)
rapid development	LoFert	Low	Low	Medium	High (FT-GET)
	Rich-OECD	Medium	Low	Medium	High (FT-GET)
SSP2:	HiFert	Medium	Medium	Medium	Medium (GET)
medium	LoFert	Medium	Medium	Medium	Medium (GET)
	Rich-OECD	Medium	Medium	Medium	Medium (GET)
SSP3:	HiFert	High	High	Low	Low (CER)
stalled development	LoFert	High	High	Low	Low (CER)
	Rich-OECD	Low	High	Low	Low (CER)
SSP4:	HiFert	High	High	Medium	CER-10%/GET
inequality	LoFert	Low	Medium	Medium	CER-10%/GET
	Rich-OECD	Low	Medium	Medium	CER/CER-20%
SSP5:	HiFert	Low	Low	High	High (FT-GET)
conventional	LoFert	Low	Low	High	High (FT-GET)
development	Rich-OECD	High	Low	High	High (FT-GET)

HiFert: high fertility; LoFert: low fertility; OECD: Organisation for Economic Co-operation and Development; FT: fast track; GET: global education trend; CER: constant enrolment rates.

differentiated, with relatively high fertility assumed for the rich OECD countries (as a consequence of high technology and a very high standard of living that allows for easier combination of work and family, and possibly for immigrant domestic assistants) and low fertility assumed for all other countries. The emphasis on market solutions and globalization also implies the assumption of high migration for all countries.

Some of the education scenario choices presented in Table 12.1 for different SSPs are combinations of the earlier described stylized scenarios: fast track (FT)–GET for SSP1 and SSP5 has been calculated for each country by taking the arithmetic mean of the education progression rates implied under the GET and FT scenarios. For SSP4 a more complex combination was chosen in order to reflect the increasing within-country inequality that this storyline implies: 'constant enrolment rate (CER)–10 per cent/GET' implies that the educational attainment progression ratio is further reduced by 10 per cent compared with CER (and hence still more pessimistic), for the transitions from no education to incomplete primary, incomplete primary to completed primary, and completed primary to completed lower secondary. The GET transition ratios are assumed for the higher educational categories, which will produce larger groups of elites in these countries. Under 'CER/CER–20 per cent', for the high-income OECD countries, it is assumed that for these higher education groups the transition rates are 20 per cent lower than under CER and hence produce a more polarized society.

12.3 SSP SCENARIO RESULTS

The calculations supporting the scenarios resulted in an enormous number of data points. For every country and for every scenario, population and education pyramids are produced for every point in time (five-year steps) from 2010 to 2100. The data result in 18 pyramids for each of the 195 countries (plus for 6 world regions and the world total), times five scenarios, plus a pyramid for the starting year. Each pyramid contains three age groups below the age of 15 and 18 age groups above the age of 15. The age groups are each subdivided by sex and six different educational attainment categories. This entire exercise results in 3,939,390 data points, which obviously cannot be presented here, but are available online at: <https://secure.iiasa.ac.at/web-apps/ene/SspDb/>.

In presenting results, there is an overlap with Chapters 10 and 11, which also present and discuss the results of some of the scenarios for population and human capital in the twenty-first century. The main difference is that the previous chapters largely focused on the medium scenario, which is identical to SSP2, and on the differences that are induced through alternative education scenarios that assume medium fertility, mortality, and migration assumptions. Here, in contrast, we will significantly expand the scope of the scenario by including high and low fertility, mortality, migration trends, and alternative education scenarios. In addition to the uncertainty introduced through alternative education scenarios, we also assume additional fertility, mortality, and migration uncertainty that is reflected in high and low sets of education-specific fertility, mortality, and migration assumptions, as summarized in Chapter 9. For this reason, the differences between, for example, SSP1 and SSP3, tend to be much bigger than the differences between the other scenarios discussed in Chapter 10. Those scenarios consider only education-induced differences with otherwise identical sets of education-specific trajectories.

Figure 12.3 gives, as an example, the age and education pyramids projected for India for 2050 under the SSP1, SSP2, and SSP3 scenarios. While SSP2 is identical to the me-

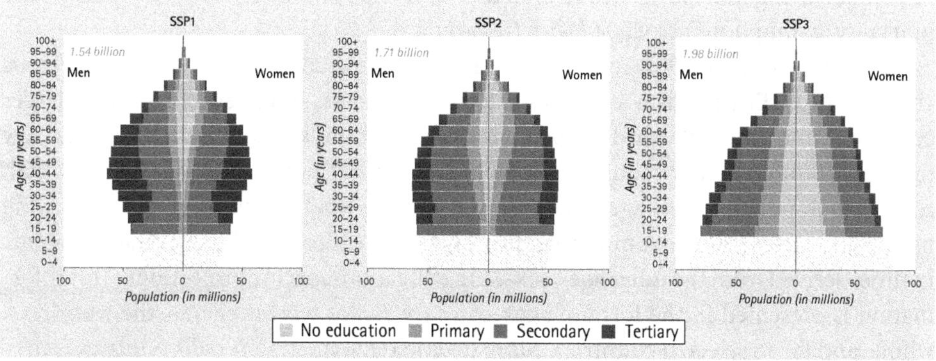

FIGURE 12.3 Age and education pyramids for India in 2050 under Shared Socio-economic Pathway (SSP) 1, SSP2, and SSP3.

dium scenario discussed in Chapter 10, SSP1 shows a rapidly ageing India, which will be highly educated and growing to 1.54 billion by mid-century. SSP3 shows a young and uneducated India growing to 1.98 billion over the next four decades. As most of the scenario assumptions (except for mortality) affect younger age groups and the time horizon is only 40 years, the three pyramids are very similar for the elderly populations, but differ greatly for the younger ones. As shown in Table 12.2, the difference in total population size between SSP1 and SSP3 for India alone will be around 439 million by 2050 and increase to 1.56 billion people by 2100, much higher than India's total population today.

India is highlighted here as the biggest country in the twenty-first century. Another country that will likely be among the top three in the world is Nigeria. As already discussed in Chapter 10, Nigeria, in many respects, stands at the crossroads. The experts consulted about future trends in Nigeria were divided, seeing two very different futures. Some saw the country on the brink of a major development upsurge with rapid economic growth, major investments in education, and likely significant improvements in the quality of governance. Several spoke of an 'African Lion' following the path of the 'Asian Tiger'. Other experts, however, saw a high probability of complete development stalemate and a downward spiral of excessive population growth, worsening school enrolment rates, declining health conditions, and possibly violent conflict that reinforces these trends. These differing views of the future are well reflected in SSP1 (rapid development) versus SSP3 (stalled development) scenarios, as depicted in Figure 12.4. In both cases Nigeria will see very significant population growth, which is, in part, pre-programmed in its current high levels of fertility and very young age structure. Even under SSP1 the population would increase almost by a factor of three, reaching about 440 million before levelling off by the end of the century. SSP3, however, would result in growth to almost 880 million people by 2100, more than the 754 million that China is expected to have under the SSP2 scenario. Also, the resulting human capital patterns differ substantially. Under SSP1 Nigeria could, indeed, follow in the footsteps of the Asian Tigers during the second half of the century. SSP3, however, would most likely bring all kinds of disasters that might, in fact, through feedbacks with food security, eroding health infrastructure or conflict, bring mortality rates to even higher levels than the already very pessimistic mortality assumptions associated with this scenario.

Table 12.2 shows the SSP results in the form of the standard table used in previous chapters, providing the data for the world, the continents, and a set of 12 selected larger countries from different world regions. Appendix II provides a comprehensive overview for every country, both in tabular and graphical form, of the results for the five SSPs with respect to population size, age structure, and average level of education. The following figures and tables provide summary indicators for the different SSPs and different points in time, derived from the fuller age-, sex-, and education-specific projections. This information is presented in the form of aggregates for major world regions, the world as a whole, and for 12 selected countries. More detailed information for all countries is provided in the online appendix.

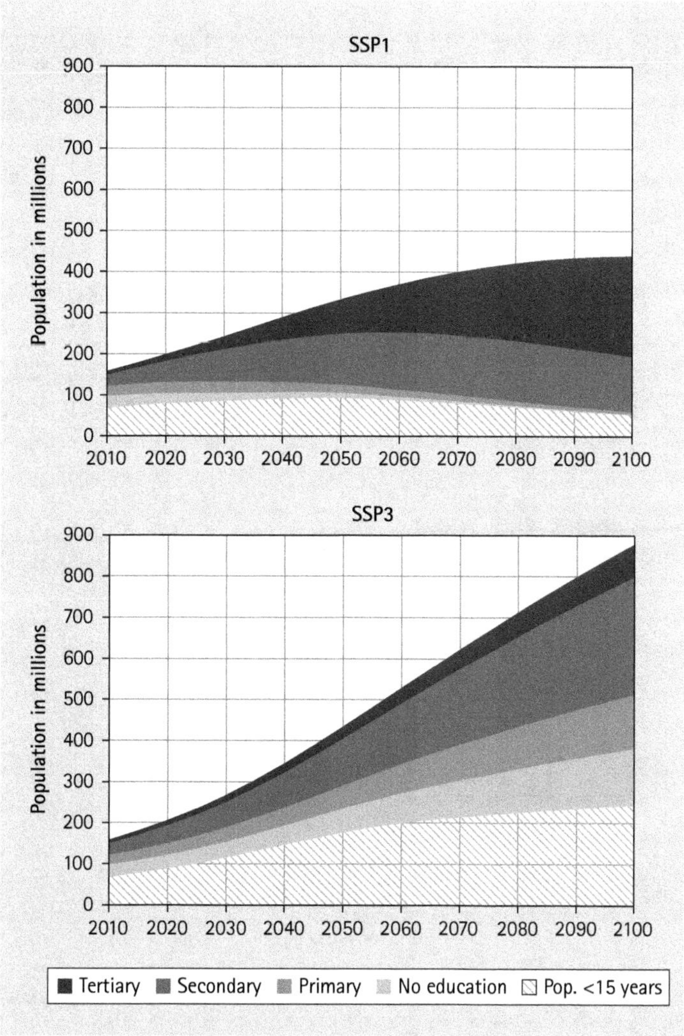

FIGURE 12.4 Nigeria under Shared Socio-economic Pathway (SSP) 1 (rapid development) and SSP3 (stalled development).

The rest of this section describes the results for the world and its six continents. Beginning with the global pattern, Figure 12.5 (and Table 12.3) shows the full range of future trajectories of world population growth across the different SSPs. Starting from about 7 billion today, the range opens to 8.5–10.0 billion in 2050 and 7.1–12.8 billion in 2100. SSP3 (stalled development), which combines high fertility assumptions with high mortality and low education, stands out as the top trajectory. The other SSPs come in pairs in term of global population size: the medium scenario, SSP2, path is almost identical to that of SSP4 until the middle of the century, then declines more quickly than SSP4, which is almost flat during the second half of the century.

Table 12.2 Results for Major World Regions and Selected Countries

		Population in millions					MYS, age 25+				
		SSP1	SSP2	SSP3	SSP4	SSP5	SSP1	SSP2	SSP3	SSP4	SSP5
World	2010	6,896	6,896	6,896	6,896	6,896	7.90	7.90	7.90	7.90	7.90
	2050	8,525	9,162	9,989	9,161	8,626	11.35	10.42	8.79	8.59	11.39
	2100	7,096	8,963	12,774	9,355	7,616	13.78	12.87	8.28	8.44	13.89
Africa	2010	1,022	1,022	1,022	1,022	1,022	5.38	5.38	5.38	5.38	5.38
	2050	1,801	2,018	2,324	2,252	1,779	10.59	9.24	6.72	6.40	10.58
	2100	1,925	2,622	3,924	3,614	1,869	13.46	12.25	6.69	6.54	13.46
Asia	2010	4,164	4,164	4,164	4,164	4,164	7.06	7.06	7.06	7.06	7.06
	2050	4,746	5,126	5,702	4,997	4,723	10.93	9.98	8.41	8.22	10.95
	2100	3,330	4,368	6,877	4,148	3,316	13.54	12.72	8.20	8.58	13.58
Europe	2010	738	738	738	738	738	10.93	10.93	10.93	10.93	10.93
	2050	764	755	678	709	841	13.29	12.88	12.19	11.75	13.35
	2100	699	703	539	536	976	14.91	14.31	12.33	11.89	15.02
Latin America and the Caribbean	2010	590	590	590	590	590	7.97	7.97	7.97	7.97	7.97
	2050	696	758	865	724	678	11.44	10.74	9.44	9.10	11.41
	2100	520	684	1,094	580	490	13.53	12.87	9.53	9.47	13.51
North America	2010	345	345	345	345	345	12.93	12.93	12.93	12.93	12.93
	2050	461	447	369	422	537	14.20	13.81	13.30	12.71	14.23
	2100	556	521	289	413	863	14.98	14.57	13.32	12.46	15.01
Oceania	2010	37	37	37	37	37	12.03	12.03	12.03	12.03	12.03
	2050	57	58	51	57	67	14.62	14.31	13.66	13.24	14.72
	2100	66	67	50	64	101	15.96	15.60	13.99	13.46	16.01
Brazil	2010	195	195	195	195	195	6.97	6.97	6.97	6.97	6.97
	2050	217	233	255	217	216	10.46	9.85	8.92	8.56	10.45
	2100	148	189	279	138	145	12.79	12.04	9.25	9.35	12.78
China	2010	1,341	1,341	1,341	1,341	1,341	7.36	7.36	7.36	7.36	7.36
	2050	1,219	1,255	1,310	1,178	1,214	10.42	9.86	9.16	9.03	10.41

	2100	644	754	1,046	550	637	12.79	12.21	9.40	10.48	12.78
Egypt	2010	81	81	81	81	81	6.77	6.77	6.77	6.77	6.77
	2050	115	126	142	114	113	12.29	11.70	10.14	9.63	12.28
	2100	100	134	202	93	97	14.53	14.02	10.56	10.59	14.52
Germany	2010	82	82	82	82	82	13.71	13.71	13.71	13.71	13.71
	2050	82	79	67	75	92	14.99	14.72	14.25	13.77	15.02
	2100	75	69	38	54	111	15.94	15.58	14.17	13.37	15.97
India	2010	1,225	1,225	1,225	1,225	1,225	5.53	5.53	5.53	5.53	5.53
	2050	1,543	1,715	1,982	1,605	1,532	10.77	9.32	7.13	6.89	10.76
	2100	1,131	1,569	2,687	1,190	1,112	13.66	12.65	7.27	7.48	13.66
Indonesia	2010	240	240	240	240	240	7.96	7.96	7.96	7.96	7.96
	2050	269	285	306	260	265	11.61	11.10	10.07	9.65	11.60
	2100	182	225	292	152	176	13.98	13.39	10.33	10.55	13.98
Iran	2010	74	74	74	74	74	7.20	7.20	7.20	7.20	7.20
	2050	92	98	108	92	91	11.63	11.16	9.37	9.32	11.63
	2100	66	81	122	63	66	14.22	13.90	9.64	10.41	14.22
Kenya	2010	41	41	41	41	41	7.68	7.68	7.68	7.68	7.68
	2050	73	80	95	92	71	12.25	11.39	8.03	8.17	12.24
	2100	75	98	157	146	72	13.94	12.99	7.99	8.72	13.94
Nigeria	2010	158	158	158	158	158	6.13	6.13	6.13	6.13	6.13
	2050	333	371	435	434	330	12.35	11.62	8.57	8.30	12.34
	2100	439	576	879	863	430	14.66	14.29	8.67	8.98	14.66
Republic of Korea	2010	48	48	48	48	48	11.85	11.85	11.85	11.85	11.85
	2050	49	46	41	44	51	14.48	14.55	14.28	13.60	14.49
	2100	35	30	19	24	45	15.48	15.47	14.68	13.60	15.48
Russian Federation	2010	143	143	143	143	143	10.44	10.44	10.44	10.44	10.44
	2050	126	132	133	123	131	12.36	11.80	11.45	10.95	12.38
	2100	88	115	144	82	94	13.50	12.73	11.70	11.46	13.50

(*continued*)

Table 12.2 Continued

		Population in millions					MYS, age 25+				
		SSP1	SSP2	SSP3	SSP4	SSP5	SSP1	SSP2	SSP3	SSP4	SSP5
South Africa	2010	50	50	50	50	50	8.94	8.94	8.94	8.94	8.94
	2050	62	63	61	56	65	12.08	11.24	10.20	9.96	12.09
	2100	50	59	70	39	53	13.63	12.54	10.23	10.67	13.63
Spain	2010	46	46	46	46	46	8.99	8.99	8.99	8.99	8.99
	2050	53	52	44	50	61	12.51	12.25	11.15	10.88	12.63
	2100	51	47	28	40	78	14.78	14.46	11.78	11.35	14.85
USA	2010	310	310	310	310	310	12.86	12.86	12.86	12.86	12.86
	2050	411	400	332	377	477	14.11	13.69	13.19	12.63	14.13
	2100	496	466	261	369	761	14.93	14.48	13.22	12.39	14.95

MYS: mean years of schooling; SSP: Shared Socio-economic Pathway.

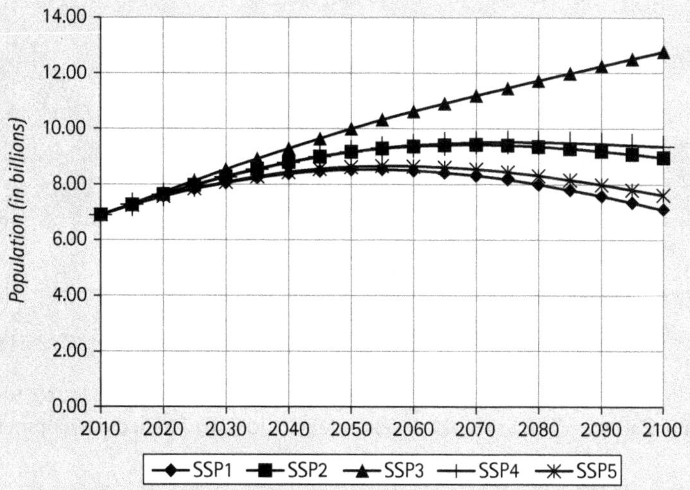

FIGURE 12.5 Trajectories of world population under the five different Shared Socio-economic Pathways (SSPs) to 2100.

The definitions of these scenarios reveal an interesting offset. While SSP2 assumes medium assumptions for all countries, SSP4 assumes a high fertility (and mortality) trajectory for the current high fertility countries and a low fertility trajectory for the low fertility countries (including India and China). Until the middle of the century these opposing trends seem to compensate for each other, although later in the century the successively higher weight of the more rapidly growing high fertility countries dominates and results in a somewhat higher path. At the lower end, the similarity of SSP1 (rapid

Table 12.3 Time Series of World Population Size to 2100 Under the Different Shared Socio-economic Pathways (SSPs)

	SSP1	SSP2	SSP3	SSP4	SSP5
2010	6,896	6,896	6,896	6,896	6,896
2020	7,560	7,636	7,719	7,633	7,568
2030	8,048	8,280	8,536	8,267	8,078
2040	8,380	8,795	9,284	8,778	8,438
2050	8,525	9,162	9,989	9,161	8,626
2060	8,492	9,361	10,619	9,398	8,649
2070	8,309	9,416	11,181	9,501	8,537
2080	7,997	9,352	11,723	9,510	8,309
2090	7,579	9,189	12,255	9,452	7,988
2100	7,096	8,963	12,774	9,355	7,616

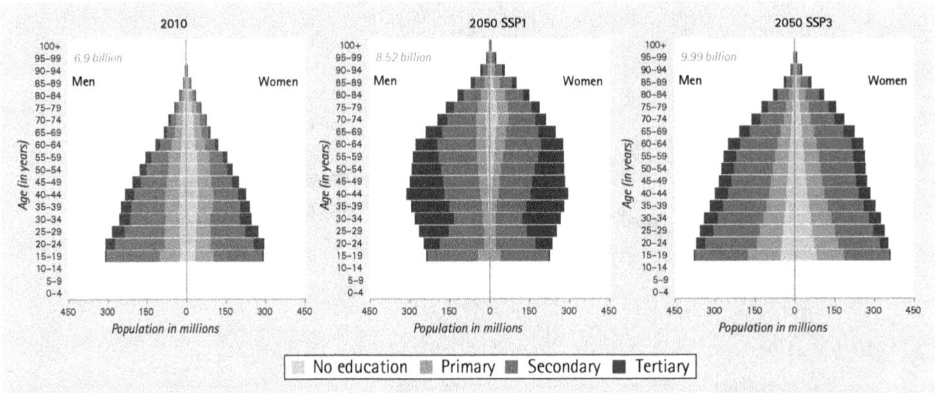

FIGURE 12.6 Age and education pyramids for the world in 2010 and 2050 under Shared Socio-economic Pathway (SSP) 1 (rapid development) and SSP3 (stalled development).

development) and SSP5 (conventional development) is not surprising because of almost identical demographic assumptions for fertility and mortality trajectories. Only in the case of the rich OECD countries does SSP5 assume high instead of low fertility, resulting in a somewhat higher trajectory of world population growth.

Moving to the age and education structure of the world population, Figure 12.6 shows the two contrasting scenarios on the high and low side of SSP2 for the coming four decades. SSP1 shows a world that is likely to greatly benefit from the demographic dividend. The age structure is dominated by a large group of highly educated young to middle-aged adults, which according to the literature in population economics is a key for stimulating economic growth (Crespo Cuaresma et al., 2014). SSP2, in sharp contrast, will result in a much larger population that is significantly less educated and has many more children to support. Table 12.4 shows that the proportion of the total world population that will be below the age of 20 will range from 20 per cent under SSP1 to 31 per cent under SSP3 by 2050. By 2100 this gap will widen further, with only 11 per cent in SSP1 being below the age of 20 compared with 29 per cent under SSP3. This gap illustrates the universal trend of population ageing in which even under the highest population growth scenario, the proportion of people below the age of 20 will decline throughout this century and be always lower than the current level of 36 per cent.

Neither SSP1 nor SSP3 are likely to happen, but they span the range that the community defining these assumptions considered plausible. It is worth noting that the continental and global aggregations of the country-level SSPs being presented here show the cases in which all countries that are being aggregated follow the same SSP storyline. This is comparable to the way the United Nations (UN) population projections aggregate the high and low variants of all individual countries. In the case that some countries follow one variant and others another, there are likely to be compensating effects with the aggregate trend coming to lie between the two extremes.

Figure 12.7 shows that for the world as a whole the different SSPs cover not only a broad range of total population sizes, but also education distributions. SSP2, which is considered the most likely population and education trajectory, shows a continuous decrease of the adult population with no education or only some primary education.

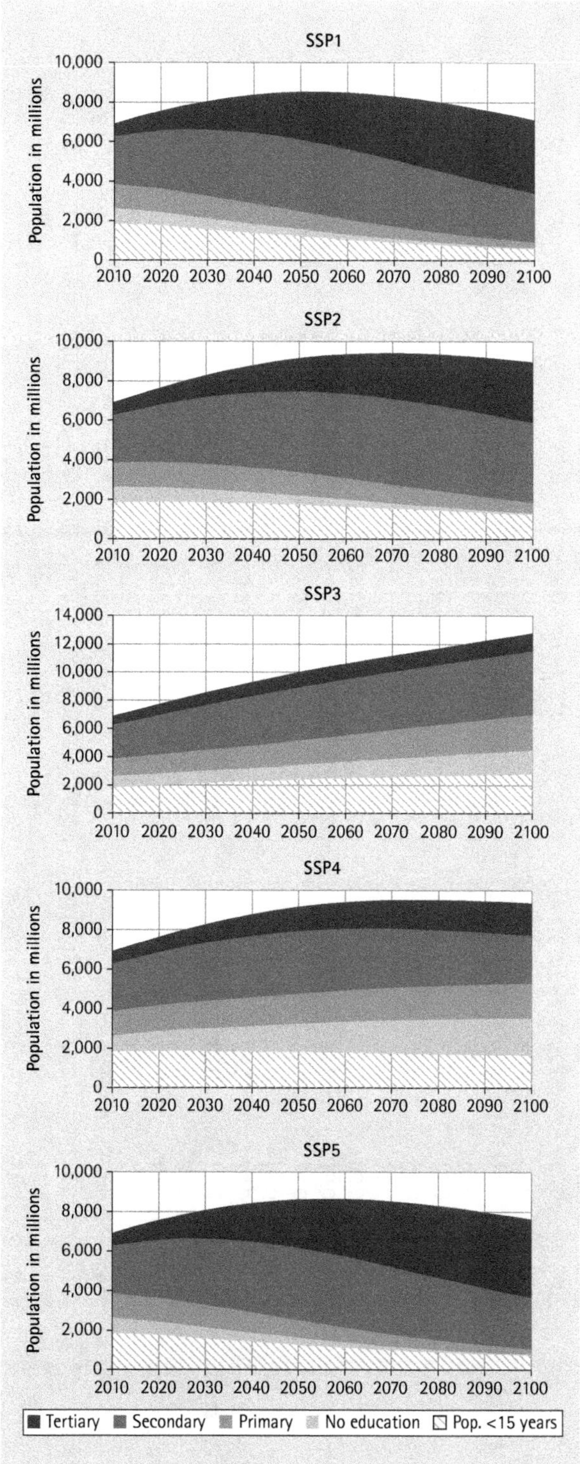

FIGURE 12.7 Line charts of future world population trends by level of education up to 2100 for the five different Shared Socio-economic Pathways (SSPs).

Table 12.4 Proportions of the Population Below the Age of 20 and Above the Age of 65

		Proportion below age 20					Proportion aged 65+				
		SSP1	SSP2	SSP3	SSP4	SSP5	SSP1	SSP2	SSP3	SSP4	SSP5
World	2010	0.36	0.36	0.36	0.36	0.36	0.08	0.08	0.08	0.08	0.08
	2050	0.20	0.26	0.31	0.26	0.20	0.21	0.18	0.14	0.17	0.21
	2100	0.11	0.19	0.29	0.24	0.13	0.47	0.30	0.16	0.24	0.44
Africa	2010	0.51	0.51	0.51	0.51	0.51	0.04	0.04	0.04	0.04	0.04
	2050	0.30	0.38	0.44	0.43	0.30	0.09	0.07	0.05	0.06	0.10
	2100	0.13	0.23	0.34	0.33	0.13	0.37	0.19	0.10	0.11	0.37
Asia	2010	0.35	0.35	0.35	0.35	0.35	0.07	0.07	0.07	0.07	0.07
	2050	0.17	0.22	0.29	0.22	0.17	0.23	0.19	0.15	0.20	0.23
	2100	0.09	0.17	0.28	0.19	0.09	0.52	0.33	0.17	0.30	0.52
Europe	2010	0.21	0.21	0.21	0.21	0.21	0.16	0.16	0.16	0.16	0.16
	2050	0.17	0.19	0.19	0.16	0.20	0.32	0.29	0.28	0.31	0.30
	2100	0.14	0.17	0.19	0.13	0.19	0.46	0.37	0.30	0.44	0.38
Latin America and the Caribbean	2010	0.37	0.37	0.37	0.37	0.37	0.07	0.07	0.07	0.07	0.07
	2050	0.17	0.23	0.30	0.21	0.17	0.24	0.20	0.16	0.21	0.25
	2100	0.08	0.16	0.27	0.15	0.08	0.56	0.37	0.20	0.39	0.57
Northern America	2010	0.27	0.27	0.27	0.27	0.27	0.13	0.13	0.13	0.13	0.13
	2050	0.22	0.23	0.19	0.20	0.26	0.25	0.23	0.24	0.24	0.22
	2100	0.17	0.19	0.15	0.15	0.23	0.40	0.34	0.35	0.39	0.31
Oceania	2010	0.32	0.32	0.32	0.32	0.32	0.11	0.11	0.11	0.11	0.11
	2050	0.21	0.23	0.23	0.23	0.24	0.22	0.20	0.20	0.20	0.20
	2100	0.15	0.18	0.21	0.18	0.20	0.43	0.35	0.28	0.34	0.35
Brazil	2010	0.34	0.34	0.34	0.34	0.34	0.07	0.07	0.07	0.07	0.07
	2050	0.15	0.20	0.26	0.16	0.15	0.28	0.23	0.19	0.25	0.28
	2100	0.07	0.15	0.26	0.10	0.07	0.59	0.39	0.23	0.48	0.59
China	2010	0.27	0.27	0.27	0.27	0.27	0.08	0.08	0.08	0.08	0.08

	2050	0.11	0.15	0.20	0.12	0.11	0.33	0.28	0.24	0.30	0.33
	2100	0.07	0.13	0.24	0.09	0.07	0.63	0.43	0.24	0.51	0.63
Egypt	2010	0.41	0.41	0.41	0.41	0.41	0.05	0.05	0.05	0.05	0.05
	2050	0.21	0.27	0.33	0.23	0.21	0.17	0.14	0.11	0.15	0.17
	2100	0.10	0.18	0.28	0.13	0.10	0.49	0.31	0.17	0.38	0.49
Germany	2010	0.19	0.19	0.19	0.19	0.19	0.20	0.20	0.20	0.20	0.20
	2050	0.16	0.16	0.14	0.14	0.19	0.37	0.34	0.34	0.36	0.33
	2100	0.14	0.15	0.12	0.11	0.19	0.48	0.41	0.43	0.48	0.38
India	2010	0.40	0.40	0.40	0.40	0.40	0.05	0.05	0.05	0.05	0.05
	2050	0.19	0.25	0.33	0.22	0.19	0.18	0.15	0.11	0.16	0.18
	2100	0.09	0.17	0.29	0.14	0.09	0.50	0.31	0.15	0.35	0.50
Indonesia	2010	0.36	0.36	0.36	0.36	0.36	0.06	0.06	0.06	0.06	0.06
	2050	0.16	0.21	0.26	0.17	0.16	0.23	0.19	0.16	0.21	0.23
	2100	0.09	0.16	0.24	0.11	0.09	0.52	0.35	0.21	0.43	0.53
Iran	2010	0.33	0.33	0.33	0.33	0.33	0.05	0.05	0.05	0.05	0.05
	2050	0.15	0.19	0.26	0.17	0.15	0.27	0.23	0.19	0.25	0.27
	2100	0.07	0.14	0.25	0.11	0.07	0.60	0.41	0.23	0.48	0.60
Kenya	2010	0.53	0.53	0.53	0.53	0.53	0.03	0.03	0.03	0.03	0.03
	2050	0.30	0.37	0.45	0.45	0.30	0.09	0.06	0.05	0.05	0.09
	2100	0.13	0.23	0.34	0.33	0.13	0.39	0.19	0.09	0.10	0.39
Nigeria	2010	0.53	0.53	0.53	0.53	0.53	0.03	0.03	0.03	0.03	0.03
	2050	0.37	0.44	0.51	0.51	0.37	0.07	0.05	0.04	0.04	0.07
	2100	0.17	0.26	0.36	0.36	0.17	0.29	0.14	0.07	0.07	0.29
Republic of Korea	2010	0.24	0.24	0.24	0.24	0.24	0.11	0.11	0.11	0.11	0.11
	2050	0.13	0.14	0.12	0.12	0.16	0.40	0.37	0.36	0.39	0.37
	2100	0.11	0.13	0.10	0.10	0.16	0.53	0.46	0.47	0.53	0.44
Russian Federation	2010	0.21	0.21	0.21	0.21	0.21	0.13	0.13	0.13	0.13	0.13
	2050	0.15	0.20	0.25	0.16	0.15	0.29	0.24	0.21	0.26	0.28
	2100	0.10	0.18	0.27	0.13	0.10	0.51	0.32	0.19	0.40	0.51

(continued)

Table 12.4 Continued

		Proportion below age 20					Proportion aged 65+				
		SSP1	SSP2	SSP3	SSP4	SSP5	SSP1	SSP2	SSP3	SSP4	SSP5
South Africa	2010	0.40	0.40	0.40	0.40	0.40	0.05	0.05	0.05	0.05	0.05
	2050	0.21	0.29	0.35	0.24	0.21	0.13	0.09	0.08	0.10	0.13
	2100	0.10	0.20	0.33	0.15	0.10	0.45	0.22	0.10	0.28	0.45
Spain	2010	0.20	0.20	0.20	0.20	0.20	0.17	0.17	0.17	0.17	0.17
	2050	0.16	0.17	0.15	0.15	0.19	0.37	0.35	0.36	0.36	0.33
	2100	0.14	0.16	0.14	0.13	0.19	0.47	0.40	0.40	0.45	0.38
USA	2010	0.27	0.27	0.27	0.27	0.27	0.13	0.13	0.13	0.13	0.13
	2050	0.22	0.23	0.20	0.20	0.26	0.24	0.22	0.23	0.24	0.21
	2100	0.17	0.19	0.16	0.15	0.23	0.39	0.33	0.35	0.39	0.31

SSP: Shared Socio-economic Pathway.

The proportion with tertiary education under this scenario is on an expanding trajectory. Numerical information on the proportions in different education categories at different points in time are given in Table 12.5 for the female population aged 20–39, which is particularly relevant for education. Under SSP2, the combined proportion of younger women in the two lowest education categories (no education and some primary education) declines from the current level of 35 per cent to 17 per cent by 2050, and a low 4 per cent in 2100 under the global education trend scenario. While the decline is even faster under the SSP1 scenario, under SSP3 the proportion actually increases to 44 per cent in 2050 and 50 per cent in 2100. Under this scenario of stalled development, much of the educational gains of the past decades will be undone over the coming decades in a rather slow process caused by the inertia of education changes.

In all the higher education categories, the absolute number of people with secondary or tertiary education will increase over the coming decades. This trend is already preprogrammed into today's education structures, where, in almost all cases, the younger age groups are better educated than the older ones. This momentum of educational improvement leads to better future education of the elderly, even under the scenarios that assume no further increase in school enrolment rates (such as under SSP3). Under SSP1 and SSP5 the global proportion of people with higher education will increase dramatically and the global mean years of schooling (MYS; Table 12.2) of the total adult population will be 11.4 years by 2050, which is slightly higher than the current level in Europe (10.9 years) and below that in North America (12.9 MYS). In other words, under these scenarios the whole world will be slightly more educated in 40 years than Europe is today and will most likely experience the many positive consequences associated with higher education. Even under the most likely SSP2 scenario the global MYS will reach 10.4 years by mid-century. But SSP3 and SSP4 draw a much more pessimistic picture based on the assumption that the increase in school enrolment stagnates. In both instances the average education of the world population will experience a minor increase in the nearer future due to the earlier described momentum, then decline slightly during the second half of the century.

SSP4 is an interesting scenario in that it describes a world of inequality that is reflected in the education assumptions as described earlier. Although for total population size the trajectory is quite similar to that of the medium SSP2, the education composition of the population comes out very differently. As Figure 12.4 shows for SSP4, both the highest and the lowest education categories are on a growing trajectory, while the number of people with primary education is nearly constant over time. The group with secondary education first expands owing to the momentum of education, then declines. For the education distribution of younger women Table 12.5 shows, for SSP4, an increase in the proportion without any formal schooling from the current 15 per cent at the global level to 27 per cent in 2050, and 33 per cent in 2100. At the same time, the proportion of younger women with post-secondary/tertiary education—which is currently almost the same 15 per cent as for women without any schooling—will increase to 19 per cent by the end of the century. That is in sharp contrast to SSP1 and SSP5, where this proportion is assumed to increase to above 60 per cent by 2100.

Table 12.5 Proportion of the Female Population Aged 20–39 in the Region, Year, and Socio-economic Pathway (SSP) Stated by Level of Educational Attainment (in Percent for the Four Stated Categories)

		SSP1				SSP2				SSP2				SSP4				SSP5			
Region	Year	No education	Primary	Secondary	Tertiary	No education	Primary	Secondary	Tertiary	No education	Primary	Secondary	Tertiary	No education	Primary	Secondary	Tertiary	No education	Primary	Secondary	Tertiary
World	2010	15	20	49	16	15	20	49	16	15	20	49	16	15	20	49	16	15	20	49	16
	2050	2	7	46	45	4	13	55	29	20	24	44	12	27	22	34	17	2	7	46	45
	2100	0	2	39	59	0	4	50	46	23	26	40	10	33	25	23	19	0	2	38	60
Africa	2010	33	30	31	6	33	30	31	6	33	30	31	6	33	30	31	6	33	30	31	6
	2050	4	14	51	30	7	25	53	15	32	33	29	5	39	31	23	7	4	14	51	30
	2100	0	5	46	49	0	9	59	32	33	34	28	5	41	31	17	11	0	5	46	49
Asia	2010	16	21	49	14	16	21	49	14	16	21	49	14	16	21	49	14	16	21	49	14
	2050	2	6	45	48	3	10	56	31	19	23	46	12	27	21	33	19	2	5	45	48
	2100	0	1	35	63	0	2	47	52	22	24	43	11	32	22	21	25	0	1	35	64
Europe	2010	0	3	69	28	0	3	69	28	0	3	69	28	0	3	69	28	0	3	69	28
	2050	0	0	42	58	0	1	55	44	1	3	69	27	4	3	66	27	0	0	42	57
	2100	0	0	34	66	0	0	42	57	1	3	71	26	3	4	64	29	0	0	34	66
Latin America and the Caribbean	2010	4	27	52	17	4	27	52	17	4	27	52	17	4	27	52	17	4	27	52	17
	2050	0	5	46	49	0	9	57	33	4	26	54	17	13	24	40	23	0	5	46	49
	2100	0	1	38	61	0	1	48	51	4	26	53	17	16	28	27	29	0	1	38	61
North America	2010	0	2	57	41	0	2	57	41	0	2	57	41	0	2	57	41	0	2	57	41
	2050	0	0	38	61	0	1	47	52	0	2	58	40	0	2	65	32	0	0	39	61
	2100	0	0	34	66	0	0	38	62	0	2	58	40	0	2	66	32	0	0	34	66
Oceania	2010	2	9	53	36	2	9	53	36	2	9	53	36	2	9	53	36	2	9	53	36
	2050	0	3	38	59	0	6	46	48	3	12	53	32	5	10	55	29	0	2	38	60
	2100	0	0	31	69	0	1	38	61	3	15	52	29	7	12	50	31	0	0	30	69

We conclude with a look at alternative pathways of population ageing across the SSPs. Chapter 11 is dedicated to measuring population ageing and describing the ageing-related results of the WIC projections, primarily with reference to the medium scenario (SSP2) and alternative education scenarios that use identical medium education-specific fertility and mortality trends. Chapter 11 emphasizes redefining age and ageing indicators to reflect changing patterns of longevity and health. The chapter suggests that the old age dependency ratio be retired. For this reason, the following discussion does not refer to dependency ratios, but instead uses the neutral indicators of proportions of the total population below and above specific critical ages when presenting a conventional review of ageing results across the SSPs. These indicators are based on the conventional definition of chronological age. Table 12.4 gives these proportions in terms of the fraction of the populations that is below the age of 20 and above the age of 65. The data are for all continents and the selected 14 larger countries that are shown in other results tables in this volume (results for all individual countries are given in Appendix II).

Figure 12.8 shows the global-level proportions above the age of 65 for the five SSP scenarios. The resulting pattern is due to underlying mortality assumptions, with minor contributions from the fertility, migration, and education assumptions. SSP2 and SSP4 are based on medium mortality assumptions. In SSP3 (stalled development), high mortality is combined with high fertility, which results in a moderate increase in the proportion of the population above the age of 65. That increase levels off at about 16 per cent during the second half of the century. SSP1 (rapid development) and SSP5

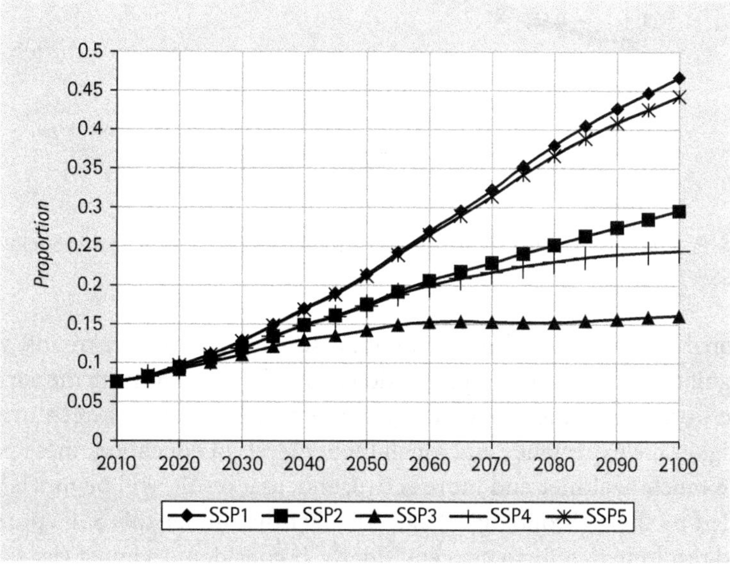

FIGURE 12.8 Projected proportions of people above the age of 65 for all Shared Socio-economic Pathways (SSPs) at the global level to 2100.

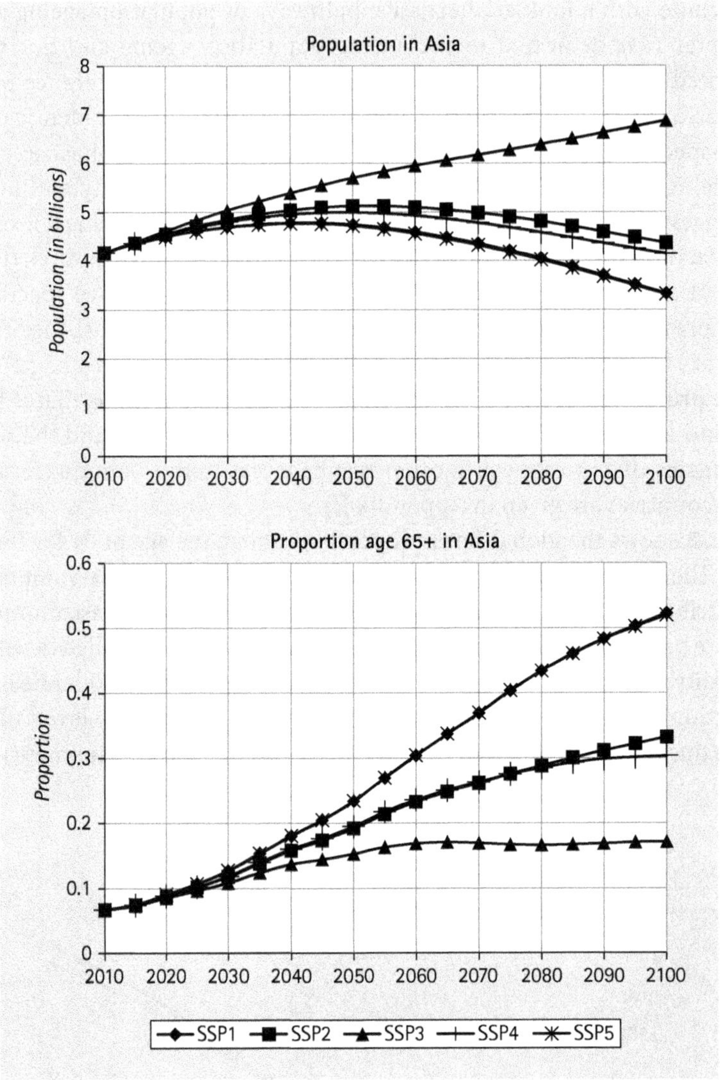

FIGURE 12.9 Population size and proportion above the age of 65 across all Shared Socio-economic Pathways (SSPs) in Asia.

(conventional development), however, both assume low mortality trends, which result in a significant increase in the proportion above the age of 65 from the current 8 per cent of the world population to about 45 per cent by the end of the century. But because of higher life expectancy and much higher levels of education, these people are likely to be much healthier and more active, and, as a result, will be much 'younger' than implied by their chronological age. The fact that under this SSP approach, the SSP3 world resulting in only 16 per cent 'elderly' is considered a much less sustainable and less desirable world than SSP1, with more than 45 per cent, poses serious challenges to the conventional view that societies with less ageing have a brighter future than those with more ageing.

The SSP scenario results by continents show that Asia is by far the most populous continent, home to about 60 per cent of the world population. Under all scenarios the population of Asia will increase until mid-century and then, except in the SSP3 scenario, start to decline. According to the medium scenario, Asia's population in 2100 will not be significantly different from today. In all likelihood, Asia will continue to be the most populous continent to end of the century. This could change if Asia were to follow the rapid development of the SSP1 scenario and Africa followed the stalled development of the SSP3 scenario. In that event, Africa's population in 2100 (Figure 12.10) would be bigger (3.92 billion) than Asia's (3.3 billion).

With respect to the proportion above the age of 65, Figure 12.9 shows a picture across scenarios similar to the pattern just described for the world as a whole. Table 12.2 shows that Asia's current adult population is still less educated than the global average (7.1 years of schooling compared with 7.9 years for the world). Owing to the recent rapid expansion of education in some Asian countries (China, in particular), the momentum of education increase will result under all scenarios in a quicker improvement than at the global level, and, by the end of the century, the average education in Asia under each scenario will be very close to the global average in those scenarios.

For all of Europe (including Russia), the medium SSP2 scenario portrays an almost constant population size for the rest of the century (Figure 12.11). This is due to a fertility level somewhat below replacement level that is compensated for by immigration and increases in life expectancy. Not surprisingly, the SSP5 scenario results in a visible increase of Europe's population to almost one billion by the end of the century owing to high assumed migration gains and high fertility levels in rich OECD countries. SSP3 (stalled development) and SSP4 (inequality) result in a decrease of total population from about 740 million now to about 540 million by the end of the century owing to the assumption of lower fertility. Given the low starting levels in fertility together with a decades-long low fertility history and assumed further increases in life expectancy, it is not surprising that the proportion of the popualtion above the age of 65 shows a strongly increasing trend across all scenarios (Figure 12.11). There is very little difference across scenarios up to the middle of the century because the trend is largely preprogrammed by the age structure, but afterwards the trend flattens under SSP3 and continues to increase almost lineary under SSP1. This is primarily the consequence of alternative mortality assumptions. The differences in average educational attainment among scenarios are rather modest because the young population in Europe today is well educated.

In North America the patterns of population growth, ageing, and educational attainment across scenarios are very similar to those in Europe. One notable difference is that the medium SSP2 scenario is not flat like Europe's, but shows a moderate increase from about 350 million today to more than 520 million in 2100 (Figure 12.12). This is due to

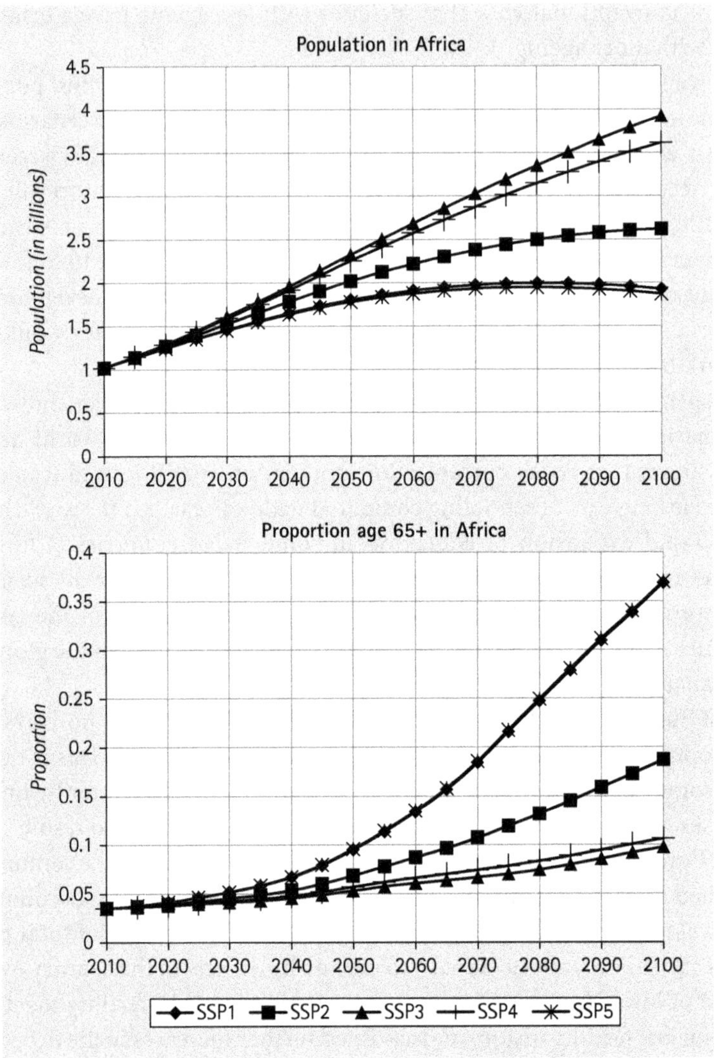

FIGURE 12.10 Population size and proportion above the age of 65 across all Shared Socioeconomic Pathways (SSPs) in Africa.

significantly higher assumed migration and somewhat higher assumed fertility compared with Europe. Another difference can be observed with respect to SSP1 (rapid development), which, in North America, comes out slightly higher than SSP2. This is a consequence of the differentiation (see Table 12.1) between rich OECD countries (including the USA and Canada), for which medium fertility is assumed, and other low fertility countries (including many Eastern European countries) for which low fertility is assumed. SSP3 (stalled development) combines the assumption of low fertility with low migration gains and hence results in an actual decline of the North American population to below 300 million by the end of the century.

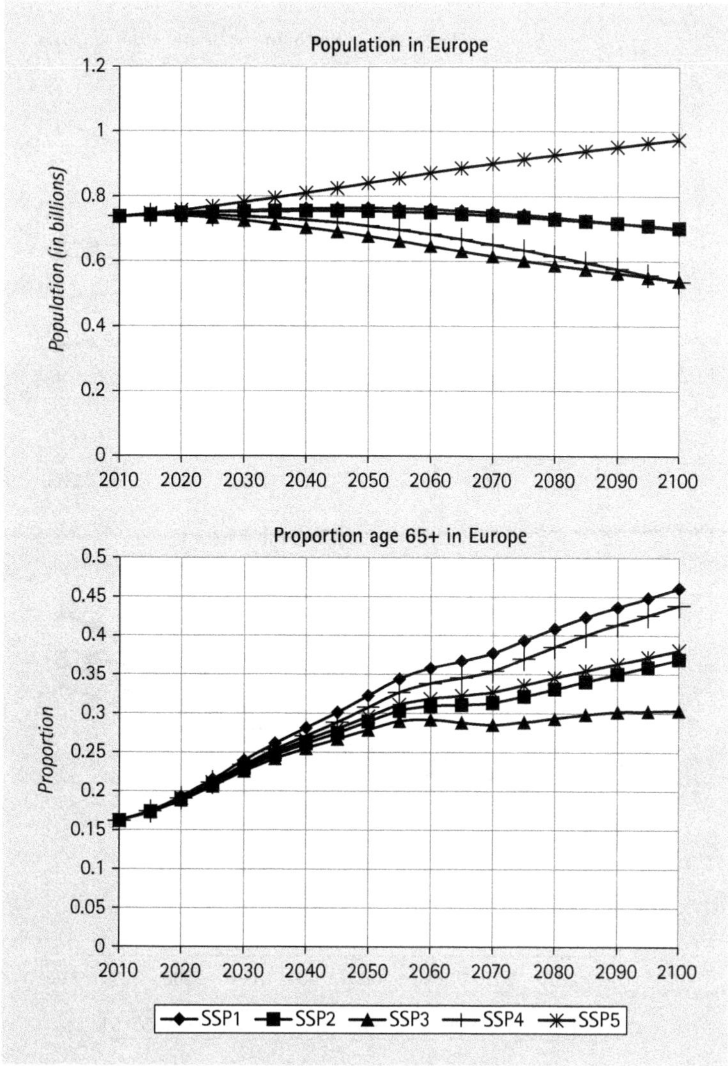

FIGURE 12.11 Population size and proportion above the age of 65 across all Shared Socio-economic Pathways (SSPs) in Europe.

Figure 12.13 compares the inter-scenario ranges for two of the world regions that have not yet been discussed, Latin America (including the Carribean) and Oceania (primarily Australia). What is notable in this comparison is the much wider inter-scenario range in Latin America. While the pattern in Oceania is similar to that of North America as discussed in the previous paragraph (Australia also belongs to the group of rich OECD countries), the pattern for Latin America resembles that for much of the rest of the world and for Asia, as shown in Figures 12.8 and 12.9. The combination of low fertility and low mortality in SSP1 and SSP5 results in a rapidly increasing proportion of the

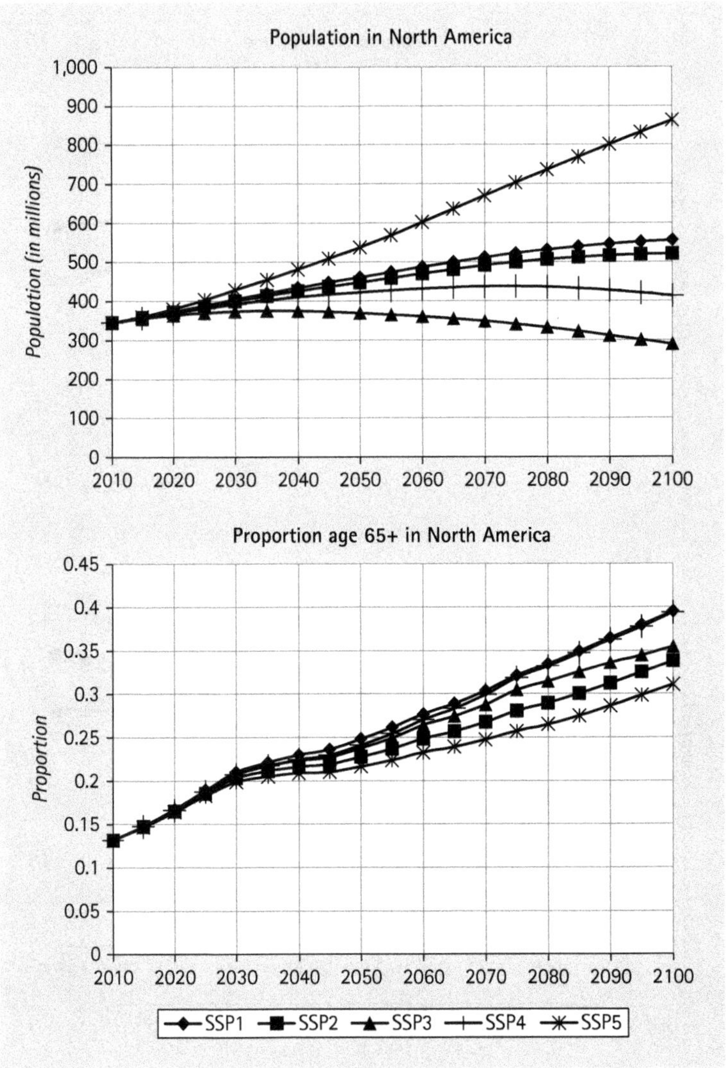

FIGURE 12.12 Population size and proportion above the age of 65 across all Shared Socio-economic Pathways (SSPs) in North America.

population above the age of 65. Under SSP3, this region has high fertility combined with slow increases in life expectancy, together resulting in a flattening of the proportion above the age of 65 over the second half of the century. In terms of average educational attainment, Latin America will see significant improvements under all five scenarios because in most countries in the region the young cohorts are already much better educated than the older cohorts, causing education momentum to dominate the future. Even under the most pessimistic SSP3 and SSP4 scenarios, the MYS of the adult population will increase from the current 8.0 to about 9.5 years by the end of the century.

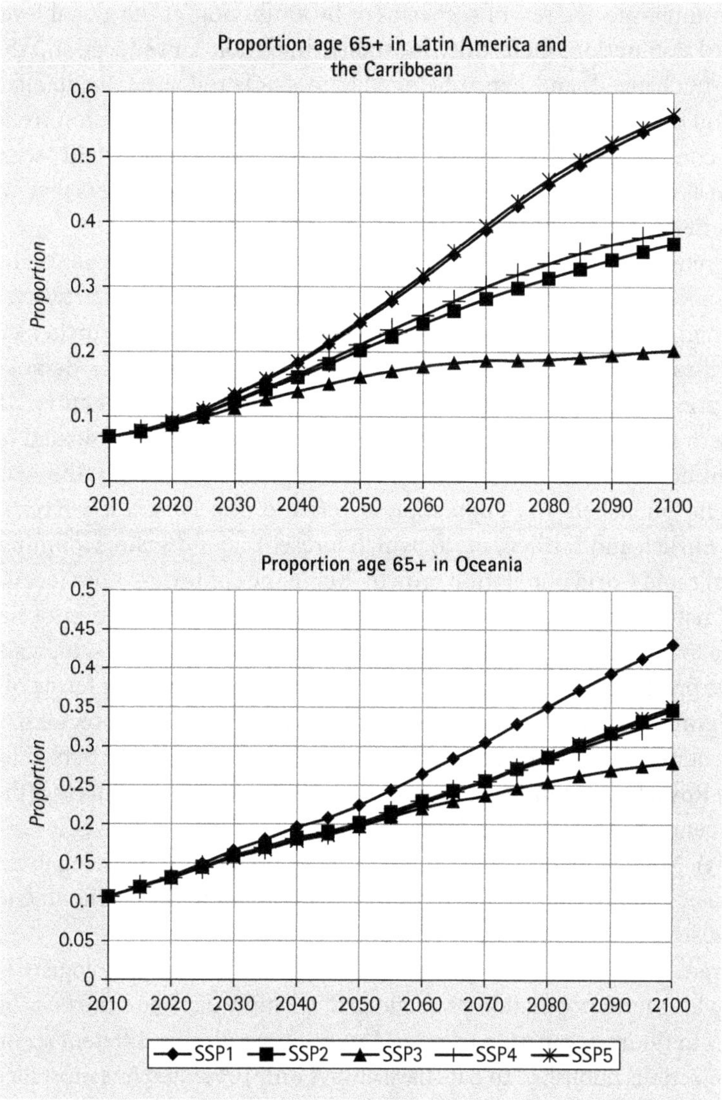

FIGURE 12.13 Comparison of trends in the proportions above the age of 65 in Latin America and the Caribbean (left side) and Oceania (right side) across Shared Socio-economic Pathways (SSP) scenarios.

12.4 POSSIBLE DISASTER SCENARIOS

The earlier described set of shared scenarios (SSPs) provides a broad framework within which many more specific scenarios can be defined and evaluated by different research groups. This can be either done by zooming into specific world regions or countries and defining country-specific sets of scenarios or by modifying, at the global level, some of the standard assumptions for fertility, mortality, migration, and education, while leaving the others unchanged, and hence being able to single out the specific effects of this modification of assumptions on the bigger picture of world population trends. In this section we conduct the latter exercise by defining some extreme mortality scenarios that can be seen as examples of possible, but not necessarily likely, disasters that humankind might experience over the course of the twenty-first century.

In conferences addressing the global twenty-first century challenges there often is a clash of projections that reflect very different underlying paradigms between ecologists who see a high probability of major disasters threatening even the further existence of human civilizations on the planet and social scientists—in particular, demographers—who only present business-as-usual scenarios for the rest of the century. There is no space here to review all of the doomsday scenarios that are being floated in the ecological community. Best known among demographers is probably the work of Paul Ehrlich, who published *The Population Bomb* and *The Population Explosion* (Ehrlich, 1968; Ehrlich and Ehrlich, 1990), which foresee major disasters looming as a consequence of rapid world population growth. But in the context of more recent concerns around climate change and the destruction of biodiversity the notion of humankind being close to falling over the cliff is frequently used as a metaphor—typically without being more precise about what exactly this cliff fall would imply in terms of mortality or other significant negative impacts in human well-being. More precise has been the prominent statement by one of the most distinguished British scientists, former president of the Royal Society and Astronomer Royal, Lord Rees of Ludlow that there is only a 50 per cent chance that the human race will survive the twenty-first century (Rees, 2003). More recently, he has qualified this statement to referring to the survival of 'human society as we know it' (2012), which, in our view, makes the statement more likely, but also much less precise.

The extreme opposite to this pessimistic view held by many ecologists is the view reflected in long term population projections that simply disregard the possibility of any uncertainty in future population trends. Most prominently, the different scenarios of all the UN projections published to date have always only presented one mortality scenario, which then was combined with different fertility assumptions. In other words, the entire uncertainty range presented by the UN population projections only reflects fertility uncertainty, while under all scenarios identical rates of future increases in life expectancy are assumed. In contrast, IIASA's population projections have, since their beginning (Lutz, 1991), always considered mortality and migration uncertainty along with fertility uncertainty. While in all these projections, as well as the scenarios described in this book so far, mortality was considered to be uncertain within a range covering roughly 80 per cent of plausible trajectories, in the 1994 IIASA book *The Future Population of the World: What Can We Assume Today?* (Lutz, 1994) there was even a separate chapter on 'Special World Population Scenarios to 2100', which tried to quantify some possible extreme examples of major mortality crises, as well as possible new inter-continental migration flows in the form of specific scenarios. The problem with any such quantitative scenarios

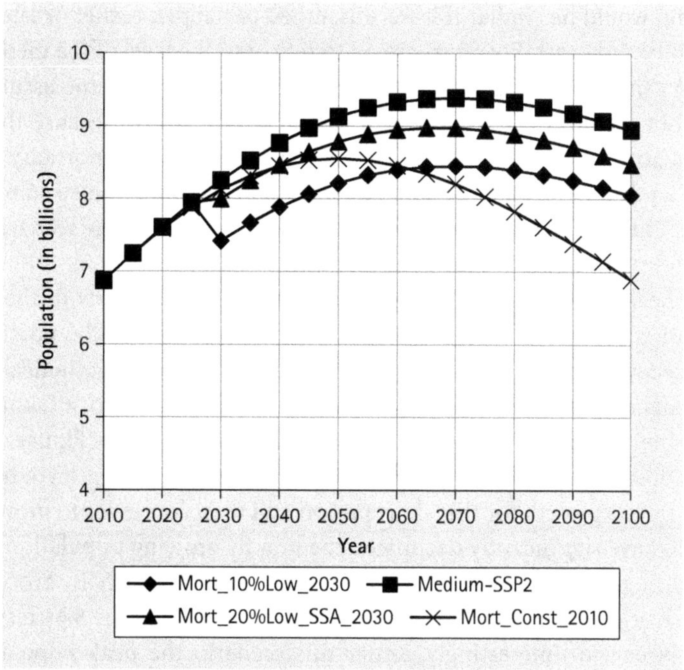

FIGURE 12.14 World population under possible disaster scenario.

Mort_10%Low_2030: in addition to medium mortality scenario 10% of the world population die in the period 2025–30; Mort_20%Low_SSA_2030: in addition to medium mortality scenario 20% of the population in sub-Saharan Africa die in the period 2025–30; Mort_Const_2010: mortality rates remain constant at the level in the period 2010–2015.

of possible disasters is that, by definition, they must be somewhat arbitrary because we have virtually no scientific basis for making informed assumptions about the timing and the extent of such crises.

When looking through the population-related literature there is, indeed, very little in terms of systematic assessments of what are main threats to human health and survival in the twenty-first century that could serve as the basis for defining informed alternative mortality scenarios. The most important contribution of this sort is a series of articles by Vaclav Smil (2005) on 'Fatal Discontinuities' published in *Population and Development Review* where he systematically assesses risks arising from pandemic influenza to climate change to changes in biodiversity. Inspired by Smil's writing, we defined for this book a set of three different 'disaster scenarios' that assume more extreme negative assumptions on future trends in life expectancy than even the high mortality trajectory in the earlier described set of projections.

The first disaster scenario attempts to describe the case of a one-time major global increase in mortality as the consequence of a deadly influenza pandemic or a global war with so far unprecedented mortality consequences. It is assumed to kill over a period of 5 years 10 per cent of the entire world population in a random manner. The timing of this unprecedented disaster was chosen to be in 2025–30, but the consequences, as depicted in Figure 12.14, would be similar if it were assumed to happen earlier or later. After the disaster, fertility and mortality are assumed to return to the level of the medium trajectory again. As shown in Figure 12.14 the result of this very extreme assumption is a downward shift in the trajectory of world population growth. Because the base line population in 2030 is reduced, the assumed medium fertility and mortality trajectories will result in a peaking of world population at a level of 8.5 billion instead of 9.4 billion around 2070. The total world population in 2100 under this extreme scenario would be 0.9 billion lower than under the medium scenario.

As public health capabilities are very different in different parts of the world this assumption of equal effects may not be meaningful for many of the possible threats. Hence, in a second disaster scenario it was assumed that this hypothetical 2030 mortality crisis kills 20 per cent of the population of sub-Saharan Africa (assumed to the most vulnerable) instead of 10 per cent of the world population. As Figure 12.14 shows, this scenario does not even result in a decline in world population growth from 2025 to 2030, it only arrests growth for this short period and then continues to grow again. But because it will have significantly decimated the rapidly growing population it will have significant consequences on longer-term world population growth. By 2100, under this scenario, the world population would be 8.48 billion instead of the 8.95 resulting from the medium scenario. Interestingly, under this scenario the peak population of the world would have already been reached in 2065 instead of 2070.

A third scenario defines a chronic mortality disaster by simply assuming no further mortality improvements, that is, freezing all mortality rates at their current levels, while other assumptions follow the medium trajectory. It is interesting to see from Figure 12.14 that this lack of further improvement would have a much more dramatic impact on future world population size than the death of 10 per cent of the world population or 20 per cent of Africa's population. Under the simple assumption of no further increases in life expectancy the world population would reach 6.89 billion in 2100 and thus be lower than today's world population. Also, the peak population would have already been reached in 2050 at a level of 8.56 billion.

These are just three rather simplistic scenarios about what could be the effects of different possible disasters on global population trends. One could, of course, also make much more refined assumptions about fertility and migration responses to such disasters or, alternatively, make the plausible assumption that the less educated are disproportionally affected by such disasters, which would also affect the educational composition of populations and therefore their overall fertility and mortality levels. But the more specific the scenario assumptions are, the more arbitrary they look in the absence of any specific scientific basis. This is also the reason why, in this section of special scenarios, we refrained from defining any scenarios of mass migration as a consequence of future climate change, for example from Africa and South Asia into Russia and Canada, where climate change might open up massive, previously unusable fertile lands. After an analysis of the work of the UN University Institute on Environment and Human Security in Bonn (Warner et al., 2013), as well as the UK Government Office of Science Foresight Report on Migration and Environmental Change (Black et al., 2011), we came to the conclusion that there simply is no basis for making specific numerical assumptions about specific bilateral migration flows in the distant future that are very different from today's flows. Chapter 7 discusses this topic in more detail.

In sum, there are two interesting lessons to be learned from the rather speculative disaster scenario exercise described. First, future world population trends are essentially shaped by the long-term levels of fertility and mortality. Even inconceivably large, tragic, one-time events, such as the sudden death of hundreds of millions of people, do not fundamentally alter the major patterns of world population trends. This was also true for World War II, which was hardly visible as a discontinuity in the trend of world population growth. The second, very interesting, insight is that the widely spread notion that future population growth is exclusively the consequence of future birth rates is not correct. Assumed mortality improvements also play a significant role. As shown earlier, the assumptions of no further improvements results in a world population that is two billion lower by the end of the century. As shown by Basten et al. (2013), the role of future mortality improvements becomes even more important when scenarios are extended beyond the twenty-first century.

12.5 Conclusions

The new population scenarios by age, sex, and level of educational attainment represent a major step forward compared with the earlier SRES scenarios used in the environmental change research community, which only considered total population size (Nakicenovic et al., 2000). From a social science perspective they provide a much richer picture of major social changes, as described along the three key dimensions of age, gender, and level of education. These dimensions, as explicitly and quantitatively modelled and projected in the scenarios, can also be related to many of the Millennium Development Goals (MDG) and to the main components of the Human Development Index (HDI). Level of educational attainment by gender, as well as health and mortality by age for men and women separately (which form two of the three components of the HDI), are explicitly included in the set of indicators that shape the human core of the SSPs. As a next step, these alternative pathways of population and human capital are being translated by other research teams into alternative trajectories of future economic growth in individual countries. Identifying those trajectories can help project the third component of the HDI (in addition to the education and life expectancy components given here) and to derive several of the other technology- and environment-related dimensions of the SSPs. Together, this new family of scenarios provides a powerful analytical tool to deal with multiple social and economic dimensions of global environmental change in the twenty-first century.

APPENDIX 12.1

Country groupings

High fertility countries (TFR >2.9)	Low fertility countries (TFR ≤2.9)	
	Rich OECD	Others
Afghanistan, Angola, Belize, Benin, Bolivia (Plurinational State of), Burkina Faso, Burundi, Cameroon, Central African Republic, Chad, Comoros, Congo, Côte d'Ivoire, Democratic Republic of the Congo, Djibouti, Equatorial Guinea, Eritrea, Ethiopia, French Guiana, Gabon, Gambia, Ghana, Guatemala, Guinea, Guinea-Bissau, Haiti, Honduras, Iraq, Jordan, Kenya, Lao People's Democratic Republic, Lesotho, Liberia, Madagascar, Malawi, Mali, Mauritania, Mayotte, Micronesia (Federal States of), Mozambique, Namibia, Nepal, Niger, Nigeria, Occupied Palestinian Territory, Pakistan, Papua New Guinea, Paraguay, Philippines, Rwanda, Samoa, Sao Tome and Principe, Saudi Arabia, Senegal, Sierra Leone, Solomon Islands, Somalia, Sudan, Swaziland, Syrian Arab Republic, Tajikistan, Timor-Leste, Togo, Tonga, Uganda, United Republic of Tanzania, Vanuatu, Yemen, Zambia, Zimbabwe	Australia, Austria, Belgium, Canada, Czech Republic, Denmark, Estonia, Finland, France, Germany, Greece, Hungary, Iceland, Ireland, Israel, Italy, Japan, Luxembourg, Netherlands, New Zealand, Norway, Poland, Portugal, Republic of Korea, Slovakia, Slovenia, Spain, Sweden, Switzerland, UK, USA	Albania, Algeria, Argentina, Armenia, Aruba, Azerbaijan, Bahamas, Bahrain, Bangladesh, Barbados, Belarus, Bhutan, Bosnia and Herzegovina, Botswana, Brazil, Brunei Darussalam, Bulgaria, Cambodia, Cape Verde, Channel Islands, Chile, China, China, Hong Kong Special Administrative Region, China, Macao Special Administrative Region, Colombia, Costa Rica, Croatia, Cuba, Cyprus, Democratic People's Republic of Korea, Dominican Republic, Ecuador, Egypt, El Salvador, Fiji, French Polynesia, Georgia, Grenada, Guadeloupe, Guam, Guyana, India, Indonesia, Iran (Islamic Republic of), Jamaica, Kazakhstan, Kuwait, Kyrgyzstan, Latvia, Lebanon, Libyan Arab Jamahiriya, Lithuania, Malaysia, Maldives, Malta, Martinique, Mauritius, Mexico, Mongolia, Montenegro, Morocco, Myanmar, Netherlands Antilles, New Caledonia, Nicaragua, Oman, Panama, Peru, Puerto Rico, Qatar, Republic of Moldova, Réunion, Romania, Russian Federation, Saint Lucia, Saint Vincent and the Grenadines, Serbia, Singapore, South Africa, Sri Lanka, Suriname, Thailand, The Former Yugoslav Republic of Macedonia, Trinidad and Tobago, Tunisia, Turkey, Turkmenistan, Ukraine, United Arab Emirates, United States Virgin Islands, Uruguay, Uzbekistan, Venezuela (Bolivarian Republic of), Viet Nam

TFR: total fertility rate; OECD: Organisation for Economic Co-operation and Development.

References

Arnell, N., Kram, T., Carter, T., Ebi, K., Edmonds, J., Hallegatte, S., et al. 2011 'A Framework For a New Generation of Socioeconomic Scenarios for Climate Change Impact, Adaptation, Vulnerability and Mitigation Research' (Scenario Framework Paper). Potsdam Institute for Climate Impact Research: Potsdam.

Basten, S., Lutz, W. and Scherbov, S. 2013 'Very Long Range Global Population Scenarios to 2300 and the Implications of Sustained Low Fertility'. *Demographic Research*, 28: 1145–66.

Biraben, J.-N. 2003 'L'évolution du nombre des hommes'. *Population et Sociétés*, 394: 1–4.

Black, R., Adger, N., Arnell, N., Dercon, S., Geddes, A. and Thomas, D. 2011 'Migration and Global Environmental Change: Future Challenges and Opportunities' (Final Project Report). Available at: <http://www.bis.gov.uk/foresight/our-work/projects> (accessed 3 February 2014).

Crespo Cuaresma, J., Lutz, W. and Sanderson, W. C. 2013. 'Is the Demographic Dividend an Education Dividend?' *Demography*, 51: 299–315.

Ehrlich, P.R. 1968 *The Population Bomb*. Ballantine: New York.

Ehrlich, P.R. and Holdren, J.P. 1971 'Impact of Population Growth'. *Science*, 171: 1212–17.

Ehrlich, P.R. and Ehrlich, A.H. 1990 *The Population Explosion*. Simon & Schuster: New York.

Lutz, W. (ed.) 1991 *Future Demographic Trends in Europe and North America. What Can We Assume Today?* Academic Press: London.

Lutz, W. (ed.) 1994 *The Future Population of the World. What Can We Assume Today?* Earthscan: London.

Lutz, W. 2009 'What Can Demographers Contribute to Understanding the Link Between Population and Climate Change'. *POPNET*, 41: 1–2.

Moss, R.H., Edmonds, J.A., Hibbard, K.A., Manning, M.R., Rose, S.K., van Vuuren, D.P., et al. 2010 'The Next Generation of Scenarios for Climate Change Research and Assessment'. *Nature*, 463: 747–56.

Nakicenovic, N., Alcamo, J., Grubler, A., Riahi, K., Roehrl, R.A., Rogner, H.-H. and Victor, N. 2000 'Special Report on Emissions Scenarios (SRES), A Special Report of Working Group III of the Intergovernmental Panel on Climate Change, IPCC Special Reports on Climate Change'. Cambridge University Press: Cambridge.

O'Neill, B.C., Dalton, M., Fuchs, R., Jiang, L., Pachauri, S. and Zigova, K. 2010 'Global Demographic Trends and Future Carbon Emissions'. *Proceedings of the National Academy of Sciences of the United States of America*, 107: 17521–6.

O'Neill, B.C., Kriegler, E., Riahi, K., Ebi, K., Hallegatte, S., Carter, T.R., et al. 2014 'A New Scenario Framework for Climate Change Research: The Concept of Shared Socio-economic Pathways'. *Climate Change*, 122: 387–400.

Rees, M.J. 2003 *Our Final Hour: A Scientist's Warning: How Terror, Error, and Environmental Disaster Threaten Humankind's Future in this Century—On Earth and Beyond*. Basic Books: New York.

Smil, V. 2005 'The Next 50 Years: Fatal Discontinuities'. *Population and Development Review*, 31: 201–36.

Vuuren, D.P. van, Edmonds, J.A., Kainuma, M., Riahi, K. and Weyant, J. 2011 'A Special Issue on the RCPs'. *Climatic Change*, 109: 1–4.

Warner, K., Afifi, T., Kalin, W., Leckie, S., Ferris, B., Martin, S. and Wrathall, D. 2013 'Changing Climate, Moving People: Framing Migration, Displacement and Planned Relocation' (No. Policy Brief 8). United Nations University Institute for Environment and Human Security.

EPILOGUE

With Education the Future Looks Different

WOLFGANG LUTZ[1]

THE title of the epilogue to this book on twenty-first century world population and human capital can be read in three different ways. Each relates to the book's content. 'With Education the Future Looks Different' can first be read as referring to the cognitive processes of perceiving the world and thinking about the future, processes that education helps shape. Second, the title can be understood in the more specific demographic modelling context of this book, where we show that explicitly adding education to the conventional demographic approach, which differentiates only by age and sex, produces a population outlook to the future that does, indeed, look very different when accounting for education heterogeneity compared with assuming homogeneity. Finally, the title can be read as referring to the improved life chances and development opportunities that result from education, at the level of both individuals and societies, where at both levels the future looks better with education.

I here discuss the first meaning only briefly because research about the effects of education on perception is still in its infancy, and the topic really belongs to the field of cognitive science and experimental psychology, rather than demography. I then address the second meaning referring to education as a decisive source of population heterogeneity, and give examples of how the anticipated challenges associated with population ageing look very different when education is factored in. Finally, I address the multiple benefits of education and provide a brief overview of how the new data of educational attainment by age and sex allow for a much richer and much more convincing assessment of the returns to education in terms of desirable individual and social futures. I conclude with some policy-relevant considerations.

[1] Some parts of the text in this epilogue are taken from Lutz (2009), as well as some of the other cited papers co-authored by Lutz.

E.1 Education changes our cognition and the way we think about the future

The foundations of the effects of education on human behaviour are covered in Chapter 2, which summarizes the evidence base for assuming functional causality in the effects of education on demographic outcomes. There, I refer to modern brain research, which leaves no doubt that every learning experience and, in particular, repeated experiences physiologically changes our brains by building new synapses that not only store the information content of our experiences, but also become an integral part of what forms our sense of personality (Kandel, 2007). While neuroscience still seems to be far away from a full understanding of the process of learning, neurological studies have confirmed, beyond doubt, that brain volumes, cortical thickness, and neurological structures can be affected by more education. Hence, it seems reasonable to assume that cognitive functions that relate to our perception of the environment around us, our view of the future, and our degree of rationality are related to our previous education experiences. In particular, empirical studies show that better educated individuals tend to have a longer investment horizon and be more risk adverse (van der Pol, 2011).

Given the empirical evidence of manifest behaviour, as well as stated preferences as a function of levels of education, it is surprising how little systematic scientific research exists on the more specific mechanisms and forms in which education changes our brains, our cognition, and, ultimately, our behaviour. When screening (as an interested outsider) the neuroscience literature on the topic of how education changes our brains and talking to some leading experts in the field, I arrived at the impression that this research question simply is not on the table as something interesting to be studied in that community. It even seems hard to conduct secondary analysis of existing samples because most of the participants tend to be rather homogenous with respect their education background (most often college students who are readily available and willing to engage in brain scanning tests). Interestingly, the most explicit treatment I have found of different behaviour resulting from differences in cognition of people with greatly differing levels of education is in a study of literacy and mothering (LeVine et al., 2012) that deals with the effects of basic female education on child health and survival in developing countries.

Levine et al. (2012) present a broad discussion about what formal (Western-type) schooling and different aspects of literacy imply for cognitive functions, based on several empirical studies in different parts of the developing world. They take a socio-linguistic approach. In addition to measuring the ability to read text, they also assess the ability to engage in metalinguistic speech, that is, the ability to provide verbal explanations of activities and to treat words as objects. This is operationalized through noun definition measures where women were asked to define, for example, what a dog or a knife is, and the responses scored for the presence of superordinate category membership (e.g. 'A dog is an animal…' or 'A knife is an instrument…'). The results show a high correlation of such ability for metalinguistic speech with the level of formal education. After ruling out alternative explanations, they conclude that, indeed, there is something about Western-type schooling that leads to metalinguistic awareness and the use of abstract terms in speech, as well as in writing. They attribute this, in part, to the classroom setting, where children pay attention to an expert and respond verbally to questions by an adult, while in traditional agrarian societies it is rare for adults to talk to children except to direct their activities through commands. And they see the use of abstraction as a cardinal feature of standardized communicative norms in bureaucratic organizations, including schools and health care systems. This is also why young women who went to school are shown to be better able to deliver intelligible illness narratives of their children to clinic or health workers, and are better able and willing to follow the instructions given by them, thus having a higher probability of saving the lives of their children. This cognitive mechanism is seen as an important reason for the markedly lower child mortality for women who attended school, even if only for a short period, compared with women who never attended school. Hence, in addition to literacy and language skills, schools also transmit cognitive schemas that influence the way these women communicate with other adults and with their own children, as well as how they prepare for the future.

Clearly, there is a need for much more systematic interdisciplinary research about how education changes our brains, our cognition, our ways of communication, and our behaviour. This is a field in which enhanced collaboration among social scientists, neuroscientists, and experimental psychologists is absolutely essential because it has far-reaching policy consequences for the urgency, strength, and orientation of public, as well as private, education programmes. Interestingly, in the last paragraph of their conclusions Levine et al. (2012)—coming from an education background—explicitly refer to demography: 'Our analysis challenges the field of population studies, including demography and epidemiology, to integrate educational research and literacy assessment into its empirical research program as well as its theories and policy analyses.' At least in this respect there seems to be some progress in interdisciplinary collaboration because this volume tries to do precisely what Levine et al. (2012) are calling for.

E.2 When education is factored in, future population ageing looks less challenging

Conventionally, population trends have been studied with respect to the two basic demographic dimensions of age and sex/gender. In Chapter 2 the point is made that in twenty-first-century demography traditional age and gender distinctions are in the process of losing their previously unquestioned position as presumably natural factors, with education considered to be socially constructed. Instead, we now understand that all three factors—age, gender, and education—have elements of social construction, as well as of underlying physiological differences. In Chapter 11, entitled 'Re-measuring Twenty-first Century Population Ageing', alternative definitions of age and ageing are introduced that take account of changing life expectancies, and refer to both the changing social construction of age ('60 is the new 50') and the changing physiological meaning of age as more and more people stay in good health at higher, conventionally-measured (chronological), ages. The increases in life expectancy and, in particular, disability-free life expectancy to which these new definitions of age refer, are likely to also reflect a consequence of the improving educational composition of the populations studied; this implicit contribution of education can be made explicit.

Even before affecting the average health status of the elderly, education is also known to improve the labour productivity of the working age population. Conventional age-dependency ratios assume that every person of a given age is equally productive by giving equal weights to all people in the denominator. Here, also, the future of old age dependency looks very different when the productivity-enhancing effect of education is explicitly factored in through constructing alternative education-weighted dependency ratios. As a further consequence of explicitly including education, it can be shown that the optimal level of fertility in terms of minimizing the long-term dependency ratios (or maximizing support ratios) turns out to lie below replacement level, which is lower than when education is omitted from the analysis. I now illustrate these two aspects of how the future looks different with education by summarizing work published elsewhere by members of this book's author team.

E.2.1 With education we expect fewer disabled people in the future

Samir KC and Harold Lentzner (2010) present overwhelming empirical evidence from virtually all countries for which data exist that the risk of falling into disability and of dying at any given age varies greatly by level of education for both men and women. For male life expectancies these differences between the highest and lowest educational groups in various countries range from a high of 12 years in Eastern Europe to some 3–4 years in Mediterranean countries. What is less well known and documented is that the prevalence of disability also tends to vary greatly with the level of education. Data from the World Health Survey (WHS)[2] were analysed by KC and Lentzner for educational differentials in disability of the adult population above the age of 30. WHS data had been collected in 2002/03 with personal interviews conducted in the local language using standardized survey instruments. Respondents provided information on demographic characteristics, health status, risk factors, access to and utilization of health services, and health care expenditure. In this analysis, two health status indicators measuring

[2] The WHS is a collection of sample surveys of the adult population of 18 years of age and older in 70 countries around the globe.

disability (presence or absence) were defined based on responses on activity of daily living (ADL) and self-reported health.

Table E.1 shows the result of their regression of ADL disability on age and education, separately for women and men, for five world regions. The odds of reporting severe or extreme difficulty in mobility or self-care increase with age and decline with level of education. For Eastern European women the odds increase rapidly with age, almost nine times larger at the age of 60–69 as at the age of 30–39, and almost three times larger for Asian and Latin American women. For men, as age increases, the odds at the age of 60–69 increase by as much as six times in Western and Eastern Europe compared with the odds at the age of 30–39. For both sexes and in all five regions (except for Eastern European men with at least secondary education), the decline in the prevalence of disability with increasing education is statistically significant. The odds of reporting ADL disability for a woman with no education compared with a woman with primary education is the highest (more than double) in Latin America (2.43 times) and least in Africa (1.19 times); for women with at least secondary education, the odds ratio is least (less than half) in Asia (0.46) and highest in Eastern Europe (0.82).

As the analysis shows, these significant health differentials by level of education affect not only the elderly population beyond working age, but also the working age population itself. While the first is primarily relevant in order to assess the future need for care

Table E.1 Results of Regression of Activities of Daily Living on Age and Education: Odds Ratio (For Data Source See Text)

	Africa	Asia	Western Europe	Latin America	Eastern Europe
Women					
30–39	1.00	1.00	1.00	1.00	1.00
40–49	1.39	1.27	1.62	1.55	2.58
50–59	2.08	1.82	3.39	1.91	3.82
60–69	3.49	2.92	4.07	2.92	8.77
70–74	5.74	6.37	11.07	4.81	21.3
Education					
None	1.19	1.74	1.93	2.43	1.73
Primary	1.00	1.00	1.00	1.00	1.00
At least secondary	0.62	0.46	0.53	0.52	0.82
Men					
30–39	1.00	1.00	1.00	1.00	1.00
40–49	1.09	1.58	1.39	0.93	2.87
50–59	1.8ns	2.80	3.93^{ns}	1.85^{ns}	3.89
60–69	3.26	4.50	6.02	3.16	6.19
70–74	5.65	6.41	7.89	6.46	14.45
Education					
None	1.38	1.21	2.00	2.35	2.56
Primary	1.00	1.00	1.00	1.00	1.00
At least secondary	0.75	0.65	0.88	0.61	0.64^{ns}

Note: All values are significant at the 0.05 level or higher except for those identified by *ns* (not significant).

for the disabled, the latter also directly matters for the ability to work and be productive as a member of the work force. KC and Lentzner (2010) also estimated from their model the proportion of older adults disabled, per education level, among men and women by age groups (for the age range 30–74) for major world regions. They then applied this constant age-, sex-, and education-specific prevalence matrix of disability to an earlier version of International Institute for Applied Systems Analysis' (IIASA) world population projections by age, sex, and education for the period 2000–50 (KC et al., 2010) and estimated adult disability up to 2050 in two different ways. They first applied a constant age/sex profile of ADL disability without considering our observed educational differentials. This reflects the conventional demographic approach, which is the basis on which most governments assume a future increase in overall disability. In Figure E.1 the line labelled 'NES' (no education scenario) does, indeed, show an increasing trend for the future. This is simply the consequence of projected population ageing together with the increase of disability with age in current and recent populations.

In a second set of projections they enriched the model by factoring in the education/disability relationships obtained from the WHS analysis and applying them to three different educational attainment scenarios over the same time horizon. More than 100 countries (covering approximately 90 per cent of the world's population) grouped into regions were used in this exercise. These multidimensional projections that are based on the same empirical baseline, but also cover the education heterogeneity, are given in the three additional lines shown in Figure E.1. Under all three wide-ranging education scenarios the projections of future disability in the age group 30–74 come out clearly lower than when education heterogeneity is disregarded. Even under the most pessimistic constant enrolment number (CEN) scenario (that assumes constant school enrolment numbers in the future) the resulting projections show declining proportions disabled in Asia, Latin America, and Europe. Only in Africa does the high rate of population growth imply that if the school system is not expanded the average educational attainment will actually deteriorate over time and hence lead to an increase in average disability after an initial decline.

The reason for this result—that even in the absence of further education improvements the average disability projection is significantly lower than in the case of disregarding education heterogeneity—is that in most parts of the world the improvement is already pre-programmed in today's population structure. In Asia and Latin America, in particular, the young generations are much better educated than the older ones; therefore, we know with certainty that future older adults will be better educated than today's older adults, implying that their average disability will be lower if the differentials by level of education are factored in.

Under the middle-of-the-road global education trend (GET) scenario and the very optimistic fast track scenario the future prevalence of disability comes out accordingly lower than under the very pessimistic CEN scenario.

In conclusion, it is clear that the vulnerability of men and women falling into disability not only varies greatly among countries and world regions, but that significant and consistent differences with respect to the level of education also emerge within

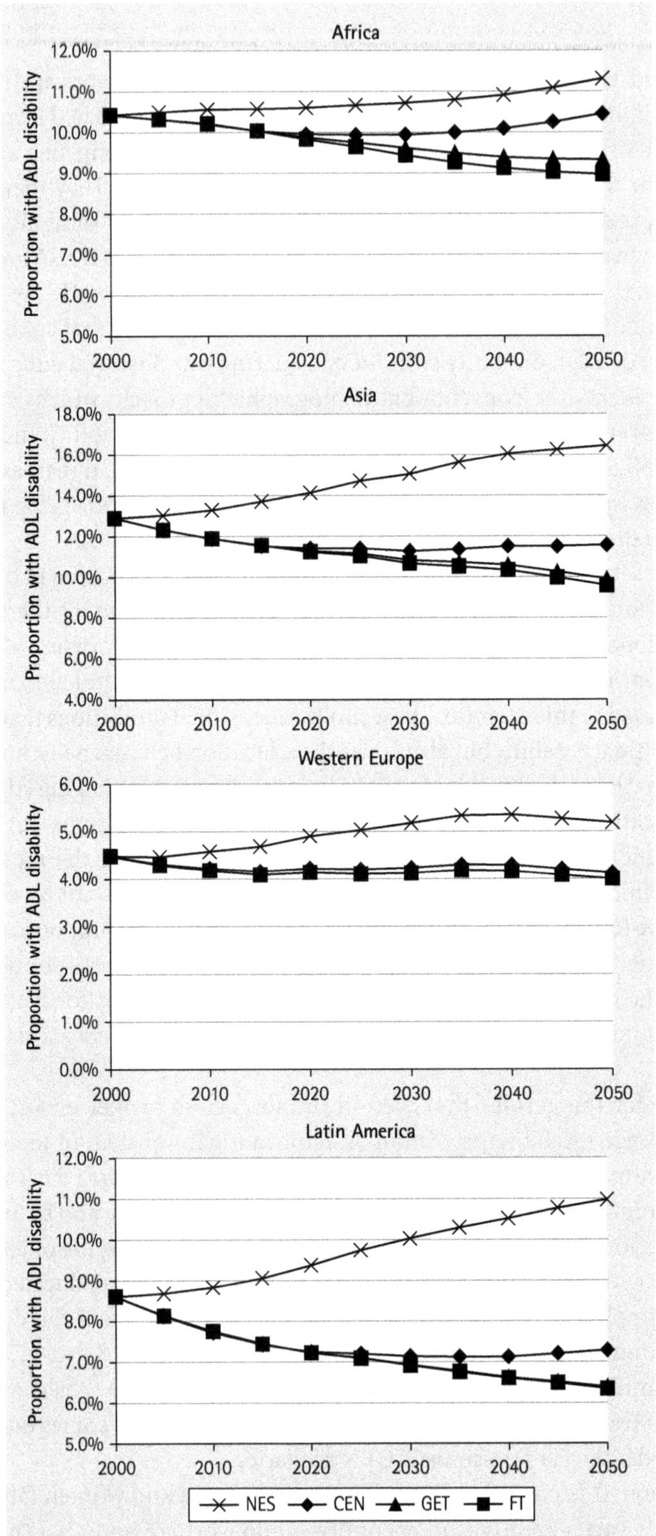

FIGURE E.1 Projected prevalence of activities of daily living (ADL) disability for the age group 30–74 in four world regions. NES: no education scenario; CEN: constant enrolment number scenario; GET: global education trend scenario; FT: fast track scenario.

countries. This is not only a matter of individual risk and vulnerability, but it also occurs at the population level, where broadly expected increases in the future prevalence of disability are a major public health and financial concern. An explicit accounting for education heterogeneity at a given age makes the future look different.

E.2.2 With more education 'optimal' fertility will be below replacement level

Another recent line of research has studied the implications of explicitly addressing heterogeneity by level of education attainment in the context of analysing the socially desirable level of fertility for any given low fertility country. Already in the concluding chapter of the 2004 IIASA book on world population projections (Lutz et al., 2004), a model was presented that calculated the levels of a welfare indicator based on an education-weighted support ratio for stable populations at different levels of fertility and with different educational attainment distributions. Education was assumed to present a cost for young people, but also to result in higher productivity of adults. As the benefits of education outweigh the cost, the results showed, unsurprisingly, that in better educated populations at every level of fertility, overall welfare was higher than in the less educated case. What was somewhat surprising, however, was the result that the 'optimal' level of fertility, as implied by the stable total fertility rate (TFR) yielding the highest welfare indicator, was below the replacement level of 2.1, with the optimum moving lower under higher education assumptions. This is a consequence of the relatively lower total education cost in the case of fewer children.

This finding challenges the widespread view that replacement level fertility is the most desirable long-term level of fertility for any society. When asked about what a desirable fertility level for populations might be, most politicians, journalists, and even demographers would spontaneously answer that it is slightly above two children per woman—a level sometimes called 'replacement level fertility'. The reasons stated in support of this level of fertility (which in most European countries is higher than the current rates) usually refer to some vague notions of maintaining the size of the labour force and stabilizing the dependency ratio. But a closer look at the demographic models that underlie this reasoning reveals that this supposedly precise level of 2.1 (actually more like 2.06 under low mortality conditions) is only derived from a highly stylized theoretical model of stationary population. It has little to do with actually maintaining the size of the labour force in contemporary *real* societies. These have an age structure that is often quite irregular and the size of the working age population is influenced by migration and mortality changes in addition to fertility.

Even in the hypothetical absence of migration and under constant mortality conditions, in countries with a high share of young people (positive momentum of population growth), fertility should be well below replacement level if the goal is to keep the absolute size of the working age population constant. Conversely, in countries with relatively few younger people (i.e. that have already entered a phase of negative momentum) fertility should be significantly above replacement level if, again, the goal is to maintain the working age population. Lutz et al. (2003) showed that Europe's population entered the phase of negative momentum around the year 2000. Hence, in this context of real European populations and their empirically given age structures, a reference to replacement level fertility makes little sense in terms of the stated goal of maintaining the labour force at its current size. On top of this, all real populations in Europe and elsewhere do experience mortality change and migration, which renders the 2.1 goal even less relevant as a path toward a supposedly desirable constant working age population.

To account for these existing realities in population structures, Striessnig and Lutz (2013) recently calculated a set of models similar to Lutz et al. (2004) for a number of European countries, based on existing current age and education structures, as well as long-term scenarios that correspond to the education scenarios as presented in this volume. In terms of costs of education, returns to education, and different ages of labour force entry and exit by level of education, they tried to make assumptions as close as possible to reality. The results show that in the short run (over the coming two decades) the education-weighted support ratio is always highest when there are no children at all because in this case there are no education costs while the adults are still around and productive—a situation that is clearly not sustainable in the longer term. Over the subsequent decades there are still some irregularities in the resulting patterns due to the uneven age structures described earlier. In the very long run, though, the pattern becomes smoother. Accordingly, Figure E.2 shows the results for Germany for a large number of alternative stable TFRs that are assumed to be constant from the current date until the end of the century. For simplicity, the country is assumed to be closed to migration, while mortality is assumed to further decline as in the usual projections.

Note the resulting education-weighted support ratios (defined as the inverse of the total dependency ratio) for Germany for two alternative education scenarios. The assumed education costs and education-specific productivity weights are given in the upper right box. The resulting curves show that at very low fertility levels (i.e. below a TFR of 1.0) the support ratio rapidly declines and can in no way be compensated by higher education. At the high end of simulated fertility levels, the support ratio also falls, but less rapidly and it is always higher under the GET scenario (assuming a trend of further improving education) compared with the constant enrolment rate (CER) scenario. The highest (or optimal) level of the support ratio is reached at a TFR of around 2.0 (again: assuming no migration and further gains in life expectancy) for the low education CER scenario, while under the likely GET scenario it is reached at a TFR of 1.78.

While the details of the model, together with extensive sensitivity analyses, are given in Striessnig and Lutz (2013), this brief summary clearly indicates that the most desirable level of fertility from a societal macro-economic support ratio perspective is different once education is explicitly factored in. Hence, this is another important case where the fears associated with population decline and population ageing look very different with education considered than under a conventional demographic approach that considers only the changing age structure of the population and implicitly assumes that every person at a given age is equality productive.

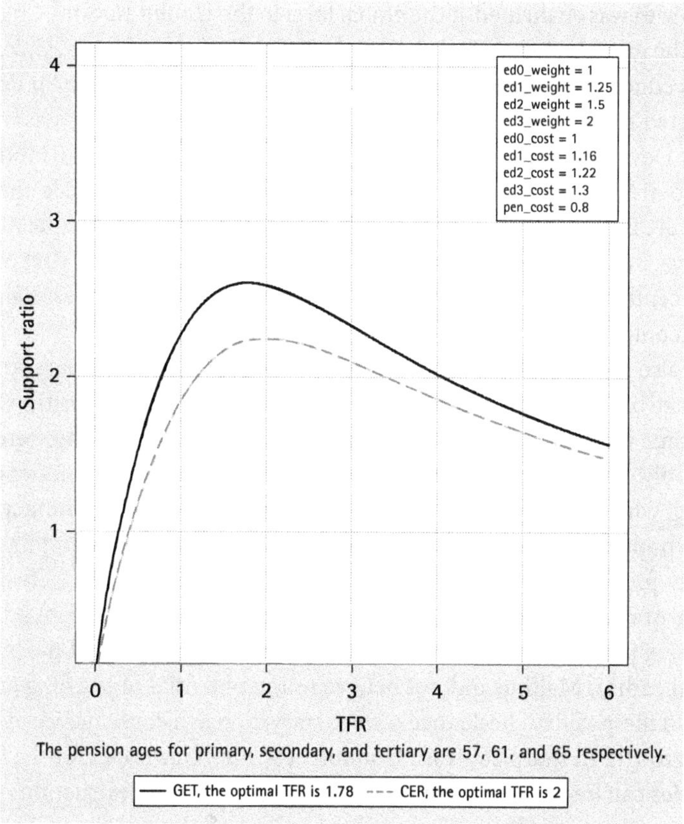

FIGURE E.2 Model calculations of the education-weighted support ratio in Germany in 2100 under the global education trend (GET) and constant enrolment rate (CER) education scenarios for different levels of total fertility rates (TFRs) that are assumed to stay constant over the entire period.

E.3 Education empowers individuals and societies for a healthier, wealthier, more democratic, and resilient future

The value of education for enhancing human well-being has been a major topic of writings since antiquity. During the age of enlightenment the view that the development of cognitive skills, the acquisition of more knowledge, and the practice of critical and self-reflective thinking can help humanity to move towards a brighter future became a powerful and highly influential perspective across much of Europe. It later spread around the rest of the world and was blended with non-European traditions, such as Confucianism, which also put great emphasis on scholarship and education. More recently, the idea was enshrined at the global level in the United Nations Charter in 1945, as well as in the 1948 Universal Declaration of Human Rights (Jones and Coleman, 2005). In the 1960s education became one of the key priorities of international development. This is reflected more recently in the global 'Education For All' policy, as well as in the Millennium Development Goals (MDG). From early on the calls for more education have had two distinctly different justifications: a human rights rationale and a development rationale. Both favour priority investments in universal basic education for both girls and boys, as well as higher education wherever possible. This is part of the reason why, until recently, the view that education at all levels is a priority investment seemed to be nearly uncontested.

But there also is a long tradition of dissenting views critical of the value of education. During the age of enlightenment and humanism in Europe this opposition to universal education came mostly from Roman Catholic Church authorities who were afraid that their monopoly on interpreting church doctrine was endangered by independent critical thinking, while the protestant reformation put a high value on literacy in order to enable everybody to read the bible. For demographers, it is interesting that one of the oldest widely publicized disputes about the value of education was between Malthus (a forefather of demography) and Condorcet. While Condorcet (1795) advocated the 'Enlightenment project for human improvement through progress of the human mind' (LeVine et al., 2012), Malthus did not believe in the potential of learning and avoiding what he called the 'positive check', that is, mass starvation as a consequence of exponential population growth. In sharp contrast, Condorcet wrote: 'Our hopes for the future of the human species can be reduced to three important points: the destruction of inequality among nations; the progress of equality within each people; and the real betterment of humankind', with the last point clearly referring to universal and well-organized instruction (i.e. formal education), including gender equity, according to Levine et al. (2012). Indeed, this reads like a modern development agenda. In contrast, the position of Malthus is similar to that of a conventional demographic approach, which only focuses on human numbers without differentiation by education.

A recent review article entitled '*Sola Schola et Sanitate*: Human Capital as the Root Cause and Priority for International Development' (Lutz, 2009) summarizes many of the contemporary arguments that point to broad-based basic education and basic health as development priorities. Yet, the paper also finds that many of the recent influential books on global development—ranging from William Easterly's (2006) *The White Man's Burden*, to Paul Collier's (2007) *Bottom Billion* to J. Glennie's (2008) *The Trouble with Aid*—do not even mention education, or treat it only as a minor aspect of social development. This low priority for basic education is also reflected in the Organisation for Economic Co-operation and Development statistics of financial flows of official development assistance, which shows that in 2011, on average, only 2.1 per cent of bilateral development assistance went to basic education. For the World Bank the proportion for basic education was only 1.7 per cent and for regional development banks, on average, 2.3 per cent, while most of the spending went on infrastructure (OECD, 2013) Both aspects viewed together—the lack of attention to education by prominent development economists and the lack of funding by donors—can be taken as an indication that the aforementioned near consensus about the value of universal basic education seems to have significantly weakened recently.

Education sceptics and the various reasons behind their views cannot be comprehensively reviewed here; I will only address some of the intellectual arguments that may have contributed to this development by cautioning against too much optimism with respect to the positive effects of education. An important contribution and frequent reference in the field of education sceptics is Philip Coombs' book *The World Education Crisis: A Systems Analysis* (1968). In 1983 Coombs updated his analysis in the book *The World Crisis in Education: The View from the Eighties* (Coombs, 1985). Based on his first-hand experience as director of UNESCO's International Institute for Education Planning, Coombs—in both assessments—stresses the unrealistic nature of the naïve belief that investments in education expansion would automatically lead to better and more developed societies. But reading through his extensive analyses, it becomes apparent that his main criticism is directed to the inefficient and often misguided ways in which the international education programmes were conducted, so that they often did not reach their goals of actually improving human capital. He does not claim that effective high-quality education has no benefits, but only that good intention and financial spending alone do not necessarily result in better human capital. Unfortunately, people referring to his work often throw the baby out with the bathwater by concluding that as the spending in education did not produce the expected results, improvements in education levels as such may not be a good investment.

Another frequent reference regarding education sceptics is the writing of Harvey Graff since the 1970s on the 'literacy myth' (Graff, 1991), which—according to the Encyclopedia of Language and Education—refers to the belief that the acquisition of literacy is a necessary precursor to and invariable cause of economic development, democratic practice, cognitive enhancement, and upward social mobility (Hornberger, 2008). In 2010 the guest editors of the *Vienna Yearbook of Population Research* (Bilal Barakat and Hans-Peter Blossfeld) invited Harvey Graff, along with Alaka Basu, to contribute to the 'Demographic Debate' section of the *Yearbook* by critically commenting on an introductory statement by myself, which was entitled 'Education Will be at the Heart of 21st Century Demography' (Lutz, 2010). In his contribution, Graff (2010) summarizes and updates his views, and relates them to demography. He stresses that his criticism is primarily directed to the assumption of some sort of automatism and that he does not at all deny the many benefits of literacy. In his words: 'I never claimed that there was no relationship between literacy and economic success, income and literacy skill, labor force attainment and literacy and occupational change and literacy. To the contrary, we emphasized their complexity, variability and contradictoriness in relationships among key factors and in more general explanatory and interpretive terms that shape expectations, theory and policy. Never did we allege that literacy was unimportant' (Graff, 2010, p. 20). Finally, in direct reaction to my proposal to systematically introduce educational attainment as a third demographic dimension Graff writes: 'The idea of treating educational attainment as an individual's single most important socio-economic characteristic, not in response to its proven discriminatory power in a given time and place bound population, but a priori, is an act of myth-making par excellence' (2010, p. 22). But he also extends this assessment to the conventional demographic dimensions by writing: 'Other myths surround biological sex and age, without diminishing their utility as dimensions of disaggregation in demographic research' (2010, p. 22).

The main conclusion I draw from this commentary by Graff is that the choice to focus on educational attainment should not be made simply in an 'a priori' manner, but rather focus on the 'proven discriminatory power' at different times and different places. This is exactly the main focus of this book analysing educational differentials in all countries of the world over time.

Another important distinction between my earlier mentioned '*sola schola et sanitate*' proposition and what is described as the 'literacy myth' is that I do consider education (including literacy) a necessary precondition for development, but not always a sufficient one. There is no automatism by which more and better education always translates into the desired individual and social outcomes. Other factors, including culture, institutions, economic structures, path dependencies of earlier choices, and last, but not least, pure randomness also play their parts. Hence, we should look for significant correlations (assuming the appropriate lag structures), rather than pure determination. As discussed in Chapter 2 with respect to functional causality, we should address plausible narratives that explain the effect. I now turn to this task by reviewing published empirical findings.

The title of this section, 'Education Empowers Individuals and Societies for a Healthier, Wealthier, More Democratic, and Resilient Future', alludes to four important areas where better education can be expected to have positive impacts for the future: health and mortality, economic growth, democracy and civil liberties, and adaptive capacity to already unavoidable climate change. As the education effects on reducing mortality and disability and enhancing health have already been extensively discussed in several chapters of this book, as well as in the section E.2 of this epilogue, I now address the evidence on the other three aspects.

E.3.1 Education and economic growth

It is commonly assumed in economic theory that education has an important positive effect on economic growth, but, until recently, the statistical evidence for this assumption has been surprisingly weak. Evidence shows beyond any reasonable doubt that, at the individual level, more years of schooling generally lead to higher income. But at the macro-economic level, empirical evidence relating changes in education measures to economic growth has, until recently, been ambiguous. Many authors suggest that this may be due to problems with the global empirical data on human capital (Barro and Lee, 1996; Benhabib and Spiegel, 1994; Cohen and Soto, 2007; de la Fuente and Doménech, 2006; Pritchett, 2001).

In a more recent study published in *Science*, Lutz et al. (2008) provide, for the first time, the unambiguous statistical evidence (based on econometric models) that education is a consistently significant determinant of a country's aggregate level of economic growth. The key to these new results lies in the more detailed and more consistent nature of the new IIASA–Vienna Institute for Demography (VID) data set on educational attainment by age and sex for 120 countries back to 1970 (Lutz et al., 2007). While in most previous studies (e.g. Barro and Lee, 1996) the educational attainment of the entire population above the age of 25 was considered as the human capital variable (which is relatively insensitive to rapid improvements in the education of the younger, working age population), the new data provide information by five-year age groups and the full attainment distribution (which includes more information for statistical analysis). In addition to greater detail, the consideration of differential mortality by level of education and the strict consistency over time of the definition of educational categories evidently turned out to be decisive advantages of the new data set over previous ones.

While the new study and the specific models estimated cannot be described in any detail here, I only want to point out one important finding of great policy importance: for poor countries with low human capital, only the combination of universal primary education with broadly-based secondary education results in the kind of rapid economic growth that has the potential to push countries out of poverty. This additional investment in secondary education provides a huge boost to economic growth, much greater than universal primary education alone. In these simulations the effect of secondary education works primarily through the adoption of new technologies. From this we can conclude that the current MDG focus on universal primary education is important, but insufficient. It needs to be complemented with the goal of giving broad segments of the population at least a completed junior secondary education or, even better, universal secondary education.

Most recently another follow-up study by Crespo et al. (2013) published in *Demography* addresses the role of education in the context of models studying the demographic dividend. Entitled 'Is the Demographic Dividend an Education Dividend?' the article answers the question with 'yes'. The literature on the demographic dividend, such as Kelley and Schmidt (2005) and Bloom et al. (2009), tends to assume that, in addition to the so-called accounting effect (a smaller population in the denominator results in a high growth domestic product (GDP) per capita), there is also a positive effect of fertility decline on productivity that results in a lower youth dependency ratio. Crespo et al. (2013) reassess the empirical evidence on the associations among economic growth, changes in age structure, labour force participation, and educational attainment using a global panel of countries. They find that after the effect of human capital dynamics is controlled for, no evidence exists that changes in age structure affect labour productivity. These results clearly imply that improvements in educational attainment are the key to explaining productivity and income growth, and that a substantial proportion of the demographic dividend is an education dividend. When addressing aggregate economic growth rather than growth in per capita GDP, even the accounting effect plays no role, which implies that age structure becomes irrelevant, leaving education along with physical investment as the key driver of a country's economic growth.

E.3.2 Education and democracy

Another study by Lutz et al. (2010) in *Population and Development Review* applies the IIASA–VID education reconstructions by age and sex for 120 countries to reassess the relationship between improving educational attainment of the population, education differentials between men and women, and indicators of civil liberties and the quality of democratic institutions. The results are highly statistically significant and reaffirm, on a broader and more consistent basis, the findings from earlier studies in the field.

The theoretical arguments relating education to democracy are manifold. At the individual level, education is a determinant of political participation. As the educational level increases, individuals tend to develop a stronger sense of civic duty and a greater interest in politics. However, to the extent that education causes economic growth, it is also an indirect determinant of democracy through the link between wealth at the macro-economic level and democracy. Recent contributions to the theoretical literature on the link between educational attainment and democracy emphasize the increase in the benefits of political participation caused by education as the catalytic link relating changes in educational measures to changes in democracy. Glaeser et al. (2007) present a theoretical model where the effect of education on the (otherwise weak) incentives faced by individuals to support democratic regimes leads to higher stability of democratic regimes in more educated societies. The empirical evidence on the effect of education on democracy lends support to a positive relationship between these two variables when differences across countries are exploited. Barro (1997) and Glaeser et al. (2007) find a positive effect of education on the level of democracy by exploiting differences across countries from panel data. Already, a simple scatterplot showing the average level of democracy against average years of schooling for all countries for which data exist in the period 1970–2004 shows a clear positive relationship. The index of democracy used in the study by Lutz et al. (2010) summarizes information on the existence of electoral freedom, based on the level of adult suffrage and the existence of competition for public offices, political accountability, and lack of corruption.

The positive relationship also appears when the focus is on variations within countries over time. While the previous empirical evidence on the effect of changes in education on democracy within countries is more mixed (Arellano and Bond, 1991; Blundell and Bond, 1998; Bobba and Coviello, 2007), the richer information of the IIASA–VID data set allows evaluation of the differential effect of educational attainment depending on its distribution across age groups and genders. The multivariate econometric studies by Lutz et al. (2010) are based on educational attainment for age groups of men and women in 5-year steps for 120 countries in the period 1970–2000. These studies also control for GDP per capita, the investment rate, life expectancy, the urbanization rate, the share of agricultural output on total output, and the change in the young age dependency ratio. Among the interesting findings are the following: societies with high proportions of young people tend to have a lower probability of achieving democratic regimes; increases in urbanization and investment tend to lead to political changes in the direction of democratization; and education turns out to be a significant and robust determinant of democracy. This was tested for mean years of schooling, as well as the full educational attainment distribution. With respect to gender differentials the findings also show that an increase in female relative to male education is a robust predictor of changes towards more democratic rights.

Hence, of all the variables studied, increases in human capital and, in particular, the improvement of female education relative to male education turned out to be the most important systematic social change associated with the move towards more democracy and higher levels of civil rights and liberties. As the education efforts that later result in higher human capital levels come well before the evaluated improvements in democracy, this temporal sequences suggests that the primary direction of causation goes from education to democracy. Again, this does not imply a deterministic view in which better education automatically translates into more democracy. But the analysis shows that education clearly increases the probability of changes in a democratic direction.

E.3.3 Education and adaptive capacity to already unavoidable climate change

The Intergovernmental Panel on Climate Change (IPCC) is currently finalizing its Fifth Assessment Report (IPCC-AR5), which, by all indications, will demonstrate with high certainty that global climate change is an ongoing reality. While there are some uncertainties remaining about what factors contribute to what degree to this ongoing change, almost nobody denies any more that such change is actually ongoing. Hence, no matter how successful the world community will be in reducing future greenhouse gas emissions, a certain degree of climate change is already unavoidable and we have to prepare to cope with it. As one of the IPCC-AR5 lead authors for the section on sustainable development I also got the strong sense that, for this reason, the attention is now not only focused on mitigating climate change, but is also moving increasingly to aspects of adaptation and strengthening the future adaptive capacity to already unavoidable climate change. The international community has already pledged the significant sum of US$100 billion/year to be spent on climate change adaptation in developing countries from 2020 onwards. But it seems to be still quite unclear what precisely should happen with this money. Recent work conducted at IIASA suggests that investments in universal primary and secondary education would be a good and efficient way to strengthen adaptive capacity through enhancing general resilience, particularly in a situation in which the precise consequences of climate change in specific areas are still uncertain.

But what is the empirical evidence base for claiming that education enhances adaptive capacity and reduces vulnerability to climate change? The problem is that climate change is just starting to show its first consequences so that it is hard to find solid empirical evidence about what factors are best to reduce the vulnerabilities to this kind of change. One possible strategy is to study differential vulnerability to natural disasters, such as flooding, droughts, and storms, that have occurred over long periods and for which abundant empirical data exist. In this sense, vulnerability to natural disasters is not only of significant interest in its own right as a source of premature death in developing countries, but it can also be seen as isomorphic to the likely future risks associated with unavoidable climate change. In other words, if we have a better understanding of the risk factors associated with currently observed vulnerabilities to natural disasters, we can draw conclusions about the risk factors associated with future climate change, in particular with respect to the likely higher frequency and intensity of tropical storms, extreme flooding events, and severe droughts.

An international scientific panel on population and the environment recently produced a statement that was published in *Science* (Lutz et al., 2012). It summarizes as follows: 'The evidence is clear that demographic differences fundamentally affect people's contributions to environmental burdens, their ability to participate in sustainable development, and their adaptability to a changing environment'. But the empirical basis for assessing the role of educational differences has been very scant until recently, mostly because the hypothesis has not been on the table and therefore no data have been collected to test it. The theoretical argument is quite clear: education is an important way through which individuals acquire knowledge, skills, and competencies that can directly or indirectly influence their adaptive capacity. First, and most directly, literacy and numerical skills obtained through formal education imply better access to relevant information, such as early warnings for tropical storms or seasonal prediction of drought (Moser and Ekstrom, 2010; Patt et al., 2007). Second, there is evidence that education also enhances cognitive skills and the willingness to change risky behaviour, while at the same time extending the personal planning horizon (Behrman and Stacey, 1997; Neisser et al., 1996; Nisbett, 2009). Education also enhances the acquisition of knowledge, influencing values and priorities, as well as the capacity to plan for the future and improve allocation of resources (Glewwe, 1999; Thomas et al., 1991). Besides that, as described extensively in this book, education leads to better health and physical well-being. Consequently, it is reasonable to assume that when facing natural hazards or climate risks, educated individuals are more empowered and hence more adaptive in their response to, preparation for, and recovery from disasters. At the aggregate level it can be argued that better educated societies have greater social, economic, and institutional capabilities necessary for successful adaptation to climatic change (KC and Lutz, 2013).

Taking the earlier described approach of seeing disaster vulnerability as proxy for climate change vulnerability, a recent series of studies has focused on identifying the relative role of education in reducing such vulnerabilities, and hence provides the basis for recommending strategies for reducing vulnerability and enhancing the adaptive capacities of populations to unavoidable climate change. A special issue of *Ecology and Society*

(2013) is entirely dedicated to studying the empirical evidence on this issue with data from different parts of the world. Muttarak and Pothisiri (2013) present an individual-level study of disaster preparedness of 557 households located along the Andaman coast in Phang Nga province during the 2012 Indian Ocean earthquakes. They find that formal education—measured at the individual, household, and community levels—increases the likelihood of preparedness actions being taken. Having been affected by the 2004 tsunami clearly increases emergency preparedness, but for the group of persons without such disaster experience, education turned out to be a relevant factor in anticipating the risk and taking preparedness actions. Another tsunami-related study by Frankenberg et al. (2013) uses individual level data from the Indonesian Household Panel to examine the extent to which education serves as a means of protection against natural disaster, using longitudinal survey data collected in two provinces on the island of Sumatra, before and after the 2004 Indian Ocean tsunami. They find that education clearly plays a role in coping with the disaster over the longer term, with the better educated being of better psycho-social health five years after the tsunami. They are less likely than others to live under precarious living conditions and appear to be better at compensating for loss of income following the tsunami.

Similar evidence on the association between education and vulnerability has been reported at the community level by KC (2013). Using comprehensive village-level data in Nepal (a micro-sample of the 2001 census covering 2.5 million individuals together with disaster data for 2000–09) on damages due to floods and landslides in terms of human lives lost, animals lost, and other damage to households, he finds strong effects of education. Comparing the effect of education with those of income and wealth, the author concludes that education has stronger and more consistent impacts in reducing damage due to floods and landslides in Nepal.

In addition to further studies based on individual-level data that essentially show the same picture, the special issue also includes some country comparisons. Pichler and Striessnig (2013) use data from qualitative interviews conducted in Cuba and the Dominican Republic to compare these two island states with regard to disaster vulnerability. Even though they usually experience the same hurricanes passing with similar strength over Cuba and Hispaniola, the outcomes vary greatly between the two countries. While effective disaster response is strongly embedded in the entire Cuban population, which is one of the most educated in the developing world, the interviews strongly confirm that lack of education and literacy in the Dominican Republic makes people more vulnerable and prevents them from even understanding warnings about upcoming danger.

At a highly aggregate level Striessnig and Lutz (2013) use national-level time series of disaster fatalities around the world, regressing them against a number of socio-economic variables, also including the three components of the Human Development Index. Different models with alternative specifications all find significant effects of education—particularly female education—in reducing disaster fatalities, while there is no support for the widely assumed role of income per capita in reducing vulnerability. These findings suggest that education is the more relevant dimension of socio-economic development compared with income when it comes to enhancing adaptive capacity to natural disasters and hence, by implication, to future unavoidable climate change.

E.4 Human capital can be seen as a population policy priority

Many of the population-related policies developed during the second half of the twentieth century are no longer responding to emerging population-related concerns of the twenty-first century. In large parts of the world the concerns about too-rapid population growth have been replaced by broad concerns about rapid population ageing, in some cases even population shrinking, and the implications of international migration. This shift has become quite apparent in the preparations for the 20-year review of the 1994 International Conference on Population and Development in Cairo, Egypt. The shift has occurred both at the level of government views as reflected in a comprehensive global survey of government views on population priorities and policies (Vobecká et al., 2013), as well as in the scientific population research community as reflected in a recent survey taken among International Union for the Scientific Study of Population members (Van Dalen and Henkens, 2012).

At the same time, concerns about reproductive health and rights continue to be high on the international population agenda. But, as their names say, these are primarily health and human rights concerns that are not directly related to population in its core meaning, namely referring to aggregates of people with respect to their changing sizes and structures. It is with respect to these questions of population shrinking, ageing, and other important changes in population composition that there is a need to rethink population policies. Governments of some Eastern European countries that are deeply concerned about population shrinking even call this trend the most serious national security crisis. They can find no help from the currently existing arsenal of population policies as offered by the international population community. A much larger group of countries worried about the consequences of rapid population ageing for the sustainability of their health care, and pension and social support system; equally, future economic growth, in general, finds no help from existing international population policy paradigms. There is a clear need for a new population policy paradigm, one—as this book suggests—that explicitly includes human capital, in addition to the conventional focus on human numbers and age structure.

This book presents and discusses the science of what is known about the drivers of fertility, mortality, migration, and education in different parts of the world and what this knowledge implies for the course of population and human capital over the rest of the century. Specifically, we have attempted to illustrate how the population future looks different when education is systematically added as a core demographic dimension. Such an analysis provides the scientific and numerical basis for a new population policy paradigm. But this is not a book on population policy. We refrain from entering the population policy domain and developing specific population policy suggestions that address the aforementioned deficits in the current arsenal of policies and that take appropriate account of the important new insights that have been shown to arise when education is explicitly factored in. Such policy recommendations are a task for another occasion.

This broader view of population and human capital that this book presents has already been carried beyond the field of demography into the sustainable development modelling community. As discussed in the context of the Shared Socio-economic Pathways (see Chapter 12) the new paradigm has the potential not only to refocus population policies in the narrower sense, but more generally to quantitatively describe and therefore make tangible the human core of long-term global sustainable development strategies. As such, the new paradigm may contribute centrally to developing integrated strategies for improving the quality of life of current and future generations through enhancement of human capabilities of all segments of the population, hence fostering the human resource base for achieving broadly shared development.

Such efforts need to integrate the knowledge base from a wide array of other disciplines, far beyond demography. But demography, as the mathematical description of the human population, can make a distinct and visible, albeit limited, contribution in this effort. This book—by expanding demography to explicitly include education—tries to make this limited demographic contribution more relevant and useful for the rest of the world.

REFERENCES

Arellano, M. and Bond, S. 1991 'Some Tests of Specification for Panel Data: Monte Carlo Evidence and an Application to Employment Equations'. *The Review of Economic Studies*, 58: 277–97.

Barro, R.J. 1997 *Determinants of Economic Growth: A Cross-Country Empirical Study*. MIT Press: Cambridge, MA.

Barro, R.J. and Lee, J.W. 1996 'International Measures of Schooling Years and Schooling Quality'. *American Economic Review*, 86: 218–23.

Behrman, J.R. and Stacey, N. 1997 *The Social Benefits of Education, The Economics of Education*. University of Michigan Press: Ann Arbor, MI.

Benhabib, J. and Spiegel, M. 1994 'The Role of Human Capital in Economic Development. Evidence From Aggregate Cross-country Data'. *Journal of Monetary Economics*, 34: 143–73.

Bloom, D.E., Canning, D., Fink, G. and Finlay, J.E. 2009 'Fertility, Female Labor Force Participation, and the Demographic Dividend'. *Journal of Economic Growth*, 14: 79–101.

Blundell, R.W. and Bond, S.R. 1998 'Initial Conditions and Moment Restrictions in Dynamic Panel Data Models'. *Journal of Econometrics*, 87: 115–43.

Bobba, M. and Coviello, D. 2007 'Weak Instruments and Weak Identification, in Estimating the Effects of Education, on Democracy'. *Economics Letters*, 96: 301–6.

Cohen, D. and Soto, M. 2007 'Growth and Human Capital: Good Data, Good Results'. *Journal of Economic Growth*, 12: 51–76.

Collier, P. 2007 *The Bottom Billion: Why the Poorest Countries are Failing and What Can be Done About it*. Oxford University Press: Oxford.

Coombs, P.H. 1968 *The World Educational Crisis: A Systems Analysis*. Oxford University Press: Oxford.

Coombs, P.H. 1985 *The World Crisis in Education: The View from the Eighties*. Oxford University Press: Oxford.

Crespo Cuaresma, J., Lutz, W. and Sanderson, W.C. 2013 'Is the Demographic Dividend an Education Dividend?' *Demography*, epub ahead of print 4 December.

De la Fuente, A. and Doménech, R. 2006 'Human Capital in Growth Regressions: How Much Difference Does Data Quality Make?' *Journal of the European Economics Association*, 4: 1–36.

Easterly, W. 2006 *The White Man's Burden: Why the West's Efforts to Aid the Rest Have Done so Much Ill and so Little Good*. Penguin Press: New York.

Frankenberg, E., Sikoki, B., Sumantri, C., Suriastini, W. and Thomas, D. 2013 'Education, Vulnerability, and Resilience after a Natural Disaster'. *Ecology and Society*, 18: 16.

Glaeser, E.L., Ponzetto, G.A.M. and Shleifer, A. 2007 'Why Does Democracy Need Education?' *Journal of Economic Growth*, 12: 77–99.

Glennie, J. 2008 *The Trouble With Aid: Why Less Could Mean More for Africa*. Zed Books: London.

Glewwe, P. 1999 'Why Does Mother's Schooling raise Child Health in Developing Countries? Evidence from Morocco'. *The Journal of Human Resources*, 34: 124–59.

Graff, H.J. 1991 *The Literacy Myth: Cultural Integration and Social Structure in the Nineteenth Century*. Transaction Publishers: New Brunswick, NJ.

Graff, H.J. 2010 'The Literacy Myth: Literacy, Education and Demography'. *Vienna Yearbook of Population Research*, 8: 17–23.

Hornberger, N.H. (ed.) 2008 *Encyclopedia of Language and Education*, 2nd edn. Springer: Dordrecht.

Jones, P.W. and Coleman, D. 2005 *The United Nations and Education: Multilateralism, Development and Globalisation*. Routledge: London.

Kandel, E.R. 2007 *In Search of Memory: The Emergence of a New Science of Mind*. W.W. Norton & Co.: New York.

KC, S. 2013 'Community Vulnerability to Floods and Landslides in Nepal'. *Ecology and Society*, 18: 8.

KC, S. and Lentzner, H. 2010 'The Effect of Education on Adult Mortality and Disability: A Global Perspective. *Vienna Yearbook of Population Research*, 8: 201–35.

KC, S. and Lutz, W. 2013 'The Human Core of the SSPs: Population Scenarios by Age, Sex and Level of Education for all Countries to 2100'. Submitted.

KC, S., Barakat, B., Goujon, A., Skirbekk, V., Sanderson, W.C. and Lutz, W. 2010 'Projection of Populations by Level of Educational Attainment, Age, and Sex for 120 Countries for 2005–2050'. *Demographic Research*, 22: 383–472.

Kelley, A. and Schmidt, R. 2005 'Evolution of Recent Economic-Demographic Modeling: A Synthesis'. *Journal of Population Economics*, 18: 275–300.

LeVine, R.A., LeVine, S.E., Schnell-Anzola, B., Rowe, M.L. and Dexter, E. 2012 *Literacy and Mothering: How Women's Schooling Changes the Lives of the World's Children*. Oxford University Press: Oxford.

Lutz, W. 2009 'Sola Schola et Sanitate: Human Capital as the Root Cause and Priority for International Development?' *Philosophical Transactions of the Royal Society*, 364: 3031–47.

Lutz, W. 2010 'Education Will be at the Heart of 21st Century Demography'. *Vienna Yearbook of Population Research*, 8: 9–16.

Lutz, W., O'Neill, B.C. and Scherbov, S. 2003 'Europe's Population at a Turning Point'. *Science*, 299: 1991–2.

Lutz, W., Sanderson, W.C. and Scherbov, S. (eds) 2004 *The End of World Population Growth in the 21st Century: New Challenges for Human Capital Formation and Sustainable Development*. Earthscan: London.

Lutz, W., Goujon, A., KC, S. and Sanderson, W.C. 2007 'Reconstruction of Populations by Age, Sex and Level of Educational Attainment for 120 Countries for 1970–2000'. *Vienna Yearbook of Population Research*, 2007: 193–235.

Lutz, W., Crespo Cuaresma, J. and Sanderson, W.C. 2008 'The Demography of Educational Attainment and Economic Growth'. *Science*, 319: 1047–8.

Lutz, W., Cuaresma, J.C. and Abbasi-Shavazi, M.J. 2010 'Demography, Education, and Democracy: Global Trends and the Case of Iran'. *Population and Development Review*, 36: 253–81.

Lutz, W., Butz, W.P., Castro, M., Dasgupta, P., Demeny, P.G., Ehrlich, I., et al. 2012 'Demography's Role in Sustainable Development'. *Science*, 335: 918.

Moser, S.C. and Ekstrom, J.A. 2010 'A Framework to Diagnose Barriers to Climate Change Adaptation'. *Proceedings of the National Academy of Science of the United States of America*, 107: 22026–31.

Muttarak, R. and Pothisiri, W. 2013 'The Role of Education on Disaster Preparedness: Case Study of 2012 Indian Ocean Earthquakes on Thailand's Andaman Coast'. *Ecology and Society*, 18: 4.

Neisser, U., Boodoo, G., Bouchard, T.J., Boykin, A.W., Brody, N., Ceci, S.J., et al. 1996 'Intelligence: Knowns and Unknowns'. *American Psychologist*, 51: 77–101.

Nisbett, R.E. 2009 *Intelligence and How to Get it: Why Schools and Cultures Count*, 1st ed. W. W. Norton: New York.

OECD 2013 *Aid Statistics: Charts, Tables and Databases*. OECD, Paris.

Patt, A.G., Ogallo, L. and Hellmuth, M. 2007 'Learning from 10 Years of Climate Outlook Forums in Africa'. *Science*, 318: 49–50.

Pichler, A. and Striessnig, E. 2013 'Differential Vulnerability to Hurricanes in Cuba, Haiti and the Dominican Republic: The Contribution of Education'. *Ecology and Society*, 18: 31.

Pritchett, L. 2001 'Where Has all the Education Gone?' *World Bank Economic Review*, 15: 367–91.

Striessnig, E. and Lutz, W. 2013 'Can Below-replacement Fertility be Desirable?' *Empirica*, 40: 409–25.

Thomas, D., Strauss, J. and Henriques, M.-H. 1991 'How Does Mother's Education Affect Child Height?' *The Journal of Human Resources*, 26: 183–211.

Van Dalen, H.P. and Henkens, K. 2012 'What is on a Demographer's Mind? *Demographic Research*, 26: 363–408.

Van der Pol, M. 2011 'Health, Education and Time Preference'. *Health Economics*, 20: 917–29.

Vobecká, J., Butz, W.P. and Reyes, G.C. 2013 *Population Trends and Policies in the UNECE Region: Outcomes, Policies and Possibilities*. UNFPA and IIASA: Laxenburg.

Appendix I

Forecasting Mortality Convergence up to 2100

ALESSANDRA GARBERO AND WARREN C. SANDERSON

1 Introduction

In summer 2011, a global Internet survey on the likely future trends in fertility, mortality, and migration and the main factors behind them was conducted among the members of major population associations and selected other professional organizations. The survey, a collaboration between the International Institute for Applied Systems Analysis' (IIASA) World Population Program and Oxford University, constitutes a basis for new population forecasts by age, sex, and level of education for most of the countries of the world and the provinces of India and China. By allowing a large number of experts to participate and by providing an 'argument-based' underpinning of numerical estimates about future trends in life expectancy in high and low mortality countries, the survey addresses two common weaknesses of population projection-making: (1) a very limited or no theoretical foundation, and (2) a participation of a small and often closed group of experts formulating the parameters of projection scenarios.

This 'argument-based' approach to producing probabilistic population projections has been developed and refined at IIASA over the last decade. Nathan Keyfitz and Andrei Rogers laid out the methodological foundations during the 1970s and early 1980s, and, later, Wolfgang Lutz translated these concepts into sets of systematic numerical population forecasts for world regions. In general, introducing experts' opinions within population forecasting offers the useful advantage of providing a wealth of information, demographic as well as epidemiological, at least in a qualitative way. A limitation is its potential of being prone to bias, namely experts' subjectivity or their need to conform (for a review see Booth and Tickle, 2008).

In order to reduce bias, Lutz and Scherbov (1998) proposed Delphi methods to draw on a wider expertise, thereby averaging out expert opinions.

In this appendix, we put greater emphasis on experts' arguments rather than opinions as in successive developments of the methodology (Lutz and Goldstein, 2004; Lutz et al., 2001). Experts' arguments have been shown to increase the range of expectations. Experts' expectations approximate population-level behaviour and have been found to be particularly suited for medium- to longer-term forecasting (Booth and Tickle, 2008).

As part of this endeavour to produce a new set of argument-based population forecasts, a number of workshops were organized to validate ex post the estimates in the survey given by the source experts. Leading experts in the field were asked to comment upon and reach consensus about the future of life expectancy in high and low mortality[1] countries in two meetings, held, respectively, in Cape Town, South Africa (February 2012) and in San Jose, Costa Rica (February 2012). At the meeting in Costa Rica, the majority of experts agreed on a general paradigm of mortality convergence.

The concept of convergence is central to the demographic transition theory, and the presence of a global mortality convergence has been largely documented (Wilson, 2001). This idea initially arose from analyses that were performed on mortality data starting from the 1960s mostly coming from developed countries (McMichael et al., 2004). In addition, the occurrence of a common pattern, named the 'epidemiological transition' (Omran, 1971), with the latter term broadly indicating falling death rates from infectious diseases (mostly linked to young age and premature mortality) to increasing deaths from non-communicable disease (largely occurring in old age), also gave some expectation of a rapid decline of mortality in high mortality countries, and stagnation for countries that have already achieved a relatively low level of mortality.

Although the idea of a global mortality convergence is widely acknowledged (Wilson, 2001), there have been relatively few attempts made to deal with convergence explicitly (Heuveline, 1999; Wilson, 2001; Oeppen, 2006). However, the concept of convergence has been largely employed in the economics literature and particularly in the empirical literature on economic growth (Barro and Sala-I-Martin, 1995; Landau et al., 1996). In the latter there are two main concepts of convergence; the first one, beta-convergence, occurs when the growth rate of the variable of interest (normally the growth rate in gross domestic product) depends negatively on its prior value. Controlling for the influence of other factors, this produces the case of conditional convergence, where the level of convergence depends on those other factors. The second concept is sigma-convergence, which occurs when the dispersion of the indicator decreases. It is just a description, without any assumption about the functional relation, in contrast to the beta-convergence. In the literature (Anand and Ravallion, 1993; Bidani and Ravallion, 1997) there are different sub-concepts of sigma convergence.

Using the concept of sigma-convergence in absolute terms, this appendix produces female life expectancy forecasts for 159 countries in the world.

Specifically, we develop a multi-pronged methodology that takes into account country-specific heterogeneity in life expectancy, historical trajectories of life-expectancies, between-country heterogeneity across life expectancy gains, and argument-based expert judgement (Lutz et al., 1998, 2001).

The literature on forecasting mortality has usually focused on forecasting mortality for a single population (for a review see Hyndman et al., 2011). An exception to this rule is the work by Li and Lee (2005), in which the authors argue that mortality trajectories and patterns are increasingly becoming more similar in closely related populations and therefore develop mortality forecasts that take into account patterns in a larger group using the Lee and Carter model (1992). In this appendix, we go a step further and forecast country-specific life expectancy within a regional framework.

In addition, we take into account existing work by several authors (Oeppen and Vaupel, 2002; White, 2002; Lee, 2003; Torri and Vaupel, 2012). The latter have stressed three major points: the first is that life expectancy (record or average) appears to have changed linearly over

[1] High and low mortality populations were separated on the basis of the level of child mortality in the year 2010 according to the revised estimates from the Inter-agency Group for Child Mortality Estimation, with the threshold being 40 deaths per 1,000 children below the age of 5.

long periods of time. The second is that 'national mortality trends should be viewed in a larger international context rather than being analysed and projected individually' (Lee, 2003). The third is that life expectancy in different countries tends to be positively correlated. Torri and Vaupel (2012) forecast life expectancies in individual countries by forecasting the best practice level and the gap between the national performance and the best practice level.

We build upon the work by Torri and Vaupel (2012) by explicitly varying the speed of convergence, that is, taking into account differential rates of linear increase in life expectancy across groups of countries. Other authors (Lalic and Raftery, 2011; Raftery et al., 2012) have already stressed this point and highlighted that life expectancy has been increasing most quickly for countries with middle life expectancy (i.e. around 60 years), and more slowly for countries with lower or higher levels. With respect to these authors, we subdivide countries between forerunners and laggards, propose a one-sex model, and generate life expectancy forecasts that are a function of country-specific stochastic and structural trends in life expectancy, as well as a function of stochastic and structural differences between forerunners and non-forerunners. Hence, we explicitly take into account different forms of heterogeneity: (1) the heterogeneity among forerunner-specific gains, as well as among non-forerunner/laggard ones; (2) the relationship between the two; and (3) the heterogeneity across countries and regions. The model is explained in detail in the next section.

2 Methodology

Our forecasts are based on estimates of female life expectancy from 1950 to 2005 (United Nations, 2011).

Specifically, we assume a specification that allows country-specific life expectancy to converge toward that of the appropriate regional forerunner. The global forerunner has been defined as 'the best practice life expectancy' (BPL), a time series that includes Japan, as well as other countries that historically exhibited the highest level of life expectancy during the period 1950–2005. The forecast for the global forerunner is based on a linear increase in life expectancy of two years per decade until 2100 (Oeppen and Vaupel, 2002; Sanderson and Scherbov, 2004).

Although it is plausible to believe that low mortality countries will exhibit linear increases in life expectancy and will converge to an upper bound level of life expectancy by 2100, the paradigm is less applicable to high mortality countries. To this end, we developed the idea of a two-step convergence process, where countries were subdivided into regional forerunners and laggards vis-à-vis the global forerunner. The idea is that laggards' life expectancy will continue to grow as fast as in the regional forerunner. Regional forerunners were defined as countries that exhibited the highest life expectancies in 2005–10 within each geographical region.

The model is implemented as a dynamic panel data model, autoregressive of order 1, with fixed effects, which is estimated with two-step generalized method of moments (GMM). The specification is as follows and is estimated over the period 1980–2005:

$$\Delta e0_{ct,t-1} = \gamma \Delta e0_{it,t-1} + \beta(e0_{i,t-1} - e0_{c,t-1}) + \varepsilon_{c,t} + \in_c$$

where $e0_{i,t}$ is the female life expectancy at birth for the forerunner i at time t; $e0_{c,t}$ is the female life expectancy at birth for the country c at time t; $\Delta e0_{ct,t-1}$ is the change in female life expectancy at birth for the country c between t and $t-1$; $\Delta e0_{it,t-1}$ is the change in female life expectancy at birth for the forerunner i between t and $t-1$; $\varepsilon_{c,t}$ is the time-varying error component; and $\in_c$ are country-specific fixed effects.

It is important to note that the equilibrium is reached when:

$$(e0_{i,t-1} - e0_{c,t-1}) = \frac{(\gamma - 1)\Delta e0_{it,t-1} + \epsilon_c}{\beta}$$

The 'beta term' is endogenous. In order to correct for the dynamic panel bias and auto-correlation, we instrument this term with its fourth and fifth lags. The Sargan–Hansen test indicates that the instruments are valid, and the result from the endogeneity test corroborates the fact that the beta term is endogenous (the latter is defined as the difference of two Sargan–Hansen statistics: one for the equation with the smaller set of instruments, where the suspect regressors are treated as endogenous; and one for the equation with the larger set of instruments, where the suspect regressors are treated as exogenous).

In summary, we are trying to estimate a model where life expectancy gains (or changes between *t* and *t–1*) for each country are regressed against the forerunner life expectancy gains controlling for the gap (the 'beta term') between the forerunner life expectancy and that of the country itself observed in the previous period (*t–1*). The lags are computed over the period 1950–2005.

Hence, convergence is achieved when the difference between country-specific life expectancy and the forerunner is no longer changing. In essence, we have a model in which only the mean of the distribution of life expectancies changes over time, but the variance remains constant. In addition, our model does not impose an upper limit. There is no convergence to the level of the forerunner, in part because the level is always changing.

The added value of this convergence model lies in the fact that it is based on empirical data. In addition, it takes into account the heterogeneous country-specific historical experience, as well as differences in gains between forerunners and laggards over time and across regions. Thus, it takes into account structural, as well as stochastic, components that contribute to life expectancy trends over time, and it is able to generate unbiased parameters upon which the new forecasts are based.

3 Estimation procedure

The estimation procedure encompasses five steps.

1. The first step involved generating the forerunners' life expectancy forecasts (2010–2100).
2. The second step involved generating life expectancy forecasts for the non-forerunners. Separate regressions were conducted for Southern and South East Asia to obtain region-specific parameters (2010–2100).
3. The third step involved generating life expectancy forecasts for HIV-affected countries, as well as high mortality countries such as Afghanistan (2050–2100).
4. The fourth step involved incorporating source experts' and meta-experts' opinions in the form of net gains in life expectancy, from the low and high mortality surveys (2020–50).
5. The final step consisted of recalibrating the future trajectories (2050–95) based on new trend and estimated parameters, as expert opinions were only given until 2050.

Step 1: generating forerunners' life expectancy forecasts

In order to generate the forerunners' life expectancy forecasts, we estimated the model using, as the global forerunner, a BPL that includes Japan, as well as other countries that historically

Table 1 Estimation Sample

Region	Country
Oceania	Australia
Caribbean	Martinique
Central America	Costa Rica
Central Asia	Kazakhstan
Eastern Africa	Réunion; Mauritius; Mayotte; Madagascar
Eastern Asia	Japan
Eastern Europe	Czech Republic
Melanesia	New Caledonia
Micronesia	Guam
Middle Africa	São Tomé and Principe; Gabon
North America	Canada
North Africa	Libyan Arab Jamahiriya; Tunisia
Northern Europe	Iceland
Polynesia	French Polynesia
South America	Chile
South East Asia	Singapore
Southern Africa	Namibia
Southern Asia	Sri Lanka
Southern Europe	Italy
Western Africa	Cape Verde; Ghana
Western Asia	Israel
Western Europe	France

exhibited the highest life expectancies during the period spanning from 1950 to 2005.[2] The estimation sample for the first stage regressions included the countries listed in Table 1.

This model fits the data well and succeeds in capturing historical converging trends across this set of countries. Exceptions are, however, some African countries (Madagascar and Ghana, but the fit for Namibia and Gabon is largely acceptable and surprisingly converging towards the United Nations (UN) forecast value in 2100). Given the presence of HIV and AIDS, we do not assume convergence for the period 2010–50 for HIV and AIDS-affected countries, as well as high mortality countries, such as Haiti and Afghanistan. The latter are exceptions to the convergence theory owing to the occurrence of mortality reversals over the last two decades. Factors such as conflicts, failure of health systems, and the impact of the HIV and AIDS epidemic have largely impeded progress in life expectancy in the last 20 years and will probably continue to impede it in the short term. For this subset of countries, the UN's medium variant was adopted up to 2050 (United Nations, 2011).[3] Therefore, we use the UN's medium scenario as the correct forecast, given the impact of the mortality crisis, which the model cannot capture.

[2] Specifically: Norway (1950–55/1955–60); Iceland (1960–65), Sweden (1965–70/1970–75); Iceland (1975–80); Japan (1980–85 to 2005–10).

[3] Although India is considered an HIV and AIDS-affected country in the UN medium variant scenario, we decided to also explicitly model convergence for India, given the low prevalence of HIV.

Table 2 Forerunners for Second-stage Regression

Europe and North America: Japan
North Africa (including Sudan): Tunisia
East Africa: Madagascar
Western Africa: Ghana
Middle Africa: Gabon
Southern Africa: Namibia
Southern Asia: Sri Lanka
Polynesia: French Polynesia
Micronesia: Guam
Melanesia: New Caledonia
South-Eastern Asia: Singapore
South America/Central America: Costa Rica
Caribbean: Martinique
Western Asia: Israel
Central Asia: Kazakhstan
Hybrid group (including Cape Verde, Comoros, Mauritius, Mayotte, São Tomé and Principe): Réunion

Therefore, based on the parameters obtained from this model, we produced forecasts for the regional leaders (Japan, Tunisia, Sri Lanka, French Polynesia, Guam, New Caledonia, Singapore, Costa Rica, Martinique, Kazakhstan, Israel, Réunion and Madagascar). As Madagascar represents an outlier in terms of its past mortality experience (Ranis and Stewart, 2000), we imposed an average parameter that summarizes the historical experience of the African forerunners (i.e. Tunisia, Réunion, Mauritius, Gabon, Ghana, São Tomé and Principe, and Cape Verde) (Table 2).

Step 2: generating non-forerunners' life expectancy forecasts

The second step involved running the model on all the remaining countries. We stratified the model by region, that is, Southern Asia, South East Asia, and the remaining countries (excluding countries that belong to the HIV-affected group, as well as Haiti and Afghanistan). This time the regional forerunners' life expectancies were chosen as BPLs for each region. Based on the parameters obtained from the second-stage regression, we generated forecasts up to 2100.

Step 3: generating non-forerunners' life expectancy forecasts (HIV and AIDS-affected countries and Afghanistan)

The third step involved generating life expectancy forecasts from 2050 to 2100, for HIV-affected countries and high mortality countries, such as Haiti and Afghanistan. We explicitly assume convergence for this projection interval. Namibia was chosen as a forerunner for this set of countries for three reasons. First, for its high life expectancy across the period 2005–10 in the entire sub-Saharan Africa region (United Nations, 2011); second, for its high levels of antiretroviral treatment provision in 2010 to the large percentage of affected population (UNAIDS, 2010); and, third, for its large investments in the health sector (GHI, 2011). We retrieved the structural parameter that is implicit from the first-step regression and imposed it for the period 2050–2100. This parameter embodies all unobserved characteristics (e.g. success of health care system, economic growth, education expansion) that characterize life expectancy gains in Namibia. By retrieving this parameter and using the Namibian forecast, as well the parameters beta and gamma from the second-stage regression, we generated the structural parameters for the countries falling in this group and produced our forecasts from 2050–2100. Remarkably, these forecasts are quite close to the UN ones for the period 2050–2100.

Step 4: incorporating uncertainty through an expert-based argument approach

The fourth, and quite important, step involved the reweighting of these forecasts in order to incorporate source experts' and meta-experts' arguments in the form of life expectancy net gains. Through this step, we aim to incorporate uncertainty in our forecasts based on an expert-based argument methodology (Lutz et al., 2001).

In order to take into account source experts' (i.e. experts that answered the survey) and meta-experts' (i.e. experts that attended the workshops) numerical estimates (decadal gains in life expectancy), we implemented a framework that operationalizes source experts' and meta-experts' arguments, and combines their estimates with our life expectancy forecasts.

Analytically, given model gains $e0_{mc,t}$, which consist of the model gains implied by our forecasts for all countries except sub-Saharan Africa, Haiti, and Afghanistan, and the ones implied by UN medium scenario for the other set of countries, we reweighted model gains (from 2010 to 2050) to obtain new model gains $e_{0nmc,t}$:

$$e_{0nmc,t} = 1 * e0_{mc,t} + 0.2$$
$$* IndSourceExpGains_{c,t} + 1 * AvgMetaExpGain_{c,t}) / \Sigma Weights$$

where $IndSourceExpGains_{c,t}$ are the net gains as given by the source experts in the low and high mortality surveys—the latter were given a weight of 0.2; $AvgMetaExpGain_{c,t}$ is the average of the net gains as given by the meta-experts[4] in the low and high mortality surveys—the latter are given a weight of 1; model gains $e0_{mc,t}$ are also given a weight of 1. The magnitude of these weights was assessed through a sensitivity analysis.

The new model gains were then employed to adjust the model forecasts up to 2050.

Step 5: generating forecasts for all countries for the period 2050–2100

The final step consisted of modifying the future trajectories (2050–95) based on the new trend implied by the reweighted forecasts up to 2050. We computed the structural parameter (fixed effect), which is implied by the new forecast (2010–50), and combined it with the parameters

[4] One additional complication was that the metric was different (gains vs life expectancy point estimates) as meta-experts gave only predicted life expectancy for both sexes for two point estimates (i.e. 2030 and 2050) for high mortality countries. Therefore, we calculated the e_0 differential (female life expectancy—total) in 2005 and derived predicted female life expectancy (assuming that this difference remains constant to the 2005 level). We then performed quadratic interpolation to reconstruct 'missing' net gains. In addition, we kept the model gains until 2015 for HIV and AIDS-affected countries and then interpolated between 2015 and the first available gain (2020) given by the experts; hence, there is a difference in the magnitude of gains between our predicted gains and the ones implied by the UN's medium scenario until 2050.

(beta and gamma) that have been estimated throughout the various phases of our procedure to obtain forecasts for the period 2050–2100.

4 Results

We present results after the first step for the forerunners (Figure 1), and the overall procedure for the USA, Brazil, Botswana, Tajikistan, Ethiopia, China, and Ghana (Figures 2–8). Figures 2–8 present our final forecast (*final*), that is, after step 5; the model value obtained after step 3 (*model*); the UN life expectancy value (*UN*); and the forerunner life expectancy (*BPL*). For countries with no experts' numerical estimates,[5] the procedure stops after the third step (i.e. model values coincide with our final forecast value) hence the resulting three lines in the figures.

Figure 1 shows the forerunners forecasts after the first step of the procedure. For HIV and AIDS-affected countries this first step is only illustrative of how the model fits the data and how the forecasts would look had we employed the parameters to generate the forecasts. For instance, the final forecast for Ghana is presented in Figure 8 after step 5 is implemented (i.e. reweighting owing to experts' predicted decadal gains and calibration of trend after 2050).

Figure 2 (USA) shows how, historically, the USA diverged from Japan. However, our model is generally optimistic in generating linear gains and a parallel line. For this country, we had the largest number of experts in the low mortality survey. The latter provided a distribution of decadal gains in life expectancy for 2020–30 and 2040–50. After adjusting the model forecast taking into account experts' numerical estimates, the forecast is adjusted downward, indicating their pessimistic view.

In Brazil (Figure 3) experts provided a more optimistic outlook about the future of life expectancy, which results in an upward adjustment of our model forecast.

As far as Botswana, Ghana, and Ethiopia were concerned, experts were largely pessimistic (resulting in a downward adjustment of the line). However, our model results did not exclude a possible catch up in the period 2050–2100.

In general, our forecasts are largely optimistic when compared with the ones of the UN. Exceptions are HIV and AIDS-affected countries, sub-Saharan Africa, and high mortality countries such as Afghanistan. In these instances, our final forecast values are either lower or in substantial agreement (i.e. Afghanistan and Haiti).

5 Discussion

We have developed an econometric model that operationalizes the concept of mortality convergence for 159 countries in the world, explicitly varying the speed of convergence, that is, taking into account differential rates of linear increase in life expectancy across the group of countries. The model is grounded on empirical data and produces life expectancy forecasts that are a function of country-specific stochastic and structural trends in female life expectancy, as well as a function of stochastic and structural differences between forerunners and non-forerunners. Therefore, the model takes into account country-specific and between-countries heterogeneity at various levels, and it is econometrically unbiased.

[5] The low and high mortality surveys provided data only for 30 and 14 countries respectively.

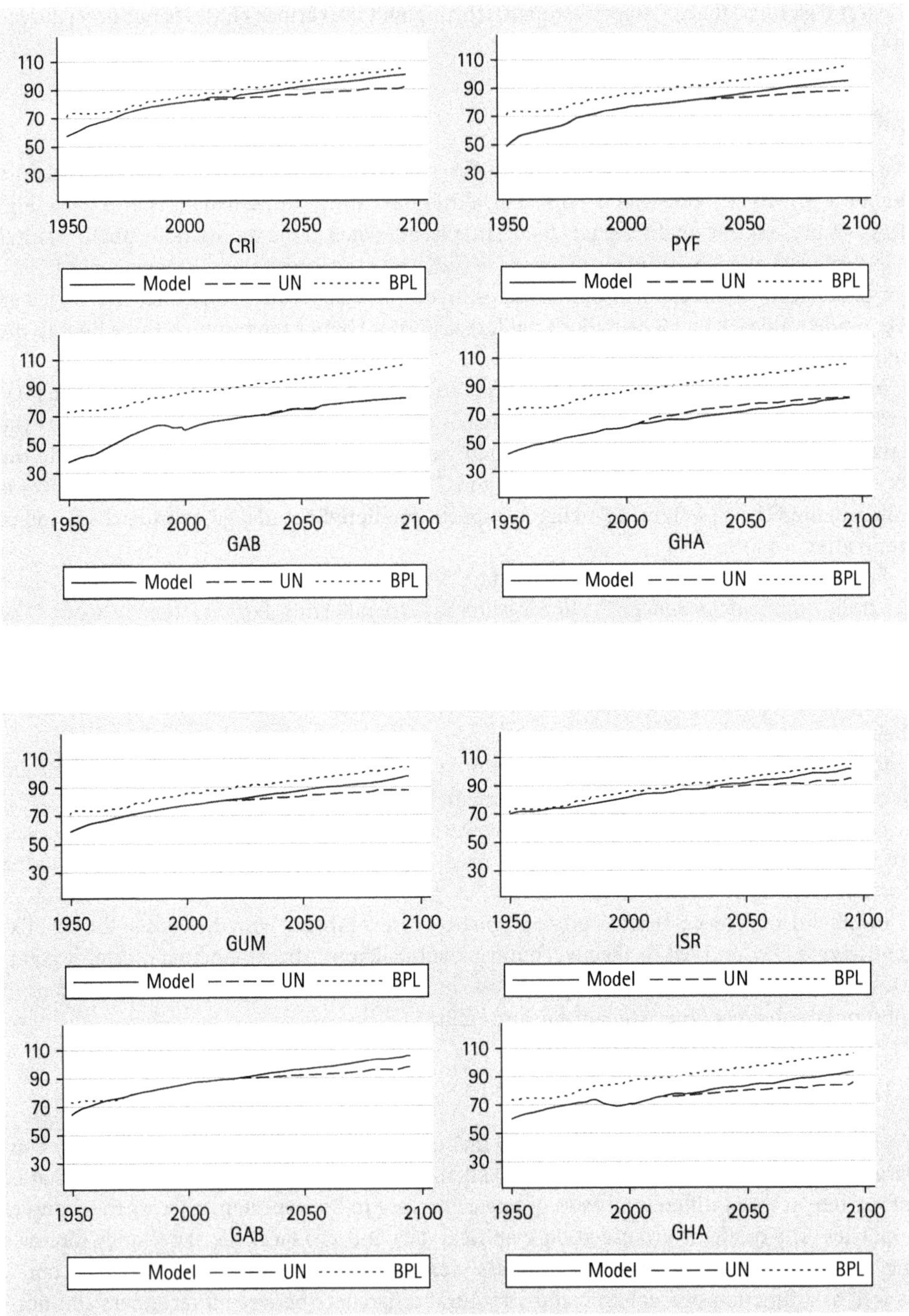

FIGURE 1 (a–d) Step 1—forerunners' forecasts (model forecast, United Nations (UN) medium scenario vs global forerunner e_0 – best practice life expectancy (BPL)). CRI: Costa Rica; PYF: French Polynesia; GAB: Gabon; GHA: Ghana; GUM: Guam; ISR: Israel; JPN: Japan; KAZ: Kazakhstan; MDG: Madagascar; MTQ: Martinique; NAM: Namibia; NCL: New Caledonia; REU: Réunion; SGP: Singapore; LKA: Sri Lanka; TUN: Tunisia.

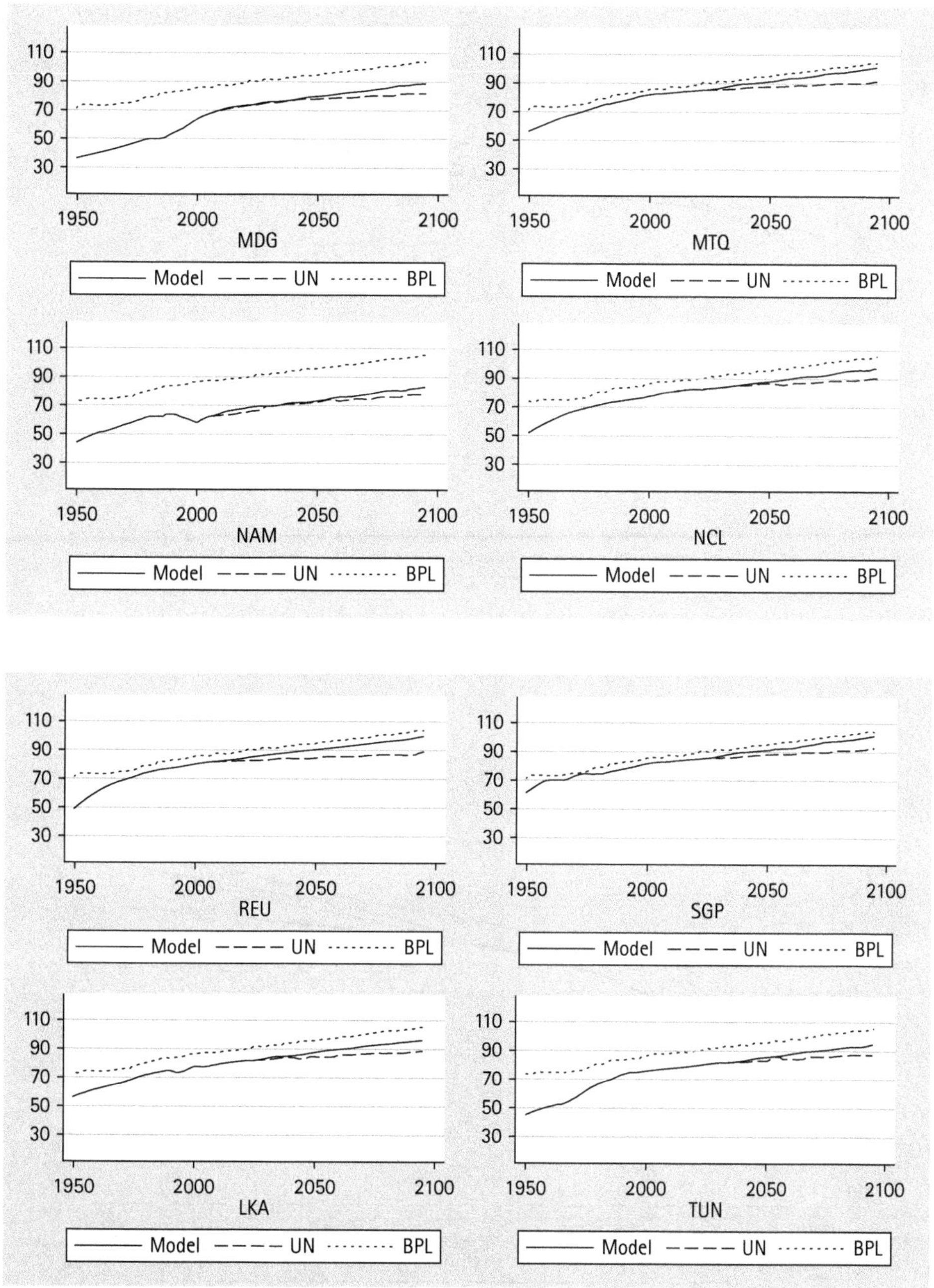

FIGURE 1 Continued

For countries with generalized HIV and AIDS epidemics (38 countries), we do not assume convergence for the period 2010–50. For the latter, we endorse the UN's medium scenario, which explicitly models the impact of HIV and AIDS with an epidemiological model (Alkema et al., 2007; Brown et al., 2010; Raftery and Bao, 2010).

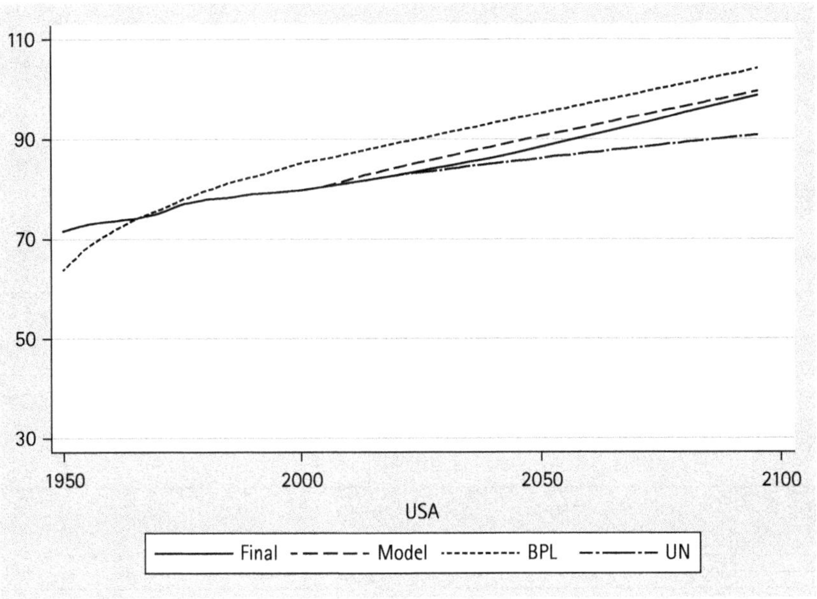

FIGURE 2 USA (best practice life expectancy (BPL): Japan). UN: United Nations.

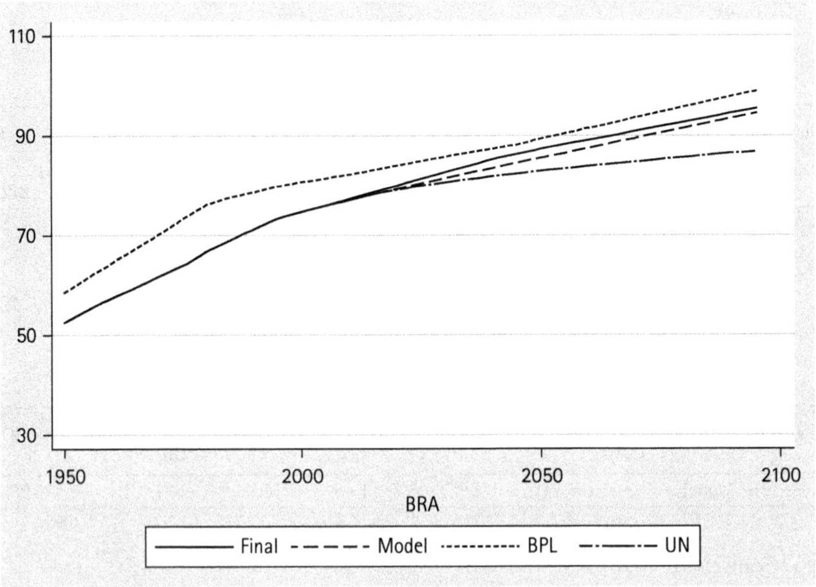

FIGURE 3 Brazil (BRA) (best practice life expectancy (BPL): Costa Rica). UN: United Nations.

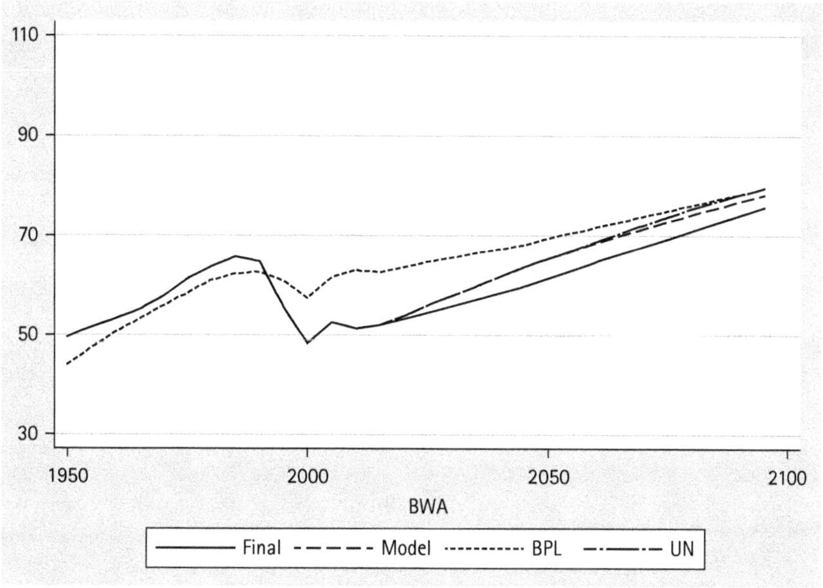

FIGURE 4 Botswana (BWA) (best practice life expectancy (BPL): Namibia). UN: United Nations.

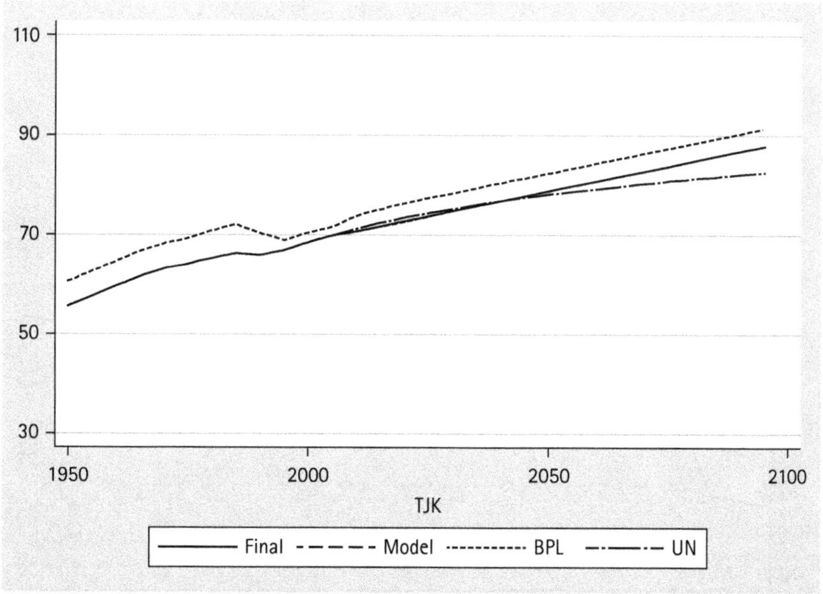

FIGURE 5 Tajikistan (TJK) (best practice life expectancy (BPL): Kazakhstan). UN: United Nations.

Our model incorporates uncertainty through an expert-based approach. To this end, experts were asked to participate and provide an argument-based underpinning of numerical estimates about future trends in life expectancy in high and low mortality countries. Therefore, we develop a framework that operationalizes source experts' and meta-experts' opinions, and combines their estimates with our life expectancy forecasts.

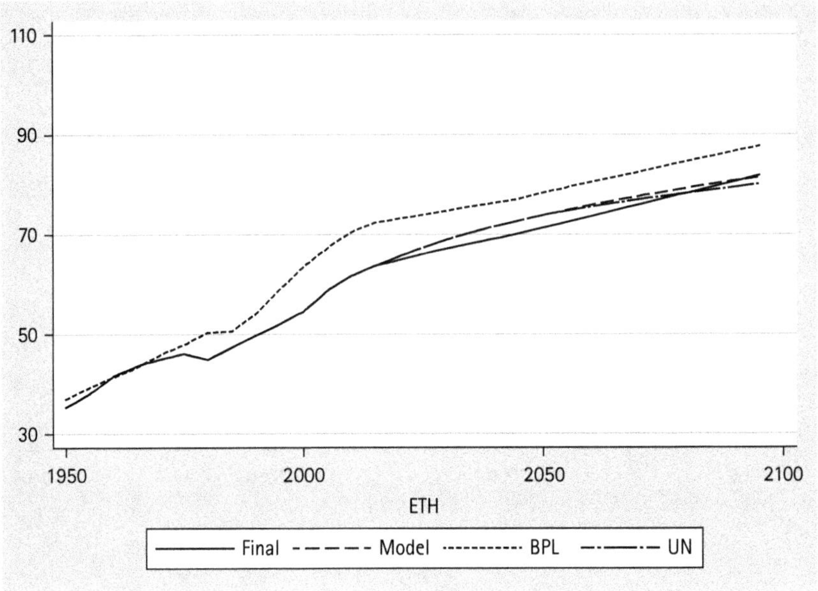

FIGURE 6 Ethiopia (ETH) (best practice life expectancy (BPL): Madagascar). UN: United Nations.

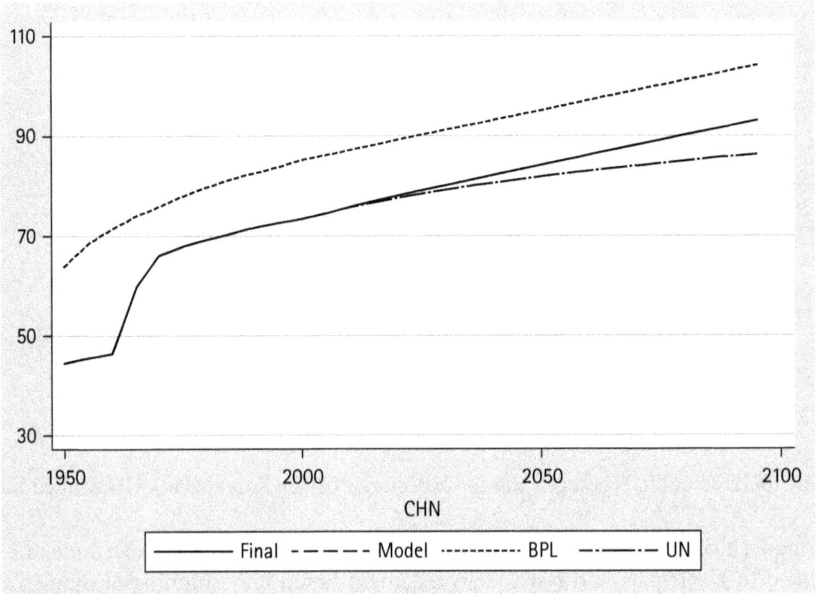

FIGURE 7 China (CHN) (best practice life expectancy (BPL): Japan). UN: United Nations.

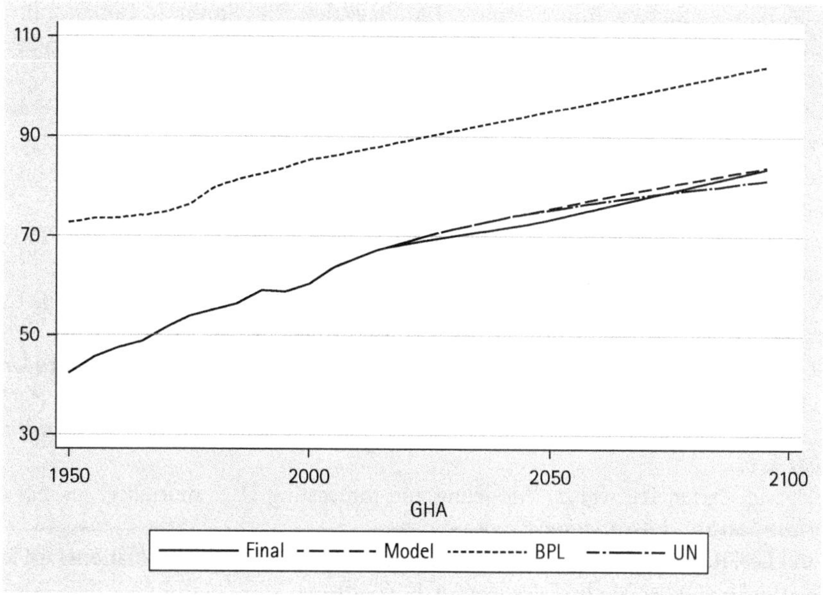

FIGURE 8 Ghana (GHA) (best practice life expectancy (BPL): Global forerunner). UN: United Nations.

The methodology proposed essentially presents a formal framework where extrapolative methods are combined with expert-based argument approaches. In addition, it is based on empirical data, it is replicable, relatively simple, and transparent.

Acknowledgement

Reproduced with permission of IIASA. First published as: Garbero, A. and Sanderson, W. C. (2012) 'Forecasting Mortality Convergence up to 2100. IIASA Interim Report IR-12-013'. International Institute for Applied Systems Analysis (IIASA): Laxenburg.

References

Alkema, L., Raftery, A.E. and Clark, S.J. (2007) 'Probabilistic Projections of HIV Prevalence Using Bayesian Melding'. *The Annals of Applied Statistics*, 1: 229–48.

Anand, S. and Ravallion, M. (1993) 'Human Development in Poor Countries: On the Role of Private Incomes and Public Services'. *The Journal of Economic Perspectives*, 7: 133–50.

Barro, R.J. and Sala-I-Martin, X. (1995) *Economic Growth*. McGraw Hill: London.

Bidani, B. and Ravallion, M. (1997) 'Decomposing Social Indicators Using Distributional Data'. *Journal of Econometrics*, 77: 125–39.

Booth, H. and Tickle, L. (2008) 'Mortality Modelling and Forecasting: A Review of Methods'. *Annals of Actuarial Science*, 3: 3–43.

Brown, T., Bao, L., Raftery, A.E., Salomon, J.A., Baggaley, R.F., Stover, J., Gerland, P. (2010) 'Modelling HIV Epidemics in the Antiretroviral Era: The UNAIDS Estimation and Projection Package 2009'. *Sexually Transmitted Infections*, 86: ii3–ii10.

GHI (2011) 'Namibia: Global Health Initiative 2011–2015/16'. Available at: <http://www.ghi.gov/whereWeWork/docs/NamibiaStrategy.pdf> (accessed 2012).

Heuveline, P. (1999) 'The Global and Regional Impact of Mortality and Fertility Transitions, 1950–2000'. *Population and Development Review*, 25: 681–702.

Hyndman, R.J., Booth, H. and Yasmeen, F. (2011) 'Coherent Mortality Forecasting: The Product-ratio Method With Functional Time Series Models'. *Demography*, 50: 261–83.

Lalic, N. and Raftery, A.E. (2011) *Joint Probabilistic Projection of Female and Male Life Expectancy*. Population Association of America: San Francisco, CA.

Landau, R., Taylor, T. and Wright, G. (1996) *The Mosaic of Economic Growth*. Stanford University Press: Stanford, CA.

Lee, R. (2003) 'Mortality Forecasts and Linear Life Expectancy Trends'. *Social Insurance Studies*, 3: 19.

Lee, R.D. and Carter, L.R. (1992) 'Modeling and forecasting U. S. mortality'. *Journal of the American Statistical Association*, 87: 659–71.

Li, N., and Lee, R. 2005 'Coherent Mortality Forecasts For a Group of Populations: An Extension of the Lee-Carter Method'. *Demography*, 42: 575–94.

Lutz, W. and Scherbov, S. (1998) 'An Expert-based Framework for Probabilistic National Population Projections: The Example of Austria'. *European Journal of Population*, 14: 1–17.

Lutz, W. and Goldstein, J.R. (2004) 'Introduction: How to Deal with Uncertainty in Population Forecasting?' *International Statistical Review*, 72: 1–4.

Lutz, W., Sanderson, W.C. and Scherbov, S. (1998) 'Expert-based Probabilistic Population Projections'. *Population and Development Review*, 24: 139–55.

Lutz, W., Sanderson, W. and Scherbov, S. (2001) *The End of World Population Growth*. International Institute for Applied Systems Analysis (IIASA): Laxenburg.

McMichael, A.J., McKee, M., Shkolnikov, V. and Valkonen, T. (2004) 'Mortality Trends and Setbacks: Global Convergence or Divergence?' *The Lancet*, 363: 1155–9.

Oeppen, J. (2006) 'Life Expectancy Convergence Among Nations Since 1820: Separating the Effects of Technology and Income'. In: Bengtsson, T. (ed.) *Perspectives on Mortality Forecasting-III. The Linear Rise in Life Expectancy: History and Prospects*, pp. 55–82. Swedish Social Insurance Agency: Försäkringskassan.

Oeppen, J. and Vaupel, J.W. (2002) 'Broken Limits to Life Expectancy'. *Science*, 296: 1029–31.

Omran, A.R. (1971) 'The Epidemiologic Transition: A Theory of the Epidemiology of Population Change'. *The Milbank Memorial Fund Quarterly*, 49: 509–38.

Raftery, A.E. and Bao, L. (2010) 'Estimating and Projecting Trends in HIV/AIDS Generalized Epidemics Using Incremental Mixture Importance Sampling'. *Biometrics*, 66: 1162–73.

Raftery, A.E., Li, N., Ševčíková, H., Gerland, P. and Heilig, G.K. (2012) 'Bayesian Probabilistic Population Projections for all Countries'. *Proceedings of the National Academy of Sciences of the United States of America*, 109: 13915–21.

Ranis, G. and Stewart, F. (2000) 'Strategies for Success in Human Development'. *Journal of Human Development*, 1: 49–69.

Sanderson, W. and Scherbov, S. (2004) 'Putting Oeppen and Vaupel to Work: On the Road to New Stochastic Mortality Forecasts'. (IIASA Interim Report IR-04-049). International Institute for Applied Systems Analysis (IIASA): Laxenburg.

Torri, T. and Vaupel, J.W. (2012) 'Forecasting Life Expectancy in an International Context'. *International Journal of Forecasting*, 28: 519–31.

UNAIDS (2010) 'UNAIDS Global Report on the AIDS Epidemic'. Available at: <http://www.unaids.org/globalreport/global_report.htm> (accessed 27 January 2014).

United Nations (2011) *World Population Prospects: The 2010 Revision*. United Nations: New York.

White, K.M. (2002) 'Longevity Advances in High-income Countries, 1955–96'. *Population and Development Review*, 28: 59–76.

Wilson, C. (2001) 'On the Scale of Global Demographic Convergence 1950–2000'. *Population and Development Review*, 27: 155–71.

Appendix II

Introduction

The following tables list key results of the different scenarios for 171 individual countries for which education-specific projections could be carried out, as well as for aggregate regions. For the remaining 24 of 195 countries, the education distributions were approximated in order to calculate the regional and global distributions. The membership of the regions follows standard United Nations definitions.

For each country/region these key results are presented on two pages.

Page 1

The top left table, entitled 'Detailed Human Capital Projections to 2060,' summarizes the results of the detailed population and human capital projections by age and sex until 2060. It presents the medium scenario, which is also identical to the Shared Socio-economic Pathway (SSP) 2 scenario discussed in the context of the SSPs in Chapter 12. This is the most likely trajectory from today's perspective. The upper part of this table presents standard demographic indicators as listed. The migration flow data give the cumulative flow over a five-year period and hence are correspondingly higher than annual flows.

The table immediately below, entitled 'Human Capital Indicators', presents the full educational attainment distributions for six education categories for the adult population aged 25 years and above. Mean years of schooling is a summary indicator averaged across the attainment distributions. Their calculation follows the procedure described in Chapter 9. The 'Gender gap' section presents an indicator of gender inequality, namely the ratio of men to women in each education category. A ratio <1.0 indicates more women than men, while a ratio >1.0 indicates more men than women. The bottom of this table details the educational attainment distributions of women aged 20–39—demographically, a particularly relevant group.

The first page of each country set also contains two sets of graphs. At the upper right are population pyramids in which the grey shading shows the numbers of persons in each age group, separately for men and women, by level of educational attainment. Children below the age of 15, having not necessarily completed their schooling, are all shown in light grey. Total population size in the indicated year is shown in the upper left corner of each picture.

At the bottom of the first page are line charts showing changes in the absolute size of educational attainment groups of men and women over time. The data for the period 1970–2010 are based on a reconstruction following the procedure described in Lutz et al. (2007). The chart on the left-hand side shows projected trends according to the medium global education trend scenario, followed to the right by the alternative constant enrolment rates and fast track education scenarios. These scenarios are described in detail in Chapters 8–10.

Page 2

Except at the very bottom, all tables and figures on this page compare results across the five SSP scenarios, as described in detail in Chapter 12. As they are also based on high and low fertility and mortality trajectories, in addition to different education scenarios, these projections span a wide range of possible future population trends. The upper part of the table, entitled 'Alternative Scenarios to 2100,' lists the conventional demographic indicators: population size, proportion aged 65+, and proportion below the age of 20, and two human capital indicators, proportion of women aged 20–39 with at least secondary education, and mean years of schooling of the adult population aged 25+. The middle part of the table, entitled 'Demographic Assumptions Underlying SSPs', specifies the underlying fertility, mortality, and migration assumptions for the five different SSP scenarios. The upper three graphs to the left depict visually the information given in the upper part of the table in terms of total population size, mean years of schooling of the adult population, and proportion of the population in different age groups, across all five scenarios.

The table and graph at the very bottom of the second page refer to the analysis on re-measuring ageing in Chapter 11. The table entitled 'Ageing Indicators, Medium Scenario (SSP2)' compares two alternative ageing indicators, prospective median age, and proportion with remaining life expectancy (RLE) <15 years, to the conventional indicators, medium age and proportion aged 65+. The graph in the lower left corner illustrates the different projected trajectories of the conventional proportion aged 65+ and the proportion with a remaining life expectancy of <15 years.

References

Lutz, W., Goujon, A., KC, S. and Sanderson, W.C. 2007 'Reconstruction of Populations by Age, Sex and Level of Educational Attainment for 120 Countries for 1970–2000'. *Vienna Yearbook of Population Research*, 5: 193–235.

World

Detailed Human Capital Projections to 2060

Demographic indicators, Medium Scenario (SSP2)	2010	2020	2030	2040	2050	2060
Population (in millions)	6895.89	7636.49	8280.34	8795.44	9162.26	9361.10
Proportion age 65+	0.08	0.09	0.12	0.15	0.18	0.21
Proportion below age 20	0.36	0.33	0.30	0.27	0.26	0.24
	2005–10	2015–20	2025–30	2035–40	2045–50	2055–60
Total Fertility Rate	2.52	2.34	2.22	2.11	2.00	1.90
Life expectancy at birth (in years)						
Men	65.71	68.37	70.46	72.38	74.32	76.21
Women	70.14	72.98	75.22	77.25	79.19	81.05
Five-year immigration flow (in '000)	40214.35	32400.36	33659.35	34432.81	34447.55	33944.90
Five-year emigration flow (in '000)	40214.35	32400.36	33659.35	34432.81	34447.55	33944.90

Human Capital indicators, Medium Scenario (SSP2)	2010	2020	2030	2040	2050	2060
Population age 25+: highest educational attainment						
E1 - no education	0.18	0.14	0.11	0.09	0.07	0.05
E2 - incomplete primary	0.07	0.06	0.05	0.04	0.03	0.02
E3 - primary	0.19	0.17	0.15	0.14	0.13	0.12
E4 - lower secondary	0.20	0.21	0.21	0.19	0.18	0.16
E5 - upper secondary	0.24	0.26	0.29	0.32	0.35	0.37
E6 - post-secondary	0.14	0.16	0.19	0.22	0.25	0.28
Mean years of schooling (in years)	7.90	8.60	9.23	9.83	10.42	10.99
Gender gap (population age 25+): highest educational attainment (ratio male/female)						
E1 - no education	0.57	0.58	0.60	0.63	0.66	0.70
E2 - incomplete primary	1.00	0.99	0.98	0.97	0.96	0.95
E3 - primary	0.98	0.94	0.92	0.92	0.93	0.94
E4 - lower secondary	1.22	1.18	1.15	1.11	1.08	1.04
E5 - upper secondary	1.18	1.15	1.13	1.10	1.08	1.06
E6 - post-secondary	1.16	1.08	1.03	1.00	0.99	1.00
Mean years of schooling (male minus female)	1.08	0.86	0.66	0.48	0.34	0.24
Women age 20–39: highest educational attainment						
E1 - no education	0.15	0.11	0.08	0.06	0.04	0.02
E2 - incomplete primary	0.05	0.04	0.03	0.03	0.02	0.01
E3 - primary	0.15	0.14	0.13	0.12	0.11	0.09
E4 - lower secondary	0.22	0.20	0.17	0.14	0.12	0.11
E5 - upper secondary	0.27	0.31	0.35	0.39	0.42	0.44
E6 - post-secondary	0.16	0.19	0.22	0.26	0.29	0.32
Mean years of schooling (in years)	8.58	9.44	10.16	10.85	11.44	11.95

Education scenarios

GET: global education trend scenario (medium assumption also used for SSP2)

CER: constant enrolment rates scenario (assumption of no future improvements)

FT: Fast track scenario (assumption of education expansion according to fastest historical experience)

Pyramids by Education, Medium Scenario

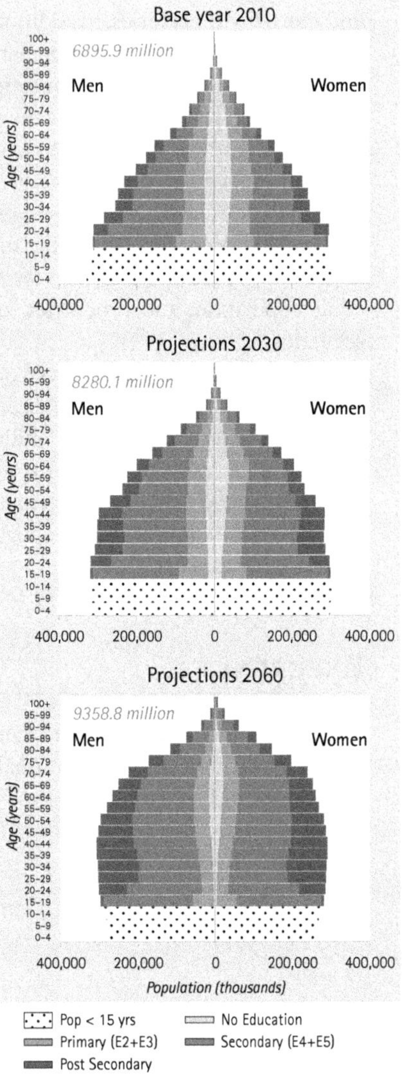

Population Size by Educational Attainment According to Three Education Scenarios: GET, CER, and FT

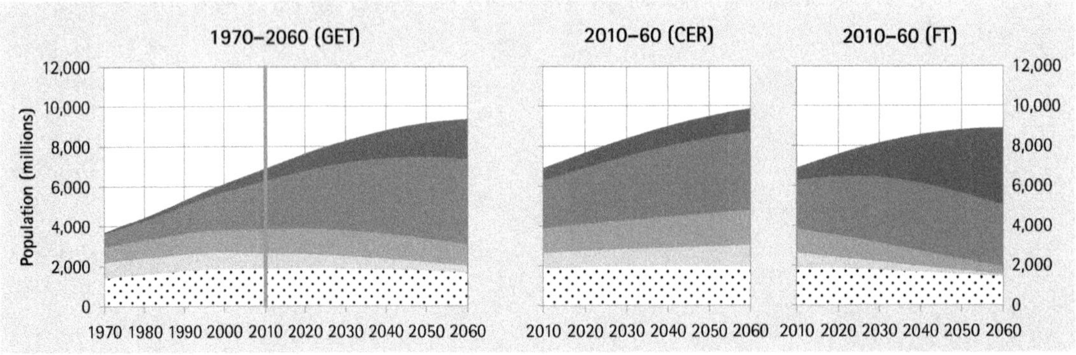

World (Continued)

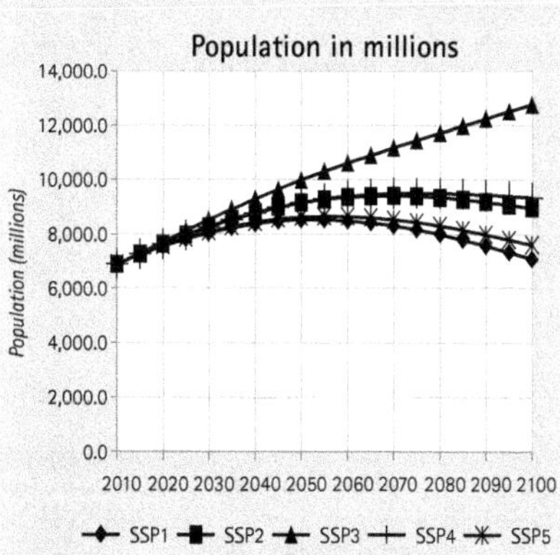

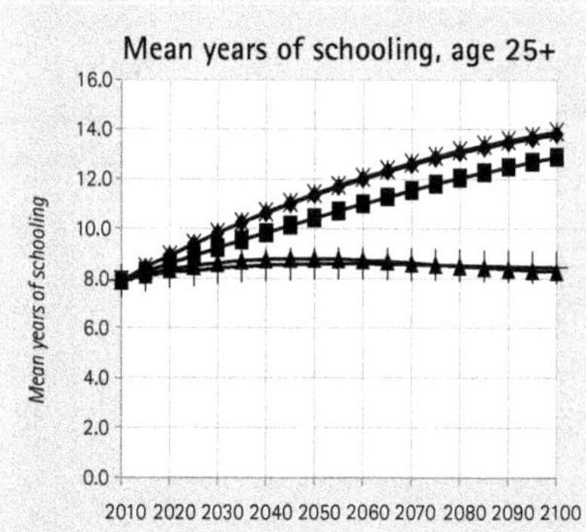

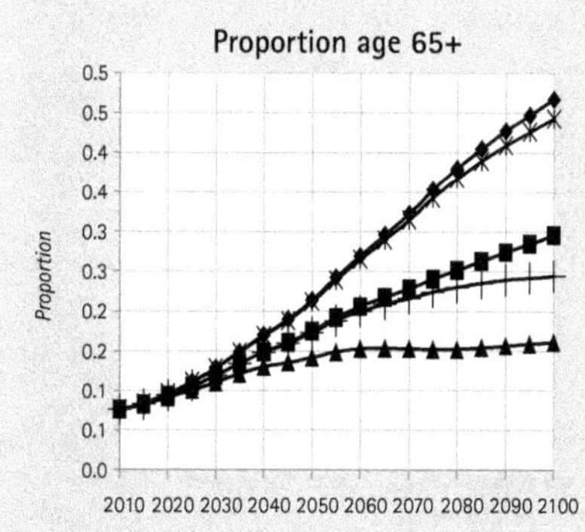

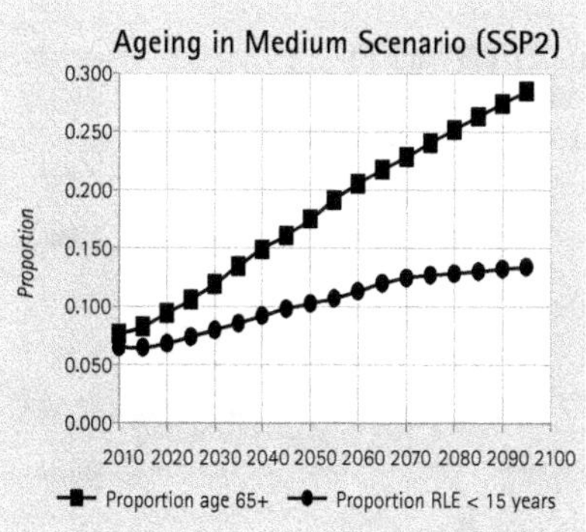

Alternative Scenarios to 2100

Projection Results by Scenario (SSP1–5)

	2010	2020	2030	2040	2050	2075	2100
Population (in millions)							
SSP1 - Rapid development	6895.89	7559.65	8048.36	8379.67	8525.46	8168.61	7095.93
SSP2 - Medium	6895.89	7636.49	8280.34	8795.44	9162.26	9398.11	8963.33
SSP3 - Stalled development	6895.89	7718.73	8535.75	9283.91	9989.16	11453.65	12774.20
SSP4 - Inequality	6895.89	7632.90	8266.66	8777.85	9161.17	9515.61	9355.06
SSP5 - Conventional development	6895.89	7567.94	8077.54	8438.19	8625.58	8436.32	7615.64
Proportion age 65+							
SSP1 - Rapid development	0.08	0.10	0.13	0.17	0.21	0.35	0.47
SSP2 - Medium	0.08	0.09	0.12	0.15	0.18	0.24	0.30
SSP3 - Stalled development	0.08	0.09	0.11	0.13	0.14	0.15	0.16
SSP4 - Inequality	0.08	0.09	0.12	0.15	0.17	0.22	0.24
SSP5 - Conventional development	0.08	0.10	0.13	0.17	0.21	0.34	0.44
Proportion below age 20							
SSP1 - Rapid development	0.36	0.31	0.27	0.23	0.20	0.14	0.11
SSP2 - Medium	0.36	0.33	0.30	0.27	0.26	0.22	0.19
SSP3 - Stalled development	0.36	0.34	0.33	0.32	0.31	0.30	0.29
SSP4 - Inequality	0.36	0.33	0.30	0.28	0.26	0.24	0.24
SSP5 - Conventional development	0.36	0.32	0.27	0.23	0.20	0.16	0.13
Proportion of Women age 20–39 with at least secondary education							
SSP1 - Rapid development	0.65	0.77	0.83	0.88	0.91	0.95	0.98
SSP2 - Medium	0.65	0.71	0.75	0.79	0.83	0.91	0.96
SSP3 - Stalled development	0.65	0.64	0.61	0.58	0.56	0.52	0.50
SSP4 - Inequality	0.65	0.61	0.56	0.54	0.51	0.46	0.42
SSP5 - Conventional development	0.65	0.77	0.83	0.88	0.91	0.96	0.98
Mean years of schooling, age 25+							
SSP1 - Rapid development	7.90	8.91	9.80	10.63	11.35	12.82	13.78
SSP2 - Medium	7.90	8.60	9.23	9.83	10.42	11.79	12.87
SSP3 - Stalled development	7.90	8.35	8.62	8.77	8.79	8.56	8.28
SSP4 - Inequality	7.90	8.24	8.41	8.53	8.59	8.54	8.44
SSP5 - Conventional development	7.90	8.92	9.82	10.65	11.39	12.89	13.89

Demographic Assumptions Underlying SSPs

	2010–15	2020–25	2030–35	2040–45	2050–55	2075–80	2095–2100
Total fertility rate							
SSP1 - Rapid development	2.27	1.90	1.67	1.54	1.45	1.36	1.33
SSP2 - Medium	2.40	2.28	2.16	2.05	1.95	1.76	1.68
SSP3 - Stalled development	2.55	2.71	2.75	2.72	2.64	2.45	2.38
SSP4 - Inequality	2.41	2.34	2.27	2.25	2.24	2.16	2.14
SSP5 - Conventional development	2.28	1.93	1.71	1.59	1.53	1.48	1.52
Life expectancy at birth for females (in years)							
SSP1 - Rapid development	72.49	76.55	80.17	83.67	86.88	94.09	99.84
SSP2 - Medium	71.66	74.14	76.25	78.22	80.15	84.68	88.38
SSP3 - Stalled development	71.10	70.83	71.36	71.74	72.07	73.04	74.31
SSP4 - Inequality	71.46	71.87	72.74	73.40	73.81	75.05	76.25
SSP5 - Conventional development	72.50	76.58	80.22	83.72	86.94	94.17	99.93
Migration – net flow over five years (in thousands)							
SSP1 - Rapid development	0	0	0	0	0	0	0
SSP2 - Medium	0	0	0	0	0	0	0
SSP3 - Stalled development	0	0	0	0	0	0	0
SSP4 - Inequality	0	0	0	0	0	0	0
SSP5 - Conventional development	0	0	0	0	0	0	0

Ageing Indicators, Medium Scenario (SSP2)

	2010	2020	2030	2040	2050	2075	2095
Median age	28.39	31.15	33.86	36.20	38.52	43.62	47.27
Propspective median age	28.39	29.38	30.52	31.36	32.30	34.25	35.06
Proportion age 65+	0.08	0.09	0.12	0.15	0.18	0.24	0.28
Proportion RLE < 15 years	0.06	0.07	0.08	0.09	0.10	0.13	0.13

Africa

Detailed Human Capital Projections to 2060

Demographic indicators, Medium Scenario (SSP2)	2010	2020	2030	2040	2050	2060
Population (in millions)	1022.23	1268.39	1526.97	1781.86	2018.18	2216.69
Proportion age 65+	0.04	0.04	0.05	0.05	0.07	0.09
Proportion below age 20	0.51	0.48	0.45	0.41	0.38	0.34
	2005–10	2015–20	2025–30	2035–40	2045–50	2055–60
Total Fertility Rate	4.64	3.98	3.42	2.96	2.59	2.30
Life expectancy at birth (in years)						
Men	53.99	57.63	59.52	61.17	62.97	65.40
Women	56.33	60.39	62.86	65.08	67.24	69.83
Five-year immigration flow (in '000)	4029.78	3769.25	3910.00	3993.29	3989.29	3927.79
Five-year emigration flow (in '000)	7117.06	6321.27	7407.88	8354.95	9025.57	9470.04

Human Capital indicators, Medium Scenario (SSP2)	2010	2020	2030	2040	2050	2060
Population age 25+: highest educational attainment						
E1 - no education	0.40	0.30	0.24	0.18	0.13	0.10
E2 - incomplete primary	0.13	0.12	0.10	0.08	0.07	0.05
E3 - primary	0.15	0.17	0.18	0.19	0.19	0.19
E4 - lower secondary	0.11	0.14	0.15	0.15	0.15	0.14
E5 - upper secondary	0.14	0.19	0.23	0.27	0.31	0.35
E6 - post-secondary	0.06	0.08	0.10	0.12	0.15	0.17
Mean years of schooling (in years)	5.38	6.52	7.51	8.42	9.24	9.98
Gender gap (population age 25+): highest educational attainment (ratio male/female)						
E1 - no education	0.64	0.64	0.66	0.69	0.73	0.77
E2 - incomplete primary	1.11	1.04	1.03	1.02	1.01	0.99
E3 - primary	1.23	1.10	1.03	0.99	0.98	0.97
E4 - lower secondary	1.39	1.24	1.14	1.08	1.04	1.01
E5 - upper secondary	1.53	1.35	1.24	1.16	1.10	1.06
E6 - post-secondary	1.71	1.41	1.24	1.13	1.07	1.05
Mean years of schooling (male minus female)	1.88	1.52	1.17	0.82	0.55	0.36
Women age 20–39: highest educational attainment						
E1 - no education	0.33	0.23	0.16	0.11	0.07	0.05
E2 - incomplete primary	0.13	0.12	0.09	0.07	0.05	0.04
E3 - primary	0.17	0.19	0.20	0.20	0.19	0.18
E4 - lower secondary	0.14	0.16	0.17	0.17	0.17	0.16
E5 - upper secondary	0.17	0.22	0.27	0.32	0.36	0.40
E6 - post-secondary	0.06	0.08	0.10	0.13	0.15	0.18
Mean years of schooling (in years)	6.06	7.35	8.36	9.29	10.10	10.79

Education scenarios

GET: global education trend scenario (medium assumption also used for SSP2)

CER: constant enrolment rates scenario (assumption of no future improvements)

FT: Fast track scenario (assumption of education expansion according to fastest historical experience)

Pyramids by Education, Medium Scenario

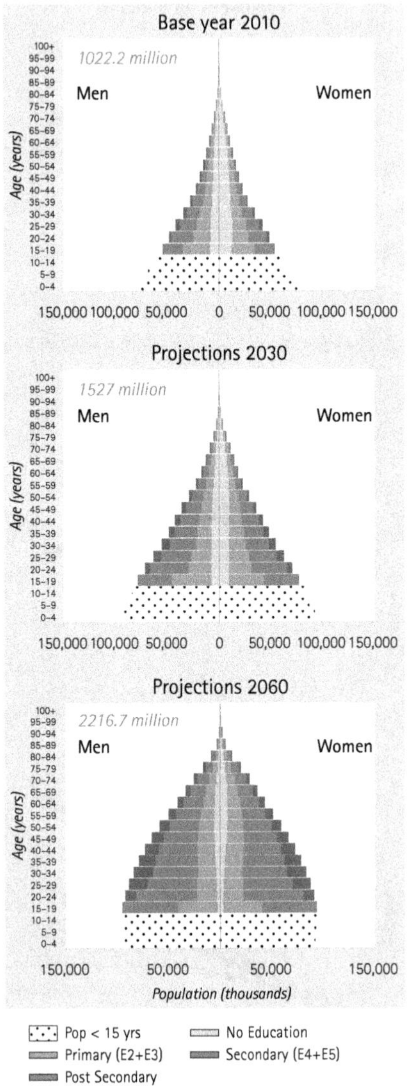

Population Size by Educational Attainment According to Three Education Scenarios: GET, CER, and FT

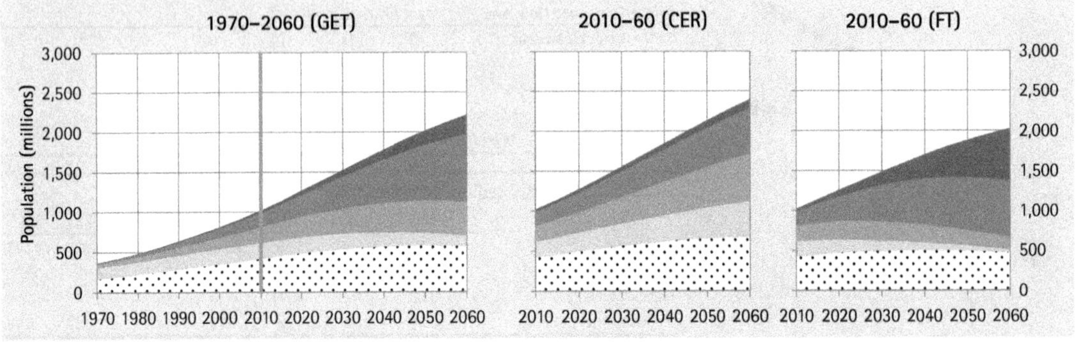

Africa (Continued)

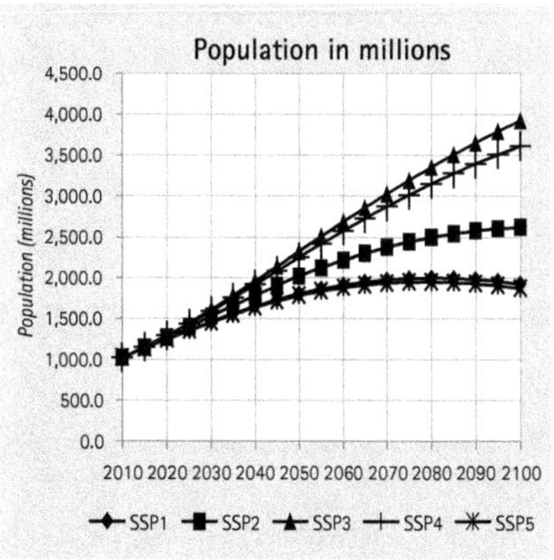

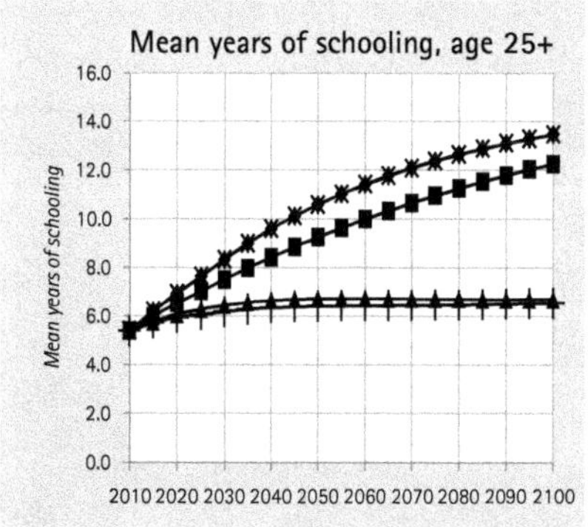

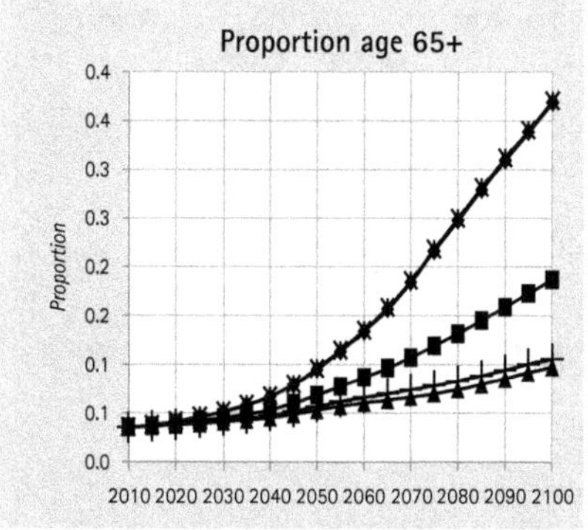

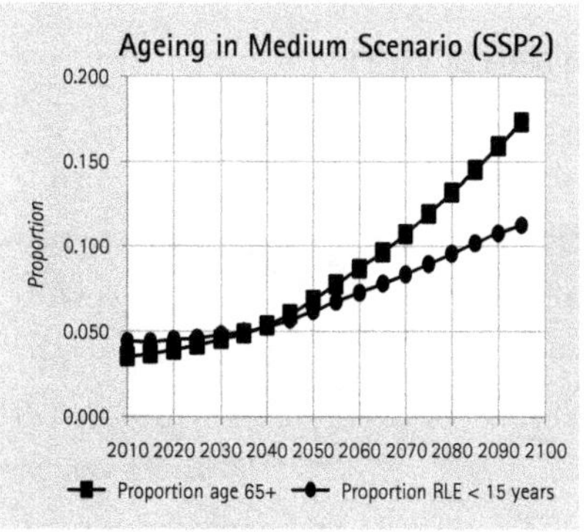

Alternative Scenarios to 2100

Projection Results by Scenario (SSP1–5)

	2010	2020	2030	2040	2050	2075	2100
Population (in millions)							
SSP1 - Rapid development	1022.23	1248.16	1459.07	1649.20	1801.01	1989.63	1924.50
SSP2 - Medium	1022.23	1268.39	1526.97	1781.86	2018.18	2442.86	2621.53
SSP3 - Stalled development	1022.23	1292.97	1611.11	1957.53	2323.85	3193.20	3923.95
SSP4 - Inequality	1022.23	1287.17	1591.00	1915.77	2251.50	3014.66	3613.55
SSP5 - Conventional development	1022.23	1246.56	1452.84	1636.18	1779.24	1943.63	1869.26
Proportion age 65+							
SSP1 - Rapid development	0.04	0.04	0.05	0.07	0.09	0.22	0.37
SSP2 - Medium	0.04	0.04	0.05	0.05	0.07	0.12	0.19
SSP3 - Stalled development	0.04	0.04	0.04	0.05	0.05	0.07	0.10
SSP4 - Inequality	0.04	0.04	0.04	0.05	0.06	0.08	0.11
SSP5 - Conventional development	0.04	0.04	0.05	0.07	0.10	0.22	0.37
Proportion below age 20							
SSP1 - Rapid development	0.51	0.47	0.41	0.35	0.30	0.20	0.13
SSP2 - Medium	0.51	0.48	0.45	0.41	0.38	0.29	0.23
SSP3 - Stalled development	0.51	0.50	0.49	0.47	0.44	0.38	0.34
SSP4 - Inequality	0.51	0.49	0.48	0.46	0.43	0.37	0.33
SSP5 - Conventional development	0.51	0.47	0.41	0.35	0.30	0.20	0.13
Proportion of Women age 20–39 with at least secondary education							
SSP1 - Rapid development	0.37	0.54	0.66	0.75	0.82	0.90	0.95
SSP2 - Medium	0.37	0.47	0.54	0.61	0.68	0.82	0.91
SSP3 - Stalled development	0.37	0.37	0.36	0.35	0.34	0.34	0.34
SSP4 - Inequality	0.37	0.35	0.33	0.31	0.30	0.29	0.28
SSP5 - Conventional development	0.37	0.54	0.66	0.76	0.82	0.90	0.95
Mean years of schooling, age 25+							
SSP1 - Rapid development	5.38	6.93	8.32	9.58	10.59	12.38	13.46
SSP2 - Medium	5.38	6.52	7.51	8.42	9.24	10.96	12.25
SSP3 - Stalled development	5.38	6.07	6.44	6.64	6.72	6.70	6.69
SSP4 - Inequality	5.38	5.94	6.18	6.34	6.40	6.45	6.54
SSP5 - Conventional development	5.38	6.93	8.32	9.57	10.58	12.37	13.46

Demographic Assumptions Underlying SSPs

	2010–15	2020–25	2030–35	2040–45	2050–55	2075–80	2095–2100
Total fertility rate							
SSP1 - Rapid development	4.02	3.00	2.35	1.98	1.72	1.39	1.28
SSP2 - Medium	4.28	3.69	3.18	2.77	2.44	1.93	1.75
SSP3 - Stalled development	4.57	4.50	4.24	3.85	3.46	2.76	2.54
SSP4 - Inequality	4.51	4.39	4.11	3.74	3.38	2.70	2.49
SSP5 - Conventional development	4.02	3.00	2.35	1.98	1.72	1.39	1.28
Life expectancy at birth for females (in years)							
SSP1 - Rapid development	60.12	66.60	70.95	75.11	79.10	88.13	95.12
SSP2 - Medium	58.48	61.65	64.00	66.11	68.52	74.93	79.86
SSP3 - Stalled development	57.79	56.59	57.45	58.01	58.69	61.62	64.32
SSP4 - Inequality	57.92	56.77	57.64	58.25	58.96	61.88	64.42
SSP5 - Conventional development	60.12	66.60	70.95	75.11	79.10	88.13	95.12
Migration – net flow over five years (in thousands)							
SSP1 - Rapid development	−2611	−2994	−3893	−4509	−4874	−2151	0
SSP2 - Medium	−2640	−3015	−3953	−4721	−5314	−2597	0
SSP3 - Stalled development	−2170	−1468	−1883	−2224	−2506	−1247	0
SSP4 - Inequality	−2600	−2958	−3890	−4732	−5468	−2827	0
SSP5 - Conventional development	−3048	−4556	−6097	−7352	−8291	−4132	0

Ageing Indicators, Medium Scenario (SSP2)

	2010	2020	2030	2040	2050	2075	2095
Median age	19.58	20.84	22.67	24.86	27.25	33.85	39.21
Propspective median age	19.58	19.11	19.61	20.60	21.64	24.22	26.12
Proportion age 65+	0.04	0.04	0.05	0.05	0.07	0.12	0.17
Proportion RLE < 15 years	0.04	0.05	0.05	0.05	0.06	0.09	0.11

Asia

Detailed Human Capital Projections to 2060

Demographic indicators, Medium Scenario (SSP2)	2010	2020	2030	2040	2050	2060
Population (in millions)	4164.25	4554.49	4850.06	5041.54	5125.97	5100.39
Proportion age 65+	0.07	0.09	0.12	0.16	0.19	0.23
Proportion below age 20	0.35	0.31	0.27	0.25	0.22	0.21
	2005–10	2015–20	2025–30	2035–40	2045–50	2055–60
Total Fertility Rate	2.28	2.07	1.95	1.85	1.77	1.72
Life expectancy at birth (in years)						
Men	67.22	69.79	72.18	74.52	76.83	78.65
Women	70.89	73.89	76.50	78.91	81.19	82.95
Five-year immigration flow (in '000)	12644.66	9103.71	9453.73	9665.31	9666.90	9528.79
Five-year emigration flow (in '000)	20529.80	16653.60	17033.82	17123.54	16775.11	16161.85

Human Capital indicators, Medium Scenario (SSP2)	2010	2020	2030	2040	2050	2060
Population age 25+: highest educational attainment						
E1 - no education	0.21	0.16	0.13	0.10	0.08	0.06
E2 - incomplete primary	0.06	0.05	0.04	0.03	0.02	0.02
E3 - primary	0.22	0.20	0.18	0.15	0.13	0.12
E4 - lower secondary	0.23	0.25	0.25	0.23	0.21	0.19
E5 - upper secondary	0.18	0.21	0.25	0.29	0.32	0.35
E6 - post-secondary	0.11	0.14	0.17	0.20	0.23	0.27
Mean years of schooling (in years)	7.06	7.90	8.62	9.32	9.98	10.62
Gender gap (population age 25+): highest educational attainment (ratio male/female)						
E1 - no education	0.52	0.53	0.56	0.58	0.61	0.65
E2 - incomplete primary	0.97	0.97	0.96	0.95	0.94	0.93
E3 - primary	0.95	0.90	0.87	0.87	0.88	0.90
E4 - lower secondary	1.29	1.21	1.16	1.12	1.08	1.04
E5 - upper secondary	1.34	1.24	1.17	1.12	1.09	1.06
E6 - post-secondary	1.37	1.22	1.14	1.09	1.05	1.04
Mean years of schooling (male minus female)	1.48	1.19	0.93	0.71	0.52	0.38
Women age 20–39: highest educational attainment						
E1 - no education	0.16	0.11	0.08	0.05	0.03	0.02
E2 - incomplete primary	0.04	0.03	0.02	0.01	0.01	0.01
E3 - primary	0.17	0.15	0.14	0.12	0.09	0.07
E4 - lower secondary	0.27	0.24	0.20	0.16	0.12	0.10
E5 - upper secondary	0.22	0.28	0.34	0.40	0.43	0.46
E6 - post-secondary	0.14	0.18	0.22	0.27	0.31	0.35
Mean years of schooling (in years)	8.07	9.07	9.95	10.78	11.49	12.08

Education scenarios

GET: global education trend scenario (medium assumption also used for SSP2)

CER: constant enrolment rates scenario (assumption of no future improvements)

FT: Fast track scenario (assumption of education expansion according to fastest historical experience)

Pyramids by Education, Medium Scenario

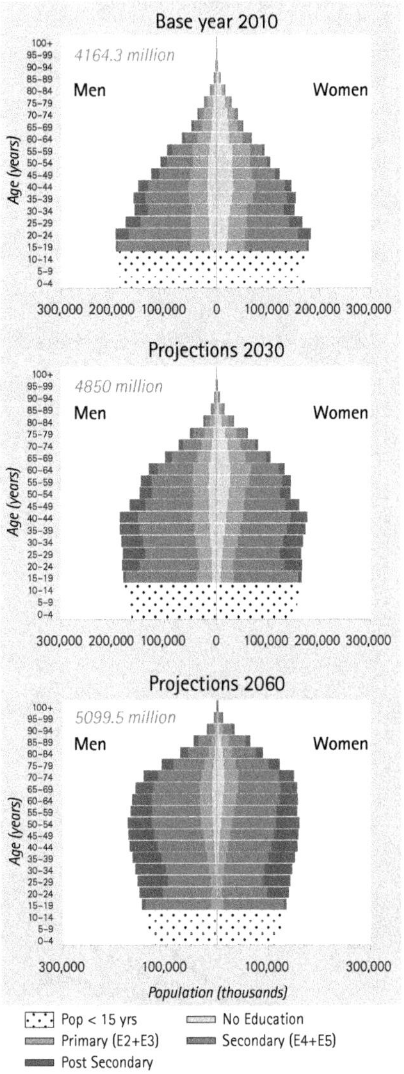

Population Size by Educational Attainment According to Three Education Scenarios: GET, CER, and FT

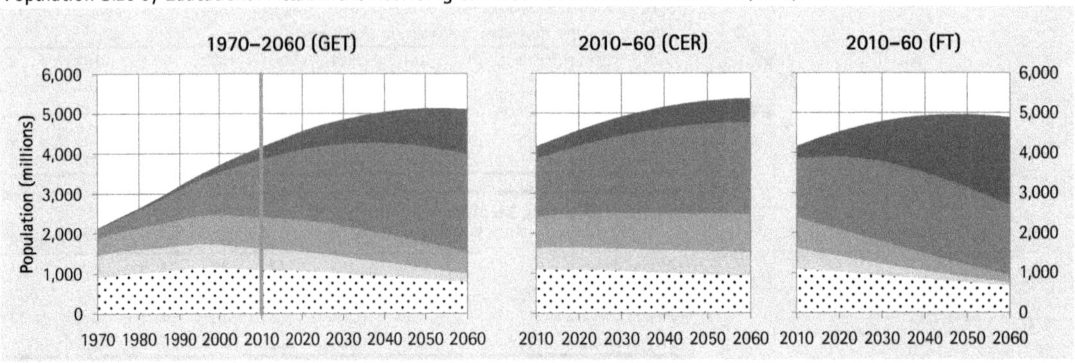

Asia (Continued)

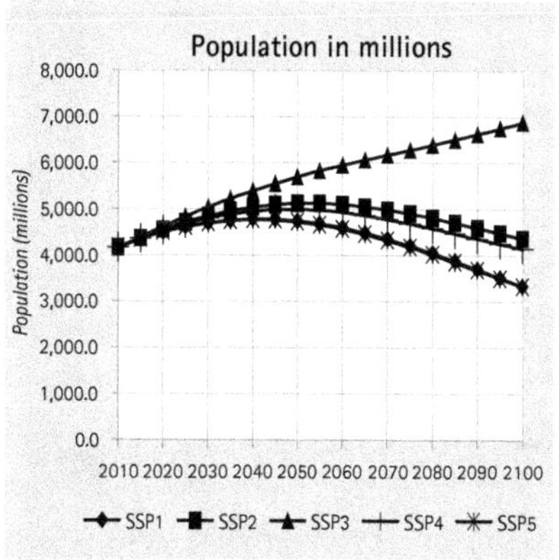

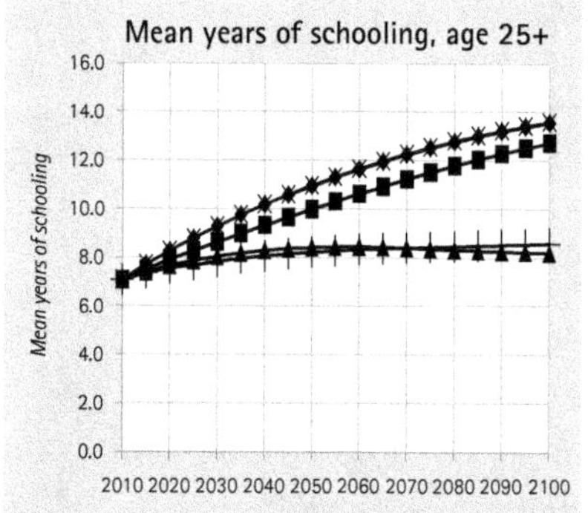

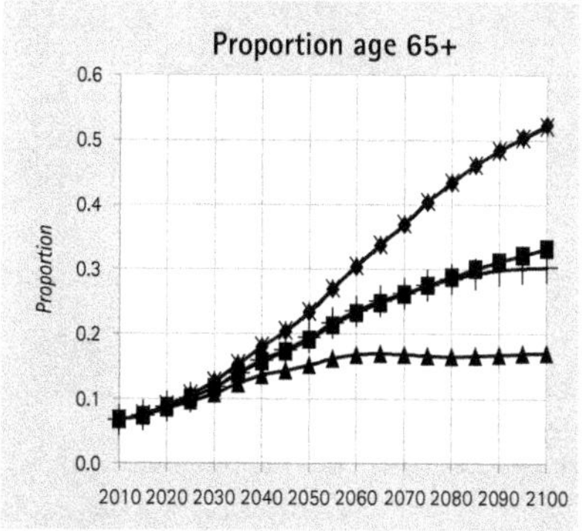

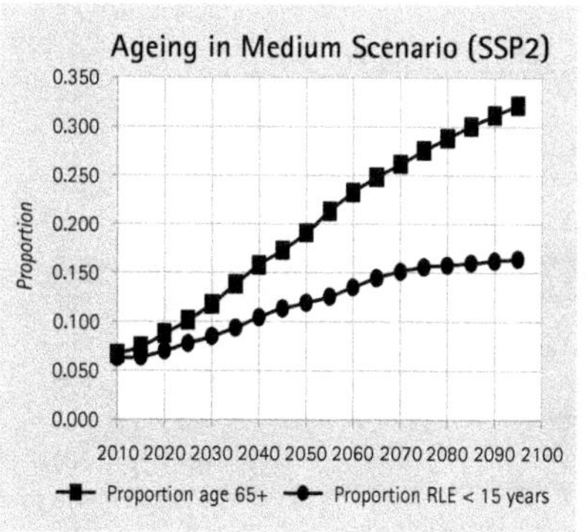

Alternative Scenarios to 2100

Projection Results by Scenario (SSP1–5)

	2010	2020	2030	2040	2050	2075	2100
Population (in millions)							
SSP1 - Rapid development	4164.25	4502.65	4701.96	4784.94	4746.10	4213.59	3329.69
SSP2 - Medium	4164.25	4554.49	4850.06	5041.54	5125.97	4907.36	4367.64
SSP3 - Stalled development	4164.25	4617.16	5041.50	5393.30	5702.07	6281.56	6877.42
SSP4 - Inequality	4164.25	4541.50	4804.98	4954.05	4996.84	4689.45	4148.29
SSP5 - Conventional development	4164.25	4499.55	4692.20	4768.41	4722.95	4181.67	3316.05
Proportion age 65+							
SSP1 - Rapid development	0.07	0.09	0.13	0.18	0.23	0.40	0.52
SSP2 - Medium	0.07	0.09	0.12	0.16	0.19	0.28	0.33
SSP3 - Stalled development	0.07	0.09	0.11	0.14	0.15	0.17	0.17
SSP4 - Inequality	0.07	0.09	0.12	0.16	0.20	0.28	0.30
SSP5 - Conventional development	0.07	0.09	0.13	0.18	0.23	0.40	0.52
Proportion below age 20							
SSP1 - Rapid development	0.35	0.30	0.24	0.20	0.17	0.12	0.09
SSP2 - Medium	0.35	0.31	0.27	0.25	0.22	0.19	0.17
SSP3 - Stalled development	0.35	0.32	0.31	0.30	0.29	0.28	0.28
SSP4 - Inequality	0.35	0.30	0.27	0.24	0.22	0.19	0.19
SSP5 - Conventional development	0.35	0.30	0.24	0.20	0.17	0.12	0.09
Proportion of Women age 20–39 with at least secondary education							
SSP1 - Rapid development	0.63	0.78	0.85	0.90	0.93	0.97	0.99
SSP2 - Medium	0.63	0.70	0.76	0.82	0.86	0.95	0.98
SSP3 - Stalled development	0.63	0.63	0.61	0.59	0.58	0.55	0.54
SSP4 - Inequality	0.63	0.59	0.55	0.54	0.52	0.49	0.46
SSP5 - Conventional development	0.63	0.78	0.85	0.90	0.93	0.97	0.99
Mean years of schooling, age 25+							
SSP1 - Rapid development	7.06	8.26	9.27	10.17	10.93	12.50	13.54
SSP2 - Medium	7.06	7.90	8.62	9.32	9.98	11.51	12.72
SSP3 - Stalled development	7.06	7.66	8.04	8.28	8.41	8.36	8.20
SSP4 - Inequality	7.06	7.55	7.83	8.06	8.22	8.43	8.58
SSP5 - Conventional development	7.06	8.26	9.27	10.17	10.95	12.53	13.58

Demographic Assumptions Underlying SSPs

	2010–15	2020–25	2030–35	2040–45	2050–55	2075–80	2095–2100
Total fertility rate							
SSP1 - Rapid development	2.00	1.65	1.44	1.33	1.27	1.22	1.20
SSP2 - Medium	2.14	2.00	1.90	1.81	1.74	1.65	1.60
SSP3 - Stalled development	2.29	2.43	2.47	2.46	2.43	2.39	2.36
SSP4 - Inequality	2.11	1.94	1.81	1.77	1.77	1.84	1.89
SSP5 - Conventional development	2.01	1.65	1.45	1.34	1.28	1.25	1.25
Life expectancy at birth for females (in years)							
SSP1 - Rapid development	73.14	76.66	80.30	83.81	86.94	93.77	99.05
SSP2 - Medium	72.50	75.22	77.70	80.08	82.13	86.23	89.47
SSP3 - Stalled development	72.05	72.94	74.15	75.23	76.05	76.86	77.69
SSP4 - Inequality	72.44	74.47	76.42	78.19	79.53	81.69	83.16
SSP5 - Conventional development	73.14	76.67	80.31	83.82	86.96	93.79	99.08
Migration – net flow over five years (in thousands)							
SSP1 - Rapid development	-7423	-7532	-7396	-6999	-6387	-2488	0
SSP2 - Medium	-7484	-7599	-7536	-7313	-6873	-2987	0
SSP3 - Stalled development	-6181	-3781	-3738	-3569	-3266	-1380	0
SSP4 - Inequality	-7425	-7522	-7345	-6893	-6218	-2532	0
SSP5 - Conventional development	-8662	-11285	-11213	-11069	-10679	-4845	0

Ageing Indicators, Medium Scenario (SSP2)

	2010	2020	2030	2040	2050	2075	2095
Median age	28.50	31.98	35.61	38.78	41.62	47.43	50.73
Propspective median age	28.50	30.16	32.13	33.61	34.90	37.42	37.88
Proportion age 65+	0.07	0.09	0.12	0.16	0.19	0.28	0.32
Proportion RLE < 15 years	0.06	0.07	0.08	0.10	0.12	0.16	0.16

Europe

Detailed Human Capital Projections to 2060

Demographic indicators, Medium Scenario (SSP2)	2010	2020	2030	2040	2050	2060
Population (in millions)	738.20	748.41	753.46	755.41	754.77	750.15
Proportion age 65+	0.16	0.19	0.23	0.26	0.29	0.31
Proportion below age 20	0.21	0.21	0.20	0.19	0.19	0.19
	2005–10	2015–20	2025–30	2035–40	2045–50	2055–60
Total Fertility Rate	1.53	1.57	1.64	1.70	1.71	1.73
Life expectancy at birth (in years)						
Men	71.40	74.47	77.35	79.73	82.05	84.34
Women	79.32	81.52	83.75	85.78	87.84	89.94
Five-year immigration flow (in '000)	13419.83	9784.28	10171.53	10411.00	10424.55	10278.80
Five-year emigration flow (in '000)	4402.39	2949.59	2696.92	2554.64	2444.57	2365.57

Human Capital indicators, Medium Scenario (SSP2)	2010	2020	2030	2040	2050	2060
Population age 25+: highest educational attainment						
E1 - no education	0.01	0.01	0.01	0.00	0.00	0.00
E2 - incomplete primary	0.02	0.01	0.01	0.00	0.00	0.00
E3 - primary	0.11	0.08	0.05	0.04	0.03	0.02
E4 - lower secondary	0.18	0.16	0.15	0.13	0.10	0.08
E5 - upper secondary	0.46	0.49	0.50	0.50	0.49	0.48
E6 - post-secondary	0.22	0.25	0.29	0.33	0.37	0.42
Mean years of schooling (in years)	10.93	11.53	12.03	12.47	12.88	13.26
Gender gap (population age 25+): highest educational attainment (ratio male/female)						
E1 - no education	0.65	0.71	0.78	0.80	0.79	0.79
E2 - incomplete primary	0.71	0.71	0.74	0.78	0.82	0.89
E3 - primary	0.81	0.83	0.86	0.92	0.99	1.06
E4 - lower secondary	0.93	0.99	1.04	1.08	1.09	1.09
E5 - upper secondary	1.10	1.08	1.07	1.07	1.07	1.06
E6 - post-secondary	1.01	0.94	0.90	0.89	0.90	0.92
Mean years of schooling (male minus female)	0.39	0.19	0.04	−0.05	−0.09	−0.08
Women age 20–39: highest educational attainment						
E1 - no education	0.00	0.00	0.00	0.00	0.00	0.00
E2 - incomplete primary	0.00	0.00	0.00	0.00	0.00	0.00
E3 - primary	0.03	0.02	0.01	0.01	0.01	0.01
E4 - lower secondary	0.14	0.10	0.08	0.06	0.05	0.04
E5 - upper secondary	0.55	0.54	0.53	0.51	0.50	0.49
E6 - post-secondary	0.28	0.34	0.38	0.41	0.44	0.46
Mean years of schooling (in years)	12.10	12.75	13.19	13.41	13.61	13.77

Education scenarios

GET : global education trend scenario (medium assumption also used for SSP2)

CER: constant enrolment rates scenario (assumption of no future improvements)

FT: Fast track scenario (assumption of education expansion according to fastest historical experience)

Pyramids by Education, Medium Scenario

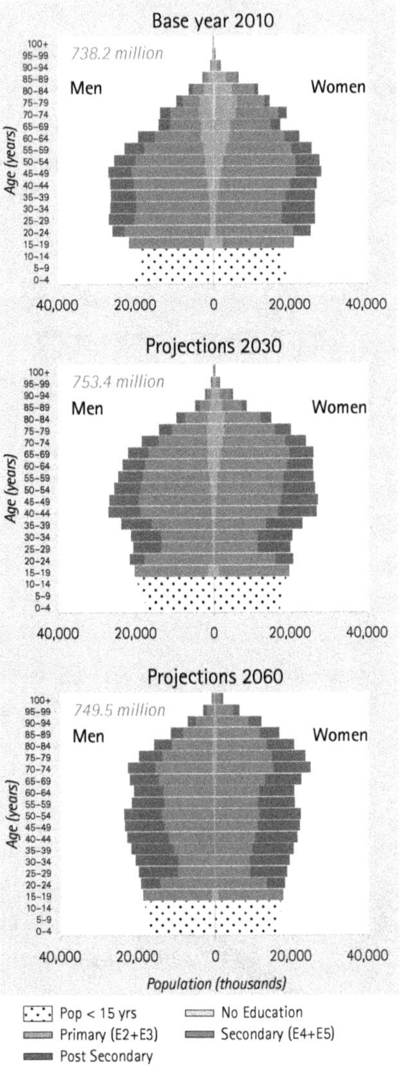

Population Size by Educational Attainment According to Three Education Scenarios: GET, CER, and FT

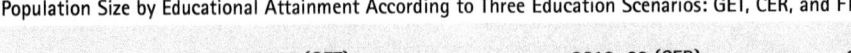

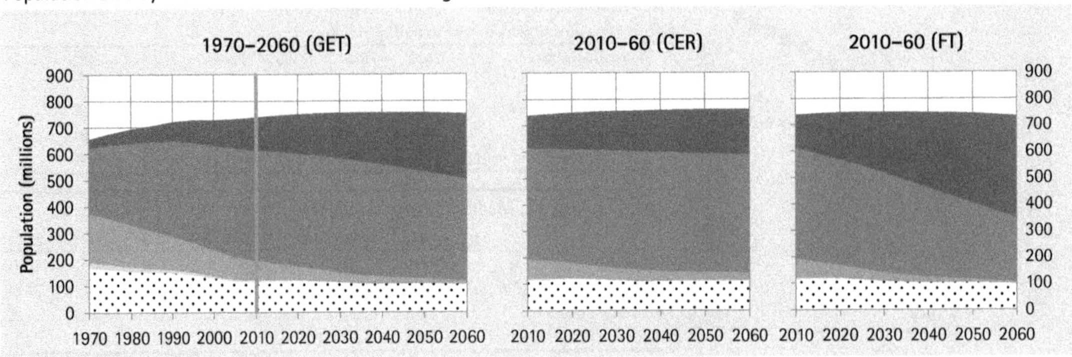

Europe (Continued)

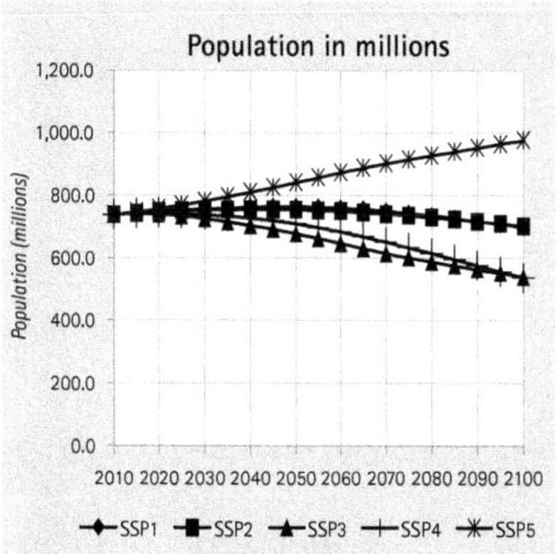

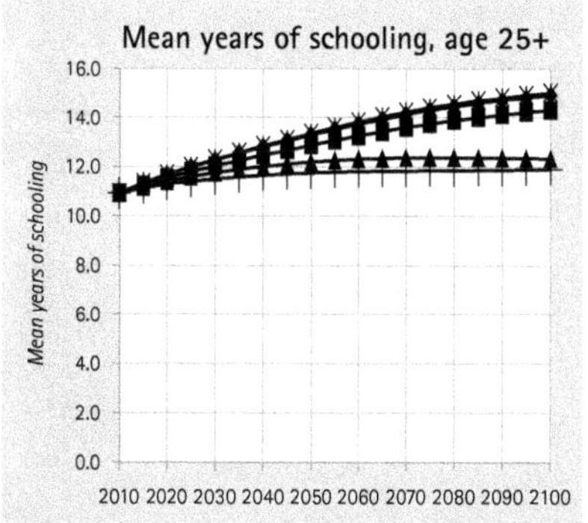

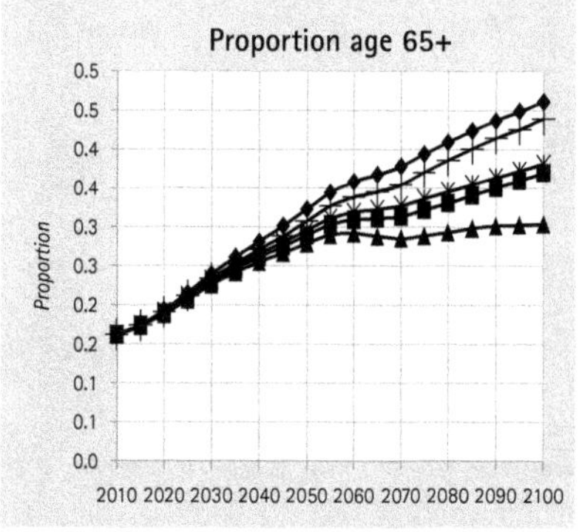

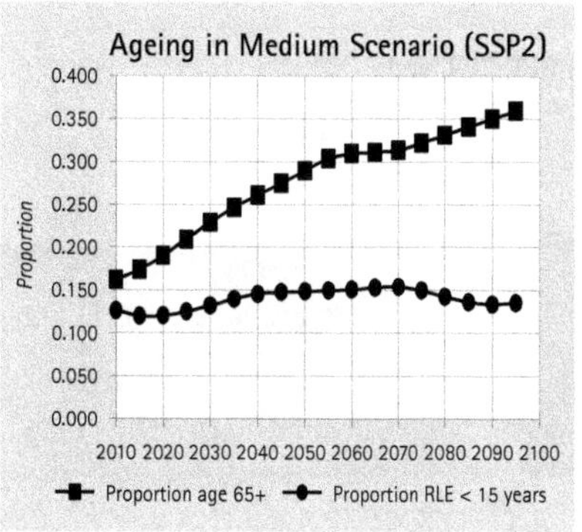

Alternative Scenarios to 2100

Projection Results by Scenario (SSP1–5)

	2010	2020	2030	2040	2050	2075	2100
Population (in millions)							
SSP1 - Rapid development	738.20	749.73	756.97	762.50	764.29	743.79	699.30
SSP2 - Medium	738.20	748.41	753.46	755.41	754.77	736.11	702.55
SSP3 - Stalled development	738.20	740.01	725.83	704.04	677.94	601.47	539.42
SSP4 - Inequality	738.20	743.83	738.81	727.69	709.47	633.95	536.25
SSP5 - Conventional development	738.20	757.32	782.30	810.40	840.97	914.80	975.74
Proportion age 65+							
SSP1 - Rapid development	0.16	0.19	0.24	0.28	0.32	0.39	0.46
SSP2 - Medium	0.16	0.19	0.23	0.26	0.29	0.32	0.37
SSP3 - Stalled development	0.16	0.19	0.23	0.25	0.28	0.29	0.30
SSP4 - Inequality	0.16	0.19	0.23	0.27	0.31	0.37	0.44
SSP5 - Conventional development	0.16	0.19	0.23	0.27	0.30	0.34	0.38
Proportion below age 20							
SSP1 - Rapid development	0.21	0.20	0.19	0.17	0.17	0.15	0.14
SSP2 - Medium	0.21	0.21	0.20	0.19	0.19	0.18	0.17
SSP3 - Stalled development	0.21	0.21	0.20	0.18	0.19	0.19	0.19
SSP4 - Inequality	0.21	0.20	0.18	0.16	0.16	0.14	0.13
SSP5 - Conventional development	0.21	0.21	0.20	0.19	0.20	0.20	0.19
Proportion of Women age 20–39 with at least secondary education							
SSP1 - Rapid development	0.97	0.99	0.99	0.99	0.99	1.00	1.00
SSP2 - Medium	0.97	0.98	0.98	0.99	0.99	1.00	1.00
SSP3 - Stalled development	0.97	0.96	0.96	0.96	0.96	0.96	0.97
SSP4 - Inequality	0.97	0.94	0.93	0.93	0.93	0.93	0.93
SSP5 - Conventional development	0.97	0.99	0.99	0.99	0.99	1.00	1.00
Mean years of schooling, age 25+							
SSP1 - Rapid development	10.93	11.67	12.27	12.81	13.29	14.30	14.91
SSP2 - Medium	10.93	11.53	12.03	12.47	12.88	13.75	14.31
SSP3 - Stalled development	10.93	11.40	11.75	12.01	12.19	12.37	12.33
SSP4 - Inequality	10.93	11.29	11.50	11.65	11.75	11.84	11.89
SSP5 - Conventional development	10.93	11.67	12.29	12.84	13.35	14.40	15.02

Demographic Assumptions Underlying SSPs

	2010–15	2020–25	2030–35	2040–45	2050–55	2075–80	2095–2100
Total fertility rate							
SSP1 - Rapid development	1.52	1.49	1.54	1.55	1.58	1.63	1.66
SSP2 - Medium	1.56	1.60	1.68	1.70	1.72	1.74	1.75
SSP3 - Stalled development	1.55	1.55	1.59	1.64	1.67	1.77	1.84
SSP4 - Inequality	1.49	1.41	1.39	1.37	1.37	1.39	1.41
SSP5 - Conventional development	1.57	1.65	1.79	1.84	1.91	2.02	2.08
Life expectancy at birth for females (in years)							
SSP1 - Rapid development	80.92	84.13	87.27	90.28	93.38	101.20	108.06
SSP2 - Medium	80.43	82.63	84.78	86.79	88.89	94.16	98.57
SSP3 - Stalled development	79.92	81.02	82.08	82.99	83.98	86.41	88.26
SSP4 - Inequality	80.43	82.56	84.64	86.62	88.65	93.67	97.94
SSP5 - Conventional development	80.92	84.14	87.29	90.30	93.41	101.23	108.11
Migration – net flow over five years (in thousands)							
SSP1 - Rapid development	7390	7124	7521	7472	7137	2691	0
SSP2 - Medium	7448	7189	7695	7949	7965	3438	0
SSP3 - Stalled development	6150	3572	3839	4019	4106	1934	0
SSP4 - Inequality	7384	7106	7516	7590	7440	3112	0
SSP5 - Conventional development	8624	10699	11421	11700	11622	4935	0

Ageing Indicators, Medium Scenario (SSP2)

	2010	2020	2030	2040	2050	2075	2095
Median age	40.20	42.49	45.14	47.40	47.77	50.04	52.53
Propspective median age	40.20	40.15	40.74	41.07	39.38	36.45	34.62
Proportion age 65+	0.16	0.19	0.23	0.26	0.29	0.32	0.36
Proportion RLE < 15 years	0.13	0.12	0.13	0.15	0.15	0.15	0.14

Latin America and the Caribbean

Detailed Human Capital Projections to 2060

Demographic indicators, Medium Scenario (SSP2)	2010	2020	2030	2040	2050	2060
Population (in millions)	590.08	651.34	702.03	738.06	758.28	762.42
Proportion age 65+	0.07	0.09	0.12	0.16	0.20	0.24
Proportion below age 20	0.37	0.33	0.29	0.26	0.23	0.21
	2005–10	2015–20	2025–30	2035–40	2045–50	2055–60
Total Fertility Rate	2.30	2.07	1.93	1.83	1.76	1.70
Life expectancy at birth (in years)						
Men	70.22	73.03	75.58	77.97	80.19	82.23
Women	76.66	79.18	81.52	83.75	85.83	87.76
Five-year immigration flow (in '000)	905.39	888.82	923.27	944.56	945.33	931.96
Five-year emigration flow (in '000)	6126.27	4953.54	4980.66	4854.30	4629.86	4344.50

Human Capital indicators, Medium Scenario (SSP2)	2010	2020	2030	2040	2050	2060
Population age 25+: highest educational attainment						
E1 - no education	0.09	0.06	0.04	0.03	0.02	0.01
E2 - incomplete primary	0.16	0.13	0.09	0.07	0.05	0.03
E3 - primary	0.22	0.20	0.18	0.16	0.14	0.12
E4 - lower secondary	0.16	0.18	0.18	0.17	0.16	0.14
E5 - upper secondary	0.22	0.26	0.30	0.34	0.37	0.40
E6 - post-secondary	0.14	0.17	0.20	0.23	0.26	0.30
Mean years of schooling (in years)	7.97	8.81	9.53	10.17	10.74	11.26
Gender gap (population age 25+): highest educational attainment (ratio male/female)						
E1 - no education	0.84	0.84	0.84	0.85	0.86	0.86
E2 - incomplete primary	1.01	0.99	0.97	0.95	0.93	0.91
E3 - primary	1.05	1.06	1.07	1.08	1.07	1.05
E4 - lower secondary	1.06	1.07	1.07	1.07	1.06	1.03
E5 - upper secondary	1.03	1.04	1.05	1.05	1.05	1.05
E6 - post-secondary	0.92	0.88	0.86	0.87	0.89	0.92
Mean years of schooling (male minus female)	0.06	−0.04	−0.10	−0.14	−0.13	−0.09
Women age 20–39: highest educational attainment						
E1 - no education	0.04	0.02	0.01	0.01	0.00	0.00
E2 - incomplete primary	0.09	0.05	0.03	0.02	0.01	0.01
E3 - primary	0.19	0.15	0.13	0.10	0.08	0.06
E4 - lower secondary	0.20	0.19	0.16	0.13	0.10	0.08
E5 - upper secondary	0.32	0.37	0.41	0.45	0.47	0.49
E6 - post-secondary	0.17	0.21	0.26	0.29	0.33	0.36
Mean years of schooling (in years)	9.54	10.37	11.00	11.56	12.01	12.35

Education scenarios

GET: global education trend scenario (medium assumption also used for SSP2)

CER: constant enrolment rates scenario (assumption of no future improvements)

FT: Fast track scenario (assumption of education expansion according to fastest historical experience)

Pyramids by Education, Medium Scenario

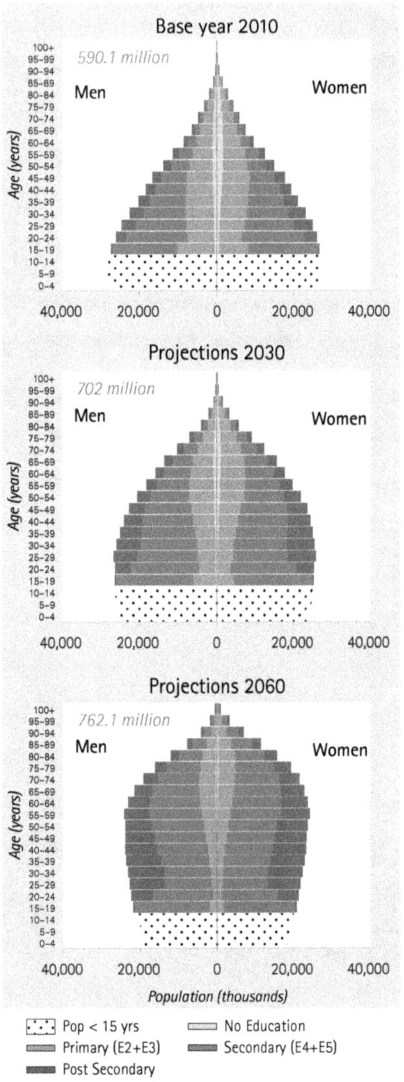

Population Size by Educational Attainment According to Three Education Scenarios: GET, CER, and FT

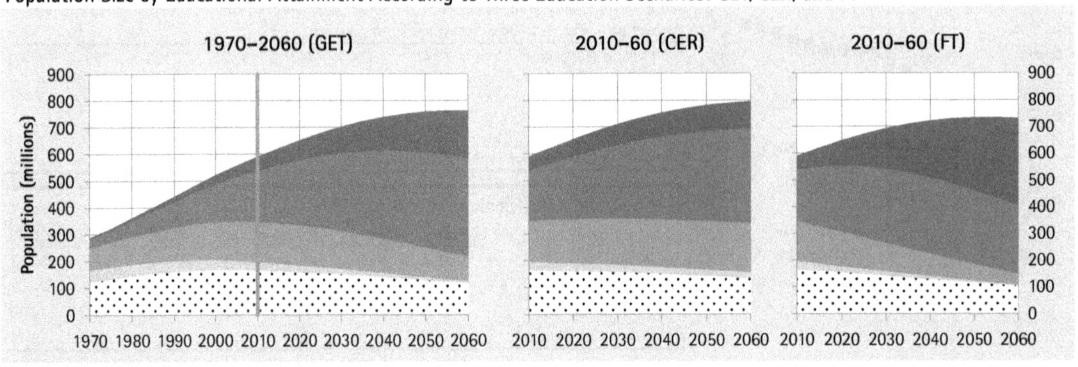

Latin America and the Caribbean (Continued)

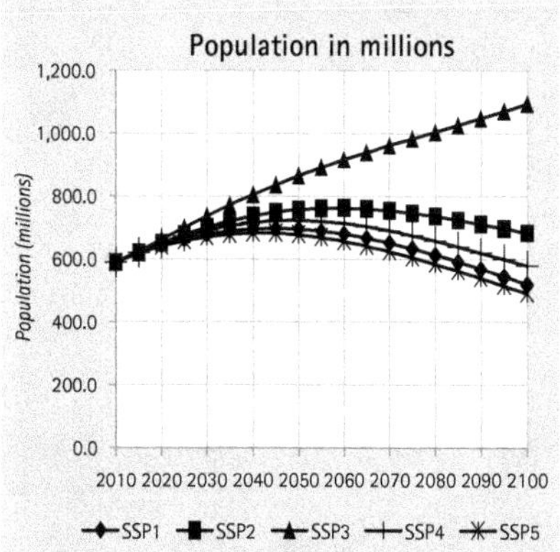

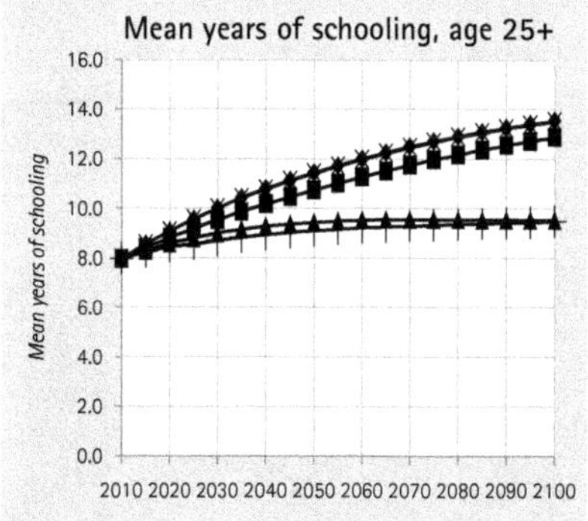

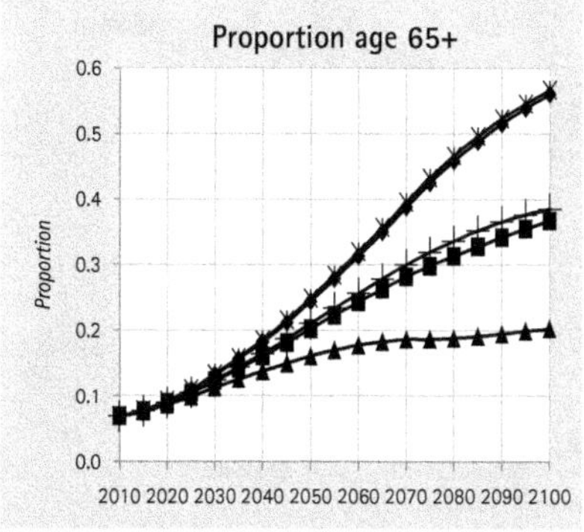

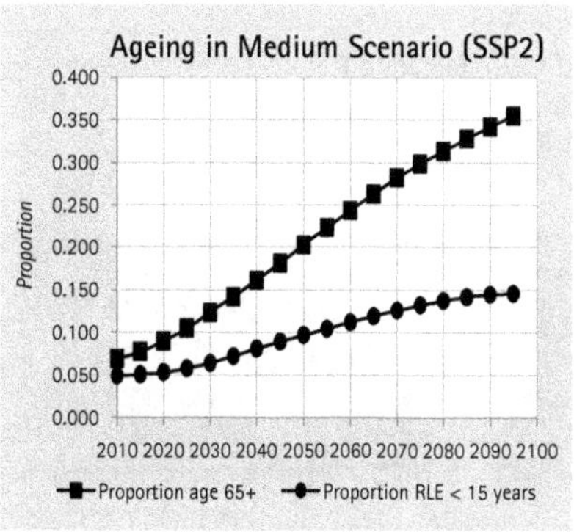

Alternative Scenarios to 2100

Projection Results by Scenario (SSP1–5)

	2010	2020	2030	2040	2050	2075	2100
Population (in millions)							
SSP1 - Rapid development	590.08	643.70	678.31	696.08	696.12	634.41	520.25
SSP2 - Medium	590.08	651.34	702.03	738.06	758.28	746.78	684.22
SSP3 - Stalled development	590.08	663.12	738.35	805.27	865.10	983.49	1,094.09
SSP4 - Inequality	590.08	648.77	691.85	717.10	723.98	675.86	580.34
SSP5 - Conventional development	590.08	641.34	670.93	683.35	678.04	605.76	490.26
Proportion age 65+							
SSP1 - Rapid development	0.07	0.09	0.13	0.18	0.24	0.42	0.56
SSP2 - Medium	0.07	0.09	0.12	0.16	0.20	0.30	0.37
SSP3 - Stalled development	0.07	0.09	0.11	0.14	0.16	0.19	0.20
SSP4 - Inequality	0.07	0.09	0.12	0.17	0.21	0.32	0.39
SSP5 - Conventional development	0.07	0.09	0.13	0.19	0.25	0.43	0.57
Proportion below age 20							
SSP1 - Rapid development	0.37	0.31	0.25	0.21	0.17	0.11	0.08
SSP2 - Medium	0.37	0.33	0.29	0.26	0.23	0.19	0.16
SSP3 - Stalled development	0.37	0.34	0.32	0.31	0.30	0.28	0.27
SSP4 - Inequality	0.37	0.32	0.28	0.24	0.21	0.17	0.15
SSP5 - Conventional development	0.37	0.31	0.25	0.21	0.17	0.11	0.08
Proportion of Women age 20–39 with at least secondary education							
SSP1 - Rapid development	0.69	0.83	0.90	0.93	0.95	0.98	0.99
SSP2 - Medium	0.69	0.77	0.83	0.87	0.90	0.96	0.99
SSP3 - Stalled development	0.69	0.72	0.72	0.71	0.71	0.70	0.70
SSP4 - Inequality	0.69	0.67	0.64	0.64	0.63	0.60	0.56
SSP5 - Conventional development	0.69	0.83	0.90	0.93	0.95	0.98	0.99
Mean years of schooling, age 25+							
SSP1 - Rapid development	7.97	9.07	10.01	10.79	11.44	12.69	13.53
SSP2 - Medium	7.97	8.81	9.53	10.17	10.74	11.96	12.87
SSP3 - Stalled development	7.97	8.58	8.99	9.27	9.44	9.55	9.53
SSP4 - Inequality	7.97	8.44	8.70	8.94	9.10	9.32	9.47
SSP5 - Conventional development	7.97	9.07	9.99	10.77	11.41	12.67	13.51

Demographic Assumptions Underlying SSPs

	2010–15	2020–25	2030–35	2040–45	2050–55	2075–80	2095–2100
Total fertility rate							
SSP1 - Rapid development	2.03	1.64	1.43	1.32	1.26	1.20	1.19
SSP2 - Medium	2.16	1.99	1.88	1.79	1.72	1.63	1.60
SSP3 - Stalled development	2.30	2.41	2.43	2.38	2.33	2.26	2.26
SSP4 - Inequality	2.12	1.89	1.71	1.61	1.56	1.58	1.64
SSP5 - Conventional development	2.03	1.64	1.43	1.32	1.26	1.20	1.19
Life expectancy at birth for females (in years)							
SSP1 - Rapid development	78.48	81.80	85.18	88.45	91.49	98.83	104.89
SSP2 - Medium	77.97	80.37	82.66	84.81	86.82	91.51	95.33
SSP3 - Stalled development	77.50	78.46	79.66	80.70	81.59	83.47	85.12
SSP4 - Inequality	77.91	79.87	81.85	83.68	85.29	88.71	91.22
SSP5 - Conventional development	78.48	81.80	85.18	88.45	91.49	98.83	104.89
Migration – net flow over five years (in thousands)							
SSP1 - Rapid development	-4368	-4047	-3891	-3527	-3092	-1010	0
SSP2 - Medium	-4392	-4083	-3995	-3806	-3551	-1352	0
SSP3 - Stalled development	-3636	-2023	-1990	-1948	-1891	-828	0
SSP4 - Inequality	-4366	-4045	-3898	-3564	-3145	-1056	0
SSP5 - Conventional development	-5097	-6117	-5977	-5554	-5016	-1790	0

Ageing Indicators, Medium Scenario (SSP2)

	2010	2020	2030	2040	2050	2075	2095
Median age	27.42	30.85	34.38	37.98	41.35	48.43	52.76
Propspective median age	27.42	28.80	30.35	32.14	33.79	36.67	37.49
Proportion age 65+	0.07	0.09	0.12	0.16	0.20	0.30	0.35
Proportion RLE < 15 years	0.05	0.05	0.06	0.08	0.10	0.13	0.15

Northern America

Detailed Human Capital Projections to 2060

Demographic indicators, Medium Scenario (SSP2)	2010	2020	2030	2040	2050	2060
Population (in millions)	344.53	371.51	399.86	425.52	447.48	469.89
Proportion age 65+	0.13	0.16	0.20	0.22	0.23	0.25
Proportion below age 20	0.27	0.25	0.24	0.23	0.23	0.22
	2005–10	2015–20	2025–30	2035–40	2045–50	2055–60
Total Fertility Rate	2.03	1.88	1.90	1.91	1.90	1.89
Life expectancy at birth (in years)						
Men	75.63	76.92	78.65	80.50	82.45	84.68
Women	80.73	82.06	83.80	85.56	87.49	89.71
Five-year immigration flow (in '000)	7780.70	7661.91	7961.98	8151.07	8152.70	8026.77
Five-year emigration flow (in '000)	1736.86	1287.81	1298.48	1300.62	1327.60	1360.56

Human Capital indicators, Medium Scenario (SSP2)	2010	2020	2030	2040	2050	2060
Population age 25+: highest educational attainment						
E1 - no education	0.01	0.01	0.00	0.00	0.00	0.00
E2 - incomplete primary	0.01	0.00	0.00	0.00	0.00	0.00
E3 - primary	0.04	0.03	0.02	0.02	0.01	0.01
E4 - lower secondary	0.07	0.06	0.06	0.05	0.04	0.04
E5 - upper secondary	0.49	0.48	0.46	0.45	0.43	0.41
E6 - post-secondary	0.38	0.42	0.45	0.48	0.51	0.55
Mean years of schooling (in years)	12.93	13.20	13.42	13.62	13.81	13.99
Gender gap (population age 25+): highest educational attainment (ratio male/female)						
E1 - no education	0.99	1.00	1.01	1.01	0.99	0.97
E2 - incomplete primary	1.13	1.17	1.19	1.19	1.17	1.12
E3 - primary	1.06	1.12	1.17	1.19	1.20	1.17
E4 - lower secondary	1.03	1.09	1.13	1.15	1.14	1.10
E5 - upper secondary	0.98	1.03	1.07	1.10	1.11	1.10
E6 - post-secondary	1.01	0.95	0.91	0.90	0.90	0.93
Mean years of schooling (male minus female)	−0.01	−0.13	−0.21	−0.25	−0.24	−0.19
Women age 20–39: highest educational attainment						
E1 - no education	0.00	0.00	0.00	0.00	0.00	0.00
E2 - incomplete primary	0.00	0.00	0.00	0.00	0.00	0.00
E3 - primary	0.02	0.02	0.01	0.01	0.01	0.00
E4 - lower secondary	0.06	0.05	0.04	0.03	0.02	0.02
E5 - upper secondary	0.50	0.48	0.47	0.45	0.45	0.44
E6 - post-secondary	0.41	0.45	0.48	0.51	0.52	0.53
Mean years of schooling (in years)	13.26	13.53	13.70	13.86	13.95	14.03

Education scenarios

GET: global education trend scenario (medium assumption also used for SSP2)

CER: constant enrolment rates scenario (assumption of no future improvements)

FT: Fast track scenario (assumption of education expansion according to fastest historical experience)

Pyramids by Education, Medium Scenario

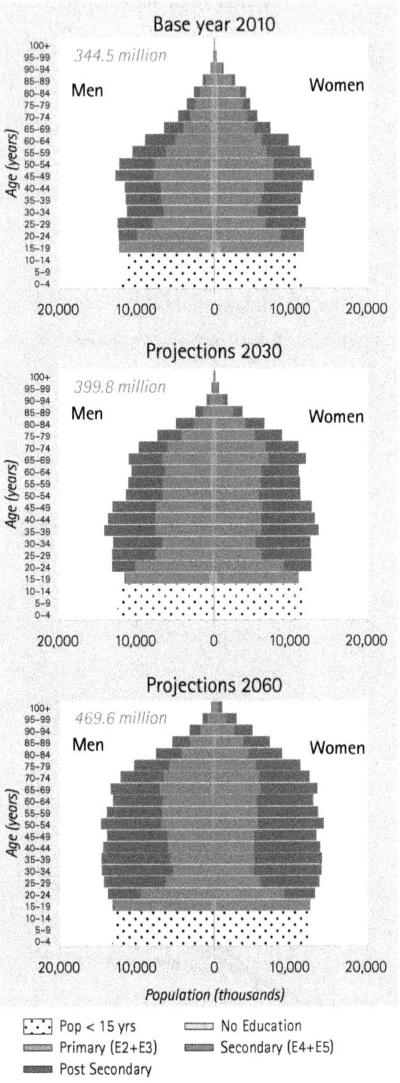

Population Size by Educational Attainment According to Three Education Scenarios: GET, CER, and FT

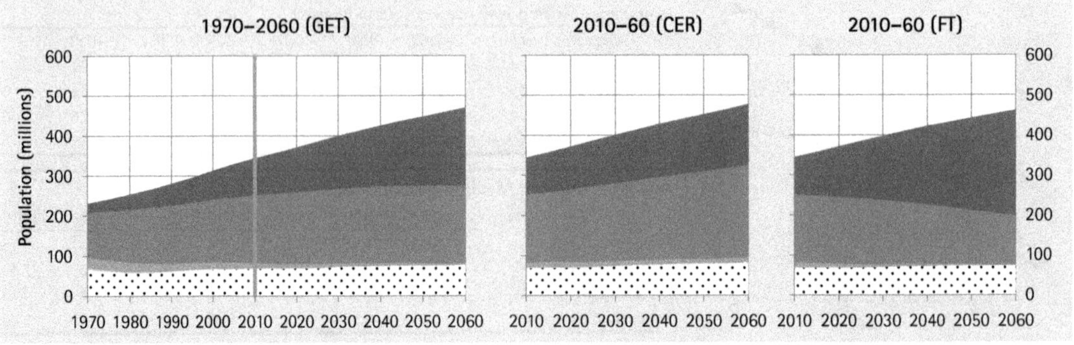

Northern America (Continued)

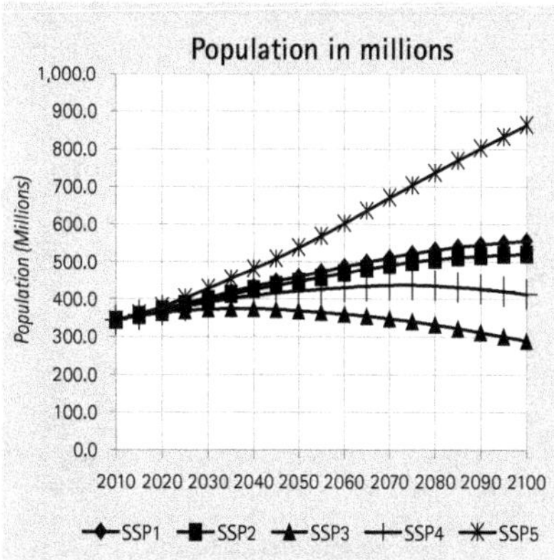

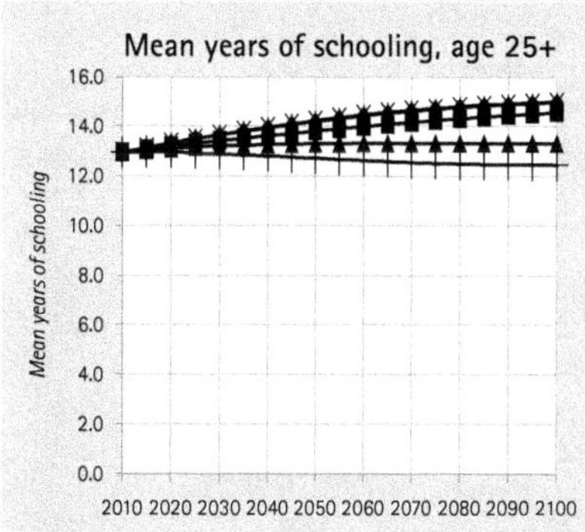

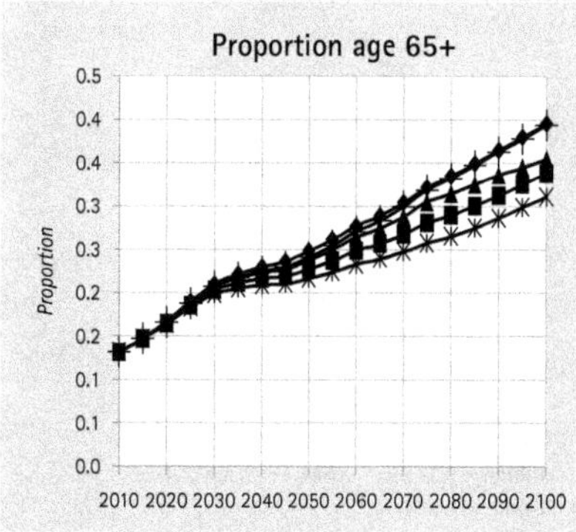

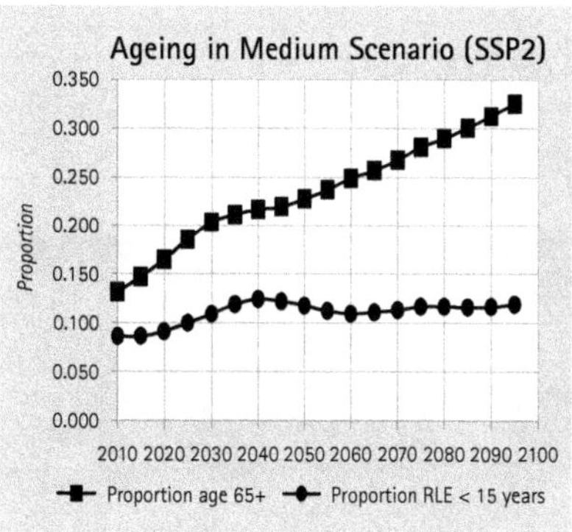

Alternative Scenarios to 2100

Projection Results by Scenario (SSP1–5)

	2010	2020	2030	2040	2050	2075	2100
Population (in millions)							
SSP1 - Rapid development	344.53	373.06	404.16	434.03	460.60	522.19	556.05
SSP2 - Medium	344.53	371.51	399.86	425.52	447.48	499.39	520.66
SSP3 - Stalled development	344.53	363.76	373.19	374.88	369.05	340.88	289.14
SSP4 - Inequality	344.53	369.23	391.96	410.15	421.96	437.30	412.87
SSP5 - Conventional development	344.53	379.97	428.37	481.07	537.45	703.39	862.89
Proportion age 65+							
SSP1 - Rapid development	0.13	0.17	0.21	0.23	0.25	0.32	0.40
SSP2 - Medium	0.13	0.16	0.20	0.22	0.23	0.28	0.34
SSP3 - Stalled development	0.13	0.17	0.21	0.22	0.24	0.30	0.35
SSP4 - Inequality	0.13	0.17	0.21	0.22	0.24	0.32	0.39
SSP5 - Conventional development	0.13	0.16	0.20	0.21	0.22	0.26	0.31
Proportion below age 20							
SSP1 - Rapid development	0.27	0.25	0.23	0.23	0.22	0.19	0.17
SSP2 - Medium	0.27	0.25	0.24	0.23	0.23	0.21	0.19
SSP3 - Stalled development	0.27	0.24	0.22	0.20	0.19	0.17	0.15
SSP4 - Inequality	0.27	0.24	0.22	0.21	0.20	0.17	0.15
SSP5 - Conventional development	0.27	0.25	0.25	0.26	0.26	0.25	0.23
Proportion of Women age 20–39 with at least secondary education							
SSP1 - Rapid development	0.97	0.99	0.99	0.99	1.00	1.00	1.00
SSP2 - Medium	0.97	0.98	0.99	0.99	0.99	1.00	1.00
SSP3 - Stalled development	0.97	0.97	0.97	0.97	0.97	0.97	0.97
SSP4 - Inequality	0.97	0.97	0.97	0.97	0.97	0.97	0.97
SSP5 - Conventional development	0.97	0.99	0.99	0.99	1.00	1.00	1.00
Mean years of schooling, age 25+							
SSP1 - Rapid development	12.93	13.32	13.65	13.94	14.20	14.70	14.98
SSP2 - Medium	12.93	13.20	13.42	13.62	13.81	14.24	14.57
SSP3 - Stalled development	12.93	13.10	13.21	13.27	13.30	13.32	13.32
SSP4 - Inequality	12.93	12.96	12.88	12.80	12.71	12.51	12.46
SSP5 - Conventional development	12.93	13.33	13.66	13.96	14.23	14.74	15.01

Demographic Assumptions Underlying SSPs

	2010–15	2020–25	2030–35	2040–45	2050–55	2075–80	2095–2100
Total fertility rate							
SSP1 - Rapid development	1.85	1.87	1.88	1.87	1.86	1.84	1.83
SSP2 - Medium	1.86	1.90	1.91	1.91	1.89	1.86	1.85
SSP3 - Stalled development	1.77	1.64	1.55	1.50	1.47	1.47	1.46
SSP4 - Inequality	1.78	1.70	1.64	1.59	1.56	1.55	1.54
SSP5 - Conventional development	1.94	2.14	2.27	2.32	2.33	2.30	2.29
Life expectancy at birth for females (in years)							
SSP1 - Rapid development	81.86	84.48	87.17	89.90	92.95	101.33	108.32
SSP2 - Medium	81.36	82.98	84.68	86.47	88.60	94.28	98.84
SSP3 - Stalled development	80.86	81.45	82.15	82.84	83.93	87.02	89.49
SSP4 - Inequality	81.37	82.93	84.56	86.31	88.41	93.93	98.39
SSP5 - Conventional development	81.85	84.47	87.16	89.89	92.94	101.33	108.33
Migration – net flow over five years (in thousands)							
SSP1 - Rapid development	6008	6477	6665	6582	6276	2586	0
SSP2 - Medium	6058	6530	6777	6865	6755	3051	0
SSP3 - Stalled development	5000	3223	3296	3258	3117	1339	0
SSP4 - Inequality	6003	6451	6626	6607	6418	2874	0
SSP5 - Conventional development	7011	9771	10276	10614	10662	5048	0

Ageing Indicators, Medium Scenario (SSP2)

	2010	2020	2030	2040	2050	2075	2095
Median age	37.17	38.41	40.13	41.53	42.63	45.79	49.31
Propspective median age	37.17	36.88	36.99	36.70	35.79	33.68	32.88
Proportion age 65+	0.13	0.16	0.20	0.22	0.23	0.28	0.32
Proportion RLE < 15 years	0.09	0.09	0.11	0.12	0.12	0.12	0.12

Oceania

Detailed Human Capital Projections to 2060

Demographic indicators, Medium Scenario (SSP2)	2010	2020	2030	2040	2050	2060
Population (in millions)	36.59	42.34	47.96	53.05	57.58	61.57
Proportion age 65+	0.11	0.13	0.16	0.18	0.20	0.23
Proportion below age 20	0.32	0.29	0.27	0.25	0.23	0.22
	2005–10	2015–20	2025–30	2035–40	2045–50	2055–60
Total Fertility Rate	2.49	2.24	2.08	1.94	1.86	1.82
Life expectancy at birth (in years)						
Men	74.32	77.17	79.35	81.22	83.14	85.08
Women	79.00	81.58	83.79	85.69	87.54	89.41
Five-year immigration flow (in '000)	1433.98	1192.39	1238.84	1267.58	1268.79	1250.78
Five-year emigration flow (in '000)	301.98	234.54	241.59	244.75	244.84	242.37

Human Capital indicators, Medium Scenario (SSP2)	2010	2020	2030	2040	2050	2060
Population age 25+: highest educational attainment						
E1 - no education	0.03	0.02	0.01	0.01	0.01	0.00
E2 - incomplete primary	0.03	0.03	0.02	0.02	0.01	0.01
E3 - primary	0.13	0.10	0.08	0.07	0.06	0.05
E4 - lower secondary	0.15	0.14	0.12	0.10	0.08	0.07
E5 - upper secondary	0.36	0.38	0.39	0.40	0.40	0.39
E6 - post-secondary	0.30	0.34	0.37	0.41	0.44	0.48
Mean years of schooling (in years)	12.03	12.73	13.32	13.84	14.31	14.70
Gender gap (population age 25+): highest educational attainment (ratio male/female)						
E1 - no education	0.80	0.81	0.84	0.87	0.87	0.87
E2 - incomplete primary	0.88	0.91	0.94	0.97	0.98	0.96
E3 - primary	0.80	0.82	0.85	0.90	0.94	0.97
E4 - lower secondary	0.83	0.89	0.93	0.97	1.00	1.01
E5 - upper secondary	1.30	1.25	1.21	1.18	1.15	1.11
E6 - post-secondary	0.92	0.88	0.87	0.88	0.89	0.92
Mean years of schooling (male minus female)	0.26	0.10	−0.01	−0.08	−0.11	−0.10
Women age 20–39: highest educational attainment						
E1 - no education	0.02	0.02	0.01	0.01	0.00	0.00
E2 - incomplete primary	0.03	0.03	0.02	0.01	0.01	0.01
E3 - primary	0.07	0.06	0.06	0.06	0.05	0.04
E4 - lower secondary	0.11	0.09	0.08	0.06	0.05	0.04
E5 - upper secondary	0.41	0.42	0.41	0.41	0.41	0.41
E6 - post-secondary	0.36	0.40	0.42	0.45	0.48	0.50
Mean years of schooling (in years)	13.56	14.27	14.76	14.95	15.10	15.20

Education scenarios

GET: global education trend scenario (medium assumption also used for SSP2)

CER: constant enrolment rates scenario (assumption of no future improvements)

FT: Fast track scenario (assumption of education expansion according to fastest historical experience)

Pyramids by Education, Medium Scenario

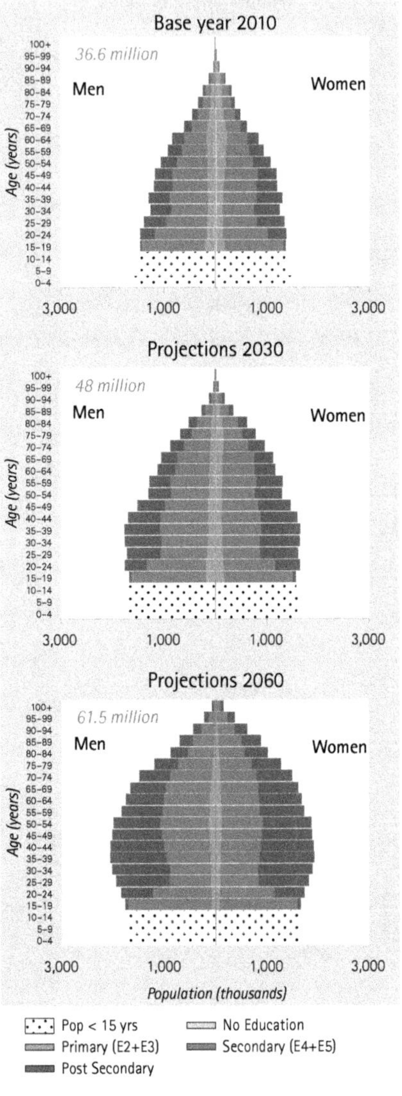

Population Size by Educational Attainment According to Three Education Scenarios: GET, CER, and FT

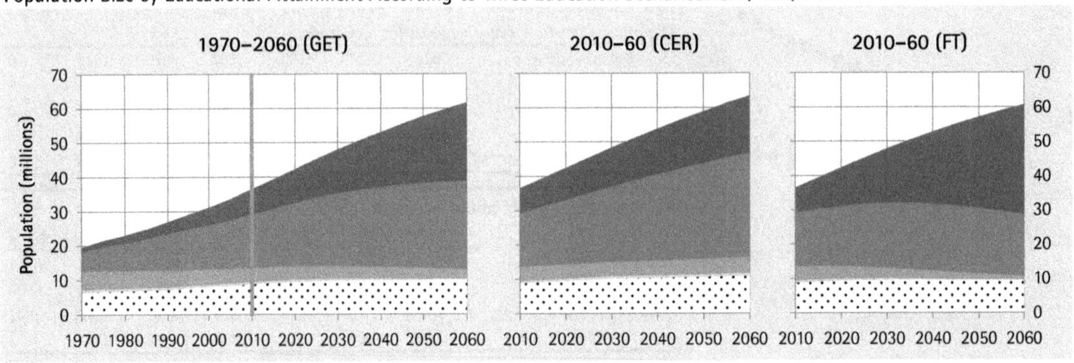

Oceania (Continued)

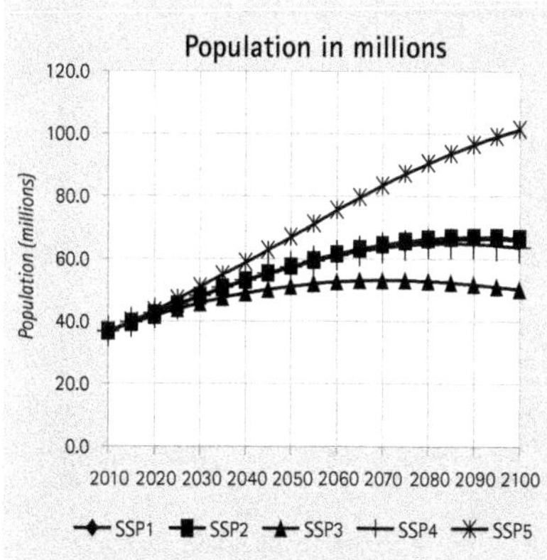

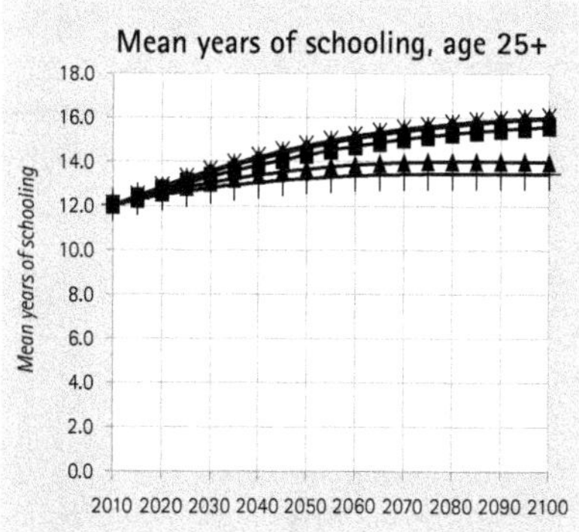

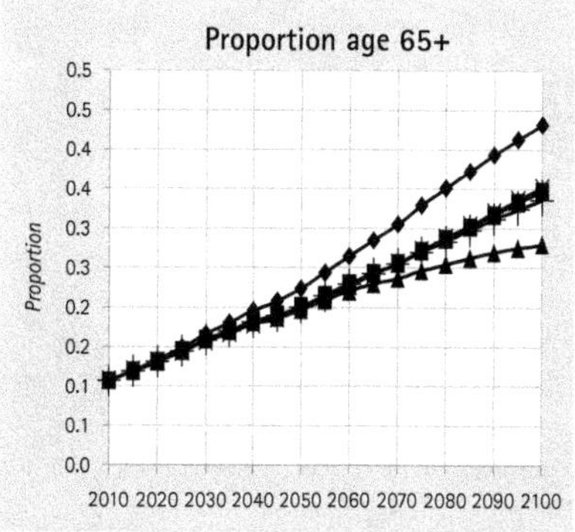

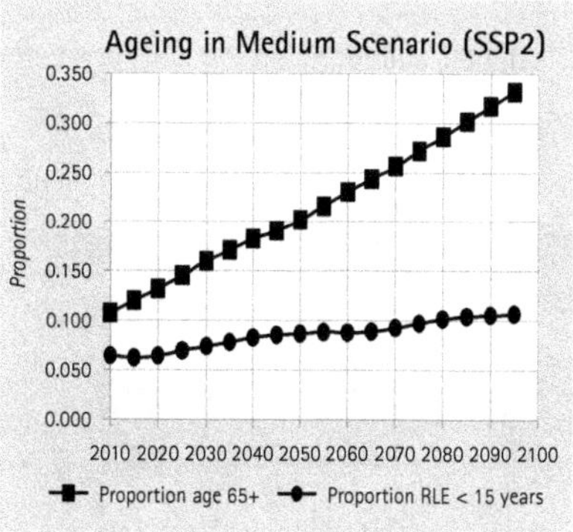

Alternative Scenarios to 2100

Projection Results by Scenario (SSP1–5)

	2010	2020	2030	2040	2050	2075	2100
Population (in millions)							
SSP1 - Rapid development	36.59	42.34	47.89	52.92	57.35	65.01	66.13
SSP2 - Medium	36.59	42.34	47.96	53.05	57.58	65.61	66.72
SSP3 - Stalled development	36.59	41.71	45.78	48.89	51.14	53.05	50.18
SSP4 - Inequality	36.59	42.40	48.07	53.09	57.42	64.39	63.77
SSP5 - Conventional development	36.59	43.20	50.90	58.78	66.93	87.08	101.44
Proportion age 65+							
SSP1 - Rapid development	0.11	0.13	0.17	0.20	0.22	0.33	0.43
SSP2 - Medium	0.11	0.13	0.16	0.18	0.20	0.27	0.35
SSP3 - Stalled development	0.11	0.13	0.16	0.18	0.20	0.25	0.28
SSP4 - Inequality	0.11	0.13	0.16	0.18	0.20	0.27	0.34
SSP5 - Conventional development	0.11	0.13	0.16	0.18	0.20	0.27	0.35
Proportion below age 20							
SSP1 - Rapid development	0.32	0.29	0.26	0.23	0.21	0.17	0.15
SSP2 - Medium	0.32	0.29	0.27	0.25	0.23	0.20	0.18
SSP3 - Stalled development	0.32	0.29	0.27	0.25	0.23	0.21	0.21
SSP4 - Inequality	0.32	0.29	0.27	0.25	0.23	0.20	0.18
SSP5 - Conventional development	0.32	0.29	0.27	0.26	0.24	0.22	0.20
Proportion of Women age 20–39 with at least secondary education							
SSP1 - Rapid development	0.89	0.93	0.94	0.96	0.97	0.99	1.00
SSP2 - Medium	0.89	0.90	0.91	0.92	0.94	0.97	0.99
SSP3 - Stalled development	0.89	0.89	0.87	0.86	0.85	0.83	0.81
SSP4 - Inequality	0.89	0.88	0.86	0.85	0.84	0.83	0.81
SSP5 - Conventional development	0.89	0.93	0.95	0.96	0.98	0.99	1.00
Mean years of schooling, age 25+							
SSP1 - Rapid development	12.03	12.84	13.52	14.11	14.62	15.51	15.96
SSP2 - Medium	12.03	12.73	13.32	13.84	14.31	15.15	15.60
SSP3 - Stalled development	12.03	12.60	13.04	13.39	13.66	13.99	13.99
SSP4 - Inequality	12.03	12.50	12.81	13.06	13.24	13.44	13.46
SSP5 - Conventional development	12.03	12.86	13.58	14.20	14.72	15.61	16.01

Demographic Assumptions Underlying SSPs

	2010–15	2020–25	2030–35	2040–45	2050–55	2075–80	2095–2100
Total fertility rate							
SSP1 - Rapid development	2.25	2.00	1.79	1.69	1.66	1.66	1.67
SSP2 - Medium	2.31	2.17	2.00	1.89	1.84	1.77	1.74
SSP3 - Stalled development	2.30	2.14	1.99	1.91	1.87	1.86	1.88
SSP4 - Inequality	2.29	2.16	2.00	1.89	1.83	1.79	1.80
SSP5 - Conventional development	2.31	2.19	2.07	2.02	2.03	2.08	2.12
Life expectancy at birth for females (in years)							
SSP1 - Rapid development	81.04	84.25	87.29	90.13	92.88	99.77	106.69
SSP2 - Medium	80.41	82.75	84.74	86.62	88.48	93.18	97.13
SSP3 - Stalled development	79.92	80.45	80.84	81.12	81.39	81.94	82.54
SSP4 - Inequality	80.32	81.56	82.70	83.65	84.49	86.20	87.54
SSP5 - Conventional development	81.06	84.34	87.41	90.24	93.00	99.92	106.95
Migration – net flow over five years (in thousands)							
SSP1 - Rapid development	1005	971	995	980	940	371	0
SSP2 - Medium	1011	978	1012	1027	1018	446	0
SSP3 - Stalled development	836	477	476	464	441	182	0
SSP4 - Inequality	1004	969	992	991	973	428	0
SSP5 - Conventional development	1172	1488	1589	1661	1701	784	0

Ageing Indicators, Medium Scenario (SSP2)

	2010	2020	2030	2040	2050	2075	2095
Median age	32.28	33.89	36.22	38.40	40.53	46.07	50.42
Propspective median age	32.28	31.87	32.58	33.33	33.96	35.51	36.16
Proportion age 65+	0.11	0.13	0.16	0.18	0.20	0.27	0.33
Proportion RLE < 15 years	0.06	0.06	0.07	0.08	0.09	0.10	0.11

Albania

Detailed Human Capital Projections to 2060

Demographic indicators, Medium Scenario (SSP2)

	2010	2020	2030	2040	2050	2060
Population (in millions)	3.20	3.32	3.39	3.38	3.31	3.19
Proportion age 65+	0.10	0.12	0.17	0.21	0.26	0.33
Proportion below age 20	0.32	0.25	0.21	0.19	0.16	0.15
	2005–10	2015–20	2025–30	2035–40	2045–50	2055–60
Total Fertility Rate	1.60	1.44	1.49	1.50	1.50	1.51
Life expectancy at birth (in years)						
Men	73.43	75.71	77.88	80.02	82.17	84.25
Women	79.73	81.79	83.79	85.81	87.81	89.80
Five-year immigration flow (in '000)	30.99	30.53	31.74	32.52	32.59	32.15
Five-year emigration flow (in '000)	78.78	58.97	51.05	43.35	38.10	33.10

Human Capital indicators, Medium Scenario (SSP2)

	2010	2020	2030	2040	2050	2060
Population age 25+: highest educational attainment						
E1 - no education	0.03	0.01	0.01	0.00	0.00	0.00
E2 - incomplete primary	0.01	0.00	0.00	0.00	0.00	0.00
E3 - primary	0.08	0.05	0.03	0.02	0.02	0.01
E4 - lower secondary	0.39	0.36	0.32	0.28	0.24	0.19
E5 - upper secondary	0.40	0.47	0.53	0.58	0.61	0.65
E6 - post-secondary	0.09	0.10	0.11	0.12	0.13	0.15
Mean years of schooling (in years)	9.85	10.46	10.94	11.25	11.53	11.80
Gender gap (population age 25+): highest educational attainment (ratio male/female)						
E1 - no education	0.41	0.50	0.74	0.98	1.07	1.06
E2 - incomplete primary	0.82	0.77	0.84	0.93	0.94	0.96
E3 - primary	0.78	0.72	0.82	1.18	1.52	1.55
E4 - lower secondary	0.97	1.01	1.01	1.01	1.03	1.06
E5 - upper secondary	1.08	1.04	1.02	1.01	1.01	1.01
E6 - post-secondary	1.35	1.10	0.95	0.88	0.85	0.87
Mean years of schooling (male minus female)	0.69	0.31	0.07	-0.07	-0.13	-0.14
Women age 20–39: highest educational attainment						
E1 - no education	0.01	0.00	0.00	0.00	0.00	0.00
E2 - incomplete primary	0.00	0.00	0.00	0.00	0.00	0.00
E3 - primary	0.02	0.01	0.01	0.01	0.01	0.00
E4 - lower secondary	0.41	0.31	0.24	0.22	0.20	0.18
E5 - upper secondary	0.47	0.56	0.60	0.62	0.62	0.63
E6 - post-secondary	0.10	0.12	0.14	0.16	0.17	0.19
Mean years of schooling (in years)	10.64	11.24	11.69	11.91	12.04	12.17

Education scenarios

GET : global education trend scenario (medium assumption also used for SSP2)

CER: constant enrolment rates scenario (assumption of no future improvements)

FT: Fast track scenario (assumption of education expansion according to fastest historical experience)

Pyramids by Education, Medium Scenario

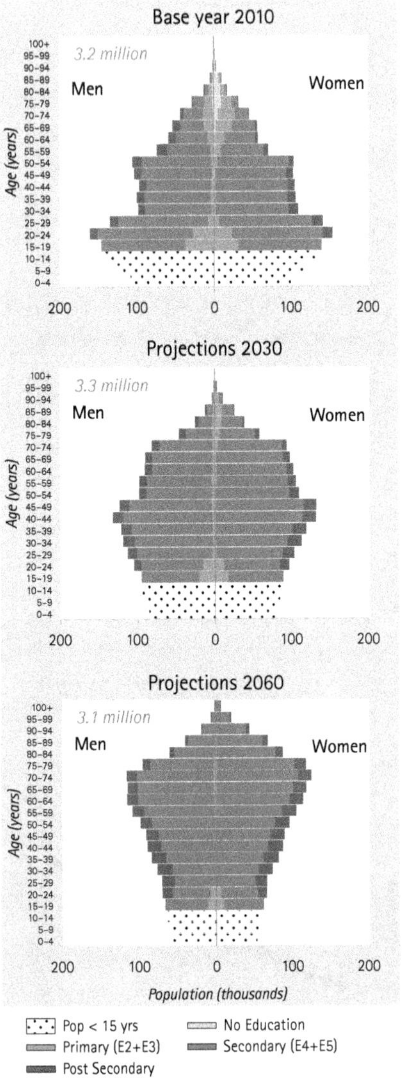

Population Size by Educational Attainment According to Three Education Scenarios: GET, CER, and FT

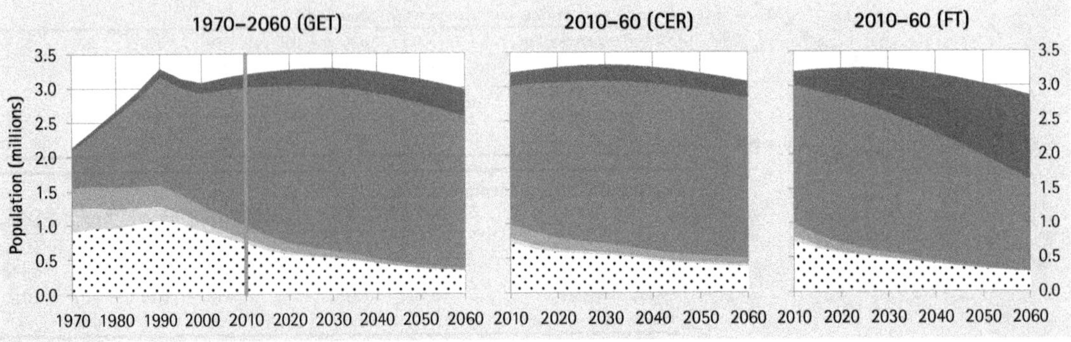

Albania (Continued)

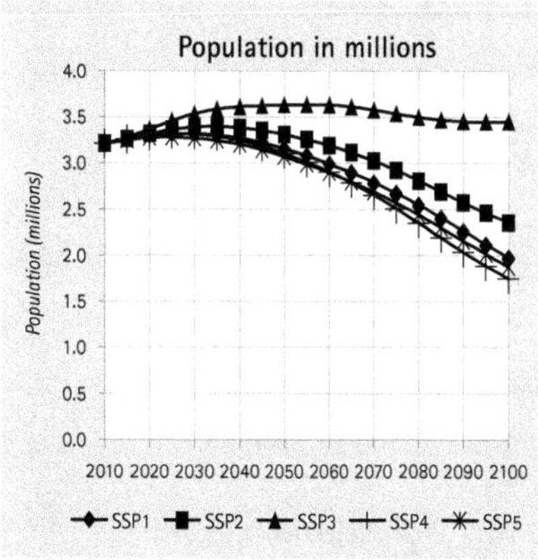

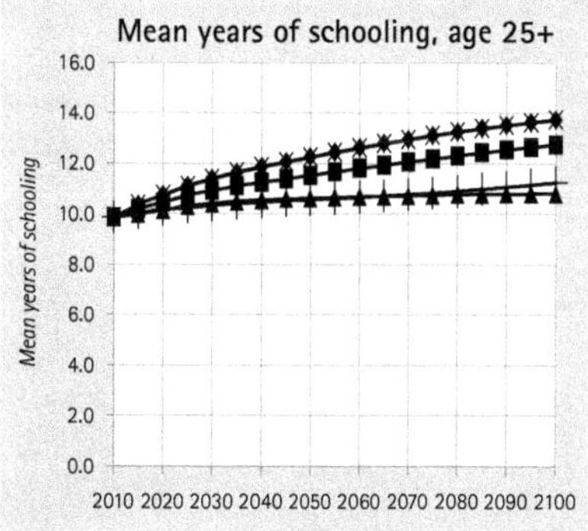

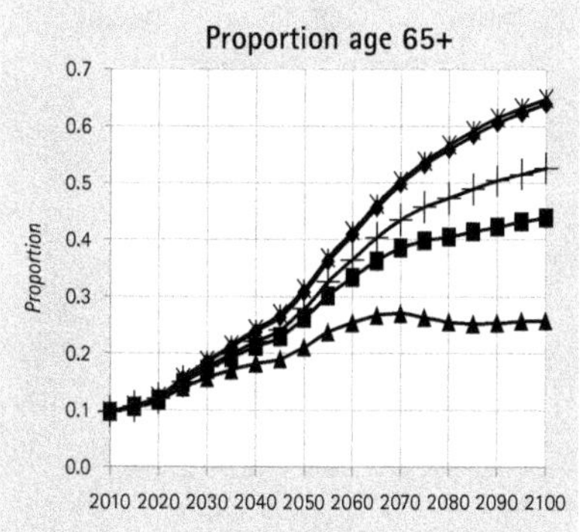

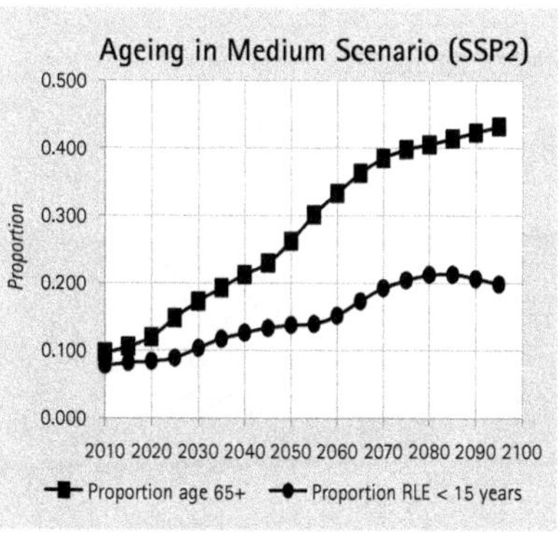

Alternative Scenarios to 2100

Projection Results by Scenario (SSP1–5)

	2010	2020	2030	2040	2050	2075	2100
Population (in millions)							
SSP1 - Rapid development	3.20	3.29	3.32	3.27	3.16	2.67	1.98
SSP2 - Medium	3.20	3.32	3.39	3.38	3.31	2.92	2.36
SSP3 - Stalled development	3.20	3.37	3.53	3.61	3.63	3.53	3.45
SSP4 - Inequality	3.20	3.29	3.31	3.25	3.10	2.51	1.74
SSP5 - Conventional development	3.20	3.27	3.27	3.20	3.07	2.57	1.87
Proportion age 65+							
SSP1 - Rapid development	0.10	0.12	0.18	0.24	0.31	0.53	0.64
SSP2 - Medium	0.10	0.12	0.17	0.21	0.26	0.40	0.44
SSP3 - Stalled development	0.10	0.12	0.16	0.18	0.21	0.26	0.26
SSP4 - Inequality	0.10	0.12	0.18	0.22	0.28	0.46	0.53
SSP5 - Conventional development	0.10	0.12	0.19	0.24	0.31	0.54	0.65
Proportion below age 20							
SSP1 - Rapid development	0.32	0.24	0.19	0.15	0.12	0.08	0.06
SSP2 - Medium	0.32	0.25	0.21	0.19	0.16	0.14	0.14
SSP3 - Stalled development	0.32	0.26	0.24	0.23	0.22	0.22	0.23
SSP4 - Inequality	0.32	0.24	0.19	0.16	0.13	0.10	0.09
SSP5 - Conventional development	0.32	0.24	0.18	0.15	0.12	0.08	0.06
Proportion of Women age 20–39 with at least secondary education							
SSP1 - Rapid development	0.98	0.99	0.99	0.99	1.00	1.00	1.00
SSP2 - Medium	0.98	0.98	0.99	0.99	0.99	1.00	1.00
SSP3 - Stalled development	0.98	0.96	0.96	0.96	0.96	0.96	0.96
SSP4 - Inequality	0.98	0.91	0.87	0.87	0.87	0.87	0.87
SSP5 - Conventional development	0.98	0.99	0.99	0.99	1.00	1.00	1.00
Mean years of schooling, age 25+							
SSP1 - Rapid development	9.85	10.75	11.40	11.87	12.26	13.11	13.74
SSP2 - Medium	9.85	10.46	10.94	11.25	11.53	12.18	12.74
SSP3 - Stalled development	9.85	10.15	10.43	10.56	10.63	10.76	10.81
SSP4 - Inequality	9.85	10.16	10.34	10.47	10.57	10.84	11.24
SSP5 - Conventional development	9.85	10.74	11.39	11.85	12.24	13.09	13.73

Demographic Assumptions Underlying SSPs

	2010–15	2020–25	2030–35	2040–45	2050–55	2075–80	2095–2100
Total fertility rate							
SSP1 - Rapid development	1.33	1.19	1.13	1.10	1.09	1.12	1.15
SSP2 - Medium	1.41	1.46	1.50	1.50	1.50	1.55	1.58
SSP3 - Stalled development	1.52	1.78	1.93	1.98	2.02	2.11	2.18
SSP4 - Inequality	1.36	1.27	1.21	1.18	1.16	1.20	1.23
SSP5 - Conventional development	1.33	1.19	1.13	1.10	1.09	1.12	1.15
Life expectancy at birth for females (in years)							
SSP1 - Rapid development	82.60	85.08	87.80	90.67	93.56	100.98	107.02
SSP2 - Medium	80.69	82.79	84.79	86.81	88.81	93.81	97.80
SSP3 - Stalled development	81.82	82.48	83.21	84.07	84.91	87.05	88.86
SSP4 - Inequality	82.17	83.83	85.49	87.35	89.21	93.71	97.52
SSP5 - Conventional development	82.60	85.08	87.80	90.67	93.56	100.98	107.02
Migration – net flow over five years (in thousands)							
SSP1 - Rapid development	−36	−24	−14	−7	−3	0	0
SSP2 - Medium	−36	−24	−15	−8	−3	0	0
SSP3 - Stalled development	−30	−12	−7	−4	−1	1	0
SSP4 - Inequality	−36	−24	−14	−7	−2	1	0
SSP5 - Conventional development	−42	−36	−22	−12	−5	0	0

Ageing Indicators, Medium Scenario (SSP2)

	2010	2020	2030	2040	2050	2075	2095
Median age	29.97	35.08	40.46	45.38	49.86	56.58	59.32
Propspective median age	29.97	33.38	37.00	40.09	42.78	45.14	44.12
Proportion age 65+	0.10	0.12	0.17	0.21	0.26	0.40	0.43
Proportion RLE < 15 years	0.08	0.08	0.10	0.13	0.14	0.20	0.20

Algeria

Detailed Human Capital Projections to 2060

Demographic indicators, Medium Scenario (SSP2)	2010	2020	2030	2040	2050	2060
Population (in millions)	35.47	40.66	44.80	47.89	50.14	50.91
Proportion age 65+	0.05	0.06	0.09	0.13	0.19	0.24
Proportion below age 20	0.37	0.33	0.30	0.25	0.23	0.22
	2005–10	2015–20	2025–30	2035–40	2045–50	2055–60
Total Fertility Rate	2.38	2.10	1.95	1.87	1.80	1.72
Life expectancy at birth (in years)						
Men	70.86	73.18	75.22	77.18	79.10	81.09
Women	73.70	76.50	78.80	80.89	82.89	84.91
Five-year immigration flow (in '000)	55.75	54.70	56.82	58.10	58.11	57.28
Five-year emigration flow (in '000)	194.98	148.78	148.73	149.03	142.22	134.22

Human Capital indicators, Medium Scenario (SSP2)	2010	2020	2030	2040	2050	2060
Population age 25+: highest educational attainment						
E1 - no education	0.25	0.16	0.10	0.06	0.03	0.02
E2 - incomplete primary	0.05	0.03	0.02	0.02	0.01	0.01
E3 - primary	0.12	0.10	0.09	0.07	0.05	0.04
E4 - lower secondary	0.26	0.27	0.25	0.23	0.19	0.16
E5 - upper secondary	0.23	0.30	0.36	0.41	0.45	0.48
E6 - post-secondary	0.10	0.13	0.17	0.21	0.26	0.30
Mean years of schooling (in years)	7.97	9.34	10.28	11.12	11.82	12.39
Gender gap (population age 25+): highest educational attainment (ratio male/female)						
E1 - no education	0.44	0.38	0.33	0.28	0.25	0.24
E2 - incomplete primary	1.04	0.94	0.85	0.74	0.61	0.50
E3 - primary	1.22	1.12	1.05	0.98	0.91	0.87
E4 - lower secondary	1.55	1.44	1.38	1.32	1.25	1.17
E5 - upper secondary	1.28	1.19	1.16	1.13	1.11	1.08
E6 - post-secondary	1.01	0.88	0.84	0.84	0.87	0.91
Mean years of schooling (male minus female)	2.01	1.41	0.98	0.60	0.31	0.14
Women age 20–39: highest educational attainment						
E1 - no education	0.12	0.04	0.01	0.00	0.00	0.00
E2 - incomplete primary	0.04	0.02	0.01	0.00	0.00	0.00
E3 - primary	0.10	0.07	0.05	0.03	0.02	0.01
E4 - lower secondary	0.27	0.24	0.18	0.13	0.10	0.08
E5 - upper secondary	0.30	0.39	0.44	0.47	0.48	0.47
E6 - post-secondary	0.18	0.24	0.30	0.36	0.41	0.45
Mean years of schooling (in years)	9.93	11.33	12.30	12.92	13.30	13.56

Education scenarios

GET: global education trend scenario (medium assumption also used for SSP2)

CER: constant enrolment rates scenario (assumption of no future improvements)

FT: Fast track scenario (assumption of education expansion according to fastest historical experience)

Pyramids by Education, Medium Scenario

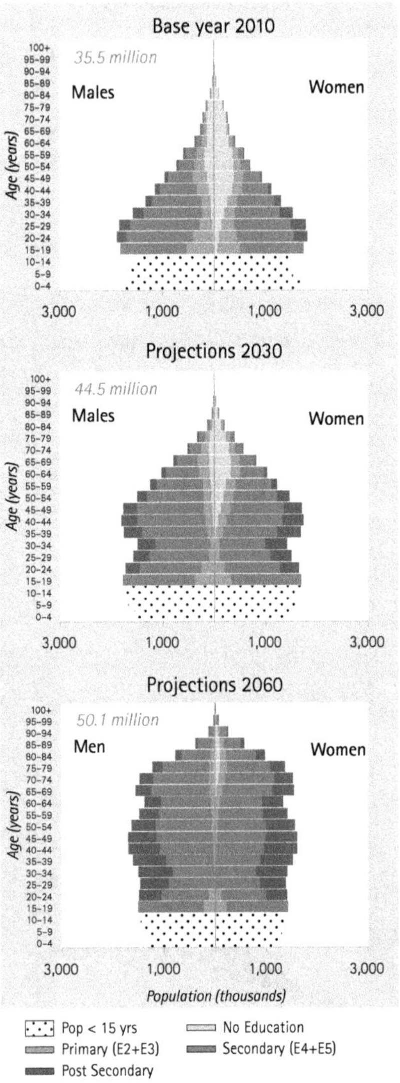

Population Size by Educational Attainment According to Three Education Scenarios: GET, CER, and FT

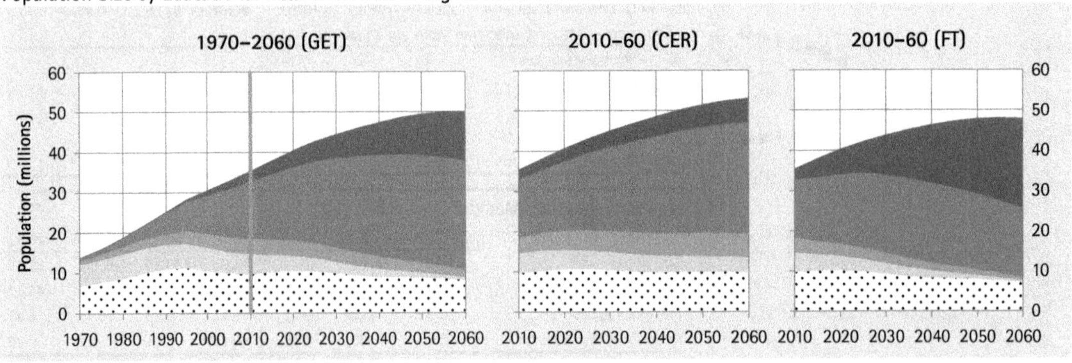

Algeria (Continued)

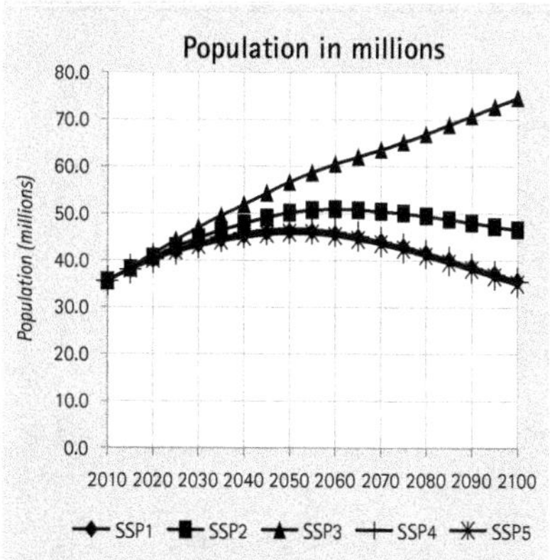

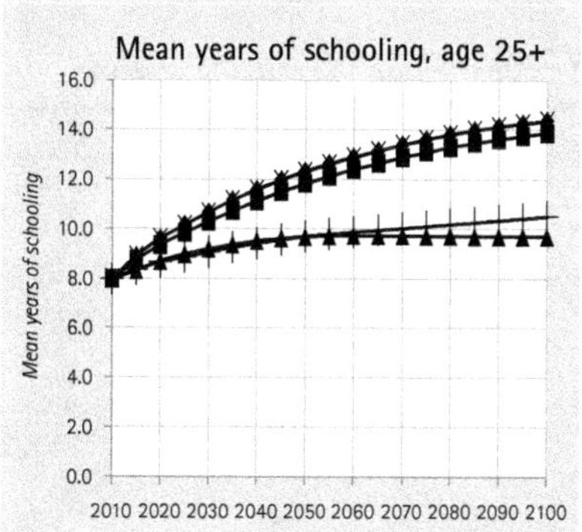

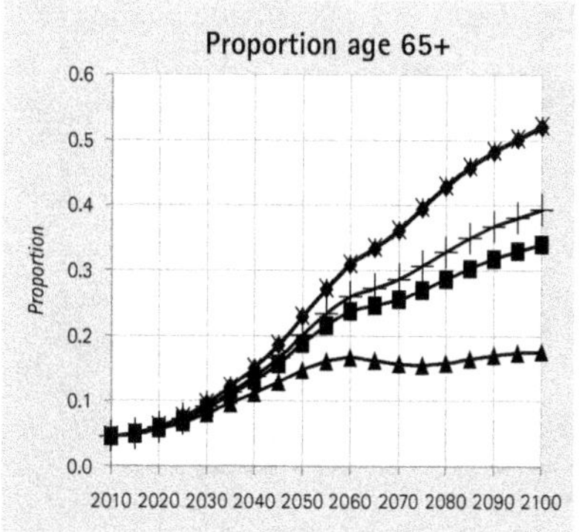

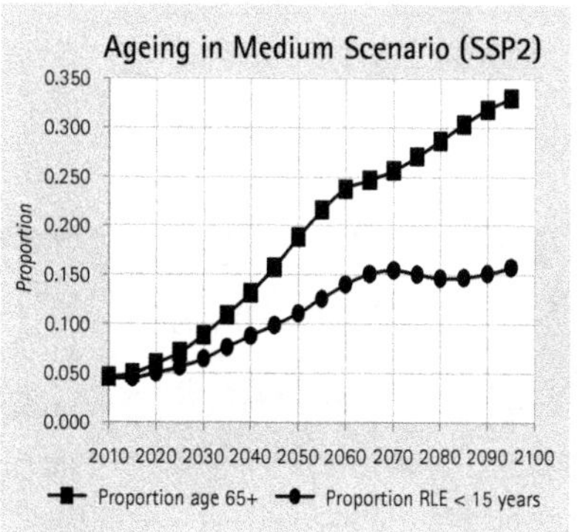

Alternative Scenarios to 2100

Projection Results by Scenario (SSP1–5)

	2010	2020	2030	2040	2050	2075	2100
Population (in millions)							
SSP1 - Rapid development	35.47	40.11	43.23	45.24	46.20	42.98	35.62
SSP2 - Medium	35.47	40.66	44.80	47.89	50.14	50.04	46.54
SSP3 - Stalled development	35.47	41.39	47.06	51.93	56.65	65.19	74.63
SSP4 - Inequality	35.47	40.30	43.70	45.82	46.73	42.70	35.37
SSP5 - Conventional development	35.47	40.05	43.06	44.94	45.76	42.27	34.86
Proportion age 65+							
SSP1 - Rapid development	0.05	0.06	0.10	0.15	0.23	0.39	0.52
SSP2 - Medium	0.05	0.06	0.09	0.13	0.19	0.27	0.34
SSP3 - Stalled development	0.05	0.06	0.08	0.11	0.15	0.16	0.18
SSP4 - Inequality	0.05	0.06	0.09	0.14	0.20	0.31	0.39
SSP5 - Conventional development	0.05	0.06	0.10	0.15	0.23	0.40	0.52
Proportion below age 20							
SSP1 - Rapid development	0.37	0.32	0.26	0.21	0.18	0.12	0.09
SSP2 - Medium	0.37	0.33	0.30	0.25	0.23	0.19	0.17
SSP3 - Stalled development	0.37	0.35	0.33	0.31	0.30	0.29	0.28
SSP4 - Inequality	0.37	0.33	0.28	0.23	0.20	0.16	0.13
SSP5 - Conventional development	0.37	0.32	0.26	0.21	0.18	0.12	0.09
Proportion of Women age 20–39 with at least secondary education							
SSP1 - Rapid development	0.75	0.90	0.96	0.98	0.99	1.00	1.00
SSP2 - Medium	0.75	0.86	0.93	0.97	0.98	1.00	1.00
SSP3 - Stalled development	0.75	0.73	0.73	0.73	0.73	0.73	0.73
SSP4 - Inequality	0.75	0.69	0.66	0.66	0.66	0.66	0.66
SSP5 - Conventional development	0.75	0.90	0.96	0.98	0.99	1.00	1.00
Mean years of schooling, age 25+							
SSP1 - Rapid development	7.97	9.60	10.66	11.58	12.31	13.61	14.37
SSP2 - Medium	7.97	9.34	10.28	11.12	11.82	13.10	13.87
SSP3 - Stalled development	7.97	8.69	9.19	9.51	9.68	9.72	9.71
SSP4 - Inequality	7.97	8.65	9.06	9.42	9.68	10.10	10.51
SSP5 - Conventional development	7.97	9.60	10.66	11.58	12.30	13.61	14.36

Demographic Assumptions Underlying SSPs

	2010–15	2020–25	2030–35	2040–45	2050–55	2075–80	2095–2100
Total fertility rate							
SSP1 - Rapid development	2.07	1.67	1.45	1.35	1.28	1.17	1.17
SSP2 - Medium	2.20	2.03	1.90	1.85	1.75	1.60	1.60
SSP3 - Stalled development	2.35	2.49	2.56	2.56	2.51	2.35	2.36
SSP4 - Inequality	2.12	1.83	1.63	1.53	1.45	1.33	1.33
SSP5 - Conventional development	2.07	1.67	1.45	1.35	1.28	1.17	1.17
Life expectancy at birth for females (in years)							
SSP1 - Rapid development	77.27	80.29	83.24	86.13	88.97	96.29	102.19
SSP2 - Medium	75.21	77.70	79.89	81.89	83.89	89.00	92.99
SSP3 - Stalled development	76.57	77.59	78.65	79.45	80.14	81.81	83.47
SSP4 - Inequality	76.91	78.98	80.94	82.65	84.32	88.57	92.20
SSP5 - Conventional development	77.27	80.29	83.24	86.13	88.97	96.29	102.19
Migration – net flow over five years (in thousands)							
SSP1 - Rapid development	−109	−91	−89	−82	−71	−24	0
SSP2 - Medium	−107	−91	−91	−88	−80	−31	0
SSP3 - Stalled development	−91	−46	−46	−45	−42	−19	0
SSP4 - Inequality	−109	−91	−88	−80	−67	−21	0
SSP5 - Conventional development	−127	−139	−140	−134	−120	−46	0

Ageing Indicators, Medium Scenario (SSP2)

	2010	2020	2030	2040	2050	2075	2095
Median age	26.14	30.43	34.58	37.50	40.47	47.09	50.91
Propspective median age	26.14	28.80	31.29	32.65	33.95	36.11	36.24
Proportion age 65+	0.05	0.06	0.09	0.13	0.19	0.27	0.33
Proportion RLE < 15 years	0.05	0.05	0.06	0.09	0.11	0.15	0.16

Argentina

Detailed Human Capital Projections to 2060

Demographic indicators, Medium Scenario (SSP2)	2010	2020	2030	2040	2050	2060
Population (in millions)	40.41	43.70	46.44	48.59	49.98	50.56
Proportion age 65+	0.11	0.12	0.14	0.16	0.20	0.24
Proportion below age 20	0.33	0.30	0.28	0.25	0.23	0.21
	2005–10	2015–20	2025–30	2035–40	2045–50	2055–60
Total Fertility Rate	2.25	2.08	1.97	1.91	1.81	1.72
Life expectancy at birth (in years)						
Men	71.52	73.49	75.37	77.32	79.32	81.67
Women	79.06	81.09	82.99	84.81	86.61	88.69
Five-year immigration flow (in '000)	78.54	76.94	79.88	81.66	81.65	80.46
Five-year emigration flow (in '000)	277.86	212.91	209.44	204.46	195.63	186.13

Human Capital indicators, Medium Scenario (SSP2)	2010	2020	2030	2040	2050	2060
Population age 25+: highest educational attainment						
E1 - no education	0.03	0.02	0.01	0.01	0.01	0.00
E2 - incomplete primary	0.12	0.08	0.06	0.04	0.02	0.02
E3 - primary	0.30	0.26	0.23	0.19	0.16	0.13
E4 - lower secondary	0.13	0.14	0.13	0.12	0.11	0.09
E5 - upper secondary	0.28	0.33	0.37	0.40	0.43	0.45
E6 - post-secondary	0.14	0.17	0.20	0.24	0.27	0.31
Mean years of schooling (in years)	9.72	10.37	10.92	11.42	11.87	12.27
Gender gap (population age 25+): highest educational attainment (ratio male/female)						
E1 - no education	0.87	0.87	0.85	0.83	0.81	0.78
E2 - incomplete primary	0.95	0.93	0.92	0.89	0.87	0.84
E3 - primary	1.08	1.11	1.13	1.13	1.12	1.10
E4 - lower secondary	1.27	1.25	1.22	1.19	1.15	1.10
E5 - upper secondary	1.05	1.09	1.13	1.14	1.14	1.12
E6 - post-secondary	0.65	0.63	0.63	0.67	0.73	0.80
Mean years of schooling (male minus female)	-0.27	-0.40	-0.48	-0.49	-0.44	-0.34
Women age 20–39: highest educational attainment						
E1 - no education	0.01	0.01	0.00	0.00	0.00	0.00
E2 - incomplete primary	0.05	0.03	0.01	0.01	0.00	0.00
E3 - primary	0.21	0.17	0.14	0.10	0.08	0.06
E4 - lower secondary	0.14	0.12	0.10	0.09	0.07	0.06
E5 - upper secondary	0.42	0.46	0.49	0.52	0.54	0.56
E6 - post-secondary	0.18	0.21	0.25	0.28	0.30	0.32
Mean years of schooling (in years)	11.11	11.51	11.90	12.31	12.63	12.85

Education scenarios

GET: global education trend scenario (medium assumption also used for SSP2)

CER: constant enrolment rates scenario (assumption of no future improvements)

FT: Fast track scenario (assumption of education expansion according to fastest historical experience)

Pyramids by Education, Medium Scenario

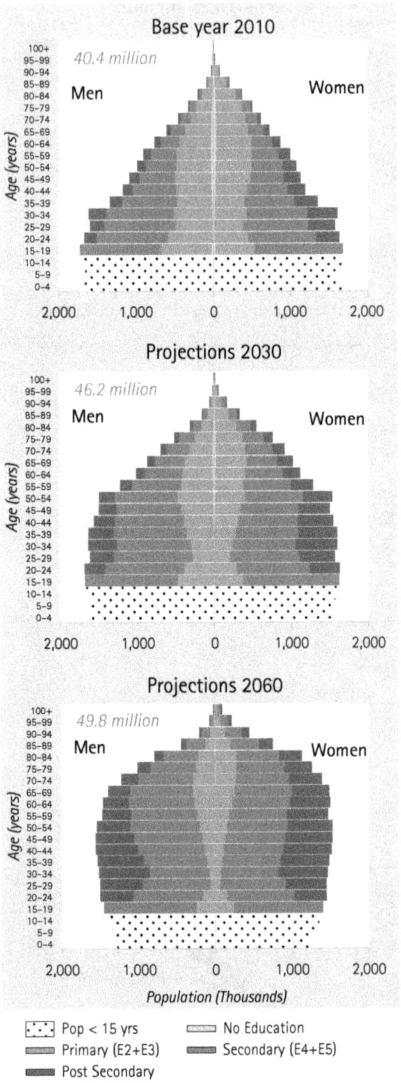

Population Size by Educational Attainment According to Three Education Scenarios: GET, CER, and FT

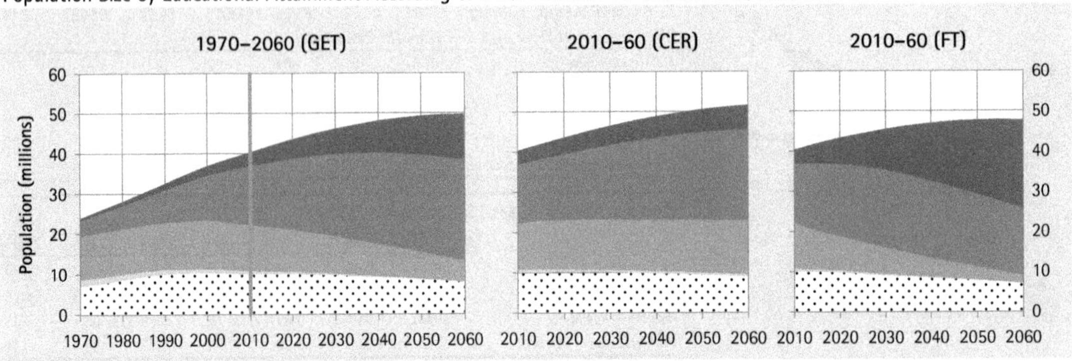

Argentina (Continued)

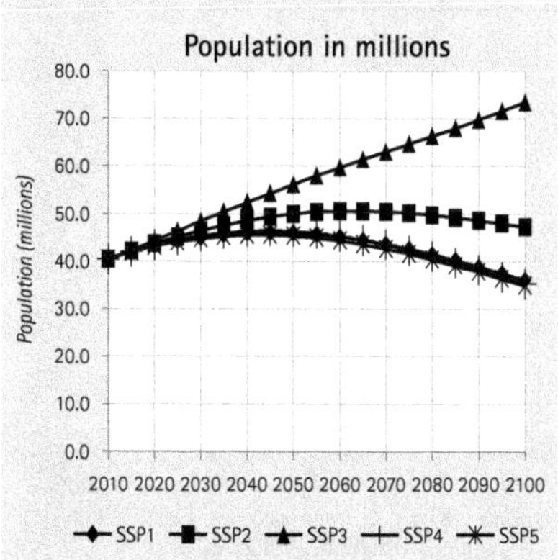

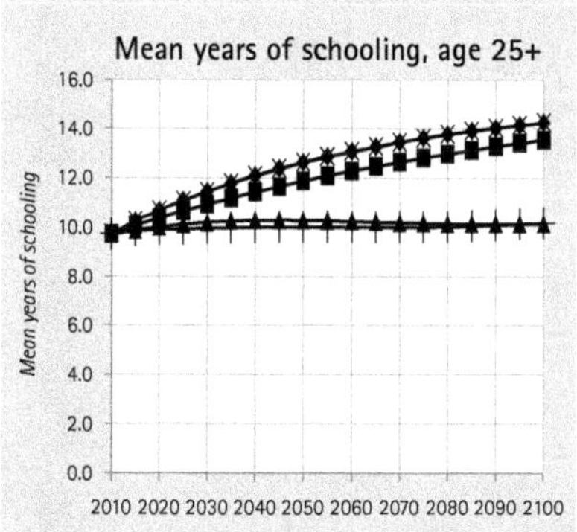

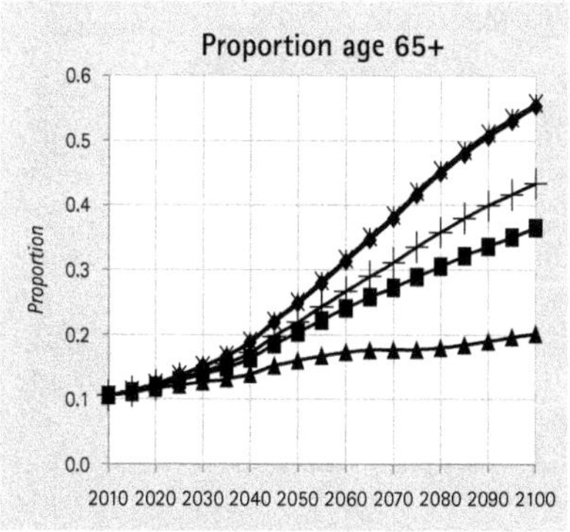

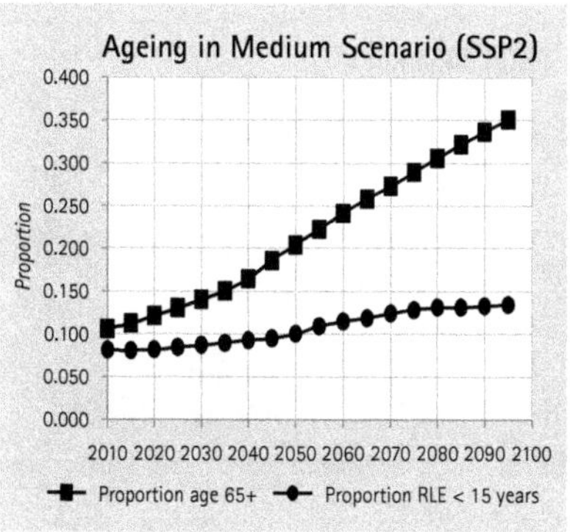

Alternative Scenarios to 2100

Projection Results by Scenario (SSP1–5)

	2010	2020	2030	2040	2050	2075	2100
Population (in millions)							
SSP1 - Rapid development	40.41	43.23	44.99	45.96	45.96	42.64	36.01
SSP2 - Medium	40.41	43.70	46.44	48.59	49.98	50.19	47.29
SSP3 - Stalled development	40.41	44.31	48.44	52.36	56.17	64.65	73.43
SSP4 - Inequality	40.41	43.36	45.29	46.31	46.28	42.31	35.18
SSP5 - Conventional development	40.41	43.14	44.74	45.51	45.32	41.57	34.81
Proportion age 65+							
SSP1 - Rapid development	0.11	0.12	0.15	0.19	0.25	0.42	0.55
SSP2 - Medium	0.11	0.12	0.14	0.16	0.20	0.29	0.37
SSP3 - Stalled development	0.11	0.12	0.13	0.14	0.16	0.18	0.20
SSP4 - Inequality	0.11	0.12	0.14	0.17	0.22	0.34	0.43
SSP5 - Conventional development	0.11	0.12	0.15	0.19	0.25	0.42	0.56
Proportion below age 20							
SSP1 - Rapid development	0.33	0.29	0.25	0.21	0.18	0.12	0.08
SSP2 - Medium	0.33	0.30	0.28	0.25	0.23	0.19	0.16
SSP3 - Stalled development	0.33	0.32	0.31	0.31	0.30	0.28	0.27
SSP4 - Inequality	0.33	0.30	0.26	0.23	0.20	0.15	0.12
SSP5 - Conventional development	0.33	0.29	0.25	0.20	0.17	0.11	0.08
Proportion of Women age 20–39 with at least secondary education							
SSP1 - Rapid development	0.74	0.87	0.91	0.94	0.95	0.98	0.99
SSP2 - Medium	0.74	0.80	0.85	0.89	0.92	0.97	0.99
SSP3 - Stalled development	0.74	0.70	0.70	0.70	0.70	0.70	0.70
SSP4 - Inequality	0.74	0.66	0.63	0.63	0.63	0.63	0.63
SSP5 - Conventional development	0.74	0.87	0.91	0.94	0.95	0.98	0.99
Mean years of schooling, age 25+							
SSP1 - Rapid development	9.72	10.67	11.43	12.09	12.62	13.62	14.24
SSP2 - Medium	9.72	10.37	10.92	11.42	11.87	12.81	13.54
SSP3 - Stalled development	9.72	10.00	10.19	10.27	10.28	10.16	10.14
SSP4 - Inequality	9.72	9.90	9.94	9.99	10.00	10.00	10.18
SSP5 - Conventional development	9.72	10.67	11.43	12.08	12.62	13.61	14.24

Demographic Assumptions Underlying SSPs

	2010–15	2020–25	2030–35	2040–45	2050–55	2075–80	2095–2100
Total fertility rate							
SSP1 - Rapid development	2.01	1.66	1.47	1.37	1.29	1.19	1.20
SSP2 - Medium	2.14	2.02	1.93	1.85	1.76	1.60	1.62
SSP3 - Stalled development	2.28	2.44	2.50	2.46	2.39	2.23	2.27
SSP4 - Inequality	2.06	1.81	1.62	1.51	1.42	1.32	1.33
SSP5 - Conventional development	2.01	1.66	1.47	1.37	1.29	1.19	1.20
Life expectancy at birth for females (in years)							
SSP1 - Rapid development	81.51	84.17	86.89	89.53	92.43	100.51	106.98
SSP2 - Medium	80.09	82.09	83.89	85.61	87.61	93.20	97.70
SSP3 - Stalled development	80.64	81.39	82.13	82.73	83.51	86.05	88.21
SSP4 - Inequality	81.07	82.83	84.44	85.99	87.78	92.81	97.03
SSP5 - Conventional development	81.51	84.17	86.89	89.53	92.43	100.51	106.98
Migration – net flow over five years (in thousands)							
SSP1 - Rapid development	−155	−131	−122	−108	−94	−30	0
SSP2 - Medium	−152	−131	−126	−118	−109	−42	0
SSP3 - Stalled development	−129	−66	−63	−61	−59	−26	0
SSP4 - Inequality	−155	−131	−121	−106	−88	−25	0
SSP5 - Conventional development	−181	−200	−192	−176	−160	−58	0

Ageing Indicators, Medium Scenario (SSP2)

	2010	2020	2030	2040	2050	2075	2095
Median age	30.35	32.95	35.82	38.54	41.13	47.70	52.47
Propspective median age	30.35	31.25	32.51	33.67	34.36	35.67	36.10
Proportion age 65+	0.11	0.12	0.14	0.16	0.20	0.29	0.35
Proportion RLE < 15 years	0.08	0.08	0.09	0.09	0.10	0.13	0.13

Armenia

Detailed Human Capital Projections to 2060

Demographic indicators, Medium Scenario (SSP2)	2010	2020	2030	2040	2050	2060
Population (in millions)	3.09	3.09	3.04	2.99	2.88	2.77
Proportion age 65+	0.11	0.13	0.19	0.20	0.24	0.30
Proportion below age 20	0.29	0.26	0.23	0.21	0.20	0.19
	2005–10	2015–20	2025–30	2035–40	2045–50	2055–60
Total Fertility Rate	1.74	1.56	1.67	1.70	1.70	1.70
Life expectancy at birth (in years)						
Men	70.21	72.01	74.08	76.26	78.31	80.42
Women	76.73	78.19	79.99	81.99	83.89	85.92
Five-year immigration flow (in '000)	23.91	23.47	24.34	24.94	25.03	24.72
Five-year emigration flow (in '000)	98.72	70.59	61.49	53.99	48.05	43.32

Human Capital indicators, Medium Scenario (SSP2)	2010	2020	2030	2040	2050	2060
Population age 25+: highest educational attainment						
E1 - no education	0.01	0.00	0.00	0.00	0.00	0.00
E2 - incomplete primary	0.01	0.00	0.00	0.00	0.00	0.00
E3 - primary	0.03	0.02	0.01	0.00	0.00	0.00
E4 - lower secondary	0.08	0.06	0.04	0.03	0.02	0.01
E5 - upper secondary	0.65	0.68	0.69	0.69	0.69	0.67
E6 - post-secondary	0.22	0.24	0.25	0.27	0.29	0.31
Mean years of schooling (in years)	10.35	10.67	10.84	10.96	11.06	11.17
Gender gap (population age 25+): highest educational attainment (ratio male/female)						
E1 - no education	0.55	0.55	0.67	0.81	0.87	0.93
E2 - incomplete primary	0.51	0.51	0.55	0.61	0.68	0.78
E3 - primary	0.90	0.88	1.05	1.27	1.35	1.36
E4 - lower secondary	1.16	1.20	1.26	1.29	1.29	1.30
E5 - upper secondary	1.00	1.02	1.03	1.04	1.04	1.04
E6 - post-secondary	1.01	0.93	0.89	0.88	0.88	0.90
Mean years of schooling (male minus female)	0.09	−0.04	−0.12	−0.15	−0.16	−0.13
Women age 20–39: highest educational attainment						
E1 - no education	0.00	0.00	0.00	0.00	0.00	0.00
E2 - incomplete primary	0.00	0.00	0.00	0.00	0.00	0.00
E3 - primary	0.01	0.00	0.00	0.00	0.00	0.00
E4 - lower secondary	0.05	0.03	0.03	0.03	0.02	0.03
E5 - upper secondary	0.70	0.69	0.68	0.66	0.64	0.62
E6 - post-secondary	0.25	0.28	0.29	0.31	0.33	0.35
Mean years of schooling (in years)	10.84	11.00	11.07	11.18	11.26	11.32

Education scenarios

GET : global education trend scenario (medium assumption also used for SSP2)

CER: constant enrolment rates scenario (assumption of no future improvements)

FT: Fast track scenario (assumption of education expansion according to fastest historical experience)

Pyramids by Education, Medium Scenario

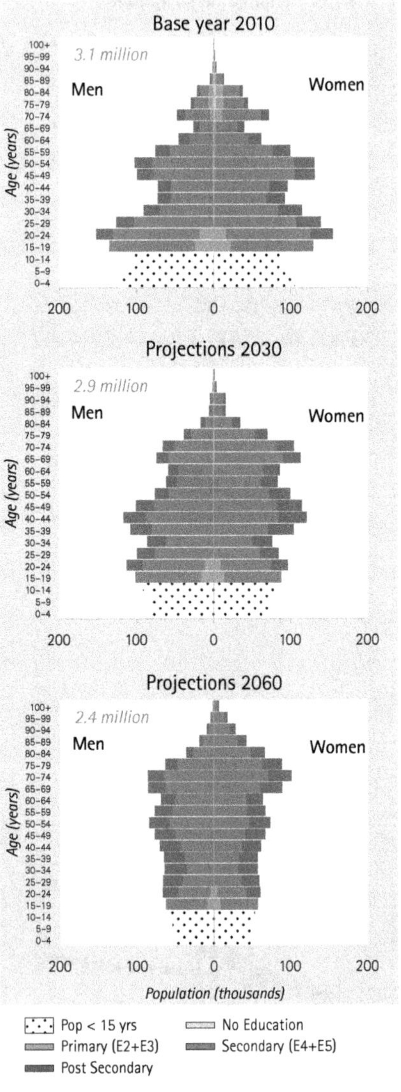

Population Size by Educational Attainment According to Three Education Scenarios: GET, CER, and FT

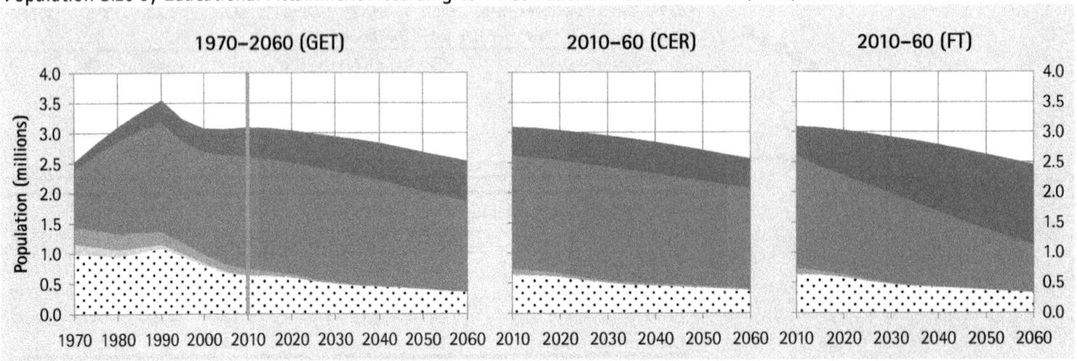

Armenia (Continued)

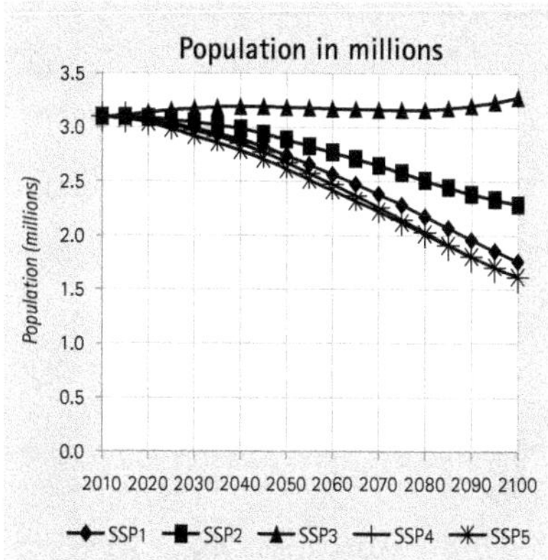

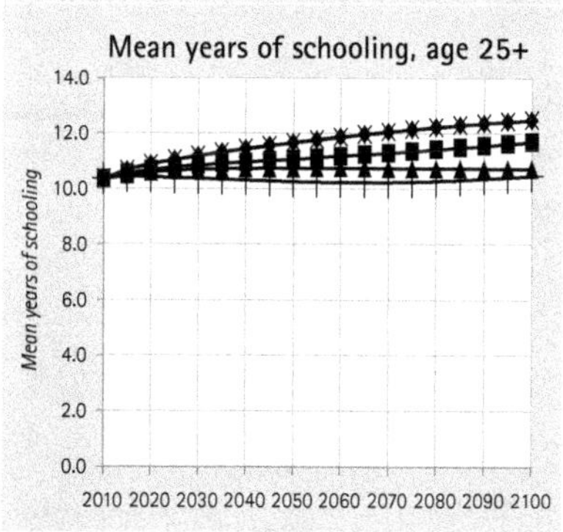

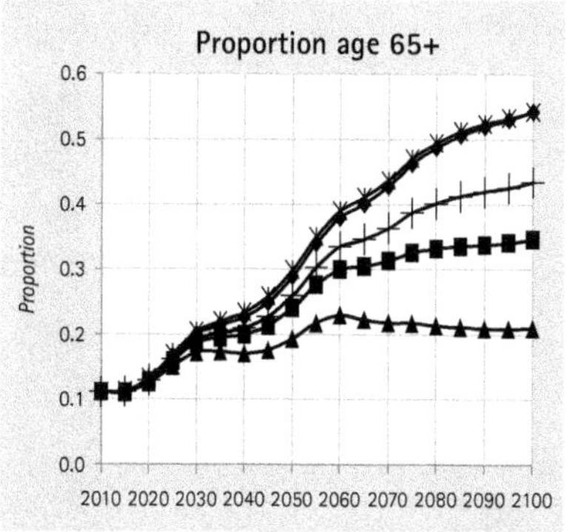

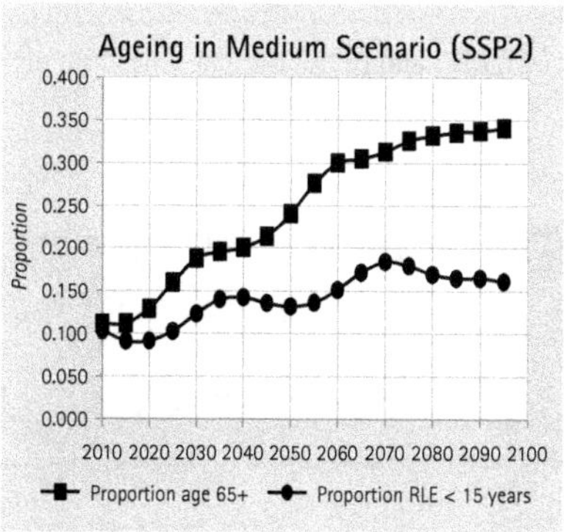

Alternative Scenarios to 2100

Projection Results by Scenario (SSP1–5)

	2010	2020	2030	2040	2050	2075	2100
Population (in millions)							
SSP1 - Rapid development	3.09	3.07	2.99	2.89	2.74	2.28	1.76
SSP2 - Medium	3.09	3.09	3.04	2.99	2.88	2.58	2.29
SSP3 - Stalled development	3.09	3.14	3.17	3.19	3.18	3.16	3.27
SSP4 - Inequality	3.09	3.06	2.97	2.85	2.67	2.14	1.61
SSP5 - Conventional development	3.09	3.04	2.92	2.78	2.61	2.12	1.62
Proportion age 65+							
SSP1 - Rapid development	0.11	0.13	0.20	0.23	0.29	0.46	0.54
SSP2 - Medium	0.11	0.13	0.19	0.20	0.24	0.33	0.35
SSP3 - Stalled development	0.11	0.12	0.17	0.17	0.19	0.22	0.21
SSP4 - Inequality	0.11	0.13	0.19	0.21	0.26	0.39	0.43
SSP5 - Conventional development	0.11	0.13	0.20	0.23	0.30	0.47	0.54
Proportion below age 20							
SSP1 - Rapid development	0.29	0.25	0.20	0.17	0.15	0.11	0.09
SSP2 - Medium	0.29	0.26	0.23	0.21	0.20	0.19	0.18
SSP3 - Stalled development	0.29	0.27	0.25	0.24	0.25	0.25	0.26
SSP4 - Inequality	0.29	0.25	0.21	0.18	0.16	0.13	0.12
SSP5 - Conventional development	0.29	0.25	0.20	0.17	0.15	0.11	0.10
Proportion of Women age 20–39 with at least secondary education							
SSP1 - Rapid development	0.99	1.00	1.00	1.00	1.00	1.00	1.00
SSP2 - Medium	0.99	1.00	1.00	1.00	1.00	1.00	1.00
SSP3 - Stalled development	0.99	0.99	0.99	0.99	0.99	0.99	0.99
SSP4 - Inequality	0.99	0.93	0.89	0.89	0.89	0.89	0.89
SSP5 - Conventional development	0.99	1.00	1.00	1.00	1.00	1.00	1.00
Mean years of schooling, age 25+							
SSP1 - Rapid development	10.35	10.88	11.19	11.44	11.66	12.13	12.47
SSP2 - Medium	10.35	10.67	10.84	10.96	11.06	11.35	11.69
SSP3 - Stalled development	10.35	10.59	10.69	10.72	10.74	10.73	10.73
SSP4 - Inequality	10.35	10.42	10.37	10.31	10.26	10.25	10.47
SSP5 - Conventional development	10.35	10.88	11.18	11.43	11.65	12.13	12.47

Demographic Assumptions Underlying SSPs

	2010–15	2020–25	2030–35	2040–45	2050–55	2075–80	2095–2100
Total fertility rate							
SSP1 - Rapid development	1.42	1.34	1.30	1.27	1.25	1.26	1.27
SSP2 - Medium	1.50	1.61	1.70	1.70	1.70	1.71	1.72
SSP3 - Stalled development	1.59	1.88	2.08	2.15	2.18	2.20	2.23
SSP4 - Inequality	1.44	1.40	1.36	1.34	1.32	1.33	1.33
SSP5 - Conventional development	1.42	1.34	1.30	1.27	1.25	1.26	1.27
Life expectancy at birth for females (in years)							
SSP1 - Rapid development	79.72	81.82	84.32	87.09	89.90	97.19	103.15
SSP2 - Medium	77.40	79.09	80.99	82.89	84.89	89.89	93.91
SSP3 - Stalled development	78.93	79.28	80.03	80.79	81.60	83.72	85.50
SSP4 - Inequality	79.29	80.51	82.09	83.74	85.49	89.98	93.79
SSP5 - Conventional development	79.72	81.82	84.32	87.09	89.90	97.19	103.15
Migration – net flow over five years (in thousands)							
SSP1 - Rapid development	–59	–42	–32	–24	–18	–5	0
SSP2 - Medium	–59	–42	–33	–26	–21	–7	0
SSP3 - Stalled development	–49	–21	–17	–13	–11	–3	0
SSP4 - Inequality	–59	–41	–31	–23	–16	–4	0
SSP5 - Conventional development	–69	–62	–48	–37	–29	–10	0

Ageing Indicators, Medium Scenario (SSP2)

	2010	2020	2030	2040	2050	2075	2095
Median age	31.90	35.86	40.78	44.66	46.18	50.28	51.13
Propspective median age	31.90	34.44	37.65	39.95	39.68	39.38	36.32
Proportion age 65+	0.11	0.13	0.19	0.20	0.24	0.33	0.34
Proportion RLE < 15 years	0.10	0.09	0.12	0.14	0.13	0.18	0.16

Aruba

Detailed Human Capital Projections to 2060

Demographic indicators, Medium Scenario (SSP2)	2010	2020	2030	2040	2050	2060
Population (in millions)	0.11	0.12	0.13	0.14	0.15	0.15
Proportion age 65+	0.10	0.13	0.20	0.23	0.23	0.26
Proportion below age 20	0.27	0.22	0.21	0.20	0.18	0.17
	2005–10	2015–20	2025–30	2035–40	2045–50	2055–60
Total Fertility Rate	1.74	1.58	1.53	1.48	1.44	1.47
Life expectancy at birth (in years)						
Men	72.29	75.38	77.78	79.89	82.00	84.07
Women	77.09	80.09	82.39	84.49	86.61	88.61
Five-year immigration flow (in '000)	4.68	4.59	4.76	4.87	4.88	4.81
Five-year emigration flow (in '000)	0.69	0.56	0.55	0.54	0.56	0.55

Human Capital indicators, Medium Scenario (SSP2)	2010	2020	2030	2040	2050	2060
Population age 25+: highest educational attainment						
E1 - no education	0.08	0.06	0.04	0.03	0.02	0.01
E2 - incomplete primary	0.08	0.05	0.03	0.02	0.01	0.01
E3 - primary	0.23	0.20	0.18	0.15	0.13	0.10
E4 - lower secondary	0.29	0.30	0.29	0.27	0.24	0.21
E5 - upper secondary	0.09	0.11	0.13	0.15	0.16	0.18
E6 - post-secondary	0.23	0.28	0.33	0.39	0.44	0.49
Mean years of schooling (in years)	8.59	9.35	10.06	10.69	11.28	11.82
Gender gap (population age 25+): highest educational attainment (ratio male/female)						
E1 - no education	0.82	0.83	0.85	0.87	0.91	0.97
E2 - incomplete primary	0.88	0.87	0.89	0.91	0.92	0.94
E3 - primary	0.92	0.97	1.02	1.07	1.11	1.13
E4 - lower secondary	1.17	1.17	1.17	1.17	1.17	1.15
E5 - upper secondary	0.80	0.82	0.86	0.90	0.94	0.97
E6 - post-secondary	1.08	0.99	0.95	0.92	0.92	0.93
Mean years of schooling (male minus female)	0.29	0.07	−0.11	−0.23	−0.28	−0.26
Women age 20–39: highest educational attainment						
E1 - no education	0.03	0.01	0.01	0.00	0.00	0.00
E2 - incomplete primary	0.02	0.01	0.00	0.00	0.00	0.00
E3 - primary	0.19	0.14	0.11	0.08	0.06	0.05
E4 - lower secondary	0.29	0.29	0.25	0.22	0.20	0.17
E5 - upper secondary	0.19	0.22	0.23	0.26	0.27	0.28
E6 - post-secondary	0.27	0.33	0.40	0.43	0.46	0.50
Mean years of schooling (in years)	9.96	10.68	11.36	11.75	12.04	12.30

Education scenarios

GET: global education trend scenario (medium assumption also used for SSP2)

CER: constant enrolment rates scenario (assumption of no future improvements)

FT: Fast track scenario (assumption of education expansion according to fastest historical experience)

Pyramids by Education, Medium Scenario

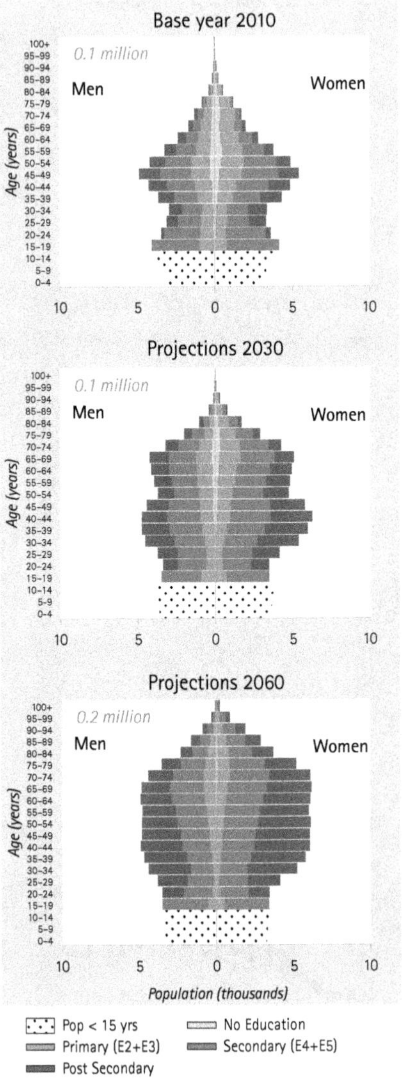

Population Size by Educational Attainment According to Three Education Scenarios: GET, CER, and FT

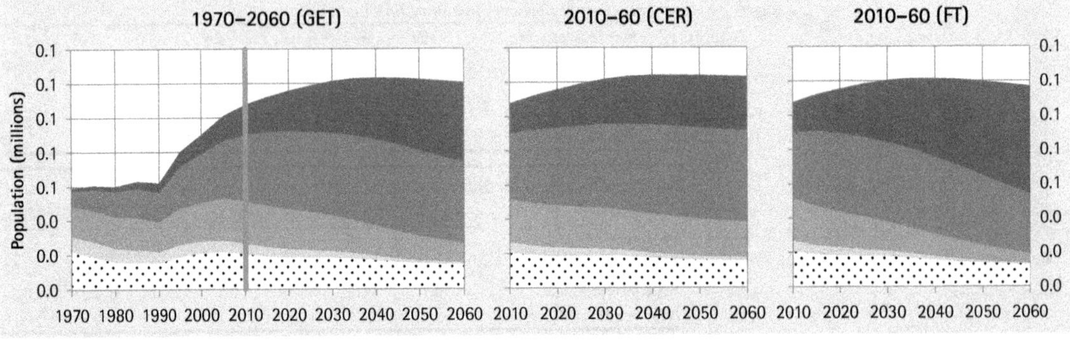

Aruba (Continued)

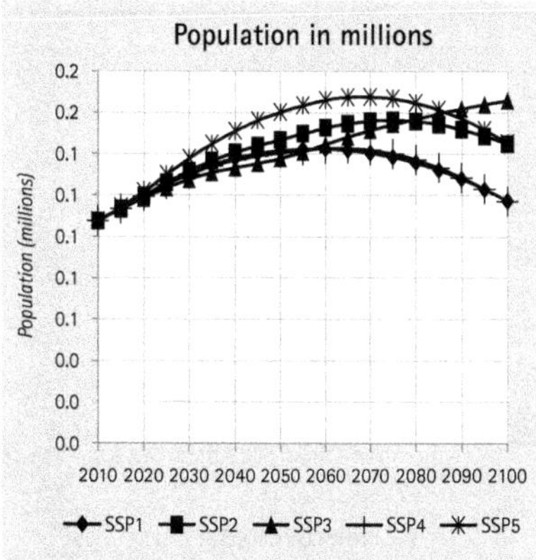

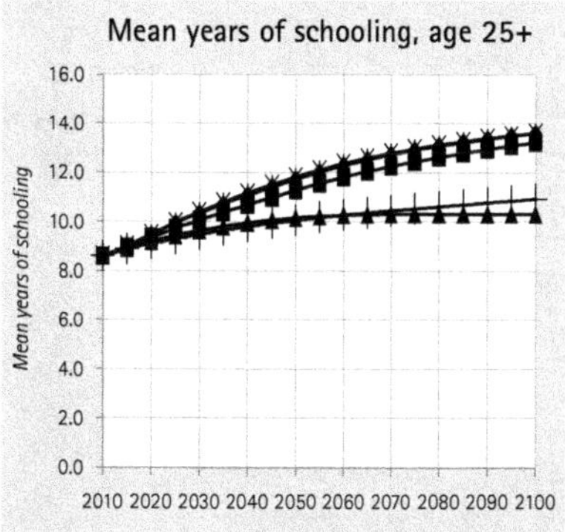

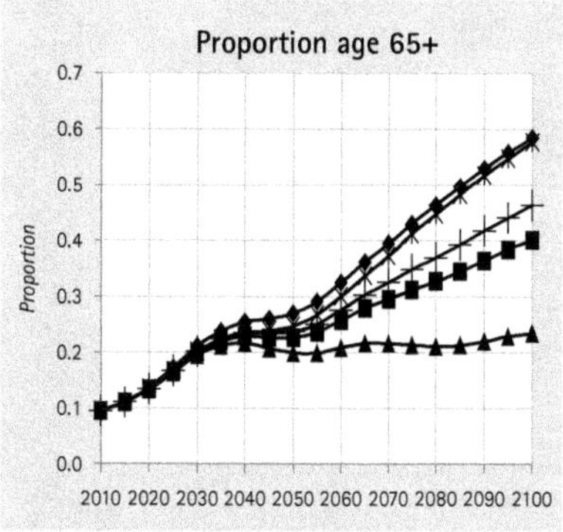

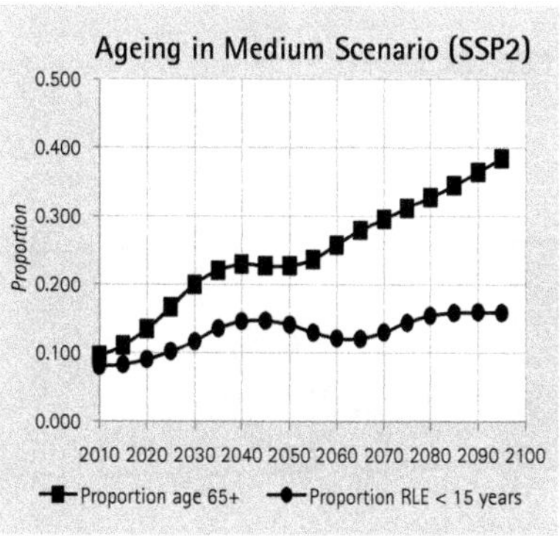

Alternative Scenarios to 2100

Projection Results by Scenario (SSP1–5)

	2010	2020	2030	2040	2050	2075	2100
Population (in millions)							
SSP1 - Rapid development	0.11	0.12	0.13	0.14	0.14	0.14	0.12
SSP2 - Medium	0.11	0.12	0.13	0.14	0.15	0.16	0.14
SSP3 - Stalled development	0.11	0.12	0.13	0.13	0.14	0.15	0.17
SSP4 - Inequality	0.11	0.12	0.13	0.14	0.14	0.14	0.12
SSP5 - Conventional development	0.11	0.12	0.14	0.15	0.16	0.17	0.15
Proportion age 65+							
SSP1 - Rapid development	0.10	0.14	0.21	0.25	0.27	0.43	0.58
SSP2 - Medium	0.10	0.13	0.20	0.23	0.23	0.31	0.40
SSP3 - Stalled development	0.10	0.13	0.20	0.22	0.20	0.21	0.24
SSP4 - Inequality	0.10	0.13	0.20	0.24	0.24	0.35	0.46
SSP5 - Conventional development	0.10	0.13	0.20	0.24	0.25	0.41	0.58
Proportion below age 20							
SSP1 - Rapid development	0.27	0.21	0.18	0.16	0.14	0.10	0.08
SSP2 - Medium	0.27	0.22	0.21	0.20	0.18	0.16	0.15
SSP3 - Stalled development	0.27	0.23	0.23	0.24	0.23	0.24	0.25
SSP4 - Inequality	0.27	0.21	0.19	0.17	0.15	0.13	0.11
SSP5 - Conventional development	0.27	0.21	0.19	0.16	0.14	0.10	0.08
Proportion of Women age 20–39 with at least secondary education							
SSP1 - Rapid development	0.76	0.88	0.93	0.95	0.97	0.98	0.99
SSP2 - Medium	0.76	0.83	0.88	0.91	0.93	0.97	0.99
SSP3 - Stalled development	0.76	0.81	0.82	0.82	0.82	0.82	0.82
SSP4 - Inequality	0.76	0.76	0.74	0.74	0.74	0.74	0.74
SSP5 - Conventional development	0.76	0.88	0.93	0.95	0.97	0.98	0.99
Mean years of schooling, age 25+							
SSP1 - Rapid development	8.59	9.47	10.34	11.08	11.73	12.92	13.60
SSP2 - Medium	8.59	9.35	10.06	10.69	11.28	12.45	13.22
SSP3 - Stalled development	8.59	9.19	9.64	9.95	10.16	10.32	10.32
SSP4 - Inequality	8.59	9.12	9.49	9.81	10.07	10.53	10.93
SSP5 - Conventional development	8.59	9.49	10.40	11.16	11.82	12.97	13.61

Demographic Assumptions Underlying SSPs

	2010–15	2020–25	2030–35	2040–45	2050–55	2075–80	2095–2100
Total fertility rate							
SSP1 - Rapid development	1.52	1.29	1.15	1.08	1.06	1.11	1.15
SSP2 - Medium	1.61	1.54	1.50	1.46	1.45	1.51	1.55
SSP3 - Stalled development	1.70	1.83	1.91	1.93	1.97	2.09	2.18
SSP4 - Inequality	1.55	1.37	1.24	1.17	1.15	1.21	1.25
SSP5 - Conventional development	1.52	1.29	1.15	1.08	1.06	1.11	1.15
Life expectancy at birth for females (in years)							
SSP1 - Rapid development	80.20	83.44	86.50	89.43	92.35	99.81	105.82
SSP2 - Medium	78.69	81.29	83.49	85.51	87.61	92.61	96.60
SSP3 - Stalled development	79.33	80.65	81.77	82.73	83.63	85.67	87.37
SSP4 - Inequality	79.73	82.09	84.13	86.01	87.94	92.41	96.15
SSP5 - Conventional development	80.20	83.44	86.50	89.43	92.35	99.81	105.82
Migration – net flow over five years (in thousands)							
SSP1 - Rapid development	4	4	4	4	3	1	0
SSP2 - Medium	4	4	4	4	4	1	0
SSP3 - Stalled development	3	2	2	2	3	1	0
SSP4 - Inequality	4	4	4	4	4	1	0
SSP5 - Conventional development	5	6	6	6	5	1	0

Ageing Indicators, Medium Scenario (SSP2)

	2010	2020	2030	2040	2050	2075	2095
Median age	38.35	39.40	40.57	43.54	45.58	50.49	55.78
Propspective median age	38.35	37.24	36.43	37.68	37.78	38.08	39.68
Proportion age 65+	0.09	0.13	0.20	0.23	0.23	0.31	0.38
Proportion RLE < 15 years	0.08	0.09	0.12	0.15	0.14	0.14	0.16

Australia

Detailed Human Capital Projections to 2060

Demographic indicators, Medium Scenario (SSP2)						
	2010	2020	2030	2040	2050	2060
Population (in millions)	22.27	25.72	29.18	32.41	35.50	38.44
Proportion age 65+	0.13	0.17	0.20	0.22	0.24	0.27
Proportion below age 20	0.26	0.24	0.23	0.22	0.21	0.20
	2005–10	2015–20	2025–30	2035–40	2045–50	2055–60
Total Fertility Rate	1.93	1.88	1.86	1.83	1.81	1.80
Life expectancy at birth (in years)						
Men	79.12	81.91	84.19	86.21	88.18	90.18
Women	83.75	86.11	88.31	90.31	92.29	94.29
Five-year immigration flow (in '000)	1161.94	925.65	961.86	984.35	985.47	971.55
Five-year emigration flow (in '000)	39.66	30.45	31.72	33.70	35.64	36.93

Human Capital indicators, Medium Scenario (SSP2)	2010	2020	2030	2040	2050	2060
Population age 25+: highest educational attainment						
E1 - no education	0.01	0.01	0.00	0.00	0.00	0.00
E2 - incomplete primary	0.01	0.01	0.00	0.00	0.00	0.00
E3 - primary	0.12	0.08	0.05	0.03	0.02	0.01
E4 - lower secondary	0.15	0.13	0.10	0.08	0.06	0.04
E5 - upper secondary	0.38	0.41	0.42	0.42	0.41	0.39
E6 - post-secondary	0.33	0.38	0.42	0.46	0.51	0.55
Mean years of schooling (in years)	11.96	12.71	13.34	13.90	14.39	14.79
Gender gap (population age 25+): highest educational attainment (ratio male/female)						
E1 - no education	0.79	0.78	0.77	0.74	0.73	0.73
E2 - incomplete primary	0.61	0.64	0.66	0.69	0.76	0.86
E3 - primary	0.69	0.69	0.70	0.72	0.79	0.88
E4 - lower secondary	0.73	0.78	0.82	0.87	0.91	0.96
E5 - upper secondary	1.46	1.37	1.32	1.27	1.22	1.16
E6 - post-secondary	0.87	0.85	0.84	0.85	0.87	0.90
Mean years of schooling (male minus female)	0.31	0.11	−0.01	−0.09	−0.13	−0.13
Women age 20–39: highest educational attainment						
E1 - no education	0.00	0.00	0.00	0.00	0.00	0.00
E2 - incomplete primary	0.00	0.00	0.00	0.00	0.00	0.00
E3 - primary	0.03	0.02	0.01	0.01	0.00	0.00
E4 - lower secondary	0.09	0.06	0.04	0.02	0.02	0.01
E5 - upper secondary	0.45	0.45	0.44	0.42	0.41	0.40
E6 - post-secondary	0.43	0.48	0.52	0.55	0.57	0.59
Mean years of schooling (in years)	13.69	14.43	14.94	15.10	15.22	15.30

Education scenarios

GET: global education trend scenario (medium assumption also used for SSP2)

CER: constant enrolment rates scenario (assumption of no future improvements)

FT: Fast track scenario (assumption of education expansion according to fastest historical experience)

Pyramids by Education, Medium Scenario

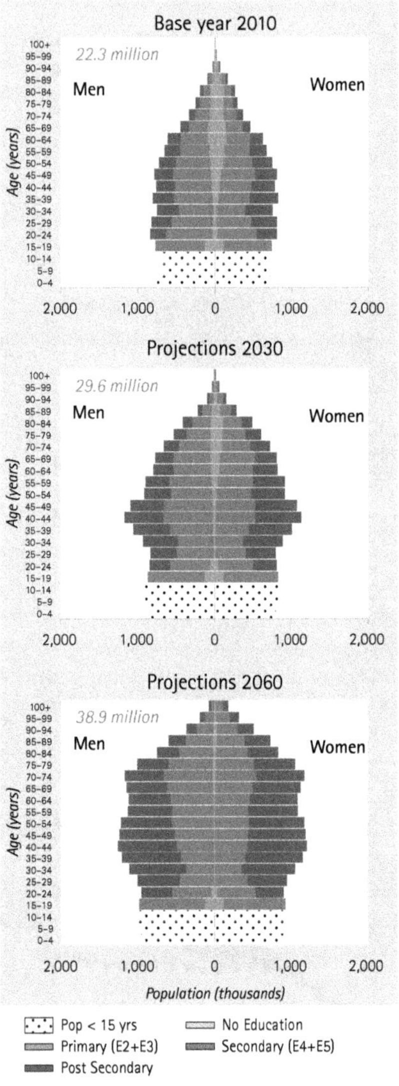

Population Size by Educational Attainment According to Three Education Scenarios: GET, CER, and FT

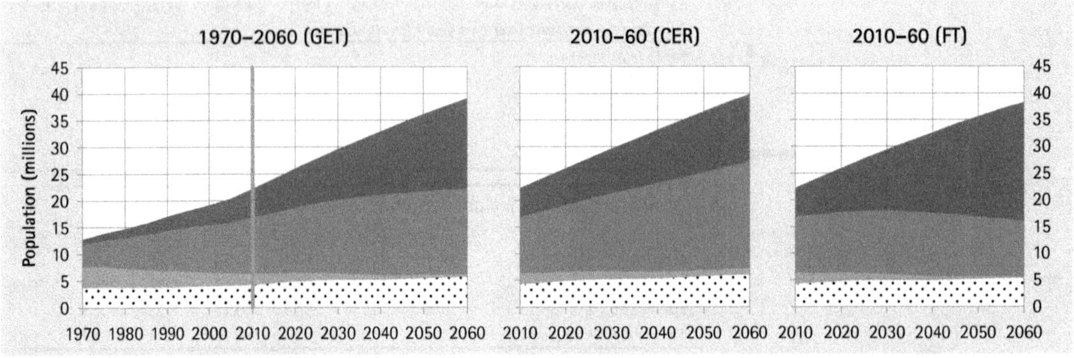

Australia (Continued)

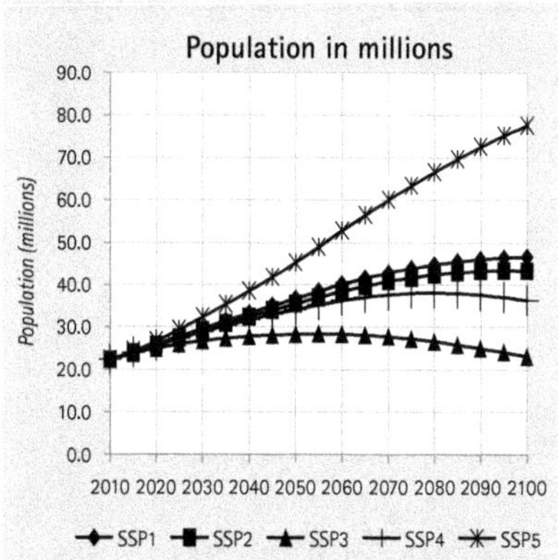

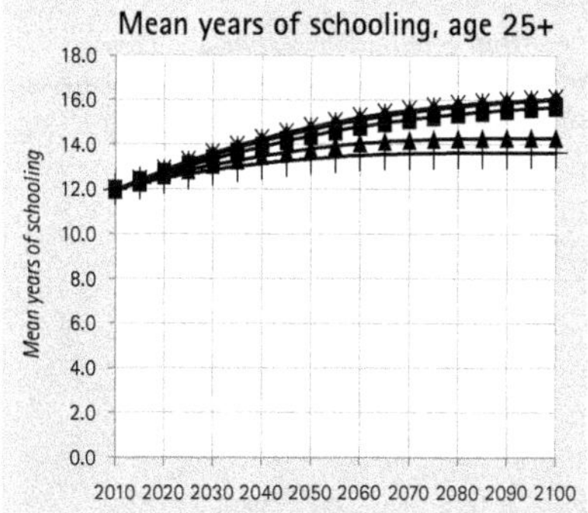

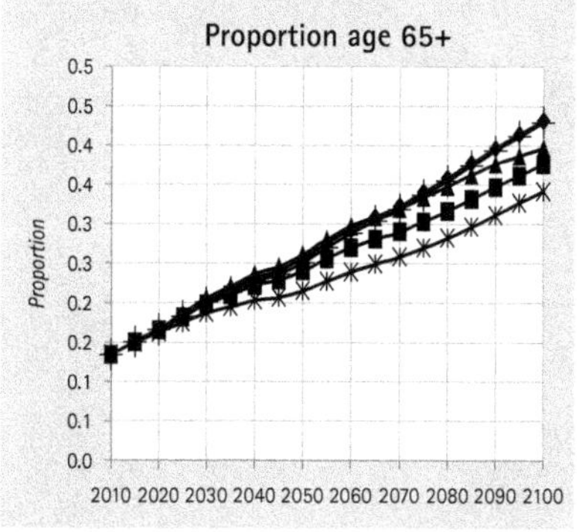

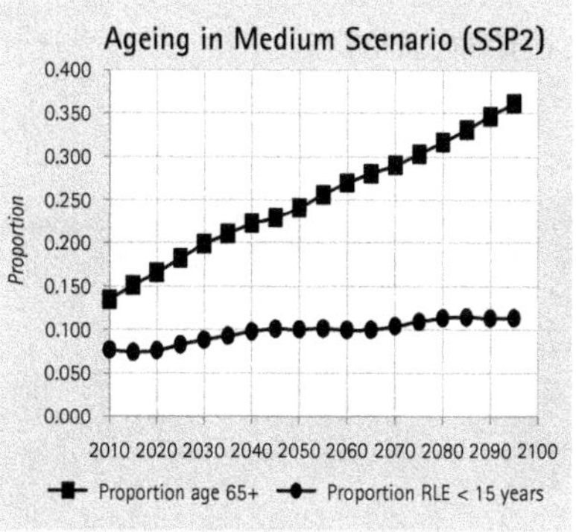

Alternative Scenarios to 2100

Projection Results by Scenario (SSP1–5)

	2010	2020	2030	2040	2050	2075	2100
Population (in millions)							
SSP1 - Rapid development	22.27	25.90	29.64	33.26	36.76	43.87	46.67
SSP2 - Medium	22.27	25.72	29.18	32.41	35.50	41.68	43.33
SSP3 - Stalled development	22.27	25.01	26.74	27.79	28.30	27.25	23.15
SSP4 - Inequality	22.27	25.65	28.85	31.68	34.14	37.97	36.35
SSP5 - Conventional development	22.27	26.67	32.33	38.48	45.26	63.36	77.63
Proportion age 65+							
SSP1 - Rapid development	0.13	0.17	0.20	0.23	0.26	0.34	0.43
SSP2 - Medium	0.13	0.17	0.20	0.22	0.24	0.30	0.38
SSP3 - Stalled development	0.13	0.17	0.21	0.24	0.26	0.33	0.40
SSP4 - Inequality	0.13	0.17	0.20	0.23	0.25	0.34	0.43
SSP5 - Conventional development	0.13	0.16	0.19	0.20	0.22	0.27	0.34
Proportion below age 20							
SSP1 - Rapid development	0.26	0.24	0.23	0.21	0.20	0.18	0.16
SSP2 - Medium	0.26	0.24	0.23	0.22	0.21	0.19	0.17
SSP3 - Stalled development	0.26	0.24	0.21	0.19	0.18	0.15	0.14
SSP4 - Inequality	0.26	0.24	0.22	0.20	0.18	0.16	0.14
SSP5 - Conventional development	0.26	0.25	0.25	0.25	0.24	0.23	0.21
Proportion of Women age 20–39 with at least secondary education							
SSP1 - Rapid development	0.97	0.99	0.99	1.00	1.00	1.00	1.00
SSP2 - Medium	0.97	0.98	0.99	0.99	1.00	1.00	1.00
SSP3 - Stalled development	0.97	0.97	0.97	0.97	0.97	0.97	0.97
SSP4 - Inequality	0.97	0.97	0.97	0.97	0.97	0.97	0.97
SSP5 - Conventional development	0.97	0.99	0.99	1.00	1.00	1.00	1.00
Mean years of schooling, age 25+							
SSP1 - Rapid development	11.96	12.81	13.53	14.14	14.66	15.57	16.00
SSP2 - Medium	11.96	12.71	13.34	13.90	14.39	15.25	15.68
SSP3 - Stalled development	11.96	12.60	13.08	13.48	13.80	14.22	14.29
SSP4 - Inequality	11.96	12.50	12.86	13.15	13.36	13.61	13.64
SSP5 - Conventional development	11.96	12.84	13.60	14.23	14.77	15.65	16.04

Demographic Assumptions Underlying SSPs

	2010–15	2020–25	2030–35	2040–45	2050–55	2075–80	2095–2100
Total fertility rate							
SSP1 - Rapid development	1.88	1.84	1.81	1.79	1.78	1.77	1.77
SSP2 - Medium	1.88	1.87	1.84	1.82	1.80	1.79	1.78
SSP3 - Stalled development	1.80	1.62	1.50	1.44	1.41	1.42	1.42
SSP4 - Inequality	1.81	1.67	1.57	1.52	1.48	1.49	1.49
SSP5 - Conventional development	1.98	2.11	2.20	2.22	2.22	2.22	2.22
Life expectancy at birth for females (in years)							
SSP1 - Rapid development	85.94	89.05	92.07	94.99	97.96	105.42	111.46
SSP2 - Medium	84.99	87.21	89.31	91.31	93.29	98.31	102.29
SSP3 - Stalled development	84.95	86.15	87.20	88.15	89.11	91.40	93.27
SSP4 - Inequality	85.47	87.59	89.62	91.54	93.46	98.17	101.97
SSP5 - Conventional development	85.94	89.05	92.07	94.99	97.96	105.42	111.46
Migration – net flow over five years (in thousands)							
SSP1 - Rapid development	963	907	927	910	870	343	0
SSP2 - Medium	916	859	883	889	875	382	0
SSP3 - Stalled development	801	446	443	431	410	168	0
SSP4 - Inequality	962	905	925	921	903	395	0
SSP5 - Conventional development	1123	1389	1479	1540	1574	724	0

Ageing Indicators, Medium Scenario (SSP2)

	2010	2020	2030	2040	2050	2075	2095
Median age	36.97	38.08	40.35	42.44	43.63	48.20	52.39
Propspective median age	36.97	35.79	36.11	36.36	35.67	35.61	36.00
Proportion age 65+	0.13	0.17	0.20	0.22	0.24	0.30	0.36
Proportion RLE < 15 years	0.08	0.08	0.09	0.10	0.10	0.11	0.11

Austria

Detailed Human Capital Projections to 2060

Demographic indicators, Medium Scenario (SSP2)	2010	2020	2030	2040	2050	2060
Population (in millions)	8.39	8.69	8.95	9.12	9.22	9.22
Proportion age 65+	0.18	0.20	0.26	0.30	0.33	0.35
Proportion below age 20	0.21	0.19	0.18	0.17	0.16	0.16
	2005–10	2015–20	2025–30	2035–40	2045–50	2055–60
Total Fertility Rate	1.38	1.45	1.49	1.54	1.59	1.61
Life expectancy at birth (in years)						
Men	77.41	80.33	82.89	85.31	87.59	89.49
Women	82.89	85.21	87.41	89.79	92.09	93.99
Five-year immigration flow (in '000)	212.40	169.96	176.85	181.30	181.85	179.48
Five-year emigration flow (in '000)	52.93	36.03	32.66	30.73	29.70	28.67

Human Capital indicators, Medium Scenario (SSP2)	2010	2020	2030	2040	2050	2060
Population age 25+: highest educational attainment						
E1 - no education	0.00	0.00	0.00	0.00	0.00	0.00
E2 - incomplete primary	0.00	0.00	0.00	0.00	0.00	0.00
E3 - primary	0.03	0.02	0.02	0.01	0.01	0.01
E4 - lower secondary	0.23	0.19	0.15	0.11	0.09	0.07
E5 - upper secondary	0.50	0.51	0.50	0.49	0.46	0.43
E6 - post-secondary	0.24	0.28	0.33	0.38	0.44	0.49
Mean years of schooling (in years)	12.03	12.47	12.83	13.16	13.47	13.77
Gender gap (population age 25+): highest educational attainment (ratio male/female)						
E1 - no education	NA	NA	NA	NA	NA	NA
E2 - incomplete primary	NA	NA	1.11	1.10	1.10	1.09
E3 - primary	0.66	0.68	0.69	0.71	0.72	0.73
E4 - lower secondary	0.51	0.54	0.57	0.62	0.67	0.73
E5 - upper secondary	1.25	1.20	1.17	1.15	1.13	1.10
E6 - post-secondary	1.25	1.11	1.03	0.98	0.96	0.96
Mean years of schooling (male minus female)	0.94	0.64	0.40	0.21	0.07	−0.01
Women age 20–39: highest educational attainment						
E1 - no education	0.00	0.00	0.00	0.00	0.00	0.00
E2 - incomplete primary	0.00	0.00	0.00	0.00	0.00	0.00
E3 - primary	0.02	0.01	0.01	0.00	0.00	0.00
E4 - lower secondary	0.15	0.10	0.07	0.04	0.03	0.02
E5 - upper secondary	0.49	0.47	0.44	0.42	0.39	0.38
E6 - post-secondary	0.35	0.42	0.49	0.54	0.57	0.59
Mean years of schooling (in years)	12.99	13.45	13.63	13.92	14.12	14.25

Education scenarios

GET: global education trend scenario (medium assumption also used for SSP2)

CER: constant enrolment rates scenario (assumption of no future improvements)

FT: Fast track scenario (assumption of education expansion according to fastest historical experience)

Pyramids by Education, Medium Scenario

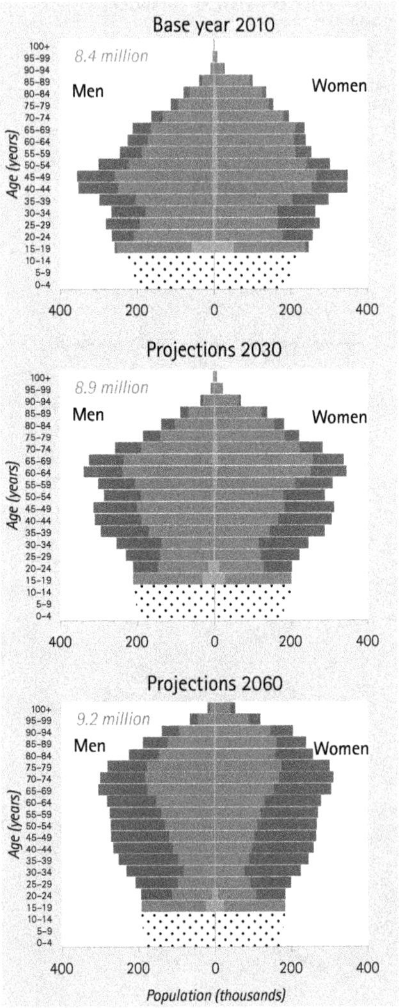

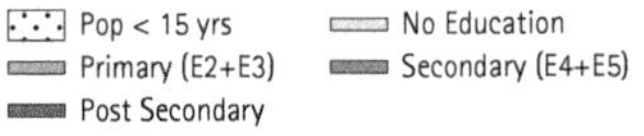

Population Size by Educational Attainment According to Three Education Scenarios: GET, CER, and FT

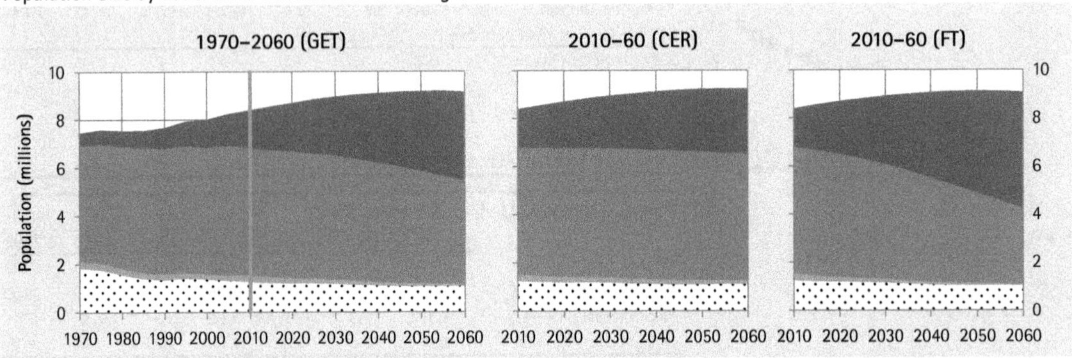

Austria (Continued)

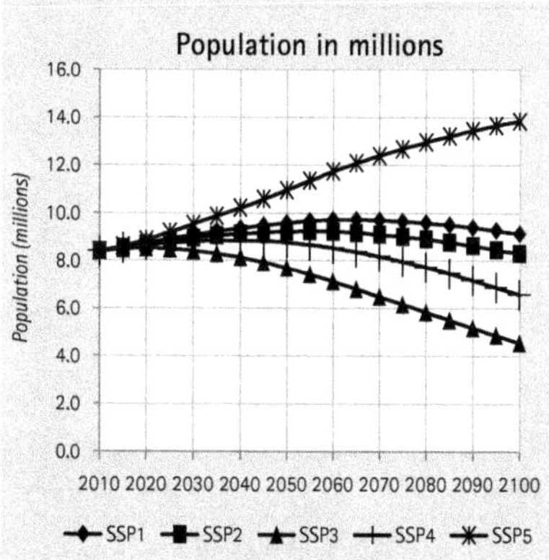

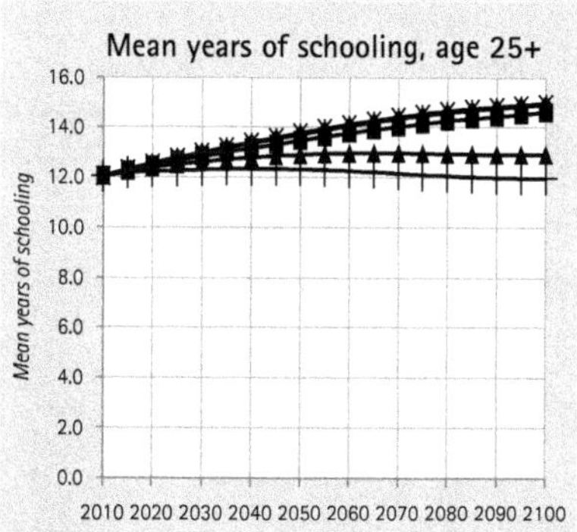

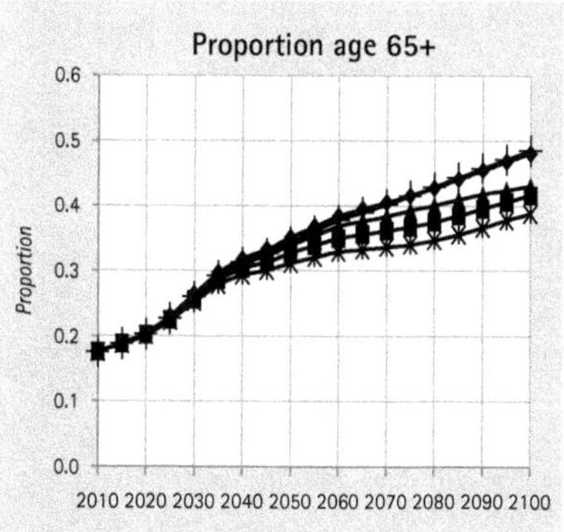

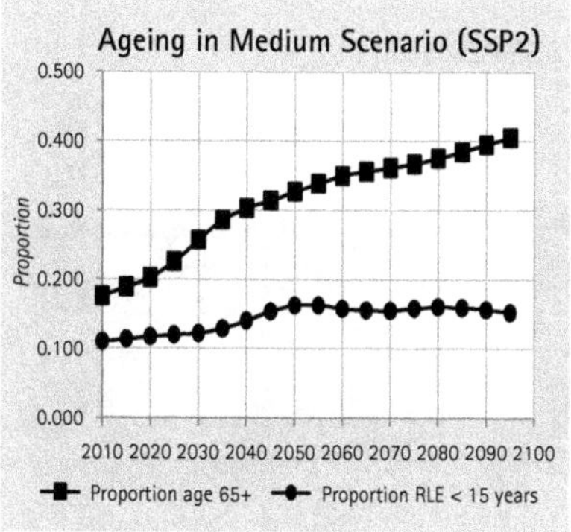

Alternative Scenarios to 2100

Projection Results by Scenario (SSP1–5)

	2010	2020	2030	2040	2050	2075	2100
Population (in millions)							
SSP1 - Rapid development	8.39	8.73	9.08	9.36	9.59	9.65	9.14
SSP2 - Medium	8.39	8.69	8.95	9.12	9.22	9.01	8.30
SSP3 - Stalled development	8.39	8.52	8.41	8.13	7.69	6.16	4.55
SSP4 - Inequality	8.39	8.64	8.80	8.84	8.76	7.96	6.58
SSP5 - Conventional development	8.39	8.87	9.53	10.21	10.96	12.69	13.85
Proportion age 65+							
SSP1 - Rapid development	0.18	0.21	0.26	0.32	0.35	0.42	0.48
SSP2 - Medium	0.18	0.20	0.26	0.30	0.33	0.37	0.42
SSP3 - Stalled development	0.18	0.20	0.26	0.31	0.34	0.39	0.43
SSP4 - Inequality	0.18	0.20	0.26	0.31	0.34	0.42	0.49
SSP5 - Conventional development	0.18	0.20	0.25	0.29	0.31	0.34	0.39
Proportion below age 20							
SSP1 - Rapid development	0.21	0.18	0.18	0.16	0.16	0.15	0.13
SSP2 - Medium	0.21	0.19	0.18	0.17	0.16	0.16	0.15
SSP3 - Stalled development	0.21	0.18	0.16	0.14	0.13	0.13	0.12
SSP4 - Inequality	0.21	0.18	0.16	0.15	0.14	0.12	0.11
SSP5 - Conventional development	0.21	0.19	0.19	0.19	0.19	0.20	0.19
Proportion of Women age 20–39 with at least secondary education							
SSP1 - Rapid development	0.98	0.99	1.00	1.00	1.00	1.00	1.00
SSP2 - Medium	0.98	0.99	0.99	1.00	1.00	1.00	1.00
SSP3 - Stalled development	0.98	0.99	0.99	0.99	0.99	0.99	0.99
SSP4 - Inequality	0.98	0.99	0.99	0.99	0.99	0.99	0.99
SSP5 - Conventional development	0.98	0.99	1.00	1.00	1.00	1.00	1.00
Mean years of schooling, age 25+							
SSP1 - Rapid development	12.03	12.54	12.97	13.36	13.72	14.47	14.91
SSP2 - Medium	12.03	12.47	12.83	13.16	13.47	14.14	14.60
SSP3 - Stalled development	12.03	12.38	12.62	12.79	12.90	12.96	12.91
SSP4 - Inequality	12.03	12.23	12.30	12.33	12.31	12.11	11.97
SSP5 - Conventional development	12.03	12.55	12.99	13.39	13.77	14.54	14.96

Demographic Assumptions Underlying SSPs

	2010–15	2020–25	2030–35	2040–45	2050–55	2075–80	2095–2100
Total fertility rate							
SSP1 - Rapid development	1.43	1.46	1.50	1.55	1.58	1.62	1.64
SSP2 - Medium	1.43	1.47	1.51	1.56	1.60	1.63	1.65
SSP3 - Stalled development	1.36	1.26	1.22	1.22	1.24	1.27	1.29
SSP4 - Inequality	1.37	1.29	1.25	1.26	1.27	1.30	1.33
SSP5 - Conventional development	1.50	1.68	1.82	1.92	1.98	2.02	2.05
Life expectancy at birth for females (in years)							
SSP1 - Rapid development	84.89	88.09	91.26	94.57	97.63	104.69	110.36
SSP2 - Medium	84.09	86.31	88.61	90.99	93.10	97.59	101.30
SSP3 - Stalled development	83.92	85.15	86.37	87.70	88.77	90.64	92.15
SSP4 - Inequality	84.44	86.61	88.83	91.16	93.22	97.47	100.98
SSP5 - Conventional development	84.89	88.09	91.26	94.57	97.63	104.69	110.36
Migration – net flow over five years (in thousands)							
SSP1 - Rapid development	142	138	146	146	142	52	0
SSP2 - Medium	141	136	144	146	145	58	0
SSP3 - Stalled development	118	69	72	72	70	26	0
SSP4 - Inequality	142	138	145	145	142	56	0
SSP5 - Conventional development	166	208	224	235	241	102	0

Ageing Indicators, Medium Scenario (SSP2)

	2010	2020	2030	2040	2050	2075	2095
Median age	41.85	44.90	47.10	49.65	51.61	53.68	56.56
Propspective median age	41.85	42.64	42.67	43.03	43.07	40.79	40.09
Proportion age 65+	0.18	0.20	0.26	0.30	0.33	0.37	0.41
Proportion RLE < 15 years	0.11	0.12	0.12	0.14	0.16	0.16	0.15

Azerbaijan

Detailed Human Capital Projections to 2060

Demographic indicators, Medium Scenario (SSP2)	2010	2020	2030	2040	2050	2060
Population (in millions)	9.19	10.49	11.09	11.49	11.72	11.64
Proportion age 65+	0.07	0.07	0.13	0.15	0.18	0.24
Proportion below age 20	0.31	0.30	0.28	0.22	0.22	0.20
	2005–10	2015–20	2025–30	2035–40	2045–50	2055–60
Total Fertility Rate	2.16	2.19	1.80	1.70	1.70	1.70
Life expectancy at birth (in years)						
Men	67.09	69.22	71.33	73.34	75.42	77.51
Women	73.14	74.81	76.70	78.60	80.59	82.59
Five-year immigration flow (in '000)	67.70	66.35	68.91	70.41	70.38	69.33
Five-year emigration flow (in '000)	14.40	11.14	10.19	10.49	9.64	8.67

Human Capital indicators, Medium Scenario (SSP2)	2010	2020	2030	2040	2050	2060
Population age 25+: highest educational attainment						
E1 - no education	0.02	0.01	0.00	0.00	0.00	0.00
E2 - incomplete primary	0.01	0.01	0.00	0.00	0.00	0.00
E3 - primary	0.05	0.03	0.02	0.02	0.01	0.01
E4 - lower secondary	0.12	0.10	0.08	0.07	0.05	0.04
E5 - upper secondary	0.65	0.69	0.72	0.72	0.73	0.74
E6 - post-secondary	0.14	0.16	0.17	0.19	0.20	0.22
Mean years of schooling (in years)	9.94	10.61	10.96	11.23	11.48	11.66
Gender gap (population age 25+): highest educational attainment (ratio male/female)						
E1 - no education	0.32	0.31	0.35	0.37	0.42	0.56
E2 - incomplete primary	0.39	0.35	0.35	0.41	0.45	0.59
E3 - primary	0.53	0.61	0.78	0.90	0.90	0.87
E4 - lower secondary	0.73	0.80	0.83	0.91	0.93	0.97
E5 - upper secondary	1.05	1.00	0.98	0.98	0.98	0.99
E6 - post-secondary	1.65	1.40	1.29	1.18	1.11	1.06
Mean years of schooling (male minus female)	0.89	0.55	0.38	0.26	0.18	0.10
Women age 20–39: highest educational attainment						
E1 - no education	0.00	0.00	0.00	0.00	0.00	0.00
E2 - incomplete primary	0.01	0.00	0.00	0.00	0.00	0.00
E3 - primary	0.07	0.04	0.03	0.02	0.01	0.01
E4 - lower secondary	0.15	0.11	0.10	0.12	0.08	0.09
E5 - upper secondary	0.63	0.66	0.67	0.64	0.67	0.64
E6 - post-secondary	0.15	0.19	0.20	0.22	0.24	0.26
Mean years of schooling (in years)	10.55	11.24	11.42	11.51	11.68	11.73

Education scenarios

GET: global education trend scenario (medium assumption also used for SSP2)

CER: constant enrolment rates scenario (assumption of no future improvements)

FT: Fast track scenario (assumption of education expansion according to fastest historical experience)

Pyramids by Education, Medium Scenario

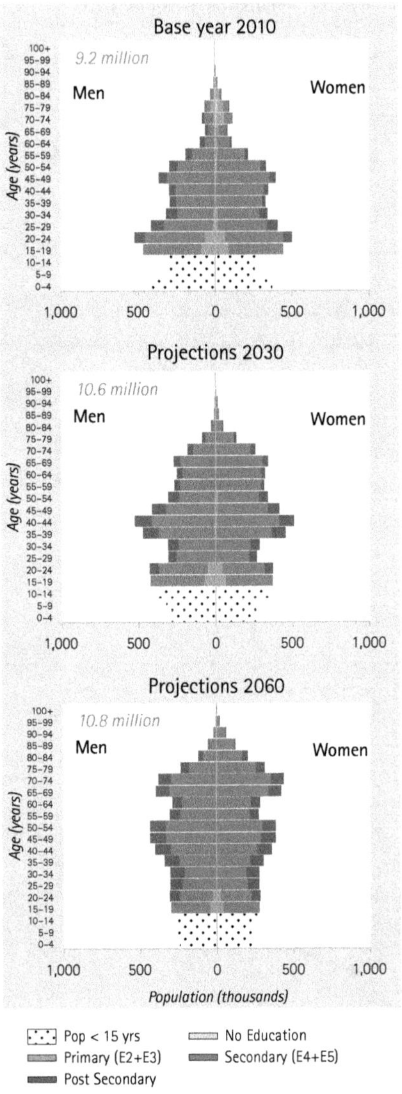

Population Size by Educational Attainment According to Three Education Scenarios: GET, CER, and FT

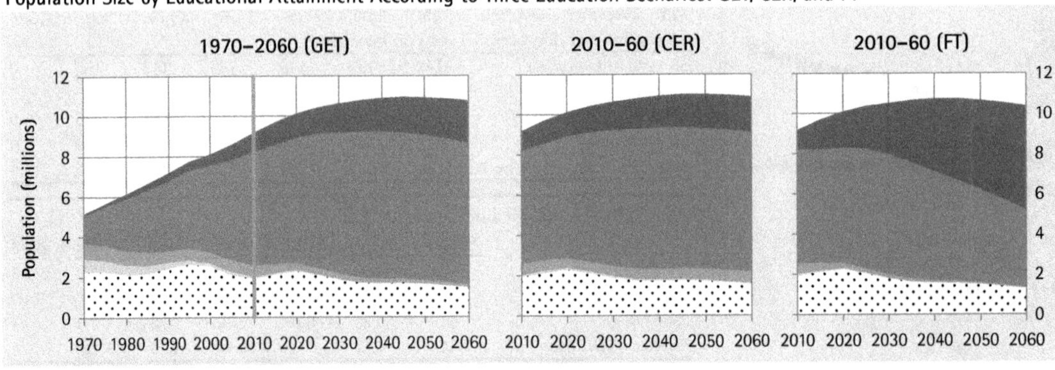

Azerbaijan (Continued)

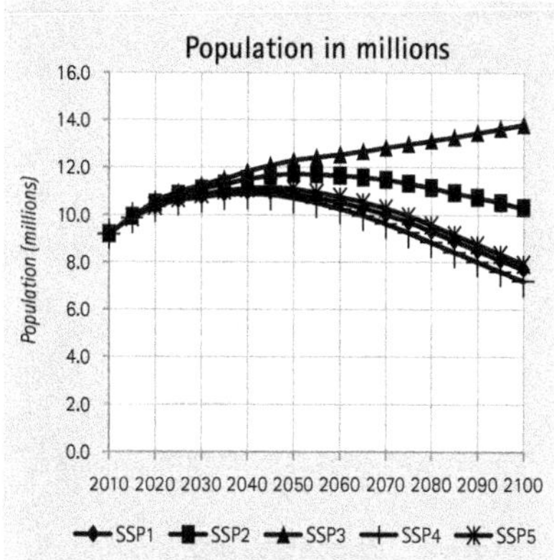

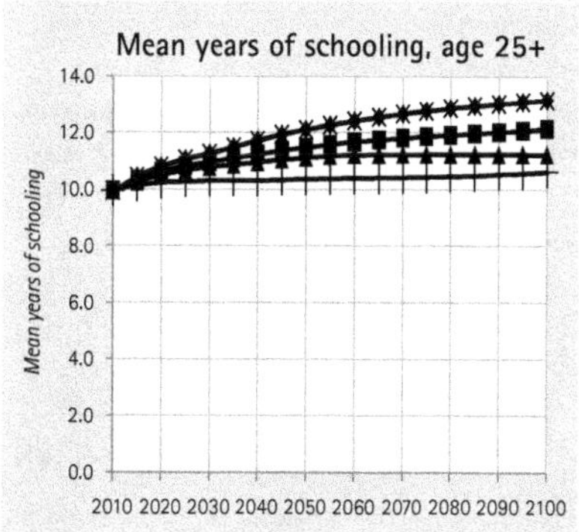

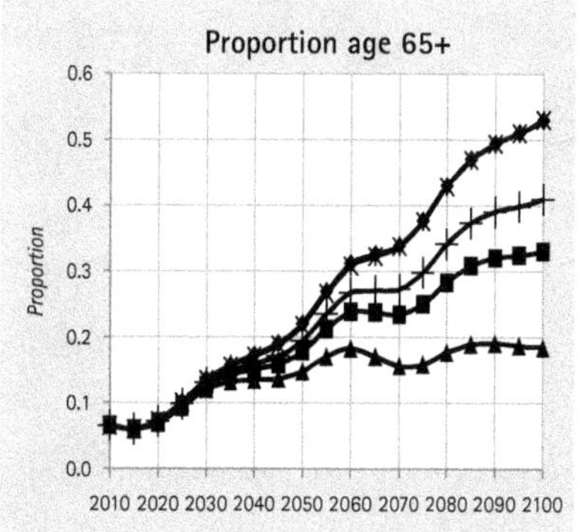

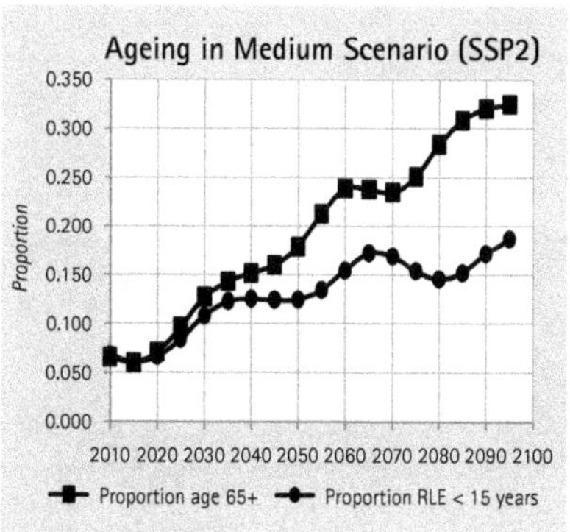

Alternative Scenarios to 2100

Projection Results by Scenario (SSP1–5)

	2010	2020	2030	2040	2050	2075	2100
Population (in millions)							
SSP1 - Rapid development	9.19	10.34	10.77	10.97	10.88	9.69	7.72
SSP2 - Medium	9.19	10.49	11.09	11.49	11.72	11.32	10.30
SSP3 - Stalled development	9.19	10.54	11.25	11.81	12.28	12.97	13.80
SSP4 - Inequality	9.19	10.33	10.74	10.87	10.70	9.24	7.19
SSP5 - Conventional development	9.19	10.36	10.86	11.11	11.08	9.95	7.95
Proportion age 65+							
SSP1 - Rapid development	0.07	0.07	0.14	0.17	0.22	0.38	0.53
SSP2 - Medium	0.07	0.07	0.13	0.15	0.18	0.25	0.33
SSP3 - Stalled development	0.07	0.07	0.12	0.14	0.15	0.16	0.19
SSP4 - Inequality	0.07	0.07	0.13	0.16	0.20	0.30	0.41
SSP5 - Conventional development	0.07	0.07	0.14	0.17	0.22	0.38	0.53
Proportion below age 20							
SSP1 - Rapid development	0.31	0.29	0.25	0.18	0.16	0.11	0.09
SSP2 - Medium	0.31	0.30	0.28	0.22	0.22	0.18	0.17
SSP3 - Stalled development	0.31	0.31	0.31	0.26	0.27	0.26	0.27
SSP4 - Inequality	0.31	0.30	0.26	0.19	0.18	0.14	0.12
SSP5 - Conventional development	0.31	0.29	0.25	0.18	0.16	0.11	0.09
Proportion of Women age 20–39 with at least secondary education							
SSP1 - Rapid development	0.92	0.96	0.98	0.98	0.99	0.99	0.99
SSP2 - Medium	0.92	0.96	0.97	0.98	0.99	0.99	0.99
SSP3 - Stalled development	0.92	0.89	0.88	0.87	0.89	0.88	0.88
SSP4 - Inequality	0.92	0.84	0.79	0.79	0.80	0.80	0.80
SSP5 - Conventional development	0.92	0.96	0.98	0.98	0.99	0.99	0.99
Mean years of schooling, age 25+							
SSP1 - Rapid development	9.94	10.79	11.26	11.71	12.10	12.77	13.15
SSP2 - Medium	9.94	10.61	10.96	11.23	11.48	11.86	12.13
SSP3 - Stalled development	9.94	10.49	10.77	10.95	11.11	11.23	11.23
SSP4 - Inequality	9.94	10.22	10.30	10.30	10.35	10.43	10.61
SSP5 - Conventional development	9.94	10.80	11.26	11.72	12.11	12.77	13.15

Demographic Assumptions Underlying SSPs

	2010–15	2020–25	2030–35	2040–45	2050–55	2075–80	2095–2100
Total fertility rate							
SSP1 - Rapid development	2.22	1.65	1.33	1.24	1.22	1.23	1.24
SSP2 - Medium	2.38	1.99	1.70	1.70	1.70	1.71	1.72
SSP3 - Stalled development	2.49	2.33	2.18	2.16	2.20	2.25	2.29
SSP4 - Inequality	2.25	1.74	1.43	1.34	1.33	1.35	1.36
SSP5 - Conventional development	2.22	1.65	1.33	1.24	1.22	1.23	1.24
Life expectancy at birth for females (in years)							
SSP1 - Rapid development	76.97	78.82	81.22	83.86	86.68	93.88	99.84
SSP2 - Medium	73.89	75.71	77.70	79.59	81.59	86.61	90.60
SSP3 - Stalled development	76.36	76.48	77.23	78.01	78.72	80.60	82.28
SSP4 - Inequality	76.68	77.68	79.14	80.70	82.36	86.69	90.43
SSP5 - Conventional development	76.97	78.82	81.22	83.86	86.68	93.88	99.84
Migration – net flow over five years (in thousands)							
SSP1 - Rapid development	52	56	56	52	47	14	0
SSP2 - Medium	54	58	60	61	61	25	0
SSP3 - Stalled development	43	29	32	37	43	26	0
SSP4 - Inequality	52	56	58	57	56	22	0
SSP5 - Conventional development	61	83	82	73	65	19	0

Ageing Indicators, Medium Scenario (SSP2)

	2010	2020	2030	2040	2050	2075	2095
Median age	29.47	32.50	37.52	39.21	40.59	48.05	51.13
Propspective median age	29.47	31.38	35.11	35.40	35.09	38.45	37.86
Proportion age 65+	0.07	0.07	0.13	0.15	0.18	0.25	0.32
Proportion RLE < 15 years	0.07	0.07	0.11	0.13	0.12	0.15	0.19

Bahamas

Detailed Human Capital Projections to 2060

Demographic indicators, Medium Scenario (SSP2)	2010	2020	2030	2040	2050	2060
Population (in millions)	0.34	0.39	0.42	0.46	0.48	0.49
Proportion age 65+	0.07	0.10	0.14	0.18	0.21	0.25
Proportion below age 20	0.32	0.26	0.24	0.22	0.21	0.20
	2005–10	2015–20	2025–30	2035–40	2045–50	2055–60
Total Fertility Rate	1.91	1.73	1.72	1.73	1.71	1.68
Life expectancy at birth (in years)						
Men	71.60	73.45	75.43	77.93	79.61	81.44
Women	77.83	79.80	81.69	83.69	85.61	87.61
Five-year immigration flow (in '000)	6.88	6.76	7.03	7.19	7.20	7.10
Five-year emigration flow (in '000)	0.47	0.35	0.34	0.34	0.33	0.33

Human Capital indicators, Medium Scenario (SSP2)	2010	2020	2030	2040	2050	2060
Population age 25+: highest educational attainment						
E1 - no education	0.01	0.01	0.01	0.00	0.00	0.00
E2 - incomplete primary	0.06	0.04	0.02	0.01	0.01	0.00
E3 - primary	0.17	0.14	0.12	0.10	0.09	0.08
E4 - lower secondary	0.53	0.56	0.57	0.56	0.53	0.49
E5 - upper secondary	0.09	0.11	0.14	0.16	0.19	0.23
E6 - post-secondary	0.13	0.14	0.15	0.16	0.18	0.20
Mean years of schooling (in years)	9.46	9.86	10.19	10.46	10.74	11.03
Gender gap (population age 25+): highest educational attainment (ratio male/female)						
E1 - no education	1.13	1.06	0.97	0.89	0.87	0.91
E2 - incomplete primary	0.98	1.03	1.11	1.25	1.46	1.51
E3 - primary	1.20	1.24	1.28	1.32	1.32	1.27
E4 - lower secondary	1.06	1.09	1.10	1.10	1.10	1.08
E5 - upper secondary	0.66	0.69	0.74	0.80	0.86	0.92
E6 - post-secondary	0.84	0.77	0.73	0.73	0.76	0.83
Mean years of schooling (male minus female)	-0.34	-0.45	-0.51	-0.52	-0.48	-0.37
Women age 20–39: highest educational attainment						
E1 - no education	0.00	0.00	0.00	0.00	0.00	0.00
E2 - incomplete primary	0.01	0.00	0.00	0.00	0.00	0.00
E3 - primary	0.08	0.08	0.08	0.07	0.07	0.06
E4 - lower secondary	0.60	0.56	0.51	0.46	0.42	0.38
E5 - upper secondary	0.16	0.19	0.22	0.26	0.29	0.33
E6 - post-secondary	0.14	0.16	0.18	0.20	0.22	0.23
Mean years of schooling (in years)	10.42	10.68	10.93	11.17	11.40	11.60

Education scenarios

GET: global education trend scenario (medium assumption also used for SSP2)

CER: constant enrolment rates scenario (assumption of no future improvements)

FT: Fast track scenario (assumption of education expansion according to fastest historical experience)

Pyramids by Education, Medium Scenario

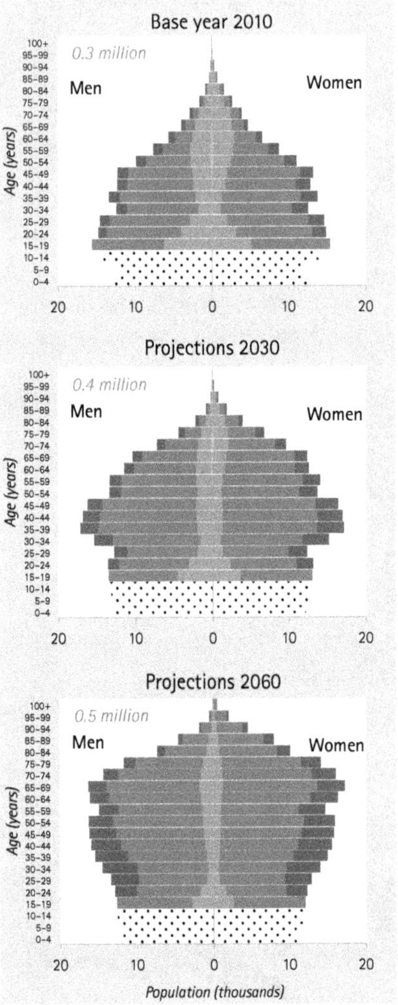

Pop < 15 yrs; No Education; Primary (E2+E3); Secondary (E4+E5); Post Secondary

Population Size by Educational Attainment According to Three Education Scenarios: GET, CER, and FT

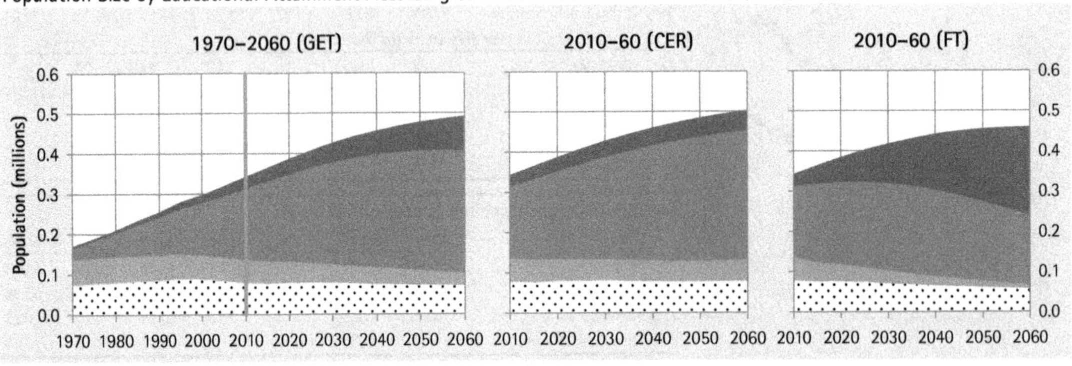

Bahamas (Continued)

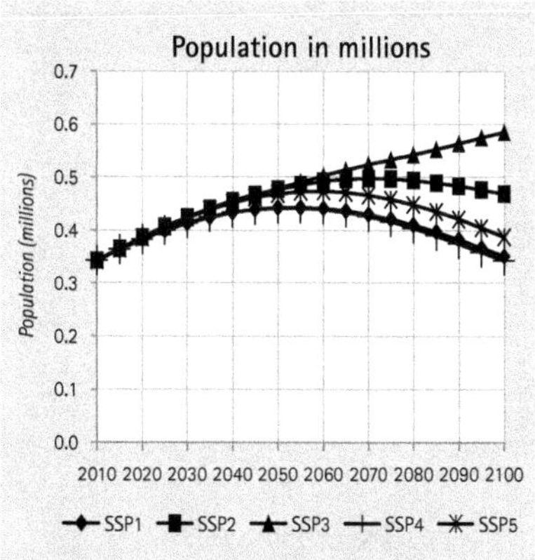

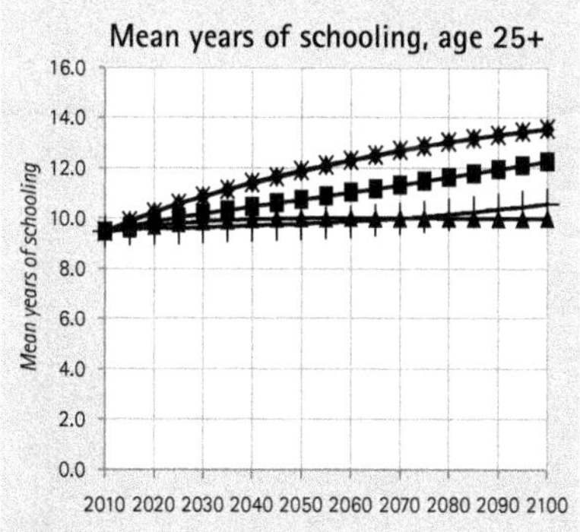

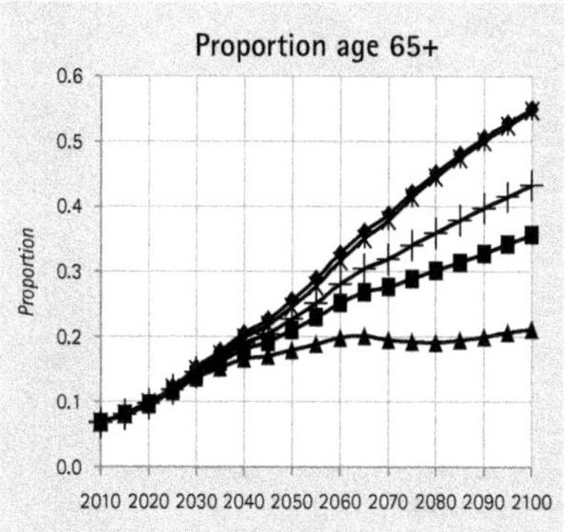

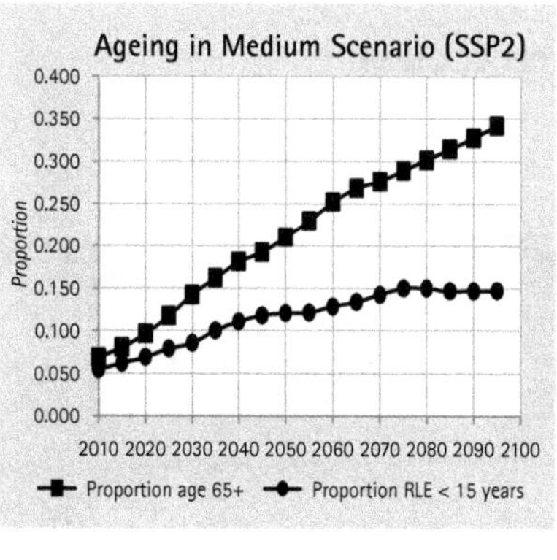

Alternative Scenarios to 2100

Projection Results by Scenario (SSP1–5)

	2010	2020	2030	2040	2050	2075	2100
Population (in millions)							
SSP1 - Rapid development	0.34	0.38	0.41	0.43	0.44	0.42	0.35
SSP2 - Medium	0.34	0.39	0.42	0.46	0.48	0.50	0.47
SSP3 - Stalled development	0.34	0.39	0.42	0.45	0.48	0.53	0.58
SSP4 - Inequality	0.34	0.38	0.41	0.43	0.44	0.42	0.34
SSP5 - Conventional development	0.34	0.39	0.42	0.45	0.47	0.46	0.39
Proportion age 65+							
SSP1 - Rapid development	0.07	0.10	0.15	0.21	0.26	0.42	0.55
SSP2 - Medium	0.07	0.10	0.14	0.18	0.21	0.29	0.36
SSP3 - Stalled development	0.07	0.10	0.14	0.17	0.18	0.19	0.21
SSP4 - Inequality	0.07	0.10	0.15	0.19	0.23	0.34	0.43
SSP5 - Conventional development	0.07	0.10	0.15	0.20	0.25	0.41	0.55
Proportion below age 20							
SSP1 - Rapid development	0.32	0.25	0.21	0.18	0.15	0.11	0.09
SSP2 - Medium	0.32	0.26	0.24	0.22	0.21	0.18	0.16
SSP3 - Stalled development	0.32	0.27	0.27	0.26	0.26	0.26	0.26
SSP4 - Inequality	0.32	0.26	0.22	0.19	0.17	0.14	0.12
SSP5 - Conventional development	0.32	0.25	0.21	0.18	0.16	0.11	0.09
Proportion of Women age 20–39 with at least secondary education							
SSP1 - Rapid development	0.91	0.95	0.96	0.96	0.96	0.98	0.99
SSP2 - Medium	0.91	0.91	0.92	0.93	0.93	0.95	0.98
SSP3 - Stalled development	0.91	0.90	0.90	0.90	0.90	0.90	0.90
SSP4 - Inequality	0.91	0.84	0.81	0.81	0.81	0.81	0.81
SSP5 - Conventional development	0.91	0.95	0.96	0.96	0.96	0.98	0.99
Mean years of schooling, age 25+							
SSP1 - Rapid development	9.46	10.23	10.85	11.39	11.86	12.85	13.55
SSP2 - Medium	9.46	9.86	10.19	10.46	10.74	11.47	12.25
SSP3 - Stalled development	9.46	9.70	9.87	9.96	10.00	10.01	10.00
SSP4 - Inequality	9.46	9.59	9.64	9.71	9.78	10.07	10.57
SSP5 - Conventional development	9.46	10.24	10.87	11.41	11.89	12.87	13.55

Demographic Assumptions Underlying SSPs

	2010–15	2020–25	2030–35	2040–45	2050–55	2075–80	2095–2100
Total fertility rate							
SSP1 - Rapid development	1.67	1.40	1.27	1.23	1.19	1.13	1.16
SSP2 - Medium	1.80	1.72	1.72	1.71	1.70	1.58	1.61
SSP3 - Stalled development	1.88	2.04	2.15	2.21	2.22	2.17	2.27
SSP4 - Inequality	1.70	1.50	1.38	1.33	1.29	1.23	1.26
SSP5 - Conventional development	1.67	1.40	1.27	1.23	1.19	1.13	1.16
Life expectancy at birth for females (in years)							
SSP1 - Rapid development	80.21	82.77	85.67	88.58	91.44	98.97	105.05
SSP2 - Medium	78.79	80.69	82.69	84.59	86.61	91.60	95.61
SSP3 - Stalled development	79.34	80.07	80.94	81.81	82.56	84.86	86.66
SSP4 - Inequality	79.74	81.48	83.22	85.03	86.92	91.51	95.36
SSP5 - Conventional development	80.21	82.77	85.67	88.58	91.44	98.97	105.05
Migration – net flow over five years (in thousands)							
SSP1 - Rapid development	6	6	6	6	5	2	0
SSP2 - Medium	6	6	7	7	7	3	0
SSP3 - Stalled development	5	3	4	4	5	3	0
SSP4 - Inequality	6	6	7	6	6	2	0
SSP5 - Conventional development	7	10	10	9	7	2	0

Ageing Indicators, Medium Scenario (SSP2)

	2010	2020	2030	2040	2050	2075	2095
Median age	30.85	34.45	38.12	41.64	43.38	48.16	51.97
Propspective median age	30.85	33.22	35.17	37.16	37.26	37.57	37.48
Proportion age 65+	0.07	0.10	0.14	0.18	0.21	0.29	0.34
Proportion RLE < 15 years	0.05	0.07	0.09	0.11	0.12	0.15	0.15

Bahrain

Detailed Human Capital Projections to 2060

Demographic indicators, Medium Scenario (SSP2)	2010	2020	2030	2040	2050	2060
Population (in millions)	1.26	1.79	2.23	2.66	3.05	3.36
Proportion age 65+	0.02	0.04	0.08	0.14	0.21	0.24
Proportion below age 20	0.25	0.26	0.24	0.21	0.20	0.19
	2005–10	2015–20	2025–30	2035–40	2045–50	2055–60
Total Fertility Rate	2.63	2.21	2.03	1.90	1.84	1.74
Life expectancy at birth (in years)						
Men	74.03	76.91	78.86	80.66	82.55	84.43
Women	75.37	78.29	80.61	82.69	84.81	86.81
Five-year immigration flow (in '000)	446.94	157.94	164.15	167.75	167.63	165.10
Five-year emigration flow (in '000)	0.00	0.00	0.00	0.00	0.00	0.00

Human Capital indicators, Medium Scenario (SSP2)	2010	2020	2030	2040	2050	2060
Population age 25+: highest educational attainment						
E1 - no education	0.09	0.06	0.04	0.03	0.01	0.01
E2 - incomplete primary	0.09	0.07	0.05	0.03	0.02	0.01
E3 - primary	0.10	0.10	0.09	0.08	0.07	0.06
E4 - lower secondary	0.19	0.19	0.18	0.17	0.15	0.13
E5 - upper secondary	0.33	0.36	0.38	0.40	0.42	0.42
E6 - post-secondary	0.20	0.23	0.26	0.29	0.33	0.37
Mean years of schooling (in years)	9.63	10.35	10.95	11.54	12.10	12.58
Gender gap (population age 25+): highest educational attainment (ratio male/female)						
E1 - no education	0.73	0.93	1.12	1.29	1.42	1.48
E2 - incomplete primary	1.02	1.11	1.19	1.25	1.29	1.29
E3 - primary	1.47	1.73	1.88	1.94	1.92	1.80
E4 - lower secondary	1.71	1.76	1.83	1.87	1.84	1.74
E5 - upper secondary	0.95	0.93	0.96	1.01	1.04	1.05
E6 - post-secondary	0.68	0.61	0.59	0.60	0.65	0.73
Mean years of schooling (male minus female)	−0.36	−0.93	−1.19	−1.22	−1.09	−0.85
Women age 20–39: highest educational attainment						
E1 - no education	0.02	0.01	0.00	0.00	0.00	0.00
E2 - incomplete primary	0.04	0.01	0.00	0.00	0.00	0.00
E3 - primary	0.07	0.05	0.04	0.03	0.03	0.03
E4 - lower secondary	0.14	0.12	0.10	0.08	0.08	0.07
E5 - upper secondary	0.45	0.47	0.47	0.46	0.46	0.48
E6 - post-secondary	0.27	0.34	0.39	0.42	0.43	0.42
Mean years of schooling (in years)	11.42	12.40	12.99	13.18	13.29	13.28

Education scenarios

GET: global education trend scenario (medium assumption also used for SSP2)

CER: constant enrolment rates scenario (assumption of no future improvements)

FT: Fast track scenario (assumption of education expansion according to fastest historical experience)

Pyramids by Education, Medium Scenario

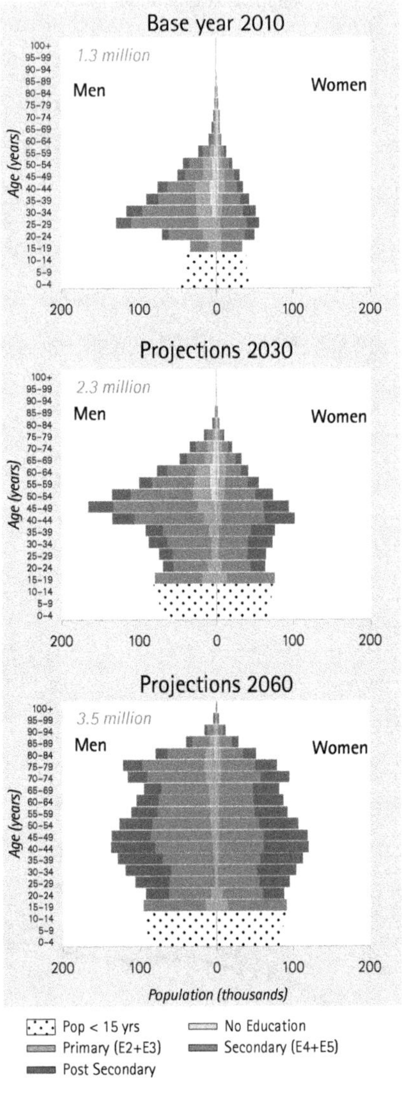

Population Size by Educational Attainment According to Three Education Scenarios: GET, CER, and FT

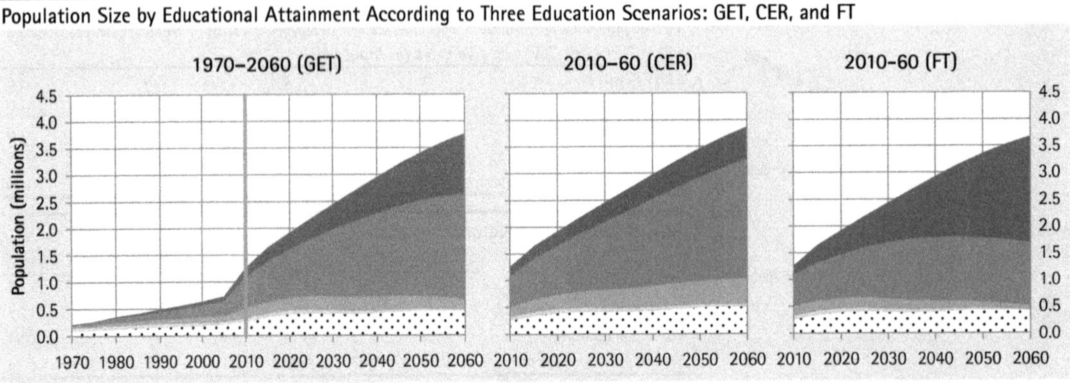

Bahrain (Continued)

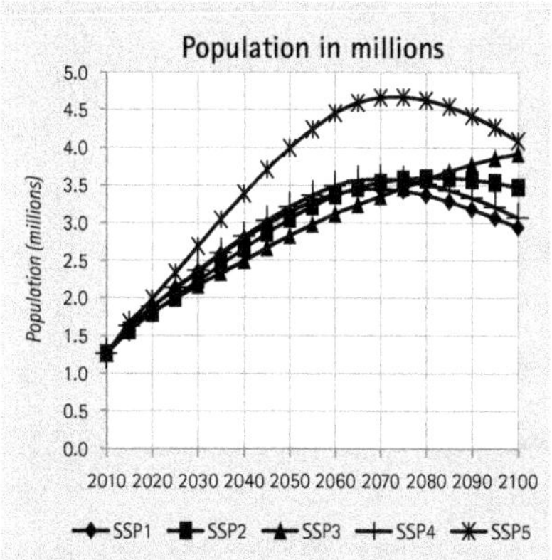

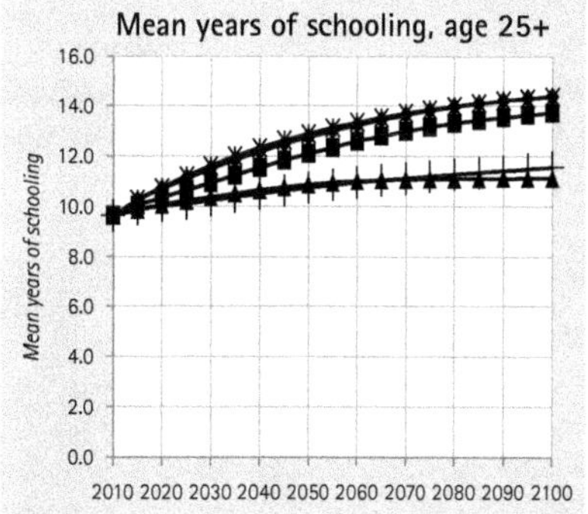

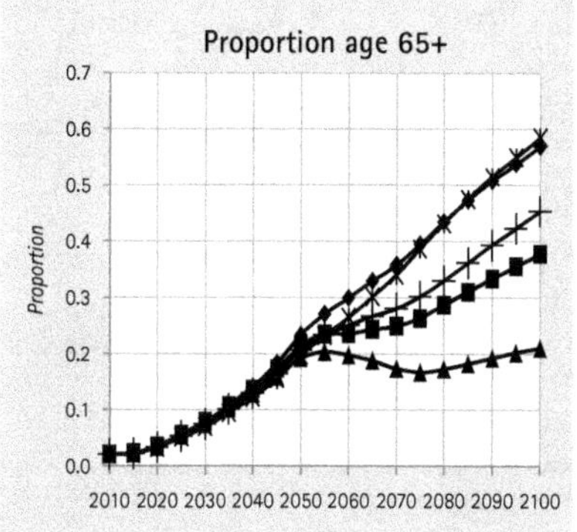

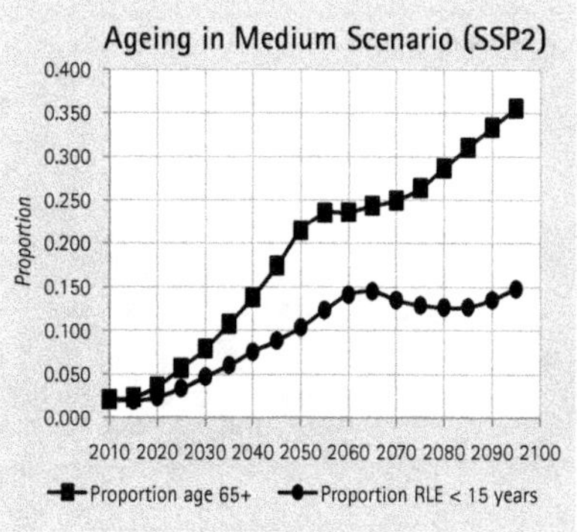

Alternative Scenarios to 2100

Projection Results by Scenario (SSP1–5)

	2010	2020	2030	2040	2050	2075	2100
Population (in millions)							
SSP1 - Rapid development	1.26	1.88	2.35	2.79	3.14	3.42	2.94
SSP2 - Medium	1.26	1.79	2.23	2.66	3.05	3.58	3.47
SSP3 - Stalled development	1.26	1.81	2.16	2.50	2.83	3.47	3.92
SSP4 - Inequality	1.26	1.88	2.37	2.82	3.21	3.57	3.07
SSP5 - Conventional development	1.26	1.99	2.69	3.39	3.99	4.67	4.09
Proportion age 65+							
SSP1 - Rapid development	0.02	0.03	0.08	0.14	0.23	0.39	0.57
SSP2 - Medium	0.02	0.04	0.08	0.14	0.21	0.26	0.38
SSP3 - Stalled development	0.02	0.03	0.08	0.13	0.19	0.17	0.21
SSP4 - Inequality	0.02	0.03	0.07	0.13	0.21	0.30	0.45
SSP5 - Conventional development	0.02	0.03	0.07	0.12	0.20	0.39	0.59
Proportion below age 20							
SSP1 - Rapid development	0.25	0.24	0.21	0.16	0.14	0.10	0.07
SSP2 - Medium	0.25	0.26	0.24	0.21	0.20	0.17	0.15
SSP3 - Stalled development	0.25	0.27	0.27	0.25	0.25	0.26	0.25
SSP4 - Inequality	0.25	0.25	0.22	0.18	0.16	0.13	0.10
SSP5 - Conventional development	0.25	0.24	0.20	0.16	0.14	0.10	0.07
Proportion of Women age 20–39 with at least secondary education							
SSP1 - Rapid development	0.86	0.96	0.97	0.98	0.98	0.99	1.00
SSP2 - Medium	0.86	0.93	0.95	0.96	0.97	0.98	0.99
SSP3 - Stalled development	0.86	0.89	0.89	0.89	0.89	0.89	0.89
SSP4 - Inequality	0.86	0.84	0.80	0.80	0.80	0.80	0.80
SSP5 - Conventional development	0.86	0.96	0.97	0.98	0.98	0.99	1.00
Mean years of schooling, age 25+							
SSP1 - Rapid development	9.63	10.70	11.49	12.18	12.76	13.82	14.39
SSP2 - Medium	9.63	10.35	10.95	11.54	12.10	13.17	13.73
SSP3 - Stalled development	9.63	10.06	10.37	10.65	10.87	11.09	11.14
SSP4 - Inequality	9.63	10.01	10.24	10.50	10.74	11.20	11.56
SSP5 - Conventional development	9.63	10.75	11.61	12.33	12.89	13.86	14.38

Demographic Assumptions Underlying SSPs

	2010–15	2020–25	2030–35	2040–45	2050–55	2075–80	2095–2100
Total fertility rate							
SSP1 - Rapid development	2.23	1.77	1.51	1.39	1.31	1.21	1.17
SSP2 - Medium	2.37	2.10	1.94	1.87	1.80	1.65	1.60
SSP3 - Stalled development	2.49	2.50	2.50	2.45	2.39	2.23	2.17
SSP4 - Inequality	2.29	1.92	1.65	1.50	1.41	1.30	1.26
SSP5 - Conventional development	2.23	1.77	1.51	1.39	1.31	1.21	1.17
Life expectancy at birth for females (in years)							
SSP1 - Rapid development	77.84	81.12	84.39	87.53	90.52	97.97	103.96
SSP2 - Medium	76.89	79.49	81.69	83.69	85.79	90.80	94.80
SSP3 - Stalled development	76.91	78.27	79.59	80.65	81.54	83.66	85.56
SSP4 - Inequality	77.33	79.70	81.99	83.99	85.95	90.48	94.35
SSP5 - Conventional development	77.84	81.12	84.39	87.53	90.52	97.97	103.96
Migration – net flow over five years (in thousands)							
SSP1 - Rapid development	254	159	158	145	128	33	0
SSP2 - Medium	194	127	134	136	134	51	0
SSP3 - Stalled development	212	75	76	83	91	47	0
SSP4 - Inequality	254	160	163	164	160	55	0
SSP5 - Conventional development	297	255	270	254	227	57	0

Ageing Indicators, Medium Scenario (SSP2)

	2010	2020	2030	2040	2050	2075	2095
Median age	30.13	35.24	39.12	40.71	42.15	47.91	54.05
Propspective median age	30.13	32.78	34.87	34.85	34.48	35.67	37.99
Proportion age 65+	0.02	0.04	0.08	0.14	0.21	0.26	0.36
Proportion RLE < 15 years	0.02	0.02	0.05	0.08	0.10	0.13	0.15

Bangladesh

Detailed Human Capital Projections to 2060

Demographic indicators, Medium Scenario (SSP2)	2010	2020	2030	2040	2050	2060
Population (in millions)	148.69	165.18	178.65	187.22	190.67	189.05
Proportion age 65+	0.05	0.05	0.08	0.11	0.16	0.21
Proportion below age 20	0.42	0.36	0.31	0.27	0.24	0.22
	2005–10	2015–20	2025–30	2035–40	2045–50	2055–60
Total Fertility Rate	2.38	2.11	1.91	1.78	1.67	1.60
Life expectancy at birth (in years)						
Men	67.41	69.89	72.12	74.22	76.30	78.37
Women	68.29	72.09	75.00	77.49	79.79	81.99
Five-year immigration flow (in '000)	62.56	61.47	64.01	65.45	65.40	64.45
Five-year emigration flow (in '000)	2954.69	2370.00	2341.54	2251.96	2117.18	1942.53

Human Capital indicators, Medium Scenario (SSP2)	2010	2020	2030	2040	2050	2060
Population age 25+: highest educational attainment						
E1 - no education	0.40	0.30	0.23	0.17	0.12	0.09
E2 - incomplete primary	0.17	0.16	0.14	0.12	0.10	0.08
E3 - primary	0.17	0.20	0.22	0.24	0.24	0.23
E4 - lower secondary	0.12	0.16	0.18	0.20	0.20	0.20
E5 - upper secondary	0.06	0.08	0.10	0.12	0.15	0.18
E6 - post-secondary	0.08	0.10	0.13	0.15	0.18	0.21
Mean years of schooling (in years)	4.67	5.63	6.49	7.27	8.07	8.85
Gender gap (population age 25+): highest educational attainment (ratio male/female)						
E1 - no education	0.78	0.85	0.91	0.96	1.00	1.05
E2 - incomplete primary	0.89	0.94	0.97	0.99	1.00	1.01
E3 - primary	1.06	0.98	0.97	0.98	0.98	0.98
E4 - lower secondary	1.21	1.00	0.95	0.94	0.94	0.93
E5 - upper secondary	1.57	1.21	1.04	0.98	0.96	0.98
E6 - post-secondary	2.18	1.64	1.36	1.22	1.13	1.09
Mean years of schooling (male minus female)	1.37	0.85	0.48	0.25	0.13	0.09
Women age 20–39: highest educational attainment						
E1 - no education	0.21	0.11	0.08	0.06	0.04	0.03
E2 - incomplete primary	0.18	0.12	0.08	0.05	0.04	0.03
E3 - primary	0.25	0.28	0.27	0.25	0.22	0.19
E4 - lower secondary	0.19	0.25	0.24	0.22	0.20	0.17
E5 - upper secondary	0.08	0.12	0.17	0.21	0.25	0.28
E6 - post-secondary	0.08	0.12	0.16	0.21	0.26	0.30
Mean years of schooling (in years)	6.06	7.44	8.34	9.21	10.01	10.71

Education scenarios

GET: global education trend scenario (medium assumption also used for SSP2)

CER: constant enrolment rates scenario (assumption of no future improvements)

FT: Fast track scenario (assumption of education expansion according to fastest historical experience)

Pyramids by Education, Medium Scenario

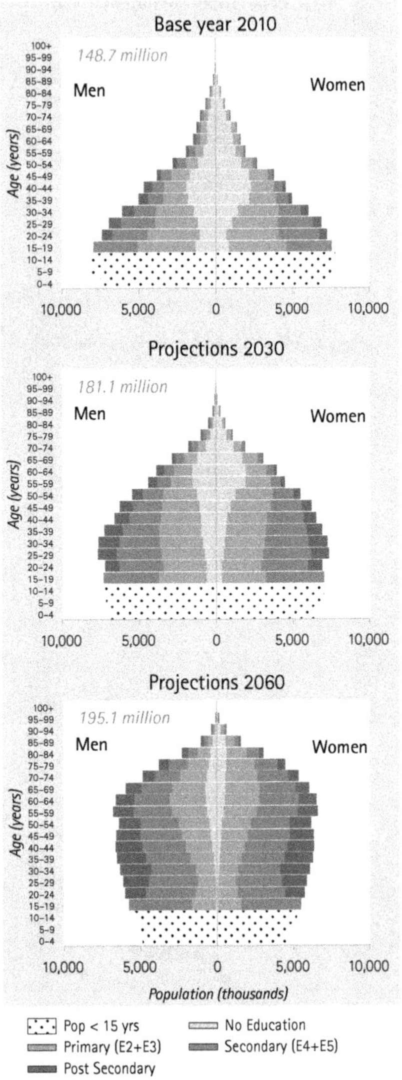

Population Size by Educational Attainment According to Three Education Scenarios: GET, CER, and FT

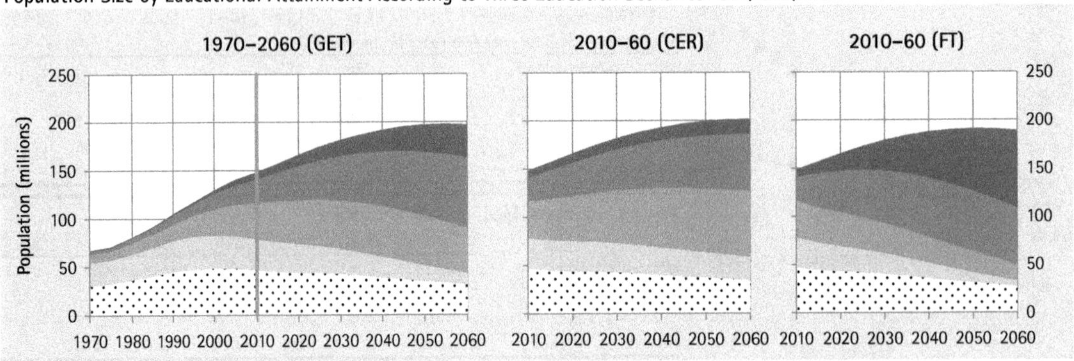

Bangladesh (Continued)

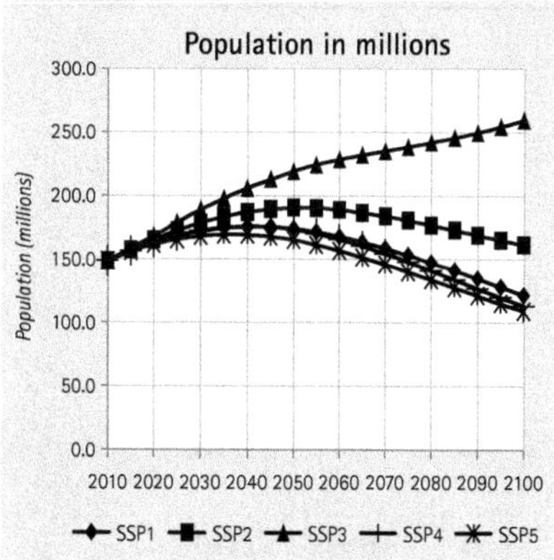

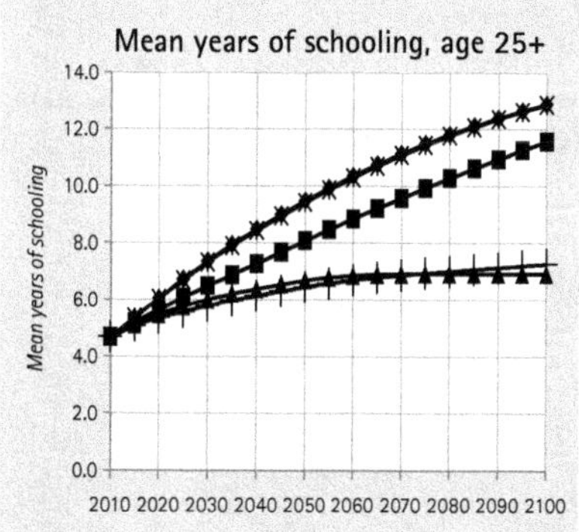

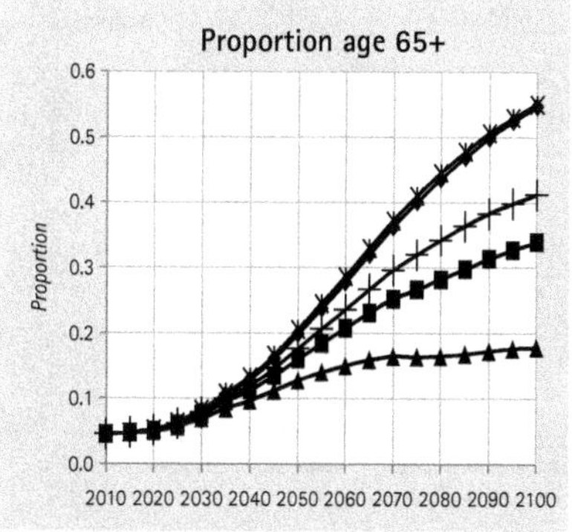

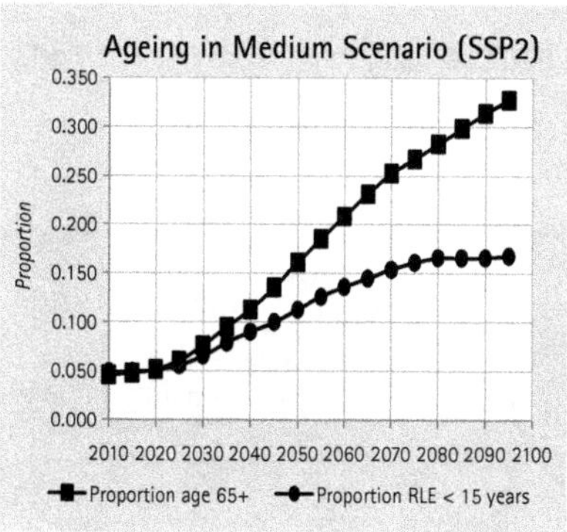

Alternative Scenarios to 2100

Projection Results by Scenario (SSP1–5)

	2010	2020	2030	2040	2050	2075	2100
Population (in millions)							
SSP1 - Rapid development	148.69	162.91	171.99	175.78	174.21	153.34	121.53
SSP2 - Medium	148.69	165.18	178.65	187.22	190.67	180.68	161.61
SSP3 - Stalled development	148.69	168.47	189.03	205.89	219.32	238.72	259.59
SSP4 - Inequality	148.69	163.23	172.51	175.99	173.51	147.97	113.26
SSP5 - Conventional development	148.69	161.64	168.12	169.30	165.21	140.08	108.94
Proportion age 65+							
SSP1 - Rapid development	0.05	0.05	0.08	0.13	0.20	0.40	0.55
SSP2 - Medium	0.05	0.05	0.08	0.11	0.16	0.27	0.34
SSP3 - Stalled development	0.05	0.05	0.07	0.10	0.13	0.16	0.18
SSP4 - Inequality	0.05	0.05	0.08	0.12	0.18	0.32	0.41
SSP5 - Conventional development	0.05	0.05	0.08	0.13	0.21	0.41	0.55
Proportion below age 20							
SSP1 - Rapid development	0.42	0.35	0.28	0.22	0.18	0.11	0.08
SSP2 - Medium	0.42	0.36	0.31	0.27	0.24	0.19	0.17
SSP3 - Stalled development	0.42	0.36	0.34	0.31	0.29	0.28	0.28
SSP4 - Inequality	0.42	0.35	0.29	0.24	0.20	0.14	0.12
SSP5 - Conventional development	0.42	0.35	0.28	0.23	0.18	0.11	0.08
Proportion of Women age 20–39 with at least secondary education							
SSP1 - Rapid development	0.36	0.59	0.72	0.80	0.84	0.91	0.96
SSP2 - Medium	0.36	0.49	0.57	0.64	0.70	0.83	0.93
SSP3 - Stalled development	0.36	0.45	0.46	0.46	0.46	0.46	0.46
SSP4 - Inequality	0.36	0.42	0.41	0.41	0.41	0.41	0.41
SSP5 - Conventional development	0.36	0.59	0.72	0.80	0.84	0.91	0.96
Mean years of schooling, age 25+							
SSP1 - Rapid development	4.67	6.04	7.36	8.48	9.47	11.48	12.87
SSP2 - Medium	4.67	5.63	6.49	7.27	8.07	9.93	11.57
SSP3 - Stalled development	4.67	5.46	6.00	6.38	6.68	6.92	6.92
SSP4 - Inequality	4.67	5.35	5.78	6.14	6.45	6.95	7.28
SSP5 - Conventional development	4.67	6.03	7.32	8.44	9.42	11.44	12.86

Demographic Assumptions Underlying SSPs

	2010–15	2020–25	2030–35	2040–45	2050–55	2075–80	2095–2100
Total fertility rate							
SSP1 - Rapid development	2.10	1.67	1.40	1.26	1.17	1.16	1.20
SSP2 - Medium	2.23	2.01	1.83	1.72	1.64	1.59	1.62
SSP3 - Stalled development	2.34	2.35	2.32	2.25	2.20	2.23	2.34
SSP4 - Inequality	2.12	1.74	1.49	1.36	1.29	1.30	1.36
SSP5 - Conventional development	2.10	1.67	1.40	1.26	1.17	1.16	1.20
Life expectancy at birth for females (in years)							
SSP1 - Rapid development	73.29	76.44	79.87	83.09	86.17	93.93	100.34
SSP2 - Medium	70.38	73.61	76.29	78.59	80.89	86.31	90.70
SSP3 - Stalled development	72.59	74.10	75.56	76.68	77.59	79.75	81.55
SSP4 - Inequality	72.89	75.43	77.71	79.75	81.73	86.34	90.21
SSP5 - Conventional development	73.29	76.44	79.87	83.09	86.17	93.93	100.34
Migration – net flow over five years (in thousands)							
SSP1 - Rapid development	−2453	−2294	−2173	−1972	−1714	−531	0
SSP2 - Medium	−2456	−2323	−2248	−2146	−1989	−743	0
SSP3 - Stalled development	−2042	−1146	−1110	−1079	−1034	−445	0
SSP4 - Inequality	−2453	−2287	−2140	−1891	−1590	−450	0
SSP5 - Conventional development	−2863	−3464	−3329	−3094	−2766	−940	0

Ageing Indicators, Medium Scenario (SSP2)

	2010	2020	2030	2040	2050	2075	2095
Median age	24.18	27.98	31.99	36.13	39.59	47.21	51.21
Propspective median age	24.18	26.49	28.93	31.60	33.35	36.43	36.46
Proportion age 65+	0.05	0.05	0.08	0.11	0.16	0.27	0.33
Proportion RLE < 15 years	0.05	0.05	0.07	0.09	0.11	0.16	0.17

Belarus

Detailed Human Capital Projections to 2060

Demographic indicators, Medium Scenario (SSP2)	2010	2020	2030	2040	2050	2060
Population (in millions)	9.60	9.32	8.96	8.57	8.17	7.72
Proportion age 65+	0.14	0.15	0.20	0.23	0.28	0.31
Proportion below age 20	0.21	0.21	0.20	0.18	0.18	0.18
	2005–10	2015–20	2025–30	2035–40	2045–50	2055–60
Total Fertility Rate	1.39	1.51	1.50	1.54	1.59	1.61
Life expectancy at birth (in years)						
Men	63.60	67.47	70.66	73.49	76.07	78.67
Women	75.52	78.09	80.29	82.39	84.41	86.51
Five-year immigration flow (in '000)	58.45	57.26	59.44	60.78	60.79	59.91
Five-year emigration flow (in '000)	108.53	67.79	58.05	52.74	46.28	41.63

Human Capital indicators, Medium Scenario (SSP2)	2010	2020	2030	2040	2050	2060
Population age 25+: highest educational attainment						
E1 - no education	0.00	0.00	0.00	0.00	0.00	0.00
E2 - incomplete primary	0.00	0.00	0.00	0.00	0.00	0.00
E3 - primary	0.08	0.03	0.01	0.00	0.00	0.00
E4 - lower secondary	0.07	0.04	0.02	0.01	0.01	0.00
E5 - upper secondary	0.66	0.71	0.72	0.72	0.69	0.66
E6 - post-secondary	0.19	0.22	0.24	0.27	0.30	0.33
Mean years of schooling (in years)	10.77	11.36	11.70	11.96	12.17	12.35
Gender gap (population age 25+): highest educational attainment (ratio male/female)						
E1 - no education	0.64	0.95	1.03	1.01	0.99	0.98
E2 - incomplete primary	0.33	0.42	0.65	0.79	0.82	0.84
E3 - primary	0.49	0.39	0.36	0.46	0.62	0.65
E4 - lower secondary	1.00	0.92	0.92	1.03	1.11	1.14
E5 - upper secondary	1.11	1.10	1.09	1.09	1.08	1.07
E6 - post-secondary	0.93	0.85	0.81	0.81	0.83	0.87
Mean years of schooling (male minus female)	0.26	0.04	−0.10	−0.16	−0.19	−0.20
Women age 20–39: highest educational attainment						
E1 - no education	0.00	0.00	0.00	0.00	0.00	0.00
E2 - incomplete primary	0.00	0.00	0.00	0.00	0.00	0.00
E3 - primary	0.00	0.00	0.00	0.00	0.00	0.00
E4 - lower secondary	0.02	0.01	0.02	0.02	0.02	0.02
E5 - upper secondary	0.76	0.71	0.69	0.66	0.63	0.62
E6 - post-secondary	0.22	0.27	0.29	0.32	0.36	0.37
Mean years of schooling (in years)	12.03	12.22	12.12	12.24	12.37	12.40

Education scenarios

GET : global education trend scenario (medium assumption also used for SSP2)

CER: constant enrolment rates scenario (assumption of no future improvements)

FT: Fast track scenario (assumption of education expansion according to fastest historical experience)

Pyramids by Education, Medium Scenario

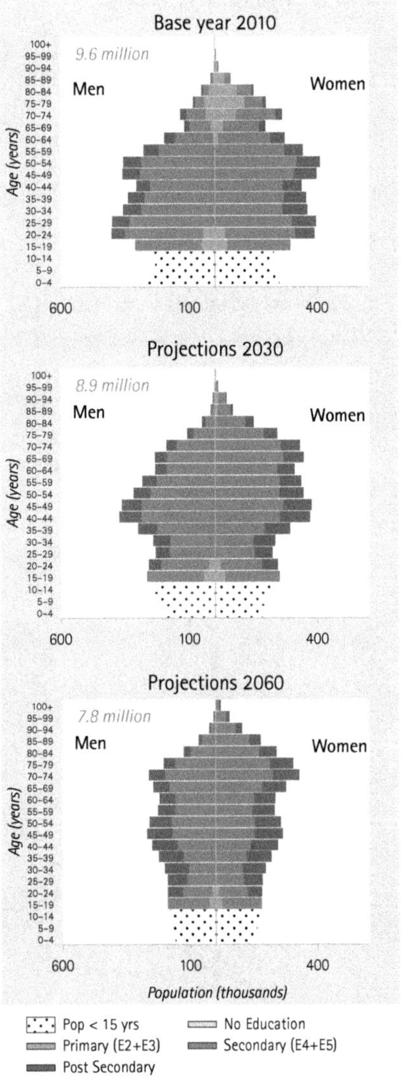

Population Size by Educational Attainment According to Three Education Scenarios: GET, CER, and FT

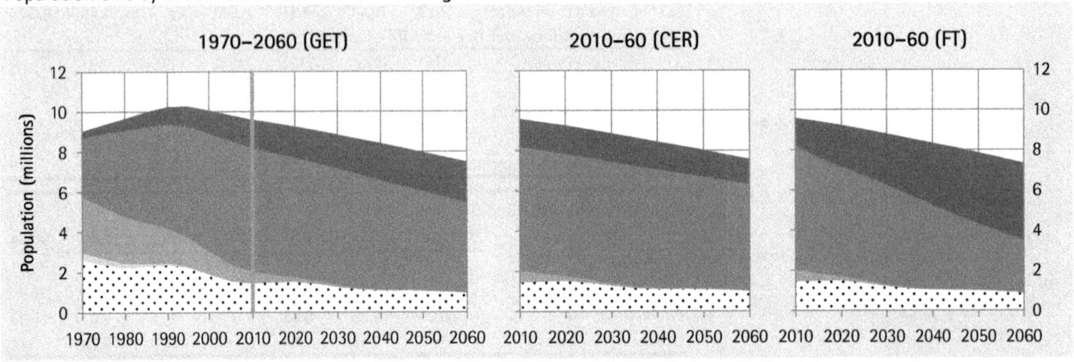

Belarus (Continued)

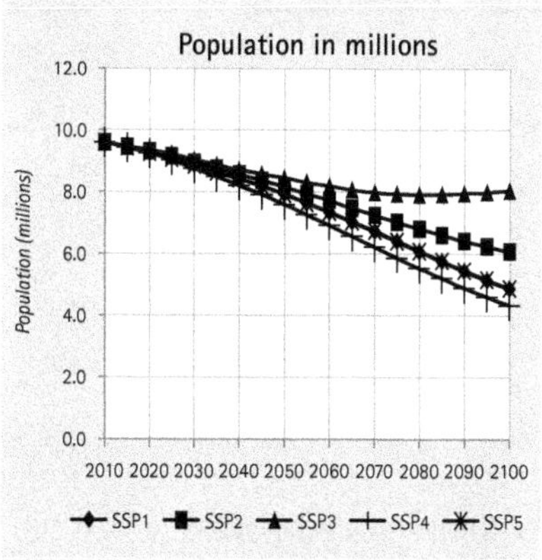

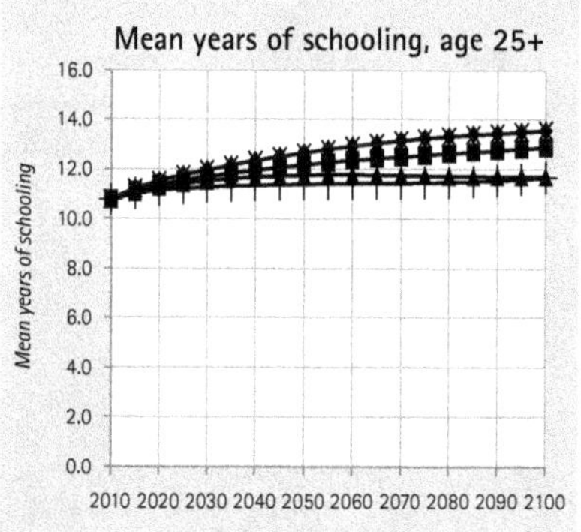

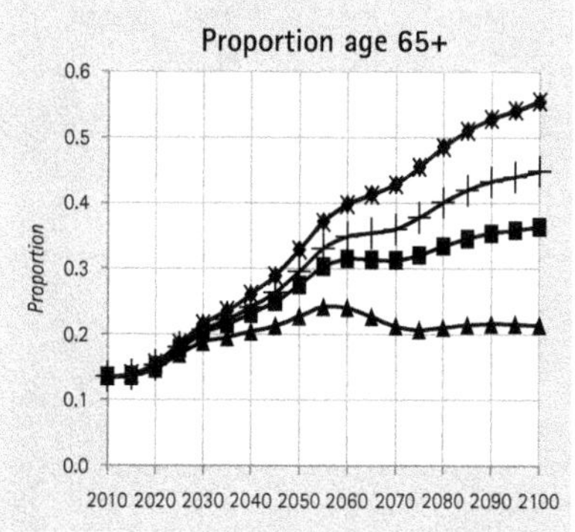

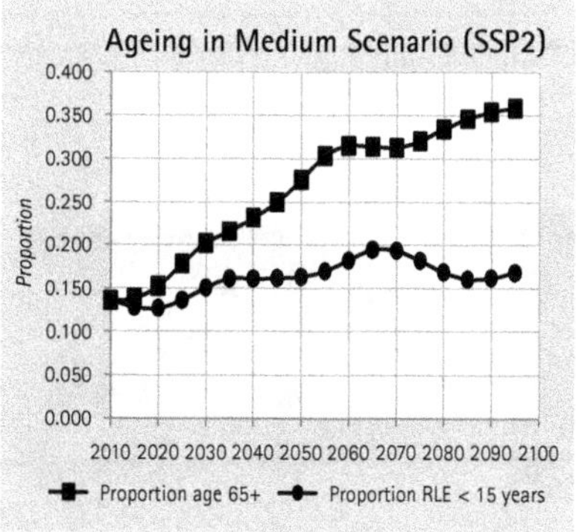

Alternative Scenarios to 2100

Projection Results by Scenario (SSP1–5)

	2010	2020	2030	2040	2050	2075	2100
Population (in millions)							
SSP1 - Rapid development	9.60	9.29	8.88	8.43	7.93	6.40	4.86
SSP2 - Medium	9.60	9.32	8.96	8.57	8.17	7.04	6.09
SSP3 - Stalled development	9.60	9.36	9.06	8.72	8.45	7.94	8.05
SSP4 - Inequality	9.60	9.25	8.76	8.21	7.60	5.87	4.33
SSP5 - Conventional development	9.60	9.28	8.87	8.43	7.93	6.42	4.88
Proportion age 65+							
SSP1 - Rapid development	0.14	0.16	0.22	0.26	0.33	0.46	0.55
SSP2 - Medium	0.14	0.15	0.20	0.23	0.28	0.32	0.36
SSP3 - Stalled development	0.14	0.15	0.19	0.20	0.23	0.21	0.21
SSP4 - Inequality	0.14	0.15	0.21	0.24	0.30	0.38	0.45
SSP5 - Conventional development	0.14	0.16	0.22	0.26	0.33	0.46	0.56
Proportion below age 20							
SSP1 - Rapid development	0.21	0.20	0.18	0.14	0.13	0.10	0.08
SSP2 - Medium	0.21	0.21	0.20	0.18	0.18	0.17	0.16
SSP3 - Stalled development	0.21	0.22	0.23	0.21	0.23	0.24	0.25
SSP4 - Inequality	0.21	0.21	0.18	0.15	0.14	0.12	0.11
SSP5 - Conventional development	0.21	0.20	0.18	0.14	0.13	0.10	0.08
Proportion of Women age 20–39 with at least secondary education							
SSP1 - Rapid development	1.00	1.00	1.00	1.00	1.00	1.00	1.00
SSP2 - Medium	1.00	1.00	1.00	1.00	1.00	1.00	1.00
SSP3 - Stalled development	1.00	1.00	1.00	1.00	1.00	1.00	1.00
SSP4 - Inequality	1.00	0.94	0.90	0.90	0.90	0.90	0.90
SSP5 - Conventional development	1.00	1.00	1.00	1.00	1.00	1.00	1.00
Mean years of schooling, age 25+							
SSP1 - Rapid development	10.77	11.52	11.97	12.33	12.65	13.24	13.56
SSP2 - Medium	10.77	11.36	11.70	11.96	12.17	12.56	12.89
SSP3 - Stalled development	10.77	11.26	11.53	11.67	11.75	11.73	11.71
SSP4 - Inequality	10.77	11.14	11.28	11.34	11.39	11.45	11.67
SSP5 - Conventional development	10.77	11.52	11.97	12.33	12.66	13.24	13.56

Demographic Assumptions Underlying SSPs

	2010–15	2020–25	2030–35	2040–45	2050–55	2075–80	2095–2100
Total fertility rate							
SSP1 - Rapid development	1.43	1.26	1.17	1.17	1.17	1.20	1.22
SSP2 - Medium	1.52	1.51	1.51	1.56	1.60	1.63	1.65
SSP3 - Stalled development	1.60	1.76	1.88	1.97	2.05	2.11	2.15
SSP4 - Inequality	1.44	1.30	1.23	1.23	1.23	1.26	1.28
SSP5 - Conventional development	1.43	1.26	1.17	1.17	1.17	1.20	1.22
Life expectancy at birth for females (in years)							
SSP1 - Rapid development	78.09	81.16	84.17	87.15	90.11	97.61	103.62
SSP2 - Medium	76.89	79.19	81.39	83.39	85.51	90.51	94.49
SSP3 - Stalled development	77.11	78.16	79.24	80.27	81.24	83.61	85.56
SSP4 - Inequality	77.63	79.61	81.66	83.59	85.62	90.33	94.22
SSP5 - Conventional development	78.09	81.16	84.17	87.15	90.11	97.61	103.62
Migration – net flow over five years (in thousands)							
SSP1 - Rapid development	−25	−3	5	10	14	5	0
SSP2 - Medium	−25	−3	5	12	17	8	0
SSP3 - Stalled development	−21	−2	2	7	12	8	0
SSP4 - Inequality	−25	−3	5	11	16	7	0
SSP5 - Conventional development	−30	−5	7	14	18	6	0

Ageing Indicators, Medium Scenario (SSP2)

	2010	2020	2030	2040	2050	2075	2095
Median age	38.21	40.51	44.36	47.97	48.36	51.72	53.02
Propspective median age	38.21	37.87	39.42	41.05	39.20	37.54	34.68
Proportion age 65+	0.14	0.15	0.20	0.23	0.28	0.32	0.36
Proportion RLE < 15 years	0.14	0.13	0.15	0.16	0.16	0.18	0.17

Belgium

Detailed Human Capital Projections to 2060

Demographic indicators, Medium Scenario (SSP2)	2010	2020	2030	2040	2050	2060
Population (in millions)	10.71	11.30	11.92	12.50	13.02	13.49
Proportion age 65+	0.17	0.20	0.24	0.26	0.27	0.29
Proportion below age 20	0.23	0.22	0.21	0.21	0.20	0.20
	2005–10	2015–20	2025–30	2035–40	2045–50	2055–60
Total Fertility Rate	1.79	1.81	1.80	1.80	1.80	1.80
Life expectancy at birth (in years)						
Men	76.95	79.36	81.64	83.79	85.82	87.83
Women	82.49	84.89	87.11	89.21	91.19	93.19
Five-year immigration flow (in '000)	217.19	214.75	223.47	229.16	229.94	226.99
Five-year emigration flow (in '000)	17.76	12.46	12.41	12.51	12.59	12.73

Human Capital indicators, Medium Scenario (SSP2)	2010	2020	2030	2040	2050	2060
Population age 25+: highest educational attainment						
E1 - no education	0.03	0.02	0.02	0.01	0.01	0.00
E2 - incomplete primary	0.00	0.00	0.00	0.00	0.00	0.00
E3 - primary	0.13	0.08	0.05	0.03	0.01	0.01
E4 - lower secondary	0.22	0.19	0.15	0.11	0.07	0.04
E5 - upper secondary	0.29	0.32	0.33	0.33	0.32	0.31
E6 - post-secondary	0.33	0.39	0.46	0.52	0.58	0.64
Mean years of schooling (in years)	11.51	12.28	12.94	13.49	13.95	14.31
Gender gap (population age 25+): highest educational attainment (ratio male/female)						
E1 - no education	0.83	0.79	0.75	0.72	0.68	0.66
E2 - incomplete primary	NA	NA	NA	NA	NA	NA
E3 - primary	0.77	0.76	0.77	0.80	0.84	0.91
E4 - lower secondary	1.04	1.06	1.08	1.09	1.10	1.12
E5 - upper secondary	1.14	1.16	1.18	1.19	1.18	1.15
E6 - post-secondary	0.98	0.92	0.90	0.90	0.91	0.93
Mean years of schooling (male minus female)	0.20	0.02	−0.12	−0.20	−0.22	−0.20
Women age 20–39: highest educational attainment						
E1 - no education	0.01	0.00	0.00	0.00	0.00	0.00
E2 - incomplete primary	0.00	0.00	0.00	0.00	0.00	0.00
E3 - primary	0.01	0.01	0.00	0.00	0.00	0.00
E4 - lower secondary	0.09	0.05	0.03	0.01	0.01	0.01
E5 - upper secondary	0.37	0.36	0.34	0.32	0.30	0.29
E6 - post-secondary	0.52	0.59	0.63	0.67	0.69	0.70
Mean years of schooling (in years)	13.61	14.09	14.39	14.57	14.68	14.74

Education scenarios

GET: global education trend scenario (medium assumption also used for SSP2)

CER: constant enrolment rates scenario (assumption of no future improvements)

FT: Fast track scenario (assumption of education expansion according to fastest historical experience)

Pyramids by Education, Medium Scenario

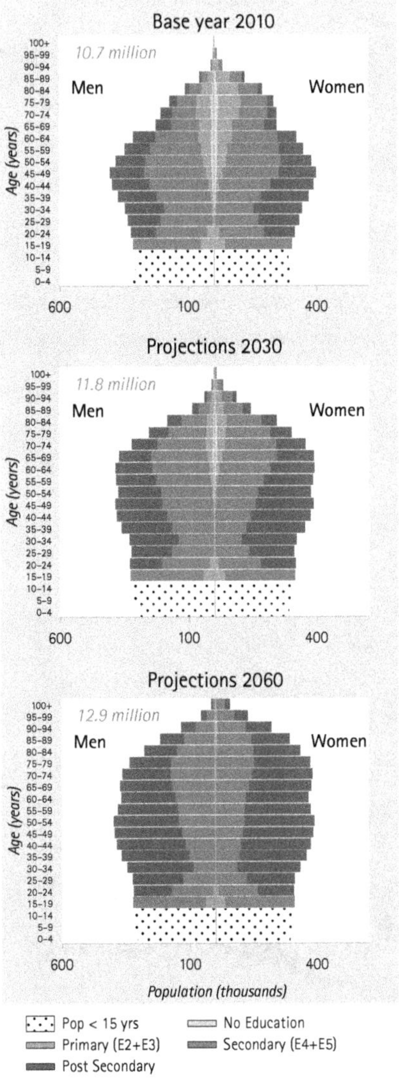

Population Size by Educational Attainment According to Three Education Scenarios: GET, CER, and FT

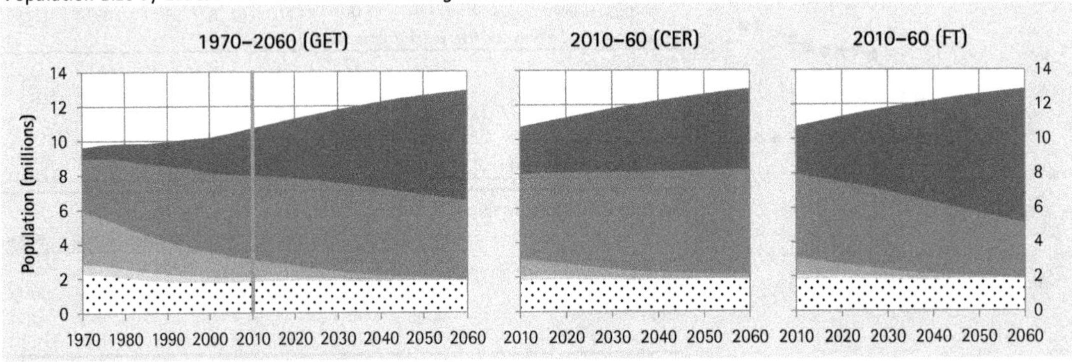

Belgium (Continued)

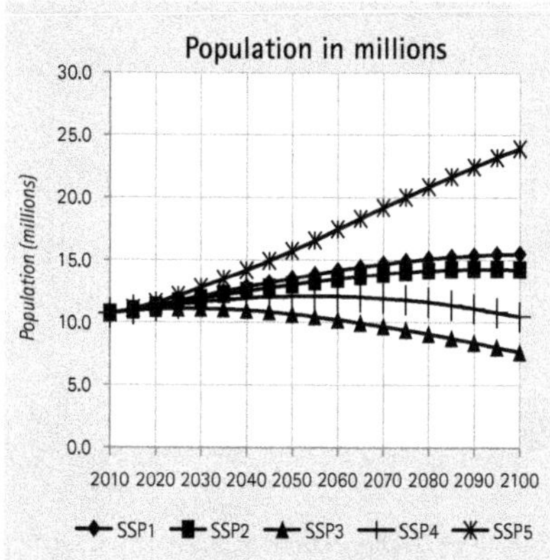

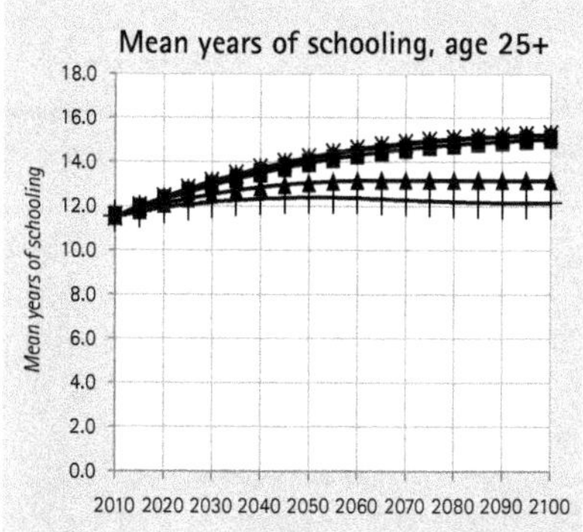

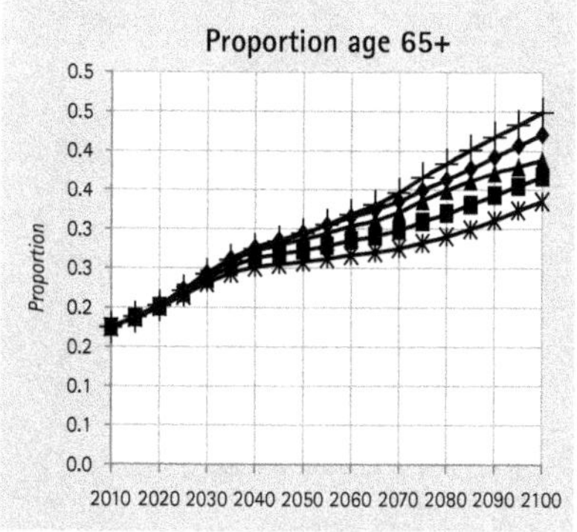

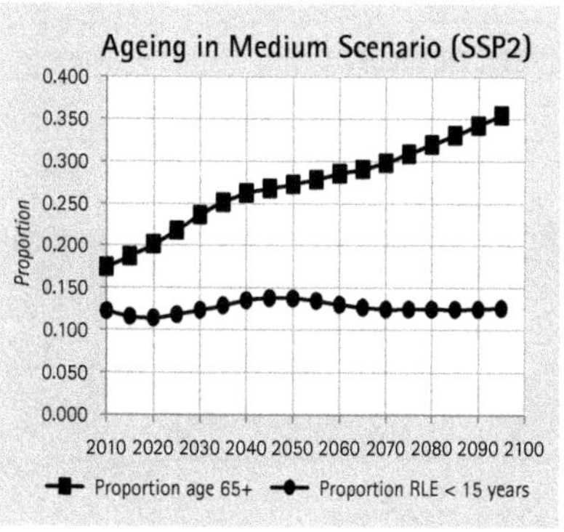

Alternative Scenarios to 2100

Projection Results by Scenario (SSP1–5)

	2010	2020	2030	2040	2050	2075	2100
Population (in millions)							
SSP1 - Rapid development	10.71	11.37	12.10	12.84	13.53	14.91	15.51
SSP2 - Medium	10.71	11.30	11.92	12.50	13.02	14.03	14.25
SSP3 - Stalled development	10.71	11.05	11.10	10.97	10.66	9.39	7.64
SSP4 - Inequality	10.71	11.22	11.63	11.94	12.09	11.80	10.46
SSP5 - Conventional development	10.71	11.57	12.81	14.21	15.75	20.04	23.93
Proportion age 65+							
SSP1 - Rapid development	0.17	0.20	0.24	0.28	0.29	0.35	0.42
SSP2 - Medium	0.17	0.20	0.24	0.26	0.27	0.31	0.37
SSP3 - Stalled development	0.17	0.20	0.24	0.27	0.29	0.34	0.39
SSP4 - Inequality	0.17	0.20	0.24	0.27	0.29	0.37	0.45
SSP5 - Conventional development	0.17	0.20	0.23	0.25	0.26	0.28	0.34
Proportion below age 20							
SSP1 - Rapid development	0.23	0.22	0.21	0.20	0.20	0.18	0.16
SSP2 - Medium	0.23	0.22	0.21	0.21	0.20	0.19	0.18
SSP3 - Stalled development	0.23	0.21	0.19	0.18	0.17	0.15	0.14
SSP4 - Inequality	0.23	0.21	0.19	0.18	0.17	0.14	0.12
SSP5 - Conventional development	0.23	0.23	0.23	0.24	0.24	0.23	0.22
Proportion of Women age 20–39 with at least secondary education							
SSP1 - Rapid development	0.98	0.99	1.00	1.00	1.00	1.00	1.00
SSP2 - Medium	0.98	0.99	1.00	1.00	1.00	1.00	1.00
SSP3 - Stalled development	0.98	0.98	0.98	0.98	0.98	0.98	0.98
SSP4 - Inequality	0.98	0.98	0.98	0.98	0.98	0.98	0.98
SSP5 - Conventional development	0.98	0.99	1.00	1.00	1.00	1.00	1.00
Mean years of schooling, age 25+							
SSP1 - Rapid development	11.51	12.37	13.07	13.66	14.13	14.91	15.23
SSP2 - Medium	11.51	12.28	12.94	13.49	13.95	14.69	15.04
SSP3 - Stalled development	11.51	12.08	12.54	12.85	13.06	13.17	13.17
SSP4 - Inequality	11.51	11.93	12.18	12.33	12.39	12.24	12.15
SSP5 - Conventional development	11.51	12.38	13.11	13.70	14.20	14.96	15.26

Demographic Assumptions Underlying SSPs

	2010–15	2020–25	2030–35	2040–45	2050–55	2075–80	2095–2100
Total fertility rate							
SSP1 - Rapid development	1.81	1.81	1.80	1.80	1.80	1.79	1.78
SSP2 - Medium	1.81	1.81	1.80	1.80	1.80	1.79	1.78
SSP3 - Stalled development	1.72	1.54	1.42	1.38	1.36	1.35	1.35
SSP4 - Inequality	1.72	1.54	1.43	1.39	1.37	1.36	1.36
SSP5 - Conventional development	1.90	2.08	2.18	2.22	2.24	2.24	2.23
Life expectancy at birth for females (in years)							
SSP1 - Rapid development	84.80	87.94	90.90	93.86	96.83	104.27	110.27
SSP2 - Medium	83.79	86.01	88.11	90.19	92.19	97.19	101.20
SSP3 - Stalled development	83.84	84.99	86.03	87.00	87.92	90.15	92.05
SSP4 - Inequality	84.35	86.45	88.42	90.44	92.35	96.99	100.82
SSP5 - Conventional development	84.80	87.94	90.90	93.86	96.83	104.27	110.27
Migration – net flow over five years (in thousands)							
SSP1 - Rapid development	193	206	212	211	203	83	0
SSP2 - Medium	192	202	208	210	208	92	0
SSP3 - Stalled development	161	102	104	103	99	41	0
SSP4 - Inequality	193	205	209	205	197	83	0
SSP5 - Conventional development	226	310	326	338	345	161	0

Ageing Indicators, Medium Scenario (SSP2)

	2010	2020	2030	2040	2050	2075	2095
Median age	41.24	42.77	43.84	45.01	45.65	48.41	51.83
Propspective median age	41.24	40.64	39.74	39.00	37.76	35.73	35.28
Proportion age 65+	0.17	0.20	0.24	0.26	0.27	0.31	0.35
Proportion RLE < 15 years	0.12	0.11	0.12	0.14	0.14	0.12	0.13

Belize

Detailed Human Capital Projections to 2060

Demographic indicators, Medium Scenario (SSP2)	2010	2020	2030	2040	2050	2060
Population (in millions)	0.31	0.38	0.44	0.49	0.54	0.57
Proportion age 65+	0.04	0.05	0.07	0.11	0.14	0.19
Proportion below age 20	0.46	0.40	0.35	0.30	0.27	0.24
	2005–10	2015–20	2025–30	2035–40	2045–50	2055–60
Total Fertility Rate	2.94	2.42	2.15	1.98	1.88	1.81
Life expectancy at birth (in years)						
Men	73.93	76.55	78.17	80.37	82.55	84.70
Women	76.79	79.41	81.71	83.79	85.91	87.90
Five-year immigration flow (in '000)	6.86	6.71	6.96	7.11	7.11	7.00
Five-year emigration flow (in '000)	7.79	7.12	7.77	8.18	8.33	8.21

Human Capital indicators, Medium Scenario (SSP2)	2010	2020	2030	2040	2050	2060
Population age 25+: highest educational attainment						
E1 - no education	0.08	0.06	0.05	0.04	0.03	0.02
E2 - incomplete primary	0.32	0.29	0.26	0.22	0.18	0.15
E3 - primary	0.33	0.33	0.33	0.32	0.32	0.31
E4 - lower secondary	0.13	0.15	0.16	0.16	0.17	0.16
E5 - upper secondary	0.03	0.04	0.06	0.08	0.10	0.13
E6 - post-secondary	0.11	0.13	0.16	0.18	0.20	0.23
Mean years of schooling (in years)	6.53	7.11	7.70	8.27	8.86	9.45
Gender gap (population age 25+): highest educational attainment (ratio male/female)						
E1 - no education	1.00	0.98	0.98	0.96	0.95	0.94
E2 - incomplete primary	0.96	0.98	0.99	0.99	0.98	0.97
E3 - primary	1.06	1.08	1.09	1.09	1.08	1.06
E4 - lower secondary	0.95	0.95	0.95	0.96	0.96	0.96
E5 - upper secondary	0.76	0.78	0.81	0.87	0.92	0.97
E6 - post-secondary	1.06	1.01	0.98	0.97	0.98	0.99
Mean years of schooling (male minus female)	0.04	−0.04	−0.10	−0.11	−0.09	−0.03
Women age 20–39: highest educational attainment						
E1 - no education	0.04	0.04	0.03	0.02	0.01	0.01
E2 - incomplete primary	0.30	0.24	0.18	0.13	0.09	0.05
E3 - primary	0.30	0.31	0.31	0.31	0.29	0.27
E4 - lower secondary	0.17	0.17	0.17	0.17	0.17	0.16
E5 - upper secondary	0.06	0.08	0.11	0.15	0.18	0.22
E6 - post-secondary	0.13	0.16	0.19	0.23	0.26	0.29
Mean years of schooling (in years)	7.42	8.09	8.89	9.64	10.34	10.96

Education scenarios

GET: global education trend scenario (medium assumption also used for SSP2)

CER: constant enrolment rates scenario (assumption of no future improvements)

FT: Fast track scenario (assumption of education expansion according to fastest historical experience)

Pyramids by Education, Medium Scenario

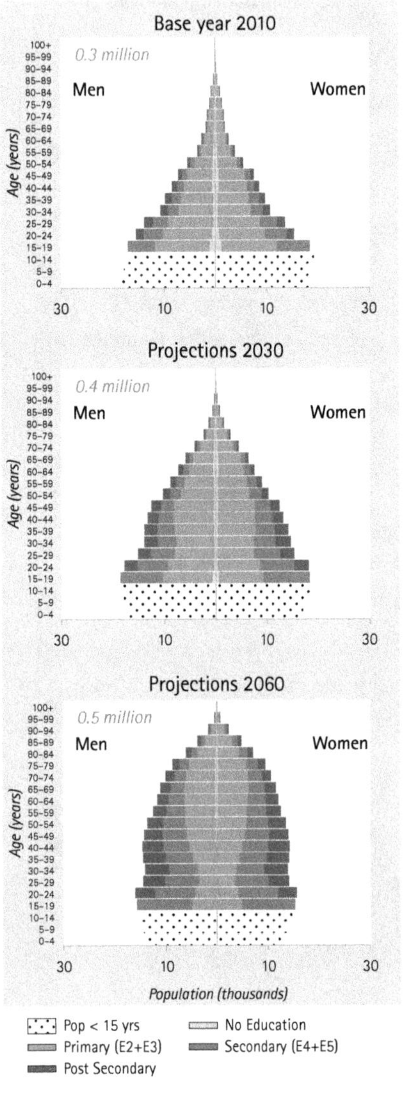

Population Size by Educational Attainment According to Three Education Scenarios: GET, CER, and FT

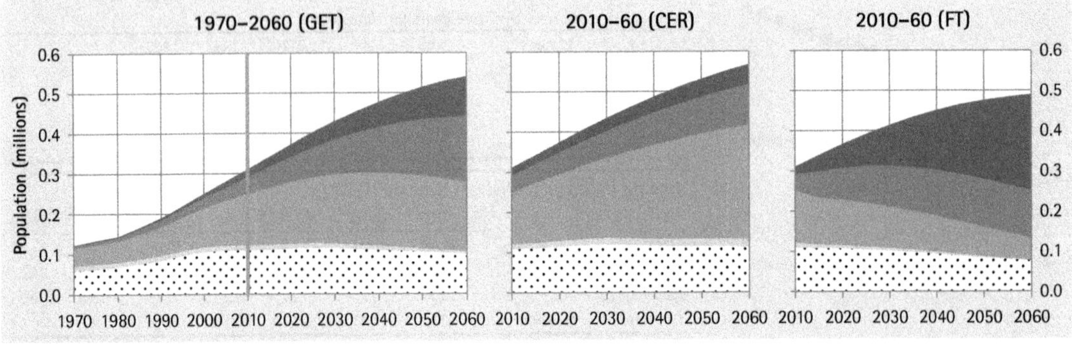

Belize (Continued)

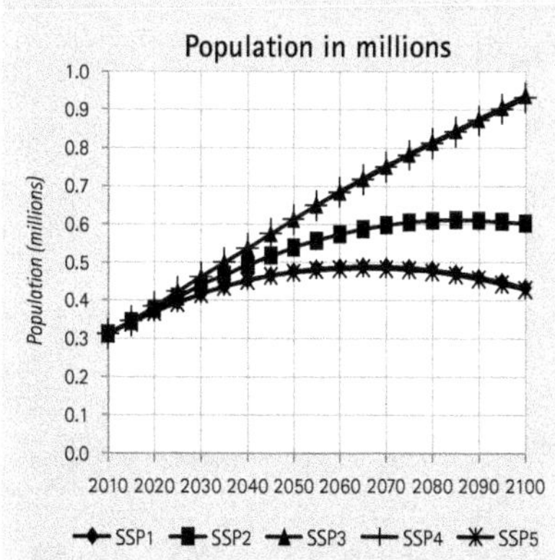

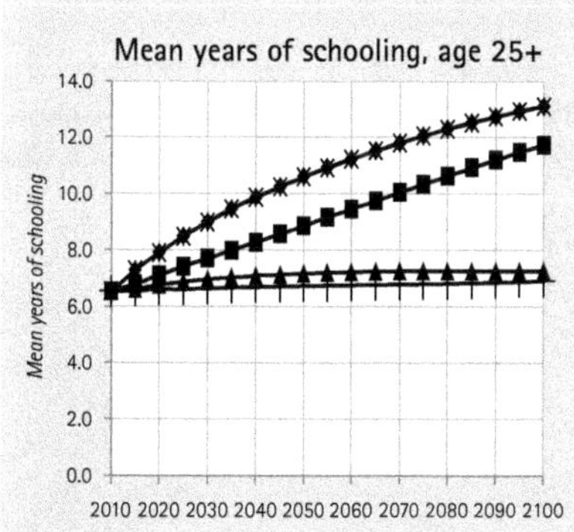

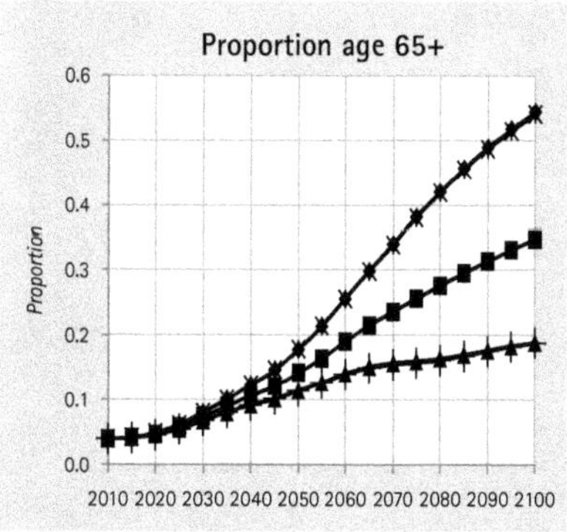

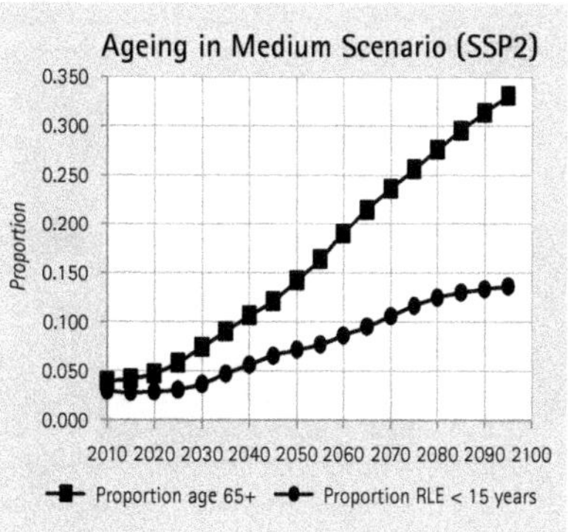

Alternative Scenarios to 2100

Projection Results by Scenario (SSP1–5)

	2010	2020	2030	2040	2050	2075	2100
Population (in millions)							
SSP1 - Rapid development	0.31	0.37	0.42	0.45	0.48	0.49	0.43
SSP2 - Medium	0.31	0.38	0.44	0.49	0.54	0.61	0.60
SSP3 - Stalled development	0.31	0.38	0.46	0.54	0.61	0.78	0.94
SSP4 - Inequality	0.31	0.38	0.46	0.54	0.61	0.78	0.93
SSP5 - Conventional development	0.31	0.37	0.42	0.45	0.47	0.48	0.43
Proportion age 65+							
SSP1 - Rapid development	0.04	0.05	0.08	0.12	0.18	0.38	0.54
SSP2 - Medium	0.04	0.05	0.07	0.11	0.14	0.26	0.35
SSP3 - Stalled development	0.04	0.05	0.07	0.09	0.11	0.16	0.19
SSP4 - Inequality	0.04	0.05	0.07	0.09	0.11	0.16	0.19
SSP5 - Conventional development	0.04	0.05	0.08	0.12	0.18	0.38	0.54
Proportion below age 20							
SSP1 - Rapid development	0.46	0.38	0.31	0.25	0.20	0.13	0.09
SSP2 - Medium	0.46	0.40	0.35	0.30	0.27	0.21	0.17
SSP3 - Stalled development	0.46	0.41	0.39	0.36	0.33	0.30	0.28
SSP4 - Inequality	0.46	0.41	0.39	0.36	0.33	0.30	0.28
SSP5 - Conventional development	0.46	0.38	0.31	0.25	0.20	0.13	0.09
Proportion of Women age 20–39 with at least secondary education							
SSP1 - Rapid development	0.37	0.60	0.70	0.76	0.80	0.88	0.94
SSP2 - Medium	0.37	0.42	0.48	0.54	0.61	0.77	0.90
SSP3 - Stalled development	0.37	0.35	0.35	0.35	0.35	0.35	0.35
SSP4 - Inequality	0.37	0.33	0.32	0.32	0.32	0.32	0.32
SSP5 - Conventional development	0.37	0.60	0.70	0.76	0.80	0.88	0.94
Mean years of schooling, age 25+							
SSP1 - Rapid development	6.53	7.90	8.99	9.87	10.59	12.05	13.10
SSP2 - Medium	6.53	7.11	7.70	8.27	8.86	10.33	11.73
SSP3 - Stalled development	6.53	6.77	6.97	7.09	7.18	7.26	7.27
SSP4 - Inequality	6.53	6.62	6.65	6.70	6.74	6.80	6.91
SSP5 - Conventional development	6.53	7.90	8.99	9.87	10.59	12.05	13.11

Demographic Assumptions Underlying SSPs

	2010–15	2020–25	2030–35	2040–45	2050–55	2075–80	2095–2100
Total fertility rate							
SSP1 - Rapid development	2.40	1.82	1.52	1.38	1.31	1.20	1.18
SSP2 - Medium	2.63	2.24	2.05	1.92	1.84	1.66	1.61
SSP3 - Stalled development	2.75	2.71	2.62	2.53	2.47	2.33	2.33
SSP4 - Inequality	2.76	2.74	2.63	2.53	2.46	2.30	2.29
SSP5 - Conventional development	2.40	1.82	1.52	1.38	1.31	1.20	1.18
Life expectancy at birth for females (in years)							
SSP1 - Rapid development	79.71	82.84	85.72	88.77	91.72	99.45	105.65
SSP2 - Medium	78.21	80.59	82.80	84.89	86.91	91.90	95.90
SSP3 - Stalled development	78.75	80.02	81.20	82.14	82.95	84.93	86.45
SSP4 - Inequality	78.75	80.00	81.17	82.10	82.90	84.82	86.36
SSP5 - Conventional development	79.71	82.84	85.72	88.77	91.72	99.45	105.65
Migration – net flow over five years (in thousands)							
SSP1 - Rapid development	−1	−1	−1	−1	−1	0	0
SSP2 - Medium	−1	−1	−1	−1	−1	0	0
SSP3 - Stalled development	0	0	0	−1	−1	0	0
SSP4 - Inequality	−1	−1	−1	−1	−1	0	0
SSP5 - Conventional development	−1	−1	−1	−2	−2	−1	0

Ageing Indicators, Medium Scenario (SSP2)

	2010	2020	2030	2040	2050	2075	2095
Median age	21.73	25.37	29.12	32.76	36.38	45.05	50.64
Propspective median age	21.73	23.29	25.13	27.18	29.24	33.70	35.68
Proportion age 65+	0.04	0.05	0.07	0.11	0.14	0.26	0.33
Proportion RLE < 15 years	0.03	0.03	0.04	0.06	0.07	0.12	0.14

Benin

Detailed Human Capital Projections to 2060

Demographic indicators, Medium Scenario (SSP2)	2010	2020	2030	2040	2050	2060
Population (in millions)	8.85	11.50	14.21	16.76	19.04	20.90
Proportion age 65+	0.03	0.03	0.04	0.05	0.06	0.08
Proportion below age 20	0.54	0.51	0.46	0.41	0.36	0.32
	2005–10	2015–20	2025–30	2035–40	2045–50	2055–60
Total Fertility Rate	5.48	4.40	3.39	2.73	2.34	2.08
Life expectancy at birth (in years)						
Men	52.72	56.79	59.15	61.25	63.22	65.72
Women	56.50	60.68	63.42	65.78	67.88	70.38
Five-year immigration flow (in '000)	79.43	77.73	80.66	82.38	82.30	81.05
Five-year emigration flow (in '000)	28.77	28.48	36.16	43.09	47.70	50.22

Human Capital indicators, Medium Scenario (SSP2)	2010	2020	2030	2040	2050	2060
Population age 25+: highest educational attainment						
E1 - no education	0.59	0.48	0.40	0.32	0.26	0.20
E2 - incomplete primary	0.18	0.18	0.16	0.14	0.11	0.09
E3 - primary	0.11	0.15	0.19	0.22	0.24	0.25
E4 - lower secondary	0.07	0.12	0.15	0.18	0.20	0.22
E5 - upper secondary	0.03	0.05	0.08	0.11	0.14	0.19
E6 - post-secondary	0.02	0.02	0.03	0.03	0.04	0.05
Mean years of schooling (in years)	2.81	3.88	4.87	5.82	6.73	7.60
Gender gap (population age 25+): highest educational attainment (ratio male/female)						
E1 - no education	0.62	0.62	0.64	0.67	0.72	0.77
E2 - incomplete primary	1.60	1.40	1.26	1.16	1.09	1.03
E3 - primary	1.87	1.33	1.15	1.06	1.02	1.00
E4 - lower secondary	2.55	1.80	1.52	1.34	1.23	1.14
E5 - upper secondary	2.89	1.96	1.53	1.29	1.17	1.10
E6 - post-secondary	4.41	2.79	1.89	1.41	1.18	1.09
Mean years of schooling (male minus female)	2.22	1.98	1.65	1.26	0.91	0.61
Women age 20–39: highest educational attainment						
E1 - no education	0.55	0.42	0.33	0.25	0.17	0.11
E2 - incomplete primary	0.20	0.15	0.12	0.09	0.07	0.05
E3 - primary	0.13	0.20	0.24	0.26	0.27	0.26
E4 - lower secondary	0.08	0.14	0.18	0.20	0.22	0.22
E5 - upper secondary	0.04	0.07	0.11	0.16	0.23	0.30
E6 - post-secondary	0.01	0.01	0.02	0.03	0.04	0.05
Mean years of schooling (in years)	2.98	4.53	5.78	6.93	8.07	9.16

Education scenarios

GET: global education trend scenario (medium assumption also used for SSP2)

CER: constant enrolment rates scenario (assumption of no future improvements)

FT: Fast track scenario (assumption of education expansion according to fastest historical experience)

Pyramids by Education, Medium Scenario

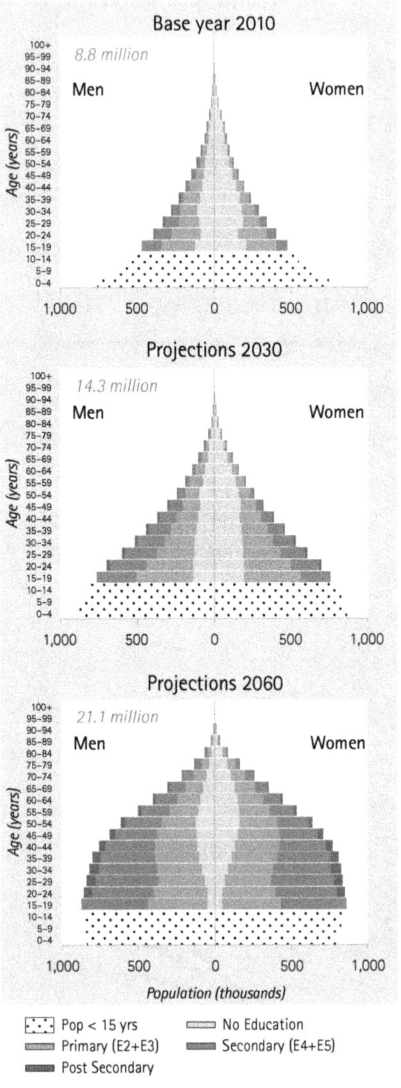

Population Size by Educational Attainment According To Three Education Scenarios: GET, CER, and FT

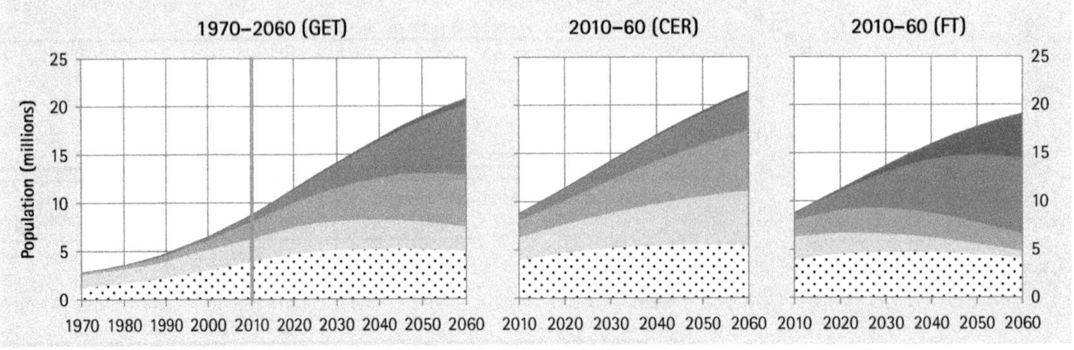

Benin (Continued)

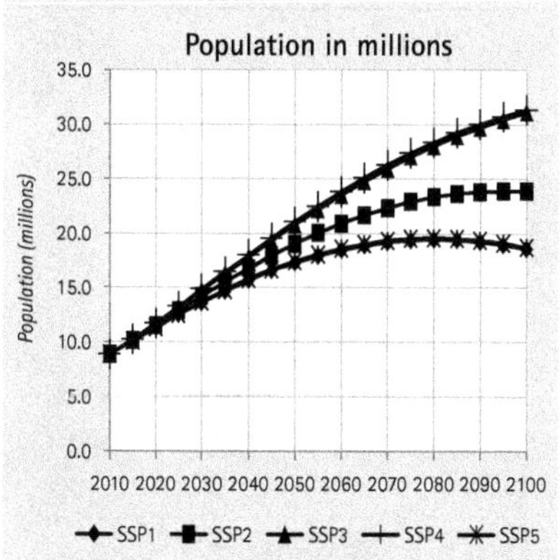

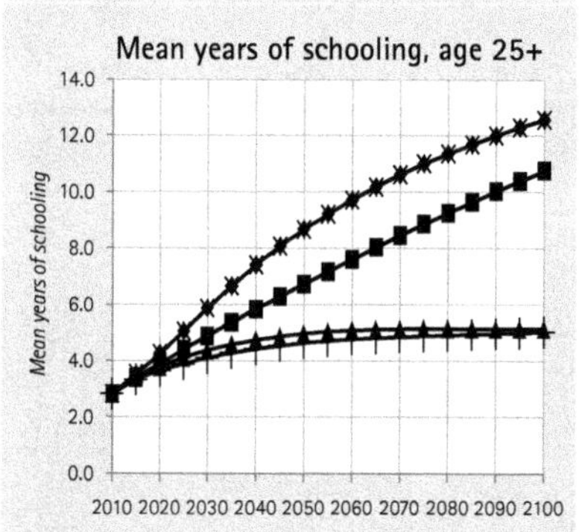

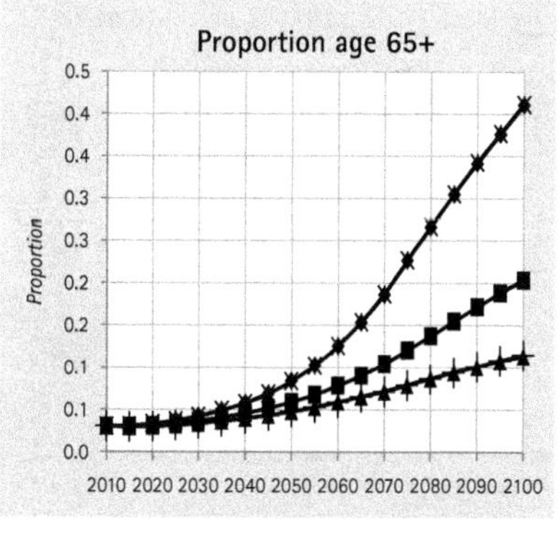

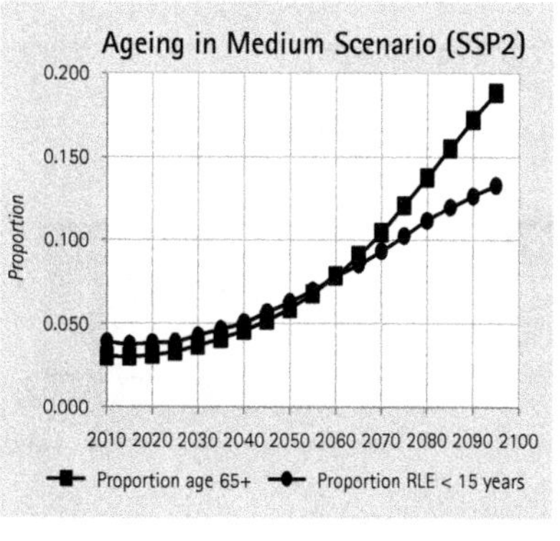

Alternative Scenarios to 2100

Projection Results by Scenario (SSP1–5)

	2010	2020	2030	2040	2050	2075	2100
Population (in millions)							
SSP1 - Rapid development	8.85	11.30	13.60	15.65	17.28	19.37	18.60
SSP2 - Medium	8.85	11.50	14.21	16.76	19.04	22.90	23.88
SSP3 - Stalled development	8.85	11.67	14.73	17.82	20.79	27.04	31.12
SSP4 - Inequality	8.85	11.71	14.86	18.02	21.06	27.38	31.34
SSP5 - Conventional development	8.85	11.33	13.67	15.77	17.43	19.53	18.74
Proportion age 65+							
SSP1 - Rapid development	0.03	0.03	0.04	0.06	0.08	0.23	0.41
SSP2 - Medium	0.03	0.03	0.04	0.05	0.06	0.12	0.20
SSP3 - Stalled development	0.03	0.03	0.03	0.04	0.05	0.08	0.11
SSP4 - Inequality	0.03	0.03	0.03	0.04	0.05	0.08	0.11
SSP5 - Conventional development	0.03	0.03	0.04	0.06	0.08	0.23	0.41
Proportion below age 20							
SSP1 - Rapid development	0.54	0.50	0.42	0.35	0.29	0.18	0.12
SSP2 - Medium	0.54	0.51	0.46	0.41	0.36	0.27	0.22
SSP3 - Stalled development	0.54	0.52	0.49	0.45	0.41	0.35	0.31
SSP4 - Inequality	0.54	0.52	0.49	0.45	0.41	0.34	0.31
SSP5 - Conventional development	0.54	0.50	0.42	0.35	0.29	0.18	0.12
Proportion of Women age 20–39 with at least secondary education							
SSP1 - Rapid development	0.13	0.29	0.46	0.60	0.71	0.84	0.92
SSP2 - Medium	0.13	0.23	0.31	0.40	0.49	0.69	0.85
SSP3 - Stalled development	0.13	0.15	0.17	0.17	0.17	0.17	0.17
SSP4 - Inequality	0.13	0.14	0.15	0.15	0.15	0.15	0.15
SSP5 - Conventional development	0.13	0.29	0.46	0.60	0.71	0.84	0.92
Mean years of schooling, age 25+							
SSP1 - Rapid development	2.81	4.24	5.85	7.40	8.66	10.99	12.56
SSP2 - Medium	2.81	3.88	4.87	5.82	6.73	8.85	10.75
SSP3 - Stalled development	2.81	3.75	4.35	4.73	4.95	5.13	5.13
SSP4 - Inequality	2.81	3.63	4.09	4.41	4.62	4.87	5.02
SSP5 - Conventional development	2.81	4.24	5.86	7.40	8.67	10.99	12.56

Demographic Assumptions Underlying SSPs

	2010–15	2020–25	2030–35	2040–45	2050–55	2075–80	2095–2100
Total fertility rate							
SSP1 - Rapid development	4.64	3.17	2.28	1.81	1.54	1.30	1.21
SSP2 - Medium	4.91	3.89	3.00	2.52	2.18	1.85	1.71
SSP3 - Stalled development	5.23	4.62	3.91	3.33	2.95	2.57	2.46
SSP4 - Inequality	5.24	4.66	3.94	3.34	2.95	2.54	2.43
SSP5 - Conventional development	4.64	3.17	2.28	1.81	1.54	1.30	1.21
Life expectancy at birth for females (in years)							
SSP1 - Rapid development	63.46	69.84	74.12	78.14	81.79	90.19	97.17
SSP2 - Medium	58.68	62.08	64.62	66.82	69.08	75.29	80.29
SSP3 - Stalled development	61.36	60.06	61.02	62.20	63.11	65.60	68.17
SSP4 - Inequality	61.36	60.05	60.98	62.16	63.07	65.56	68.14
SSP5 - Conventional development	63.46	69.84	74.12	78.14	81.79	90.19	97.17
Migration – net flow over five years (in thousands)							
SSP1 - Rapid development	48	46	40	33	26	11	0
SSP2 - Medium	50	48	43	38	33	17	0
SSP3 - Stalled development	39	23	22	22	22	16	0
SSP4 - Inequality	47	46	42	40	39	26	0
SSP5 - Conventional development	56	68	57	45	36	14	0

Ageing Indicators, Medium Scenario (SSP2)

	2010	2020	2030	2040	2050	2075	2095
Median age	17.85	19.39	21.87	24.93	28.14	35.76	41.10
Propspective median age	17.85	17.75	18.80	20.69	22.98	27.11	28.91
Proportion age 65+	0.03	0.03	0.04	0.05	0.06	0.12	0.19
Proportion RLE < 15 years	0.04	0.04	0.04	0.05	0.06	0.10	0.13

Bhutan

Detailed Human Capital Projections to 2060

Demographic indicators, Medium Scenario (SSP2)	2010	2020	2030	2040	2050	2060
Population (in millions)	0.73	0.86	0.99	1.11	1.21	1.28
Proportion age 65+	0.05	0.05	0.07	0.10	0.15	0.21
Proportion below age 20	0.40	0.34	0.30	0.26	0.23	0.21
	2005–10	2015–20	2025–30	2035–40	2045–50	2055–60
Total Fertility Rate	2.61	2.20	2.03	1.90	1.84	1.74
Life expectancy at birth (in years)						
Men	64.08	67.72	70.85	73.72	76.31	78.79
Women	67.77	71.92	75.30	78.29	80.91	83.40
Five-year immigration flow (in '000)	19.40	19.04	19.79	20.22	20.20	19.89
Five-year emigration flow (in '000)	2.57	2.12	2.22	2.29	2.29	2.25

Human Capital indicators, Medium Scenario (SSP2)	2010	2020	2030	2040	2050	2060
Population age 25+: highest educational attainment						
E1 - no education	0.60	0.46	0.35	0.27	0.20	0.14
E2 - incomplete primary	0.17	0.16	0.14	0.12	0.09	0.07
E3 - primary	0.01	0.02	0.02	0.03	0.03	0.03
E4 - lower secondary	0.13	0.22	0.29	0.35	0.38	0.40
E5 - upper secondary	0.03	0.05	0.08	0.11	0.15	0.19
E6 - post-secondary	0.06	0.08	0.10	0.12	0.15	0.17
Mean years of schooling (in years)	3.22	4.98	6.52	7.89	9.13	10.22
Gender gap (population age 25+): highest educational attainment (ratio male/female)						
E1 - no education	0.66	0.67	0.66	0.66	0.67	0.67
E2 - incomplete primary	2.10	1.81	1.63	1.49	1.34	1.19
E3 - primary	2.10	1.45	1.32	1.25	1.19	1.14
E4 - lower secondary	1.67	1.19	1.09	1.05	1.03	1.02
E5 - upper secondary	1.47	0.98	0.91	0.91	0.93	0.97
E6 - post-secondary	2.48	1.98	1.74	1.56	1.40	1.27
Mean years of schooling (male minus female)	2.02	1.58	1.33	1.12	0.91	0.74
Women age 20–39: highest educational attainment						
E1 - no education	0.48	0.30	0.18	0.10	0.05	0.02
E2 - incomplete primary	0.15	0.11	0.07	0.04	0.02	0.01
E3 - primary	0.02	0.03	0.03	0.04	0.03	0.03
E4 - lower secondary	0.23	0.36	0.45	0.46	0.43	0.38
E5 - upper secondary	0.06	0.11	0.16	0.22	0.28	0.34
E6 - post-secondary	0.06	0.08	0.11	0.14	0.18	0.22
Mean years of schooling (in years)	4.50	7.27	9.48	10.89	11.90	12.64

Education scenarios

GET: global education trend scenario (medium assumption also used for SSP2)

CER: constant enrolment rates scenario (assumption of no future improvements)

FT: Fast track scenario (assumption of education expansion according to fastest historical experience)

Pyramids by Education, Medium Scenario

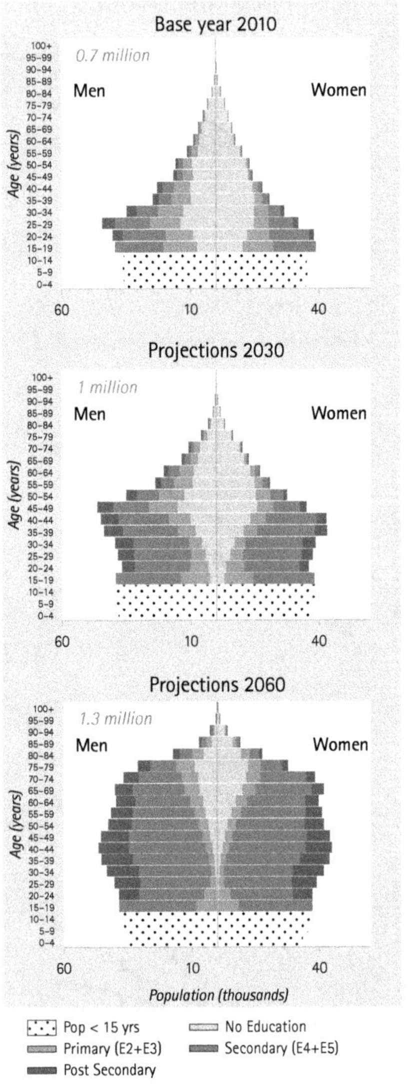

Population Size by Educational Attainment According to Three Education Scenarios: GET, CER, and FT

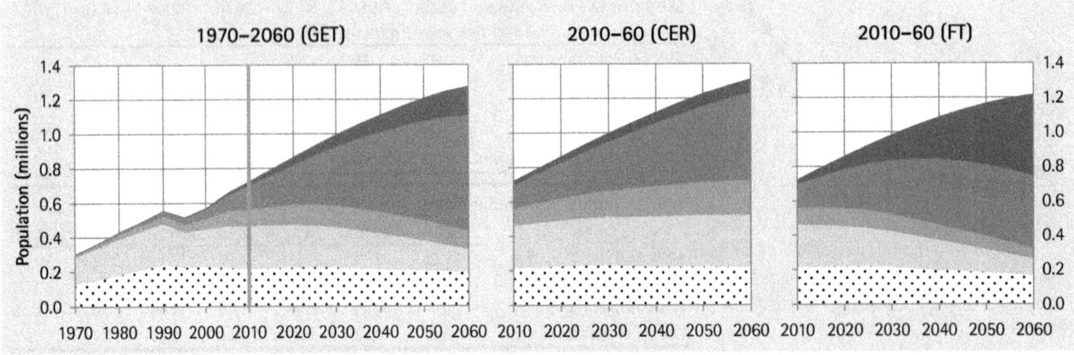

Bhutan (Continued)

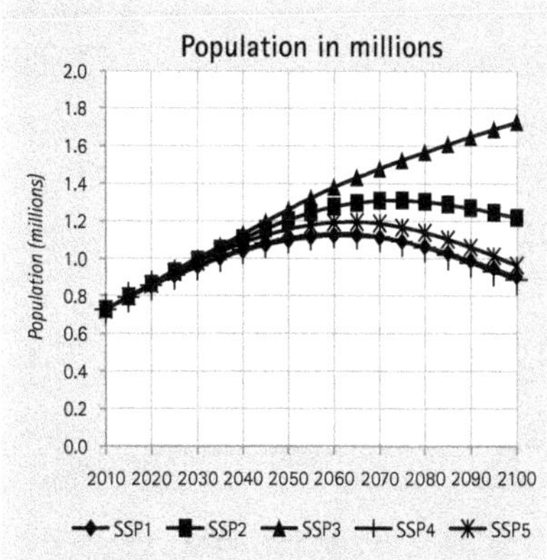

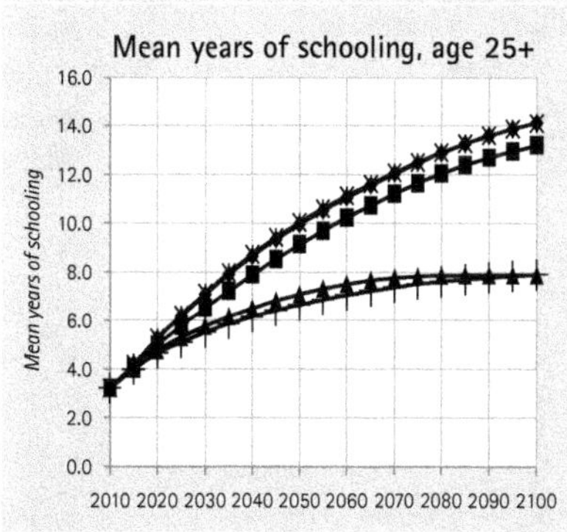

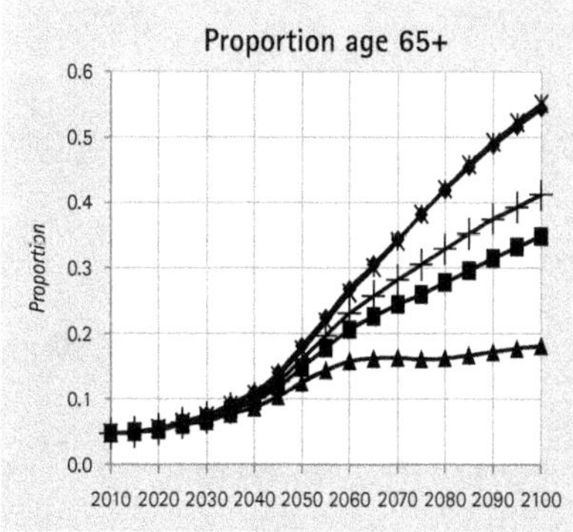

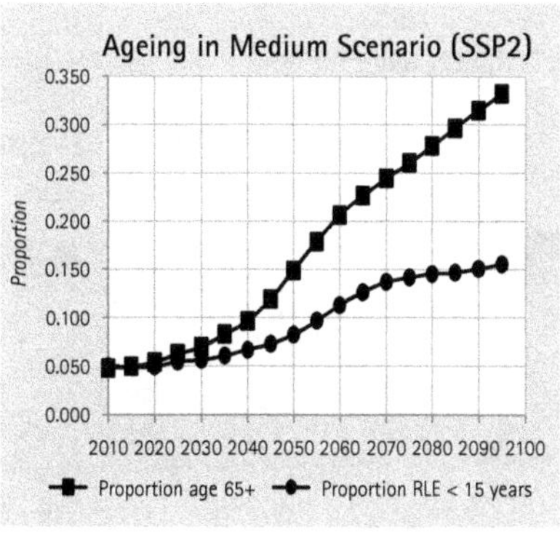

Alternative Scenarios to 2100

Projection Results by Scenario (SSP1–5)

	2010	2020	2030	2040	2050	2075	2100
Population (in millions)							
SSP1 - Rapid development	0.73	0.85	0.96	1.04	1.10	1.09	0.90
SSP2 - Medium	0.73	0.86	0.99	1.11	1.21	1.31	1.22
SSP3 - Stalled development	0.73	0.87	1.00	1.13	1.26	1.52	1.73
SSP4 - Inequality	0.73	0.85	0.96	1.05	1.11	1.09	0.89
SSP5 - Conventional development	0.73	0.86	0.98	1.08	1.16	1.17	0.97
Proportion age 65+							
SSP1 - Rapid development	0.05	0.06	0.08	0.11	0.18	0.38	0.54
SSP2 - Medium	0.05	0.05	0.07	0.10	0.15	0.26	0.35
SSP3 - Stalled development	0.05	0.05	0.07	0.09	0.13	0.16	0.18
SSP4 - Inequality	0.05	0.05	0.07	0.10	0.16	0.31	0.41
SSP5 - Conventional development	0.05	0.06	0.07	0.11	0.18	0.38	0.55
Proportion below age 20							
SSP1 - Rapid development	0.40	0.33	0.27	0.21	0.17	0.11	0.08
SSP2 - Medium	0.40	0.34	0.30	0.26	0.23	0.18	0.16
SSP3 - Stalled development	0.40	0.35	0.34	0.31	0.30	0.28	0.28
SSP4 - Inequality	0.40	0.33	0.28	0.23	0.19	0.14	0.12
SSP5 - Conventional development	0.40	0.33	0.27	0.21	0.17	0.11	0.08
Proportion of Women age 20–39 with at least secondary education							
SSP1 - Rapid development	0.35	0.58	0.77	0.89	0.94	0.98	0.99
SSP2 - Medium	0.35	0.56	0.72	0.83	0.90	0.97	0.99
SSP3 - Stalled development	0.35	0.49	0.53	0.53	0.53	0.53	0.53
SSP4 - Inequality	0.35	0.46	0.48	0.48	0.48	0.48	0.48
SSP5 - Conventional development	0.35	0.58	0.77	0.89	0.94	0.98	0.99
Mean years of schooling, age 25+							
SSP1 - Rapid development	3.22	5.24	7.07	8.64	9.95	12.48	14.12
SSP2 - Medium	3.22	4.98	6.52	7.89	9.13	11.65	13.20
SSP3 - Stalled development	3.22	4.76	5.76	6.50	7.08	7.83	7.87
SSP4 - Inequality	3.22	4.65	5.51	6.16	6.65	7.51	7.91
SSP5 - Conventional development	3.22	5.26	7.13	8.73	10.04	12.51	14.11

Demographic Assumptions Underlying SSPs

	2010–15	2020–25	2030–35	2040–45	2050–55	2075–80	2095–2100
Total fertility rate							
SSP1 - Rapid development	2.22	1.75	1.48	1.36	1.27	1.18	1.16
SSP2 - Medium	2.36	2.10	1.94	1.87	1.80	1.65	1.60
SSP3 - Stalled development	2.49	2.49	2.49	2.46	2.43	2.33	2.33
SSP4 - Inequality	2.25	1.85	1.62	1.51	1.43	1.35	1.33
SSP5 - Conventional development	2.22	1.75	1.48	1.36	1.27	1.18	1.16
Life expectancy at birth for females (in years)							
SSP1 - Rapid development	72.64	76.47	80.53	84.12	87.46	95.33	101.58
SSP2 - Medium	69.92	73.72	76.89	79.69	82.20	87.91	92.11
SSP3 - Stalled development	71.90	73.96	75.84	77.50	78.78	81.02	82.52
SSP4 - Inequality	72.02	75.37	78.23	80.79	83.03	87.78	91.26
SSP5 - Conventional development	72.64	76.47	80.53	84.12	87.46	95.33	101.58
Migration – net flow over five years (in thousands)							
SSP1 - Rapid development	16	17	17	15	14	4	0
SSP2 - Medium	16	17	17	18	17	7	0
SSP3 - Stalled development	13	9	9	11	12	7	0
SSP4 - Inequality	16	17	17	17	16	6	0
SSP5 - Conventional development	19	25	25	23	19	5	0

Ageing Indicators, Medium Scenario (SSP2)

	2010	2020	2030	2040	2050	2075	2095
Median age	24.55	28.71	32.64	36.14	39.30	46.87	51.85
Propspective median age	24.55	26.47	28.36	29.71	30.82	33.92	35.36
Proportion age 65+	0.05	0.05	0.07	0.10	0.15	0.26	0.33
Proportion RLE < 15 years	0.05	0.05	0.06	0.07	0.08	0.14	0.16

Bolivia

Detailed Human Capital Projections to 2060

Demographic indicators, Medium Scenario (SSP2)	2010	2020	2030	2040	2050	2060
Population (in millions)	9.93	11.41	12.76	13.83	14.58	15.00
Proportion age 65+	0.05	0.06	0.07	0.09	0.11	0.15
Proportion below age 20	0.47	0.42	0.37	0.33	0.30	0.27
	2005–10	2015–20	2025–30	2035–40	2045–50	2055–60
Total Fertility Rate	3.50	2.84	2.47	2.21	2.03	1.91
Life expectancy at birth (in years)						
Men	#N/A	65.31	67.44	69.54	71.55	73.47
Women	#N/A	69.82	71.88	73.98	75.99	77.99
Five-year immigration flow (in '000)	#N/A	28.37	29.48	30.16	30.18	29.75
Five-year emigration flow (in '000)	#N/A	171.98	186.74	191.46	191.14	185.56

Human Capital indicators, Medium Scenario (SSP2)	2010	2020	2030	2040	2050	2060
Population age 25+: highest educational attainment						
E1 - no education	0.11	0.06	0.04	0.02	0.01	0.01
E2 - incomplete primary	0.22	0.15	0.11	0.07	0.04	0.03
E3 - primary	0.17	0.16	0.15	0.13	0.11	0.09
E4 - lower secondary	0.17	0.18	0.18	0.17	0.15	0.13
E5 - upper secondary	0.18	0.26	0.32	0.36	0.40	0.43
E6 - post-secondary	0.15	0.18	0.21	0.24	0.28	0.32
Mean years of schooling (in years)	7.83	9.15	10.10	10.87	11.53	12.11
Gender gap (population age 25+): highest educational attainment (ratio male/female)						
E1 - no education	0.35	0.33	0.33	0.36	0.38	0.39
E2 - incomplete primary	0.75	0.67	0.60	0.55	0.53	0.51
E3 - primary	1.10	1.02	0.96	0.92	0.90	0.89
E4 - lower secondary	1.29	1.25	1.20	1.15	1.10	1.06
E5 - upper secondary	1.21	1.20	1.16	1.12	1.09	1.06
E6 - post-secondary	1.67	1.20	1.09	1.03	1.00	0.99
Mean years of schooling (male minus female)	1.96	1.31	0.92	0.62	0.39	0.24
Women age 20–39: highest educational attainment						
E1 - no education	0.07	0.02	0.01	0.00	0.00	0.00
E2 - incomplete primary	0.18	0.08	0.04	0.02	0.01	0.00
E3 - primary	0.19	0.15	0.12	0.09	0.07	0.04
E4 - lower secondary	0.20	0.18	0.15	0.12	0.09	0.06
E5 - upper secondary	0.24	0.38	0.43	0.48	0.51	0.53
E6 - post-secondary	0.11	0.20	0.25	0.29	0.33	0.36
Mean years of schooling (in years)	8.30	10.64	11.41	12.10	12.64	13.05

Education scenarios

GET: global education trend scenario (medium assumption also used for SSP2)

CER: constant enrolment rates scenario (assumption of no future improvements)

FT: Fast track scenario (assumption of education expansion according to fastest historical experience)

Pyramids by Education, Medium Scenario

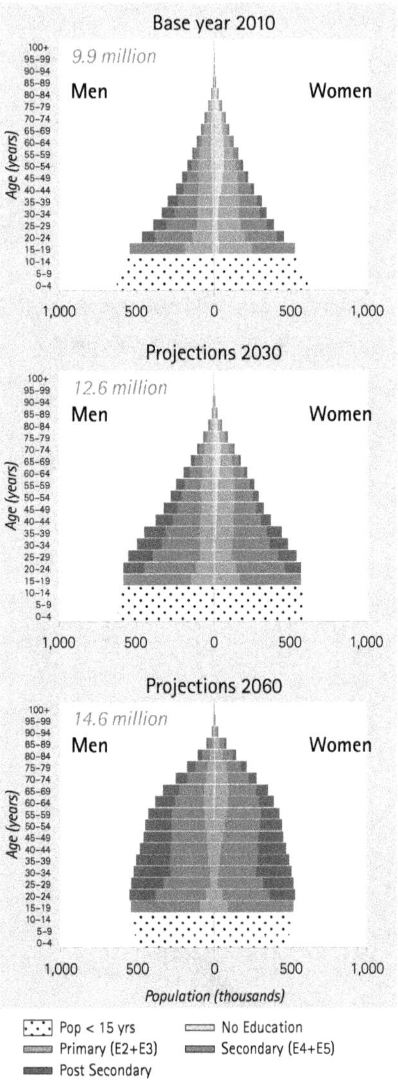

Population Size by Educational Attainment According to Three Education Scenarios: GET, CER, and FT

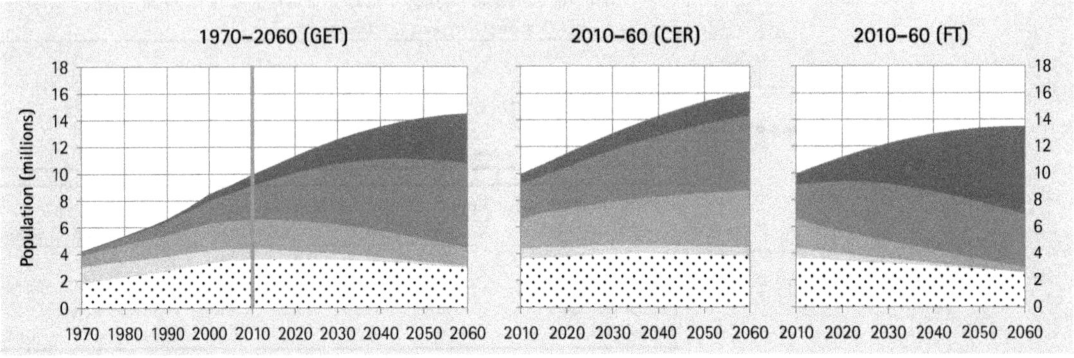

Bolivia (Continued)

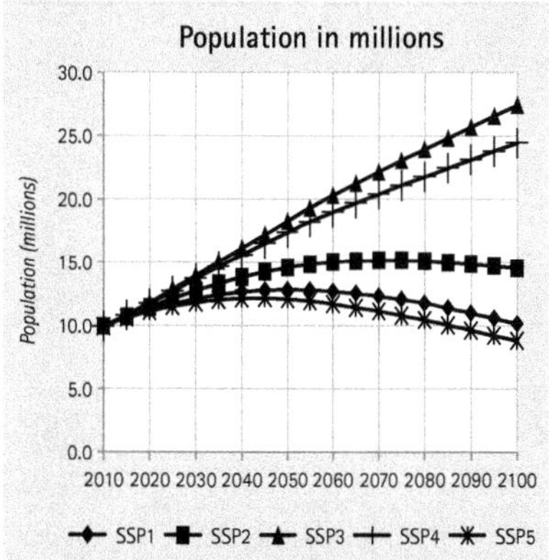

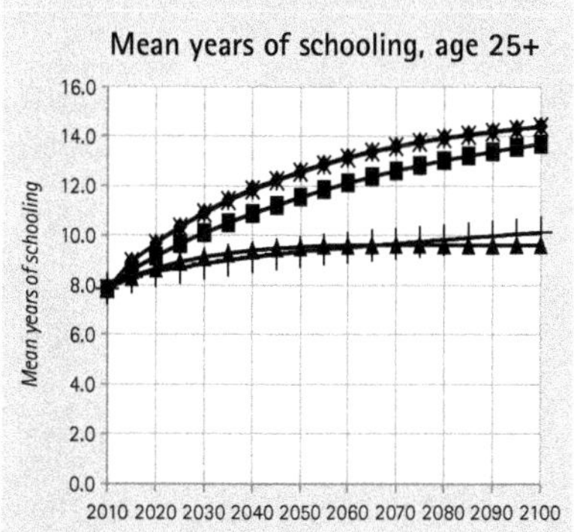

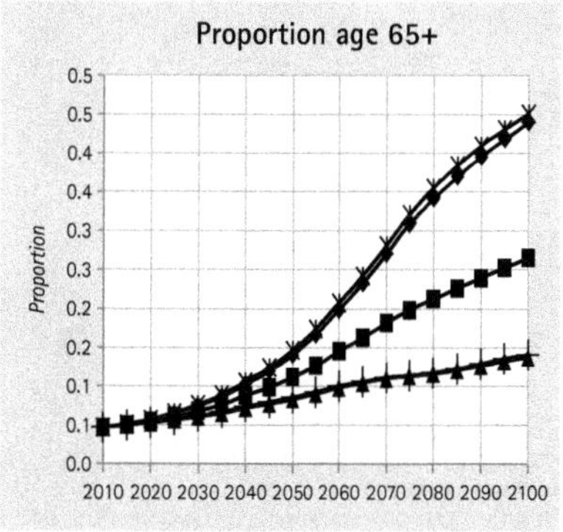

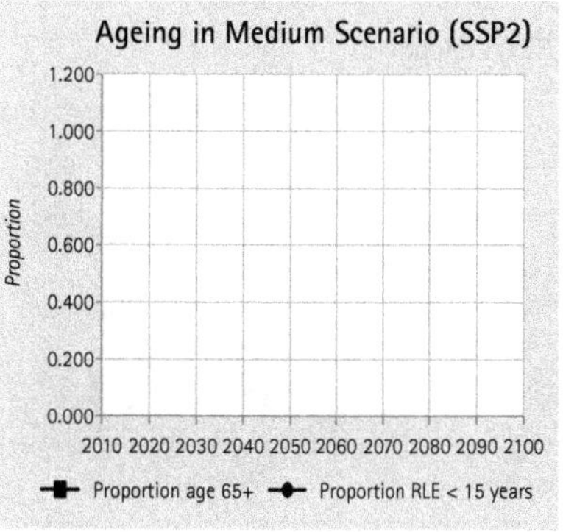

Alternative Scenarios to 2100

Projection Results by Scenario (SSP1–5)

	2010	2020	2030	2040	2050	2075	2100
Population (in millions)							
SSP1 - Rapid development	9.93	11.20	12.09	12.65	12.84	12.05	10.16
SSP2 - Medium	9.93	11.41	12.76	13.83	14.58	15.15	14.57
SSP3 - Stalled development	9.93	11.80	13.98	16.15	18.28	23.08	27.43
SSP4 - Inequality	9.93	11.72	13.72	15.61	17.39	21.11	24.48
SSP5 - Conventional development	9.93	11.11	11.81	12.14	12.08	10.79	8.82
Proportion age 65+							
SSP1 - Rapid development	0.05	0.06	0.07	0.10	0.14	0.31	0.44
SSP2 - Medium	0.05	0.06	0.07	0.09	0.11	0.20	0.27
SSP3 - Stalled development	0.05	0.05	0.06	0.07	0.08	0.11	0.14
SSP4 - Inequality	0.05	0.05	0.06	0.07	0.09	0.11	0.14
SSP5 - Conventional development	0.05	0.06	0.08	0.11	0.15	0.32	0.45
Proportion below age 20							
SSP1 - Rapid development	0.47	0.40	0.33	0.28	0.23	0.15	0.11
SSP2 - Medium	0.47	0.42	0.37	0.33	0.30	0.23	0.20
SSP3 - Stalled development	0.47	0.43	0.41	0.40	0.37	0.33	0.31
SSP4 - Inequality	0.47	0.43	0.42	0.40	0.37	0.33	0.30
SSP5 - Conventional development	0.47	0.41	0.33	0.28	0.23	0.15	0.11
Proportion of Women age 20–39 with at least secondary education							
SSP1 - Rapid development	0.55	0.84	0.91	0.94	0.96	0.99	1.00
SSP2 - Medium	0.55	0.76	0.83	0.89	0.93	0.98	0.99
SSP3 - Stalled development	0.55	0.64	0.64	0.64	0.64	0.64	0.64
SSP4 - Inequality	0.55	0.60	0.58	0.58	0.58	0.58	0.58
SSP5 - Conventional development	0.55	0.84	0.91	0.94	0.96	0.99	1.00
Mean years of schooling, age 25+							
SSP1 - Rapid development	7.83	9.68	10.92	11.86	12.57	13.77	14.40
SSP2 - Medium	7.83	9.15	10.10	10.87	11.53	12.81	13.69
SSP3 - Stalled development	7.83	8.66	9.13	9.40	9.54	9.62	9.62
SSP4 - Inequality	7.83	8.55	8.86	9.13	9.34	9.75	10.13
SSP5 - Conventional development	7.83	9.67	10.89	11.83	12.54	13.75	14.39

Demographic Assumptions Underlying SSPs

	2010–15	2020–25	2030–35	2040–45	2050–55	2075–80	2095–2100
Total fertility rate							
SSP1 - Rapid development	2.90	2.11	1.74	1.55	1.43	1.29	1.26
SSP2 - Medium	3.09	2.64	2.33	2.11	1.96	1.73	1.68
SSP3 - Stalled development	3.36	3.29	3.15	2.95	2.76	2.46	2.43
SSP4 - Inequality	3.36	3.34	3.19	2.94	2.73	2.40	2.35
SSP5 - Conventional development	2.90	2.11	1.74	1.55	1.43	1.29	1.26
Life expectancy at birth for females (in years)							
SSP1 - Rapid development	71.51	73.83	76.52	79.30	82.13	89.45	95.33
SSP2 - Medium	68.68	70.92	72.92	74.99	77.00	81.99	86.02
SSP3 - Stalled development	71.07	71.54	72.08	73.02	73.63	75.15	76.68
SSP4 - Inequality	71.07	71.51	72.02	72.94	73.53	75.05	76.62
SSP5 - Conventional development	71.51	73.83	76.52	79.30	82.13	89.45	95.33
Migration – net flow over five years (in thousands)							
SSP1 - Rapid development	−145	−150	−155	−147	−136	−47	0
SSP2 - Medium	−147	−153	−161	−163	−161	−66	0
SSP3 - Stalled development	−121	−75	−80	−85	−89	−43	0
SSP4 - Inequality	−145	−151	−165	−178	−187	−89	0
SSP5 - Conventional development	−170	−226	−237	−231	−219	−82	0

Ageing Indicators, Medium Scenario (SSP2)

	2010	2020	2030	2040	2050	2075	2095
Median age	#N/A	#N/A	#N/A	#N/A	#N/A	#N/A	#N/A
Propspective median age	#N/A	#N/A	#N/A	#N/A	#N/A	#N/A	#N/A
Proportion age 65+	#N/A	#N/A	#N/A	#N/A	#N/A	#N/A	#N/A
Proportion RLE < 15 years	#N/A	#N/A	#N/A	#N/A	#N/A	#N/A	#N/A

Bosnia and Herzegovina

Detailed Human Capital Projections to 2060

Demographic indicators, Medium Scenario (SSP2)	2010	2020	2030	2040	2050	2060
Population (in millions)	3.76	3.74	3.66	3.52	3.33	3.11
Proportion age 65+	0.14	0.18	0.23	0.28	0.32	0.36
Proportion below age 20	0.21	0.19	0.18	0.16	0.15	0.15
	2005–10	2015–20	2025–30	2035–40	2045–50	2055–60
Total Fertility Rate	1.18	1.38	1.48	1.50	1.50	1.51
Life expectancy at birth (in years)						
Men	72.42	75.06	77.26	79.41	81.49	83.57
Women	77.70	80.09	82.19	84.29	86.31	88.31
Five-year immigration flow (in '000)	20.55	20.11	20.87	21.33	21.32	21.01
Five-year emigration flow (in '000)	30.42	19.40	15.99	14.14	12.57	11.12

Human Capital indicators, Medium Scenario (SSP2)	2010	2020	2030	2040	2050	2060
Population age 25+: highest educational attainment						
E1 - no education	0.09	0.05	0.02	0.01	0.01	0.00
E2 - incomplete primary	0.04	0.03	0.02	0.01	0.00	0.00
E3 - primary	0.12	0.09	0.07	0.05	0.03	0.02
E4 - lower secondary	0.16	0.15	0.13	0.11	0.09	0.06
E5 - upper secondary	0.49	0.57	0.63	0.68	0.71	0.73
E6 - post-secondary	0.09	0.11	0.13	0.14	0.16	0.19
Mean years of schooling (in years)	9.31	10.40	11.25	11.90	12.46	12.95
Gender gap (population age 25+): highest educational attainment (ratio male/female)						
E1 - no education	0.25	0.20	0.20	0.23	0.28	0.31
E2 - incomplete primary	0.48	0.35	0.26	0.25	0.36	0.61
E3 - primary	0.64	0.53	0.45	0.43	0.46	0.52
E4 - lower secondary	0.73	0.69	0.65	0.61	0.60	0.60
E5 - upper secondary	1.55	1.40	1.30	1.23	1.17	1.11
E6 - post-secondary	1.25	1.02	0.89	0.82	0.81	0.83
Mean years of schooling (male minus female)	2.23	1.62	1.10	0.67	0.36	0.17
Women age 20–39: highest educational attainment						
E1 - no education	0.01	0.00	0.00	0.00	0.00	0.00
E2 - incomplete primary	0.00	0.00	0.00	0.00	0.00	0.00
E3 - primary	0.05	0.02	0.01	0.00	0.00	0.00
E4 - lower secondary	0.16	0.07	0.03	0.01	0.01	0.00
E5 - upper secondary	0.64	0.74	0.77	0.78	0.77	0.76
E6 - post-secondary	0.13	0.17	0.19	0.21	0.23	0.24
Mean years of schooling (in years)	11.25	12.67	13.55	13.72	13.83	13.88

Education scenarios

GET: global education trend scenario (medium assumption also used for SSP2)

CER: constant enrolment rates scenario (assumption of no future improvements)

FT: Fast track scenario (assumption of education expansion according to fastest historical experience)

Pyramids by Education, Medium Scenario

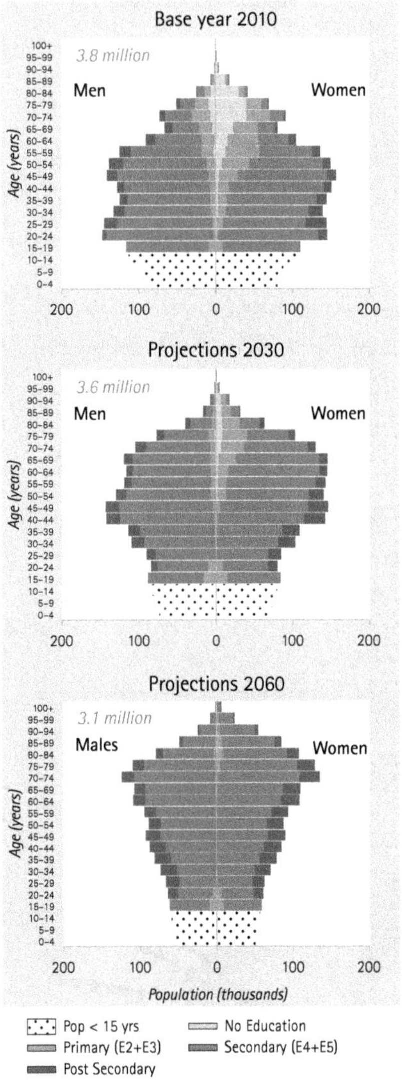

Population Size by Educational Attainment According to Three Education Scenarios: GET, CER, and FT

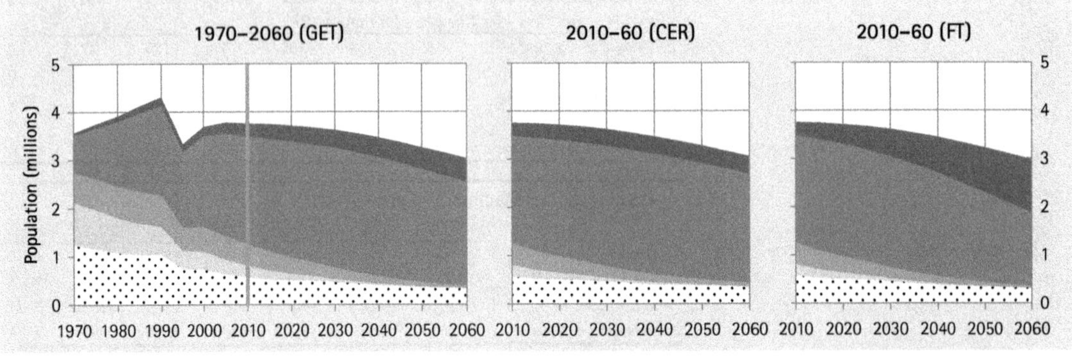

Bosnia and Herzegovina (Continued)

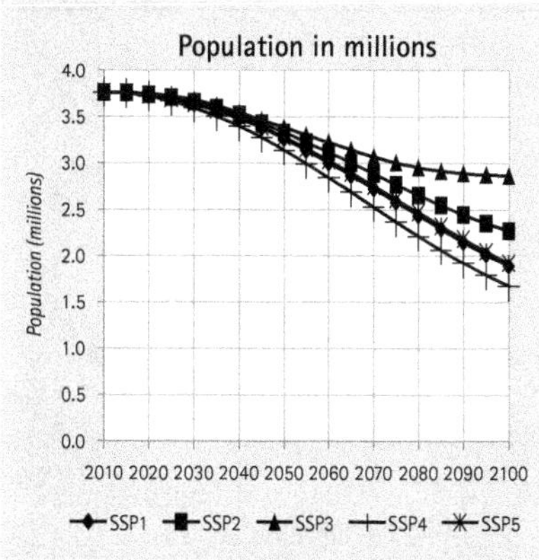

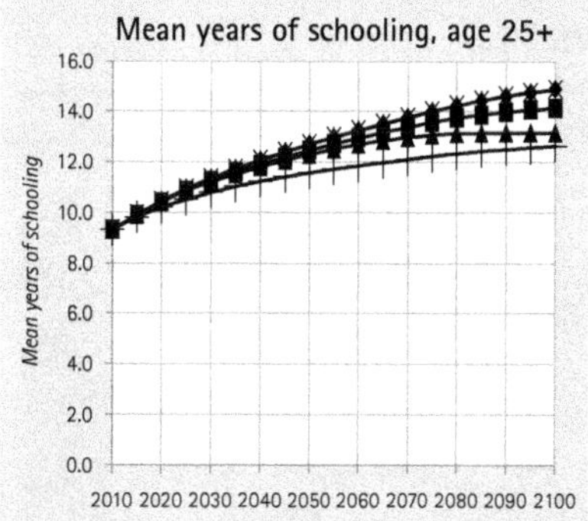

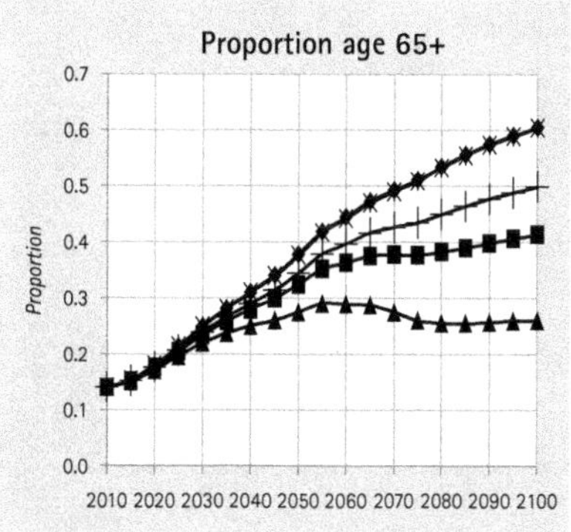

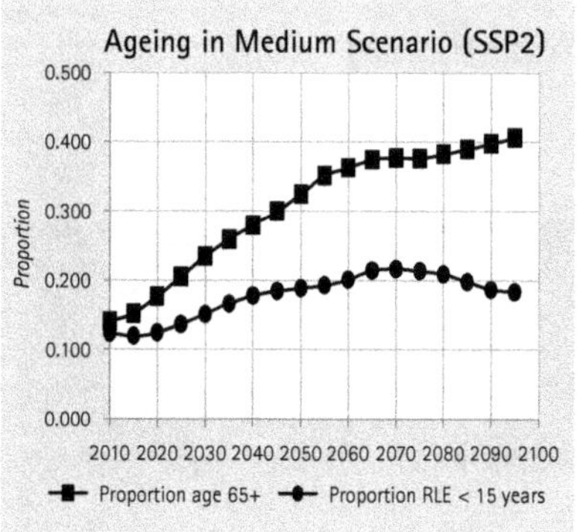

Alternative Scenarios to 2100

Projection Results by Scenario (SSP1–5)

	2010	2020	2030	2040	2050	2075	2100
Population (in millions)							
SSP1 - Rapid development	3.76	3.73	3.63	3.47	3.26	2.58	1.89
SSP2 - Medium	3.76	3.74	3.66	3.52	3.33	2.77	2.27
SSP3 - Stalled development	3.76	3.75	3.68	3.54	3.38	3.01	2.87
SSP4 - Inequality	3.76	3.72	3.59	3.39	3.14	2.37	1.67
SSP5 - Conventional development	3.76	3.73	3.64	3.49	3.28	2.61	1.92
Proportion age 65+							
SSP1 - Rapid development	0.14	0.18	0.25	0.31	0.38	0.51	0.60
SSP2 - Medium	0.14	0.18	0.23	0.28	0.32	0.38	0.41
SSP3 - Stalled development	0.14	0.17	0.22	0.25	0.28	0.26	0.26
SSP4 - Inequality	0.14	0.18	0.24	0.29	0.34	0.43	0.50
SSP5 - Conventional development	0.14	0.18	0.25	0.31	0.38	0.51	0.60
Proportion below age 20							
SSP1 - Rapid development	0.21	0.18	0.16	0.13	0.11	0.09	0.07
SSP2 - Medium	0.21	0.19	0.18	0.16	0.15	0.15	0.14
SSP3 - Stalled development	0.21	0.19	0.20	0.19	0.20	0.21	0.22
SSP4 - Inequality	0.21	0.18	0.16	0.14	0.12	0.11	0.10
SSP5 - Conventional development	0.21	0.18	0.16	0.13	0.11	0.09	0.07
Proportion of Women age 20–39 with at least secondary education							
SSP1 - Rapid development	0.93	0.98	0.99	1.00	1.00	1.00	1.00
SSP2 - Medium	0.93	0.98	0.99	1.00	1.00	1.00	1.00
SSP3 - Stalled development	0.93	0.97	0.98	0.98	0.98	0.98	0.98
SSP4 - Inequality	0.93	0.91	0.88	0.88	0.88	0.88	0.88
SSP5 - Conventional development	0.93	0.98	0.99	1.00	1.00	1.00	1.00
Mean years of schooling, age 25+							
SSP1 - Rapid development	9.31	10.44	11.35	12.07	12.69	14.00	14.89
SSP2 - Medium	9.31	10.40	11.25	11.90	12.46	13.58	14.15
SSP3 - Stalled development	9.31	10.40	11.21	11.80	12.30	13.07	13.16
SSP4 - Inequality	9.31	10.19	10.79	11.24	11.58	12.22	12.63
SSP5 - Conventional development	9.31	10.44	11.35	12.07	12.70	14.01	14.89

Demographic Assumptions Underlying SSPs

	2010–15	2020–25	2030–35	2040–45	2050–55	2075–80	2095–2100
Total fertility rate							
SSP1 - Rapid development	1.27	1.19	1.15	1.12	1.10	1.13	1.16
SSP2 - Medium	1.32	1.43	1.50	1.50	1.50	1.55	1.58
SSP3 - Stalled development	1.41	1.65	1.83	1.90	1.93	2.00	2.06
SSP4 - Inequality	1.28	1.24	1.21	1.19	1.17	1.20	1.23
SSP5 - Conventional development	1.27	1.19	1.15	1.12	1.10	1.13	1.16
Life expectancy at birth for females (in years)							
SSP1 - Rapid development	80.66	83.56	86.38	89.21	92.05	99.41	105.42
SSP2 - Medium	78.89	81.09	83.19	85.31	87.31	92.30	96.30
SSP3 - Stalled development	79.70	80.68	81.64	82.56	83.46	85.72	87.58
SSP4 - Inequality	80.17	82.09	83.95	85.91	87.74	92.19	96.02
SSP5 - Conventional development	80.66	83.56	86.38	89.21	92.05	99.41	105.42
Migration – net flow over five years (in thousands)							
SSP1 - Rapid development	−3	3	6	7	8	2	0
SSP2 - Medium	−3	3	6	8	9	4	0
SSP3 - Stalled development	−3	2	3	5	6	4	0
SSP4 - Inequality	−3	3	6	8	9	4	0
SSP5 - Conventional development	−4	4	9	10	10	3	0

Ageing Indicators, Medium Scenario (SSP2)

	2010	2020	2030	2040	2050	2075	2095
Median age	39.40	42.84	46.59	50.75	53.02	55.34	57.00
Propspective median age	39.40	40.82	42.65	44.93	45.40	43.39	41.22
Proportion age 65+	0.14	0.18	0.23	0.28	0.32	0.38	0.41
Proportion RLE < 15 years	0.12	0.12	0.15	0.18	0.19	0.21	0.18

Brazil

Detailed Human Capital Projections to 2060

Demographic indicators, Medium Scenario (SSP2)	2010	2020	2030	2040	2050	2060
Population (in millions)	194.95	210.99	223.31	230.54	232.72	229.65
Proportion age 65+	0.07	0.10	0.14	0.18	0.23	0.28
Proportion below age 20	0.34	0.29	0.25	0.22	0.20	0.18
	2005–10	2015–20	2025–30	2035–40	2045–50	2055–60
Total Fertility Rate	1.90	1.80	1.72	1.67	1.61	1.59
Life expectancy at birth (in years)						
Men	68.66	72.07	75.12	77.90	80.35	82.34
Women	75.94	78.60	81.29	83.89	86.29	88.21
Five-year immigration flow (in '000)	5.29	5.19	5.39	5.52	5.53	5.45
Five-year emigration flow (in '000)	507.08	378.13	359.12	332.98	306.60	278.37

Human Capital indicators, Medium Scenario (SSP2)	2010	2020	2030	2040	2050	2060
Population age 25+: highest educational attainment						
E1 - no education	0.11	0.08	0.05	0.04	0.03	0.02
E2 - incomplete primary	0.17	0.13	0.10	0.07	0.05	0.03
E3 - primary	0.21	0.19	0.17	0.15	0.13	0.11
E4 - lower secondary	0.15	0.16	0.17	0.16	0.15	0.13
E5 - upper secondary	0.25	0.30	0.36	0.40	0.45	0.48
E6 - post-secondary	0.11	0.13	0.15	0.17	0.19	0.22
Mean years of schooling (in years)	6.97	7.83	8.60	9.25	9.85	10.40
Gender gap (population age 25+): highest educational attainment (ratio male/female)						
E1 - no education	1.02	1.02	1.04	1.06	1.08	1.06
E2 - incomplete primary	1.09	1.08	1.07	1.06	1.05	1.05
E3 - primary	1.06	1.08	1.09	1.10	1.09	1.08
E4 - lower secondary	1.04	1.06	1.07	1.07	1.06	1.04
E5 - upper secondary	0.96	0.99	1.00	1.02	1.03	1.02
E6 - post-secondary	0.79	0.79	0.78	0.80	0.83	0.88
Mean years of schooling (male minus female)	−0.35	−0.35	−0.36	−0.34	−0.28	−0.20
Women age 20–39: highest educational attainment						
E1 - no education	0.04	0.02	0.01	0.01	0.00	0.00
E2 - incomplete primary	0.08	0.04	0.02	0.01	0.01	0.00
E3 - primary	0.17	0.14	0.11	0.09	0.06	0.05
E4 - lower secondary	0.19	0.18	0.15	0.12	0.10	0.08
E5 - upper secondary	0.39	0.46	0.52	0.56	0.59	0.61
E6 - post-secondary	0.13	0.15	0.18	0.21	0.24	0.26
Mean years of schooling (in years)	8.83	9.69	10.36	10.87	11.27	11.57

Education scenarios

GET: global education trend scenario (medium assumption also used for SSP2)

CER: constant enrolment rates scenario (assumption of no future improvements)

FT: Fast track scenario (assumption of education expansion according to fastest historical experience)

Pyramids by Education, Medium Scenario

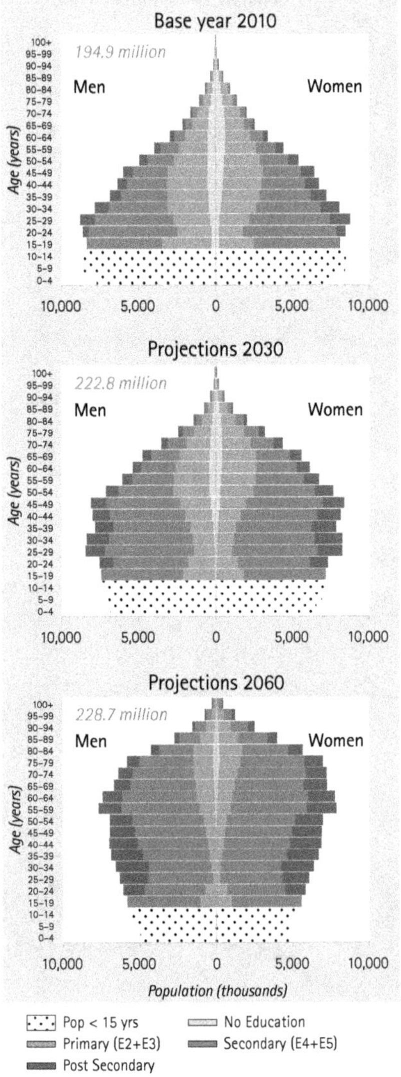

Population Size by Educational Attainment According to Three Education Scenarios: GET, CER, and FT

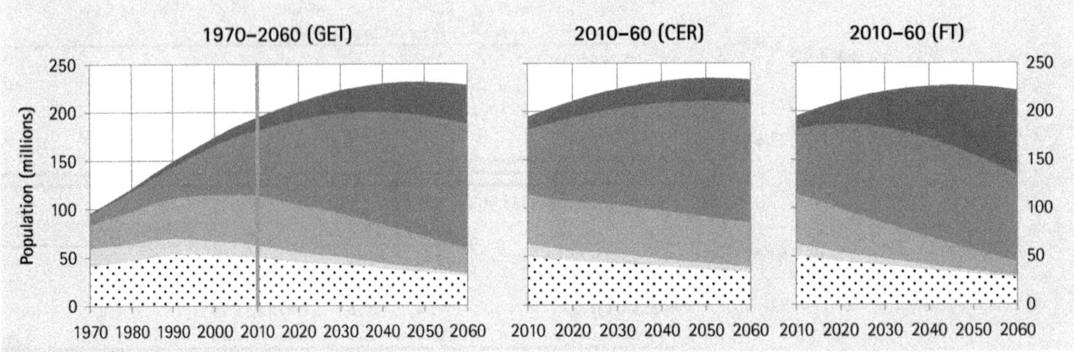

Brazil (Continued)

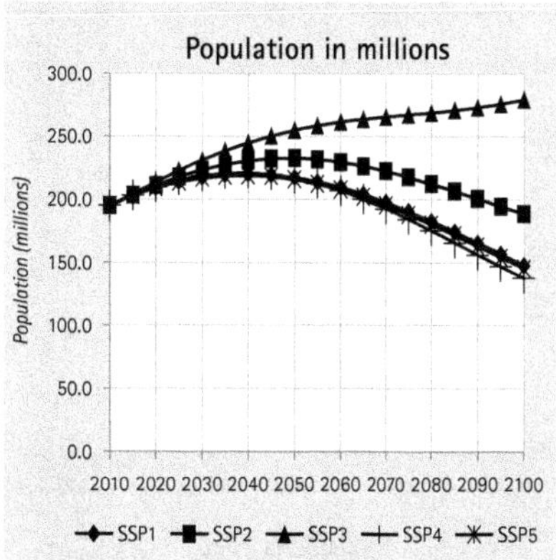

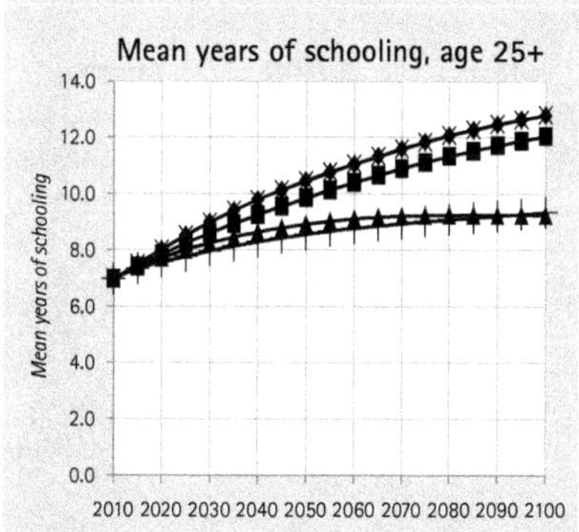

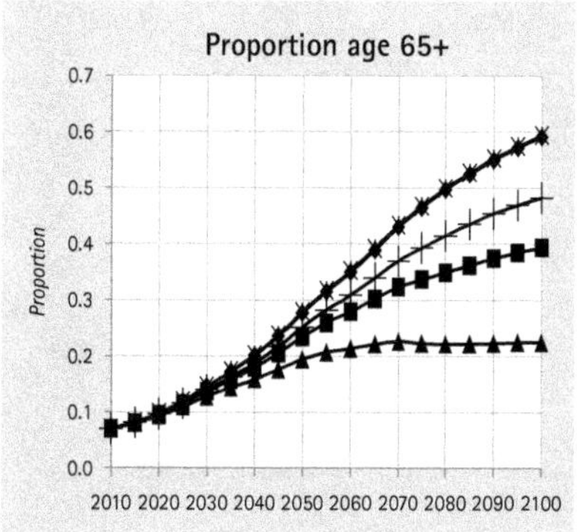

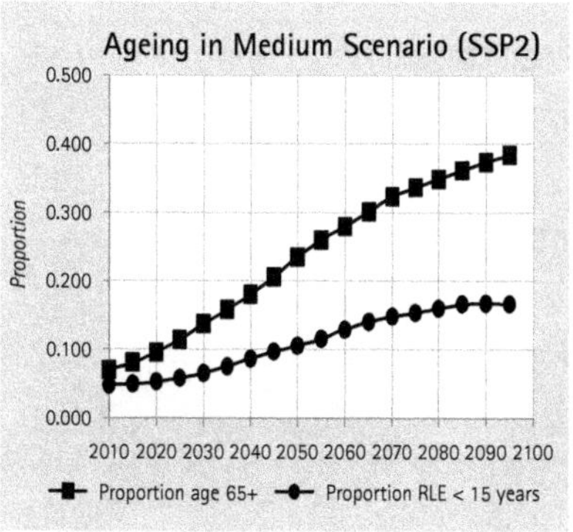

Alternative Scenarios to 2100

Projection Results by Scenario (SSP1–5)

	2010	2020	2030	2040	2050	2075	2100
Population (in millions)							
SSP1 - Rapid development	194.95	209.12	217.25	219.93	217.31	190.50	147.98
SSP2 - Medium	194.95	210.99	223.31	230.54	232.72	217.77	188.79
SSP3 - Stalled development	194.95	213.72	231.17	244.67	254.90	267.21	279.23
SSP4 - Inequality	194.95	209.78	218.53	220.79	216.77	184.29	137.59
SSP5 - Conventional development	194.95	208.90	216.59	218.80	215.71	187.96	145.33
Proportion age 65+							
SSP1 - Rapid development	0.07	0.10	0.15	0.20	0.28	0.46	0.59
SSP2 - Medium	0.07	0.10	0.14	0.18	0.23	0.34	0.39
SSP3 - Stalled development	0.07	0.09	0.13	0.16	0.19	0.22	0.23
SSP4 - Inequality	0.07	0.10	0.14	0.19	0.25	0.39	0.48
SSP5 - Conventional development	0.07	0.10	0.15	0.20	0.28	0.47	0.59
Proportion below age 20							
SSP1 - Rapid development	0.34	0.28	0.22	0.18	0.15	0.10	0.07
SSP2 - Medium	0.34	0.29	0.25	0.22	0.20	0.17	0.15
SSP3 - Stalled development	0.34	0.30	0.28	0.27	0.26	0.25	0.26
SSP4 - Inequality	0.34	0.29	0.24	0.20	0.16	0.12	0.10
SSP5 - Conventional development	0.34	0.28	0.22	0.18	0.15	0.10	0.07
Proportion of Women age 20–39 with at least secondary education							
SSP1 - Rapid development	0.71	0.85	0.92	0.94	0.96	0.99	1.00
SSP2 - Medium	0.71	0.80	0.86	0.90	0.93	0.97	0.99
SSP3 - Stalled development	0.71	0.77	0.78	0.78	0.78	0.78	0.78
SSP4 - Inequality	0.71	0.73	0.70	0.70	0.70	0.70	0.70
SSP5 - Conventional development	0.71	0.85	0.92	0.94	0.96	0.99	1.00
Mean years of schooling, age 25+							
SSP1 - Rapid development	6.97	8.02	8.99	9.79	10.46	11.84	12.79
SSP2 - Medium	6.97	7.83	8.60	9.25	9.85	11.12	12.04
SSP3 - Stalled development	6.97	7.72	8.26	8.64	8.92	9.24	9.25
SSP4 - Inequality	6.97	7.58	7.97	8.30	8.56	9.02	9.35
SSP5 - Conventional development	6.97	8.01	8.98	9.78	10.45	11.83	12.78

Demographic Assumptions Underlying SSPs

	2010–15	2020–25	2030–35	2040–45	2050–55	2075–80	2095–2100
Total fertility rate							
SSP1 - Rapid development	1.75	1.45	1.29	1.22	1.17	1.19	1.22
SSP2 - Medium	1.83	1.76	1.69	1.64	1.58	1.61	1.63
SSP3 - Stalled development	1.97	2.09	2.14	2.12	2.11	2.18	2.25
SSP4 - Inequality	1.79	1.58	1.40	1.30	1.25	1.28	1.32
SSP5 - Conventional development	1.75	1.45	1.29	1.22	1.17	1.19	1.22
Life expectancy at birth for females (in years)							
SSP1 - Rapid development	79.00	82.13	85.52	89.05	92.11	99.05	104.70
SSP2 - Medium	77.30	79.99	82.59	85.19	87.32	91.80	95.41
SSP3 - Stalled development	78.15	79.51	80.99	82.36	83.30	84.82	86.11
SSP4 - Inequality	78.58	80.91	83.22	85.58	87.55	91.60	94.94
SSP5 - Conventional development	79.00	82.13	85.52	89.05	92.11	99.05	104.70
Migration – net flow over five years (in thousands)							
SSP1 - Rapid development	−402	−363	−331	−290	−248	−77	0
SSP2 - Medium	−396	−362	−337	−312	−285	−108	0
SSP3 - Stalled development	−335	−180	−167	−157	−148	−63	0
SSP4 - Inequality	−402	−363	−328	−283	−233	−64	0
SSP5 - Conventional development	−470	−554	−520	−474	−425	−152	0

Ageing Indicators, Medium Scenario (SSP2)

	2010	2020	2030	2040	2050	2075	2095
Median age	29.05	33.33	37.17	41.11	45.07	51.77	55.28
Propspective median age	29.05	30.91	32.44	34.21	36.42	39.18	39.45
Proportion age 65+	0.07	0.10	0.14	0.18	0.23	0.34	0.38
Proportion RLE < 15 years	0.05	0.05	0.07	0.09	0.11	0.15	0.17

Bulgaria

Detailed Human Capital Projections to 2060

Demographic indicators, Medium Scenario (SSP2)

	2010	2020	2030	2040	2050	2060
Population (in millions)	7.49	7.01	6.56	6.14	5.73	5.32
Proportion age 65+	0.18	0.20	0.23	0.26	0.31	0.34
Proportion below age 20	0.19	0.19	0.18	0.17	0.17	0.17
	2005–10	2015–20	2025–30	2035–40	2045–50	2055–60
Total Fertility Rate	1.46	1.46	1.57	1.60	1.60	1.61
Life expectancy at birth (in years)						
Men	69.20	71.58	73.91	76.08	78.34	80.55
Women	76.34	78.29	80.39	82.39	84.51	86.61
Five-year immigration flow (in '000)	33.94	33.36	34.67	35.48	35.51	35.01
Five-year emigration flow (in '000)	83.97	50.22	43.37	38.13	33.49	30.41

Human Capital indicators, Medium Scenario (SSP2)

	2010	2020	2030	2040	2050	2060
Population age 25+: highest educational attainment						
E1 - no education	0.01	0.01	0.00	0.00	0.00	0.00
E2 - incomplete primary	0.01	0.00	0.00	0.00	0.00	0.00
E3 - primary	0.05	0.03	0.02	0.02	0.01	0.01
E4 - lower secondary	0.23	0.17	0.12	0.09	0.06	0.04
E5 - upper secondary	0.49	0.54	0.57	0.59	0.59	0.58
E6 - post-secondary	0.21	0.25	0.27	0.30	0.34	0.37
Mean years of schooling (in years)	10.67	11.32	11.80	12.23	12.63	13.02
Gender gap (population age 25+): highest educational attainment (ratio male/female)						
E1 - no education	0.52	0.55	0.58	0.59	0.58	0.62
E2 - incomplete primary	0.63	0.66	0.67	0.67	0.66	0.68
E3 - primary	0.61	0.67	0.75	0.80	0.80	0.77
E4 - lower secondary	1.06	1.03	1.02	1.01	0.98	0.95
E5 - upper secondary	1.18	1.19	1.19	1.19	1.17	1.14
E6 - post-secondary	0.76	0.72	0.71	0.73	0.77	0.82
Mean years of schooling (male minus female)	−0.01	−0.18	−0.26	−0.28	−0.25	−0.19
Women age 20–39: highest educational attainment						
E1 - no education	0.01	0.00	0.00	0.00	0.00	0.00
E2 - incomplete primary	0.00	0.00	0.00	0.00	0.00	0.00
E3 - primary	0.03	0.02	0.01	0.00	0.00	0.00
E4 - lower secondary	0.11	0.08	0.06	0.05	0.04	0.04
E5 - upper secondary	0.57	0.58	0.59	0.57	0.57	0.56
E6 - post-secondary	0.28	0.33	0.34	0.37	0.39	0.40
Mean years of schooling (in years)	11.80	12.68	13.02	13.24	13.36	13.39

Education scenarios

GET: global education trend scenario (medium assumption also used for SSP2)

CER: constant enrolment rates scenario (assumption of no future improvements)

FT: Fast track scenario (assumption of education expansion according to fastest historical experience)

Pyramids by Education, Medium Scenario

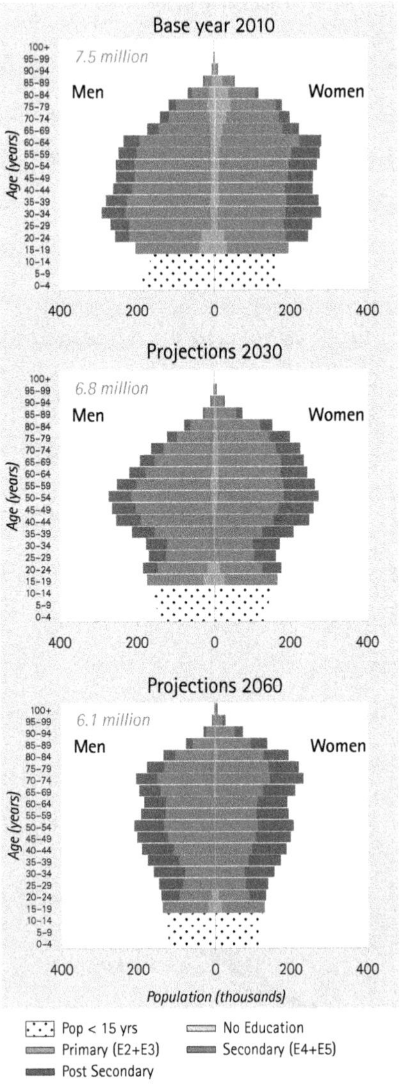

Population Size by Educational Attainment According to Three Education Scenarios: GET, CER, and FT

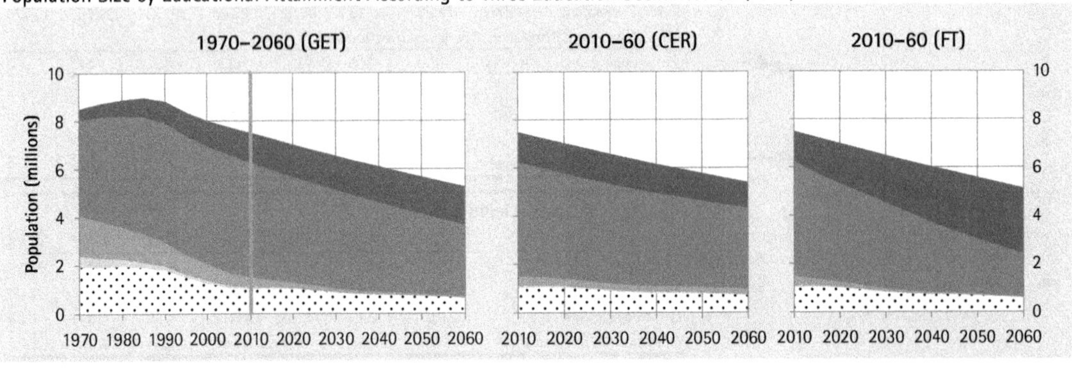

Bulgaria (Continued)

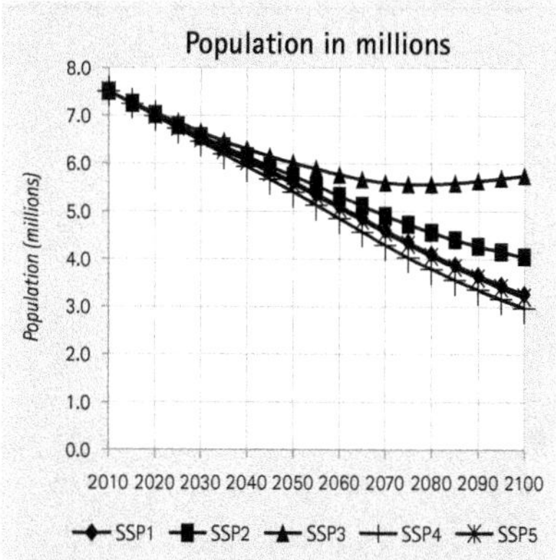

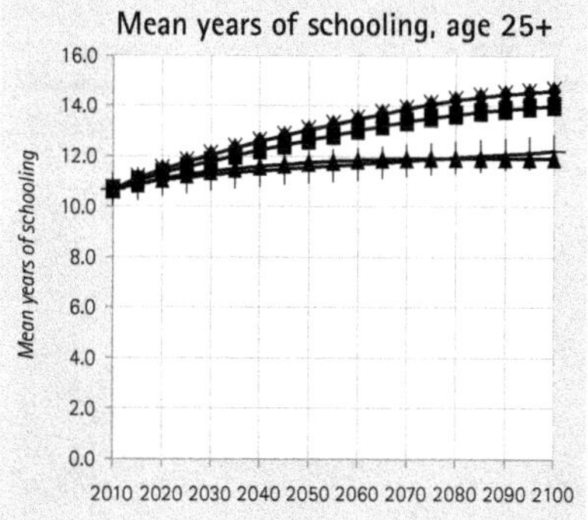

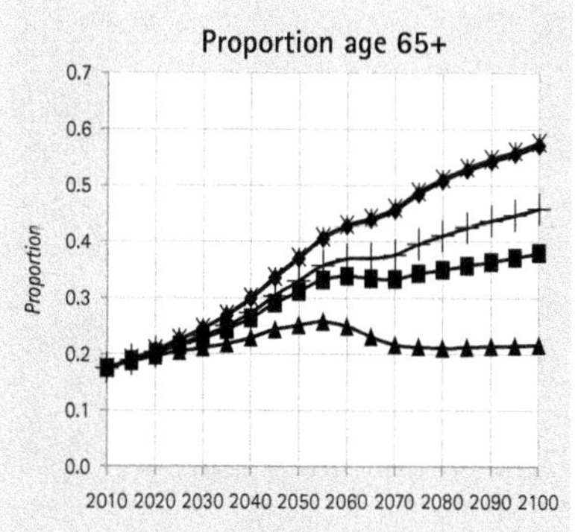

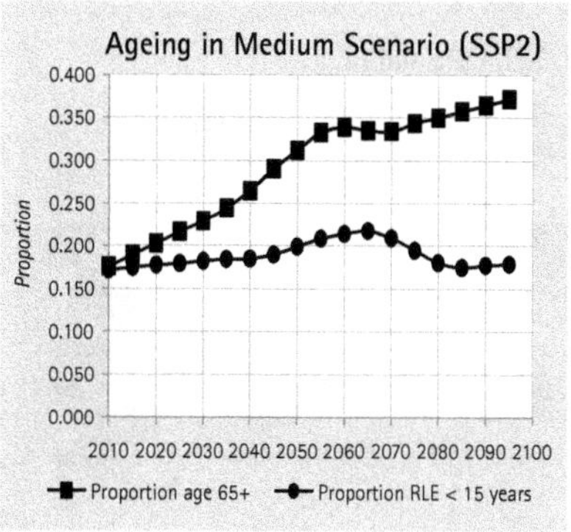

Alternative Scenarios to 2100

Projection Results by Scenario (SSP1–5)

	2010	2020	2030	2040	2050	2075	2100
Population (in millions)							
SSP1 - Rapid development	7.49	7.01	6.53	6.07	5.60	4.35	3.26
SSP2 - Medium	7.49	7.01	6.56	6.14	5.73	4.73	4.04
SSP3 - Stalled development	7.49	7.05	6.65	6.29	6.01	5.57	5.75
SSP4 - Inequality	7.49	6.98	6.45	5.93	5.40	4.03	2.97
SSP5 - Conventional development	7.49	7.00	6.50	6.04	5.56	4.30	3.20
Proportion age 65+							
SSP1 - Rapid development	0.18	0.21	0.25	0.30	0.37	0.48	0.57
SSP2 - Medium	0.18	0.20	0.23	0.26	0.31	0.34	0.38
SSP3 - Stalled development	0.18	0.20	0.21	0.23	0.25	0.21	0.22
SSP4 - Inequality	0.18	0.20	0.23	0.27	0.33	0.40	0.46
SSP5 - Conventional development	0.18	0.21	0.25	0.30	0.37	0.49	0.58
Proportion below age 20							
SSP1 - Rapid development	0.19	0.18	0.15	0.13	0.12	0.10	0.08
SSP2 - Medium	0.19	0.19	0.18	0.17	0.17	0.16	0.16
SSP3 - Stalled development	0.19	0.20	0.21	0.21	0.23	0.25	0.25
SSP4 - Inequality	0.19	0.19	0.16	0.15	0.14	0.12	0.11
SSP5 - Conventional development	0.19	0.18	0.15	0.13	0.12	0.09	0.08
Proportion of Women age 20–39 with at least secondary education							
SSP1 - Rapid development	0.96	0.99	0.99	1.00	1.00	1.00	1.00
SSP2 - Medium	0.96	0.98	0.99	1.00	1.00	1.00	1.00
SSP3 - Stalled development	0.96	0.94	0.93	0.93	0.93	0.93	0.93
SSP4 - Inequality	0.96	0.88	0.84	0.84	0.84	0.84	0.84
SSP5 - Conventional development	0.96	0.99	0.99	1.00	1.00	1.00	1.00
Mean years of schooling, age 25+							
SSP1 - Rapid development	10.67	11.47	12.04	12.58	13.04	14.07	14.60
SSP2 - Medium	10.67	11.32	11.80	12.23	12.63	13.53	14.01
SSP3 - Stalled development	10.67	11.10	11.40	11.60	11.74	11.92	11.92
SSP4 - Inequality	10.67	11.05	11.26	11.42	11.55	11.89	12.20
SSP5 - Conventional development	10.67	11.47	12.04	12.57	13.04	14.06	14.60

Demographic Assumptions Underlying SSPs

	2010–15	2020–25	2030–35	2040–45	2050–55	2075–80	2095–2100
Total fertility rate							
SSP1 - Rapid development	1.34	1.25	1.22	1.20	1.18	1.20	1.22
SSP2 - Medium	1.40	1.52	1.60	1.60	1.60	1.63	1.65
SSP3 - Stalled development	1.51	1.82	2.02	2.09	2.12	2.16	2.21
SSP4 - Inequality	1.36	1.34	1.31	1.28	1.26	1.28	1.30
SSP5 - Conventional development	1.34	1.25	1.22	1.20	1.18	1.20	1.22
Life expectancy at birth for females (in years)							
SSP1 - Rapid development	78.53	81.33	84.23	87.21	90.23	98.09	104.39
SSP2 - Medium	77.29	79.29	81.39	83.51	85.61	90.90	95.20
SSP3 - Stalled development	77.62	78.43	79.43	80.35	81.35	83.93	86.14
SSP4 - Inequality	78.09	79.84	81.75	83.73	85.73	90.61	94.78
SSP5 - Conventional development	78.53	81.33	84.23	87.21	90.23	98.09	104.39
Migration – net flow over five years (in thousands)							
SSP1 - Rapid development	−29	−12	−5	0	3	2	0
SSP2 - Medium	−29	−12	−6	0	4	2	0
SSP3 - Stalled development	−24	−6	−3	0	3	3	0
SSP4 - Inequality	−29	−12	−5	1	4	3	0
SSP5 - Conventional development	−34	−18	−8	0	3	1	0

Ageing Indicators, Medium Scenario (SSP2)

	2010	2020	2030	2040	2050	2075	2095
Median age	41.56	44.14	47.39	50.25	50.90	52.66	54.40
Propspective median age	41.56	42.25	43.52	44.35	42.98	39.71	37.26
Proportion age 65+	0.18	0.20	0.23	0.26	0.31	0.34	0.37
Proportion RLE < 15 years	0.17	0.18	0.18	0.18	0.20	0.19	0.18

Burkina Faso

Detailed Human Capital Projections to 2060

Demographic indicators, Medium Scenario (SSP2)	2010	2020	2030	2040	2050	2060
Population (in millions)	16.47	21.68	27.44	33.15	38.33	42.68
Proportion age 65+	0.02	0.02	0.03	0.04	0.05	0.06
Proportion below age 20	0.56	0.54	0.50	0.46	0.41	0.37
	2005–10	2015–20	2025–30	2035–40	2045–50	2055–60
Total Fertility Rate	5.94	5.05	4.24	3.45	2.86	2.44
Life expectancy at birth (in years)						
Men	52.84	56.90	59.46	61.73	63.81	66.03
Women	54.78	59.12	62.02	64.72	67.21	69.72
Five-year immigration flow (in '000)	262.52	256.65	266.14	271.72	271.37	267.16
Five-year emigration flow (in '000)	385.84	380.74	488.22	598.84	695.21	767.09

Human Capital indicators, Medium Scenario (SSP2)	2010	2020	2030	2040	2050	2060
Population age 25+: highest educational attainment						
E1 - no education	0.79	0.70	0.61	0.52	0.43	0.35
E2 - incomplete primary	0.07	0.09	0.10	0.10	0.09	0.08
E3 - primary	0.05	0.07	0.09	0.12	0.15	0.17
E4 - lower secondary	0.05	0.08	0.10	0.13	0.16	0.18
E5 - upper secondary	0.03	0.04	0.07	0.10	0.13	0.18
E6 - post-secondary	0.01	0.02	0.02	0.03	0.04	0.04
Mean years of schooling (in years)	1.68	2.41	3.27	4.25	5.31	6.42
Gender gap (population age 25+): highest educational attainment (ratio male/female)						
E1 - no education	0.84	0.81	0.80	0.80	0.81	0.84
E2 - incomplete primary	1.57	1.42	1.29	1.19	1.12	1.05
E3 - primary	1.93	1.63	1.40	1.23	1.13	1.07
E4 - lower secondary	1.81	1.55	1.35	1.21	1.12	1.07
E5 - upper secondary	2.65	2.24	1.87	1.57	1.35	1.19
E6 - post-secondary	3.13	2.16	1.58	1.25	1.09	1.05
Mean years of schooling (male minus female)	1.20	1.33	1.31	1.16	0.92	0.65
Women age 20–39: highest educational attainment						
E1 - no education	0.76	0.66	0.56	0.44	0.32	0.21
E2 - incomplete primary	0.09	0.11	0.11	0.11	0.11	0.10
E3 - primary	0.06	0.09	0.13	0.16	0.19	0.21
E4 - lower secondary	0.06	0.09	0.13	0.18	0.23	0.27
E5 - upper secondary	0.02	0.03	0.05	0.08	0.12	0.18
E6 - post-secondary	0.01	0.01	0.02	0.02	0.03	0.04
Mean years of schooling (in years)	1.68	2.53	3.61	4.88	6.24	7.58

Education scenarios

GET: global education trend scenario (medium assumption also used for SSP2)

CER: constant enrolment rates scenario (assumption of no future improvements)

FT: Fast track scenario (assumption of education expansion according to fastest historical experience)

Pyramids by Education, Medium Scenario

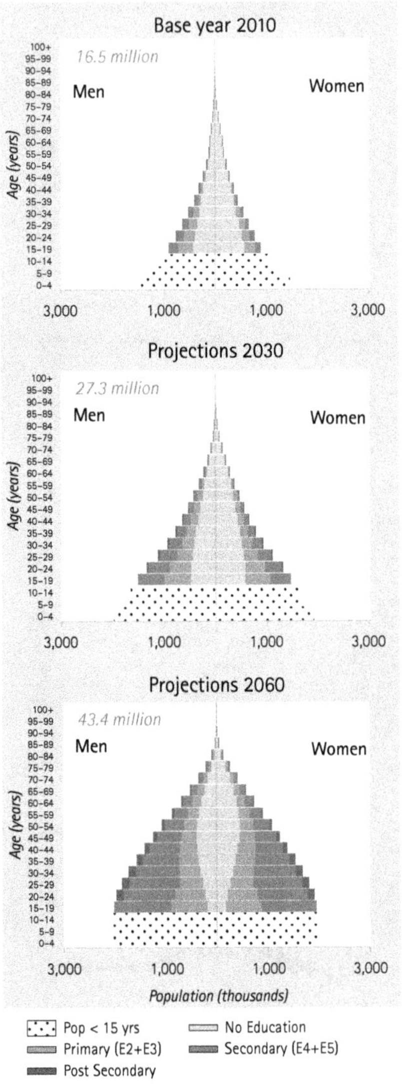

Population Size by Educational Attainment According to Three Education Scenarios: GET, CER, and FT

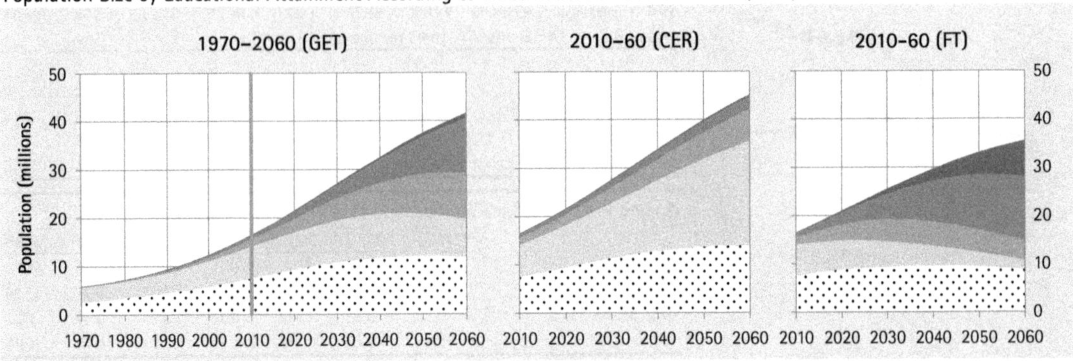

Burkina Faso (Continued)

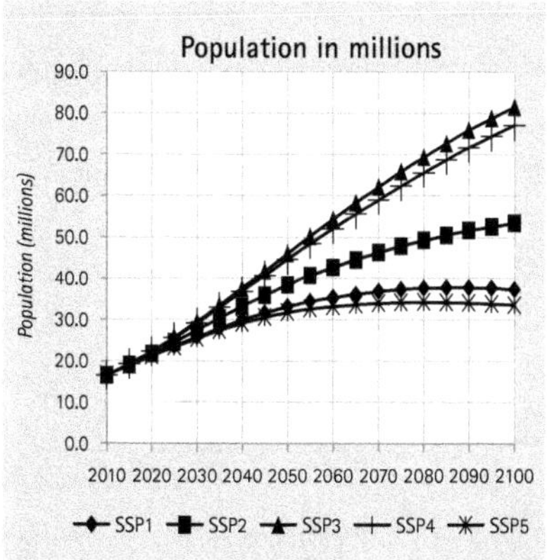

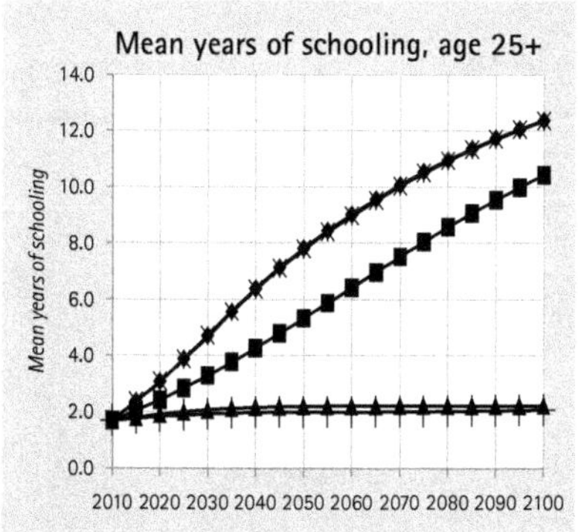

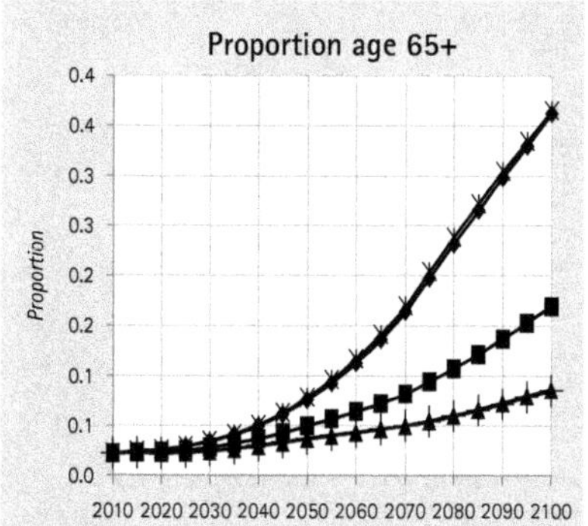

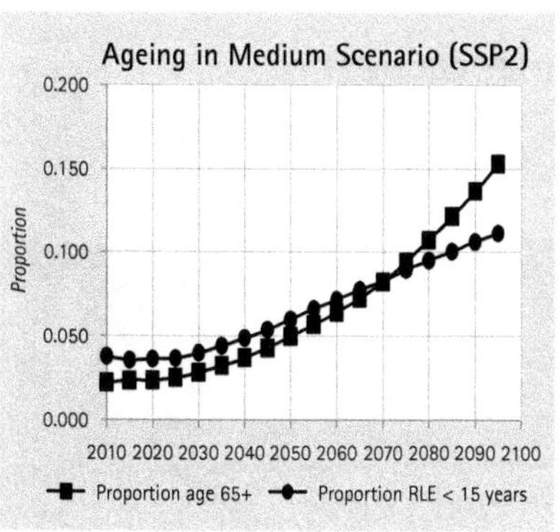

Alternative Scenarios to 2100

Projection Results by Scenario (SSP1–5)

	2010	2020	2030	2040	2050	2075	2100
Population (in millions)							
SSP1 - Rapid development	16.47	21.19	25.73	29.84	33.09	37.27	37.28
SSP2 - Medium	16.47	21.68	27.44	33.15	38.33	47.84	53.36
SSP3 - Stalled development	16.47	22.28	29.44	37.51	45.98	65.77	81.42
SSP4 - Inequality	16.47	22.22	29.15	36.78	44.59	62.33	76.98
SSP5 - Conventional development	16.47	21.12	25.40	29.06	31.69	34.09	33.47
Proportion age 65+							
SSP1 - Rapid development	0.02	0.03	0.03	0.05	0.08	0.20	0.36
SSP2 - Medium	0.02	0.02	0.03	0.04	0.05	0.09	0.17
SSP3 - Stalled development	0.02	0.02	0.02	0.03	0.04	0.05	0.09
SSP4 - Inequality	0.02	0.02	0.02	0.03	0.04	0.05	0.09
SSP5 - Conventional development	0.02	0.03	0.03	0.05	0.08	0.20	0.36
Proportion below age 20							
SSP1 - Rapid development	0.56	0.52	0.45	0.39	0.33	0.21	0.14
SSP2 - Medium	0.56	0.54	0.50	0.46	0.41	0.31	0.24
SSP3 - Stalled development	0.56	0.55	0.53	0.51	0.47	0.38	0.33
SSP4 - Inequality	0.56	0.55	0.54	0.51	0.48	0.39	0.33
SSP5 - Conventional development	0.56	0.52	0.45	0.39	0.33	0.21	0.14
Proportion of Women age 20–39 with at least secondary education							
SSP1 - Rapid development	0.09	0.22	0.38	0.53	0.63	0.80	0.90
SSP2 - Medium	0.09	0.13	0.20	0.29	0.38	0.63	0.82
SSP3 - Stalled development	0.09	0.07	0.07	0.07	0.07	0.07	0.07
SSP4 - Inequality	0.09	0.06	0.06	0.06	0.06	0.06	0.06
SSP5 - Conventional development	0.09	0.22	0.38	0.53	0.63	0.80	0.90
Mean years of schooling, age 25+							
SSP1 - Rapid development	1.68	3.06	4.70	6.38	7.81	10.53	12.36
SSP2 - Medium	1.68	2.41	3.27	4.25	5.31	8.05	10.42
SSP3 - Stalled development	1.68	1.90	2.06	2.16	2.19	2.21	2.22
SSP4 - Inequality	1.68	1.83	1.92	1.97	1.99	2.01	2.07
SSP5 - Conventional development	1.68	3.06	4.68	6.35	7.77	10.48	12.34

Demographic Assumptions Underlying SSPs

	2010–15	2020–25	2030–35	2040–45	2050–55	2075–80	2095–2100
Total fertility rate							
SSP1 - Rapid development	5.14	3.69	2.74	2.17	1.82	1.40	1.29
SSP2 - Medium	5.47	4.66	3.82	3.11	2.63	1.98	1.81
SSP3 - Stalled development	5.86	5.67	5.10	4.35	3.70	2.76	2.53
SSP4 - Inequality	5.87	5.70	5.13	4.37	3.71	2.75	2.53
SSP5 - Conventional development	5.14	3.70	2.74	2.18	1.82	1.40	1.29
Life expectancy at birth for females (in years)							
SSP1 - Rapid development	61.41	68.05	72.37	77.12	81.06	89.72	96.72
SSP2 - Medium	56.97	60.47	63.42	65.98	68.52	74.69	79.69
SSP3 - Stalled development	59.57	58.00	59.68	60.65	62.16	64.89	66.98
SSP4 - Inequality	59.57	58.00	59.66	60.64	62.14	64.87	66.97
SSP5 - Conventional development	61.41	68.05	72.37	77.12	81.06	89.72	96.72
Migration – net flow over five years (in thousands)							
SSP1 - Rapid development	−110	−169	−267	−351	−409	−181	0
SSP2 - Medium	−109	−169	−275	−379	−469	−242	0
SSP3 - Stalled development	−91	−83	−132	−183	−232	−129	0
SSP4 - Inequality	−109	−168	−274	−387	−496	−274	0
SSP5 - Conventional development	−128	−256	−416	−563	−677	−326	0

Ageing Indicators, Medium Scenario (SSP2)

	2010	2020	2030	2040	2050	2075	2095
Median age	17.05	18.18	19.94	22.15	24.77	32.12	38.00
Propspective median age	17.05	16.65	16.89	17.95	19.40	23.53	25.78
Proportion age 65+	0.02	0.02	0.03	0.04	0.05	0.09	0.15
Proportion RLE < 15 years	0.04	0.04	0.04	0.05	0.06	0.09	0.11

Burundi

Detailed Human Capital Projections to 2060

Demographic indicators, Medium Scenario (SSP2)	2010	2020	2030	2040	2050	2060
Population (in millions)	8.38	10.88	13.17	15.25	17.12	18.61
Proportion age 65+	0.03	0.03	0.04	0.05	0.07	0.10
Proportion below age 20	0.49	0.45	0.41	0.36	0.32	0.29
	2005–10	2015–20	2025–30	2035–40	2045–50	2055–60
Total Fertility Rate	4.66	3.59	2.87	2.45	2.16	1.98
Life expectancy at birth (in years)						
Men	47.49	51.37	53.11	55.73	58.36	61.55
Women	50.05	54.80	57.03	59.08	61.18	64.08
Five-year immigration flow (in '000)	369.31	292.57	303.55	310.08	309.86	305.20
Five-year emigration flow (in '000)	0.00	0.00	0.00	0.00	0.00	0.00

Human Capital indicators, Medium Scenario (SSP2)	2010	2020	2030	2040	2050	2060
Population age 25+: highest educational attainment						
E1 - no education	0.55	0.39	0.31	0.24	0.17	0.13
E2 - incomplete primary	0.22	0.25	0.22	0.20	0.16	0.13
E3 - primary	0.17	0.24	0.30	0.34	0.38	0.41
E4 - lower secondary	0.03	0.06	0.09	0.11	0.13	0.14
E5 - upper secondary	0.02	0.03	0.05	0.07	0.09	0.12
E6 - post-secondary	0.02	0.03	0.03	0.04	0.06	0.07
Mean years of schooling (in years)	2.77	4.03	4.93	5.84	6.74	7.55
Gender gap (population age 25+): highest educational attainment (ratio male/female)						
E1 - no education	0.69	0.69	0.74	0.78	0.82	0.86
E2 - incomplete primary	1.41	1.19	1.13	1.10	1.09	1.08
E3 - primary	1.60	1.20	1.04	0.98	0.95	0.96
E4 - lower secondary	1.68	1.54	1.30	1.18	1.10	1.05
E5 - upper secondary	1.91	1.59	1.47	1.34	1.23	1.15
E6 - post-secondary	2.68	1.81	1.45	1.22	1.10	1.06
Mean years of schooling (male minus female)	1.42	1.18	0.87	0.61	0.40	0.27
Women age 20–39: highest educational attainment						
E1 - no education	0.46	0.27	0.20	0.13	0.09	0.06
E2 - incomplete primary	0.25	0.30	0.24	0.21	0.16	0.13
E3 - primary	0.21	0.29	0.36	0.40	0.42	0.41
E4 - lower secondary	0.05	0.08	0.11	0.14	0.17	0.19
E5 - upper secondary	0.02	0.04	0.05	0.08	0.11	0.15
E6 - post-secondary	0.01	0.02	0.03	0.04	0.06	0.07
Mean years of schooling (in years)	3.20	4.71	5.71	6.69	7.60	8.41

Education scenarios

GET : global education trend scenario (medium assumption also used for SSP2)

CER: constant enrolment rates scenario (assumption of no future improvements)

FT: Fast track scenario (assumption of education expansion according to fastest historical experience)

Pyramids by Education, Medium Scenario

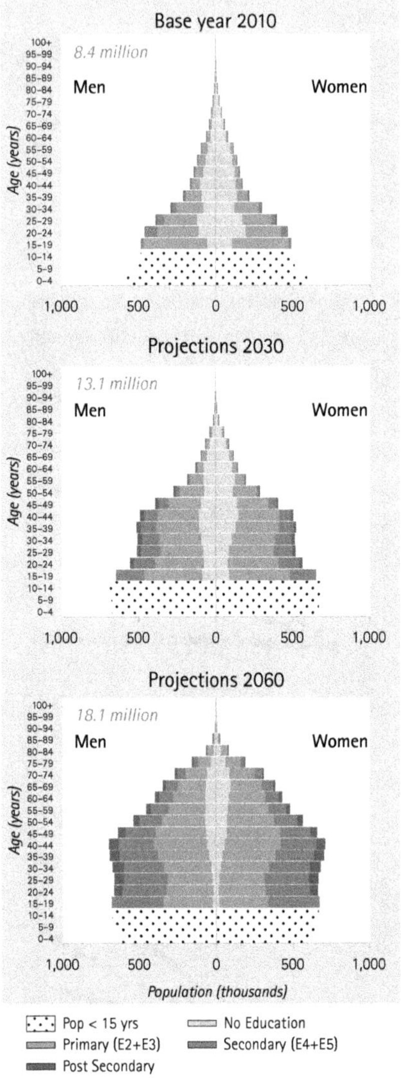

Population Size by Educational Attainment According to Three Education Scenarios: GET, CER, and FT

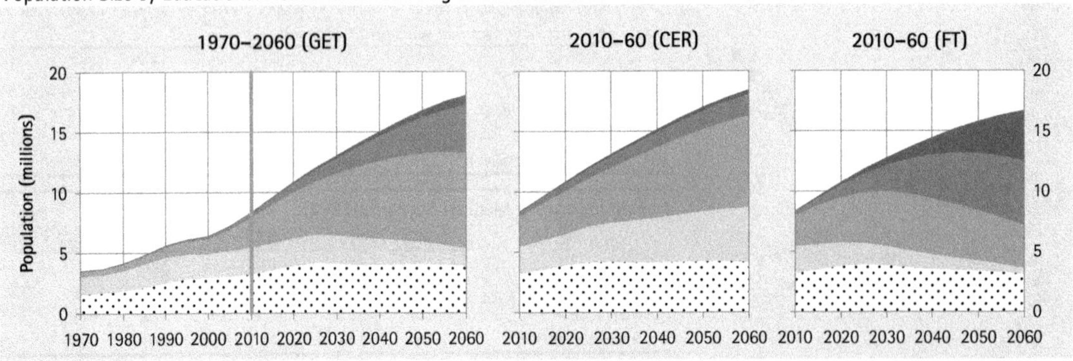

Burundi (Continued)

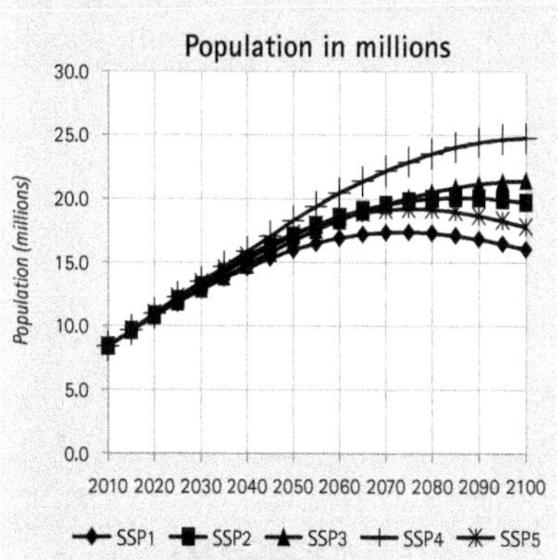

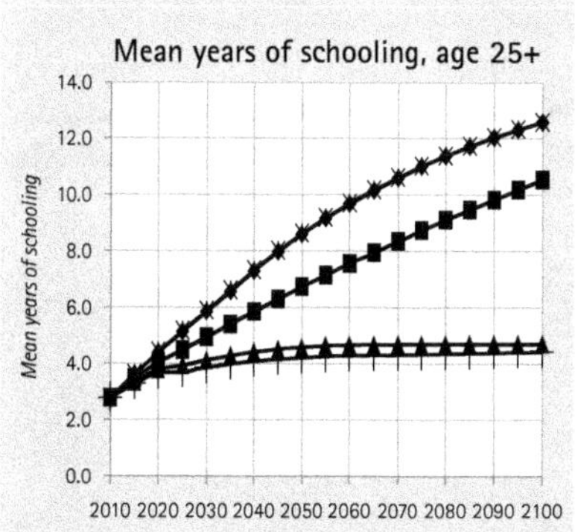

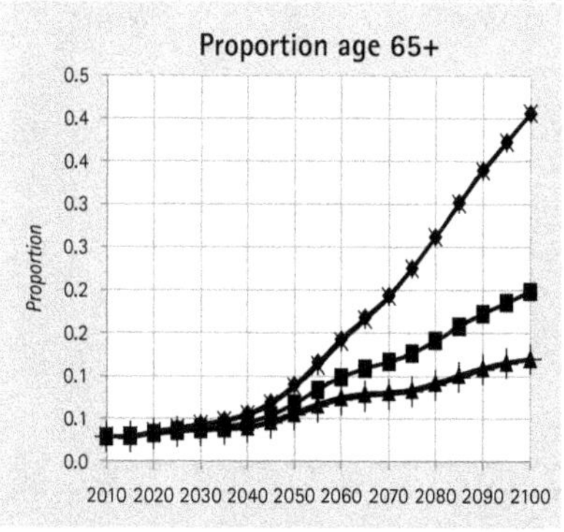

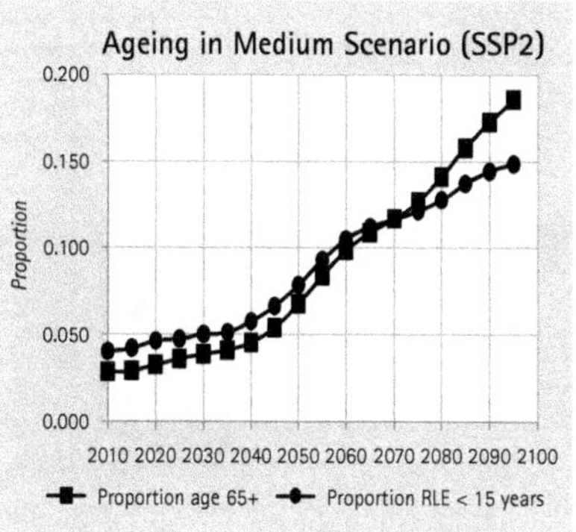

Alternative Scenarios to 2100

Projection Results by Scenario (SSP1–5)

	2010	2020	2030	2040	2050	2075	2100
Population (in millions)							
SSP1 - Rapid development	8.38	10.76	12.83	14.57	15.98	17.39	16.05
SSP2 - Medium	8.38	10.88	13.17	15.25	17.12	19.84	19.74
SSP3 - Stalled development	8.38	10.78	12.89	14.81	16.72	20.07	21.45
SSP4 - Inequality	8.38	10.97	13.49	15.87	18.29	22.90	24.77
SSP5 - Conventional development	8.38	10.93	13.39	15.51	17.26	19.22	17.81
Proportion age 65+							
SSP1 - Rapid development	0.03	0.03	0.04	0.06	0.09	0.23	0.41
SSP2 - Medium	0.03	0.03	0.04	0.05	0.07	0.13	0.20
SSP3 - Stalled development	0.03	0.03	0.04	0.04	0.06	0.08	0.12
SSP4 - Inequality	0.03	0.03	0.04	0.04	0.05	0.08	0.12
SSP5 - Conventional development	0.03	0.03	0.04	0.05	0.09	0.22	0.41
Proportion below age 20							
SSP1 - Rapid development	0.49	0.43	0.38	0.30	0.25	0.17	0.11
SSP2 - Medium	0.49	0.45	0.41	0.36	0.32	0.26	0.22
SSP3 - Stalled development	0.49	0.46	0.45	0.41	0.38	0.32	0.30
SSP4 - Inequality	0.49	0.46	0.45	0.41	0.38	0.32	0.30
SSP5 - Conventional development	0.49	0.43	0.37	0.30	0.25	0.17	0.11
Proportion of Women age 20–39 with at least secondary education							
SSP1 - Rapid development	0.08	0.19	0.34	0.48	0.60	0.75	0.86
SSP2 - Medium	0.08	0.14	0.20	0.26	0.33	0.53	0.74
SSP3 - Stalled development	0.08	0.10	0.11	0.10	0.11	0.11	0.11
SSP4 - Inequality	0.08	0.10	0.10	0.09	0.10	0.10	0.10
SSP5 - Conventional development	0.08	0.19	0.34	0.48	0.60	0.75	0.86
Mean years of schooling, age 25+							
SSP1 - Rapid development	2.77	4.38	5.84	7.28	8.59	11.00	12.57
SSP2 - Medium	2.77	4.03	4.93	5.84	6.74	8.73	10.53
SSP3 - Stalled development	2.77	3.77	4.11	4.40	4.58	4.68	4.70
SSP4 - Inequality	2.77	3.64	3.85	4.07	4.21	4.33	4.42
SSP5 - Conventional development	2.77	4.39	5.87	7.32	8.62	11.01	12.58

Demographic Assumptions Underlying SSPs

	2010–15	2020–25	2030–35	2040–45	2050–55	2075–80	2095–2100
Total fertility rate							
SSP1 - Rapid development	3.83	2.63	1.96	1.62	1.43	1.25	1.17
SSP2 - Medium	4.10	3.16	2.64	2.27	2.07	1.79	1.65
SSP3 - Stalled development	4.29	3.81	3.37	3.00	2.74	2.40	2.31
SSP4 - Inequality	4.29	3.84	3.40	3.01	2.74	2.40	2.30
SSP5 - Conventional development	3.83	2.63	1.96	1.62	1.43	1.25	1.17
Life expectancy at birth for females (in years)							
SSP1 - Rapid development	57.85	63.91	67.86	71.39	75.64	85.24	93.01
SSP2 - Medium	52.63	55.90	58.12	59.98	62.58	70.08	76.02
SSP3 - Stalled development	54.83	53.60	54.88	55.56	56.48	60.82	64.08
SSP4 - Inequality	54.83	53.57	54.84	55.51	56.42	60.76	64.03
SSP5 - Conventional development	57.85	63.91	67.86	71.39	75.64	85.24	93.01
Migration – net flow over five years (in thousands)							
SSP1 - Rapid development	306	289	291	275	249	88	0
SSP2 - Medium	309	291	300	304	300	137	0
SSP3 - Stalled development	253	142	151	167	184	111	0
SSP4 - Inequality	303	285	300	327	356	211	0
SSP5 - Conventional development	357	434	435	406	363	125	0

Ageing Indicators, Medium Scenario (SSP2)

	2010	2020	2030	2040	2050	2075	2095
Median age	20.22	22.73	24.92	27.69	30.78	36.81	41.37
Propspective median age	20.22	21.04	21.87	23.34	24.75	27.14	27.81
Proportion age 65+	0.03	0.03	0.04	0.05	0.07	0.13	0.19
Proportion RLE < 15 years	0.04	0.05	0.05	0.06	0.08	0.12	0.15

Cambodia

Detailed Human Capital Projections to 2060

Demographic indicators, Medium Scenario (SSP2)	2010	2020	2030	2040	2050	2060
Population (in millions)	14.14	15.82	17.14	18.00	18.55	18.64
Proportion age 65+	0.04	0.05	0.07	0.09	0.12	0.17
Proportion below age 20	0.44	0.37	0.34	0.30	0.27	0.25
	2005–10	2015–20	2025–30	2035–40	2045–50	2055–60
Total Fertility Rate	2.80	2.34	2.08	1.94	1.85	1.75
Life expectancy at birth (in years)						
Men	60.21	64.63	67.34	69.55	71.56	73.65
Women	62.62	67.88	71.19	73.81	76.00	78.10
Five-year immigration flow (in '000)	0.30	0.29	0.30	0.31	0.31	0.30
Five-year emigration flow (in '000)	254.34	222.49	221.77	218.91	211.49	198.25

Human Capital indicators, Medium Scenario (SSP2)	2010	2020	2030	2040	2050	2060
Population age 25+: highest educational attainment						
E1 - no education	0.28	0.20	0.16	0.12	0.09	0.06
E2 - incomplete primary	0.27	0.25	0.20	0.16	0.12	0.09
E3 - primary	0.24	0.28	0.31	0.33	0.34	0.34
E4 - lower secondary	0.13	0.16	0.19	0.20	0.21	0.21
E5 - upper secondary	0.06	0.08	0.11	0.14	0.18	0.22
E6 - post-secondary	0.02	0.03	0.04	0.05	0.06	0.08
Mean years of schooling (in years)	4.18	5.17	6.01	6.81	7.58	8.29
Gender gap (population age 25+): highest educational attainment (ratio male/female)						
E1 - no education	0.49	0.55	0.61	0.65	0.69	0.71
E2 - incomplete primary	0.93	0.87	0.85	0.84	0.85	0.86
E3 - primary	1.36	1.11	0.99	0.93	0.91	0.91
E4 - lower secondary	1.60	1.40	1.26	1.17	1.11	1.06
E5 - upper secondary	2.63	1.92	1.70	1.52	1.36	1.24
E6 - post-secondary	3.20	1.83	1.43	1.22	1.11	1.07
Mean years of schooling (male minus female)	1.84	1.41	1.13	0.89	0.69	0.54
Women age 20–39: highest educational attainment						
E1 - no education	0.25	0.13	0.08	0.05	0.03	0.01
E2 - incomplete primary	0.22	0.22	0.16	0.11	0.07	0.05
E3 - primary	0.29	0.34	0.37	0.37	0.34	0.30
E4 - lower secondary	0.16	0.18	0.20	0.21	0.21	0.20
E5 - upper secondary	0.06	0.09	0.13	0.19	0.25	0.32
E6 - post-secondary	0.02	0.04	0.06	0.08	0.10	0.12
Mean years of schooling (in years)	4.44	6.16	7.38	8.26	9.01	9.70

Education scenarios

GET: global education trend scenario (medium assumption also used for SSP2)

CER: constant enrolment rates scenario (assumption of no future improvements)

FT: Fast track scenario (assumption of education expansion according to fastest historical experience)

Pyramids by Education, Medium Scenario

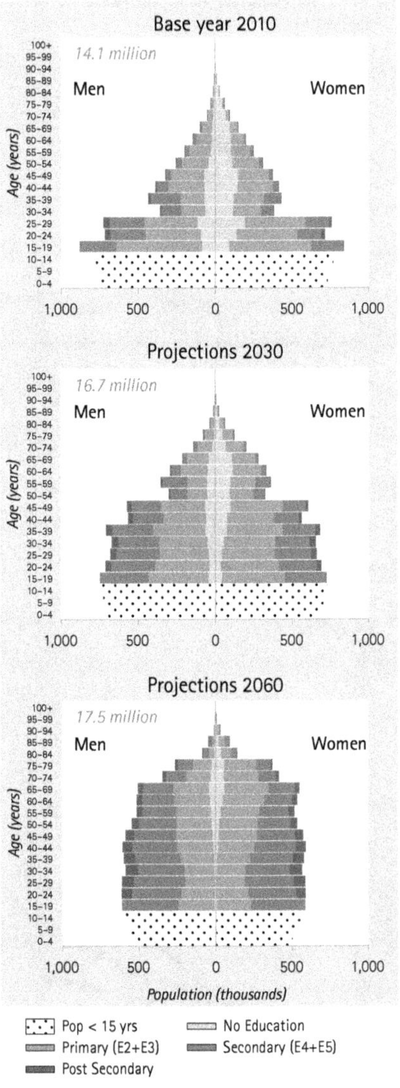

Population Size by Educational Attainment According to Three Education Scenarios: GET, CER, and FT

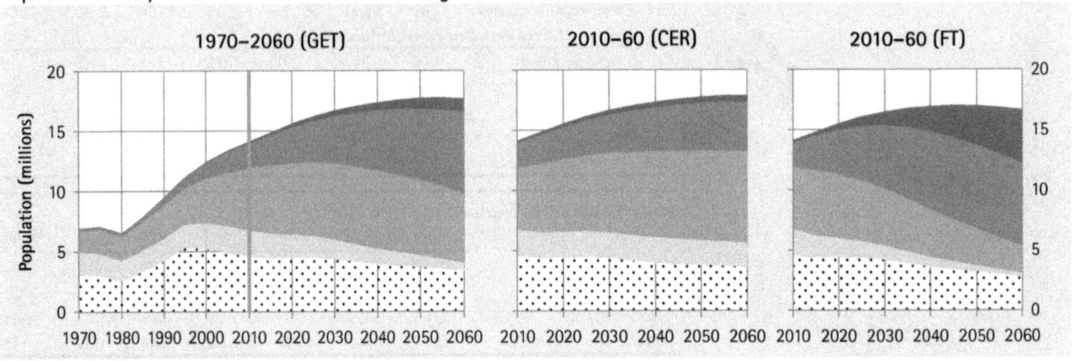

Cambodia (Continued)

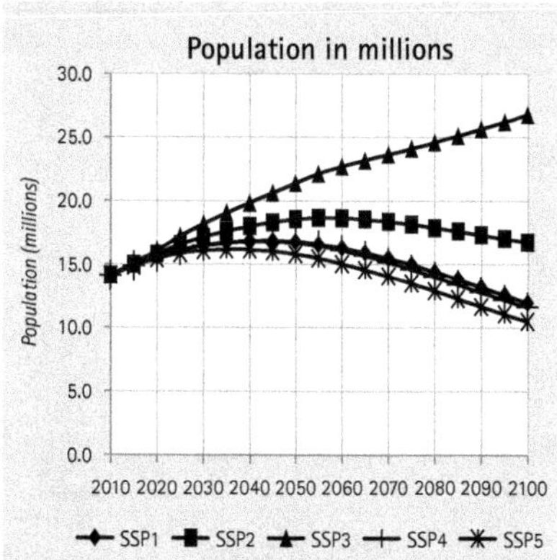

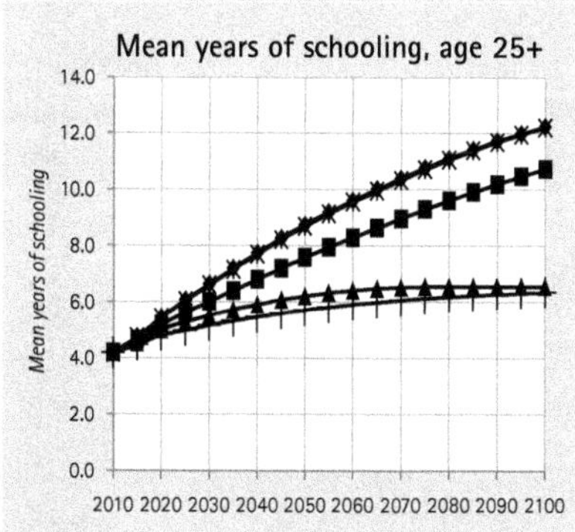

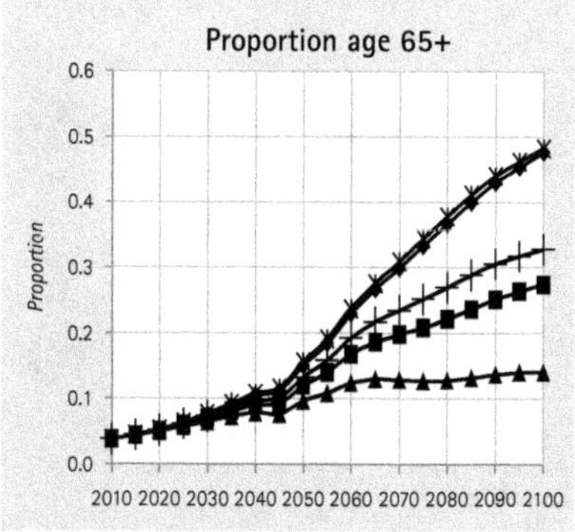

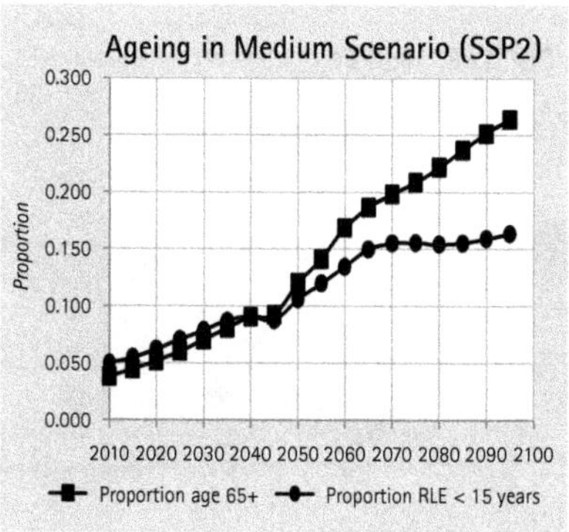

Alternative Scenarios to 2100

Projection Results by Scenario (SSP1–5)

	2010	2020	2030	2040	2050	2075	2100
Population (in millions)							
SSP1 - Rapid development	14.14	15.59	16.49	16.84	16.78	14.99	11.97
SSP2 - Medium	14.14	15.82	17.14	18.00	18.55	18.15	16.75
SSP3 - Stalled development	14.14	16.14	18.19	19.84	21.41	24.11	26.77
SSP4 - Inequality	14.14	15.60	16.48	16.81	16.70	14.61	11.63
SSP5 - Conventional development	14.14	15.46	16.09	16.16	15.81	13.50	10.51
Proportion age 65+							
SSP1 - Rapid development	0.04	0.05	0.08	0.11	0.15	0.33	0.48
SSP2 - Medium	0.04	0.05	0.07	0.09	0.12	0.21	0.27
SSP3 - Stalled development	0.04	0.05	0.07	0.08	0.10	0.13	0.14
SSP4 - Inequality	0.04	0.05	0.07	0.10	0.13	0.25	0.33
SSP5 - Conventional development	0.04	0.05	0.08	0.11	0.16	0.34	0.48
Proportion below age 20							
SSP1 - Rapid development	0.44	0.36	0.31	0.25	0.21	0.13	0.10
SSP2 - Medium	0.44	0.37	0.34	0.30	0.27	0.22	0.19
SSP3 - Stalled development	0.44	0.38	0.37	0.34	0.32	0.30	0.30
SSP4 - Inequality	0.44	0.37	0.31	0.26	0.23	0.17	0.15
SSP5 - Conventional development	0.44	0.36	0.31	0.25	0.21	0.13	0.10
Proportion of Women age 20–39 with at least secondary education							
SSP1 - Rapid development	0.24	0.37	0.54	0.67	0.75	0.87	0.94
SSP2 - Medium	0.24	0.31	0.39	0.47	0.55	0.74	0.88
SSP3 - Stalled development	0.24	0.26	0.29	0.29	0.29	0.29	0.29
SSP4 - Inequality	0.24	0.25	0.26	0.26	0.26	0.26	0.26
SSP5 - Conventional development	0.24	0.37	0.54	0.67	0.75	0.87	0.94
Mean years of schooling, age 25+							
SSP1 - Rapid development	4.18	5.43	6.64	7.74	8.75	10.75	12.23
SSP2 - Medium	4.18	5.17	6.01	6.81	7.58	9.30	10.73
SSP3 - Stalled development	4.18	4.99	5.51	5.91	6.21	6.55	6.56
SSP4 - Inequality	4.18	4.80	5.16	5.46	5.71	6.13	6.36
SSP5 - Conventional development	4.18	5.42	6.61	7.70	8.70	10.70	12.21

Demographic Assumptions Underlying SSPs

	2010–15	2020–25	2030–35	2040–45	2050–55	2075–80	2095–2100
Total fertility rate							
SSP1 - Rapid development	2.37	1.85	1.53	1.36	1.25	1.15	1.14
SSP2 - Medium	2.53	2.18	2.01	1.91	1.79	1.65	1.61
SSP3 - Stalled development	2.63	2.57	2.50	2.44	2.39	2.32	2.35
SSP4 - Inequality	2.38	1.90	1.62	1.50	1.42	1.37	1.38
SSP5 - Conventional development	2.37	1.85	1.53	1.36	1.25	1.15	1.14
Life expectancy at birth for females (in years)							
SSP1 - Rapid development	68.97	72.64	76.26	79.49	82.45	89.93	95.93
SSP2 - Medium	65.58	69.68	72.61	74.90	77.10	82.19	86.20
SSP3 - Stalled development	68.26	70.43	71.99	73.02	73.77	75.70	77.14
SSP4 - Inequality	68.33	71.72	74.16	76.04	77.86	82.25	85.68
SSP5 - Conventional development	68.97	72.64	76.26	79.49	82.45	89.93	95.93
Migration – net flow over five years (in thousands)							
SSP1 - Rapid development	−233	−222	−213	−202	−180	−60	0
SSP2 - Medium	−235	−226	−221	−218	−207	−84	0
SSP3 - Stalled development	−194	−110	−108	−108	−105	−48	0
SSP4 - Inequality	−233	−220	−209	−192	−165	−51	0
SSP5 - Conventional development	−272	−335	−328	−317	−291	−106	0

Ageing Indicators, Medium Scenario (SSP2)

	2010	2020	2030	2040	2050	2075	2095
Median age	22.93	26.57	30.14	33.08	36.08	42.77	46.59
Propspective median age	22.93	24.64	26.84	28.40	30.00	32.78	33.01
Proportion age 65+	0.04	0.05	0.07	0.09	0.12	0.21	0.26
Proportion RLE < 15 years	0.05	0.06	0.08	0.09	0.11	0.16	0.16

Cameroon

Detailed Human Capital Projections to 2060

Demographic indicators, Medium Scenario (SSP2)	2010	2020	2030	2040	2050	2060
Population (in millions)	19.60	23.67	27.34	30.63	33.14	34.90
Proportion age 65+	0.04	0.04	0.04	0.05	0.07	0.09
Proportion below age 20	0.52	0.48	0.43	0.38	0.34	0.30
	2005–10	2015–20	2025–30	2035–40	2045–50	2055–60
Total Fertility Rate	4.67	3.60	2.87	2.45	2.16	1.98
Life expectancy at birth (in years)						
Men	49.01	53.25	55.03	56.80	58.89	61.44
Women	50.89	55.70	58.20	60.52	62.88	65.58
Five-year immigration flow (in '000)	35.66	34.87	36.17	36.95	36.92	36.36
Five-year emigration flow (in '000)	53.37	48.84	57.50	63.67	66.08	66.96

Human Capital indicators, Medium Scenario (SSP2)	2010	2020	2030	2040	2050	2060
Population age 25+: highest educational attainment						
E1 - no education	0.26	0.16	0.10	0.06	0.03	0.02
E2 - incomplete primary	0.18	0.15	0.11	0.08	0.05	0.03
E3 - primary	0.33	0.38	0.40	0.39	0.37	0.33
E4 - lower secondary	0.10	0.13	0.14	0.15	0.14	0.13
E5 - upper secondary	0.08	0.13	0.18	0.25	0.31	0.38
E6 - post-secondary	0.04	0.05	0.07	0.08	0.09	0.11
Mean years of schooling (in years)	5.71	7.00	8.12	9.09	9.89	10.61
Gender gap (population age 25+): highest educational attainment (ratio male/female)						
E1 - no education	0.52	0.53	0.55	0.58	0.61	0.66
E2 - incomplete primary	0.88	0.87	0.88	0.90	0.94	0.99
E3 - primary	1.17	0.98	0.89	0.86	0.86	0.87
E4 - lower secondary	1.44	1.25	1.14	1.07	1.03	1.01
E5 - upper secondary	2.10	1.74	1.48	1.30	1.19	1.12
E6 - post-secondary	2.32	1.81	1.51	1.31	1.19	1.11
Mean years of schooling (male minus female)	1.98	1.57	1.20	0.88	0.63	0.43
Women age 20–39: highest educational attainment						
E1 - no education	0.17	0.08	0.03	0.01	0.01	0.00
E2 - incomplete primary	0.18	0.12	0.08	0.05	0.03	0.02
E3 - primary	0.41	0.46	0.44	0.39	0.32	0.23
E4 - lower secondary	0.12	0.16	0.18	0.18	0.18	0.18
E5 - upper secondary	0.09	0.14	0.20	0.28	0.36	0.44
E6 - post-secondary	0.03	0.05	0.06	0.08	0.10	0.12
Mean years of schooling (in years)	6.36	7.77	8.92	9.86	10.68	11.43

Education scenarios

GET: global education trend scenario (medium assumption also used for SSP2)

CER: constant enrolment rates scenario (assumption of no future improvements)

FT: Fast track scenario (assumption of education expansion according to fastest historical experience)

Pyramids by Education, Medium Scenario

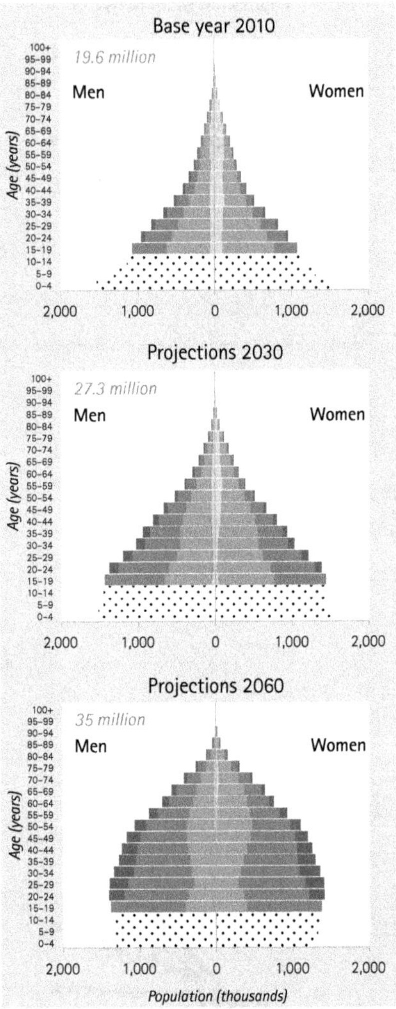

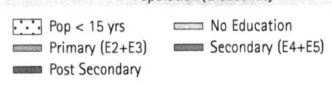

Population Size by Educational Attainment According to Three Education Scenarios: GET, CER, and FT

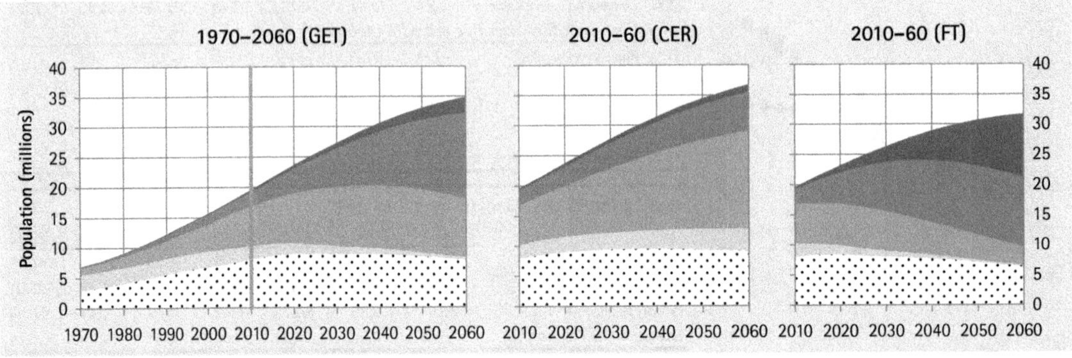

Cameroon (Continued)

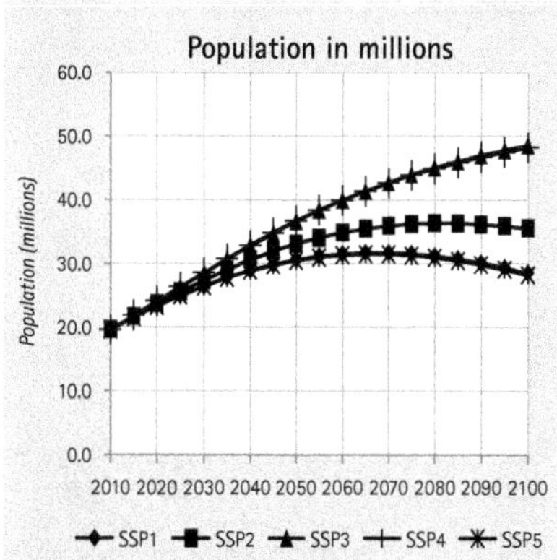

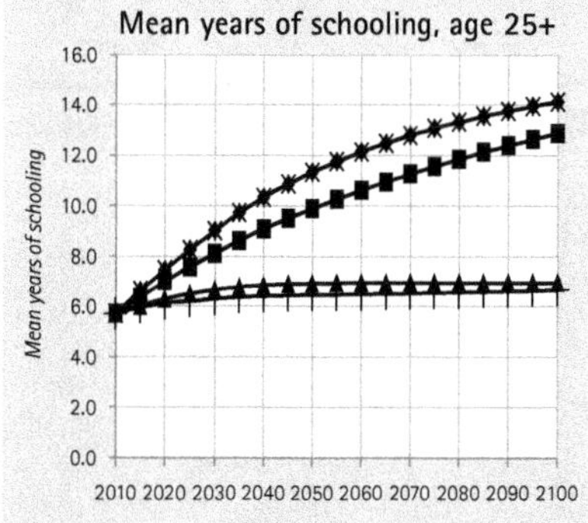

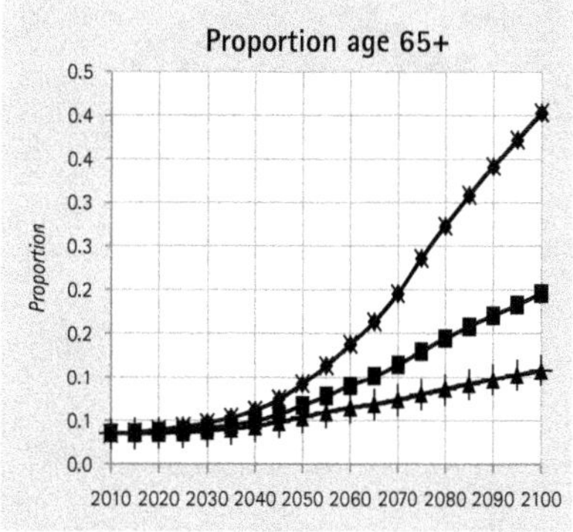

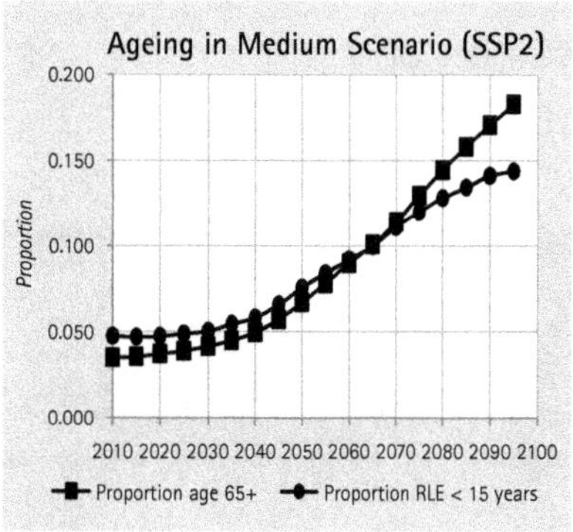

Alternative Scenarios to 2100

Projection Results by Scenario (SSP1–5)

	2010	2020	2030	2040	2050	2075	2100
Population (in millions)							
SSP1 - Rapid development	19.60	23.31	26.42	28.93	30.62	31.58	28.53
SSP2 - Medium	19.60	23.67	27.34	30.63	33.14	36.24	35.60
SSP3 - Stalled development	19.60	24.05	28.55	32.84	36.68	43.99	48.62
SSP4 - Inequality	19.60	24.07	28.61	32.89	36.71	43.87	48.28
SSP5 - Conventional development	19.60	23.31	26.38	28.85	30.49	31.31	28.22
Proportion age 65+							
SSP1 - Rapid development	0.04	0.04	0.05	0.06	0.09	0.24	0.40
SSP2 - Medium	0.04	0.04	0.04	0.05	0.07	0.13	0.20
SSP3 - Stalled development	0.04	0.04	0.04	0.04	0.05	0.08	0.11
SSP4 - Inequality	0.04	0.04	0.04	0.04	0.05	0.08	0.11
SSP5 - Conventional development	0.04	0.04	0.05	0.06	0.09	0.24	0.40
Proportion below age 20							
SSP1 - Rapid development	0.52	0.46	0.38	0.32	0.27	0.17	0.12
SSP2 - Medium	0.52	0.48	0.43	0.38	0.34	0.27	0.22
SSP3 - Stalled development	0.52	0.50	0.47	0.43	0.40	0.35	0.32
SSP4 - Inequality	0.52	0.50	0.47	0.44	0.40	0.35	0.32
SSP5 - Conventional development	0.52	0.46	0.38	0.32	0.27	0.17	0.12
Proportion of Women age 20–39 with at least secondary education							
SSP1 - Rapid development	0.24	0.45	0.61	0.72	0.80	0.92	0.97
SSP2 - Medium	0.24	0.34	0.44	0.54	0.65	0.85	0.95
SSP3 - Stalled development	0.24	0.21	0.21	0.21	0.21	0.21	0.21
SSP4 - Inequality	0.24	0.20	0.19	0.19	0.19	0.19	0.19
SSP5 - Conventional development	0.24	0.45	0.61	0.72	0.80	0.92	0.97
Mean years of schooling, age 25+							
SSP1 - Rapid development	5.71	7.46	9.01	10.34	11.34	13.08	14.13
SSP2 - Medium	5.71	7.00	8.12	9.09	9.89	11.57	12.87
SSP3 - Stalled development	5.71	6.30	6.67	6.85	6.93	6.96	6.96
SSP4 - Inequality	5.71	6.13	6.31	6.42	6.46	6.54	6.66
SSP5 - Conventional development	5.71	7.46	9.01	10.34	11.33	13.07	14.13

Demographic Assumptions Underlying SSPs

	2010–15	2020–25	2030–35	2040–45	2050–55	2075–80	2095–2100
Total fertility rate							
SSP1 - Rapid development	3.79	2.58	1.96	1.64	1.46	1.29	1.21
SSP2 - Medium	4.11	3.16	2.64	2.28	2.08	1.80	1.67
SSP3 - Stalled development	4.37	3.97	3.52	3.13	2.87	2.56	2.43
SSP4 - Inequality	4.38	4.02	3.55	3.14	2.86	2.54	2.41
SSP5 - Conventional development	3.79	2.58	1.96	1.64	1.46	1.29	1.21
Life expectancy at birth for females (in years)							
SSP1 - Rapid development	58.49	64.84	68.73	73.11	77.16	86.22	93.49
SSP2 - Medium	53.57	57.00	59.38	61.58	64.18	71.18	76.68
SSP3 - Stalled development	55.84	54.65	55.71	56.72	57.91	61.12	64.30
SSP4 - Inequality	55.84	54.62	55.64	56.64	57.83	61.04	64.23
SSP5 - Conventional development	58.49	64.84	68.73	73.11	77.16	86.22	93.49
Migration – net flow over five years (in thousands)							
SSP1 - Rapid development	−14	−17	−24	−27	−28	−10	0
SSP2 - Medium	−14	−17	−24	−28	−30	−13	0
SSP3 - Stalled development	−11	−8	−11	−13	−14	−6	0
SSP4 - Inequality	−14	−17	−24	−28	−31	−14	0
SSP5 - Conventional development	−16	−26	−38	−44	−47	−20	0

Ageing Indicators, Medium Scenario (SSP2)

	2010	2020	2030	2040	2050	2075	2095
Median age	19.28	20.94	23.54	26.57	29.56	36.32	40.76
Propspective median age	19.28	19.15	20.50	22.38	24.22	26.74	27.32
Proportion age 65+	0.04	0.04	0.04	0.05	0.07	0.13	0.18
Proportion RLE < 15 years	0.05	0.05	0.05	0.06	0.08	0.12	0.14

Canada

Detailed Human Capital Projections to 2060

Demographic indicators, Medium Scenario (SSP2)	2010	2020	2030	2040	2050	2060
Population (in millions)	34.02	37.40	40.90	43.99	46.91	49.83
Proportion age 65+	0.14	0.18	0.23	0.24	0.26	0.28
Proportion below age 20	0.23	0.21	0.21	0.20	0.20	0.20
	2005–10	2015–20	2025–30	2035–40	2045–50	2055–60
Total Fertility Rate	1.65	1.64	1.69	1.74	1.79	1.80
Life expectancy at birth (in years)						
Men	78.18	79.94	82.01	84.14	86.25	88.42
Women	82.82	84.59	86.71	88.81	90.89	93.09
Five-year immigration flow (in '000)	1395.21	1368.04	1420.50	1452.46	1452.63	1431.33
Five-year emigration flow (in '000)	298.76	221.06	219.32	223.80	233.75	241.54

Human Capital indicators, Medium Scenario (SSP2)	2010	2020	2030	2040	2050	2060
Population age 25+: highest educational attainment						
E1 - no education	0.01	0.01	0.00	0.00	0.00	0.00
E2 - incomplete primary	0.00	0.00	0.00	0.00	0.00	0.00
E3 - primary	0.05	0.03	0.02	0.01	0.01	0.00
E4 - lower secondary	0.07	0.05	0.04	0.03	0.02	0.01
E5 - upper secondary	0.32	0.31	0.29	0.28	0.25	0.23
E6 - post-secondary	0.55	0.60	0.64	0.68	0.72	0.75
Mean years of schooling (in years)	13.54	13.98	14.29	14.55	14.77	14.95
Gender gap (population age 25+): highest educational attainment (ratio male/female)						
E1 - no education	0.83	0.84	0.83	0.82	0.83	0.85
E2 - incomplete primary	0.87	0.85	0.83	0.83	0.84	0.88
E3 - primary	0.95	0.94	0.94	0.94	0.97	0.99
E4 - lower secondary	1.05	1.10	1.13	1.14	1.13	1.11
E5 - upper secondary	0.96	1.02	1.06	1.10	1.12	1.11
E6 - post-secondary	1.03	0.99	0.97	0.96	0.96	0.97
Mean years of schooling (male minus female)	0.09	−0.02	−0.08	−0.11	−0.12	−0.11
Women age 20–39: highest educational attainment						
E1 - no education	0.00	0.00	0.00	0.00	0.00	0.00
E2 - incomplete primary	0.00	0.00	0.00	0.00	0.00	0.00
E3 - primary	0.01	0.00	0.00	0.00	0.00	0.00
E4 - lower secondary	0.03	0.02	0.01	0.01	0.01	0.00
E5 - upper secondary	0.33	0.30	0.28	0.27	0.26	0.25
E6 - post-secondary	0.63	0.68	0.71	0.72	0.73	0.74
Mean years of schooling (in years)	14.37	14.63	14.76	14.83	14.89	14.92

Education scenarios

GET: global education trend scenario (medium assumption also used for SSP2)

CER: constant enrolment rates scenario (assumption of no future improvements)

FT: Fast track scenario (assumption of education expansion according to fastest historical experience)

Pyramids by Education, Medium Scenario

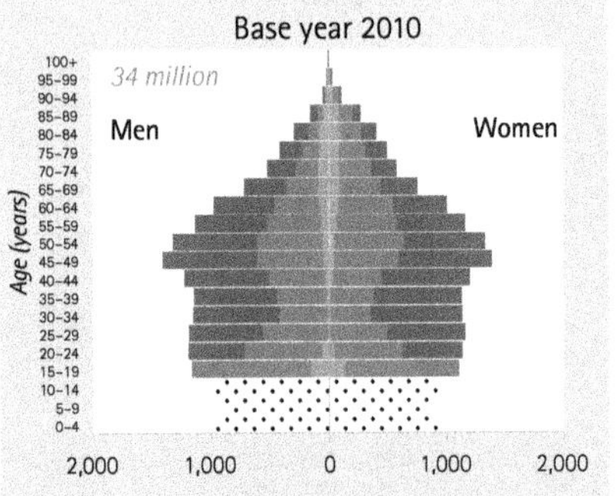

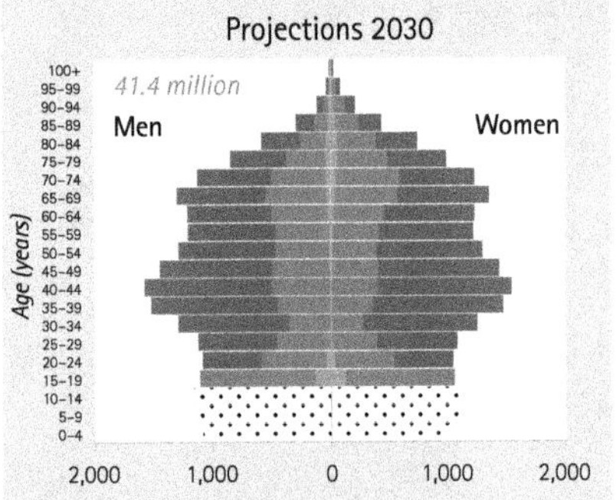

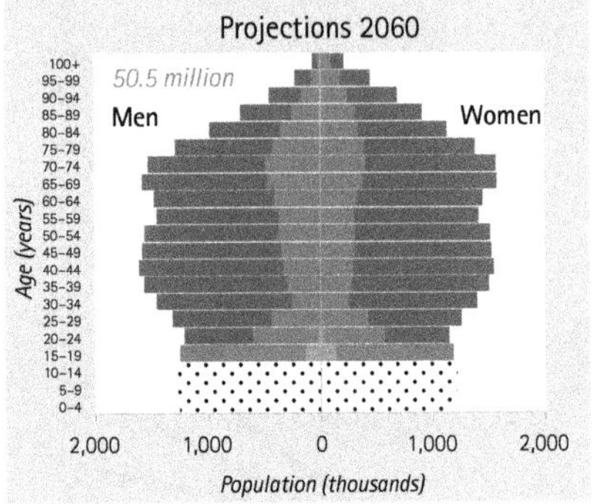

Pop < 15 yrs | No Education | Primary (E2+E3) | Secondary (E4+E5) | Post Secondary

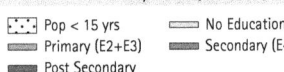

Population Size by Educational Attainment According to Three Education Scenarios: GET, CER, and FT

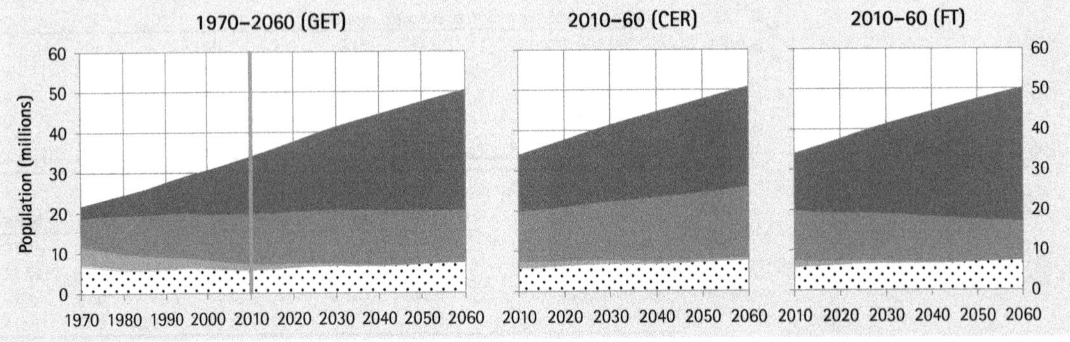

Canada (Continued)

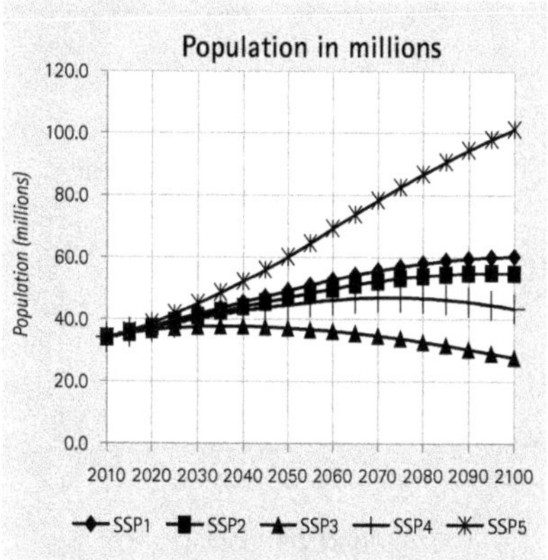

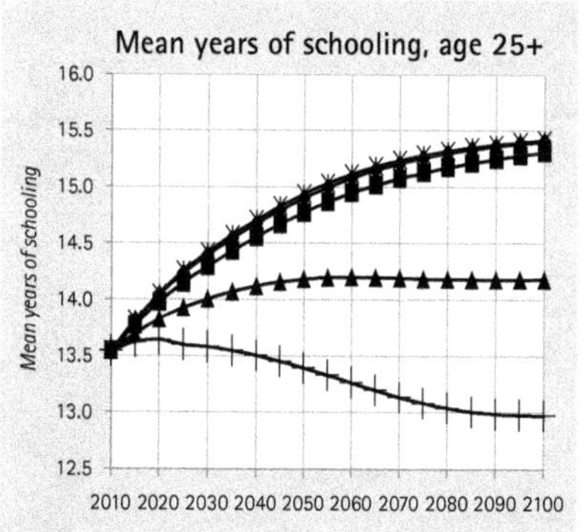

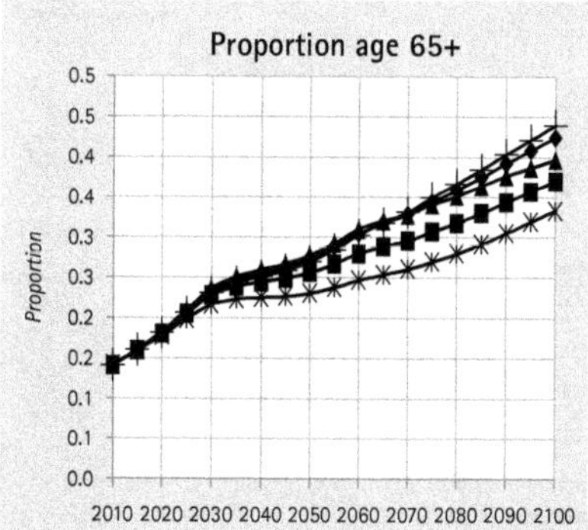

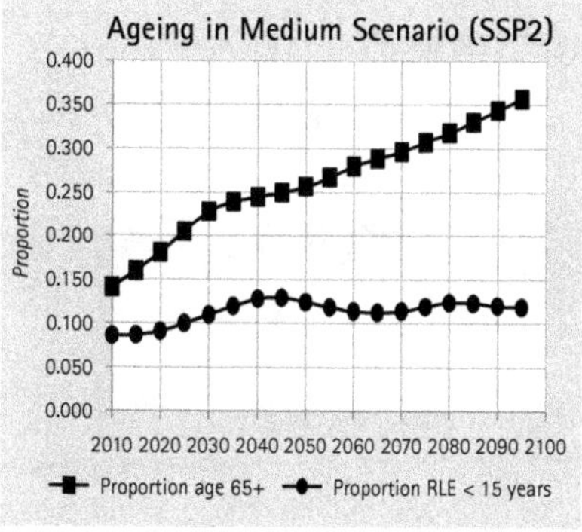

Alternative Scenarios to 2100

Projection Results by Scenario (SSP1–5)

	2010	2020	2030	2040	2050	2075	2100
Population (in millions)							
SSP1 - Rapid development	34.02	37.66	41.66	45.47	49.15	57.03	60.31
SSP2 - Medium	34.02	37.40	40.90	43.99	46.91	53.21	54.81
SSP3 - Stalled development	34.02	36.45	37.59	37.73	37.14	33.77	27.75
SSP4 - Inequality	34.02	37.24	40.28	42.73	44.62	47.02	43.44
SSP5 - Conventional development	34.02	38.60	45.03	52.13	60.11	82.57	101.22
Proportion age 65+							
SSP1 - Rapid development	0.14	0.18	0.23	0.26	0.27	0.34	0.42
SSP2 - Medium	0.14	0.18	0.23	0.24	0.26	0.31	0.37
SSP3 - Stalled development	0.14	0.18	0.24	0.26	0.28	0.34	0.40
SSP4 - Inequality	0.14	0.18	0.23	0.25	0.27	0.35	0.44
SSP5 - Conventional development	0.14	0.18	0.22	0.23	0.23	0.27	0.33
Proportion below age 20							
SSP1 - Rapid development	0.23	0.21	0.21	0.20	0.19	0.18	0.16
SSP2 - Medium	0.23	0.21	0.21	0.20	0.20	0.19	0.17
SSP3 - Stalled development	0.23	0.20	0.19	0.17	0.16	0.15	0.14
SSP4 - Inequality	0.23	0.20	0.19	0.18	0.17	0.15	0.13
SSP5 - Conventional development	0.23	0.22	0.23	0.24	0.24	0.24	0.22
Proportion of Women age 20–39 with at least secondary education							
SSP1 - Rapid development	0.99	1.00	1.00	1.00	1.00	1.00	1.00
SSP2 - Medium	0.99	0.99	1.00	1.00	1.00	1.00	1.00
SSP3 - Stalled development	0.99	0.98	0.98	0.98	0.98	0.98	0.98
SSP4 - Inequality	0.99	0.98	0.98	0.98	0.98	0.98	0.98
SSP5 - Conventional development	0.99	1.00	1.00	1.00	1.00	1.00	1.00
Mean years of schooling, age 25+							
SSP1 - Rapid development	13.54	14.04	14.40	14.67	14.90	15.26	15.40
SSP2 - Medium	13.54	13.98	14.29	14.55	14.77	15.13	15.31
SSP3 - Stalled development	13.54	13.82	14.01	14.12	14.18	14.19	14.18
SSP4 - Inequality	13.54	13.64	13.58	13.50	13.39	13.08	12.97
SSP5 - Conventional development	13.54	14.05	14.42	14.71	14.94	15.28	15.41

Demographic Assumptions Underlying SSPs

	2010–15	2020–25	2030–35	2040–45	2050–55	2075–80	2095–2100
Total fertility rate							
SSP1 - Rapid development	1.61	1.66	1.71	1.76	1.79	1.79	1.78
SSP2 - Medium	1.61	1.66	1.71	1.76	1.80	1.79	1.78
SSP3 - Stalled development	1.53	1.42	1.37	1.37	1.37	1.37	1.37
SSP4 - Inequality	1.54	1.46	1.41	1.41	1.41	1.41	1.41
SSP5 - Conventional development	1.69	1.91	2.07	2.18	2.24	2.24	2.23
Life expectancy at birth for females (in years)							
SSP1 - Rapid development	84.61	87.48	90.47	93.50	96.61	104.51	110.86
SSP2 - Medium	83.69	85.71	87.71	89.89	91.99	97.51	101.80
SSP3 - Stalled development	83.66	84.54	85.61	86.67	87.75	90.49	92.77
SSP4 - Inequality	84.15	86.07	87.99	90.09	92.12	97.32	101.47
SSP5 - Conventional development	84.61	87.48	90.47	93.50	96.61	104.51	110.86
Migration – net flow over five years (in thousands)							
SSP1 - Rapid development	1090	1170	1203	1183	1128	435	0
SSP2 - Medium	1054	1109	1141	1145	1118	476	0
SSP3 - Stalled development	907	574	572	550	515	200	0
SSP4 - Inequality	1089	1163	1190	1171	1127	465	0
SSP5 - Conventional development	1272	1786	1920	2007	2049	927	0

Ageing Indicators, Medium Scenario (SSP2)

	2010	2020	2030	2040	2050	2075	2095
Median age	39.86	41.14	42.74	44.79	45.37	48.37	51.91
Propspective median age	39.86	39.31	39.11	39.20	37.82	35.56	34.92
Proportion age 65+	0.14	0.18	0.23	0.24	0.26	0.31	0.36
Proportion RLE < 15 years	0.09	0.09	0.11	0.13	0.12	0.12	0.12

Cape Verde

Detailed Human Capital Projections to 2060

Demographic indicators, Medium Scenario (SSP2)	2010	2020	2030	2040	2050	2060
Population (in millions)	0.50	0.54	0.57	0.59	0.60	0.59
Proportion age 65+	0.06	0.05	0.08	0.12	0.16	0.23
Proportion below age 20	0.44	0.37	0.32	0.27	0.24	0.21
	2005–10	2015–20	2025–30	2035–40	2045–50	2055–60
Total Fertility Rate	2.60	2.18	2.01	1.90	1.84	1.76
Life expectancy at birth (in years)						
Men	69.42	72.03	74.28	76.55	78.75	80.91
Women	77.36	78.99	80.89	82.89	84.91	86.91
Five-year immigration flow (in '000)	3.68	3.61	3.75	3.84	3.84	3.78
Five-year emigration flow (in '000)	20.96	18.15	17.55	16.59	15.43	13.91

Human Capital indicators, Medium Scenario (SSP2)	2010	2020	2030	2040	2050	2060
Population age 25+: highest educational attainment						
E1 - no education	0.17	0.09	0.06	0.03	0.02	0.01
E2 - incomplete primary	0.43	0.37	0.31	0.25	0.20	0.15
E3 - primary	0.16	0.22	0.25	0.27	0.28	0.28
E4 - lower secondary	0.16	0.21	0.25	0.27	0.29	0.30
E5 - upper secondary	0.05	0.07	0.09	0.12	0.15	0.19
E6 - post-secondary	0.04	0.04	0.05	0.05	0.06	0.07
Mean years of schooling (in years)	5.21	6.26	6.99	7.60	8.16	8.69
Gender gap (population age 25+): highest educational attainment (ratio male/female)						
E1 - no education	0.39	0.35	0.35	0.40	0.50	0.70
E2 - incomplete primary	1.13	1.07	1.03	0.99	0.96	0.94
E3 - primary	1.23	1.12	1.06	1.03	1.01	1.00
E4 - lower secondary	1.14	1.06	1.01	1.00	0.99	0.97
E5 - upper secondary	1.53	1.27	1.21	1.18	1.14	1.11
E6 - post-secondary	1.63	1.35	1.19	1.09	1.04	1.03
Mean years of schooling (male minus female)	1.14	0.79	0.54	0.37	0.25	0.17
Women age 20–39: highest educational attainment						
E1 - no education	0.02	0.01	0.01	0.01	0.00	0.00
E2 - incomplete primary	0.35	0.20	0.13	0.08	0.05	0.03
E3 - primary	0.21	0.30	0.31	0.31	0.29	0.26
E4 - lower secondary	0.30	0.33	0.35	0.35	0.33	0.30
E5 - upper secondary	0.08	0.12	0.15	0.20	0.26	0.32
E6 - post-secondary	0.03	0.04	0.05	0.06	0.07	0.08
Mean years of schooling (in years)	7.06	7.96	8.49	9.01	9.47	9.91

Education scenarios

GET: global education trend scenario (medium assumption also used for SSP2)

CER: constant enrolment rates scenario (assumption of no future improvements)

FT: Fast track scenario (assumption of education expansion according to fastest historical experience)

Pyramids by Education, Medium Scenario

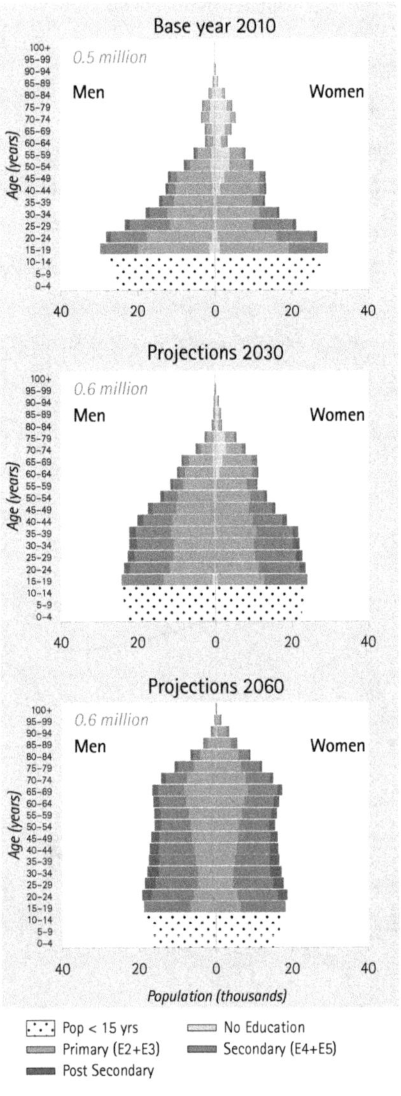

Population Size by Educational Attainment According to Three Education Scenarios: GET, CER, and FT

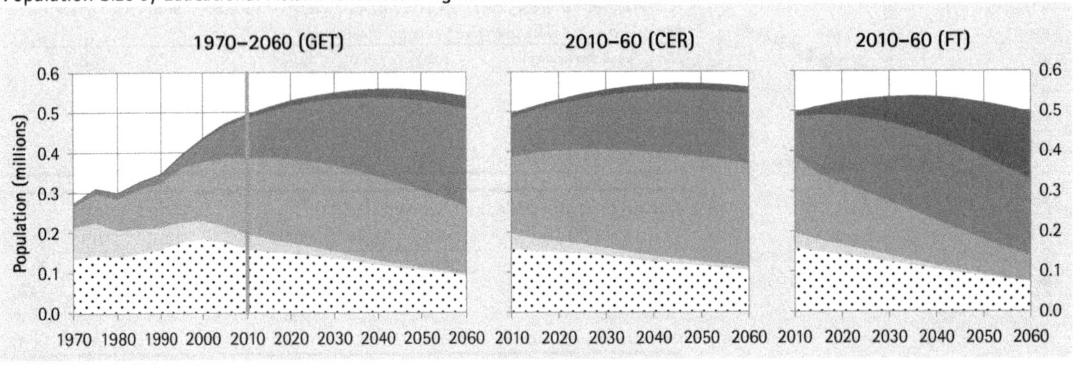

Cape Verde (Continued)

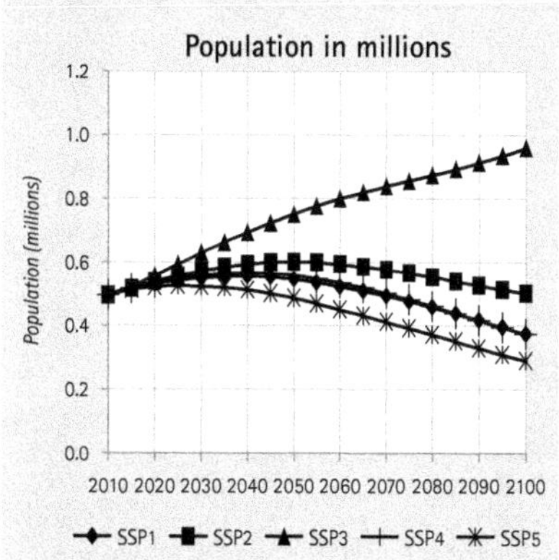

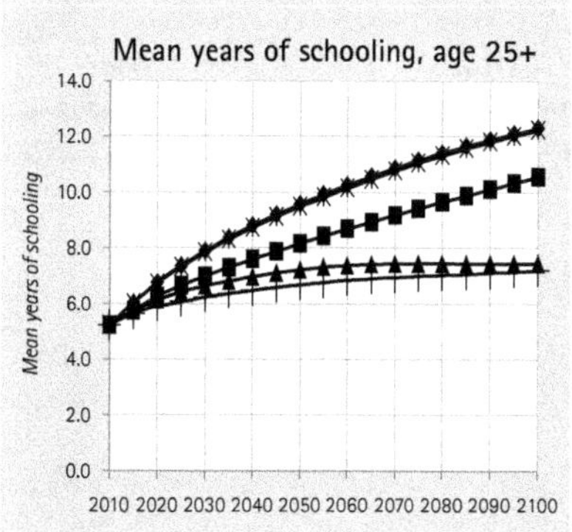

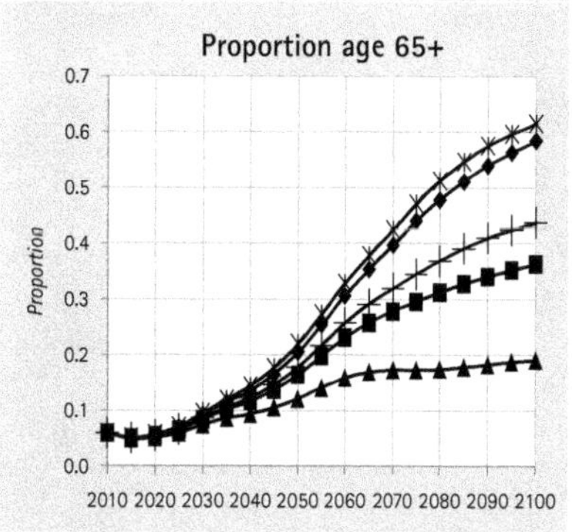

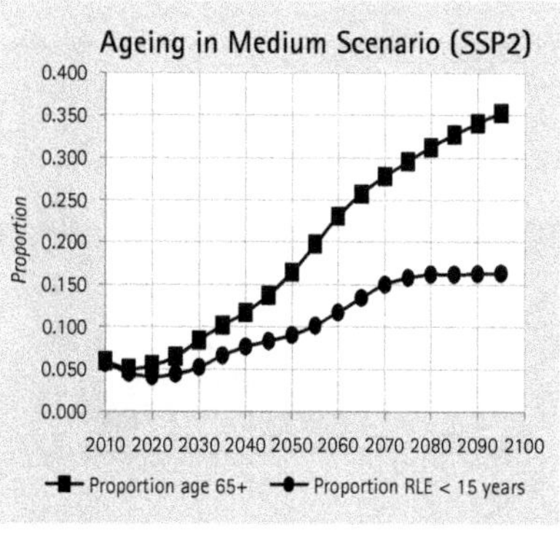

Alternative Scenarios to 2100

Projection Results by Scenario (SSP1–5)

	2010	2020	2030	2040	2050	2075	2100
Population (in millions)							
SSP1 - Rapid development	0.50	0.53	0.55	0.56	0.55	0.48	0.37
SSP2 - Medium	0.50	0.54	0.57	0.59	0.60	0.57	0.50
SSP3 - Stalled development	0.50	0.56	0.63	0.69	0.75	0.86	0.96
SSP4 - Inequality	0.50	0.53	0.56	0.57	0.56	0.48	0.37
SSP5 - Conventional development	0.50	0.52	0.52	0.51	0.49	0.39	0.29
Proportion age 65+							
SSP1 - Rapid development	0.06	0.06	0.09	0.14	0.20	0.44	0.58
SSP2 - Medium	0.06	0.05	0.08	0.12	0.16	0.30	0.36
SSP3 - Stalled development	0.06	0.05	0.07	0.09	0.12	0.17	0.19
SSP4 - Inequality	0.06	0.05	0.09	0.12	0.18	0.34	0.44
SSP5 - Conventional development	0.06	0.06	0.10	0.14	0.22	0.47	0.62
Proportion below age 20							
SSP1 - Rapid development	0.44	0.35	0.28	0.22	0.18	0.10	0.07
SSP2 - Medium	0.44	0.37	0.32	0.27	0.24	0.18	0.16
SSP3 - Stalled development	0.44	0.38	0.35	0.33	0.31	0.28	0.27
SSP4 - Inequality	0.44	0.36	0.30	0.24	0.20	0.14	0.11
SSP5 - Conventional development	0.44	0.35	0.28	0.22	0.17	0.09	0.06
Proportion of Women age 20–39 with at least secondary education							
SSP1 - Rapid development	0.42	0.61	0.72	0.78	0.82	0.89	0.94
SSP2 - Medium	0.42	0.49	0.55	0.60	0.65	0.78	0.89
SSP3 - Stalled development	0.42	0.44	0.44	0.44	0.44	0.44	0.44
SSP4 - Inequality	0.42	0.41	0.39	0.39	0.39	0.39	0.39
SSP5 - Conventional development	0.42	0.61	0.72	0.78	0.82	0.89	0.94
Mean years of schooling, age 25+							
SSP1 - Rapid development	5.21	6.75	7.89	8.80	9.57	11.14	12.29
SSP2 - Medium	5.21	6.26	6.99	7.60	8.16	9.42	10.56
SSP3 - Stalled development	5.21	6.13	6.64	6.98	7.23	7.45	7.45
SSP4 - Inequality	5.21	5.90	6.24	6.49	6.69	7.00	7.21
SSP5 - Conventional development	5.21	6.73	7.83	8.72	9.47	11.05	12.23

Demographic Assumptions Underlying SSPs

	2010–15	2020–25	2030–35	2040–45	2050–55	2075–80	2095–2100
Total fertility rate							
SSP1 - Rapid development	2.14	1.68	1.44	1.33	1.26	1.16	1.16
SSP2 - Medium	2.33	2.08	1.93	1.87	1.81	1.63	1.62
SSP3 - Stalled development	2.44	2.47	2.45	2.42	2.38	2.25	2.31
SSP4 - Inequality	2.22	1.84	1.60	1.48	1.41	1.32	1.34
SSP5 - Conventional development	2.14	1.68	1.44	1.33	1.26	1.16	1.16
Life expectancy at birth for females (in years)							
SSP1 - Rapid development	79.69	82.24	85.00	87.91	90.82	98.52	104.93
SSP2 - Medium	78.09	79.89	81.89	83.89	85.91	91.10	95.30
SSP3 - Stalled development	78.82	79.44	80.31	81.21	82.01	84.24	86.06
SSP4 - Inequality	79.19	80.80	82.66	84.56	86.40	90.96	94.81
SSP5 - Conventional development	79.69	82.24	85.00	87.91	90.82	98.52	104.93
Migration – net flow over five years (in thousands)							
SSP1 - Rapid development	−16	−14	−13	−11	−9	−3	0
SSP2 - Medium	−16	−15	−14	−12	−11	−4	0
SSP3 - Stalled development	−13	−7	−7	−7	−6	−3	0
SSP4 - Inequality	−16	−14	−13	−11	−9	−2	0
SSP5 - Conventional development	−18	−21	−19	−16	−14	−4	0

Ageing Indicators, Medium Scenario (SSP2)

	2010	2020	2030	2040	2050	2075	2095
Median age	22.73	27.07	31.52	35.90	39.96	48.69	52.67
Propspective median age	22.73	25.40	28.09	30.91	33.29	37.48	37.42
Proportion age 65+	0.06	0.05	0.08	0.12	0.16	0.30	0.35
Proportion RLE < 15 years	0.06	0.04	0.05	0.08	0.09	0.16	0.16

Central African Republic

Detailed Human Capital Projections to 2060

Demographic indicators, Medium Scenario (SSP2)	2010	2020	2030	2040	2050	2060
Population (in millions)	4.40	5.26	6.10	6.82	7.38	7.77
Proportion age 65+	0.04	0.04	0.04	0.05	0.06	0.09
Proportion below age 20	0.51	0.47	0.43	0.38	0.34	0.30
	2005–10	2015–20	2025–30	2035–40	2045–50	2055–60
Total Fertility Rate	4.85	3.72	2.97	2.51	2.17	1.99
Life expectancy at birth (in years)						
Men	44.48	50.15	51.88	53.62	55.72	58.72
Women	47.32	54.38	57.13	59.28	61.48	64.42
Five-year immigration flow (in '000)	39.23	38.39	39.83	40.70	40.69	40.08
Five-year emigration flow (in '000)	34.11	31.34	36.47	40.18	42.04	42.40

Human Capital indicators, Medium Scenario (SSP2)	2010	2020	2030	2040	2050	2060
Population age 25+: highest educational attainment						
E1 - no education	0.38	0.26	0.17	0.11	0.07	0.05
E2 - incomplete primary	0.28	0.24	0.19	0.14	0.10	0.06
E3 - primary	0.21	0.31	0.38	0.43	0.45	0.44
E4 - lower secondary	0.08	0.11	0.14	0.15	0.16	0.16
E5 - upper secondary	0.03	0.06	0.09	0.13	0.18	0.24
E6 - post-secondary	0.01	0.02	0.03	0.03	0.04	0.06
Mean years of schooling (in years)	3.91	5.18	6.32	7.31	8.17	8.96
Gender gap (population age 25+): highest educational attainment (ratio male/female)						
E1 - no education	0.44	0.40	0.40	0.42	0.45	0.49
E2 - incomplete primary	1.43	1.22	1.09	1.01	0.96	0.91
E3 - primary	1.51	1.25	1.12	1.05	1.02	1.00
E4 - lower secondary	2.40	1.86	1.55	1.36	1.25	1.16
E5 - upper secondary	2.52	1.73	1.37	1.19	1.10	1.06
E6 - post-secondary	2.13	1.48	1.15	1.00	0.96	0.99
Mean years of schooling (male minus female)	2.22	1.87	1.38	0.93	0.61	0.40
Women age 20–39: highest educational attainment						
E1 - no education	0.32	0.20	0.11	0.05	0.02	0.01
E2 - incomplete primary	0.27	0.22	0.17	0.13	0.09	0.07
E3 - primary	0.30	0.39	0.44	0.45	0.41	0.36
E4 - lower secondary	0.08	0.13	0.17	0.21	0.23	0.25
E5 - upper secondary	0.03	0.05	0.09	0.14	0.19	0.26
E6 - post-secondary	0.01	0.02	0.02	0.03	0.04	0.05
Mean years of schooling (in years)	4.32	5.69	6.98	8.04	8.92	9.65

Education scenarios

GET : global education trend scenario (medium assumption also used for SSP2)

CER: constant enrolment rates scenario (assumption of no future improvements)

FT: Fast track scenario (assumption of education expansion according to fastest historical experience)

Pyramids by Education, Medium Scenario

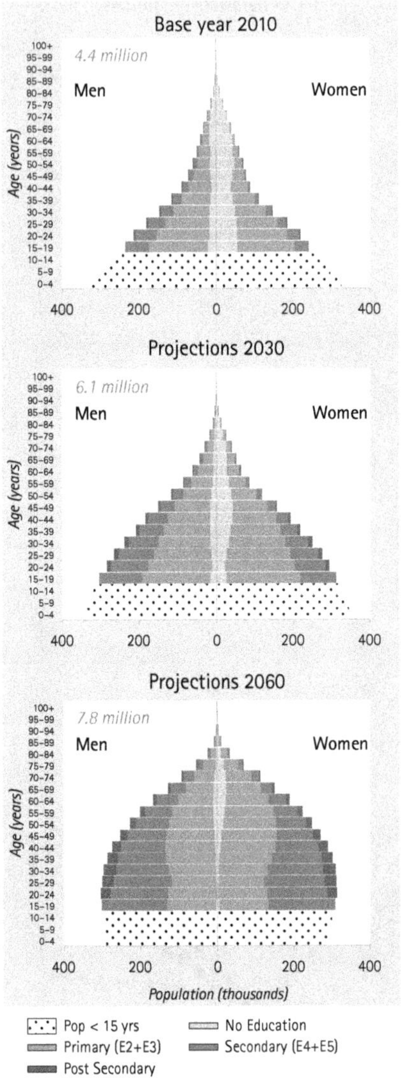

Population Size by Educational Attainment According to Three Education Scenarios: GET, CER, and FT

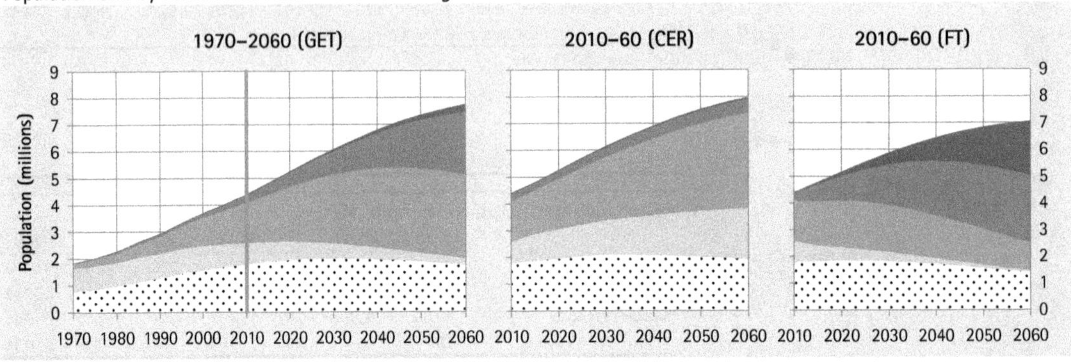

Central African Republic (Continued)

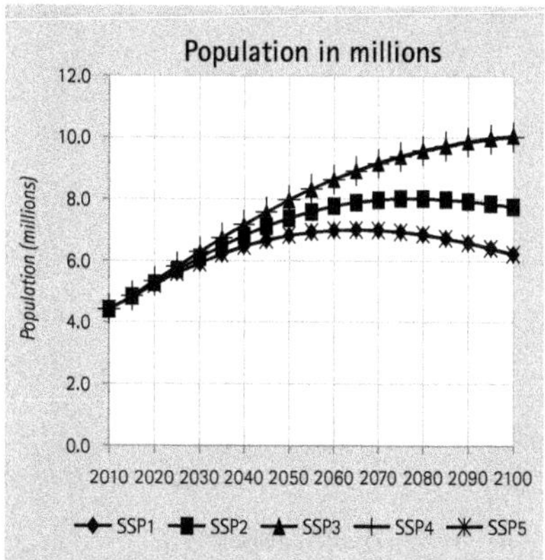

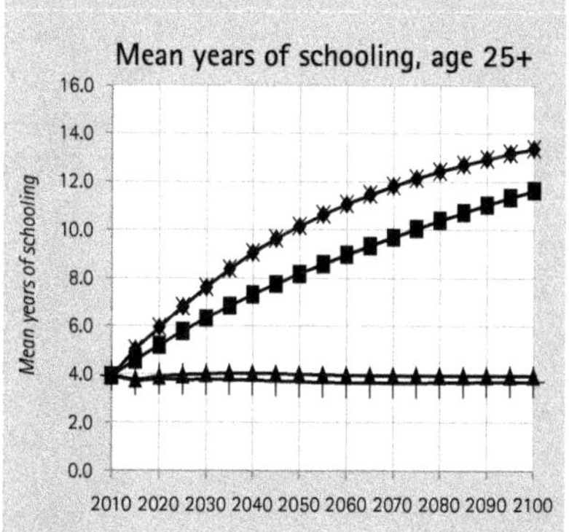

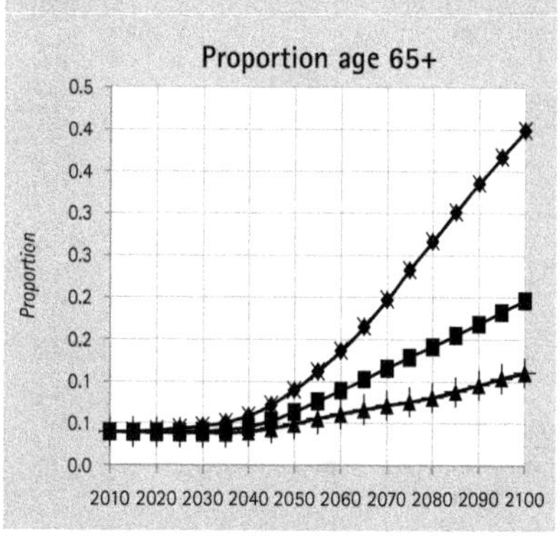

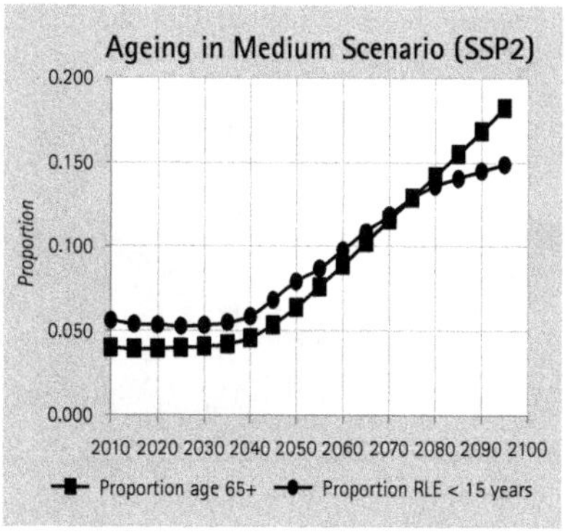

Alternative Scenarios to 2100

Projection Results by Scenario (SSP1–5)

	2010	2020	2030	2040	2050	2075	2100
Population (in millions)							
SSP1 - Rapid development	4.40	5.20	5.91	6.46	6.82	6.95	6.23
SSP2 - Medium	4.40	5.26	6.10	6.82	7.38	8.02	7.76
SSP3 - Stalled development	4.40	5.32	6.28	7.16	7.97	9.40	10.06
SSP4 - Inequality	4.40	5.32	6.29	7.17	7.97	9.38	10.03
SSP5 - Conventional development	4.40	5.21	5.92	6.47	6.82	6.94	6.21
Proportion age 65+							
SSP1 - Rapid development	0.04	0.04	0.05	0.06	0.09	0.23	0.40
SSP2 - Medium	0.04	0.04	0.04	0.05	0.06	0.13	0.20
SSP3 - Stalled development	0.04	0.04	0.04	0.04	0.05	0.08	0.11
SSP4 - Inequality	0.04	0.04	0.04	0.04	0.05	0.08	0.11
SSP5 - Conventional development	0.04	0.04	0.05	0.06	0.09	0.23	0.40
Proportion below age 20							
SSP1 - Rapid development	0.51	0.46	0.38	0.32	0.27	0.17	0.12
SSP2 - Medium	0.51	0.47	0.43	0.38	0.34	0.26	0.22
SSP3 - Stalled development	0.51	0.49	0.47	0.44	0.40	0.34	0.31
SSP4 - Inequality	0.51	0.49	0.47	0.44	0.40	0.34	0.31
SSP5 - Conventional development	0.51	0.46	0.38	0.32	0.27	0.17	0.12
Proportion of Women age 20–39 with at least secondary education							
SSP1 - Rapid development	0.12	0.34	0.49	0.61	0.70	0.83	0.92
SSP2 - Medium	0.12	0.19	0.28	0.38	0.47	0.70	0.87
SSP3 - Stalled development	0.12	0.05	0.05	0.05	0.05	0.05	0.05
SSP4 - Inequality	0.12	0.05	0.05	0.05	0.05	0.05	0.05
SSP5 - Conventional development	0.12	0.34	0.49	0.61	0.70	0.83	0.92
Mean years of schooling, age 25+							
SSP1 - Rapid development	3.91	5.91	7.61	9.03	10.15	12.13	13.36
SSP2 - Medium	3.91	5.18	6.32	7.31	8.17	10.04	11.63
SSP3 - Stalled development	3.91	3.89	4.01	4.03	4.00	3.94	3.93
SSP4 - Inequality	3.91	3.78	3.77	3.75	3.69	3.65	3.70
SSP5 - Conventional development	3.91	5.91	7.61	9.03	10.15	12.13	13.36

Demographic Assumptions Underlying SSPs

	2010–15	2020–25	2030–35	2040–45	2050–55	2075–80	2095–2100
Total fertility rate							
SSP1 - Rapid development	3.92	2.68	2.00	1.66	1.46	1.27	1.18
SSP2 - Medium	4.24	3.29	2.70	2.33	2.08	1.77	1.63
SSP3 - Stalled development	4.48	4.07	3.56	3.12	2.82	2.42	2.30
SSP4 - Inequality	4.48	4.08	3.56	3.12	2.81	2.41	2.30
SSP5 - Conventional development	3.92	2.68	2.00	1.66	1.46	1.27	1.18
Life expectancy at birth for females (in years)							
SSP1 - Rapid development	56.71	64.02	68.18	72.03	76.02	85.63	93.28
SSP2 - Medium	51.31	55.80	58.21	60.28	62.88	70.42	76.28
SSP3 - Stalled development	52.83	53.30	54.38	55.13	56.45	60.64	63.57
SSP4 - Inequality	52.83	53.28	54.35	55.10	56.41	60.60	63.53
SSP5 - Conventional development	56.71	64.02	68.18	72.03	76.02	85.63	93.28
Migration – net flow over five years (in thousands)							
SSP1 - Rapid development	6	5	2	−1	−2	0	0
SSP2 - Medium	7	5	2	−1	−2	0	0
SSP3 - Stalled development	5	2	1	0	0	1	0
SSP4 - Inequality	6	5	2	0	−1	1	0
SSP5 - Conventional development	8	7	2	−2	−4	−1	0

Ageing Indicators, Medium Scenario (SSP2)

	2010	2020	2030	2040	2050	2075	2095
Median age	19.42	21.27	23.77	26.57	29.62	36.63	41.11
Propspective median age	19.42	17.90	18.91	20.28	22.15	25.32	26.20
Proportion age 65+	0.04	0.04	0.04	0.05	0.06	0.13	0.18
Proportion RLE < 15 years	0.06	0.05	0.05	0.06	0.08	0.13	0.15

Chad

Detailed Human Capital Projections to 2060

Demographic indicators, Medium Scenario (SSP2)						
	2010	2020	2030	2040	2050	2060
Population (in millions)	11.23	14.55	18.23	21.76	24.88	27.49
Proportion age 65+	0.03	0.03	0.03	0.03	0.04	0.06
Proportion below age 20	0.56	0.54	0.51	0.46	0.41	0.36
	2005–10	2015–20	2025–30	2035–40	2045–50	2055–60
Total Fertility Rate	6.20	5.25	4.30	3.35	2.73	2.34
Life expectancy at birth (in years)						
Men	47.15	50.12	52.52	54.62	56.90	59.71
Women	49.90	53.27	56.07	58.58	61.23	64.22
Five-year immigration flow (in '000)	74.29	72.80	75.57	77.21	77.16	75.99
Five-year emigration flow (in '000)	148.41	145.87	187.01	229.00	264.74	287.78

Human Capital indicators, Medium Scenario (SSP2)						
	2010	2020	2030	2040	2050	2060
Population age 25+: highest educational attainment						
E1 - no education	0.69	0.61	0.54	0.47	0.41	0.35
E2 - incomplete primary	0.16	0.18	0.18	0.16	0.15	0.12
E3 - primary	0.07	0.10	0.13	0.15	0.17	0.19
E4 - lower secondary	0.04	0.05	0.07	0.09	0.10	0.11
E5 - upper secondary	0.02	0.04	0.06	0.10	0.14	0.19
E6 - post-secondary	0.01	0.02	0.02	0.03	0.03	0.04
Mean years of schooling (in years)	1.89	2.65	3.43	4.25	5.14	6.07
Gender gap (population age 25+): highest educational attainment (ratio male/female)						
E1 - no education	0.72	0.69	0.68	0.70	0.74	0.80
E2 - incomplete primary	1.50	1.26	1.11	1.02	0.97	0.96
E3 - primary	3.01	2.25	1.83	1.54	1.33	1.18
E4 - lower secondary	3.68	2.63	2.07	1.70	1.43	1.25
E5 - upper secondary	4.90	2.99	2.05	1.56	1.29	1.14
E6 - post-secondary	4.98	3.07	2.07	1.53	1.25	1.13
Mean years of schooling (male minus female)	1.83	2.02	1.96	1.69	1.29	0.86
Women age 20–39: highest educational attainment						
E1 - no education	0.68	0.61	0.53	0.45	0.35	0.25
E2 - incomplete primary	0.20	0.18	0.17	0.14	0.11	0.09
E3 - primary	0.07	0.10	0.13	0.17	0.19	0.21
E4 - lower secondary	0.03	0.06	0.09	0.12	0.15	0.18
E5 - upper secondary	0.01	0.03	0.06	0.10	0.16	0.23
E6 - post-secondary	0.01	0.01	0.02	0.03	0.03	0.05
Mean years of schooling (in years)	1.73	2.51	3.47	4.64	6.00	7.42

Education scenarios

GET: global education trend scenario (medium assumption also used for SSP2)

CER: constant enrolment rates scenario (assumption of no future improvements)

FT: Fast track scenario (assumption of education expansion according to fastest historical experience)

Pyramids by Education, Medium Scenario

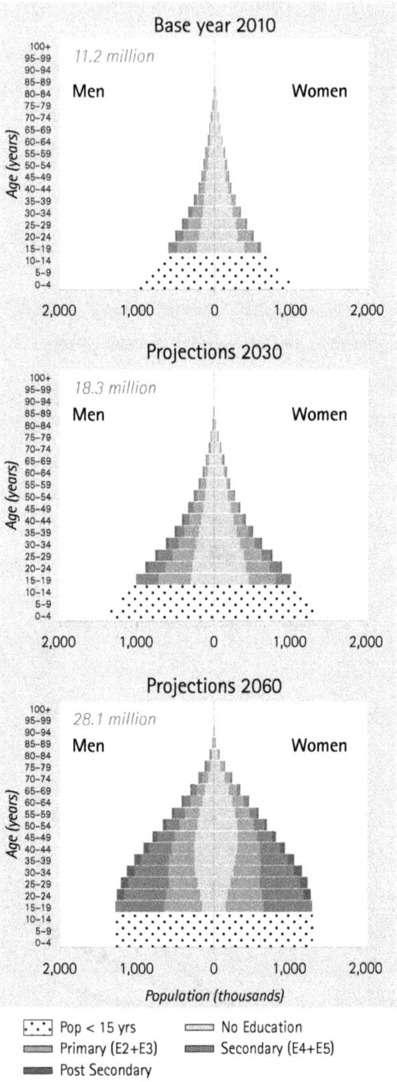

Population Size by Educational Attainment According to Three Education Scenarios: GET, CER, and FT

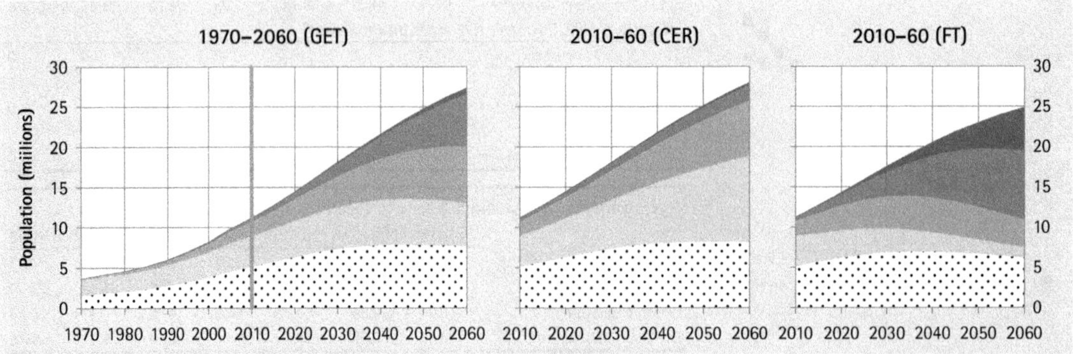

Chad (Continued)

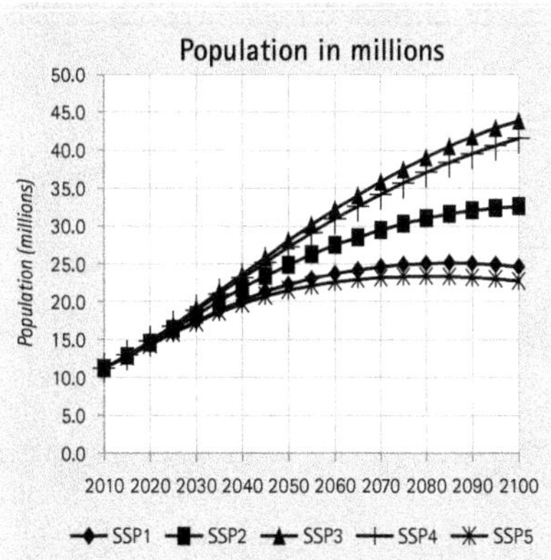

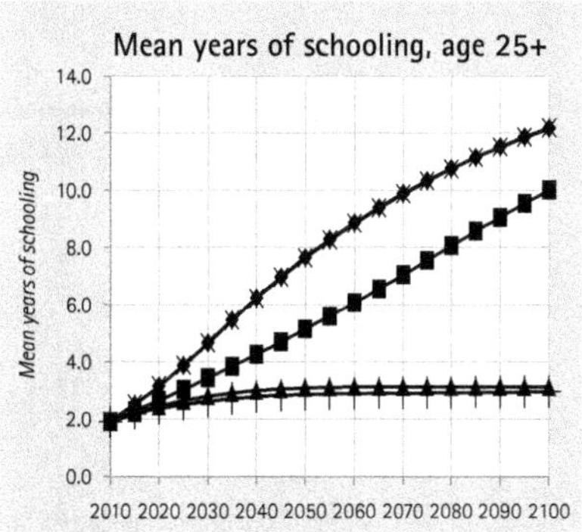

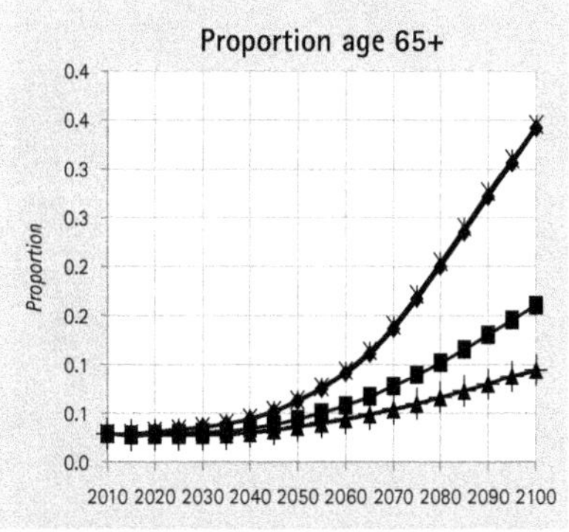

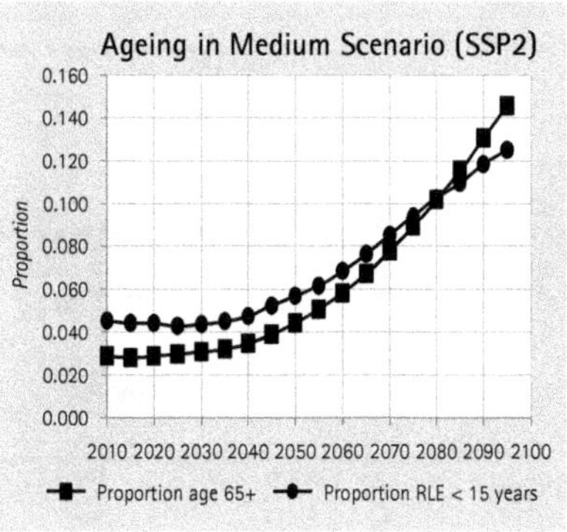

Alternative Scenarios to 2100

Projection Results by Scenario (SSP1–5)

	2010	2020	2030	2040	2050	2075	2100
Population (in millions)							
SSP1 - Rapid development	11.23	14.33	17.41	20.14	22.23	24.92	24.67
SSP2 - Medium	11.23	14.55	18.23	21.76	24.88	30.33	32.61
SSP3 - Stalled development	11.23	14.81	19.06	23.59	28.05	37.50	43.92
SSP4 - Inequality	11.23	14.76	18.85	23.11	27.22	35.68	41.56
SSP5 - Conventional development	11.23	14.28	17.21	19.71	21.48	23.29	22.72
Proportion age 65+							
SSP1 - Rapid development	0.03	0.03	0.04	0.04	0.06	0.17	0.34
SSP2 - Medium	0.03	0.03	0.03	0.03	0.04	0.09	0.16
SSP3 - Stalled development	0.03	0.03	0.03	0.03	0.04	0.06	0.09
SSP4 - Inequality	0.03	0.03	0.03	0.03	0.04	0.06	0.09
SSP5 - Conventional development	0.03	0.03	0.04	0.04	0.06	0.17	0.34
Proportion below age 20							
SSP1 - Rapid development	0.56	0.53	0.47	0.40	0.34	0.21	0.14
SSP2 - Medium	0.56	0.54	0.51	0.46	0.41	0.31	0.24
SSP3 - Stalled development	0.56	0.55	0.53	0.50	0.46	0.37	0.33
SSP4 - Inequality	0.56	0.55	0.53	0.50	0.46	0.37	0.33
SSP5 - Conventional development	0.56	0.53	0.47	0.41	0.34	0.21	0.14
Proportion of Women age 20–39 with at least secondary education							
SSP1 - Rapid development	0.05	0.16	0.30	0.46	0.59	0.79	0.90
SSP2 - Medium	0.05	0.10	0.16	0.25	0.35	0.60	0.82
SSP3 - Stalled development	0.05	0.05	0.05	0.05	0.05	0.05	0.05
SSP4 - Inequality	0.05	0.05	0.05	0.05	0.05	0.05	0.05
SSP5 - Conventional development	0.05	0.16	0.30	0.46	0.59	0.79	0.90
Mean years of schooling, age 25+							
SSP1 - Rapid development	1.89	3.14	4.65	6.22	7.64	10.34	12.17
SSP2 - Medium	1.89	2.65	3.43	4.25	5.14	7.55	10.02
SSP3 - Stalled development	1.89	2.45	2.80	2.99	3.09	3.13	3.12
SSP4 - Inequality	1.89	2.37	2.62	2.78	2.86	2.91	2.96
SSP5 - Conventional development	1.89	3.14	4.64	6.21	7.62	10.31	12.16

Demographic Assumptions Underlying SSPs

	2010–15	2020–25	2030–35	2040–45	2050–55	2075–80	2095–2100
Total fertility rate							
SSP1 - Rapid development	5.43	3.93	2.83	2.15	1.75	1.38	1.26
SSP2 - Medium	5.73	4.80	3.81	3.00	2.53	1.95	1.76
SSP3 - Stalled development	6.07	5.62	4.85	4.01	3.41	2.72	2.51
SSP4 - Inequality	6.07	5.62	4.84	4.01	3.40	2.71	2.50
SSP5 - Conventional development	5.43	3.93	2.83	2.15	1.75	1.38	1.26
Life expectancy at birth for females (in years)							
SSP1 - Rapid development	57.96	63.52	68.02	71.75	76.06	85.52	93.22
SSP2 - Medium	51.57	54.68	57.38	59.92	62.68	70.12	76.09
SSP3 - Stalled development	55.90	54.46	55.70	56.92	58.14	61.53	64.41
SSP4 - Inequality	55.90	54.45	55.69	56.90	58.12	61.51	64.39
SSP5 - Conventional development	57.96	63.52	68.02	71.75	76.06	85.52	93.22
Migration – net flow over five years (in thousands)							
SSP1 - Rapid development	−66	−90	−129	−163	−185	−82	0
SSP2 - Medium	−67	−91	−131	−171	−203	−102	0
SSP3 - Stalled development	−55	−44	−62	−79	−94	−49	0
SSP4 - Inequality	−65	−89	−128	−167	−200	−103	0
SSP5 - Conventional development	−77	−137	−201	−263	−309	−152	0

Ageing Indicators, Medium Scenario (SSP2)

	2010	2020	2030	2040	2050	2075	2095
Median age	17.03	17.93	19.53	21.82	24.66	32.34	37.88
Propspective median age	17.03	16.81	17.15	18.18	19.76	23.79	25.86
Proportion age 65+	0.03	0.03	0.03	0.03	0.04	0.09	0.15
Proportion RLE < 15 years	0.05	0.04	0.04	0.05	0.06	0.09	0.13

Chile*

Detailed Human Capital Projections to 2060

Demographic indicators, Medium Scenario (SSP2)	2010	2020	2030	2040	2050	2060
Population (in millions)	17.11	18.58	19.74	20.44	20.67	20.54
Proportion age 65+	0.09	0.12	0.18	0.22	0.26	0.31
Proportion below age 20	0.31	0.26	0.23	0.21	0.19	0.17
	2005–10	2015–20	2025–30	2035–40	2045–50	2055–60
Total Fertility Rate	1.90	1.73	1.67	1.61	1.53	1.54
Life expectancy at birth (in years)						
Men	75.54	78.02	80.19	82.32	84.44	86.55
Women	81.68	84.21	86.41	88.49	90.51	92.50
Five-year immigration flow (in '000)	101.10	99.04	102.82	105.14	105.18	103.67
Five-year emigration flow (in '000)	71.20	55.11	51.56	48.07	44.81	41.11

Human Capital indicators, Medium Scenario (SSP2)	2010	2020	2030	2040	2050	2060
Population age 25+: highest educational attainment						
E1 - no education	0.03	0.02	0.01	0.01	0.01	0.00
E2 - incomplete primary	0.11	0.07	0.05	0.03	0.02	0.01
E3 - primary	0.18	0.15	0.13	0.11	0.09	0.07
E4 - lower secondary	0.17	0.16	0.15	0.13	0.11	0.09
E5 - upper secondary	0.37	0.41	0.44	0.47	0.49	0.50
E6 - post-secondary	0.15	0.18	0.22	0.25	0.29	0.33
Mean years of schooling (in years)	10.21	10.89	11.43	11.91	12.35	12.74
Gender gap (population age 25+): highest educational attainment (ratio male/female)						
E1 - no education	0.83	0.82	0.82	0.82	0.81	0.80
E2 - incomplete primary	0.87	0.86	0.84	0.83	0.83	0.83
E3 - primary	0.99	1.00	1.00	1.00	0.99	0.99
E4 - lower secondary	0.98	1.01	1.03	1.04	1.03	1.02
E5 - upper secondary	1.03	1.02	1.02	1.02	1.02	1.01
E6 - post-secondary	1.11	1.04	1.00	0.98	0.98	0.99
Mean years of schooling (male minus female)	0.30	0.17	0.09	0.03	-0.01	-0.02
Women age 20–39: highest educational attainment						
E1 - no education	0.01	0.00	0.00	0.00	0.00	0.00
E2 - incomplete primary	0.03	0.01	0.01	0.00	0.00	0.00
E3 - primary	0.11	0.08	0.06	0.04	0.03	0.02
E4 - lower secondary	0.15	0.11	0.08	0.05	0.04	0.02
E5 - upper secondary	0.51	0.54	0.56	0.56	0.55	0.53
E6 - post-secondary	0.20	0.25	0.30	0.35	0.39	0.43
Mean years of schooling (in years)	11.81	12.28	12.62	13.06	13.39	13.64

Education scenarios

GET : global education trend scenario (medium assumption also used for SSP2)

CER: constant enrolment rates scenario (assumption of no future improvements)

FT: Fast track scenario (assumption of education expansion according to fastest historical experience)

Pyramids by Education, Medium Scenario

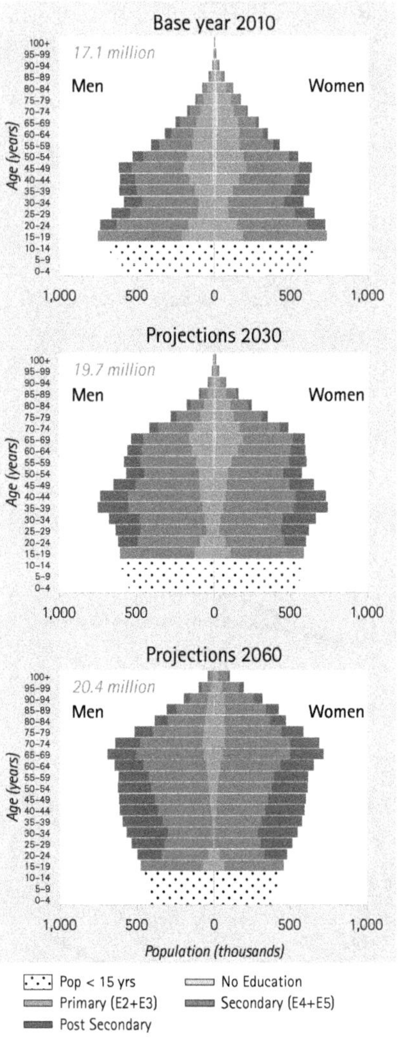

Population Size by Educational Attainment According to Three Education Scenarios: GET, CER, and FT

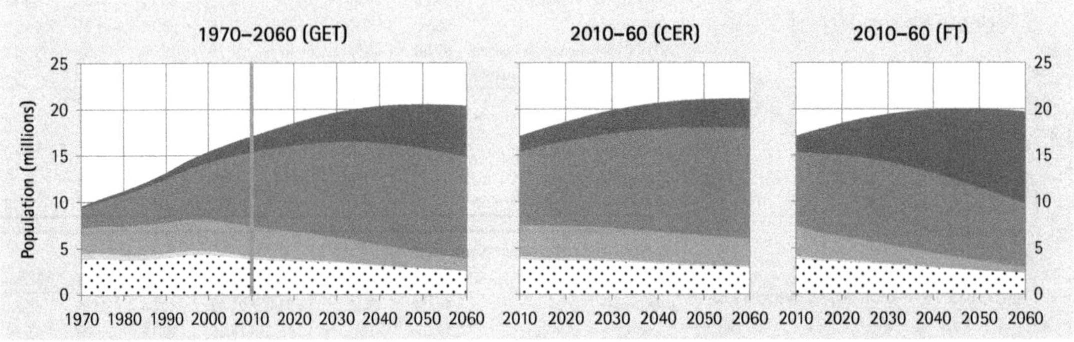

*Updated data for Chile is provided on the WIC Data Explorer <http://www.wittgensteincentre.org/dataexplorer>. The data was adjusted to account for corrections in the education category definitions and changes over time.

Chile (Continued)

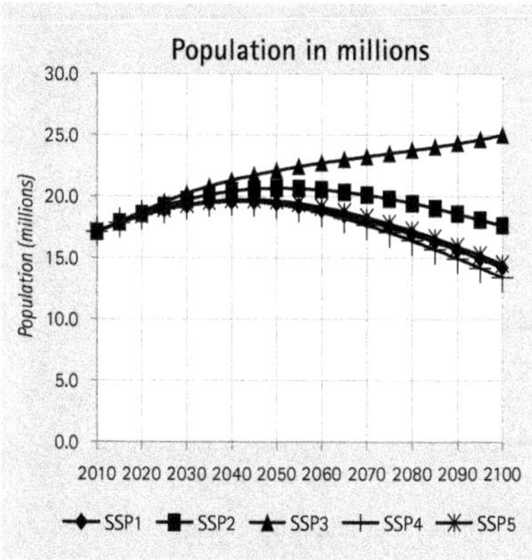

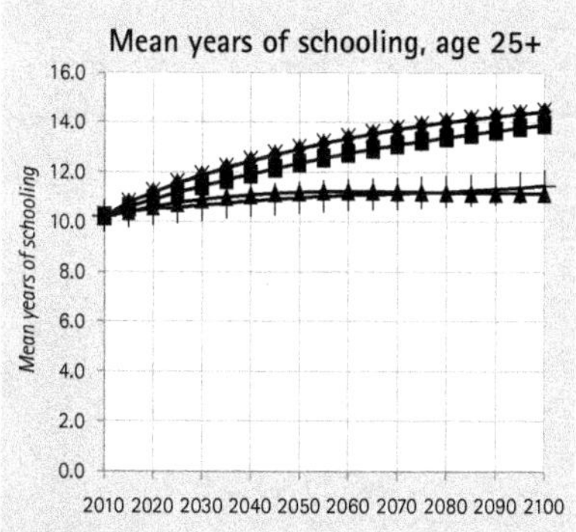

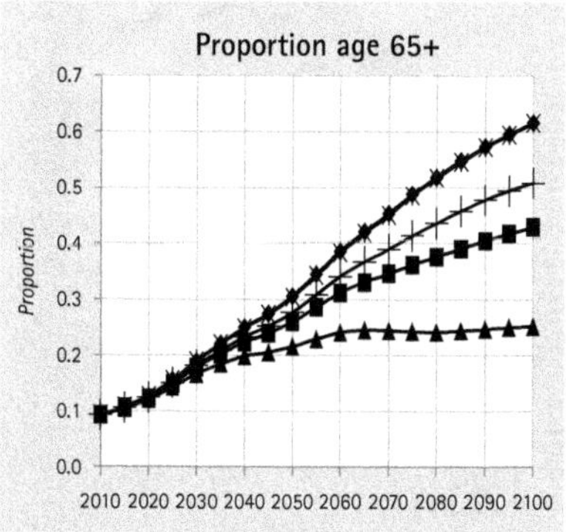

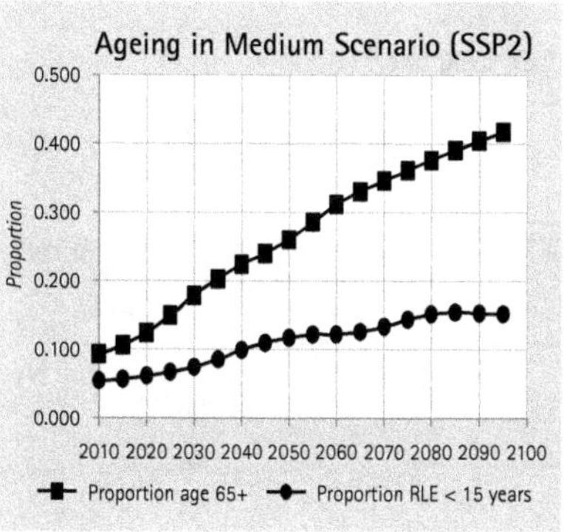

Alternative Scenarios to 2100

Projection Results by Scenario (SSP1–5)

	2010	2020	2030	2040	2050	2075	2100
Population (in millions)							
SSP1 - Rapid development	17.11	18.42	19.25	19.59	19.46	17.52	14.24
SSP2 - Medium	17.11	18.58	19.74	20.44	20.67	19.82	17.66
SSP3 - Stalled development	17.11	18.76	20.25	21.32	22.12	23.52	25.01
SSP4 - Inequality	17.11	18.47	19.33	19.63	19.40	17.08	13.42
SSP5 - Conventional development	17.11	18.44	19.32	19.73	19.65	17.80	14.53
Proportion age 65+							
SSP1 - Rapid development	0.09	0.13	0.19	0.25	0.31	0.49	0.62
SSP2 - Medium	0.09	0.12	0.18	0.22	0.26	0.36	0.43
SSP3 - Stalled development	0.09	0.12	0.17	0.20	0.22	0.24	0.25
SSP4 - Inequality	0.09	0.12	0.18	0.23	0.28	0.41	0.51
SSP5 - Conventional development	0.09	0.13	0.19	0.25	0.30	0.48	0.61
Proportion below age 20							
SSP1 - Rapid development	0.31	0.25	0.20	0.17	0.14	0.09	0.07
SSP2 - Medium	0.31	0.26	0.23	0.21	0.19	0.16	0.14
SSP3 - Stalled development	0.31	0.27	0.26	0.25	0.24	0.24	0.25
SSP4 - Inequality	0.31	0.26	0.22	0.18	0.15	0.12	0.10
SSP5 - Conventional development	0.31	0.25	0.20	0.17	0.14	0.09	0.07
Proportion of Women age 20–39 with at least secondary education							
SSP1 - Rapid development	0.85	0.94	0.97	0.98	0.99	1.00	1.00
SSP2 - Medium	0.85	0.90	0.93	0.96	0.97	0.99	1.00
SSP3 - Stalled development	0.85	0.84	0.84	0.84	0.84	0.84	0.84
SSP4 - Inequality	0.85	0.79	0.75	0.75	0.75	0.75	0.75
SSP5 - Conventional development	0.85	0.94	0.97	0.98	0.99	1.00	1.00
Mean years of schooling, age 25+							
SSP1 - Rapid development	10.21	11.17	11.86	12.43	12.92	13.86	14.43
SSP2 - Medium	10.21	10.89	11.43	11.91	12.35	13.23	13.90
SSP3 - Stalled development	10.21	10.60	10.89	11.08	11.19	11.19	11.16
SSP4 - Inequality	10.21	10.51	10.67	10.84	10.97	11.17	11.45
SSP5 - Conventional development	10.21	11.17	11.86	12.44	12.93	13.86	14.43

Demographic Assumptions Underlying SSPs

	2010–15	2020–25	2030–35	2040–45	2050–55	2075–80	2095–2100
Total fertility rate							
SSP1 - Rapid development	1.68	1.40	1.25	1.17	1.13	1.17	1.20
SSP2 - Medium	1.79	1.70	1.64	1.58	1.54	1.57	1.60
SSP3 - Stalled development	1.91	2.05	2.10	2.08	2.08	2.17	2.24
SSP4 - Inequality	1.73	1.52	1.36	1.26	1.22	1.26	1.29
SSP5 - Conventional development	1.68	1.40	1.25	1.17	1.13	1.17	1.20
Life expectancy at birth for females (in years)							
SSP1 - Rapid development	83.97	87.19	90.25	93.25	96.27	103.75	109.80
SSP2 - Medium	82.89	85.31	87.49	89.51	91.50	96.50	100.60
SSP3 - Stalled development	83.07	84.30	85.40	86.43	87.34	89.46	91.21
SSP4 - Inequality	83.46	85.75	87.84	89.79	91.69	96.21	100.08
SSP5 - Conventional development	83.97	87.19	90.25	93.25	96.27	103.75	109.80
Migration – net flow over five years (in thousands)							
SSP1 - Rapid development	37	47	51	50	47	14	0
SSP2 - Medium	38	48	55	59	62	26	0
SSP3 - Stalled development	31	24	30	38	46	30	0
SSP4 - Inequality	37	47	53	57	57	23	0
SSP5 - Conventional development	43	69	74	70	64	19	0

Ageing Indicators, Medium Scenario (SSP2)

	2010	2020	2030	2040	2050	2075	2095
Median age	32.12	35.56	39.73	43.90	47.10	53.63	57.89
Propspective median age	32.12	33.35	35.54	37.84	39.19	41.05	41.37
Proportion age 65+	0.09	0.12	0.18	0.22	0.26	0.36	0.42
Proportion RLE < 15 years	0.05	0.06	0.07	0.10	0.12	0.14	0.15

China, Hong Kong SAR

Detailed Human Capital Projections to 2060

Demographic indicators, Medium Scenario (SSP2)	2010	2020	2030	2040	2050	2060
Population (in millions)	7.05	7.63	8.12	8.43	8.66	8.80
Proportion age 65+	0.13	0.18	0.27	0.32	0.34	0.37
Proportion below age 20	0.18	0.16	0.17	0.15	0.14	0.16
	2005–10	2015–20	2025–30	2035–40	2045–50	2055–60
Total Fertility Rate	0.98	1.24	1.21	1.28	1.38	1.42
Life expectancy at birth (in years)						
Men	79.05	80.54	82.80	84.84	86.97	89.01
Women	84.29	86.69	88.89	90.89	93.00	95.00
Five-year immigration flow (in '000)	#N/A	316.09	327.87	335.04	334.93	330.01
Five-year emigration flow (in '000)	#N/A	99.97	86.59	89.76	89.43	88.80

Human Capital indicators, Medium Scenario (SSP2)	2010	2020	2030	2040	2050	2060
Population age 25+: highest educational attainment						
E1 - no education	0.06	0.03	0.02	0.01	0.00	0.00
E2 - incomplete primary	0.08	0.06	0.04	0.02	0.01	0.01
E3 - primary	0.16	0.13	0.10	0.07	0.05	0.02
E4 - lower secondary	0.15	0.15	0.13	0.11	0.09	0.06
E5 - upper secondary	0.30	0.33	0.35	0.35	0.34	0.33
E6 - post-secondary	0.23	0.30	0.36	0.43	0.50	0.58
Mean years of schooling (in years)	10.93	11.99	12.83	13.57	14.26	14.82
Gender gap (population age 25+): highest educational attainment (ratio male/female)						
E1 - no education	0.40	0.36	0.34	0.33	0.33	0.36
E2 - incomplete primary	0.86	0.72	0.60	0.50	0.42	0.36
E3 - primary	1.07	0.99	0.90	0.80	0.70	0.65
E4 - lower secondary	1.20	1.17	1.13	1.08	1.01	0.95
E5 - upper secondary	0.94	0.94	0.94	0.94	0.94	0.93
E6 - post-secondary	1.21	1.17	1.15	1.13	1.11	1.08
Mean years of schooling (male minus female)	0.85	0.73	0.62	0.53	0.43	0.29
Women age 20–39: highest educational attainment						
E1 - no education	0.01	0.00	0.00	0.00	0.00	0.00
E2 - incomplete primary	0.01	0.00	0.00	0.00	0.00	0.00
E3 - primary	0.05	0.02	0.01	0.00	0.00	0.00
E4 - lower secondary	0.13	0.07	0.04	0.02	0.01	0.00
E5 - upper secondary	0.44	0.44	0.41	0.39	0.34	0.31
E6 - post-secondary	0.36	0.46	0.54	0.59	0.65	0.68
Mean years of schooling (in years)	13.56	14.18	14.91	15.25	15.53	15.69

Education scenarios

GET: global education trend scenario (medium assumption also used for SSP2)

CER: constant enrolment rates scenario (assumption of no future improvements)

FT: Fast track scenario (assumption of education expansion according to fastest historical experience)

Pyramids by Education, Medium Scenario

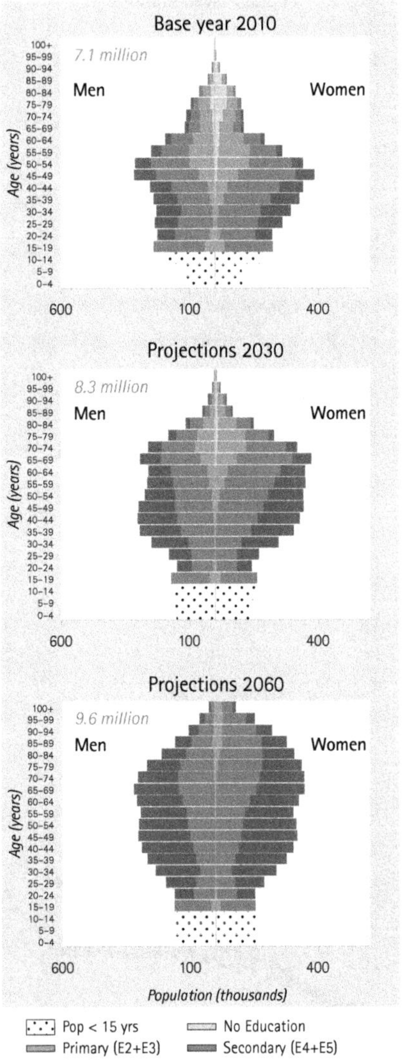

Population Size by Educational Attainment According to Three Education Scenarios: GET, CER, and FT

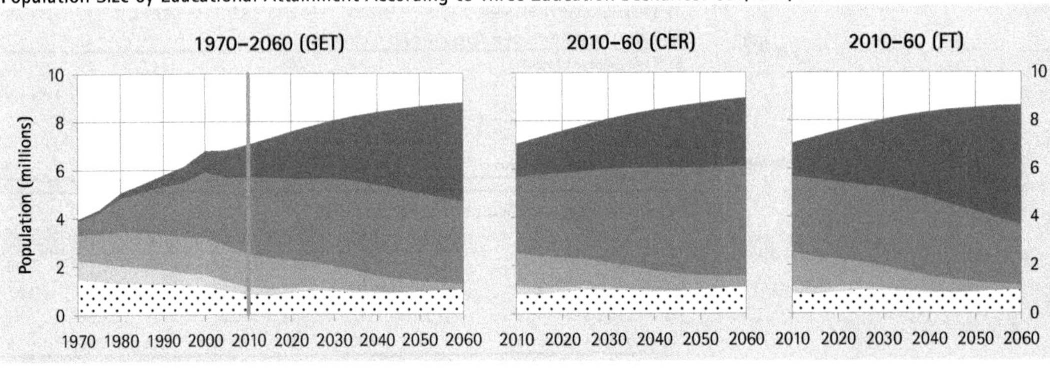

China, Hong Kong SAR (Continued)

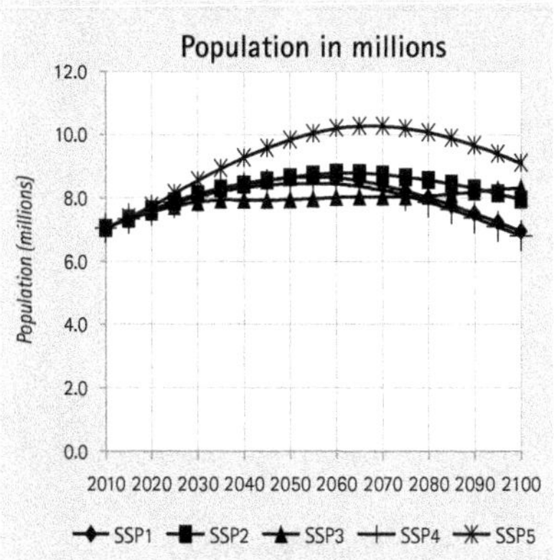

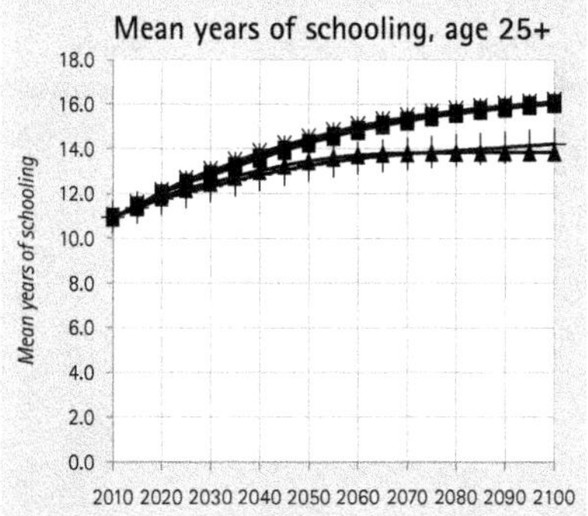

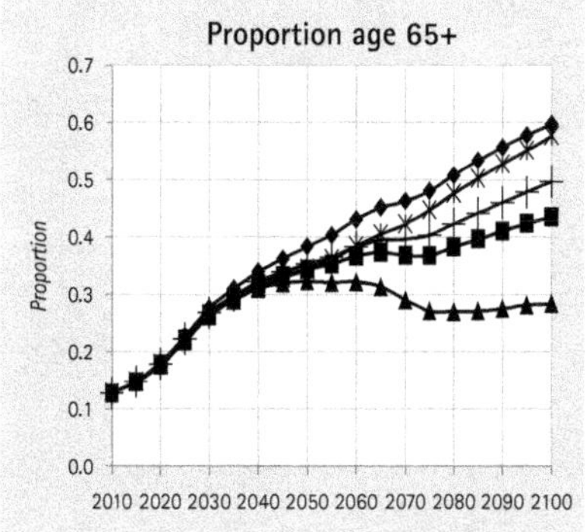

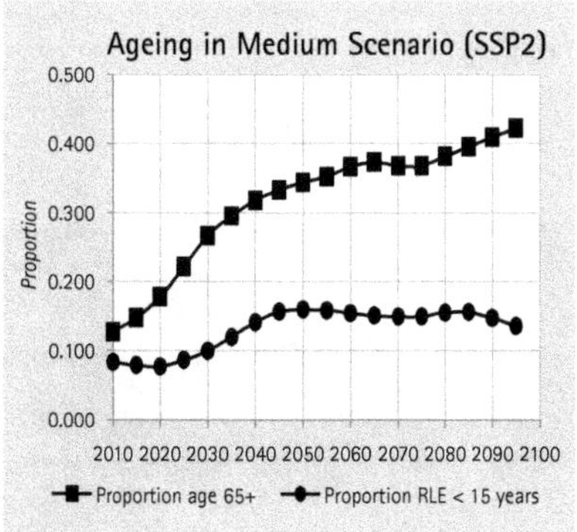

Alternative Scenarios to 2100

Projection Results by Scenario (SSP1–5)

	2010	2020	2030	2040	2050	2075	2100
Population (in millions)							
SSP1 - Rapid development	7.05	7.63	8.13	8.47	8.65	8.23	6.96
SSP2 - Medium	7.05	7.63	8.12	8.43	8.66	8.67	7.97
SSP3 - Stalled development	7.05	7.56	7.88	7.95	7.96	8.05	8.34
SSP4 - Inequality	7.05	7.61	8.06	8.33	8.45	8.08	6.81
SSP5 - Conventional development	7.05	7.75	8.55	9.27	9.84	10.20	9.10
Proportion age 65+							
SSP1 - Rapid development	0.13	0.18	0.28	0.34	0.38	0.48	0.60
SSP2 - Medium	0.13	0.18	0.27	0.32	0.34	0.37	0.43
SSP3 - Stalled development	0.13	0.18	0.26	0.31	0.32	0.27	0.28
SSP4 - Inequality	0.13	0.18	0.27	0.32	0.35	0.40	0.50
SSP5 - Conventional development	0.13	0.18	0.26	0.31	0.34	0.45	0.58
Proportion below age 20							
SSP1 - Rapid development	0.18	0.15	0.15	0.12	0.11	0.10	0.08
SSP2 - Medium	0.18	0.16	0.17	0.15	0.14	0.15	0.14
SSP3 - Stalled development	0.18	0.16	0.19	0.17	0.18	0.22	0.23
SSP4 - Inequality	0.18	0.15	0.15	0.13	0.12	0.12	0.10
SSP5 - Conventional development	0.18	0.15	0.15	0.13	0.13	0.11	0.08
Proportion of Women age 20–39 with at least secondary education							
SSP1 - Rapid development	0.94	0.98	0.99	1.00	1.00	1.00	1.00
SSP2 - Medium	0.94	0.98	0.99	1.00	1.00	1.00	1.00
SSP3 - Stalled development	0.94	0.96	0.96	0.96	0.96	0.96	0.96
SSP4 - Inequality	0.94	0.91	0.87	0.87	0.87	0.87	0.87
SSP5 - Conventional development	0.94	0.98	0.99	1.00	1.00	1.00	1.00
Mean years of schooling, age 25+							
SSP1 - Rapid development	10.93	12.05	12.93	13.68	14.34	15.48	16.06
SSP2 - Medium	10.93	11.99	12.83	13.57	14.26	15.42	16.01
SSP3 - Stalled development	10.93	11.84	12.50	13.03	13.46	13.83	13.85
SSP4 - Inequality	10.93	11.76	12.33	12.83	13.25	13.84	14.21
SSP5 - Conventional development	10.93	12.07	13.02	13.81	14.47	15.57	16.09

Demographic Assumptions Underlying SSPs

	2010–15	2020–25	2030–35	2040–45	2050–55	2075–80	2095–2100
Total fertility rate							
SSP1 - Rapid development	1.18	1.03	0.97	1.00	1.04	1.10	1.13
SSP2 - Medium	1.25	1.22	1.23	1.33	1.41	1.47	1.51
SSP3 - Stalled development	1.31	1.44	1.58	1.73	1.87	1.99	2.06
SSP4 - Inequality	1.19	1.06	1.01	1.04	1.09	1.15	1.18
SSP5 - Conventional development	1.18	1.03	0.97	1.00	1.04	1.10	1.13
Life expectancy at birth for females (in years)							
SSP1 - Rapid development	86.57	89.65	92.68	95.75	98.69	106.11	112.11
SSP2 - Medium	85.59	87.79	89.89	91.99	94.00	99.01	103.01
SSP3 - Stalled development	85.56	86.66	87.77	88.81	89.76	91.98	93.81
SSP4 - Inequality	86.14	88.12	90.18	92.31	94.26	98.85	102.65
SSP5 - Conventional development	86.57	89.65	92.68	95.75	98.69	106.11	112.11
Migration – net flow over five years (in thousands)							
SSP1 - Rapid development	196	229	233	215	192	52	0
SSP2 - Medium	188	210	218	220	213	77	0
SSP3 - Stalled development	163	114	119	131	140	67	0
SSP4 - Inequality	196	229	238	234	229	81	0
SSP5 - Conventional development	229	351	373	348	319	88	0

Ageing Indicators, Medium Scenario (SSP2)

	2010	2020	2030	2040	2050	2075	2095
Median age	41.90	45.46	48.50	51.30	53.65	54.62	57.90
Propspective median age	41.90	43.20	44.01	44.72	45.16	41.40	40.78
Proportion age 65+	0.13	0.18	0.27	0.32	0.34	0.37	0.42
Proportion RLE < 15 years	0.08	0.08	0.10	0.14	0.16	0.15	0.14

China, Macao SAR

Detailed Human Capital Projections to 2060

Demographic indicators, Medium Scenario (SSP2)	2010	2020	2030	2040	2050	2060
Population (in millions)	0.54	0.65	0.75	0.83	0.90	0.95
Proportion age 65+	0.07	0.11	0.20	0.26	0.29	0.33
Proportion below age 20	0.20	0.17	0.17	0.15	0.15	0.16
	2005–10	2015–20	2025–30	2035–40	2045–50	2055–60
Total Fertility Rate	1.02	1.13	1.19	1.27	1.37	1.41
Life expectancy at birth (in years)						
Men	77.74	80.30	82.37	84.47	86.48	88.46
Women	82.57	85.01	87.11	89.19	91.20	93.20
Five-year immigration flow (in '000)	#N/A	43.86	45.52	46.51	46.48	45.79
Five-year emigration flow (in '000)	#N/A	3.41	3.40	3.66	3.85	4.05

Human Capital indicators, Medium Scenario (SSP2)	2010	2020	2030	2040	2050	2060
Population age 25+: highest educational attainment						
E1 - no education	0.04	0.02	0.01	0.01	0.00	0.00
E2 - incomplete primary	0.09	0.06	0.04	0.03	0.02	0.01
E3 - primary	0.20	0.16	0.13	0.10	0.08	0.05
E4 - lower secondary	0.26	0.25	0.23	0.20	0.17	0.14
E5 - upper secondary	0.23	0.25	0.26	0.26	0.27	0.26
E6 - post-secondary	0.18	0.26	0.32	0.39	0.47	0.54
Mean years of schooling (in years)	9.67	10.71	11.41	12.10	12.80	13.41
Gender gap (population age 25+): highest educational attainment (ratio male/female)						
E1 - no education	0.38	0.39	0.39	0.37	0.37	0.40
E2 - incomplete primary	0.90	0.90	0.87	0.85	0.87	1.02
E3 - primary	1.06	1.04	1.00	0.96	0.94	1.00
E4 - lower secondary	1.03	1.02	1.01	0.98	0.94	0.92
E5 - upper secondary	1.07	1.03	1.02	1.01	1.00	0.98
E6 - post-secondary	1.04	1.01	1.03	1.04	1.04	1.03
Mean years of schooling (male minus female)	0.44	0.21	0.19	0.20	0.18	0.11
Women age 20–39: highest educational attainment						
E1 - no education	0.00	0.00	0.00	0.00	0.00	0.00
E2 - incomplete primary	0.01	0.00	0.00	0.00	0.00	0.00
E3 - primary	0.08	0.05	0.04	0.03	0.02	0.01
E4 - lower secondary	0.25	0.18	0.13	0.08	0.05	0.04
E5 - upper secondary	0.34	0.34	0.34	0.34	0.32	0.31
E6 - post-secondary	0.31	0.42	0.49	0.55	0.61	0.64
Mean years of schooling (in years)	11.90	12.81	13.35	13.82	14.18	14.39

Education scenarios

GET: global education trend scenario (medium assumption also used for SSP2)

CER: constant enrolment rates scenario (assumption of no future improvements)

FT: Fast track scenario (assumption of education expansion according to fastest historical experience)

Pyramids by Education, Medium Scenario

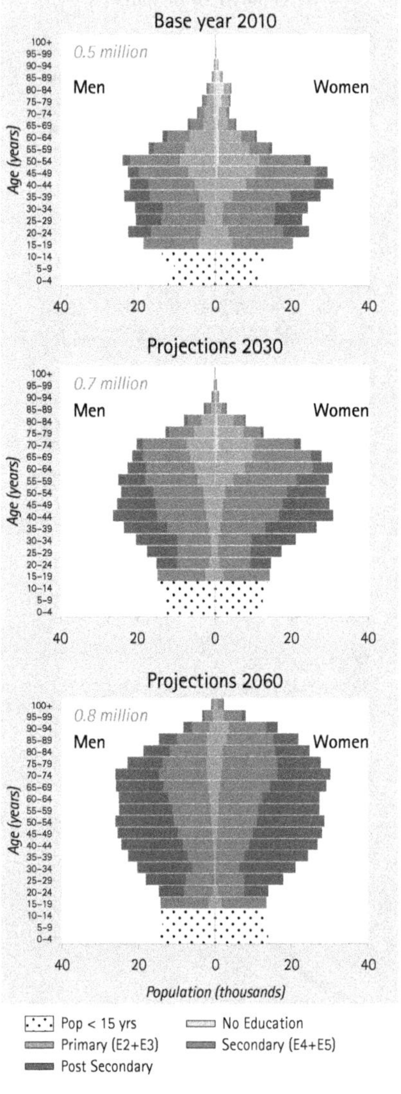

Population Size by Educational Attainment According to Three Education Scenarios: GET, CER, and FT

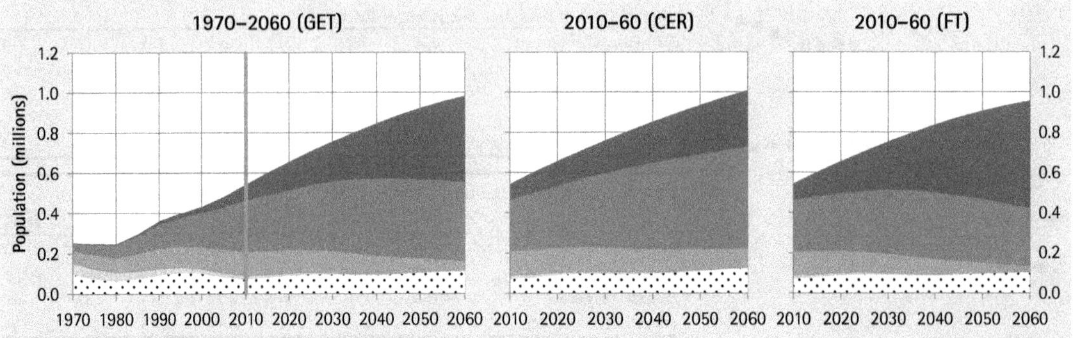

China, Macao SAR (Continued)

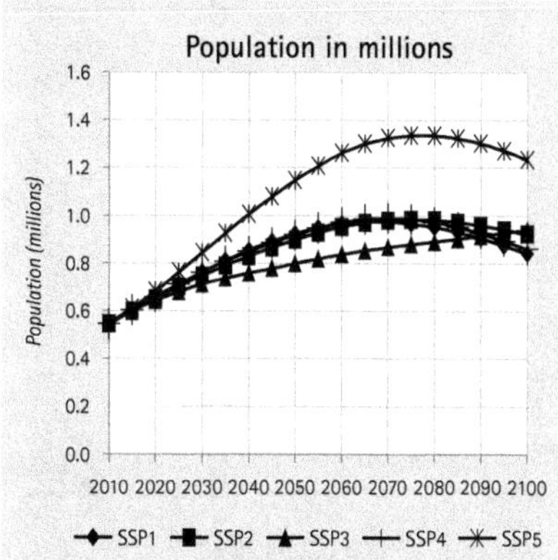

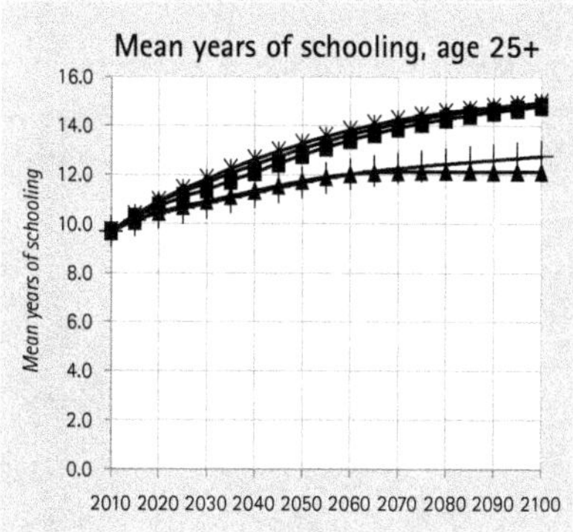

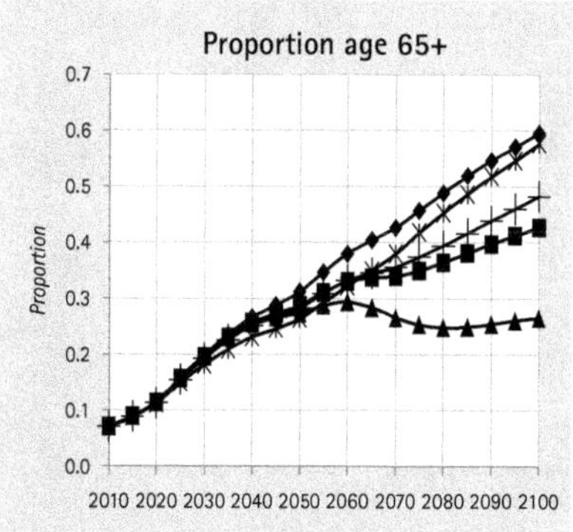

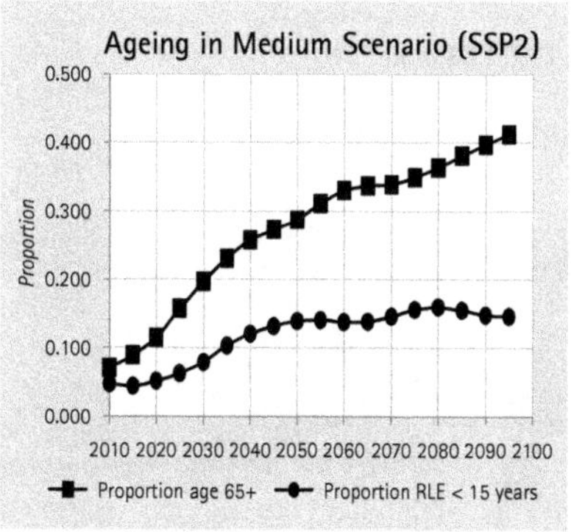

Alternative Scenarios to 2100

Projection Results by Scenario (SSP1–5)

	2010	2020	2030	2040	2050	2075	2100
Population (in millions)							
SSP1 - Rapid development	0.54	0.66	0.76	0.85	0.92	0.97	0.84
SSP2 - Medium	0.54	0.65	0.75	0.83	0.90	0.98	0.92
SSP3 - Stalled development	0.54	0.64	0.71	0.76	0.80	0.88	0.94
SSP4 - Inequality	0.54	0.66	0.76	0.85	0.92	0.99	0.86
SSP5 - Conventional development	0.54	0.68	0.84	1.00	1.15	1.33	1.23
Proportion age 65+							
SSP1 - Rapid development	0.07	0.12	0.20	0.27	0.31	0.46	0.60
SSP2 - Medium	0.07	0.11	0.20	0.26	0.29	0.35	0.43
SSP3 - Stalled development	0.07	0.11	0.20	0.26	0.27	0.25	0.27
SSP4 - Inequality	0.07	0.11	0.19	0.25	0.28	0.37	0.48
SSP5 - Conventional development	0.07	0.11	0.18	0.23	0.26	0.42	0.58
Proportion below age 20							
SSP1 - Rapid development	0.20	0.17	0.15	0.13	0.12	0.10	0.08
SSP2 - Medium	0.20	0.17	0.17	0.15	0.15	0.15	0.14
SSP3 - Stalled development	0.20	0.18	0.19	0.18	0.19	0.23	0.23
SSP4 - Inequality	0.20	0.17	0.16	0.14	0.13	0.12	0.11
SSP5 - Conventional development	0.20	0.17	0.16	0.14	0.13	0.11	0.08
Proportion of Women age 20–39 with at least secondary education							
SSP1 - Rapid development	0.90	0.96	0.98	0.99	0.99	1.00	1.00
SSP2 - Medium	0.90	0.94	0.96	0.97	0.98	0.99	1.00
SSP3 - Stalled development	0.90	0.93	0.93	0.93	0.93	0.93	0.93
SSP4 - Inequality	0.90	0.87	0.83	0.83	0.83	0.83	0.83
SSP5 - Conventional development	0.90	0.96	0.98	0.99	0.99	1.00	1.00
Mean years of schooling, age 25+							
SSP1 - Rapid development	9.67	10.87	11.68	12.41	13.06	14.29	14.91
SSP2 - Medium	9.67	10.71	11.41	12.10	12.80	14.10	14.79
SSP3 - Stalled development	9.67	10.47	10.93	11.35	11.75	12.13	12.13
SSP4 - Inequality	9.67	10.43	10.84	11.27	11.68	12.35	12.76
SSP5 - Conventional development	9.67	10.92	11.83	12.61	13.27	14.40	14.94

Demographic Assumptions Underlying SSPs

	2010–15	2020–25	2030–35	2040–45	2050–55	2075–80	2095–2100
Total fertility rate							
SSP1 - Rapid development	1.05	0.97	0.95	0.99	1.03	1.09	1.13
SSP2 - Medium	1.11	1.16	1.22	1.32	1.40	1.46	1.51
SSP3 - Stalled development	1.17	1.37	1.57	1.75	1.89	2.03	2.12
SSP4 - Inequality	1.05	1.00	1.00	1.04	1.09	1.15	1.19
SSP5 - Conventional development	1.05	0.97	0.95	0.99	1.03	1.09	1.13
Life expectancy at birth for females (in years)							
SSP1 - Rapid development	84.91	87.79	90.92	93.93	96.91	104.33	110.40
SSP2 - Medium	83.81	86.11	88.19	90.19	92.20	97.20	101.20
SSP3 - Stalled development	83.92	84.89	86.09	87.15	88.12	90.21	91.97
SSP4 - Inequality	84.40	86.37	88.52	90.52	92.50	97.01	100.82
SSP5 - Conventional development	84.91	87.79	90.92	93.93	96.91	104.33	110.40
Migration – net flow over five years (in thousands)							
SSP1 - Rapid development	44	41	40	37	32	9	0
SSP2 - Medium	39	35	35	35	33	12	0
SSP3 - Stalled development	36	20	20	21	22	11	0
SSP4 - Inequality	44	41	41	41	39	14	0
SSP5 - Conventional development	51	64	68	64	59	16	0

Ageing Indicators, Medium Scenario (SSP2)

	2010	2020	2030	2040	2050	2075	2095
Median age	37.70	40.83	44.19	48.26	50.27	53.29	57.39
Propspective median age	37.70	38.54	39.76	41.95	42.05	40.48	40.71
Proportion age 65+	0.07	0.11	0.20	0.26	0.29	0.35	0.41
Proportion RLE < 15 years	0.05	0.05	0.08	0.12	0.14	0.16	0.15

China

Detailed Human Capital Projections to 2060

Demographic indicators, Medium Scenario (SSP2)

	2010	2020	2030	2040	2050	2060
Population (in millions)	1341.34	1378.80	1377.72	1334.09	1255.26	1153.92
Proportion age 65+	0.08	0.12	0.17	0.25	0.28	0.34
Proportion below age 20	0.27	0.22	0.19	0.16	0.15	0.14
	2005–10	2015–20	2025–30	2035–40	2045–50	2055–60
Total Fertility Rate	1.64	1.40	1.40	1.40	1.40	1.41
Life expectancy at birth (in years)						
Men	71.10	73.20	75.24	77.14	79.23	81.22
Women	74.45	76.90	79.09	81.09	83.19	85.21
Five-year immigration flow (in '000)	126.24	126.98	136.09	142.92	146.07	146.38
Five-year emigration flow (in '000)	2011.35	1405.93	1187.67	1008.03	846.22	717.63

Human Capital indicators, Medium Scenario (SSP2)

	2010	2020	2030	2040	2050	2060
Population age 25+: highest educational attainment						
E1 - no education	0.10	0.06	0.03	0.02	0.01	0.01
E2 - incomplete primary	0.00	0.00	0.00	0.00	0.00	0.00
E3 - primary	0.28	0.23	0.18	0.14	0.11	0.08
E4 - lower secondary	0.42	0.45	0.46	0.46	0.43	0.39
E5 - upper secondary	0.13	0.16	0.19	0.21	0.24	0.27
E6 - post-secondary	0.07	0.10	0.13	0.17	0.21	0.25
Mean years of schooling (in years)	7.36	8.16	8.78	9.34	9.86	10.38
Gender gap (population age 25+): highest educational attainment (ratio male/female)						
E1 - no education	0.32	0.29	0.27	0.27	0.30	0.35
E2 - incomplete primary	NA	NA	NA	NA	NA	NA
E3 - primary	0.85	0.76	0.70	0.68	0.69	0.75
E4 - lower secondary	1.23	1.17	1.12	1.08	1.03	1.00
E5 - upper secondary	1.37	1.27	1.21	1.16	1.12	1.09
E6 - post-secondary	1.36	1.18	1.11	1.07	1.04	1.02
Mean years of schooling (male minus female)	1.18	0.87	0.66	0.48	0.32	0.21
Women age 20–39: highest educational attainment						
E1 - no education	0.02	0.01	0.00	0.00	0.00	0.00
E2 - incomplete primary	0.00	0.00	0.00	0.00	0.00	0.00
E3 - primary	0.15	0.10	0.08	0.06	0.05	0.03
E4 - lower secondary	0.54	0.48	0.40	0.31	0.24	0.18
E5 - upper secondary	0.16	0.22	0.26	0.31	0.34	0.36
E6 - post-secondary	0.13	0.19	0.25	0.31	0.37	0.43
Mean years of schooling (in years)	8.91	9.70	10.34	10.96	11.51	11.98

Education scenarios

GET : global education trend scenario (medium assumption also used for SSP2)

CER: constant enrolment rates scenario (assumption of no future improvements)

FT: Fast track scenario (assumption of education expansion according to fastest historical experience)

Pyramids by Education, Medium Scenario

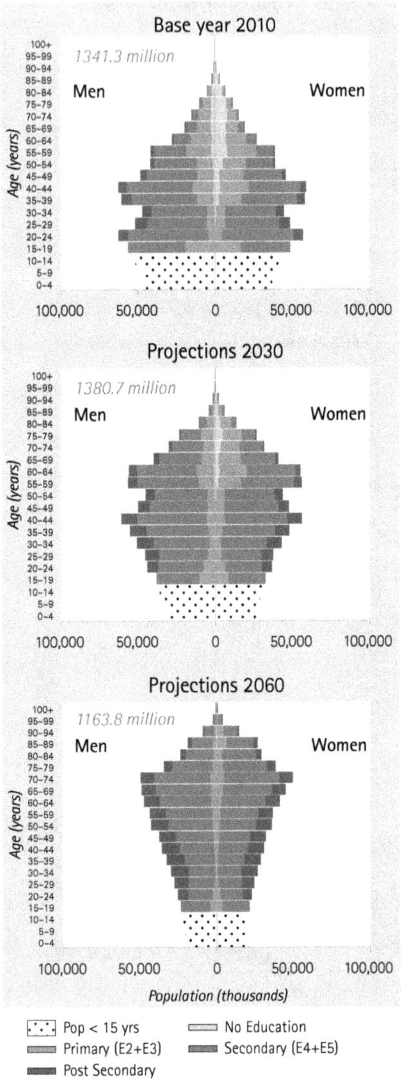

Population Size by Educational Attainment According to Three Education Scenarios: GET, CER, and FT

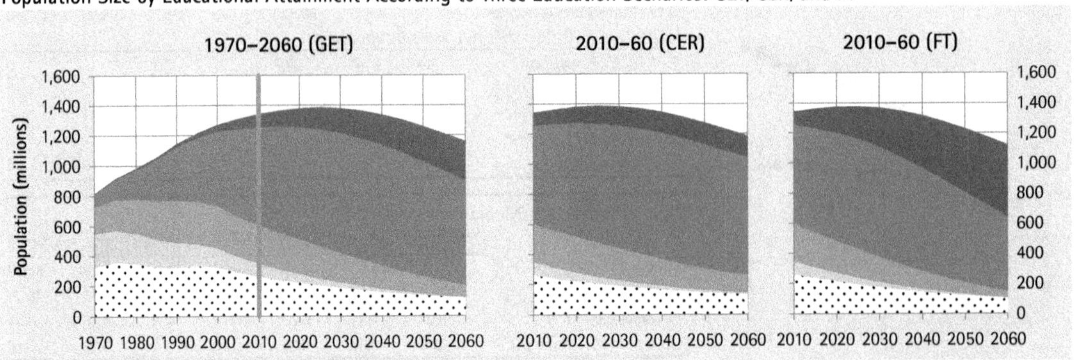

China (Continued)

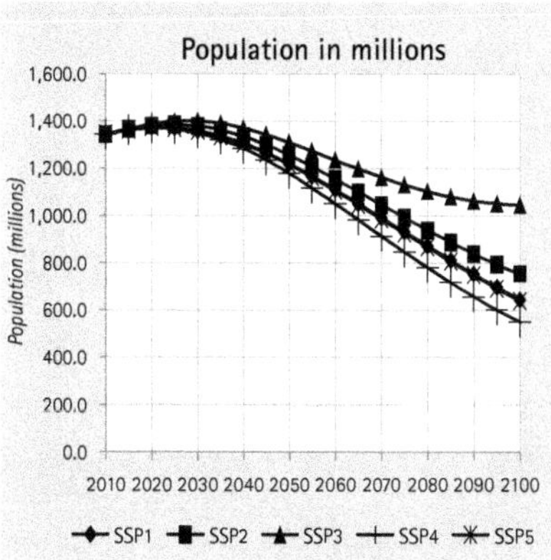

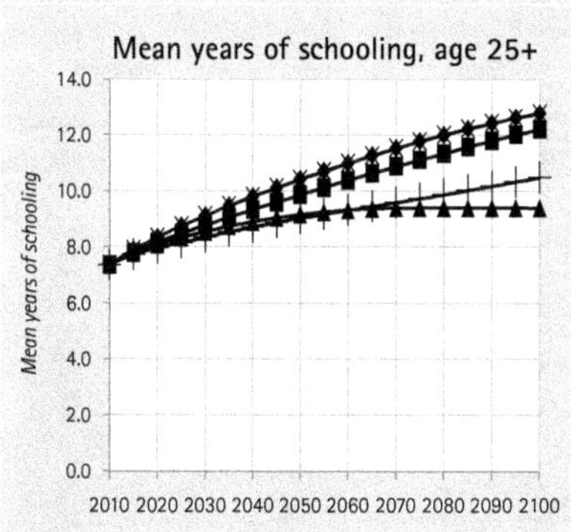

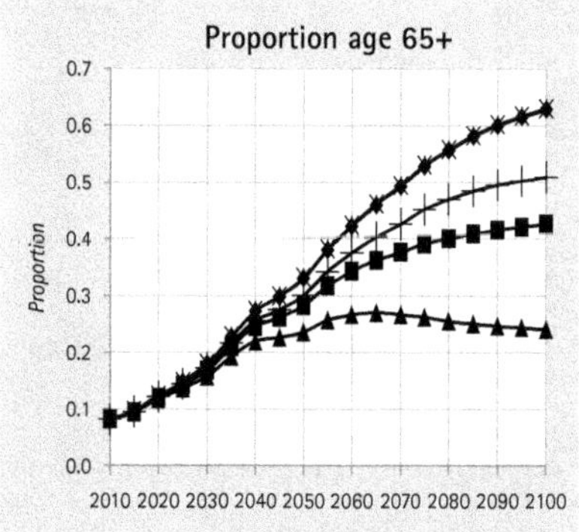

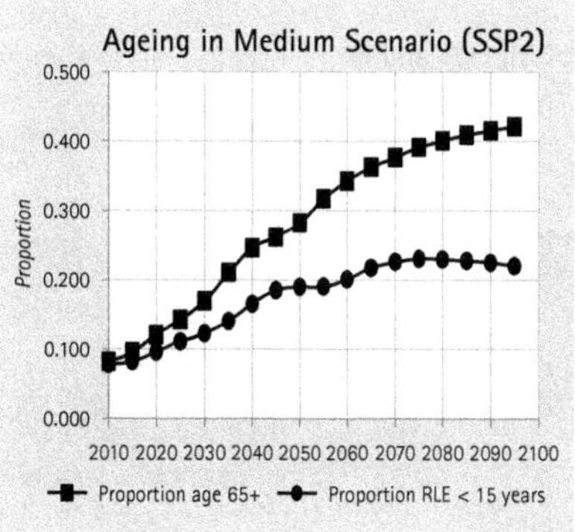

Alternative Scenarios to 2100

Projection Results by Scenario (SSP1–5)

	2010	2020	2030	2040	2050	2075	2100
Population (in millions)							
SSP1 - Rapid development	1,341.34	1,371.06	1,357.27	1,304.94	1,218.80	931.20	643.59
SSP2 - Medium	1,341.34	1,378.80	1,377.72	1,334.09	1,255.26	992.05	754.13
SSP3 - Stalled development	1,341.34	1,386.54	1,399.60	1,369.81	1,309.80	1,131.22	1,046.14
SSP4 - Inequality	1,341.34	1,368.80	1,348.12	1,282.01	1,178.01	846.29	549.55
SSP5 - Conventional development	1,341.34	1,370.32	1,355.16	1,301.57	1,214.31	924.82	637.36
Proportion age 65+							
SSP1 - Rapid development	0.08	0.12	0.18	0.27	0.33	0.53	0.63
SSP2 - Medium	0.08	0.12	0.17	0.25	0.28	0.39	0.43
SSP3 - Stalled development	0.08	0.12	0.16	0.22	0.24	0.26	0.24
SSP4 - Inequality	0.08	0.12	0.17	0.26	0.30	0.45	0.51
SSP5 - Conventional development	0.08	0.12	0.18	0.27	0.33	0.53	0.63
Proportion below age 20							
SSP1 - Rapid development	0.27	0.21	0.16	0.13	0.11	0.08	0.07
SSP2 - Medium	0.27	0.22	0.19	0.16	0.15	0.13	0.13
SSP3 - Stalled development	0.27	0.23	0.21	0.20	0.20	0.22	0.24
SSP4 - Inequality	0.27	0.21	0.17	0.14	0.12	0.10	0.09
SSP5 - Conventional development	0.27	0.21	0.16	0.13	0.11	0.08	0.07
Proportion of Women age 20–39 with at least secondary education							
SSP1 - Rapid development	0.83	0.91	0.94	0.96	0.97	0.99	1.00
SSP2 - Medium	0.83	0.89	0.91	0.93	0.95	0.98	0.99
SSP3 - Stalled development	0.83	0.87	0.87	0.87	0.87	0.87	0.87
SSP4 - Inequality	0.83	0.82	0.78	0.78	0.78	0.78	0.78
SSP5 - Conventional development	0.83	0.91	0.94	0.96	0.97	0.99	1.00
Mean years of schooling, age 25+							
SSP1 - Rapid development	7.36	8.34	9.11	9.80	10.42	11.77	12.79
SSP2 - Medium	7.36	8.16	8.78	9.34	9.86	11.11	12.21
SSP3 - Stalled development	7.36	8.08	8.55	8.90	9.16	9.41	9.40
SSP4 - Inequality	7.36	7.96	8.35	8.72	9.03	9.73	10.48
SSP5 - Conventional development	7.36	8.34	9.11	9.80	10.41	11.77	12.78

Demographic Assumptions Underlying SSPs

	2010–15	2020–25	2030–35	2040–45	2050–55	2075–80	2095–2100
Total fertility rate							
SSP1 - Rapid development	1.33	1.16	1.06	1.02	1.01	1.07	1.12
SSP2 - Medium	1.42	1.40	1.40	1.40	1.40	1.46	1.51
SSP3 - Stalled development	1.50	1.65	1.78	1.86	1.93	2.10	2.22
SSP4 - Inequality	1.35	1.20	1.12	1.09	1.09	1.15	1.20
SSP5 - Conventional development	1.33	1.16	1.06	1.02	1.01	1.07	1.12
Life expectancy at birth for females (in years)							
SSP1 - Rapid development	78.03	80.73	83.51	86.28	89.19	96.50	102.51
SSP2 - Medium	75.71	78.00	80.09	82.09	84.21	89.20	93.19
SSP3 - Stalled development	77.29	78.21	79.12	80.01	80.81	82.68	84.27
SSP4 - Inequality	77.66	79.52	81.30	83.01	84.90	89.22	92.95
SSP5 - Conventional development	78.03	80.73	83.51	86.28	89.19	96.50	102.51
Migration – net flow over five years (in thousands)							
SSP1 - Rapid development	−1480	−1150	−928	−718	−545	−147	0
SSP2 - Medium	−1448	−1143	−944	−771	−627	−202	0
SSP3 - Stalled development	−1232	−570	−465	−385	−322	−117	0
SSP4 - Inequality	−1480	−1146	−914	−684	−497	−117	0
SSP5 - Conventional development	−1727	−1756	−1462	−1177	−939	−292	0

Ageing Indicators, Medium Scenario (SSP2)

	2010	2020	2030	2040	2050	2075	2095
Median age	34.58	38.31	43.06	47.90	51.56	56.95	58.72
Propspective median age	34.58	36.62	39.80	43.08	45.05	46.27	44.31
Proportion age 65+	0.08	0.12	0.17	0.25	0.28	0.39	0.42
Proportion RLE < 15 years	0.08	0.10	0.12	0.17	0.19	0.23	0.22

Colombia

Detailed Human Capital Projections to 2060

Demographic indicators, Medium Scenario (SSP2)	2010	2020	2030	2040	2050	2060
Population (in millions)	46.29	52.30	57.48	61.47	64.23	65.71
Proportion age 65+	0.06	0.08	0.12	0.15	0.19	0.23
Proportion below age 20	0.38	0.34	0.30	0.26	0.24	0.22
	2005–10	2015–20	2025–30	2035–40	2045–50	2055–60
Total Fertility Rate	2.45	2.16	1.99	1.88	1.81	1.75
Life expectancy at birth (in years)						
Men	69.24	72.01	74.46	76.84	79.23	81.40
Women	76.67	79.29	81.59	83.71	85.81	87.81
Five-year immigration flow (in '000)	20.23	19.88	20.65	21.13	21.16	20.86
Five-year emigration flow (in '000)	139.43	111.21	113.37	112.09	108.50	103.76

Human Capital indicators, Medium Scenario (SSP2)	2010	2020	2030	2040	2050	2060
Population age 25+: highest educational attainment						
E1 - no education	0.08	0.06	0.04	0.03	0.02	0.01
E2 - incomplete primary	0.18	0.14	0.10	0.07	0.05	0.03
E3 - primary	0.28	0.25	0.22	0.18	0.15	0.12
E4 - lower secondary	0.07	0.07	0.07	0.06	0.06	0.05
E5 - upper secondary	0.21	0.27	0.31	0.35	0.38	0.40
E6 - post-secondary	0.18	0.22	0.26	0.30	0.35	0.39
Mean years of schooling (in years)	7.83	8.78	9.60	10.33	10.98	11.55
Gender gap (population age 25+): highest educational attainment (ratio male/female)						
E1 - no education	1.04	1.06	1.08	1.08	1.08	1.05
E2 - incomplete primary	1.03	1.02	1.01	1.01	0.99	0.97
E3 - primary	1.02	1.04	1.06	1.06	1.06	1.04
E4 - lower secondary	1.01	1.03	1.05	1.06	1.06	1.04
E5 - upper secondary	1.00	1.02	1.04	1.05	1.05	1.04
E6 - post-secondary	0.93	0.90	0.88	0.89	0.91	0.94
Mean years of schooling (male minus female)	−0.16	−0.23	−0.26	−0.25	−0.21	−0.14
Women age 20–39: highest educational attainment						
E1 - no education	0.03	0.02	0.01	0.01	0.00	0.00
E2 - incomplete primary	0.09	0.05	0.03	0.01	0.01	0.00
E3 - primary	0.22	0.17	0.12	0.09	0.06	0.04
E4 - lower secondary	0.08	0.07	0.05	0.04	0.03	0.02
E5 - upper secondary	0.34	0.39	0.42	0.43	0.44	0.43
E6 - post-secondary	0.24	0.31	0.37	0.42	0.47	0.50
Mean years of schooling (in years)	9.82	10.77	11.42	12.03	12.47	12.77

Education scenarios

GET: global education trend scenario (medium assumption also used for SSP2)

CER: constant enrolment rates scenario (assumption of no future improvements)

FT: Fast track scenario (assumption of education expansion according to fastest historical experience)

Pyramids by Education, Medium Scenario

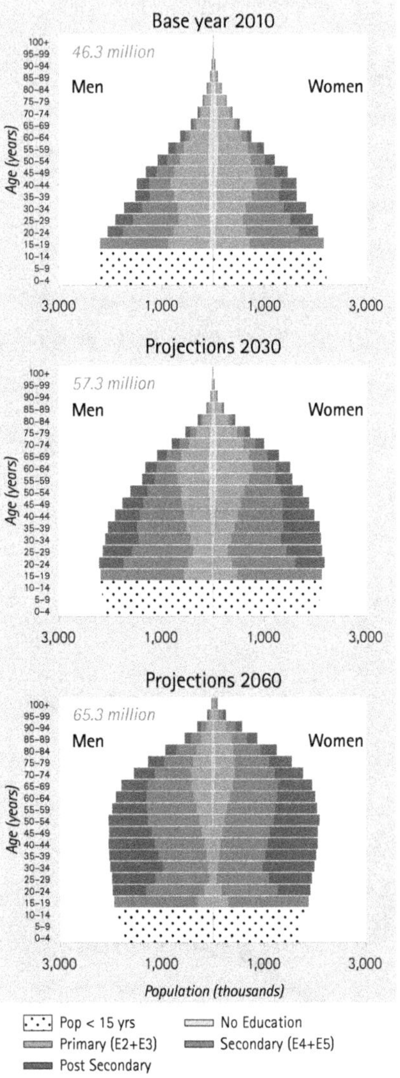

Population Size by Educational Attainment According to Three Education Scenarios: GET, CER, and FT

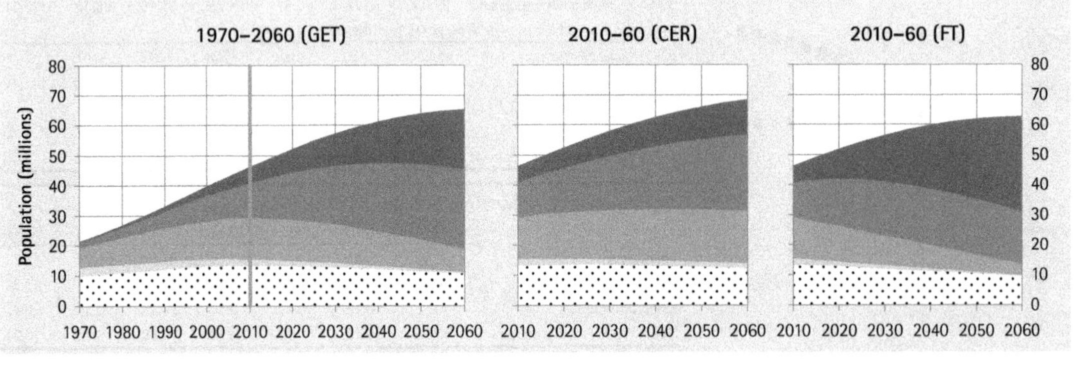

Colombia (Continued)

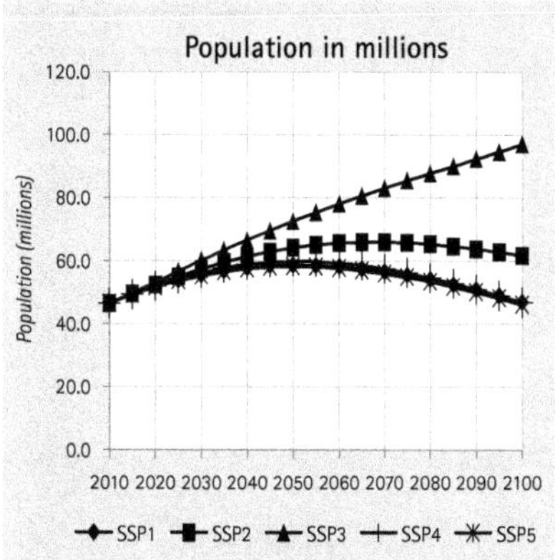

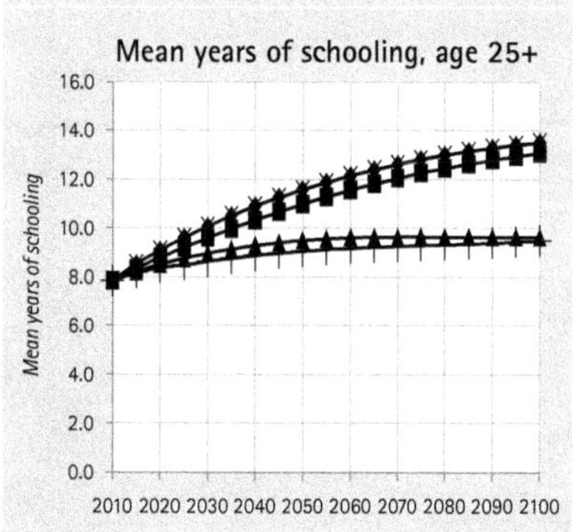

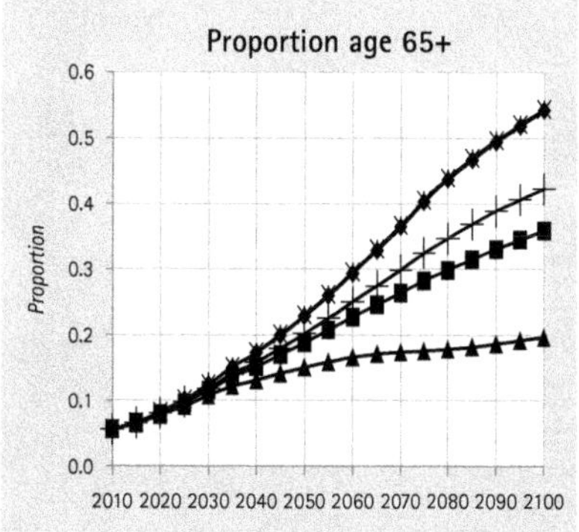

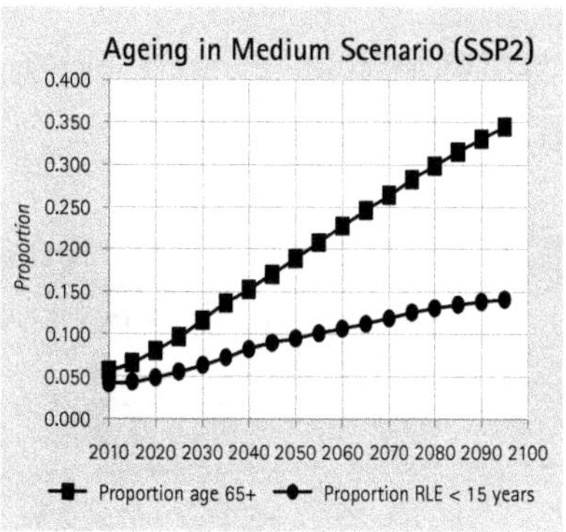

Alternative Scenarios to 2100

Projection Results by Scenario (SSP1–5)

	2010	2020	2030	2040	2050	2075	2100
Population (in millions)							
SSP1 - Rapid development	46.29	51.64	55.43	57.83	58.70	55.48	46.87
SSP2 - Medium	46.29	52.30	57.48	61.47	64.23	65.83	61.79
SSP3 - Stalled development	46.29	53.18	60.18	66.62	72.62	85.49	97.02
SSP4 - Inequality	46.29	51.95	56.21	58.90	59.90	56.21	46.80
SSP5 - Conventional development	46.29	51.59	55.26	57.53	58.26	54.73	46.06
Proportion age 65+							
SSP1 - Rapid development	0.06	0.08	0.13	0.17	0.23	0.40	0.54
SSP2 - Medium	0.06	0.08	0.12	0.15	0.19	0.28	0.36
SSP3 - Stalled development	0.06	0.08	0.11	0.13	0.15	0.18	0.20
SSP4 - Inequality	0.06	0.08	0.12	0.16	0.20	0.32	0.42
SSP5 - Conventional development	0.06	0.08	0.13	0.17	0.23	0.40	0.54
Proportion below age 20							
SSP1 - Rapid development	0.38	0.32	0.26	0.22	0.18	0.12	0.09
SSP2 - Medium	0.38	0.34	0.30	0.26	0.24	0.19	0.16
SSP3 - Stalled development	0.38	0.35	0.33	0.32	0.31	0.29	0.27
SSP4 - Inequality	0.38	0.33	0.28	0.24	0.21	0.15	0.12
SSP5 - Conventional development	0.38	0.32	0.26	0.22	0.18	0.12	0.09
Proportion of Women age 20–39 with at least secondary education							
SSP1 - Rapid development	0.66	0.83	0.90	0.94	0.96	0.99	0.99
SSP2 - Medium	0.66	0.76	0.84	0.89	0.93	0.98	1.00
SSP3 - Stalled development	0.66	0.69	0.69	0.69	0.69	0.69	0.69
SSP4 - Inequality	0.66	0.65	0.62	0.62	0.62	0.62	0.62
SSP5 - Conventional development	0.66	0.83	0.90	0.94	0.96	0.99	0.99
Mean years of schooling, age 25+							
SSP1 - Rapid development	7.83	9.09	10.07	10.90	11.58	12.82	13.51
SSP2 - Medium	7.83	8.78	9.60	10.33	10.98	12.26	13.07
SSP3 - Stalled development	7.83	8.51	8.96	9.28	9.50	9.65	9.64
SSP4 - Inequality	7.83	8.37	8.64	8.88	9.06	9.29	9.49
SSP5 - Conventional development	7.83	9.08	10.07	10.90	11.57	12.81	13.51

Demographic Assumptions Underlying SSPs

	2010–15	2020–25	2030–35	2040–45	2050–55	2075–80	2095–2100
Total fertility rate							
SSP1 - Rapid development	2.13	1.70	1.47	1.37	1.31	1.20	1.19
SSP2 - Medium	2.26	2.07	1.91	1.85	1.77	1.60	1.59
SSP3 - Stalled development	2.42	2.50	2.51	2.47	2.42	2.25	2.25
SSP4 - Inequality	2.20	1.89	1.66	1.53	1.44	1.33	1.33
SSP5 - Conventional development	2.13	1.70	1.47	1.37	1.31	1.20	1.19
Life expectancy at birth for females (in years)							
SSP1 - Rapid development	79.45	82.47	85.54	88.56	91.58	99.09	105.08
SSP2 - Medium	77.99	80.49	82.69	84.71	86.81	91.81	95.81
SSP3 - Stalled development	78.69	79.82	80.91	81.85	82.69	84.59	86.23
SSP4 - Inequality	79.07	81.22	83.22	85.08	86.98	91.40	95.07
SSP5 - Conventional development	79.45	82.47	85.54	88.56	91.58	99.09	105.08
Migration – net flow over five years (in thousands)							
SSP1 - Rapid development	−98	−91	−89	−82	−73	−25	0
SSP2 - Medium	−96	−91	−91	−88	−84	−35	0
SSP3 - Stalled development	−81	−45	−45	−45	−45	−21	0
SSP4 - Inequality	−98	−91	−89	−81	−70	−22	0
SSP5 - Conventional development	−114	−139	−140	−134	−126	−50	0

Ageing Indicators, Medium Scenario (SSP2)

	2010	2020	2030	2040	2050	2075	2095
Median age	26.75	30.08	33.61	36.96	40.16	47.18	52.00
Propspective median age	26.75	27.98	29.60	31.19	32.62	35.29	36.53
Proportion age 65+	0.06	0.08	0.12	0.15	0.19	0.28	0.34
Proportion RLE < 15 years	0.04	0.05	0.06	0.08	0.10	0.13	0.14

Comoros

Detailed Human Capital Projections to 2060

Demographic indicators, Medium Scenario (SSP2)	2010	2020	2030	2040	2050	2060
Population (in millions)	0.73	0.90	1.05	1.19	1.29	1.36
Proportion age 65+	0.03	0.03	0.04	0.05	0.07	0.08
Proportion below age 20	0.52	0.50	0.43	0.39	0.35	0.30
	2005–10	2015–20	2025–30	2035–40	2045–50	2055–60
Total Fertility Rate	5.08	3.95	3.04	2.55	2.20	2.00
Life expectancy at birth (in years)						
Men	58.34	59.85	61.25	62.73	64.27	66.43
Women	61.00	62.88	64.68	66.48	68.18	70.38
Five-year immigration flow (in '000)	0.25	0.25	0.26	0.26	0.26	0.26
Five-year emigration flow (in '000)	10.20	9.36	11.57	12.81	13.28	13.58

Human Capital indicators, Medium Scenario (SSP2)	2010	2020	2030	2040	2050	2060
Population age 25+: highest educational attainment						
E1 - no education	0.38	0.26	0.15	0.08	0.05	0.02
E2 - incomplete primary	0.13	0.12	0.09	0.06	0.04	0.02
E3 - primary	0.26	0.33	0.38	0.39	0.38	0.35
E4 - lower secondary	0.13	0.16	0.19	0.20	0.20	0.19
E5 - upper secondary	0.04	0.06	0.09	0.12	0.17	0.21
E6 - post-secondary	0.05	0.08	0.10	0.13	0.17	0.20
Mean years of schooling (in years)	4.94	6.36	7.72	8.91	9.85	10.64
Gender gap (population age 25+): highest educational attainment (ratio male/female)						
E1 - no education	0.64	0.61	0.58	0.57	0.59	0.63
E2 - incomplete primary	1.18	1.09	1.03	0.97	0.92	0.90
E3 - primary	1.24	1.09	1.01	0.97	0.95	0.94
E4 - lower secondary	1.10	0.98	0.92	0.91	0.91	0.94
E5 - upper secondary	1.92	1.47	1.23	1.08	1.02	1.00
E6 - post-secondary	2.86	2.42	2.02	1.68	1.44	1.26
Mean years of schooling (male minus female)	1.72	1.54	1.26	0.97	0.72	0.49
Women age 20–39: highest educational attainment						
E1 - no education	0.22	0.11	0.04	0.02	0.01	0.00
E2 - incomplete primary	0.15	0.10	0.07	0.04	0.03	0.02
E3 - primary	0.37	0.44	0.44	0.41	0.34	0.27
E4 - lower secondary	0.19	0.24	0.29	0.30	0.31	0.33
E5 - upper secondary	0.04	0.07	0.10	0.14	0.18	0.22
E6 - post-secondary	0.03	0.04	0.06	0.09	0.12	0.15
Mean years of schooling (in years)	6.02	7.47	8.61	9.52	10.26	10.91

Education scenarios

GET: global education trend scenario (medium assumption also used for SSP2)

CER: constant enrolment rates scenario (assumption of no future improvements)

FT: Fast track scenario (assumption of education expansion according to fastest historical experience)

Pyramids by Education, Medium Scenario

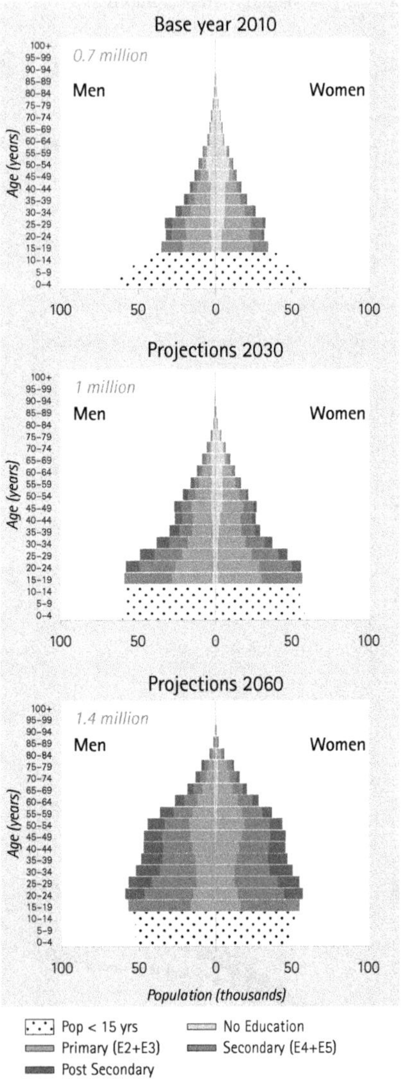

Population Size by Educational Attainment According to Three Education Scenarios: GET, CER, and FT

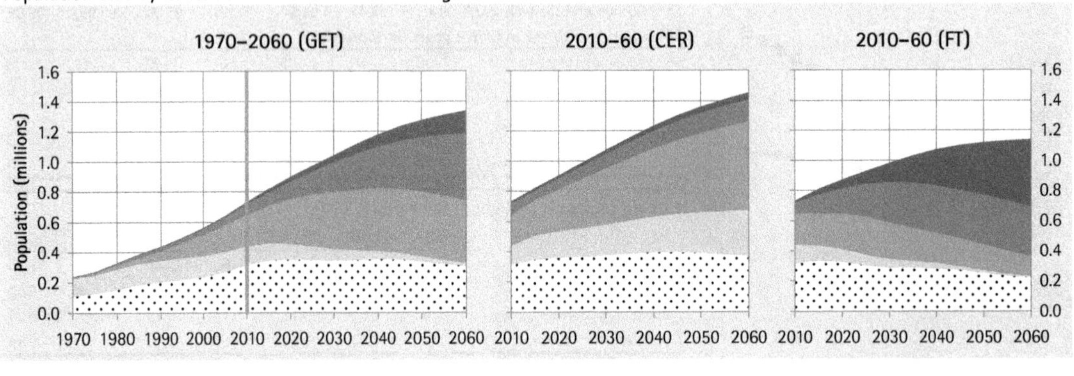

Comoros (Continued)

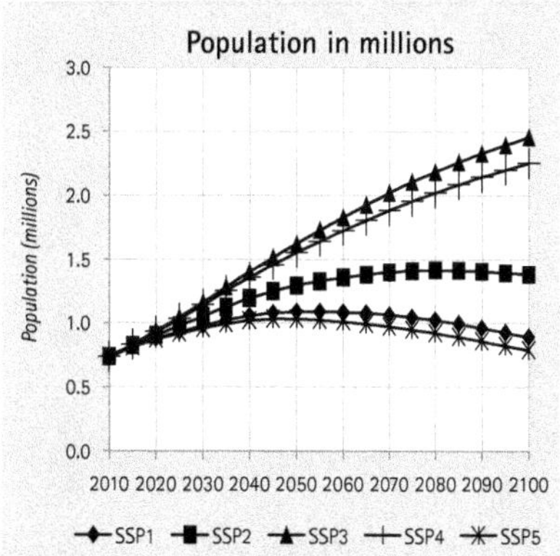

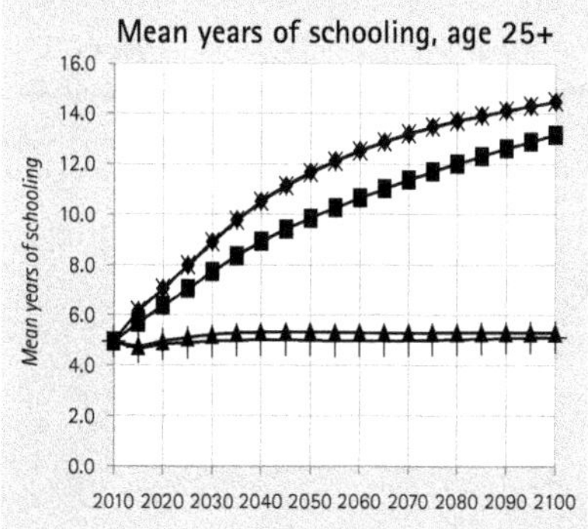

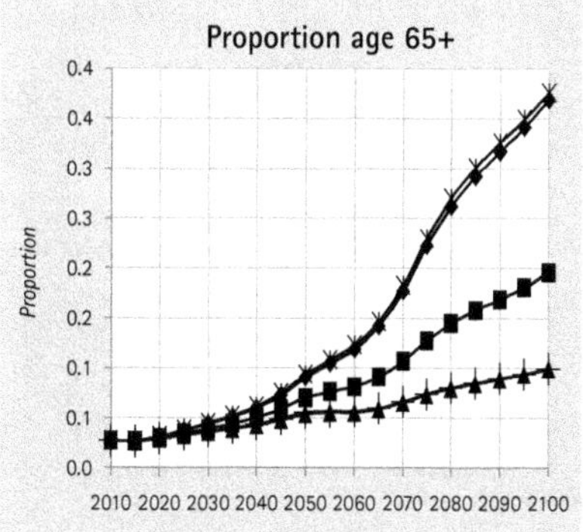

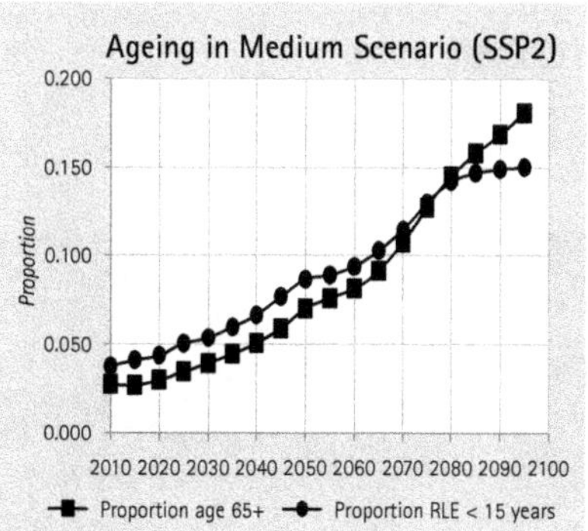

Alternative Scenarios to 2100

Projection Results by Scenario (SSP1–5)

	2010	2020	2030	2040	2050	2075	2100
Population (in millions)							
SSP1 - Rapid development	0.73	0.88	0.98	1.06	1.09	1.05	0.89
SSP2 - Medium	0.73	0.90	1.05	1.19	1.29	1.41	1.38
SSP3 - Stalled development	0.73	0.94	1.16	1.40	1.63	2.11	2.46
SSP4 - Inequality	0.73	0.93	1.14	1.36	1.55	1.96	2.26
SSP5 - Conventional development	0.73	0.87	0.96	1.02	1.03	0.95	0.79
Proportion age 65+							
SSP1 - Rapid development	0.03	0.03	0.04	0.06	0.09	0.22	0.37
SSP2 - Medium	0.03	0.03	0.04	0.05	0.07	0.13	0.20
SSP3 - Stalled development	0.03	0.03	0.04	0.04	0.05	0.07	0.10
SSP4 - Inequality	0.03	0.03	0.04	0.04	0.06	0.07	0.10
SSP5 - Conventional development	0.03	0.03	0.04	0.06	0.09	0.23	0.38
Proportion below age 20							
SSP1 - Rapid development	0.52	0.48	0.38	0.32	0.27	0.18	0.12
SSP2 - Medium	0.52	0.50	0.43	0.39	0.35	0.26	0.21
SSP3 - Stalled development	0.52	0.52	0.48	0.45	0.42	0.35	0.32
SSP4 - Inequality	0.52	0.52	0.48	0.45	0.42	0.35	0.32
SSP5 - Conventional development	0.52	0.49	0.38	0.32	0.27	0.17	0.12
Proportion of Women age 20–39 with at least secondary education							
SSP1 - Rapid development	0.26	0.52	0.65	0.74	0.79	0.90	0.96
SSP2 - Medium	0.26	0.35	0.45	0.54	0.62	0.81	0.93
SSP3 - Stalled development	0.26	0.15	0.15	0.15	0.15	0.15	0.15
SSP4 - Inequality	0.26	0.14	0.14	0.14	0.14	0.14	0.14
SSP5 - Conventional development	0.26	0.52	0.65	0.74	0.79	0.90	0.96
Mean years of schooling, age 25+							
SSP1 - Rapid development	4.94	7.05	8.90	10.52	11.66	13.47	14.47
SSP2 - Medium	4.94	6.36	7.72	8.91	9.85	11.70	13.15
SSP3 - Stalled development	4.94	4.95	5.21	5.32	5.32	5.29	5.30
SSP4 - Inequality	4.94	4.83	4.95	5.01	4.99	5.01	5.12
SSP5 - Conventional development	4.94	7.04	8.88	10.49	11.63	13.45	14.46

Demographic Assumptions Underlying SSPs

	2010–15	2020–25	2030–35	2040–45	2050–55	2075–80	2095–2100
Total fertility rate							
SSP1 - Rapid development	4.11	2.66	1.95	1.63	1.46	1.28	1.20
SSP2 - Medium	4.51	3.44	2.76	2.36	2.08	1.77	1.63
SSP3 - Stalled development	4.82	4.39	3.78	3.30	2.96	2.50	2.38
SSP4 - Inequality	4.83	4.41	3.79	3.29	2.95	2.48	2.36
SSP5 - Conventional development	4.11	2.66	1.95	1.63	1.46	1.28	1.20
Life expectancy at birth for females (in years)							
SSP1 - Rapid development	65.72	68.10	70.38	72.77	75.53	83.11	89.19
SSP2 - Medium	62.02	63.82	65.62	67.28	69.30	74.90	79.29
SSP3 - Stalled development	65.52	65.49	66.20	66.46	66.86	68.42	70.29
SSP4 - Inequality	65.52	65.47	66.17	66.42	66.82	68.38	70.27
SSP5 - Conventional development	65.72	68.10	70.38	72.77	75.53	83.11	89.19
Migration – net flow over five years (in thousands)							
SSP1 - Rapid development	−9	−10	−12	−11	−11	−4	0
SSP2 - Medium	−9	−10	−12	−13	−13	−6	0
SSP3 - Stalled development	−7	−5	−6	−7	−7	−4	0
SSP4 - Inequality	−9	−10	−12	−14	−15	−8	0
SSP5 - Conventional development	−10	−15	−18	−18	−18	−7	0

Ageing Indicators, Medium Scenario (SSP2)

	2010	2020	2030	2040	2050	2075	2095
Median age	18.85	19.88	23.11	26.41	29.41	36.74	41.44
Propspective median age	18.85	19.02	21.44	24.05	26.33	30.80	32.40
Proportion age 65+	0.03	0.03	0.04	0.05	0.07	0.13	0.18
Proportion RLE < 15 years	0.04	0.04	0.05	0.07	0.09	0.13	0.15

Congo

Detailed Human Capital Projections to 2060

Demographic indicators, Medium Scenario (SSP2)

	2010	2020	2030	2040	2050	2060
Population (in millions)	4.04	5.07	6.08	7.04	7.85	8.50
Proportion age 65+	0.04	0.04	0.04	0.06	0.07	0.09
Proportion below age 20	0.51	0.47	0.42	0.37	0.33	0.30
	2005–10	2015–20	2025–30	2035–40	2045–50	2055–60
Total Fertility Rate	4.64	3.58	2.85	2.44	2.16	1.99
Life expectancy at birth (in years)						
Men	54.89	58.18	59.76	61.44	63.12	65.49
Women	57.16	61.18	63.42	65.48	67.38	69.78
Five-year immigration flow (in '000)	49.84	48.80	50.66	51.77	51.76	50.99
Five-year emigration flow (in '000)	0.00	0.00	0.00	0.00	0.00	0.00

Human Capital indicators, Medium Scenario (SSP2)

	2010	2020	2030	2040	2050	2060
Population age 25+: highest educational attainment						
E1 – no education	0.13	0.06	0.03	0.01	0.00	0.00
E2 – incomplete primary	0.16	0.12	0.08	0.05	0.03	0.02
E3 – primary	0.38	0.43	0.44	0.43	0.40	0.35
E4 – lower secondary	0.19	0.21	0.22	0.22	0.21	0.19
E5 – upper secondary	0.08	0.11	0.15	0.20	0.26	0.31
E6 – post-secondary	0.06	0.07	0.08	0.09	0.11	0.13
Mean years of schooling (in years)	7.19	8.17	8.95	9.59	10.16	10.71
Gender gap (population age 25+): highest educational attainment (ratio male/female)						
E1 – no education	0.29	0.27	0.29	0.37	0.49	0.62
E2 – incomplete primary	0.83	0.74	0.71	0.73	0.80	0.92
E3 – primary	0.93	0.85	0.82	0.82	0.83	0.86
E4 – lower secondary	1.46	1.23	1.11	1.03	0.98	0.95
E5 – upper secondary	2.10	1.74	1.47	1.29	1.18	1.12
E6 – post-secondary	3.85	2.93	2.29	1.83	1.52	1.30
Mean years of schooling (male minus female)	2.35	1.75	1.31	0.97	0.73	0.51
Women age 20–39: highest educational attainment						
E1 – no education	0.04	0.01	0.00	0.00	0.00	0.00
E2 – incomplete primary	0.18	0.11	0.09	0.06	0.05	0.03
E3 – primary	0.49	0.49	0.45	0.39	0.32	0.25
E4 – lower secondary	0.21	0.24	0.26	0.26	0.27	0.27
E5 – upper secondary	0.06	0.10	0.15	0.21	0.28	0.34
E6 – post-secondary	0.02	0.03	0.05	0.07	0.09	0.12
Mean years of schooling (in years)	7.40	8.26	8.94	9.62	10.30	11.00

Education scenarios

GET: global education trend scenario (medium assumption also used for SSP2)

CER: constant enrolment rates scenario (assumption of no future improvements)

FT: Fast track scenario (assumption of education expansion according to fastest historical experience)

Pyramids by Education, Medium Scenario

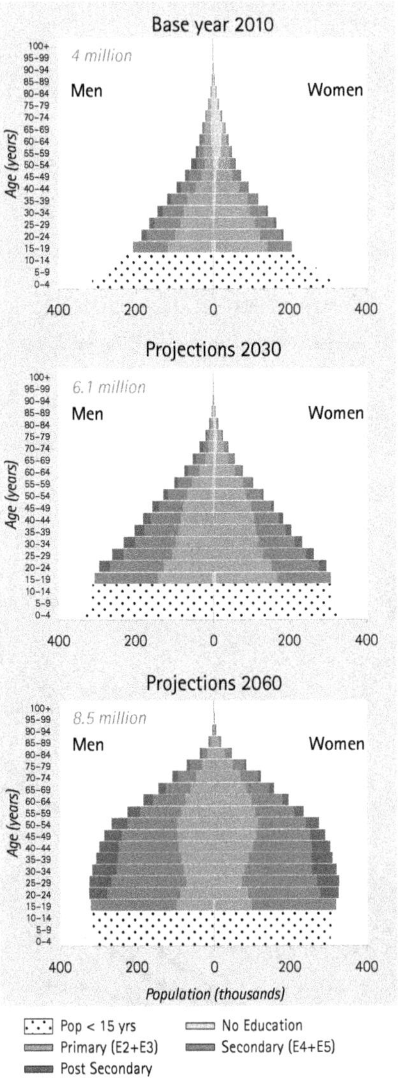

Population Size by Educational Attainment According to Three Education Scenarios: GET, CER, and FT

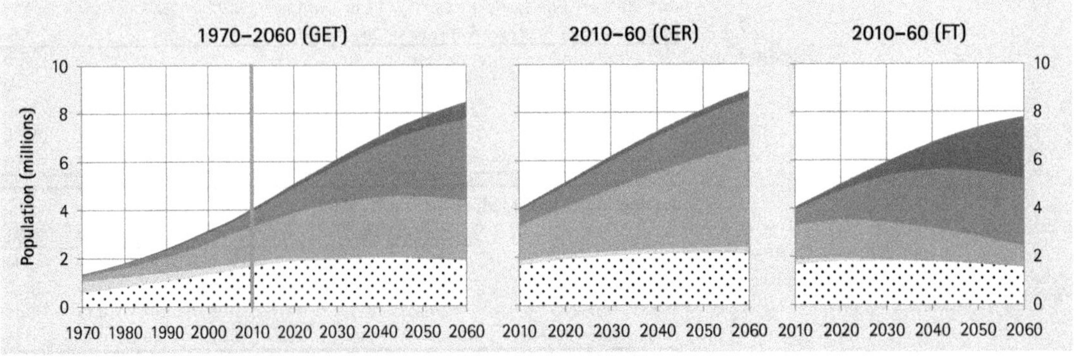

Congo (Continued)

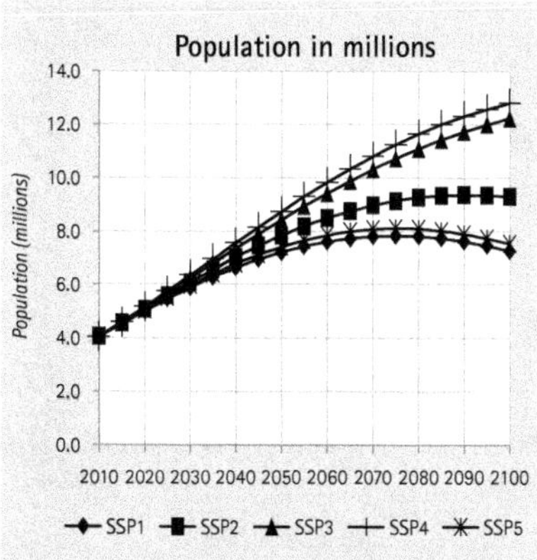

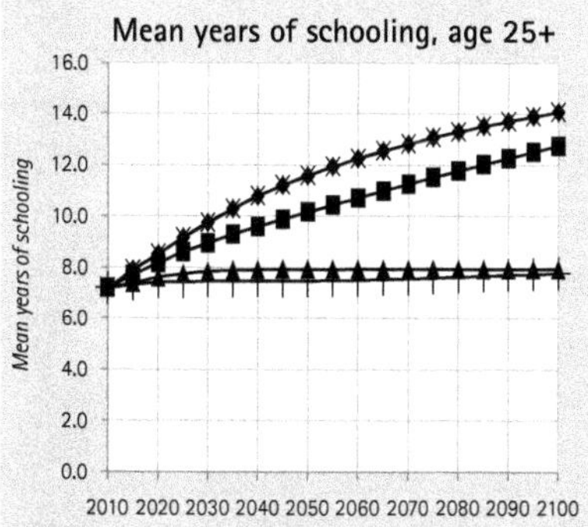

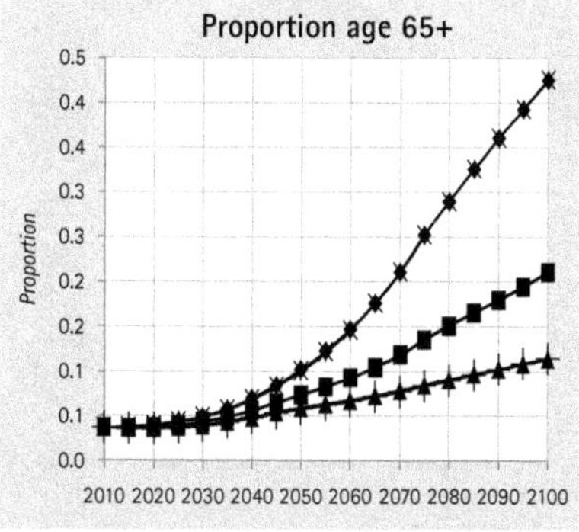

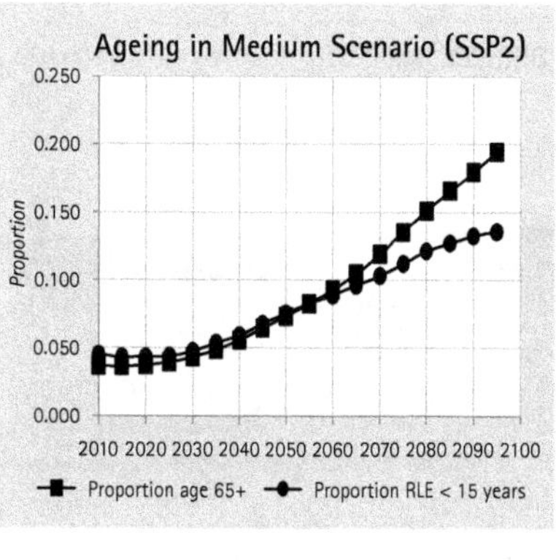

Alternative Scenarios to 2100

Projection Results by Scenario (SSP1–5)

	2010	2020	2030	2040	2050	2075	2100
Population (in millions)							
SSP1 - Rapid development	4.04	5.00	5.87	6.64	7.22	7.84	7.27
SSP2 - Medium	4.04	5.07	6.08	7.04	7.85	9.15	9.30
SSP3 - Stalled development	4.04	5.12	6.25	7.36	8.44	10.72	12.23
SSP4 - Inequality	4.04	5.16	6.37	7.57	8.74	11.24	12.80
SSP5 - Conventional development	4.04	5.03	5.96	6.79	7.42	8.12	7.54
Proportion age 65+							
SSP1 - Rapid development	0.04	0.04	0.05	0.07	0.10	0.25	0.42
SSP2 - Medium	0.04	0.04	0.04	0.06	0.07	0.14	0.21
SSP3 - Stalled development	0.04	0.04	0.04	0.05	0.06	0.08	0.11
SSP4 - Inequality	0.04	0.04	0.04	0.05	0.06	0.08	0.11
SSP5 - Conventional development	0.04	0.04	0.05	0.07	0.10	0.25	0.43
Proportion below age 20							
SSP1 - Rapid development	0.51	0.46	0.38	0.31	0.26	0.17	0.11
SSP2 - Medium	0.51	0.47	0.42	0.37	0.33	0.26	0.21
SSP3 - Stalled development	0.51	0.49	0.46	0.43	0.40	0.34	0.32
SSP4 - Inequality	0.51	0.49	0.46	0.43	0.40	0.34	0.31
SSP5 - Conventional development	0.51	0.46	0.38	0.31	0.26	0.17	0.11
Proportion of Women age 20–39 with at least secondary education							
SSP1 - Rapid development	0.29	0.49	0.63	0.73	0.80	0.91	0.96
SSP2 - Medium	0.29	0.38	0.46	0.54	0.63	0.82	0.94
SSP3 - Stalled development	0.29	0.26	0.26	0.26	0.26	0.26	0.26
SSP4 - Inequality	0.29	0.25	0.24	0.24	0.24	0.24	0.24
SSP5 - Conventional development	0.29	0.49	0.63	0.73	0.80	0.91	0.96
Mean years of schooling, age 25+							
SSP1 - Rapid development	7.19	8.52	9.73	10.77	11.57	13.06	14.05
SSP2 - Medium	7.19	8.17	8.95	9.59	10.16	11.51	12.73
SSP3 - Stalled development	7.19	7.60	7.84	7.91	7.93	7.94	7.95
SSP4 - Inequality	7.19	7.42	7.46	7.48	7.48	7.60	7.77
SSP5 - Conventional development	7.19	8.52	9.74	10.78	11.58	13.07	14.05

Demographic Assumptions Underlying SSPs

	2010–15	2020–25	2030–35	2040–45	2050–55	2075–80	2095–2100
Total fertility rate							
SSP1 - Rapid development	3.78	2.61	1.96	1.64	1.47	1.30	1.21
SSP2 - Medium	4.08	3.14	2.63	2.26	2.08	1.81	1.66
SSP3 - Stalled development	4.32	3.91	3.43	3.05	2.82	2.52	2.37
SSP4 - Inequality	4.34	3.96	3.46	3.06	2.81	2.48	2.33
SSP5 - Conventional development	3.78	2.61	1.96	1.64	1.47	1.30	1.21
Life expectancy at birth for females (in years)							
SSP1 - Rapid development	63.89	69.58	73.81	77.64	81.19	89.58	96.45
SSP2 - Medium	59.28	62.28	64.48	66.42	68.58	74.82	79.81
SSP3 - Stalled development	61.08	59.94	60.77	61.49	62.26	64.82	67.50
SSP4 - Inequality	61.08	59.90	60.71	61.42	62.18	64.76	67.46
SSP5 - Conventional development	63.89	69.58	73.81	77.64	81.19	89.58	96.45
Migration – net flow over five years (in thousands)							
SSP1 - Rapid development	46	49	49	46	41	15	0
SSP2 - Medium	48	50	52	52	51	25	0
SSP3 - Stalled development	38	24	27	30	34	23	0
SSP4 - Inequality	46	48	51	57	63	41	0
SSP5 - Conventional development	54	72	71	65	57	20	0

Ageing Indicators, Medium Scenario (SSP2)

	2010	2020	2030	2040	2050	2075	2095
Median age	19.58	21.40	24.15	27.17	30.07	36.78	41.61
Propspective median age	19.58	19.83	21.47	23.54	25.59	28.31	29.36
Proportion age 65+	0.04	0.04	0.04	0.06	0.07	0.14	0.19
Proportion RLE < 15 years	0.05	0.04	0.05	0.06	0.08	0.11	0.14

Costa Rica

Detailed Human Capital Projections to 2060

Demographic indicators, Medium Scenario (SSP2)

	2010	2020	2030	2040	2050	2060
Population (in millions)	4.66	5.34	5.96	6.47	6.85	7.12
Proportion age 65+	0.07	0.09	0.14	0.17	0.22	0.27
Proportion below age 20	0.34	0.28	0.25	0.22	0.20	0.19
	2005–10	2015–20	2025–30	2035–40	2045–50	2055–60
Total Fertility Rate	1.92	1.74	1.73	1.73	1.71	1.68
Life expectancy at birth (in years)						
Men	76.51	78.29	80.13	81.69	83.29	85.31
Women	81.36	83.09	84.91	86.51	88.19	90.29
Five-year immigration flow (in '000)	119.09	116.57	121.01	123.65	123.59	121.74
Five-year emigration flow (in '000)	43.49	33.90	33.33	32.39	31.50	30.55

Human Capital indicators, Medium Scenario (SSP2)

	2010	2020	2030	2040	2050	2060
Population age 25+: highest educational attainment						
E1 - no education	0.04	0.03	0.02	0.01	0.01	0.00
E2 - incomplete primary	0.16	0.11	0.07	0.05	0.03	0.02
E3 - primary	0.39	0.39	0.37	0.35	0.31	0.28
E4 - lower secondary	0.10	0.11	0.11	0.11	0.10	0.09
E5 - upper secondary	0.14	0.18	0.21	0.24	0.27	0.30
E6 - post-secondary	0.17	0.19	0.22	0.24	0.27	0.30
Mean years of schooling (in years)	8.10	8.76	9.30	9.78	10.24	10.69
Gender gap (population age 25+): highest educational attainment (ratio male/female)						
E1 - no education	1.06	1.06	1.09	1.12	1.14	1.14
E2 - incomplete primary	0.93	0.96	0.97	0.99	0.99	0.99
E3 - primary	1.05	1.06	1.07	1.07	1.07	1.05
E4 - lower secondary	1.00	1.01	1.03	1.03	1.03	1.03
E5 - upper secondary	0.92	0.92	0.93	0.95	0.97	0.98
E6 - post-secondary	0.99	0.96	0.94	0.94	0.95	0.97
Mean years of schooling (male minus female)	−0.04	−0.12	−0.16	−0.18	−0.16	−0.11
Women age 20–39: highest educational attainment						
E1 - no education	0.01	0.01	0.00	0.00	0.00	0.00
E2 - incomplete primary	0.09	0.05	0.03	0.02	0.01	0.01
E3 - primary	0.37	0.34	0.29	0.23	0.18	0.14
E4 - lower secondary	0.12	0.12	0.11	0.10	0.09	0.08
E5 - upper secondary	0.20	0.24	0.28	0.32	0.35	0.37
E6 - post-secondary	0.21	0.24	0.28	0.33	0.36	0.40
Mean years of schooling (in years)	9.20	9.89	10.48	11.00	11.45	11.82

Education scenarios

GET: global education trend scenario (medium assumption also used for SSP2)

CER: constant enrolment rates scenario (assumption of no future improvements)

FT: Fast track scenario (assumption of education expansion according to fastest historical experience)

Pyramids by Education, Medium Scenario

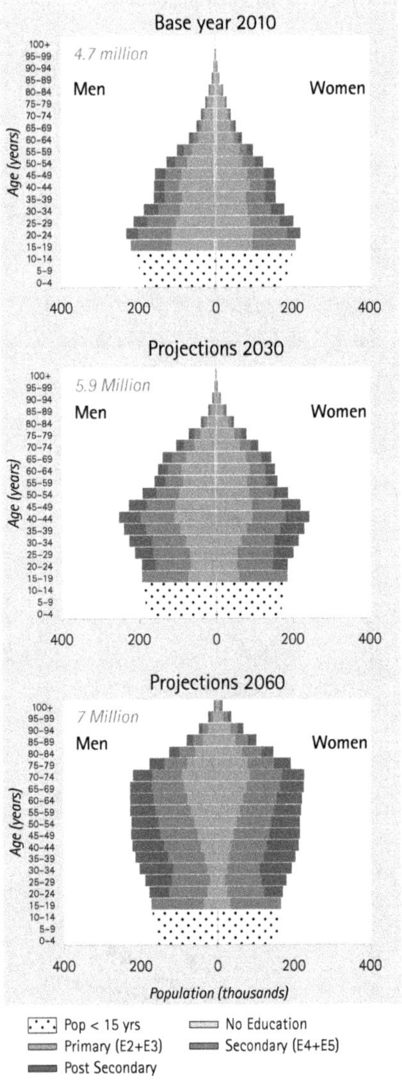

Population Size by Educational Attainment According to Three Education Scenarios: GET, CER, and FT

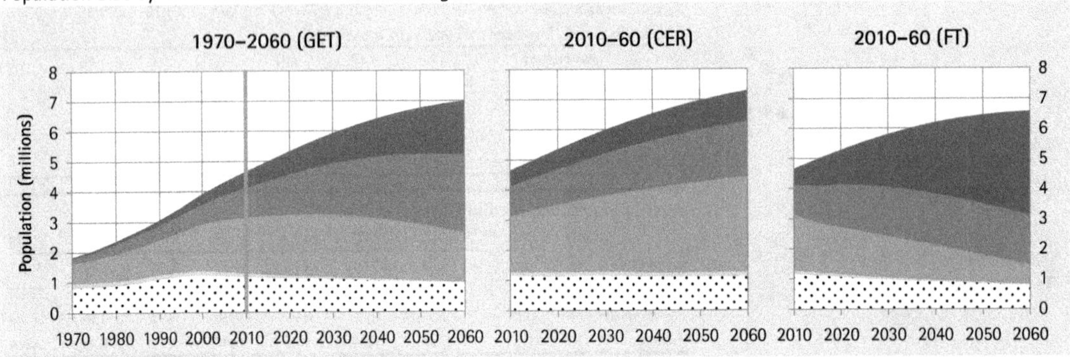

Costa Rica (Continued)

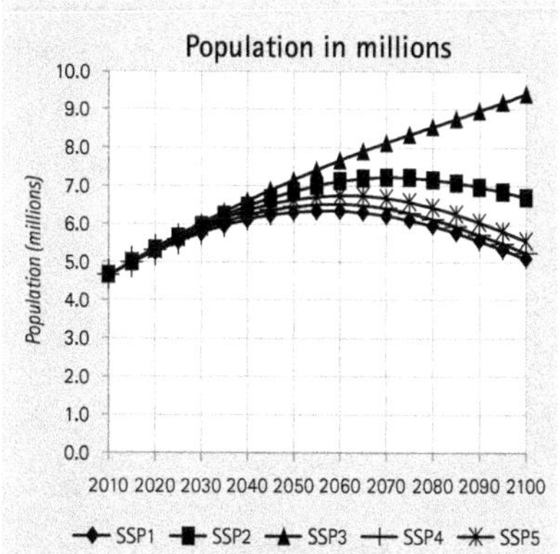

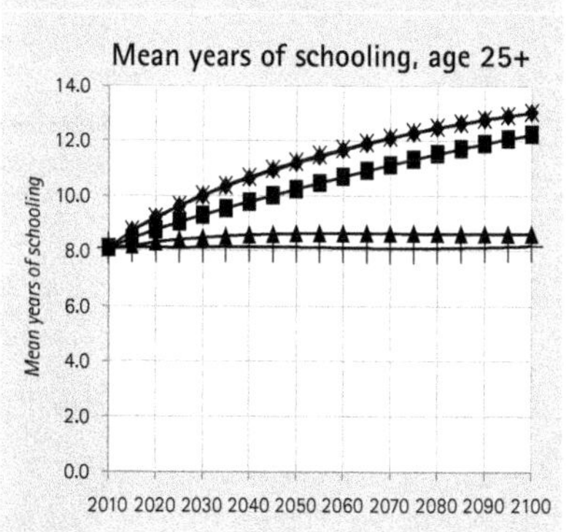

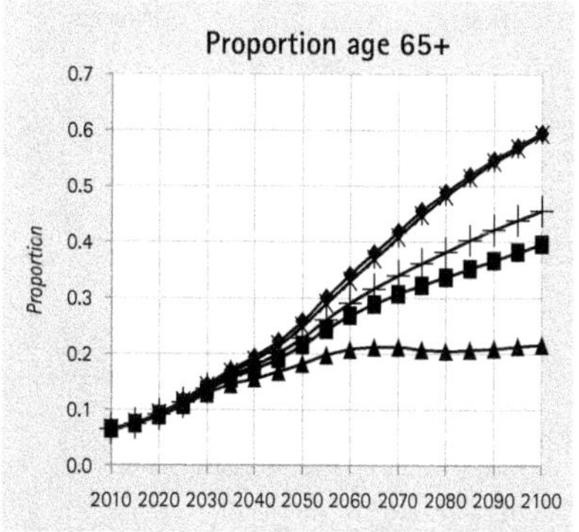

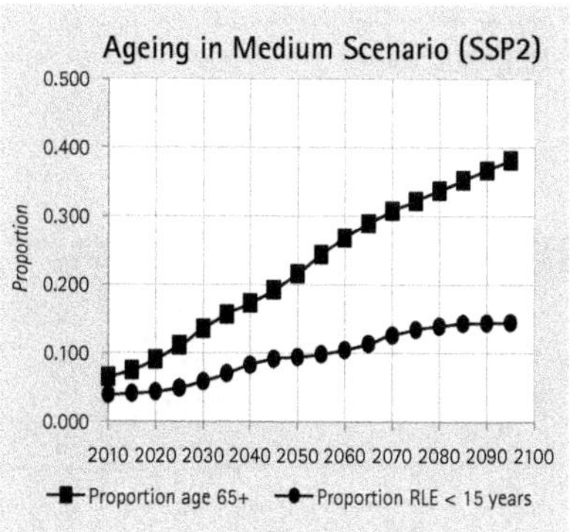

Alternative Scenarios to 2100

Projection Results by Scenario (SSP1–5)

	2010	2020	2030	2040	2050	2075	2100
Population (in millions)							
SSP1 - Rapid development	4.66	5.27	5.76	6.12	6.30	6.10	5.09
SSP2 - Medium	4.66	5.34	5.96	6.47	6.85	7.21	6.70
SSP3 - Stalled development	4.66	5.37	6.03	6.61	7.15	8.34	9.41
SSP4 - Inequality	4.66	5.31	5.85	6.23	6.45	6.29	5.25
SSP5 - Conventional development	4.66	5.32	5.90	6.35	6.63	6.57	5.56
Proportion age 65+							
SSP1 - Rapid development	0.07	0.09	0.15	0.19	0.26	0.46	0.59
SSP2 - Medium	0.07	0.09	0.14	0.17	0.22	0.32	0.40
SSP3 - Stalled development	0.07	0.09	0.13	0.16	0.18	0.21	0.22
SSP4 - Inequality	0.07	0.09	0.14	0.18	0.23	0.36	0.46
SSP5 - Conventional development	0.07	0.09	0.14	0.19	0.25	0.45	0.59
Proportion below age 20							
SSP1 - Rapid development	0.34	0.27	0.21	0.17	0.15	0.10	0.07
SSP2 - Medium	0.34	0.28	0.25	0.22	0.20	0.17	0.15
SSP3 - Stalled development	0.34	0.29	0.28	0.27	0.26	0.26	0.26
SSP4 - Inequality	0.34	0.28	0.23	0.20	0.17	0.13	0.11
SSP5 - Conventional development	0.34	0.27	0.21	0.18	0.15	0.10	0.07
Proportion of Women age 20–39 with at least secondary education							
SSP1 - Rapid development	0.53	0.73	0.81	0.86	0.89	0.95	0.98
SSP2 - Medium	0.53	0.60	0.68	0.75	0.80	0.91	0.97
SSP3 - Stalled development	0.53	0.47	0.47	0.47	0.47	0.47	0.47
SSP4 - Inequality	0.53	0.44	0.42	0.42	0.42	0.42	0.42
SSP5 - Conventional development	0.53	0.73	0.81	0.86	0.89	0.95	0.98
Mean years of schooling, age 25+							
SSP1 - Rapid development	8.10	9.20	9.99	10.63	11.18	12.28	13.02
SSP2 - Medium	8.10	8.76	9.30	9.78	10.24	11.32	12.23
SSP3 - Stalled development	8.10	8.31	8.49	8.59	8.63	8.63	8.62
SSP4 - Inequality	8.10	8.14	8.14	8.15	8.14	8.10	8.19
SSP5 - Conventional development	8.10	9.20	10.01	10.67	11.22	12.30	13.03

Demographic Assumptions Underlying SSPs

	2010–15	2020–25	2030–35	2040–45	2050–55	2075–80	2095–2100
Total fertility rate							
SSP1 - Rapid development	1.67	1.39	1.29	1.26	1.23	1.17	1.20
SSP2 - Medium	1.81	1.72	1.72	1.71	1.70	1.59	1.61
SSP3 - Stalled development	1.92	2.11	2.23	2.28	2.30	2.25	2.33
SSP4 - Inequality	1.74	1.57	1.45	1.41	1.38	1.34	1.39
SSP5 - Conventional development	1.67	1.39	1.29	1.26	1.23	1.17	1.20
Life expectancy at birth for females (in years)							
SSP1 - Rapid development	83.30	85.88	88.49	91.06	94.02	101.99	108.33
SSP2 - Medium	82.19	84.01	85.71	87.31	89.29	94.60	98.81
SSP3 - Stalled development	82.41	83.03	83.70	84.27	85.04	87.30	89.13
SSP4 - Inequality	82.86	84.48	86.05	87.54	89.38	94.10	97.95
SSP5 - Conventional development	83.30	85.88	88.49	91.06	94.02	101.99	108.33
Migration – net flow over five years (in thousands)							
SSP1 - Rapid development	77	84	84	78	68	20	0
SSP2 - Medium	78	84	88	90	90	36	0
SSP3 - Stalled development	64	43	48	57	65	40	0
SSP4 - Inequality	77	84	88	89	87	34	0
SSP5 - Conventional development	90	125	125	113	98	27	0

Ageing Indicators, Medium Scenario (SSP2)

	2010	2020	2030	2040	2050	2075	2095
Median age	28.38	32.81	37.28	41.14	44.24	50.46	55.09
Propspective median age	28.38	31.18	34.11	36.65	38.01	39.51	40.29
Proportion age 65+	0.07	0.09	0.14	0.17	0.22	0.32	0.38
Proportion RLE < 15 years	0.04	0.04	0.06	0.08	0.09	0.13	0.14

Côte d'Ivoire

Detailed Human Capital Projections to 2060

Demographic indicators, Medium Scenario (SSP2)	2010	2020	2030	2040	2050	2060
Population (in millions)	19.74	23.29	26.36	28.91	30.67	31.67
Proportion age 65+	0.04	0.04	0.05	0.05	0.07	0.10
Proportion below age 20	0.52	0.48	0.43	0.38	0.34	0.30
	2005–10	2015–20	2025–30	2035–40	2045–50	2055–60
Total Fertility Rate	4.65	3.58	2.85	2.44	2.15	1.98
Life expectancy at birth (in years)						
Men	52.14	57.81	59.75	61.34	63.07	65.47
Women	54.05	60.58	63.18	65.32	67.22	69.62
Five-year immigration flow (in '000)	207.14	202.6	210.3	214.8	214.6	211.4
Five-year emigration flow (in '000)	564.97	521.0	603.3	651.0	661.3	652.9

Human Capital indicators, Medium Scenario (SSP2)	2010	2020	2030	2040	2050	2060
Population age 25+: highest educational attainment						
E1 - no education	0.53	0.41	0.31	0.22	0.16	0.11
E2 - incomplete primary	0.19	0.19	0.17	0.14	0.11	0.08
E3 - primary	0.12	0.16	0.20	0.23	0.24	0.24
E4 - lower secondary	0.08	0.11	0.15	0.17	0.19	0.20
E5 - upper secondary	0.03	0.05	0.08	0.12	0.17	0.21
E6 - post-secondary	0.05	0.07	0.09	0.12	0.14	0.17
Mean years of schooling (in years)	3.41	4.71	6.10	7.40	8.56	9.58
Gender gap (population age 25+): highest educational attainment (ratio male/female)						
E1 - no education	0.74	0.72	0.71	0.71	0.72	0.74
E2 - incomplete primary	1.06	1.01	0.97	0.96	0.96	0.97
E3 - primary	1.32	1.10	0.99	0.95	0.94	0.94
E4 - lower secondary	1.90	1.40	1.13	1.01	0.98	0.98
E5 - upper secondary	3.91	2.95	2.17	1.69	1.39	1.20
E6 - post-secondary	2.21	1.67	1.42	1.26	1.15	1.08
Mean years of schooling (male minus female)	1.75	1.70	1.49	1.18	0.88	0.60
Women age 20–39: highest educational attainment						
E1 - no education	0.45	0.33	0.21	0.12	0.06	0.03
E2 - incomplete primary	0.24	0.22	0.19	0.15	0.11	0.07
E3 - primary	0.16	0.21	0.25	0.27	0.25	0.21
E4 - lower secondary	0.08	0.14	0.19	0.24	0.26	0.27
E5 - upper secondary	0.02	0.05	0.08	0.13	0.19	0.25
E6 - post-secondary	0.04	0.06	0.08	0.10	0.13	0.17
Mean years of schooling (in years)	3.68	5.19	6.82	8.30	9.59	10.67

Education scenarios

GET: global education trend scenario (medium assumption also used for SSP2)

CER: constant enrolment rates scenario (assumption of no future improvements)

FT: Fast track scenario (assumption of education expansion according to fastest historical experience)

Pyramids by Education, Medium Scenario

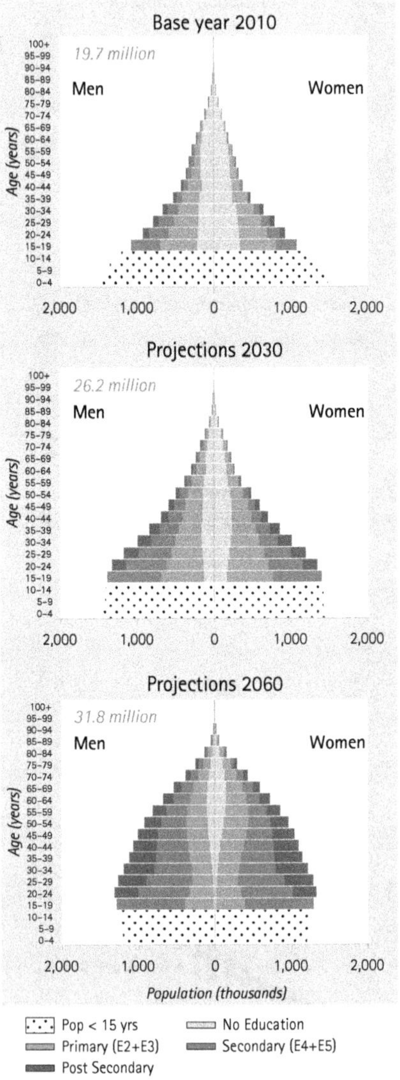

Population Size by Educational Attainment According to Three Education Scenarios: GET, CER, and FT

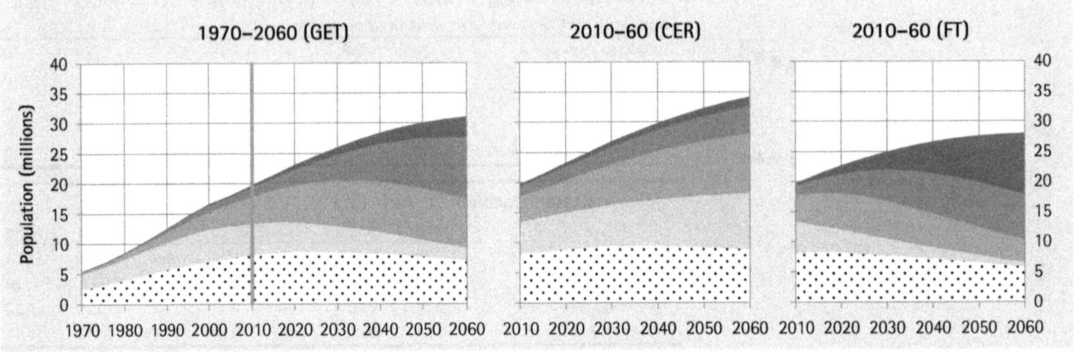

Côte d'Ivoire (Continued)

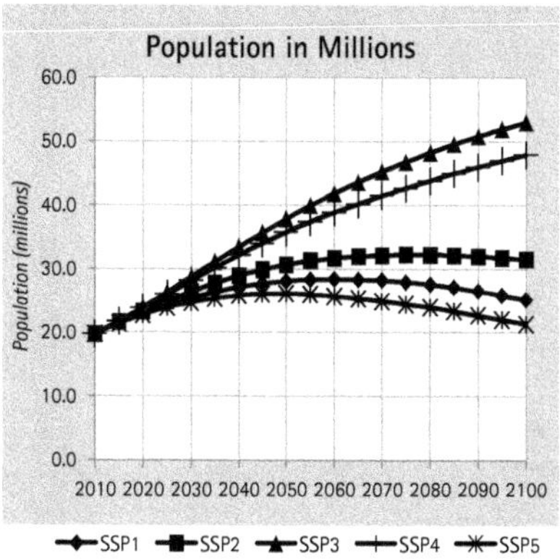

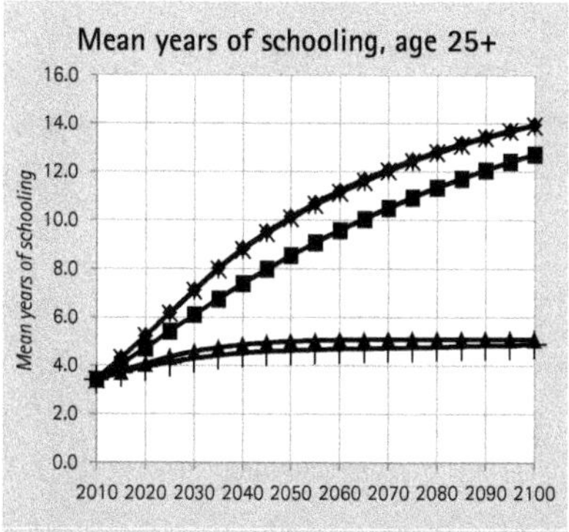

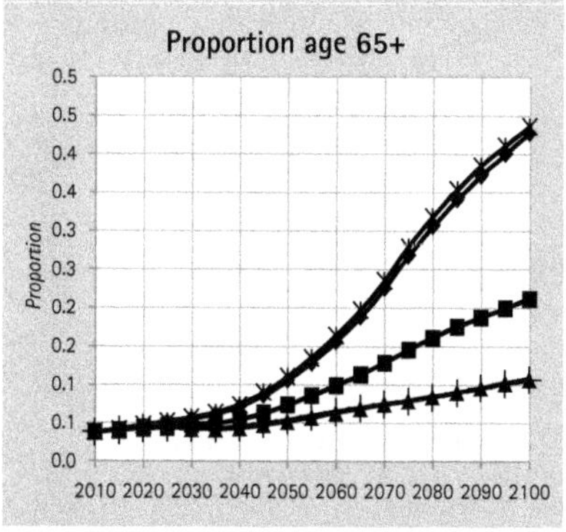

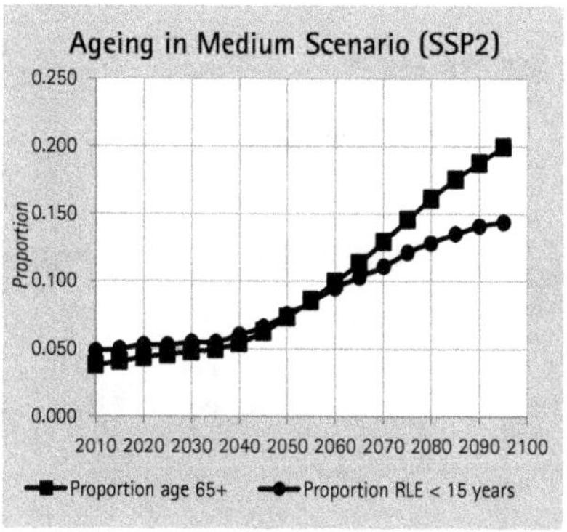

Alternative Scenarios to 2100

Projection Results by Scenario (SSP1–5)

	2010	2020	2030	2040	2050	2075	2100
Population (in millions)							
SSP1 - Rapid development	19.74	22.94	25.36	27.11	28.09	27.91	25.08
SSP2 - Medium	19.74	23.29	26.36	28.91	30.67	32.27	31.50
SSP3 - Stalled development	19.74	23.96	28.75	33.44	37.85	46.76	52.97
SSP4 - Inequality	19.74	23.80	28.11	32.13	35.76	42.66	47.88
SSP5 - Conventional development	19.74	22.74	24.67	25.80	26.10	24.45	21.32
Proportion age 65+							
SSP1 - Rapid development	0.04	0.05	0.06	0.07	0.11	0.27	0.43
SSP2 - Medium	0.04	0.04	0.05	0.05	0.07	0.15	0.21
SSP3 - Stalled development	0.04	0.04	0.04	0.04	0.05	0.08	0.11
SSP4 - Inequality	0.04	0.04	0.04	0.04	0.05	0.08	0.11
SSP5 - Conventional development	0.04	0.05	0.06	0.07	0.11	0.28	0.44
Proportion below age 20							
SSP1 - Rapid development	0.52	0.46	0.38	0.32	0.27	0.17	0.12
SSP2 - Medium	0.52	0.48	0.43	0.38	0.34	0.26	0.21
SSP3 - Stalled development	0.52	0.50	0.48	0.45	0.42	0.35	0.32
SSP4 - Inequality	0.52	0.50	0.48	0.45	0.42	0.35	0.32
SSP5 - Conventional development	0.52	0.47	0.39	0.32	0.27	0.17	0.11
Proportion of Women age 20–39 with at least secondary education							
SSP1 - Rapid development	0.15	0.31	0.46	0.60	0.70	0.84	0.91
SSP2 - Medium	0.15	0.25	0.35	0.47	0.58	0.80	0.93
SSP3 - Stalled development	0.15	0.14	0.14	0.14	0.14	0.15	0.15
SSP4 - Inequality	0.15	0.13	0.13	0.13	0.13	0.13	0.13
SSP5 - Conventional development	0.15	0.31	0.46	0.60	0.70	0.84	0.91
Mean years of schooling, age 25+							
SSP1 - Rapid development	3.41	5.21	7.13	8.83	10.16	12.49	13.94
SSP2 - Medium	3.41	4.71	6.10	7.40	8.56	10.94	12.73
SSP3 - Stalled development	3.41	4.06	4.57	4.86	5.00	5.08	5.09
SSP4 - Inequality	3.41	3.93	4.28	4.51	4.62	4.75	4.88
SSP5 - Conventional development	3.41	5.20	7.09	8.78	10.09	12.43	13.92

Demographic Assumptions Underlying SSPs

	2010–15	2020–25	2030–35	2040–45	2050–55	2075–80	2095–2100
Total fertility rate							
SSP1 - Rapid development	3.78	2.55	1.92	1.63	1.46	1.29	1.21
SSP2 - Medium	4.09	3.15	2.63	2.26	2.05	1.76	1.63
SSP3 - Stalled development	4.38	4.07	3.66	3.26	2.95	2.51	2.40
SSP4 - Inequality	4.39	4.12	3.70	3.28	2.96	2.50	2.39
SSP5 - Conventional development	3.78	2.55	1.92	1.63	1.46	1.29	1.21
Life expectancy at birth for females (in years)							
SSP1 - Rapid development	62.5	69.2	73.7	77.5	81.1	89.6	96.5
SSP2 - Medium	57.7	61.9	64.3	66.2	68.4	74.6	79.6
SSP3 - Stalled development	59.1	59.4	60.3	60.9	61.8	64.5	66.7
SSP4 - Inequality	59.1	59.3	60.3	60.8	61.7	64.5	66.7
SSP5 - Conventional development	62.5	69.2	73.7	77.5	81.1	89.6	96.5
Migration – net flow over five years (in thousands)							
SSP1 - Rapid development	-312	-354	-409	-419	-402	-139	0
SSP2 - Medium	-319	-361	-425	-450	-454	-180	0
SSP3 - Stalled development	-257	-173	-204	-224	-237	-107	0
SSP4 - Inequality	-309	-348	-416	-464	-493	-218	0
SSP5 - Conventional development	-364	-534	-627	-654	-641	-238	0

Ageing Indicators, Medium Scenario (SSP2)

	2010	2020	2030	2040	2050	2075	2095
Median age	19.10	20.87	23.58	26.59	29.75	37.02	41.69
Propspective median age	19.10	18.31	19.71	21.68	23.42	27.00	28.03
Proportion age 65+	0.04	0.04	0.05	0.05	0.07	0.15	0.20
Proportion RLE < 15 years	0.05	0.05	0.05	0.06	0.08	0.12	0.14

Croatia

Detailed Human Capital Projections to 2060

Demographic indicators, Medium Scenario (SSP2)

	2010	2020	2030	2040	2050	2060
Population (in millions)	4.40	4.32	4.21	4.08	3.93	3.76
Proportion age 65+	0.17	0.20	0.24	0.27	0.31	0.34
Proportion below age 20	0.21	0.19	0.18	0.17	0.16	0.16
	2005–10	2015–20	2025–30	2035–40	2045–50	2055–60
Total Fertility Rate	1.42	1.43	1.49	1.52	1.54	1.56
Life expectancy at birth (in years)						
Men	72.46	74.91	77.28	79.71	81.98	84.21
Women	79.49	81.81	83.91	86.01	87.99	90.01
Five-year immigration flow (in '000)	37.54	37.02	38.51	39.46	39.55	39.02
Five-year emigration flow (in '000)	27.58	17.97	15.62	14.03	12.71	11.63

Human Capital indicators, Medium Scenario (SSP2)

	2010	2020	2030	2040	2050	2060
Population age 25+: highest educational attainment						
E1 - no education	0.02	0.01	0.00	0.00	0.00	0.00
E2 - incomplete primary	0.03	0.02	0.01	0.00	0.00	0.00
E3 - primary	0.08	0.05	0.02	0.01	0.01	0.00
E4 - lower secondary	0.17	0.15	0.12	0.09	0.07	0.04
E5 - upper secondary	0.54	0.60	0.65	0.67	0.69	0.69
E6 - post-secondary	0.16	0.18	0.20	0.21	0.24	0.26
Mean years of schooling (in years)	10.79	11.49	11.98	12.32	12.58	12.81
Gender gap (population age 25+): highest educational attainment (ratio male/female)						
E1 - no education	0.26	0.29	0.41	0.53	0.60	0.68
E2 - incomplete primary	0.41	0.38	0.42	0.50	0.58	0.71
E3 - primary	0.51	0.46	0.50	0.65	0.94	1.25
E4 - lower secondary	0.74	0.75	0.76	0.79	0.85	0.93
E5 - upper secondary	1.33	1.25	1.19	1.15	1.12	1.09
E6 - post-secondary	0.97	0.83	0.76	0.73	0.75	0.80
Mean years of schooling (male minus female)	1.06	0.54	0.13	−0.11	−0.21	−0.23
Women age 20–39: highest educational attainment						
E1 - no education	0.00	0.00	0.00	0.00	0.00	0.00
E2 - incomplete primary	0.00	0.00	0.00	0.00	0.00	0.00
E3 - primary	0.01	0.00	0.00	0.00	0.00	0.00
E4 - lower secondary	0.09	0.05	0.02	0.01	0.01	0.01
E5 - upper secondary	0.71	0.73	0.73	0.72	0.70	0.70
E6 - post-secondary	0.19	0.22	0.24	0.27	0.28	0.30
Mean years of schooling (in years)	12.30	12.61	12.82	12.95	13.05	13.10

Education scenarios

GET : global education trend scenario (medium assumption also used for SSP2)

CER: constant enrolment rates scenario (assumption of no future improvements)

FT: Fast track scenario (assumption of education expansion according to fastest historical experience)

Pyramids by Education, Medium Scenario

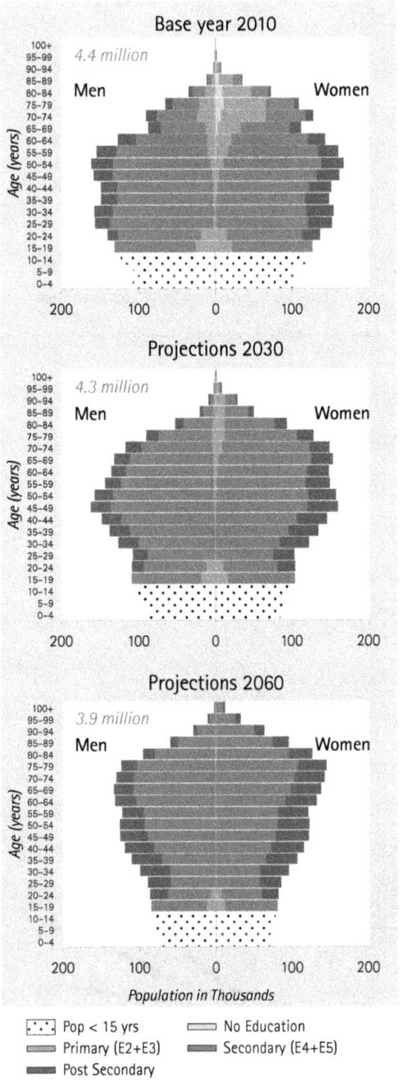

Population Size by Educational Attainment According to Three Education Scenarios: GET, CER, and FT

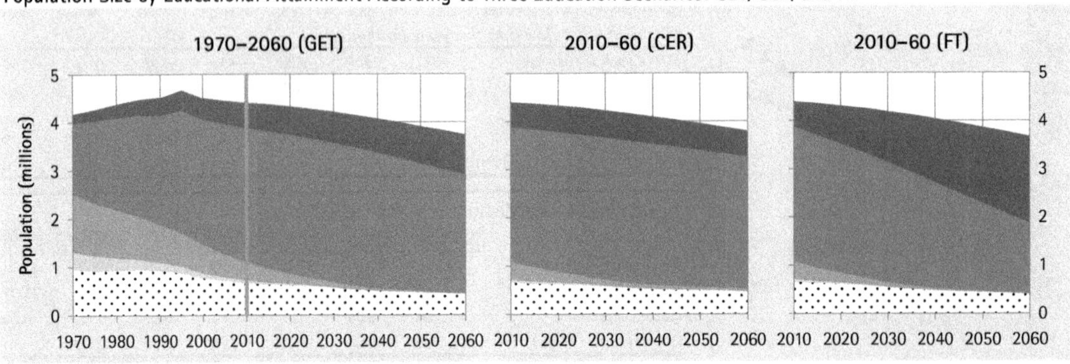

Croatia (Continued)

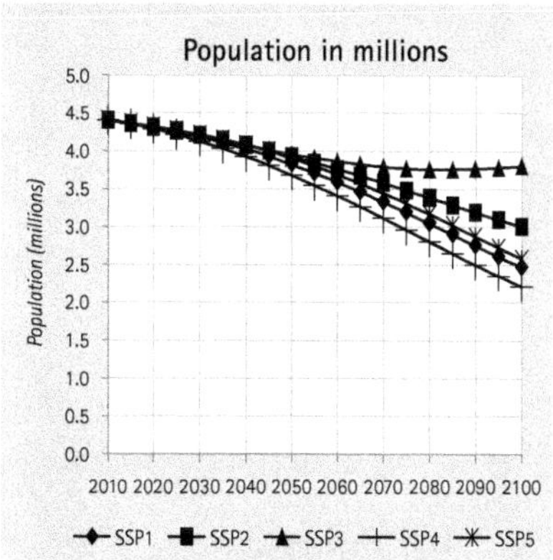

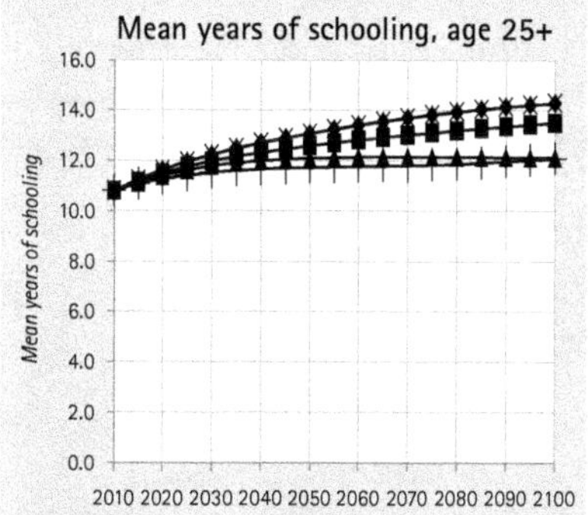

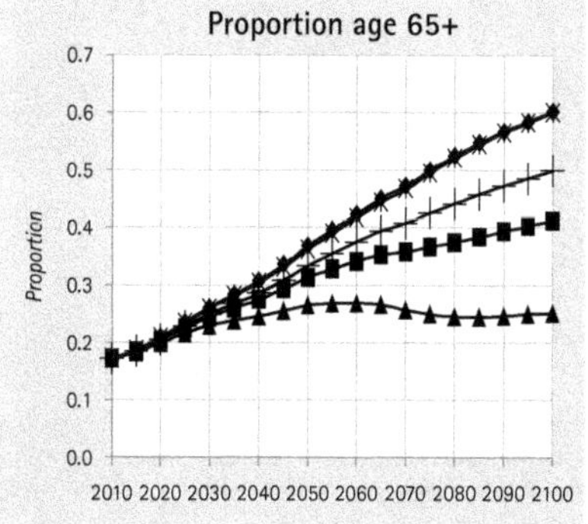

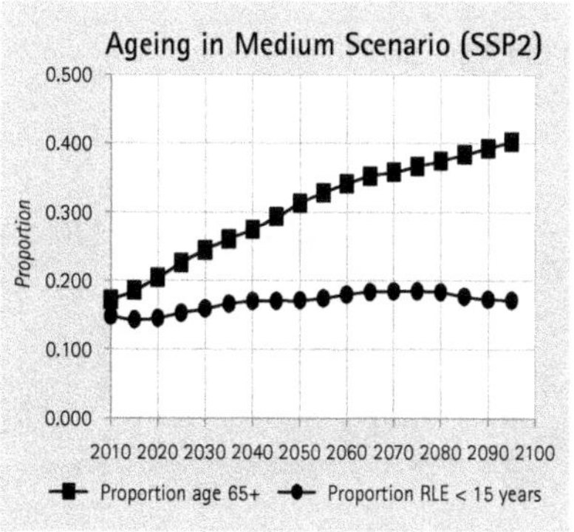

Alternative Scenarios to 2100

Projection Results by Scenario (SSP1–5)

	2010	2020	2030	2040	2050	2075	2100
Population (in millions)							
SSP1 - Rapid development	4.40	4.31	4.18	4.02	3.82	3.19	2.47
SSP2 - Medium	4.40	4.32	4.21	4.08	3.93	3.49	3.01
SSP3 - Stalled development	4.40	4.31	4.21	4.07	3.95	3.77	3.80
SSP4 - Inequality	4.40	4.29	4.12	3.92	3.68	2.96	2.21
SSP5 - Conventional development	4.40	4.32	4.21	4.08	3.91	3.31	2.58
Proportion age 65+							
SSP1 - Rapid development	0.17	0.21	0.26	0.31	0.37	0.50	0.60
SSP2 - Medium	0.17	0.20	0.24	0.27	0.31	0.37	0.41
SSP3 - Stalled development	0.17	0.20	0.23	0.25	0.27	0.25	0.25
SSP4 - Inequality	0.17	0.21	0.25	0.29	0.33	0.43	0.50
SSP5 - Conventional development	0.17	0.21	0.26	0.30	0.36	0.49	0.60
Proportion below age 20							
SSP1 - Rapid development	0.21	0.18	0.16	0.13	0.12	0.09	0.07
SSP2 - Medium	0.21	0.19	0.18	0.17	0.16	0.15	0.15
SSP3 - Stalled development	0.21	0.20	0.20	0.20	0.21	0.23	0.23
SSP4 - Inequality	0.21	0.18	0.16	0.14	0.13	0.11	0.10
SSP5 - Conventional development	0.21	0.18	0.16	0.13	0.12	0.09	0.07
Proportion of Women age 20–39 with at least secondary education							
SSP1 - Rapid development	0.99	1.00	1.00	1.00	1.00	1.00	1.00
SSP2 - Medium	0.99	0.99	1.00	1.00	1.00	1.00	1.00
SSP3 - Stalled development	0.99	0.99	0.99	0.99	0.99	0.99	0.99
SSP4 - Inequality	0.99	0.93	0.89	0.89	0.89	0.89	0.89
SSP5 - Conventional development	0.99	1.00	1.00	1.00	1.00	1.00	1.00
Mean years of schooling, age 25+							
SSP1 - Rapid development	10.79	11.62	12.23	12.69	13.07	13.81	14.28
SSP2 - Medium	10.79	11.49	11.98	12.32	12.58	13.11	13.50
SSP3 - Stalled development	10.79	11.39	11.78	11.98	12.09	12.14	12.13
SSP4 - Inequality	10.79	11.28	11.53	11.66	11.72	11.83	12.09
SSP5 - Conventional development	10.79	11.62	12.24	12.70	13.08	13.82	14.28

Demographic Assumptions Underlying SSPs

	2010–15	2020–25	2030–35	2040–45	2050–55	2075–80	2095–2100
Total fertility rate							
SSP1 - Rapid development	1.32	1.22	1.16	1.14	1.14	1.17	1.19
SSP2 - Medium	1.40	1.46	1.51	1.53	1.55	1.59	1.62
SSP3 - Stalled development	1.48	1.71	1.88	1.96	2.02	2.08	2.13
SSP4 - Inequality	1.34	1.26	1.22	1.20	1.20	1.23	1.25
SSP5 - Conventional development	1.32	1.22	1.16	1.14	1.14	1.17	1.19
Life expectancy at birth for females (in years)							
SSP1 - Rapid development	82.01	84.88	87.73	90.69	93.65	101.14	107.17
SSP2 - Medium	80.71	82.91	85.01	87.01	88.99	94.00	97.99
SSP3 - Stalled development	81.05	81.94	82.88	83.83	84.76	87.09	88.99
SSP4 - Inequality	81.54	83.42	85.32	87.24	89.12	93.78	97.67
SSP5 - Conventional development	82.01	84.88	87.73	90.69	93.65	101.14	107.17
Migration – net flow over five years (in thousands)							
SSP1 - Rapid development	15	21	23	23	22	6	0
SSP2 - Medium	15	21	24	26	27	11	0
SSP3 - Stalled development	12	11	13	16	19	11	0
SSP4 - Inequality	15	21	24	25	25	9	0
SSP5 - Conventional development	17	31	34	33	30	9	0

Ageing Indicators, Medium Scenario (SSP2)

	2010	2020	2030	2040	2050	2075	2095
Median age	41.52	43.83	46.77	49.37	51.32	54.24	56.69
Propspective median age	41.52	41.73	42.59	43.22	43.17	41.19	39.60
Proportion age 65+	0.17	0.20	0.24	0.27	0.31	0.37	0.40
Proportion RLE < 15 years	0.15	0.15	0.16	0.17	0.17	0.18	0.17

Cuba

Detailed Human Capital Projections to 2060

Demographic indicators, Medium Scenario (SSP2)

	2010	2020	2030	2040	2050	2060
Population (in millions)	11.26	11.15	10.84	10.26	9.43	8.42
Proportion age 65+	0.12	0.16	0.24	0.34	0.38	0.42
Proportion below age 20	0.24	0.20	0.17	0.15	0.13	0.12
	2005–10	2015–20	2025–30	2035–40	2045–50	2055–60
Total Fertility Rate	1.50	1.43	1.43	1.41	1.40	1.42
Life expectancy at birth (in years)						
Men	76.55	78.78	80.59	82.64	84.58	86.43
Women	80.52	82.91	84.89	87.09	89.19	91.21
Five-year immigration flow (in '000)	0.16	0.16	0.16	0.17	0.17	0.17
Five-year emigration flow (in '000)	189.72	128.63	105.36	85.93	71.25	58.42

Human Capital indicators, Medium Scenario (SSP2)

	2010	2020	2030	2040	2050	2060
Population age 25+: highest educational attainment						
E1 - no education	0.02	0.01	0.01	0.00	0.00	0.00
E2 - incomplete primary	0.06	0.04	0.02	0.01	0.01	0.00
E3 - primary	0.14	0.11	0.09	0.07	0.05	0.04
E4 - lower secondary	0.29	0.28	0.26	0.23	0.20	0.16
E5 - upper secondary	0.38	0.43	0.48	0.52	0.56	0.58
E6 - post-secondary	0.11	0.13	0.14	0.16	0.18	0.21
Mean years of schooling (in years)	10.51	11.06	11.47	11.77	12.03	12.31
Gender gap (population age 25+): highest educational attainment (ratio male/female)						
E1 - no education	0.89	0.89	0.99	1.15	1.25	1.24
E2 - incomplete primary	0.72	0.71	0.74	0.84	0.99	1.14
E3 - primary	0.85	0.87	0.90	0.96	1.04	1.12
E4 - lower secondary	1.25	1.27	1.27	1.27	1.27	1.26
E5 - upper secondary	0.98	0.98	0.98	0.99	0.99	1.00
E6 - post-secondary	0.88	0.82	0.78	0.77	0.78	0.82
Mean years of schooling (male minus female)	0.14	−0.06	−0.22	−0.33	−0.37	−0.34
Women age 20–39: highest educational attainment						
E1 - no education	0.00	0.00	0.00	0.00	0.00	0.00
E2 - incomplete primary	0.01	0.00	0.00	0.00	0.00	0.00
E3 - primary	0.06	0.04	0.03	0.02	0.01	0.01
E4 - lower secondary	0.26	0.20	0.16	0.13	0.11	0.10
E5 - upper secondary	0.54	0.59	0.61	0.62	0.62	0.61
E6 - post-secondary	0.13	0.16	0.20	0.23	0.25	0.28
Mean years of schooling (in years)	11.58	12.05	12.30	12.54	12.71	12.86

Education scenarios

GET: global education trend scenario (medium assumption also used for SSP2)

CER: constant enrolment rates scenario (assumption of no future improvements)

FT: Fast track scenario (assumption of education expansion according to fastest historical experience)

Pyramids by Education, Medium Scenario

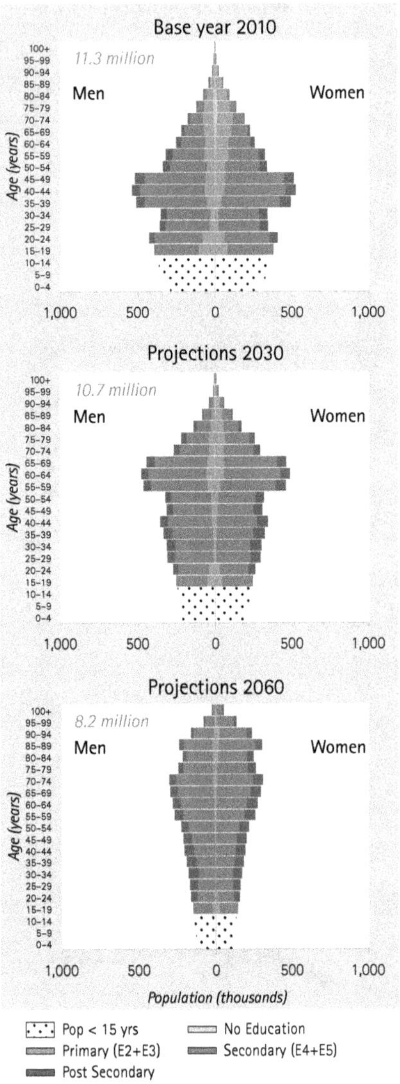

Population Size by Educational Attainment According to Three Education Scenarios: GET, CER, and FT

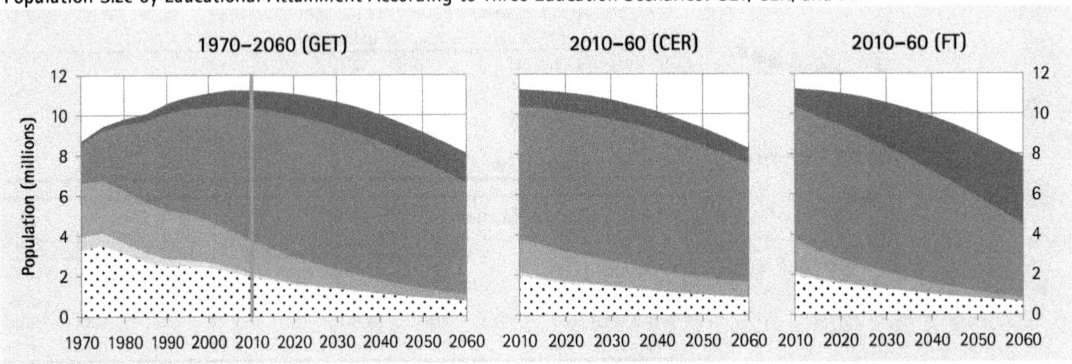

Cuba (Continued)

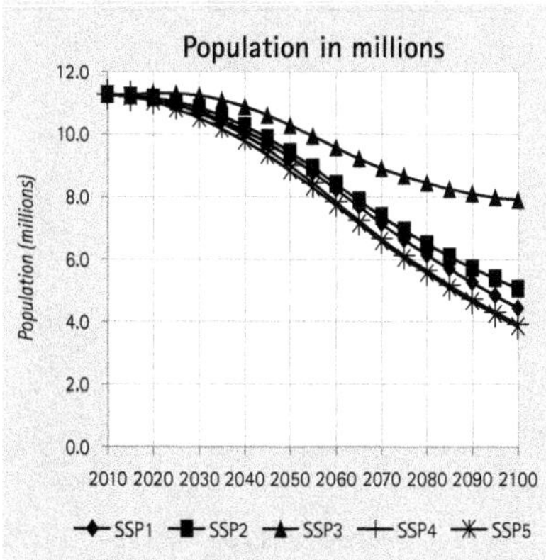

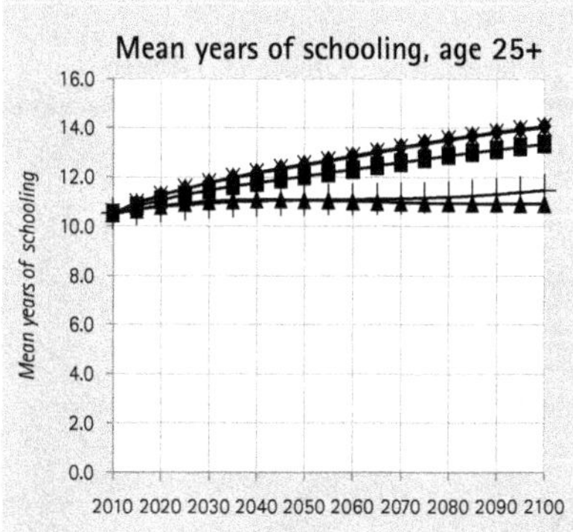

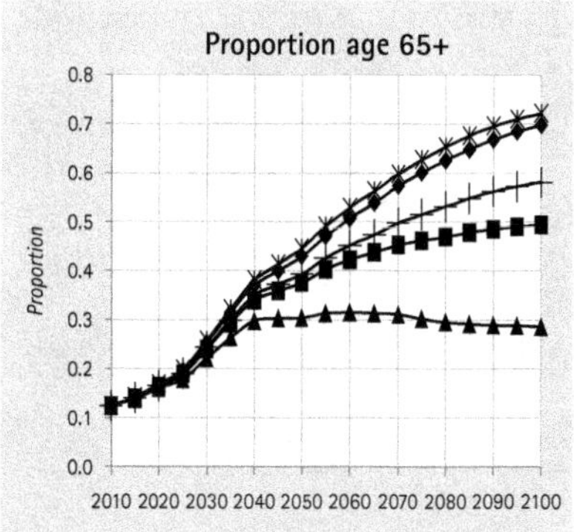

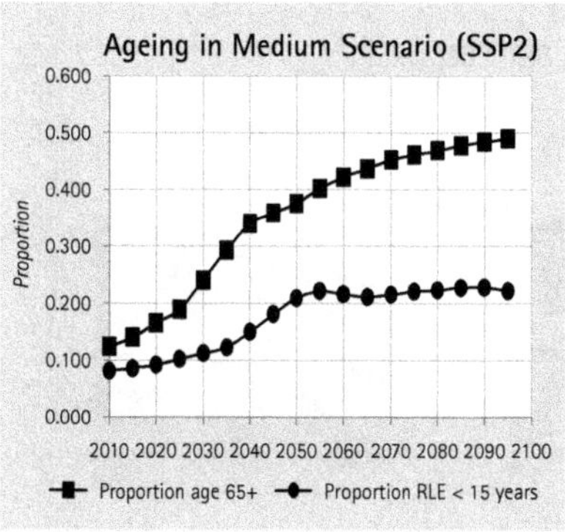

Alternative Scenarios to 2100

Projection Results by Scenario (SSP1–5)

	2010	2020	2030	2040	2050	2075	2100
Population (in millions)							
SSP1 - Rapid development	11.26	11.11	10.72	10.10	9.27	6.63	4.44
SSP2 - Medium	11.26	11.15	10.84	10.26	9.43	6.93	5.06
SSP3 - Stalled development	11.26	11.29	11.23	10.88	10.29	8.66	7.90
SSP4 - Inequality	11.26	11.11	10.68	9.97	9.01	6.13	3.92
SSP5 - Conventional development	11.26	11.03	10.51	9.77	8.84	6.04	3.86
Proportion age 65+							
SSP1 - Rapid development	0.12	0.17	0.25	0.37	0.43	0.60	0.70
SSP2 - Medium	0.12	0.16	0.24	0.34	0.38	0.46	0.49
SSP3 - Stalled development	0.12	0.16	0.22	0.30	0.30	0.30	0.29
SSP4 - Inequality	0.12	0.17	0.24	0.35	0.39	0.51	0.58
SSP5 - Conventional development	0.12	0.17	0.26	0.38	0.45	0.63	0.72
Proportion below age 20							
SSP1 - Rapid development	0.24	0.19	0.15	0.12	0.09	0.06	0.05
SSP2 - Medium	0.24	0.20	0.17	0.15	0.13	0.12	0.12
SSP3 - Stalled development	0.24	0.21	0.20	0.19	0.19	0.20	0.22
SSP4 - Inequality	0.24	0.19	0.16	0.13	0.11	0.08	0.07
SSP5 - Conventional development	0.24	0.19	0.15	0.11	0.09	0.06	0.04
Proportion of Women age 20–39 with at least secondary education							
SSP1 - Rapid development	0.93	0.97	0.98	0.99	0.99	1.00	1.00
SSP2 - Medium	0.93	0.96	0.97	0.98	0.99	0.99	1.00
SSP3 - Stalled development	0.93	0.90	0.90	0.90	0.90	0.90	0.90
SSP4 - Inequality	0.93	0.84	0.81	0.81	0.81	0.81	0.81
SSP5 - Conventional development	0.93	0.97	0.98	0.99	0.99	1.00	1.00
Mean years of schooling, age 25+							
SSP1 - Rapid development	10.51	11.25	11.77	12.18	12.52	13.39	14.05
SSP2 - Medium	10.51	11.06	11.47	11.77	12.03	12.74	13.34
SSP3 - Stalled development	10.51	10.82	11.02	11.09	11.07	10.95	10.92
SSP4 - Inequality	10.51	10.80	10.94	11.03	11.07	11.16	11.46
SSP5 - Conventional development	10.51	11.24	11.75	12.15	12.48	13.34	14.02

Demographic Assumptions Underlying SSPs

	2010–15	2020–25	2030–35	2040–45	2050–55	2075–80	2095–2100
Total fertility rate							
SSP1 - Rapid development	1.34	1.17	1.08	1.04	1.03	1.07	1.11
SSP2 - Medium	1.42	1.42	1.42	1.41	1.41	1.47	1.52
SSP3 - Stalled development	1.53	1.72	1.81	1.85	1.88	1.99	2.08
SSP4 - Inequality	1.38	1.27	1.17	1.12	1.10	1.15	1.19
SSP5 - Conventional development	1.34	1.17	1.08	1.04	1.03	1.07	1.11
Life expectancy at birth for females (in years)							
SSP1 - Rapid development	82.79	85.81	88.79	91.89	94.90	102.20	108.08
SSP2 - Medium	81.71	83.89	86.01	88.21	90.19	95.01	98.90
SSP3 - Stalled development	81.81	82.83	83.84	84.95	85.93	87.88	89.58
SSP4 - Inequality	82.27	84.31	86.30	88.43	90.35	94.75	98.47
SSP5 - Conventional development	82.79	85.81	88.79	91.89	94.90	102.20	108.08
Migration – net flow over five years (in thousands)							
SSP1 - Rapid development	−150	−116	−92	−71	−54	−14	0
SSP2 - Medium	−150	−118	−96	−79	−65	−20	0
SSP3 - Stalled development	−125	−59	−48	−42	−37	−14	0
SSP4 - Inequality	−150	−116	−91	−70	−52	−12	0
SSP5 - Conventional development	−175	−175	−140	−110	−86	−23	0

Ageing Indicators, Medium Scenario (SSP2)

	2010	2020	2030	2040	2050	2075	2095
Median age	38.49	44.25	48.08	52.42	56.49	61.87	64.18
Propspective median age	38.49	42.38	44.33	46.74	49.12	50.27	49.12
Proportion age 65+	0.12	0.16	0.24	0.34	0.38	0.46	0.49
Proportion RLE < 15 years	0.08	0.09	0.11	0.15	0.21	0.22	0.22

Cyprus

Detailed Human Capital Projections to 2060

Demographic indicators, Medium Scenario (SSP2)	2010	2020	2030	2040	2050	2060
Population (in millions)	1.10	1.24	1.37	1.49	1.59	1.67
Proportion age 65+	0.12	0.14	0.17	0.21	0.26	0.31
Proportion below age 20	0.25	0.21	0.20	0.18	0.17	0.16
	2005–10	2015–20	2025–30	2035–40	2045–50	2055–60
Total Fertility Rate	1.51	1.42	1.57	1.60	1.60	1.61
Life expectancy at birth (in years)						
Men	76.85	79.22	81.48	83.50	85.64	87.65
Women	81.08	83.69	85.89	87.89	89.99	91.99
Five-year immigration flow (in '000)	45.99	45.39	47.24	48.39	48.50	47.84
Five-year emigration flow (in '000)	1.93	1.38	1.31	1.29	1.29	1.28

Human Capital indicators, Medium Scenario (SSP2)	2010	2020	2030	2040	2050	2060
Population age 25+: highest educational attainment						
E1 - no education	0.01	0.00	0.00	0.00	0.00	0.00
E2 - incomplete primary	0.04	0.02	0.01	0.00	0.00	0.00
E3 - primary	0.16	0.11	0.07	0.04	0.02	0.01
E4 - lower secondary	0.08	0.07	0.05	0.04	0.03	0.02
E5 - upper secondary	0.37	0.39	0.39	0.38	0.35	0.32
E6 - post-secondary	0.34	0.42	0.48	0.54	0.60	0.65
Mean years of schooling (in years)	11.77	12.71	13.33	13.81	14.17	14.46
Gender gap (population age 25+): highest educational attainment (ratio male/female)						
E1 - no education	0.31	0.48	0.76	1.00	1.06	1.03
E2 - incomplete primary	0.39	0.32	0.34	0.48	0.78	0.99
E3 - primary	0.85	0.76	0.72	0.74	0.85	1.07
E4 - lower secondary	1.15	1.12	1.08	1.04	1.03	1.05
E5 - upper secondary	1.18	1.20	1.21	1.21	1.20	1.18
E6 - post-secondary	0.99	0.93	0.91	0.90	0.90	0.92
Mean years of schooling (male minus female)	0.53	0.20	−0.03	−0.17	−0.23	−0.23
Women age 20–39: highest educational attainment						
E1 - no education	0.00	0.00	0.00	0.00	0.00	0.00
E2 - incomplete primary	0.00	0.00	0.00	0.00	0.00	0.00
E3 - primary	0.02	0.01	0.00	0.00	0.00	0.00
E4 - lower secondary	0.05	0.03	0.01	0.01	0.01	0.01
E5 - upper secondary	0.42	0.37	0.34	0.33	0.31	0.31
E6 - post-secondary	0.51	0.59	0.64	0.66	0.68	0.69
Mean years of schooling (in years)	13.75	14.23	14.47	14.59	14.66	14.70

Education scenarios

GET: global education trend scenario (medium assumption also used for SSP2)

CER: constant enrolment rates scenario (assumption of no future improvements)

FT: Fast track scenario (assumption of education expansion according to fastest historical experience)

Pyramids by Education, Medium Scenario

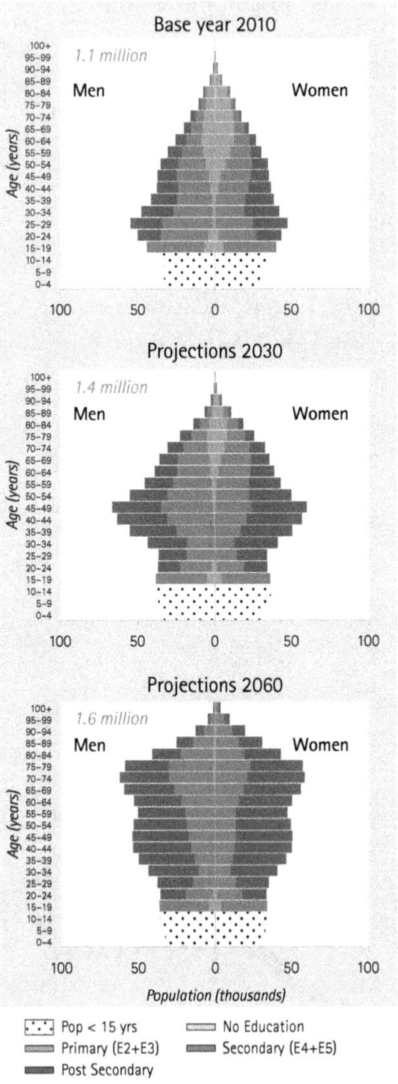

Population Size by Educational Attainment According to Three Education Scenarios: GET, CER, and FT

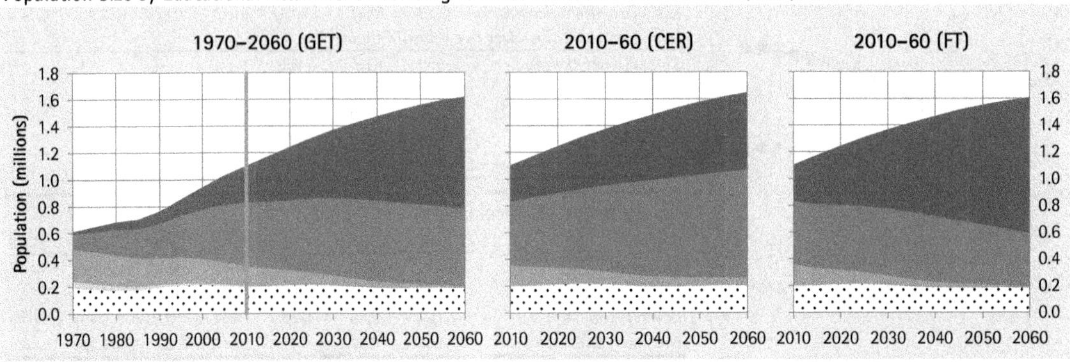

Cyprus (Continued)

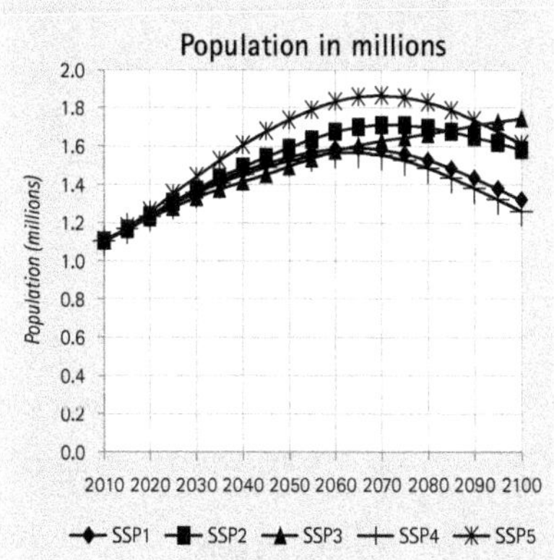

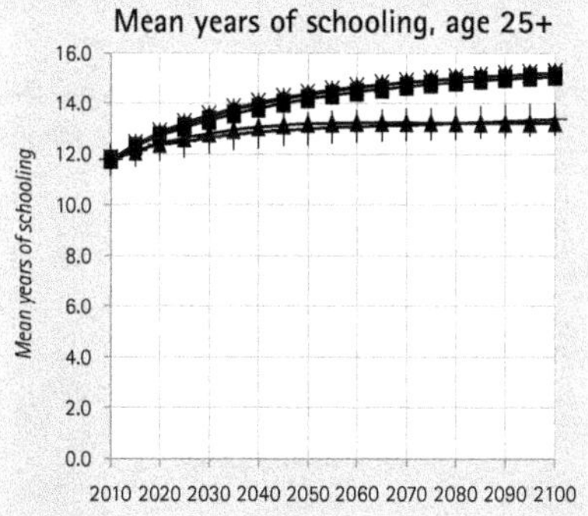

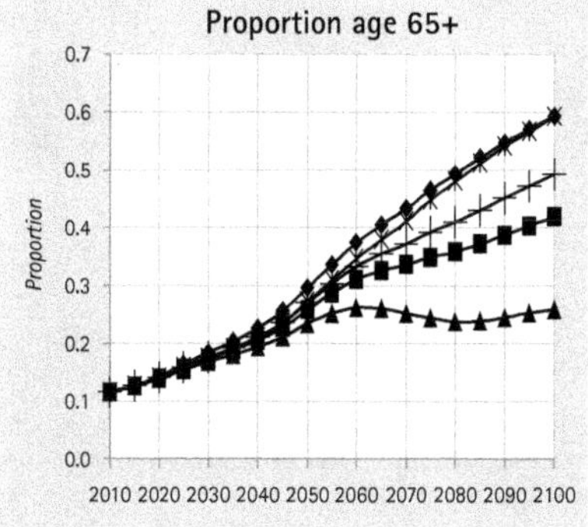

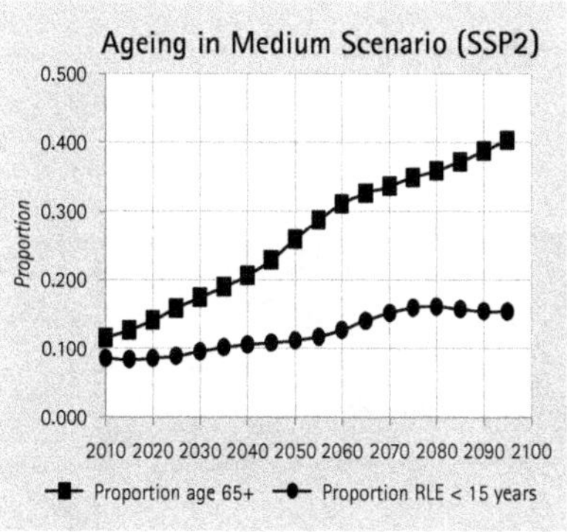

Alternative Scenarios to 2100

Projection Results by Scenario (SSP1–5)

	2010	2020	2030	2040	2050	2075	2100
Population (in millions)							
SSP1 - Rapid development	1.10	1.24	1.36	1.47	1.54	1.56	1.32
SSP2 - Medium	1.10	1.24	1.37	1.49	1.59	1.71	1.58
SSP3 - Stalled development	1.10	1.23	1.33	1.41	1.49	1.65	1.75
SSP4 - Inequality	1.10	1.23	1.36	1.45	1.52	1.52	1.26
SSP5 - Conventional development	1.10	1.26	1.44	1.61	1.74	1.85	1.61
Proportion age 65+							
SSP1 - Rapid development	0.12	0.14	0.18	0.23	0.30	0.47	0.59
SSP2 - Medium	0.12	0.14	0.17	0.21	0.26	0.35	0.42
SSP3 - Stalled development	0.12	0.14	0.17	0.19	0.23	0.24	0.26
SSP4 - Inequality	0.12	0.14	0.18	0.21	0.27	0.39	0.49
SSP5 - Conventional development	0.12	0.14	0.18	0.21	0.27	0.45	0.59
Proportion below age 20							
SSP1 - Rapid development	0.25	0.21	0.18	0.15	0.13	0.10	0.08
SSP2 - Medium	0.25	0.21	0.20	0.18	0.17	0.16	0.15
SSP3 - Stalled development	0.25	0.22	0.22	0.22	0.21	0.23	0.23
SSP4 - Inequality	0.25	0.21	0.18	0.16	0.14	0.12	0.10
SSP5 - Conventional development	0.25	0.20	0.18	0.15	0.13	0.10	0.08
Proportion of Women age 20–39 with at least secondary education							
SSP1 - Rapid development	0.98	0.99	1.00	1.00	1.00	1.00	1.00
SSP2 - Medium	0.98	0.99	1.00	1.00	1.00	1.00	1.00
SSP3 - Stalled development	0.98	0.97	0.97	0.97	0.97	0.97	0.97
SSP4 - Inequality	0.98	0.92	0.88	0.88	0.88	0.88	0.88
SSP5 - Conventional development	0.98	0.99	1.00	1.00	1.00	1.00	1.00
Mean years of schooling, age 25+							
SSP1 - Rapid development	11.77	12.81	13.47	13.97	14.34	14.92	15.22
SSP2 - Medium	11.77	12.71	13.33	13.81	14.17	14.77	15.09
SSP3 - Stalled development	11.77	12.40	12.81	13.06	13.20	13.24	13.23
SSP4 - Inequality	11.77	12.36	12.64	12.86	13.00	13.18	13.38
SSP5 - Conventional development	11.77	12.83	13.52	14.02	14.39	14.95	15.22

Demographic Assumptions Underlying SSPs

	2010–15	2020–25	2030–35	2040–45	2050–55	2075–80	2095–2100
Total fertility rate							
SSP1 - Rapid development	1.29	1.26	1.24	1.22	1.20	1.22	1.23
SSP2 - Medium	1.35	1.49	1.60	1.60	1.60	1.63	1.65
SSP3 - Stalled development	1.44	1.76	1.99	2.07	2.10	2.14	2.17
SSP4 - Inequality	1.30	1.30	1.29	1.27	1.25	1.27	1.29
SSP5 - Conventional development	1.29	1.26	1.24	1.22	1.20	1.22	1.23
Life expectancy at birth for females (in years)							
SSP1 - Rapid development	83.49	86.70	89.77	92.69	95.62	103.05	109.05
SSP2 - Medium	82.39	84.79	86.89	88.99	90.99	96.00	100.00
SSP3 - Stalled development	82.54	83.77	84.82	85.80	86.71	89.00	90.89
SSP4 - Inequality	82.97	85.25	87.28	89.29	91.16	95.75	99.61
SSP5 - Conventional development	83.49	86.70	89.77	92.69	95.62	103.05	109.05
Migration – net flow over five years (in thousands)							
SSP1 - Rapid development	42	45	45	42	37	10	0
SSP2 - Medium	41	42	43	44	43	16	0
SSP3 - Stalled development	35	22	24	26	29	15	0
SSP4 - Inequality	42	45	46	45	44	16	0
SSP5 - Conventional development	49	68	69	65	58	16	0

Ageing Indicators, Medium Scenario (SSP2)

	2010	2020	2030	2040	2050	2075	2095
Median age	34.13	37.80	41.86	45.60	48.03	52.70	56.92
Propspective median age	34.13	35.48	37.57	39.35	39.93	39.99	40.27
Proportion age 65+	0.12	0.14	0.17	0.21	0.26	0.35	0.40
Proportion RLE < 15 years	0.09	0.09	0.10	0.11	0.11	0.16	0.15

Czech Republic

Detailed Human Capital Projections to 2060

Demographic indicators, Medium Scenario (SSP2)	2010	2020	2030	2040	2050	2060
Population (in millions)	10.49	10.94	11.27	11.48	11.71	11.88
Proportion age 65+	0.15	0.20	0.22	0.25	0.30	0.32
Proportion below age 20	0.20	0.20	0.20	0.18	0.18	0.18
	2005–10	2015–20	2025–30	2035–40	2045–50	2055–60
Total Fertility Rate	1.41	1.51	1.62	1.67	1.69	1.70
Life expectancy at birth (in years)						
Men	73.77	76.40	78.93	81.43	83.77	85.64
Women	80.16	82.61	85.01	87.41	89.69	91.49
Five-year immigration flow (in '000)	240.34	191.75	199.42	204.15	204.44	201.59
Five-year emigration flow (in '000)	0.58	0.39	0.35	0.34	0.33	0.32

Human Capital indicators, Medium Scenario (SSP2)	2010	2020	2030	2040	2050	2060
Population age 25+: highest educational attainment						
E1 - no education	0.00	0.00	0.00	0.00	0.00	0.00
E2 - incomplete primary	0.00	0.00	0.00	0.00	0.00	0.00
E3 - primary	0.00	0.00	0.00	0.00	0.00	0.00
E4 - lower secondary	0.14	0.10	0.07	0.05	0.03	0.02
E5 - upper secondary	0.70	0.73	0.74	0.74	0.73	0.72
E6 - post-secondary	0.16	0.17	0.19	0.21	0.24	0.26
Mean years of schooling (in years)	12.29	12.71	13.01	13.30	13.58	13.84
Gender gap (population age 25+): highest educational attainment (ratio male/female)						
E1 - no education	0.87	0.92	0.94	0.93	0.93	0.94
E2 - incomplete primary	0.83	0.88	0.83	0.75	0.70	0.71
E3 - primary	0.99	1.16	1.21	1.20	1.20	1.24
E4 - lower secondary	0.44	0.49	0.56	0.65	0.80	0.96
E5 - upper secondary	1.14	1.10	1.08	1.06	1.05	1.04
E6 - post-secondary	1.09	0.97	0.91	0.88	0.88	0.91
Mean years of schooling (male minus female)	0.48	0.26	0.12	0.02	−0.04	−0.05
Women age 20–39: highest educational attainment						
E1 - no education	0.00	0.00	0.00	0.00	0.00	0.00
E2 - incomplete primary	0.00	0.00	0.00	0.00	0.00	0.00
E3 - primary	0.00	0.00	0.00	0.00	0.00	0.00
E4 - lower secondary	0.05	0.03	0.02	0.02	0.02	0.02
E5 - upper secondary	0.76	0.75	0.73	0.70	0.68	0.66
E6 - post-secondary	0.19	0.22	0.24	0.27	0.30	0.32
Mean years of schooling (in years)	13.18	13.82	13.83	13.97	14.09	14.18

Education scenarios

GET: global education trend scenario (medium assumption also used for SSP2)

CER: constant enrolment rates scenario (assumption of no future improvements)

FT: Fast track scenario (assumption of education expansion according to fastest historical experience)

Pyramids by Education, Medium Scenario

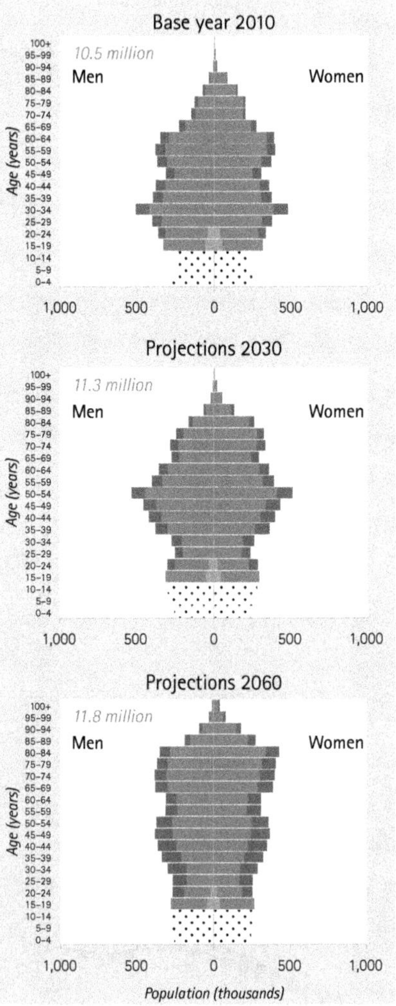

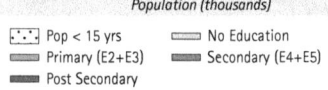

Population Size by Educational Attainment According to Three Education Scenarios: GET, CER, and FT

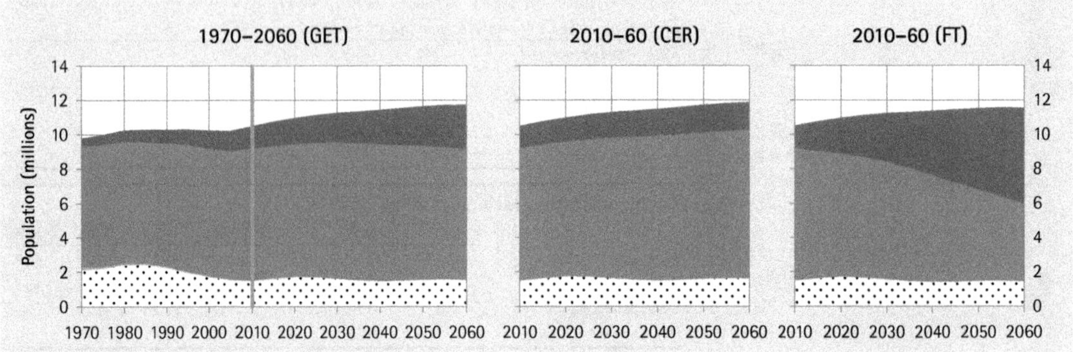

Czech Republic (Continued)

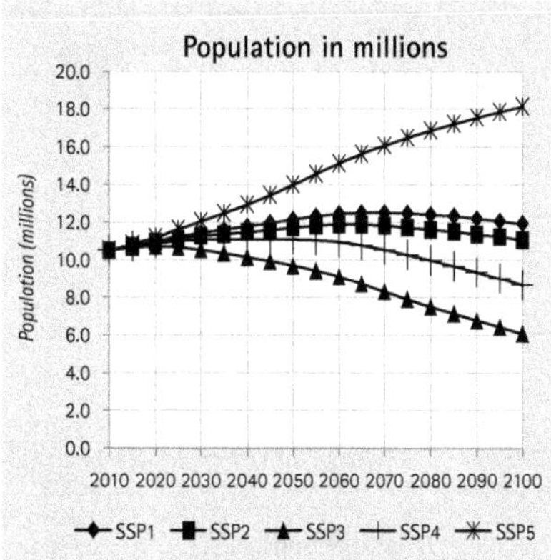

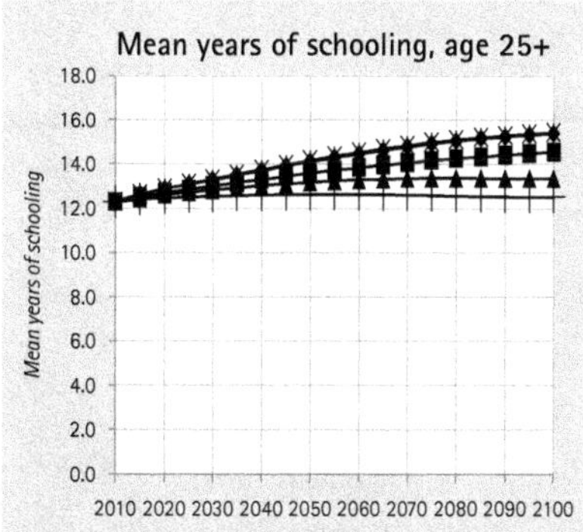

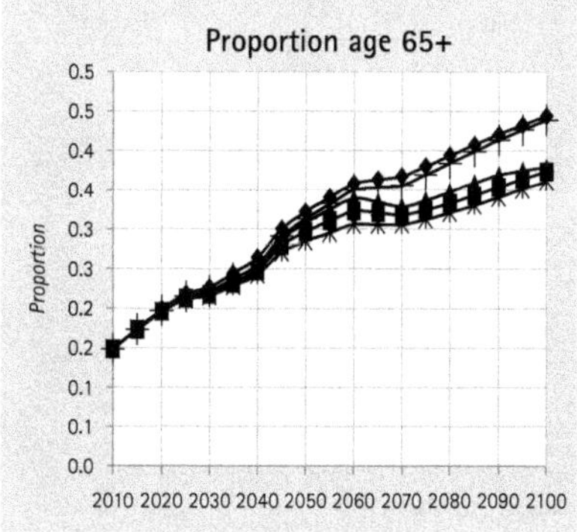

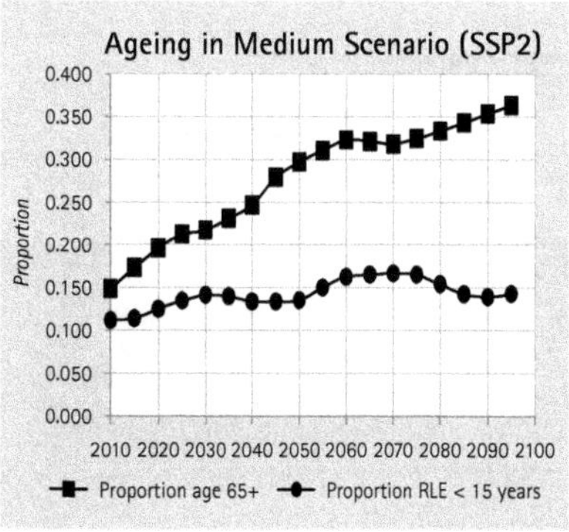

Alternative Scenarios to 2100

Projection Results by Scenario (SSP1–5)

	2010	2020	2030	2040	2050	2075	2100
Population (in millions)							
SSP1 - Rapid development	10.49	11.00	11.43	11.78	12.15	12.48	11.93
SSP2 - Medium	10.49	10.94	11.27	11.48	11.71	11.72	11.07
SSP3 - Stalled development	10.49	10.71	10.54	10.14	9.69	7.89	6.07
SSP4 - Inequality	10.49	10.88	11.07	11.10	11.09	10.27	8.67
SSP5 - Conventional development	10.49	11.19	12.05	12.92	13.98	16.47	18.13
Proportion age 65+							
SSP1 - Rapid development	0.15	0.20	0.23	0.26	0.32	0.38	0.44
SSP2 - Medium	0.15	0.20	0.22	0.25	0.30	0.32	0.37
SSP3 - Stalled development	0.15	0.20	0.22	0.25	0.31	0.34	0.38
SSP4 - Inequality	0.15	0.20	0.22	0.26	0.31	0.37	0.44
SSP5 - Conventional development	0.15	0.20	0.22	0.24	0.28	0.31	0.36
Proportion below age 20							
SSP1 - Rapid development	0.20	0.20	0.19	0.17	0.17	0.16	0.15
SSP2 - Medium	0.20	0.20	0.20	0.18	0.18	0.17	0.17
SSP3 - Stalled development	0.20	0.19	0.18	0.16	0.15	0.14	0.14
SSP4 - Inequality	0.20	0.19	0.18	0.16	0.15	0.14	0.13
SSP5 - Conventional development	0.20	0.20	0.21	0.20	0.20	0.20	0.20
Proportion of Women age 20–39 with at least secondary education							
SSP1 - Rapid development	1.00	1.00	1.00	1.00	1.00	1.00	1.00
SSP2 - Medium	1.00	1.00	1.00	1.00	1.00	1.00	1.00
SSP3 - Stalled development	1.00	1.00	1.00	1.00	1.00	1.00	1.00
SSP4 - Inequality	1.00	1.00	1.00	1.00	1.00	1.00	1.00
SSP5 - Conventional development	1.00	1.00	1.00	1.00	1.00	1.00	1.00
Mean years of schooling, age 25+							
SSP1 - Rapid development	12.29	12.87	13.28	13.71	14.10	14.92	15.38
SSP2 - Medium	12.29	12.71	13.01	13.30	13.58	14.17	14.56
SSP3 - Stalled development	12.29	12.61	12.83	13.02	13.18	13.36	13.36
SSP4 - Inequality	12.29	12.47	12.54	12.60	12.63	12.59	12.52
SSP5 - Conventional development	12.29	12.88	13.31	13.75	14.16	14.98	15.42

Demographic Assumptions Underlying SSPs

	2010–15	2020–25	2030–35	2040–45	2050–55	2075–80	2095–2100
Total fertility rate							
SSP1 - Rapid development	1.45	1.54	1.61	1.65	1.66	1.68	1.69
SSP2 - Medium	1.45	1.56	1.66	1.68	1.70	1.71	1.72
SSP3 - Stalled development	1.39	1.35	1.32	1.31	1.31	1.33	1.34
SSP4 - Inequality	1.39	1.38	1.36	1.36	1.35	1.37	1.39
SSP5 - Conventional development	1.52	1.77	1.96	2.04	2.08	2.10	2.11
Life expectancy at birth for females (in years)							
SSP1 - Rapid development	82.13	85.50	88.88	92.22	95.22	102.22	107.87
SSP2 - Medium	81.39	83.81	86.19	88.59	90.59	95.10	98.71
SSP3 - Stalled development	81.13	82.53	83.92	85.29	86.27	88.16	89.67
SSP4 - Inequality	81.66	84.01	86.37	88.73	90.68	94.97	98.46
SSP5 - Conventional development	82.13	85.50	88.88	92.22	95.22	102.22	107.87
Migration – net flow over five years (in thousands)							
SSP1 - Rapid development	205	194	199	196	188	71	0
SSP2 - Medium	204	190	196	197	195	82	0
SSP3 - Stalled development	171	96	98	97	93	38	0
SSP4 - Inequality	205	193	197	195	189	78	0
SSP5 - Conventional development	239	293	308	317	320	139	0

Ageing Indicators, Medium Scenario (SSP2)

	2010	2020	2030	2040	2050	2075	2095
Median age	39.35	42.36	45.72	48.13	48.46	50.81	52.89
Propspective median age	39.35	39.96	41.05	41.17	39.54	37.72	36.19
Proportion age 65+	0.15	0.20	0.22	0.25	0.30	0.32	0.36
Proportion RLE < 15 years	0.11	0.12	0.14	0.13	0.14	0.17	0.14

Democratic Republic of the Congo

Detailed Human Capital Projections to 2060

Demographic indicators, Medium Scenario (SSP2)	2010	2020	2030	2040	2050	2060
Population (in millions)	65.97	85.79	107.37	127.36	145.51	160.49
Proportion age 65+	0.03	0.03	0.03	0.03	0.04	0.06
Proportion below age 20	0.57	0.54	0.51	0.45	0.40	0.35
	2005-10	2015-20	2025-30	2035-40	2045-50	2055-60
Total Fertility Rate	6.07	5.09	4.06	3.13	2.62	2.25
Life expectancy at birth (in years)						
Men	45.93	48.68	50.86	53.02	55.41	58.23
Women	48.91	52.18	54.80	57.32	59.88	62.88
Five-year immigration flow (in '000)	77.36	75.64	78.34	79.82	79.56	78.23
Five-year emigration flow (in '000)	99.84	100.37	128.49	156.90	180.44	193.88

Human Capital indicators, Medium Scenario (SSP2)	2010	2020	2030	2040	2050	2060
Population age 25+: highest educational attainment						
E1 - no education	0.19	0.12	0.08	0.05	0.03	0.02
E2 - incomplete primary	0.22	0.18	0.13	0.09	0.06	0.03
E3 - primary	0.14	0.15	0.16	0.15	0.14	0.13
E4 - lower secondary	0.25	0.29	0.31	0.31	0.29	0.26
E5 - upper secondary	0.15	0.20	0.26	0.32	0.39	0.46
E6 - post-secondary	0.05	0.05	0.06	0.07	0.09	0.10
Mean years of schooling (in years)	6.29	7.33	8.27	9.08	9.77	10.37
Gender gap (population age 25+): highest educational attainment (ratio male/female)						
E1 - no education	0.28	0.30	0.35	0.41	0.47	0.53
E2 - incomplete primary	0.72	0.69	0.70	0.74	0.78	0.83
E3 - primary	1.05	0.90	0.84	0.83	0.85	0.87
E4 - lower secondary	1.52	1.20	1.05	0.98	0.95	0.94
E5 - upper secondary	2.40	1.77	1.42	1.23	1.13	1.07
E6 - post-secondary	3.70	2.58	1.96	1.59	1.35	1.19
Mean years of schooling (male minus female)	3.00	2.20	1.51	1.00	0.64	0.39
Women age 20–39: highest educational attainment						
E1 - no education	0.17	0.09	0.04	0.02	0.01	0.00
E2 - incomplete primary	0.25	0.18	0.13	0.08	0.05	0.03
E3 - primary	0.16	0.18	0.17	0.15	0.12	0.09
E4 - lower secondary	0.28	0.33	0.36	0.35	0.32	0.29
E5 - upper secondary	0.12	0.19	0.26	0.34	0.41	0.48
E6 - post-secondary	0.02	0.03	0.05	0.06	0.08	0.10
Mean years of schooling (in years)	6.07	7.38	8.45	9.30	10.01	10.62

Education scenarios

GET: global education trend scenario (medium assumption also used for SSP2)

CER: constant enrolment rates scenario (assumption of no future improvements)

FT: Fast track scenario (assumption of education expansion according to fastest historical experience)

Pyramids by Education, Medium Scenario

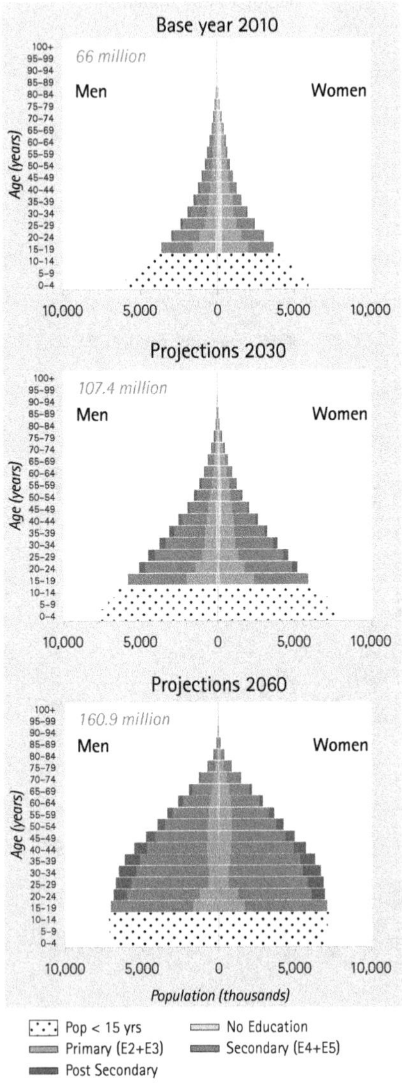

Population Size by Educational Attainment According to Three Education Scenarios: GET, CER, and FT

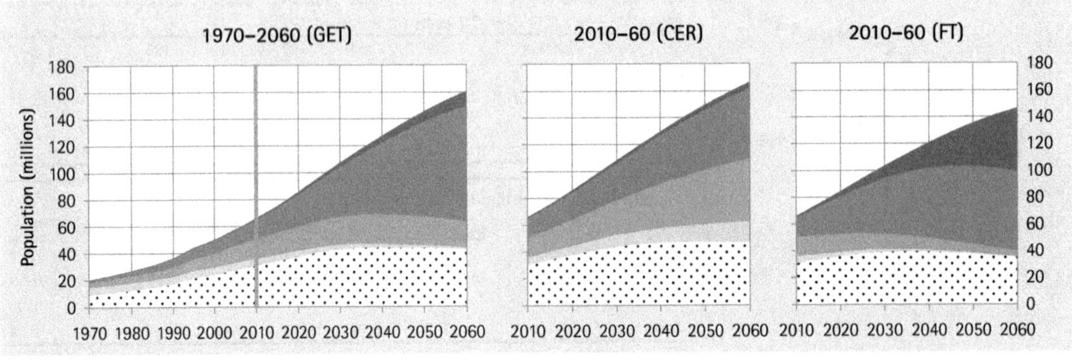

Democratic Republic of the Congo (Continued)

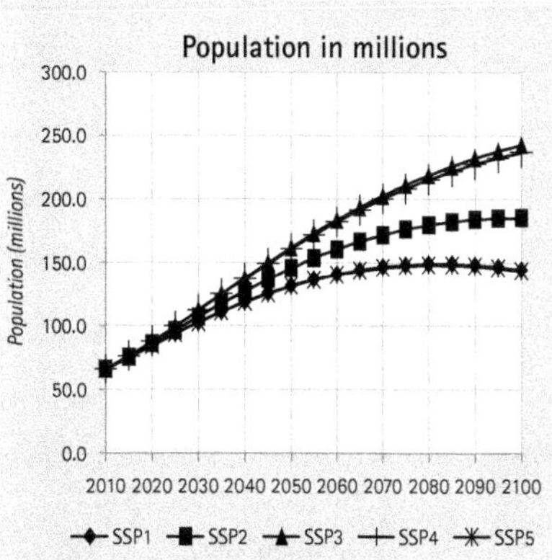

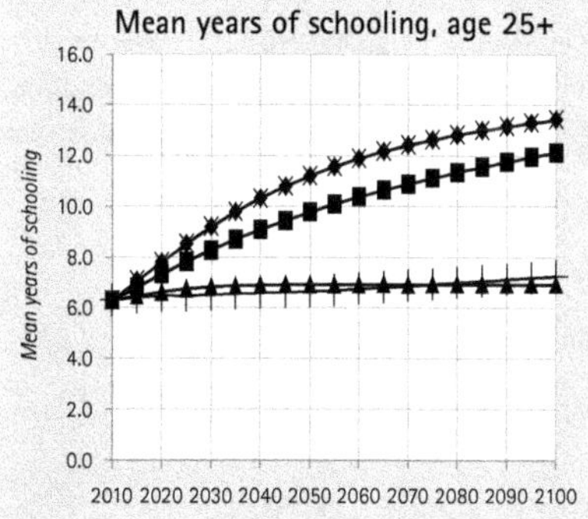

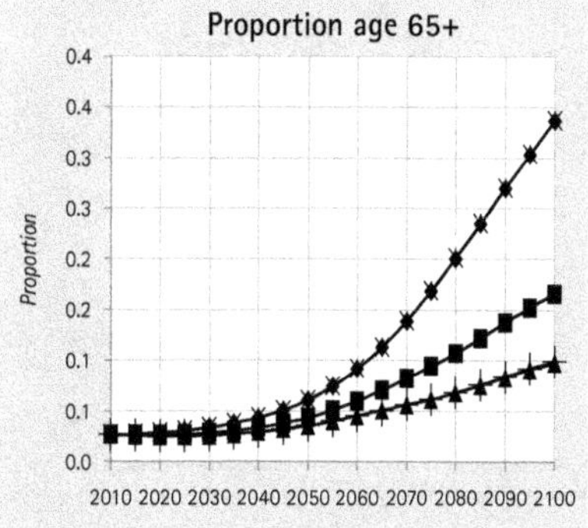

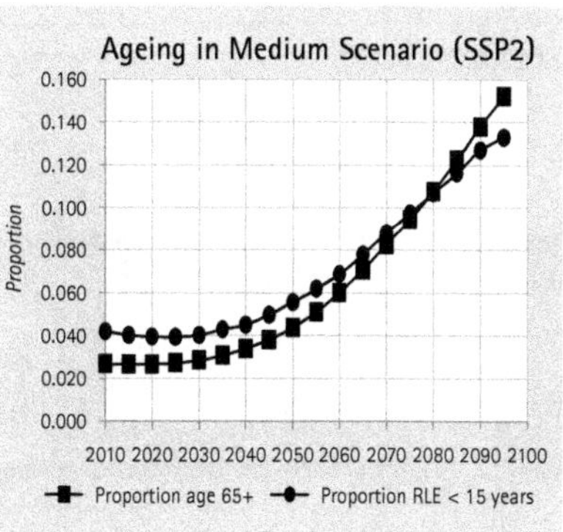

Alternative Scenarios to 2100

Projection Results by Scenario (SSP1–5)

	2010	2020	2030	2040	2050	2075	2100
Population (in millions)							
SSP1 - Rapid development	65.97	84.52	102.72	118.87	131.65	148.25	144.67
SSP2 - Medium	65.97	85.79	107.37	127.36	145.51	176.37	185.38
SSP3 - Stalled development	65.97	87.68	112.54	137.67	161.90	211.09	242.89
SSP4 - Inequality	65.97	87.68	112.45	137.28	161.01	208.15	236.98
SSP5 - Conventional development	65.97	84.50	102.62	118.63	131.22	147.23	143.38
Proportion age 65+							
SSP1 - Rapid development	0.03	0.03	0.03	0.04	0.06	0.17	0.34
SSP2 - Medium	0.03	0.03	0.03	0.03	0.04	0.09	0.17
SSP3 - Stalled development	0.03	0.03	0.03	0.03	0.04	0.06	0.10
SSP4 - Inequality	0.03	0.03	0.03	0.03	0.04	0.06	0.10
SSP5 - Conventional development	0.03	0.03	0.03	0.04	0.06	0.17	0.34
Proportion below age 20							
SSP1 - Rapid development	0.57	0.53	0.46	0.39	0.33	0.21	0.14
SSP2 - Medium	0.57	0.54	0.51	0.45	0.40	0.30	0.24
SSP3 - Stalled development	0.57	0.56	0.53	0.50	0.45	0.37	0.33
SSP4 - Inequality	0.57	0.56	0.53	0.50	0.45	0.37	0.32
SSP5 - Conventional development	0.57	0.53	0.46	0.39	0.33	0.21	0.14
Proportion of Women age 20–39 with at least secondary education							
SSP1 - Rapid development	0.42	0.65	0.78	0.86	0.91	0.96	0.99
SSP2 - Medium	0.42	0.55	0.66	0.75	0.82	0.93	0.98
SSP3 - Stalled development	0.42	0.37	0.37	0.37	0.37	0.37	0.37
SSP4 - Inequality	0.42	0.35	0.33	0.33	0.33	0.33	0.33
SSP5 - Conventional development	0.42	0.65	0.78	0.86	0.91	0.96	0.99
Mean years of schooling, age 25+							
SSP1 - Rapid development	6.29	7.81	9.18	10.31	11.19	12.62	13.42
SSP2 - Medium	6.29	7.33	8.27	9.08	9.77	11.12	12.12
SSP3 - Stalled development	6.29	6.62	6.83	6.91	6.93	6.93	6.94
SSP4 - Inequality	6.29	6.46	6.51	6.58	6.65	6.94	7.26
SSP5 - Conventional development	6.29	7.81	9.18	10.30	11.19	12.62	13.41

Demographic Assumptions Underlying SSPs

	2010–15	2020–25	2030–35	2040–45	2050–55	2075–80	2095–2100
Total fertility rate							
SSP1 - Rapid development	5.27	3.69	2.65	2.05	1.71	1.39	1.28
SSP2 - Medium	5.57	4.60	3.56	2.83	2.42	1.93	1.77
SSP3 - Stalled development	5.97	5.53	4.73	3.91	3.36	2.74	2.54
SSP4 - Inequality	5.98	5.55	4.73	3.89	3.33	2.69	2.49
SSP5 - Conventional development	5.27	3.69	2.65	2.05	1.71	1.39	1.28
Life expectancy at birth for females (in years)							
SSP1 - Rapid development	55.88	62.24	66.35	70.01	74.31	83.95	91.60
SSP2 - Medium	50.63	53.50	56.03	58.48	61.38	69.02	74.98
SSP3 - Stalled development	54.22	52.10	53.18	54.25	55.51	59.61	62.97
SSP4 - Inequality	54.22	52.07	53.13	54.18	55.44	59.56	62.95
SSP5 - Conventional development	55.88	62.24	66.35	70.01	74.31	83.96	91.60
Migration – net flow over five years (in thousands)							
SSP1 - Rapid development	−20	−37	−62	−86	−101	−45	0
SSP2 - Medium	−20	−37	−63	−90	−109	−55	0
SSP3 - Stalled development	−16	−18	−30	−41	−50	−26	0
SSP4 - Inequality	−20	−36	−62	−88	−109	−56	0
SSP5 - Conventional development	−23	−56	−98	−141	−174	−90	0

Ageing Indicators, Medium Scenario (SSP2)

	2010	2020	2030	2040	2050	2075	2095
Median age	16.59	17.94	19.76	22.43	25.56	33.23	38.34
Propspective median age	16.59	16.57	17.00	18.27	20.13	24.16	26.33
Proportion age 65+	0.03	0.03	0.03	0.03	0.04	0.09	0.15
Proportion RLE < 15 years	0.04	0.04	0.04	0.04	0.06	0.10	0.13

Denmark

Detailed Human Capital Projections to 2060

Demographic indicators, Medium Scenario (SSP2)	2010	2020	2030	2040	2050	2060
Population (in millions)	5.55	5.79	6.12	6.45	6.74	7.07
Proportion age 65+	0.16	0.20	0.22	0.24	0.24	0.26
Proportion below age 20	0.24	0.22	0.22	0.23	0.22	0.22
	2005–10	2015–20	2025–30	2035–40	2045–50	2055–60
Total Fertility Rate	1.85	1.81	1.96	2.00	2.00	1.99
Life expectancy at birth (in years)						
Men	75.99	78.11	80.19	82.17	84.17	86.20
Women	80.50	82.81	84.91	86.91	88.91	90.91
Five-year immigration flow (in '000)	109.59	107.71	111.91	114.54	114.68	113.07
Five-year emigration flow (in '000)	19.58	14.53	14.46	14.15	14.83	15.55

Human Capital indicators, Medium Scenario (SSP2)	2010	2020	2030	2040	2050	2060
Population age 25+: highest educational attainment						
E1 - no education	0.00	0.00	0.00	0.00	0.00	0.00
E2 - incomplete primary	0.00	0.00	0.00	0.00	0.00	0.00
E3 - primary	0.00	0.00	0.00	0.00	0.00	0.00
E4 - lower secondary	0.29	0.23	0.19	0.15	0.11	0.08
E5 - upper secondary	0.45	0.48	0.49	0.49	0.49	0.48
E6 - post-secondary	0.25	0.29	0.32	0.36	0.40	0.44
Mean years of schooling (in years)	12.13	12.43	12.72	12.98	13.23	13.49
Gender gap (population age 25+): highest educational attainment (ratio male/female)						
E1 - no education	NA	NA	NA	NA	NA	NA
E2 - incomplete primary	NA	1.08	1.08	1.08	1.07	1.05
E3 - primary	0.73	0.66	0.61	0.55	0.49	0.48
E4 - lower secondary	0.83	0.92	1.01	1.11	1.19	1.23
E5 - upper secondary	1.20	1.16	1.13	1.11	1.10	1.07
E6 - post-secondary	0.89	0.85	0.82	0.83	0.85	0.89
Mean years of schooling (male minus female)	0.04	−0.13	−0.25	−0.31	−0.31	−0.25
Women age 20–39: highest educational attainment						
E1 - no education	0.00	0.00	0.00	0.00	0.00	0.00
E2 - incomplete primary	0.00	0.00	0.00	0.00	0.00	0.00
E3 - primary	0.00	0.00	0.00	0.00	0.00	0.00
E4 - lower secondary	0.18	0.14	0.11	0.08	0.07	0.06
E5 - upper secondary	0.55	0.56	0.55	0.55	0.55	0.54
E6 - post-secondary	0.27	0.30	0.34	0.37	0.38	0.40
Mean years of schooling (in years)	12.50	12.75	13.03	13.20	13.27	13.41

Education scenarios

GET: global education trend scenario (medium assumption also used for SSP2)

CER: constant enrolment rates scenario (assumption of no future improvements)

FT: Fast track scenario (assumption of education expansion according to fastest historical experience)

Pyramids by Education, Medium Scenario

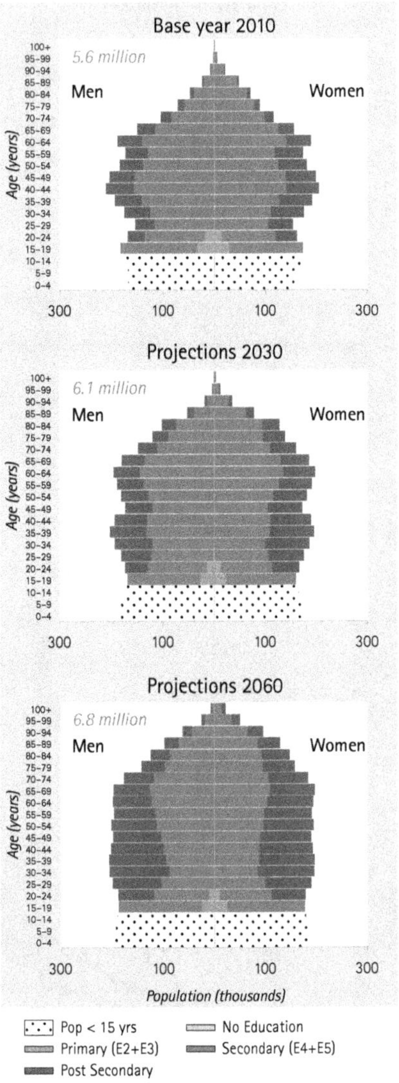

Population Size by Educational Attainment According to Three Education Scenarios: GET, CER, and FT

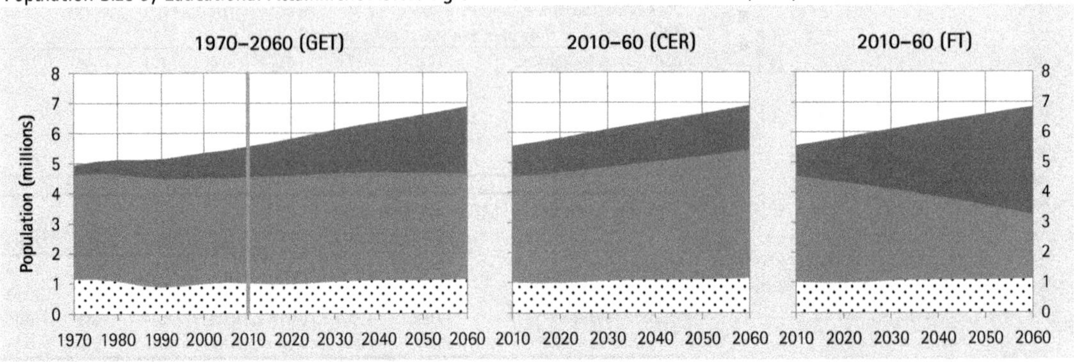

Denmark (Continued)

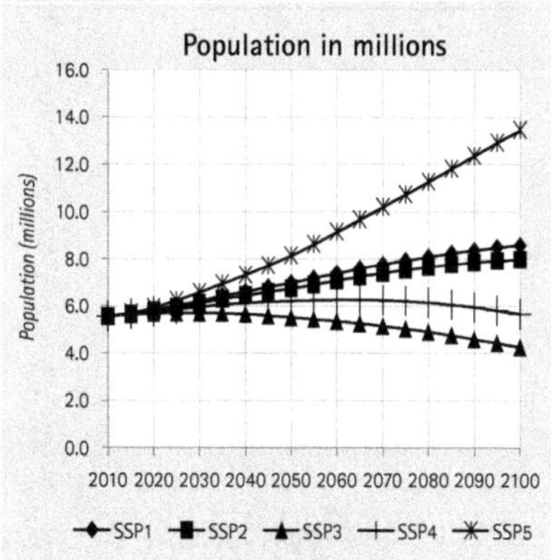

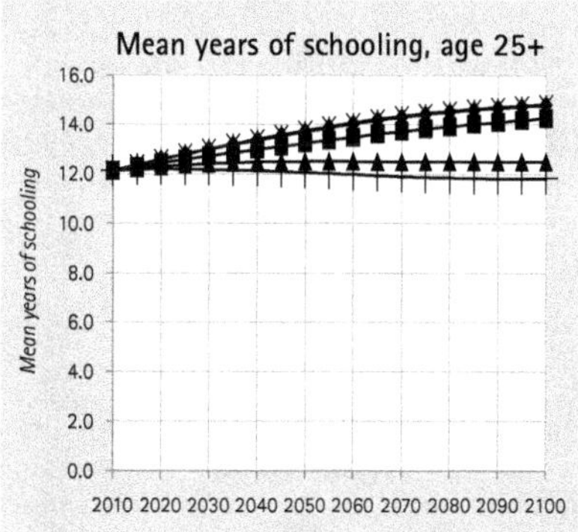

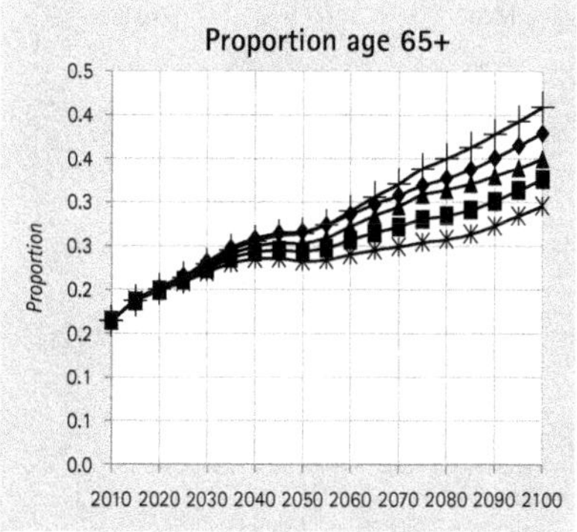

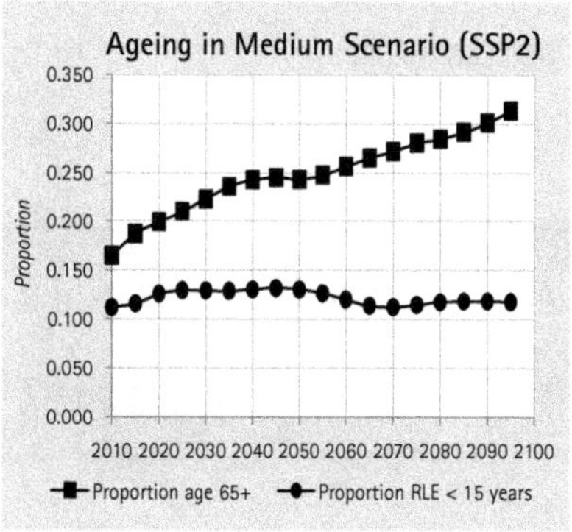

Alternative Scenarios to 2100

Projection Results by Scenario (SSP1–5)

	2010	2020	2030	2040	2050	2075	2100
Population (in millions)							
SSP1 - Rapid development	5.55	5.82	6.21	6.61	6.98	7.93	8.59
SSP2 - Medium	5.55	5.79	6.12	6.45	6.74	7.53	7.98
SSP3 - Stalled development	5.55	5.67	5.70	5.65	5.51	5.04	4.26
SSP4 - Inequality	5.55	5.75	5.96	6.12	6.20	6.20	5.66
SSP5 - Conventional development	5.55	5.92	6.57	7.31	8.13	10.73	13.45
Proportion age 65+							
SSP1 - Rapid development	0.16	0.20	0.23	0.26	0.27	0.32	0.38
SSP2 - Medium	0.16	0.20	0.22	0.24	0.24	0.28	0.33
SSP3 - Stalled development	0.16	0.20	0.23	0.25	0.25	0.31	0.35
SSP4 - Inequality	0.16	0.20	0.23	0.26	0.26	0.34	0.41
SSP5 - Conventional development	0.16	0.20	0.22	0.23	0.23	0.25	0.30
Proportion below age 20							
SSP1 - Rapid development	0.24	0.22	0.22	0.23	0.22	0.21	0.18
SSP2 - Medium	0.24	0.22	0.22	0.23	0.22	0.22	0.20
SSP3 - Stalled development	0.24	0.22	0.20	0.20	0.19	0.17	0.16
SSP4 - Inequality	0.24	0.22	0.20	0.20	0.19	0.16	0.14
SSP5 - Conventional development	0.24	0.23	0.24	0.26	0.26	0.26	0.24
Proportion of Women age 20–39 with at least secondary education							
SSP1 - Rapid development	1.00	1.00	1.00	1.00	1.00	1.00	1.00
SSP2 - Medium	1.00	1.00	1.00	1.00	1.00	1.00	1.00
SSP3 - Stalled development	1.00	1.00	1.00	1.00	1.00	1.00	1.00
SSP4 - Inequality	1.00	1.00	1.00	1.00	1.00	1.00	1.00
SSP5 - Conventional development	1.00	1.00	1.00	1.00	1.00	1.00	1.00
Mean years of schooling, age 25+							
SSP1 - Rapid development	12.13	12.58	13.00	13.37	13.71	14.41	14.79
SSP2 - Medium	12.13	12.43	12.72	12.98	13.23	13.82	14.26
SSP3 - Stalled development	12.13	12.29	12.41	12.48	12.50	12.48	12.48
SSP4 - Inequality	12.13	12.19	12.17	12.13	12.06	11.87	11.81
SSP5 - Conventional development	12.13	12.58	13.01	13.40	13.74	14.45	14.81

Demographic Assumptions Underlying SSPs

	2010–15	2020–25	2030–35	2040–45	2050–55	2075–80	2095–2100
Total fertility rate							
SSP1 - Rapid development	1.74	1.88	1.97	2.00	1.99	1.95	1.92
SSP2 - Medium	1.73	1.88	2.00	2.00	2.00	1.95	1.92
SSP3 - Stalled development	1.66	1.61	1.57	1.54	1.51	1.48	1.46
SSP4 - Inequality	1.66	1.61	1.58	1.55	1.52	1.49	1.47
SSP5 - Conventional development	1.83	2.16	2.39	2.47	2.49	2.44	2.40
Life expectancy at birth for females (in years)							
SSP1 - Rapid development	82.50	85.60	88.62	91.60	94.54	102.05	108.08
SSP2 - Medium	81.71	83.81	85.91	87.91	89.91	94.89	98.90
SSP3 - Stalled development	81.49	82.61	83.67	84.67	85.63	87.92	89.85
SSP4 - Inequality	82.03	84.09	86.13	88.08	90.02	94.70	98.56
SSP5 - Conventional development	82.50	85.60	88.62	91.60	94.54	102.05	108.08
Migration – net flow over five years (in thousands)							
SSP1 - Rapid development	89	95	98	97	92	40	0
SSP2 - Medium	88	94	97	98	96	44	0
SSP3 - Stalled development	74	47	48	48	45	20	0
SSP4 - Inequality	89	94	96	95	89	39	0
SSP5 - Conventional development	103	143	150	155	156	77	0

Ageing Indicators, Medium Scenario (SSP2)

	2010	2020	2030	2040	2050	2075	2095
Median age	40.56	42.20	41.94	42.90	43.64	45.09	47.91
Propspective median age	40.56	40.11	37.84	36.82	35.57	32.30	31.32
Proportion age 65+	0.16	0.20	0.22	0.24	0.24	0.28	0.31
Proportion RLE < 15 years	0.11	0.13	0.13	0.13	0.13	0.11	0.12

Dominican Republic

Detailed Human Capital Projections to 2060

Demographic indicators, Medium Scenario (SSP2)	2010	2020	2030	2040	2050	2060
Population (in millions)	9.93	11.14	12.16	12.95	13.47	13.71
Proportion age 65+	0.06	0.08	0.11	0.14	0.17	0.21
Proportion below age 20	0.41	0.36	0.32	0.28	0.25	0.23
	2005–10	2015–20	2025–30	2035–40	2045–50	2055–60
Total Fertility Rate	2.67	2.25	2.06	1.92	1.86	1.76
Life expectancy at birth (in years)						
Men	69.84	72.68	74.77	77.01	79.02	81.10
Women	75.44	77.90	80.00	82.09	84.09	86.09
Five-year immigration flow (in '000)	65.49	64.11	66.55	68.01	67.97	66.96
Five-year emigration flow (in '000)	204.87	168.43	174.56	172.30	165.60	156.79

Human Capital indicators, Medium Scenario (SSP2)	2010	2020	2030	2040	2050	2060
Population age 25+: highest educational attainment						
E1 - no education	0.01	0.01	0.01	0.00	0.00	0.00
E2 - incomplete primary	0.25	0.18	0.12	0.08	0.05	0.03
E3 - primary	0.11	0.10	0.09	0.08	0.07	0.06
E4 - lower secondary	0.27	0.28	0.28	0.26	0.23	0.20
E5 - upper secondary	0.19	0.23	0.27	0.30	0.32	0.34
E6 - post-secondary	0.16	0.20	0.24	0.28	0.32	0.36
Mean years of schooling (in years)	8.65	9.53	10.31	11.01	11.61	12.15
Gender gap (population age 25+): highest educational attainment (ratio male/female)						
E1 - no education	0.99	1.02	1.05	1.07	1.08	1.10
E2 - incomplete primary	1.04	1.05	1.07	1.09	1.10	1.11
E3 - primary	1.12	1.14	1.18	1.20	1.20	1.18
E4 - lower secondary	1.14	1.20	1.22	1.23	1.22	1.19
E5 - upper secondary	0.91	0.93	0.96	0.99	1.01	1.02
E6 - post-secondary	0.79	0.75	0.74	0.77	0.81	0.86
Mean years of schooling (male minus female)	−0.43	−0.58	−0.65	−0.64	−0.56	−0.43
Women age 20–39: highest educational attainment						
E1 - no education	0.00	0.00	0.00	0.00	0.00	0.00
E2 - incomplete primary	0.10	0.06	0.03	0.02	0.01	0.01
E3 - primary	0.09	0.07	0.06	0.05	0.04	0.03
E4 - lower secondary	0.28	0.24	0.19	0.16	0.12	0.10
E5 - upper secondary	0.30	0.35	0.38	0.40	0.41	0.42
E6 - post-secondary	0.22	0.28	0.34	0.38	0.42	0.45
Mean years of schooling (in years)	10.49	11.38	12.09	12.62	13.00	13.28

Education scenarios

GET: global education trend scenario (medium assumption also used for SSP2)

CER: constant enrolment rates scenario (assumption of no future improvements)

FT: Fast track scenario (assumption of education expansion according to fastest historical experience)

Pyramids by Education, Medium Scenario

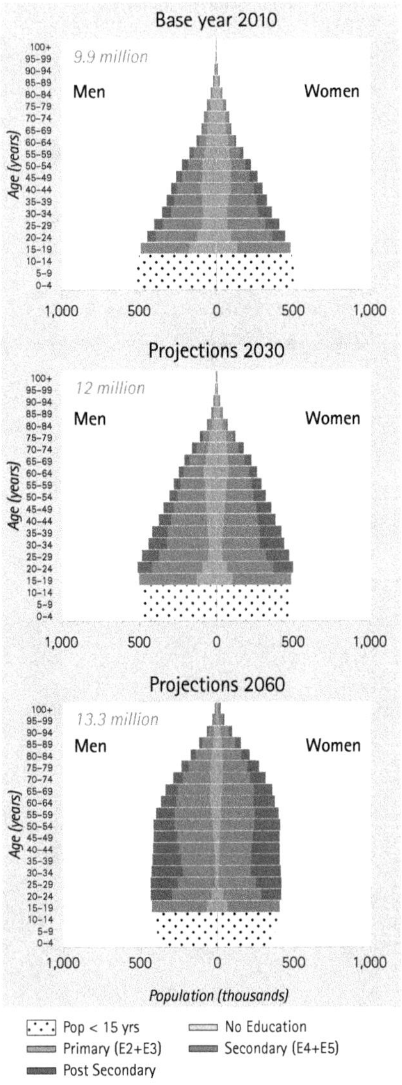

Population Size by Educational Attainment According to Three Education Scenarios: GET, CER, and FT

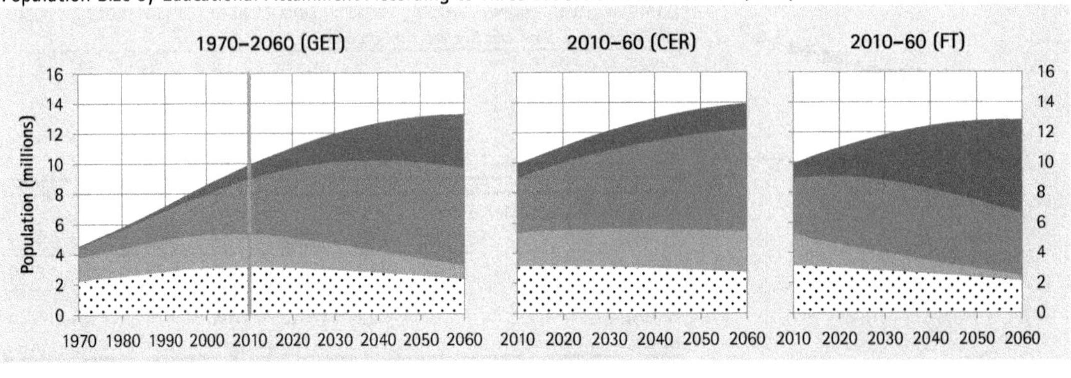

Dominican Republic (Continued)

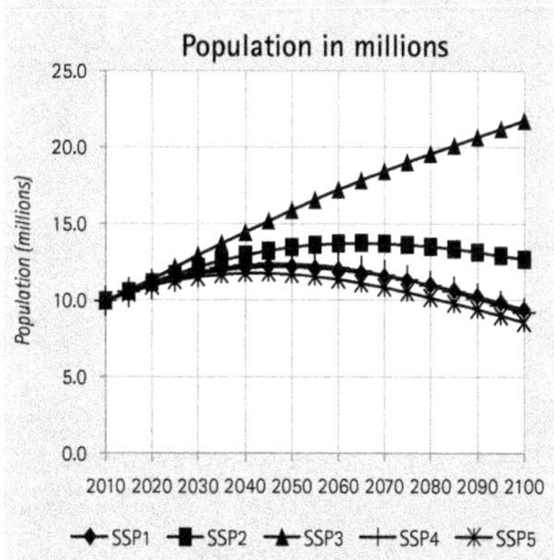

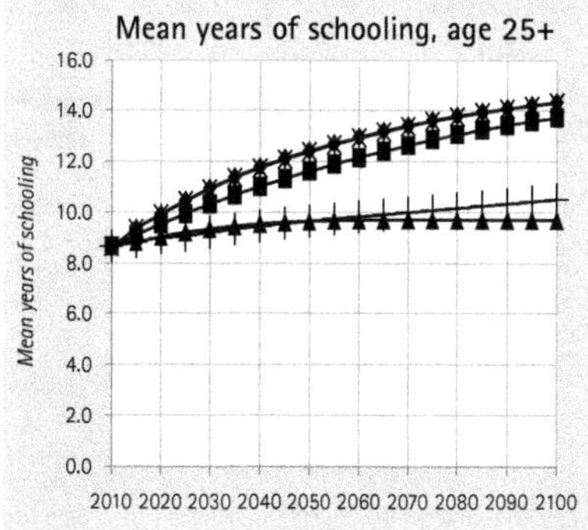

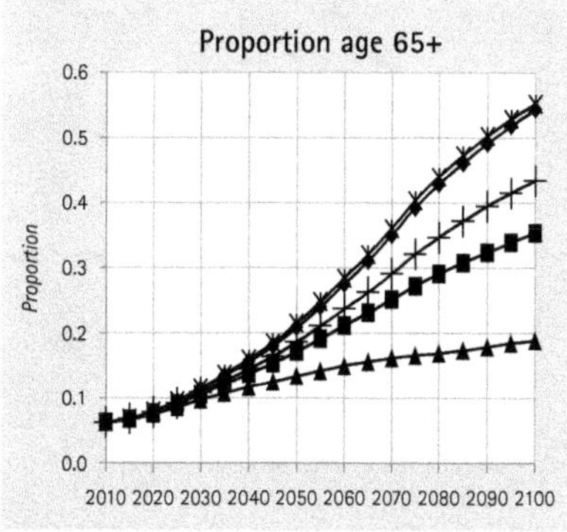

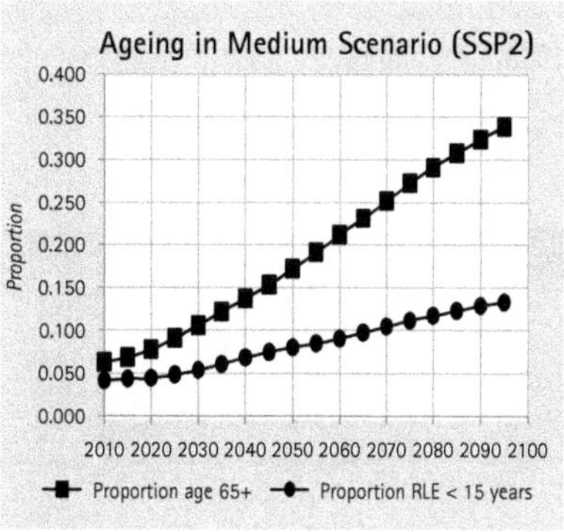

Alternative Scenarios to 2100

Projection Results by Scenario (SSP1–5)

	2010	2020	2030	2040	2050	2075	2100
Population (in millions)							
SSP1 - Rapid development	9.93	10.98	11.70	12.11	12.19	11.30	9.40
SSP2 - Medium	9.93	11.14	12.16	12.95	13.47	13.63	12.69
SSP3 - Stalled development	9.93	11.38	12.95	14.44	15.89	19.00	21.73
SSP4 - Inequality	9.93	11.04	11.84	12.29	12.38	11.32	9.17
SSP5 - Conventional development	9.93	10.92	11.50	11.76	11.69	10.50	8.56
Proportion age 65+							
SSP1 - Rapid development	0.06	0.08	0.11	0.16	0.21	0.39	0.54
SSP2 - Medium	0.06	0.08	0.11	0.14	0.17	0.27	0.35
SSP3 - Stalled development	0.06	0.08	0.10	0.12	0.13	0.17	0.19
SSP4 - Inequality	0.06	0.08	0.11	0.14	0.19	0.32	0.43
SSP5 - Conventional development	0.06	0.08	0.12	0.16	0.22	0.40	0.55
Proportion below age 20							
SSP1 - Rapid development	0.41	0.35	0.28	0.23	0.19	0.12	0.08
SSP2 - Medium	0.41	0.36	0.32	0.28	0.25	0.20	0.16
SSP3 - Stalled development	0.41	0.37	0.35	0.34	0.32	0.30	0.27
SSP4 - Inequality	0.41	0.36	0.30	0.25	0.21	0.15	0.11
SSP5 - Conventional development	0.41	0.35	0.28	0.23	0.19	0.12	0.08
Proportion of Women age 20–39 with at least secondary education							
SSP1 - Rapid development	0.81	0.92	0.95	0.97	0.98	0.99	1.00
SSP2 - Medium	0.81	0.87	0.91	0.94	0.95	0.98	0.99
SSP3 - Stalled development	0.81	0.78	0.78	0.78	0.78	0.78	0.78
SSP4 - Inequality	0.81	0.74	0.71	0.71	0.71	0.71	0.71
SSP5 - Conventional development	0.81	0.92	0.95	0.97	0.98	0.99	1.00
Mean years of schooling, age 25+							
SSP1 - Rapid development	8.65	9.92	10.94	11.76	12.41	13.61	14.33
SSP2 - Medium	8.65	9.53	10.31	11.01	11.61	12.85	13.73
SSP3 - Stalled development	8.65	9.03	9.34	9.54	9.64	9.70	9.70
SSP4 - Inequality	8.65	8.98	9.21	9.45	9.65	10.08	10.51
SSP5 - Conventional development	8.65	9.91	10.91	11.73	12.38	13.58	14.31

Demographic Assumptions Underlying SSPs

	2010–15	2020–25	2030–35	2040–45	2050–55	2075–80	2095–2100
Total fertility rate							
SSP1 - Rapid development	2.25	1.78	1.53	1.41	1.33	1.20	1.20
SSP2 - Medium	2.42	2.13	1.99	1.88	1.80	1.61	1.60
SSP3 - Stalled development	2.55	2.60	2.57	2.51	2.44	2.24	2.24
SSP4 - Inequality	2.31	1.94	1.67	1.53	1.43	1.29	1.29
SSP5 - Conventional development	2.25	1.78	1.53	1.41	1.33	1.20	1.20
Life expectancy at birth for females (in years)							
SSP1 - Rapid development	78.53	81.37	84.17	87.04	90.03	97.45	103.40
SSP2 - Medium	76.81	79.00	81.09	83.09	85.09	90.11	94.09
SSP3 - Stalled development	77.89	78.64	79.57	80.45	81.18	83.06	84.72
SSP4 - Inequality	78.24	80.08	81.83	83.58	85.31	89.78	93.53
SSP5 - Conventional development	78.53	81.37	84.17	87.04	90.03	97.45	103.40
Migration – net flow over five years (in thousands)							
SSP1 - Rapid development	−114	−106	−104	−93	−81	−24	0
SSP2 - Medium	−114	−107	−107	−102	−95	−34	0
SSP3 - Stalled development	−95	−53	−53	−52	−51	−22	0
SSP4 - Inequality	−114	−106	−103	−91	−77	−21	0
SSP5 - Conventional development	−133	−160	−160	−148	−133	−44	0

Ageing Indicators, Medium Scenario (SSP2)

	2010	2020	2030	2040	2050	2075	2095
Median age	25.08	28.13	31.43	34.97	38.52	46.35	51.60
Propspective median age	25.08	26.37	27.96	29.80	31.68	35.19	36.98
Proportion age 65+	0.06	0.08	0.11	0.14	0.17	0.27	0.34
Proportion RLE < 15 years	0.04	0.04	0.05	0.07	0.08	0.11	0.13

Ecuador

Detailed Human Capital Projections to 2060

Demographic indicators, Medium Scenario (SSP2)

	2010	2020	2030	2040	2050	2060
Population (in millions)	14.46	16.45	18.20	19.62	20.62	21.18
Proportion age 65+	0.06	0.08	0.11	0.14	0.19	0.23
Proportion below age 20	0.40	0.35	0.31	0.27	0.24	0.22
	2005-10	2015-20	2025-30	2035-40	2045-50	2055-60
Total Fertility Rate	2.58	2.22	2.04	1.92	1.81	1.73
Life expectancy at birth (in years)						
Men	72.15	74.61	76.91	79.22	81.33	83.41
Women	78.06	80.41	82.49	84.59	86.61	88.61
Five-year immigration flow (in '000)	138.77	136.20	141.46	144.70	144.80	142.74
Five-year emigration flow (in '000)	258.45	210.64	217.09	215.22	208.61	198.84

Human Capital indicators, Medium Scenario (SSP2)

	2010	2020	2030	2040	2050	2060
Population age 25+: highest educational attainment						
E1 - no education	0.09	0.06	0.04	0.02	0.02	0.01
E2 - incomplete primary	0.16	0.12	0.09	0.06	0.04	0.02
E3 - primary	0.28	0.26	0.24	0.21	0.17	0.14
E4 - lower secondary	0.12	0.12	0.12	0.11	0.09	0.08
E5 - upper secondary	0.15	0.19	0.22	0.24	0.26	0.28
E6 - post-secondary	0.20	0.25	0.30	0.36	0.41	0.46
Mean years of schooling (in years)	8.07	9.11	10.13	11.01	11.77	12.44
Gender gap (population age 25+): highest educational attainment (ratio male/female)						
E1 - no education	0.74	0.74	0.74	0.75	0.78	0.80
E2 - incomplete primary	0.93	0.92	0.90	0.88	0.87	0.85
E3 - primary	1.15	1.16	1.16	1.15	1.13	1.10
E4 - lower secondary	1.09	1.09	1.10	1.10	1.08	1.06
E5 - upper secondary	0.98	1.03	1.08	1.10	1.11	1.09
E6 - post-secondary	0.97	0.90	0.87	0.87	0.89	0.92
Mean years of schooling (male minus female)	0.17	0.01	−0.12	−0.18	−0.18	−0.13
Women age 20–39: highest educational attainment						
E1 - no education	0.03	0.02	0.01	0.00	0.00	0.00
E2 - incomplete primary	0.09	0.05	0.03	0.01	0.01	0.00
E3 - primary	0.25	0.20	0.15	0.11	0.08	0.05
E4 - lower secondary	0.14	0.13	0.12	0.10	0.09	0.07
E5 - upper secondary	0.22	0.26	0.29	0.31	0.33	0.34
E6 - post-secondary	0.26	0.34	0.40	0.46	0.50	0.53
Mean years of schooling (in years)	9.61	10.93	12.19	12.87	13.34	13.66

Education scenarios

GET: global education trend scenario (medium assumption also used for SSP2)

CER: constant enrolment rates scenario (assumption of no future improvements)

FT: Fast track scenario (assumption of education expansion according to fastest historical experience)

Pyramids by Education, Medium Scenario

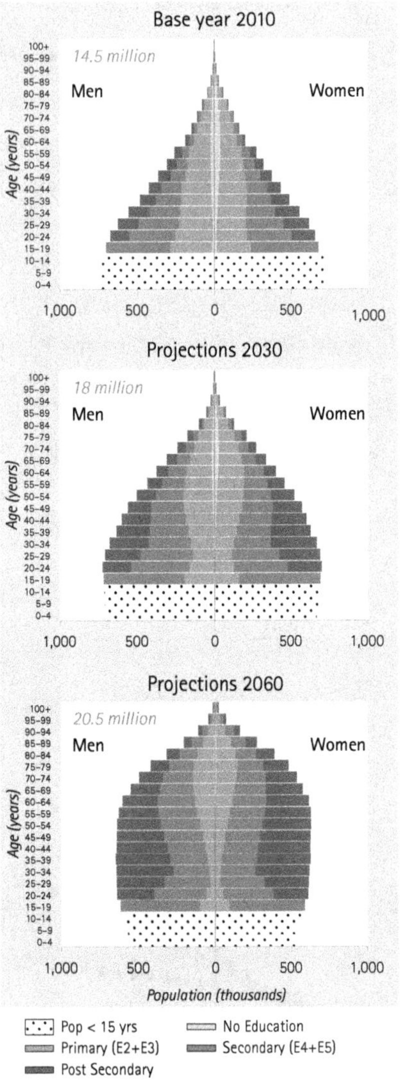

Population Size by Educational Attainment According to Three Education Scenarios: GET, CER, and FT

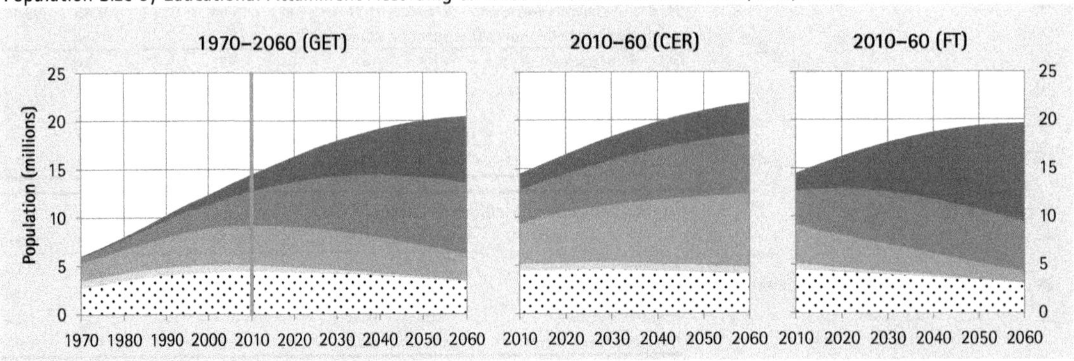

Ecuador (Continued)

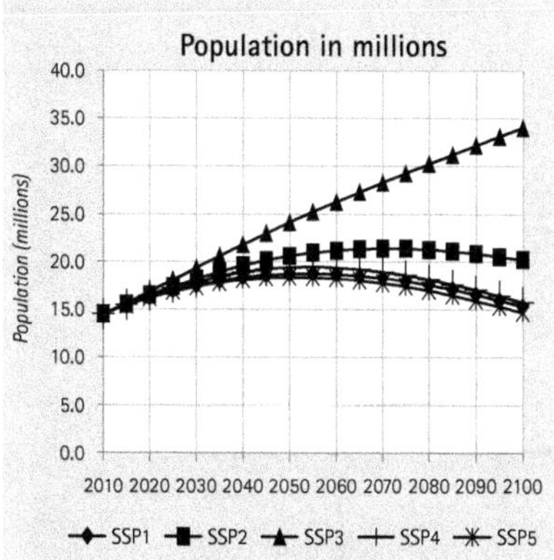

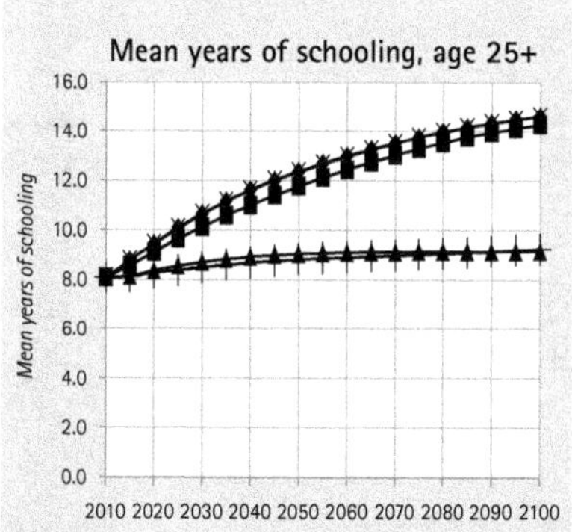

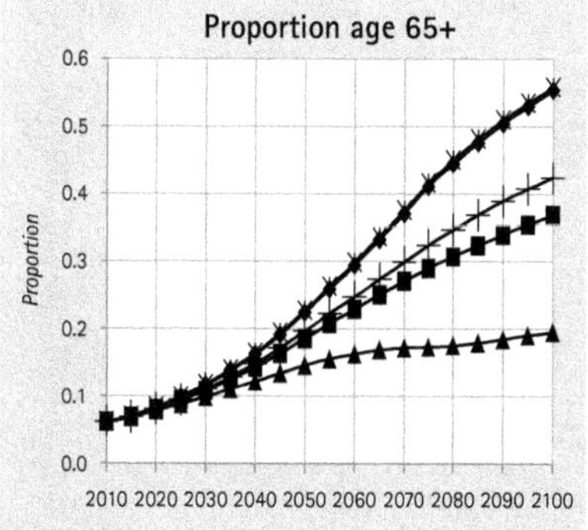

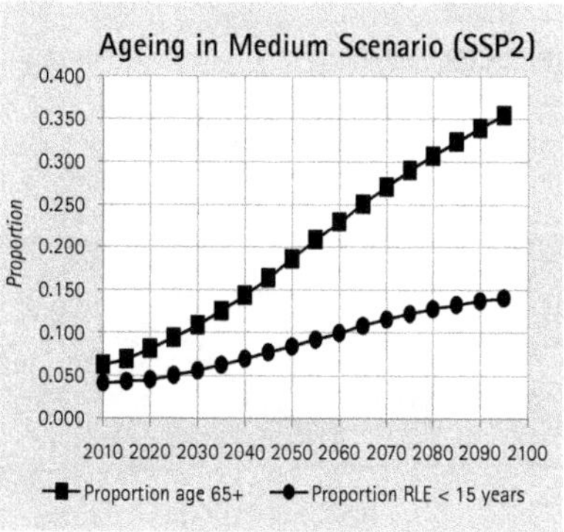

Alternative Scenarios to 2100

Projection Results by Scenario (SSP1–5)

	2010	2020	2030	2040	2050	2075	2100
Population (in millions)							
SSP1 - Rapid development	14.46	16.22	17.50	18.36	18.74	17.97	15.31
SSP2 - Medium	14.46	16.45	18.20	19.62	20.62	21.39	20.22
SSP3 - Stalled development	14.46	16.83	19.38	21.81	24.13	29.26	34.03
SSP4 - Inequality	14.46	16.38	17.89	18.91	19.41	18.59	15.76
SSP5 - Conventional development	14.46	16.17	17.36	18.10	18.38	17.38	14.69
Proportion age 65+							
SSP1 - Rapid development	0.06	0.08	0.12	0.16	0.22	0.41	0.55
SSP2 - Medium	0.06	0.08	0.11	0.14	0.19	0.29	0.37
SSP3 - Stalled development	0.06	0.08	0.10	0.12	0.15	0.17	0.20
SSP4 - Inequality	0.06	0.08	0.11	0.15	0.20	0.32	0.42
SSP5 - Conventional development	0.06	0.08	0.12	0.16	0.23	0.42	0.56
Proportion below age 20							
SSP1 - Rapid development	0.40	0.34	0.27	0.22	0.18	0.12	0.08
SSP2 - Medium	0.40	0.35	0.31	0.27	0.24	0.19	0.16
SSP3 - Stalled development	0.40	0.36	0.35	0.33	0.32	0.29	0.28
SSP4 - Inequality	0.40	0.35	0.29	0.25	0.21	0.15	0.12
SSP5 - Conventional development	0.40	0.34	0.27	0.22	0.18	0.12	0.08
Proportion of Women age 20–39 with at least secondary education							
SSP1 - Rapid development	0.62	0.81	0.88	0.92	0.95	0.98	0.99
SSP2 - Medium	0.62	0.73	0.81	0.87	0.91	0.97	0.99
SSP3 - Stalled development	0.62	0.53	0.53	0.53	0.53	0.53	0.53
SSP4 - Inequality	0.62	0.50	0.48	0.48	0.48	0.48	0.48
SSP5 - Conventional development	0.62	0.81	0.88	0.92	0.95	0.98	0.99
Mean years of schooling, age 25+							
SSP1 - Rapid development	8.07	9.44	10.65	11.62	12.37	13.76	14.61
SSP2 - Medium	8.07	9.11	10.13	11.01	11.77	13.30	14.27
SSP3 - Stalled development	8.07	8.36	8.70	8.92	9.04	9.13	9.15
SSP4 - Inequality	8.07	8.26	8.49	8.68	8.81	9.01	9.23
SSP5 - Conventional development	8.07	9.43	10.64	11.60	12.35	13.75	14.60

Demographic Assumptions Underlying SSPs

	2010–15	2020–25	2030–35	2040–45	2050–55	2075–80	2095–2100
Total fertility rate							
SSP1 - Rapid development	2.22	1.75	1.51	1.38	1.31	1.24	1.18
SSP2 - Medium	2.37	2.13	1.96	1.85	1.76	1.68	1.58
SSP3 - Stalled development	2.56	2.66	2.64	2.54	2.46	2.37	2.26
SSP4 - Inequality	2.32	2.00	1.73	1.57	1.47	1.41	1.34
SSP5 - Conventional development	2.22	1.75	1.51	1.38	1.31	1.24	1.18
Life expectancy at birth for females (in years)							
SSP1 - Rapid development	80.93	83.71	86.55	89.51	92.48	99.99	105.97
SSP2 - Medium	79.19	81.50	83.59	85.59	87.61	92.71	96.69
SSP3 - Stalled development	80.15	81.07	81.93	82.74	83.45	85.08	86.68
SSP4 - Inequality	80.49	82.39	84.17	85.92	87.68	92.00	95.59
SSP5 - Conventional development	80.93	83.71	86.55	89.51	92.48	99.99	105.97
Migration – net flow over five years (in thousands)							
SSP1 - Rapid development	–88	–75	–71	–62	–52	–13	0
SSP2 - Medium	–87	–76	–73	–67	–60	–18	0
SSP3 - Stalled development	–73	–38	–37	–35	–33	–12	0
SSP4 - Inequality	–88	–75	–71	–62	–51	–12	0
SSP5 - Conventional development	–103	–114	–111	–100	–87	–25	0

Ageing Indicators, Medium Scenario (SSP2)

	2010	2020	2030	2040	2050	2075	2095
Median age	25.53	29.00	32.56	36.26	39.85	47.65	52.66
Propspective median age	25.53	27.11	28.90	30.93	32.86	36.24	37.69
Proportion age 65+	0.06	0.08	0.11	0.14	0.19	0.29	0.35
Proportion RLE < 15 years	0.04	0.05	0.06	0.07	0.08	0.12	0.14

Egypt

Detailed Human Capital Projections to 2060

Demographic indicators, Medium Scenario (SSP2)

	2010	2020	2030	2040	2050	2060
Population (in millions)	81.12	95.05	107.38	117.98	126.47	132.62
Proportion age 65+	0.05	0.07	0.09	0.10	0.14	0.18
Proportion below age 20	0.41	0.38	0.34	0.30	0.27	0.25
	2005–10	2015–20	2025–30	2035–40	2045–50	2055–60
Total Fertility Rate	2.85	2.52	2.28	2.07	1.90	1.85
Life expectancy at birth (in years)						
Men	70.46	71.94	73.71	75.56	77.54	79.53
Women	74.25	75.99	77.89	79.79	81.79	83.79
Five-year immigration flow (in '000)	52.92	51.84	53.79	54.97	54.96	54.15
Five-year emigration flow (in '000)	395.34	328.62	351.56	367.97	369.11	362.68

Human Capital indicators, Medium Scenario (SSP2)

	2010	2020	2030	2040	2050	2060
Population age 25+: highest educational attainment						
E1 - no education	0.40	0.29	0.21	0.14	0.09	0.06
E2 - incomplete primary	0.07	0.05	0.04	0.03	0.02	0.01
E3 - primary	0.04	0.04	0.04	0.03	0.03	0.02
E4 - lower secondary	0.04	0.05	0.04	0.04	0.03	0.03
E5 - upper secondary	0.31	0.39	0.46	0.51	0.54	0.55
E6 - post-secondary	0.14	0.18	0.22	0.26	0.30	0.34
Mean years of schooling (in years)	6.77	8.36	9.67	10.79	11.70	12.43
Gender gap (population age 25+): highest educational attainment (ratio male/female)						
E1 - no education	0.60	0.59	0.59	0.58	0.59	0.60
E2 - incomplete primary	1.58	1.41	1.26	1.13	1.01	0.93
E3 - primary	1.37	1.24	1.18	1.13	1.08	1.01
E4 - lower secondary	1.41	1.21	1.13	1.08	1.02	0.97
E5 - upper secondary	1.31	1.20	1.14	1.10	1.07	1.04
E6 - post-secondary	1.47	1.25	1.13	1.05	1.02	1.02
Mean years of schooling (male minus female)	2.20	1.68	1.25	0.87	0.57	0.37
Women age 20–39: highest educational attainment						
E1 - no education	0.25	0.14	0.06	0.03	0.01	0.00
E2 - incomplete primary	0.04	0.02	0.01	0.01	0.00	0.00
E3 - primary	0.04	0.04	0.03	0.02	0.01	0.01
E4 - lower secondary	0.05	0.05	0.04	0.02	0.01	0.01
E5 - upper secondary	0.46	0.54	0.58	0.59	0.58	0.56
E6 - post-secondary	0.17	0.22	0.28	0.33	0.38	0.42
Mean years of schooling (in years)	8.70	10.67	12.07	12.85	13.33	13.64

Education scenarios

GET: global education trend scenario (medium assumption also used for SSP2)

CER: constant enrolment rates scenario (assumption of no future improvements)

FT: Fast track scenario (assumption of education expansion according to fastest historical experience)

Pyramids by Education, Medium Scenario

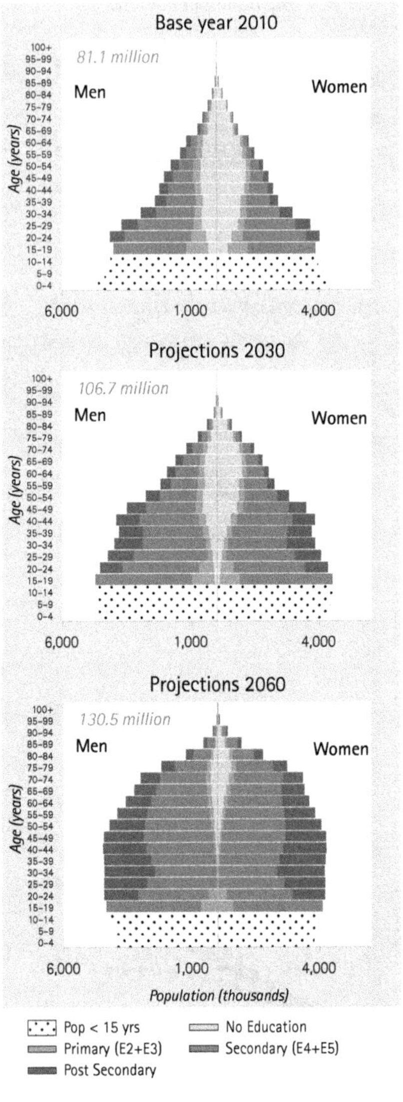

Population Size by Educational Attainment According to Three Education Scenarios: GET, CER, and FT

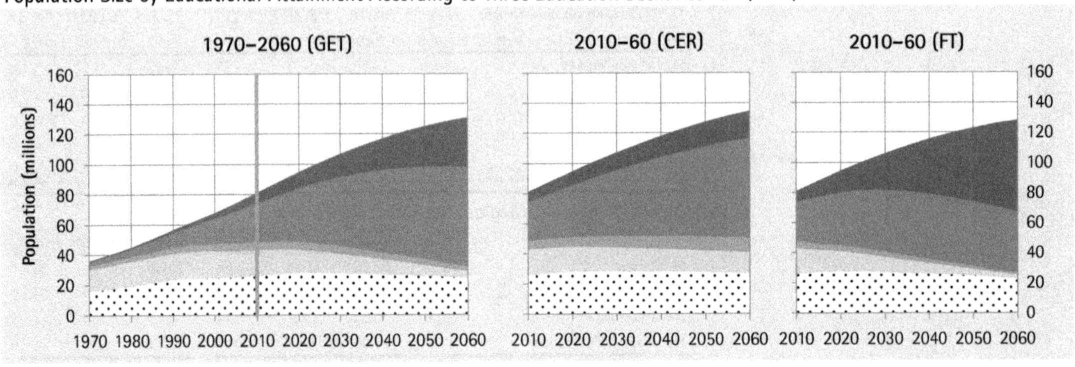

Egypt (Continued)

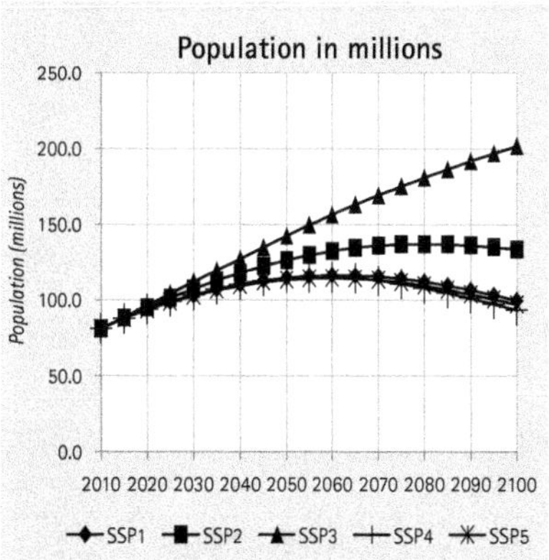

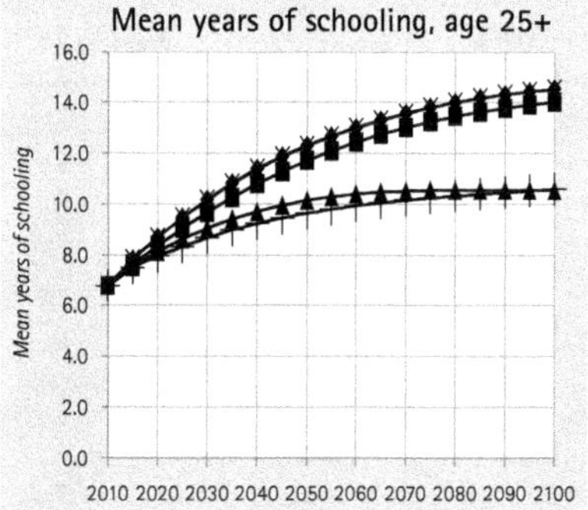

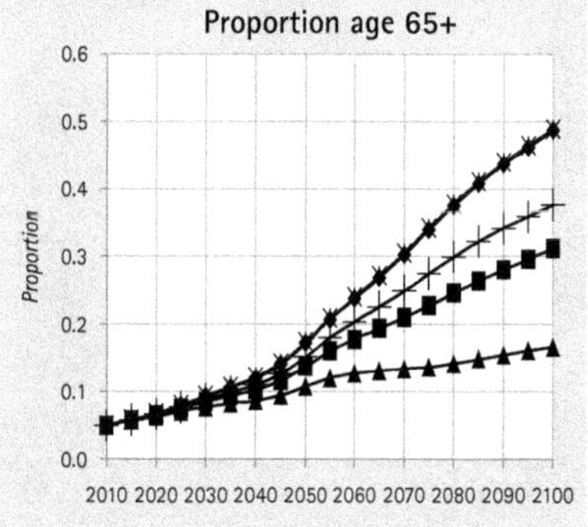

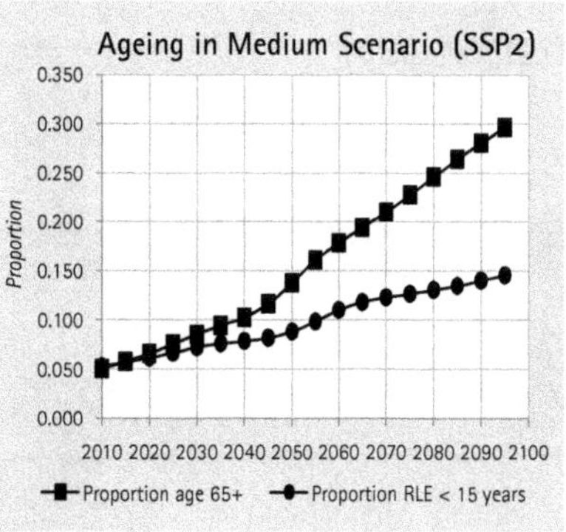

Alternative Scenarios to 2100

Projection Results by Scenario (SSP1–5)

	2010	2020	2030	2040	2050	2075	2100
Population (in millions)							
SSP1 - Rapid development	81.12	93.74	103.23	110.35	114.69	114.09	99.80
SSP2 - Medium	81.12	95.05	107.38	117.98	126.47	136.97	133.87
SSP3 - Stalled development	81.12	96.46	112.13	127.38	142.49	175.15	201.83
SSP4 - Inequality	81.12	93.72	103.22	110.19	114.17	110.69	93.46
SSP5 - Conventional development	81.12	93.58	102.70	109.39	113.25	111.57	97.09
Proportion age 65+							
SSP1 - Rapid development	0.05	0.07	0.09	0.12	0.17	0.34	0.49
SSP2 - Medium	0.05	0.07	0.09	0.10	0.14	0.23	0.31
SSP3 - Stalled development	0.05	0.06	0.08	0.09	0.11	0.14	0.17
SSP4 - Inequality	0.05	0.07	0.09	0.11	0.15	0.27	0.38
SSP5 - Conventional development	0.05	0.07	0.09	0.12	0.17	0.34	0.49
Proportion below age 20							
SSP1 - Rapid development	0.41	0.37	0.31	0.25	0.21	0.14	0.10
SSP2 - Medium	0.41	0.38	0.34	0.30	0.27	0.22	0.18
SSP3 - Stalled development	0.41	0.39	0.37	0.35	0.33	0.30	0.28
SSP4 - Inequality	0.41	0.37	0.31	0.27	0.23	0.17	0.13
SSP5 - Conventional development	0.41	0.37	0.31	0.25	0.21	0.14	0.10
Proportion of Women age 20–39 with at least secondary education							
SSP1 - Rapid development	0.67	0.84	0.93	0.97	0.98	0.99	1.00
SSP2 - Medium	0.67	0.81	0.90	0.95	0.97	1.00	1.00
SSP3 - Stalled development	0.67	0.74	0.76	0.76	0.76	0.76	0.76
SSP4 - Inequality	0.67	0.70	0.68	0.68	0.68	0.68	0.68
SSP5 - Conventional development	0.67	0.84	0.93	0.97	0.98	0.99	1.00
Mean years of schooling, age 25+							
SSP1 - Rapid development	6.77	8.69	10.17	11.38	12.29	13.80	14.53
SSP2 - Medium	6.77	8.36	9.67	10.79	11.70	13.25	14.02
SSP3 - Stalled development	6.77	8.12	9.04	9.70	10.14	10.54	10.56
SSP4 - Inequality	6.77	7.96	8.67	9.23	9.63	10.24	10.59
SSP5 - Conventional development	6.77	8.68	10.16	11.37	12.28	13.79	14.52

Demographic Assumptions Underlying SSPs

	2010–15	2020–25	2030–35	2040–45	2050–55	2075–80	2095–2100
Total fertility rate							
SSP1 - Rapid development	2.52	2.01	1.68	1.49	1.38	1.25	1.19
SSP2 - Medium	2.67	2.39	2.17	1.99	1.87	1.69	1.60
SSP3 - Stalled development	2.80	2.81	2.74	2.61	2.51	2.30	2.19
SSP4 - Inequality	2.53	2.08	1.78	1.60	1.50	1.36	1.29
SSP5 - Conventional development	2.52	2.01	1.68	1.49	1.38	1.25	1.19
Life expectancy at birth for females (in years)							
SSP1 - Rapid development	77.38	79.79	82.46	85.19	87.96	95.17	101.03
SSP2 - Medium	75.11	76.90	78.80	80.79	82.79	87.81	91.81
SSP3 - Stalled development	76.65	77.25	78.02	78.74	79.42	81.06	82.63
SSP4 - Inequality	76.97	78.51	80.18	81.89	83.53	87.60	91.13
SSP5 - Conventional development	77.38	79.79	82.46	85.19	87.96	95.17	101.03
Migration – net flow over five years (in thousands)							
SSP1 - Rapid development	−290	−286	−299	−294	−275	−102	0
SSP2 - Medium	−283	−284	−304	−313	−311	−136	0
SSP3 - Stalled development	−241	−142	−150	−156	−159	−77	0
SSP4 - Inequality	−290	−284	−294	−280	−251	−82	0
SSP5 - Conventional development	−338	−435	−471	−481	−470	−198	0

Ageing Indicators, Medium Scenario (SSP2)

	2010	2020	2030	2040	2050	2075	2095
Median age	24.36	27.32	29.97	32.88	36.12	43.46	48.53
Propspective median age	24.36	25.98	27.21	28.43	29.98	32.96	34.36
Proportion age 65+	0.05	0.07	0.09	0.10	0.14	0.23	0.30
Proportion RLE < 15 years	0.05	0.06	0.07	0.08	0.09	0.13	0.15

El Salvador

Detailed Human Capital Projections to 2060

Demographic indicators, Medium Scenario (SSP2)	2010	2020	2030	2040	2050	2060
Population (in millions)	6.19	6.46	6.61	6.63	6.52	6.29
Proportion age 65+	0.07	0.08	0.11	0.14	0.18	0.24
Proportion below age 20	0.44	0.37	0.33	0.29	0.26	0.23
	2015–10	2015–20	2025–30	2035–40	2045–50	2055–60
Total Fertility Rate	2.35	2.07	1.92	1.86	1.76	1.69
Life expectancy at birth (in years)						
Men	66.55	69.34	71.99	74.33	76.53	78.75
Women	76.09	78.60	80.89	82.99	84.99	87.11
Five-year immigration flow (in '000)	4.13	4.04	4.20	4.29	4.29	4.22
Five-year emigration flow (in '000)	295.03	249.73	233.65	215.87	195.65	173.50

Human Capital indicators, Medium Scenario (SSP2)	2010	2020	2030	2040	2050	2060
Population age 25+: highest educational attainment						
E1 - no education	0.21	0.15	0.11	0.08	0.06	0.04
E2 - incomplete primary	0.24	0.20	0.17	0.13	0.10	0.08
E3 - primary	0.15	0.14	0.14	0.13	0.11	0.10
E4 - lower secondary	0.15	0.17	0.18	0.19	0.18	0.17
E5 - upper secondary	0.14	0.19	0.23	0.27	0.31	0.34
E6 - post-secondary	0.11	0.14	0.17	0.20	0.23	0.27
Mean years of schooling (in years)	6.39	7.60	8.62	9.48	10.28	10.98
Gender gap (population age 25+): highest educational attainment (ratio male/female)						
E1 - no education	0.78	0.76	0.75	0.75	0.76	0.77
E2 - incomplete primary	0.93	0.89	0.85	0.82	0.79	0.77
E3 - primary	1.08	1.05	1.03	1.01	0.99	0.97
E4 - lower secondary	1.28	1.25	1.22	1.19	1.14	1.10
E5 - upper secondary	1.06	1.07	1.07	1.07	1.07	1.06
E6 - post-secondary	1.13	1.04	1.00	0.98	0.98	1.00
Mean years of schooling (male minus female)	0.66	0.57	0.49	0.40	0.33	0.28
Women age 20–39: highest educational attainment						
E1 - no education	0.09	0.06	0.04	0.02	0.01	0.01
E2 - incomplete primary	0.20	0.13	0.08	0.05	0.02	0.01
E3 - primary	0.16	0.14	0.12	0.10	0.08	0.06
E4 - lower secondary	0.21	0.22	0.21	0.19	0.17	0.14
E5 - upper secondary	0.22	0.28	0.33	0.38	0.41	0.44
E6 - post-secondary	0.13	0.17	0.22	0.26	0.30	0.34
Mean years of schooling (in years)	8.27	9.56	10.50	11.38	12.06	12.57

Education scenarios

GET: global education trend scenario (medium assumption also used for SSP2)

CER: constant enrolment rates scenario (assumption of no future improvements)

FT: Fast track scenario (assumption of education expansion according to fastest historical experience)

Pyramids by Education, Medium Scenario

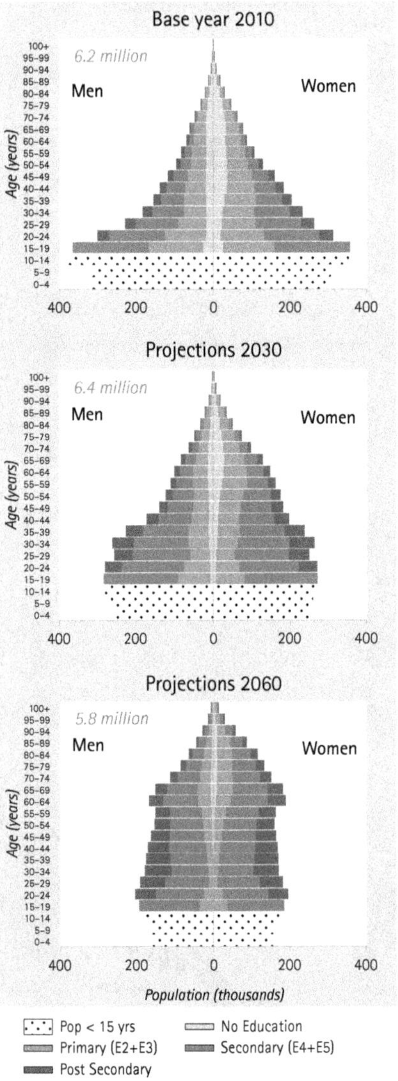

Population Size by Educational Attainment According to Three Education Scenarios: GET, CER, and FT

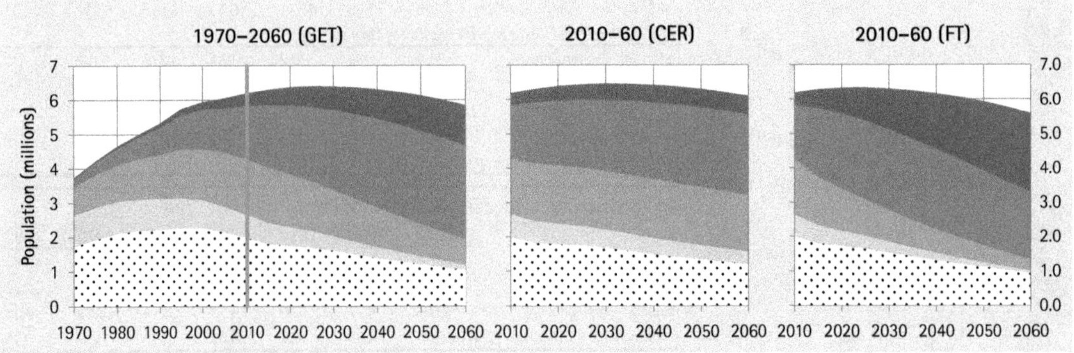

El Salvador (Continued)

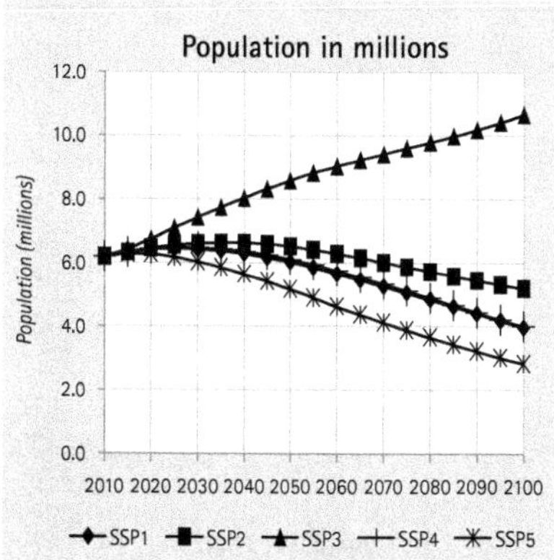

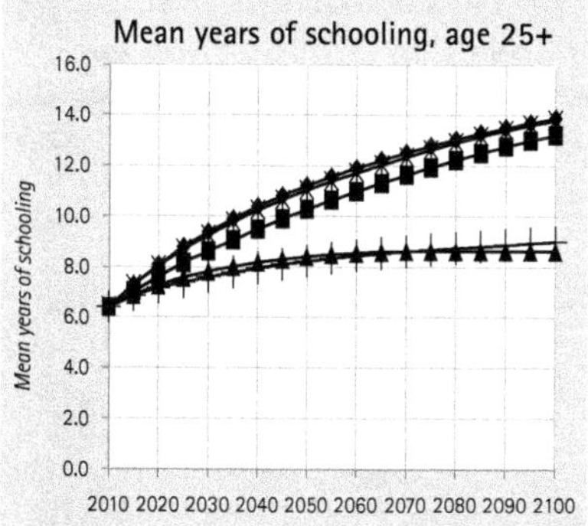

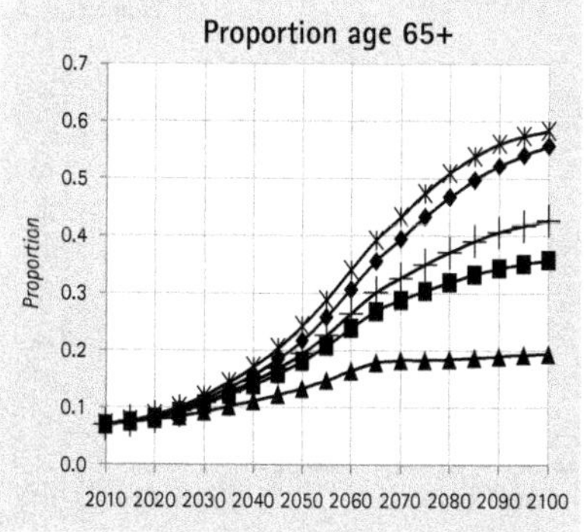

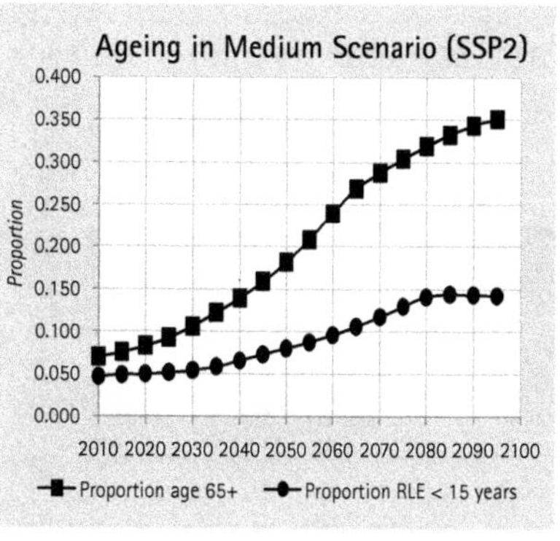

Alternative Scenarios to 2100

Projection Results by Scenario (SSP1–5)

	2010	2020	2030	2040	2050	2075	2100
Population (in millions)							
SSP1 - Rapid development	6.19	6.41	6.42	6.28	6.02	5.05	3.97
SSP2 - Medium	6.19	6.46	6.61	6.63	6.52	5.87	5.19
SSP3 - Stalled development	6.19	6.75	7.44	8.04	8.59	9.60	10.67
SSP4 - Inequality	6.19	6.43	6.48	6.36	6.11	5.12	4.00
SSP5 - Conventional development	6.19	6.27	6.02	5.64	5.17	3.88	2.83
Proportion age 65+							
SSP1 - Rapid development	0.07	0.08	0.11	0.16	0.22	0.43	0.56
SSP2 - Medium	0.07	0.08	0.11	0.14	0.18	0.30	0.36
SSP3 - Stalled development	0.07	0.08	0.09	0.11	0.13	0.18	0.19
SSP4 - Inequality	0.07	0.08	0.11	0.15	0.20	0.35	0.43
SSP5 - Conventional development	0.07	0.09	0.12	0.17	0.24	0.47	0.58
Proportion below age 20							
SSP1 - Rapid development	0.44	0.35	0.29	0.24	0.19	0.12	0.09
SSP2 - Medium	0.44	0.37	0.33	0.29	0.26	0.19	0.17
SSP3 - Stalled development	0.44	0.37	0.36	0.34	0.32	0.29	0.28
SSP4 - Inequality	0.44	0.36	0.31	0.26	0.22	0.15	0.13
SSP5 - Conventional development	0.44	0.36	0.30	0.24	0.19	0.11	0.08
Proportion of Women age 20–39 with at least secondary education							
SSP1 - Rapid development	0.55	0.76	0.85	0.91	0.94	0.98	0.99
SSP2 - Medium	0.55	0.67	0.75	0.83	0.89	0.96	0.99
SSP3 - Stalled development	0.55	0.57	0.58	0.58	0.58	0.58	0.58
SSP4 - Inequality	0.55	0.54	0.52	0.52	0.52	0.52	0.52
SSP5 - Conventional development	0.55	0.76	0.85	0.91	0.94	0.98	0.99
Mean years of schooling, age 25+							
SSP1 - Rapid development	6.39	8.06	9.36	10.38	11.20	12.78	13.87
SSP2 - Medium	6.39	7.60	8.62	9.48	10.28	11.93	13.21
SSP3 - Stalled development	6.39	7.25	7.82	8.18	8.42	8.64	8.64
SSP4 - Inequality	6.39	7.17	7.60	7.96	8.23	8.68	9.00
SSP5 - Conventional development	6.39	8.02	9.25	10.23	11.03	12.63	13.80

Demographic Assumptions Underlying SSPs

	2010–15	2020–25	2030–35	2040–45	2050–55	2075–80	2095–2100
Total fertility rate							
SSP1 - Rapid development	2.03	1.64	1.43	1.33	1.25	1.18	1.21
SSP2 - Medium	2.16	2.00	1.88	1.81	1.71	1.60	1.62
SSP3 - Stalled development	2.30	2.39	2.43	2.40	2.34	2.26	2.33
SSP4 - Inequality	2.08	1.78	1.57	1.46	1.38	1.32	1.36
SSP5 - Conventional development	2.03	1.64	1.43	1.33	1.25	1.18	1.21
Life expectancy at birth for females (in years)							
SSP1 - Rapid development	79.19	82.07	84.99	87.98	90.97	98.52	104.54
SSP2 - Medium	77.40	79.79	81.99	83.99	85.99	91.11	95.09
SSP3 - Stalled development	78.43	79.48	80.38	81.28	82.04	83.84	85.32
SSP4 - Inequality	78.77	80.79	82.68	84.44	86.22	90.75	94.31
SSP5 - Conventional development	79.19	82.07	84.99	87.98	90.97	98.52	104.54
Migration – net flow over five years (in thousands)							
SSP1 - Rapid development	−260	−236	−214	−187	−155	−45	0
SSP2 - Medium	−275	−249	−228	−209	−186	−63	0
SSP3 - Stalled development	−217	−120	−114	−112	−107	−46	0
SSP4 - Inequality	−260	−235	−211	−182	−148	−40	0
SSP5 - Conventional development	−304	−351	−312	−271	−223	−63	0

Ageing Indicators, Medium Scenario (SSP2)

	2010	2020	2030	2040	2050	2075	2095
Median age	23.07	26.82	31.23	35.20	39.16	48.21	51.82
Propspective median age	23.07	24.50	26.77	28.93	31.20	36.06	36.25
Proportion age 65+	0.07	0.08	0.11	0.14	0.18	0.30	0.35
Proportion RLE < 15 years	0.05	0.05	0.05	0.07	0.08	0.13	0.14

Equatorial Guinea

Detailed Human Capital Projections to 2060

Demographic indicators, Medium Scenario (SSP2)	2010	2020	2030	2040	2050	2060
Population (in millions)	0.70	0.90	1.09	1.27	1.43	1.57
Proportion age 65+	0.03	0.03	0.06	0.06	0.06	0.08
Proportion below age 20	0.50	0.47	0.43	0.39	0.35	0.32
	2005–10	2015–20	2025–30	2035–40	2045–50	2055–60
Total Fertility Rate	5.36	4.21	3.22	2.67	2.31	2.07
Life expectancy at birth (in years)						
Men	48.87	51.95	54.26	56.25	58.29	61.02
Women	51.48	54.40	57.00	59.52	61.98	64.88
Five-year immigration flow (in '000)	19.99	19.59	20.34	20.79	20.78	20.47
Five-year emigration flow (in '000)	0.00	0.00	0.00	0.00	0.00	0.00

Human Capital indicators, Medium Scenario (SSP2)	2010	2020	2030	2040	2050	2060
Population age 25+: highest educational attainment						
E1 - no education	0.09	0.07	0.05	0.03	0.02	0.01
E2 - incomplete primary	0.11	0.08	0.05	0.04	0.02	0.01
E3 - primary	0.24	0.21	0.18	0.16	0.13	0.11
E4 - lower secondary	0.31	0.33	0.32	0.30	0.27	0.24
E5 - upper secondary	0.19	0.24	0.30	0.35	0.40	0.44
E6 - post-secondary	0.06	0.08	0.10	0.12	0.15	0.19
Mean years of schooling (in years)	7.81	8.61	9.49	10.28	10.93	11.46
Gender gap (population age 25+): highest educational attainment (ratio male/female)						
E1 - no education	0.26	0.27	0.29	0.33	0.38	0.45
E2 - incomplete primary	0.46	0.44	0.44	0.46	0.50	0.55
E3 - primary	0.61	0.59	0.60	0.64	0.70	0.78
E4 - lower secondary	1.45	1.18	1.02	0.93	0.88	0.88
E5 - upper secondary	2.00	1.68	1.46	1.29	1.17	1.10
E6 - post-secondary	4.31	2.92	2.16	1.68	1.40	1.22
Mean years of schooling (male minus female)	2.71	2.27	1.78	1.30	0.87	0.55
Women age 20–39: highest educational attainment						
E1 - no education	0.08	0.06	0.03	0.02	0.01	0.00
E2 - incomplete primary	0.09	0.06	0.04	0.02	0.01	0.01
E3 - primary	0.24	0.23	0.20	0.16	0.13	0.09
E4 - lower secondary	0.34	0.34	0.32	0.28	0.24	0.19
E5 - upper secondary	0.21	0.27	0.34	0.41	0.48	0.53
E6 - post-secondary	0.03	0.05	0.07	0.10	0.14	0.18
Mean years of schooling (in years)	7.89	8.80	9.92	10.78	11.39	11.91

Education scenarios

GET: global education trend scenario (medium assumption also used for SSP2)

CER: constant enrolment rates scenario (assumption of no future improvements)

FT: Fast track scenario (assumption of education expansion according to fastest historical experience)

Pyramids by Education, Medium Scenario

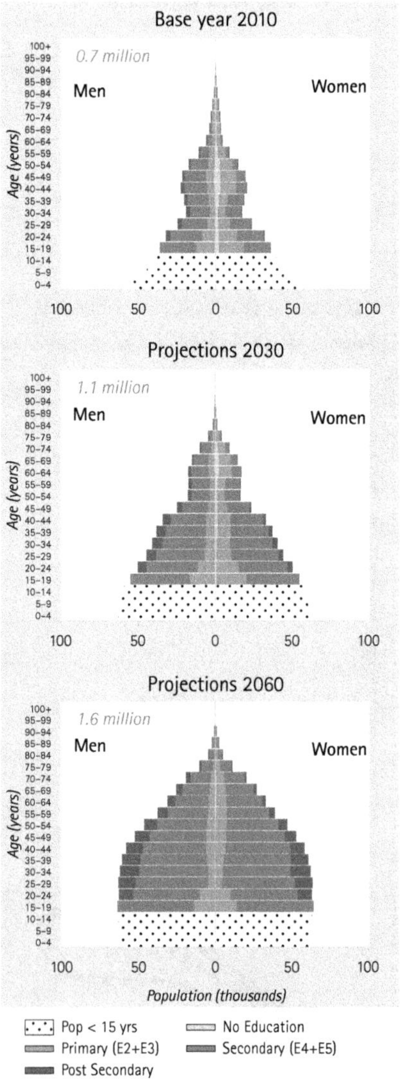

Population Size by Educational Attainment According to Three Education Scenarios: GET, CER, and FT

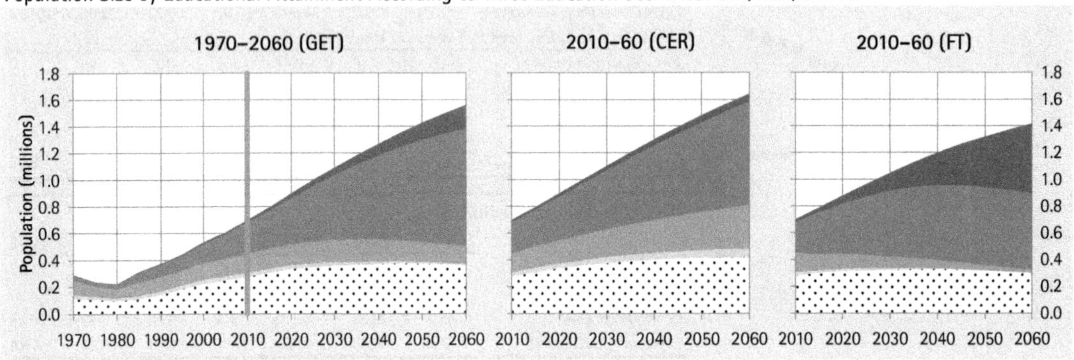

Equatorial Guinea (Continued)

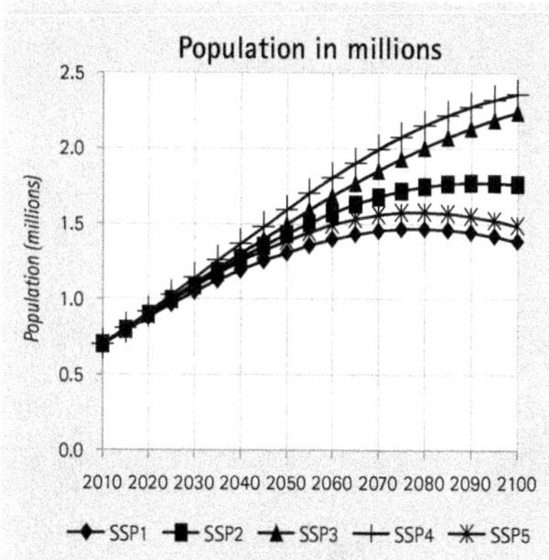

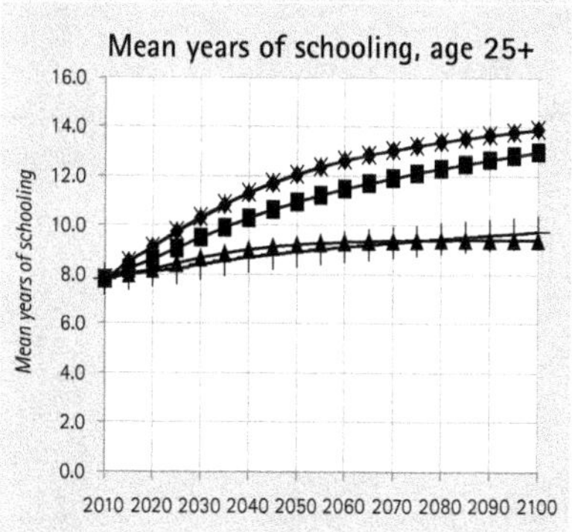

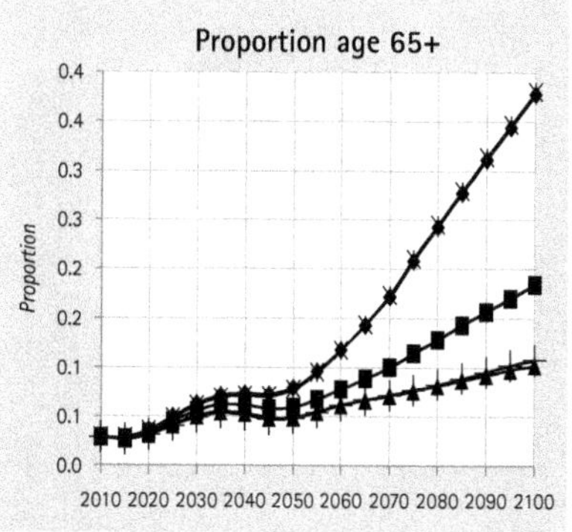

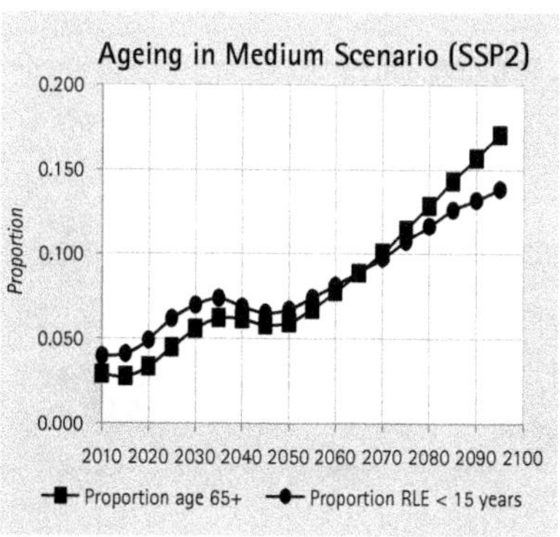

Alternative Scenarios to 2100

Projection Results by Scenario (SSP1–5)

	2010	2020	2030	2040	2050	2075	2100
Population (in millions)							
SSP1 - Rapid development	0.70	0.88	1.05	1.19	1.31	1.47	1.39
SSP2 - Medium	0.70	0.90	1.09	1.27	1.43	1.72	1.76
SSP3 - Stalled development	0.70	0.90	1.10	1.30	1.50	1.93	2.24
SSP4 - Inequality	0.70	0.91	1.14	1.37	1.59	2.08	2.36
SSP5 - Conventional development	0.70	0.89	1.08	1.25	1.39	1.57	1.49
Proportion age 65+							
SSP1 - Rapid development	0.03	0.04	0.06	0.07	0.08	0.21	0.38
SSP2 - Medium	0.03	0.03	0.06	0.06	0.06	0.11	0.18
SSP3 - Stalled development	0.03	0.03	0.05	0.05	0.05	0.08	0.10
SSP4 - Inequality	0.03	0.03	0.05	0.05	0.05	0.08	0.11
SSP5 - Conventional development	0.03	0.04	0.06	0.07	0.08	0.21	0.38
Proportion below age 20							
SSP1 - Rapid development	0.50	0.45	0.39	0.33	0.28	0.18	0.13
SSP2 - Medium	0.50	0.47	0.43	0.39	0.35	0.27	0.23
SSP3 - Stalled development	0.50	0.48	0.47	0.44	0.41	0.36	0.33
SSP4 - Inequality	0.50	0.48	0.47	0.44	0.41	0.35	0.32
SSP5 - Conventional development	0.50	0.45	0.38	0.33	0.28	0.18	0.13
Proportion of Women age 20–39 with at least secondary education							
SSP1 - Rapid development	0.58	0.77	0.85	0.89	0.93	0.97	0.99
SSP2 - Medium	0.58	0.66	0.73	0.80	0.85	0.94	0.98
SSP3 - Stalled development	0.58	0.58	0.58	0.58	0.58	0.58	0.58
SSP4 - Inequality	0.58	0.54	0.52	0.52	0.52	0.52	0.52
SSP5 - Conventional development	0.58	0.77	0.85	0.89	0.93	0.97	0.99
Mean years of schooling, age 25+							
SSP1 - Rapid development	7.81	9.10	10.28	11.28	12.04	13.22	13.88
SSP2 - Medium	7.81	8.61	9.49	10.28	10.93	12.11	12.97
SSP3 - Stalled development	7.81	8.21	8.67	9.01	9.21	9.39	9.40
SSP4 - Inequality	7.81	8.12	8.40	8.69	8.92	9.36	9.74
SSP5 - Conventional development	7.81	9.11	10.31	11.30	12.05	13.22	13.88

Demographic Assumptions Underlying SSPs

	2010–15	2020–25	2030–35	2040–45	2050–55	2075–80	2095–2100
Total fertility rate							
SSP1 - Rapid development	4.38	2.93	2.17	1.79	1.56	1.35	1.26
SSP2 - Medium	4.75	3.66	2.92	2.48	2.18	1.87	1.71
SSP3 - Stalled development	5.08	4.53	3.92	3.42	3.08	2.68	2.51
SSP4 - Inequality	5.08	4.58	3.93	3.38	3.00	2.57	2.38
SSP5 - Conventional development	4.38	2.93	2.17	1.79	1.56	1.35	1.26
Life expectancy at birth for females (in years)							
SSP1 - Rapid development	57.07	63.74	67.80	72.32	76.35	85.63	93.08
SSP2 - Medium	52.88	55.70	58.33	60.68	63.38	70.72	76.50
SSP3 - Stalled development	56.44	54.16	55.44	56.31	57.47	60.97	64.16
SSP4 - Inequality	56.44	54.13	55.38	56.25	57.43	60.99	64.24
SSP5 - Conventional development	57.07	63.74	67.80	72.32	76.35	85.63	93.08
Migration – net flow over five years (in thousands)							
SSP1 - Rapid development	18	19	19	18	17	6	0
SSP2 - Medium	19	20	20	21	20	10	0
SSP3 - Stalled development	15	10	10	12	13	9	0
SSP4 - Inequality	18	19	20	22	24	15	0
SSP5 - Conventional development	21	29	29	26	24	9	0

Ageing Indicators, Medium Scenario (SSP2)

	2010	2020	2030	2040	2050	2075	2095
Median age	20.25	21.72	23.57	25.95	28.54	35.27	40.03
Propspective median age	20.25	20.97	21.62	22.77	24.11	26.44	27.47
Proportion age 65+	0.03	0.03	0.06	0.06	0.06	0.11	0.17
Proportion RLE < 15 years	0.04	0.05	0.07	0.07	0.07	0.11	0.14

Estonia

Detailed Human Capital Projections to 2060

Demographic indicators, Medium Scenario (SSP2)	2010	2020	2030	2040	2050	2060
Population (in millions)	1.34	1.32	1.28	1.24	1.21	1.18
Proportion age 65+	0.17	0.19	0.22	0.24	0.27	0.31
Proportion below age 20	0.21	0.22	0.21	0.19	0.19	0.19
	2005–10	2015–20	2025–30	2035–40	2045–50	2055–60
Total Fertility Rate	1.64	1.55	1.63	1.67	1.70	1.70
Life expectancy at birth (in years)						
Men	68.35	70.98	73.59	76.01	78.39	80.68
Women	79.17	80.69	82.59	84.49	86.51	88.51
Five-year immigration flow (in '000)	4.99	4.92	5.12	5.25	5.27	5.20
Five-year emigration flow (in '000)	5.00	3.31	2.87	2.68	2.46	2.26

Human Capital indicators, Medium Scenario (SSP2)	2010	2020	2030	2040	2050	2060
Population age 25+: highest educational attainment						
E1 - no education	0.00	0.00	0.00	0.00	0.00	0.00
E2 - incomplete primary	0.00	0.00	0.00	0.00	0.00	0.00
E3 - primary	0.05	0.02	0.01	0.00	0.00	0.00
E4 - lower secondary	0.13	0.09	0.06	0.04	0.02	0.01
E5 - upper secondary	0.46	0.50	0.51	0.51	0.50	0.48
E6 - post-secondary	0.35	0.39	0.42	0.45	0.48	0.51
Mean years of schooling (in years)	12.67	13.14	13.43	13.64	13.81	13.96
Gender gap (population age 25+): highest educational attainment (ratio male/female)						
E1 - no education	1.07	1.09	1.06	0.98	0.93	0.92
E2 - incomplete primary	0.56	0.69	0.95	1.07	1.05	1.02
E3 - primary	0.71	0.74	0.95	1.34	1.63	1.71
E4 - lower secondary	1.25	1.23	1.28	1.35	1.35	1.26
E5 - upper secondary	1.25	1.31	1.34	1.34	1.32	1.26
E6 - post-secondary	0.71	0.67	0.67	0.69	0.73	0.79
Mean years of schooling (male minus female)	-0.44	-0.61	-0.70	-0.69	-0.61	-0.48
Women age 20–39: highest educational attainment						
E1 - no education	0.00	0.00	0.00	0.00	0.00	0.00
E2 - incomplete primary	0.00	0.00	0.00	0.00	0.00	0.00
E3 - primary	0.00	0.00	0.00	0.00	0.00	0.00
E4 - lower secondary	0.07	0.04	0.05	0.05	0.04	0.05
E5 - upper secondary	0.52	0.48	0.48	0.47	0.46	0.46
E6 - post-secondary	0.41	0.47	0.46	0.48	0.50	0.49
Mean years of schooling (in years)	13.41	13.73	13.68	13.78	13.84	13.79

Education scenarios

GET: global education trend scenario (medium assumption also used for SSP2)

CER: constant enrolment rates scenario (assumption of no future improvements)

FT: Fast track scenario (assumption of education expansion according to fastest historical experience)

Pyramids by Education, Medium Scenario

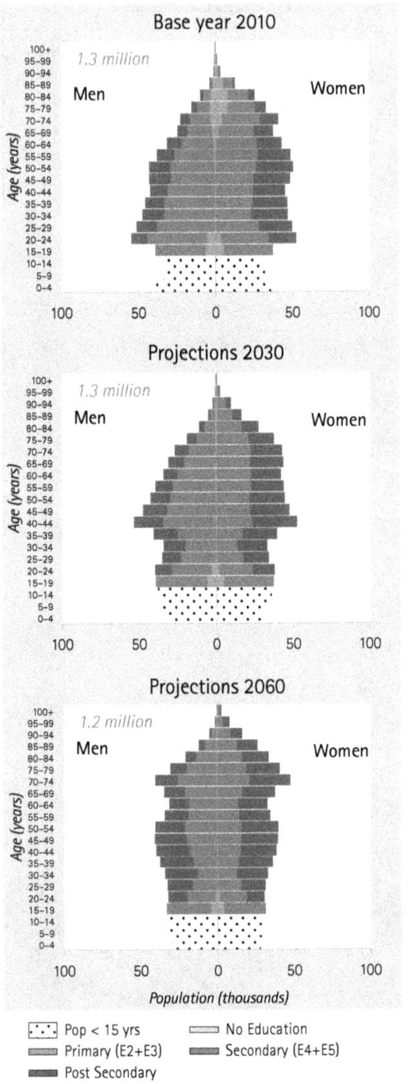

Population Size by Educational Attainment According to Three Education Scenarios: GET, CER, and FT

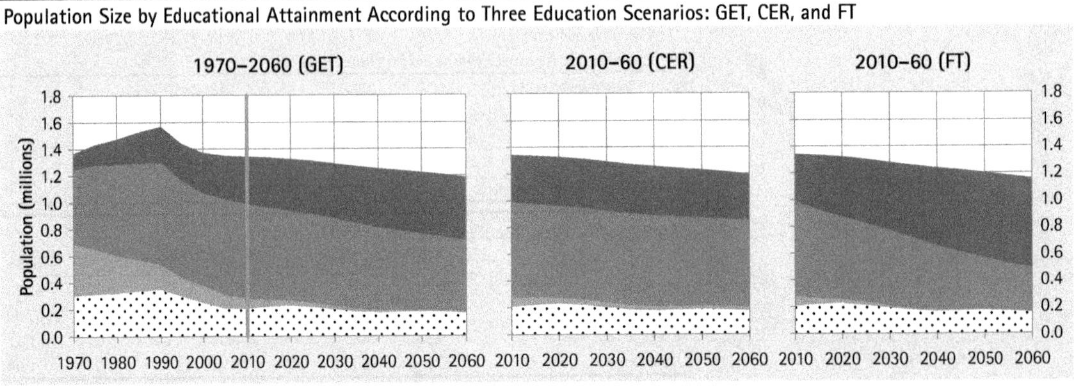

Estonia (Continued)

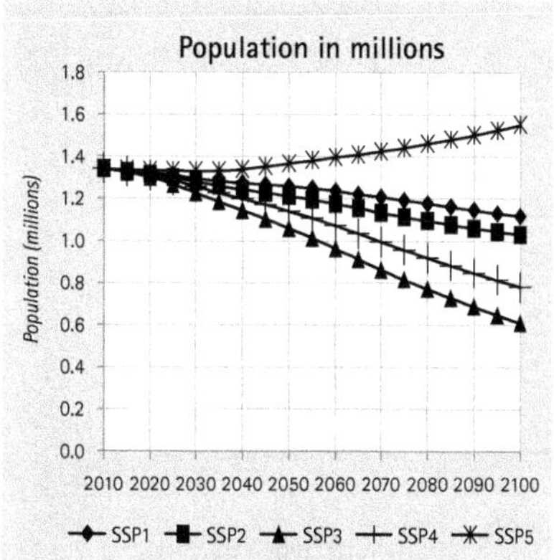

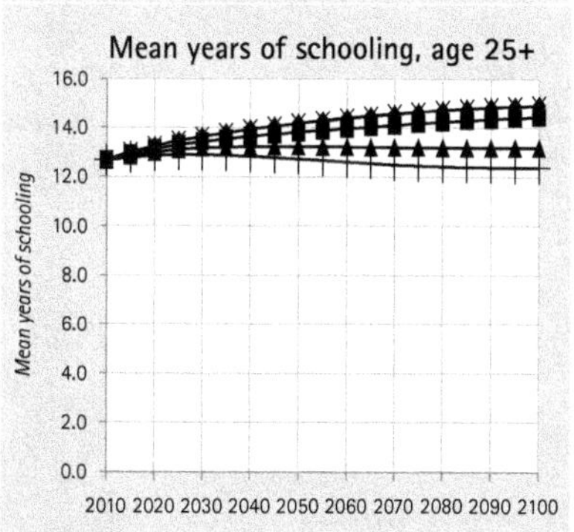

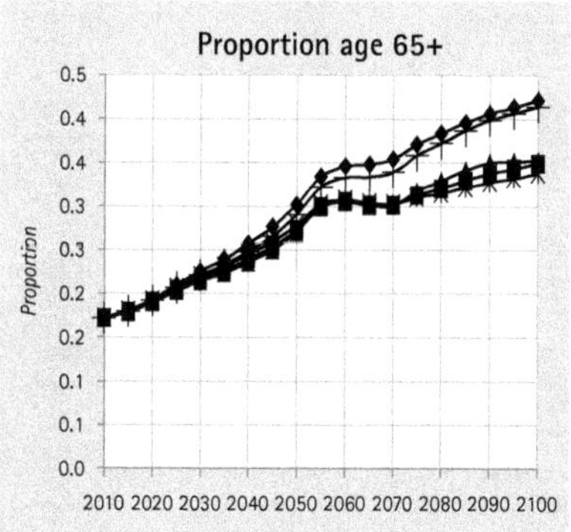

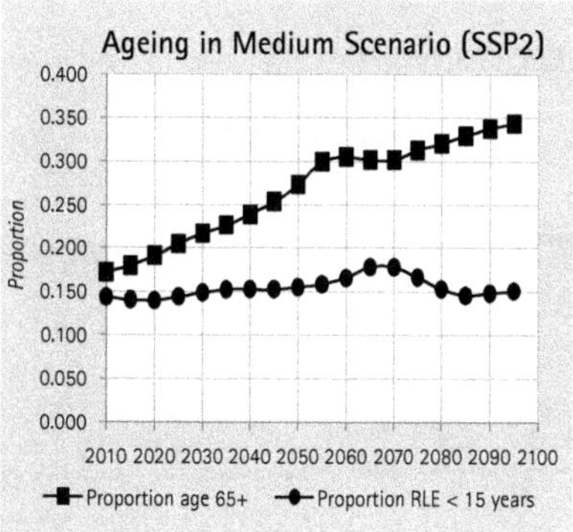

Alternative Scenarios to 2100

Projection Results by Scenario (SSP1–5)

	2010	2020	2030	2040	2050	2075	2100
Population (in millions)							
SSP1 - Rapid development	1.34	1.32	1.30	1.27	1.26	1.19	1.12
SSP2 - Medium	1.34	1.32	1.28	1.24	1.21	1.11	1.03
SSP3 - Stalled development	1.34	1.30	1.23	1.14	1.06	0.82	0.61
SSP4 - Inequality	1.34	1.31	1.26	1.20	1.14	0.96	0.78
SSP5 - Conventional development	1.34	1.33	1.33	1.34	1.37	1.44	1.55
Proportion age 65+							
SSP1 - Rapid development	0.17	0.19	0.23	0.26	0.30	0.37	0.42
SSP2 - Medium	0.17	0.19	0.22	0.24	0.27	0.31	0.35
SSP3 - Stalled development	0.17	0.19	0.21	0.24	0.27	0.32	0.35
SSP4 - Inequality	0.17	0.19	0.22	0.25	0.29	0.36	0.41
SSP5 - Conventional development	0.17	0.19	0.22	0.24	0.28	0.31	0.34
Proportion below age 20							
SSP1 - Rapid development	0.21	0.21	0.20	0.18	0.18	0.16	0.15
SSP2 - Medium	0.21	0.22	0.21	0.19	0.19	0.18	0.17
SSP3 - Stalled development	0.21	0.21	0.19	0.17	0.17	0.15	0.14
SSP4 - Inequality	0.21	0.21	0.19	0.17	0.17	0.14	0.13
SSP5 - Conventional development	0.21	0.22	0.22	0.21	0.22	0.21	0.21
Proportion of Women age 20–39 with at least secondary education							
SSP1 - Rapid development	1.00	1.00	1.00	1.00	1.00	1.00	1.00
SSP2 - Medium	1.00	1.00	1.00	1.00	1.00	1.00	1.00
SSP3 - Stalled development	1.00	0.99	0.99	0.99	0.99	0.99	0.99
SSP4 - Inequality	1.00	0.99	0.99	0.99	0.99	0.99	0.99
SSP5 - Conventional development	1.00	1.00	1.00	1.00	1.00	1.00	1.00
Mean years of schooling, age 25+							
SSP1 - Rapid development	12.67	13.25	13.63	13.93	14.18	14.65	14.92
SSP2 - Medium	12.67	13.14	13.43	13.64	13.81	14.17	14.45
SSP3 - Stalled development	12.67	12.99	13.17	13.23	13.23	13.20	13.19
SSP4 - Inequality	12.67	12.86	12.90	12.84	12.73	12.45	12.38
SSP5 - Conventional development	12.67	13.25	13.63	13.93	14.19	14.67	14.93

Demographic Assumptions Underlying SSPs

	2010–15	2020–25	2030–35	2040–45	2050–55	2075–80	2095–2100
Total fertility rate							
SSP1 - Rapid development	1.51	1.56	1.62	1.66	1.67	1.69	1.70
SSP2 - Medium	1.52	1.59	1.66	1.68	1.70	1.71	1.72
SSP3 - Stalled development	1.46	1.38	1.33	1.32	1.31	1.32	1.34
SSP4 - Inequality	1.46	1.43	1.40	1.39	1.38	1.39	1.41
SSP5 - Conventional development	1.59	1.80	1.96	2.05	2.09	2.11	2.12
Life expectancy at birth for females (in years)							
SSP1 - Rapid development	80.89	83.44	86.26	89.17	92.11	99.60	105.62
SSP2 - Medium	79.89	81.69	83.59	85.51	87.51	92.50	96.49
SSP3 - Stalled development	79.91	80.47	81.30	82.21	83.17	85.57	87.53
SSP4 - Inequality	80.40	82.02	83.79	85.65	87.60	92.32	96.22
SSP5 - Conventional development	80.89	83.44	86.26	89.17	92.11	99.60	105.62
Migration – net flow over five years (in thousands)							
SSP1 - Rapid development	1	2	2	3	3	1	0
SSP2 - Medium	1	2	2	3	3	1	0
SSP3 - Stalled development	1	1	1	1	1	1	0
SSP4 - Inequality	1	2	2	3	3	1	0
SSP5 - Conventional development	1	3	4	4	4	2	0

Ageing Indicators, Medium Scenario (SSP2)

	2010	2020	2030	2040	2050	2075	2095
Median age	39.66	41.50	44.37	47.30	46.73	49.78	51.25
Propspective median age	39.66	39.56	40.55	41.64	39.00	37.17	34.56
Proportion age 65+	0.17	0.19	0.22	0.24	0.27	0.31	0.34
Proportion RLE < 15 years	0.14	0.14	0.15	0.15	0.16	0.17	0.15

Ethiopia

Detailed Human Capital Projections to 2060

Demographic indicators, Medium Scenario (SSP2)

	2010	2020	2030	2040	2050	2060
Population (in millions)	82.95	103.17	124.25	142.97	159.23	172.49
Proportion age 65+	0.03	0.04	0.04	0.05	0.07	0.09
Proportion below age 20	0.53	0.48	0.44	0.39	0.34	0.31
	2005–10	2015–20	2025–30	2035–40	2045–50	2055–60
Total Fertility Rate	4.60	3.73	3.04	2.58	2.21	2.04
Life expectancy at birth (in years)						
Men	55.71	60.16	62.18	64.01	65.87	68.07
Women	58.74	63.58	66.12	68.18	70.18	72.38
Five-year immigration flow (in '000)	0.09	0.09	0.09	0.09	0.09	0.09
Five-year emigration flow (in '000)	296.65	291.92	344.96	390.85	426.07	438.59

Human Capital indicators, Medium Scenario (SSP2)

	2010	2020	2030	2040	2050	2060
Population age 25+: highest educational attainment						
E1 - no education	0.65	0.46	0.37	0.28	0.21	0.15
E2 - incomplete primary	0.18	0.25	0.22	0.20	0.16	0.13
E3 - primary	0.09	0.14	0.20	0.24	0.27	0.29
E4 - lower secondary	0.02	0.05	0.08	0.10	0.12	0.13
E5 - upper secondary	0.03	0.05	0.08	0.11	0.15	0.20
E6 - post-secondary	0.03	0.04	0.06	0.07	0.09	0.11
Mean years of schooling (in years)	2.23	3.65	4.79	5.87	6.94	7.91
Gender gap (population age 25+): highest educational attainment (ratio male/female)						
E1 - no education	0.65	0.65	0.64	0.66	0.69	0.73
E2 - incomplete primary	2.12	1.34	1.30	1.20	1.11	1.04
E3 - primary	2.61	1.58	1.28	1.14	1.07	1.04
E4 - lower secondary	2.43	1.29	1.10	1.03	1.00	1.00
E5 - upper secondary	1.89	1.41	1.30	1.23	1.16	1.09
E6 - post-secondary	2.82	2.01	1.61	1.36	1.21	1.13
Mean years of schooling (male minus female)	1.83	1.50	1.30	1.01	0.74	0.52
Women age 20–39: highest educational attainment						
E1 - no education	0.58	0.31	0.25	0.17	0.10	0.05
E2 - incomplete primary	0.20	0.27	0.18	0.13	0.08	0.05
E3 - primary	0.11	0.20	0.27	0.32	0.33	0.32
E4 - lower secondary	0.04	0.09	0.13	0.15	0.17	0.17
E5 - upper secondary	0.04	0.07	0.10	0.15	0.21	0.27
E6 - post-secondary	0.03	0.05	0.07	0.09	0.11	0.14
Mean years of schooling (in years)	2.79	4.89	6.14	7.46	8.64	9.62

Education scenarios

GET: global education trend scenario (medium assumption also used for SSP2)

CER: constant enrolment Rates Scenario (assumption of no future improvements)

FT: Fast track scenario (assumption of education expansion according to fastest historical experience)

Pyramids by Education, Medium Scenario

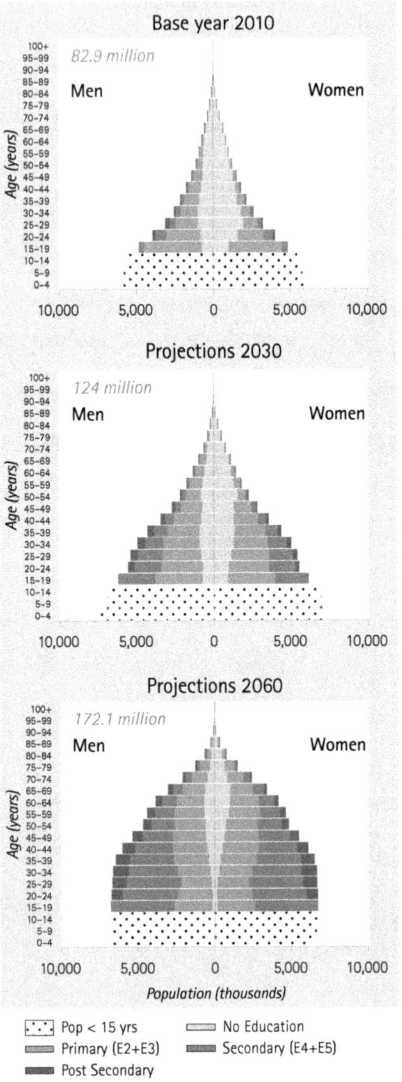

Population Size by Educational Attainment According to Three Education Scenarios: GET, CER, and FT

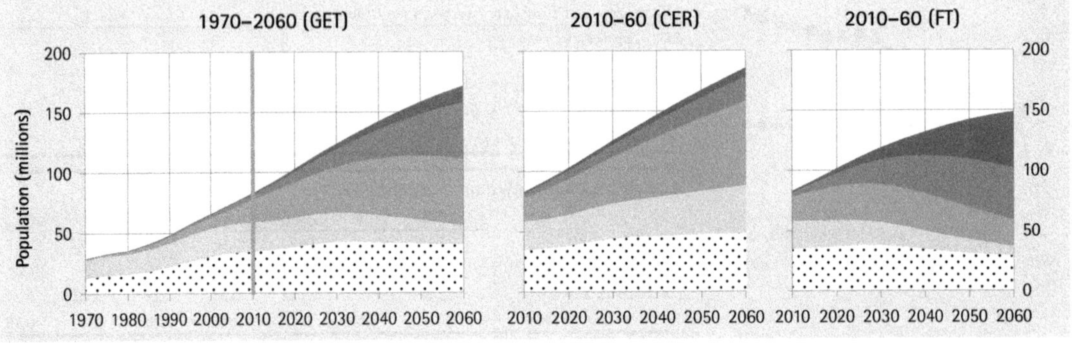

Ethiopia (Continued)

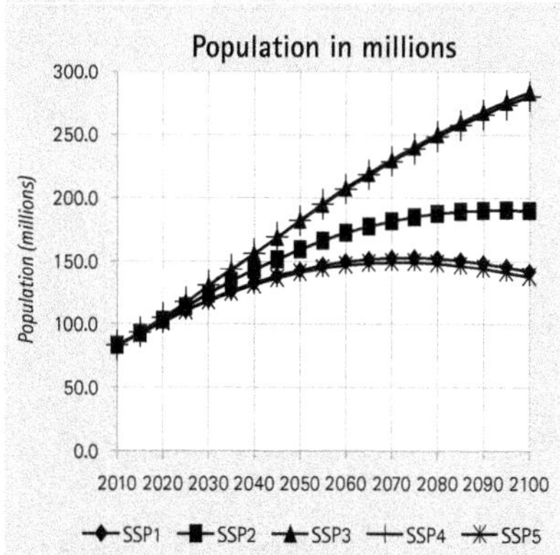

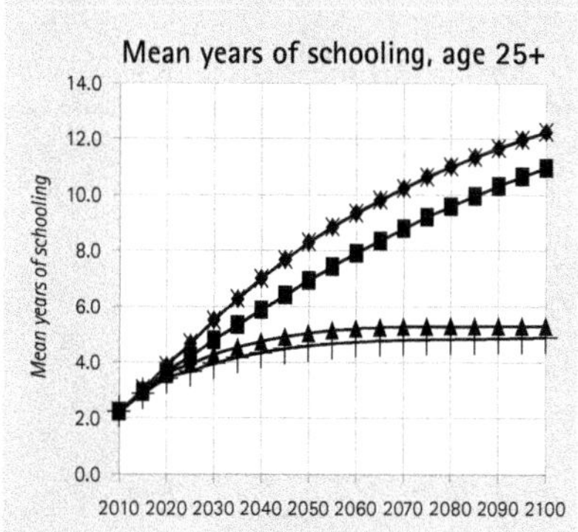

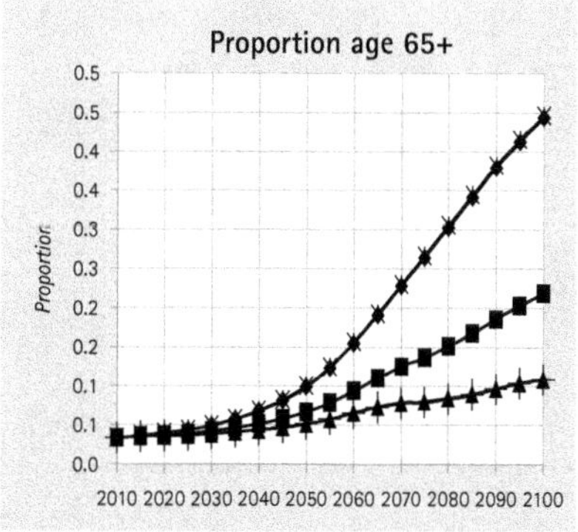

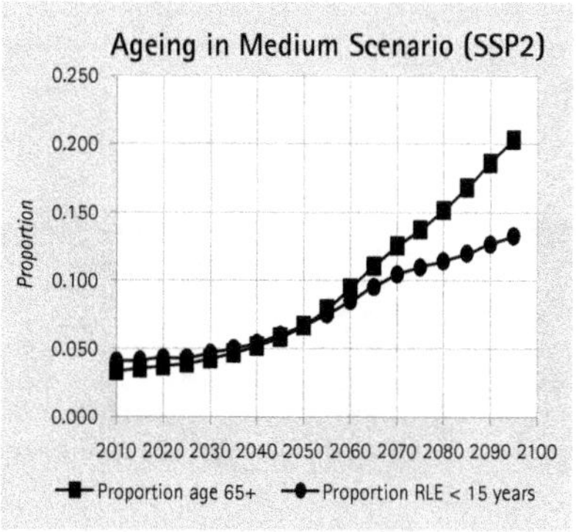

Alternative Scenarios to 2100

Projection Results by Scenario (SSP1-5)

	2010	2020	2030	2040	2050	2075	2100
Population (in millions)							
SSP1 - Rapid development	82.95	101.73	118.83	132.44	142.78	152.93	141.82
SSP2 - Medium	82.95	103.17	124.25	142.97	159.23	185.29	190.27
SSP3 - Stalled development	82.95	104.93	130.58	156.19	182.57	240.72	283.80
SSP4 - Inequality	82.95	104.94	130.62	156.06	182.14	238.96	280.56
SSP5 - Conventional development	82.95	101.55	118.16	131.15	140.76	149.07	137.39
Proportion age 65+							
SSP1 - Rapid development	0.03	0.04	0.05	0.07	0.10	0.26	0.44
SSP2 - Medium	0.03	0.04	0.04	0.05	0.07	0.14	0.22
SSP3 - Stalled development	0.03	0.04	0.04	0.04	0.05	0.08	0.11
SSP4 - Inequality	0.03	0.04	0.04	0.04	0.05	0.08	0.11
SSP5 - Conventional development	0.03	0.04	0.05	0.07	0.10	0.27	0.45
Proportion below age 20							
SSP1 - Rapid development	0.53	0.46	0.39	0.32	0.26	0.16	0.11
SSP2 - Medium	0.53	0.48	0.44	0.39	0.34	0.26	0.21
SSP3 - Stalled development	0.53	0.49	0.47	0.45	0.41	0.35	0.32
SSP4 - Inequality	0.53	0.49	0.48	0.45	0.42	0.36	0.32
SSP5 - Conventional development	0.53	0.46	0.39	0.32	0.26	0.16	0.11
Proportion of Women age 20-39 with at least secondary education							
SSP1 - Rapid development	0.11	0.26	0.43	0.58	0.69	0.84	0.93
SSP2 - Medium	0.11	0.21	0.30	0.39	0.49	0.71	0.87
SSP3 - Stalled development	0.11	0.18	0.20	0.20	0.20	0.20	0.20
SSP4 - Inequality	0.11	0.17	0.18	0.18	0.18	0.18	0.18
SSP5 - Conventional development	0.11	0.26	0.43	0.58	0.69	0.84	0.93
Mean years of schooling, age 25+							
SSP1 - Rapid development	2.23	3.87	5.49	7.00	8.30	10.63	12.24
SSP2 - Medium	2.23	3.65	4.79	5.87	6.94	9.20	10.97
SSP3 - Stalled development	2.23	3.57	4.27	4.74	5.04	5.29	5.30
SSP4 - Inequality	2.23	3.42	3.95	4.34	4.59	4.82	4.89
SSP5 - Conventional development	2.23	3.86	5.49	6.99	8.29	10.62	12.24

Demographic assumptions underlying SSPs

	2010–15	2020–25	2030–35	2040–45	2050–55	2075–80	2095–2100
Total fertility rate							
SSP1 - Rapid development	3.92	2.72	1.99	1.62	1.43	1.27	1.18
SSP2 - Medium	4.14	3.37	2.79	2.38	2.11	1.80	1.65
SSP3 - Stalled development	4.40	4.05	3.75	3.39	3.07	2.57	2.44
SSP4 - Inequality	4.41	4.12	3.82	3.43	3.08	2.55	2.41
SSP5 - Conventional development	3.92	2.72	1.99	1.62	1.43	1.27	1.18
Life expectancy at birth for females (in years)							
SSP1 - Rapid development	66.18	72.34	76.45	80.32	83.74	91.80	98.51
SSP2 - Medium	61.58	64.78	67.22	69.22	71.28	77.09	81.71
SSP3 - Stalled development	63.69	62.39	63.25	64.37	64.81	67.55	69.08
SSP4 - Inequality	63.69	62.37	63.21	64.32	64.75	67.49	69.03
SSP5 - Conventional development	66.18	72.34	76.45	80.32	83.74	91.80	98.51
Migration – net flow over five years (in thousands)							
SSP1 - Rapid development	−274	−318	−362	−389	−387	−157	0
SSP2 - Medium	−273	−318	−365	−410	−435	−212	0
SSP3 - Stalled development	−227	−155	−174	−195	−212	−113	0
SSP4 - Inequality	−272	−314	−364	−421	−467	−251	0
SSP5 - Conventional development	−320	−485	−567	−633	−658	−301	0

Ageing Indicators, Medium Scenario (SSP2)

	2010	2020	2030	2040	2050	2075	2095
Median age	18.59	21.06	23.42	26.02	29.23	36.78	41.89
Propspective median age	18.59	19.48	20.42	21.87	24.12	28.01	29.63
Proportion age 65+	0.03	0.04	0.04	0.05	0.07	0.14	0.20
Proportion RLE < 15 years	0.04	0.04	0.05	0.05	0.07	0.11	0.13

Finland

Detailed Human Capital Projections to 2060

Demographic indicators, Medium Scenario (SSP2)

	2010	2020	2030	2040	2050	2060
Population (in millions)	5.36	5.62	5.88	6.08	6.29	6.53
Proportion age 65+	0.17	0.23	0.25	0.26	0.27	0.28
Proportion below age 20	0.23	0.22	0.22	0.22	0.22	0.22
	2005–10	2015–20	2025–30	2035–40	2045–50	2055–60
Total Fertility Rate	1.84	1.88	1.98	2.00	2.00	1.99
Life expectancy at birth (in years)						
Men	75.90	79.35	81.65	83.67	85.81	87.85
Women	82.75	85.09	87.21	89.21	91.31	93.31
Five-year immigration flow (in '000)	72.62	71.50	74.34	76.12	76.24	75.18
Five-year emigration flow (in '000)	0.31	0.22	0.21	0.21	0.22	0.22

Human Capital indicators, Medium Scenario (SSP2)

	2010	2020	2030	2040	2050	2060
Population age 25+: highest educational attainment						
E1 - no education	0.00	0.00	0.00	0.00	0.00	0.00
E2 - incomplete primary	0.00	0.00	0.00	0.00	0.00	0.00
E3 - primary	0.00	0.00	0.00	0.00	0.00	0.00
E4 - lower secondary	0.19	0.17	0.16	0.14	0.12	0.11
E5 - upper secondary	0.36	0.35	0.35	0.34	0.34	0.33
E6 - post-secondary	0.45	0.47	0.49	0.51	0.54	0.56
Mean years of schooling (in years)	14.15	14.23	14.22	14.21	14.22	14.23
Gender gap (population age 25+): highest educational attainment (ratio male/female)						
E1 - no education	NA	NA	1.11	NA	NA	NA
E2 - incomplete primary	NA	1.11	1.11	1.11	1.10	1.08
E3 - primary	0.91	0.89	0.85	0.79	0.71	0.64
E4 - lower secondary	0.94	1.04	1.13	1.19	1.22	1.21
E5 - upper secondary	1.17	1.23	1.28	1.31	1.30	1.25
E6 - post-secondary	0.91	0.84	0.81	0.79	0.81	0.84
Mean years of schooling (male minus female)	−0.22	−0.48	−0.65	−0.72	−0.69	−0.58
Women age 20–39: highest educational attainment						
E1 - no education	0.00	0.00	0.00	0.00	0.00	0.00
E2 - incomplete primary	0.00	0.00	0.00	0.00	0.00	0.00
E3 - primary	0.00	0.00	0.00	0.00	0.00	0.00
E4 - lower secondary	0.18	0.17	0.15	0.13	0.12	0.11
E5 - upper secondary	0.37	0.38	0.39	0.41	0.42	0.44
E6 - post-secondary	0.44	0.45	0.46	0.46	0.46	0.45
Mean years of schooling (in years)	14.07	13.88	13.38	13.42	13.45	13.48

Pyramids by Education, Medium Scenario

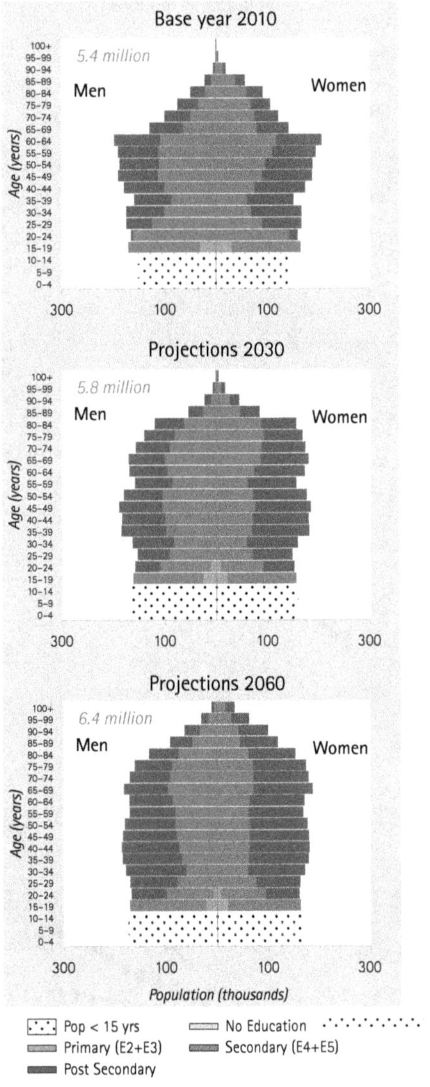

Education scenarios

GET : global education trend scenario (medium assumption also used for SSP2)

CER: constant enrolment rates scenario (assumption of no future improvements)

FT: Fast track scenario (assumption of education expansion according to fastest historical experience)

Population Size by Educational Attainment According to Three Education Scenarios: GET, CER, and FT

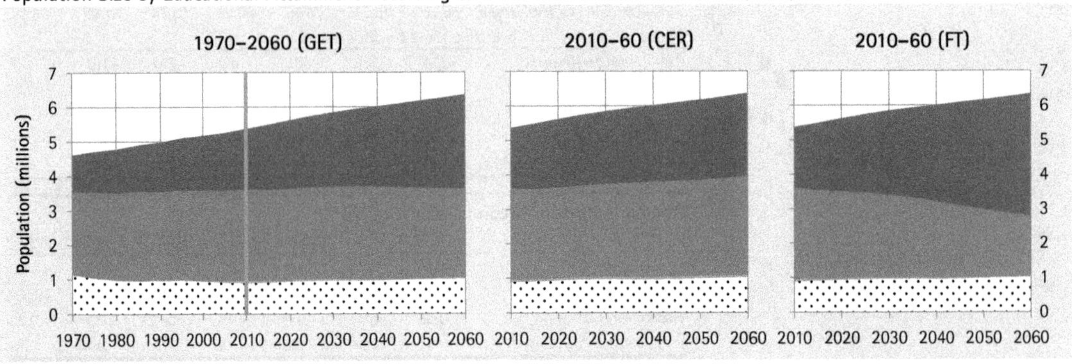

Finland (Continued)

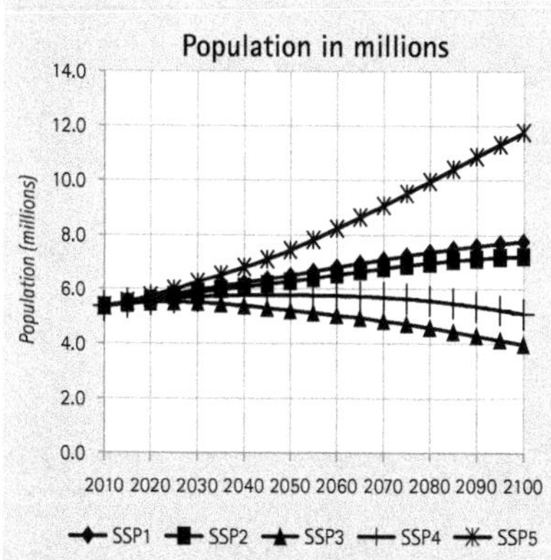

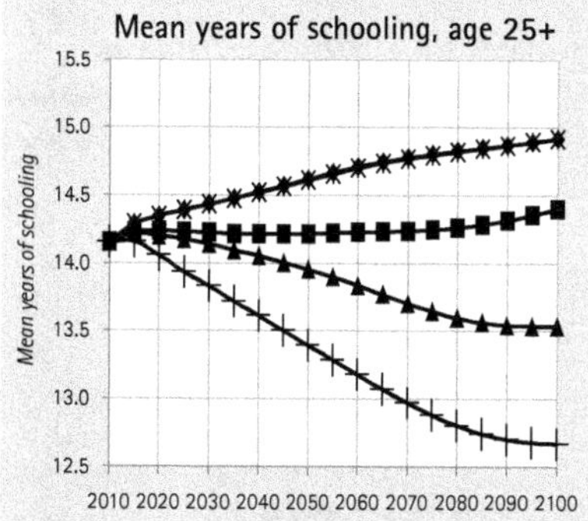

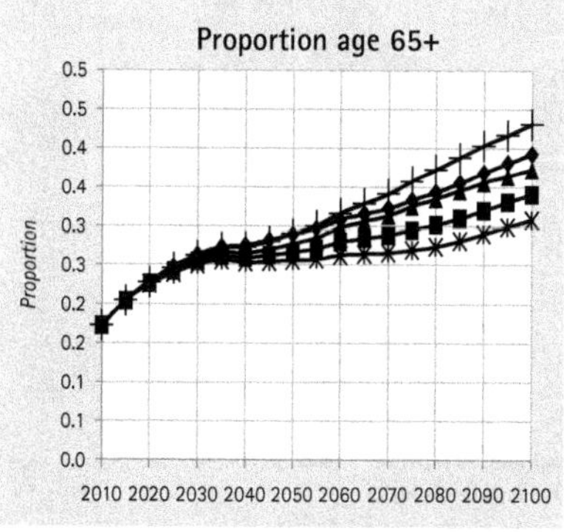

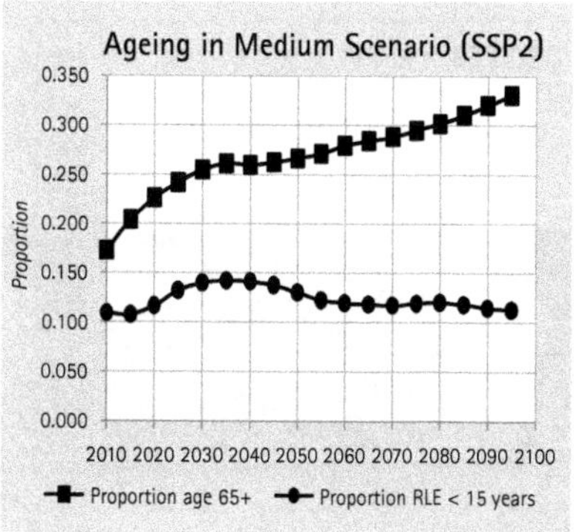

Alternative Scenarios to 2100

Projection Results by Scenario (SSP1–5)

	2010	2020	2030	2040	2050	2075	2100
Population (in millions)							
SSP1 - Rapid development	5.36	5.65	5.96	6.24	6.51	7.24	7.77
SSP2 - Medium	5.36	5.62	5.88	6.08	6.29	6.88	7.22
SSP3 - Stalled development	5.36	5.51	5.51	5.39	5.22	4.72	3.98
SSP4 - Inequality	5.36	5.57	5.72	5.78	5.78	5.65	5.10
SSP5 - Conventional development	5.36	5.73	6.26	6.81	7.45	9.51	11.76
Proportion age 65+							
SSP1 - Rapid development	0.17	0.23	0.26	0.28	0.29	0.33	0.39
SSP2 - Medium	0.17	0.23	0.25	0.26	0.27	0.29	0.34
SSP3 - Stalled development	0.17	0.23	0.26	0.27	0.28	0.33	0.37
SSP4 - Inequality	0.17	0.23	0.26	0.27	0.29	0.36	0.43
SSP5 - Conventional development	0.17	0.23	0.25	0.25	0.26	0.27	0.31
Proportion below age 20							
SSP1 - Rapid development	0.23	0.22	0.22	0.21	0.21	0.20	0.18
SSP2 - Medium	0.23	0.22	0.22	0.22	0.22	0.21	0.19
SSP3 - Stalled development	0.23	0.21	0.20	0.19	0.18	0.16	0.15
SSP4 - Inequality	0.23	0.21	0.20	0.19	0.18	0.15	0.13
SSP5 - Conventional development	0.23	0.22	0.24	0.25	0.25	0.25	0.24
Proportion of Women age 20–39 with at least secondary education							
SSP1 - Rapid development	1.00	1.00	1.00	1.00	1.00	1.00	1.00
SSP2 - Medium	1.00	1.00	1.00	1.00	1.00	1.00	1.00
SSP3 - Stalled development	1.00	1.00	1.00	1.00	1.00	1.00	1.00
SSP4 - Inequality	1.00	1.00	1.00	1.00	1.00	1.00	1.00
SSP5 - Conventional development	1.00	1.00	1.00	1.00	1.00	1.00	1.00
Mean years of schooling, age 25+							
SSP1 - Rapid development	14.15	14.34	14.43	14.52	14.62	14.80	14.91
SSP2 - Medium	14.15	14.23	14.22	14.21	14.22	14.25	14.40
SSP3 - Stalled development	14.15	14.20	14.14	14.05	13.95	13.64	13.53
SSP4 - Inequality	14.15	14.06	13.83	13.61	13.39	12.88	12.67
SSP5 - Conventional development	14.15	14.34	14.43	14.52	14.61	14.79	14.92

Demographic Assumptions Underlying SSPs

	2010–15	2020–25	2030–35	2040–45	2050–55	2075–80	2095–2100
Total fertility rate							
SSP1 - Rapid development	1.83	1.92	1.98	2.00	1.99	1.95	1.92
SSP2 - Medium	1.83	1.93	2.00	2.00	2.00	1.95	1.92
SSP3 - Stalled development	1.74	1.64	1.57	1.53	1.50	1.47	1.45
SSP4 - Inequality	1.74	1.64	1.58	1.54	1.51	1.48	1.46
SSP5 - Conventional development	1.92	2.21	2.41	2.47	2.49	2.44	2.40
Life expectancy at birth for females (in years)							
SSP1 - Rapid development	84.63	87.82	90.88	93.85	96.83	104.32	110.37
SSP2 - Medium	83.89	86.09	88.21	90.31	92.29	97.30	101.31
SSP3 - Stalled development	83.64	84.81	85.89	86.93	87.91	90.36	92.29
SSP4 - Inequality	84.09	86.27	88.36	90.44	92.38	97.19	101.08
SSP5 - Conventional development	84.63	87.82	90.88	93.85	96.83	104.32	110.37
Migration – net flow over five years (in thousands)							
SSP1 - Rapid development	69	72	74	73	71	31	0
SSP2 - Medium	69	72	74	75	74	35	0
SSP3 - Stalled development	57	36	37	37	35	16	0
SSP4 - Inequality	69	72	73	71	68	30	0
SSP5 - Conventional development	80	108	113	116	117	59	0

Ageing Indicators, Medium Scenario (SSP2)

	2010	2020	2030	2040	2050	2075	2095
Median age	42.07	42.79	43.77	44.72	44.61	46.52	49.08
Propspective median age	42.07	40.37	39.36	38.32	36.22	33.38	32.03
Proportion age 65+	0.17	0.23	0.25	0.26	0.27	0.29	0.33
Proportion RLE < 15 years	0.11	0.12	0.14	0.14	0.13	0.12	0.11

France

Detailed Human Capital Projections to 2060

Demographic indicators, Medium Scenario (SSP2)	2010	2020	2030	2040	2050	2060
Population (in millions)	62.79	66.45	69.99	73.24	75.88	78.16
Proportion age 65+	0.17	0.21	0.24	0.26	0.27	0.29
Proportion below age 20	0.24	0.24	0.23	0.22	0.22	0.21
	2005–10	2015–20	2025–30	2035–40	2045–50	2055–60
Total Fertility Rate	1.97	2.00	2.00	1.96	1.91	1.89
Life expectancy at birth (in years)						
Men	77.48	80.57	83.17	85.24	87.36	89.37
Women	84.31	86.71	88.91	90.91	93.00	95.00
Five-year immigration flow (in '000)	752.55	739.25	768.01	785.65	786.17	774.84
Five-year emigration flow (in '000)	253.17	181.35	180.41	181.80	181.03	181.21

Human Capital indicators, Medium Scenario (SSP2)	2010	2020	2030	2040	2050	2060
Population age 25+: highest educational attainment						
E1 - no education	0.02	0.02	0.01	0.01	0.01	0.00
E2 - incomplete primary	0.00	0.00	0.00	0.00	0.00	0.00
E3 - primary	0.25	0.18	0.12	0.08	0.05	0.03
E4 - lower secondary	0.09	0.09	0.08	0.07	0.05	0.04
E5 - upper secondary	0.39	0.41	0.41	0.40	0.38	0.36
E6 - post-secondary	0.24	0.31	0.37	0.44	0.51	0.57
Mean years of schooling (in years)	10.53	11.34	12.09	12.75	13.33	13.82
Gender gap (population age 25+): highest educational attainment (ratio male/female)						
E1 - no education	1.02	0.87	0.75	0.67	0.63	0.62
E2 - incomplete primary	NA	NA	NA	NA	NA	NA
E3 - primary	0.77	0.75	0.74	0.73	0.75	0.78
E4 - lower secondary	0.85	0.87	0.89	0.90	0.91	0.92
E5 - upper secondary	1.25	1.22	1.19	1.17	1.13	1.10
E6 - post-secondary	0.98	0.95	0.94	0.94	0.95	0.96
Mean years of schooling (male minus female)	0.46	0.35	0.22	0.13	0.06	0.02
Women age 20–39: highest educational attainment						
E1 - no education	0.01	0.01	0.00	0.00	0.00	0.00
E2 - incomplete primary	0.00	0.00	0.00	0.00	0.00	0.00
E3 - primary	0.07	0.03	0.02	0.01	0.00	0.00
E4 - lower secondary	0.09	0.07	0.05	0.04	0.03	0.02
E5 - upper secondary	0.43	0.41	0.40	0.38	0.36	0.35
E6 - post-secondary	0.40	0.48	0.53	0.57	0.61	0.63
Mean years of schooling (in years)	12.35	13.13	13.80	14.10	14.29	14.40

Education scenarios

GET: global education trend scenario (medium assumption also used for SSP2)

CER: constant enrolment rates scenario (assumption of no future improvements)

FT: Fast track scenario (assumption of education expansion according to fastest historical experience)

Pyramids by Education, Medium Scenario

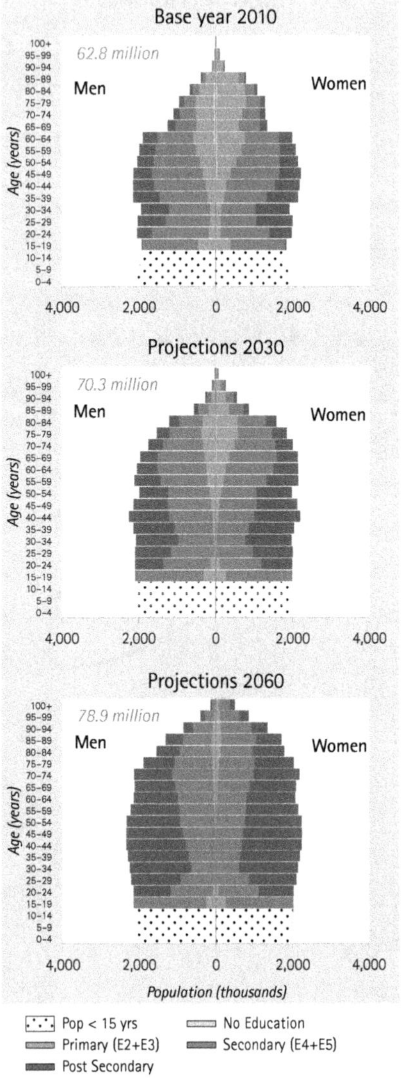

Population Size by Educational Attainment According to Three Education Scenarios: GET, CER, and FT

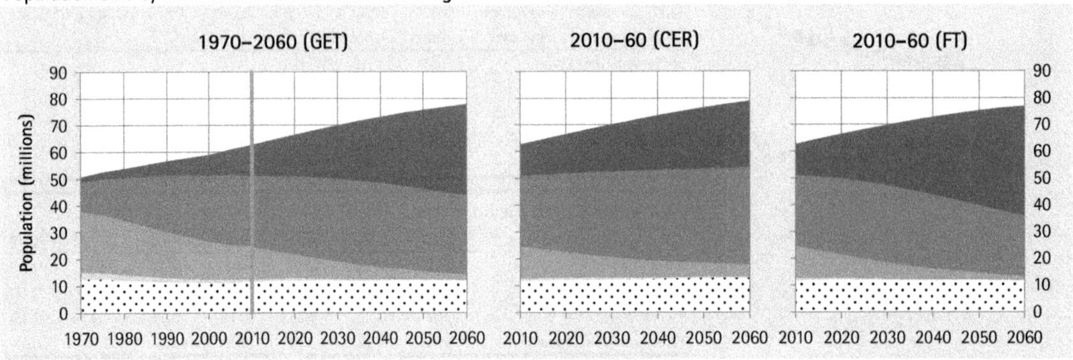

France (Continued)

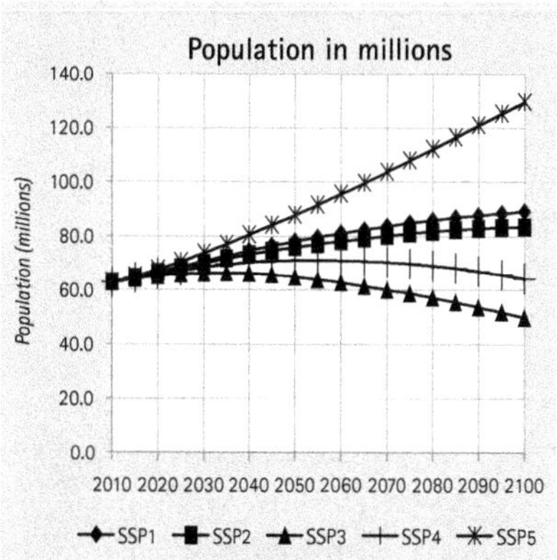

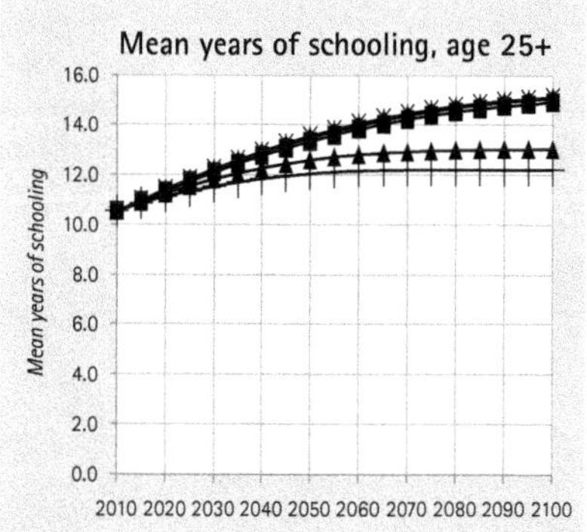

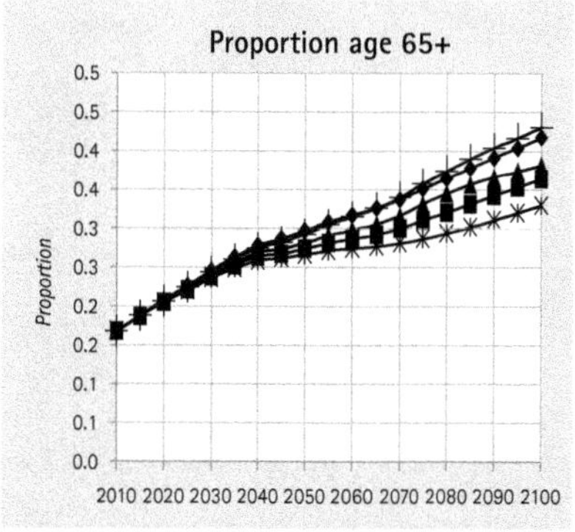

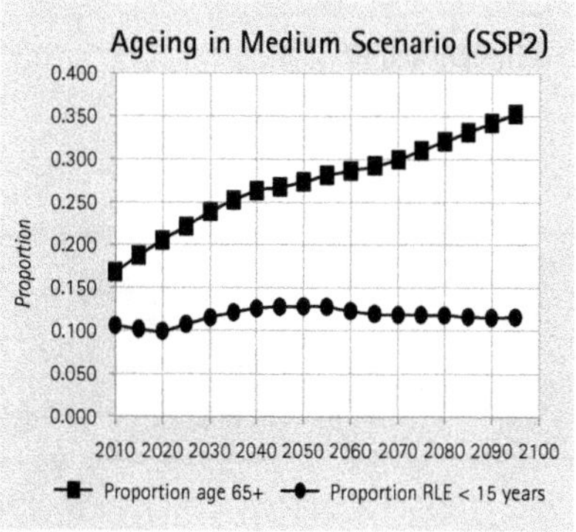

Alternative Scenarios to 2100

Projection Results by Scenario (SSP1-5)

	2010	2020	2030	2040	2050	2075	2100
Population (in millions)							
SSP1 - Rapid development	62.79	66.70	70.70	74.63	78.10	84.93	89.14
SSP2 - Medium	62.79	66.45	69.99	73.24	75.88	81.07	83.46
SSP3 - Stalled development	62.79	65.30	66.26	66.22	64.94	58.79	49.88
SSP4 - Inequality	62.79	65.97	68.43	70.24	71.01	69.78	64.29
SSP5 - Conventional development	62.79	67.61	73.76	80.50	87.73	107.94	129.61
Proportion age 65+							
SSP1 - Rapid development	0.17	0.21	0.25	0.28	0.30	0.35	0.42
SSP2 - Medium	0.17	0.21	0.24	0.26	0.27	0.31	0.36
SSP3 - Stalled development	0.17	0.21	0.24	0.27	0.28	0.33	0.38
SSP4 - Inequality	0.17	0.21	0.24	0.27	0.29	0.36	0.43
SSP5 - Conventional development	0.17	0.20	0.24	0.26	0.27	0.29	0.33
Proportion below age 20							
SSP1 - Rapid development	0.24	0.24	0.23	0.22	0.21	0.19	0.17
SSP2 - Medium	0.24	0.24	0.23	0.22	0.22	0.20	0.18
SSP3 - Stalled development	0.24	0.23	0.21	0.19	0.18	0.16	0.15
SSP4 - Inequality	0.24	0.23	0.21	0.20	0.19	0.16	0.14
SSP5 - Conventional development	0.24	0.25	0.25	0.25	0.25	0.24	0.22
Proportion of Women age 20-39 with at least secondary education							
SSP1 - Rapid development	0.92	0.97	0.99	0.99	0.99	1.00	1.00
SSP2 - Medium	0.92	0.96	0.98	0.99	0.99	1.00	1.00
SSP3 - Stalled development	0.92	0.94	0.94	0.94	0.94	0.94	0.94
SSP4 - Inequality	0.92	0.94	0.94	0.94	0.94	0.94	0.94
SSP5 - Conventional development	0.92	0.97	0.99	0.99	0.99	1.00	1.00
Mean years of schooling, age 25+							
SSP1 - Rapid development	10.53	11.39	12.19	12.88	13.48	14.54	15.08
SSP2 - Medium	10.53	11.34	12.09	12.75	13.33	14.38	14.91
SSP3 - Stalled development	10.53	11.24	11.81	12.25	12.58	12.96	13.03
SSP4 - Inequality	10.53	11.12	11.53	11.83	12.03	12.20	12.20
SSP5 - Conventional development	10.53	11.40	12.21	12.92	13.53	14.62	15.12

Demographic Assumptions Underlying SSPs

	2010–15	2020–25	2030–35	2040–45	2050–55	2075–80	2095–2100
Total fertility rate							
SSP1 - Rapid development	2.00	1.98	1.96	1.92	1.89	1.86	1.85
SSP2 - Medium	2.00	2.00	1.99	1.94	1.90	1.87	1.85
SSP3 - Stalled development	1.91	1.72	1.60	1.53	1.49	1.48	1.47
SSP4 - Inequality	1.92	1.77	1.66	1.59	1.55	1.53	1.52
SSP5 - Conventional development	2.10	2.28	2.38	2.38	2.36	2.33	2.31
Life expectancy at birth for females (in years)							
SSP1 - Rapid development	86.58	89.68	92.65	95.63	98.59	106.05	112.07
SSP2 - Medium	85.59	87.81	89.91	91.89	94.00	98.99	103.00
SSP3 - Stalled development	85.61	86.76	87.81	88.79	89.72	91.93	93.77
SSP4 - Inequality	86.13	88.22	90.22	92.15	94.17	98.84	102.61
SSP5 - Conventional development	86.58	89.68	92.65	95.63	98.59	106.05	112.07
Migration – net flow over five years (in thousands)							
SSP1 - Rapid development	517	571	589	584	561	240	0
SSP2 - Medium	526	574	595	603	595	273	0
SSP3 - Stalled development	430	287	299	300	293	133	0
SSP4 - Inequality	517	569	585	582	565	257	0
SSP5 - Conventional development	603	854	888	910	911	442	0

Ageing Indicators, Medium Scenario (SSP2)

	2010	2020	2030	2040	2050	2075	2095
Median age	39.92	41.45	42.83	43.89	44.70	47.90	51.35
Propspective median age	39.92	39.13	38.48	37.73	36.56	34.97	34.53
Proportion age 65+	0.17	0.21	0.24	0.26	0.27	0.31	0.35
Proportion RLE < 15 years	0.11	0.10	0.12	0.13	0.13	0.12	0.12

French Guiana

Detailed Human Capital Projections to 2060

Demographic indicators, Medium Scenario (SSP2)	2010	2020	2030	2040	2050	2060
Population (in millions)	0.23	0.29	0.35	0.40	0.45	0.49
Proportion age 65+	0.04	0.07	0.10	0.13	0.15	0.19
Proportion below age 20	0.43	0.38	0.33	0.30	0.26	0.24
	2005–10	2015–20	2025–30	2035–40	2045–50	2055–60
Total Fertility Rate	3.27	2.60	2.24	2.04	1.88	1.83
Life expectancy at birth (in years)						
Men	72.56	75.50	78.16	80.47	82.62	84.76
Women	79.89	82.29	84.51	86.61	88.61	90.60
Five-year immigration flow (in '000)	9.60	9.44	9.81	10.05	10.06	9.92
Five-year emigration flow (in '000)	3.58	3.29	3.88	4.18	4.39	4.49

Human Capital indicators, Medium Scenario (SSP2)	2010	2020	2030	2040	2050	2060
Population age 25+: highest educational attainment						
E1 - no education	0.16	0.14	0.12	0.10	0.08	0.06
E2 - incomplete primary	0.00	0.00	0.00	0.00	0.00	0.00
E3 - primary	0.29	0.26	0.24	0.21	0.19	0.17
E4 - lower secondary	0.13	0.14	0.14	0.14	0.14	0.13
E5 - upper secondary	0.27	0.28	0.31	0.33	0.36	0.38
E6 - post-secondary	0.16	0.18	0.19	0.21	0.24	0.26
Mean years of schooling (in years)	8.38	8.85	9.38	9.90	10.41	10.91
Gender gap (population age 25+): highest educational attainment (ratio male/female)						
E1 - no education	0.87	0.87	0.89	0.91	0.91	0.90
E2 - incomplete primary	NA	NA	NA	NA	NA	NA
E3 - primary	0.95	0.96	0.96	0.96	0.96	0.95
E4 - lower secondary	0.98	1.02	1.05	1.07	1.07	1.05
E5 - upper secondary	1.14	1.12	1.10	1.09	1.08	1.06
E6 - post-secondary	1.03	0.97	0.93	0.91	0.92	0.95
Mean years of schooling (male minus female)	0.39	0.27	0.15	0.08	0.05	0.07
Women age 20–39: highest educational attainment						
E1 - no education	0.15	0.12	0.08	0.06	0.04	0.02
E2 - incomplete primary	0.00	0.00	0.00	0.00	0.00	0.00
E3 - primary	0.28	0.24	0.21	0.18	0.15	0.12
E4 - lower secondary	0.15	0.17	0.16	0.15	0.14	0.13
E5 - upper secondary	0.27	0.30	0.34	0.39	0.42	0.46
E6 - post-secondary	0.15	0.17	0.20	0.23	0.25	0.27
Mean years of schooling (in years)	8.51	9.27	10.07	10.73	11.29	11.77

Education scenarios

GET: global education trend scenario (medium assumption also used for SSP2)

CER: constant enrolment rates scenario (assumption of no future improvements)

FT: Fast track scenario (assumption of education expansion according to fastest historical experience)

Pyramids by Education, Medium Scenario

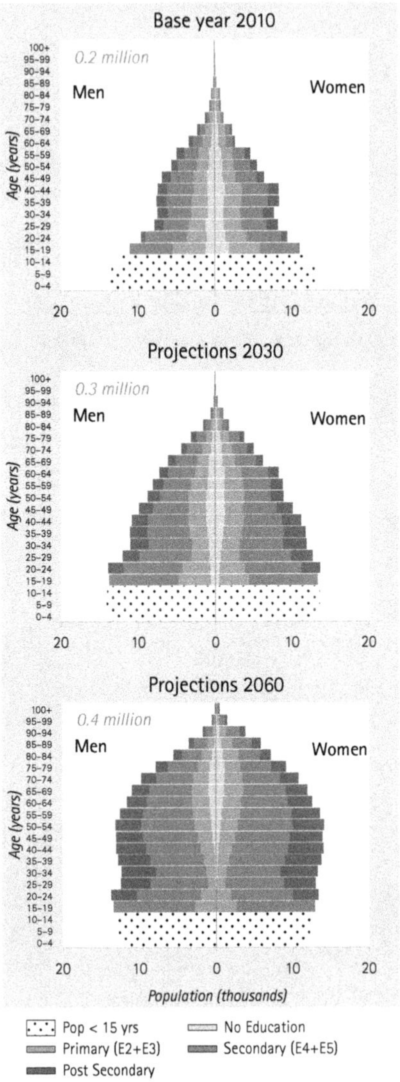

Population Size by Educational Attainment According to Three Education Scenarios: GET, CER, and FT

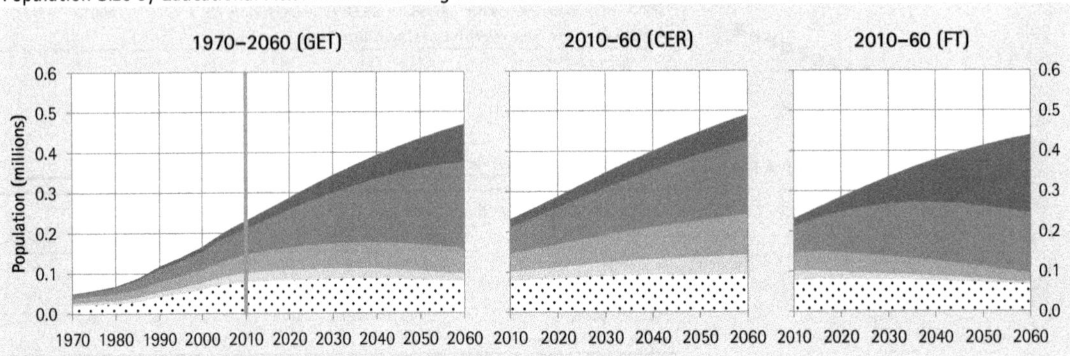

French Guiana (Continued)

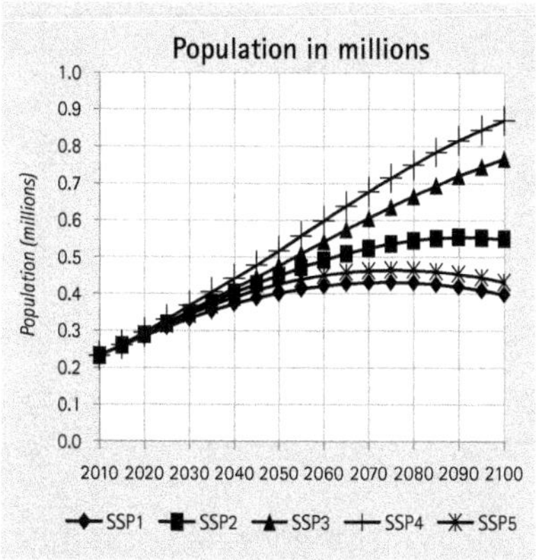

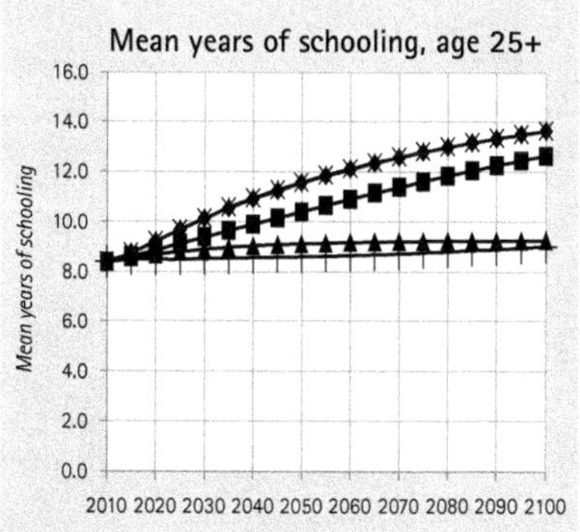

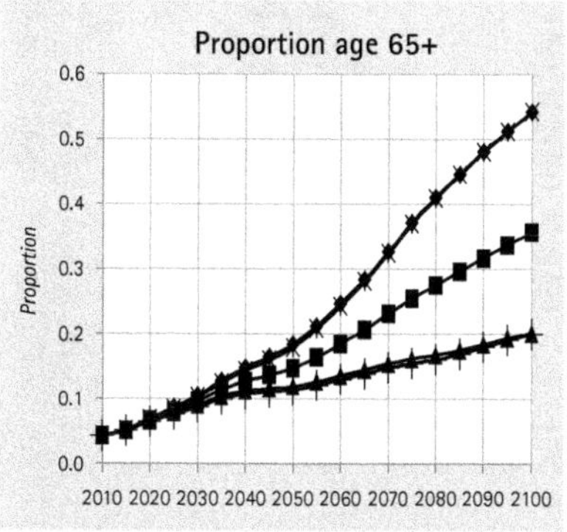

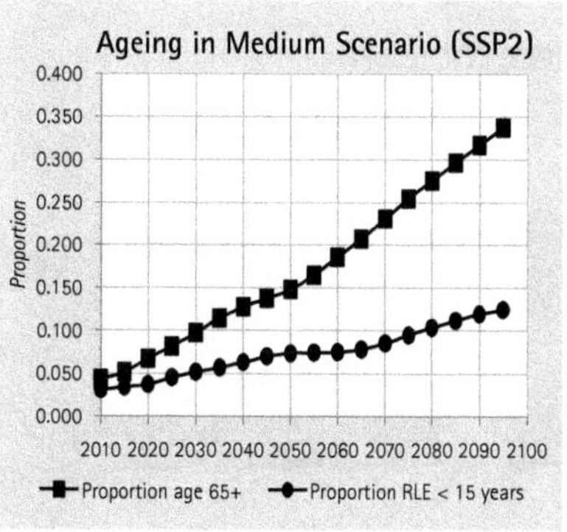

Alternative Scenarios to 2100

Projection Results by Scenario (SSP1-5)

	2010	2020	2030	2040	2050	2075	2100
Population (in millions)							
SSP1 - Rapid development	0.23	0.28	0.33	0.37	0.40	0.43	0.40
SSP2 - Medium	0.23	0.29	0.35	0.40	0.45	0.54	0.55
SSP3 - Stalled development	0.23	0.29	0.35	0.41	0.48	0.64	0.77
SSP4 - Inequality	0.23	0.29	0.37	0.44	0.52	0.71	0.87
SSP5 - Conventional development	0.23	0.29	0.34	0.39	0.43	0.47	0.43
Proportion age 65+							
SSP1 - Rapid development	0.04	0.07	0.11	0.15	0.18	0.37	0.54
SSP2 - Medium	0.04	0.07	0.10	0.13	0.15	0.25	0.36
SSP3 - Stalled development	0.04	0.07	0.09	0.11	0.12	0.16	0.20
SSP4 - Inequality	0.04	0.06	0.09	0.11	0.11	0.16	0.20
SSP5 - Conventional development	0.04	0.07	0.10	0.14	0.18	0.37	0.54
Proportion below age 20							
SSP1 - Rapid development	0.43	0.36	0.29	0.24	0.20	0.13	0.09
SSP2 - Medium	0.43	0.38	0.33	0.30	0.26	0.21	0.16
SSP3 - Stalled development	0.43	0.39	0.37	0.35	0.33	0.29	0.27
SSP4 - Inequality	0.43	0.39	0.37	0.35	0.33	0.29	0.27
SSP5 - Conventional development	0.43	0.36	0.29	0.24	0.20	0.13	0.09
Proportion of Women age 20-39 with at least secondary education							
SSP1 - Rapid development	0.57	0.72	0.81	0.87	0.90	0.95	0.98
SSP2 - Medium	0.57	0.64	0.71	0.76	0.82	0.92	0.97
SSP3 - Stalled development	0.57	0.59	0.59	0.59	0.59	0.59	0.59
SSP4 - Inequality	0.57	0.55	0.53	0.53	0.53	0.53	0.53
SSP5 - Conventional development	0.57	0.72	0.81	0.87	0.90	0.95	0.98
Mean years of schooling, age 25+							
SSP1 - Rapid development	8.38	9.20	10.12	10.91	11.55	12.78	13.63
SSP2 - Medium	8.38	8.85	9.38	9.90	10.41	11.61	12.63
SSP3 - Stalled development	8.38	8.68	8.89	9.03	9.12	9.22	9.24
SSP4 - Inequality	8.38	8.50	8.51	8.56	8.60	8.76	9.00
SSP5 - Conventional development	8.38	9.20	10.14	10.93	11.57	12.79	13.63

Demographic Assumptions Underlying SSPs

	2010–15	2020–25	2030–35	2040–45	2050–55	2075–80	2095–2100
Total fertility rate							
SSP1 - Rapid development	2.65	1.96	1.58	1.41	1.32	1.22	1.16
SSP2 - Medium	2.85	2.40	2.12	1.95	1.85	1.68	1.59
SSP3 - Stalled development	2.99	2.88	2.73	2.58	2.49	2.33	2.26
SSP4 - Inequality	3.02	2.97	2.79	2.61	2.50	2.31	2.23
SSP5 - Conventional development	2.65	1.96	1.58	1.41	1.32	1.22	1.16
Life expectancy at birth for females (in years)							
SSP1 - Rapid development	82.24	85.37	88.39	91.34	94.31	101.93	108.07
SSP2 - Medium	81.09	83.39	85.51	87.61	89.60	94.61	98.59
SSP3 - Stalled development	81.34	82.52	83.58	84.55	85.50	87.58	89.20
SSP4 - Inequality	81.34	82.51	83.55	84.50	85.42	87.41	89.05
SSP5 - Conventional development	82.24	85.37	88.39	91.34	94.31	101.93	108.07
Migration – net flow over five years (in thousands)							
SSP1 - Rapid development	6	6	6	5	4	1	0
SSP2 - Medium	6	6	6	6	5	2	0
SSP3 - Stalled development	5	3	3	3	4	3	0
SSP4 - Inequality	6	6	6	7	7	5	0
SSP5 - Conventional development	7	9	8	7	6	2	0

Ageing Indicators, Medium Scenario (SSP2)

	2010	2020	2030	2040	2050	2075	2095
Median age	24.21	27.03	30.26	33.72	37.00	45.06	51.32
Propspective median age	24.21	24.61	25.79	27.20	28.54	31.86	34.36
Proportion age 65+	0.04	0.07	0.10	0.13	0.15	0.25	0.34
Proportion RLE < 15 years	0.03	0.04	0.05	0.06	0.07	0.09	0.12

French Polynesia

Detailed Human Capital Projections to 2060

Demographic indicators, Medium Scenario (SSP2)

	2010	2020	2030	2040	2050	2060
Population (in millions)	0.27	0.30	0.33	0.34	0.36	0.36
Proportion age 65+	0.06	0.09	0.12	0.16	0.19	0.23
Proportion below age 20	0.34	0.30	0.28	0.25	0.23	0.22
	2005–10	2015–20	2025–30	2035–40	2045–50	2055–60
Total Fertility Rate	2.16	2.06	2.01	1.96	1.91	1.89
Life expectancy at birth (in years)						
Men	72.21	73.88	75.96	77.99	80.00	81.99
Women	77.09	78.79	80.69	82.71	84.71	86.71
Five-year immigration flow (in '000)	0.95	0.93	0.97	1.00	1.00	0.98
Five-year emigration flow (in '000)	1.38	1.09	1.04	1.02	1.00	0.95

Human Capital indicators, Medium Scenario (SSP2)

	2010	2020	2030	2040	2050	2060
Population age 25+: highest educational attainment						
E1 - no education	0.04	0.02	0.01	0.01	0.01	0.00
E2 - incomplete primary	0.05	0.03	0.02	0.01	0.00	0.00
E3 - primary	0.16	0.12	0.09	0.06	0.04	0.03
E4 - lower secondary	0.20	0.19	0.17	0.15	0.12	0.10
E5 - upper secondary	0.35	0.41	0.45	0.47	0.49	0.50
E6 - post-secondary	0.19	0.23	0.26	0.29	0.33	0.37
Mean years of schooling (in years)	9.97	10.81	11.48	12.02	12.51	12.92
Gender gap (population age 25+): highest educational attainment (ratio male/female)						
E1 - no education	1.09	1.10	1.15	1.17	1.13	1.04
E2 - incomplete primary	1.12	1.13	1.18	1.20	1.17	1.12
E3 - primary	1.20	1.25	1.30	1.33	1.35	1.37
E4 - lower secondary	0.98	1.08	1.14	1.18	1.21	1.21
E5 - upper secondary	0.96	0.99	1.02	1.05	1.06	1.05
E6 - post-secondary	0.90	0.82	0.79	0.79	0.82	0.87
Mean years of schooling (male minus female)	−0.33	−0.42	−0.47	−0.46	−0.39	−0.29
Women age 20–39: highest educational attainment						
E1 - no education	0.01	0.00	0.00	0.00	0.00	0.00
E2 - incomplete primary	0.00	0.00	0.00	0.00	0.00	0.00
E3 - primary	0.04	0.03	0.02	0.01	0.01	0.01
E4 - lower secondary	0.18	0.12	0.08	0.05	0.04	0.03
E5 - upper secondary	0.49	0.52	0.52	0.52	0.51	0.50
E6 - post-secondary	0.27	0.33	0.38	0.42	0.44	0.46
Mean years of schooling (in years)	11.87	12.58	13.12	13.39	13.57	13.69

Education scenarios

GET: global education trend scenario (medium assumption also used for SSP2)

CER: constant enrolment rates scenario (assumption of no future improvements)

FT: Fast track scenario (assumption of education expansion according to fastest historical experience)

Pyramids by Education, Medium Scenario

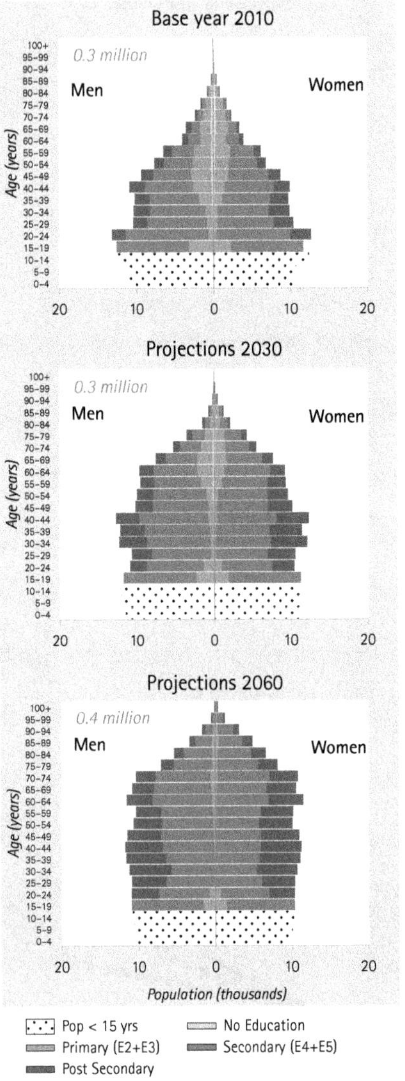

Population Size by Educational Attainment According to Three Education Scenarios: GET, CER, and FT

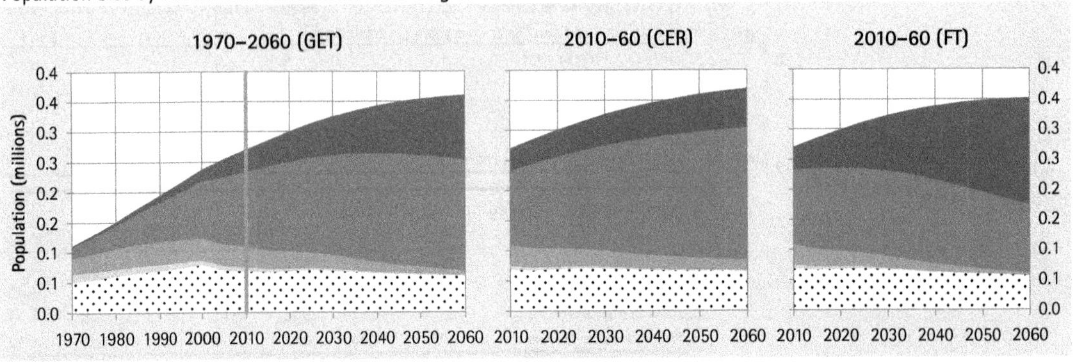

French Polynesia (Continued)

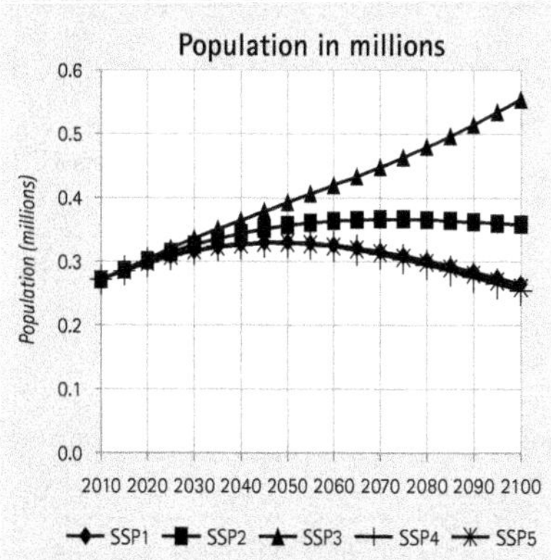

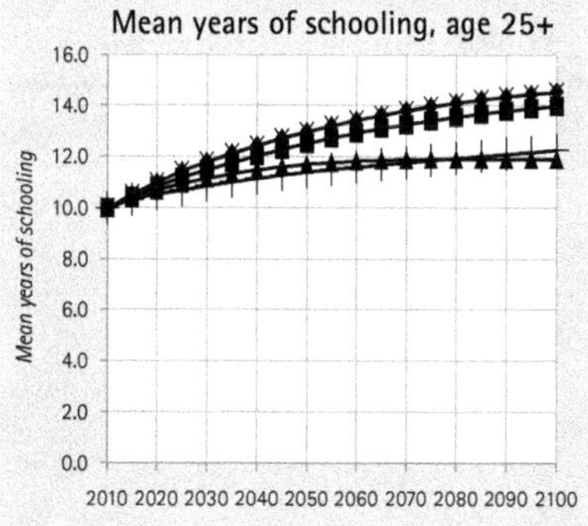

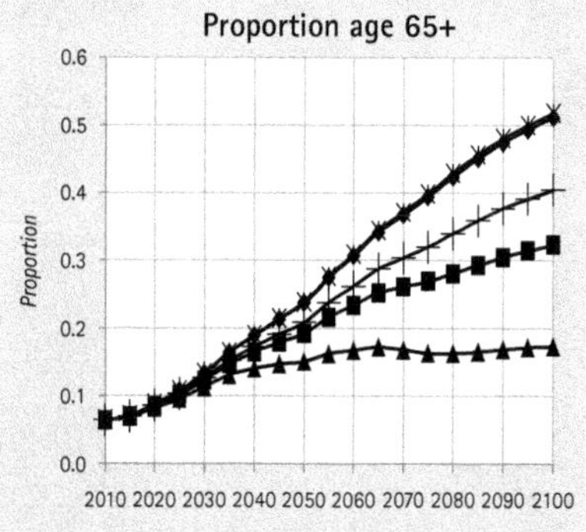

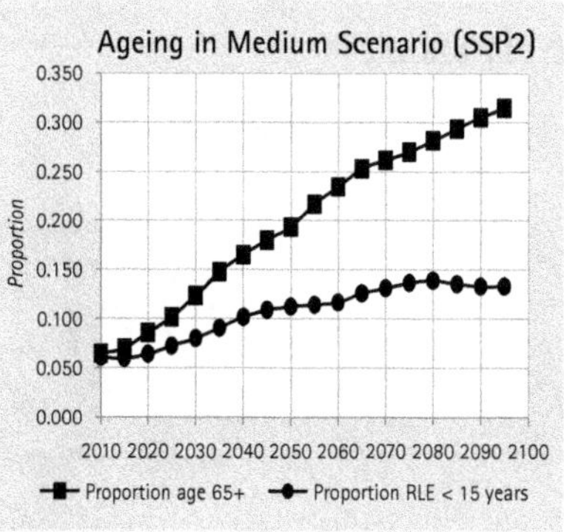

Alternative Scenarios to 2100

Projection Results by Scenario (SSP1–5)

	2010	2020	2030	2040	2050	2075	2100
Population (in millions)							
SSP1 - Rapid development	0.27	0.30	0.32	0.33	0.33	0.31	0.26
SSP2 - Medium	0.27	0.30	0.33	0.34	0.36	0.37	0.36
SSP3 - Stalled development	0.27	0.30	0.34	0.37	0.39	0.46	0.55
SSP4 - Inequality	0.27	0.30	0.32	0.33	0.33	0.30	0.25
SSP5 - Conventional development	0.27	0.30	0.32	0.33	0.33	0.31	0.26
Proportion age 65+							
SSP1 - Rapid development	0.06	0.09	0.13	0.19	0.24	0.39	0.51
SSP2 - Medium	0.06	0.09	0.12	0.16	0.19	0.27	0.32
SSP3 - Stalled development	0.06	0.08	0.11	0.14	0.15	0.16	0.17
SSP4 - Inequality	0.06	0.09	0.13	0.17	0.21	0.32	0.40
SSP5 - Conventional development	0.06	0.09	0.13	0.19	0.24	0.40	0.52
Proportion below age 20							
SSP1 - Rapid development	0.34	0.29	0.25	0.21	0.18	0.13	0.10
SSP2 - Medium	0.34	0.30	0.28	0.25	0.23	0.21	0.19
SSP3 - Stalled development	0.34	0.31	0.31	0.30	0.30	0.30	0.30
SSP4 - Inequality	0.34	0.29	0.26	0.22	0.20	0.16	0.13
SSP5 - Conventional development	0.34	0.29	0.25	0.21	0.17	0.13	0.10
Proportion of Women age 20–39 with at least secondary education							
SSP1 - Rapid development	0.94	0.98	0.99	0.99	0.99	1.00	1.00
SSP2 - Medium	0.94	0.97	0.98	0.99	0.99	1.00	1.00
SSP3 - Stalled development	0.94	0.96	0.96	0.96	0.96	0.96	0.96
SSP4 - Inequality	0.94	0.91	0.87	0.87	0.87	0.87	0.87
SSP5 - Conventional development	0.94	0.98	0.99	0.99	0.99	1.00	1.00
Mean years of schooling, age 25+							
SSP1 - Rapid development	9.97	10.98	11.78	12.43	12.97	13.96	14.53
SSP2 - Medium	9.97	10.81	11.48	12.02	12.51	13.41	13.98
SSP3 - Stalled development	9.97	10.67	11.15	11.47	11.70	11.89	11.90
SSP4 - Inequality	9.97	10.52	10.85	11.15	11.39	11.85	12.25
SSP5 - Conventional development	9.97	10.98	11.78	12.42	12.96	13.95	14.52

Demographic Assumptions Underlying SSPs

	2010–15	2020–25	2030–35	2040–45	2050–55	2075–80	2095–2100
Total fertility rate							
SSP1 - Rapid development	1.98	1.70	1.53	1.45	1.40	1.39	1.38
SSP2 - Medium	2.09	2.04	1.99	1.94	1.90	1.87	1.85
SSP3 - Stalled development	2.21	2.39	2.50	2.51	2.50	2.50	2.49
SSP4 - Inequality	2.01	1.82	1.67	1.57	1.51	1.48	1.46
SSP5 - Conventional development	1.98	1.70	1.53	1.45	1.40	1.39	1.38
Life expectancy at birth for females (in years)							
SSP1 - Rapid development	78.89	81.66	84.60	87.57	90.50	97.92	103.93
SSP2 - Medium	77.79	79.79	81.71	83.71	85.71	90.70	94.71
SSP3 - Stalled development	77.95	78.76	79.75	80.69	81.58	83.85	85.72
SSP4 - Inequality	78.40	80.24	82.10	84.04	85.92	90.55	94.41
SSP5 - Conventional development	78.89	81.66	84.60	87.57	90.50	97.92	103.93
Migration – net flow over five years (in thousands)							
SSP1 - Rapid development	0	0	0	0	0	0	0
SSP2 - Medium	0	0	0	0	0	0	0
SSP3 - Stalled development	0	0	0	0	0	0	0
SSP4 - Inequality	0	0	0	0	0	0	0
SSP5 - Conventional development	0	0	0	0	0	0	0

Ageing Indicators, Medium Scenario (SSP2)

	2010	2020	2030	2040	2050	2075	2095
Median age	29.04	32.31	35.89	39.17	40.96	46.12	48.82
Propspective median age	29.04	30.32	32.04	33.44	33.38	33.98	33.07
Proportion age 65+	0.06	0.09	0.12	0.16	0.19	0.27	0.31
Proportion RLE < 15 years	0.06	0.06	0.08	0.10	0.11	0.14	0.13

Gabon

Detailed Human Capital Projections to 2060

Demographic indicators, Medium Scenario (SSP2)	2010	2020	2030	2040	2050	2060
Population (in millions)	1.51	1.77	2.01	2.20	2.35	2.45
Proportion age 65+	0.04	0.05	0.06	0.08	0.10	0.14
Proportion below age 20	0.47	0.41	0.36	0.32	0.29	0.26
	2005–10	2015–20	2025–30	2035–40	2045–50	2055–60
Total Fertility Rate	3.35	2.61	2.25	2.05	1.91	1.85
Life expectancy at birth (in years)						
Men	60.24	63.89	65.20	66.56	68.00	70.05
Women	62.35	65.98	68.02	69.78	71.48	73.72
Five-year immigration flow (in '000)	35.28	34.53	35.84	36.62	36.59	36.04
Five-year emigration flow (in '000)	30.16	27.03	29.62	30.79	30.90	30.31

Human Capital indicators, Medium Scenario (SSP2)	2010	2020	2030	2040	2050	2060
Population age 25+: highest educational attainment						
E1 - no education	0.14	0.07	0.03	0.02	0.01	0.00
E2 - incomplete primary	0.19	0.13	0.09	0.05	0.03	0.02
E3 - primary	0.34	0.38	0.40	0.38	0.36	0.32
E4 - lower secondary	0.18	0.21	0.22	0.22	0.21	0.19
E5 - upper secondary	0.09	0.13	0.18	0.23	0.29	0.34
E6 - post-secondary	0.06	0.07	0.08	0.09	0.11	0.13
Mean years of schooling (in years)	6.96	8.06	8.71	9.18	9.62	10.05
Gender gap (population age 25+): highest educational attainment (ratio male/female)						
E1 - no education	0.69	0.77	0.94	1.15	1.22	1.23
E2 - incomplete primary	0.78	0.75	0.74	0.79	0.91	1.06
E3 - primary	0.85	0.78	0.76	0.76	0.78	0.81
E4 - lower secondary	1.39	1.23	1.13	1.07	1.02	0.98
E5 - upper secondary	1.83	1.63	1.47	1.34	1.23	1.15
E6 - post-secondary	2.25	1.89	1.62	1.42	1.28	1.18
Mean years of schooling (male minus female)	1.42	1.14	0.92	0.75	0.60	0.45
Women age 20–39: highest educational attainment						
E1 - no education	0.03	0.01	0.00	0.00	0.00	0.00
E2 - incomplete primary	0.15	0.10	0.07	0.06	0.04	0.03
E3 - primary	0.46	0.46	0.41	0.35	0.28	0.21
E4 - lower secondary	0.24	0.26	0.27	0.27	0.26	0.25
E5 - upper secondary	0.09	0.13	0.18	0.25	0.32	0.38
E6 - post-secondary	0.03	0.04	0.06	0.08	0.10	0.13
Mean years of schooling (in years)	7.87	8.41	8.61	8.95	9.65	10.33

Pyramids by Education, Medium Scenario

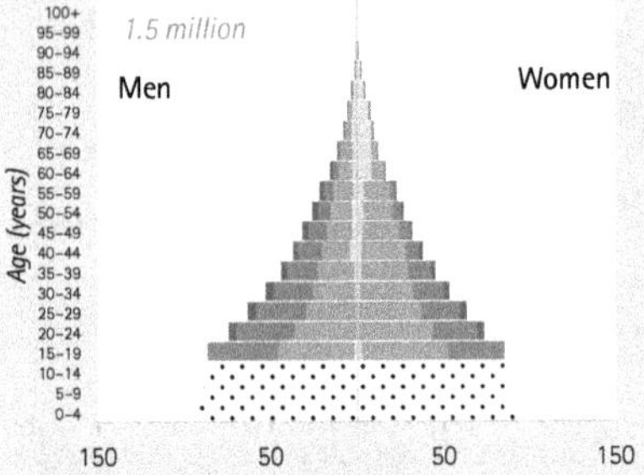

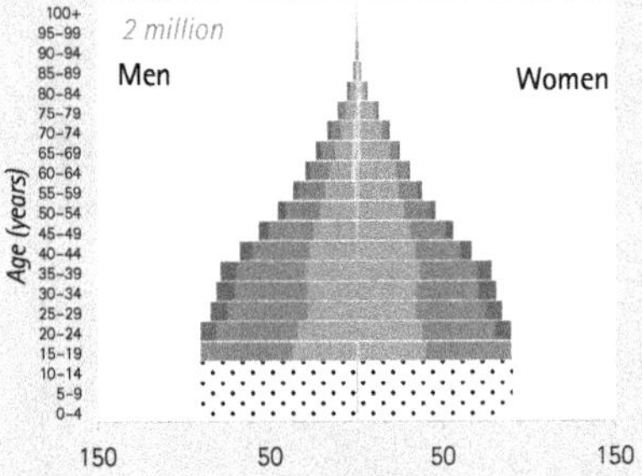

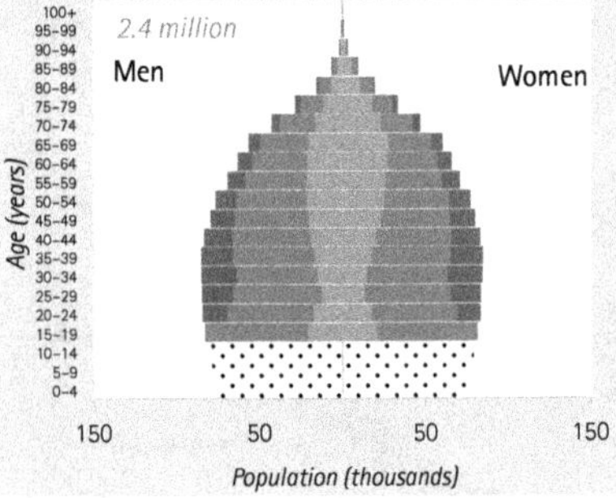

Pop < 15 yrs
No Education
Primary (E2+E3)
Secondary (E4+E5)
Post Secondary

Education scenarios

GET: global education trend scenario (Medium assumption also used for SSP2)

CER: constant enrolment rates scenario (assumption of no future improvements)

FT: Fast track scenario (assumption of education expansion according to fastest historical experience)

Population Size by Educational Attainment According to Three Education Scenarios: GET, CER, and FT

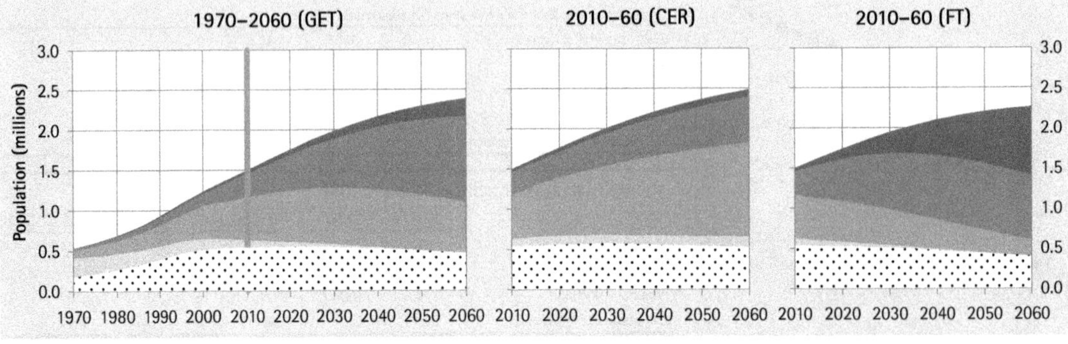

Gabon (Continued)

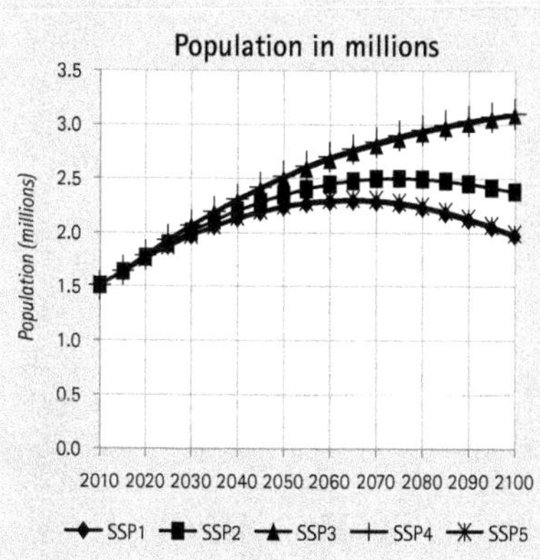

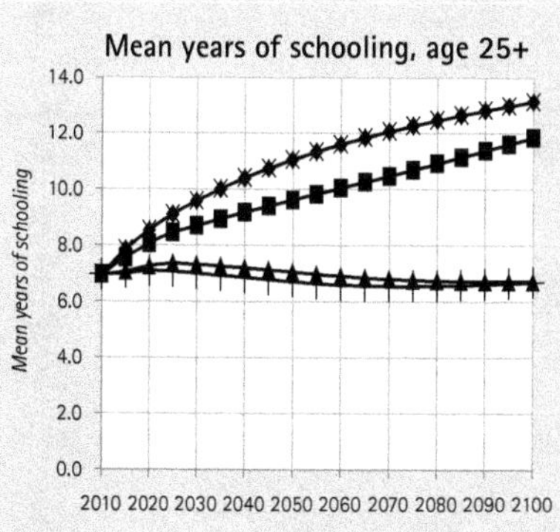

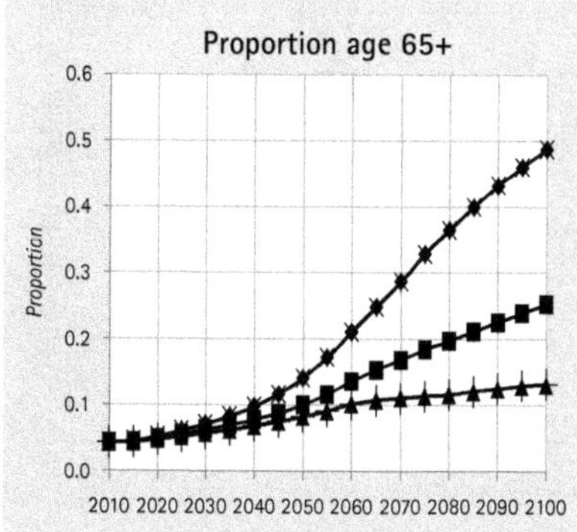

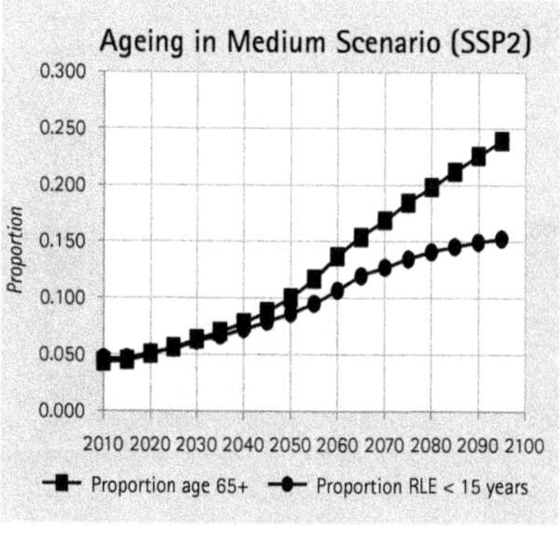

Alternative Scenarios to 2100

Projection Results by Scenario (SSP1–5)

	2010	2020	2030	2040	2050	2075	2100
Population (in millions)							
SSP1 - Rapid development	1.51	1.75	1.97	2.13	2.23	2.26	1.97
SSP2 - Medium	1.51	1.77	2.01	2.20	2.35	2.50	2.38
SSP3 - Stalled development	1.51	1.79	2.06	2.29	2.50	2.87	3.09
SSP4 - Inequality	1.51	1.79	2.07	2.31	2.52	2.90	3.10
SSP5 - Conventional development	1.51	1.76	1.98	2.14	2.25	2.28	1.99
Proportion age 65+							
SSP1 - Rapid development	0.04	0.05	0.07	0.10	0.14	0.33	0.49
SSP2 - Medium	0.04	0.05	0.06	0.08	0.10	0.18	0.25
SSP3 - Stalled development	0.04	0.05	0.06	0.07	0.08	0.11	0.13
SSP4 - Inequality	0.04	0.05	0.06	0.07	0.08	0.11	0.13
SSP5 - Conventional development	0.04	0.05	0.07	0.10	0.14	0.33	0.49
Proportion below age 20							
SSP1 - Rapid development	0.47	0.39	0.32	0.26	0.21	0.14	0.10
SSP2 - Medium	0.47	0.41	0.36	0.32	0.29	0.23	0.19
SSP3 - Stalled development	0.47	0.42	0.40	0.37	0.35	0.32	0.30
SSP4 - Inequality	0.47	0.42	0.40	0.37	0.35	0.31	0.30
SSP5 - Conventional development	0.47	0.39	0.32	0.26	0.21	0.14	0.10
Proportion of Women age 20–39 with at least secondary education							
SSP1 - Rapid development	0.36	0.58	0.69	0.77	0.83	0.92	0.97
SSP2 - Medium	0.36	0.43	0.51	0.59	0.68	0.85	0.95
SSP3 - Stalled development	0.36	0.27	0.27	0.27	0.27	0.27	0.27
SSP4 - Inequality	0.36	0.25	0.24	0.24	0.24	0.24	0.24
SSP5 - Conventional development	0.36	0.58	0.69	0.77	0.83	0.92	0.97
Mean years of schooling, age 25+							
SSP1 - Rapid development	6.96	8.53	9.57	10.39	11.05	12.26	13.13
SSP2 - Medium	6.96	8.06	8.71	9.18	9.62	10.69	11.84
SSP3 - Stalled development	6.96	7.26	7.32	7.20	7.06	6.77	6.73
SSP4 - Inequality	6.96	7.10	7.01	6.86	6.72	6.56	6.69
SSP5 - Conventional development	6.96	8.53	9.58	10.39	11.05	12.27	13.13

Demographic Assumptions Underlying SSPs

	2010–15	2020–25	2030–35	2040–45	2050–55	2075–80	2095–2100
Total fertility rate							
SSP1 - Rapid development	2.67	1.99	1.61	1.44	1.34	1.22	1.16
SSP2 - Medium	2.87	2.42	2.13	1.98	1.87	1.69	1.60
SSP3 - Stalled development	3.06	2.96	2.76	2.60	2.52	2.34	2.27
SSP4 - Inequality	3.06	2.97	2.77	2.60	2.50	2.31	2.23
SSP5 - Conventional development	2.67	1.99	1.61	1.44	1.34	1.22	1.16
Life expectancy at birth for females (in years)							
SSP1 - Rapid development	67.82	74.23	78.03	81.57	84.87	92.94	99.43
SSP2 - Medium	64.28	66.98	68.88	70.62	72.48	78.19	82.71
SSP3 - Stalled development	65.36	63.76	64.45	64.95	65.48	67.67	69.82
SSP4 - Inequality	65.36	63.72	64.38	64.87	65.40	67.60	69.77
SSP5 - Conventional development	67.82	74.23	78.03	81.57	84.87	92.94	99.43
Migration – net flow over five years (in thousands)							
SSP1 - Rapid development	6	7	6	5	4	2	0
SSP2 - Medium	7	7	6	6	6	3	0
SSP3 - Stalled development	5	3	3	4	4	3	0
SSP4 - Inequality	6	7	6	7	7	5	0
SSP5 - Conventional development	8	10	8	7	6	2	0

Ageing Indicators, Medium Scenario (SSP2)

	2010	2020	2030	2040	2050	2075	2095
Median age	21.52	24.79	27.91	31.05	34.00	40.60	44.97
Propspective median age	21.52	23.38	25.38	27.47	29.14	31.56	32.66
Proportion age 65+	0.04	0.05	0.06	0.08	0.10	0.18	0.24
Proportion RLE < 15 years	0.05	0.05	0.06	0.07	0.09	0.13	0.15

Gambia

Detailed Human Capital Projections to 2060

Demographic indicators, Medium Scenario (SSP2)	2010	2020	2030	2040	2050	2060
Population (in millions)	1.73	2.20	2.65	3.05	3.39	3.63
Proportion age 65+	0.02	0.02	0.03	0.04	0.06	0.08
Proportion below age 20	0.55	0.51	0.45	0.40	0.36	0.32
	2005–10	2015–20	2025–30	2035–40	2045–50	2055–60
Total Fertility Rate	5.10	3.99	3.08	2.59	2.24	2.05
Life expectancy at birth (in years)						
Men	56.24	59.00	60.77	62.54	64.29	66.54
Women	58.50	61.88	64.22	66.29	68.29	70.71
Five-year immigration flow (in '000)	23.04	22.58	23.45	23.95	23.93	23.57
Five-year emigration flow (in '000)	36.64	35.37	43.93	50.63	54.15	56.17

Human Capital indicators, Medium Scenario (SSP2)	2010	2020	2030	2040	2050	2060
Population age 25+: highest educational attainment						
E1 - no education	0.47	0.37	0.28	0.20	0.15	0.10
E2 - incomplete primary	0.14	0.11	0.08	0.06	0.04	0.03
E3 - primary	0.09	0.12	0.14	0.16	0.16	0.16
E4 - lower secondary	0.16	0.22	0.26	0.28	0.29	0.28
E5 - upper secondary	0.08	0.11	0.15	0.19	0.23	0.27
E6 - post-secondary	0.05	0.07	0.09	0.11	0.13	0.16
Mean years of schooling (in years)	4.57	5.81	6.95	7.98	8.86	9.63
Gender gap (population age 25+): highest educational attainment (ratio male/female)						
E1 - no education	0.61	0.54	0.49	0.49	0.51	0.55
E2 - incomplete primary	1.35	1.32	1.19	1.06	0.94	0.85
E3 - primary	1.13	1.05	0.99	0.94	0.92	0.93
E4 - lower secondary	1.55	1.36	1.21	1.10	1.04	1.01
E5 - upper secondary	1.89	1.66	1.49	1.33	1.21	1.13
E6 - post-secondary	2.80	2.56	2.19	1.82	1.52	1.30
Mean years of schooling (male minus female)	2.43	2.53	2.33	1.91	1.43	0.96
Women age 20–39: highest educational attainment						
E1 - no education	0.45	0.33	0.22	0.14	0.08	0.04
E2 - incomplete primary	0.09	0.07	0.05	0.04	0.03	0.02
E3 - primary	0.13	0.16	0.18	0.18	0.17	0.14
E4 - lower secondary	0.20	0.26	0.29	0.30	0.29	0.25
E5 - upper secondary	0.09	0.13	0.19	0.25	0.31	0.38
E6 - post-secondary	0.03	0.04	0.06	0.09	0.12	0.16
Mean years of schooling (in years)	4.78	6.15	7.46	8.65	9.71	10.62

Education scenarios

GET: global education trend scenario (medium assumption also used for SSP2)

CER: constant enrolment rates scenario (assumption of no future improvements)

FT: Fast track scenario (assumption of education expansion according to fastest historical experience)

Pyramids by Education, Medium Scenario

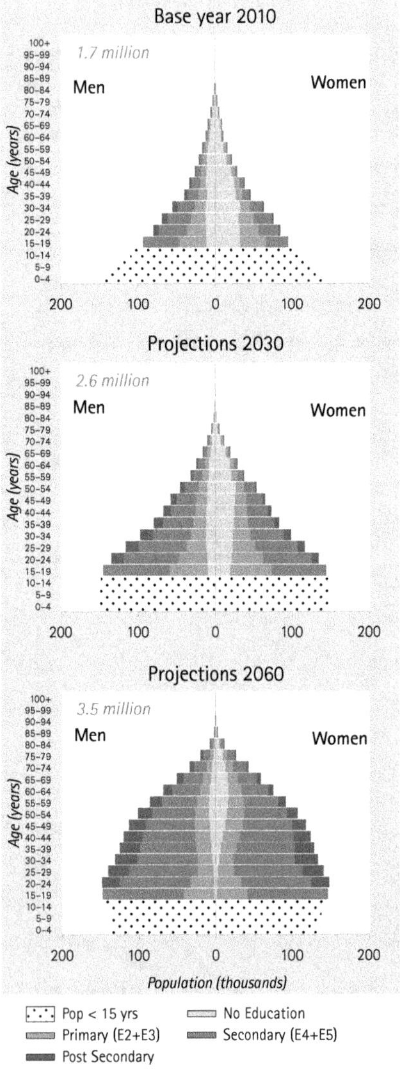

Population Size by Educational Attainment According to Three Education Scenarios: GET, CER, and FT

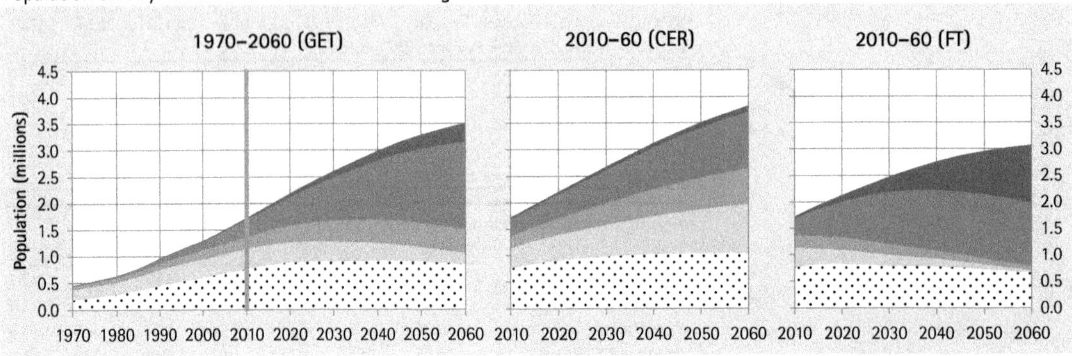

Gambia (Continued)

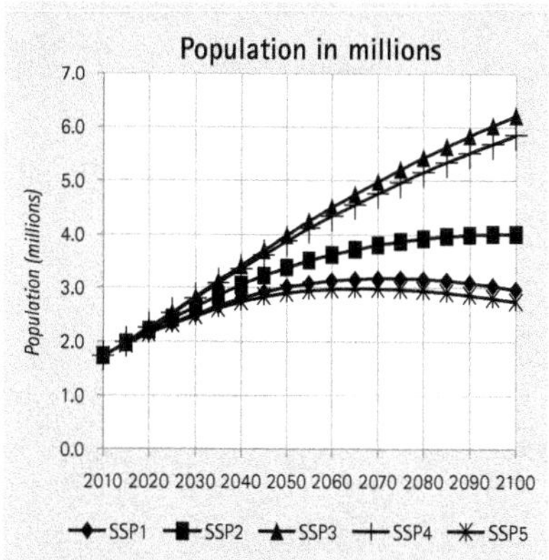

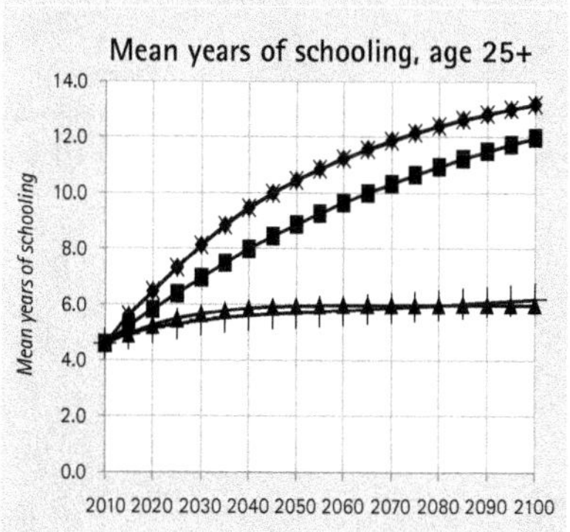

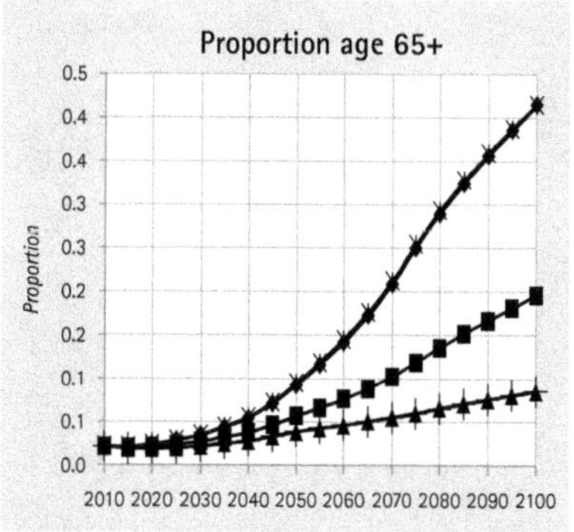

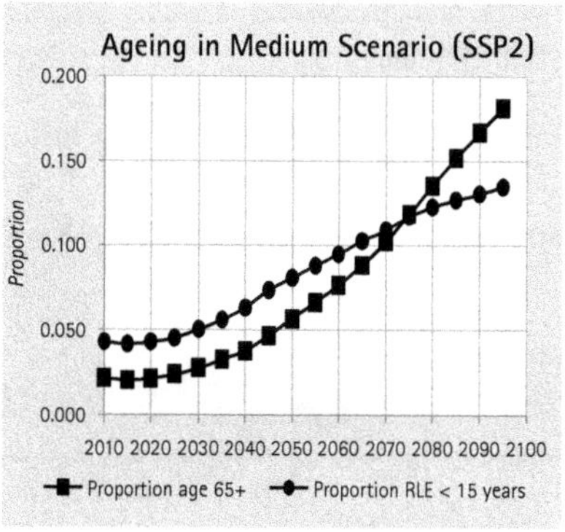

Alternative Scenarios to 2100

Projection Results by Scenario (SSP1–5)

	2010	2020	2030	2040	2050	2075	2100
Population (in millions)							
SSP1 - Rapid development	1.73	2.15	2.51	2.80	3.01	3.18	2.97
SSP2 - Medium	1.73	2.20	2.65	3.05	3.39	3.88	4.01
SSP3 - Stalled development	1.73	2.26	2.83	3.42	3.98	5.21	6.21
SSP4 - Inequality	1.73	2.25	2.81	3.36	3.88	4.97	5.85
SSP5 - Conventional development	1.73	2.14	2.48	2.74	2.90	2.97	2.74
Proportion age 65+							
SSP1 - Rapid development	0.02	0.02	0.04	0.05	0.09	0.25	0.41
SSP2 - Medium	0.02	0.02	0.03	0.04	0.06	0.12	0.20
SSP3 - Stalled development	0.02	0.02	0.02	0.03	0.04	0.06	0.09
SSP4 - Inequality	0.02	0.02	0.02	0.03	0.04	0.06	0.09
SSP5 - Conventional development	0.02	0.02	0.04	0.06	0.09	0.25	0.41
Proportion below age 20							
SSP1 - Rapid development	0.55	0.49	0.40	0.33	0.28	0.18	0.12
SSP2 - Medium	0.55	0.51	0.45	0.40	0.36	0.28	0.22
SSP3 - Stalled development	0.55	0.53	0.49	0.46	0.42	0.36	0.33
SSP4 - Inequality	0.55	0.53	0.50	0.46	0.43	0.36	0.33
SSP5 - Conventional development	0.55	0.49	0.41	0.33	0.28	0.18	0.12
Proportion of Women age 20–39 with at least secondary education							
SSP1 - Rapid development	0.33	0.57	0.72	0.80	0.86	0.93	0.97
SSP2 - Medium	0.33	0.44	0.54	0.64	0.72	0.87	0.94
SSP3 - Stalled development	0.33	0.33	0.33	0.33	0.33	0.33	0.33
SSP4 - Inequality	0.33	0.31	0.30	0.30	0.30	0.30	0.30
SSP5 - Conventional development	0.33	0.57	0.72	0.80	0.86	0.93	0.97
Mean years of schooling, age 25+							
SSP1 - Rapid development	4.57	6.47	8.11	9.46	10.44	12.15	13.18
SSP2 - Medium	4.57	5.81	6.95	7.98	8.86	10.64	11.97
SSP3 - Stalled development	4.57	5.24	5.65	5.86	5.95	5.98	6.00
SSP4 - Inequality	4.57	5.14	5.42	5.60	5.70	5.92	6.20
SSP5 - Conventional development	4.57	6.47	8.09	9.43	10.42	12.12	13.18

Demographic Assumptions Underlying SSPs

	2010–15	2020–25	2030–35	2040–45	2050–55	2075–80	2095–2100
Total fertility rate							
SSP1 - Rapid development	4.18	2.76	2.03	1.69	1.49	1.30	1.22
SSP2 - Medium	4.53	3.50	2.79	2.40	2.12	1.81	1.67
SSP3 - Stalled development	4.83	4.33	3.78	3.33	3.02	2.62	2.50
SSP4 - Inequality	4.84	4.36	3.81	3.33	2.99	2.56	2.43
SSP5 - Conventional development	4.18	2.76	2.03	1.69	1.49	1.30	1.22
Life expectancy at birth for females (in years)							
SSP1 - Rapid development	65.17	70.71	74.72	78.52	82.00	90.48	97.26
SSP2 - Medium	60.28	63.08	65.28	67.28	69.49	75.60	80.48
SSP3 - Stalled development	62.67	61.37	62.21	62.64	63.50	65.64	67.89
SSP4 - Inequality	62.67	61.35	62.17	62.59	63.45	65.61	67.89
SSP5 - Conventional development	65.17	70.71	74.72	78.52	82.00	90.48	97.26
Migration – net flow over five years (in thousands)							
SSP1 - Rapid development	−12	−16	−23	−27	−28	−11	0
SSP2 - Medium	−12	−17	−24	−29	−32	−14	0
SSP3 - Stalled development	−10	−8	−12	−14	−16	−8	0
SSP4 - Inequality	−12	−16	−24	−30	−34	−16	0
SSP5 - Conventional development	−14	−25	−36	−43	−46	−20	0

Ageing Indicators, Medium Scenario (SSP2)

	2010	2020	2030	2040	2050	2075	2095
Median age	17.67	19.41	22.28	25.40	28.46	35.50	40.57
Propspective median age	17.67	17.84	19.35	21.33	23.22	26.19	27.17
Proportion age 65+	0.02	0.02	0.03	0.04	0.06	0.12	0.18
Proportion RLE < 15 years	0.04	0.04	0.05	0.06	0.08	0.12	0.13

Georgia

Detailed Human Capital Projections to 2060

Demographic indicators, Medium Scenario (SSP2)

	2010	2020	2030	2040	2050	2060
Population (in millions)	4.35	4.15	3.89	3.59	3.28	2.95
Proportion age 65+	0.14	0.17	0.23	0.26	0.30	0.36
Proportion below age 20	0.24	0.23	0.21	0.18	0.18	0.17
	2005–10	2015–20	2025–30	2035–40	2045–50	2055–60
Total Fertility Rate	1.58	1.67	1.69	1.70	1.70	1.70
Life expectancy at birth (in years)						
Men	69.36	72.28	74.71	76.97	79.25	81.41
Women	76.50	78.90	80.99	82.99	85.09	87.11
Five-year immigration flow (in '000)	1.43	1.41	1.46	1.49	1.50	1.47
Five-year emigration flow (in '000)	151.08	98.69	80.04	69.86	58.37	49.34

Human Capital indicators, Medium Scenario (SSP2)

	2010	2020	2030	2040	2050	2060
Population age 25+: highest educational attainment						
E1 - no education	0.00	0.00	0.00	0.00	0.00	0.00
E2 - incomplete primary	0.01	0.00	0.00	0.00	0.00	0.00
E3 - primary	0.04	0.02	0.01	0.01	0.01	0.00
E4 - lower secondary	0.06	0.05	0.04	0.03	0.02	0.01
E5 - upper secondary	0.36	0.35	0.34	0.33	0.31	0.29
E6 - post-secondary	0.53	0.57	0.60	0.63	0.66	0.69
Mean years of schooling (in years)	12.66	13.18	13.52	13.83	14.12	14.40
Gender gap (population age 25+): highest educational attainment (ratio male/female)						
E1 - no education	0.57	0.75	0.93	0.99	1.00	1.01
E2 - incomplete primary	0.50	0.50	0.56	0.65	0.73	0.82
E3 - primary	0.73	0.70	0.73	0.78	0.79	0.80
E4 - lower secondary	0.97	0.98	1.00	1.00	0.99	0.98
E5 - upper secondary	1.13	1.17	1.20	1.21	1.21	1.18
E6 - post-secondary	0.95	0.92	0.91	0.91	0.92	0.93
Mean years of schooling (male minus female)	0.02	–0.10	–0.15	–0.15	–0.12	–0.10
Women age 20–39: highest educational attainment						
E1 - no education	0.00	0.00	0.00	0.00	0.00	0.00
E2 - incomplete primary	0.00	0.00	0.00	0.00	0.00	0.00
E3 - primary	0.01	0.01	0.00	0.00	0.00	0.00
E4 - lower secondary	0.04	0.03	0.02	0.02	0.01	0.01
E5 - upper secondary	0.31	0.29	0.27	0.26	0.25	0.25
E6 - post-secondary	0.63	0.68	0.70	0.72	0.73	0.74
Mean years of schooling (in years)	13.53	14.22	14.70	14.80	14.87	14.90

Education scenarios

GET: global education trend scenario (medium assumption also used for SSP2)

CER: constant enrolment rates scenario (assumption of no future improvements)

FT: Fast track scenario (assumption of education expansion according to fastest historical experience)

Pyramids by Education, Medium Scenario

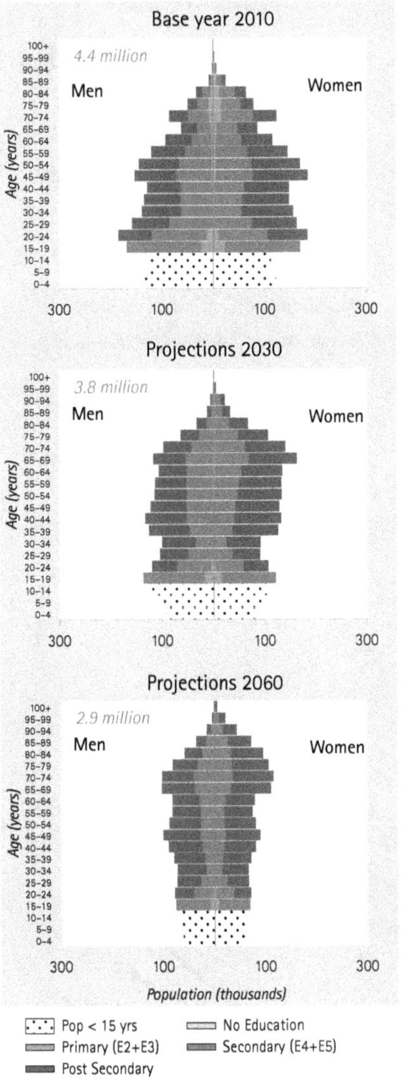

Population Size by Educational Attainment According to Three Education Scenarios: GET, CER, and FT

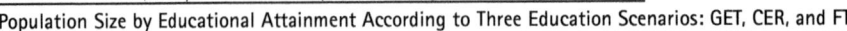

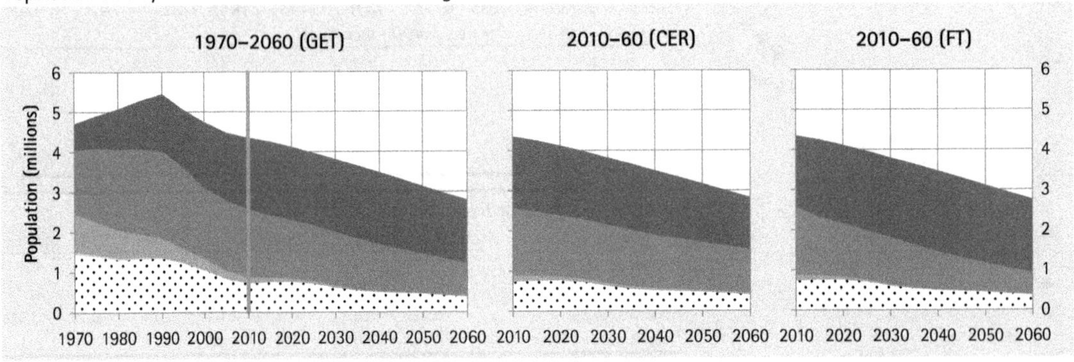

Georgia (Continued)

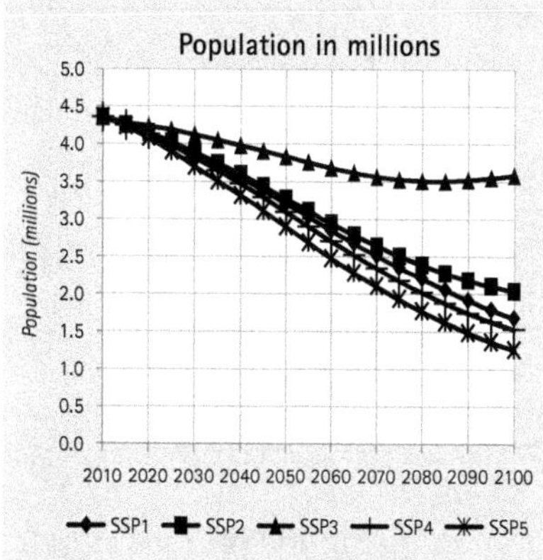

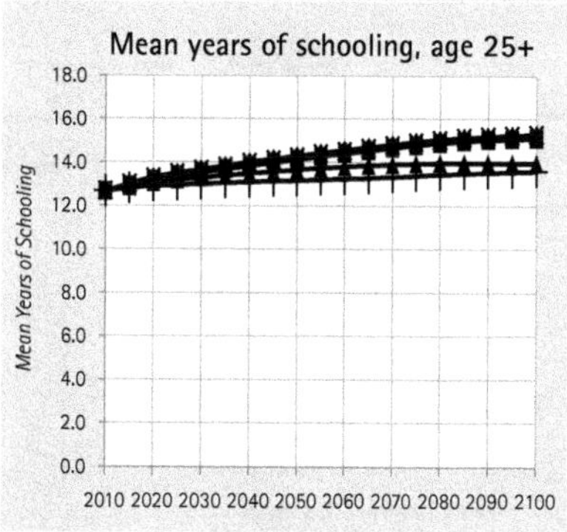

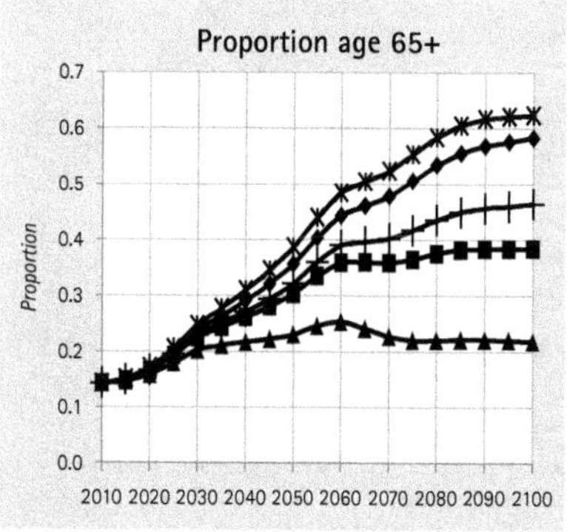

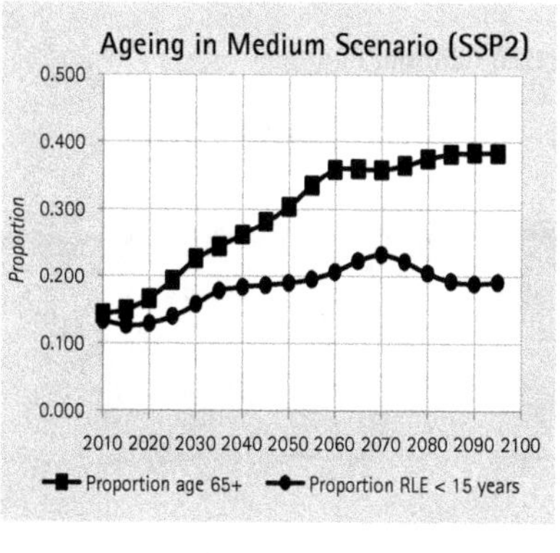

Alternative Scenarios to 2100

Projection Results by Scenario (SSP1–5)

	2010	2020	2030	2040	2050	2075	2100
Population (in millions)							
SSP1 - Rapid development	4.35	4.13	3.85	3.55	3.21	2.36	1.68
SSP2 - Medium	4.35	4.15	3.89	3.59	3.28	2.51	2.04
SSP3 - Stalled development	4.35	4.23	4.12	3.98	3.83	3.53	3.59
SSP4 - Inequality	4.35	4.12	3.82	3.47	3.10	2.18	1.53
SSP5 - Conventional development	4.35	4.08	3.70	3.31	2.90	1.93	1.26
Proportion age 65+							
SSP1 - Rapid development	0.14	0.17	0.24	0.29	0.36	0.51	0.58
SSP2 - Medium	0.14	0.17	0.23	0.26	0.30	0.37	0.38
SSP3 - Stalled development	0.14	0.16	0.20	0.22	0.23	0.22	0.22
SSP4 - Inequality	0.14	0.17	0.23	0.27	0.32	0.42	0.46
SSP5 - Conventional development	0.14	0.17	0.25	0.31	0.39	0.55	0.62
Proportion below age 20							
SSP1 - Rapid development	0.24	0.22	0.19	0.15	0.13	0.10	0.08
SSP2 - Medium	0.24	0.23	0.21	0.18	0.18	0.16	0.16
SSP3 - Stalled development	0.24	0.24	0.24	0.23	0.24	0.25	0.25
SSP4 - Inequality	0.24	0.22	0.19	0.16	0.15	0.12	0.11
SSP5 - Conventional development	0.24	0.22	0.19	0.14	0.12	0.08	0.07
Proportion of Women age 20–39 with at least secondary education							
SSP1 - Rapid development	0.99	0.99	1.00	1.00	1.00	1.00	1.00
SSP2 - Medium	0.99	0.99	1.00	1.00	1.00	1.00	1.00
SSP3 - Stalled development	0.99	0.98	0.98	0.98	0.98	0.98	0.98
SSP4 - Inequality	0.99	0.92	0.88	0.88	0.88	0.88	0.88
SSP5 - Conventional development	0.99	0.99	1.00	1.00	1.00	1.00	1.00
Mean years of schooling, age 25+							
SSP1 - Rapid development	12.66	13.28	13.66	14.00	14.29	14.94	15.28
SSP2 - Medium	12.66	13.18	13.52	13.83	14.12	14.79	15.11
SSP3 - Stalled development	12.66	13.03	13.29	13.48	13.65	13.94	13.97
SSP4 - Inequality	12.66	12.90	13.00	13.08	13.15	13.38	13.59
SSP5 - Conventional development	12.66	13.27	13.63	13.95	14.23	14.90	15.27

Demographic Assumptions Underlying SSPs

	2010–15	2020–25	2030–35	2040–45	2050–55	2075–80	2095–2100
Total fertility rate							
SSP1 - Rapid development	1.57	1.42	1.33	1.29	1.27	1.28	1.29
SSP2 - Medium	1.65	1.68	1.70	1.70	1.70	1.71	1.72
SSP3 - Stalled development	1.75	1.97	2.11	2.17	2.20	2.22	2.23
SSP4 - Inequality	1.58	1.46	1.39	1.35	1.33	1.34	1.34
SSP5 - Conventional development	1.57	1.42	1.33	1.29	1.27	1.28	1.29
Life expectancy at birth for females (in years)							
SSP1 - Rapid development	80.04	82.48	85.11	87.98	90.85	98.20	104.15
SSP2 - Medium	77.70	79.99	81.99	84.09	86.11	91.10	95.10
SSP3 - Stalled development	79.28	80.10	80.84	81.67	82.44	84.56	86.42
SSP4 - Inequality	79.61	81.26	82.85	84.71	86.53	90.99	94.82
SSP5 - Conventional development	80.04	82.48	85.11	87.98	90.85	98.20	104.15
Migration – net flow over five years (in thousands)							
SSP1 - Rapid development	−119	−85	−71	−58	−45	−13	0
SSP2 - Medium	−123	−88	−75	−64	−53	−17	0
SSP3 - Stalled development	−99	−43	−38	−34	−30	−12	0
SSP4 - Inequality	−119	−85	−70	−55	−41	−10	0
SSP5 - Conventional development	−139	−127	−106	−85	−66	−18	0

Ageing Indicators, Medium Scenario (SSP2)

	2010	2020	2030	2040	2050	2075	2095
Median age	37.29	40.52	44.59	49.06	51.42	54.86	54.62
Propspective median age	37.29	38.70	41.11	43.89	44.48	43.54	39.30
Proportion age 65+	0.14	0.17	0.23	0.26	0.30	0.37	0.38
Proportion RLE < 15 years	0.13	0.13	0.16	0.18	0.19	0.22	0.19

Germany

Detailed Human Capital Projections to 2060

Demographic indicators, Medium Scenario (SSP2)	2010	2020	2030	2040	2050	2060
Population (in millions)	82.30	81.86	81.39	80.41	78.91	77.06
Proportion age 65+	0.20	0.23	0.29	0.32	0.34	0.35
Proportion below age 20	0.19	0.17	0.17	0.17	0.16	0.17
	2005–10	2015–20	2025–30	2035–40	2045–50	2055–60
Total Fertility Rate	1.36	1.42	1.52	1.57	1.59	1.61
Life expectancy at birth (in years)						
Men	77.20	79.99	82.45	84.41	86.52	88.51
Women	82.39	84.49	86.61	88.61	90.69	92.69
Five-year immigration flow (in '000)	1337.09	1317.05	1370.19	1403.55	1406.05	1386.89
Five-year emigration flow (in '000)	788.07	516.16	458.30	423.84	407.43	392.42

Human Capital indicators, Medium Scenario (SSP2)	2010	2020	2030	2040	2050	2060
Population age 25+: highest educational attainment						
E1 - no education	0.01	0.01	0.01	0.01	0.00	0.00
E2 - incomplete primary	0.00	0.00	0.00	0.00	0.00	0.00
E3 - primary	0.03	0.02	0.02	0.02	0.01	0.01
E4 - lower secondary	0.16	0.13	0.11	0.09	0.08	0.07
E5 - upper secondary	0.51	0.50	0.48	0.46	0.43	0.40
E6 - post-secondary	0.30	0.34	0.39	0.43	0.48	0.52
Mean years of schooling (in years)	13.71	14.03	14.28	14.50	14.72	14.93
Gender gap (population age 25+): highest educational attainment (ratio male/female)						
E1 - no education	0.81	0.82	0.80	0.77	0.74	0.71
E2 - incomplete primary	NA	NA	NA	NA	NA	NA
E3 - primary	0.78	0.81	0.83	0.85	0.86	0.88
E4 - lower secondary	0.44	0.55	0.69	0.82	0.92	0.97
E5 - upper secondary	1.06	1.03	1.03	1.04	1.06	1.06
E6 - post-secondary	1.38	1.20	1.08	1.01	0.97	0.96
Mean years of schooling (male minus female)	0.90	0.58	0.31	0.11	−0.01	−0.07
Women age 20–39: highest educational attainment						
E1 - no education	0.01	0.01	0.00	0.00	0.00	0.00
E2 - incomplete primary	0.00	0.00	0.00	0.00	0.00	0.00
E3 - primary	0.02	0.01	0.01	0.01	0.00	0.00
E4 - lower secondary	0.13	0.11	0.09	0.07	0.06	0.05
E5 - upper secondary	0.50	0.47	0.45	0.44	0.43	0.42
E6 - post-secondary	0.34	0.41	0.46	0.49	0.51	0.53
Mean years of schooling (in years)	13.94	14.39	14.46	14.66	14.80	14.91

Education scenarios

GET: global education trend scenario (medium assumption also used for SSP2)

CER: constant enrolment rates scenario (assumption of no future improvements)

FT: Fast track scenario (assumption of education expansion according to fastest historical experience)

Pyramids by Education, Medium Scenario

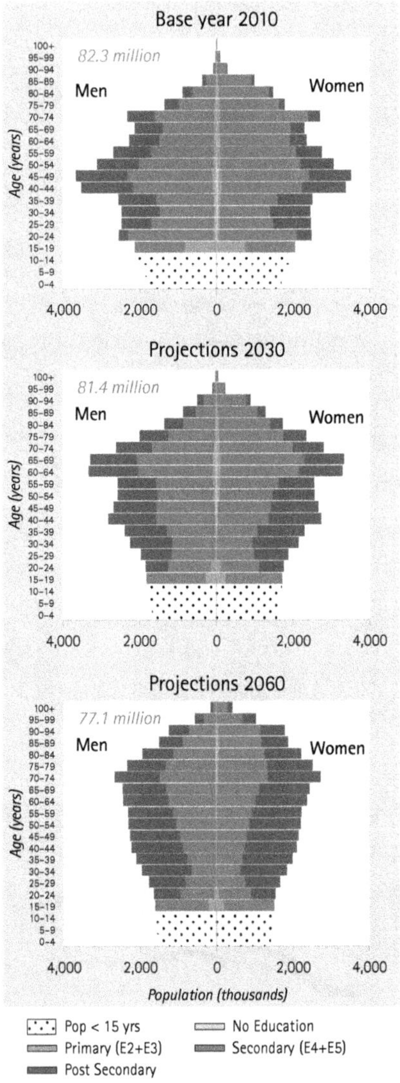

Population Size by Educational Attainment According to Three Education Scenarios: GET, CER, and FT

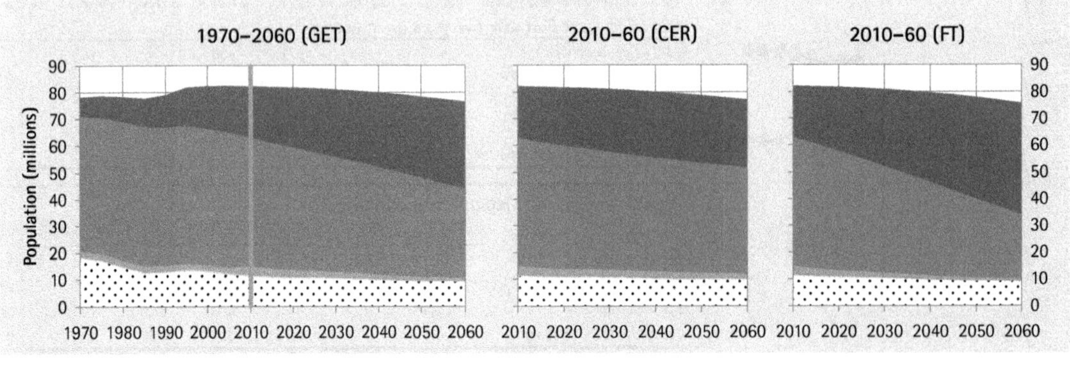

Germany (Continued)

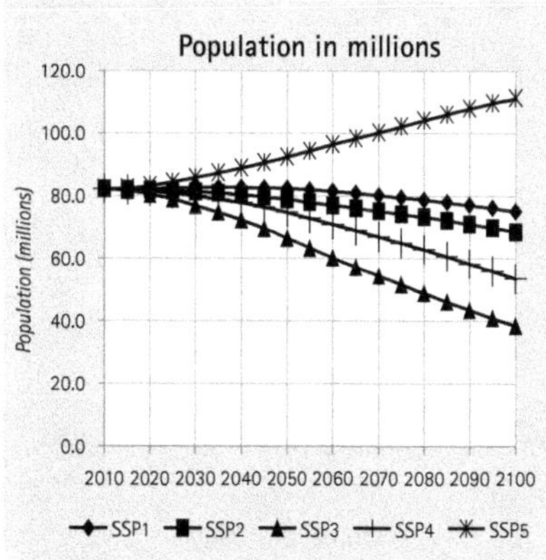

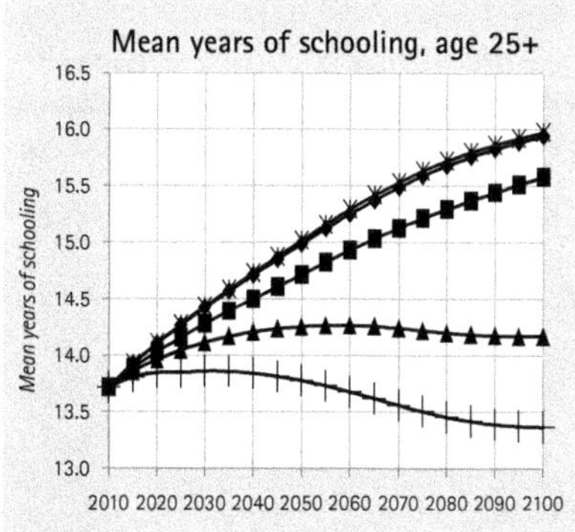

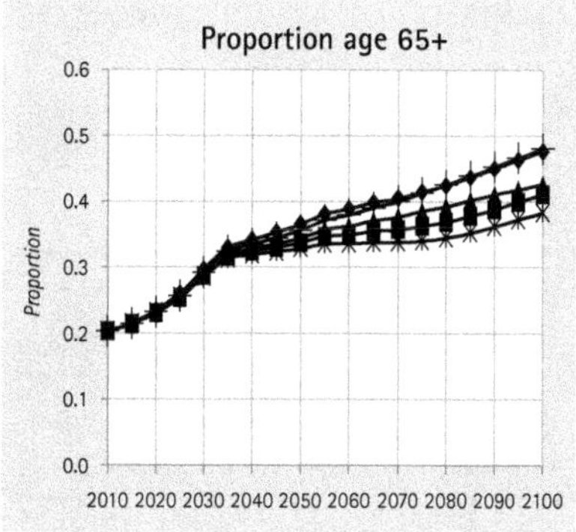

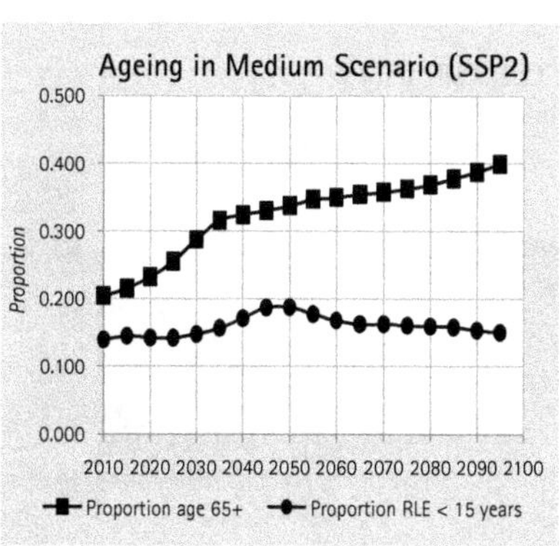

Alternative Scenarios to 2100

Projection Results by Scenario (SSP1–5)

	2010	2020	2030	2040	2050	2075	2100
Population (in millions)							
SSP1 - Rapid development	82.30	82.33	82.65	82.69	82.37	79.51	75.14
SSP2 - Medium	82.30	81.86	81.39	80.41	78.91	74.26	68.61
SSP3 - Stalled development	82.30	80.49	76.95	72.31	66.52	51.67	38.43
SSP4 - Inequality	82.30	81.43	79.96	77.78	74.74	64.97	53.60
SSP5 - Conventional development	82.30	83.26	85.90	88.92	92.45	102.21	111.26
Proportion age 65+							
SSP1 - Rapid development	0.20	0.23	0.30	0.34	0.37	0.41	0.48
SSP2 - Medium	0.20	0.23	0.29	0.32	0.34	0.36	0.41
SSP3 - Stalled development	0.20	0.23	0.29	0.33	0.34	0.39	0.43
SSP4 - Inequality	0.20	0.23	0.29	0.34	0.36	0.41	0.48
SSP5 - Conventional development	0.20	0.23	0.29	0.32	0.33	0.34	0.38
Proportion below age 20							
SSP1 - Rapid development	0.19	0.17	0.17	0.16	0.16	0.15	0.14
SSP2 - Medium	0.19	0.17	0.17	0.17	0.16	0.16	0.15
SSP3 - Stalled development	0.19	0.17	0.15	0.14	0.14	0.13	0.12
SSP4 - Inequality	0.19	0.17	0.15	0.14	0.14	0.13	0.11
SSP5 - Conventional development	0.19	0.18	0.18	0.19	0.19	0.20	0.19
Proportion of Women age 20–39 with at least secondary education							
SSP1 - Rapid development	0.97	0.99	0.99	1.00	1.00	1.00	1.00
SSP2 - Medium	0.97	0.98	0.99	0.99	0.99	1.00	1.00
SSP3 - Stalled development	0.97	0.98	0.98	0.98	0.98	0.98	0.98
SSP4 - Inequality	0.97	0.98	0.98	0.98	0.98	0.98	0.98
SSP5 - Conventional development	0.97	0.99	0.99	1.00	1.00	1.00	1.00
Mean years of schooling, age 25+							
SSP1 - Rapid development	13.71	14.10	14.42	14.71	14.99	15.59	15.94
SSP2 - Medium	13.71	14.03	14.28	14.50	14.72	15.21	15.58
SSP3 - Stalled development	13.71	13.96	14.11	14.21	14.25	14.22	14.17
SSP4 - Inequality	13.71	13.84	13.86	13.84	13.77	13.50	13.37
SSP5 - Conventional development	13.71	14.10	14.43	14.73	15.02	15.63	15.97

Demographic Assumptions Underlying SSPs

	2010–15	2020–25	2030–35	2040–45	2050–55	2075–80	2095–2100
Total fertility rate							
SSP1 - Rapid development	1.37	1.46	1.53	1.57	1.59	1.62	1.64
SSP2 - Medium	1.36	1.47	1.56	1.58	1.60	1.63	1.65
SSP3 - Stalled development	1.30	1.26	1.24	1.24	1.24	1.27	1.29
SSP4 - Inequality	1.31	1.29	1.28	1.28	1.27	1.30	1.33
SSP5 - Conventional development	1.44	1.68	1.85	1.94	1.98	2.02	2.05
Life expectancy at birth for females (in years)							
SSP1 - Rapid development	84.24	87.28	90.28	93.26	96.27	103.96	110.13
SSP2 - Medium	83.39	85.51	87.61	89.71	91.69	96.91	101.00
SSP3 - Stalled development	83.26	84.32	85.37	86.36	87.39	89.88	91.91
SSP4 - Inequality	83.73	85.78	87.80	89.85	91.79	96.75	100.67
SSP5 - Conventional development	84.24	87.28	90.28	93.26	96.27	103.96	110.13
Migration – net flow over five years (in thousands)							
SSP1 - Rapid development	682	854	939	956	929	346	0
SSP2 - Medium	689	849	932	968	967	391	0
SSP3 - Stalled development	568	428	470	480	469	181	0
SSP4 - Inequality	682	851	931	948	929	368	0
SSP5 - Conventional development	796	1281	1431	1517	1550	665	0

Ageing Indicators, Medium Scenario (SSP2)

	2010	2020	2030	2040	2050	2075	2095
Median age	44.35	47.90	49.28	51.18	52.19	53.09	56.06
Propspective median age	44.35	45.72	45.08	45.06	44.24	40.00	38.99
Proportion age 65+	0.20	0.23	0.29	0.32	0.34	0.36	0.40
Proportion RLE < 15 years	0.14	0.14	0.15	0.17	0.19	0.16	0.15

Ghana

Detailed Human Capital Projections to 2060

Demographic indicators, Medium Scenario (SSP2)	2010	2020	2030	2040	2050	2060
Population (in millions)	24.39	30.27	36.17	41.85	46.80	50.73
Proportion age 65+	0.04	0.04	0.05	0.06	0.08	0.10
Proportion below age 20	0.49	0.46	0.42	0.38	0.35	0.31
	2005–10	2015–20	2025–30	2035–40	2045–50	2055–60
Total Fertility Rate	4.34	3.66	3.12	2.72	2.38	2.12
Life expectancy at birth (in years)						
Men	61.84	64.91	66.22	67.44	68.85	70.90
Women	63.61	67.42	69.22	70.82	72.38	74.48
Five-year immigration flow (in '000)	261.25	255.53	265.05	270.64	270.32	266.15
Five-year emigration flow (in '000)	310.52	282.06	334.63	380.56	411.79	433.36

Human Capital indicators, Medium Scenario (SSP2)	2010	2020	2030	2040	2050	2060
Population age 25+: highest educational attainment						
E1 - no education	0.41	0.33	0.26	0.20	0.14	0.10
E2 - incomplete primary	0.04	0.04	0.03	0.03	0.02	0.01
E3 - primary	0.10	0.10	0.11	0.11	0.11	0.10
E4 - lower secondary	0.25	0.29	0.33	0.35	0.35	0.34
E5 - upper secondary	0.14	0.17	0.21	0.25	0.30	0.35
E6 - post-secondary	0.06	0.06	0.07	0.07	0.08	0.09
Mean years of schooling (in years)	6.16	6.97	7.81	8.63	9.41	10.13
Gender gap (population age 25+): highest educational attainment (ratio male/female)						
E1 - no education	0.70	0.73	0.76	0.79	0.82	0.84
E2 - incomplete primary	0.82	0.79	0.81	0.83	0.86	0.89
E3 - primary	1.03	0.96	0.91	0.89	0.90	0.91
E4 - lower secondary	1.26	1.13	1.06	1.03	1.01	1.00
E5 - upper secondary	1.66	1.46	1.31	1.20	1.13	1.08
E6 - post-secondary	1.56	1.39	1.23	1.12	1.05	1.03
Mean years of schooling (male minus female)	1.91	1.47	1.06	0.72	0.48	0.32
Women age 20–39: highest educational attainment						
E1 - no education	0.35	0.25	0.17	0.10	0.06	0.04
E2 - incomplete primary	0.04	0.04	0.03	0.02	0.02	0.01
E3 - primary	0.12	0.12	0.12	0.12	0.11	0.09
E4 - lower secondary	0.29	0.34	0.35	0.35	0.32	0.28
E5 - upper secondary	0.15	0.20	0.26	0.32	0.39	0.47
E6 - post-secondary	0.05	0.06	0.07	0.08	0.10	0.11
Mean years of schooling (in years)	6.54	7.67	8.79	9.77	10.62	11.35

Education scenarios

GET: global education trend scenario (medium assumption also used for SSP2)

CER: constant enrolment rates scenario (assumption of no future improvements)

FT: Fast track scenario (assumption of education expansion according to fastest historical experience)

Pyramids by Education, Medium Scenario

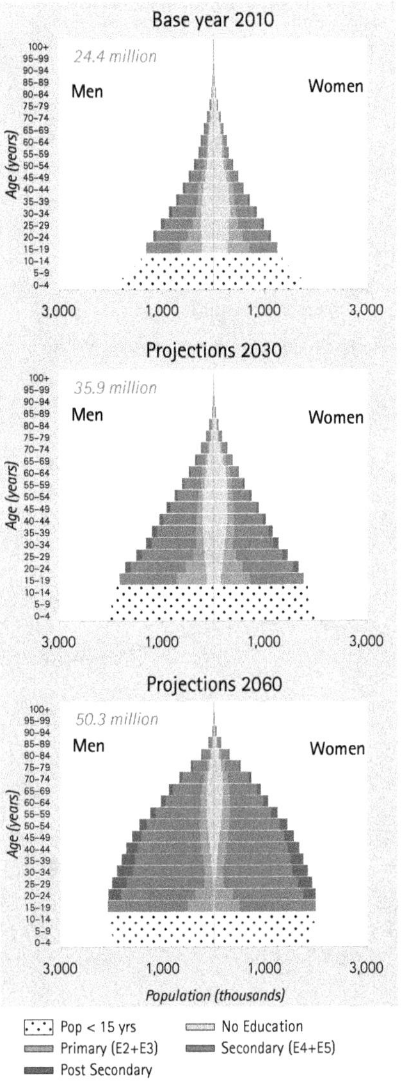

Population Size by Educational Attainment According to Three Education Scenarios: GET, CER, and FT

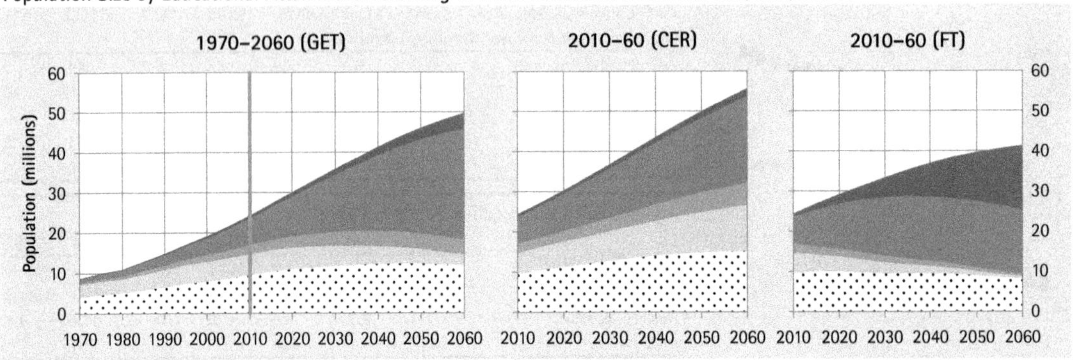

Ghana (Continued)

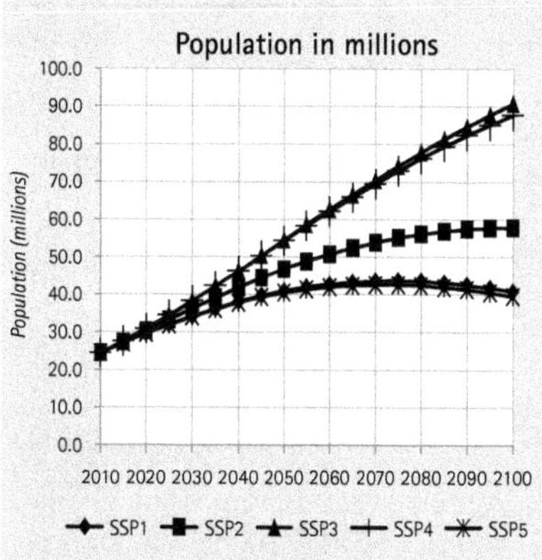

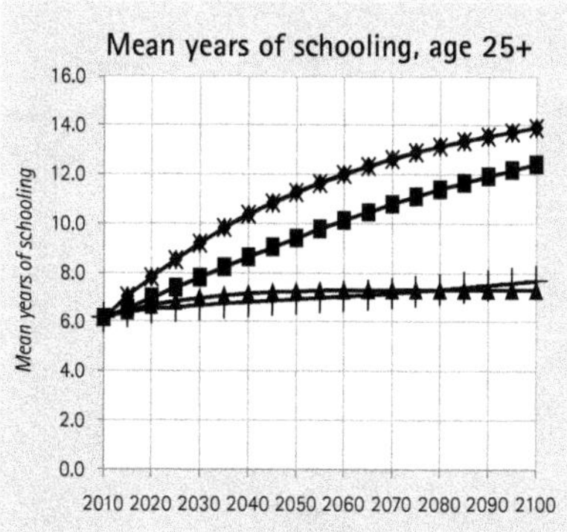

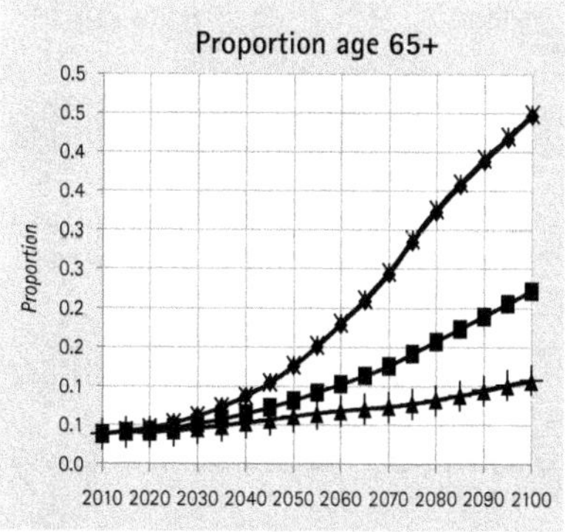

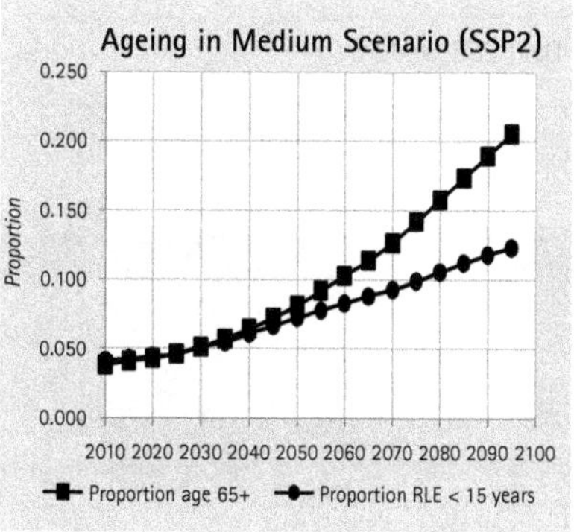

Alternative Scenarios to 2100

Projection Results by Scenario (SSP1–5)

	2010	2020	2030	2040	2050	2075	2100
Population (in millions)							
SSP1 - Rapid development	24.39	29.59	34.09	38.03	40.92	43.65	40.82
SSP2 - Medium	24.39	30.27	36.17	41.85	46.80	55.15	57.90
SSP3 - Stalled development	24.39	30.85	38.24	46.27	54.57	74.20	90.74
SSP4 - Inequality	24.39	30.86	38.31	46.27	54.38	72.90	87.64
SSP5 - Conventional development	24.39	29.57	33.99	37.78	40.45	42.56	39.51
Proportion age 65+							
SSP1 - Rapid development	0.04	0.05	0.06	0.09	0.13	0.28	0.45
SSP2 - Medium	0.04	0.04	0.05	0.06	0.08	0.14	0.22
SSP3 - Stalled development	0.04	0.04	0.05	0.05	0.06	0.08	0.11
SSP4 - Inequality	0.04	0.04	0.05	0.05	0.06	0.08	0.11
SSP5 - Conventional development	0.04	0.05	0.06	0.09	0.13	0.29	0.45
Proportion below age 20							
SSP1 - Rapid development	0.49	0.44	0.37	0.31	0.26	0.16	0.11
SSP2 - Medium	0.49	0.46	0.42	0.38	0.35	0.27	0.21
SSP3 - Stalled development	0.49	0.48	0.47	0.45	0.43	0.37	0.32
SSP4 - Inequality	0.49	0.48	0.47	0.45	0.43	0.36	0.32
SSP5 - Conventional development	0.49	0.44	0.37	0.31	0.26	0.16	0.11
Proportion of Women age 20-39 with at least secondary education							
SSP1 - Rapid development	0.49	0.72	0.82	0.87	0.90	0.96	0.98
SSP2 - Medium	0.49	0.59	0.68	0.75	0.81	0.91	0.97
SSP3 - Stalled development	0.49	0.52	0.52	0.52	0.52	0.52	0.52
SSP4 - Inequality	0.49	0.48	0.46	0.46	0.46	0.46	0.46
SSP5 - Conventional development	0.49	0.72	0.82	0.87	0.90	0.96	0.98
Mean years of schooling, age 25+							
SSP1 - Rapid development	6.16	7.80	9.19	10.37	11.26	12.90	13.90
SSP2 - Medium	6.16	6.97	7.81	8.63	9.41	11.10	12.41
SSP3 - Stalled development	6.16	6.66	6.98	7.16	7.26	7.31	7.32
SSP4 - Inequality	6.16	6.53	6.68	6.81	6.93	7.25	7.68
SSP5 - Conventional development	6.16	7.80	9.19	10.36	11.25	12.88	13.90

Demographic Assumptions Underlying SSPs

	2010–15	2020–25	2030–35	2040–45	2050–55	2075–80	2095–2100
Total fertility rate							
SSP1 - Rapid development	3.65	2.55	2.01	1.72	1.53	1.32	1.23
SSP2 - Medium	3.98	3.37	2.90	2.54	2.22	1.84	1.71
SSP3 - Stalled development	4.26	4.18	3.97	3.62	3.24	2.63	2.48
SSP4 - Inequality	4.27	4.24	4.03	3.63	3.22	2.56	2.38
SSP5 - Conventional development	3.65	2.55	2.01	1.72	1.53	1.32	1.23
Life expectancy at birth for females (in years)							
SSP1 - Rapid development	69.54	75.65	79.26	82.57	85.82	93.80	100.21
SSP2 - Medium	65.82	68.28	69.98	71.48	73.38	78.99	83.50
SSP3 - Stalled development	66.84	65.39	65.95	66.26	66.56	69.14	71.04
SSP4 - Inequality	66.84	65.36	65.88	66.19	66.48	69.08	71.02
SSP5 - Conventional development	69.54	75.65	79.26	82.57	85.82	93.80	100.21
Migration – net flow over five years (in thousands)							
SSP1 - Rapid development	−30	−47	−88	−114	−130	−47	0
SSP2 - Medium	−29	−47	−90	−126	−155	−69	0
SSP3 - Stalled development	−24	−23	−44	−62	−78	−39	0
SSP4 - Inequality	−29	−47	−91	−133	−173	−86	0
SSP5 - Conventional development	−35	−71	−138	−187	−223	−92	0

Ageing Indicators, Medium Scenario (SSP2)

	2010	2020	2030	2040	2050	2075	2095
Median age	20.46	22.06	24.12	26.64	29.24	36.33	42.02
Propspective median age	20.46	20.81	21.94	23.56	24.92	27.81	30.08
Proportion age 65+	0.04	0.04	0.05	0.06	0.08	0.14	0.21
Proportion RLE < 15 years	0.04	0.04	0.05	0.06	0.07	0.10	0.12

Greece

Detailed Human Capital Projections to 2060

Demographic indicators, Medium Scenario (SSP2)

	2010	2020	2030	2040	2050	2060
Population (in millions)	11.36	11.57	11.68	11.77	11.75	11.57
Proportion age 65+	0.19	0.21	0.25	0.31	0.35	0.36
Proportion below age 20	0.19	0.19	0.17	0.17	0.17	0.16
	2005–10	2015–20	2025–30	2035–40	2045–50	2055–60
Total Fertility Rate	1.46	1.47	1.58	1.60	1.60	1.61
Life expectancy at birth (in years)						
Men	77.01	79.85	82.21	84.35	86.43	88.58
Women	82.00	84.81	87.11	89.21	91.21	93.30
Five-year immigration flow (in '000)	212.21	168.84	175.38	179.44	179.61	177.07
Five-year emigration flow (in '000)	58.40	37.28	34.54	32.36	30.24	29.23

Human Capital indicators, Medium Scenario (SSP2)

	2010	2020	2030	2040	2050	2060
Population age 25+: highest educational attainment						
E1 - no education	0.03	0.01	0.01	0.00	0.00	0.00
E2 - incomplete primary	0.05	0.03	0.01	0.00	0.00	0.00
E3 - primary	0.28	0.22	0.16	0.11	0.07	0.04
E4 - lower secondary	0.09	0.09	0.08	0.07	0.06	0.05
E5 - upper secondary	0.36	0.40	0.44	0.46	0.46	0.45
E6 - post-secondary	0.20	0.25	0.30	0.35	0.40	0.46
Mean years of schooling (in years)	10.28	11.14	11.87	12.50	13.01	13.45
Gender gap (population age 25+): highest educational attainment (ratio male/female)						
E1 - no education	0.40	0.48	0.66	0.91	1.06	1.13
E2 - incomplete primary	0.56	0.50	0.52	0.70	0.95	1.16
E3 - primary	0.90	0.86	0.83	0.83	0.89	0.98
E4 - lower secondary	1.33	1.31	1.28	1.25	1.21	1.18
E5 - upper secondary	1.11	1.11	1.12	1.12	1.12	1.10
E6 - post-secondary	1.08	0.98	0.91	0.88	0.88	0.89
Mean years of schooling (male minus female)	0.66	0.37	0.10	−0.10	−0.20	−0.23
Women age 20–39: highest educational attainment						
E1 - no education	0.00	0.00	0.00	0.00	0.00	0.00
E2 - incomplete primary	0.00	0.00	0.00	0.00	0.00	0.00
E3 - primary	0.07	0.04	0.02	0.01	0.00	0.00
E4 - lower secondary	0.08	0.05	0.03	0.02	0.02	0.01
E5 - upper secondary	0.54	0.54	0.53	0.49	0.47	0.46
E6 - post-secondary	0.30	0.37	0.42	0.47	0.50	0.52
Mean years of schooling (in years)	12.49	13.10	13.46	13.76	13.92	14.00

Education scenarios

GET: global education trend scenario (medium assumption also used for SSP2)

CER: constant enrolment rates scenario (assumption of no future improvements)

FT: Fast track scenario (assumption of education expansion according to fastest historical experience)

Pyramids by Education, Medium Scenario

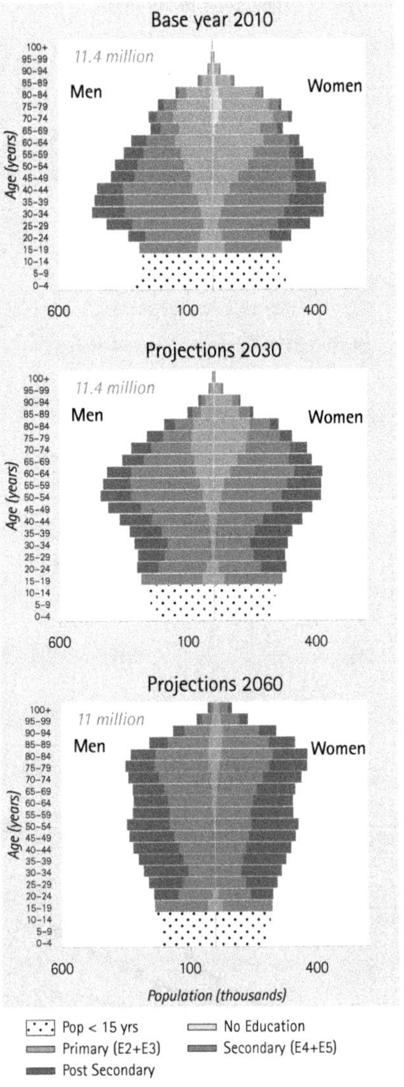

Population Size by Educational Attainment According to Three Education Scenarios: GET, CER, and FT

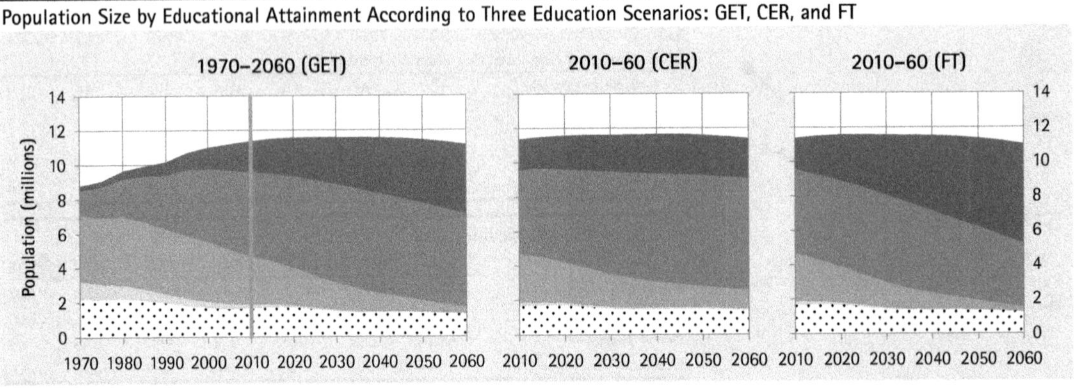

Greece (Continued)

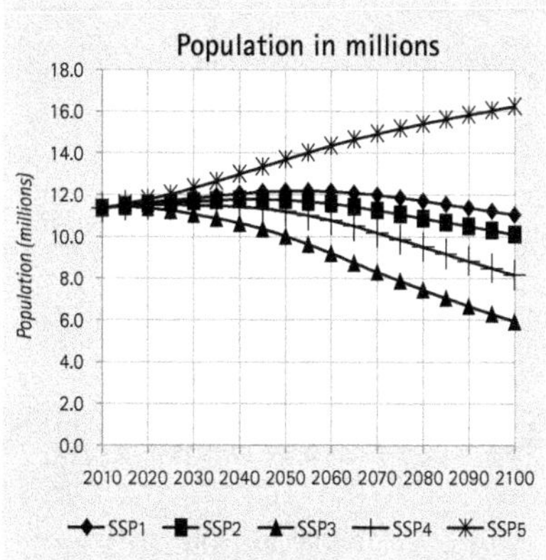

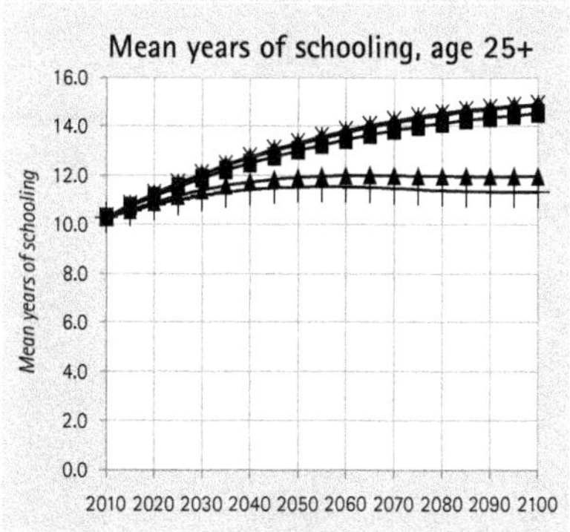

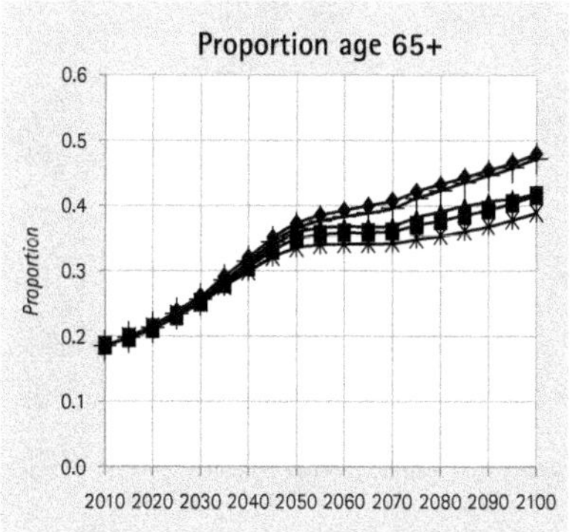

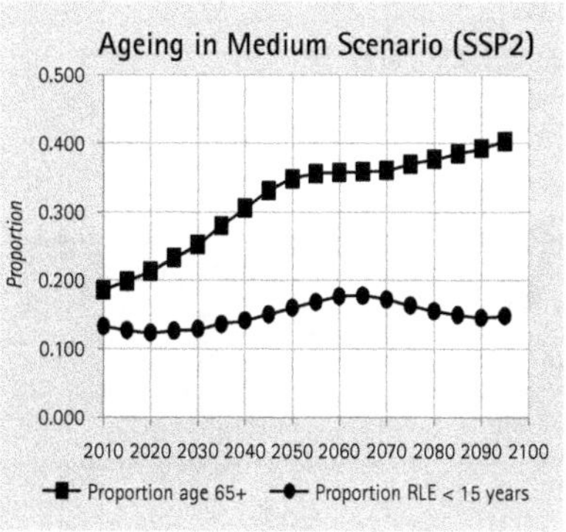

Alternative Scenarios to 2100

Projection Results by Scenario (SSP1–5)

	2010	2020	2030	2040	2050	2075	2100
Population (in millions)							
SSP1 - Rapid development	11.36	11.63	11.84	12.05	12.18	11.86	11.05
SSP2 - Medium	11.36	11.57	11.68	11.77	11.75	11.08	10.12
SSP3 - Stalled development	11.36	11.38	11.07	10.65	10.03	7.86	5.93
SSP4 - Inequality	11.36	11.52	11.50	11.43	11.20	9.86	8.15
SSP5 - Conventional development	11.36	11.78	12.33	12.99	13.68	15.17	16.24
Proportion age 65+							
SSP1 - Rapid development	0.19	0.22	0.26	0.32	0.37	0.42	0.48
SSP2 - Medium	0.19	0.21	0.25	0.31	0.35	0.37	0.42
SSP3 - Stalled development	0.19	0.21	0.25	0.31	0.36	0.38	0.42
SSP4 - Inequality	0.19	0.21	0.26	0.31	0.37	0.41	0.47
SSP5 - Conventional development	0.19	0.21	0.25	0.30	0.33	0.35	0.39
Proportion below age 20							
SSP1 - Rapid development	0.19	0.19	0.17	0.16	0.16	0.14	0.13
SSP2 - Medium	0.19	0.19	0.17	0.17	0.17	0.16	0.15
SSP3 - Stalled development	0.19	0.19	0.16	0.15	0.14	0.13	0.12
SSP4 - Inequality	0.19	0.19	0.16	0.15	0.14	0.13	0.11
SSP5 - Conventional development	0.19	0.19	0.19	0.19	0.19	0.19	0.18
Proportion of Women age 20–39 with at least secondary education							
SSP1 - Rapid development	0.92	0.98	0.99	0.99	1.00	1.00	1.00
SSP2 - Medium	0.92	0.96	0.98	0.99	0.99	1.00	1.00
SSP3 - Stalled development	0.92	0.90	0.90	0.90	0.90	0.90	0.90
SSP4 - Inequality	0.92	0.90	0.90	0.90	0.90	0.90	0.90
SSP5 - Conventional development	0.92	0.98	0.99	0.99	1.00	1.00	1.00
Mean years of schooling, age 25+							
SSP1 - Rapid development	10.28	11.23	12.02	12.70	13.26	14.32	14.87
SSP2 - Medium	10.28	11.14	11.87	12.50	13.01	13.99	14.53
SSP3 - Stalled development	10.28	10.89	11.39	11.72	11.91	11.97	11.96
SSP4 - Inequality	10.28	10.79	11.18	11.41	11.52	11.43	11.33
SSP5 - Conventional development	10.28	11.24	12.05	12.75	13.32	14.39	14.91

Demographic Assumptions Underlying SSPs

	2010–15	2020–25	2030–35	2040–45	2050–55	2075–80	2095–2100
Total fertility rate							
SSP1 - Rapid development	1.43	1.51	1.57	1.59	1.59	1.62	1.64
SSP2 - Medium	1.42	1.52	1.60	1.60	1.60	1.63	1.65
SSP3 - Stalled development	1.37	1.34	1.31	1.29	1.28	1.31	1.33
SSP4 - Inequality	1.37	1.36	1.34	1.33	1.32	1.34	1.37
SSP5 - Conventional development	1.50	1.73	1.90	1.96	1.99	2.02	2.05
Life expectancy at birth for females (in years)							
SSP1 - Rapid development	84.68	88.07	91.05	93.95	96.91	104.38	110.40
SSP2 - Medium	83.51	86.01	88.21	90.21	92.30	97.30	101.30
SSP3 - Stalled development	83.73	85.13	86.14	87.12	87.98	90.10	91.91
SSP4 - Inequality	84.21	86.60	88.62	90.50	92.46	97.01	100.76
SSP5 - Conventional development	84.68	88.07	91.05	93.95	96.91	104.38	110.40
Migration – net flow over five years (in thousands)							
SSP1 - Rapid development	139	136	142	143	138	51	0
SSP2 - Medium	139	135	142	145	145	58	0
SSP3 - Stalled development	115	68	71	73	71	28	0
SSP4 - Inequality	139	136	141	143	141	57	0
SSP5 - Conventional development	162	205	217	227	231	98	0

Ageing Indicators, Medium Scenario (SSP2)

	2010	2020	2030	2040	2050	2075	2095
Median age	41.35	44.95	48.68	51.00	51.82	53.78	56.60
Propspective median age	41.35	42.58	44.22	44.72	43.67	40.99	39.91
Proportion age 65+	0.19	0.21	0.25	0.31	0.35	0.37	0.40
Proportion RLE < 15 years	0.13	0.12	0.13	0.14	0.16	0.16	0.15

Guadeloupe

Detailed Human Capital Projections to 2060

Demographic indicators, Medium Scenario (SSP2)	2010	2020	2030	2040	2050	2060
Population (in millions)	0.46	0.49	0.51	0.53	0.54	0.54
Proportion age 65+	0.12	0.16	0.21	0.26	0.26	0.28
Proportion below age 20	0.30	0.27	0.25	0.24	0.23	0.22
	2005–10	2015–20	2025–30	2035–40	2045–50	2055–60
Total Fertility Rate	2.14	2.13	2.03	1.96	1.91	1.89
Life expectancy at birth (in years)						
Man	75.70	77.89	80.29	82.71	84.99	87.29
Women	82.88	85.19	87.31	89.41	91.41	93.40
Five-year immigration flow (in '000)	2.31	2.26	2.34	2.39	2.39	2.36
Five-year emigration flow (in '000)	5.78	4.66	4.57	4.35	4.26	4.15

Human Capital indicators, Medium Scenario (SSP2)	2010	2020	2030	2040	2050	2060
Population age 25+: highest educational attainment						
E1 - no education	0.02	0.02	0.01	0.01	0.01	0.00
E2 - incomplete primary	0.11	0.07	0.04	0.03	0.02	0.01
E3 - primary	0.25	0.20	0.16	0.12	0.08	0.05
E4 - lower secondary	0.14	0.13	0.12	0.10	0.08	0.06
E5 - upper secondary	0.32	0.38	0.43	0.46	0.49	0.49
E6 - post-secondary	0.16	0.20	0.24	0.28	0.33	0.38
Mean years of schooling (in years)	9.27	10.16	10.99	11.69	12.31	12.87
Gender gap (population age 25+): highest educational attainment (ratio male/female)						
E1 - no education	1.36	1.15	0.99	0.88	0.80	0.75
E2 - incomplete primary	0.97	0.94	0.91	0.89	0.87	0.86
E3 - primary	1.06	1.02	0.99	0.96	0.93	0.93
E4 - lower secondary	0.94	0.97	0.98	0.98	0.97	0.96
E5 - upper secondary	1.03	1.07	1.09	1.10	1.09	1.07
E6 - post-secondary	0.89	0.88	0.88	0.89	0.91	0.93
Mean years of schooling (male minus female)	−0.16	−0.08	−0.03	−0.01	−0.01	−0.01
Women age 20–39: highest educational attainment						
E1 - no education	0.01	0.01	0.00	0.00	0.00	0.00
E2 - incomplete primary	0.02	0.01	0.00	0.00	0.00	0.00
E3 - primary	0.12	0.06	0.04	0.02	0.01	0.01
E4 - lower secondary	0.13	0.12	0.08	0.06	0.05	0.04
E5 - upper secondary	0.47	0.52	0.53	0.53	0.52	0.51
E6 - post-secondary	0.25	0.29	0.34	0.38	0.41	0.44
Mean years of schooling (in years)	11.40	12.27	12.93	13.28	13.50	13.67

Education scenarios

GET: global education trend scenario (medium assumption also used for SSP2)

CER: constant enrolment rates scenario (assumption of no future improvements)

FT: Fast track scenario (assumption of education expansion according to fastest historical experience)

Pyramids by Education, Medium Scenario

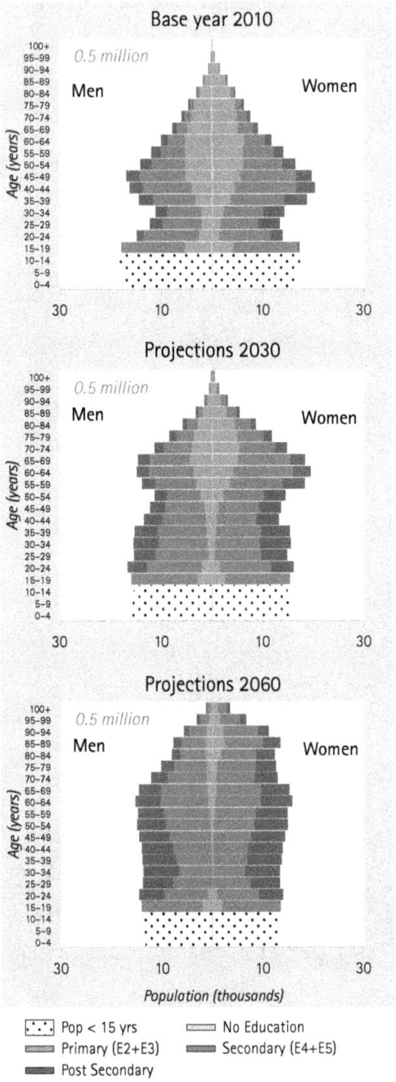

Population Size by Educational Attainment According to Three Education Scenarios: GET, CER, and FT

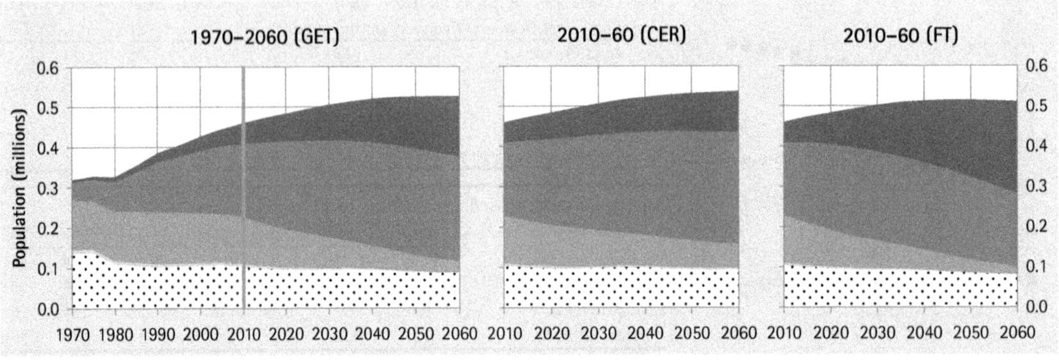

Guadeloupe (Continued)

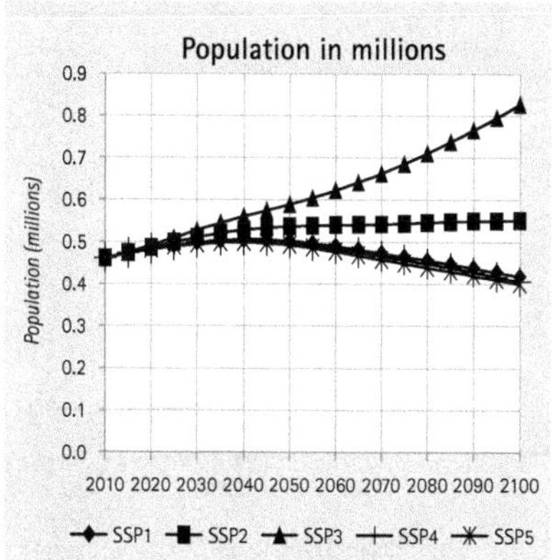

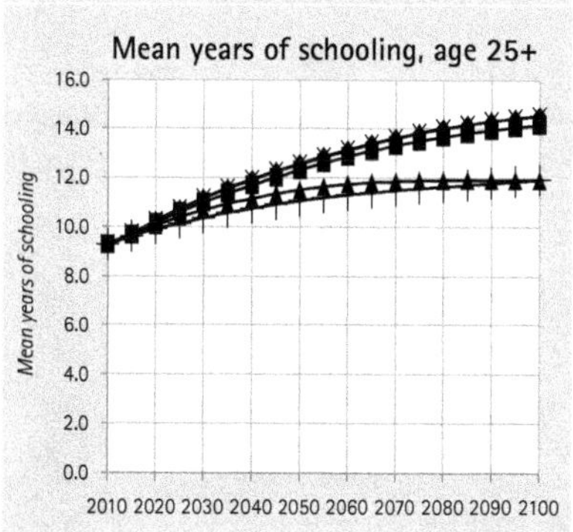

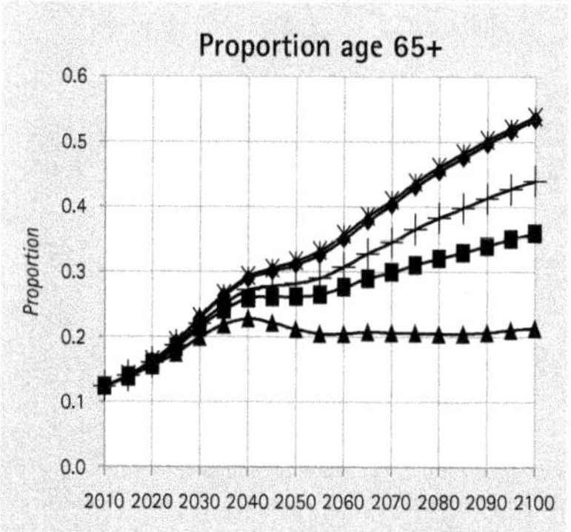

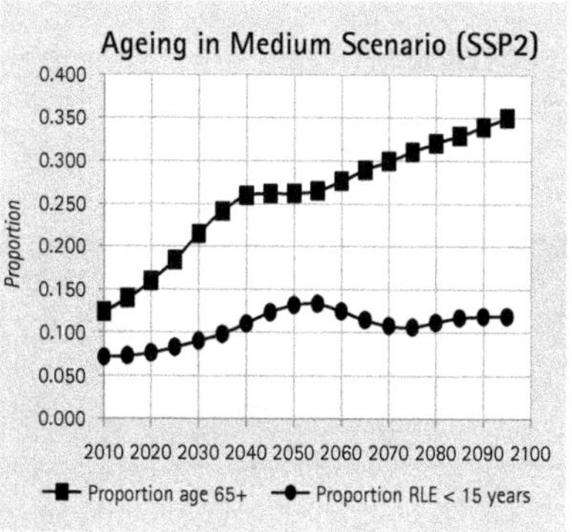

Alternative Scenarios to 2100

Projection Results by Scenario (SSP1–5)

	2010	2020	2030	2040	2050	2075	2100
Population (in millions)							
SSP1 - Rapid development	0.46	0.48	0.50	0.51	0.50	0.47	0.42
SSP2 - Medium	0.46	0.49	0.51	0.53	0.54	0.54	0.55
SSP3 - Stalled development	0.46	0.49	0.53	0.56	0.59	0.69	0.83
SSP4 - Inequality	0.46	0.48	0.50	0.50	0.50	0.46	0.41
SSP5 - Conventional development	0.46	0.48	0.49	0.50	0.49	0.45	0.40
Proportion age 65+							
SSP1 - Rapid development	0.12	0.16	0.23	0.29	0.31	0.43	0.53
SSP2 - Medium	0.12	0.16	0.21	0.26	0.26	0.31	0.36
SSP3 - Stalled development	0.12	0.16	0.20	0.23	0.21	0.21	0.21
SSP4 - Inequality	0.12	0.16	0.22	0.27	0.28	0.37	0.44
SSP5 - Conventional development	0.12	0.16	0.23	0.29	0.32	0.44	0.54
Proportion below age 20							
SSP1 - Rapid development	0.30	0.26	0.22	0.20	0.17	0.13	0.11
SSP2 - Medium	0.30	0.27	0.25	0.24	0.23	0.21	0.19
SSP3 - Stalled development	0.30	0.28	0.28	0.29	0.28	0.29	0.29
SSP4 - Inequality	0.30	0.26	0.23	0.21	0.19	0.16	0.14
SSP5 - Conventional development	0.30	0.26	0.22	0.20	0.17	0.13	0.11
Proportion of Women age 20–39 with at least secondary education							
SSP1 - Rapid development	0.85	0.95	0.97	0.99	0.99	1.00	1.00
SSP2 - Medium	0.85	0.93	0.96	0.98	0.99	1.00	1.00
SSP3 - Stalled development	0.85	0.89	0.90	0.90	0.90	0.90	0.90
SSP4 - Inequality	0.85	0.84	0.81	0.81	0.81	0.81	0.81
SSP5 - Conventional development	0.85	0.95	0.97	0.99	0.99	1.00	1.00
Mean years of schooling, age 25+							
SSP1 - Rapid development	9.27	10.23	11.16	11.93	12.58	13.84	14.54
SSP2 - Medium	9.27	10.16	10.99	11.69	12.31	13.50	14.16
SSP3 - Stalled development	9.27	10.05	10.69	11.16	11.51	11.88	11.91
SSP4 - Inequality	9.27	9.90	10.36	10.76	11.07	11.57	11.92
SSP5 - Conventional development	9.27	10.23	11.15	11.91	12.56	13.82	14.53

Demographic Assumptions Underlying SSPs

	2010–15	2020–25	2030–35	2040–45	2050–55	2075–80	2095–2100
Total fertility rate							
SSP1 - Rapid development	2.06	1.73	1.53	1.44	1.40	1.38	1.38
SSP2 - Medium	2.17	2.08	1.99	1.94	1.90	1.87	1.85
SSP3 - Stalled development	2.29	2.43	2.51	2.52	2.52	2.53	2.53
SSP4 - Inequality	2.09	1.84	1.65	1.55	1.50	1.49	1.48
SSP5 - Conventional development	2.06	1.73	1.53	1.44	1.40	1.38	1.38
Life expectancy at birth for females (in years)							
SSP1 - Rapid development	85.23	88.26	91.22	94.14	97.09	104.52	110.53
SSP2 - Medium	84.09	86.29	88.31	90.41	92.40	97.41	101.40
SSP3 - Stalled development	84.30	85.35	86.36	87.35	88.29	90.43	92.22
SSP4 - Inequality	84.73	86.80	88.74	90.75	92.65	97.22	100.99
SSP5 - Conventional development	85.23	88.26	91.22	94.14	97.09	104.52	110.53
Migration – net flow over five years (in thousands)							
SSP1 - Rapid development	−3	−2	−2	−2	−2	0	0
SSP2 - Medium	−3	−2	−2	−2	−2	−1	0
SSP3 - Stalled development	−2	−1	−1	−1	−1	0	0
SSP4 - Inequality	−3	−2	−2	−2	−1	0	0
SSP5 - Conventional development	−3	−4	−3	−3	−3	−1	0

Ageing Indicators, Medium Scenario (SSP2)

	2010	2020	2030	2040	2050	2075	2095
Median age	36.88	38.38	39.50	42.07	44.07	47.59	50.79
Propspective median age	36.88	36.15	35.22	35.76	35.84	34.43	33.71
Proportion age 65+	0.12	0.16	0.21	0.26	0.26	0.31	0.35
Proportion RLE < 15 years	0.07	0.08	0.09	0.11	0.13	0.11	0.12

Guatemala

Detailed Human Capital Projections to 2060

Demographic indicators, Medium Scenario (SSP2)

	2010	2020	2030	2040	2050	2060
Population (in millions)	14.39	17.64	20.75	23.55	25.93	27.80
Proportion age 65+	0.04	0.05	0.06	0.07	0.10	0.13
Proportion below age 20	0.53	0.48	0.42	0.37	0.32	0.29
	2005–10	2015–20	2025–30	2035–40	2045–50	2055–60
Total Fertility Rate	4.15	3.14	2.61	2.25	2.05	1.92
Life expectancy at birth (in years)						
Men	66.73	68.29	70.27	72.38	74.72	76.99
Women	73.79	75.48	77.49	79.51	81.50	83.49
Five-year immigration flow (in '000)	6.43	6.30	6.54	6.69	6.69	6.60
Five-year emigration flow (in '000)	205.50	198.23	238.11	262.63	274.57	277.09

Human Capital indicators, Medium Scenario (SSP2)

	2010	2020	2030	2040	2050	2060
Population age 25+: highest educational attainment						
E1 - no education	0.29	0.23	0.17	0.13	0.10	0.07
E2 - incomplete primary	0.28	0.25	0.21	0.17	0.14	0.11
E3 - primary	0.19	0.21	0.23	0.24	0.24	0.23
E4 - lower secondary	0.09	0.11	0.12	0.13	0.13	0.13
E5 - upper secondary	0.10	0.14	0.18	0.22	0.27	0.31
E6 - post-secondary	0.06	0.07	0.09	0.10	0.12	0.15
Mean years of schooling (in years)	5.01	5.83	6.65	7.42	8.11	8.75
Gender gap (population age 25+): highest educational attainment (ratio male/female)						
E1 - no education	0.66	0.63	0.62	0.63	0.65	0.67
E2 - incomplete primary	1.09	1.03	0.97	0.92	0.88	0.85
E3 - primary	1.30	1.26	1.21	1.16	1.12	1.07
E4 - lower secondary	1.26	1.24	1.20	1.15	1.11	1.07
E5 - upper secondary	1.03	1.05	1.05	1.04	1.04	1.04
E6 - post-secondary	1.39	1.26	1.16	1.10	1.07	1.06
Mean years of schooling (male minus female)	0.95	0.91	0.78	0.63	0.50	0.40
Women age 20–39: highest educational attainment						
E1 - no education	0.21	0.16	0.12	0.08	0.04	0.02
E2 - incomplete primary	0.27	0.21	0.15	0.11	0.07	0.04
E3 - primary	0.21	0.23	0.25	0.25	0.23	0.20
E4 - lower secondary	0.11	0.12	0.13	0.14	0.14	0.13
E5 - upper secondary	0.15	0.19	0.25	0.31	0.37	0.43
E6 - post-secondary	0.06	0.08	0.10	0.12	0.15	0.18
Mean years of schooling (in years)	5.81	6.64	7.61	8.55	9.39	10.09

Education scenarios

GET: global education trend scenario (medium assumption also used for SSP2)

CER: constant enrolment rates scenario (assumption of no future improvements)

FT: Fast track scenario (assumption of education expansion according to fastest historical experience)

Pyramids by Education, Medium Scenario

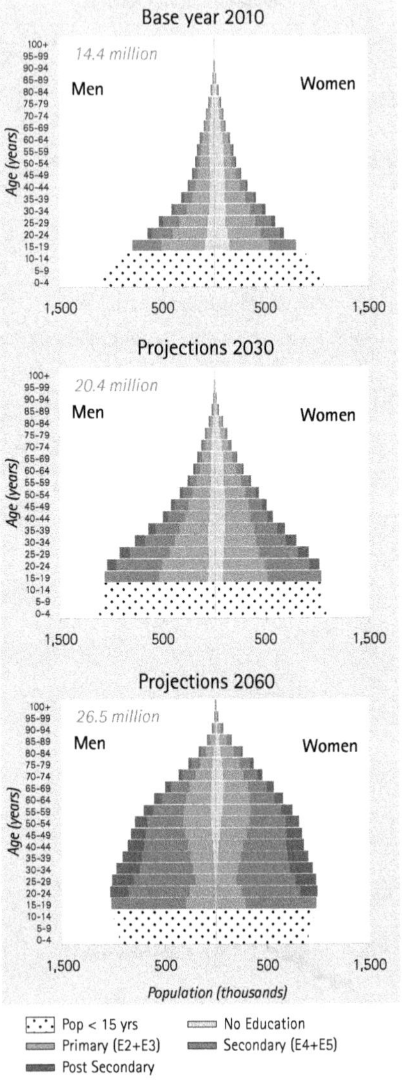

Population Size by Educational Attainment According to Three Education Scenarios: GET, CER, and FT

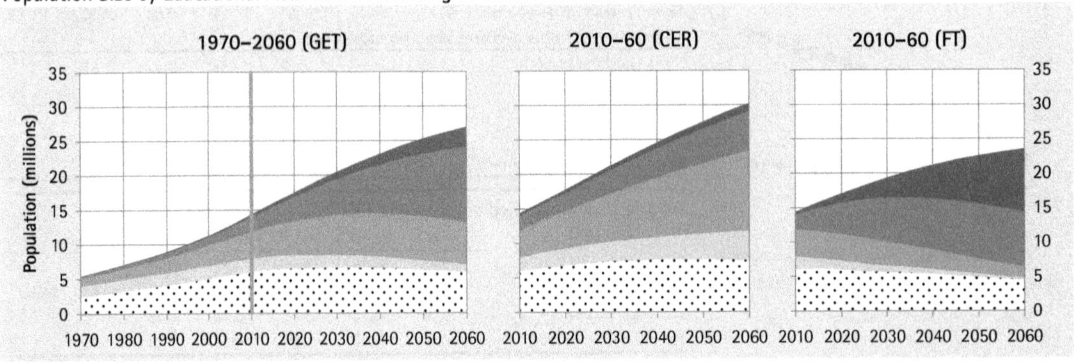

Guatemala (Continued)

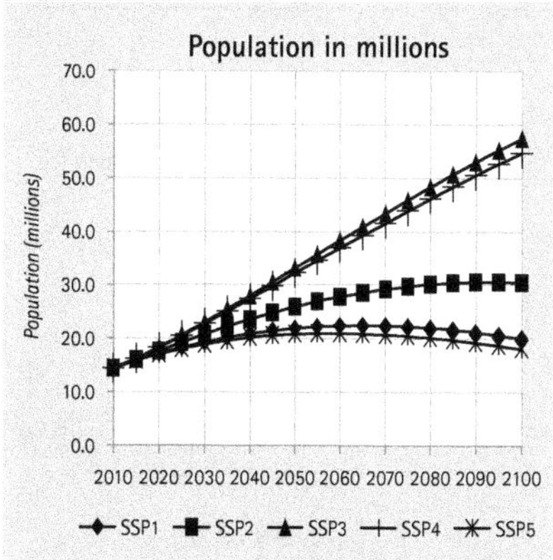

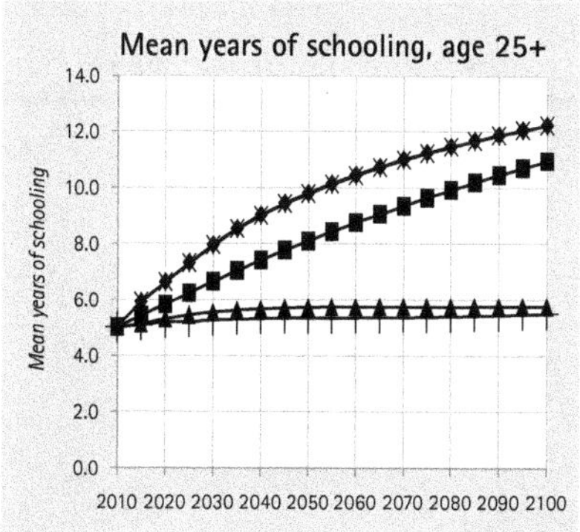

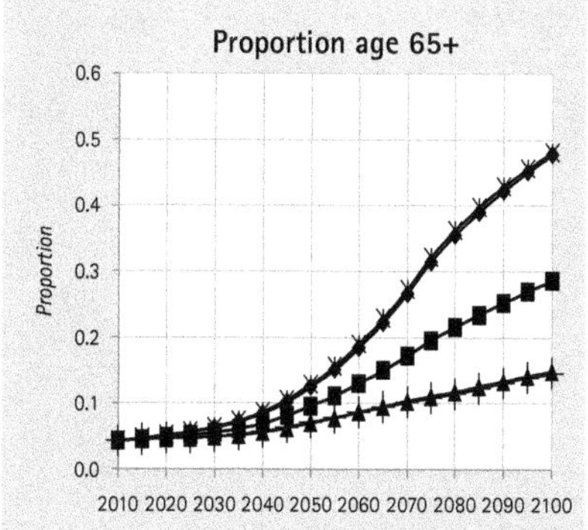

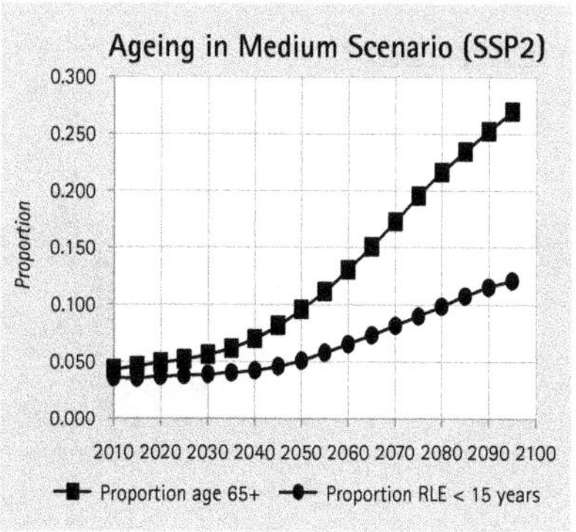

Alternative Scenarios to 2100

Projection Results by Scenario (SSP1–5)

	2010	2020	2030	2040	2050	2075	2100
Population (in millions)							
SSP1 - Rapid development	14.39	17.14	19.28	20.88	21.88	22.29	20.01
SSP2 - Medium	14.39	17.64	20.75	23.55	25.93	29.76	30.52
SSP3 - Stalled development	14.39	18.35	23.05	27.99	33.18	45.96	57.43
SSP4 - Inequality	14.39	18.27	22.79	27.44	32.25	43.93	54.78
SSP5 - Conventional development	14.39	17.03	18.90	20.18	20.83	20.47	18.09
Proportion age 65+							
SSP1 - Rapid development	0.04	0.05	0.06	0.08	0.13	0.31	0.48
SSP2 - Medium	0.04	0.05	0.06	0.07	0.10	0.20	0.29
SSP3 - Stalled development	0.04	0.05	0.05	0.06	0.07	0.11	0.15
SSP4 - Inequality	0.04	0.05	0.05	0.06	0.07	0.11	0.15
SSP5 - Conventional development	0.04	0.05	0.06	0.09	0.13	0.32	0.48
Proportion below age 20							
SSP1 - Rapid development	0.53	0.46	0.37	0.30	0.24	0.15	0.10
SSP2 - Medium	0.53	0.48	0.42	0.37	0.32	0.24	0.19
SSP3 - Stalled development	0.53	0.49	0.47	0.44	0.40	0.34	0.30
SSP4 - Inequality	0.53	0.50	0.47	0.44	0.41	0.35	0.30
SSP5 - Conventional development	0.53	0.46	0.37	0.30	0.25	0.15	0.10
Proportion of Women age 20–39 with at least secondary education							
SSP1 - Rapid development	0.31	0.56	0.68	0.76	0.81	0.91	0.96
SSP2 - Medium	0.31	0.39	0.48	0.57	0.66	0.83	0.94
SSP3 - Stalled development	0.31	0.28	0.28	0.28	0.28	0.28	0.28
SSP4 - Inequality	0.31	0.26	0.25	0.25	0.25	0.25	0.25
SSP5 - Conventional development	0.31	0.56	0.68	0.76	0.81	0.91	0.96
Mean years of schooling, age 25+							
SSP1 - Rapid development	5.01	6.64	7.96	9.02	9.81	11.25	12.23
SSP2 - Medium	5.01	5.83	6.65	7.42	8.11	9.64	10.95
SSP3 - Stalled development	5.01	5.31	5.54	5.67	5.72	5.75	5.76
SSP4 - Inequality	5.01	5.18	5.26	5.32	5.35	5.39	5.50
SSP5 - Conventional development	5.01	6.63	7.93	8.99	9.78	11.22	12.22

Demographic Assumptions Underlying SSPs

	2010–15	2020–25	2030–35	2040–45	2050–55	2075–80	2095–2100
Total fertility rate							
SSP1 - Rapid development	3.25	2.21	1.73	1.51	1.40	1.27	1.18
SSP2 - Medium	3.60	2.84	2.42	2.15	1.99	1.76	1.61
SSP3 - Stalled development	3.84	3.62	3.30	3.00	2.79	2.48	2.33
SSP4 - Inequality	3.86	3.69	3.35	3.03	2.80	2.46	2.31
SSP5 - Conventional development	3.25	2.21	1.73	1.51	1.40	1.27	1.18
Life expectancy at birth for females (in years)							
SSP1 - Rapid development	76.70	79.06	81.79	84.59	87.59	95.29	101.29
SSP2 - Medium	74.59	76.48	78.49	80.50	82.49	87.51	91.50
SSP3 - Stalled development	76.08	76.52	77.17	77.93	78.67	80.39	81.69
SSP4 - Inequality	76.08	76.51	77.14	77.88	78.61	80.30	81.61
SSP5 - Conventional development	76.70	79.06	81.79	84.59	87.59	95.29	101.29
Migration – net flow over five years (in thousands)							
SSP1 - Rapid development	−184	−210	−235	−235	−224	−83	0
SSP2 - Medium	−184	−213	−247	−264	−273	−124	0
SSP3 - Stalled development	−153	−105	−123	−139	−152	−82	0
SSP4 - Inequality	−184	−212	−253	−293	−325	−176	0
SSP5 - Conventional development	−215	−317	−363	−373	−367	−150	0

Ageing Indicators, Medium Scenario (SSP2)

	2010	2020	2030	2040	2050	2075	2095
Median age	18.78	21.09	24.18	27.66	31.18	39.99	45.86
Propspective median age	18.78	19.52	21.04	22.63	24.35	29.05	31.60
Proportion age 65+	0.04	0.05	0.06	0.07	0.10	0.20	0.27
Proportion RLE < 15 years	0.04	0.04	0.04	0.04	0.05	0.09	0.12

Guinea

Detailed Human Capital Projections to 2060

Demographic indicators, Medium Scenario (SSP2)	2010	2020	2030	2040	2050	2060
Population (in millions)	9.98	11.86	13.48	14.76	15.62	16.02
Proportion age 65+	0.03	0.04	0.04	0.05	0.07	0.08
Proportion below age 20	0.54	0.52	0.46	0.41	0.37	0.32
	2005–10	2015–20	2025–30	2035–40	2045–50	2055–60
Total Fertility Rate	5.45	4.33	3.37	2.73	2.34	2.08
Life expectancy at birth (in years)						
Men	50.93	55.17	57.63	59.86	61.99	64.39
Women	54.02	58.48	61.27	63.88	66.32	68.78
Five-year immigration flow (in '000)	4.03	3.94	4.08	4.17	4.17	4.11
Five-year emigration flow (in '000)	302.54	279.32	330.28	365.95	376.13	372.19

Human Capital indicators, Medium Scenario (SSP2)	2010	2020	2030	2040	2050	2060
Population age 25+: highest educational attainment						
E1 - no education	0.73	0.65	0.55	0.44	0.35	0.27
E2 - incomplete primary	0.05	0.05	0.05	0.05	0.04	0.03
E3 - primary	0.08	0.10	0.12	0.14	0.16	0.17
E4 - lower secondary	0.08	0.13	0.17	0.22	0.25	0.28
E5 - upper secondary	0.03	0.04	0.06	0.09	0.12	0.16
E6 - post-secondary	0.04	0.04	0.05	0.06	0.08	0.09
Mean years of schooling (in years)	2.31	3.28	4.37	5.56	6.71	7.80
Gender gap (population age 25+): highest educational attainment (ratio male/female)						
E1 - no education	0.75	0.72	0.70	0.70	0.71	0.74
E2 - incomplete primary	1.65	1.37	1.17	1.06	1.01	1.02
E3 - primary	1.84	1.53	1.27	1.11	1.03	1.00
E4 - lower secondary	2.44	1.88	1.53	1.30	1.16	1.08
E5 - upper secondary	3.64	3.24	2.61	2.04	1.64	1.34
E6 - post-secondary	3.41	2.47	1.86	1.47	1.26	1.14
Mean years of schooling (male minus female)	2.00	2.22	2.16	1.86	1.47	1.04
Women age 20–39: highest educational attainment						
E1 - no education	0.74	0.63	0.49	0.35	0.23	0.13
E2 - incomplete primary	0.07	0.07	0.08	0.08	0.08	0.07
E3 - primary	0.10	0.11	0.14	0.17	0.18	0.18
E4 - lower secondary	0.06	0.14	0.20	0.26	0.31	0.35
E5 - upper secondary	0.02	0.03	0.05	0.08	0.13	0.18
E6 - post-secondary	0.02	0.02	0.04	0.05	0.07	0.09
Mean years of schooling (in years)	2.01	3.17	4.62	6.13	7.61	8.94

Education scenarios

GET: global education trend scenario (medium assumption also used for SSP2)

CER: constant enrolment rates scenario (assumption of no future improvements)

FT: Fast track scenario (assumption of education expansion according to fastest historical experience)

Pyramids by Education, Medium Scenario

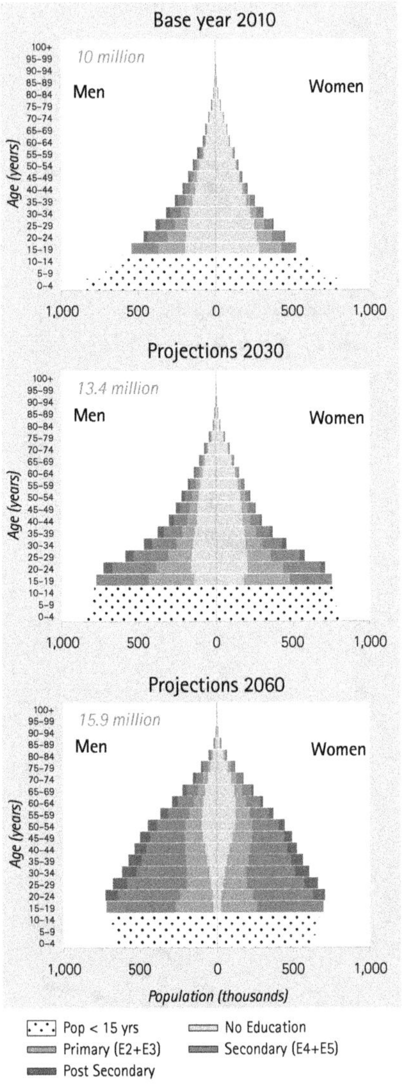

Population Size by Educational Attainment According to Three Education Scenarios: GET, CER, and FT

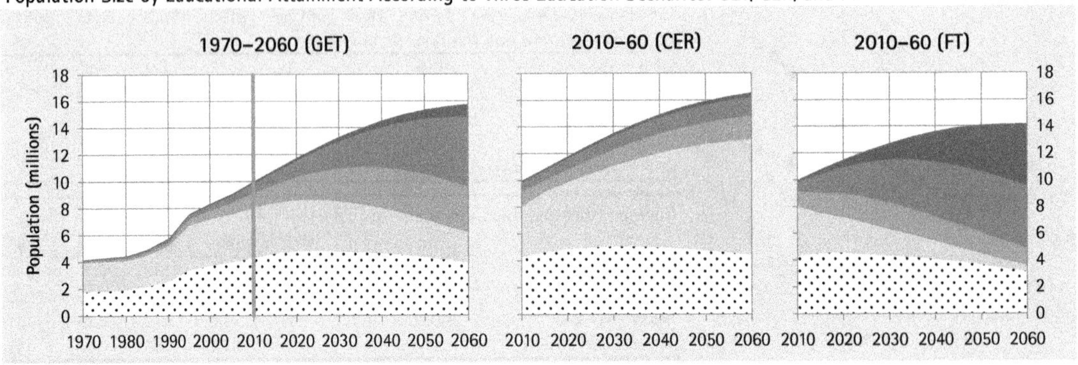

Guinea (Continued)

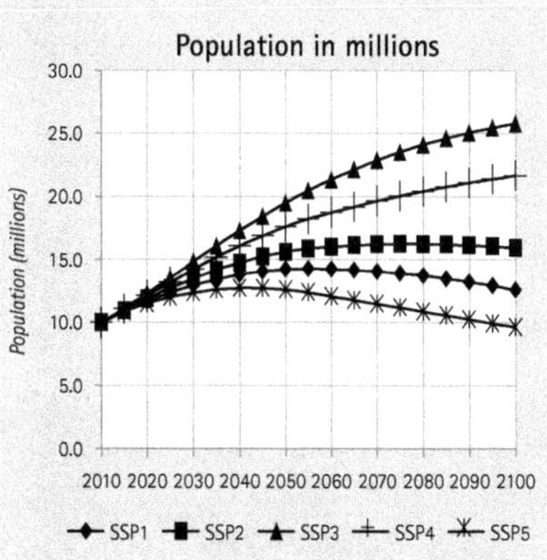

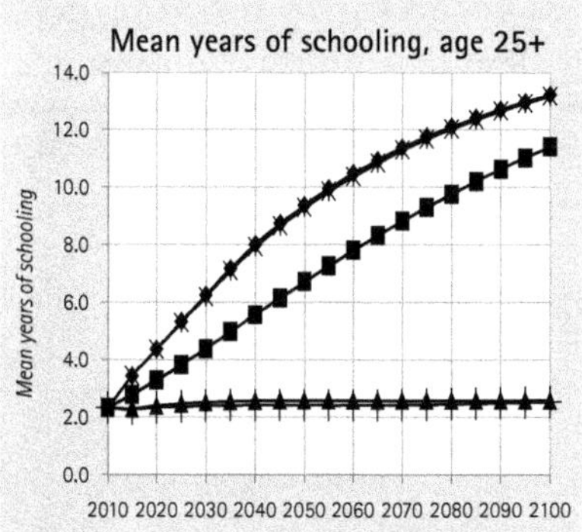

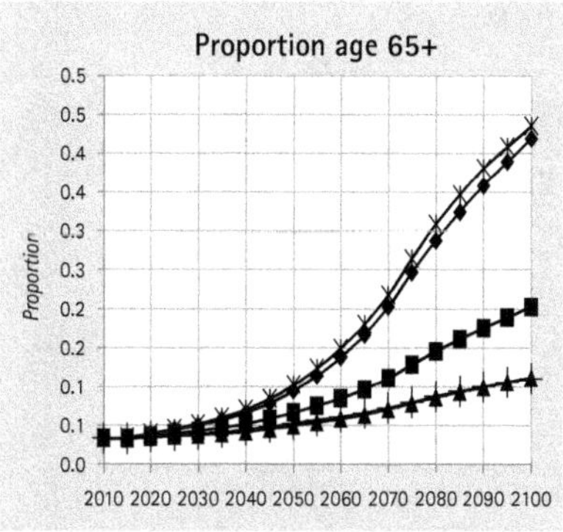

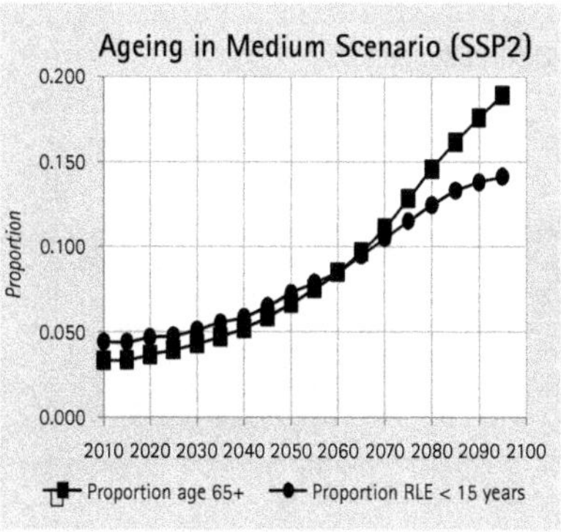

Alternative Scenarios to 2100

Projection Results by Scenario (SSP1–5)

	2010	2020	2030	2040	2050	2075	2100
Population (in millions)							
SSP1 - Rapid development	9.98	11.66	12.93	13.80	14.21	13.91	12.58
SSP2 - Medium	9.98	11.86	13.48	14.76	15.62	16.26	15.97
SSP3 - Stalled development	9.98	12.30	14.85	17.31	19.51	23.52	25.79
SSP4 - Inequality	9.98	12.13	14.23	16.09	17.62	20.05	21.67
SSP5 - Conventional development	9.98	11.49	12.34	12.71	12.59	11.17	9.62
Proportion age 65+							
SSP1 - Rapid development	0.03	0.04	0.05	0.07	0.09	0.25	0.42
SSP2 - Medium	0.03	0.04	0.04	0.05	0.07	0.13	0.20
SSP3 - Stalled development	0.03	0.03	0.04	0.04	0.05	0.08	0.11
SSP4 - Inequality	0.03	0.04	0.04	0.04	0.05	0.08	0.11
SSP5 - Conventional development	0.03	0.04	0.05	0.07	0.10	0.26	0.43
Proportion below age 20							
SSP1 - Rapid development	0.54	0.50	0.42	0.35	0.29	0.18	0.12
SSP2 - Medium	0.54	0.52	0.46	0.41	0.37	0.27	0.22
SSP3 - Stalled development	0.54	0.53	0.50	0.46	0.42	0.35	0.31
SSP4 - Inequality	0.54	0.53	0.50	0.46	0.42	0.35	0.31
SSP5 - Conventional development	0.54	0.50	0.42	0.35	0.29	0.17	0.11
Proportion of Women age 20–39 with at least secondary education							
SSP1 - Rapid development	0.10	0.36	0.51	0.63	0.71	0.85	0.93
SSP2 - Medium	0.10	0.19	0.29	0.39	0.51	0.73	0.88
SSP3 - Stalled development	0.10	0.07	0.07	0.07	0.08	0.08	0.08
SSP4 - Inequality	0.10	0.07	0.07	0.07	0.07	0.07	0.07
SSP5 - Conventional development	0.10	0.36	0.51	0.63	0.71	0.85	0.93
Mean years of schooling, age 25+							
SSP1 - Rapid development	2.31	4.35	6.25	8.00	9.37	11.75	13.21
SSP2 - Medium	2.31	3.28	4.37	5.56	6.71	9.30	11.40
SSP3 - Stalled development	2.31	2.39	2.51	2.56	2.58	2.57	2.58
SSP4 - Inequality	2.31	2.34	2.39	2.41	2.41	2.44	2.53
SSP5 - Conventional development	2.31	4.33	6.18	7.91	9.27	11.67	13.17

Demographic Assumptions Underlying SSPs

	2010–15	2020–25	2030–35	2040–45	2050–55	2075–80	2095–2100
Total fertility rate							
SSP1 - Rapid development	4.50	3.05	2.22	1.79	1.54	1.29	1.20
SSP2 - Medium	4.87	3.83	3.01	2.52	2.18	1.81	1.66
SSP3 - Stalled development	5.18	4.68	3.98	3.39	2.99	2.51	2.37
SSP4 - Inequality	5.18	4.69	3.99	3.40	2.99	2.50	2.36
SSP5 - Conventional development	4.50	3.05	2.22	1.79	1.54	1.29	1.20
Life expectancy at birth for females (in years)							
SSP1 - Rapid development	61.39	67.92	72.05	76.58	80.50	89.34	96.28
SSP2 - Medium	56.43	59.88	62.58	65.02	67.48	73.98	79.19
SSP3 - Stalled development	59.21	57.88	59.31	59.95	61.24	64.10	66.40
SSP4 - Inequality	59.21	57.87	59.30	59.93	61.22	64.09	66.39
SSP5 - Conventional development	61.39	67.92	72.05	76.58	80.50	89.34	96.28
Migration – net flow over five years (in thousands)							
SSP1 - Rapid development	−269	−296	−339	−347	−334	−124	0
SSP2 - Medium	−281	−307	−356	−378	−381	−160	0
SSP3 - Stalled development	−223	−146	−171	−186	−195	−91	0
SSP4 - Inequality	−267	−292	−342	−373	−388	−174	0
SSP5 - Conventional development	−314	−444	−509	−525	−509	−192	0

Ageing Indicators, Medium Scenario (SSP2)

	2010	2020	2030	2040	2050	2075	2095
Median age	18.24	19.24	21.69	24.69	27.83	35.90	41.20
Propspective median age	18.24	17.48	18.41	20.12	22.27	27.09	28.93
Proportion age 65+	0.03	0.04	0.04	0.05	0.07	0.13	0.19
Proportion RLE < 15 years	0.04	0.05	0.05	0.06	0.07	0.12	0.14

Guinea-Bissau

Detailed Human Capital Projections to 2060

Demographic indicators, Medium Scenario (SSP2)	2010	2020	2030	2040	2050	2060
Population (in millions)	1.52	1.82	2.08	2.31	2.49	2.60
Proportion age 65+	0.03	0.04	0.04	0.05	0.06	0.08
Proportion below age 20	0.52	0.49	0.44	0.39	0.35	0.31
	2005–10	2015–20	2025–30	2035–40	2045–50	2055–60
Total Fertility Rate	5.27	4.15	3.19	2.66	2.29	2.08
Life expectancy at birth (in years)						
Men	45.33	49.24	51.66	53.94	56.27	59.07
Women	48.22	52.38	55.07	57.82	60.38	63.52
Five-year immigration flow (in '000)	8.18	8.01	8.32	8.50	8.49	8.37
Five-year emigration flow (in '000)	18.10	16.63	19.53	21.65	22.42	22.51

Human Capital indicators, Medium Scenario (SSP2)	2010	2020	2030	2040	2050	2060
Population age 25+: highest educational attainment						
E1 - no education	0.58	0.48	0.38	0.30	0.23	0.17
E2 - incomplete primary	0.09	0.09	0.08	0.07	0.05	0.04
E3 - primary	0.13	0.14	0.16	0.17	0.17	0.16
E4 - lower secondary	0.10	0.13	0.16	0.17	0.18	0.17
E5 - upper secondary	0.08	0.13	0.20	0.27	0.34	0.41
E6 - post-secondary	0.02	0.02	0.02	0.02	0.03	0.04
Mean years of schooling (in years)	3.27	4.31	5.36	6.36	7.26	8.07
Gender gap (population age 25+): highest educational attainment (ratio male/female)						
E1 - no education	0.56	0.51	0.50	0.51	0.55	0.60
E2 - incomplete primary	1.69	1.62	1.39	1.21	1.08	0.99
E3 - primary	2.34	1.70	1.33	1.12	1.03	0.99
E4 - lower secondary	2.17	1.70	1.40	1.20	1.09	1.03
E5 - upper secondary	2.99	2.40	1.96	1.62	1.40	1.23
E6 - post-secondary	2.65	1.70	1.17	0.92	0.85	0.89
Mean years of schooling (male minus female)	2.71	2.70	2.38	1.88	1.37	0.92
Women age 20–39: highest educational attainment						
E1 - no education	0.58	0.46	0.34	0.23	0.14	0.07
E2 - incomplete primary	0.10	0.08	0.06	0.05	0.03	0.02
E3 - primary	0.12	0.15	0.17	0.18	0.17	0.14
E4 - lower secondary	0.11	0.15	0.19	0.21	0.21	0.20
E5 - upper secondary	0.08	0.14	0.22	0.31	0.42	0.52
E6 - post-secondary	0.01	0.01	0.02	0.02	0.03	0.04
Mean years of schooling (in years)	3.23	4.51	5.87	7.19	8.36	9.32

Education scenarios

GET: global education trend scenario (medium assumption also used for SSP2)

CER: constant enrolment rates scenario (assumption of no future improvements)

FT: Fast track scenario (assumption of education expansion according to fastest historical experience)

Pyramids by Education, Medium Scenario

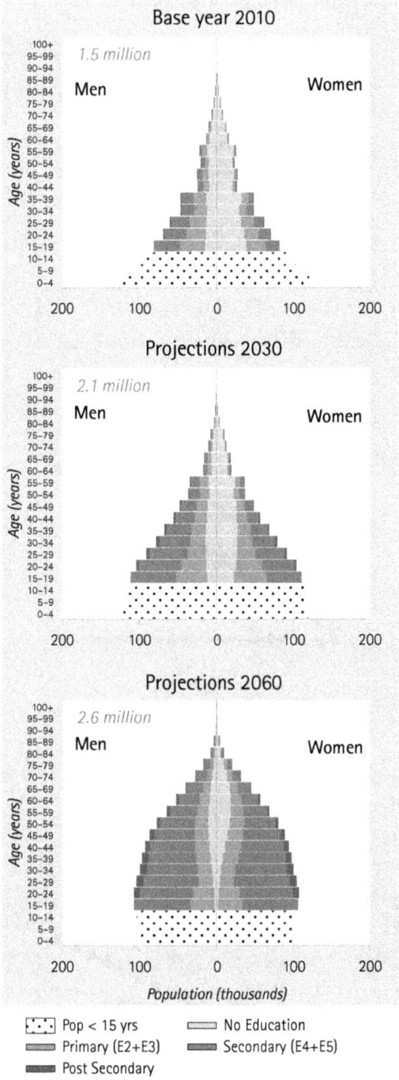

Population Size by Educational Attainment According to Three Education Scenarios: GET, CER, and FT

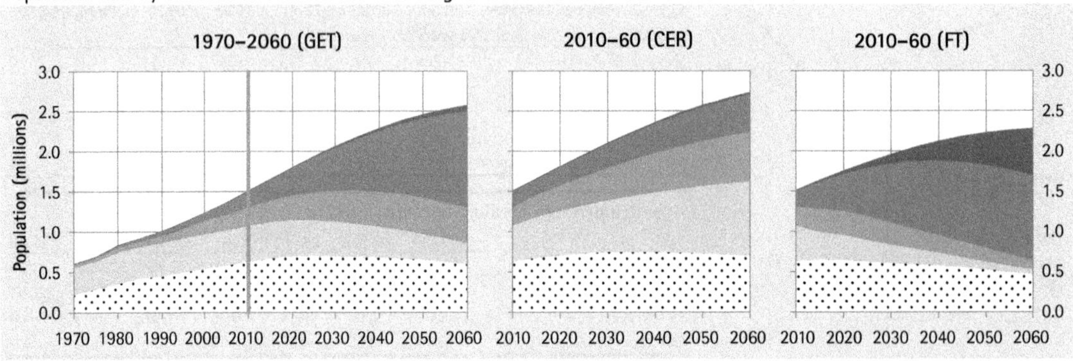

Guinea-Bissau (Continued)

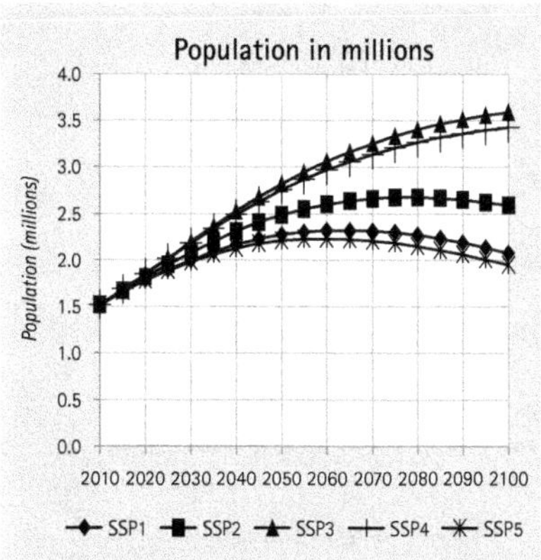

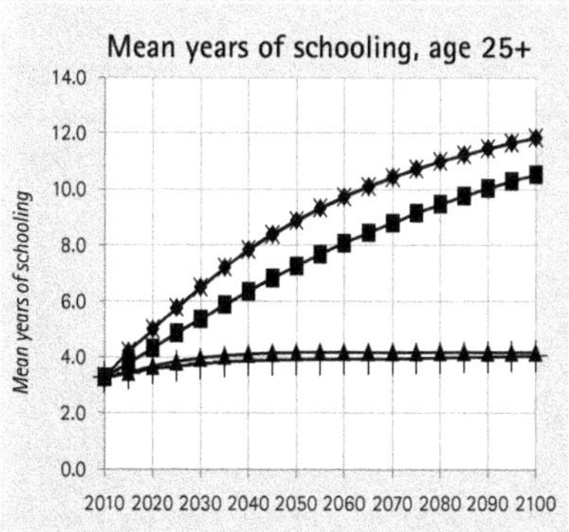

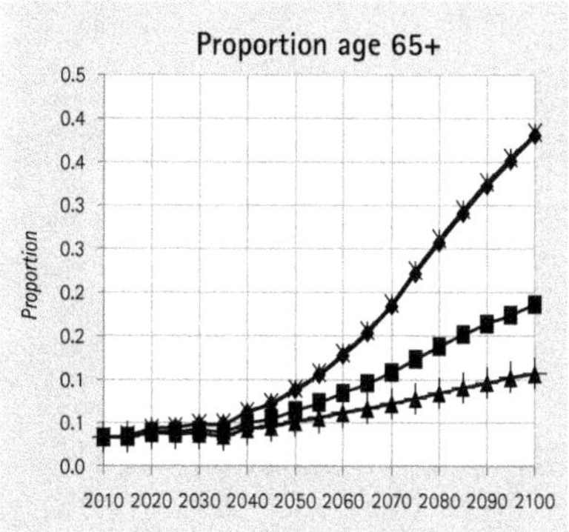

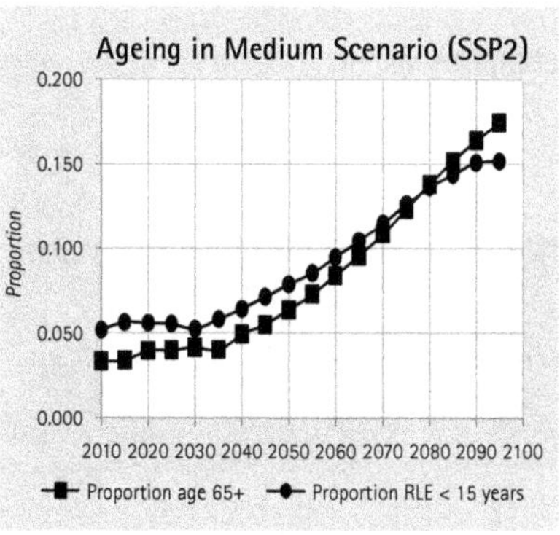

Alternative Scenarios to 2100

Projection Results by Scenario (SSP1–5)

	2010	2020	2030	2040	2050	2075	2100
Population (in millions)							
SSP1 - Rapid development	1.52	1.78	2.00	2.17	2.27	2.30	2.08
SSP2 - Medium	1.52	1.82	2.08	2.31	2.49	2.67	2.59
SSP3 - Stalled development	1.52	1.86	2.20	2.53	2.82	3.33	3.59
SSP4 - Inequality	1.52	1.85	2.18	2.49	2.75	3.21	3.42
SSP5 - Conventional development	1.52	1.78	1.98	2.13	2.21	2.18	1.95
Proportion age 65+							
SSP1 - Rapid development	0.03	0.04	0.05	0.06	0.09	0.22	0.38
SSP2 - Medium	0.03	0.04	0.04	0.05	0.06	0.12	0.19
SSP3 - Stalled development	0.03	0.04	0.04	0.04	0.05	0.08	0.11
SSP4 - Inequality	0.03	0.04	0.04	0.04	0.05	0.08	0.11
SSP5 - Conventional development	0.03	0.04	0.05	0.06	0.09	0.22	0.38
Proportion below age 20							
SSP1 - Rapid development	0.52	0.47	0.39	0.33	0.28	0.18	0.13
SSP2 - Medium	0.52	0.49	0.44	0.39	0.35	0.27	0.22
SSP3 - Stalled development	0.52	0.50	0.47	0.44	0.41	0.35	0.31
SSP4 - Inequality	0.52	0.50	0.48	0.44	0.41	0.34	0.31
SSP5 - Conventional development	0.52	0.47	0.39	0.33	0.28	0.18	0.12
Proportion of Women age 20–39 with at least secondary education							
SSP1 - Rapid development	0.20	0.45	0.62	0.74	0.82	0.93	0.98
SSP2 - Medium	0.20	0.31	0.42	0.54	0.66	0.86	0.95
SSP3 - Stalled development	0.20	0.18	0.18	0.18	0.18	0.18	0.18
SSP4 - Inequality	0.20	0.17	0.16	0.16	0.16	0.16	0.16
SSP5 - Conventional development	0.20	0.45	0.62	0.74	0.82	0.93	0.98
Mean years of schooling, age 25+							
SSP1 - Rapid development	3.27	4.97	6.50	7.83	8.88	10.72	11.83
SSP2 - Medium	3.27	4.31	5.36	6.36	7.26	9.14	10.52
SSP3 - Stalled development	3.27	3.66	3.95	4.11	4.16	4.17	4.17
SSP4 - Inequality	3.27	3.57	3.75	3.86	3.90	3.95	4.04
SSP5 - Conventional development	3.27	4.97	6.49	7.82	8.86	10.71	11.83

Demographic Assumptions Underlying SSPs

	2010–15	2020–25	2030–35	2040–45	2050–55	2075–80	2095–2100
Total fertility rate							
SSP1 - Rapid development	4.32	2.87	2.10	1.73	1.52	1.30	1.20
SSP2 - Medium	4.70	3.63	2.90	2.46	2.17	1.81	1.66
SSP3 - Stalled development	5.01	4.53	3.94	3.45	3.10	2.60	2.45
SSP4 - Inequality	5.02	4.55	3.96	3.45	3.09	2.58	2.42
SSP5 - Conventional development	4.32	2.87	2.10	1.73	1.52	1.30	1.20
Life expectancy at birth for females (in years)							
SSP1 - Rapid development	55.57	61.93	66.64	70.59	75.11	84.86	92.47
SSP2 - Medium	50.42	53.80	56.53	58.98	61.88	69.52	75.49
SSP3 - Stalled development	53.70	51.98	53.10	54.23	55.61	59.68	62.83
SSP4 - Inequality	53.70	51.96	53.07	54.20	55.58	59.65	62.82
SSP5 - Conventional development	55.57	61.93	66.64	70.59	75.11	84.86	92.47
Migration – net flow over five years (in thousands)							
SSP1 - Rapid development	−8	−10	−12	−13	−13	−5	0
SSP2 - Medium	−9	−10	−12	−14	−14	−6	0
SSP3 - Stalled development	−7	−5	−6	−6	−7	−3	0
SSP4 - Inequality	−8	−10	−12	−14	−14	−6	0
SSP5 - Conventional development	−10	−15	−19	−21	−21	−9	0

Ageing Indicators, Medium Scenario (SSP2)

	2010	2020	2030	2040	2050	2075	2095
Median age	18.99	20.51	23.01	26.01	29.09	36.09	40.49
Propspective median age	18.99	18.83	19.78	21.41	23.20	26.88	28.19
Proportion age 65+	0.03	0.04	0.04	0.05	0.06	0.12	0.17
Proportion RLE < 15 years	0.05	0.06	0.05	0.06	0.08	0.13	0.15

Guyana

Detailed Human Capital Projections to 2060

Demographic indicators, Medium Scenario (SSP2)	2010	2020	2030	2040	2050	2060
Population (in millions)	0.75	0.76	0.76	0.73	0.69	0.64
Proportion age 65+	0.04	0.06	0.10	0.15	0.19	0.22
Proportion below age 20	0.44	0.35	0.30	0.27	0.23	0.21
	2005–10	2015–20	2025–30	2035–40	2045–50	2055–60
Total Fertility Rate	2.33	2.07	1.92	1.86	1.77	1.69
Life expectancy at birth (in years)						
Men	65.53	67.18	69.09	71.35	73.41	75.49
Women	71.93	73.29	75.09	77.09	79.01	81.00
Five-year immigration flow (in '000)	3.51	3.47	3.61	3.70	3.71	3.67
Five-year emigration flow (in '000)	43.44	37.30	33.66	28.55	25.51	21.78

Human Capital indicators, Medium Scenario (SSP2)	2010	2020	2030	2040	2050	2060
Population age 25+: highest educational attainment						
E1 - no education	0.02	0.02	0.01	0.01	0.01	0.00
E2 - incomplete primary	0.05	0.03	0.02	0.01	0.01	0.00
E3 - primary	0.16	0.14	0.12	0.10	0.08	0.06
E4 - lower secondary	0.29	0.28	0.25	0.23	0.20	0.17
E5 - upper secondary	0.37	0.41	0.47	0.51	0.55	0.58
E6 - post-secondary	0.10	0.12	0.13	0.14	0.16	0.18
Mean years of schooling (in years)	9.46	9.87	10.28	10.57	10.86	11.12
Gender gap (population age 25+): highest educational attainment (ratio male/female)						
E1 - no education	1.13	1.22	1.25	1.24	1.20	1.16
E2 - incomplete primary	1.21	1.32	1.46	1.60	1.65	1.59
E3 - primary	1.36	1.52	1.60	1.64	1.64	1.57
E4 - lower secondary	1.11	1.13	1.17	1.19	1.19	1.17
E5 - upper secondary	0.82	0.82	0.85	0.88	0.91	0.94
E6 - post-secondary	0.83	0.81	0.80	0.81	0.84	0.89
Mean years of schooling (male minus female)	−0.44	−0.50	−0.49	−0.44	−0.36	−0.26
Women age 20–39: highest educational attainment						
E1 - no education	0.01	0.01	0.00	0.00	0.00	0.00
E2 - incomplete primary	0.01	0.00	0.00	0.00	0.00	0.00
E3 - primary	0.08	0.06	0.05	0.05	0.04	0.03
E4 - lower secondary	0.27	0.22	0.17	0.14	0.12	0.09
E5 - upper secondary	0.50	0.56	0.60	0.63	0.64	0.65
E6 - post-secondary	0.13	0.15	0.17	0.18	0.20	0.22
Mean years of schooling (in years)	10.44	10.81	11.15	11.33	11.48	11.62

Education scenarios

GET: global education trend scenario (medium assumption also used for SSP2)

CER: constant enrolment rates scenario (assumption of no future improvements)

FT: Fast track scenario (assumption of education expansion according to fastest historical experience)

Pyramids by Education, Medium Scenario

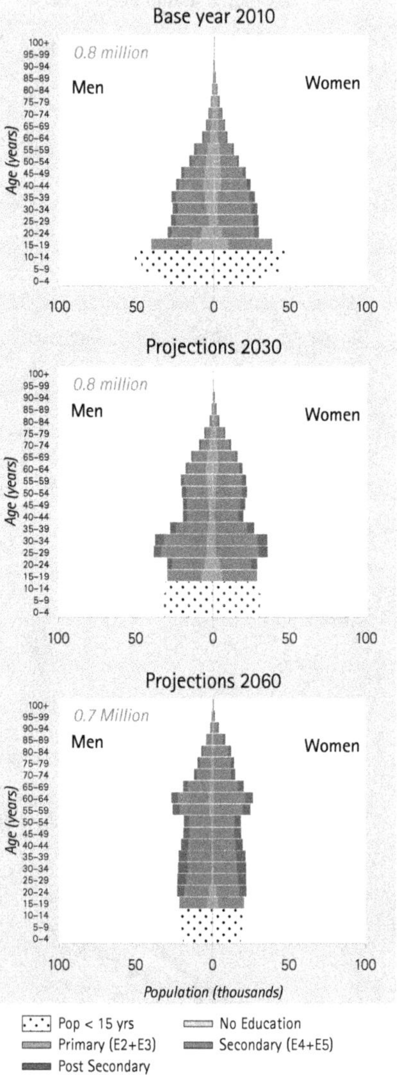

Population Size by Educational Attainment According to Three Education Scenarios: GET, CER, and FT

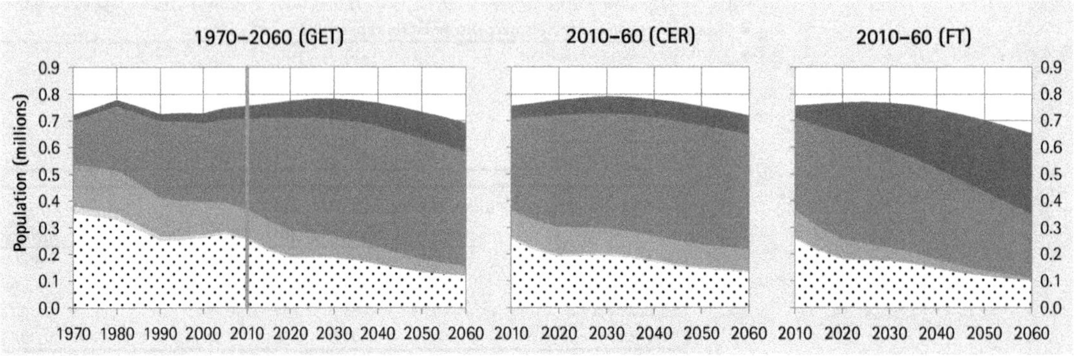

Guyana (Continued)

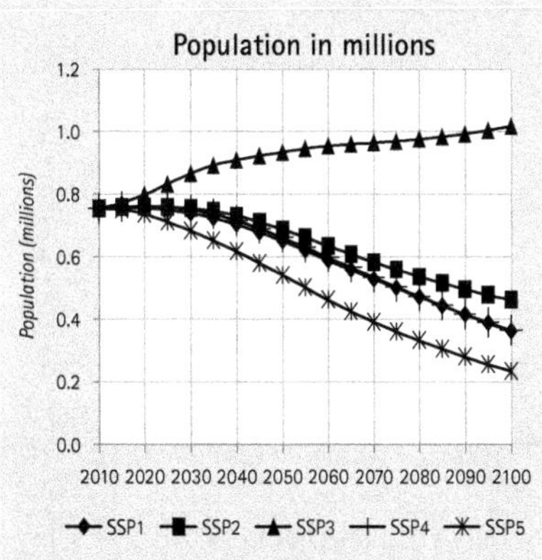

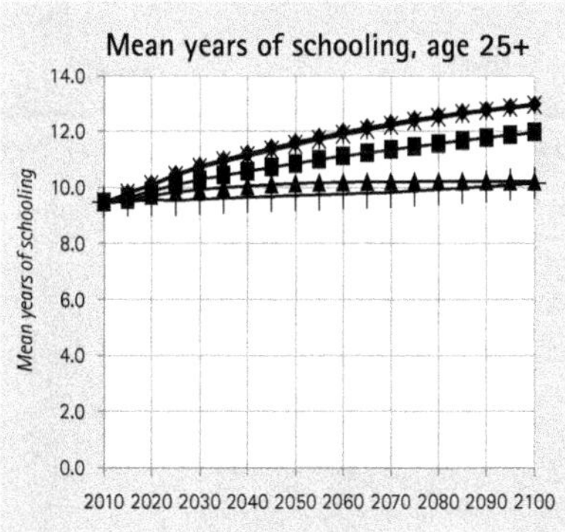

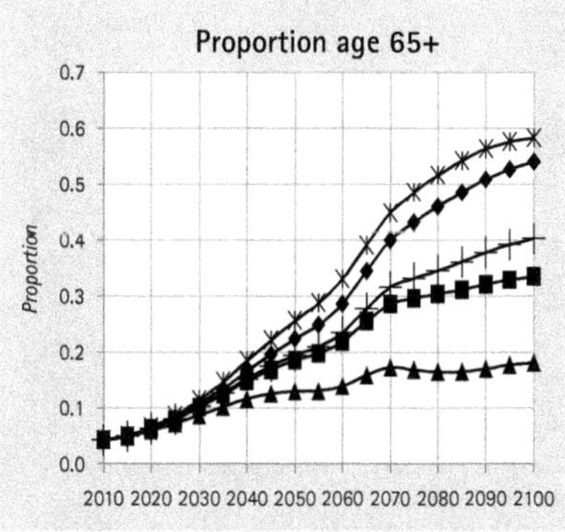

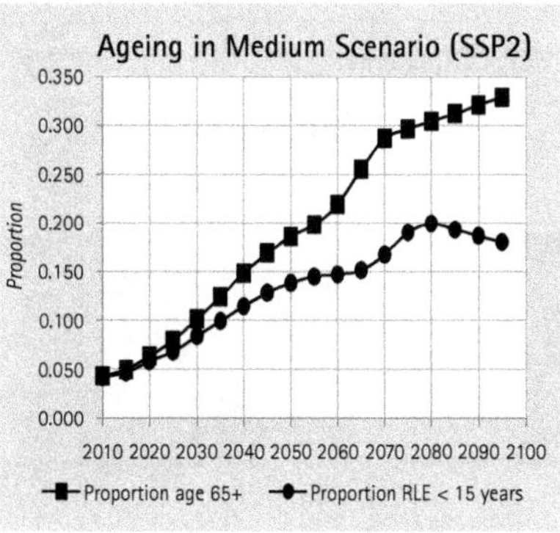

Alternative Scenarios to 2100

Projection Results by Scenario (SSP1–5)

	2010	2020	2030	2040	2050	2075	2100
Population (in millions)							
SSP1 - Rapid development	0.75	0.76	0.74	0.70	0.65	0.50	0.36
SSP2 - Medium	0.75	0.76	0.76	0.73	0.69	0.56	0.46
SSP3 - Stalled development	0.75	0.80	0.87	0.91	0.93	0.97	1.02
SSP4 - Inequality	0.75	0.76	0.75	0.72	0.66	0.50	0.36
SSP5 - Conventional development	0.75	0.74	0.68	0.62	0.54	0.36	0.23
Proportion age 65+							
SSP1 - Rapid development	0.04	0.06	0.11	0.17	0.22	0.43	0.54
SSP2 - Medium	0.04	0.06	0.10	0.15	0.19	0.30	0.34
SSP3 - Stalled development	0.04	0.06	0.09	0.12	0.13	0.17	0.18
SSP4 - Inequality	0.04	0.06	0.10	0.15	0.19	0.33	0.40
SSP5 - Conventional development	0.04	0.07	0.11	0.18	0.26	0.48	0.58
Proportion below age 20							
SSP1 - Rapid development	0.44	0.34	0.27	0.22	0.18	0.11	0.09
SSP2 - Medium	0.44	0.35	0.30	0.27	0.23	0.18	0.17
SSP3 - Stalled development	0.44	0.36	0.34	0.33	0.30	0.28	0.27
SSP4 - Inequality	0.44	0.35	0.29	0.24	0.20	0.14	0.12
SSP5 - Conventional development	0.44	0.34	0.27	0.22	0.17	0.10	0.08
Proportion of Women age 20–39 with at least secondary education							
SSP1 - Rapid development	0.90	0.96	0.97	0.98	0.98	0.99	1.00
SSP2 - Medium	0.90	0.93	0.94	0.95	0.96	0.98	0.99
SSP3 - Stalled development	0.90	0.88	0.88	0.88	0.88	0.88	0.88
SSP4 - Inequality	0.90	0.83	0.79	0.79	0.79	0.79	0.80
SSP5 - Conventional development	0.90	0.96	0.97	0.98	0.98	0.99	1.00
Mean years of schooling, age 25+							
SSP1 - Rapid development	9.46	10.11	10.75	11.20	11.61	12.43	12.98
SSP2 - Medium	9.46	9.87	10.28	10.57	10.86	11.46	11.97
SSP3 - Stalled development	9.46	9.70	9.92	10.06	10.14	10.21	10.21
SSP4 - Inequality	9.46	9.55	9.58	9.65	9.71	9.87	10.15
SSP5 - Conventional development	9.46	10.09	10.69	11.12	11.51	12.35	12.94

Demographic Assumptions Underlying SSPs

	2010–15	2020–25	2030–35	2040–45	2050–55	2075–80	2095–2100
Total fertility rate							
SSP1 - Rapid development	2.01	1.62	1.42	1.32	1.25	1.17	1.19
SSP2 - Medium	2.15	1.99	1.89	1.81	1.72	1.60	1.63
SSP3 - Stalled development	2.31	2.43	2.44	2.38	2.30	2.19	2.26
SSP4 - Inequality	2.10	1.82	1.59	1.44	1.35	1.27	1.29
SSP5 - Conventional development	2.01	1.62	1.42	1.32	1.25	1.17	1.19
Life expectancy at birth for females (in years)							
SSP1 - Rapid development	75.08	77.51	80.05	82.78	85.51	92.62	98.44
SSP2 - Medium	72.48	74.20	76.09	78.01	80.01	84.99	89.00
SSP3 - Stalled development	74.41	74.84	75.61	76.39	77.18	79.23	80.94
SSP4 - Inequality	74.74	76.25	77.90	79.51	81.17	85.48	89.13
SSP5 - Conventional development	75.08	77.51	80.05	82.78	85.51	92.62	98.44
Migration – net flow over five years (in thousands)							
SSP1 - Rapid development	−35	−33	−26	−21	−17	−4	0
SSP2 - Medium	−37	−35	−28	−24	−20	−6	0
SSP3 - Stalled development	−29	−17	−14	−13	−12	−5	0
SSP4 - Inequality	−35	−33	−26	−21	−17	−4	0
SSP5 - Conventional development	−41	−49	−38	−30	−23	−5	0

Ageing Indicators, Medium Scenario (SSP2)

	2010	2020	2030	2040	2050	2075	2095
Median age	23.75	27.51	32.53	37.95	42.19	48.85	51.05
Propspective median age	23.75	26.48	30.02	34.20	37.01	39.82	38.44
Proportion age 65+	0.04	0.06	0.10	0.15	0.19	0.30	0.33
Proportion RLE < 15 years	0.04	0.06	0.08	0.11	0.14	0.19	0.18

Haiti

Detailed Human Capital Projections to 2060

Demographic indicators, Medium Scenario (SSP2)

	2010	2020	2030	2040	2050	2060
Population (in millions)	9.99	11.19	12.17	12.88	13.29	13.37
Proportion age 65+	0.04	0.05	0.06	0.07	0.11	0.15
Proportion below age 20	0.47	0.42	0.37	0.32	0.29	0.26
	2005–10	2015–20	2025–30	2035–40	2045–50	2055–60
Total Fertility Rate	3.55	2.73	2.31	2.07	1.90	1.79
Life expectancy at birth (in years)						
Men	59.94	62.28	64.97	67.66	69.77	71.86
Women	62.02	65.38	68.38	71.28	73.48	75.59
Five-year immigration flow (in '000)	1.67	1.63	1.69	1.73	1.73	1.71
Five-year emigration flow (in '000)	240.86	209.15	220.48	220.74	212.86	200.40

Human Capital indicators, Medium Scenario (SSP2)

	2010	2020	2030	2040	2050	2060
Population age 25+: highest educational attainment						
E1 - no education	0.33	0.21	0.13	0.08	0.05	0.03
E2 - incomplete primary	0.26	0.24	0.19	0.15	0.11	0.08
E3 - primary	0.13	0.15	0.16	0.16	0.15	0.13
E4 - lower secondary	0.14	0.18	0.20	0.20	0.19	0.17
E5 - upper secondary	0.09	0.16	0.23	0.31	0.39	0.46
E6 - post-secondary	0.04	0.06	0.08	0.10	0.12	0.15
Mean years of schooling (in years)	4.77	6.44	7.91	9.17	10.25	11.16
Gender gap (population age 25+): highest educational attainment (ratio male/female)						
E1 - no education	0.67	0.64	0.61	0.59	0.60	0.64
E2 - incomplete primary	1.10	1.00	0.93	0.86	0.81	0.76
E3 - primary	1.06	0.97	0.92	0.90	0.89	0.88
E4 - lower secondary	1.27	1.16	1.10	1.05	1.01	0.97
E5 - upper secondary	1.60	1.32	1.19	1.11	1.07	1.05
E6 - post-secondary	1.70	1.66	1.56	1.44	1.33	1.23
Mean years of schooling (male minus female)	1.32	1.27	1.14	0.97	0.78	0.61
Women age 20–39: highest educational attainment						
E1 - no education	0.13	0.07	0.04	0.02	0.01	0.00
E2 - incomplete primary	0.28	0.20	0.11	0.06	0.03	0.01
E3 - primary	0.20	0.20	0.19	0.15	0.11	0.07
E4 - lower secondary	0.23	0.26	0.27	0.25	0.23	0.20
E5 - upper secondary	0.13	0.22	0.32	0.42	0.50	0.56
E6 - post-secondary	0.04	0.05	0.07	0.10	0.13	0.16
Mean years of schooling (in years)	6.60	8.18	9.59	10.77	11.70	12.39

Education scenarios

GET: global education trend scenario (medium assumption also used for SSP2)

CER: constant enrolment rates scenario (assumption of no future improvements)

FT: Fast track scenario (assumption of education expansion according to fastest historical experience)

Pyramids by Education, Medium Scenario

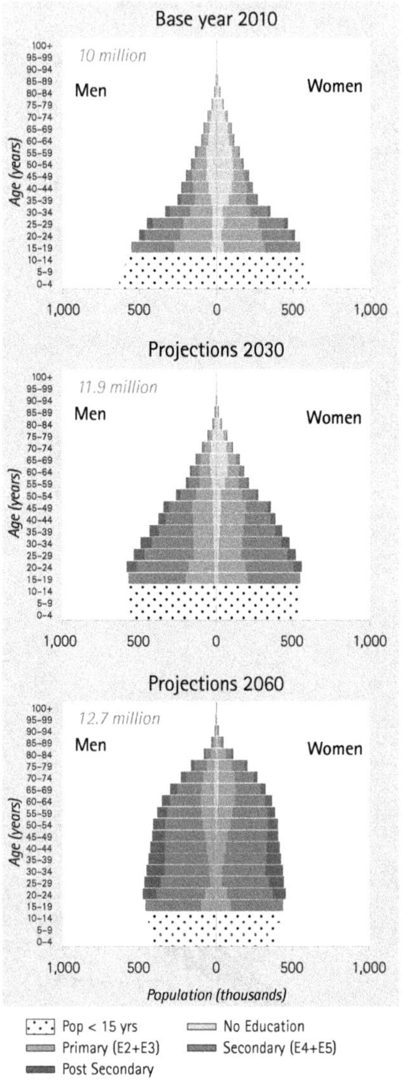

Population Size by Educational Attainment According to Three Education Scenarios: GET, CER, and FT

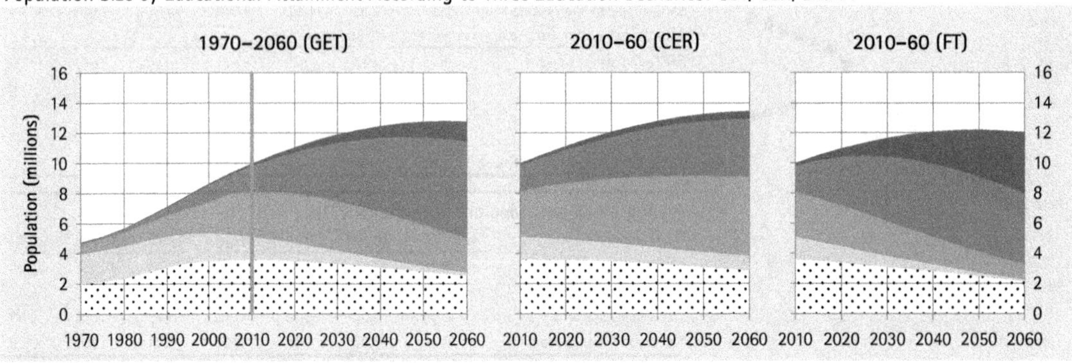

Haiti (Continued)

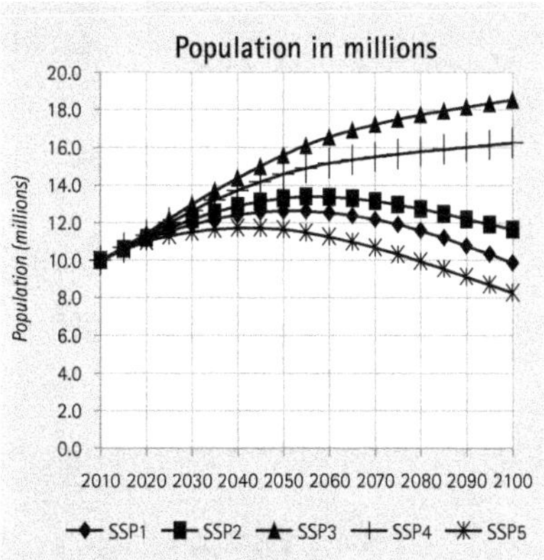

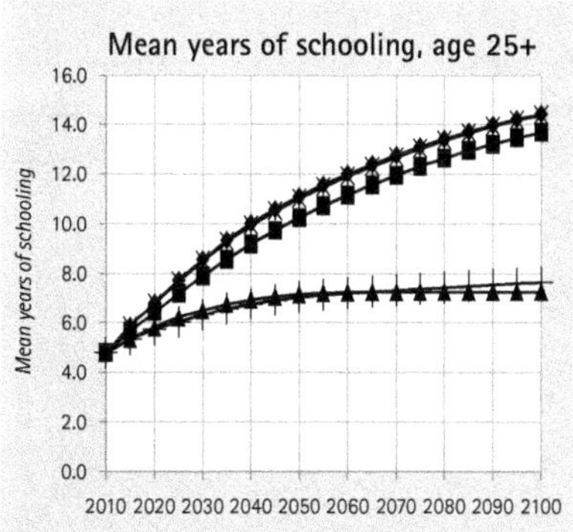

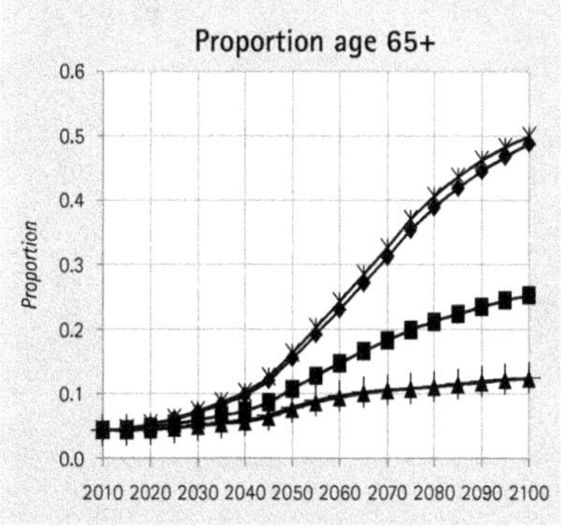

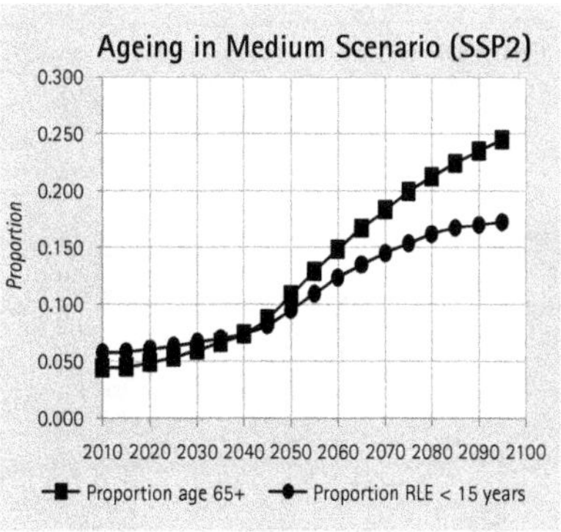

Alternative Scenarios to 2100

Projection Results by Scenario (SSP1–5)

	2010	2020	2030	2040	2050	2075	2100
Population (in millions)							
SSP1 - Rapid development	9.99	11.10	11.89	12.40	12.63	11.91	9.88
SSP2 - Medium	9.99	11.19	12.17	12.88	13.29	12.96	11.66
SSP3 - Stalled development	9.99	11.44	12.98	14.37	15.59	17.49	18.53
SSP4 - Inequality	9.99	11.34	12.63	13.71	14.57	15.65	16.25
SSP5 - Conventional development	9.99	10.98	11.50	11.72	11.64	10.33	8.26
Proportion age 65+							
SSP1 - Rapid development	0.04	0.05	0.07	0.10	0.16	0.35	0.49
SSP2 - Medium	0.04	0.05	0.06	0.07	0.11	0.20	0.25
SSP3 - Stalled development	0.04	0.05	0.05	0.06	0.08	0.11	0.12
SSP4 - Inequality	0.04	0.05	0.05	0.06	0.08	0.11	0.13
SSP5 - Conventional development	0.04	0.05	0.07	0.10	0.16	0.37	0.50
Proportion below age 20							
SSP1 - Rapid development	0.47	0.40	0.33	0.27	0.22	0.14	0.10
SSP2 - Medium	0.47	0.42	0.37	0.32	0.29	0.23	0.19
SSP3 - Stalled development	0.47	0.43	0.40	0.38	0.35	0.31	0.30
SSP4 - Inequality	0.47	0.43	0.41	0.38	0.35	0.31	0.29
SSP5 - Conventional development	0.47	0.40	0.33	0.27	0.22	0.13	0.10
Proportion of Women age 20–39 with at least secondary education							
SSP1 - Rapid development	0.40	0.62	0.77	0.87	0.92	0.98	1.00
SSP2 - Medium	0.40	0.53	0.66	0.77	0.85	0.96	0.99
SSP3 - Stalled development	0.40	0.38	0.38	0.38	0.38	0.38	0.38
SSP4 - Inequality	0.40	0.36	0.35	0.35	0.35	0.35	0.35
SSP5 - Conventional development	0.40	0.62	0.77	0.87	0.92	0.98	1.00
Mean years of schooling, age 25+							
SSP1 - Rapid development	4.77	6.82	8.57	10.00	11.10	13.10	14.43
SSP2 - Medium	4.77	6.44	7.91	9.17	10.25	12.31	13.69
SSP3 - Stalled development	4.77	5.81	6.51	6.93	7.16	7.26	7.27
SSP4 - Inequality	4.77	5.72	6.32	6.76	7.04	7.38	7.65
SSP5 - Conventional development	4.77	6.79	8.51	9.93	11.02	13.03	14.39

Demographic Assumptions Underlying SSPs

	2010–15	2020–25	2030–35	2040–45	2050–55	2075–80	2095–2100
Total fertility rate							
SSP1 - Rapid development	2.84	2.05	1.64	1.44	1.33	1.18	1.15
SSP2 - Medium	3.04	2.50	2.16	1.98	1.86	1.64	1.59
SSP3 - Stalled development	3.24	3.05	2.87	2.70	2.58	2.37	2.34
SSP4 - Inequality	3.25	3.10	2.90	2.69	2.54	2.31	2.27
SSP5 - Conventional development	2.84	2.05	1.64	1.44	1.33	1.18	1.15
Life expectancy at birth for females (in years)							
SSP1 - Rapid development	68.56	74.27	78.76	83.10	86.60	93.53	98.53
SSP2 - Medium	63.88	66.88	69.88	72.38	74.59	79.00	82.00
SSP3 - Stalled development	65.43	64.53	66.19	67.20	68.12	68.98	69.53
SSP4 - Inequality	65.43	64.50	66.14	67.14	68.06	68.94	69.53
SSP5 - Conventional development	68.56	74.27	78.76	83.10	86.60	93.53	98.53
Migration – net flow over five years (in thousands)							
SSP1 - Rapid development	−212	−213	−216	−205	−186	−64	0
SSP2 - Medium	−215	−217	−223	−219	−208	−82	0
SSP3 - Stalled development	−175	−105	−108	−109	−107	−47	0
SSP4 - Inequality	−210	−210	−219	−224	−221	−95	0
SSP5 - Conventional development	−247	−321	−329	−317	−293	−107	0

Ageing Indicators, Medium Scenario (SSP2)

	2010	2020	2030	2040	2050	2075	2095
Median age	21.47	24.26	27.45	30.98	34.45	41.69	45.36
Propspective median age	21.47	22.51	23.83	25.77	27.78	32.21	33.77
Proportion age 65+	0.04	0.05	0.06	0.07	0.11	0.20	0.24
Proportion RLE < 15 years	0.06	0.06	0.07	0.07	0.09	0.15	0.17

Honduras

Detailed Human Capital Projections to 2060

Demographic indicators, Medium Scenario (SSP2)

	2010	2020	2030	2040	2050	2060
Population (in millions)	7.60	8.99	10.24	11.30	12.10	12.65
Proportion age 65+	0.04	0.05	0.07	0.09	0.13	0.18
Proportion below age 20	0.48	0.42	0.36	0.32	0.28	0.25
	2005–10	2015–20	2025–30	2035–40	2045–50	2055–60
Total Fertility Rate	3.31	2.62	2.26	2.08	1.91	1.85
Life expectancy at birth (in years)						
Men	69.74	72.27	74.37	76.38	78.47	80.65
Women	74.50	76.98	79.29	81.41	83.39	85.49
Five-year immigration flow (in '000)	1.27	1.25	1.30	1.33	1.33	1.31
Five-year emigration flow (in '000)	100.77	91.85	100.62	104.26	103.59	100.50

Human Capital indicators, Medium Scenario (SSP2)

	2010	2020	2030	2040	2050	2060
Population age 25+: highest educational attainment						
E1 - no education	0.20	0.14	0.10	0.07	0.05	0.03
E2 - incomplete primary	0.26	0.20	0.16	0.12	0.09	0.06
E3 - primary	0.30	0.35	0.38	0.38	0.38	0.36
E4 - lower secondary	0.07	0.09	0.09	0.10	0.10	0.09
E5 - upper secondary	0.11	0.14	0.18	0.21	0.25	0.29
E6 - post-secondary	0.06	0.08	0.10	0.12	0.14	0.16
Mean years of schooling (in years)	5.71	6.62	7.37	8.03	8.62	9.17
Gender gap (population age 25+): highest educational attainment (ratio male/female)						
E1 - no education	0.99	1.01	1.03	1.04	1.04	1.03
E2 - incomplete primary	1.03	1.05	1.04	1.02	1.00	0.98
E3 - primary	1.08	1.07	1.09	1.09	1.08	1.06
E4 - lower secondary	0.99	0.99	1.00	1.02	1.02	1.01
E5 - upper secondary	0.75	0.78	0.82	0.86	0.91	0.94
E6 - post-secondary	1.10	1.01	0.96	0.94	0.95	0.97
Mean years of schooling (male minus female)	−0.11	−0.21	−0.23	−0.23	−0.19	−0.12
Women age 20–39: highest educational attainment						
E1 - no education	0.10	0.06	0.04	0.02	0.01	0.00
E2 - incomplete primary	0.20	0.13	0.08	0.05	0.04	0.02
E3 - primary	0.37	0.40	0.39	0.36	0.32	0.27
E4 - lower secondary	0.10	0.12	0.13	0.13	0.13	0.13
E5 - upper secondary	0.16	0.20	0.24	0.28	0.32	0.36
E6 - post-secondary	0.07	0.10	0.12	0.15	0.18	0.21
Mean years of schooling (in years)	7.04	7.90	8.57	9.22	9.76	10.23

Education scenarios

GET : global education trend scenario (medium assumption also used for SSP2)

CER: constant enrolment rates scenario (assumption of no future improvements)

FT: Fast track scenario (assumption of education expansion according to fastest historical experience)

Pyramids by Education, Medium Scenario

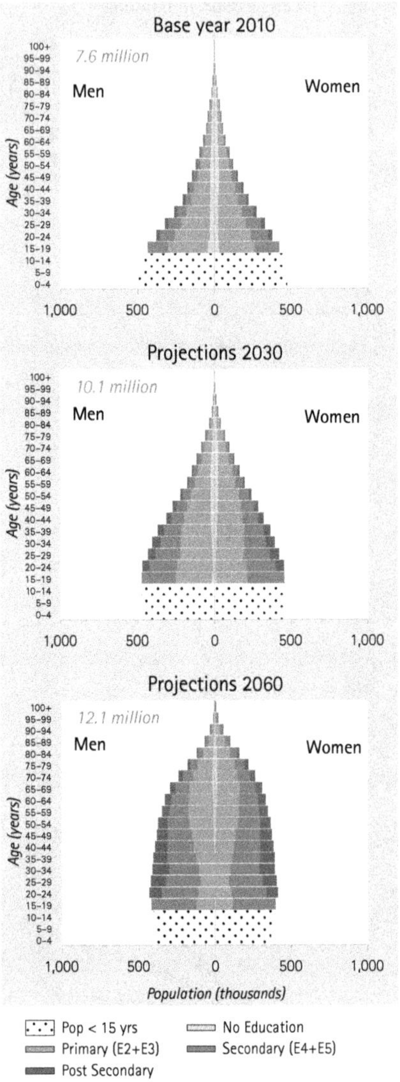

Population Size by Educational Attainment According to Three Education Scenarios: GET, CER, and FT

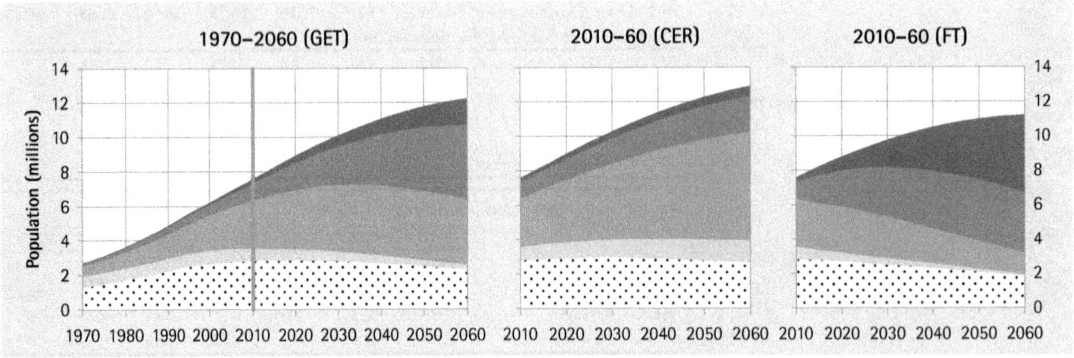

Honduras (Continued)

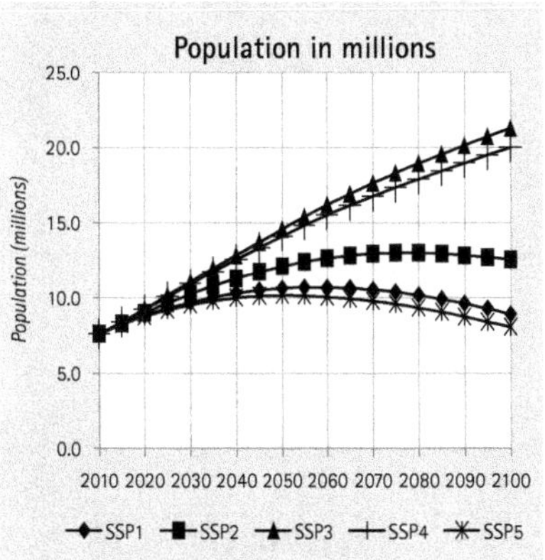

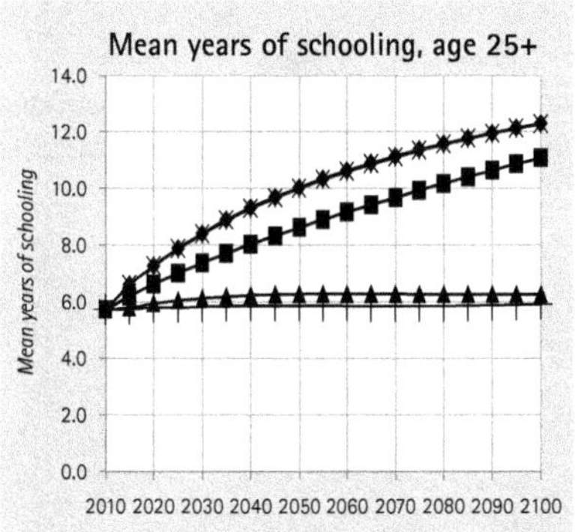

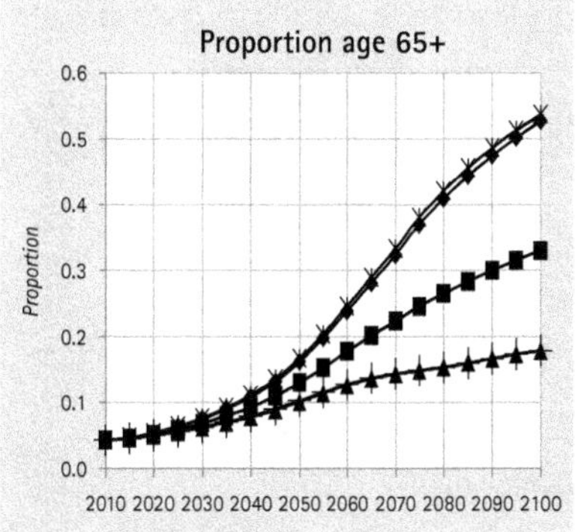

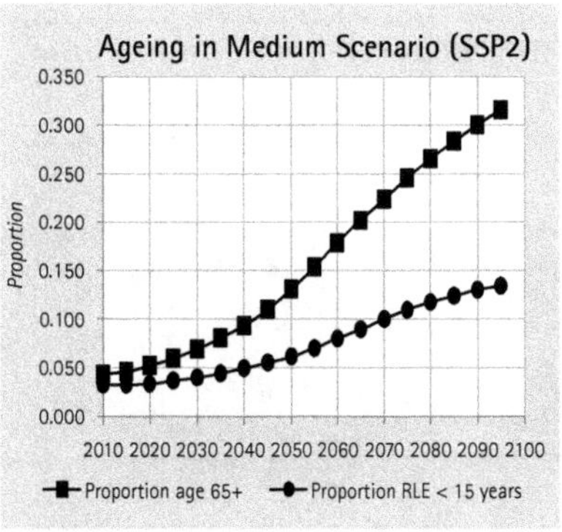

Alternative Scenarios to 2100

Projection Results by Scenario (SSP1–5)

	2010	2020	2030	2040	2050	2075	2100
Population (in millions)							
SSP1 - Rapid development	7.60	8.80	9.69	10.31	10.63	10.38	8.91
SSP2 - Medium	7.60	8.99	10.24	11.30	12.10	13.00	12.56
SSP3 - Stalled development	7.60	9.25	11.08	12.85	14.58	18.30	21.29
SSP4 - Inequality	7.60	9.22	10.93	12.56	14.11	17.34	20.01
SSP5 - Conventional development	7.60	8.75	9.51	9.98	10.15	9.57	8.04
Proportion age 65+							
SSP1 - Rapid development	0.04	0.05	0.08	0.11	0.16	0.37	0.53
SSP2 - Medium	0.04	0.05	0.07	0.09	0.13	0.25	0.33
SSP3 - Stalled development	0.04	0.05	0.06	0.08	0.10	0.15	0.18
SSP4 - Inequality	0.04	0.05	0.06	0.08	0.10	0.15	0.18
SSP5 - Conventional development	0.04	0.05	0.08	0.11	0.17	0.38	0.54
Proportion below age 20							
SSP1 - Rapid development	0.48	0.40	0.32	0.26	0.21	0.13	0.09
SSP2 - Medium	0.48	0.42	0.36	0.32	0.28	0.21	0.17
SSP3 - Stalled development	0.48	0.43	0.40	0.37	0.35	0.30	0.28
SSP4 - Inequality	0.48	0.43	0.41	0.38	0.35	0.30	0.28
SSP5 - Conventional development	0.48	0.40	0.32	0.26	0.21	0.13	0.09
Proportion of Women age 20–39 with at least secondary education							
SSP1 - Rapid development	0.34	0.57	0.68	0.75	0.80	0.89	0.95
SSP2 - Medium	0.34	0.41	0.49	0.56	0.64	0.80	0.92
SSP3 - Stalled development	0.34	0.28	0.28	0.28	0.28	0.28	0.28
SSP4 - Inequality	0.34	0.26	0.25	0.25	0.25	0.25	0.25
SSP5 - Conventional development	0.34	0.57	0.68	0.75	0.80	0.89	0.95
Mean years of schooling, age 25+							
SSP1 - Rapid development	5.71	7.27	8.40	9.31	10.02	11.36	12.29
SSP2 - Medium	5.71	6.62	7.37	8.03	8.62	9.93	11.08
SSP3 - Stalled development	5.71	5.94	6.13	6.23	6.28	6.27	6.27
SSP4 - Inequality	5.71	5.79	5.83	5.86	5.86	5.84	5.92
SSP5 - Conventional development	5.71	7.27	8.38	9.29	9.99	11.33	12.27

Demographic Assumptions Underlying SSPs

	2010–15	2020–25	2030–35	2040–45	2050–55	2075–80	2095–2100
Total fertility rate							
SSP1 - Rapid development	2.66	1.95	1.60	1.43	1.33	1.21	1.16
SSP2 - Medium	2.89	2.43	2.16	1.98	1.88	1.69	1.60
SSP3 - Stalled development	3.08	2.99	2.82	2.65	2.54	2.34	2.27
SSP4 - Inequality	3.09	3.04	2.86	2.67	2.55	2.33	2.26
SSP5 - Conventional development	2.66	1.95	1.60	1.43	1.33	1.21	1.16
Life expectancy at birth for females (in years)							
SSP1 - Rapid development	77.76	80.46	83.40	86.35	89.41	97.09	103.15
SSP2 - Medium	75.78	78.18	80.39	82.40	84.49	89.51	93.51
SSP3 - Stalled development	76.96	77.80	78.76	79.67	80.39	82.20	83.69
SSP4 - Inequality	76.96	77.78	78.73	79.62	80.33	82.10	83.60
SSP5 - Conventional development	77.76	80.46	83.40	86.35	89.41	97.09	103.15
Migration – net flow over five years (in thousands)							
SSP1 - Rapid development	−90	−94	−98	−94	−86	−30	0
SSP2 - Medium	−90	−96	−102	−104	−102	−43	0
SSP3 - Stalled development	−75	−47	−51	−53	−55	−27	0
SSP4 - Inequality	−90	−96	−104	−112	−116	−57	0
SSP5 - Conventional development	−105	−143	−152	−149	−141	−54	0

Ageing Indicators, Medium Scenario (SSP2)

	2010	2020	2030	2040	2050	2075	2095
Median age	20.91	24.27	27.89	31.69	35.58	44.28	49.66
Propspective median age	20.91	22.57	24.58	26.81	29.02	33.61	35.52
Proportion age 65+	0.04	0.05	0.07	0.09	0.13	0.25	0.32
Proportion RLE < 15 years	0.03	0.03	0.04	0.05	0.06	0.11	0.13

Hungary

Detailed Human Capital Projections to 2060

Demographic indicators, Medium Scenario (SSP2)	2010	2020	2030	2040	2050	2060
Population (in millions)	9.98	9.72	9.48	9.20	8.90	8.59
Proportion age 65+	0.17	0.20	0.21	0.25	0.29	0.32
Proportion below age 20	0.21	0.19	0.18	0.18	0.17	0.17
	2005–10	2015–20	2025–30	2035–40	2045–50	2055–60
Total Fertility Rate	1.34	1.30	1.42	1.49	1.54	1.56
Life expectancy at birth (in years)						
Men	69.54	72.40	74.76	76.87	78.93	80.94
Women	77.64	79.79	81.79	83.79	85.81	87.81
Five-year immigration flow (in '000)	83.97	83.11	86.52	88.77	89.11	87.98
Five-year emigration flow (in '000)	9.21	5.97	5.19	4.61	4.23	3.94

Human Capital indicators, Medium Scenario (SSP2)	2010	2020	2030	2040	2050	2060
Population age 25+: highest educational attainment						
E1 - no education	0.01	0.00	0.00	0.00	0.00	0.00
E2 - incomplete primary	0.00	0.00	0.00	0.00	0.00	0.00
E3 - primary	0.05	0.02	0.01	0.01	0.01	0.00
E4 - lower secondary	0.27	0.21	0.15	0.11	0.07	0.05
E5 - upper secondary	0.52	0.60	0.65	0.68	0.69	0.69
E6 - post-secondary	0.15	0.16	0.18	0.20	0.23	0.26
Mean years of schooling (in years)	11.13	11.71	12.10	12.38	12.62	12.83
Gender gap (population age 25+): highest educational attainment (ratio male/female)						
E1 - no education	0.78	0.78	0.79	0.80	0.83	0.88
E2 - incomplete primary	0.70	0.65	0.63	0.63	0.69	0.85
E3 - primary	0.45	0.48	0.59	0.66	0.67	0.66
E4 - lower secondary	0.78	0.73	0.72	0.75	0.78	0.79
E5 - upper secondary	1.25	1.21	1.18	1.15	1.13	1.10
E6 - post-secondary	0.95	0.82	0.75	0.74	0.76	0.82
Mean years of schooling (male minus female)	0.56	0.23	0.00	−0.14	−0.20	−0.19
Women age 20–39: highest educational attainment						
E1 – no education	0.00	0.00	0.00	0.00	0.00	0.00
E2 – incomplete primary	0.00	0.00	0.00	0.00	0.00	0.00
E3 – primary	0.01	0.01	0.00	0.00	0.00	0.00
E4 – lower secondary	0.13	0.08	0.05	0.04	0.03	0.03
E5 – upper secondary	0.68	0.71	0.71	0.70	0.69	0.68
E6 – post-secondary	0.18	0.21	0.24	0.26	0.28	0.29
Mean years of schooling (in years)	12.25	12.59	12.69	12.86	12.96	13.02

Education scenarios

GET: global education trend scenario (medium assumption also used for SSP2)

CER: constant enrolment rates scenario (assumption of no future improvements)

FT: Fast track scenario (assumption of education expansion according to fastest historical experience)

Pyramids by Education, Medium Scenario

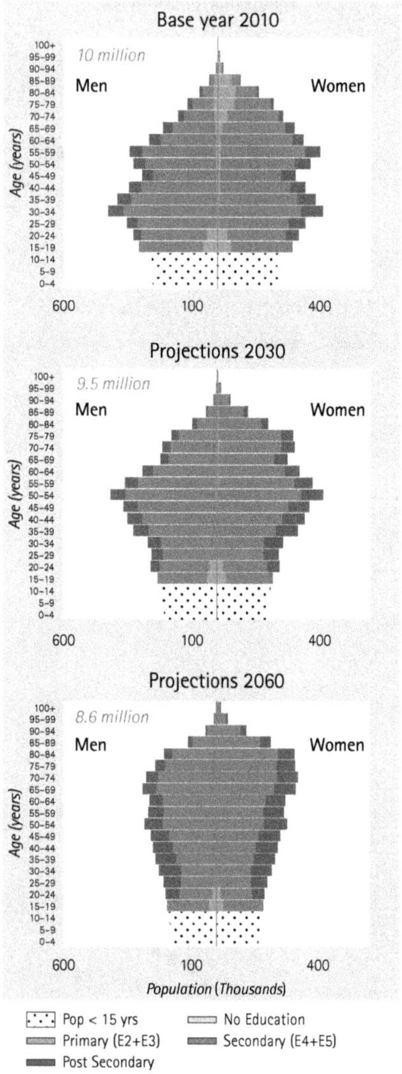

Population Size by Educational Attainment According to Three Education Scenarios: GET, CER, and FT

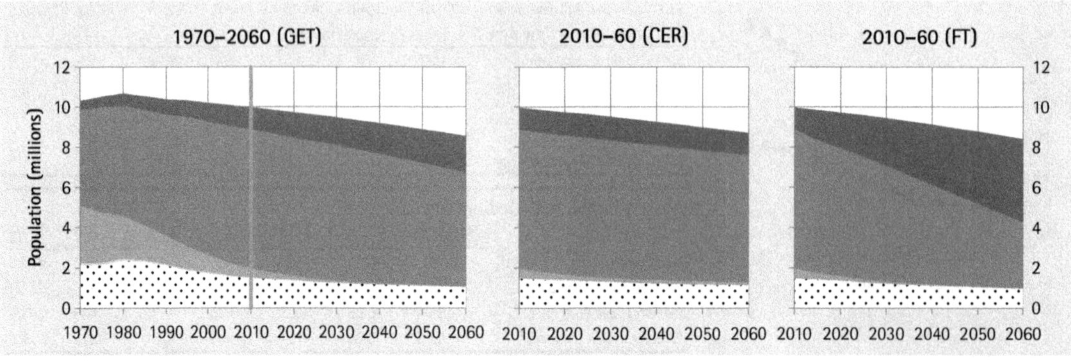

Hungary (Continued)

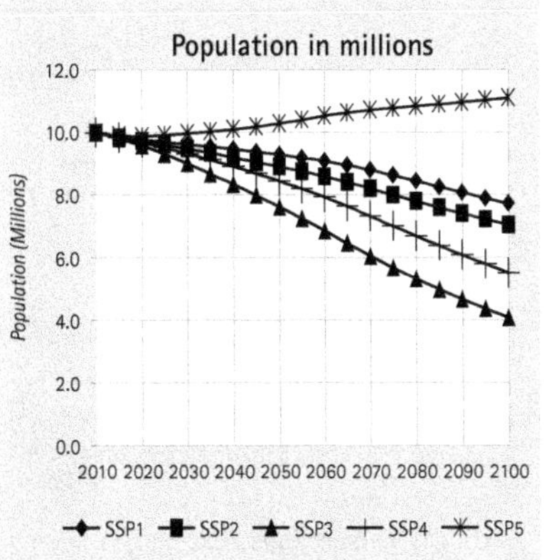

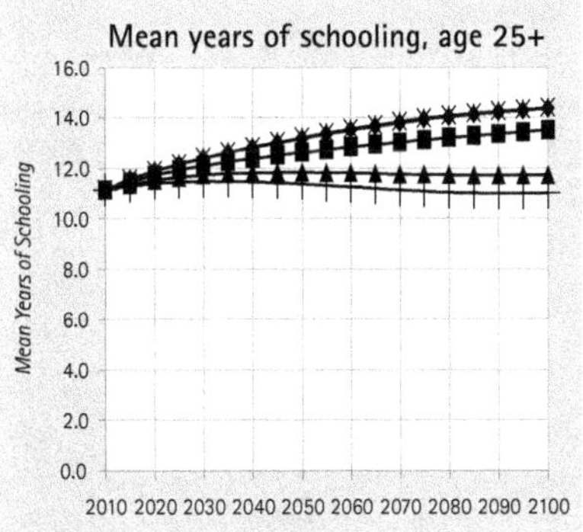

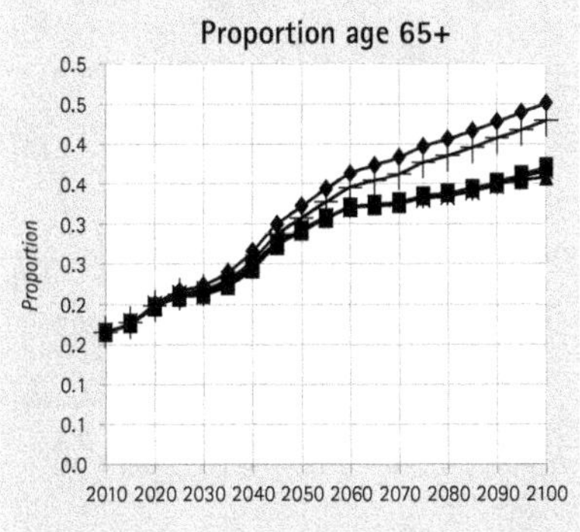

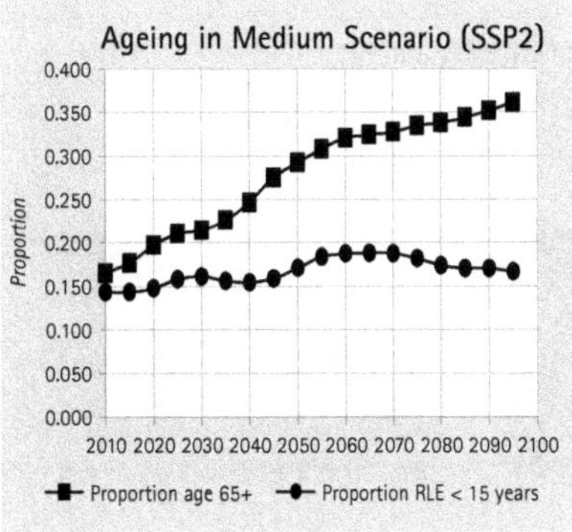

Alternative Scenarios to 2100

Projection Results by Scenario (SSP1–5)

	2010	2020	2030	2040	2050	2075	2100
Population (in millions)							
SSP1 - Rapid development	9.98	9.77	9.62	9.46	9.28	8.62	7.72
SSP2 - Medium	9.98	9.72	9.48	9.20	8.90	8.00	7.05
SSP3 - Stalled development	9.98	9.57	9.00	8.34	7.62	5.67	4.07
SSP4 - Inequality	9.98	9.67	9.32	8.91	8.44	7.01	5.51
SSP5 - Conventional development	9.98	9.88	9.97	10.09	10.28	10.77	11.09
Proportion age 65+							
SSP1 - Rapid development	0.17	0.20	0.22	0.27	0.32	0.40	0.45
SSP2 - Medium	0.17	0.20	0.21	0.25	0.29	0.33	0.37
SSP3 - Stalled development	0.17	0.20	0.21	0.24	0.29	0.33	0.36
SSP4 - Inequality	0.17	0.20	0.22	0.25	0.31	0.38	0.43
SSP5 - Conventional development	0.17	0.20	0.22	0.25	0.29	0.33	0.37
Proportion below age 20							
SSP1 - Rapid development	0.21	0.19	0.17	0.17	0.16	0.15	0.14
SSP2 - Medium	0.21	0.19	0.18	0.18	0.17	0.17	0.16
SSP3 - Stalled development	0.21	0.19	0.17	0.15	0.15	0.14	0.14
SSP4 - Inequality	0.21	0.19	0.17	0.15	0.15	0.13	0.12
SSP5 - Conventional development	0.21	0.19	0.19	0.19	0.19	0.20	0.19
Proportion of Women age 20–39 with at least secondary education							
SSP1 - Rapid development	0.99	1.00	1.00	1.00	1.00	1.00	1.00
SSP2 - Medium	0.99	0.99	1.00	1.00	1.00	1.00	1.00
SSP3 - Stalled development	0.99	0.98	0.98	0.98	0.98	0.98	0.98
SSP4 - Inequality	0.99	0.98	0.98	0.98	0.98	0.98	0.98
SSP5 - Conventional development	0.99	1.00	1.00	1.00	1.00	1.00	1.00
Mean years of schooling, age 25+							
SSP1 - Rapid development	11.13	11.88	12.39	12.81	13.17	13.92	14.35
SSP2 - Medium	11.13	11.71	12.10	12.38	12.62	13.11	13.50
SSP3 - Stalled development	11.13	11.52	11.73	11.81	11.83	11.74	11.72
SSP4 - Inequality	11.13	11.40	11.47	11.45	11.37	11.08	10.99
SSP5 - Conventional development	11.13	11.88	12.40	12.83	13.20	13.96	14.38

Demographic Assumptions Underlying SSPs

	2010–15	2020–25	2030–35	2040–45	2050–55	2075–80	2095–2100
Total fertility rate							
SSP1 - Rapid development	1.24	1.34	1.43	1.48	1.52	1.55	1.59
SSP2 - Medium	1.23	1.36	1.46	1.51	1.55	1.59	1.61
SSP3 - Stalled development	1.19	1.19	1.19	1.20	1.22	1.25	1.28
SSP4 - Inequality	1.19	1.21	1.22	1.24	1.25	1.29	1.32
SSP5 - Conventional development	1.30	1.54	1.73	1.84	1.89	1.94	1.98
Life expectancy at birth for females (in years)							
SSP1 - Rapid development	79.78	82.66	85.61	88.60	91.52	99.00	105.02
SSP2 - Medium	78.69	80.79	82.79	84.81	86.81	91.80	95.80
SSP3 - Stalled development	78.81	79.73	80.70	81.64	82.54	84.88	86.79
SSP4 - Inequality	79.26	81.18	83.09	85.03	86.95	91.63	95.48
SSP5 - Conventional development	79.78	82.66	85.61	88.60	91.52	99.00	105.02
Migration – net flow over five years (in thousands)							
SSP1 - Rapid development	73	79	82	82	79	29	0
SSP2 - Medium	74	79	82	84	83	34	0
SSP3 - Stalled development	61	40	41	42	41	16	0
SSP4 - Inequality	73	78	81	82	80	32	0
SSP5 - Conventional development	85	118	123	127	127	54	0

Ageing Indicators, Medium Scenario (SSP2)

	2010	2020	2030	2040	2050	2075	2095
Median age	39.83	42.96	46.03	48.37	49.72	51.44	53.44
Propspective median age	39.83	40.74	41.88	42.26	41.71	38.73	36.93
Proportion age 65+	0.17	0.20	0.21	0.25	0.29	0.33	0.36
Proportion RLE < 15 years	0.14	0.15	0.16	0.15	0.17	0.18	0.17

Iceland

Detailed Human Capital Projections to 2060

Demographic indicators, Medium Scenario (SSP2)	2010	2020	2030	2040	2050	2060
Population (in millions)	0.32	0.37	0.41	0.46	0.50	0.54
Proportion age 65+	0.12	0.15	0.19	0.21	0.23	0.26
Proportion below age 20	0.28	0.26	0.25	0.24	0.23	0.22
	2005–10	2015–20	2025–30	2035–40	2045–50	2055–60
Total Fertility Rate	2.10	2.03	2.01	2.00	2.00	1.99
Life expectancy at birth (in years)						
Men	79.48	81.93	84.00	86.09	88.04	90.03
Women	83.05	85.51	87.61	89.69	91.69	93.69
Five-year immigration flow (in '000)	13.17	10.55	10.98	11.26	11.30	11.15
Five-year emigration flow (in '000)	2.90	2.24	2.30	2.41	2.52	2.60

Human Capital indicators, Medium Scenario (SSP2)	2010	2020	2030	2040	2050	2060
Population age 25+: highest educational attainment						
E1 - no education	0.00	0.00	0.00	0.00	0.00	0.00
E2 - incomplete primary	0.00	0.00	0.00	0.00	0.00	0.00
E3 - primary	0.31	0.27	0.23	0.20	0.17	0.14
E4 - lower secondary	0.01	0.01	0.00	0.00	0.00	0.00
E5 - upper secondary	0.34	0.33	0.32	0.31	0.30	0.28
E6 - post-secondary	0.34	0.39	0.44	0.49	0.53	0.58
Mean years of schooling (in years)	12.20	12.91	13.54	14.15	14.70	15.20
Gender gap (population age 25+): highest educational attainment (ratio male/female)						
E1 - no education	NA	0.00	0.34	0.47	0.59	0.72
E2 - incomplete primary	NA	Inf	3.09	2.40	1.95	1.60
E3 - primary	0.77	0.90	1.02	1.14	1.23	1.27
E4 - lower secondary	1.06	0.99	0.98	1.00	1.03	1.03
E5 - upper secondary	1.29	1.25	1.24	1.23	1.21	1.17
E6 - post-secondary	0.98	0.89	0.85	0.83	0.85	0.88
Mean years of schooling (male minus female)	0.48	0.03	−0.28	−0.45	−0.51	−0.45
Women age 20–39: highest educational attainment						
E1 - no education	0.00	0.00	0.00	0.00	0.00	0.00
E2 - incomplete primary	0.00	0.00	0.00	0.00	0.00	0.00
E3 - primary	0.18	0.14	0.11	0.09	0.08	0.07
E4 - lower secondary	0.00	0.00	0.00	0.00	0.00	0.00
E5 - upper secondary	0.34	0.31	0.29	0.28	0.28	0.28
E6 - post-secondary	0.48	0.54	0.59	0.62	0.64	0.65
Mean years of schooling (in years)	14.04	14.92	15.63	15.88	16.04	16.13

Education scenarios

GET: global education trend scenario (Medium assumption also used for SSP2)

CER: constant enrolment rates scenario (assumption of no future improvements)

FT: Fast track scenario (assumption of education expansion according to fastest historical experience)

Pyramids by Education, Medium Scenario

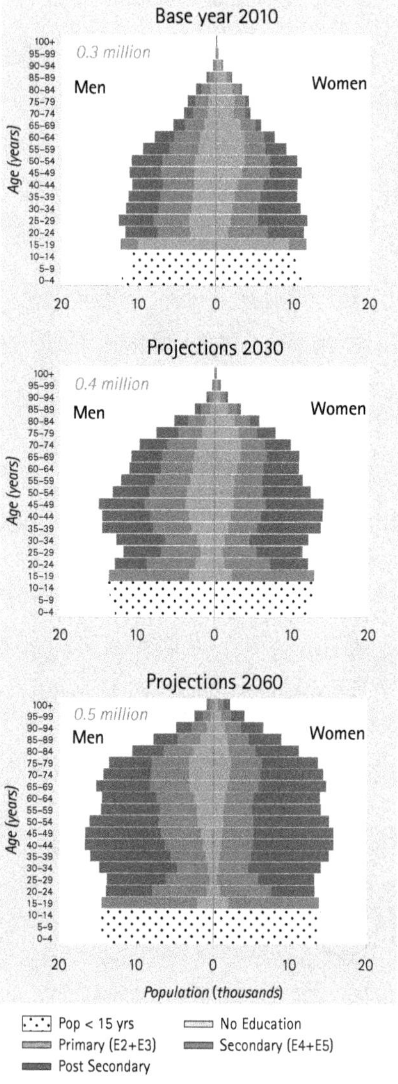

Population Size by Educational Attainment According to Three Education Scenarios: GET, CER, and FT

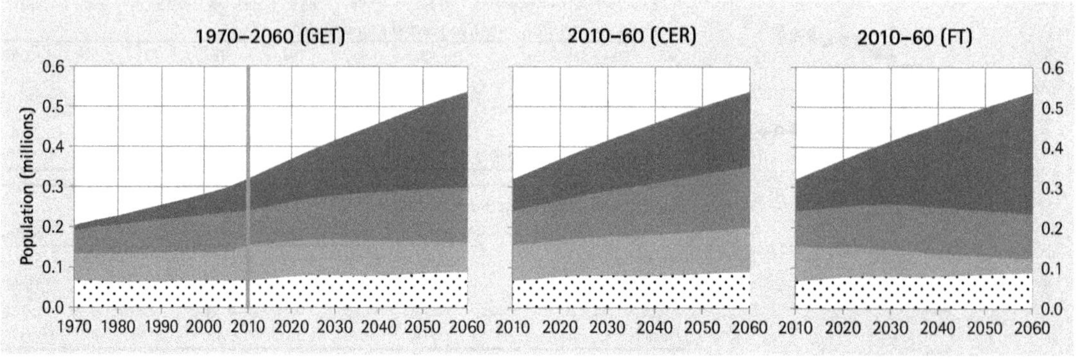

Iceland (Continued)

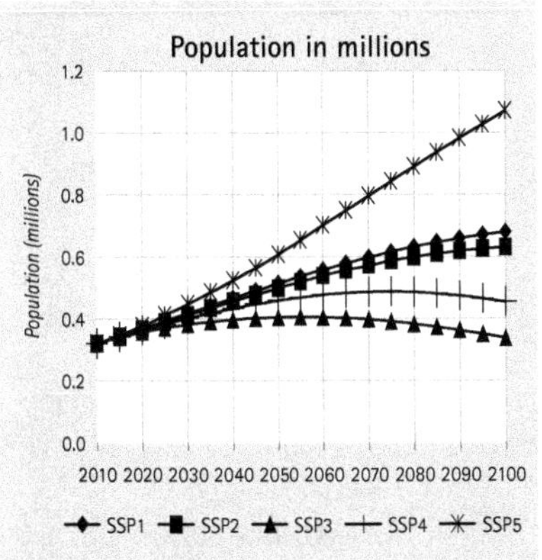

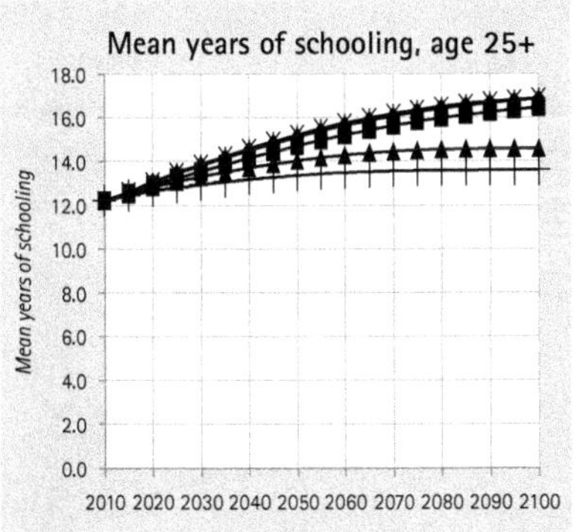

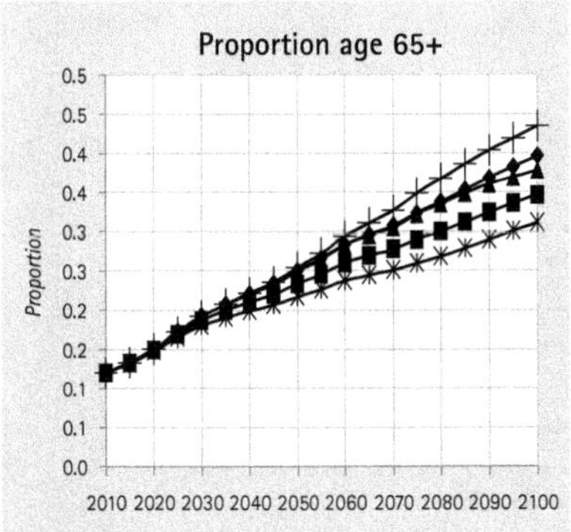

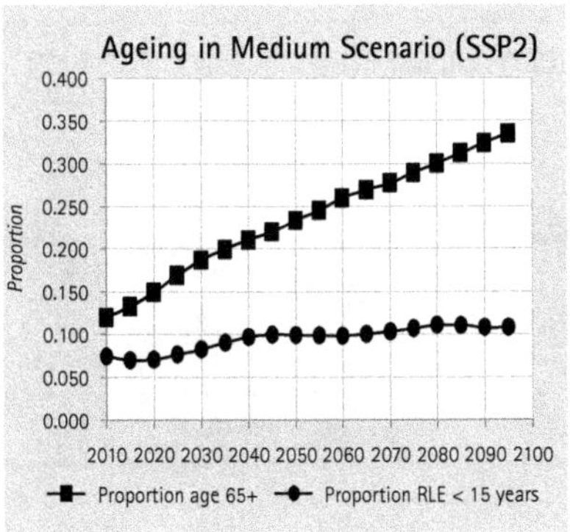

Alternative Scenarios to 2100

Projection Results by Scenario (SSP1–5)

	2010	2020	2030	2040	2050	2075	2100
Population (in millions)							
SSP1 - Rapid development	0.32	0.37	0.42	0.47	0.51	0.62	0.68
SSP2 - Medium	0.32	0.37	0.41	0.46	0.50	0.59	0.63
SSP3 - Stalled development	0.32	0.36	0.38	0.40	0.40	0.39	0.34
SSP4 - Inequality	0.32	0.36	0.40	0.43	0.46	0.49	0.45
SSP5 - Conventional development	0.32	0.38	0.45	0.52	0.61	0.84	1.07
Proportion age 65+							
SSP1 - Rapid development	0.12	0.15	0.19	0.22	0.25	0.32	0.40
SSP2 - Medium	0.12	0.15	0.19	0.21	0.23	0.29	0.35
SSP3 - Stalled development	0.12	0.15	0.19	0.22	0.25	0.32	0.38
SSP4 - Inequality	0.12	0.15	0.19	0.22	0.25	0.35	0.43
SSP5 - Conventional development	0.12	0.15	0.18	0.20	0.22	0.26	0.31
Proportion below age 20							
SSP1 - Rapid development	0.28	0.26	0.25	0.23	0.22	0.20	0.18
SSP2 - Medium	0.28	0.26	0.25	0.24	0.23	0.21	0.19
SSP3 - Stalled development	0.28	0.26	0.23	0.20	0.19	0.16	0.15
SSP4 - Inequality	0.28	0.25	0.23	0.20	0.19	0.16	0.13
SSP5 - Conventional development	0.28	0.27	0.27	0.27	0.26	0.25	0.24
Proportion of Women age 20–39 with at least secondary education							
SSP1 - Rapid development	0.82	0.89	0.93	0.94	0.95	0.97	0.98
SSP2 - Medium	0.82	0.86	0.89	0.91	0.92	0.96	0.98
SSP3 - Stalled development	0.82	0.85	0.86	0.86	0.86	0.86	0.86
SSP4 - Inequality	0.82	0.85	0.86	0.86	0.86	0.86	0.86
SSP5 - Conventional development	0.82	0.89	0.93	0.94	0.95	0.97	0.98
Mean years of schooling, age 25+							
SSP1 - Rapid development	12.20	13.05	13.81	14.50	15.11	16.24	16.85
SSP2 - Medium	12.20	12.91	13.54	14.15	14.70	15.80	16.45
SSP3 - Stalled development	12.20	12.82	13.30	13.70	14.03	14.50	14.58
SSP4 - Inequality	12.20	12.66	12.94	13.17	13.35	13.56	13.60
SSP5 - Conventional development	12.20	13.06	13.86	14.57	15.20	16.34	16.90

Demographic Assumptions Underlying SSPs

	2010–15	2020–25	2030–35	2040–45	2050–55	2075–80	2095–2100
Total fertility rate							
SSP1 - Rapid development	2.03	2.01	2.00	1.99	1.99	1.95	1.92
SSP2 - Medium	2.04	2.02	2.00	2.00	2.00	1.95	1.92
SSP3 - Stalled development	1.93	1.72	1.58	1.53	1.50	1.47	1.45
SSP4 - Inequality	1.94	1.72	1.59	1.54	1.51	1.49	1.46
SSP5 - Conventional development	2.14	2.31	2.42	2.47	2.49	2.44	2.40
Life expectancy at birth for females (in years)							
SSP1 - Rapid development	85.05	88.30	91.38	94.34	97.34	104.84	110.90
SSP2 - Medium	84.31	86.61	88.71	90.69	92.69	97.70	101.69
SSP3 - Stalled development	84.05	85.30	86.40	87.41	88.39	90.73	92.61
SSP4 - Inequality	84.55	86.83	88.91	90.86	92.83	97.59	101.38
SSP5 - Conventional development	85.05	88.30	91.38	94.34	97.34	104.84	110.90
Migration – net flow over five years (in thousands)							
SSP1 - Rapid development	9	8	9	9	8	3	0
SSP2 - Medium	9	8	9	9	8	4	0
SSP3 - Stalled development	7	4	4	4	4	2	0
SSP4 - Inequality	9	8	9	8	8	3	0
SSP5 - Conventional development	10	13	13	14	14	7	0

Ageing Indicators, Medium Scenario (SSP2)

	2010	2020	2030	2040	2050	2075	2095
Median age	34.83	36.73	39.00	41.14	42.33	46.27	49.47
Propspective median age	34.83	34.49	34.78	35.07	34.32	33.50	32.81
Proportion age 65+	0.12	0.15	0.19	0.21	0.23	0.29	0.34
Proportion RLE < 15 years	0.07	0.07	0.08	0.10	0.10	0.11	0.11

India

Detailed Human Capital Projections to 2060

Demographic indicators, Medium Scenario (SSP2)	2010	2020	2030	2040	2050	2060
Population (in millions)	1224.61	1385.24	1520.63	1632.48	1714.61	1754.56
Proportion age 65+	0.05	0.06	0.08	0.11	0.15	0.19
Proportion below age 20	0.40	0.36	0.32	0.28	0.25	0.23
	2005–20	2015–20	2025–20	2035–20	2045–20	2055–60
Total Fertility Rate	2.73	2.37	2.10	1.97	1.85	1.75
Life expectancy at birth (in years)						
Men	62.80	66.12	69.22	72.54	75.56	77.25
Women	65.73	69.48	72.88	76.39	79.50	81.19
Five-year immigration flow (in '000)	792.18	767.73	792.68	809.73	811.67	802.81
Five-year emigration flow (in '000)	3696.67	3014.55	3122.82	3130.62	3031.22	2896.89

Human Capital indicators, Medium Scenario (SSP2)	2010	2020	2030	2040	2050	2060
Population age 25+: highest educational attainment						
E1 - no education	0.39	0.32	0.25	0.19	0.15	0.11
E2 - incomplete primary	0.08	0.07	0.05	0.04	0.03	0.02
E3 - primary	0.14	0.15	0.15	0.14	0.14	0.12
E4 - lower secondary	0.11	0.13	0.13	0.13	0.13	0.12
E5 - upper secondary	0.18	0.23	0.27	0.32	0.37	0.41
E6 - post-secondary	0.09	0.11	0.14	0.16	0.19	0.22
Mean years of schooling (in years)	5.53	6.56	7.53	8.46	9.32	10.12
Gender gap (population age 25+): highest educational attainment (ratio male/female)						
E1 - no education	0.54	0.54	0.56	0.58	0.60	0.62
E2 - incomplete primary	1.21	1.17	1.10	1.04	0.99	0.96
E3 - primary	1.19	1.07	1.00	0.97	0.95	0.93
E4 - lower secondary	1.54	1.36	1.25	1.18	1.12	1.07
E5 - upper secondary	1.70	1.41	1.24	1.15	1.09	1.06
E6 - post-secondary	1.91	1.63	1.43	1.29	1.20	1.14
Mean years of schooling (male minus female)	2.56	2.15	1.73	1.34	1.01	0.74
Women age 20–39: highest educational attainment						
E1 - no education	0.34	0.23	0.15	0.09	0.05	0.03
E2 - incomplete primary	0.06	0.04	0.03	0.02	0.01	0.01
E3 - primary	0.15	0.16	0.15	0.13	0.11	0.08
E4 - lower secondary	0.13	0.14	0.13	0.12	0.10	0.08
E5 - upper secondary	0.23	0.31	0.38	0.44	0.49	0.52
E6 - post-secondary	0.09	0.12	0.16	0.20	0.24	0.29
Mean years of schooling (in years)	6.26	7.79	9.08	10.23	11.18	11.95

Education scenarios

GET: global education trend scenario (Medium assumption also used for SSP2)

CER: constant enrolment rates scenario (assumption of no future improvements)

FT: Fast track scenario (assumption of education expansion according to fastest historical experience)

Pyramids by Education, Medium Scenario

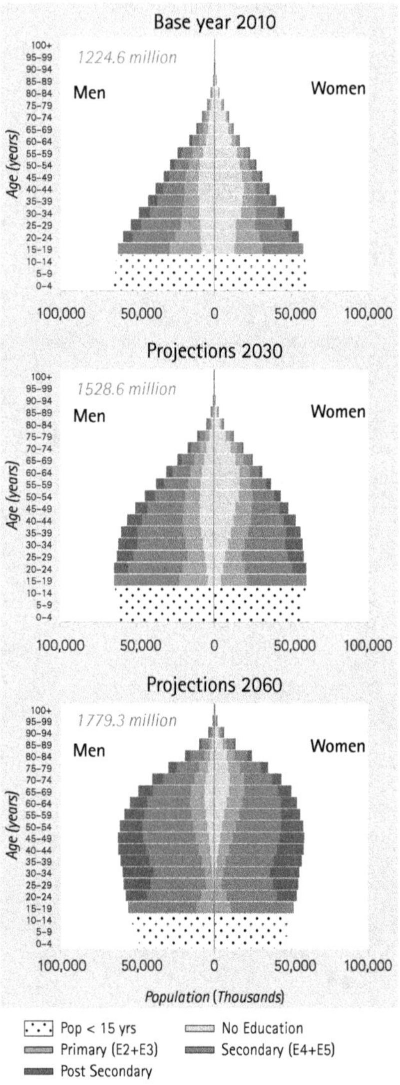

Population Size by Educational Attainment According to Three Education Scenarios: GET, CER, and FT

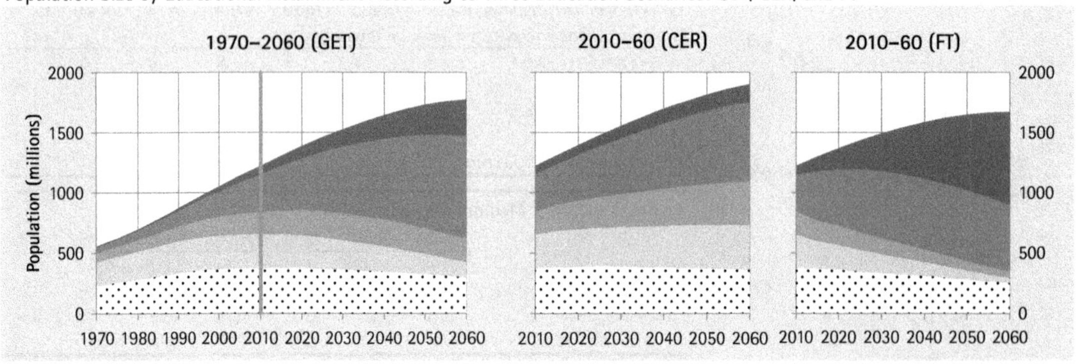

India (Continued)

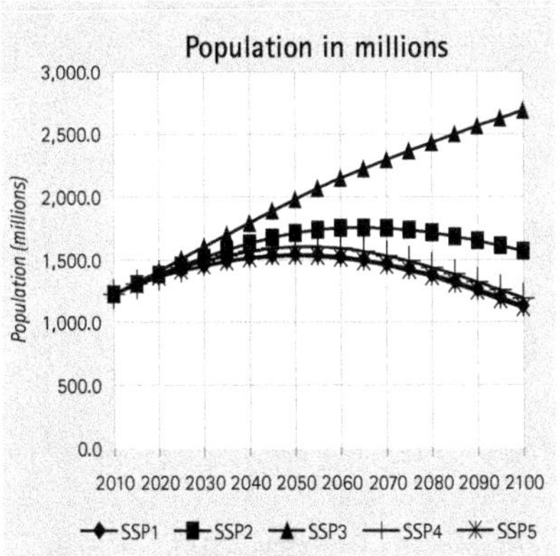

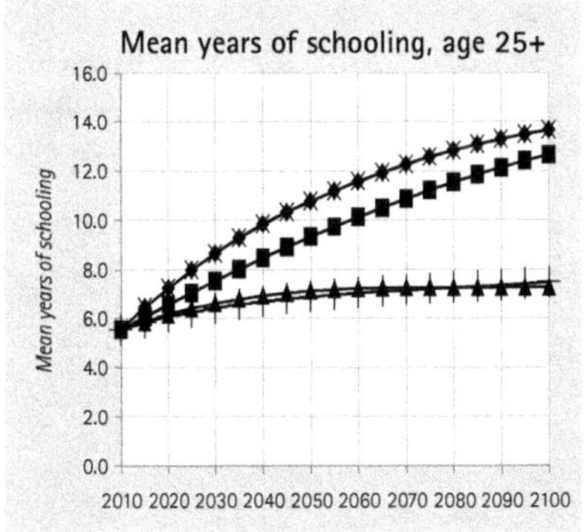

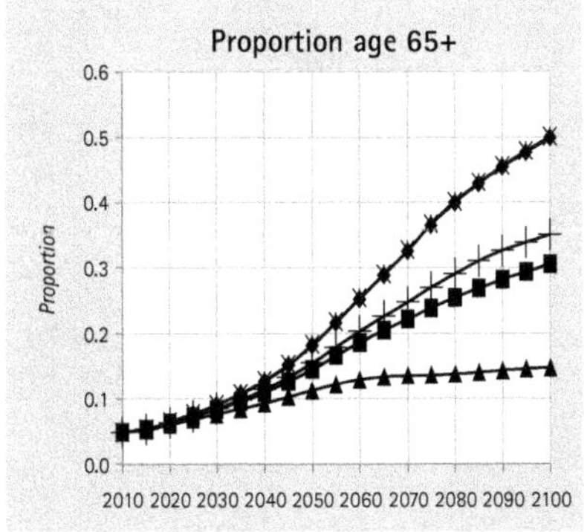

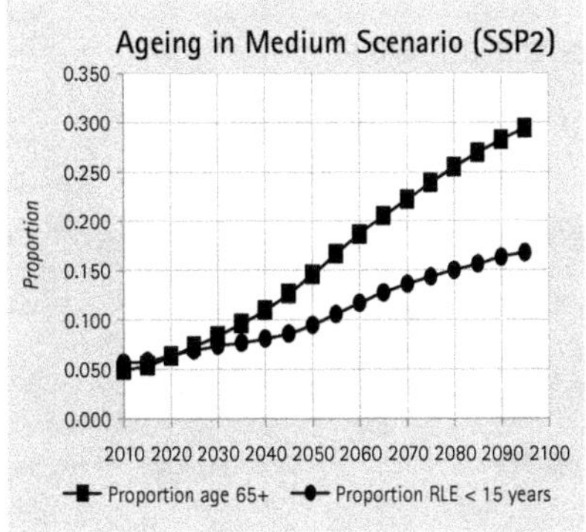

Alternative Scenarios to 2100

Projection Results by Scenario (SSP1–5)

	2010	2020	2030	2040	2050	2075	2100
Population (in millions)							
SSP1 - Rapid development	1,224.61	1,361.85	1,456.61	1,518.60	1,543.02	1,429.58	1,130.90
SSP2 - Medium	1,224.61	1,385.24	1,520.63	1,632.48	1,714.61	1,738.46	1,569.46
SSP3 - Stalled development	1,224.61	1,414.01	1,607.98	1,795.49	1,982.47	2,367.65	2,686.57
SSP4 - Inequality	1,224.61	1,378.21	1,491.13	1,567.97	1,604.86	1,490.47	1,189.56
SSP5 - Conventional development	1,224.61	1,360.52	1,452.27	1,510.85	1,531.68	1,410.79	1,111.50
Proportion age 65+							
SSP1 - Rapid development	0.05	0.07	0.09	0.13	0.18	0.36	0.50
SSP2 - Medium	0.05	0.06	0.08	0.11	0.15	0.24	0.31
SSP3 - Stalled development	0.05	0.06	0.08	0.09	0.11	0.14	0.15
SSP4 - Inequality	0.05	0.06	0.09	0.11	0.16	0.27	0.35
SSP5 - Conventional development	0.05	0.07	0.09	0.13	0.18	0.37	0.50
Proportion below age 20							
SSP1 - Rapid development	0.40	0.35	0.28	0.23	0.19	0.12	0.09
SSP2 - Medium	0.40	0.36	0.32	0.28	0.25	0.20	0.17
SSP3 - Stalled development	0.40	0.37	0.36	0.34	0.33	0.30	0.29
SSP4 - Inequality	0.40	0.36	0.30	0.26	0.22	0.16	0.14
SSP5 - Conventional development	0.40	0.35	0.28	0.23	0.19	0.12	0.09
Proportion of Women age 20–39 with at least secondary education							
SSP1 - Rapid development	0.45	0.69	0.80	0.87	0.91	0.97	0.99
SSP2 - Medium	0.45	0.57	0.67	0.76	0.83	0.94	0.98
SSP3 - Stalled development	0.45	0.44	0.44	0.44	0.44	0.44	0.44
SSP4 - Inequality	0.45	0.41	0.39	0.39	0.39	0.39	0.39
SSP5 - Conventional development	0.45	0.69	0.80	0.87	0.91	0.97	0.99
Mean years of schooling, age 25+							
SSP1 - Rapid development	5.53	7.24	8.65	9.83	10.77	12.56	13.66
SSP2 - Medium	5.53	6.56	7.53	8.46	9.32	11.21	12.65
SSP3 - Stalled development	5.53	6.16	6.61	6.92	7.13	7.27	7.27
SSP4 - Inequality	5.53	6.07	6.41	6.69	6.89	7.20	7.48
SSP5 - Conventional development	5.53	7.24	8.64	9.82	10.76	12.56	13.66

Demographic Assumptions Underlying SSPs

	2010–15	2020–25	2030–35	2040–45	2050–55	2075–80	2095–2100
Total fertility rate							
SSP1 - Rapid development	2.35	1.81	1.53	1.39	1.30	1.23	1.18
SSP2 - Medium	2.53	2.22	2.03	1.91	1.81	1.69	1.60
SSP3 - Stalled development	2.74	2.78	2.72	2.63	2.55	2.46	2.40
SSP4 - Inequality	2.48	2.07	1.77	1.61	1.51	1.45	1.40
SSP5 - Conventional development	2.35	1.81	1.53	1.39	1.30	1.23	1.18
Life expectancy at birth for females (in years)							
SSP1 - Rapid development	71.30	74.87	78.91	82.98	86.15	91.97	96.47
SSP2 - Medium	67.68	71.22	74.60	78.09	80.50	84.00	86.70
SSP3 - Stalled development	70.62	72.44	74.47	76.57	77.68	77.79	78.02
SSP4 - Inequality	70.83	73.92	76.85	79.77	81.69	84.09	86.09
SSP5 - Conventional development	71.30	74.87	78.91	82.98	86.15	91.97	96.47
Migration – net flow over five years (in thousands)							
SSP1 - Rapid development	−2380	−2271	−2260	−2085	−1855	−612	0
SSP2 - Medium	−2348	−2270	−2317	−2266	−2155	−861	0
SSP3 - Stalled development	−1981	−1129	−1152	−1162	−1152	−539	0
SSP4 - Inequality	−2380	−2274	−2272	−2100	−1831	−566	0
SSP5 - Conventional development	−2777	−3463	−3553	−3410	−3177	−1198	0

Ageing Indicators, Medium Scenario (SSP2)

	2010	2020	2030	2040	2050	2075	2095
Median age	25.14	28.13	31.39	34.64	38.02	45.02	49.12
Propspective median age	25.14	25.86	26.95	27.76	29.37	33.79	35.71
Proportion age 65+	0.05	0.06	0.08	0.11	0.15	0.24	0.29
Proportion RLE < 15 years	0.06	0.06	0.07	0.08	0.09	0.14	0.17

Indonesia

Detailed Human Capital Projections to 2060

Demographic indicators, Medium Scenario (SSP2)	2010	2020	2030	2040	2050	2060
Population (in millions)	239.87	261.32	276.37	284.81	285.50	279.59
Proportion age 65+	0.06	0.07	0.10	0.14	0.19	0.23
Proportion below age 20	0.36	0.32	0.27	0.24	0.21	0.19
	2005–10	2015–20	2025–30	2035–40	2045–50	2055–60
Total Fertility Rate	2.19	1.94	1.75	1.63	1.52	1.53
Life expectancy at birth (in years)						
Men	66.29	68.43	70.58	73.16	75.51	77.50
Women	69.43	72.22	74.68	77.41	79.80	81.80
Five-year immigration flow (in '000)	0.83	0.81	0.83	0.86	0.86	0.85
Five-year emigration flow (in '000)	1273.77	948.12	930.09	876.64	801.21	724.38

Human Capital indicators, Medium Scenario (SSP2)	2010	2020	2030	2040	2050	2060
Population age 25+: highest educational attainment						
E1 - no education	0.10	0.06	0.04	0.02	0.01	0.01
E2 - incomplete primary	0.09	0.06	0.04	0.03	0.02	0.01
E3 - primary	0.36	0.32	0.28	0.23	0.18	0.14
E4 - lower secondary	0.16	0.17	0.17	0.16	0.14	0.12
E5 - upper secondary	0.21	0.28	0.35	0.40	0.45	0.49
E6 - post-secondary	0.08	0.10	0.13	0.16	0.19	0.23
Mean years of schooling (in years)	7.96	8.93	9.75	10.47	11.10	11.67
Gender gap (population age 25+): highest educational attainment (ratio male/female)						
E1 - no education	0.55	0.53	0.52	0.52	0.53	0.57
E2 - incomplete primary	0.80	0.78	0.76	0.75	0.74	0.76
E3 - primary	0.94	0.92	0.91	0.89	0.89	0.89
E4 - lower secondary	1.14	1.09	1.07	1.05	1.02	0.98
E5 - upper secondary	1.38	1.23	1.16	1.12	1.10	1.07
E6 - post-secondary	1.14	1.03	0.97	0.94	0.95	0.97
Mean years of schooling (male minus female)	0.96	0.68	0.46	0.30	0.19	0.12
Women age 20–39: highest educational attainment						
E1 - no education	0.03	0.01	0.01	0.01	0.01	0.01
E2 - incomplete primary	0.04	0.02	0.01	0.00	0.00	0.00
E3 - primary	0.31	0.22	0.16	0.11	0.07	0.04
E4 - lower secondary	0.21	0.19	0.14	0.10	0.06	0.04
E5 - upper secondary	0.32	0.43	0.52	0.57	0.60	0.60
E6 - post-secondary	0.10	0.13	0.17	0.22	0.27	0.31
Mean years of schooling (in years)	9.47	10.48	11.30	11.93	12.42	12.78

Education scenarios

GET: global education trend scenario (Medium assumption also used for SSP2)

CER: constant enrolment rates scenario (assumption of no future improvements)

FT: Fast track scenario (assumption of education expansion according to fastest historical experience)

Pyramids by Education, Medium Scenario

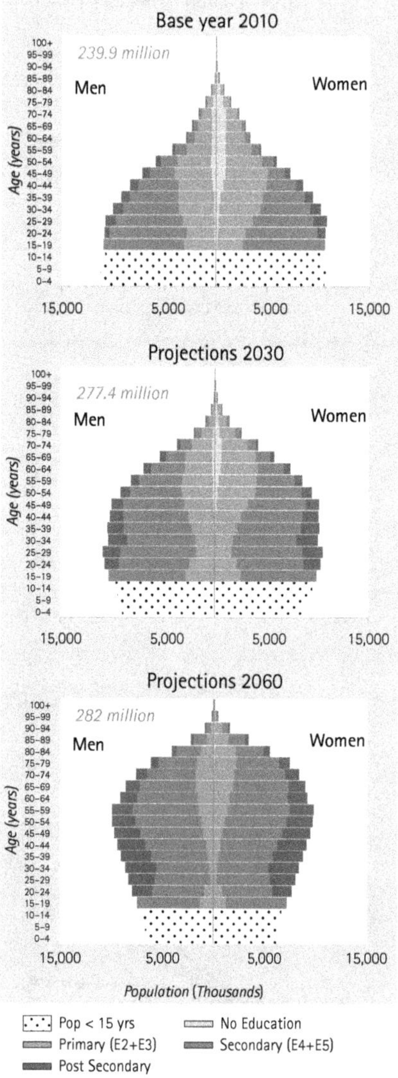

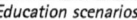

Population Size by Educational Attainment According to Three Education Scenarios: GET, CER, and FT

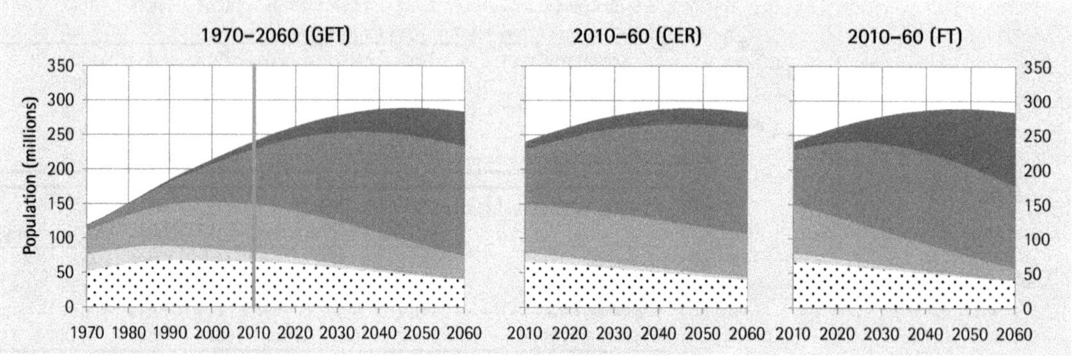

Indonesia (Continued)

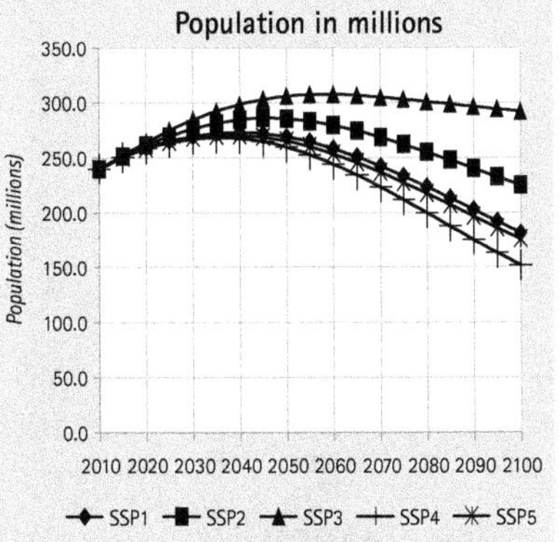

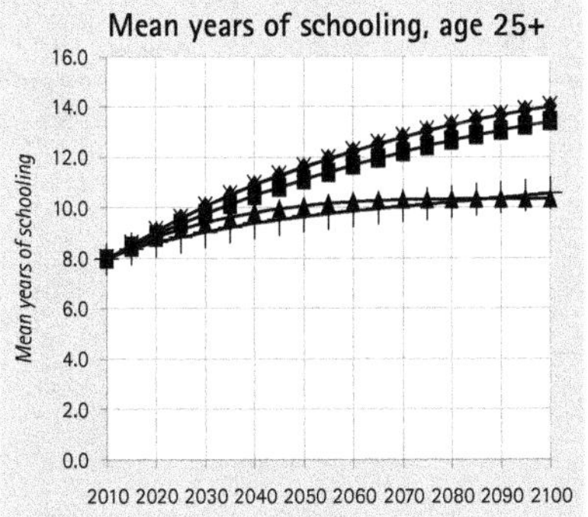

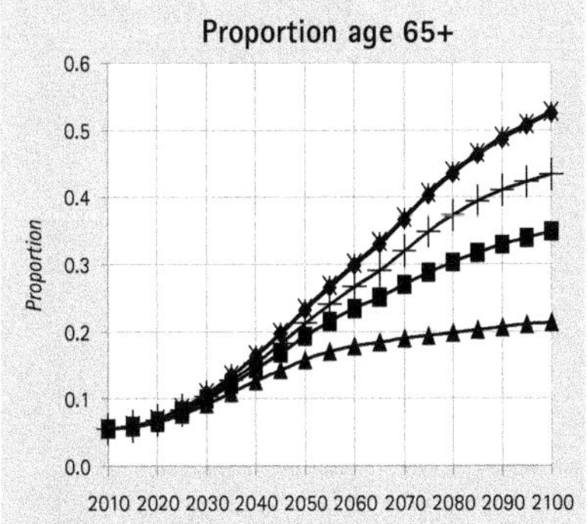

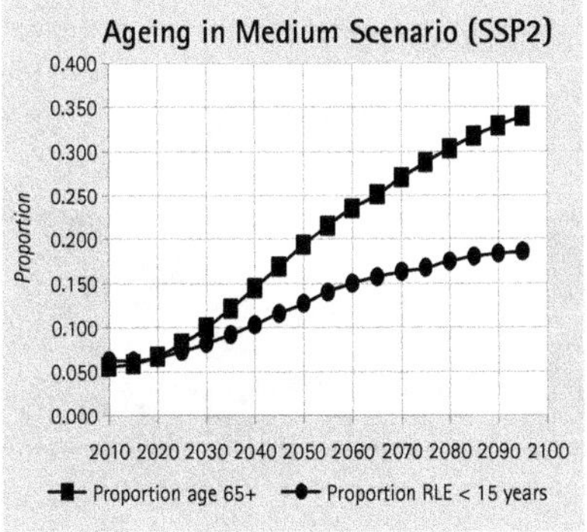

Alternative Scenarios to 2100

Projection Results by Scenario (SSP1–5)

	2010	2020	2030	2040	2050	2075	2100
Population (in millions)							
SSP1 - Rapid development	239.87	258.99	269.53	273.07	269.18	233.32	181.59
SSP2 - Medium	239.87	261.32	276.37	284.81	285.50	262.13	225.10
SSP3 - Stalled development	239.87	264.00	284.61	298.63	306.17	303.16	292.13
SSP4 - Inequality	239.87	258.22	266.98	267.61	259.72	211.71	151.54
SSP5 - Conventional development	239.87	258.46	267.91	270.31	265.31	227.37	175.79
Proportion age 65+							
SSP1 - Rapid development	0.06	0.07	0.11	0.16	0.23	0.40	0.52
SSP2 - Medium	0.06	0.07	0.10	0.14	0.19	0.29	0.35
SSP3 - Stalled development	0.06	0.07	0.09	0.13	0.16	0.19	0.21
SSP4 - Inequality	0.06	0.07	0.10	0.15	0.21	0.35	0.43
SSP5 - Conventional development	0.06	0.07	0.11	0.17	0.23	0.41	0.53
Proportion below age 20							
SSP1 - Rapid development	0.36	0.31	0.25	0.20	0.16	0.11	0.09
SSP2 - Medium	0.36	0.32	0.27	0.24	0.21	0.18	0.16
SSP3 - Stalled development	0.36	0.33	0.30	0.28	0.26	0.24	0.24
SSP4 - Inequality	0.36	0.31	0.25	0.20	0.17	0.13	0.11
SSP5 - Conventional development	0.36	0.31	0.25	0.20	0.16	0.11	0.09
Proportion of Women age 20–39 with at least secondary education							
SSP1 - Rapid development	0.62	0.79	0.89	0.94	0.96	0.99	1.00
SSP2 - Medium	0.62	0.75	0.83	0.88	0.93	0.98	0.99
SSP3 - Stalled development	0.62	0.72	0.73	0.73	0.73	0.73	0.73
SSP4 - Inequality	0.62	0.68	0.66	0.66	0.66	0.66	0.66
SSP5 - Conventional development	0.62	0.79	0.89	0.94	0.96	0.99	1.00
Mean years of schooling, age 25+							
SSP1 - Rapid development	7.96	9.07	10.05	10.90	11.61	13.03	13.98
SSP2 - Medium	7.96	8.93	9.75	10.47	11.10	12.43	13.39
SSP3 - Stalled development	7.96	8.83	9.41	9.80	10.07	10.32	10.33
SSP4 - Inequality	7.96	8.64	9.04	9.38	9.65	10.12	10.55
SSP5 - Conventional development	7.96	9.07	10.04	10.89	11.60	13.02	13.98

Demographic Assumptions Underlying SSPs

	2010–15	2020–25	2030–35	2040–45	2050–55	2075–80	2095–2100
Total fertility rate							
SSP1 - Rapid development	1.94	1.56	1.32	1.20	1.14	1.17	1.20
SSP2 - Medium	2.05	1.84	1.68	1.57	1.52	1.56	1.59
SSP3 - Stalled development	2.14	2.13	2.05	1.96	1.93	1.98	2.03
SSP4 - Inequality	1.94	1.57	1.33	1.21	1.15	1.18	1.21
SSP5 - Conventional development	1.94	1.56	1.32	1.20	1.14	1.17	1.20
Life expectancy at birth for females (in years)							
SSP1 - Rapid development	72.95	76.16	79.59	83.05	86.09	92.90	98.41
SSP2 - Medium	70.81	73.48	76.02	78.71	80.90	85.39	88.99
SSP3 - Stalled development	72.09	73.46	74.90	76.37	77.41	78.88	80.13
SSP4 - Inequality	72.46	74.87	77.21	79.67	81.63	85.44	88.64
SSP5 - Conventional development	72.95	76.16	79.59	83.05	86.09	92.90	98.41
Migration – net flow over five years (in thousands)							
SSP1 - Rapid development	−1027	−932	−883	−785	−678	−220	0
SSP2 - Medium	−1010	−929	−897	−833	−758	−282	0
SSP3 - Stalled development	−855	−461	−440	−410	−378	−148	0
SSP4 - Inequality	−1027	−927	−861	−732	−597	−162	0
SSP5 - Conventional development	−1198	−1419	−1383	−1277	−1152	−425	0

Ageing Indicators, Medium Scenario (SSP2)

	2010	2020	2030	2040	2050	2075	2095
Median age	27.75	31.39	35.05	38.62	42.34	49.11	52.29
Propspective median age	27.75	29.25	30.86	32.19	34.10	37.14	37.27
Proportion age 65+	0.06	0.07	0.10	0.14	0.19	0.29	0.34
Proportion RLE < 15 years	0.06	0.07	0.08	0.10	0.13	0.17	0.19

Iran (Islamic Republic of)

Detailed Human Capital Projections to 2060

Demographic indicators, Medium Scenario (SSP2)	2010	2020	2030	2040	2050	2060
Population (in millions)	73.97	83.81	90.49	95.19	98.07	97.82
Proportion age 65+	0.05	0.06	0.10	0.15	0.23	0.31
Proportion below age 20	0.33	0.30	0.27	0.22	0.19	0.18
	2005–10	2015–20	2025–30	2035–40	2045–50	2055–60
Total Fertility Rate	1.77	1.82	1.72	1.62	1.53	1.51
Life expectancy at birth (in years)						
Men	70.33	73.60	76.54	79.16	81.62	84.03
Women	73.91	77.50	80.59	83.29	85.81	88.21
Fivevyear immigration flow (in '000)	291.66	285.71	296.82	303.29	303.34	299.03
Five-year emigration flow (in '000)	474.45	348.84	327.27	318.13	293.58	263.96

Human Capital indicators, Medium Scenario (SSP2)	2010	2020	2030	2040	2050	2060
Population age 25+: highest educational attainment						
E1 - no education	0.23	0.14	0.10	0.06	0.04	0.02
E2 - incomplete primary	0.08	0.06	0.05	0.03	0.02	0.01
E3 - primary	0.20	0.19	0.17	0.15	0.12	0.10
E4 - lower secondary	0.16	0.17	0.17	0.16	0.14	0.13
E5 - upper secondary	0.21	0.27	0.31	0.35	0.37	0.39
E6 - post-secondary	0.12	0.17	0.20	0.25	0.30	0.35
Mean years of schooling (in years)	7.20	8.58	9.46	10.35	11.16	11.86
Gender gap (population age 25+): highest educational attainment (ratio male/female)						
E1 - no education	0.58	0.53	0.49	0.46	0.46	0.46
E2 - incomplete primary	0.67	0.62	0.57	0.51	0.46	0.44
E3 - primary	1.17	1.09	1.03	0.98	0.93	0.89
E4 - lower secondary	1.44	1.35	1.30	1.26	1.20	1.13
E5 - upper secondary	1.18	1.11	1.09	1.08	1.06	1.04
E6 - post-secondary	1.28	1.13	1.08	1.03	1.02	1.02
Mean years of schooling (male minus female)	1.43	1.08	0.87	0.63	0.45	0.32
Women age 20–39: highest educational attainment						
E1 - no education	0.08	0.04	0.01	0.00	0.00	0.00
E2 - incomplete primary	0.05	0.02	0.01	0.00	0.00	0.00
E3 - primary	0.19	0.16	0.11	0.07	0.04	0.02
E4 - lower secondary	0.18	0.17	0.13	0.09	0.07	0.05
E5 - upper secondary	0.33	0.39	0.45	0.47	0.46	0.46
E6 - post-secondary	0.16	0.22	0.29	0.36	0.42	0.46
Mean years of schooling (in years)	9.23	10.59	11.72	12.55	13.09	13.44

Education scenarios

GET: global education trend scenario (Medium assumption also used for SSP2)

CER: constant enrolment rates scenario (assumption of no future improvements)

FT: Fast track scenario (assumption of education expansion according to fastest historical experience)

Pyramids by Education, Medium Scenario

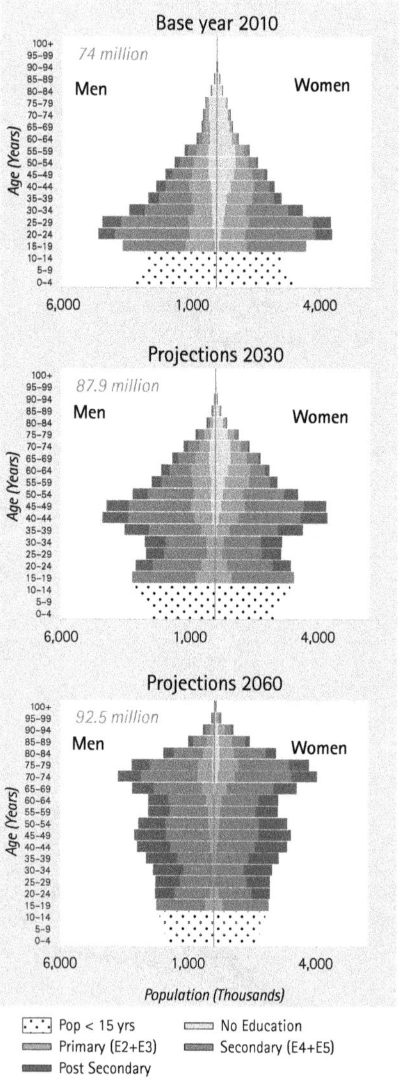

Population Size by Educational Attainment According to Three Education Scenarios: GET, CER, and FT

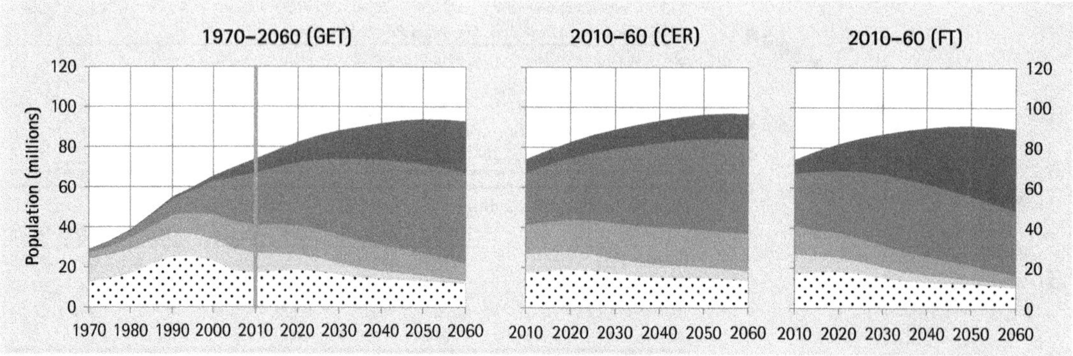

Iran (Islamic Republic of) (Continued)

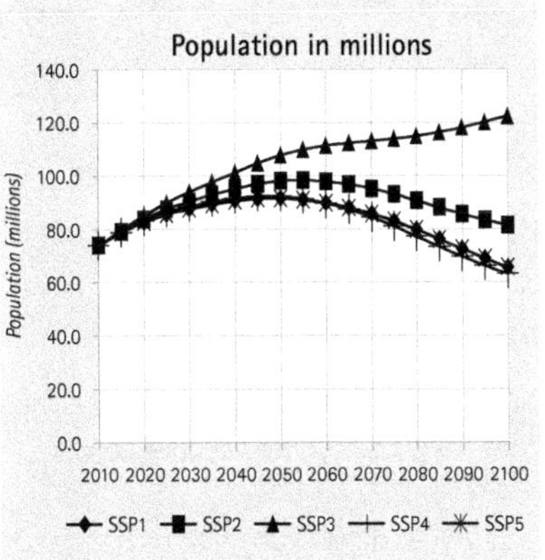

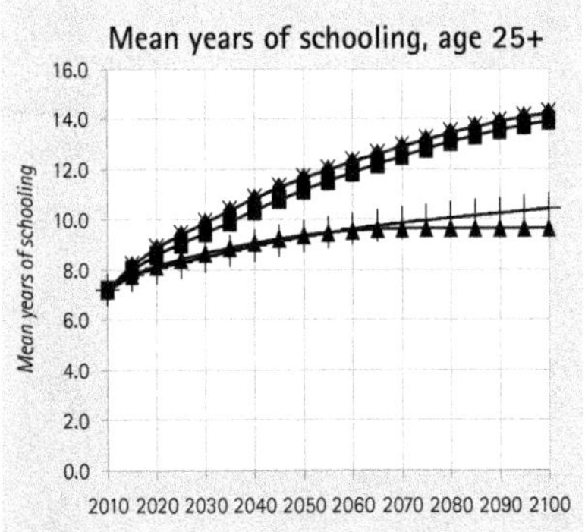

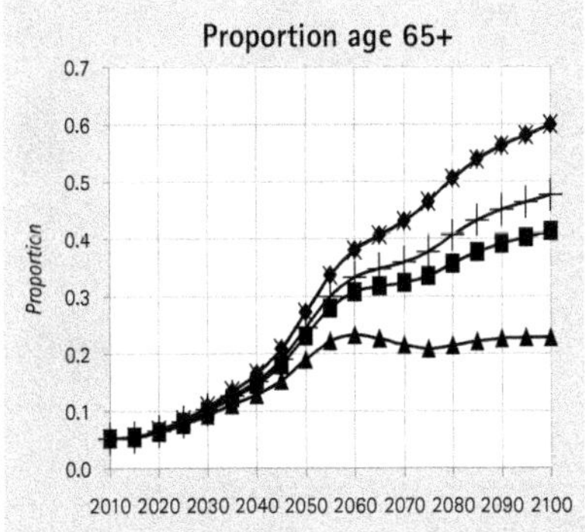

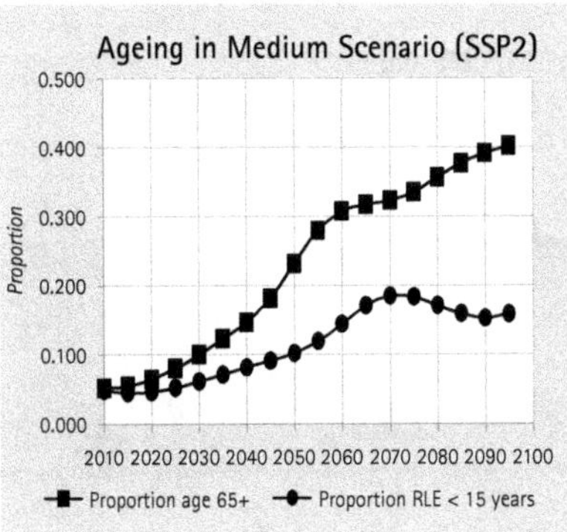

Alternative Scenarios to 2100

Projection Results by Scenario (SSP1–5)

	2010	2020	2030	2040	2050	2075	2100
Population (in millions)							
SSP1 - Rapid development	73.97	82.79	87.66	90.61	91.59	83.06	65.58
SSP2 - Medium	73.97	83.81	90.49	95.19	98.07	93.09	81.38
SSP3 - Stalled development	73.97	85.14	93.98	101.26	107.70	113.88	122.31
SSP4 - Inequality	73.97	83.22	88.60	91.60	92.29	81.01	63.01
SSP5 - Conventional development	73.97	82.75	87.58	90.50	91.46	82.98	65.56
Proportion age 65+							
SSP1 - Rapid development	0.05	0.07	0.11	0.17	0.27	0.46	0.60
SSP2 - Medium	0.05	0.06	0.10	0.15	0.23	0.34	0.41
SSP3 - Stalled development	0.05	0.06	0.09	0.13	0.19	0.21	0.23
SSP4 - Inequality	0.05	0.07	0.10	0.15	0.25	0.38	0.48
SSP5 - Conventional development	0.05	0.07	0.11	0.17	0.27	0.46	0.60
Proportion below age 20							
SSP1 - Rapid development	0.33	0.29	0.24	0.17	0.15	0.09	0.07
SSP2 - Medium	0.33	0.30	0.27	0.22	0.19	0.16	0.14
SSP3 - Stalled development	0.33	0.31	0.30	0.26	0.26	0.25	0.25
SSP4 - Inequality	0.33	0.29	0.25	0.19	0.17	0.12	0.11
SSP5 - Conventional development	0.33	0.29	0.24	0.17	0.15	0.09	0.07
Proportion of Women age 20–39 with at least secondary education							
SSP1 - Rapid development	0.67	0.83	0.92	0.96	0.98	0.99	1.00
SSP2 - Medium	0.67	0.79	0.87	0.93	0.95	0.99	1.00
SSP3 - Stalled development	0.67	0.71	0.72	0.72	0.72	0.72	0.72
SSP4 - Inequality	0.67	0.67	0.64	0.64	0.64	0.64	0.64
SSP5 - Conventional development	0.67	0.83	0.92	0.96	0.98	0.99	1.00
Mean years of schooling, age 25+							
SSP1 - Rapid development	7.20	8.86	9.87	10.83	11.63	13.17	14.22
SSP2 - Medium	7.20	8.58	9.46	10.35	11.16	12.80	13.90
SSP3 - Stalled development	7.20	8.14	8.65	9.07	9.37	9.64	9.64
SSP4 - Inequality	7.20	8.06	8.51	8.95	9.32	9.96	10.41
SSP5 - Conventional development	7.20	8.86	9.87	10.84	11.63	13.17	14.22

Demographic Assumptions Underlying SSPs

	2010–15	2020–25	2030–35	2040–45	2050–55	2075–80	2095–2100
Total fertility rate							
SSP1 - Rapid development	1.77	1.45	1.27	1.17	1.11	1.14	1.18
SSP2 - Medium	1.87	1.77	1.67	1.58	1.51	1.55	1.58
SSP3 - Stalled development	2.02	2.16	2.20	2.15	2.12	2.23	2.31
SSP4 - Inequality	1.83	1.61	1.42	1.30	1.24	1.29	1.33
SSP5 - Conventional development	1.77	1.45	1.27	1.17	1.11	1.14	1.18
Life expectancy at birth for females (in years)							
SSP1 - Rapid development	77.78	81.46	85.15	88.67	91.93	100.06	106.69
SSP2 - Medium	75.80	78.99	81.99	84.59	87.01	92.81	97.39
SSP3 - Stalled development	77.06	78.77	80.57	82.03	83.17	85.80	87.93
SSP4 - Inequality	77.41	80.16	82.91	85.30	87.43	92.53	96.67
SSP5 - Conventional development	77.78	81.46	85.15	88.67	91.93	100.06	106.69
Migration – net flow over five years (in thousands)							
SSP1 - Rapid development	−109	−43	−22	−8	10	8	0
SSP2 - Medium	−108	−43	−23	−4	24	20	0
SSP3 - Stalled development	−91	−22	−11	3	27	30	0
SSP4 - Inequality	−109	−43	−21	−3	23	19	0
SSP5 - Conventional development	−127	−67	−37	−18	5	6	0

Ageing Indicators, Medium Scenario (SSP2)

	2010	2020	2030	2040	2050	2075	2095
Median age	27.02	32.48	38.04	42.06	44.63	53.25	56.59
Propspective median age	27.02	30.14	33.44	35.36	35.88	39.49	38.40
Proportion age 65+	0.05	0.06	0.10	0.15	0.23	0.34	0.40
Proportion RLE < 15 years	0.05	0.05	0.06	0.08	0.10	0.18	0.16

Iraq

Detailed Human Capital Projections to 2060

Demographic indicators, Medium Scenario (SSP2)

	2010	2020	2030	2040	2050	2060
Population (in millions)	31.67	40.85	50.35	59.87	68.29	75.40
Proportion age 65+	0.03	0.04	0.04	0.06	0.09	0.12
Proportion below age 20	0.54	0.50	0.43	0.38	0.33	0.29
	2005–10	2015–20	2025–30	2035–40	2045–50	2055–60
Total Fertility Rate	4.86	3.74	2.99	2.52	2.18	2.01
Life expectancy at birth (in years)						
Men	63.36	70.93	73.78	76.08	78.24	80.40
Women	71.70	75.91	78.81	81.10	83.19	85.28
Five-year immigration flow (in '000)	0.73	0.71	0.74	0.75	0.75	0.74
Five-year emigration flow (in '000)	148.73	146.91	186.32	215.71	235.11	247.87

Human Capital indicators, Medium Scenario (SSP2)

	2010	2020	2030	2040	2050	2060
Population age 25+: highest educational attainment						
E1 - no education	0.21	0.13	0.07	0.04	0.02	0.01
E2 - incomplete primary	0.09	0.07	0.05	0.03	0.02	0.01
E3 - primary	0.27	0.27	0.25	0.22	0.18	0.15
E4 - lower secondary	0.10	0.11	0.11	0.10	0.08	0.07
E5 - upper secondary	0.14	0.18	0.22	0.25	0.28	0.29
E6 - post-secondary	0.19	0.24	0.30	0.36	0.41	0.47
Mean years of schooling (in years)	7.46	8.80	10.05	11.08	11.89	12.56
Gender gap (population age 25+): highest educational attainment (ratio male/female)						
E1 - no education	0.44	0.40	0.38	0.38	0.39	0.40
E2 - incomplete primary	0.61	0.56	0.52	0.47	0.44	0.43
E3 - primary	1.13	1.02	0.96	0.93	0.91	0.88
E4 - lower secondary	1.42	1.23	1.13	1.07	1.02	0.98
E5 - upper secondary	1.48	1.30	1.18	1.12	1.08	1.05
E6 - post-secondary	1.55	1.34	1.20	1.12	1.08	1.06
Mean years of schooling (male minus female)	2.14	1.63	1.17	0.80	0.56	0.40
Women age 20–39: highest educational attainment						
E1 - no education	0.11	0.05	0.02	0.01	0.00	0.00
E2 - incomplete primary	0.09	0.05	0.03	0.02	0.01	0.01
E3 - primary	0.33	0.30	0.24	0.18	0.13	0.09
E4 - lower secondary	0.13	0.14	0.15	0.13	0.12	0.11
E5 - upper secondary	0.16	0.21	0.25	0.29	0.31	0.32
E6 - post-secondary	0.18	0.24	0.31	0.37	0.43	0.47
Mean years of schooling (in years)	8.22	9.73	11.05	11.93	12.57	13.03

Education scenarios

GET: global education trend scenario (medium assumption also used for SSP2)

CER: constant enrolment rates scenario (assumption of no future improvements)

FT: Fast track scenario (assumption of education expansion according to fastest historical experience)

Pyramids by Education, Medium Scenario

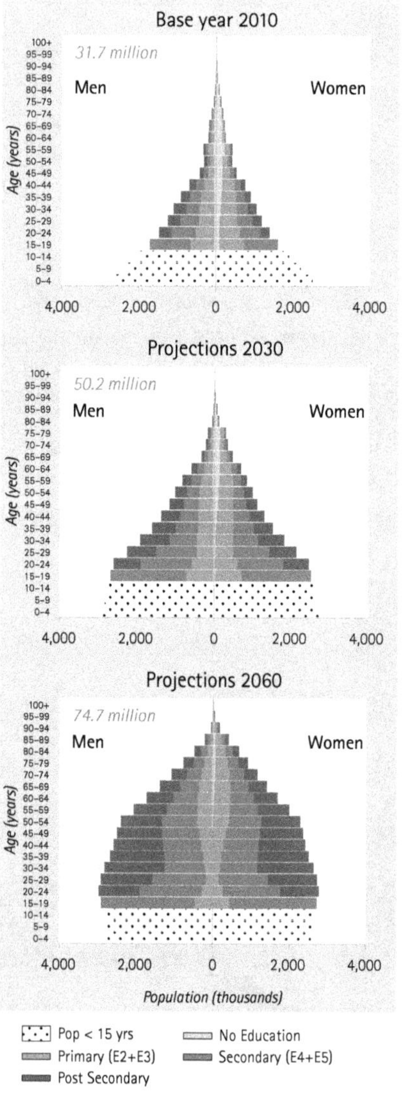

Population Size by Educational Attainment According to Three Education Scenarios: GET, CER, and FT

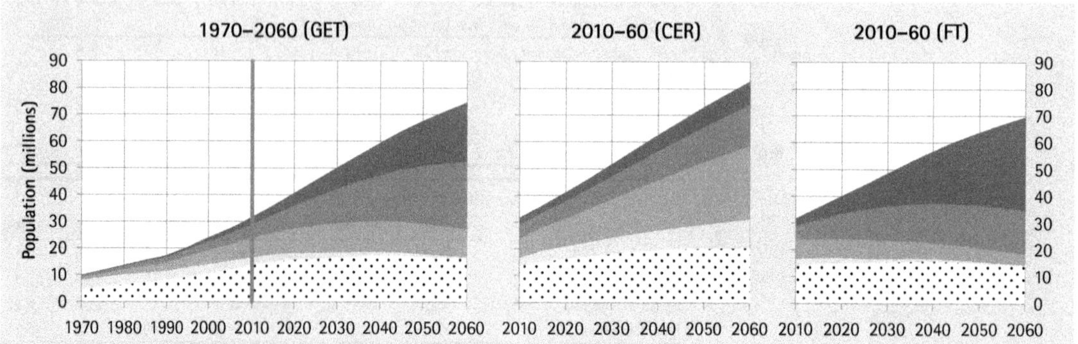

Iraq (Continued)

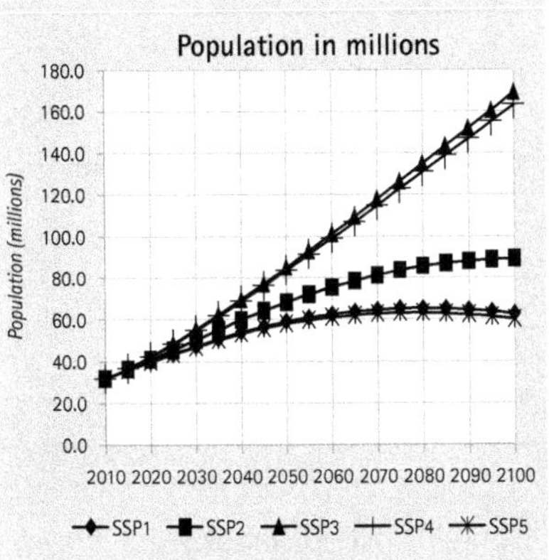

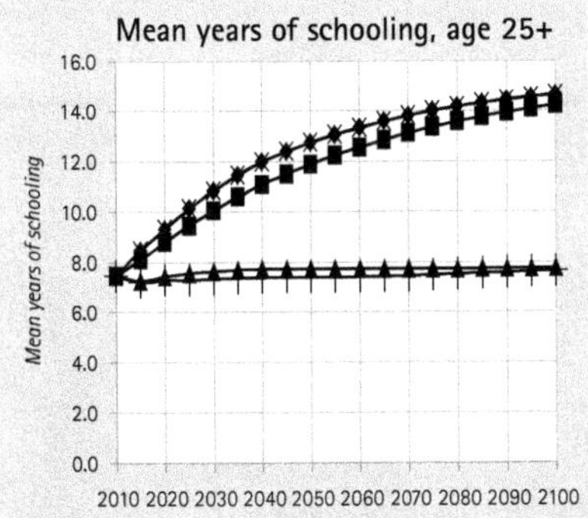

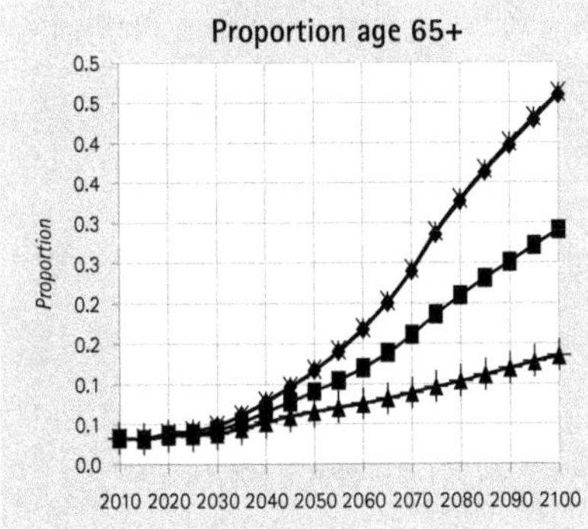

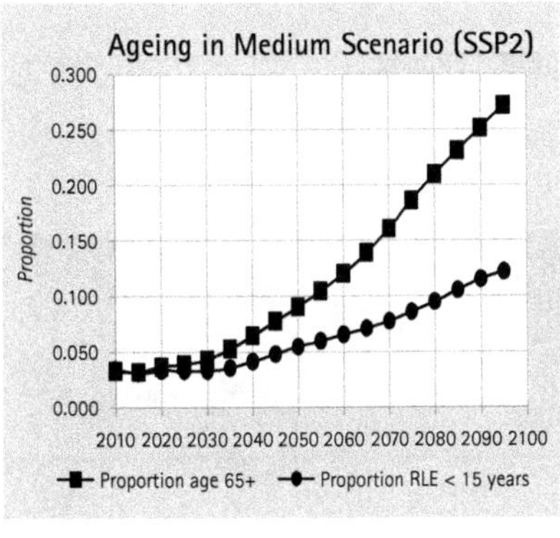

Alternative Scenarios to 2100

Projection Results by Scenario (SSP1–5)

	2010	2020	2030	2040	2050	2075	2100
Population (in millions)							
SSP1 - Rapid development	31.67	39.82	47.22	53.91	58.96	65.12	62.45
SSP2 - Medium	31.67	40.85	50.35	59.87	68.29	83.62	89.15
SSP3 - Stalled development	31.67	42.26	55.25	69.66	85.12	126.39	168.96
SSP4 - Inequality	31.67	42.18	54.92	68.92	83.80	122.89	163.01
SSP5 - Conventional development	31.67	39.73	46.89	53.24	57.90	63.04	60.02
Proportion age 65+							
SSP1 - Rapid development	0.03	0.04	0.05	0.08	0.12	0.29	0.46
SSP2 - Medium	0.03	0.04	0.04	0.06	0.09	0.19	0.29
SSP3 - Stalled development	0.03	0.04	0.04	0.05	0.06	0.10	0.13
SSP4 - Inequality	0.03	0.04	0.04	0.05	0.07	0.10	0.14
SSP5 - Conventional development	0.03	0.04	0.05	0.08	0.12	0.29	0.46
Proportion below age 20							
SSP1 - Rapid development	0.54	0.48	0.39	0.32	0.27	0.16	0.11
SSP2 - Medium	0.54	0.50	0.43	0.38	0.33	0.24	0.19
SSP3 - Stalled development	0.54	0.51	0.48	0.45	0.42	0.36	0.32
SSP4 - Inequality	0.54	0.51	0.48	0.45	0.42	0.36	0.32
SSP5 - Conventional development	0.54	0.48	0.39	0.32	0.27	0.16	0.11
Proportion of Women age 20–39 with at least secondary education							
SSP1 - Rapid development	0.47	0.71	0.81	0.87	0.91	0.96	0.97
SSP2 - Medium	0.47	0.60	0.71	0.80	0.86	0.95	0.98
SSP3 - Stalled development	0.47	0.30	0.30	0.30	0.30	0.30	0.30
SSP4 - Inequality	0.47	0.28	0.27	0.27	0.27	0.27	0.27
SSP5 - Conventional development	0.47	0.71	0.81	0.87	0.91	0.96	0.97
Mean years of schooling, age 25+							
SSP1 - Rapid development	7.46	9.31	10.85	11.98	12.75	14.01	14.66
SSP2 - Medium	7.46	8.80	10.05	11.08	11.89	13.36	14.24
SSP3 - Stalled development	7.46	7.44	7.64	7.73	7.74	7.74	7.76
SSP4 - Inequality	7.46	7.29	7.35	7.39	7.41	7.49	7.65
SSP5 - Conventional development	7.46	9.31	10.84	11.97	12.74	14.00	14.66

Demographic Assumptions Underlying SSPs

	2010–15	2020–25	2030–35	2040–45	2050–55	2075–80	2095–2100
Total fertility rate							
SSP1 - Rapid development	3.94	2.72	2.06	1.72	1.52	1.34	1.27
SSP2 - Medium	4.27	3.31	2.71	2.34	2.08	1.81	1.71
SSP3 - Stalled development	4.59	4.28	3.78	3.35	3.08	2.73	2.61
SSP4 - Inequality	4.59	4.29	3.78	3.35	3.06	2.70	2.58
SSP5 - Conventional development	3.94	2.72	2.06	1.72	1.52	1.34	1.27
Life expectancy at birth for females (in years)							
SSP1 - Rapid development	76.58	80.12	83.37	86.33	89.27	96.76	102.65
SSP2 - Medium	74.11	77.49	79.99	82.19	84.19	89.30	93.31
SSP3 - Stalled development	75.98	77.40	78.60	79.48	80.16	81.48	82.95
SSP4 - Inequality	75.98	77.39	78.57	79.45	80.11	81.40	82.89
SSP5 - Conventional development	76.58	80.12	83.37	86.33	89.27	96.76	102.65
Migration – net flow over five years (in thousands)							
SSP1 - Rapid development	−138	−164	−196	−208	−211	−88	0
SSP2 - Medium	−136	−164	−201	−225	−242	−119	0
SSP3 - Stalled development	−115	−82	−100	−117	−133	−78	0
SSP4 - Inequality	−138	−166	−209	−250	−287	−170	0
SSP5 - Conventional development	−161	−250	−307	−337	−357	−168	0

Ageing Indicators, Medium Scenario (SSP2)

	2010	2020	2030	2040	2050	2075	2095
Median age	18.16	20.21	23.39	26.93	30.53	39.73	46.40
Propspective median age	18.16	17.76	18.91	20.64	22.65	27.59	30.77
Proportion age 65+	0.03	0.04	0.04	0.06	0.09	0.19	0.27
Proportion RLE < 15 years	0.03	0.03	0.03	0.04	0.05	0.09	0.12

Ireland

Detailed Human Capital Projections to 2060

Demographic indicators, Medium Scenario (SSP2)

	2010	2020	2030	2040	2050	2060
Population (in millions)	4.47	5.02	5.52	6.00	6.44	6.80
Proportion age 65+	0.12	0.14	0.17	0.21	0.25	0.26
Proportion below age 20	0.27	0.27	0.25	0.23	0.22	0.21
	2005–10	2015–20	2025–30	2035–40	2045–50	2055–60
Total Fertility Rate	2.10	1.98	2.00	1.96	1.91	1.89
Life expectancy at birth (in years)						
Men	77.33	79.38	81.37	83.39	85.37	87.38
Women	82.02	84.11	86.11	88.11	90.09	92.09
Five-year immigration flow (in '000)	167.51	134.01	139.41	142.91	143.34	141.47
Five-year emigration flow (in '000)	67.73	48.71	50.80	52.45	52.57	53.37

Human Capital indicators, Medium Scenario (SSP2)

	2010	2020	2030	2040	2050	2060
Population age 25+: highest educational attainment						
E1 - no education	0.00	0.00	0.00	0.00	0.00	0.00
E2 - incomplete primary	0.00	0.00	0.00	0.00	0.00	0.00
E3 - primary	0.15	0.10	0.06	0.03	0.02	0.01
E4 - lower secondary	0.20	0.18	0.14	0.11	0.08	0.05
E5 - upper secondary	0.21	0.22	0.22	0.22	0.21	0.19
E6 - post-secondary	0.43	0.50	0.57	0.64	0.69	0.74
Mean years of schooling (in years)	11.95	12.92	13.75	14.49	15.08	15.56
Gender gap (population age 25+): highest educational attainment (ratio male/female)						
E1 - no education	1.23	1.16	1.09	1.03	0.99	0.97
E2 - incomplete primary	NA	NA	NA	NA	NA	NA
E3 - primary	1.08	1.06	1.03	1.03	1.10	1.15
E4 - lower secondary	1.12	1.17	1.20	1.22	1.22	1.22
E5 - upper secondary	0.84	0.90	0.95	0.99	1.02	1.04
E6 - post-secondary	1.01	0.98	0.97	0.97	0.97	0.97
Mean years of schooling (male minus female)	−0.11	−0.11	−0.10	−0.07	−0.06	−0.04
Women age 20–39: highest educational attainment						
E1 - no education	0.00	0.00	0.00	0.00	0.00	0.00
E2 - incomplete primary	0.00	0.00	0.00	0.00	0.00	0.00
E3 - primary	0.02	0.01	0.01	0.00	0.00	0.00
E4 - lower secondary	0.10	0.06	0.03	0.02	0.01	0.01
E5 - upper secondary	0.26	0.25	0.25	0.23	0.22	0.21
E6 - post-secondary	0.62	0.68	0.71	0.75	0.77	0.78
Mean years of schooling (in years)	14.41	15.46	15.75	15.93	16.02	16.07

Education scenarios

GET: global education trend scenario (medium assumption also used for SSP2)

CER: constant enrolment rates scenario (assumption of no future improvements)

FT: Fast track scenario (assumption of education expansion according to fastest historical experience)

Pyramids by Education, Medium Scenario

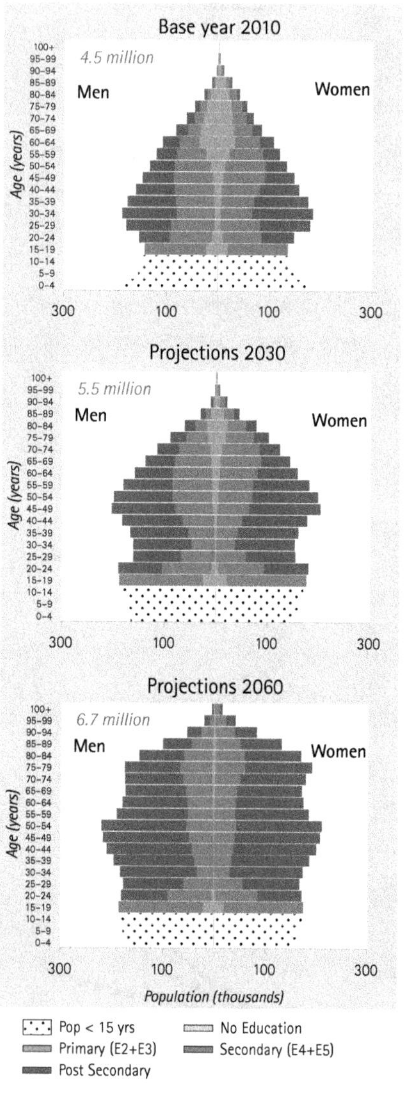

Population Size by Educational Attainment According to Three Education Scenarios: GET, CER, and FT

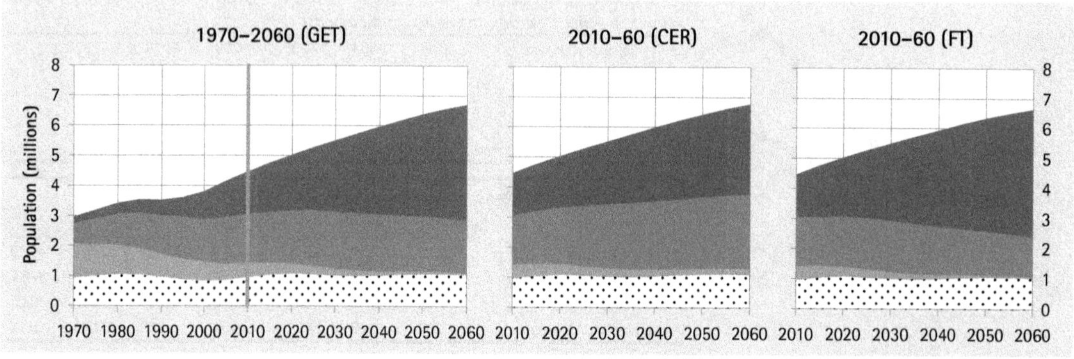

Ireland (Continued)

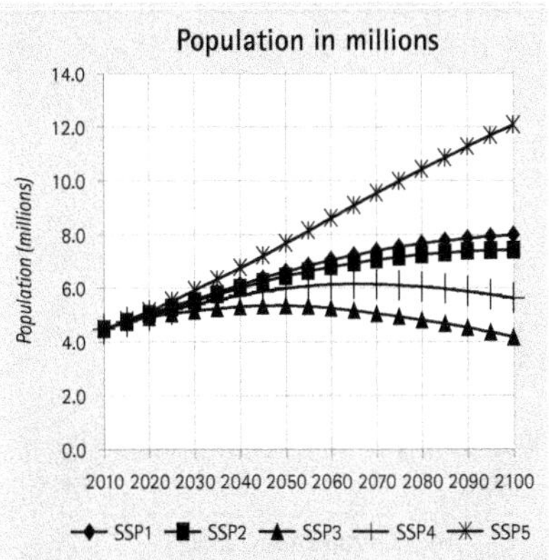

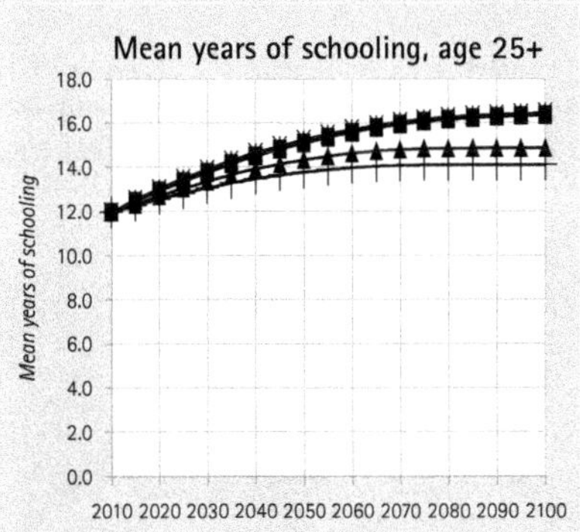

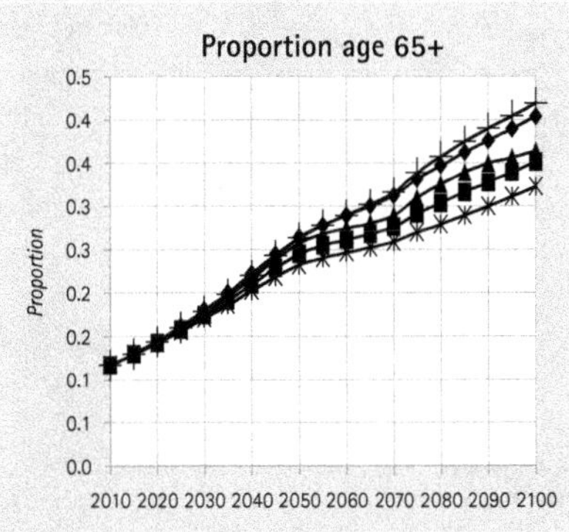

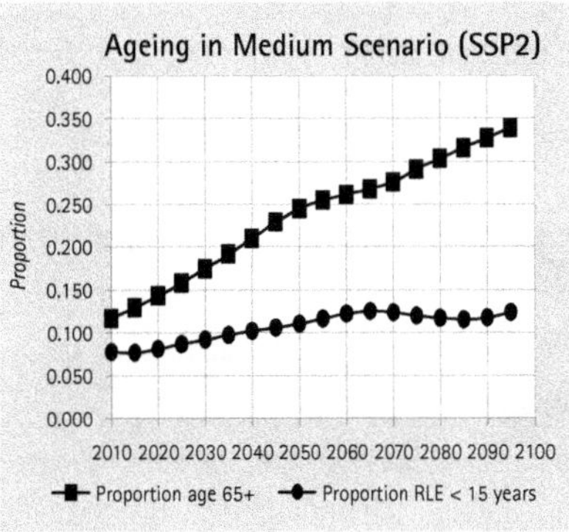

Alternative Scenarios to 2100

Projection Results by Scenario (SSP1–5)

	2010	2020	2030	2040	2050	2075	2100
Population (in millions)							
SSP1 - Rapid development	4.47	5.04	5.58	6.11	6.62	7.55	7.99
SSP2 - Medium	4.47	5.02	5.52	6.00	6.44	7.17	7.42
SSP3 - Stalled development	4.47	4.91	5.15	5.30	5.34	4.94	4.18
SSP4 - Inequality	4.47	4.98	5.38	5.73	5.99	6.11	5.61
SSP5 - Conventional development	4.47	5.14	5.91	6.76	7.67	9.99	12.07
Proportion age 65+							
SSP1 - Rapid development	0.12	0.14	0.18	0.22	0.26	0.33	0.40
SSP2 - Medium	0.12	0.14	0.17	0.21	0.25	0.29	0.35
SSP3 - Stalled development	0.12	0.14	0.18	0.22	0.26	0.31	0.36
SSP4 - Inequality	0.12	0.14	0.18	0.22	0.26	0.34	0.42
SSP5 - Conventional development	0.12	0.14	0.17	0.20	0.23	0.27	0.32
Proportion below age 20							
SSP1 - Rapid development	0.27	0.27	0.24	0.23	0.22	0.19	0.17
SSP2 - Medium	0.27	0.27	0.25	0.23	0.22	0.20	0.18
SSP3 - Stalled development	0.27	0.26	0.23	0.20	0.19	0.16	0.15
SSP4 - Inequality	0.27	0.26	0.23	0.20	0.19	0.16	0.14
SSP5 - Conventional development	0.27	0.28	0.27	0.26	0.26	0.24	0.22
Proportion of Women age 20–39 with at least secondary education							
SSP1 - Rapid development	0.97	0.99	1.00	1.00	1.00	1.00	1.00
SSP2 - Medium	0.97	0.99	0.99	1.00	1.00	1.00	1.00
SSP3 - Stalled development	0.97	0.97	0.97	0.97	0.97	0.97	0.97
SSP4 - Inequality	0.97	0.97	0.97	0.97	0.97	0.97	0.97
SSP5 - Conventional development	0.97	0.99	1.00	1.00	1.00	1.00	1.00
Mean years of schooling, age 25+							
SSP1 - Rapid development	11.95	13.00	13.84	14.57	15.15	16.11	16.41
SSP2 - Medium	11.95	12.92	13.75	14.49	15.08	16.05	16.34
SSP3 - Stalled development	11.95	12.70	13.35	13.90	14.32	14.82	14.85
SSP4 - Inequality	11.95	12.56	13.06	13.47	13.76	14.09	14.09
SSP5 - Conventional development	11.95	13.02	13.89	14.63	15.22	16.15	16.43

Demographic assumptions underlying SSPs

	2010–15	2020–25	2030–35	2040–45	2050–55	2075–80	2095–2100
Total fertility rate							
SSP1 - Rapid development	1.98	1.98	1.97	1.93	1.90	1.87	1.85
SSP2 - Medium	1.98	1.99	1.99	1.94	1.90	1.87	1.85
SSP3 - Stalled development	1.89	1.71	1.59	1.52	1.47	1.45	1.44
SSP4 - Inequality	1.90	1.74	1.64	1.56	1.51	1.49	1.48
SSP5 - Conventional development	2.08	2.28	2.38	2.39	2.37	2.34	2.31
Life expectancy at birth for females (in years)							
SSP1 - Rapid development	84.00	86.99	89.96	92.88	95.78	103.19	109.17
SSP2 - Medium	82.99	85.11	87.11	89.11	91.09	96.10	100.10
SSP3 - Stalled development	83.03	84.03	85.01	85.94	86.86	89.15	91.05
SSP4 - Inequality	83.47	85.53	87.48	89.39	91.29	95.92	99.73
SSP5 - Conventional development	84.00	86.99	89.96	92.88	95.78	103.19	109.17
Migration – net flow over five years (in thousands)							
SSP1 - Rapid development	91	87	88	88	84	35	0
SSP2 - Medium	90	86	88	89	88	39	0
SSP3 - Stalled development	76	43	44	44	42	18	0
SSP4 - Inequality	91	87	88	87	84	36	0
SSP5 - Conventional development	106	132	135	139	140	65	0

Ageing Indicators, Medium Scenario (SSP2)

	2010	2020	2030	2040	2050	2075	2095
Median age	34.68	37.58	39.82	41.15	42.69	46.85	50.57
Propspective median age	34.68	35.58	35.98	35.46	35.13	34.66	34.50
Proportion age 65+	0.12	0.14	0.17	0.21	0.25	0.29	0.34
Proportion RLE < 15 years	0.08	0.08	0.09	0.10	0.11	0.12	0.12

Israel

Detailed Human Capital Projections to 2060

Demographic indicators, Medium Scenario (SSP2)	2010	2020	2030	2040	2050	2060
Population (in millions)	7.42	9.26	11.30	13.52	15.90	18.38
Proportion age 65+	0.10	0.12	0.13	0.14	0.15	0.17
Proportion below age 20	0.35	0.35	0.34	0.32	0.31	0.30
	2005–10	2015–20	2025–30	2035–40	2045–50	2055–60
Total Fertility Rate	2.91	2.91	2.74	2.63	2.53	2.46
Life expectancy at birth (in years)						
Men	78.36	80.19	82.12	84.14	86.16	88.04
Women	82.87	85.11	87.21	89.19	91.19	93.10
Five-year immigration flow (in '000)	363.00	356.01	369.59	377.96	378.13	372.65
Five-year emigration flow (in '000)	89.88	76.76	91.22	107.66	122.69	137.21

Human Capital indicators, Medium Scenario (SSP2)	2010	2020	2030	2040	2050	2060
Population age 25+: highest educational attainment						
E1 - no education	0.03	0.02	0.01	0.01	0.00	0.00
E2 - incomplete primary	0.05	0.03	0.02	0.01	0.01	0.00
E3 - primary	0.16	0.14	0.12	0.10	0.09	0.07
E4 - lower secondary	0.18	0.18	0.17	0.16	0.14	0.12
E5 - upper secondary	0.24	0.30	0.35	0.39	0.43	0.46
E6 - post-secondary	0.33	0.33	0.33	0.33	0.33	0.34
Mean years of schooling (in years)	11.47	11.85	12.08	12.27	12.46	12.65
Gender gap (population age 25+): highest educational attainment (ratio male/female)						
E1 - no education	0.39	0.38	0.38	0.39	0.41	0.46
E2 - incomplete primary	0.98	1.00	1.07	1.12	1.15	1.15
E3 - primary	1.29	1.34	1.37	1.38	1.35	1.29
E4 - lower secondary	1.33	1.34	1.34	1.33	1.29	1.23
E5 - upper secondary	0.93	0.96	0.98	1.01	1.02	1.02
E6 - post-secondary	0.86	0.81	0.79	0.79	0.81	0.86
Mean years of schooling (male minus female)	-0.31	-0.52	-0.62	-0.61	-0.53	-0.39
Women age 20–39: highest educational attainment						
E1 - no education	0.01	0.00	0.00	0.00	0.00	0.00
E2 - incomplete primary	0.01	0.01	0.00	0.00	0.00	0.00
E3 - primary	0.10	0.08	0.07	0.06	0.05	0.04
E4 - lower secondary	0.17	0.15	0.13	0.11	0.09	0.08
E5 - upper secondary	0.38	0.43	0.46	0.48	0.50	0.52
E6 - post-secondary	0.33	0.33	0.34	0.35	0.36	0.37
Mean years of schooling (in years)	12.43	12.53	12.58	12.75	12.90	13.01

Education scenarios

GET: global education trend scenario (medium assumption also used for SSP2)

CER: constant enrolment rates scenario (assumption of no future improvements)

FT: fast track scenario (assumption of education expansion according to fastest historical experience)

Pyramids by Education, Medium Scenario

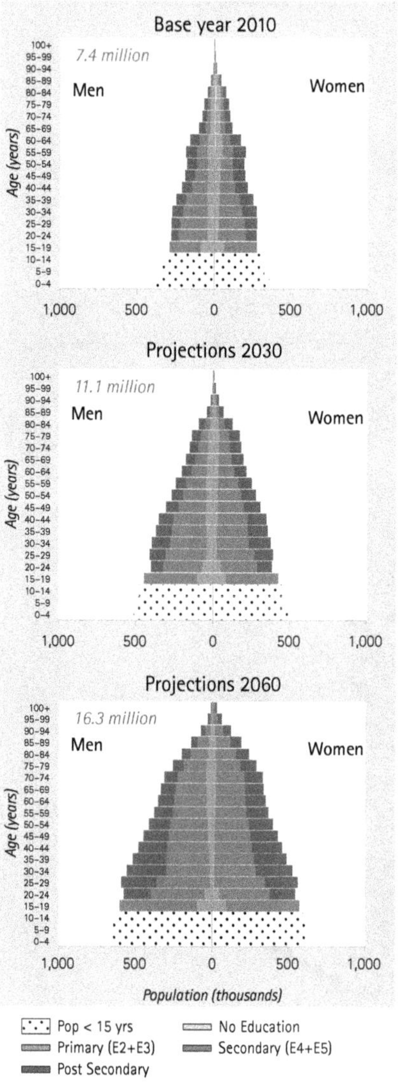

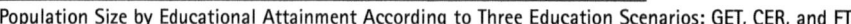

Population Size by Educational Attainment According to Three Education Scenarios: GET, CER, and FT

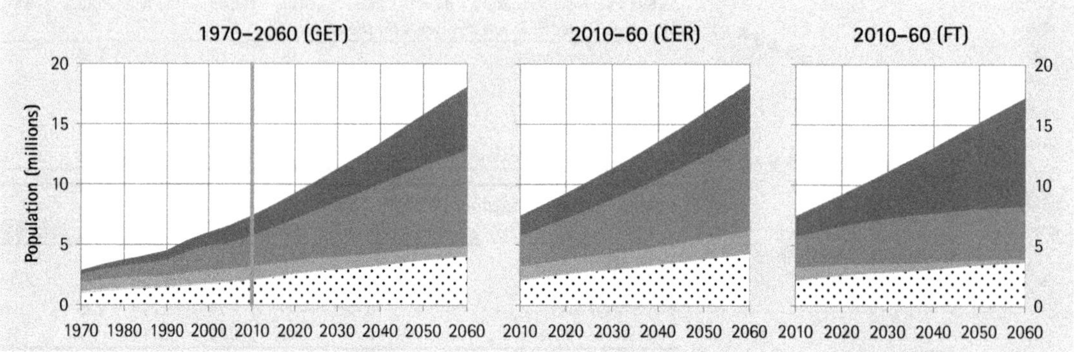

Israel (Continued)

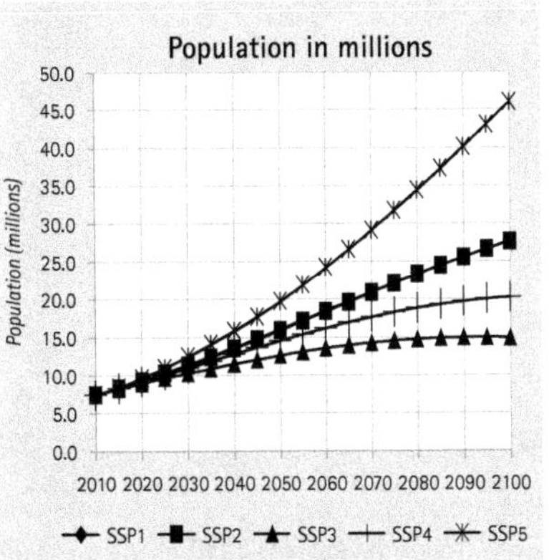

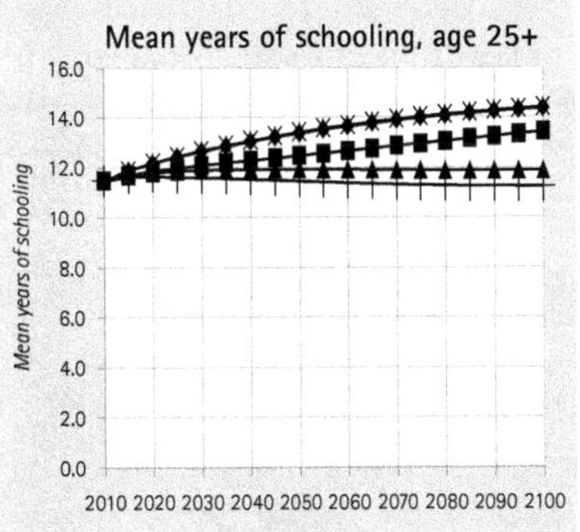

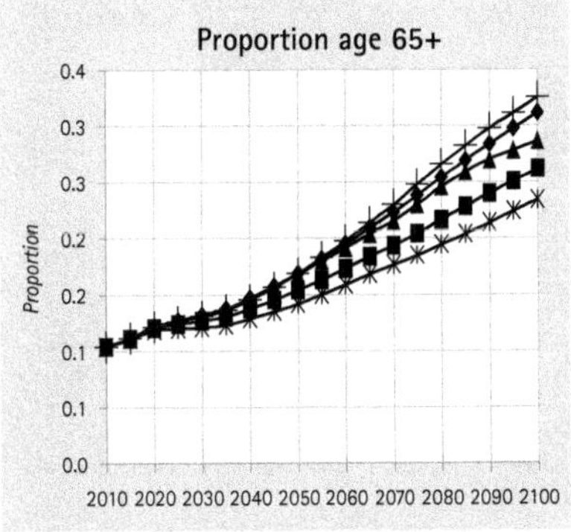

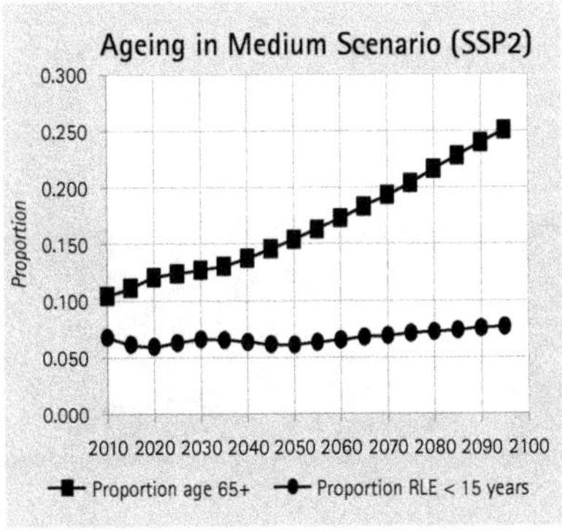

Alternative Scenarios to 2100

Projection Results by Scenario (SSP1–5)

	2010	2020	2030	2040	2050	2075	2100
Population (in millions)							
SSP1 - Rapid development	7.42	9.29	11.36	13.62	16.00	22.12	27.63
SSP2 - Medium	7.42	9.26	11.30	13.52	15.90	22.10	27.62
SSP3 - Stalled development	7.42	8.97	10.27	11.49	12.61	14.52	14.88
SSP4 - Inequality	7.42	9.17	10.95	12.76	14.52	18.27	20.23
SSP5 - Conventional development	7.42	9.60	12.46	15.81	19.70	31.70	45.96
Proportion age 65+							
SSP1 - Rapid development	0.10	0.12	0.13	0.15	0.17	0.24	0.31
SSP2 - Medium	0.10	0.12	0.13	0.14	0.15	0.20	0.26
SSP3 - Stalled development	0.10	0.12	0.13	0.15	0.17	0.23	0.29
SSP4 - Inequality	0.10	0.12	0.13	0.15	0.17	0.25	0.33
SSP5 - Conventional development	0.10	0.12	0.12	0.13	0.14	0.18	0.23
Proportion below age 20							
SSP1 - Rapid development	0.35	0.34	0.33	0.31	0.30	0.26	0.23
SSP2 - Medium	0.35	0.35	0.34	0.32	0.31	0.28	0.25
SSP3 - Stalled development	0.35	0.34	0.31	0.28	0.26	0.22	0.20
SSP4 - Inequality	0.35	0.34	0.31	0.29	0.27	0.22	0.20
SSP5 - Conventional development	0.35	0.35	0.36	0.35	0.34	0.32	0.29
Proportion of Women age 20–39 with at least secondary education							
SSP1 - Rapid development	0.88	0.94	0.96	0.97	0.97	0.99	0.99
SSP2 - Medium	0.88	0.91	0.93	0.94	0.95	0.98	0.99
SSP3 - Stalled development	0.88	0.90	0.90	0.90	0.90	0.90	0.90
SSP4 - Inequality	0.88	0.90	0.90	0.90	0.90	0.90	0.90
SSP5 - Conventional development	0.88	0.94	0.96	0.97	0.97	0.99	0.99
Mean years of schooling, age 25+							
SSP1 - Rapid development	11.47	12.16	12.64	13.03	13.36	13.97	14.36
SSP2 - Medium	11.47	11.85	12.08	12.27	12.46	12.94	13.42
SSP3 - Stalled development	11.47	11.78	11.89	11.92	11.92	11.88	11.87
SSP4 - Inequality	11.47	11.64	11.60	11.52	11.45	11.29	11.24
SSP5 - Conventional development	11.47	12.17	12.66	13.06	13.39	14.01	14.39

Demographic Assumptions Underlying SSPs

	2010–15	2020–25	2030–35	2040–45	2050–55	2075–80	2095–2100
Total fertility rate							
SSP1 - Rapid development	2.98	2.75	2.59	2.48	2.40	2.30	2.22
SSP2 - Medium	3.00	2.83	2.68	2.58	2.49	2.36	2.26
SSP3 - Stalled development	2.85	2.42	2.15	2.01	1.93	1.87	1.81
SSP4 - Inequality	2.86	2.47	2.22	2.08	2.00	1.93	1.88
SSP5 - Conventional development	3.12	3.16	3.14	3.06	3.00	2.87	2.77
Life expectancy at birth for females (in years)							
SSP1 - Rapid development	84.92	87.86	90.86	93.84	96.76	104.11	110.01
SSP2 - Medium	84.01	86.21	88.19	90.19	92.20	96.90	100.80
SSP3 - Stalled development	83.97	84.95	85.97	86.94	87.85	89.96	91.66
SSP4 - Inequality	84.43	86.46	88.38	90.32	92.27	96.79	100.54
SSP5 - Conventional development	84.92	87.86	90.86	93.84	96.76	104.11	110.01
Migration – net flow over five years (in thousands)							
SSP1 - Rapid development	270	277	270	250	225	107	0
SSP2 - Medium	261	268	266	255	238	125	0
SSP3 - Stalled development	225	137	132	123	112	56	0
SSP4 - Inequality	270	276	268	250	229	117	0
SSP5 - Conventional development	315	422	422	409	388	212	0

Ageing Indicators, Medium Scenario (SSP2)

	2010	2020	2030	2040	2050	2075	2095
Median age	30.10	30.25	31.13	32.19	33.71	37.65	41.10
Propspective median age	30.10	28.46	27.46	26.62	26.18	25.61	25.24
Proportion age 65+	0.10	0.12	0.13	0.14	0.15	0.20	0.25
Proportion RLE < 15 years	0.07	0.06	0.07	0.06	0.06	0.07	0.08

Italy

Detailed Human Capital Projections to 2060

Demographic indicators, Medium Scenario (SSP2)						
	2010	2020	2030	2040	2050	2060
Population (in millions)	60.55	61.53	61.74	61.77	61.14	59.83
Proportion age 65+	0.20	0.23	0.27	0.33	0.36	0.36
Proportion below age 20	0.19	0.18	0.17	0.16	0.16	0.16
	2005–10	2015–20	2025–30	2035–40	2045–50	2055–60
Total Fertility Rate	1.38	1.45	1.57	1.60	1.60	1.61
Life expectancy at birth (in years)						
Men	78.59	80.81	82.91	85.08	87.08	89.09
Women	83.97	86.21	88.31	90.41	92.39	94.40
Five-year immigration flow (in '000)	2009.17	711.92	740.37	757.97	758.94	748.31
Five-year emigration flow (in '000)	14.54	9.76	9.00	8.33	7.85	7.61

Human Capital indicators, Medium Scenario (SSP2)						
	2010	2020	2030	2040	2050	2060
Population age 25+: highest educational attainment						
E1 - no education	0.01	0.01	0.00	0.00	0.00	0.00
E2 - incomplete primary	0.04	0.02	0.01	0.01	0.00	0.00
E3 - primary	0.20	0.14	0.09	0.05	0.03	0.01
E4 - lower secondary	0.31	0.30	0.28	0.25	0.21	0.16
E5 - upper secondary	0.33	0.39	0.45	0.50	0.53	0.56
E6 - post-secondary	0.12	0.14	0.17	0.20	0.23	0.27
Mean years of schooling (in years)	9.81	10.61	11.35	12.00	12.56	13.09
Gender gap (population age 25+): highest educational attainment (ratio male/female)						
E1 - no education	0.61	0.66	0.79	0.94	0.99	0.98
E2 - incomplete primary	0.47	0.45	0.52	0.67	0.80	0.86
E3 - primary	0.72	0.65	0.60	0.61	0.73	0.90
E4 - lower secondary	1.28	1.27	1.24	1.20	1.17	1.15
E5 - upper secondary	1.09	1.07	1.06	1.05	1.04	1.04
E6 - post-secondary	0.93	0.86	0.81	0.80	0.82	0.86
Mean years of schooling (male minus female)	0.42	0.20	-0.01	-0.17	-0.25	-0.22
Women age 20–39: highest educational attainment						
E1 - no education	0.00	0.00	0.00	0.00	0.00	0.00
E2 - incomplete primary	0.00	0.00	0.00	0.00	0.00	0.00
E3 - primary	0.02	0.01	0.01	0.01	0.00	0.00
E4 - lower secondary	0.24	0.15	0.09	0.06	0.04	0.03
E5 - upper secondary	0.56	0.62	0.64	0.64	0.63	0.63
E6 - post-secondary	0.18	0.22	0.26	0.30	0.32	0.34
Mean years of schooling (in years)	12.15	12.89	13.48	13.81	14.03	14.18

Education scenarios

GET : global education trend scenario (medium assumption also used for SSP2)

CER: constant enrolment rates scenario (assumption of no future improvements)

FT: fast track scenario (assumption of education expansion according to fastest historical experience)

Pyramids by Education, Medium Scenario

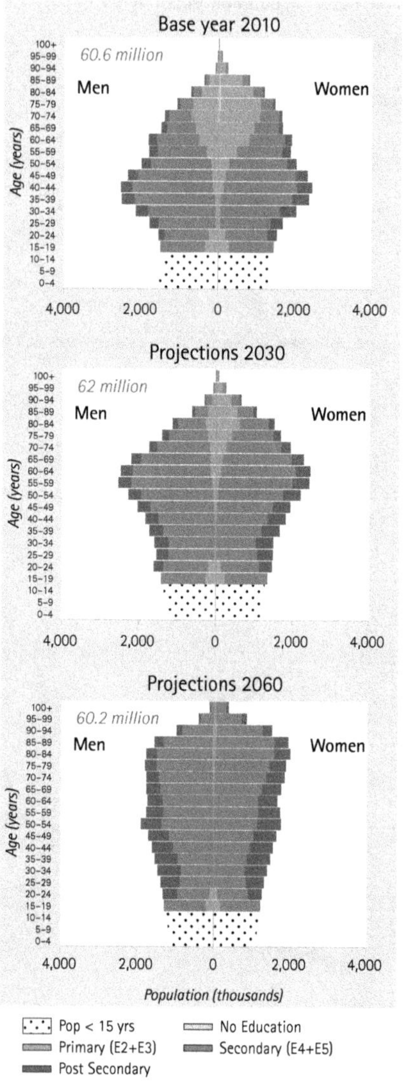

Population Size by Educational Attainment According to Three Education Scenarios: GET, CER, and FT

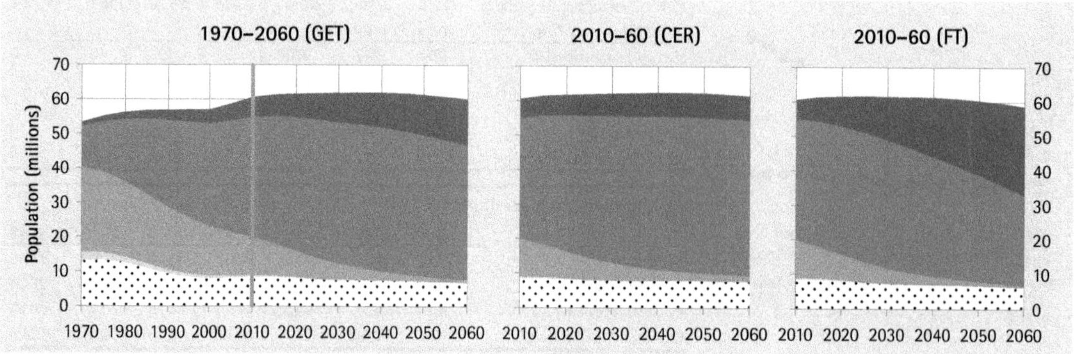

Italy (Continued)

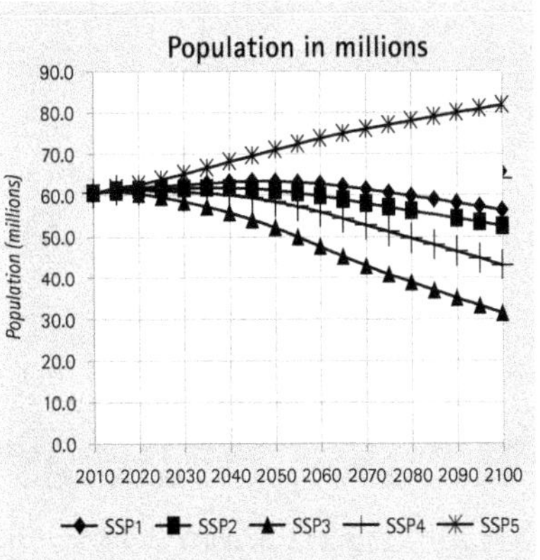

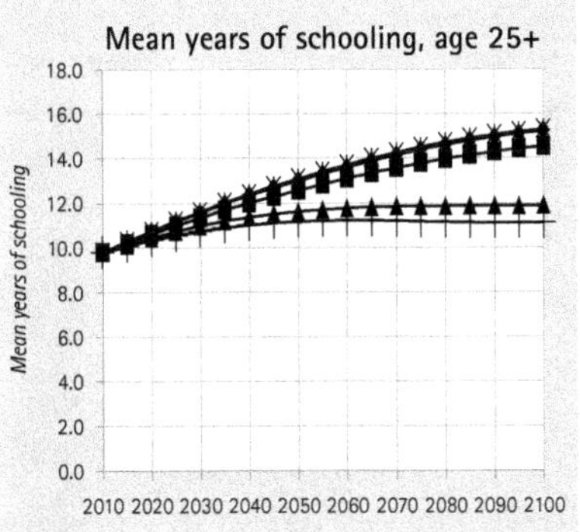

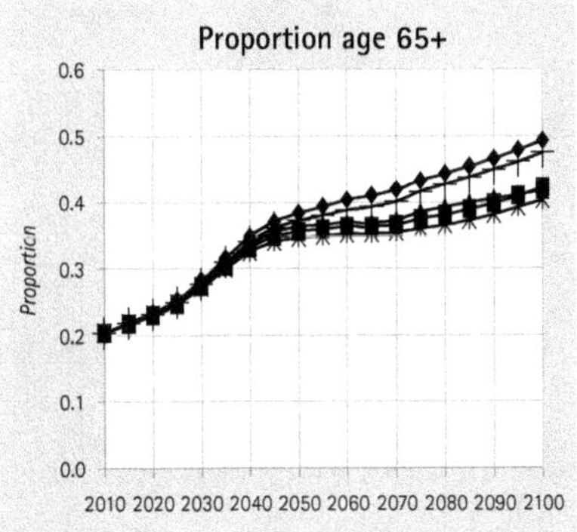

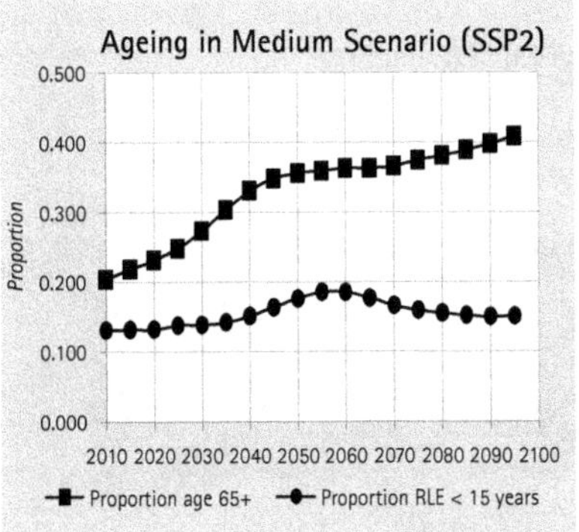

Alternative Scenarios to 2100

Projection Results by Scenario (SSP1–5)

	2010	2020	2030	2040	2050	2075	2100
Population (in millions)							
SSP1 - Rapid development	60.55	61.86	62.57	63.23	63.36	60.65	56.39
SSP2 - Medium	60.55	61.53	61.74	61.77	61.14	57.10	52.54
SSP3 - Stalled development	60.55	60.44	58.44	55.79	52.14	40.87	31.43
SSP4 - Inequality	60.55	61.27	60.82	60.04	58.44	51.20	43.09
SSP5 - Conventional development	60.55	62.71	65.19	68.07	70.96	76.98	81.68
Proportion age 65+							
SSP1 - Rapid development	0.20	0.23	0.28	0.35	0.38	0.43	0.49
SSP2 - Medium	0.20	0.23	0.27	0.33	0.36	0.37	0.42
SSP3 - Stalled development	0.20	0.23	0.27	0.34	0.36	0.39	0.42
SSP4 - Inequality	0.20	0.23	0.28	0.34	0.37	0.42	0.47
SSP5 - Conventional development	0.20	0.23	0.27	0.33	0.35	0.36	0.40
Proportion below age 20							
SSP1 - Rapid development	0.19	0.18	0.16	0.16	0.15	0.14	0.13
SSP2 - Medium	0.19	0.18	0.17	0.16	0.16	0.16	0.15
SSP3 - Stalled development	0.19	0.18	0.15	0.14	0.14	0.13	0.13
SSP4 - Inequality	0.19	0.18	0.15	0.15	0.14	0.13	0.12
SSP5 - Conventional development	0.19	0.18	0.18	0.18	0.19	0.19	0.18
Proportion of Women age 20–39 with at least secondary education							
SSP1 - Rapid development	0.97	0.99	0.99	1.00	1.00	1.00	1.00
SSP2 - Medium	0.97	0.99	0.99	0.99	1.00	1.00	1.00
SSP3 - Stalled development	0.97	0.97	0.97	0.97	0.97	0.97	0.97
SSP4 - Inequality	0.97	0.97	0.97	0.97	0.97	0.97	0.97
SSP5 - Conventional development	0.97	0.99	0.99	1.00	1.00	1.00	1.00
Mean years of schooling, age 25+							
SSP1 - Rapid development	9.81	10.72	11.58	12.34	12.99	14.38	15.22
SSP2 - Medium	9.81	10.61	11.35	12.00	12.56	13.78	14.54
SSP3 - Stalled development	9.81	10.44	10.98	11.37	11.62	11.85	11.88
SSP4 - Inequality	9.81	10.34	10.74	11.02	11.16	11.17	11.11
SSP5 - Conventional development	9.81	10.74	11.61	12.39	13.08	14.50	15.29

Demographic Assumptions Underlying SSPs

	2010–15	2020–25	2030–35	2040–45	2050–55	2075–80	2095–2100
Total fertility rate							
SSP1 - Rapid development	1.40	1.48	1.54	1.56	1.56	1.59	1.62
SSP2 - Medium	1.39	1.51	1.60	1.60	1.60	1.63	1.65
SSP3 - Stalled development	1.34	1.32	1.31	1.30	1.29	1.33	1.36
SSP4 - Inequality	1.34	1.34	1.34	1.34	1.33	1.37	1.40
SSP5 - Conventional development	1.47	1.70	1.87	1.93	1.95	1.99	2.03
Life expectancy at birth for females (in years)							
SSP1 - Rapid development	86.17	89.27	92.26	95.10	98.00	105.61	111.75
SSP2 - Medium	85.11	87.31	89.41	91.39	93.40	98.50	102.59
SSP3 - Stalled development	85.19	86.34	87.32	88.19	89.14	91.48	93.42
SSP4 - Inequality	85.71	87.86	89.82	91.67	93.60	98.37	102.24
SSP5 - Conventional development	86.17	89.27	92.26	95.10	98.00	105.61	111.75
Migration – net flow over five years (in thousands)							
SSP1 - Rapid development	1136	713	730	719	686	252	0
SSP2 - Medium	1119	709	730	735	726	294	0
SSP3 - Stalled development	946	356	367	366	358	145	0
SSP4 - Inequality	1135	711	727	723	706	291	0
SSP5 - Conventional development	1326	1074	1117	1145	1146	481	0

Ageing Indicators, Medium Scenario (SSP2)

	2010	2020	2030	2040	2050	2075	2095
Median age	43.17	46.98	50.11	51.57	52.56	53.93	57.06
Propspective median age	43.17	44.99	46.27	45.92	45.08	41.63	40.78
Proportion age 65+	0.20	0.23	0.27	0.33	0.36	0.37	0.41
Proportion RLE < 15 years	0.13	0.13	0.14	0.15	0.18	0.16	0.15

Jamaica

Detailed Human Capital Projections to 2060

Demographic indicators, Medium Scenario (SSP2)	2010	2020	2030	2040	2050	2060
Population (in millions)	2.74	2.85	2.93	2.93	2.87	2.75
Proportion age 65+	0.08	0.09	0.13	0.18	0.21	0.25
Proportion below age 20	0.39	0.33	0.30	0.26	0.24	0.22
	2005–10	2015–20	2025–30	2035–40	2045–50	2055–60
Total Fertility Rate	2.40	2.11	1.95	1.87	1.81	1.76
Life expectancy at birth (in years)						
Men	69.56	72.69	75.50	78.00	80.13	82.13
Women	74.97	77.69	80.01	82.10	84.09	86.08
Five-year immigration flow (in '000)	2.61	2.57	2.67	2.74	2.74	2.70
Five-year emigration flow (in '000)	102.37	84.03	78.48	71.84	65.37	57.99

Human Capital indicators, Medium Scenario (SSP2)	2010	2020	2030	2040	2050	2060
Population age 25+: highest educational attainment						
E1 - no education	0.01	0.00	0.00	0.00	0.00	0.00
E2 - incomplete primary	0.08	0.04	0.02	0.01	0.01	0.00
E3 - primary	0.17	0.13	0.10	0.08	0.07	0.06
E4 - lower secondary	0.50	0.53	0.52	0.51	0.47	0.43
E5 - upper secondary	0.09	0.11	0.13	0.16	0.18	0.21
E6 - post-secondary	0.16	0.18	0.21	0.24	0.27	0.30
Mean years of schooling (in years)	9.23	9.78	10.26	10.62	10.94	11.21
Gender gap (population age 25+): highest educational attainment (ratio male/female)						
E1 - no education	1.35	1.35	1.34	1.32	1.28	1.22
E2 - incomplete primary	1.05	1.09	1.17	1.30	1.48	1.57
E3 - primary	1.26	1.31	1.36	1.39	1.40	1.36
E4 - lower secondary	1.12	1.14	1.16	1.16	1.14	1.12
E5 - upper secondary	0.72	0.77	0.82	0.88	0.93	0.96
E6 - post-secondary	0.63	0.63	0.66	0.70	0.75	0.82
Mean years of schooling (male minus female)	−0.68	−0.69	−0.68	−0.64	−0.55	−0.42
Women age 20–39: highest educational attainment						
E1 - no education	0.00	0.00	0.00	0.00	0.00	0.00
E2 - incomplete primary	0.01	0.00	0.00	0.00	0.00	0.00
E3 - primary	0.05	0.05	0.05	0.04	0.04	0.04
E4 - lower secondary	0.55	0.48	0.42	0.36	0.31	0.26
E5 - upper secondary	0.15	0.18	0.21	0.23	0.26	0.29
E6 - post-secondary	0.25	0.29	0.33	0.36	0.39	0.41
Mean years of schooling (in years)	10.79	10.99	11.38	11.64	11.86	12.03

Education scenarios

GET: global education trend scenario (medium assumption also used for SSP2)

CER: constant enrolment rates scenario (assumption of no future improvements)

FT: Fast track scenario (assumption of education expansion according to fastest historical experience)

Pyramids by Education, Medium Scenario

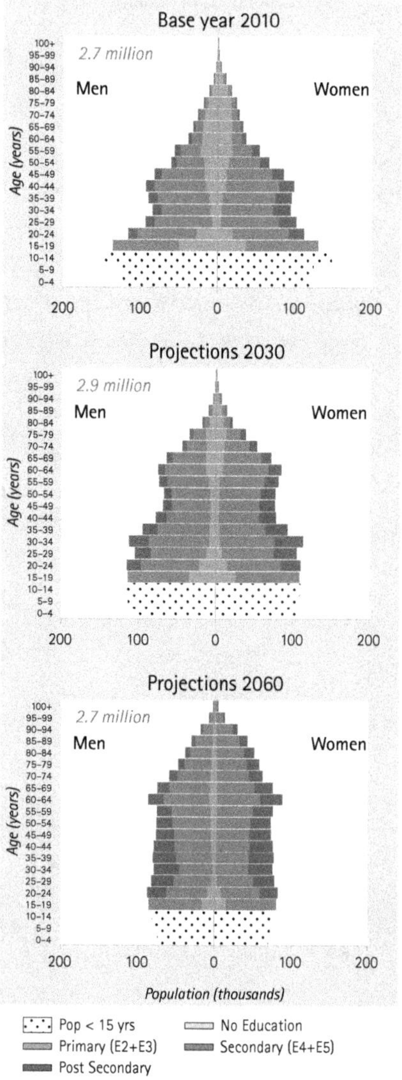

Population Size by Educational Attainment According to Three Education Scenarios: GET, CER, and FT

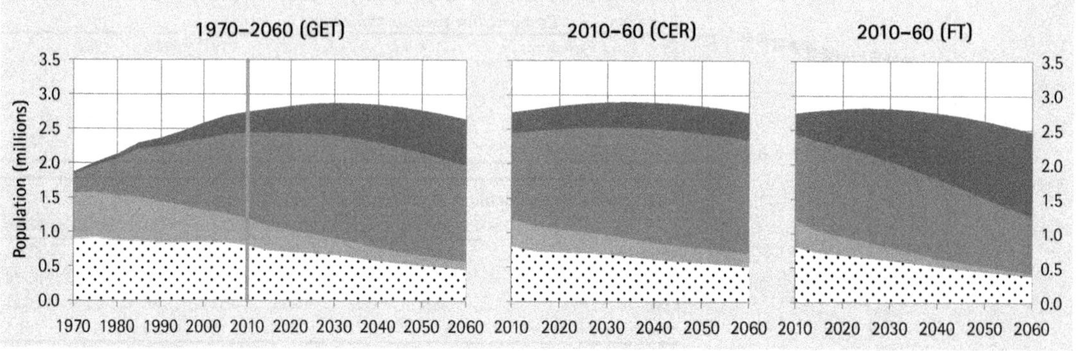

Jamaica (Continued)

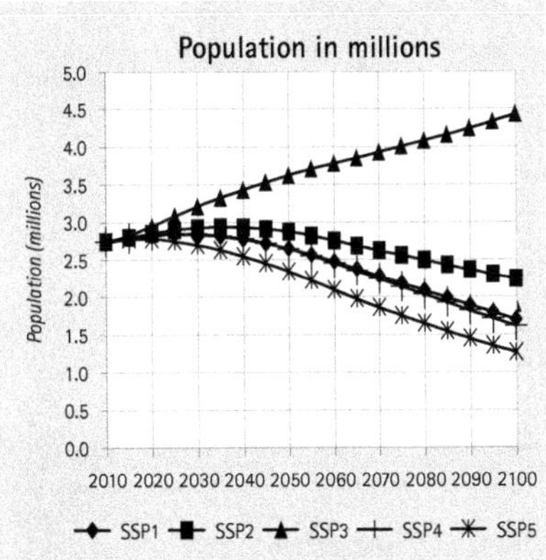

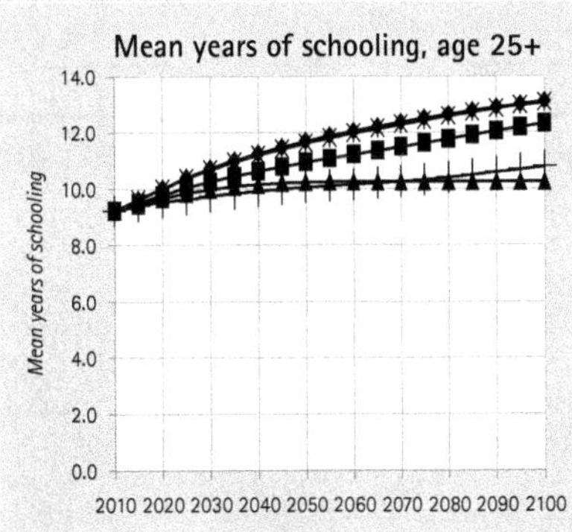

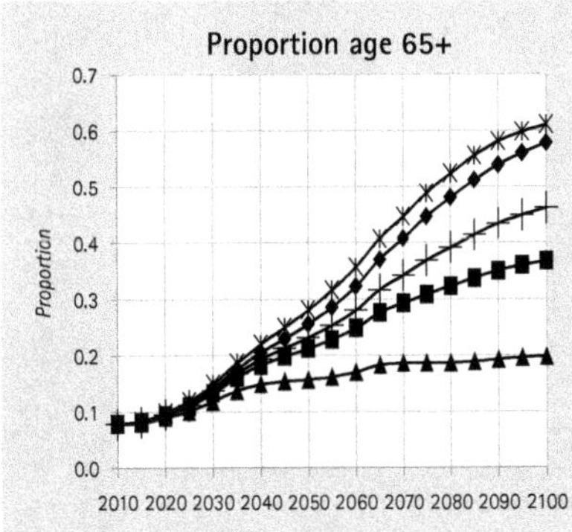

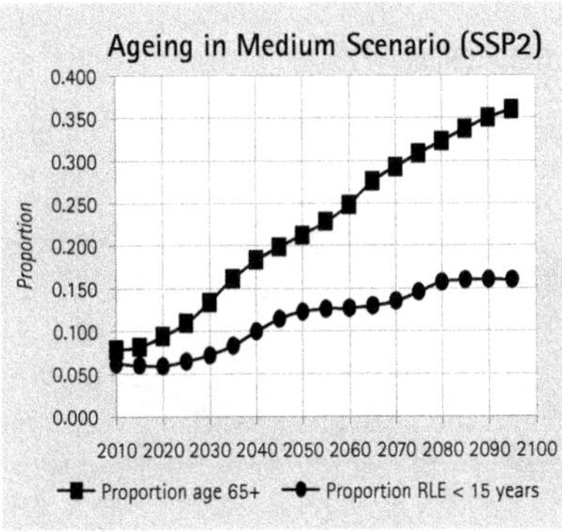

Alternative Scenarios to 2100

Projection Results by Scenario (SSP1–5)

	2010	2020	2030	2040	2050	2075	2100
Population (in millions)							
SSP1 - Rapid development	2.74	2.82	2.83	2.77	2.65	2.18	1.69
SSP2 - Medium	2.74	2.85	2.93	2.93	2.87	2.56	2.24
SSP3 - Stalled development	2.74	2.95	3.21	3.43	3.62	4.00	4.43
SSP4 - Inequality	2.74	2.83	2.84	2.78	2.64	2.14	1.61
SSP5 - Conventional development	2.74	2.78	2.69	2.55	2.34	1.75	1.26
Proportion age 65+							
SSP1 - Rapid development	0.08	0.10	0.14	0.21	0.26	0.45	0.58
SSP2 - Medium	0.08	0.09	0.13	0.18	0.21	0.31	0.37
SSP3 - Stalled development	0.08	0.09	0.12	0.15	0.16	0.19	0.20
SSP4 - Inequality	0.08	0.09	0.14	0.19	0.23	0.37	0.46
SSP5 - Conventional development	0.08	0.10	0.15	0.22	0.28	0.49	0.61
Proportion below age 20							
SSP1 - Rapid development	0.39	0.32	0.26	0.21	0.17	0.11	0.08
SSP2 - Medium	0.39	0.33	0.30	0.26	0.24	0.19	0.16
SSP3 - Stalled development	0.39	0.34	0.33	0.32	0.30	0.28	0.27
SSP4 - Inequality	0.39	0.32	0.27	0.23	0.19	0.13	0.10
SSP5 - Conventional development	0.39	0.32	0.26	0.21	0.17	0.10	0.07
Proportion of Women age 20–39 with at least secondary education							
SSP1 - Rapid development	0.95	0.97	0.97	0.97	0.98	0.98	0.99
SSP2 - Medium	0.95	0.94	0.95	0.95	0.96	0.97	0.99
SSP3 - Stalled development	0.95	0.94	0.94	0.94	0.94	0.94	0.94
SSP4 - Inequality	0.95	0.88	0.85	0.85	0.85	0.85	0.85
SSP5 - Conventional development	0.95	0.97	0.97	0.97	0.98	0.98	0.99
Mean years of schooling, age 25+							
SSP1 - Rapid development	9.23	10.01	10.71	11.25	11.68	12.50	13.11
SSP2 - Medium	9.23	9.78	10.26	10.62	10.94	11.62	12.31
SSP3 - Stalled development	9.23	9.66	9.98	10.15	10.23	10.25	10.25
SSP4 - Inequality	9.23	9.55	9.74	9.92	10.05	10.32	10.78
SSP5 - Conventional development	9.23	10.00	10.67	11.19	11.61	12.43	13.07

Demographic Assumptions Underlying SSPs

	2010–15	2020–25	2030–35	2040–45	2050–55	2075–80	2095–2100
Total fertility rate							
SSP1 - Rapid development	2.06	1.65	1.43	1.34	1.28	1.18	1.18
SSP2 - Medium	2.21	2.04	1.90	1.85	1.77	1.61	1.60
SSP3 - Stalled development	2.34	2.42	2.44	2.42	2.39	2.24	2.27
SSP4 - Inequality	2.10	1.75	1.53	1.43	1.36	1.24	1.24
SSP5 - Conventional development	2.06	1.65	1.43	1.34	1.28	1.18	1.18
Life expectancy at birth for females (in years)							
SSP1 - Rapid development	78.44	81.23	84.10	87.03	89.98	97.45	103.47
SSP2 - Medium	76.49	78.89	81.01	83.09	85.09	90.09	94.10
SSP3 - Stalled development	77.75	78.66	79.50	80.46	81.29	83.41	85.15
SSP4 - Inequality	78.07	79.93	81.72	83.61	85.42	90.06	93.91
SSP5 - Conventional development	78.44	81.23	84.10	87.03	89.98	97.45	103.47
Migration – net flow over five years (in thousands)							
SSP1 - Rapid development	−87	−79	−70	−60	−50	−14	0
SSP2 - Medium	−90	−82	−74	−68	−60	−21	0
SSP3 - Stalled development	−72	−40	−37	−36	−35	−15	0
SSP4 - Inequality	−87	−78	−69	−58	−46	−12	0
SSP5 - Conventional development	−101	−117	−103	−89	−73	−21	0

Ageing Indicators, Medium Scenario (SSP2)

	2010	2020	2030	2040	2050	2075	2095
Median age	26.95	29.96	33.93	38.42	41.76	49.24	52.85
Propspective median age	26.95	27.88	29.81	32.57	34.40	37.78	37.89
Proportion age 65+	0.08	0.09	0.13	0.18	0.21	0.31	0.36
Proportion RLE < 15 years	0.06	0.06	0.07	0.10	0.12	0.15	0.16

Japan

Detailed Human Capital Projections to 2060

Demographic indicators, Medium Scenario (SSP2)	2010	2020	2030	2040	2050	2060
Population (in millions)	126.54	124.53	119.93	114.02	107.48	100.85
Proportion age 65+	0.23	0.29	0.31	0.36	0.40	0.42
Proportion below age 20	0.18	0.17	0.15	0.14	0.14	0.14
	2005–10	2015–20	2025–30	2035–40	2045–50	2055–60
Total Fertility Rate	1.32	1.38	1.40	1.40	1.40	1.42
Life expectancy at birth (in years)						
Men	79.24	81.04	83.18	85.25	87.26	89.32
Women	86.05	88.11	90.21	92.19	94.19	96.20
Five-year immigration flow (in '000)	439.12	430.97	448.07	458.58	459.01	452.63
Five-year emigration flow (in '000)	170.93	108.65	94.84	83.64	73.16	65.64

Human Capital indicators, Medium Scenario (SSP2)	2010	2020	2030	2040	2050	2060
Population age 25+: highest educational attainment						
E1 - no education	0.00	0.00	0.00	0.00	0.00	0.00
E2 - incomplete primary	0.01	0.01	0.00	0.00	0.00	0.00
E3 - primary	0.11	0.07	0.04	0.02	0.01	0.00
E4 - lower secondary	0.06	0.05	0.04	0.03	0.02	0.02
E5 - upper secondary	0.46	0.44	0.42	0.38	0.33	0.29
E6 - post-secondary	0.35	0.42	0.50	0.57	0.64	0.69
Mean years of schooling (in years)	12.46	13.05	13.59	14.06	14.42	14.69
Gender gap (population age 25+): highest educational attainment (ratio male/female)						
E1 - no education	0.71	0.78	0.85	0.91	0.94	0.95
E2 - incomplete primary	0.34	0.33	0.34	0.45	0.78	1.04
E3 - primary	0.68	0.62	0.58	0.62	0.81	1.05
E4 - lower secondary	1.48	1.39	1.30	1.25	1.28	1.28
E5 - upper secondary	0.94	0.95	0.96	0.97	1.00	1.02
E6 - post-secondary	1.18	1.11	1.06	1.02	0.99	0.98
Mean years of schooling (male minus female)	0.51	0.38	0.23	0.09	−0.02	−0.06
Women age 20–39: highest educational attainment						
E1 - no education	0.00	0.00	0.00	0.00	0.00	0.00
E2 - incomplete primary	0.00	0.00	0.00	0.00	0.00	0.00
E3 - primary	0.01	0.00	0.00	0.00	0.00	0.00
E4 - lower secondary	0.03	0.02	0.01	0.01	0.01	0.00
E5 - upper secondary	0.41	0.34	0.29	0.26	0.24	0.23
E6 - post-secondary	0.55	0.64	0.69	0.73	0.75	0.77
Mean years of schooling (in years)	14.03	14.46	14.72	14.89	14.98	15.03

Education scenarios

GET: global education trend scenario (medium assumption also used for SSP2)

CER: constant enrolment rates scenario (assumption of no future improvements)

FT: Fast track scenario (assumption of education expansion according to fastest historical experience)

Pyramids by Education, Medium Scenario

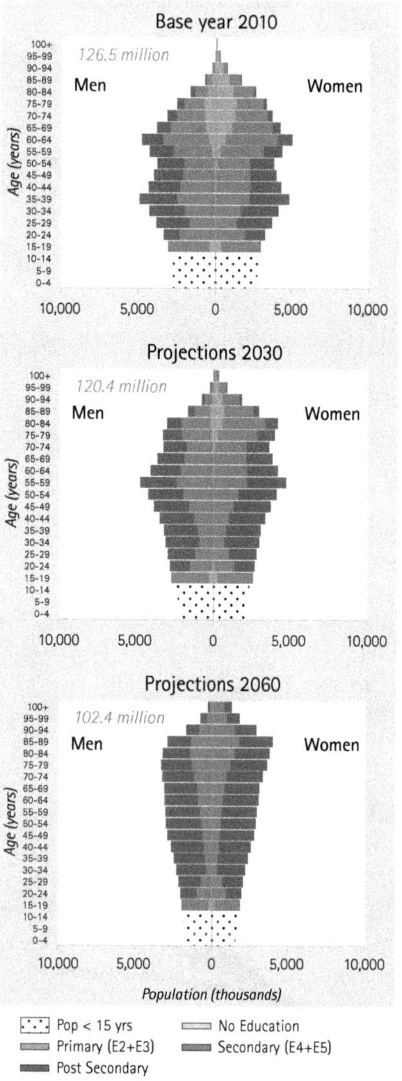

Population Size by Educational Attainment According to Three Education Scenarios: GET, CER, and FT

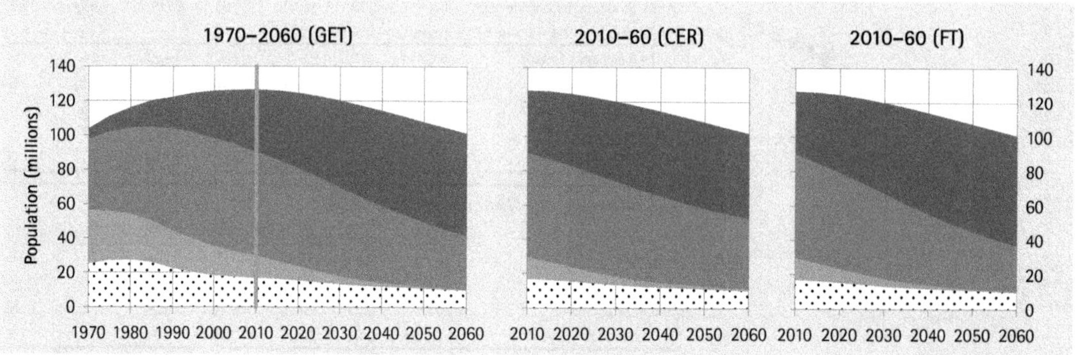

Japan (Continued)

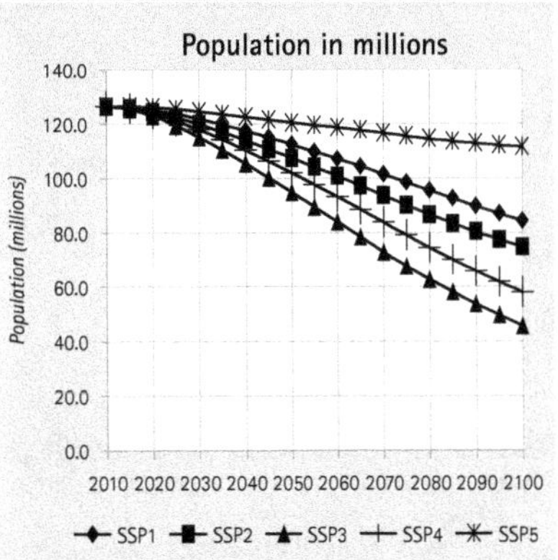

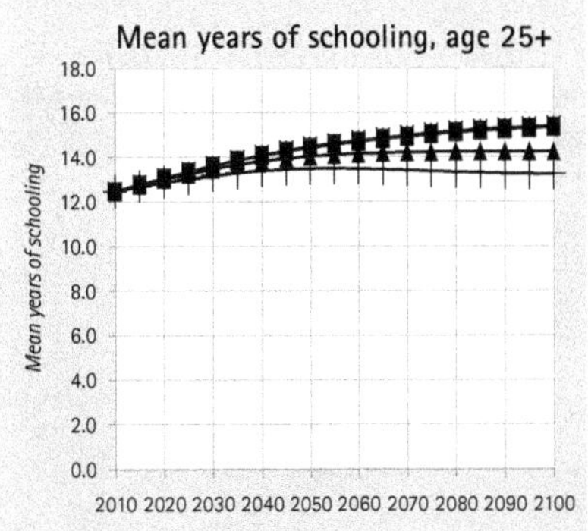

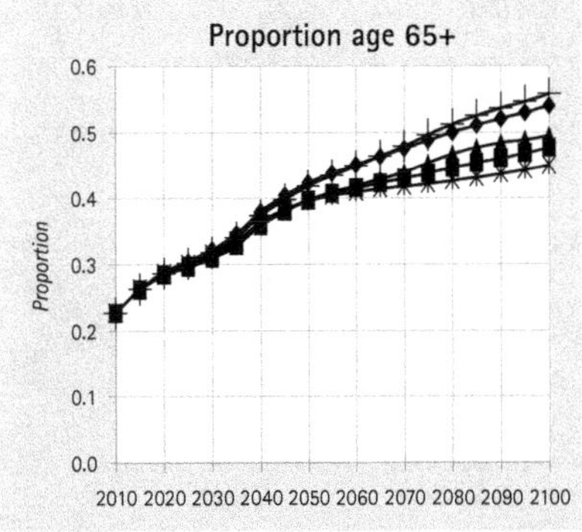

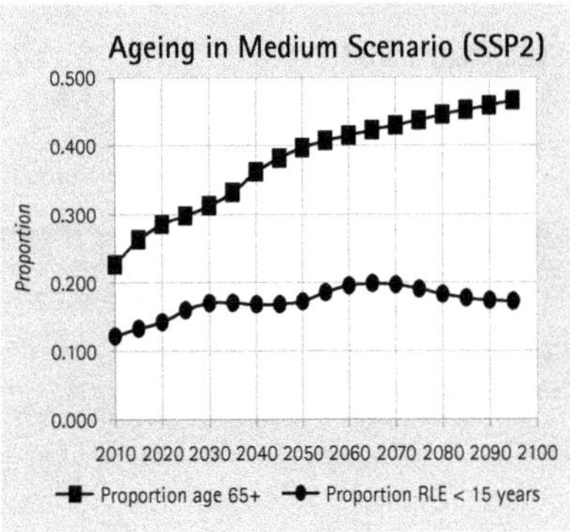

Alternative Scenarios to 2100

Projection Results by Senario (SSP1–5)

	2010	2020	2030	2040	2050	2075	2100
Population (in millions)							
SSP1 - Rapid development	126.54	125.24	121.85	117.47	112.49	98.52	84.43
SSP2 - Medium	126.54	124.53	119.93	114.02	107.48	90.16	74.74
SSP3 - Stalled development	126.54	123.00	115.12	105.37	94.85	67.63	45.66
SSP4 - Inequality	126.54	123.86	117.92	110.41	102.00	79.10	57.99
SSP5 - Conventional development	126.54	126.13	124.65	122.57	120.45	115.53	111.56
Proportion age 65+							
SSP1 - Rapid development	0.23	0.29	0.32	0.38	0.42	0.49	0.54
SSP2 - Medium	0.23	0.29	0.31	0.36	0.40	0.44	0.48
SSP3 - Stalled development	0.23	0.28	0.31	0.36	0.40	0.45	0.49
SSP4 - Inequality	0.23	0.29	0.32	0.37	0.42	0.50	0.56
SSP5 - Conventional development	0.23	0.29	0.32	0.36	0.40	0.42	0.45
Proportion below age 20							
SSP1 - Rapid development	0.18	0.17	0.15	0.14	0.13	0.12	0.11
SSP2 - Medium	0.18	0.17	0.15	0.14	0.14	0.13	0.13
SSP3 - Stalled development	0.18	0.16	0.14	0.12	0.12	0.10	0.10
SSP4 - Inequality	0.18	0.16	0.14	0.12	0.12	0.10	0.09
SSP5 - Conventional development	0.18	0.17	0.17	0.16	0.16	0.16	0.16
Proportion of Women age 20–39 with at least secondary education							
SSP1 - Rapid development	0.99	1.00	1.00	1.00	1.00	1.00	1.00
SSP2 - Medium	0.99	1.00	1.00	1.00	1.00	1.00	1.00
SSP3 - Stalled development	0.99	0.99	0.99	0.99	0.99	0.99	0.99
SSP4 - Inequality	0.99	0.99	0.99	0.99	0.99	0.99	0.99
SSP5 - Conventional development	0.99	1.00	1.00	1.00	1.00	1.00	1.00
Mean years of schooling, age 25+							
SSP1 - Rapid development	12.46	13.06	13.60	14.07	14.43	15.02	15.36
SSP2 - Medium	12.46	13.05	13.59	14.06	14.42	15.01	15.32
SSP3 - Stalled development	12.46	13.00	13.46	13.81	14.03	14.21	14.23
SSP4 - Inequality	12.46	12.87	13.16	13.37	13.47	13.36	13.23
SSP5 - Conventional development	12.46	13.06	13.60	14.08	14.45	15.06	15.38

Demographic Assumptions Underlying SSPs

	2010–15	2020–25	2030–35	2040–45	2050–55	2075–80	2095–2100
Total fertility rate							
SSP1 - Rapid development	1.37	1.38	1.39	1.40	1.41	1.46	1.51
SSP2 - Medium	1.37	1.39	1.40	1.40	1.41	1.47	1.51
SSP3 - Stalled development	1.31	1.19	1.11	1.08	1.07	1.12	1.15
SSP4 - Inequality	1.31	1.20	1.14	1.11	1.10	1.14	1.18
SSP5 - Conventional development	1.44	1.59	1.69	1.73	1.76	1.83	1.89
Life expectancy at birth for females (in years)							
SSP1 - Rapid development	88.10	91.08	93.99	96.89	99.76	107.20	113.20
SSP2 - Medium	87.11	89.21	91.21	93.19	95.20	100.19	104.21
SSP3 - Stalled development	87.12	88.14	89.05	89.93	90.86	93.22	95.15
SSP4 - Inequality	87.58	89.66	91.57	93.45	95.35	100.10	103.89
SSP5 - Conventional development	88.10	91.08	93.99	96.89	99.76	107.20	113.20
Migration – net flow over five years (in thousands)							
SSP1 - Rapid development	291	337	360	368	363	132	0
SSP2 - Medium	300	342	368	383	386	150	0
SSP3 - Stalled development	242	170	185	192	192	73	0
SSP4 - Inequality	291	336	356	361	356	134	0
SSP5 - Conventional development	340	501	537	565	578	237	0

Ageing Indicators, Medium Scenario (SSP2)

	2010	2020	2030	2040	2050	2075	2095
Median age	44.67	48.40	52.31	54.90	56.38	59.81	62.09
Propspective median age	44.67	46.45	48.56	49.35	48.93	47.70	46.03
Proportion age 65+	0.23	0.29	0.31	0.36	0.40	0.44	0.47
Proportion RLE < 15 years	0.12	0.14	0.17	0.17	0.17	0.19	0.17

Jordan

Detailed Human Capital Projections to 2060

Demographic indicators, Medium Scenario (SSP2)	2010	2020	2030	2040	2050	2060
Population (in millions)	6.19	7.98	9.84	11.60	13.21	14.58
Proportion age 65+	0.04	0.04	0.05	0.08	0.11	0.16
Proportion below age 20	0.48	0.41	0.35	0.31	0.27	0.25
	2005–10	2015–20	2025–30	2035–40	2045–50	2055–60
Total Fertility Rate	3.27	2.60	2.24	2.05	1.92	1.84
Life expectancy at birth (in years)						
Men	71.65	74.03	76.14	78.02	80.02	81.98
Women	74.29	77.09	79.39	81.49	83.59	85.61
Five-year immigration flow (in '000)	379.88	371.71	385.74	394.11	393.85	387.94
Five-year emigration flow (in '000)	176.87	168.36	201.66	222.72	237.65	244.85

Human Capital indicators, Medium Scenario (SSP2)	2010	2020	2030	2040	2050	2060
Population age 25+: highest educational attainment						
E1 - no education	0.15	0.08	0.04	0.02	0.01	0.01
E2 - incomplete primary	0.05	0.04	0.02	0.01	0.01	0.00
E3 - primary	0.14	0.12	0.10	0.08	0.06	0.04
E4 - lower secondary	0.15	0.15	0.15	0.13	0.11	0.09
E5 - upper secondary	0.23	0.27	0.29	0.30	0.31	0.30
E6 - post-secondary	0.28	0.34	0.40	0.45	0.50	0.55
Mean years of schooling (in years)	9.57	10.93	11.93	12.63	13.16	13.59
Gender gap (population age 25+): highest educational attainment (ratio male/female)						
E1 - no education	0.59	0.64	0.73	0.88	1.01	1.11
E2 - incomplete primary	1.04	1.04	1.04	1.07	1.14	1.21
E3 - primary	1.13	1.20	1.23	1.24	1.24	1.23
E4 - lower secondary	1.26	1.32	1.37	1.40	1.38	1.33
E5 - upper secondary	1.07	1.04	1.06	1.09	1.09	1.08
E6 - post-secondary	1.03	0.88	0.84	0.84	0.86	0.90
Mean years of schooling (male minus female)	0.79	0.07	-0.30	-0.44	-0.43	-0.33
Women age 20–39: highest educational attainment						
E1 - no education	0.05	0.02	0.01	0.00	0.00	0.00
E2 - incomplete primary	0.03	0.01	0.01	0.00	0.00	0.00
E3 - primary	0.11	0.07	0.05	0.03	0.02	0.02
E4 - lower secondary	0.17	0.14	0.10	0.08	0.06	0.05
E5 - upper secondary	0.33	0.35	0.36	0.36	0.36	0.36
E6 - post-secondary	0.31	0.41	0.48	0.52	0.55	0.57
Mean years of schooling (in years)	11.21	12.46	13.32	13.70	13.90	14.04

Education scenarios

GET: global education trend scenario (medium assumption also used for SSP2)

CER: constant enrolment rates scenario (assumption of no future improvements)

FT: Fast track scenario (assumption of education expansion according to fastest historical experience)

Pyramids by Education, Medium Scenario

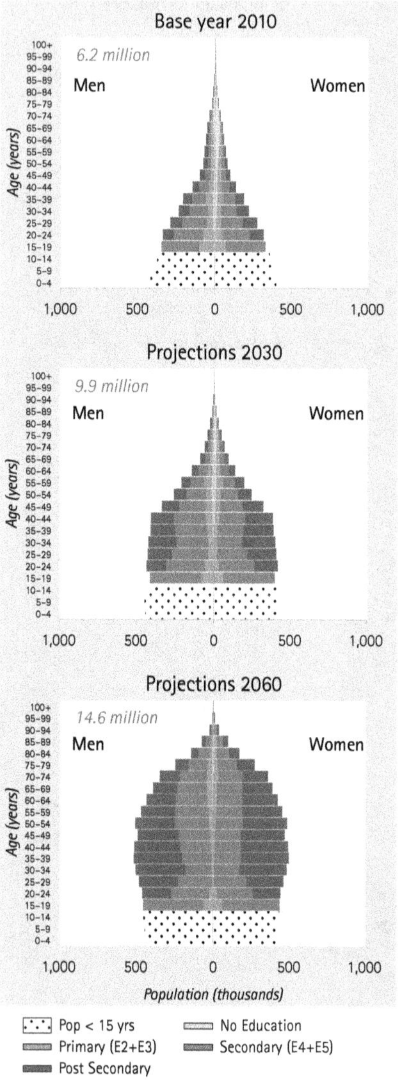

Population Size by Educational Attainment According to Three Education Scenarios: GET, CER, and FT

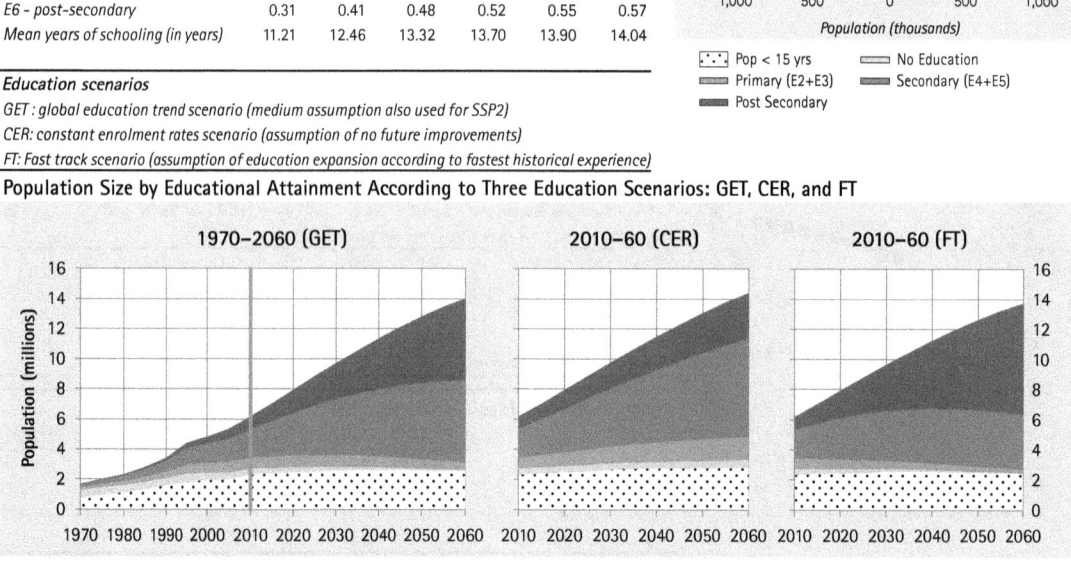

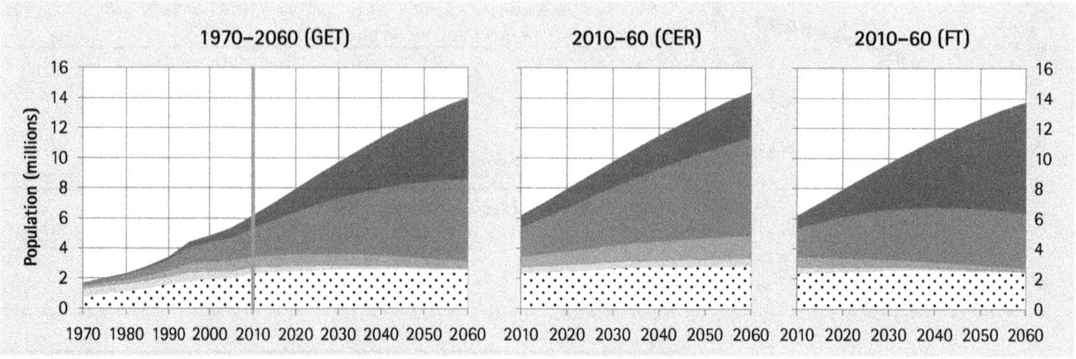

Jordan (Continued)

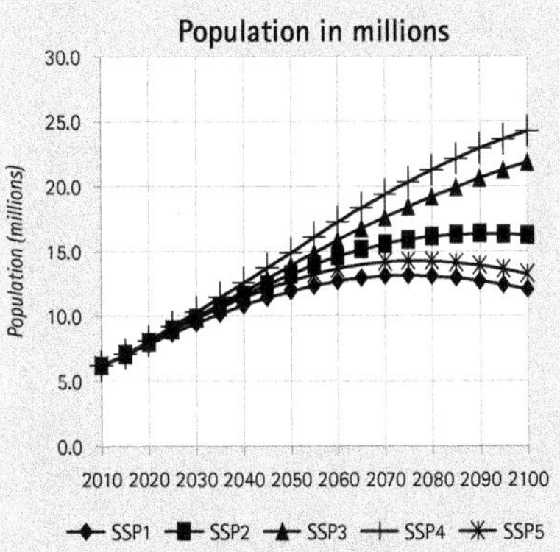

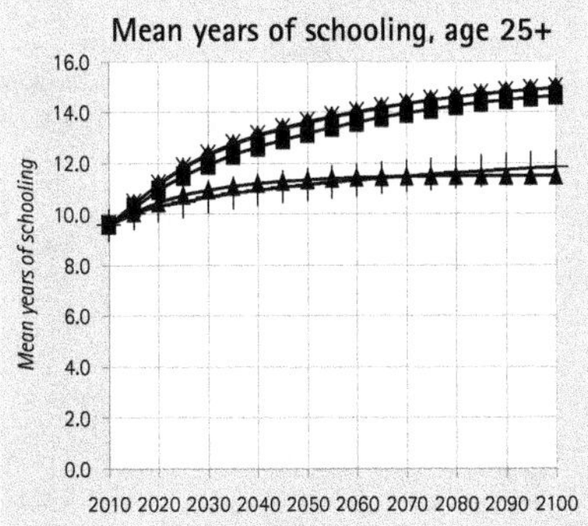

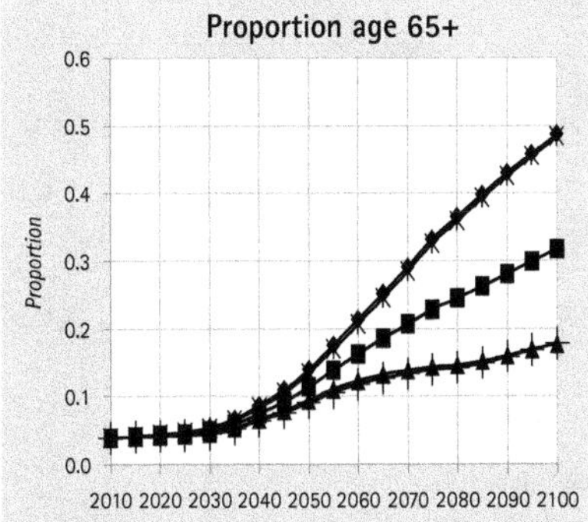

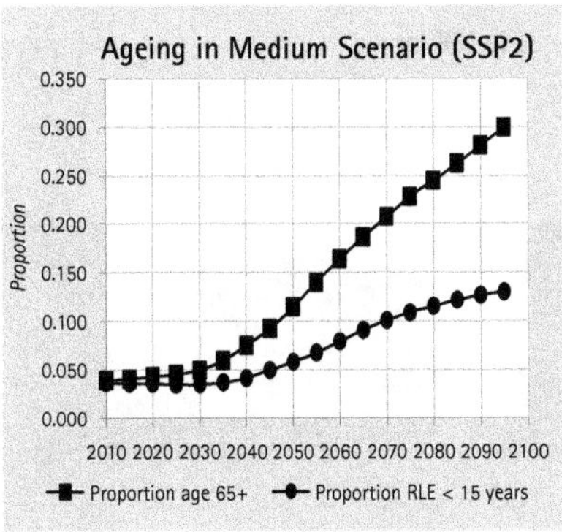

Alternative Scenarios to 2100

Projection Results by Scenario (SSP1–5)

	2010	2020	2030	2040	2050	2075	2100
Population (in millions)							
SSP1 - Rapid development	6.19	7.86	9.44	10.82	11.90	13.11	12.05
SSP2 - Medium	6.19	7.98	9.84	11.60	13.21	15.92	16.23
SSP3 - Stalled development	6.19	7.99	9.94	11.89	13.89	18.43	21.84
SSP4 - Inequality	6.19	8.10	10.31	12.56	14.90	20.35	24.23
SSP5 - Conventional development	6.19	7.98	9.80	11.41	12.69	14.24	13.21
Proportion age 65+							
SSP1 - Rapid development	0.04	0.04	0.05	0.09	0.14	0.33	0.49
SSP2 - Medium	0.04	0.04	0.05	0.08	0.11	0.23	0.32
SSP3 - Stalled development	0.04	0.04	0.05	0.07	0.09	0.14	0.18
SSP4 - Inequality	0.04	0.04	0.05	0.06	0.09	0.14	0.18
SSP5 - Conventional development	0.04	0.04	0.05	0.08	0.13	0.33	0.48
Proportion below age 20							
SSP1 - Rapid development	0.48	0.40	0.32	0.27	0.22	0.14	0.10
SSP2 - Medium	0.48	0.41	0.35	0.31	0.27	0.22	0.18
SSP3 - Stalled development	0.48	0.42	0.39	0.36	0.33	0.30	0.27
SSP4 - Inequality	0.48	0.42	0.38	0.36	0.33	0.30	0.27
SSP5 - Conventional development	0.48	0.40	0.32	0.27	0.22	0.15	0.10
Proportion of Women age 20–39 with at least secondary education							
SSP1 - Rapid development	0.81	0.93	0.97	0.98	0.99	0.99	1.00
SSP2 - Medium	0.81	0.90	0.94	0.96	0.97	0.99	1.00
SSP3 - Stalled development	0.81	0.81	0.82	0.82	0.82	0.82	0.82
SSP4 - Inequality	0.81	0.76	0.74	0.74	0.73	0.74	0.74
SSP5 - Conventional development	0.81	0.93	0.97	0.98	0.99	0.99	1.00
Mean years of schooling, age 25+							
SSP1 - Rapid development	9.57	11.16	12.30	13.06	13.58	14.45	14.93
SSP2 - Medium	9.57	10.93	11.93	12.63	13.16	14.11	14.64
SSP3 - Stalled development	9.57	10.45	10.94	11.21	11.35	11.49	11.50
SSP4 - Inequality	9.57	10.31	10.66	10.95	11.15	11.56	11.83
SSP5 - Conventional development	9.57	11.18	12.33	13.09	13.61	14.47	14.94

Demographic Assumptions Underlying SSPs

	2010–15	2020–25	2030–35	2040–45	2050–55	2075–80	2095–2100
Total fertility rate							
SSP1 - Rapid development	2.67	2.04	1.66	1.48	1.39	1.26	1.19
SSP2 - Medium	2.86	2.41	2.12	1.97	1.88	1.70	1.60
SSP3 - Stalled development	2.98	2.86	2.72	2.60	2.51	2.29	2.17
SSP4 - Inequality	2.97	2.85	2.70	2.57	2.48	2.25	2.12
SSP5 - Conventional development	2.67	2.04	1.66	1.48	1.39	1.26	1.19
Life expectancy at birth for females (in years)							
SSP1 - Rapid development	77.63	80.73	83.62	86.50	89.43	96.81	102.76
SSP2 - Medium	75.80	78.29	80.49	82.59	84.61	89.60	93.59
SSP3 - Stalled development	76.83	77.93	78.84	79.75	80.61	82.58	84.37
SSP4 - Inequality	76.83	77.91	78.80	79.69	80.53	82.49	84.32
SSP5 - Conventional development	77.63	80.73	83.62	86.50	89.43	96.81	102.76
Migration – net flow over five years (in thousands)							
SSP1 - Rapid development	200	189	167	138	110	35	0
SSP2 - Medium	198	189	175	161	146	62	0
SSP3 - Stalled development	167	97	95	100	107	67	0
SSP4 - Inequality	200	193	187	194	203	125	0
SSP5 - Conventional development	234	284	248	202	158	48	0

Ageing Indicators, Medium Scenario (SSP2)

	2010	2020	2030	2040	2050	2075	2095
Median age	20.72	24.61	28.24	31.93	35.25	43.04	48.56
Propspective median age	20.72	22.76	24.57	26.45	28.05	31.51	33.35
Proportion age 65+	0.04	0.04	0.05	0.08	0.11	0.23	0.30
Proportion RLE < 15 years	0.04	0.04	0.03	0.04	0.06	0.11	0.13

Kazakhstan

Detailed Human Capital Projections to 2060

Demographic indicators, Medium Scenario (SSP2)	2010	2020	2030	2040	2050	2060
Population (in millions)	16.03	17.75	19.00	20.04	20.83	21.20
Proportion age 65+	0.07	0.08	0.11	0.13	0.16	0.20
Proportion below age 20	0.33	0.33	0.29	0.26	0.24	0.22
	2005–10	2015–20	2025–30	2035–40	2045–50	2055–60
Total Fertility Rate	2.54	2.17	1.99	1.84	1.75	1.70
Life expectancy at birth (in years)						
Men	60.19	65.18	68.33	71.09	73.68	76.14
Women	71.52	75.21	77.40	79.39	81.39	83.39
Five-year immigration flow (in '000)	340.91	334.25	347.06	354.85	354.94	349.80
Five-year emigration flow (in '000)	333.87	249.90	254.31	259.10	245.63	234.34

Human Capital indicators, Medium Scenario (SSP2)	2010	2020	2030	2040	2050	2060
Population age 25+: highest educational attainment						
E1 - no education	0.00	0.00	0.00	0.00	0.00	0.00
E2 - incomplete primary	0.01	0.01	0.00	0.00	0.00	0.00
E3 - primary	0.03	0.01	0.01	0.00	0.00	0.00
E4 - lower secondary	0.10	0.08	0.06	0.04	0.03	0.02
E5 - upper secondary	0.61	0.61	0.60	0.58	0.55	0.52
E6 - post-secondary	0.24	0.29	0.33	0.37	0.42	0.46
Mean years of schooling (in years)	10.57	11.26	11.69	12.10	12.42	12.69
Gender gap (population age 25+): highest educational attainment (ratio male/female)						
E1 - no education	0.56	0.73	0.92	0.97	0.93	0.91
E2 - incomplete primary	0.57	0.61	0.75	0.93	0.95	0.91
E3 - primary	0.55	0.54	0.72	1.00	1.11	1.07
E4 - lower secondary	1.06	1.10	1.15	1.15	1.11	1.04
E5 - upper secondary	1.08	1.07	1.07	1.08	1.08	1.06
E6 - post-secondary	0.89	0.87	0.86	0.88	0.90	0.93
Mean years of schooling (male minus female)	0.09	-0.04	-0.10	-0.11	-0.10	-0.08
Women age 20–39: highest educational attainment						
E1 - no education	0.00	0.00	0.00	0.00	0.00	0.00
E2 - incomplete primary	0.00	0.00	0.00	0.00	0.00	0.00
E3 - primary	0.00	0.00	0.00	0.00	0.00	0.00
E4 - lower secondary	0.06	0.04	0.03	0.02	0.01	0.01
E5 - upper secondary	0.58	0.54	0.51	0.48	0.46	0.45
E6 - post-secondary	0.35	0.41	0.46	0.50	0.52	0.54
Mean years of schooling (in years)	11.81	12.51	12.76	12.94	13.05	13.13

Education scenarios

GET: global education trend scenario (medium assumption also used for SSP2)

CER: constant enrolment rates scenario (assumption of no future improvements)

FT: Fast track scenario (assumption of education expansion according to fastest historical experience)

Pyramids by Education, Medium Scenario

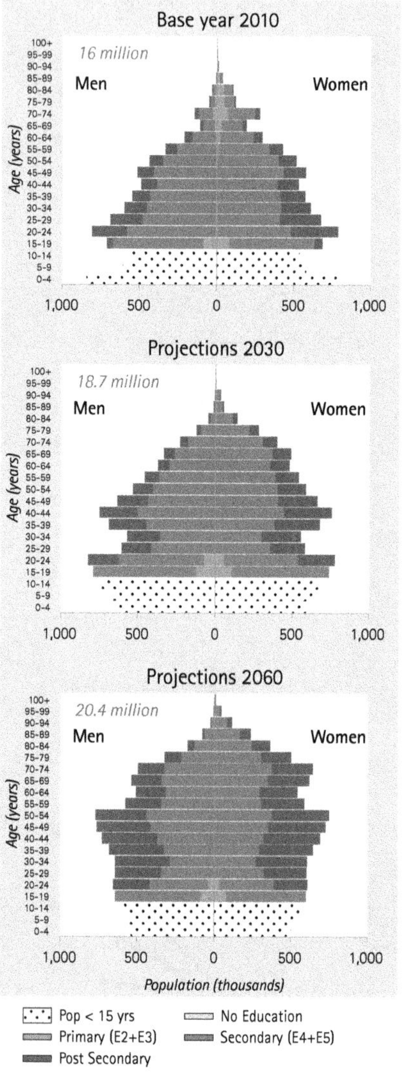

Population Size by Educational Attainment According to Three Education Scenarios: GET, CER, and FT

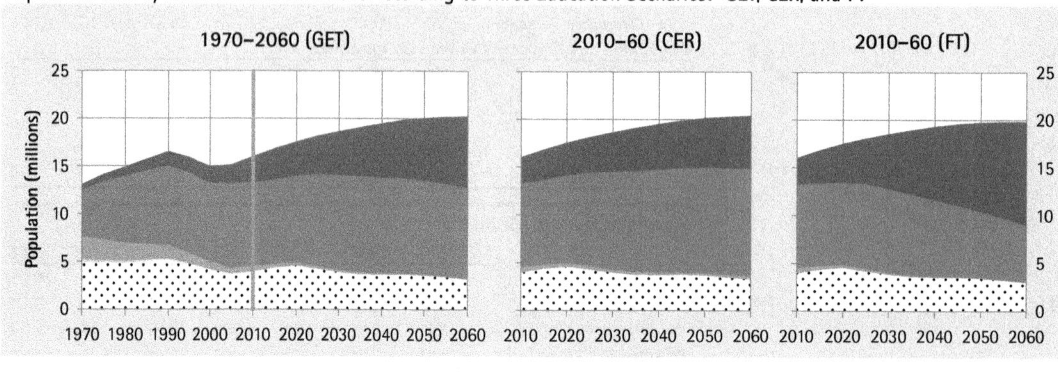

Kazakhstan (Continued)

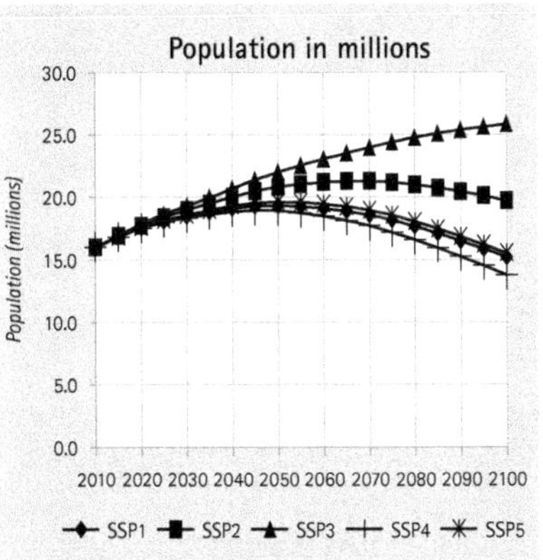

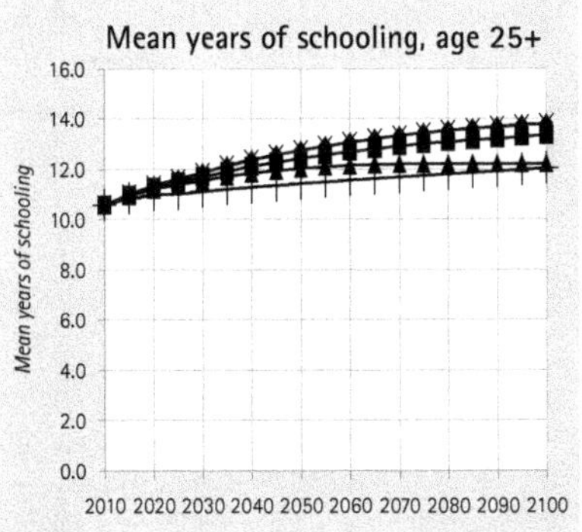

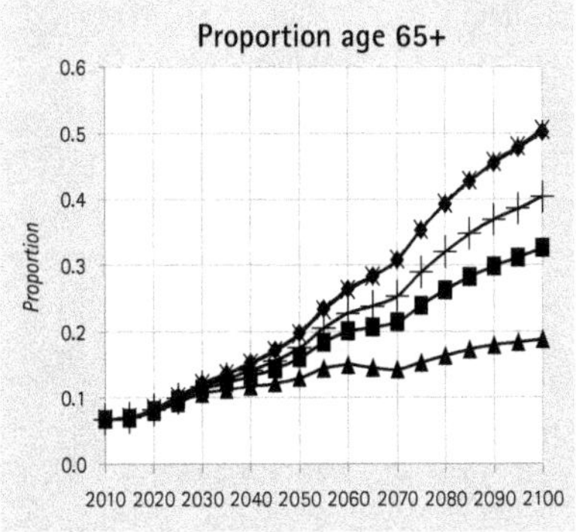

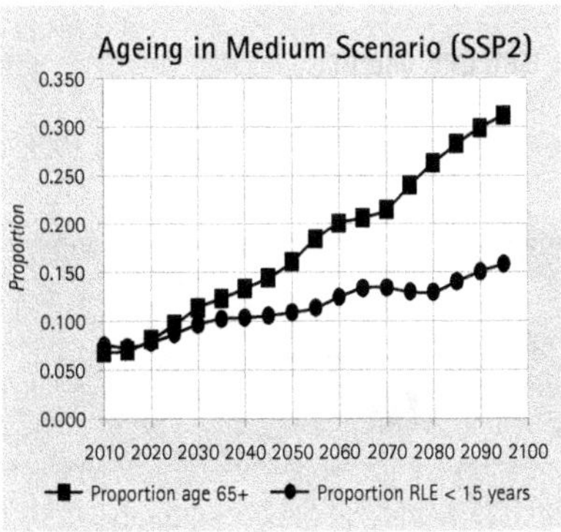

Alternative Scenarios to 2100

Projection Results by Scenario (SSP1–5)

	2010	2020	2030	2040	2050	2075	2100
Population (in millions)							
SSP1 - Rapid development	16.03	17.56	18.47	19.09	19.34	18.16	15.21
SSP2 - Medium	16.03	17.75	19.00	20.04	20.83	21.20	19.71
SSP3 - Stalled development	16.03	17.87	19.33	20.69	22.02	24.40	25.84
SSP4 - Inequality	16.03	17.53	18.37	18.85	18.92	17.20	13.78
SSP5 - Conventional development	16.03	17.60	18.60	19.31	19.62	18.55	15.52
Proportion age 65+							
SSP1 - Rapid development	0.07	0.08	0.12	0.15	0.20	0.35	0.50
SSP2 - Medium	0.07	0.08	0.11	0.13	0.16	0.24	0.33
SSP3 - Stalled development	0.07	0.08	0.11	0.12	0.13	0.15	0.19
SSP4 - Inequality	0.07	0.08	0.12	0.14	0.18	0.29	0.40
SSP5 - Conventional development	0.07	0.08	0.12	0.15	0.20	0.35	0.50
Proportion below age 20							
SSP1 - Rapid development	0.33	0.32	0.26	0.21	0.19	0.12	0.09
SSP2 - Medium	0.33	0.33	0.29	0.26	0.24	0.19	0.17
SSP3 - Stalled development	0.33	0.34	0.32	0.30	0.30	0.27	0.25
SSP4 - Inequality	0.33	0.32	0.27	0.22	0.20	0.14	0.12
SSP5 - Conventional development	0.33	0.32	0.26	0.21	0.19	0.12	0.09
Proportion of Women age 20–39 with at least secondary education							
SSP1 - Rapid development	0.99	1.00	1.00	1.00	1.00	1.00	1.00
SSP2 - Medium	0.99	1.00	1.00	1.00	1.00	1.00	1.00
SSP3 - Stalled development	0.99	0.99	0.99	0.99	0.99	0.99	0.99
SSP4 - Inequality	0.99	0.93	0.89	0.89	0.89	0.89	0.89
SSP5 - Conventional development	0.99	1.00	1.00	1.00	1.00	1.00	1.00
Mean years of schooling, age 25+							
SSP1 - Rapid development	10.57	11.34	11.85	12.36	12.75	13.44	13.80
SSP2 - Medium	10.57	11.26	11.69	12.10	12.42	13.00	13.34
SSP3 - Stalled development	10.57	11.20	11.55	11.83	12.02	12.20	12.21
SSP4 - Inequality	10.57	10.96	11.11	11.28	11.42	11.74	12.03
SSP5 - Conventional development	10.57	11.34	11.86	12.37	12.75	13.44	13.80

Demographic Assumptions Underlying SSPs

	2010–15	2020–25	2030–35	2040–45	2050–55	2075–80	2095–2100
Total fertility rate							
SSP1 - Rapid development	2.18	1.75	1.48	1.35	1.27	1.18	1.19
SSP2 - Medium	2.32	2.07	1.92	1.79	1.71	1.58	1.61
SSP3 - Stalled development	2.42	2.41	2.36	2.27	2.20	2.07	2.09
SSP4 - Inequality	2.19	1.80	1.55	1.41	1.33	1.24	1.25
SSP5 - Conventional development	2.18	1.75	1.48	1.35	1.27	1.18	1.19
Life expectancy at birth for females (in years)							
SSP1 - Rapid development	75.79	78.83	81.59	84.39	87.27	94.58	100.53
SSP2 - Medium	73.81	76.30	78.40	80.39	82.39	87.40	91.40
SSP3 - Stalled development	74.96	76.10	77.07	77.98	78.88	81.02	82.82
SSP4 - Inequality	75.33	77.45	79.28	81.05	82.85	87.41	91.24
SSP5 - Conventional development	75.79	78.83	81.59	84.39	87.27	94.58	100.53
Migration – net flow over five years (in thousands)							
SSP1 - Rapid development	47	93	89	91	91	31	0
SSP2 - Medium	50	95	93	103	114	51	0
SSP3 - Stalled development	39	47	48	61	77	50	0
SSP4 - Inequality	47	92	89	97	104	44	0
SSP5 - Conventional development	55	137	128	127	124	40	0

Ageing Indicators, Medium Scenario (SSP2)

	2010	2020	2030	2040	2050	2075	2095
Median age	28.94	31.62	34.63	35.77	39.01	45.51	50.57
Propspective median age	28.94	29.02	29.99	29.17	30.55	32.44	33.77
Proportion age 65+	0.07	0.08	0.11	0.13	0.16	0.24	0.31
Proportion RLE < 15 years	0.08	0.08	0.10	0.10	0.11	0.13	0.16

Kenya

Detailed Human Capital Projections to 2060

Demographic indicators, Medium Scenario (SSP2)	2010	2020	2030	2040	2050	2060
Population (in millions)	40.51	50.91	61.25	71.27	79.95	86.66
Proportion age 65+	0.03	0.03	0.04	0.04	0.06	0.08
Proportion below age 20	0.53	0.51	0.46	0.41	0.37	0.33
	2005–10	2015–20	2025–30	2035–40	2045–50	2055–60
Total Fertility Rate	4.80	3.89	3.18	2.70	2.36	2.10
Life expectancy at birth (in years)						
Men	53.95	58.22	59.64	60.99	62.60	64.95
Women	55.93	61.02	63.28	65.18	66.98	69.28
Five-year immigration flow (in '000)	81.12	79.20	82.03	83.72	83.60	82.30
Five-year emigration flow (in '000)	268.77	250.05	306.11	354.29	387.51	410.61

Human Capital indicators, Medium Scenario (SSP2)	2010	2020	2030	2040	2050	2060
Population age 25+: highest educational attainment						
E1 - no education	0.16	0.09	0.05	0.02	0.01	0.00
E2 - incomplete primary	0.14	0.09	0.06	0.03	0.02	0.01
E3 - primary	0.17	0.15	0.12	0.09	0.07	0.05
E4 - lower secondary	0.22	0.24	0.22	0.19	0.15	0.12
E5 - upper secondary	0.26	0.38	0.48	0.57	0.64	0.69
E6 - post-secondary	0.04	0.06	0.07	0.09	0.11	0.13
Mean years of schooling (in years)	7.68	8.97	9.97	10.79	11.39	11.85
Gender gap (population age 25+): highest educational attainment (ratio male/female)						
E1 - no education	0.47	0.46	0.48	0.52	0.59	0.66
E2 - incomplete primary	0.87	0.83	0.81	0.81	0.83	0.86
E3 - primary	0.99	0.91	0.87	0.85	0.85	0.84
E4 - lower secondary	1.10	1.00	0.97	0.95	0.94	0.93
E5 - upper secondary	1.38	1.17	1.07	1.02	1.00	1.00
E6 - post-secondary	2.14	1.94	1.66	1.44	1.28	1.16
Mean years of schooling (male minus female)	1.72	1.21	0.78	0.47	0.29	0.18
Women age 20–39: highest educational attainment						
E1 - no education	0.06	0.02	0.01	0.00	0.00	0.00
E2 - incomplete primary	0.12	0.06	0.03	0.01	0.01	0.00
E3 - primary	0.15	0.12	0.08	0.05	0.03	0.01
E4 - lower secondary	0.34	0.32	0.30	0.25	0.22	0.19
E5 - upper secondary	0.30	0.44	0.54	0.62	0.66	0.67
E6 - post-secondary	0.03	0.04	0.05	0.07	0.09	0.11
Mean years of schooling (in years)	8.51	9.61	10.42	11.03	11.45	11.73

Education scenarios

GET: global education trend scenario (medium assumption also used for SSP2)

CER: constant enrolment rates scenario (assumption of no future improvements)

FT: Fast track scenario (assumption of education expansion according to fastest historical experience)

Pyramids by Education, Medium Scenario

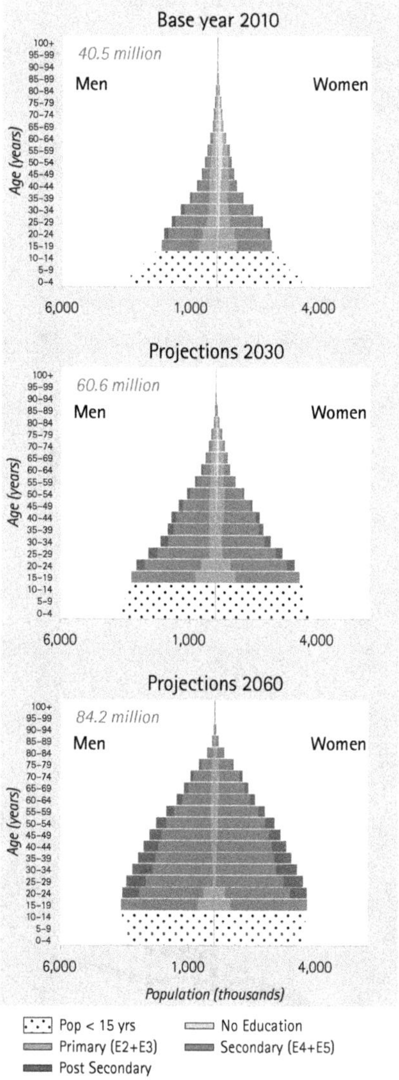

Population Size by Educational Attainment According to Three Education Scenarios: GET, CER, and FT

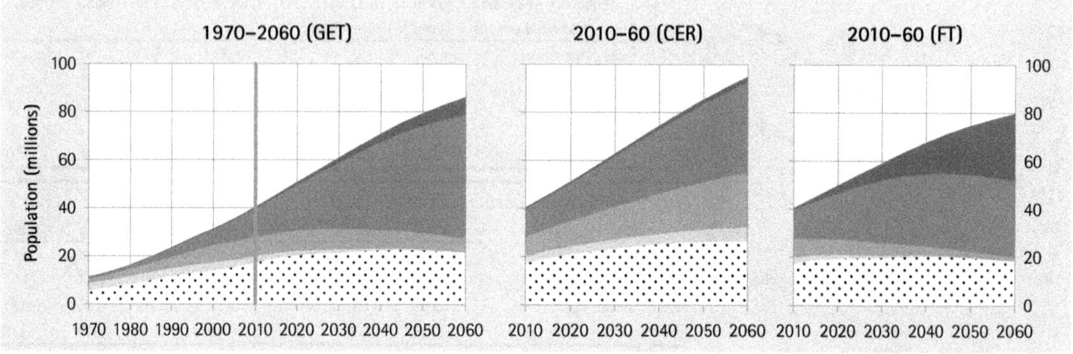

Kenya (Continued)

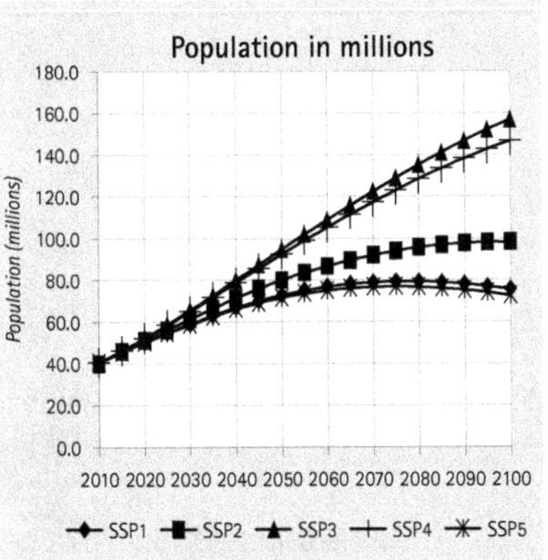

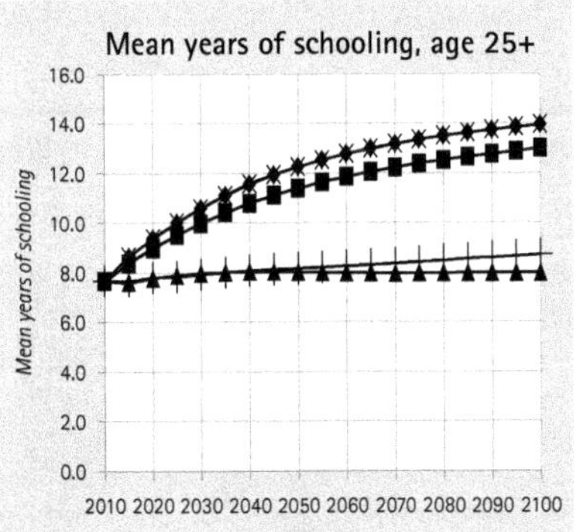

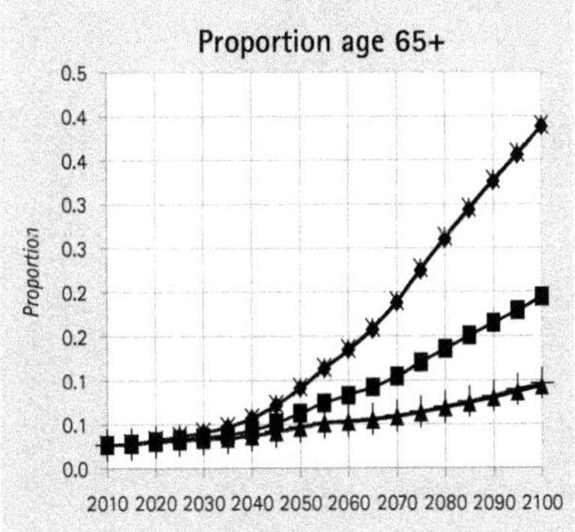

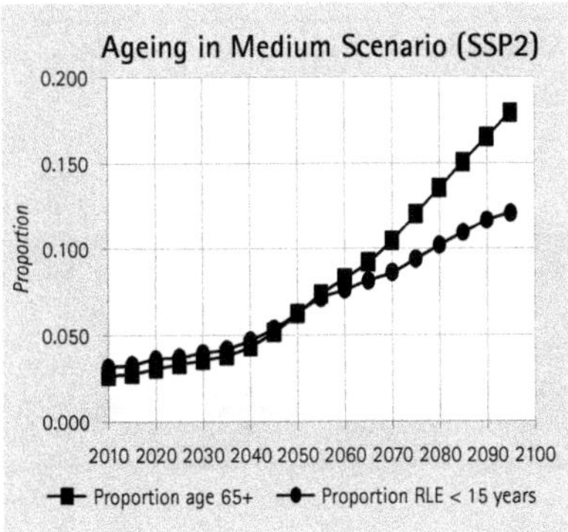

Alternative Scenarios to 2100

Projection Results by Scenario (SSP1–5)

	2010	2020	2030	2040	2050	2075	2100
Population (in millions)							
SSP1 - Rapid development	40.51	50.14	58.88	66.75	72.68	79.19	75.29
SSP2 - Medium	40.51	50.91	61.25	71.27	79.95	94.01	98.25
SSP3 - Stalled development	40.51	52.26	65.56	79.98	94.76	128.86	156.67
SSP4 - Inequality	40.51	52.08	64.98	78.70	92.46	122.94	146.40
SSP5 - Conventional development	40.51	50.04	58.49	65.97	71.43	76.66	72.38
Proportion age 65+							
SSP1 - Rapid development	0.03	0.03	0.04	0.06	0.09	0.22	0.39
SSP2 - Medium	0.03	0.03	0.04	0.04	0.06	0.12	0.19
SSP3 - Stalled development	0.03	0.03	0.03	0.04	0.05	0.06	0.09
SSP4 - Inequality	0.03	0.03	0.03	0.04	0.05	0.06	0.10
SSP5 - Conventional development	0.03	0.03	0.04	0.06	0.09	0.23	0.39
Proportion below age 20							
SSP1 - Rapid development	0.53	0.49	0.41	0.35	0.30	0.19	0.13
SSP2 - Medium	0.53	0.51	0.46	0.41	0.37	0.29	0.23
SSP3 - Stalled development	0.53	0.53	0.51	0.48	0.45	0.38	0.34
SSP4 - Inequality	0.53	0.53	0.51	0.48	0.45	0.38	0.33
SSP5 - Conventional development	0.53	0.49	0.41	0.35	0.30	0.19	0.13
Proportion of Women age 20–39 with at least secondary education							
SSP1 - Rapid development	0.67	0.86	0.93	0.96	0.98	1.00	1.00
SSP2 - Medium	0.67	0.79	0.88	0.93	0.96	0.99	1.00
SSP3 - Stalled development	0.67	0.55	0.55	0.55	0.55	0.55	0.55
SSP4 - Inequality	0.67	0.52	0.50	0.50	0.50	0.50	0.50
SSP5 - Conventional development	0.67	0.86	0.93	0.96	0.98	1.00	1.00
Mean years of schooling, age 25+							
SSP1 - Rapid development	7.68	9.37	10.58	11.56	12.25	13.35	13.94
SSP2 - Medium	7.68	8.97	9.97	10.79	11.39	12.38	12.99
SSP3 - Stalled development	7.68	7.78	7.97	8.04	8.03	7.99	7.99
SSP4 - Inequality	7.68	7.79	7.93	8.07	8.17	8.43	8.72
SSP5 - Conventional development	7.68	9.37	10.58	11.55	12.24	13.34	13.94

Demographic Assumptions Underlying SSPs

	2010–15	2020–25	2030–35	2040–45	2050–55	2075–80	2095–2100
Total fertility rate							
SSP1 - Rapid development	4.04	2.87	2.21	1.85	1.61	1.35	1.23
SSP2 - Medium	4.30	3.52	2.93	2.52	2.20	1.86	1.69
SSP3 - Stalled development	4.69	4.53	4.11	3.61	3.19	2.64	2.41
SSP4 - Inequality	4.67	4.50	4.06	3.54	3.12	2.56	2.33
SSP5 - Conventional development	4.04	2.87	2.21	1.85	1.61	1.35	1.23
Life expectancy at birth for females (in years)							
SSP1 - Rapid development	63.31	69.51	73.47	77.09	80.54	88.86	95.58
SSP2 - Medium	59.20	62.21	64.28	65.98	68.08	74.28	79.21
SSP3 - Stalled development	59.91	58.77	59.92	60.40	61.13	64.13	66.41
SSP4 - Inequality	59.91	58.75	59.86	60.35	61.09	64.13	66.44
SSP5 - Conventional development	63.31	69.51	73.47	77.09	80.54	88.86	95.58
Migration – net flow over five years (in thousands)							
SSP1 - Rapid development	−164	−194	−244	−274	−290	−127	0
SSP2 - Medium	−164	−195	−247	−287	−317	−159	0
SSP3 - Stalled development	−135	−93	−118	−139	−158	−87	0
SSP4 - Inequality	−162	−190	−244	−295	−339	−186	0
SSP5 - Conventional development	−191	−295	−382	−446	−493	−243	0

Ageing Indicators, Medium Scenario (SSP2)

	2010	2020	2030	2040	2050	2075	2095
Median age	18.52	19.69	22.10	24.77	27.43	34.42	39.82
Propspective median age	18.52	18.05	19.08	20.74	22.09	24.42	25.77
Proportion age 65+	0.03	0.03	0.04	0.04	0.06	0.12	0.18
Proportion RLE < 15 years	0.03	0.04	0.04	0.05	0.06	0.09	0.12

Kuwait

Detailed Human Capital Projections to 2060

Demographic indicators, Medium Scenario (SSP2)

	2010	2020	2030	2040	2050	2060
Population (in millions)	2.74	3.55	4.34	5.11	5.75	6.26
Proportion age 65+	0.03	0.03	0.06	0.12	0.18	0.21
Proportion below age 20	0.33	0.30	0.25	0.23	0.22	0.20
	2005–10	2015–20	2025–30	2035–40	2045–50	2055–60
Total Fertility Rate	2.32	2.06	1.93	1.86	1.77	1.71
Life expectancy at birth (in years)						
Men	73.47	76.10	78.15	79.93	81.86	83.77
Women	75.20	78.11	80.39	82.49	84.59	86.61
Five-year immigration flow (in '000)	396.35	314.66	326.81	333.88	333.57	328.49
Five-year emigration flow (in '000)	119.08	95.71	117.14	129.63	137.08	141.91

Human Capital indicators, Medium Scenario (SSP2)

	2010	2020	2030	2040	2050	2060
Population age 25+: highest educational attainment						
E1 - no education	0.14	0.10	0.07	0.05	0.03	0.02
E2 - incomplete primary	0.27	0.20	0.14	0.10	0.07	0.04
E3 - primary	0.04	0.05	0.05	0.05	0.05	0.05
E4 - lower secondary	0.17	0.22	0.26	0.27	0.27	0.26
E5 - upper secondary	0.20	0.22	0.25	0.27	0.29	0.31
E6 - post-secondary	0.19	0.21	0.23	0.26	0.29	0.32
Mean years of schooling (in years)	7.74	8.67	9.52	10.28	10.95	11.59
Gender gap (population age 25+): highest educational attainment (ratio male/female)						
E1 - no education	0.93	1.07	1.18	1.24	1.24	1.18
E2 - incomplete primary	1.22	1.28	1.34	1.36	1.32	1.24
E3 - primary	1.11	1.17	1.23	1.27	1.27	1.24
E4 - lower secondary	1.10	1.12	1.18	1.23	1.25	1.23
E5 - upper secondary	1.01	1.03	1.04	1.05	1.07	1.06
E6 - post-secondary	0.73	0.65	0.62	0.63	0.68	0.75
Mean years of schooling (male minus female)	−0.65	−1.01	−1.17	−1.14	−0.98	−0.71
Women age 20–39: highest educational attainment						
E1 - no education	0.08	0.03	0.01	0.01	0.00	0.00
E2 - incomplete primary	0.18	0.06	0.01	0.01	0.00	0.00
E3 - primary	0.04	0.05	0.05	0.04	0.04	0.03
E4 - lower secondary	0.20	0.27	0.27	0.23	0.20	0.18
E5 - upper secondary	0.27	0.31	0.35	0.37	0.39	0.41
E6 - post-secondary	0.23	0.28	0.31	0.35	0.36	0.36
Mean years of schooling (in years)	9.24	10.90	11.94	12.30	12.50	12.62

Education scenarios

GET: global education trend scenario (medium assumption also used for SSP2)

CER: constant enrolment rates scenario (assumption of no future improvements)

FT: Fast track scenario (assumption of education expansion according to fastest historical experience)

Pyramids by Education, Medium Scenario

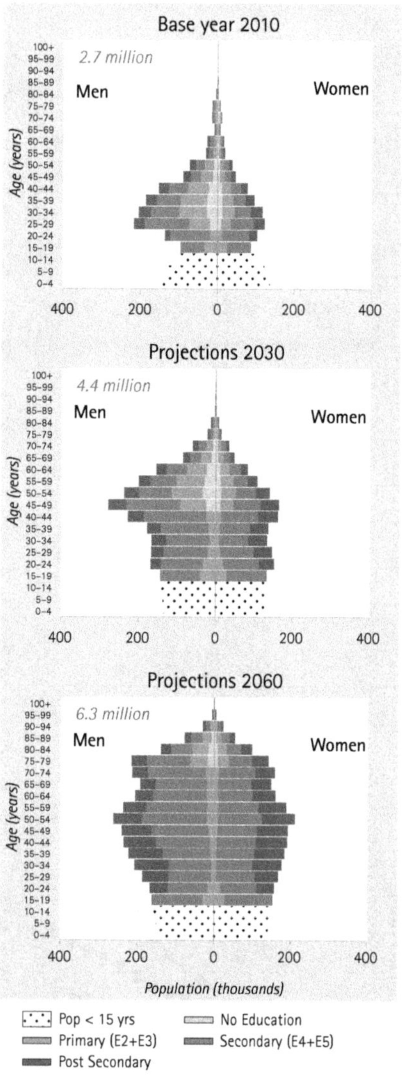

Population Size by Educational Attainment According to Three Education Scenarios: GET, CER, and FT

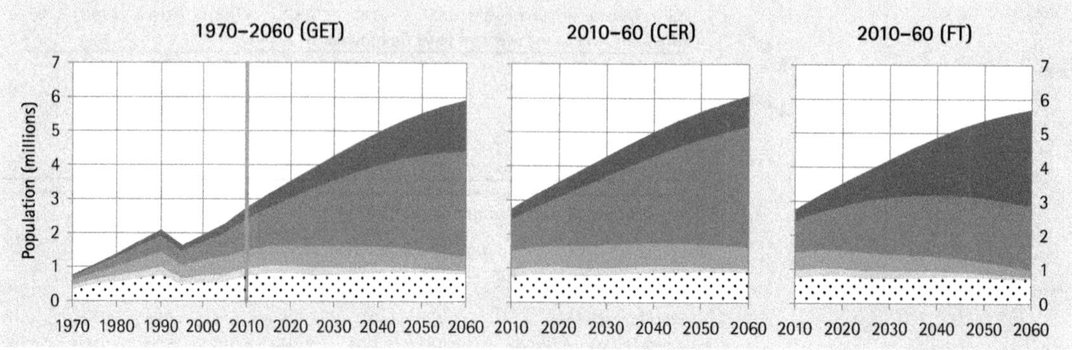

Kuwait (Continued)

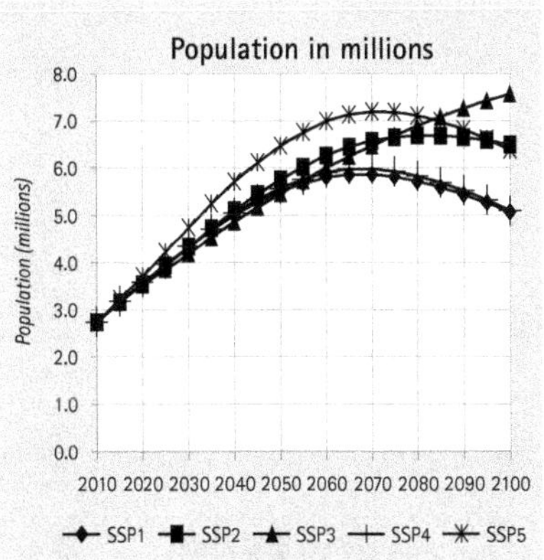

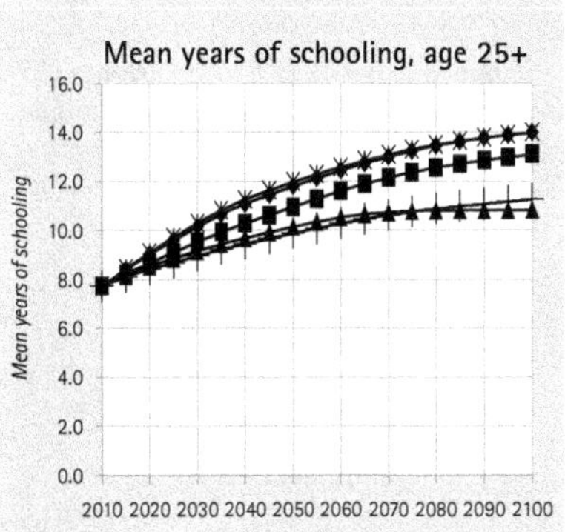

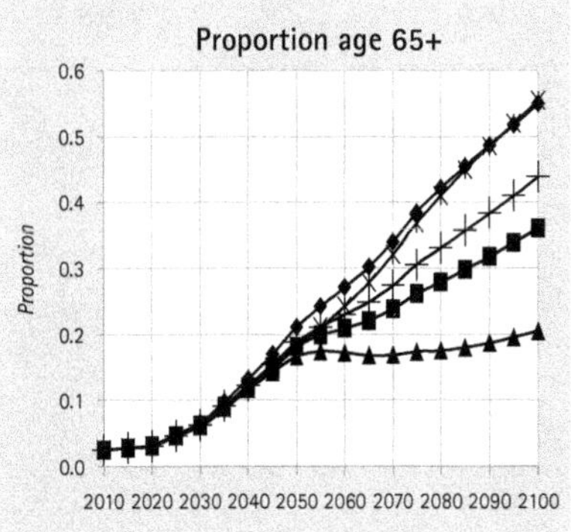

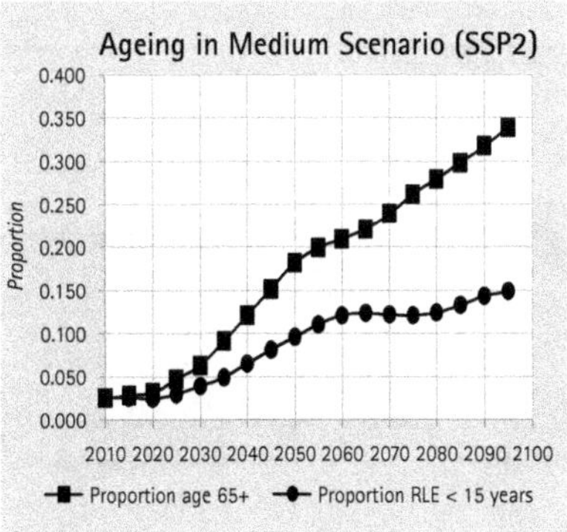

Alternative Scenarios to 2100

Projection Results by Scenario (SSP1–5)

	2010	2020	2030	2040	2050	2075	2100
Population (in millions)							
SSP1 - Rapid development	2.74	3.57	4.33	5.00	5.50	5.81	5.06
SSP2 - Medium	2.74	3.55	4.34	5.11	5.75	6.65	6.49
SSP3 - Stalled development	2.74	3.52	4.19	4.86	5.46	6.68	7.56
SSP4 - Inequality	2.74	3.58	4.35	5.04	5.56	5.92	5.09
SSP5 - Conventional development	2.74	3.70	4.74	5.70	6.46	7.18	6.37
Proportion age 65+							
SSP1 - Rapid development	0.03	0.03	0.07	0.13	0.21	0.38	0.55
SSP2 - Medium	0.03	0.03	0.06	0.12	0.18	0.26	0.36
SSP3 - Stalled development	0.03	0.03	0.06	0.12	0.17	0.17	0.21
SSP4 - Inequality	0.03	0.03	0.06	0.12	0.19	0.31	0.44
SSP5 - Conventional development	0.03	0.03	0.06	0.12	0.18	0.37	0.55
Proportion below age 20							
SSP1 - Rapid development	0.33	0.29	0.22	0.19	0.16	0.11	0.08
SSP2 - Medium	0.33	0.30	0.25	0.23	0.22	0.18	0.16
SSP3 - Stalled development	0.33	0.31	0.28	0.27	0.27	0.27	0.25
SSP4 - Inequality	0.33	0.29	0.23	0.20	0.18	0.14	0.11
SSP5 - Conventional development	0.33	0.29	0.22	0.19	0.16	0.11	0.08
Proportion of Women age 20–39 with at least secondary education							
SSP1 - Rapid development	0.70	0.89	0.96	0.97	0.97	0.98	0.99
SSP2 - Medium	0.70	0.86	0.93	0.94	0.95	0.97	0.99
SSP3 - Stalled development	0.70	0.85	0.90	0.90	0.90	0.90	0.90
SSP4 - Inequality	0.70	0.80	0.81	0.81	0.81	0.81	0.81
SSP5 - Conventional development	0.70	0.89	0.96	0.97	0.97	0.98	0.99
Mean years of schooling, age 25+							
SSP1 - Rapid development	7.74	9.03	10.14	11.07	11.79	13.23	13.99
SSP2 - Medium	7.74	8.67	9.52	10.28	10.95	12.36	13.10
SSP3 - Stalled development	7.74	8.54	9.16	9.68	10.13	10.78	10.83
SSP4 - Inequality	7.74	8.43	8.96	9.45	9.87	10.75	11.26
SSP5 - Conventional development	7.74	9.07	10.28	11.24	11.95	13.29	13.98

Demographic Assumptions Underlying SSPs

	2010–15	2020–25	2030–35	2040–45	2050–55	2075–80	2095–2100
Total fertility rate							
SSP1 - Rapid development	2.03	1.64	1.43	1.33	1.26	1.20	1.16
SSP2 - Medium	2.15	1.99	1.89	1.82	1.73	1.65	1.59
SSP3 - Stalled development	2.27	2.34	2.38	2.35	2.31	2.22	2.18
SSP4 - Inequality	2.05	1.73	1.54	1.43	1.35	1.28	1.24
SSP5 - Conventional development	2.03	1.64	1.43	1.33	1.26	1.20	1.16
Life expectancy at birth for females (in years)							
SSP1 - Rapid development	77.76	81.01	84.26	87.38	90.41	97.93	103.88
SSP2 - Medium	76.79	79.29	81.51	83.59	85.59	90.59	94.60
SSP3 - Stalled development	76.84	78.15	79.45	80.56	81.57	83.61	85.45
SSP4 - Inequality	77.34	79.59	81.86	83.96	85.91	90.38	94.24
SSP5 - Conventional development	77.76	81.01	84.26	87.38	90.41	97.93	103.88
Migration – net flow over five years (in thousands)							
SSP1 - Rapid development	245	211	194	167	137	29	0
SSP2 - Medium	215	187	182	175	168	54	0
SSP3 - Stalled development	204	103	101	109	119	55	0
SSP4 - Inequality	245	212	201	190	175	52	0
SSP5 - Conventional development	286	329	314	274	223	43	0

Ageing Indicators, Medium Scenario (SSP2)

	2010	2020	2030	2040	2050	2075	2095
Median age	28.22	32.55	35.24	37.78	41.02	46.53	52.78
Propspective median age	28.22	30.23	30.99	31.79	33.25	34.32	36.81
Proportion age 65+	0.03	0.03	0.06	0.12	0.18	0.26	0.34
Proportion RLE < 15 years	0.03	0.02	0.04	0.07	0.10	0.12	0.15

Kyrgyzstan

Detailed Human Capital Pojections to 2060

Demographic indicators, Medium Scenario (SSP2)	2010	2020	2030	2040	2050	2060
Population (in millions)	5.33	5.92	6.34	6.63	6.75	6.71
Proportion age 65+	0.04	0.05	0.08	0.11	0.14	0.20
Proportion below age 20	0.41	0.37	0.33	0.29	0.26	0.23
	2005–10	2015–20	2025–30	2035–40	2045–50	2055–60
Total Fertility Rate	2.70	2.27	2.05	1.92	1.81	1.72
Life expectancy at birth (in years)						
Men	62.66	65.95	68.80	71.46	73.93	76.22
Women	71.05	73.71	76.00	78.20	80.29	82.29
Five-year immigration flow (in '000)	0.84	0.82	0.86	0.88	0.88	0.87
Five-year emigration flow (in '000)	132.04	110.09	107.52	107.28	100.49	92.77

Human Capital indicators, Medium Scenario (SSP2)	2010	2020	2030	2040	2050	2060
Population age 25+: highest educational attainment						
E1 - no education	0.01	0.00	0.00	0.00	0.00	0.00
E2 - incomplete primary	0.01	0.00	0.00	0.00	0.00	0.00
E3 - primary	0.03	0.01	0.01	0.00	0.00	0.00
E4 - lower secondary	0.09	0.06	0.04	0.03	0.02	0.01
E5 - upper secondary	0.72	0.77	0.79	0.80	0.79	0.78
E6 - post-secondary	0.15	0.15	0.16	0.17	0.19	0.21
Mean years of schooling (in years)	10.26	10.84	11.14	11.36	11.56	11.72
Gender gap (population age 25+): highest educational attainment (ratio male/female)						
E1 - no education	0.38	0.48	0.70	0.88	0.94	0.96
E2 - incomplete primary	0.44	0.37	0.43	0.61	0.74	0.85
E3 - primary	0.66	0.65	0.81	1.07	1.26	1.35
E4 - lower secondary	1.14	1.18	1.20	1.20	1.20	1.21
E5 - upper secondary	1.06	1.06	1.07	1.07	1.07	1.05
E6 - post-secondary	0.82	0.73	0.70	0.71	0.75	0.82
Mean years of schooling (male minus female)	0.05	−0.11	−0.18	−0.19	−0.17	−0.14
Women age 20–39: highest educational attainment						
E1 - no education	0.00	0.00	0.00	0.00	0.00	0.00
E2 - incomplete primary	0.00	0.00	0.00	0.00	0.00	0.00
E3 - primary	0.00	0.00	0.00	0.00	0.00	0.00
E4 - lower secondary	0.06	0.04	0.04	0.03	0.03	0.03
E5 - upper secondary	0.80	0.80	0.79	0.78	0.77	0.76
E6 - post-secondary	0.13	0.16	0.17	0.19	0.20	0.21
Mean years of schooling (in years)	10.98	11.51	11.59	11.65	11.73	11.76

Education scenarios

GET: global education trend scenario (medium assumption also used for SSP2)

CER: constant enrolment rates scenario (assumption of no future improvements)

FT: Fast track scenario (assumption of education expansion according to fastest historical experience)

Pyramids by Education, Medium Scenario

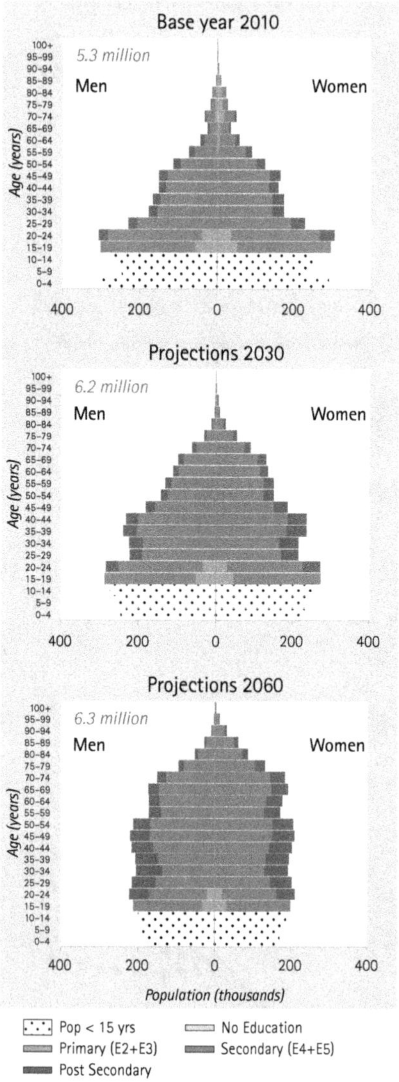

Population Size by Educational Attainment According to Three Education Scenarios: GET, CER, and FT

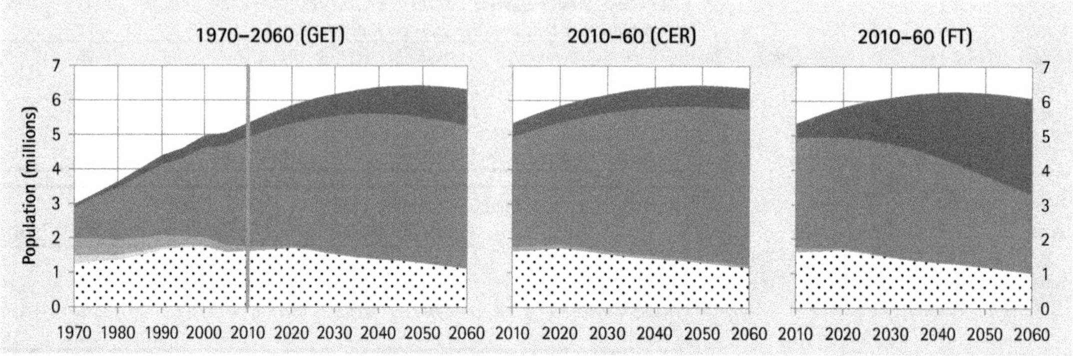

Kyrgyzstan (Continued)

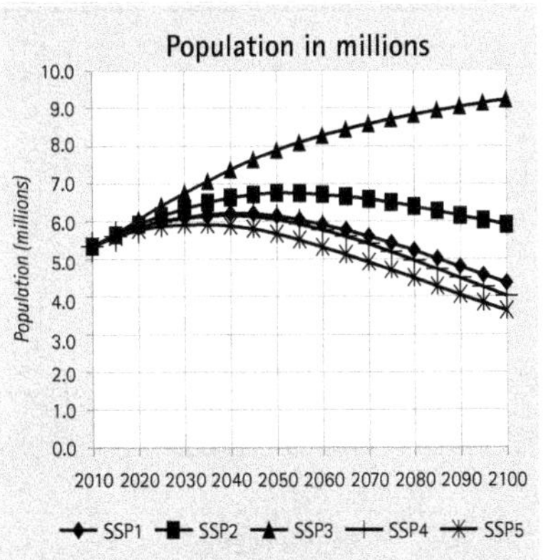

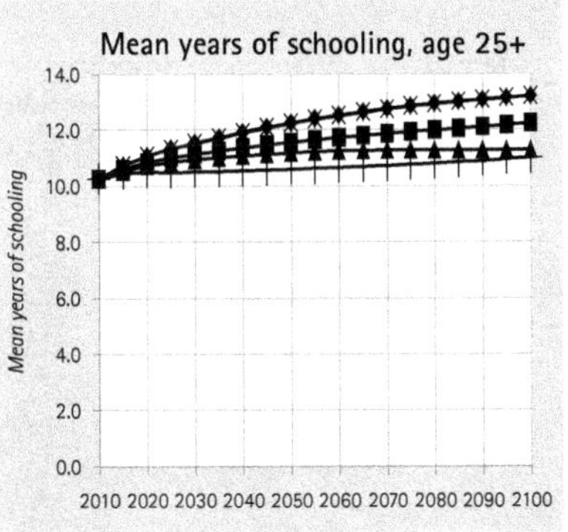

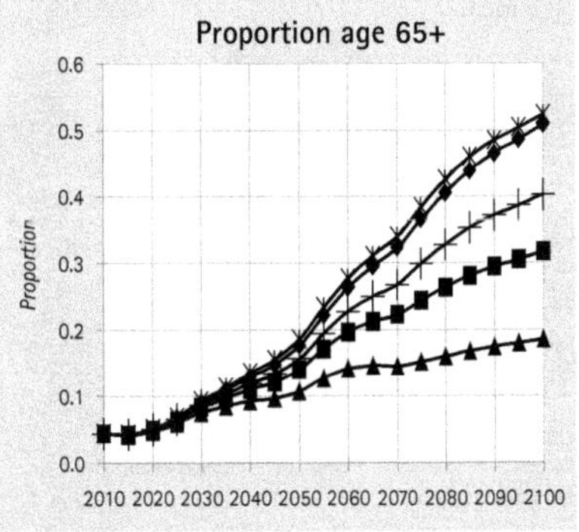

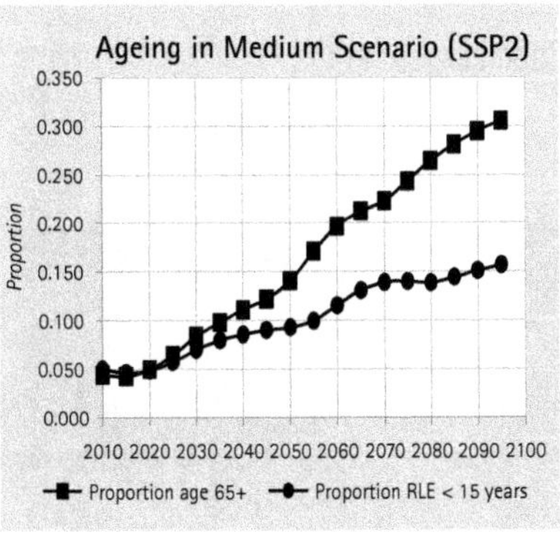

Alternative Scenarios to 2100

Projection Results by Scenario (SSP1–5)

	2010	2020	2030	2040	2050	2075	2100
Population (in millions)							
SSP1 - Rapid development	5.33	5.84	6.11	6.22	6.14	5.42	4.35
SSP2 - Medium	5.33	5.92	6.34	6.63	6.75	6.50	5.92
SSP3 - Stalled development	5.33	6.05	6.75	7.37	7.88	8.71	9.23
SSP4 - Inequality	5.33	5.83	6.08	6.16	6.05	5.19	4.01
SSP5 - Conventional development	5.33	5.78	5.91	5.88	5.67	4.70	3.62
Proportion age 65+							
SSP1 - Rapid development	0.04	0.05	0.09	0.13	0.18	0.37	0.51
SSP2 - Medium	0.04	0.05	0.08	0.11	0.14	0.24	0.32
SSP3 - Stalled development	0.04	0.05	0.08	0.09	0.11	0.15	0.19
SSP4 - Inequality	0.04	0.05	0.09	0.12	0.16	0.30	0.40
SSP5 - Conventional development	0.04	0.05	0.09	0.14	0.19	0.38	0.52
Proportion below age 20							
SSP1 - Rapid development	0.41	0.36	0.30	0.24	0.20	0.13	0.09
SSP2 - Medium	0.41	0.37	0.33	0.29	0.26	0.20	0.17
SSP3 - Stalled development	0.41	0.38	0.36	0.33	0.31	0.28	0.25
SSP4 - Inequality	0.41	0.36	0.30	0.25	0.21	0.15	0.12
SSP5 - Conventional development	0.41	0.36	0.30	0.24	0.20	0.12	0.09
Proportion of Women age 20–39 with at least secondary education							
SSP1 - Rapid development	1.00	1.00	1.00	1.00	1.00	1.00	1.00
SSP2 - Medium	1.00	1.00	1.00	1.00	1.00	1.00	1.00
SSP3 - Stalled development	1.00	0.99	0.99	0.99	0.99	0.99	0.99
SSP4 - Inequality	1.00	0.93	0.89	0.89	0.89	0.89	0.89
SSP5 - Conventional development	1.00	1.00	1.00	1.00	1.00	1.00	1.00
Mean years of schooling, age 25+							
SSP1 - Rapid development	10.26	11.07	11.54	11.92	12.25	12.85	13.20
SSP2 - Medium	10.26	10.84	11.14	11.36	11.56	11.93	12.23
SSP3 - Stalled development	10.26	10.71	10.94	11.07	11.18	11.28	11.28
SSP4 - Inequality	10.26	10.50	10.51	10.54	10.59	10.76	11.00
SSP5 - Conventional development	10.26	11.06	11.52	11.90	12.22	12.83	13.19

Demographic Assumptions Underlying SSPs

	2010–15	2020–25	2030–35	2040–45	2050–55	2075–80	2095–2100
Total fertility rate							
SSP1 - Rapid development	2.28	1.80	1.52	1.38	1.29	1.20	1.16
SSP2 - Medium	2.45	2.15	1.98	1.85	1.76	1.65	1.60
SSP3 - Stalled development	2.54	2.51	2.43	2.33	2.25	2.11	2.06
SSP4 - Inequality	2.30	1.86	1.59	1.45	1.36	1.27	1.23
SSP5 - Conventional development	2.28	1.80	1.52	1.38	1.29	1.20	1.16
Life expectancy at birth for females (in years)							
SSP1 - Rapid development	74.87	77.84	80.83	83.68	86.48	93.68	99.57
SSP2 - Medium	72.31	74.91	77.10	79.20	81.29	86.31	90.28
SSP3 - Stalled development	74.09	75.22	76.36	77.34	78.22	80.43	82.20
SSP4 - Inequality	74.41	76.58	78.50	80.38	82.19	86.62	90.33
SSP5 - Conventional development	74.87	77.84	80.83	83.68	86.48	93.68	99.57
Migration – net flow over five years (in thousands)							
SSP1 - Rapid development	−116	−106	−104	−96	−84	−27	0
SSP2 - Medium	−118	−109	−109	−106	−98	−38	0
SSP3 - Stalled development	−97	−53	−53	−53	−51	−22	0
SSP4 - Inequality	−116	−105	−102	−91	−76	−22	0
SSP5 - Conventional development	−136	−160	−158	−149	−132	−45	0

Ageing Indicators, Medium Scenario (SSP2)

	2010	2020	2030	2040	2050	2075	2095
Median age	23.73	27.54	30.95	33.64	37.50	45.08	49.49
Propspective median age	23.73	25.05	26.49	27.30	29.25	32.43	33.20
Proportion age 65+	0.04	0.05	0.08	0.11	0.14	0.24	0.31
Proportion RLE < 15 years	0.05	0.05	0.07	0.09	0.09	0.14	0.16

Lao People's Democratic Republic

Detailed Human Capital Projections to 2060

Demographic indicators, Medium Scenario (SSP2)	2010	2020	2030	2040	2050	2060
Population (in millions)	6.20	7.11	7.90	8.45	8.82	8.97
Proportion age 65+	0.04	0.04	0.06	0.08	0.10	0.15
Proportion below age 20	0.47	0.39	0.35	0.31	0.27	0.25
	2005–10	2015–20	2025–30	2035–40	2045–50	2055–60
Total Fertility Rate	3.02	2.44	2.16	1.99	1.89	1.82
Life expectancy at birth (in years)						
Men	64.78	65.67	66.91	68.54	70.30	72.24
Women	67.31	69.00	70.69	72.61	74.50	76.49
Five-year immigration flow (in '000)	0.30	0.29	0.30	0.31	0.31	0.30
Five-year emigration flow (in '000)	74.95	67.63	69.59	69.56	68.23	64.66

Human Capital indicators, Medium Scenario (SSP2)	2010	2020	2030	2040	2050	2060
Population age 25+: highest educational attainment						
E1 - no education	0.27	0.19	0.14	0.10	0.07	0.04
E2 - incomplete primary	0.21	0.18	0.14	0.11	0.08	0.06
E3 - primary	0.22	0.25	0.27	0.27	0.27	0.26
E4 - lower secondary	0.14	0.18	0.21	0.23	0.23	0.23
E5 - upper secondary	0.10	0.14	0.18	0.22	0.27	0.32
E6 - post-secondary	0.06	0.06	0.07	0.07	0.08	0.09
Mean years of schooling (in years)	5.18	5.96	6.70	7.33	7.93	8.50
Gender gap (population age 25+): highest educational attainment (ratio male/female)						
E1 - no education	0.44	0.52	0.59	0.66	0.72	0.77
E2 - incomplete primary	0.98	0.96	0.99	1.02	1.07	1.08
E3 - primary	1.20	1.00	0.93	0.90	0.91	0.91
E4 - lower secondary	1.50	1.24	1.13	1.08	1.05	1.02
E5 - upper secondary	1.76	1.43	1.22	1.12	1.06	1.05
E6 - post-secondary	2.70	1.93	1.57	1.36	1.21	1.13
Mean years of schooling (male minus female)	2.25	1.48	0.95	0.60	0.38	0.26
Women age 20–39: highest educational attainment						
E1 - no education	0.23	0.13	0.07	0.04	0.03	0.02
E2 - incomplete primary	0.17	0.14	0.10	0.07	0.05	0.03
E3 - primary	0.24	0.29	0.30	0.28	0.25	0.21
E4 - lower secondary	0.19	0.21	0.23	0.22	0.20	0.18
E5 - upper secondary	0.12	0.18	0.24	0.32	0.38	0.45
E6 - post-secondary	0.05	0.06	0.07	0.08	0.09	0.11
Mean years of schooling (in years)	5.40	6.61	7.64	8.43	9.02	9.51

Education scenarios

GET: global education trend scenario (medium assumption also used for SSP2)

CER: constant enrolment rates scenario (assumption of no future improvements)

FT: Fast track scenario (assumption of education expansion according to fastest historical experience)

Pyramids by Education, Medium Scenario

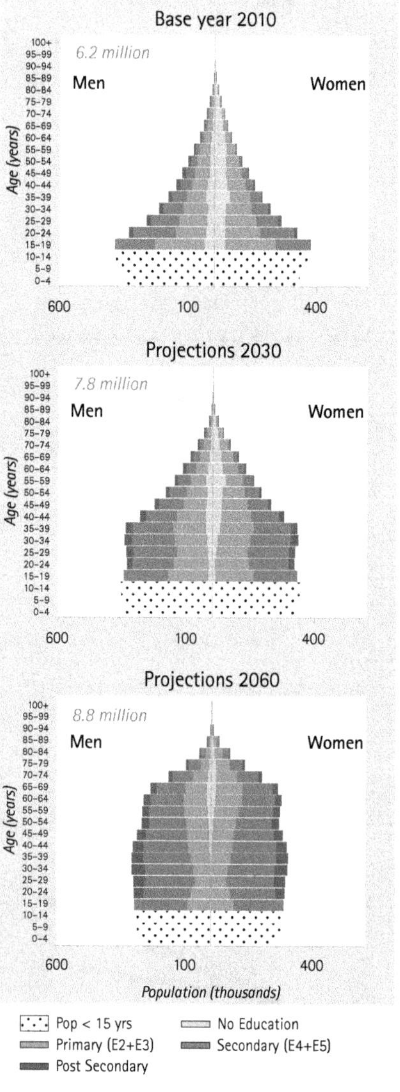

Population Size by Educational Attainment According to Three Education Scenarios: GET, CER, and FT

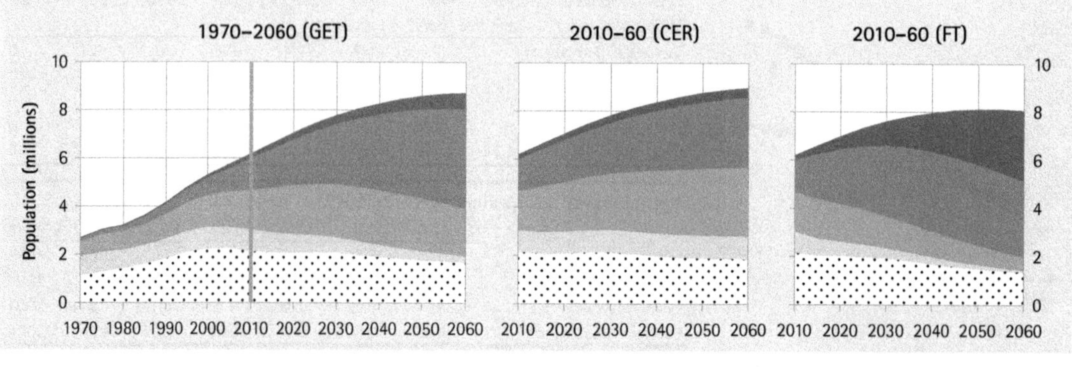

Lao People's Democratic Republic (Continued)

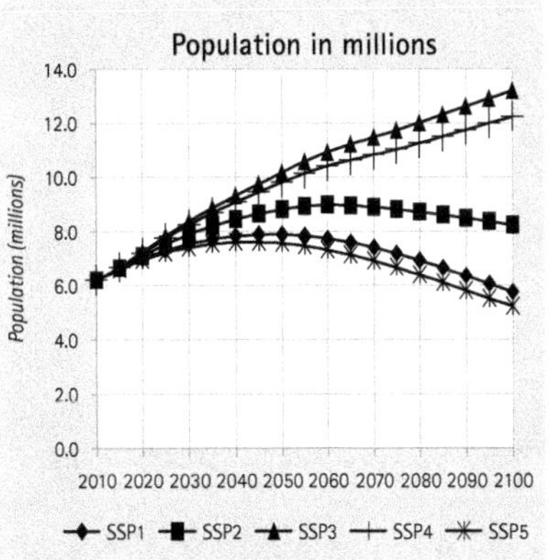

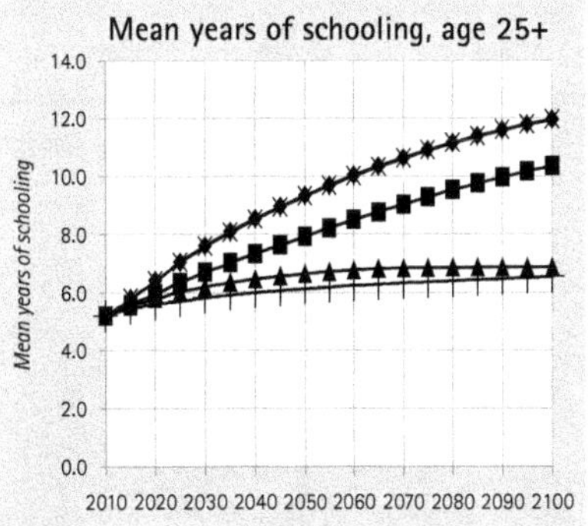

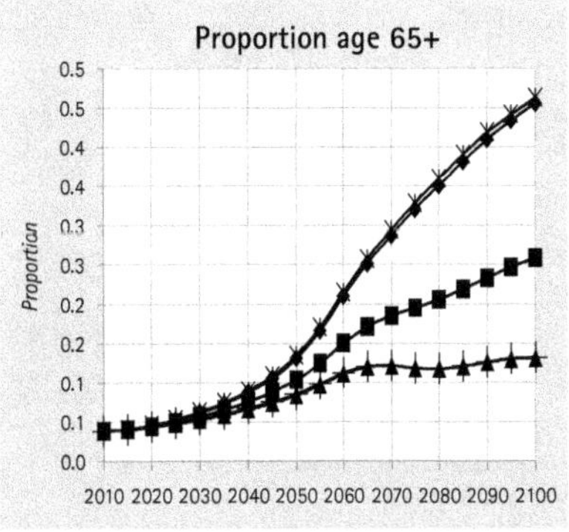

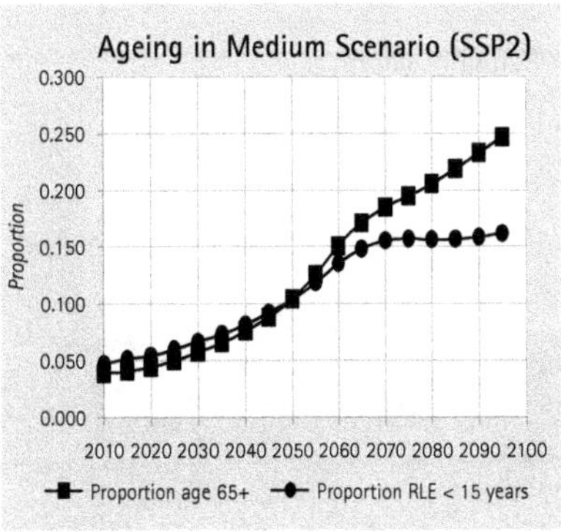

Alternative Scenarios to 2100

Projection Results by Scenario (SSP1–5)

	2010	2020	2030	2040	2050	2075	2100
Population (in millions)							
SSP1 - Rapid development	6.20	6.99	7.54	7.83	7.89	7.19	5.75
SSP2 - Medium	6.20	7.11	7.90	8.45	8.82	8.82	8.23
SSP3 - Stalled development	6.20	7.25	8.38	9.32	10.18	11.73	13.19
SSP4 - Inequality	6.20	7.22	8.26	9.09	9.81	11.03	12.22
SSP5 - Conventional development	6.20	6.95	7.41	7.60	7.56	6.67	5.23
Proportion age 65+							
SSP1 - Rapid development	0.04	0.05	0.06	0.09	0.13	0.32	0.46
SSP2 - Medium	0.04	0.04	0.06	0.08	0.10	0.19	0.26
SSP3 - Stalled development	0.04	0.04	0.05	0.07	0.08	0.12	0.13
SSP4 - Inequality	0.04	0.04	0.05	0.07	0.09	0.12	0.13
SSP5 - Conventional development	0.04	0.05	0.06	0.09	0.13	0.33	0.46
Proportion below age 20							
SSP1 - Rapid development	0.47	0.38	0.31	0.25	0.21	0.14	0.10
SSP2 - Medium	0.47	0.39	0.35	0.31	0.27	0.22	0.19
SSP3 - Stalled development	0.47	0.40	0.38	0.35	0.33	0.31	0.30
SSP4 - Inequality	0.47	0.40	0.38	0.35	0.33	0.31	0.30
SSP5 - Conventional development	0.47	0.38	0.31	0.25	0.21	0.14	0.10
Proportion of Women age 20–39 with at least secondary education							
SSP1 - Rapid development	0.36	0.56	0.70	0.79	0.84	0.91	0.96
SSP2 - Medium	0.36	0.45	0.54	0.61	0.68	0.82	0.91
SSP3 - Stalled development	0.36	0.39	0.40	0.40	0.40	0.40	0.40
SSP4 - Inequality	0.36	0.36	0.36	0.36	0.36	0.36	0.36
SSP5 - Conventional development	0.36	0.56	0.70	0.79	0.84	0.91	0.96
Mean years of schooling, age 25+							
SSP1 - Rapid development	5.18	6.41	7.60	8.54	9.34	10.90	11.95
SSP2 - Medium	5.18	5.96	6.70	7.33	7.93	9.29	10.36
SSP3 - Stalled development	5.18	5.79	6.21	6.47	6.66	6.86	6.87
SSP4 - Inequality	5.18	5.59	5.82	6.00	6.14	6.37	6.55
SSP5 - Conventional development	5.18	6.41	7.58	8.52	9.32	10.88	11.94

Demographic Assumptions Underlying SSPs

	2010–15	2020–25	2030–35	2040–45	2050–55	2075–80	2095–2100
Total fertility rate							
SSP1 - Rapid development	2.47	1.86	1.53	1.38	1.29	1.21	1.16
SSP2 - Medium	2.66	2.26	2.06	1.93	1.86	1.71	1.61
SSP3 - Stalled development	2.78	2.70	2.61	2.54	2.49	2.40	2.36
SSP4 - Inequality	2.78	2.71	2.62	2.54	2.48	2.36	2.31
SSP5 - Conventional development	2.47	1.86	1.53	1.38	1.29	1.21	1.16
Life expectancy at birth for females (in years)							
SSP1 - Rapid development	70.77	72.94	75.53	78.23	81.08	88.38	94.22
SSP2 - Medium	68.12	69.78	71.59	73.59	75.50	80.49	84.51
SSP3 - Stalled development	70.52	70.81	71.28	71.97	72.54	74.17	75.57
SSP4 - Inequality	70.52	70.79	71.23	71.89	72.44	74.04	75.47
SSP5 - Conventional development	70.77	72.94	75.53	78.23	81.08	88.38	94.22
Migration – net flow over five years (in thousands)							
SSP1 - Rapid development	−68	−68	−67	−64	−58	−20	0
SSP2 - Medium	−68	−69	−69	−69	−67	−28	0
SSP3 - Stalled development	−56	−34	−34	−34	−34	−16	0
SSP4 - Inequality	−68	−69	−70	−72	−72	−33	0
SSP5 - Conventional development	−79	−104	−104	−102	−95	−36	0

Ageing Indicators, Medium Scenario (SSP2)

	2010	2020	2030	2040	2050	2075	2095
Median age	21.39	25.44	29.21	32.53	35.48	41.96	45.31
Propspective median age	21.39	24.78	27.73	29.91	31.84	34.62	34.38
Proportion age 65+	0.04	0.04	0.06	0.08	0.10	0.19	0.25
Proportion RLE < 15 years	0.05	0.05	0.07	0.08	0.10	0.16	0.16

Latvia

Detailed Human Capital Projections to 2060

Demographic indicators, Medium Scenario (SSP2)	2010	2020	2030	2040	2050	2060
Population (in millions)	2.25	2.15	2.03	1.90	1.78	1.65
Proportion age 65+	0.18	0.19	0.23	0.26	0.31	0.36
Proportion below age 20	0.20	0.20	0.18	0.17	0.16	0.16
	2005–10	2015–20	2025–30	2035–40	2045–50	2055–60
Total Fertility Rate	1.41	1.34	1.43	1.49	1.54	1.56
Life expectancy at birth (in years)						
Men	66.88	70.55	73.36	75.99	78.36	80.65
Women	77.45	79.79	81.89	83.99	86.01	88.01
Five-year immigration flow (in '000)	0.75	0.74	0.77	0.79	0.79	0.78
Five-year emigration flow (in '000)	10.72	6.58	5.50	4.84	4.19	3.67

Human Capital indicators, Medium Scenario (SSP2)	2010	2020	2030	2040	2050	2060
Population age 25+: highest educational attainment						
E1 - no education	0.01	0.00	0.00	0.00	0.00	0.00
E2 - incomplete primary	0.00	0.00	0.00	0.00	0.00	0.00
E3 - primary	0.04	0.02	0.01	0.00	0.00	0.00
E4 - lower secondary	0.19	0.13	0.08	0.05	0.03	0.02
E5 - upper secondary	0.44	0.49	0.51	0.51	0.50	0.48
E6 - post-secondary	0.32	0.36	0.40	0.43	0.47	0.50
Mean years of schooling (in years)	12.33	12.90	13.26	13.52	13.73	13.92
Gender gap (population age 25+): highest educational attainment (ratio male/female)						
E1 - no education	0.68	0.85	0.95	0.95	0.91	0.91
E2 - incomplete primary	0.54	0.64	0.84	0.94	0.92	0.92
E3 - primary	0.67	0.69	0.88	1.32	1.56	1.60
E4 - lower secondary	1.13	1.12	1.16	1.23	1.25	1.20
E5 - upper secondary	1.14	1.16	1.16	1.15	1.14	1.11
E6 - post-secondary	0.81	0.80	0.80	0.82	0.86	0.90
Mean years of schooling (male minus female)	−0.18	−0.31	−0.38	−0.37	−0.31	−0.23
Women age 20–39: highest educational attainment						
E1 - no education	0.00	0.00	0.00	0.00	0.00	0.00
E2 - incomplete primary	0.00	0.00	0.00	0.00	0.00	0.00
E3 - primary	0.00	0.00	0.00	0.00	0.00	0.00
E4 - lower secondary	0.11	0.07	0.07	0.07	0.06	0.06
E5 - upper secondary	0.53	0.50	0.49	0.46	0.43	0.42
E6 - post-secondary	0.36	0.43	0.44	0.47	0.51	0.52
Mean years of schooling (in years)	13.08	13.50	13.51	13.67	13.82	13.88

Education scenarios

GET: global education trend scenario (medium assumption also used for SSP2)

CER: constant enrolment rates scenario (assumption of no future improvements)

FT: Fast track scenario (assumption of education expansion according to fastest historical experience)

Pyramids by Education, Medium Scenario

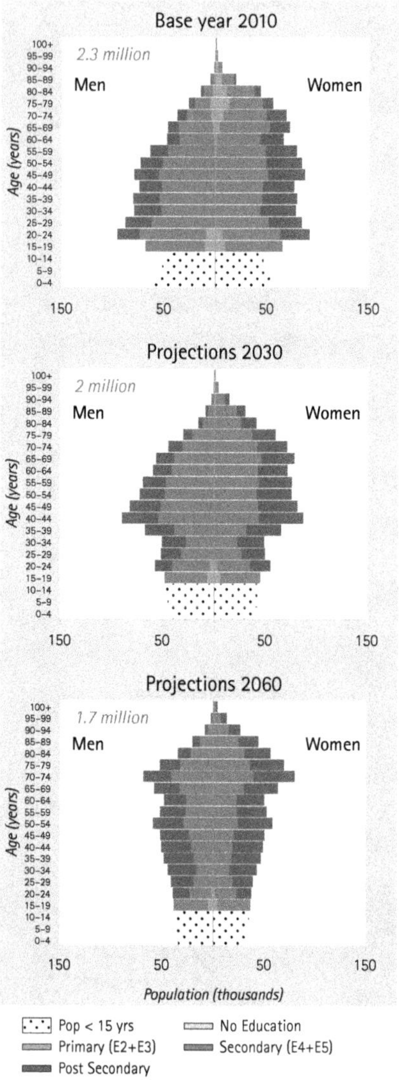

Population Size by Educational Attainment According to Three Education Scenarios: GET, CER, and FT

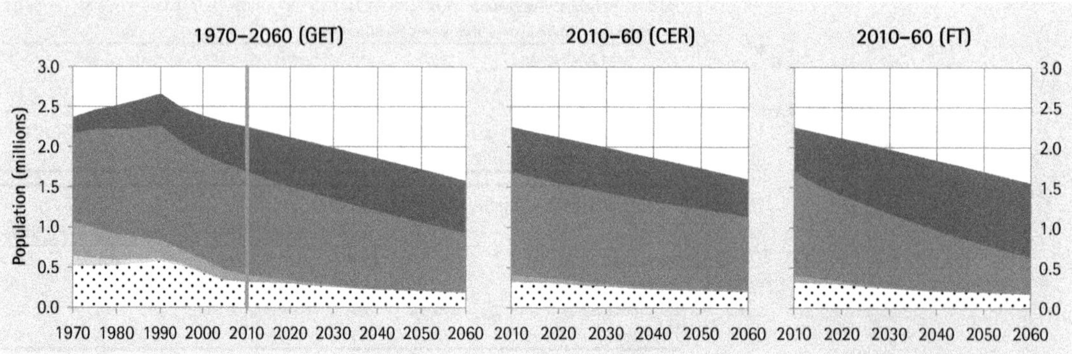

Latvia (Continued)

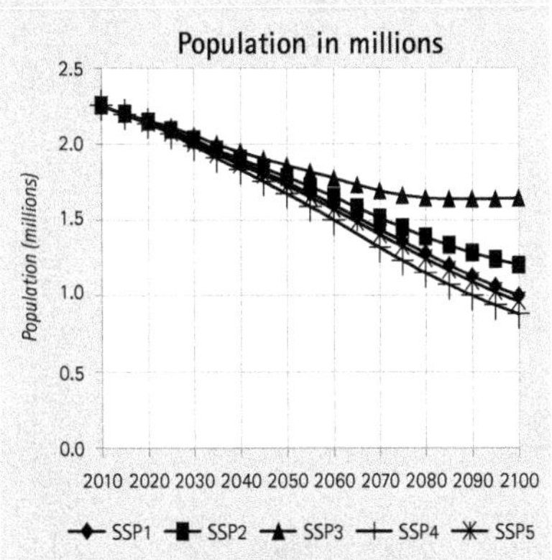

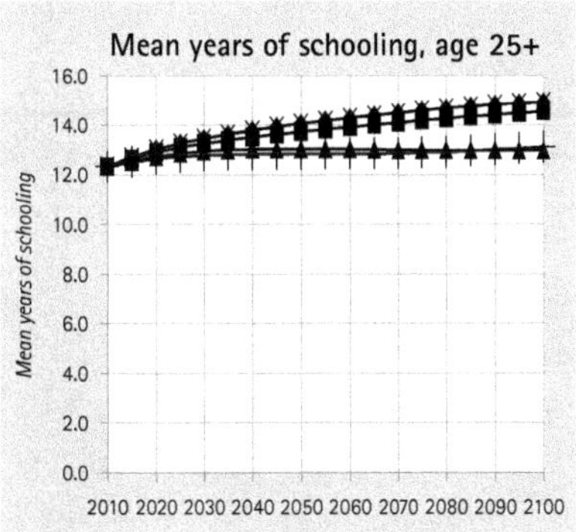

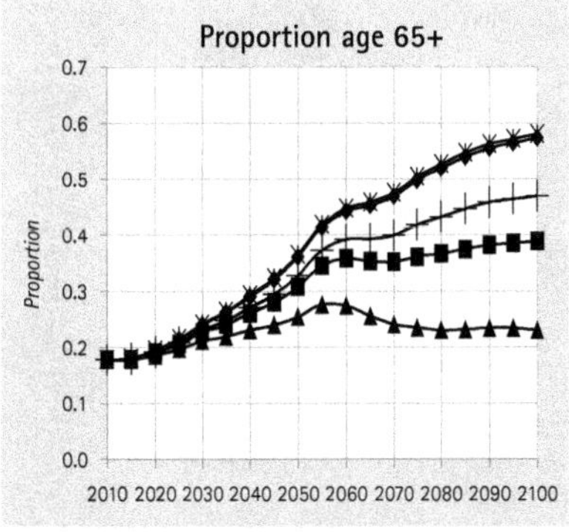

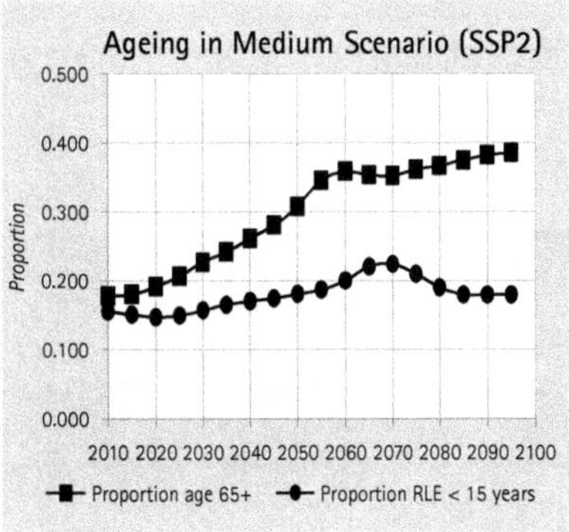

Alternative Scenarios to 2100

Projection Results by Scenario (SSP1–5)

	2010	2020	2030	2040	2050	2075	2100
Population (in millions)							
SSP1 - Rapid development	2.25	2.14	2.01	1.88	1.75	1.36	1.00
SSP2 - Medium	2.25	2.15	2.03	1.90	1.78	1.45	1.20
SSP3 - Stalled development	2.25	2.15	2.06	1.95	1.86	1.66	1.64
SSP4 - Inequality	2.25	2.13	1.99	1.83	1.67	1.23	0.88
SSP5 - Conventional development	2.25	2.14	2.00	1.86	1.73	1.33	0.96
Proportion age 65+							
SSP1 - Rapid development	0.18	0.19	0.24	0.29	0.36	0.50	0.57
SSP2 - Medium	0.18	0.19	0.23	0.26	0.31	0.36	0.39
SSP3 - Stalled development	0.18	0.19	0.21	0.23	0.25	0.24	0.23
SSP4 - Inequality	0.18	0.19	0.23	0.27	0.33	0.42	0.47
SSP5 - Conventional development	0.18	0.20	0.24	0.29	0.36	0.50	0.58
Proportion below age 20							
SSP1 - Rapid development	0.20	0.19	0.16	0.13	0.12	0.09	0.08
SSP2 - Medium	0.20	0.20	0.18	0.17	0.16	0.16	0.15
SSP3 - Stalled development	0.20	0.20	0.21	0.20	0.21	0.23	0.24
SSP4 - Inequality	0.20	0.19	0.17	0.14	0.13	0.11	0.11
SSP5 - Conventional development	0.20	0.19	0.16	0.13	0.12	0.09	0.08
Proportion of Women age 20–39 with at least secondary education							
SSP1 - Rapid development	0.99	1.00	1.00	1.00	1.00	1.00	1.00
SSP2 - Medium	0.99	1.00	1.00	1.00	1.00	1.00	1.00
SSP3 - Stalled development	0.99	0.99	0.99	0.99	0.99	0.99	0.99
SSP4 - Inequality	0.99	0.93	0.89	0.89	0.89	0.89	0.89
SSP5 - Conventional development	0.99	1.00	1.00	1.00	1.00	1.00	1.00
Mean years of schooling, age 25+							
SSP1 - Rapid development	12.33	13.02	13.46	13.80	14.07	14.60	14.94
SSP2 - Medium	12.33	12.90	13.26	13.52	13.73	14.19	14.55
SSP3 - Stalled development	12.33	12.72	12.95	13.03	13.04	12.99	12.98
SSP4 - Inequality	12.33	12.65	12.78	12.83	12.84	12.88	13.12
SSP5 - Conventional development	12.33	13.02	13.46	13.79	14.06	14.60	14.94

Demographic Assumptions Underlying SSPs

	2010–15	2020–25	2030–35	2040–45	2050–55	2075–80	2095–2100
Total fertility rate							
SSP1 - Rapid development	1.23	1.16	1.13	1.14	1.14	1.18	1.20
SSP2 - Medium	1.30	1.39	1.46	1.51	1.55	1.59	1.62
SSP3 - Stalled development	1.38	1.63	1.83	1.94	2.02	2.09	2.14
SSP4 - Inequality	1.24	1.20	1.18	1.19	1.20	1.23	1.25
SSP5 - Conventional development	1.23	1.16	1.13	1.14	1.14	1.18	1.20
Life expectancy at birth for females (in years)							
SSP1 - Rapid development	79.85	82.79	85.71	88.65	91.61	99.09	105.09
SSP2 - Medium	78.59	80.89	82.89	84.99	87.01	92.00	95.99
SSP3 - Stalled development	78.90	79.90	80.83	81.78	82.72	85.05	86.99
SSP4 - Inequality	79.32	81.36	83.18	85.17	87.11	91.78	95.68
SSP5 - Conventional development	79.85	82.79	85.71	88.65	91.61	99.09	105.09
Migration – net flow over five years (in thousands)							
SSP1 - Rapid development	−7	−5	−4	−3	−3	−1	0
SSP2 - Medium	−7	−5	−4	−4	−3	−1	0
SSP3 - Stalled development	−6	−3	−2	−2	−2	−1	0
SSP4 - Inequality	−7	−5	−4	−3	−2	−1	0
SSP5 - Conventional development	−9	−8	−7	−6	−5	−2	0

Ageing Indicators, Medium Scenario (SSP2)

	2010	2020	2030	2040	2050	2075	2095
Median age	40.17	42.59	45.88	50.37	51.89	54.36	54.79
Propspective median age	40.17	40.22	41.54	44.10	43.66	41.30	37.57
Proportion age 65+	0.18	0.19	0.23	0.26	0.31	0.36	0.39
Proportion RLE < 15 years	0.16	0.15	0.16	0.17	0.18	0.21	0.18

Lebanon

Detailed Human Capital Projections to 2060

Demographic indicators, Medium Scenario (SSP2)	2010	2020	2030	2040	2050	2060
Population (in millions)	4.23	4.58	4.90	5.10	5.19	5.20
Proportion age 65+	0.07	0.09	0.12	0.16	0.21	0.25
Proportion below age 20	0.34	0.28	0.25	0.23	0.20	0.19
	2005–10	2015–20	2025–30	2035–40	2045–50	2055–60
Total Fertility Rate	1.86	1.71	1.69	1.63	1.56	1.58
Life expectancy at birth (in years)						
Men	69.87	72.23	74.34	76.30	78.32	80.35
Women	74.17	76.60	78.79	80.79	82.79	84.81
Five-year immigration flow (in '000)	86.11	84.28	87.49	89.40	89.35	88.01
Five-year emigration flow (in '000)	98.39	74.83	70.18	66.01	62.30	57.46

Human Capital indicators, Medium Scenario (SSP2)	2010	2020	2030	2040	2050	2060
Population age 25+: highest educational attainment						
E1 - no education	0.10	0.06	0.03	0.02	0.01	0.00
E2 - incomplete primary	0.05	0.03	0.01	0.01	0.00	0.00
E3 - primary	0.22	0.20	0.17	0.14	0.11	0.08
E4 - lower secondary	0.28	0.28	0.25	0.22	0.18	0.14
E5 - upper secondary	0.17	0.21	0.24	0.26	0.28	0.29
E6 - post-secondary	0.17	0.23	0.29	0.36	0.42	0.48
Mean years of schooling (in years)	8.69	9.86	10.83	11.62	12.33	12.96
Gender gap (population age 25+): highest educational attainment (ratio male/female)						
E1 - no education	0.53	0.50	0.50	0.53	0.58	0.66
E2 - incomplete primary	1.16	0.93	0.78	0.69	0.65	0.64
E3 - primary	1.23	1.21	1.20	1.19	1.18	1.17
E4 - lower secondary	0.93	0.96	0.98	0.98	0.98	0.99
E5 - upper secondary	1.02	0.99	0.99	1.00	1.01	1.00
E6 - post-secondary	1.16	1.06	1.01	0.98	0.97	0.98
Mean years of schooling (male minus female)	0.53	0.30	0.12	0.00	-0.06	-0.07
Women age 20–39: highest educational attainment						
E1 - no education	0.02	0.01	0.01	0.01	0.00	0.00
E2 - incomplete primary	0.01	0.00	0.00	0.00	0.00	0.00
E3 - primary	0.15	0.10	0.07	0.05	0.04	0.03
E4 - lower secondary	0.29	0.20	0.13	0.09	0.06	0.04
E5 - upper secondary	0.26	0.30	0.31	0.30	0.29	0.28
E6 - post-secondary	0.28	0.38	0.47	0.55	0.61	0.65
Mean years of schooling (in years)	11.02	12.19	13.00	13.61	14.00	14.26

Education scenarios

GET: global education trend scenario (medium assumption also used for SSP2)

CER: constant enrolment rates scenario (assumption of no future improvements)

FT: Fast track scenario (assumption of education expansion according to fastest historical experience)

Pyramids by Education, Medium Scenario

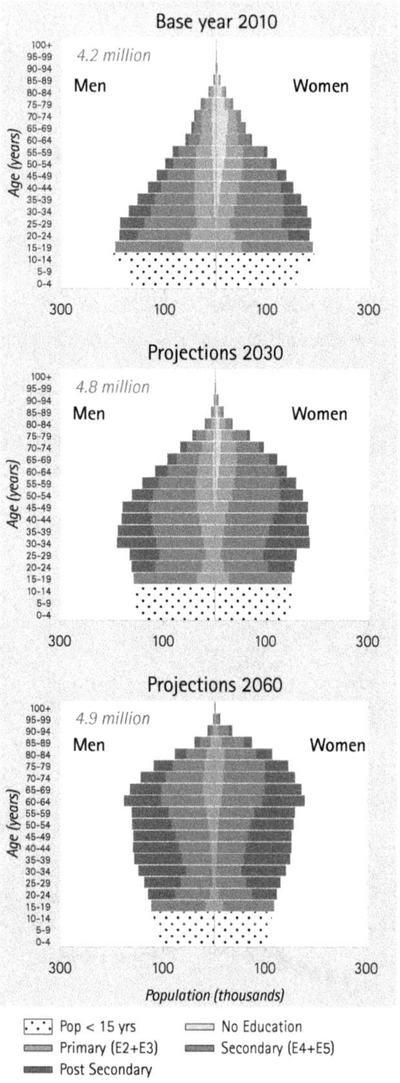

Population Size by Educational Attainment According to Three Education Scenarios: GET, CER, and FT

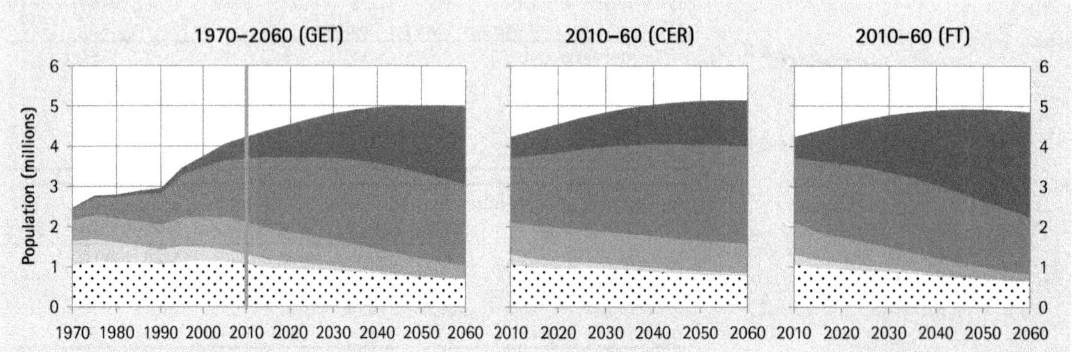

Lebanon (Continued)

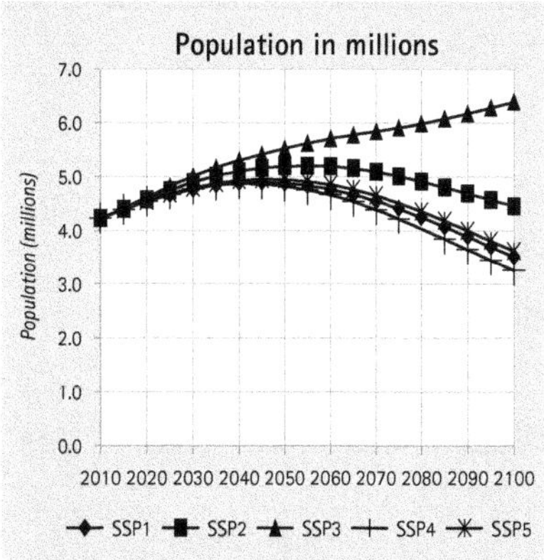

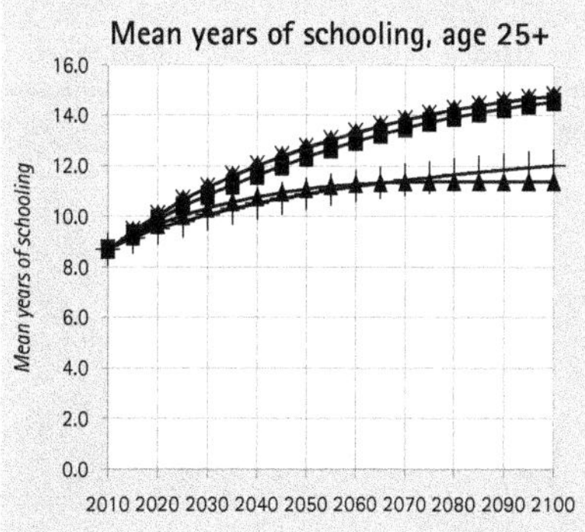

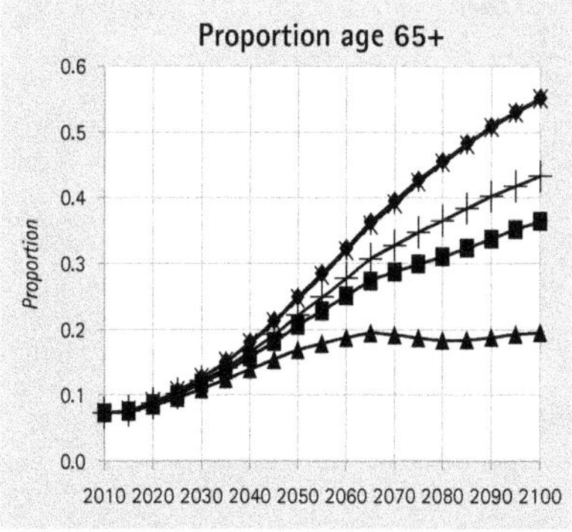

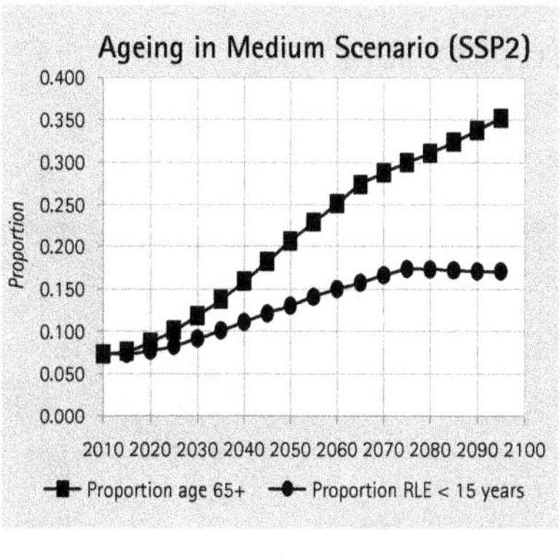

Alternative Scenarios to 2100

Projection Results by Scenario (SSP1–5)

	2010	2020	2030	2040	2050	2075	2100
Population (in millions)							
SSP1 - Rapid development	4.23	4.54	4.77	4.89	4.88	4.41	3.51
SSP2 - Medium	4.23	4.58	4.90	5.10	5.19	5.01	4.46
SSP3 - Stalled development	4.23	4.62	5.01	5.30	5.53	5.91	6.39
SSP4 - Inequality	4.23	4.54	4.77	4.87	4.82	4.22	3.26
SSP5 - Conventional development	4.23	4.54	4.79	4.93	4.94	4.51	3.62
Proportion age 65+							
SSP1 - Rapid development	0.07	0.09	0.13	0.18	0.25	0.43	0.55
SSP2 - Medium	0.07	0.09	0.12	0.16	0.21	0.30	0.36
SSP3 - Stalled development	0.07	0.08	0.11	0.14	0.17	0.19	0.20
SSP4 - Inequality	0.07	0.09	0.12	0.17	0.22	0.35	0.43
SSP5 - Conventional development	0.07	0.09	0.13	0.18	0.25	0.42	0.55
Proportion below age 20							
SSP1 - Rapid development	0.34	0.27	0.22	0.18	0.15	0.11	0.09
SSP2 - Medium	0.34	0.28	0.25	0.23	0.20	0.17	0.16
SSP3 - Stalled development	0.34	0.29	0.28	0.27	0.26	0.26	0.27
SSP4 - Inequality	0.34	0.27	0.23	0.20	0.17	0.13	0.12
SSP5 - Conventional development	0.34	0.27	0.22	0.18	0.15	0.11	0.09
Proportion of Women age 20–39 with at least secondary education							
SSP1 - Rapid development	0.83	0.92	0.95	0.97	0.98	0.99	1.00
SSP2 - Medium	0.83	0.88	0.92	0.94	0.96	0.98	0.99
SSP3 - Stalled development	0.83	0.86	0.86	0.86	0.86	0.86	0.86
SSP4 - Inequality	0.83	0.81	0.77	0.77	0.77	0.77	0.77
SSP5 - Conventional development	0.83	0.92	0.95	0.97	0.98	0.99	1.00
Mean years of schooling, age 25+							
SSP1 - Rapid development	8.69	10.04	11.13	11.98	12.69	14.02	14.76
SSP2 - Medium	8.69	9.86	10.83	11.62	12.33	13.72	14.53
SSP3 - Stalled development	8.69	9.66	10.32	10.77	11.08	11.37	11.38
SSP4 - Inequality	8.69	9.51	10.06	10.51	10.88	11.55	12.01
SSP5 - Conventional development	8.69	10.04	11.14	12.00	12.71	14.03	14.76

Demographic Assumptions Underlying SSPs

	2010–15	2020–25	2030–35	2040–45	2050–55	2075–80	2095–2100
Total fertility rate							
SSP1 - Rapid development	1.65	1.41	1.27	1.19	1.16	1.19	1.22
SSP2 - Medium	1.74	1.70	1.66	1.59	1.57	1.60	1.63
SSP3 - Stalled development	1.84	2.02	2.13	2.14	2.16	2.25	2.31
SSP4 - Inequality	1.67	1.50	1.37	1.28	1.25	1.29	1.32
SSP5 - Conventional development	1.65	1.41	1.27	1.19	1.16	1.19	1.22
Life expectancy at birth for females (in years)							
SSP1 - Rapid development	77.32	80.17	83.04	85.94	88.81	96.12	102.06
SSP2 - Medium	75.50	77.69	79.79	81.79	83.79	88.80	92.79
SSP3 - Stalled development	76.51	77.44	78.40	79.29	80.15	82.10	83.78
SSP4 - Inequality	76.95	78.80	80.69	82.51	84.30	88.70	92.41
SSP5 - Conventional development	77.32	80.17	83.04	85.94	88.81	96.12	102.06
Migration – net flow over five years (in thousands)							
SSP1 - Rapid development	1	13	20	22	22	7	0
SSP2 - Medium	1	13	21	25	29	13	0
SSP3 - Stalled development	1	7	11	16	21	14	0
SSP4 - Inequality	1	13	20	24	27	11	0
SSP5 - Conventional development	1	19	28	31	30	9	0

Ageing Indicators, Medium Scenario (SSP2)

	2010	2020	2030	2040	2050	2075	2095
Median age	29.10	33.12	36.96	41.02	44.01	49.61	53.07
Propspective median age	29.10	31.54	33.68	36.10	37.37	38.59	38.36
Proportion age 65+	0.07	0.09	0.12	0.16	0.21	0.30	0.35
Proportion RLE < 15 years	0.07	0.08	0.09	0.11	0.13	0.17	0.17

Lesotho

Detailed Human Capital Projections to 2060

Demographic indicators, Medium Scenario (SSP2)	2010	2020	2030	2040	2050	2060
Population (in millions)	2.17	2.37	2.52	2.60	2.64	2.64
Proportion age 65+	0.04	0.04	0.04	0.04	0.06	0.09
Proportion below age 20	0.49	0.44	0.41	0.37	0.34	0.31
	2005–10	2015–20	2025–30	2035–40	2045–50	2055–60
Total Fertility Rate	3.37	2.68	2.32	2.08	1.91	1.81
Life expectancy at birth (in years)						
Men	46.46	51.12	52.89	54.17	55.97	58.61
Women	45.19	49.30	52.08	54.70	57.30	60.20
Five-year immigration flow (in '000)	1.41	1.38	1.43	1.47	1.46	1.44
Five-year emigration flow (in '000)	21.33	18.46	19.48	19.63	19.17	18.34

Human Capital indicators, Medium Scenario (SSP2)	2010	2020	2030	2040	2050	2060
Population age 25+: highest educational attainment						
E1 - no education	0.13	0.08	0.05	0.04	0.02	0.01
E2 - incomplete primary	0.37	0.28	0.19	0.13	0.09	0.06
E3 - primary	0.28	0.33	0.36	0.35	0.33	0.30
E4 - lower secondary	0.09	0.12	0.14	0.14	0.14	0.14
E5 - upper secondary	0.07	0.12	0.17	0.23	0.29	0.35
E6 - post-secondary	0.06	0.07	0.09	0.11	0.13	0.15
Mean years of schooling (in years)	6.45	7.65	8.60	9.39	10.05	10.62
Gender gap (population age 25+): highest educational attainment (ratio male/female)						
E1 - no education	4.31	4.21	4.05	3.65	3.07	2.38
E2 - incomplete primary	0.96	1.15	1.34	1.55	1.66	1.58
E3 - primary	0.63	0.75	0.81	0.87	0.91	0.93
E4 - lower secondary	0.74	0.74	0.81	0.86	0.92	0.95
E5 - upper secondary	1.01	0.99	0.96	0.95	0.96	0.99
E6 - post-secondary	0.99	0.93	0.90	0.90	0.91	0.96
Mean years of schooling (male minus female)	−1.38	−1.07	−0.90	−0.72	−0.51	−0.27
Women age 20–39: highest educational attainment						
E1 - no education	0.01	0.01	0.01	0.01	0.01	0.00
E2 - incomplete primary	0.20	0.14	0.09	0.07	0.05	0.03
E3 - primary	0.45	0.41	0.38	0.33	0.28	0.22
E4 - lower secondary	0.15	0.17	0.18	0.18	0.17	0.16
E5 - upper secondary	0.13	0.18	0.24	0.30	0.37	0.42
E6 - post-secondary	0.06	0.08	0.09	0.11	0.13	0.15
Mean years of schooling (in years)	8.54	9.14	9.73	10.24	10.74	11.19

Education scenarios

GET : global education trend scenario (medium assumption also used for SSP2)

CER: constant enrolment rates scenario (assumption of no future improvements)

FT: fast track scenario (assumption of education expansion according to fastest historical experience)

Pyramids by Education, Medium Scenario

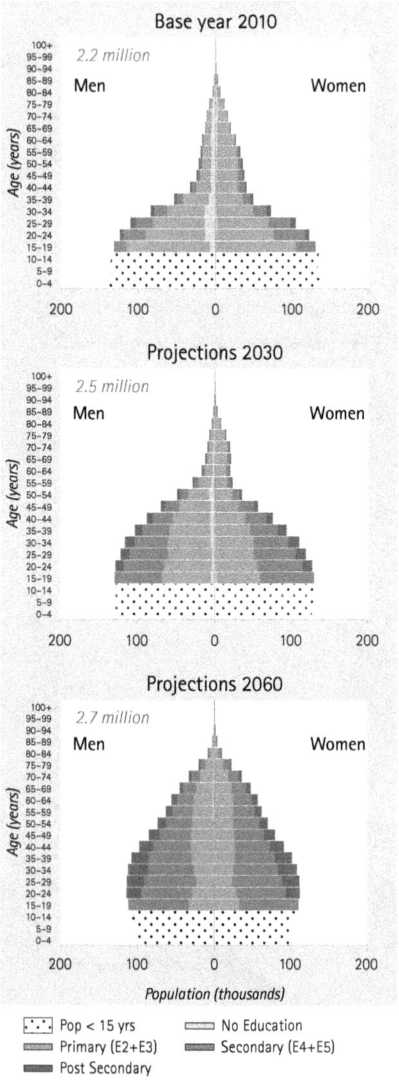

Population Size by Educational Attainment According to Three Education Scenarios: GET, CER, and FT

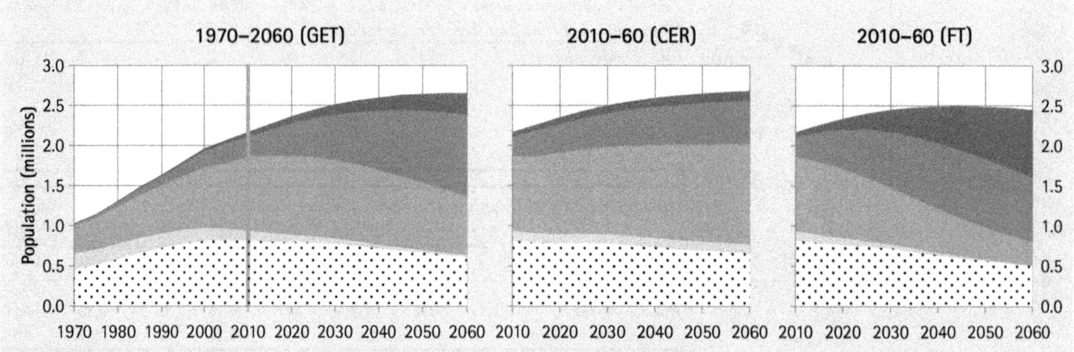

Lesotho (Continued)

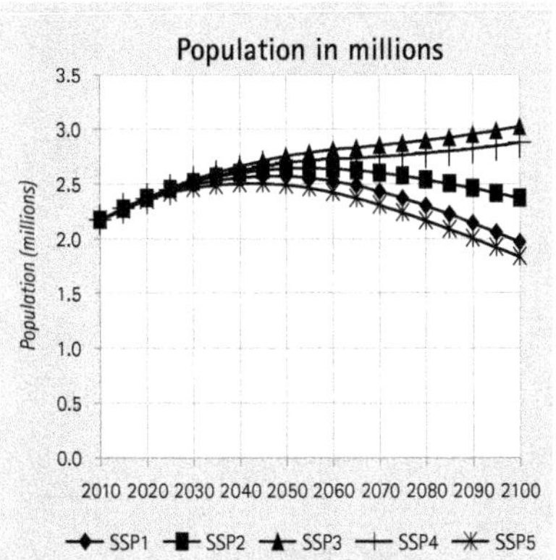

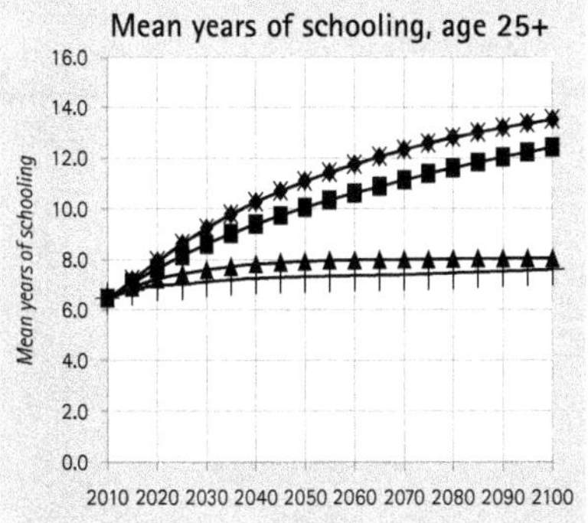

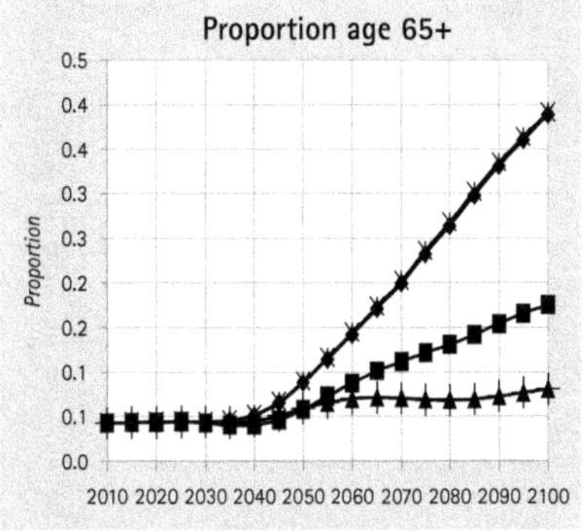

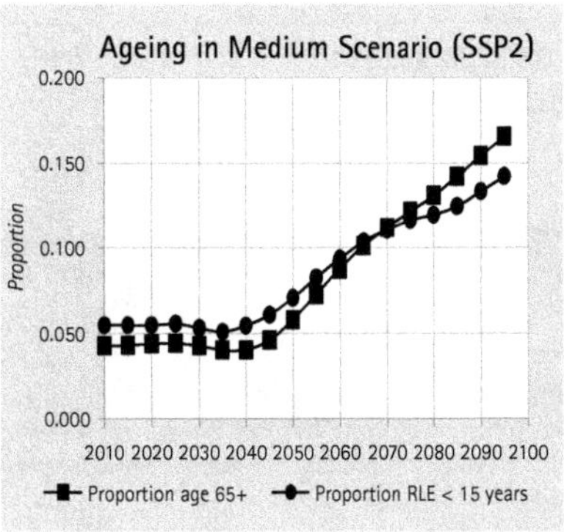

Alternative Scenarios to 2100

Projection Results by Scenario (SSP1–5)

	2010	2020	2030	2040	2050	2075	2100
Population (in millions)							
SSP1 - Rapid development	2.17	2.36	2.49	2.56	2.57	2.37	1.97
SSP2 - Medium	2.17	2.37	2.52	2.60	2.64	2.57	2.37
SSP3 - Stalled development	2.17	2.37	2.54	2.66	2.75	2.88	3.02
SSP4 - Inequality	2.17	2.37	2.52	2.62	2.69	2.76	2.88
SSP5 - Conventional development	2.17	2.35	2.46	2.50	2.49	2.24	1.84
Proportion age 65+							
SSP1 - Rapid development	0.04	0.04	0.04	0.05	0.09	0.23	0.39
SSP2 - Medium	0.04	0.04	0.04	0.04	0.06	0.12	0.18
SSP3 - Stalled development	0.04	0.04	0.04	0.04	0.06	0.07	0.08
SSP4 - Inequality	0.04	0.04	0.04	0.05	0.06	0.07	0.08
SSP5 - Conventional development	0.04	0.04	0.04	0.05	0.09	0.24	0.39
Proportion below age 20							
SSP1 - Rapid development	0.49	0.43	0.36	0.30	0.25	0.16	0.12
SSP2 - Medium	0.49	0.44	0.41	0.37	0.34	0.28	0.23
SSP3 - Stalled development	0.49	0.45	0.43	0.41	0.39	0.37	0.36
SSP4 - Inequality	0.49	0.46	0.44	0.42	0.40	0.37	0.36
SSP5 - Conventional development	0.49	0.43	0.37	0.30	0.25	0.16	0.11
Proportion of Women age 20–39 with at least secondary education							
SSP1 - Rapid development	0.34	0.52	0.66	0.76	0.82	0.91	0.96
SSP2 - Medium	0.34	0.43	0.51	0.59	0.67	0.84	0.94
SSP3 - Stalled development	0.34	0.38	0.38	0.38	0.38	0.38	0.38
SSP4 - Inequality	0.34	0.35	0.34	0.34	0.34	0.34	0.34
SSP5 - Conventional development	0.34	0.52	0.66	0.76	0.82	0.91	0.96
Mean years of schooling, age 25+							
SSP1 - Rapid development	6.45	7.94	9.23	10.26	11.08	12.58	13.51
SSP2 - Medium	6.45	7.65	8.60	9.39	10.05	11.38	12.41
SSP3 - Stalled development	6.45	7.24	7.60	7.82	7.93	8.02	8.06
SSP4 - Inequality	6.45	6.99	7.13	7.27	7.33	7.44	7.60
SSP5 - Conventional development	6.45	7.93	9.22	10.25	11.07	12.57	13.50

Demographic Assumptions Underlying SSPs

	2010–15	2020–25	2030–35	2040–45	2050–55	2075–80	2095–2100
Total fertility rate							
SSP1 - Rapid development	2.74	2.04	1.63	1.42	1.31	1.20	1.15
SSP2 - Medium	2.93	2.49	2.18	2.00	1.85	1.67	1.59
SSP3 - Stalled development	3.06	2.94	2.78	2.61	2.50	2.35	2.28
SSP4 - Inequality	3.07	2.98	2.81	2.62	2.49	2.32	2.24
SSP5 - Conventional development	2.74	2.05	1.63	1.42	1.31	1.20	1.15
Life expectancy at birth for females (in years)							
SSP1 - Rapid development	51.25	57.87	62.58	67.07	71.31	81.00	88.42
SSP2 - Medium	48.09	50.70	53.52	56.00	58.80	65.89	71.58
SSP3 - Stalled development	49.04	47.64	48.63	50.26	51.13	55.42	58.43
SSP4 - Inequality	49.04	47.56	48.51	50.13	51.01	55.31	58.35
SSP5 - Conventional development	51.25	57.87	62.58	67.07	71.31	81.00	88.42
Migration – net flow over five years (in thousands)							
SSP1 - Rapid development	−17	−17	−18	−17	−16	−6	0
SSP2 - Medium	−17	−18	−18	−18	−17	−7	0
SSP3 - Stalled development	−14	−8	−8	−8	−7	−3	0
SSP4 - Inequality	−16	−16	−16	−16	−16	−7	0
SSP5 - Conventional development	−19	−26	−28	−28	−27	−11	0

Ageing Indicators, Medium Scenario (SSP2)

	2010	2020	2030	2040	2050	2075	2095
Median age	20.25	22.58	24.60	26.70	28.98	34.61	39.00
Propspective median age	20.25	21.80	22.54	23.13	23.02	21.20	20.43
Proportion age 65+	0.04	0.04	0.04	0.04	0.06	0.12	0.17
Proportion RLE < 15 years	0.05	0.05	0.05	0.05	0.07	0.12	0.14

Liberia

Detailed Human Capital Projections to 2060

Demographic indicators, Medium Scenario (SSP2)	2010	2020	2030	2040	2050	2060
Population (in millions)	3.99	5.72	7.59	9.45	11.21	12.74
Proportion age 65+	0.03	0.03	0.03	0.04	0.05	0.07
Proportion below age 20	0.54	0.50	0.45	0.40	0.35	0.31
	2005–10	2015–20	2025–30	2035–40	2045–50	2055–60
Total Fertility Rate	5.42	4.32	3.36	2.73	2.34	2.08
Life expectancy at birth (in years)						
Men	53.45	58.63	60.53	62.37	64.24	66.51
Women	55.35	61.08	63.68	65.92	67.98	70.29
Five-year immigration flow (in '000)	321.52	254.87	264.47	270.23	270.08	266.04
Five-year emigration flow (in '000)	21.90	22.71	31.20	39.35	45.97	50.60

Human Capital indicators, Medium Scenario (SSP2)	2010	2020	2030	2040	2050	2060
Population age 25+: highest educational attainment						
E1 - no education	0.78	0.70	0.62	0.54	0.45	0.36
E2 - incomplete primary	0.09	0.09	0.09	0.09	0.08	0.06
E3 - primary	0.05	0.06	0.09	0.11	0.13	0.15
E4 - lower secondary	0.05	0.07	0.11	0.15	0.18	0.22
E5 - upper secondary	0.03	0.05	0.07	0.10	0.13	0.17
E6 - post-secondary	0.01	0.02	0.02	0.02	0.03	0.04
Mean years of schooling (in years)	1.61	2.26	3.05	3.95	4.94	5.97
Gender gap (population age 25+): highest educational attainment (ratio male/female)						
E1 - no education	0.86	0.84	0.84	0.85	0.86	0.87
E2 - incomplete primary	1.36	1.19	1.10	1.04	1.02	1.02
E3 - primary	1.54	1.24	1.11	1.04	1.01	1.00
E4 - lower secondary	2.05	1.79	1.51	1.32	1.19	1.11
E5 - upper secondary	2.66	2.16	1.78	1.50	1.30	1.17
E6 - post-secondary	3.65	2.21	1.48	1.13	0.99	0.98
Mean years of schooling (male minus female)	1.11	1.16	1.09	0.93	0.73	0.53
Women age 20–39: highest educational attainment						
E1 - no education	0.77	0.68	0.56	0.43	0.31	0.20
E2 - incomplete primary	0.10	0.11	0.12	0.12	0.11	0.10
E3 - primary	0.06	0.08	0.12	0.15	0.17	0.18
E4 - lower secondary	0.04	0.08	0.12	0.17	0.21	0.25
E5 - upper secondary	0.03	0.04	0.07	0.11	0.16	0.23
E6 - post-secondary	0.01	0.01	0.02	0.02	0.03	0.04
Mean years of schooling (in years)	1.54	2.33	3.42	4.69	6.04	7.34

Education scenarios

GET: global education trend scenario (medium assumption also used for SSP2)

CER: constant enrolment rates scenario (assumption of no future improvements)

FT: Fast track scenario (assumption of education expansion according to fastest historical experience)

Pyramids by Education, Medium Scenario

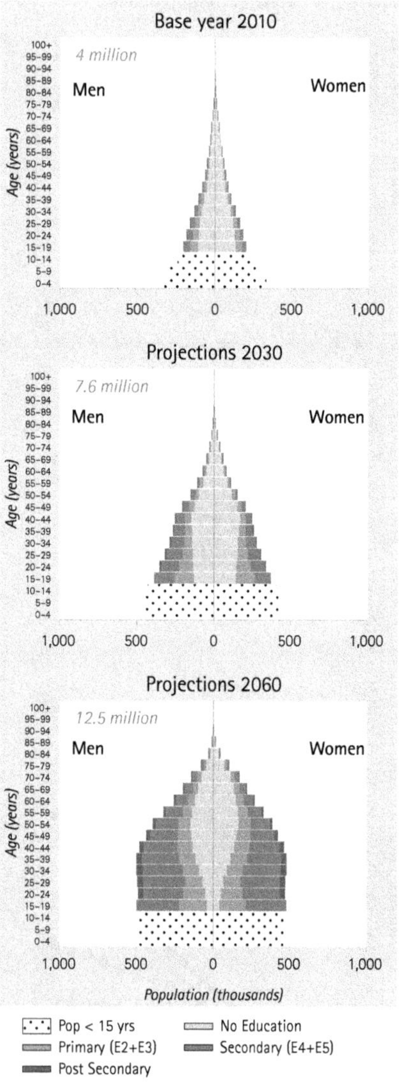

Population Size by Educational Attainment According to Three Education Scenarios: GET, CER, and FT

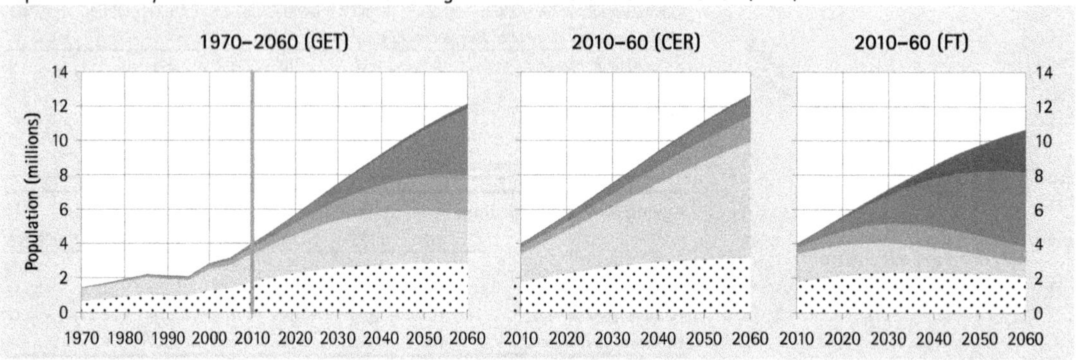

Liberia (Continued)

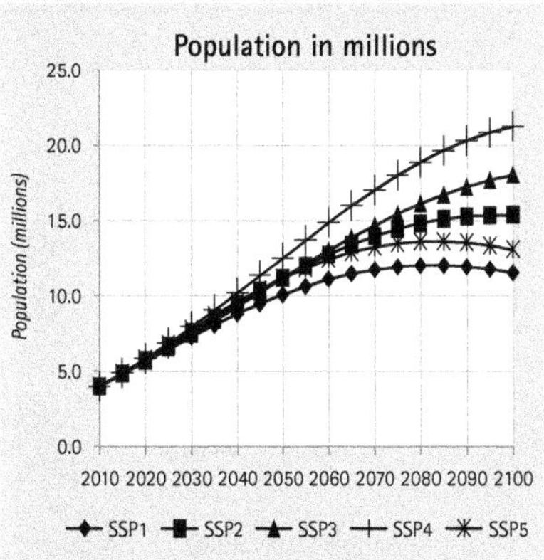

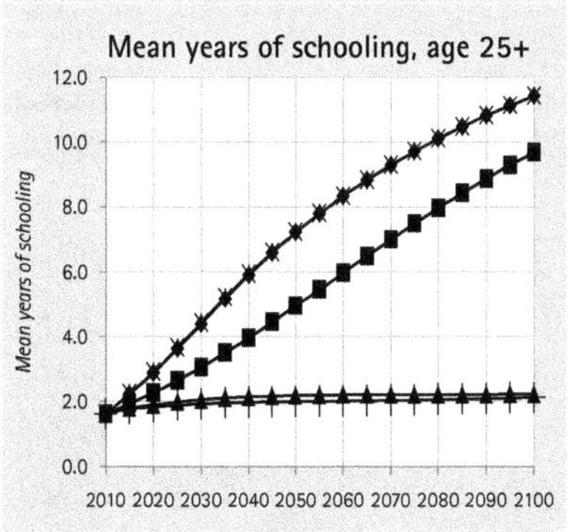

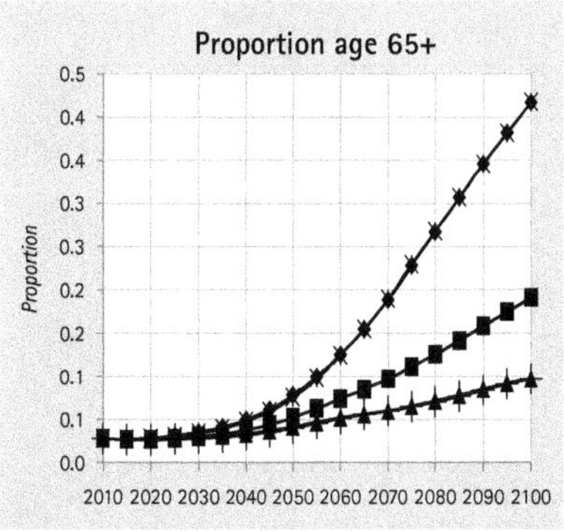

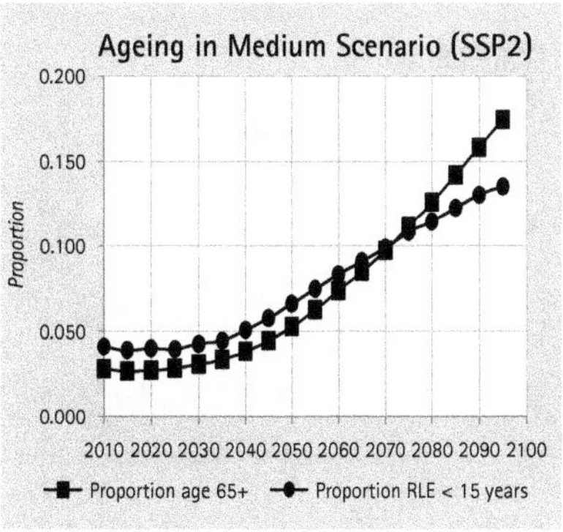

Alternative Scenarios to 2100

Projection Results by Scenario (SSP1–5)

	2010	2020	2030	2040	2050	2075	2100
Population (in millions)							
SSP1 - Rapid development	3.99	5.64	7.28	8.79	10.07	11.91	11.52
SSP2 - Medium	3.99	5.72	7.59	9.45	11.21	14.45	15.37
SSP3 - Stalled development	3.99	5.67	7.45	9.29	11.18	15.44	18.03
SSP4 - Inequality	3.99	5.82	7.95	10.19	12.53	18.00	21.24
SSP5 - Conventional development	3.99	5.79	7.75	9.58	11.16	13.48	13.08
Proportion age 65+							
SSP1 - Rapid development	0.03	0.03	0.04	0.05	0.08	0.23	0.42
SSP2 - Medium	0.03	0.03	0.03	0.04	0.05	0.11	0.19
SSP3 - Stalled development	0.03	0.03	0.03	0.03	0.04	0.07	0.10
SSP4 - Inequality	0.03	0.03	0.03	0.03	0.04	0.06	0.10
SSP5 - Conventional development	0.03	0.03	0.03	0.05	0.08	0.23	0.42
Proportion below age 20							
SSP1 - Rapid development	0.54	0.48	0.40	0.33	0.27	0.17	0.12
SSP2 - Medium	0.54	0.50	0.45	0.40	0.35	0.27	0.22
SSP3 - Stalled development	0.54	0.51	0.49	0.45	0.42	0.35	0.32
SSP4 - Inequality	0.54	0.51	0.48	0.45	0.41	0.35	0.32
SSP5 - Conventional development	0.54	0.47	0.40	0.33	0.27	0.17	0.12
Proportion of Women age 20–39 with at least secondary education							
SSP1 - Rapid development	0.08	0.22	0.38	0.53	0.64	0.81	0.91
SSP2 - Medium	0.08	0.13	0.21	0.30	0.41	0.65	0.84
SSP3 - Stalled development	0.08	0.09	0.09	0.09	0.09	0.09	0.09
SSP4 - Inequality	0.08	0.08	0.08	0.08	0.08	0.08	0.08
SSP5 - Conventional development	0.08	0.22	0.38	0.53	0.64	0.81	0.91
Mean years of schooling, age 25+							
SSP1 - Rapid development	1.61	2.88	4.37	5.89	7.21	9.70	11.42
SSP2 - Medium	1.61	2.26	3.05	3.95	4.94	7.48	9.68
SSP3 - Stalled development	1.61	1.88	2.05	2.14	2.18	2.21	2.22
SSP4 - Inequality	1.61	1.83	1.92	1.97	1.99	2.04	2.12
SSP5 - Conventional development	1.61	2.89	4.41	5.92	7.22	9.70	11.42

Demographic Assumptions Underlying SSPs

	2010–15	2020–25	2030–35	2040–45	2050–55	2075–80	2095–2100
Total fertility rate							
SSP1 - Rapid development	4.52	3.08	2.18	1.74	1.50	1.29	1.21
SSP2 - Medium	4.85	3.82	3.00	2.52	2.18	1.85	1.71
SSP3 - Stalled development	5.11	4.58	3.93	3.38	3.00	2.55	2.41
SSP4 - Inequality	5.11	4.59	3.94	3.38	3.00	2.54	2.39
SSP5 - Conventional development	4.52	3.07	2.18	1.74	1.50	1.29	1.21
Life expectancy at birth for females (in years)							
SSP1 - Rapid development	64.05	70.24	74.10	78.03	81.65	90.14	97.00
SSP2 - Medium	58.61	62.41	64.78	66.88	69.08	75.19	79.99
SSP3 - Stalled development	61.16	60.70	61.97	62.61	63.49	65.90	67.62
SSP4 - Inequality	61.16	60.69	61.96	62.59	63.47	65.87	67.60
SSP5 - Conventional development	64.05	70.24	74.10	78.03	81.64	90.14	97.00
Migration – net flow over five years (in thousands)							
SSP1 - Rapid development	250	228	220	198	172	63	0
SSP2 - Medium	239	222	224	220	212	103	0
SSP3 - Stalled development	206	111	114	123	134	88	0
SSP4 - Inequality	248	225	231	245	265	171	0
SSP5 - Conventional development	292	346	335	298	255	91	0

Ageing Indicators, Medium Scenario (SSP2)

	2010	2020	2030	2040	2050	2075	2095
Median age	18.09	20.14	22.66	25.54	28.53	35.46	40.60
Propspective median age	18.09	18.00	19.33	21.23	23.42	26.60	28.12
Proportion age 65+	0.03	0.03	0.03	0.04	0.05	0.11	0.17
Proportion RLE < 15 years	0.04	0.04	0.04	0.05	0.07	0.11	0.14

Lithuania

Detailed Human Capital Projections to 2060

Demographic indicators, Medium Scenario (SSP2)	2010	2020	2030	2040	2050	2060
Population (in millions)	3.32	3.22	3.10	2.95	2.80	2.64
Proportion age 65+	0.16	0.17	0.22	0.25	0.28	0.33
Proportion below age 20	0.22	0.21	0.22	0.19	0.18	0.19
	2005–10	2015–20	2025–30	2035–40	2045–50	2055–60
Total Fertility Rate	1.41	1.62	1.64	1.67	1.70	1.70
Life expectancy at birth (in years)						
Men	65.45	69.45	72.55	75.41	78.06	80.44
Women	77.24	79.99	82.19	84.29	86.41	88.41
Five-year immigration flow (in '000)	0.88	0.87	0.91	0.93	0.93	0.92
Five-year emigration flow (in '000)	36.31	23.72	19.55	18.16	16.32	14.26

Human Capital indicators, Medium Scenario (SSP2)	2010	2020	2030	2040	2050	2060
Population age 25+: highest educational attainment						
E1 - no education	0.00	0.00	0.00	0.00	0.00	0.00
E2 - incomplete primary	0.01	0.00	0.00	0.00	0.00	0.00
E3 - primary	0.07	0.03	0.01	0.00	0.00	0.00
E4 - lower secondary	0.09	0.07	0.04	0.03	0.02	0.01
E5 - upper secondary	0.37	0.39	0.39	0.38	0.36	0.33
E6 - post-secondary	0.45	0.51	0.55	0.59	0.62	0.66
Mean years of schooling (in years)	12.79	13.55	14.00	14.23	14.41	14.58
Gender gap (population age 25+): highest educational attainment (ratio male/female)						
E1 - no education	0.92	0.88	0.85	0.82	0.81	0.87
E2 - incomplete primary	0.35	0.32	0.41	0.72	0.87	0.92
E3 - primary	0.57	0.49	0.51	0.90	1.45	1.53
E4 - lower secondary	1.27	1.21	1.20	1.30	1.27	1.14
E5 - upper secondary	1.53	1.52	1.49	1.43	1.37	1.31
E6 - post-secondary	0.74	0.73	0.75	0.78	0.82	0.87
Mean years of schooling (male minus female)	−0.17	−0.45	−0.60	−0.59	−0.49	−0.37
Women age 20–39: highest educational attainment						
E1 - no education	0.00	0.00	0.00	0.00	0.00	0.00
E2 - incomplete primary	0.00	0.00	0.00	0.00	0.00	0.00
E3 - primary	0.00	0.00	0.00	0.00	0.00	0.00
E4 - lower secondary	0.09	0.06	0.05	0.06	0.05	0.05
E5 - upper secondary	0.42	0.38	0.37	0.38	0.35	0.35
E6 - post-secondary	0.48	0.56	0.57	0.55	0.59	0.60
Mean years of schooling (in years)	13.67	14.08	14.14	14.06	14.24	14.27

Education scenarios

GET: global education trend scenario (medium assumption also used for SSP2)

CER: constant enrolment rates scenario (assumption of no future improvements)

FT: Fast track scenario (assumption of education expansion according to fastest historical experience)

Pyramids by Education, Medium Scenario

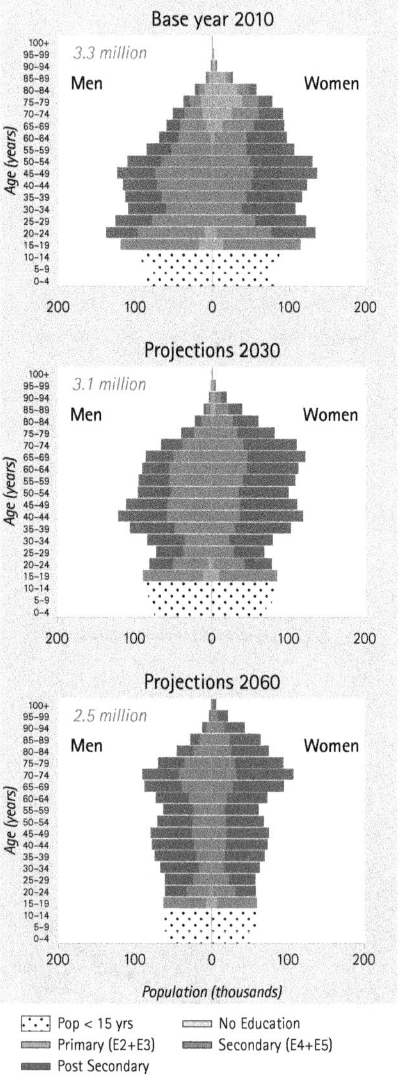

Population Size by Educational Attainment According to Three Education Scenarios: GET, CER, and FT

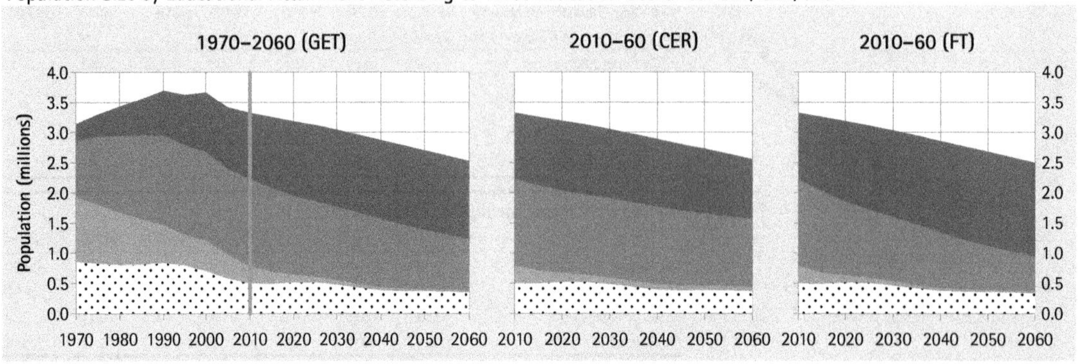

Lithuania (Continued)

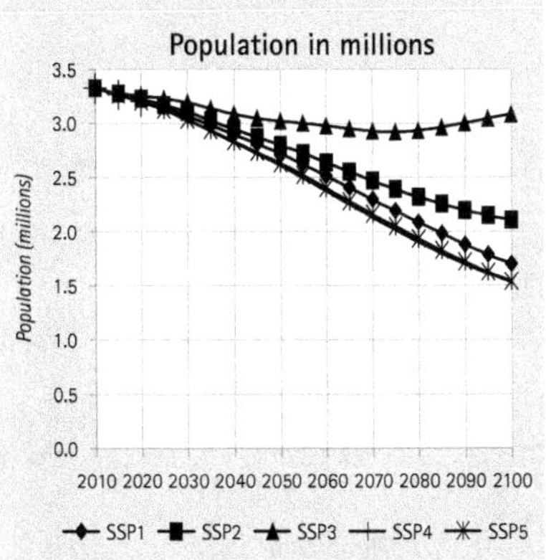

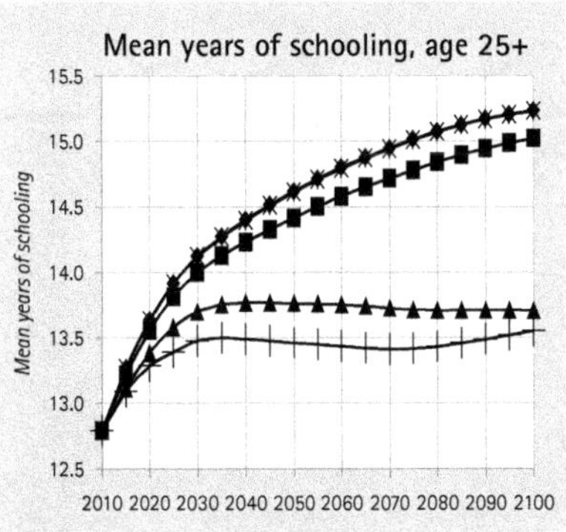

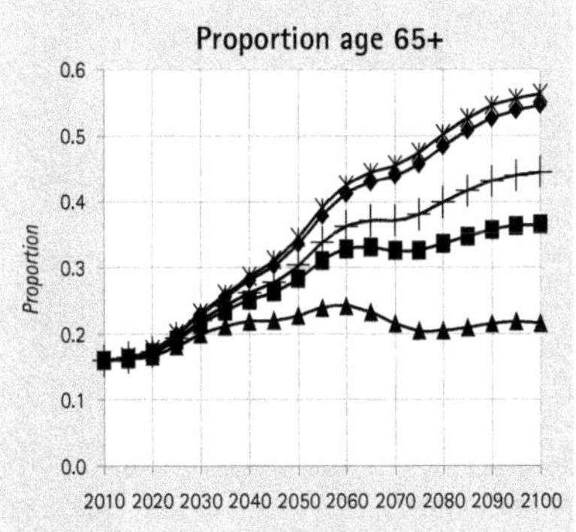

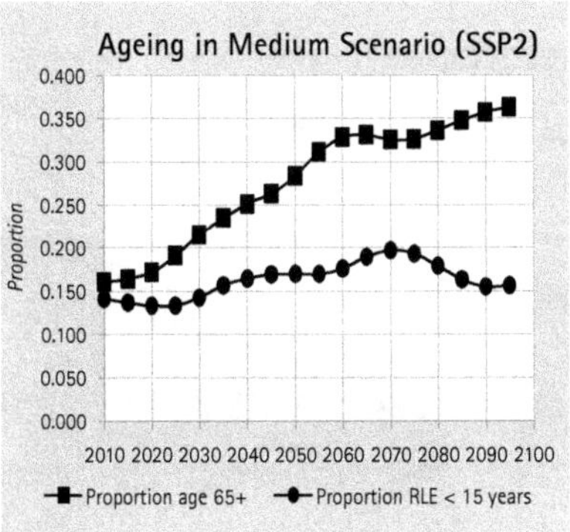

Alternative Scenarios to 2100

Projection Results by Scenario (SSP1–5)

	2010	2020	2030	2040	2050	2075	2100
Population (in millions)							
SSP1 - Rapid development	3.32	3.21	3.07	2.90	2.72	2.19	1.70
SSP2 - Medium	3.32	3.22	3.10	2.95	2.80	2.39	2.10
SSP3 - Stalled development	3.32	3.25	3.19	3.08	3.02	2.92	3.08
SSP4 - Inequality	3.32	3.20	3.03	2.82	2.61	2.02	1.53
SSP5 - Conventional development	3.32	3.20	3.03	2.83	2.63	2.05	1.54
Proportion age 65+							
SSP1 - Rapid development	0.16	0.18	0.23	0.28	0.34	0.46	0.55
SSP2 - Medium	0.16	0.17	0.22	0.25	0.28	0.33	0.37
SSP3 - Stalled development	0.16	0.17	0.20	0.22	0.23	0.20	0.22
SSP4 - Inequality	0.16	0.17	0.22	0.26	0.30	0.38	0.44
SSP5 - Conventional development	0.16	0.18	0.23	0.29	0.35	0.47	0.56
Proportion below age 20							
SSP1 - Rapid development	0.22	0.20	0.19	0.15	0.14	0.11	0.10
SSP2 - Medium	0.22	0.21	0.22	0.19	0.18	0.17	0.17
SSP3 - Stalled development	0.22	0.22	0.25	0.23	0.24	0.25	0.26
SSP4 - Inequality	0.22	0.20	0.20	0.16	0.15	0.13	0.12
SSP5 - Conventional development	0.22	0.20	0.19	0.15	0.13	0.10	0.09
Proportion of Women age 20–39 with at least secondary education							
SSP1 - Rapid development	0.99	1.00	1.00	1.00	1.00	1.00	1.00
SSP2 - Medium	0.99	1.00	1.00	1.00	1.00	1.00	1.00
SSP3 - Stalled development	0.99	0.99	0.99	0.99	0.99	0.99	0.99
SSP4 - Inequality	0.99	0.93	0.89	0.89	0.89	0.89	0.89
SSP5 - Conventional development	0.99	1.00	1.00	1.00	1.00	1.00	1.00
Mean years of schooling, age 25+							
SSP1 - Rapid development	12.79	13.63	14.12	14.40	14.62	15.01	15.23
SSP2 - Medium	12.79	13.55	14.00	14.23	14.41	14.78	15.02
SSP3 - Stalled development	12.79	13.38	13.70	13.77	13.76	13.71	13.71
SSP4 - Inequality	12.79	13.28	13.47	13.49	13.46	13.42	13.55
SSP5 - Conventional development	12.79	13.63	14.12	14.39	14.61	15.01	15.23

Demographic Assumptions Underlying SSPs

	2010–15	2020–25	2030–35	2040–45	2050–55	2075–80	2095–2100
Total fertility rate							
SSP1 - Rapid development	1.52	1.37	1.29	1.27	1.26	1.28	1.28
SSP2 - Medium	1.60	1.63	1.66	1.68	1.70	1.71	1.72
SSP3 - Stalled development	1.70	1.91	2.06	2.15	2.19	2.22	2.23
SSP4 - Inequality	1.53	1.42	1.35	1.33	1.32	1.33	1.33
SSP5 - Conventional development	1.52	1.37	1.29	1.27	1.26	1.28	1.28
Life expectancy at birth for females (in years)							
SSP1 - Rapid development	80.00	83.09	86.06	89.01	92.00	99.47	105.46
SSP2 - Medium	78.70	81.09	83.29	85.39	87.41	92.40	96.40
SSP3 - Stalled development	79.02	80.12	81.12	82.12	83.11	85.48	87.45
SSP4 - Inequality	79.53	81.56	83.53	85.54	87.49	92.15	96.06
SSP5 - Conventional development	80.00	83.09	86.06	89.01	92.00	99.47	105.46
Migration – net flow over five years (in thousands)							
SSP1 - Rapid development	−27	−20	−17	−15	−12	−4	0
SSP2 - Medium	−27	−20	−18	−17	−14	−6	0
SSP3 - Stalled development	−23	−10	−9	−8	−8	−3	0
SSP4 - Inequality	−27	−20	−17	−14	−11	−3	0
SSP5 - Conventional development	−32	−30	−27	−24	−21	−8	0

Ageing Indicators, Medium Scenario (SSP2)

	2010	2020	2030	2040	2050	2075	2095
Median age	39.30	41.08	44.08	48.05	49.27	51.84	52.16
Propspective median age	39.30	38.61	39.29	41.24	40.42	38.07	34.12
Proportion age 65+	0.16	0.17	0.22	0.25	0.28	0.33	0.36
Proportion RLE < 15 years	0.14	0.13	0.14	0.16	0.17	0.19	0.16

Luxembourg

Detailed Human Capital Projections to 2060

Demographic indicators, Medium Scenario (SSP2)	2010	2020	2030	2040	2050	2060
Population (in millions)	0.51	0.59	0.68	0.78	0.86	0.95
Proportion age 65+	0.14	0.16	0.19	0.22	0.24	0.26
Proportion below age 20	0.24	0.21	0.21	0.21	0.21	0.20
	2005–10	2015–20	2025–30	2035–40	2045–50	2055–60
Total Fertility Rate	1.62	1.60	1.76	1.80	1.80	1.80
Life expectancy at birth (in years)						
Men	76.70	79.67	82.16	84.22	86.25	88.21
Women	81.99	84.39	86.51	88.61	90.61	92.61
Five-year immigration flow (in '000)	42.92	34.17	35.50	36.33	36.37	35.86
Five-year emigration flow (in '000)	0.61	0.47	0.51	0.55	0.61	0.67

Human Capital indicators, Medium Scenario (SSP2)	2010	2020	2030	2040	2050	2060
Population age 25+: highest educational attainment						
E1 - no education	0.06	0.05	0.04	0.02	0.02	0.01
E2 - incomplete primary	0.00	0.00	0.00	0.00	0.00	0.00
E3 - primary	0.19	0.14	0.10	0.07	0.06	0.04
E4 - lower secondary	0.19	0.19	0.18	0.16	0.14	0.12
E5 - upper secondary	0.31	0.33	0.35	0.36	0.37	0.37
E6 - post-secondary	0.25	0.29	0.33	0.38	0.42	0.47
Mean years of schooling (in years)	11.20	11.90	12.53	13.06	13.56	14.03
Gender gap (population age 25+): highest educational attainment (ratio male/female)						
E1 - no education	0.80	0.79	0.78	0.75	0.71	0.67
E2 - incomplete primary	NA	NA	NA	NA	NA	NA
E3 - primary	0.76	0.83	0.92	1.00	1.06	1.11
E4 - lower secondary	0.84	0.91	0.98	1.03	1.07	1.09
E5 - upper secondary	1.07	1.02	1.01	1.01	1.01	1.01
E6 - post-secondary	1.37	1.17	1.06	1.00	0.97	0.97
Mean years of schooling (male minus female)	0.96	0.56	0.26	0.07	-0.03	-0.07
Women age 20–39: highest educational attainment						
E1 - no education	0.03	0.01	0.00	0.00	0.00	0.00
E2 - incomplete primary	0.00	0.00	0.00	0.00	0.00	0.00
E3 - primary	0.07	0.05	0.04	0.03	0.02	0.02
E4 - lower secondary	0.20	0.16	0.12	0.09	0.07	0.06
E5 - upper secondary	0.40	0.43	0.43	0.43	0.43	0.42
E6 - post-secondary	0.30	0.35	0.41	0.45	0.48	0.50
Mean years of schooling (in years)	12.52	13.32	13.83	14.20	14.44	14.65

Education scenarios

GET: global education trend scenario (medium assumption also used for SSP2)

CER: constant enrolment rates scenario (assumption of no future improvements)

FT: Fast track scenario (assumption of education expansion according to fastest historical experience)

Pyramids by Education, Medium Scenario

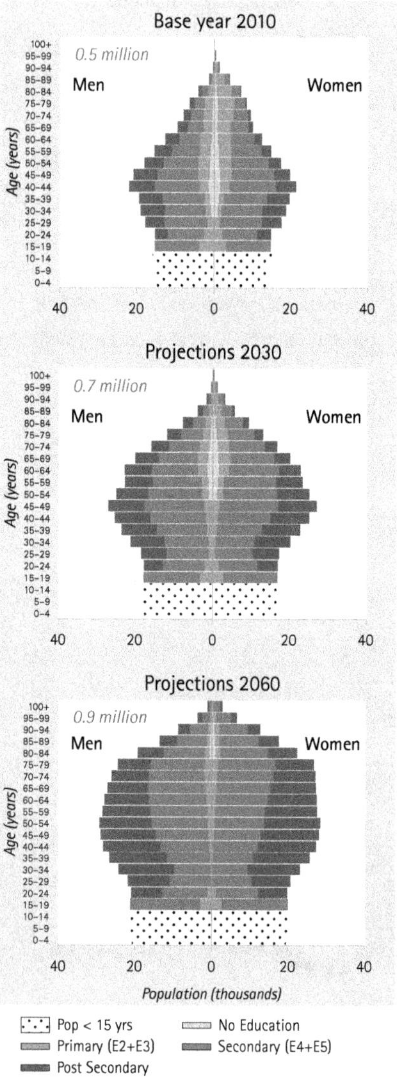

Population Size by Educational Attainment According to Three Education Scenarios: GET, CER, and FT

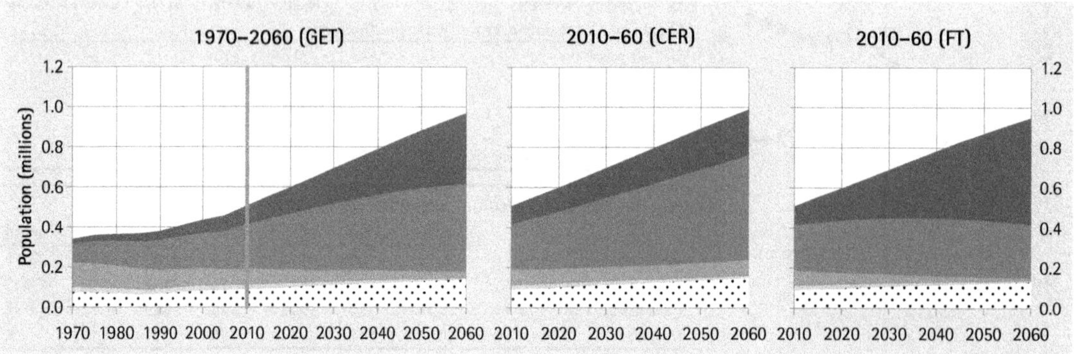

Luxembourg (Continued)

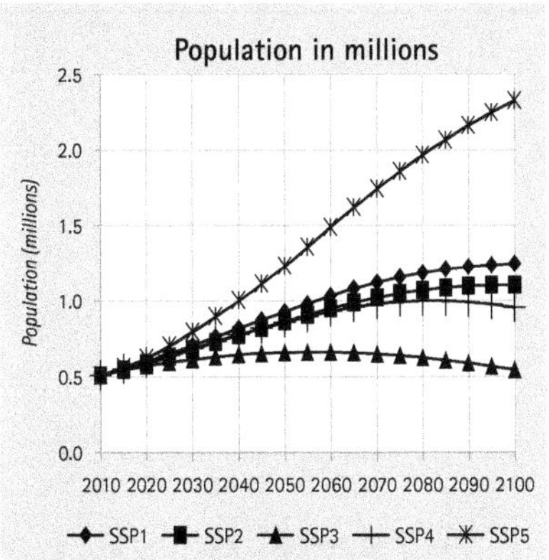

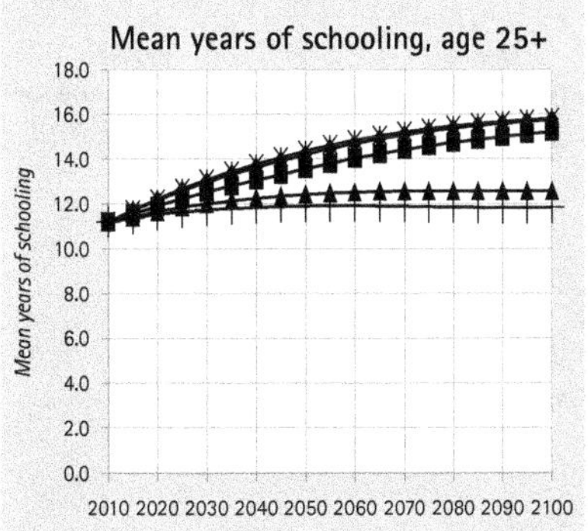

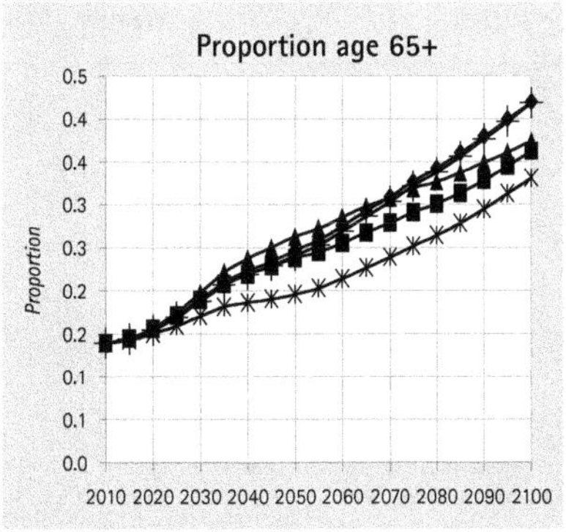

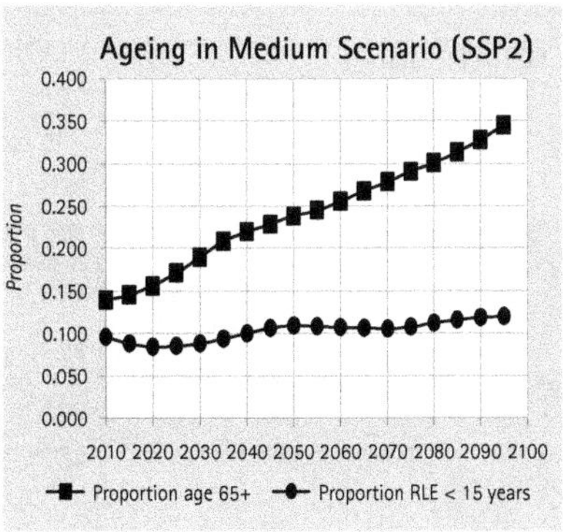

Alternative Scenarios to 2100

Projection Results by Scenario (SSP1–5)

	2010	2020	2030	2040	2050	2075	2100
Population (in millions)							
SSP1 - Rapid development	0.51	0.60	0.71	0.82	0.93	1.16	1.25
SSP2 - Medium	0.51	0.59	0.68	0.78	0.86	1.05	1.10
SSP3 - Stalled development	0.51	0.57	0.61	0.65	0.66	0.64	0.55
SSP4 - Inequality	0.51	0.59	0.69	0.78	0.86	0.99	0.96
SSP5 - Conventional development	0.51	0.62	0.80	1.00	1.23	1.86	2.32
Proportion age 65+							
SSP1 - Rapid development	0.14	0.16	0.19	0.22	0.25	0.33	0.42
SSP2 - Medium	0.14	0.16	0.19	0.22	0.24	0.29	0.36
SSP3 - Stalled development	0.14	0.16	0.20	0.24	0.26	0.32	0.37
SSP4 - Inequality	0.14	0.15	0.19	0.22	0.24	0.32	0.42
SSP5 - Conventional development	0.14	0.15	0.17	0.19	0.20	0.25	0.33
Proportion below age 20							
SSP1 - Rapid development	0.24	0.21	0.21	0.21	0.20	0.18	0.16
SSP2 - Medium	0.24	0.21	0.21	0.21	0.21	0.20	0.18
SSP3 - Stalled development	0.24	0.21	0.19	0.18	0.17	0.16	0.15
SSP4 - Inequality	0.24	0.21	0.20	0.19	0.18	0.16	0.14
SSP5 - Conventional development	0.24	0.22	0.23	0.25	0.25	0.24	0.22
Proportion of Women age 20–39 with at least secondary education							
SSP1 - Rapid development	0.90	0.97	0.98	0.98	0.99	0.99	1.00
SSP2 - Medium	0.90	0.94	0.96	0.97	0.98	0.99	1.00
SSP3 - Stalled development	0.90	0.90	0.90	0.90	0.90	0.90	0.90
SSP4 - Inequality	0.90	0.90	0.90	0.90	0.90	0.90	0.90
SSP5 - Conventional development	0.90	0.97	0.98	0.98	0.99	0.99	1.00
Mean years of schooling, age 25+							
SSP1 - Rapid development	11.20	12.16	12.98	13.63	14.19	15.23	15.74
SSP2 - Medium	11.20	11.90	12.53	13.06	13.56	14.57	15.21
SSP3 - Stalled development	11.20	11.66	12.01	12.25	12.42	12.57	12.57
SSP4 - Inequality	11.20	11.54	11.73	11.84	11.90	11.87	11.83
SSP5 - Conventional development	11.20	12.21	13.08	13.77	14.35	15.34	15.80

Demographic Assumptions Underlying SSPs

	2010–15	2020–25	2030–35	2040–45	2050–55	2075–80	2095–2100
Total fertility rate							
SSP1 - Rapid development	1.53	1.66	1.75	1.78	1.78	1.78	1.78
SSP2 - Medium	1.52	1.68	1.80	1.80	1.80	1.79	1.78
SSP3 - Stalled development	1.47	1.46	1.45	1.44	1.42	1.43	1.43
SSP4 - Inequality	1.47	1.48	1.48	1.46	1.45	1.45	1.46
SSP5 - Conventional development	1.60	1.91	2.12	2.20	2.22	2.22	2.22
Life expectancy at birth for females (in years)							
SSP1 - Rapid development	84.09	87.26	90.29	93.30	96.29	103.79	109.82
SSP2 - Medium	83.19	85.51	87.61	89.61	91.59	96.60	100.59
SSP3 - Stalled development	83.09	84.23	85.30	86.33	87.29	89.47	91.30
SSP4 - Inequality	83.57	85.79	87.82	89.79	91.75	96.36	100.13
SSP5 - Conventional development	84.09	87.26	90.29	93.30	96.29	103.79	109.82
Migration – net flow over five years (in thousands)							
SSP1 - Rapid development	36	34	35	34	32	12	0
SSP2 - Medium	32	30	31	31	31	13	0
SSP3 - Stalled development	30	16	16	15	14	5	0
SSP4 - Inequality	36	34	35	34	33	14	0
SSP5 - Conventional development	42	53	58	62	64	29	0

Ageing Indicators, Medium Scenario (SSP2)

	2010	2020	2030	2040	2050	2075	2095
Median age	38.96	40.14	41.14	42.67	44.04	46.95	51.52
Propspective median age	38.96	37.61	36.52	36.17	35.62	33.84	34.63
Proportion age 65+	0.14	0.16	0.19	0.22	0.24	0.29	0.34
Proportion RLE < 15 years	0.10	0.08	0.09	0.10	0.11	0.11	0.12

Madagascar

Detailed Human Capital Projections to 2060

Demographic indicators, Medium Scenario (SSP2)						
	2010	2020	2030	2040	2050	2060
Population (in millions)	20.71	26.87	33.29	39.54	45.17	50.09
Proportion age 65+	0.03	0.04	0.05	0.06	0.07	0.10
Proportion below age 20	0.54	0.49	0.44	0.39	0.34	0.30
	2005–10	2015–20	2025–30	2035–40	2045–50	2055–60
Total Fertility Rate	4.83	3.71	2.97	2.51	2.18	2.00
Life expectancy at birth (in years)						
Men	64.27	68.70	69.93	71.38	73.08	75.20
Women	67.30	72.38	73.98	75.49	77.19	79.29
Five-year immigration flow (in '000)	2.70	2.63	2.73	2.79	2.78	2.74
Five-year emigration flow (in '000)	8.49	8.61	10.86	12.73	14.05	14.88

Human Capital indicators, Medium Scenario (SSP2)						
	2010	2020	2030	2040	2050	2060
Population age 25+: highest educational attainment						
E1 - no education	0.25	0.20	0.18	0.15	0.13	0.10
E2 - incomplete primary	0.42	0.41	0.38	0.34	0.29	0.24
E3 - primary	0.19	0.23	0.27	0.31	0.35	0.38
E4 - lower secondary	0.08	0.09	0.11	0.12	0.14	0.15
E5 - upper secondary	0.03	0.03	0.04	0.05	0.06	0.08
E6 - post-secondary	0.02	0.03	0.03	0.04	0.04	0.05
Mean years of schooling (in years)	4.02	4.32	4.65	5.08	5.55	6.07
Gender gap (population age 25+): highest educational attainment (ratio male/female)						
E1 - no education	0.74	0.80	0.86	0.91	0.95	0.95
E2 - incomplete primary	1.04	1.05	1.06	1.07	1.07	1.06
E3 - primary	1.05	0.96	0.93	0.92	0.93	0.95
E4 - lower secondary	1.35	1.24	1.16	1.11	1.07	1.05
E5 - upper secondary	1.43	1.25	1.15	1.07	1.04	1.04
E6 - post-secondary	1.58	1.29	1.11	1.01	0.98	0.99
Mean years of schooling (male minus female)	0.68	0.41	0.21	0.07	0.02	0.03
Women age 20–39: highest educational attainment						
E1 - no education	0.22	0.17	0.14	0.11	0.08	0.06
E2 - incomplete primary	0.43	0.39	0.34	0.27	0.22	0.16
E3 - primary	0.23	0.29	0.33	0.38	0.41	0.42
E4 - lower secondary	0.07	0.09	0.11	0.13	0.15	0.16
E5 - upper secondary	0.03	0.04	0.05	0.07	0.10	0.14
E6 - post-secondary	0.02	0.03	0.03	0.04	0.05	0.06
Mean years of schooling (in years)	3.84	4.48	5.08	5.74	6.41	7.07

Education scenarios

GET: global education trend scenario (medium assumption also used for SSP2)

CER: constant enrolment rates scenario (assumption of no future improvements)

FT: Fast track scenario (assumption of education expansion according to fastest historical experience)

Pyramids by Education, Medium Scenario

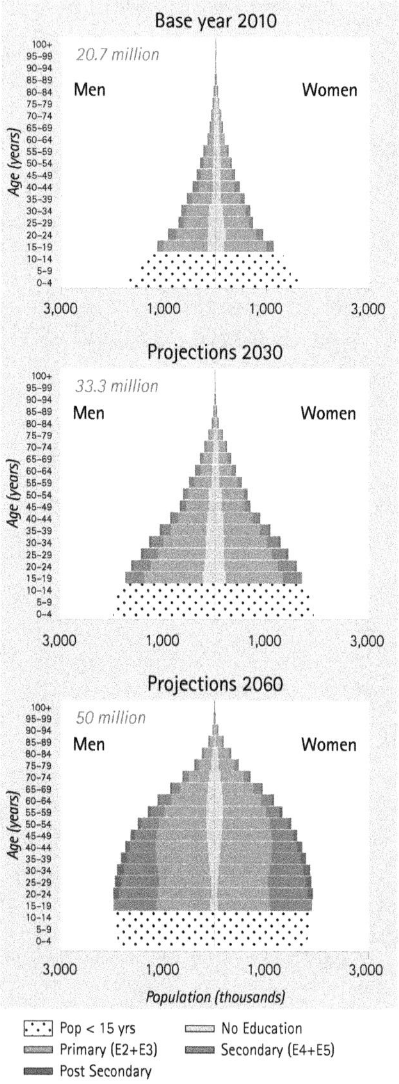

Population Size by Educational Attainment According to Three Education Scenarios: GET, CER, and FT

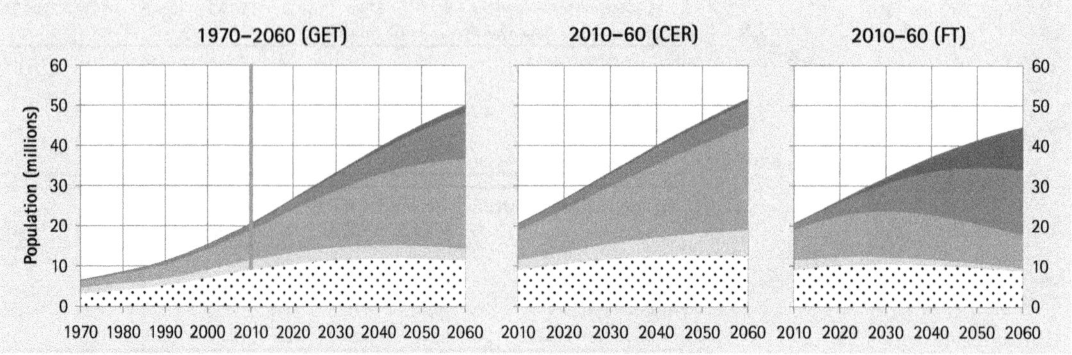

Madagascar (Continued)

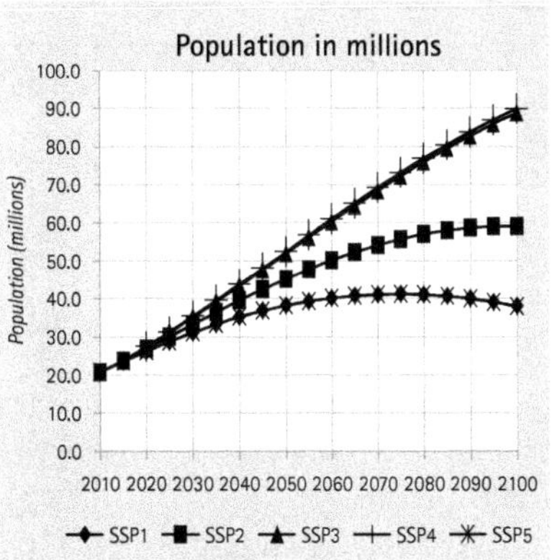

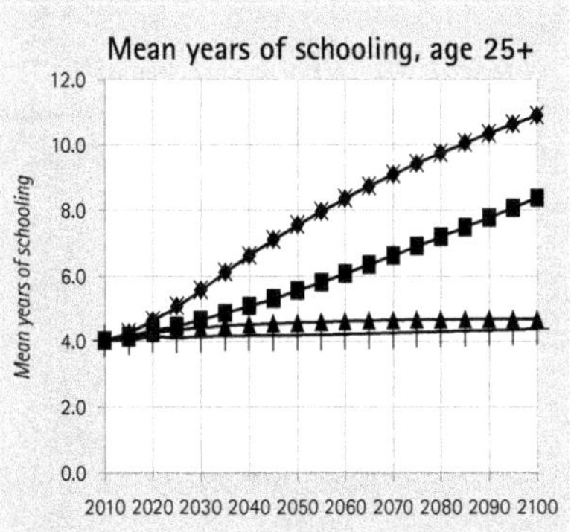

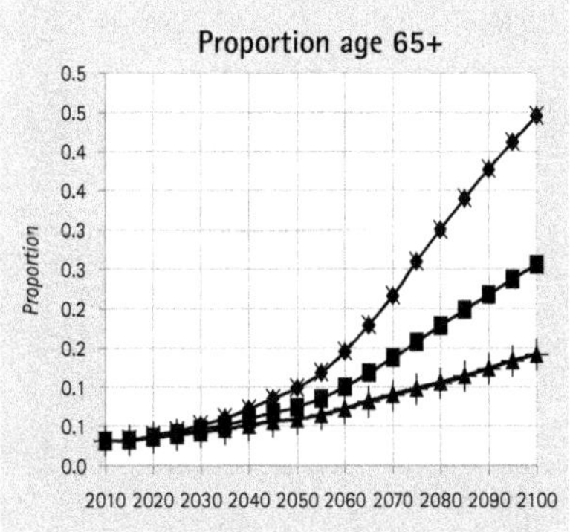

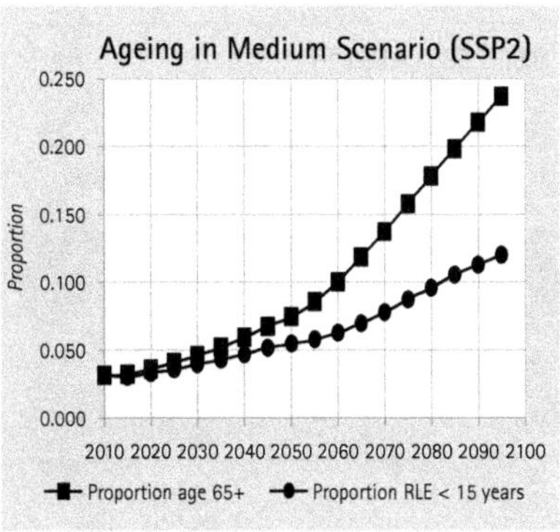

Alternative Scenarios to 2100

Projection Results by Scenario (SSP1–5)

	2010	2020	2030	2040	2050	2075	2100
Population (in millions)							
SSP1 - Rapid development	20.71	26.18	31.09	35.21	38.19	41.21	38.03
SSP2 - Medium	20.71	26.87	33.29	39.54	45.17	55.73	59.17
SSP3 - Stalled development	20.71	27.35	35.21	43.44	51.91	72.28	88.81
SSP4 - Inequality	20.71	27.40	35.41	43.77	52.41	73.14	89.87
SSP5 - Conventional Development	20.71	26.17	31.08	35.18	38.14	41.12	37.92
Proportion age 65+							
SSP1 - Rapid development	0.03	0.04	0.05	0.07	0.10	0.26	0.45
SSP2 - Medium	0.03	0.04	0.05	0.06	0.07	0.16	0.26
SSP3 - Stalled development	0.03	0.04	0.04	0.05	0.06	0.10	0.14
SSP4 - Inequality	0.03	0.04	0.04	0.05	0.06	0.10	0.14
SSP5 - Conventional Development	0.03	0.04	0.05	0.07	0.10	0.26	0.45
Proportion below age 20							
SSP1 - Rapid development	0.54	0.48	0.40	0.33	0.27	0.16	0.11
SSP2 - Medium	0.54	0.49	0.44	0.39	0.34	0.26	0.20
SSP3 - Stalled development	0.54	0.50	0.47	0.44	0.40	0.34	0.30
SSP4 - Inequality	0.54	0.50	0.48	0.44	0.41	0.34	0.30
SSP5 - Conventional Development	0.54	0.48	0.40	0.33	0.27	0.16	0.11
Proportion of Women age 20–39 with at least secondary education							
SSP1 - Rapid development	0.12	0.23	0.37	0.51	0.60	0.72	0.82
SSP2 - Medium	0.12	0.15	0.20	0.24	0.30	0.46	0.65
SSP3 - Stalled development	0.12	0.15	0.16	0.16	0.16	0.16	0.16
SSP4 - Inequality	0.12	0.14	0.14	0.14	0.14	0.14	0.14
SSP5 - Conventional Development	0.12	0.23	0.37	0.51	0.60	0.72	0.82
Mean years of schooling, age 25+							
SSP1 - Rapid development	4.02	4.63	5.58	6.62	7.54	9.42	10.88
SSP2 - Medium	4.02	4.32	4.65	5.08	5.55	6.90	8.37
SSP3 - Stalled development	4.02	4.25	4.41	4.51	4.56	4.66	4.67
SSP4 - Inequality	4.02	4.13	4.15	4.17	4.19	4.28	4.37
SSP5 - Conventional Development	4.02	4.63	5.58	6.62	7.54	9.42	10.88

Demographic Assumptions Underlying SSPs

	2010–15	2020–25	2030–35	2040–45	2050–55	2075–80	2095–2100
Total fertility rate							
SSP1 - Rapid development	3.92	2.69	1.98	1.63	1.43	1.25	1.16
SSP2 - Medium	4.24	3.28	2.70	2.33	2.08	1.81	1.66
SSP3 - Stalled development	4.38	3.89	3.39	2.99	2.72	2.39	2.27
SSP4 - Inequality	4.40	3.95	3.44	3.02	2.73	2.38	2.26
SSP5 - Conventional Development	3.92	2.69	1.98	1.63	1.43	1.25	1.16
Life expectancy at birth for females (in years)							
SSP1 - Rapid development	73.08	76.08	78.47	80.90	83.68	91.36	97.65
SSP2 - Medium	70.38	73.19	74.69	76.29	78.29	83.49	87.69
SSP3 - Stalled development	72.34	73.30	74.01	74.47	75.16	77.36	79.07
SSP4 - Inequality	72.34	73.29	73.97	74.42	75.09	77.26	78.97
SSP5 - Conventional development	73.08	76.08	78.47	80.90	83.68	91.36	97.65
Migration – net flow over five years (in thousands)							
SSP1 - Rapid development	−5	−7	−9	−10	−10	−4	0
SSP2 - Medium	−5	−7	−9	−11	−12	−6	0
SSP3 - Stalled development	−5	−3	−4	−5	−6	−3	0
SSP4 - Inequality	−5	−7	−9	−11	−13	−7	0
SSP5 - Conventional development	−6	−11	−14	−16	−17	−8	0

Ageing Indicators, Medium Scenario (SSP2)

	2010	2020	2030	2040	2050	2075	2095
Median age	18.06	20.25	22.97	26.04	29.33	37.93	44.09
Propspective median age	18.06	18.69	20.37	22.32	24.00	28.46	31.26
Proportion age 65+	0.03	0.04	0.05	0.06	0.07	0.16	0.24
Proportion RLE < 15 years	0.03	0.03	0.04	0.05	0.05	0.09	0.12

Malawi

Detailed Human Capital Projections to 2060

Demographic indicators, Medium Scenario (SSP2)	2010	2020	2030	2040	2050	2060
Population (in millions)	14.90	20.04	26.32	33.50	40.99	48.12
Proportion age 65+	0.03	0.03	0.03	0.03	0.04	0.05
Proportion below age 20	0.57	0.56	0.53	0.50	0.46	0.41
	2005–10	2015–20	2025–30	2035–40	2045–50	2055–60
Total Fertility Rate	6.00	5.22	4.53	3.79	3.15	2.63
Life expectancy at birth (in years)						
Men	51.51	56.57	58.64	60.33	62.37	64.84
Women	51.48	56.98	60.22	62.98	65.62	68.21
Five-year immigration flow (in '000)	18.82	18.37	19.03	19.43	19.40	19.10
Five-year emigration flow (in '000)	38.32	39.16	51.91	67.31	83.45	98.84

Human Capital indicators, Medium Scenario (SSP2)	2010	2020	2030	2040	2050	2060
Population age 25+: highest educational attainment						
E1 - no education	0.32	0.23	0.17	0.12	0.08	0.06
E2 - incomplete primary	0.24	0.23	0.19	0.15	0.11	0.08
E3 - primary	0.13	0.15	0.16	0.16	0.16	0.15
E4 - lower secondary	0.20	0.24	0.27	0.28	0.28	0.26
E5 - upper secondary	0.09	0.14	0.20	0.26	0.33	0.41
E6 - post-secondary	0.01	0.02	0.02	0.03	0.04	0.05
Mean years of schooling (in years)	5.11	6.27	7.26	8.19	9.00	9.70
Gender gap (population age 25+): highest educational attainment (ratio male/female)						
E1 - no education	0.49	0.54	0.58	0.65	0.71	0.76
E2 - incomplete primary	0.98	0.88	0.88	0.88	0.88	0.87
E3 - primary	1.22	1.01	0.90	0.86	0.87	0.90
E4 - lower secondary	1.76	1.36	1.16	1.06	1.01	0.99
E5 - upper secondary	2.49	1.88	1.57	1.36	1.22	1.12
E6 - post-secondary	2.21	1.52	1.14	0.95	0.90	0.95
Mean years of schooling (male minus female)	2.45	1.84	1.34	0.89	0.56	0.35
Women age 20–39: highest educational attainment						
E1 - no education	0.27	0.15	0.11	0.07	0.04	0.02
E2 - incomplete primary	0.25	0.22	0.15	0.10	0.06	0.04
E3 - primary	0.16	0.18	0.19	0.19	0.17	0.14
E4 - lower secondary	0.22	0.28	0.31	0.31	0.30	0.27
E5 - upper secondary	0.09	0.15	0.22	0.30	0.39	0.48
E6 - post-secondary	0.01	0.02	0.02	0.03	0.04	0.05
Mean years of schooling (in years)	5.44	7.03	8.05	9.03	9.87	10.55

Education scenarios

GET : global education trend scenario (medium assumption also used for SSP2)

CER: constant enrolment rates scenario (assumption of no future improvements)

FT: Fast Track Scenario (assumption of education expansion according to fastest historical experience)

Pyramids by Education, Medium Scenario

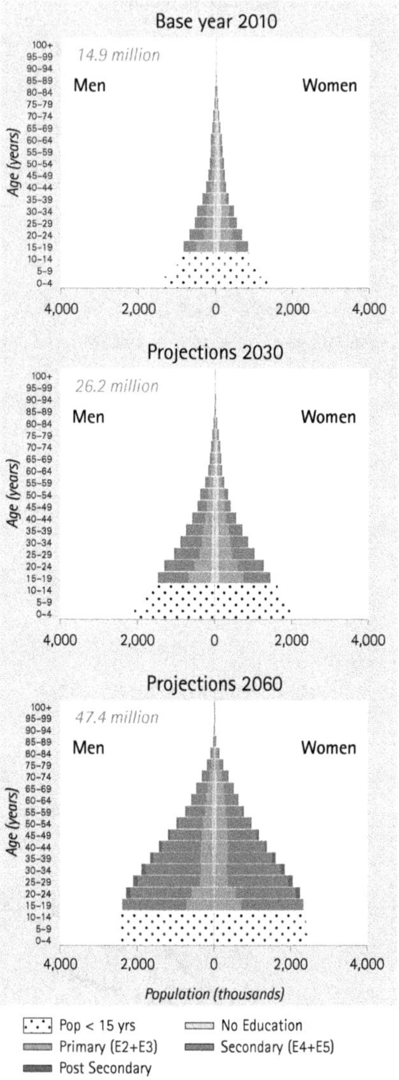

Population Size by Educational Attainment According to Three Education Scenarios: GET, CER, and FT

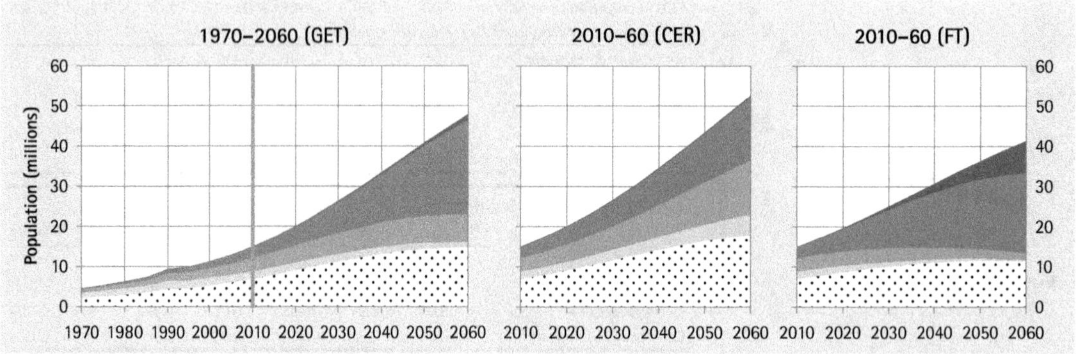

Malawi (Continued)

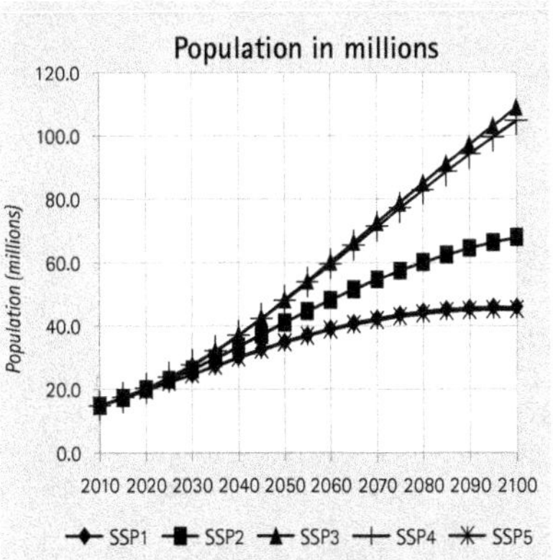

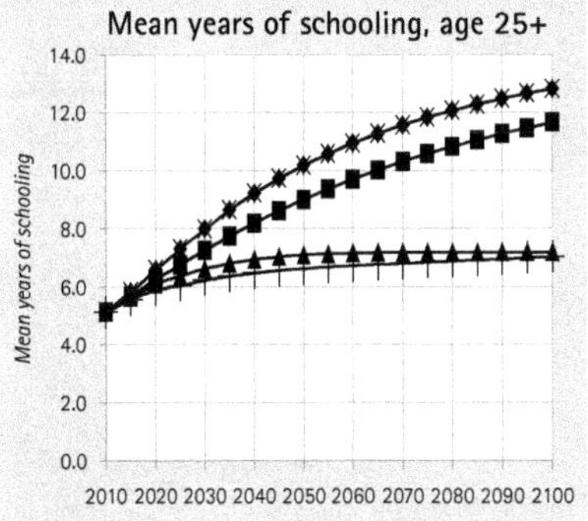

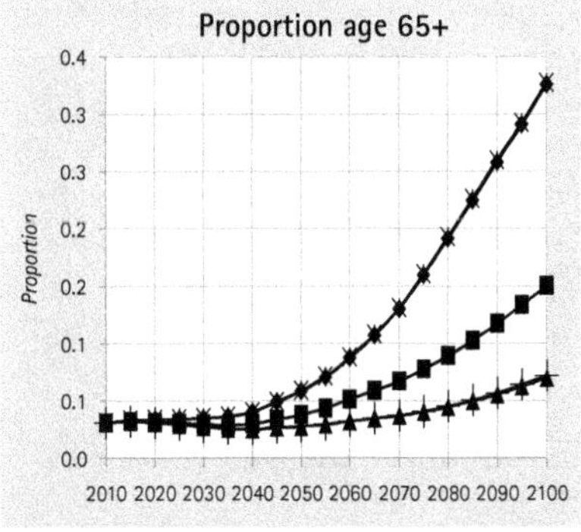

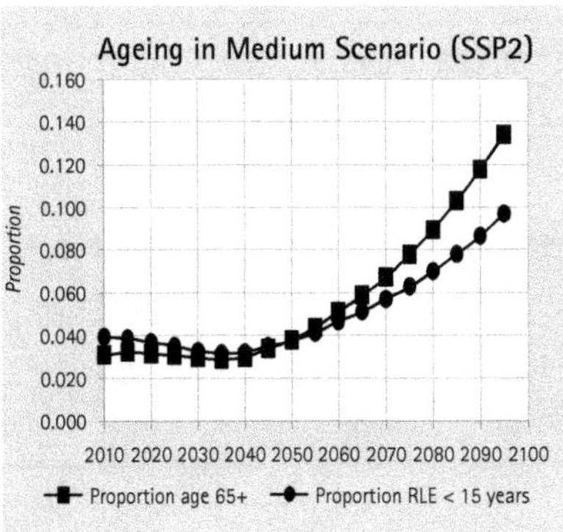

Alternative Scenarios to 2100

Projection results by scenario (SSP1–5)

	2010	2020	2030	2040	2050	2075	2100
Population (in millions)							
SSP1 - Rapid	14.90	19.66	24.76	30.07	34.95	43.54	45.84
SSP2 - Medium	14.90	20.04	26.32	33.50	40.99	57.45	67.97
SSP3 - Stalled development	14.90	20.39	27.75	37.16	48.27	78.99	108.96
SSP4 - Inequality	14.90	20.39	27.75	37.05	47.93	77.30	104.80
SSP5 - Conventional	14.90	19.65	24.70	29.93	34.69	42.88	44.97
Proportion age 65+							
SSP1 - Rapid development	0.03	0.03	0.03	0.04	0.06	0.16	0.33
SSP2 - Medium	0.03	0.03	0.03	0.03	0.04	0.08	0.15
SSP3 - Stalled development	0.03	0.03	0.03	0.03	0.03	0.04	0.07
SSP4 - Inequality	0.03	0.03	0.03	0.03	0.03	0.04	0.07
SSP5 - Conventional development	0.03	0.03	0.03	0.04	0.06	0.16	0.33
Proportion below age 20							
SSP1 - Rapid development	0.57	0.54	0.49	0.42	0.37	0.23	0.15
SSP2 - Medium	0.57	0.56	0.53	0.50	0.46	0.34	0.25
SSP3 - Stalled development	0.57	0.57	0.57	0.56	0.53	0.44	0.37
SSP4 - Inequality	0.57	0.57	0.57	0.56	0.53	0.44	0.37
SSP5 - Conventional development	0.57	0.54	0.49	0.42	0.37	0.23	0.15
Proportion of Women age 20–39 with at least secondary education							
SSP1 - Rapid development	0.31	0.51	0.68	0.79	0.85	0.94	0.98
SSP2 - Medium	0.31	0.44	0.55	0.64	0.73	0.88	0.96
SSP3 - Stalled development	0.31	0.39	0.40	0.40	0.40	0.40	0.40
SSP4 - Inequality	0.31	0.36	0.36	0.36	0.36	0.36	0.36
SSP5 - Conventional development	0.31	0.51	0.68	0.79	0.85	0.94	0.98
Mean years of schooling, age 25+							
SSP1 - Rapid development	5.11	6.59	7.99	9.21	10.17	11.83	12.82
SSP2 - Medium	5.11	6.27	7.26	8.19	9.00	10.57	11.65
SSP3 - Stalled development	5.11	6.09	6.62	6.94	7.10	7.18	7.19
SSP4 - Inequality	5.11	5.89	6.22	6.48	6.63	6.84	7.04
SSP5 - Conventional development	5.11	6.59	7.98	9.21	10.17	11.83	12.82

Demographic Assumptions Underlying SSPs

	2010–15	2020–25	2030–35	2040–45	2050–55	2075–80	2095–2100
Total fertility rate							
SSP1 - Rapid development	5.30	3.94	3.00	2.41	1.99	1.46	1.33
SSP2 - Medium	5.59	4.87	4.15	3.46	2.85	2.05	1.86
SSP3 - Stalled development	5.95	5.85	5.52	4.88	4.17	2.98	2.70
SSP4 - Inequality	5.96	5.90	5.53	4.85	4.11	2.91	2.62
SSP5 - Conventional development	5.30	3.94	3.00	2.41	1.99	1.46	1.33
Life expectancy at birth for females (in years)							
SSP1 - Rapid development	60.59	67.26	72.05	76.41	80.35	88.46	95.18
SSP2 - Medium	55.18	58.63	61.68	64.32	66.92	73.32	78.39
SSP3 - Stalled development	57.43	56.77	58.85	59.62	60.98	64.34	67.01
SSP4 - Inequality	57.43	56.73	58.78	59.54	60.91	64.29	67.01
SSP5 - Conventional development	60.59	67.26	72.05	76.41	80.35	88.46	95.18
Migration – net flow over five years (in thousands)							
SSP1 - Rapid development	−18	−26	−39	−52	−64	−34	0
SSP2 - Medium	−18	−26	−40	−56	−72	−46	0
SSP3 - Stalled development	−15	−12	−19	−26	−35	−24	0
SSP4 - Inequality	−18	−25	−39	−56	−76	−53	0
SSP5 - Conventional development	−21	−40	−62	−86	−109	−66	0

Ageing Indicators, Medium Scenario (SSP2)

	2010	2020	2030	2040	2050	2075	2095
Median age	16.77	17.27	18.43	20.06	22.24	29.67	36.24
Propspective median age	16.77	15.67	15.16	15.27	15.61	17.71	20.22
Proportion age 65+	0.03	0.03	0.03	0.03	0.04	0.08	0.13
Proportion RLE < 15 years	0.04	0.04	0.03	0.03	0.04	0.06	0.10

Malaysia

Detailed Human Capital Projections to 2060

Demographic indicators, Medium Scenario (SSP2)	2010	2020	2030	2040	2050	2060
Population (in millions)	28.40	33.13	37.59	41.36	44.26	46.43
Proportion age 65+	0.05	0.07	0.11	0.14	0.17	0.20
Proportion below age 20	0.40	0.35	0.31	0.28	0.25	0.23
	2005–10	2015–20	2025–30	2035–40	2045–50	2055–60
Total Fertility Rate	2.72	2.37	2.13	1.95	1.84	1.75
Life expectancy at birth (in years)						
Men	71.25	74.23	76.50	78.60	80.59	82.68
Women	75.73	78.61	80.91	83.01	85.01	87.09
Five-year immigration flow (in '000)	720.89	705.69	732.51	748.35	747.71	736.41
Five-year emigration flow (in '000)	635.07	525.67	560.34	570.87	571.78	561.20

Human Capital indicators, Medium Scenario (SSP2)	2010	2020	2030	2040	2050	2060
Population age 25+: highest educational attainment						
E1 - no education	0.09	0.05	0.03	0.02	0.01	0.00
E2 - incomplete primary	0.07	0.05	0.03	0.02	0.01	0.00
E3 - primary	0.13	0.10	0.07	0.05	0.03	0.02
E4 - lower secondary	0.21	0.19	0.16	0.13	0.09	0.07
E5 - upper secondary	0.35	0.41	0.44	0.46	0.46	0.44
E6 - post-secondary	0.14	0.21	0.27	0.34	0.40	0.47
Mean years of schooling (in years)	9.89	11.17	12.25	13.09	13.79	14.34
Gender gap (population age 25+): highest educational attainment (ratio male/female)						
E1 - no education	0.54	0.55	0.58	0.64	0.72	0.85
E2 - incomplete primary	0.84	0.80	0.78	0.82	0.89	0.98
E3 - primary	1.01	0.96	0.89	0.87	0.90	0.95
E4 - lower secondary	1.21	1.19	1.18	1.15	1.13	1.12
E5 - upper secondary	1.04	1.03	1.03	1.03	1.02	1.01
E6 - post-secondary	1.09	1.00	0.96	0.96	0.96	0.97
Mean years of schooling (male minus female)	0.70	0.38	0.17	0.04	-0.04	-0.05
Women age 20–39: highest educational attainment						
E1 - no education	0.02	0.01	0.01	0.01	0.01	0.01
E2 - incomplete primary	0.02	0.01	0.00	0.00	0.00	0.00
E3 - primary	0.05	0.03	0.01	0.01	0.00	0.00
E4 - lower secondary	0.17	0.11	0.06	0.04	0.03	0.02
E5 - upper secondary	0.47	0.48	0.47	0.43	0.38	0.35
E6 - post-secondary	0.27	0.37	0.45	0.52	0.58	0.63
Mean years of schooling (in years)	12.34	13.48	14.32	14.78	15.10	15.32

Education scenarios

GET: global education trend scenario (medium assumption also used for SSP2)

CER: constant enrolment rates scenario (assumption of no future improvements)

FT: Fast track scenario (assumption of education expansion according to fastest historical experience)

Pyramids by Education, Medium Scenario

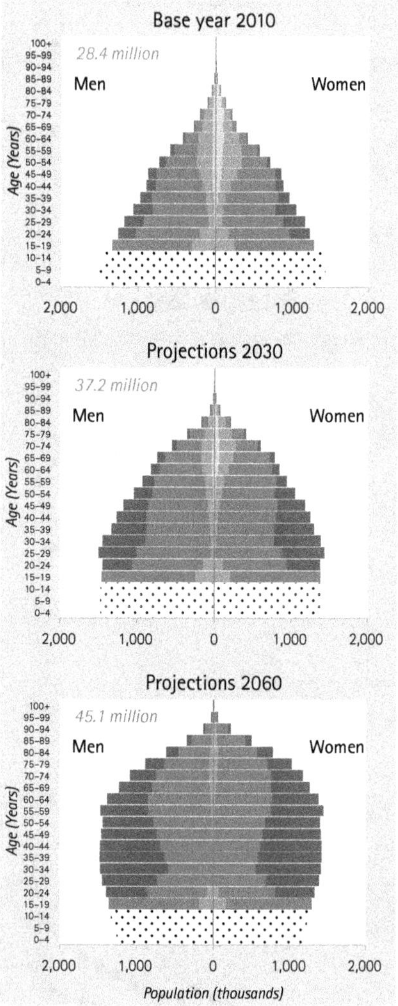

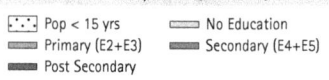

Population Size by Educational Attainment According to Three Education Scenarios: GET, CER, and FT

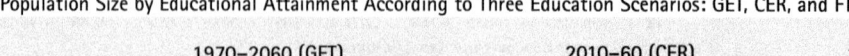

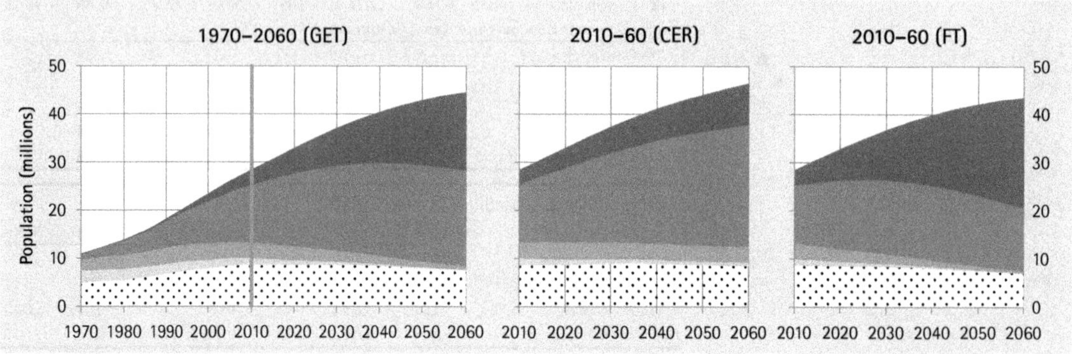

Malaysia (Continued)

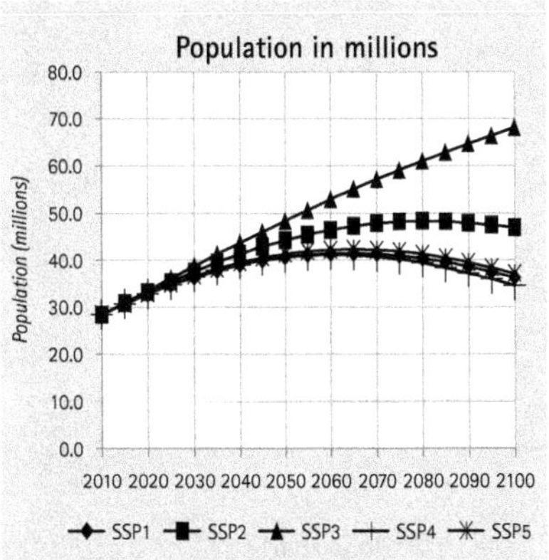

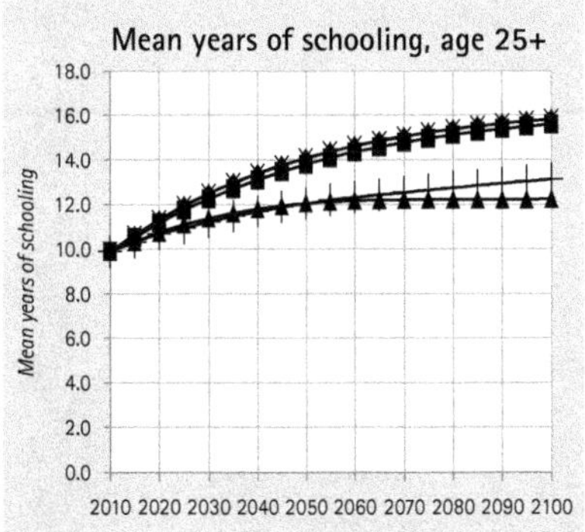

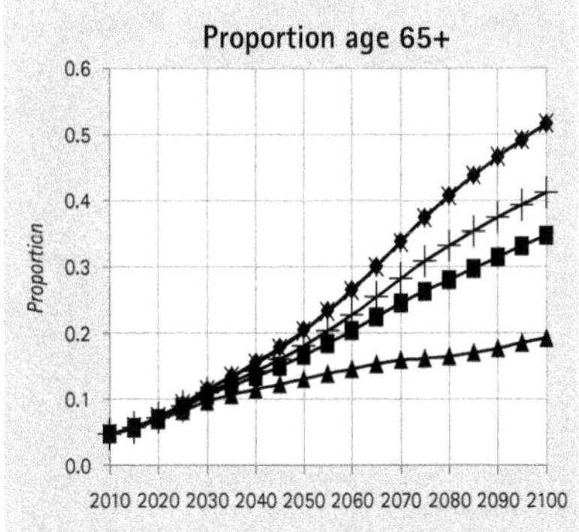

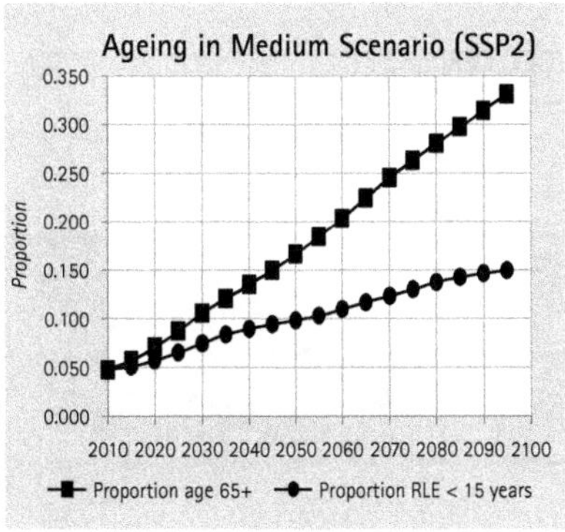

Alternative Scenarios to 2100

Projection Results by Scenario (SSP1–5)

	2010	2020	2030	2040	2050	2075	2100
Population (in millions)							
SSP1 - Rapid development	28.40	32.72	36.30	39.04	40.70	40.97	36.24
SSP2 - Medium	28.40	33.13	37.59	41.36	44.26	48.18	46.85
SSP3 - Stalled development	28.40	33.46	38.80	43.73	48.32	59.10	68.10
SSP4 - Inequality	28.40	32.75	36.38	39.08	40.61	40.20	34.52
SSP5 - Conventional development	28.40	32.81	36.58	39.51	41.34	41.87	37.11
Proportion age 65+							
SSP1 - Rapid development	0.05	0.07	0.12	0.16	0.21	0.37	0.52
SSP2 - Medium	0.05	0.07	0.11	0.14	0.17	0.26	0.35
SSP3 - Stalled development	0.05	0.07	0.10	0.12	0.13	0.16	0.19
SSP4 - Inequality	0.05	0.07	0.11	0.14	0.18	0.31	0.41
SSP5 - Conventional development	0.05	0.07	0.11	0.15	0.20	0.37	0.52
Proportion below age 20							
SSP1 - Rapid development	0.40	0.34	0.28	0.23	0.19	0.13	0.10
SSP2 - Medium	0.40	0.35	0.31	0.28	0.25	0.20	0.17
SSP3 - Stalled development	0.40	0.36	0.34	0.33	0.31	0.29	0.27
SSP4 - Inequality	0.40	0.34	0.29	0.25	0.21	0.16	0.12
SSP5 - Conventional development	0.40	0.34	0.28	0.23	0.19	0.13	0.10
Proportion of Women age 20–39 with at least secondary education							
SSP1 - Rapid development	0.91	0.97	0.99	0.99	0.99	1.00	1.00
SSP2 - Medium	0.91	0.95	0.98	0.99	0.99	0.99	0.99
SSP3 - Stalled development	0.91	0.90	0.90	0.90	0.90	0.90	0.90
SSP4 - Inequality	0.91	0.84	0.81	0.81	0.81	0.81	0.81
SSP5 - Conventional development	0.91	0.97	0.99	0.99	0.99	1.00	1.00
Mean years of schooling, age 25+							
SSP1 - Rapid development	9.89	11.31	12.48	13.37	14.06	15.21	15.81
SSP2 - Medium	9.89	11.17	12.25	13.09	13.79	14.95	15.58
SSP3 - Stalled development	9.89	10.74	11.38	11.79	12.05	12.22	12.23
SSP4 - Inequality	9.89	10.67	11.22	11.69	12.05	12.64	13.12
SSP5 - Conventional development	9.89	11.31	12.49	13.38	14.07	15.22	15.81

Demographic Assumptions Underlying SSPs

	2010–15	2020–25	2030–35	2040–45	2050–55	2075–80	2095–2100
Total fertility rate							
SSP1 - Rapid development	2.37	1.88	1.57	1.42	1.32	1.22	1.18
SSP2 - Medium	2.52	2.23	2.04	1.89	1.79	1.65	1.59
SSP3 - Stalled development	2.66	2.68	2.63	2.54	2.46	2.30	2.24
SSP4 - Inequality	2.40	1.97	1.69	1.53	1.43	1.31	1.27
SSP5 - Conventional development	2.37	1.88	1.57	1.42	1.32	1.22	1.18
Life expectancy at birth for females (in years)							
SSP1 - Rapid development	78.35	81.65	84.78	87.79	90.75	98.18	104.18
SSP2 - Medium	77.31	79.81	81.91	84.01	85.99	91.10	95.10
SSP3 - Stalled development	77.44	78.77	79.94	80.90	81.73	83.81	85.64
SSP4 - Inequality	77.92	80.28	82.32	84.30	86.10	90.69	94.55
SSP5 - Conventional development	78.35	81.65	84.78	87.79	90.75	98.18	104.18
Migration – net flow over five years (in thousands)							
SSP1 - Rapid development	147	168	166	155	137	52	0
SSP2 - Medium	152	173	177	179	176	87	0
SSP3 - Stalled development	123	88	96	111	127	96	0
SSP4 - Inequality	147	169	171	169	162	79	0
SSP5 - Conventional development	172	249	240	217	187	67	0

Ageing Indicators, Medium Scenario (SSP2)

	2010	2020	2030	2040	2050	2075	2095
Median age	26.00	29.03	32.27	35.68	38.70	45.91	51.07
Propspective median age	26.00	26.69	27.99	29.50	30.73	33.30	34.71
Proportion age 65+	0.05	0.07	0.11	0.14	0.17	0.26	0.33
Proportion RLE < 15 years	0.05	0.06	0.07	0.09	0.10	0.13	0.15

Maldives

Detailed Human Capital Projections to 2060

Demographic indicators, Medium Scenario (SSP2)	2010	2020	2030	2040	2050	2060
Population (in millions)	0.32	0.36	0.40	0.44	0.46	0.48
Proportion age 65+	0.05	0.06	0.09	0.14	0.22	0.32
Proportion below age 20	0.39	0.31	0.28	0.23	0.19	0.18
	2005–10	2015–20	2025–30	2035–40	2045–50	2055–60
Total Fertility Rate	1.90	1.73	1.69	1.63	1.57	1.59
Life expectancy at birth (in years)						
Men	74.63	78.03	81.15	84.41	87.18	89.76
Women	76.51	81.39	85.31	88.61	91.39	94.01
Five-year immigration flow (in '000)	0.57	0.56	0.58	0.59	0.59	0.58
Five-year emigration flow (in '000)	0.60	0.49	0.47	0.45	0.43	0.39

Human Capital indicators, Medium Scenario (SSP2)	2010	2020	2030	2040	2050	2060
Population age 25+: highest educational attainment						
E1 - no education	0.21	0.12	0.08	0.05	0.03	0.02
E2 - incomplete primary	0.25	0.17	0.13	0.10	0.07	0.05
E3 - primary	0.27	0.29	0.29	0.28	0.27	0.25
E4 - lower secondary	0.21	0.31	0.36	0.38	0.39	0.39
E5 - upper secondary	0.02	0.03	0.05	0.08	0.11	0.14
E6 - post-secondary	0.05	0.07	0.09	0.11	0.13	0.16
Mean years of schooling (in years)	5.52	7.06	7.98	8.71	9.40	10.03
Gender gap (population age 25+): highest educational attainment (ratio male/female)						
E1 - no education	1.05	0.96	0.88	0.79	0.68	0.57
E2 - incomplete primary	0.86	0.85	0.83	0.79	0.75	0.71
E3 - primary	1.11	1.12	1.11	1.09	1.07	1.04
E4 - lower secondary	0.89	0.92	0.95	0.97	0.98	0.98
E5 - upper secondary	1.45	1.11	1.02	0.99	1.00	1.02
E6 - post-secondary	1.45	1.35	1.30	1.24	1.19	1.15
Mean years of schooling (male minus female)	0.07	0.18	0.27	0.31	0.33	0.31
Women age 20–39: highest educational attainment						
E1 - no education	0.03	0.01	0.01	0.00	0.00	0.00
E2 - incomplete primary	0.13	0.05	0.02	0.01	0.00	0.00
E3 - primary	0.29	0.28	0.26	0.23	0.20	0.16
E4 - lower secondary	0.43	0.50	0.47	0.41	0.35	0.29
E5 - upper secondary	0.05	0.08	0.13	0.20	0.25	0.31
E6 - post-secondary	0.06	0.09	0.12	0.15	0.19	0.23
Mean years of schooling (in years)	7.99	9.37	10.25	10.75	11.21	11.64

Education scenarios

GET: global education trend scenario (medium assumption also used for SSP2)

CER: constant enrolment rates scenario (assumption of no future improvements)

FT: Fast track scenario (assumption of education expansion according to fastest historical experience)

Pyramids by Education, Medium Scenario

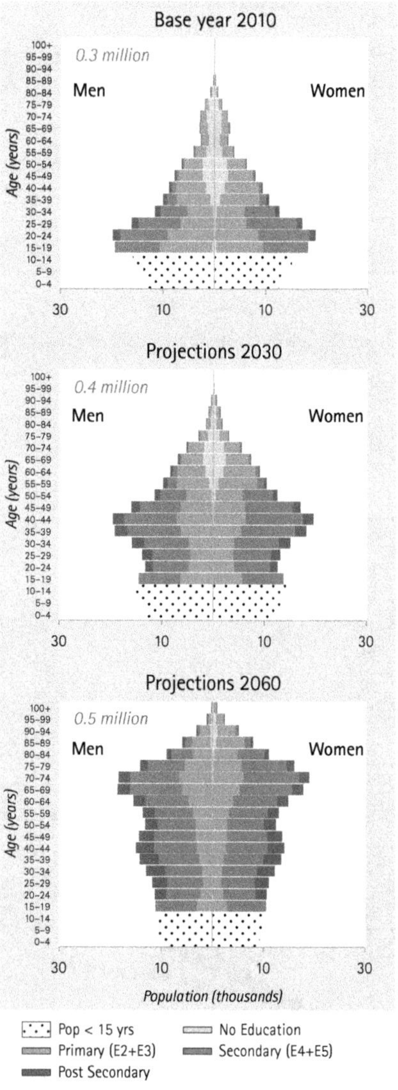

Population Size by Educational Attainment According to Three Education Scenarios: GET, CER, and FT

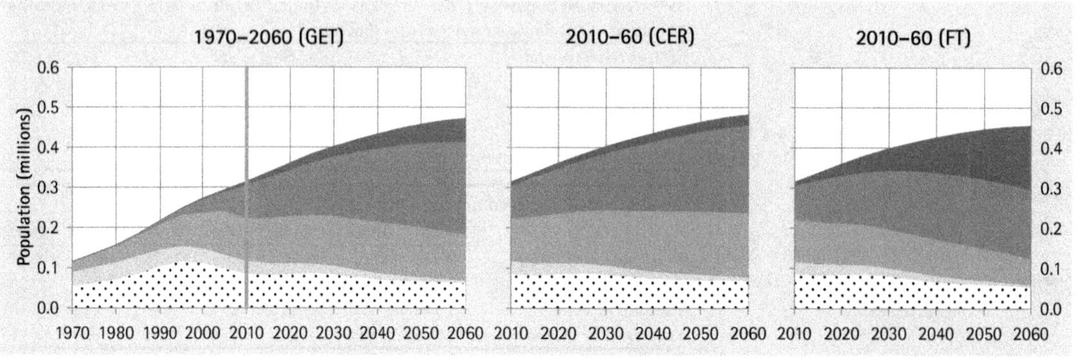

Maldives (Continued)

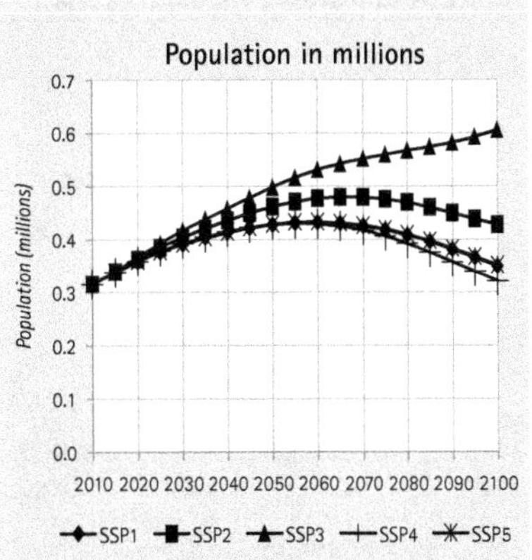

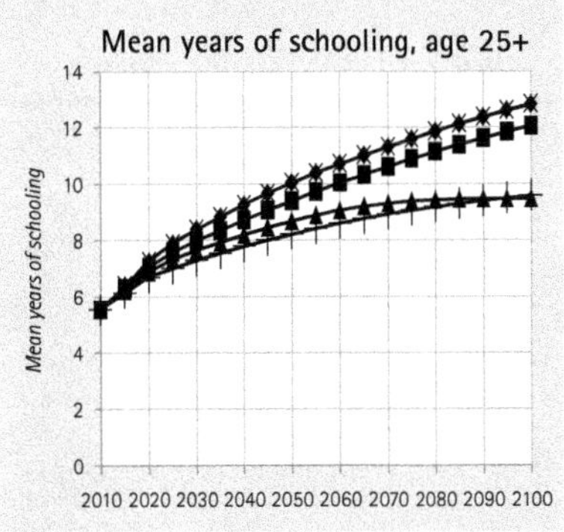

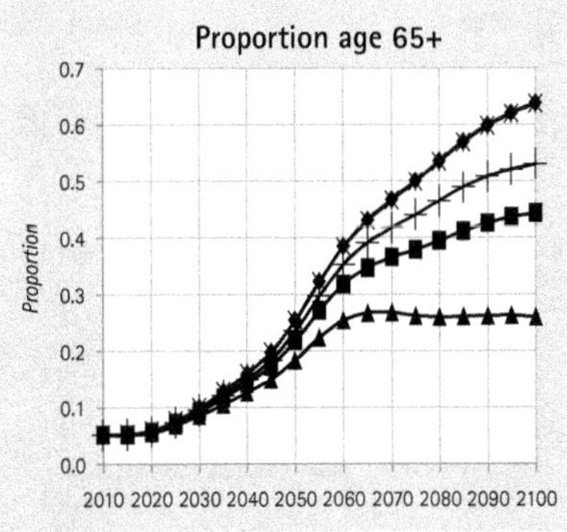

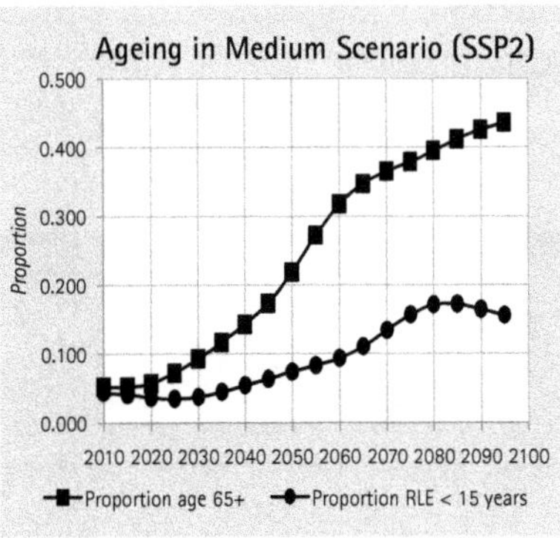

Alternative Scenarios to 2100

Projection Results by Scenario (SSP1–5)

	2010	2020	2030	2040	2050	2075	2100
Population (in millions)							
SSP1 - Rapid development	0.32	0.36	0.39	0.41	0.43	0.42	0.35
SSP2 - Medium	0.32	0.36	0.40	0.44	0.46	0.48	0.43
SSP3 - Stalled development	0.32	0.37	0.42	0.46	0.50	0.56	0.61
SSP4 - Inequality	0.32	0.36	0.39	0.41	0.43	0.41	0.32
SSP5 - Conventional development	0.32	0.36	0.39	0.41	0.43	0.42	0.35
Proportion age 65+							
SSP1 - Rapid development	0.05	0.06	0.10	0.16	0.25	0.50	0.64
SSP2 - Medium	0.05	0.06	0.09	0.14	0.22	0.38	0.44
SSP3 - Stalled development	0.05	0.06	0.09	0.13	0.18	0.26	0.26
SSP4 - Inequality	0.05	0.06	0.10	0.15	0.24	0.44	0.53
SSP5 - Conventional development	0.05	0.06	0.10	0.16	0.25	0.50	0.64
Proportion below age 20							
SSP1 - Rapid development	0.39	0.30	0.25	0.19	0.14	0.09	0.07
SSP2 - Medium	0.39	0.31	0.28	0.23	0.19	0.15	0.14
SSP3 - Stalled development	0.39	0.31	0.30	0.27	0.24	0.24	0.25
SSP4 - Inequality	0.39	0.30	0.25	0.20	0.16	0.11	0.10
SSP5 - Conventional development	0.39	0.30	0.25	0.19	0.15	0.09	0.07
Proportion of Women age 20–39 with at least secondary education							
SSP1 - Rapid development	0.54	0.71	0.80	0.86	0.89	0.94	0.98
SSP2 - Medium	0.54	0.67	0.71	0.76	0.80	0.89	0.96
SSP3 - Stalled development	0.54	0.62	0.63	0.63	0.63	0.63	0.63
SSP4 - Inequality	0.54	0.59	0.57	0.57	0.57	0.57	0.57
SSP5 - Conventional development	0.54	0.71	0.80	0.86	0.89	0.94	0.98
Mean years of schooling, age 25+							
SSP1 - Rapid development	5.52	7.26	8.39	9.26	10.04	11.59	12.82
SSP2 - Medium	5.52	7.06	7.98	8.71	9.40	10.88	12.05
SSP3 - Stalled development	5.52	6.89	7.65	8.20	8.68	9.38	9.48
SSP4 - Inequality	5.52	6.69	7.30	7.79	8.22	9.06	9.58
SSP5 - Conventional development	5.52	7.26	8.39	9.26	10.04	11.59	12.82

Demographic Assumptions Underlying SSPs

	2010–15	2020–25	2030–35	2040–45	2050–55	2075–80	2095–2100
Total fertility rate							
SSP1 - Rapid development	1.69	1.42	1.25	1.16	1.13	1.16	1.20
SSP2 - Medium	1.78	1.70	1.65	1.60	1.58	1.61	1.64
SSP3 - Stalled development	1.88	1.99	2.07	2.10	2.15	2.31	2.44
SSP4 - Inequality	1.70	1.48	1.34	1.26	1.24	1.30	1.36
SSP5 - Conventional development	1.69	1.42	1.25	1.16	1.13	1.16	1.20
Life expectancy at birth for females (in years)							
SSP1 - Rapid development	80.13	85.20	89.71	93.75	97.44	105.65	112.29
SSP2 - Medium	79.09	83.41	87.01	89.99	92.71	98.61	102.90
SSP3 - Stalled development	79.20	82.30	84.88	86.96	88.59	91.61	93.58
SSP4 - Inequality	79.64	83.84	87.36	90.34	92.99	98.45	102.55
SSP5 - Conventional development	80.13	85.20	89.71	93.75	97.44	105.65	112.29
Migration – net flow over five years (in thousands)							
SSP1 - Rapid development	0	0	0	0	0	0	0
SSP2 - Medium	0	0	0	0	0	0	0
SSP3 - Stalled development	0	0	0	0	0	0	0
SSP4 - Inequality	0	0	0	0	0	0	0
SSP5 - Conventional development	0	0	0	0	0	0	0

Ageing Indicators, Medium Scenario (SSP2)

	2010	2020	2030	2040	2050	2075	2095
Median age	24.56	30.26	35.97	41.38	45.71	55.02	58.97
Propspective median age	24.56	26.94	29.25	31.79	33.71	37.65	37.34
Proportion age 65+	0.05	0.06	0.09	0.14	0.22	0.38	0.44
Proportion RLE < 15 years	0.04	0.04	0.04	0.05	0.07	0.16	0.16

Mali

Detailed Human Capital Projections to 2060

Demographic indicators, Medium Scenario (SSP2)	2010	2020	2030	2040	2050	2060
Population (in millions)	15.37	20.40	25.90	31.29	36.14	40.12
Proportion age 65+	0.02	0.02	0.02	0.03	0.04	0.06
Proportion below age 20	0.58	0.56	0.51	0.46	0.40	0.35
	2005–10	2015–20	2025–30	2035–40	2045–50	2055–60
Total Fertility Rate	6.46	5.41	4.28	3.31	2.67	2.28
Life expectancy at birth (in years)						
Men	48.89	52.79	55.69	58.19	60.56	63.01
Women	51.00	55.08	58.18	60.98	63.82	66.58
Five-year immigration flow (in '000)	16.69	16.33	16.94	17.29	17.27	17.00
Five-year emigration flow (in '000)	115.87	115.82	152.63	190.10	220.73	241.37

Human Capital indicators, Medium Scenario (SSP2)	2010	2020	2030	2040	2050	2060
Population age 25+: highest educational attainment						
E1 - no education	0.80	0.74	0.67	0.59	0.50	0.41
E2 - incomplete primary	0.07	0.08	0.08	0.07	0.07	0.06
E3 - primary	0.05	0.07	0.09	0.12	0.14	0.16
E4 - lower secondary	0.03	0.05	0.07	0.09	0.11	0.13
E5 - upper secondary	0.03	0.05	0.08	0.11	0.16	0.22
E6 - post-secondary	0.01	0.01	0.01	0.02	0.02	0.03
Mean years of schooling (in years)	1.40	1.95	2.66	3.54	4.52	5.57
Gender gap (population age 25+): highest educational attainment (ratio male/female)						
E1 - no education	0.86	0.85	0.85	0.86	0.87	0.89
E2 - incomplete primary	1.63	1.39	1.27	1.18	1.10	1.03
E3 - primary	1.83	1.80	1.61	1.44	1.28	1.15
E4 - lower secondary	1.90	1.78	1.60	1.45	1.32	1.21
E5 - upper secondary	2.02	1.44	1.15	1.02	0.98	0.99
E6 - post-secondary	3.34	2.14	1.48	1.16	1.03	1.01
Mean years of schooling (male minus female)	0.93	0.95	0.86	0.70	0.52	0.38
Women age 20–39: highest educational attainment						
E1 - no education	0.80	0.73	0.62	0.50	0.38	0.26
E2 - incomplete primary	0.07	0.08	0.09	0.09	0.09	0.09
E3 - primary	0.05	0.06	0.09	0.12	0.15	0.17
E4 - lower secondary	0.03	0.05	0.08	0.10	0.13	0.15
E5 - upper secondary	0.04	0.07	0.11	0.16	0.23	0.29
E6 - post-secondary	0.00	0.01	0.01	0.02	0.03	0.03
Mean years of schooling (in years)	1.40	2.11	3.14	4.35	5.67	6.97

Education scenarios

GET: global education trend scenario (medium assumption also used for SSP2)

CER: constant enrolment rates scenario (assumption of no future improvements)

FT: Fast track scenario (assumption of education expansion according to fastest historical experience)

Pyramids by Education, Medium Scenario

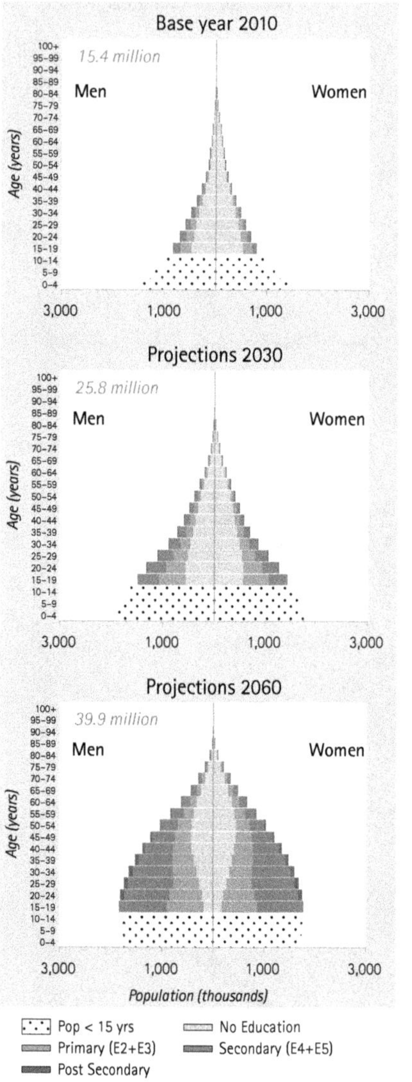

Population Size by Educational Attainment According to Three Education Scenarios: GET, CER, and FT

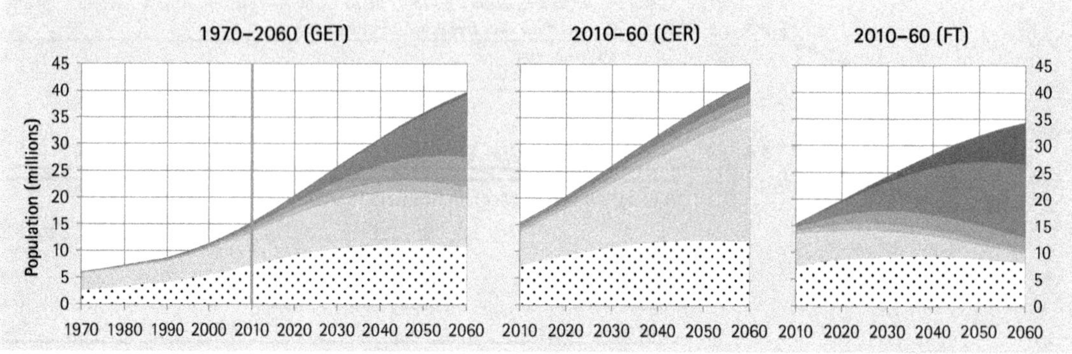

Mali (Continued)

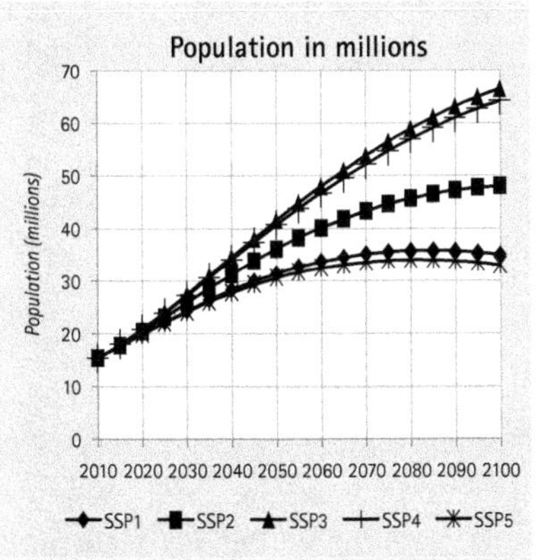

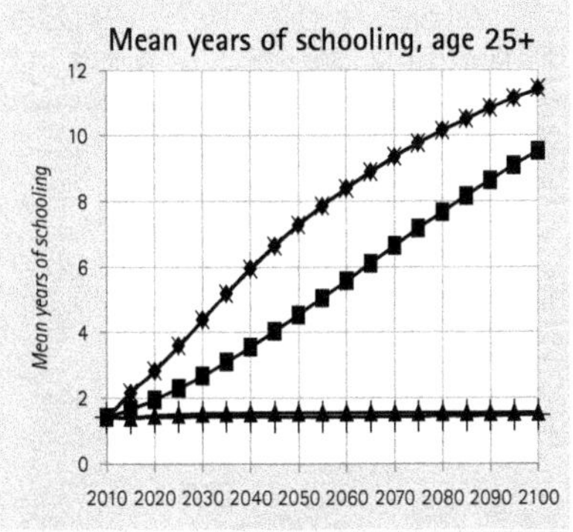

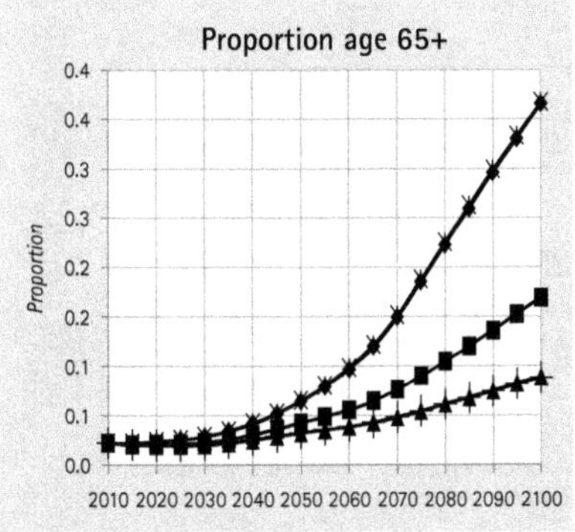

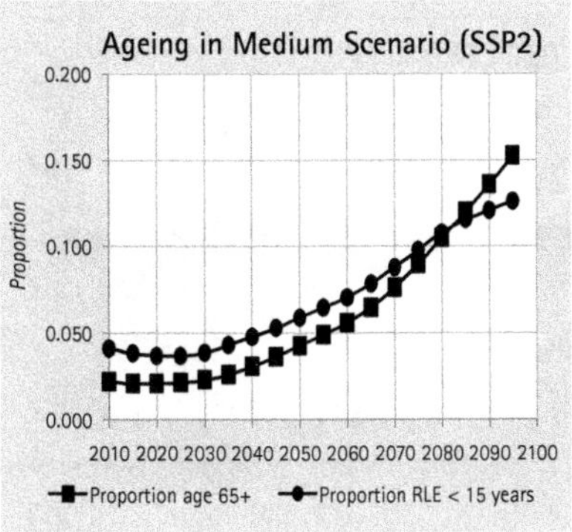

Alternative Scenarios to 2100

Projection Results by Scenario (SSP1–5)

	2010	2020	2030	2040	2050	2075	2100
Population (in millions)							
SSP1 - Rapid development	15.37	19.93	24.34	28.32	31.46	35.54	34.96
SSP2 - Medium	15.37	20.40	25.90	31.29	36.14	44.65	48.07
SSP3 - Stalled development	15.37	20.91	27.49	34.58	41.54	56.46	66.49
SSP4 - Inequality	15.37	20.86	27.26	34.09	40.70	54.67	64.24
SSP5 - Conventional development	15.37	19.87	24.10	27.83	30.64	33.85	32.99
Proportion age 65+							
SSP1 - Rapid development	0.02	0.02	0.03	0.04	0.06	0.19	0.37
SSP2 - Medium	0.02	0.02	0.02	0.03	0.04	0.09	0.17
SSP3 - Stalled development	0.02	0.02	0.02	0.03	0.03	0.05	0.09
SSP4 - Inequality	0.02	0.02	0.02	0.03	0.03	0.05	0.09
SSP5 - Conventional development	0.02	0.02	0.03	0.04	0.07	0.19	0.37
Proportion below age 20							
SSP1 - Rapid development	0.58	0.54	0.46	0.39	0.33	0.20	0.13
SSP2 - Medium	0.58	0.56	0.51	0.46	0.40	0.30	0.24
SSP3 - Stalled development	0.58	0.57	0.54	0.50	0.46	0.37	0.33
SSP4 - Inequality	0.58	0.57	0.54	0.51	0.46	0.37	0.33
SSP5 - Conventional development	0.58	0.54	0.47	0.39	0.33	0.20	0.13
Proportion of Women age 20–39 with at least secondary education							
SSP1 - Rapid development	0.07	0.23	0.38	0.52	0.62	0.79	0.89
SSP2 - Medium	0.07	0.13	0.20	0.28	0.38	0.63	0.82
SSP3 - Stalled development	0.07	0.05	0.05	0.05	0.05	0.05	0.05
SSP4 - Inequality	0.07	0.05	0.05	0.05	0.05	0.05	0.05
SSP5 - Conventional development	0.07	0.23	0.38	0.52	0.62	0.79	0.89
Mean years of schooling, age 25+							
SSP1 - Rapid development	1.40	2.82	4.38	5.94	7.27	9.76	11.42
SSP2 - Medium	1.40	1.95	2.66	3.54	4.52	7.15	9.51
SSP3 - Stalled development	1.40	1.46	1.52	1.54	1.54	1.54	1.55
SSP4 - Inequality	1.40	1.41	1.43	1.42	1.42	1.43	1.47
SSP5 - Conventional development	1.40	2.82	4.37	5.93	7.25	9.75	11.42

Demographic Assumptions Underlying SSPs

	2010–15	2020–25	2030–35	2040–45	2050–55	2075–80	2095–2100
Total fertility rate							
SSP1 - Rapid development	5.58	3.83	2.71	2.06	1.69	1.36	1.25
SSP2 - Medium	5.97	4.85	3.75	2.97	2.46	1.93	1.77
SSP3 - Stalled development	6.36	5.82	4.93	4.02	3.38	2.72	2.54
SSP4 - Inequality	6.36	5.83	4.94	4.03	3.38	2.72	2.54
SSP5 - Conventional development	5.58	3.83	2.71	2.06	1.69	1.36	1.25
Life expectancy at birth for females (in years)							
SSP1 - Rapid development	58.39	64.67	69.50	73.81	78.23	87.33	94.63
SSP2 - Medium	53.13	56.68	59.62	62.38	65.22	72.00	77.41
SSP3 - Stalled development	56.59	55.06	56.77	57.80	59.14	62.38	64.83
SSP4 - Inequality	56.59	55.06	56.76	57.79	59.12	62.37	64.82
SSP5 - Conventional development	58.39	64.67	69.50	73.81	78.23	87.33	94.63
Migration – net flow over five years (in thousands)							
SSP1 - Rapid development	−91	−115	−151	−177	−192	−88	0
SSP2 - Medium	−91	−116	−154	−189	−215	−114	0
SSP3 - Stalled development	−75	−56	−73	−89	−103	−56	0
SSP4 - Inequality	−90	−114	−152	−189	−221	−121	0
SSP5 - Conventional development	−106	−175	−235	−286	−323	−165	0

Ageing Indicators, Medium Scenario (SSP2)

	2010	2020	2030	2040	2050	2075	2095
Median age	16.25	17.29	19.39	22.08	25.14	33.17	38.62
Propspective median age	16.25	15.55	16.05	17.42	19.14	24.05	26.00
Proportion age 65+	0.02	0.02	0.02	0.03	0.04	0.09	0.15
Proportion RLE < 15 years	0.04	0.04	0.04	0.05	0.06	0.10	0.13

Malta

Detailed Human Capital Projections to 2060

Demographic indicators, Medium Scenario (SSP2)	2010	2020	2030	2040	2050	2060
Population (in millions)	0.42	0.43	0.45	0.45	0.45	0.44
Proportion age 65+	0.14	0.20	0.25	0.26	0.30	0.34
Proportion below age 20	0.22	0.19	0.19	0.18	0.17	0.17
	2005–10	2015–20	2025–30	2035–40	2045–50	2055–60
Total Fertility Rate	1.33	1.49	1.58	1.60	1.60	1.61
Life expectancy at birth (in years)						
Men	76.34	78.91	80.99	83.05	85.08	87.10
Women	81.20	83.61	85.69	87.79	89.79	91.80
Five-year immigration flow (in '000)	4.96	4.92	5.12	5.26	5.28	5.21
Five-year emigration flow (in '000)	0.00	0.00	0.00	0.00	0.00	0.00

Human Capital indicators, Medium Scenario (SSP2)	2010	2020	2030	2040	2050	2060
Population age 25+: highest educational attainment						
E1 - no education	0.01	0.00	0.00	0.00	0.00	0.00
E2 - incomplete primary	0.05	0.02	0.01	0.01	0.00	0.00
E3 - primary	0.25	0.17	0.11	0.06	0.02	0.01
E4 - lower secondary	0.44	0.47	0.47	0.45	0.40	0.34
E5 - upper secondary	0.06	0.08	0.10	0.12	0.14	0.16
E6 - post-secondary	0.19	0.25	0.30	0.36	0.43	0.49
Mean years of schooling (in years)	9.61	10.76	11.62	12.45	13.26	13.95
Gender gap (population age 25+): highest educational attainment (ratio male/female)						
E1 - no education	1.06	0.94	0.82	0.73	0.71	0.78
E2 - incomplete primary	0.30	0.38	0.45	0.51	0.71	1.13
E3 - primary	0.83	0.76	0.72	0.69	0.77	1.13
E4 - lower secondary	1.05	1.05	1.04	1.03	1.02	1.03
E5 - upper secondary	1.06	0.91	0.86	0.86	0.86	0.88
E6 - post-secondary	1.45	1.25	1.16	1.09	1.05	1.02
Mean years of schooling (male minus female)	1.04	0.77	0.58	0.43	0.26	0.12
Women age 20–39: highest educational attainment						
E1 - no education	0.00	0.00	0.00	0.00	0.00	0.00
E2 - incomplete primary	0.00	0.00	0.00	0.00	0.00	0.00
E3 - primary	0.01	0.00	0.00	0.00	0.00	0.00
E4 - lower secondary	0.51	0.40	0.30	0.22	0.17	0.13
E5 - upper secondary	0.16	0.19	0.22	0.24	0.23	0.23
E6 - post-secondary	0.31	0.40	0.48	0.54	0.60	0.64
Mean years of schooling (in years)	12.26	13.61	14.30	14.71	15.03	15.27

Education scenarios

GET: global education trend scenario (medium assumption also used for SSP2)

CER: constant enrolment rates scenario (assumption of no future improvements)

FT: Fast track scenario (assumption of education expansion according to fastest historical experience)

Pyramids by Education, Medium Scenario

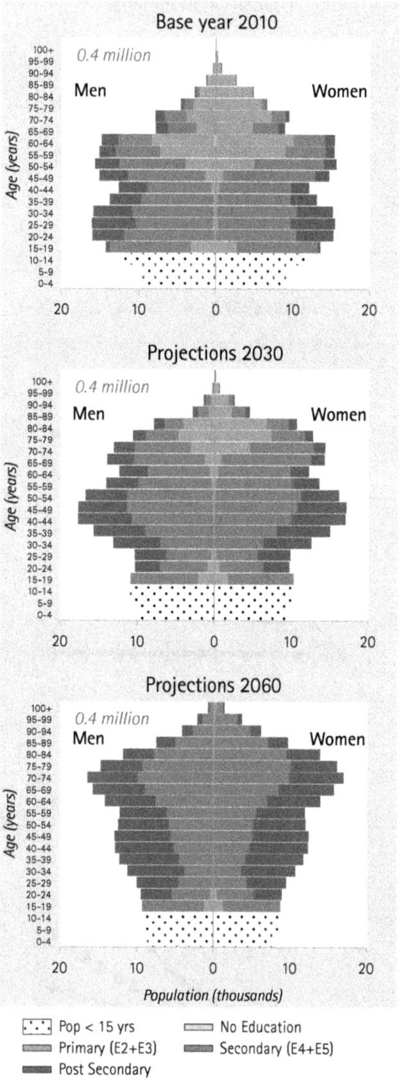

Population Size by Educational Attainment According to Three Education Scenarios: GET, CER, and FT

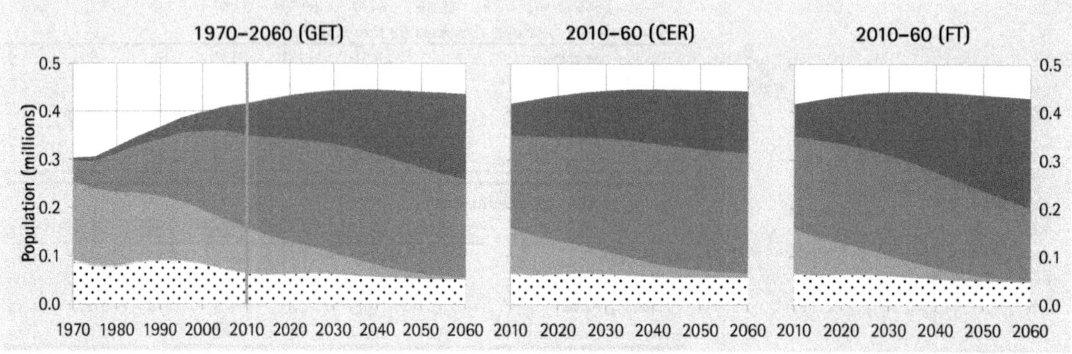

Malta (Continued)

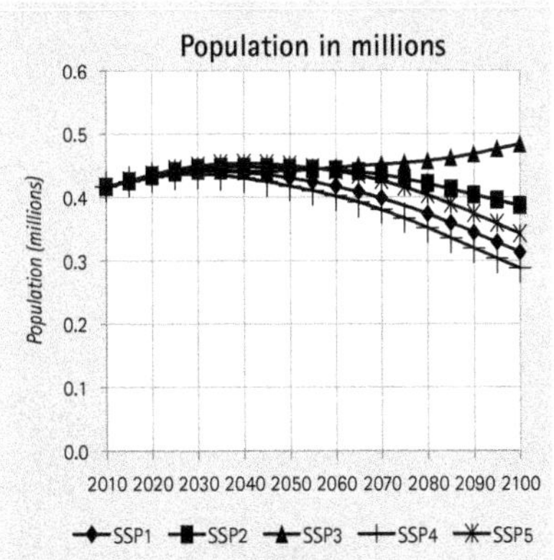

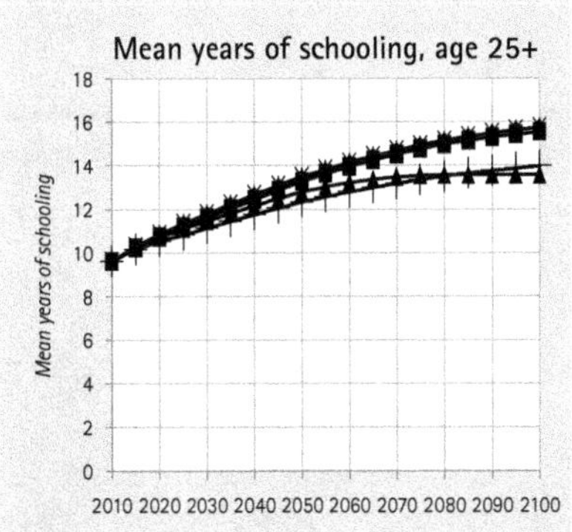

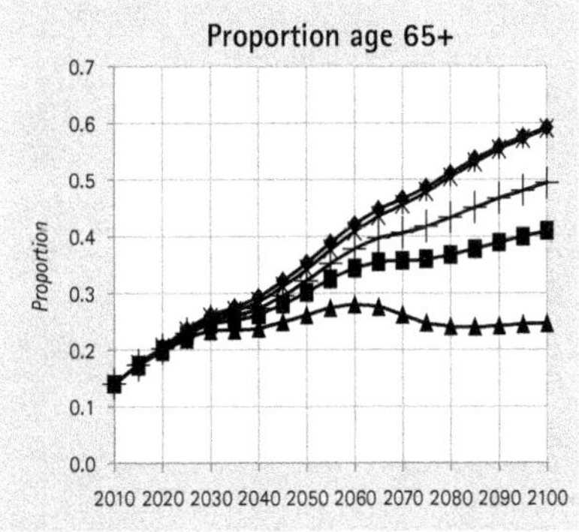

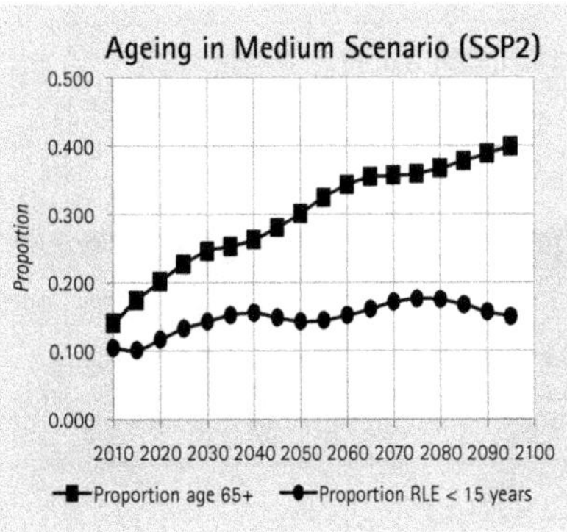

Alternative Scenarios to 2100

Projection Results by Scenario (SSP1–5)

	2010	2020	2030	2040	2050	2075	2100
Population (in millions)							
SSP1 - Rapid development	0.42	0.43	0.44	0.44	0.43	0.39	0.31
SSP2 - Medium	0.42	0.43	0.45	0.45	0.45	0.43	0.39
SSP3 - Stalled development	0.42	0.43	0.44	0.44	0.44	0.45	0.48
SSP4 - Inequality	0.42	0.43	0.44	0.43	0.42	0.37	0.29
SSP5 - Conventional development	0.42	0.44	0.45	0.45	0.45	0.42	0.34
Proportion age 65+							
SSP1 - Rapid development	0.14	0.21	0.26	0.29	0.35	0.49	0.59
SSP2 - Medium	0.14	0.20	0.25	0.26	0.30	0.36	0.41
SSP3 - Stalled development	0.14	0.20	0.23	0.24	0.26	0.25	0.25
SSP4 - Inequality	0.14	0.20	0.25	0.27	0.32	0.42	0.49
SSP5 - Conventional development	0.14	0.20	0.26	0.29	0.34	0.48	0.59
Proportion below age 20							
SSP1 - Rapid development	0.22	0.18	0.17	0.14	0.12	0.10	0.08
SSP2 - Medium	0.22	0.19	0.19	0.18	0.17	0.16	0.15
SSP3 - Stalled development	0.22	0.20	0.21	0.21	0.22	0.24	0.25
SSP4 - Inequality	0.22	0.19	0.17	0.15	0.14	0.12	0.10
SSP5 - Conventional development	0.22	0.18	0.17	0.14	0.13	0.10	0.08
Proportion of Women age 20–39 with at least secondary education							
SSP1 - Rapid development	0.99	0.99	1.00	1.00	1.00	1.00	1.00
SSP2 - Medium	0.99	0.99	0.99	0.99	1.00	1.00	1.00
SSP3 - Stalled development	0.99	0.99	0.99	0.99	0.99	0.99	0.99
SSP4 - Inequality	0.99	0.93	0.89	0.89	0.89	0.89	0.89
SSP5 - Conventional development	0.99	0.99	1.00	1.00	1.00	1.00	1.00
Mean years of schooling, age 25+							
SSP1 - Rapid development	9.61	10.85	11.76	12.61	13.42	14.89	15.72
SSP2 - Medium	9.61	10.76	11.62	12.45	13.26	14.75	15.53
SSP3 - Stalled development	9.61	10.70	11.46	12.16	12.78	13.53	13.57
SSP4 - Inequality	9.61	10.53	11.14	11.75	12.33	13.34	13.96
SSP5 - Conventional development	9.61	10.86	11.80	12.66	13.47	14.93	15.73

Demographic Assumptions Underlying SSPs

	2010–15	2020–25	2030–35	2040–45	2050–55	2075–80	2095–2100
Total fertility rate							
SSP1 - Rapid development	1.38	1.29	1.23	1.19	1.18	1.21	1.23
SSP2 - Medium	1.45	1.54	1.60	1.60	1.60	1.63	1.65
SSP3 - Stalled development	1.53	1.78	1.98	2.08	2.13	2.22	2.28
SSP4 - Inequality	1.39	1.33	1.28	1.25	1.24	1.26	1.28
SSP5 - Conventional development	1.38	1.29	1.23	1.19	1.18	1.21	1.23
Life expectancy at birth for females (in years)							
SSP1 - Rapid development	83.44	86.56	89.69	92.67	95.51	102.93	108.99
SSP2 - Medium	82.41	84.71	86.79	88.79	90.80	95.80	99.80
SSP3 - Stalled development	82.48	83.69	84.87	85.76	86.61	88.91	90.69
SSP4 - Inequality	82.93	85.17	87.31	89.20	91.01	95.66	99.51
SSP5 - Conventional development	83.44	86.56	89.69	92.67	95.51	102.93	108.99
Migration – net flow over five years (in thousands)							
SSP1 - Rapid development	5	5	5	5	4	1	0
SSP2 - Medium	5	5	5	5	5	2	0
SSP3 - Stalled development	4	3	3	3	3	2	0
SSP4 - Inequality	5	5	5	5	5	2	0
SSP5 - Conventional development	6	7	7	7	6	2	0

Ageing Indicators, Medium Scenario (SSP2)

	2010	2020	2030	2040	2050	2075	2095
Median age	39.42	42.09	45.44	48.79	50.94	53.52	56.08
Propspective median age	39.42	39.89	41.27	42.87	43.18	41.09	39.71
Proportion age 65+	0.14	0.20	0.25	0.26	0.30	0.36	0.40
Proportion RLE < 15 years	0.10	0.12	0.14	0.16	0.14	0.18	0.15

Martinique

Detailed Human Capital Projections to 2060

Demographic indicators, Medium Scenario (SSP2)	2010	2020	2030	2040	2050	2060
Population (in millions)	0.41	0.42	0.44	0.45	0.45	0.45
Proportion age 65+	0.15	0.18	0.24	0.27	0.27	0.29
Proportion below age 20	0.27	0.24	0.24	0.23	0.22	0.21
	2005–10	2015–20	2025–30	2035–40	2045–50	2055–60
Total Fertility Rate	1.91	2.00	2.00	1.96	1.91	1.89
Life expectancy at birth (in years)						
Men	76.68	78.18	80.33	82.43	84.53	86.63
Women	83.17	84.49	86.51	88.51	90.49	92.51
Five-year immigration flow (in '000)	2.80	2.74	2.84	2.91	2.90	2.86
Five-year emigration flow (in '000)	4.79	3.69	3.46	3.33	3.28	3.17

Human Capital indicators, Medium Scenario (SSP2)	2010	2020	2030	2040	2050	2060
Population age 25+: highest educational attainment						
E1 - no education	0.01	0.01	0.01	0.00	0.00	0.00
E2 - incomplete primary	0.11	0.07	0.04	0.03	0.01	0.01
E3 - primary	0.24	0.19	0.14	0.10	0.07	0.04
E4 - lower secondary	0.14	0.13	0.12	0.10	0.07	0.05
E5 - upper secondary	0.32	0.38	0.43	0.46	0.47	0.47
E6 - post-secondary	0.18	0.22	0.27	0.32	0.37	0.43
Mean years of schooling (in years)	9.43	10.42	11.27	12.00	12.65	13.22
Gender gap (population age 25+): highest educational attainment (ratio male/female)						
E1 - no education	1.21	1.23	1.21	1.15	1.08	1.00
E2 - incomplete primary	0.97	0.94	0.91	0.88	0.86	0.83
E3 - primary	1.09	1.05	1.00	0.96	0.94	0.94
E4 - lower secondary	0.96	0.99	1.01	1.01	1.01	1.02
E5 - upper secondary	1.04	1.08	1.10	1.11	1.09	1.07
E6 - post-secondary	0.86	0.86	0.87	0.88	0.90	0.93
Mean years of schooling (male minus female)	−0.19	−0.13	−0.09	−0.07	−0.06	−0.05
Women age 20–39: highest educational attainment						
E1 - no education	0.01	0.00	0.00	0.00	0.00	0.00
E2 - incomplete primary	0.01	0.00	0.00	0.00	0.00	0.00
E3 - primary	0.09	0.04	0.02	0.01	0.01	0.00
E4 - lower secondary	0.12	0.10	0.07	0.05	0.04	0.04
E5 - upper secondary	0.50	0.52	0.52	0.51	0.50	0.48
E6 - post-secondary	0.28	0.34	0.39	0.42	0.45	0.48
Mean years of schooling (in years)	11.88	12.67	13.28	13.53	13.72	13.86

Education scenarios

GET: global education trend scenario (medium assumption also used for SSP2)

CER: constant enrolment rates scenario (assumption of no future improvements)

FT: Fast track scenario (assumption of education expansion according to fastest historical experience)

Pyramids by Education, Medium Scenario

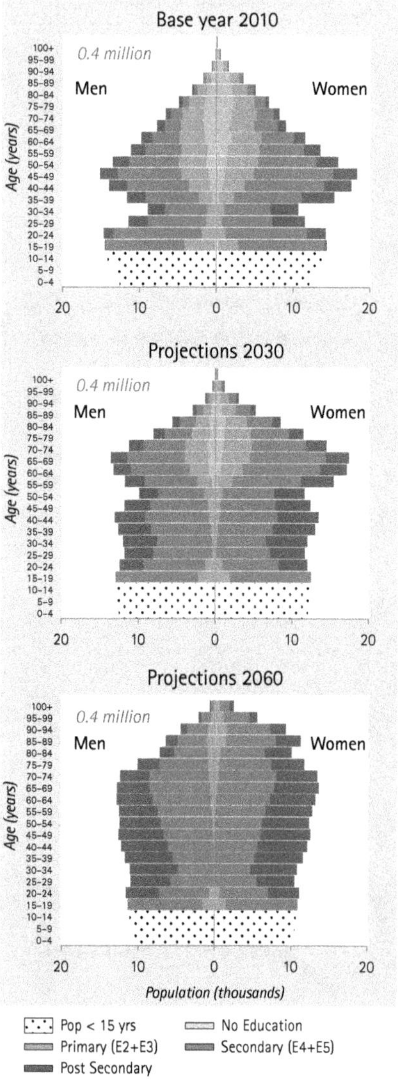

Population Size by Educational Attainment According to Three Education Scenarios: GET, CER, and FT

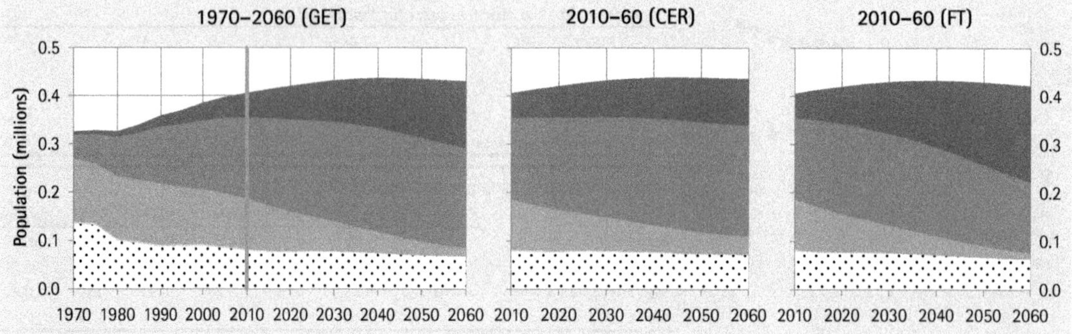

Martinique (Continued)

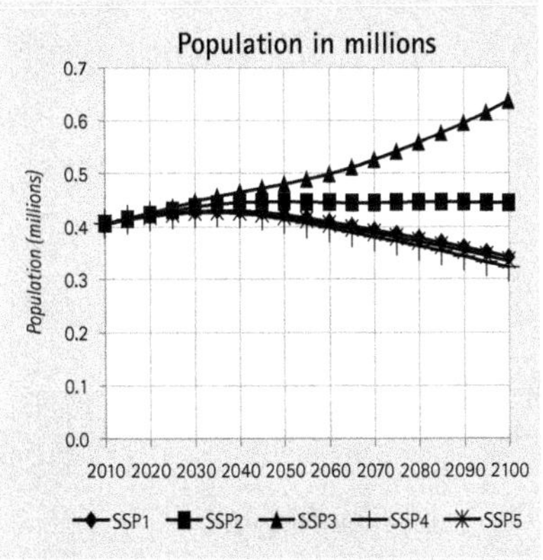

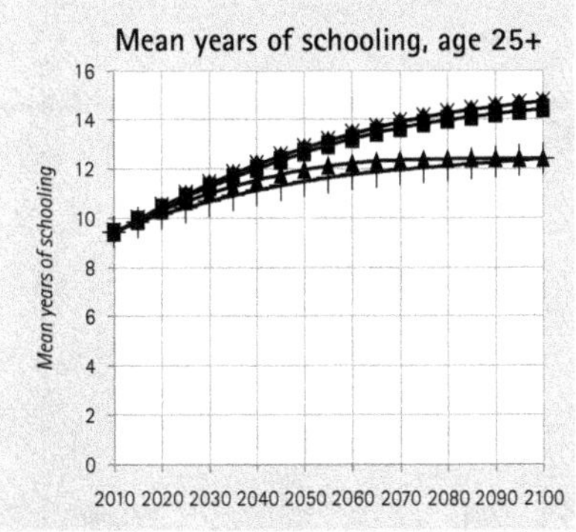

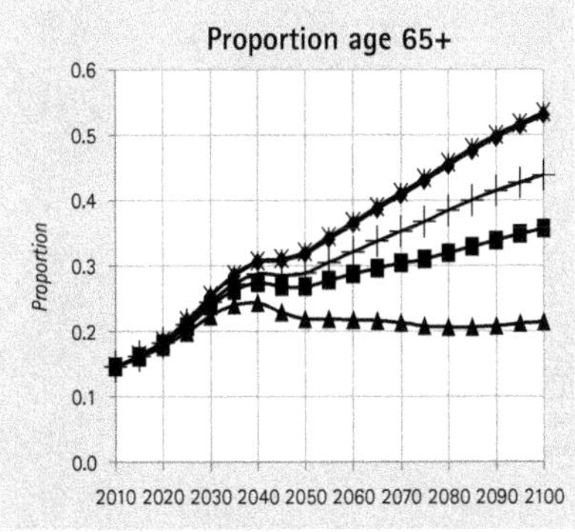

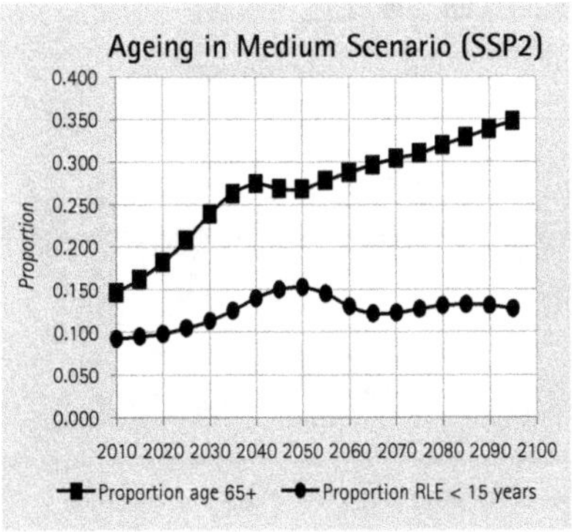

Alternative Scenarios to 2100

Projection Results by Scenario (SSP1–5)

	2010	2020	2030	2040	2050	2075	2100
Population (in millions)							
SSP1 - Rapid development	0.41	0.42	0.43	0.43	0.42	0.39	0.34
SSP2 - Medium	0.41	0.42	0.44	0.45	0.45	0.45	0.44
SSP3 - Stalled development	0.41	0.43	0.45	0.47	0.48	0.54	0.64
SSP4 - Inequality	0.41	0.42	0.43	0.42	0.41	0.37	0.32
SSP5 - Conventional development	0.41	0.42	0.43	0.43	0.42	0.38	0.33
Proportion age 65+							
SSP1 - Rapid development	0.15	0.19	0.25	0.31	0.32	0.43	0.53
SSP2 - Medium	0.15	0.18	0.24	0.27	0.27	0.31	0.36
SSP3 - Stalled development	0.15	0.18	0.22	0.24	0.22	0.21	0.21
SSP4 - Inequality	0.15	0.18	0.24	0.29	0.29	0.37	0.44
SSP5 - Conventional development	0.15	0.19	0.25	0.31	0.32	0.43	0.53
Proportion below age 20							
SSP1 - Rapid development	0.27	0.23	0.21	0.18	0.16	0.13	0.11
SSP2 - Medium	0.27	0.24	0.24	0.23	0.22	0.20	0.19
SSP3 - Stalled development	0.27	0.25	0.26	0.27	0.27	0.28	0.28
SSP4 - Inequality	0.27	0.24	0.22	0.20	0.18	0.15	0.13
SSP5 - Conventional development	0.27	0.23	0.21	0.18	0.16	0.13	0.10
Proportion of Women age 20–39 with at least secondary education							
SSP1 - Rapid development	0.90	0.96	0.98	0.99	0.99	1.00	1.00
SSP2 - Medium	0.90	0.95	0.97	0.99	0.99	1.00	1.00
SSP3 - Stalled development	0.90	0.93	0.93	0.93	0.93	0.93	0.93
SSP4 - Inequality	0.90	0.87	0.84	0.84	0.84	0.84	0.84
SSP5 - Conventional development	0.90	0.96	0.98	0.99	0.99	1.00	1.00
Mean years of schooling, age 25+							
SSP1 - Rapid development	9.43	10.47	11.40	12.17	12.84	14.09	14.73
SSP2 - Medium	9.43	10.42	11.27	12.00	12.65	13.83	14.42
SSP3 - Stalled development	9.43	10.32	11.01	11.54	11.95	12.38	12.40
SSP4 - Inequality	9.43	10.16	10.69	11.13	11.49	12.04	12.40
SSP5 - Conventional development	9.43	10.47	11.39	12.16	12.83	14.08	14.72

Demographic Assumptions Underlying SSPs

	2010–15	2020–25	2030–35	2040–45	2050–55	2075–80	2095–2100
Total fertility rate							
SSP1 - Rapid development	1.90	1.67	1.53	1.45	1.40	1.38	1.37
SSP2 - Medium	2.00	2.00	1.98	1.93	1.89	1.87	1.85
SSP3 - Stalled development	2.11	2.32	2.46	2.49	2.49	2.48	2.48
SSP4 - Inequality	1.92	1.75	1.63	1.54	1.49	1.47	1.46
SSP5 - Conventional development	1.90	1.67	1.53	1.45	1.40	1.38	1.37
Life expectancy at birth for females (in years)							
SSP1 - Rapid development	84.91	87.53	90.36	93.26	96.21	103.58	109.61
SSP2 - Medium	83.69	85.49	87.51	89.51	91.51	96.50	100.50
SSP3 - Stalled development	84.01	84.69	85.58	86.51	87.46	89.55	91.38
SSP4 - Inequality	84.48	86.11	87.98	89.87	91.78	96.29	100.10
SSP5 - Conventional development	84.91	87.53	90.36	93.26	96.21	103.58	109.61
Migration – net flow over five years (in thousands)							
SSP1 - Rapid development	−1	−1	0	0	0	0	0
SSP2 - Medium	−1	−1	0	0	0	0	0
SSP3 - Stalled development	−1	0	0	0	0	0	0
SSP4 - Inequality	−1	−1	0	0	0	0	0
SSP5 - Conventional development	−2	−1	−1	−1	−1	0	0

Ageing Indicators, Medium Scenario (SSP2)

	2010	2020	2030	2040	2050	2075	2095
Median age	39.47	40.81	41.96	44.12	45.41	48.08	50.82
Propspective median age	39.47	39.15	38.48	38.85	38.34	36.43	35.42
Proportion age 65+	0.15	0.18	0.24	0.27	0.27	0.31	0.35
Proportion RLE < 15 years	0.09	0.10	0.11	0.14	0.15	0.13	0.13

Mauritius*

Detailed Human Capital Projections to 2060

Demographic indicators, Medium Scenario (SSP2)	2010	2020	2030	2040	2050	2060
Population (in millions)	1.30	1.37	1.42	1.45	1.45	1.43
Proportion age 65+	0.07	0.11	0.16	0.20	0.24	0.28
Proportion below age 20	0.30	0.25	0.22	0.21	0.20	0.19
	2005–10	2015–20	2025–30	2035–40	2045–50	2055–60
Total Fertility Rate	1.67	1.53	1.66	1.70	1.70	1.70
Life expectancy at birth (in years)						
Men	69.49	72.48	74.98	77.26	79.50	81.65
Women	76.18	78.79	80.99	83.09	85.21	87.21
Five-year immigration flow (in '000)	9.21	9.01	9.35	9.55	9.55	9.41
Five-year emigration flow (in '000)	9.23	6.76	6.12	5.47	5.19	4.89

Human Capital indicators, Medium Scenario (SSP2)	2010	2020	2030	2040	2050	2060
Population age 25+: highest educational attainment						
E1 - no education	0.07	0.04	0.02	0.01	0.01	0.00
E2 - incomplete primary	0.33	0.27	0.21	0.16	0.12	0.08
E3 - primary	0.34	0.37	0.38	0.39	0.38	0.35
E4 - lower secondary	0.15	0.16	0.17	0.17	0.17	0.16
E5 - upper secondary	0.08	0.12	0.17	0.22	0.27	0.33
E6 - post-secondary	0.03	0.04	0.04	0.05	0.06	0.07
Mean years of schooling (in years)	6.46	7.22	7.91	8.53	9.18	9.84
Gender gap (population age 25+): highest educational attainment (ratio male/female)						
E1 - no education	0.36	0.36	0.37	0.43	0.55	0.69
E2 - incomplete primary	0.94	0.93	0.93	0.93	0.94	0.96
E3 - primary	1.13	1.09	1.07	1.06	1.04	1.02
E4 - lower secondary	1.16	1.10	1.06	1.04	1.03	1.01
E5 - upper secondary	1.06	0.97	0.94	0.95	0.96	0.98
E6 - post-secondary	1.85	1.47	1.25	1.13	1.05	1.03
Mean years of schooling (male minus female)	0.80	0.50	0.28	0.12	0.03	0.01
Women age 20–39: highest educational attainment						
E1 - no education	0.01	0.00	0.00	0.00	0.00	0.00
E2 - incomplete primary	0.20	0.11	0.06	0.04	0.02	0.02
E3 - primary	0.41	0.40	0.38	0.33	0.28	0.23
E4 - lower secondary	0.17	0.17	0.16	0.14	0.12	0.10
E5 - upper secondary	0.18	0.26	0.34	0.42	0.50	0.55
E6 - post-secondary	0.03	0.05	0.06	0.07	0.09	0.10
Mean years of schooling (in years)	8.07	9.01	9.79	10.48	11.10	11.60

Education scenarios

GET: global education trend scenario (medium assumption also used for SSP2)

CER: constant enrolment rates scenario (assumption of no future improvements)

FT: Fast track scenario (assumption of education expansion according to fastest historical experience)

Pyramids by Education, Medium Scenario

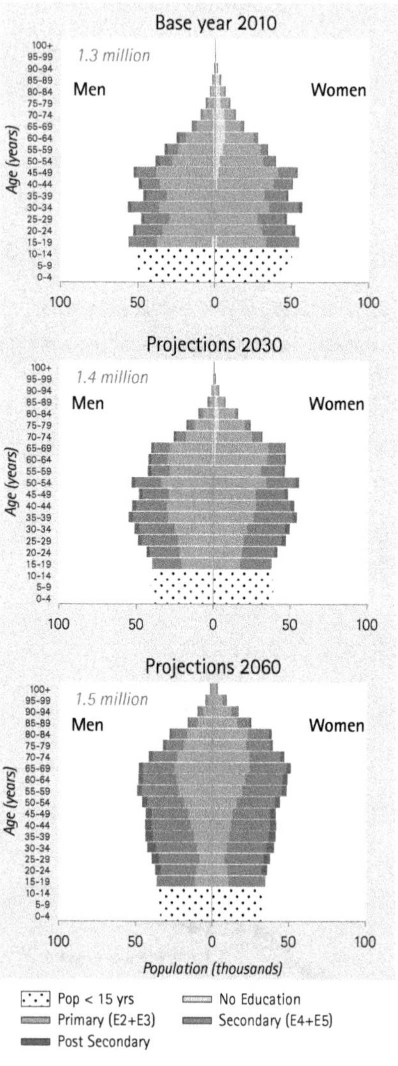

Population Size by Educational Attainment According to Three Education Scenarios: GET, CER, and FT

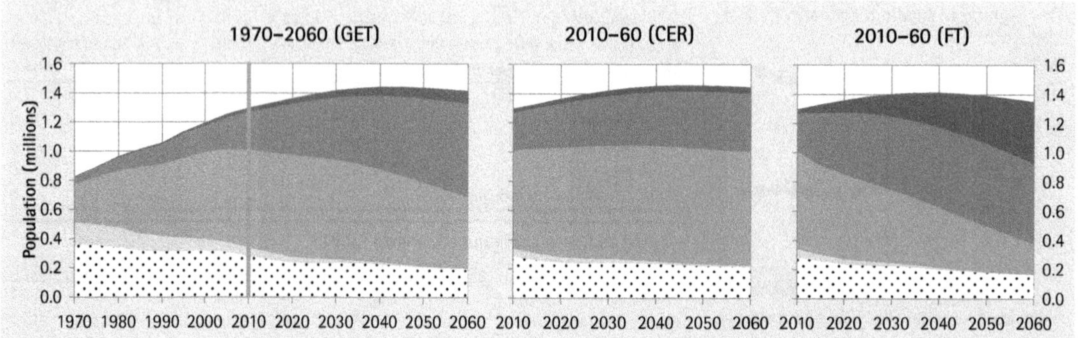

*Updated data for Mauritius is provided on the WIC Data Explorer <http://www.wittgensteincentre.org/dataexplorer>. The data was adjusted to account for corrections in the education category definitions and changes over time.

Mauritius (Continued)

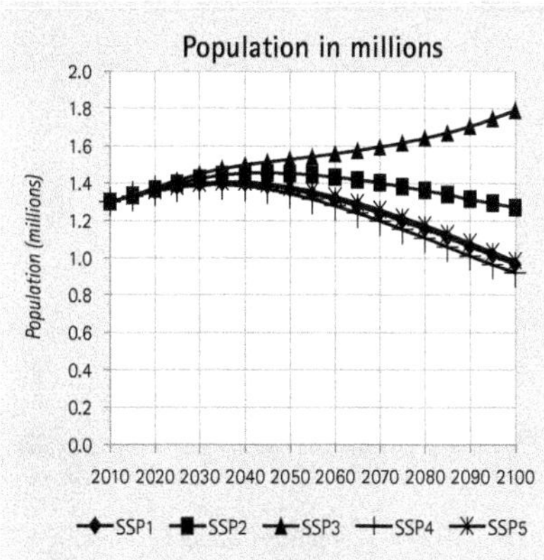

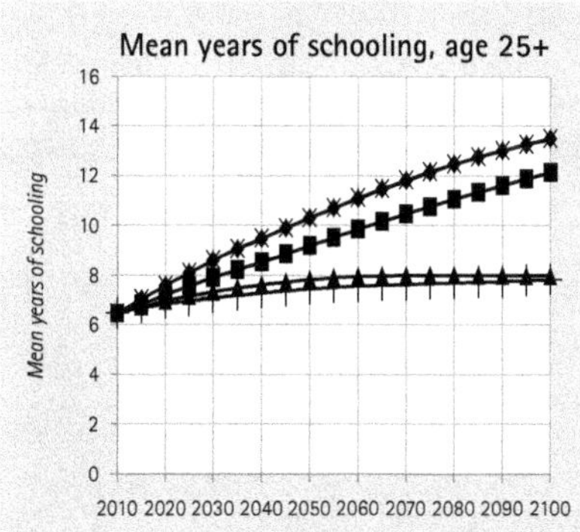

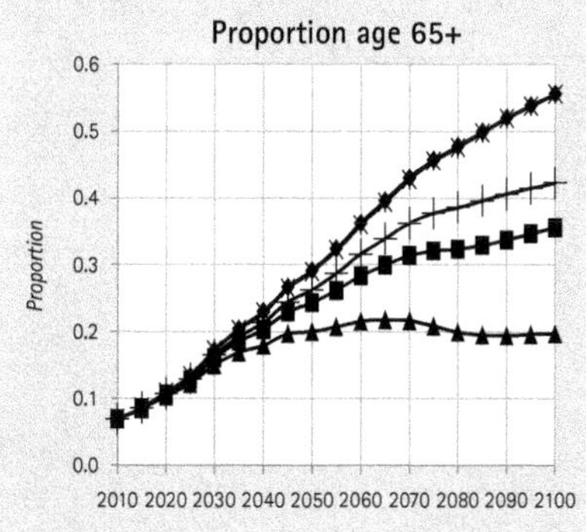

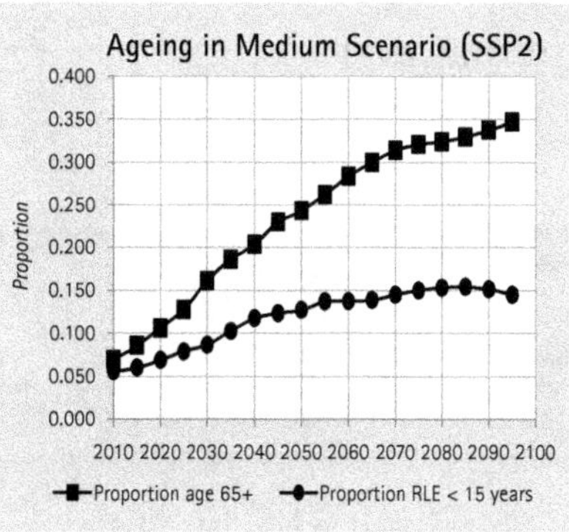

Alternative Scenarios to 2100

Projection Results by Scenario (SSP1–5)

	2010	2020	2030	2040	2050	2075	2100
Population (in millions)							
SSP1 - Rapid development	1.30	1.36	1.39	1.40	1.37	1.20	0.97
SSP2 - Medium	1.30	1.37	1.42	1.45	1.45	1.38	1.27
SSP3 - Stalled development	1.30	1.37	1.45	1.50	1.53	1.62	1.79
SSP4 - Inequality	1.30	1.36	1.39	1.38	1.34	1.15	0.92
SSP5 - Conventional development	1.30	1.36	1.40	1.41	1.38	1.22	0.98
Proportion age 65+							
SSP1 - Rapid development	0.07	0.11	0.17	0.23	0.29	0.46	0.56
SSP2 - Medium	0.07	0.11	0.16	0.20	0.24	0.32	0.36
SSP3 - Stalled development	0.07	0.10	0.15	0.18	0.20	0.21	0.20
SSP4 - Inequality	0.07	0.11	0.17	0.21	0.26	0.38	0.42
SSP5 - Conventional development	0.07	0.11	0.17	0.23	0.29	0.45	0.55
Proportion below age 20							
SSP1 - Rapid development	0.30	0.24	0.19	0.17	0.14	0.11	0.09
SSP2 - Medium	0.30	0.25	0.22	0.21	0.20	0.18	0.17
SSP3 - Stalled development	0.30	0.26	0.25	0.25	0.25	0.27	0.28
SSP4 - Inequality	0.30	0.24	0.20	0.18	0.16	0.14	0.13
SSP5 - Conventional development	0.30	0.24	0.19	0.17	0.14	0.11	0.09
Proportion of Women age 20–39 with at least secondary education							
SSP1 - Rapid development	0.39	0.62	0.73	0.80	0.85	0.92	0.97
SSP2 - Medium	0.39	0.48	0.56	0.63	0.70	0.84	0.93
SSP3 - Stalled development	0.39	0.39	0.39	0.39	0.39	0.39	0.39
SSP4 - Inequality	0.39	0.36	0.35	0.35	0.35	0.35	0.35
SSP5 - Conventional development	0.39	0.62	0.73	0.80	0.85	0.92	0.97
Mean years of schooling, age 25+							
SSP1 - Rapid development	6.46	7.58	8.59	9.46	10.29	12.14	13.49
SSP2 - Medium	6.46	7.22	7.91	8.53	9.18	10.77	12.13
SSP3 - Stalled development	6.46	6.97	7.35	7.62	7.83	8.00	8.00
SSP4 - Inequality	6.46	6.85	7.09	7.29	7.45	7.67	7.84
SSP5 - Conventional development	6.46	7.58	8.59	9.47	10.30	12.15	13.49

Demographic Assumptions Underlying SSPs

	2010–15	2020–25	2030–35	2040–45	2050–55	2075–80	2095–2100
Total fertility rate							
SSP1 - Rapid development	1.41	1.32	1.26	1.23	1.20	1.21	1.23
SSP2 - Medium	1.50	1.60	1.70	1.70	1.70	1.71	1.71
SSP3 - Stalled development	1.58	1.88	2.11	2.22	2.27	2.38	2.46
SSP4 - Inequality	1.43	1.39	1.36	1.35	1.34	1.39	1.44
SSP5 - Conventional development	1.41	1.32	1.26	1.23	1.20	1.21	1.23
Life expectancy at birth for females (in years)							
SSP1 - Rapid development	78.87	82.09	85.19	88.19	91.18	98.78	104.93
SSP2 - Medium	77.59	79.89	82.09	84.11	86.21	91.30	95.31
SSP3 - Stalled development	77.95	79.21	80.32	81.32	82.20	84.27	85.94
SSP4 - Inequality	78.44	80.61	82.73	84.66	86.61	91.07	94.67
SSP5 - Conventional development	78.87	82.09	85.19	88.19	91.18	98.78	104.93
Migration – net flow over five years (in thousands)							
SSP1 - Rapid development	1	3	4	4	3	1	0
SSP2 - Medium	1	3	4	4	4	2	0
SSP3 - Stalled development	1	1	2	3	3	2	0
SSP4 - Inequality	1	3	4	4	4	2	0
SSP5 - Conventional development	1	4	5	5	5	1	0

Ageing Indicators, Medium Scenario (SSP2)

	2010	2020	2030	2040	2050	2075	2095
Median age	32.38	36.47	39.99	43.63	46.50	49.44	51.76
Propspective median age	32.38	34.13	35.49	37.18	38.03	36.11	34.56
Proportion age 65+	0.07	0.11	0.16	0.20	0.24	0.32	0.35
Proportion RLE < 15 years	0.06	0.07	0.09	0.12	0.13	0.15	0.15

Mexico

Detailed Human Capital Projections to 2060

Demographic indicators, Medium Scenario (SSP2)

	2010	2020	2030	2040	2050	2060
Population (in millions)	113.42	126.86	138.31	146.91	152.18	154.10
Proportion age 65+	0.06	0.08	0.12	0.16	0.20	0.23
Proportion below age 20	0.39	0.34	0.30	0.27	0.25	0.22
	2005–10	2015–20	2025–30	2035–40	2045–50	2055–60
Total Fertility Rate	2.41	2.20	2.04	1.93	1.84	1.74
Life expectancy at birth (in years)						
Men	73.73	76.21	78.30	80.23	82.19	84.23
Women	78.62	80.99	83.09	85.01	86.91	88.91
Five-year immigration flow (in '000)	123.09	121.82	126.81	130.12	130.67	129.07
Five-year emigration flow (in '000)	1921.45	1553.50	1586.09	1567.93	1511.91	1433.81

Human Capital indicators, Medium Scenario (SSP2)

	2010	2020	2030	2040	2050	2060
Population age 25+: highest educational attainment						
E1 - no education	0.09	0.06	0.04	0.02	0.01	0.01
E2 - incomplete primary	0.16	0.12	0.08	0.06	0.04	0.02
E3 - primary	0.22	0.20	0.18	0.16	0.13	0.11
E4 - lower secondary	0.26	0.30	0.30	0.29	0.27	0.25
E5 - upper secondary	0.13	0.16	0.20	0.23	0.26	0.29
E6 - post-secondary	0.14	0.17	0.20	0.24	0.28	0.32
Mean years of schooling (in years)	8.29	9.22	10.00	10.67	11.28	11.83
Gender gap (population age 25+): highest educational attainment (ratio male/female)						
E1 - no education	0.74	0.71	0.69	0.67	0.68	0.69
E2 - incomplete primary	0.95	0.93	0.89	0.85	0.82	0.80
E3 - primary	0.97	0.99	0.99	0.98	0.98	0.97
E4 - lower secondary	0.99	0.99	1.01	1.01	1.01	0.99
E5 - upper secondary	1.16	1.12	1.10	1.09	1.08	1.06
E6 - post-secondary	1.21	1.09	1.03	0.99	0.98	0.99
Mean years of schooling (male minus female)	0.60	0.43	0.30	0.20	0.12	0.09
Women age 20–39: highest educational attainment						
E1 - no education	0.03	0.02	0.01	0.00	0.00	0.00
E2 - incomplete primary	0.07	0.04	0.02	0.01	0.00	0.00
E3 - primary	0.19	0.14	0.12	0.09	0.07	0.05
E4 - lower secondary	0.35	0.33	0.28	0.22	0.16	0.12
E5 - upper secondary	0.20	0.26	0.31	0.35	0.39	0.41
E6 - post-secondary	0.16	0.22	0.27	0.33	0.38	0.42
Mean years of schooling (in years)	9.93	10.87	11.54	12.18	12.69	13.10

Education scenarios

GET: global education trend scenario (medium assumption also used for SSP2)

CER: constant enrolment rates scenario (assumption of no future improvements)

FT: Fast track scenario (assumption of education expansion according to fastest historical experience)

Pyramids by Education, Medium Scenario

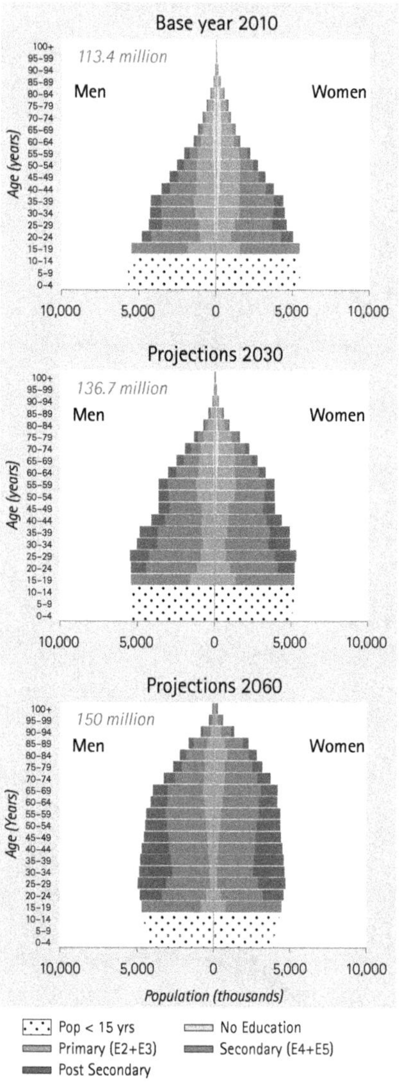

Population Size by Educational Attainment According to Three Education Scenarios: GET, CER, and FT

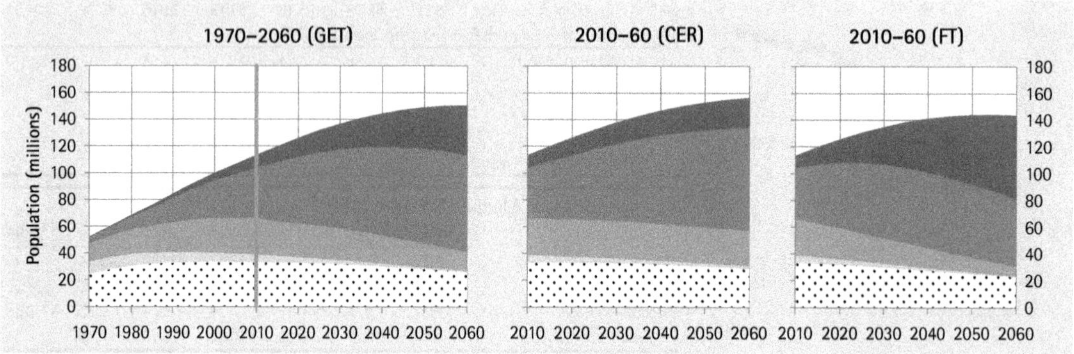

Mexico (Continued)

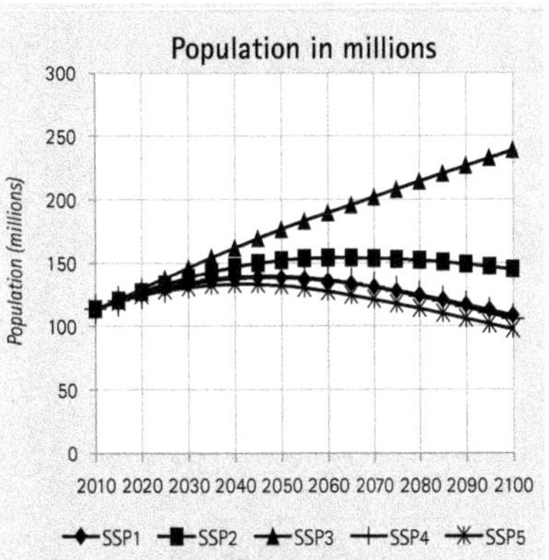

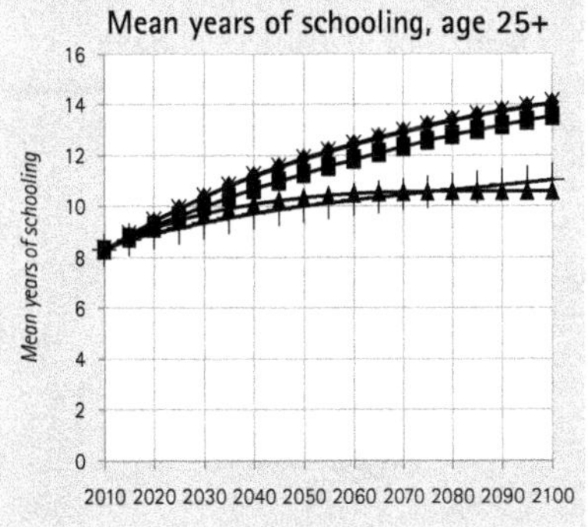

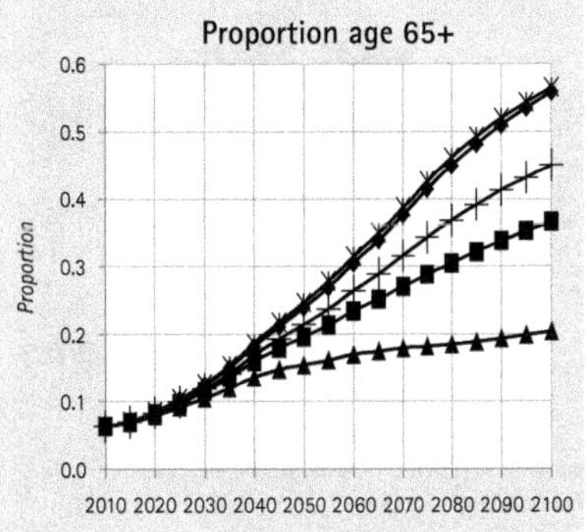

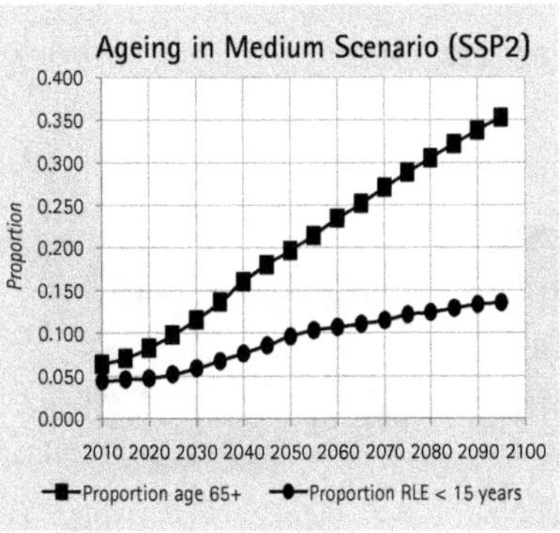

Alternative Scenarios to 2100

Projection Results by Scenario (SSP1–5)

	2010	2020	2030	2040	2050	2075	2100
Population (in millions)							
SSP1 - Rapid development	113.42	125.18	133.07	137.55	138.23	127.79	108.28
SSP2 - Medium	113.42	126.86	138.31	146.91	152.18	153.28	145.08
SSP3 - Stalled development	113.42	129.27	146.28	162.13	176.69	208.35	238.99
SSP4 - Inequality	113.42	125.56	134.11	138.91	139.47	127.36	105.34
SSP5 - Conventional development	113.42	124.36	130.48	133.05	131.80	117.48	97.50
Proportion age 65+							
SSP1 - Rapid development	0.06	0.08	0.12	0.18	0.24	0.41	0.56
SSP2 - Medium	0.06	0.08	0.12	0.16	0.20	0.29	0.37
SSP3 - Stalled development	0.06	0.08	0.11	0.14	0.16	0.18	0.20
SSP4 - Inequality	0.06	0.08	0.12	0.17	0.21	0.34	0.45
SSP5 - Conventional development	0.06	0.09	0.13	0.19	0.25	0.43	0.56
Proportion below age 20							
SSP1 - Rapid development	0.39	0.33	0.27	0.22	0.18	0.12	0.08
SSP2 - Medium	0.39	0.34	0.30	0.27	0.25	0.19	0.16
SSP3 - Stalled development	0.39	0.35	0.34	0.32	0.31	0.29	0.27
SSP4 - Inequality	0.39	0.34	0.28	0.24	0.21	0.15	0.11
SSP5 - Conventional development	0.39	0.33	0.27	0.22	0.19	0.12	0.08
Proportion of Women age 20–39 with at least secondary education							
SSP1 - Rapid development	0.71	0.85	0.91	0.94	0.96	0.98	0.99
SSP2 - Medium	0.71	0.81	0.86	0.90	0.93	0.97	0.99
SSP3 - Stalled development	0.71	0.79	0.81	0.81	0.81	0.81	0.81
SSP4 - Inequality	0.71	0.75	0.73	0.73	0.73	0.73	0.73
SSP5 - Conventional development	0.71	0.85	0.91	0.94	0.96	0.98	0.99
Mean years of schooling, age 25+							
SSP1 - Rapid development	8.29	9.40	10.38	11.20	11.87	13.17	14.05
SSP2 - Medium	8.29	9.22	10.00	10.67	11.28	12.56	13.53
SSP3 - Stalled development	8.29	9.15	9.71	10.09	10.34	10.58	10.59
SSP4 - Inequality	8.29	8.96	9.36	9.72	10.01	10.55	11.03
SSP5 - Conventional development	8.29	9.39	10.35	11.17	11.84	13.14	14.03

Demographic Assumptions Underlying SSPs

	2010–15	2020–25	2030–35	2040–45	2050–55	2075–80	2095–2100
Total fertility rate							
SSP1 - Rapid development	2.16	1.74	1.50	1.38	1.30	1.21	1.18
SSP2 - Medium	2.29	2.12	1.98	1.88	1.80	1.64	1.59
SSP3 - Stalled development	2.42	2.49	2.52	2.48	2.41	2.28	2.24
SSP4 - Inequality	2.20	1.87	1.64	1.50	1.41	1.31	1.27
SSP5 - Conventional development	2.16	1.74	1.50	1.38	1.30	1.21	1.18
Life expectancy at birth for females (in years)							
SSP1 - Rapid development	81.26	84.02	86.90	89.70	92.64	100.36	106.59
SSP2 - Medium	79.79	81.99	84.11	85.91	87.91	93.10	97.29
SSP3 - Stalled development	80.45	81.38	82.29	83.08	83.93	86.17	87.93
SSP4 - Inequality	80.85	82.73	84.63	86.27	88.13	92.92	96.87
SSP5 - Conventional development	81.26	84.02	86.90	89.70	92.64	100.36	106.59
Migration – net flow over five years (in thousands)							
SSP1 - Rapid development	−1521	−1440	−1421	−1313	−1167	−390	0
SSP2 - Medium	−1520	−1456	−1462	−1424	−1356	−544	0
SSP3 - Stalled development	−1266	−719	−721	−718	−714	−334	0
SSP4 - Inequality	−1521	−1438	−1410	−1280	−1107	−335	0
SSP5 - Conventional development	−1775	−2181	−2190	−2075	−1903	−697	0

Ageing Indicators, Medium Scenario (SSP2)

	2010	2020	2030	2040	2050	2075	2095
Median age	26.60	29.60	33.10	36.52	39.83	47.23	52.34
Propspective median age	26.60	27.84	29.55	31.42	32.95	35.54	36.73
Proportion age 65+	0.06	0.08	0.12	0.16	0.20	0.29	0.35
Proportion RLE < 15 years	0.04	0.05	0.06	0.08	0.10	0.12	0.14

Mongolia

Detailed Human Capital Projections to 2060

Demographic indicators, Medium Scenario (SSP2)	2010	2020	2030	2040	2050	2060
Population (in millions)	2.76	3.15	3.42	3.62	3.78	3.82
Proportion age 65+	0.04	0.05	0.08	0.11	0.14	0.18
Proportion below age 20	0.38	0.35	0.32	0.28	0.27	0.25
	200-10	2015-20	2025-30	2035-40	2045-50	2055-60
Total Fertility Rate	2.50	2.28	2.11	2.00	1.92	1.80
Life expectancy at birth (in years)						
Men	63.41	64.40	66.15	68.59	70.90	73.21
Women	71.47	72.31	73.90	75.80	77.69	79.69
Five-year immigration flow (in '000)	0.80	0.79	0.82	0.84	0.84	0.82
Five-year emigration flow (in '000)	15.79	12.39	12.31	12.72	12.22	11.66

Human Capital indicators, Medium Scenario (SSP2)	2010	2020	2030	2040	2050	2060
Population age 25+: highest educational attainment						
E1 - no education	0.01	0.01	0.00	0.00	0.00	0.00
E2 - incomplete primary	0.02	0.01	0.01	0.00	0.00	0.00
E3 - primary	0.11	0.07	0.06	0.04	0.03	0.03
E4 - lower secondary	0.24	0.21	0.18	0.14	0.11	0.09
E5 - upper secondary	0.50	0.58	0.62	0.66	0.69	0.70
E6 - post-secondary	0.12	0.13	0.13	0.15	0.16	0.18
Mean years of schooling (in years)	9.22	9.85	10.27	10.65	10.99	11.27
Gender gap (population age 25+): highest educational attainment (ratio male/female)						
E1 - no education	0.52	1.02	0.87	0.83	0.68	0.63
E2 - incomplete primary	0.76	0.99	1.26	1.40	1.43	1.37
E3 - primary	1.09	1.36	1.71	1.97	2.00	1.80
E4 - lower secondary	1.52	1.62	1.68	1.67	1.63	1.55
E5 - upper secondary	0.86	0.87	0.90	0.94	0.97	0.99
E6 - post-secondary	0.85	0.70	0.65	0.64	0.70	0.79
Mean years of schooling (male minus female)	−0.28	−0.55	−0.60	−0.55	−0.44	−0.30
Women age 20–39: highest educational attainment						
E1 - no education	0.00	0.00	0.00	0.00	0.00	0.00
E2 - incomplete primary	0.01	0.00	0.00	0.00	0.00	0.00
E3 - primary	0.04	0.02	0.02	0.02	0.02	0.01
E4 - lower secondary	0.21	0.16	0.15	0.14	0.12	0.12
E5 - upper secondary	0.62	0.66	0.66	0.65	0.66	0.65
E6 - post-secondary	0.12	0.15	0.17	0.19	0.20	0.21
Mean years of schooling (in years)	10.06	10.85	11.20	11.33	11.45	11.49

Education scenarios

GET: global education trend scenario (medium assumption also used for SSP2)

CER: constant enrolment rates scenario (assumption of no future improvements)

FT: Fast track scenario (assumption of education expansion according to fastest historical experience)

Pyramids by Education, Medium Scenario

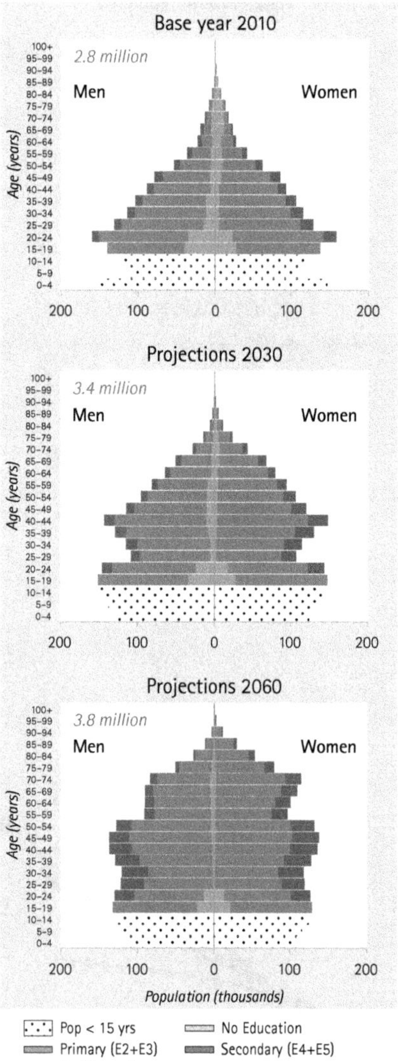

Population Size by Educational Attainment According to Three Education Scenarios: GET, CER, and FT

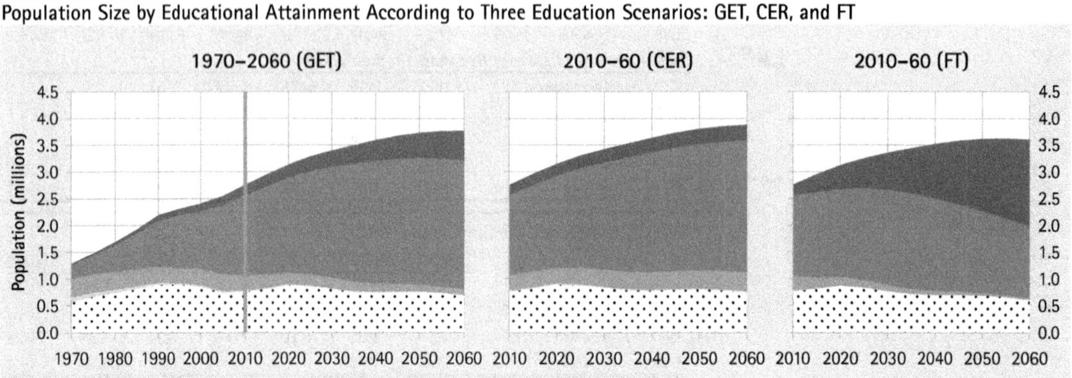

Mongolia (Continued)

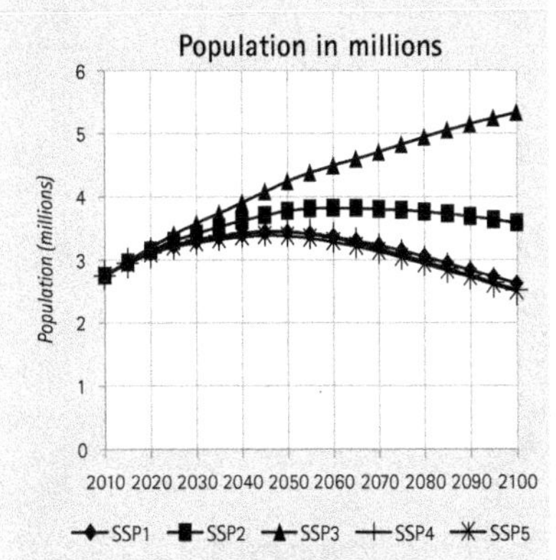

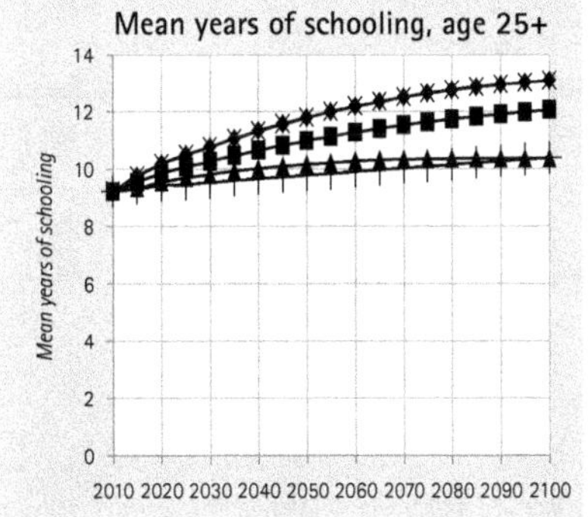

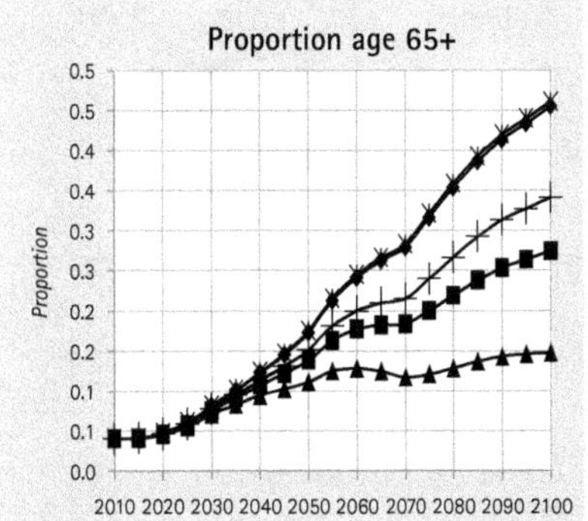

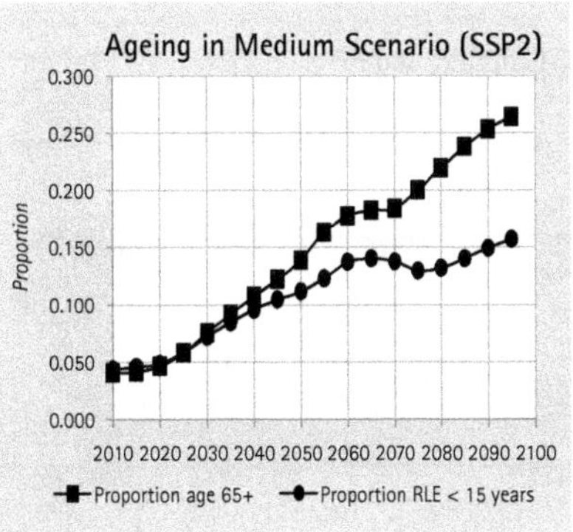

Alternative Scenarios to 2100

Projection Results by Scenario (SSP1–5)

	2010	2020	2030	2040	2050	2075	2100
Population (in millions)							
SSP1 - Rapid development	2.76	3.11	3.30	3.41	3.44	3.15	2.62
SSP2 - Medium	2.76	3.15	3.42	3.62	3.78	3.79	3.59
SSP3 - Stalled development	2.76	3.20	3.58	3.91	4.24	4.83	5.33
SSP4 - Inequality	2.76	3.12	3.32	3.43	3.45	3.08	2.51
SSP5 - Conventional development	2.76	3.10	3.27	3.37	3.38	3.04	2.50
Proportion age 65+							
SSP1 - Rapid development	0.04	0.05	0.08	0.12	0.17	0.32	0.45
SSP2 - Medium	0.04	0.05	0.08	0.11	0.14	0.20	0.27
SSP3 - Stalled development	0.04	0.05	0.07	0.09	0.11	0.12	0.15
SSP4 - Inequality	0.04	0.05	0.08	0.11	0.15	0.24	0.34
SSP5 - Conventional development	0.04	0.05	0.08	0.12	0.18	0.32	0.46
Proportion below age 20							
SSP1 - Rapid development	0.38	0.34	0.29	0.23	0.21	0.14	0.10
SSP2 - Medium	0.38	0.35	0.32	0.28	0.27	0.22	0.18
SSP3 - Stalled development	0.38	0.36	0.36	0.33	0.33	0.30	0.28
SSP4 - Inequality	0.38	0.35	0.30	0.25	0.23	0.17	0.13
SSP5 - Conventional development	0.38	0.34	0.29	0.23	0.21	0.14	0.10
Proportion of Women age 20–39 with at least secondary education							
SSP1 - Rapid development	0.95	0.98	0.99	0.99	0.99	0.99	1.00
SSP2 - Medium	0.95	0.97	0.97	0.98	0.98	0.99	1.00
SSP3 - Stalled development	0.95	0.93	0.93	0.93	0.93	0.93	0.93
SSP4 - Inequality	0.95	0.87	0.83	0.83	0.84	0.84	0.84
SSP5 - Conventional development	0.95	0.98	0.99	0.99	0.99	0.99	1.00
Mean years of schooling, age 25+							
SSP1 - Rapid development	9.22	10.17	10.77	11.32	11.79	12.64	13.09
SSP2 - Medium	9.22	9.85	10.27	10.65	10.99	11.64	12.06
SSP3 - Stalled development	9.22	9.55	9.81	10.02	10.16	10.35	10.37
SSP4 - Inequality	9.22	9.43	9.54	9.66	9.78	10.10	10.39
SSP5 - Conventional development	9.22	10.17	10.77	11.32	11.79	12.64	13.09

Demographic Assumptions Underlying SSPs

	2010–15	2020–25	2030–35	2040–45	2050–55	2075–80	2095–2100
Total fertility rate							
SSP1 - Rapid development	2.23	1.82	1.57	1.44	1.34	1.19	1.16
SSP2 - Medium	2.37	2.20	2.05	1.95	1.86	1.65	1.60
SSP3 - Stalled development	2.51	2.61	2.60	2.53	2.44	2.18	2.13
SSP4 - Inequality	2.28	1.97	1.72	1.57	1.45	1.28	1.24
SSP5 - Conventional development	2.23	1.82	1.57	1.44	1.34	1.19	1.16
Life expectancy at birth for females (in years)							
SSP1 - Rapid development	74.07	76.02	78.46	81.17	83.94	91.13	97.00
SSP2 - Medium	71.82	73.11	74.80	76.70	78.69	83.69	87.71
SSP3 - Stalled development	73.54	73.70	74.08	74.95	75.64	77.64	79.37
SSP4 - Inequality	73.93	74.88	76.27	77.82	79.50	83.93	87.69
SSP5 - Conventional development	74.07	76.02	78.46	81.17	83.94	91.13	97.00
Migration – net flow over five years (in thousands)							
SSP1 - Rapid development	−13	−11	−11	−11	−10	−4	0
SSP2 - Medium	−13	−11	−12	−12	−11	−5	0
SSP3 - Stalled development	−11	−6	−6	−6	−6	−3	0
SSP4 - Inequality	−13	−11	−11	−10	−9	−3	0
SSP5 - Conventional development	−15	−17	−18	−18	−16	−7	0

Ageing Indicators, Medium Scenario (SSP2)

	2010	2020	2030	2040	2050	2075	2095
Median age	25.38	29.28	32.22	33.73	36.60	41.99	46.84
Propspective median age	25.38	28.45	29.99	29.96	31.16	32.07	33.29
Proportion age 65+	0.04	0.05	0.08	0.11	0.14	0.20	0.26
Proportion RLE < 15 years	0.04	0.05	0.07	0.10	0.11	0.13	0.16

Montenegro

Detailed Human Capital Projections to 2060

Demographic indicators, Medium Scenario (SSP2)	2010	2020	2030	2040	2050	2060
Population (in millions)	0.63	0.65	0.67	0.69	0.69	0.70
Proportion age 65+	0.12	0.16	0.20	0.22	0.26	0.29
Proportion below age 20	0.26	0.24	0.22	0.20	0.19	0.18
	2005–10	2015–20	2025–30	2035–40	2045–50	2055–60
Total Fertility Rate	1.69	1.64	1.61	1.60	1.60	1.61
Life expectancy at birth (in years)						
Men	71.54	75.33	78.05	80.29	82.44	84.49
Women	76.47	80.19	82.91	85.11	87.21	89.20
Five-year immigration flow (in '000)	18.17	17.85	18.53	18.97	19.00	18.74
Five-year emigration flow (in '000)	20.70	14.38	13.38	12.56	11.79	11.18

Human Capital indicators, Medium Scenario (SSP2)	2010	2020	2030	2040	2050	2060
Population age 25+: highest educational attainment						
E1 - no education	0.03	0.01	0.01	0.00	0.00	0.00
E2 - incomplete primary	0.01	0.01	0.00	0.00	0.00	0.00
E3 - primary	0.08	0.05	0.03	0.01	0.01	0.00
E4 - lower secondary	0.18	0.16	0.13	0.10	0.07	0.05
E5 - upper secondary	0.53	0.60	0.65	0.67	0.69	0.69
E6 - post-secondary	0.16	0.18	0.19	0.21	0.23	0.26
Mean years of schooling (in years)	10.80	11.47	11.93	12.26	12.52	12.75
Gender gap (population age 25+): highest educational attainment (ratio male/female)						
E1 - no education	0.25	0.33	0.48	0.61	0.68	0.76
E2 - incomplete primary	0.29	0.25	0.29	0.43	0.60	0.76
E3 - primary	0.45	0.34	0.31	0.36	0.51	0.69
E4 - lower secondary	0.78	0.78	0.79	0.82	0.87	0.92
E5 - upper secondary	1.24	1.20	1.17	1.15	1.13	1.11
E6 - post-secondary	1.29	0.99	0.83	0.75	0.73	0.77
Mean years of schooling (male minus female)	1.38	0.74	0.27	−0.04	−0.20	−0.23
Women age 20–39: highest educational attainment						
E1 - no education	0.01	0.00	0.00	0.00	0.00	0.00
E2 - incomplete primary	0.00	0.00	0.00	0.00	0.00	0.00
E3 - primary	0.01	0.01	0.00	0.00	0.00	0.00
E4 - lower secondary	0.13	0.07	0.05	0.03	0.03	0.02
E5 - upper secondary	0.68	0.71	0.71	0.71	0.70	0.69
E6 - post-secondary	0.17	0.21	0.23	0.26	0.27	0.28
Mean years of schooling (in years)	11.93	12.41	12.68	12.84	12.94	12.98

Education scenarios

GET: global education trend scenario (medium assumption also used for SSP2)

CER: constant enrolment rates scenario (assumption of no future improvements)

FT: Fast track scenario (assumption of education expansion according to fastest historical experience)

Pyramids by Education, Medium Scenario

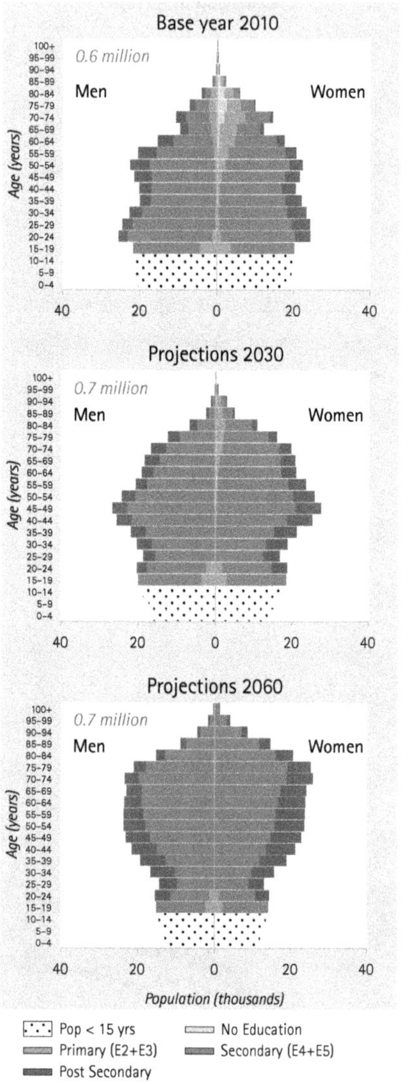

Population Size by Educational Attainment According to Three Education Scenarios: GET, CER, and FT

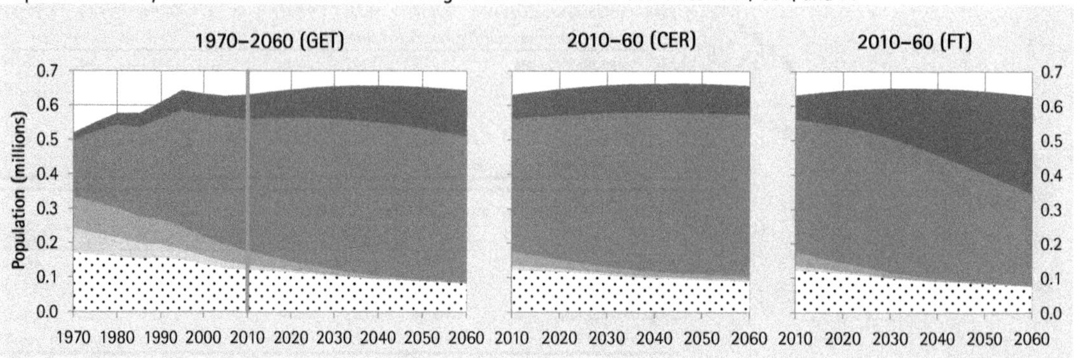

Montenegro (Continued)

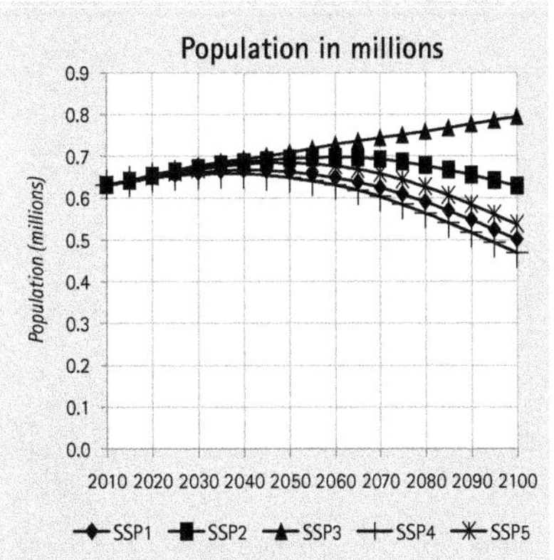

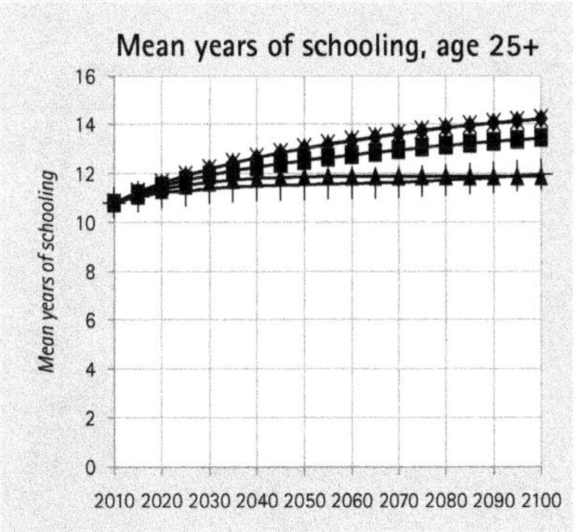

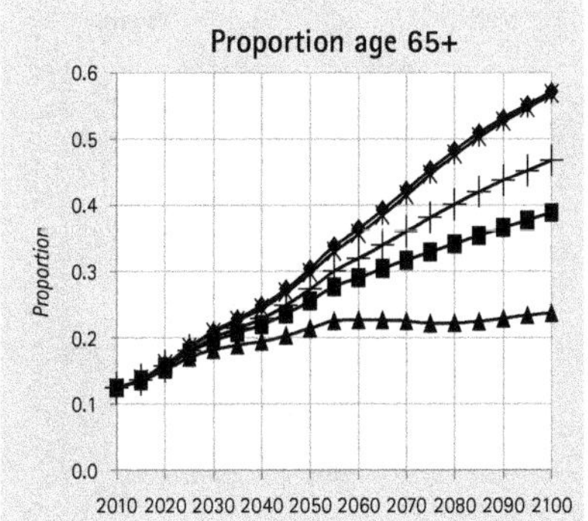

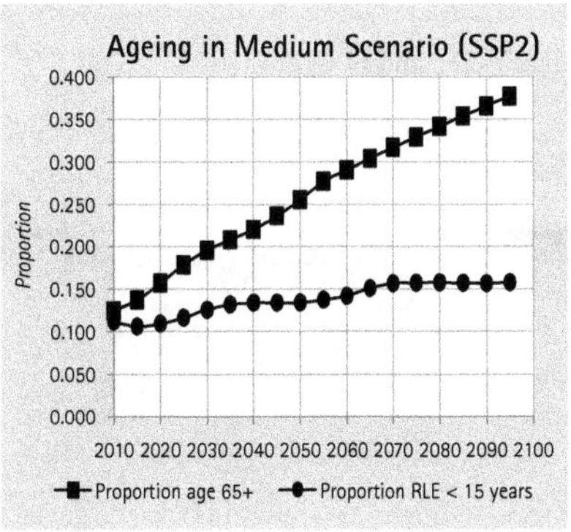

Alternative Scenarios to 2100

Projection Results by Scenario (SSP1–5)

	2010	2020	2030	2040	2050	2075	2100
Population (in millions)							
SSP1 - Rapid development	0.63	0.65	0.66	0.67	0.66	0.61	0.50
SSP2 - Medium	0.63	0.65	0.67	0.69	0.69	0.69	0.63
SSP3 - Stalled development	0.63	0.66	0.68	0.69	0.71	0.75	0.79
SSP4 - Inequality	0.63	0.65	0.66	0.66	0.65	0.58	0.47
SSP5 - Conventional development	0.63	0.65	0.67	0.68	0.68	0.64	0.54
Proportion age 65+							
SSP1 - Rapid development	0.12	0.16	0.21	0.25	0.30	0.45	0.57
SSP2 - Medium	0.12	0.16	0.20	0.22	0.26	0.33	0.39
SSP3 - Stalled development	0.12	0.15	0.18	0.20	0.21	0.22	0.24
SSP4 - Inequality	0.12	0.16	0.20	0.23	0.27	0.38	0.47
SSP5 - Conventional development	0.12	0.16	0.21	0.24	0.30	0.45	0.57
Proportion below age 20							
SSP1 - Rapid development	0.26	0.23	0.19	0.16	0.14	0.11	0.08
SSP2 - Medium	0.26	0.24	0.22	0.20	0.19	0.17	0.16
SSP3 - Stalled development	0.26	0.25	0.25	0.24	0.24	0.24	0.24
SSP4 - Inequality	0.26	0.23	0.20	0.17	0.16	0.13	0.11
SSP5 - Conventional development	0.26	0.23	0.19	0.16	0.14	0.11	0.08
Proportion of Women age 20–39 with at least secondary education							
SSP1 - Rapid development	0.98	0.99	1.00	1.00	1.00	1.00	1.00
SSP2 - Medium	0.98	0.99	1.00	1.00	1.00	1.00	1.00
SSP3 - Stalled development	0.98	0.97	0.97	0.97	0.97	0.97	0.97
SSP4 - Inequality	0.98	0.91	0.87	0.87	0.87	0.87	0.87
SSP5 - Conventional development	0.98	0.99	1.00	1.00	1.00	1.00	1.00
Mean years of schooling, age 25+							
SSP1 - Rapid development	10.80	11.59	12.17	12.63	13.01	13.73	14.21
SSP2 - Medium	10.80	11.47	11.93	12.26	12.52	13.04	13.44
SSP3 - Stalled development	10.80	11.33	11.64	11.79	11.86	11.87	11.87
SSP4 - Inequality	10.80	11.21	11.38	11.49	11.54	11.67	11.95
SSP5 - Conventional development	10.80	11.59	12.18	12.65	13.02	13.75	14.22

Demographic Assumptions Underlying SSPs

	2010–15	2020–25	2030–35	2040–45	2050–55	2075–80	2095–2100
Total fertility rate							
SSP1 - Rapid development	1.57	1.35	1.23	1.19	1.18	1.19	1.21
SSP2 - Medium	1.65	1.62	1.60	1.60	1.60	1.63	1.65
SSP3 - Stalled development	1.76	1.93	2.02	2.06	2.09	2.14	2.19
SSP4 - Inequality	1.58	1.42	1.31	1.26	1.25	1.27	1.28
SSP5 - Conventional development	1.57	1.35	1.23	1.19	1.18	1.19	1.21
Life expectancy at birth for females (in years)							
SSP1 - Rapid development	79.91	83.69	86.88	89.91	92.90	100.39	106.42
SSP2 - Medium	78.61	81.61	84.01	86.21	88.20	93.30	97.30
SSP3 - Stalled development	78.96	80.76	82.01	83.08	84.05	86.34	88.22
SSP4 - Inequality	79.49	82.19	84.39	86.48	88.35	93.07	96.94
SSP5 - Conventional development	79.91	83.69	86.88	89.91	92.90	100.39	106.42
Migration – net flow over five years (in thousands)							
SSP1 - Rapid development	1	4	6	6	6	2	0
SSP2 - Medium	1	4	6	7	7	3	0
SSP3 - Stalled development	1	2	3	4	5	3	0
SSP4 - Inequality	1	4	6	7	7	3	0
SSP5 - Conventional development	1	6	8	9	9	2	0

Ageing Indicators, Medium Scenario (SSP2)

	2010	2020	2030	2040	2050	2075	2095
Median age	35.90	38.59	41.95	44.51	46.56	51.24	54.51
Propspective median age	35.90	35.83	36.94	37.43	37.52	37.44	36.86
Proportion age 65+	0.12	0.16	0.20	0.22	0.26	0.33	0.38
Proportion RLE < 15 years	0.11	0.11	0.13	0.13	0.13	0.16	0.16

Morocco

Detailed Human Capital Projections to 2060

Demographic indicators, Medium Scenario (SSP2)	2010	2020	2030	2040	2050	2060
Population (in millions)	31.95	35.04	37.39	38.72	39.23	38.97
Proportion age 65+	0.05	0.07	0.10	0.14	0.18	0.23
Proportion below age 20	0.38	0.33	0.30	0.27	0.24	0.22
	2005–10	2015–20	2025–30	2035–40	2045–50	2055–60
Total Fertility Rate	2.38	2.11	1.95	1.86	1.75	1.70
Life expectancy at birth (in years)						
Men	68.96	71.39	73.42	75.52	77.52	79.59
Women	73.45	76.00	78.09	80.19	82.19	84.19
Five-year immigration flow (in '000)	2.40	2.36	2.45	2.51	2.51	2.47
Five-year emigration flow (in '000)	675.48	524.64	509.75	492.58	462.21	424.56

Human Capital indicators, Medium Scenario (SSP2)	2010	2020	2030	2040	2050	2060
Population age 25+: highest educational attainment						
E1 - no education	0.52	0.40	0.30	0.22	0.16	0.10
E2 - incomplete primary	0.08	0.09	0.08	0.07	0.06	0.04
E3 - primary	0.16	0.18	0.19	0.19	0.18	0.17
E4 - lower secondary	0.11	0.15	0.18	0.19	0.20	0.20
E5 - upper secondary	0.07	0.10	0.14	0.18	0.23	0.27
E6 - post-secondary	0.06	0.09	0.11	0.14	0.18	0.22
Mean years of schooling (in years)	4.10	5.45	6.64	7.79	8.90	9.91
Gender gap (population age 25+): highest educational attainment (ratio male/female)						
E1 - no education	0.65	0.61	0.57	0.54	0.51	0.50
E2 - incomplete primary	1.50	1.33	1.25	1.18	1.09	0.99
E3 - primary	1.79	1.56	1.41	1.29	1.20	1.11
E4 - lower secondary	1.40	1.25	1.18	1.13	1.09	1.05
E5 - upper secondary	1.50	1.30	1.19	1.13	1.10	1.08
E6 - post-secondary	1.56	1.38	1.28	1.20	1.14	1.11
Mean years of schooling (male minus female)	1.77	1.64	1.47	1.26	1.04	0.81
Women age 20–39: highest educational attainment						
E1 - no education	0.41	0.25	0.14	0.07	0.03	0.01
E2 - incomplete primary	0.12	0.11	0.09	0.06	0.04	0.03
E3 - primary	0.16	0.17	0.18	0.16	0.14	0.10
E4 - lower secondary	0.15	0.20	0.22	0.21	0.20	0.17
E5 - upper secondary	0.10	0.16	0.23	0.30	0.35	0.39
E6 - post-secondary	0.07	0.11	0.15	0.19	0.24	0.29
Mean years of schooling (in years)	5.21	7.11	8.79	10.12	11.13	11.88

Education scenarios

GET: global education trend scenario (medium assumption also used for SSP2)

CER: constant enrolment rates scenario (assumption of no future improvements)

FT: Fast track scenario (assumption of education expansion according to fastest historical experience)

Pyramids by Education, Medium Scenario

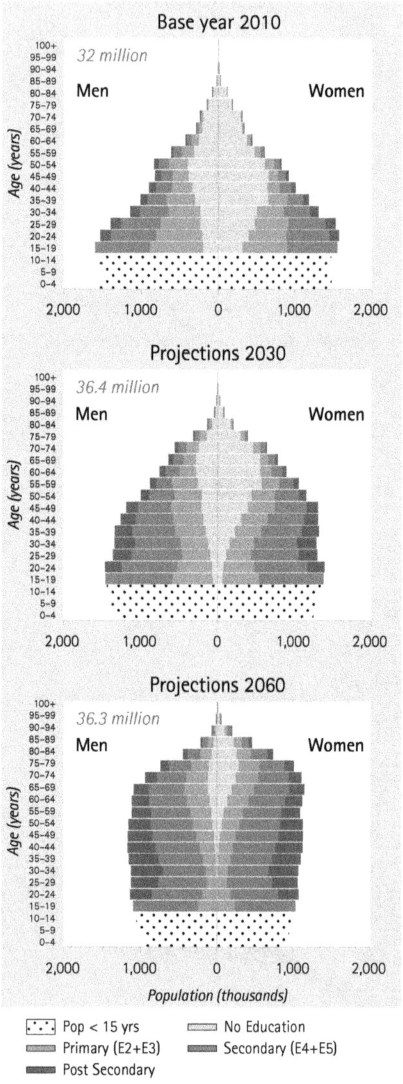

Population Size by Educational Attainment According to Three Education Scenarios: GET, CER, and FT

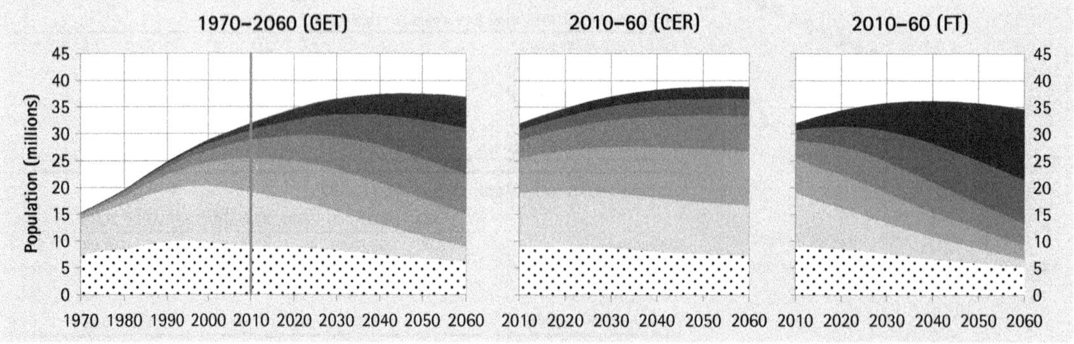

Morocco (Continued)

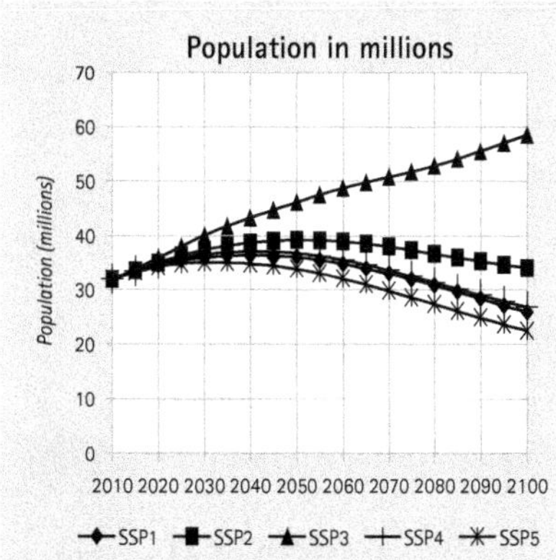

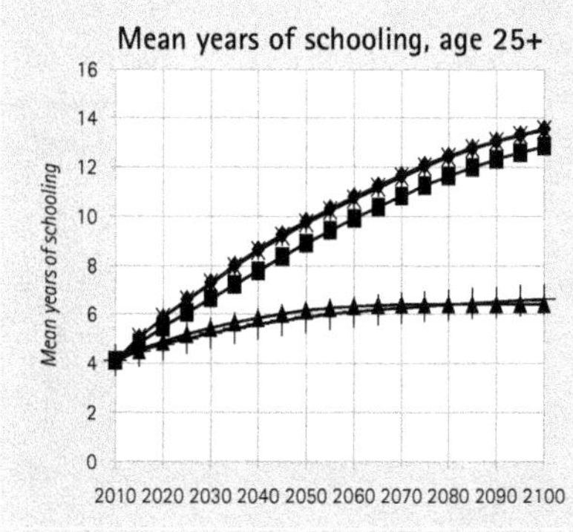

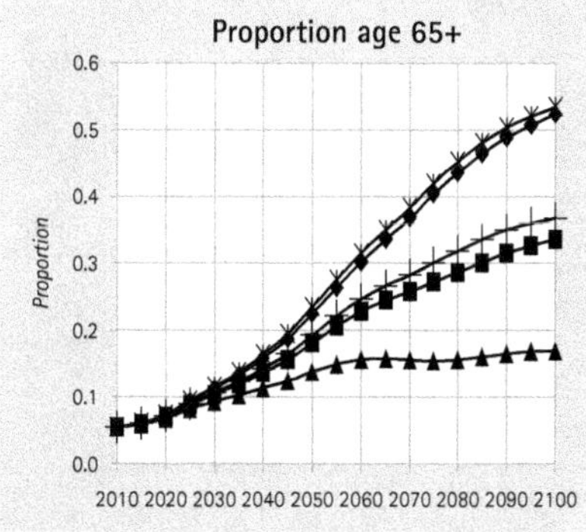

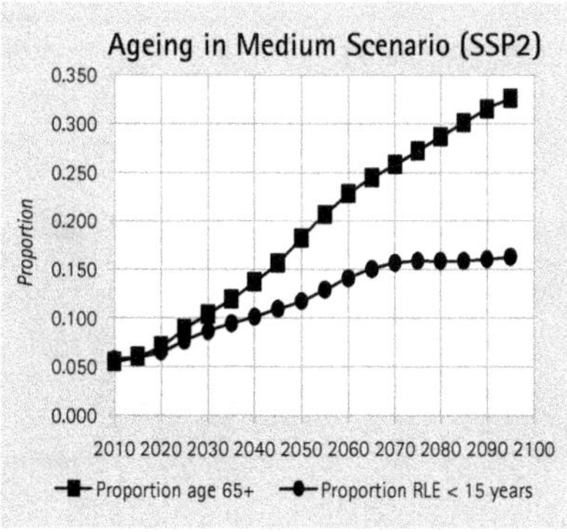

Alternative Scenarios to 2100

Projection Results by Scenario (SSP1-5)

	2010	2020	2030	2040	2050	2075	2100
Population (in millions)							
SSP1 - Rapid development	31.95	34.58	35.99	36.42	36.04	31.96	25.92
SSP2 - Medium	31.95	35.04	37.39	38.72	39.23	37.38	34.08
SSP3 - Stalled development	31.95	35.93	40.09	43.31	46.17	51.77	58.61
SSP4 - Inequality	31.95	34.81	36.56	37.12	36.79	32.53	26.85
SSP5 - Conventional development	31.95	34.28	35.08	34.88	33.88	28.61	22.49
Proportion age 65+							
SSP1 - Rapid development	0.05	0.07	0.11	0.16	0.22	0.40	0.52
SSP2 - Medium	0.05	0.07	0.10	0.14	0.18	0.27	0.34
SSP3 - Stalled development	0.05	0.07	0.09	0.11	0.14	0.16	0.17
SSP4 - Inequality	0.05	0.07	0.11	0.14	0.19	0.30	0.37
SSP5 - Conventional development	0.05	0.07	0.12	0.16	0.23	0.42	0.53
Proportion below age 20							
SSP1 - Rapid development	0.38	0.32	0.27	0.21	0.18	0.12	0.09
SSP2 - Medium	0.38	0.33	0.30	0.27	0.24	0.19	0.17
SSP3 - Stalled development	0.38	0.35	0.34	0.32	0.30	0.29	0.29
SSP4 - Inequality	0.38	0.33	0.29	0.24	0.21	0.17	0.15
SSP5 - Conventional development	0.38	0.32	0.27	0.21	0.18	0.12	0.09
Proportion of Women age 20–39 with at least secondary education							
SSP1 - Rapid development	0.32	0.56	0.72	0.82	0.88	0.96	0.98
SSP2 - Medium	0.32	0.46	0.59	0.71	0.79	0.93	0.98
SSP3 - Stalled development	0.32	0.33	0.35	0.35	0.35	0.35	0.35
SSP4 - Inequality	0.32	0.31	0.31	0.31	0.31	0.31	0.31
SSP5 - Conventional development	0.32	0.56	0.72	0.82	0.88	0.96	0.98
Mean years of schooling, age 25+							
SSP1 - Rapid development	4.10	5.85	7.32	8.66	9.80	12.09	13.55
SSP2 - Medium	4.10	5.45	6.64	7.79	8.90	11.25	12.85
SSP3 - Stalled development	4.10	4.87	5.43	5.85	6.15	6.40	6.42
SSP4 - Inequality	4.10	4.76	5.22	5.59	5.88	6.32	6.61
SSP5 - Conventional development	4.10	5.83	7.27	8.58	9.71	12.01	13.52

Demographic Assumptions Underlying SSPs

	2010–15	2020–25	2030–35	2040–45	2050–55	2075–80	2095–2100
Total fertility rate							
SSP1 - Rapid development	2.08	1.64	1.41	1.30	1.22	1.15	1.17
SSP2 - Medium	2.20	2.03	1.90	1.80	1.72	1.57	1.60
SSP3 - Stalled development	2.37	2.48	2.50	2.46	2.43	2.39	2.49
SSP4 - Inequality	2.15	1.85	1.62	1.50	1.44	1.40	1.45
SSP5 - Conventional development	2.08	1.65	1.41	1.30	1.22	1.15	1.17
Life expectancy at birth for females (in years)							
SSP1 - Rapid development	77.05	79.82	82.70	85.59	88.45	95.84	101.78
SSP2 - Medium	74.81	77.10	79.19	81.19	83.19	88.21	92.20
SSP3 - Stalled development	76.28	77.19	78.14	78.95	79.63	80.99	82.26
SSP4 - Inequality	76.67	78.54	80.38	82.14	83.80	87.68	90.93
SSP5 - Conventional development	77.05	79.82	82.70	85.59	88.45	95.84	101.78
Migration – net flow over five years (in thousands)							
SSP1 - Rapid development	−568	−510	−484	−437	−379	−126	0
SSP2 - Medium	−570	−518	−504	−483	−447	−174	0
SSP3 - Stalled development	−473	−256	−253	−252	−244	−112	0
SSP4 - Inequality	−568	−510	−483	−435	−370	−116	0
SSP5 - Conventional development	−663	−770	−740	−683	−606	−219	0

Ageing Indicators, Medium Scenario (SSP2)

	2010	2020	2030	2040	2050	2075	2095
Median age	26.24	30.10	33.80	37.11	40.21	47.12	50.47
Propspective median age	26.24	28.52	30.64	32.28	33.62	36.20	35.89
Proportion age 65+	0.05	0.07	0.10	0.14	0.18	0.27	0.33
Proportion RLE < 15 years	0.06	0.07	0.09	0.10	0.12	0.16	0.16

Mozambique

Detailed Human Capital Projections to 2060

Demographic indicators, Medium Scenario (SSP2)	2010	2020	2030	2040	2050	2060
Population (in millions)	23.39	28.67	33.89	38.63	42.50	45.58
Proportion age 65+	0.03	0.04	0.04	0.04	0.05	0.07
Proportion below age 20	0.55	0.52	0.46	0.42	0.37	0.33
	2005–10	2015–20	2025–30	2035–40	2045–50	2055–60
Total Fertility Rate	5.11	3.98	3.08	2.60	2.25	2.05
Life expectancy at birth (in years)						
Men	47.55	52.45	54.69	56.35	58.49	61.25
Women	49.89	54.11	57.01	59.63	62.10	64.91
Five-year immigration flow (in '000)	115.31	112.68	116.82	119.29	119.18	117.37
Five-year emigration flow (in '000)	134.61	128.11	159.43	180.97	194.70	202.34

Human Capital indicators, Medium Scenario (SSP2)	2010	2020	2030	2040	2050	2060
Population age 25+: highest educational attainment						
E1 - no education	0.69	0.61	0.52	0.44	0.36	0.28
E2 - incomplete primary	0.14	0.15	0.14	0.13	0.11	0.09
E3 - primary	0.04	0.05	0.07	0.08	0.09	0.10
E4 - lower secondary	0.08	0.12	0.18	0.23	0.27	0.31
E5 - upper secondary	0.04	0.06	0.08	0.11	0.14	0.18
E6 - post-secondary	0.01	0.01	0.01	0.02	0.02	0.03
Mean years of schooling (in years)	1.67	2.67	3.83	4.95	6.04	7.08
Gender gap (population age 25+): highest educational attainment (ratio male/female)						
E1 - no education	0.73	0.72	0.74	0.76	0.80	0.83
E2 - incomplete primary	1.83	1.53	1.33	1.21	1.13	1.07
E3 - primary	2.18	1.66	1.34	1.17	1.09	1.05
E4 - lower secondary	2.14	1.71	1.41	1.23	1.13	1.08
E5 - upper secondary	2.21	1.84	1.54	1.34	1.20	1.11
E6 - post-secondary	2.19	1.58	1.20	1.03	0.97	1.00
Mean years of schooling (male minus female)	1.23	1.38	1.27	1.02	0.75	0.53
Women age 20–39: highest educational attainment						
E1 - no education	0.66	0.57	0.46	0.35	0.24	0.16
E2 - incomplete primary	0.16	0.14	0.12	0.09	0.07	0.05
E3 - primary	0.04	0.06	0.09	0.11	0.12	0.13
E4 - lower secondary	0.10	0.16	0.23	0.29	0.34	0.36
E5 - upper secondary	0.04	0.07	0.10	0.14	0.20	0.27
E6 - post-secondary	0.00	0.01	0.01	0.02	0.03	0.04
Mean years of schooling (in years)	2.06	3.48	4.92	6.26	7.62	8.81

Education scenarios

GET: global education trend scenario (medium assumption also used for SSP2)

CER: constant enrolment rates scenario (assumption of no future improvements)

FT: Fast track scenario (assumption of education expansion according to fastest historical experience)

Pyramids by Education, Medium Scenario

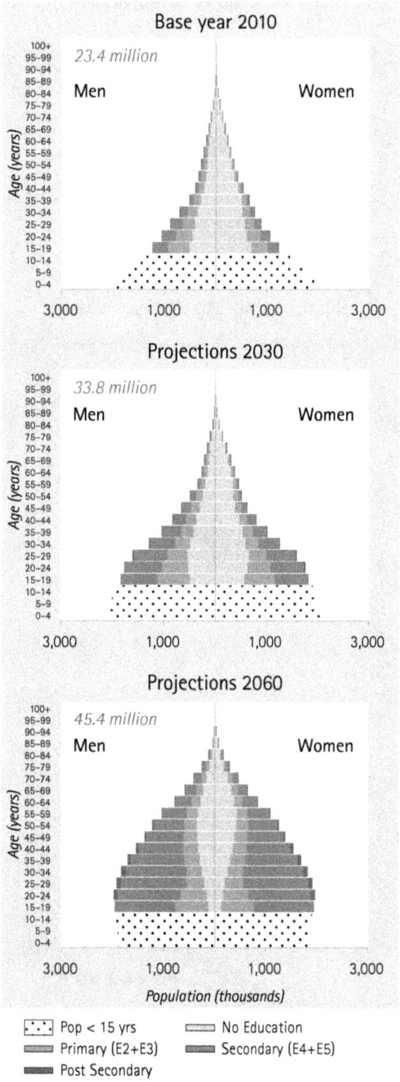

Population Size by Educational Attainment According to Three Education Scenarios: GET, CER, and FT

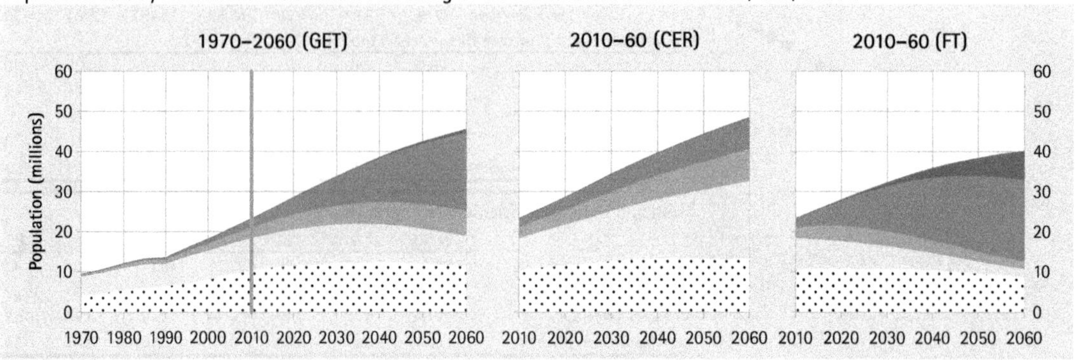

Mozambique (Continued)

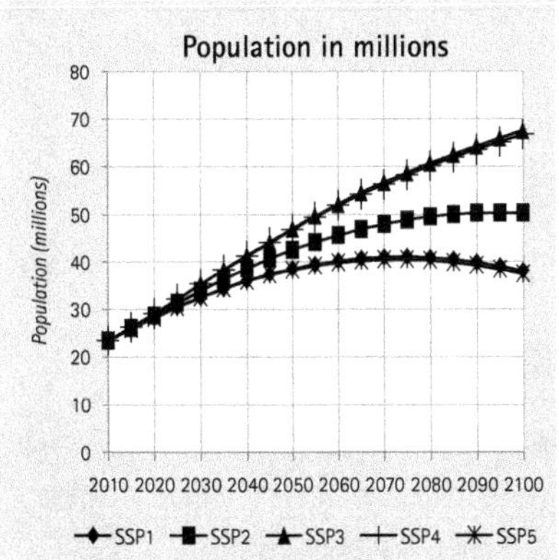

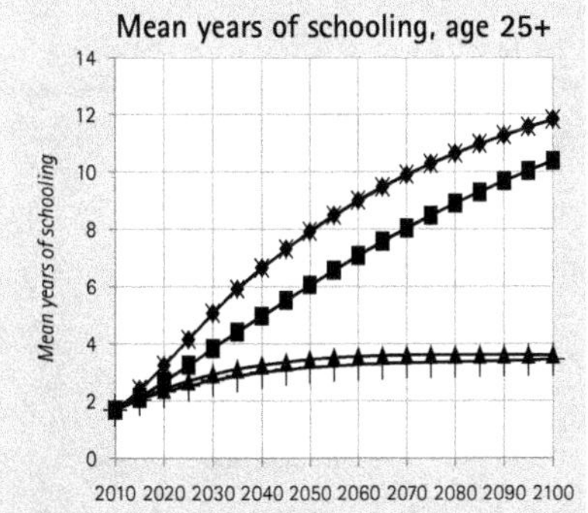

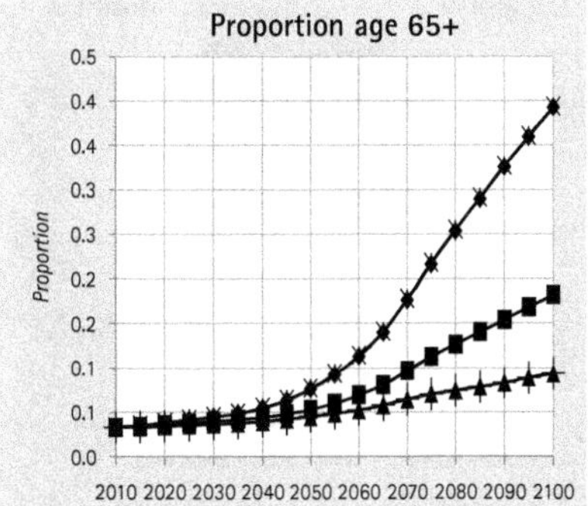

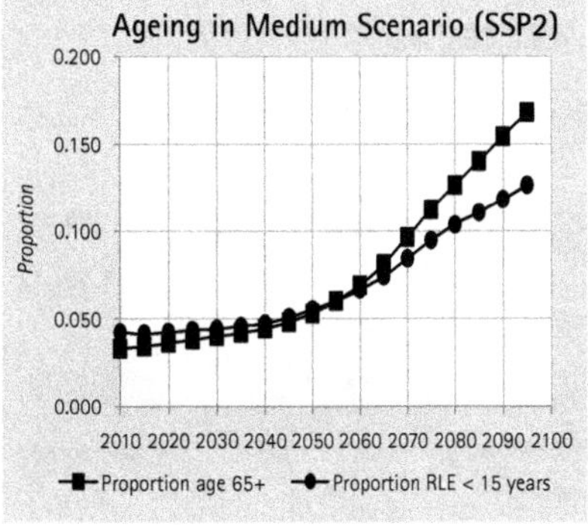

Alternative Scenarios to 2100

Projection Results by Scenario (SSP1–5)

	2010	2020	2030	2040	2050	2075	2100
Population (in millions)							
SSP1 - Rapid development	23.39	28.15	32.49	36.04	38.54	41.05	38.06
SSP2 - Medium	23.39	28.67	33.89	38.63	42.50	48.81	50.20
SSP3 - Stalled development	23.39	29.07	35.30	41.34	46.97	58.73	67.53
SSP4 - Inequality	23.39	29.07	35.30	41.28	46.80	58.23	66.68
SSP5 - Conventional development	23.39	28.14	32.43	35.89	38.27	40.45	37.38
Proportion age 65+							
SSP1 - Rapid development	0.03	0.04	0.04	0.05	0.08	0.22	0.39
SSP2 - Medium	0.03	0.04	0.04	0.04	0.05	0.11	0.18
SSP3 - Stalled development	0.03	0.03	0.04	0.04	0.05	0.07	0.09
SSP4 - Inequality	0.03	0.03	0.04	0.04	0.05	0.07	0.09
SSP5 - Conventional development	0.03	0.04	0.04	0.05	0.08	0.22	0.39
Proportion below age 20							
SSP1 - Rapid development	0.55	0.50	0.41	0.35	0.29	0.18	0.12
SSP2 - Medium	0.55	0.52	0.46	0.42	0.37	0.29	0.23
SSP3 - Stalled development	0.55	0.53	0.50	0.47	0.44	0.38	0.35
SSP4 - Inequality	0.55	0.53	0.50	0.47	0.44	0.38	0.35
SSP5 - Conventional development	0.55	0.50	0.41	0.35	0.29	0.18	0.12
Proportion of Women age 20–39 with at least secondary education							
SSP1 - Rapid development	0.15	0.35	0.53	0.67	0.77	0.89	0.95
SSP2 - Medium	0.15	0.24	0.34	0.45	0.57	0.79	0.91
SSP3 - Stalled development	0.15	0.16	0.16	0.16	0.16	0.16	0.16
SSP4 - Inequality	0.15	0.15	0.14	0.14	0.14	0.14	0.14
SSP5 - Conventional development	0.15	0.35	0.53	0.67	0.77	0.89	0.95
Mean years of schooling, age 25+							
SSP1 - Rapid development	1.67	3.24	5.05	6.65	7.92	10.28	11.81
SSP2 - Medium	1.67	2.67	3.83	4.95	6.04	8.47	10.38
SSP3 - Stalled development	1.67	2.40	2.93	3.25	3.44	3.60	3.59
SSP4 - Inequality	1.67	2.31	2.72	2.99	3.16	3.34	3.44
SSP5 - Conventional development	1.67	3.23	5.04	6.64	7.91	10.27	11.81

Demographic Assumptions Underlying SSPs

	2010–15	2020–25	2030–35	2040–45	2050–55	2075–80	2095–2100
Total fertility rate							
SSP1 - Rapid development	4.19	2.82	2.05	1.68	1.48	1.30	1.22
SSP2 - Medium	4.53	3.49	2.80	2.41	2.13	1.85	1.71
SSP3 - Stalled development	4.78	4.27	3.71	3.27	2.95	2.57	2.46
SSP4 - Inequality	4.78	4.29	3.73	3.27	2.95	2.56	2.43
SSP5 - Conventional development	4.19	2.82	2.05	1.68	1.48	1.30	1.22
Life expectancy at birth for females (in years)							
SSP1 - Rapid development	56.13	63.20	67.76	72.27	76.44	85.81	93.16
SSP2 - Medium	51.80	55.51	58.32	60.79	63.40	70.52	76.02
SSP3 - Stalled development	54.06	53.16	54.33	54.91	56.61	59.76	62.72
SSP4 - Inequality	54.06	53.14	54.30	54.88	56.57	59.72	62.70
SSP5 - Conventional development	56.13	63.20	67.76	72.27	76.44	85.81	93.16
Migration – net flow over five years (in thousands)							
SSP1 - Rapid development	−12	−29	−52	−65	−73	−27	0
SSP2 - Medium	−12	−29	−52	−68	−80	−36	0
SSP3 - Stalled development	−10	−14	−24	−31	−37	−17	0
SSP4 - Inequality	−12	−28	−51	−67	−81	−37	0
SSP5 - Conventional development	−14	−44	−81	−107	−125	−53	0

Ageing Indicators, Medium Scenario (SSP2)

	2010	2020	2030	2040	2050	2075	2095
Median age	17.69	19.23	21.80	24.24	26.87	33.95	39.03
Propspective median age	17.69	17.38	18.53	19.45	20.29	20.96	21.45
Proportion age 65+	0.03	0.04	0.04	0.04	0.05	0.11	0.17
Proportion RLE < 15 years	0.04	0.04	0.04	0.05	0.06	0.09	0.13

Myanmar

Detailed Human Capital Projections to 2060

Demographic indicators, Medium Scenario (SSP2)

	2010	2020	2030	2040	2050	2060
Population (in millions)	47.96	50.48	51.77	51.48	49.84	47.36
Proportion age 65+	0.05	0.07	0.10	0.13	0.17	0.20
Proportion below age 20	0.35	0.30	0.27	0.24	0.22	0.21
	2005–10	2015–20	2025–30	2035–40	2045–50	2055–60
Total Fertility Rate	2.08	1.79	1.72	1.66	1.60	1.61
Life expectancy at birth (in years)						
Men	62.09	63.40	65.17	66.97	68.89	70.86
Women	64.98	67.38	69.50	71.49	73.51	75.50
Five-year immigration flow (in '000)	3.92	3.82	3.95	4.04	4.05	3.99
Five-year emigration flow (in '000)	501.41	366.48	337.32	307.90	279.79	252.65

Human Capital indicators, Medium Scenario (SSP2)

	2010	2020	2030	2040	2050	2060
Population age 25+: highest educational attainment						
E1 - no education	0.10	0.07	0.04	0.02	0.01	0.01
E2 - incomplete primary	0.08	0.06	0.04	0.03	0.02	0.01
E3 - primary	0.41	0.41	0.39	0.37	0.34	0.30
E4 - lower secondary	0.20	0.20	0.21	0.20	0.19	0.17
E5 - upper secondary	0.11	0.13	0.15	0.16	0.18	0.19
E6 - post-secondary	0.10	0.13	0.17	0.21	0.26	0.31
Mean years of schooling (in years)	6.88	7.64	8.29	8.91	9.50	10.08
Gender gap (population age 25+): highest educational attainment (ratio male/female)						
E1 - no education	1.18	1.17	1.15	1.13	1.08	1.01
E2 - incomplete primary	0.58	0.63	0.68	0.74	0.79	0.82
E3 - primary	0.85	0.88	0.91	0.93	0.96	0.97
E4 - lower secondary	1.44	1.36	1.30	1.24	1.18	1.12
E5 - upper secondary	1.40	1.32	1.28	1.24	1.20	1.15
E6 - post-secondary	0.83	0.80	0.79	0.80	0.84	0.90
Mean years of schooling (male minus female)	0.33	0.18	0.04	−0.07	−0.12	−0.08
Women age 20–39: highest educational attainment						
E1 - no education	0.03	0.02	0.01	0.00	0.00	0.00
E2 - incomplete primary	0.05	0.03	0.02	0.01	0.01	0.00
E3 - primary	0.41	0.38	0.34	0.30	0.25	0.21
E4 - lower secondary	0.20	0.19	0.17	0.16	0.14	0.12
E5 - upper secondary	0.13	0.16	0.17	0.19	0.21	0.24
E6 - post-secondary	0.17	0.24	0.29	0.35	0.39	0.43
Mean years of schooling (in years)	8.20	9.06	9.82	10.41	10.89	11.29

Education scenarios

GET: global education trend scenario (medium assumption also used for SSP2)

CER: constant enrolment rates scenario (assumption of no future improvements)

FT: Fast track scenario (assumption of education expansion according to fastest historical experience)

Pyramids by Education, Medium Scenario

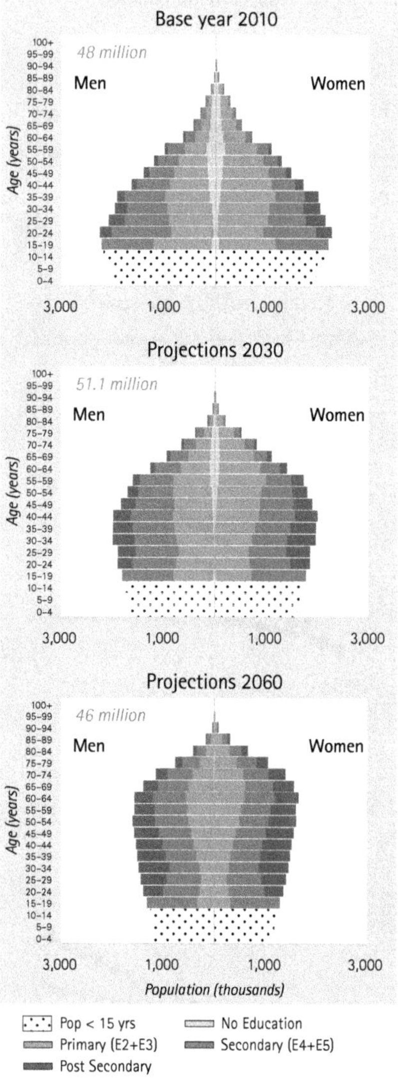

Population Size by Educational Attainment According to Three Education Scenarios: GET, CER, and FT

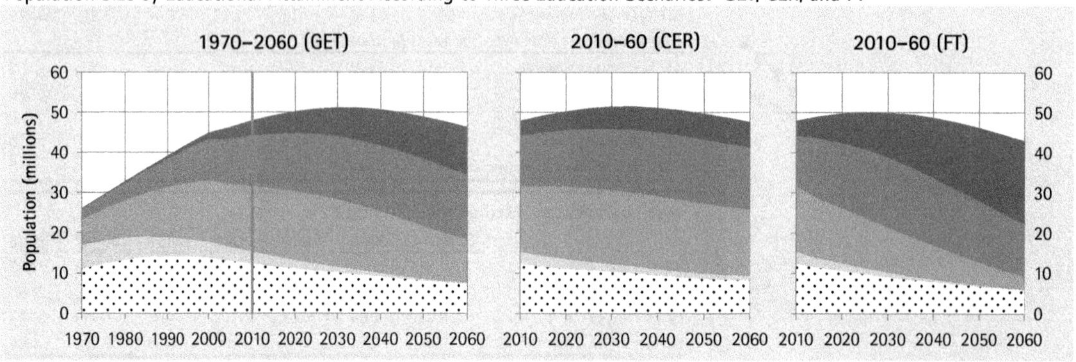

Myanmar (Continued)

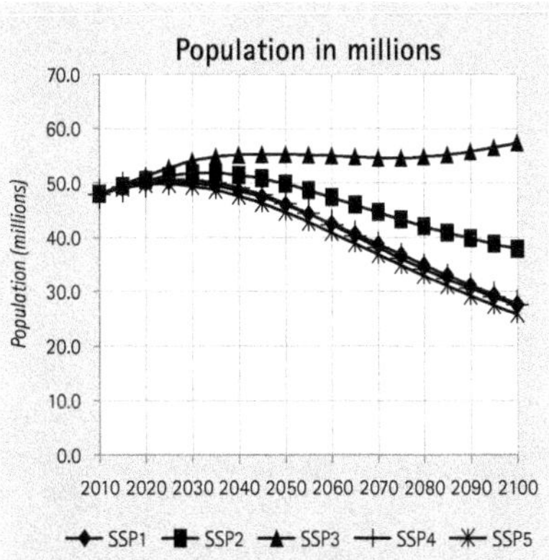

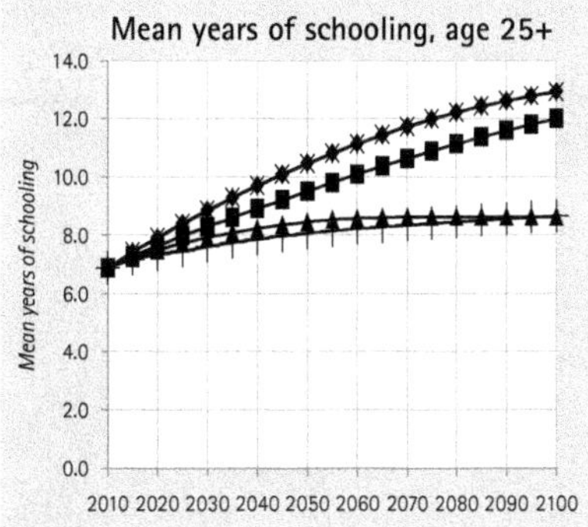

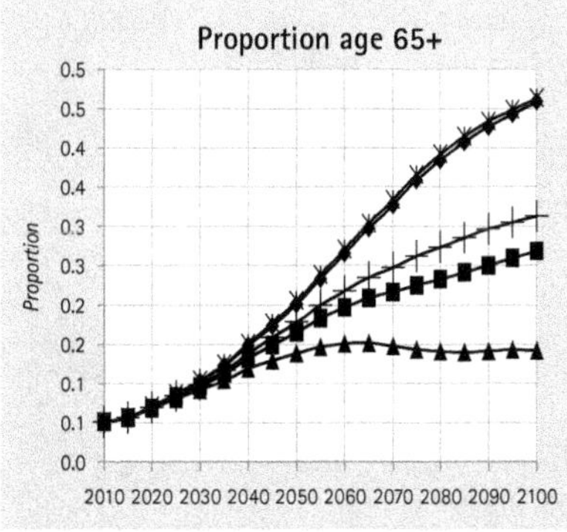

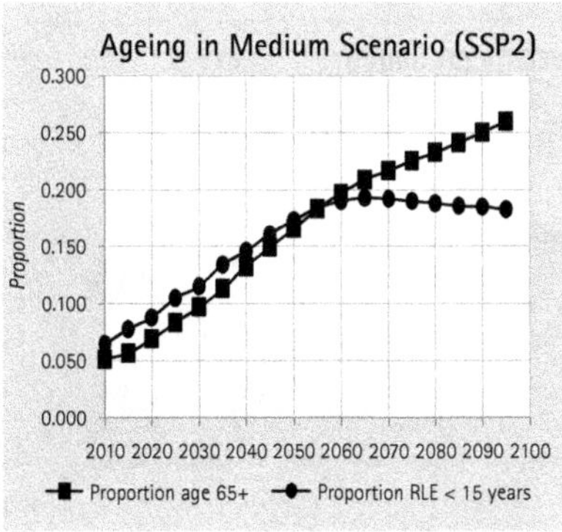

Alternative Scenarios to 2100

Projection Results by Scenario (SSP1–5)

	2010	2020	2030	2040	2050	2075	2100
Population (in millions)							
SSP1 - Rapid development	47.96	49.90	50.00	48.61	46.00	36.90	27.72
SSP2 - Medium	47.96	50.48	51.77	51.48	49.84	43.32	37.93
SSP3 - Stalled development	47.96	51.28	54.06	55.21	55.27	54.60	57.36
SSP4 - Inequality	47.96	50.09	50.51	49.11	46.23	36.14	27.51
SSP5 - Conventional development	47.96	49.70	49.40	47.62	44.64	34.93	25.84
Proportion age 65+							
SSP1 - Rapid development	0.05	0.07	0.10	0.15	0.20	0.36	0.46
SSP2 - Medium	0.05	0.07	0.10	0.13	0.17	0.23	0.27
SSP3 - Stalled development	0.05	0.07	0.09	0.12	0.14	0.14	0.14
SSP4 - Inequality	0.05	0.07	0.10	0.14	0.18	0.26	0.31
SSP5 - Conventional development	0.05	0.07	0.10	0.15	0.21	0.37	0.46
Proportion below age 20							
SSP1 - Rapid development	0.35	0.29	0.23	0.19	0.17	0.13	0.11
SSP2 - Medium	0.35	0.30	0.27	0.24	0.22	0.21	0.19
SSP3 - Stalled development	0.35	0.31	0.29	0.28	0.27	0.29	0.30
SSP4 - Inequality	0.35	0.29	0.25	0.22	0.19	0.17	0.16
SSP5 - Conventional development	0.35	0.29	0.23	0.19	0.17	0.13	0.11
Proportion of Women age 20–39 with at least secondary education							
SSP1 - Rapid development	0.51	0.69	0.78	0.84	0.87	0.92	0.96
SSP2 - Medium	0.51	0.58	0.64	0.69	0.74	0.85	0.93
SSP3 - Stalled development	0.51	0.52	0.52	0.52	0.52	0.52	0.52
SSP4 - Inequality	0.51	0.49	0.47	0.47	0.47	0.47	0.47
SSP5 - Conventional development	0.51	0.69	0.78	0.84	0.87	0.92	0.96
Mean years of schooling, age 25+							
SSP1 - Rapid development	6.88	7.92	8.85	9.70	10.46	11.98	12.92
SSP2 - Medium	6.88	7.64	8.29	8.91	9.50	10.88	11.99
SSP3 - Stalled development	6.88	7.49	7.92	8.23	8.46	8.63	8.63
SSP4 - Inequality	6.88	7.33	7.61	7.87	8.07	8.40	8.66
SSP5 - Conventional development	6.88	7.91	8.84	9.69	10.44	11.97	12.92

Demographic Assumptions Underlying SSPs

	2010–15	2020–25	2030–35	2040–45	2050–55	2075–80	2095–2100
Total fertility rate							
SSP1 - Rapid development	1.76	1.40	1.23	1.16	1.13	1.17	1.20
SSP2 - Medium	1.89	1.74	1.69	1.63	1.60	1.63	1.65
SSP3 - Stalled development	2.00	2.09	2.15	2.15	2.17	2.31	2.43
SSP4 - Inequality	1.81	1.57	1.40	1.31	1.29	1.36	1.42
SSP5 - Conventional development	1.76	1.40	1.23	1.16	1.13	1.17	1.20
Life expectancy at birth for females (in years)							
SSP1 - Rapid development	68.98	71.67	74.50	77.28	80.11	87.34	93.12
SSP2 - Medium	66.32	68.38	70.48	72.49	74.50	79.49	83.49
SSP3 - Stalled development	68.92	69.06	70.41	70.78	71.82	73.52	74.94
SSP4 - Inequality	69.16	70.83	72.49	74.04	75.55	79.69	83.23
SSP5 - Conventional development	68.98	71.67	74.50	77.28	80.11	87.34	93.12
Migration – net flow over five years (in thousands)							
SSP1 - Rapid development	−399	−342	−306	−263	−223	−72	0
SSP2 - Medium	−397	−346	−317	−290	−263	−100	0
SSP3 - Stalled development	−332	−170	−155	−144	−133	−56	0
SSP4 - Inequality	−399	−342	−303	−258	−213	−62	0
SSP5 - Conventional development	−466	−520	−476	−422	−373	−135	0

Ageing Indicators, Medium Scenario (SSP2)

	2010	2020	2030	2040	2050	2075	2095
Median age	28.19	32.21	35.94	39.07	41.36	44.74	46.45
Propspective median age	28.19	31.49	34.42	36.64	38.09	37.81	35.88
Proportion age 65+	0.05	0.07	0.10	0.13	0.17	0.23	0.26
Proportion RLE < 15 years	0.06	0.09	0.11	0.15	0.17	0.19	0.18

Namibia

Detailed Human Capital Projections to 2060

Demographic indicators, Medium Scenario (SSP2)	2010	2020	2030	2040	2050	2060
Population (in millions)	2.28	2.65	2.96	3.20	3.37	3.48
Proportion age 65+	0.04	0.04	0.06	0.07	0.09	0.12
Proportion below age 20	0.48	0.42	0.37	0.34	0.30	0.27
	2005–10	2015–20	2025–30	2035–40	2045–50	2055–60
Total Fertility Rate	3.40	2.61	2.23	2.04	1.91	1.80
Life expectancy at birth (in years)						
Men	60.34	62.06	63.24	64.14	65.41	67.74
Women	61.63	62.60	64.70	66.50	68.18	70.48
Five-year immigration flow (in '000)	19.62	19.20	19.93	20.37	20.36	20.07
Five-year emigration flow (in '000)	21.09	18.70	20.40	20.94	20.92	20.48

Human Capital indicators, Medium Scenario (SSP2)	2010	2020	2030	2040	2050	2060
Population age 25+: highest educational attainment						
E1 - no education	0.14	0.09	0.05	0.03	0.02	0.01
E2 - incomplete primary	0.23	0.17	0.11	0.07	0.05	0.03
E3 - primary	0.13	0.12	0.11	0.10	0.09	0.07
E4 - lower secondary	0.25	0.29	0.30	0.29	0.26	0.23
E5 - upper secondary	0.18	0.24	0.31	0.38	0.44	0.49
E6 - post-secondary	0.08	0.09	0.11	0.13	0.15	0.17
Mean years of schooling (in years)	7.87	9.01	9.95	10.68	11.26	11.72
Gender gap (population age 25+): highest educational attainment (ratio male/female)						
E1 - no education	1.07	1.08	1.09	1.12	1.12	1.10
E2 - incomplete primary	0.98	1.02	1.03	1.05	1.06	1.05
E3 - primary	0.83	0.85	0.90	0.94	0.97	0.97
E4 - lower secondary	0.94	0.94	0.95	0.95	0.95	0.95
E5 - upper secondary	1.16	1.12	1.10	1.08	1.07	1.06
E6 - post-secondary	1.12	0.99	0.91	0.87	0.88	0.92
Mean years of schooling (male minus female)	0.08	0.01	-0.04	-0.08	-0.08	-0.04
Women age 20–39: highest educational attainment						
E1 - no education	0.05	0.03	0.01	0.01	0.00	0.00
E2 - incomplete primary	0.12	0.07	0.04	0.02	0.02	0.01
E3 - primary	0.12	0.11	0.10	0.08	0.06	0.04
E4 - lower secondary	0.40	0.40	0.36	0.31	0.27	0.23
E5 - upper secondary	0.24	0.31	0.38	0.45	0.50	0.55
E6 - post-secondary	0.07	0.09	0.11	0.13	0.15	0.17
Mean years of schooling (in years)	9.53	10.36	11.00	11.46	11.81	12.09

Education scenarios

GET: global education trend scenario (medium assumption also used for SSP2)

CER: constant enrolment rates scenario (assumption of no future improvements)

FT: Fast track scenario (assumption of education expansion according to fastest historical experience)

Pyramids by Education, Medium Scenario

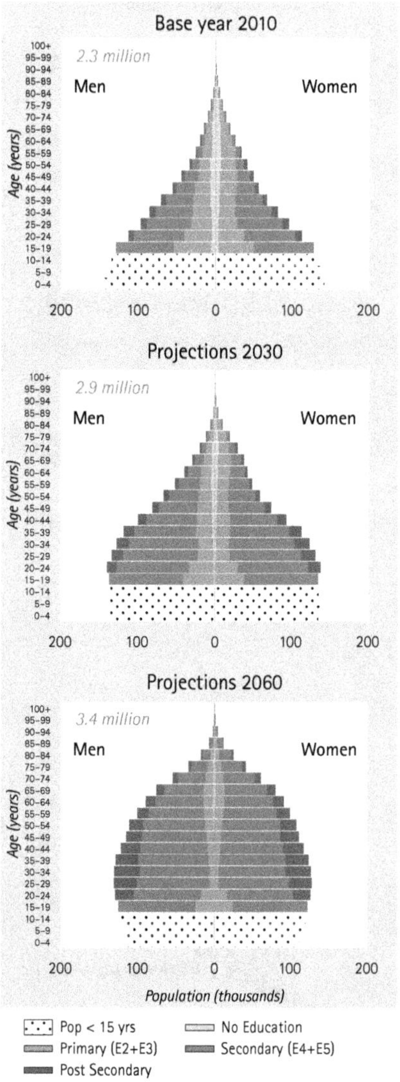

Population Size by Educational Attainment According to Three Education Scenarios: GET, CER, and FT

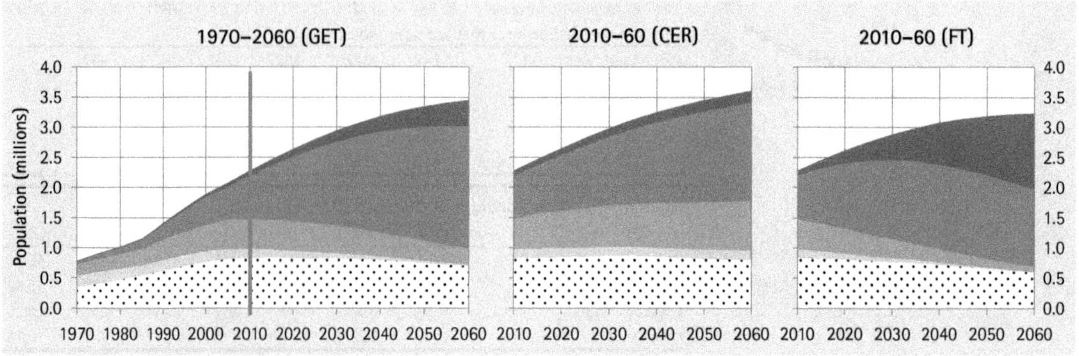

Namibia (Continued)

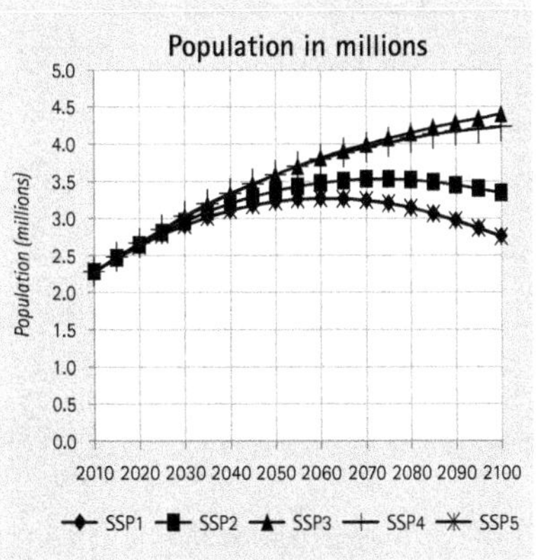

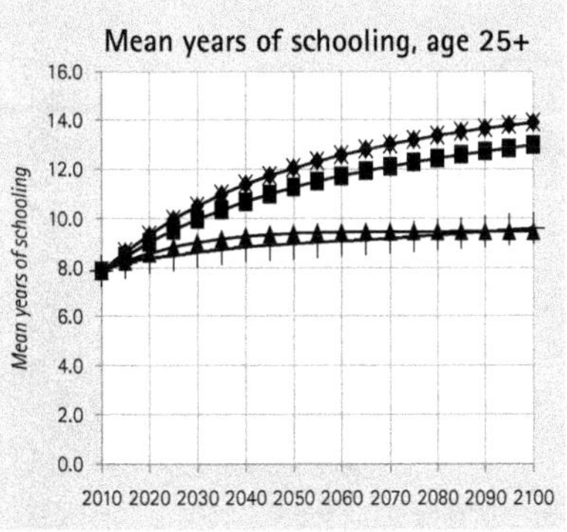

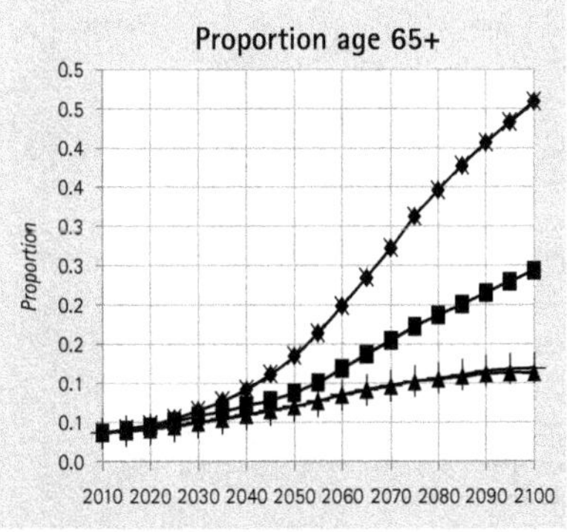

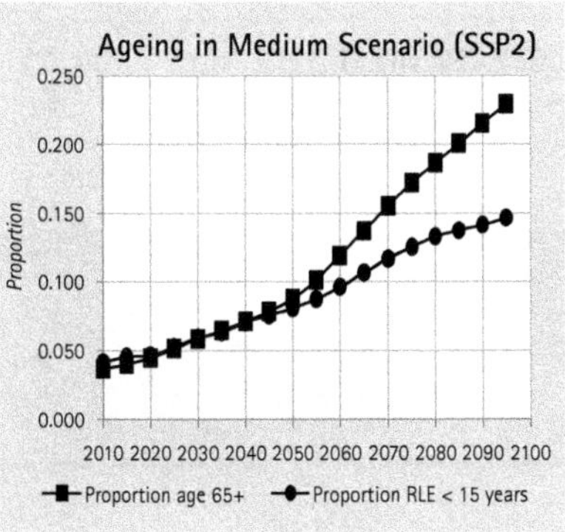

Alternative Scenarios to 2100

Projection Results by Scenario (SSP1-5)

	2010	2020	2030	2040	2050	2075	2100
Population (in millions)							
SSP1 - Rapid development	2.28	2.63	2.91	3.11	3.23	3.20	2.76
SSP2 - Medium	2.28	2.65	2.96	3.20	3.37	3.53	3.34
SSP3 - Stalled development	2.28	2.66	3.02	3.33	3.58	4.08	4.40
SSP4 - Inequality	2.28	2.67	3.04	3.34	3.59	4.02	4.23
SSP5 - Conventional development	2.28	2.63	2.90	3.11	3.22	3.20	2.75
Proportion age 65+							
SSP1 - Rapid development	0.04	0.05	0.07	0.09	0.13	0.31	0.46
SSP2 - Medium	0.04	0.04	0.06	0.07	0.09	0.17	0.24
SSP3 - Stalled development	0.04	0.04	0.05	0.06	0.07	0.10	0.11
SSP4 - Inequality	0.04	0.04	0.05	0.06	0.07	0.10	0.12
SSP5 - Conventional development	0.04	0.05	0.07	0.09	0.14	0.31	0.46
Proportion below age 20							
SSP1 - Rapid development	0.48	0.40	0.33	0.27	0.23	0.15	0.11
SSP2 - Medium	0.48	0.42	0.37	0.34	0.30	0.24	0.20
SSP3 - Stalled development	0.48	0.43	0.41	0.39	0.37	0.33	0.32
SSP4 - Inequality	0.48	0.43	0.41	0.39	0.36	0.33	0.31
SSP5 - Conventional development	0.48	0.40	0.33	0.27	0.23	0.15	0.11
Proportion of Women age 20–39 with at least secondary education							
SSP1 - Rapid development	0.71	0.85	0.91	0.94	0.96	0.99	1.00
SSP2 - Medium	0.71	0.79	0.85	0.89	0.92	0.97	0.99
SSP3 - Stalled development	0.71	0.70	0.70	0.70	0.70	0.70	0.70
SSP4 - Inequality	0.71	0.66	0.63	0.63	0.63	0.63	0.63
SSP5 - Conventional development	0.71	0.85	0.91	0.94	0.96	0.99	1.00
Mean years of schooling, age 25+							
SSP1 - Rapid development	7.87	9.32	10.49	11.37	12.04	13.19	13.89
SSP2 - Medium	7.87	9.01	9.95	10.68	11.26	12.27	12.98
SSP3 - Stalled development	7.87	8.57	9.02	9.27	9.39	9.46	9.47
SSP4 - Inequality	7.87	8.38	8.63	8.83	8.97	9.25	9.58
SSP5 - Conventional development	7.87	9.32	10.49	11.37	12.04	13.19	13.89

Demographic Assumptions Underlying SSPs

	2010–15	2020–25	2030–35	2040–45	2050–55	2075–80	2095–2100
Total fertility rate							
SSP1 - Rapid development	2.70	1.98	1.60	1.43	1.32	1.21	1.16
SSP2 - Medium	2.91	2.40	2.13	1.96	1.84	1.68	1.60
SSP3 - Stalled development	3.06	2.92	2.77	2.64	2.53	2.37	2.30
SSP4 - Inequality	3.08	2.97	2.78	2.60	2.46	2.26	2.18
SSP5 - Conventional development	2.70	1.98	1.60	1.43	1.32	1.21	1.16
Life expectancy at birth for females (in years)							
SSP1 - Rapid development	66.05	70.51	74.42	78.04	81.60	89.66	95.94
SSP2 - Medium	63.00	63.62	65.60	67.30	69.28	75.01	79.49
SSP3 - Stalled development	62.84	59.88	60.69	61.17	62.04	64.22	66.53
SSP4 - Inequality	62.84	59.83	60.59	61.07	61.96	64.21	66.58
SSP5 - Conventional development	66.05	70.51	74.42	78.04	81.60	89.66	95.94
Migration – net flow over five years (in thousands)							
SSP1 - Rapid development	0	0	−1	−1	−1	0	0
SSP2 - Medium	0	0	−1	−1	−1	0	0
SSP3 - Stalled development	0	0	0	0	0	1	0
SSP4 - Inequality	0	0	0	0	0	1	0
SSP5 - Conventional development	0	0	−1	−1	−1	0	0

Ageing Indicators, Medium Scenario (SSP2)

	2010	2020	2030	2040	2050	2075	2095
Median age	21.11	24.06	26.90	29.77	32.37	39.14	43.67
Propspective median age	21.11	23.99	25.48	27.05	27.70	28.29	28.58
Proportion age 65+	0.04	0.04	0.06	0.07	0.09	0.17	0.23
Proportion RLE < 15 years	0.04	0.05	0.06	0.07	0.08	0.13	0.15

Nepal

Detailed Human Capital Projections to 2060

Demographic indicators, Medium Scenario (SSP2)	2010	2020	2030	2040	2050	2060
Population (in millions)	29.96	35.91	41.71	46.91	51.38	54.71
Proportion age 65+	0.04	0.05	0.06	0.09	0.12	0.17
Proportion below age 20	0.47	0.41	0.36	0.31	0.28	0.25
	2005–10	2015–20	2025–30	2035–40	2045–50	2055–60
Total Fertility Rate	2.95	2.52	2.19	2.02	1.87	1.80
Life expectancy at birth (in years)						
Men	66.72	71.63	74.57	77.39	80.00	81.68
Women	68.04	74.00	77.59	80.79	83.59	85.41
Five-year immigration flow (in '000)	99.09	96.34	99.66	101.84	101.88	100.44
Five-year emigration flow (in '000)	196.74	179.62	198.75	209.79	214.02	210.84

Human Capital indicators, Medium Scenario (SSP2)	2010	2020	2030	2040	2050	2060
Population age 25+: highest educational attainment						
E1 - no education	0.54	0.41	0.30	0.22	0.15	0.10
E2 - incomplete primary	0.06	0.05	0.04	0.03	0.02	0.02
E3 - primary	0.10	0.11	0.12	0.12	0.11	0.10
E4 - lower secondary	0.07	0.09	0.10	0.10	0.09	0.08
E5 - upper secondary	0.19	0.28	0.36	0.44	0.50	0.55
E6 - post-secondary	0.04	0.06	0.08	0.10	0.12	0.15
Mean years of schooling (in years)	3.84	5.50	6.99	8.19	9.26	10.17
Gender gap (population age 25+): highest educational attainment (ratio male/female)						
E1 - no education	0.59	0.55	0.53	0.52	0.52	0.53
E2 - incomplete primary	1.52	1.51	1.34	1.22	1.10	1.00
E3 - primary	1.49	1.13	0.98	0.91	0.87	0.85
E4 - lower secondary	1.64	1.24	1.08	1.00	0.95	0.90
E5 - upper secondary	1.94	1.54	1.32	1.21	1.13	1.09
E6 - post-secondary	4.03	2.92	2.23	1.82	1.52	1.33
Mean years of schooling (male minus female)	2.58	2.47	2.14	1.78	1.40	1.05
Women age 20–39: highest educational attainment						
E1 - no education	0.42	0.26	0.15	0.07	0.03	0.01
E2 - incomplete primary	0.06	0.03	0.02	0.01	0.00	0.00
E3 - primary	0.14	0.16	0.14	0.12	0.08	0.05
E4 - lower secondary	0.10	0.12	0.11	0.10	0.08	0.06
E5 - upper secondary	0.26	0.39	0.50	0.60	0.66	0.69
E6 - post-secondary	0.03	0.05	0.07	0.10	0.14	0.18
Mean years of schooling (in years)	5.05	7.31	8.94	10.29	11.29	11.97

Education scenarios

GET: global education trend scenario (medium assumption also used for SSP2)

CER: constant enrolment rates scenario (assumption of no future improvements)

FT: Fast track scenario (assumption of education expansion according to fastest historical experience)

Pyramids by Education, Medium Scenario

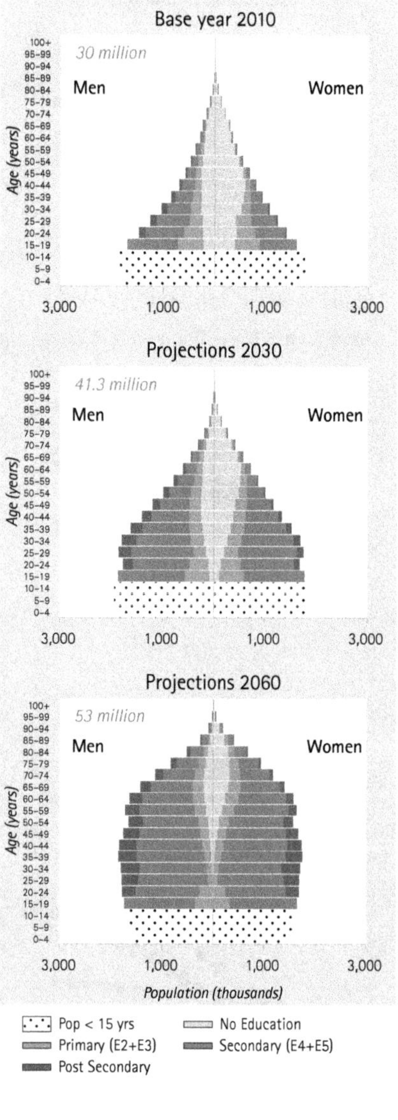

Population Size by Educational Attainment According to Three Education Scenarios: GET, CER, and FT

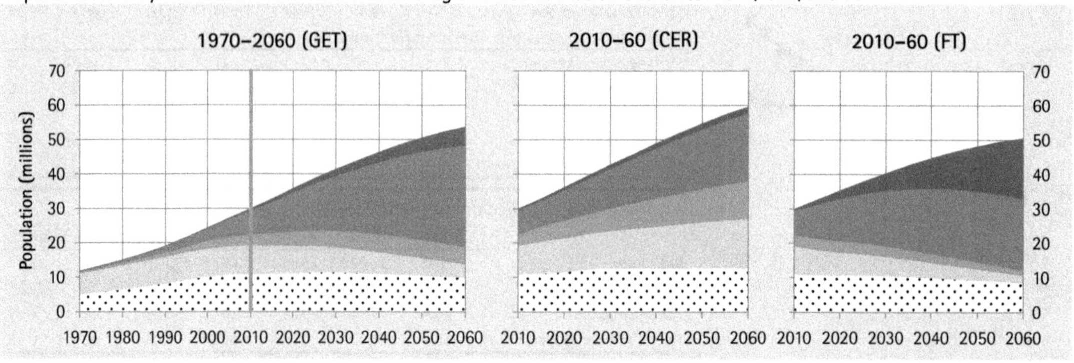

Nepal (Continued)

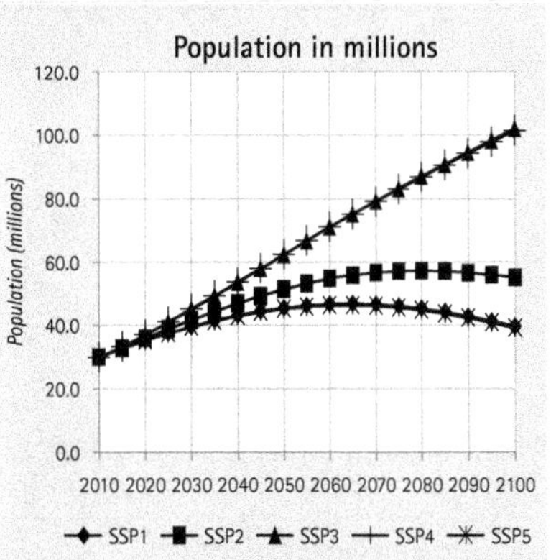

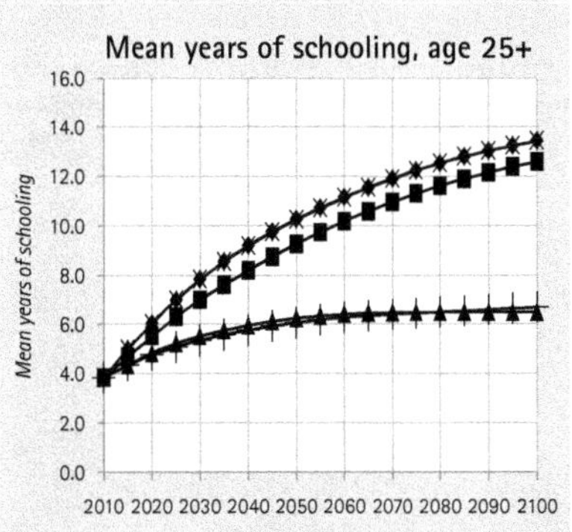

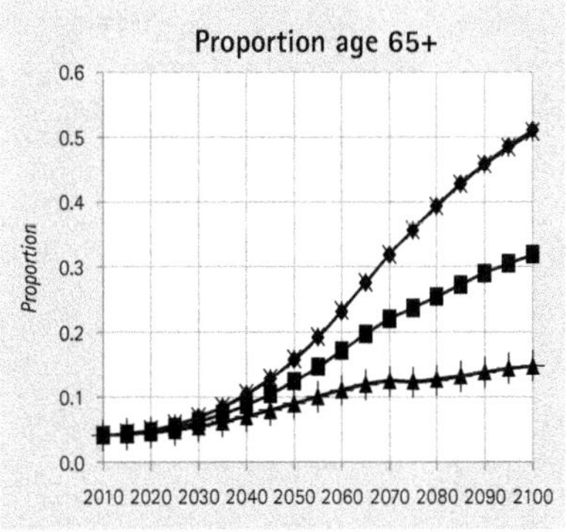

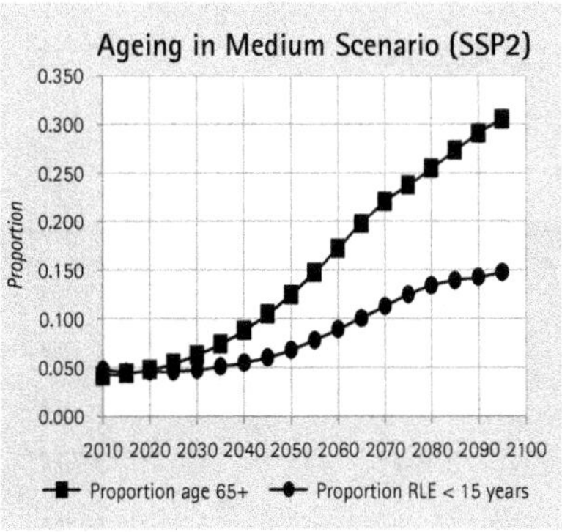

Alternative Scenarios to 2100

Projection Results by Scenario (SSP1–5)

	2010	2020	2030	2040	2050	2075	2100
Population (in millions)							
SSP1 - Rapid development	29.96	35.19	39.62	43.10	45.49	46.08	39.61
SSP2 - Medium	29.96	35.91	41.71	46.91	51.38	57.09	55.13
SSP3 - Stalled development	29.96	37.04	45.16	53.52	62.48	83.25	102.10
SSP4 - Inequality	29.96	37.06	45.21	53.58	62.50	83.05	101.49
SSP5 - Conventional development	29.96	35.15	39.49	42.86	45.13	45.49	39.12
Proportion age 65+							
SSP1 - Rapid development	0.04	0.05	0.07	0.10	0.16	0.36	0.51
SSP2 - Medium	0.04	0.05	0.06	0.09	0.12	0.24	0.32
SSP3 - Stalled development	0.04	0.05	0.06	0.07	0.09	0.13	0.15
SSP4 - Inequality	0.04	0.05	0.06	0.07	0.09	0.12	0.15
SSP5 - Conventional development	0.04	0.05	0.07	0.10	0.16	0.36	0.51
Proportion below age 20							
SSP1 - Rapid development	0.47	0.40	0.32	0.26	0.21	0.13	0.09
SSP2 - Medium	0.47	0.41	0.36	0.31	0.28	0.21	0.17
SSP3 - Stalled development	0.47	0.43	0.41	0.39	0.36	0.32	0.30
SSP4 - Inequality	0.47	0.43	0.42	0.39	0.36	0.32	0.30
SSP5 - Conventional development	0.47	0.40	0.32	0.26	0.21	0.13	0.09
Proportion of Women age 20–39 with at least secondary education							
SSP1 - Rapid development	0.39	0.65	0.79	0.88	0.93	0.98	1.00
SSP2 - Medium	0.39	0.56	0.69	0.80	0.88	0.97	1.00
SSP3 - Stalled development	0.39	0.37	0.37	0.37	0.37	0.37	0.37
SSP4 - Inequality	0.39	0.35	0.33	0.33	0.33	0.33	0.33
SSP5 - Conventional development	0.39	0.65	0.79	0.88	0.93	0.98	1.00
Mean years of schooling, age 25+							
SSP1 - Rapid development	3.84	6.01	7.84	9.19	10.26	12.24	13.43
SSP2 - Medium	3.84	5.50	6.99	8.19	9.26	11.30	12.59
SSP3 - Stalled development	3.84	4.82	5.51	5.94	6.23	6.47	6.49
SSP4 - Inequality	3.84	4.76	5.34	5.75	6.05	6.44	6.68
SSP5 - Conventional development	3.84	6.00	7.82	9.17	10.24	12.23	13.43

Demographic Assumptions Underlying SSPs

	2010–15	2020–25	2030–35	2040–45	2050–55	2075–80	2095–2100
Total fertility rate							
SSP1 - Rapid development	2.54	1.92	1.60	1.43	1.34	1.21	1.17
SSP2 - Medium	2.71	2.35	2.10	1.94	1.84	1.65	1.60
SSP3 - Stalled development	3.00	3.03	2.91	2.76	2.64	2.44	2.39
SSP4 - Inequality	3.01	3.06	2.93	2.75	2.61	2.40	2.35
SSP5 - Conventional development	2.54	1.92	1.60	1.43	1.34	1.21	1.17
Life expectancy at birth for females (in years)							
SSP1 - Rapid development	73.73	78.31	82.59	86.52	89.63	96.08	101.21
SSP2 - Medium	71.39	75.80	79.29	82.29	84.61	88.60	91.69
SSP3 - Stalled development	73.25	75.58	77.84	79.70	80.63	81.06	81.59
SSP4 - Inequality	73.25	75.57	77.82	79.68	80.59	81.00	81.56
SSP5 - Conventional development	73.73	78.31	82.59	86.52	89.63	96.08	101.21
Migration – net flow over five years (in thousands)							
SSP1 - Rapid development	−83	−93	−102	−104	−99	−36	0
SSP2 - Medium	−80	−91	−101	−110	−110	−47	0
SSP3 - Stalled development	−69	−46	−50	−55	−56	−24	0
SSP4 - Inequality	−83	−94	−107	−122	−130	−62	0
SSP5 - Conventional development	−97	−143	−162	−173	−173	−72	0

Ageing indicators, Medium Scenario (SSP2)

	2010	2020	2030	2040	2050	2075	2095
Median age	21.36	24.55	28.27	31.89	35.48	44.10	49.20
Propspective median age	21.36	21.63	22.57	23.66	25.32	30.67	33.02
Proportion age 65+	0.04	0.05	0.06	0.09	0.12	0.24	0.31
Proportion RLE < 15 years	0.05	0.05	0.05	0.05	0.07	0.12	0.15

Netherlands Antilles

Detailed Human Capital Projections to 2060

Demographic Indicators, Medium Scenario (SSP2)	2010	2020	2030	2040	2050	2060
Population (in millions)	0.20	0.23	0.26	0.28	0.31	0.33
Proportion age 65+	0.10	0.14	0.19	0.23	0.24	0.24
Proportion below age 20	0.26	0.24	0.22	0.22	0.21	0.20
	2005–10	2015–20	2025–30	2035–40	2045–50	2055–60
Total Fertility Rate	1.98	1.77	1.72	1.72	1.71	1.71
Life expectancy at birth (in years)						
Men	72.65	76.24	79.00	81.48	83.85	86.06
Women	79.36	82.29	84.61	86.71	88.71	90.79
Five-year immigration flow (in '000)	11.43	11.22	11.66	11.93	11.95	11.78
Five-year emigration flow (in '000)	3.04	2.36	2.60	2.67	2.82	2.98

Human Capital indicators, Medium Scenario (SSP2)	2010	2020	2030	2040	2050	2060
Population age 25+: highest educational attainment						
E1 - no education	0.01	0.00	0.00	0.00	0.00	0.00
E2 - incomplete primary	0.08	0.06	0.04	0.03	0.02	0.01
E3 - primary	0.29	0.28	0.27	0.26	0.24	0.22
E4 - lower secondary	0.36	0.35	0.34	0.32	0.29	0.25
E5 - upper secondary	0.17	0.20	0.24	0.28	0.33	0.37
E6 - post-secondary	0.10	0.10	0.11	0.11	0.13	0.14
Mean years of schooling (in years)	8.46	8.80	9.17	9.55	9.93	10.34
Gender gap (population age 25+): highest educational attainment (ratio male/female)						
E1 - no education	0.67	0.63	0.60	0.60	0.63	0.70
E2 - incomplete primary	0.94	0.98	1.01	1.04	1.07	1.10
E3 - primary	0.97	1.04	1.11	1.15	1.16	1.14
E4 - lower secondary	1.02	1.02	1.03	1.04	1.04	1.04
E5 - upper secondary	0.95	0.88	0.86	0.87	0.89	0.93
E6 - post-secondary	1.19	1.07	0.98	0.92	0.90	0.92
Mean years of schooling (male minus female)	0.15	–0.04	–0.18	–0.27	–0.29	–0.24
Women age 20–39: highest educational attainment						
E1 - no education	0.00	0.00	0.00	0.00	0.00	0.00
E2 - incomplete primary	0.02	0.01	0.01	0.00	0.00	0.00
E3 - primary	0.30	0.27	0.23	0.20	0.17	0.15
E4 - lower secondary	0.38	0.32	0.30	0.27	0.25	0.24
E5 - upper secondary	0.22	0.31	0.36	0.41	0.44	0.46
E6 - post-secondary	0.08	0.09	0.10	0.12	0.13	0.15
Mean years of schooling (in years)	8.91	9.64	10.04	10.43	10.71	10.96

Education scenarios

GET : global education trend scenario (medium assumption also used for SSP2)

CER: constant enrolment rates scenario (assumption of no future improvements)

FT: Fast Track scenario (assumption of education expansion according to fastest historical experience)

Pyramids by Education, Medium Scenario

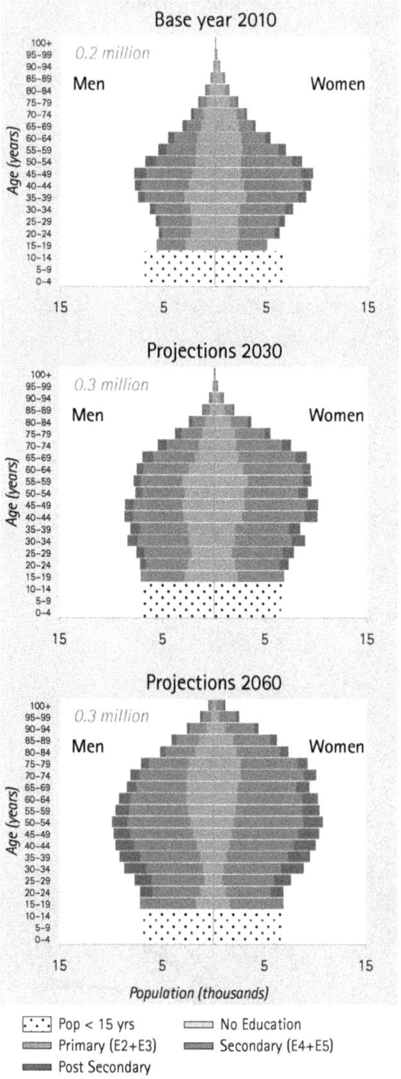

Population Size by Educational Attainment According to Three Education Scenarios: GET, CER, and FT

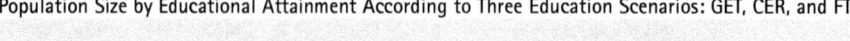

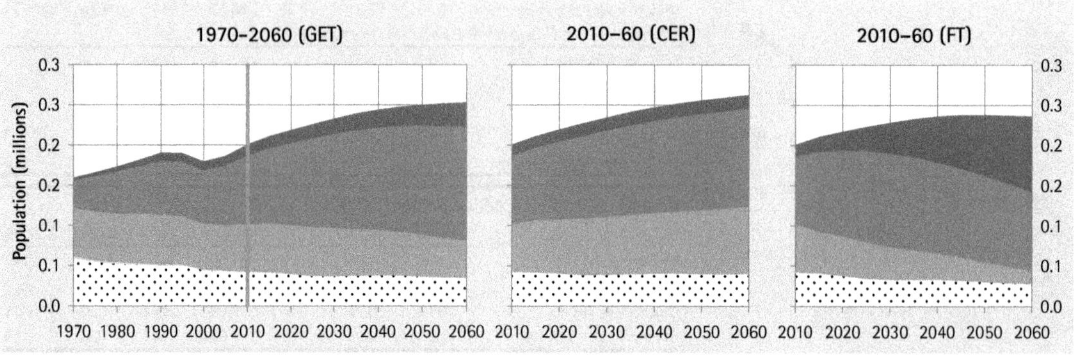

Netherlands Antilles (Continued)

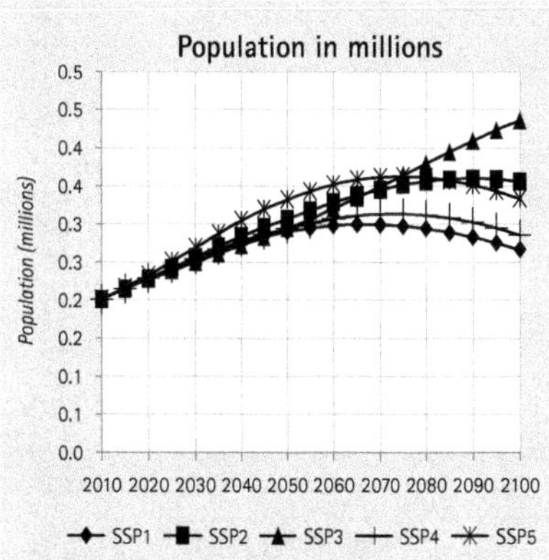

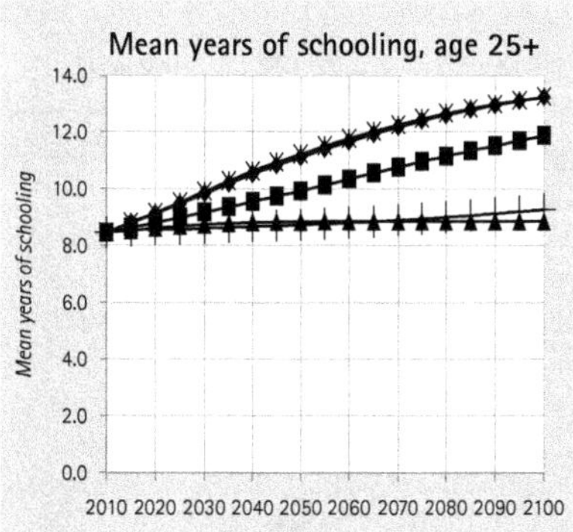

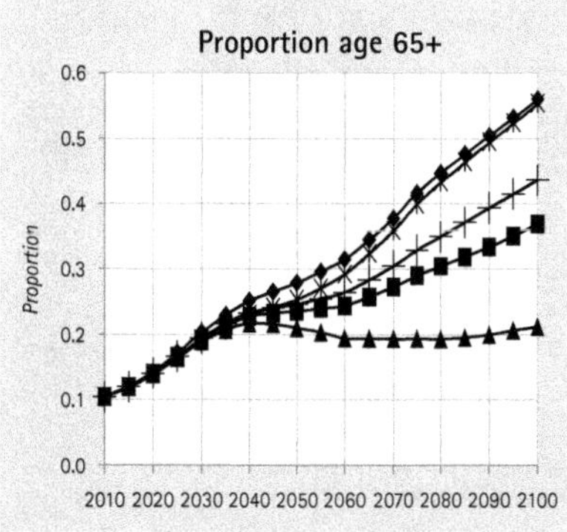

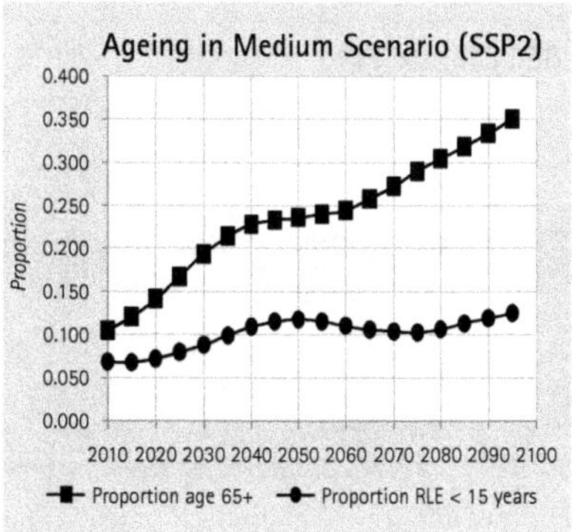

Alternative Scenarios to 2100

Projection Results by Scenario (SSP1–5)

	2010	2020	2030	2040	2050	2075	2100
Population (in millions)							
SSP1 - Rapid development	0.20	0.23	0.25	0.28	0.29	0.30	0.27
SSP2 - Medium	0.20	0.23	0.26	0.28	0.31	0.35	0.36
SSP3 - Stalled development	0.20	0.23	0.25	0.27	0.29	0.36	0.44
SSP4 - Inequality	0.20	0.23	0.25	0.28	0.29	0.31	0.29
SSP5 - Conventional development	0.20	0.23	0.27	0.30	0.33	0.36	0.33
Proportion age 65+							
SSP1 - Rapid development	0.10	0.14	0.20	0.25	0.28	0.42	0.56
SSP2 - Medium	0.10	0.14	0.19	0.23	0.24	0.29	0.37
SSP3 - Stalled development	0.10	0.14	0.19	0.22	0.21	0.19	0.21
SSP4 - Inequality	0.10	0.14	0.19	0.23	0.25	0.33	0.44
SSP5 - Conventional development	0.10	0.14	0.19	0.23	0.25	0.40	0.55
Proportion below age 20							
SSP1 - Rapid development	0.26	0.23	0.19	0.17	0.16	0.12	0.09
SSP2 - Medium	0.26	0.24	0.22	0.22	0.21	0.19	0.17
SSP3 - Stalled development	0.26	0.25	0.25	0.26	0.27	0.28	0.27
SSP4 - Inequality	0.26	0.24	0.21	0.19	0.18	0.15	0.12
SSP5 - Conventional development	0.26	0.23	0.20	0.18	0.16	0.12	0.09
Proportion of Women age 20–39 with at least secondary education							
SSP1 - Rapid development	0.67	0.82	0.87	0.89	0.91	0.95	0.98
SSP2 - Medium	0.67	0.72	0.76	0.80	0.83	0.90	0.96
SSP3 - Stalled development	0.67	0.63	0.63	0.63	0.63	0.63	0.63
SSP4 - Inequality	0.67	0.60	0.57	0.57	0.57	0.57	0.57
SSP5 - Conventional development	0.67	0.82	0.87	0.89	0.91	0.95	0.98
Mean years of schooling, age 25+							
SSP1 - Rapid development	8.46	9.12	9.83	10.52	11.11	12.40	13.23
SSP2 - Medium	8.46	8.80	9.17	9.55	9.93	10.96	11.88
SSP3 - Stalled development	8.46	8.62	8.74	8.82	8.85	8.86	8.86
SSP4 - Inequality	8.46	8.57	8.61	8.68	8.74	8.95	9.27
SSP5 - Conventional development	8.46	9.14	9.90	10.61	11.21	12.46	13.25

Demographic Assumptions Underlying SSPs

	2010–15	2020–25	2030–35	2040–45	2050–55	2075–80	2095–2100
Total fertility rate							
SSP1 - Rapid development	1.70	1.40	1.28	1.24	1.22	1.22	1.17
SSP2 - Medium	1.84	1.73	1.72	1.72	1.72	1.71	1.61
SSP3 - Stalled development	1.95	2.11	2.21	2.26	2.31	2.37	2.31
SSP4 - Inequality	1.76	1.55	1.41	1.37	1.35	1.37	1.32
SSP5 - Conventional development	1.70	1.40	1.28	1.24	1.22	1.22	1.17
Life expectancy at birth for females (in years)							
SSP1 - Rapid development	82.18	85.43	88.45	91.42	94.43	102.11	108.22
SSP2 - Medium	80.99	83.51	85.71	87.71	89.70	94.80	98.80
SSP3 - Stalled development	81.30	82.59	83.66	84.61	85.55	87.67	89.41
SSP4 - Inequality	81.76	84.04	86.04	87.91	89.81	94.54	98.30
SSP5 - Conventional development	82.18	85.43	88.45	91.42	94.43	102.11	108.22
Migration – net flow over five years (in thousands)							
SSP1 - Rapid development	8	9	9	8	7	2	0
SSP2 - Medium	8	8	8	8	8	3	0
SSP3 - Stalled development	7	4	5	5	5	3	0
SSP4 - Inequality	8	9	9	9	8	3	0
SSP5 - Conventional development	10	13	14	13	11	3	0

Ageing Indicators, Medium Scenario (SSP2)

	2010	2020	2030	2040	2050	2075	2095
Median age	37.94	39.74	40.65	41.71	43.52	47.31	52.31
Propspective median age	37.94	37.43	36.32	35.49	35.37	34.25	35.56
Proportion age 65+	0.10	0.14	0.19	0.23	0.24	0.29	0.35
Proportion RLE < 15 years	0.07	0.07	0.09	0.11	0.12	0.10	0.12

Netherlands

Detailed Human Capital Projections to 2060

Demographic indicators, Medium Scenario (SSP2)

	2010	2020	2030	2040	2050	2060
Population (in millions)	16.61	17.14	17.65	17.99	18.09	18.15
Proportion age 65+	0.15	0.20	0.25	0.28	0.29	0.30
Proportion below age 20	0.24	0.22	0.20	0.20	0.20	0.19
	2005–10	2015–20	2025–30	2035–40	2045–50	2055–60
Total Fertility Rate	1.75	1.75	1.79	1.80	1.80	1.80
Life expectancy at birth (in years)						
Men	78.05	80.13	82.21	84.14	86.21	88.31
Women	82.20	83.99	86.01	88.01	90.09	92.19
Five-year immigration flow (in '000)	296.40	290.70	301.92	308.75	308.82	304.33
Five-year emigration flow (in '000)	245.97	174.95	169.13	158.75	154.80	153.64

Human Capital indicators, Medium Scenario (SSP2)

	2010	2020	2030	2040	2050	2060
Population age 25+: highest educational attainment						
E1 - no education	0.03	0.03	0.02	0.02	0.01	0.01
E2 - incomplete primary	0.00	0.00	0.00	0.00	0.00	0.00
E3 - primary	0.10	0.07	0.05	0.04	0.03	0.02
E4 - lower secondary	0.22	0.19	0.16	0.13	0.10	0.07
E5 - upper secondary	0.38	0.41	0.43	0.44	0.44	0.44
E6 - post-secondary	0.27	0.30	0.34	0.38	0.42	0.46
Mean years of schooling (in years)	11.49	11.93	12.34	12.71	13.07	13.41
Gender gap (population age 25+): highest educational attainment (ratio male/female)						
E1 - no education	0.82	0.84	0.85	0.86	0.87	0.87
E2 - incomplete primary	NA	NA	NA	NA	NA	NA
E3 - primary	0.72	0.81	0.89	0.98	1.08	1.18
E4 - lower secondary	0.78	0.86	0.94	1.03	1.12	1.19
E5 - upper secondary	1.11	1.06	1.04	1.03	1.03	1.02
E6 - post-secondary	1.21	1.09	1.01	0.96	0.94	0.95
Mean years of schooling (male minus female)	0.61	0.33	0.11	−0.03	−0.12	−0.13
Women age 20–39: highest educational attainment						
E1 - no education	0.02	0.01	0.01	0.00	0.00	0.00
E2 - incomplete primary	0.00	0.00	0.00	0.00	0.00	0.00
E3 - primary	0.03	0.02	0.01	0.01	0.01	0.01
E4 - lower secondary	0.13	0.09	0.07	0.05	0.04	0.03
E5 - upper secondary	0.49	0.50	0.49	0.47	0.45	0.44
E6 - post-secondary	0.32	0.38	0.43	0.47	0.49	0.52
Mean years of schooling (in years)	12.46	12.95	13.33	13.59	13.77	13.92

Education scenarios

GET: global education trend scenario (medium assumption also used for SSP2)

CER: constant enrolment rates scenario (assumption of no future improvements)

FT: Fast Track scenario (assumption of education expansion according to fastest historical experience)

Pyramids by Education, Medium Scenario

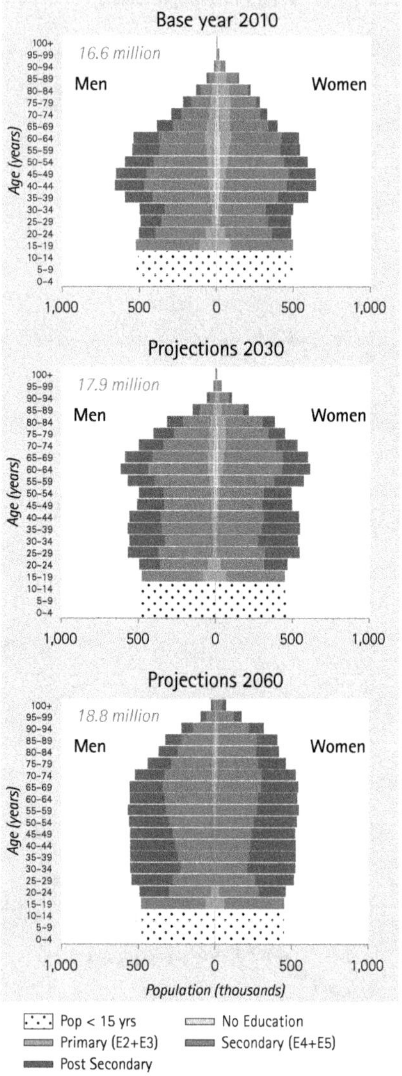

Population Size by Educational Attainment According to Three Education Scenarios: GET, CER, and FT

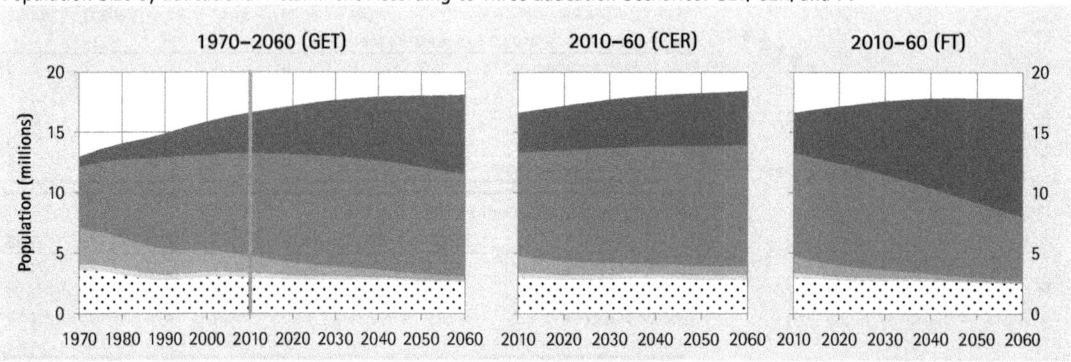

Netherlands (Continued)

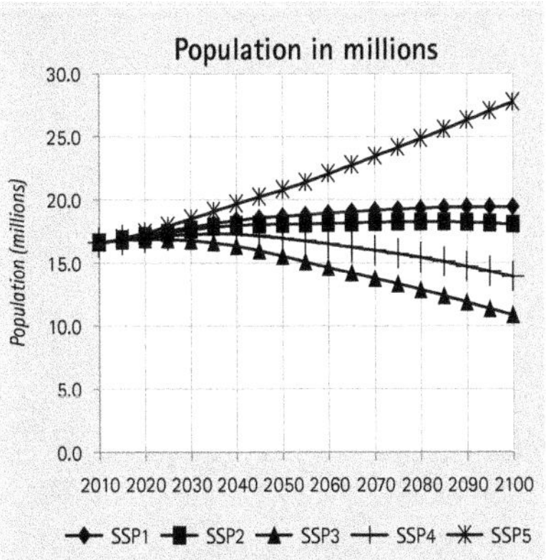

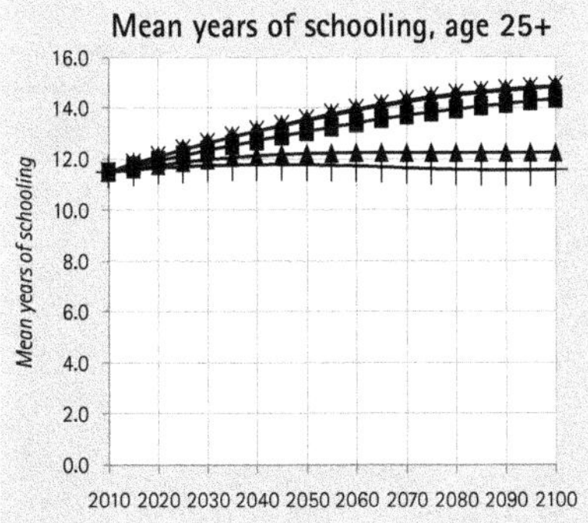

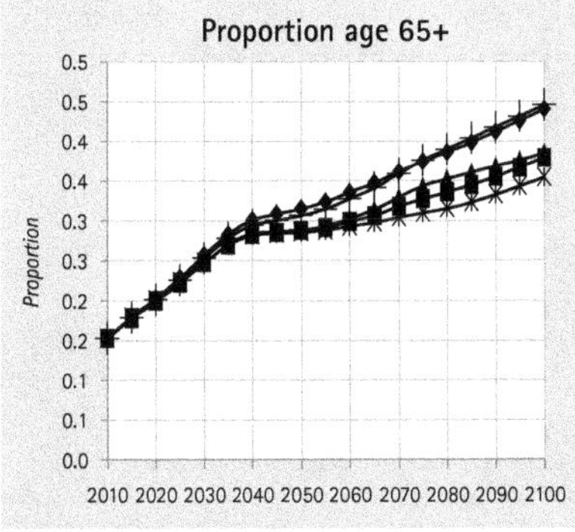

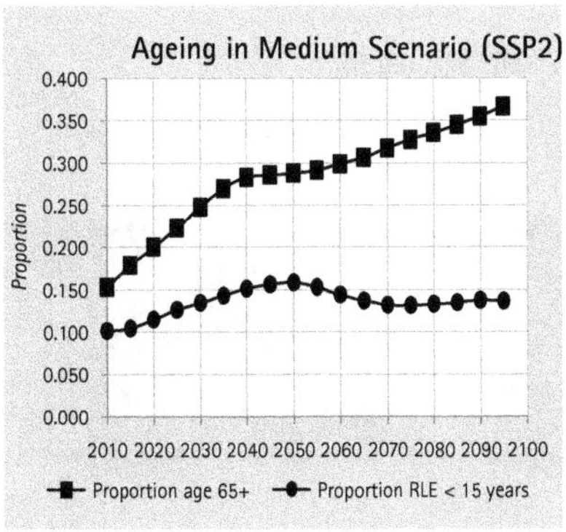

Alternative Scenarios to 2100

Projection Results by Scenario (SSP1–5)

	2010	2020	2030	2040	2050	2075	2100
Population (in millions)							
SSP1 - Rapid development	16.61	17.21	17.86	18.40	18.72	19.27	19.44
SSP2 - Medium	16.61	17.14	17.65	17.99	18.09	18.28	18.06
SSP3 - Stalled development	16.61	16.89	16.79	16.35	15.56	13.34	10.84
SSP4 - Inequality	16.61	17.03	17.28	17.29	16.98	15.74	13.88
SSP5 - Conventional development	16.61	17.40	18.51	19.68	20.80	24.14	27.73
Proportion age 65+							
SSP1 - Rapid development	0.15	0.20	0.26	0.30	0.32	0.37	0.44
SSP2 - Medium	0.15	0.20	0.25	0.28	0.29	0.33	0.38
SSP3 - Stalled development	0.15	0.20	0.25	0.28	0.29	0.34	0.39
SSP4 - Inequality	0.15	0.20	0.25	0.29	0.31	0.38	0.45
SSP5 - Conventional development	0.15	0.20	0.25	0.28	0.29	0.31	0.35
Proportion below age 20							
SSP1 - Rapid development	0.24	0.22	0.20	0.20	0.19	0.17	0.15
SSP2 - Medium	0.24	0.22	0.20	0.20	0.20	0.19	0.17
SSP3 - Stalled development	0.24	0.21	0.19	0.18	0.17	0.15	0.14
SSP4 - Inequality	0.24	0.21	0.19	0.18	0.17	0.15	0.13
SSP5 - Conventional development	0.24	0.22	0.22	0.23	0.22	0.22	0.21
Proportion of Women age 20–39 with at least secondary education							
SSP1 - Rapid development	0.95	0.98	0.99	0.99	0.99	1.00	1.00
SSP2 - Medium	0.95	0.97	0.98	0.99	0.99	1.00	1.00
SSP3 - Stalled development	0.95	0.93	0.93	0.93	0.93	0.93	0.93
SSP4 - Inequality	0.95	0.93	0.93	0.93	0.93	0.93	0.93
SSP5 - Conventional development	0.95	0.98	0.99	0.99	0.99	1.00	1.00
Mean years of schooling, age 25+							
SSP1 - Rapid development	11.49	12.09	12.62	13.08	13.50	14.37	14.82
SSP2 - Medium	11.49	11.93	12.34	12.71	13.07	13.83	14.34
SSP3 - Stalled development	11.49	11.76	11.98	12.12	12.21	12.24	12.24
SSP4 - Inequality	11.49	11.66	11.74	11.78	11.77	11.62	11.55
SSP5 - Conventional development	11.49	12.09	12.63	13.10	13.54	14.43	14.86

Demographic Assumptions Underlying SSPs

	2010–15	2020–25	2030–35	2040–45	2050–55	2075–80	2095–2100
Total fertility rate							
SSP1 - Rapid development	1.72	1.74	1.77	1.78	1.78	1.78	1.77
SSP2 - Medium	1.72	1.77	1.80	1.80	1.80	1.79	1.78
SSP3 - Stalled development	1.65	1.54	1.46	1.43	1.41	1.42	1.42
SSP4 - Inequality	1.65	1.56	1.49	1.46	1.44	1.45	1.45
SSP5 - Conventional development	1.81	2.00	2.14	2.20	2.22	2.22	2.22
Life expectancy at birth for females (in years)							
SSP1 - Rapid development	84.03	86.86	89.77	92.71	95.78	103.75	110.15
SSP2 - Medium	83.09	85.01	87.01	88.99	91.09	96.61	101.00
SSP3 - Stalled development	83.06	83.91	84.88	85.82	86.85	89.50	91.73
SSP4 - Inequality	83.56	85.36	87.29	89.20	91.22	96.36	100.55
SSP5 - Conventional development	84.03	86.86	89.77	92.71	95.78	103.75	110.15
Migration – net flow over five years (in thousands)							
SSP1 - Rapid development	90	123	140	148	142	58	0
SSP2 - Medium	92	124	142	153	151	66	0
SSP3 - Stalled development	75	62	71	76	75	33	0
SSP4 - Inequality	90	123	139	147	143	62	0
SSP5 - Conventional development	105	184	211	230	229	105	0

Ageing Indicators, Medium Scenario (SSP2)

	2010	2020	2030	2040	2050	2075	2095
Median age	40.76	43.76	44.89	46.01	47.22	49.44	53.05
Propspective median age	40.76	41.97	41.29	40.57	39.79	36.70	36.08
Proportion age 65+	0.15	0.20	0.25	0.28	0.29	0.33	0.37
Proportion RLE < 15 years	0.10	0.11	0.13	0.15	0.16	0.13	0.14

New Caledonia

Detailed Human Capital Projections to 2060

Demographic indicators, Medium Scenario (SSP2)	2010	2020	2030	2040	2050	2060
Population (in millions)	0.25	0.29	0.33	0.36	0.39	0.42
Proportion age 65+	0.08	0.10	0.12	0.15	0.18	0.22
Proportion below age 20	0.34	0.30	0.28	0.25	0.23	0.22
	2005–10	2015–20	2025–30	2035–40	2045–50	2055–60
Total Fertility Rate	2.19	2.06	1.89	1.83	1.80	1.79
Life expectancy at birth (in years)						
Men	72.31	73.62	75.72	77.89	80.04	82.16
Women	78.71	80.19	82.09	84.09	86.09	88.09
Five-year immigration flow (in '000)	6.65	6.53	6.79	6.94	6.95	6.86
Five-year emigration flow (in '000)	0.29	0.23	0.24	0.25	0.25	0.26

Human Capital indicators, Medium Scenario (SSP2)	2010	2020	2030	2040	2050	2060
Population age 25+: highest educational attainment						
E1 - no education	0.07	0.04	0.02	0.01	0.01	0.00
E2 - incomplete primary	0.05	0.03	0.02	0.01	0.00	0.00
E3 - primary	0.14	0.09	0.06	0.04	0.02	0.01
E4 - lower secondary	0.19	0.17	0.15	0.12	0.10	0.07
E5 - upper secondary	0.30	0.36	0.40	0.41	0.42	0.41
E6 - post-secondary	0.25	0.30	0.35	0.40	0.45	0.50
Mean years of schooling (in years)	10.01	11.07	11.94	12.62	13.16	13.59
Gender gap (population age 25+): highest educational attainment (ratio male/female)						
E1 - no education	0.82	0.79	0.79	0.80	0.82	0.85
E2 - incomplete primary	0.91	0.87	0.81	0.76	0.71	0.68
E3 - primary	0.95	0.91	0.86	0.81	0.78	0.79
E4 - lower secondary	1.04	1.10	1.13	1.13	1.12	1.10
E5 - upper secondary	1.08	1.09	1.10	1.10	1.09	1.06
E6 - post-secondary	0.97	0.92	0.90	0.90	0.92	0.94
Mean years of schooling (male minus female)	0.20	0.08	−0.02	−0.08	−0.10	−0.08
Women age 20–39: highest educational attainment						
E1 - no education	0.02	0.01	0.00	0.00	0.00	0.00
E2 - incomplete primary	0.00	0.00	0.00	0.00	0.00	0.00
E3 - primary	0.03	0.01	0.00	0.00	0.00	0.00
E4 - lower secondary	0.17	0.11	0.07	0.04	0.03	0.02
E5 - upper secondary	0.44	0.47	0.45	0.43	0.41	0.39
E6 - post-secondary	0.35	0.41	0.48	0.53	0.57	0.59
Mean years of schooling (in years)	12.13	13.01	13.64	13.94	14.15	14.29

Education scenarios

GET : global education trend scenario (medium assumption also used for SSP2)

CER: constant enrolment rates scenario (assumption of no future improvements)

FT: Fast track scenario (assumption of education expansion according to fastest historical experience)

Pyramids by Education, Medium Scenario

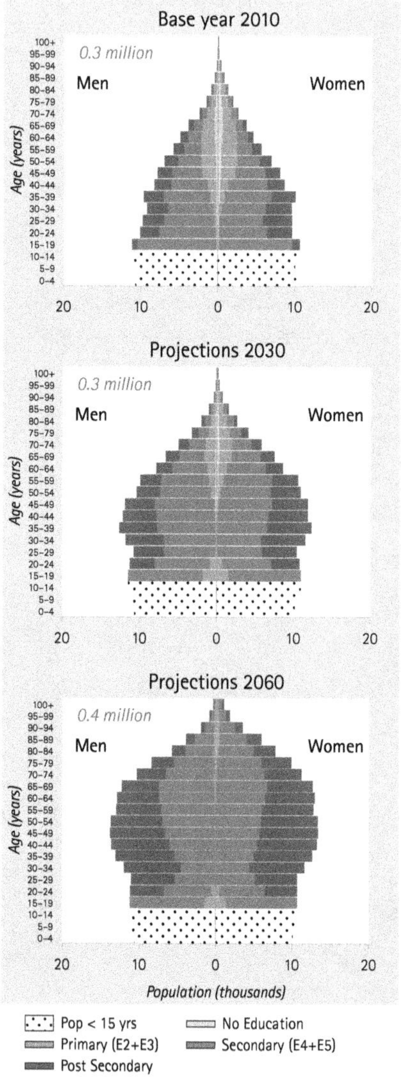

Population Size by Educational Attainment According to Three Education Scenarios: GET, CER, and FT

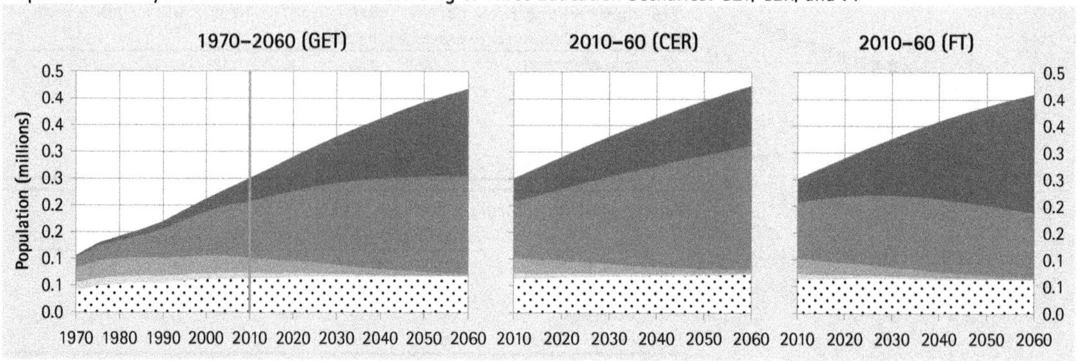

New Caledonia (Continued)

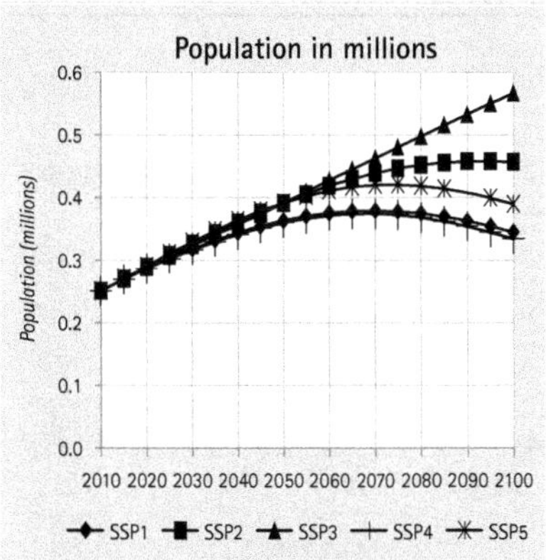

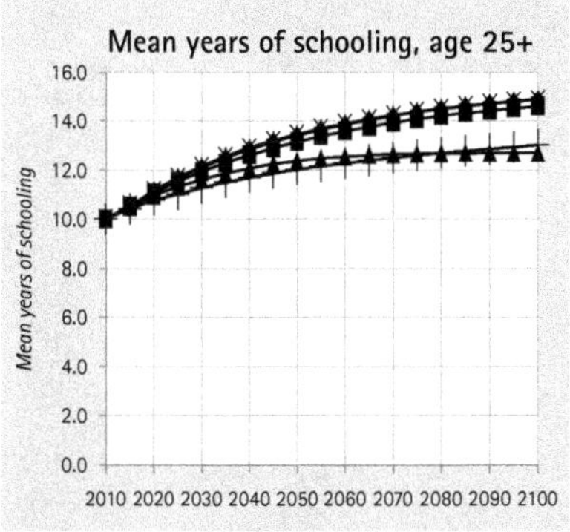

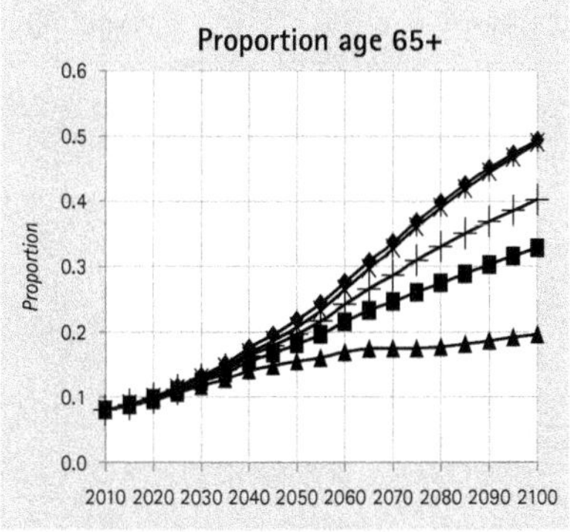

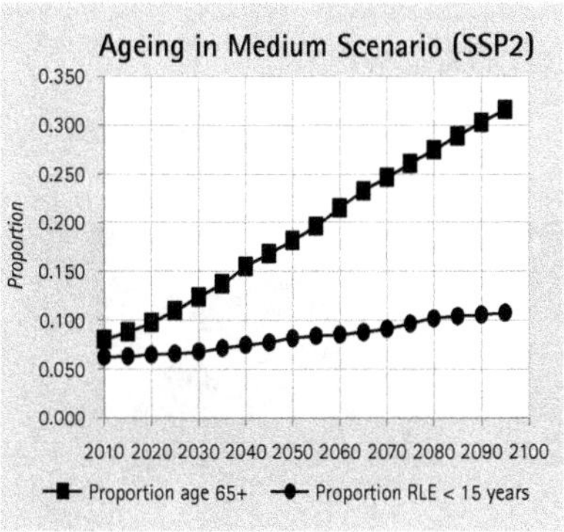

Alternative Scenarios to 2100

Projection Results by Scenario (SSP1–5)

	2010	2020	2030	2040	2050	2075	2100
Population (in millions)							
SSP1 - Rapid development	0.25	0.29	0.32	0.34	0.36	0.38	0.35
SSP2 - Medium	0.25	0.29	0.33	0.36	0.39	0.45	0.46
SSP3 - Stalled development	0.25	0.29	0.32	0.36	0.39	0.48	0.57
SSP4 - Inequality	0.25	0.29	0.32	0.34	0.36	0.37	0.33
SSP5 - Conventional development	0.25	0.29	0.33	0.36	0.39	0.42	0.39
Proportion age 65+							
SSP1 - Rapid development	0.08	0.10	0.13	0.18	0.22	0.37	0.49
SSP2 - Medium	0.08	0.10	0.12	0.15	0.18	0.26	0.33
SSP3 - Stalled development	0.08	0.10	0.12	0.14	0.16	0.18	0.20
SSP4 - Inequality	0.08	0.10	0.13	0.16	0.20	0.31	0.40
SSP5 - Conventional development	0.08	0.10	0.13	0.17	0.21	0.36	0.49
Proportion below age 20							
SSP1 - Rapid development	0.34	0.29	0.25	0.21	0.18	0.14	0.11
SSP2 - Medium	0.34	0.30	0.28	0.25	0.23	0.21	0.19
SSP3 - Stalled development	0.34	0.31	0.30	0.29	0.29	0.28	0.28
SSP4 - Inequality	0.34	0.29	0.25	0.22	0.20	0.16	0.14
SSP5 - Conventional development	0.34	0.29	0.25	0.21	0.19	0.14	0.11
Proportion of Women age 20–39 with at least secondary education							
SSP1 - Rapid development	0.95	0.99	1.00	1.00	1.00	1.00	1.00
SSP2 - Medium	0.95	0.99	0.99	1.00	1.00	1.00	1.00
SSP3 - Stalled development	0.95	0.98	0.98	0.98	0.98	0.98	0.98
SSP4 - Inequality	0.95	0.92	0.88	0.88	0.88	0.88	0.88
SSP5 - Conventional development	0.95	0.99	1.00	1.00	1.00	1.00	1.00
Mean years of schooling, age 25+							
SSP1 - Rapid development	10.01	11.14	12.11	12.86	13.42	14.36	14.87
SSP2 - Medium	10.01	11.07	11.94	12.62	13.16	14.08	14.60
SSP3 - Stalled development	10.01	10.95	11.62	12.08	12.38	12.67	12.70
SSP4 - Inequality	10.01	10.78	11.28	11.71	12.03	12.60	13.01
SSP5 - Conventional development	10.01	11.16	12.15	12.90	13.47	14.39	14.88

Demographic Assumptions Underlying SSPs

	2010–15	2020–25	2030–35	2040–45	2050–55	2075–80	2095–2100
Total fertility rate							
SSP1 - Rapid development	2.03	1.66	1.44	1.35	1.32	1.33	1.33
SSP2 - Medium	2.15	1.98	1.84	1.82	1.80	1.79	1.78
SSP3 - Stalled development	2.25	2.29	2.30	2.32	2.35	2.38	2.39
SSP4 - Inequality	2.04	1.70	1.50	1.42	1.39	1.39	1.39
SSP5 - Conventional development	2.03	1.66	1.44	1.35	1.32	1.33	1.33
Life expectancy at birth for females (in years)							
SSP1 - Rapid development	80.26	82.98	85.95	88.95	91.88	99.28	105.27
SSP2 - Medium	79.29	81.09	83.09	85.09	87.09	92.11	96.09
SSP3 - Stalled development	79.24	80.07	80.97	81.97	82.89	85.20	87.11
SSP4 - Inequality	79.70	81.46	83.41	85.35	87.27	91.97	95.82
SSP5 - Conventional development	80.26	82.98	85.95	88.95	91.88	99.28	105.27
Migration – net flow over five years (in thousands)							
SSP1 - Rapid development	6	6	6	6	5	2	0
SSP2 - Medium	6	6	6	7	6	3	0
SSP3 - Stalled development	5	3	3	4	4	3	0
SSP4 - Inequality	6	6	6	6	6	3	0
SSP5 - Conventional development	7	9	9	9	8	2	0

Ageing Indicators, Medium Scenario (SSP2)

	2010	2020	2030	2040	2050	2075	2095
Median age	30.31	32.36	35.22	37.94	40.15	45.33	48.96
Propspective median age	30.31	30.38	31.13	31.85	32.06	32.41	32.24
Proportion age 65+	0.08	0.10	0.12	0.15	0.18	0.26	0.32
Proportion RLE < 15 years	0.06	0.06	0.07	0.07	0.08	0.10	0.11

New Zealand

Detailed Human Capital Projections to 2060

Demographic indicators, Medium Scenario (SSP2)	2010	2020	2030	2040	2050	2060
Population (in millions)	4.37	4.87	5.38	5.83	6.23	6.59
Proportion age 65+	0.13	0.16	0.20	0.22	0.24	0.26
Proportion below age 20	0.28	0.26	0.24	0.23	0.22	0.21
	2005–10	2015–20	2025–30	2035–40	2045–50	2055–60
Total Fertility Rate	2.14	1.99	1.88	1.83	1.81	1.80
Life expectancy at birth (in years)						
Men	78.03	80.69	82.87	84.93	86.91	88.88
Women	82.16	84.39	86.51	88.61	90.61	92.61
Five-year immigration flow (in '000)	246.55	241.74	251.00	256.67	256.76	253.05
Five-year emigration flow (in '000)	181.69	142.54	147.10	151.70	154.48	155.34

Human Capital indicators, Medium Scenario (SSP2)	2010	2020	2030	2040	2050	2060
Population age 25+: highest educational attainment						
E1 - no education	0.01	0.00	0.00	0.00	0.00	0.00
E2 - incomplete primary	0.01	0.01	0.00	0.00	0.00	0.00
E3 - primary	0.09	0.06	0.04	0.03	0.02	0.01
E4 - lower secondary	0.14	0.12	0.10	0.08	0.06	0.04
E5 - upper secondary	0.42	0.44	0.44	0.45	0.44	0.42
E6 - post-secondary	0.34	0.38	0.41	0.45	0.48	0.52
Mean years of schooling (in years)	12.92	13.34	13.75	14.11	14.44	14.73
Gender gap (population age 25+): highest educational attainment (ratio male/female)						
E1 - no education	1.14	1.10	1.04	0.97	0.90	0.84
E2 - incomplete primary	0.94	0.97	0.99	1.03	1.08	1.07
E3 - primary	0.99	1.00	1.01	1.05	1.09	1.12
E4 - lower secondary	1.06	1.10	1.14	1.16	1.17	1.17
E5 - upper secondary	0.88	0.89	0.91	0.93	0.94	0.95
E6 - post-secondary	1.15	1.11	1.08	1.05	1.03	1.02
Mean years of schooling (male minus female)	0.12	0.08	0.06	0.04	0.03	0.03
Women age 20–39: highest educational attainment						
E1 - no education	0.00	0.00	0.00	0.00	0.00	0.00
E2 - incomplete primary	0.00	0.00	0.00	0.00	0.00	0.00
E3 - primary	0.02	0.02	0.01	0.01	0.00	0.00
E4 - lower secondary	0.08	0.05	0.03	0.02	0.01	0.01
E5 - upper secondary	0.52	0.51	0.49	0.46	0.44	0.41
E6 - post-secondary	0.37	0.42	0.47	0.51	0.55	0.58
Mean years of schooling (in years)	13.69	14.21	14.68	14.91	15.09	15.24

Education scenarios

GET : global education trend scenario (medium assumption also used for SSP2)

CER: constant enrolment rates scenario (assumption of no future improvements)

FT: Fast track scenario (assumption of education expansion according to fastest historical experience)

Pyramids by Education, Medium Scenario

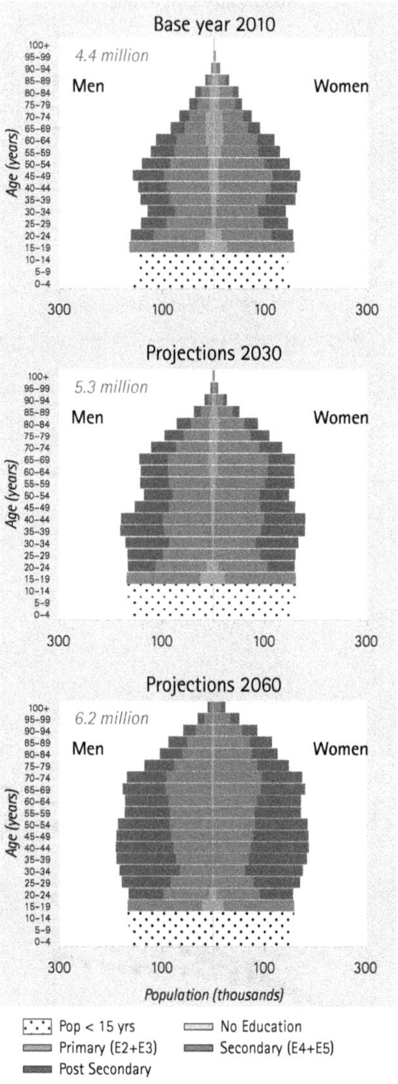

Population Size by Educational Attainment According to Three Education Scenarios: GET, CER, and FT

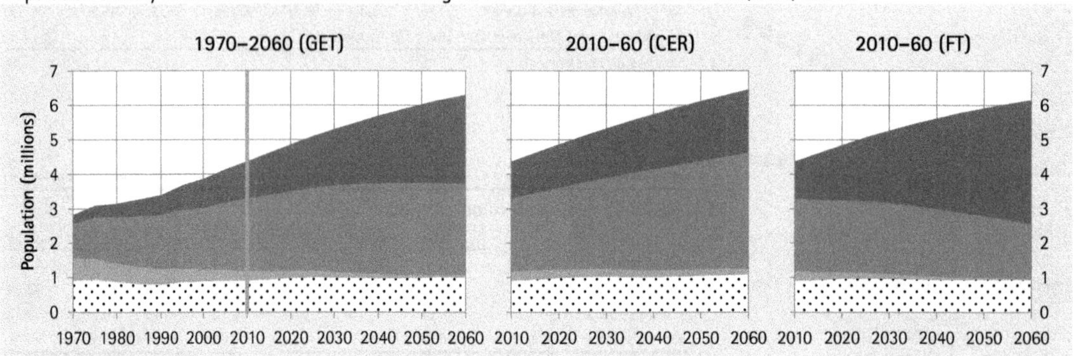

New Zealand (Continued)

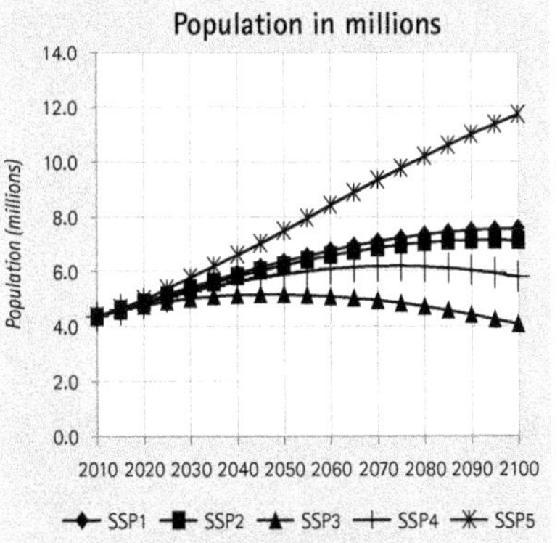

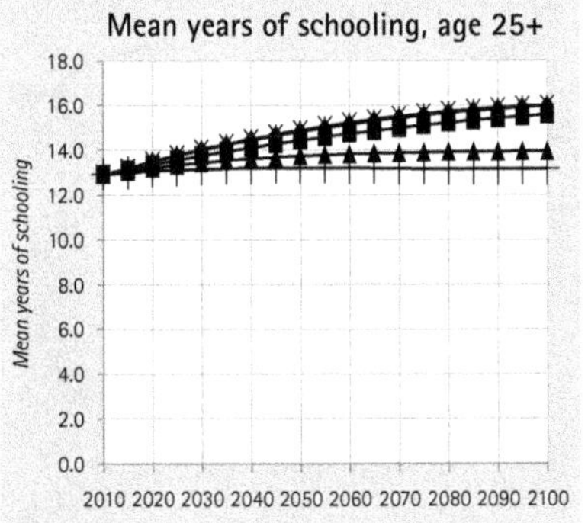

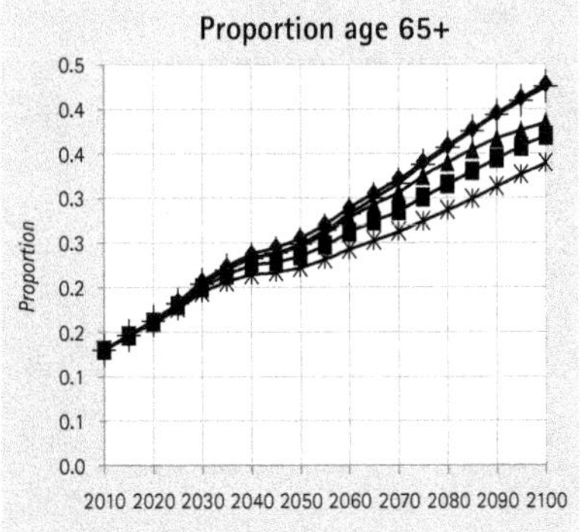

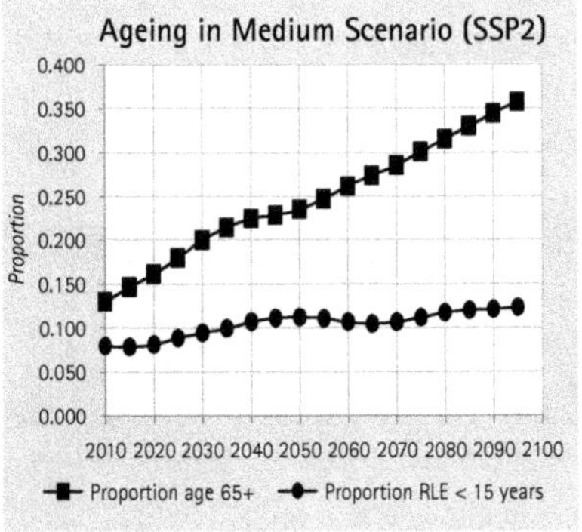

Alternative Scenarios to 2100

Projection Results by Scenario (SSP1–5)

	2010	2020	2030	2040	2050	2075	2100
Population (in millions)							
SSP1 - Rapid development	4.37	4.88	5.42	5.92	6.38	7.24	7.58
SSP2 - Medium	4.37	4.87	5.38	5.83	6.23	6.98	7.13
SSP3 - Stalled development	4.37	4.76	5.01	5.14	5.16	4.85	4.07
SSP4 - Inequality	4.37	4.84	5.28	5.63	5.90	6.20	5.79
SSP5 - Conventional development	4.37	4.99	5.78	6.61	7.49	9.77	11.71
Proportion age 65+							
SSP1 - Rapid development	0.13	0.16	0.21	0.24	0.26	0.34	0.43
SSP2 - Medium	0.13	0.16	0.20	0.22	0.24	0.30	0.37
SSP3 - Stalled development	0.13	0.16	0.20	0.23	0.25	0.32	0.38
SSP4 - Inequality	0.13	0.16	0.20	0.23	0.25	0.34	0.42
SSP5 - Conventional development	0.13	0.16	0.19	0.21	0.22	0.27	0.34
Proportion below age 20							
SSP1 - Rapid development	0.28	0.26	0.24	0.22	0.21	0.18	0.16
SSP2 - Medium	0.28	0.26	0.24	0.23	0.22	0.19	0.17
SSP3 - Stalled development	0.28	0.25	0.22	0.20	0.18	0.16	0.14
SSP4 - Inequality	0.28	0.25	0.23	0.21	0.19	0.16	0.14
SSP5 - Conventional development	0.28	0.26	0.26	0.26	0.25	0.23	0.21
Proportion of Women age 20–39 with at least secondary education							
SSP1 - Rapid development	0.97	0.99	0.99	1.00	1.00	1.00	1.00
SSP2 - Medium	0.97	0.98	0.99	0.99	1.00	1.00	1.00
SSP3 - Stalled development	0.97	0.97	0.97	0.97	0.97	0.97	0.97
SSP4 - Inequality	0.97	0.97	0.97	0.97	0.97	0.97	0.97
SSP5 - Conventional development	0.97	0.99	0.99	1.00	1.00	1.00	1.00
Mean years of schooling, age 25+							
SSP1 - Rapid development	12.92	13.48	14.00	14.45	14.83	15.55	15.96
SSP2 - Medium	12.92	13.34	13.75	14.11	14.44	15.11	15.57
SSP3 - Stalled development	12.92	13.20	13.44	13.62	13.73	13.89	13.93
SSP4 - Inequality	12.92	13.07	13.14	13.20	13.21	13.17	13.16
SSP5 - Conventional development	12.92	13.49	14.02	14.49	14.89	15.61	16.00

Demographic Assumptions Underlying SSPs

	2010–15	2020–25	2030–35	2040–45	2050–55	2075–80	2095–2100
Total fertility rate							
SSP1 - Rapid development	2.04	1.90	1.81	1.78	1.77	1.77	1.77
SSP2 - Medium	2.05	1.94	1.84	1.82	1.80	1.79	1.78
SSP3 - Stalled development	1.96	1.68	1.51	1.45	1.42	1.44	1.44
SSP4 - Inequality	1.97	1.74	1.58	1.52	1.49	1.50	1.51
SSP5 - Conventional development	2.14	2.18	2.20	2.20	2.21	2.22	2.22
Life expectancy at birth for females (in years)							
SSP1 - Rapid development	84.22	87.32	90.29	93.22	96.19	103.70	109.72
SSP2 - Medium	83.29	85.49	87.51	89.61	91.61	96.60	100.59
SSP3 - Stalled development	83.23	84.37	85.37	86.34	87.33	89.62	91.50
SSP4 - Inequality	83.71	85.85	87.78	89.80	91.75	96.45	100.26
SSP5 - Conventional development	84.22	87.32	90.29	93.22	96.19	103.70	109.72
Migration – net flow over five years (in thousands)							
SSP1 - Rapid development	86	101	102	99	93	35	0
SSP2 - Medium	85	99	101	100	97	40	0
SSP3 - Stalled development	72	50	51	49	47	18	0
SSP4 - Inequality	86	101	103	100	96	39	0
SSP5 - Conventional development	100	153	159	161	159	68	0

Ageing Indicators, Medium Scenario (SSP2)

	2010	2020	2030	2040	2050	2075	2095
Median age	36.61	37.37	39.24	41.41	42.99	47.93	52.09
Propspective median age	36.61	35.11	35.17	35.41	35.14	35.48	35.89
Proportion age 65+	0.13	0.16	0.20	0.22	0.24	0.30	0.36
Proportion RLE < 15 years	0.08	0.08	0.09	0.11	0.11	0.11	0.12

Nicaragua

Detailed Human Capital Projections to 2060

Demographic indicators, Medium Scenario (SSP2)	2010	2020	2030	2040	2050	2060
Population (in millions)	5.79	6.45	6.95	7.29	7.44	7.41
Proportion age 65+	0.05	0.06	0.08	0.11	0.15	0.20
Proportion below age 20	0.46	0.40	0.35	0.30	0.27	0.24
	2005–10	2015–20	2025–30	2035–40	2045–50	2055–60
Total Fertility Rate	2.76	2.30	2.08	1.92	1.82	1.73
Life expectancy at birth (in years)						
Men	69.92	71.67	73.67	75.83	77.85	79.96
Women	76.12	77.60	79.39	81.39	83.29	85.29
Five-year immigration flow (in '000)	0.78	0.76	0.79	0.80	0.80	0.79
Five-year emigration flow (in '000)	200.18	171.19	174.42	170.66	161.00	148.64

Human Capital indicators, Medium Scenario (SSP2)	2010	2020	2030	2040	2050	2060
Population age 25+: highest educational attainment						
E1 - no education	0.23	0.18	0.14	0.10	0.08	0.06
E2 - incomplete primary	0.25	0.22	0.18	0.15	0.12	0.09
E3 - primary	0.21	0.23	0.24	0.23	0.22	0.21
E4 - lower secondary	0.08	0.10	0.10	0.10	0.10	0.10
E5 - upper secondary	0.12	0.16	0.20	0.24	0.28	0.32
E6 - post-secondary	0.10	0.12	0.14	0.17	0.20	0.23
Mean years of schooling (in years)	5.86	6.74	7.54	8.29	8.98	9.62
Gender gap (population age 25+): highest educational attainment (ratio male/female)						
E1 - no education	0.97	0.99	1.01	1.03	1.04	1.04
E2 - incomplete primary	1.07	1.09	1.09	1.08	1.06	1.03
E3 - primary	1.03	1.06	1.09	1.10	1.09	1.07
E4 - lower secondary	1.03	1.04	1.06	1.07	1.07	1.06
E5 - upper secondary	0.87	0.87	0.90	0.93	0.95	0.98
E6 - post-secondary	1.00	0.91	0.87	0.87	0.89	0.93
Mean years of schooling (male minus female)	−0.08	−0.25	−0.33	−0.34	−0.30	−0.20
Women age 20–39: highest educational attainment						
E1 - no education	0.13	0.09	0.06	0.04	0.02	0.01
E2 - incomplete primary	0.21	0.15	0.10	0.07	0.04	0.03
E3 - primary	0.24	0.24	0.22	0.20	0.17	0.14
E4 - lower secondary	0.11	0.11	0.11	0.10	0.09	0.08
E5 - upper secondary	0.20	0.25	0.31	0.36	0.40	0.43
E6 - post-secondary	0.12	0.16	0.20	0.24	0.28	0.31
Mean years of schooling (in years)	7.32	8.36	9.25	10.07	10.72	11.22

Education scenarios

GET: global education trend scenario (medium assumption also used for SSP2)

CER: constant enrolment rates scenario (assumption of no future improvements)

FT: Fast track scenario (assumption of education expansion according to fastest historical experience)

Pyramids by Education, Medium Scenario

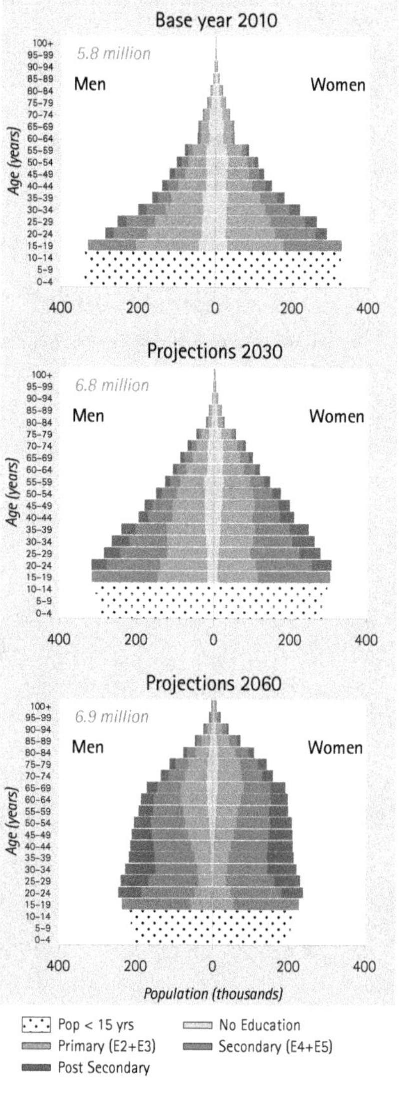

Population Size by Educational Attainment According to Three Education Scenarios: GET, CER, and FT

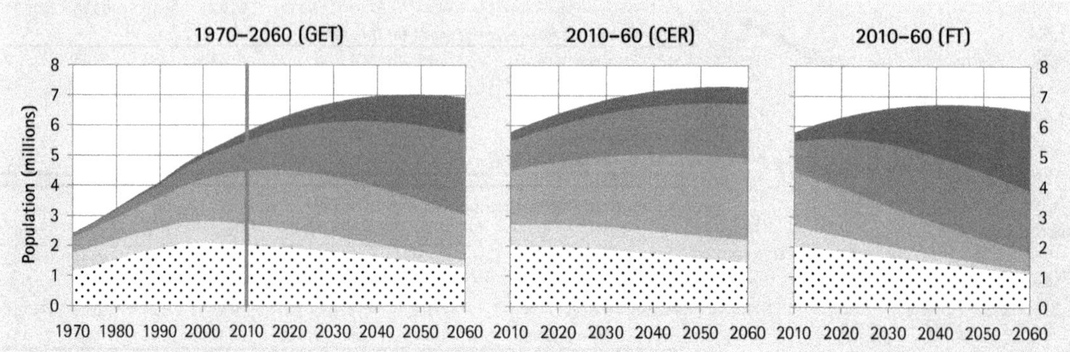

Nicaragua (Continued)

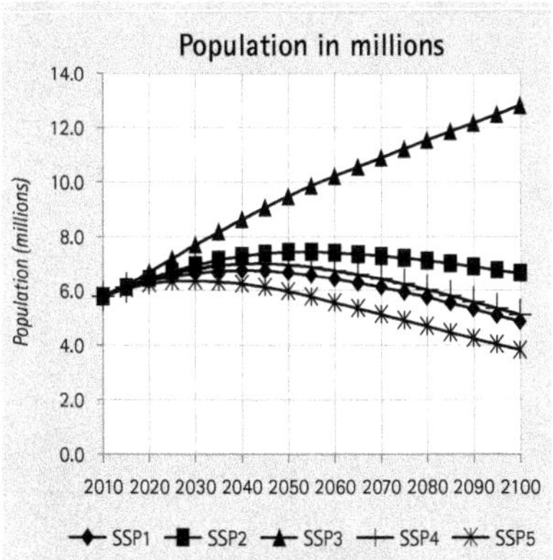

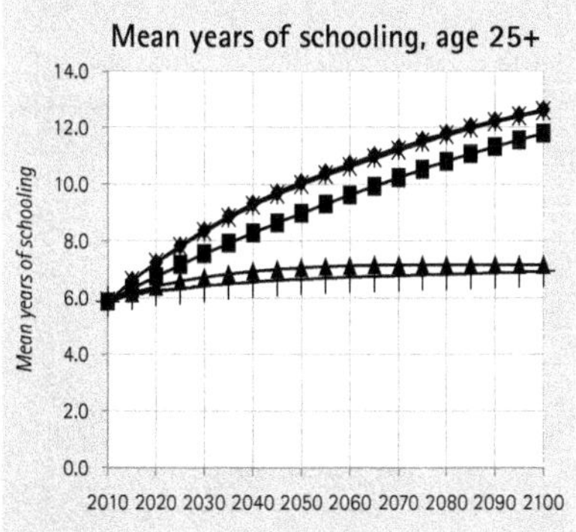

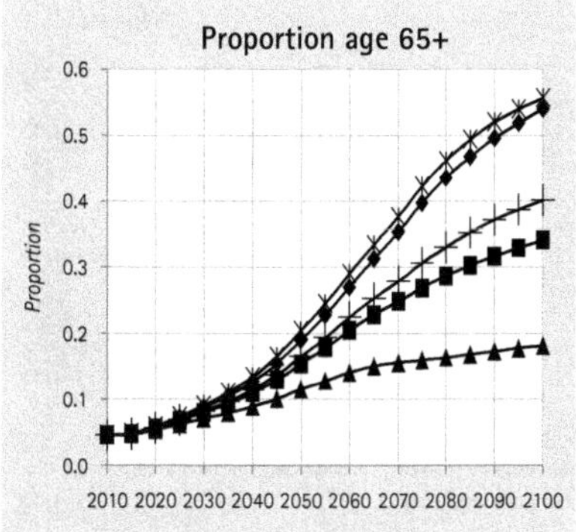

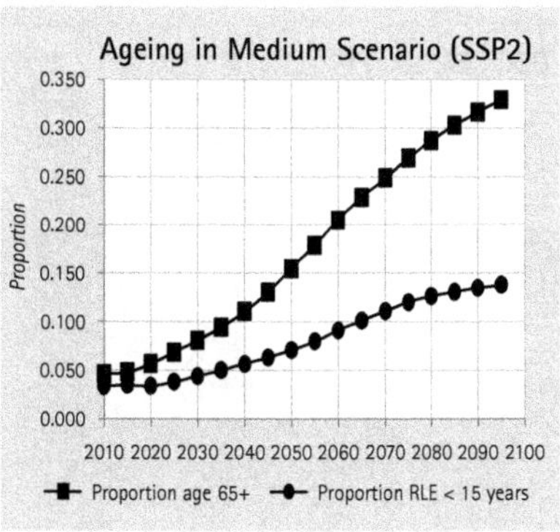

Alternative Scenarios to 2100

Projection Results by Scenario (SSP1–5)

	2010	2020	2030	2040	2050	2075	2100
Population (in millions)							
SSP1 - Rapid development	5.79	6.34	6.65	6.75	6.67	5.95	4.87
SSP2 - Medium	5.79	6.45	6.95	7.29	7.44	7.22	6.66
SSP3 - Stalled development	5.79	6.69	7.70	8.63	9.48	11.22	12.82
SSP4 - Inequality	5.79	6.42	6.82	7.00	6.96	6.25	5.12
SSP5 - Conventional development	5.79	6.25	6.35	6.25	5.97	4.91	3.82
Proportion age 65+							
SSP1 - Rapid development	0.05	0.06	0.09	0.13	0.19	0.40	0.54
SSP2 - Medium	0.05	0.06	0.08	0.11	0.15	0.27	0.34
SSP3 - Stalled development	0.05	0.05	0.07	0.09	0.12	0.16	0.18
SSP4 - Inequality	0.05	0.06	0.08	0.12	0.17	0.31	0.40
SSP5 - Conventional development	0.05	0.06	0.09	0.13	0.20	0.42	0.56
Proportion below age 20							
SSP1 - Rapid development	0.46	0.38	0.31	0.25	0.20	0.12	0.09
SSP2 - Medium	0.46	0.40	0.35	0.30	0.27	0.20	0.17
SSP3 - Stalled development	0.46	0.41	0.38	0.36	0.33	0.30	0.28
SSP4 - Inequality	0.46	0.39	0.33	0.28	0.23	0.16	0.13
SSP5 - Conventional development	0.46	0.39	0.31	0.25	0.20	0.12	0.09
Proportion of Women age 20–39 with at least secondary education							
SSP1 - Rapid development	0.42	0.64	0.76	0.83	0.87	0.94	0.97
SSP2 - Medium	0.42	0.52	0.62	0.70	0.77	0.89	0.96
SSP3 - Stalled development	0.42	0.43	0.44	0.44	0.44	0.44	0.44
SSP4 - Inequality	0.42	0.41	0.39	0.39	0.39	0.39	0.39
SSP5 - Conventional development	0.42	0.64	0.76	0.83	0.87	0.94	0.97
Mean years of schooling, age 25+							
SSP1 - Rapid development	5.86	7.24	8.37	9.31	10.07	11.55	12.61
SSP2 - Medium	5.86	6.74	7.54	8.29	8.98	10.52	11.78
SSP3 - Stalled development	5.86	6.40	6.73	6.94	7.06	7.17	7.17
SSP4 - Inequality	5.86	6.24	6.42	6.56	6.66	6.81	6.94
SSP5 - Conventional development	5.86	7.22	8.31	9.24	9.98	11.46	12.57

Demographic assumptions underlying SSPs

	2010–15	2020–25	2030–35	2040–45	2050–55	2075–80	2095–2100
Total fertility rate							
SSP1 - Rapid development	2.30	1.77	1.50	1.36	1.28	1.23	1.17
SSP2 - Medium	2.48	2.17	2.00	1.86	1.77	1.68	1.58
SSP3 - Stalled development	2.64	2.66	2.60	2.48	2.40	2.34	2.26
SSP4 - Inequality	2.40	2.01	1.72	1.54	1.44	1.39	1.34
SSP5 - Conventional development	2.30	1.77	1.50	1.36	1.28	1.23	1.17
Life expectancy at birth for females (in years)							
SSP1 - Rapid development	78.47	80.80	83.50	86.35	89.35	96.93	102.92
SSP2 - Medium	76.70	78.49	80.39	82.29	84.29	89.31	93.29
SSP3 - Stalled development	77.72	78.11	78.93	79.69	80.48	82.26	83.71
SSP4 - Inequality	77.97	79.49	81.15	82.84	84.60	88.95	92.46
SSP5 - Conventional development	78.47	80.80	83.50	86.35	89.35	96.93	102.92
Migration – net flow over five years (in thousands)							
SSP1 - Rapid development	−178	−171	−167	−152	−132	−41	0
SSP2 - Medium	−183	−177	−177	−169	−158	−59	0
SSP3 - Stalled development	−148	−86	−88	−89	−89	−41	0
SSP4 - Inequality	−178	−171	−167	−152	−131	−39	0
SSP5 - Conventional development	−208	−256	−250	−229	−200	−65	0

Ageing Indicators, Medium Scenario (SSP2)

	2010	2020	2030	2040	2050	2075	2095
Median age	21.99	25.47	29.20	33.07	37.16	45.88	50.45
Propspective median age	21.99	23.84	25.85	28.03	30.38	34.77	35.79
Proportion age 65+	0.05	0.06	0.08	0.11	0.15	0.27	0.33
Proportion RLE < 15 years	0.03	0.03	0.04	0.06	0.07	0.12	0.14

Niger

Detailed Human Capital Projections to 2060

Demographic indicators, Medium Scenario (SSP2)	2010	2020	2030	2040	2050	2060
Population (in millions)	15.51	21.85	29.91	39.86	51.23	62.44
Proportion age 65+	0.02	0.02	0.03	0.03	0.03	0.04
Proportion below age 20	0.59	0.59	0.56	0.53	0.50	0.45
	2005–10	2015–20	2025–30	2035–40	2045–50	2055–60
Total Fertility Rate	7.19	6.38	5.51	4.82	4.11	3.20
Life expectancy at birth (in years)						
Men	52.66	56.90	58.62	60.08	61.49	63.54
Women	53.55	57.97	60.12	62.12	64.12	66.58
Five-year immigration flow (in '000)	31.60	30.88	32.00	32.66	32.59	32.05
Five-year emigration flow (in '000)	58.46	62.98	90.00	122.34	158.47	198.61

Human Capital indicators, Medium Scenario (SSP2)	2010	2020	2030	2040	2050	2060
Population age 25+: highest educational attainment						
E1 - no education	0.81	0.74	0.66	0.57	0.47	0.38
E2 - incomplete primary	0.10	0.11	0.12	0.11	0.10	0.09
E3 - primary	0.05	0.08	0.13	0.18	0.22	0.26
E4 - lower secondary	0.02	0.04	0.06	0.09	0.12	0.14
E5 - upper secondary	0.01	0.01	0.02	0.04	0.06	0.10
E6 - post-secondary	0.01	0.01	0.02	0.02	0.03	0.04
Mean years of schooling (in years)	1.15	1.68	2.44	3.34	4.34	5.43
Gender gap (population age 25+): highest educational attainment (ratio male/female)						
E1 - no education	0.89	0.86	0.83	0.82	0.84	0.87
E2 - incomplete primary	1.40	1.31	1.22	1.14	1.08	1.02
E3 - primary	1.84	1.82	1.65	1.45	1.28	1.13
E4 - lower secondary	2.28	1.72	1.52	1.36	1.24	1.16
E5 - upper secondary	2.43	1.63	1.22	1.02	0.95	0.96
E6 - post-secondary	3.62	2.19	1.47	1.12	0.99	0.98
Mean years of schooling (male minus female)	0.76	0.87	0.93	0.83	0.62	0.40
Women age 20–39: highest educational attainment						
E1 - no education	0.78	0.71	0.61	0.49	0.37	0.25
E2 - incomplete primary	0.12	0.12	0.12	0.12	0.11	0.10
E3 - primary	0.06	0.10	0.15	0.21	0.27	0.32
E4 - lower secondary	0.02	0.05	0.08	0.12	0.17	0.21
E5 - upper secondary	0.01	0.01	0.03	0.04	0.07	0.10
E6 - post-secondary	0.00	0.01	0.01	0.02	0.02	0.03
Mean years of schooling (in years)	1.23	1.89	2.82	3.97	5.25	6.53

Education scenarios

GET: global education trend scenario (medium assumption also used for SSP2)

CER: constant enrolment rates scenario (assumption of no future improvements)

FT: Fast track scenario (assumption of education expansion according to fastest historical experience)

Pyramids by Education, Medium Scenario

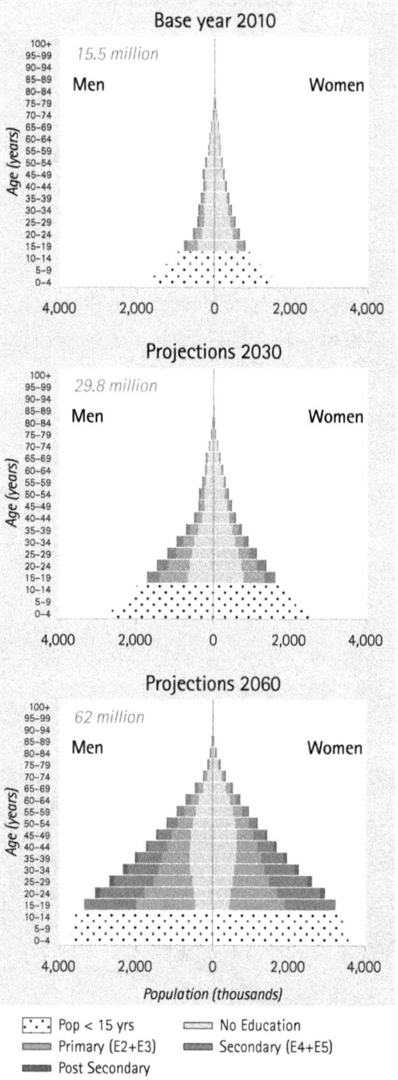

Population Size by Educational Attainment According to Three Education Scenarios: GET, CER, and FT

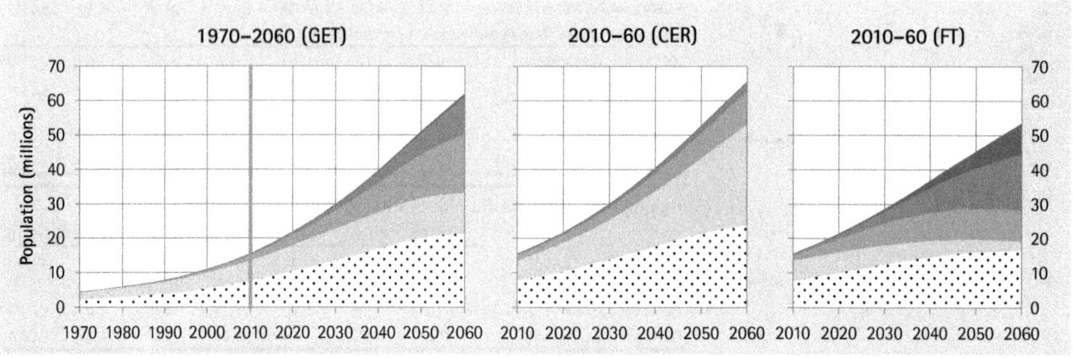

Niger (Continued)

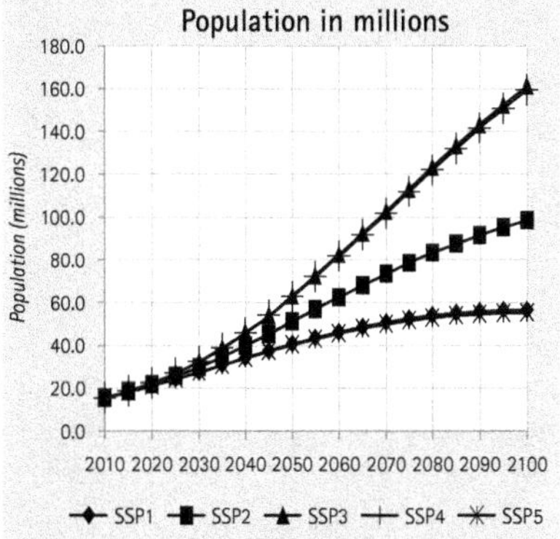

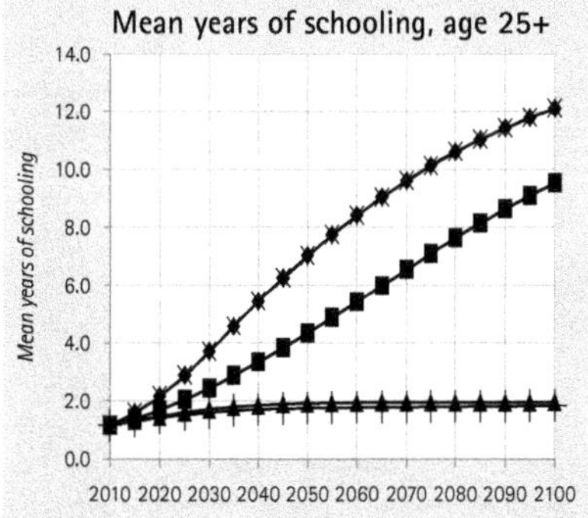

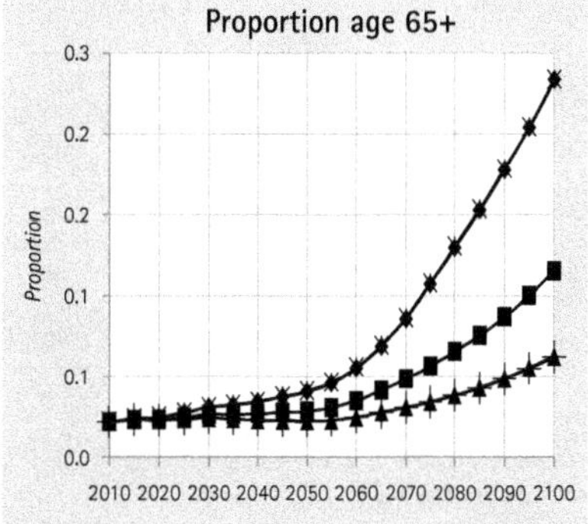

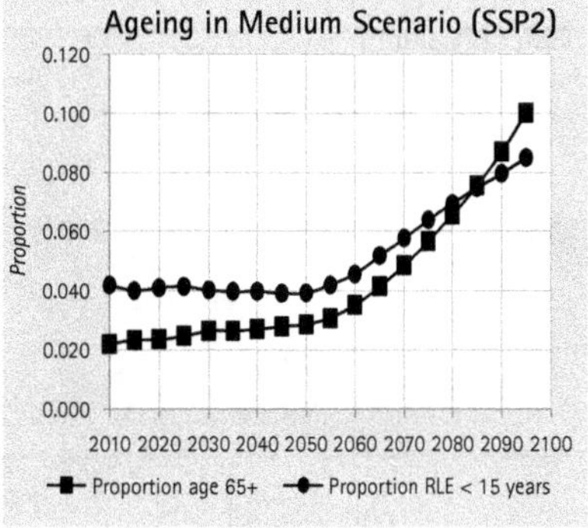

Alternative Scenarios to 2100

Projection Results by Scenario (SSP1–5)

	2010	2020	2030	2040	2050	2075	2100
Population (in millions)							
SSP1 - Rapid development	15.51	21.19	27.46	34.22	40.68	52.57	56.51
SSP2 - Medium	15.51	21.85	29.91	39.86	51.23	78.47	98.40
SSP3 - Stalled development	15.51	22.48	32.57	46.05	63.14	113.15	161.19
SSP4 - Inequality	15.51	22.46	32.50	45.86	62.75	111.93	159.33
SSP5 - Conventional development	15.51	21.17	27.37	34.01	40.27	51.50	55.16
Proportion age 65+							
SSP1 - Rapid development	0.02	0.03	0.03	0.03	0.04	0.11	0.23
SSP2 - Medium	0.02	0.02	0.03	0.03	0.03	0.06	0.12
SSP3 - Stalled development	0.02	0.02	0.02	0.02	0.02	0.03	0.06
SSP4 - Inequality	0.02	0.02	0.02	0.02	0.02	0.03	0.06
SSP5 - Conventional development	0.02	0.03	0.03	0.03	0.04	0.11	0.23
Proportion below age 20							
SSP1 - Rapid development	0.59	0.57	0.52	0.46	0.41	0.28	0.18
SSP2 - Medium	0.59	0.59	0.56	0.53	0.50	0.37	0.28
SSP3 - Stalled development	0.59	0.60	0.59	0.58	0.56	0.45	0.36
SSP4 - Inequality	0.59	0.60	0.60	0.58	0.56	0.45	0.36
SSP5 - Conventional development	0.59	0.57	0.52	0.46	0.41	0.28	0.18
Proportion of Women age 20–39 with at least secondary education							
SSP1 - Rapid development	0.04	0.12	0.24	0.38	0.51	0.70	0.82
SSP2 - Medium	0.04	0.07	0.12	0.18	0.26	0.47	0.69
SSP3 - Stalled development	0.04	0.04	0.04	0.04	0.04	0.04	0.04
SSP4 - Inequality	0.04	0.03	0.03	0.03	0.03	0.04	0.04
SSP5 - Conventional development	0.04	0.12	0.24	0.38	0.51	0.70	0.82
Mean years of schooling, age 25+							
SSP1 - Rapid development	1.15	2.16	3.70	5.43	7.02	10.13	12.11
SSP2 - Medium	1.15	1.68	2.44	3.34	4.34	7.10	9.54
SSP3 - Stalled development	1.15	1.46	1.71	1.85	1.91	1.94	1.95
SSP4 - Inequality	1.15	1.42	1.59	1.70	1.75	1.79	1.83
SSP5 - Conventional development	1.15	2.15	3.69	5.42	7.01	10.12	12.11

Demographic Assumptions Underlying SSPs

	2010–15	2020–25	2030–35	2040–45	2050–55	2075–80	2095–2100
Total fertility rate							
SSP1 - Rapid development	6.41	4.88	3.80	3.07	2.47	1.61	1.36
SSP2 - Medium	6.81	5.94	5.16	4.47	3.62	2.29	1.92
SSP3 - Stalled development	7.18	7.04	6.62	5.94	5.00	3.17	2.63
SSP4 - Inequality	7.18	7.05	6.64	5.94	5.00	3.17	2.63
SSP5 - Conventional development	6.41	4.88	3.80	3.07	2.47	1.61	1.36
Life expectancy at birth for females (in years)							
SSP1 - Rapid development	60.80	64.00	66.44	68.97	71.63	80.47	87.17
SSP2 - Medium	56.18	59.08	61.18	63.08	65.32	71.69	76.69
SSP3 - Stalled development	60.31	61.58	62.42	63.03	63.84	66.41	68.48
SSP4 - Inequality	60.31	61.58	62.41	63.02	63.82	66.39	68.46
SSP5 - Conventional development	60.80	64.00	66.44	68.97	71.63	80.47	87.17
Migration – net flow over five years (in thousands)							
SSP1 - Rapid development	−26	−43	−70	−97	−122	−71	0
SSP2 - Medium	−25	−43	−72	−106	−145	−103	0
SSP3 - Stalled development	−22	−21	−35	−53	−74	−57	0
SSP4 - Inequality	−26	−44	−74	−113	−162	−126	0
SSP5 - Conventional development	−30	−66	−111	−159	−211	−141	0

Ageing Indicators, Medium Scenario (SSP2)

	2010	2020	2030	2040	2050	2075	2095
Median age	15.45	16.04	17.17	18.47	20.08	27.16	33.41
Propspective median age	15.45	14.76	14.72	15.20	15.71	19.55	22.43
Proportion age 65+	0.02	0.02	0.03	0.03	0.03	0.06	0.10
Proportion RLE < 15 years	0.04	0.04	0.04	0.04	0.04	0.06	0.09

Nigeria

Detailed Human Capital Projections to 2060

Demographic indicators, Medium Scenario (SSP2)	2010	2020	2030	2040	2050	2060
Population (in millions)	158.42	201.62	252.76	310.28	370.67	425.29
Proportion age 65+	0.03	0.03	0.04	0.04	0.05	0.06
Proportion below age 20	0.53	0.52	0.50	0.47	0.44	0.40
	2005–10	2015–20	2025–30	2035–40	2045–50	2055–60
Total Fertility Rate	5.61	4.99	4.45	3.93	3.46	2.79
Life expectancy at birth (in years)						
Men	49.50	53.74	55.89	57.38	59.03	61.57
Women	51.02	55.60	58.18	60.28	62.38	65.18
Five-year immigration flow (in '000)	151.32	147.31	151.85	154.00	152.60	148.96
Five-year emigration flow (in '000)	435.57	408.11	512.09	626.24	744.31	862.14

Human Capital indicators, Medium Scenario (SSP2)	2010	2020	2030	2040	2050	2060
Population age 25+: highest educational attainment						
E1 - no education	0.40	0.29	0.20	0.13	0.08	0.05
E2 - incomplete primary	0.06	0.05	0.03	0.02	0.01	0.01
E3 - primary	0.19	0.17	0.14	0.11	0.09	0.06
E4 - lower secondary	0.05	0.08	0.09	0.09	0.08	0.06
E5 - upper secondary	0.19	0.26	0.33	0.38	0.42	0.44
E6 - post-secondary	0.12	0.16	0.21	0.26	0.32	0.38
Mean years of schooling (in years)	6.13	7.71	9.22	10.54	11.62	12.48
Gender gap (population age 25+): highest educational attainment (ratio male/female)						
E1 - no education	0.60	0.59	0.59	0.60	0.62	0.65
E2 - incomplete primary	0.73	0.73	0.74	0.76	0.79	0.81
E3 - primary	1.15	0.98	0.88	0.83	0.82	0.83
E4 - lower secondary	1.33	1.21	1.10	1.03	1.00	0.97
E5 - upper secondary	1.80	1.45	1.26	1.15	1.09	1.05
E6 - post-secondary	1.81	1.46	1.27	1.14	1.08	1.04
Mean years of schooling (male minus female)	2.63	2.16	1.61	1.08	0.66	0.38
Women age 20–39: highest educational attainment						
E1 - no education	0.34	0.21	0.11	0.05	0.02	0.01
E2 - incomplete primary	0.05	0.04	0.03	0.01	0.01	0.00
E3 - primary	0.19	0.16	0.13	0.09	0.06	0.03
E4 - lower secondary	0.09	0.11	0.11	0.10	0.08	0.07
E5 - upper secondary	0.24	0.34	0.43	0.48	0.51	0.52
E6 - post-secondary	0.10	0.15	0.20	0.26	0.32	0.37
Mean years of schooling (in years)	6.70	8.70	10.35	11.60	12.48	13.07

Education scenarios

GET: global education trend scenario (medium assumption also used for SSP2)

CER: constant enrolment rates scenario (assumption of no future improvements)

FT: Fast track scenario (assumption of education expansion according to fastest historical experience)

Pyramids by Education, Medium Scenario

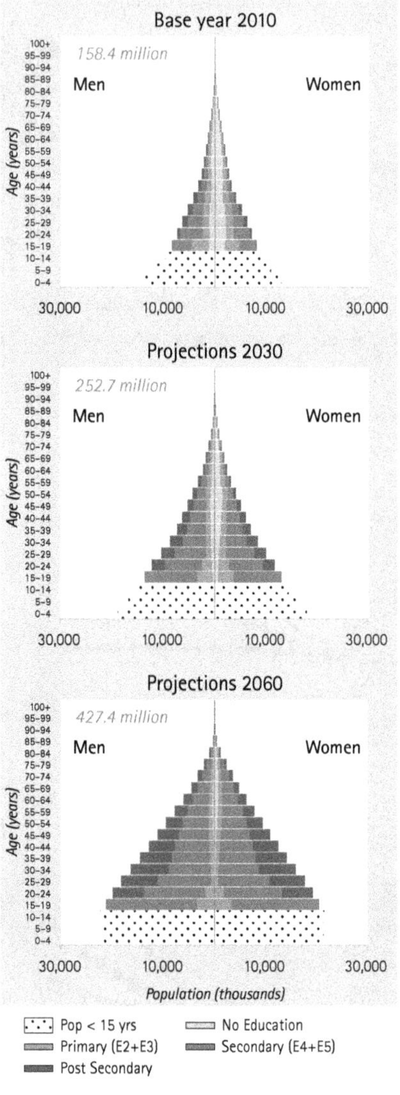

Population Size by Educational Attainment According to Three Education Scenarios: GET, CER, and FT

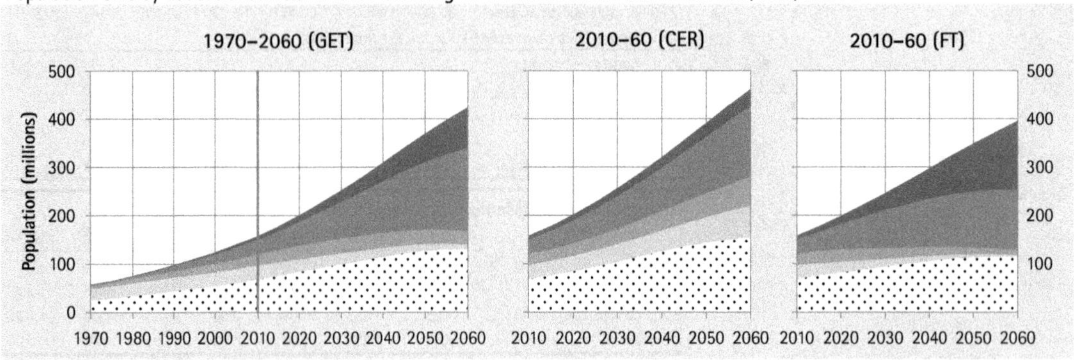

Nigeria (Continued)

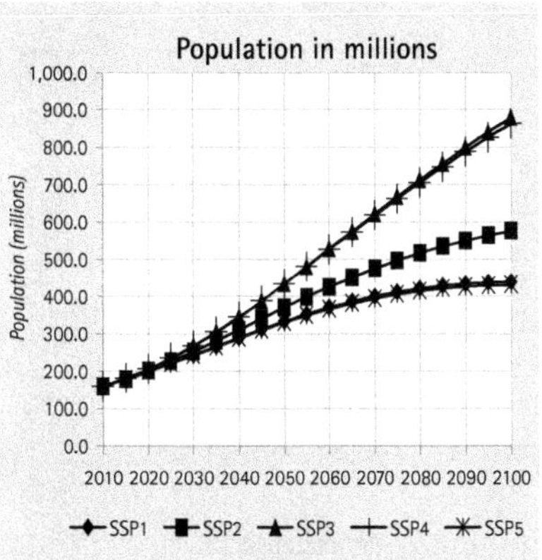

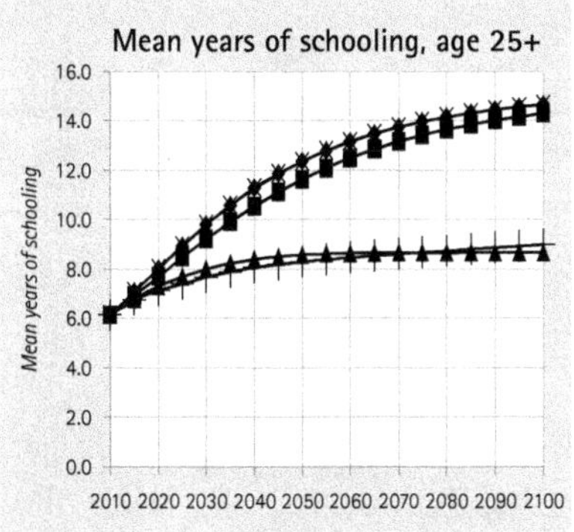

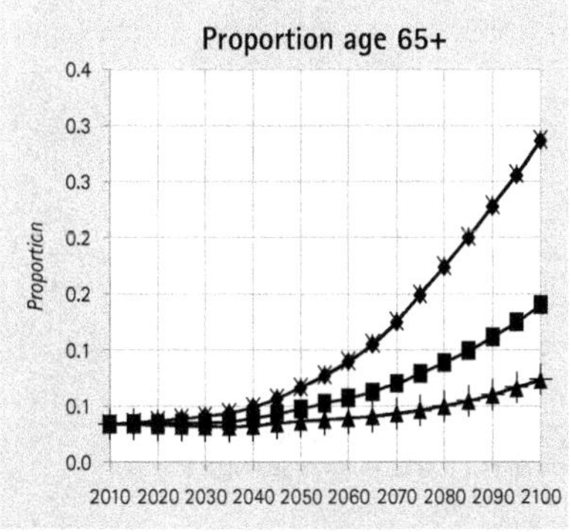

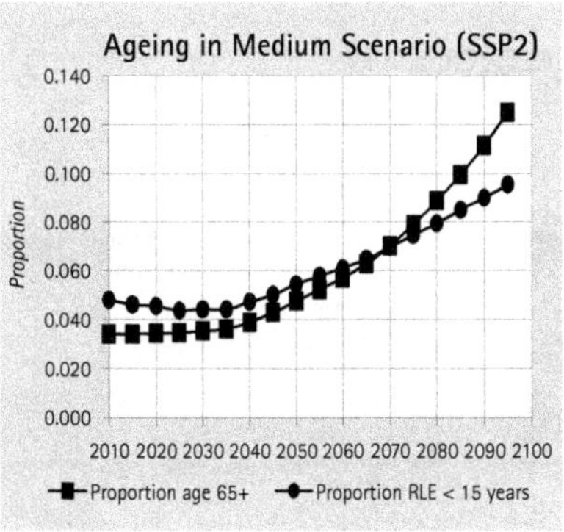

Alternative Scenarios to 2100

Projection Results by Scenario (SSP1–5)

	2010	2020	2030	2040	2050	2075	2100
Population (in millions)							
SSP1 - Rapid development	158.42	199.14	242.96	289.16	332.77	411.59	438.71
SSP2 - Medium	158.42	201.62	252.76	310.28	370.67	496.64	576.13
SSP3 - Stalled development	158.42	205.74	267.95	345.15	434.57	668.10	879.43
SSP4 - Inequality	158.42	205.81	268.21	345.17	433.84	661.92	862.98
SSP5 - Conventional development	158.42	198.98	242.30	287.70	330.19	405.26	430.39
Proportion age 65+							
SSP1 - Rapid development	0.03	0.04	0.04	0.05	0.07	0.15	0.29
SSP2 - Medium	0.03	0.03	0.04	0.04	0.05	0.08	0.14
SSP3 - Stalled development	0.03	0.03	0.03	0.03	0.04	0.05	0.07
SSP4 - Inequality	0.03	0.03	0.03	0.03	0.04	0.05	0.07
SSP5 - Conventional development	0.03	0.04	0.04	0.05	0.07	0.15	0.29
Proportion below age 20							
SSP1 - Rapid development	0.53	0.51	0.46	0.41	0.37	0.25	0.17
SSP2 - Medium	0.53	0.52	0.50	0.47	0.44	0.34	0.26
SSP3 - Stalled development	0.53	0.53	0.53	0.53	0.51	0.43	0.36
SSP4 - Inequality	0.53	0.53	0.54	0.53	0.51	0.43	0.36
SSP5 - Conventional development	0.53	0.51	0.46	0.41	0.37	0.25	0.17
Proportion of Women age 20–39 with at least secondary education							
SSP1 - Rapid development	0.42	0.64	0.80	0.89	0.94	0.98	0.99
SSP2 - Medium	0.42	0.59	0.73	0.84	0.91	0.98	1.00
SSP3 - Stalled development	0.42	0.49	0.50	0.50	0.50	0.50	0.50
SSP4 - Inequality	0.42	0.46	0.45	0.45	0.45	0.45	0.45
SSP5 - Conventional development	0.42	0.64	0.80	0.89	0.94	0.98	0.99
Mean years of schooling, age 25+							
SSP1 - Rapid development	6.13	8.02	9.80	11.27	12.35	13.96	14.66
SSP2 - Medium	6.13	7.71	9.22	10.54	11.62	13.42	14.29
SSP3 - Stalled development	6.13	7.31	8.00	8.39	8.57	8.66	8.67
SSP4 - Inequality	6.13	7.15	7.68	8.06	8.30	8.67	8.98
SSP5 - Conventional development	6.13	8.01	9.79	11.26	12.34	13.96	14.66

Demographic Assumptions Underlying SSPs

	2010–15	2020–25	2030–35	2040–45	2050–55	2075–80	2095–2100
Total fertility rate							
SSP1 - Rapid development	5.01	3.90	3.15	2.67	2.24	1.56	1.38
SSP2 - Medium	5.27	4.72	4.18	3.69	3.08	2.11	1.87
SSP3 - Stalled development	5.63	5.79	5.74	5.35	4.66	3.16	2.77
SSP4 - Inequality	5.64	5.85	5.80	5.37	4.65	3.11	2.72
SSP5 - Conventional development	5.01	3.90	3.16	2.67	2.24	1.56	1.38
Life expectancy at birth for females (in years)							
SSP1 - Rapid development	58.45	64.96	69.09	72.88	76.68	85.85	93.30
SSP2 - Medium	53.38	56.90	59.32	61.18	63.68	71.12	76.89
SSP3 - Stalled development	55.99	54.95	55.98	56.82	57.48	61.38	64.50
SSP4 - Inequality	55.99	54.91	55.91	56.74	57.40	61.32	64.47
SSP5 - Conventional development	58.45	64.96	69.09	72.88	76.68	85.85	93.30
Migration – net flow over five years (in thousands)							
SSP1 - Rapid development	−244	−303	−407	−509	−604	−335	0
SSP2 - Medium	−245	−303	−410	−527	−650	−401	0
SSP3 - Stalled development	−202	−146	−194	−250	−315	−209	0
SSP4 - Inequality	−242	−298	−407	−539	−694	−462	0
SSP5 - Conventional development	−285	−462	−642	−836	−1043	−661	0

Ageing Indicators, Medium Scenario (SSP2)

	2010	2020	2030	2040	2050	2075	2095
Median age	18.41	18.96	20.15	21.49	23.09	29.54	35.54
Propspective median age	18.41	17.17	17.11	17.28	17.59	19.60	21.53
Proportion age 65+	0.03	0.03	0.04	0.04	0.05	0.08	0.13
Proportion RLE < 15 years	0.05	0.05	0.04	0.05	0.05	0.07	0.10

Norway

Detailed Human Capital Projections to 2060

Demographic indicators, Medium Scenario (SSP2)

	2010	2020	2030	2040	2050	2060
Population (in millions)	4.88	5.37	5.92	6.44	6.92	7.42
Proportion age 65+	0.15	0.18	0.21	0.23	0.24	0.26
Proportion below age 20	0.25	0.23	0.23	0.23	0.22	0.22
	2005–10	2015–20	2025–30	2035–40	2045–50	2055–60
Total Fertility Rate	1.92	1.91	1.98	2.00	2.00	1.99
Life expectancy at birth (in years)						
Men	78.13	80.34	82.42	84.48	86.49	88.60
Women	82.71	84.59	86.71	88.81	90.79	92.89
Five-year immigration flow (in '000)	174.83	139.37	144.90	148.33	148.52	146.45
Five-year emigration flow (in '000)	4.14	3.25	3.29	3.35	3.53	3.69

Human Capital indicators, Medium Scenario (SSP2)

	2010	2020	2030	2040	2050	2060
Population age 25+: highest educational attainment						
E1 - no education	0.00	0.00	0.00	0.00	0.00	0.00
E2 - incomplete primary	0.00	0.00	0.00	0.00	0.00	0.00
E3 - primary	0.00	0.00	0.00	0.00	0.00	0.00
E4 - lower secondary	0.24	0.21	0.18	0.15	0.13	0.11
E5 - upper secondary	0.44	0.42	0.39	0.36	0.33	0.31
E6 - post-secondary	0.32	0.37	0.43	0.48	0.53	0.58
Mean years of schooling (in years)	12.65	13.19	13.66	14.09	14.49	14.87
Gender gap (population age 25+): highest educational attainment (ratio male/female)						
E1 - no education	NA	Inf	3.22	2.50	2.01	1.63
E2 - incomplete primary	NA	NA	0.36	0.46	0.57	0.69
E3 - primary	0.79	0.76	0.75	0.71	0.66	0.60
E4 - lower secondary	0.91	1.00	1.07	1.12	1.15	1.16
E5 - upper secondary	1.16	1.19	1.23	1.25	1.26	1.22
E6 - post-secondary	0.88	0.83	0.81	0.82	0.84	0.88
Mean years of schooling (male minus female)	−0.11	−0.28	−0.38	−0.42	−0.40	−0.32
Women age 20–39: highest educational attainment						
E1 - no education	0.00	0.00	0.00	0.00	0.00	0.00
E2 - incomplete primary	0.00	0.00	0.00	0.00	0.00	0.00
E3 - primary	0.00	0.00	0.00	0.00	0.00	0.00
E4 - lower secondary	0.18	0.16	0.13	0.11	0.09	0.08
E5 - upper secondary	0.37	0.35	0.34	0.34	0.35	0.35
E6 - post-secondary	0.44	0.49	0.53	0.55	0.56	0.57
Mean years of schooling (in years)	13.78	14.42	14.73	14.87	14.95	15.04

Education scenarios

GET: global education trend scenario (medium assumption also used for SSP2)

CER: constant enrolment rates scenario (assumption of no future improvements)

FT: Fast track scenario (assumption of education expansion according to fastest historical experience)

Pyramids by Education, Medium Scenario

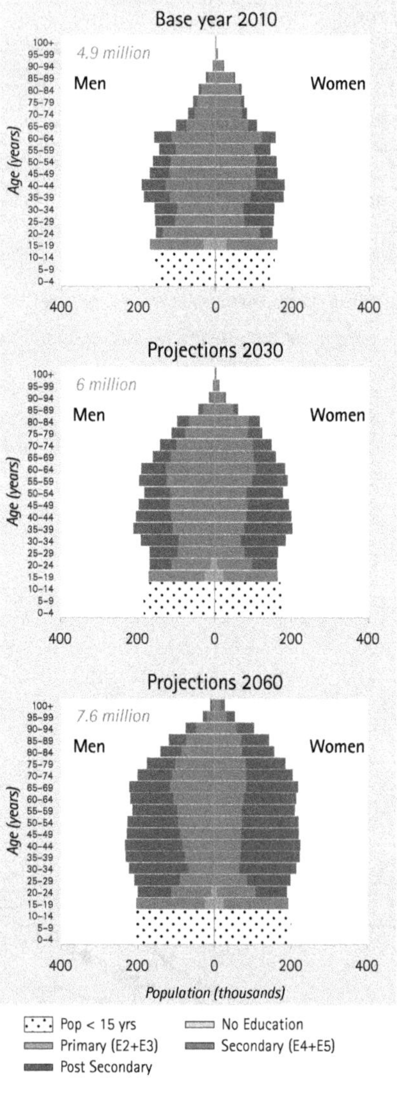

Population Size by Educational Attainment According to Three Education Scenarios: GET, CER, and FT

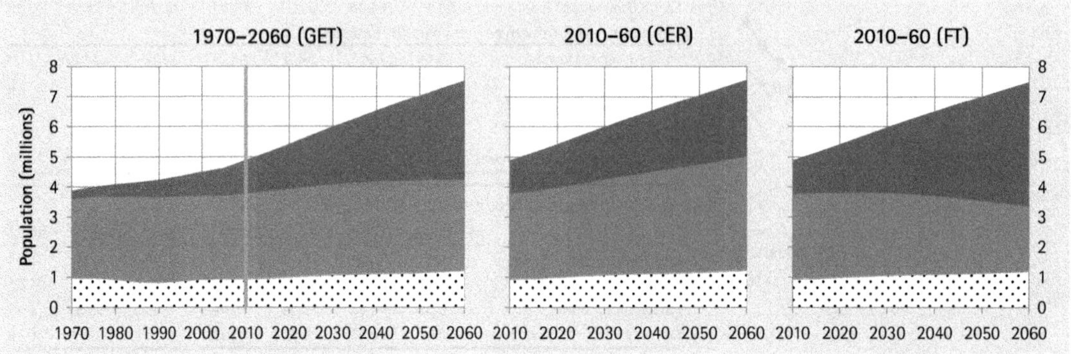

Norway (Continued)

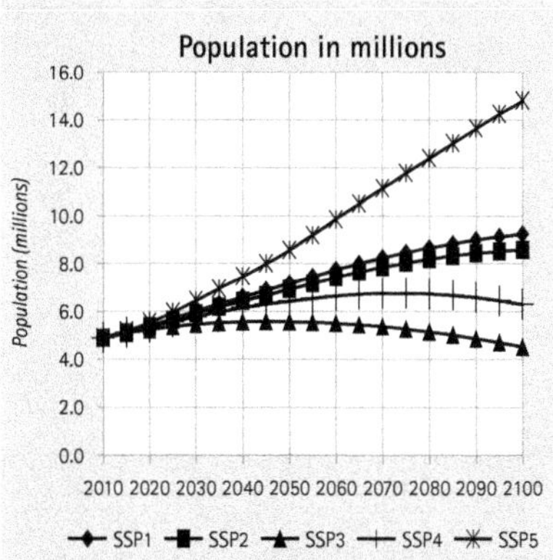

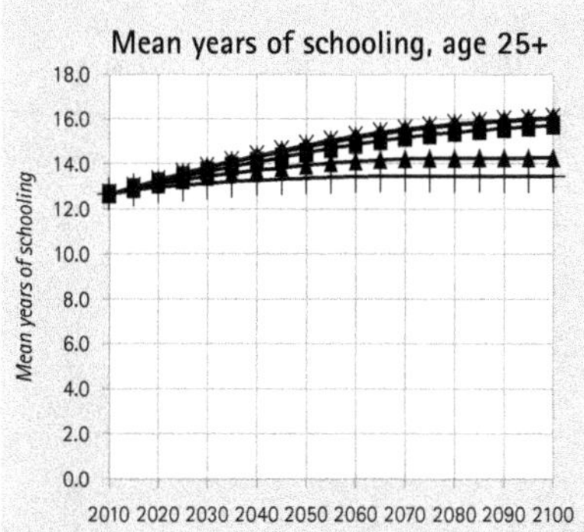

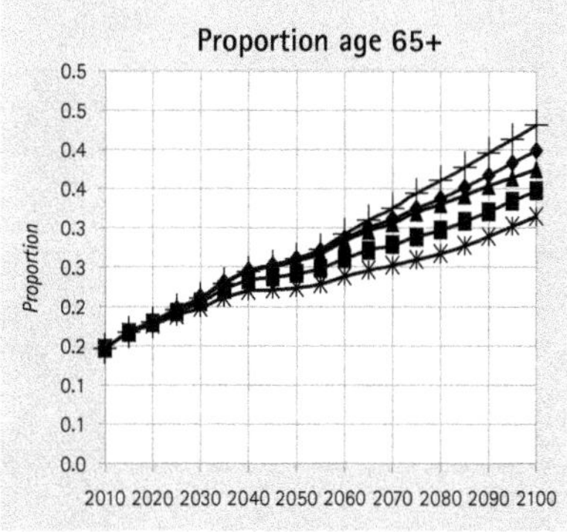

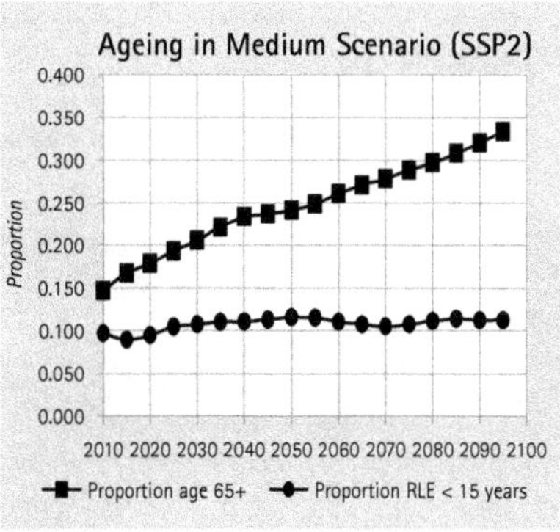

Alternative Scenarios to 2100

Projection Results by Scenario (SSP1-5)

	2010	2020	2030	2040	2050	2075	2100
Population (in millions)							
SSP1 - Rapid development	4.88	5.40	6.00	6.60	7.17	8.47	9.24
SSP2 - Medium	4.88	5.37	5.92	6.44	6.92	8.04	8.58
SSP3 - Stalled development	4.88	5.23	5.45	5.56	5.56	5.26	4.52
SSP4 - Inequality	4.88	5.33	5.78	6.15	6.43	6.76	6.29
SSP5 - Conventional development	4.88	5.53	6.45	7.46	8.56	11.77	14.80
Proportion age 65+							
SSP1 - Rapid development	0.15	0.18	0.21	0.25	0.26	0.32	0.40
SSP2 - Medium	0.15	0.18	0.21	0.23	0.24	0.29	0.35
SSP3 - Stalled development	0.15	0.18	0.21	0.25	0.26	0.32	0.38
SSP4 - Inequality	0.15	0.18	0.21	0.24	0.26	0.34	0.43
SSP5 - Conventional development	0.15	0.18	0.20	0.22	0.22	0.26	0.31
Proportion below age 20							
SSP1 - Rapid development	0.25	0.23	0.23	0.22	0.21	0.20	0.18
SSP2 - Medium	0.25	0.23	0.23	0.23	0.22	0.21	0.19
SSP3 - Stalled development	0.25	0.23	0.21	0.20	0.18	0.16	0.15
SSP4 - Inequality	0.25	0.23	0.21	0.20	0.18	0.16	0.13
SSP5 - Conventional development	0.25	0.24	0.25	0.26	0.25	0.25	0.23
Proportion of Women age 20-39 with at least secondary education							
SSP1 - Rapid development	1.00	1.00	1.00	1.00	1.00	1.00	1.00
SSP2 - Medium	1.00	1.00	1.00	1.00	1.00	1.00	1.00
SSP3 - Stalled development	1.00	1.00	1.00	1.00	1.00	1.00	1.00
SSP4 - Inequality	1.00	1.00	1.00	1.00	1.00	1.00	1.00
SSP5 - Conventional development	1.00	1.00	1.00	1.00	1.00	1.00	1.00
Mean years of schooling, age 25+							
SSP1 - Rapid development	12.65	13.26	13.82	14.31	14.75	15.61	16.02
SSP2 - Medium	12.65	13.19	13.66	14.09	14.49	15.30	15.72
SSP3 - Stalled development	12.65	13.10	13.44	13.71	13.94	14.25	14.27
SSP4 - Inequality	12.65	12.96	13.13	13.27	13.37	13.46	13.44
SSP5 - Conventional development	12.65	13.27	13.86	14.36	14.82	15.67	16.05

Demographic Assumptions Underlying SSPs

	2010–15	2020–25	2030–35	2040–45	2050–55	2075–80	2095–2100
Total fertility rate							
SSP1 - Rapid development	1.88	1.94	1.98	2.00	1.99	1.95	1.92
SSP2 - Medium	1.88	1.95	2.00	2.00	2.00	1.95	1.92
SSP3 - Stalled development	1.79	1.66	1.58	1.54	1.51	1.48	1.46
SSP4 - Inequality	1.79	1.67	1.59	1.56	1.53	1.50	1.48
SSP5 - Conventional development	1.98	2.23	2.41	2.47	2.49	2.44	2.40
Life expectancy at birth for females (in years)							
SSP1 - Rapid development	84.37	87.36	90.43	93.41	96.44	104.19	110.42
SSP2 - Medium	83.59	85.71	87.71	89.81	91.79	97.10	101.29
SSP3 - Stalled development	83.40	84.36	85.47	86.51	87.54	90.16	92.28
SSP4 - Inequality	83.86	85.93	87.90	89.97	91.91	96.97	101.00
SSP5 - Conventional development	84.37	87.36	90.43	93.41	96.44	104.19	110.42
Migration – net flow over five years (in thousands)							
SSP1 - Rapid development	146	138	141	140	134	56	0
SSP2 - Medium	142	134	138	139	137	63	0
SSP3 - Stalled development	122	68	69	67	64	27	0
SSP4 - Inequality	146	137	140	137	131	57	0
SSP5 - Conventional development	171	210	221	230	234	113	0

Ageing Indicators, Medium Scenario (SSP2)

	2010	2020	2030	2040	2050	2075	2095
Median age	38.78	39.95	40.76	42.50	43.42	46.24	49.67
Propspective median age	38.78	37.86	36.82	36.56	35.53	33.37	32.81
Proportion age 65+	0.15	0.18	0.21	0.23	0.24	0.29	0.33
Proportion RLE < 15 years	0.10	0.09	0.11	0.11	0.12	0.11	0.11

Occupied Palestinian Territory

Detailed Human Capital Projections to 2060

Demographic indicators, Medium Scenario (SSP2)						
	2010	2020	2030	2040	2050	2060
Population (in millions)	4.04	5.04	5.98	6.84	7.54	8.07
Proportion age 65+	0.03	0.03	0.05	0.07	0.10	0.13
Proportion below age 20	0.55	0.49	0.43	0.38	0.33	0.29
	2005–10	2015–20	2025–30	2035–40	2045–50	2055–60
Total Fertility Rate	4.65	3.59	2.86	2.44	2.16	1.98
Life expectancy at birth (in years)						
Men	70.60	72.61	74.97	77.41	79.91	81.88
Women	73.81	75.99	78.49	81.09	83.69	85.71
Five-year immigration flow (in '000)	0.07	0.07	0.07	0.07	0.07	0.07
Five-year emigration flow (in '000)	89.67	89.57	106.24	118.81	124.59	125.93

Human Capital indicators, Medium Scenario (SSP2)						
	2010	2020	2030	2040	2050	2060
Population age 25+: highest educational attainment						
E1 - no education	0.14	0.07	0.04	0.02	0.01	0.00
E2 - incomplete primary	0.10	0.07	0.04	0.02	0.01	0.01
E3 - primary	0.20	0.17	0.14	0.11	0.08	0.06
E4 - lower secondary	0.21	0.22	0.20	0.17	0.14	0.11
E5 - upper secondary	0.17	0.23	0.27	0.30	0.32	0.32
E6 - post-secondary	0.18	0.24	0.31	0.38	0.44	0.50
Mean years of schooling (in years)	8.26	9.79	11.02	11.95	12.67	13.24
Gender gap (population age 25+): highest educational attainment (ratio male/female)						
E1 - no education	0.33	0.30	0.30	0.33	0.39	0.46
E2 - incomplete primary	1.08	0.93	0.81	0.72	0.67	0.65
E3 - primary	1.06	1.00	0.96	0.93	0.90	0.88
E4 - lower secondary	1.05	1.02	1.02	1.02	1.01	0.99
E5 - upper secondary	1.16	1.04	0.98	0.97	0.97	0.97
E6 - post-secondary	1.61	1.34	1.19	1.11	1.07	1.05
Mean years of schooling (male minus female)	1.82	1.24	0.80	0.49	0.32	0.21
Women age 20–39: highest educational attainment						
E1 - no education	0.03	0.01	0.00	0.00	0.00	0.00
E2 - incomplete primary	0.07	0.03	0.01	0.01	0.00	0.00
E3 - primary	0.20	0.14	0.09	0.05	0.03	0.02
E4 - lower secondary	0.29	0.26	0.20	0.14	0.10	0.08
E5 - upper secondary	0.25	0.34	0.40	0.43	0.43	0.43
E6 - post-secondary	0.16	0.23	0.31	0.37	0.43	0.48
Mean years of schooling (in years)	9.59	11.07	12.08	12.79	13.30	13.63

Education scenarios

GET: global education trend scenario (medium assumption also used for SSP2)

CER: constant enrolment rates scenario (assumption of no future improvements)

FT: Fast track scenario (assumption of education expansion according to fastest historical experience)

Pyramids by Education, Medium Scenario

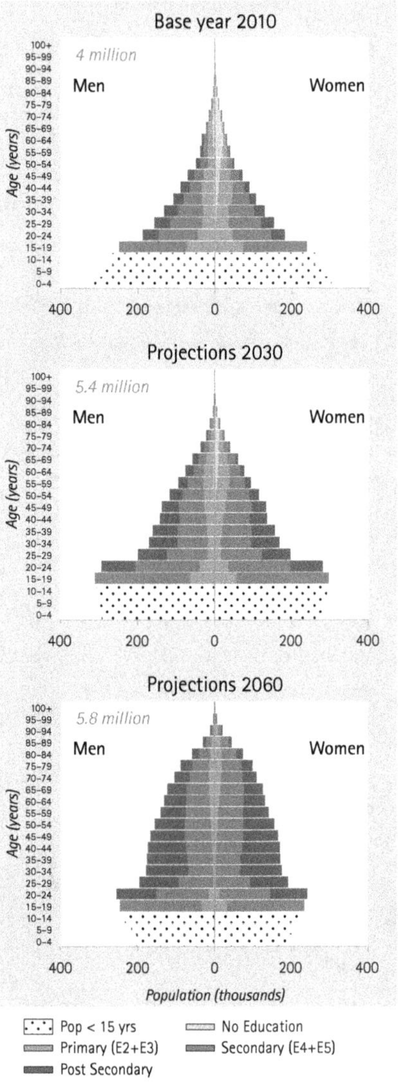

Population size by educational attainment according to three education scenarios: GET, CER, and FT

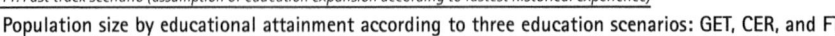

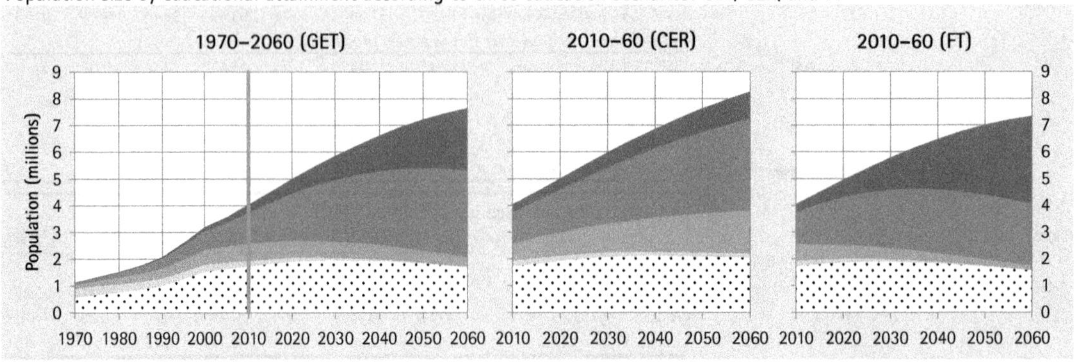

Occupied Palestinian Territory (Continued)

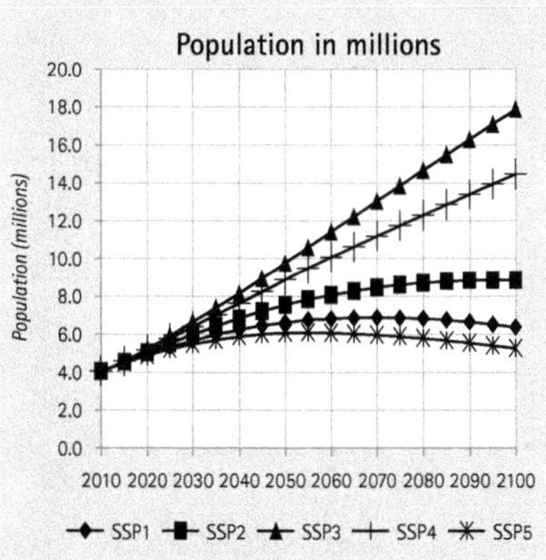

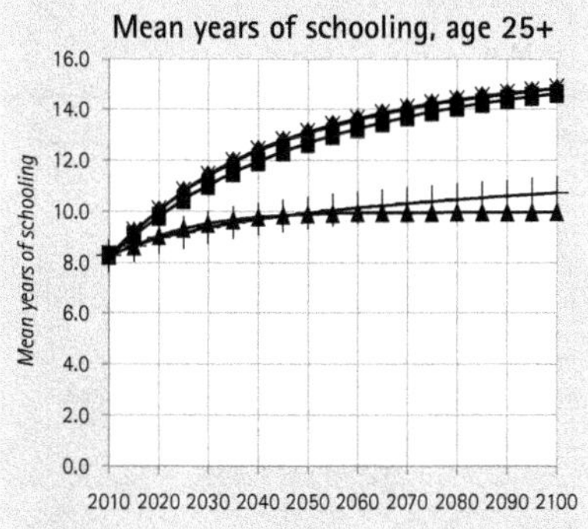

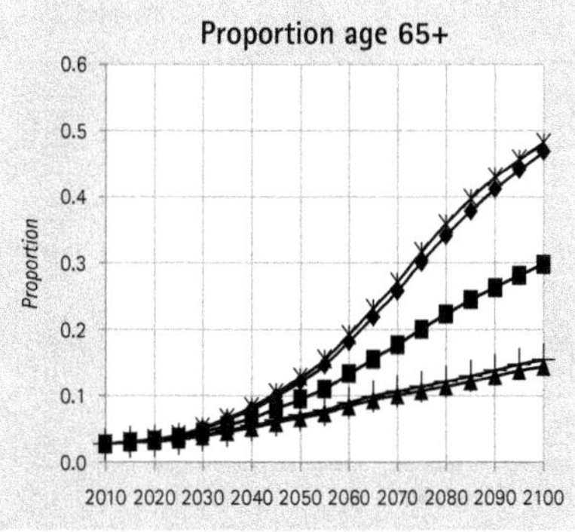

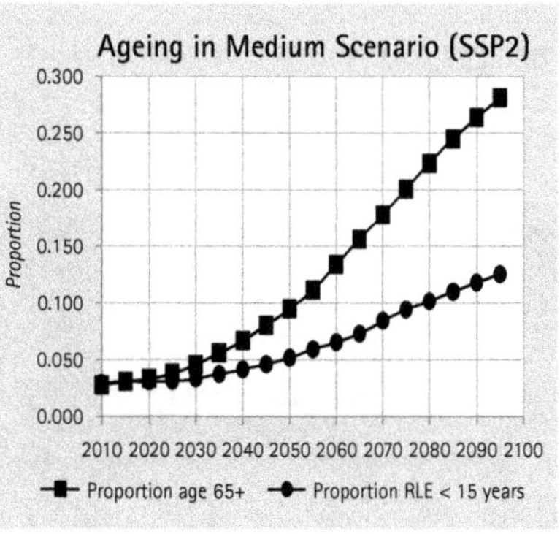

Alternative Scenarios to 2100

Projection Results by Scenario (SSP1–5)

	2010	2020	2030	2040	2050	2075	2100
Population (in millions)							
SSP1 - Rapid development	4.04	4.93	5.66	6.24	6.62	6.86	6.35
SSP2 - Medium	4.04	5.04	5.98	6.84	7.54	8.61	8.86
SSP3 - Stalled development	4.04	5.22	6.66	8.16	9.77	13.86	17.88
SSP4 - Inequality	4.04	5.15	6.40	7.63	8.88	11.75	14.46
SSP5 - Conventional development	4.04	4.88	5.47	5.87	6.06	5.87	5.25
Proportion age 65+							
SSP1 - Rapid development	0.03	0.03	0.05	0.08	0.12	0.30	0.47
SSP2 - Medium	0.03	0.03	0.05	0.07	0.10	0.20	0.30
SSP3 - Stalled development	0.03	0.03	0.04	0.05	0.07	0.11	0.15
SSP4 - Inequality	0.03	0.03	0.04	0.06	0.07	0.11	0.15
SSP5 - Conventional development	0.03	0.04	0.05	0.08	0.13	0.32	0.48
Proportion below age 20							
SSP1 - Rapid development	0.55	0.48	0.39	0.32	0.26	0.16	0.11
SSP2 - Medium	0.55	0.49	0.43	0.38	0.33	0.24	0.19
SSP3 - Stalled development	0.55	0.50	0.47	0.44	0.40	0.35	0.31
SSP4 - Inequality	0.55	0.50	0.47	0.43	0.40	0.33	0.29
SSP5 - Conventional development	0.55	0.48	0.40	0.32	0.27	0.16	0.11
Proportion of Women age 20–39 with at least secondary education							
SSP1 - Rapid development	0.70	0.87	0.94	0.97	0.98	1.00	1.00
SSP2 - Medium	0.70	0.83	0.90	0.94	0.97	0.99	1.00
SSP3 - Stalled development	0.70	0.69	0.70	0.70	0.70	0.70	0.70
SSP4 - Inequality	0.70	0.65	0.63	0.63	0.63	0.63	0.63
SSP5 - Conventional development	0.70	0.87	0.94	0.97	0.98	1.00	1.00
Mean years of schooling, age 25+							
SSP1 - Rapid development	8.26	10.05	11.42	12.41	13.11	14.23	14.84
SSP2 - Medium	8.26	9.79	11.02	11.95	12.67	13.90	14.62
SSP3 - Stalled development	8.26	9.03	9.52	9.77	9.89	9.96	9.98
SSP4 - Inequality	8.26	8.96	9.37	9.69	9.94	10.39	10.73
SSP5 - Conventional development	8.26	10.03	11.38	12.37	13.06	14.19	14.82

Demographic Assumptions Underlying SSPs

	2010–15	2020–25	2030–35	2040–45	2050–55	2075–80	2095–2100
Total fertility rate							
SSP1 - Rapid development	3.81	2.67	2.02	1.70	1.51	1.31	1.22
SSP2 - Medium	4.09	3.15	2.63	2.27	2.05	1.76	1.63
SSP3 - Stalled development	4.30	3.92	3.52	3.18	2.95	2.60	2.43
SSP4 - Inequality	4.28	3.86	3.42	3.06	2.82	2.45	2.28
SSP5 - Conventional development	3.81	2.67	2.02	1.70	1.51	1.31	1.22
Life expectancy at birth for females (in years)							
SSP1 - Rapid development	76.75	79.70	82.94	86.52	89.71	96.68	102.34
SSP2 - Medium	74.80	77.19	79.79	82.49	84.81	89.40	93.10
SSP3 - Stalled development	75.95	76.94	78.21	79.76	80.76	82.18	83.53
SSP4 - Inequality	75.95	76.93	78.19	79.74	80.74	82.21	83.65
SSP5 - Conventional development	76.75	79.70	82.94	86.52	89.71	96.68	102.34
Migration – net flow over five years (in thousands)							
SSP1 - Rapid development	−86	−97	−110	−114	−111	−43	0
SSP2 - Medium	−87	−99	−115	−124	−128	−57	0
SSP3 - Stalled development	−72	−49	−57	−65	−72	−40	0
SSP4 - Inequality	−86	−98	−116	−132	−143	−75	0
SSP5 - Conventional development	−100	−147	−168	−177	−174	−71	0

Ageing Indicators, Medium Scenario (SSP2)

	2010	2020	2030	2040	2050	2075	2095
Median age	17.98	20.57	23.50	27.04	30.92	40.54	46.89
Propspective median age	17.98	18.73	19.44	20.58	22.45	28.09	31.09
Proportion age 65+	0.03	0.03	0.05	0.07	0.10	0.20	0.28
Proportion RLE < 15 years	0.03	0.03	0.03	0.04	0.05	0.09	0.13

Pakistan

Detailed Human Capital Projections to 2060

Demographic indicators, Medium Scenario (SSP2)	2010	2020	2030	2040	2050	2060
Population (in millions)	173.59	206.52	237.24	263.76	286.35	301.69
Proportion age 65+	0.04	0.05	0.06	0.07	0.10	0.13
Proportion below age 20	0.47	0.42	0.39	0.34	0.31	0.28
	2005-10	2015-20	2025-30	2035-40	2045-50	2055-60
Total Fertility Rate	3.65	3.07	2.65	2.40	2.19	1.99
Life expectancy at birth (in years)						
Men	63.78	65.28	67.03	68.85	70.70	72.73
Women	65.42	67.62	69.88	72.12	74.18	76.39
Five-year immigration flow (in '000)	43.67	42.63	44.19	45.04	44.93	44.21
Five-year emigration flow (in '000)	2028.65	1808.09	1958.58	2107.09	2174.74	2172.43

Human Capital indicators, Medium Scenario (SSP2)	2010	2020	2030	2040	2050	2060
Population age 25+: highest educational attainment						
E1 - no education	0.57	0.49	0.41	0.34	0.27	0.20
E2 - incomplete primary	0.05	0.04	0.04	0.03	0.03	0.02
E3 - primary	0.10	0.11	0.12	0.12	0.12	0.12
E4 - lower secondary	0.09	0.11	0.11	0.12	0.12	0.12
E5 - upper secondary	0.14	0.18	0.23	0.29	0.34	0.40
E6 - post-secondary	0.05	0.07	0.08	0.10	0.12	0.14
Mean years of schooling (in years)	3.78	4.76	5.73	6.72	7.74	8.70
Gender gap (population age 25+): highest educational attainment (ratio male/female)						
E1 - no education	0.65	0.65	0.66	0.68	0.70	0.72
E2 - incomplete primary	1.51	1.48	1.36	1.26	1.17	1.09
E3 - primary	1.49	1.28	1.16	1.09	1.04	1.01
E4 - lower secondary	2.26	1.84	1.61	1.44	1.31	1.20
E5 - upper secondary	1.82	1.44	1.25	1.14	1.08	1.05
E6 - post-secondary	2.01	1.75	1.55	1.39	1.26	1.17
Mean years of schooling (male minus female)	2.26	2.02	1.71	1.37	1.04	0.78
Women age 20-39: highest educational attainment						
E1 - no education	0.56	0.44	0.32	0.22	0.14	0.08
E2 - incomplete primary	0.04	0.03	0.02	0.02	0.01	0.01
E3 - primary	0.11	0.12	0.13	0.13	0.12	0.10
E4 - lower secondary	0.08	0.10	0.11	0.11	0.11	0.10
E5 - upper secondary	0.17	0.25	0.33	0.41	0.49	0.54
E6 - post-secondary	0.05	0.07	0.09	0.11	0.15	0.18
Mean years of schooling (in years)	4.05	5.51	6.97	8.43	9.67	10.72

Education scenarios

GET: global education trend scenario (medium assumption also used for SSP2)

CER: constant enrolment rates scenario (assumption of no future improvements)

FT: Fast track scenario (assumption of education expansion according to fastest historical experience)

Pyramids by Education, Medium Scenario

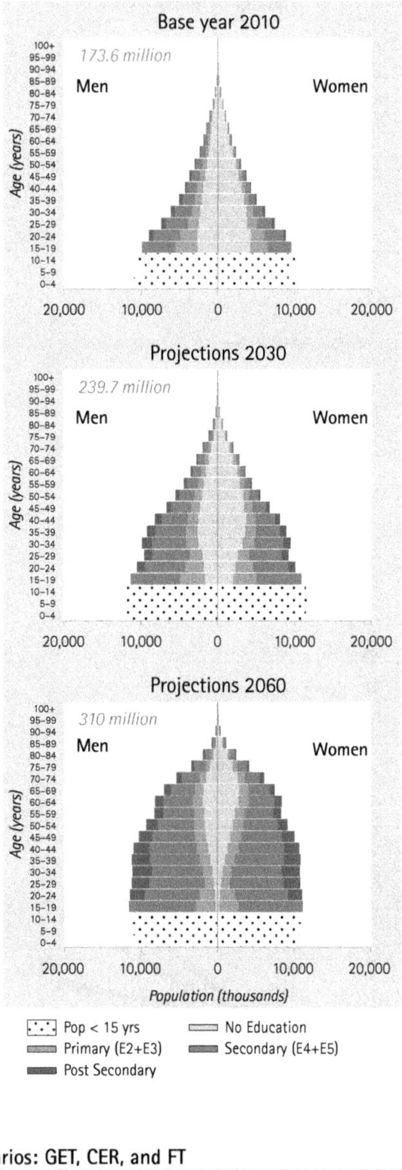

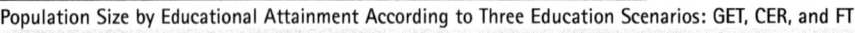

Population Size by Educational Attainment According to Three Education Scenarios: GET, CER, and FT

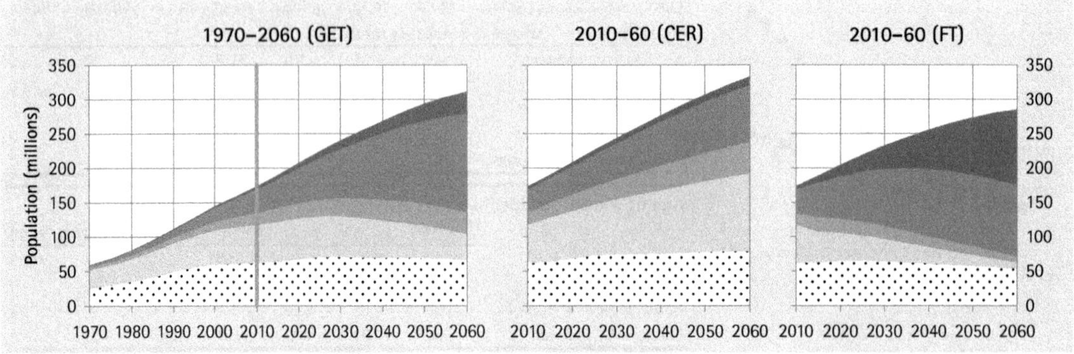

Pakistan (Continued)

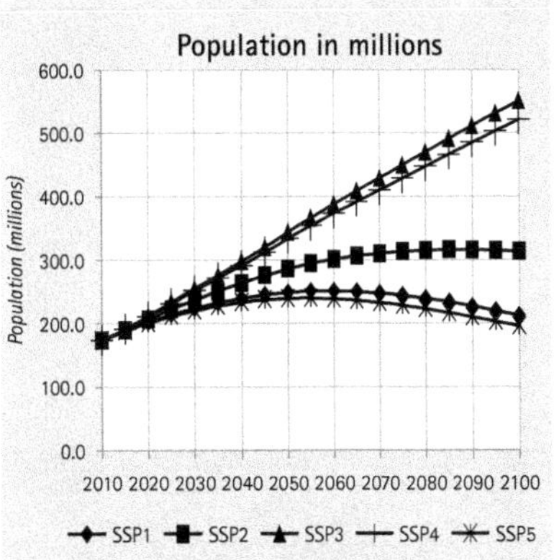

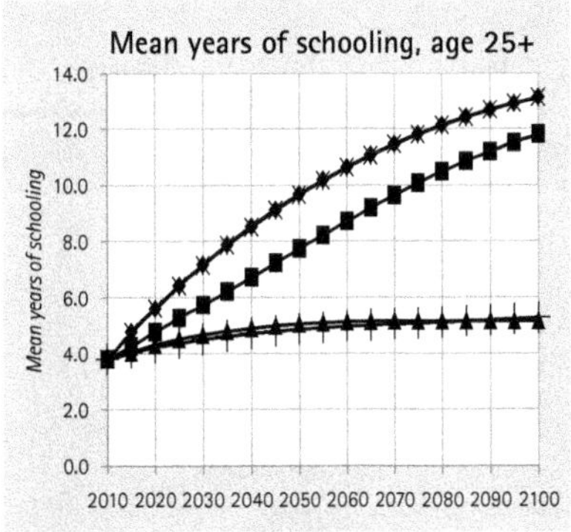

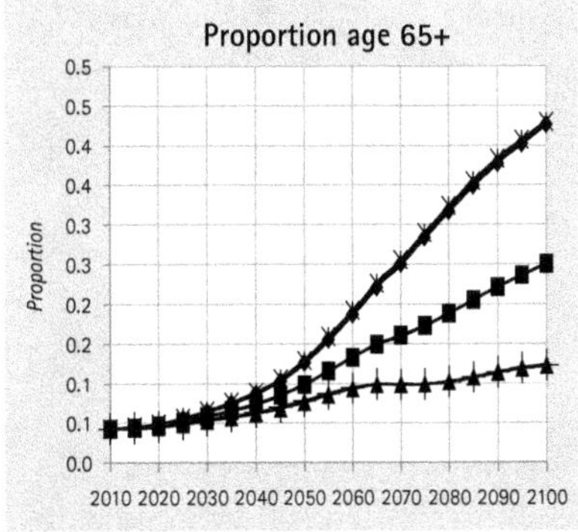

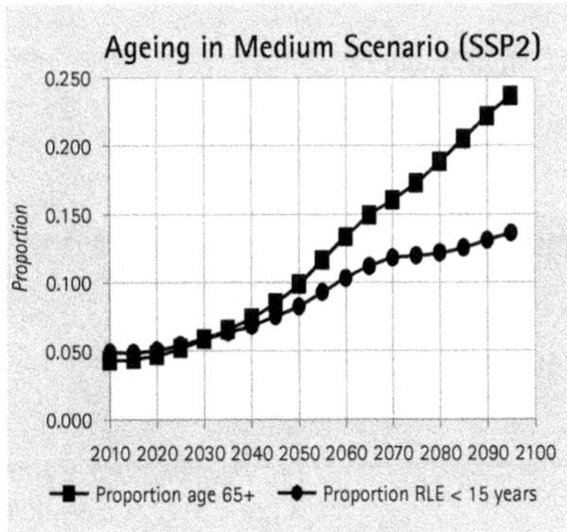

Alternative Scenarios to 2100

Projection Results by Scenario (SSP1-5)

	2010	2020	2030	2040	2050	2075	2100
Population (in millions)							
SSP1 - Rapid development	173.59	202.00	223.81	239.42	248.62	243.97	212.16
SSP2 - Medium	173.59	206.52	237.24	263.76	286.35	313.69	313.97
SSP3 - Stalled development	173.59	211.83	255.17	298.14	344.12	449.70	550.59
SSP4 - Inequality	173.59	210.89	251.90	291.81	333.95	428.47	521.04
SSP5 - Conventional development	173.59	200.98	220.40	233.23	239.38	228.13	195.47
Proportion age 65+							
SSP1 - Rapid development	0.04	0.05	0.06	0.09	0.13	0.28	0.43
SSP2 - Medium	0.04	0.05	0.06	0.07	0.10	0.17	0.25
SSP3 - Stalled development	0.04	0.05	0.05	0.06	0.08	0.10	0.12
SSP4 - Inequality	0.04	0.05	0.05	0.06	0.08	0.10	0.12
SSP5 - Conventional development	0.04	0.05	0.07	0.09	0.13	0.29	0.43
Proportion below age 20							
SSP1 - Rapid development	0.47	0.40	0.34	0.28	0.24	0.16	0.11
SSP2 - Medium	0.47	0.42	0.39	0.34	0.31	0.24	0.20
SSP3 - Stalled development	0.47	0.43	0.42	0.40	0.38	0.34	0.31
SSP4 - Inequality	0.47	0.43	0.43	0.40	0.38	0.34	0.31
SSP5 - Conventional development	0.47	0.40	0.35	0.29	0.24	0.16	0.11
Proportion of Women age 20-39 with at least secondary education							
SSP1 - Rapid development	0.30	0.54	0.69	0.78	0.85	0.94	0.98
SSP2 - Medium	0.30	0.41	0.52	0.64	0.74	0.90	0.97
SSP3 - Stalled development	0.30	0.28	0.28	0.28	0.28	0.28	0.28
SSP4 - Inequality	0.30	0.26	0.25	0.25	0.25	0.25	0.25
SSP5 - Conventional development	0.30	0.54	0.69	0.78	0.85	0.94	0.98
Mean years of schooling, age 25+							
SSP1 - Rapid development	3.78	5.60	7.16	8.53	9.68	11.81	13.13
SSP2 - Medium	3.78	4.76	5.73	6.72	7.74	10.07	11.80
SSP3 - Stalled development	3.78	4.30	4.66	4.89	5.04	5.14	5.15
SSP4 - Inequality	3.78	4.22	4.49	4.70	4.85	5.06	5.26
SSP5 - Conventional development	3.78	5.59	7.14	8.49	9.64	11.79	13.12

Demographic assumptions underlying SSPs

	2010–15	2020–25	2030–35	2040–45	2050–55	2075–80	2095–2100
Total fertility rate							
SSP1 - Rapid development	3.08	2.29	1.85	1.62	1.47	1.28	1.20
SSP2 - Medium	3.32	2.85	2.52	2.29	2.08	1.77	1.64
SSP3 - Stalled development	3.52	3.48	3.35	3.17	2.98	2.63	2.51
SSP4 - Inequality	3.53	3.50	3.36	3.18	2.97	2.60	2.47
SSP5 - Conventional development	3.08	2.29	1.85	1.62	1.47	1.28	1.20
Life expectancy at birth for females (in years)							
SSP1 - Rapid development	70.85	73.17	76.11	78.91	81.75	89.31	95.30
SSP2 - Medium	66.52	68.68	71.02	73.12	75.28	80.91	85.40
SSP3 - Stalled development	70.36	70.90	71.93	72.80	73.48	75.28	76.73
SSP4 - Inequality	70.36	70.89	71.91	72.77	73.44	75.21	76.68
SSP5 - Conventional development	70.85	73.17	76.11	78.91	81.75	89.31	95.30
Migration – net flow over five years (in thousands)							
SSP1 - Rapid development	−1775	−1820	−1921	−1926	−1823	−697	0
SSP2 - Medium	−1763	−1835	−1988	−2114	−2142	−984	0
SSP3 - Stalled development	−1477	−908	−983	−1074	−1134	−602	0
SSP4 - Inequality	−1774	−1839	−2032	−2265	−2423	−1282	0
SSP5 - Conventional development	−2071	−2763	−2984	−3084	−3026	−1286	0

Ageing Indicators, Medium Scenario (SSP2)

	2010	2020	2030	2040	2050	2075	2095
Median age	21.61	24.32	26.89	29.49	32.41	39.26	44.36
Propspective median age	21.61	23.19	24.61	26.07	27.76	30.90	32.47
Proportion age 65+	0.04	0.05	0.06	0.07	0.10	0.17	0.24
Proportion RLE < 15 years	0.05	0.05	0.06	0.07	0.08	0.12	0.14

Panama

Detailed Human Capital Projections to 2060

Demographic indicators, Medium Scenario (SSP2)	2010	2020	2030	2040	2050	2060
Population (in millions)	3.52	4.03	4.50	4.90	5.18	5.36
Proportion age 65+	0.07	0.09	0.12	0.16	0.19	0.23
Proportion below age 20	0.38	0.33	0.29	0.26	0.24	0.21
	2005-10	2015-20	2025-30	2035-40	2045-50	2055-60
Total Fertility Rate	2.56	2.18	2.01	1.90	1.79	1.71
Life expectancy at birth (in years)						
Men	72.99	75.64	78.10	80.27	82.18	84.19
Women	78.21	80.80	83.09	85.21	87.21	89.31
Five-year immigration flow (in '000)	28.77	28.20	29.28	29.94	29.95	29.52
Five-year emigration flow (in '000)	17.80	14.54	15.24	15.16	14.86	14.36

Human Capital indicators, Medium Scenario (SSP2)	2010	2020	2030	2040	2050	2060
Population age 25+: highest educational attainment						
E1 - no education	0.07	0.05	0.03	0.02	0.02	0.01
E2 - incomplete primary	0.10	0.07	0.05	0.04	0.03	0.02
E3 - primary	0.26	0.23	0.20	0.17	0.14	0.11
E4 - lower secondary	0.12	0.13	0.13	0.12	0.11	0.09
E5 - upper secondary	0.25	0.28	0.31	0.33	0.34	0.35
E6 - post-secondary	0.20	0.24	0.28	0.32	0.37	0.41
Mean years of schooling (in years)	9.41	10.19	10.90	11.52	12.07	12.58
Gender gap (population age 25+): highest educational attainment (ratio male/female)						
E1 - no education	0.81	0.76	0.72	0.70	0.69	0.68
E2 - incomplete primary	1.10	1.08	1.06	1.04	1.01	0.96
E3 - primary	1.17	1.18	1.18	1.17	1.15	1.11
E4 - lower secondary	1.14	1.16	1.17	1.16	1.15	1.12
E5 - upper secondary	1.02	1.07	1.10	1.12	1.12	1.10
E6 - post-secondary	0.75	0.76	0.77	0.79	0.83	0.88
Mean years of schooling (male minus female)	-0.39	-0.41	-0.42	-0.40	-0.35	-0.25
Women age 20–39: highest educational attainment						
E1 - no education	0.04	0.02	0.01	0.00	0.00	0.00
E2 - incomplete primary	0.05	0.03	0.02	0.01	0.00	0.00
E3 - primary	0.19	0.15	0.12	0.09	0.07	0.05
E4 - lower secondary	0.13	0.13	0.11	0.09	0.07	0.06
E5 - upper secondary	0.33	0.36	0.39	0.41	0.42	0.43
E6 - post-secondary	0.26	0.30	0.35	0.40	0.43	0.46
Mean years of schooling (in years)	10.78	11.57	12.25	12.79	13.17	13.46

Education scenarios

GET: global education trend scenario (medium assumption also used for SSP2)

CER: constant enrolment rates scenario (assumption of no future improvements)

FT: Fast Track scenario (assumption of education expansion according to fastest historical experience)

Pyramids by Education, Medium Scenario

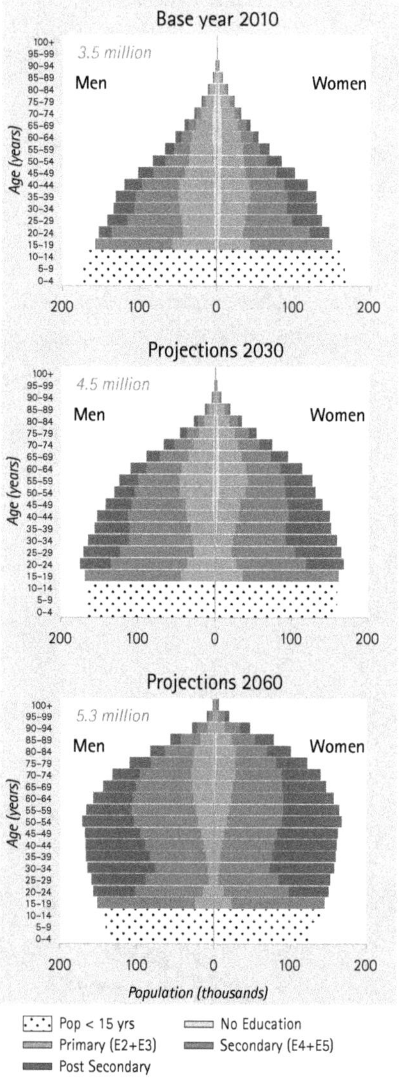

Population Size by Educational Attainment According to Three Education Scenarios: GET, CER, and FT

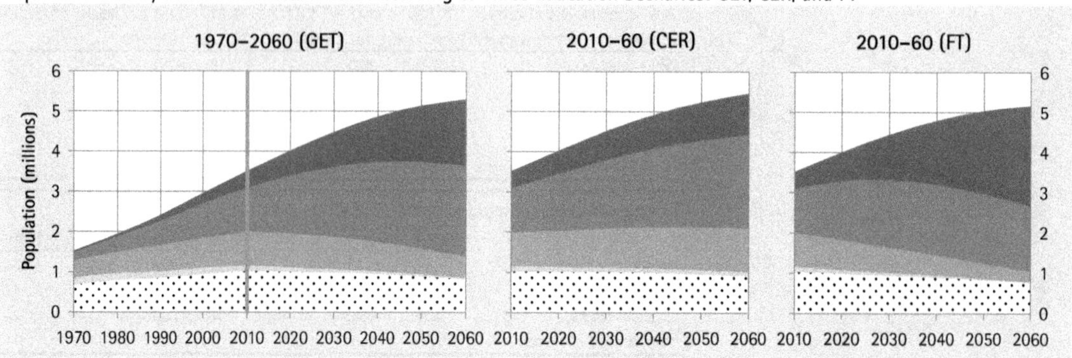

Panama (Continued)

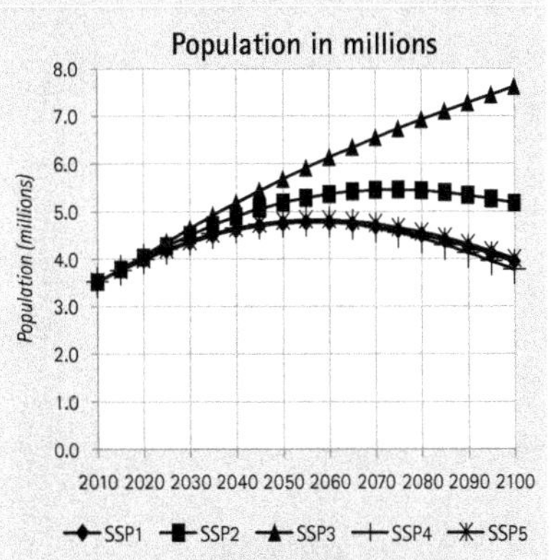

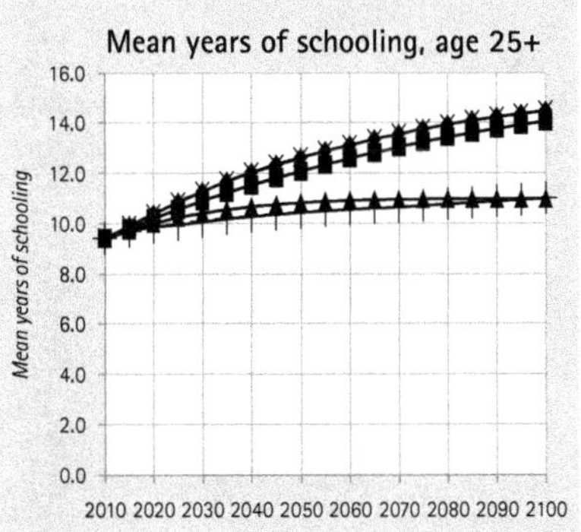

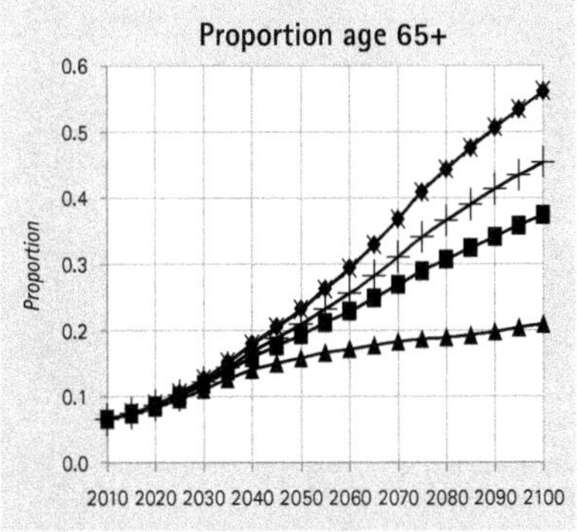

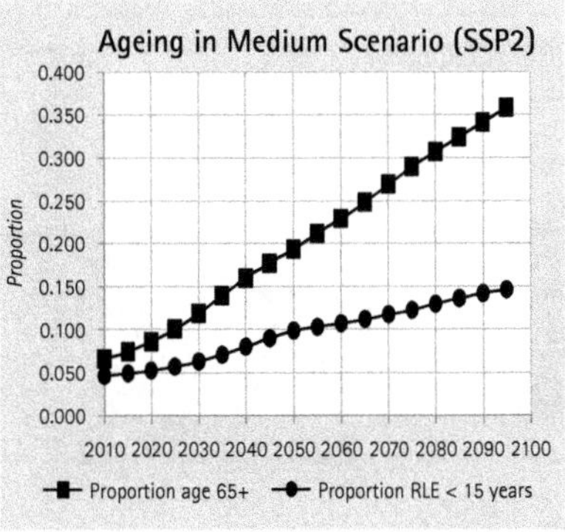

Alternative Scenarios to 2100

Projection Results by Scenario (SSP1–5)

	2010	2020	2030	2040	2050	2075	2100
Population (in millions)							
SSP1 - Rapid development	3.52	3.98	4.35	4.61	4.75	4.60	3.94
SSP2 - Medium	3.52	4.03	4.50	4.90	5.18	5.45	5.17
SSP3 - Stalled development	3.52	4.07	4.64	5.18	5.68	6.74	7.61
SSP4 - Inequality	3.52	3.99	4.38	4.65	4.78	4.55	3.77
SSP5 - Conventional development	3.52	3.99	4.37	4.65	4.79	4.66	4.00
Proportion age 65+							
SSP1 - Rapid development	0.07	0.09	0.13	0.18	0.23	0.41	0.56
SSP2 - Medium	0.07	0.09	0.12	0.16	0.19	0.29	0.37
SSP3 - Stalled development	0.07	0.08	0.11	0.14	0.16	0.19	0.21
SSP4 - Inequality	0.07	0.09	0.12	0.17	0.21	0.34	0.45
SSP5 - Conventional development	0.07	0.09	0.13	0.18	0.23	0.41	0.56
Proportion below age 20							
SSP1 - Rapid development	0.38	0.32	0.26	0.22	0.18	0.11	0.08
SSP2 - Medium	0.38	0.33	0.29	0.26	0.24	0.19	0.15
SSP3 - Stalled development	0.38	0.34	0.32	0.31	0.30	0.28	0.26
SSP4 - Inequality	0.38	0.33	0.27	0.23	0.20	0.14	0.11
SSP5 - Conventional development	0.38	0.32	0.26	0.21	0.18	0.11	0.08
Proportion of Women age 20–39 with at least secondary education							
SSP1 - Rapid development	0.72	0.85	0.91	0.94	0.96	0.98	0.99
SSP2 - Medium	0.72	0.80	0.85	0.89	0.93	0.98	0.99
SSP3 - Stalled development	0.72	0.77	0.77	0.77	0.77	0.77	0.77
SSP4 - Inequality	0.72	0.72	0.69	0.69	0.69	0.69	0.69
SSP5 - Conventional development	0.72	0.85	0.91	0.94	0.96	0.98	0.99
Mean years of schooling, age 25+							
SSP1 - Rapid development	9.41	10.38	11.27	12.02	12.61	13.75	14.47
SSP2 - Medium	9.41	10.19	10.90	11.52	12.07	13.24	14.04
SSP3 - Stalled development	9.41	10.01	10.41	10.67	10.83	10.97	10.98
SSP4 - Inequality	9.41	9.85	10.08	10.28	10.43	10.71	11.01
SSP5 - Conventional development	9.41	10.38	11.28	12.02	12.61	13.75	14.47

Demographic Assumptions Underlying SSPs

	2010–15	2020–25	2030–35	2040–45	2050–55	2075–80	2095–2100
Total fertility rate							
SSP1 - Rapid development	2.18	1.73	1.49	1.38	1.30	1.21	1.21
SSP2 - Medium	2.33	2.08	1.94	1.85	1.75	1.63	1.62
SSP3 - Stalled development	2.44	2.48	2.47	2.41	2.34	2.22	2.22
SSP4 - Inequality	2.22	1.87	1.63	1.49	1.40	1.32	1.31
SSP5 - Conventional development	2.18	1.73	1.49	1.38	1.30	1.21	1.21
Life expectancy at birth for females (in years)							
SSP1 - Rapid development	81.02	83.98	86.99	89.93	92.93	100.49	106.53
SSP2 - Medium	79.50	81.99	84.19	86.21	88.21	93.29	97.29
SSP3 - Stalled development	80.23	81.32	82.33	83.27	84.19	86.22	87.90
SSP4 - Inequality	80.55	82.74	84.67	86.51	88.38	92.99	96.72
SSP5 - Conventional development	81.02	83.98	86.99	89.93	92.93	100.49	106.53
Migration – net flow over five years (in thousands)							
SSP1 - Rapid development	12	14	14	13	12	4	0
SSP2 - Medium	13	14	15	15	15	7	0
SSP3 - Stalled development	10	7	8	9	11	8	0
SSP4 - Inequality	12	14	14	14	14	6	0
SSP5 - Conventional development	14	20	20	18	16	5	0

Ageing Indicators, Medium Scenario (SSP2)

	2010	2020	2030	2040	2050	2075	2095
Median age	27.29	30.41	33.64	37.12	40.53	47.78	53.25
Propspective median age	27.29	28.34	29.78	31.65	33.42	36.26	38.24
Proportion age 65+	0.07	0.09	0.12	0.16	0.19	0.29	0.36
Proportion RLE < 15 years	0.05	0.05	0.06	0.08	0.10	0.12	0.15

Paraguay

Detailed Human Capital Projections to 2060

Demographic indicators, Medium Scenario (SSP2)	2010	2020	2030	2040	2050	2060
Population (in millions)	6.45	7.53	8.49	9.30	9.90	10.31
Proportion age 65+	0.05	0.07	0.08	0.10	0.14	0.19
Proportion below age 20	0.44	0.39	0.34	0.30	0.27	0.24
	2005–10	2015–20	2025–30	2035–40	2045–50	2055–60
Total Fertility Rate	3.08	2.50	2.17	2.00	1.85	1.76
Life expectancy at birth (in years)						
Men	69.67	72.00	74.19	76.24	78.40	80.38
Women	73.91	76.09	78.20	80.19	82.29	84.29
Five-year immigration flow (in '000)	6.18	6.04	6.26	6.40	6.40	6.30
Five-year emigration flow (in '000)	45.94	39.78	42.66	43.73	43.34	42.03

Human Capital indicators, Medium Scenario (SSP2)	2010	2020	2030	2040	2050	2060
Population age 25+: highest educational attainment						
E1 - no education	0.04	0.03	0.02	0.01	0.01	0.01
E2 - incomplete primary	0.26	0.19	0.14	0.10	0.06	0.04
E3 - primary	0.31	0.31	0.30	0.28	0.26	0.23
E4 - lower secondary	0.12	0.13	0.14	0.13	0.13	0.11
E5 - upper secondary	0.14	0.18	0.22	0.25	0.28	0.31
E6 - post-secondary	0.13	0.16	0.19	0.22	0.26	0.29
Mean years of schooling (in years)	7.77	8.64	9.41	10.09	10.71	11.27
Gender gap (population age 25+): highest educational attainment (ratio male/female)						
E1 - no education	0.70	0.72	0.74	0.74	0.75	0.74
E2 - incomplete primary	0.96	0.94	0.92	0.90	0.88	0.86
E3 - primary	1.07	1.07	1.07	1.07	1.06	1.04
E4 - lower secondary	1.19	1.21	1.19	1.17	1.14	1.10
E5 - upper secondary	1.07	1.07	1.08	1.08	1.08	1.06
E6 - post-secondary	0.82	0.79	0.79	0.82	0.85	0.90
Mean years of schooling (male minus female)	0.00	−0.12	−0.18	−0.21	−0.19	−0.12
Women age 20–39: highest educational attainment						
E1 - no education	0.02	0.02	0.01	0.01	0.01	0.01
E2 - incomplete primary	0.14	0.09	0.05	0.03	0.01	0.01
E3 - primary	0.30	0.29	0.26	0.22	0.18	0.14
E4 - lower secondary	0.14	0.13	0.12	0.10	0.08	0.07
E5 - upper secondary	0.22	0.26	0.30	0.34	0.38	0.41
E6 - post-secondary	0.18	0.22	0.26	0.31	0.34	0.37
Mean years of schooling (in years)	9.35	10.07	10.84	11.50	12.06	12.51

Education scenarios

GET: global education trend scenario (medium assumption also used for SSP2)

CER: constant enrolment rates scenario (assumption of no future improvements)

FT: Fast track scenario (assumption of education expansion according to fastest historical experience)

Pyramids by Education, Medium Scenario

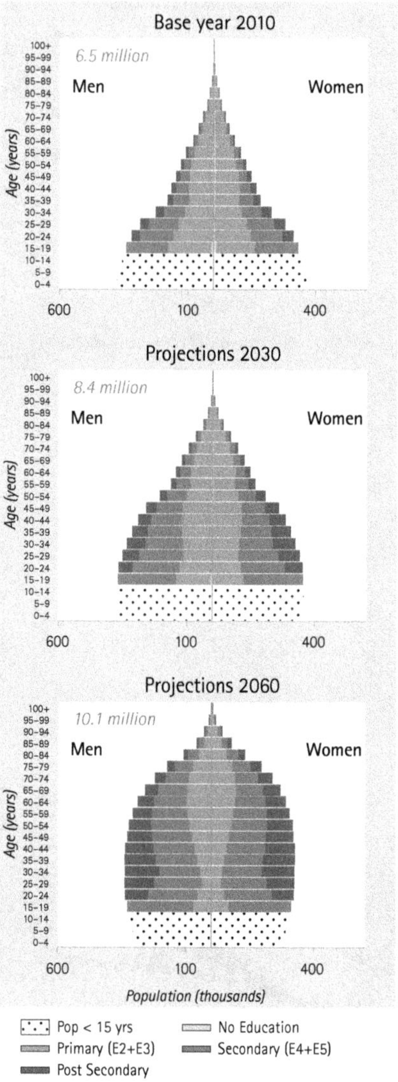

Population Size by Educational Attainment According to Three Education Scenarios: GET, CER, and FT

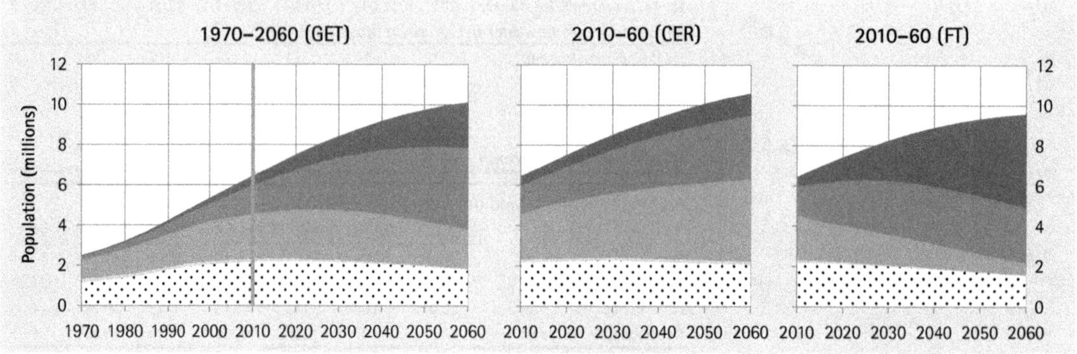

Paraguay (Continued)

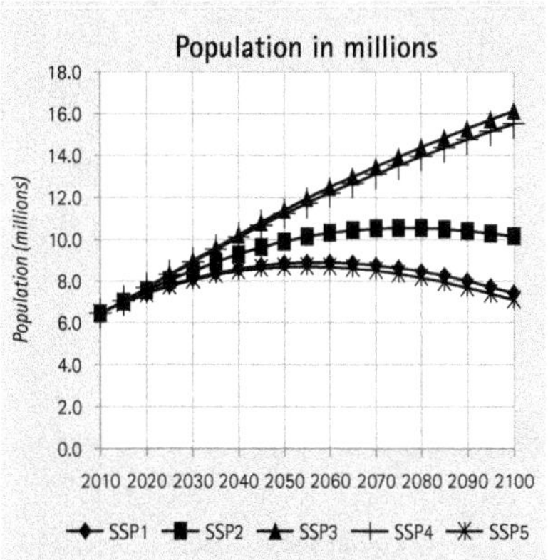

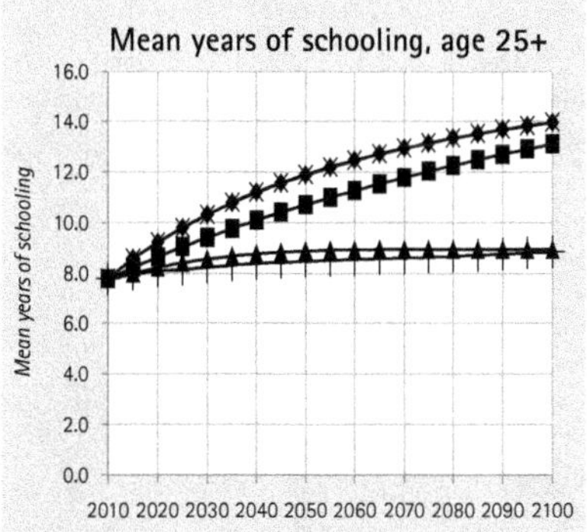

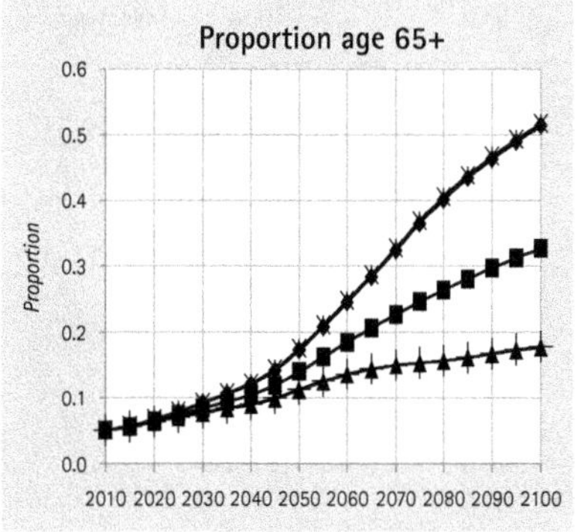

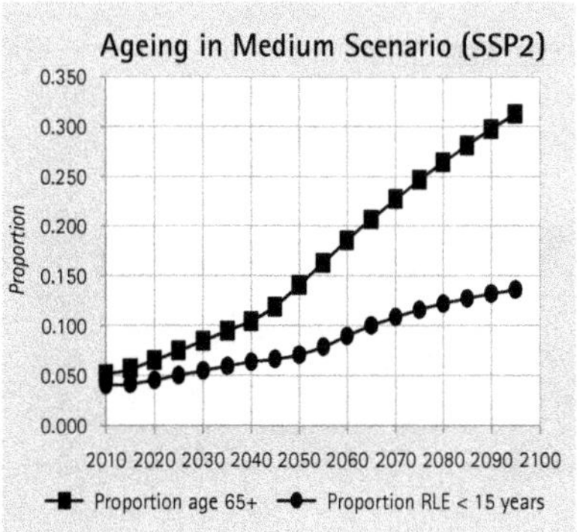

Alternative Scenarios to 2100

Projection Results by Scenario (SSP1–5)

	2010	2020	2030	2040	2050	2075	2100
Population (in millions)							
SSP1 - Rapid development	6.45	7.40	8.10	8.59	8.85	8.63	7.41
SSP2 - Medium	6.45	7.53	8.49	9.30	9.90	10.55	10.15
SSP3 - Stalled development	6.45	7.68	8.98	10.21	11.39	13.94	16.12
SSP4 - Inequality	6.45	7.66	8.92	10.10	11.21	13.54	15.52
SSP5 - Conventional development	6.45	7.38	8.04	8.48	8.68	8.34	7.10
Proportion age 65+							
SSP1 - Rapid development	0.05	0.07	0.09	0.12	0.17	0.36	0.51
SSP2 - Medium	0.05	0.07	0.08	0.10	0.14	0.25	0.33
SSP3 - Stalled development	0.05	0.06	0.08	0.09	0.11	0.15	0.18
SSP4 - Inequality	0.05	0.06	0.08	0.09	0.11	0.15	0.18
SSP5 - Conventional development	0.05	0.07	0.09	0.12	0.18	0.37	0.52
Proportion below age 20							
SSP1 - Rapid development	0.44	0.37	0.30	0.25	0.20	0.13	0.09
SSP2 - Medium	0.44	0.39	0.34	0.30	0.27	0.21	0.17
SSP3 - Stalled development	0.44	0.40	0.38	0.35	0.33	0.30	0.28
SSP4 - Inequality	0.44	0.40	0.38	0.35	0.33	0.30	0.28
SSP5 - Conventional development	0.44	0.37	0.30	0.25	0.20	0.13	0.09
Proportion of Women age 20–39 with at least secondary education							
SSP1 - Rapid development	0.53	0.74	0.82	0.86	0.89	0.95	0.98
SSP2 - Medium	0.53	0.61	0.68	0.74	0.80	0.91	0.97
SSP3 - Stalled development	0.53	0.52	0.52	0.52	0.52	0.52	0.52
SSP4 - Inequality	0.53	0.49	0.47	0.47	0.47	0.47	0.47
SSP5 - Conventional development	0.53	0.74	0.82	0.86	0.89	0.95	0.98
Mean years of schooling, age 25+							
SSP1 - Rapid development	7.77	9.21	10.31	11.20	11.90	13.16	13.97
SSP2 - Medium	7.77	8.64	9.41	10.09	10.71	12.03	13.11
SSP3 - Stalled development	7.77	8.23	8.55	8.76	8.87	8.94	8.95
SSP4 - Inequality	7.77	8.08	8.23	8.38	8.47	8.64	8.85
SSP5 - Conventional development	7.77	9.21	10.30	11.19	11.88	13.14	13.96

Demographic Assumptions Underlying SSPs

	2010–15	2020–25	2030–35	2040–45	2050–55	2075–80	2095–2100
Total fertility rate							
SSP1 - Rapid development	2.52	1.90	1.56	1.40	1.30	1.24	1.17
SSP2 - Medium	2.71	2.32	2.08	1.92	1.81	1.70	1.57
SSP3 - Stalled development	2.86	2.79	2.67	2.55	2.45	2.38	2.28
SSP4 - Inequality	2.86	2.81	2.68	2.54	2.44	2.35	2.24
SSP5 - Conventional development	2.52	1.90	1.56	1.40	1.30	1.24	1.17
Life expectancy at birth for females (in years)							
SSP1 - Rapid development	77.03	79.62	82.36	85.19	88.21	95.80	101.78
SSP2 - Medium	74.99	77.11	79.20	81.19	83.29	88.31	92.32
SSP3 - Stalled development	76.38	77.10	78.02	78.71	79.40	81.17	82.69
SSP4 - Inequality	76.38	77.08	77.97	78.64	79.31	81.03	82.58
SSP5 - Conventional development	77.03	79.62	82.36	85.19	88.21	95.80	101.78
Migration – net flow over five years (in thousands)							
SSP1 - Rapid development	−34	−35	−36	−34	−31	−11	0
SSP2 - Medium	−34	−35	−37	−37	−36	−15	0
SSP3 - Stalled development	−29	−17	−18	−19	−19	−9	0
SSP4 - Inequality	−34	−35	−38	−40	−41	−19	0
SSP5 - Conventional development	−40	−53	−56	−56	−53	−21	0

Ageing Indicators, Medium Scenario (SSP2)

	2010	2020	2030	2040	2050	2075	2095
Median age	23.02	26.24	29.60	33.09	36.58	44.61	49.56
Propspective median age	23.02	24.75	26.51	28.54	30.33	34.16	35.53
Proportion age 65+	0.05	0.07	0.08	0.10	0.14	0.25	0.31
Proportion RLE < 15 years	0.04	0.05	0.05	0.06	0.07	0.12	0.14

Peru

Detailed Human Capital Projections to 2060

Demographic indicators, Medium Scenario (SSP2)	2010	2020	2030	2040	2050	2060
Population (in millions)	29.08	31.74	33.71	34.87	35.20	34.67
Proportion age 65+	0.06	0.08	0.11	0.15	0.19	0.23
Proportion below age 20	0.40	0.35	0.30	0.27	0.24	0.22
	2005–10	2015–20	2025–30	2035–40	2045–50	2055–60
Total Fertility Rate	2.60	2.21	2.02	1.88	1.79	1.71
Life expectancy at birth (in years)						
Men	70.57	72.71	74.82	76.86	78.73	80.65
Women	75.90	77.81	79.80	81.79	83.79	85.79
Five-year immigration flow (in '000)	0.03	0.03	0.03	0.03	0.03	0.03
Five-year emigration flow (in '000)	722.92	577.16	568.60	539.97	500.50	457.82

Human Capital indicators, Medium Scenario (SSP2)	2010	2020	2030	2040	2050	2060
Population age 25+: highest educational attainment						
E1 - no education	0.08	0.05	0.03	0.02	0.01	0.01
E2 - incomplete primary	0.18	0.13	0.09	0.06	0.04	0.02
E3 - primary	0.10	0.10	0.09	0.08	0.07	0.06
E4 - lower secondary	0.07	0.07	0.07	0.06	0.05	0.04
E5 - upper secondary	0.33	0.37	0.40	0.42	0.43	0.43
E6 - post-secondary	0.25	0.28	0.32	0.36	0.40	0.44
Mean years of schooling (in years)	9.40	10.26	10.91	11.44	11.89	12.28
Gender gap (population age 25+): highest educational attainment (ratio male/female)						
E1 - no education	0.34	0.34	0.35	0.38	0.40	0.44
E2 - incomplete primary	0.87	0.79	0.72	0.67	0.63	0.60
E3 - primary	1.01	0.98	0.95	0.93	0.91	0.88
E4 - lower secondary	1.22	1.16	1.11	1.07	1.03	0.99
E5 - upper secondary	1.29	1.25	1.21	1.18	1.15	1.11
E6 - post-secondary	1.00	0.96	0.94	0.93	0.94	0.96
Mean years of schooling (male minus female)	1.01	0.73	0.49	0.31	0.18	0.11
Women age 20–39: highest educational attainment						
E1 - no education	0.03	0.01	0.01	0.00	0.00	0.00
E2 - incomplete primary	0.09	0.05	0.02	0.01	0.00	0.00
E3 - primary	0.12	0.10	0.07	0.05	0.03	0.02
E4 - lower secondary	0.07	0.07	0.06	0.04	0.03	0.02
E5 - upper secondary	0.42	0.47	0.49	0.50	0.50	0.50
E6 - post-secondary	0.25	0.30	0.35	0.39	0.43	0.46
Mean years of schooling (in years)	10.55	11.35	11.81	12.25	12.55	12.76

Education scenarios

GET: global education trend scenario (medium assumption also used for SSP2)

CER: constant enrolment rates scenario (assumption of no future improvements)

FT: Fast track scenario (assumption of education expansion according to fastest historical experience)

Pyramids by Education, Medium Scenario

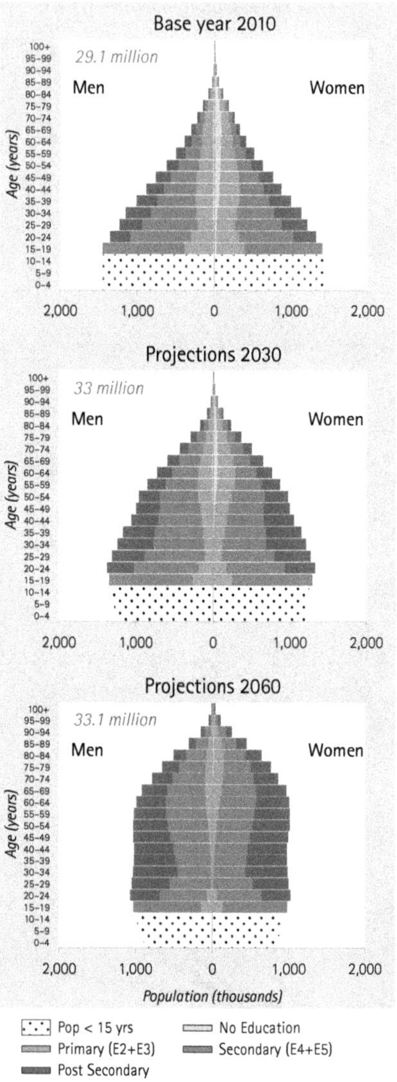

Population Size by Educational Attainment According to Three Education Scenarios: GET, CER, and FT

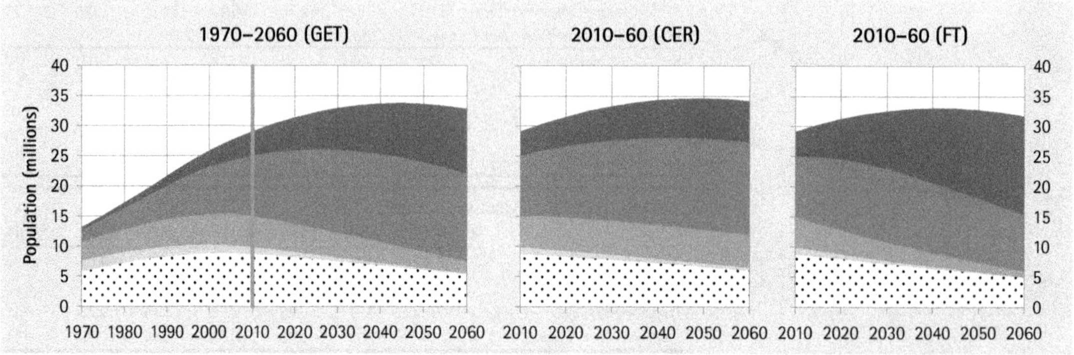

Peru (Continued)

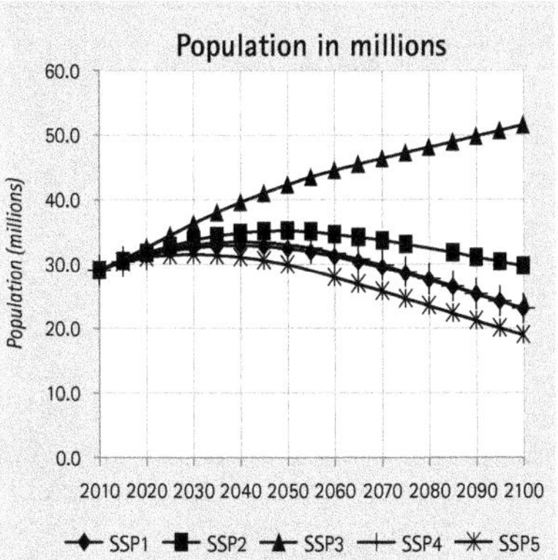

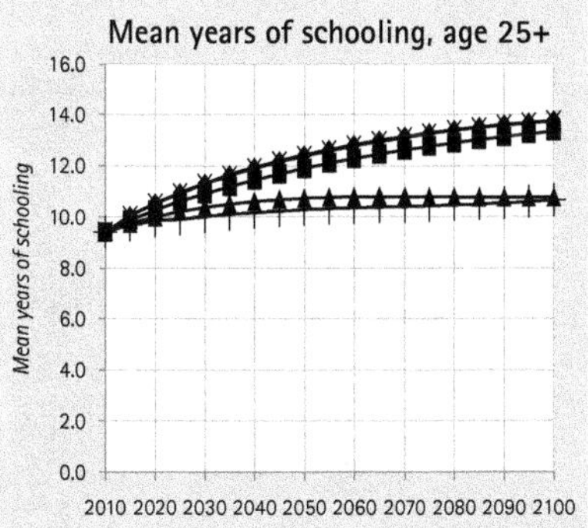

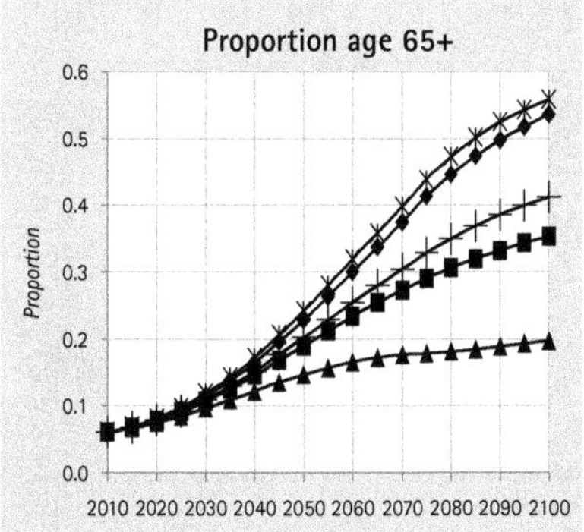

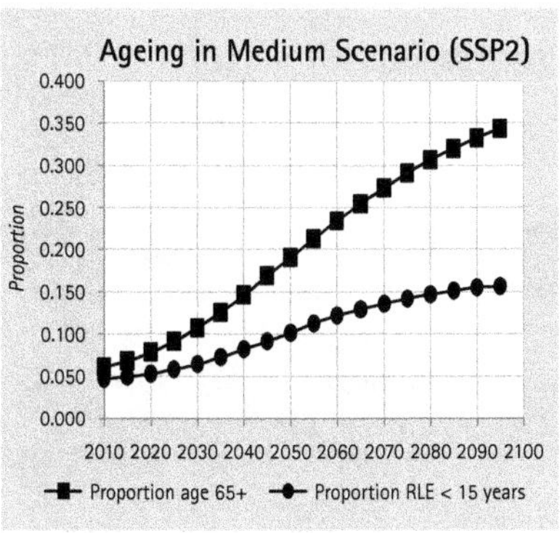

Alternative Scenarios to 2100

Projection Results by Scenario (SSP1–5)

	2010	2020	2030	2040	2050	2075	2100
Population (in millions)							
SSP1 - Rapid development	29.08	31.36	32.54	32.90	32.41	28.54	23.03
SSP2 - Medium	29.08	31.74	33.71	34.87	35.20	33.14	29.73
SSP3 - Stalled development	29.08	32.59	36.34	39.61	42.34	47.29	51.60
SSP4 - Inequality	29.08	31.55	33.00	33.49	33.01	28.79	23.07
SSP5 - Conventional development	29.08	31.02	31.50	31.11	29.90	24.66	18.96
Proportion age 65+							
SSP1 - Rapid development	0.06	0.08	0.12	0.17	0.23	0.41	0.54
SSP2 - Medium	0.06	0.08	0.11	0.15	0.19	0.29	0.35
SSP3 - Stalled development	0.06	0.08	0.10	0.12	0.15	0.18	0.20
SSP4 - Inequality	0.06	0.08	0.11	0.15	0.20	0.33	0.41
SSP5 - Conventional development	0.06	0.08	0.12	0.17	0.24	0.44	0.56
Proportion below age 20							
SSP1 - Rapid development	0.40	0.34	0.27	0.22	0.18	0.12	0.09
SSP2 - Medium	0.40	0.35	0.30	0.27	0.24	0.19	0.16
SSP3 - Stalled development	0.40	0.36	0.34	0.32	0.30	0.28	0.27
SSP4 - Inequality	0.40	0.34	0.29	0.24	0.21	0.15	0.13
SSP5 - Conventional development	0.40	0.34	0.27	0.22	0.18	0.11	0.09
Proportion of Women age 20–39 with at least secondary education							
SSP1 - Rapid development	0.75	0.88	0.94	0.96	0.98	0.99	0.99
SSP2 - Medium	0.75	0.84	0.90	0.94	0.97	0.99	1.00
SSP3 - Stalled development	0.75	0.76	0.77	0.77	0.77	0.77	0.77
SSP4 - Inequality	0.75	0.72	0.69	0.69	0.69	0.69	0.69
SSP5 - Conventional development	0.75	0.88	0.94	0.96	0.98	0.99	0.99
Mean years of schooling, age 25+							
SSP1 - Rapid development	9.40	10.52	11.31	11.94	12.42	13.29	13.76
SSP2 - Medium	9.40	10.26	10.91	11.44	11.89	12.75	13.34
SSP3 - Stalled development	9.40	10.00	10.37	10.60	10.73	10.78	10.77
SSP4 - Inequality	9.40	9.83	10.01	10.17	10.28	10.43	10.64
SSP5 - Conventional development	9.40	10.51	11.28	11.90	12.38	13.25	13.74

Demographic Assumptions Underlying SSPs

	2010–15	2020–25	2030–35	2040–45	2050–55	2075–80	2095–2100
Total fertility rate							
SSP1 - Rapid Development	2.22	1.74	1.49	1.37	1.29	1.22	1.18
SSP2 - Medium	2.37	2.10	1.94	1.84	1.75	1.64	1.59
SSP3 - Stalled Development	2.52	2.54	2.51	2.44	2.37	2.26	2.21
SSP4 - Inequality	2.29	1.92	1.66	1.51	1.42	1.34	1.30
SSP5 - Conventional development	2.22	1.74	1.49	1.37	1.29	1.22	1.18
Life expectancy at birth for females (in years)							
SSP1 - Rapid development	78.49	80.99	83.79	86.67	89.65	97.10	103.04
SSP2 - Medium	76.79	78.81	80.79	82.79	84.78	89.80	93.81
SSP3 - Stalled development	77.75	78.39	79.21	80.06	80.87	82.74	84.40
SSP4 - Inequality	78.06	79.77	81.50	83.27	85.03	89.42	93.14
SSP5 - Conventional development	78.49	80.99	83.79	86.67	89.65	97.10	103.04
Migration – net flow over five years (in thousands)							
SSP1 - Rapid development	−618	−570	−540	−480	−416	−134	0
SSP2 - Medium	−626	−584	−565	−528	−486	−181	0
SSP3 - Stalled development	−514	−287	−282	−276	−268	−119	0
SSP4 - Inequality	−618	−570	−538	−473	−400	−118	0
SSP5 - Conventional development	−721	−858	−819	−738	−649	−220	0

Ageing Indicators, Medium Scenario (SSP2)

	2010	2020	2030	2040	2050	2075	2095
Median age	25.55	29.17	33.00	36.86	40.57	47.94	51.80
Propspective median age	25.55	27.60	29.87	32.26	34.45	37.70	38.07
Proportion age 65+	0.06	0.08	0.11	0.15	0.19	0.29	0.34
Proportion RLE < 15 years	0.05	0.05	0.06	0.08	0.10	0.14	0.16

Philippines

Detailed Human Capital Projections to 2060

Demographic indicators, Medium Scenario (SSP2)	2010	2020	2030	2040	2050	2060
Population (in millions)	93.26	108.37	122.00	133.16	141.44	147.00
Proportion age 65+	0.04	0.05	0.07	0.09	0.12	0.15
Proportion below age 20	0.46	0.41	0.36	0.32	0.29	0.26
	2005–10	2015–20	2025–30	2035–40	2045–50	2055–60
Total Fertility Rate	3.27	2.72	2.33	2.11	1.94	1.87
Life expectancy at birth (in years)						
Men	64.53	66.80	69.17	71.43	73.71	76.08
Women	71.30	73.21	75.31	77.31	79.40	81.59
Five-year immigration flow (in '000)	32.23	31.56	32.73	33.45	33.45	32.97
Five-year emigration flow (in '000)	1260.09	1097.21	1197.67	1235.42	1233.32	1201.97

Human Capital indicators, Medium Scenario (SSP2)	2010	2020	2030	2040	2050	2060
Population age 25+: highest educational attainment						
E1 - no education	0.02	0.02	0.01	0.01	0.00	0.00
E2 - incomplete primary	0.13	0.09	0.06	0.04	0.02	0.02
E3 - primary	0.25	0.20	0.16	0.12	0.09	0.07
E4 - lower secondary	0.04	0.04	0.04	0.03	0.03	0.02
E5 - upper secondary	0.28	0.31	0.34	0.35	0.36	0.35
E6 - post-secondary	0.29	0.34	0.40	0.45	0.50	0.54
Mean years of schooling (in years)	9.27	9.96	10.55	11.04	11.45	11.80
Gender gap (population age 25+): highest educational attainment (ratio male/female)						
E1 - no education	0.82	0.85	0.86	0.86	0.86	0.88
E2 - incomplete primary	1.17	1.21	1.23	1.23	1.21	1.18
E3 - primary	0.96	0.99	1.03	1.05	1.06	1.05
E4 - lower secondary	1.07	1.09	1.10	1.09	1.07	1.04
E5 - upper secondary	1.04	1.05	1.06	1.06	1.06	1.04
E6 - post-secondary	0.93	0.91	0.91	0.92	0.94	0.96
Mean years of schooling (male minus female)	−0.13	−0.20	−0.22	−0.20	−0.17	−0.11
Women age 20–39: highest educational attainment						
E1 - no education	0.01	0.01	0.00	0.00	0.00	0.00
E2 - incomplete primary	0.06	0.03	0.02	0.01	0.01	0.00
E3 - primary	0.17	0.12	0.08	0.06	0.04	0.02
E4 - lower secondary	0.05	0.04	0.03	0.03	0.02	0.02
E5 - upper secondary	0.34	0.35	0.35	0.34	0.33	0.31
E6 - post-secondary	0.38	0.45	0.51	0.56	0.61	0.64
Mean years of schooling (in years)	10.46	11.10	11.60	11.96	12.24	12.43

Education scenarios

GET: global education trend scenario (medium assumption also used for SSP2)

CER: constant enrolment rates scenario (assumption of no future improvements)

FT: Fast track scenario (assumption of education expansion according to fastest historical experience)

Pyramids by Education, Medium Scenario

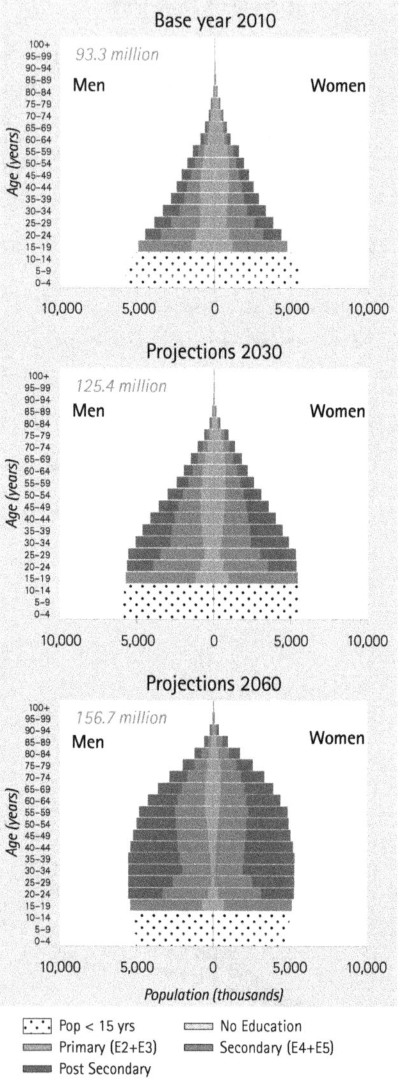

Population Size by Educational Attainment According to Three Education Scenarios: GET, CER, and FT

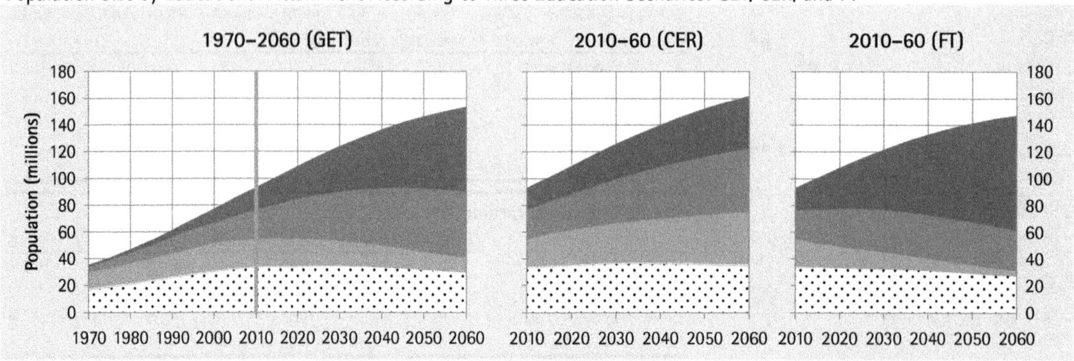

Philippines (Continued)

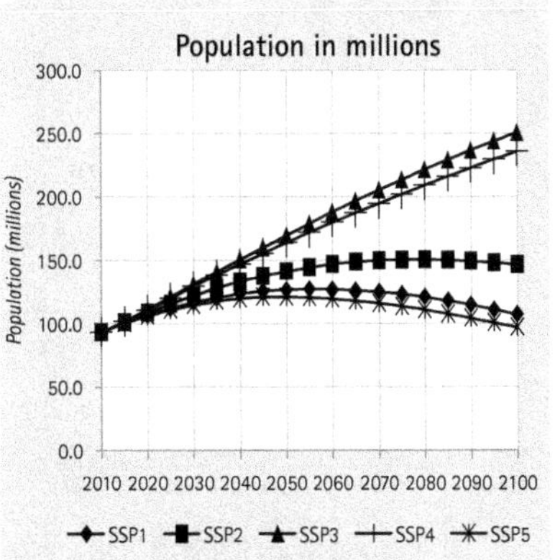

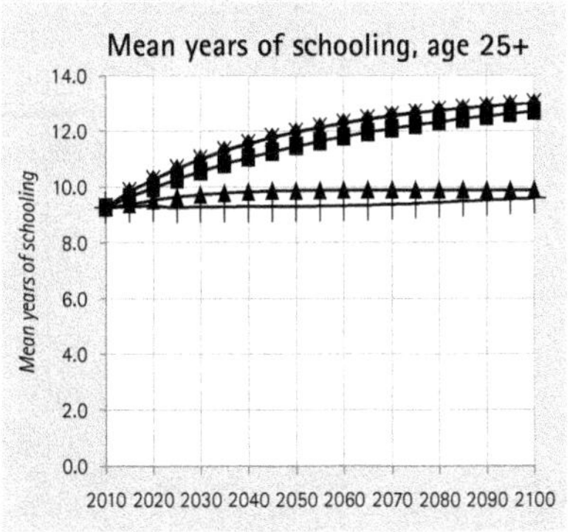

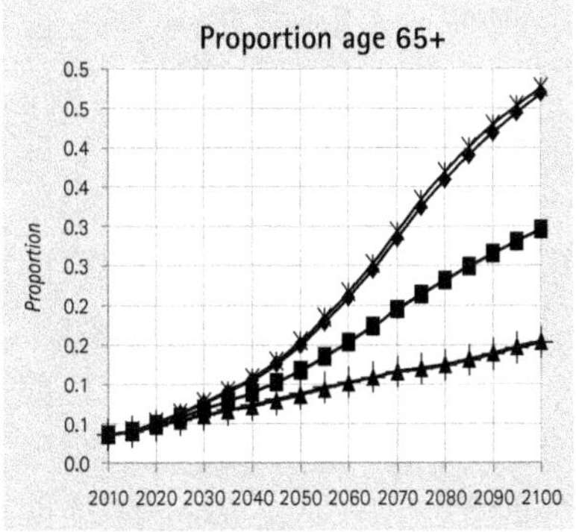

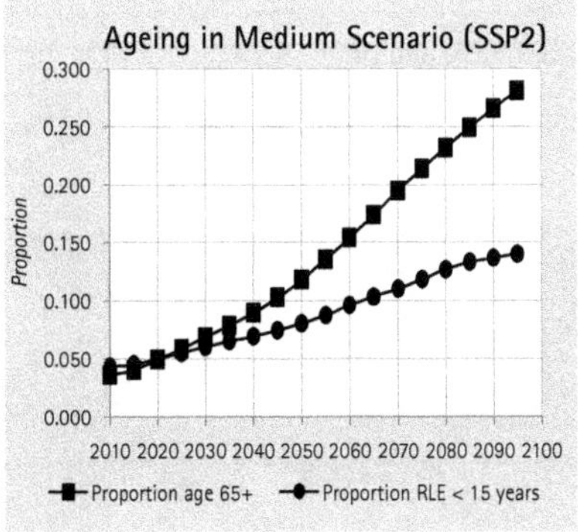

Alternative Scenarios to 2100

Projection Results by Scenario (SSP1–5)

	2010	2020	2030	2040	2050	2075	2100
Population (in millions)							
SSP1 - Rapid development	93.26	106.55	116.55	123.36	126.60	123.07	107.03
SSP2 - Medium	93.26	108.37	122.00	133.16	141.44	150.65	146.63
SSP3 - Stalled development	93.26	111.12	131.22	150.58	169.73	213.56	250.60
SSP4 - Inequality	93.26	110.56	129.35	146.96	164.00	202.06	235.74
SSP5 - Conventional development	93.26	105.93	114.45	119.58	121.02	113.55	96.72
Proportion age 65+							
SSP1 - Rapid development	0.04	0.05	0.08	0.11	0.15	0.32	0.47
SSP2 - Medium	0.04	0.05	0.07	0.09	0.12	0.21	0.30
SSP3 - Stalled development	0.04	0.05	0.06	0.07	0.09	0.12	0.15
SSP4 - Inequality	0.04	0.05	0.06	0.07	0.09	0.12	0.15
SSP5 - Conventional development	0.04	0.05	0.08	0.11	0.15	0.33	0.48
Proportion below age 20							
SSP1 - Rapid development	0.46	0.40	0.33	0.27	0.23	0.15	0.11
SSP2 - Medium	0.46	0.41	0.36	0.32	0.29	0.22	0.18
SSP3 - Stalled development	0.46	0.42	0.40	0.38	0.36	0.32	0.29
SSP4 - Inequality	0.46	0.43	0.41	0.39	0.36	0.32	0.29
SSP5 - Conventional development	0.46	0.40	0.33	0.27	0.23	0.15	0.11
Proportion of Women age 20–39 with at least secondary education							
SSP1 - Rapid development	0.76	0.89	0.93	0.96	0.97	0.99	0.99
SSP2 - Medium	0.76	0.84	0.90	0.93	0.96	0.99	1.00
SSP3 - Stalled development	0.76	0.72	0.72	0.72	0.72	0.72	0.72
SSP4 - Inequality	0.76	0.68	0.65	0.65	0.65	0.65	0.65
SSP5 - Conventional development	0.76	0.89	0.93	0.96	0.97	0.99	0.99
Mean years of schooling, age 25+							
SSP1 - Rapid development	9.27	10.26	10.99	11.55	11.97	12.65	13.01
SSP2 - Medium	9.27	9.96	10.55	11.04	11.45	12.21	12.70
SSP3 - Stalled development	9.27	9.52	9.72	9.82	9.87	9.88	9.89
SSP4 - Inequality	9.27	9.31	9.28	9.30	9.31	9.41	9.59
SSP5 - Conventional development	9.27	10.25	10.98	11.54	11.95	12.64	13.00

Demographic Assumptions Underlying SSPs

	2010–15	2020–25	2030–35	2040–45	2050–55	2075–80	2095–2100
Total fertility rate							
SSP1 - Rapid development	2.76	2.07	1.69	1.51	1.40	1.27	1.18
SSP2 - Medium	2.96	2.51	2.21	2.03	1.90	1.70	1.57
SSP3 - Stalled development	3.14	3.07	2.90	2.74	2.61	2.38	2.22
SSP4 - Inequality	3.15	3.10	2.94	2.76	2.62	2.37	2.20
SSP5 - Conventional development	2.76	2.07	1.69	1.51	1.40	1.27	1.18
Life expectancy at birth for females (in years)							
SSP1 - Rapid development	73.95	76.72	79.65	82.54	85.51	93.23	99.43
SSP2 - Medium	72.21	74.31	76.31	78.40	80.50	85.92	90.19
SSP3 - Stalled development	73.11	73.92	74.85	75.69	76.58	78.97	81.00
SSP4 - Inequality	73.11	73.89	74.78	75.58	76.42	78.76	80.81
SSP5 - Conventional development	73.95	76.72	79.65	82.54	85.51	93.23	99.43
Migration – net flow over five years (in thousands)							
SSP1 - Rapid development	−1076	−1111	−1152	−1113	−1035	−381	0
SSP2 - Medium	−1075	−1123	−1191	−1211	−1196	−513	0
SSP3 - Stalled development	−896	−554	−590	−621	−643	−320	0
SSP4 - Inequality	−1075	−1121	−1215	−1306	−1369	−679	0
SSP5 - Conventional development	−1255	−1685	−1782	−1771	−1702	−688	0

Ageing Indicators, Medium Scenario (SSP2)

	2010	2020	2030	2040	2050	2075	2095
Median age	22.12	24.73	27.85	31.17	34.43	42.20	47.25
Propspective median age	22.12	22.64	23.83	25.21	26.54	29.55	30.80
Proportion age 65+	0.04	0.05	0.07	0.09	0.12	0.21	0.28
Proportion RLE < 15 years	0.04	0.05	0.06	0.07	0.08	0.12	0.14

Poland

Detailed Human Capital Projections to 2060

Demographic indicators, Medium Scenario (SSP2)	2010	2020	2030	2040	2050	2060
Population (in millions)	38.28	38.30	38.08	37.13	35.98	34.88
Proportion age 65+	0.14	0.18	0.22	0.25	0.30	0.34
Proportion below age 20	0.21	0.20	0.20	0.19	0.18	0.18
	2005–10	2015–20	2025–30	2035–40	2045–50	2055–60
Total Fertility Rate	1.32	1.40	1.60	1.67	1.69	1.70
Life expectancy at birth (in years)						
Men	71.17	73.65	76.09	78.41	80.66	82.84
Women	79.86	81.79	83.79	85.81	87.81	89.81
Five-year immigration flow (in '000)	91.93	90.61	94.27	96.56	96.76	95.46
Five-year emigration flow (in '000)	36.50	23.66	19.95	18.00	16.95	15.67

Human Capital indicators, Medium Scenario (SSP2)	2010	2020	2030	2040	2050	2060
Population age 25+: highest educational attainment						
E1 - no education	0.01	0.00	0.00	0.00	0.00	0.00
E2 - incomplete primary	0.00	0.00	0.00	0.00	0.00	0.00
E3 - primary	0.00	0.00	0.00	0.00	0.00	0.00
E4 - lower secondary	0.17	0.12	0.08	0.05	0.03	0.02
E5 - upper secondary	0.61	0.64	0.65	0.65	0.63	0.61
E6 - post-secondary	0.20	0.24	0.27	0.30	0.34	0.37
Mean years of schooling (in years)	11.93	12.39	12.70	12.96	13.19	13.39
Gender gap (population age 25+): highest educational attainment (ratio male/female)						
E1 - no education	0.40	0.53	0.83	0.94	0.92	0.92
E2 - incomplete primary	0.78	0.78	0.92	1.02	1.02	1.01
E3 - primary	1.86	1.98	1.97	1.79	1.56	1.40
E4 - lower secondary	0.77	0.78	0.83	0.90	0.98	1.03
E5 - upper secondary	1.21	1.20	1.18	1.17	1.16	1.13
E6 - post-secondary	0.71	0.69	0.69	0.72	0.76	0.81
Mean years of schooling (male minus female)	0.00	−0.21	−0.33	−0.38	−0.37	−0.31
Women age 20–39: highest educational attainment						
E1 - no education	0.00	0.00	0.00	0.00	0.00	0.00
E2 - incomplete primary	0.00	0.00	0.00	0.00	0.00	0.00
E3 - primary	0.00	0.00	0.00	0.00	0.00	0.00
E4 - lower secondary	0.05	0.03	0.02	0.02	0.01	0.01
E5 - upper secondary	0.65	0.62	0.61	0.60	0.58	0.57
E6 - post-secondary	0.30	0.35	0.37	0.39	0.41	0.42
Mean years of schooling (in years)	12.98	13.27	13.38	13.46	13.55	13.59

Education scenarios

GET: global education trend scenario (medium assumption also used for SSP2)

CER: constant enrolment rates scenario (assumption of no future improvements)

FT: Fast track scenario (assumption of education expansion according to fastest historical experience)

Pyramids by Education, Medium Scenario

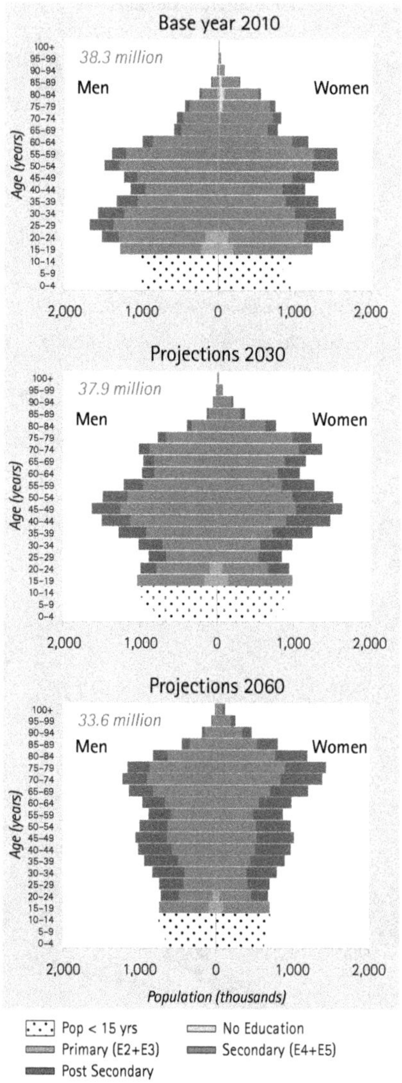

Population Size by Educational Attainment According to Three Education Scenarios: GET, CER, and FT

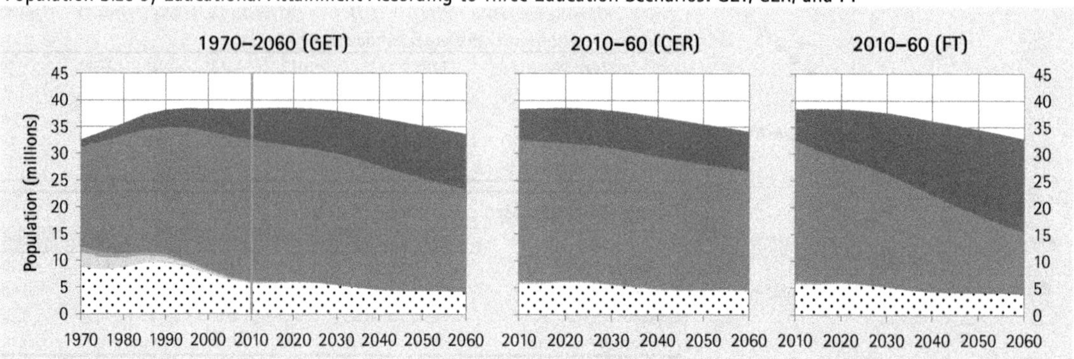

Poland (Continued)

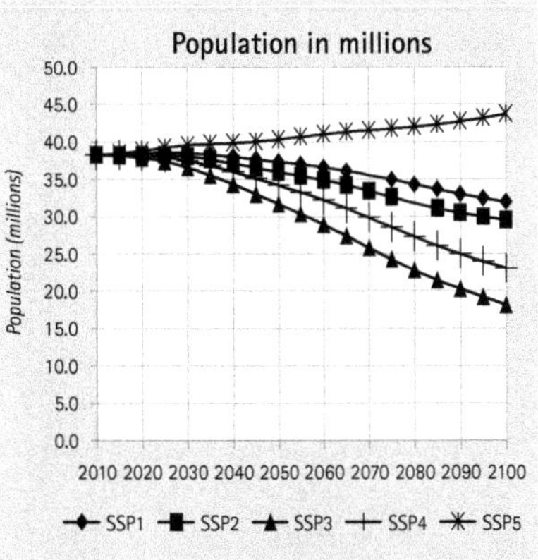

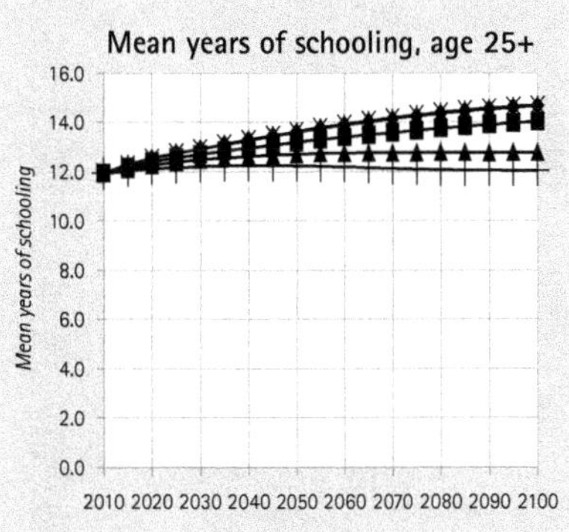

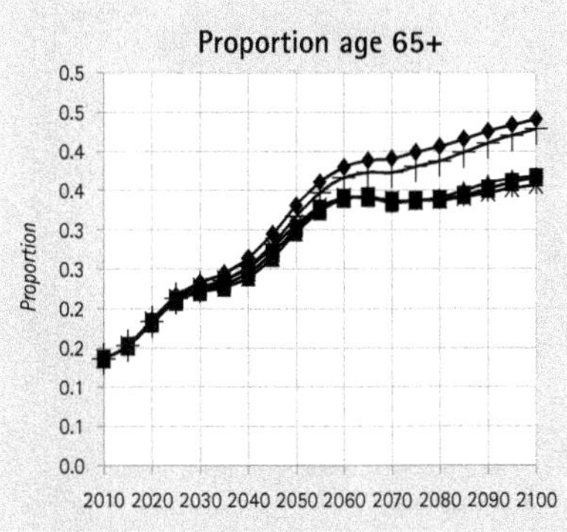

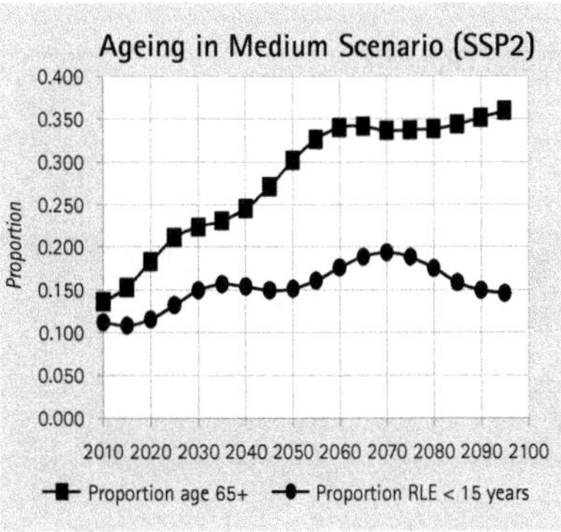

Alternative Scenarios to 2100

Projection Results by Scenario (SSP1–5)

	2010	2020	2030	2040	2050	2075	2100
Population (in millions)							
SSP1 - Rapid development	38.28	38.49	38.53	38.00	37.33	34.94	31.95
SSP2 - Medium	38.28	38.30	38.08	37.13	35.98	32.60	29.53
SSP3 - Stalled development	38.28	37.87	36.59	34.32	31.70	24.25	18.11
SSP4 - Inequality	38.28	38.15	37.49	36.02	34.19	28.59	23.05
SSP5 - Conventional development	38.28	38.81	39.57	39.86	40.32	41.76	43.72
Proportion age 65+							
SSP1 - Rapid development	0.14	0.19	0.23	0.26	0.33	0.40	0.44
SSP2 - Medium	0.14	0.18	0.22	0.25	0.30	0.34	0.37
SSP3 - Stalled development	0.14	0.18	0.22	0.24	0.30	0.34	0.37
SSP4 - Inequality	0.14	0.18	0.23	0.25	0.32	0.38	0.43
SSP5 - Conventional development	0.14	0.18	0.23	0.25	0.31	0.34	0.36
Proportion below age 20							
SSP1 - Rapid development	0.21	0.20	0.19	0.18	0.17	0.16	0.15
SSP2 - Medium	0.21	0.20	0.20	0.19	0.18	0.18	0.17
SSP3 - Stalled development	0.21	0.19	0.18	0.16	0.15	0.15	0.14
SSP4 - Inequality	0.21	0.19	0.19	0.17	0.15	0.14	0.13
SSP5 - Conventional development	0.21	0.20	0.21	0.20	0.20	0.20	0.20
Proportion of Women age 20–39 with at least secondary education							
SSP1 - Rapid development	1.00	1.00	1.00	1.00	1.00	1.00	1.00
SSP2 - Medium	1.00	1.00	1.00	1.00	1.00	1.00	1.00
SSP3 - Stalled development	1.00	1.00	1.00	1.00	1.00	1.00	1.00
SSP4 - Inequality	1.00	1.00	1.00	1.00	1.00	1.00	1.00
SSP5 - Conventional development	1.00	1.00	1.00	1.00	1.00	1.00	1.00
Mean years of schooling, age 25+							
SSP1 - Rapid development	11.93	12.53	12.92	13.27	13.60	14.25	14.66
SSP2 - Medium	11.93	12.39	12.70	12.96	13.19	13.66	14.02
SSP3 - Stalled development	11.93	12.26	12.48	12.62	12.71	12.76	12.76
SSP4 - Inequality	11.93	12.11	12.20	12.24	12.23	12.09	12.03
SSP5 - Conventional development	11.93	12.53	12.93	13.28	13.62	14.29	14.69

Demographic Assumptions Underlying SSPs

	2010–15	2020–25	2030–35	2040–45	2050–55	2075–80	2095–2100
Total fertility rate							
SSP1 - Rapid development	1.30	1.47	1.59	1.65	1.66	1.67	1.69
SSP2 - Medium	1.30	1.50	1.66	1.68	1.70	1.71	1.72
SSP3 - Stalled development	1.26	1.31	1.32	1.33	1.32	1.33	1.35
SSP4 - Inequality	1.27	1.36	1.40	1.39	1.38	1.40	1.42
SSP5 - Conventional development	1.37	1.69	1.93	2.04	2.08	2.09	2.11
Life expectancy at birth for females (in years)							
SSP1 - Rapid development	81.85	84.64	87.56	90.49	93.45	100.92	106.94
SSP2 - Medium	80.79	82.79	84.81	86.81	88.81	93.81	97.80
SSP3 - Stalled development	80.89	81.72	82.68	83.63	84.55	86.93	88.85
SSP4 - Inequality	81.33	83.17	85.11	87.04	88.96	93.67	97.54
SSP5 - Conventional development	81.85	84.64	87.56	90.49	93.45	100.92	106.94
Migration – net flow over five years (in thousands)							
SSP1 - Rapid development	60	70	76	76	74	31	0
SSP2 - Medium	61	72	78	80	80	36	0
SSP3 - Stalled development	50	36	39	41	40	18	0
SSP4 - Inequality	60	70	76	77	76	34	0
SSP5 - Conventional development	70	105	112	115	116	54	0

Ageing Indicators, Medium Scenario (SSP2)

	2010	2020	2030	2040	2050	2075	2095
Median age	37.92	41.26	45.37	48.99	50.31	51.38	52.08
Propspective median age	37.92	39.11	41.22	42.91	42.22	38.43	35.02
Proportion age 65+	0.14	0.18	0.22	0.25	0.30	0.34	0.36
Proportion RLE < 15 years	0.11	0.12	0.15	0.15	0.15	0.19	0.15

Portugal

Detailed Human Capital Projections to 2060

Demographic indicators, Medium Scenario (SSP2)

	2010	2020	2030	2040	2050	2060
Population (in millions)	10.68	10.90	11.17	11.46	11.68	11.81
Proportion age 65+	0.18	0.21	0.24	0.28	0.32	0.33
Proportion below age 20	0.20	0.19	0.17	0.17	0.17	0.17
	2005–10	2015–20	2025–30	2035–40	2045–50	2055–60
Total Fertility Rate	1.36	1.33	1.47	1.58	1.68	1.70
Life expectancy at birth (in years)						
Men	75.31	78.31	80.60	82.82	84.93	87.00
Women	81.79	84.19	86.41	88.51	90.49	92.51
Five-year immigration flow (in '000)	314.63	309.37	321.49	329.09	329.57	324.99
Five-year emigration flow (in '000)	164.99	107.26	100.99	93.68	91.07	91.73

Human Capital indicators, Medium Scenario (SSP2)

	2010	2020	2030	2040	2050	2060
Population age 25+: highest educational attainment						
E1 - no education	0.06	0.03	0.02	0.01	0.01	0.00
E2 - incomplete primary	0.34	0.26	0.18	0.11	0.06	0.03
E3 - primary	0.11	0.13	0.14	0.13	0.12	0.10
E4 - lower secondary	0.21	0.22	0.23	0.23	0.22	0.19
E5 - upper secondary	0.15	0.20	0.25	0.29	0.33	0.37
E6 - post-secondary	0.13	0.16	0.19	0.23	0.27	0.31
Mean years of schooling (in years)	7.27	8.31	9.37	10.30	11.12	11.82
Gender gap (population age 25+): highest educational attainment (ratio male/female)						
E1 - no education	0.55	0.58	0.73	0.97	1.06	1.04
E2 - incomplete primary	0.94	0.89	0.83	0.78	0.76	0.82
E3 - primary	1.21	1.27	1.28	1.26	1.25	1.25
E4 - lower secondary	1.34	1.33	1.32	1.31	1.27	1.21
E5 - upper secondary	1.07	1.05	1.05	1.05	1.05	1.04
E6 - post-secondary	0.75	0.71	0.70	0.71	0.75	0.81
Mean years of schooling (male minus female)	0.24	0.01	−0.19	−0.33	−0.40	−0.40
Women age 20–39: highest educational attainment						
E1 - no education	0.01	0.01	0.00	0.00	0.00	0.00
E2 - incomplete primary	0.01	0.03	0.01	0.00	0.00	0.00
E3 - primary	0.06	0.13	0.11	0.08	0.06	0.05
E4 - lower secondary	0.37	0.17	0.14	0.11	0.09	0.07
E5 - upper secondary	0.34	0.40	0.44	0.46	0.48	0.49
E6 - post-secondary	0.22	0.26	0.30	0.34	0.36	0.38
Mean years of schooling (in years)	11.12	11.39	12.15	12.55	12.82	13.00

Education scenarios

GET : global education trend scenario (medium assumption also used for SSP2)

CER: constant enrolment rates scenario (assumption of no future improvements)

FT: Fast track scenario (assumption of education expansion according to fastest historical experience)

Pyramids by Education, Medium Scenario

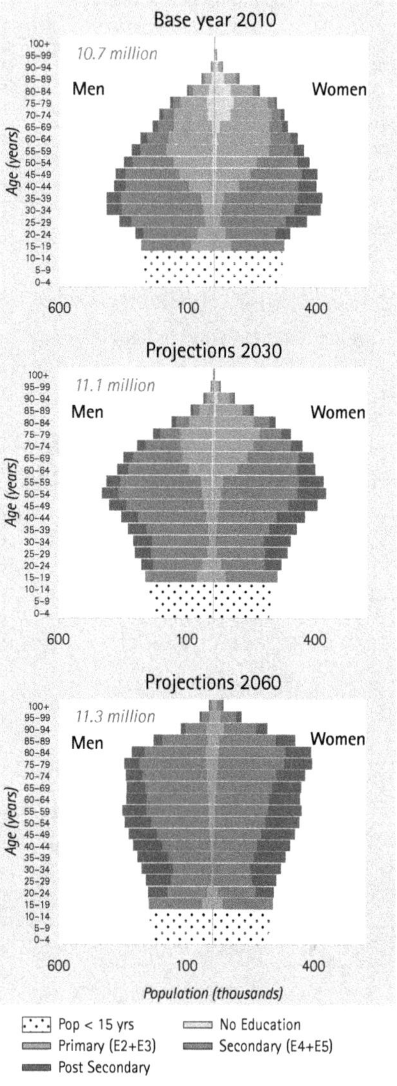

Population Size by Educational Attainment According to Three Education Scenarios: GET, CER, and FT

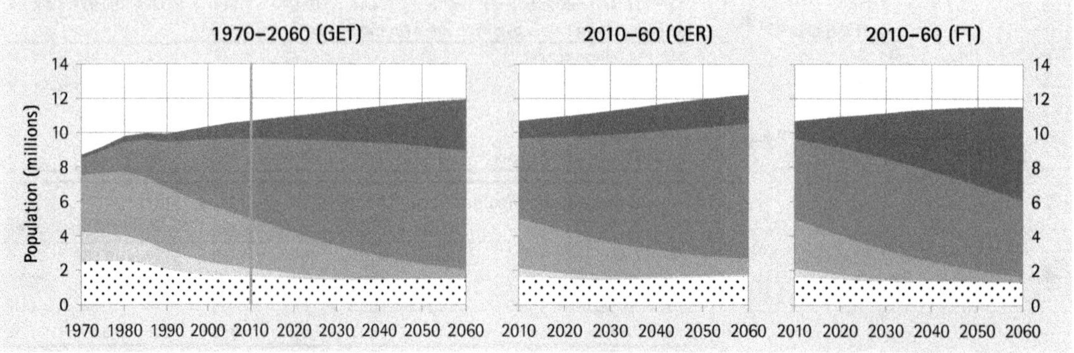

Portugal (Continued)

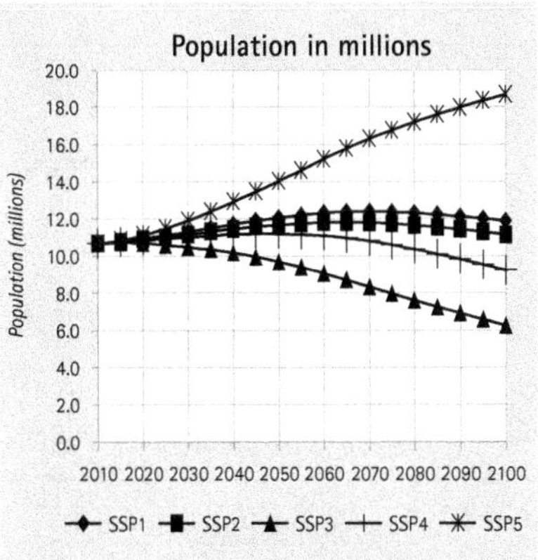

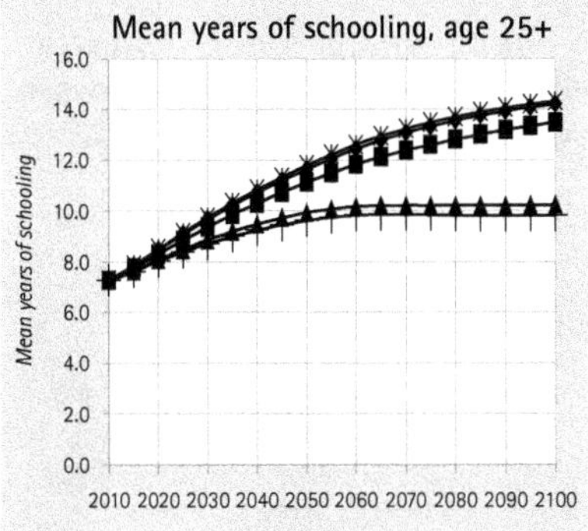

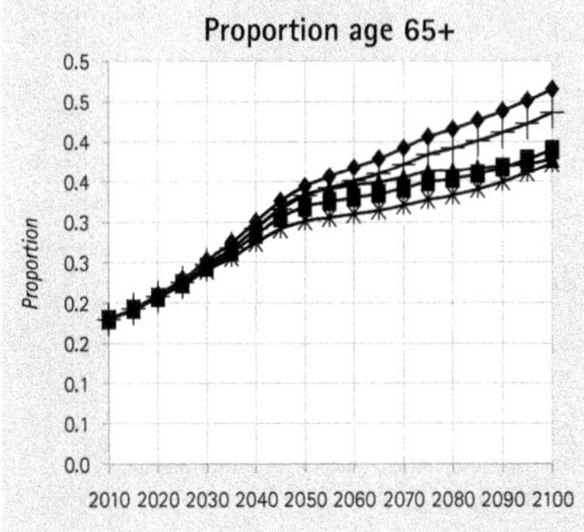

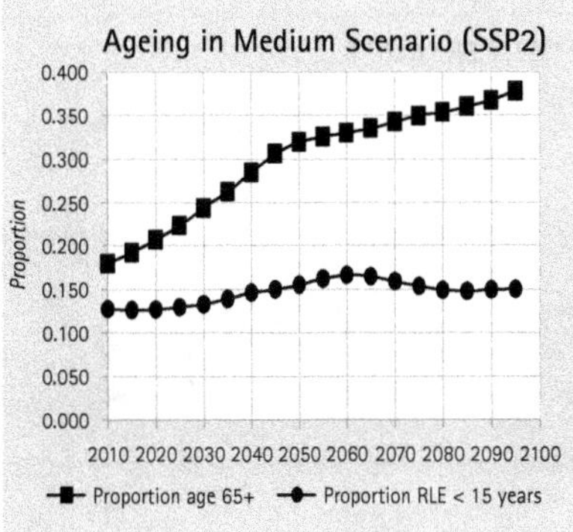

Alternative Scenarios to 2100

Projection Results by Scenario (SSP1–5)

	2010	2020	2030	2040	2050	2075	2100
Population (in millions)							
SSP1 - Rapid development	10.68	10.96	11.31	11.72	12.06	12.38	11.89
SSP2 - Medium	10.68	10.90	11.17	11.46	11.68	11.74	11.15
SSP3 - Stalled development	10.68	10.69	10.48	10.18	9.69	7.96	6.24
SSP4 - Inequality	10.68	10.86	11.01	11.17	11.20	10.60	9.22
SSP5 - Conventional development	10.68	11.13	11.92	12.91	14.01	16.76	18.68
Proportion age 65+							
SSP1 - Rapid development	0.18	0.21	0.25	0.30	0.34	0.41	0.46
SSP2 - Medium	0.18	0.21	0.24	0.28	0.32	0.35	0.39
SSP3 - Stalled development	0.18	0.21	0.25	0.29	0.33	0.36	0.38
SSP4 - Inequality	0.18	0.21	0.25	0.29	0.33	0.38	0.44
SSP5 - Conventional development	0.18	0.21	0.24	0.27	0.30	0.33	0.37
Proportion below age 20							
SSP1 - Rapid development	0.20	0.18	0.16	0.16	0.16	0.15	0.14
SSP2 - Medium	0.20	0.19	0.17	0.17	0.17	0.17	0.16
SSP3 - Stalled development	0.20	0.18	0.16	0.15	0.15	0.15	0.14
SSP4 - Inequality	0.20	0.18	0.16	0.15	0.15	0.14	0.13
SSP5 - Conventional development	0.20	0.19	0.18	0.19	0.20	0.21	0.19
Proportion of Women age 20–39 with at least secondary education							
SSP1 - Rapid development	0.93	0.89	0.94	0.96	0.97	0.98	0.99
SSP2 - Medium	0.93	0.84	0.88	0.91	0.93	0.97	0.99
SSP3 - Stalled development	0.93	0.77	0.77	0.77	0.77	0.77	0.77
SSP4 - Inequality	0.93	0.77	0.77	0.77	0.77	0.77	0.77
SSP5 - Conventional development	0.93	0.89	0.94	0.96	0.97	0.98	0.99
Mean years of schooling, age 25+							
SSP1 - Rapid development	7.27	8.48	9.68	10.72	11.63	13.33	14.21
SSP2 - Medium	7.27	8.31	9.37	10.30	11.12	12.60	13.48
SSP3 - Stalled development	7.27	8.08	8.86	9.47	9.92	10.21	10.23
SSP4 - Inequality	7.27	8.02	8.72	9.24	9.62	9.84	9.81
SSP5 - Conventional development	7.27	8.51	9.74	10.83	11.78	13.48	14.30

Demographic Assumptions Underlying SSPs

	2010–15	2020–25	2030–35	2040–45	2050–55	2075–80	2095–2100
Total fertility rate							
SSP1 - Rapid development	1.25	1.36	1.47	1.57	1.63	1.67	1.69
SSP2 - Medium	1.26	1.40	1.53	1.63	1.70	1.71	1.72
SSP3 - Stalled development	1.20	1.23	1.27	1.33	1.38	1.43	1.45
SSP4 - Inequality	1.21	1.25	1.29	1.36	1.40	1.46	1.48
SSP5 - Conventional development	1.31	1.57	1.78	1.94	2.04	2.09	2.11
Life expectancy at birth for females (in years)							
SSP1 - Rapid development	84.20	87.38	90.39	93.35	96.31	103.67	109.80
SSP2 - Medium	83.09	85.31	87.51	89.51	91.51	96.50	100.50
SSP3 - Stalled development	83.26	84.46	85.54	86.53	87.31	89.33	91.08
SSP4 - Inequality	83.76	85.90	88.01	89.95	91.82	96.23	99.92
SSP5 - Conventional development	84.20	87.38	90.39	93.35	96.31	103.67	109.80
Migration – net flow over five years (in thousands)							
SSP1 - Rapid development	178	210	225	227	216	76	0
SSP2 - Medium	177	205	220	226	223	88	0
SSP3 - Stalled development	148	105	111	112	109	41	0
SSP4 - Inequality	178	210	224	230	225	90	0
SSP5 - Conventional development	208	318	349	372	376	154	0

Ageing Indicators, Medium Scenario (SSP2)

	2010	2020	2030	2040	2050	2075	2095
Median age	40.98	44.41	47.48	49.11	50.23	51.58	54.36
Propspective median age	40.98	42.31	43.28	43.07	42.49	39.16	38.08
Proportion age 65+	0.18	0.21	0.24	0.28	0.32	0.35	0.38
Proportion RLE < 15 years	0.13	0.13	0.13	0.15	0.16	0.15	0.15

Puerto Rico

Detailed Human Capital Projections to 2060

Demographic indicators, Medium Scenario (SSP2)	2010	2020	2030	2040	2050	2060
Population (in millions)	3.75	3.68	3.54	3.34	3.07	2.78
Proportion age 65+	0.13	0.17	0.23	0.29	0.34	0.40
Proportion below age 20	0.29	0.25	0.21	0.18	0.16	0.14
	2005–10	2015–20	2025–30	2035–40	2045–50	2055–60
Total Fertility Rate	1.83	1.69	1.63	1.57	1.52	1.54
Life expectancy at birth (in years)						
Men	74.70	77.31	79.66	81.85	84.04	86.20
Women	82.67	85.01	87.11	89.11	91.11	93.11
Five-year immigration flow (in '000)	1.43	1.40	1.45	1.48	1.48	1.46
Five-year emigration flow (in '000)	146.05	102.11	86.48	72.33	59.09	48.13

Human Capital indicators, Medium Scenario (SSP2)	2010	2020	2030	2040	2050	2060
Population age 25+: highest educational attainment						
E1 - no education	0.03	0.02	0.01	0.01	0.01	0.00
E2 - incomplete primary	0.04	0.02	0.01	0.01	0.00	0.00
E3 - primary	0.11	0.08	0.06	0.04	0.03	0.02
E4 - lower secondary	0.09	0.08	0.07	0.05	0.04	0.03
E5 - upper secondary	0.42	0.44	0.44	0.43	0.41	0.39
E6 - post-secondary	0.31	0.36	0.42	0.47	0.51	0.56
Mean years of schooling (in years)	11.81	12.48	13.00	13.43	13.79	14.08
Gender gap (population age 25+): highest educational attainment (ratio male/female)						
E1 - no education	0.95	0.99	1.05	1.10	1.11	1.08
E2 - incomplete primary	0.93	0.91	0.93	0.98	1.07	1.17
E3 - primary	1.08	1.07	1.06	1.09	1.14	1.19
E4 - lower secondary	1.21	1.18	1.13	1.09	1.06	1.04
E5 - upper secondary	1.14	1.16	1.17	1.17	1.16	1.15
E6 - post-secondary	0.78	0.80	0.82	0.85	0.87	0.90
Mean years of schooling (male minus female)	−0.32	−0.34	−0.33	−0.32	−0.29	−0.24
Women age 20–39: highest educational attainment						
E1 - no education	0.01	0.00	0.00	0.00	0.00	0.00
E2 - incomplete primary	0.00	0.00	0.00	0.00	0.00	0.00
E3 - primary	0.03	0.02	0.01	0.00	0.00	0.00
E4 - lower secondary	0.06	0.04	0.03	0.02	0.02	0.02
E5 - upper secondary	0.48	0.45	0.43	0.40	0.39	0.38
E6 - post-secondary	0.42	0.49	0.53	0.57	0.59	0.60
Mean years of schooling (in years)	13.40	13.79	14.03	14.22	14.34	14.40

Education scenarios

GET : global education trend scenario (medium assumption also used for SSP2)

CER: constant enrolment rates scenario (assumption of no future improvements)

FT: Fast track scenario (assumption of education expansion according to fastest historical experience)

Pyramids by Education, Medium Scenario

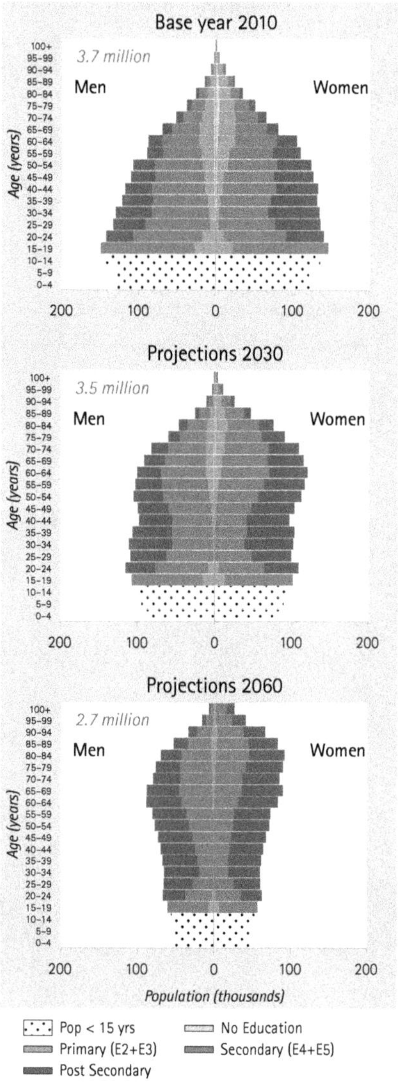

Population Size by Educational Attainment According to Three Education Scenarios: GET, CER, and FT

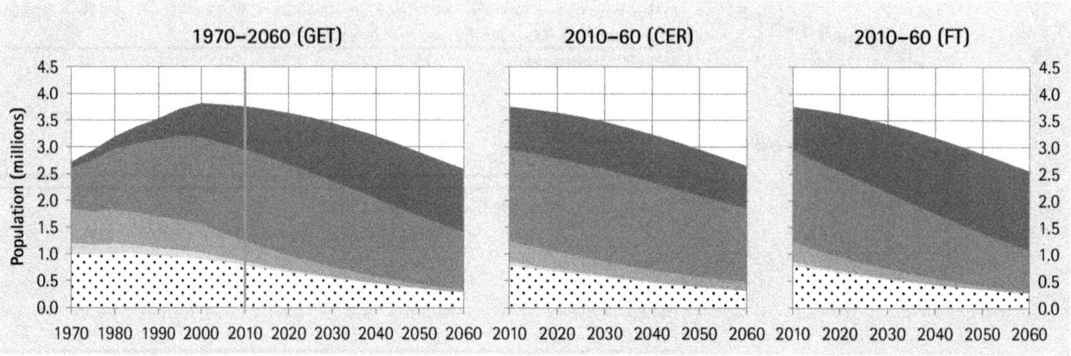

Puerto Rico (Continued)

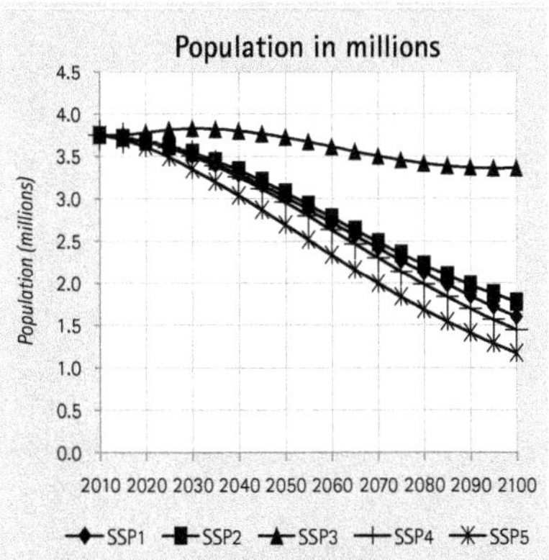

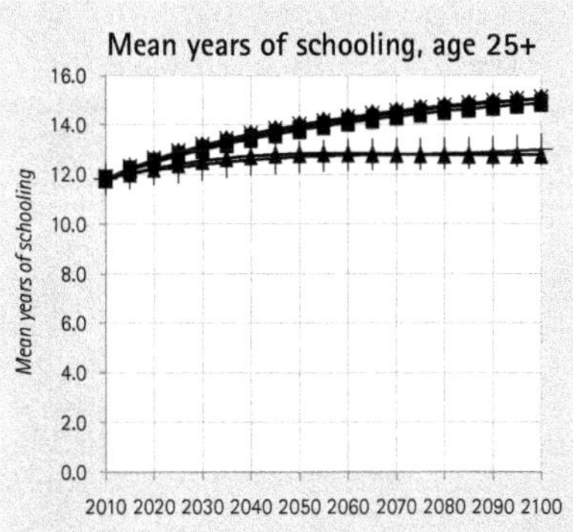

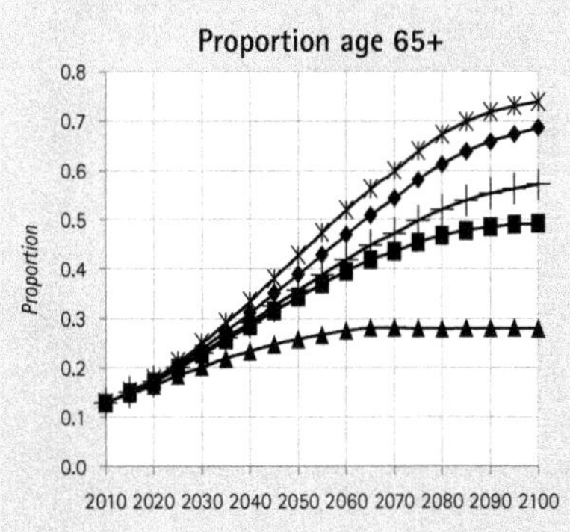

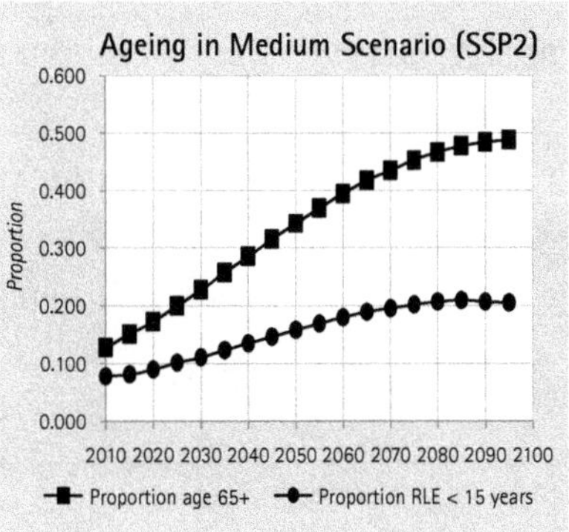

Alternative Scenarios to 2100

Projection Results by Scenario (SSP1–5)

	2010	2020	2030	2040	2050	2075	2100
Population (in millions)							
SSP1 - Rapid development	3.75	3.67	3.51	3.29	3.02	2.27	1.60
SSP2 - Medium	3.75	3.68	3.54	3.34	3.07	2.35	1.78
SSP3 - Stalled development	3.75	3.78	3.83	3.80	3.72	3.46	3.36
SSP4 - Inequality	3.75	3.67	3.50	3.26	2.96	2.14	1.44
SSP5 - Conventional development	3.75	3.61	3.35	3.03	2.69	1.83	1.17
Proportion age 65+							
SSP1 - Rapid development	0.13	0.18	0.24	0.31	0.39	0.58	0.69
SSP2 - Medium	0.13	0.17	0.23	0.29	0.34	0.45	0.49
SSP3 - Stalled development	0.13	0.16	0.20	0.23	0.26	0.28	0.28
SSP4 - Inequality	0.13	0.17	0.23	0.29	0.36	0.50	0.57
SSP5 - Conventional development	0.13	0.18	0.25	0.33	0.43	0.64	0.74
Proportion below age 20							
SSP1 - Rapid development	0.29	0.24	0.19	0.15	0.12	0.07	0.06
SSP2 - Medium	0.29	0.25	0.21	0.18	0.16	0.13	0.12
SSP3 - Stalled development	0.29	0.26	0.24	0.23	0.22	0.22	0.23
SSP4 - Inequality	0.29	0.24	0.20	0.16	0.13	0.09	0.08
SSP5 - Conventional development	0.29	0.24	0.18	0.14	0.11	0.06	0.04
Proportion of Women age 20–39 with at least secondary education							
SSP1 - Rapid development	0.96	0.99	0.99	1.00	1.00	1.00	1.00
SSP2 - Medium	0.96	0.98	0.99	0.99	1.00	1.00	1.00
SSP3 - Stalled development	0.96	0.94	0.94	0.94	0.94	0.94	0.94
SSP4 - Inequality	0.96	0.89	0.85	0.85	0.85	0.85	0.85
SSP5 - Conventional development	0.96	0.99	0.99	1.00	1.00	1.00	1.00
Mean years of schooling, age 25+							
SSP1 - Rapid development	11.81	12.58	13.15	13.62	13.98	14.66	15.06
SSP2 - Medium	11.81	12.48	13.00	13.43	13.79	14.44	14.86
SSP3 - Stalled development	11.81	12.24	12.54	12.74	12.83	12.80	12.77
SSP4 - Inequality	11.81	12.18	12.39	12.58	12.70	12.80	12.98
SSP5 - Conventional development	11.81	12.56	13.11	13.55	13.91	14.59	15.03

Demographic Assumptions Underlying SSPs

	2010–15	2020–25	2030–35	2040–45	2050–55	2075–80	2095–2100
Total fertility rate							
SSP1 - Rapid development	1.63	1.39	1.25	1.17	1.14	1.17	1.20
SSP2 - Medium	1.72	1.67	1.60	1.52	1.53	1.57	1.60
SSP3 - Stalled development	1.85	2.00	2.03	2.01	2.01	2.08	2.13
SSP4 - Inequality	1.67	1.49	1.32	1.23	1.20	1.23	1.26
SSP5 - Conventional development	1.63	1.39	1.25	1.17	1.14	1.17	1.20
Life expectancy at birth for females (in years)							
SSP1 - Rapid development	85.12	88.08	90.97	93.87	96.80	104.23	110.23
SSP2 - Medium	83.91	86.11	88.11	90.11	92.11	97.11	101.10
SSP3 - Stalled development	84.16	85.20	86.15	87.06	87.96	90.15	92.00
SSP4 - Inequality	84.64	86.68	88.55	90.43	92.30	96.89	100.70
SSP5 - Conventional development	85.12	88.08	90.97	93.87	96.80	104.23	110.23
Migration – net flow over five years (in thousands)							
SSP1 - Rapid development	−118	−92	−76	−59	−45	−11	0
SSP2 - Medium	−123	−96	−81	−66	−53	−15	0
SSP3 - Stalled development	−98	−47	−41	−37	−32	−12	0
SSP4 - Inequality	−118	−92	−75	−57	−42	−9	0
SSP5 - Conventional development	−137	−136	−111	−85	−63	−14	0

Ageing Indicators, Medium Scenario (SSP2)

	2010	2020	2030	2040	2050	2075	2095
Median age	34.43	39.27	44.16	48.85	53.25	61.35	64.03
Propspective median age	34.43	37.05	40.04	42.94	45.57	49.38	48.31
Proportion age 65+	0.13	0.17	0.23	0.29	0.34	0.45	0.49
Proportion RLE < 15 years	0.08	0.09	0.11	0.13	0.16	0.20	0.21

Qatar

Detailed Human Capital Projections to 2060

Demographic indicators, Medium Scenario (SSP2)	2010	2020	2030	2040	2050	2060
Population (in millions)	1.76	2.47	3.01	3.52	3.94	4.23
Proportion age 65+	0.01	0.03	0.08	0.18	0.30	0.32
Proportion below age 20	0.17	0.19	0.17	0.15	0.14	0.13
	2005–10	2015–20	2025–30	2035–40	2045–50	2055–60
Total Fertility Rate	2.40	2.12	1.96	1.85	1.77	1.70
Life expectancy at birth (in years)						
Men	78.07	80.07	81.91	83.73	85.67	87.52
Women	77.29	79.89	82.09	84.19	86.29	88.31
Five-year immigration flow (in '000)	864.23	305.80	318.02	324.97	324.64	319.66
Five-year emigration flow (in '000)	8.89	9.88	12.40	15.01	16.76	17.51

Human Capital indicators, Medium Scenario (SSP2)	2010	2020	2030	2040	2050	2060
Population age 25+: highest educational attainment						
E1 - no education	0.04	0.03	0.03	0.02	0.02	0.01
E2 - incomplete primary	0.24	0.22	0.20	0.16	0.13	0.10
E3 - primary	0.21	0.20	0.20	0.19	0.18	0.17
E4 - lower secondary	0.11	0.12	0.12	0.13	0.12	0.12
E5 - upper secondary	0.21	0.23	0.24	0.26	0.28	0.30
E6 - post-secondary	0.18	0.19	0.21	0.23	0.26	0.30
Mean years of schooling (in years)	9.07	9.38	9.66	10.06	10.52	11.02
Gender gap (population age 25+): highest educational attainment (ratio male/female)						
E1 - no education	0.62	0.78	1.00	1.24	1.47	1.62
E2 - incomplete primary	1.31	1.37	1.53	1.68	1.78	1.82
E3 - primary	2.07	2.21	2.23	2.15	1.97	1.75
E4 - lower secondary	1.15	1.13	1.15	1.20	1.24	1.23
E5 - upper secondary	0.98	0.98	0.96	0.98	1.01	1.02
E6 - post-secondary	0.47	0.45	0.45	0.47	0.52	0.61
Mean years of schooling (male minus female)	−1.60	−1.87	−2.11	−2.14	−1.98	−1.63
Women age 20–39: highest educational attainment						
E1 - no education	0.02	0.02	0.01	0.01	0.00	0.00
E2 - incomplete primary	0.16	0.11	0.07	0.05	0.04	0.03
E3 - primary	0.11	0.09	0.10	0.11	0.12	0.12
E4 - lower secondary	0.14	0.16	0.14	0.12	0.11	0.11
E5 - upper secondary	0.27	0.30	0.33	0.34	0.35	0.38
E6 - post-secondary	0.29	0.32	0.35	0.37	0.38	0.36
Mean years of schooling (in years)	10.77	11.31	11.82	12.12	12.25	12.20

Education scenarios

GET: global education trend scenario (medium assumption also used for SSP2)

CER: constant enrolment rates scenario (assumption of no future improvements)

FT: Fast track scenario (assumption of education expansion according to fastest historical experience)

Pyramids by Education, Medium Scenario

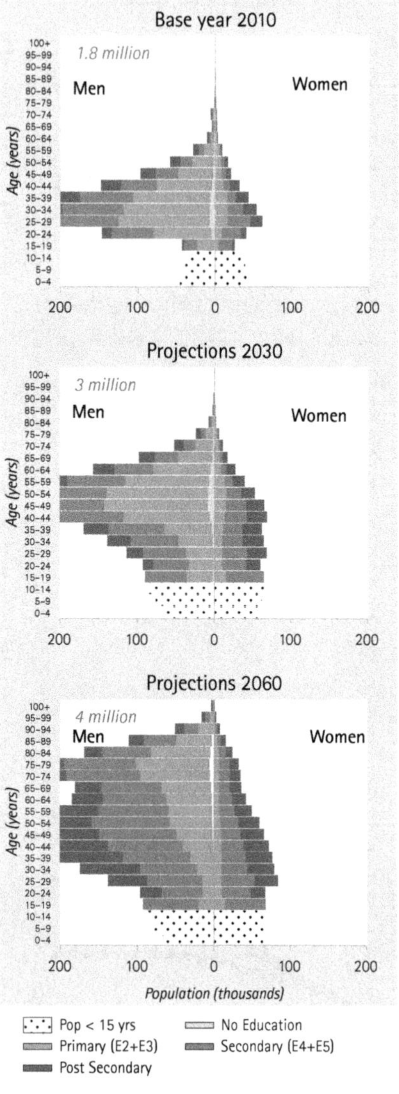

Population Size by Educational Attainment According to Three Education Scenarios: GET, CER, and FT

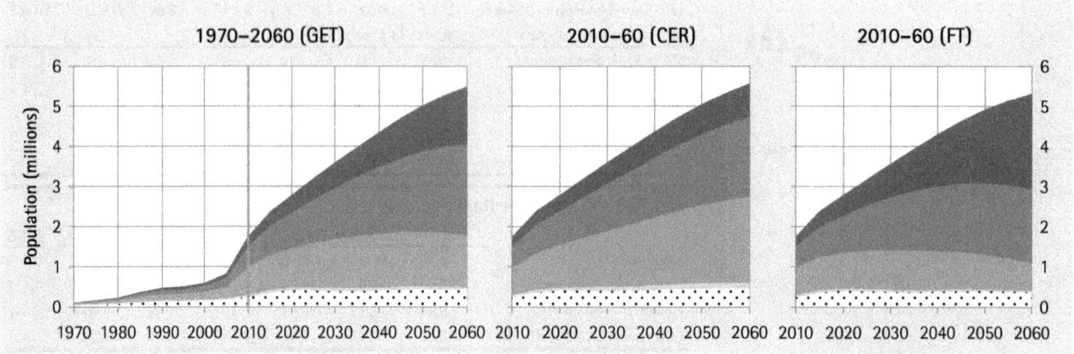

Qatar (Continued)

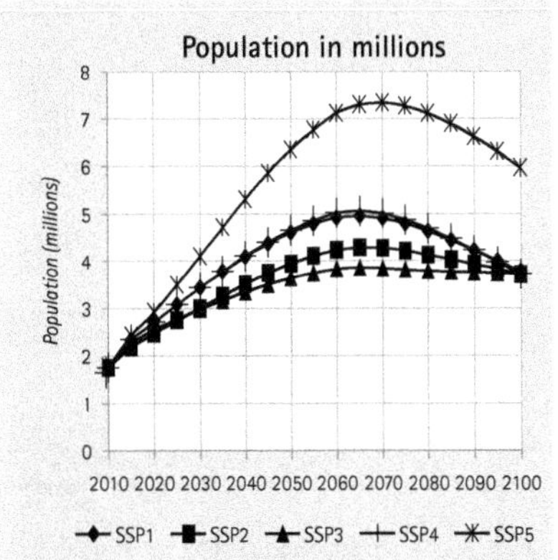

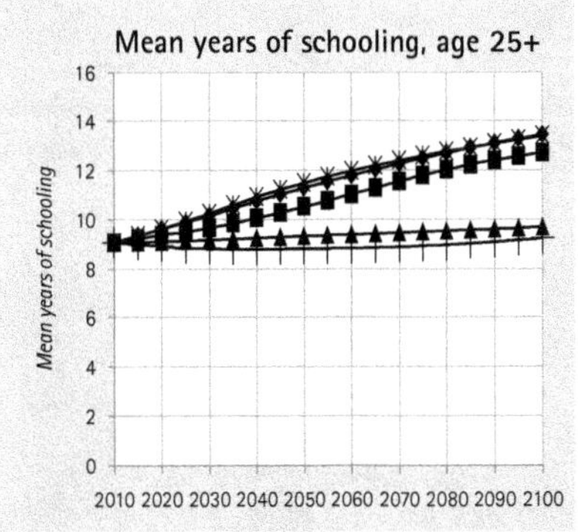

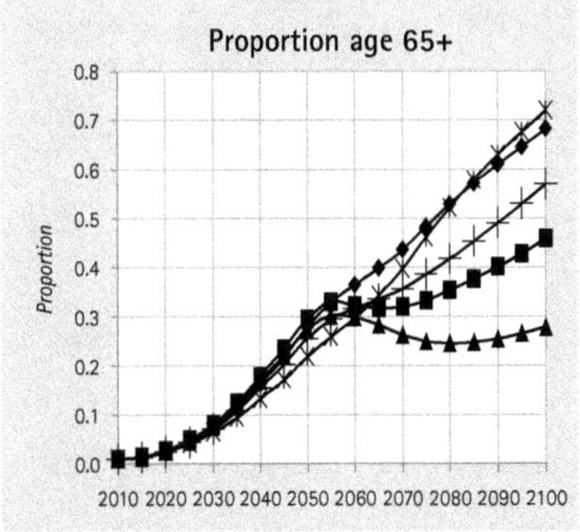

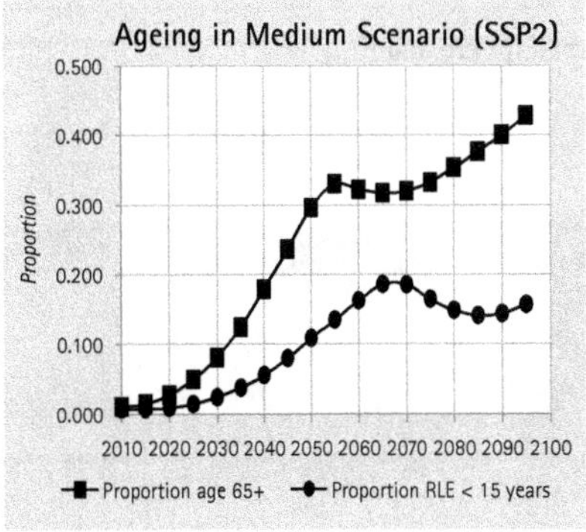

Alternative Scenarios to 2100

Projection Results by Scenario (SSP1–5)

	2010	2020	2030	2040	2050	2075	2100
Population (in millions)							
SSP1 - Rapid development	1.76	2.72	3.44	4.09	4.60	4.79	3.77
SSP2 - Medium	1.76	2.47	3.01	3.52	3.94	4.22	3.71
SSP3 - Stalled development	1.76	2.55	2.98	3.35	3.64	3.82	3.73
SSP4 - Inequality	1.76	2.72	3.44	4.10	4.65	4.87	3.71
SSP5 - Conventional development	1.76	2.92	4.10	5.30	6.34	7.27	5.96
Proportion age 65+							
SSP1 - Rapid development	0.01	0.03	0.07	0.16	0.28	0.48	0.68
SSP2 - Medium	0.01	0.03	0.08	0.18	0.30	0.33	0.46
SSP3 - Stalled development	0.01	0.03	0.08	0.17	0.27	0.25	0.28
SSP4 - Inequality	0.01	0.02	0.07	0.15	0.26	0.39	0.57
SSP5 - Conventional development	0.01	0.02	0.06	0.13	0.22	0.46	0.72
Proportion below age 20							
SSP1 - Rapid development	0.17	0.17	0.14	0.11	0.09	0.06	0.05
SSP2 - Medium	0.17	0.19	0.17	0.15	0.14	0.12	0.11
SSP3 - Stalled development	0.17	0.19	0.18	0.17	0.18	0.19	0.21
SSP4 - Inequality	0.17	0.18	0.14	0.12	0.10	0.08	0.07
SSP5 - Conventional development	0.17	0.17	0.13	0.10	0.08	0.05	0.04
Proportion of Women age 20–39 with at least secondary education							
SSP1 - Rapid development	0.71	0.84	0.90	0.91	0.92	0.94	0.97
SSP2 - Medium	0.71	0.78	0.82	0.84	0.84	0.88	0.94
SSP3 - Stalled development	0.71	0.78	0.79	0.79	0.79	0.79	0.79
SSP4 - Inequality	0.71	0.74	0.71	0.71	0.71	0.71	0.71
SSP5 - Conventional development	0.71	0.84	0.90	0.91	0.92	0.94	0.97
Mean years of schooling, age 25+							
SSP1 - Rapid development	9.07	9.62	10.16	10.75	11.29	12.48	13.44
SSP2 - Medium	9.07	9.38	9.66	10.06	10.52	11.79	12.71
SSP3 - Stalled development	9.07	9.10	9.17	9.24	9.32	9.50	9.69
SSP4 - Inequality	9.07	8.92	8.82	8.80	8.81	8.92	9.23
SSP5 - Conventional development	9.07	9.63	10.25	10.91	11.48	12.58	13.39

Demographic Assumptions Underlying SSPs

	2010–15	2020–25	2030–35	2040–45	2050–55	2075–80	2095–2100
Total fertility rate							
SSP1 - Rapid development	2.09	1.69	1.45	1.33	1.26	1.16	1.17
SSP2 - Medium	2.22	2.04	1.91	1.81	1.76	1.58	1.61
SSP3 - Stalled development	2.32	2.39	2.39	2.34	2.27	2.11	2.16
SSP4 - Inequality	2.10	1.77	1.55	1.43	1.35	1.25	1.28
SSP5 - Conventional development	2.09	1.69	1.45	1.33	1.26	1.16	1.17
Life expectancy at birth for females (in years)							
SSP1 - Rapid development	79.38	82.63	85.79	88.91	91.96	99.58	105.60
SSP2 - Medium	78.69	81.09	83.19	85.29	87.29	92.30	96.30
SSP3 - Stalled development	78.47	79.82	81.01	82.14	83.16	85.32	87.17
SSP4 - Inequality	78.94	81.27	83.39	85.52	87.49	92.10	95.91
SSP5 - Conventional development	79.38	82.63	85.79	88.91	91.96	99.58	105.60
Migration – net flow over five years (in thousands)							
SSP1 - Rapid development	484	296	291	263	227	41	0
SSP2 - Medium	326	194	200	201	199	59	0
SSP3 - Stalled development	403	134	127	132	144	52	0
SSP4 - Inequality	484	297	299	295	287	69	0
SSP5 - Conventional development	565	496	548	522	458	78	0

Ageing Indicators, Medium Scenario (SSP2)

	2010	2020	2030	2040	2050	2075	2095
Median age	31.57	37.90	44.46	49.03	48.84	53.44	60.06
Propspective median age	31.57	35.94	40.87	43.83	42.10	42.29	45.06
Proportion age 65+	0.01	0.03	0.08	0.18	0.30	0.33	0.43
Proportion RLE < 15 years	0.01	0.01	0.02	0.06	0.11	0.16	0.16

Republic of Korea

Detailed Human Capital Projections to 2060

Demographic indicators, Medium Scenario (SSP2)	2010	2020	2030	2040	2050	2060
Population (in millions)	48.18	49.61	49.95	48.88	46.39	43.04
Proportion age 65+	0.11	0.16	0.24	0.32	0.37	0.40
Proportion below age 20	0.24	0.18	0.17	0.16	0.14	0.14
	2005–10	2015–20	2025–30	2035–40	2045–50	2055–60
Total Fertility Rate	1.29	1.32	1.38	1.40	1.40	1.41
Life expectancy at birth (in years)						
Men	76.48	78.36	80.40	82.36	84.41	86.45
Women	83.26	85.01	86.91	88.81	90.79	92.80
Five-year immigration flow (in '000)	80.03	78.59	81.68	83.63	83.75	82.61
Five-year emigration flow (in '000)	109.96	74.57	62.15	53.20	46.83	41.04

Human Capital indicators, Medium Scenario (SSP2)	2010	2020	2030	2040	2050	2060
Population age 25+: highest educational attainment						
E1 – no education	0.05	0.02	0.01	0.00	0.00	0.00
E2 – incomplete primary	0.01	0.01	0.00	0.00	0.00	0.00
E3 – primary	0.11	0.08	0.05	0.03	0.01	0.00
E4 – lower secondary	0.10	0.08	0.06	0.04	0.02	0.01
E5 – upper secondary	0.37	0.36	0.34	0.32	0.28	0.24
E6 – post-secondary	0.36	0.45	0.53	0.60	0.68	0.75
Mean years of schooling (in years)	11.85	12.76	13.50	14.08	14.55	14.93
Gender gap (population age 25+): highest educational attainment (ratio male/female)						
E1 – no education	0.25	0.22	0.24	0.37	0.57	0.77
E2 – incomplete primary	0.41	0.35	0.32	0.35	0.40	0.54
E3 – primary	0.60	0.49	0.41	0.35	0.32	0.34
E4 – lower secondary	0.87	0.77	0.66	0.55	0.48	0.50
E5 – upper secondary	1.07	1.03	0.97	0.92	0.87	0.87
E6 – post-secondary	1.35	1.25	1.19	1.15	1.10	1.06
Mean years of schooling (male minus female)	1.51	1.17	0.85	0.60	0.39	0.21
Women age 20–39: highest educational attainment						
E1 – no education	0.00	0.00	0.00	0.00	0.00	0.00
E2 – incomplete primary	0.00	0.00	0.00	0.00	0.00	0.00
E3 – primary	0.00	0.00	0.00	0.00	0.00	0.00
E4 – lower secondary	0.01	0.01	0.00	0.00	0.00	0.00
E5 – upper secondary	0.43	0.34	0.29	0.29	0.28	0.28
E6 – post-secondary	0.55	0.65	0.71	0.71	0.71	0.72
Mean years of schooling (in years)	14.12	14.56	14.80	14.81	14.82	14.86

Education scenarios

GET: global education trend scenario (medium assumption also used for SSP2)

CER: constant enrolment rates scenario (assumption of no future improvements)

FT: Fast track scenario (assumption of education expansion according to fastest historical experience)

Pyramids by Education, Medium Scenario

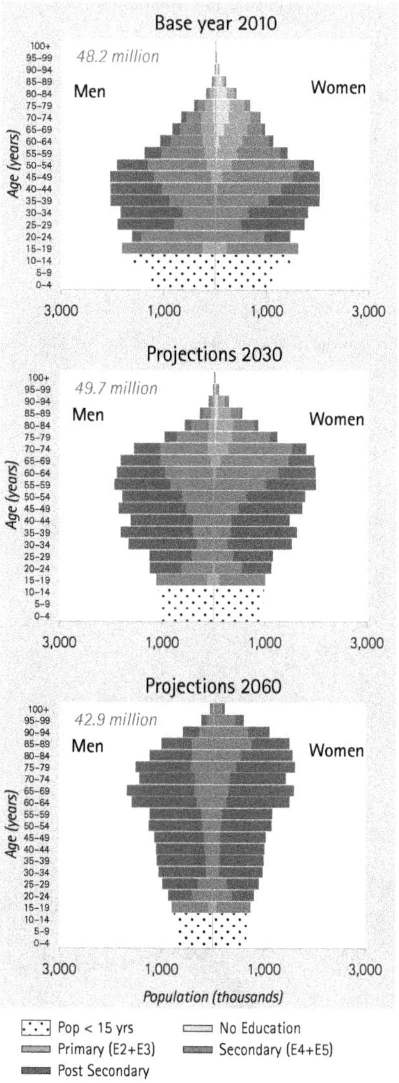

Population Size by Educational Attainment According to Three Education Scenarios: GET, CER, and FT

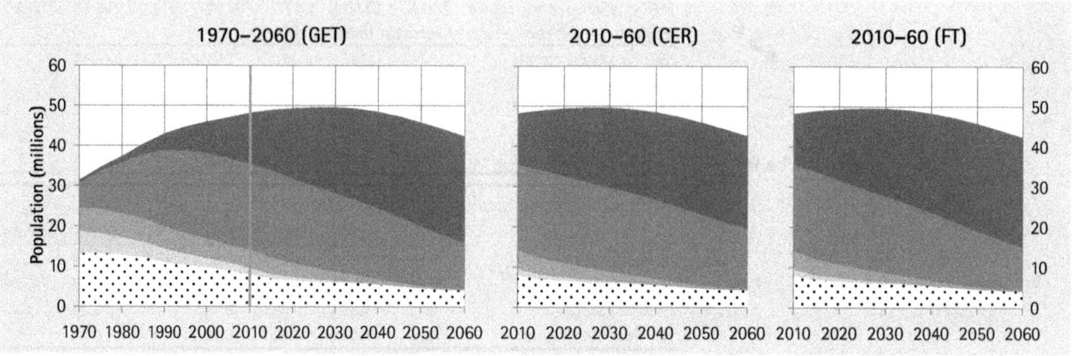

Republic of Korea (Continued)

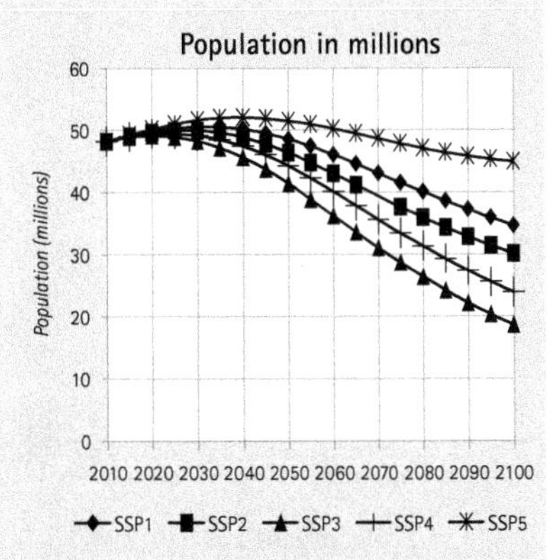

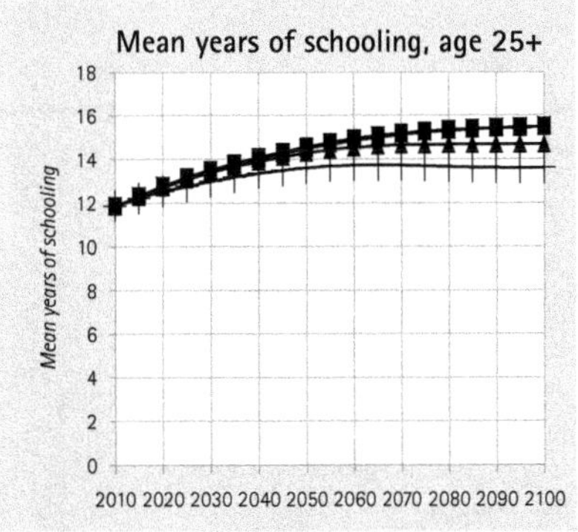

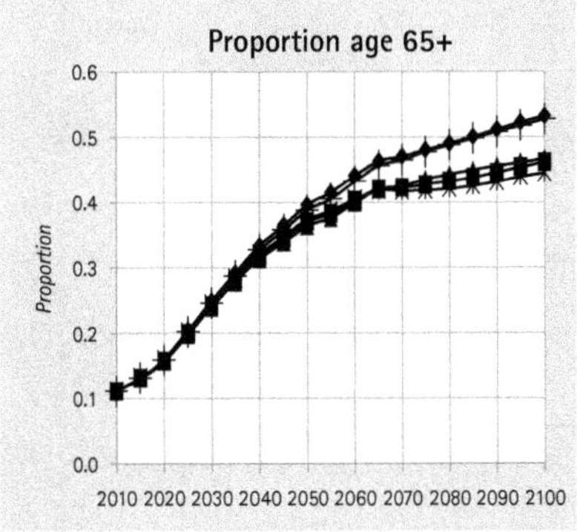

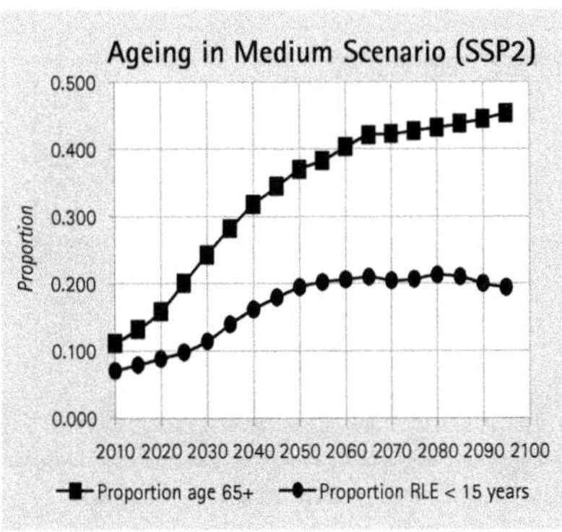

Alternative Scenarios to 2100

Projection Results by Scenario (SSP1–5)

	2010	2020	2030	2040	2050	2075	2100
Population (in millions)							
SSP1 - Rapid development	48.18	49.81	50.56	50.15	48.57	41.58	34.68
SSP2 - Medium	48.18	49.61	49.95	48.88	46.39	37.66	30.15
SSP3 - Stalled development	48.18	49.10	48.26	45.66	41.40	28.68	18.63
SSP4 - Inequality	48.18	49.34	49.10	47.43	44.27	33.45	23.89
SSP5 - Conventional development	48.18	50.14	51.62	52.05	51.48	47.83	44.89
Proportion age 65+							
SSP1 - Rapid development	0.11	0.16	0.25	0.33	0.40	0.48	0.53
SSP2 - Medium	0.11	0.16	0.24	0.32	0.37	0.43	0.46
SSP3 - Stalled development	0.11	0.16	0.24	0.31	0.36	0.43	0.47
SSP4 - Inequality	0.11	0.16	0.25	0.33	0.39	0.48	0.53
SSP5 - Conventional development	0.11	0.16	0.24	0.32	0.37	0.42	0.44
Proportion below age 20							
SSP1 - Rapid development	0.24	0.18	0.17	0.15	0.13	0.12	0.11
SSP2 - Medium	0.24	0.18	0.17	0.16	0.14	0.13	0.13
SSP3 - Stalled development	0.24	0.18	0.15	0.13	0.12	0.11	0.10
SSP4 - Inequality	0.24	0.18	0.16	0.14	0.12	0.10	0.10
SSP5 - Conventional development	0.24	0.19	0.18	0.17	0.16	0.16	0.16
Proportion of Women age 20–39 with at least secondary education							
SSP1 - Rapid development	1.00	1.00	1.00	1.00	1.00	1.00	1.00
SSP2 - Medium	1.00	1.00	1.00	1.00	1.00	1.00	1.00
SSP3 - Stalled development	1.00	1.00	1.00	1.00	1.00	1.00	1.00
SSP4 - Inequality	1.00	1.00	1.00	1.00	1.00	1.00	1.00
SSP5 - Conventional development	1.00	1.00	1.00	1.00	1.00	1.00	1.00
Mean years of schooling, age 25+							
SSP1 - Rapid development	11.85	12.76	13.47	14.02	14.48	15.22	15.48
SSP2 - Medium	11.85	12.76	13.50	14.08	14.55	15.27	15.47
SSP3 - Stalled development	11.85	12.71	13.38	13.90	14.28	14.67	14.68
SSP4 - Inequality	11.85	12.53	12.99	13.35	13.60	13.69	13.60
SSP5 - Conventional development	11.85	12.76	13.47	14.03	14.49	15.24	15.48

Demographic Assumptions Underlying SSPs

	2010–15	2020–25	2030–35	2040–45	2050–55	2075–80	2095–2100
Total fertility rate							
SSP1 - Rapid development	1.30	1.35	1.38	1.39	1.40	1.46	1.51
SSP2 - Medium	1.30	1.35	1.40	1.40	1.40	1.46	1.51
SSP3 - Stalled development	1.24	1.15	1.11	1.08	1.07	1.12	1.15
SSP4 - Inequality	1.24	1.19	1.17	1.15	1.14	1.18	1.22
SSP5 - Conventional development	1.37	1.55	1.68	1.73	1.75	1.82	1.88
Life expectancy at birth for females (in years)							
SSP1 - Rapid development	85.26	88.01	90.73	93.59	96.50	103.86	109.83
SSP2 - Medium	84.09	85.91	87.91	89.81	91.79	96.80	100.80
SSP3 - Stalled development	84.31	85.08	85.84	86.75	87.64	89.95	91.88
SSP4 - Inequality	84.81	86.55	88.34	90.16	92.06	96.69	100.52
SSP5 - Conventional development	85.26	88.01	90.73	93.59	96.50	103.86	109.83
Migration – net flow over five years (in thousands)							
SSP1 - Rapid development	−9	12	25	33	37	15	0
SSP2 - Medium	−8	12	26	34	39	17	0
SSP3 - Stalled development	−7	6	13	17	20	9	0
SSP4 - Inequality	−9	12	25	33	37	16	0
SSP5 - Conventional development	−10	18	38	50	58	26	0

Ageing Indicators, Medium Scenario (SSP2)

	2010	2020	2030	2040	2050	2075	2095
Median age	37.93	43.32	48.01	51.93	55.40	58.80	61.07
Propspective median age	37.93	41.59	44.44	46.66	48.41	47.22	45.61
Proportion age 65+	0.11	0.16	0.24	0.32	0.37	0.43	0.45
Proportion RLE < 15 years	0.07	0.09	0.11	0.16	0.19	0.21	0.19

Republic of Moldova

Detailed Human Capital Projections to 2060

Demographic indicators, Medium Scenario (SSP2)	2010	2020	2030	2040	2050	2060
Population (in millions)	3.57	3.22	2.89	2.56	2.24	1.94
Proportion age 65+	0.11	0.15	0.21	0.23	0.29	0.37
Proportion below age 20	0.25	0.22	0.19	0.17	0.16	0.15
	2005–10	2015–20	2025–30	2035–40	2045–50	2055–60
Total Fertility Rate	1.50	1.33	1.47	1.50	1.50	1.51
Life expectancy at birth (in years)						
Men	64.42	67.59	70.25	72.69	75.03	77.22
Women	72.06	74.69	76.89	78.99	81.09	83.09
Five-year immigration flow (in '000)	10.97	10.80	11.24	11.49	11.48	11.31
Five-year emigration flow (in '000)	182.41	116.66	88.12	70.12	55.86	44.69

Human Capital indicators, Medium Scenario (SSP2)	2010	2020	2030	2040	2050	2060
Population age 25+: highest educational attainment						
E1 - no education	0.00	0.00	0.00	0.00	0.00	0.00
E2 - incomplete primary	0.02	0.01	0.00	0.00	0.00	0.00
E3 - primary	0.09	0.04	0.02	0.01	0.01	0.01
E4 - lower secondary	0.26	0.24	0.21	0.18	0.14	0.11
E5 - upper secondary	0.48	0.55	0.59	0.62	0.65	0.66
E6 - post-secondary	0.14	0.16	0.17	0.18	0.20	0.22
Mean years of schooling (in years)	10.29	10.82	11.09	11.28	11.44	11.59
Gender gap (population age 25+): highest educational attainment (ratio male/female)						
E1 - no education	0.42	0.51	0.76	0.93	0.89	0.87
E2 - incomplete primary	0.46	0.53	0.66	0.80	0.83	0.84
E3 - primary	0.64	0.64	0.80	1.10	1.29	1.30
E4 - lower secondary	1.22	1.23	1.23	1.24	1.23	1.19
E5 - upper secondary	1.04	1.01	1.00	1.00	1.01	1.01
E6 - post-secondary	0.89	0.83	0.81	0.81	0.83	0.87
Mean years of schooling (male minus female)	0.24	−0.03	−0.17	−0.22	−0.21	−0.16
Women age 20–39: highest educational attainment						
E1 - no education	0.00	0.00	0.00	0.00	0.00	0.00
E2 - incomplete primary	0.00	0.00	0.00	0.00	0.00	0.00
E3 - primary	0.01	0.01	0.01	0.00	0.00	0.00
E4 - lower secondary	0.26	0.18	0.15	0.12	0.10	0.09
E5 - upper secondary	0.56	0.61	0.64	0.65	0.65	0.65
E6 - post-secondary	0.16	0.20	0.21	0.23	0.24	0.25
Mean years of schooling (in years)	11.03	11.36	11.49	11.62	11.74	11.81

Education scenarios

GET: global education trend scenario (medium assumption also used for SSP2)

CER: constant enrolment rates scenario (assumption of no future improvements)

FT: Fast track scenario (assumption of education expansion according to fastest historical experience)

Pyramids by Education, Medium Scenario

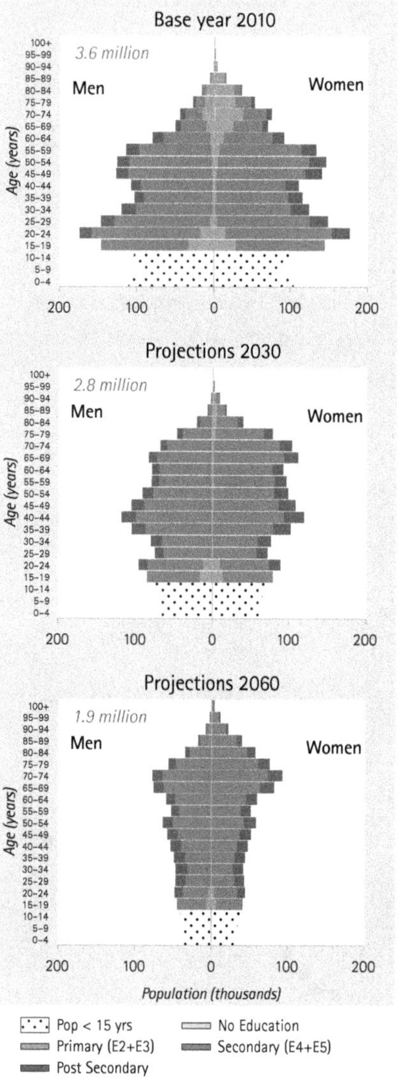

Population Size by Educational Attainment According to Three Education Scenarios: GET, CER, and FT

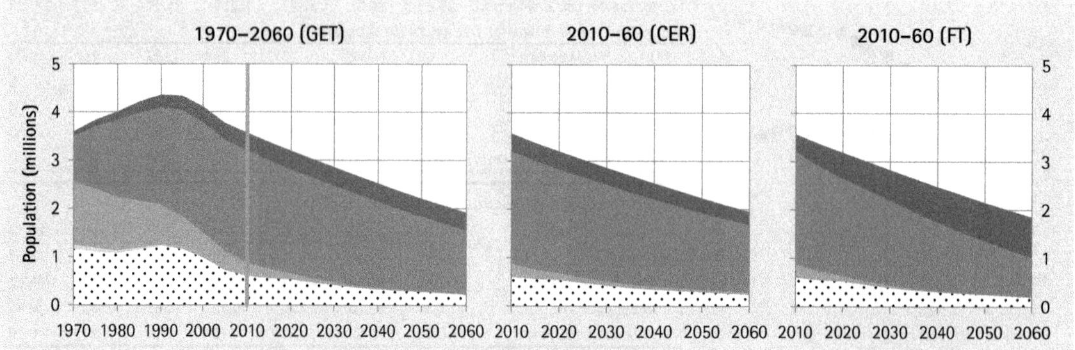

Republic of Moldova (Continued)

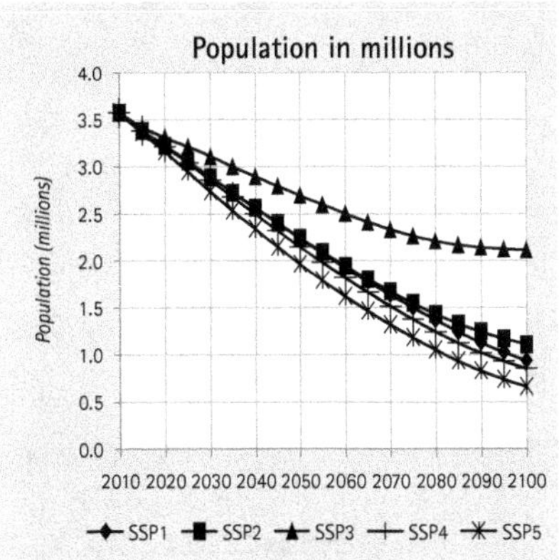

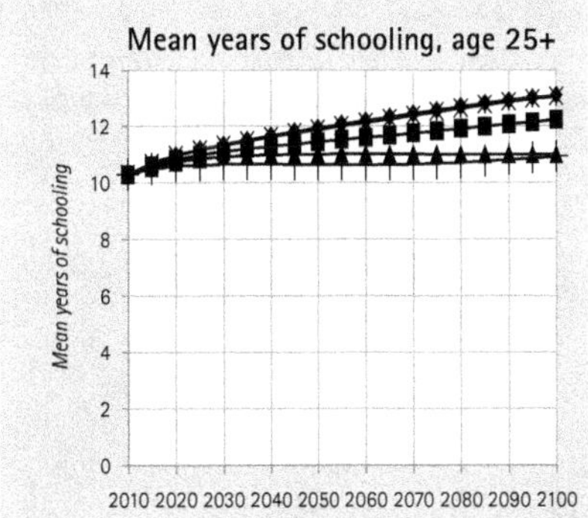

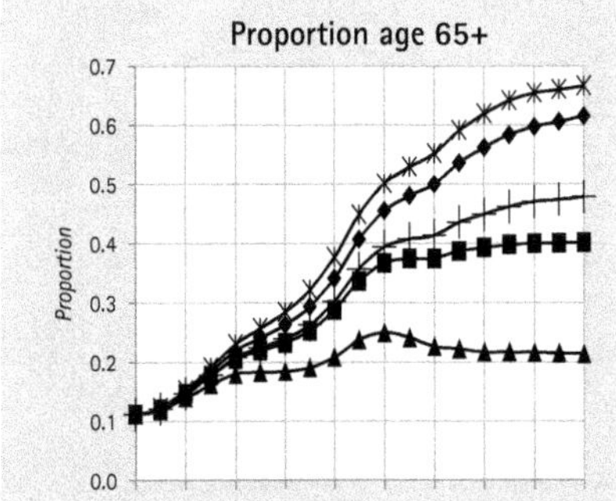

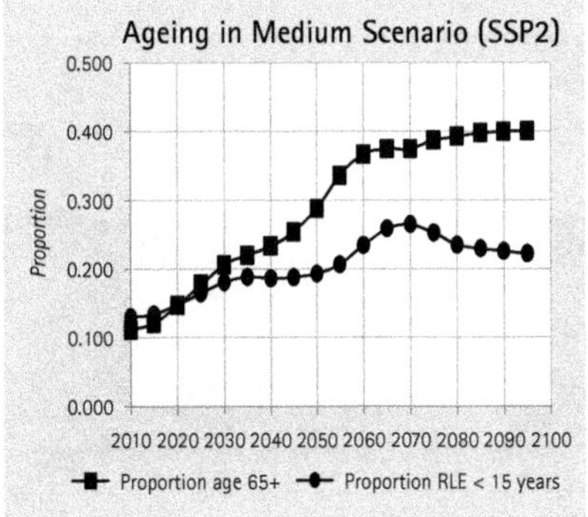

Alternative Scenarios to 2100

Projection Results by Scenario (SSP1–5)

	2010	2020	2030	2040	2050	2075	2100
Population (in millions)							
SSP1 - Rapid development	3.57	3.22	2.89	2.56	2.24	1.50	0.94
SSP2 - Medium	3.57	3.22	2.89	2.56	2.24	1.55	1.11
SSP3 - Stalled development	3.57	3.31	3.11	2.89	2.69	2.26	2.12
SSP4 - Inequality	3.57	3.21	2.86	2.50	2.15	1.37	0.85
SSP5 - Conventional development	3.57	3.16	2.74	2.34	1.96	1.18	0.66
Proportion age 65+							
SSP1 - Rapid development	0.11	0.15	0.22	0.26	0.34	0.54	0.62
SSP2 - Medium	0.11	0.15	0.21	0.23	0.29	0.39	0.40
SSP3 - Stalled development	0.11	0.14	0.18	0.18	0.21	0.22	0.21
SSP4 - Inequality	0.11	0.15	0.21	0.24	0.30	0.44	0.48
SSP5 - Conventional development	0.11	0.15	0.23	0.28	0.38	0.59	0.67
Proportion below age 20							
SSP1 - Rapid development	0.25	0.21	0.17	0.13	0.11	0.07	0.07
SSP2 - Medium	0.25	0.22	0.19	0.17	0.16	0.14	0.14
SSP3 - Stalled development	0.25	0.23	0.22	0.22	0.22	0.23	0.24
SSP4 - Inequality	0.25	0.21	0.18	0.15	0.13	0.10	0.10
SSP5 - Conventional development	0.25	0.21	0.17	0.13	0.10	0.06	0.05
Proportion of Women age 20–39 with at least secondary education							
SSP1 - Rapid development	0.98	0.99	1.00	1.00	1.00	1.00	1.00
SSP2 - Medium	0.98	0.99	0.99	0.99	1.00	1.00	1.00
SSP3 - Stalled development	0.98	0.98	0.98	0.98	0.98	0.98	0.98
SSP4 - Inequality	0.98	0.92	0.88	0.88	0.88	0.88	0.88
SSP5 - Conventional development	0.98	0.99	1.00	1.00	1.00	1.00	1.00
Mean years of schooling, age 25+							
SSP1 - Rapid development	10.29	10.96	11.34	11.66	11.93	12.57	13.09
SSP2 - Medium	10.29	10.82	11.09	11.28	11.44	11.83	12.22
SSP3 - Stalled development	10.29	10.72	10.91	10.98	11.00	11.00	10.99
SSP4 - Inequality	10.29	10.58	10.65	10.65	10.64	10.68	10.92
SSP5 - Conventional development	10.29	10.95	11.32	11.62	11.88	12.50	13.05

Demographic Assumptions Underlying SSPs

	2010–15	2020–25	2030–35	2040–45	2050–55	2075–80	2095–2100
Total fertility rate							
SSP1 - Rapid development	1.20	1.16	1.13	1.11	1.10	1.13	1.16
SSP2 - Medium	1.27	1.40	1.50	1.50	1.51	1.55	1.58
SSP3 - Stalled development	1.35	1.65	1.86	1.93	1.97	2.04	2.11
SSP4 - Inequality	1.22	1.22	1.20	1.18	1.17	1.20	1.23
SSP5 - Conventional development	1.20	1.16	1.13	1.11	1.10	1.13	1.16
Life expectancy at birth for females (in years)							
SSP1 - Rapid development	74.96	78.08	81.20	84.13	87.04	94.38	100.34
SSP2 - Medium	73.49	75.89	77.99	80.09	82.09	87.11	91.09
SSP3 - Stalled development	74.08	75.23	76.28	77.33	78.28	80.58	82.44
SSP4 - Inequality	74.56	76.71	78.69	80.68	82.54	87.19	90.98
SSP5 - Conventional development	74.96	78.08	81.20	84.13	87.04	94.38	100.34
Migration – net flow over five years (in thousands)							
SSP1 - Rapid development	−135	−88	−65	−47	−33	−7	0
SSP2 - Medium	−143	−92	−69	−52	−39	−10	0
SSP3 - Stalled development	−112	−45	−35	−29	−23	−8	0
SSP4 - Inequality	−135	−88	−64	−45	−31	−6	0
SSP5 - Conventional development	−158	−130	−94	−67	−46	−9	0

Ageing Indicators, Medium Scenario (SSP2)

	2010	2020	2030	2040	2050	2075	2095
Median age	35.16	39.04	44.03	49.27	52.74	56.82	57.00
Propspective median age	35.16	36.61	39.51	42.75	44.31	43.83	40.20
Proportion age 65+	0.11	0.15	0.21	0.23	0.29	0.39	0.40
Proportion RLE < 15 years	0.13	0.15	0.18	0.19	0.19	0.25	0.22

Réunion

Detailed Human Capital Projections to 2060

Demographic indicators, Medium Scenario (SSP2)	2010	2020	2030	2040	2050	2060
Population (in millions)	0.85	0.94	1.03	1.10	1.16	1.20
Proportion age 65+	0.08	0.11	0.16	0.19	0.21	0.24
Proportion below age 20	0.34	0.31	0.28	0.26	0.24	0.23
	2005-10	2015-20	2025-30	2035-40	2045-50	2055-60
Total Fertility Rate	2.40	2.19	2.04	1.96	1.91	1.89
Life expectancy at birth (in years)						
Male	73.69	75.97	78.28	80.50	82.65	84.79
Female	81.08	83.21	85.21	87.21	89.21	91.20
Five-year immigration flow (in '000)	3.4	3.3	3.4	3.5	3.5	3.5
Five-year emigration flow (in '000)	3.4	2.6	2.7	2.7	2.6	2.6

Human Capital indicators, Medium Scenario (SSP2)	2010	2020	2030	2040	2050	2060
Population age 25+: highest educational attainment						
E1 - no education	0.06	0.04	0.02	0.01	0.01	0.00
E2 - incomplete primary	0.10	0.07	0.05	0.03	0.02	0.01
E3 - primary	0.29	0.23	0.18	0.13	0.09	0.06
E4 - lower secondary	0.13	0.14	0.13	0.11	0.09	0.08
E5 - upper secondary	0.27	0.34	0.39	0.43	0.46	0.48
E6 - post-secondary	0.15	0.19	0.24	0.28	0.33	0.37
Mean years of schooling (in years)	8.70	9.82	10.75	11.54	12.21	12.78
Gender gap (population age 25+): highest educational attainment (ratio male/female)						
E1 - no education	1.00	1.00	0.95	0.89	0.83	0.80
E2 - incomplete primary	0.83	0.85	0.87	0.88	0.90	0.97
E3 - primary	0.94	0.92	0.91	0.90	0.91	0.95
E4 - lower secondary	0.90	0.93	0.94	0.94	0.93	0.93
E5 - upper secondary	1.18	1.15	1.14	1.13	1.11	1.07
E6 - post-secondary	1.02	0.95	0.92	0.91	0.92	0.94
Mean years of schooling (male minus female)	0.33	0.22	0.14	0.07	0.02	-0.03
Women age 20–39: highest educational attainment						
E1 - no education	0.01	0.00	0.00	0.00	0.00	0.00
E2 - incomplete primary	0.02	0.01	0.00	0.00	0.00	0.00
E3 - primary	0.15	0.08	0.05	0.03	0.02	0.01
E4 - lower secondary	0.18	0.16	0.11	0.08	0.06	0.05
E5 - upper secondary	0.42	0.48	0.52	0.53	0.53	0.52
E6 - post-secondary	0.22	0.27	0.32	0.36	0.40	0.42
Mean years of schooling (in years)	10.96	11.98	12.70	13.11	13.38	13.56

Education scenarios

GET: global education trend scenario (medium assumption also used for SSP2)

CER: constant enrolment rates scenario (assumption of no future improvements)

FT: Fast track scenario (assumption of education expansion according to fastest historical experience)

Pyramids by Education, Medium Scenario

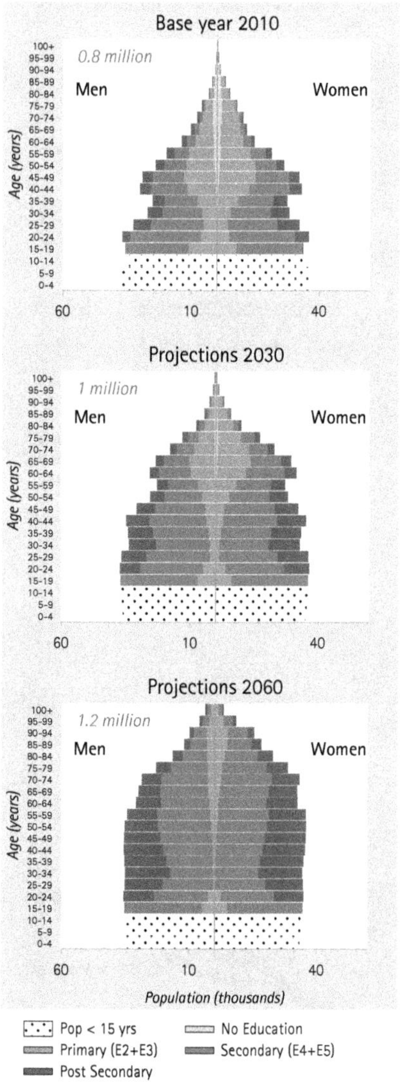

Population Size by Educational Attainment According to Three Education Scenarios: GET, CER, and FT

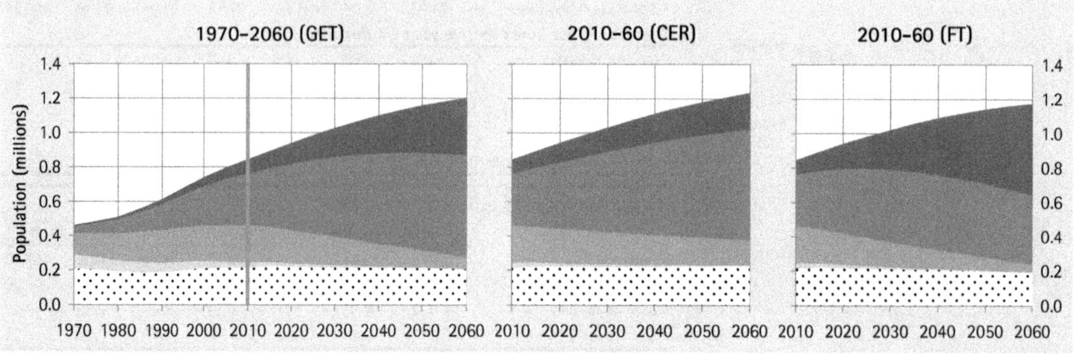

Réunion (Continued)

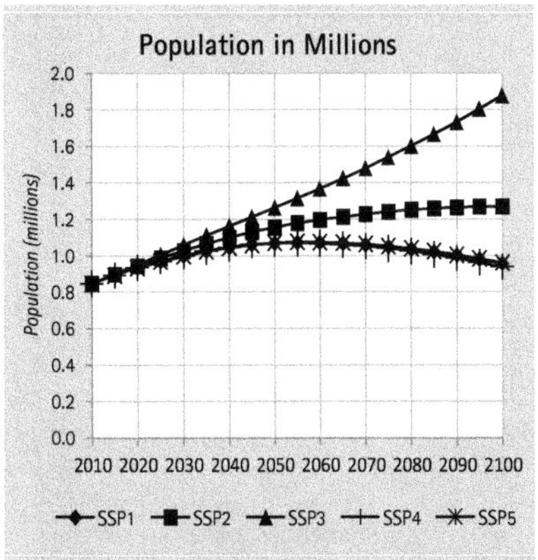

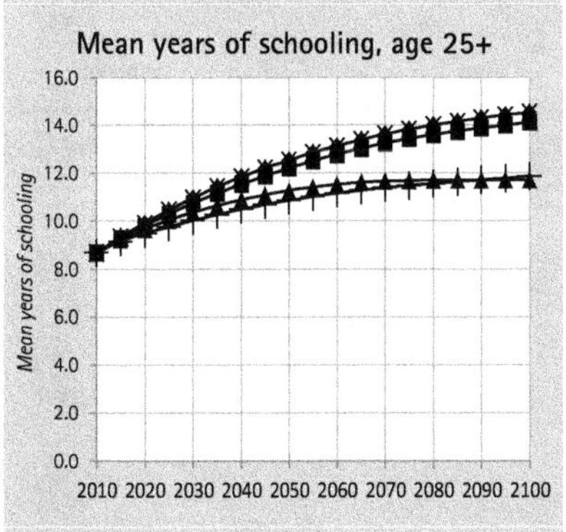

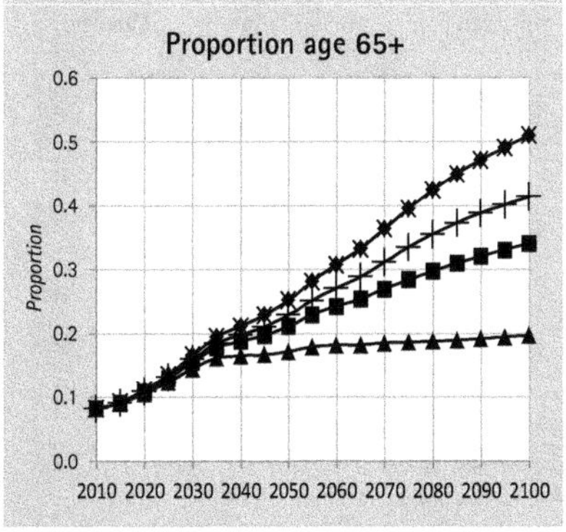

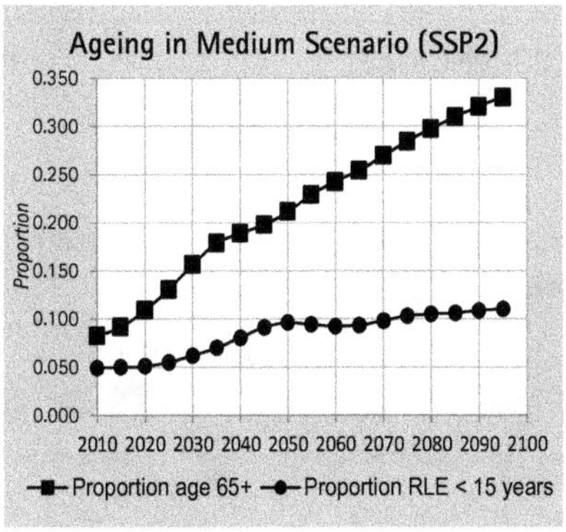

Alternative Scenarios to 2100

Projection Results by Scenario (SSP1–5)

	2010	2020	2030	2040	2050	2075	2100
Population (in millions)							
SSP1 - Rapid development	0.85	0.93	1.00	1.04	1.07	1.05	0.96
SSP2 - Medium	0.85	0.94	1.03	1.10	1.16	1.24	1.27
SSP3 - Stalled development	0.85	0.95	1.06	1.16	1.26	1.54	1.88
SSP4 - Inequality	0.85	0.93	1.00	1.05	1.07	1.04	0.94
SSP5 - Conventional development	0.85	0.93	1.00	1.05	1.07	1.05	0.96
Proportion age 65+							
SSP1 - Rapid development	0.08	0.11	0.17	0.21	0.25	0.40	0.51
SSP2 - Medium	0.08	0.11	0.16	0.19	0.21	0.28	0.34
SSP3 - Stalled development	0.08	0.11	0.15	0.17	0.17	0.19	0.20
SSP4 - Inequality	0.08	0.11	0.16	0.20	0.23	0.34	0.41
SSP5 - Conventional development	0.08	0.11	0.17	0.21	0.25	0.40	0.51
Proportion below age 20							
SSP1 - Rapid development	0.34	0.30	0.25	0.21	0.19	0.14	0.11
SSP2 - Medium	0.34	0.31	0.28	0.26	0.24	0.21	0.19
SSP3 - Stalled development	0.34	0.32	0.31	0.31	0.30	0.30	0.29
SSP4 - Inequality	0.34	0.31	0.26	0.23	0.20	0.17	0.14
SSP5 - Conventional development	0.34	0.30	0.25	0.21	0.19	0.14	0.11
Proportion of Women age 20–39 with at least secondary education							
SSP1 - Rapid development	0.82	0.93	0.97	0.98	0.99	1.00	1.00
SSP2 - Medium	0.82	0.91	0.95	0.97	0.98	1.00	1.00
SSP3 - Stalled development	0.82	0.88	0.88	0.88	0.88	0.88	0.88
SSP4 - Inequality	0.82	0.83	0.79	0.80	0.80	0.80	0.80
SSP5 - Conventional development	0.82	0.93	0.97	0.98	0.99	1.00	1.00
Mean years of schooling, age 25+							
SSP1 - Rapid development	8.70	9.92	10.97	11.84	12.54	13.82	14.52
SSP2 - Medium	8.70	9.82	10.75	11.54	12.21	13.43	14.11
SSP3 - Stalled development	8.70	9.67	10.37	10.89	11.28	11.69	11.72
SSP4 - Inequality	8.70	9.50	10.04	10.50	10.87	11.49	11.86
SSP5 - Conventional development	8.70	9.92	10.97	11.84	12.54	13.82	14.52

Demographic Assumptions Underlying SSPs

	2010–15	2020–25	2030–35	2040–45	2050–55	2075–80	2095–2100
Total fertility rate							
SSP1 - Rapid development	2.14	1.76	1.54	1.44	1.39	1.38	1.37
SSP2 - Medium	2.26	2.11	1.98	1.93	1.89	1.87	1.85
SSP3 - Stalled development	2.38	2.47	2.52	2.53	2.54	2.56	2.56
SSP4 - Inequality	2.17	1.87	1.67	1.57	1.52	1.50	1.49
SSP5 - Conventional development	2.14	1.76	1.54	1.44	1.39	1.38	1.37
Life expectancy at birth for females (in years)							
SSP1 - Rapid development	83.1	86.1	89.1	92.0	95.0	102.3	108.4
SSP2 - Medium	82.1	84.2	86.2	88.2	90.2	95.2	99.2
SSP3 - Stalled development	82.1	83.1	84.2	85.2	86.1	88.2	90.0
SSP4 - Inequality	82.6	84.6	86.6	88.6	90.5	95.0	98.8
SSP5 - Conventional development	83.1	86.1	89.1	92.0	95.0	102.3	108.4
Migration – net flow over five years (in thousands)							
SSP1 - Rapid development	0	1	1	1	1	0	0
SSP2 - Medium	0	1	1	1	1	0	0
SSP3 - Stalled development	0	0	0	1	1	1	0
SSP4 - Inequality	0	1	1	1	1	0	0
SSP5 - Conventional development	0	1	1	1	1	0	0

Ageing Indicators, Medium Scenario (SSP2)

	2010	2020	2030	2040	2050	2075	2095
Median age	29.92	32.68	35.61	38.10	40.75	45.98	49.36
Propspective median age	29.92	30.29	30.98	31.33	32.03	32.44	31.94
Proportion age 65+	0.08	0.11	0.16	0.19	0.21	0.28	0.33
Proportion RLE < 15 years	0.05	0.05	0.06	0.08	0.10	0.10	0.11

Romania

Detailed Human Capital Projections to 2060

Demographic indicators, Medium Scenario (SSP2)	2010	2020	2030	2040	2050	2060
Population (in millions)	21.49	20.77	19.96	19.00	17.84	16.45
Proportion age 65+	0.15	0.18	0.21	0.27	0.33	0.37
Proportion below age 20	0.21	0.19	0.17	0.16	0.16	0.15
	2005–10	2015–20	2025–30	2035–40	2045–50	2055–60
Total Fertility Rate	1.33	1.32	1.47	1.50	1.50	1.51
Life expectancy at birth (in years)						
Men	69.57	72.48	75.15	77.62	79.93	81.91
Women	76.82	79.59	81.89	84.09	86.21	88.01
Five-year immigration flow (in '000)	42.49	41.85	43.52	44.57	44.65	44.04
Five-year emigration flow (in '000)	142.36	87.01	73.28	62.86	54.54	48.11

Human Capital indicators, Medium Scenario (SSP2)	2010	2020	2030	2040	2050	2060
Population age 25+: highest educational attainment						
E1 - no education	0.03	0.01	0.01	0.01	0.00	0.00
E2 - incomplete primary	0.01	0.01	0.00	0.00	0.00	0.00
E3 - primary	0.10	0.06	0.03	0.02	0.01	0.01
E4 - lower secondary	0.23	0.19	0.15	0.12	0.09	0.06
E5 - upper secondary	0.50	0.58	0.64	0.68	0.70	0.72
E6 - post-secondary	0.14	0.16	0.17	0.18	0.19	0.21
Mean years of schooling (in years)	10.52	11.21	11.67	11.99	12.25	12.49
Gender gap (population age 25+): highest educational attainment (ratio male/female)						
E1 - no education	0.44	0.49	0.57	0.60	0.59	0.60
E2 - incomplete primary	0.60	0.54	0.56	0.66	0.74	0.77
E3 - primary	0.55	0.50	0.57	0.72	0.83	0.83
E4 - lower secondary	0.77	0.72	0.69	0.70	0.72	0.74
E5 - upper secondary	1.29	1.24	1.19	1.15	1.12	1.10
E6 - post-secondary	1.08	0.92	0.82	0.77	0.77	0.80
Mean years of schooling (male minus female)	0.97	0.60	0.28	0.06	−0.06	−0.10
Women age 20–39: highest educational attainment						
E1 - no education	0.01	0.00	0.00	0.00	0.00	0.00
E2 - incomplete primary	0.00	0.00	0.00	0.00	0.00	0.00
E3 - primary	0.03	0.01	0.01	0.00	0.00	0.00
E4 - lower secondary	0.18	0.12	0.10	0.09	0.08	0.08
E5 - upper secondary	0.61	0.66	0.68	0.69	0.68	0.68
E6 - post-secondary	0.18	0.20	0.21	0.22	0.24	0.24
Mean years of schooling (in years)	11.66	12.14	12.34	12.50	12.59	12.64

Education scenarios

GET: global education trend scenario (medium assumption also used for SSP2)

CER: constant enrolment rates scenario (assumption of no future improvements)

FT: Fast track scenario (assumption of education expansion according to fastest historical experience)

Pyramids by Education, Medium Scenario

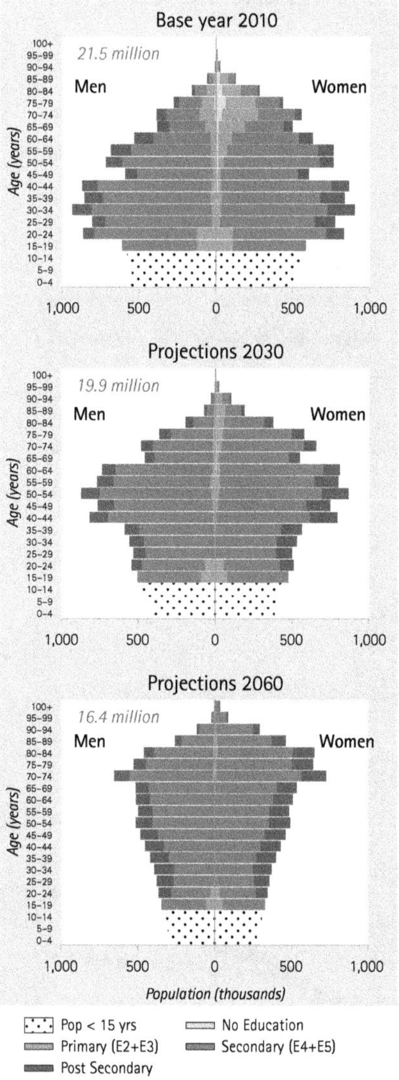

Population Size by Educational Attainment According to Three Education Scenarios: GET, CER, and FT

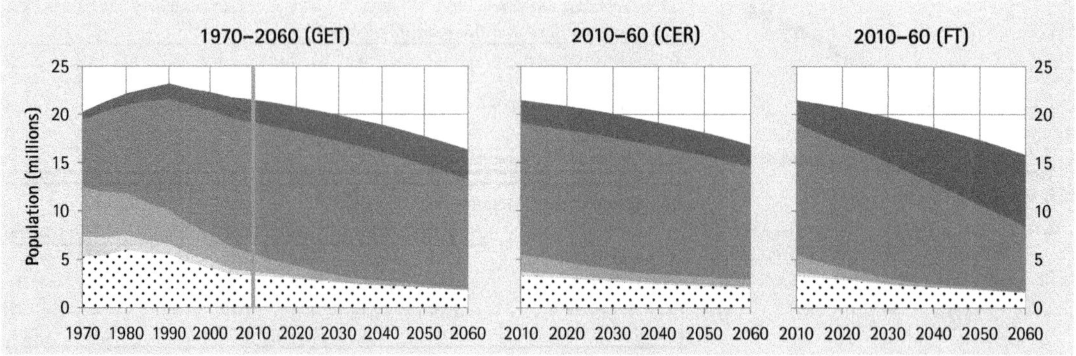

Romania (Continued)

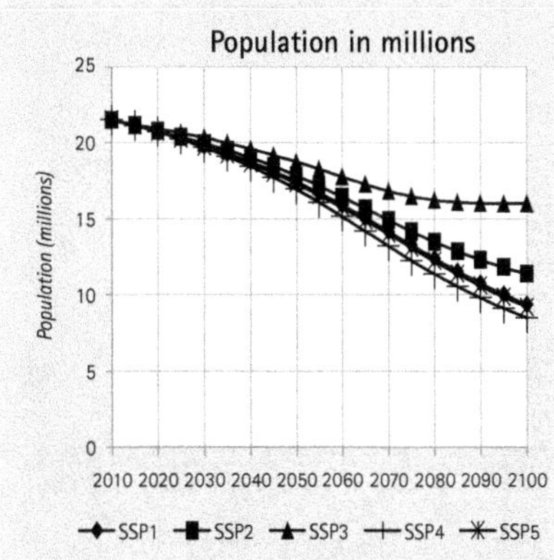

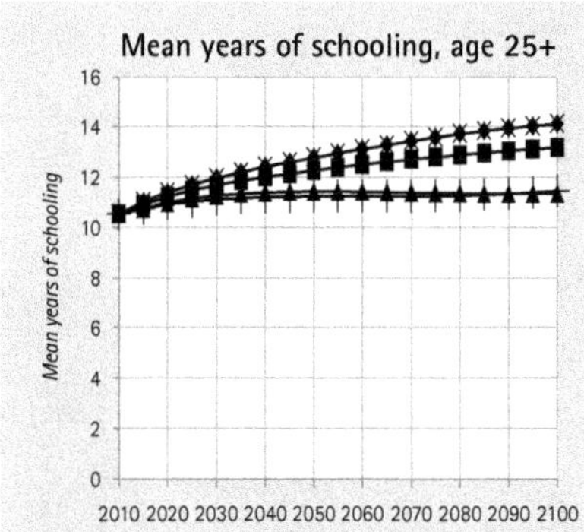

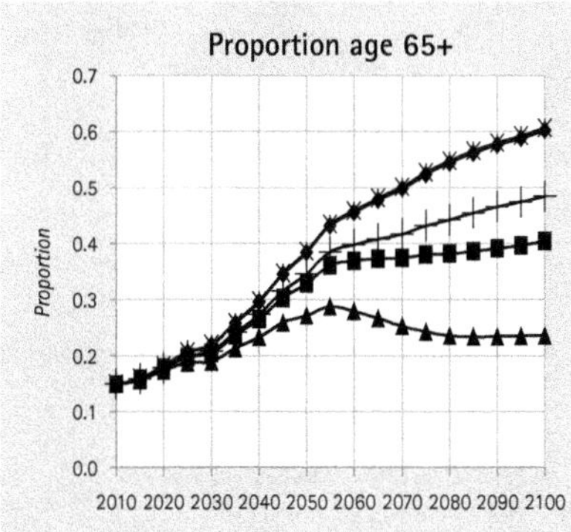

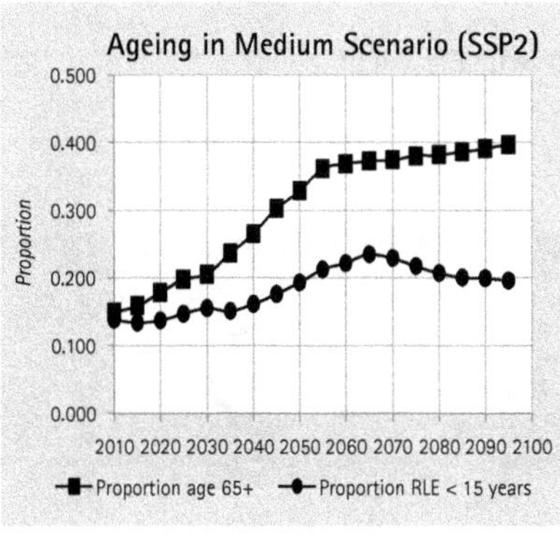

Alternative Scenarios to 2100

Projection Results by Scenario (SSP1–5)

	2010	2020	2030	2040	2050	2075	2100
Population (in millions)							
SSP1 - Rapid development	21.49	20.72	19.78	18.73	17.44	13.28	9.36
SSP2 - Medium	21.49	20.77	19.96	19.00	17.84	14.19	11.37
SSP3 - Stalled development	21.49	20.91	20.32	19.58	18.74	16.48	16.02
SSP4 - Inequality	21.49	20.70	19.67	18.43	16.93	12.27	8.49
SSP5 - Conventional development	21.49	20.69	19.71	18.62	17.31	13.11	9.18
Proportion age 65+							
SSP1 - Rapid development	0.15	0.18	0.22	0.30	0.38	0.52	0.60
SSP2 - Medium	0.15	0.18	0.21	0.27	0.33	0.38	0.40
SSP3 - Stalled development	0.15	0.17	0.19	0.23	0.27	0.24	0.24
SSP4 - Inequality	0.15	0.18	0.21	0.27	0.35	0.43	0.48
SSP5 - Conventional development	0.15	0.18	0.22	0.30	0.39	0.53	0.61
Proportion below age 20							
SSP1 - Rapid development	0.21	0.18	0.15	0.13	0.11	0.08	0.07
SSP2 - Medium	0.21	0.19	0.17	0.16	0.16	0.15	0.15
SSP3 - Stalled development	0.21	0.20	0.20	0.20	0.21	0.23	0.24
SSP4 - Inequality	0.21	0.19	0.16	0.14	0.13	0.11	0.10
SSP5 - Conventional development	0.21	0.18	0.15	0.13	0.11	0.08	0.07
Proportion of Women age 20–39 with at least secondary education							
SSP1 - Rapid development	0.96	0.99	1.00	1.00	1.00	1.00	1.00
SSP2 - Medium	0.96	0.98	0.99	1.00	1.00	1.00	1.00
SSP3 - Stalled development	0.96	0.93	0.93	0.93	0.93	0.93	0.93
SSP4 - Inequality	0.96	0.88	0.84	0.84	0.84	0.84	0.84
SSP5 - Conventional development	0.96	0.99	1.00	1.00	1.00	1.00	1.00
Mean years of schooling, age 25+							
SSP1 - Rapid development	10.52	11.38	11.95	12.40	12.77	13.58	14.11
SSP2 - Medium	10.52	11.21	11.67	11.99	12.25	12.80	13.18
SSP3 - Stalled development	10.52	10.98	11.26	11.38	11.42	11.37	11.35
SSP4 - Inequality	10.52	10.92	11.11	11.20	11.23	11.25	11.45
SSP5 - Conventional development	10.52	11.38	11.95	12.40	12.76	13.58	14.11

Demographic Assumptions Underlying SSPs

	2010–15	2020–25	2030–35	2040–45	2050–55	2075–80	2095–2100
Total fertility rate							
SSP1 - Rapid development	1.20	1.14	1.13	1.11	1.10	1.12	1.15
SSP2 - Medium	1.25	1.40	1.50	1.50	1.50	1.55	1.58
SSP3 - Stalled development	1.36	1.70	1.90	1.96	1.99	2.06	2.12
SSP4 - Inequality	1.23	1.25	1.23	1.20	1.18	1.21	1.24
SSP5 - Conventional development	1.20	1.14	1.13	1.11	1.10	1.12	1.15
Life expectancy at birth for females (in years)							
SSP1 - Rapid development	79.89	82.88	85.90	88.99	91.86	98.84	104.49
SSP2 - Medium	78.29	80.69	82.99	85.21	87.11	91.70	95.30
SSP3 - Stalled development	79.01	80.09	81.14	82.18	83.00	84.75	86.29
SSP4 - Inequality	79.45	81.45	83.46	85.55	87.31	91.45	94.91
SSP5 - Conventional development	79.89	82.88	85.90	88.99	91.86	98.84	104.49
Migration – net flow over five years (in thousands)							
SSP1 - Rapid development	−65	−36	−23	−12	−5	0	0
SSP2 - Medium	−64	−37	−24	−14	−7	−1	0
SSP3 - Stalled development	−54	−18	−12	−7	−4	0	0
SSP4 - Inequality	−65	−36	−23	−11	−4	1	0
SSP5 - Conventional development	−76	−55	−36	−20	−10	−2	0

Ageing Indicators, Medium Scenario (SSP2)

	2010	2020	2030	2040	2050	2075	2095
Median age	38.46	42.54	46.69	50.96	53.14	55.38	56.54
Propspective median age	38.46	40.34	42.39	44.62	45.03	43.00	40.58
Proportion age 65+	0.15	0.18	0.21	0.27	0.33	0.38	0.40
Proportion RLE < 15 years	0.14	0.14	0.16	0.16	0.19	0.22	0.20

Russian Federation

Detailed Human Capital Projections to 2060

Demographic indicators, Medium Scenario (SSP2)	2010	2020	2030	2040	2050	2060
Population (in millions)	142.96	142.09	138.45	134.88	132.18	128.95
Proportion age 65+	0.13	0.15	0.19	0.20	0.24	0.27
Proportion below age 20	0.21	0.22	0.21	0.19	0.20	0.20
	2005–10	2015–20	2025–30	2035–40	2045–50	2055–60
Total Fertility Rate	1.44	1.56	1.51	1.58	1.68	1.70
Life expectancy at birth (in years)						
Men	61.56	64.94	68.13	70.90	73.45	76.10
Women	74.03	76.00	78.09	79.99	81.89	83.99
Five-year immigration flow (in '000)	1,399.32	1,376.28	1,431.37	1,464.16	1,465.78	1,445.09
Five-year emigration flow (in '000)	267.00	167.41	150.93	141.79	129.26	122.45

Human Capital indicators, Medium Scenario (SSP2)	2010	2020	2030	2040	2050	2060
Population age 25+: highest educational attainment						
E1 - no education	0.00	0.00	0.00	0.00	0.00	0.00
E2 - incomplete primary	0.00	0.00	0.00	0.00	0.00	0.00
E3 - primary	0.04	0.01	0.01	0.00	0.00	0.00
E4 - lower secondary	0.08	0.05	0.03	0.02	0.01	0.01
E5 - upper secondary	0.67	0.71	0.72	0.71	0.69	0.68
E6 - post-secondary	0.21	0.23	0.25	0.27	0.29	0.31
Mean years of schooling (in years)	10.44	10.93	11.24	11.53	11.80	12.05
Gender gap (population age 25+): highest educational attainment (ratio male/female)						
E1 - no education	0.65	0.80	0.89	0.89	0.90	0.93
E2 - incomplete primary	0.56	0.69	0.83	0.87	0.88	0.91
E3 - primary	0.62	0.66	0.86	1.13	1.21	1.20
E4 - lower secondary	0.92	1.00	1.15	1.24	1.21	1.14
E5 - upper secondary	1.08	1.08	1.08	1.08	1.08	1.07
E6 - post-secondary	0.88	0.81	0.79	0.79	0.82	0.87
Mean years of schooling (male minus female)	0.03	–0.10	–0.16	–0.15	–0.13	–0.09
Women age 20–39: highest educational attainment						
E1 - no education	0.00	0.00	0.00	0.00	0.00	0.00
E2 - incomplete primary	0.00	0.00	0.00	0.00	0.00	0.00
E3 - primary	0.00	0.00	0.00	0.00	0.00	0.00
E4 - lower secondary	0.04	0.03	0.03	0.03	0.02	0.03
E5 - upper secondary	0.72	0.70	0.68	0.66	0.64	0.63
E6 - post-secondary	0.24	0.28	0.29	0.31	0.34	0.34
Mean years of schooling (in years)	11.15	11.80	12.06	12.17	12.27	12.29

Education scenarios

GET: global education trend scenario (medium assumption also used for SSP2)

CER: constant enrolment rates scenario (assumption of no future improvements)

FT: Fast track scenario (assumption of education expansion according to fastest historical experience)

Pyramids by Education, Medium Scenario

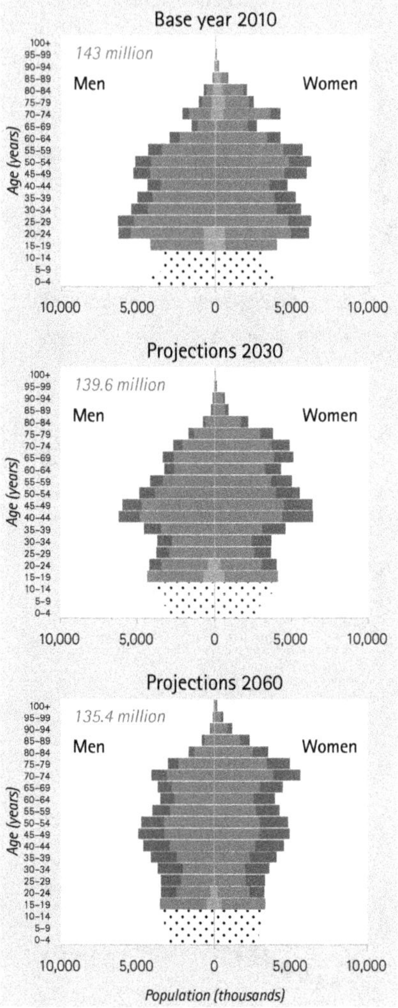

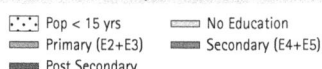

Pop < 15 yrs · No Education · Primary (E2+E3) · Secondary (E4+E5) · Post Secondary

Population Size by Educational Attainment According to Three Education Scenarios: GET, CER, and FT

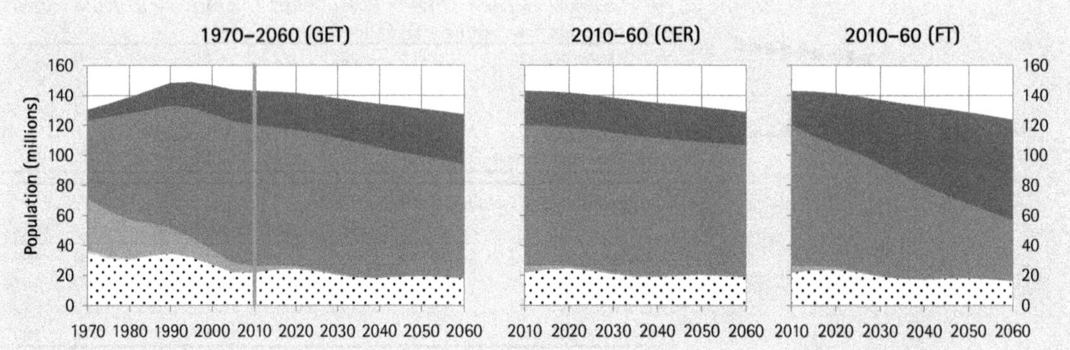

Russian Federation (Continued)

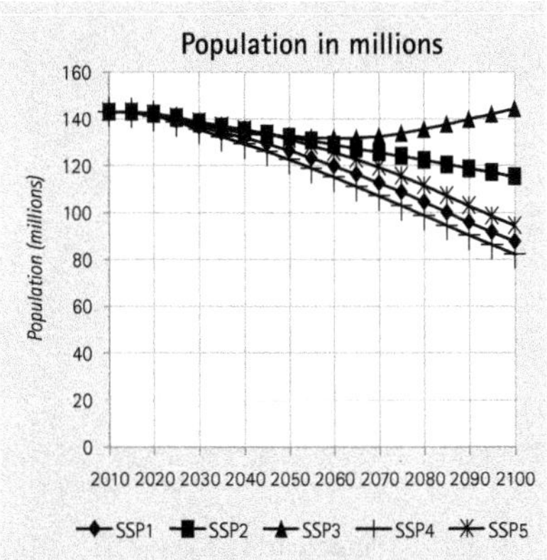

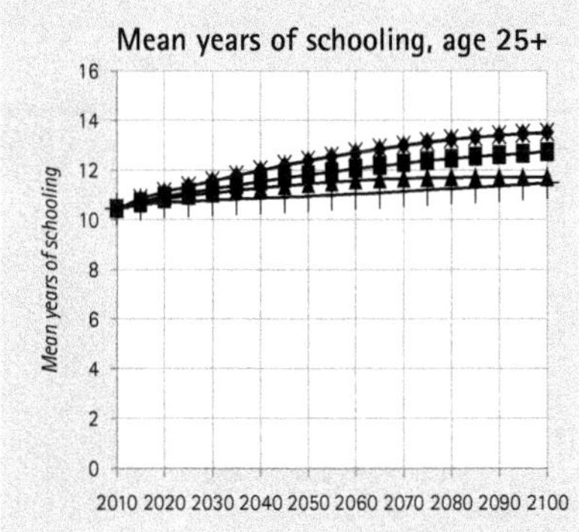

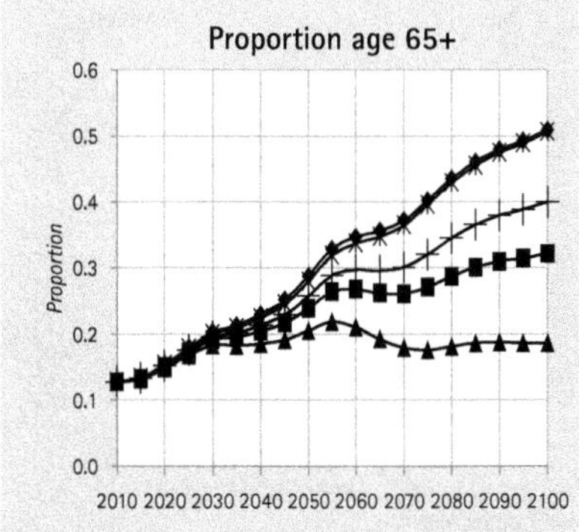

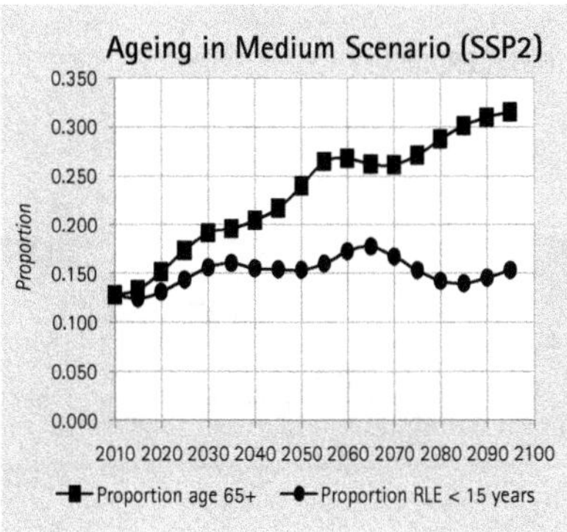

Alternative Scenarios to 2100

Projection Results by Rcenario (SSP1–5)

	2010	2020	2030	2040	2050	2075	2100
Population (in millions)							
SSP1 - Rapid development	142.96	141.28	136.60	131.77	126.41	108.68	87.68
SSP2 - Medium	142.96	142.09	138.45	134.88	132.18	124.00	115.25
SSP3 - Stalled development	142.96	141.94	137.85	134.01	132.52	133.81	144.13
SSP4 - Inequality	142.96	140.92	135.41	129.20	122.58	102.98	82.29
SSP5 - Conventional development	142.96	141.91	138.64	135.25	131.17	115.56	94.37
Proportion age 65+							
SSP1 - Rapid development	0.13	0.15	0.20	0.23	0.29	0.40	0.51
SSP2 - Medium	0.13	0.15	0.19	0.20	0.24	0.27	0.32
SSP3 - Stalled development	0.13	0.15	0.18	0.19	0.21	0.18	0.19
SSP4 - Inequality	0.13	0.15	0.20	0.21	0.26	0.32	0.40
SSP5 - Conventional development	0.13	0.15	0.20	0.22	0.28	0.40	0.51
Proportion below age 20							
SSP1 - Rapid development	0.21	0.21	0.19	0.15	0.15	0.12	0.10
SSP2 - Medium	0.21	0.22	0.21	0.19	0.20	0.19	0.18
SSP3 - Stalled development	0.21	0.23	0.24	0.22	0.25	0.26	0.27
SSP4 - Inequality	0.21	0.22	0.19	0.16	0.16	0.14	0.13
SSP5 - Conventional development	0.21	0.21	0.19	0.15	0.15	0.12	0.10
Proportion of Women age 20–39 with at least secondary education							
SSP1 - Rapid development	1.00	1.00	1.00	1.00	1.00	1.00	1.00
SSP2 - Medium	1.00	1.00	1.00	1.00	1.00	1.00	1.00
SSP3 - Stalled development	1.00	0.99	0.99	0.99	0.99	0.99	0.99
SSP4 - Inequality	1.00	0.94	0.89	0.89	0.89	0.89	0.89
SSP5 - Conventional development	1.00	1.00	1.00	1.00	1.00	1.00	1.00
Mean years of schooling, age 25+							
SSP1 - Rapid development	10.44	11.11	11.55	11.98	12.36	13.11	13.50
SSP2 - Medium	10.44	10.93	11.24	11.53	11.80	12.37	12.73
SSP3 - Stalled development	10.44	10.83	11.08	11.28	11.45	11.68	11.70
SSP4 - Inequality	10.44	10.70	10.79	10.87	10.95	11.20	11.46
SSP5 - Conventional development	10.44	11.12	11.56	11.99	12.38	13.12	13.50

Demographic Assumptions Underlying SSPs

	2010–15	2020–25	2030–35	2040–45	2050–55	2075–80	2095–2100
Total fertility rate							
SSP1 - Rapid development	1.49	1.28	1.19	1.21	1.24	1.26	1.27
SSP2 - Medium	1.58	1.54	1.53	1.63	1.70	1.71	1.72
SSP3 - Stalled development	1.66	1.80	1.91	2.05	2.16	2.21	2.23
SSP4 - Inequality	1.50	1.34	1.26	1.27	1.30	1.32	1.33
SSP5 - Conventional development	1.49	1.28	1.19	1.21	1.24	1.26	1.27
Life expectancy at birth for females (in years)							
SSP1 - Rapid development	76.25	79.04	81.95	84.73	87.68	95.52	101.86
SSP2 - Medium	75.00	77.00	78.99	80.89	82.89	88.30	92.71
SSP3 - Stalled development	75.31	76.14	77.10	77.93	78.89	81.63	83.86
SSP4 - Inequality	75.79	77.58	79.45	81.22	83.08	88.19	92.47
SSP5 - Conventional development	76.25	79.04	81.95	84.73	87.68	95.52	101.86
Migration – net flow over five years (in thousands)							
SSP1 - Rapid development	1120	1223	1232	1150	1035	323	0
SSP2 - Medium	1155	1243	1296	1318	1308	557	0
SSP3 - Stalled development	932	624	689	791	899	545	0
SSP4 - Inequality	1119	1224	1261	1255	1222	491	0
SSP5 - Conventional development	1308	1819	1808	1656	1467	444	0

Ageing Indicators, Medium Scenario (SSP2)

	2010	2020	2030	2040	2050	2075	2095
Median age	37.81	39.63	43.37	45.59	44.59	47.57	49.76
Propspective median age	37.81	37.36	39.16	39.64	36.41	33.92	31.60
Proportion age 65+	0.13	0.15	0.19	0.20	0.24	0.27	0.31
Proportion RLE < 15 years	0.13	0.13	0.16	0.15	0.15	0.15	0.15

Rwanda

Detailed Human Capital Projections to 2060

Demographic indicators, Medium Scenario (SSP2)	2010	2020	2030	2040	2050	2060
Population (in millions)	10.62	13.79	16.95	20.21	23.32	25.85
Proportion age 65+	0.03	0.03	0.03	0.04	0.06	0.07
Proportion below age 20	0.53	0.52	0.47	0.43	0.39	0.35
	2005–10	2015–20	2025–30	2035–40	2045–50	2055–60
Total Fertility Rate	5.43	4.55	3.72	3.09	2.66	2.28
Life expectancy at birth (in years)						
Men	52.70	55.87	57.76	59.45	61.18	63.70
Women	55.15	58.72	61.08	63.28	65.32	67.88
Five-year immigration flow (in '000)	61.36	59.97	62.18	63.51	63.47	62.51
Five-year emigration flow (in '000)	46.13	43.47	54.16	65.28	73.38	80.15

Human Capital indicators, Medium Scenario (SSP2)	2010	2020	2030	2040	2050	2060
Population age 25+: highest educational attainment						
E1 - no education	0.33	0.24	0.18	0.13	0.09	0.06
E2 - incomplete primary	0.33	0.30	0.25	0.20	0.15	0.11
E3 - primary	0.25	0.31	0.37	0.41	0.43	0.43
E4 - lower secondary	0.04	0.06	0.07	0.08	0.09	0.09
E5 - upper secondary	0.04	0.07	0.11	0.16	0.21	0.28
E6 - post-secondary	0.01	0.01	0.02	0.02	0.03	0.04
Mean years of schooling (in years)	3.88	4.81	5.69	6.59	7.39	8.13
Gender gap (population age 25+): highest educational attainment (ratio male/female)						
E1 - no education	0.76	0.84	0.93	1.01	1.06	1.06
E2 - incomplete primary	1.10	1.08	1.09	1.11	1.11	1.10
E3 - primary	1.06	0.92	0.87	0.87	0.88	0.91
E4 - lower secondary	1.36	1.12	1.02	0.98	0.96	0.95
E5 - upper secondary	1.58	1.49	1.36	1.25	1.16	1.10
E6 - post-secondary	2.91	2.04	1.55	1.25	1.11	1.07
Mean years of schooling (male minus female)	0.70	0.44	0.26	0.14	0.10	0.09
Women age 20–39: highest educational attainment						
E1 - no education	0.21	0.15	0.09	0.06	0.04	0.02
E2 - incomplete primary	0.33	0.25	0.18	0.12	0.09	0.06
E3 - primary	0.34	0.42	0.48	0.48	0.45	0.39
E4 - lower secondary	0.07	0.09	0.11	0.13	0.14	0.16
E5 - upper secondary	0.05	0.08	0.12	0.18	0.25	0.32
E6 - post-secondary	0.01	0.01	0.01	0.02	0.03	0.04
Mean years of schooling (in years)	4.81	5.78	6.74	7.57	8.31	9.00

Education scenarios

GET: global education trend scenario (medium assumption also used for SSP2)

CER: constant enrolment rates scenario (assumption of no future improvements)

FT: Fast track scenario (assumption of education expansion according to fastest historical experience)

Pyramids by Education, Medium Scenario

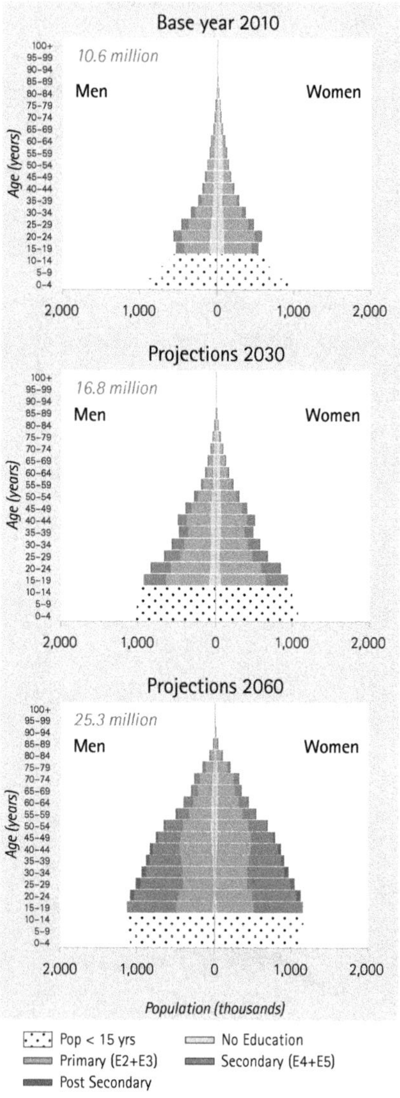

Population Size by Educational Attainment According to Three Education Scenarios: GET, CER, and FT

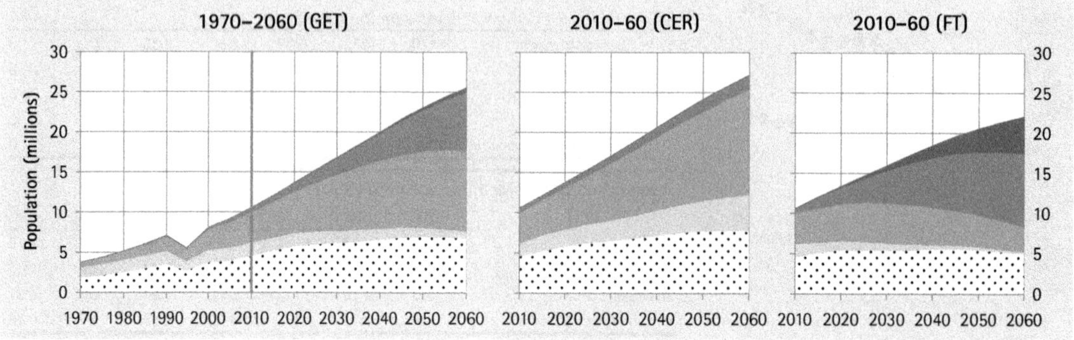

Rwanda (Continued)

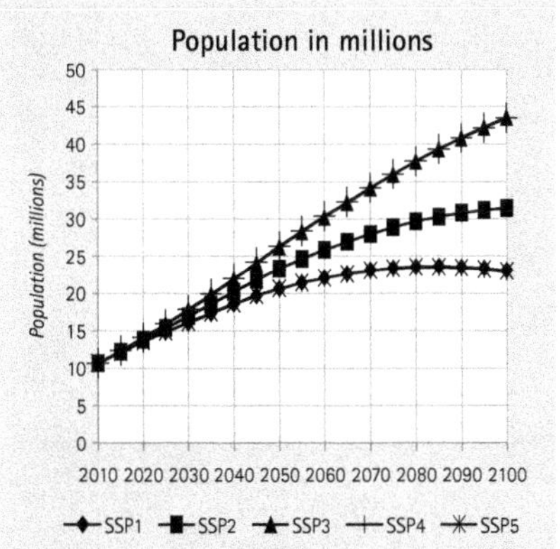

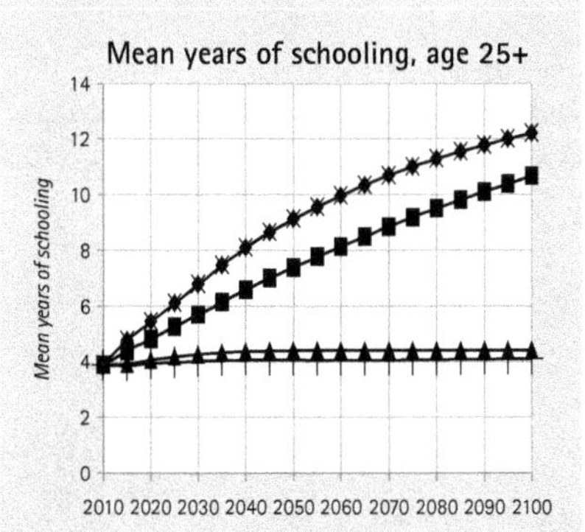

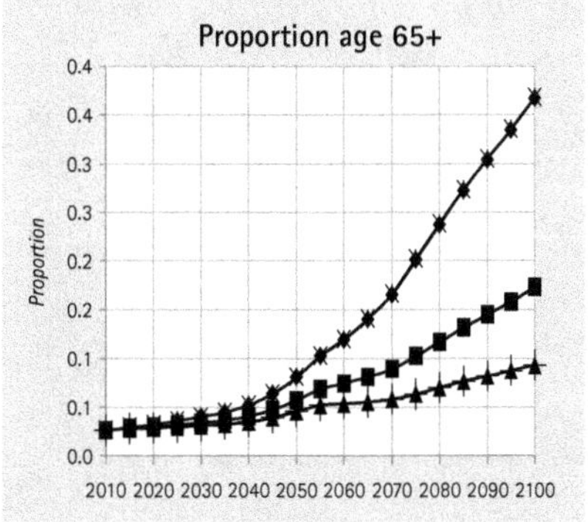

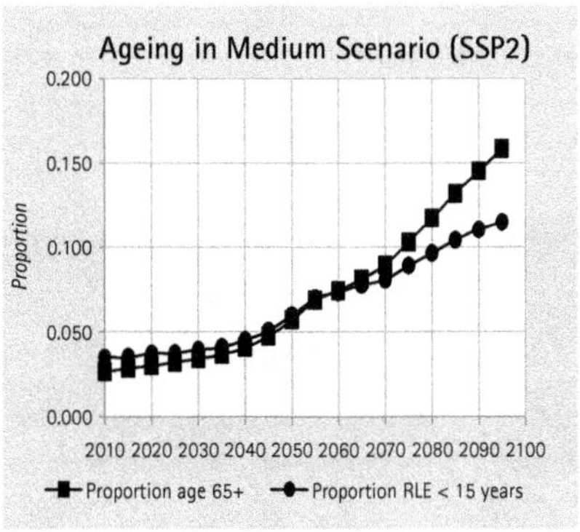

Alternative Scenarios to 2100

Projection Results by Scenario (SSP1–5)

	2010	2020	2030	2040	2050	2075	2100
Population (in millions)							
SSP1 - Rapid development	10.62	13.50	16.08	18.56	20.63	23.39	23.03
SSP2 - Medium	10.62	13.79	16.95	20.21	23.32	28.89	31.45
SSP3 - Stalled development	10.62	14.07	17.80	21.93	26.28	35.95	43.55
SSP4 - Inequality	10.62	14.09	17.86	22.01	26.36	35.97	43.46
SSP5 - Conventional development	10.62	13.51	16.10	18.58	20.63	23.31	22.90
Proportion age 65+							
SSP1 - Rapid development	0.03	0.03	0.04	0.05	0.08	0.20	0.37
SSP2 - Medium	0.03	0.03	0.03	0.04	0.06	0.10	0.17
SSP3 - Stalled development	0.03	0.03	0.03	0.03	0.05	0.06	0.09
SSP4 - Inequality	0.03	0.03	0.03	0.03	0.05	0.06	0.09
SSP5 - Conventional development	0.03	0.03	0.04	0.05	0.08	0.20	0.37
Proportion below age 20							
SSP1 - Rapid development	0.53	0.50	0.43	0.36	0.31	0.20	0.13
SSP2 - Medium	0.53	0.52	0.47	0.43	0.39	0.30	0.24
SSP3 - Stalled development	0.53	0.53	0.51	0.48	0.45	0.38	0.34
SSP4 - Inequality	0.53	0.53	0.51	0.48	0.45	0.38	0.33
SSP5 - Conventional development	0.53	0.50	0.43	0.36	0.31	0.20	0.13
Proportion of Women age 20–39 with at least secondary education							
SSP1 - Rapid development	0.12	0.32	0.47	0.59	0.67	0.81	0.91
SSP2 - Medium	0.12	0.18	0.25	0.33	0.42	0.66	0.85
SSP3 - Stalled development	0.12	0.08	0.08	0.08	0.08	0.08	0.08
SSP4 - Inequality	0.12	0.08	0.08	0.08	0.08	0.08	0.08
SSP5 - Conventional development	0.12	0.32	0.47	0.59	0.67	0.81	0.91
Mean years of schooling, age 25+							
SSP1 - Rapid development	3.88	5.44	6.79	8.09	9.12	11.00	12.20
SSP2 - Medium	3.88	4.81	5.69	6.59	7.39	9.19	10.66
SSP3 - Stalled development	3.88	4.06	4.25	4.36	4.39	4.40	4.40
SSP4 - Inequality	3.88	3.93	4.01	4.05	4.06	4.06	4.10
SSP5 - Conventional development	3.88	5.44	6.79	8.09	9.12	10.99	12.20

Demographic Assumptions Underlying SSPs

	2010–15	2020–25	2030–35	2040–45	2050–55	2075–80	2095–2100
Total fertility rate							
SSP1 - Rapid development	4.64	3.26	2.44	1.98	1.69	1.35	1.22
SSP2 - Medium	4.97	4.11	3.38	2.85	2.46	1.91	1.71
SSP3 - Stalled development	5.32	5.04	4.50	3.92	3.43	2.72	2.49
SSP4 - Inequality	5.33	5.07	4.53	3.93	3.44	2.71	2.48
SSP5 - Conventional development	4.64	3.26	2.44	1.98	1.69	1.35	1.22
Life expectancy at birth for females (in years)							
SSP1 - Rapid development	62.41	67.99	72.14	76.00	79.62	88.44	95.61
SSP2 - Medium	57.13	59.92	62.18	64.18	66.62	73.28	78.69
SSP3 - Stalled development	60.38	58.50	59.66	60.35	60.72	64.04	66.58
SSP4 - Inequality	60.38	58.48	59.62	60.30	60.67	63.98	66.52
SSP5 - Conventional development	62.41	67.99	72.14	76.00	79.62	88.44	95.61
Migration – net flow over five years (in thousands)							
SSP1 - Rapid development	16	12	3	−6	−13	−6	0
SSP2 - Medium	17	13	3	−6	−14	−7	0
SSP3 - Stalled development	13	6	2	−2	−6	−3	0
SSP4 - Inequality	16	12	3	−6	−14	−7	0
SSP5 - Conventional development	18	18	3	−11	−23	−12	0

Ageing Indicators, Medium Scenario (SSP2)

	2010	2020	2030	2040	2050	2075	2095
Median age	18.67	19.12	21.24	23.87	26.30	32.91	38.44
Propspective median age	18.67	18.03	18.74	20.39	21.61	24.34	25.87
Proportion age 65+	0.03	0.03	0.03	0.04	0.06	0.10	0.16
Proportion RLE < 15 years	0.03	0.04	0.04	0.05	0.06	0.09	0.11

Saint Lucia

Detailed Human Capital Projections to 2060

Demographic indicators, Medium Scenario (SSP2)

	2010	2020	2030	2040	2050	2060
Population (in millions)	0.17	0.19	0.21	0.21	0.22	0.22
Proportion age 65+	0.07	0.08	0.12	0.16	0.21	0.27
Proportion below age 20	0.36	0.30	0.27	0.23	0.21	0.19
	2005–10	2015–20	2025–30	2035–40	2045–50	2055–60
Total Fertility Rate	2.05	1.79	1.71	1.65	1.58	1.59
Life expectancy at birth (in years)						
Men	71.41	73.53	75.50	77.65	79.74	81.82
Women	76.59	78.99	81.09	83.09	85.08	87.11
Five-year immigration flow (in '000)	1.36	1.33	1.38	1.41	1.42	1.40
Five-year emigration flow (in '000)	2.36	1.82	1.73	1.64	1.52	1.39

Human Capital indicators, Medium Scenario (SSP2)

	2010	2020	2030	2040	2050	2060
Population age 25+: highest educational attainment						
E1 - no education	0.03	0.01	0.01	0.00	0.00	0.00
E2 - incomplete primary	0.03	0.02	0.01	0.01	0.00	0.00
E3 - primary	0.47	0.40	0.34	0.28	0.23	0.18
E4 - lower secondary	0.14	0.15	0.15	0.15	0.13	0.12
E5 - upper secondary	0.18	0.23	0.28	0.33	0.37	0.40
E6 - post-secondary	0.16	0.18	0.21	0.24	0.27	0.30
Mean years of schooling (in years)	9.60	10.30	10.84	11.32	11.76	12.17
Gender gap (population age 25+): highest educational attainment (ratio male/female)						
E1 - no education	1.11	1.06	1.03	1.06	1.09	1.06
E2 - incomplete primary	1.19	1.20	1.21	1.24	1.24	1.18
E3 - primary	1.15	1.20	1.23	1.25	1.25	1.23
E4 - lower secondary	0.89	0.95	0.99	1.00	1.01	0.99
E5 - upper secondary	0.81	0.87	0.91	0.95	0.98	1.00
E6 - post-secondary	0.86	0.81	0.80	0.81	0.84	0.89
Mean years of schooling (male minus female)	−0.41	−0.46	−0.47	−0.45	−0.38	−0.28
Women age 20–39: highest educational attainment						
E1 - no education	0.00	0.00	0.00	0.00	0.00	0.00
E2 - incomplete primary	0.01	0.00	0.00	0.00	0.00	0.00
E3 - primary	0.25	0.20	0.16	0.12	0.10	0.08
E4 - lower secondary	0.20	0.15	0.11	0.08	0.06	0.04
E5 - upper secondary	0.32	0.38	0.42	0.45	0.47	0.48
E6 - post-secondary	0.22	0.26	0.30	0.34	0.38	0.40
Mean years of schooling (in years)	11.22	11.77	12.34	12.72	13.01	13.24

Education scenarios

GET: global education trend scenario (medium assumption also used for SSP2)

CER: constant enrolment rates scenario (assumption of no future improvements)

FT: Fast track scenario (assumption of education expansion according to fastest historical experience)

Pyramids by Education, Medium Scenario

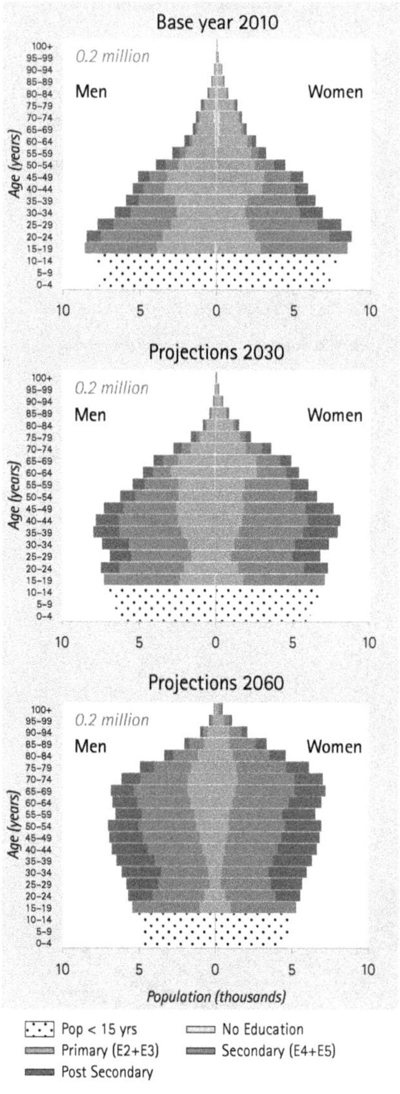

Population Size by Educational Attainment According to Three Education Scenarios: GET, CER, and FT

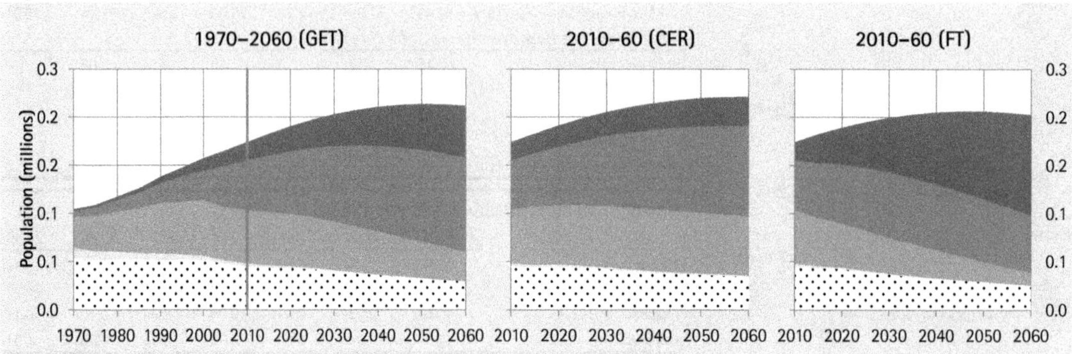

Saint Lucia (Continued)

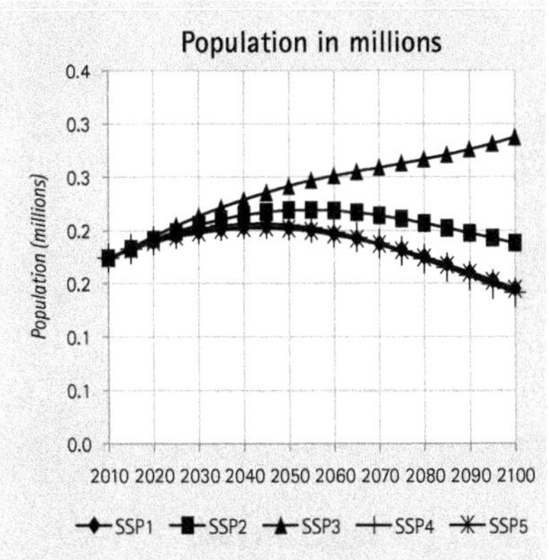

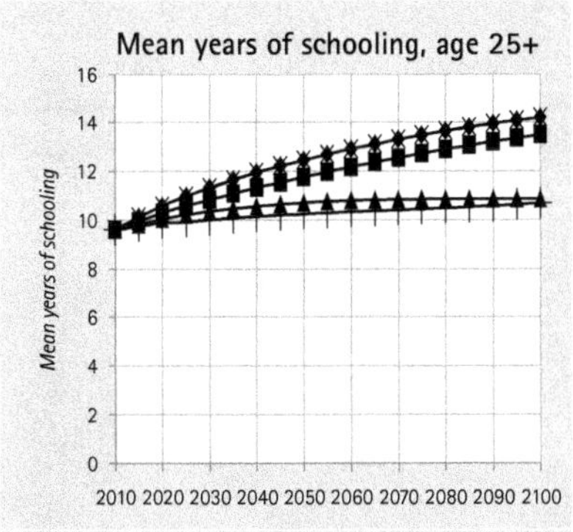

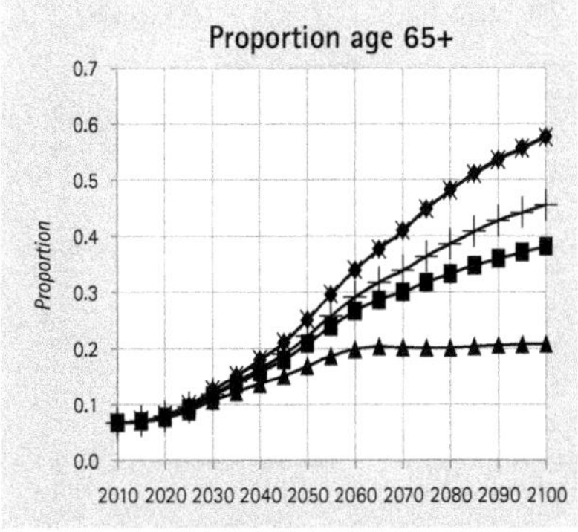

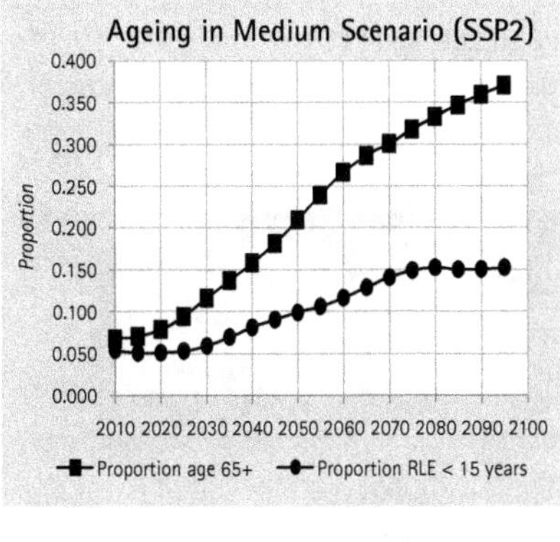

Alternative Scenarios to 2100

Projection Results by Scenario (SSP1–5)

	2010	2020	2030	2040	2050	2075	2100
Population (in millions)							
SSP1 - Rapid development	0.17	0.19	0.20	0.20	0.20	0.18	0.14
SSP2 - Medium	0.17	0.19	0.21	0.21	0.22	0.21	0.19
SSP3 - Stalled development	0.17	0.19	0.21	0.23	0.24	0.26	0.29
SSP4 - Inequality	0.17	0.19	0.20	0.21	0.21	0.18	0.14
SSP5 - Conventional development	0.17	0.19	0.20	0.20	0.20	0.18	0.14
Proportion age 65+							
SSP1 - Rapid development	0.07	0.08	0.13	0.18	0.25	0.45	0.58
SSP2 - Medium	0.07	0.08	0.12	0.16	0.21	0.32	0.38
SSP3 - Stalled development	0.07	0.08	0.11	0.14	0.17	0.20	0.21
SSP4 - Inequality	0.07	0.08	0.12	0.16	0.22	0.36	0.45
SSP5 - Conventional development	0.07	0.08	0.13	0.18	0.25	0.45	0.58
Proportionbelowage20							
SSP1 - Rapid development	0.36	0.29	0.23	0.19	0.15	0.10	0.08
SSP2 - Medium	0.36	0.30	0.27	0.23	0.21	0.17	0.16
SSP3 - Stalled development	0.36	0.31	0.30	0.28	0.27	0.26	0.27
SSP4 - Inequality	0.36	0.30	0.25	0.21	0.17	0.13	0.12
SSP5 - Conventional development	0.36	0.29	0.23	0.19	0.15	0.10	0.08
Proportion of Women age 20–39 with at least secondary education							
SSP1 - Rapid development	0.74	0.87	0.91	0.93	0.95	0.98	0.99
SSP2 - Medium	0.74	0.79	0.84	0.87	0.90	0.96	0.99
SSP3 - Stalled development	0.74	0.74	0.74	0.74	0.74	0.74	0.74
SSP4 - Inequality	0.74	0.69	0.66	0.66	0.66	0.66	0.66
SSP5 - Conventional development	0.74	0.87	0.91	0.93	0.95	0.98	0.99
Mean years of schooling, age 25+							
SSP1 - Rapid development	9.60	10.58	11.32	11.95	12.46	13.48	14.19
SSP2 - Medium	9.60	10.30	10.84	11.32	11.76	12.72	13.49
SSP3 - Stalled development	9.60	10.04	10.35	10.56	10.71	10.85	10.86
SSP4 - Inequality	9.60	9.87	10.00	10.14	10.25	10.45	10.68
SSP5 - Conventional development	9.60	10.58	11.32	11.94	12.46	13.49	14.19

Demographic Assumptions Underlying SSPs

	2010–15	2020–25	2030–35	2040–45	2050–55	2075–80	2095–2100
Total fertility rate							
SSP1 - Rapid development	1.75	1.42	1.26	1.19	1.16	1.19	1.22
SSP2 - Medium	1.88	1.74	1.67	1.61	1.59	1.61	1.64
SSP3 - Stalled development	1.99	2.11	2.16	2.15	2.16	2.27	2.34
SSP4 - Inequality	1.82	1.61	1.41	1.31	1.27	1.32	1.36
SSP5 - Conventional development	1.75	1.42	1.26	1.19	1.16	1.19	1.22
Life expectancy at birth for females (in years)							
SSP1 - Rapid development	79.14	82.11	85.07	88.08	91.04	98.49	104.49
SSP2 - Medium	77.89	79.99	82.09	84.09	86.09	91.11	95.09
SSP3 - Stalled development	78.25	79.22	80.22	81.17	82.02	84.14	85.88
SSP4 - Inequality	78.66	80.62	82.60	84.51	86.35	90.90	94.62
SSP5 - Conventional development	79.14	82.11	85.07	88.08	91.04	98.49	104.49
Migration – net flow over five years (in thousands)							
SSP1 - Rapid development	−1	0	0	0	0	0	0
SSP2 - Medium	−1	0	0	0	0	0	0
SSP3 - Stalled development	−1	0	0	0	0	0	0
SSP4 - Inequality	−1	0	0	0	0	0	0
SSP5 - Conventional development	−1	−1	0	0	0	0	0

Ageing Indicators, Medium Scenario (SSP2)

	2010	2020	2030	2040	2050	2075	2095
Median age	27.34	31.67	36.20	40.24	43.51	50.64	54.12
Propspective median age	27.34	29.76	32.32	34.54	36.06	38.73	38.50
Proportion age 65+	0.07	0.08	0.12	0.16	0.21	0.32	0.37
Proportion RLE < 15 years	0.05	0.05	0.06	0.08	0.10	0.15	0.15

Saint Vincent and the Grenadines

Detailed Human Capital Projections to 2060

Demographic indicators, Medium Scenario (SSP2)	2010	2020	2030	2040	2050	2060
Population (in millions)	0.11	0.11	0.11	0.11	0.10	0.10
Proportion age 65+	0.07	0.08	0.13	0.18	0.23	0.28
Proportion below age 20	0.36	0.31	0.27	0.24	0.21	0.20
	2005–10	2015–20	2025–30	2035–40	2045–50	2055–60
Total Fertility Rate	2.13	1.90	1.85	1.75	1.71	1.68
Life expectancy at birth (in years)						
Men	69.60	72.86	75.28	77.41	79.55	81.61
Women	73.79	77.09	79.49	81.59	83.69	85.71
Five-year immigration flow (in '000)	0.40	0.40	0.41	0.42	0.42	0.42
Five-year emigration flow (in '000)	5.39	4.04	3.62	3.20	2.81	2.43

Human Capital indicators, Medium Scenario (SSP2)	2010	2020	2030	2040	2050	2060
Population age 25+: highest educational attainment						
E1 - no education	0.01	0.01	0.00	0.00	0.00	0.00
E2 - incomplete primary	0.05	0.03	0.02	0.01	0.01	0.01
E3 - primary	0.53	0.48	0.43	0.37	0.32	0.27
E4 - lower secondary	0.13	0.13	0.13	0.13	0.12	0.11
E5 - upper secondary	0.17	0.21	0.26	0.30	0.35	0.39
E6 - post-secondary	0.13	0.14	0.16	0.18	0.20	0.22
Mean years of schooling (in years)	9.97	10.27	10.61	10.94	11.26	11.56
Gender gap (population age 25+): highest educational attainment (ratio male/female)						
E1 - no education	1.21	1.39	1.50	1.53	1.50	1.45
E2 - incomplete primary	1.31	1.46	1.62	1.75	1.78	1.72
E3 - primary	1.20	1.27	1.32	1.35	1.36	1.33
E4 - lower secondary	0.82	0.83	0.87	0.90	0.92	0.94
E5 - upper secondary	0.71	0.74	0.78	0.83	0.88	0.92
E6 - post-secondary	0.80	0.75	0.74	0.75	0.78	0.84
Mean years of schooling (male minus female)	−0.69	−0.80	−0.83	−0.79	−0.70	−0.54
Women age 20–39: highest educational attainment						
E1 - no education	0.01	0.00	0.00	0.00	0.00	0.00
E2 - incomplete primary	0.01	0.01	0.00	0.00	0.00	0.00
E3 - primary	0.30	0.27	0.23	0.20	0.17	0.14
E4 - lower secondary	0.20	0.15	0.11	0.09	0.07	0.06
E5 - upper secondary	0.31	0.37	0.42	0.46	0.48	0.50
E6 - post-secondary	0.17	0.20	0.22	0.25	0.27	0.29
Mean years of schooling (in years)	11.19	11.20	11.69	12.01	12.27	12.48

Education scenarios

GET : global education trend scenario (medium assumption also used for SSP2)

CER: constant enrolment rates scenario (assumption of no future improvements)

FT: Fast track scenario (assumption of education expansion according to fastest historical experience)

Pyramids by Education, Medium Scenario

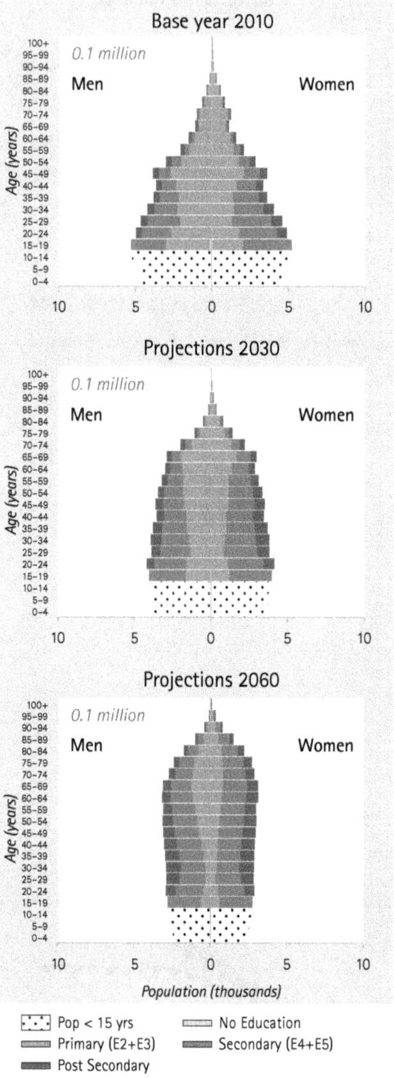

Population Size by Educational Attainment According to Three Education Scenarios: GET, CER, and FT

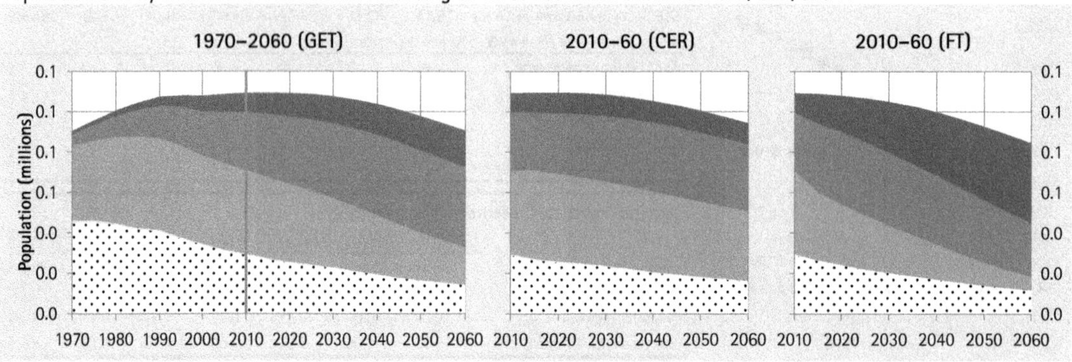

Saint Vincent and the Grenadines (Continued)

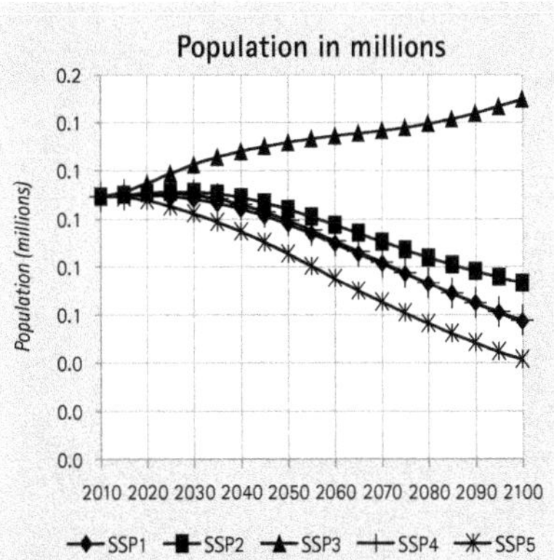

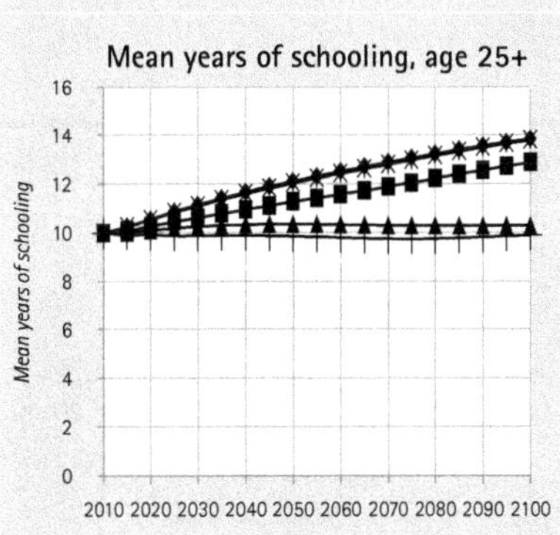

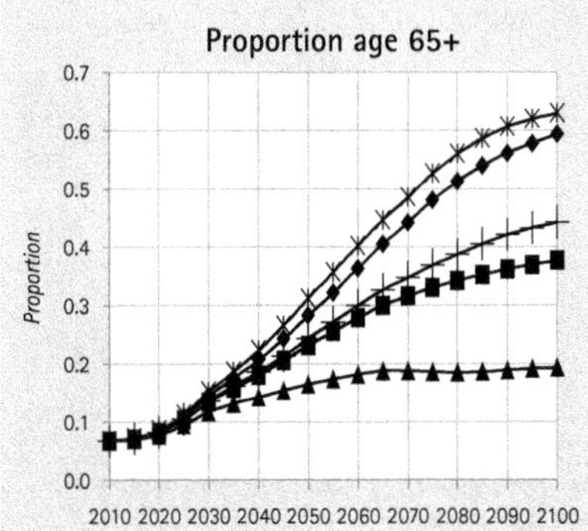

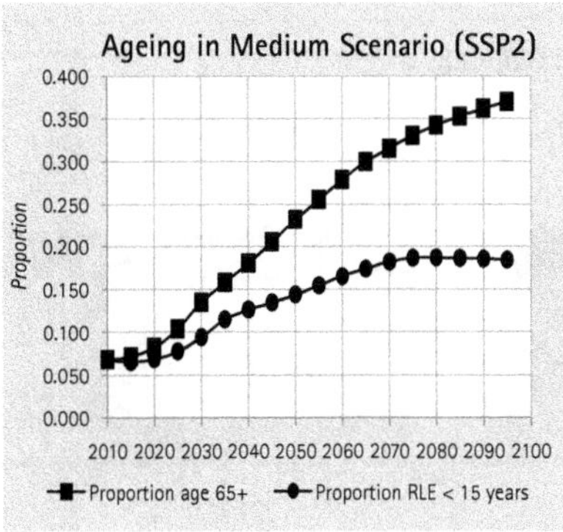

Alternative Scenarios to 2100

Projection Results by Scenario (SSP1–5)

	2010	2020	2030	2040	2050	2075	2100
Population (in millions)							
SSP1 - Rapid development	0.11	0.11	0.11	0.10	0.10	0.08	0.06
SSP2 - Medium	0.11	0.11	0.11	0.11	0.10	0.09	0.07
SSP3 - Stalled development	0.11	0.11	0.12	0.13	0.13	0.14	0.15
SSP4 - Inequality	0.11	0.11	0.11	0.11	0.10	0.08	0.06
SSP5 - Conventional development	0.11	0.11	0.10	0.09	0.09	0.06	0.04
Proportion age 65+							
SSP1 - Rapid development	0.07	0.08	0.15	0.21	0.28	0.48	0.59
SSP2 - Medium	0.07	0.08	0.13	0.18	0.23	0.33	0.38
SSP3 - Stalled development	0.07	0.08	0.12	0.14	0.17	0.19	0.19
SSP4 - Inequality	0.07	0.08	0.14	0.19	0.24	0.37	0.44
SSP5 - Conventional development	0.07	0.09	0.15	0.22	0.31	0.53	0.63
Proportion below age 20							
SSP1 - Rapid development	0.36	0.30	0.24	0.19	0.15	0.10	0.07
SSP2 - Medium	0.36	0.31	0.27	0.24	0.21	0.17	0.16
SSP3 - Stalled development	0.36	0.32	0.31	0.29	0.28	0.27	0.27
SSP4 - Inequality	0.36	0.31	0.26	0.21	0.18	0.13	0.12
SSP5 - Conventional development	0.36	0.30	0.24	0.19	0.15	0.09	0.07
Proportion of Women age 20–39 with at least secondary education							
SSP1 - Rapid development	0.68	0.82	0.87	0.90	0.91	0.95	0.98
SSP2 - Medium	0.68	0.72	0.76	0.80	0.83	0.90	0.96
SSP3 - Stalled development	0.68	0.65	0.65	0.65	0.65	0.65	0.65
SSP4 - Inequality	0.68	0.62	0.59	0.59	0.59	0.59	0.59
SSP5 - Conventional development	0.68	0.82	0.87	0.90	0.91	0.95	0.98
Mean years of schooling, age 25+							
SSP1 - Rapid development	9.97	10.54	11.14	11.65	12.10	13.06	13.83
SSP2 - Medium	9.97	10.27	10.61	10.94	11.26	12.04	12.87
SSP3 - Stalled development	9.97	10.10	10.24	10.32	10.34	10.29	10.29
SSP4 - Inequality	9.97	9.91	9.88	9.88	9.85	9.73	9.89
SSP5 - Conventional development	9.97	10.53	11.10	11.59	12.02	12.97	13.79

Demographic Assumptions Underlying SSPs

	2010–15	2020–25	2030–35	2040–45	2050–55	2075–80	2095–2100
Total fertility rate							
SSP1 - Rapid development	1.82	1.50	1.34	1.26	1.22	1.16	1.19
SSP2 - Medium	1.97	1.87	1.80	1.71	1.70	1.59	1.61
SSP3 - Stalled development	2.10	2.26	2.30	2.29	2.28	2.21	2.30
SSP4 - Inequality	1.91	1.72	1.51	1.40	1.35	1.30	1.34
SSP5 - Conventional development	1.82	1.50	1.34	1.26	1.22	1.16	1.19
Life expectancy at birth for females (in years)							
SSP1 - Rapid development	77.31	80.64	83.71	86.69	89.62	97.14	103.14
SSP2 - Medium	75.60	78.29	80.59	82.59	84.71	89.70	93.70
SSP3 - Stalled development	76.52	77.85	79.01	79.98	80.82	82.91	84.63
SSP4 - Inequality	76.88	79.25	81.36	83.22	85.11	89.52	93.23
SSP5 - Conventional development	77.31	80.64	83.71	86.69	89.62	97.14	103.14
Migration – net flow over five years (in thousands)							
SSP1 - Rapid development	−4	−3	−3	−2	−2	0	0
SSP2 - Medium	−4	−4	−3	−3	−2	−1	0
SSP3 - Stalled development	−3	−2	−2	−1	−1	−1	0
SSP4 - Inequality	−4	−3	−3	−2	−2	0	0
SSP5 - Conventional development	−5	−5	−4	−3	−3	−1	0

Ageing Indicators, Medium Scenario (SSP2)

	2010	2020	2030	2040	2050	2075	2095
Median age	27.81	32.15	36.62	41.03	44.64	51.41	53.93
Propspective median age	27.81	30.10	32.64	35.37	37.15	39.42	38.15
Proportion age 65+	0.07	0.08	0.13	0.18	0.23	0.33	0.37
Proportion RLE < 15 years	0.07	0.07	0.09	0.13	0.14	0.19	0.18

Samoa

Detailed Human Capital Projections to 2060

Demographic indicators, Medium Scenario (SSP2)	2010	2020	2030	2040	2050	2060
Population (in millions)	0.18	0.18	0.18	0.17	0.16	0.15
Proportion age 65+	0.05	0.07	0.10	0.14	0.17	0.20
Proportion below age 20	0.49	0.43	0.36	0.32	0.28	0.24
	2005–10	2015–20	2025–30	2035–40	2045–50	2055–60
Total Fertility Rate	3.99	2.99	2.52	2.18	2.02	1.90
Life expectancy at birth (in years)						
Men	68.61	71.18	73.48	75.75	77.88	79.99
Women	74.89	77.19	79.29	81.39	83.39	85.39
Five-year immigration flow (in '000)	1.03	1.02	1.06	1.09	1.09	1.08
Five-year emigration flow (in '000)	16.74	12.00	12.21	10.69	9.43	8.28

Human Capital indicators, Medium Scenario (SSP2)	2010	2020	2030	2040	2050	2060
Population age 25+: highest educational attainment						
E1 - no education	0.01	0.00	0.00	0.00	0.00	0.00
E2 - incomplete primary	0.01	0.01	0.01	0.00	0.00	0.00
E3 - primary	0.41	0.35	0.30	0.26	0.23	0.20
E4 - lower secondary	0.34	0.36	0.35	0.34	0.31	0.28
E5 - upper secondary	0.08	0.11	0.15	0.19	0.22	0.26
E6 - post-secondary	0.15	0.17	0.19	0.21	0.24	0.27
Mean years of schooling (in years)	9.98	10.22	10.56	10.89	11.22	11.57
Gender gap (population age 25+): highest educational attainment (ratio male/female)						
E1 - no education	1.25	1.17	1.07	0.98	0.93	0.91
E2 - incomplete primary	1.21	1.18	1.15	1.09	1.03	0.97
E3 - primary	1.10	1.15	1.19	1.23	1.23	1.19
E4 - lower secondary	0.91	0.93	0.95	0.95	0.96	0.96
E5 - upper secondary	0.73	0.75	0.80	0.85	0.90	0.93
E6 - post-secondary	1.11	1.04	0.99	0.97	0.97	0.98
Mean years of schooling (male minus female)	−0.18	−0.30	−0.39	−0.41	−0.37	−0.27
Women age 20–39: highest educational attainment						
E1 - no education	0.00	0.00	0.00	0.00	0.00	0.00
E2 - incomplete primary	0.00	0.00	0.00	0.00	0.00	0.00
E3 - primary	0.26	0.23	0.20	0.18	0.15	0.13
E4 - lower secondary	0.40	0.36	0.31	0.27	0.23	0.20
E5 - upper secondary	0.18	0.22	0.26	0.30	0.33	0.36
E6 - post-secondary	0.16	0.19	0.22	0.26	0.28	0.31
Mean years of schooling (in years)	10.70	10.65	11.05	11.56	12.02	12.46

Education scenarios

GET: global education trend scenario (medium assumption also used for SSP2)

CER: constant enrolment rates scenario (assumption of no future improvements)

FT: Fast track scenario (assumption of education expansion according to fastest historical experience)

Pyramids by Education, Medium Scenario

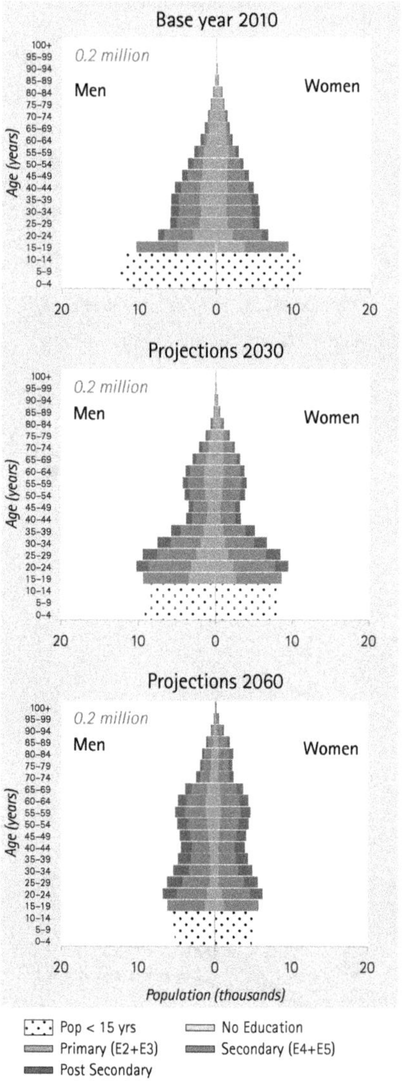

Population Size by Aducational Attainment According to Three Education Scenarios: GET, CER, and FT

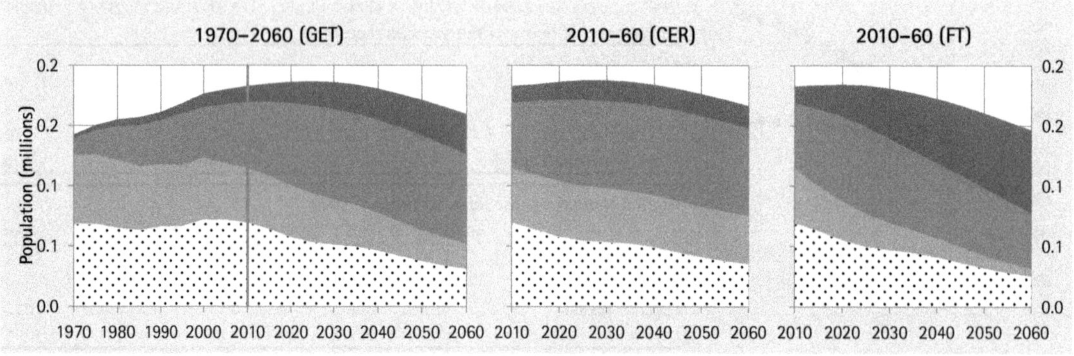

Samoa (Continued)

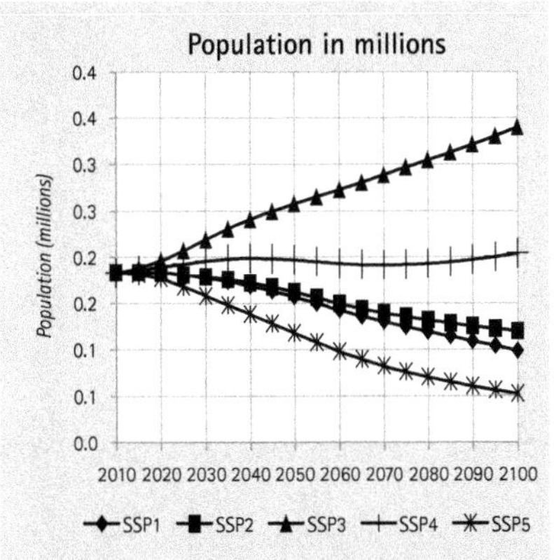

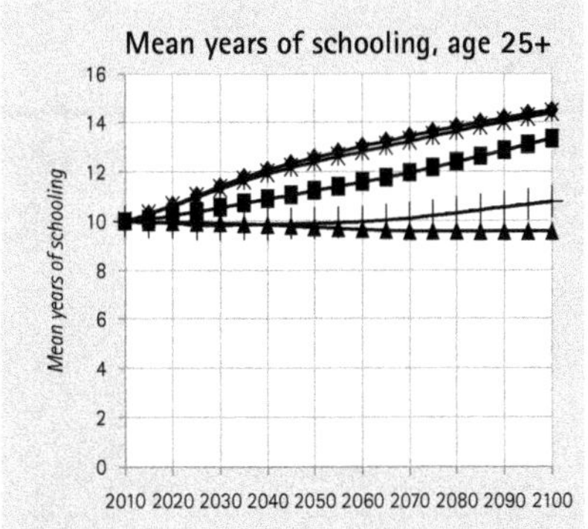

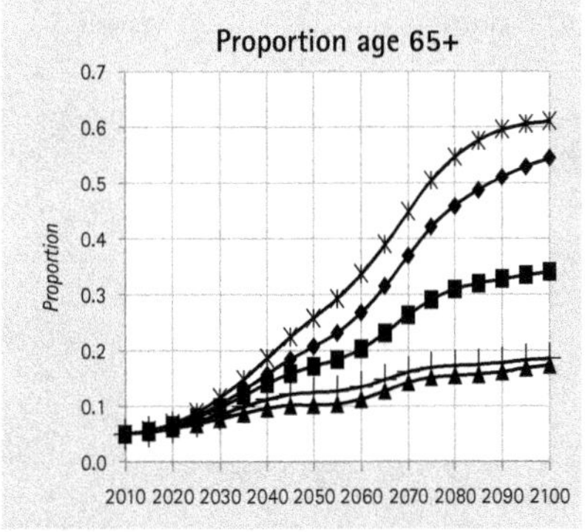

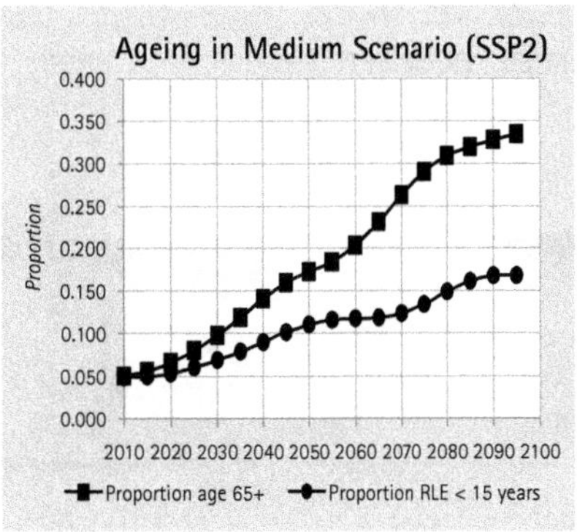

Alternative Scenarios to 2100

Projection Results by Scenario (SSP1–5)

	2010	2020	2030	2040	2050	2075	2100
Population (in millions)							
SSP1 - Rapid development	0.18	0.18	0.18	0.17	0.16	0.12	0.10
SSP2 - Medium	0.18	0.18	0.18	0.17	0.16	0.14	0.12
SSP3 - Stalled development	0.18	0.20	0.22	0.24	0.26	0.30	0.34
SSP4 - Inequality	0.18	0.19	0.20	0.20	0.20	0.19	0.20
SSP5 - Conventional development	0.18	0.18	0.16	0.14	0.12	0.08	0.05
Proportion age 65+							
SSP1 - Rapid development	0.05	0.07	0.10	0.16	0.21	0.42	0.54
SSP2 - Medium	0.05	0.07	0.10	0.14	0.17	0.29	0.34
SSP3 - Stalled development	0.05	0.06	0.08	0.10	0.10	0.15	0.17
SSP4 - Inequality	0.05	0.06	0.09	0.11	0.12	0.17	0.19
SSP5 - Conventional development	0.05	0.07	0.12	0.19	0.26	0.50	0.61
Proportion below age 20							
SSP1 - Rapid development	0.49	0.42	0.32	0.27	0.22	0.12	0.09
SSP2 - Medium	0.49	0.43	0.36	0.32	0.28	0.20	0.17
SSP3 - Stalled development	0.49	0.44	0.39	0.38	0.35	0.30	0.28
SSP4 - Inequality	0.49	0.44	0.40	0.38	0.34	0.29	0.27
SSP5 - Conventional development	0.49	0.42	0.32	0.26	0.21	0.10	0.08
Proportion of Women age 20–39 with at least secondary education							
SSP1 - Rapid development	0.74	0.85	0.89	0.91	0.92	0.96	0.98
SSP2 - Medium	0.74	0.77	0.80	0.82	0.85	0.91	0.96
SSP3 - Stalled development	0.74	0.72	0.72	0.72	0.72	0.72	0.72
SSP4 - Inequality	0.74	0.68	0.65	0.65	0.65	0.65	0.65
SSP5 - Conventional development	0.74	0.85	0.89	0.91	0.92	0.96	0.98
Mean years of schooling, age 25+							
SSP1 - Rapid development	9.98	10.64	11.41	12.06	12.57	13.64	14.50
SSP2 - Medium	9.98	10.22	10.56	10.89	11.22	12.16	13.33
SSP3 - Stalled development	9.98	9.95	9.90	9.84	9.74	9.58	9.57
SSP4 - Inequality	9.98	9.91	9.83	9.86	9.89	10.21	10.77
SSP5 - Conventional development	9.98	10.61	11.31	11.92	12.39	13.44	14.38

Demographic Assumptions Underlying SSPs

	2010–15	2020–25	2030–35	2040–45	2050–55	2075–80	2095–2100
Total fertility rate							
SSP1 - Rapid development	3.15	2.22	1.72	1.49	1.37	1.24	1.20
SSP2 - Medium	3.45	2.72	2.34	2.08	1.95	1.71	1.64
SSP3 - Stalled development	3.57	3.28	2.98	2.76	2.63	2.43	2.40
SSP4 - Inequality	3.57	3.30	2.97	2.71	2.55	2.30	2.24
SSP5 - Conventional development	3.15	2.22	1.73	1.49	1.37	1.24	1.20
Life expectancy at birth for females (in years)							
SSP1 - Rapid development	78.06	80.88	83.71	86.58	89.47	96.87	102.86
SSP2 - Medium	76.09	78.29	80.29	82.39	84.38	89.40	93.41
SSP3 - Stalled development	77.24	78.14	79.06	79.95	80.80	82.90	84.57
SSP4 - Inequality	77.24	78.13	79.04	79.91	80.73	82.82	84.57
SSP5 - Conventional development	78.06	80.88	83.71	86.58	89.47	96.87	102.86
Migration – net flow over five years (in thousands)							
SSP1 - Rapid development	−13	−11	−10	−8	−7	−2	0
SSP2 - Medium	−15	−12	−11	−9	−8	−2	0
SSP3 - Stalled development	−11	−6	−6	−5	−5	−2	0
SSP4 - Inequality	−13	−11	−11	−10	−9	−3	0
SSP5 - Conventional development	−15	−16	−14	−10	−8	−2	0

Ageing Indicators, Medium Scenario (SSP2)

	2010	2020	2030	2040	2050	2075	2095
Median age	20.75	23.35	27.96	32.88	37.76	47.14	50.71
Propspective median age	20.75	21.35	24.22	27.29	30.38	35.16	34.99
Proportion age 65+	0.05	0.07	0.10	0.14	0.17	0.29	0.33
Proportion RLE < 15 years	0.05	0.05	0.07	0.09	0.11	0.13	0.17

São Tomé and Principe

Detailed Human Capital Projections to 2060

Demographic indicators, Medium Scenario (SSP2)	2010	2020	2030	2040	2050	2060
Population (in millions)	0.17	0.19	0.20	0.21	0.22	0.22
Proportion age 65+	0.04	0.04	0.05	0.06	0.10	0.13
Proportion below age 20	0.52	0.47	0.40	0.35	0.32	0.28
	2005–10	2015–20	2025–30	2035–40	2045–50	2055–60
Total Fertility Rate	3.85	2.92	2.45	2.16	2.00	1.88
Life expectancy at birth (in years)						
Men	#N/A	63.64	64.95	66.42	68.00	70.19
Women	#N/A	66.92	68.58	70.32	72.02	74.19
Five-year immigration flow (in '000)	0.97	0.95	0.99	1.01	1.01	0.99
Five-year emigration flow (in '000)	7.45	6.79	7.39	7.49	7.26	6.85

Human Capital indicators, Medium Scenario (SSP2)	2010	2020	2030	2040	2050	2060
Population age 25+: highest educational attainment						
E1 - no education	0.13	0.08	0.04	0.03	0.02	0.01
E2 - incomplete primary	0.49	0.42	0.34	0.26	0.19	0.13
E3 - primary	0.23	0.30	0.35	0.40	0.43	0.44
E4 - lower secondary	0.08	0.12	0.16	0.19	0.21	0.22
E5 - upper secondary	0.04	0.07	0.09	0.11	0.13	0.16
E6 - post-secondary	0.01	0.01	0.02	0.02	0.03	0.04
Mean years of schooling (in years)	3.59	4.59	5.62	6.43	7.10	7.70
Gender gap (population age 25+): highest educational attainment (ratio male/female)						
E1 - no education	0.31	0.31	0.36	0.45	0.56	0.64
E2 - incomplete primary	0.97	0.94	0.91	0.91	0.91	0.92
E3 - primary	1.30	1.18	1.13	1.09	1.06	1.04
E4 - lower secondary	1.55	1.16	1.04	0.99	0.98	0.97
E5 - upper secondary	2.83	1.67	1.39	1.22	1.14	1.10
E6 - post-secondary	2.12	1.23	0.87	0.70	0.68	0.76
Mean years of schooling (male minus female)	1.19	0.77	0.50	0.27	0.12	0.07
Women age 20–39: highest educational attainment						
E1 - no education	0.04	0.04	0.03	0.02	0.01	0.01
E2 - incomplete primary	0.49	0.33	0.20	0.13	0.08	0.05
E3 - primary	0.29	0.37	0.43	0.46	0.46	0.44
E4 - lower secondary	0.12	0.16	0.20	0.21	0.21	0.20
E5 - upper secondary	0.05	0.09	0.13	0.16	0.21	0.27
E6 - post-secondary	0.01	0.01	0.01	0.02	0.03	0.03
Mean years of schooling (in years)	4.12	5.78	7.12	7.75	8.18	8.54

Education scenarios

GET: global education trend scenario (medium assumption also used for SSP2)

CER: constant enrolment rates scenario (assumption of no future improvements)

FT: Fast track scenario (assumption of education expansion according to fastest historical experience)

Pyramids by Education, Medium Scenario

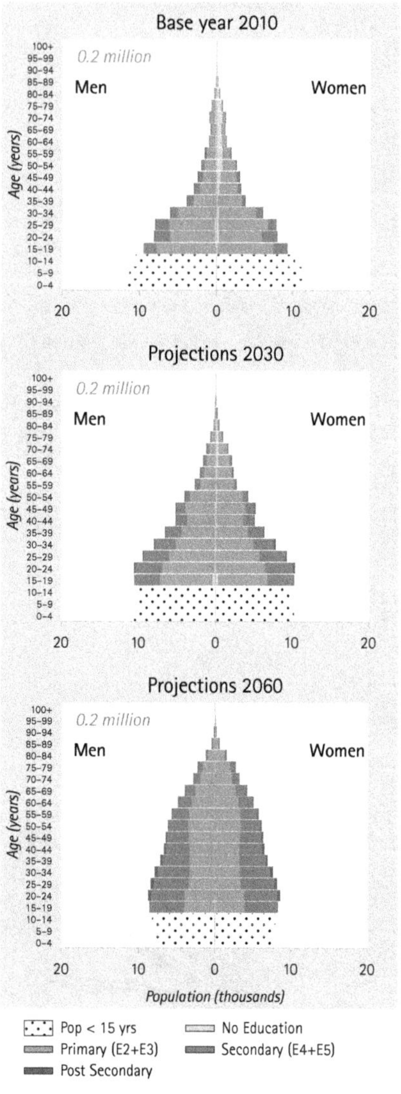

Population Size by Educational Attainment According to Three Education Scenarios: GET, CER, and FT

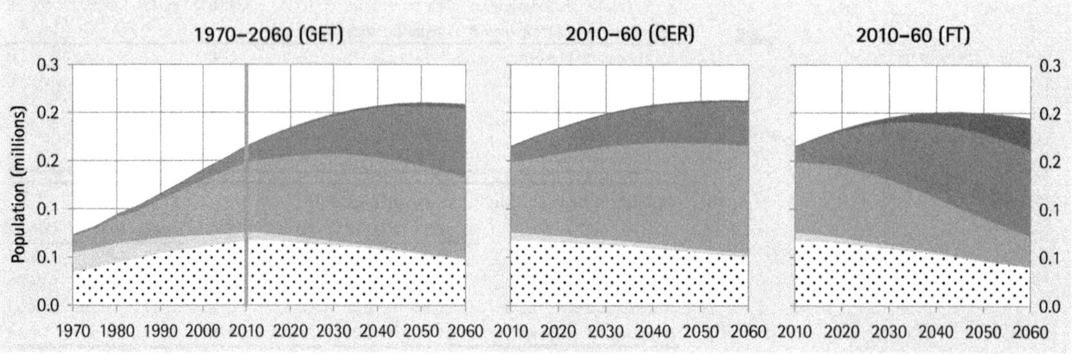

São Tomé and Principe (Continued)

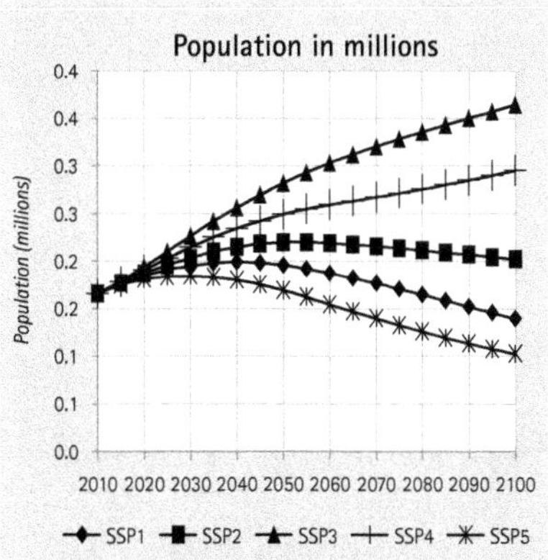

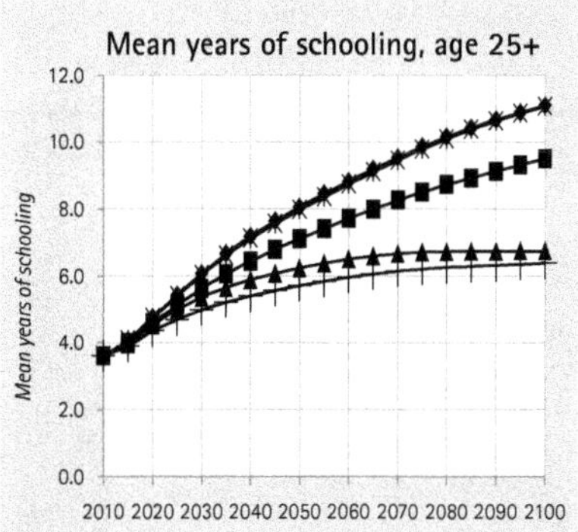

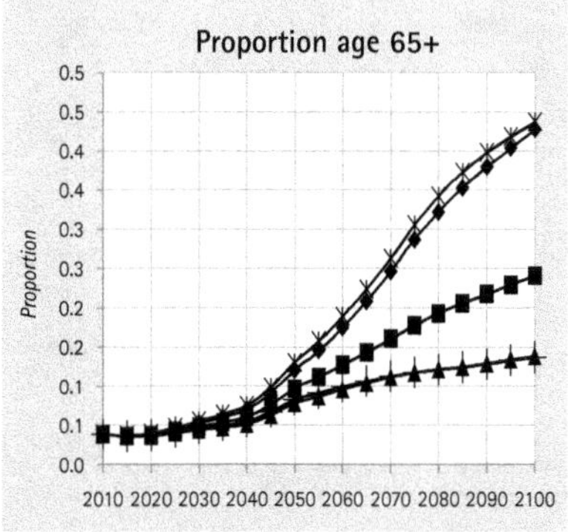

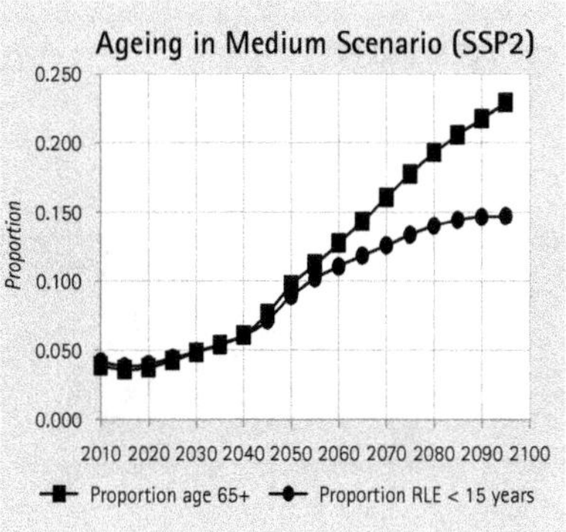

Alternative Scenarios to 2100

Projection Results by Scenario (SSP1–5)

	2010	2020	2030	2040	2050	2075	2100
Population (in millions)							
SSP1 - Rapid development	0.17	0.18	0.20	0.20	0.20	0.17	0.14
SSP2 - Medium	0.17	0.19	0.20	0.21	0.22	0.21	0.20
SSP3 - Stalled development	0.17	0.19	0.23	0.26	0.28	0.33	0.36
SSP4 - Inequality	0.17	0.19	0.21	0.23	0.25	0.27	0.30
SSP5 - Conventional development	0.17	0.18	0.18	0.18	0.17	0.13	0.10
Proportion age 65+							
SSP1 - Rapid development	0.04	0.04	0.05	0.07	0.12	0.29	0.43
SSP2 - Medium	0.04	0.04	0.05	0.06	0.10	0.18	0.24
SSP3 - Stalled development	0.04	0.04	0.04	0.05	0.08	0.12	0.14
SSP4 - Inequality	0.04	0.04	0.05	0.05	0.08	0.12	0.14
SSP5 - Conventional development	0.04	0.04	0.06	0.08	0.13	0.31	0.44
Proportion below age 20							
SSP1 - Rapid development	0.52	0.45	0.36	0.30	0.25	0.16	0.11
SSP2 - Medium	0.52	0.47	0.40	0.35	0.32	0.25	0.20
SSP3 - Stalled development	0.52	0.47	0.42	0.39	0.36	0.32	0.29
SSP4 - Inequality	0.52	0.47	0.43	0.40	0.37	0.32	0.29
SSP5 - Conventional development	0.52	0.46	0.37	0.30	0.25	0.16	0.11
Proportion of Women age 20–39 with at least secondary education							
SSP1 - Rapid development	0.17	0.34	0.51	0.63	0.70	0.79	0.86
SSP2 - Medium	0.17	0.26	0.34	0.40	0.45	0.59	0.74
SSP3 - Stalled development	0.17	0.28	0.32	0.32	0.32	0.32	0.32
SSP4 - Inequality	0.17	0.26	0.29	0.29	0.29	0.29	0.29
SSP5 - Conventional development	0.17	0.34	0.51	0.63	0.70	0.79	0.86
Mean years of schooling, age 25+							
SSP1 - Rapid development	3.59	4.76	6.07	7.17	8.05	9.85	11.09
SSP2 - Medium	3.59	4.59	5.62	6.43	7.10	8.50	9.50
SSP3 - Stalled development	3.59	4.51	5.36	5.88	6.23	6.71	6.74
SSP4 - Inequality	3.59	4.34	4.97	5.40	5.71	6.21	6.38
SSP5 - Conventional development	3.59	4.74	6.02	7.11	7.97	9.77	11.07

Demographic Assumptions Underlying SSPs

	2010–15	2020–25	2030–35	2040–45	2050–55	2075–80	2095–2100
Total fertility rate							
SSP1 - Rapid development	3.07	2.21	1.73	1.50	1.37	1.22	1.15
SSP2 - Medium	3.30	2.65	2.28	2.09	1.92	1.71	1.59
SSP3 - Stalled development	3.41	3.09	2.83	2.64	2.52	2.32	2.23
SSP4 - Inequality	3.41	3.10	2.83	2.63	2.49	2.28	2.18
SSP5 - Conventional development	3.07	2.21	1.73	1.50	1.37	1.22	1.15
Life expectancy at birth for females (in years)							
SSP1 - Rapid development	69.36	71.22	73.54	76.07	78.91	86.63	92.94
SSP2 - Medium	66.12	67.82	69.42	71.08	73.12	78.59	83.01
SSP3 - Stalled development	69.00	69.02	69.42	69.89	70.37	72.98	74.83
SSP4 - Inequality	69.00	69.00	69.37	69.83	70.29	72.87	74.75
SSP5 - Conventional development	69.36	71.22	73.54	76.07	78.91	86.63	92.94
Migration – net flow over five years (in thousands)							
SSP1 - Rapid development	−6	−6	−6	−6	−5	−2	0
SSP2 - Medium	−6	−6	−7	−7	−6	−2	0
SSP3 - Stalled development	−5	−3	−3	−3	−3	−1	0
SSP4 - Inequality	−6	−6	−7	−7	−6	−3	0
SSP5 - Conventional development	−7	−9	−9	−9	−8	−3	0

Ageing Indicators, Medium Scenario (SSP2)

	2010	2020	2030	2040	2050	2075	2095
Median age	19.22	21.67	25.01	28.60	32.01	39.17	43.63
Propspective median age	19.22	20.73	23.22	26.24	28.45	32.17	33.09
Proportion age 65+	0.04	0.04	0.05	0.06	0.10	0.18	0.23
Proportion RLE < 15 years	0.04	0.04	0.05	0.06	0.09	0.13	0.15

Saudi Arabia

Detailed Human Capital Projections to 2060

Demographic indicators, Medium Scenario (SSP2)	2010	2020	2030	2040	2050	2060
Population (in millions)	27.45	34.60	41.77	48.68	54.72	59.75
Proportion age 65+	0.03	0.04	0.07	0.12	0.16	0.19
Proportion below age 20	0.39	0.35	0.31	0.28	0.25	0.23
	2005–10	2015–20	2025–30	2035–40	2045–50	2055–60
Total Fertility Rate	3.03	2.45	2.16	1.99	1.89	1.81
Life expectancy at birth (in years)						
Men	72.24	74.69	76.67	78.57	80.55	82.49
Women	74.41	77.29	79.59	81.69	83.79	85.81
Five-year immigration flow (in '000)	1304.56	1277.64	1325.82	1354.08	1352.60	1331.71
Five-year emigration flow (in '000)	249.83	198.76	229.92	252.47	265.15	274.93

Human Capital indicators, Medium Scenario (SSP2)	2010	2020	2030	2040	2050	2060
Population age 25+: highest educational attainment						
E1 - no education	0.16	0.10	0.06	0.03	0.02	0.01
E2 - incomplete primary	0.06	0.04	0.03	0.02	0.01	0.01
E3 - primary	0.15	0.12	0.09	0.07	0.05	0.03
E4 - lower secondary	0.16	0.16	0.14	0.11	0.09	0.06
E5 - upper secondary	0.19	0.23	0.25	0.27	0.27	0.26
E6 - post-secondary	0.27	0.35	0.43	0.50	0.57	0.63
Mean years of schooling (in years)	9.42	10.80	11.87	12.77	13.47	14.03
Gender gap (population age 25+): highest educational attainment (ratio male/female)						
E1 - no education	0.30	0.29	0.27	0.25	0.23	0.23
E2 - incomplete primary	0.65	0.62	0.57	0.50	0.44	0.40
E3 - primary	1.43	1.40	1.37	1.30	1.20	1.11
E4 - lower secondary	1.64	1.56	1.54	1.50	1.43	1.32
E5 - upper secondary	1.36	1.18	1.14	1.12	1.10	1.07
E6 - post-secondary	1.15	0.99	0.94	0.93	0.94	0.96
Mean years of schooling (male minus female)	2.19	1.14	0.58	0.25	0.07	0.00
Women age 20–39: highest educational attainment						
E1 - no education	0.08	0.02	0.00	0.00	0.00	0.00
E2 - incomplete primary	0.04	0.01	0.00	0.00	0.00	0.00
E3 - primary	0.10	0.06	0.03	0.02	0.01	0.00
E4 - lower secondary	0.16	0.12	0.08	0.05	0.04	0.03
E5 - upper secondary	0.32	0.38	0.40	0.39	0.38	0.37
E6 - post-secondary	0.31	0.41	0.48	0.55	0.58	0.60
Mean years of schooling (in years)	10.98	12.65	13.43	13.92	14.14	14.27

Education scenarios

GET: global education trend scenario (medium assumption also used for SSP2)

CER: constant enrolment rates scenario (assumption of no future improvements)

FT: Fast track scenario (assumption of education expansion according to fastest historical experience)

Pyramids by Education, Medium Scenario

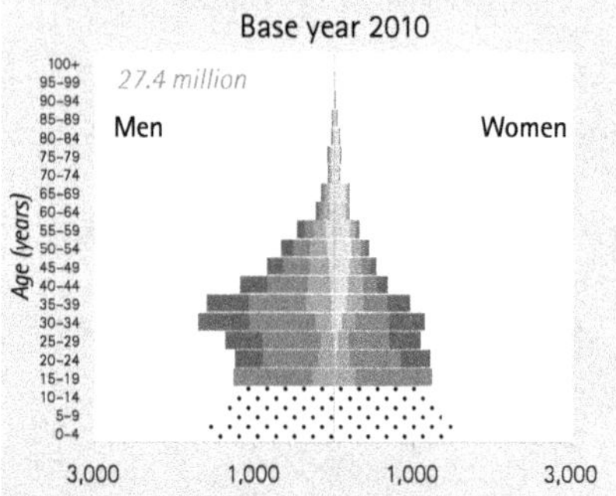

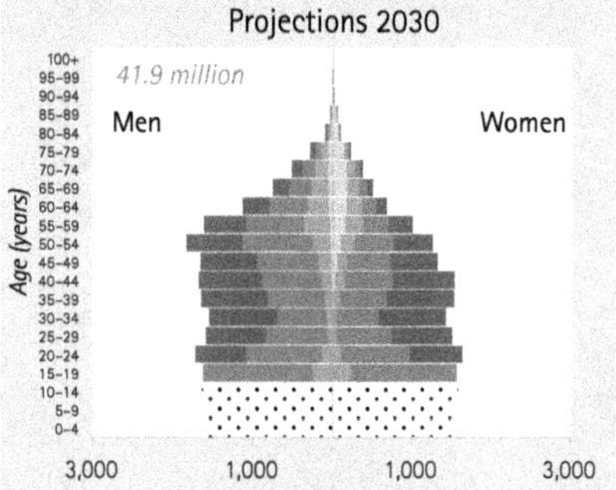

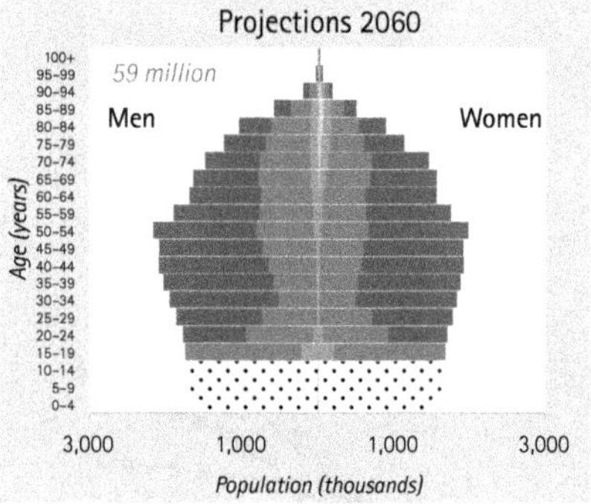

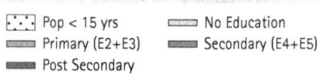

Population Size by Educational Attainment According to Three Education Scenarios: GET, CER, and FT

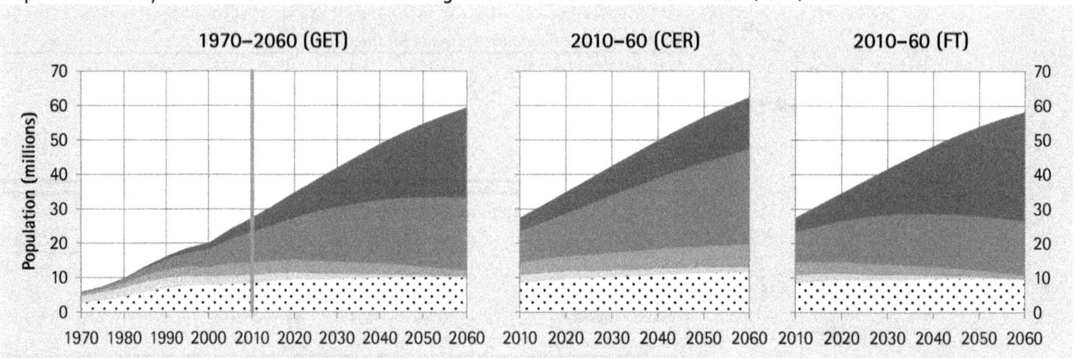

Saudi Arabia (Continued)

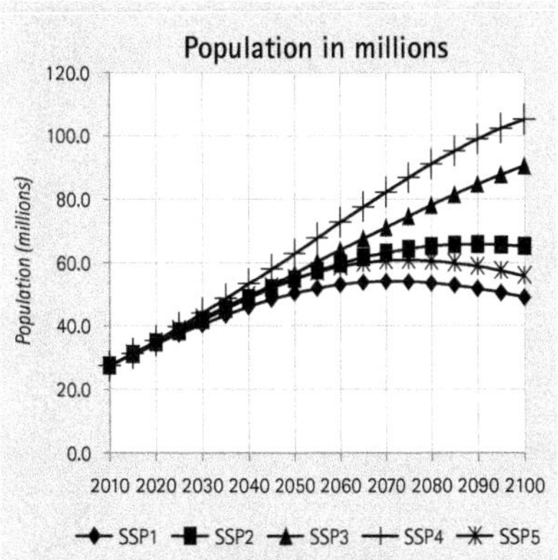

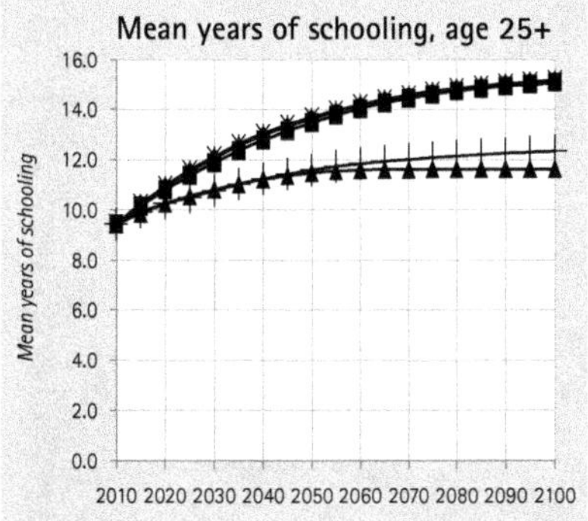

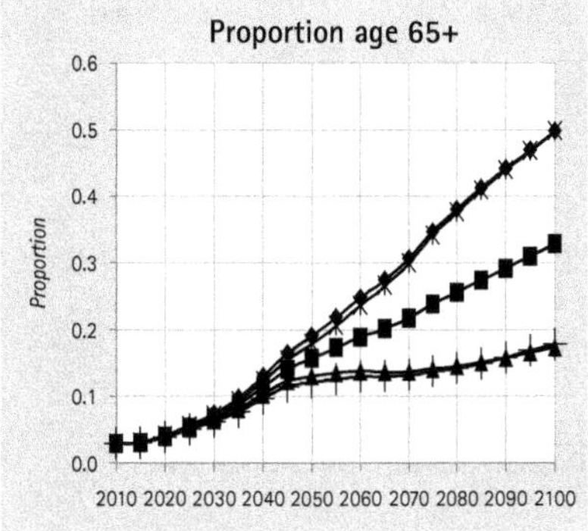

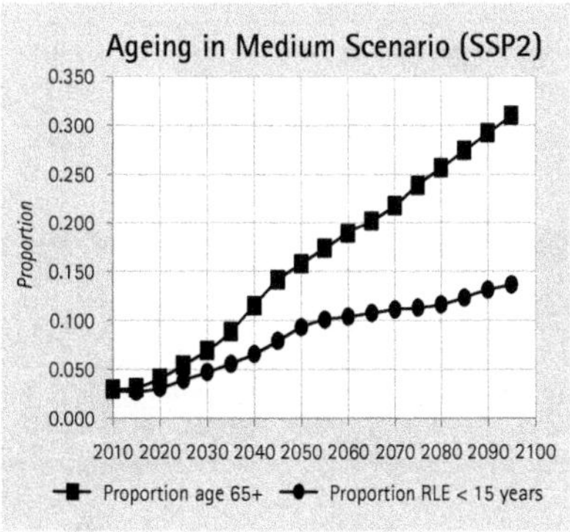

Alternative Scenarios to 2100

Projection Results by Scenario (SSP1–5)

	2010	2020	2030	2040	2050	2075	2100
Population (in millions)							
SSP1 - Rapid development	27.45	34.23	40.47	46.06	50.28	53.95	48.97
SSP2 - Medium	27.45	34.60	41.77	48.68	54.72	64.44	65.15
SSP3 - Stalled development	27.45	34.63	41.85	49.22	56.66	74.72	90.52
SSP4 - Inequality	27.45	35.26	44.05	53.25	62.86	86.81	105.23
SSP5 - Conventional development	27.45	34.83	42.43	49.45	54.97	60.89	55.86
Proportion age 65+							
SSP1 - Rapid development	0.03	0.04	0.07	0.13	0.19	0.35	0.50
SSP2 - Medium	0.03	0.04	0.07	0.12	0.16	0.24	0.33
SSP3 - Stalled development	0.03	0.04	0.07	0.10	0.13	0.14	0.17
SSP4 - Inequality	0.03	0.04	0.06	0.10	0.12	0.14	0.18
SSP5 - Conventional development	0.03	0.04	0.07	0.12	0.18	0.34	0.50
Proportion below age 20							
SSP1 - Rapid development	0.39	0.34	0.27	0.23	0.20	0.14	0.10
SSP2 - Medium	0.39	0.35	0.31	0.28	0.25	0.21	0.17
SSP3 - Stalled development	0.39	0.37	0.34	0.33	0.32	0.30	0.28
SSP4 - Inequality	0.39	0.37	0.34	0.33	0.32	0.30	0.27
SSP5 - Conventional development	0.39	0.34	0.27	0.23	0.20	0.14	0.10
Proportion of Women age 20–39 with at least secondary education							
SSP1 - Rapid development	0.78	0.93	0.97	0.99	0.99	1.00	1.00
SSP2 - Medium	0.78	0.91	0.96	0.98	0.99	1.00	1.00
SSP3 - Stalled development	0.78	0.82	0.82	0.82	0.82	0.82	0.82
SSP4 - Inequality	0.78	0.77	0.74	0.74	0.74	0.74	0.74
SSP5 - Conventional development	0.78	0.93	0.97	0.99	0.99	1.00	1.00
Mean years of schooling, age 25+							
SSP1 - Rapid development	9.42	10.93	12.07	12.98	13.64	14.72	15.17
SSP2 - Medium	9.42	10.80	11.87	12.77	13.47	14.60	15.08
SSP3 - Stalled development	9.42	10.25	10.81	11.22	11.48	11.62	11.63
SSP4 - Inequality	9.42	10.26	10.77	11.24	11.59	12.08	12.34
SSP5 - Conventional development	9.42	10.96	12.13	13.04	13.70	14.74	15.18

Demographic Assumptions Underlying SSPs

	2010–15	2020–25	2030–35	2040–45	2050–55	2075–80	2095–2100
Total fertility rate							
SSP1 - Rapid development	2.53	1.92	1.61	1.46	1.38	1.24	1.20
SSP2 - Medium	2.68	2.27	2.07	1.92	1.87	1.66	1.61
SSP3 - Stalled development	2.84	2.78	2.73	2.65	2.57	2.32	2.25
SSP4 - Inequality	2.85	2.80	2.73	2.61	2.51	2.25	2.18
SSP5 - Conventional development	2.52	1.92	1.61	1.46	1.38	1.24	1.20
Life expectancy at birth for females (in years)							
SSP1 - Rapid development	77.54	80.78	83.85	86.79	89.66	96.99	102.90
SSP2 - Medium	75.99	78.49	80.69	82.79	84.81	89.80	93.80
SSP3 - Stalled development	76.70	78.01	79.14	80.04	80.85	82.67	84.45
SSP4 - Inequality	76.70	78.00	79.11	80.00	80.79	82.60	84.42
SSP5 - Conventional development	77.54	80.78	83.85	86.79	89.66	96.99	102.90
Migration – net flow over five years (in thousands)							
SSP1 - Rapid development	1034	1075	1041	945	825	259	0
SSP2 - Medium	1010	1051	1061	1055	1030	441	0
SSP3 - Stalled development	861	544	576	651	737	476	0
SSP4 - Inequality	1033	1093	1159	1302	1462	921	0
SSP5 - Conventional development	1207	1622	1575	1418	1225	374	0

Ageing Indicators, Medium Scenario (SSP2)

	2010	2020	2030	2040	2050	2075	2095
Median age	25.94	28.92	32.01	34.85	38.02	44.11	49.74
Propspective median age	25.94	26.92	28.25	29.28	30.65	32.16	34.11
Proportion age 65+	0.03	0.04	0.07	0.12	0.16	0.24	0.31
Proportion RLE < 15 years	0.03	0.03	0.05	0.07	0.09	0.11	0.14

Senegal

Detailed Human Capital Projections to 2060

Demographic indicators, Medium Scenario (SSP2)	2010	2020	2030	2040	2050	2060
Population (in millions)	12.43	15.77	19.09	22.32	25.09	27.32
Proportion age 65+	0.02	0.02	0.03	0.04	0.05	0.07
Proportion below age 20	0.55	0.52	0.46	0.41	0.37	0.33
	2005–10	2015–20	2025–30	2035–40	2045–50	2055–60
Total Fertility Rate	5.03	4.06	3.26	2.75	2.39	2.12
Life expectancy at birth (in years)						
Men	57.18	59.28	61.10	62.82	64.64	67.61
Women	59.13	61.88	64.32	66.42	68.49	71.60
Five-year immigration flow (in '000)	18.00	17.62	18.28	18.67	18.66	18.37
Five-year emigration flow (in '000)	149.82	144.31	178.69	208.16	227.38	241.30

Human Capital indicators, Medium Scenario (SSP2)	2010	2020	2030	2040	2050	2060
Population age 25+: highest educational attainment						
E1 - no education	0.64	0.54	0.45	0.35	0.27	0.20
E2 - incomplete primary	0.06	0.07	0.06	0.06	0.05	0.04
E3 - primary	0.16	0.21	0.26	0.30	0.34	0.35
E4 - lower secondary	0.06	0.08	0.10	0.11	0.13	0.14
E5 - upper secondary	0.04	0.06	0.08	0.11	0.14	0.18
E6 - post-secondary	0.03	0.04	0.05	0.06	0.08	0.10
Mean years of schooling (in years)	3.05	3.96	4.94	5.98	6.99	7.97
Gender gap (population age 25+): highest educational attainment (ratio male/female)						
E1 - no education	0.84	0.85	0.88	0.91	0.93	0.94
E2 - incomplete primary	1.05	1.09	1.08	1.07	1.06	1.03
E3 - primary	1.19	1.02	0.95	0.93	0.93	0.95
E4 - lower secondary	1.54	1.32	1.18	1.11	1.06	1.03
E5 - upper secondary	2.14	1.88	1.65	1.44	1.29	1.17
E6 - post-secondary	2.02	1.47	1.15	1.00	0.95	0.97
Mean years of schooling (male minus female)	1.26	1.00	0.73	0.49	0.32	0.25
Women age 20–39: highest educational attainment						
E1 - no education	0.57	0.44	0.32	0.22	0.14	0.09
E2 - incomplete primary	0.08	0.08	0.07	0.07	0.06	0.05
E3 - primary	0.20	0.28	0.33	0.37	0.37	0.35
E4 - lower secondary	0.07	0.09	0.12	0.13	0.15	0.15
E5 - upper secondary	0.04	0.06	0.09	0.13	0.18	0.24
E6 - post-secondary	0.03	0.05	0.06	0.08	0.10	0.12
Mean years of schooling (in years)	3.45	4.74	6.09	7.32	8.44	9.43

Education scenarios

GET: global education trend scenario (medium assumption also used for SSP2)

CER: constant enrollment rates scenario (assumption of no future improvements)

FT: Fast track scenario (assumption of education expansion according to fastest historical experience)

Pyramids by Education, Medium Scenario

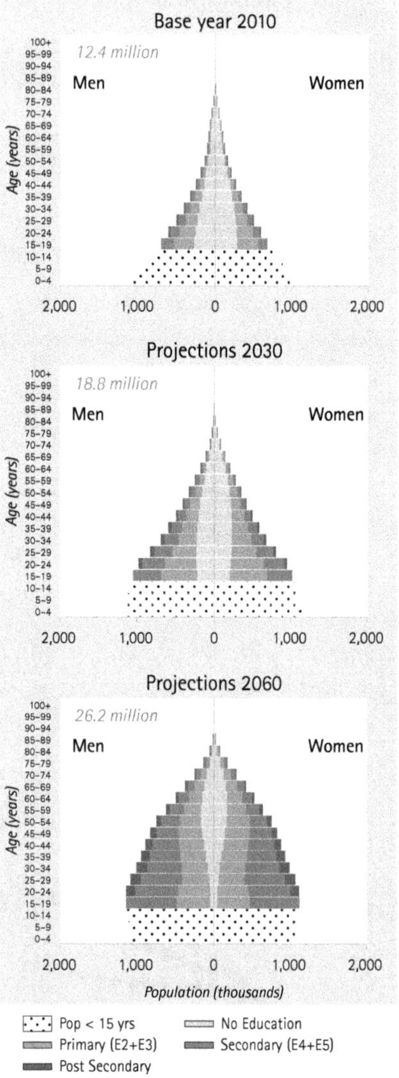

Population Size by Educational Attainment According to Three Education Scenarios: GET, CER, and FT

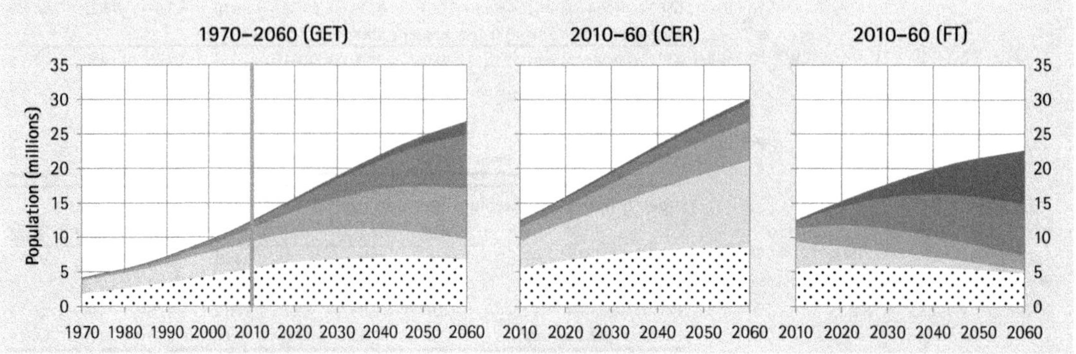

Senegal (Continued)

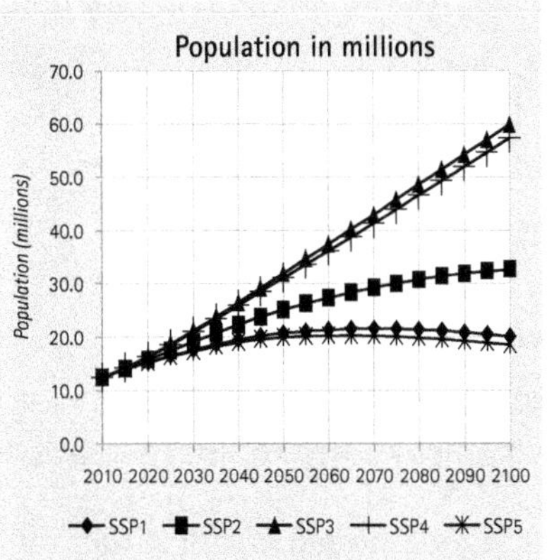

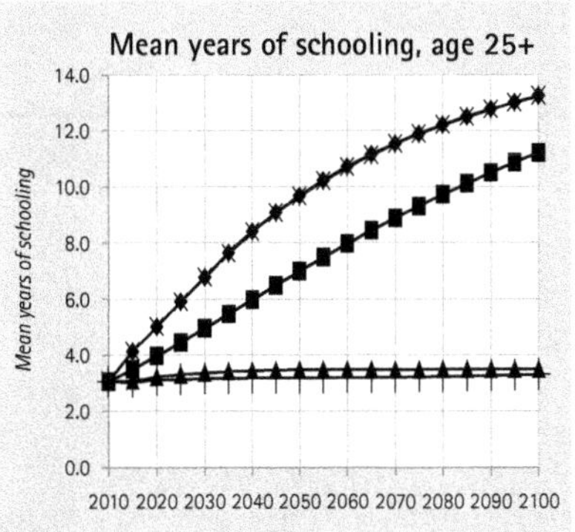

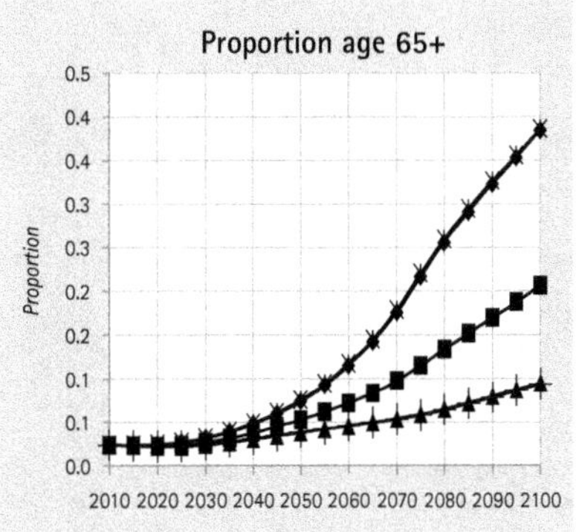

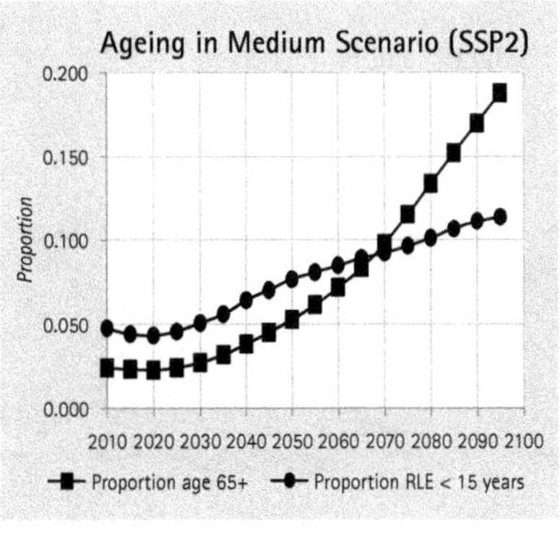

Alternative Scenarios to 2100

Projection Results by Scenario (SSP1–5)

	2010	2020	2030	2040	2050	2075	2100
Population (in millions)							
SSP1 - Rapid development	12.43	15.29	17.61	19.51	20.70	21.51	20.06
SSP2 - Medium	12.43	15.77	19.09	22.32	25.09	30.04	32.70
SSP3 - Stalled development	12.43	16.41	21.22	26.46	31.96	45.83	59.82
SSP4 - Inequality	12.43	16.35	20.99	25.96	31.12	43.98	57.32
SSP5 - Conventional development	12.43	15.21	17.35	19.00	19.91	20.06	18.48
Proportion age 65+							
SSP1 - Rapid development	0.02	0.02	0.03	0.05	0.07	0.22	0.38
SSP2 - Medium	0.02	0.02	0.03	0.04	0.05	0.12	0.21
SSP3 - Stalled development	0.02	0.02	0.02	0.03	0.04	0.06	0.09
SSP4 - Inequality	0.02	0.02	0.02	0.03	0.04	0.06	0.09
SSP5 - Conventional development	0.02	0.02	0.03	0.05	0.08	0.22	0.39
Proportion below age 20							
SSP1 - Rapid development	0.55	0.50	0.41	0.34	0.29	0.19	0.13
SSP2 - Medium	0.55	0.52	0.46	0.41	0.37	0.28	0.22
SSP3 - Stalled development	0.55	0.53	0.51	0.48	0.45	0.38	0.34
SSP4 - Inequality	0.55	0.53	0.51	0.48	0.45	0.38	0.34
SSP5 - Conventional development	0.55	0.50	0.41	0.34	0.29	0.19	0.13
Proportion of Women age 20–39 with at least secondary education							
SSP1 - Rapid development	0.14	0.35	0.50	0.61	0.68	0.81	0.90
SSP2 - Medium	0.14	0.20	0.27	0.35	0.43	0.64	0.83
SSP3 - Stalled development	0.14	0.11	0.11	0.11	0.11	0.11	0.11
SSP4 - Inequality	0.14	0.11	0.10	0.10	0.10	0.10	0.10
SSP5 - Conventional development	0.14	0.35	0.50	0.61	0.68	0.81	0.90
Mean years of schooling, age 25+							
SSP1 - Rapid development	3.05	5.00	6.79	8.40	9.68	11.89	13.25
SSP2 - Medium	3.05	3.96	4.94	5.98	6.99	9.31	11.21
SSP3 - Stalled development	3.05	3.21	3.36	3.44	3.47	3.48	3.49
SSP4 - Inequality	3.05	3.11	3.15	3.18	3.18	3.22	3.29
SSP5 - Conventional development	3.05	4.99	6.77	8.38	9.66	11.87	13.24

Demographic Assumptions Underlying SSPs

	2010–15	2020–25	2030–35	2040–45	2050–55	2075–80	2095–2100
Total fertility rate							
SSP1 - Rapid development	4.17	2.81	2.10	1.74	1.53	1.31	1.23
SSP2 - Medium	4.53	3.63	2.99	2.56	2.24	1.87	1.71
SSP3 - Stalled development	4.87	4.59	4.11	3.61	3.20	2.65	2.49
SSP4 - Inequality	4.88	4.63	4.14	3.62	3.21	2.64	2.48
SSP5 - Conventional development	4.17	2.81	2.10	1.74	1.53	1.31	1.23
Life expectancy at birth for females (in years)							
SSP1 - Rapid development	63.66	66.42	69.42	72.29	75.95	86.07	94.10
SSP2 - Medium	60.58	63.12	65.38	67.29	70.01	77.89	84.09
SSP3 - Stalled development	63.06	63.90	64.92	65.55	66.46	70.92	74.36
SSP4 - Inequality	63.06	63.89	64.90	65.52	66.42	70.87	74.32
SSP5 - Conventional development	63.66	66.42	69.42	72.29	75.95	86.07	94.10
Migration – net flow over five years (in thousands)							
SSP1 - Rapid development	−120	−140	−168	−179	−180	−75	0
SSP2 - Medium	−121	−142	−176	−200	−218	−110	0
SSP3 - Stalled development	−100	−70	−87	−103	−117	−68	0
SSP4 - Inequality	−120	−142	−180	−218	−252	−146	0
SSP5 - Conventional development	−140	−213	−261	−286	−298	−137	0

Ageing indicators, Medium Scenario (SSP2)

	2010	2020	2030	2040	2050	2075	2095
Median Age	17.77	19.27	21.81	24.62	27.39	34.74	40.59
Propspective Median Age	17.77	17.75	19.09	20.87	22.12	23.35	23.86
Proportion age 65+	0.02	0.02	0.03	0.04	0.05	0.12	0.19
Proportion RLE < 15 years	0.05	0.04	0.05	0.06	0.08	0.10	0.11

Serbia

Detailed Human Capital Projections to 2060

Demographic indicators, Medium Scenario (SSP2)	2010	2020	2030	2040	2050	2060
Population (in millions)	9.86	9.75	9.72	9.67	9.52	9.33
Proportion age 65+	0.14	0.17	0.19	0.22	0.26	0.30
Proportion below age 20	0.24	0.21	0.19	0.19	0.18	0.17
	2005–10	2015–20	2025–30	2035–40	2045–50	2055–60
Total Fertility Rate	1.62	1.42	1.57	1.60	1.60	1.61
Life expectancy at birth (in years)						
Men	71.69	73.72	75.89	77.87	79.99	82.13
Women	76.34	78.29	80.39	82.41	84.51	86.61
Five-year immigration flow (in '000)	174.35	172.91	180.08	184.88	185.74	183.48
Five-year emigration flow (in '000)	174.38	116.03	104.37	92.49	85.88	80.54

Human Capital indicators, Medium Scenario (SSP2)	2010	2020	2030	2040	2050	2060
Population age 25+: highest educational attainment						
E1 - no education	0.02	0.01	0.00	0.00	0.00	0.00
E2 - incomplete primary	0.02	0.01	0.00	0.00	0.00	0.00
E3 - primary	0.11	0.06	0.03	0.02	0.01	0.01
E4 - lower secondary	0.20	0.17	0.14	0.10	0.07	0.05
E5 - upper secondary	0.51	0.59	0.65	0.68	0.70	0.70
E6 - post-secondary	0.15	0.16	0.18	0.20	0.22	0.24
Mean years of schooling (in years)	10.55	11.36	11.86	12.19	12.45	12.68
Gender gap (population age 25+): highest educational attainment (ratio male/female)						
E1 - no education	0.16	0.30	0.49	0.60	0.70	0.82
E2 - incomplete primary	0.24	0.41	0.69	0.83	0.88	0.95
E3 - primary	0.55	0.52	0.60	0.77	0.99	1.13
E4 - lower secondary	0.98	0.94	0.94	0.99	1.06	1.13
E5 - upper secondary	1.26	1.18	1.15	1.13	1.12	1.10
E6 - post-secondary	1.00	0.79	0.70	0.67	0.69	0.75
Mean years of schooling (male minus female)	1.05	0.32	−0.08	−0.26	−0.34	−0.31
Women age 20–39: highest educational attainment						
E1 - no education	0.00	0.00	0.00	0.00	0.00	0.00
E2 - incomplete primary	0.00	0.00	0.00	0.00	0.00	0.00
E3 - primary	0.01	0.01	0.00	0.00	0.00	0.00
E4 - lower secondary	0.12	0.07	0.04	0.03	0.02	0.02
E5 - upper secondary	0.69	0.72	0.73	0.72	0.72	0.71
E6 - post-secondary	0.17	0.20	0.22	0.25	0.26	0.27
Mean years of schooling (in years)	12.03	12.43	12.65	12.81	12.88	12.94

Education scenarios

GET: global education trend scenario (medium assumption also used for SSP2)

CER: constant enrolment rates scenario (assumption of no future improvements)

FT: Fast track scenario (assumption of education expansion according to fastest historical experience)

Pyramids by Education, Medium Scenario

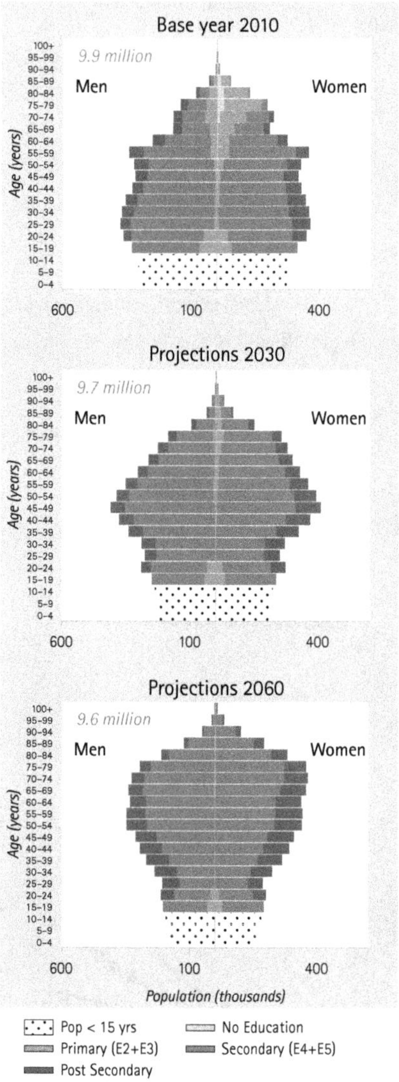

Population Size by Educational Attainment According to Three Education Scenarios: GET, CER, and FT

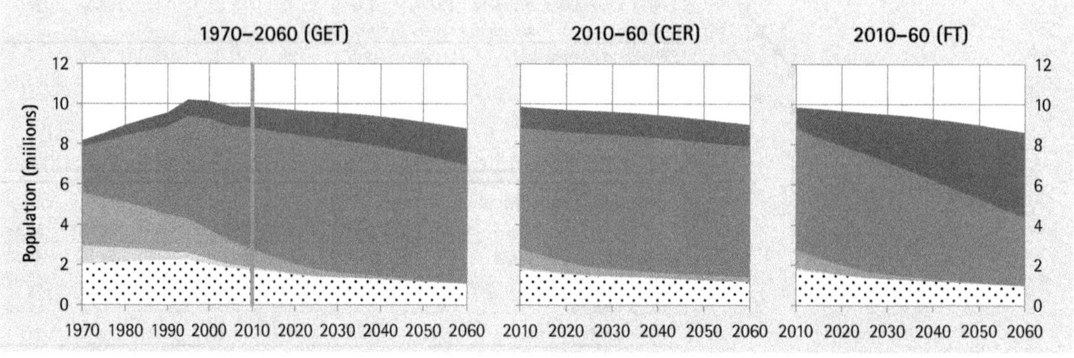

Serbia (Continued)

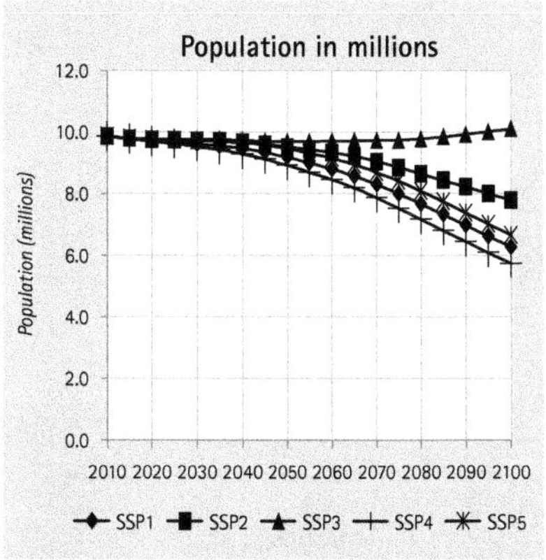

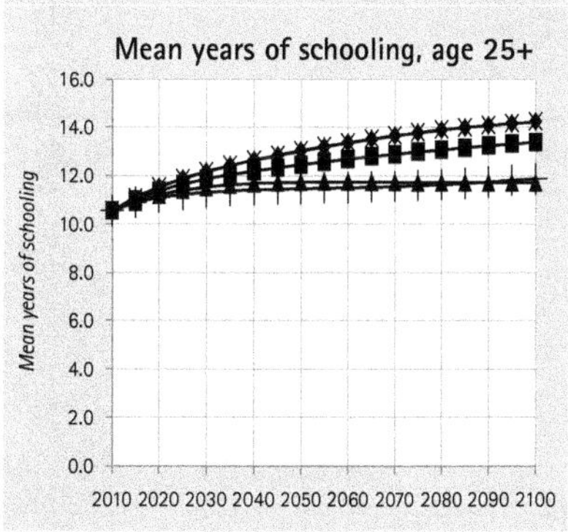

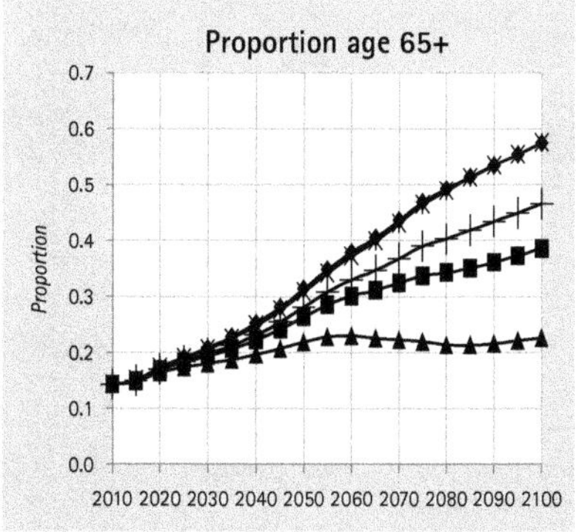

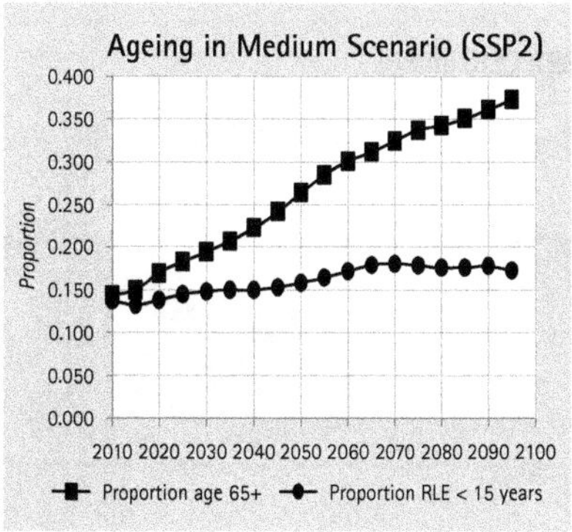

Alternative Scenarios to 2100

Projection Results by Scenario (SSP1–5)

	2010	2020	2030	2040	2050	2075	2100
Population (in millions)							
SSP1 - Rapid development	9.86	9.72	9.61	9.46	9.18	8.00	6.28
SSP2 - Medium	9.86	9.75	9.72	9.67	9.52	8.86	7.79
SSP3 - Stalled development	9.86	9.77	9.77	9.73	9.69	9.74	10.11
SSP4 - Inequality	9.86	9.69	9.53	9.29	8.92	7.53	5.74
SSP5 - Conventional development	9.86	9.75	9.71	9.65	9.45	8.41	6.66
Proportion age 65+							
SSP1 - Rapid development	0.14	0.17	0.21	0.25	0.31	0.47	0.57
SSP2 - Medium	0.14	0.17	0.19	0.22	0.26	0.34	0.39
SSP3 - Stalled development	0.14	0.16	0.18	0.20	0.22	0.22	0.23
SSP4 - Inequality	0.14	0.17	0.20	0.23	0.28	0.39	0.47
SSP5 - Conventional development	0.14	0.17	0.21	0.25	0.31	0.46	0.57
Proportion below age 20							
SSP1 - Rapid development	0.24	0.21	0.17	0.15	0.13	0.10	0.08
SSP2 - Medium	0.24	0.21	0.19	0.19	0.18	0.16	0.16
SSP3 - Stalled development	0.24	0.22	0.22	0.23	0.23	0.24	0.25
SSP4 - Inequality	0.24	0.21	0.18	0.16	0.15	0.12	0.11
SSP5 - Conventional development	0.24	0.21	0.17	0.15	0.13	0.10	0.08
Proportion of Women age 20–39 with at least secondary education							
SSP1 - Rapid development	0.98	0.99	1.00	1.00	1.00	1.00	1.00
SSP2 - Medium	0.98	0.99	0.99	1.00	1.00	1.00	1.00
SSP3 - Stalled development	0.98	0.97	0.97	0.97	0.97	0.97	0.97
SSP4 - Inequality	0.98	0.91	0.87	0.87	0.87	0.87	0.87
SSP5 - Conventional development	0.98	0.99	1.00	1.00	1.00	1.00	1.00
Mean years of schooling, age 25+							
SSP1 - Rapid development	10.55	11.52	12.16	12.64	13.02	13.77	14.23
SSP2 - Medium	10.55	11.36	11.86	12.19	12.45	12.98	13.38
SSP3 - Stalled development	10.55	11.20	11.53	11.68	11.73	11.72	11.72
SSP4 - Inequality	10.55	11.10	11.31	11.42	11.47	11.59	11.87
SSP5 - Conventional development	10.55	11.52	12.17	12.65	13.03	13.78	14.23

Demographic Assumptions Underlying SSPs

	2010–15	2020–25	2030–35	2040–45	2050–55	2075–80	2095–2100
Total fertility rate							
SSP1 - Rapid development	1.30	1.25	1.22	1.20	1.18	1.20	1.22
SSP2 - Medium	1.35	1.50	1.60	1.60	1.60	1.63	1.65
SSP3 - Stalled development	1.46	1.80	2.00	2.08	2.10	2.15	2.19
SSP4 - Inequality	1.31	1.31	1.29	1.27	1.25	1.27	1.28
SSP5 - Conventional development	1.30	1.25	1.22	1.20	1.18	1.20	1.22
Life expectancy at birth for females (in years)							
SSP1 - Rapid development	78.90	81.45	84.37	87.31	90.26	98.00	104.25
SSP2 - Medium	77.29	79.29	81.39	83.51	85.51	90.80	95.10
SSP3 - Stalled development	77.98	78.57	79.57	80.47	81.45	84.00	86.12
SSP4 - Inequality	78.46	79.99	81.92	83.87	85.72	90.60	94.77
SSP5 - Conventional development	78.90	81.45	84.37	87.31	90.26	98.00	104.25
Migration – net flow over five years (in thousands)							
SSP1 - Rapid development	33	65	83	88	83	24	0
SSP2 - Medium	34	67	85	95	99	39	0
SSP3 - Stalled development	27	34	45	57	68	38	0
SSP4 - Inequality	33	66	84	94	95	35	0
SSP5 - Conventional development	38	97	120	126	116	33	0

Ageing Indicators, Medium Scenario (SSP2)

	2010	2020	2030	2040	2050	2075	2095
Median age	37.54	40.39	43.52	46.25	48.18	51.71	54.76
Propspective median age	37.54	38.69	39.92	40.74	40.78	39.42	38.35
Proportion age 65+	0.14	0.17	0.19	0.22	0.26	0.34	0.37
Proportion RLE < 15 years	0.14	0.14	0.15	0.15	0.16	0.18	0.17

Sierra Leone

Detailed Human Capital Projections to 2060

Demographic indicators, Medium Scenario (SSP2)

	2010	2020	2030	2040	2050	2060
Population (in millions)	5.87	7.32	8.76	10.14	11.31	12.24
Proportion age 65+	0.02	0.02	0.02	0.03	0.04	0.06
Proportion below age 20	0.53	0.50	0.45	0.40	0.36	0.32
	2005-10	2015-20	2025-30	2035-40	2045-50	2055-60
Total Fertility Rate	5.22	4.09	3.15	2.64	2.27	2.07
Life expectancy at birth (in years)						
Men	45.64	49.36	52.21	55.01	57.67	60.19
Women	46.88	50.80	53.81	56.82	59.82	62.78
Five-year immigration flow (in '000)	74.99	73.34	76.08	77.73	77.68	76.51
Five-year emigration flow (in '000)	14.69	13.86	17.23	19.77	21.37	22.40

Human Capital indicators, Medium Scenario (SSP2)

	2010	2020	2030	2040	2050	2060
Population age 25+: highest educational attainment						
E1 - no education	0.64	0.55	0.47	0.38	0.31	0.24
E2 - incomplete primary	0.10	0.11	0.10	0.09	0.08	0.06
E3 - primary	0.08	0.10	0.13	0.15	0.17	0.18
E4 - lower secondary	0.09	0.11	0.14	0.17	0.20	0.21
E5 - upper secondary	0.07	0.09	0.11	0.14	0.17	0.21
E6 - post-secondary	0.04	0.04	0.05	0.06	0.08	0.10
Mean years of schooling (in years)	3.59	4.22	4.95	5.78	6.65	7.54
Gender gap (population age 25+): highest educational attainment (ratio male/female)						
E1 - no education	0.74	0.73	0.74	0.76	0.79	0.82
E2 - incomplete primary	1.16	1.10	1.04	1.01	0.99	0.98
E3 - primary	1.65	1.39	1.21	1.10	1.04	1.01
E4 - lower secondary	1.96	1.59	1.35	1.19	1.10	1.05
E5 - upper secondary	2.13	1.85	1.60	1.41	1.27	1.15
E6 - post-secondary	2.59	1.92	1.46	1.21	1.09	1.05
Mean years of schooling (male minus female)	2.31	2.03	1.63	1.22	0.85	0.55
Women age 20-39: highest educational attainment						
E1 - no education	0.60	0.52	0.41	0.30	0.21	0.13
E2 - incomplete primary	0.15	0.12	0.11	0.09	0.08	0.06
E3 - primary	0.09	0.12	0.15	0.18	0.19	0.20
E4 - lower secondary	0.09	0.13	0.17	0.20	0.23	0.24
E5 - upper secondary	0.06	0.09	0.12	0.16	0.21	0.27
E6 - post-secondary	0.02	0.03	0.04	0.06	0.08	0.10
Mean years of schooling (in years)	3.35	4.08	5.15	6.40	7.64	8.77

Education scenarios

GET: global education trend scenario (medium assumption also used for SSP2)

CER: constant enrolment rates scenario (assumption of no future improvements)

FT: Fast track scenario (assumption of education expansion according to fastest historical experience)

Pyramids by Education, Medium Scenario

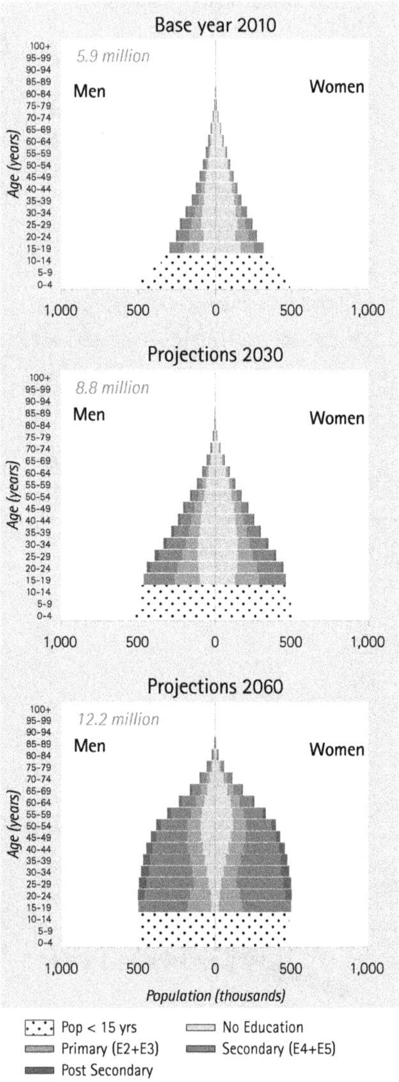

Population size by educational attainment according to three education scenarios: GET, CER, and FT

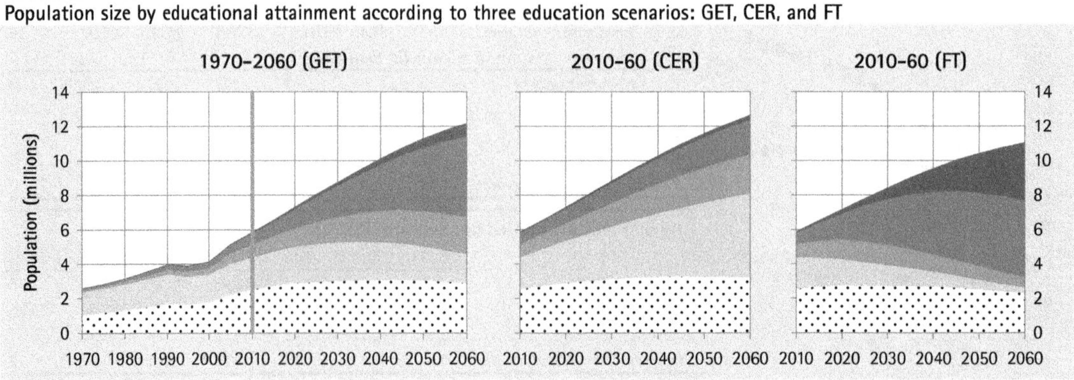

Sierra Leone (Continued)

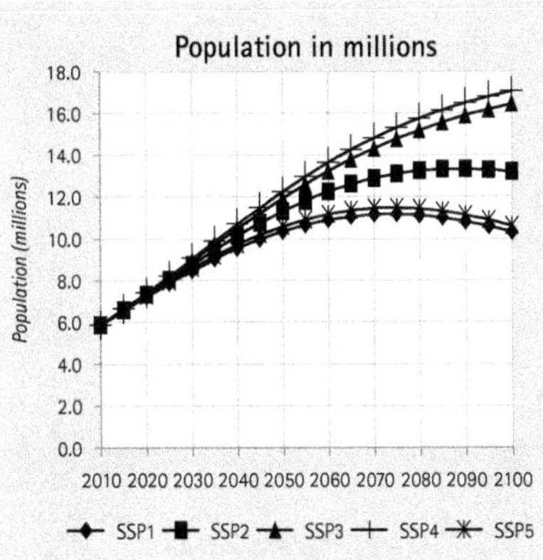

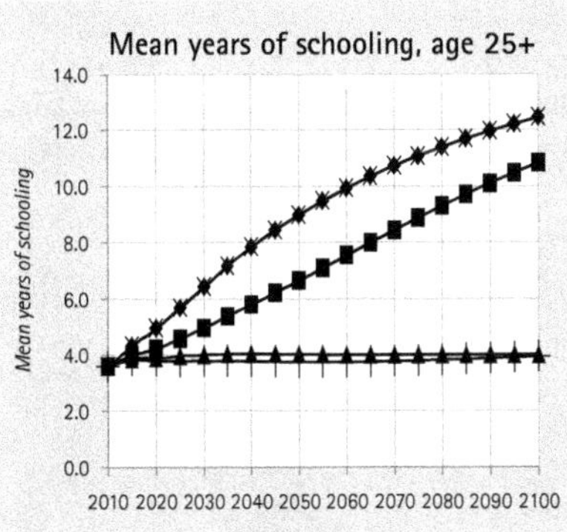

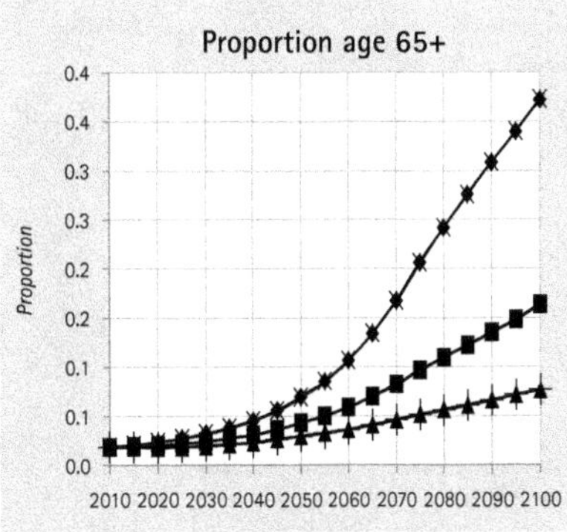

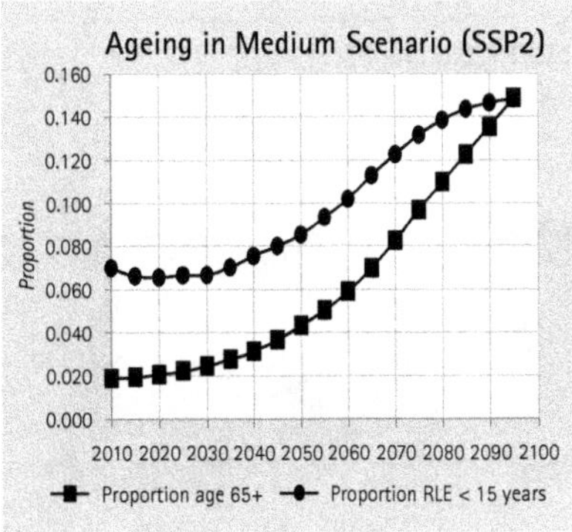

Alternative Scenarios to 2100

Projection Results by Scenario (SSP1–5)

	2010	2020	2030	2040	2050	2075	2100
Population (in millions)							
SSP1 - Rapid development	5.87	7.22	8.46	9.54	10.35	11.17	10.32
SSP2 - Medium	5.87	7.32	8.76	10.14	11.31	13.10	13.22
SSP3 - Stalled development	5.87	7.37	8.94	10.49	11.93	14.77	16.44
SSP4 - Inequality	5.87	7.41	9.07	10.71	12.25	15.30	17.04
SSP5 - Conventional development	5.87	7.25	8.57	9.72	10.58	11.48	10.61
Proportion age 65+							
SSP1 - Rapid development	0.02	0.02	0.03	0.05	0.07	0.21	0.37
SSP2 - Medium	0.02	0.02	0.02	0.03	0.04	0.10	0.16
SSP3 - Stalled development	0.02	0.02	0.02	0.02	0.03	0.05	0.08
SSP4 - Inequality	0.02	0.02	0.02	0.02	0.03	0.05	0.08
SSP5 - Conventional development	0.02	0.02	0.03	0.05	0.07	0.21	0.37
Proportion below age 20							
SSP1 - Rapid development	0.53	0.48	0.40	0.34	0.28	0.18	0.13
SSP2 - Medium	0.53	0.50	0.45	0.40	0.36	0.28	0.23
SSP3 - Stalled development	0.53	0.52	0.48	0.45	0.42	0.36	0.33
SSP4 - Inequality	0.53	0.52	0.48	0.45	0.42	0.36	0.33
SSP5 - Conventional development	0.53	0.48	0.40	0.34	0.28	0.18	0.13
Proportion of Women age 20–39 with at least secondary education							
SSP1 - Rapid development	0.17	0.36	0.52	0.64	0.73	0.86	0.93
SSP2 - Medium	0.17	0.24	0.33	0.43	0.52	0.74	0.88
SSP3 - Stalled development	0.17	0.17	0.18	0.18	0.18	0.18	0.18
SSP4 - Inequality	0.17	0.16	0.16	0.16	0.16	0.16	0.16
SSP5 - Conventional development	0.17	0.36	0.52	0.64	0.73	0.86	0.93
Mean years of schooling, age 25+							
SSP1 - Rapid development	3.59	4.94	6.42	7.84	8.98	11.07	12.45
SSP2 - Medium	3.59	4.22	4.95	5.78	6.65	8.87	10.82
SSP3 - Stalled development	3.59	3.88	4.00	4.02	4.01	3.99	4.00
SSP4 - Inequality	3.59	3.78	3.78	3.76	3.74	3.79	3.93
SSP5 - Conventional development	3.59	4.94	6.43	7.84	8.98	11.07	12.45

Demographic Assumptions Underlying SSPs

	2010–15	2020–25	2030–35	2040–45	2050–55	2075–80	2095–2100
Total fertility rate							
SSP1 - Rapid development	4.30	2.89	2.11	1.72	1.50	1.29	1.21
SSP2 - Medium	4.64	3.59	2.86	2.44	2.15	1.83	1.69
SSP3 - Stalled development	4.89	4.34	3.73	3.26	2.94	2.55	2.45
SSP4 - Inequality	4.90	4.36	3.75	3.26	2.94	2.54	2.43
SSP5 - Conventional development	4.30	2.89	2.11	1.72	1.50	1.29	1.21
Life expectancy at birth for females (in years)							
SSP1 - Rapid development	54.56	60.89	65.35	69.95	74.45	84.04	91.62
SSP2 - Medium	48.90	52.31	55.32	58.32	61.29	68.70	74.59
SSP3 - Stalled development	51.99	50.96	52.41	53.82	55.49	59.17	62.11
SSP4 - Inequality	51.99	50.94	52.37	53.78	55.45	59.14	62.09
SSP5 - Conventional development	54.56	60.89	65.35	69.95	74.45	84.04	91.62
Migration – net flow over five years (in thousands)							
SSP1 - Rapid development	56	58	55	50	44	17	0
SSP2 - Medium	59	60	59	58	55	27	0
SSP3 - Stalled development	46	29	30	33	36	24	0
SSP4 - Inequality	56	57	57	61	65	41	0
SSP5 - Conventional development	66	85	80	71	61	22	0

Ageing Indicators, Medium Scenario (SSP2)

	2010	2020	2030	2040	2050	2075	2095
Median age	18.27	19.87	22.51	25.31	28.15	34.88	39.17
Propspective median age	18.27	17.67	18.20	19.18	20.14	23.04	23.44
Proportion age 65+	0.02	0.02	0.02	0.03	0.04	0.10	0.15
Proportion RLE < 15 years	0.07	0.07	0.07	0.08	0.09	0.13	0.15

Singapore

Detailed Human Capital Projections to 2060

Demographic indicators, Medium Scenario (SSP2)						
	2010	2020	2030	2040	2050	2060
Population (in millions)	5.09	5.92	6.64	7.21	7.63	8.00
Proportion age 65+	0.09	0.14	0.20	0.24	0.27	0.30
Proportion below age 20	0.25	0.19	0.18	0.18	0.16	0.16
	2005–10	2015–20	2025–30	2035–40	2045–50	2055–60
Total Fertility Rate	1.25	1.31	1.38	1.40	1.40	1.42
Life expectancy at birth (in years)						
Men	78.48	79.63	81.58	83.59	85.59	87.59
Women	82.71	84.39	86.39	88.39	90.39	92.40
Five-year immigration flow (in '000)	720.34	253.72	263.32	269.06	268.91	264.89
Five-year emigration flow (in '000)	0.00	0.00	0.00	0.00	0.00	0.00

Human Capital indicators, Medium Scenario (SSP2)						
	2010	2020	2030	2040	2050	2060
Population age 25+: highest educational attainment						
E1 - no education	0.07	0.04	0.02	0.01	0.00	0.00
E2 - incomplete primary	0.09	0.06	0.04	0.02	0.01	0.00
E3 - primary	0.07	0.05	0.04	0.03	0.01	0.01
E4 - lower secondary	0.11	0.08	0.06	0.05	0.03	0.02
E5 - upper secondary	0.19	0.18	0.16	0.15	0.13	0.12
E6 - post-secondary	0.47	0.59	0.68	0.75	0.81	0.85
Mean years of schooling (in years)	11.04	11.95	12.45	12.78	12.98	13.04
Gender gap (population age 25+): highest educational attainment (ratio male/female)						
E1 - no education	0.40	0.36	0.35	0.36	0.39	0.45
E2 - incomplete primary	0.89	0.78	0.69	0.62	0.56	0.51
E3 - primary	0.93	0.84	0.75	0.66	0.58	0.51
E4 - lower secondary	1.06	0.98	0.90	0.79	0.68	0.59
E5 - upper secondary	0.87	0.87	0.86	0.85	0.87	0.91
E6 - post-secondary	1.23	1.16	1.12	1.09	1.06	1.03
Mean years of schooling (male minus female)	1.21	0.90	0.63	0.41	0.21	0.04
Women age 20–39: highest educational attainment						
E1 - no education	0.01	0.00	0.00	0.00	0.00	0.00
E2 - incomplete primary	0.01	0.00	0.00	0.00	0.00	0.00
E3 - primary	0.02	0.00	0.00	0.00	0.00	0.00
E4 - lower secondary	0.05	0.02	0.01	0.00	0.00	0.00
E5 - upper secondary	0.16	0.14	0.13	0.13	0.13	0.12
E6 - post-secondary	0.76	0.84	0.86	0.87	0.87	0.87
Mean years of schooling (in years)	13.63	13.26	12.75	12.77	12.77	12.79

Education scenarios

GET : global education trend scenario (medium assumption also used for SSP2)

CER: constant enrolment rates scenario (assumption of no future improvements)

FT: Fast track scenario (assumption of education expansion according to fastest historical experience)

Pyramids by Education, Medium Scenario

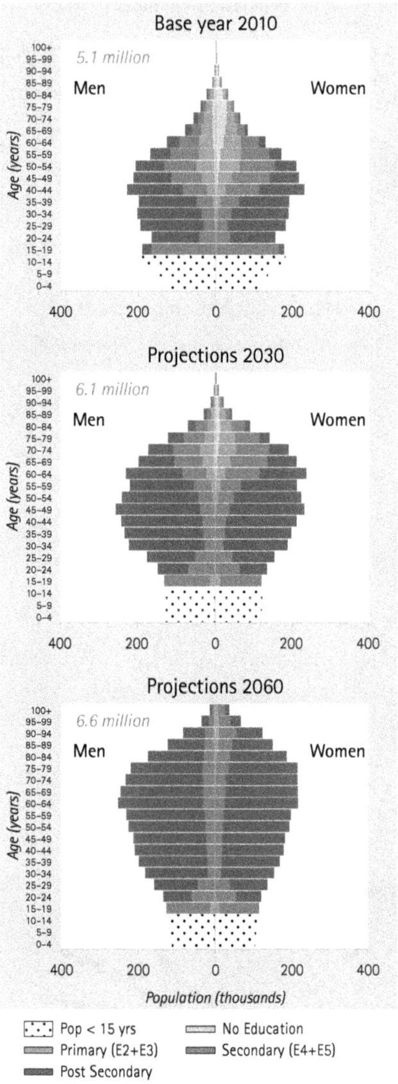

Population Size by Educational Attainment According to Three Education Scenarios: GET, CER, and FT

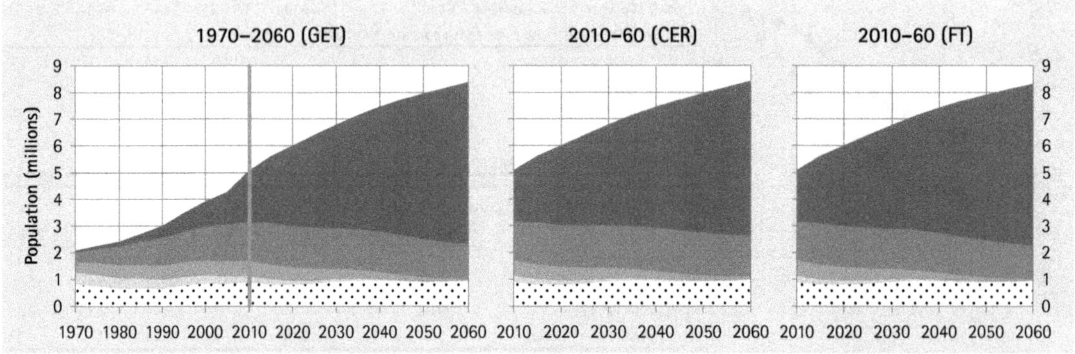

Singapore (Continued)

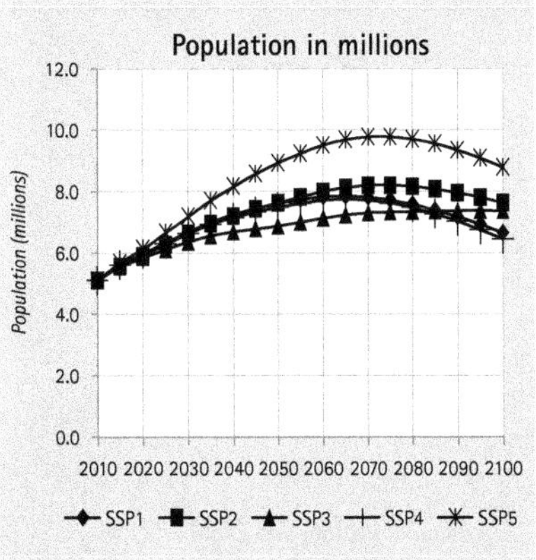

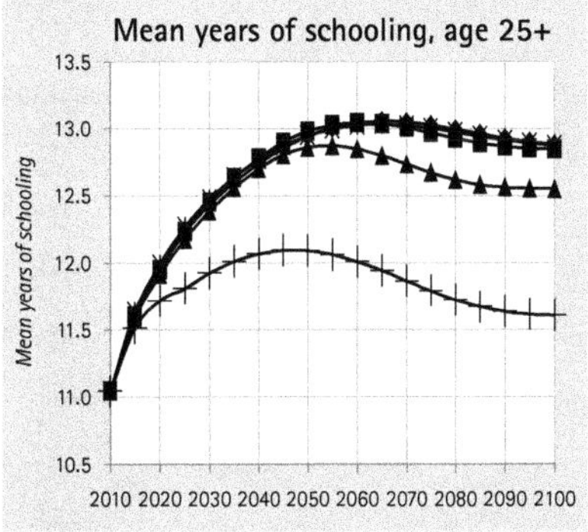

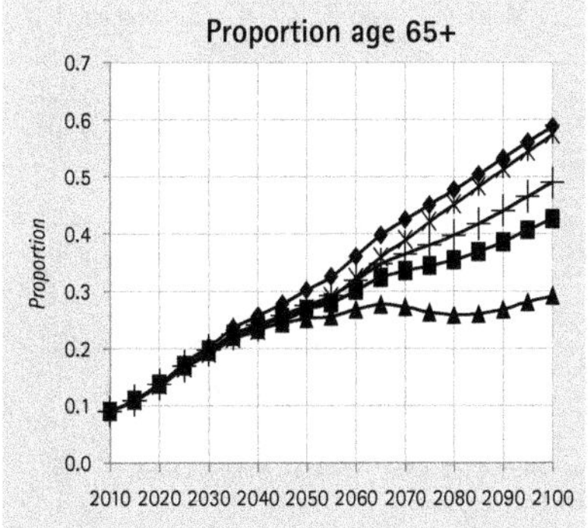

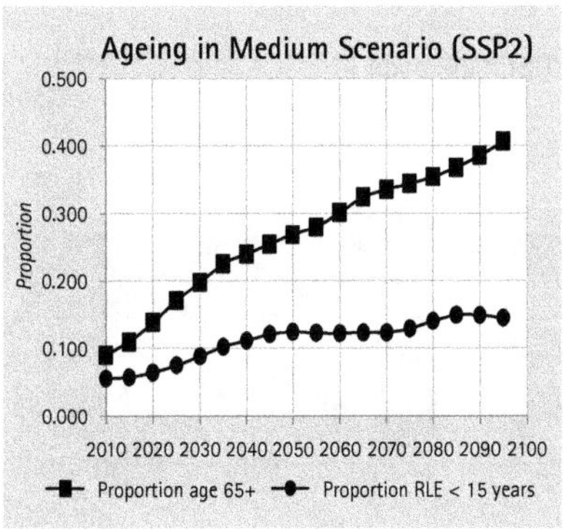

Alternative Scenarios to 2100

Projection Results by Scenario (SSP1–5)

	2010	2020	2030	2040	2050	2075	2100
Population (in millions)							
SSP1 - Rapid development	5.09	5.97	6.69	7.25	7.62	7.72	6.66
SSP2 - Medium	5.09	5.92	6.64	7.21	7.63	8.20	7.63
SSP3 - Stalled development	5.09	5.85	6.36	6.69	6.89	7.33	7.37
SSP4 - Inequality	5.09	5.96	6.64	7.16	7.49	7.62	6.45
SSP5 - Conventional development	5.09	6.14	7.20	8.16	8.92	9.77	8.78
Proportion age 65+							
SSP1 - Rapid development	0.09	0.14	0.20	0.26	0.30	0.45	0.59
SSP2 - Medium	0.09	0.14	0.20	0.24	0.27	0.34	0.43
SSP3 - Stalled development	0.09	0.14	0.20	0.23	0.25	0.26	0.29
SSP4 - Inequality	0.09	0.14	0.20	0.24	0.28	0.38	0.49
SSP5 - Conventional development	0.09	0.14	0.19	0.23	0.27	0.42	0.57
Proportion below age 20							
SSP1 - Rapid development	0.25	0.18	0.17	0.15	0.13	0.10	0.08
SSP2 - Medium	0.25	0.19	0.18	0.18	0.16	0.16	0.14
SSP3 - Stalled development	0.25	0.19	0.21	0.21	0.19	0.21	0.21
SSP4 - Inequality	0.25	0.18	0.17	0.16	0.14	0.12	0.10
SSP5 - Conventional development	0.25	0.18	0.17	0.16	0.14	0.11	0.08
Proportion of Women age 20–39 with at least secondary education							
SSP1 - Rapid development	0.97	0.99	1.00	1.00	1.00	1.00	1.00
SSP2 - Medium	0.97	0.99	1.00	1.00	1.00	1.00	1.00
SSP3 - Stalled development	0.97	0.99	0.99	0.99	0.99	0.99	0.99
SSP4 - Inequality	0.97	0.93	0.89	0.89	0.89	0.89	0.89
SSP5 - Conventional development	0.97	0.99	1.00	1.00	1.00	1.00	1.00
Mean years of schooling, age 25+							
SSP1 - Rapid development	11.04	11.96	12.43	12.74	12.94	13.03	12.88
SSP2 - Medium	11.04	11.95	12.45	12.78	12.98	12.97	12.84
SSP3 - Stalled development	11.04	11.91	12.38	12.70	12.86	12.67	12.55
SSP4 - Inequality	11.04	11.72	11.92	12.07	12.09	11.79	11.61
SSP5 - Conventional development	11.04	11.99	12.47	12.77	12.94	13.00	12.87

Demographic Assumptions Underlying SSPs

	2010–15	2020–25	2030–35	2040–45	2050–55	2075–80	2095–2100
Total fertility rate							
SSP1 - Rapid development	1.22	1.14	1.09	1.07	1.06	1.10	1.13
SSP2 - Medium	1.28	1.35	1.40	1.40	1.41	1.47	1.51
SSP3 - Stalled development	1.36	1.56	1.71	1.76	1.79	1.86	1.92
SSP4 - Inequality	1.23	1.17	1.13	1.11	1.10	1.14	1.18
SSP5 - Conventional development	1.22	1.14	1.09	1.07	1.06	1.10	1.13
Life expectancy at birth for females (in years)							
SSP1 - Rapid development	84.27	87.12	90.13	93.19	96.17	103.45	109.42
SSP2 - Medium	83.49	85.39	87.39	89.39	91.39	96.41	100.41
SSP3 - Stalled development	83.29	84.15	85.23	86.26	87.18	89.48	91.46
SSP4 - Inequality	83.79	85.61	87.65	89.68	91.60	96.16	100.04
SSP5 - Conventional development	84.27	87.12	90.13	93.19	96.17	103.45	109.42
Migration – net flow over five years (in thousands)							
SSP1 - Rapid development	410	256	254	235	209	58	0
SSP2 - Medium	363	237	238	238	235	89	0
SSP3 - Stalled development	341	127	130	140	150	73	0
SSP4 - Inequality	410	256	260	256	248	91	0
SSP5 - Conventional development	478	394	407	385	347	99	0

Ageing Indicators, Medium Scenario (SSP2)

	2010	2020	2030	2040	2050	2075	2095
Median age	37.69	40.18	42.66	45.70	48.85	52.00	57.58
Propspective median age	37.69	38.30	38.76	39.86	41.13	39.57	41.30
Proportion age 65+	0.09	0.14	0.20	0.24	0.27	0.34	0.41
Proportion RLE < 15 years	0.06	0.06	0.09	0.11	0.12	0.13	0.14

Slovakia

Detailed Human Capital Projections to 2060

Demographic indicators, Medium Scenario (SSP2)

	2010	2020	2030	2040	2050	2060
Population (in millions)	5.46	5.63	5.72	5.69	5.64	5.55
Proportion age 65+	0.12	0.16	0.20	0.23	0.29	0.32
Proportion below age 20	0.22	0.21	0.21	0.19	0.18	0.18
	2005–10	2015–20	2025–30	2035–40	2045–50	2055–60
Total Fertility Rate	1.27	1.51	1.62	1.67	1.69	1.70
Life expectancy at birth (in years)						
Men	70.74	73.73	76.31	78.55	80.84	83.02
Women	78.66	81.01	83.11	85.11	87.21	89.21
Five-year immigration flow (in '000)	40.72	40.26	41.91	42.96	43.08	42.51
Five-year emigration flow (in '000)	4.25	2.89	2.45	2.29	2.16	2.00

Human Capital indicators, Medium Scenario (SSP2)

	2010	2020	2030	2040	2050	2060
Population age 25+: highest educational attainment						
E1 - no education	0.00	0.00	0.00	0.00	0.00	0.00
E2 - incomplete primary	0.00	0.00	0.00	0.00	0.00	0.00
E3 - primary	0.00	0.00	0.00	0.00	0.00	0.00
E4 - lower secondary	0.16	0.11	0.07	0.05	0.03	0.02
E5 - upper secondary	0.69	0.73	0.75	0.76	0.75	0.74
E6 - post-secondary	0.14	0.16	0.17	0.19	0.22	0.24
Mean years of schooling (in years)	12.13	12.61	12.93	13.22	13.51	13.76
Gender gap (population age 25+): highest educational attainment (ratio male/female)						
E1 - no education	0.95	1.00	1.01	0.99	0.97	0.97
E2 - incomplete primary	1.00	1.02	0.93	0.80	0.73	0.75
E3 - primary	1.21	1.34	1.35	1.27	1.20	1.20
E4 - lower secondary	0.53	0.57	0.63	0.71	0.83	0.94
E5 - upper secondary	1.13	1.09	1.07	1.06	1.05	1.04
E6 - post-secondary	1.11	0.97	0.90	0.86	0.87	0.90
Mean years of schooling (male minus female)	0.47	0.24	0.10	0.00	−0.05	−0.06
Women age 20–39: highest educational attainment						
E1 - no education	0.00	0.00	0.00	0.00	0.00	0.00
E2 - incomplete primary	0.00	0.00	0.00	0.00	0.00	0.00
E3 - primary	0.00	0.00	0.00	0.00	0.00	0.00
E4 - lower secondary	0.05	0.03	0.02	0.02	0.02	0.01
E5 - upper secondary	0.79	0.78	0.76	0.74	0.71	0.70
E6 - post-secondary	0.16	0.19	0.22	0.24	0.27	0.29
Mean years of schooling (in years)	13.04	13.71	13.73	13.83	13.97	14.05

Education scenarios

GET : global education trend scenario (medium assumption also used for SSP2)

CER: constant enrolment rates scenario (assumption of no future improvements)

FT: Fast track scenario (assumption of education expansion according to fastest historical experience)

Pyramids by Education, Medium Scenario

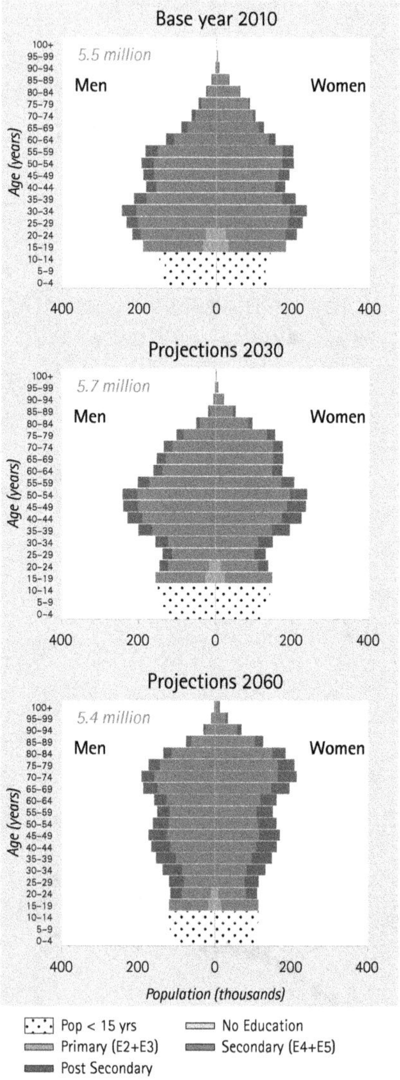

Population Size by Educational Attainment According to Three Education Scenarios: GET, CER, and FT

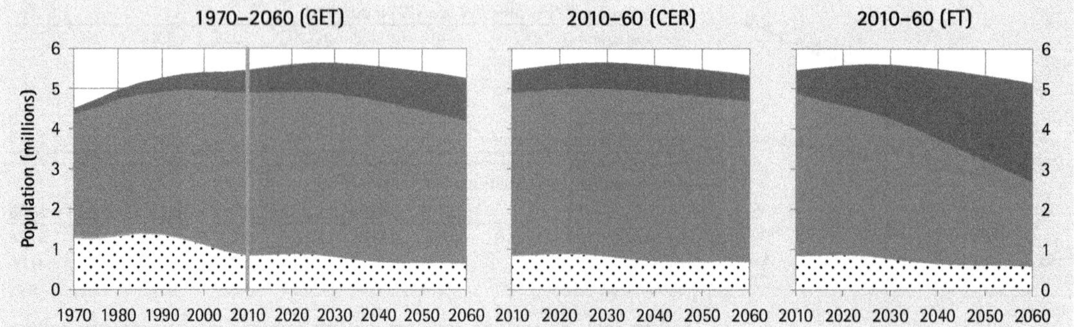

Slovakia (Continued)

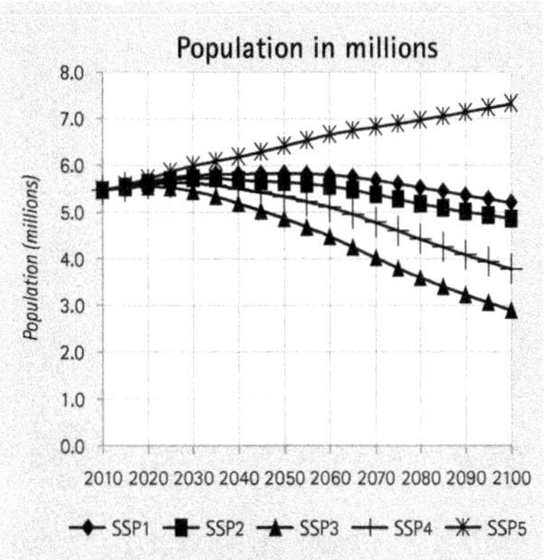

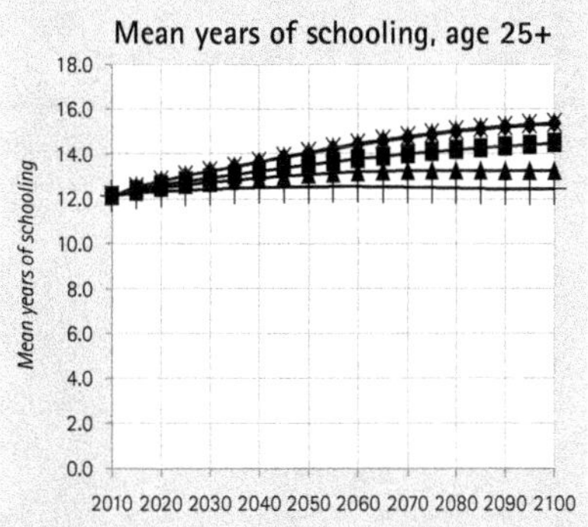

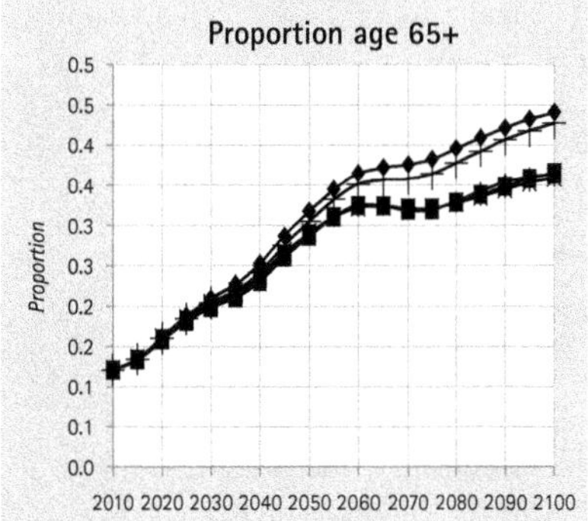

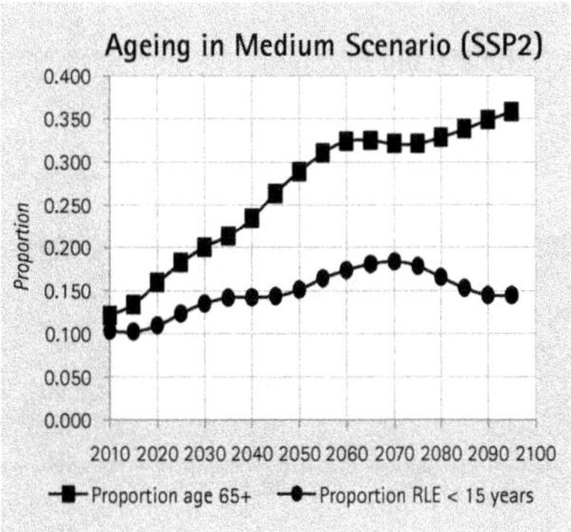

Alternative Scenarios to 2100

Projection Results by Scenario (SSP1–5)

	2010	2020	2030	2040	2050	2075	2100
Population (in millions)							
SSP1 - Rapid development	5.46	5.65	5.78	5.81	5.82	5.60	5.20
SSP2 - Medium	5.46	5.63	5.72	5.69	5.64	5.27	4.86
SSP3 - Stalled development	5.46	5.54	5.45	5.19	4.86	3.80	2.89
SSP4 - Inequality	5.46	5.59	5.62	5.50	5.33	4.60	3.78
SSP5 - Conventional development	5.46	5.71	5.99	6.18	6.41	6.89	7.31
Proportion age 65+							
SSP1 - Rapid development	0.12	0.16	0.21	0.25	0.32	0.38	0.44
SSP2 - Medium	0.12	0.16	0.20	0.23	0.29	0.32	0.37
SSP3 - Stalled development	0.12	0.16	0.20	0.23	0.29	0.32	0.36
SSP4 - Inequality	0.12	0.16	0.20	0.24	0.31	0.36	0.43
SSP5 - Conventional development	0.12	0.16	0.20	0.24	0.29	0.32	0.36
Proportion below age 20							
SSP1 - Rapid development	0.22	0.20	0.20	0.18	0.17	0.16	0.15
SSP2 - Medium	0.22	0.21	0.21	0.19	0.18	0.18	0.17
SSP3 - Stalled development	0.22	0.20	0.19	0.16	0.15	0.15	0.14
SSP4 - Inequality	0.22	0.20	0.19	0.17	0.15	0.14	0.13
SSP5 - Conventional development	0.22	0.21	0.22	0.20	0.20	0.20	0.20
Proportion of Women age 20–39 with at least secondary education							
SSP1 - Rapid development	1.00	1.00	1.00	1.00	1.00	1.00	1.00
SSP2 - Medium	1.00	1.00	1.00	1.00	1.00	1.00	1.00
SSP3 - Stalled development	1.00	1.00	1.00	1.00	1.00	1.00	1.00
SSP4 - Inequality	1.00	1.00	1.00	1.00	1.00	1.00	1.00
SSP5 - Conventional development	1.00	1.00	1.00	1.00	1.00	1.00	1.00
Mean years of schooling, age 25+							
SSP1 - Rapid development	12.13	12.79	13.22	13.63	14.03	14.86	15.33
SSP2 - Medium	12.13	12.61	12.93	13.22	13.51	14.09	14.48
SSP3 - Stalled development	12.13	12.49	12.73	12.92	13.08	13.25	13.25
SSP4 - Inequality	12.13	12.34	12.43	12.50	12.53	12.50	12.44
SSP5 - Conventional development	12.13	12.79	13.23	13.64	14.06	14.91	15.37

Demographic Assumptions Underlying SSPs

	2010–15	2020–25	2030–35	2040–45	2050–55	2075–80	2095–2100
Total fertility rate							
SSP1 - Rapid development	1.45	1.53	1.60	1.64	1.65	1.66	1.68
SSP2 - Medium	1.45	1.56	1.66	1.68	1.70	1.71	1.72
SSP3 - Stalled development	1.40	1.36	1.33	1.32	1.32	1.34	1.36
SSP4 - Inequality	1.40	1.40	1.39	1.38	1.38	1.40	1.42
SSP5 - Conventional development	1.52	1.76	1.94	2.03	2.06	2.08	2.10
Life expectancy at birth for females (in years)							
SSP1 - Rapid development	80.81	83.86	86.86	89.83	92.78	100.29	106.33
SSP2 - Medium	79.81	82.01	84.11	86.21	88.21	93.21	97.20
SSP3 - Stalled development	79.83	80.93	81.99	82.96	83.91	86.28	88.19
SSP4 - Inequality	80.27	82.36	84.39	86.42	88.36	93.09	96.96
SSP5 - Conventional development	80.81	83.86	86.86	89.83	92.78	100.29	106.33
Migration – net flow over five years (in thousands)							
SSP1 - Rapid development	35	38	40	39	38	15	0
SSP2 - Medium	36	39	40	41	41	17	0
SSP3 - Stalled development	29	19	20	20	20	9	0
SSP4 - Inequality	35	38	39	39	38	17	0
SSP5 - Conventional development	41	57	59	60	60	27	0

Ageing Indicators, Medium Scenario (SSP2)

	2010	2020	2030	2040	2050	2075	2095
Median age	36.83	40.65	44.50	47.95	48.96	50.85	52.07
Propspective median age	36.83	38.29	40.06	41.49	40.50	37.64	34.80
Proportion age 65+	0.12	0.16	0.20	0.23	0.29	0.32	0.36
Proportion RLE < 15 years	0.10	0.11	0.14	0.14	0.15	0.18	0.14

Slovenia

Detailed Human Capital Projections to 2060

Demographic indicators, Medium Scenario (SSP2)	2010	2020	2030	2040	2050	2060
Population (in millions)	2.03	2.08	2.09	2.08	2.06	2.04
Proportion age 65+	0.16	0.21	0.25	0.28	0.32	0.33
Proportion below age 20	0.19	0.19	0.19	0.17	0.18	0.18
	2005–10	2015–20	2025–30	2035–40	2045–50	2055–60
Total Fertility Rate	1.39	1.59	1.64	1.67	1.69	1.70
Life expectancy at birth (in years)						
Men	74.97	77.12	79.24	81.33	83.41	85.44
Women	81.99	83.79	85.81	87.81	89.79	91.79
Five-year immigration flow (in '000)	24.87	24.47	25.44	26.03	26.06	25.70
Five-year emigration flow (in '000)	2.96	1.88	1.70	1.65	1.57	1.50

Human Capital indicators, Medium Scenario (SSP2)	2010	2020	2030	2040	2050	2060
Population age 25+: highest educational attainment						
E1 - no education	0.00	0.00	0.00	0.00	0.00	0.00
E2 - incomplete primary	0.01	0.01	0.00	0.00	0.00	0.00
E3 - primary	0.02	0.01	0.01	0.00	0.00	0.00
E4 - lower secondary	0.19	0.16	0.12	0.09	0.07	0.05
E5 - upper secondary	0.59	0.61	0.63	0.63	0.63	0.61
E6 - post-secondary	0.18	0.21	0.23	0.27	0.30	0.34
Mean years of schooling (in years)	11.85	12.39	12.81	13.22	13.61	13.96
Gender gap (population age 25+): highest educational attainment (ratio male/female)						
E1 - no education	0.47	0.53	0.56	0.54	0.47	0.35
E2 - incomplete primary	0.70	0.89	1.06	1.11	1.09	1.03
E3 - primary	2.75	3.14	3.37	3.07	2.58	2.16
E4 - lower secondary	0.57	0.67	0.78	0.88	0.99	1.11
E5 - upper secondary	1.25	1.22	1.20	1.19	1.17	1.14
E6 - post-secondary	0.79	0.71	0.67	0.68	0.71	0.77
Mean years of schooling (male minus female)	0.09	−0.18	−0.35	−0.43	−0.43	−0.38
Women age 20–39: highest educational attainment						
E1 - no education	0.00	0.00	0.00	0.00	0.00	0.00
E2 - incomplete primary	0.00	0.00	0.00	0.00	0.00	0.00
E3 - primary	0.00	0.00	0.00	0.00	0.00	0.00
E4 - lower secondary	0.07	0.04	0.03	0.02	0.01	0.01
E5 - upper secondary	0.69	0.67	0.68	0.67	0.65	0.65
E6 - post-secondary	0.24	0.28	0.29	0.31	0.34	0.33
Mean years of schooling (in years)	13.14	13.88	14.01	14.14	14.26	14.26

Education scenarios

GET : global education trend scenario (medium assumption also used for SSP2)

CER: constant enrolment rates scenario (assumption of no future improvements)

FT: Fast track scenario (assumption of education expansion according to fastest historical experience)

Pyramids by Education, Medium Scenario

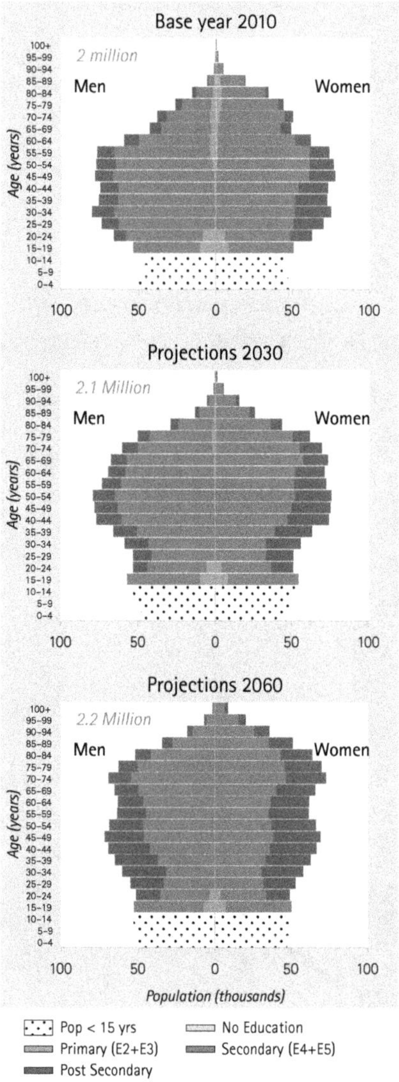

Population Size by Educational Attainment According to Three Education Scenarios: GET, CER, and FT

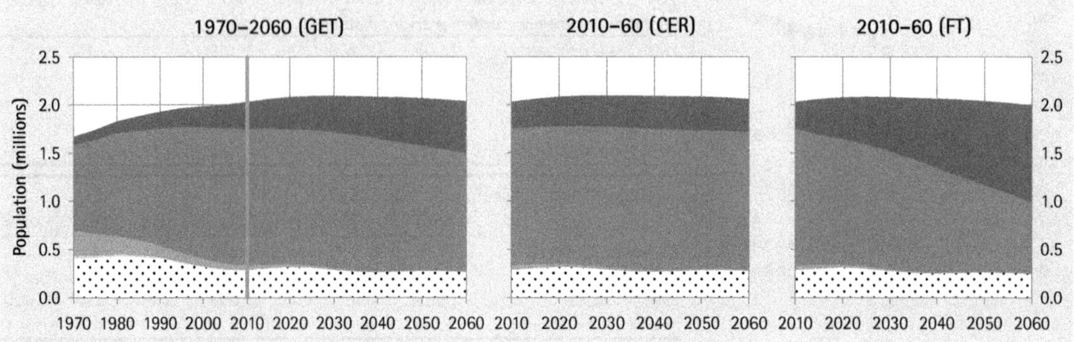

Slovenia (Continued)

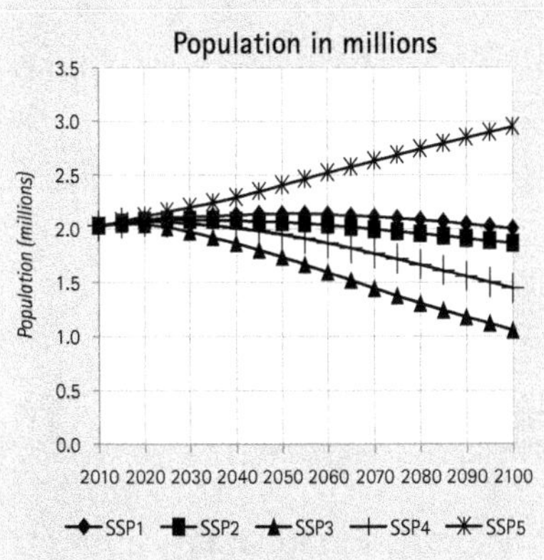

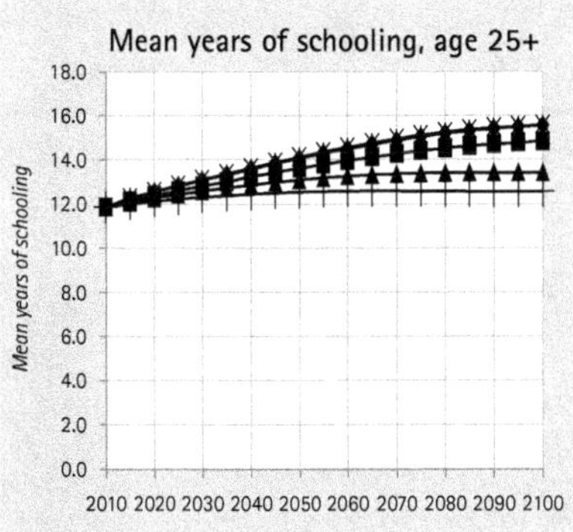

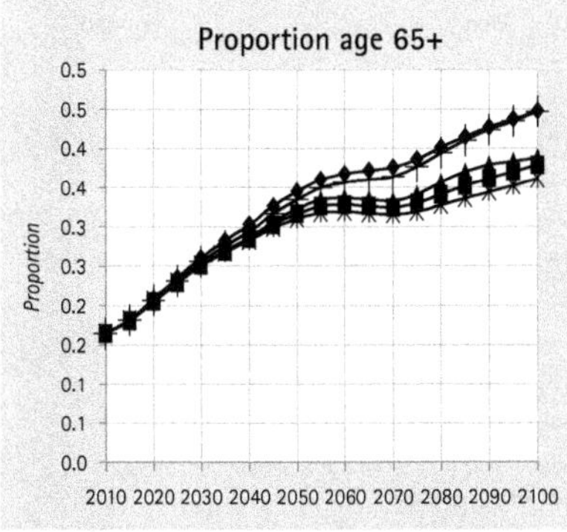

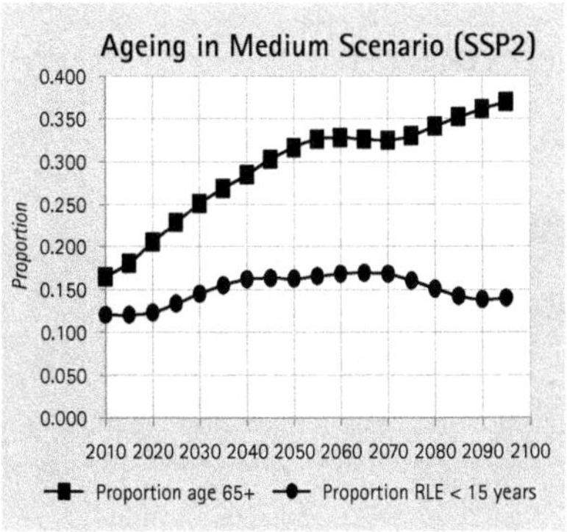

Alternative Scenarios to 2100

Projection Results by Scenario (SSP1–5)

	2010	2020	2030	2040	2050	2075	2100
Population (in millions)							
SSP1 - Rapid development	2.03	2.09	2.12	2.13	2.14	2.10	2.00
SSP2 - Medium	2.03	2.08	2.09	2.08	2.06	1.98	1.86
SSP3 - Stalled development	2.03	2.04	1.97	1.87	1.74	1.38	1.06
SSP4 - Inequality	2.03	2.07	2.05	2.01	1.95	1.72	1.45
SSP5 - Conventional development	2.03	2.12	2.20	2.29	2.41	2.69	2.95
Proportion age 65+							
SSP1 - Rapid development	0.16	0.21	0.26	0.30	0.35	0.39	0.45
SSP2 - Medium	0.16	0.21	0.25	0.28	0.32	0.33	0.38
SSP3 - Stalled development	0.16	0.20	0.25	0.29	0.32	0.34	0.39
SSP4 - Inequality	0.16	0.21	0.26	0.29	0.33	0.38	0.45
SSP5 - Conventional development	0.16	0.21	0.25	0.28	0.31	0.32	0.36
Proportion below age 20							
SSP1 - Rapid development	0.19	0.19	0.18	0.17	0.17	0.16	0.14
SSP2 - Medium	0.19	0.19	0.19	0.17	0.18	0.17	0.16
SSP3 - Stalled development	0.19	0.19	0.17	0.15	0.15	0.14	0.13
SSP4 - Inequality	0.19	0.19	0.17	0.15	0.15	0.13	0.12
SSP5 - Conventional development	0.19	0.20	0.20	0.20	0.20	0.20	0.20
Proportion of Women age 20–39 with at least secondary education							
SSP1 - Rapid development	1.00	1.00	1.00	1.00	1.00	1.00	1.00
SSP2 - Medium	1.00	1.00	1.00	1.00	1.00	1.00	1.00
SSP3 - Stalled development	1.00	1.00	1.00	1.00	1.00	1.00	1.00
SSP4 - Inequality	1.00	1.00	1.00	1.00	1.00	1.00	1.00
SSP5 - Conventional development	1.00	1.00	1.00	1.00	1.00	1.00	1.00
Mean years of schooling, age 25+							
SSP1 - Rapid development	11.85	12.55	13.07	13.58	14.06	15.04	15.53
SSP2 - Medium	11.85	12.39	12.81	13.22	13.61	14.40	14.83
SSP3 - Stalled development	11.85	12.26	12.59	12.86	13.08	13.39	13.41
SSP4 - Inequality	11.85	12.13	12.31	12.44	12.53	12.58	12.55
SSP5 - Conventional development	11.85	12.56	13.09	13.61	14.11	15.10	15.56

Demographic Assumptions Underlying SSPs

	2010–15	2020–25	2030–35	2040–45	2050–55	2075–80	2095–2100
Total fertility rate							
SSP1 - Rapid development	1.56	1.59	1.62	1.65	1.67	1.68	1.69
SSP2 - Medium	1.56	1.61	1.66	1.68	1.70	1.71	1.72
SSP3 - Stalled development	1.49	1.39	1.33	1.32	1.31	1.33	1.34
SSP4 - Inequality	1.50	1.42	1.38	1.37	1.36	1.38	1.39
SSP5 - Conventional development	1.64	1.82	1.97	2.04	2.08	2.10	2.12
Life expectancy at birth for females (in years)							
SSP1 - Rapid development	83.75	86.59	89.48	92.43	95.38	102.88	108.92
SSP2 - Medium	82.89	84.81	86.81	88.79	90.79	95.80	99.80
SSP3 - Stalled development	82.78	83.61	84.56	85.52	86.47	88.80	90.73
SSP4 - Inequality	83.26	85.09	87.03	88.97	90.91	95.66	99.53
SSP5 - Conventional development	83.75	86.59	89.48	92.43	95.38	102.88	108.92
Migration – net flow over five years (in thousands)							
SSP1 - Rapid development	21	23	24	23	23	9	0
SSP2 - Medium	22	23	24	24	24	10	0
SSP3 - Stalled development	18	12	12	12	12	5	0
SSP4 - Inequality	21	23	24	23	23	10	0
SSP5 - Conventional development	25	35	36	37	37	17	0

Ageing Indicators, Medium Scenario (SSP2)

	2010	2020	2030	2040	2050	2075	2095
Median age	41.72	44.37	47.46	49.68	49.53	51.25	53.30
Propspective median age	41.72	42.57	43.74	44.12	42.04	38.96	37.05
Proportion age 65+	0.16	0.21	0.25	0.28	0.32	0.33	0.37
Proportion RLE < 15 years	0.12	0.12	0.15	0.16	0.16	0.16	0.14

Somalia

Detailed Human Capital Projections to 2060

Demographic indicators, Medium Scenario (SSP2)

	2010	2020	2030	2040	2050	2060
Population (in millions)	9.33	11.30	13.21	14.89	15.99	16.69
Proportion age 65+	0.03	0.03	0.04	0.05	0.05	0.06
Proportion below age 20	0.55	0.54	0.50	0.46	0.41	0.36
	2005–10	2015–20	2025–30	2035–40	2045–50	2055–60
Total Fertility Rate	6.40	5.45	4.41	3.41	2.74	2.34
Life expectancy at birth (in years)						
Men	48.71	51.20	53.35	55.14	56.97	59.85
Women	51.78	54.61	56.98	58.98	61.08	64.22
Five-year immigration flow (in '000)	0.00	0.00	0.00	0.00	0.00	0.00
Five-year emigration flow (in '000)	298.94	278.05	342.53	392.99	424.79	439.45

Human Capital indicators, Medium Scenario (SSP2)

	2010	2020	2030	2040	2050	2060
Population age 25+: highest educational attainment						
E1 - no education	0.59	0.50	0.39	0.29	0.20	0.14
E2 - incomplete primary	0.04	0.04	0.04	0.04	0.03	0.02
E3 - primary	0.14	0.19	0.25	0.29	0.32	0.32
E4 - lower secondary	0.08	0.08	0.08	0.08	0.08	0.08
E5 - upper secondary	0.12	0.15	0.19	0.24	0.30	0.35
E6 - post-secondary	0.03	0.04	0.05	0.06	0.08	0.10
Mean years of schooling (in years)	3.49	4.43	5.54	6.69	7.74	8.69
Gender gap (population age 25+): highest educational attainment (ratio male/female)						
E1 - no education	0.60	0.58	0.58	0.59	0.62	0.66
E2 - incomplete primary	1.12	0.90	0.82	0.79	0.80	0.85
E3 - primary	1.53	1.25	1.06	0.96	0.92	0.93
E4 - lower secondary	1.91	1.53	1.22	1.04	0.95	0.92
E5 - upper secondary	3.75	2.94	2.25	1.76	1.45	1.24
E6 - post-secondary	5.68	3.59	2.35	1.69	1.36	1.18
Mean years of schooling (male minus female)	3.08	2.95	2.56	2.01	1.45	0.93
Women age 20–39: highest educational attainment						
E1 - no education	0.61	0.46	0.31	0.20	0.11	0.06
E2 - incomplete primary	0.05	0.06	0.06	0.05	0.04	0.03
E3 - primary	0.20	0.28	0.33	0.35	0.34	0.29
E4 - lower secondary	0.06	0.06	0.08	0.09	0.09	0.09
E5 - upper secondary	0.07	0.12	0.18	0.25	0.33	0.40
E6 - post-secondary	0.01	0.03	0.05	0.07	0.09	0.12
Mean years of schooling (in years)	3.05	4.48	6.02	7.42	8.68	9.75

Education scenarios

GET: global education trend scenario (medium assumption also used for SSP2)

CER: constant enrolment rates scenario (assumption of no future improvements)

FT: Fast track scenario (assumption of education expansion according to fastest historical experience)

Pyramids by Education, Medium Scenario

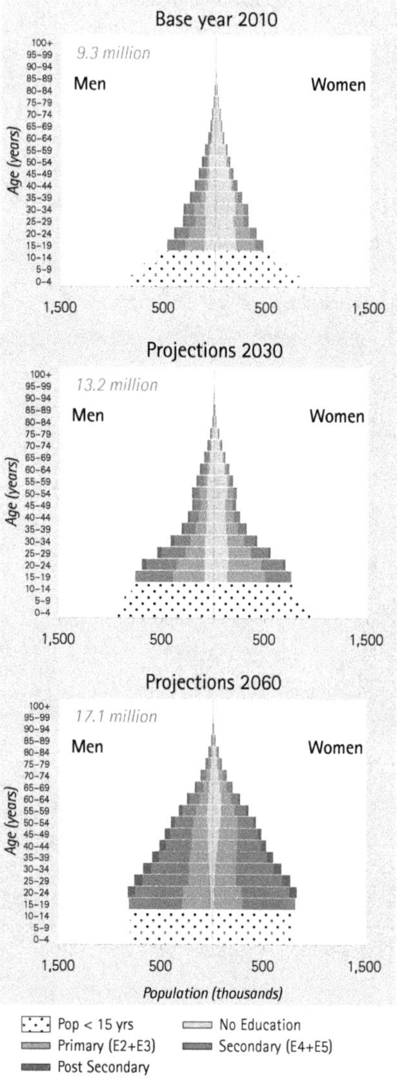

Population Size by Educational Attainment According to Three Education Scenarios: GET, CER, and FT

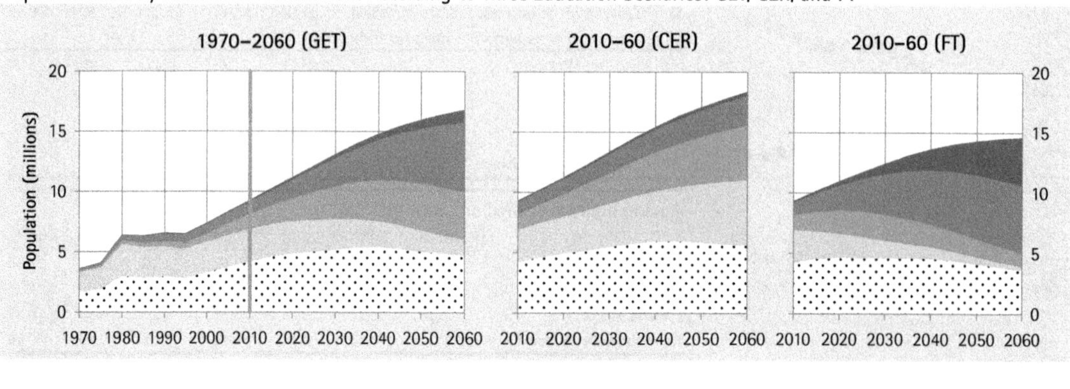

Somalia (Continued)

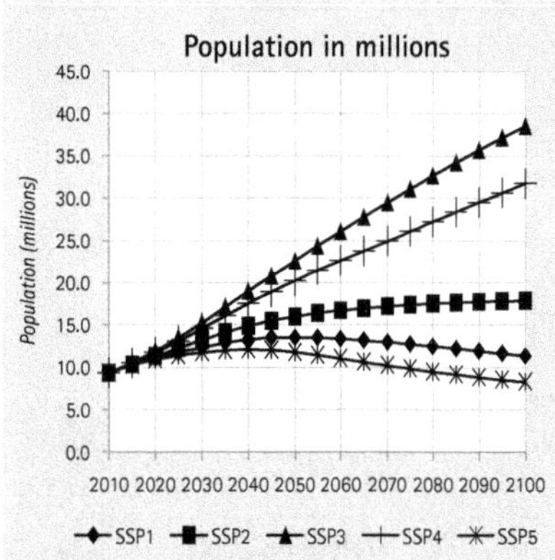

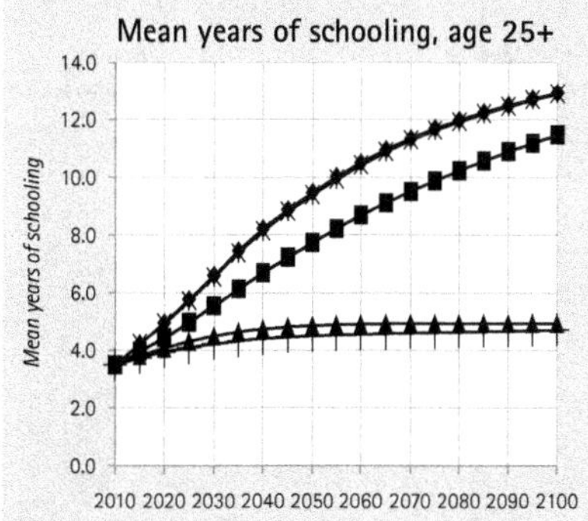

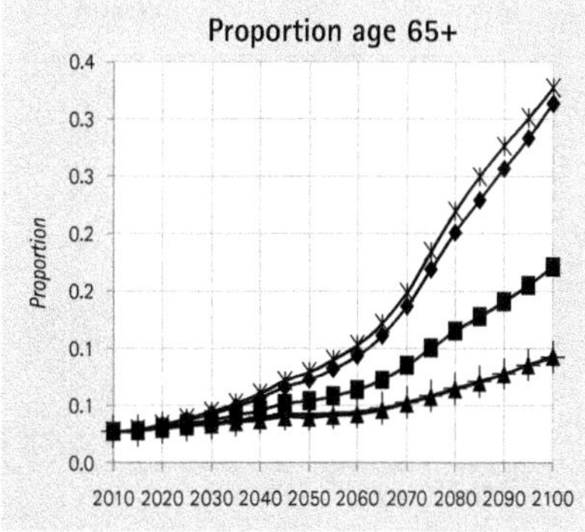

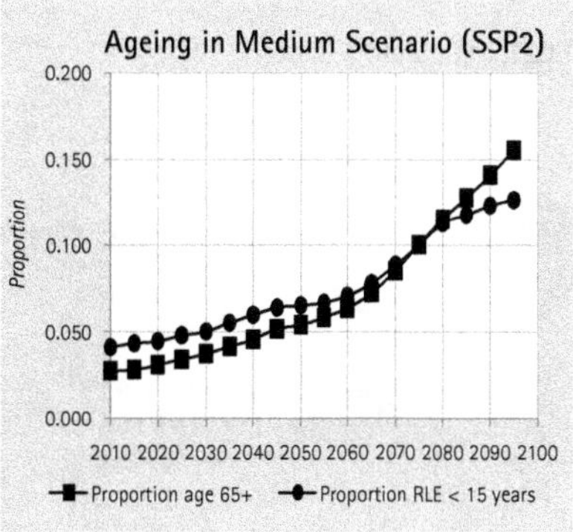

Alternative Scenarios to 2100

Projection Results by Scenario (SSP1–5)

	2010	2020	2030	2040	2050	2075	2100
Population (in millions)							
SSP1 - Rapid development	9.33	11.08	12.35	13.26	13.53	12.73	11.33
SSP2 - Medium	9.33	11.30	13.21	14.89	15.99	17.38	17.86
SSP3 - Stalled development	9.33	11.92	15.27	18.98	22.60	31.09	38.52
SSP4 - Inequality	9.33	11.74	14.58	17.54	20.24	26.07	31.75
SSP5 - Conventional development	9.33	10.90	11.73	12.08	11.78	9.84	8.25
Proportion age 65+							
SSP1 - Rapid development	0.03	0.03	0.04	0.06	0.07	0.17	0.31
SSP2 - Medium	0.03	0.03	0.04	0.05	0.05	0.10	0.17
SSP3 - Stalled development	0.03	0.03	0.03	0.04	0.04	0.06	0.09
SSP4 - Inequality	0.03	0.03	0.03	0.04	0.04	0.06	0.09
SSP5 - Conventional development	0.03	0.03	0.04	0.06	0.08	0.18	0.33
Proportion below age 20							
SSP1 - Rapid development	0.55	0.53	0.45	0.39	0.33	0.21	0.14
SSP2 - Medium	0.55	0.54	0.50	0.46	0.41	0.30	0.24
SSP3 - Stalled development	0.55	0.55	0.54	0.52	0.48	0.39	0.33
SSP4 - Inequality	0.55	0.56	0.54	0.52	0.49	0.39	0.33
SSP5 - Conventional development	0.55	0.53	0.46	0.39	0.34	0.21	0.14
Proportion of Women age 20–39 with at least secondary education							
SSP1 - Rapid development	0.14	0.30	0.46	0.60	0.70	0.85	0.93
SSP2 - Medium	0.14	0.21	0.30	0.40	0.51	0.74	0.88
SSP3 - Stalled development	0.14	0.13	0.13	0.13	0.13	0.13	0.13
SSP4 - Inequality	0.14	0.12	0.12	0.12	0.12	0.12	0.12
SSP5 - Conventional development	0.14	0.30	0.46	0.60	0.70	0.85	0.93
Mean years of schooling, age 25+							
SSP1 - Rapid development	3.49	4.94	6.60	8.21	9.48	11.68	12.93
SSP2 - Medium	3.49	4.43	5.54	6.69	7.74	9.88	11.47
SSP3 - Stalled development	3.49	4.07	4.49	4.73	4.85	4.93	4.93
SSP4 - Inequality	3.49	3.93	4.22	4.40	4.50	4.61	4.70
SSP5 - Conventional development	3.49	4.92	6.54	8.13	9.39	11.62	12.90

Demographic Assumptions Underlying SSPs

	2010–15	2020–25	2030–35	2040–45	2050–55	2075–80	2095–2100
Total fertility rate							
SSP1 - Rapid development	5.63	3.92	2.79	2.14	1.75	1.35	1.22
SSP2 - Medium	5.96	4.93	3.91	3.02	2.53	1.91	1.70
SSP3 - Stalled development	6.39	6.01	5.26	4.35	3.66	2.80	2.56
SSP4 - Inequality	6.40	6.05	5.30	4.37	3.66	2.79	2.54
SSP5 - Conventional development	5.63	3.92	2.79	2.14	1.75	1.35	1.22
Life expectancy at birth for females (in years)							
SSP1 - Rapid development	57.87	60.51	63.58	66.25	69.42	79.31	87.00
SSP2 - Medium	53.30	55.78	58.08	59.87	62.58	70.62	76.89
SSP3 - Stalled development	57.39	57.97	59.27	59.50	60.77	64.94	67.92
SSP4 - Inequality	57.39	57.96	59.24	59.47	60.72	64.89	67.88
SSP5 - Conventional development	57.87	60.51	63.58	66.25	69.42	79.31	87.00
Migration – net flow over five years (in thousands)							
SSP1 - Rapid development	−268	−302	−355	−368	−366	−141	0
SSP2 - Medium	−283	−318	−382	−421	−448	−199	0
SSP3 - Stalled development	−223	−152	−188	−220	−253	−139	0
SSP4 - Inequality	−267	−304	−376	−440	−498	−260	0
SSP5 - Conventional development	−312	−452	−532	−553	−549	−212	0

Ageing Indicators, Medium Scenario (SSP2)

	2010	2020	2030	2040	2050	2075	2095
Median age	17.43	17.92	19.85	21.98	24.67	33.09	38.58
Propspective median age	17.43	16.48	17.17	18.42	19.81	24.62	26.96
Proportion age 65+	0.03	0.03	0.04	0.05	0.05	0.10	0.16
Proportion RLE < 15 years	0.04	0.04	0.05	0.06	0.07	0.10	0.13

South Africa

Detailed Human Capital Projections to 2060

Demographic indicators, Medium Scenario (SSP2)	2010	2020	2030	2040	2050	2060
Population (in millions)	50.13	54.73	58.58	61.29	63.15	64.25
Proportion age 65+	0.05	0.06	0.07	0.08	0.09	0.12
Proportion below age 20	0.40	0.37	0.34	0.31	0.29	0.27
	2005–10	2015–20	2025–30	2035–40	2045–50	2055–60
Total Fertility Rate	2.55	2.25	2.03	1.91	1.81	1.71
Life expectancy at birth (in years)						
Men	50.12	55.45	57.79	58.76	60.42	62.72
Women	52.08	55.80	58.50	61.00	63.60	66.41
Five-year immigration flow (in '000)	796.11	781.15	811.30	829.59	829.73	817.66
Five-year emigration flow (in '000)	97.18	75.97	77.78	77.80	76.50	74.43

Human Capital indicators, Medium Scenario (SSP2)	2010	2020	2030	2040	2050	2060
Population age 25+: highest educational attainment						
E1 - no education	0.09	0.05	0.03	0.01	0.01	0.00
E2 - incomplete primary	0.15	0.10	0.07	0.04	0.02	0.01
E3 - primary	0.13	0.11	0.09	0.07	0.06	0.05
E4 - lower secondary	0.29	0.31	0.31	0.29	0.26	0.22
E5 - upper secondary	0.29	0.37	0.44	0.51	0.57	0.63
E6 - post-secondary	0.05	0.06	0.06	0.07	0.08	0.10
Mean years of schooling (in years)	8.94	9.71	10.33	10.83	11.24	11.56
Gender gap (population age 25+): highest educational attainment (ratio male/female)						
E1 - no education	0.67	0.61	0.58	0.59	0.67	0.75
E2 - incomplete primary	1.00	0.94	0.89	0.89	0.93	0.93
E3 - primary	0.96	0.96	0.97	1.00	1.03	1.02
E4 - lower secondary	1.02	1.04	1.05	1.05	1.04	1.01
E5 - upper secondary	1.09	1.06	1.04	1.02	1.02	1.02
E6 - post-secondary	1.15	0.97	0.87	0.82	0.83	0.90
Mean years of schooling (male minus female)	0.45	0.33	0.17	0.03	−0.05	−0.04
Women age 20–39: highest educational attainment						
E1 - no education	0.02	0.01	0.00	0.00	0.00	0.00
E2 - incomplete primary	0.06	0.03	0.01	0.01	0.00	0.00
E3 - primary	0.09	0.08	0.07	0.05	0.04	0.03
E4 - lower secondary	0.39	0.36	0.31	0.26	0.21	0.17
E5 - upper secondary	0.39	0.47	0.54	0.60	0.65	0.69
E6 - post-secondary	0.04	0.06	0.07	0.08	0.09	0.10
Mean years of schooling (in years)	10.31	10.69	11.07	11.40	11.67	11.89

Education scenarios

GET: global education trend scenario (medium assumption also used for SSP2)

CER: constant enrolment rates scenario (assumption of no future improvements)

FT: Fast track scenario (assumption of education expansion according to fastest historical experience)

Pyramids by Education, Medium Scenario

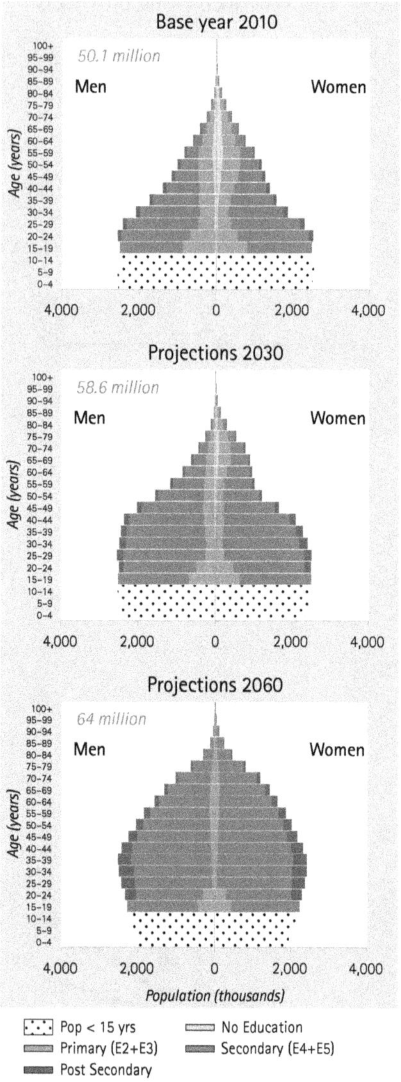

Population Size by Educational Attainment According to Three Education Scenarios: GET, CER, and FT

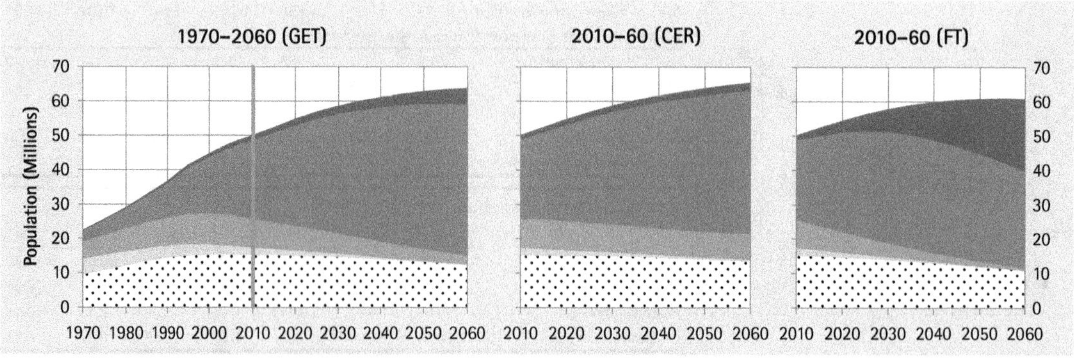

South Africa (Continued)

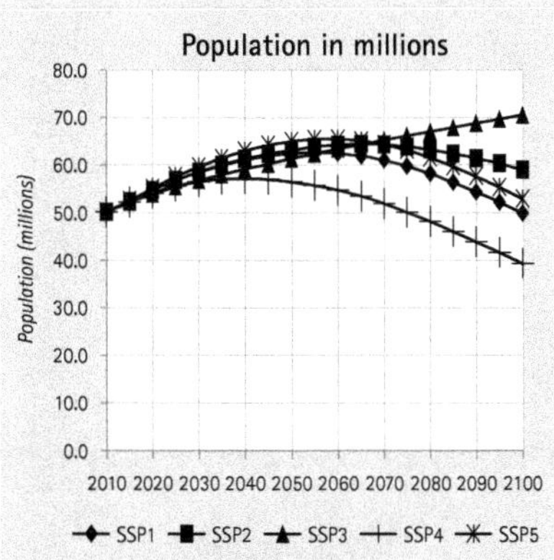

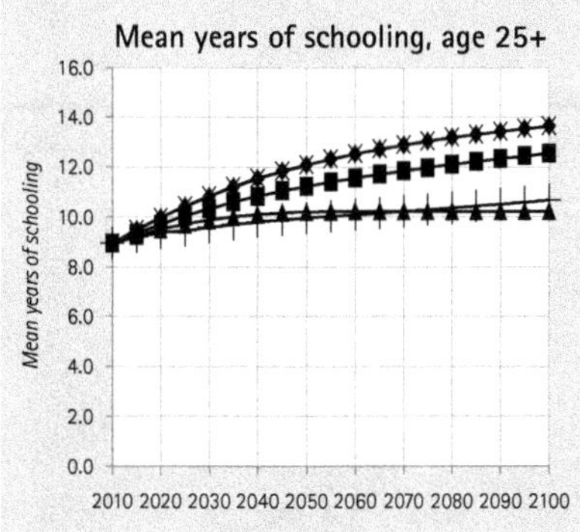

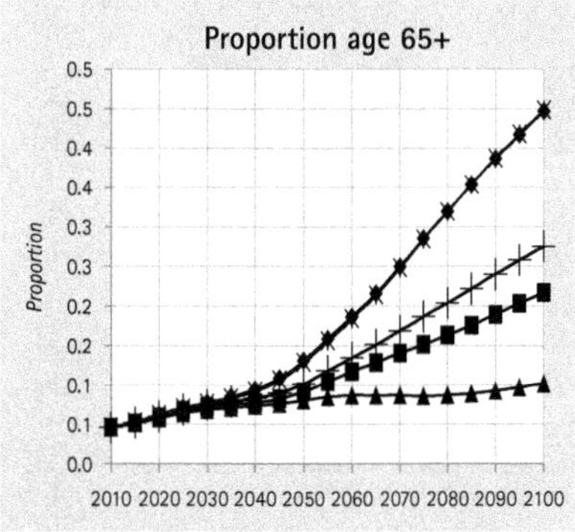

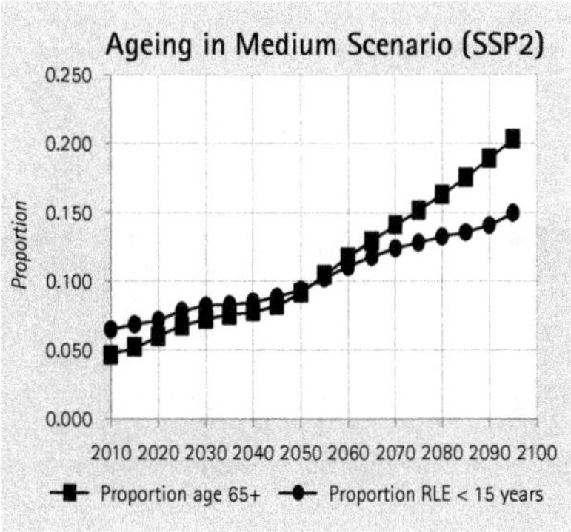

Alternative Scenarios to 2100

Projection Results by Scenario (SSP1–5)

	2010	2020	2030	2040	2050	2075	2100
Population (in millions)							
SSP1 - Rapid development	50.13	54.74	58.51	61.08	62.44	59.75	49.94
SSP2 - Medium	50.13	54.73	58.58	61.29	63.15	63.88	58.99
SSP3 - Stalled development	50.13	53.93	56.87	59.17	61.35	66.17	70.48
SSP4 - Inequality	50.13	54.09	56.51	57.19	56.45	50.12	39.31
SSP5 - Conventional development	50.13	55.10	59.65	62.97	64.97	63.10	52.89
Proportion age 65+							
SSP1 - Rapid development	0.05	0.06	0.08	0.09	0.13	0.29	0.45
SSP2 - Medium	0.05	0.06	0.07	0.08	0.09	0.15	0.22
SSP3 - Stalled development	0.05	0.06	0.07	0.07	0.08	0.09	0.10
SSP4 - Inequality	0.05	0.06	0.07	0.08	0.10	0.19	0.28
SSP5 - Conventional development	0.05	0.06	0.08	0.09	0.13	0.28	0.45
Proportion below age 20							
SSP1 - Rapid development	0.40	0.35	0.30	0.25	0.21	0.14	0.10
SSP2 - Medium	0.40	0.37	0.34	0.31	0.29	0.24	0.20
SSP3 - Stalled development	0.40	0.38	0.37	0.36	0.35	0.34	0.33
SSP4 - Inequality	0.40	0.36	0.32	0.28	0.24	0.19	0.15
SSP5 - Conventional development	0.40	0.35	0.30	0.25	0.21	0.14	0.10
Proportion of Women age 20–39 with at least secondary education							
SSP1 - Rapid development	0.83	0.92	0.95	0.97	0.98	0.99	1.00
SSP2 - Medium	0.83	0.88	0.92	0.94	0.96	0.98	0.99
SSP3 - Stalled development	0.83	0.86	0.86	0.86	0.86	0.86	0.86
SSP4 - Inequality	0.83	0.80	0.78	0.78	0.78	0.78	0.78
SSP5 - Conventional development	0.83	0.92	0.95	0.97	0.98	0.99	1.00
Mean years of schooling, age 25+							
SSP1 - Rapid development	8.94	9.97	10.82	11.53	12.08	13.03	13.63
SSP2 - Medium	8.94	9.71	10.33	10.83	11.24	11.97	12.54
SSP3 - Stalled development	8.94	9.50	9.88	10.10	10.20	10.23	10.23
SSP4 - Inequality	8.94	9.36	9.58	9.80	9.96	10.29	10.67
SSP5 - Conventional development	8.94	9.97	10.84	11.54	12.09	13.04	13.63

Demographic Assumptions Underlying SSPs

	2010–15	2020–25	2030–35	2040–45	2050–55	2075–80	2095–2100
Total fertility rate							
SSP1 - Rapid development	2.23	1.77	1.50	1.36	1.27	1.17	1.18
SSP2 - Medium	2.38	2.14	1.97	1.86	1.76	1.59	1.62
SSP3 - Stalled development	2.51	2.53	2.50	2.43	2.35	2.21	2.26
SSP4 - Inequality	2.28	1.90	1.63	1.47	1.37	1.27	1.28
SSP5 - Conventional development	2.23	1.77	1.50	1.36	1.27	1.17	1.18
Life expectancy at birth for females (in years)							
SSP1 - Rapid development	57.53	64.43	68.99	73.47	77.59	86.63	93.81
SSP2 - Medium	54.10	57.20	59.80	62.30	65.00	71.90	77.30
SSP3 - Stalled development	54.13	53.74	54.96	56.30	57.43	61.77	64.99
SSP4 - Inequality	55.86	58.60	61.00	63.33	65.87	72.55	77.73
SSP5 - Conventional development	57.53	64.43	68.99	73.47	77.59	86.63	93.81
Migration – net flow over five years (in thousands)							
SSP1 - Rapid development	653	700	711	674	611	199	0
SSP2 - Medium	688	720	742	749	742	313	0
SSP3 - Stalled development	534	340	367	406	455	272	0
SSP4 - Inequality	647	687	701	694	668	267	0
SSP5 - Conventional development	762	1040	1039	965	858	268	0

Ageing Indicators, Medium Scenario (SSP2)

	2010	2020	2030	2040	2050	2075	2095
Median age	24.90	27.21	29.27	31.26	33.21	38.54	42.99
Propspective median age	24.90	24.26	24.80	24.99	24.72	23.54	23.64
Proportion age 65+	0.05	0.06	0.07	0.08	0.09	0.15	0.20
Proportion RLE < 15 years	0.06	0.07	0.08	0.08	0.09	0.13	0.15

Spain

Detailed Human Capital Projections to 2060

Demographic indicators, Medium Scenario (SSP2)

	2010	2020	2030	2040	2050	2060
Population (in millions)	46.08	48.22	49.43	50.72	51.53	51.53
Proportion age 65+	0.17	0.19	0.24	0.30	0.35	0.36
Proportion below age 20	0.20	0.19	0.17	0.16	0.17	0.17
	2005–10	2015–20	2025–30	2035–40	2045–50	2055–60
Total Fertility Rate	1.41	1.37	1.47	1.58	1.68	1.70
Life expectancy at birth (in years)						
Men	77.22	80.03	82.51	84.65	86.69	88.89
Women	83.75	85.71	87.81	89.91	91.89	94.10
Five-year immigration flow (in '000)	2402.21	850.74	884.25	905.09	906.25	893.48
Five-year emigration flow (in '000)	157.11	100.48	95.59	89.13	83.47	82.88

Human Capital indicators, Medium Scenario (SSP2)

	2010	2020	2030	2040	2050	2060
Population age 25+: highest educational attainment						
E1 - no education	0.02	0.01	0.01	0.00	0.00	0.00
E2 - incomplete primary	0.09	0.06	0.03	0.02	0.01	0.00
E3 - primary	0.20	0.16	0.12	0.09	0.06	0.05
E4 - lower secondary	0.32	0.32	0.30	0.26	0.22	0.18
E5 - upper secondary	0.18	0.22	0.25	0.27	0.29	0.31
E6 - post-secondary	0.20	0.24	0.30	0.35	0.41	0.46
Mean years of schooling (in years)	8.99	9.95	10.80	11.58	12.25	12.86
Gender gap (population age 25+): highest educational attainment (ratio male/female)						
E1 - no education	0.45	0.50	0.61	0.74	0.82	0.83
E2 - incomplete primary	0.76	0.72	0.72	0.78	0.87	0.94
E3 - primary	0.94	0.95	0.99	1.06	1.16	1.24
E4 - lower secondary	1.15	1.15	1.15	1.15	1.16	1.16
E5 - upper secondary	1.18	1.17	1.16	1.15	1.14	1.12
E6 - post-secondary	0.89	0.83	0.80	0.80	0.82	0.86
Mean years of schooling (male minus female)	0.23	0.03	−0.18	−0.31	−0.35	−0.31
Women age 20–39: highest educational attainment						
E1 - no education	0.00	0.00	0.00	0.00	0.00	0.00
E2 - incomplete primary	0.01	0.00	0.00	0.00	0.00	0.00
E3 - primary	0.06	0.04	0.03	0.02	0.01	0.01
E4 - lower secondary	0.28	0.20	0.14	0.10	0.08	0.07
E5 - upper secondary	0.30	0.34	0.36	0.35	0.35	0.36
E6 - post-secondary	0.34	0.42	0.48	0.53	0.56	0.56
Mean years of schooling (in years)	11.53	12.63	13.49	13.82	13.99	14.06

Education scenarios

GET: global education trend scenario (medium assumption also used for SSP2)

CER: constant enrolment rates scenario (assumption of no future improvements)

FT: Fast track scenario (assumption of education expansion according to fastest historical experience)

Pyramids by Education, Medium Scenario

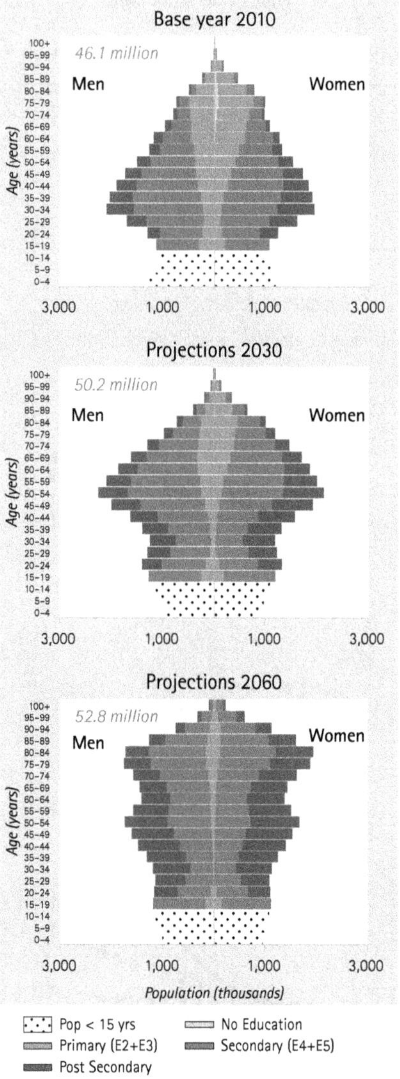

Population Size by Educational Attainment According to Three Education Scenarios: GET, CER, and FT

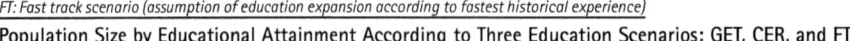

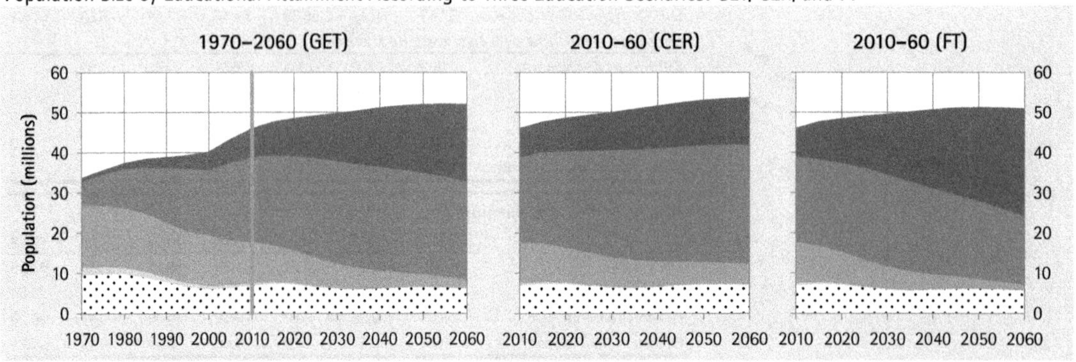

Spain (Continued)

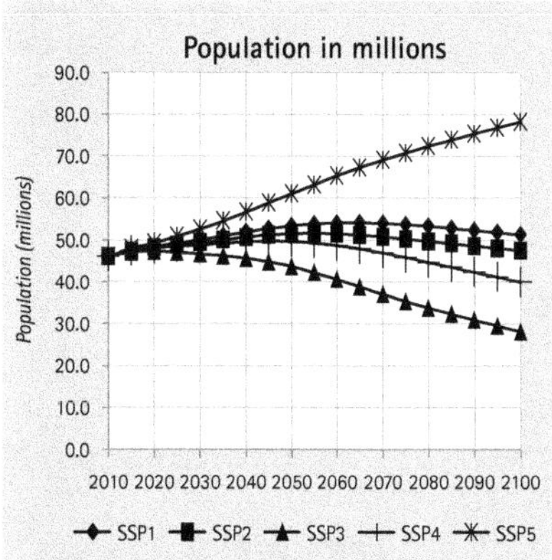

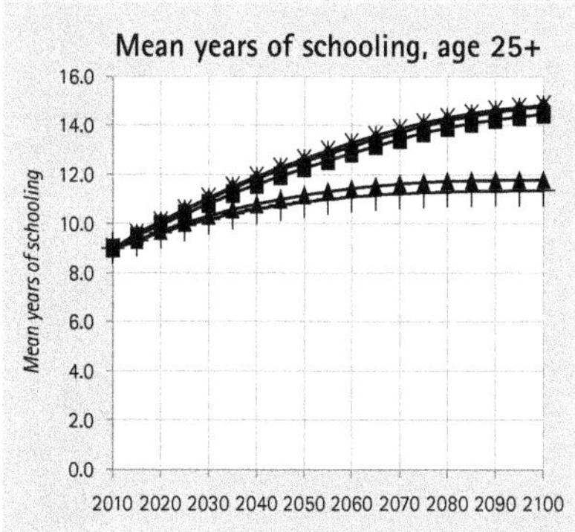

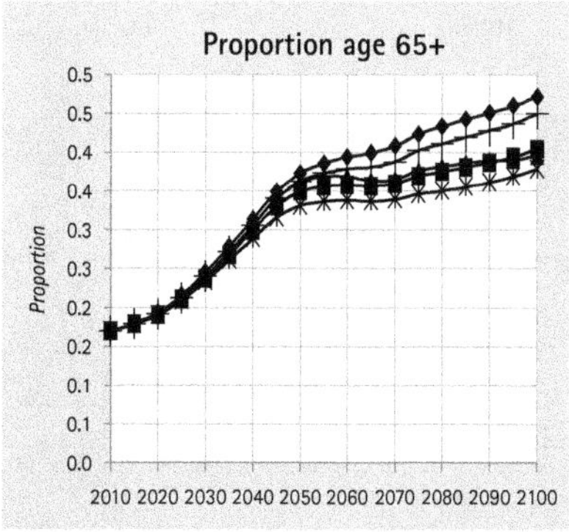

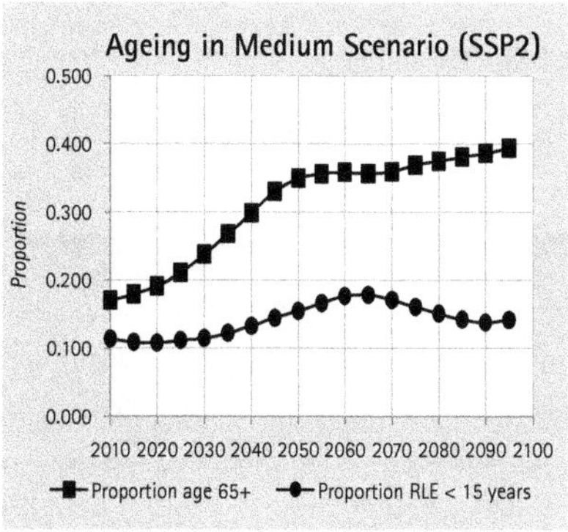

Alternative Scenarios to 2100

Projection Results by Scenario (SSP1–5)

	2010	2020	2030	2040	2050	2075	2100
Population (in millions)							
SSP1 - Rapid development	46.08	48.47	50.09	51.93	53.40	53.75	51.32
SSP2 - Medium	46.08	48.22	49.43	50.72	51.53	50.30	47.49
SSP3 - Stalled development	46.08	47.30	46.70	45.66	43.68	35.36	28.10
SSP4 - Inequality	46.08	48.06	48.88	49.60	49.65	45.89	39.96
SSP5 - Conventional development	46.08	49.30	52.61	56.67	61.03	70.78	78.20
Proportion age 65+							
SSP1 - Rapid development	0.17	0.19	0.25	0.31	0.37	0.42	0.47
SSP2 - Medium	0.17	0.19	0.24	0.30	0.35	0.37	0.40
SSP3 - Stalled development	0.17	0.19	0.24	0.31	0.36	0.38	0.40
SSP4 - Inequality	0.17	0.19	0.24	0.31	0.36	0.40	0.45
SSP5 - Conventional development	0.17	0.19	0.23	0.29	0.33	0.35	0.38
Proportion below age 20							
SSP1 - Rapid development	0.20	0.19	0.16	0.16	0.16	0.15	0.14
SSP2 - Medium	0.20	0.19	0.17	0.16	0.17	0.17	0.16
SSP3 - Stalled development	0.20	0.19	0.16	0.14	0.15	0.14	0.14
SSP4 - Inequality	0.20	0.19	0.16	0.15	0.15	0.14	0.13
SSP5 - Conventional development	0.20	0.20	0.18	0.19	0.19	0.20	0.19
Proportion of Women age 20–39 with at least secondary education							
SSP1 - Rapid development	0.93	0.97	0.98	0.99	0.99	1.00	1.00
SSP2 - Medium	0.93	0.95	0.97	0.98	0.99	0.99	1.00
SSP3 - Stalled development	0.93	0.90	0.90	0.90	0.90	0.90	0.90
SSP4 - Inequality	0.93	0.90	0.90	0.90	0.90	0.90	0.90
SSP5 - Conventional development	0.93	0.97	0.98	0.99	0.99	1.00	1.00
Mean years of schooling, age 25+							
SSP1 - Rapid development	8.99	10.07	10.99	11.82	12.51	13.96	14.78
SSP2 - Medium	8.99	9.95	10.80	11.58	12.25	13.68	14.46
SSP3 - Stalled development	8.99	9.69	10.31	10.80	11.15	11.68	11.78
SSP4 - Inequality	8.99	9.63	10.17	10.59	10.88	11.27	11.35
SSP5 - Conventional development	8.99	10.09	11.04	11.90	12.63	14.10	14.85

Demographic Assumptions Underlying SSPs

	2010–15	2020–25	2030–35	2040–45	2050–55	2075–80	2095–2100
Total fertility rate							
SSP1 - Rapid development	1.31	1.40	1.49	1.59	1.66	1.69	1.70
SSP2 - Medium	1.32	1.42	1.53	1.63	1.70	1.71	1.72
SSP3 - Stalled development	1.27	1.27	1.29	1.35	1.39	1.43	1.45
SSP4 - Inequality	1.27	1.28	1.32	1.38	1.43	1.47	1.48
SSP5 - Conventional development	1.38	1.61	1.81	1.97	2.07	2.11	2.13
Life expectancy at birth for females (in years)							
SSP1 - Rapid development	85.78	88.80	91.76	94.66	97.64	105.53	111.90
SSP2 - Medium	84.69	86.81	88.91	90.89	93.00	98.40	102.70
SSP3 - Stalled development	84.81	85.82	86.84	87.74	88.73	91.24	93.37
SSP4 - Inequality	85.33	87.36	89.32	91.18	93.20	98.15	102.15
SSP5 - Conventional development	85.78	88.80	91.76	94.66	97.64	105.53	111.90
Migration – net flow over five years (in thousands)							
SSP1 - Rapid development	1257	767	790	785	755	283	0
SSP2 - Medium	1216	752	780	790	781	324	0
SSP3 - Stalled development	1047	381	393	396	388	160	0
SSP4 - Inequality	1257	765	789	798	789	334	0
SSP5 - Conventional development	1467	1161	1222	1274	1297	562	0

Ageing Indicators, Medium Scenario (SSP2)

	2010	2020	2030	2040	2050	2075	2095
Median age	40.09	44.04	48.44	50.98	51.69	53.39	55.45
Propspective median age	40.09	41.85	44.26	44.99	43.79	40.39	38.21
Proportion age 65+	0.17	0.19	0.24	0.30	0.35	0.37	0.39
Proportion RLE < 15 years	0.11	0.11	0.11	0.13	0.15	0.16	0.14

Sudan

Detailed Human Capital Projections to 2060

Demographic indicators, Medium Scenario (SSP2)	2010	2020	2030	2040	2050	2060
Population (in millions)	43.55	54.19	64.56	74.10	81.83	87.70
Proportion age 65+	0.04	0.04	0.05	0.06	0.08	0.10
Proportion below age 20	0.51	0.47	0.41	0.37	0.33	0.29
	2005–10	2015–20	2025–30	2035–40	2045–50	2055–60
Total Fertility Rate	4.60	3.61	2.92	2.47	2.15	1.98
Life expectancy at birth (in years)						
Men	58.59	61.40	62.56	63.64	64.42	65.91
Women	62.00	65.22	66.62	68.11	69.71	71.62
Five-year immigration flow (in '000)	199.58	195.27	202.49	206.75	206.52	203.35
Five-year emigration flow (in '000)	62.94	59.22	70.93	79.54	84.49	86.71

Human Capital indicators, Medium Scenario (SSP2)	2010	2020	2030	2040	2050	2060
Population age 25+: highest educational attainment						
E1 - no education	0.68	0.57	0.47	0.36	0.27	0.20
E2 - incomplete primary	0.08	0.10	0.10	0.09	0.08	0.06
E3 - primary	0.05	0.08	0.11	0.13	0.15	0.15
E4 - lower secondary	0.04	0.04	0.04	0.04	0.04	0.04
E5 - upper secondary	0.09	0.13	0.18	0.24	0.30	0.35
E6 - post-secondary	0.06	0.08	0.11	0.13	0.16	0.20
Mean years of schooling (in years)	2.86	3.88	5.08	6.29	7.44	8.53
Gender gap (population age 25+): highest educational attainment (ratio male/female)						
E1 - no education	0.81	0.81	0.82	0.83	0.84	0.85
E2 - incomplete primary	1.50	1.31	1.21	1.15	1.12	1.07
E3 - primary	1.55	1.32	1.21	1.15	1.10	1.06
E4 - lower secondary	1.71	1.45	1.24	1.11	1.04	1.01
E5 - upper secondary	1.62	1.33	1.18	1.10	1.06	1.04
E6 - post-secondary	1.62	1.32	1.16	1.07	1.03	1.02
Mean years of schooling (male minus female)	1.34	1.11	0.85	0.60	0.42	0.31
Women age 20–39: highest educational attainment						
E1 - no education	0.64	0.47	0.34	0.22	0.13	0.07
E2 - incomplete primary	0.08	0.13	0.12	0.10	0.08	0.06
E3 - primary	0.07	0.10	0.12	0.14	0.14	0.13
E4 - lower secondary	0.03	0.03	0.04	0.05	0.05	0.05
E5 - upper secondary	0.12	0.18	0.26	0.34	0.41	0.46
E6 - post-secondary	0.06	0.09	0.12	0.16	0.20	0.23
Mean years of schooling (in years)	3.30	4.87	6.47	7.92	9.17	10.15

Education scenarios

GET: global education trend scenario (medium assumption also used for SSP2)

CER: constant enrolment rates scenario (assumption of no future improvements)

FT: Fast track scenario (assumption of education expansion according to fastest historical experience)

Pyramids by Education, Medium Scenario

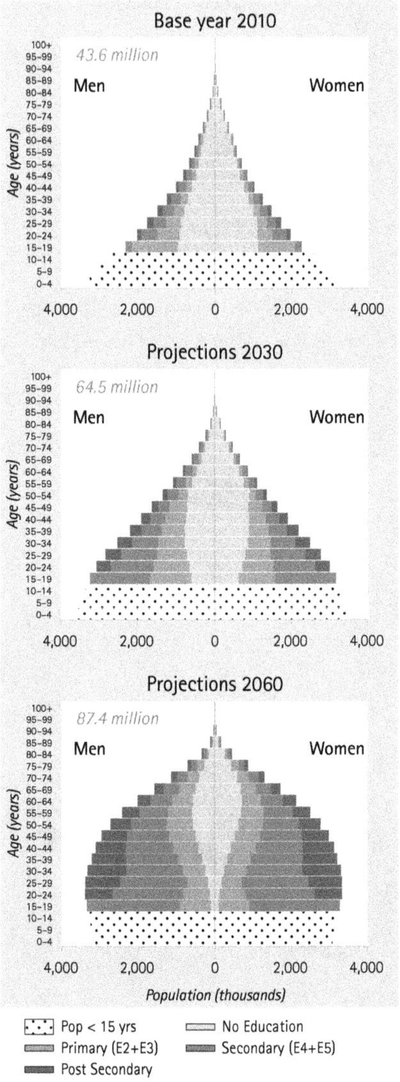

Population Size by Educational Attainment According to Three Education Scenarios: GET, CER, and FT

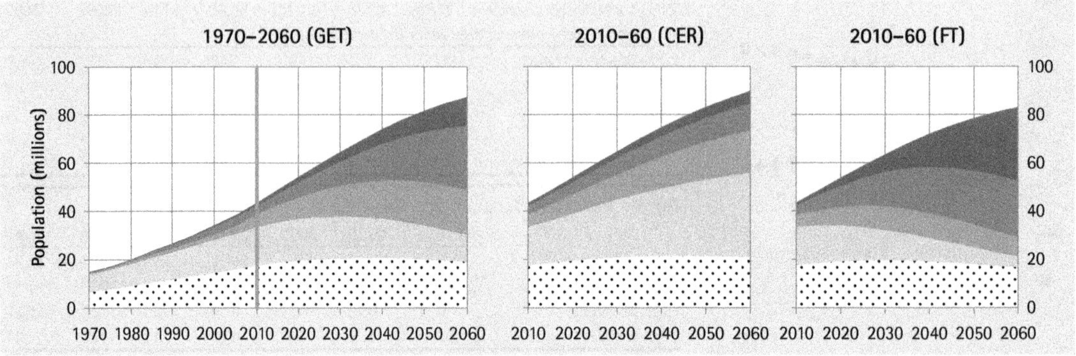

Sudan (Continued)

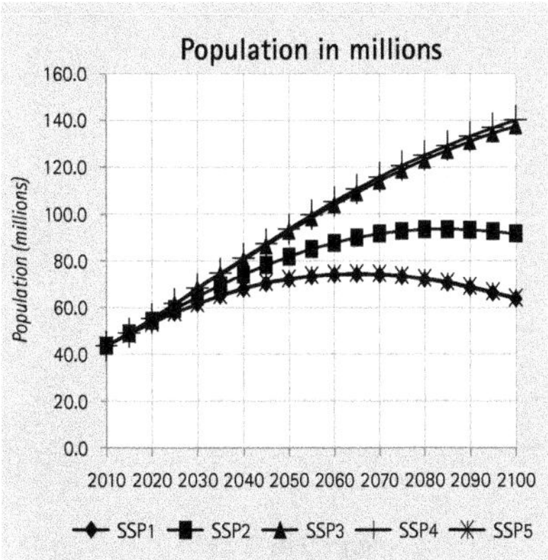

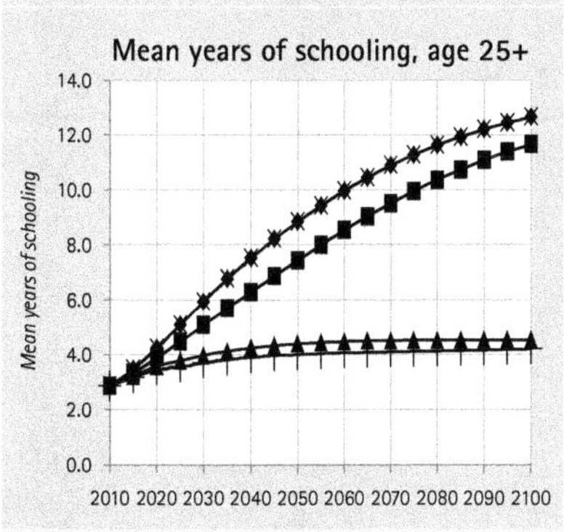

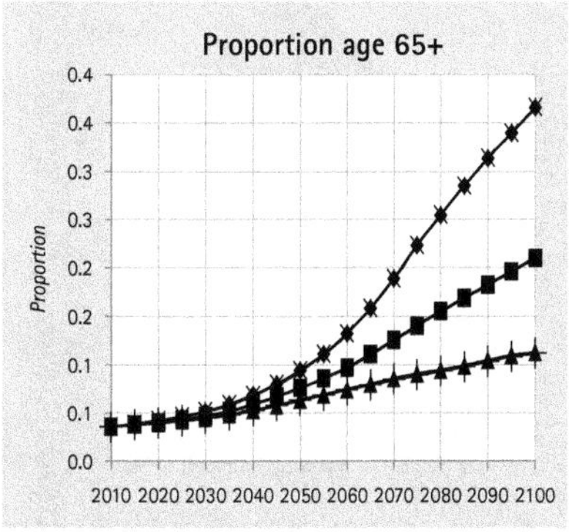

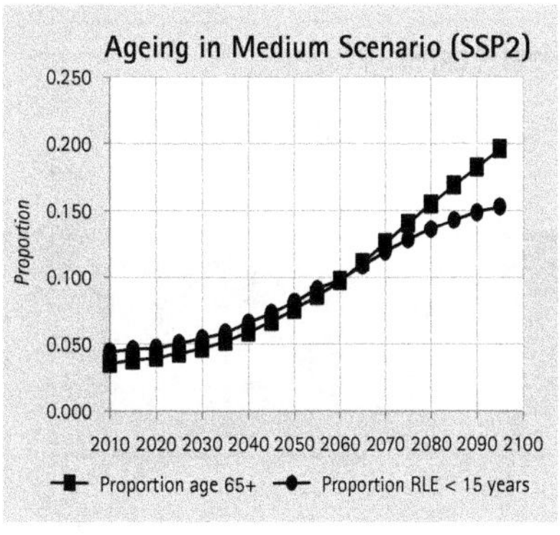

Alternative Scenarios to 2100

Projection Results by Scenario (SSP1–5)

	2010	2020	2030	2040	2050	2075	2100
Population (in millions)							
SSP1 - Rapid development	43.55	53.19	61.35	67.84	71.90	73.09	63.50
SSP2 - Medium	43.55	54.19	64.56	74.10	81.83	92.76	91.57
SSP3 - Stalled development	43.55	55.11	67.94	80.54	92.67	118.68	137.54
SSP4 - Inequality	43.55	55.22	68.30	81.18	93.61	120.45	139.97
SSP5 - Conventional development	43.55	53.27	61.58	68.19	72.35	73.65	63.98
Proportion age 65+							
SSP1 - Rapid development	0.04	0.04	0.05	0.07	0.09	0.22	0.37
SSP2 - Medium	0.04	0.04	0.05	0.06	0.08	0.14	0.21
SSP3 - Stalled development	0.04	0.04	0.04	0.05	0.06	0.09	0.11
SSP4 - Inequality	0.04	0.04	0.04	0.05	0.06	0.09	0.11
SSP5 - Conventional development	0.04	0.04	0.05	0.07	0.09	0.22	0.37
Proportion below age 20							
SSP1 - Rapid development	0.51	0.45	0.38	0.32	0.26	0.18	0.13
SSP2 - Medium	0.51	0.47	0.41	0.37	0.33	0.26	0.21
SSP3 - Stalled development	0.51	0.47	0.45	0.42	0.39	0.34	0.32
SSP4 - Inequality	0.51	0.47	0.45	0.42	0.39	0.34	0.32
SSP5 - Conventional development	0.51	0.45	0.38	0.31	0.26	0.17	0.13
Proportion of Women age 20–39 with at least secondary education							
SSP1 - Rapid development	0.21	0.36	0.54	0.69	0.78	0.91	0.96
SSP2 - Medium	0.21	0.30	0.42	0.54	0.65	0.85	0.94
SSP3 - Stalled development	0.21	0.23	0.24	0.24	0.24	0.24	0.24
SSP4 - Inequality	0.21	0.21	0.21	0.21	0.21	0.21	0.21
SSP5 - Conventional development	0.21	0.36	0.54	0.69	0.78	0.91	0.96
Mean years of schooling, age 25+							
SSP1 - Rapid development	2.86	4.23	5.93	7.52	8.85	11.27	12.65
SSP2 - Medium	2.86	3.88	5.08	6.29	7.44	9.95	11.66
SSP3 - Stalled development	2.86	3.58	3.97	4.24	4.39	4.52	4.53
SSP4 - Inequality	2.86	3.44	3.70	3.90	4.00	4.11	4.19
SSP5 - Conventional development	2.86	4.23	5.93	7.52	8.85	11.27	12.65

Demographic Assumptions Underlying SSPs

	2010–15	2020–25	2030–35	2040–45	2050–55	2075–80	2095–2100
Total fertility rate							
SSP1 - Rapid development	3.81	2.70	2.02	1.66	1.47	1.30	1.22
SSP2 - Medium	4.08	3.21	2.67	2.29	2.07	1.80	1.66
SSP3 - Stalled development	4.24	3.83	3.42	3.07	2.85	2.60	2.49
SSP4 - Inequality	4.24	3.86	3.44	3.09	2.86	2.61	2.49
SSP5 - Conventional development	3.81	2.70	2.02	1.66	1.47	1.30	1.22
Life expectancy at birth for females (in years)							
SSP1 - Rapid development	67.41	69.55	71.77	74.05	76.79	83.97	89.58
SSP2 - Medium	63.92	65.91	67.32	68.82	70.61	75.59	79.59
SSP3 - Stalled development	66.82	67.39	67.25	67.76	68.13	69.15	70.61
SSP4 - Inequality	66.82	67.38	67.21	67.71	68.06	69.06	70.53
SSP5 - Conventional development	67.41	69.55	71.77	74.05	76.79	83.97	89.58
Migration – net flow over five years (in thousands)							
SSP1 - Rapid development	130	130	121	108	92	35	0
SSP2 - Medium	137	136	132	127	121	59	0
SSP3 - Stalled development	108	67	69	76	84	60	0
SSP4 - Inequality	130	132	132	140	150	103	0
SSP5 - Conventional development	152	192	174	150	125	45	0

Ageing Indicators, Medium Scenario (SSP2)

	2010	2020	2030	2040	2050	2075	2095
Median age	19.70	21.76	24.52	27.50	30.58	37.64	42.00
Propspective median age	19.70	20.69	22.86	25.17	27.53	32.28	34.06
Proportion age 65+	0.04	0.04	0.05	0.06	0.08	0.14	0.20
Proportion RLE < 15 years	0.04	0.05	0.05	0.07	0.08	0.13	0.15

Suriname

Detailed Human Capital Projections to 2060

Demographic indicators, Medium Scenario (SSP2)	2010	2020	2030	2040	2050	2060
Population (in millions)	0.52	0.57	0.62	0.65	0.67	0.67
Proportion age 65+	0.06	0.08	0.11	0.15	0.18	0.21
Proportion below age 20	0.37	0.33	0.30	0.27	0.25	0.23
	2005–10	2015–20	2025–30	2035–40	2045–50	2055–60
Total Fertility Rate	2.42	2.19	2.04	1.95	1.90	1.84
Life expectancy at birth (in years)						
Men	66.42	69.59	72.26	74.60	76.81	79.06
Women	73.11	75.70	77.99	80.19	82.19	84.19
Five-year immigration flow (in '000)	1.42	1.41	1.46	1.50	1.51	1.49
Five-year emigration flow (in '000)	6.37	5.03	5.04	4.86	4.68	4.44

Human Capital indicators, Medium Scenario (SSP2)	2010	2020	2030	2040	2050	2060
Population age 25+: highest educational attainment						
E1 - no education	0.00	0.00	0.00	0.00	0.00	0.00
E2 - incomplete primary	0.08	0.06	0.04	0.02	0.01	0.01
E3 - primary	0.30	0.26	0.23	0.20	0.18	0.15
E4 - lower secondary	0.39	0.41	0.40	0.39	0.36	0.32
E5 - upper secondary	0.16	0.20	0.25	0.29	0.34	0.39
E6 - post-secondary	0.06	0.07	0.08	0.10	0.11	0.13
Mean years of schooling (in years)	9.30	9.85	10.36	10.78	11.18	11.59
Gender gap (population age 25+): highest educational attainment (ratio male/female)						
E1 - no education	0.47	0.47	0.47	0.47	0.47	0.48
E2 - incomplete primary	0.53	0.51	0.51	0.51	0.51	0.52
E3 - primary	1.08	1.10	1.12	1.13	1.13	1.10
E4 - lower secondary	1.12	1.10	1.08	1.07	1.05	1.03
E5 - upper secondary	0.93	0.95	0.96	0.98	1.00	1.01
E6 - post-secondary	1.00	0.83	0.74	0.72	0.75	0.82
Mean years of schooling (male minus female)	0.30	0.09	−0.09	−0.17	−0.19	−0.14
Women age 20–39: highest educational attainment						
E1 - no education	0.00	0.00	0.00	0.00	0.00	0.00
E2 - incomplete primary	0.05	0.03	0.01	0.01	0.01	0.00
E3 - primary	0.20	0.18	0.16	0.14	0.12	0.10
E4 - lower secondary	0.42	0.38	0.34	0.29	0.24	0.20
E5 - upper secondary	0.25	0.30	0.36	0.42	0.48	0.52
E6 - post-secondary	0.09	0.11	0.13	0.14	0.16	0.17
Mean years of schooling (in years)	10.30	10.94	11.54	11.91	12.26	12.55

Education scenarios

GET: global education trend scenario (medium assumption also used for SSP2)

CER: constant enrolment rates scenario (assumption of no future improvements)

FT: Fast track scenario (assumption of education expansion according to fastest historical experience)

Pyramids by Education, Medium Scenario

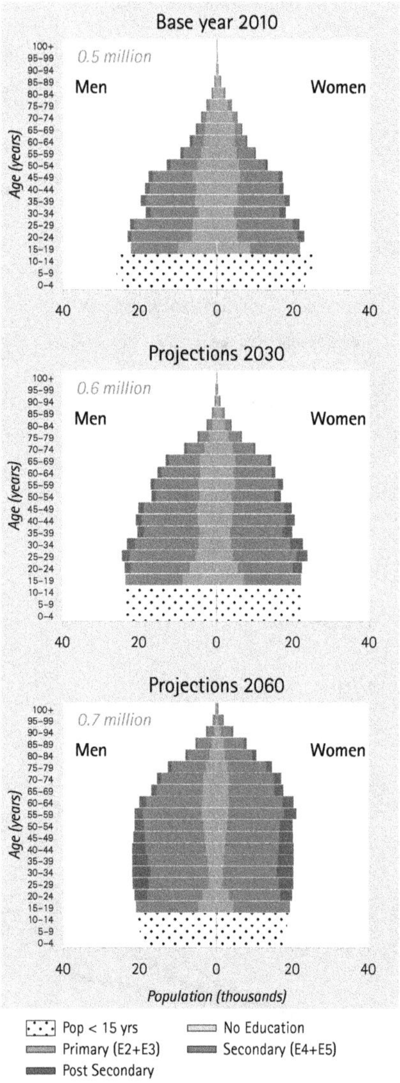

Population Size by Educational Attainment According to Three Education Scenarios: GET, CER, and FT

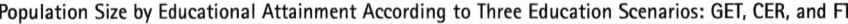

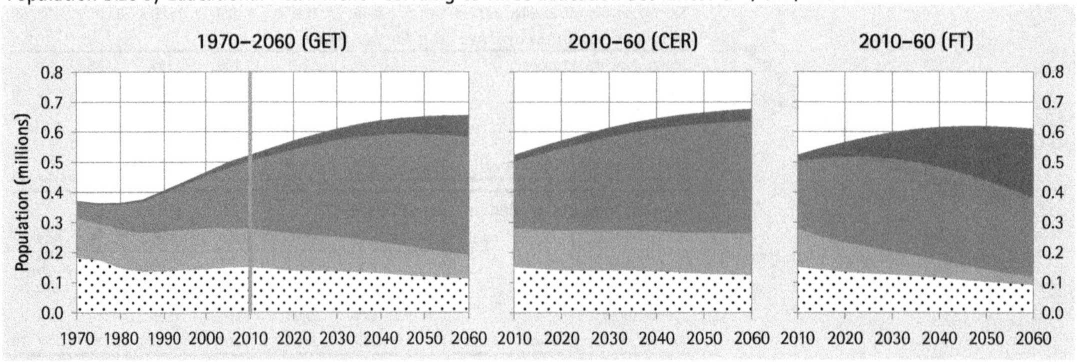

Suriname (Continued)

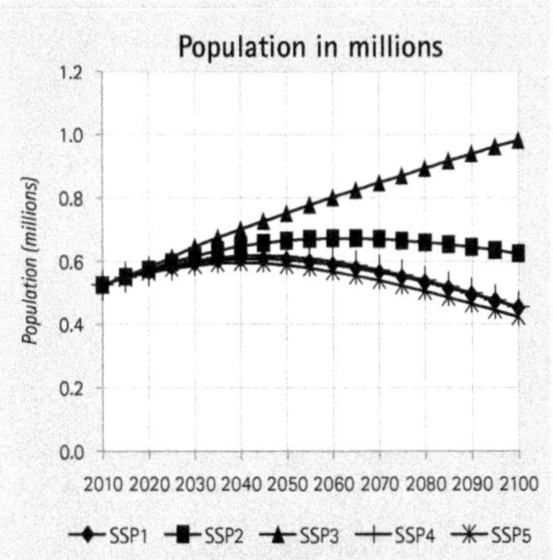

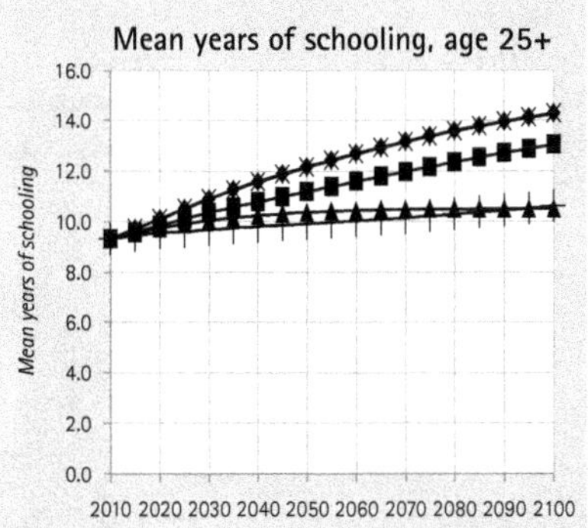

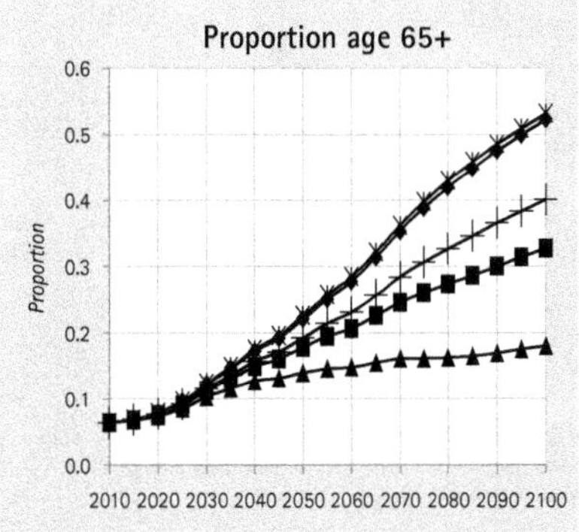

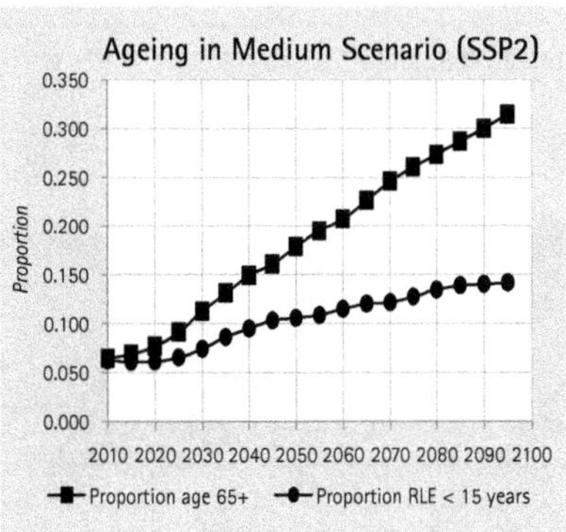

Alternative Scenarios to 2100

Projection Results by Scenario (SSP1–5)

	2010	2020	2030	2040	2050	2075	2100
Population (in millions)							
SSP1 - Rapid development	0.52	0.57	0.59	0.61	0.61	0.55	0.45
SSP2 - Medium	0.52	0.57	0.62	0.65	0.67	0.67	0.62
SSP3 - Stalled development	0.52	0.58	0.65	0.70	0.75	0.87	0.98
SSP4 - Inequality	0.52	0.57	0.60	0.62	0.62	0.56	0.45
SSP5 - Conventional development	0.52	0.56	0.59	0.60	0.59	0.52	0.42
Proportion age 65+							
SSP1 - Rapid development	0.06	0.08	0.12	0.17	0.22	0.39	0.52
SSP2 - Medium	0.06	0.08	0.11	0.15	0.18	0.26	0.33
SSP3 - Stalled development	0.06	0.07	0.10	0.13	0.14	0.16	0.18
SSP4 - Inequality	0.06	0.08	0.12	0.16	0.19	0.31	0.40
SSP5 - Conventional development	0.06	0.08	0.12	0.18	0.23	0.40	0.53
Proportion below age 20							
SSP1 - Rapid development	0.37	0.32	0.26	0.22	0.18	0.12	0.09
SSP2 - Medium	0.37	0.33	0.30	0.27	0.25	0.20	0.17
SSP3 - Stalled development	0.37	0.34	0.33	0.32	0.31	0.29	0.28
SSP4 - Inequality	0.37	0.33	0.28	0.24	0.21	0.16	0.13
SSP5 - Conventional development	0.37	0.32	0.26	0.22	0.18	0.12	0.09
Proportion of Women age 20–39 with at least secondary education							
SSP1 - Rapid development	0.75	0.86	0.90	0.92	0.94	0.96	0.99
SSP2 - Medium	0.75	0.80	0.83	0.85	0.88	0.93	0.97
SSP3 - Stalled development	0.75	0.77	0.77	0.77	0.77	0.77	0.77
SSP4 - Inequality	0.75	0.72	0.70	0.70	0.70	0.70	0.70
SSP5 - Conventional development	0.75	0.86	0.90	0.92	0.94	0.96	0.99
Mean years of schooling, age 25+							
SSP1 - Rapid development	9.30	10.10	10.90	11.58	12.16	13.39	14.28
SSP2 - Medium	9.30	9.85	10.36	10.78	11.18	12.16	13.05
SSP3 - Stalled development	9.30	9.73	10.05	10.24	10.37	10.50	10.51
SSP4 - Inequality	9.30	9.55	9.68	9.81	9.92	10.22	10.61
SSP5 - Conventional development	9.30	10.10	10.89	11.56	12.14	13.37	14.26

Demographic Assumptions Underlying SSPs

	2010–15	2020–25	2030–35	2040–45	2050–55	2075–80	2095–2100
Total fertility rate							
SSP1 - Rapid development	2.12	1.71	1.48	1.38	1.32	1.22	1.15
SSP2 - Medium	2.27	2.10	1.99	1.92	1.87	1.70	1.58
SSP3 - Stalled development	2.40	2.49	2.52	2.52	2.49	2.34	2.24
SSP4 - Inequality	2.19	1.90	1.68	1.56	1.47	1.34	1.27
SSP5 - Conventional development	2.12	1.71	1.48	1.38	1.32	1.22	1.15
Life expectancy at birth for females (in years)							
SSP1 - Rapid development	76.11	79.14	82.14	85.13	88.13	95.63	101.66
SSP2 - Medium	74.50	76.89	79.09	81.19	83.19	88.21	92.21
SSP3 - Stalled development	75.29	76.44	77.49	78.44	79.35	81.49	83.20
SSP4 - Inequality	75.71	77.79	79.79	81.71	83.53	88.11	91.91
SSP5 - Conventional development	76.11	79.14	82.14	85.13	88.13	95.63	101.66
Migration – net flow over five years (in thousands)							
SSP1 - Rapid development	−4	−4	−3	−3	−3	−1	0
SSP2 - Medium	−4	−4	−3	−3	−3	−1	0
SSP3 - Stalled development	−3	−2	−2	−2	−2	−1	0
SSP4 - Inequality	−4	−4	−3	−3	−2	−1	0
SSP5 - Conventional development	−5	−5	−5	−5	−4	−2	0

Ageing Indicators, Medium Scenario (SSP2)

	2010	2020	2030	2040	2050	2075	2095
Median age	27.48	30.68	33.31	36.75	39.47	45.48	49.56
Propspective median age	27.48	28.36	29.05	30.70	31.61	33.09	33.54
Proportion age 65+	0.06	0.08	0.11	0.15	0.18	0.26	0.31
Proportion RLE < 15 years	0.06	0.06	0.07	0.10	0.11	0.13	0.14

Swaziland

Detailed Human Capital Projections to 2060

Demographic indicators, Medium Scenario (SSP2)

	2010	2020	2030	2040	2050	2060
Population (in millions)	1.19	1.33	1.43	1.50	1.55	1.58
Proportion age 65+	0.03	0.04	0.04	0.04	0.05	0.07
Proportion below age 20	0.51	0.45	0.42	0.38	0.34	0.32
	2005–10	2015–20	2025–30	2035–40	2045–50	2055–60
Total Fertility Rate	3.58	2.78	2.35	2.09	1.95	1.86
Life expectancy at birth (in years)						
Men	47.56	49.54	52.30	53.79	55.25	58.10
Women	47.05	47.70	51.20	54.30	57.20	60.70
Five-year immigration flow (in '000)	11.44	11.19	11.61	11.87	11.86	11.68
Five-year emigration flow (in '000)	17.41	15.71	16.95	17.44	17.35	16.89

Human Capital indicators, Medium Scenario (SSP2)

	2010	2020	2030	2040	2050	2060
Population age 25+: highest educational attainment						
E1 - no education	0.15	0.08	0.04	0.02	0.01	0.00
E2 - incomplete primary	0.20	0.14	0.09	0.05	0.03	0.02
E3 - primary	0.22	0.21	0.18	0.14	0.11	0.08
E4 - lower secondary	0.13	0.14	0.13	0.11	0.09	0.07
E5 - upper secondary	0.19	0.30	0.39	0.46	0.51	0.53
E6 - post-secondary	0.11	0.14	0.18	0.21	0.25	0.30
Mean years of schooling (in years)	7.98	9.50	10.63	11.47	12.12	12.60
Gender gap (population age 25+): highest educational attainment (ratio male/female)						
E1 - no education	0.86	0.82	0.83	0.91	1.05	1.16
E2 - incomplete primary	0.95	1.00	1.07	1.18	1.31	1.37
E3 - primary	0.82	0.73	0.70	0.71	0.73	0.75
E4 - lower secondary	0.90	0.87	0.83	0.83	0.83	0.82
E5 - upper secondary	1.38	1.31	1.22	1.14	1.09	1.06
E6 - post-secondary	1.30	1.15	1.07	1.01	0.99	0.99
Mean years of schooling (male minus female)	0.68	0.57	0.39	0.20	0.08	0.06
Women age 20–39: highest educational attainment						
E1 - no education	0.04	0.02	0.01	0.00	0.00	0.00
E2 - incomplete primary	0.14	0.08	0.04	0.02	0.01	0.01
E3 - primary	0.29	0.24	0.18	0.13	0.08	0.06
E4 - lower secondary	0.20	0.20	0.19	0.17	0.15	0.13
E5 - upper secondary	0.24	0.34	0.42	0.48	0.52	0.53
E6 - post-secondary	0.09	0.12	0.16	0.20	0.24	0.28
Mean years of schooling (in years)	9.31	10.42	11.23	11.85	12.32	12.66

Education scenarios

GET: global education trend scenario (medium assumption also used for SSP2)

CER: constant enrolment rates scenario (assumption of no future improvements)

FT: Fast track scenario (assumption of education expansion according to fastest historical experience)

Pyramids by Education, Medium Scenario

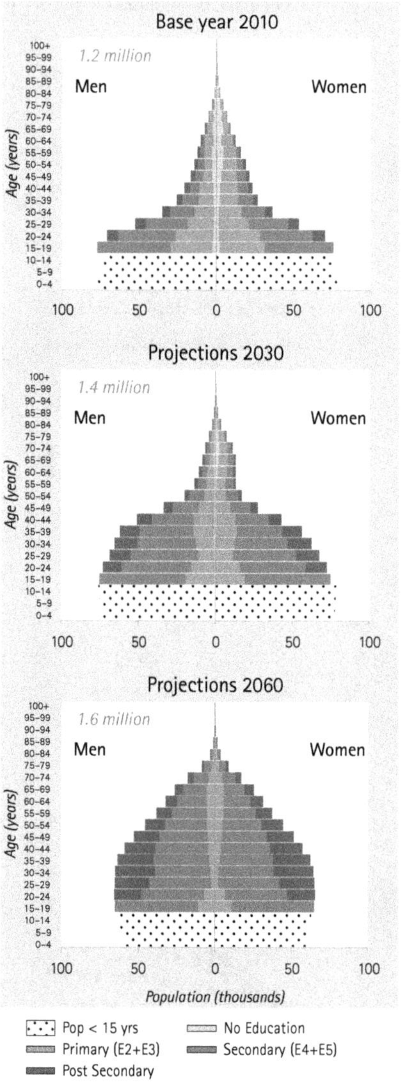

Population Size by Educational Attainment According to Three Education Scenarios: GET, CER, and FT

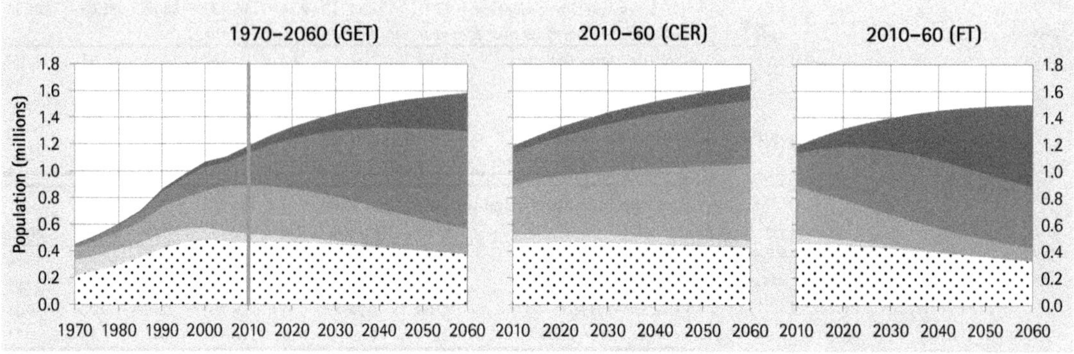

Swaziland (Continued)

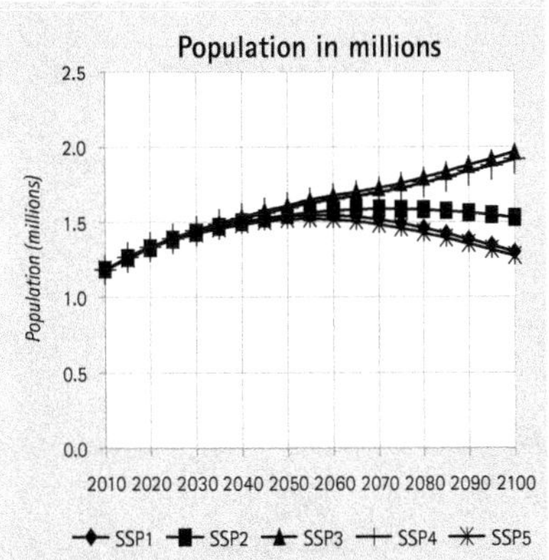

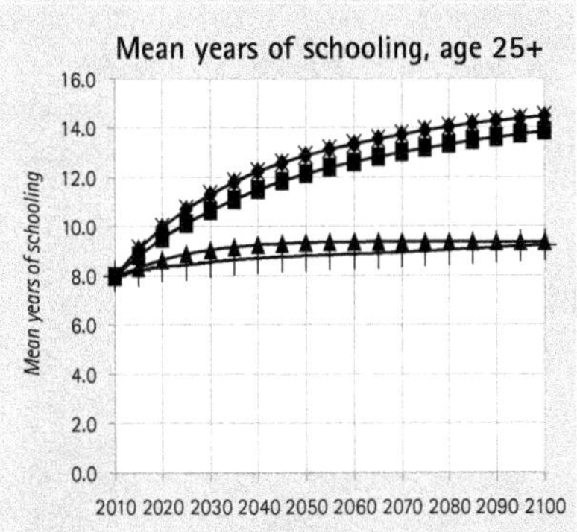

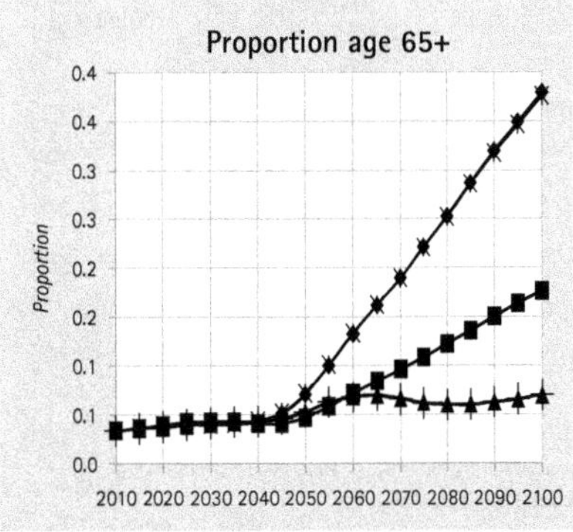

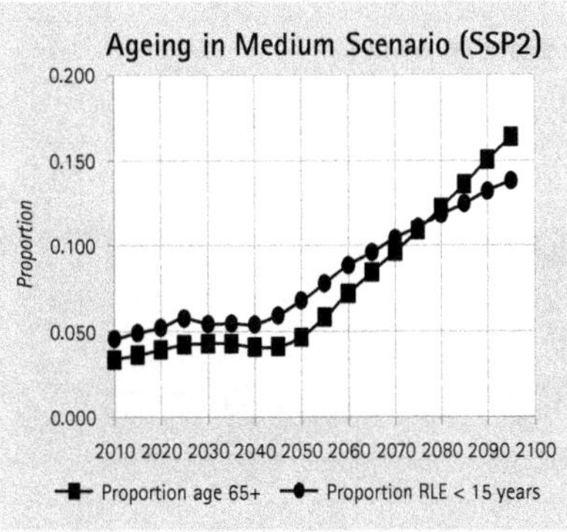

Alternative Scenarios to 2100

Projection Results by Scenario (SSP1–5)

	2010	2020	2030	2040	2050	2075	2100
Population (in millions)							
SSP1 - Rapid development	1.19	1.33	1.43	1.50	1.54	1.49	1.30
SSP2 - Medium	1.19	1.33	1.43	1.50	1.55	1.59	1.53
SSP3 - Stalled development	1.19	1.34	1.45	1.54	1.61	1.76	1.97
SSP4 - Inequality	1.19	1.34	1.44	1.53	1.59	1.73	1.92
SSP5 - Conventional development	1.19	1.33	1.42	1.49	1.52	1.46	1.27
Proportion age 65+							
SSP1 - Rapid development	0.03	0.04	0.04	0.04	0.07	0.22	0.38
SSP2 - Medium	0.03	0.04	0.04	0.04	0.05	0.11	0.18
SSP3 - Stalled development	0.03	0.04	0.04	0.04	0.05	0.06	0.07
SSP4 - Inequality	0.03	0.04	0.04	0.04	0.05	0.06	0.07
SSP5 - Conventional development	0.03	0.04	0.04	0.04	0.07	0.22	0.38
Proportion below age 20							
SSP1 - Rapid development	0.51	0.44	0.38	0.31	0.26	0.17	0.12
SSP2 - Medium	0.51	0.45	0.42	0.38	0.34	0.28	0.22
SSP3 - Stalled development	0.51	0.47	0.45	0.42	0.40	0.39	0.36
SSP4 - Inequality	0.51	0.47	0.45	0.42	0.41	0.39	0.36
SSP5 - Conventional development	0.51	0.44	0.38	0.31	0.26	0.18	0.12
Proportion of Women age 20–39 with at least secondary education							
SSP1 - Rapid development	0.53	0.73	0.84	0.91	0.94	0.98	0.99
SSP2 - Medium	0.53	0.66	0.77	0.85	0.90	0.97	0.98
SSP3 - Stalled development	0.53	0.49	0.49	0.49	0.49	0.49	0.49
SSP4 - Inequality	0.53	0.46	0.44	0.44	0.44	0.44	0.44
SSP5 - Conventional development	0.53	0.73	0.84	0.91	0.94	0.98	0.99
Mean years of schooling, age 25+							
SSP1 - Rapid development	7.98	9.96	11.29	12.21	12.85	13.88	14.45
SSP2 - Medium	7.98	9.50	10.63	11.47	12.12	13.16	13.84
SSP3 - Stalled development	7.98	8.64	9.04	9.24	9.33	9.36	9.36
SSP4 - Inequality	7.98	8.37	8.56	8.71	8.80	8.99	9.23
SSP5 - Conventional development	7.98	9.96	11.28	12.20	12.85	13.88	14.45

Demographic Assumptions Underlying SSPs

	2010–15	2020–25	2030–35	2040–45	2050–55	2075–80	2095–2100
Total fertility rate							
SSP1 - Rapid development	2.87	2.10	1.68	1.48	1.38	1.23	1.17
SSP2 - Medium	3.09	2.54	2.19	2.02	1.91	1.67	1.59
SSP3 - Stalled development	3.26	3.11	2.91	2.77	2.67	2.41	2.30
SSP4 - Inequality	3.26	3.13	2.92	2.76	2.65	2.37	2.25
SSP5 - Conventional development	2.87	2.10	1.68	1.48	1.38	1.23	1.17
Life expectancy at birth for females (in years)							
SSP1 - Rapid development	51.52	56.77	62.06	66.80	71.41	82.19	90.45
SSP2 - Medium	48.51	49.40	52.82	55.70	58.90	67.40	74.02
SSP3 - Stalled development	50.03	46.48	48.46	49.32	51.26	56.54	60.84
SSP4 - Inequality	50.03	46.41	48.34	49.20	51.15	56.47	60.80
SSP5 - Conventional development	51.52	56.77	62.06	66.80	71.41	82.19	90.45
Migration – net flow over five years (in thousands)							
SSP1 - Rapid development	−5	−5	−5	−6	−5	−2	0
SSP2 - Medium	−5	−5	−5	−6	−5	−2	0
SSP3 - Stalled development	−4	−2	−2	−2	−2	−1	0
SSP4 - Inequality	−5	−4	−5	−5	−5	−2	0
SSP5 - Conventional development	−6	−8	−9	−9	−9	−3	0

Ageing Indicators, Medium Scenario (SSP2)

	2010	2020	2030	2040	2050	2075	2095
Median age	19.47	22.12	24.05	26.29	28.55	34.37	39.36
Propspective median age	19.47	22.88	22.46	22.83	22.47	19.84	18.99
Proportion age 65+	0.03	0.04	0.04	0.04	0.05	0.11	0.16
Proportion RLE < 15 years	0.05	0.05	0.05	0.05	0.07	0.11	0.14

Sweden

Detailed Human Capital Projections to 2060

Demographic indicators, Medium Scenario (SSP2)	2010	2020	2030	2040	2050	2060
Population (in millions)	9.38	10.09	10.88	11.61	12.40	13.23
Proportion age 65+	0.18	0.21	0.22	0.24	0.24	0.27
Proportion below age 20	0.23	0.23	0.23	0.23	0.22	0.22
	2005–10	2015–20	2025–30	2035–40	2045–50	2055–60
Total Fertility Rate	1.90	1.94	1.99	2.00	2.00	1.99
Life expectancy at birth (in years)						
Men	78.77	80.73	82.77	84.75	86.74	88.80
Women	82.93	84.51	86.51	88.51	90.49	92.59
Five-year immigration flow (in '000)	318.38	253.10	262.89	268.89	269.02	265.15
Five-year emigration flow (in '000)	53.37	40.18	39.67	41.61	43.75	45.10

Human Capital indicators, Medium Scenario (SSP2)	2010	2020	2030	2040	2050	2060
Population age 25+: highest educational attainment						
E1 - no education	0.00	0.00	0.00	0.00	0.00	0.00
E2 - incomplete primary	0.00	0.00	0.00	0.00	0.00	0.00
E3 - primary	0.11	0.06	0.03	0.02	0.01	0.01
E4 - lower secondary	0.10	0.09	0.08	0.07	0.05	0.04
E5 - upper secondary	0.44	0.44	0.43	0.41	0.38	0.35
E6 - post-secondary	0.35	0.41	0.46	0.51	0.56	0.60
Mean years of schooling (in years)	12.50	13.03	13.41	13.74	14.02	14.26
Gender gap (population age 25+): highest educational attainment (ratio male/female)						
E1 - no education	NA	Inf	3.22	2.45	1.96	1.60
E2 - incomplete primary	NA	NA	0.36	0.46	0.57	0.69
E3 - primary	1.03	0.99	0.91	0.80	0.75	0.74
E4 - lower secondary	1.27	1.30	1.33	1.32	1.28	1.22
E5 - upper secondary	1.08	1.11	1.14	1.15	1.16	1.14
E6 - post-secondary	0.85	0.84	0.85	0.87	0.89	0.92
Mean years of schooling (male minus female)	−0.32	−0.35	−0.35	−0.33	−0.28	−0.22
Women age 20–39: highest educational attainment						
E1 - no education	0.00	0.00	0.00	0.00	0.00	0.00
E2 - incomplete primary	0.00	0.00	0.00	0.00	0.00	0.00
E3 - primary	0.02	0.01	0.01	0.00	0.00	0.00
E4 - lower secondary	0.07	0.06	0.05	0.03	0.02	0.02
E5 - upper secondary	0.44	0.41	0.40	0.39	0.38	0.37
E6 - post-secondary	0.47	0.52	0.54	0.57	0.59	0.61
Mean years of schooling (in years)	13.53	13.81	14.00	14.15	14.28	14.37

Education scenarios

GET: global education trend scenario (medium assumption also used for SSP2)

CER: constant enrolment rates scenario (assumption of no future improvements)

FT: Fast track scenario (assumption of education expansion according to fastest historical experience)

Pyramids by Education, Medium Scenario

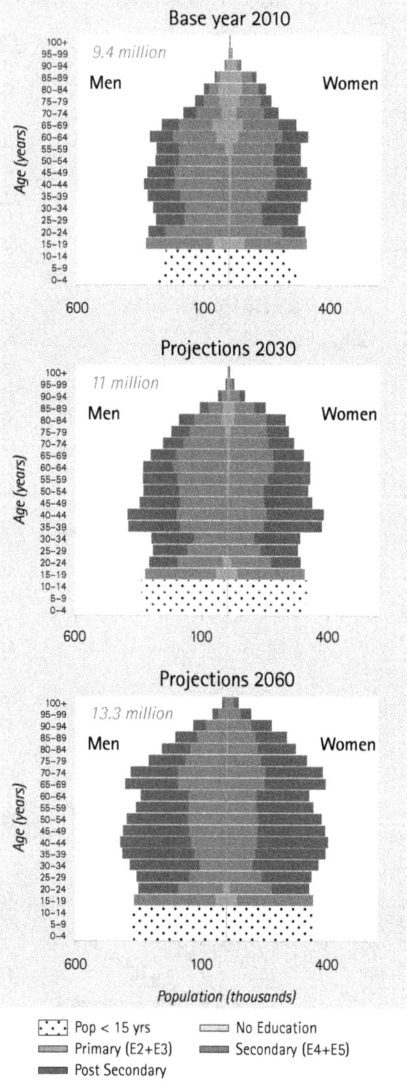

Population Size by Educational Attainment According to Three Education Scenarios: GET, CER, and FT

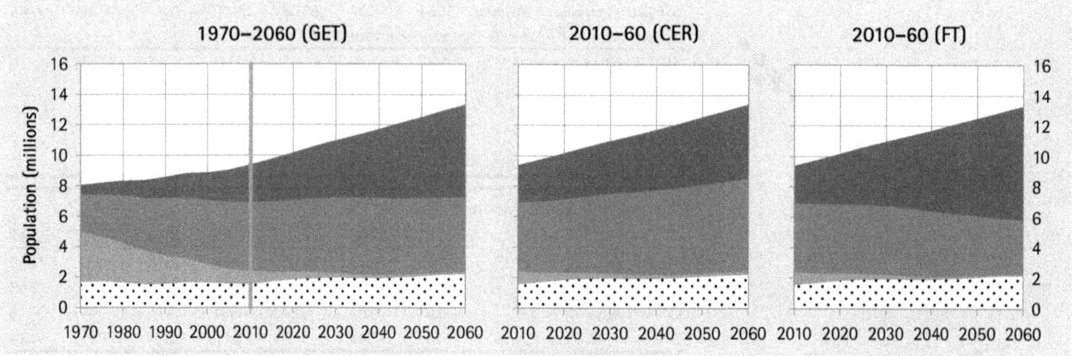

Sweden (Continued)

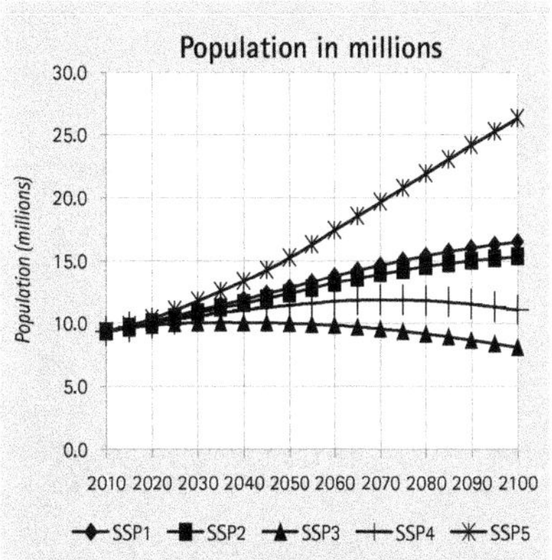

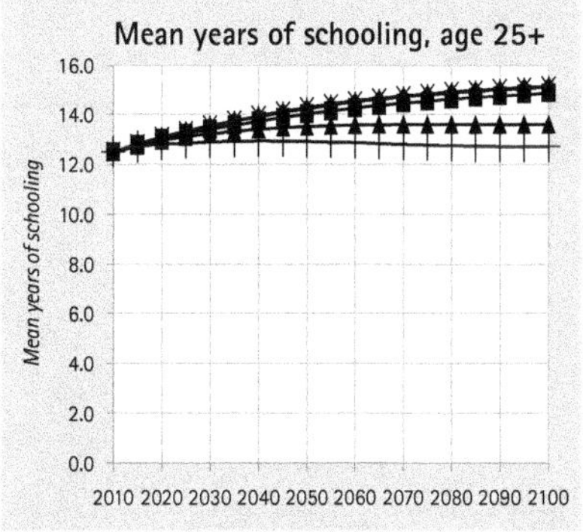

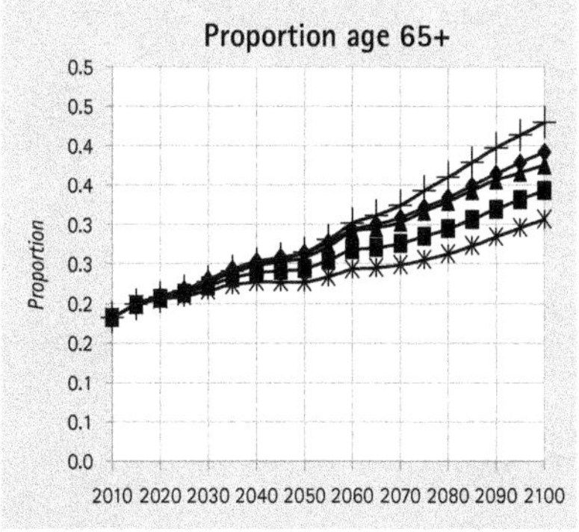

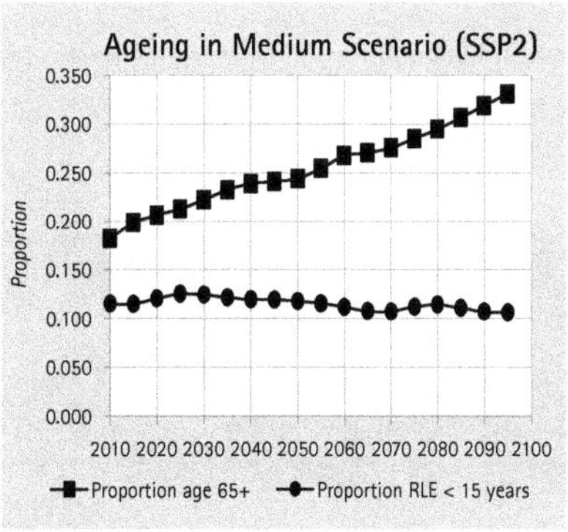

Alternative Scenarios to 2100

Projection Results by Scenario (SSP1–5)	2010	2020	2030	2040	2050	2075	2100
Population (in millions)							
SSP1 - Rapid development	9.38	10.16	11.05	11.92	12.84	15.05	16.50
SSP2 - Medium	9.38	10.09	10.88	11.61	12.40	14.27	15.33
SSP3 - Stalled development	9.38	9.85	10.05	10.06	10.00	9.40	8.11
SSP4 - Inequality	9.38	10.02	10.60	11.06	11.45	11.87	11.07
SSP5 - Conventional development	9.38	10.37	11.80	13.37	15.24	20.79	26.32
Proportion age 65+							
SSP1 - Rapid development	0.18	0.21	0.23	0.25	0.26	0.32	0.39
SSP2 - Medium	0.18	0.21	0.22	0.24	0.24	0.29	0.34
SSP3 - Stalled development	0.18	0.21	0.23	0.25	0.26	0.32	0.38
SSP4 - Inequality	0.18	0.21	0.23	0.25	0.26	0.34	0.43
SSP5 - Conventional development	0.18	0.21	0.22	0.23	0.23	0.26	0.31
Proportion below age 20							
SSP1 - Rapid development	0.23	0.23	0.23	0.22	0.22	0.20	0.18
SSP2 - Medium	0.23	0.23	0.23	0.23	0.22	0.21	0.19
SSP3 - Stalled development	0.23	0.22	0.21	0.19	0.18	0.16	0.15
SSP4 - Inequality	0.23	0.22	0.21	0.19	0.18	0.16	0.13
SSP5 - Conventional development	0.23	0.23	0.25	0.26	0.26	0.26	0.24
Proportion of Women age 20–39 with at least secondary education							
SSP1 - Rapid development	0.98	0.99	1.00	1.00	1.00	1.00	1.00
SSP2 - Medium	0.98	0.99	0.99	1.00	1.00	1.00	1.00
SSP3 - Stalled development	0.98	0.98	0.98	0.98	0.98	0.98	0.98
SSP4 - Inequality	0.98	0.98	0.98	0.98	0.98	0.98	0.98
SSP5 - Conventional development	0.98	0.99	1.00	1.00	1.00	1.00	1.00
Mean years of schooling, age 25+							
SSP1 - Rapid development	12.50	13.09	13.53	13.91	14.24	14.82	15.13
SSP2 - Medium	12.50	13.03	13.41	13.74	14.02	14.55	14.89
SSP3 - Stalled development	12.50	12.96	13.23	13.41	13.52	13.61	13.61
SSP4 - Inequality	12.50	12.81	12.90	12.94	12.92	12.78	12.72
SSP5 - Conventional development	12.50	13.10	13.55	13.95	14.29	14.86	15.16

Demographic Assumptions Underlying SSPs	2010–15	2020–25	2030–35	2040–45	2050–55	2075–80	2095–2100
Total fertility rate							
SSP1 - Rapid development	1.91	1.96	1.99	2.00	1.99	1.95	1.92
SSP2 - Medium	1.91	1.96	2.00	2.00	2.00	1.95	1.92
SSP3 - Stalled development	1.82	1.67	1.58	1.53	1.50	1.47	1.45
SSP4 - Inequality	1.82	1.68	1.59	1.54	1.51	1.49	1.46
SSP5 - Conventional development	2.01	2.25	2.41	2.47	2.49	2.44	2.40
Life expectancy at birth for females (in years)							
SSP1 - Rapid development	84.52	87.30	90.25	93.10	96.14	104.08	110.45
SSP2 - Medium	83.71	85.51	87.51	89.51	91.59	97.00	101.41
SSP3 - Stalled development	83.51	84.31	85.25	86.16	87.23	90.07	92.33
SSP4 - Inequality	84.05	85.78	87.74	89.66	91.70	96.87	101.12
SSP5 - Conventional development	84.52	87.30	90.25	93.10	96.14	104.08	110.45
Migration – net flow over five years (in thousands)							
SSP1 - Rapid development	229	217	223	218	208	89	0
SSP2 - Medium	225	211	218	218	214	99	0
SSP3 - Stalled development	191	108	109	106	100	43	0
SSP4 - Inequality	229	216	220	213	202	88	0
SSP5 - Conventional development	268	329	347	357	360	176	0

Ageing Indicators, Medium Scenario (SSP2)

	2010	2020	2030	2040	2050	2075	2095
Median age	40.72	41.25	41.68	43.18	43.09	46.02	49.12
Propspective median age	40.72	39.34	37.90	37.53	35.41	33.23	32.06
Proportion age 65+	0.18	0.21	0.22	0.24	0.24	0.29	0.33
Proportion RLE < 15 years	0.12	0.12	0.12	0.12	0.12	0.11	0.11

Switzerland

Detailed Human Capital Projections to 2060

Demographic indicators, Medium Scenario (SSP2)	2010	2020	2030	2040	2050	2060
Population (in millions)	7.66	8.15	8.63	9.03	9.34	9.60
Proportion age 65+	0.17	0.20	0.25	0.30	0.31	0.33
Proportion below age 20	0.21	0.19	0.19	0.19	0.18	0.18
	2005–10	2015–20	2025–30	2035–40	2045–50	2055–60
Total Fertility Rate	1.46	1.57	1.67	1.72	1.74	1.75
Life expectancy at birth (in years)						
Men	79.31	82.17	84.67	86.64	88.73	90.74
Women	84.11	86.51	88.71	90.69	92.80	94.80
Five-year immigration flow (in '000)	304.92	243.99	253.89	260.26	261.02	257.60
Five-year emigration flow (in '000)	122.63	85.73	80.63	79.39	80.04	80.36

Human Capital indicators, Medium Scenario (SSP2)	2010	2020	2030	2040	2050	2060
Population age 25+: highest educational attainment						
E1 - no education	0.00	0.00	0.00	0.00	0.00	0.00
E2 - incomplete primary	0.00	0.00	0.00	0.00	0.00	0.00
E3 - primary	0.03	0.02	0.02	0.01	0.01	0.01
E4 - lower secondary	0.22	0.18	0.15	0.12	0.09	0.07
E5 - upper secondary	0.52	0.53	0.53	0.53	0.52	0.51
E6 - post-secondary	0.24	0.27	0.30	0.33	0.37	0.42
Mean years of schooling (in years)	12.66	12.96	13.28	13.58	13.89	14.21
Gender gap (population age 25+): highest educational attainment (ratio male/female)						
E1 - no education	NA	NA	NA	NA	NA	NA
E2 - incomplete primary	NA	1.10	1.10	1.09	1.08	1.07
E3 - primary	0.76	0.79	0.80	0.81	0.81	0.84
E4 - lower secondary	0.61	0.65	0.71	0.76	0.80	0.85
E5 - upper secondary	0.93	0.90	0.89	0.89	0.90	0.92
E6 - post-secondary	1.93	1.66	1.47	1.33	1.22	1.14
Mean years of schooling (male minus female)	0.91	0.73	0.59	0.46	0.35	0.26
Women age 20–39: highest educational attainment						
E1 - no education	0.00	0.00	0.00	0.00	0.00	0.00
E2 - incomplete primary	0.00	0.00	0.00	0.00	0.00	0.00
E3 - primary	0.01	0.01	0.01	0.00	0.00	0.00
E4 - lower secondary	0.15	0.11	0.08	0.05	0.04	0.03
E5 - upper secondary	0.64	0.63	0.62	0.60	0.58	0.55
E6 - post-secondary	0.20	0.25	0.30	0.34	0.38	0.42
Mean years of schooling (in years)	12.91	13.33	13.83	14.09	14.31	14.52

Education scenarios

GET: global education trend scenario (medium assumption also used for SSP2)

CER: constant enrolment rates scenario (assumption of no future improvements)

FT: Fast track scenario (assumption of education expansion according to fastest historical experience)

Pyramids by Education, Medium Scenario

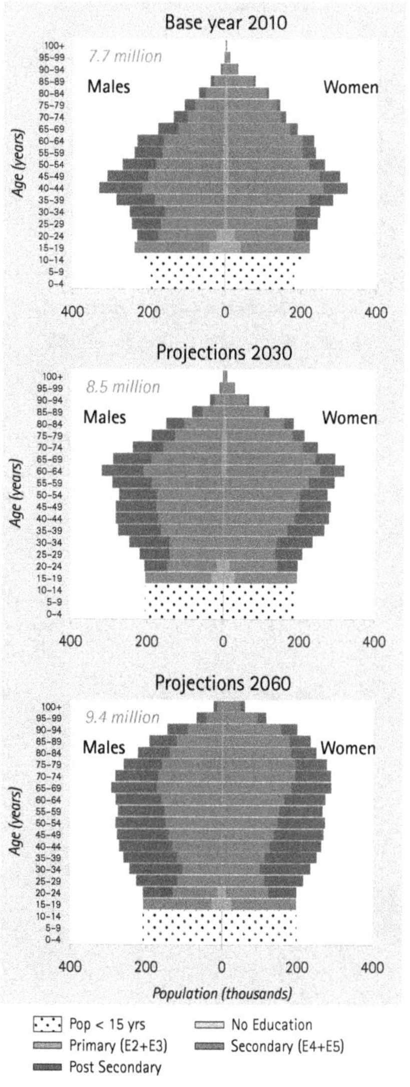

Population Size by Educational Attainment According to Three Education Scenarios: GET, CER, and FT

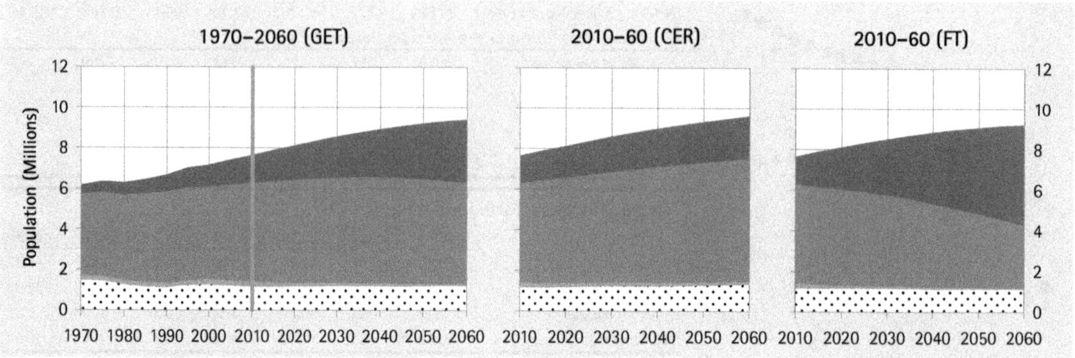

Switzerland (Continued)

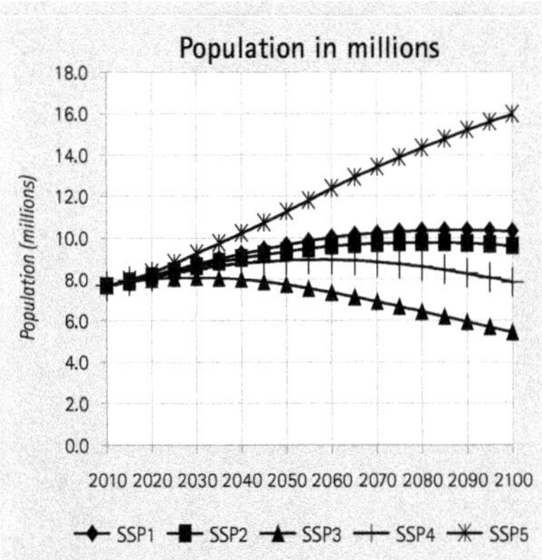

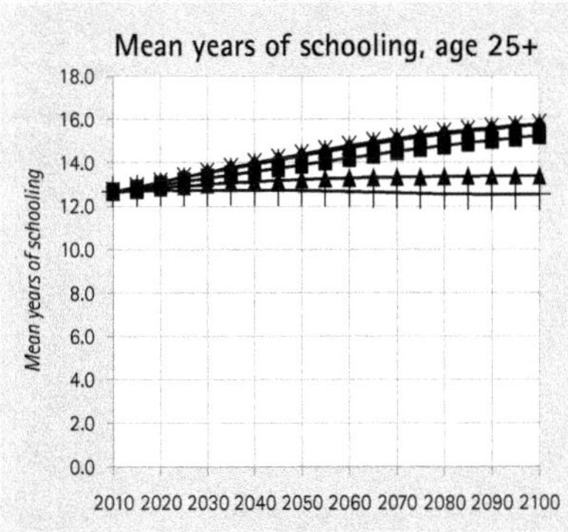

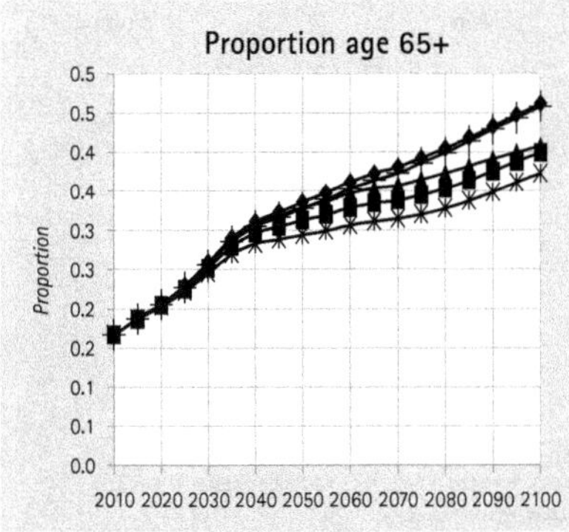

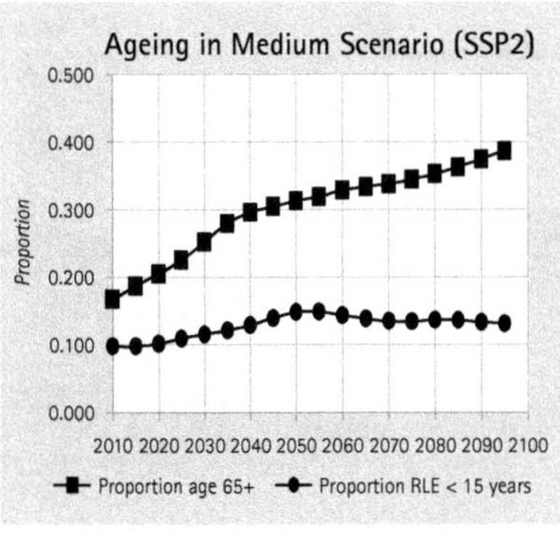

Alternative Scenarios to 2100

Projection Results by Scenario (SSP1–5)

	2010	2020	2030	2040	2050	2075	2100
Population (in millions)							
SSP1 - Rapid development	7.66	8.19	8.74	9.23	9.66	10.30	10.31
SSP2 - Medium	7.66	8.15	8.63	9.03	9.34	9.76	9.60
SSP3 - Stalled development	7.66	7.98	8.08	7.99	7.73	6.67	5.42
SSP4 - Inequality	7.66	8.11	8.50	8.77	8.91	8.74	7.84
SSP5 - Conventional development	7.66	8.33	9.25	10.22	11.25	13.87	15.93
Proportion age 65+							
SSP1 - Rapid development	0.17	0.21	0.26	0.31	0.34	0.39	0.46
SSP2 - Medium	0.17	0.20	0.25	0.30	0.31	0.35	0.40
SSP3 - Stalled development	0.17	0.20	0.26	0.31	0.33	0.36	0.41
SSP4 - Inequality	0.17	0.21	0.26	0.31	0.33	0.39	0.46
SSP5 - Conventional development	0.17	0.20	0.25	0.28	0.29	0.32	0.37
Proportion below age 20							
SSP1 - Rapid development	0.21	0.19	0.19	0.18	0.17	0.16	0.15
SSP2 - Medium	0.21	0.19	0.19	0.19	0.18	0.18	0.16
SSP3 - Stalled development	0.21	0.19	0.17	0.16	0.15	0.14	0.14
SSP4 - Inequality	0.21	0.19	0.17	0.16	0.15	0.14	0.13
SSP5 - Conventional development	0.21	0.20	0.21	0.21	0.21	0.21	0.20
Proportion of Women age 20–39 with at least secondary education							
SSP1 - Rapid development	0.99	0.99	1.00	1.00	1.00	1.00	1.00
SSP2 - Medium	0.99	0.99	0.99	1.00	1.00	1.00	1.00
SSP3 - Stalled development	0.99	0.98	0.98	0.98	0.98	0.98	0.98
SSP4 - Inequality	0.99	0.98	0.98	0.98	0.98	0.98	0.98
SSP5 - Conventional development	0.99	0.99	1.00	1.00	1.00	1.00	1.00
Mean years of schooling, age 25+							
SSP1 - Rapid development	12.66	13.09	13.53	13.93	14.32	15.17	15.71
SSP2 - Medium	12.66	12.96	13.28	13.58	13.89	14.65	15.22
SSP3 - Stalled development	12.66	12.83	13.00	13.12	13.22	13.34	13.37
SSP4 - Inequality	12.66	12.72	12.73	12.73	12.71	12.58	12.53
SSP5 - Conventional development	12.66	13.10	13.55	13.98	14.39	15.25	15.76

Demographic Assumptions Underlying SSPs

	2010–15	2020–25	2030–35	2040–45	2050–55	2075–80	2095–2100
Total fertility rate							
SSP1 - Rapid development	1.52	1.59	1.66	1.70	1.72	1.73	1.74
SSP2 - Medium	1.52	1.62	1.71	1.73	1.75	1.75	1.75
SSP3 - Stalled development	1.45	1.41	1.39	1.39	1.38	1.41	1.42
SSP4 - Inequality	1.46	1.44	1.43	1.43	1.43	1.45	1.46
SSP5 - Conventional development	1.59	1.83	2.02	2.11	2.15	2.16	2.17
Life expectancy at birth for females (in years)							
SSP1 - Rapid development	86.17	89.31	92.35	95.35	98.34	105.86	111.93
SSP2 - Medium	85.41	87.61	89.71	91.79	93.80	98.79	102.80
SSP3 - Stalled development	85.19	86.39	87.45	88.46	89.42	91.72	93.58
SSP4 - Inequality	85.72	87.85	89.90	91.95	93.90	98.63	102.44
SSP5 - Conventional development	86.17	89.31	92.35	95.35	98.34	105.86	111.93
Migration – net flow over five years (in thousands)							
SSP1 - Rapid development	168	165	175	174	166	62	0
SSP2 - Medium	166	161	171	174	171	70	0
SSP3 - Stalled development	140	82	86	86	82	32	0
SSP4 - Inequality	168	165	175	175	170	69	0
SSP5 - Conventional development	196	250	272	284	285	121	0

Ageing Indicators, Medium Scenario (SSP2)

	2010	2020	2030	2040	2050	2075	2095
Median age	41.47	44.61	46.49	48.26	49.61	51.35	54.64
Propspective median age	41.47	42.48	42.45	42.34	41.83	38.72	38.12
Proportion age 65+	0.17	0.20	0.25	0.30	0.31	0.34	0.39
Proportion RLE < 15 years	0.10	0.10	0.12	0.13	0.15	0.13	0.13

Syrian Arab Republic

Detailed Human Capital Projections to 2060

Demographic indicators, Medium Scenario (SSP2)	2010	2020	2030	2040	2050	2060
Population (in millions)	20.41	24.31	28.28	31.77	34.54	36.73
Proportion age 65+	0.04	0.05	0.07	0.10	0.14	0.19
Proportion below age 20	0.48	0.40	0.34	0.31	0.27	0.24
	2005–10	2015–20	2025–30	2035–40	2045–50	2055–60
Total Fertility Rate	3.10	2.50	2.17	2.00	1.85	1.77
Life expectancy at birth (in years)						
Men	73.91	76.01	78.09	80.09	82.08	84.06
Women	76.86	79.39	81.59	83.69	85.71	87.71
Five-year immigration flow (in '000)	390.69	381.82	396.02	404.66	404.44	398.44
Five-year emigration flow (in '000)	445.45	413.68	462.30	470.66	478.25	472.95

Human Capital indicators, Medium Scenario (SSP2)	2010	2020	2030	2040	2050	2060
Population age 25+: highest educational attainment						
E1 - no education	0.22	0.15	0.11	0.08	0.05	0.04
E2 - incomplete primary	0.31	0.28	0.23	0.19	0.15	0.11
E3 - primary	0.17	0.21	0.23	0.25	0.25	0.24
E4 - lower secondary	0.10	0.11	0.12	0.12	0.12	0.11
E5 - upper secondary	0.08	0.11	0.14	0.17	0.19	0.22
E6 - post-secondary	0.11	0.14	0.17	0.20	0.24	0.28
Mean years of schooling (in years)	6.01	6.90	7.61	8.31	9.01	9.72
Gender gap (population age 25+): highest educational attainment (ratio male/female)						
E1 - no education	0.45	0.45	0.48	0.52	0.57	0.64
E2 - incomplete primary	1.12	1.09	1.06	1.04	1.01	0.98
E3 - primary	1.29	1.20	1.17	1.15	1.12	1.09
E4 - lower secondary	1.30	1.20	1.15	1.13	1.11	1.08
E5 - upper secondary	1.39	1.18	1.08	1.04	1.03	1.02
E6 - post-secondary	1.36	1.11	0.99	0.94	0.92	0.95
Mean years of schooling (male minus female)	1.44	0.93	0.46	0.17	0.00	-0.03
Women age 20–39: highest educational attainment						
E1 - no education	0.12	0.08	0.05	0.03	0.01	0.01
E2 - incomplete primary	0.30	0.22	0.15	0.09	0.06	0.04
E3 - primary	0.22	0.25	0.25	0.23	0.20	0.17
E4 - lower secondary	0.13	0.14	0.15	0.15	0.15	0.14
E5 - upper secondary	0.13	0.17	0.21	0.26	0.30	0.32
E6 - post-secondary	0.11	0.15	0.20	0.24	0.28	0.32
Mean years of schooling (in years)	6.91	7.89	8.82	9.65	10.48	11.14

Education scenarios

GET: global education trend scenario (medium assumption also used for SSP2)

CER: constant enrolment rates scenario (assumption of no future improvements)

FT: Fast track scenario (assumption of education expansion according to fastest historical experience)

Pyramids by Education, Medium Scenario

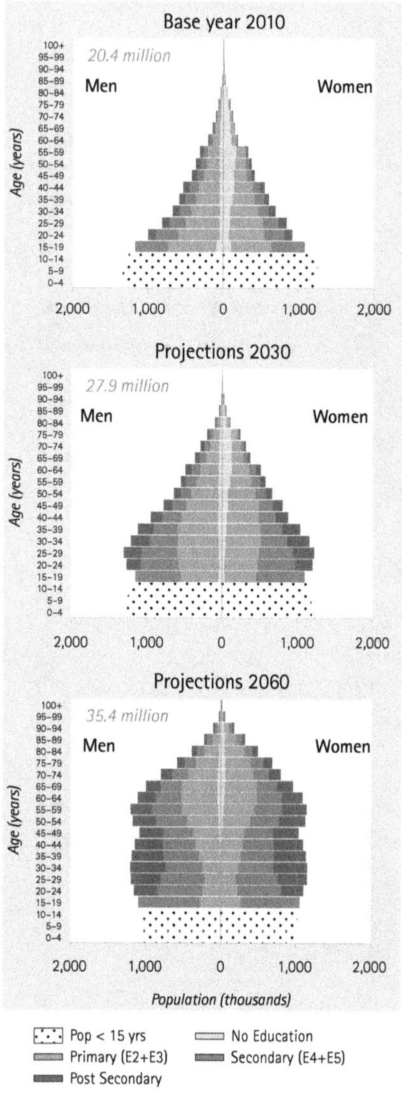

Population Size by Educational Attainment According to Three Education Scenarios: GET, CER, and FT

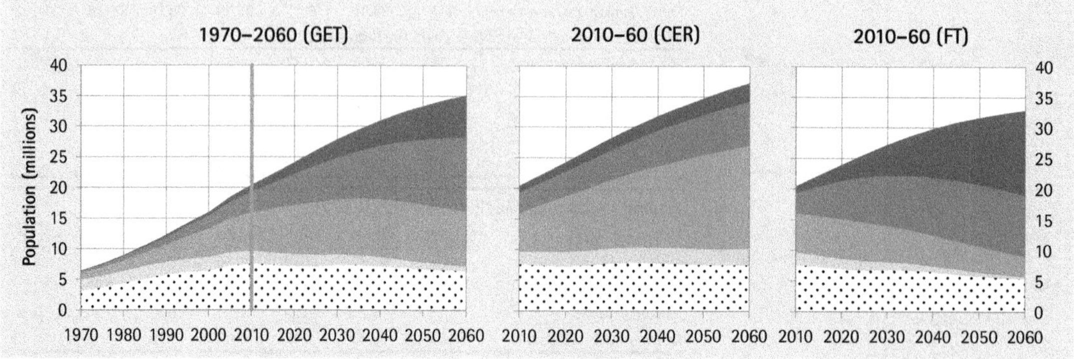

Syrian Arab Republic (Continued)

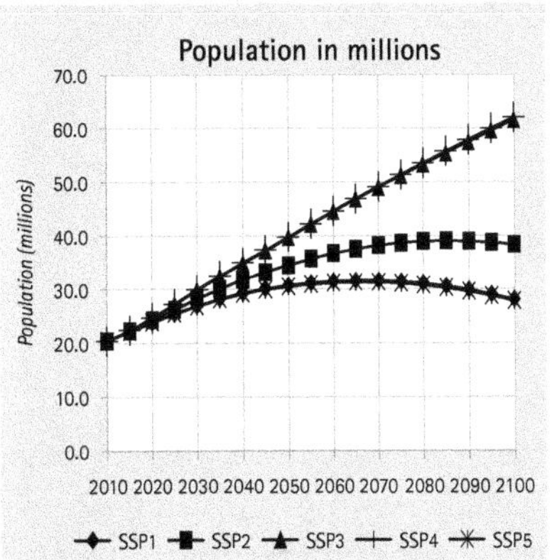

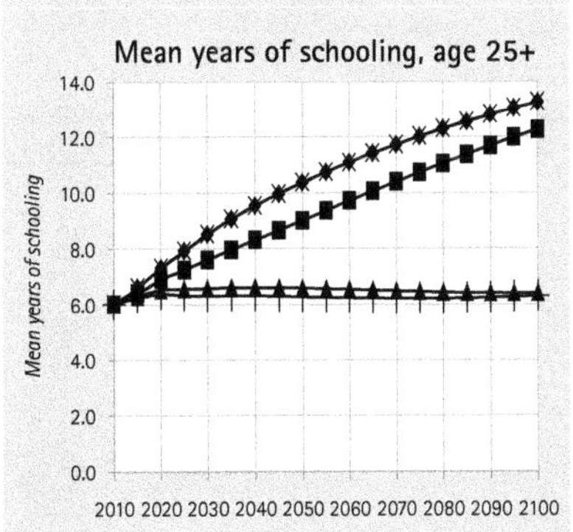

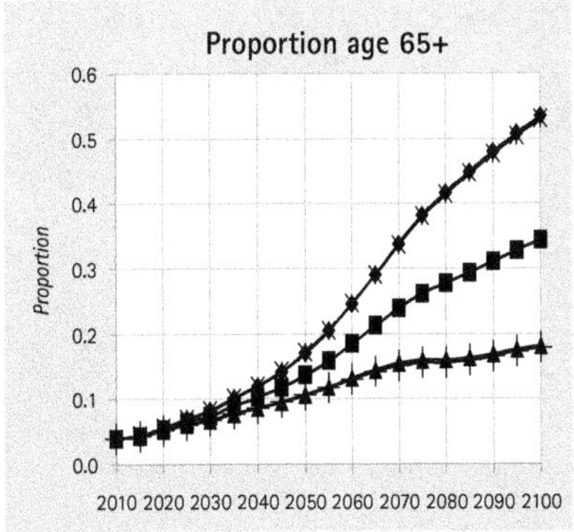

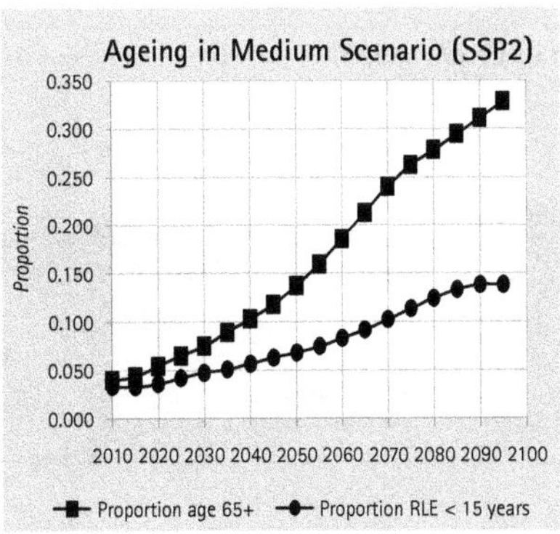

Alternative Scenarios to 2100

Projection Results by Scenario (SSP1-5)

	2010	2020	2030	2040	2050	2075	2100
Population (in millions)							
SSP1 - Rapid development	20.41	23.89	26.94	29.29	30.75	31.46	28.09
SSP2 - Medium	20.41	24.31	28.28	31.77	34.54	38.67	38.34
SSP3 - Stalled development	20.41	24.76	29.93	34.90	39.71	51.15	61.54
SSP4 - Inequality	20.41	24.78	29.96	34.94	39.76	51.31	61.99
SSP5 - Conventional development	20.41	23.87	26.86	29.14	30.52	31.09	27.80
Proportion age 65+							
SSP1 - Rapid development	0.04	0.06	0.08	0.12	0.17	0.38	0.53
SSP2 - Medium	0.04	0.05	0.07	0.10	0.14	0.26	0.34
SSP3 - Stalled development	0.04	0.05	0.07	0.09	0.11	0.16	0.18
SSP4 - Inequality	0.04	0.05	0.07	0.09	0.11	0.16	0.18
SSP5 - Conventional development	0.04	0.06	0.08	0.12	0.17	0.38	0.53
Proportion below age 20							
SSP1 - Rapid development	0.48	0.39	0.30	0.25	0.20	0.13	0.09
SSP2 - Medium	0.48	0.40	0.34	0.31	0.27	0.21	0.17
SSP3 - Stalled development	0.48	0.41	0.38	0.36	0.33	0.30	0.29
SSP4 - Inequality	0.48	0.41	0.38	0.37	0.34	0.31	0.29
SSP5 - Conventional development	0.48	0.39	0.30	0.25	0.21	0.13	0.09
Proportion of Women age 20–39 with at least secondary education							
SSP1 - Rapid development	0.36	0.56	0.70	0.79	0.84	0.92	0.96
SSP2 - Medium	0.36	0.46	0.56	0.65	0.72	0.86	0.95
SSP3 - Stalled development	0.36	0.33	0.33	0.33	0.33	0.33	0.33
SSP4 - Inequality	0.36	0.31	0.30	0.30	0.30	0.30	0.30
SSP5 - Conventional development	0.36	0.56	0.70	0.79	0.84	0.92	0.96
Mean years of schooling, age 25+							
SSP1 - Rapid development	6.01	7.31	8.52	9.54	10.37	12.02	13.25
SSP2 - Medium	6.01	6.90	7.61	8.31	9.01	10.73	12.28
SSP3 - Stalled development	6.01	6.53	6.59	6.61	6.59	6.46	6.41
SSP4 - Inequality	6.01	6.38	6.32	6.31	6.28	6.21	6.30
SSP5 - Conventional development	6.01	7.31	8.52	9.54	10.37	12.02	13.26

Demographic Assumptions Underlying SSPs

	2010–15	2020–25	2030–35	2040–45	2050–55	2075–80	2095–2100
Total fertility rate							
SSP1 - Rapid development	2.53	1.90	1.56	1.39	1.29	1.23	1.17
SSP2 - Medium	2.72	2.32	2.08	1.92	1.81	1.70	1.58
SSP3 - Stalled development	2.88	2.83	2.73	2.60	2.51	2.45	2.36
SSP4 - Inequality	2.88	2.86	2.75	2.61	2.50	2.43	2.34
SSP5 - Conventional development	2.53	1.90	1.56	1.39	1.29	1.23	1.17
Life expectancy at birth for females (in years)							
SSP1 - Rapid development	79.61	82.69	85.72	88.64	91.56	99.17	105.28
SSP2 - Medium	78.19	80.49	82.59	84.71	86.71	91.70	95.70
SSP3 - Stalled development	78.74	79.89	80.92	81.81	82.65	84.38	85.82
SSP4 - Inequality	78.74	79.88	80.90	81.78	82.60	84.28	85.73
SSP5 - Conventional development	79.61	82.69	85.72	88.64	91.56	99.17	105.28
Migration – net flow over five years (in thousands)							
SSP1 - Rapid development	−35	−56	−67	−68	−71	−18	0
SSP2 - Medium	−33	−54	−65	−69	−75	−20	0
SSP3 - Stalled development	−29	−26	−29	−31	−34	−4	0
SSP4 - Inequality	−35	−54	−63	−69	−79	−16	0
SSP5 - Conventional development	−41	−86	−107	−114	−122	−36	0

Ageing Indicators, Medium Scenario (SSP2)

	2010	2020	2030	2040	2050	2075	2095
Median age	21.03	25.00	29.01	33.09	36.69	45.17	50.47
Propspective median age	21.03	23.04	25.22	27.42	29.19	33.21	34.80
Proportion age 65+	0.04	0.05	0.07	0.10	0.14	0.26	0.33
Proportion RLE < 15 years	0.03	0.04	0.05	0.06	0.07	0.11	0.14

Tajikistan

Detailed Human Capital Projections to 2060

Demographic indicators, Medium Scenario (SSP2)	2010	2020	2030	2040	2050	2060
Population (in millions)	6.88	7.68	8.27	8.62	8.76	8.69
Proportion age 65+	0.03	0.04	0.06	0.09	0.11	0.16
Proportion below age 20	0.49	0.43	0.38	0.33	0.30	0.27
	2005–10	2015–20	2025–30	2035–40	2045–50	2055–60
Total Fertility Rate	3.45	2.68	2.28	2.09	1.93	1.87
Life expectancy at birth (in years)						
Men	63.29	65.37	67.76	70.02	72.24	74.46
Women	69.91	71.72	73.82	75.79	77.78	79.79
Five-year immigration flow (in '000)	0.19	0.19	0.20	0.20	0.20	0.20
Five-year emigration flow (in '000)	295.48	269.87	278.79	277.12	265.27	245.53

Human Capital indicators, Medium Scenario (SSP2)	2010	2020	2030	2040	2050	2060
Population age 25+: highest educational attainment						
E1 - no education	0.03	0.02	0.01	0.01	0.01	0.00
E2 - incomplete primary	0.00	0.00	0.00	0.00	0.00	0.00
E3 - primary	0.05	0.04	0.02	0.02	0.01	0.01
E4 - lower secondary	0.15	0.12	0.10	0.08	0.06	0.04
E5 - upper secondary	0.63	0.68	0.71	0.73	0.73	0.74
E6 - post-secondary	0.13	0.14	0.15	0.17	0.19	0.21
Mean years of schooling (in years)	10.50	10.85	11.10	11.29	11.46	11.61
Gender gap (population age 25+): highest educational attainment (ratio male/female)						
E1 - no education	0.47	0.49	0.49	0.47	0.43	0.42
E2 - incomplete primary	0.00	0.04	0.09	0.13	0.18	0.21
E3 - primary	0.36	0.40	0.47	0.52	0.56	0.58
E4 - lower secondary	0.63	0.65	0.68	0.71	0.74	0.77
E5 - upper secondary	1.04	0.98	0.96	0.95	0.95	0.96
E6 - post-secondary	2.75	2.21	1.88	1.62	1.42	1.28
Mean years of schooling (male minus female)	1.26	0.92	0.69	0.53	0.41	0.30
Women age 20–39: highest educational attainment						
E1 - no education	0.03	0.01	0.01	0.00	0.00	0.00
E2 - incomplete primary	0.00	0.00	0.00	0.00	0.00	0.00
E3 - primary	0.06	0.03	0.02	0.01	0.00	0.00
E4 - lower secondary	0.18	0.14	0.10	0.08	0.06	0.05
E5 - upper secondary	0.67	0.72	0.75	0.76	0.75	0.73
E6 - post-secondary	0.06	0.09	0.12	0.15	0.18	0.22
Mean years of schooling (in years)	10.20	10.71	11.07	11.34	11.56	11.74

Education scenarios

GET: global education trend scenario (medium assumption also used for SSP2)

CER: constant enrolment rates scenario (assumption of no future improvements)

FT: Fast track scenario (assumption of education expansion according to fastest historical experience)

Pyramids by Education, Medium Scenario

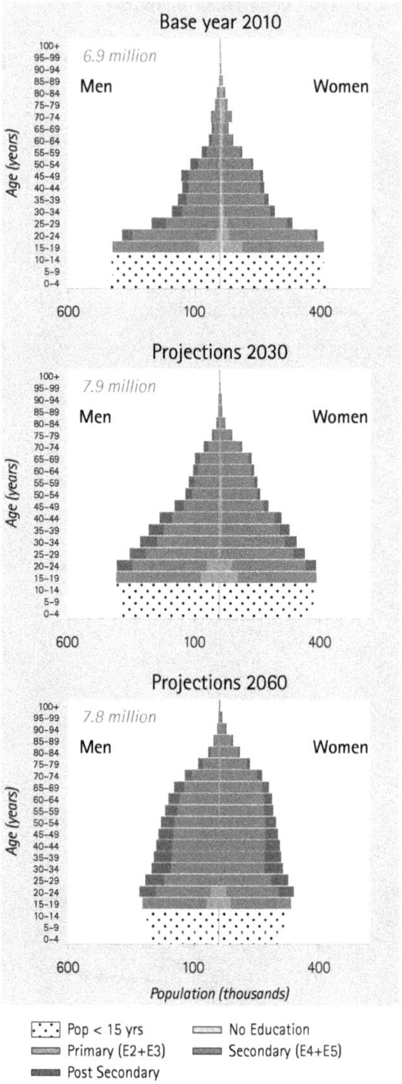

Population Size by Educational Attainment According to Three Education Scenarios: GET, CER, and FT

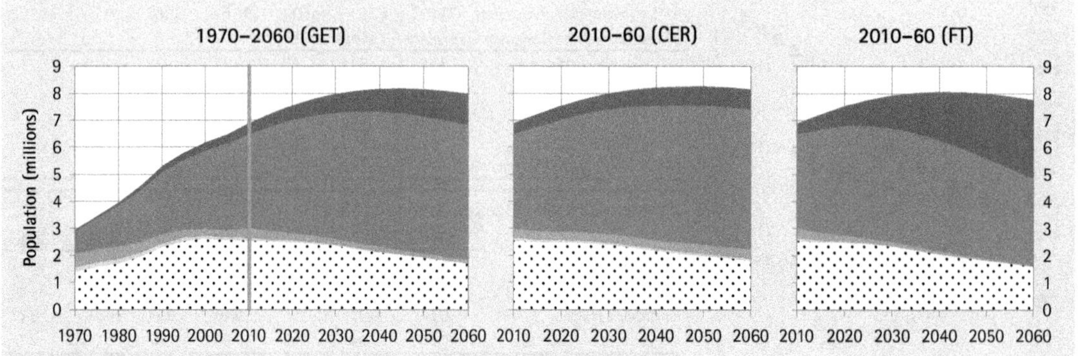

Tajikistan (Continued)

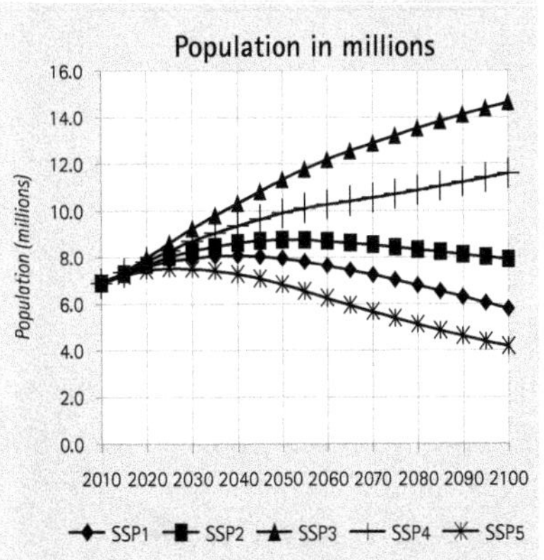

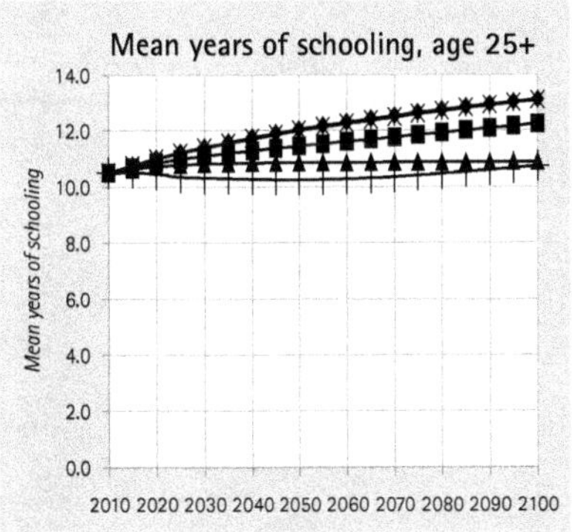

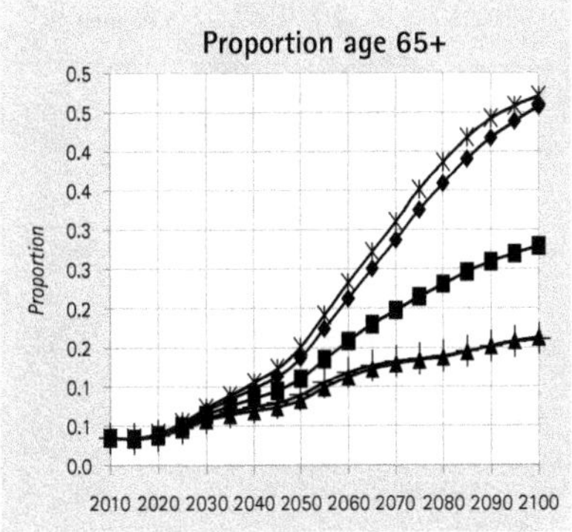

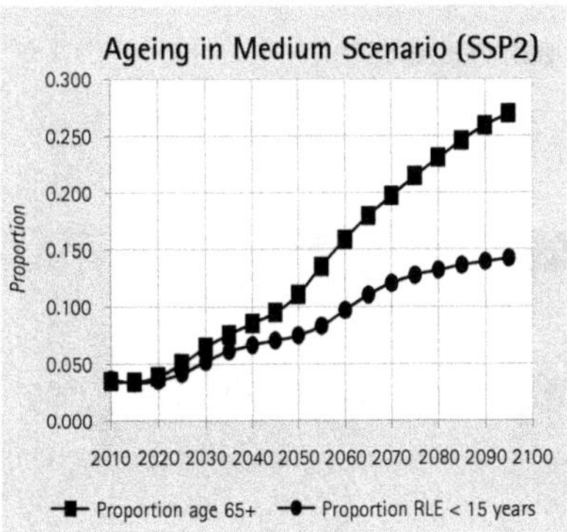

Alternative Scenarios to 2100

Projection Results by Scenario (SSP1–5)

	2010	2020	2030	2040	2050	2075	2100
Population (in millions)							
SSP1 - Rapid development	6.88	7.58	7.97	8.08	7.95	7.01	5.77
SSP2 - Medium	6.88	7.68	8.27	8.62	8.76	8.44	7.90
SSP3 - Stalled development	6.88	7.98	9.24	10.32	11.32	13.21	14.62
SSP4 - Inequality	6.88	7.81	8.70	9.36	9.89	10.71	11.58
SSP5 - Conventional development	6.88	7.42	7.49	7.26	6.82	5.37	4.17
Proportion age 65+							
SSP1 - Rapid development	0.03	0.04	0.07	0.10	0.14	0.32	0.46
SSP2 - Medium	0.03	0.04	0.06	0.09	0.11	0.21	0.28
SSP3 - Stalled development	0.03	0.04	0.06	0.07	0.08	0.13	0.16
SSP4 - Inequality	0.03	0.04	0.06	0.07	0.09	0.14	0.16
SSP5 - Conventional development	0.03	0.04	0.07	0.11	0.15	0.35	0.47
Proportion below age 20							
SSP1 - Rapid development	0.49	0.42	0.35	0.28	0.24	0.15	0.11
SSP2 - Medium	0.49	0.43	0.38	0.33	0.30	0.23	0.19
SSP3 - Stalled development	0.49	0.44	0.41	0.37	0.34	0.30	0.27
SSP4 - Inequality	0.49	0.44	0.41	0.38	0.35	0.31	0.27
SSP5 - Conventional development	0.49	0.42	0.35	0.29	0.24	0.15	0.11
Proportion of Women age 20–39 with at least secondary education							
SSP1 - Rapid development	0.91	0.96	0.98	0.99	1.00	1.00	1.00
SSP2 - Medium	0.91	0.95	0.97	0.99	0.99	1.00	1.00
SSP3 - Stalled development	0.91	0.91	0.91	0.91	0.91	0.91	0.91
SSP4 - Inequality	0.91	0.86	0.82	0.82	0.82	0.82	0.82
SSP5 - Conventional development	0.91	0.96	0.98	0.99	1.00	1.00	1.00
Mean years of schooling, age 25+							
SSP1 - Rapid development	10.50	11.00	11.41	11.75	12.04	12.64	13.11
SSP2 - Medium	10.50	10.85	11.10	11.29	11.46	11.85	12.24
SSP3 - Stalled development	10.50	10.73	10.82	10.85	10.86	10.87	10.88
SSP4 - Inequality	10.50	10.46	10.32	10.27	10.26	10.40	10.74
SSP5 - Conventional development	10.50	10.99	11.38	11.72	12.00	12.59	13.09

Demographic Assumptions Underlying SSPs

	2010–15	2020–25	2030–35	2040–45	2050–55	2075–80	2095–2100
Total fertility rate							
SSP1 - Rapid development	2.77	2.09	1.69	1.50	1.39	1.26	1.17
SSP2 - Medium	2.97	2.46	2.16	2.00	1.90	1.71	1.58
SSP3 - Stalled development	3.07	2.91	2.73	2.58	2.49	2.28	2.13
SSP4 - Inequality	3.07	2.90	2.71	2.56	2.46	2.23	2.07
SSP5 - Conventional development	2.77	2.09	1.69	1.50	1.39	1.26	1.17
Life expectancy at birth for females (in years)							
SSP1 - Rapid development	74.42	76.58	79.19	81.81	84.50	91.46	97.21
SSP2 - Medium	70.68	72.72	74.78	76.79	78.79	83.79	87.79
SSP3 - Stalled development	73.92	74.34	75.11	75.99	76.77	78.63	80.21
SSP4 - Inequality	73.92	74.31	75.05	75.90	76.64	78.48	80.11
SSP5 - Conventional development	74.42	76.58	79.19	81.81	84.50	91.46	97.21
Migration – net flow over five years (in thousands)							
SSP1 - Rapid development	−276	−273	−271	−255	−227	−75	0
SSP2 - Medium	−288	−286	−288	−281	−263	−100	0
SSP3 - Stalled development	−230	−138	−143	−146	−145	−65	0
SSP4 - Inequality	−276	−275	−280	−284	−277	−119	0
SSP5 - Conventional development	−322	−407	−399	−375	−331	−109	0

Ageing Indicators, Medium Scenario (SSP2)

	2010	2020	2030	2040	2050	2075	2095
Median age	20.34	23.39	26.56	30.10	33.80	41.77	46.00
Propspective median age	20.34	21.77	23.41	25.58	27.78	31.86	32.66
Proportion age 65+	0.03	0.04	0.06	0.09	0.11	0.21	0.27
Proportion RLE < 15 years	0.04	0.04	0.05	0.07	0.07	0.13	0.14

TFYR Macedonia

Detailed Human Capital Projections to 2060

Demographic indicators, Medium Scenario (SSP2)	2010	2020	2030	2040	2050	2060
Population (in millions)	2.06	2.10	2.12	2.11	2.08	2.02
Proportion age 65+	0.12	0.15	0.19	0.22	0.27	0.32
Proportion below age 20	0.25	0.22	0.20	0.19	0.18	0.17
	2005–10	2015–20	2025–30	2035–40	2045–50	2055–60
Total Fertility Rate	1.46	1.50	1.58	1.60	1.60	1.61
Life expectancy at birth (in years)						
Men	72.12	74.20	76.50	78.85	81.12	83.15
Women	76.33	78.29	80.59	83.01	85.31	87.31
Five-year immigration flow (in '000)	#N/A	17.84	18.57	19.05	19.12	18.88
Five-year emigration flow (in '000)	#N/A	10.88	9.44	8.57	7.86	7.18

Human Capital indicators, Medium Scenario (SSP2)	2010	2020	2030	2040	2050	2060
Population age 25+: highest educational attainment						
E1 - no education	0.04	0.02	0.01	0.01	0.01	0.00
E2 - incomplete primary	0.13	0.08	0.04	0.03	0.01	0.01
E3 - primary	0.09	0.07	0.05	0.03	0.02	0.02
E4 - lower secondary	0.21	0.21	0.20	0.18	0.15	0.12
E5 - upper secondary	0.40	0.48	0.53	0.58	0.61	0.64
E6 - post-secondary	0.12	0.14	0.16	0.17	0.19	0.21
Mean years of schooling (in years)	9.22	10.29	11.11	11.74	12.30	12.80
Gender gap (population age 25+): highest educational attainment (ratio male/female)						
E1 - no education	0.24	0.31	0.37	0.41	0.42	0.42
E2 - incomplete primary	0.48	0.40	0.36	0.36	0.39	0.42
E3 - primary	0.84	0.70	0.61	0.60	0.65	0.73
E4 - lower secondary	0.92	0.89	0.86	0.83	0.81	0.80
E5 - upper secondary	1.45	1.33	1.26	1.21	1.16	1.12
E6 - post-secondary	1.23	1.03	0.91	0.85	0.84	0.87
Mean years of schooling (male minus female)	1.78	1.25	0.83	0.51	0.30	0.18
Women age 20–39: highest educational attainment						
E1 - no education	0.02	0.01	0.00	0.00	0.00	0.00
E2 - incomplete primary	0.04	0.01	0.01	0.00	0.00	0.00
E3 - primary	0.03	0.02	0.02	0.01	0.01	0.00
E4 - lower secondary	0.27	0.17	0.11	0.07	0.04	0.02
E5 - upper secondary	0.51	0.60	0.66	0.70	0.72	0.73
E6 - post-secondary	0.13	0.19	0.20	0.22	0.23	0.25
Mean years of schooling (in years)	10.65	12.12	13.11	13.48	13.70	13.83

Education scenarios

GET: global education trend scenario (medium assumption also used for SSP2)

CER: constant enrolment rates scenario (assumption of no future improvements)

FT: Fast track scenario (assumption of education expansion according to fastest historical experience)

Pyramids by Education, Medium Scenario

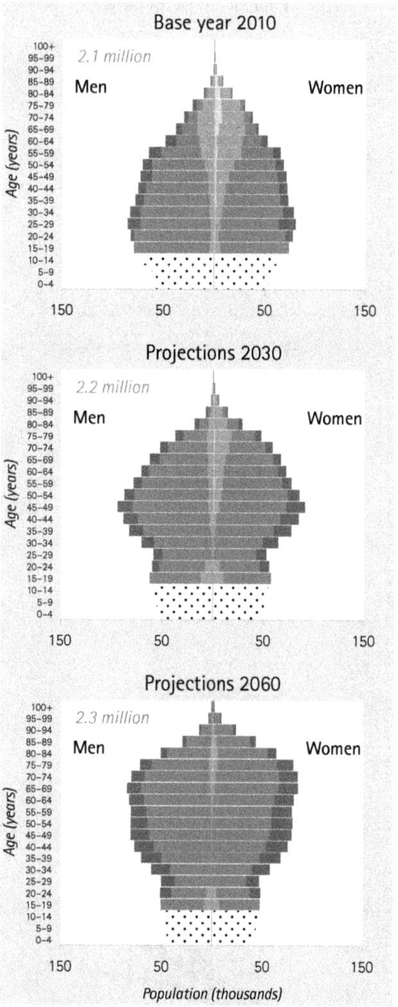

Population Size by Educational Attainment According to Three Education Scenarios: GET, CER, and FT

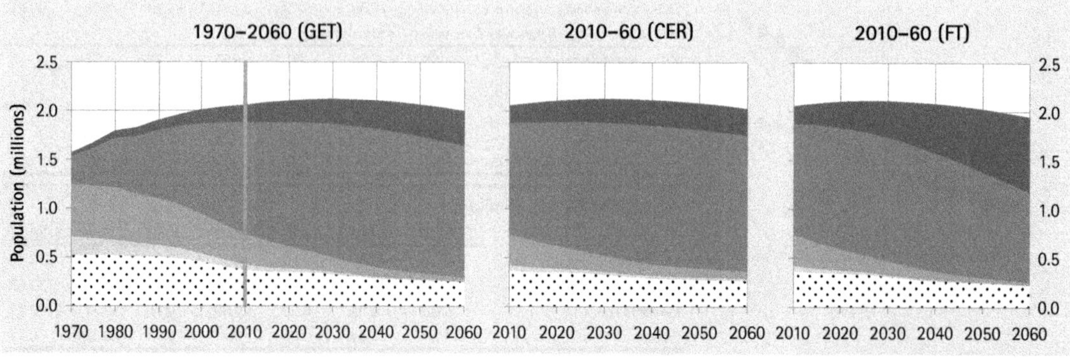

TFYR Macedonia (Continued)

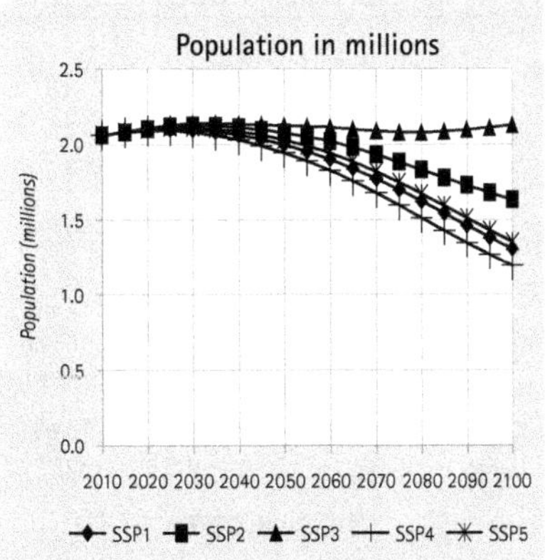

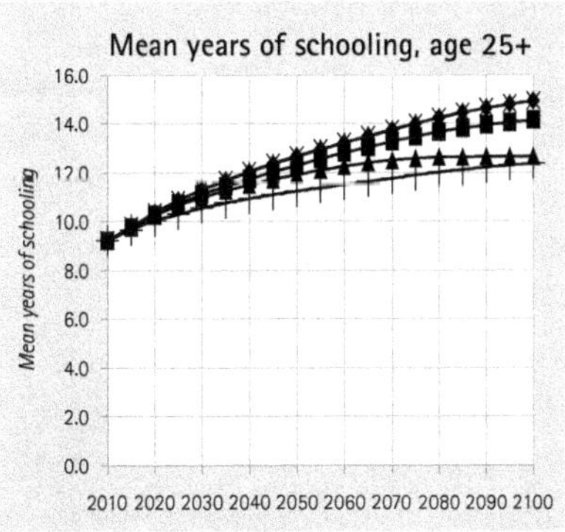

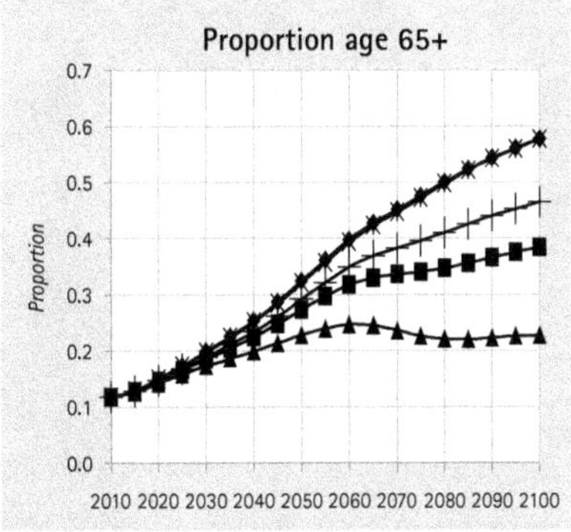

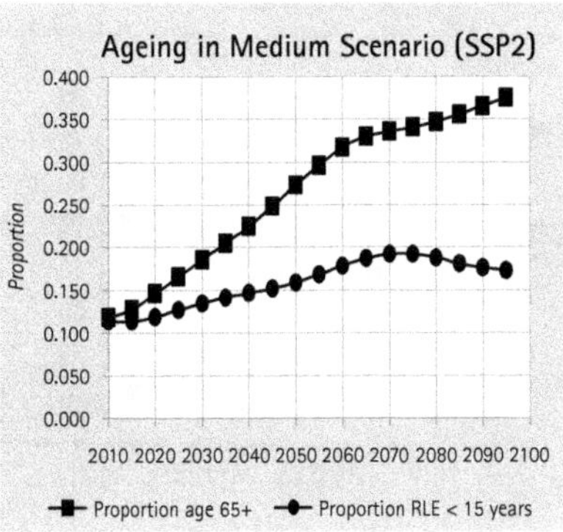

Alternative Scenarios to 2100

Projection Results by Scenario (SSP1–5)

	2010	2020	2030	2040	2050	2075	2100
Population (in millions)							
SSP1 - Rapid development	2.06	2.09	2.10	2.06	2.00	1.70	1.30
SSP2 - Medium	2.06	2.10	2.12	2.11	2.08	1.88	1.63
SSP3 - Stalled development	2.06	2.11	2.14	2.13	2.13	2.08	2.13
SSP4 - Inequality	2.06	2.09	2.08	2.03	1.94	1.59	1.19
SSP5 - Conventional development	2.06	2.10	2.11	2.08	2.03	1.75	1.35
Proportion age 65+							
SSP1 - Rapid development	0.12	0.15	0.20	0.25	0.32	0.48	0.58
SSP2 - Medium	0.12	0.15	0.19	0.22	0.27	0.34	0.38
SSP3 - Stalled development	0.12	0.14	0.17	0.20	0.23	0.23	0.23
SSP4 - Inequality	0.12	0.15	0.19	0.23	0.29	0.40	0.46
SSP5 - Conventional development	0.12	0.15	0.20	0.25	0.32	0.47	0.58
Proportion below age 20							
SSP1 - Rapid development	0.25	0.21	0.18	0.15	0.13	0.10	0.08
SSP2 - Medium	0.25	0.22	0.20	0.19	0.18	0.16	0.16
SSP3 - Stalled development	0.25	0.22	0.23	0.22	0.22	0.24	0.25
SSP4 - Inequality	0.25	0.21	0.19	0.16	0.14	0.12	0.11
SSP5 - Conventional development	0.25	0.21	0.18	0.15	0.13	0.10	0.08
Proportion of Women age 20–39 with at least secondary education							
SSP1 - Rapid development	0.91	0.96	0.98	0.99	1.00	1.00	1.00
SSP2 - Medium	0.91	0.95	0.98	0.99	0.99	1.00	1.00
SSP3 - Stalled development	0.91	0.93	0.94	0.94	0.94	0.94	0.94
SSP4 - Inequality	0.91	0.88	0.85	0.85	0.85	0.85	0.85
SSP5 - Conventional development	0.91	0.96	0.98	0.99	1.00	1.00	1.00
Mean years of schooling, age 25+							
SSP1 - Rapid development	9.22	10.37	11.29	12.03	12.65	13.99	14.91
SSP2 - Medium	9.22	10.29	11.11	11.74	12.30	13.47	14.14
SSP3 - Stalled development	9.22	10.25	10.98	11.50	11.92	12.57	12.64
SSP4 - Inequality	9.22	10.04	10.55	10.94	11.24	11.89	12.36
SSP5 - Conventional development	9.22	10.37	11.30	12.04	12.67	14.01	14.91

Demographic Assumptions Underlying SSPs

	2010–15	2020–25	2030–35	2040–45	2050–55	2075–80	2095–2100
Total fertility rate							
SSP1 - Rapid development	1.40	1.28	1.22	1.19	1.17	1.19	1.21
SSP2 - Medium	1.46	1.54	1.60	1.60	1.60	1.63	1.65
SSP3 - Stalled development	1.55	1.79	1.98	2.06	2.10	2.16	2.21
SSP4 - Inequality	1.41	1.34	1.30	1.27	1.25	1.27	1.29
SSP5 - Conventional development	1.40	1.28	1.22	1.19	1.17	1.19	1.21
Life expectancy at birth for females (in years)							
SSP1 - Rapid development	78.92	81.66	84.75	88.00	91.05	98.30	104.18
SSP2 - Medium	77.19	79.39	81.79	84.21	86.31	91.20	95.00
SSP3 - Stalled development	78.05	78.93	80.06	81.30	82.37	84.38	86.05
SSP4 - Inequality	78.46	80.25	82.39	84.63	86.59	91.01	94.64
SSP5 - Conventional development	78.92	81.66	84.75	88.00	91.05	98.30	104.18
Migration – net flow over five years (in thousands)							
SSP1 - Rapid development	5	8	10	10	9	3	0
SSP2 - Medium	5	8	10	11	11	5	0
SSP3 - Stalled development	4	4	5	6	8	5	0
SSP4 - Inequality	5	8	10	10	11	4	0
SSP5 - Conventional development	6	12	14	14	13	4	0

Ageing Indicators, Medium Scenario (SSP2)

	2010	2020	2030	2040	2050	2075	2095
Median age	35.86	39.39	43.11	46.67	49.15	52.36	54.44
Propspective median age	35.86	37.57	39.22	40.64	41.20	39.93	38.32
Proportion age 65+	0.12	0.15	0.19	0.22	0.27	0.34	0.38
Proportion RLE < 15 years	0.11	0.12	0.13	0.15	0.16	0.19	0.17

Thailand*

Detailed Human Capital Projections to 2060

Demographic indicators, Medium Scenario (SSP2)	2010	2020	2030	2040	2050	2060
Population (in millions)	69.12	72.72	74.76	74.76	72.82	69.88
Proportion age 65+	0.09	0.12	0.17	0.22	0.24	0.27
Proportion below age 20	0.28	0.24	0.21	0.19	0.18	0.17
	2005–10	2015–20	2025–30	2035–40	2045–50	2055–60
Total Fertility Rate	1.63	1.58	1.54	1.53	1.52	1.53
Life expectancy at birth (in years)						
Men	70.16	71.62	73.29	74.70	76.05	77.70
Women	77.06	78.10	79.50	80.69	81.89	83.39
Five-year immigration flow (in '000)	518.08	507.76	527.57	539.52	539.50	531.67
Five-year emigration flow (in '000)	25.93	18.74	16.98	15.23	13.83	12.54

Human Capital indicators, Medium Scenario (SSP2)	2010	2020	2030	2040	2050	2060
Population age 25+: highest educational attainment						
E1 - no education	0.06	0.04	0.02	0.01	0.01	0.00
E2 - incomplete primary	0.37	0.26	0.17	0.10	0.04	0.01
E3 - primary	0.20	0.22	0.23	0.22	0.20	0.16
E4 - lower secondary	0.13	0.15	0.16	0.16	0.15	0.13
E5 - upper secondary	0.11	0.15	0.20	0.24	0.28	0.31
E6 - post-secondary	0.13	0.17	0.22	0.27	0.32	0.39
Mean years of schooling (in years)	7.51	8.59	9.59	10.51	11.39	12.16
Gender gap (population age 25+): highest educational attainment (ratio male/female)						
E1 - no education	0.53	0.54	0.54	0.54	0.54	0.54
E2 - incomplete primary	0.88	0.81	0.72	0.62	0.52	0.51
E3 - primary	1.35	1.37	1.36	1.33	1.27	1.20
E4 - lower secondary	0.95	0.92	0.90	0.87	0.83	0.79
E5 - upper secondary	1.33	1.25	1.22	1.19	1.16	1.11
E6 - post-secondary	0.96	0.91	0.89	0.90	0.91	0.94
Mean years of schooling (male minus female)	0.52	0.34	0.21	0.09	−0.02	−0.07
Women age 20–39: highest educational attainment						
E1 - no education	0.02	0.01	0.00	0.00	0.00	0.00
E2 - incomplete primary	0.03	0.01	0.00	0.00	0.00	0.00
E3 - primary	0.24	0.20	0.15	0.11	0.08	0.06
E4 - lower secondary	0.28	0.21	0.15	0.10	0.06	0.04
E5 - upper secondary	0.26	0.33	0.38	0.41	0.43	0.43
E6 - post-secondary	0.18	0.25	0.32	0.38	0.43	0.47
Mean years of schooling (in years)	10.13	11.19	11.98	12.59	13.07	13.42

Education scenarios

GET: global education trend scenario (medium assumption also used for SSP2)

CER: constant enrolment rates scenario (assumption of no future improvements)

FT: Fast track scenario (assumption of education expansion according to fastest historical experience)

Pyramids by Education, Medium Scenario

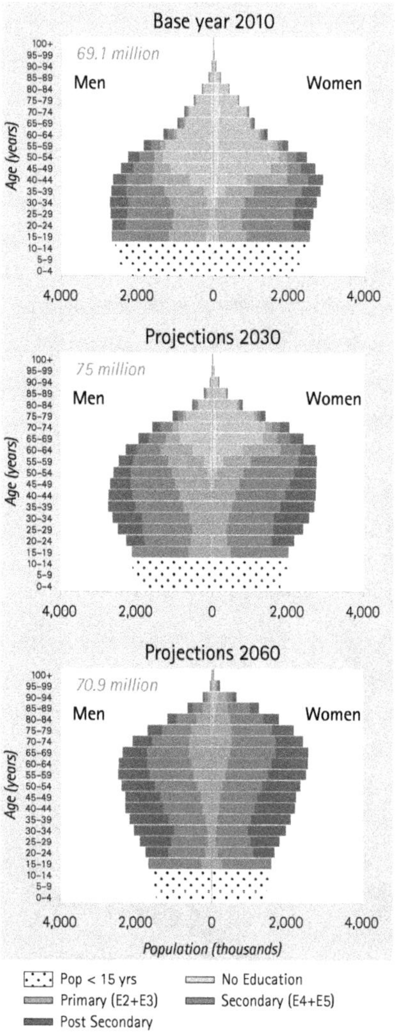

Population Size by Educational Attainment According to Three Education Scenarios: GET, CER, and FT

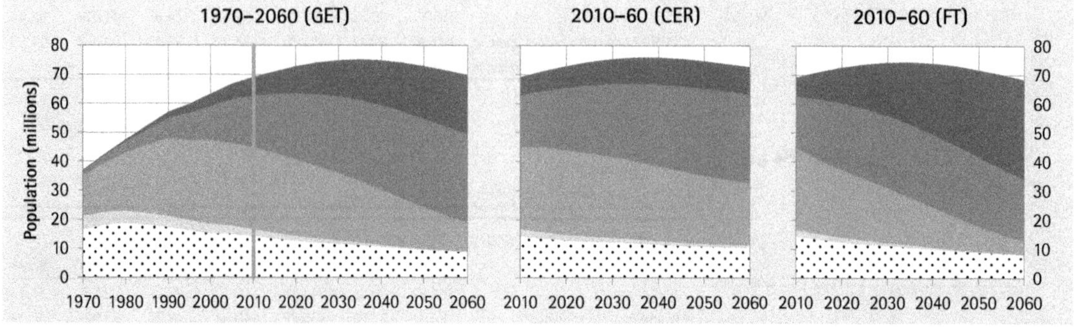

* Updated data for Thailand is provided on the WIC Data Explorer <http://www.wittgensteincentre.org/dataexplorer>. The data was adjusted to account for corrections in the education category definitions and changes over time.

Thailand (Continued)

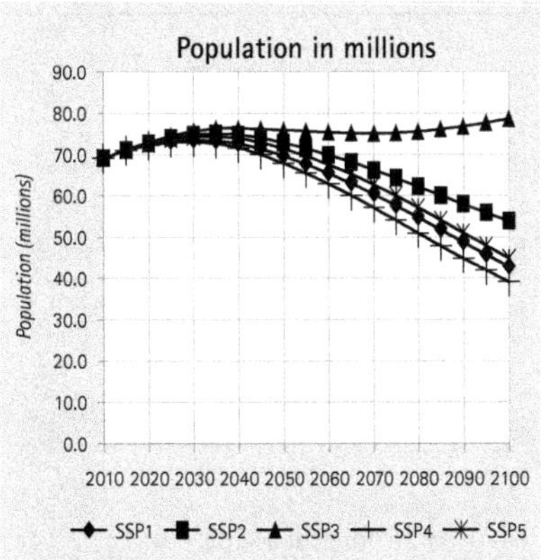

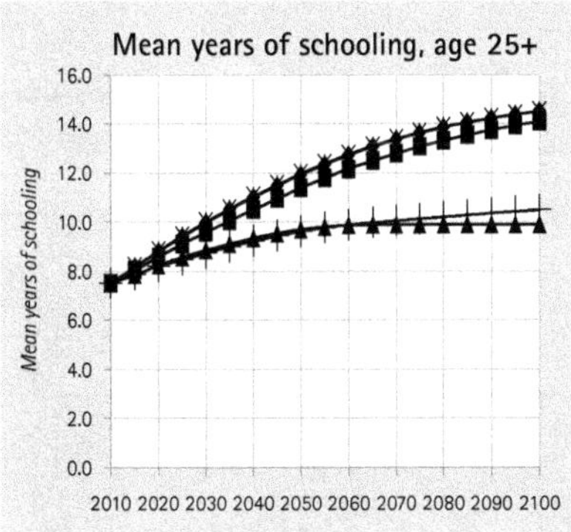

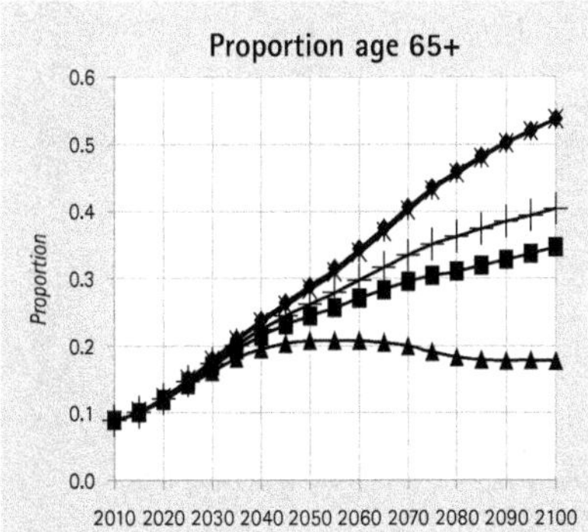

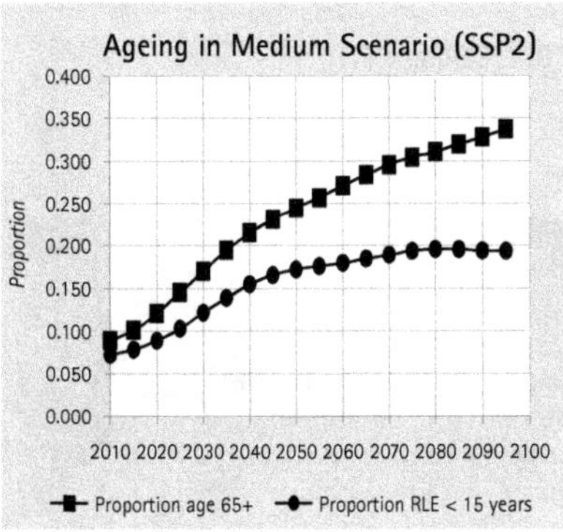

Alternative Scenarios to 2100

Projection Results by Scenario (SSP1–5)

	2010	2020	2030	2040	2050	2075	2100
Population (in millions)							
SSP1 - Rapid development	69.12	72.24	73.42	72.57	69.65	57.57	42.66
SSP2 - Medium	69.12	72.72	74.76	74.76	72.82	64.25	53.83
SSP3 - Stalled development	69.12	72.97	75.61	76.35	75.90	75.20	78.53
SSP4 - Inequality	69.12	72.14	73.01	71.57	67.86	54.02	39.01
SSP5 - Conventional development	69.12	72.50	74.21	73.89	71.42	59.97	44.78
Proportion age 65+							
SSP1 - Rapid development	0.09	0.12	0.18	0.24	0.29	0.43	0.54
SSP2 - Medium	0.09	0.12	0.17	0.22	0.24	0.30	0.35
SSP3 - Stalled development	0.09	0.12	0.16	0.20	0.21	0.19	0.18
SSP4 - Inequality	0.09	0.12	0.17	0.22	0.26	0.35	0.40
SSP5 - Conventional development	0.09	0.12	0.18	0.23	0.28	0.43	0.54
Proportion below age 20							
SSP1 - Rapid development	0.28	0.23	0.19	0.16	0.13	0.10	0.09
SSP2 - Medium	0.28	0.24	0.21	0.19	0.18	0.17	0.16
SSP3 - Stalled development	0.28	0.25	0.24	0.24	0.24	0.27	0.28
SSP4 - Inequality	0.28	0.23	0.19	0.17	0.15	0.13	0.12
SSP5 - Conventional development	0.28	0.23	0.19	0.16	0.13	0.10	0.09
Proportion of Women age 20–39 with at least secondary education							
SSP1 - Rapid development	0.71	0.85	0.91	0.94	0.96	0.98	0.99
SSP2 - Medium	0.71	0.79	0.84	0.88	0.92	0.97	0.99
SSP3 - Stalled development	0.71	0.71	0.71	0.71	0.71	0.71	0.71
SSP4 - Inequality	0.71	0.67	0.64	0.64	0.64	0.64	0.64
SSP5 - Conventional development	0.71	0.85	0.91	0.94	0.96	0.98	0.99
Mean years of schooling, age 25+							
SSP1 - Rapid development	7.51	8.82	9.98	11.01	11.93	13.62	14.50
SSP2 - Medium	7.51	8.59	9.59	10.51	11.39	13.06	14.08
SSP3 - Stalled development	7.51	8.24	8.86	9.35	9.70	9.90	9.89
SSP4 - Inequality	7.51	8.21	8.75	9.24	9.63	10.13	10.49
SSP5 - Conventional development	7.51	8.82	10.00	11.04	11.96	13.63	14.50

Demographic Assumptions Underlying SSPs

	2010–15	2020–25	2030–35	2040–45	2050–55	2075–80	2095–2100
Total fertility rate							
SSP1 - Rapid development	1.48	1.29	1.17	1.13	1.12	1.16	1.19
SSP2 - Medium	1.56	1.54	1.53	1.52	1.52	1.56	1.60
SSP3 - Stalled development	1.67	1.87	2.00	2.08	2.14	2.26	2.34
SSP4 - Inequality	1.50	1.35	1.26	1.23	1.22	1.28	1.32
SSP5 - Conventional development	1.48	1.29	1.17	1.13	1.12	1.16	1.19
Life expectancy at birth for females (in years)							
SSP1 - Rapid development	79.02	81.23	83.51	85.65	87.85	93.78	98.61
SSP2 - Medium	77.60	78.80	80.10	81.29	82.59	86.31	89.31
SSP3 - Stalled development	78.15	78.38	78.72	78.79	78.79	79.32	79.95
SSP4 - Inequality	78.62	79.77	81.04	82.13	83.12	86.12	88.78
SSP5 - Conventional development	79.02	81.23	83.51	85.65	87.85	93.78	98.61
Migration – net flow over five years (in thousands)							
SSP1 - Rapid development	468	492	493	456	406	117	0
SSP2 - Medium	483	504	521	526	521	202	0
SSP3 - Stalled development	389	253	280	325	377	230	0
SSP4 - Inequality	468	492	504	496	479	180	0
SSP5 - Conventional development	546	729	717	649	565	156	0

Ageing Indicators, Medium Scenario (SSP2)

	2010	2020	2030	2040	2050	2075	2095
Median age	34.16	37.92	41.26	44.36	46.77	50.11	52.35
Propspective median age	34.16	36.82	38.96	41.20	42.66	43.01	42.58
Proportion age 65+	0.09	0.12	0.17	0.22	0.24	0.30	0.34
Proportion RLE < 15 years	0.07	0.09	0.12	0.15	0.17	0.19	0.19

Timor-Leste

Detailed Human Capital Projections to 2060

Demographic indicators, Medium Scenario (SSP2)	2010	2020	2030	2040	2050	2060
Population (in millions)	1.12	1.38	1.65	1.88	2.06	2.17
Proportion age 65+	0.03	0.03	0.04	0.04	0.05	0.06
Proportion below age 20	0.58	0.55	0.53	0.49	0.43	0.39
	2005–10	2015–20	2025–30	2035–40	2045–50	2055–60
Total Fertility Rate	6.53	5.62	4.66	3.61	2.88	2.46
Life expectancy at birth (in years)						
Men	59.95	61.88	63.31	64.78	66.60	68.47
Women	61.68	64.28	66.48	68.48	70.60	72.61
Five-year immigration flow (in '000)	0.00	0.00	0.00	0.00	0.00	0.00
Five-year emigration flow (in '000)	49.71	51.68	63.01	74.23	83.82	87.82

Human Capital indicators, Medium Scenario (SSP2)	2010	2020	2030	2040	2050	2060
Population age 25+: highest educational attainment						
E1 - no education	0.48	0.30	0.17	0.08	0.04	0.02
E2 - incomplete primary	0.14	0.13	0.09	0.06	0.03	0.02
E3 - primary	0.11	0.12	0.12	0.10	0.08	0.06
E4 - lower secondary	0.07	0.12	0.14	0.14	0.12	0.10
E5 - upper secondary	0.16	0.26	0.38	0.48	0.55	0.60
E6 - post-secondary	0.04	0.07	0.10	0.14	0.17	0.21
Mean years of schooling (in years)	4.36	6.50	8.52	10.05	11.14	11.88
Gender gap (population age 25+): highest educational attainment (ratio male/female)						
E1 - no education	0.69	0.67	0.64	0.64	0.70	0.77
E2 - incomplete primary	1.53	1.24	1.13	1.04	0.97	0.93
E3 - primary	1.04	0.91	0.83	0.79	0.78	0.77
E4 - lower secondary	1.00	0.88	0.84	0.83	0.82	0.81
E5 - upper secondary	1.69	1.35	1.18	1.08	1.04	1.02
E6 - post-secondary	2.37	1.88	1.62	1.41	1.26	1.14
Mean years of schooling (male minus female)	1.68	1.45	1.15	0.80	0.50	0.31
Women age 20–39: highest educational attainment						
E1 - no education	0.25	0.09	0.03	0.01	0.00	0.00
E2 - incomplete primary	0.14	0.11	0.06	0.03	0.02	0.01
E3 - primary	0.17	0.15	0.12	0.08	0.05	0.03
E4 - lower secondary	0.17	0.22	0.21	0.18	0.15	0.12
E5 - upper secondary	0.24	0.37	0.49	0.58	0.62	0.64
E6 - post-secondary	0.03	0.06	0.09	0.12	0.16	0.20
Mean years of schooling (in years)	6.53	8.74	10.20	11.12	11.75	12.21

Education scenarios

GET: global education trend scenario (medium assumption also used for SSP2)

CER: constant enrolment rates scenario (assumption of no future improvements)

FT: Fast track scenario (assumption of education expansion according to fastest historical experience)

Pyramids by Education, Medium Scenario

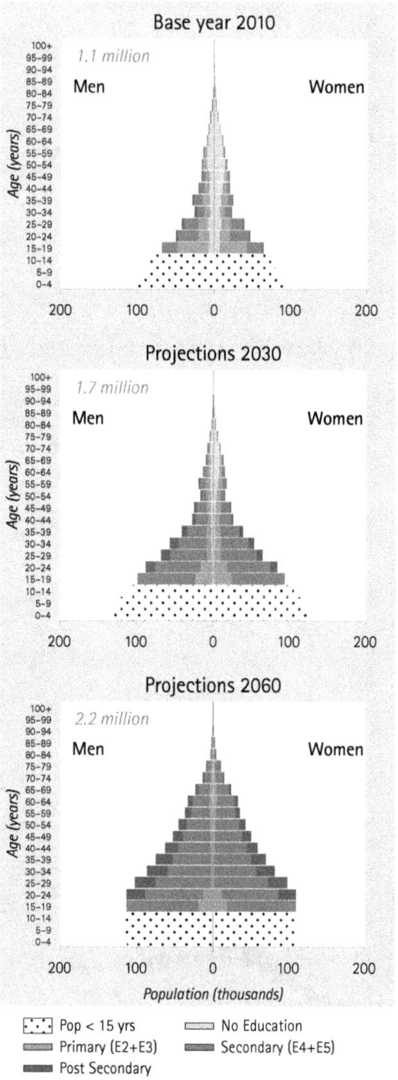

Population Size by Educational Attainment According to Three Education Scenarios: GET, CER, and FT

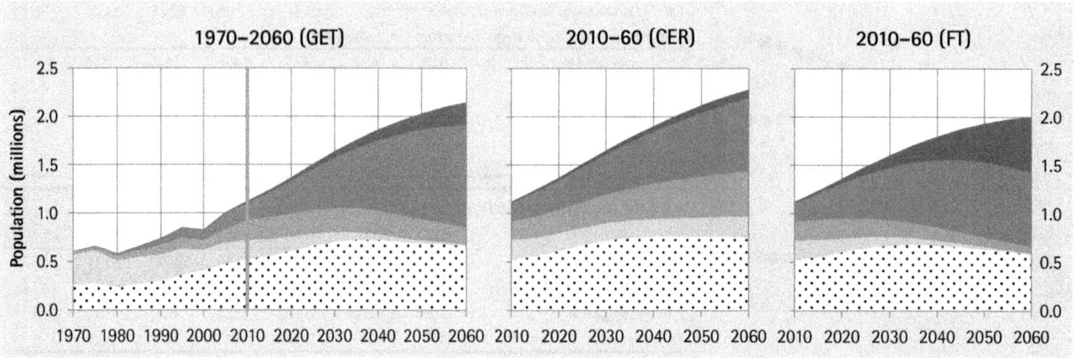

Timor-Leste (Continued)

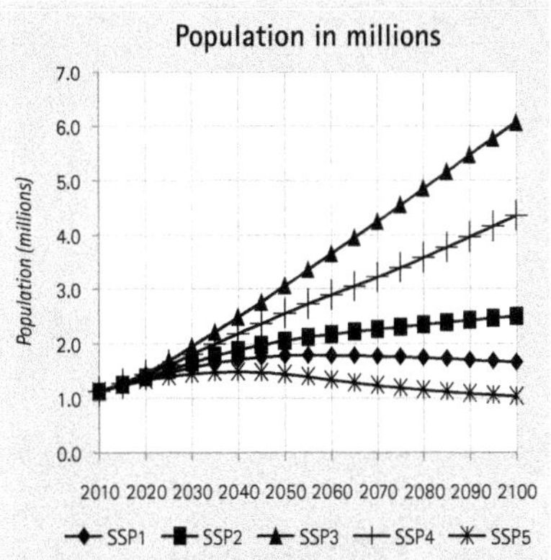

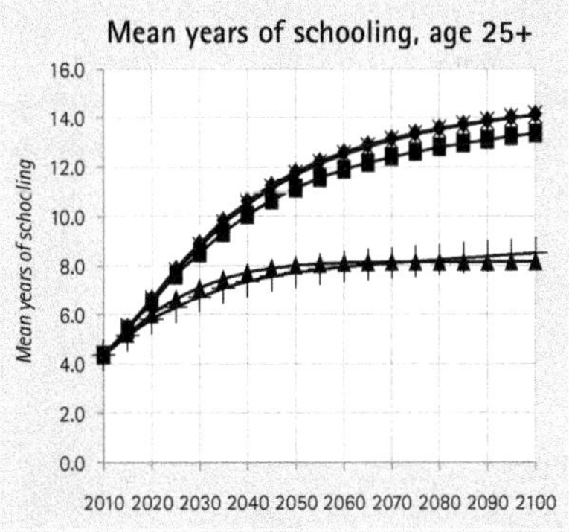

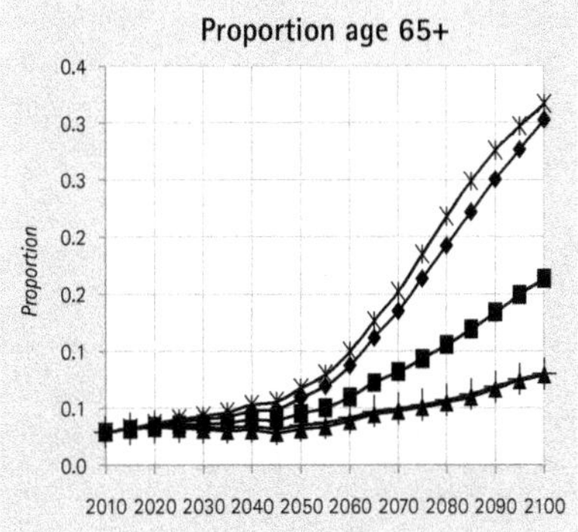

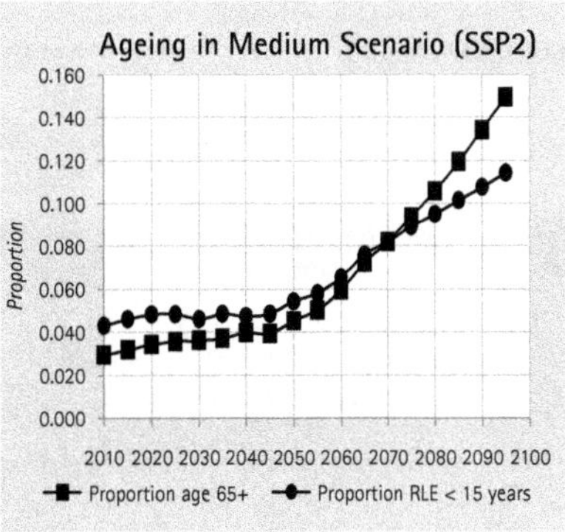

Alternative Scenarios to 2100

Projection Results by Scenario (SSP1-5)

	2010	2020	2030	2040	2050	2075	2100
Population (in millions)							
SSP1 - Rapid development	1.12	1.36	1.56	1.71	1.78	1.76	1.66
SSP2 - Medium	1.12	1.38	1.65	1.88	2.06	2.31	2.50
SSP3 - Stalled development	1.12	1.46	1.95	2.48	3.06	4.55	6.07
SSP4 - Inequality	1.12	1.43	1.80	2.18	2.55	3.40	4.36
SSP5 - Conventional development.	1.12	1.33	1.44	1.48	1.44	1.19	1.03
Proportion age 65+							
SSP1 - Rapid development	0.03	0.04	0.04	0.05	0.06	0.16	0.30
SSP2 - Medium	0.03	0.03	0.04	0.04	0.05	0.09	0.16
SSP3 - Stalled development	0.03	0.03	0.03	0.03	0.03	0.05	0.08
SSP4 - Inequality	0.03	0.03	0.03	0.03	0.04	0.05	0.08
SSP5 - Conventional development.	0.03	0.04	0.04	0.05	0.07	0.18	0.32
Proportion below age 20							
SSP1 - Rapid development	0.58	0.54	0.49	0.43	0.37	0.23	0.16
SSP2 - Medium	0.58	0.55	0.53	0.49	0.43	0.32	0.25
SSP3 - Stalled development	0.58	0.56	0.56	0.54	0.49	0.41	0.35
SSP4 - Inequality	0.58	0.56	0.57	0.54	0.50	0.41	0.34
SSP5 - Conventional development.	0.58	0.55	0.50	0.44	0.38	0.23	0.15
Proportion of Women age 20–39 with at least secondary education							
SSP1 - Rapid development	0.44	0.69	0.85	0.93	0.96	0.99	1.00
SSP2 - Medium	0.44	0.65	0.79	0.88	0.93	0.99	1.00
SSP3 - Stalled development	0.44	0.55	0.56	0.56	0.56	0.56	0.56
SSP4 - Inequality	0.44	0.51	0.50	0.50	0.50	0.50	0.50
SSP5 - Conventional development.	0.44	0.69	0.85	0.93	0.96	0.99	1.00
Mean years of schooling, age 25+							
SSP1 - Rapid development	4.36	6.66	8.91	10.61	11.79	13.38	14.12
SSP2 - Medium	4.36	6.50	8.52	10.05	11.14	12.61	13.37
SSP3 - Stalled development	4.36	6.01	7.11	7.72	8.01	8.15	8.17
SSP4 - Inequality	4.36	5.81	6.73	7.36	7.73	8.17	8.50
SSP5 - Conventional development.	4.36	6.60	8.76	10.47	11.67	13.30	14.10

Demographic Assumptions Underlying SSPs

	2010–15	2020–25	2030–35	2040–45	2050–55	2075–80	2095–2100
Total fertility rate							
SSP1 - Rapid development	5.83	4.25	3.12	2.37	1.92	1.45	1.30
SSP2 - Medium	6.11	5.13	4.11	3.17	2.65	1.99	1.77
SSP3 - Stalled development	6.49	6.09	5.37	4.47	3.78	2.90	2.61
SSP4 - Inequality	6.49	6.07	5.32	4.39	3.69	2.81	2.51
SSP5 - Conventional development.	5.83	4.25	3.12	2.37	1.92	1.45	1.30
Life expectancy at birth for females (in years)							
SSP1 - Rapid development	67.36	69.36	71.96	74.49	77.20	84.36	90.06
SSP2 - Medium	63.11	65.41	67.52	69.58	71.61	76.59	80.59
SSP3 - Stalled development	67.29	67.38	68.16	68.63	69.12	70.52	71.64
SSP4 - Inequality	67.29	67.35	68.10	68.56	69.04	70.48	71.65
SSP5 - Conventional development.	67.36	69.36	71.96	74.49	77.20	84.36	90.06
Migration – net flow over five years (in thousands)							
SSP1 - Rapid development	−49	−57	−67	−74	−76	−30	0
SSP2 - Medium	−53	−60	−72	−83	−90	−41	0
SSP3 - Stalled development	−41	−29	−36	−44	−52	−31	0
SSP4 - Inequality	−49	−57	−69	−84	−96	−51	0
SSP5 - Conventional development.	−57	−84	−97	−106	−105	−40	0

Ageing Indicators, Medium Scenario (SSP2)

	2010	2020	2030	2040	2050	2075	2095
Median age	16.46	17.51	18.44	20.41	23.24	31.19	37.46
Propspective median age	16.46	16.48	16.30	17.31	19.24	24.14	27.43
Proportion age 65+	0.03	0.03	0.04	0.04	0.05	0.09	0.15
Proportion RLE < 15 years	0.04	0.05	0.05	0.05	0.05	0.09	0.11

Tonga

Detailed Human Capital Projections to 2060

Demographic indicators, Medium Scenario (SSP2)	2010	2020	2030	2040	2050	2060
Population (in millions)	0.10	0.11	0.11	0.11	0.10	0.10
Proportion age 65+	0.06	0.06	0.09	0.12	0.16	0.19
Proportion below age 20	0.48	0.44	0.37	0.32	0.29	0.25
	2005–10	2015–20	2025–30	2035–40	2045–50	2055–60
Total Fertility Rate	4.03	3.02	2.53	2.19	2.02	1.91
Life expectancy at birth (in years)						
Men	69.04	71.56	73.87	76.06	78.33	80.49
Women	74.70	77.19	79.39	81.39	83.49	85.52
Five-year immigration flow (in '000)	0.00	0.00	0.00	0.00	0.00	0.00
Five-year emigration flow (in '000)	8.17	5.68	5.98	5.50	4.86	4.36

Human Capital indicators, Medium Scenario (SSP2)	2010	2020	2030	2040	2050	2060
Population age 25+: highest educational attainment						
E1 - no education	0.01	0.01	0.01	0.00	0.00	0.00
E2 - incomplete primary	0.01	0.01	0.00	0.00	0.00	0.00
E3 - primary	0.23	0.17	0.12	0.09	0.07	0.05
E4 - lower secondary	0.49	0.50	0.48	0.45	0.41	0.36
E5 - upper secondary	0.13	0.17	0.21	0.25	0.29	0.32
E6 - post-secondary	0.13	0.16	0.18	0.21	0.24	0.27
Mean years of schooling (in years)	10.14	10.61	11.08	11.47	11.79	12.09
Gender gap (population age 25+): highest educational attainment (ratio male/female)						
E1 - no education	0.85	0.81	0.75	0.72	0.69	0.69
E2 - incomplete primary	0.97	0.96	0.92	0.86	0.82	0.82
E3 - primary	0.92	0.91	0.93	0.99	1.07	1.13
E4 - lower secondary	1.01	1.02	1.03	1.02	1.00	0.98
E5 - upper secondary	0.97	0.98	1.00	1.01	1.02	1.02
E6 - post-secondary	1.19	1.08	1.00	0.96	0.96	0.97
Mean years of schooling (male minus female)	0.21	0.13	0.04	−0.03	−0.05	−0.04
Women age 20–39: highest educational attainment						
E1 - no education	0.01	0.00	0.00	0.00	0.00	0.00
E2 - incomplete primary	0.00	0.00	0.00	0.00	0.00	0.00
E3 - primary	0.07	0.06	0.05	0.04	0.04	0.03
E4 - lower secondary	0.55	0.47	0.39	0.32	0.26	0.22
E5 - upper secondary	0.21	0.27	0.32	0.35	0.39	0.41
E6 - post-secondary	0.16	0.20	0.24	0.28	0.31	0.34
Mean years of schooling (in years)	11.10	11.47	11.92	12.25	12.54	12.79

Education scenarios

GET : global education trend scenario (medium assumption also used for SSP2)

CER: constant enrolment rates scenario (assumption of no future improvements)

FT: Fast track scenario (assumption of education expansion according to fastest historical experience)

Pyramids by Education, Medium Scenario

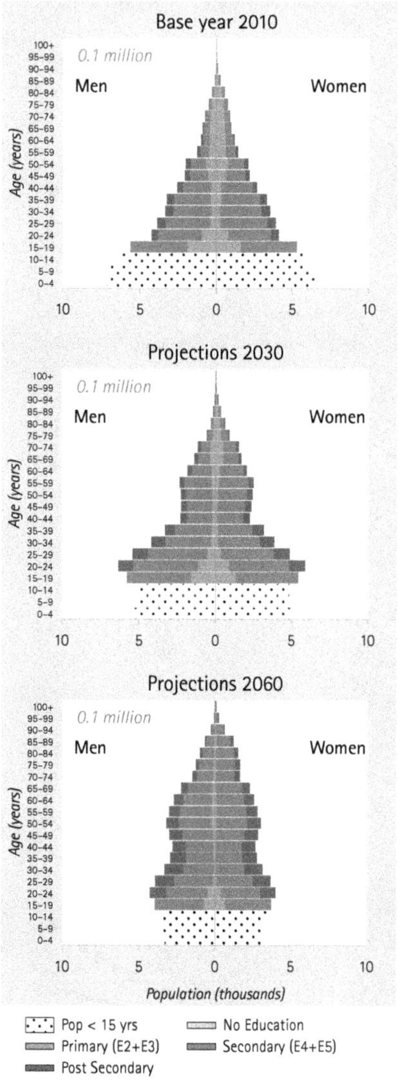

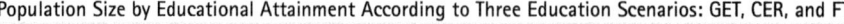

Population Size by Educational Attainment According to Three Education Scenarios: GET, CER, and FT

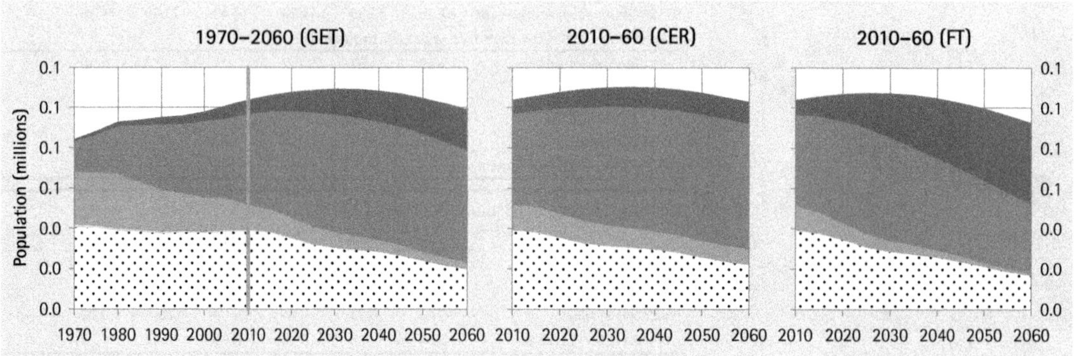

Tonga (Continued)

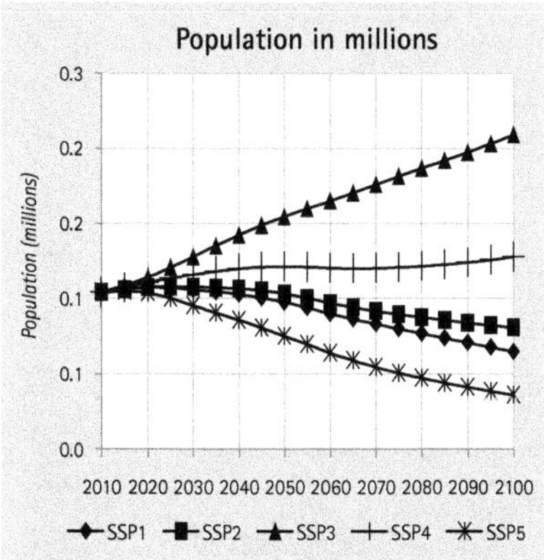

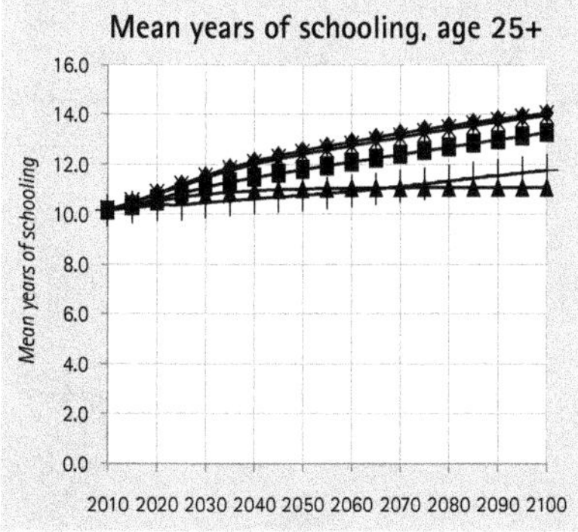

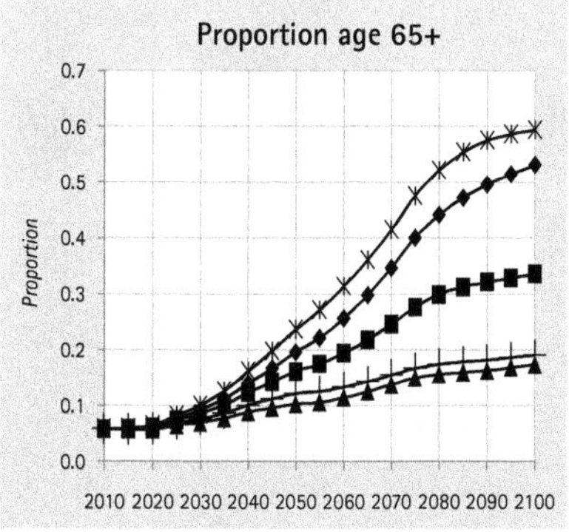

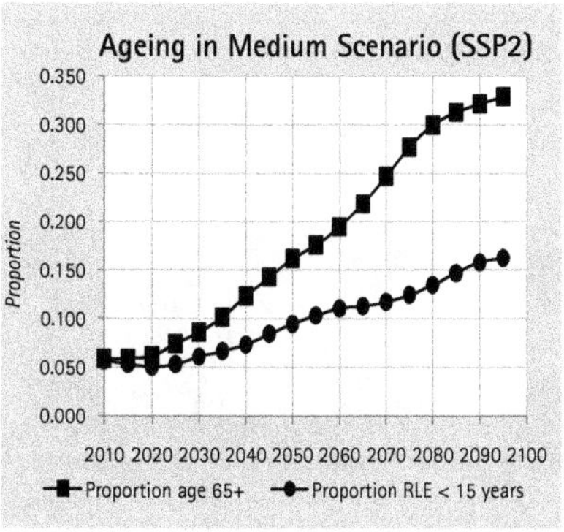

Alternative Scenarios to 2100

Projection Results by Scenario (SSP1–5)

	2010	2020	2030	2040	2050	2075	2100
Population (in millions)							
SSP1 - Rapid development	0.10	0.11	0.11	0.10	0.10	0.08	0.06
SSP2 - Medium	0.10	0.11	0.11	0.11	0.10	0.09	0.08
SSP3 - Stalled development	0.10	0.11	0.13	0.14	0.15	0.18	0.21
SSP4 - Inequality	0.10	0.11	0.12	0.12	0.12	0.12	0.13
SSP5 - Conventional development.	0.10	0.10	0.10	0.09	0.08	0.05	0.04
Proportion age 65+							
SSP1 - Rapid development	0.06	0.06	0.09	0.14	0.20	0.40	0.53
SSP2 - Medium	0.06	0.06	0.09	0.12	0.16	0.28	0.34
SSP3 - Stalled development	0.06	0.06	0.07	0.09	0.10	0.15	0.17
SSP4 - Inequality	0.06	0.06	0.08	0.10	0.12	0.17	0.19
SSP5 - Conventional development.	0.06	0.07	0.10	0.16	0.24	0.48	0.59
Proportion below age 20							
SSP1 - Rapid development	0.48	0.43	0.33	0.27	0.23	0.13	0.09
SSP2 - Medium	0.48	0.44	0.37	0.32	0.29	0.21	0.17
SSP3 - Stalled development	0.48	0.45	0.40	0.38	0.35	0.31	0.28
SSP4 - Inequality	0.48	0.45	0.40	0.38	0.35	0.29	0.26
SSP5 - Conventional development.	0.48	0.43	0.33	0.27	0.22	0.11	0.08
Proportion of Women age 20–39 with at least secondary education							
SSP1 - Rapid development	0.92	0.96	0.97	0.98	0.98	0.99	1.00
SSP2 - Medium	0.92	0.94	0.95	0.96	0.96	0.98	0.99
SSP3 - Stalled development	0.92	0.94	0.94	0.94	0.94	0.94	0.94
SSP4 - Inequality	0.92	0.88	0.84	0.84	0.84	0.84	0.84
SSP5 - Conventional development.	0.92	0.96	0.97	0.98	0.98	0.99	1.00
Mean years of schooling, age 25+							
SSP1 - Rapid development	10.14	10.83	11.53	12.11	12.54	13.39	14.04
SSP2 - Medium	10.14	10.61	11.08	11.47	11.79	12.54	13.27
SSP3 - Stalled development	10.14	10.52	10.79	10.94	11.02	11.07	11.07
SSP4 - Inequality	10.14	10.35	10.46	10.62	10.76	11.21	11.76
SSP5 - Conventional development.	10.14	10.80	11.45	12.00	12.40	13.24	13.95

Demographic Assumptions Underlying SSPs

	2010–15	2020–25	2030–35	2040–45	2050–55	2075–80	2095–2100
Total fertility rate							
SSP1 - Rapid development	3.20	2.28	1.75	1.51	1.39	1.24	1.17
SSP2 - Medium	3.47	2.74	2.35	2.09	1.94	1.71	1.59
SSP3 - Stalled development	3.58	3.26	2.97	2.76	2.63	2.42	2.30
SSP4 - Inequality	3.59	3.30	2.96	2.68	2.52	2.23	2.08
SSP5 - Conventional development.	3.20	2.28	1.75	1.51	1.39	1.24	1.17
Life expectancy at birth for females (in years)							
SSP1 - Rapid development	78.03	80.92	83.79	86.66	89.49	96.85	102.83
SSP2 - Medium	75.99	78.29	80.39	82.49	84.48	89.50	93.50
SSP3 - Stalled development	77.21	78.21	79.17	80.08	80.96	83.08	84.78
SSP4 - Inequality	77.21	78.20	79.14	80.02	80.87	83.01	84.82
SSP5 - Conventional development.	78.03	80.92	83.79	86.66	89.49	96.85	102.83
Migration – net flow over five years (in thousands)							
SSP1 - Rapid development	−7	−6	−6	−5	−4	−1	0
SSP2 - Medium	−7	−6	−6	−5	−5	−1	0
SSP3 - Stalled development	−6	−3	−3	−3	−3	−1	0
SSP4 - Inequality	−7	−6	−6	−6	−5	−2	0
SSP5 - Conventional development.	−8	−9	−8	−6	−5	−1	0

Ageing Indicators, Medium Scenario (SSP2)

	2010	2020	2030	2040	2050	2075	2095
Median age	21.16	23.00	27.00	31.70	36.55	45.94	50.38
Propspective median age	21.16	20.97	23.07	25.91	28.97	33.81	34.52
Proportion age 65+	0.06	0.06	0.09	0.12	0.16	0.28	0.33
Proportion RLE < 15 years	0.06	0.05	0.06	0.07	0.09	0.12	0.16

Trinidad and Tobago

Detailed Human Capital Projections to 2060

Demographic indicators, Medium Scenario (SSP2)	2010	2020	2030	2040	2050	2060
Population (in millions)	1.34	1.38	1.38	1.35	1.28	1.19
Proportion age 65+	0.07	0.10	0.16	0.20	0.27	0.33
Proportion below age 20	0.28	0.25	0.22	0.19	0.17	0.16
	2005–10	2015–20	2025–30	2035–40	2045–50	2055–60
Total Fertility Rate	1.64	1.53	1.47	1.45	1.42	1.45
Life expectancy at birth (in years)						
Men	65.80	69.48	72.15	74.63	76.95	79.08
Women	72.90	76.30	78.80	80.89	82.99	84.98
Five-year immigration flow (in '000)	1.05	1.02	1.06	1.09	1.08	1.07
Five-year emigration flow (in '000)	20.78	13.84	12.04	10.59	9.00	7.69

Human Capital indicators, Medium Scenario (SSP2)	2010	2020	2030	2040	2050	2060
Population age 25+: highest educational attainment						
E1 - no education	0.02	0.01	0.01	0.01	0.00	0.00
E2 - incomplete primary	0.07	0.04	0.03	0.01	0.01	0.00
E3 - primary	0.27	0.22	0.18	0.15	0.12	0.09
E4 - lower secondary	0.40	0.42	0.42	0.40	0.38	0.34
E5 - upper secondary	0.19	0.24	0.29	0.34	0.40	0.45
E6 - post-secondary	0.06	0.07	0.08	0.09	0.10	0.11
Mean years of schooling (in years)	9.60	10.11	10.48	10.83	11.15	11.43
Gender gap (population age 25+): highest educational attainment (ratio male/female)						
E1 - no education	0.73	0.83	0.91	0.95	0.96	0.96
E2 - incomplete primary	0.95	0.94	0.93	0.90	0.89	0.94
E3 - primary	0.99	0.99	0.99	1.00	1.02	1.04
E4 - lower secondary	1.09	1.09	1.09	1.08	1.06	1.04
E5 - upper secondary	0.90	0.94	0.96	0.99	1.00	1.01
E6 - post-secondary	0.94	0.83	0.78	0.76	0.78	0.83
Mean years of schooling (male minus female)	0.04	−0.04	−0.09	−0.12	−0.12	−0.10
Women age 20–39: highest educational attainment						
E1 - no education	0.01	0.00	0.00	0.00	0.00	0.00
E2 - incomplete primary	0.01	0.00	0.00	0.00	0.00	0.00
E3 - primary	0.12	0.11	0.09	0.07	0.06	0.05
E4 - lower secondary	0.45	0.40	0.33	0.27	0.22	0.18
E5 - upper secondary	0.33	0.39	0.46	0.52	0.57	0.61
E6 - post-secondary	0.08	0.10	0.12	0.13	0.15	0.17
Mean years of schooling (in years)	10.86	11.17	11.53	11.79	12.01	12.21

Education scenarios

GET: global education trend scenario (medium assumption also used for SSP2)

CER: constant enrolment rates scenario (assumption of no future improvements)

FT: Fast track scenario (assumption of education expansion according to fastest historical experience)

Pyramids by Education, Medium Scenario

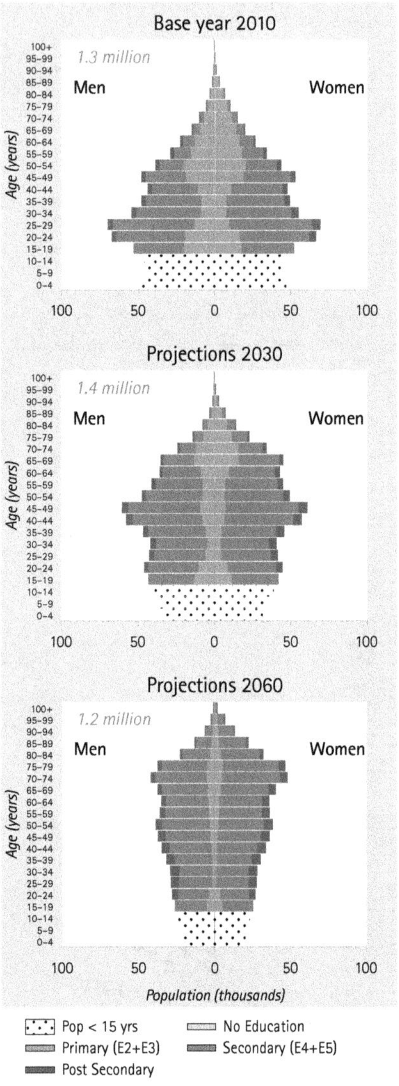

Population Size by Educational Attainment According to Three Education Scenarios: GET, CER, and FT

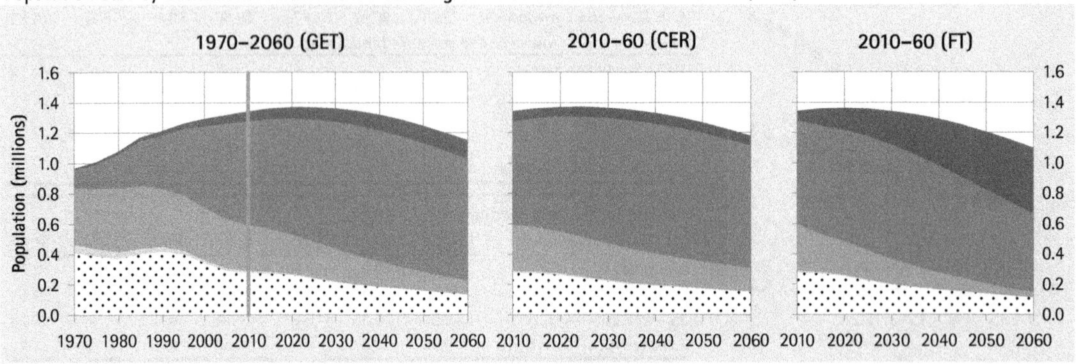

Trinidad and Tobago (Continued)

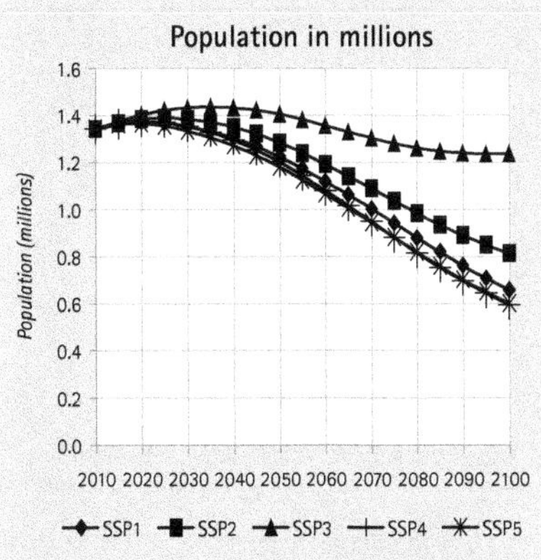

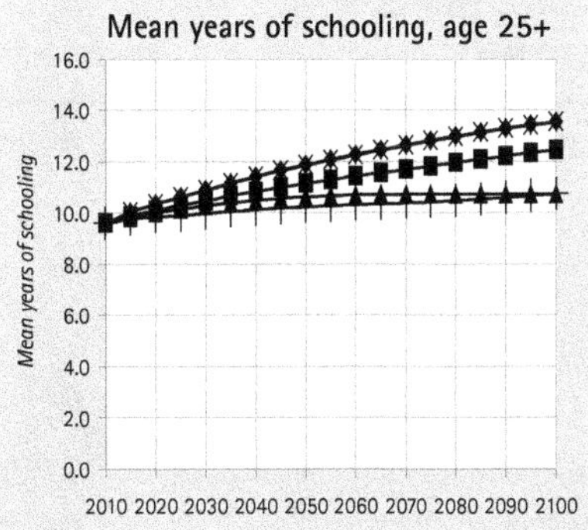

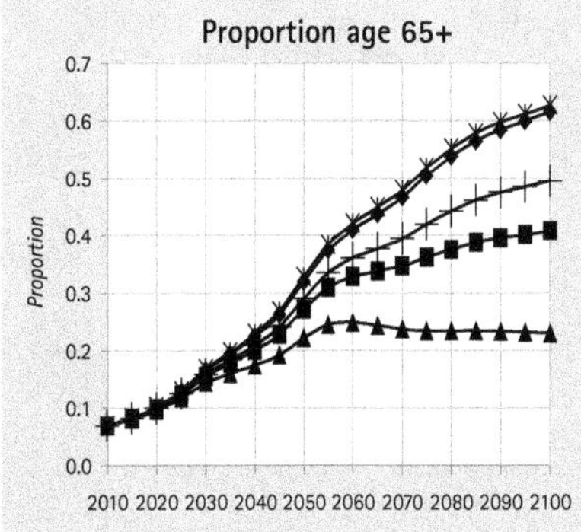

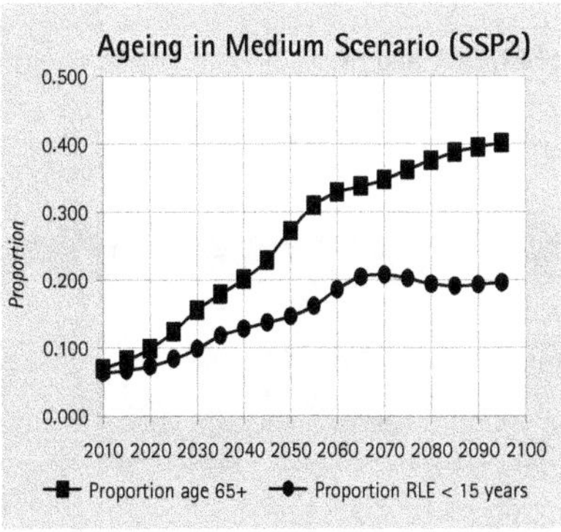

Alternative Scenarios to 2100

Projection Results by Scenario (SSP1–5)

	2010	2020	2030	2040	2050	2075	2100
Population (in millions)							
SSP1 - Rapid development	1.34	1.37	1.35	1.30	1.22	0.94	0.66
SSP2 - Medium	1.34	1.38	1.38	1.35	1.28	1.04	0.81
SSP3 - Stalled development	1.34	1.40	1.43	1.43	1.40	1.28	1.24
SSP4 - Inequality	1.34	1.37	1.35	1.29	1.20	0.88	0.59
SSP5 - Conventional development.	1.34	1.36	1.33	1.27	1.18	0.88	0.60
Proportion age 65+							
SSP1 - Rapid development	0.07	0.10	0.17	0.23	0.32	0.50	0.62
SSP2 - Medium	0.07	0.10	0.16	0.20	0.27	0.36	0.41
SSP3 - Stalled development	0.07	0.10	0.14	0.18	0.22	0.24	0.23
SSP4 - Inequality	0.07	0.10	0.16	0.21	0.29	0.42	0.49
SSP5 - Conventional development.	0.07	0.10	0.17	0.23	0.33	0.52	0.63
Proportion below age 20							
SSP1 - Rapid development	0.28	0.24	0.19	0.15	0.12	0.08	0.07
SSP2 - Medium	0.28	0.25	0.22	0.19	0.17	0.15	0.14
SSP3 - Stalled development	0.28	0.26	0.24	0.23	0.22	0.23	0.25
SSP4 - Inequality	0.28	0.25	0.20	0.16	0.14	0.10	0.09
SSP5 - Conventional development.	0.28	0.24	0.19	0.14	0.12	0.08	0.06
Proportion of Women age 20–39 with at least secondary education							
SSP1 - Rapid development	0.87	0.93	0.95	0.96	0.97	0.98	0.99
SSP2 - Medium	0.87	0.89	0.91	0.93	0.94	0.97	0.99
SSP3 - Stalled development	0.87	0.86	0.86	0.86	0.86	0.86	0.86
SSP4 - Inequality	0.87	0.82	0.78	0.78	0.78	0.78	0.78
SSP5 - Conventional development.	0.87	0.93	0.95	0.96	0.97	0.98	0.99
Mean years of schooling, age 25+							
SSP1 - Rapid development	9.60	10.34	10.89	11.42	11.87	12.82	13.54
SSP2 - Medium	9.60	10.11	10.48	10.83	11.15	11.83	12.45
SSP3 - Stalled development	9.60	10.00	10.28	10.49	10.62	10.72	10.72
SSP4 - Inequality	9.60	9.84	9.98	10.12	10.23	10.42	10.74
SSP5 - Conventional development.	9.60	10.34	10.88	11.40	11.85	12.79	13.53

Demographic Assumptions Underlying SSPs

	2010–15	2020–25	2030–35	2040–45	2050–55	2075–80	2095–2100
Total fertility rate							
SSP1 - Rapid development	1.45	1.22	1.09	1.04	1.03	1.08	1.13
SSP2 - Medium	1.54	1.50	1.46	1.43	1.44	1.49	1.54
SSP3 - Stalled development	1.64	1.78	1.85	1.88	1.93	2.07	2.18
SSP4 - Inequality	1.48	1.31	1.19	1.13	1.11	1.17	1.22
SSP5 - Conventional development.	1.45	1.22	1.09	1.04	1.03	1.08	1.13
Life expectancy at birth for females (in years)							
SSP1 - Rapid development	76.81	80.18	83.24	86.20	89.07	96.48	102.45
SSP2 - Medium	74.81	77.60	79.90	81.99	83.99	89.01	93.01
SSP3 - Stalled development	75.99	77.48	78.64	79.56	80.40	82.52	84.22
SSP4 - Inequality	76.38	78.85	80.91	82.78	84.51	89.08	92.83
SSP5 - Conventional development.	76.81	80.18	83.24	86.20	89.07	96.48	102.45
Migration – net flow over five years (in thousands)							
SSP1 - Rapid development	−15	−12	−10	−8	−6	−2	0
SSP2 - Medium	−15	−12	−10	−9	−7	−2	0
SSP3 - Stalled development	−13	−6	−5	−4	−4	−1	0
SSP4 - Inequality	−15	−12	−10	−8	−6	−1	0
SSP5 - Conventional development.	−18	−18	−15	−13	−10	−3	0

Ageing Indicators, Medium Scenario (SSP2)

	2010	2020	2030	2040	2050	2075	2095
Median age	30.69	36.05	41.75	46.14	48.86	55.01	56.99
Propspective median age	30.69	33.51	37.29	40.01	41.14	42.93	41.13
Proportion age 65+	0.07	0.10	0.16	0.20	0.27	0.36	0.40
Proportion RLE < 15 years	0.06	0.07	0.10	0.13	0.15	0.20	0.20

Tunisia

Detailed Human Capital Projections to 2060

Demographic indicators, Medium Scenario (SSP2)	2010	2020	2030	2040	2050	2060
Population (in millions)	10.48	11.49	12.24	12.64	12.79	12.66
Proportion age 65+	0.07	0.09	0.12	0.16	0.22	0.28
Proportion below age 20	0.33	0.29	0.26	0.22	0.20	0.19
	2005–10	2015–20	2025–30	2035–40	2045–50	2055–60
Total Fertility Rate	2.04	1.77	1.69	1.63	1.57	1.59
Life expectancy at birth (in years)						
Men	71.90	73.07	75.03	77.06	79.08	81.10
Women	76.03	77.59	79.60	81.59	83.59	85.61
Five-year immigration flow (in '000)	9.00	8.83	9.17	9.38	9.38	9.24
Five-year emigration flow (in '000)	28.86	21.01	19.86	18.91	17.35	15.68

Human Capital indicators, Medium Scenario (SSP2)	2010	2020	2030	2040	2050	2060
Population age 25+: highest educational attainment						
E1 - no education	0.29	0.19	0.12	0.08	0.05	0.02
E2 - incomplete primary	0.01	0.01	0.00	0.00	0.00	0.00
E3 - primary	0.31	0.23	0.19	0.14	0.09	0.05
E4 - lower secondary	0.18	0.27	0.30	0.29	0.28	0.25
E5 - upper secondary	0.10	0.14	0.17	0.21	0.23	0.26
E6 - post-secondary	0.11	0.16	0.22	0.28	0.35	0.42
Mean years of schooling (in years)	6.98	8.78	10.03	11.19	12.24	13.14
Gender gap (population age 25+): highest educational attainment (ratio male/female)						
E1 - no education	0.43	0.35	0.28	0.24	0.22	0.22
E2 - incomplete primary	7.98	4.25	2.36	1.40	1.04	0.81
E3 - primary	1.23	1.17	1.07	0.94	0.81	0.69
E4 - lower secondary	1.61	1.36	1.29	1.24	1.18	1.10
E5 - upper secondary	1.54	1.42	1.37	1.32	1.26	1.19
E6 - post-secondary	1.23	1.02	0.96	0.93	0.94	0.95
Mean years of schooling (male minus female)	2.24	1.75	1.36	0.95	0.60	0.33
Women age 20–39: highest educational attainment						
E1 - no education	0.13	0.05	0.02	0.01	0.00	0.00
E2 - incomplete primary	0.00	0.00	0.00	0.00	0.00	0.00
E3 - primary	0.23	0.04	0.03	0.02	0.01	0.01
E4 - lower secondary	0.27	0.40	0.29	0.20	0.14	0.09
E5 - upper secondary	0.19	0.23	0.30	0.33	0.35	0.36
E6 - post-secondary	0.18	0.29	0.37	0.44	0.50	0.54
Mean years of schooling (in years)	9.56	11.83	13.05	13.88	14.42	14.77

Education scenarios

GET: global education trend scenario (medium assumption also used for SSP2)

CER: constant enrolment rates scenario (assumption of no future improvements)

FT: Fast track scenario (assumption of education expansion according to fastest historical experience)

Pyramids by Education, Medium Scenario

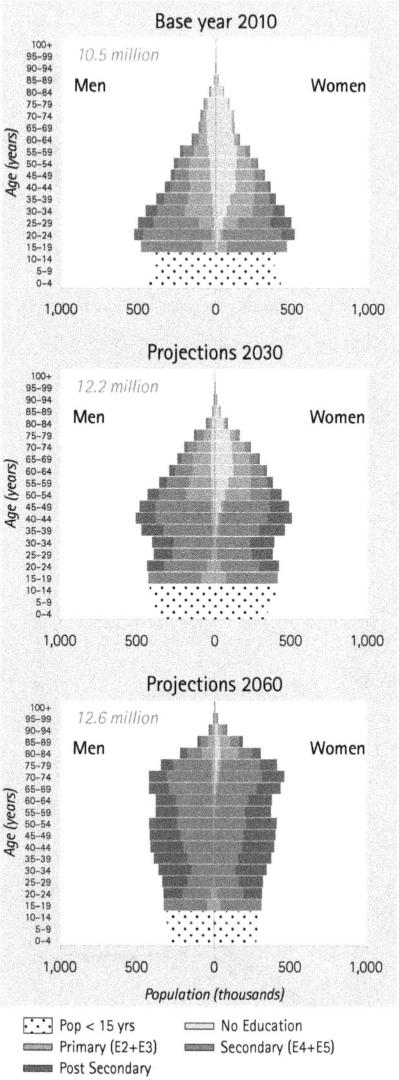

Population Size by Educational Attainment According to Three Education Scenarios: GET, CER, and FT

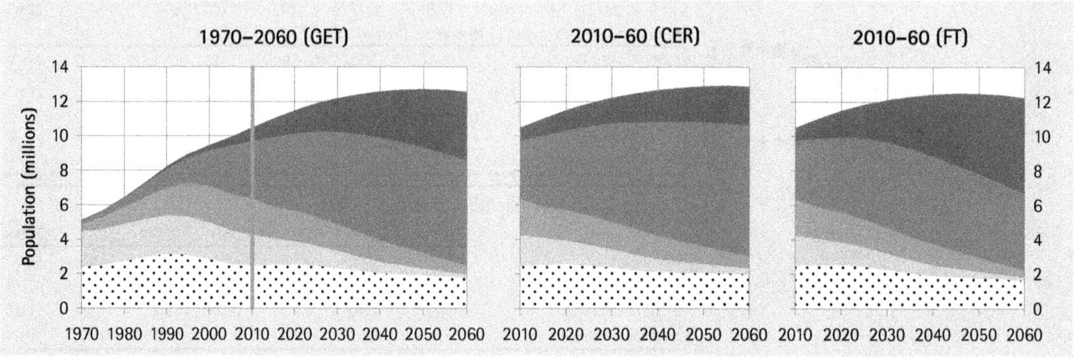

Tunisia (Continued)

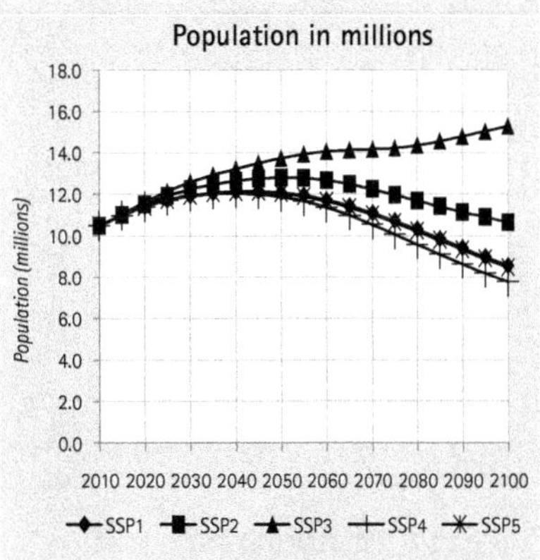

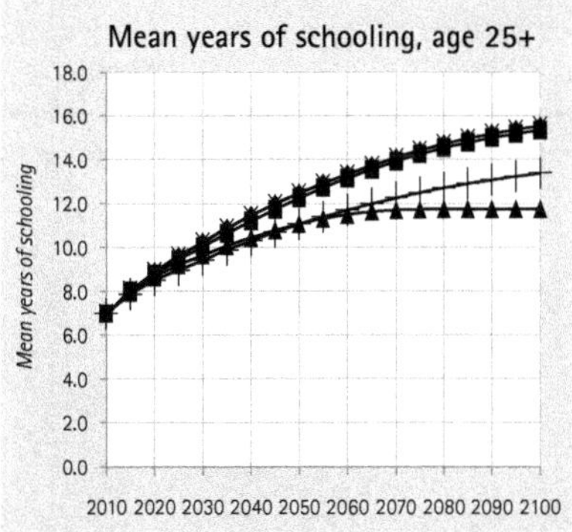

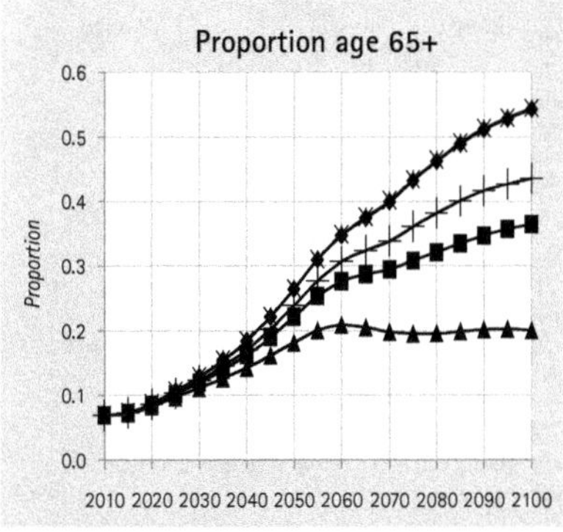

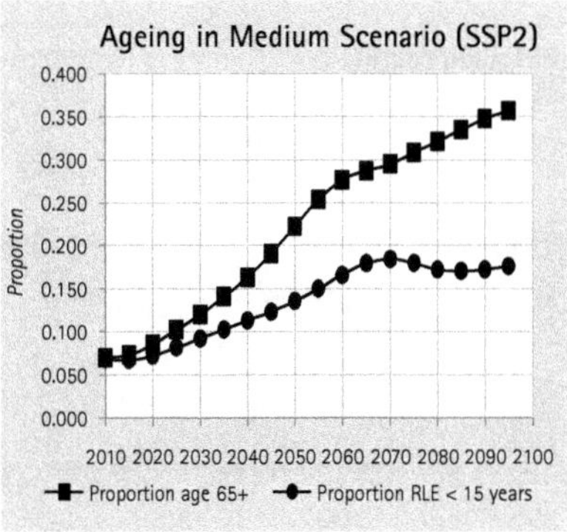

Alternative Scenarios to 2100

Projection Results by Scenario (SSP1–5)

	2010	2020	2030	2040	2050	2075	2100
Population (in millions)							
SSP1 - Rapid development	10.48	11.40	11.93	12.13	12.08	10.71	8.55
SSP2 - Medium	10.48	11.49	12.24	12.64	12.79	11.97	10.65
SSP3 - Stalled development	10.48	11.61	12.58	13.22	13.73	14.23	15.28
SSP4 - Inequality	10.48	11.39	11.90	12.04	11.87	10.06	7.76
SSP5 - Conventional development.	10.48	11.39	11.91	12.09	12.02	10.63	8.47
Proportion age 65+							
SSP1 - Rapid development	0.07	0.09	0.13	0.18	0.26	0.43	0.54
SSP2 - Medium	0.07	0.09	0.12	0.16	0.22	0.31	0.36
SSP3 - Stalled development	0.07	0.08	0.11	0.14	0.18	0.20	0.20
SSP4 - Inequality	0.07	0.09	0.12	0.17	0.24	0.36	0.44
SSP5 - Conventional development.	0.07	0.09	0.13	0.19	0.26	0.43	0.54
Proportion below age 20							
SSP1 - Rapid development	0.33	0.28	0.23	0.18	0.15	0.11	0.09
SSP2 - Medium	0.33	0.29	0.26	0.22	0.20	0.17	0.16
SSP3 - Stalled development	0.33	0.30	0.28	0.26	0.25	0.26	0.27
SSP4 - Inequality	0.33	0.28	0.24	0.19	0.17	0.13	0.12
SSP5 - Conventional development.	0.33	0.28	0.23	0.18	0.15	0.11	0.09
Proportion of Women age 20–39 with at least secondary education							
SSP1 - Rapid development	0.63	0.92	0.97	0.99	0.99	1.00	1.00
SSP2 - Medium	0.63	0.91	0.96	0.98	0.99	0.99	1.00
SSP3 - Stalled development	0.63	0.91	0.94	0.94	0.94	0.94	0.94
SSP4 - Inequality	0.63	0.86	0.84	0.84	0.84	0.84	0.84
SSP5 - Conventional development.	0.63	0.92	0.97	0.99	0.99	1.00	1.00
Mean years of schooling, age 25+							
SSP1 - Rapid development	6.98	8.88	10.24	11.45	12.46	14.41	15.52
SSP2 - Medium	6.98	8.78	10.03	11.19	12.24	14.24	15.32
SSP3 - Stalled development	6.98	8.65	9.64	10.44	11.06	11.73	11.74
SSP4 - Inequality	6.98	8.50	9.42	10.30	11.05	12.49	13.36
SSP5 - Conventional development.	6.98	8.88	10.23	11.45	12.46	14.41	15.52

Demographic Assumptions Underlying SSPs

	2010–15	2020–25	2030–35	2040–45	2050–55	2075–80	2095–2100
Total fertility rate							
SSP1 - Rapid development	1.77	1.43	1.27	1.18	1.15	1.19	1.21
SSP2 - Medium	1.86	1.72	1.66	1.60	1.58	1.61	1.63
SSP3 - Stalled development	1.96	2.00	2.10	2.14	2.18	2.30	2.37
SSP4 - Inequality	1.78	1.49	1.35	1.27	1.24	1.27	1.29
SSP5 - Conventional development.	1.77	1.43	1.27	1.18	1.15	1.19	1.21
Life expectancy at birth for females (in years)							
SSP1 - Rapid development	78.76	81.27	84.01	86.88	89.71	96.78	102.75
SSP2 - Medium	76.69	78.61	80.60	82.59	84.59	89.60	93.60
SSP3 - Stalled development	78.03	78.66	79.59	80.52	81.31	82.99	84.58
SSP4 - Inequality	78.37	80.03	81.84	83.68	85.45	89.61	93.31
SSP5 - Conventional development.	78.76	81.27	84.01	86.88	89.71	96.78	102.75
Migration – net flow over five years (in thousands)							
SSP1 - Rapid development	−15	−11	−10	−8	−6	−2	0
SSP2 - Medium	−15	−11	−10	−9	−7	−2	0
SSP3 - Stalled development	−12	−6	−5	−4	−4	−1	0
SSP4 - Inequality	−15	−11	−10	−8	−6	−1	0
SSP5 - Conventional development.	−17	−17	−16	−13	−11	−4	0

Ageing Indicators, Medium Scenario (SSP2)

	2010	2020	2030	2040	2050	2075	2095
Median age	28.91	33.34	37.98	41.68	44.22	50.50	52.73
Propspective median age	28.91	31.88	34.89	36.92	37.70	39.78	38.27
Proportion age 65+	0.07	0.09	0.12	0.16	0.22	0.31	0.36
Proportion RLE < 15 years	0.07	0.07	0.09	0.11	0.14	0.18	0.18

Turkey

Detailed Human Capital Projections to 2060

Demographic indicators, Medium Scenario (SSP2)						
	2010	2020	2030	2040	2050	2060
Population (in millions)	72.75	80.74	87.05	91.17	92.98	92.76
Proportion age 65+	0.06	0.08	0.11	0.15	0.20	0.24
Proportion below age 20	0.35	0.31	0.27	0.24	0.22	0.20
	2005–10	2015–20	2025–30	2035–40	2045–50	2055–60
Total Fertility Rate	2.15	1.96	1.83	1.73	1.63	1.61
Life expectancy at birth (in years)						
Men	70.70	72.23	74.11	76.02	78.03	79.99
Women	75.28	76.80	78.70	80.59	82.59	84.51
Five-year immigration flow (in '000)	111.32	110.06	114.56	117.50	117.92	116.44
Five-year emigration flow (in '000)	160.26	124.34	122.77	118.65	111.95	103.90

Human Capital indicators, Medium Scenario (SSP2)						
	2010	2020	2030	2040	2050	2060
Population age 25+: highest educational attainment						
E1 - no education	0.11	0.07	0.04	0.02	0.01	0.01
E2 - incomplete primary	0.04	0.03	0.02	0.01	0.01	0.00
E3 - primary	0.47	0.44	0.40	0.34	0.29	0.23
E4 - lower secondary	0.09	0.10	0.09	0.08	0.07	0.06
E5 - upper secondary	0.19	0.25	0.30	0.36	0.41	0.45
E6 - post-secondary	0.10	0.12	0.15	0.18	0.21	0.25
Mean years of schooling (in years)	7.04	7.96	8.81	9.59	10.34	11.04
Gender gap (population age 25+): highest educational attainment (ratio male/female)						
E1 - no education	0.22	0.19	0.18	0.18	0.19	0.22
E2 - incomplete primary	0.56	0.45	0.38	0.36	0.37	0.38
E3 - primary	0.96	0.88	0.83	0.79	0.77	0.76
E4 - lower secondary	1.92	1.76	1.63	1.50	1.37	1.25
E5 - upper secondary	1.50	1.37	1.28	1.21	1.16	1.11
E6 - post-secondary	1.54	1.35	1.21	1.13	1.08	1.06
Mean years of schooling (male minus female)	1.79	1.47	1.18	0.92	0.71	0.54
Women age 20–39: highest educational attainment						
E1 - no education	0.05	0.02	0.01	0.00	0.00	0.00
E2 - incomplete primary	0.02	0.01	0.01	0.00	0.00	0.00
E3 - primary	0.47	0.38	0.29	0.20	0.13	0.08
E4 - lower secondary	0.08	0.07	0.06	0.04	0.03	0.02
E5 - upper secondary	0.27	0.37	0.45	0.51	0.55	0.57
E6 - post-secondary	0.11	0.15	0.19	0.24	0.28	0.32
Mean years of schooling (in years)	8.01	9.35	10.54	11.40	12.10	12.64

Education scenarios

GET: global education trend scenario (medium assumption also used for SSP2)

CER: constant enrolment rates scenario (assumption of no future improvements)

FT: Fast track scenario (assumption of education expansion according to fastest historical experience)

Pyramids by Education, Medium Scenario

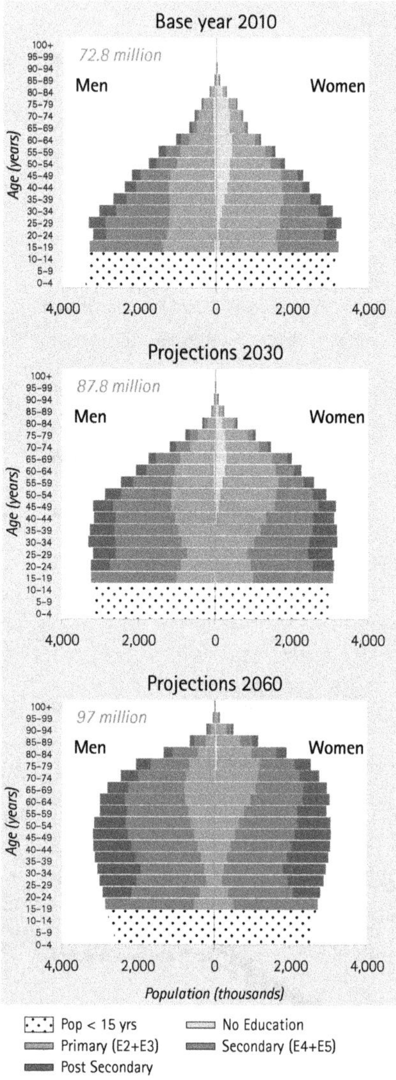

Population Size by Educational Attainment According to Three Education Scenarios: GET, CER, and FT

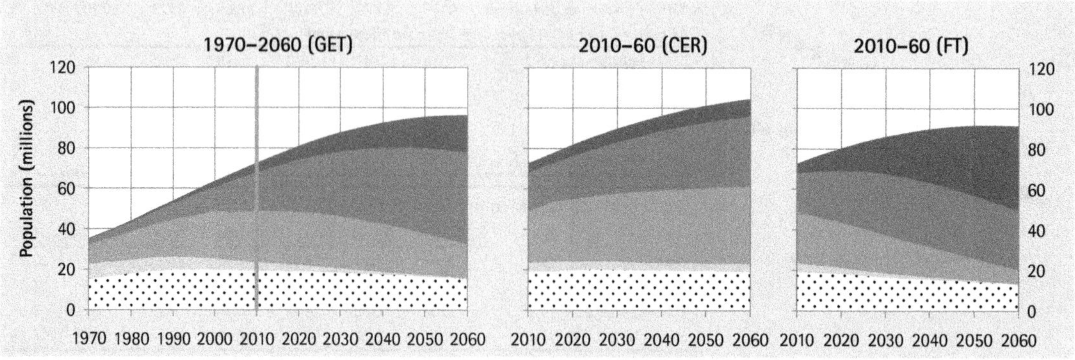

Turkey (Continued)

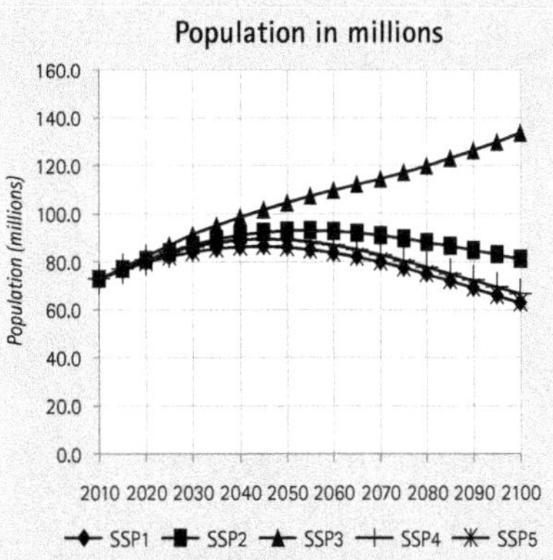

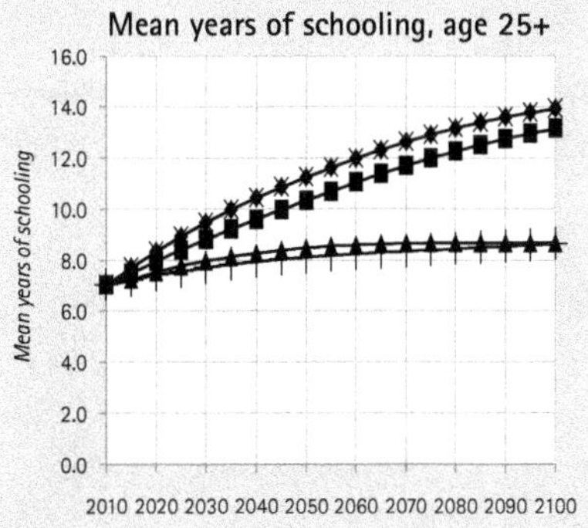

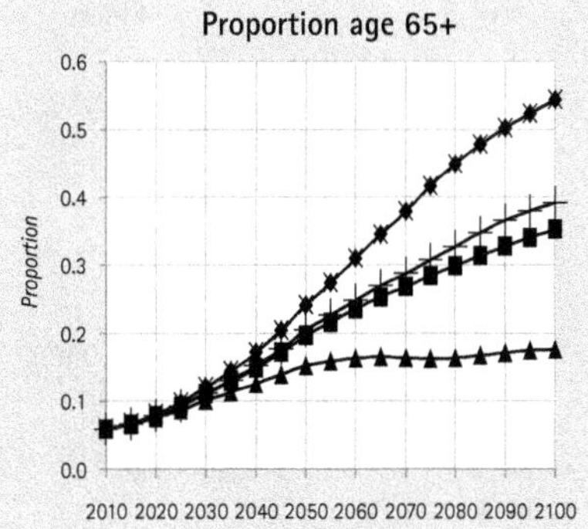

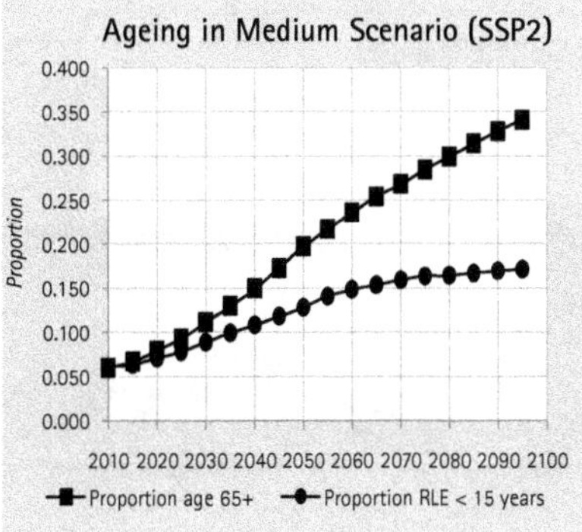

Alternative Scenarios to 2100

Projection Results by Scenario (SSP1–5)

	2010	2020	2030	2040	2050	2075	2100
Population (in millions)							
SSP1 - Rapid development	72.75	79.75	84.06	86.28	86.09	77.52	62.63
SSP2 - Medium	72.75	80.74	87.05	91.17	92.98	89.69	81.19
SSP3 - Stalled development	72.75	82.35	91.37	98.53	104.64	117.12	133.54
SSP4 - Inequality	72.75	80.76	86.31	89.06	89.21	80.46	66.38
SSP5 - Conventional development.	72.75	79.74	84.04	86.25	86.05	77.49	62.61
Proportion age 65+							
SSP1 - Rapid development	0.06	0.08	0.12	0.17	0.24	0.42	0.54
SSP2 - Medium	0.06	0.08	0.11	0.15	0.20	0.28	0.35
SSP3 - Stalled development	0.06	0.08	0.10	0.13	0.15	0.16	0.18
SSP4 - Inequality	0.06	0.08	0.11	0.15	0.20	0.31	0.39
SSP5 - Conventional development.	0.06	0.08	0.12	0.17	0.24	0.42	0.54
Proportion below age 20							
SSP1 - Rapid development	0.35	0.30	0.24	0.19	0.16	0.11	0.09
SSP2 - Medium	0.35	0.31	0.27	0.24	0.22	0.18	0.17
SSP3 - Stalled development	0.35	0.32	0.31	0.30	0.29	0.28	0.29
SSP4 - Inequality	0.35	0.31	0.27	0.22	0.19	0.15	0.14
SSP5 - Conventional development.	0.35	0.30	0.24	0.19	0.16	0.11	0.09
Proportion of Women age 20–39 with at least secondary education							
SSP1 - Rapid development	0.46	0.69	0.81	0.88	0.92	0.98	0.99
SSP2 - Medium	0.46	0.58	0.70	0.79	0.86	0.96	0.99
SSP3 - Stalled development	0.46	0.42	0.42	0.42	0.42	0.42	0.42
SSP4 - Inequality	0.46	0.40	0.38	0.38	0.38	0.38	0.38
SSP5 - Conventional development.	0.46	0.69	0.81	0.88	0.92	0.98	0.99
Mean years of schooling, age 25+							
SSP1 - Rapid development	7.04	8.34	9.46	10.43	11.24	12.90	13.91
SSP2 - Medium	7.04	7.96	8.81	9.59	10.34	11.98	13.14
SSP3 - Stalled development	7.04	7.54	7.97	8.27	8.48	8.67	8.68
SSP4 - Inequality	7.04	7.43	7.71	7.94	8.12	8.39	8.64
SSP5 - Conventional development.	7.04	8.34	9.46	10.43	11.24	12.90	13.91

Demographic Assumptions Underlying SSPs

	2010–15	2020–25	2030–35	2040–45	2050–55	2075–80	2095–2100
Total fertility rate							
SSP1 - Rapid development	1.89	1.52	1.32	1.23	1.17	1.20	1.22
SSP2 - Medium	2.02	1.90	1.78	1.68	1.60	1.63	1.65
SSP3 - Stalled development	2.22	2.39	2.39	2.32	2.30	2.42	2.50
SSP4 - Inequality	2.03	1.83	1.58	1.43	1.37	1.44	1.48
SSP5 - Conventional development.	1.89	1.52	1.32	1.23	1.17	1.20	1.22
Life expectancy at birth for females (in years)							
SSP1 - Rapid development	78.11	80.43	83.08	85.86	88.69	96.07	102.00
SSP2 - Medium	76.01	77.70	79.59	81.59	83.59	88.51	92.50
SSP3 - Stalled development	77.33	77.78	78.51	79.30	79.98	81.59	83.04
SSP4 - Inequality	77.69	79.07	80.73	82.47	84.15	88.09	91.53
SSP5 - Conventional development.	78.11	80.43	83.08	85.86	88.69	96.07	102.00
Migration – net flow over five years (in thousands)							
SSP1 - Rapid development	−26	−11	−5	1	6	4	0
SSP2 - Medium	−26	−11	−5	3	10	8	0
SSP3 - Stalled development	−22	−6	−2	3	8	11	0
SSP4 - Inequality	−26	−11	−5	3	9	8	0
SSP5 - Conventional development.	−31	−17	−8	0	8	5	0

Ageing Indicators, Medium Scenario (SSP2)

	2010	2020	2030	2040	2050	2075	2095
Median age	28.25	32.02	35.59	39.04	42.10	48.45	52.14
Propspective median age	28.25	30.65	32.76	34.55	35.89	37.88	37.85
Proportion age 65+	0.06	0.08	0.11	0.15	0.20	0.28	0.34
Proportion RLE < 15 years	0.06	0.07	0.09	0.11	0.13	0.16	0.17

Turkmenistan

Detailed Human Capital Projections to 2060

Demographic indicators, Medium Scenario (SSP2)	2010	2020	2030	2040	2050	2060
Population (in millions)	5.04	5.63	6.09	6.37	6.51	6.49
Proportion age 65+	0.04	0.05	0.08	0.11	0.14	0.19
Proportion below age 20	0.40	0.35	0.32	0.28	0.25	0.23
	2005–10	2015–20	2025–30	2035–40	2045–50	2055–60
Total Fertility Rate	2.50	2.17	2.00	1.87	1.77	1.69
Life expectancy at birth (in years)						
Men	60.62	63.29	66.11	68.69	71.10	73.42
Women	68.90	71.18	73.48	75.60	77.58	79.61
Five-year immigration flow (in '000)	2.18	2.14	2.22	2.27	2.27	2.24
Five-year emigration flow (in '000)	56.51	45.53	45.03	44.38	42.21	39.15

Human Capital indicators, Medium Scenario (SSP2)	2010	2020	2030	2040	2050	2060
Population age 25+: highest educational attainment						
E1 - no education	0.00	0.00	0.00	0.00	0.00	0.00
E2 - incomplete primary	0.00	0.00	0.00	0.00	0.00	0.00
E3 - primary	0.02	0.01	0.00	0.00	0.00	0.00
E4 - lower secondary	0.07	0.04	0.02	0.01	0.01	0.00
E5 - upper secondary	0.76	0.80	0.82	0.82	0.81	0.80
E6 - post-secondary	0.14	0.14	0.15	0.16	0.18	0.20
Mean years of schooling (in years)	10.79	10.64	10.64	10.63	10.64	10.69
Gender gap (population age 25+): highest educational attainment (ratio male/female)						
E1 - no education	0.34	0.42	0.57	0.75	0.90	0.98
E2 - incomplete primary	0.38	0.41	0.50	0.64	0.79	0.89
E3 - primary	0.50	0.46	0.48	0.53	0.60	0.72
E4 - lower secondary	0.80	0.81	0.84	0.89	0.96	1.03
E5 - upper secondary	0.99	0.98	0.98	0.99	0.99	0.99
E6 - post-secondary	1.39	1.24	1.15	1.08	1.04	1.03
Mean years of schooling (male minus female)	0.34	0.14	0.05	0.00	0.00	0.02
Women age 20–39: highest educational attainment						
E1 - no education	0.00	0.00	0.00	0.00	0.00	0.00
E2 - incomplete primary	0.00	0.00	0.00	0.00	0.00	0.00
E3 - primary	0.00	0.00	0.00	0.00	0.00	0.00
E4 - lower secondary	0.03	0.02	0.02	0.02	0.02	0.02
E5 - upper secondary	0.87	0.86	0.84	0.82	0.80	0.78
E6 - post-secondary	0.10	0.12	0.14	0.16	0.18	0.20
Mean years of schooling (in years)	10.17	9.99	10.50	10.58	10.68	10.76

Education scenarios

GET : global education trend scenario (medium assumption also used for SSP2)

CER: constant enrolment rates senario (assumption of no future improvements)

FT: Fast track scenario (assumption of education expansion according to fastest historical experience)

Pyramids by Education, Medium Scenario

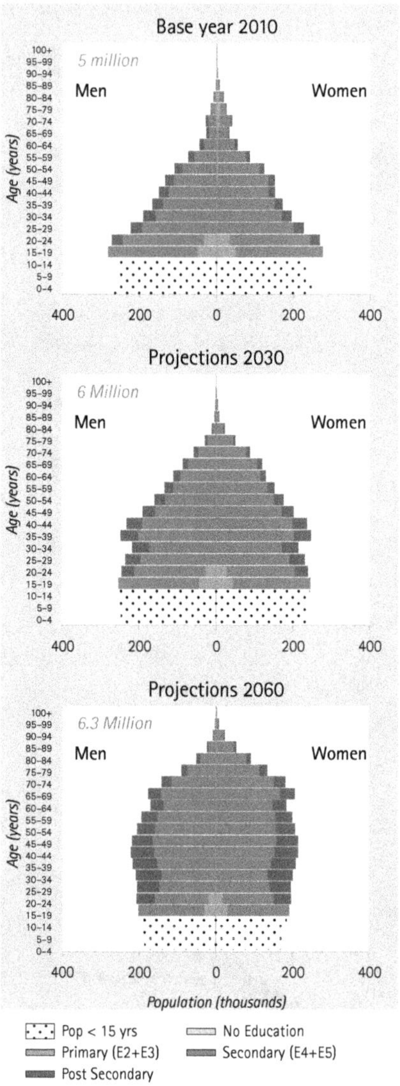

Population Size by Educational Attainment According to Three Education Scenarios: GET, CER, and FT

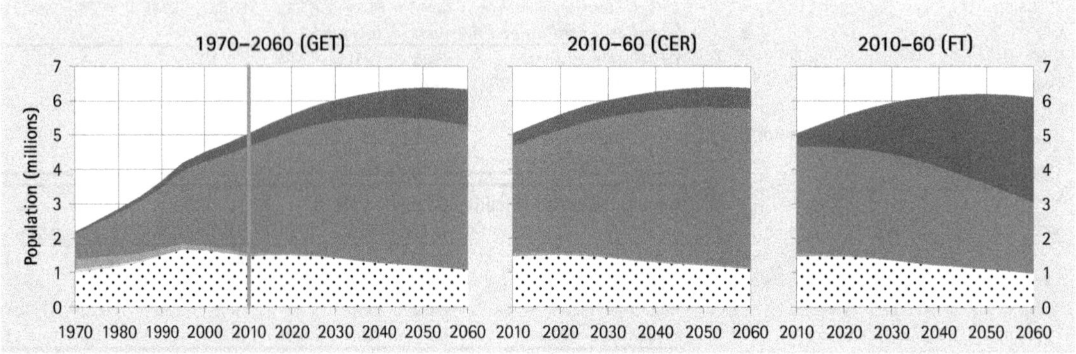

Turkmenistan (Continued)

Population in millions

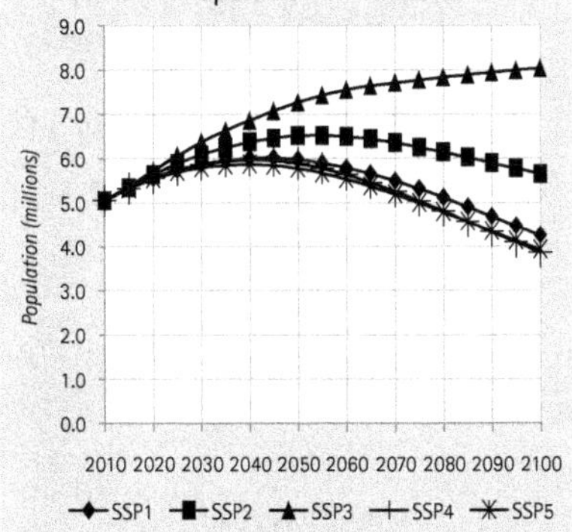

Mean years of schooling, age 25+

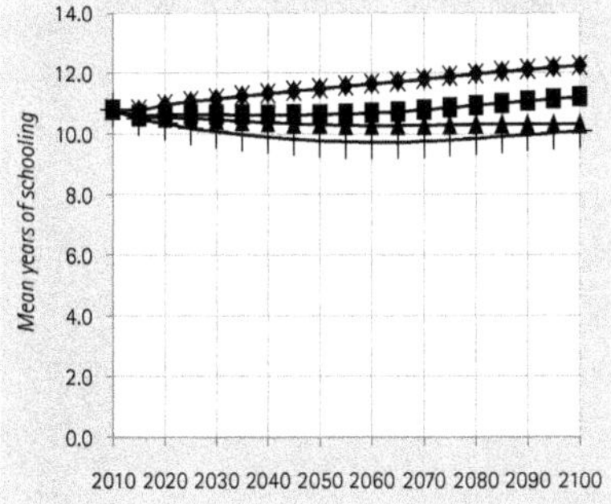

Proportion age 65+

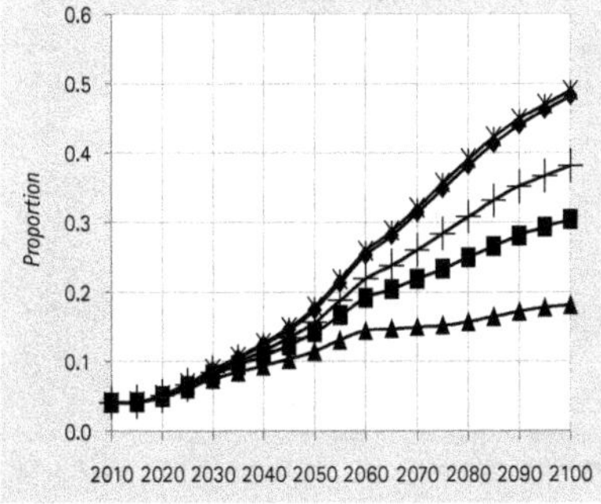

Ageing in Medium Scenario (SSP2)

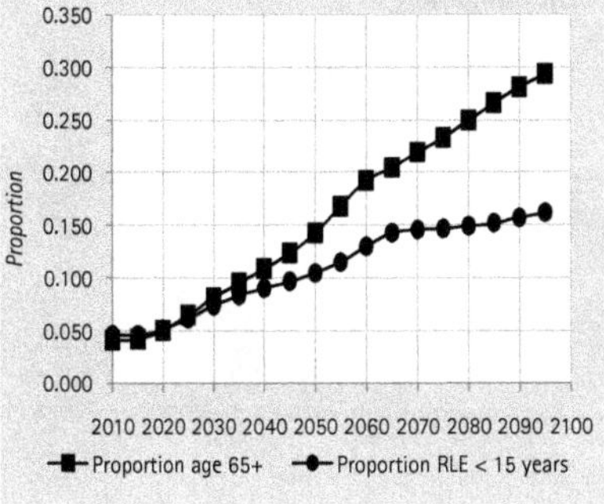

Alternative Scenarios to 2100

Projection Results by Scenario (SSP1–5)

	2010	2020	2030	2040	2050	2075	2100
Population (in millions)							
SSP1 - Rapid development	5.04	5.56	5.87	6.00	5.97	5.31	4.25
SSP2 - Medium	5.04	5.63	6.09	6.37	6.51	6.25	5.64
SSP3 - Stalled development	5.04	5.72	6.37	6.86	7.27	7.77	8.03
SSP4 - Inequality	5.04	5.56	5.86	5.96	5.89	5.03	3.86
SSP5 - Conventional development.	5.04	5.53	5.79	5.86	5.77	4.99	3.92
Proportion age 65+							
SSP1 - Rapid development	0.04	0.05	0.09	0.12	0.17	0.35	0.48
SSP2 - Medium	0.04	0.05	0.08	0.11	0.14	0.23	0.30
SSP3 - Stalled development	0.04	0.05	0.08	0.09	0.12	0.15	0.18
SSP4 - Inequality	0.04	0.05	0.08	0.12	0.16	0.28	0.38
SSP5 - Conventional development.	0.04	0.05	0.09	0.13	0.18	0.36	0.49
Proportion below age 20							
SSP1 - Rapid development	0.40	0.34	0.28	0.23	0.19	0.13	0.10
SSP2 - Medium	0.40	0.35	0.32	0.28	0.25	0.20	0.18
SSP3 - Stalled development	0.40	0.36	0.34	0.32	0.30	0.27	0.26
SSP4 - Inequality	0.40	0.35	0.29	0.24	0.21	0.15	0.12
SSP5 - Conventional development.	0.40	0.34	0.28	0.23	0.19	0.13	0.10
Proportion of Women age 20–39 with at least secondary education							
SSP1 - Rapid development	1.00	1.00	1.00	1.00	1.00	1.00	1.00
SSP2 - Medium	1.00	1.00	1.00	1.00	1.00	1.00	1.00
SSP3 - Stalled development	1.00	0.99	0.99	0.99	0.99	0.99	0.99
SSP4 - Inequality	1.00	0.93	0.89	0.89	0.89	0.89	0.89
SSP5 - Conventional development.	1.00	1.00	1.00	1.00	1.00	1.00	1.00
Mean years of schooling, age 25+							
SSP1 - Rapid development	10.79	10.95	11.15	11.33	11.49	11.89	12.23
SSP2 - Medium	10.79	10.64	10.64	10.63	10.64	10.86	11.20
SSP3 - Stalled development	10.79	10.55	10.47	10.38	10.30	10.30	10.32
SSP4 - Inequality	10.79	10.35	10.07	9.90	9.78	9.80	10.08
SSP5 - Conventional development.	10.79	10.95	11.15	11.32	11.48	11.88	12.23

Demographic Assumptions Underlying SSPs

	2010–15	2020–25	2030–35	2040–45	2050–55	2075–80	2095–2100
Total fertility rate							
SSP1 - Rapid development	2.16	1.74	1.48	1.35	1.26	1.18	1.20
SSP2 - Medium	2.31	2.09	1.92	1.81	1.72	1.60	1.63
SSP3 - Stalled development	2.41	2.43	2.38	2.28	2.20	2.07	2.11
SSP4 - Inequality	2.18	1.80	1.56	1.42	1.33	1.24	1.26
SSP5 - Conventional development.	2.16	1.74	1.48	1.35	1.26	1.18	1.20
Life expectancy at birth for females (in years)							
SSP1 - Rapid development	72.98	75.77	78.65	81.46	84.18	91.22	97.02
SSP2 - Medium	69.98	72.38	74.49	76.59	78.61	83.60	87.60
SSP3 - Stalled development	72.30	73.27	74.32	75.24	76.11	78.25	80.02
SSP4 - Inequality	72.56	74.65	76.47	78.26	79.97	84.28	87.92
SSP5 - Conventional development.	72.98	75.77	78.65	81.46	84.18	91.22	97.02
Migration – net flow over five years (in thousands)							
SSP1 - Rapid development	−46	−43	−41	−38	−34	−11	0
SSP2 - Medium	−46	−43	−43	−41	−39	−15	0
SSP3 - Stalled development	−39	−21	−21	−20	−19	−8	0
SSP4 - Inequality	−46	−42	−40	−36	−31	−9	0
SSP5 - Conventional development.	−54	−65	−64	−61	−56	−21	0

Ageing Indicators, Medium Scenario (SSP2)

	2010	2020	2030	2040	2050	2075	2095
Median age	24.47	28.44	32.00	35.09	38.09	45.02	48.80
Propspective median age	24.47	26.48	28.41	29.96	31.39	34.21	34.43
Proportion age 65+	0.04	0.05	0.08	0.11	0.14	0.23	0.29
Proportion RLE < 15 years	0.05	0.05	0.07	0.09	0.10	0.15	0.16

Uganda

Detailed Human Capital Projections to 2060

Demographic indicators, Medium Scenario (SSP2)	2010	2020	2030	2040	2050	2060
Population (in millions)	33.42	45.49	60.01	76.34	93.12	108.98
Proportion age 65+	0.03	0.02	0.02	0.03	0.04	0.05
Proportion below age 20	0.59	0.58	0.55	0.51	0.47	0.42
	2005–10	2015–20	2025–30	2035–40	2045–50	2055–60
Total Fertility Rate	6.38	5.47	4.64	3.87	3.21	2.67
Life expectancy at birth (in years)						
Men	51.68	55.07	56.76	58.41	60.38	62.93
Women	52.73	57.00	59.60	62.02	64.28	66.88
Five-year immigration flow (in '000)	13.71	13.40	13.88	14.15	14.11	13.86
Five-year emigration flow (in '000)	147.09	151.98	205.23	266.69	330.51	392.09

Human Capital indicators, Medium Scenario (SSP2)	2010	2020	2030	2040	2050	2060
Population age 25+: highest educational attainment						
E1 - no education	0.24	0.19	0.14	0.10	0.07	0.05
E2 - incomplete primary	0.36	0.31	0.26	0.20	0.15	0.10
E3 - primary	0.25	0.31	0.36	0.40	0.42	0.42
E4 - lower secondary	0.10	0.11	0.13	0.15	0.15	0.16
E5 - upper secondary	0.03	0.04	0.06	0.09	0.13	0.17
E6 - post-secondary	0.03	0.04	0.05	0.06	0.08	0.10
Mean years of schooling (in years)	5.36	6.24	7.16	8.04	8.84	9.59
Gender gap (population age 25+): highest educational attainment (ratio male/female)						
E1 - no education	0.48	0.53	0.61	0.69	0.76	0.80
E2 - incomplete primary	1.01	0.99	0.99	0.99	0.99	0.98
E3 - primary	1.35	1.15	1.04	1.00	0.99	0.99
E4 - lower secondary	1.68	1.34	1.16	1.08	1.04	1.02
E5 - upper secondary	2.67	2.02	1.61	1.36	1.20	1.10
E6 - post-secondary	1.83	1.36	1.09	0.96	0.94	0.98
Mean years of schooling (male minus female)	1.81	1.30	0.81	0.46	0.25	0.16
Women age 20–39: highest educational attainment						
E1 - no education	0.18	0.14	0.09	0.06	0.03	0.02
E2 - incomplete primary	0.37	0.27	0.20	0.14	0.09	0.06
E3 - primary	0.29	0.37	0.42	0.44	0.43	0.40
E4 - lower secondary	0.10	0.13	0.15	0.17	0.18	0.19
E5 - upper secondary	0.03	0.05	0.08	0.12	0.17	0.23
E6 - post-secondary	0.03	0.04	0.06	0.08	0.09	0.11
Mean years of schooling (in years)	5.84	6.91	8.00	8.94	9.75	10.45

Education scenarios

GET: global education trend scenario (medium assumption also used for SSP2)

CER: constant enrolment rates scenario (assumption of no future improvements)

FT: Fast track scenario (assumption of education expansion according to fastest historical experience)

Pyramids by Education, Medium Scenario

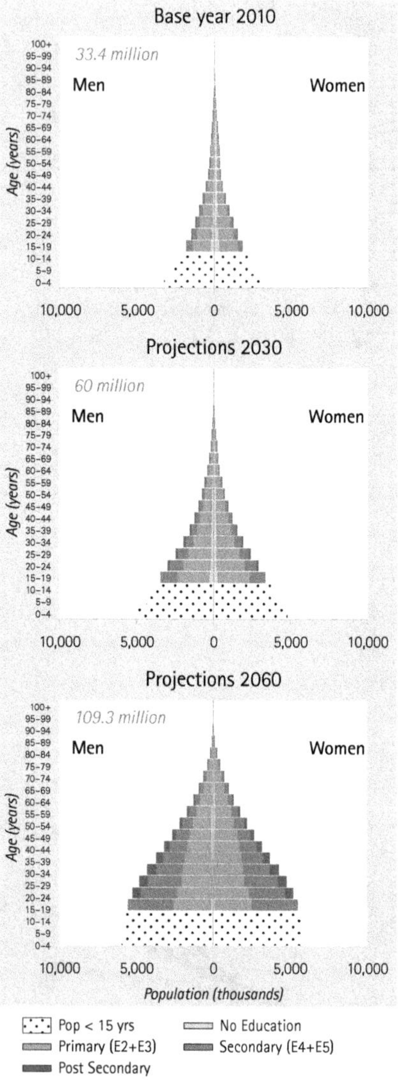

Population Size by Educational Attainment According to Three Education Scenarios: GET, CER, and FT

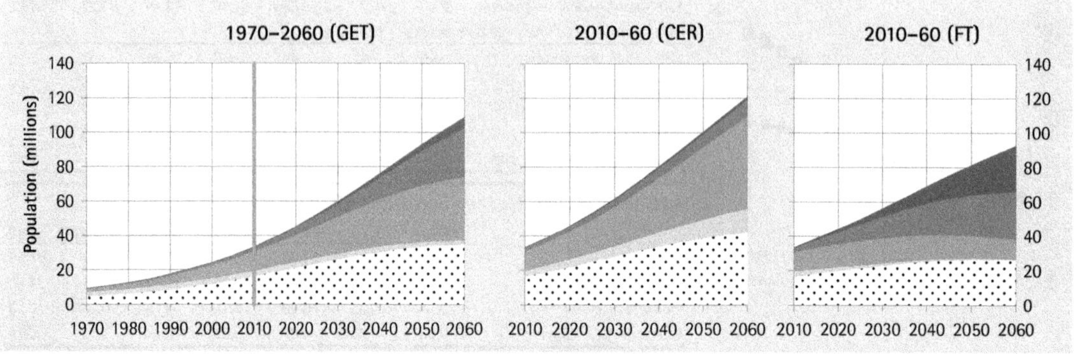

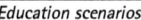

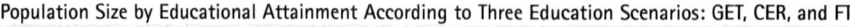

Uganda (Continued)

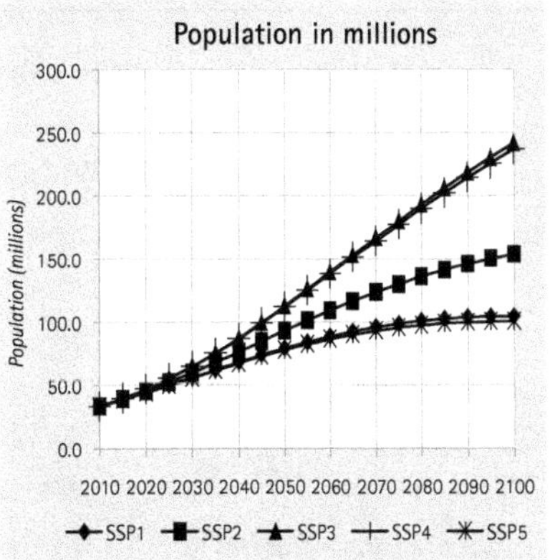

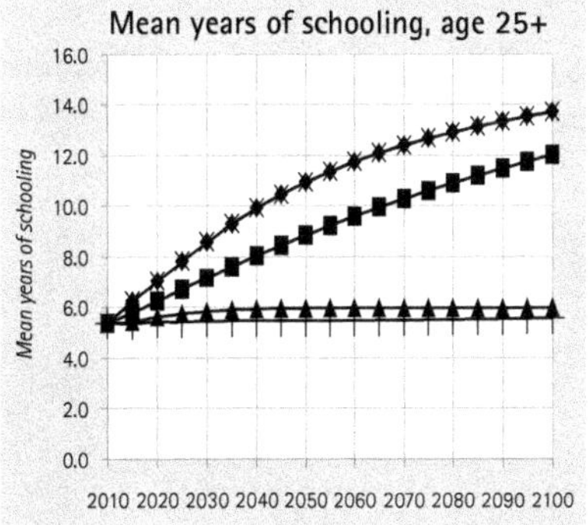

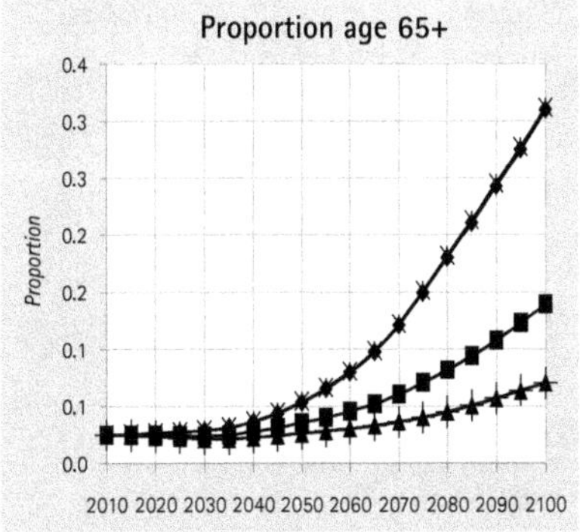

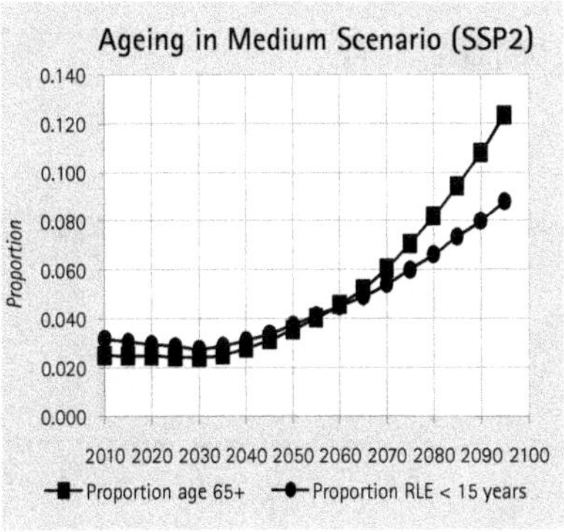

Alternative Scenarios to 2100

Projection Results by Scenario (SSP1–5)

	2010	2020	2030	2040	2050	2075	2100
Population (in millions)							
SSP1 - Rapid development	33.42	44.37	56.08	68.23	79.23	98.60	104.28
SSP2 - Medium	33.42	45.49	60.01	76.34	93.12	129.91	153.76
SSP3 - Stalled development	33.42	47.08	65.11	87.26	112.89	180.38	241.98
SSP4 - Inequality	33.42	47.06	64.97	86.84	112.00	177.42	236.78
SSP5 - Conventional 'development.	33.42	44.28	55.72	67.44	77.85	95.40	100.18
Proportion age 65+							
SSP1 - Rapid development	0.03	0.03	0.03	0.04	0.05	0.15	0.31
SSP2 - Medium	0.03	0.02	0.02	0.03	0.04	0.07	0.14
SSP3 - Stalled development	0.03	0.02	0.02	0.02	0.03	0.04	0.07
SSP4 - Inequality	0.03	0.02	0.02	0.02	0.03	0.04	0.07
SSP5 - Conventional 'development.	0.03	0.03	0.03	0.04	0.05	0.15	0.31
Proportion below age 20							
SSP1 - Rapid development	0.59	0.56	0.50	0.44	0.38	0.24	0.15
SSP2 - Medium	0.59	0.58	0.55	0.51	0.47	0.35	0.26
SSP3 - Stalled development	0.59	0.60	0.59	0.57	0.53	0.44	0.37
SSP4 - Inequality	0.59	0.60	0.59	0.57	0.54	0.44	0.37
SSP5 - Conventional 'development.	0.59	0.56	0.50	0.44	0.38	0.24	0.15
Proportion of Women age 20–39 with at least secondary education							
SSP1 - Rapid development	0.16	0.38	0.52	0.63	0.70	0.81	0.91
SSP2 - Medium	0.16	0.22	0.29	0.36	0.44	0.64	0.82
SSP3 - Stalled development	0.16	0.13	0.13	0.13	0.13	0.13	0.13
SSP4 - Inequality	0.16	0.12	0.12	0.12	0.12	0.12	0.12
SSP5 - Conventional 'development.	0.16	0.38	0.52	0.63	0.70	0.81	0.91
Mean years of schooling, age 25+							
SSP1 - Rapid development	5.36	7.03	8.58	9.91	10.93	12.66	13.70
SSP2 - Medium	5.36	6.24	7.16	8.04	8.84	10.60	12.01
SSP3 - Stalled development	5.36	5.61	5.82	5.92	5.96	5.97	5.97
SSP4 - Inequality	5.36	5.42	5.44	5.46	5.46	5.49	5.56
SSP5 - Conventional 'development.	5.36	7.03	8.57	9.90	10.92	12.65	13.70

Demographic Assumptions Underlying SSPs

	2010–15	2020–25	2030–35	2040–45	2050–55	2075–80	2095–2100
Total fertility rate							
SSP1 - Rapid development	5.53	3.99	3.05	2.46	2.03	1.48	1.31
SSP2 - Medium	5.93	5.05	4.25	3.52	2.91	2.08	1.82
SSP3 - Stalled development	6.41	6.26	5.70	4.91	4.13	2.95	2.63
SSP4 - Inequality	6.42	6.32	5.76	4.93	4.13	2.93	2.60
SSP5 - Conventional 'development.	5.53	4.00	3.05	2.46	2.03	1.48	1.31
Life expectancy at birth for females (in years)							
SSP1 - Rapid development	59.74	66.10	70.41	74.59	78.50	87.36	94.49
SSP2 - Medium	55.38	58.30	60.78	63.11	65.58	72.22	77.49
SSP3 - Stalled development	57.43	56.02	57.20	58.26	59.31	62.05	64.96
SSP4 - Inequality	57.43	56.00	57.15	58.21	59.25	61.99	64.91
SSP5 - Conventional 'development.	59.74	66.10	70.41	74.59	78.50	87.36	94.49
Migration – net flow over five years (in thousands)							
SSP1 - Rapid development	−124	−160	−215	−266	−309	−168	0
SSP2 - Medium	−125	−162	−220	−283	−348	−223	0
SSP3 - Stalled development	−103	−78	−105	−136	−170	−117	0
SSP4 - Inequality	−123	−158	−218	−292	−372	−257	0
SSP5 - Conventional 'development.	−145	−244	−338	−433	−526	−323	0

Ageing Indicators, Medium Scenario (SSP2)

	2010	2020	2030	2040	2050	2075	2095
Median age	15.66	16.44	17.86	19.57	21.71	28.80	35.17
Propspective median age	15.66	15.19	15.37	15.98	16.59	18.64	20.61
Proportion age 65+	0.03	0.02	0.02	0.03	0.04	0.07	0.12
Proportion RLE < 15 years	0.03	0.03	0.03	0.03	0.04	0.06	0.09

Ukraine

Detailed Human Capital Projections to 2060

Demographic indicators, Medium Scenario (SSP2)						
	2010	2020	2030	2040	2050	2060
Population (in millions)	45.45	42.97	40.59	38.44	36.62	34.83
Proportion age 65+	0.15	0.16	0.19	0.21	0.25	0.28
Proportion below age 20	0.20	0.21	0.20	0.18	0.19	0.19
	2005-10	2015-20	2025-30	2035-40	2045-50	2055-60
Total Fertility Rate	1.39	1.47	1.49	1.54	1.59	1.61
Life expectancy at birth (in years)						
Men	61.78	64.43	67.54	70.24	72.88	75.67
Women	73.55	74.89	76.99	78.89	80.89	83.19
Five-year immigration flow (in '000)	381.39	373.88	388.35	397.12	397.28	391.58
Five-year emigration flow (in '000)	421.66	259.65	223.00	203.15	180.95	165.92

Human Capital indicators, Medium Scenario (SSP2)						
	2010	2020	2030	2040	2050	2060
Population age 25+: highest educational attainment						
E1 - no education	0.00	0.00	0.00	0.00	0.00	0.00
E2 - incomplete primary	0.01	0.00	0.00	0.00	0.00	0.00
E3 - primary	0.05	0.02	0.00	0.00	0.00	0.00
E4 - lower secondary	0.09	0.07	0.05	0.03	0.02	0.01
E5 - upper secondary	0.66	0.71	0.73	0.73	0.71	0.70
E6 - post-secondary	0.18	0.20	0.22	0.24	0.26	0.29
Mean years of schooling (in years)	10.07	10.61	10.96	11.28	11.59	11.87
Gender gap (population age 25+): highest educational attainment (ratio male/female)						
E1 - no education	0.54	0.75	0.90	0.91	0.92	0.94
E2 - incomplete primary	0.30	0.38	0.63	0.84	0.88	0.92
E3 - primary	0.72	0.70	0.91	2.40	4.43	3.48
E4 - lower secondary	0.86	0.94	1.07	1.15	1.15	1.12
E5 - upper secondary	1.08	1.06	1.06	1.06	1.06	1.05
E6 - post-secondary	0.95	0.86	0.82	0.81	0.83	0.88
Mean years of schooling (male minus female)	0.15	0.01	−0.05	−0.06	−0.04	−0.02
Women age 20–39: highest educational attainment						
E1 - no education	0.00	0.00	0.00	0.00	0.00	0.00
E2 - incomplete primary	0.00	0.00	0.00	0.00	0.00	0.00
E3 - primary	0.00	0.00	0.00	0.00	0.00	0.00
E4 - lower secondary	0.05	0.03	0.03	0.02	0.02	0.02
E5 - upper secondary	0.74	0.73	0.71	0.69	0.67	0.66
E6 - post-secondary	0.21	0.24	0.26	0.29	0.31	0.32
Mean years of schooling (in years)	10.80	11.50	11.97	12.07	12.18	12.23

Education scenarios

GET: global education trend scenario (medium assumption also used for SSP2)

CER: constant enrolment rates scenario (assumption of no future improvements)

FT: Fast track scenario (assumption of education expansion according to fastest historical experience)

Pyramids by Education, Medium Scenario

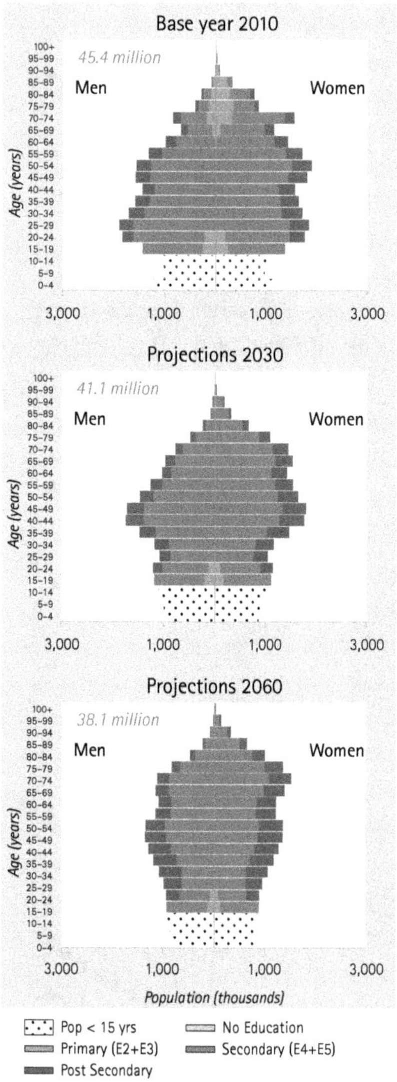

Population Size by Educational Attainment According to Three Education Scenarios: GET, CER, and FT

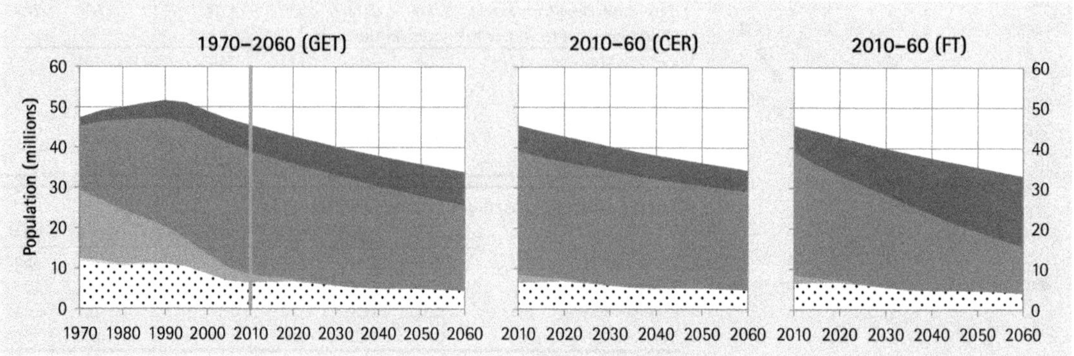

Ukraine (Continued)

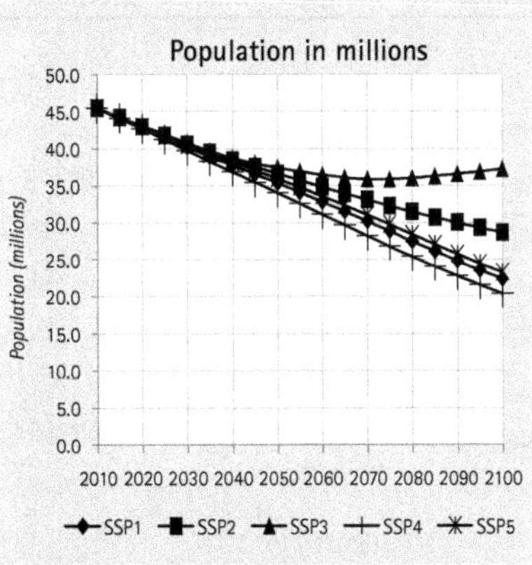

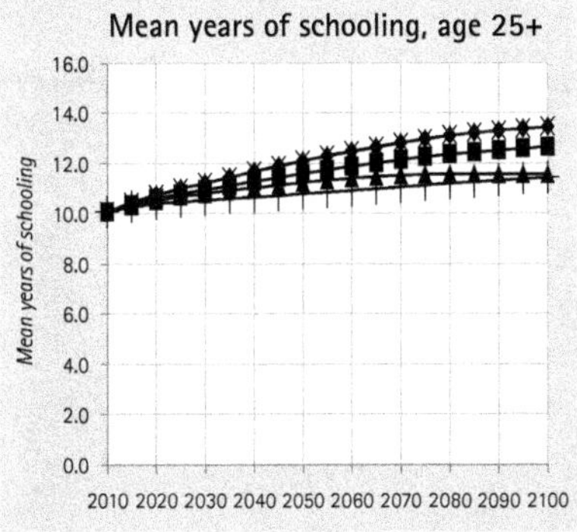

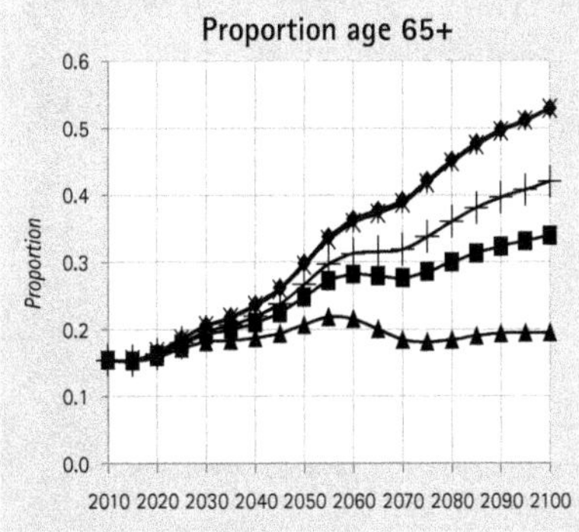

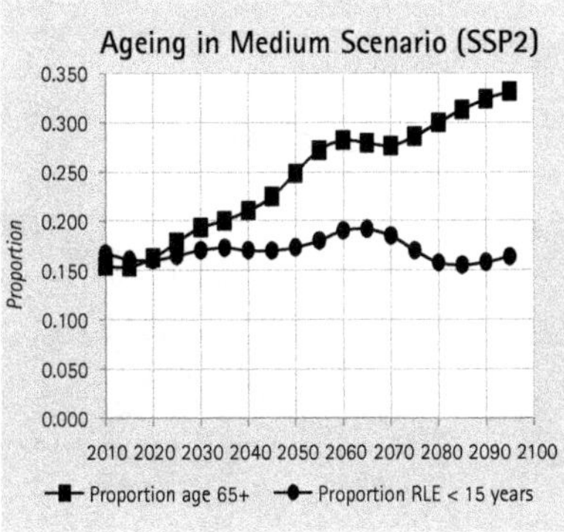

Alternative Scenarios to 2100

Projection Results by Scenario (SSP1–5)

	2010	2020	2030	2040	2050	2075	2100
Population (in millions)							
SSP1 - Rapid development	45.45	42.86	40.20	37.76	35.36	28.86	22.35
SSP2 - Medium	45.45	42.97	40.59	38.44	36.62	32.25	28.65
SSP3 - Stalled development	45.45	43.09	40.78	38.75	37.44	35.88	37.24
SSP4 - Inequality	45.45	42.67	39.72	36.84	34.02	26.78	20.38
SSP5 - Conventional development.	45.45	42.91	40.42	38.17	35.96	29.77	23.23
Proportion age 65+							
SSP1 - Rapid development	0.15	0.17	0.21	0.24	0.30	0.42	0.53
SSP2 - Medium	0.15	0.16	0.19	0.21	0.25	0.29	0.34
SSP3 - Stalled development	0.15	0.16	0.18	0.19	0.21	0.18	0.20
SSP4 - Inequality	0.15	0.16	0.20	0.22	0.27	0.34	0.42
SSP5 - Conventional development.	0.15	0.17	0.21	0.24	0.29	0.42	0.53
Proportion below age 20							
SSP1 - Rapid development	0.20	0.20	0.18	0.15	0.14	0.11	0.09
SSP2 - Medium	0.20	0.21	0.20	0.18	0.19	0.18	0.17
SSP3 - Stalled development	0.20	0.22	0.23	0.22	0.24	0.25	0.26
SSP4 - Inequality	0.20	0.20	0.19	0.16	0.15	0.13	0.12
SSP5 - Conventional development.	0.20	0.20	0.18	0.15	0.14	0.11	0.09
Proportion of Women age 20–39 with at least secondary education							
SSP1 - Rapid development	1.00	1.00	1.00	1.00	1.00	1.00	1.00
SSP2 - Medium	1.00	1.00	1.00	1.00	1.00	1.00	1.00
SSP3 - Stalled development	1.00	1.00	1.00	1.00	1.00	1.00	1.00
SSP4 - Inequality	1.00	0.94	0.90	0.90	0.90	0.90	0.90
SSP5 - Conventional development.	1.00	1.00	1.00	1.00	1.00	1.00	1.00
Mean years of schooling, age 25+							
SSP1 - Rapid development	10.07	10.74	11.22	11.67	12.09	12.95	13.43
SSP2 - Medium	10.07	10.61	10.96	11.28	11.59	12.25	12.64
SSP3 - Stalled development	10.07	10.52	10.80	11.03	11.23	11.55	11.57
SSP4 - Inequality	10.07	10.40	10.54	10.66	10.78	11.12	11.43
SSP5 - Conventional development.	10.07	10.74	11.22	11.68	12.10	12.96	13.43

Demographic Assumptions Underlying SSPs

	2010–15	2020–25	2030–35	2040–45	2050–55	2075–80	2095–2100
Total fertility rate							
SSP1 - Rapid development	1.38	1.23	1.17	1.16	1.17	1.20	1.22
SSP2 - Medium	1.46	1.48	1.51	1.56	1.60	1.63	1.65
SSP3 - Stalled development	1.55	1.75	1.89	1.99	2.06	2.12	2.16
SSP4 - Inequality	1.40	1.29	1.23	1.23	1.23	1.26	1.28
SSP5 - Conventional development.	1.38	1.23	1.17	1.16	1.17	1.20	1.22
Life expectancy at birth for females (in years)							
SSP1 - Rapid development	75.51	78.10	81.00	83.77	86.83	94.96	101.52
SSP2 - Medium	74.10	75.89	77.99	79.89	81.99	87.81	92.31
SSP3 - Stalled development	74.57	75.17	76.15	76.99	78.06	81.10	83.53
SSP4 - Inequality	75.07	76.60	78.53	80.29	82.25	87.73	92.10
SSP5 - Conventional development.	75.51	78.10	81.00	83.77	86.83	94.96	101.52
Migration – net flow over five years (in thousands)							
SSP1 - Rapid development	49	144	173	181	177	55	0
SSP2 - Medium	52	147	181	206	221	92	0
SSP3 - Stalled development	41	72	95	123	152	92	0
SSP4 - Inequality	49	143	175	195	204	81	0
SSP5 - Conventional development.	57	213	251	256	244	73	0

Ageing Indicators, Medium Scenario (SSP2)

	2010	2020	2030	2040	2050	2075	2095
Median age	39.25	40.71	43.94	46.65	46.12	49.11	51.27
Propspective median age	39.25	38.60	39.66	40.66	37.87	34.99	32.58
Proportion age 65+	0.15	0.16	0.19	0.21	0.25	0.29	0.33
Proportion RLE < 15 years	0.17	0.16	0.17	0.17	0.17	0.17	0.16

United Arab Emirates

Detailed Human Capital Projections to 2060

Demographic indicators, Medium Scenario (SSP2)

	2010	2020	2030	2040	2050	2060
Population (in millions)	7.51	10.61	13.10	15.38	17.29	18.67
Proportion age 65+	0.00	0.02	0.06	0.15	0.26	0.29
Proportion below age 20	0.23	0.21	0.19	0.16	0.15	0.15
	2005–10	2015–20	2025–30	2035–40	2045–50	2055–60
Total Fertility Rate	1.86	1.70	1.64	1.57	1.52	1.53
Life expectancy at birth (in years)						
Men	75.25	77.39	79.35	81.30	83.22	85.17
Women	77.05	79.59	81.79	83.89	85.89	87.91
Five-year immigration flow (in '000)	3070.49	1085.48	1128.18	1152.90	1152.06	1134.59
Five-year emigration flow (in '000)	0.11	0.11	0.16	0.21	0.26	0.26

Human Capital indicators, Medium Scenario (SSP2)

	2010	2020	2030	2040	2050	2060
Population age 25+: highest educational attainment						
E1 - no education	0.09	0.07	0.05	0.04	0.03	0.02
E2 - incomplete primary	0.13	0.10	0.08	0.06	0.04	0.03
E3 - primary	0.12	0.12	0.12	0.11	0.11	0.10
E4 - lower secondary	0.17	0.17	0.18	0.17	0.16	0.15
E5 - upper secondary	0.32	0.34	0.36	0.37	0.38	0.40
E6 - post-secondary	0.18	0.20	0.22	0.24	0.28	0.31
Mean years of schooling (in years)	9.36	9.90	10.34	10.79	11.27	11.75
Gender gap (population age 25+): highest educational attainment (ratio male/female)						
E1 - no education	1.40	1.68	1.94	2.16	2.32	2.29
E2 - incomplete primary	1.63	1.72	1.89	1.99	2.02	1.92
E3 - primary	1.66	2.02	2.09	2.06	1.94	1.76
E4 - lower secondary	1.57	1.70	1.78	1.81	1.77	1.67
E5 - upper secondary	0.80	0.82	0.85	0.90	0.95	0.98
E6 - post-secondary	0.54	0.50	0.49	0.51	0.56	0.65
Mean years of schooling (male minus female)	−1.59	−1.84	−1.95	−1.88	−1.64	−1.28
Women age 20–39: highest educational attainment						
E1 - no education	0.03	0.02	0.01	0.00	0.00	0.00
E2 - incomplete primary	0.06	0.04	0.02	0.01	0.01	0.01
E3 - primary	0.08	0.06	0.06	0.06	0.06	0.06
E4 - lower secondary	0.13	0.12	0.12	0.11	0.11	0.10
E5 - upper secondary	0.44	0.45	0.46	0.45	0.45	0.47
E6 - post-secondary	0.25	0.31	0.34	0.36	0.37	0.36
Mean years of schooling (in years)	11.06	11.85	12.46	12.60	12.67	12.65

Education scenarios

GET: global education trend scenario (medium assumption also used for SSP2)

CER: constant enrolment rates scenario (assumption of no future improvements)

FT: Fast track scenario (assumption of education expansion according to fastest historical experience)

Pyramids by Education, Medium Scenario

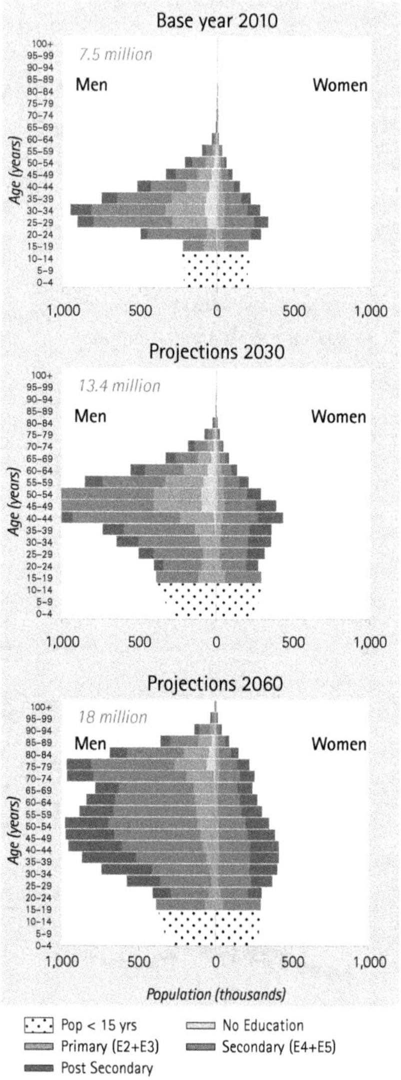

Population Size by Educational Attainment According to Three Education Scenarios: GET, CER, and FT

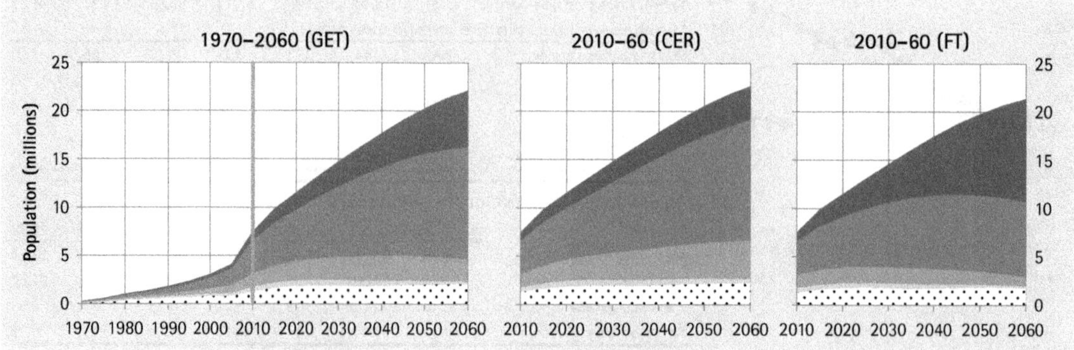

United Arab Emirates (Continued)

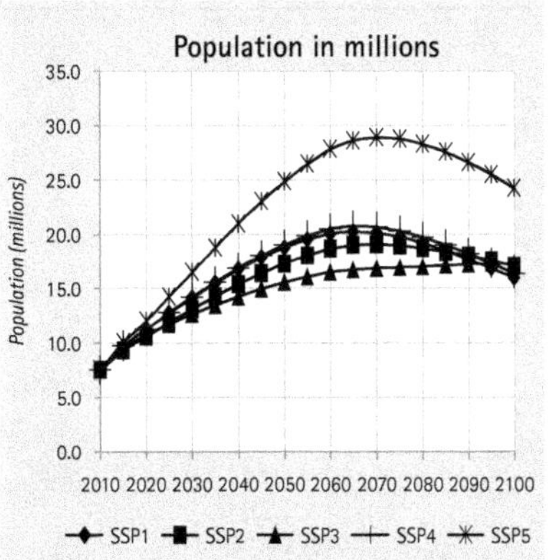

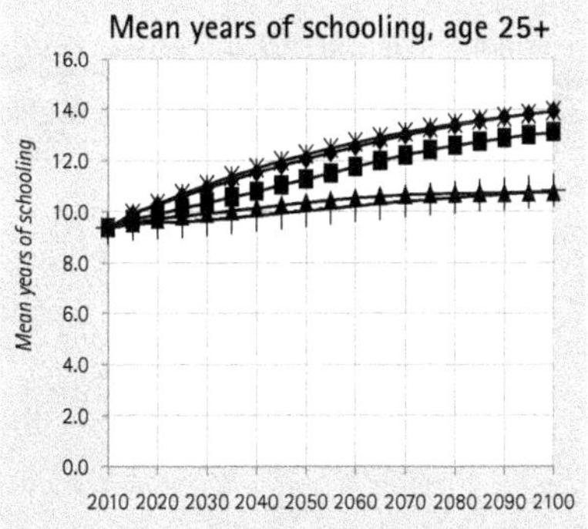

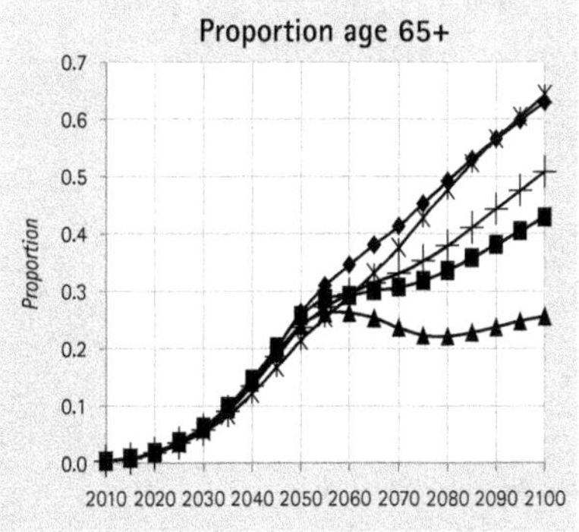

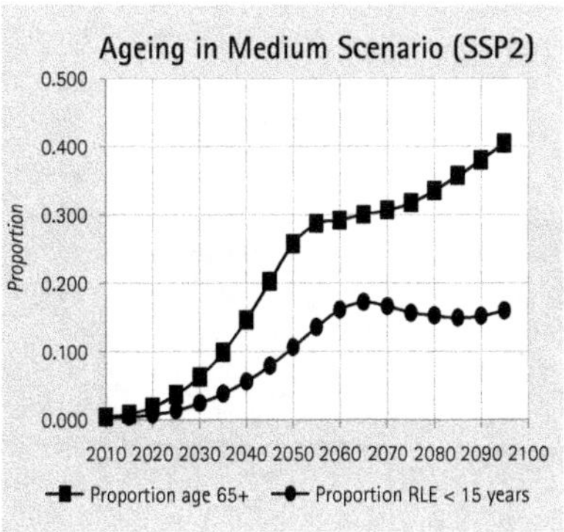

Alternative Scenarios to 2100

Projection Results by Scenario (SSP1–5)

	2010	2020	2030	2040	2050	2075	2100
Population (in millions)							
SSP1 - Rapid development	7.51	11.26	14.16	16.76	18.79	19.77	15.98
SSP2 - Medium	7.51	10.61	13.10	15.38	17.29	18.96	17.09
SSP3 - Stalled development	7.51	10.72	12.65	14.25	15.57	16.94	17.34
SSP4 - Inequality	7.51	11.28	14.22	16.86	19.03	20.31	16.38
SSP5 - Conventional development	7.51	12.00	16.50	20.98	24.85	28.77	24.24
Proportion age 65+							
SSP1 - Rapid development	0.00	0.02	0.06	0.14	0.26	0.45	0.63
SSP2 - Medium	0.00	0.02	0.06	0.15	0.26	0.32	0.43
SSP3 - Stalled development	0.00	0.02	0.06	0.14	0.24	0.22	0.26
SSP4 - Inequality	0.00	0.02	0.06	0.13	0.24	0.35	0.51
SSP5 - Conventional development	0.00	0.02	0.05	0.12	0.21	0.43	0.64
Proportion below age 20							
SSP1 - Rapid development	0.23	0.20	0.16	0.13	0.11	0.08	0.06
SSP2 - Medium	0.23	0.21	0.19	0.16	0.15	0.14	0.13
SSP3 - Stalled development	0.23	0.21	0.21	0.19	0.19	0.21	0.22
SSP4 - Inequality	0.23	0.20	0.17	0.14	0.12	0.10	0.09
SSP5 - Conventional development	0.23	0.20	0.16	0.13	0.11	0.08	0.06
Proportion of Women age 20–39 with at least secondary education							
SSP1 - Rapid development	0.82	0.92	0.95	0.96	0.96	0.97	0.98
SSP2 - Medium	0.82	0.88	0.92	0.93	0.93	0.95	0.98
SSP3 - Stalled development	0.82	0.85	0.86	0.86	0.86	0.86	0.86
SSP4 - Inequality	0.82	0.80	0.78	0.78	0.78	0.78	0.78
SSP5 - Conventional development	0.82	0.92	0.95	0.96	0.96	0.97	0.98
Mean years of schooling, age 25+							
SSP1 - Rapid development	9.36	10.26	10.92	11.52	12.05	13.18	13.93
SSP2 - Medium	9.36	9.90	10.34	10.79	11.27	12.40	13.10
SSP3 - Stalled development	9.36	9.71	9.93	10.13	10.35	10.69	10.76
SSP4 - Inequality	9.36	9.56	9.68	9.84	10.03	10.47	10.81
SSP5 - Conventional development	9.36	10.29	11.03	11.69	12.23	13.27	13.91

Demographic Assumptions Underlying SSPs

	2010–15	2020–25	2030–35	2040–45	2050–55	2075–80	2095–2100
Total fertility rate							
SSP1 - Rapid development	1.63	1.38	1.22	1.14	1.11	1.14	1.18
SSP2 - Medium	1.73	1.67	1.60	1.53	1.53	1.57	1.60
SSP3 - Stalled development	1.84	1.97	2.02	1.99	1.99	2.08	2.15
SSP4 - Inequality	1.67	1.47	1.31	1.22	1.19	1.23	1.27
SSP5 - Conventional development	1.63	1.38	1.22	1.14	1.11	1.14	1.18
Life expectancy at birth for females (in years)							
SSP1 - Rapid development	78.70	82.07	85.35	88.52	91.58	99.13	105.13
SSP2 - Medium	78.39	80.69	82.79	84.89	86.89	91.90	95.91
SSP3 - Stalled development	77.79	79.27	80.56	81.64	82.63	84.87	86.77
SSP4 - Inequality	78.13	80.65	82.90	85.04	86.99	91.62	95.48
SSP5 - Conventional development	78.70	82.07	85.35	88.52	91.58	99.13	105.13
Migration – net flow over five years (in thousands)							
SSP1 - Rapid development	1747	1089	1079	984	858	191	0
SSP2 - Medium	1304	835	853	856	841	282	0
SSP3 - Stalled development	1454	511	500	531	571	244	0
SSP4 - Inequality	1746	1093	1114	1105	1077	325	0
SSP5 - Conventional development	2039	1765	1916	1825	1634	364	0

Ageing Indicators, Medium Scenario (SSP2)

	2010	2020	2030	2040	2050	2075	2095
Median age	30.10	36.41	42.11	45.15	47.34	52.18	58.06
Propspective median age	30.10	34.35	38.40	39.77	40.17	40.31	42.28
Proportion age 65+	0.00	0.02	0.06	0.15	0.26	0.32	0.40
Proportion RLE < 15 years	0.00	0.01	0.03	0.06	0.11	0.16	0.16

United Kingdom

Detailed Human Capital Projections to 2060

Demographic indicators, Medium Scenario (SSP2)	2010	2020	2030	2040	2050	2060
Population (in millions)	62.04	66.20	70.28	73.92	77.35	80.46
Proportion age 65+	0.17	0.19	0.22	0.25	0.26	0.27
Proportion below age 20	0.24	0.23	0.23	0.22	0.22	0.21
	2005–10	2015–20	2025–30	2035–40	2045–50	2055–60
Total Fertility Rate	1.83	1.97	2.00	1.96	1.91	1.89
Life expectancy at birth (in years)						
Men	77.39	79.79	81.97	83.93	85.93	87.94
Women	81.69	83.99	86.21	88.21	90.21	92.19
Five-year immigration flow (in '000)	#N/A	1378.36	1431.50	1463.74	1464.14	1442.83
Five-year emigration flow (in '000)	#N/A	521.50	505.66	520.63	528.48	530.00

Human Capital indicators, Medium Scenario (SSP2)	2010	2020	2030	2040	2050	2060
Population age 25+: highest educational attainment						
E1 - no education	0.01	0.01	0.01	0.00	0.00	0.00
E2 - incomplete primary	0.00	0.00	0.00	0.00	0.00	0.00
E3 - primary	0.28	0.21	0.15	0.11	0.08	0.06
E4 - lower secondary	0.36	0.37	0.36	0.34	0.30	0.25
E5 - upper secondary	0.08	0.10	0.12	0.15	0.17	0.19
E6 - post-secondary	0.26	0.31	0.35	0.40	0.45	0.49
Mean years of schooling (in years)	10.44	11.10	11.72	12.33	12.91	13.46
Gender gap (population age 25+): highest educational attainment (ratio male/female)						
E1 - no education	1.03	1.01	0.98	0.94	0.90	0.89
E2 - incomplete primary	NA	NA	NA	NA	NA	NA
E3 - primary	0.90	0.90	0.91	0.95	1.00	1.03
E4 - lower secondary	1.01	1.01	1.01	1.00	0.99	0.99
E5 - upper secondary	1.05	1.00	0.99	0.98	0.99	0.99
E6 - post-secondary	1.10	1.06	1.04	1.02	1.01	1.01
Mean years of schooling (male minus female)	0.27	0.19	0.13	0.07	0.03	0.03
Women age 20–39: highest educational attainment						
E1 - no education	0.00	0.00	0.00	0.00	0.00	0.00
E2 - incomplete primary	0.00	0.00	0.00	0.00	0.00	0.00
E3 - primary	0.09	0.07	0.06	0.05	0.04	0.03
E4 - lower secondary	0.37	0.31	0.25	0.20	0.15	0.11
E5 - upper secondary	0.19	0.22	0.25	0.27	0.29	0.30
E6 - post-secondary	0.34	0.40	0.44	0.48	0.52	0.56
Mean years of schooling (in years)	11.96	12.65	13.35	13.82	14.23	14.57

Education scenarios

GET: global education trend scenario (medium assumption also used for SSP2)

CER: constant enrolment rates scenario (assumption of no future improvements)

FT: Fast track scenario (assumption of education expansion according to fastest historical experience)

Pyramids by Education, Medium Scenario

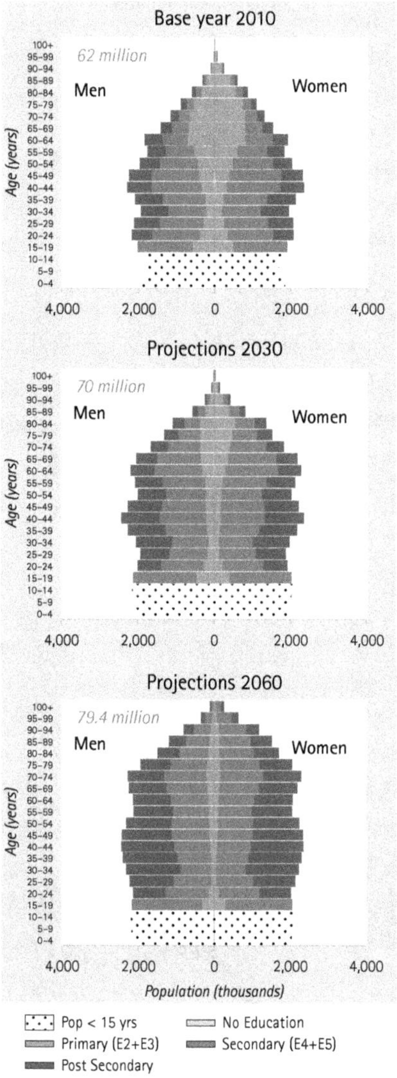

Population Size by Educational Attainment According to Three Education Scenarios: GET, CER, and FT

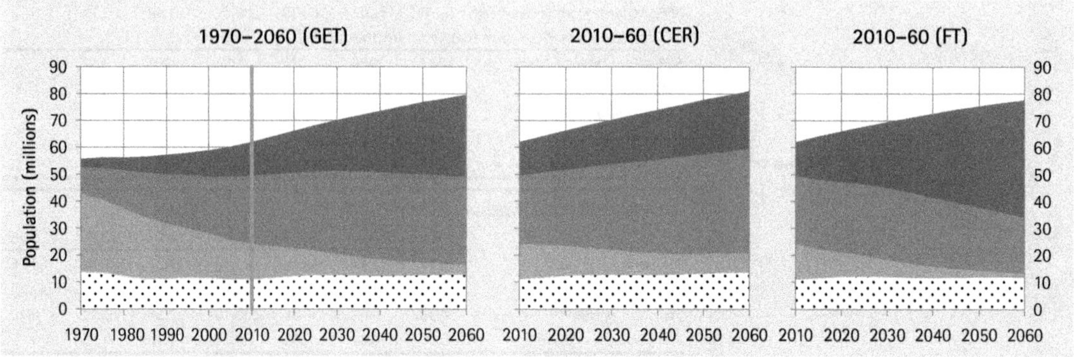

United Kingdom (Continued)

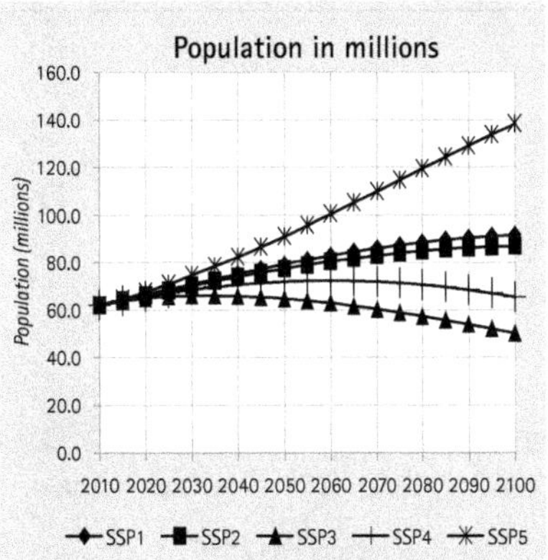

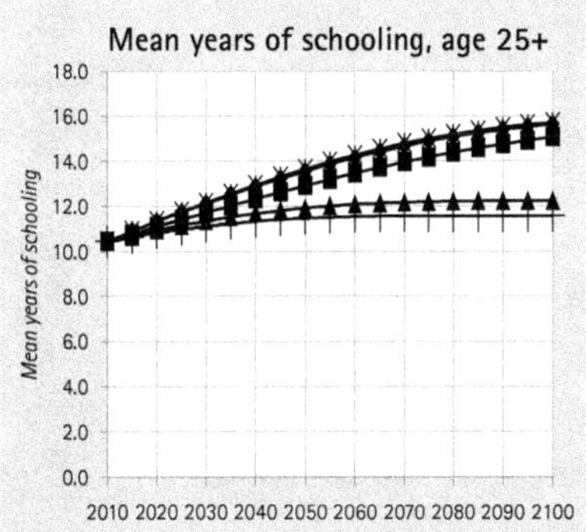

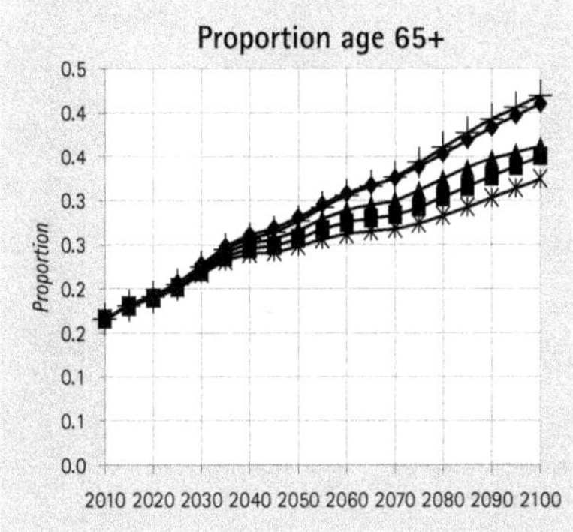

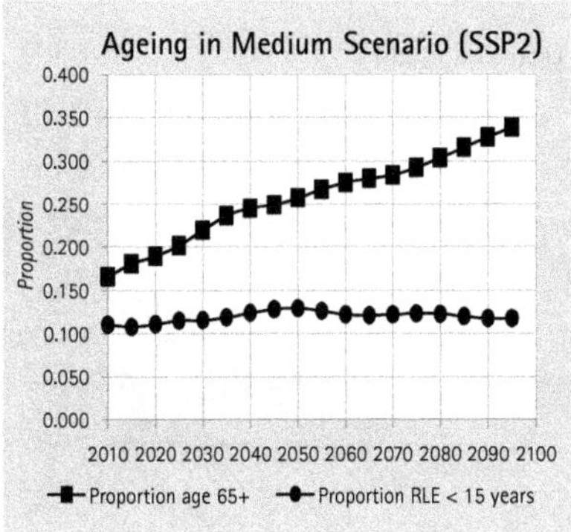

Alternative Scenarios to 2100

Projection Results by Scenario (SSP1–5)

	2010	2020	2030	2040	2050	2075	2100
Population (in millions)							
SSP1 - Rapid development	62.04	66.45	70.93	75.16	79.27	87.34	91.67
SSP2 - Medium	62.04	66.20	70.28	73.92	77.35	84.08	86.87
SSP3 - Stalled development	62.04	64.88	65.93	65.78	64.76	58.88	50.10
SSP4 - Inequality	62.04	65.69	68.54	70.57	71.86	71.28	65.37
SSP5 - Conventional development	62.04	67.54	74.65	82.33	90.97	114.67	138.17
Proportion age 65+							
SSP1 - Rapid development	0.17	0.19	0.23	0.26	0.28	0.34	0.41
SSP2 - Medium	0.17	0.19	0.22	0.25	0.26	0.29	0.35
SSP3 - Stalled development	0.17	0.19	0.22	0.25	0.27	0.31	0.36
SSP4 - Inequality	0.17	0.19	0.22	0.26	0.28	0.34	0.42
SSP5 - Conventional development	0.17	0.19	0.22	0.24	0.25	0.27	0.32
Proportion below age 20							
SSP1 - Rapid development	0.24	0.23	0.23	0.21	0.21	0.19	0.17
SSP2 - Medium	0.24	0.23	0.23	0.22	0.22	0.20	0.19
SSP3 - Stalled development	0.24	0.23	0.22	0.19	0.18	0.16	0.15
SSP4 - Inequality	0.24	0.23	0.21	0.19	0.18	0.16	0.14
SSP5 - Conventional development	0.24	0.24	0.25	0.25	0.25	0.24	0.23
Proportion of Women age 20–39 with at least secondary education							
SSP1 - Rapid development	0.91	0.95	0.97	0.97	0.98	0.99	1.00
SSP2 - Medium	0.91	0.92	0.94	0.95	0.96	0.98	0.99
SSP3 - Stalled development	0.91	0.91	0.91	0.91	0.91	0.91	0.91
SSP4 - Inequality	0.91	0.91	0.91	0.91	0.91	0.91	0.91
SSP5 - Conventional development	0.91	0.95	0.97	0.97	0.98	0.99	1.00
Mean years of schooling, age 25+							
SSP1 - Rapid development	10.44	11.33	12.12	12.88	13.55	14.88	15.63
SSP2 - Medium	10.44	11.10	11.72	12.33	12.91	14.17	15.05
SSP3 - Stalled development	10.44	10.94	11.36	11.68	11.92	12.20	12.24
SSP4 - Inequality	10.44	10.83	11.12	11.33	11.47	11.56	11.56
SSP5 - Conventional development	10.44	11.34	12.16	12.93	13.64	14.99	15.71

Demographic Assumptions Underlying SSPs

	2010–15	2020–25	2030–35	2040–45	2050–55	2075–80	2095–2100
Total fertility rate							
SSP1 - Rapid development	1.96	1.95	1.93	1.90	1.87	1.85	1.84
SSP2 - Medium	1.96	1.98	1.99	1.94	1.90	1.87	1.85
SSP3 - Stalled development	1.88	1.71	1.60	1.53	1.49	1.49	1.50
SSP4 - Inequality	1.88	1.73	1.62	1.56	1.51	1.52	1.52
SSP5 - Conventional development	2.06	2.24	2.34	2.35	2.34	2.31	2.30
Life expectancy at birth for females (in years)							
SSP1 - Rapid development	83.89	87.05	90.05	92.98	95.94	103.43	109.50
SSP2 - Medium	82.89	85.11	87.21	89.21	91.19	96.20	100.21
SSP3 - Stalled development	82.92	84.08	85.12	86.10	87.04	89.27	91.05
SSP4 - Inequality	83.42	85.57	87.58	89.50	91.43	96.07	99.84
SSP5 - Conventional development	83.89	87.05	90.05	92.98	95.94	103.43	109.50
Migration – net flow over five years (in thousands)							
SSP1 - Rapid development	918	891	923	899	855	353	0
SSP2 - Medium	920	884	924	925	907	406	0
SSP3 - Stalled development	764	446	463	456	439	193	0
SSP4 - Inequality	918	889	917	894	856	375	0
SSP5 - Conventional development	1072	1340	1410	1428	1423	668	0

Ageing Indicators, Medium Scenario (SSP2)

	2010	2020	2030	2040	2050	2075	2095
Median age	39.79	40.69	42.12	43.49	43.80	47.02	50.20
Propspective median age	39.79	38.66	38.17	37.70	36.11	34.66	33.96
Proportion age 65+	0.17	0.19	0.22	0.25	0.26	0.29	0.34
Proportion RLE < 15 years	0.11	0.11	0.12	0.12	0.13	0.12	0.12

United Republic of Tanzania

Detailed Human Capital Projections to 2060

Demographic indicators, Medium Scenario (SSP2)	2010	2020	2030	2040	2050	2060
Population (in millions)	44.84	58.41	73.05	87.98	101.91	113.69
Proportion age 65+	0.03	0.03	0.04	0.04	0.05	0.07
Proportion below age 20	0.55	0.54	0.50	0.45	0.40	0.36
	2005–10	2015–20	2025–30	2035–40	2045–50	2055–60
Total Fertility Rate	5.58	4.60	3.66	2.99	2.54	2.19
Life expectancy at birth (in years)						
Men	54.62	60.86	62.53	64.08	65.80	67.98
Women	56.19	63.28	65.78	67.88	69.78	72.02
Five-year immigration flow (in '000)	67.35	65.89	68.27	69.64	69.50	68.37
Five-year emigration flow (in '000)	365.94	356.45	462.37	566.56	649.86	714.26

Human Capital indicators, Medium Scenario (SSP2)	2010	2020	2030	2040	2050	2060
Population age 25+: highest educational attainment						
E1 - no education	0.21	0.12	0.06	0.03	0.01	0.01
E2 - incomplete primary	0.12	0.08	0.05	0.04	0.02	0.02
E3 - primary	0.57	0.68	0.73	0.74	0.73	0.69
E4 - lower secondary	0.06	0.08	0.08	0.09	0.09	0.09
E5 - upper secondary	0.02	0.03	0.04	0.07	0.10	0.14
E6 - post-secondary	0.01	0.02	0.02	0.03	0.04	0.06
Mean years of schooling (in years)	6.27	7.31	8.06	8.62	9.06	9.45
Gender gap (population age 25+): highest educational attainment (ratio male/female)						
E1 - no education	0.50	0.49	0.51	0.57	0.67	0.79
E2 - incomplete primary	1.21	1.12	1.08	1.09	1.09	1.04
E3 - primary	1.16	1.08	1.05	1.04	1.03	1.02
E4 - lower secondary	1.44	1.25	1.15	1.10	1.08	1.07
E5 - upper secondary	1.56	0.99	0.79	0.76	0.81	0.91
E6 - post-secondary	1.42	1.12	0.96	0.89	0.90	0.96
Mean years of schooling (male minus female)	1.20	0.69	0.29	0.02	−0.08	−0.06
Women age 20–39: highest educational attainment						
E1 - no education	0.12	0.06	0.04	0.03	0.02	0.02
E2 - incomplete primary	0.08	0.07	0.07	0.06	0.05	0.05
E3 - primary	0.69	0.72	0.69	0.65	0.61	0.56
E4 - lower secondary	0.08	0.10	0.11	0.12	0.13	0.14
E5 - upper secondary	0.02	0.04	0.07	0.10	0.14	0.18
E6 - post-secondary	0.01	0.02	0.03	0.04	0.05	0.06
Mean years of schooling (in years)	7.29	8.01	8.44	8.87	9.27	9.66

Education scenarios

GET: global education trend scenario (medium assumption also used for SSP2)

CER: constant enrolment rates scenario (assumption of no future improvements)

FT: Fast track scenario (assumption of education expansion according to fastest historical experience)

Pyramids by Education, Medium Scenario

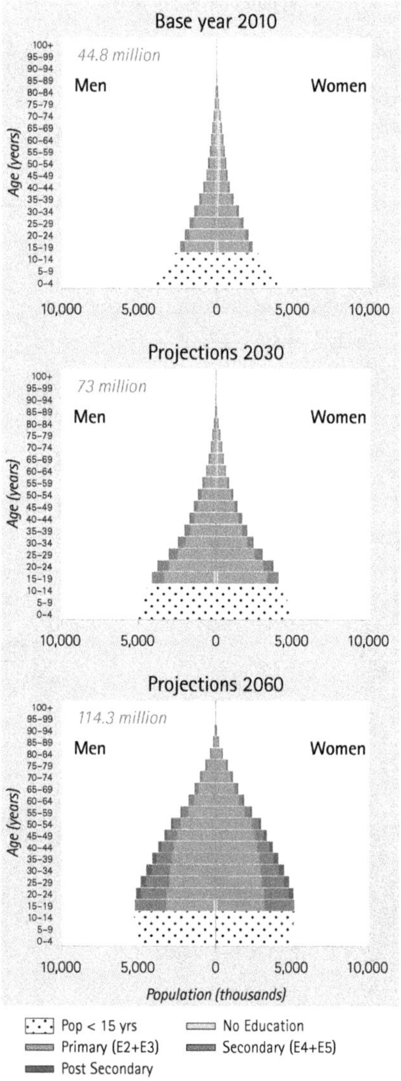

Population Size by Educational Attainment According to Three Education Scenarios: GET, CER, and FT

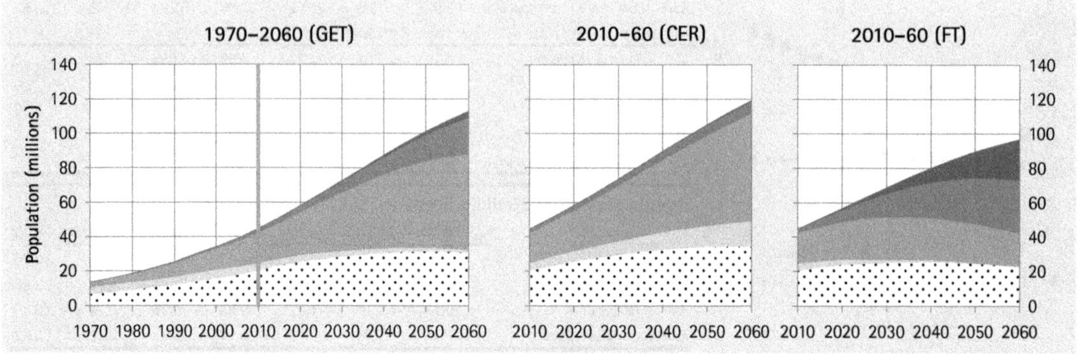

United Republic of Tanzania (Continued)

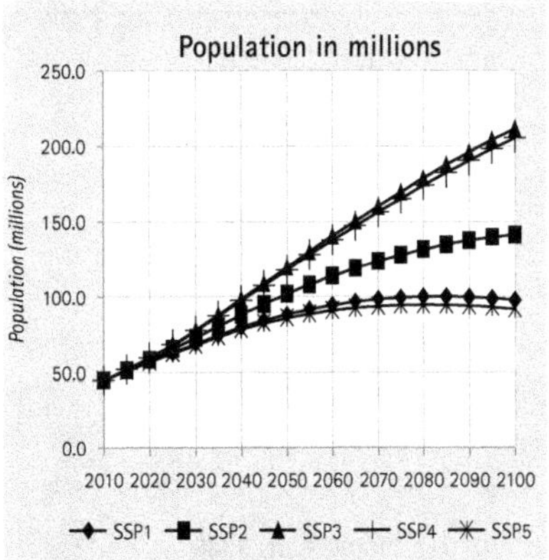

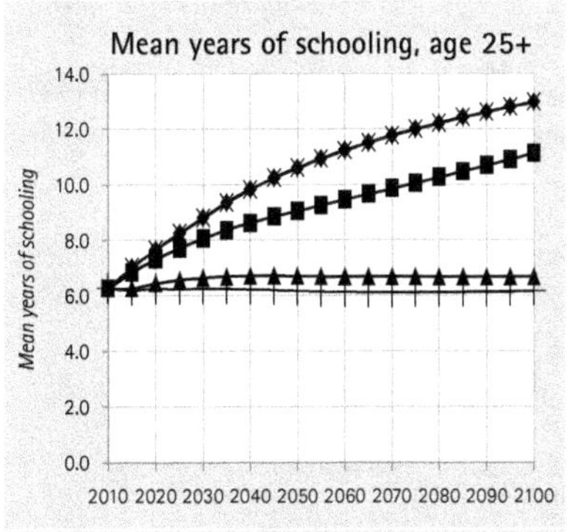

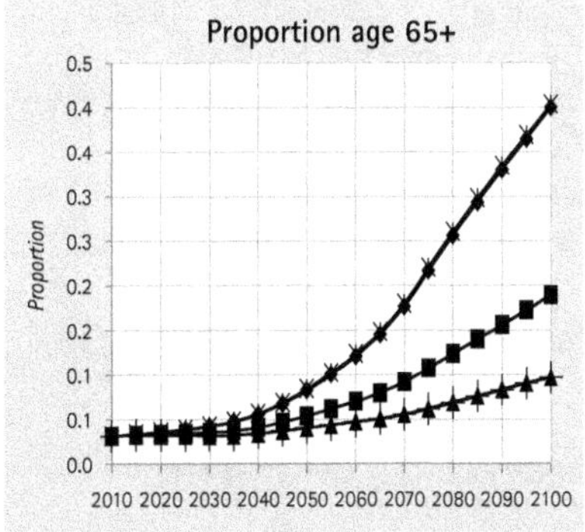

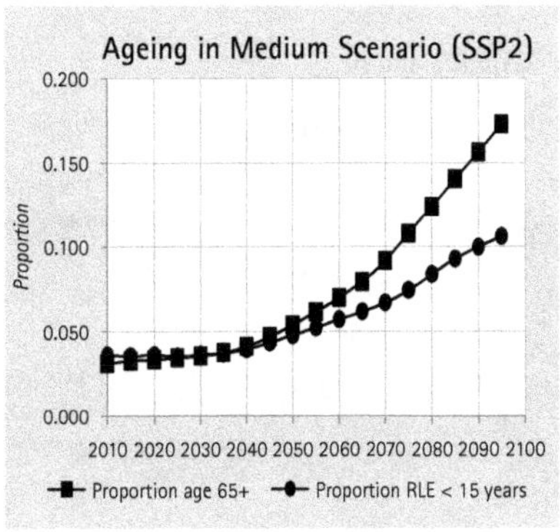

Alternative Scenarios to 2100

Projection Results by Scenario (SSP1–5)

	2010	2020	2030	2040	2050	2075	2100
Population (in millions)							
SSP1 - Rapid development	44.84	57.09	68.90	79.77	88.31	99.37	97.69
SSP2 - Medium	44.84	58.41	73.05	87.98	101.91	127.81	141.18
SSP3 - Stalled development	44.84	59.84	78.07	98.44	119.69	169.52	211.58
SSP4 - Inequality	44.84	59.76	77.69	97.50	117.95	165.10	205.32
SSP5 - Conventional development	44.84	56.91	68.19	78.30	85.87	94.35	91.71
Proportion age 65+							
SSP1 - Rapid development	0.03	0.04	0.04	0.06	0.08	0.22	0.40
SSP2 - Medium	0.03	0.03	0.04	0.04	0.05	0.11	0.19
SSP3 - Stalled development	0.03	0.03	0.03	0.03	0.04	0.06	0.10
SSP4 - Inequality	0.03	0.03	0.03	0.03	0.04	0.06	0.10
SSP5 - Conventional development	0.03	0.04	0.04	0.06	0.08	0.22	0.40
Proportion below age 20							
SSP1 - Rapid development	0.55	0.52	0.45	0.38	0.31	0.19	0.12
SSP2 - Medium	0.55	0.54	0.50	0.45	0.40	0.30	0.24
SSP3 - Stalled development	0.55	0.55	0.53	0.50	0.47	0.38	0.34
SSP4 - Inequality	0.55	0.55	0.54	0.51	0.47	0.38	0.34
SSP5 - Conventional development	0.55	0.52	0.45	0.38	0.31	0.19	0.12
Proportion of Women age 20–39 with at least secondary education							
SSP1 - Rapid development	0.11	0.28	0.43	0.54	0.62	0.74	0.84
SSP2 - Medium	0.11	0.15	0.20	0.26	0.32	0.50	0.69
SSP3 - Stalled development	0.11	0.08	0.08	0.08	0.08	0.08	0.08
SSP4 - Inequality	0.11	0.07	0.07	0.07	0.07	0.07	0.07
SSP5 - Conventional development	0.11	0.28	0.43	0.54	0.62	0.74	0.84
Mean years of schooling, age 25+							
SSP1 - Rapid development	6.27	7.66	8.81	9.82	10.60	11.99	12.97
SSP2 - Medium	6.27	7.31	8.06	8.62	9.06	10.06	11.12
SSP3 - Stalled development	6.27	6.45	6.65	6.72	6.71	6.69	6.69
SSP4 - Inequality	6.27	6.25	6.25	6.23	6.17	6.13	6.17
SSP5 - Conventional development	6.27	7.66	8.81	9.81	10.59	11.98	12.96

Demographic Assumptions Underlying SSPs

	2010–15	2020–25	2030–35	2040–45	2050–55	2075–80	2095–2100
Total fertility rate							
SSP1 - Rapid development	4.74	3.29	2.40	1.92	1.62	1.34	1.27
SSP2 - Medium	5.06	4.11	3.28	2.73	2.36	1.90	1.77
SSP3 - Stalled development	5.45	5.05	4.33	3.66	3.16	2.58	2.46
SSP4 - Inequality	5.46	5.11	4.39	3.68	3.17	2.58	2.45
SSP5 - Conventional development	4.74	3.29	2.40	1.92	1.62	1.34	1.27
Life expectancy at birth for females (in years)							
SSP1 - Rapid development	64.34	71.81	76.05	79.83	83.24	91.34	97.98
SSP2 - Medium	60.32	64.51	66.88	68.78	70.88	76.62	81.11
SSP3 - Stalled development	61.49	61.58	62.69	63.31	64.14	66.56	68.44
SSP4 - Inequality	61.49	61.56	62.64	63.25	64.07	66.48	68.37
SSP5 - Conventional development	64.34	71.81	76.05	79.83	83.24	91.34	97.98
Migration – net flow over five years (in thousands)							
SSP1 - Rapid development	−270	−334	−436	−502	−539	−237	0
SSP2 - Medium	−272	−337	−446	−540	−617	−330	0
SSP3 - Stalled development	−223	−163	−213	−260	−303	−173	0
SSP4 - Inequality	−268	−330	−443	−555	−657	−377	0
SSP5 - Conventional development	−316	−508	−680	−812	−907	−445	0

Ageing Indicators, Medium Scenario (SSP2)

	2010	2020	2030	2040	2050	2075	2095
Median age	17.43	18.10	20.22	22.61	25.24	33.09	39.19
Propspective median age	17.43	15.93	16.76	17.91	19.06	21.89	24.25
Proportion age 65+	0.03	0.03	0.04	0.04	0.05	0.11	0.17
Proportion RLE < 15 years	0.04	0.04	0.04	0.04	0.05	0.07	0.11

United States of America

Detailed Human Capital Projections to 2060

Demographic indicators, Medium Scenario (SSP2)

	2010	2020	2030	2040	2050	2060
Population (in millions)	310.38	333.97	358.81	381.37	400.41	419.88
Proportion age 65+	0.13	0.16	0.20	0.21	0.22	0.24
Proportion below age 20	0.27	0.25	0.24	0.24	0.23	0.22
	2005–10	2015–20	2025–30	2035–40	2045–50	2055–60
Total Fertility Rate	2.07	1.90	1.94	1.93	1.91	1.89
Life expectancy at birth (in years)						
Men	75.36	76.76	78.47	80.30	82.20	84.40
Women	80.51	81.89	83.59	85.39	87.31	89.51
Five-year immigration flow (in '000)	6385.49	6293.87	6541.48	6698.61	6700.08	6595.45
Five-year emigration flow (in '000)	1438.10	1066.75	1079.16	1076.83	1093.85	1119.02

Human Capital indicators, Medium Scenario (SSP2)

	2010	2020	2030	2040	2050	2060
Population age 25+: highest educational attainment						
E1 - no education	0.01	0.01	0.00	0.00	0.00	0.00
E2 - incomplete primary	0.01	0.01	0.00	0.00	0.00	0.00
E3 - primary	0.04	0.03	0.02	0.02	0.02	0.01
E4 - lower secondary	0.07	0.06	0.06	0.05	0.05	0.04
E5 - upper secondary	0.52	0.50	0.49	0.47	0.45	0.43
E6 - post-secondary	0.36	0.39	0.42	0.46	0.49	0.52
Mean years of schooling (in years)	12.86	13.11	13.31	13.50	13.69	13.88
Gender gap (population age 25+): highest educational attainment (ratio male/female)						
E1 - no education	1.01	1.03	1.04	1.03	1.01	0.98
E2 - incomplete primary	1.15	1.19	1.21	1.22	1.19	1.14
E3 - primary	1.08	1.14	1.19	1.21	1.21	1.18
E4 - lower secondary	1.03	1.09	1.13	1.15	1.14	1.10
E5 - upper secondary	0.98	1.03	1.07	1.10	1.11	1.10
E6 - post-secondary	1.00	0.94	0.90	0.89	0.89	0.92
Mean years of schooling (male minus female)	−0.02	−0.14	−0.23	−0.27	−0.26	−0.20
Women age 20–39: highest educational attainment						
E1 - no education	0.00	0.00	0.00	0.00	0.00	0.00
E2 - incomplete primary	0.00	0.00	0.00	0.00	0.00	0.00
E3 - primary	0.02	0.02	0.01	0.01	0.01	0.00
E4 - lower secondary	0.07	0.06	0.04	0.03	0.03	0.02
E5 - upper secondary	0.52	0.50	0.49	0.47	0.47	0.46
E6 - post-secondary	0.38	0.43	0.45	0.48	0.50	0.51
Mean years of schooling (in years)	13.14	13.40	13.58	13.75	13.85	13.93

Education scenarios

GET : global education trend scenario (medium assumption also used for SSP2)

CER: constant enrolment rates scenario (assumption of no future improvements)

FT: Fast track scenario (assumption of education expansion according to fastest historical experience)

Pyramids by Education, Medium Scenario

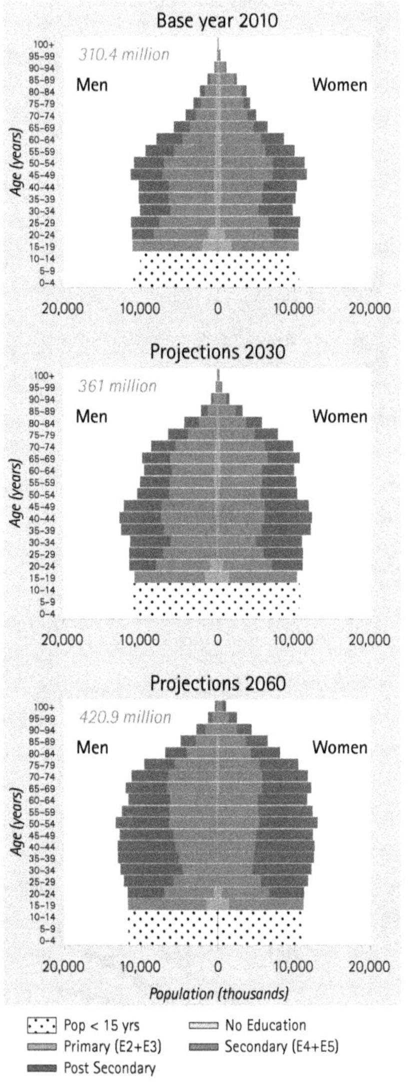

Population Size by Educational Attainment According to Three Education Scenarios: GET, CER, and FT

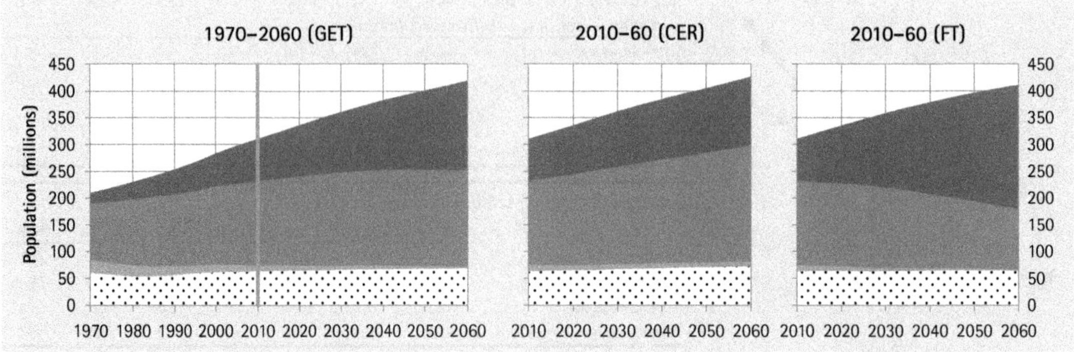

United States of America (Continued)

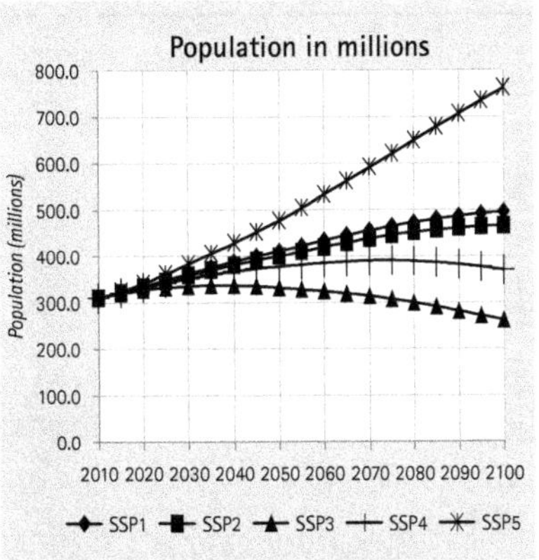

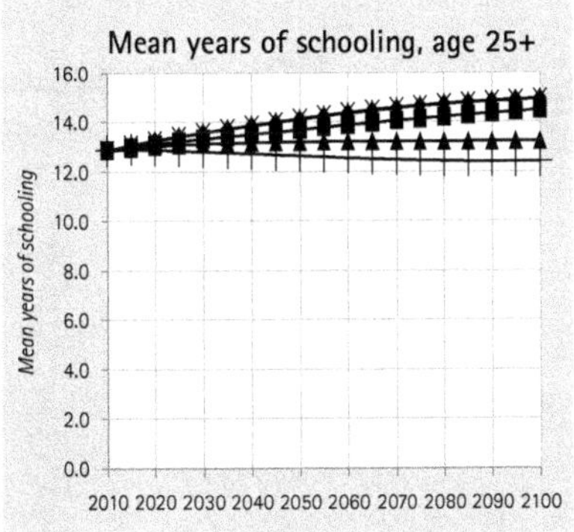

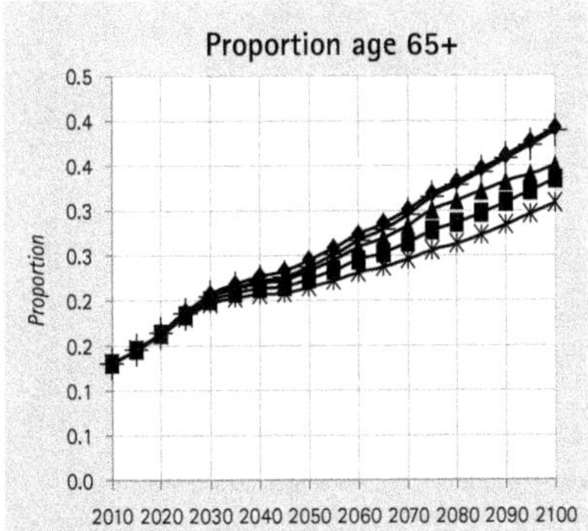

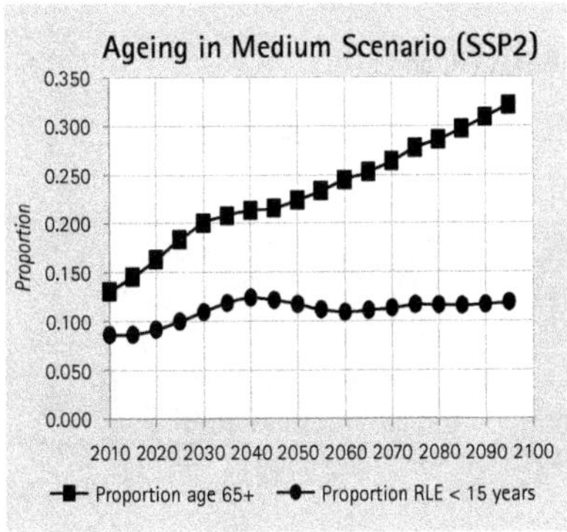

Alternative Scenarios to 2100

Projection Results by Scenario (SSP1–5)

	2010	2020	2030	2040	2050	2075	2100
Population (in millions)							
SSP1 - Rapid development	310.38	335.27	362.35	388.39	411.28	464.98	495.54
SSP2 - Medium	310.38	333.97	358.81	381.37	400.41	446.00	465.67
SSP3 - Stalled development	310.38	327.18	335.46	337.00	331.78	306.99	261.29
SSP4 - Inequality	310.38	331.85	351.53	367.26	377.18	390.12	369.28
SSP5 - Conventional development	310.38	341.23	383.18	428.76	477.14	620.56	761.36
Proportion age 65+							
SSP1 - Rapid development	0.13	0.17	0.21	0.23	0.24	0.32	0.39
SSP2 - Medium	0.13	0.16	0.20	0.21	0.22	0.28	0.33
SSP3 - Stalled development	0.13	0.16	0.20	0.22	0.23	0.30	0.35
SSP4 - Inequality	0.13	0.16	0.20	0.22	0.24	0.31	0.39
SSP5 - Conventional development	0.13	0.16	0.20	0.21	0.21	0.26	0.31
Proportion below age 20							
SSP1 - Rapid development	0.27	0.25	0.23	0.23	0.22	0.20	0.17
SSP2 - Medium	0.27	0.25	0.24	0.24	0.23	0.21	0.19
SSP3 - Stalled development	0.27	0.25	0.22	0.21	0.20	0.17	0.16
SSP4 - Inequality	0.27	0.25	0.22	0.21	0.20	0.17	0.15
SSP5 - Conventional development	0.27	0.26	0.26	0.26	0.26	0.25	0.23
Proportion of Women age 20–39 with at least secondary education							
SSP1 - Rapid development	0.97	0.99	0.99	0.99	1.00	1.00	1.00
SSP2 - Medium	0.97	0.98	0.99	0.99	0.99	1.00	1.00
SSP3 - Stalled development	0.97	0.97	0.97	0.97	0.97	0.97	0.97
SSP4 - Inequality	0.97	0.97	0.97	0.97	0.97	0.97	0.97
SSP5 - Conventional development	0.97	0.99	0.99	0.99	1.00	1.00	1.00
Mean years of schooling, age 25+							
SSP1 - Rapid development	12.86	13.24	13.56	13.85	14.11	14.63	14.93
SSP2 - Medium	12.86	13.11	13.31	13.50	13.69	14.13	14.48
SSP3 - Stalled development	12.86	13.02	13.11	13.17	13.19	13.22	13.22
SSP4 - Inequality	12.86	12.87	12.80	12.72	12.63	12.44	12.39
SSP5 - Conventional development	12.86	13.24	13.57	13.87	14.13	14.66	14.95

Demographic Assumptions Underlying SSPs

	2010–15	2020–25	2030–35	2040–45	2050–55	2075–80	2095–2100
Total fertility rate							
SSP1 - Rapid development	1.88	1.89	1.90	1.89	1.87	1.85	1.84
SSP2 - Medium	1.88	1.92	1.95	1.92	1.90	1.87	1.85
SSP3 - Stalled development	1.80	1.66	1.56	1.52	1.48	1.47	1.47
SSP4 - Inequality	1.81	1.73	1.67	1.61	1.57	1.56	1.55
SSP5 - Conventional development	1.97	2.17	2.30	2.33	2.34	2.31	2.30
Life expectancy at birth for females (in years)							
SSP1 - Rapid development	82.18	84.68	87.30	90.01	93.02	101.23	107.84
SSP2 - Medium	81.19	82.79	84.49	86.28	88.41	94.10	98.71
SSP3 - Stalled development	81.17	81.72	82.43	83.14	84.19	87.28	89.74
SSP4 - Inequality	81.69	83.19	84.81	86.54	88.59	93.99	98.44
SSP5 - Conventional development	82.18	84.68	87.30	90.01	93.02	101.23	107.84
Migration – net flow over five years (in thousands)							
SSP1 - Rapid development	4918	5308	5462	5400	5149	2151	0
SSP2 - Medium	4939	5269	5449	5508	5412	2449	0
SSP3 - Stalled development	4093	2649	2724	2708	2602	1139	0
SSP4 - Inequality	4914	5287	5436	5436	5291	2410	0
SSP5 - Conventional development	5739	7985	8356	8607	8613	4121	0

Ageing Indicators, Medium Scenario (SSP2)

	2010	2020	2030	2040	2050	2075	2095
Median age	36.88	38.11	39.82	41.13	42.33	45.49	49.01
Propspective median age	36.88	36.61	36.75	36.40	35.59	33.48	32.66
Proportion age 65+	0.13	0.16	0.20	0.21	0.22	0.28	0.32
Proportion RLE < 15 years	0.09	0.09	0.11	0.12	0.12	0.12	0.12

Uruguay

Detailed Human Capital Projections to 2060

Demographic indicators, Medium Scenario (SSP2)

	2010	2020	2030	2040	2050	2060
Population (in millions)	3.37	3.45	3.50	3.50	3.44	3.34
Proportion age 65+	0.14	0.15	0.18	0.22	0.25	0.29
Proportion below age 20	0.30	0.27	0.25	0.22	0.20	0.18
	2005–10	2015–20	2025–30	2035–40	2045–50	2055–60
Total Fertility Rate	2.12	1.89	1.79	1.69	1.62	1.60
Life expectancy at birth (in years)						
Men	72.72	75.37	77.82	80.07	82.24	84.48
Women	79.86	82.19	84.41	86.51	88.51	90.61
Five-year immigration flow (in '000)	3.12	3.06	3.17	3.25	3.25	3.20
Five-year emigration flow (in '000)	52.92	39.43	36.94	33.81	30.72	27.50

Human Capital indicators, Medium Scenario (SSP2)

	2010	2020	2030	2040	2050	2060
Population age 25+: highest educational attainment						
E1 - no education	0.01	0.01	0.00	0.00	0.00	0.00
E2 - incomplete primary	0.12	0.07	0.04	0.03	0.02	0.01
E3 - primary	0.36	0.34	0.32	0.30	0.28	0.25
E4 - lower secondary	0.26	0.28	0.29	0.29	0.28	0.26
E5 - upper secondary	0.12	0.14	0.16	0.18	0.20	0.23
E6 - post-secondary	0.13	0.15	0.17	0.20	0.23	0.26
Mean years of schooling (in years)	8.54	9.12	9.63	10.06	10.46	10.86
Gender gap (population age 25+): highest educational attainment (ratio male/female)						
E1 - no education	0.79	0.82	0.89	0.96	1.00	0.97
E2 - incomplete primary	1.00	0.96	0.96	0.97	0.97	0.96
E3 - primary	1.05	1.08	1.11	1.13	1.13	1.11
E4 - lower secondary	1.21	1.20	1.18	1.17	1.15	1.11
E5 - upper secondary	0.83	0.83	0.84	0.87	0.91	0.95
E6 - post-secondary	0.72	0.72	0.73	0.75	0.79	0.85
Mean years of schooling (male minus female)	−0.30	−0.39	−0.47	−0.49	−0.45	−0.35
Women age 20–39: highest educational attainment						
E1 - no education	0.00	0.00	0.00	0.00	0.00	0.00
E2 - incomplete primary	0.03	0.01	0.01	0.01	0.00	0.00
E3 - primary	0.29	0.27	0.24	0.22	0.19	0.16
E4 - lower secondary	0.31	0.28	0.26	0.23	0.20	0.17
E5 - upper secondary	0.21	0.23	0.26	0.29	0.32	0.35
E6 - post-secondary	0.17	0.20	0.23	0.26	0.29	0.31
Mean years of schooling (in years)	9.91	10.39	10.89	11.25	11.59	11.89

Education scenarios

GET: global education trend scenario (medium assumption also used for SSP2)

CER: constant enrolment rates scenario (assumption of no future improvements)

FT: Fast track scenario (assumption of education expansion according to fastest historical experience)

Pyramids by Education, Medium Scenario

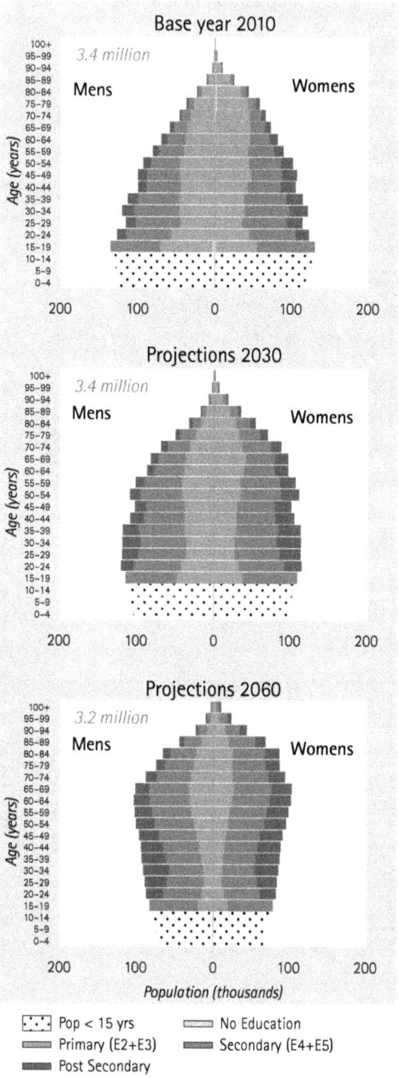

Population Size by Educational Attainment According to Three Education Scenarios: GET, CER, and FT

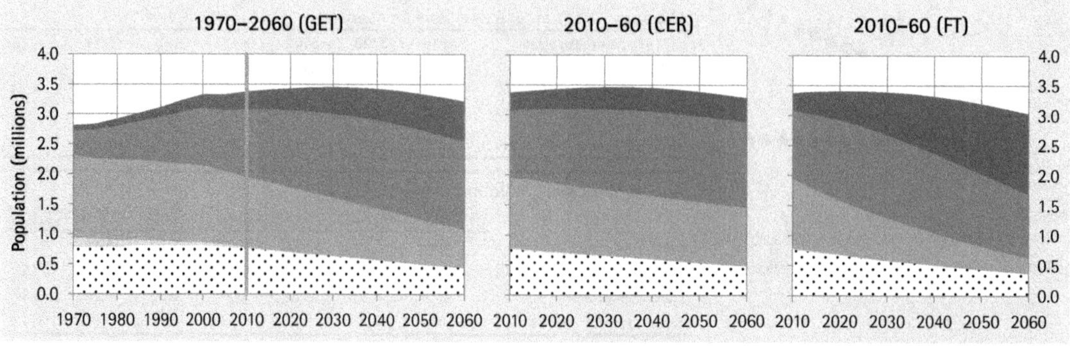

Uruguay (Continued)

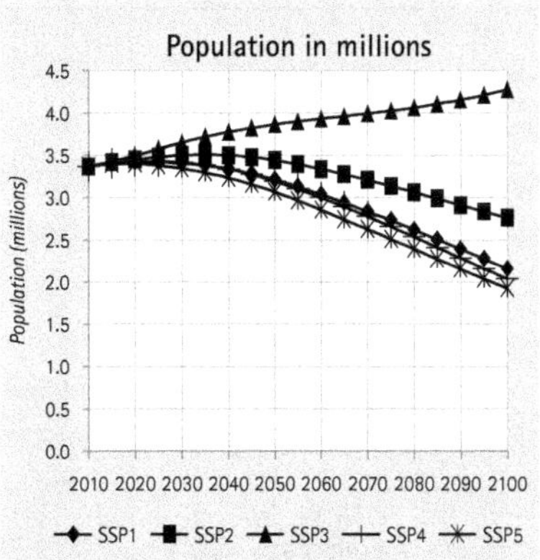

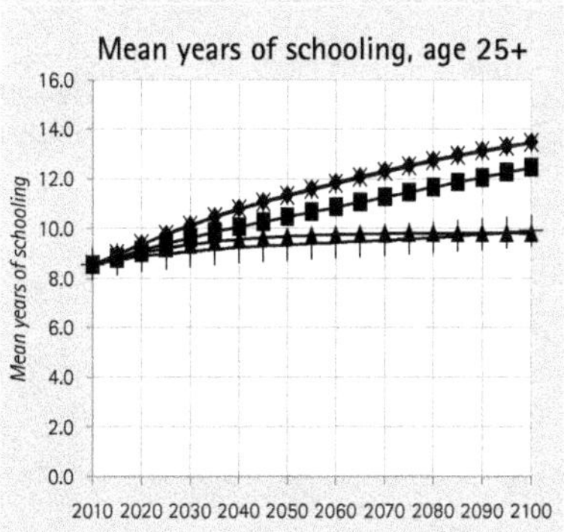

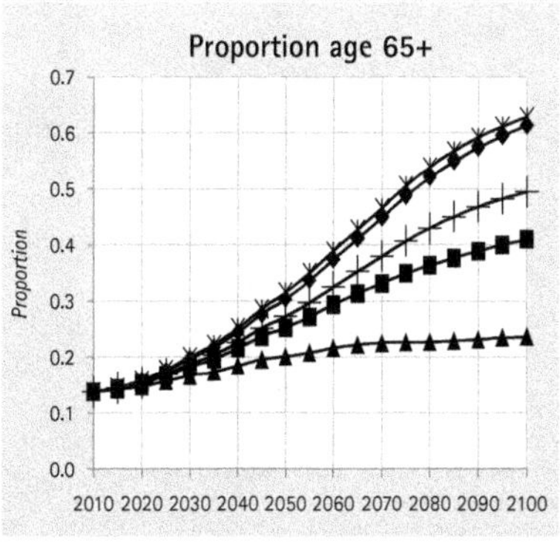

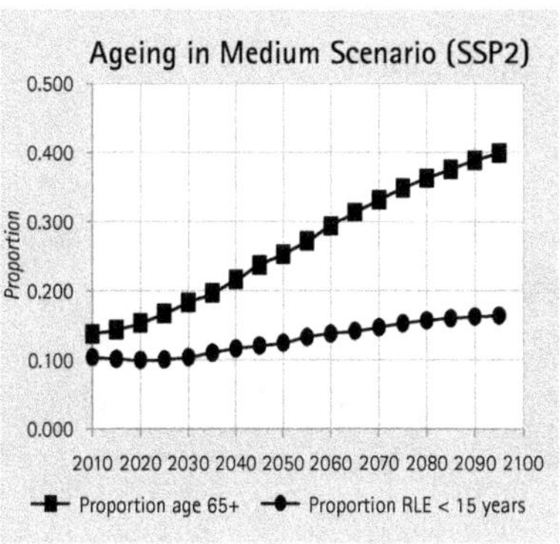

Alternative Scenarios to 2100

Projection Results by Scenario (SSP1–5)

	2010	2020	2030	2040	2050	2075	2100
Population (in millions)							
SSP1 - Rapid development	3.37	3.42	3.41	3.34	3.21	2.73	2.16
SSP2 - Medium	3.37	3.45	3.50	3.50	3.44	3.14	2.76
SSP3 - Stalled development	3.37	3.50	3.65	3.77	3.86	4.03	4.28
SSP4 - Inequality	3.37	3.42	3.41	3.34	3.19	2.66	2.04
SSP5 - Conventional development	3.37	3.40	3.34	3.23	3.07	2.51	1.92
Proportion age 65+							
SSP1 - Rapid development	0.14	0.16	0.20	0.24	0.30	0.49	0.61
SSP2 - Medium	0.14	0.15	0.18	0.22	0.25	0.35	0.41
SSP3 - Stalled development	0.14	0.15	0.17	0.18	0.20	0.23	0.24
SSP4 - Inequality	0.14	0.15	0.19	0.23	0.27	0.41	0.49
SSP5 - Conventional development	0.14	0.16	0.20	0.25	0.32	0.51	0.63
Proportion below age 20							
SSP1 - Rapid development	0.30	0.26	0.21	0.18	0.15	0.09	0.07
SSP2 - Medium	0.30	0.27	0.25	0.22	0.20	0.17	0.15
SSP3 - Stalled development	0.30	0.28	0.27	0.27	0.26	0.25	0.25
SSP4 - Inequality	0.30	0.27	0.23	0.19	0.16	0.12	0.11
SSP5 - Conventional development	0.30	0.26	0.21	0.17	0.14	0.09	0.07
Proportion of Women age 20–39 with at least secondary education							
SSP1 - Rapid development	0.68	0.81	0.86	0.89	0.90	0.94	0.97
SSP2 - Medium	0.68	0.72	0.75	0.78	0.81	0.88	0.94
SSP3 - Stalled development	0.68	0.69	0.69	0.69	0.69	0.69	0.69
SSP4 - Inequality	0.68	0.65	0.62	0.62	0.62	0.62	0.62
SSP5 - Conventional development	0.68	0.81	0.86	0.89	0.90	0.94	0.97
Mean years of schooling, age 25+							
SSP1 - Rapid development	8.54	9.36	10.13	10.79	11.34	12.53	13.46
SSP2 - Medium	8.54	9.12	9.63	10.06	10.46	11.46	12.43
SSP3 - Stalled development	8.54	9.02	9.35	9.55	9.68	9.80	9.81
SSP4 - Inequality	8.54	8.88	9.07	9.23	9.34	9.57	9.90
SSP5 - Conventional development	8.54	9.36	10.11	10.76	11.30	12.49	13.44

Demographic Assumptions Underlying SSPs

	2010–15	2020–25	2030–35	2040–45	2050–55	2075–80	2095–2100
Total fertility rate							
SSP1 - Rapid development	1.83	1.49	1.30	1.20	1.15	1.17	1.21
SSP2 - Medium	1.96	1.84	1.74	1.66	1.59	1.62	1.64
SSP3 - Stalled development	2.07	2.16	2.17	2.13	2.11	2.20	2.29
SSP4 - Inequality	1.88	1.61	1.41	1.30	1.25	1.29	1.33
SSP5 - Conventional development	1.83	1.49	1.30	1.20	1.15	1.17	1.21
Life expectancy at birth for females (in years)							
SSP1 - Rapid development	82.43	85.37	88.29	91.25	94.25	101.86	108.01
SSP2 - Medium	81.09	83.39	85.51	87.51	89.61	94.61	98.60
SSP3 - Stalled development	81.59	82.60	83.58	84.53	85.44	87.60	89.34
SSP4 - Inequality	82.03	84.04	85.93	87.77	89.75	94.40	98.19
SSP5 - Conventional development	82.43	85.37	88.29	91.25	94.25	101.86	108.01
Migration – net flow over five years (in thousands)							
SSP1 - Rapid development	−41	−35	−31	−26	−22	−6	0
SSP2 - Medium	−40	−35	−32	−29	−26	−9	0
SSP3 - Stalled development	−34	−17	−16	−15	−14	−6	0
SSP4 - Inequality	−41	−35	−31	−26	−20	−5	0
SSP5 - Conventional development	−47	−53	−48	−41	−35	−11	0

Ageing Indicators, Medium Scenario (SSP2)

	2010	2020	2030	2040	2050	2075	2095
Median age	33.72	36.28	39.14	42.49	45.70	52.58	56.33
Propspective median age	33.72	34.27	35.26	36.81	38.11	40.22	40.11
Proportion age 65+	0.14	0.15	0.18	0.22	0.25	0.35	0.40
Proportion RLE < 15 years	0.10	0.10	0.10	0.12	0.13	0.15	0.16

Vanuatu

Detailed Human Capital Projections to 2060

Demographic indicators, Medium Scenario (SSP2)	2010	2020	2030	2040	2050	2060
Population (in millions)	0.24	0.29	0.35	0.39	0.43	0.46
Proportion age 65+	0.03	0.04	0.06	0.08	0.10	0.14
Proportion below age 20	0.49	0.44	0.38	0.33	0.29	0.26
	2005–10	2015–20	2025–30	2035–40	2045–50	2055–60
Total Fertility Rate	4.00	3.00	2.51	2.17	1.98	1.85
Life expectancy at birth (in years)						
Men	68.21	69.94	71.77	73.70	75.63	77.66
Women	72.06	74.10	76.10	78.09	80.09	82.09
Five-year immigration flow (in '000)	0.12	0.12	0.12	0.13	0.13	0.12
Five-year emigration flow (in '000)	0.10	0.09	0.11	0.12	0.12	0.12

Human Capital indicators, Medium Scenario (SSP2)	2010	2020	2030	2040	2050	2060
Population age 25+: highest educational attainment						
E1 - no education	0.20	0.14	0.09	0.06	0.04	0.03
E2 - incomplete primary	0.22	0.19	0.15	0.11	0.08	0.05
E3 - primary	0.30	0.31	0.33	0.32	0.31	0.29
E4 - lower secondary	0.14	0.18	0.21	0.22	0.22	0.21
E5 - upper secondary	0.10	0.14	0.18	0.23	0.28	0.33
E6 - post-secondary	0.04	0.04	0.05	0.06	0.07	0.08
Mean years of schooling (in years)	6.12	7.05	7.92	8.68	9.33	9.94
Gender gap (population age 25+): highest educational attainment (ratio male/female)						
E1 - no education	0.74	0.75	0.78	0.82	0.84	0.86
E2 - incomplete primary	0.96	0.95	0.96	0.96	0.96	0.95
E3 - primary	0.99	0.98	0.96	0.96	0.96	0.97
E4 - lower secondary	1.12	1.05	1.02	1.00	0.99	0.98
E5 - upper secondary	1.43	1.26	1.15	1.10	1.07	1.06
E6 - post-secondary	1.63	1.40	1.26	1.16	1.10	1.07
Mean years of schooling (male minus female)	0.88	0.65	0.45	0.31	0.22	0.18
Women age 20–39: highest educational attainment						
E1 - no education	0.13	0.07	0.04	0.02	0.01	0.00
E2 - incomplete primary	0.19	0.15	0.10	0.07	0.05	0.03
E3 - primary	0.33	0.32	0.32	0.30	0.27	0.22
E4 - lower secondary	0.19	0.23	0.23	0.22	0.20	0.18
E5 - upper secondary	0.14	0.19	0.26	0.33	0.40	0.47
E6 - post-secondary	0.03	0.04	0.05	0.06	0.07	0.09
Mean years of schooling (in years)	6.99	8.10	9.05	9.80	10.45	11.04

Education scenarios

GET: global education trend scenario (medium assumption also used for SSP2)

CER: constant enrolment rates scenario (assumption of no future improvements)

FT: Fast track scenario (assumption of education expansion according to fastest historical experience)

Pyramids by Education, Medium Scenario

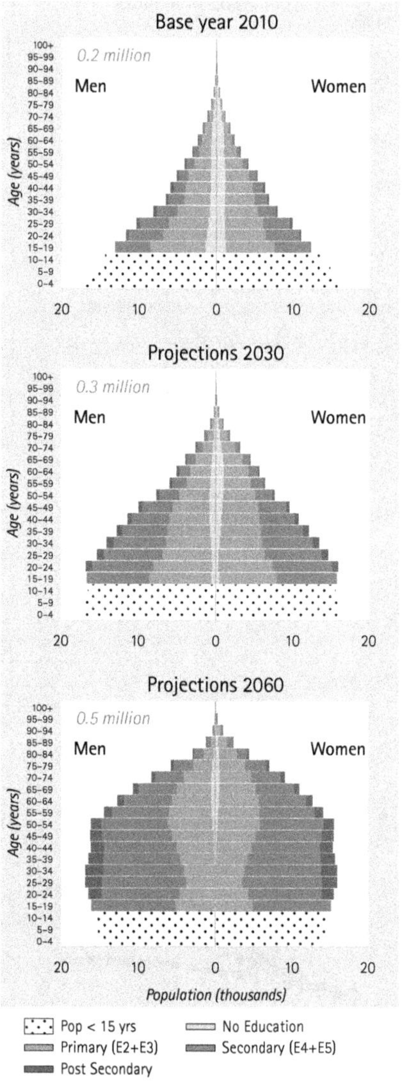

Population Size by Educational Attainment According to Three Education Scenarios: GET, CER, and FT

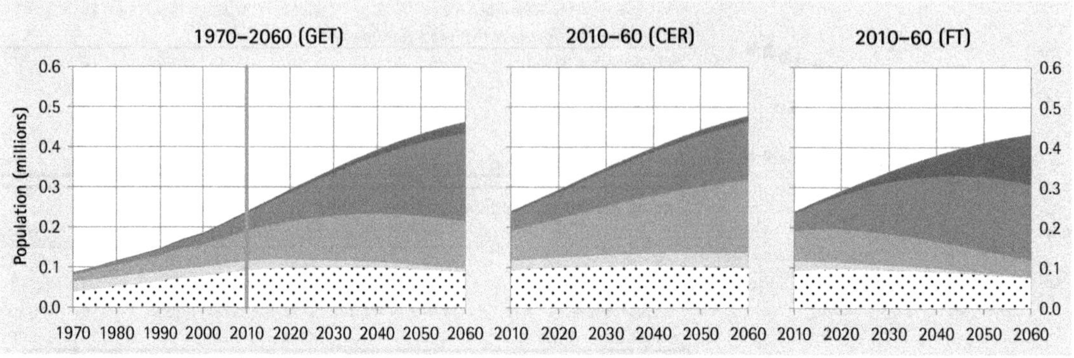

Vanuatu (Continued)

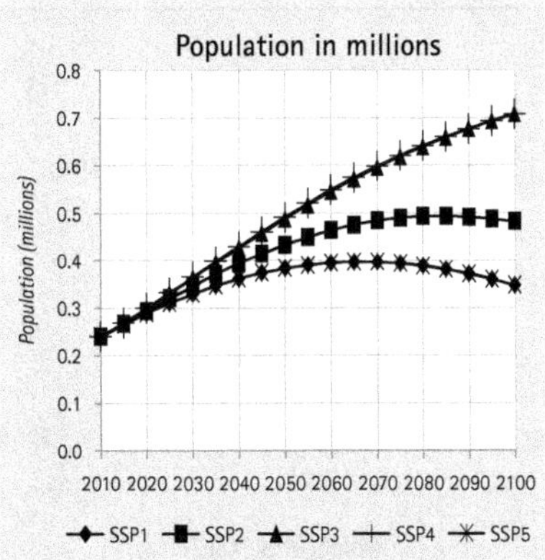

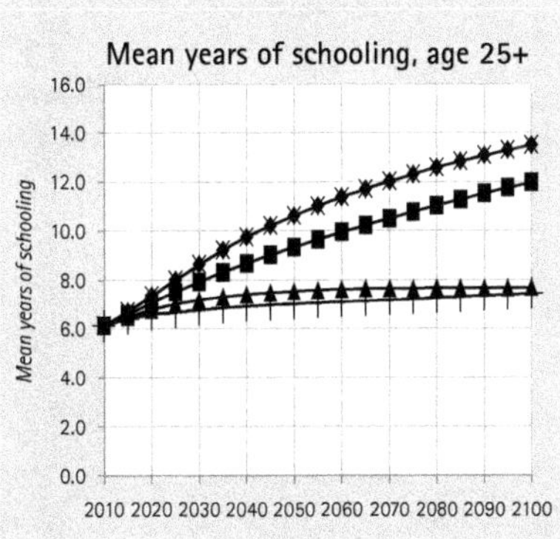

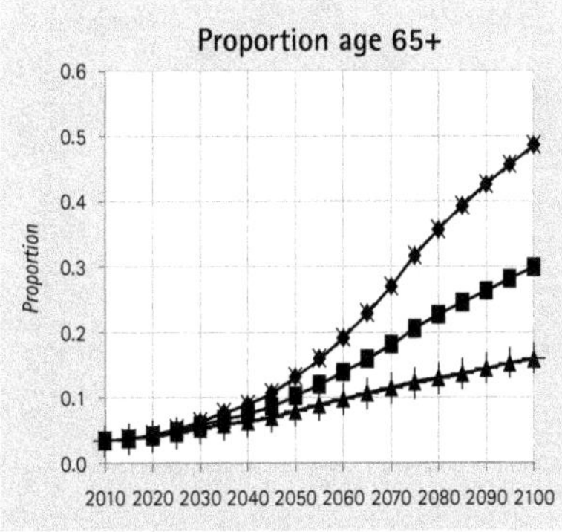

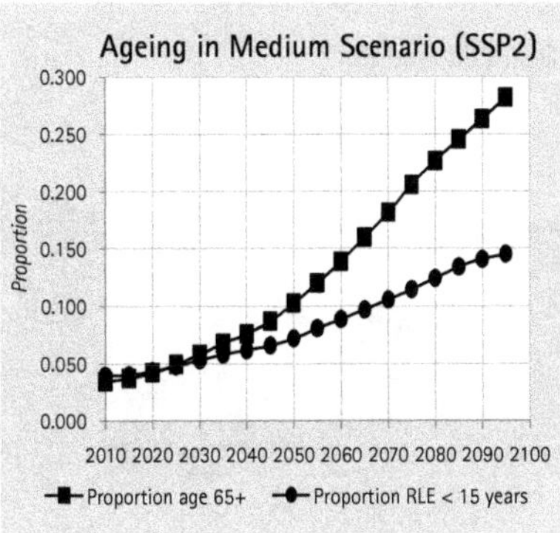

Alternative Scenarios to 2100

Projection Results by Scenario (SSP1–5)

	2010	2020	2030	2040	2050	2075	2100
Population (in millions)							
SSP1 - Rapid development	0.24	0.29	0.33	0.36	0.38	0.39	0.35
SSP2 - Medium	0.24	0.29	0.35	0.39	0.43	0.49	0.48
SSP3 - Stalled development	0.24	0.30	0.36	0.43	0.49	0.62	0.71
SSP4 - Inequality	0.24	0.30	0.37	0.43	0.49	0.62	0.71
SSP5 - Conventional development	0.24	0.29	0.33	0.36	0.38	0.39	0.35
Proportion age 65+							
SSP1 - Rapid development	0.03	0.04	0.06	0.09	0.13	0.32	0.49
SSP2 - Medium	0.03	0.04	0.06	0.08	0.10	0.21	0.30
SSP3 - Stalled development	0.03	0.04	0.05	0.06	0.08	0.12	0.16
SSP4 - Inequality	0.03	0.04	0.05	0.06	0.08	0.12	0.16
SSP5 - Conventional development	0.03	0.04	0.06	0.09	0.13	0.32	0.49
Proportion below age 20							
SSP1 - Rapid development	0.49	0.42	0.34	0.28	0.23	0.14	0.10
SSP2 - Medium	0.49	0.44	0.38	0.33	0.29	0.22	0.18
SSP3 - Stalled development	0.49	0.45	0.41	0.38	0.35	0.30	0.28
SSP4 - Inequality	0.49	0.45	0.41	0.39	0.35	0.30	0.27
SSP5 - Conventional development	0.49	0.42	0.34	0.28	0.23	0.14	0.10
Proportion of Women age 20–39 with at least secondary education							
SSP1 - Rapid development	0.36	0.55	0.69	0.78	0.83	0.91	0.96
SSP2 - Medium	0.36	0.46	0.54	0.61	0.68	0.82	0.93
SSP3 - Stalled development	0.36	0.41	0.41	0.41	0.41	0.41	0.41
SSP4 - Inequality	0.36	0.39	0.37	0.37	0.37	0.37	0.37
SSP5 - Conventional development	0.36	0.55	0.69	0.78	0.83	0.91	0.96
Mean years of schooling, age 25+							
SSP1 - Rapid development	6.12	7.34	8.62	9.74	10.62	12.30	13.48
SSP2 - Medium	6.12	7.05	7.92	8.68	9.33	10.77	11.97
SSP3 - Stalled development	6.12	6.77	7.17	7.40	7.53	7.65	7.67
SSP4 - Inequality	6.12	6.57	6.76	6.91	7.01	7.21	7.43
SSP5 - Conventional development	6.12	7.34	8.62	9.74	10.62	12.30	13.48

Demographic Assumptions Underlying SSPs

	2010–15	2020–25	2030–35	2040–45	2050–55	2075–80	2095–2100
Total fertility rate							
SSP1 - Rapid development	3.18	2.26	1.75	1.49	1.34	1.18	1.12
SSP2 - Medium	3.44	2.72	2.33	2.06	1.90	1.66	1.58
SSP3 - Stalled development	3.57	3.25	2.95	2.70	2.53	2.29	2.23
SSP4 - Inequality	3.58	3.29	2.98	2.71	2.52	2.26	2.18
SSP5 - Conventional development	3.18	2.26	1.75	1.49	1.34	1.18	1.12
Life expectancy at birth for females (in years)							
SSP1 - Rapid development	75.09	77.61	80.44	83.30	86.21	93.60	99.64
SSP2 - Medium	73.11	75.10	77.09	79.09	81.09	86.11	90.09
SSP3 - Stalled development	74.44	75.05	75.79	76.65	77.42	79.27	80.81
SSP4 - Inequality	74.44	75.03	75.75	76.59	77.33	79.14	80.72
SSP5 - Conventional development	75.09	77.61	80.44	83.30	86.21	93.60	99.64
Migration – net flow over five years (in thousands)							
SSP1 - Rapid development	0	0	0	0	0	0	0
SSP2 - Medium	0	0	0	0	0	0	0
SSP3 - Stalled development	0	0	0	0	0	0	0
SSP4 - Inequality	0	0	0	0	0	0	0
SSP5 - Conventional development	0	0	0	0	0	0	0

Ageing Indicators, Medium Scenario (SSP2)

	2010	2020	2030	2040	2050	2075	2095
Median age	20.59	23.34	26.60	30.28	33.85	42.19	47.90
Propspective median age	20.59	21.87	23.65	25.71	27.62	31.65	33.80
Proportion age 65+	0.03	0.04	0.06	0.08	0.10	0.21	0.28
Proportion RLE < 15 years	0.04	0.04	0.05	0.06	0.07	0.11	0.14

Venezuela (Bolivarian Republic of)

Detailed Human Capital Projections to 2060

Demographic indicators, Medium Scenario (SSP2)

	2010	2020	2030	2040	2050	2060
Population (in millions)	28.98	33.22	36.91	39.82	41.85	43.01
Proportion age 65+	0.06	0.08	0.11	0.14	0.18	0.22
Proportion below age 20	0.39	0.34	0.30	0.26	0.23	0.21
	2005–10	2015–20	2025–30	2035–40	2045–50	2055–60
Total Fertility Rate	2.55	2.16	1.97	1.82	1.73	1.67
Life expectancy at birth (in years)						
Men	70.83	73.33	75.58	77.70	79.95	82.10
Women	76.78	79.29	81.59	83.69	85.81	87.81
Five-year immigration flow (in '000)	112.22	110.19	114.46	117.09	117.17	115.50
Five-year emigration flow (in '000)	72.01	58.38	60.66	60.50	58.58	55.72

Human Capital indicators, Medium Scenario (SSP2)

	2010	2020	2030	2040	2050	2060
Population age 25+: highest educational attainment						
E1 - no education	0.06	0.04	0.03	0.02	0.01	0.01
E2 - incomplete primary	0.12	0.09	0.07	0.05	0.03	0.02
E3 - primary	0.29	0.27	0.24	0.22	0.19	0.16
E4 - lower secondary	0.13	0.14	0.13	0.12	0.11	0.10
E5 - upper secondary	0.19	0.21	0.24	0.26	0.28	0.29
E6 - post-secondary	0.21	0.25	0.30	0.34	0.38	0.42
Mean years of schooling (in years)	8.94	9.70	10.29	10.82	11.29	11.71
Gender gap (population age 25+): highest educational attainment (ratio male/female)						
E1 - no education	0.94	1.02	1.12	1.20	1.27	1.30
E2 - incomplete primary	1.15	1.19	1.22	1.24	1.25	1.25
E3 - primary	1.13	1.19	1.23	1.25	1.25	1.22
E4 - lower secondary	1.07	1.10	1.12	1.13	1.12	1.10
E5 - upper secondary	1.00	1.02	1.06	1.09	1.10	1.09
E6 - post-secondary	0.77	0.72	0.72	0.74	0.78	0.84
Mean years of schooling (male minus female)	−0.53	−0.75	−0.82	−0.80	−0.69	−0.53
Women age 20–39: highest educational attainment						
E1 - no education	0.02	0.01	0.00	0.00	0.00	0.00
E2 - incomplete primary	0.06	0.04	0.02	0.01	0.01	0.01
E3 - primary	0.22	0.19	0.15	0.13	0.10	0.08
E4 - lower secondary	0.14	0.13	0.11	0.09	0.08	0.07
E5 - upper secondary	0.24	0.26	0.28	0.29	0.31	0.32
E6 - post-secondary	0.32	0.38	0.44	0.48	0.50	0.52
Mean years of schooling (in years)	10.77	11.36	11.72	12.12	12.39	12.57

Education scenarios

GET : global education trend scenario (medium assumption also used for SSP2)

CER: constant enrolment rates scenario (assumption of no future improvements)

FT: Fast track scenario (assumption of education expansion according to fastest historical experience)

Pyramids by Education, Medium Scenario

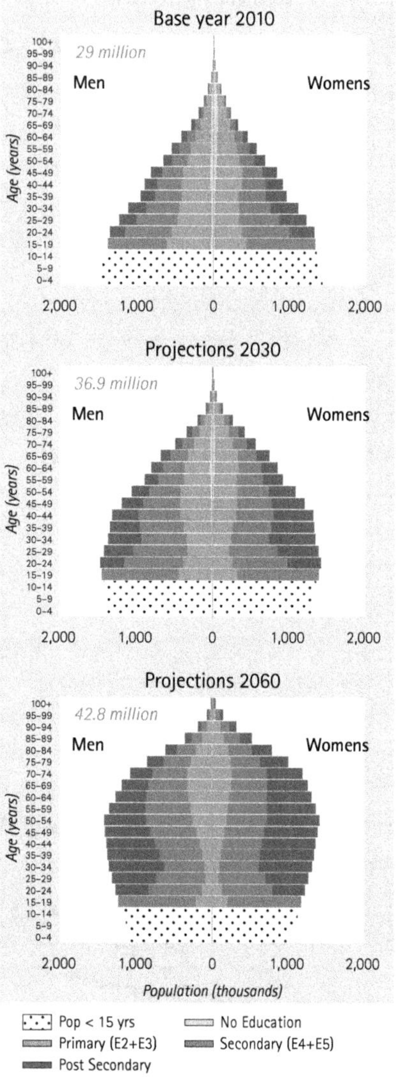

Population Size by Educational Attainment According to Three Education Scenarios: GET, CER, and FT

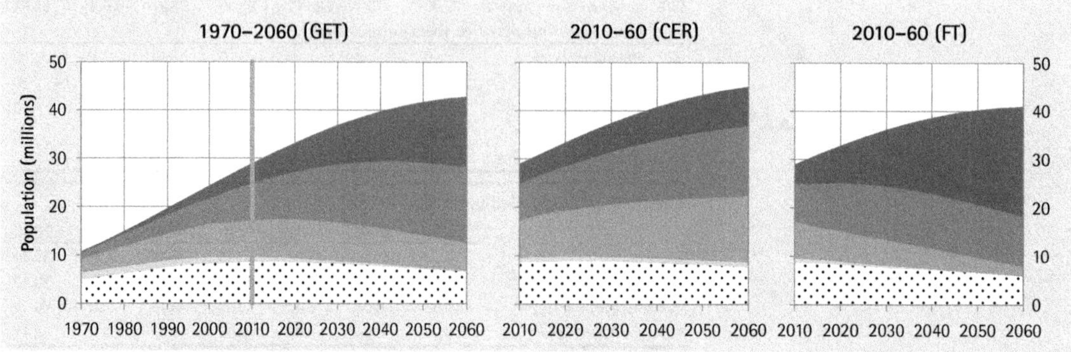

Venezuela (Bolivarian Republic of) (Continued)

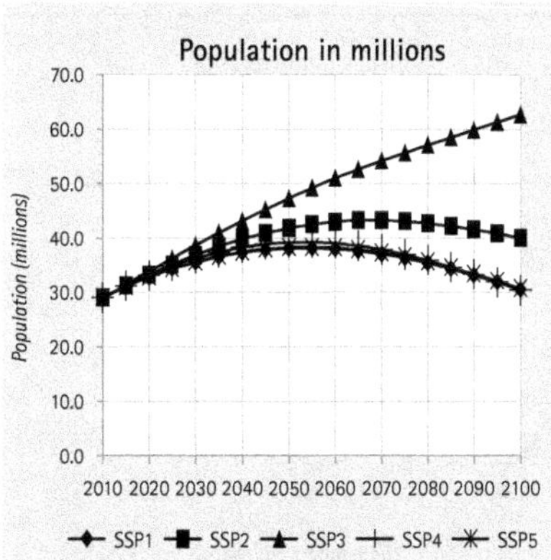

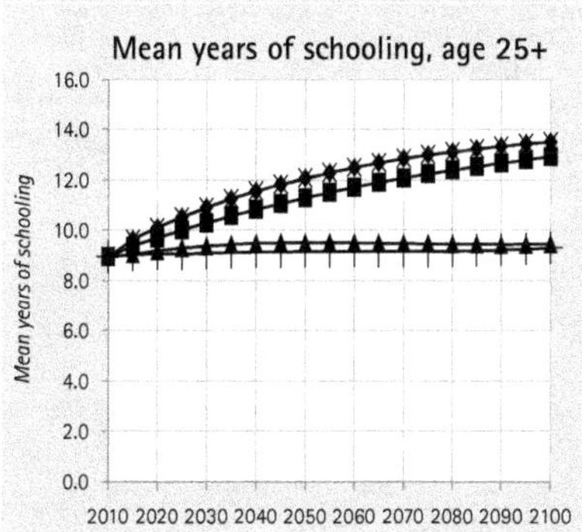

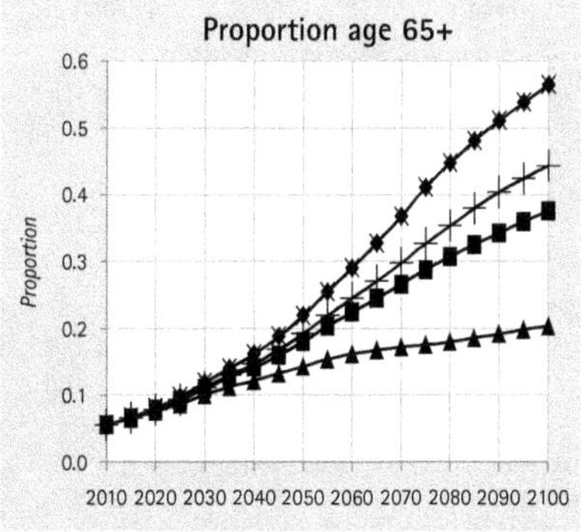

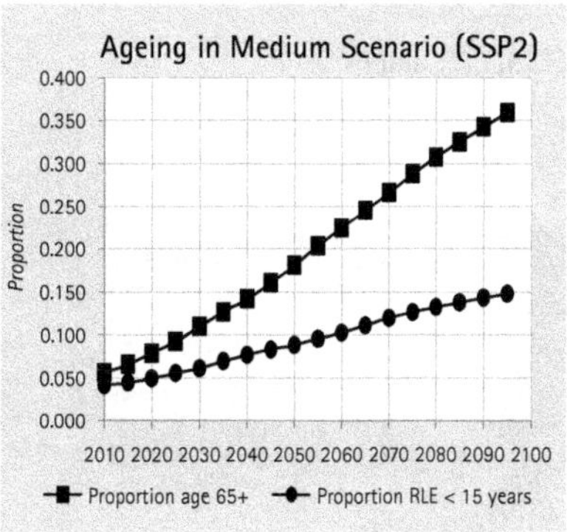

Alternative Scenarios to 2100

Projection Results by Scenario (SSP1-5)

	2010	2020	2030	2040	2050	2075	2100
Population (in millions)							
SSP1 - Rapid development	28.98	32.76	35.53	37.35	38.13	36.33	30.45
SSP2 - Medium	28.98	33.22	36.91	39.82	41.85	43.09	40.00
SSP3 - Stalled development	28.98	33.85	38.73	43.19	47.30	55.65	62.65
SSP4 - Inequality	28.98	33.10	36.26	38.31	39.21	36.98	30.38
SSP5 - Conventional development	28.98	32.79	35.61	37.48	38.31	36.57	30.67
Proportion age 65+							
SSP1 - Rapid development	0.06	0.08	0.12	0.16	0.22	0.41	0.56
SSP2 - Medium	0.06	0.08	0.11	0.14	0.18	0.29	0.38
SSP3 - Stalled development	0.06	0.08	0.10	0.12	0.14	0.18	0.20
SSP4 - Inequality	0.06	0.08	0.11	0.15	0.19	0.33	0.44
SSP5 - Conventional development	0.06	0.08	0.12	0.16	0.22	0.41	0.56
Proportion below age 20							
SSP1 - Rapid development	0.39	0.33	0.26	0.21	0.18	0.11	0.08
SSP2 - Medium	0.39	0.34	0.30	0.26	0.23	0.18	0.15
SSP3 - Stalled development	0.39	0.36	0.34	0.32	0.30	0.28	0.27
SSP4 - Inequality	0.39	0.34	0.29	0.24	0.20	0.14	0.11
SSP5 - Conventional development	0.39	0.33	0.26	0.21	0.18	0.11	0.08
Proportion of Women age 20-39 with at least secondary education							
SSP1 - Rapid development	0.70	0.86	0.90	0.92	0.94	0.97	0.99
SSP2 - Medium	0.70	0.77	0.82	0.86	0.89	0.95	0.98
SSP3 - Stalled development	0.70	0.66	0.66	0.66	0.66	0.66	0.66
SSP4 - Inequality	0.70	0.62	0.59	0.59	0.59	0.59	0.59
SSP5 - Conventional development	0.70	0.86	0.90	0.92	0.94	0.97	0.99
Mean years of schooling, age 25+							
SSP1 - Rapid development	8.94	10.10	10.89	11.54	12.06	12.99	13.51
SSP2 - Medium	8.94	9.70	10.29	10.82	11.29	12.23	12.91
SSP3 - Stalled development	8.94	9.19	9.37	9.47	9.51	9.46	9.44
SSP4 - Inequality	8.94	9.06	9.09	9.13	9.15	9.16	9.29
SSP5 - Conventional development	8.94	10.10	10.89	11.55	12.06	12.99	13.51

Demographic Assumptions Underlying SSPs

	2010–15	2020–25	2030–35	2040–45	2050–55	2075–80	2095–2100
Total fertility rate							
SSP1 - Rapid development	2.16	1.69	1.44	1.32	1.25	1.18	1.21
SSP2 - Medium	2.32	2.06	1.89	1.77	1.69	1.58	1.61
SSP3 - Stalled development	2.50	2.56	2.48	2.37	2.30	2.20	2.27
SSP4 - Inequality	2.27	1.93	1.62	1.45	1.37	1.31	1.34
SSP5 - Conventional development	2.16	1.69	1.44	1.32	1.25	1.18	1.21
Life expectancy at birth for females (in years)							
SSP1 - Rapid development	79.54	82.60	85.65	88.63	91.60	99.13	105.11
SSP2 - Medium	78.09	80.49	82.69	84.81	86.81	91.81	95.79
SSP3 - Stalled development	78.71	79.85	80.91	81.83	82.64	84.60	86.31
SSP4 - Inequality	79.11	81.23	83.24	85.18	86.96	91.35	95.05
SSP5 - Conventional development	79.54	82.60	85.65	88.63	91.60	99.13	105.11
Migration – net flow over five years (in thousands)							
SSP1 - Rapid development	45	52	52	50	45	15	0
SSP2 - Medium	48	54	56	59	60	27	0
SSP3 - Stalled development	38	27	30	37	45	32	0
SSP4 - Inequality	45	52	54	57	57	25	0
SSP5 - Conventional development	53	76	75	69	61	19	0

Ageing Indicators, Medium Scenario (SSP2)

	2010	2020	2030	2040	2050	2075	2095
Median age	26.08	29.57	33.04	36.54	40.16	48.19	53.53
Propspective median age	26.08	27.58	29.18	30.85	32.75	36.37	38.09
Proportion age 65+	0.06	0.08	0.11	0.14	0.18	0.29	0.36
Proportion RLE < 15 years	0.04	0.05	0.06	0.08	0.09	0.13	0.15

Viet Nam

Detailed Human Capital Projections to 2060

Demographic indicators, Medium Scenario (SSP2)	2010	2020	2030	2040	2050	2060
Population (in millions)	87.85	96.67	102.45	105.33	105.14	102.10
Proportion age 65+	0.06	0.08	0.13	0.19	0.24	0.32
Proportion below age 20	0.34	0.29	0.25	0.21	0.18	0.16
	2005–10	2015–20	2025–30	2035–40	2045–50	2055–60
Total Fertility Rate	1.89	1.72	1.62	1.53	1.43	1.45
Life expectancy at birth (in years)						
Men	72.33	75.06	77.17	79.25	81.16	83.37
Women	76.21	79.19	81.40	83.49	85.39	87.62
Five-year immigration flow (in '000)	20.68	20.31	21.13	21.60	21.61	21.30
Five-year emigration flow (in '000)	449.43	335.41	308.27	287.82	255.92	223.69

Human Capital indicators, Medium Scenario (SSP2)	2010	2020	2030	2040	2050	2060
Population age 25+: highest educational attainment						
E1 - no education	0.06	0.05	0.04	0.03	0.02	0.02
E2 - incomplete primary	0.17	0.13	0.10	0.07	0.06	0.04
E3 - primary	0.29	0.27	0.26	0.25	0.23	0.22
E4 - lower secondary	0.30	0.33	0.33	0.33	0.32	0.30
E5 - upper secondary	0.10	0.13	0.16	0.19	0.23	0.26
E6 - post-secondary	0.07	0.09	0.11	0.12	0.14	0.16
Mean years of schooling (in years)	7.18	7.97	8.43	8.90	9.36	9.82
Gender gap (population age 25+): highest educational attainment (ratio male/female)						
E1 - no education	0.48	0.57	0.64	0.69	0.72	0.72
E2 - incomplete primary	0.70	0.73	0.77	0.82	0.87	0.91
E3 - primary	1.06	1.03	1.02	1.02	1.02	1.01
E4 - lower secondary	1.16	1.08	1.06	1.04	1.03	1.02
E5 - upper secondary	1.30	1.16	1.09	1.05	1.03	1.03
E6 - post-secondary	1.30	1.11	1.02	0.97	0.95	0.96
Mean years of schooling (male minus female)	0.91	0.56	0.34	0.17	0.08	0.05
Women age 20–39: highest educational attainment						
E1 - no education	0.05	0.03	0.01	0.01	0.00	0.00
E2 - incomplete primary	0.10	0.06	0.03	0.02	0.01	0.01
E3 - primary	0.29	0.21	0.21	0.19	0.17	0.15
E4 - lower secondary	0.31	0.36	0.32	0.28	0.25	0.21
E5 - upper secondary	0.15	0.21	0.28	0.33	0.38	0.42
E6 - post-secondary	0.09	0.13	0.15	0.17	0.19	0.21
Mean years of schooling (in years)	8.13	9.27	9.89	10.42	10.83	11.19

Education scenarios

GET: global education trend scenario (medium assumption also used for SSP2)

CER: constant enrolment rates scenario (assumption of no future improvements)

FT: Fast track scenario (assumption of education expansion according to fastest historical experience)

Pyramids by Education, Medium Scenario

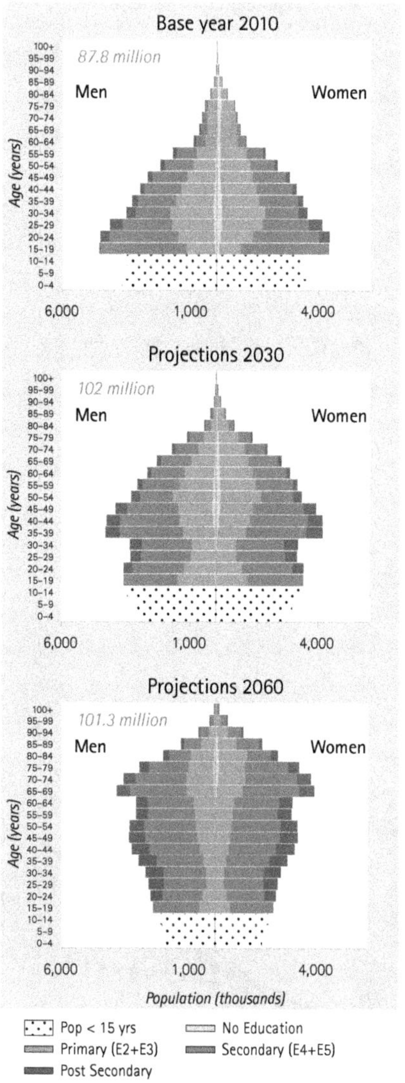

Population Size by Educational Attainment According to Three Education Scenarios: GET, CER, and FT

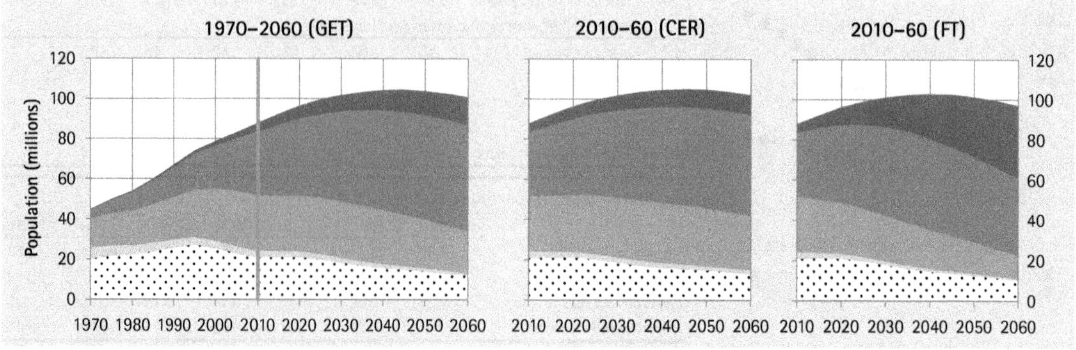

Viet Nam (Continued)

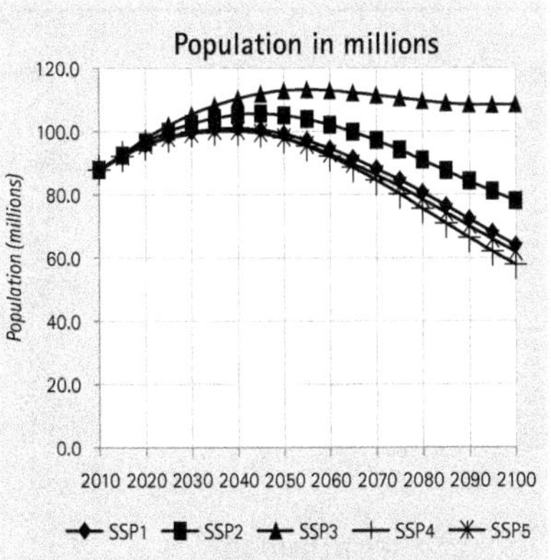

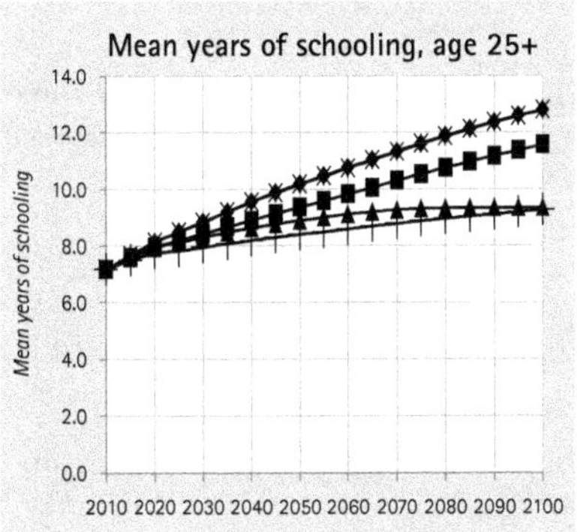

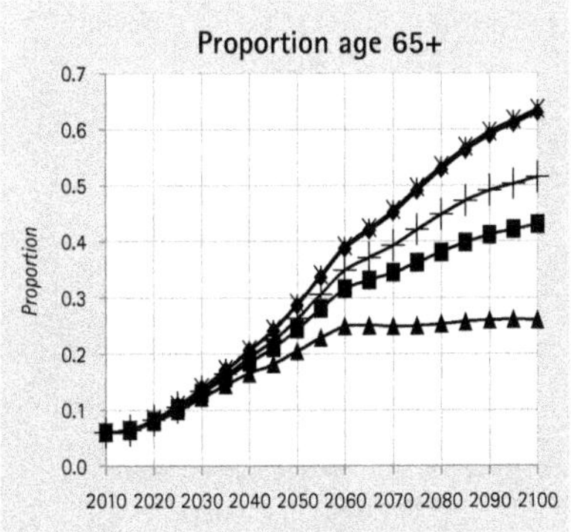

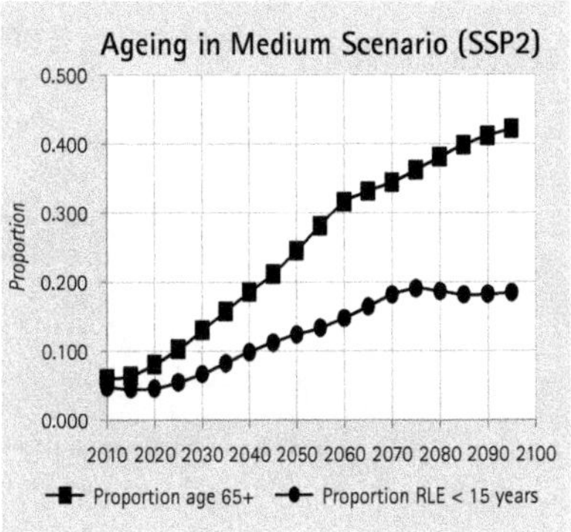

Alternative Scenarios to 2100

Projection Results by Scenario (SSP1–5)

	2010	2020	2030	2040	2050	2075	2100
Population (in millions)							
SSP1 - Rapid development	87.85	95.79	99.88	101.03	99.20	84.65	64.03
SSP2 - Medium	87.85	96.67	102.45	105.33	105.14	94.18	78.09
SSP3 - Stalled development	87.85	97.71	105.42	110.39	112.92	110.57	108.52
SSP4 - Inequality	87.85	95.76	99.74	100.48	97.83	80.24	57.84
SSP5 - Conventional development	87.85	95.60	99.31	100.06	97.83	82.54	61.82
Proportion age 65+							
SSP1 - Rapid development	0.06	0.08	0.14	0.21	0.29	0.49	0.63
SSP2 - Medium	0.06	0.08	0.13	0.19	0.24	0.36	0.43
SSP3 - Stalled development	0.06	0.08	0.12	0.17	0.21	0.25	0.26
SSP4 - Inequality	0.06	0.08	0.13	0.19	0.26	0.42	0.51
SSP5 - Conventional development	0.06	0.08	0.14	0.21	0.29	0.50	0.64
Proportion below age 20							
SSP1 - Rapid development	0.34	0.28	0.22	0.17	0.13	0.08	0.06
SSP2 - Medium	0.34	0.29	0.25	0.21	0.18	0.15	0.13
SSP3 - Stalled development	0.34	0.29	0.27	0.24	0.23	0.22	0.23
SSP4 - Inequality	0.34	0.28	0.23	0.18	0.15	0.11	0.09
SSP5 - Conventional development	0.34	0.28	0.22	0.16	0.13	0.08	0.06
Proportion of Women age 20–39 with at least secondary education							
SSP1 - Rapid development	0.56	0.73	0.82	0.88	0.90	0.94	0.97
SSP2 - Medium	0.56	0.70	0.75	0.79	0.82	0.89	0.95
SSP3 - Stalled development	0.56	0.69	0.70	0.70	0.70	0.70	0.70
SSP4 - Inequality	0.56	0.65	0.63	0.63	0.63	0.63	0.63
SSP5 - Conventional development	0.56	0.73	0.82	0.88	0.90	0.94	0.97
Mean years of schooling, age 25+							
SSP1 - Rapid development	7.18	8.13	8.84	9.55	10.18	11.60	12.78
SSP2 - Medium	7.18	7.97	8.43	8.90	9.36	10.52	11.55
SSP3 - Stalled development	7.18	7.94	8.31	8.63	8.89	9.31	9.34
SSP4 - Inequality	7.18	7.75	7.96	8.19	8.40	8.88	9.26
SSP5 - Conventional development	7.18	8.13	8.83	9.54	10.17	11.58	12.77

Demographic Assumptions Underlying SSPs

	2010–15	2020–25	2030–35	2040–45	2050–55	2075–80	2095–2100
Total fertility rate							
SSP1 - Rapid development	1.68	1.40	1.19	1.07	1.02	1.07	1.12
SSP2 - Medium	1.78	1.67	1.57	1.49	1.44	1.50	1.54
SSP3 - Stalled development	1.87	1.94	1.95	1.92	1.92	2.07	2.20
SSP4 - Inequality	1.70	1.46	1.27	1.17	1.13	1.20	1.26
SSP5 - Conventional development	1.68	1.40	1.19	1.07	1.02	1.07	1.12
Life expectancy at birth for females (in years)							
SSP1 - Rapid development	79.62	82.64	85.55	88.45	91.40	99.20	105.63
SSP2 - Medium	77.89	80.29	82.50	84.39	86.49	91.90	96.20
SSP3 - Stalled development	78.76	79.88	80.98	81.88	82.86	85.30	87.26
SSP4 - Inequality	79.18	81.26	83.28	85.06	87.02	91.91	95.90
SSP5 - Conventional development	79.62	82.64	85.55	88.45	91.40	99.20	105.63
Migration – net flow over five years (in thousands)							
SSP1 - Rapid development	−354	−297	−270	−234	−191	−55	0
SSP2 - Medium	−350	−298	−277	−252	−218	−76	0
SSP3 - Stalled development	−295	−148	−136	−124	−110	−43	0
SSP4 - Inequality	−354	−296	−266	−224	−176	−46	0
SSP5 - Conventional development	−413	−452	−422	−379	−322	−105	0

Ageing Indicators, Medium Scenario (SSP2)

	2010	2020	2030	2040	2050	2075	2095
Median age	28.11	32.98	38.46	43.47	46.69	54.89	58.42
Propspective median age	28.11	31.02	34.71	38.26	39.73	43.57	43.21
Proportion age 65+	0.06	0.08	0.13	0.19	0.24	0.36	0.42
Proportion RLE < 15 years	0.05	0.05	0.07	0.10	0.12	0.19	0.18

Zambia

Detailed Human Capital Projections to 2060

Demographic indicators, Medium Scenario (SSP2)	2010	2020	2030	2040	2050	2060
Population (in millions)	13.09	16.99	21.37	25.84	29.90	33.44
Proportion age 65+	0.03	0.03	0.03	0.03	0.04	0.05
Proportion below age 20	0.57	0.57	0.54	0.50	0.45	0.40
	2005–10	2015–20	2025–30	2035–40	2045–50	2055–60
Total Fertility Rate	6.20	5.27	4.40	3.49	2.84	2.43
Life expectancy at birth (in years)						
Men	46.49	50.49	52.08	53.31	55.12	58.15
Women	47.27	51.30	54.00	56.40	58.92	62.09
Five-year immigration flow (in '000)	42.11	41.19	42.72	43.62	43.58	42.90
Five-year emigration flow (in '000)	126.56	122.74	158.36	198.18	233.79	262.34

Human Capital indicators, Medium Scenario (SSP2)	2010	2020	2030	2040	2050	2060
Population age 25+: highest educational attainment						
E1 - no education	0.12	0.06	0.03	0.01	0.01	0.00
E2 - incomplete primary	0.24	0.17	0.11	0.07	0.04	0.02
E3 - primary	0.28	0.31	0.33	0.32	0.30	0.27
E4 - lower secondary	0.20	0.23	0.25	0.25	0.24	0.22
E5 - upper secondary	0.11	0.15	0.20	0.25	0.31	0.36
E6 - post-secondary	0.06	0.07	0.08	0.10	0.11	0.13
Mean years of schooling (in years)	7.32	8.34	9.14	9.76	10.25	10.69
Gender gap (population age 25+): highest educational attainment (ratio male/female)						
E1 - no education	0.37	0.39	0.45	0.54	0.61	0.67
E2 - incomplete primary	0.68	0.68	0.71	0.77	0.84	0.93
E3 - primary	0.99	0.85	0.80	0.79	0.81	0.86
E4 - lower secondary	1.33	1.07	0.96	0.91	0.90	0.90
E5 - upper secondary	2.79	2.17	1.74	1.45	1.26	1.14
E6 - post-secondary	2.03	1.86	1.63	1.43	1.27	1.16
Mean years of schooling (male minus female)	2.05	1.53	1.08	0.76	0.53	0.33
Women age 20–39: highest educational attainment						
E1 - no education	0.06	0.02	0.01	0.00	0.00	0.00
E2 - incomplete primary	0.25	0.17	0.13	0.09	0.07	0.05
E3 - primary	0.33	0.36	0.34	0.30	0.25	0.20
E4 - lower secondary	0.23	0.26	0.26	0.25	0.24	0.22
E5 - upper secondary	0.10	0.15	0.21	0.27	0.35	0.42
E6 - post-secondary	0.04	0.05	0.06	0.07	0.09	0.11
Mean years of schooling (in years)	7.61	8.50	9.13	9.67	10.21	10.73

Education scenarios

GET: global education trend scenario (medium assumption also used for SSP2)

CER: constant enrolment rates scenario (assumption of no future improvements)

FT: Fast track scenario (assumption of education expansion according to fastest historical experience)

Pyramids by Education, Medium Scenario

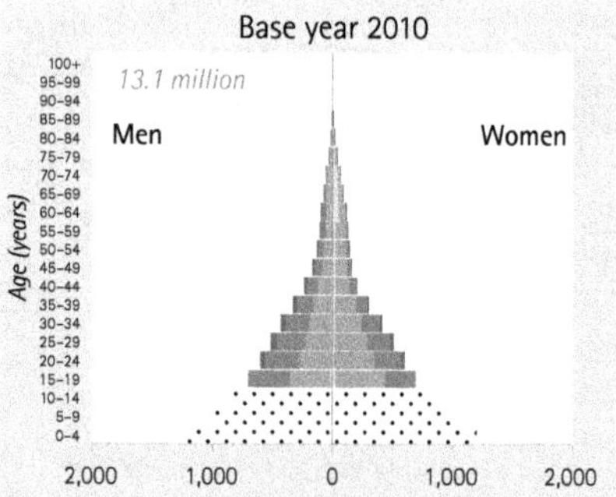

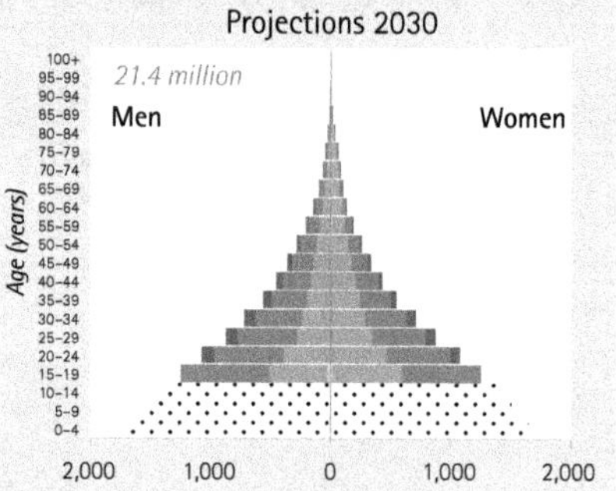

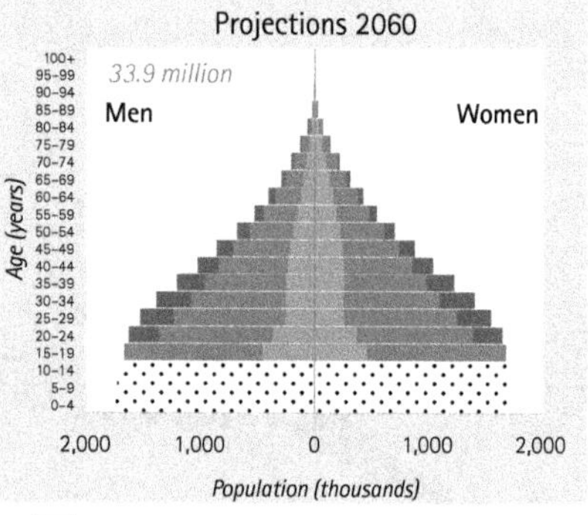

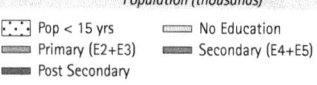

Population Size by Educational Attainment According to Three Education Scenarios: GET, CER, and FT

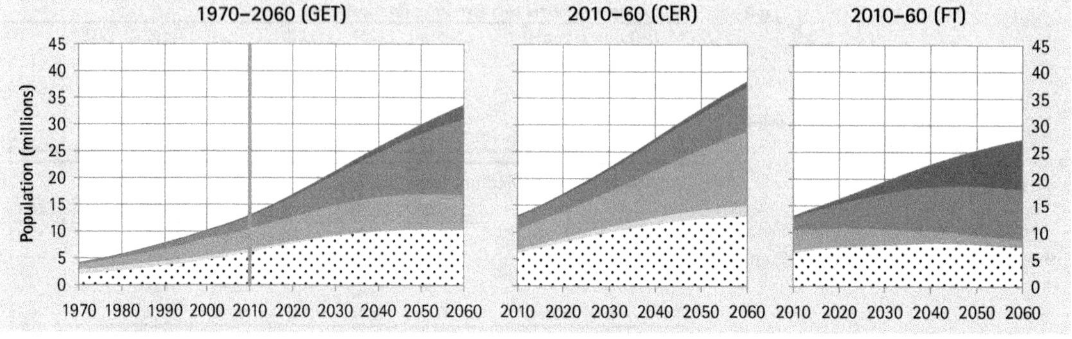

Zambia (Continued)

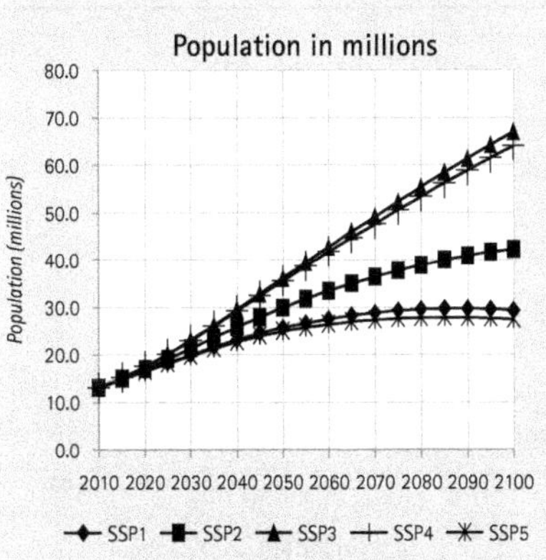

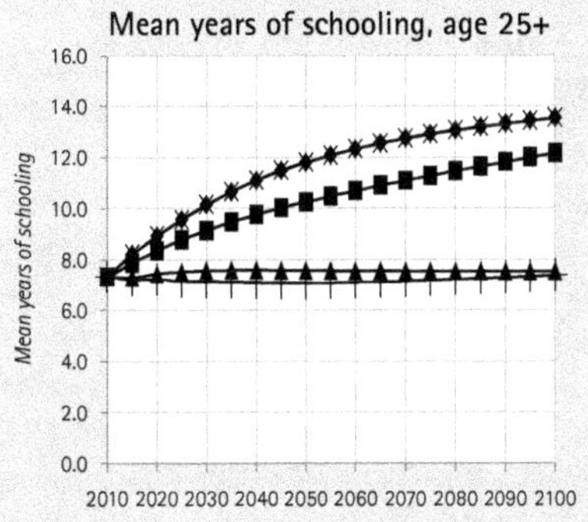

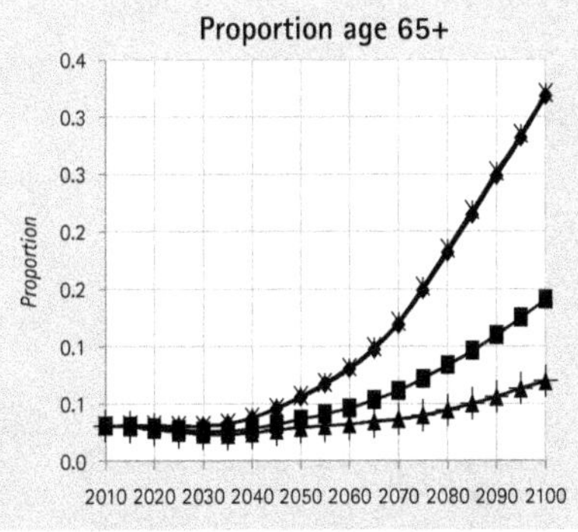

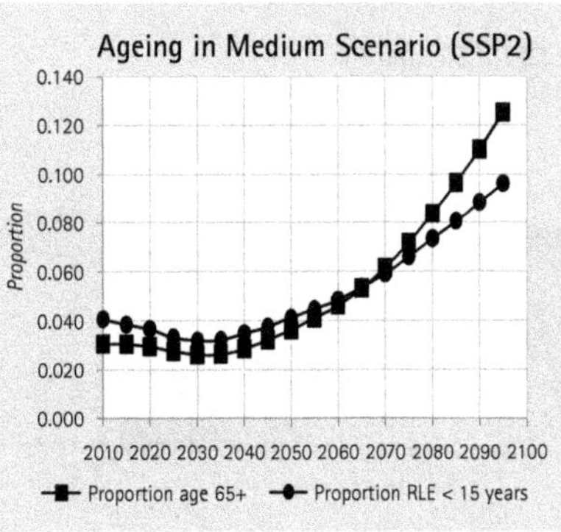

Alternative Scenarios to 2100

Projection Results by Scenario (SSP1-5)

	2010	2020	2030	2040	2050	2075	2100
Population (in millions)							
SSP1 - Rapid development	13.09	16.58	19.96	23.17	25.68	29.23	29.37
SSP2 - Medium	13.09	16.99	21.37	25.84	29.90	37.73	42.25
SSP3 - Stalled development	13.09	17.62	23.17	29.53	36.18	52.33	66.99
SSP4 - Inequality	13.09	17.60	23.07	29.23	35.58	50.55	64.01
SSP5 - Conventional development	13.09	16.53	19.76	22.73	24.94	27.61	27.40
Proportion age 65+							
SSP1 - Rapid development	0.03	0.03	0.03	0.04	0.06	0.15	0.32
SSP2 - Medium	0.03	0.03	0.03	0.03	0.04	0.07	0.14
SSP3 - Stalled development	0.03	0.03	0.02	0.02	0.03	0.04	0.07
SSP4 - Inequality	0.03	0.03	0.02	0.02	0.03	0.04	0.07
SSP5 - Conventional development	0.03	0.03	0.03	0.04	0.06	0.15	0.32
Proportion below age 20							
SSP1 - Rapid development	0.57	0.55	0.48	0.42	0.36	0.23	0.15
SSP2 - Medium	0.57	0.57	0.54	0.50	0.45	0.34	0.26
SSP3 - Stalled development	0.57	0.58	0.58	0.55	0.52	0.43	0.38
SSP4 - Inequality	0.57	0.58	0.58	0.56	0.52	0.43	0.37
SSP5 - Conventional development	0.57	0.55	0.48	0.42	0.36	0.23	0.15
Proportion of Women age 20-39 with at least secondary education							
SSP1 - Rapid development	0.37	0.61	0.72	0.79	0.83	0.92	0.97
SSP2 - Medium	0.37	0.45	0.53	0.60	0.68	0.83	0.94
SSP3 - Stalled development	0.37	0.29	0.29	0.29	0.29	0.29	0.29
SSP4 - Inequality	0.37	0.27	0.26	0.26	0.26	0.26	0.26
SSP5 - Conventional development	0.37	0.61	0.72	0.79	0.83	0.92	0.97
Mean years of schooling, age 25+							
SSP1 - Rapid development	7.32	8.92	10.14	11.10	11.80	12.90	13.53
SSP2 - Medium	7.32	8.34	9.14	9.76	10.25	11.27	12.16
SSP3 - Stalled development	7.32	7.43	7.56	7.58	7.57	7.54	7.53
SSP4 - Inequality	7.32	7.20	7.12	7.08	7.07	7.18	7.37
SSP5 - Conventional development	7.32	8.91	10.13	11.09	11.79	12.90	13.53

Demographic Assumptions Underlying SSPs

	2010–15	2020–25	2030–35	2040–45	2050–55	2075–80	2095–2100
Total fertility rate							
SSP1 - Rapid development	5.34	3.71	2.75	2.17	1.81	1.41	1.27
SSP2 - Medium	5.74	4.85	3.93	3.12	2.62	1.97	1.75
SSP3 - Stalled development	6.30	6.18	5.47	4.54	3.80	2.85	2.57
SSP4 - Inequality	6.32	6.27	5.54	4.55	3.79	2.82	2.53
SSP5 - Conventional development	5.34	3.71	2.75	2.17	1.81	1.41	1.27
Life expectancy at birth for females (in years)							
SSP1 - Rapid development	53.70	60.56	64.81	69.20	73.46	83.80	92.00
SSP2 - Medium	50.00	52.70	55.30	57.61	60.48	68.68	75.22
SSP3 - Stalled development	52.42	50.23	50.81	52.39	53.69	58.24	62.20
SSP4 - Inequality	52.42	50.19	50.73	52.30	53.60	58.17	62.15
SSP5 - Conventional development	53.70	60.56	64.81	69.20	73.46	83.80	92.00
Migration – net flow over five years (in thousands)							
SSP1 - Rapid development	−74	−95	−130	−159	−180	−86	0
SSP2 - Medium	−76	−97	−135	−173	−206	−115	0
SSP3 - Stalled development	−61	−46	−63	−82	−99	−60	0
SSP4 - Inequality	−73	−93	−132	−174	−215	−130	0
SSP5 - Conventional development	−86	−144	−204	−257	−302	−161	0

Ageing Indicators, Medium Scenario (SSP2)

	2010	2020	2030	2040	2050	2075	2095
Median age	16.60	16.93	18.24	20.17	22.52	29.51	35.59
Propspective median age	16.60	16.22	15.98	16.82	17.42	17.77	18.12
Proportion age 65+	0.03	0.03	0.03	0.03	0.04	0.07	0.13
Proportion RLE < 15 years	0.04	0.04	0.03	0.03	0.04	0.07	0.10

Zimbabwe

Detailed Human Capital Projections to 2060

Demographic indicators, Medium Scenario (SSP2)	2010	2020	2030	2040	2050	2060
Population (in millions)	12.57	12.96	13.07	12.87	12.45	11.85
Proportion age 65+	0.04	0.05	0.05	0.05	0.07	0.12
Proportion below age 20	0.52	0.47	0.43	0.39	0.35	0.32
	2005–10	2015–20	2025–30	2035–40	2045–50	2055–60
Total Fertility Rate	3.47	2.68	2.28	2.07	1.91	1.81
Life expectancy at birth (in years)						
Men	47.45	57.52	58.32	59.37	60.69	63.41
Women	45.43	56.90	59.20	61.41	63.58	66.52
Five-year immigration flow (in '000)	0.00	0.00	0.00	0.00	0.00	0.00
Five-year emigration flow (in '000)	897.92	638.18	650.25	623.38	574.60	520.29

Human Capital indicators, Medium Scenario (SSP2)	2010	2020	2030	2040	2050	2060
Population age 25+: highest educational attainment						
E1 - no education	0.09	0.04	0.02	0.01	0.00	0.00
E2 - incomplete primary	0.17	0.10	0.05	0.03	0.01	0.01
E3 - primary	0.19	0.15	0.11	0.08	0.05	0.04
E4 - lower secondary	0.13	0.12	0.10	0.08	0.06	0.05
E5 - upper secondary	0.37	0.52	0.62	0.70	0.74	0.76
E6 - post-secondary	0.06	0.07	0.09	0.11	0.13	0.15
Mean years of schooling (in years)	9.16	10.69	11.76	12.51	12.99	13.30
Gender gap (population age 25+): highest educational attainment (ratio male/female)						
E1 - no education	0.38	0.32	0.27	0.25	0.29	0.41
E2 - incomplete primary	0.65	0.59	0.52	0.49	0.51	0.53
E3 - primary	0.91	0.81	0.76	0.74	0.72	0.68
E4 - lower secondary	0.99	0.89	0.83	0.80	0.77	0.75
E5 - upper secondary	1.42	1.21	1.11	1.04	1.02	1.01
E6 - post-secondary	2.00	1.77	1.58	1.41	1.27	1.18
Mean years of schooling (male minus female)	1.87	1.38	0.96	0.59	0.37	0.26
Women age 20–39: highest educational attainment						
E1 - no education	0.01	0.00	0.00	0.00	0.00	0.00
E2 - incomplete primary	0.08	0.03	0.01	0.00	0.00	0.00
E3 - primary	0.19	0.12	0.07	0.04	0.02	0.01
E4 - lower secondary	0.17	0.14	0.11	0.09	0.07	0.06
E5 - upper secondary	0.52	0.65	0.74	0.78	0.78	0.76
E6 - post-secondary	0.04	0.05	0.07	0.10	0.13	0.16
Mean years of schooling (in years)	10.86	11.87	12.57	12.99	13.26	13.46

Education scenarios

GET : global education trend scenario (medium assumption also used for SSP2)

CER: constant enrolment rates scenario (assumption of no future improvements)

FT: Fast track scenario (assumption of education expansion according to fastest historical experience)

Pyramids by Education, Medium Scenario

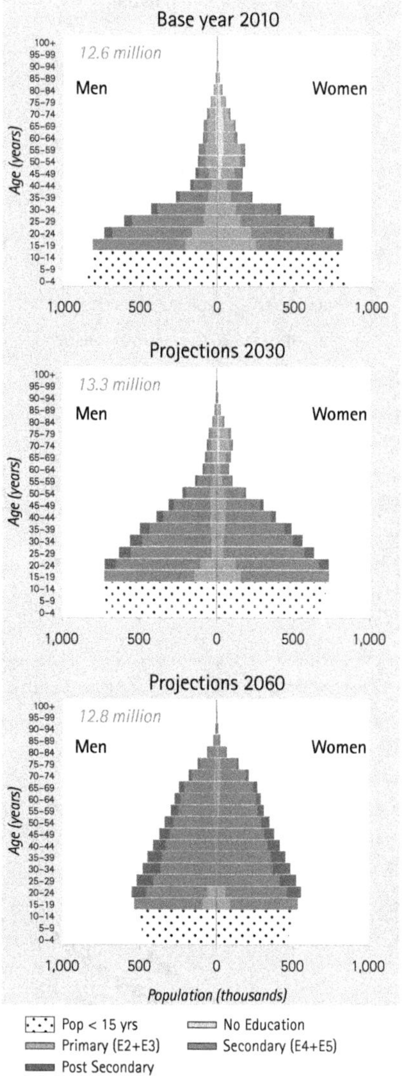

Population Size by Educational Attainment According to Three Education Scenarios: GET, CER, and FT

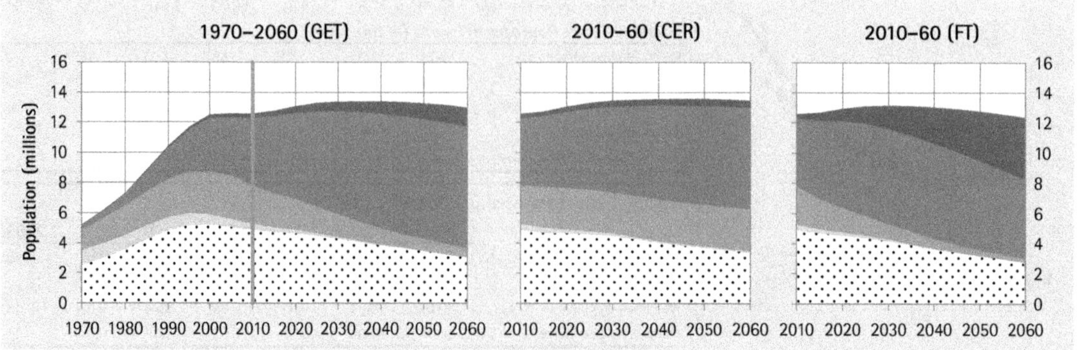

Zimbabwe (Continued)

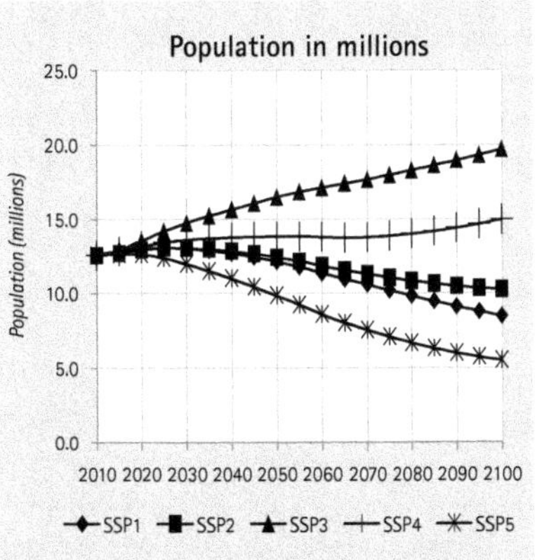

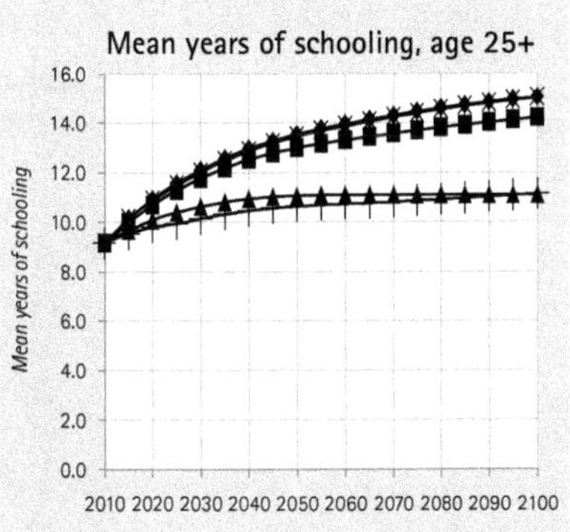

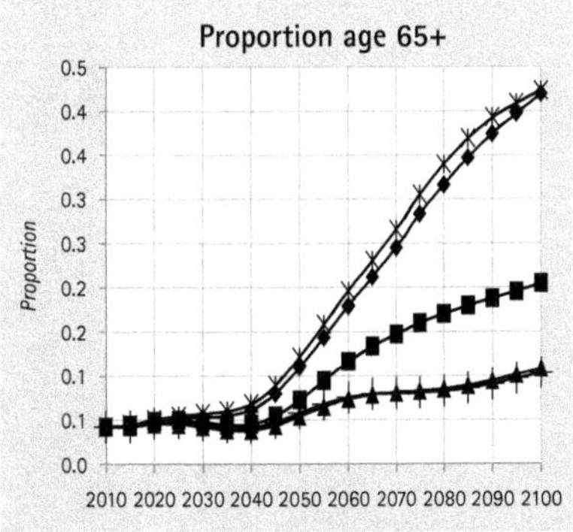

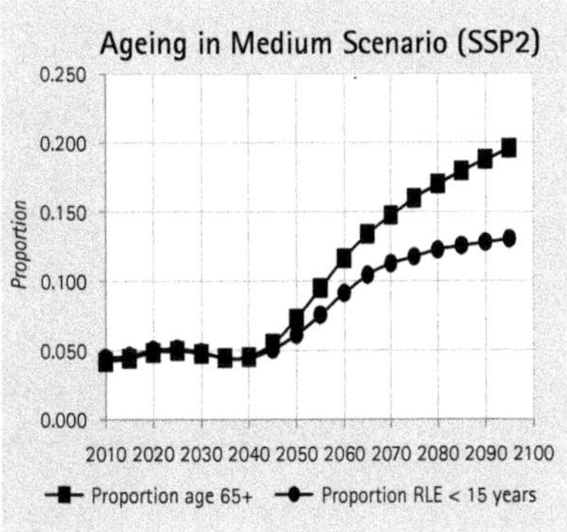

Alternative scenarios to 2100

Projection Results by Scenario (SSP1–5)

	2010	2020	2030	2040	2050	2075	2100
Population (in millions)							
SSP1 - Rapid development	12.57	12.99	13.03	12.71	12.14	10.20	8.47
SSP2 - Medium	12.57	12.96	13.07	12.87	12.45	11.06	10.26
SSP3 - Stalled development	12.57	13.57	14.77	15.67	16.49	17.98	19.69
SSP4 - Inequality	12.57	13.20	13.64	13.79	13.87	13.89	14.98
SSP5 - Conventional development	12.57	12.63	11.97	10.99	9.84	7.08	5.50
Proportion age 65+							
SSP1 - Rapid development	0.04	0.05	0.05	0.06	0.11	0.28	0.42
SSP2 - Medium	0.04	0.05	0.05	0.05	0.07	0.16	0.20
SSP3 - Stalled development	0.04	0.05	0.04	0.04	0.05	0.08	0.11
SSP4 - Inequality	0.04	0.05	0.05	0.04	0.06	0.08	0.10
SSP5 - Conventional development	0.04	0.05	0.06	0.07	0.12	0.30	0.42
Proportion below age 20							
SSP1 - Rapid development	0.52	0.45	0.38	0.32	0.27	0.17	0.12
SSP2 - Medium	0.52	0.47	0.43	0.39	0.35	0.27	0.22
SSP3 - Stalled development	0.52	0.48	0.46	0.43	0.41	0.36	0.33
SSP4 - Inequality	0.52	0.48	0.47	0.44	0.42	0.37	0.33
SSP5 - Conventional development	0.52	0.46	0.40	0.33	0.28	0.18	0.12
Proportion of Women age 20–39 with at least secondary education							
SSP1 - Rapid development	0.73	0.88	0.95	0.98	0.99	0.99	1.00
SSP2 - Medium	0.73	0.84	0.92	0.96	0.98	0.99	0.99
SSP3 - Stalled development	0.73	0.70	0.70	0.70	0.70	0.70	0.70
SSP4 - Inequality	0.73	0.66	0.63	0.63	0.63	0.63	0.63
SSP5 - Conventional development	0.73	0.88	0.95	0.98	0.99	0.99	1.00
Mean years of schooling, age 25+							
SSP1 - Rapid development	9.16	10.92	12.10	12.95	13.53	14.45	15.03
SSP2 - Medium	9.16	10.69	11.76	12.51	12.99	13.69	14.20
SSP3 - Stalled development	9.16	10.07	10.62	10.93	11.06	11.09	11.09
SSP4 - Inequality	9.16	9.79	10.14	10.45	10.64	10.86	11.13
SSP5 - Conventional development	9.16	10.88	12.01	12.86	13.45	14.39	15.01

Demographic Assumptions Underlying SSPs

	2010–15	2020–25	2030–35	2040–45	2050–55	2075–80	2095–2100
Total fertility rate							
SSP1 - Rapid development	2.77	2.07	1.67	1.47	1.36	1.22	1.16
SSP2 - Medium	2.98	2.46	2.17	1.99	1.85	1.67	1.59
SSP3 - Stalled development	3.12	2.98	2.82	2.66	2.54	2.32	2.21
SSP4 - Inequality	3.12	2.98	2.81	2.64	2.52	2.28	2.16
SSP5 - Conventional development	2.78	2.07	1.67	1.47	1.36	1.22	1.16
Life expectancy at birth for females (in years)							
SSP1 - Rapid development	56.77	65.08	69.18	73.19	77.29	86.90	94.53
SSP2 - Medium	52.70	58.10	60.30	62.42	65.00	72.42	78.21
SSP3 - Stalled development	52.84	54.03	55.06	55.84	57.52	62.04	65.57
SSP4 - Inequality	52.84	53.97	54.92	55.70	57.38	61.94	65.50
SSP5 - Conventional development	56.77	65.08	69.18	73.19	77.29	86.90	94.53
Migration – net flow over five years (in thousands)							
SSP1 - Rapid development	−726	−637	−628	−581	−513	−165	0
SSP2 - Medium	−803	−683	−671	−628	−571	−205	0
SSP3 - Stalled development	−597	−312	−314	−307	−298	−130	0
SSP4 - Inequality	−717	−615	−603	−581	−551	−227	0
SSP5 - Conventional development	−847	−939	−903	−821	−711	−221	0

Ageing Indicators, Medium Scenario (SSP2)

	2010	2020	2030	2040	2050	2075	2095
Median age	19.30	21.25	23.35	25.94	28.66	35.36	40.26
Propspective median age	19.30	17.30	18.30	19.37	19.94	19.45	19.43
Proportion age 65+	0.04	0.05	0.05	0.05	0.07	0.16	0.20
Proportion RLE < 15 years	0.04	0.05	0.05	0.04	0.06	0.12	0.13

Index